WEBSTER'S GUIDE TO
AMERICAN HISTORY

EDITORS: CHARLES VAN DOREN AND ROBERT McHENRY
ASSISTANT EDITOR: CAROLEE BENEFICO
GENERAL EDITOR: MORTIMER J. ADLER
CONSULTING EDITOR: JOHN WILLIAM WARD

WEBSTER'S GUIDE TO AMERICAN HISTORY

A CHRONOLOGICAL, GEOGRAPHICAL, AND BIOGRAPHICAL SURVEY AND COMPENDIUM

G. & C. MERRIAM COMPANY, PUBLISHERS
SPRINGFIELD, MASSACHUSETTS, U.S.A.

The editors wish to express their gratitude for permission to reprint material from the following sources:

Amsco Music Publishing Company for "Away With Rum," from *This Singing Land,* EFS #127, comp. and ed. by Irwin Silber, © 1965 Amsco Music Publishing Company, New York.

Basic Books Inc., for Letter by Albert Einstein to President Roosevelt—August 2, 1939, as found in *The Atomic Age,* ed. by Morton Grodzins and Eugene Rabinowitch, © 1939 by Educational Foundation for Nuclear Science, Inc., © 1963 by Basic Books, Inc., Publishers, New York.

Consumers Union of U.S., Inc., for "The Clorox Case: A Washday Miracle," from *Consumer Reports,* July 1967, Copyright © 1967 by Consumers Union of U.S., Inc.

Continued after the Index—

CONTENTS

PREFACE

A work of this size and scope is necessarily the product of many minds and hands. It is a pleasure to acknowledge the help of the following persons and institutions.

We are indebted to Carolyn Amundson, Martha Mackey, Cynthia Peterson, David Ross-Robertson, and Richard Thompson for their work on the design of the book, and for their ingenuity in finding, identifying, and laying out the many pictures and the other illustrative material in the volume.

We are grateful to Patty Mote, Richard O'Connor, Karen Padderud, and Celia Wittenber for assistance provided in the production process. Janet L. Warner was active in the creation of the index.

We owe a major debt of gratitude to Andrew Ross and Glila Sharp for research on the biographies. These were first written by the editors and then checked by Mrs. Sharp and Mr. Ross against all of the available reference sources. The editors hope that the biographies contain no errors, but they do not really expect that this will turn out to be so, particularly since, in a surprisingly large number of cases, the principal sources disagree even on such apparently simple matters as birth and death dates. Every effort has been made, however, to make the biographies as accurate and dependable as possible.

We are grateful to Helen Hanson for her capable work in obtaining permission to reprint various copyrighted materials. Acknowledgements for such use appear in the customary place in the volume.

We are particularly grateful to Otto Bird, Joseph Epstein, Clifton Fadiman, and John Van Doren for advice on the biographical subjects that should be included. The editors admit, however, that they did not always take that advice, and so the choice of subjects must finally be laid at their door.

We are grateful to several Chicago institutions and to their staffs—notably the Chicago Public Library, the library of McCormick Seminary, and the library of the University of Chicago—for their cooperation in allowing us to reproduce materials and in providing access to their research facilities.

Finally, we wish to point out that certain materials in this book are adapted from *The Annals of America* (20 volumes, 1969). These materials include the major portion of the chronologies as well as many maps.

INTRODUCTION
by John William Ward

The root meaning of the word "refer," if one refers to that basic reference book, a good dictionary, is to bear or carry something back. *Webster's Guide to American History* is a one-volume reference book on American history. Its aim is to carry essential information back from the past and make it readily available to anyone interested in American history. The word "essential" begs a large question, of course. How great a burden can a single volume carry? The design of the *Guide* embodies the attempt to answer that important question.

Webster's Guide to American History is divided into three main parts. Part I is a detailed and illustrated chronology of American history from the discovery of the new world by Columbus to the end of the 1960s. The elementary task that confronts anyone interested in the past is to know when something happened, the chronology or sequence of events. The discrete fact, however, has meaning not only in relation to other events which happened at the same time but also in relation to other events of the same kind over time. Part II is a series of maps and tables that provide in visual and tabular form a ready review of the sequence of events in a common category, ranging from the routes of the earliest explorers to popular tastes in reading. Finally, there are the individual human beings who are the bearers of the meaning of the past. Part III consists of the biographies of 1035 notable Americans. The index allows the reader to move between these three major parts.

Part I, the detailed, illustrated chronology, consists of the sequence of significant moments and events in our history from the time of the Discovery. Within a single year, events are described in the order of occurrence; where the specific day and month are known they are noted. Certain events—for example, the publication of a famous book—can be known only by year, and appear at the end of the chronology for the year of their occurrence; other events—for example, a war—extend over a number of years and when that is the case it is clearly indicated.

A special feature of Part I makes it unique among the many chronologies of American history that are in print. A glance at the pages of Part I will show that in parallel columns, alongside the chronology of events, appear quotations from the primary documents of the past that bear upon one or more of the particular events noted on the page. The quotations, each chosen for its connection with an event in American history, number about a thousand. They provide, at one level, a handy collection of great American quotations. Further, the words of contemporaries help to bring to life the reality of a bare notation in the chronology. Most important, they remind anyone who uses the chronology that the meaning of an event lies in the minds of men and women who experience it and that history is more than names and dates. The editors hope that the relevant quotations will be provocative and encourage anyone who uses the chronology to want to dig further into the sources of the American past and not to rest content with the mere facts.

Part II consists of a collection of maps and tables that provide the kind of information that can be presented best in visual and tabular form. As the Table of Contents indicates, Part II is divided into chronological and topical sections or chapters. Chapters 1 through 8 are organized around the conventional periods of American history from the "Exploration of the New World" to the period of "International Conflict 1946-1970." Chapters 9 through 14 present statistical tables and charts on topics from "Population" to "Natural Resources" and "The City." Chapter 15, "Additional Information," is itself a compendium of information ranging from "Presidents and Presidential Candidates" to popular songs and movies and best selling books.

It is fair to say that Part II offered the greatest challenge to the editors. What maps and what data would a modern student of American history most wish to have? The answer to that question depends finally on what questions are asked of the past. The questions will determine what is important and not important. *The Historical Statistics of the United States: Colonial Times to 1957,* published by the Government Printing Office, Washington, D.C., the best single source on its subject, runs to 789 finely printed pages, and is itself an "abstract" of historical statistics. Similarly, C. O. Paullin's *Atlas of the Historical Geography of the United States* (Washington, 1932), the best single collection of maps, but long out of print, will suggest to a student who is lucky enough to put his hands on a copy the immense number of maps one might include in a guide to the study of the past.

The editors of *Webster's Guide,* in other words, had to pick and choose. It seemed sensible to do two things: first, provide maps for traditional historical periods; second, provide tables for the information one considers "standard," the kind of information one expects to have at hand in a basic reference work. Yet, having said that, one must also say that the potential for the imaginative inquirer is perhaps greatest in Part II. To move from the titles of popular books and songs to who was the President and what was taking place in population shifts and the productive power of the United States is to start to raise fascinating and important questions about aspects of our social history that are not immediately evident in the neat and ordered information there on the page. Again, the editors hope that *Webster's Guide* will lead the student on a quest for more knowledge and greater understanding.

Part III, Biographies, is exactly what its title says. In alphabetical order, from Francis E. Abbott to Vladimir Zworykin, biographies of 1035 notable Americans— 1008 as main entries, 27 covered within the body of biographies of others—are included. Even with so large a number, considerably more than in any other single-volume reference work on American history, selectivity again was necessary. Everyone has some favorite, unsung hero from out of our past who he feels must be included among "notable" Americans, but not everyone will agree on what "notable" means. Even a work in many volumes like the *Dictionary of American Biography,* the basic biographical reference for American history, faces the problem of defining what criteria to establish for inclusion or exclusion, but the problem becomes crucial when one wishes to settle upon a thousand or so historically significant persons. The editors followed two broad criteria: first, if a person filled an important office, for example, President of the United States, he was automatically included; second, a much more relative and subjective criterion, the editors asked themselves what subjects one might, in the 1970s, wish to look up. In other words, the editors bore in mind that the importance of the past is related to the concerns of the present and tried to make their list of 1035 reflect that fact.

A special word about the Index is in order. For a reference work like *Webster's Guide,* a good index is crucial, and the editors believe the lengthy, cross-referenced Index meets the test. The Index, in one sense, ties the entire *Guide* together. It will lead the reader to all three parts of the *Guide.* For example, George Washington is not only the subject of a biographical entry, but he appears in the biographies of other Americans, is the author of some of the contemporary quotations and receives mention in others, and is included in various tables and even mentioned on some maps. The Index captures all the many allusions to Washington and makes them readily available to the reader who wishes to pursue them all. The same is true for each and every subject and event in the *Guide*. Thus the Index should make it an eminently usable book.

There is one element in the study of the past that does not have a place in *Webster's Guide,* that is, reference to the secondary literature and the interpretation of the past by historians. The aim of the *Guide* is to provide in concise and usable form essential information about the American past in a single volume. The editors recognize that the meaning of that information becomes finally a matter of scholarly interpretation, but they do not believe that a basic reference work can or should go beyond the limits of basic information. Also, there are a number of books and pamphlets readily available for the student who wishes to explore interpretations of American history by American historians. A comprehensive and useful guide to the literature on American history since the Discovery, aimed at the general reader and the beginning student, is Oscar Handlin, *et al., Harvard Guide to American History* (Cambridge, 1955); it includes a chapter, "Aids to Historical Research," which leads to more specialized bibliographies. Under the auspices of the American Historical Association, the Service Center for Teachers of History publishes bibliographic and interpretive pamphlets on major problems and periods that maintain uniformly high standards; a list of titles is available free from the Center, and individual pamphlets may be ordered directly from the Center (400 A Street, S.E., Washington, D.C., 20003). The Library of Congress has published a classified and annotated guide that is useful for recent scholarship, *A Guide to the Study of the United States of America: Representative Books Reflecting the Development of American Life and Thought;* it may be ordered from the Superintendent of Documents, U.S. Government Printing Office, Washington, D.C., 20005.

Finally, the test of the worth of *Webster's Guide to American History* will lie in its use, not in what those who made it think of it. The editors, aware that the *Guide* might still be improved, are confident that it is a good and useful book. But the reader must be the final judge of that.

PART I
Chronology

Fighting Indians in Florida, from Montanus'
"New World," 1671

CHRISTOPHER COLUMBUS
Letter to Sanchez, 1493

I have decided upon writing you this letter to acquaint you with all the events which have occurred in my voyage, and the discoveries which have resulted from it. Thirty-three days after my departure from [Gomera] I reached the Indian Sea, where I discovered many islands, thickly peopled, of which I took possession without resistance in the name of our most illustrious monarch, by public proclamation and with unfurled banners. To the first of these islands, which is called by the Indians Guanahani, I gave the name of the blessed Savior (San Salvador), relying upon whose protection I had reached this as well as the other islands; to each of these I also gave a name, ordering that one should be called Santa Maria de la Concepcion, another Fernandina, the third Isabella, the fourth Juana [Cuba], and so with all the rest. . . .

As soon as we arrived at that, which as I have said was named Juana, I proceeded along its coast a short distance westward and found it to be so large and apparently without termination that I could not suppose it to be an island, but the continental province of Cathay. . . .

In the meantime I had learned from some Indians whom I had seized that

1492

Oct. 12. Christopher Columbus makes first discovery of America that leads to permanent European settlement. The Bahama Islands are sighted on the first of four voyages (1492-1504) sponsored by the Spanish Crown in search of a western route to Asia. Columbus believes various Caribbean Islands and parts of Central and South America he discovers are outlying regions of Asia, but others are convinced that a New World exists. First settlement is La Navidad on island of Santo Domingo. It is found destroyed on second voyage in 1496, when city of Santo Domingo is founded.

1493

May 3-4. Pope Alexander VI settles dispute between Spain and Portugal by allocating to Spanish monarchs Ferdinand and Isabella exclusive rights to all lands not under Christian rule west of a line drawn north and south 100 leagues west of the Azores, called the Line of Demarcation. Portuguese claims to lands east of this line are recognized as valid.

1494

June 7. Treaty of Tordesillas is signed by Spain and Portugal. Terms of treaty move Line of Demarcation westward to 370 leagues west of Cape Verde Islands, placing Brazil in Portuguese zone. Supposition is that Portuguese had already discovered Brazil and that Spain did not know of it.

1496

Spanish introduce growing of sugar cane, cotton, and cattle in Santo Domingo, which proves also a source of gold, exported at a rate of $1 million a year by 1512.

1497

May 2-Aug. 6. John Cabot, Venetian resident of England, explores Newfoundland coast for Henry VII in further search of Asia. In 1498, subsequent voyage by Cabot in search of Japan and the Spice Islands reaches Delaware.

1501

May 13. Amerigo Vespucci begins second voyage to South America. Letter by Vespucci to his former patron asserts that not Asia but a New World has been found.

1507

Martin Waldseemüller, mapmaker, suggests that newly found land be called America after Amerigo Vespucci.

1508 - 1511

Spanish conquest of Caribbean Islands, including Puerto Rico, Jamaica, and Cuba.

that country was certainly an island, and therefore I sailed toward the east, coasting to the distance of 322 miles, which brought us to the extremity of it; from this point I saw lying eastward another island, 54 miles distant from Juana, to which I gave the name of Española [Hispaniola]. I went thither and steered my course eastward as I had done at Juana, even to the distance of 564 miles along the north coast. . . .

Finally, to compress into few words the entire summary of my voyage and speedy return and of the advantages derivable therefrom, I promise, that with a little assistance afforded me by our most invincible sovereigns, I will procure them as much gold as they need, as great a quantity of spices, of cotton, and of mastic (which is only found in Chios), and as many men for the service of the navy as Their Majesties may require. I promise also rhubarb and other sorts of drugs, which I am persuaded the men whom I have left in the aforesaid fortress have found already and will continue to find; for I myself have tarried nowhere longer than I was compelled to do by the winds, except in the city of Navidad, while I provided for the building of the fortress and took the necessary precautions for the perfect security of the men I left there.

View of the Spanish settlement at
St. Augustine in the late 1500s

Montezuma, last Aztec emperor of Mexico

JOHN SPARKE
Principal Navigations, etc., 1589
The Floridians, when they travel, have a kind of herb dried [tobacco], which, with a cane and an earthen cup in the end, with fire, and the dried herbs put together, do suck through the cane the smoke thereof, which smoke satisfies their hunger; and therewith they live four or five days without meat or drink; and this all the Frenchmen used for this purpose. Yet do they hold opinion withal, that it causes water and phlegm to void from their stomachs.

The commodities of this land are more than are yet known to any man; for besides the land itself whereof there is more than any king Christian is able to inhabit, it flourishes with meadow, pasture ground, with woods of cedar and cypress, and other sorts, as better cannot be in the world. They have for apothecary herbs, trees, roots, and gum, great store, as liquid storax, turpentine, gum, myrrh, and frankincense, with many others, whereof I know not the names. Colors, both red, black, yellow, and russet, very perfect, wherewith they paint their bodies, and deer skins which they wear about them, that with water it nei-

1513

March 3. Juan Ponce de León, sailing from Puerto Rico, explores coast of Florida.

Vasco Núñez de Balboa discovers Pacific Ocean at Panama, thus proving that Columbus was wrong in thinking he had reached Asia and confirming the opinion of Vespucci and others that lands were in the Western Hemisphere.

1519

March. Hernando Cortés leads expedition into Mexico. By August, 1521, he has crushed all resistance, established Spanish power in Central America, and secured treasure of the Aztecs.

September. Ferdinand Magellan, a Portuguese sailing for Spain, begins attempt to circumnavigate the globe. His ships sail down South American coast and into the Pacific through strait now named for him. Magellan is killed in Philippines, but one of his ships reaches Spain.

1523 - 1524

December. French-sponsored expedition sails to North America with Giovanni de Verrazano as pilot; explores coast from Carolina to Nova Scotia; enters New York harbor and discovers the Hudson River.

1527

June 10. Beginning of first exploration sponsored by the English Crown: the *Mary Guildford* explores the North American coast from Labrador to Florida and reaches the West Indies.

1534

April 20. Jacques Cartier begins first of

three voyages (1534-1542) during which he explores the St. Lawrence River for France. He takes back to France a cargo of worthless iron pyrites (fool's gold). All attempts to found a colony at Quebec fail until the seventeenth century.

1539 - 1542

May 28, 1539. Hernando de Soto, for Spain, lands in Florida, explores the interior of North America. **May, 1541.** De Soto reaches and crosses the Mississippi River; he travels west to Oklahoma, returns and dies at the Mississippi in 1542. During same period, Francisco Vázquez de Coronado, starting from Mexico, explores region west of the Mississippi and north of Mexico as far as Kansas. Other expeditions claim the California coast for Spain, but there are no permanent Spanish settlements until the eighteenth century.

1562 - 1586

Struggle between France and Spain for control of Florida and route of Spanish treasure ships. **1564.** French Huguenots settle on St. Johns River at Fort Caroline. **Sept. 20, 1565.** Defenders of settlement massacred by Spanish forces and name is changed to San Mateo. **1565-67.** Spanish found St. Augustine and other Florida settlements. **1568.** Spanish occupants of San Mateo massacred by French with help of Indians. Further destruction of settlements continues to 1581, intermixed with Indian hostilities. **June-July 1586.** St. Augustine burned by Sir Francis Drake, English explorer and privateer.

1564

Beginning of permanent Spanish occupation of the Philippine Islands begins after landing of expedition led by Miguel López de Legazpi.

ther fades away, nor alters color.

Gold and silver they want not; for at the Frenchmen first coming thither, they had the same offered them for little or nothing, for they received for a hatchet two pound weight of gold, because they knew not the estimation thereof. But the soldiers, being greedy of the same, did take it from them, giving them nothing for it; the which, they perceiving, that both the Frenchmen did greatly esteem it and also did rigorously deal with them, at last would not be known they had any more, neither dared they wear the same for fear of being taken away; so that saving at their first coming, they could get none of them. . . .

The Floridians have pieces of unicorns' horns, which they wear about their necks, whereof the Frenchmen obtained many pieces. Of those unicorns they have many, for that they do affirm it to be a beast with one horn, which coming to the river to drink, puts the same into the water before she drinks. . . .

Of beasts in this country, besides deer, foxes, hares, polecats, cunnies [rabbits], ownces [lynx], leopards, I am not able certainly to say; but it is thought that there are lions and tigers as well as unicorns, lions especially, if it be true that it is said of the enmity between them and the unicorns. . . . And seeing I have made mention of the beasts of this country, it shall not be from my purpose to speak also of the venomous beasts, as crocodiles, whereof there is a great abundance; adders of great bigness, whereof our men killed some of a yard and a half long. . . . On these adders the Frenchmen did feed to no little admiration of us, and affirmed the same to be a delicate meat. And [their] captain . . . saw also a serpent with three heads and four feet, of the bigness of a great spaniel, which for want of a harquebus he dared not attempt to slay.

Reasons for Founding Colonies, London, 1607

That realm is more complete and wealthy which either has the sufficiency to serve itself, or can find the means to export its natural commodities, than if it has occasion necessarily to import, for, consequently, it must ensue that by public consent a colony transported into a good and plentiful climate able to furnish our wants, our moneys, and wares, that now run into the hands of our adversaries or cold friends, shall pass unto our friends and natural kinsmen and from them likewise we shall receive such things as shall be most available to our necessities. This intercourse of trade may rather be called a homebred traffic than a foreign exchange. . . .

The want of our fresh and present supply of our discoveries has in a manner taken away the title which the law of nations gives us unto the coast first found out by our industry, forasmuch as whatsoever a man relinquishes may be claimed by the next finder as his own property. Neither is it sufficient to set foot in a country but to possess and hold it, in defense of an invading force (for want whereof) the king of Denmark intends to a northwest voyage (as it is reported). It is also reported that the French intend to inhabit Virginia, which they may safely achieve if their second voyage proves strong and there does not languish for want of sufficient and timely supplies, which cannot be had but by the means of a large contribution.

1576 - 1606

Eight English expeditions search for a Northwest Passage to Asia, some reaching Hudson Bay and Baffin Bay.

1578 - 1583

Queen Elizabeth grants patent to Sir Humphrey Gilbert for discovery and colonization in North America. Gilbert dies during second voyage when his ship sinks on the way home.

1581

Spain's conquest of Portugal extends to overseas possessions when Spain under Philip II claims dominion over entire non-European world.

1585 - 1590

July 27, 1585. Sir Walter Raleigh, granted a renewal of the patent of his half-brother, Sir Humphrey Gilbert, attempts to found English colony on Roanoke Island in what he calls "Virginia." **1586.** First settlers abandon colony. **1587.** Another group, including 17 women, lands on Roanoke Island. **Aug. 18.** Virginia Dare born there, first English child born in North America. Governor John White goes to England for supplies, is delayed; on return in 1590 finds entire colony gone without a trace.

1585 - 1604

Spain's war against England and France begins long decline of Spanish Empire. Series of treaties from 1604 to 1701 forces Spanish acceptance of English and French rights in New World.

1598

Spanish settlement of the Southwest begins in New Mexico; Santa Fe is founded in 1609.

1603 - 1615

1603. Samuel de Champlain of France explores St. Lawrence River on the first of eleven voyages. **1604.** Port Royal, Nova Scotia, is founded. **1608.** Champlain founds Quebec. Further exploration of Canada by Champlain creates a fur-trade route extending as far as Georgian Bay. French and Huron attacks on Iroquois "Five Nations" (later six) drive these powerful tribes eventually to ally themselves with the British.

1606

Merchants of London and Plymouth form two joint-stock companies and receive crown patents for the settlement of "Virginia." The London, or South Virginia, Company is given rights to settle an area now between Washington, D. C., and New York City; the Plymouth, or North Virginia, Company to settle New England, but neither may settle within 100 miles of the other.

1607 - 1610

1607. Jamestown Colony, sponsored by the London Company, established at head of James River, Virginia. **1610.** This first successful English colony, held together through the efforts of Captain John Smith, is increased by 400 new settlers under Thomas West, Lord Delaware (De La Warr).

1608

Captain John Smith publishes *A True Relation of Occurrences in Virginia*. This and other writings by the adventurer, explorer, pioneer of the Jamestown colony are influential in promoting colonial settlement.

JOHN SMITH
Generall Historie of Virginia, 1624
As for corn provision and contribution from the savages, we had nothing but mortal wounds, with clubs and arrows. As for our hogs, hens, goats, sheep, horses, or what lived, our commanders, officers, and savages daily consumed them; some small proportions sometimes we tasted, till all was devoured. Then swords, arms, pieces, or anything we traded with the savages, whose cruel fingers were so oft imbrued in our blood, that what by their cruelty, our governor's indiscretion, and the loss of our ships, of 500 within six months after Captain Smith's departure there remained not past 60 men, women, and children — most miserable and poor creatures. And those were preserved for the most part by roots, herbs, acorns, walnuts, berries, now and then a little fish. They that had starch in these extremities made no small use of it; yea, even the very skins of our horses.

Nay, so great was our famine that a savage we slew and buried, the poorer sort took him up again and ate him; and so did diverse one another boiled and stewed with roots and herbs. And one among the rest did kill his wife, powdered [salted] her, and had eaten part of her before it was known; for which he was executed, as he well deserved. Now, whether she was better roasted, boiled, or carbonadoed [broiled], I know not; but of such a dish as powdered wife I never heard.

This was that time, which still to this day, we called the starving time.

ANDREW MARVELL
Bermudas, c. 1655

Where the remote Bermudas ride
In the ocean's bosom unespied,
From a small boat that rowed along,
The listening winds received this song:
"What should we do but sing His praise,
That led us through the watery maze,
Unto an isle so long unknown,
And yet far kinder than our own?
Where He the huge sea monsters wracks,
That lift the deep upon their backs,
He lands us on a grassy stage,
Safe from the storms, and prelate's rage.
He gave us this eternal spring,
Which here enamels everything,
And sends the fowls to us in care,
On daily visits through the air;
He hangs in shades the orange bright,
Like golden lamps in a green night,
And does in the pomegranates close
Jewels more rich than Ormus shows;
He makes the figs our mouths to meet,
And throws the melons at our feet;
But apples plants of such a price,
No tree could ever bear them twice;
With cedars chosen by His hand,
From Lebanon, He stores the land,
And makes the hollow seas, that roar,
Proclaim the ambergris on shore.
He cast (of which we rather boast)
The gospel's pearl upon our coast,
And in these rocks for us did frame
A temple where to sound His name.
Oh! let our voice His praise exalt,
Till it arrive at heaven's vault,
Which, thence perhaps rebounding, may
Echo beyond the Mexique Bay."
Thus sung they, in the English boat,
An holy and a cheerful note;
And all the way, to guide their chime,
With falling oars they kept the time.

1609

Henry Hudson, Englishman employed by the Dutch East India Company, explores Hudson River to Albany; explorations lead to establishment of Fort Orange (Albany, 1624) and a fur-trading post on Manhattan Island (1625).

Church of England established by law in Virginia but in no other colony until 1693.

First cultivation of maize (corn) by white colonists in Virginia at insistence of Captain John Smith on the necessity for farming.

1612

Bermuda settled by the English, who establish themselves also on other West Indian islands; population 20,000 by 1640. Tobacco growing is introduced in Virginia around this time.

1613

French settlements around the Bay of Fundy are destroyed by English raiders commanded by Captain Samuel Argall.

1615

Four Récollect (Franciscan) friars arrive in Quebec, the beginning of French missionary activity in Canada. First Jesuits arrive in 1625.

1616

Captain John Smith publishes *A Description of New England* after exploring New England coast, thus establishing the name for that part of North America.

1618

Headrights instituted in Virginia; persons

immigrating with their families and persons paying an immigrating worker's passage are granted 50 acres of land per head for workers brought to Virginia. This arrangement becomes basis of land tenure in all southern colonies, attracting settlers uninterested in sharecropping larger Virginia grants called "hundreds." New England uses different form of settlement, by communities; groups receive land grants from the legislature; these grants are then formed into townships.

1619

July-August. General Assembly of Virginia, first colonial legislature in the New World, meets for first time; English common law is introduced into the colony.

August. Twenty Negroes, the first brought to America, come to Jamestown, Virginia, as indentured servants, same status as many white immigrants. Chattel slavery is not legally recognized until after 1650.

1619 - 1624

Struggle for control of Virginia Company. Capable but conservative merchant-governor, Sir Thomas Smith, is replaced by Sir Edwin Sandys on motion of small stockholders. Sandys' well-meant efforts to increase colony's prosperity strain its resources and lead to dissolution of the Company by James I, who revokes charter. **May 24, 1624.** Virginia becomes a Royal Colony.

1620

Sept. 16. Separatist "Pilgrims," chartered by Virginia Company to settle in Virginia, sail from Plymouth, England in *Mayflower*. Pilgrims are called Separatists because they repudiate liturgy and Episcopal organization of Church of England, practise "congrega-

JOHN PORY
Proceedings of the First Assembly of Virginia, 1619
The most convenient place we could find to sit in was the choir of the church, where Sir George Yeardley, the governor, being set down in his accustomed place, those of the Council of Estate sat next him on both hands, except only the secretary, then appointed speaker, who sat right before him. John Twine, clerk of the General Assembly, being placed next the speaker, and Thomas Pierse, the sergeant, standing at the bar to be ready for any service the Assembly should command him. . . .

Prayer being ended, to the intent that as we had begun at God Almighty so we might proceed w[ith] awful and due respect toward his lieutenant, our most gracious and dread sovereign, all the burgesses were entreated to retire themselves into the body of the church; which being done, before they were fully admitted, they were called in order and by name, and so every man (none staggering at it) took the oath of supremacy, and then entered the Assembly. . . .

And whereas the speaker had propounded four several objects for the Assembly to consider on; namely, first the Great Charter of orders, laws, and privileges; second, which of the instructions given by the Council in England to My Lord La Warre, Captain Argall, or Sir George Yeardley might conveniently put on the habit of laws; third, what laws might issue out of the private concept of any of the burgesses or any other of the colony; and, lastly, what petitions were fit to be sent home for England.

The Mayflower Compact, 1620

In the name of God, Amen. We whose names are underwritten, the loyal subjects of our dread sovereign lord, King James, by the grace of God, of Great Britain, France, and Ireland, King, Defender of the Faith, etc.

Having undertaken for the glory of God, and advancement of the Christian faith and honor of our king and country, a voyage to plant the first colony in the northern parts of Virginia, do by these present, solemnly and mutually, in the presence of God and one of another, covenant and combine ourselves together into a civil body politic, for our better ordering and preservation and furtherance of the ends aforesaid; and by virtue hereof to enact, constitute, and frame such just and equal laws, ordinances, acts, constitutions, offices from time to time as shall be thought most meet and convenient for the general good of the colony; unto which we promise all due submission and obedience. In witness whereof we have hereunder subscribed our names, Cape Cod, 11th of November, in the year of the reign of our sovereign lord, King James, of England, France, and Ireland 18, and of Scotland 54. Anno Domini 1620.

tionalism" based on doctrines of John Calvin. **Nov. 19.** *Mayflower* reaches Cape Cod. After sailing along coast, Pilgrims decide to settle because of lateness of season, but since this region is outside territory for which their charter is valid, they have no legal basis for a government. **Nov. 21.** (New Style date; Old Style date given in text is Nov. 11). While still on shipboard, Pilgrims bind themselves together into a "civil body politick" by Mayflower Compact, signed by all adult males except one invalid and eight servants. **Dec. 26.** Plymouth Plantation is established under first governor, John Carver. **April.** Carver dies and is succeeded by William Bradford.

1621

"Triangular Trade" from American colonies to West Indies to England begins about this time. Colonies cannot sell directly to England enough of what they produce to pay for necessary English manufactures (tools, textiles), but these can be purchased with sugar, molasses, and rum obtained in West Indies. Tobacco is chief direct export to England.

1623 - 1631

Settlements are established at Portsmouth, New Hampshire, and Saco Bay, Maine, sponsored by the Council for New England, successor to the Plymouth Company.

1625

Population of colonies is now 1,980 (Virginia 1,800; Plymouth, 180).

1626

Peter Minuit with new immigrants from Holland lands on Manhattan Island, occupied by Dutch colonists in 1624. They build 30 houses during summer. Minuit buys island from the Indians and renames it New Amsterdam.

1628

Dutch Reformed Church organized in New Amsterdam. Presbyterian in form and Calvinist in faith, it is governed by a council of ministers and elders who remain technically under the jurisdiction of the parent church in Holland until after the Revolution.

1628 - 1629

Sept. 6, 1628. John Endecott with 50-60 colonists establishes colony at Salem, Massachusetts. **June 27, 1629.** 420 more settlers join first group, vanguard of the Massachusetts Bay Colony.

1629

March 10. Charles I dissolves Parliament and rules personally. This, and rising influence of William Laud, Bishop of London, who leads persecution of Puritans, persuades eminent English Puritans to emigrate with their many followers to America. Rather than a mere commercial company, they create an entire society that is defiant of British control.

March 14. Massachusetts Bay Company chartered with rights of settlement between the Charles and Merrimack rivers. Charter does not specify place for annual meetings, so control of Company is transferred to New England when its officers go there, taking the charter with them. Company becomes self-governing commonwealth organized on corporate rather than parliamentary lines.

June 7. Dutch West India Company grants patroonships, giving feudal rights and

Charter of Freedoms and Exemptions for New Netherland, 1629
All such shall be acknowledged patroons of New Netherland who shall, within the space of four years next after they have given notice to any of the chambers of the Company here, or to the commander or council there, undertake to plant a colony there of fifty souls, upward of fifteen years old; one-fourth part within one year, and within three years after the sending of the first, making together four years, the remainder, to the full number of fifty persons, to be shipped from hence, on pain, in case of willful neglect, of being deprived of the privileges obtained; but it is to be observed that the Company reserve the island of the Manhattes [Manhattan] to themselves. . . .

Inasmuch as it is intended to people the island of the Manhattes first, all fruits and wares that are produced on the lands situate[d] on the North River and lying thereabout shall, for the present, be brought there before they may be sent elsewhere; excepting such as are from their nature unnecessary there, or such as cannot, without great loss to the owner thereof be brought there. . . .

Whosoever shall settle any colony out of the limits of the Manhattes Island shall be obliged to satisfy the Indians for the land they shall settle upon, and they may extend or enlarge the limits of their colonies if they settle a proportionate number of colonists thereon.

JOHN WINTHROP

A Modell of Christian Charity, 1630
*So shall we keep the unity of the spirit
in the bond of peace. The Lord will be
our God and delight to dwell among us
as His own people. He will command a
blessing on us in all our ways, so that
we shall see much more of His wisdom,
power, goodness, and truth than we
have formerly known. We shall find that
the God of Israel is among us, and ten
of us shall be able to resist a thousand
of our enemies. The Lord will make our
name a praise and glory, so that men
shall say of succeeding plantations:
"The Lord make it like that of New England." For we must consider that we
shall be like a City upon a Hill; the eyes
of all people are on us.*

*If we deal falsely with our God in this
work we have undertaken and so cause
Him to withdraw His present help from
us, we shall be made a story and a by-
word throughout the world; we shall
open the mouths of enemies to speak
evil of the ways of God and all believers
in God; we shall shame the faces of
many of God's worthy servants and
cause their prayers to be turned into
curses upon us, till we are forced out of
the new land where we are going.*

GEORGE BERKELEY

On the Prospect of Planting Arts and
Learning in America
*Westward the course of empire takes
    its way;
  The four first acts already past,
A fifth shall close the drama with the
    day:
  Time's noblest offspring is the last.*

privileges to wealthy individuals who will transport settlers to New Netherland. Vast estates are granted along the Hudson, Connecticut, and Delaware rivers.

July 20. During war between France and England (1627-1629), British take Quebec, unaware that treaty has been signed in April.

1630

June 12. First of eleven ships from England lands at Salem, Massachusetts. Massachusetts Bay Colony is established along Massachusetts coast north of Plymouth under the leadership of Governor John Winthrop. The first 1,000 settlers have been joined by 16,000 others by 1642, the so-called Great Migration.

Massachusetts becomes "Bible Commonwealth" in which ruling magistrates are in fact, though not by law, Puritan divines. Their influence declines as population gradually disperses. Civil rights are restricted to church members — those who have made public testament of their conversion. This is in violation of the charter, but remains in effect until 1664.

1630 - 1635

Civil government is established in Massachusetts Bay Colony. Governor and assistants (originally Company board of directors) are at first independent of legislature, or General Court, but after 1632, legislature elects governor and assistants.

1630 - 1649

John Winthrop writes his *Journal*, describing the affairs of Massachusetts Bay Colony and including his General Court speech of 1645 on the nature of liberty. First two volumes published in 1790; published in full in 1825-1826 as *The History of New England.*

1630 - 1651

Governor William Bradford writes his *History of Plimouth Plantation*, not published until 1856. This account of the Plymouth Colony is best known of colonial histories.

1632

France and England recognize each other's North American colonies in Treaty of St. Germain-en-Laye, which does not specify boundaries.

1634

First American saw mill constructed in Maine.

1634 - 1654

Feb. 27, 1634. Settlers arrive in Virginia and travel to St. Mary's, founding Maryland as Catholic colony under patent applied for by George Calvert, first Lord Baltimore, and granted to Cecilius Calvert, second Lord Baltimore. Maryland is first English colony to practise religious toleration, confirmed by law for all Christians. **Oct. 1654.** Protestant majority, inspired by English revolution, repeals Toleration Act and denies protection to Catholics; Catholic toleration is later restored. Although tolerated for a brief period in New York (1687-1688), outside Maryland Catholics have religious and civil rights only in Rhode Island and Pennsylvania by 1700.

1635 - 1636

October. Roger Williams, having protested control of civil affairs by church, is banished from Salem; he spends winter with Indians. **June.** Williams founds Provi-

WILLIAM BRADFORD

Of Plymouth Plantation 1620–1647

All this while no supply was heard of, neither knew they when they might expect any. So they began to think how they might raise as much corn as they could and obtain a better crop than they had done, that they might not still thus languish in misery. At length, after much debate of things, the governor (with the advice of the chief among them) gave way that they should set corn, every man for his own particular, and in that regard trust to themselves; in all other things to go on in the general way as before. And so [was] assigned to every family a parcel of land, according to the proportion of their number, for that end, only for present use (but made no division for inheritance), and ranged all boys and youth under some family. This had very good success, for it made all hands very industrious, so as much more corn was planted than otherwise would have been by any means the governor or any other could use, and saved him a great deal of trouble and gave far better content. . . .

The experience that was had in this common course and condition, tried sundry years and that among godly and sober men, may well evince the vanity of that conceit of Plato's and other ancients applauded by some of later times —that the taking away of property and bringing in community into a commonwealth would make them happy and flourishing, as if they were wiser than God. For this community (so far as it was) was found to breed much confusion and discontent and retard much employment that would have been to their benefit and comfort. . . . Let none object this is men's corruption, and nothing to the course itself. I answer, seeing all men have this corruption in them, God in His wisdom saw another course fitter for them.

Massachusetts Bay School Law, 1642

Forasmuch as the good education of children is of singular behoof and benefit to any commonwealth, and whereas many parents and masters are too indulgent and negligent of their duty in that kind:

It is ordered that the selectmen of every town, in the several precincts and quarters where they dwell, shall have a vigilant eye over their brethren and neighbors to see, first, that none of them shall suffer so much barbarism in any of their families as not to endeavor to teach, by themselves or others, their children and apprentices so much learning as may enable them perfectly to read the English tongue, and knowledge of the capital laws; upon penalty of 20s. for each neglect therein.

Also that all masters of families do once a week (at the least) catechize their children and servants in the grounds and principles of religion; and if any be unable to do so much, that then at the least they procure such children and apprentices to learn some short orthodox catechism without book that they may be able to answer unto the questions that shall be propounded to them out of such catechism by their parents or masters, or any of the selectmen when they shall call them to a trial, of what they have learned in that kind.

And, further, that all parents and masters do breed and bring up their children and apprentices in some honest lawful calling, labor, or employment, either in husbandry or some other trade, profitable for themselves and the Commonwealth, if they will not or cannot train them up in learning, to fit them for higher employments.

dence, Rhode Island; democratic government includes separation of church and state.

1635 - 1656

French occupy some West Indian islands; first settlement is on St. Christopher, followed by Guadeloupe, Martinique, Tortuga, and seven other islands by 1656.

1636 - 1637

Connecticut expedition against Pequot Indians to avenge murder of New England trader destroys main Pequot village near Stonington, Connecticut. Retreating survivors are slaughtered at New Haven by Connecticut and Plymouth forces.

1636 - 1689

Compulsory education in New England. **1636.** Latin grammar school established in Boston. **1647.** Law requires similar schools for all Massachusetts towns with more than 100 families. Similar acts are voted by Connecticut (1650), Plymouth (1671), and New Hampshire (1689). Literacy in Massachusetts estimated at 95 percent between 1640 and 1700, as compared with estimated 54-60 percent in Virginia during same period.

Beginning of higher education. General Court of Massachusetts votes (1636) £400 toward founding of Congregational college begun at Cambridge with one building and a tutor (1638); college is named Harvard College in 1639 upon gift of money and books from John Harvard.

1637 - 1638

Nov. 12, 1637. Anne Hutchinson tried for sedition and contempt in Massachusetts Bay Colony. Her claim of divine guidance by personal revelation and stress upon "grace" rather than "works" challenges role of clergy in Puritan society. **Nov. 17.** She is sentenced to banishment. **March 1638.** She is excommunicated and sentence is carried out. **March 7.** With her husband and fourteen children, she founds town of Pocasset, later Portsmouth, Rhode Island.

1638

March. Swedish settlements established by arrangement with Dutch authorities, and despite protests of Dutch colonists, at Fort Christina (now Wilmington), Delaware; occupied by the Dutch themselves in 1655 after years of hostile action on both sides.

1638 - 1710

1638. Parochial school system of Middle Colonies begins with Dutch Reformed school at New Amsterdam, supported by town. **1659.** Classical school established at New Amsterdam. **1689.** Friends School (Quaker) opens in Pennsylvania. **1702.** New York act authorizes free grammar school, but is not implemented because of established practice of schooling by apprenticeship for the poor. **1710.** Trinity School established in New York under the auspices of the Society for the Propagation of the Gospel (S.P.G.). No real public school system during colonial times in the Middle Colonies, where emphasis is on charity schools for the poor and private schools for the rich. Public education lags in Southern Colonies, where most children are educated at home.

1639

Roger Williams organizes Baptist Church in Providence, Rhode Island; Baptist faith spreads widely by middle of eighteenth century as its leaders advocate religious liberty and separation of church and state.

JOHN WINTHROP
Reply to Sir Henry Vane, 1637
Seeing it must be granted that there may come such persons (suppose Jesuits, etc.), which by consent of all ought to be rejected, it will follow that by this law (being only for notice to be taken of all that come to us, without which we cannot avoid such as indeed are to be kept out) is no other but just and needful. . . . The intent of the law is to preserve the welfare of the body; and for this end to have none received into any fellowship with it who are likely to disturb the same, and this intent (I am sure) is lawful and good. . . .

I would demand then in the case in question (for it is bootless curiosity to refrain openness in things public), whereas it is said that this law was made of purpose to keep away such as are of Mr. Wheelwright his judgment (admit it were so which yet I cannot confess), where is the evil of it? If we conceive and find by sad experience that his opinions are such, as by his own profession cannot stand with external peace, may we not provide for our peace by keeping of such as would strengthen him and infect others with such dangerous tenets? And if we find his opinions such as will cause divisions and make people look at their magistrates, ministers, and brethren as enemies to Christ and antichrists, etc., were it not sin and unfaithfulness in us to receive more of those opinions, which we already find the evil fruit of?

NATHANIEL WARD

The Simple Cobler of Aggawam, 1645

He that is willing to tolerate any religion, or discrepant way of religion, besides his own, unless it be in matters merely indifferent, either doubts of his own or is not sincere in it.

He that is willing to tolerate any unsound opinion, that his own may also be tolerated, though never so sound, will for a need hang God's Bible at the devil's girdle.

Every toleration of false religions or opinions has as many errors and sins in it as all the false religions and opinions it tolerates, and one sound one more.

That state that will give liberty of conscience in matters of religion must give liberty of conscience and conversation in their moral laws, or else the fiddle will be out of tune and some of the strings crack. . . .

Experience will teach churches and Christians that it is far better to live in a state united, though a little corrupt, than in a state whereof some part is incorrupt and all the rest divided. . . .

There is talk of a universal toleration, I would talk as loud as I could against it, did I know what more apt and reasonable sacrifice England could offer to God for His late performing all His heavenly truths than a universal toleration of all hellish errors, or how they shall make a universal reformation, but by making Christ's academy the devil's university, where any man may commence heretic per saltum [by a leap]; where he that is filius diabolicus [the devil's son], or simpliciter pessimus [outrightly most evil], may have his grace to go to hell cum publico privilegio [as a public right]; and carry as many after him as he can.

First printing done in the colonies: "The Freeman's Oath," a single sheet printed by Stephen Daye in Cambridge, Massachusetts.

1640

First log cabins, introduced from Sweden, constructed in Swedish settlements on the Delaware River; after about 1700 they become the common frontier dwelling.

The Bay Psalm Book (The Whole Booke of Psalmes Faithfully Translated into English Metre), the first book printed in the colonies, becomes the hymnal, without tunes, of New England; translation is by Thomas Welde, Richard Mather, and John Eliot; printing is by Stephen Daye, at Cambridge Massachusetts.

First Lutheran minister arrives in New Sweden, on the Delaware River, but church is not formally organized until 1748, when the Ministerium of Pennsylvania is formed

1640 - 1660

English Civil War (1642-1651) and period of Protectorate (1653-1659) under Oliver Cromwell increase sense of independence from England in American colonies, either because, as in New England, English Puritans are considered too tolerant, or because, as in Virginia, the prevailing sympathy is royalist. **Oct. 1652.** Massachusetts Bay Colony declares itself independent of Parliament; distributes pine-tree shilling (minted in June), first money minted in America. **1660.** All English colonies proclaim Charles II at the Restoration.

1640 - 1700

Colonial style of house, more weatherproof than European houses, developed in New England; characteristics are clapboard or shingle walls, leaded casement windows, second-story overhang, and steep salt-box roof. Jacobean style, with geometric gables, central stair tower, and clustered chimneys is introduced in the South, especially Virginia.

1641

December. Adoption of Body of Liberties, a code of 100 laws, by General Court of Massachusetts Bay Colony, affirming the authority of ecclesiastical magistrates. Criminal provisions of this code are based upon the Old Testament rather than on English common law.

Montreal, Canada, founded on site laid out by Champlain in 1611.

1642

Massachusetts law imposes fines for neglect of education.

Sugar-cane cultivation, introduced into British West Indies from Brazil, transforms economy and social system of islands from a struggling community of white employers to a prosperous slave-supported society.

1643

May 19. New England Confederation formed; Massachusetts Bay, Plymouth, Connecticut, and New Haven join as the United Colonies of New England for common defense against Indians and to resist threat of Dutch expansion from Hudson River valley. Government, consisting of two commissioners from each colony who meet annually, is empowered to declare war, adjust intercolonial quarrels, punish fugitive criminals, and apprehend bound servants. Confederation is especially active until 1664 and during King Philip's War (1675-1676), but is dissolved in 1684.

First mill powered by tidal currents built in Massachusetts.

Champlain, portrait by Ducornet

Massachusetts Body of Liberties, 1641
The free fruition of such liberties, immunities, and privileges as humanity, civility, and Christianity call for as due to every man in his place and proportion without impeachment and infringement, has ever been and ever will be the tranquillity and stability of churches and commonwealths; and the denial or deprival thereof, the disturbance if not the ruin of both.

We hold it, therefore, our duty and safety, while we are about the further establishing of this government, to collect and express all such freedoms as for [the] present we foresee may concern us, and our posterity after us, and to ratify them with our solemn consent. We do, therefore, this day, religiously and unanimously decree and confirm these following rights, liberties, and privileges concerning our churches and civil state, to be respectively, impartially, and inviolably enjoyed and observed throughout our jurisdiction forever.

(Left) Christopher Columbus; (above) a facsimile of earliest reproduction of the landing of Columbus, in Dati, "Narrative of Columbus," 1493; (below) French pirates looting a Spanish settlement: engraving by Theodore de Bry

(Above) Roanoke, after drawing by John White, governor of the
island; (below) German woodcut of American Indians, c. 1505

ADRIAEN VAN DER DONCK
Report on New Netherland, 1650

As we shall speak of the reasons and causes which have brought New Netherland into the ruinous condition in which it is now found to be, we deem it necessary to state the very first difficulties and, for this purpose, regard it as we see and find it in our daily experience. As far as our understanding goes, to describe it in one word (and none better presents itself), it is bad government, with its attendants and consequences, that is the true and only foundation stone of the decay and ruin of New Netherland. This government from which so much abuse proceeds is twofold; that is, in the fatherland by the managers and in this country. . . .

Besides this, the country of the Company is so taxed, and is burdened and kept down in such a manner, that the inhabitants are not able to appear beside their neighbors of Virginia or New England or to undertake any enterprise. It seems — and thus much is known by us — that all the inhabitants of New Netherland admit that the managers have scarce any care or regard for New Netherland, except when there is something to receive, for which reason, however, they receive less. . . .

In our opinion this country will never flourish under the government of the Honorable Company but will pass away and come to an end of itself, unless the Honorable Company be reformed.

1644

Roger Williams publishes *The Bloudy Tenent of Persecution for the Cause of Conscience* to protest doctrines of Massachusetts Bay Colony, especially those of John Cotton, who defends persecution of defiant souls.

1646 - 1655

Joseph Jenks of Massachusetts experiments with design and manufacture of curved scythe handle (snath), increasing efficiency of farm labor in harvesting.

1647

May 29-31. Under charter granted in 1644, Rhode Island adopts constitution establishing freedom of conscience, separation of church and state, provision for town referendums on laws passed by the assembly, and right of towns to initiate laws.

1647 - 1664

Struggle against autocratic Dutch rule in New Amsterdam leads to establishment of local self-government in 1653, but failure of administration of Peter Stuyvesant to satisfy varied interests and diversified population forces capitulation to English authority in 1664, when colony is renamed New York.

1648

Survey of the Summe of Church Discipline, by Thomas Hooker, argues the absolute authority of God in human affairs. Hooker and John Cotton are the most distinguished scholars and chief spokesmen of New England theocracy.

1650

The Tenth Muse, earliest collection of poems by a colonial poet, Anne Bradstreet, is published in London; does not include *Contemplations*, by which she is best known, published after her death in 1678.

1650 - 1700

Earliest American painters (limners). Self-taught, they are traveling portraitists whose knowledge of anatomy is limited but who paint in fine detail. *The Mason Children* (1670) and *Mrs. Freake and Baby Mary* (1674) are two of best-known paintings.

1654

First Jews, seven of whom are stockholders of Dutch West India Company, arrive in New Amsterdam. Denied the right of public worship until 1685, they are earlier, in 1655-1656, permitted to engage in wholesale trade and in 1657 admitted to retail trades. First New York synagogue known to exist in 1695, but as late as 1737 Jews are prohibited from voting for New York assembly. Civil rights granted in Rhode Island in 1655 are withdrawn in 1728, and elsewhere in the colonies vote is mostly denied until after the Revolution — in Maryland until 1828, and in North Carolina as late as 1868.

July. Acadia (Nova Scotia) captured from French by colonials under Major Robert Sedgwick of Boston; purpose is to take over fishing and fur trade to eliminate French competition with New England. Acadia ceded back to France in 1667.

1656 - 1671

July-August. Society of Friends (Quakers) first represented in Boston, where its members are immediately persecuted and expelled. **May 1658.** Quaker meetings banned by Massachusetts. **Oct.** Death penalty imposed for returning after expulsion. **Oct. 1659-March 1661.** Four executions

ANNE BRADSTREET
To My Dear and Loving Husband, c. 1660
If ever two were one, then surely we.
If ever man were loved by wife, then thee;
If ever wife was happy in a man,
Compare with me ye women if you can.
I prize thy love more than whole mines of gold,
Or all the riches that the East doth hold.
My love is such that rivers cannot quench,
Nor ought but love from thee, give recompense.
Thy love is such I can no way repay,
The heavens reward thee manifold I pray.
Then while we live, in love let's so persevere,
That when we live no more, we may live ever.

Connecticut Code, 1650
If any man have a stubborn and rebellious son of sufficient years and understanding, viz., sixteen years of age, which will not obey the voice of his father or the voice of his mother, and that when they have chastened him will not hearken unto them, then may his father and mother, being his natural parents, lay hold on him and bring him to the magistrates assembled in Court, and testify unto them that their son is stubborn and rebellious and will not obey their voice and chastisement, but lives in sundry notorious crimes, such a son shall be put to death.

The Flushing Remonstrance, New York, 1657
You have been pleased to send up unto us a certain prohibition or command that we should not receive or entertain any of those people called Quakers, because they are supposed to be, by some, seducers of the people. For our part we cannot condemn them in this case, neither can we stretch out our hands against them to punish, banish, or persecute them, for out of Christ, God is a consuming fire, and it is a fearful thing to fall into the hands of the living God . . . .

The law of love, peace, and liberty in the states extending to Jews, Turks, and Egyptians, as they are considered the sons of Adam, which is the glory of the outward state of Holland; so love, peace, and liberty, extending to all in Christ Jesus condemns hatred, war, and bondage; and because our Savior says it is impossible but that offense will come, but woe be unto him by whom they come, our desire is not to offend one of His little ones in whatsoever form, name, or title he appears in, whether Presbyterian, Independent, Baptist, or Quaker; but shall be glad to see anything of God in any of them, desiring to do unto all men as we desire all men should do unto us, which is the true law both of church and state; for our Savior says this is the law and the prophets. Therefore, if any of these said persons come in love unto us, we cannot in conscience lay violent hands upon them, but give them free egress into our town and houses as God shall persuade our consciences.

are carried out by hanging. **1671.** Visit to America of Society's founder, George Fox, causes sect to expand, particularly in Pennsylvania, where it is vigorously supported from 1682 by William Penn, himself a Quaker.

1660

July 4. Committee for Trade and Plantations of the Privy Council (known afterward as the Lords of Trade) established by Charles II to centralize colonial administration. Board of Trade exercises these functions after 1696; Secretary of State after 1766.

Oct. 1. Navigation Act of 1660. British Parliament passes one of a series of laws regulating colonial trade on mercantilist principles (the acquisition of a store of precious metals by exporting as much produce and importing as little raw material as possible in order to create a powerful, self-sufficient country or empire). Act requires shipment of goods to and from colonies in English vessels to meet Dutch and Spanish competition. It also requires enumerated articles, such as sugar, tobacco, and indigo, originating in colonies, to be shipped only to England or her colonies. One result of Act is to encourage shipbuilding, which consumes white pine forests of New England; by 1760 one-third of total British tonnage (400,000) is colonial built.

1661 - 1664

Conquest of New Netherland by England, during Anglo-Dutch wars. Dutch settlements in eastern Connecticut and Hudson River Valley are regarded as barrier to expansion of New England. **April 2, 1664.** English forces are dispatched by Duke of York (later James II), who receives grant from his brother, Charles II, of all areas between Maine and the Narrows (in New

York Bay) not already occupied by English settlers as well as land south to Delaware Bay. **Sept. 8.** English achieve easy victory over New Amsterdam Dutch authorities, who lack support of inhabitants and surrender the town. **Sept. 24.** Fort Orange (Albany) surrenders without a fight. **Oct. 4.** New Amsterdam renamed New York; British become allies of Five Nations of the Iroquois in place of Dutch.

1662

Michael Wigglesworth publishes his best-selling book, *Day of Doom,* ballad stanzas describing hellfire and damnation.

1663

Charles II grants Carolina province to eight aristocratic proprietors. Area is settled, 1669-1680, by colonists from Virginia and Barbados, as well as from England.

John Eliot, Puritan missionary, completes translation of the Bible into the language of Massachusetts Indians; he also writes an Indian grammar in 1666 and primer in 1669.

1663 - 1696

Later Navigation Acts restrict shipment of most European goods to colonies. Act of 1663 requires goods to be transferred at England and thence carried to colonists on English ships. Act of 1673 provides for appointment of customs commissioners to collect duties in the colonies on goods being exported. Act of 1696 gives these commissioners same wide powers as in England, including right of forcible entry; also extends restrictions of 1663 to all colonial trade, requires bonds to be posted on enumerated commodities, and voids colonial laws deemed contrary to the various Acts, which are a continual source of conflict and resentment, especially in Massachusetts.

JOHN ELIOT
The Day-Breaking, 1646
The observations I have gathered by conversing with them are such as these . . . .

That there is need of learning in ministers who preach to Indians, much more to Englishmen and gracious Christians, for these had sundry philosophical questions which some knowledge of the arts must help to give answer to; and without which these would not have been satisfied. Worse than Indian ignorance has blinded their eyes that renounce learning as an enemy to gospel ministries. . . .

That there is no necessity of extraordinary gifts nor miraculous signs always to convert heathens . . . for we see the Spirit of God working mightily upon the hearts of these natives in an ordinary way, and I hope will, they being but a remnant, the Lord using to show mercy to the remnant. For there be but few that are left alive from the plague and pox, which God sent into those parts; and, if one or two can understand, they usually talk of it as we do of news — it flies suddenly far and near, and truth scattered will rise in time, for ought we know . . . .

That the deepest estrangements of man from God is no hindrance to His grace nor to the spirit of grace; for what nation or people ever so deeply degenerated since Adam's fall as these Indians, and yet the Spirit of God is working upon them?

A Brief Description . . . of Carolina, 1666

Is there, therefore, any younger brother who is born of gentile blood, and whose spirit is elevated above the common sort, and yet the hard usage of our country has not allowed suitable fortune; he will not surely be afraid to leave his native soil to advance his fortunes equal to his blood and spirit, and so he will avoid these unlawful ways too many of our young gentlemen take to maintain themselves according to their high education, having but small estates. . . .

Such as are here tormented with much care how to get worth to gain a livelihood, or that with their labor can hardly get a comfortable subsistence, shall do well to go to this place, where any man whatever that is but willing to take moderate pains may be assured of a most comfortable subsistence, and be in a way to raise his fortunes far beyond what he could ever hope for in England. . . .

Therefore, all artificers, as carpenters, wheelwrights, joiners, coopers, bricklayers, smiths, or diligent husbandmen and laborers that are willing to advance their fortunes and live in a most pleasant healthful and fruitful country, where artificers are of high esteem and used with all civility and courtesy imaginable, may take notice. . . .

If any maid or single woman have a desire to go over, they will think themselves in the Golden Age, when men paid a dowry for their wives; for if they be but civil, and under fifty years of age, some honest man or other will purchase them for their wives.

1664 - 1676

Attempt by the King's Commissioners to regulate New England colonies resisted by Massachusetts, whose General Court refuses to send representatives to England to answer charges of violating English law. Edward Randolph, special agent for the Crown, arrives in Boston in 1676 to assert royal authority.

1665

March 11. Meeting of deputies in New York approves the Duke's Laws (after James, Duke of York, later James II of England). Laws provide for organization of courts and militia (not extended to predominantly Dutch areas) and freedom of conscience, but deny right to have an assembly, which the colony lacks until 1691.

Concessions and Agreements drawn up by proprietors of Carolina grant to colonists freedom of conscience, land distribution on generous terms, and an assembly of freeholders' representatives. Similar grant is made by proprietors of East Jersey in same year.

Ye Bare and Ye Cubb, first English play known to have been shown in the colonies, is performed by its authors, three Virginia amateurs. The three are charged with having "acted a play" but are acquitted.

1665 - 1694

1665. John Winthrop, Jr., makes first systematic astronomical observations in colonies. **1678.** Thomas Brattle publishes his *Almanack*, showing advanced knowledge of astronomy. **1680.** Brattle makes observations of comet that are used and acknowledged by Isaac Newton in *Principia mathematica* (1687). **1694.** Brattle writes account of solar eclipse.

1668 - 1686

Struggle between France and England for Hudson Bay. **1669.** To divert fur trade from the St. Lawrence, English trading posts are built on James Bay and Hudson Bay. **1686.** James Bay posts captured by French.

1669 - 1670

March 11, 1669. Fundamental Constitutions of Carolina drawn up; attributed to English philosopher John Locke 'in collaboration with Sir Anthony Ashley Cooper (afterward Earl of Shaftesbury), one of colony's proprietors. Enlightened in some aspects, plan of government is otherwise feudal, claiming that all power is founded on property and setting up an elaborate hierarchy of nobility. Religious freedom is granted, but revision of March 1, 1670, establishes the Church of England. Civil authority is vested in Palatine Court of proprietors in England; they appoint governor, disallow laws passed by assembly, and hear appeals. The Constitutions, never accepted by the assembly, are revised in 1682.

1670 - 1705

1670. Act of Virginia assembly formally declares "all servants not being Christian" brought in by sea to be slaves for life, status of children same as of mother. **1705.** Black Code restricts movement of slaves and forbids miscegenation with heavy penalties: the first colonial law to differentiate Negroes and whites on the basis of race as well as legal status.

1673

May 17. Father Jacques Marquette, Jesuit missionary, and Louis Jolliet, trader and explorer, start from Mackinac Straits, travel to the Mississippi River, and paddle down

Virginia Slave Laws, 1662–1669
Whereas *some doubts have arisen whether children got by any Englishman upon a Negro woman should be slave or free,* be it therefore enacted and declared . . . *that all children born in this country shall be held bond or free only according to the condition of the mother; and that if any Christian shall commit fornication with a Negro man or woman, he or she so offending shall pay double the fines imposed by the former act.*

Whereas *some doubts have arisen whether children that are slaves by birth, and by the charity and piety of their owners made partakers of the blessed sacrament of baptism, should by virtue of their baptism be made free,* it is enacted and declared . . . *that the conferring of baptism does not alter the condition of the person as to his bondage or freedom; that diverse masters, freed from this doubt may more carefully endeavor the propagation of Christianity by permitting children, though slaves, or those of greater growth if capable, to be admitted to that sacrament.*

Whereas *the only law in force for the punishment of refractory servants resisting their master, mistress, or overseer cannot be inflicted upon Negroes, nor the obstinacy of many of them be suppressed by other than violent means,* be it enacted and declared. . . *if any slave resists his master. . . and by the extremity of the correction should chance to die, that his death shall not be accounted a felony, but the master. . . be acquitted from molestation, since it cannot be presumed that premeditated malice* (which alone makes murder a felony) *should induce any man to destroy his own estate.*

SAMUEL SEWALL
Letter to Sir William Ashurst, 1700
I have met with an observation of some grave divines, that ordinarily when God intends good to a nation, He is pleased to make use of some of themselves to be instrumental in conveying of that good unto them. Now God has furnished several of the Indians with considerable abilities for the work of the ministry, and teaching school. And therefore I am apt to believe that if the Indians so qualified were more taken notice of in suitable rewards, it would conduce very much to the propagation of the Gospel among them. . . .

I should think it requisite that convenient tracts of land should be set out to them; and that by plain and natural boundaries, as much as may be—as lakes, rivers, mountains, rocks—upon which for any Englishman to encroach should be accounted a crime. Except this be done, I fear their own jealousies, and the French friars, will persuade them that the English, as they increase and think they want more room, will never leave till they have crowded them quite out of all their lands. And it will be a vain attempt for us to offer Heaven to them if they take up prejudices against us, as if we did grudge them a living upon their own earth.

the Mississippi as far as the Arkansas by July 17. Marquette is convinced that the Mississippi flows into Gulf of Mexico, not Pacific Ocean.

1673 - 1687

Struggle in New York for representative government, prohibited by Duke's Laws, which are reasserted after temporary Dutch reoccupation in 1673. **1673-1683.** Administration of Governor Sir Edmund Andros proves unpopular. **Aug. 28, 1683.** Andros' successor, Colonel Thomas Dongan, arrives in New York, calls assembly of delegates. **Oct. 30.** Assembly enacts Charter of Liberties, approved by Duke of York, but disallowed by him upon his accession to English throne as James II, February 6, 1685. **Jan. 1687.** Assembly is permanently dissolved.

1673 - 1729

Samuel Sewall, English-born Boston judge and man of affairs, writes his *Diary,* the fullest, best-known, and most humanly interesting of colonial diaries. First published 1878-1882, it omits the years 1677-1685.

1675 - 1676

June 20, 1675. Beginning of King Philip's War. Expansion of New England colonies leads to full-scale conflict with Indian tribes led by Philip, son of Massasoit, chief of the Wampanoags. **Aug. 28, 1676.** Last surrender of Indians. Indian power in New England has been broken at fearful cost to colonists and Indians in lives, devastation of settlements, and money. Philip has been run down and shot on August 12, and wife and child sold into West Indian slavery.

1675 - 1677

Bacon's Rebellion in Virginia. **1675.** Susquehannock Indians raid settlements in Virginia, are unrestrained because of Royal Governor Sir William Berkeley's private interest in the fur trade. **May 10, 1676.** Nathaniel Bacon leads uprising against autocratic rule of Berkeley in attempt to gain protection against Indians. **June 23.** Bacon's force occupies Jamestown, and other democratic reforms are sought and temporarily gained from the prominent planter interests. **Oct. 18.** Bacon dies suddenly and leaves rebellion leaderless. **Nov.-Dec.** Berkeley regains power, nullifies pardon of the rebels granted from England, and hangs 23 of them. Berkeley is characterized by Charles II as a "bloody old fool who has hanged more men . . . than I have done for the murder of my father." **April 27, 1677.** Colonel Herbert Jeffries, sent to restore order, takes over government.

1677 - 1679

Culpeper's Rebellion in Carolina. **Dec. 3, 1677.** Antiproprietary party headed by John Culpeper sets up revolutionary government in protest against arbitrary acts of proprietary governor, Thomas Miller. Miller is imprisoned, but escapes to England, where he appeals to the Privy Council. Culpeper defends rebels before proprietors, and influence of the Earl of Shaftesbury bring rebellion to end. Culpeper is tried for treason in England and acquitted.

c. 1680 - 1700

Edward Taylor, minister of Westfield, Massachusetts, writes his imaginative poems; his work is not discovered until 1937.

1681

March 4. William Penn (Quaker) receives charter for region he calls "Sylvania" from Charles II. Penn is made absolute proprietor subject to approval of laws by assembly,

Report to Investigating Commission, 1705
In these frightful times the most exposed small families withdrew into our houses of better numbers, which we fortified with palisades and redoubts. Neighbors in bodies joined their labors from each plantation to others alternately, taking their arms into the fields and setting sentinels. No man stirred out-of-doors unarmed. . . .

These at the heads of James and York rivers (having now most people destroyed by the Indians flight thither from Potomac) grew impatient at the many slaughters of their neighbors and rose for their own defense, who choosing Mr. Bacon for their leader, sent oftentimes to the Governor, humbly beseeching a commission to go against those Indians at their own charge; which His Honor as often promised, but did not send. . . . Most or all the officers, civil and military, with as many dwellers next the heads of the rivers as made up 300 men, taking Mr. Bacon for their commander, met and concerted together, the danger of going without a commission on the one part and the continual murders of their neighbors on the other part (not knowing whose or how many of their own turns might be next), and came to this resolution, viz., to prepare themselves with necessaries for a march, but interim to send again for a commission, which if could or could not be obtained by a certain day, they would proceed, commission or no commission.

This day lapsing and no commission come, they marched into the wilderness in quest of these Indians, after whom the Governor sent his proclamation, denouncing all rebels who should not return within a limited day; whereupon those of estates obeyed. But Mr. Bacon, with fifty-seven men, proceeded.

WILLIAM PENN
Frame of Government of Pennsylvania, 1682

But, lastly, when all is said, there is hardly one frame of government in the world so ill designed by its first founders that, in good hands, would not do well enough; and story tells us the best, in ill ones, can do nothing that is great or good. . . .

I know some say let us have good laws, and no matter for the men that execute them; but let them consider that though good laws do well, good men do better; for good laws may want good men, and be abolished or evaded by ill men; but good men will never want good laws, nor suffer ill ones.

Mennonite Resolution, 1683

These are the reasons why we are against the traffic of mens-body as follows: Is there any that would be done or handled at this manner, viz., to be sold or made a slave for all the time of his life?. . . Now, though they are black, we cannot conceive there is more liberty to have them slaves as it is to have other white ones. There is a saying that we shall do to all men like as we will be done ourselves, making no difference of what generation, descent, or color they are. And those who steal or rob men, and those who buy or purchase them, are they not all alike? Here is liberty of conscience, which is right and reasonable. Here ought to be likewise liberty of the body, except of evildoers, which is another case. But to bring men hither, or to rob and sell them against their will, we stand against. . . .

Pray! What thing in the world can be done worse toward us than if men should rob or steal us away and sell us for slaves to strange countries, separating husbands from their wives and children.

right of veto by Privy Council, right of judicial appeal reserved to the Crown, and right of Crown to impose taxes "by act of Parliament." Thomas Holme, Penn's surveyor general, lays out site of Philadelphia early in following year.

1682

April 9. René Robert Cavelier, Sieur de la Salle, having traveled from Illinois River to mouth of the Mississippi, claims entire region of Mississippi Valley for King of France, names it Louisiana.

May 5. Frame of Government drawn up by William Penn for Pennsylvania (name has been changed by king in honor of Penn's father). "Liberty of conscience" is established, as well as enlightened penal code. Frame provides for a governor (Penn or his deputy) and a council to initiate and enforce laws to be ratified or rejected by assembly. Assembly is granted right of initiation in 1696. **Oct. 27.** Penn arrives from England, almost immediately makes treaty with Delaware Indians and pays for land.

The Sovereignty and Goodness of God: The Narrative of the Captivity and Restoration of Mrs. Mary Rowlandson is published. It is the most widely read of Indian captivity stories by a victim of King Philip's War (1676) who had eventually been ransomed from her captors. Many editions published later under book's subtitle.

1683

Mennonites, led by Francis Daniel Pastorius, settle at Germantown, Pennsylvania. Sect is noted for pacifism and antislavery principles; they make formal protest against slavery in the colonies by resolution at Germantown, 1688. Amish are a conservative branch of the sect, retaining exclusively German language.

1683 - 1690

Rejection by Berkeley County (Charleston) of the 1682 revised Fundamental Constitutions of Carolina leads to dissolution of assembly in 1685 and subsequent uprising of antiproprietary party in 1690.

1684

June 21. Charter of Massachusetts Bay Colony is annulled by Court of Chancery for failure to support Navigation Acts, execution of British subjects for religious dissent, denying right of appeal to Privy Council, and refusing the oath of allegiance. Many attempts are made to have charter restored, but it is replaced in 1691 by a royal charter that places Maine and Plymouth within Massachusetts. Massachusetts Bay Colony contends that abrogation of its original charter was illegal and continues to operate under old charter until 1718.

1685 - 1689

James II forms Dominion of New England to include New York, New Jersey, and Pennsylvania. Centralized colonial administration is presided over by Governor Sir Edmund Andros, who becomes increasingly unpopular because of his arbitrary rulings. **1689.** Rebellions in Massachusetts and New York bring Andros' regime to an end.

1685 - 1695

Revolution in Maryland. **1685-1688.** Coincident with English rebellion against Catholic James II, antiproprietary movement becomes Protestant-Catholic conflict. Protestants protest nepotism, neglect, and restriction of their rights. **May 1689.** Uprising, after accession of William and Mary to throne, overthrows Catholic governor claiming divine right. **Aug.** Victorious Protestant Association petitions crown to take over

EDWARD RAWSON(?)
The Revolution in New-England, 1691
*Sir Edmund Andros, then governor . . .
was pleased to tell me he would
have my judgment about this question
— Whether all the lands in New England
were not the King's?. . .*

*I then said I did not understand that
the lands of New England were the
King's, but the King's subjects', who
had for more than sixty years had the
possession and use of them by a twofold right, warranted by the word of
God: (1) By a right of just occupation
from the grand charter in Genesis, first
and ninth chapters, whereby God gave
the earth to the sons of Adam and
Noah, to be subdued and replenished;
(2) By a right of purchase from the Indians, who were native inhabitants and
had possession of the land before the
English came hither. . . .*

*I told them that so far as I understood,
we received only the right and power of
government from the King's charter
within such limits and bounds. . . . I
told them I had heard it was a standing
principle in law and reason, nil dat qui
non habet [he gives nought that owns
not]; and from thence I propounded
this argument — He that has no right
can give no right to another, but the
King had no right to the lands of America before the English came hither,
therefore he could give no right to
them. . . .*

*And, at last, Sir Edmund Andros said
with indignation, "Either you are subjects or you are rebels," intimating, as I
understood him, according to the whole
scope and tendency of his speeches and
actions, that if we would not yield all
the lands of New England to be the
King's, so as to take patents for lands
and to pay rent for the same, then we
should not be accounted subjects but
rebels and treated accordingly.*

Maryland Toleration Act, 1649

And be it also further enacted . . . *that whatsoever person or persons shall from henceforth upon any occasion of offense or otherwise in a reproachful manner or way declare, call, or denominate any person or persons whatsoever inhabiting, residing, trading, or commercing within this province or within any of the ports, harbors, creeks, or havens to the same belonging, a heretic, schismatic, idolator, Puritan, independent, Presbyterian, popish priest, Jesuit, Jesuited papist, Lutheran, Calvinist, Anabaptist, Brownist, Antinomian, Barrowist, Roundhead, Separatist, or any other name or term in a reproachful manner relating to matter of religion, shall for every such offense forfeit and lose the sum of 10s. or the value thereof to be levied on the goods and chattels of every such offender and offenders. . . .*

And whereas *the enforcing of the conscience in matters of religion has frequently fallen out to be of dangerous consequence in those commonwealths where it has been practised, and for the more quiet and peaceable government of this province, and the better to preserve mutual love and amity among the inhabitants thereof, be it, therefore . . . ordained and enacted . . . that no person or persons whatsoever within this province . . . professing to believe in Jesus Christ, shall from henceforth be in any way troubled, molested, or discountenanced for or in respect of his or her religion, nor in the free exercise thereof . . . nor in any way compelled to the belief or exercise of any other religion against his or her consent.*

colony. **1692.** Maryland is made a royal province, though Lord Baltimore, a Catholic, retains property rights. **1694.** Provincial capital is moved from Catholic St. Mary's to Protestant Annapolis.

1685 - 1697

English Revolution produces various colonial struggles and upheavals. Accession of William and Mary in 1689 after abdication of James II restores peace in the colonies, but imperial reorganization proceeds. Proprietorships are transformed into royal provinces and Vice-Admiralty Courts are established to enforce Navigation Acts.

1689

Declaration of Rights passed by Parliament and accepted by William III forbids king to suspend any Parliamentary act, gives Parliament the sole right to raise taxes, and guarantees protection of the laws to every British subject. These guarantees are the basis of later colonial claims.

1689 - 1691

Leisler's Rebellion in New York. **June 12, 1689.** Jacob Leisler, German-born trader, having seized Fort James, is left in charge of New York when royal governor flees upon hearing news of overthrow of Andros in Boston. Leisler proclaims William and Mary on June 22. **July 27-Aug. 15.** Leisler holds first assembly. **Feb. 8-March 29, 1691.** He refuses to turn over control of the government to new governor appointed by Lords of Trade until he is forced to surrender. **May.** Charged with treason, he is tried and hanged, though all but one of his lieutenants are acquitted.

1689 - 1697

King William's War, American phase of

War of the League of Augsburg in Europe (1688-1697), leads to Anglo-French conflict on Hudson Bay and Iroquois-French war in Mohawk Valley and along the St. Lawrence River. New England settlements are devastated by French and allied Indians. **1690.** Port Royal, Nova Scotia, is captured by Massachusetts troops under Sir William Phips; recaptured in 1691. Colonial conflict, first of six Anglo-French wars between 1689 and 1815 challenging or altering balance of power in the New World, is indecisive.

1690

Benjamin Harris publishes his *New England Primer*, which sells an estimated 6 to 8 million copies over 150 years; it is the only textbook used in colonial grade schools for 50 years after publication. Besides illustrated ABC, book contains moral texts.

1692

Massachusetts act reviving compulsory education laws is disallowed. New system empowers town selectmen to bind out poor children as apprentices. Quality of education remains poor until after the Revolution.

1692 - 1693

Massachusetts witchcraft trials, in which 150 "witches" and "wizards" are charged with having been possessed by the devil, result in execution of 19 men and women. Trials are encouraged, but with some reservations about procedures, by Cotton Mather, last of a distinguished dynasty, who later (1702) agrees with those who assert the innocence of the condemned.

1693

William and Mary, Anglican college, founded in Virginia.

COTTON MATHER

Wonders of the Invisible World, 1693

Yea, more than twenty-one have confessed that they have signed unto a book, which the devil showed them, and engaged in his hellish design of bewitching and ruining our land. . . .

Now, by these confessions it is agreed that the devil has made a dreadful knot of witches in the country, and by the help of witches has dreadfully increased that knot . . . yea, that at prodigious witch meetings the wretches have proceeded so far as to concert and consult the methods of rooting out the Christian religion from this country, and setting up instead of it perhaps a more gross diabolism than ever the world saw before.

INCREASE MATHER

Concerning Evil Spirits, 1693

Let me premise this also, that there have been ways of trying witches long used in many nations, especially in the dark times of paganism and popery, which the righteous God never approved of, but which . . . were invented by the devil, that so innocent persons might be condemned and some notorious witches escape. . . .

It is a tempting of God when men put the innocency of their fellow creatures upon such trials; to desire the Almighty to show a miracle to clear the innocent or to convict the guilty is a most presumptuous tempting of Him. . . .

It is proof enough that such a one has that conversation and correspondence with the devil as that he or she, whoever they be, ought to be exterminated from among men. This notwithstanding I will add: It were better that ten suspected witches should escape than that one innocent person should be condemned.

A South-West View of the CITY of NEW YORK in North America.

(Above) An early 18th century view of New York City; (below left)
King Philip, chief of the Wampanoags; (below right) Sir William
Berkeley, portrait by an unknown artist

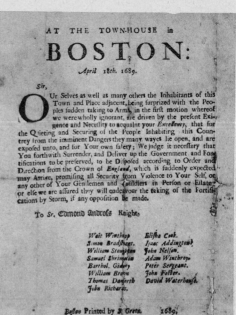

AT THE TOWN-HOUSE in

BOSTON:

April 18th. 1689.

Sir,

OUr Selves as well as many others the Inhabitants of this Town and Place adjacent, being surprized with the Peoples sudden taking to Arms, in the first motion whereof we were wholly ignorant, are driven by the present Exigence and Necessity to acquaint your *Excellency*, that for the Quieting and Securing of the People Inhabiting this Countrey from the imminent Dangers they many wayes lie open, and are exposed unto, and for Your own safety; We judge it necessary that You forthwith Surrender, and Deliver up the Government and Fortifications to be preserved, to be Disposed according to Order and Direction from the Crown of *England*, which is suddenly expected may Arrive, promising all Security from Violence to Your Self, or any other of Your Gentlemen and Souldiers in Person or Estate: or else we are assured they will endeavour the taking of the Fortifications by Storm, if any opposition be made.

To Sr. *Edmond Andross* Knight.

Wait Winthrop.	*Elisha Cook.*
Simon Bradstreet.	*Isaac Addington.*
William Stoughton	*John Nelson.*
Samuel Shrimpton	*Adam Winthrop.*
Barthol. Gidney	*Peter Sergeant.*
William Brown	*John Foster.*
Thomas Danforth	*David Waterhouse.*
John Richards.	

Boston Printed by *S. Green.* 1689.

(Above left) Increase Mather, portrait by John Vanderspriet, 1688; (above right) broadside warning Governor Andros to surrender, 1689; (below right) Sir Edmund Andros, portrait by F. S. Batcheler; (below left) title page from "An accurate description of the recently founded province of Pennsylvania" by F. D. Pastorius, who established the first German settlement in the colonies, 1700

Umständige Geographische

Beschreibung

Der zu allerletzt erfundenen Provintz

PENSYLVA-

NIÆ,

In denen End-Gräntzen

AMERICÆ

In der West-Welt gelegen/

Durch

FRANCISCUM DANIELEM

PASTORIUM,

J.V. Lic. und Friedens-Richtern daselbsten.

Worbey angehencket sind einige notable Begebenheiten / und Bericht-Schreiben an dessen Herrn Vattern

MELCHIOREM ADAMUM PASTO-

RIUM,

Und andere gute Freunde.

Franckfurt und Leipzig/

Zufinden bey Andreas Otto. 1700.

FRANCIS HIGGINSON
New England's Plantation, 1630
This country abounds naturally with store of roots of great variety and good to eat. Our turnips, parsnips, and carrots are here both bigger and sweeter than is ordinarily to be found in England. Here are also store of pumpkins, cucumbers, and other things of that nature which I know not. . . .

For beasts there are some bears, and they say some lions also, for they have been seen at Cape Anne. Also, here are several sorts of deer, some whereof bring three or four young ones at once, which is not ordinary in England. Also, wolves, foxes, beavers, otters, martens, great wildcats, and a great beast called a molke [moose] as big as an ox. I have seen the skins of all these beasts since I came to this plantation, excepting lions. Also here are great store of squirrels, some greater and some smaller and lesser; there are some of the lesser sort, they tell me, that by a certain skin will fly from tree to tree though they stand far distant. . . .

There is a fish called a bass, a most sweet and wholesome fish as ever I did eat. . . .

The temper of the air of New England is one special thing that commends this place. Experience does manifest that there is hardly a more healthful place to be found in the world that agrees better with our English bodies. . . . For here is an extraordinary clear and dry air that is of a most healing nature to all such as are of a cold, melancholy, phlegmatic, rheumatic temper of body. . . .

And, therefore, I think it is a wise course for all cold complexions to come to take physic in New England, for a sup of New England's air is better than a whole draft of old England's ale.

1693 - 1725

1693. First systematic natural history paper (on plants of Virginia) written in the colonies, the work of John Banister. Among later colonial writings in this field are Cotton Mather's 13 letters on natural history and biology in 1712 and a work on fruit trees by Paul Dudley, the first colonial horticulturalist, in 1724. Dudley's *Natural History of Whales*, published in 1725, becomes a standard work.

1693 - 1758

Church of England established by law in New York (1693), Maryland (1702), South Carolina (1706), North Carolina (1711), and Georgia (1758). Anglicanism is introduced without becoming official faith in Massachusetts (1686), Pennsylvania (1694), New Jersey (1702), and Connecticut (1706). Church lacks influence in colonial period because dissenters and colonial authorities refuse to accept a resident bishop. Since ordination cannot be administered, there is little growth of a native ministry.

1699

Wool Act passed to protect English wool industry; it prohibits intercolonial as well as overseas export of wool products from all American colonies.

Jonathan Dickinson, Quaker merchant, writes widely read account of his captivity among Florida Indians. He later becomes chief justice of Pennsylvania.

1699 - 1702

1699. French settlements established at Biloxi, Mississippi, and in present Louisiana. **1700-1701.** Forts built at Detroit and Mackinac to guard route to this area and to secure French control of fur trade in the Illinois country; other French forts and settlements and missions are established in lower Mississippi Valley and Illinois regions.

1700 - 1750

Among architectural developments are English baroque — brick, stone, or wooden houses with double-hung windows and pilastered central doorways; also Georgian, characterized by rectangular plan, dormer windows, and chimneys at each end of a central hall. Public buildings of note are Williamsburg (Virginia) College of William and Mary (1695-1702), designed from drawings supplied by London architect Christopher Wren; the capitol at Williamsburg (1701-1705); the Old State House, Boston (1713-1728); and Independence Hall, Philadelphia (1732-1741), designed by Andrew Hamilton.

1701

Thomas Bray, Maryland commissary for the Bishop of London, founds the Venerable Society for the Propagation of the Gospel in Foreign Parts. Organization engages in missionary activities and founds churches throughout the colonies. To assist poor clergy, Bray later establishes parochial libraries.

Nov. 8. Charter of Privileges granted by William Penn to Pennsylvania in effect ends proprietary rule except in the appointment of a governor empowered to enact laws with consent of assembly. Charter remains the constitution of Pennsylvania until the Revolution. Congregational college founded in Connecticut; located in New Haven in 1716; named Yale College after its benefactor, Elihu Yale, in 1718.

1702

Cotton Mather publishes his *Magnalia*

WILLIAM PENN
Plan of Union for the Colonies, 1697
That the several colonies before mentioned do meet once a year, and oftener if need be during the war, and at least once in two years in times of peace, by their stated and appointed deputies, to debate and resolve of such measures as are most advisable for their better understanding and the public tranquillity and safety. . . .

That the King's commissioner, for that purpose specially appointed, shall have the chair and preside in the said congress. . . .

That their business shall be to hear and adjust all matters of complaint or difference between province and province. As, (1) where persons quit their own province and go to another that they may avoid their just debts, though they be able to pay them; (2) where offenders fly justice or justice cannot well be had upon such offenders in the provinces that entertain them; (3) to prevent or cure injuries in point of commerce; (4) to consider the ways and means to support the union and safety of these provinces against the public enemies. In which congress the quotas of men and charges will be much easier and more equally set than it is possible for any establishment made here to do; for the provinces, knowing their own condition and one another's, can debate that matter with more freedom and satisfaction, and better adjust and balance their affairs in all respects for their common safety.

COTTON MATHER
A Christian at His Calling, 1701

A Christian should be able to give this account, that he hath an occupation . . . that so he may glorify God by doing of good for others and getting of good for himself. . . . 'Tis not honest nor Christian that a Christian should have no business to do. . . .

A Christian should follow his occupation with industry. *. . . It seems a man slothful in business is not a man serving the Lord. . . . A diligent man is very rarely an indigent man. Would a man rise by his business? I say, then, let him rise to his business. . . .*

A Christian should follow his occupation with discretion. *. . . It is a dishonor to the profession of religion if there be no discretion expressed in the affairs of its professors. . . .*

'Tis a sin, I say, 'tis ordinarily a sin, and it will at length be a shame, for a man to spend more than he gets, or make his layings out more than his comings in. . . .

A Christian should follow his occupation with honesty. *. . . Truly, justice, justice must be exactly followed in that calling by which we go to get our living. . . .*

Well, then, don't conceal from any customer that which you ought in equity or charity to acquaint him withal; and, more especially, if your customer do rely upon your sincerity. Don't exceed the truth, either in commendations or disparagements of commodities. Don't assert anything that is contrary to truth about the kind or the use or the price of them. . . .

A Christian should with piety *follow his occupation. . . . Oh, let every Christian walk with God when he works at his calling; and act in his occupation with an eye to God, act as under the eye of God.*

Christi Americana, or *The Ecclesiastical History of New England, 1620-1698;* the most ambitious of Puritan histories, it is written in praise of New England church government at a time when its power is declining.

1702 - 1713

Queen Anne's War, American phase of the War of the Spanish Succession, follows pattern of King William's War. Treaty of Utrecht (1713) fatally undermines French power in North America. England gains strategic control of Canada with possession of Hudson Bay as well as Newfoundland and Nova Scotia at the entrance to the St. Lawrence; France retains Cape Breton Island and the St. Lawrence islands. England also acquires the *asiento,* Spanish trading concession (especially slaves) granted first to the French, who are prohibited from any share in Spanish-American commerce.

1703 - 1704

Earliest known use of church organ in colonies, at the Swedish church in Philadelphia. First colonial organ is made by Dr. Thomas Witt of Philadelphia in 1704.

1704

Sarah Kemble Knight writes her *Journal* describing her journey from Boston to New York at a time when unattended travel by a woman over such distances is unheard of; published in 1825.

1704 - 1733

John Campbell begins publishing the *Boston News-Letter,* first continuous colonial newspaper; discontinued 1766. Among other colonial papers are Samuel Keimer's *Universal Instructor . . . and Pennsylvania Gazette* (1728), bought by Benjamin Franklin in 1729 and continued as *Pennsylvania Gazette;* and *New-York Weekly Journal*

(1733), edited by John Peter Zenger.

1705

Virginia Act providing for book education as distinct from apprenticeships passed. In the South the apprentice system prevails generally, though pauper schools are established. The wealthy are educated by private tutors or in private schools.

List of products to be shipped only to English ports (enumerated articles) expanded to include rice, molasses, and naval stores; trade in naval stores is encouraged by English bounties until the Revolution.

Robert Beverley publishes *The History and Present State of Virginia*, an account of provincial Virginia.

1706

Presbyterians organized at Philadelphia; they adopt constitution of the church (Adoption Act), 1729; sect expands through founding of church schools.

1708

James Logan introduces Isaac Newton's *Principia mathematica* to America. Newton's work is further explained in Cotton Mather's *Christian Philosopher* (1721).

1711 - 1713

Tuscarora War. Indians massacre 200 settlers in North Carolina, are then defeated by colonists from Virginia and North and South Carolina. Remnants of Tuscaroras move north to New York and join the Iroquois Confederation which becomes the "Six Nations."

1712 - 1741

Various Negro uprisings in New York

ROBERT BEVERLEY
History and Present State of Virginia, 1705
I can easily imagine with Sir Josiah Child, that this, as well as all the rest of the plantations, was for the most part at first peopled by persons of low circumstances, and by such as were willing to seek their fortunes in a foreign country. . . .

Those that went over to that country first were chiefly single men, who had not the encumbrance of wives and children in England. . . . From hence it came to pass that, when they were settled there in a comfortable way of subsisting a family, they grew sensible of the misfortune of wanting wives, and such as had left wives in England sent for them; but the single men were put to their shifts. . . .

Under this difficulty they had no hopes but that the plenty in which they lived might invite modest women of small fortunes to go over thither from England. However, they would not receive any but such as could carry sufficient certificate of their modesty and good behavior. Those, if they were but moderately qualified in all other respects, might depend upon marrying very well in those days, without any fortune. Nay, the first planters were so far from expecting money with a woman that 'twas a common thing for them to buy a deserving wife at the price of £100 and make themselves believe they had a hopeful bargain.

JOHN WISE
A Vindication . . . , 1717
For certainly, if Christ has settled any form of power in His church, He has done it for His church's safety and for the benefit of every member. Then He must needs be presumed to have made choice of that government as should least expose His people to hazard, either from the fraud or arbitrary measures of particular men. And it is as plain as daylight, there is no species of government like a democracy to attain this end. . . .

In the last century, God has been very admirable in the works of Providence, and has therein highly dignified our constitution. And we want no other evidence . . . than the recognition of what God has done for these famous English colonies in North America, who have all along distinguished themselves from all the world by their singular regard, both to the faith and practice of the true religion. Now, let any other constitution on earth but parallel ours in the eminent shines of Providence and in religious effects and we will resign the whole cause. But [until] then, we will go on and rejoice in the Grace of God that we, in these countries, are by His good Providence over us the subjects of the most ancient, rational, and noble constitution in church order that ever was, will be, or can be, while the laws of nature and grace remain unrepealed. For that it is a constitution which infinite wisdom has authorized and founded in the law of nature, and His omnificent Providence has eminently honored and dignified, both by the smiles and frowns of His countenance, through all the ages of the Christian world, to this very morning.

City and South Carolina result in multiple executions and fatalities. Over 100 Negroes are executed in this interval — 21 in New York in 1712 and 50 in Charleston in 1740 — while 18 Negroes and four whites are hanged and 13 Negroes are burned alive after a burglary followed by a series of fires that had spread panic through New York in 1741.

1715 - 1728

The Yamassee War. Conflict with Indians along the Carolina frontier drives Indians beyond colonial outposts at Columbia and Port Royal (South Carolina). Anglo-Spanish War (1727-1728) provides excuse for gratuitous raid by Carolinians on Yamassee village deep in Spanish Florida, near St. Augustine.

1716

First theater known to have existed in the colonies is built at Williamsburg, Virginia; it is foreclosed 1723.

1717

In his pamphlet, *A Vindication of the Government of New-England Churches*, John Wise, minister at Ipswich, Massachusetts, defends existing and relatively democratic Congregational order of New England churches against Presbyterian (centralized) form advocated by Increase and Cotton Mather.

1718 - 1729

Nov. 1718. New Orleans, Louisiana, is founded by Jean Baptiste le Moyne, Sieur de Bienville. **1719-1726.** French forts and settlements spring up in the Mississippi Valley and French Canadians move to the Illinois country. **1729.** Indian attacks force eventual confinement of French settlement to the region of present-day Louisiana.

1719 - 1729

Colonists overthrow proprietary government in South Carolina (separated from North Carolina in 1691) for, among other things, failure to guard against Spanish encroachments from Florida. **1719.** Royal rule is established. **1729.** North and South Carolina surrender their charters, formally becoming royal colonies. Period of royal control (1719-1776) is marked by increased export of rice, skins, and indigo, and is era of prosperity.

1721

Dr. Zabdiel Boylston of Massachusetts makes first inoculations against smallpox prior to general acceptance in Europe. Boylston's inoculations are given at the instigation of Cotton Mather, whose papers of 1714-1716 had contained reports of the practice published in the Royal Society of London's *Philosophical Transactions.*

First professorship in theology created, Hollis Chair in Divinity at Harvard College.

1726 - 1756

"The Great Awakening," a series of religious revivals, sweeps the country from New England to the southern colonies, encouraged by itinerant preachers. **1734.** Sermons of Jonathan Edwards, minister at Northampton, Massachusetts, lead New England movement. **1738.** English evangelist George Whitefield acquires many followers in Georgia; later tours the country from Maine to Georgia. **1748-1749.** Movement reaches a peak in Virginia under Rev. Samuel Davies. All Protestant sects are affected; various conflicts and schisms arise. Stressing the sudden illumination of grace as the condition of conversion, movement is resisted for different reasons by both conservatives ("Old Side") and liberal ("New Side")

JONATHAN EDWARDS
Sinners in the Hands of an Angry God, 1741
The God that holds you over the pit of hell, much as one holds a spider or some loathsome insect over the fire, abhors you, and is dreadfully provoked. His wrath toward you burns like fire; He looks upon you as worthy of nothing else but to be cast into the fire; He is of purer eyes than to bear to have you in His sight; you are ten thousand times so abominable in His eyes as the most hateful and venomous serpent is in ours. You have offended Him infinitely more than ever a stubborn rebel did his prince; and yet it is nothing but His hand that holds you from falling into the fire every moment. It is ascribed to nothing else that you did not go to hell the last night; that you were suffered to awake again in this world after you closed your eyes to sleep; and there is no other reason to be given why you have not dropped into hell since you arose in the morning, but that God's hand has held you up. There is no other reason to be given why you have not gone to hell, since you have sat here in the house of God, provoking His pure eyes by your sinful, wicked manner of attending His solemn worship; yea, there is nothing else that is to be given as a reason why you do not this very moment drop down into hell.

CANASSATEEGO
Address to Pennsylvania Government,
1742
*Brethren, we received from the Propri-
etors yesterday some goods in consideration of our release of the lands on the
west side of Susquehanna. It is true, we
have the full quantity according to
agreement; but if the Proprietor had
been here himself, we think, in regard
of our numbers and poverty, he would
have made an addition to them. If the
goods were only to be divided among
the Indians present, a single person
would have but a small portion; but if
you consider what numbers are left behind, equally entitled with us to a share,
there will be extremely little. . . .*

*We know our lands are now become
more valuable. The white people think
we do not know their value; but we are
sensible that the land is everlasting, and
the few goods we receive for it are soon
worn out and gone. . . . Besides, we
are not well used with respect to the
lands still unsold by us. Your people
daily settle on these lands, and spoil
our hunting. We must insist on your
removing them. . . .*

*It is customary with us to make a
present of skins whenever we renew
our treaties. We are ashamed to offer
our brethren so few, but your horses
and cows have eaten the grass our deer
used to feed on. This has made them
scarce, and will, we hope, plead in
excuse for our not bringing a larger
quantity. If we could have spared more,
we would have given more; but we are
really poor; and desire you'll not consider the quantity, but, few as they are,
accept them in testimony of our regard.*

spokesmen; among the latter is Charles
Chauncy, rationalist Boston minister whose
distrust of revelation lays foundation of later
Unitarianism.

1727

Endowment of a chair in mathematics
and natural history at Harvard, filled first
by Isaac Greenwood, who offers a course in
fluxions (calculus).

1727 - 1747

Cadwallader Colden, scientist and lieutenant governor of New York, writes *The History of the Five Indian Nations;* this account
of the Iroquois tribes is an important colonial work on the Indian.

1728

John Bartram establishes first botanical
garden in colonies at Philadelphia; it is
stocked with rare plants gathered on extensive travels through colonies and sent to
him from abroad.

William Byrd II of Westover, Virginia,
writes *History of the Dividing Line Run in
the Year 1728*, an account of the exploration and survey of the Virginia-North Carolina boundary. Among Byrd's other works
are *Journey to the Land of Eden* (a term used
sarcastically of the backwoods, whose slov-
enly inhabitants are mercilessly and wittily
described), and an uninhibited diary written
in shorthand, only part of which has ever
been deciphered and published.

1730

Benjamin Franklin publishes *Tunes in
Praise and Love of God (Gottliche Lieben und
Lobes Gethöne)*, hymns of the German Baptists (Dunkards) in Pennsylvania. At a time
when most hymns are sung in simple uni-
son, these have up to seven-part harmony;

most are the work of J. C. Beissel.

John Smibert holds first colonial art exhibition at Boston. His realistic style of portrait painting makes the earlier limners obsolete and influences the work of Robert Feke and John Singleton Copley.

1730 - 1735

Development of navigation and surveying instruments. **1730.** Thomas Godfrey, Philadelphia mathematician, invents a more precise type of mariner's quadrant than that commonly in use. **1735.** Theodolite (transit), a device for measuring horizontal angles, is improved by Roland Houghton of Massachusetts.

1730 - 1740

Development of the Long, or Pennsylvania, rifle, known later as the Kentucky rifle. Gun introduced by German immigrants in 1710-1720 is improved by Pennsylvania gunsmiths by lengthening bore, refining rifling, and adding grease patch for lubrication.

1731 - 1759

Dec. 1731. First known colonial public concert, at Boston in a private house. **1732.** Similar concert in Charleston, South Carolina. **1732-1736.** First European musician to perform in colonies (Boston and New York) is C. T. Pachelbel, harpsichordist. **1735.** First operatic performance, *Flora, or Hob in the Well*, ballad opera, at Charleston, South Carolina. **1744.** Moravians found music school at Bethlehem, Pennsylvania, perform Handel oratorios. **1750.** *The Beggar's Opera* given in New York. **1759.** Francis Hopkinson of Philadelphia writes music for first secular song by a native of the colonies, "My Days Have Been So Wondrous Free," Thomas Parnell's poem. Hopkinson is later a signer of the Declara-

WILLIAM BYRD
History of the Dividing Line, 1728
April 7. I'm sorry I can't give a better account of the state of the poor Indians with respect to Christianity, although a great deal of pains has been and still continues to be taken with them. For my part, I must be of opinion, as I hinted before, that there is but one way of converting these poor infidels and reclaiming them from barbarity, and that is, charitably to intermarry with them, according to the modern policy of the most Christian king in Canada and Louisiana. Had the English done this at the first settlement of the colony, the infidelity of the Indians had been worn out at this day, with their dark complexions, and the country had swarmed with people more than it does with insects.

It was certainly an unreasonable nicety that prevented their entering into so good-natured an alliance. All nations of men have the same natural dignity, and we all know that very bright talents may be lodged under a very dark skin. The principal difference between one people and another proceeds only from the different opportunities of improvement. The Indians by no means want understanding, and are in their figure tall and well proportioned. Even their copper-colored complexion would admit of blanching if not in the first, at the farthest in the second generation. I may safely venture to say, the Indian women would have made altogether as honest wives for the first planters as the damsels they used to purchase from aboard the ships. It is strange, therefore, that any good Christian should have refused a wholesome, straight bedfellow, when he might have had so fair a portion with her as the merit of saving her soul.

BENJAMIN FRANKLIN
Advice to a Young Tradesman, 1748
*Remember, that time is money. He that
can earn ten shillings a day by his labor,
and goes abroad, or sits idle, one-half of
that day, though he spends but sixpence
during his diversion or idleness, ought
not to reckon that the only expense; he
has really spent. or rather thrown away,
five shillings besides.*

*Remember, that credit is money. If a
man lets his money lie in my hands after
it is due, he gives me the interest, or so
much as I can make of it during that
time. . . .*

*Remember, that money is of the
prolific, generating nature. Money can
beget money, and its offspring can beget more, and so on. Five shillings
turned is six, turned again it is seven
and threepence, and so on till it becomes a hundred pounds. . . .*

*The most trifling actions that affect a
man's credit are to be regarded. The
sound of your hammer at five in the
morning or nine at night, heard by a
creditor, makes him easy six months
longer; but if he sees you at a billiard
table, or hears your voice at a tavern
when you should be at work, he sends
for his money the next day; demands it,
before he can receive it, in a lump. . . .*

*In short, the way to wealth, if you
desire it, is as plain as the way to market. It depends chiefly on two words,
"industry" and "frugality"; that is,
waste neither time nor money, but
make the best use of both. . . . He
that gets all he can honestly and saves
all he gets (necessary expenses excepted)
will certainly become rich, if that Being who governs the world, to whom all
should look for a blessing on their honest
endeavors, does not, in His wise providence, otherwise determine.*

tion of Independence.

1732

Hat Act, like Wool Act, protects English
industry; prohibits intercolonial export of
hats and restricts number of persons allowed to enter the felt trade in the colonies.
Act is only sketchily enforced.

Benjamin Franklin writes and publishes
first issue of *Poor Richard's Almanack*, signing it "Richard Saunders." Almanac is published annually until 1757.

1733

Molasses Act, designed to protect British
West Indian producers, lays a prohibitive
duty on rum, molasses, and sugar imported
from the foreign West Indies to mainland
colonies. Act cannot be enforced.

Georgia, originally part of South Carolina
and the last of the 13 English colonies on
the continent, founded by James Oglethorpe and others as a haven for imprisoned
debtors and a barrier against Spanish power
in Florida. Charter grants freedom of conscience to Protestants, prohibits slaves and
rum at first, and limits size of landholdings.
Georgia becomes Crown colony in 1753.

1734 - 1752

Small farmers in western North Carolina
withhold quitrents (rent substitutes) in protest against neglect by the tidewater government and discriminatory legislation enacted
by it. Similar east-west conflicts develop in
South Carolina, Pennsylvania, and New
Jersey.

1735

Trial of John Peter Zenger, a New York
City printer and publisher, for libel charged
to his newspaper, the *New-York Weekly*

Journal. Zenger is acquitted when his defense attorney, Andrew Hamilton of Philadelphia, is able to establish the basic doctrine underlying freedom of the press, that truth is an absolute defense in libel cases.

1739

Papers on sunspots written by John Winthrop IV, who later reports on a transit of Venus, an eclipse of the moon, Halley's comet, and other important astronomical observations.

1741

Attempt by debtor farmers of Massachusetts to establish a land bank for issuance of paper money opposed by Royal Governor Jonathan Belcher and his conservative supporters and outlawed by Act of Parliament.

No Cross, No Crown by William Penn, written in 1669 during his imprisonment in London, explains Quaker beliefs and practices. Published posthumously, it is widely read in the colonies.

1742

Benjamin Franklin invents the Franklin Stove, or Pennsylvania Fireplace; arrangement of flues allows twice as much heat using one-quarter the fuel of existing stoves.

1744

Dr. Alexander Hamilton publishes *Itinerarium*, readable and informative account of his journey from Annapolis, Maryland, to Portsmouth, New Hampshire.

1745 - 1753

Virginia settlers move into Ohio country on land granted to the Ohio Company and the Loyal Company (1749); Pennsylvania traders also travel to the region. French oc-

JAMES ALEXANDER
Narrative of the . . . Trial of John Peter Zenger, 1736

Mr. Chief Justice. *Mr. Hamilton, the Court is of opinion you ought not to be permitted to prove the facts in the papers. These are the words of the book, "It is far from being a justification of a libel that the contents thereof are true, or that the person upon whom it is made had a bad reputation, since the greater appearance there is of truth in any malicious invective, so much the more provoking it is."* . . .

Mr. Hamilton. *I beg leave to insist that the right of complaining or remonstrating is natural; and the restraint upon this natural right is the law only, and those restraints can only extend to what is false; for as it is truth alone which can excuse or justify any man for complaining of a bad administration, I as frankly agree that nothing ought to excuse a man who raises a false charge or accusation, even against a private person, and that no manner of allowance ought to be made to him who does so against a public magistrate. Truth ought to govern the whole affair of libels.* . . .

It is agreed upon by all men that this is a reign of liberty, and while men keep within the bounds of truth, I hope they may with safety both speak and write their sentiments of the conduct of men in power. I mean of that part of their conduct only which affects the liberty or property of the people under their administration. Were this to be denied, then the next step may make them slaves; for what notions can be entertained of slavery beyond that of suffering the greatest injuries and oppressions without the liberty of complaining; or if they do, to be destroyed, body and estate, for so doing?

SAMUEL DAVIES, GILBERT TENNENT
General Account of the . . . College, 1754

Nothing has a more direct tendency to advance the happiness and glory of a community than the founding of public schools and seminaries of learning for the education of youth, and adorning their minds with useful knowledge and virtue. . . .

America remained, during a long period, in the thickest darkness of ignorance and barbarism, till Christianity, at the introduction of the Europeans, enlightened her hemisphere with the salutary beams of life and immortality. . . .

At length, several gentlemen residing in and near the province of New Jersey, who were well-wishers to the felicity of their country and real friends of religion and learning, having observed the vast increase of those colonies, with the rudeness and ignorance of their inhabitants for want of the necessary means of improvement, first projected the scheme of a collegiate education in that province. . . .

Daily observation evinces that in proportion as learning makes its progress in a country, it softens the natural roughness, eradicates the prejudices, and transforms the genius and disposition of its inhabitants. New Jersey and the adjacent provinces already feel the happy effects of this useful institution. A general desire of knowledge seems to be spreading among the people. Parents are inspired with an emulation of cultivating the minds of their offspring; public stations are honorably filled by gentlemen who have received their education here; and, from hence, many Christian assemblies are furnished with men of distinguished talents for the discharge of the pastoral office.

cupants of Ohio Valley, alarmed at invasion, put up forts across Pennsylvania. Iroquois and Delaware Indians abrogate treaty that had ceded lands south of the Ohio River to Virginia and join French.

1746

Presbyterian College of New Jersey founded. Becomes Princeton in 1896.

1747

Benjamin Franklin begins experiments with electricity; he demonstrates that lightning is electricity and invents the lightning rod in 1752.

German Reformed Church organized in Pennsylvania as a subsidiary of the Dutch Reformed Church.

1749 - 1750

Thomas Kean and Walter Murray organize first American acting company in Philadelphia; plays Joseph Addison's tragedy, *Cato. Richard III* is produced in New York, one of 15 Shakespeare plays shown in the colonies, *King Lear* and *The Taming of the Shrew* being the most popular. The Kean-Murray company also performs 24 other plays including works of Dryden and Congreve.

1750

Iron Act, typical mercantilist measure, forbids production of finished iron products in colonies but encourages manufacture of pig and bar iron by duty concessions at English ports. Iron smelting process is developed by Jared Eliot of Connecticut in 1762.

First appearance, in Pennsylvania, of the flatboat for inland navigation and the Conestoga wagon, ultimately the common pioneer transportation and original form of prairie schooner.

1751

Nonsectarian Franklin's Academy founded. Becomes University of Pennsylvania in 1779.

1752

Thomas Bond establishes first general hospital in colonies in Philadelphia. Pesthouses (contagious-disease hospitals) had functioned earlier in Boston, Philadelphia, and Charleston, which also had a hospital for the chronically ill.

1754

June 19. In an effort to win over the uncertain loyalties of the Iroquois on the eve of the French and Indian War, representatives of New York, Pennsylvania, Maryland, and the four New England colonies meet at the Albany (New York) Congress to consider a treaty. Benjamin Franklin, delegate from Pennsylvania, recommends adoption of a Plan of Union for the colonies based on one he had drawn up in 1751. **July 10.** Plan is approved by Albany Congress but rejected by colonial legislatures and the British government.

King's College founded in New York, nonsectarian, Anglican controlled; most activities discontinued 1776-1784, but resumes as Columbia College in 1784.

Eighteenth century's most important work on tetanus (lockjaw) published by Lionel Chalmers.

Jonathan Edwards publishes *A Careful and Strict Enquiry into the Modern Prevailing Notions of Freedom of the Will*, most ambitious work among many by the greatest of colonial theologians.

BENJAMIN FRANKLIN
Albany Plan of Union, 1754
It is proposed that humble application be made for an act of Parliament of Great Britain by virtue of which one general government may be formed in America, including all the said colonies, within and under which government each colony may retain its present constitution. . . .

That the said general government be administered by a president general, to be appointed and supported by the Crown; and a Grand Council, to be chosen by the representatives of the people of the several colonies met in their respective assemblies. . . .

That the president general, with the advice of the Grand Council, hold or direct all Indian treaties in which the general interest of the colonies may be concerned; and make peace or declare war with Indian nations. . . .

That they make new settlements on such purchases by granting lands in the King's name, reserving a quitrent to the Crown for the use of the general treasury. . . .

That for these purposes they have power to make laws and lay and levy such general duties, imposts, or taxes as to them shall appear most equal and just (considering the ability and other circumstances of the inhabitants in the several colonies), and such as may be collected with the least inconvenience to the people; rather discouraging luxury than loading industry with unnecessary burdens. . . .

That the laws made by them for the purposes aforesaid shall not be repugnant but, as near as may be, agreeable to the laws of England and shall be transmitted to the King in Council for approbation as soon as may be after their passing.

Fanciful version of Braddock's defeat at Great Meadows depicts the general's death in battle

GEORGE WASHINGTON

Letter to his mother, 1755

Honored Madam:

As I doubt not but you have heard of our defeat, and perhaps have it represented in a worse light (if possible) than it deserves, I have taken this earliest opportunity to give you some account of the engagement. . . .

We marched on to that place without any considerable loss, having only now and then a straggler picked up by the Indian scouts of the French. When we came there, we were attacked by a body of French and Indians, whose number (I am certain) did not exceed 300 men. Ours consisted of about 1,-300 well-armed troops, chiefly of the English soldiers, who were struck with such a panic that they behaved with more cowardice than it is possible to conceive. . . .

The Virginia troops showed a good deal of bravery, and were near all killed; for I believe out of three companies that were there, there are scarce 30 men left alive. . . .

I luckily escaped without a wound, though I had four bullets through my coat, and two horses shot under me.

1755

Continuing activities in French and Indian War (begun the previous year), American hostilities phase of the global Nine Years' Great War for the Empire (1754-1763 in Europe), also called by some historians the Seven Years' War. **April.** Commander of British forces in America, General Edward Braddock and Colonel George Washington march to Fort Duquesne from Virginia with 2,000 British troops and colonials. **July 9.** Force of 900 French and Indians surround and defeat them in Battle of the Wilderness. Braddock is fatally wounded, and Washington leads survivors back to Fort Cumberland.

June. Various attacks on French posts by colonial forces result in complete British control of Bay of Fundy area by end of the month. Afraid that a French attack will be supported by Acadia, Governor Charles Lawrence orders all to leave who will not swear loyalty to Britain. **Oct. 8.** Six thousand Acadians are exiled and sent to 13 colonies. Villages at head of Bay of Fundy are burned.

1756 - 1772

John Woolman writes his *Journal*, published in 1774, the record of a New Jersey

Quaker noted for, among other things, his belief in racial equality and concern about social injustice.

1758

July 8. James Abercrombie, new British commander, having marched from Lake George with 15,000 troops, approaches Fort Ticonderoga, which is defended by Louis Joseph, Marquis de Montcalm with an outnumbered force of 3,000. British are disastrously defeated, with 1,600 casualties.

July 26. Major General Jeffrey Amherst, with Brigadier General James Wolfe, 14,000 troops, and 40 ships, takes Louisbourg. **Aug. 27.** Fort Frontenac on Lake Ontario falls to British. **Nov. 24.** French are forced to blow up Fort Duquesne to prevent its capture by British forces.

1759

July 24. In order to prevent French attacks on the West via the St. Lawrence River, British attack and take Fort Niagara and reinforce Fort Oswego. **July 26.** Outnumbered by British, French blow up Fort Ticonderoga and, on July 31, Crown Point. **Sept. 12-13.** British land and naval forces having reached the vicinity of Quebec by the St. Lawrence River, French under

JOHN WOOLMAN
Journal, 1757

I took occasion to remark on the difference in general between a people used to labor moderately for their living, training up their children in frugality and business, and those who live on the labor of slaves; the former, in my view, being the most happy life. He concurred in the remark, and mentioned the trouble arising from the untoward, slothful disposition of the Negroes, adding that one of our laborers would do as much in a day as two of their slaves. I replied that free men, whose minds were properly on their business, found a satisfaction in improving, cultivating, and providing for their families; but Negroes, laboring to support others who claim them as their property, and expecting nothing but slavery during life, had not the like inducement to be industrious. . . .

I said that men having power too often misapplied it; that though we made slaves of the Negroes, and the Turks made slaves of the Christians, I believed that liberty was the natural right of all men equally. This he did not deny, but said the lives of the Negroes were so wretched in their own country that many of them lived better here than there. I replied, "There is great odds in regard to us on what principle we act.". . . .

The slaves look like a burdensome stone to such as burden themselves with them; and . . . if the white people retain a resolution to prefer their outward prospects of gain to all other considerations and do not act conscientiously toward them as fellow creatures, I believe that burden will grow heavier and heavier, until times change in a way disagreeable to us.

The naval blockade of Louisbourg was repeatedly challenged by the French fleet until Amherst's victory

Remonstrance of . . . Frontier Inhabitants (Pennsylvania), 1764

During the late and present Indian war, the frontiers of this province have been repeatedly attacked and ravaged by skulking parties of the Indians, who have with the most savage cruelty murdered men, women, and children without distinction, and have reduced near a thousand families to the most extreme distress. . . .

We cannot but observe with sorrow and indignation that some persons in this province are at pains to extenuate the barbarous cruelties practised by these savages on our murdered brethren and relatives, which are shocking to human nature, and must pierce every heart but that of the hardened perpetrators or their abettors. . . .

We humbly conceive that it is contrary to the maxims of good policy, and extremely dangerous to our frontiers, to suffer any Indians of what tribe soever to live within the inhabited parts of this province while we are engaged in an Indian war, as experience has taught us that they are all perfidious. . . .

In the late Indian war, this province, with others of His Majesty's colonies, gave rewards for Indian scalps, to encourage the seeking them in their own country, as the most likely means of destroying or reducing them to reason; but no such encouragement has been given in this war, which has damped the spirits of many brave men who are willing to venture their lives in parties against the enemy. We therefore pray that public rewards may be proposed for Indian scalps, which may be adequate to the dangers attending enterprises of this nature.

Montcalm expect attack from the river; Wolfe, commanding the British, takes troops across the river in small boats during the night and to north of the fort. French are surprised by British troops climbing cliffs to the Plains of Abraham on which fort stands. **Sept. 18.** Quebec surrenders after Wolfe and Montcalm have both been killed.

1760 - 1761

Sept. 1-8, 1760. British forces under William Haviland march toward Montreal from Crown Point; Amherst's forces advance from Lake Ontario; Brigadier General James Murray meets them before Montreal, marching from Quebec. Hopelessness of the situation forces governor of Canada to surrender the entire province on September 8. Major Robert Rogers occupies Detroit and other posts on Great Lakes during 1760-1761.

1763

Feb. 10. Treaty of Paris ends Nine Years' Great War and breaks French power in North America. France cedes to the British all possessions in Canada and, except New Orleans, the eastern half of Louisiana (the Mississippi Valley), including navigation rights on the Mississippi River. Western half of Louisiana extending to the Rockies is granted by France to Spain along with New Orleans; this territory remains under Spanish control until 1800, when it is returned to France by secret Treaty of San Ildefonso.

May 16 - June 18. "Conspiracy of Pontiac." Indian tribes in Ohio-Great Lakes region unite in attacks on settlements and forts, now held by British. In one month all forts west of Niagara are destroyed, except Forts Pitt and Detroit; Fort Detroit is besieged by Ottawa tribe and their allies under Chief Pontiac for five months. **Oct.-Nov.** Pontiac gives up efforts to destroy Fort Detroit, but although tribes elsewhere have come to terms with British in August, he does not make peace with Indian Commissioner Sir William Johnson until July 25, 1766. Indians accept British rule, surrender white captives and some individual Indians who have been charged with personal crimes.

Oct. 7. Proclamation of 1763 is signed by George III. To conciliate Indians, end land speculation, and consolidate settlement and government on the frontier, a royal proclamation, prepared and issued in London, forbids general settlement west of the Appalachian Mountains and regulates purchases of land from Indians east of stated limits; it also orders settlers in upper Ohio country "forthwith to remove themselves." Indian territory west of the Proclamation line is put under military control. Former French territories are divided into three small provinces, East Florida, West Florida, and Quebec; and English law is established in Quebec, an unpopular move with French Catholic settlers.

1764

April 5. Sugar Act, revising Molasses Act of 1733, becomes first Parliamentary measure specifically designed to raise money in the colonies for the British Crown. The Act inaugurates the Grenville ministry policy requiring colonies to help pay costs of administering the empire, now greatly extended by the gains made in the Nine Years' Great War; the policy, never actually put in force, is calculated to make the colonies also contribute to payment of the British war debt. Actions mark the end of previous purely commercial policy of Britain toward her colonies.

A Grenville measure of the same date is designed to enforce trade laws by strength-

BENJAMIN FRANKLIN
Massacre of Friendly Indians, 1764
On Wednesday, the 14th of December, 1763, fifty-seven men from some of our frontier townships . . . came, all well mounted and armed with firelocks, hangers, and hatchets, having traveled through the country in the night, to Conestoga manor. There they surrounded the small village of Indian huts, and just at break of day broke into them all at once. Only three men, two women, and a young boy were found at home. . . . These poor defenseless creatures were immediately fired upon, stabbed, and hatcheted to death. . . . All of them were scalped and otherwise horribly mangled. Then their huts were set on fire, and most of them burned down. Then the troop, pleased with their own conduct and bravery . . . went home. . . .

Those cruel men again assembled themselves, and hearing that the remaining fourteen Indians were in the workhouse at Lancaster, they suddenly appeared in that town on the 27th of December. Fifty of them, armed as before, dismounting, went directly to the workhouse, and by violence broke open the door, and entered with the utmost fury in their countenances. When the poor wretches saw they had no protection nigh, nor could possibly escape, and being without the least weapon for defense, they divided into their little families, the children clinging to the parents; they fell on their knees, protested their innocence, declared their love to the English, and that in their whole lives they had never done them injury; and in this posture they all received the hatchet. Men, women, and little children were every one inhumanly murdered in cold blood.

JAMES OTIS
Rights of British Colonies, 1764
Every British subject born on the continent of America or in any other of the British dominions is by the law of God and nature, by the common law, and by act of Parliament (exclusive of all charters from the Crown) entitled to all the natural, essential, inherent, and inseparable rights of our fellow subjects in Great Britain. . . .

I can see no reason to doubt but that the imposition of taxes, whether on trade, or on land, or houses, or ships, on real or personal, fixed or floating property, in the colonies is absolutely irreconcilable with the rights of the colonists as British subjects and as men. I say men, for in a state of nature no man can take my property from me without my consent; if he does, he deprives me of my liberty and makes me a slave, if such a proceeding is a breach of the law of nature, no law of society can make it just. The very act of taxing exercised over those who are not represented appears to me to be depriving them of one of their most essential rights as freemen, and if continued seems to be in effect an entire disfranchisement of every civil right. For what one civil right is worth a rush after a man's property is subject to be taken from him at pleasure without his consent? If a man is not his own assessor in person or by deputy, his liberty is gone or lies entirely at the mercy of others.

PATRICK HENRY
Speech to House of Burgesses, 1765
Caesar had his Brutus, Charles the First had his Cromwell, and George the Third ("Treason!" cried the Speaker) —may profit by their example. If this be treason, make the most of it.

ening the poorly run customs service; another is the Currency Act, directed especially at Virginia, which had issued paper money during the war. This act prohibits the plantation colonies from issuing legal tender, a prohibition that had been in effect since 1751 in the commercial colonies of New England. The Act thus creates a bond of interest between these two regions.

May 24. Grenville measures are subject of Boston town meeting at which James Otis brings up for the first time the issue of taxation without representation and proposes a protest by all the colonies. **June 12.** Massachusetts House of Representatives forms a committee of correspondence to sound out other colonies.

July. Otis' *The Rights of the British Colonies Asserted and Proved* summarizes the taxation-without-representation argument.

August. Boston merchants agree to stop buying British luxury goods, thus beginning the policy of resistance by nonimportation that is taken up by all colonies within the year.

1765 - 1766

March 22. Stamp Act, Parliament's first direct tax imposed on the American colonies, requires purchase of tax stamps for most kinds of circulating paper, such as pamphlets, licenses, ship's papers, legal documents, insurance policies, and newspapers.

March 24. Quartering Act requires colonial authorities to provide food, lodging in barracks, and supplies for British troops. Various acts of this kind are passed, the last in 1774.

May 29. Virginia Resolutions proposed by Patrick Henry with "Treason" speech. To oppose the Stamp Act, which affects all classes and sections, Sons of Liberty are organized and use violence to force Crown collection agents to resign. **Aug. 26.** Mob attacks home of Massachusetts Chief Justice Thomas Hutchinson, at Boston. **Oct. 9-25.** Circular letter sent June 8 from Massachusetts Assembly to other colonies leads to Stamp Act Congress at New York City; 9 colonies are represented. **Oct. 19.** Congress adopts John Dickinson's moderate "Declaration of Rights and Grievances" to be submitted to British government. **Oct. 28-Dec. 9.** Further nonimportation agreements are signed by New York, Philadelphia, and Boston merchants, and by November 1, when Stamp Act goes into effect, business is almost stopped in all colonies. Business resumes by end of year without stamps in defiance of the law. **Jan. 17, 1766.** Merchants in Britain move for repeal of Act, citing business failures caused by shrinking American market for their goods.

Among colonial writings in opposition to Grenville policy are John Dickinson's *Considerations Upon the Rights of the Colonists to the Privileges of British Subjects*, Daniel Dulany's *Considerations on the Propriety of Imposing Taxes*, and John Adams' series of articles in the *Boston Gazette*, revised and republished in book form in 1768.

1765 - 1767

First professional training in medicine offered by College of Philadelphia (affiliated with University of Pennsylvania in 1791). King's College (later Columbia University) offers medical training in 1767.

1765 - 1781

Pennsylvania-born painter, Benjamin West, having moved permanently to England, teaches and influences visiting American artists; among them are Charles Willson Peale, Gilbert Stuart, John Singleton Copley, and Ralph Earl.

JOHN ADAMS
Protest of Braintree, Mass., 1765

In all the calamities which have ever befallen this country, we have never felt so great a concern, or such alarming apprehensions, as on this occasion. Such is our loyalty to the King, our veneration for both houses of Parliament, and our affection for all our fellow subjects in Britain that measures which discover any unkindness in that country toward us are the more sensibly and intimately felt. And we can no longer forbear complaining that many of the measures of the late Ministry, and some of the late acts of Parliament, have a tendency, in our apprehension, to divest us of our most essential rights and liberties. We shall confine ourselves, however, chiefly to the act of Parliament, commonly called the Stamp Act, by which a very burdensome and, in our opinion, unconstitutional tax is to be laid upon us all; and we [are to be] subjected to numerous and enormous penalties, to be prosecuted, sued for, and recovered at the option of an informer in a Court of Admiralty without a jury.

We have called this a burdensome tax, because the duties are so numerous and so high, and the embarrassments to business in this infant, sparsely settled country so great, that it would be totally impossible for the people to subsist under it, if we had no controversy at all about the right and authority of imposing it.

JOHN DICKINSON
Letter from a Farmer in Pennsylvania,
1767
*For it is evident that the suspension
is meant as a compulsion; and the
method of compelling is totally indifferent. It is indeed probable that the sight
of red coats and the hearing of drums
would have been most alarming, because people are generally more influenced by their eyes and ears than by
their reason. But whoever seriously
considers the matter must perceive that
a dreadful stroke is aimed at the liberty
of these colonies. I say of these colonies; for the cause of one is the cause of
all. If the Parliament may lawfully deprive New York of any of her rights, it
may deprive any or all the other colonies of their rights; and nothing can
possibly so much encourage such attempts as a mutual inattention to the
interest of each other. To divide and
thus to destroy is the first political maxim in attacking those who are powerful
by their union. He certainly is not a
wise man who folds his arms and repos-
es himself at home, seeing with uncon-
cern the flames that have invaded his
neighbor's house without using any
endeavors to extinguish them. . . .*

*With concern I have observed that
two assemblies of this province have sat
and adjourned without taking any notice of this act. It may perhaps be asked:
What would have been proper for them
to do? I am by no means fond of inflammatory measures. I detest them. I
should be sorry that anything should be
done which might justly displease our
sovereign or our mother country. But a
firm, modest exertion of a free spirit
should never be wanting on public
occasions.*

1766

March 18. Parliament repeals Stamp Act
on argument of William Pitt that colonies
should not be taxed without representation,
and on testimony of Benjamin Franklin,
agent for Pennsylvania, that colonies are
unable to pay tax, so that enforcement by
troops may lead to rebellion. Declaratory
Act of same day nevertheless affirms authority of Parliament over colonies "in all cases
whatsoever."

April 26. Nonimportation policy is abandoned when colonies learn of repeal of
Stamp Act. **June 30.** New York Assembly
votes statues to honor George III and William Pitt.

John Street Church, first colonial Methodist Church, is established in New York
City, breaking away, as elsewhere, from An-
glicans. Spreads, notably to Virginia,
through activities of itinerant preachers sent
out by English founder, John Wesley.

1766 - 1767

Aug. 11, 1766. Refusal by New York Assembly in January to support Quartering
Act of 1765 increases tension and eventually leads to clashes between British soldiers
and colonials when British destroy liberty
pole in New York. **June 6, 1767.** Assembly
finally votes appropriation for the Act, temporarily avoiding suspension ordered by
Parliament in December 1766, but suspension is nevertheless put into effect on October 1.

1766. Southwark Theatre, first permanent playhouse to be built in America,
erected in Philadelphia; opening performance is Vanbrugh and Cibber's *The Provoked Husband.* **1767.** First native play to be
professionally produced in the colonies, *The
Prince of Parthia,* by Thomas Godfrey, is
shown at same theater.

1767

Philadelphia instrument maker David Rittenhouse builds first colonial apparatus (orrery) for demonstrating the phases and motions of the planets in the solar system.

1767 - 1768

June 29. Townshend Acts (named after Charles Townshend, nominally chancellor of the exchequer, actually head of the British government) impose duties on various imports and empower Crown authorities to collect payment. These duties are "external" taxes, and thus theoretically acceptable to the colonists, but as their aim is in part to pay the cost of civil administration, the taxation-without-representation issue is raised again. **Oct. 28.** Nonimportation is revived first in Boston and then (December 2-29) in other colonies. **Nov. 5, 1767-Jan. 1768.** John Dickinson's *Letters from a Farmer in Pennsylvania to the Inhabitants of the British Colonies*, 12 essays, appear in the *Pennsylvania Chronicle*, calling Acts unconstitutional and criticizing suspension of New York Assembly.

Daniel Boone, starting from North Carolina, makes his first exploration west of Appalachians; travels along present-day Kentucky-West Virginia border. Others from the colonies have visited the region since at least 1750.

"Yankee Doodle" (from an English song with an air known as early as the 16th century in Holland) mentioned in libretto of first American opera (printed but not produced), *The Disappointment, or the Force of Credulity*; unknown librettist uses the pen name "Andrew Barton."

1768

Feb. 11. Massachusetts Circular Letter drawn up by Samuel Adams denounces

Yankee Doodle, c. 1775
*Father and I went down to camp
Along with Captain Gooding,
And there we saw the men and boys
As thick as hasty pudding.*

*Yankee Doodle keep it up,
Yankee Doodle Dandy,
Mind the music and the step,
And with the girls be handy.*

*There was Captain Washington
Upon a slapping stallion
A-giving orders to his men—
There must have been a million.*

*Then I saw a swamping gun
As large as logs of maple
Upon a very little cart,
A load for Father's cattle.*

*Every time they shot it off
It took a horn of powder
And made a noise like father's gun
Only a nation louder.*

*There I saw a wooden keg
With heads made out of leather;
They knocked upon it with some sticks
To call the folks together.*

*Then they'd fife away like fun
And play on cornstalk fiddles,
And some had ribbons red as blood
All bound around their middles.*

*I can't tell you all I saw—
They kept up such a smother.
I took my hat off, made a bow,
And scampered home to mother.*

Boston Boycott Agreement, 1768

The merchants and traders in the town of Boston having taken into consideration the deplorable situation of the trade, and the many difficulties it at present labors under on account of the scarcity of money, which is daily increasing for want of the other remittances to discharge our debts in Great Britain, and the large sums collected by the officers of the customs for duties on goods imported; the heavy taxes levied to discharge the debts contracted by the government in the late war; the embarrassments and restrictions laid on the trade by several late acts of Parliament. . . .

We, the subscribers, in order to relieve the trade under those discouragements, to promote industry, frugality, and economy, and to discourage luxury and every kind of extravagance, do promise and engage to and with each other as follows:

First, that we will not send for or import from Great Britain, either upon our own account or upon commission this fall, any other goods than what are already ordered for the fall supply.

Second, that we will not send for or import any kind of goods or merchandise from Great Britain, either on our own account or on commissions or any other wise, from the 1st of January, 1769, to the 1st of January, 1770, except salt, coals, fishhooks and lines, hemp, and duck-bar lead and shot, wool cards and card wire. . . .

Fifth, that we will not, from and after the 1st of January, 1769, import into this province any tea, paper, glass, or painter's colors until the act imposing duties on those articles shall be repealed.

Townshend Acts, urges united colonial opposition to them. **March 4.** Massachusetts Governor Sir Francis Bernard dissolves General Court after condemning Letter as seditious. **May.** By this time assemblies of New Hampshire, New Jersey, and Connecticut have upheld Massachusetts, and similar letter is sent out by Virginia Assembly. **June 30.** Massachusetts Assembly votes 92-17 to defy British command to rescind letter. Minority who vote to support Crown are denounced by Sons of Liberty, and seven are defeated in election of May 1769.

March. Proclamation of 1763 modified to allow Proclamation line to be moved west as Indian treaties are negotiated and land purchased. Most important of treaties are October 14 Treaty of Hard Labor with Cherokees and November 5 Treaty of Fort Stanwix with Iroquois; these bring former Indian lands in Virginia up to the Ohio River as well as putting western New York and western Pennsylvania under British control.

June 10. Seizure by customs officials of John Hancock's sloop *Liberty* for nonpayment of duty on Madeira wine provokes assault by crowd. **Oct. 1.** Two regiments of British troops, requested by customs officials in February, March, and June, finally arrive and are stationed in Boston.

Aug. 1-28. Further and more stringent nonimportation measures taken in Boston and New York; other colonies follow suit, and by end of 1769, only New Hampshire has not joined nonimportation protest, which all but suspends trade with England.

1768 - 1775

A number of commercial corporations are formed; several fire insurance companies, a Massachusetts wharf company, water supply companies, and a Philadelphia corporation for the purpose of promoting manufactures.

1768 - 1792

Series of strikes (rare before 1768), in which New York tailors demand higher wages, and printers strike (1778) and gain $3 per week; Philadelphia seamen strike in 1779 for higher wages and better working conditions. Philadelphia printers form a union in 1786; New York shoemakers in 1792.

1769

May 16. Virginia Resolves condemn British government for tax and other policies. **May 17.** Address to Crown by Patrick Henry and Richard Henry Lee is prevented when Governor Botetourt dissolves Assembly. **May 18.** Burgesses meet in Raleigh Tavern, Williamsburg, and form Virginia Association, a stringent nonimportation agreement. **June-Nov.** Similar associations are created in Maryland, South Carolina, Georgia, and North Carolina; nonimportation agreements are drawn up in seaport towns of Delaware, Connecticut, and Rhode Island.

Dec. 27. Grand Ohio Company organized by Samuel Wharton and other Englishmen to obtain a grant of 20 million acres under Treaty of Fort Stanwix. Grant approved by Board of Trade in May 1770, with understanding that territory is to be organized as proprietary colony of Vandalia. Project is abandoned with approach of the Revolution.

1770

Jan 31. Lord North becomes head of British government. **April 12.** Townshend Acts repealed, with exception of tea duty, and Quartering Act is not renewed. In the colonies, nonimportation is abandoned a second time, except in Boston, a center of the tea trade. Associations have been disbanded in all colonies by July 1771.

GEORGE CROGHAN
Diary, 1765
May 19th. . . . *We proceeded down the river about fifteen miles to the mouth of Little Conhawa [Kanawha], River with little or no alteration in the face of the country; here we encamped in a fine rich bottom, after having passed fourteen islands, some of them large, and mostly lying high out of the water. Here buffaloes, bears, turkeys, with all other kinds of wild game are extremely plenty. . . .*

23rd. . . . *The general course of the river from Great Conhawa to this place inclines to the southwest; the soil rich, the country level, and the banks of the river high. The soil on the banks of Scioto, for a vast distance up the country, is prodigious rich, the bottoms very wide, and in the spring of the year, many of them are flooded, so that the river appears to be two or three miles wide. . . .*

30th. *We passed the Great Miami River, about thirty miles from the little river of that name, and in the evening arrived at the place where the elephant's bones are found, where we encamped, intending to take a view of the place next morning. This day we came about seventy miles. The country on both sides level, and rich bottoms well watered. . . .*

June 6th. *We arrived at the mouth of the Ouabache [Wabash], where we found a breastwork erected, supposed to be done by the Indians. The mouth of this river is about two hundred yards wide, and in its course runs through one of the finest countries in the world, the lands being exceedingly rich, and well watered; here hemp might be raised in immense quantities. All the bottoms, and almost the whole country abounds with great plenty of the white and red mulberry tree.*

(Left) Pontiac and his embassy meeting with Major Rogers at the end of Pontiac's War; (below) wood engraving in the "Pennsylvania Gazette," 1754; (bottom) British troops under General Wolfe land upstream from Quebec and defeat the defenders on the Plains of Abraham, during the French and Indian War

JOIN, or DIE.

This is the Place to affix the STAMP.

(Above) A general view of the siege of Louisbourg, in 1758, shows the British fleet blocking the French; (right) an American parody of a tax stamp, 1765; (below) 1768 engraving by Paul Revere shows British troops landing in Boston to enforce law and order after passage of the "Townshend Duties," a tax on imported goods

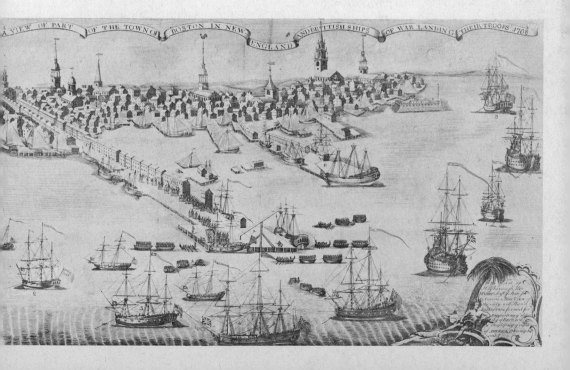

A VIEW OF PART OF THE TOWN OF BOSTON IN NEW ENGLAND AND BRITISH SHIPS OF WAR LANDING THEIR TROOPS 1768

GEN. THOMAS GAGE
Letter to Earl of Hillsborough, 1770
This party as well as the sentinel was immediately attacked, some throwing bricks, stones, pieces of ice and snowballs at them, whilst others advanced up to their bayonets, and endeavored to close with them, to use their bludgeons and clubs; calling out to them to fire if they dared, and provoking them to it by the most opprobrious language.

Captain Preston stood between the soldiers and the mob, parleying with the latter, and using every conciliating method to persuade them to retire peaceably. Some amongst them asked him if he intended to order the men to fire, he replied by no means, and observed he stood between the troops and them. All he could say had no effect, and one of the soldiers, receiving a violent blow, instantly fired. Captain Preston turned round to see who fired, and received a blow upon his arm, which was aimed at his head; and the mob, at first seeing no execution done, and imagining the soldiers had only fired powder to frighten, grew more bold and attacked with greater violence, continually striking at the soldiers and pelting them, and calling out to them to fire. The soldiers at length perceiving their lives in danger, and hearing the word fire all round them, three or four of them fired one after another, and again three more in the same hurry and confusion. Four or five persons were unfortunately killed, and more wounded. Captain Preston and the party were soon afterward delivered into the hands of the magistrates, who committed them to prison.

March 5. The Boston Massacre. Growing tension has caused frequent clashes between citizenry and quartered soldiers in New York and Massachusetts. Belligerent crowd gathers around Boston sentry who summons aid; resulting musket volley kills five citizens. Lieutenant Governor Thomas Hutchinson averts general uprising by acceding to demand to remove troops to harbor islands. **March 6.** Captain Thomas Preston and six of his men are arrested for murder. **Oct. 24-30.** They are defended by patriot lawyers John Adams and Josiah Quincy. Preston and four soldiers are acquitted; two soldiers receive only token punishment.

1771

Uprising of group called "Regulators" in North Carolina protests discriminatory laws and under-representation of western counties in state legislature. **May 16.** Climax comes at Alamance Creek, where 2,000 rebels, many unarmed, are defeated by 1,200 soldiers under command of Governor William Tryon. Thirteen rebels are found guilty of treason; seven are executed.

Philadelphia's Southwark Theatre produces *The Rising Glory of America*, from a poem of the same name written by Philip Freneau and Hugh Henry Brackenridge and read by Brackenridge at the graduation ceremonies of the College of New Jersey in the same year. Two other plays by Brackenridge, *The Battle of Bunker's Hill* and *The Death of General Montgomery*, are produced by this theater in 1776 and 1777.

1772 - 1773

June 9. Merchant John Brown and eight boatloads of followers attack customs schooner *Gaspee* aground off Providence, Rhode Island. **Sept. 2.** Commissioners of inquiry are named to identify culprits and send them to England for trial. **June 1773.** This threat to local self-rule having been thwarted by hostility of Rhode Islanders, who make it impossible to determine guilt, commission is adjourned.

1772 - 1774

June 13. Massachusetts Governor Hutchinson announces that his salary will in future be paid by the Crown. **Sept.** Policy is also applied to Massachusetts judges, rendering these officers independent of financial control of the General Court. **Nov. 2.** New standing Committee of Correspondence, headed by James Otis, is formed in Boston by Samuel Adams in response to this threat. **March 12-Feb. 1774.** Similar committees are formed in Virginia, Rhode Island, Connecticut, New Hampshire, and South Carolina; only North Carolina and Pennsylvania do not follow suit.

1773

May 10. Tea Act, passed to save British East India Company from bankruptcy threatened by overextension, authorizes selling part of huge tea surplus duty-free in colonies. This allows company to undersell both legitimate tea merchants and colonial smugglers, who have avoided the duty by buying from the Dutch, and thus to monopolize the tea trade. Opposition to the Tea Act grows in Philadelphia, Boston, and New York. **Nov. 27.** The *Dartmouth*, first of three tea ships, arrives in Boston. **Nov. 29-30.** Huge mass meetings are held in protest. **Dec. 16.** Boston Tea Party, in which a group of men disguised as Mohawk Indians boards the *Dartmouth* and dumps entire tea cargo, 342 chests, into Boston harbor.

Benjamin Franklin writes two satirical essays, "An Edict by the King of Prussia" and "Rules by Which a Great Empire May

Philadelphia Resolutions, 1774
The unanimity, spirit, and zeal which have heretofore animated all the colonies from Boston to South Carolina have been so eminently displayed in the opposition to the pernicious project of the East India Company in sending tea to America, while it remains subject to a duty, and the Americans at the same time confined by the strongest prohibitory laws to import it only from Great Britain, that a particular account of the transactions of this city cannot but be acceptable to all our readers, and every other friend of American liberty.

Upon the first advice of this measure, a general dissatisfaction was expressed that, at a time when we were struggling with this oppressive act and an agreement not to import tea while subject to the duty, our fellow subjects in England should form a measure so directly tending to enforce that act, and again embroil us with our parent state. When it was also considered that the proposed mode of disposing of the tea tended to a monopoly, ever odious in a free country, a universal disapprobation showed itself throughout the city.

BENJAMIN FRANKLIN
Rules by Which etc., 1773

An ancient sage valued himself upon this, that though he could not fiddle, he knew how to make a great city of a little one. The science that I, a modern simpleton, am about to communicate, is the very reverse.

I address myself to all ministers who have the management of extensive dominions, which from their very greatness are become troublesome to govern, because the multiplicity of their affairs leaves no time for fiddling. . . .

That the possibility of this separation may always exist, take special care the provinces are never incorporated with the mother country; that they do not enjoy the same common rights, the same privileges in commerce; and that they are governed by severer laws, all of your enacting, without allowing them any share in the choice of the legislators. . . .

However peaceably your colonies have submitted to your government, shown their affection to your interests, and patiently borne their grievances, you are to suppose them always inclined to revolt, and treat them accordingly. Quarter troops among them who by their insolence may provoke the rising of mobs, and by their bullets and bayonets suppress them. . . .

To confirm these impressions and strike them deeper, whenever the injured come to the capital with complaints of maladministration, oppression, or injustice, punish such suitors with long delay, enormous expense, and a final judgment in favor of the oppressor. This will have an admirable effect every way.

be Reduced to a Small One"; they are published in both England and America.

1773 - 1774

June 1773. Samuel Adams reads letters from Governor Thomas Hutchinson and Lieutenant Governor Andrew Oliver in session of Massachusetts House of Representatives. Letters have been sent from England secretly by Benjamin Franklin to demonstrate that objectionable acts of Britain are often owing to poor advice from Crown agents in the colonies. House petitions Crown to remove Hutchinson and Oliver. **Jan. 30, 1774.** In ensuing scandal in England, Franklin is dismissed as deputy postmaster general for America.

1774

January. Virginia Governor John Murray, earl of Dunmore, in effort to establish control of settlement in the Ohio country, appropriates Indian lands in western Pennsylvania. This and other intrusions goad Shawnee and Ottawa Indians into what becomes "Lord Dunmore's War." **Oct. 10.** Indians are defeated, cede hunting rights in Kentucky, and agree to unhindered access to and navigation on Ohio River.

March 31. First of Coercive Acts (called "Intolerable Acts" by Americans) designed to punish Massachusetts is Boston Port Bill, which prohibits loading and unloading of ships in Boston harbor until East India Company is paid for destroyed tea. **May 20.** Administration of Justice Act allows for transfer to England of legal suits against Crown officials; such trials had previously been held in provincial courts, often hostile to Crown officers or Crown authority. Massachusetts Government Act in effect annuls Massachusetts charter by greatly increasing the powers of Crown officers and reducing those of officers elected locally.

May 30. Quebec Act extends boundary of Canada south to the Ohio River, cutting off western claims of Massachusetts, Virginia, and Connecticut; Act sets up highly centralized Crown-controlled government in Canada, gives Catholic Church many privileges, provokes fear that as colonists move west they will be governed in French way and that Catholic influence will increase in Ohio Valley. This Act is also considered one of the "Intolerable" measures.

June 2. New Quartering Act authorizes troop billetings in private dwellings as well as taverns and unoccupied buildings and extends application to all colonies.

Sept. 5. First Continental Congress, with all colonies except Georgia represented, assembles at Philadelphia to consider ways of dealing with Coercive Acts. **Sept. 17.** Congress is persuaded by radical delegates to endorse Suffolk Resolves, adopted earlier by a convention of Suffolk County, Massachusetts. Resolves urge civil disobedience, self-rule, and severe economic pressure on Britain. **Sept. 28.** In an effort to establish a milder alternative to these Resolves, conservatives endorse Joseph Galloway's "Plan of Union Between Great Britain and Her Colonies," but are defeated by vote; Plan is expunged from the record on October 22. **Oct. 14.** "Declaration and Resolves" of the Congress condemn most British measures enacted since 1763. **Oct. 18.** Continental Association for nonimportation and other sanctions against Britain is formed, including machinery for enforcement. **Oct. 26.** Congress adjourns, resolving to meet again May 10, 1775, if measures voted have not been successful. Continental Association is established in all colonies by April 1775, Georgia having adopted a modified plan in January.

Loyalist argument set forth in a series of newspaper letters by Daniel Leonard using

Declaration and Resolves, 1774
The good people of the several colonies . . . justly alarmed at these arbitrary proceedings of Parliament and administration, have severally elected, constituted, and appointed deputies to meet and sit in General Congress in the city of Philadelphia in order to obtain such establishment as that their religion, laws, and liberties may not be subverted. . . .

To these grievous acts and measures Americans cannot submit, but in hopes that their fellow subjects in Great Britain will, on a revision of them, restore us to that state in which both countries found happiness and prosperity, we have for the present only resolved to pursue the following peaceable measures:

1. To enter into a nonimportation, nonconsumption, and nonexportation agreement or association.

2. To prepare an address to the people of Great Britain and a memorial to the inhabitants of British America.

3. To prepare a loyal address to His Majesty, agreeable to resolutions already entered into.

PATRICK HENRY

Speech to Virginia Assembly, 1775

Besides, sir, we shall not fight our battles alone. There is a just God who presides over the destinies of nations, and who will raise up friends to fight our battles for us. The battle, sir, is not to the strong alone; it is to the vigilant, the active, the brave. Besides, sir, we have no election. If we were base enough to desire it, it is now too late to retire from the contest. There is no retreat but in submission and slavery! Our chains are forged. Their clanking may be heard on the plains of Boston! The war is inevitable—and let it come!! I repeat it, sir, let it come!!!

It is vain, sir, to extenuate the matter. Gentlemen may cry, peace, peace; but there is no peace. The war is actually begun! The next gale that sweeps from the north will bring to our ears the clash of resounding arms! Our brethren are already in the field! Why stand we here idle? What is it that gentlemen wish? What would they have? Is life so dear or peace so sweet as to be purchased at the price of chains and slavery? Forbid it, Almighty God—I know not what course others may take; but as for me, give me liberty, or give me death!

the pen name "Massachusettensis" and refuted by patriot John Adams ("Novanglus"), extends to April 1775. Also published are James Wilson's *Considerations on the Nature and Extent of the Legislative Authority of the British Parliament* and Thomas Jefferson's *A Summary View of the Rights of British America*, both of which reject Parliamentary rule in favor of royal rule.

The Shakers, a monastic Protestant sect led by "Mother" Ann Lee, start their first communal settlement at Watervliet, New York.

Population of the colonies is estimated at 2,600,000.

1775

Feb. 1. Second Massachusetts Provincial Congress (originally formed at Salem on October 7, 1774) meets to prepare the province for war. **Feb. 9.** Having heard Declaration of the First Provincial Congress, Parliament declares Massachusetts to be in a state of rebellion. **Feb. 27.** Lord North's Conciliation Plan pledges that no new revenue bills will be passed for colonies willing to tax themselves, but refuses to recognize Continental Congress. **March 23.** Patrick Henry, in "Liberty or Death" speech before Virginia Assembly, accurately predicts early news of "the clash of resounding arms" from New England. **March 30.** Parliament passes bill forbidding New England colonies to trade with any countries except Britain and British West Indies and barring New England fishermen from the North Atlantic fisheries. **April 13.** Britain extends provisions of this act to New Jersey, Pennsylvania, Maryland, Virginia, and South Carolina upon news of their ratification of Continental Association.

March 10. Daniel Boone is sent out by the Transylvania Company to establish a trail (the Wilderness Road) through Cumberland Gap to Kentucky bluegrass country. **March 17.** Strip of land through the Gap and all lands between Kentucky River and Cumberland Valley are sold by Cherokees for £ 10,000. **April 6.** Boone founds Boonesborough, and several other Kentucky settlements are established in March and April. **Sept. 25.** Attempt to organize Transylvania as proprietary colony is frustrated when delegates to Continental Congress are rejected because Virginia claims jurisdiction over Kentucky region.

April 14. Aware that militia arms are cached at Concord, Massachusetts, General Thomas Gage dispatches British soldiers to attempt seizure. **April 18.** Seven hundred troops cross Charles River from Boston to Cambridge on way to Concord in evening. Boston Committee of Safety sends Paul Revere and William Dawes by different routes to alert the countryside; Revere reaches Lexington, but he, Dawes, and Dr. Samuel Prescott, who joins them, are stopped on way to Concord. Prescott escapes and warns Concord. **April 19.** When British arrive at Lexington at dawn, 77 armed minutemen are drawn up to greet them. Americans have almost been persuaded to retire when unidentified shot brings spontaneous volley from British, killing eight and wounding 10 minutemen. British march to Concord, seize minor arms cache, but all along return route to Boston are set upon by American militia, 4,000 of whom inflict 273 casualties before troops reach safety of Charlestown. Boston is then laid under siege by patriots (until March 1776). **April 22.** Provincial Congress authorizes raising of 30,000 men and appeals to other colonies for aid. By May 20 Rhode Island, Connecticut, and New Hampshire have voted to send 9,500 men.

May 10. Second Continental Congress convenes at Philadelphia. **May 15.** Congress resolves to put colonies in a state of defense. **May 29.** Address to the people of

JOSEPH WARREN
Address to Great Britain, 1775
Friends and Fellow Subjects:
Hostilities are at length commenced in this colony by the troops under the command of General Gage, and it being of the greatest importance, that an early, true, and authentic account of this inhuman proceeding should be known to you, the Congress of this colony have transmitted the same, and from want of a session of the honorable Continental Congress, think it proper to address you on the alarming occasion. . . .

These, brethren, are marks of ministerial vengeance against this colony for refusing, with her sister colonies, a submission to slavery; but they have not yet detached us from our royal sovereign. We profess to be his loyal and dutiful subjects, and, so hardly dealt with as we have been, are still ready, with our lives and fortunes, to defend his person, family, Crown, and dignity. Nevertheless, to the persecution and tyranny of his cruel Ministry we will not tamely submit—appealing to Heaven for the justice of our cause, we determine to die or be free.

RALPH WALDO EMERSON
Concord Hymn, 1837
By the rude bridge that arched the
flood,
Their flag to April's breeze
unfurled,
Here once the embattled farmers
stood,
And fired the shot heard 'round
the world.

GEORGE WASHINGTON
Reply to Congress, 1775
As to pay, sir, I beg to assure the Congress, that, as no pecuniary consideration could have tempted me to accept this arduous employment, at the expense of my domestic ease and happiness, I do not wish to make any profit from it. I will keep an exact account of my expenses. Those, I doubt not, they will discharge; and that is all I desire.

"Bunker's Hill, or America's Head-Dress"

THOMAS JEFFERSON, JOHN DICKINSON
Necessity of . . . Taking Up Arms, 1775
We have counted the cost of this contest and find nothing so dreadful as voluntary slavery. Honor, justice, and humanity forbid us tamely to surrender that freedom which we received from our gallant ancestors, and which our innocent posterity have a right to receive from us. We cannot endure the infamy and guilt of resigning succeeding generations to that wretchedness which inevitably awaits them, if we basely entail hereditary bondage upon them.

Our cause is just. Our union is per-

Canada is written; it asks them to join colonies as "fellow sufferers." **June 14-17.** Congress resolves to raise men for New England army in Pennsylvania, Maryland, and Virginia; unanimously votes appointment of George Washington as commander in chief; adopts plan of organization for forces now known as the Continental Army. **June 22.** Congress votes $2 million fund for support of Army, the 12 "Confederated Colonies" to share the burden according to population. (Georgia is not yet officially represented at Convention.)

May 10. Benedict Arnold and Ethan Allen lead small force that captures Fort Ticonderoga with many military supplies. **May 12.** Crown Point (north of Fort Ticonderoga) is seized. **May 16.** Arnold takes St. John's in Canada. **June 17.** British capture Charlestown peninsula and north bank of Charles River above Boston after battles of Breed's Hill and Bunker Hill. British losses are enormous. **July 3.** George Washington takes command of 14,500 troops at Cambridge.

July 5. Congress adopts John Dickinson's "Olive Branch Petition" to George III, asking for peaceful settlement of differences. **July 6.** Another Dickinson resolution, "Declaration of the Causes and Necessities of Taking Up Arms," states that colonies do not desire independence, but will not yield to enslavement. It also hints that colonies may receive foreign aid against Britain. **July 31.** Congress rejects Lord North's Conciliation Plan.

Sept. 12. Congress reconvenes with all 13 colonies represented. **Oct. 13-Nov. 10.** A navy and two battalions of marines are authorized. **Nov. 9.** Congress hears that on August 23 George III rejected "Olive Branch Petition" and declared colonies in open state of rebellion. **Nov. 29.** Committee is appointed to get in touch with "our friends abroad" and money is voted for its use. **Dec. 6.** Answer to George III affirms loyalty to Crown, but refuses allegiance to Parliament. **Dec.** French agent appears to express French interest in trade with colonies and suggest possibility of aid in war against England. **Dec. 23.** Royal proclamation closes colonies to all trade as of March 1, 1776.

Nov. 13. Expedition led by Brigadier General Richard Montgomery captures Montreal. **Dec. 11.** Governor Dunmore of Virginia is defeated by 900 Virginians and North Carolinians near Norfolk, which is ruined as a base of operations. **Dec. 31.** Benedict Arnold and 1,100 volunteers, joined by Montgomery, attack Quebec; campaign ends in disaster with Arnold wounded and Montgomery killed.

First American submarine, called *American Turtle*, constructed by David Bushnell, who in next year attempts unsuccessfully to blow up British frigate in New York Harbor.

First surgical textbook written in America is *Remarks on the Treatment of Wounds and Fractures*, by John Jones, personal physician to both Benjamin Franklin and George Washington.

Philadelphia paper, *Pennsylvania Evening Post*, published by Benjamin Towne, is first daily newspaper in America (discontinued 1784). By this year there are 37 newspapers in the colonies; political division is 23 patriot, 7 loyalist, and 7 neutral. *New York Weekly Mercury* publishes two editions during Revolution — patriot in Newark, New Jersey, and loyalist in New York City. Average weekly circulation of all papers: 3,500.

In spite of restrictions imposed by Britain in 1750, colonial iron manufacture has increased rapidly. By 1775 colonies are producing one-seventh of the world supply.

fect. Our internal resources are great; and, if necessary, foreign assistance is undoubtedly attainable. We gratefully acknowledge, as signal instances of the divine favor toward us, that His providence would not permit us to be called into this severe controversy until we were grown up to our present strength, had been previously exercised in warlike operation, and possessed of the means of defending ourselves. With hearts fortified with these animating reflections, we most solemnly, before God and the world, declare that, exerting the utmost energy of those powers which our beneficent Creator has graciously bestowed upon us, the arms we have been compelled by our enemies to assume, we will, in defiance of every hazard, with unabating firmness and perseverance, employ for the preservation of our liberties; being with one mind resolved to die free men rather than live slaves. . . .

In our own native land, in defense of the freedom that is our birthright and which we ever enjoyed till the late violation of it, for the protection of our property acquired solely by the honest industry of our forefathers and ourselves, against violence actually offered, we have taken up arms. We shall lay them down when hostilities shall cease on the part of the aggressors and all danger of their being renewed shall be removed, and not before.

TOM PAINE
Common Sense, 1776

It is the true interest of America to steer clear of European contentions which she never can do, while, by her dependence on Britain, she is made the makeweight in the scale of British politics. . . .

It is repugnant to reason and the universal order of things [and] to all examples from former ages to suppose that this continent can longer remain subject to any external power. The most sanguine in Britain do not think so. The utmost stretch of human wisdom cannot, at this time, compass a plan short of separation which can promise the continent even a year's security. Reconciliation is now a fallacious dream. Nature has deserted the connection, and art cannot supply her place. . . .

Ye that tell us of harmony and reconciliation, can ye restore to us the time that is past? Can ye give to prostitution its former innocence? Neither can ye reconcile Britain and America. The last cord now is broken; the people of England are presenting addresses against us. There are injuries which nature cannot forgive; she would cease to be nature if she did. As well can the lover forgive the ravisher of his mistress as the continent forgive the murders of Britain. . . .

O! ye that love mankind! Ye that dare oppose, not only the tyranny but the tyrant, stand forth! Every spot of the Old World is overrun with oppression. Freedom has been haunted round the globe. Asia and Africa have long expelled her. Europe regards her like a stranger, and England has given her warning to depart. O! receive the fugitive, and prepare in time an asylum for mankind.

1775 - 1776

John Trumbull publishes part of his popular satire on Tories, *M'Fingal;* first complete edition is not published until 1782.

1776

Jan. 10. Thomas Paine publishes his pamphlet, *Common Sense,* anonymously; calls George III responsible for acts against colonies, thus creating sentiment for independence among colonists, who had previously opposed Parliament but remained loyal to Crown.

March 1. French Minister Vergennes suggests to Spain that Spain join France in secret measures of aid to American colonies. **March 3.** Congress, ignorant of possible French and Spanish support, sends Silas Deane to Europe to procure military assistance. **April 6.** Congress votes to open American ports to all nations except Britain. **May 2.** Louis XVI of France authorizes the sending of one million livres' worth of munitions through secret agent Pierre de Beaumarchais. Equal amount of armaments is provided by Spain. These supplies sustain Continental Army in 1776-1777.

March 17. British and Loyalists under Sir William Howe evacuate Boston on threat of siege by General Henry Knox with 55 cannon hauled from Fort Ticonderoga.

June 7. Richard Henry Lee of Virginia proposes resolution to Congress that the United Colonies "ought to be free and independent states." **June 11.** Congress appoints committee to draft a Declaration of Independence before adopting resolution. **June 28.** Declaration, written by Thomas Jefferson, is presented, and Lee's resolution is approved by July 2. **July 4.** After making some revisions in Declaration, Congress approves it without dissent. (New York abstains, but approves on July 15.)

June 28. British attack on Charleston, South Carolina, by forces under Generals Sir Henry Clinton and Sir Peter Parker thrown back, ending British campaign in South for two years. **Aug. 22.** Howe's removal to New York from Boston and gathering of 20,000 troops on Staten Island (including 9,000 German mercenaries) leads to battle with Continental troops in Brooklyn, where bloody defeat persuades Washington to withdraw to Manhattan and fortify Harlem Heights.

Sept. 11. Peace conference held on Staten Island between representatives of Congress and Admiral Lord Howe (brother of Sir William Howe) fails when Howe insists that Declaration of Independence be revoked before discussion can begin.

Sept. 15. British occupy New York City. **Sept. 21.** Unexplained fire destroys most housing, leaving British without shelter. **Sept. 22.** Nathan Hale, caught while carrying military information, executed as American spy. **Oct. 13.** Battle for Lake Champlain results in defeat of Arnold's forces, but Sir Guy Carleton lets Ticonderoga stand over the winter. **Nov.-Dec.** Washington retreats through New Jersey, crossing Delaware River into Pennsylvania on December 11. **Dec. 12.** Congress, anticipating British attack on Philadelphia, flees to Baltimore after giving Washington dictatorial powers. **Dec. 26.** Knowing that Howe has sent most of his army back to winter quarters in New York, Washington recrosses Delaware, surprises and takes Hessian garrison at Trenton, New Jersey.

Constitutions enacted by 11 of original 13 states, with Connecticut and Rhode Island continuing under colonial charters by deleting references to British Crown. Common features of constitutions are provisions

Declaration of Independence, 1776
When, in the course of human events, it becomes necessary for one people to dissolve the political bands which have connected them with another, and to assume, among the powers of the earth, the separate and equal station to which the laws of nature and of nature's God entitle them, a decent respect to the opinions of mankind requires that they should declare the causes which impel them to the separation.

We hold these truths to be self-evident, that all men are created equal, that they are endowed by their Creator with certain unalienable rights, that among these are life, liberty, and the pursuit of happiness. That, to secure these rights, governments are instituted among men, deriving their just powers from the consent of the governed. That, whenever any form of government becomes destructive of these ends, it is the right of the people to alter or to abolish it, and to institute new government, laying its foundation on such principles, and organizing its powers in such form, as to them shall seem most likely to effect their safety and happiness. . . .

We, therefore, the representatives of the United States of America, in General Congress assembled, appealing to the Supreme Judge of the world for the rectitude of our intentions, do, in the name, and by authority of the good people of these colonies, solemnly publish and declare, that these United Colonies are, and of right ought to be free and independent states. . . . And for the support of this declaration, with a firm reliance on the protection of Divine Providence, we mutually pledge to each other our lives, our fortunes, and our sacred honor.

ALEXANDER HAMILTON
Treatment of Loyalists, 1784
Nothing is more common than for a free people, in times of heat and violence, to gratify momentary passions by letting into the government principles and precedents which afterwards prove fatal to themselves. Of this kind is the doctrine of disqualification, disfranchisement, and banishment, by acts of legislature. The dangerous consequences of this power are manifest. If the legislature can disfranchise any number of citizens at pleasure by general descriptions, it may soon confine all the votes to a small number of partisans, and establish an aristocracy or an oligarchy. If it may banish at discretion all those whom particular circumstances render obnoxious without hearing or trial, no man can be safe nor know when he may be the innocent victim of a prevailing faction. The name of liberty applied to such a government would be a mockery of common sense.

for strong legislatures and weak executives, frequent elections, property qualifications for voting and office-holding, and an appointive judiciary holding office during good behavior.

Many states adopt Bills of Rights, notably bill written by George Mason for Virginia, adopted on June 12, 1776.

1776 - 1783

"Test Acts" passed by revolutionary state governments require repudiation of loyalty to British Crown. Loyalists are variously exiled, disfranchised, barred from public office and the professions, and doubly and triply taxed. One hundred thousand Loyalists flee to Canada or England; these and many remaining are deprived of property by state confiscation acts; actual amount seized is unknown, but Crown ultimately pays them £ 3,300,000 in compensation. Division of Loyalist estates among numerous Americans after war helps shift balance of political power from owners of large estates to owners of small or middle-sized properties.

1777

Jan. 3. Washington eludes British force under Cornwallis near Trenton, New Jersey, inflicts heavy casualties on enemy at Princeton. **Jan. 6.** He establishes his 5,000 men in winter quarters near Morristown. Victories have vastly improved morale.

March 4. Congress returns to Philadelphia to discuss ways of getting foreign aid. In next few months it recruits and commissions, among others, Marquis de Lafayette, Baron Johann de Kalb, Thaddeus Kosciuszko, and "Baron" Friedrich von Steuben.

June 14. Congress specifies design of U.S. flag: "thirteen stripes alternate red and white . . . thirteen stars of white on a blue field."

June 17. General John Burgoyne begins campaign to isolate New England, capturing various posts in northern New York and around Lake Ontario by August. **Aug. 13.** Having run out of supplies, Burgoyne sends force to seize stores at Bennington, Vermont, and is frustrated by American militia. **Oct. 7.** He fails in attempt to capture Albany, where he is defeated by Arnold and others, and is forced to retreat to Saratoga, New York. **Oct. 17.** Surrounded by superior forces, Burgoyne surrenders his army of 5,700 men, who are shipped back to England on their pledge not to serve again against Americans.

Sept. 11-26. Howe occupies Philadelphia after defeating American forces guarding the city at Brandywine Creek. **Sept. 19-30.** Congress flees first to Lancaster, Pennsylvania, and then to York. **Oct. 4.** Washington is defeated with heavy losses by Howe near Germantown, and by middle of December has established winter quarters at Valley Forge.

Nov. 15. "Articles of Confederation and Perpetual Union," originally submitted to Congress July 12, 1776, are adopted after intermittent debate and submitted to the states for ratification, which is not completed by all states until March 1, 1781.

Dec. 17. France recognizes independence of U.S. on hearing news of Burgoyne's surrender.

1778

Jan. 8. French Foreign Minister Count Vergennes, unable to induce Spain to join France and America formally in war against England, offers French alliance to American commissioners Benjamin Franklin, Silas Deane, and Arthur Lee, at Paris. They sign treaties of alliance and of amity and commerce between France and U.S. **March 20.**

JOHN ADAMS
Letter to Sam Adams, 1778
The United States, therefore, will be for ages the natural bulwark of France against the hostile designs of England against her, and France is the natural defense of the United States against the rapacious spirit of Great Britain against them. France is a nation so vastly eminent, having been for so many centuries what they call the dominant power of Europe, being incomparably the most powerful at land, that united in a close alliance with our states, and enjoying the benefit of our trade, there is not the smallest reason to doubt but both will be a sufficient curb upon the naval power of Great Britain.

This connection, therefore, will forever secure a respect for our states in Spain, Portugal, and Holland too, who will always choose to be upon friendly terms with powers who have numerous cruisers at sea, and indeed, in all the rest of Europe. I presume, therefore, that sound policy as well as good faith will induce us never to renounce our alliance with France, even although it should continue us for some time in war. The French are as sensible of the benefits of this alliance to them as we are, and they are determined as much as we to cultivate it.

COUNT D'ESTAING

Declaration . . . to All the . . . French in North America, 1778

You were born French: you never could cease to be French. The late war, which was not declared but by the captivity of nearly all our seamen, and the principal advantages of which our common enemies entirely owed to the courage, the talents, and the numbers of the brave Americans, who are now fighting against them, has wrested from you that which is most dear to all men, even the name of your country.

To compel you to bear the arms of parricides against it, must be the completion of misfortunes. With this you are now threatened. . . .

Can the Canadians, who saw the brave Montcalm fall in their defense, can they become the enemies of his nephews? Can they fight against their former leaders, and arm themselves against their kinsmen? At the bare mention of their names, the weapons would fall out of their hands. . . .

I shall not urge to a whole people that to join with the United States is to secure their own happiness; since a whole people, when they acquire the right of thinking and acting for themselves, must know their own interest. But I will declare, and I now formally declare, in the name of His Majesty, who has authorized and commanded me to do it, that all his former subjects in North America, who shall no more acknowledge the supremacy of Great Britain, may depend upon his protection and support.

American commissioners received informally by Louis XVI, and immediate appointment of French Minister Conrad Gérard to U.S. leads to replacement of commission by a single minister to France. **Sept. 14.** Benjamin Franklin is elected to the post.

Feb. 17. In an effort to avert U.S. Congress ratification of the French alliance, Lord North proposes extremely wide conciliation measures, among them the appointment of a peace commission to negotiate with the Congress. **March 9.** The plan is voted by Parliament and commission sent to Philadelphia. **June 17.** Congress rejects plan with notice that only withdrawal of British troops and recognition of U.S. independence can be basis for agreement. Before leaving Philadelphia one commissioner unsuccessfully attempts to bribe three congressmen.

April 14-May 8. American privateer *Ranger*, commanded by Captain John Paul Jones, invades Irish Sea, takes two prizes, spikes guns of fort at Whitehaven, England, and captures British sloop-of-war which is taken to Brest, France. Similar raids by American privateers had taken 733 prizes by February.

June 19. Washington leaves Valley Forge in pursuit of General Sir Henry Clinton (Howe's replacement), who has marched from Philadelphia toward New York on news of approach of French fleet to America. **July 4.** After indecisive battle at Monmouth, New Jersey, American General Charles Lee is court-martialed for disobedience. **July 29-Aug. 10.** French fleet under Comte d'Estaing blockades Newport, R. I., waiting for land forces, but is forced to withdraw to Boston for repairs after battle with Admiral Howe's fleet. **Nov. 4.** D'Estaing leaves Boston for West Indies.

July 4-Feb. 25, 1779. Colonel George Rogers Clark leads 175 Virginians to capture Kaskaskia and Vincennes, gaining control of the Illinois country for Virginia.

Dec. 29. British capture Savannah, Georgia, in move by Sir Henry Clinton to shift theater of war and rally Loyalists of Southern colonies.

First American manual of standard drugs and medicines published (in Latin) by William Brown, surgeon general to the middle department of the Continental Army.

Jonathan Carver publishes *Travels Through the Interior Parts of North America*, containing information on Indian customs and natural history of Great Lakes and upper Mississippi region.

1779

January-June. British forces extend control of South despite American successes in South Carolina, Tennessee, and elsewhere. **July 16.** Clinton is thwarted in attempt to gain control of Hudson River by General Anthony Wayne's victory at Stony Point, New York. **Aug. 29-Sept. 15.** Successful expedition of Generals John Sullivan and James Clinton against Loyalists and Indians in northwestern New York reduces danger from Iroquois. **Sept. 15-Oct. 9.** Attempt to retake Savannah by D'Estaing's fleet and French and American forces under General Benjamin Lincoln fails with heavy allied losses, among them Polish Count Casimir Pulaski, who is killed.

Feb. 23-Aug. 14. Congress debates peace proposal; terms are independence, minimum boundaries, British evacuation of U.S. territory, and right of navigation on Mississippi River. **Sept. 27.** John Adams named to negotiate treaty with Britain.

June 21. Spain, opposing American independence but anxious for her own colonial possessions, joins war against England when

WILLIAM BILLINGS
Let Tyrants Shake, 1778
Let tyrants shake their iron rod,
And slavery clank her galling chains,
We fear them not, we trust in God,
New England's God forever reigns.

Howe and Burgoyne and Clinton too,
With Prescott and Cornwallis joined,
Together plot our overthrow
In one infernal league combined.

When God inspired us for the fight,
Their ranks were broke, their lines
*   were forced,*
Their ships were shattered in our sight,
Or swiftly driven from our coast.

The foe comes on with haughty stride,
Our troops advance with martial noise,
Their veterans flee before our youth,
And generals yield to beardless boys.

What grateful offering shall we bring,
What shall we render to the Lord?
Loud Hallelujahs let us sing,
And praise His name on every chord.

JOHN PAUL JONES
In Battle Against "Serapis," 1779
I have not yet begun to fight!

GEORGE WASHINGTON
Letter to Benjamin Harrison, 1778
I have seen nothing since I came here to change my opinion . . . but abundant reason to be convinced that our affairs are in a more distressed, ruinous, and deplorable condition than they have been in since the commencement of the war. . . .

If I was to be called upon to draw a picture of the times and of men from what I have seen, heard, and in part know, I should in one word say that idleness, dissipation, and extravagance seems to have laid fast hold of most of them; that speculation, peculation, and an insatiable thirst for riches seems to have got the better of every other consideration and almost of every order of men; that party disputes and personal quarrels are the great business of the day, while the momentous concerns of an empire—a great and accumulated debt, ruined finances, depreciated money, and want of credit (which in their consequences is the want of everything)—are but secondary considerations and postponed from day to day, from week to week, as if our affairs wear the most promising aspect. . . .

A great part of the officers of your Army, from absolute necessity, are quitting the service; and the more virtuous few, rather than do this, are sinking by sure degrees into beggary and want.

British refuse to give up Gibraltar as price of Spanish neutrality. **Sept. 27.** Congress President John Jay is appointed minister to Spain, but is unable to secure recognition, an alliance, or any further substantial aid during two and a half years in Madrid.

Sept. 28. John Paul Jones, in refitted French vessel renamed *Bonhomme Richard* (in honor of Benjamin Franklin's "Poor Richard"), engages British 44-gun *Serapis* off the east coast of England, captures and boards it as his own ship burns and sinks.

Despite loans from France and Spain, America is in desperate straits financially after issue of nearly $200 million in paper money ("Continentals"). In January paper currency is valued, relative to coin, at 8 to 1, but by December it has fallen to 40 to 1. At the December rate, $120 million (actually only $3 million) is accepted in payment from states in 1780, when the worthless currency is retired.

Struggle for control of West during Revolution, during which migration continues, results in various frontier clashes. Destruction of 11 Chickamauga Indian villages in the Tennessee Valley opens way to rapid expansion of settlement in Tennessee and Kentucky (whose population is 20,000 by 1780) now that settlers can move in over the Wilderness Road and down the Ohio River.

1780

May 5. Mutiny breaks out in Washington's camp at Morristown, New Jersey, after winter more severe than that at Valley Forge, but rebellious units, demanding full, instead of one-eighth rations, and five months' overdue pay, are controlled by Pennsylvania troops.

May 12. General Benjamin Lincoln surrenders Charleston, South Carolina, which has been besieged by 14,000 British for 45 days. Capture of 5,400 men and four American ships is worst defeat of the war.

Aug. 5. Benedict Arnold, having opened secret and treasonable negotiations with General Sir Henry Clinton, is placed in charge of fort at West Point on the Hudson River. **Sept. 23.** Attempt to deliver plans of the fort to the enemy through Clinton's adjutant, Major André, is frustrated by André's capture. **Sept. 25.** On hearing of this, Arnold flees to join British, with whom he campaigns until end of war. **Sept. 29.** André is convicted of spying and executed on October 2.

Aug. 16-Oct. 7. American forces suffer bloody defeat by Cornwallis at Camden, South Carolina, but partially compensate by victory of sharpshooting frontiersmen at King's Mountain, South Carolina.

Efforts of John Adams result in founding of American Academy of Arts and Sciences at Boston. Other learned societies, chiefly for promotion of agriculture, are founded in New Jersey, South Carolina, and Pennsylvania during 1781-1785.

1781

Jan. 1. Twenty-four hundred Pennsylvania Line troops in Washington's camp mutiny when unpaid veterans see new recruits being given money to enlist. **Jan. 7.** Concessions by state officials end mutiny, but 1,200 men leave the service.

Jan. 17. Americans under General Daniel Morgan defeat British force at Cowpens, South Carolina. **March 15.** British triumph at Guilford Court House, North Carolina, but Cornwallis' army is badly weakened and is forced to retire to Wilmington, North Carolina. **April 25-May 20.** Cornwallis moves north to subdue Virginia, which he raids almost at will. **June 10-19.** American reinforcements under Anthony

JAMES BOWDOIN
Address to the Academy, 1780
"Rapt into future time," and anticipating the history of our country, methinks I read in the admired pages of some American Livy or Thucydides to the following effect:

"A century is now elapsed since the commencement of American independence. What led to it, and the remarkable events of the war which preceded and followed it, have been already related in the course of this history.

"It was not to be expected that our ancestors, involved as they were in a civil war made peculiarly calamitous by British humanity, could give any attention to literature and the sciences; but, superior to their distresses and animated by the generous principles which liberty and independence inspire, they instituted the excellent society called the American Academy of Arts and Sciences. . . .

"They have particularly attended to such subjects as respected the growth, population, and improvement of their country, in which they have so happily succeeded that we now see agriculture, manufactures, navigation, and commerce in a high degree of cultivation, and all of them making swift advances in improvement as population increases. In short, they have, agreeably to the declared end of their institution, 'cultivated every art and science which might tend to advance the interest and honor of their country, the dignity and happiness of a free, independent, and virtuous people.'"

ROBERT MORRIS
Letter to the States, 1782
It affords me great satisfaction to inform you that this bank commenced its operations yesterday, and I am confident that with proper management it will answer the most sanguine expectations of those who befriend the institution. It will facilitate the management of the finances of the United States. The several states may, when their respective necessities require, and the abilities of the bank will permit, derive occasional advantages and accommodations from it. . . . It will have a tendency to increase both the internal and external commerce of North America, and undoubtedly will be infinitely useful to all the traders of every state in the Union, provided, as I have already said, it is conducted on principles of equity, justice, prudence, and economy.

Articles of Confederation, 1781
Article I. The style of this confederacy shall be "The United States of America."

Article II. Each state retains its sovereignty, freedom, and independence, and every power, jurisdiction, and right which is not by this confederation expressly delegated to the United States in Congress assembled.

Article III. The said states hereby severally enter into a firm league of friendship with each other, for their common defense, the security of their liberties, and their mutual and general welfare, binding themselves to assist each other against all force offered to, or attacks made upon them, or any of them, on account of religion, sovereignty, trade, or any other pretense whatever.

Wayne and von Steuben arrive, and Cornwallis turns back to Yorktown to establish a base, arriving on August 7. **Sept.** Helped by other American victories in South Carolina, American forces under General Nathanael Greene succeed in narrowing area of British control of South Carolina to Charleston and vicinity.

Feb. 20. Appointment of Robert Morris as superintendent of finance begins long fight by Congress to overcome inflation. **May 21.** After taking office, Morris proposes creation of first private commerical bank in U.S. **Dec. 31.** Bank is chartered as the Bank of North America. Meanwhile, new loans from France in May and Holland in November help to restore solvency.

March 1. Articles of Confederation go into effect upon ratification by last of 13 states. Delay since adoption of Articles by Congress in November 1777 has been occasioned in part by western land question, which began with proposal by John Dickinson in July 1776 that the Articles include western state boundaries. This motion was defeated, and a subsequent attempt by the states without western claims to have such boundaries drawn was again defeated in Congress in October 1777. But land bounties granted by Congress and the states as inducements to British military deserters and American soldiers who would sign up for the duration of the war had made the problem of organization of western territories acute, and in 1778 Maryland had refused to ratify Articles unless state claims were ceded to Congress. New York, Connecticut, and Virginia having ceded, Maryland signs Articles on February 27, but cessions by all states are not completed until 1802.

Aug. 30. French Admiral Count François de Grasse arrives off Yorktown, Virginia, with fleet that sets up blockade, disembarks troops that join forces with Lafayette, von Steuben, and Anthony Wayne, who have surrounded Yorktown by land. **Sept. 5-10.** British naval attack on French fleet fails. **Sept. 14-24.** De Grasse sends ships up Chesapeake Bay to bring Washington's army, which has been marching from New York, to Williamsburg to join the siege. **Sept. 28.** From Williamsburg 17,000 allied troops march against 7,500 British at Yorktown. **Oct. 18.** After various skirmishes and severe hammering by allied siege guns, Cornwallis decides his position is hopeless and surrenders his army, though Clinton is one week away with 7,000 reinforcements. **Oct. 19.** British troops lay down their arms while their bands play "The World Turned Upside Down."

1782

Feb. 27. Cornwallis' surrender at Yorktown, and British defeats by French in the West Indies, result in fall of the North ministry when Parliament votes against further prosecution of war in America. **March 22.** North is succeeded by Lord Rockingham, who immediately opens negotiations with American peace commissioners in Paris; commissioners are John Adams, Benjamin Franklin, John Jay, and Henry Laurens. **Nov. 30.** Preliminary articles signed, pending similar Anglo-French accord. Terms include recognition of U.S. independence, boundary stipulations, U.S. rights to North Atlantic fisheries, validation of debts due to citizens of both countries, and cessation of hostilities, with evacuation of British land and naval forces.

Publication of *Letters From an American Farmer*, impressions of America by J. Hector St. John [de Crèvecoeur], who has traveled through Ohio Valley and Great Lakes region before settling on farm in New York. Though enthusiastic about America, he returns to France for good in 1790.

CREVECOEUR
Letters from an American Farmer, 1782
What attachment can a poor European emigrant have for a country where he had nothing? The knowledge of the language, the love of a few kindred as poor as himself were the only cords that tied him. His country is now that which gives him land, bread, protection, and consequence. Ubi panis ibi patria [where my bread is earned, there is my country] is the motto of all emigrants. What then is the American, this new man? He is either a European or the descendant of a European; hence that strange mixture of blood which you will find in no other country. . . .He is an American who, leaving behind him all his ancient prejudices and manners, receives new ones from the new mode of life he has embraced, the new government he obeys, and the new rank he holds. He becomes an American by being received in the broad lap of our great alma mater.

Here individuals of all nations are melted into a new race of men, whose labors and posterity will one day cause great change in the world. Americans are the western pilgrims who are carrying along with them that great mass of arts, sciences, vigor, and industry which began long since in the east; they will finish the great circle. . . .

The American is a new man, who acts upon new principles; he must, therefore, entertain new ideas and form new opinions. From involuntary idleness, servile dependence, penury, and useless labor he has passed to toils of a very different nature, rewarded by ample subsistence. This is an American.

The Bloody Massacre perpetrated in King — — Street BOSTON on March 5th 1770 by a party of the 29th REG.t

Unhappy BOSTON! see thy Sons deplore,
Thy hallow'd Walks besmear'd with guiltless Gore,
While faithless P——n and his savage Bands,
With murd'rous Rancour stretch their bloody Hands,
Like fierce Barbarians grinning o'er their Prey.
Approve the Carnage and enjoy the Day.

If scalding drops from Rage from Anguish Wrung
If speechless Sorrows lab'ring for a Tongue,
Or if a weeping World can ought appease
The plaintive Ghosts of Victims such as these;
The Patriot's copious Tears for each are shed,
A glorious Tribute which embalms the Dead.

But know, Fate summons to that awful Goal,
Where Justice strips the Murd'rer of his Soul:
Should venal C——ts the scandal of the Land,
Snatch the relentless Villain from her Hand,
Keen Execrations on this Plate inscrib'd,
Shall reach a Judge who never can be brib'd.

The unhappy Sufferers were Mess.rs Sam.l Gray, Sam.l Maverick, Jam.s Caldwell, Crispus Attucks & Pat.k Carr
Killed Six wounded, two of them (Christ.r Monk & John Clark) Mortally

Engrav'd Printed & Sold by Paul Revere Boston

(Above) Paul Revere's interpretation of the incident of March 5, 1770, which he calls a "Bloody Massacre," in one of the most widely circulated pieces of propaganda before the Revolution; (below) burning of New York City in 1776; (right) colonials tar and feather a customs house agent for accepting a tea shipment

COMMON SENSE;

ADDRESSED TO THE

INHABITANTS

OF

AMERICA,

On the following interesting

SUBJECTS.

I. Of the Origin and Design of Government in general,
with concise Remarks on the English Constitution.

II. Of Monarchy and Hereditary Succession.

III. Thoughts on the present State of American Affairs.

IV. Of the present Ability of America, with some miscellaneous Reflections.

Man knows no Master save creating HEAVEN,
Or those whom choice and common good ordain.
THOMSON.

PHILADELPHIA;
Printed, and Sold, by R. BELL, in Third-Street.
MDCCLXXVI.

(Top) The battle at Concord
Bridge, 1775: engraving by Amos
Doolittle from a sketch by
Ralph Earl; (above left) Thomas
Paine and (right) title page from
his influential pamphlet, "Common
Sense"; (bottom) "Congress Voting
Independence" by Robert Edge Pine
and Edward Savage

GEORGE WASHINGTON

To the officers of the Army, 1783

For myself (and I take no merit in giving the assurance, being induced to it from principles of gratitude, veracity, and justice), a grateful sense of the confidence you have ever placed in me, a recollection of the cheerful assistance and prompt obedience I have experienced from you, under every vicissitude of fortune, and the sincere affection I feel for an Army I have so long had the honor to command, will oblige me to declare in this public and solemn manner that, in the attainment of complete justice for all your toils and dangers, and in the gratification of every wish, so far as may be done consistently with the great duty I owe my country and those powers we are bound to respect, you may freely command my services to the utmost of my abilities. . . .

Let me request you to rely on the plighted faith of your country, and place a full confidence in the purity of the intentions of Congress. . . .

By thus determining, and thus acting, you will pursue the plain and direct road to the attainment of your wishes. You will defeat the insidious designs of our enemies, who are compelled to resort from open force to secret artifice. You will give one more distinguished proof of unexampled patriotism and patient virtue, rising superior to the pressure of the most complicated sufferings; and you will, by the dignity of your conduct, afford occasion for posterity to say, when speaking of the glorious example you have exhibited to mankind, "had this day been wanting, the world had never seen the last stage of perfection to which human nature is capable of attaining."

First Catholic parochial school in U.S. is erected by St. Mary's Church, Philadelphia.

1783

Jan. 20. Britain and France reach accord, thus validating Anglo-American treaty signed November 30, 1782. **Feb. 4.** British proclaim cessation of hostilities after also signing articles of peace with Spain. **April 15.** Articles of peace ratified by Congress, Treaty of Paris signed September 3; signed treaty is ratified on January 14, 1784.

April 26. Seven thousand Loyalists, fearing American vengeance after British army is evacuated, leave from New York. **June-Nov.** Continental Army disbands. **Nov. 25.** Last British forces sail from New York. **Dec. 4.** Washington says farewell to his officers at Fraunces' Tavern, New York. **Dec. 23.** He presents himself to Congress at Annapolis, resigns his commission as commander in chief and takes "leave of all the employments of public life."

End of Revolution affirms legal changes

New Yorkers watch the Redcoats leave

Auction at Richmond: engraving from *Picture of Slavery* by G. Bourne, 1834

JUSTICE WILLIAM CUSHING
Quock Walker Case, 1783

As to the doctrine of slavery and the right of Christians to hold Africans in perpetual servitude, and sell and treat them as we do our horses and cattle, that (it is true) has been heretofore countenanced by the province laws formerly, but nowhere is it expressly enacted or established. It has been a usage—a usage which took its origin from the practice of some of the European nations, and the regulations of British government respecting the then colonies, for the benefit of trade and wealth. But whatever sentiments have formerly prevailed in this particular or slid in upon us by the example of others, a different idea has taken place with the people of America, more favorable to the natural rights of mankind, and to that natural, innate desire of liberty, which with heaven (without regard to color, complexion, or shape of noses) . . . has inspired all the human race. And upon this ground our constitution of government, by which the people of this commonwealth have solemnly bound themselves, sets out with declaring that all men are born free and equal—and that every subject is entitled to liberty, and to have it guarded by the laws, as well as life and property—and in short is totally repugnant to the idea of being born slaves. This being the case, I think the idea of slavery is inconsistent with our own conduct and constitution; and there can be no such thing as perpetual servitude of a rational creature, unless his liberty is forfeited by some criminal conduct or given up by personal consent or contract.

brought about in the several states since 1776. Among these are replacement of royal government by republican form; confiscation of royal lands and Loyalist property; abolition of quitrents, entail, and primogeniture; disestablishment of tax-supported Anglican Church; reform of penal codes; and advance of public education. Slave trade is abolished or heavily taxed in 11 states by 1786, and prohibited in Northwest Territory in 1787.

Massachusetts Medical School is founded in Boston.

Benjamin Franklin invents bifocal spectacles with both reading and distance lenses in a single frame.

Noah Webster publishes his *American Spelling Book (Blue-Backed Speller)*; estimated sale by 1883 is 70 million copies.

Continental Congress poll estimates population of United States at 2,389,300; 211,000 drop from 1774 is due to war deaths and Loyalist emigration to England and Canada.

Detroit, in 1794, part of the territory under the Northwest Ordinance

THOMAS JEFFERSON

Draft of a Territorial Ordinance, in his Journal, 1784

Resolved, that so much of the territory ceded or to be ceded by individual states to the United States as is already purchased or shall be purchased of the Indian inhabitants and offered for sale by Congress, shall be divided into distinct states. . . .

That the settlers on any territory so purchased and offered for sale shall either on their own petition, or on the order of Congress, receive authority from them with appointments of time and place for their free males of full age within the limits of their state to meet together for the purpose of establishing a temporary government, to adopt the constitution and laws of any one of the original states, so that such laws nevertheless shall be subject to alteration by their ordinary legislature. . . .

That when any such state shall have acquired 20,000 free inhabitants, on giving due proof thereof to Congress, they shall receive from them authority with appointments of time and place to call a convention of representatives to establish a permanent constitution and government for themselves. . . .

That whensoever any of the said states shall have, of free inhabitants, as many as shall then be in any one the least numerous of the thirteen original states, such state shall be admitted by its delegates into the Congress of the United States on an equal footing with the said original states. . . .Until such admission by their delegates into Congress, any of the said states after the establishment of their temporary government shall have authority to keep a member in Congress, with a right of debating, but not of voting.

1784

Feb. 22. Captain John Greene sails the *Empress of China* from New York, reaches Canton, China, by way of Cape Horn on August 30. Cargo of tea and silks brought back in 1785 leads other U.S. merchants to send more ships to China in effort to make up for losses due to shrunken British market for U.S. goods.

March 1. Committee headed by Thomas Jefferson presents to Congress a plan for interim government of Western lands, proposing eventual division of territory into states to be admitted on equal terms with original 13. **April 23.** Plan is adopted and becomes basic idea in the Northwest Ordinance of 1787.

May 28. Superintendent of Finance Robert Morris requests that he be replaced by a board of three commissioners. **Nov. 1.** He leaves office having accumulated a precarious surplus of $21,000 (after meeting army's demobilization pay in 1783 from his own pocket). Recent foreign loans are largely responsible for the surplus, since Congress has no power of taxation under the Articles of Confederation but is dependent on requisitions from states for funds. Of an $8 million requisition voted in October 1781, only about $1,500,000 has been paid by January 1784.

Aug. 23. Convention of settlers west of Appalachian Mts. organizes independent state of Franklin in area ceded to U.S. by North Carolina. After four years of nominal statehood under John Sevier settlers accept renewed jurisdiction of North Carolina.

Dec. 23. New York City selected as temporary national capital until a federal district on the Delaware River can be set up.

Potomac Company organized with George Washington as president to build route connecting Potomac River with Ohio Valley. Canal is begun, and first water locks in U.S. built, but project proves unprofitable and is never completed.

First American theological college is established in New Brunswick, New Jersey.

John Filson publishes *The Discovery, Settlement, and Present State of Kentucke* which contains, in addition to Filson's account, an alleged autobiography of Daniel Boone.

1784 - 1797

1784. Judge Tapping Reeve establishes law school in Litchfield, Connecticut; followed by Peter Van Schaack's law school at Kinderhook, New York, in 1786; law lectures at University of Pennsylvania in 1790; and Columbia College in 1797.

JOHN FILSON
"Autobiography" of Daniel Boone, 1784

It was on the 1st of May, in the year 1769, that I resigned my domestic happiness for a time, and left my family and peaceable habitation on the Yadkin River in North Carolina, to wander through the wilderness of America in quest of the country of Kentucky. . . .

We encamped and made a shelter to defend us from the inclement season, and began to hunt and reconnoiter the country. We found everywhere abundance of wild beasts of all sorts, through this vast forest. The buffalo were more frequent than I have seen cattle in the settlements, browsing on the leaves of the cane or cropping the herbage on those extensive plains, fearless, because ignorant, of the violence of man. Sometimes we saw hundreds in a drove, and the numbers about the salt springs were amazing. In this forest, the habitation of beasts of every kind natural to America, we practised hunting with great success until the 22nd day of December following. . . .

Soon after, I returned home to my family, with a determination to bring them as soon as possible to live in Kentucky, which I esteemed a second paradise, at the risk of my life and fortune.

JOHN ADAMS
Letter to John Jay, 1785

1785

The idea of thirteen plenipotentiaries meeting together in a congress at every court in Europe, each with a full power and distinct instructions from his state, presents to view such a picture of confusion, altercation, expense, and endless delay as must convince every man of its impracticability. Neither is there less absurdity in supposing that all the states should unite in the separate election of the same man, since there is not, never was, and never will be a citizen whom each state would separately prefer for conducting the negotiation. It is equally inconceivable that each state should separately send a full power and separate instructions to the ministers appointed by Congress. . . .

It behooves the United States, then, to knit themselves together in the bands of affection and mutual confidence, search their own resources to the bottom, form their foreign commerce into a system, and encourage their own navigation and seamen, and to these ends their carrying trade; and I am much afraid we shall never be able to do this unless Congress are vested with full power, under the limitations prescribed of fifteen years, and the concurrence of nine states, of forming treaties of commerce with foreign powers.

Jan. 24. Congress, being unable to obtain commercial concessions from foreign countries because Article IX of Articles of Confederation allows each state to set its own duties on foreign commerce, appoints committee to appeal to the states. Committee recommends amending Article IX but no action is taken by the states. Maryland, South Carolina, Pennsylvania, New York, Rhode Island, and North Carolina all have discriminatory duties on imports from Britain. **June 23.** Massachusetts and New Hampshire act to prohibit British ships from carrying their exports.

March 28. Commissioners from Virginia and Maryland meet at Mount Vernon, Virginia, to consider problems of navigation on Chesapeake Bay and Potomac River. Agreement recommends that Virginia and Maryland legislatures adopt uniform currency, uniform commercial regulations, and other measures of common commercial interest. **Dec. 5.** Maryland legislature endorses plan and proposes that Delaware and Pennsylvania be included.

Aug. 24. Beginning of a year of futile negotiations with Spain over U.S. right of navigation on the lower Mississippi River, which Spanish minister to U.S. refuses to concede, claiming title by virtue of 1763 Treaty of Paris. Issue is unresolved until Pinckney Treaty of 1795.

Automatic flour mill, invented by Oliver Evans, is put into operation in Maryland. New features, such as elevator and conveyor belt, cut labor needs in half.

Postwar dumping of British manufactures raises imports nearly to prewar level, but exports, no longer given preferential treatment in Britain, reach only 50 percent. British restrictions on trade with West Indies after 1783 further reduce American commerce which is only partly helped by opening of China trade and development of Pacific Northwest fur trade.

1785 - 1790

New York Society for Promoting Manumission (freeing of slaves) established with John Jay as president; similar societies established in other states, including several in the South, to 1788. Legislation to abolish slavery has been enacted in Pennsylvania in 1780, Connecticut and Rhode Island in 1784, New York in 1785, and is passed in New Jersey in 1786. Massachusetts constitution had abolished slavery in 1780. Slavery is prohibited in Northwest Territory by its ordinance. By 1790 about 93 percent of slaves in U.S. are in Southern states.

1786

Jan. 16. Virginia Assembly adopts Thomas Jefferson's Statute for Religious Freedom, model for First Amendment to the U.S. Constitution. Measure is virtually the same as one originally written and proposed in 1779 and not adopted.

Feb. 28. British notify U.S. that they will not evacuate Great Lakes posts, as promised by 1783 Treaty of Paris, until U.S. honors its debts to Britain.

June 28. Treaty with Morocco leads to suspension of Moroccan piracy on American commerce in Mediterranean Sea and off Spanish coast, but pirate raids from Algiers, Tunis, and Tripoli continue off Barbary coast until 1797.

Sept. 11-14. Following James Madison's suggestion of January 21, Virginia legislature invites all states to discuss interstate commercial problems at Annapolis, Maryland. Convention assembles at appointed

THOMAS JEFFERSON

Virginia Statute of Religious Freedom, 1786

I. Whereas *Almighty God has created the mind free, so that all attempts to influence it by temporal punishments or burdens, or by civil incapacitations, tend only to beget habits of hypocrisy and meanness, and are a departure from the plan of the Holy Author of our religion, who, being Lord both of body and mind, yet chose not to propagate it by coercions on either, as was in His almighty power to do; that the impious presumption of legislators and rulers, civil as well as ecclesiastical, who, being themselves but fallible and uninspired men, have assumed dominion over the faith of others, setting up their own opinions and modes of thinking as the only true and infallible, and as such endeavoring to impose them on others, has established and maintained false religions over the greatest part of the world, and through all time. . . .*

II. Be it . . . enacted by the General Assembly *that no man shall be compelled to frequent or support any religious worship, place, or ministry whatsoever, nor shall be enforced, restrained, molested, or burdened in his body or goods, nor shall otherwise suffer on account of his religious opinions or belief; but that all men shall be free to profess, and by argument to maintain, their opinion in matters of religion, and that the same shall in no wise diminish, enlarge, or affect their civil capacities.*

THOMAS JEFFERSON
Letter to Madison, 1787
I hold it that a little rebellion now and then is a good thing, and as necessary in the political world as storms in the physical. Unsuccessful rebellions, indeed, generally establish the encroachments on the rights of the people which have produced them. An observation of this truth should render honest republican governors so mild in their punishment of rebellions as not to discourage them too much. It is a medicine necessary for the sound health of government.

A representation of Shays's Rebellion

GEORGE WASHINGTON
Speech at Constitutional Convention
It is too probable that no plan we propose will be adopted. Perhaps another dreadful conflict is to be sustained. If to please the people, we offer what we ourselves disapprove, how can we afterwards defend our work? Let us raise a standard to which the wise and honest can repair. The event is in the hand of God.

time with only delegates from New York, New Jersey, Delaware, Pennsylvania, and Virginia present; those from New Hampshire, Massachusetts, Rhode Island, and North Carolina arrive too late to participate, and the rest of the states do not join in. Meager representation frustrates aim of convention but Alexander Hamilton, in address endorsed on September 14, calls upon the states to meet at Philadelphia in May 1787 to discuss all matters necessary "to render the constitution of the federal government adequate to the exigencies of the Union."

Imports and exports drop from 1785 levels, farm wages are down 20 percent; shortage of money, insistent creditors, and high taxes contribute to general economic depression. Pressure for paper money results in $800,000 issue from seven states, alarming creditors. They are further disturbed by the outbreak of Shays's Rebellion in Massachusetts, where debt-ridden farmers in western part of state rise in arms against constituted authorities, protesting economic injustice and legal discrimination. Rebellion led by Daniel Shays is not finally put down until February 1787, after unequal struggle with state troops.

First American steamboat, invented by John Fitch, is granted franchise for use on New Jersey waters; it is launched on Delaware River in 1787.

1787

May 25. Constitutional Convention opens at Philadelphia 11 days late, after waiting for quorum of seven states; all states except Rhode Island eventually attend. George Washington is unanimously elected to preside but takes no part in debates. William Jackson is made secretary. **May 29.** Edmund Randolph offers Virginia Plan which goes beyond revision of Articles of Confederation; Plan is debated until June 13. This proposal, in which states are represented in proportion to population, is opposed by small states, who hope to retain equality of states as under Articles of Confederation, but with enlarged powers of central government. **June 15.** Delegates of small states propose New Jersey Plan, a revision of the Articles. Plan is debated for four days. **June 19.** Virginia Plan is adopted by 7 states to 3, committing Convention to frame a new basis for central government rather than merely revise Articles.

July 13. During Convention debate on proposed Constitution, Congress of the Confederation passes Northwest Ordinance. Based on Jefferson's Report of 1784, Ordinance provides for government of territory east of the Mississippi River and north of the Ohio; it includes provision for division of territory into three to five states and their admission into the Union when population is large enough.

July 16. Convention adopts Connecticut Compromise. The work of Benjamin Franklin and others and introduced by Roger Sherman, it resolves issue of state representation by providing for equal votes for states in proposed Senate but votes according to population in House. **Aug. 6 - Sept. 10.** Draft Constitution as prepared by five-member Committee of Detail is submitted to Convention and debated on all points; the debate is led by James Madison and George Mason of Virginia, Gouverneur Morris and James Wilson of Pennsylvania, Roger Sherman of Connecticut, and Elbridge Gerry of Massachusetts. Morris is assigned to prepare final draft. **Sept. 17.** After making a few changes, state delegations approve final draft, and 39 of the 42 delegates still in attendance sign (Gerry, Mason, and Randolph refusing), transmit the Constitution to Congress of the Confederation, and adjourn.

BENJAMIN FRANKLIN
Speech to Constitutional Convention, 1787
In these sentiments, sir, I agree to this Constitution with all its faults, if they are such; because I think a general government necessary for us, and there is no form of government but what may be a blessing to the people if well administered, and believe farther that this is likely to be well administered for a course of years, and can only end in despotism, as other forms have done before it, when the people shall become so corrupted as to need despotic government, being incapable of any other. I doubt, too, whether any other convention we can obtain may be able to make a better Constitution; for when you assemble a number of men to have the advantage of their joint wisdom, you inevitably assemble with those men all their prejudices, their passions, their errors of opinion, their local interests, and their selfish views. From such an assembly can a perfect production be expected? . . .

On the whole, sir, I cannot help expressing a wish that every member of the Convention who may still have objections to it would, with me, on this occasion doubt a little of his own infallibility.

Preamble to the Constitution
We the people of the United States, in order to form a more perfect Union, establish justice, insure domestic tranquility, provide for the common defense, promote the general welfare, and secure the blessings of liberty to ourselves and our posterity, do ordain and establish this Constitution for the United States of America.

ALEXANDER HAMILTON
Federalist No. 1, 1787

After an unequivocal experience of the inefficiency of the subsisting federal government, you are called upon to deliberate on a new Constitution for the United States of America. The subject speaks its own importance; comprehending in its consequences nothing less than the existence of the Union, the safety and welfare of the parts of which it is composed, the fate of an empire in many respects the most interesting in the world. It has been frequently remarked that it seems to have been reserved to the people of this country, by their conduct and example, to decide the important question, whether societies of men are really capable or not of establishing good government from reflection and choice, or whether they are forever destined to depend for their political constitutions on accident and force. If there be any truth in the remark, the crisis at which we are arrived may with propriety be regarded as the era in which that decision is to be made; and a wrong election of the part we shall act may, in this view, deserve to be considered as the general misfortune of mankind.

This idea will add the inducements of philanthropy to those of patriotism, to heighten the solicitude which all considerate and good men must feel for the event. Happy will it be if our choice should be directed by a judicious estimate of our true interests, unperplexed and unbiased by considerations not connected with the public good. But this is a thing more ardently to be wished than seriously to be expected.

Sept. 20. Congress of the Confederation receives draft Constitution and defeats motion to censure Convention for exceeding instructions merely to revise Articles of Confederation. **Sept. 28.** Congress votes to send draft Constitution to the individual states for consideration by special ratifying conventions (ratification cannot be by legislatures or popular vote). Nine ratifications are needed for adoption.

Oct. 27. First of 85 "Federalist" papers published. Federalists, who approve the Constitution, and anti-Federalists, who oppose it, flood the states with written arguments. Most distinguished and influential are those written by "Publius" (Alexander Hamilton, James Madison, and John Jay), which appear in New York newspapers. Two-volume collection, *The Federalist*, is published in 1788.

Dec. 7. Ratification begins with convention of Delaware which ratifies unanimously.

Dec. 12. Pennsylvania convention, which has met on November 21, ratifies by vote of 46 to 23 after much delaying debate by strong anti-Federalist factions.

Dec. 18. New Jersey ratifies unanimously only a week after meeting on December 11.

Royall Tyler's comedy, *The Contrast*, is performed by a professional acting group in New York City; it is first American play with an American hero.

· 1788

Jan. 2. Georgia convention meets, ratifies Constitution unanimously. Debates on Constitution continue in other states.

Jan. 9. Connecticut convention, which has met on January 4, ratifies by vote of 128 to 40.

Feb. 6. Massachusetts convention, having met since January 9, ratifies by vote of 187 to 168. Opponents are persuaded to vote favorably when Samuel Adams proposes as condition of ratification that nine amendments be recommended at once to Congress and the other states. One of these is the basis for present-day Article X of the Bill of Rights, which reserves to the states powers not expressly delegated to the federal government.

March 24. Rhode Island rejects Constitution by direct vote. Federalists have refused to take part because a state convention has been rejected; thus only about half the qualified voters cast ballots, and only 237 out of about 3,000 voters favor ratification.

April 7. Marietta, Ohio, founded by settlers sent West by the Ohio Company, organized in 1786 for land speculation and development of land granted by Congress in exchange for Continental securities.

April 28. Maryland convention, which has met on April 21, ratifies by 63 to 11.

May 23. South Carolina anti-Federalists in legislature almost prevent holding ratifying convention, but resolution is passed, convention meets May 12 and ratifies 149 to 73.

June 21. New Hampshire convention, having met on February 13 and adjourned until June to see what action other states will take, ratifies by 57 to 47 after proposing 12 amendments. This ninth ratification is last needed for acceptance of Constitution among the ratifying states.

June 25. Virginia convention ratifies by vote of 89 to 79 after three weeks of heated argument led by Patrick Henry (against) and James Madison (for ratification). Convention recommends a bill of rights of 20 articles.

PATRICK HENRY
Speech in Virginia Ratifying Convention, 1788
What right had they to say, "We, the people"? My political curiosity, exclusive of my anxious solicitude for the public welfare, leads me to ask — Who authorized them to speak the language of "We, the people," instead of, "We, the states"? States are the characteristics and the soul of a confederation. If the states be not the agents of this compact, it must be one great, consolidated, national government of the people of all the states. . . .

This government will operate like an ambuscade. It will destroy the state governments and swallow the liberties of the people, without giving previous notice. If gentlemen are willing to run the hazard, let them run it; but I shall exculpate myself by my opposition and monitory warnings within these walls.

EDMUND PENDLETON
Speech in Virginia Ratifying Convention, 1788
But an objection is made to the form: the expression "We, the people" is thought improper. Permit me to ask the gentleman who made this objection, who but the people can delegate powers? Who but the people have a right to form government? . . . If the objection be that the Union ought to be not of the people but of the state governments, then I think the choice of the former very happy and proper. What have the state governments to do with it? Were they to determine, the people would not, in that case, be the judges upon what terms it was adopted.

Resolution of Congress, 1788
Whereas *the Convention assembled in Philadelphia pursuant to the resolution of Congress of the 21st of February, 1787, did on the 17th of September in the same year report to the United States in Congress assembled a constitution for the people of the United States. Whereupon Congress on the 28th of the same September did resolve unanimously, "That the said report with the resolutions and letter accompanying the same be transmitted to the several legislatures in order to be submitted to a convention of delegates chosen in each state by the people thereof in conformity to the resolves of the convention made and provided in that case." And whereas the constitution so reported by the Convention and by Congress transmitted to the several legislatures has been ratified in the manner therein declared to be sufficient for the establishment of the same and such ratifications duly authenticated have been received by Congress and are filed in the Office of the Secretary; therefore,* Resolved *that the first Wednesday in January next be the day for appointing electors in the several states, which before the said day shall have ratified the said constitution; that the first Wednesday in February next be the day for the electors to assemble in their respective states and vote for a president; and that the first Wednesday in March next be the time and the present seat of Congress the place for commencing proceedings under the said constitution.*

July 2. Congress of the Confederation accepts the new Constitution as ratified. **Sept. 13.** Congress arranges for conduct of government under new order to begin on March 4, 1789, when first Constitutional Congress will meet in New York. **Oct. 10.** Congress transacts its last official business under the Articles.

July 26. New York convention, having met on June 17, ratifies by 30 to 27. Anti-Federalists are majority, but Alexander Hamilton manages to delay vote until ninth ratification and Virginia's vote are announced, feeling correctly that this will sway convention. Additional factor is threat of New York City to secede from the state and ratify separately. Convention urges amendment to secure a federal bill of rights.

Aug. 2. North Carolina convention, meeting on July 21, refuses to ratify without a bill of rights, although Federalist feeling is strong.

Dec. 23. Maryland cedes 10 square miles on the Potomac River to Congress as site for federal capital of government under the new Constitution.

1789

Feb. 4. Presidential electors, chosen in each ratifying state as provided by new Constitution, cast ballots (counted in Senate on April 6) unanimously electing George Washington first President; John Adams, with 34 votes, becomes vice-president.

March 4. Majority of members of Congress for new government, elected in January and February, are still en route to New York and Congress does not have quorum present on date specified by Congress of the Confederacy. **April 1-8.** House of Representatives (30 of 59 members) and Senate (9 of 22 members) organize for conduct of business.

April 30. President Washington inaugurated at temporary capital in New York City on balcony of Federal Hall; he delivers inaugural address in Senate Chamber of Hall. Executive departments — War, Treasury, Foreign Affairs — continue temporarily as under Articles of Confederation.

May 5. Beginning of the French Revolution with meeting of Estates General at Versailles and formation by the third estate (commons) of the National Assembly. **July 14.** Paris mob storms the Bastille in attempt to get arms and to free political prisoners. Spontaneous uprisings all over France follow, as peasants revolt against feudal lords. **Aug. 27.** Assembly adopts the Declaration of Rights, preamble to first Constitution, which is largely based on American Declaration of Independence. Eventually most of Europe is involved and hostilities continue for 10 years.

July 4. New Congress passes first tariff bill, setting duties varying from 5 to 15 percent on various specified imports, to raise revenue for government expenses. A 10 percent reduction is allowed for goods imported in U.S.-owned and U.S.-built ships.

July 27. Organization of new executive departments begins with creation of Department of Foreign Affairs (later changed to Department of State). Thomas Jefferson is appointed secretary of state on September 26 but John Jay manages this department until Jefferson's return in March 1790 from post as minister to France. **Aug. 7.** War Department, created in 1785, is carried over intact to new government; General Henry Knox is appointed secretary of war on September 12. **Sept. 2.** Treasury Department is organized with Alexander Hamilton appointed secretary of the treasury on September 11. **Sept. 22.** Office of Postmaster General created and Samuel Osgood appointed on September 26, but Post Office is not permanently organized until 1795.

GEORGE WASHINGTON
First Inaugural Address, 1789
No people can be bound to acknowledge and adore the Invisible Hand which conducts the affairs of men more than those of the United States. Every step by which they have advanced to the character of an independent nation seems to have been distinguished by some token of providential agency; and in the important revolution just accomplished in the system of their united government the tranquil deliberations and voluntary consent of so many distinct communities from which the event has resulted cannot be compared with the means by which most governments have been established without some return of pious gratitude, along with a humble anticipation of the future blessings which the past seem to presage. . . .

I dwell on this prospect with every satisfaction which an ardent love for my country can inspire, since there is no truth more thoroughly established than that there exists in the economy and course of nature an indissoluble union between virtue and happiness; between duty and advantage; between the genuine maxims of an honest and magnanimous policy and the solid rewards of public prosperity and felicity, since we ought to be no less persuaded that the propitious smiles of Heaven can never be expected on a nation that disregards the eternal rules of order and right which Heaven itself has ordained; and since the preservation of the sacred fire of liberty and the destiny of the republican model of government are justly considered, perhaps, as deeply, as finally, staked on the experiment entrusted to the hands of the American people.

(Above) Benjamin West's painting, showing Jay, Adams, Franklin, Laurens, and William Franklin (peace commissioners, Paris, 1782) is unfinished because the British commissioners refused to sit with their American counterparts; (below left) Patrick Henry; (below right) Alexander Hamilton

(Above right) Edmund Randolph, the first attorney general; (above) John Jay, first chief justice of the Supreme Court; (right) Houdon's bust of Washington

JAMES MADISON
Letter to Jefferson, 1788

It is true, nevertheless, that not a few, particularly in Virginia, have contended for the proposed alterations from the most honorable and patriotic motives; and that among the advocates for the Constitution there are some who wish for further guards to public liberty and individual rights. As far as these may consist of a constitutional declaration of the most essential rights, it is probable they will be added; though there are many who think such addition unnecessary, and not a few who think it misplaced in such a Constitution. . . .

My own opinion has always been in favor of a Bill of Rights, provided it be so framed as not to imply powers not meant to be included in the enumeration. At the same time I have never thought the omission a material defect, nor been anxious to supply it even by subsequent amendment for any other reason than that it is anxiously desired by others. I have favored it because I supposed it might be of use, and if properly executed could not be of disservice.

I have not viewed it in an important light. . . .because experience proves the inefficacy of a Bill of Rights on those occasions when its control is most needed. Repeated violations of these parchment barriers have been committed by overbearing majorities in every state. . . .

Wherever the real power in a government lies, there is the danger of oppression. In our governments the real power lies in the majority of the community, and the invasion of private rights is chiefly to be apprehended, not from acts of government contrary to the sense of its constituents but from acts in which the government is the mere instrument of the major number of the constituents.

Sept. 9. House of Representatives begins action to adopt a federal bill of rights. Twelve amendments of the many proposed by various state ratifying conventions are recommended by Congress for adoption and proposed to states on September 25. Ten amendments are ratified by the necessary number of states and become part of the Constitution on December 15, 1791.

Sept. 24. Congress passes Federal Judiciary Act, setting up Supreme Court with a chief justice and five associate justices, also 13 district courts. **Sept. 26.** John Jay appointed first Chief Justice of the United States; Edmund Randolph appointed Attorney General.

Nov. 21. Submission to states by Congress of 12 amendments of a bill of rights results in second North Carolina ratifying convention which approves Constitution with amendments by vote of 194 to 77.

Georgia legislature grants to group of land companies for speculative purposes over 25 million acres in the region of the Yazoo River (Alabama and Mississippi); later grant of 35 million acres in 1795 leads eventually to Yazoo land fraud case of *Fletcher* v. *Peck* (1810), in which Supreme Court invalidates a state law for the first time.

Dr. John Jeffries, loyalist surgeon, holds first public lecture on anatomy in Boston; gathering is broken up by mob of citizens already indignant about dissection practised for study and teaching.

Protestant Episcopal Church organized independently of Church of England at first triennial convention held in Philadelphia.

Gazette of the United States, newspaper founded in New York by John Fenno and moved to Philadelphia in 1790, becomes leading Federalist weekly.

First American novel, *The Power of Sympathy,* is published; author is William Hill Brown.

University of North Carolina founded, becoming first state university to function; instruction begins in 1795.

End of Revolution and beginning of the new nation lead to a new architecture, a revival of classic Roman styles (later Greek also). Revival is inspired in part by Thomas Jefferson whose design for Virginia Capitol in Richmond is first Roman-style American building; his University of Virginia designs follow same trend. Classical influence is shown in buildings in Washington, D.C., designed by various architects, notably Benjamin Henry Latrobe, as well as a number of state capitols and commercial buildings. In spite of new style, architects such as Charles Bulfinch continue to build Adam (English) types of houses, especially in New England, for 30 years after the Revolution. Most architects of this period are not professionals but carpenter-builders.

Beginning of early period of historical, panoramic and religious painting such as "The Declaration of Independence" by John Trumbull, John Vanderlyn's "The Panorama of Versailles," and "The Bearing of the Cross" by William Dunlap.

1789 - 1796

General business depression of 1784 to 1788 halted; period of prosperity begins, stimulated by Hamilton's fiscal policies, American expansion into Ohio Valley, and opportunities for neutral trade during European wars of the French Revolution.

1790

Jan. 14. At request of Congress, Alexander Hamilton submits to House of Representatives first *Report on Public Credit* rec-

JOHN TRUMBULL
Letter to Jefferson, 1789
The greatest motive I had or have for engaging in or for continuing my pursuit of painting has been the wish of commemorating the great events of our country's Revolution. I am fully sensible that the profession, as it is generally practised, is frivolous, little useful to society, and unworthy of a man who has talents for more serious pursuits.

But to preserve and diffuse the memory of the noblest series of actions which have ever presented themselves in the history of man; to give to the present and the future sons of oppression and misfortune such glorious lessons of their rights and of the spirit with which they should assert and support them, and even to transmit to their descendants the personal resemblance of those who have been the great actors in those illustrious scenes were objects which gave a dignity to the profession peculiar to my situation. And some superiority also arose from my having borne personally a humble part in the great events which I was to describe. No one lives with me possessing this advantage, and no one can come after me to divide the honor of truth and authenticity, however easily I may hereafter be exceeded in elegance.

BENJAMIN FRANKLIN
Letter to Washington, 1780
I must soon quit the scene, but you may live to see our country flourish; as it will amazingly and rapidly after the war is over; like a field of young Indian corn, which long fair weather and sunshine had enfeebled and discolored, and which in that weak state, by a sudden gust of violent wind, hail, and rain, seemed to be threatened with absolute destruction; yet the storm being past, it recovers fresh verdure, shoots up with double vigor, and delights the eye not of its owner only, but of every observing traveler.

GEORGE WASHINGTON
Letter to Franklin, 1789
If to be venerated for benevolence: if to be admired for talents: if to be esteemed for patriotism: if to be beloved for philanthropy, can gratify the human mind, you must have the pleasing consolation that you have not lived in vain.

TURGOT
Inscription on bust of Franklin
Eripuit coelo fulmen sceptrumque tyrannis.
(He snatched the lightning from heaven and the sceptre from tyrants.)

ommending that the federal government be responsible for national debt (foreign and domestic) carried over from the Confederation (about $56 million), and assume most of the burden of debt (about $21 million) incurred by the states during the Revolution. Southern states, whose debt payments are already arranged for, object especially to U.S. assuming state debts, since they will be taxed for debts of Middle and New England states. Hamilton and Madison arrange compromise by which South agrees to accept share in debt of Northern states in return for location of national capital on Potomac River instead of at Philadelphia. **July 26.** Hamilton's proposal is passed over objection of those who have been forced to sell securities at depreciated rates.

Feb. 11. Society of Friends (Quakers) make first petition to Congress for emancipation of slaves.

April 17. Benjamin Franklin dies in Philadelphia at age 84. Half of Philadelphia, 20,000 people, attend his funeral.

May 29. Rhode Island's state convention, having first met in January, finally ratifies Constitution and becomes the thirteenth state of the United States. Decision is due in part to the passing by the Senate of a bill severing commercial relations between the United States and Rhode Island.

Dec. 6. Congress assembles at Philadelphia, voted temporary national capital until 1800.

Dec. 14. Hamilton submits report to House recommending establishment of a national bank. Bank is opposed by Jefferson but charter is signed by President Washington February 25, 1791.

Hamilton submits second *Report on Public Credit* recommending an excise tax on manufacture of liquor to increase federal revenue; tax is opposed by farmers of back-woods areas where distilling is only available means of marketing surplus grain, prohibitively expensive to transport in bulk even where roads exist. Whiskey tax bill is passed on March 3, 1791.

Dec. 21. Cotton spun for first time by water power by Samuel Slater in factory at Pawtucket, Rhode Island. Slater had emigrated from England in previous year when England prohibited export of textile machinery plans and constructed from memory Richard Arkwright's spinning machine, thus initiating cotton industry in U.S.

First national census sets United States population at 4 million (including 800,000 Negro slaves) distributed approximately 25 percent in New England, 25 percent in Middle States, and 50 percent in South. Largest city is Philadelphia, with 42,000 inhabitants; followed, in order, by New York, Boston, Charleston (South Carolina), and Baltimore; but total urban population (in towns of 2,500 or more) is only 5.4 percent. Life expectancy at birth is 34.5 years for males, 36.5 for females.

First American Roman Catholic bishop, John Carroll, is consecrated (in England) at a time when only four states have absolute religious tolerance and only Pennsylvania has Catholic churches.

Samuel Hopkins receives first federal patent for his process for manufacturing pot and pearl ash (crude and commercial carbonate of potassium) used in glass making.

1791

March 4. Vermont admitted to the Union as the fourteenth state. Claimed by Massachusetts, New Hampshire, and New York, it had, in 1777, declared itself an independent republic, but land disputes had not been settled until 1790.

JOHN CARROLL
Letter to Cardinal Antonelli, 1785
The Most Eminent Cardinal may rest assured that the greatest evils would be borne by us rather than renounce the divine authority of the Holy See; that not only we priests who are here, but the Catholic people, seem so firm In the faith that they will never withdraw from obedience to the sovereign pontiff. The Catholic body, however, think that some favor should be granted to them by the Holy Father, necessary for their permanent enjoyment of the civil rights which they now enjoy, and to avert the dangers which they fear. From what I have said, and from the framework of public affairs here, Your Eminence must see how objectionable all foreign jurisdiction will be to them. The Catholics therefore desire that no pretext be given to the enemies of our religion to accuse us of depending unnecessarily on a foreign authority; and that some plan may be adopted by which hereafter an ecclesiastical superior may be appointed for this country in such a way as to retain absolutely the spiritual jurisdiction of the Holy See, and at the same time remove all ground of objecting to us, as though we held anything hostile to the national independence.

JAMES MADISON
National Gazette, 1792
In every political society, parties are unavoidable. A difference of interests, real or supposed, is the most natural and fruitful source of them. The great object should be to combat the evil: (1) by establishing a political equality among all; (2) by witholding unnecessary opportunities from a few to increase the inequality of property by an immoderate, and especially an unmerited, accumulation of riches; (3) by the silent operation of laws, which, without violating the rights of property, reduce extreme wealth toward a state of mediocrity and raise extreme indigence toward a state of comfort; (4) by abstaining from measures which operate differently on different interests, and particularly such as favor one interest at the expense of another; (5) by making one party a check on the other, so far as the existence of parties cannot be prevented nor their views accommodated. If this is not the language of reason, it is that of republicanism. . . .

From the expediency, in politics, of making natural parties mutual checks on each other, to infer the propriety of creating artificial parties in order to form them into mutual checks is not less absurd than it would be in ethics to say that new vices ought to be promoted where they would counteract each other, because this use may be made of existing vices.

May-June. Disagreement with administration's fiscal policies leads Jefferson and Madison to establish a political alliance with anti-Federalist faction in New York. Conflict results eventually in formation from already existing smaller groups of the first two national political parties: Republicans (later Democratic-Republicans) led by Jefferson, and Federalists under Hamilton.

Oct. 31. *National Gazette*, anti-Hamilton newspaper, is founded, edited by Philip Freneau. It is soon warring with the Federalist *Gazette of the United States.*

Dec. 5. Hamilton's *Report on Manufactures* is submitted to Congress. It proposes protective tariffs for industry, agricultural subsidies, and internal improvements (chiefly roads and canals) financed by the federal government.

Dec. 12. Bank of the United States, proposed by Alexander Hamilton, opens main office at Philadelphia; eight branches are established in leading commercial centers.

Part of Benjamin Franklin's *Autobiography*, written from 1771 to 1789 and covering years to 1759, published in Paris; full text is not published until 1868.

Charlotte Temple, a sentimental novel by Susanna Rowson, is published and achieves wide popularity.

1791 - 1792

Securities exchange organized in Philadelphia in 1791, followed by New York exchange in 1792. Both deal largely in federal stock rather than local enterprise.

1792

Feb. 21. Presidential Succession Act provides that order of succession is vice-president, president pro-tempore of the Senate, speaker of the house.

April 2. Mint Act provides for decimal system of coinage, sets up two-metal standard at ratio of 15 (silver) to 1 (gold), and establishes mint at Philadelphia.

April. General Anthony Wayne appointed commander of military forces in Ohio country following defeat of General Arthur St. Clair by Indians in November 1791. **May 8.** Growing Indian hostility in Northwest Territory leads to passage of Militia Act allowing states to raise armed forces of all able-bodied free white males of 18 to 45.

June 1. Kentucky, formerly part of Virginia, is admitted to the Union as fifteenth state.

Aug. 21. Pittsburgh convention passes resolves denouncing Hamilton's whiskey tax and proposes measures to frustrate its collection; Southern states also resist this tax. **Sept. 29.** President Washington issues a proclamation insisting on enforcement.

Dec. 5. Electors cast their votes for President and vice-president: President Washington is reelected with 132 votes; Adams is also reelected (77 votes). George Clinton of New York gets substantial vote (50 out of 132), indicating anti-administration feeling.

Philadelphia-Lancaster Turnpike begun (completed in 1794); its success as a business venture leads to building of many other toll roads, especially in New England and Middle States.

Twelve-hundred-mile Columbia River (in present-day Washington) discovered by Captain Robert Gray of Boston in ship *Columbia* on fur trading expedition. Discovery becomes one basis for U.S. claim to Pacific Northwest.

PHILIP FRENEAU
National Gazette, 1792
Rules for changing a limited republican government into an unlimited hereditary one.

It being necessary, in order to effect the change, to get rid of constitutional shackles and popular prejudices, all possible means and occasions are to be used for both these purposes. . . .

But the grand nostrum will be a public debt, provided enough of it can be got and it be medicated with the proper ingredients. If by good fortune a debt be ready at hand, the most is to be made of it. . . . Assume all the debts of your neighbors—in a word, get as much debt as can be raked and scraped together, and when you have got all you can, "advertise" for more, and have the debt made as big as possible. This object being accomplished, the next will be to make it as perpetual as possible; and the next to that, to get it into as few hands as possible. . . .

The favorite few, thus possessed of it, whether within or without the government, will feel the staunchest fealty to it, and will go through thick and thin to support it in all its oppressions and usurpations. . . . A great debt will require great taxes; great taxes, many taxgatherers and other officers; and all officers are auxiliaries of power. Heavy taxes may produce discontents; these may threaten resistance; and in proportion to this danger will be the pretense for a standing army to repel it. A standing army, in its turn, will increase the moral force of the government by means of its appointments, and give it physical force by means of the sword, thus doubly forwarding the main object.

HUGH H. BRACKENRIDGE
Modern Chivalry, 1792

Teague, you are quite wrong in this matter they have put into your head. Do you know what it is to be a member of a deliberative body? What qualifications are necessary? . . .

When a man becomes a member of a public body, he is like a raccoon, or other beast that climbs up the fork of a tree; the boys pushing at him with pitchforks, or throwing stones, or shooting at him with arrows; the dogs barking in the meantime. One will find fault with your not speaking; another with your speaking, if you speak at all. They will put you in the newspapers, and ridicule you as a perfect beast. There is what they call the caricatura; that is, representing you with a dog's head, or a cat's claw. It is the devil to be exposed to the squibs and crackers of the gazette wits and publications. You know no more about these matters than a goose; and yet you would undertake rashly, without advice, to enter on the office; nay, contrary to advice. For I would not for a hundred guineas, though I have not the half to spare, that the breed of the O'Regans should come to this; bringing on them a worse stain than stealing sheep. You have nothing but your character, Teague, in a new country to depend upon. Let it never be said, that you quitted an honest livelihood, the taking care of my horse, to follow the new-fangled whims of the times, and be a statesman.

Return of portraitist Gilbert Stuart from study and professional success in England and Ireland inaugurates his career in New York, Philadelphia, Washington, and Boston as most famous of American portrait painters.

Completion of publication of Thomas Paine's *The Rights of Man*, written to defend measures used by French republicans during the early part of the French Revolution. *Modern Chivalry* by Hugh Henry Brackenridge describes frontier conditions satirically.

Russian Orthodox Church begins missionary work in Alaska; resident bishop arrives in 1798.

1793

Jan. 21. Execution of Louis XVI following proclamation of French Republic in September 1792 divides American opinion on French Revolution. **Feb. 1.** France's declaration of war on England and Holland (a month later on Spain) helps to establish party line between pro-British Federalists and anti-British Jeffersonians.

Jan. 23. Representative William Branch Giles of Virginia proposes resolutions in House for inquiry into state of Treasury; Hamilton is forced to defend himself (February 4 and 13) against charges of corruption and mismanagement. **Feb. 28.** Resolutions of censure are submitted by Giles and others, but defeated.

April. Citizen Genêt Affair. French Minister to United States, Edmond Charles Genêt, takes advantage of warm popular welcome to commission American privateers and send them to plunder British shipping. **May 18.** Genêt is coldly received by President Washington. **June 5.** He is ordered by Jefferson to cease organization of hostile projects on American soil. Genêt promises to comply but reneges, threatening to appeal to American people. **Aug. 2.** Cabinet decides to demand his recall but accession of Jacobins to power in France leads to his remaining in America as U.S. citizen.

April 22. President Washington declares American neutrality in Anglo-French war; some Americans sympathize strongly with Britain or France but Washington warns them against hostility toward either power.

July 31. President Washington's supposed partiality for the Federalists and for Hamilton's opinions on foreign affairs leads Jefferson to resign as secretary of state, effective December 31. He is succeeded by Edmund Randolph.

August-October. Yellow fever outbreak in Philadelphia becomes worst epidemic in any U.S. city; leads to improved methods of sewage disposal and more sanitary water systems.

Eli Whitney invents cotton gin for removing seed from green cotton. Mechanical process greatly increases output and revives dying slave economy of South.

1794

March 5. Congress proposes to states eleventh constitutional amendment exempting states from suits by citizens of other states and foreign countries. Amendment is declared ratified on January 8, 1798.

June 5. Neutrality Act prohibits enlistment of any U.S. citizen in service of foreign countries and forbids the supplying of foreign armed vessels in U.S. ports.

July. Whiskey Rebellion breaks out in western Pennsylvania, provoked by enforcement of excise tax. **Aug. 7.** President Wash-

ELI WHITNEY
Letter to his father, 1793
During this time I heard much said of the extreme difficulty of ginning cotton, that is, separating it from its seeds. . . . I involuntarily happened to be thinking on the subject and struck out a plan of a machine in my mind, which I communicated to Miller. . . . He was pleased with the plan and said if I would pursue it and try an experiment to see if it would answer, he would be at the whole expense; I should lose nothing but my time, and if I succeeded we would share the profits. . . .

In about ten days I made a little model, for which I was offered, if I would give up all right and title to it, 100 guineas. I concluded to relinquish my school and turn my attention to perfecting the machine. I made one before I came away which required the labor of one man to turn it and with which one man will clean ten times as much cotton as he can in any other way before known, and also cleanse it much better than in the usual mode. This machine may be turned by water or with a horse with the greatest ease, and one man and a horse will do more than fifty men with the old machines. It makes the labor fifty times less, without throwing any class of people out of business. . . .

How advantageous this business will eventually prove to me, I cannot say. It is generally said by those who know anything about it that I shall make a fortune by it. I have no expectation that I shall make an independent fortune by it, but think I had better pursue it than any other business into which I can enter.

ALEXANDER HAMILTON
"Tully" letters, 1794
Those, therefore, who preach doctrines, or set examples which undermine or subvert the authority of the laws, lead us from freedom to slavery; they incapacitate us for a government of laws, and, consequently, prepare the way for one of force, for mankind must have government of one sort or another. . . .

Such a resistance is treason against society, against liberty, against everything that ought to be dear to a free, enlightened, and prudent people. To tolerate it were to abandon your most precious interests. Not to subdue it were to tolerate it. Those who openly or covertly dissuade you from exertions adequate to the occasion are your worst enemies. They treat you either as fools or cowards, too weak to perceive your interest or your duty, or too dastardly to pursue them. They, therefore, merit and will, no doubt, meet your contempt. . . .

Fellow citizens: you are told that it will be intemperate to urge the execution of the laws which are resisted. What? Will it be indeed intemperate in your chief magistrate, sworn to maintain the Constitution, charged faithfully to execute the laws, and authorized to employ for that purpose force when the ordinary means fail — will it be intemperate in him to exert that force when the Constitution and the laws are opposed by force? Can he answer it to his conscience, to you, not to exert it? . . .

The hydra anarchy would rear its head in every quarter. The goodly fabric you have established would be rent asunder, and precipitated into the dust.

ington orders rebels to return home and calls for 15,000 volunteers from four states. **Sept. 24.** Failure of negotiations with insurrection leaders brings second proclamation ordering suppression of rebellion. Insurgents are tried for treason in May 1795; two are convicted but are pardoned by President Washington.

Aug. 20. Indian resistance broken and Northwest frontier secured by victory of General Anthony Wayne at Battle of Fallen Timbers in northwest Ohio on the Maumee River.

Nov. 19. Jay's Treaty secures promise of British withdrawal from Western military posts by June 1796, and other concessions, but fails to settle various grievances, especially the question of British interference with neutral American shipping in Anglo-French war. Treaty is bitterly criticized in the U.S. where it becomes the focus of Federalist-Republican party conflict. Treaty is ratified by Congress after prolonged debate in June 1795, but funds for its enforcement are not appropriated until April 1796.

Act of 1794 provides for additional mail routes and stage transportation. Up to 1792, Vermont, Kentucky, Tennessee, and the West have had no mail routes, and there were only 5,000 miles of post roads in all. Typical postal rates, usually paid by recipient: 6 cents up to 30 miles; 15 cents up to 200 miles; and 25 cents over 400 miles. Much mail goes by ship, usually at double fee; city deliveries involve additional fee, paid to mail carrier.

Scientific study is stimulated by arrival in U.S. of Joseph Priestley, English clergyman and chemist, who had discovered oxygen in 1774. First American chair in chemistry is established at College of New Jersey (later Princeton) in 1795.

Aurora of Philadelphia succeeds *National*

Gazette as principal Republican newspaper; *Aurora* had formerly been *General Advertiser*, founded in 1790 by Benjamin F. Bache, grandson of Benjamin Franklin. William Duane later succeeds Bache as editor.

Tammany by James Hewitt, said to be first American opera, performed in New York City.

1795

Jan. 2. Timothy Pickering of Massachusetts named secretary of war in reorganization of Cabinet. **Jan. 31.** Hamilton resigns from Treasury Department but continues as adviser and dominant voice in administration. **Aug. 19.** Edmund Randolph, having succeeded Jefferson as secretary of state, is forced to resign when President Washington becomes convinced of intrigue with French minister to prevent ratification of Jay's Treaty. Pickering succeeds to State Department, and James McHenry to War Department.

Jan. 29. Naturalization Act passed, making five-year residence a requirement for citizenship.

Aug. 3. Treaty of Greenville signed by 12 Indian tribes differentiates Indian lands and those open to settlers in Northwest Territory.

Oct. 27. Pinckney's Treaty (Treaty of San Lorenzo) with Spain gains Spanish recognition of U.S. Southern and Western boundaries (the 31st parallel and the Mississippi River) and right of navigation on Mississippi for U.S. Negotiations are by Thomas Pinckney, U.S. minister to Great Britain.

1796

May 18. Land Act passed by House providing for rectangular survey and public auction of land at minimum of $2 an acre,

TIMOTHY PICKERING
Letter to General Wayne, 1795
The overtures for peace which have been made by the Indians northwest of the Ohio bear the appearance of sincerity, and viewed in connection with the events of the last year, it is hardly to be doubted that their overtures have been made in good faith. Taking this for granted, it becomes necessary to communicate to you the ideas of the President of the United States relative to the terms on which peace is now to be negotiated. To gratify the usual expectation of Indians assembling for the purposes of treaty and thereby facilitate the negotiation, it is thought best to provide and forward a quantity of goods. These will amount to at least $25,000, but are to be delivered only in case of a successful treaty: except such small portions of them as humanity may call for pending the negotiation. . . .

As they will be collected within your power at Greenville, it will highly concern the honor and justice of the United States that strong and decided proofs be given them that they are not under even the shadow of duress. Let them feel that they are at perfect liberty to speak their sentiments, and to sign or refuse to sign such a treaty as you are now authorized to negotiate. . . .

One great principle ought to govern all public negotiations — a rigid adherence to truth — a principle that is essential in negotiations with Indians if we would gain their permanent confidence and a useful influence over them. Jealousy is strongest in minds uninformed, so that the utmost purity and candor will hardly escape suspicion. Suspicions occasion delays, and issue in discontents, and these in depredations and war.

GEORGE WASHINGTON
Farewell Address, 1796

In contemplating the causes which may disturb our Union, it occurs as matter of serious concern that any ground should have been furnished for characterizing parties by geographical discriminations: Northern and Southern; Atlantic and Western; whence designing men may endeavor to excite a belief that there is a real difference of local interests and views. . . . You cannot shield yourselves too much against the jealousies and heartburnings which spring from these misrepresentations. They tend to render alien to each other those who ought to be bound together by fraternal affection. . . .

Observe good faith and justice toward all nations. Cultivate peace and harmony with all. Religion and morality enjoin this conduct; and can it be that good policy does not equally enjoin it? It will be worthy of a free, enlightened, and, at no distant period, a great nation

and for division of public domain into townships six miles square, with half the townships further divided into 36 sections of 640 acres each. Senate defeats attempt by Westerners to allow division of half the sections into quarter sections of 160 acres.

June 1. Tennessee admitted to the Union as the sixteenth state. Formerly part of North Carolina, and since 1790 "The Territory of the United States South of the River Ohio," it is the first state to be formed out of U.S. government territory.

Sept. 19. Washington's Farewell Address, dated September 17 but never delivered orally, published in Philadelphia *Daily American Advertiser*. Written with help of Madison and Hamilton, address, among other things, warns U.S. against "permanent" alliances, but advises temporary ones in emergencies.

Dec. 7. John Adams, Federalist candidate for President, elected by narrow margin, 71 to 68, over Thomas Jefferson, Democratic-

"The Surrender of Burgoyne" by John Trumbull

"The Surrender of Lord Cornwallis" by John Trumbull

Republican; Jefferson becomes vice-president. Federalist Thomas Pinckney receives 59 votes; Democrat-Republican Aaron Burr receives 30 votes.

U.S. Supreme Court passes on and upholds constitutionality of congressional act for first time in *Hylton* v. *United States* which involves tax on carriages act passed in 1794. In *Ware* v. *Hylton* Court invalidates Virginia statute of 1777 voiding debts owed to British subjects, contrary to U.S. treaty of 1783 which provides for payment, thus maintaining supremacy of national over state law.

Congress authorizes construction of Zane's Trace, road from Wheeling (now in West Virginia) to Limestone (now Maysville), Ky. Road becomes one of the main routes traveled by westbound settlers.

Cleveland, Ohio, laid out by Moses Cleaveland, agent for Connecticut Land Company that had purchased the Western Reserve (northeastern Ohio) in 1795.

to give to mankind the magnanimous and too novel example of a people always guided by an exalted justice and benevolence. . . .

In the execution of such a plan nothing is more essential than that permanent, inveterate antipathies against particular nations and passionate attachments for others should be excluded and that in place of them just and amicable feelings toward all should be cultivated. The nation which indulges toward another an habitual hatred or an habitual fondness is in some degree a slave. It is a slave to its animosity or to its affection, either of which is sufficient to lead it astray from its duty and its interest. . . .

The great rule of conduct for us, in regard to foreign nations, is in extending our commercial relations to have with them as little political connection as possible. So far as we have already formed engagements, let them be fulfilled with perfect good faith. Here let us stop.

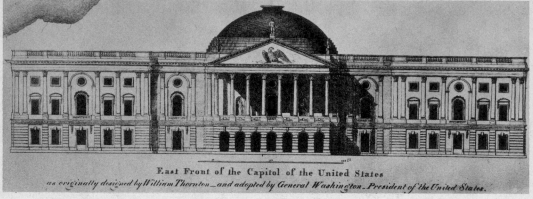

East Front of the Capitol of the United States
as originally designed by William Thornton—and adopted by General Washington President of the United States.

Design by William Thornton for the Capitol

FISHER AMES
Letter to Pickering, 1798

Why should not we play off against our foe a part of their own policy? Wage war, and call it self-defense; forbear to call it war; on the contrary, let it be said that we deprecate war, and will desist from arms, as soon as her acts shall be repealed, etc., grounding all we do on the necessity of self-preservation, etc. . . . A formal declaration would perhaps engender discords; all the thinking would come first, the action after. I would reverse this order. Not that I would conceal from the country its duties or its dangers. No, they should be fully stated and enforced. . . .

My long letter amounts to this: we must make haste to wage war, or we shall be lost. But in doing it, and, I might premise, to induce Congress to do it, and that without its ordinary slowness, we had better begin at the tail of the business and go on enacting the consequences of war, instead of declaring it at once. The latter might be the bolder measure; its adaptedness to the temper of Congress, and even of the country, is not equally clear. Something energetic and decisive must be done soon. Congress fiddles while our Rome is burning.

1797

May 31. XYZ Affair. President John Adams appoints three-man commission consisting of Charles Cotesworth Pinckney, American Minister to Britain, John Marshall and Elbridge Gerry to seek treaty of commerce and amity with France. The French Directory, convinced that Jay's Treaty shows U.S. partiality toward Britain, has refused to receive Pinckney in December 1796 and has regularly interfered with American shipping (over 300 vessels have been lost in one year). **Oct. 4.** Commissioners arrive in Paris and are visited on October 18 by three agents of French Foreign Minister Talleyrand (identified in commission reports as X, Y, and Z). Agents suggest a U.S. loan to France and a $240,000 bribe for Talleyrand himself; they also threaten war between France and U.S. Commission refuses emphatically.

Preaching of James McGready, leader of camp meeting movement, is beginning of great religious revival on Western frontier.

1798

March 19. President Adams reports to Congress only that French mission has failed and says that America must prepare for war. **April 3.** Strong pro-French and anti-British protest forces Adams to submit

XYZ correspondence to Congress, swinging public opinion against France. **March-July** In preparation for war, Congress passes 20 measures to strengthen national defense. **July 2.** George Washington is called from retirement to serve as commander in chief with Alexander Hamilton as second in command. **May 3.** Navy Department is established. **July 7.** Existing treaties with France are repealed. **Nov. 20.** Two years of undeclared war begin; isolated engagements include capture of French *L'Insurgente* by U.S. frigate *Constellation* on February 9, 1799.

Fear of war with France results in suspicion of aliens in U.S. **June-July.** Naturalization Act of June 18, Alien Act of June 25, Alien Enemies Act of July 6, and Sedition Act of July 14 passed by Federalist majority in Congress restrict activities (including freedom of speech) of citizens and European refugees, among whom are prominent supporters of Jefferson's party. Ten Republican newspaper editors are convicted, fined, and jailed for sedition.

November-December. Virginia and Kentucky Resolutions, framed by James Madison and Thomas Jefferson passed by Virginia and Kentucky legislatures; Resolutions declare that Alien and Sedition Acts are unconstitutional and that in such a case, states are "duty bound to interpose."

JAMES MADISON
Virginia Resolutions, 1798
Resolved, *that the General Assembly of Virginia . . . does explicitly and peremptorily declare that it views the powers of the federal government as resulting from the compact to which the states are parties, as limited by the plain sense and intention of the instrument constituting that compact, as no further valid than they are authorized by the grants enumerated in that compact; and that, in case of a deliberate, palpable, and dangerous exercise of other powers, not granted by the said compact, the states who are parties thereto, have the right, and are in duty bound to interpose for arresting the progress of the evil, and for maintaining, within their respective limits, the authorities, rights, and liberties, appertaining to them.*

That the General Assembly does also express its deep regret that a spirit has, in sundry instances, been manifested by the federal government to enlarge its powers by forced constructions of the constitutional charter which defines them; and that indications have appeared of a design to expound certain general phrases . . . so as to destroy the meaning and effect of the particular enumeration which necessarily explains and limits the general phrases, and so as to consolidate the states, by degrees, into one sovereignty, the obvious tendency and inevitable result of which would be to transform the present republican system of the United States into an absolute or, at best, a mixed monarchy.

The White House in 1799, prior to occupancy by John and Abigail Adams

JOSEPH HOPKINSON
Hail Columbia!, 1798
Hail Columbia, happy land!
Hail ye heroes, heav'n-born band
Who fought and bled in freedom's
cause,
Who fought and bled in freedom's
cause;
And when the storm of war was gone,
Enjoyed the peace your valor won. . . .

Immortal patriots, rise once more!
Defend your rights, defend your shore!
Let no rude foe with impious hand,
Let no rude foe with impious hand
Invade the shrine where sacred lies,
Of toil and blood, the well-earned
prize.
While off'ring peace, sincere and just,
In heav'n we place a manly trust
That truth and justice may prevail,
And ev'ry scheme of bondage fail.

Sound, sound the trump of fame!
Let Washington's great name
Ring through the world with loud
applause,
Ring through the world with loud
applause;
Let ev'ry chime to freedom dear
Listen with a joyful ear.
With equal skill, with steady pow'r,
He governs in the fearful hour
Of horrid war, or guides with ease
The happier time of honest peace.

Behold the chief who now commands!
Once more to serve his country stands
The rock on which the storm will beat,
The rock on which the storm will beat;
But armed in virtue, firm and true,
His hopes are fixed on heav'n and you.
When hope was sinking in dismay,
When gloom obscured Columbia's day,
His steady mind, from changes free,
Resolved on death or liberty.

Calder v. *Bull* declares that prohibition against *ex post facto* laws (laws passed after a crime is committed) in Article I, Section 10 of Constitution applies only to criminal, not civil, laws.

Organization of Mississippi Territory, region between Georgia's western border and Mississippi River, opens this area to settlement, but most colonization is delayed by hostility of Indians and by Spanish control of West Florida ports.

Benjamin Thompson, Count Rumford, Loyalist exile, reports on his experiments in England involving heat as a form of motion.

Words of "Hail Columbia" by Joseph Hopkinson set to music of "The President's March" (*c.* 1793) thought to be work of Philip Roth or Philip Phile. Robert Treat Paine writes words of song "Adams and Liberty."

1798 - 1800

1798. Eli Whitney begins manufacture of 10,000 muskets for U.S. **1800.** Whitney devises system of interchangeable gun parts which, with additional machinery, makes it possible to use comparatively inexperienced workmen in his factory.

1799

Feb. 18. President Adams averts war with France by nominating William Vans Murray new minister to France on Talleyrand's assurance of respectful reception; thwarts prowar faction among Federalists by appointing new members to former Commission, two of whom are Federalists.

February. John Fries and several hundred Pennsylvania men rebel against payment of property tax established in 1798 in anticipation of French War. Fries resists U.S. marshal, is convicted of treason, but is pardoned by President Adams.

Dec. 14. George Washington dies at Mount Vernon, after catching a cold that develops into a severe sore throat. He is buried at Mount Vernon.

Publication of *The Practical Navigator*, which remains a classic work of reference for seamen, by Nathaniel Bowditch; also *Arthur Mervyn*, a fictionalized but accurate account of Philadelphia's yellow fever epidemic, by Charles Brockden Brown.

First Negro minstrel act is shown in the play *Oroonoko*, produced in Boston, when an actor made up in black-face sings "The Gay Negro Boy," accompanying himself on banjo.

1800

April 4. First federal bankruptcy law, applying only to merchants and traders, allows release from prison of Robert Morris, Revolutionary superintendent of finances who personally arranged for payment of the armed forces. Financially ruined in various land speculations, he had been confined to debtor's prison since 1798.

May 10. Land Act of 1800, also known as Harrison Land Act, reduces minimum purchase of public lands from 640 to 320 acres (half sections), establishes liberal credit terms. Resulting sales in first 18 months of enactment are 400,000 acres, as compared with less than 50,000 sold under Act of 1796, but much of the purchasing is by speculators rather than settlers.

Sept. 30. Convention of 1800 (Treaty of Morfontaine) is signed by France and the

GEORGE WASHINGTON
Last Will and Testament, 1799
As it has always been a source of serious regret with me to see the youth of these United States sent to foreign countries for the purpose of education, often before their minds were formed or they had imbibed any adequate ideas of the happiness of their own, contracting too frequently not only habits of dissipation and extravagance but principles unfriendly to republican government and to the true and genuine liberties of mankind, which thereafter are rarely overcome. For these reasons it has been my ardent wish to see a plan devised on a liberal scale which would have a tendency to spread systematic ideas through all parts of this rising empire, thereby to do away local attachments and state prejudices as far as the nature of things would, or, indeed, ought to admit from our national councils. . . . My mind has not been able to contemplate any plan more likely to effect the measure than the establishment of a university in a central part of the United States to which the youth of fortune and talents from all parts thereof might be sent for the completion of their education in all the branches of polite literature in arts and sciences, in acquiring knowledge in the principles of politics and good government.

HENRY LEE
Eulogy on Washington
To the memory of the man, first in war, first in peace, and first in the hearts of his countrymen.

First page of the Louisiana Purchase treaty, French copy

MASON LOCKE WEEMS
The Life of George Washington, 1806
"George," said his father, "do you know who killed that beautiful little cherry tree yonder in the garden?" This was a tough question; and George staggered under it for a moment; but quickly recovered himself: and looking at his father with the inexpressible charm of all-conquering truth, he bravely cried out, "I can't tell a lie, Pa; you know I can't tell a lie. I did cut it with my hatchet." —"Run to my arms, you dearest boy," cried his father in transports, "run to my arms; glad am I , George, that you killed my tree; for you have payed me for it a thousand fold. Such an act of heroism in my son is more worth than a thousand trees, though blossomed with silver, and their fruits of purest gold."

U.S.; it abrogates U.S.-French Revolutionary alliance, brings French crisis of 1797-1800 to an end. Split in Federalist Party occurs over Adams' handling of French situation.

Oct. 1. Napoleon Bonaparte forces Spain to cede Louisiana to France by secret Treaty of San Ildefonso as move to revive French colonial empire in North America; France does not take possession.

Nov. 17. Congress convenes for first time in Washington, D.C.

Second U.S. census shows population of 5,308,000, an increase of 35 percent since 1790; figure includes 43,000 immigrants.

United Brethren in Christ founded by Martin Boehm and Philip E. Otterbein, who are first bishops.

Thomas Jefferson donates his private library to the federal government as initial collection in establishing Library of Congress.

Clergyman-bookseller Mason Locke ("Parson") Weems writes his widely popular but historically inaccurate *The Life and Memorable Actions of George Washington*.

1800 - 1802

1800. Cowpox vaccination to prevent smallpox introduced by Dr. Benjamin Waterhouse in Philadelphia. **Oct.-Nov. 1802.** Boston Board of Health experiments prove safety and effectiveness of vaccine.

1801

Jan. 20. John Marshall appointed Chief Justice of the Supreme Court in one of President Adams' last official acts.

Feb. 11. Count of ballots of presidential electors (cast December 3, 1800) shows a tie between Democratic-Republicans Jefferson and Aaron Burr each with 73 votes. Federalists John Adams, Charles Cotesworth Pinckney, and John Jay receive 65, 64, and 1 vote respectively. **Feb. 17.** House of Representatives, with one vote per state, elects Jefferson third President of the U.S. on thirty-sixth ballot by vote of 10 to 6 when Hamilton uses his influence against Burr, whom he considers the greater evil. Burr is elected Vice-President.

Feb. 27. Judiciary Act reduces number of Supreme Court justices to five, creates sixteen new circuit judgeships as well as positions for attorneys, marshals, and clerks. President Adams places Federalists in these positions in "midnight" appointments lasting until 9 P.M. on March 3, his last day in office, in effort to maintain Federalist power after losing presidency.

March 4. Jefferson inaugurated; first President to take office in District of Columbia. Inaugural address sets forth Democratic-Republican program, stressing economy and need for limits to power of central government.

May 14. Naval conflict with Tripoli begins when Tripolitan Pasha, demanding increase in tribute customarily paid to pirates of the Barbary States by foreign ships, declares war on U.S. President Jefferson dispatches naval vessels to Mediterranean, where blockade eventually brings war to an end. Peace treaty is signed by U.S. and Tripoli, but tribute payments to other Barbary States (Algiers, Tunis, and Morocco) are made until 1816.

New York Evening Post, Federalist newspaper, founded by Alexander Hamilton and others.

THOMAS JEFFERSON
First Inaugural Address, 1801
We have called by different names brethren of the same principle. We are all Republicans, we are all Federalists. If there be any among us who would wish to dissolve this Union or to change its republican form, let them stand undisturbed as monuments of the safety with which error of opinion may be tolerated where reason is left free to combat it. I know, indeed, that some honest men fear that a republican government cannot be strong, that this government is not strong enough; but would the honest patriot, in the full tide of successful experiment, abandon a government which has so far kept us free and firm on the theoretic and visionary fear that this government, the world's best hope, may by possibility want energy to preserve itself? I trust not. . . . Sometimes it is said that man cannot be trusted with the government of himself. Can he, then, be trusted with the government of others? Or have we found angels in the forms of kings to govern him? Let history answer this question. . . .

[Let us have] a wise and frugal government, which shall restrain men from injuring one another, which shall leave them otherwise free to regulate their own pursuits of industry and improvement, and shall not take from the mouth of labor the bread it has earned. This is the sum of good government, and this is necessary to close the circle of our felicities.

(Above) John Adams, second President of the United States: pastel portrait by Benjamin Blyth; (left) portrait of John Marshall by John Wesley Jarvis, 1825; (below) sketches submitted to the Patent Office in 1793 by Eli Whitney, showing the design and operation of the cotton gin

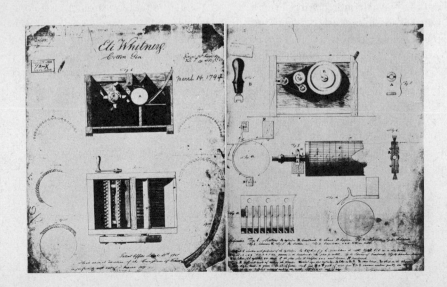

(Above) Frigate "Philadelphia" under attack in
the Tripolitan War, 1804–1805: the war ended need
for tribute to the Pasha of Tripoli, but payment
to other Barbary states continued until 1816;
(right) Thomas Jefferson, third President of the
United States: portrait by C. W. Peale; (below)
engraving from the third edition of "A Journal
of the Voyage . . . of Captain Lewis and Captain
Clarke . . ." by Patrick Gass, a member of the
expedition of 1804–1805

Resolutions of Dinwiddie County, Virginia, 1798

Resolved, *as the opinion of this meeting, that a militia, composed of the body of the people, is the proper, natural, and safe defense of a free state, and that regular armies, except in case of an invasion, or the certain prospect of an invasion, are not only highly detrimental to the public welfare but dangerous to liberty.*

Detrimental to the public welfare; *because industrious men are heavily taxed to support those who do nothing; . . . because the same object, immediate defense against a sudden invasion, might be attained infinitely cheaper by putting arms into the hands of every man capable of bearing them; and because the spirit which leads to war, the cause and the disgrace of humanity, is greatly augmented by standing armies, to whose leaders it opens a prospect of greater wealth and higher military honors; and,*

Dangerous to liberty; *because, when numerous, they have tyrannized, as the experience of all ages has proved, both over the people and the government; and when limited, have always been subservient to the views of the Executive Department, from which they derive their honors and emoluments . . . and because military establishments are in their nature progressive, the vast expense attending them, producing discontent and disturbances, and these furnishing a pretext for providing a force still more formidable; thus finally occasioning the oppression, the ruin, the slavery of the people.*

1801 - 1802

U.S. economic prosperity of 1789-1800, due largely to European wartime demand for U.S. products, is halted briefly by Peace of Amiens, temporary lull in European war.

1802

March 8. Judiciary Act of 1801 repealed in spite of opposition of Vice-President Burr. **April 29.** Act is replaced by measure that reduces number of circuit judges to six from sixteen and restores to six the number of Supreme Court judges previously reduced to five.

March 16. U.S. Military Academy established by Act of Congress; training school formally opens at West Point on July 4.

Benjamin Silliman, appointed Yale's first professor of chemistry and natural history, begins long career as influential teacher and popularizer of science.

1802 - 1809

Jefferson administration's retrenchment policy, planned and carried out by Secretary of the Treasury Albert Gallatin, increases customs duties, makes it possible to repeal excise taxes in 1802, and still reduces national debt from $83 million to $57 million by 1809.

1803

Feb. 24. Supreme Court voids an act of Congress for the first time in *Marbury* v. *Madison*, thus establishing its right to rule on the constitutionality of U.S. laws. No other congressional act is declared unconstitutional until 1857.

March 1. Ohio admitted to the Union as seventeenth state. Formerly eastern part of

Northwest Territory, and still called Northwest Territory after western region became Indiana Territory in 1800, population has grown to 70,000 since peace with Indians in 1794. Slavery is prohibited.

April 30. France cedes Louisiana (the western half of the Mississippi Valley) to U.S. for $11,250,000 plus $3,750,000 debt to U.S. citizens owed by France and assumed by U.S. Purchase of 828,000 square miles, or more than 500 million acres, doubles area of U.S. Purchase of foreign territory is resisted by Federalists as not provided for in the Constitution but is approved by Senate on October 20, eventually upheld by Supreme Court in 1828. **Dec. 20.** U.S. takes formal possession of area.

1803 - 1806

Aug. 31, 1803. Captain Meriwether Lewis, President Jefferson's secretary, and William Clark begin exploration of lands west of the Mississippi River, authorized by Congress at President Jefferson's request. Expedition follows Ohio, Missouri, and Columbia rivers to Pacific Ocean, and returns by similar route, a total of 8,000 miles. **Sept. 23, 1806.** Expedition ends on return to St. Louis, having demonstrated that an overland route to the Far West is practicable.

1804

March 12. U.S. Senate removes Judge John Pickering from his post as federal district judge in New Hampshire as unfit to serve. Justice Samuel Chase, associate justice of the Supreme Court, is impeached on charge of bias, but acquitted in trial in Senate next year. Latter case finally frustrates Jefferson's efforts to assert authority over Federalist judiciary.

March 26. Land Act of 1804 reduces minimum cash payment for Western lands

THOMAS JEFFERSON
Instructions to Captain Lewis, 1803
The object of your mission is to explore the Missouri River, and such principal stream of it, as, by its course and communication with the water of the Pacific Ocean may offer the most direct and practicable water communication across this continent, for the purposes of commerce.

Beginning at the mouth of the Missouri, you will take observations of latitude and longitude at all remarkable points on the river. . . .

Your observations are to be taken with great pains and accuracy. . . .

Other objects worthy of notice will be: the soil and face of the country, its growth and vegetable productions, especially those not of the U.S.; the animals of the country generally, and especially those not known in the U.S. . . . the mineral productions of every kind . . . volcanic appearances; climate as characterized by the thermometer, by the proportion of rainy, cloudy, and clear days, by lightning, hail, snow, ice, by the access and recess of frost, by the winds, prevailing at different seasons, the dates at which particular plants put forth or lose their flowers, or leaf, times of appearance of particular birds, reptiles, or insects. . . .

In all your intercourse with the natives, treat them in the most friendly and conciliatory manner which their own conduct will admit; allay all jealousies as to the object of your journey, satisfy them of its innocence; make them acquainted with the position, extent, character, peaceable and commercial dispositions of the U.S., of our wish to be neighborly, friendly, and useful to them.

TIMOTHY PICKERING
Letter to Rufus King, 1804
I am disgusted with the men who now rule and with their measures. At some manifestations of their malignancy I am shocked. The cowardly wretch [Jefferson] at their head, while, like a Parisian revolutionary monster, prating about humanity, would feel an infernal pleasure in the utter destruction of his opponents. We have too long witnessed his general turpitude, his cruel removals of faithful officers, and the substitution of corruption and looseness for integrity and worth. . . .

I am therefore ready to say, "Come out from among them, and be ye separate." Corruption is the object and instrument of the chief, and the tendency of his administration, for the purpose of maintaining himself in power and the accomplishment of his infidel and visionary schemes. . . .

And, if a separation should be deemed proper, the five New England states, New York, and New Jersey would naturally be united. Among those seven states, there is a sufficient congeniality of character to authorize the expectation of practicable harmony and a permanent union, [with] New York the center.

Poem dropped on Burr's doorstep and widely circulated, 1804
Oh Burr, oh Burr, what has thou done,
Thou hast shooted dead great
*   Hamilton!*
You hid behind a bunch of thistle,
And shooted him dead with a great
*   hoss pistol!*

from $2 an acre to $1.64, permits minimum purchase of a quarter section (160 acres).

Group of extremist New England Federalists, the Essex Junto, plan to organize a separate New England Confederacy (including New York and New Jersey) in alliance with Aaron Burr. **April 25.** Plan is frustrated when Burr is defeated in attempt to become governor of New York through efforts of Alexander Hamilton. **July 11.** Burr's demand for explanation of slur on his character leads to Hamilton-Burr duel in which Hamilton is mortally wounded, dying on the following day.

Sept. 25. Twelfth Amendment to Constitution, proposed by Congress in 1803, is declared ratified, providing separate voting for President and Vice-President.

Dec. 5. In first election with separate presidential and vice-presidential balloting, Jefferson is overwhelmingly reelected, with George Clinton of New York as Vice-President, both by vote of 162 to 14. Federalist opponents are Charles Cotesworth Pinckney and Rufus King.

Louisiana Purchase land is divided; area of present-day Louisiana is organized as Territory of Orleans; remainder becomes District of Louisiana.

1805

Northern section of Indiana Territory organized as Michigan Territory. District of Louisiana becomes Louisiana Territory.

Free School Society (later Public School Society) is founded in New York as a private philanthropic body concerned with establishing an alternative to the pauper school system. De Witt Clinton, mayor of New York City, is first president of board of trustees.

Lorenzo da Ponte arrives in U.S.; Italian poet, librettist of Mozart's *Don Giovanni*, he becomes professor of Italian literature at Columbia College, and actively promotes Italian opera in U.S.

Boston Athenaeum is built to house George Washington's library, bought by a group of Boston citizens.

1805 - 1806

Aug. 9, 1805-April 30, 1806. Lieutenant Zebulon Montgomery Pike explores the upper Mississippi River on orders of General James Wilkinson, commander of U.S. forces in the Mississippi Valley, but fails to find the true source of the river. He sights Pikes Peak, Colorado, in second expedition of 1806-1807, but does not climb it.

1806

Jan. 25. Secretary of State James Madison reports to Congress on results of resumption of Napoleonic wars (1803); British have renewed efforts to close French ports to neutral shipping, which results in interference (restrictions, seizures, impressment of American seamen into British service) with American vessels. **Feb. 12.** Senate passes resolution attacking "unprovoked aggression," which Britain ignores. **April 18.** Congress passes Non-Importation Act prohibiting purchase of British goods, but this is suspended after a month at President Jefferson's request. **May 16.** British declare a general blockade of European Continent. **Nov. 21.** Napoleon responds with Berlin Decree blockading British Isles and authorizing seizure of blockade-running vessels.

Dec. 31. Monroe-Pinkney Treaty is negotiated in London by Minister to Britain James Monroe and special envoy William Pinkney, who threaten to enforce Non-Importation Act; treaty achieves no signifi-

RED JACKET

Address to a Missionary, 1805
Brother, our seats were once large and yours were small. You have now become a great people, and we have scarcely a place left to spread our blankets. You have got our country but are not satisfied; you want to force your religion upon us. . . .

You say that you are sent to instruct us how to worship the Great Spirit agreeably to His mind, and, if we do not take hold of the religion which you white people teach, we shall be unhappy hereafter. You say that you are right and we are lost. How do we know this to be true? . . .

We are told that your religion was given to your forefathers and has been handed down from father to son. We also have a religion which was given to our forefathers and has been handed down to us, their children. We worship in that way. It teaches us to be thankful for all the favors we receive, to love each other, and to be united. We never quarrel about religion. . . .

Brother, we are told that you have been preaching to the white people in this place. These people are our neighbors. We are acquainted with them. We will wait a little while and see what effect your preaching has upon them. If we find it does them good, makes them honest and less disposed to cheat Indians, we will then consider again of what you have said.

GEORGE HAY
Prosecution of Burr, 1807
For the purpose of accomplishing these great designs—of establishing an empire in the West, of which New Orleans was to be the capital and the accused was to be the chief—he made two long visits to the Western country. He went to Ohio, Tennessee, and Kentucky, in fact to all the Western world, and traveled in various directions, till he went finally to New Orleans. Wherever he went, he spoke disrespectfully of the government of his country, with a view to facilitate the consummation of his own designs. He represented it as destitute of energy to support or defend our national rights against foreign enemies, and of spirit to maintain our national character. He uniformly said that we had no character, either at home or abroad. To those in whom he confided, he asserted that all the men of property and influence were dissatisfied with its arrangements, because they were not in the proper situation to which they were entitled; that with 500 men he could effect a revolution by which he could send the President to Monticello, intimidate Congress, and take the government of the United States into his own hands; that the people of the United States had so little knowledge of their rights, and so little disposition to maintain them, that they would meanly and tamely acquiesce in this shameful usurpation.

cant British concession, is never submitted to the Senate by President Jefferson, who continues to seek a more favorable agreement.

Trial of striking Philadelphia Cordwainers is first prosecution of trade union as common-law conspiracy; union is disbanded.

1807

June 22. U.S. frigate *Chesapeake* is attacked by British frigate *Leopard* off Norfolk, Virginia, after British commander demands surrender of four seamen alleged to be British subjects, and American commodore refuses to allow search. **July 2.** President Jefferson orders British warships from U.S. territorial waters. **Oct. 17.** British respond with announcement of intention to pursue impressment of British seamen from neutral ships even more rigorously.

Aug. 3-Sept. 1. Aaron Burr tried for treason after he is arrested while on mysterious western expedition thought to have as its aim either the formation of a Western empire through seizure of Spanish possessions in Mexico and the Southwest (a misdemeanor) or separating the Western states from the U.S. (treason). Tried for treason before Chief Justice Marshall, sitting in Circuit Court at Richmond, Virginia, Burr is acquitted on Marshall's narrow construction, afterward a settled principle, of U.S. law of treason. After trial, Burr goes to Europe to avoid prosecution for murder of Hamilton in New York and New Jersey and treason in Ohio, Louisiana, Mississippi, and Kentucky.

Aug. 17. First successful steamboat, the *Clermont*, built by Robert Fulton with two side paddlewheels and a Watt steam engine, sails from New York; it reaches Albany in 32 hours; return trip is made in 30 hours.

Nov. 11. British retaliate against Napoleon's Berlin Decree of 1806 by Orders in Council prohibiting all trade with ports closed to British ships and requiring duty paid at British ports from vessels bound to European ports still open. **Dec. 17.** Napoleon, in turn, issues Milan Decree declaring forfeit any shipping that obeys the Orders in Council.

Dec. 18. In response to British and French trade restrictions, President Jefferson recommends an embargo to Congress prohibiting further commerce with any foreign nation. **Dec. 22.** Act is passed by Southern and Western votes over objection of commercial states.

Eli Terry and Seth Thomas of Connecticut begin manufacture in quantity of clocks with interchangeable parts.

Agricultural fair movement, important for spread of scientific farming, begins under sponsorship of Elkanah Watson with exhibit of Merino sheep in Pittsfield, Massachusetts.

1808

Jan. 1. African slave trade prohibited by act of Congress, but illicit trade persists (estimated import of slaves from 1808 to 1860 is 250,000). By date of act, sale of unneeded slaves within U.S. from agriculturally exhausted areas to fertile ones has become more profitable than soil cultivation.

Jan. 9 and March 12. Additional embargo acts, strengthening Act of 1807, are ineffectual as domestic opposition leads to smuggling and other illegal trade. **April 17.** Napoleon, on pretext that embargo is effective, issues Bayonne Decree authorizing seizure of U.S. shipping in continental ports as presumptively British vessels with false pa-

Prohibition of slave trade, 1807
Be it enacted, by the Senate and House of Representatives of the United States of America in Congress assembled, *that from and after the 1st day of January, 1808, it shall not be lawful to import or bring into the United States or the territories thereof, from any foreign kingdom, place, or country, any Negro, mulatto, or person of color with intent to hold, sell, or dispose of such Negro, mulatto, or person of color as a slave, or to be held to service or labor.*

Section 2. And be it further enacted, that no citizen or citizens of the United States, or any other person, shall, from and after the 1st day of January, in the year of Our Lord 1808, for himself, or themselves, or any other person whatsoever, either as master, factor, or owner, build, fit, equip, load, or otherwise prepare any ship or vessel, in any port or place within the jurisdiction of the United States, nor shall cause any ship or vessel to sail from any port or place within the same, for the purpose of procuring any Negro, mulatto, or person of color from any foreign kingdom, place, or country, to be transported to any port or place whatsoever within the jurisdiction of the United States, to be held, sold, or disposed of as slaves, or to be held to service or labor.

JAMES MADISON
National Gazette, 1792
This term [Property], in its particular application, means "that dominion which one man claims and exercises over the external things of the world, in exclusion of every other individual."

In its larger and juster meaning, it embraces everything to which a man may attach a value and have a right; and which leaves to everyone else the like advantage.

In the former sense, a man's land, or merchandise, or money is called his property.

In the latter sense, a man has property in his opinions and the free communication of them.

He has a property of peculiar value in his religious opinions, and in the profession and practice dictated by them.

He has property very dear to him in the safety and liberty of his person.

He has an equal property in the free use of his faculties and free choice of the objects on which to employ them.

In a word, as a man is said to have a right to his property, he may be equally said to have a property in his rights.

pers; $10 million in U.S. goods and vessels is confiscated by French in 1808 and 1809. British economy is largely unaffected by embargo, since South America is alternative source of supply and British commerce thrives without American competition.

Dec. 7. President Jefferson, having declined to run for a third term, supports James Madison, who is elected to the presidency with 122 electoral votes over Federalist Charles Cotesworth Pinckney (47 votes) and over Vice-President George Clinton (6 votes), nominated by anti-embargo Eastern Republicans. Clinton, who also runs for the vice-presidency, is reelected.

John Jacob Astor incorporates American Fur Company, the first of several companies founded by him in the West that make him the dominant figure in the industry and, at his death, the richest man in the U.S.

1809

Stimulus to New England manufactures from embargo is outweighed by heavy shipping losses. **Jan.-Feb.** Economic distress inspires protests by town meetings and state legislatures, especially those of Massachusetts and Connecticut. State governors refuse cooperation for enforcement.

March. 1. Illinois Territory formed; region was originally part of "Territory Northwest of the River Ohio," and subsequently part of Indiana Territory.

March 1. President Jefferson, beset by criticism from both Federalists and dissidents in his own party, signs Non-Intercourse Act, repealing embargo and reopening trade with all nations except France and England as one of his last official acts before leaving office. **April 19.** On assurances by British Minister David M. Erskine that Orders in Council will be repealed, President Madison proclaims resumption of trade with Britain. **Aug. 9.** Non-Intercourse Act is revived when British government repudiates Erskine.

Publication of popular satire, *A History of New York . . . by Diedrich Knickerbocker,* the work of Washington Irving.

1810

May 1. Over solid Federalist opposition, Congress passes Macon's Bill Number 2, authorizing President Madison to reopen trade with France and England and stipulating that if either country removes its commercial restrictions before March 3, 1811, Non-Intercourse Act may be revived against the other. Napoleon, acting through French Foreign Minister the Duc de Cadore, then deceives Madison into believing that Berlin and Milan decrees are canceled, though in fact they are implemented by a fresh decree signed August 5 ordering seizure of U.S. vessels that have called at French ports before passage of Macon's Bill. **Nov. 2.** President Madison reopens trade with France and revives Non-Intercourse Act against Britain, voted by Congress March 2, 1811.

Sept. 26. Uprising of Southern expansionists against Spanish rule results in capture of fort at Baton Rouge in West Florida and proclamation of area's independence as the Republic of West Florida. **Oct. 27.** President Madison annexes West Florida (present-day southern parts of Mississippi, Alabama, and Louisiana) and announces military occupation and absorption into Orleans Territory on ground of consent by local authority.

Third U.S. census shows population of 7,239,000 — a gain of 36.4 percent since

WASHINGTON IRVING
History of New York, 1809
For what is history, in fact, but a kind of Newgate calendar, a register of the crimes and miseries that man his inflicted on his fellow-man? It is a huge libel on human nature, to which we industriously add page after page, volume after volume, as if we were building up a monument to the honor, rather than the infamy of our species. If we turn over the pages of these chronicles that man has written of himself, what are the characters dignified by the appellation of great, and held up to the admiration of posterity? Tyrants, robbers, conquerors, renowned only for the magnitude of their misdeeds, and the stupendous wrongs and miseries they have inflicted on mankind—warriors, who had hired themselves to the trade of blood, not from motives of virtuous patriotism, or to protect the injured and defenceless, but merely to gain the vaunted glory of being adroit and successful in massacring their fellow-beings! What are the great events that constitute a glorious era?—The fall of empires—the desolation of happy countries—splendid cities smoking in their ruins—the proudest works of art tumbled in the dust—the shrieks and groans of whole nations ascending unto heaven!

RICHARD M. JOHNSON
Speech in House, 1811
For God's sake, let us not again be told of the ties of religion, of laws, of blood, and of customs, which bind the two nations together, with a view to extort our love for the English government . . . let us not be told of the freedom of that corrupt government whose hands are washed alike in the blood of her own illustrious statesmen, for a manly opposition to tyranny, and the citizens of every other clime. . . .

If her energies are to be directed against the liberties of this free and happy people, against my native country, I should not drop a tear if the fast-anchored isle would sink into the waves.

JOHN RANDOLPH
Speech in House, 1811
But is war the true remedy? Who will profit by it? Speculators — a few lucky merchants who draw prizes in the lottery — commissaries and contractors. Who must suffer by it? The people. It is their blood, their taxes, that must flow to support it. . . .

Our people will not submit to be taxed for this war of conquest and dominion. The government of the United States was not calculated to wage offensive foreign war; it was instituted for the common defense and general welfare, and whosoever should embark it in a war of offense would put it to a test which it was by no means calculated to endure.

1800; figure includes 60,000 immigrants arrived since 1800 and about 1,200,000 slaves, almost entirely in the South.

Boston Philharmonic Society, first regularly performing symphony orchestra in United States, founded by Gottlieb Graupner; it is discontinued in 1824.

1811

Jan. 24-Feb. 20. Administration attempts to renew charter of Alexander Hamilton's Bank of the United States (chartered in 1791 for 20 years), but fails when combination of Old Republicans (strict Jeffersonians), Anglophobes, who resent largely British ownership of bank stock, and state banking interests anxious to remove federal competition allows recharter bill to die in House and defeats it in Senate. Lack of a federal bank leaves U.S. in financial straits during War of 1812.

May 1. British frigate *Guerrière* forcibly removes and impresses an American sailor from American vessel off Sandy Hook. **May 16.** U.S. frigate *President*, in search of *Guerrière*, mistakenly engages and disables British corvette *Little Belt*, causing 32 British casualties, upon her refusal to identify herself. **Nov. 1.** U.S. offers to compensate, but makes condition that British revoke Orders in Council.

Nov. 4. Congressional elections bring Western "War Hawks" to Congress; among them are Henry Clay and Richard M. Johnson of Kentucky, John C. Calhoun, Langdon Cheves, and William Lowndes from South Carolina, Felix Grundy from Tennessee, and Peter B. Porter from western New York. Strongly nationalist in temper, they advocate U.S. expansion, including conquest of Canada, and take the lead in protesting outrages to U.S. shipping, though the South and West are not especially affected by them. **Nov. 5.** President Madison's message to Congress encourages drive toward war with England when he requests preparations for national defense.

Tecumseh, chief of the Shawnees, actively supported by Canadian governor and fur-traders, attempts to organize a defensive confederacy of Indian tribes on Northwestern frontier to resist white settlement. **Nov. 8.** General William Henry Harrison, governor of Indiana Territory, takes advantage of Tecumseh's temporary absence to destroy, with heavy losses, the Indian capital village at Tippecanoe Creek after having been attacked by Indians the previous day. Conflict inflames Western feeling against British, who are believed to supply Indians with arms from Canada.

Beginning of Cumberland Road (the National Road) at Cumberland, Maryland. By 1840, road has reached Vandalia, Illinois, and cost $7 million. An important western route during era of westward expansion, it is present-day Highway 40.

Sidewheeler *New Orleans* is built in Pittsburgh, first steamboat built west of the Alleghenies; it makes voyage from Louisville to New Orleans, beginning Western steamboat navigation.

New York law is first to substitute general incorporation provisions for special charters from state legislatures; this leads to similar laws in other states that encourage growth in business corporations, especially those involved in transportation.

Niles Weekly Register (Whig), founded at Baltimore by Hezekiah Niles, is noted until its discontinuation in 1849 for factual reporting and the national influence of Niles' editorials.

TECUMSEH
To the messenger of the President, 1810
These lands are ours. No one has a right to remove us, because we were the first owners. The Great Spirit above has appointed this place for us, on which to light our fires, and here we will remain. As to boundaries, the Great Spirit knows no boundaries, nor will His red children acknowledge any.

HEZEKIAH NILES
Weekly Register, 1815
A high and honorable feeling generally prevails, and the people begin to assume, more and more, a national character; and to look at home for the only means, under divine goodness, of preserving their religion and liberty, with all the blessings that flow from their unrestricted enjoyment. The "bulwark" of these is in the sanctity of their principles, and the virtue and valor of these who profess to love them, and need no guarantee from the bloodstained and profligate princes and powers of Europe. Morality and good order ever prevail — canting hypocrisy has but few advocates, for the Great Architect of the universe is worshiped on the altar of men's hearts, in the way that each believes most acceptable to Him. . . .

The progress of our country in population, wealth, and resources is without parallel. . . .

It is hardly possible to imagine, with any degree of certainty, the value annually created by the recently applied industry of the people to manufactures, aided by the various laborsaving machinery adapted to large institutions or household establishments. We are friendly to the former to a given extent, but it is on the latter that we chiefly rely to accomplish a sublime independence of the New World.

1812

HENRY CLAY
Speech in House, 1813

My plan would be to call out the ample resources of the country, give them a judicious direction, prosecute the war with the utmost vigor, strike wherever we can reach the enemy, at sea or on land, and negotiate the terms of a peace at Quebec or Halifax. We are told that England is a proud and lofty nation; that disdaining to wait for danger, meets it halfway. Haughty as she is, we once triumphed over her, and if we do not listen to the councils of timidity and despair, we shall again prevail. In such a cause, with the aid of Providence, we must come out crowned with success; but if we fail, let us fail like men — lash ourselves to our gallant tars and expire together in one common struggle, fighting for "seamen's rights and free trade."

DANIEL WEBSTER
Speech in House, 1814

The administration asserts the right to fill the ranks of the regular army by compulsion. . . . Persons thus taken by force and put into an army may be compelled to serve there during the war, or for life. They may be put on any service at home or abroad for defense or for invasion, according to the will and pleasure of the government. . . .

Is this, sir, consistent with the character of a free government? Is this civil liberty? Is this the real character of our Constitution? No, sir, indeed it is not. The Constitution is libeled, foully libeled. The people of this country have not established for themselves such a fabric of despotism. They have not purchased at a vast expense of their own treasure and their own blood a Magna Carta to be slaves.

April. President Madison, in diplomatic exchange with England, insists wrongly that French commercial restrictions have been removed; Britain correctly denies that Napoleon has revoked them. **May 11.** Britain's stand on refusing to annul Orders in Council is weakening because of severe economic hardships when Prime Minister Spencer Perceval is assassinated, causing delay in considering question. **June 16.** Britain reluctantly and too late revokes Orders in Council (effective June 23). **June 18.** U S. Congress, ignorant of the revocation, declares war against England over Federalist and other opposition; Southern and Western "War Hawks" assure passage by vote of 79 to 49 in House and 19 to 13 in Senate.

April 30. Louisiana (Territory of Orleans) is admitted to the Union as the eighteenth state; state constitution allows slavery.

June 4. Name of Louisiana Territory changed to Missouri Territory.

July 2 and Aug. 5. Governors of Connecticut and Massachusetts refuse to supply militia to the federal government. **Aug. 5.** In New Hampshire, Daniel Webster prepares Rockingham memorial, which calls government measures "hasty, rash, and ruinous" and hints at disunion. **Aug. 25.** Massachusetts House of Representatives terms war against the public interest and discourages volunteers except for defensive purposes.

President Madison's War Message says nothing about Canada, listing only maritime grievances, but first U.S. effort is Canadian invasion as part of attempt to drive British from North America. **Aug. 16.** Poorly trained and badly equipped militia under

General William Hull are surrendered to Canadian force under General Isaac Brock at Detroit after a disastrous campaign that persuades Northwest Indians under Tecumseh to join the British and loses U.S. control of Lake Erie and the Michigan country. **Oct. 13.** Despite death of General Brock, their ablest leader, Canadians also defeat U.S. forces at Fort George on Niagara River, when New York militia refuse to leave New York State and cross into Canada. **Nov. 19.** U.S. effort collapses when militia under General Henry Dearborn likewise refuse to cross the frontier near Plattsburgh.

U.S. military failures are partially compensated by naval victories. **Aug. 19.** U.S. frigate *Constitution* destroys British frigate *Guerrière*. **Oct. 17.** U.S. sloop-of-war *Wasp* defeats British brig *Frolic* off Virginia. **Oct. 25.** U.S. frigate *United States* commanded by Captain Stephen Decatur captures British frigate *Macedonian*. **Dec. 29.** The *Constitution* also destroys British frigate *Java* off Brazil, earning herself the nickname "Old Ironsides" by her performance.

Aug. 24. U.S. attempts peace feeler that requires suspension of impressment and "paper" blockades and asks compensation for losses to U.S. shipping. **Aug. 29.** British Foreign Secretary Castlereagh rejects proposal. **Sept. 30.** British offer of armistice is unimplemented when Secretary of State James Monroe demands end of impressment as a condition of agreement.

Dec. 2. President Madison, Southern Republican candidate, reelected over De Witt Clinton of New York, candidate of antiwar Republicans and Federalists, by vote of 128 to 89. Elbridge Gerry of Massachusetts is elected Vice-President, succeeding George Clinton who had died in office on April 20. Vote is Gerry, 131, Charles Jared Ingersoll, Federalist, 86. Antiwar coalition wins in all

Ye Parliament of England, c. 1813
Ye Parliament of England,
  Ye Lords and Commons too,
Consider well what you're about,
  What you're about to do;
For you're to war with Yankees,
  And I'm sure you'll rue the day
You roused the sons of liberty
  In North Ameri-cay!

You first confined our commerce,
  You said our ships shan't trade,
You next impressed our seamen,
  And used them as your slaves;
You then insulted Rodgers,
  While ploughing o'er the main,
And had we not declared war,
  You'd have done it o'er again.

You tho't our frigates were but few,
  And Yankees could not fight,
Until brave Hull your Guerrière took,
  And banished her from your sight.
The Wasp then took your Frolic,
  We'll nothing say to that,
The Poictiers being of the line
  Of course she took her back.

The next, your Macedonian,
  No finer ship could swim,
Decatur took her gilt work off,
  And then he sent her in.
The Java, by a Yankee ship
  Was sunk you all must know;
The Peacock fine, in all her plume,
  By Lawrence down did go.

THOMAS JEFFERSON
Letter to John Adams, 1813
I agree with you that there is a natural aristocracy among men. . . .

There is also an artificial aristocracy, founded on wealth and birth, without either virtue or talents; for with these it would belong to the first class. The natural aristocracy I consider as the most precious gift of nature, for the instruction, the trusts, and government of society. And, indeed, it would have been inconsistent in Creation to have formed man for the social state and not to have provided virtue and wisdom enough to manage the concerns of the society. May we not even say that that form of government is the best which provides the most effectually for a pure selection of these natural aristoi into the offices of government? The artificial aristocracy is a mischievous ingredient in government, and provision should be made to prevent its ascendancy. . . .

I think the best remedy is exactly that provided by all our constitutions: to leave to the citizens the free election and separation of the aristoi from the pseudo-aristoi, of the wheat from the chaff. In general they will elect the real good and wise. In some instances, wealth may corrupt and birth blind them, but not in sufficient degree to endanger the society.

New England and Middle States except Vermont and Pennsylvania; Federalists double their strength in Congress.

Diseases of the Mind by Benjamin Rush is published, a pioneer work that contains the seeds of modern psychoanalysis.

First life insurance company in U.S., incorporated in Philadelphia, is called Pennsylvania Company for Insurance on Lives and Granting Annuities.

1813

February-August. U.S. attempt to retake Detroit and Fort Dearborn (present-day Chicago) in expedition led by General William Henry Harrison results in stand-off for lack of control of Lake Erie.

April 15. U.S. occupies West Florida, western half of which had been annexed in 1810, by taking Spanish fort at Mobile.

April 27. U.S. effort to gain control of Lake Ontario by taking York (present-day Toronto) results in destruction of the town by fire, giving British their excuse for burning Washington, D.C., in 1814. **April-November.** Campaign to conquer upper Canada, especially Montreal, fails of its object after several battles, when U.S. forces fall back on Plattsburgh, New York, for winter quarters. **Dec. 18.** British take Fort Niagara and encourage Indians to plunder Lewiston and surrounding settlements. **Dec. 30-Jan. 1, 1814.** Buffalo is burned by British along with other towns along frontier.

British blockade Chesapeake and Delaware bays, cutting off commerce, and carry out raids along coasts of Chesapeake Bay. **May 26.** Blockade is extended to ports of New York, South Carolina, Georgia, and Louisiana. **Nov. 19.** British blockade Long Island Sound, leaving only New England ports open, in effort to encourage New England protest against war. When New England fails to break away from Union, blockade is extended to New England ports in following year.

May 8. President Madison sends peace commissioners Albert Gallatin and James A. Bayard to St. Petersburg, Russia, upon hearing of Czar Alexander's offer of September 1812 to mediate war. **July 5.** British Foreign Secretary Lord Castlereagh refuses Russian offer. **Nov. 4.** Castlereagh, concerned about British defeats in Lake Erie region, sends James Monroe, secretary of state, offer of direct negotiations. President Madison accepts immediately.

June 1. U.S. frigate *Chesapeake*, with raw crew, is disabled and captured by British frigate *Shannon* off Boston. Last words of dying U.S. Captain James Lawrence, "Don't give up the ship!" are later inscribed on battle flag of flagship *Lawrence* commanded by Captain Oliver Hazard Perry, who defeats British in Battle of Lake Erie on September 10, and sends message, "We have met the enemy and they are ours." Engagement regains control of the lake and reopens prospects for conquest of Canada.

Sept. 18. Because of Perry's victory, British are forced to evacuate Detroit. **Oct. 5.** U.S. triumphs at Battle of the Thames River, north of Lake Erie. Death of Tecumseh in this battle results in collapse of Indian confederacy in Northwest, depriving British of Indian allies. U.S. regains territory lost in 1812.

Dec. 9. President Madison requests new embargo in effort to prevent sale of supplies to British forces in Canada and in New England ports by New York and New England merchants. **Dec. 17.** Congress passes measure over strong opposition, and coastal

JOHN ADAMS
Letter to Jefferson, 1813
Your distinction between the aristoi and pseudo-aristoi will not help the matter. I would trust one as well as the other with unlimited power. The law wisely refuses an oath, as a witness in his own case, to the saint as well as the sinner. . . .

I dislike and detest hereditary honors, offices, emoluments established by law. So do you. I am for excluding legal, hereditary distinctions from the United States as long as possible. So are you. I only say that mankind have not yet discovered any remedy against irresistible corruption in elections to offices of great power and profit but making them hereditary.

But will you say our elections are pure? Be it so, upon the whole; but do you recollect in history a more corrupt election than that of Aaron Burr to be President, or that of De Witt Clinton last year? By corruption here, I mean a sacrifice of every national interest and honor to private and party objects. . . . There is virtually a white rose and a red rose, a Caesar and a Pompey, in every state in this Union, and contests and dissensions will be as lasting. The rivalry of Bourbons and Noaillises produced the French Revolution, and a similar competition for consideration and influence exists and prevails in every village in the world.

DAVY CROCKETT
Account of Col. Crockett's Tour, 1835
*Next morning I rose early and started
for Lowell in a fine carriage with three
gentlemen who had agreed to accompany me. I had heard so much of this
place that I longed to see it; not because I had heard of the "mile of gals";
no, I left that for the gallantry of the
President who is admitted, on that
score, to be abler than myself; but I
wanted to see the power of machinery,
wielded by the keenest calculations of
human skill; I wanted to see how it was
that these Northerners could buy cotton, and carry it home, manufacture it,
bring it back, and sell it for half nothing; and in the meantime, be well to
live, and make money besides.*

*We stopped at the large stone house
at the head of the falls of the Merrimac
River, and having taken a little refreshment, went down among the factories.
The dinner bells were ringing, and the
folks pouring out of the houses like bees
out of a gum. I looked at them as they
passed, all well dressed, lively, and genteel in their appearance; indeed, the
girls looked as if they were coming from
a quilting frolic. . . .*

*The outdoor appearance was fully
sustained by the whole of the persons
employed in the different rooms. I went
in among the young girls, and talked
with many of them. Not one expressed
herself as tired of her employment, or
oppressed with work; all talked well,
and looked healthy. Some of them were
very handsome; and I could not help
observing that they kept the prettiest
inside, and put the homely ones on the
outside rows. . . .*

*However we, who only hear of them,
may call their houses workshops and
prisons, I assure my neighbors there is
every enjoyment of life realized by
these persons, and there can be but few
who are not happy.*

trade is stopped, but frontier trade with the
enemy persists.

Boston Manufacturing Company opens
first textile factory to perform all cloth-making operations by power in Waltham,
Massachusetts. Financed with large capital,
company recruits New England farm girls
as operatives, boards them in dormitories,
and produces a standard coarse cotton cloth
requiring minimum labor skill.

1814

Jan. 18. Senate confirms President Madison's nomination of James A. Bayard, John
Quincy Adams, Henry Clay, and Jonathan
Russell as U.S. peace commissioners. **Feb.
8.** Albert Gallatin is added to the commission. Ghent, in Flanders, is chosen for
meeting of Americans and British.

March 27. Andrew Jackson, major general of Tennessee militia, with 2,000 volunteers, wins final victory at Horseshoe Bend
of the Tallapoosa River in bloody Creek
War fought in present-day Alabama since
July 1813. **Aug. 9.** Creeks cede most of
their lands to U.S. under Treaty of Fort
Jackson. This ends Indian resistance in
southern and western Alabama. **May 22.**
Jackson is appointed major general in regular army.

March 31. President Madison, accepting
failure of nearly 10 years of commercial restrictions, recommends repeal of Embargo
and Non-Importation acts. **April 14.** Bill,
passed by large majorities in Congress, is
signed, and restrictions formally cease. U.S.
trade with enemy continues, merchants paying duty to British at captured port of Castine, Maine.

Final defeat of Napoleon in April allows
British to take offensive in U.S. war;
14,000 men of Duke of Wellington's veter-

an forces arrive during summer. Campaign of concerted attack on Lake Champlain, Chesapeake Bay, and New Orleans is planned. **July 5 and 25.** Thrust from Canada is prevented by U.S. offensive that leads to battles of Chippewa and Lundy's Lane. **Sept. 11.** Decisive victory on Lake Champlain is won by fleet of Commodore Thomas Macdonough near Plattsburgh, giving U.S. control of Great Lakes and convincing Wellington that war cannot be won.

Aug. 8. Peace negotiations begin at Ghent between U.S. and British envoys. U.S. demand for settlement on basis of prewar boundaries is met by British insistence on retaining territory acquired. **Nov. 26.** U.S. terms involving prewar boundaries are met when British hear of Macdonough's victory, and because of heavy British debt incurred in defeating Napoleon.

Aug. 19. British expeditionary force of 4,000 men lands at Chesapeake Bay, proceeds up the Patuxent River to Bladensburg and then to Washington, D.C. **Aug. 24-25.** Washington, undefended since U.S. Army has fled, is partially burned. **Sept. 12-14.** British meet greater resistance at Baltimore and are forced to withdraw; bombardment of Fort McHenry on night of September 13-14 inspires composition of "The Star Spangled Banner" by Francis Scott Key, an eyewitness.

Dec. 15. Unaware of progress of peace negotiations, Federalist representatives of Connecticut, Rhode Island, Massachusetts, New Hampshire, and Vermont meet at Hartford, Connecticut, for secret convention called on October 17 by Massachusetts legislature. Convention considers, with threat of possible disunion, revision of the Constitution that will prevent further national dominance of the sort that has led to and sustained the unpopular war. Convention is

FRANCIS SCOTT KEY

The Star-Spangled Banner, 1814

*Oh, say, can you see, by the dawn's
     early light,
  What so proudly we hailed at the
     twilight's last gleaming,
Whose broad stripes and bright stars
     through the perilous fight,
   O'er the ramparts we watched were
     so gallantly streaming?
And the rockets' red glare, the bombs
     bursting in air,
Gave proof through the night that our
     flag was still there.
Oh, say, does that star-spangled banner
     yet wave
O'er the land of the free, and the home
     of the brave?*

. . .

*Oh! thus be it ever when freemen shall
     stand
  Between their loved homes and the
     war's desolation!
Blest with victory and peace, may the
     heaven-rescued land
  Praise the Power that hath made
     and preserved us a nation!
Then conquer we must, for our cause
     it is just,
And this be our motto: "In God is our
     trust!"
And the star-spangled banner in
     triumph shall wave,
O'er the land of the free, and the home
     of the brave!*

Hartford Convention Resolutions, 1815

If the Union be destined to dissolution by reason of the multiplied abuses of bad administrations, it should, if possible, be the work of peaceable times and deliberate consent. Some new form of confederacy should be substituted among those states which shall intend to maintain a federal relation to each other. Events may prove that the causes of our calamities are deep and permanent. They may be found to proceed, not merely from the blindness of prejudice, pride of opinion, violence of party spirit, or the confusion of the times but they may be traced to implacable combinations of individuals, or of states, to monopolize power and office, and to trample without remorse upon the rights and interests of commercial sections of the Union. Whenever it shall appear that these causes are radical and permanent, a separation, by equitable arrangement, will be preferable to an alliance by constraint, among nominal friends but real enemies, inflamed by mutual hatred and jealousy, and inviting, by intestine divisions, contempt and aggression from abroad.

dominated from the outset by moderates whose influence brings about resolutions and recommendations that are not extreme, but news of Treaty of Ghent and of Battle of New Orleans two weeks after the signing causes even the moderates to be ridiculed throughout the country and constitutes fatal blow to Federalist Party.

Dec. 24. Treaty of Ghent signed; treaty is actually silent on the specific issues that have led to war, but British do not claim various rights in North America contested since 1783. This constitutes U.S. victory, since it amounts to abandonment of last serious European challenge to future American development.

Henry M. Shreve navigates steamboat *Enterprise* from Pittsburgh down the Ohio and Mississippi rivers to New Orleans, carrying supplies to General Andrew Jackson; *Enterprise* is first steamboat to travel on upper waters of Ohio-Mississippi river system. On return trip in following year, Shreve is first to ascend Mississippi and Ohio rivers to Louisville successfully.

War overturns federal economies of 1800 to 1811; national debt rises from $83 million 1811 level to $127 million in 1814. In effort to meet expenses, Congress adds to list of internally taxed items, increases tariff, doubles taxes on land, dwellings, and slaves.

1815

Jan. 1. Sir Edward Pakenham with 7,500 British veterans, having landed at mouth of the Mississippi River on December 13, 1814, attacks General Andrew Jackson with 5,000 well-fortified and experienced troops defending New Orleans; British retire after severe artillery pounding. **Jan. 8.** After waiting for reinforcements, Pakenham attacks again and is thrown back with crushing British losses — more than 2,000 casualties as opposed to 21 Americans killed or wounded. Neither British nor Americans know that war is over and treaty terms have been agreed on two weeks earlier; victory is strategically meaningless, but for America psychologically important; it wipes out at one blow the war's failures and humiliations and makes Jackson the first popular American hero.

March 3. Congress authorizes hostilities against Dey of Algiers, who has declared war on U.S. during War of 1812, saying tribute payments from U.S. ships are not great enough. June 19. Flotilla under command of Captain Stephen Decatur, dispatched May 10 from New York, enters Algiers harbor with two captured Algerine warships. June 30. Decatur exacts treaty from Dey that ends piracy and wins similar treaties from Tunis on July 26 and Tripoli on August 6, ending hostilities.

July 3. Commercial convention with Great Britain wins trade concessions for U.S., eliminates discriminatory duties and allows U.S. trade with East Indies.

Beginning of peace brings renewed western expansion into eastern half of Mississippi Valley, from the Great Lakes to the Gulf of Mexico. Population west of the Appalachian Mountains increases from 1,080,000 in 1810 to 2,236,000 in 1820.

Imports, held down by War of 1812, rise from $13 million in 1814 to $100 million average in 1815 to 1820 period. Exports, similarly affected, rise from $7 million in 1814 to $70 million average in 1815 to 1820 period. Chief imports are woolen and cotton items, sugar, and coffee; principal export is cotton.

North American Review, distinguished intellectual periodical, founded in Boston by William Tudor; discontinued 1940.

SAMUEL WOODWORTH
Hunters of Kentucky, 1815

I s'pose you've read it in the prints,
How Packenham attempted
To make Old Hickory Jackson wince,
But soon his scheme repented;
For we, with rifles ready cocked,
Thought such occasion lucky,
And soon around the general flocked
The hunters of Kentucky.

You've heard, I s'pose, how New
    Orleans
Is famed for wealth and beauty,
There's girls of every hue it seems,
From snowy white to sooty.
So Packenham he made his brags,
If he in fight was lucky,
He'd have their girls and cotton bags,
In spite of old Kentucky.

But Jackson he was wide awake,
And was not scared at trifles,
For well he knew what aim we take
With our Kentucky rifles.
So he led us down to Cypress swamp,
The ground was low and mucky;
There stood John Bull in martial pomp,
And here was old Kentucky.

A bank was raised to hide our breasts,
Not that we thought of dying,
But that we always like to rest,
Unless the game is flying.
Behind it stood our little force,
None wished it to be greater,
For every man was half a horse,
And half an alligator.

They did not let our patience tire,
Before they showed their faces;
We did not choose to waste our fire,
So snugly kept our places.
But when so near we saw them wink,
We thought it time to stop 'em,
And 'twould have done you good I
    think,
To see Kentuckians drop 'em.

(Above) Fire in Washington, D.C., set by the British in 1814, in which the White House and the Capitol were burned; (left) Tecumseh, Shawnee chief, killed at the Battle of the Thames on October 5, 1813; (below) James Madison, fourth President of the United States: portrait by Chester Harding.

TECUMSEH.

(Above) The bombing of Fort McHenry on the night of September 13–14, 1814, which inspired Francis Scott Key (right), an eyewitness, to write "The Star-Spangled Banner"; (below) Battle of Lake Champlain, New York, September 11, 1814

THOMAS JEFFERSON
Letter to Benjamin Austin, 1816

*You tell me I am quoted by those who
wish to continue our dependence on
England for manufactures. There was a
time when I might have been so quoted
with more candor, but within the thirty
years which have since elapsed, how
are circumstances changed! . . .*

*We have experienced what we did
not then believe, that there exists both
profligacy and power enough to exclude us from the field of interchange
with other nations; that to be independent for the comforts of life we must
fabricate them ourselves. We must now
place the manufacturer by the side of
the agriculturist. . . .*

*The grand inquiry now is, shall we
make our own comforts or go without
them at the will of a foreign nation? He,
therefore, who is now against domestic
manufacture must be for reducing us
either to dependence on that foreign
nation, or to be clothed in skins and to
live like wild beasts in dens and caverns. I am not one of these; experience
has taught me that manufactures are
now as necessary to our independence
as to our comfort.*

1816

March 14. Financial plight of country,
and financial needs, lead to passage of bill
chartering Second Bank of the United
States, which had been recommended by
President Madison in message of December
5, 1815. Votes in House (80 to 71) and
Senate (22 to 12) reflect opposition of both
strict Jeffersonians and Federalists who represent recently developed private banking
interests. Debate is first one led by Henry
Clay, John C. Calhoun (both taking a nationalist, pro-bank position), and Daniel
Webster, a young congressman from New
Hampshire, who opposes the measure.

April 27. Tariff of 1816 is first one enacted to protect home industry (developed
during embargo and war years) rather than
to raise revenue. New manufacturing interests oppose commercial and agricultural sectors in debate, which keeps duties moderate.
Tariff is ineffective, since lenient British
credit more than compensates for higher
cost of imported goods.

Dec. 4. Madison succeeded by James
Monroe as fifth President of the U.S. after
struggle for nomination with younger element supporting William H. Crawford,
who is defeated in Republican caucus by 65
to 54. Vote in electoral college demonstrates feeling against Federalists: 183 to 34
for Monroe over Federalist Rufus King of
New York. Republican Daniel D. Tompkins of New York is elected Vice-President.

Dec. 11. Indiana admitted to the Union
as the nineteenth state; originally part of
Northwest Territory, it had been Indiana
Territory with approximately the same
boundaries as the state since 1809. Population is 75,000; slavery is prohibited.

Supreme Court decision in *Martin* v.
Hunter's Lessee affirms right of federal courts

to review decisions of state courts, leads to controversy between Supreme Court and Virginia court led by Virginia Judge Spencer Roane.

First incorporated savings bank is chartered in Boston.

African Methodist Episcopal Church founded at Philadelphia, one of a number of churches founded by independent groups of Negroes in this period.

School for children as young as four years is established in Boston; it is included in the public school system in 1818.

1817

March 3. On his last day in office, President Madison vetoes Bonus Bill, sponsored by John C. Calhoun and passed on February 8 by the House by 86 to 84 and Senate by 20 to 15. Bill provides for federal financing of "internal improvements," chiefly roads and canals to connect the West with the Eastern Seaboard. Veto is on grounds that measure requires constitutional amendment.

March 4. President Monroe's inaugural address indicates that Jeffersonian party has adopted most of the old Hamiltonian-Federalist program involving a strong central government. **May-Sept.** President Monroe tours the Northeast and as far west as Detroit; he is enthusiastically received, which leads to characterization on July 12 of the period by a Boston newspaper as an "era of good feelings," in which political party controversies have given way to national unity.

April 28-29. Rush-Bagot Agreement, signed by Acting Secretary of State Richard Rush and Charles Bagot, British Minister to the U.S., brings to a halt naval armaments

JOHN CALHOUN
Debates . . . in Congress, 1817
Mr. Calhoun rose and observed that it seemed to be the fate of some measures to be praised but not adopted. Such, he feared, would be the fate of that on which we are now deliberating. . . . Yet it seemed to him, when he reflected how favorable was the present moment, and how confessedly important a good system of roads and canals was to our country, he might reasonably be very sanguine of success. . . .

The manner in which facility and cheapness of intercourse added to the wealth of a nation had been so often and ably discussed by writers on political economy, that he presumed the House to be perfectly acquainted with the subject. It was sufficient to observe that every branch of national industry —agricultural, manufacturing, and commercial—was greatly stimulated and rendered by it more productive. The result is, said he, that it tends to diffuse universal opulence. . . .

We are great, and rapidly—he was about to say fearfully—growing. This, said he, is our pride and danger—our weakness and our strength. . . . We are under the most imperious obligation to counteract every tendency to disunion. . . . Whatever, said Mr. C., impedes the intercourse of the extremes with this, the center of the republic, weakens the Union. The more enlarged the sphere of commercial circulation, the more extended that of social intercourse; the more strongly are we bound together; the more inseparable are our destinies.

ELIAS B. CALDWELL
Remarks to founders of Colonization Society, 1816
Among the objections which have been made, I must confess that I am most surprised at one which seems to be prevalent, to wit, that these people will be unwilling to be colonized. What, sir, are they not men? Will they not be actuated by the same motives of interest and ambition which influence other men? Or will they prefer remaining in a hopeless state of degradation for themselves and their children, to the prospect of the full enjoyment of their civil rights and a state of equality? What brought our ancestors to these shores? . . .

What is it impels many Europeans daily to seek our shores and to sell themselves — for the prime of their life — to defray the expenses of their passages? . . . If we were to add to these motives, the offer of land, and to aid in the expense of emigration and of first settling — they cannot be so blind to their own interests, so devoid of every generous and noble feeling, as to hesitate about accepting the offer. It is not a matter of speculation and opinion only. It has been satisfactorily ascertained that numbers will gladly accept of the invitation. And when once the colony is formed and flourishing, all other obstacles will be easily removed.

on the Great Lakes by limiting Britain and U.S. to eight lake ships each. Agreement implies gradual demilitarization of the Canadian frontier, but actually full disarmament of land fortifications does not take place until 1871.

Dec. 10. Mississippi Territory is divided; western part becomes Mississippi, admitted to the Union as the twentieth state, and eastern part becomes Territory of Alabama.

New York legislature authorizes construction of Erie Canal from Albany on the Hudson River to Buffalo on Lake Erie, a distance of about 360 miles. Canal, when completed in 1825, makes possible direct shipment of produce from Atlantic Ocean to Great Lakes region.

Beginning of iron production by process of puddling (to make impure pig iron more malleable) and rolling at Plumstock, Pennsylvania; method is adopted soon afterward by the industry at Pittsburgh.

First machine-made paper manufactured in U.S. is made by Thomas Gilpin near Wilmington, Delaware.

Asylum for the insane is opened in Frankford, Pennsylvania; others are opened in Boston (McLean Hospital) and New York (Bloomingdale) in 1818.

American Colonization Society for return of Negroes to Africa founded in Richmond, Virginia. Headed by a succession of distinguished Virginians, Society initially sends Negroes to Sierra Leone, then in 1822 purchases and establishes neighboring area named Liberia by Robert Goodloe Harper. Twelve thousand Negroes have been transported by 1860. Colonization movement, the early form of emancipation attempt, is widely pushed in the South until 1831, after which it sharply declines.

"Thanatopsis," poem composed by William Cullen Bryant in 1811, makes first appearance in *North American Review*.

1818

April 17-Nov. 28. After two years of intermittent conflict between Seminole Indians and U.S. forces along Georgia-Alabama border, General Andrew Jackson is dispatched to clear border area and eastern Florida of hostile Indians. He offers to take all of Spanish East Florida, but receives no reply from President Monroe. Without explicit orders, he marches into East Florida, occupies St. Marks and Pensacola and executes two British subjects, Alexander Arbuthnot and Robert Ambrister, whom he accuses of aiding the enemy. Action is condemned by the Cabinet (except for Secretary of State John Quincy Adams), the Senate, and the House, but popular approval persuades President Monroe not to punish Jackson. Adams, stating that campaign was for self-defense, sends ultimatum to Spanish government on November 28 insisting that it either control the Indians or cede the region to the U.S.

Dec. 3. Illinois becomes twenty-first state of the Union. Formerly part of Illinois Territory (present-day Illinois and Wisconsin), only southern part of state is settled, with 40,000 population, at time of admission. Slavery is prohibited.

U.S.-Canadian border is fixed at 49th parallel between Lake of the Woods and crest of the Rocky Mountains in convention between Britain and U.S.; convention leaves Oregon boundary question open to later settlement.

Transatlantic packet lines (under sail) begin operations between New York and Liverpool, England; average time in 1818 to 1822 period is 39 days.

ELIAS PYM FORDHAM
Letter from Illinois, 1818

I have consciously avoided giving to my young friends in England colored descriptions of this country; but I must beg leave to assure you that you cannot do a greater favor to any young man, who possesses from £800 to £5,000, with a proper degree of spirit, than by sending him out here. But if he has no money, if he knows no mechanical trade, and if he cannot work, he had better stay in a countinghouse in England. . . .

An emigrant who is rich may settle near a large town, find society, libraries, and a great many comforts. If he does not object to holding slaves, Kentucky offers him great advantages. But if he is not rich, or is ambitious, the Illinois and Missouri territories, and, from what I have heard, I may say, the Alabama country, will hold out advantages that will pay him for all sacrifices.

A bill is in Congress for making a state of the Illinois Territory. We shall be citizens as soon as it passes, and eligible, I believe, to any office.

Men of education and manners are much respected; and there is a large proportion of the people who have a great deal of information; which, though acquired more by conversation and observation than by reading, makes them good judges of character, and enables them to value literary and scientific acquirements.

DANIEL WEBSTER
Dartmouth College v. Woodward, 1819
It is . . . a small college, and yet there are those who love it.

JOHN MARSHALL
M'Culloch v. Maryland, 1819
We admit, as all must admit, that the powers of the government are limited, and that its limits are not to be transcended. But we think the sound construction of the Constitution must allow to the national legislature that discretion, with respect to the means by which the powers it confers are to be carried into execution, which will enable that body to perform the high duties assigned to it, in the manner most beneficial to the people. Let the end be legitimate, let it be within the scope of the Constitution, and all means which are appropriate, which are plainly adapted to that end, which are not prohibited, but consist with the letter and spirit of the Constitution, are constitutional. . . .

That the power to tax involves the power to destroy; that the power to destroy may defeat and render useless the power to create; that there is a plain repugnance in conferring on one government a power to control the constitutional measures of another, which other, with respect to those very measures, is declared to be supreme over that which exerts the control, are propositions not to be denied. . . .

The question is, in truth, a question of supremacy; and if the right of the states to tax the means employed by the general government be conceded, the declaration that the Constitution, and the laws made in pursuance thereof, shall be the supreme law of the land is empty and unmeaning declamation.

1819

Feb. 2. *Trustees of Dartmouth College* v. *Woodward* establishes that private corporate charters are contracts within the meaning of the Constitution, and therefore may not be revised or controlled by state legislatures that have granted them.

Feb. 22. Spanish government cedes East Florida to the U.S. in Adams-Onís Treaty. Border of Louisiana Purchase is agreed to as running irregularly northwest from Sabine River on Gulf of Mexico to 42nd parallel and thence due west to the Pacific Ocean. Line excludes Texas, to which U.S. relinquishes claims, and eliminates Spanish claims to Oregon country, north of treaty line. U.S. assumes $5 million claims of its citizens against Spain.

March 6. Supreme Court in *M'Culloch* v. *Maryland* unanimously disallows attempt by states to tax Bank of the United States, ("the power to tax involves the power to destroy"). Opinion of Chief Justice Marshall upholds constitutionality of the Bank and expresses nationalist doctrine on the Constitution as a document of implied powers which are to be loosely constructed: If the end is legitimate and the means are not prohibited and are consistent with the letter and spirit of the Constitution, the means are constitutional.

May 24. The *Savannah*, first steamship to cross the Atlantic Ocean, leaves from Savannah, Georgia, arriving in Liverpool, England, on June 20.

Dec. 14. Alabama admitted to the Union as twenty-second state; region had been organized as Alabama Territory in 1817; at time of admission population is 128,000. State constitution allows slavery.

Financial panic, especially in Southern

and Western states, occurs with collapse of credit on purchases, largely speculative, of Western lands. Crash is long-term result of liberal credit provisions of Land Act of 1800, but immediate cause is retraction of credit by Second Bank of the United States, which has been recklessly managed. Resulting pressure on state banks results in many failures and causes vast areas of Western land to become property of the Bank of the United States, which is henceforth characterized by Westerners as "The Monster." End of postwar European demand for U.S. food staples, sharply reducing land values, is contributing factor to what becomes general business depression lasting until 1822.

Arkansas Territory organized; area is southern part of Missouri Territory — present-day Oklahoma and Arkansas.

Because of high death rate among immigrants subjected to inhuman conditions during Atlantic crossings, federal law is passed to protect passengers; this and later acts of following thirty-five years are ineffective.

Cast-iron three-piece plow with interchangeable parts developed by Jethrow Wood of New York. Breechloading flintlock rifle invented by John Hall.

Sermon by William Ellery Channing of Boston delivered at Baltimore formulates liberal and humane Unitarian creed as opposed to orthodox Calvinist beliefs and leads to formation of Unitarian Church in Boston in 1820.

Washington Irving, during stay in England, writes *The Sketch Book of Geoffrey Crayon, Gent.*, containing, among other pieces, "Rip Van Winkle" and "The Legend of Sleepy Hollow."

American Farmer, first farm journal (discontinued 1897), founded by John P. Skin-

WILLIAM ELLERY CHANNING
Baltimore Sermon, 1819
We object, particularly on this ground, to that system which arrogates to itself the name of "Orthodoxy," and which is now industriously propagated through our country. This system, indeed, takes various shapes, but in all it casts dishonor on the Creator.

According to its old and genuine form, it teaches that God brings us into life wholly depraved, so that under the innocent features of our childhood is hidden a nature averse to all good and propense to all evil, a nature which exposes us to God's displeasure and wrath, even before we have acquired power to understand our duties or to reflect upon our actions. . . . Now, according to the plainest principles of morality, we maintain that a natural constitution of the mind, unfailingly disposing it to evil and to evil alone, would absolve it from guilt; that to give existence under this condition would argue unspeakable cruelty; and that to punish the sin of this unhappily constituted child with endless ruin would be a wrong unparalleled by the most merciless despotism. . . .

The false and dishonorable views of God which have now been stated we feel ourselves bound to resist unceasingly. Other errors we can pass over with comparative indifference. But we ask our opponents to leave to us a God worthy of our love and trust, in whom our moral sentiments may delight, in whom our weaknesses and sorrows may find refuge. We cling to the divine perfections.

Richmond (Va.) Enquirer, 1819
Whatever is indecorous in personality or unparliamentary in abuse has been abundantly poured forth by those frothy declaimers against the unavoidable domestic slavery of the South. They have assumed to themselves the power of making a form of government for others, and have supported so insolent a pretension by arguments and language no less insolent and offensive.

And when they have succeeded in excluding from the Western settlements every Southern man, and shall have sent forth in every direction swarms from the Northern hive, and missionary preachers against the cruelties and inhumanities of Southern slavery, a universal emancipation may be the next scheme suggested by visionary philanthropists or promoted by designing politicians.

With dangers such as these in prospect, can Virginia look on with stoical indifference because it is not her own case? Shall she console herself with the hope that she may be the last to be devoured? Shall she be silent when the great principles of the Constitution are assailed, when the rights of her sons, now peopling a western clime, are invaded, and principles asserted which may one day be turned with fatal effect against her own institutions?

THOMAS JEFFERSON
Letter to John Holmes, 1820
But this momentous question [the Missouri Compromise], like a firebell in the night, awakened and filled me with terror. I considered it at once as the knell of the Union.

ner at Baltimore. The *Texas Republican* published in Nacogdoches is first English-language Texan newspaper.

1819 - 1820

Feb. 13, 1819. Application of Missouri for statehood occasions move by Representative James Tallmadge of New York to prohibit further introduction of slaves (permitted by France and Spain before Louisiana Purchase) into Missouri as condition of admission. Motion threatens to upset even balance of slave and free states that has been maintained by tacit agreement since 1802 to admit free and slave states alternately. **March 3, 1820.** Extended debate and complex parliamentary maneuverings lead eventually to Missouri Compromise, in which admission of Missouri as a slave state is balanced by admission of free Maine, and which provides that slavery be henceforth prohibited in the Purchase north of latitude 36°30.' Controversy does not reflect abolitionist sentiment so much as sectional antagonism over the fact that slave states, though steadily falling behind in population and thus in House representation, maintain national power by equal representation in the Senate. With Maine (admitted on March 15, 1820) and Missouri (admitted on August 10, 1821, after extended debate about its constitution) the U.S. has 12 free and 12 slave states.

1820

April 24. Land Act of 1820 abolishes credit provisions of earlier act but reduces minimum purchase to 80 acres (⅛ section) and minimum price per acre to $1.25. General indebtedness in depression period makes act of benefit only to speculators, since settlers cannot usually pay full amount in cash.

Dec. 6. President Monroe, unopposed by any formal candidate for reelection as President, gains 231 out of 232 electoral votes cast; three electors abstain from voting and one vote is cast for John Quincy Adams (thought by some to retain for George Washington the honor of the only unanimous election). Daniel Tompkins is re-elected Vice-President, with 218 votes.

Fourth National Census shows that population is 9,638,000, a gain of more than 33 percent since 1810; figure includes 98,000 immigrants arrived since 1810. New York is largest city, with population of approximately 124,000, followed by Philadelphia (113,000), Baltimore (63,000), Boston (43,000), and New Orleans (27,000). Urban population (in places of more than 2,500) is 7.2 percent.

Responding to various American boasts of the new country's cultural importance, Sydney Smith asks in *Edinburgh Review*, "Who reads an American book?" Result is Anglo-American "Pamphlet War" on respective manners, morals, and intellect.

Edmund Kean, English tragic actor, makes American debut in New York as *Richard III*. Edwin Forrest, first native-born actor to achieve distinction, appears in tragedy *Douglas* in Philadelphia.

RUFUS KING
Niles' Weekly Register, 1819
The territory of Missouri is beyond our ancient limits, and the inquiry whether slavery shall exist there is open to many of the arguments that might be employed had slavery never existed within the United States. It is a question of no ordinary importance. Freedom and slavery are the parties which stand this day before the Senate; and upon its decision the empire of the one or the other will be established in the new state which we are about to admit into the Union. . . .

We are now about to pass our original boundary; if this can be done without affecting the principles of our free government, it can be accomplished only by the most vigilant attention to plant, cherish, and sustain the principles of liberty in the new states that may be formed beyond our ancient limits. . . .

But if, instead of freedom, slavery is to prevail and spread as we extend our dominion, can any reflecting man fail to see the necessity of giving to the general government greater powers; to enable it to afford the protection that will be demanded of it; powers that will be difficult to control and which may prove fatal to the public liberties?

View of New York from Weehawken, New Jersey

1821

NATHAN SANFORD

Debate in New York Constitutional Convention, 1821

The question before us is the right of suffrage—who shall or who shall not have the right to vote. The committee have presented the scheme they thought best; to abolish all existing distinctions and make the right of voting uniform. Is this not right? . . . To me the only qualifications seem to be the virtue and morality of the people.

JAMES KENT

Debate in New York Constitutional Convention, 1821

By the report before us, we propose to annihilate, at one stroke, all those property distinctions and to bow before the idol of universal suffrage. That extreme democratic principle, when applied to the Legislative and Executive departments of government, has been regarded with terror by the wise men of every age, because in every European republic, ancient and modern, in which it has been tried, it has terminated disastrously and been productive of corruption, injustice, violence, and tyranny. . . . If we are like other races of men, with similar follies and vices, then I greatly fear that our posterity will have reason to deplore, in sackcloth and ashes, the delusion of the day.

"March of the Caravan" from "Commerce of the Prairie" by Josiah Gregg, trader on the Santa Fe Trail

January. Spanish governor of Texas grants charter to Moses Austin for settlement of 300 families in Texas; colonization in area near Gulf of Mexico is carried out after his death by his son, Stephen F. Austin; colony is first legal settlement of Anglo-Americans in Texas.

Benjamin Lundy, promoter of Negro colonization, begins publication in Ohio of the *Genius of Universal Emancipation,* an antislavery journal, which is eventually located in Baltimore.

Aug. 10. Missouri is admitted to the Union as the twenty-fourth state and twelfth state that permits slavery.

Nov. 10. Property qualifications for voting are substantially abolished by New York Constitutional Convention after extended debate started on August 28; move follows similar action by Connecticut in 1818, Massachusetts in 1821, and by the new western states. Suffrage is also commonly extended to election of judges and many administrative officers, as well as legislators as in older state constitutions.

U.S. Supreme Court in *Cohens* v. *Virginia* affirms right of U.S. review of state court decisions.

Santa Fe Trail for commerce traveling

A scene from "The Spy" based on Cooper's novel, painted by Dunlap

between Independence, Missouri, and Santa Fe, Mexico, is mapped by Missouri trader, William Becknell; parts of route have been in use, but not continuous road.

James Fenimore Cooper publishes first of his American novels, *The Spy*, which is internationally successful. In following years, he writes the Leatherstocking series (*The Pioneers, The Last of the Mohicans, The Deerslayer*, and others).

Publication of *Poems* by Massachusetts lawyer William Cullen Bryant; volume includes "To a Waterfowl," "The Yellow Violet," and an enlarged version of "Thanatopsis."

Troy (New York) Female Seminary, first women's college-level school, is founded by Emma Willard at request of citizens of Troy. Mrs. Willard has from 1807 headed women's schools in Middlebury, Vermont, and Waterford, New York.

Junius Brutus Booth, English actor, and father of John Wilkes Booth, makes American debut in *Richard III* in Richmond, Virginia.

1821 - 1827

1821. First public high school in the U.S. is established in Boston; such schools rapidly become numerous in Massachusetts. **1827.** Massachusetts law requires a high

CHARLES J. INGERSOLL
Address to American Philosophical Society, 1823

The English language makes English reading American; and a generous, especially a parental, nationality, instead of disparaging a supposed deficiency in the creation of literature, should remember and rejoice that the idiom and ideas of England are also those of this country and of this continent, destined to be enjoyed and improved by millions of educated and thinking people, spreading from the Bay of Fundy to the mouth of the Columbia. . . .

But speaking and writing the language of an ancient and refined people, whose literature preoccupies nearly every department, is, in many respects, an unexampled disadvantage in the comparative estimate. America cannot contribute in any comparative proportion to the great British stock of literature, which almost supersedes the necessity of American subscriptions. Independent of this foreign oppression, the American mind has been called more to political, scientific, and mechanical than to literary exertion.

Trial of Denmark Vesey, 1822
Denmark Vesey—The Court, on mature consideration, have pronounced you GUILTY—You have enjoyed the advantage of able counsel, and were also heard in your own defense, in which you endeavored, with great art and plausibility, to impress a belief of your innocence. After the most patient deliberation, however, the Court were not only satisfied of your guilt, but that you were the author, and original instigator of this diabolical plot. Your professed design was to trample on all laws, human and divine; to riot in blood, outrage, rapine and conflagration, and to introduce anarchy and confusion in their most horrid forms. Your life has become, therefore, a just and necessary sacrifice, at the shrine of indignant Justice. It is difficult to imagine what infatuation could have prompted you to attempt an enterprise so wild and visionary. You were a free man; were comparatively wealthy; and enjoyed every comfort, compatible with your situation. You had, therefore, much to risk, and little to gain. From your age and experience, you ought to have known, that success was impracticable.

A moment's reflection must have convinced you, that the ruin of your race, would have been the probable result, and that years would have rolled away, before they could have recovered that confidence, which, they once enjoyed in this community. The only reparation in your power, is a full disclosure of the truth. In addition to treason, you have commited the grossest impiety, in attempting to pervert the sacred words of God into a sanction for crimes of the blackest hue.

school in every town having more than 500 families.

1821 - 1848

Kentucky legislature abolishes imprisonment for debt; eight other states have passed similar laws by 1848.

1822

May 4. President James Monroe vetoes bill authorizing collection of tolls to pay for repair of Cumberland Road, following halt in construction caused by depression of 1819-1824; veto recommends further construction of roads, but asks constitutional amendment to give federal government authority it now lacks.

May 30. Planned rebellion in Charleston, South Carolina, of city slave workers, led by free Negro Denmark Vesey, is discovered and prevented. **June 18-Aug. 9.** Vesey and 36 other Negroes are executed.

Cotton mills begin production in Massachusetts, with water-powered machinery; by 1826, in Lowell, one plant turns out 2 million yards of cloth annually. Female labor force is recruited and given many benefits under paternalistic control in company town. Woolen weaving machinery is added in 1830.

Lowell Mason compiles *Boston Handel and Haydn Society's Collection of Church Music.* Mason is known as the "father of American church music."

First patent for false teeth is issued to C. M. Graham.

Charleston (South Carolina) *Mercury* founded; it eventually becomes the leading secessionist newspaper.

1822 - 1826

March 8. In message to Congress, President Monroe proposes U.S. recognition of Latin-American republics that have broken away from Spain. **May 4.** Congressional measure provides for establishment of diplomatic relations. **June 19, 1822-May 2, 1826.** U.S. formally recognizes Colombia, Mexico, Chile, Argentina, Brazil, the Federation of Central American States, and Peru.

1823

July 17. In answer to extension to the Oregon country of Russian claims on Pacific Coast, Secretary of State John Quincy Adams informs Russian minister that the U.S. will not admit Russia's right to territory on this continent and that "the American continents are no longer subjects for any new European colonial establishments."

Aug. 20. British concern for Latin-American markets leads Foreign Minister George Canning to propose formally a joint Anglo-American declaration warning against any attempt by the Holy Alliance (France, Austria, Prussia, and Russia) to recover colonies that have broken away from Spain. **Nov. 7.** Secretary of State John Quincy Adams, anxious to prevent extension of foreign influence in Western Hemisphere, recommends independent American statement instead; proposal is agreed to in principle by President Monroe and the Cabinet. **Dec. 2.** President Monroe's Annual Message to Congress includes Adams' proposal, which becomes known afterward as the Monroe Doctrine.

Nicholas Biddle appointed third president of Second Bank of the United States, which has been restored to sound condition by administration of Langdon Cheves, second president. Under Biddle's administra-

JAMES MONROE
Message to Congress, 1823
The occasion has been judged proper for asserting, as a principle in which the rights and interests of the United States are involved, that the American continents, by the free and independent condition which they have assumed and maintain, are henceforth not to be considered as subjects for future colonization by any European powers. . . .

In the wars of the European powers in matters relating to themselves we have never taken any part, nor does it comport with our policy so to do. It is only when our rights are invaded or seriously menaced that we resent injuries or make preparation for our defense.

With the movements in this hemisphere we are of necessity more immediately connected, and by causes which must be obvious to all enlightened and impartial observers. . . . We owe it, therefore, to candor and to the amicable relations existing between the United States and those powers to declare that we should consider any attempt on their part to extend their system to any portion of this hemisphere as dangerous to our peace and safety.

With the existing colonies or dependencies of any European power we have not interfered and shall not interfere. But with the governments who have declared their independence and maintained it, and whose independence we have, on great consideration and on just principles, acknowledged, we could not view any interposition for the purpose of oppressing them, or controlling in any other manner their destiny, by any European power in any other light than as the manifestation of an unfriendly disposition toward the United States.

HENRY CLAY
Speech in House, 1824
Is this foreign market, so incompetent at present, and which, limited as its demands are, operates so unequally upon the productive labor of our country, likely to improve in future? If I am correct in the views which I have presented to the committee, it must become worse and worse. . . .

We must, then, change somewhat our course. We must give a new direction to some portion of our industry. We must speedily adopt a genuine American policy. Still cherishing the foreign market, let us create also a home market to give further scope to the consumption of the produce of American industry. Let us counteract the policy of foreigners and withdraw the support which we now give to their industry and stimulate that of our own country. . . .

But this home market, highly desirable as it is, can only be created and cherished by the protection of our own legislation against the inevitable prostration of our industry, which must ensue from the action of *foreign policy and legislation. . . . The measure of the wealth of a nation is indicated by the measure of its protection of its industry; and . . . the measure of the poverty of a nation is marked by that of the degree in which it neglects and abandons the care of its own industry, leaving it exposed to the action of foreign powers. . . .*

But there is a remedy, and that remedy consists in modifying our foreign policy, and in adopting a genuine American system. *We must naturalize the arts in our country; and we must naturalize them by the only means which the wisdom of nations has yet discovered to be effectual — by adequate protection against the otherwise overwhelming influence of foreigners.*

tion, Bank becomes dominant influence in the national economy until its charter expires in 1836.

"A Visit from St. Nicholas" (" 'Twas the night before Christmas"), written in 1822 for his children by Clement Clarke Moore, professor of Oriental and Greek literature, is published without his knowledge in *Troy* (New York) *Sentinel.*

Song "Home, Sweet Home" introduced in London and New York in *Clari, or The Maid of Milan,* a play by John Howard Payne.

1824

March 30. In speech supporting new Tariff Act, passed May 22, Henry Clay defines the "American System" as a combination of protective tariffs and internal improvements to expand the national economy and make the U.S. more independent.

April 30. Avoiding direct conflict with President Monroe's veto in 1822 of Cumberland Road project, Congress over strong opposition from New England and Southern states passes General Survey Bill authorizing federal surveys and estimates of roads judged to be necessary for national and commercial purposes. Western congressmen are unanimously in favor of Bill.

May 7. Texas incorporated into Mexican Federal Republic as part of one of its states. Several thousand Americans have settled there, but isolation of their settlements results in little identification with their adopted country.

Supreme Court in *Gibbons* v. *Ogden* disallows New York act that grants steamboat monopoly in traffic between New York and New Jersey, holding that it is a violation of commerce clause of Constitution; decision also holds that the state controls only intra-state commerce, and in effect broadens definition of what constitutes interstate commerce.

Great Salt Lake in Utah is discovered by James Bridger, fur trader and guide.

Auburn (N.Y.) Penitentiary, built in 1816, institutes what becomes known as the "Auburn System": silent prisoners housed in cell blocks and labor performed in groups. Alternative is "Pennsylvania System": solitary labor and solitary confinement.

Strike of weavers at Pawtucket, Rhode Island, is first recorded strike by women.

1824 - 1825

Competition within the Jeffersonian Republican Party (the only surviving national political party) for a successor to President Monroe leads to rejection of congressional caucus as nominating body. **Feb. 14.** Congressional caucus nominates William H. Crawford of Georgia, secretary of the treasury, but only 66 of 216 members attend. Other candidates already declared or nominated by their state legislatures are John C. Calhoun, Andrew Jackson, Henry Clay, and John Quincy Adams. Field is narrowed when Crawford is incapacitated by the effects of a stroke suffered in 1823, and Calhoun withdraws as presidential candidate, announcing his candidacy for Vice-President on both Jackson and Adams tickets. **Dec. 1.** Count in electoral college gives Jackson 99 electoral votes, Adams 84, Crawford 41, and Clay 37. As no presidential candidate has a majority, choice goes to House of Representatives, where Clay is eliminated as fourth contender and throws his support to Adams. **Feb. 9, 1825.** Adams is elected

FELIX GRUNDY
Resolutions of the Tennessee General Assembly, 1823
The General Assembly of the state of Tennessee has taken into consideration the practice . . . of members of the Congress of the United States meeting in caucus, and nominating persons to be voted for as President and Vice-President of the United States; and, upon the best view of the subject which this General Assembly has been able to take, it is believed that the practice of congressional nominations is a violation of the spirit of the Constitution of the United States. . . .

It has been said that the members of Congress in caucus only recommend to the people for whom to vote, and that such recommendation is not obligatory. This is true and clearly proves that it is a matter which does not belong to them—that, in recommending candidates, they go beyond the authority committed to them as members of Congress and thus transcend the trust delegated to them by their constituents. . . .

The following reasons . . . might be conclusively relied on to prove the impolicy and unconstitutionality of the congressional nominations. . . . 1. A caucus nomination is against the spirit of the Constitution. 2. It is both inexpedient and impolitic. 3. Members of Congress may become the final electors and therefore ought not to prejudge the case by pledging themselves previously to support particular candidates. 4. It violates the equality intended to be secured by the Constitution to the weaker states. 5. Caucus nominations may, in time (by the interference of the states), acquire the force of precedents and become authoritative and, thereby, endanger the liberties of the American people.

LORENZO DOW
Journal, 1804
*Hence to Marysville, where I spoke to
about 1,500; and many appeared to
feel the word, but about 50 felt the
jerks. At night I lodged with one of the
Nicholites, a kind of Quakers who do
not feel free to wear colored
clothes. . . . While at tea, I observed
his daughter (who sat opposite to me at
table) to have the jerks, and dropped
the teacup from her hand in the violent
agitation. I said to her, "Young woman,
what is the matter?" She replied, "I
have got the jerks." I asked her how
long she had it. She observed, "A few
days"; and that it had been the means
of the awakening and conversion of her
soul by stirring her up to serious consideration about her careless state, and so
forth.*

*Sunday, February 19, I spoke in
Knoxville to hundreds more than could
get into the courthouse, the governor
being present. About 150 appeared to
have the jerking exercise, among whom
was a circuit preacher (Johnson) who
had opposed them a little before, but he
now had them powerfully; and I believe
he would have fallen over three times
had not the auditory been so crowded
that he could not unless he fell perpen-
dicularly. . . .*

*I have seen Presbyterians, Methodists,
Quakers, Baptists, Episcopalians, and
Independents exercised with the
jerks. . . . I believe that those who are
most pious and given up to God are
rarely touched with it, and also those
naturalists who wish and try to get it to
philosophize upon it are excepted. But
the lukewarm, lazy, halfhearted, indo-
lent professor is subject to it; and many
of them I have seen who, when it came
upon them, would be alarmed and
stirred up to redouble their diligence
with God.*

sixth President of the U.S. with votes of 13 states; Jackson receives 7 votes and Craw- ford 4. Calhoun has been elected Vice- President with 182 electoral votes. When President Adams later selects Clay as secre- tary of state, Clay is charged with having made a "corrupt bargain" in supporting Adams; this charge darkens Clay's political career.

Jacksonians, resenting what they regard as "stolen" election, make immediate prepara- tions for election campaign of 1828 and formation of new political alignment: the Democratic Republicans ("Jackson's men"), opposed to the followers of Adams and Clay, who are called National Republicans.

1824 - 1830

Great success of religious revival move- ment in East led by Charles G. Finney, Presbyterian minister, whose followers adopt Congregationalism. Peter Cartwright and James B. Finley lead revivalism in Mid- dle West during same period.

1825

March 24. Texas is opened to American colonization by Mexican law.

Oct. 26. New York Governor De Witt Clinton formally opens Erie Canal, later dumping two kegs of Lake Erie water into New York Harbor. Canal immediately be- comes an important commercial route con- necting the East with the Ohio and Missis- sippi valleys. With time of travel cut to one-third and cost of shipping freight to one-tenth of previous figures, commerce via canal soon makes New York City chief At- lantic port of the U.S. West-bound emi- grants from New England settle in Great Lakes region near end of route, resulting in Northern rather than Southern dominance in the Middle West.

Dec. 6. John Quincy Adams' First Annual Message to Congress sets forth sweeping nationalist program involving government-backed construction, exploration, education, laws to improve the economy, and encouragement of the arts and sciences. Program antagonizes Southern states' rights interests, who are encouraged by Vice-President Calhoun's appointment of Senate committees unsympathetic to the administration. Only source of President Adams' strength is uneasy alliance between New England and the West, based on support of "American System."

U.S. government adopts removal policy that provides for transfer of eastern Indians to area west of the Mississippi River in order to facilitate white settlement and create a definite Indian frontier. Most Indians are settled in present-day Oklahoma and Kansas by 1835.

"Suffolk System." An early clearing house system, established by Suffolk Bank in Boston in 1816, achieves marked success; it requires rural banks to deposit funds with Suffolk Bank to back notes issued by them. Despite obvious advantages, arrangement is not widely adopted elsewhere at this time, but is eventually incorporated into National Banking System.

Francis Wright, English social reformer, establishes Nashoba community near Memphis, Tennessee; purpose is training of Negroes to make possible their colonization outside the U.S.; community is active until 1828. Robert Dale Owen, another Englishman, establishes utopian collectivist community at New Harmony, Indiana.

1825 - 1826

Dec. 6 and 26, 1825. President Adams, at the urging of Clay, sends message to Congress in attempt to arrange for consulta-

Freedom's Journal, 1827

Messrs. Editors,

Will you allow a female to offer a few remarks upon a subject that you must allow to be all-important? I don't know that in any of your papers you have said sufficient upon the education of females. I hope you are not to be classed with those who think that our mathematical knowledge should be limited to "fathoming the dish-kettle," and that we have acquired enough of history if we know that our grandfather's father lived and died. . . .

There are difficulties, and great difficulties, in the way of our advancement; but that should only stir us to greater efforts. We possess not the advantages with those of our sex whose skins are not colored like our own, but we can improve what little we have and make our one talent produce twofold. The influence that we have over the male sex demands that our minds should be instructed and improved with the principles of education and religion, in order that this influence should be properly directed. Ignorant ourselves, how can we be expected to form the minds of our youth and conduct them in the paths of knowledge? How can we "teach the young idea how to shoot" if we have none ourselves? There is a great responsibility resting somewhere, and it is time for us to be up and doing. . . .

I will not longer trespass on your time and patience. I merely throw out these hints in order that some more able pen will take up the subject.

Matilda

THIS PAGE: (Left) Henry Clay: portrait
by Samuel Osgood; (below) John C. Calhoun;
(bottom) virulent British cartoon lam-
pooning Americans and attacking Jackson's
execution of two Englishmen during his
invasion of Florida
OPPOSITE PAGE: (Top) Lifting Erie Canal
barges through the five double locks at
Lockport, New York, c. 1820; (bottom
left) James Monroe, fifth President of
the United States: portrait by Samuel
F. B. Morse; (bottom right) John Quincy
Adams, the sixth United States President

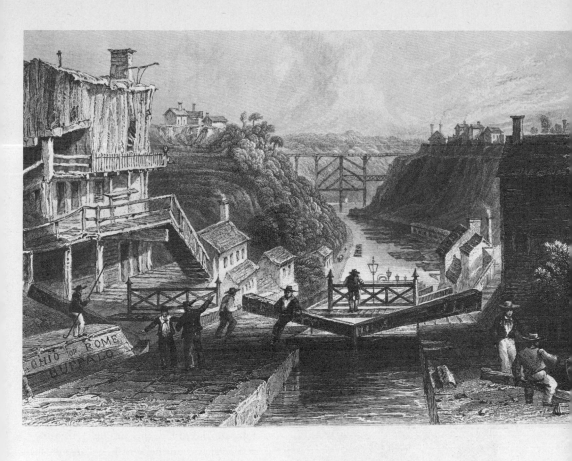

JOHN ADAMS

Last words, 1826 (Jefferson had died a few hours earlier)

Thomas Jefferson still lives.

THOMAS JEFFERSON

Directions for his tomb, found after his death, in his own handwriting, 1826

On the faces of the obelisk the following inscription, and not a word more

"*Here was buried/Thomas Jefferson/ Author of the Declaration of American Independence/of the Statute of Virginia for religious freedom/And Father of the University of Virginia.*"

because by these, as testimonials that I have lived, I wish most to be remembered.

Joseph Henry

tive U.S. participation in Panama Congress, called by Latin-American republics to consider possibilities of union among themselves. **Jan. 11-March 25, 1826.** After long debate, Congress approves sending representatives, but debate by opposition delays arrival of appointed U.S. delegates until after Panama Congress adjourns. Basis of opposition is struggle for power by anti-administration forces under Calhoun and Senator Martin Van Buren of New York.

1826

March 30. John Randolph accuses Clay of corruption from the Senate floor; Clay challenges him to a duel. **April 8.** In duel, fought in Virginia, neither man is harmed.

July 4. Thomas Jefferson dies at Monticello and John Adams at Quincy, Massachusetts, within hours of each other on the fiftieth anniversary of the Declaration of Independence.

Joseph Henry begins his first experiments in electricity, during which he invents insulated wire, the multiple-coil magnet, and other devices, one of which makes possible development of the telegraph. Henry later discovers principles of electromagnetic induction, independently arrived at during the same period by Michael Faraday in England. Henry is appointed first director of the Smithsonian Institution in 1846.

Millbury Lyceum Number 1, established at Millbury, Massachusetts, by Josiah Holbrook, inaugurates adult self-improvement and education movement in the U.S. Three thousand town lyceums exist by 1834.

United States Telegraph, Jacksonian newspaper edited by Duff Green, founded in Washington, D.C. Supported by anti-Adams congressmen, it is the chief organ of the Jacksonian forces until 1831.

1826 - 1830

James Kent, professor at Columbia University Law School and former chancellor of New York State Court of Chancery, publishes his *Commentaries on American Law*, which rapidly becomes standard manual of U.S. constitutional and common law.

1826 - 1840

1826. First railroads built in the U.S. are short-line routes, powered by cable systems, horses, or sails: the Mauch Chunk Railroad in Pennsylvania, for carrying coal, and a railroad in Massachusetts that transports granite. First passenger line incorporated is the Baltimore and Ohio Railroad, but this is not completed to Wheeling (now West Virginia) from Baltimore until 1852. By 1840, the U.S. has 3,000 miles of railroads — almost twice as much as in all of Europe.

First wave of Irish and German immigration constitutes 75 percent of total immigration to the U.S., about 620,000 in this period.

1827

July 30-Aug. 3. Advocates of a higher protective tariff, having been defeated by Southern votes in the Senate when new bill is introduced on January 10, call a convention at Harrisburg, Pennsylvania. One hundred delegates from 13 states prepare Harrisburg Memorial. **Dec. 24.** Memorial, presented to Congress, recommends extension and increase of duties to protect domestic manufactures, especially New England woolen textiles and Pennsylvania iron. Opposition of Southern interests, which depend on foreign markets for their agricultural products, has been expressed by Thomas Cooper, an early Southern sectionalist, in speech at Columbia, South Caroli-

CHANCELLOR KENT
Memoirs; when a temperance committee asked him to sign a pledge
Gentlemen, I refuse to sign any pledge. I never have been drunk, and, by the blessing of God, I never will get drunk, but I have a constitutional privilege to get drunk, and that privilege I will not sign away.

ALEXIS DE TOCQUEVILLE
Journal, 1832
America, which is the country which enjoys the greatest sum of prosperity that has ever yet been vouchsafed to any nation, is also that which, in proportion to its age and means, has made the greatest effort to supply itself with the free communications of which I was speaking above. . . .

When it seems that the population is turning toward a certain part of the country, there is a hurry to open a road thither. The road almost always comes before those whom it is intended to serve, but it encourages them to move; we have several times seen main roads opened up literally in the middle of the wilderness.

America has undertaken and finished the construction of some immense canals. It already has more railways than France. No one fails to see that the discovery of steam has incredibly increased the power and prosperity of the Union; and that is because it facilitates speedy communications between the different parts of that immense land. The states of the South, where communications are less convenient, are those which languish compared to the rest.

Preamble of the Mechanics' Union, 1827
When the disposition and efforts of one part of mankind to oppress another have become too manifest to be mistaken and too pernicious in their consequences to be endured, it has often been found necessary for those who feel aggrieved to associate for the purpose of affording to each other mutual protection from oppression.

We, the journeyman mechanics of the city and county of Philadelphia, conscious that our condition in society is lower than justice demands it should be, and feeling our inability, individually, to ward off from ourselves and families those numerous evils which result from an unequal and very excessive accumulation of wealth and power into the hands of a few, are desirous of forming an association which shall avert as much as possible those evils which poverty and incessant toil have already inflicted, and which threaten ultimately to overwhelm and destroy us. . . .

We appeal to the most intelligent of every community and ask — Do not you, and all society, depend solely for subsistence on the products of human industry? Do not those who labor, while acquiring to themselves thereby only a scanty and penurious support, likewise maintain in affluence and luxury the rich who never labor? . . .

Are we who confer almost every blessing on society never to be treated as freemen and equals and never be accounted worthy of an equivalent, in return for the products of our industry?

na, on July 2, in which he protested the prospect of higher prices for foreign manufactures and raised the possibility of secession from the Union of Southern states because of unwillingness to submit to Northern commercial ambitions. Harrisburg Memorial is eventually rejected by Congress.

Supreme Court in *Ogden* v. *Saunders* overrules Chief Justice John Marshall on a constitutional question for the first time when it upholds 4 to 3 a New York bankruptcy law against a suit brought by a citizen of another state that claims violation of contract rights. Dissent by Justices Marshall and Joseph Story argues that protection of the constitutional contract clause is absolute.

Mechanics' Union of Trade Associations, established at Philadelphia, is first city central trade council in the U.S. Twelve other cities have similar organizations by 1836.

First engravings of *The Birds of America* by ornithologist John James Audubon are published; the collection eventually contains reproductions of more than 1,000 life-size paintings of 500 species; it appears in London, is sold on subscription terms, and requires 11 years to establish.

Tamerlane and Other Poems by Edgar Allan Poe is published anonymously in Boston. First *Peter Parley* book, which teaches moral behavior to children, inaugurates a series that sells 7 million copies by 1860; books are written by various authors employed by publisher Samuel G. Goodrich.

Youth's Companion, children's magazine, founded in Boston; merges with *The American Boy* in 1929.

1828

Jan. 31. Jacksonians introduce bill in House designed to use tariff issue to defeat

President Adams in forthcoming election. Bill imposes duties so high, particularly on raw materials, that even protective tariff advocates in New England will not vote for it (the Jacksonians believe) and, lacking a tariff, will blame President Adams. **May 13.** So-called Tariff of Abominations is passed by House and Senate anyway, when protectionist interests decide it is better than nothing, but Jackson's fortunes escape damage in the resulting confusion of charges and counter-charges.

Aug. 11. First "labor" party in the U.S. is organized in Philadelphia; led by reformers and small business men rather than laborers, in 1828 election it gains temporary balance of power in city council, advocating 10-hour work day, abolition of imprisonment for debt, restrictions on monopolies (especially banks), and universal free education. Similar parties are promptly created in New York and Boston.

Election campaign of 1828 is first that resembles modern contests, because most states have passed laws since 1824 making choice of presidential electors a matter of popular vote. Jacksonians, now called Democrats, use able newspaper editors such as Amos Kendall and Duff Green to make personal attacks on President Adams, running as a National Republican; Adams' supporters reply in kind. **Dec. 3.** Though without a program, Jackson is elected, having captured New York and Pennsylvania as well as the South and West. Popular vote is 647,000 to 508,000, with Jackson receiving 178 electoral votes to Adams' 83. Calhoun, having given up nationalism, runs on the Jackson ticket, and is reelected Vice-President.

Dec. 19. South Carolina legislature adopts resolutions opposing the "Tariff of Abominations" as oppressive and unconstitutional; accompanying the resolutions is

JAMES FENIMORE COOPER
Notions of the Americans, 1828
There were three or four other passengers in the stage, men of decent and sober exterior, among whom I detected certain interchanges of queer glances, though none of them appeared to think the subject of any very engrossing interest. Provoked at their unreasonable indifference to a theme so delightful as liberty, I asked one of them if he did not apprehend there would be an end to the republic should General Jackson become the next President?

"I rather think not," was his deliberate, and somewhat laconic, answer.

"Why not? He is a soldier and a man of ambition." My unmoved yeoman did not care to dispute either of these qualities, but he still persevered in thinking there was not much danger, since he "did not know any one in his neighborhood who was much disposed to help a man in such an undertaking."

It is provoking to find a whole nation dwelling in this species of alarming security, for no other reason than that their vulgar and everyday practices teach them to rely on themselves, instead of trusting to the rational inferences of philanthropic theorists, who have so long been racking their ingenuity to demonstrate that a condition of society which has delusively endured for nearly 200 years has been in existence all that time in direct opposition to the legitimate deductions of the science of government.

MRS. SAMUEL HARRISON SMITH
Letter, 1829
Someone came and informed us the crowd before the President's house was so far lessened that they thought we might enter. This time we effected our purpose. But what a scene did we witness! The majesty of the people had disappeared, and a rabble, a mob, of boys, Negroes, women, children — scrambling, fighting, romping. What a pity, what a pity! No arrangements had been made, no police officers placed on duty, and the whole house had been inundated by the rabble mob. We came too late.

The President, after having been literally nearly pressed to death and almost suffocated and torn to pieces by the people in their eagerness to shake hands with Old Hickory, had retreated through the back way, or south front, and had escaped to his lodgings at Gadsby's. Cut glass and china to the amount of several thousand dollars had been broken in the struggle to get the refreshments. Punch and other articles had been carried out in tubs and buckets, but had it been in hogsheads it would have been insufficient. . . . Ladies fainted, men were seen with bloody noses, and such a scene of confusion took place as is impossible to describe; those who got in could not get out by the door again but had to scramble out of windows. . . .

This concourse had not been anticipated and therefore not provided against. Ladies and gentlemen only had been expected at this levee, not the people en masse. But it was the people's day, and the people's President, and the people would rule.

South Carolina Exposition and Protest, prepared anonymously by Calhoun, which upholds state sovereignty and proposes nullification of federal laws by state action; it lays early basis for secession. Protests similar to South Carolina's are later made by the legislatures of Georgia, Mississippi, and Virginia.

New York appoints Law Revision Commission to codify statutes and court decisions, and to adapt English common law to American needs and usages. Other states undertake similar reforms in this period.

Minstrel character "Jim Crow" introduced in Louisville, Kentucky, by Thomas Dartmouth Rice, known as "Daddy" Rice.

American Dictionary of the English Language is published in two volumes by Noah Webster, former journalist and pamphleteer turned lexicographer.

1829

March 4. Andrew Jackson is inaugurated seventh President of the U.S. At White House reception following inaugural, boisterous celebration by crowds, frontiersmen as well as Washington "aristocracy," suggests "the reign of King 'Mob'" to Joseph Story, associate justice of the Supreme Court. Inaugural address skirts current issues, promises economy, regard for state sovereignty, and changes in the entrenched federal civil service.

Among Jacksonian innovations is his reliance upon an unofficial "Kitchen Cabinet" of party managers, notably Amos Kendall, William B. Lewis, and Duff Green, for political advice and help in the composition of state papers; he also introduces on a national scale the "Spoils System," by which patronage is used for party purposes. The spoils system has been used moderately during the Jeffersonian "revolution" of 1800, and by President Jackson's time is already established in state politics, particularly by the "Albany Regency" in New York. But actual application by President Jackson is restrained; less than one office-holder in 10 is replaced during his first year, and fewer than 20 percent are removed for political reasons during his two terms. System at this period is a democratic device for allowing the common man a voice in the government, although later it is much abused.

William Cullen Bryant begins long career as owner and influential editor in chief until his death in 1878 of *New York Evening Post.*

Beginning of a quarter-century of agitation against Roman Catholics following several years of missionary efforts in the U.S. by European Catholic organizations, coincident with and a result of increasing immigration from Catholic countries. Among early manifestations are anti-Catholic sermons from Protestant pulpits, anti-Catholic literature, such as *Priestcraft Unmasked,* the burning of a convent, and growth of Native American movement in 1830s.

1830

Jan. 19. Speech by noted orator Senator Robert Y. Hayne of South Carolina, upholds the rights of the states against the authority of the federal government. **Jan. 20.** Senator Daniel Webster responds with criticism of Southerners who disparage the Union. **Jan. 21-27.** Exchange leads to debate between Hayne and Webster on the nature and origin of the Constitution and the federal Union. **Jan. 26-27.** Webster's reply to Hayne, rejecting the idea of a conflict in the federal system ("Liberty *and* Union, now and forever, one and inseparable!"), sets forth theory of a sovereign national government, binding upon people

DANIEL WEBSTER
Speech in Senate, 1830
While the Union lasts, we have high, exciting, gratifying prospects spread out before us, for us and our children. Beyond that I seek not to penetrate the veil.

God grant that in my day, at least, that curtain may not rise! God grant that on my vision never may be opened what lies behind! When my eyes shall be turned to behold for the last time the sun in heaven, may I not see him shining on the broken and dishonored fragments of a once glorious Union; on states dissevered, discordant, belligerent; on a land rent with civil feuds, or drenched, it may be, in fraternal blood! Let their last feeble and lingering glance rather behold the gorgeous ensign of the republic, now known and honored throughout the earth, still full high advanced, its arms and trophies streaming in their original luster, not a stripe erased or polluted, nor a single star obscured, bearing for its motto, no such miserable interrogatory as "What is all this worth?" nor those other words of delusion and folly, "Liberty first and Union afterwards"; but everywhere, spread all over in characters of living light, blazing on all its ample folds, as they float over the sea and over the land, and in every wind under the whole heavens, that other sentiment, dear to every true American heart —Liberty and Union, now and forever, one and inseparable!

ANDREW JACKSON
Veto of Maysville Road Bill, 1830

If it is expected that the people of this country, reckless of their constitutional obligations, will prefer their local interest to the principles of the Union, such expectations will in the end be disappointed; or, if it be not so, then indeed has the world but little to hope from the example of free government. When an honest observance of constitutional compacts cannot be obtained from communities like ours, it need not be anticipated elsewhere; and the cause in which there has been so much martyrdom, and from which so much was expected by the friends of liberty, may be abandoned, and the degrading truth that man is unfit for self-government admitted.

And this will be the case if expediency be made a rule of construction in interpreting the Constitution. Power in no government could desire a better shield for the insidious advances which it is ever ready to make upon the checks that are designed to restrain its action. But I do not entertain such gloomy apprehensions.

If it be the wish of the people that the construction of roads and canals should be conducted by the federal government, it is not only highly expedient but indispensably necessary that a previous amendment of the Constitution, delegating the necessary power and defining and restricting its exercise with reference to the sovereignty of the states, should be made. Without it, nothing extensively useful can be effected.

and states alike, in an oration that becomes the best-known American address for a generation afterward.

April 6. Revolutionary government in Mexico, after having restricted "rights" of U.S. settlers, finally forbids further American colonization of Texas; law also abolishes slavery.

April 13. Signifying defiance of states' rights and nullification principles, President Jackson offers toast, "Our federal Union: it must be preserved," at Jefferson Day dinner; John C. Calhoun, taken by surprise, responds: "The Union, next to our liberty, most dear."

May 27. The internal improvements program having degenerated into congressional maneuvering for federal funds, President Jackson, inspired by Van Buren, vetoes Maysville Road Bill on grounds that project lies wholly within Kentucky and federal support would require a constitutional amendment. Political object, which is to strike a blow at Clay's party and at the same time make a gesture toward Southern states' rights interests, is accomplished without offending the North or the West, since Jackson affirms belief in the principle of federal subsidy of internal improvements.

May 29. Pre-emption Act authorizes purchase of up to 160 acres of public land at minimum price of $1.25 per acre by persons who have cultivated the land within the preceding year. Act serves to encourage both homesteaders and cotton planters by making possible payment out of earnings from first year's crop. Designed as a temporary measure, the Act's provisions, politically popular, are renewed at intervals until 1862, when Homestead Act replaces it.

Dec. 7. Pro-administration *Washington Globe* starts publication with Francis P.

Blair, Sr. as editor: aim of President Jackson and Kitchen Cabinet is to replace Duff Green's *U.S. Telegraph* as chief Jacksonian paper, since Green is an ally of Calhoun, who is rapidly becoming Jackson's antagonist. *Telegraph* becomes anti-administration paper after 1831. Other newspapers established are the *Albany Evening Journal,* an influential Whig voice edited by Thurlow Weed, and the *Boston (Evening) Transcript,* a cultural organ.

Fifth national census shows population of 12,866,000, including about 150,000 immigrants arrived from 1820 to 1830, a gain of more than 33 percent since 1820; census also shows that 8.8 percent of U.S. population lives in cities of 2,500 or more.

"Tom Thumb," first steam locomotive built in America, constructed at the Canton Iron Works in Baltimore for the Baltimore and Ohio Railroad by Peter Cooper, inventor, manufacturer, and later, philanthropist.

Book of Mormon by Joseph Smith is published; in same year Church of Jesus Christ of Latter-day Saints (Mormons) is founded in Fayette, New York. Mormons are forced by opposition to their beliefs to go to Ohio, then Missouri, then Illinois, where Smith is murdered. They finally settle in Utah in 1847-1848, under the leadership of Brigham Young.

First of the "Maj. Jack Downing" letters, New England dialect political satires, written by Seba Smith, a Portland, Maine, newspaper editor. This character and his letters are taken over by Charles A. Davis.

First publication of *Lady's Book* (later *Godey's Lady's Book*), influential women's magazine, in Philadelphia; discontinued in 1898.

Poem, "Old Ironsides," published by Oliver Wendell Holmes; also "Mary Had a

JOSEPH SMITH
Pearl of Great Price, 1838
While I was thus in the act of calling upon God, I discovered a light appearing in my room, which continued to increase until the room was lighter than at noonday, when immediately a personage appeared at my bedside, standing in the air, for his feet did not touch the floor. . . .

He called me by name and said unto me that he was a messenger sent from the presence of God to me, and that his name was Moroni; that God had a work for me to do; and that my name should be had for good and evil among all nations, kindreds, and tongues, or that it should be both good and evil spoken of among all people.

He said there was a book deposited, written upon gold plates, giving an account of the former inhabitants of this continent and the source from whence they sprang. He also said that the fullness of the everlasting gospel was contained in it, as delivered by the Savior to the ancient inhabitants. Also, that there were two stones in silver bows — and these stones, fastened to a breastplate, constituted what is called the Urim and Thummim — deposited with the plates; and the possession and use of these stones were what constituted "seers" in ancient or former times; and that God had prepared them for the purpose of translating the book. . . .

While he was conversing with me about the plates, the vision was opened to my mind that I could see the place where the plates were deposited, and that so clearly and distinctly that I knew the place again when I visited it.

HORATIO GREENOUGH

Travels . . . of a Yankee Stonecutter, 1852

The above reflections have been drawn from us by the oft-repeated expressions of regret which we have listened to, "that from the constitution of our society and the nature of our institutions, no influences can be brought to bear upon art with the vivifying power of court patronage." We fully and firmly believe that these institutions are more favorable to a natural, healthful growth of art than any hotbed culture whatever. We cannot (as did Napoleon) make, by a few imperial edicts, an army of battle painters, a hierarchy of drum and fife glorifiers. Nor can we, in the lifetime of an individual, so stimulate this branch of culture, so unduly and disproportionately endow it, as to make a Valhalla start from a republican soil. The monuments, the pictures, the statues of the republic will represent what the people love and wish for, not what they can be made to accept, not how much taxation they will bear. . . .

If there be any youth toiling through the rudiments of art at the forms of the simple and efficient school at New York (whose title is the only pompous thing about it), with a chilling belief that elsewhere the difficulties he struggles with are removed or modified, we call upon him to be of good cheer, and to believe what from our hearts we are convinced of: that there is at present no country where the development and growth of an artist is more free, healthful, and happy than it is in these United States.

Little Lamb," by Sarah Josepha Hale, later, from 1837, editor of *Godey's Lady's Book.*

1830 - 1860

Underground Railroad of changing routes and places of concealment for fugitive slaves escaping to the North or to Canada is established in 14 Northern states. Railroad has been active in Western Reserve for at least a decade and its beginnings go as far back as 1790. An estimated 50,000 slaves escape, 1830-1860. Several Northern states enact "personal liberty laws" that are contrary to the federal fugitive slave law, making enforcement of it difficult.

First period in the U.S. during which sculpture becomes a profession. Horatio Greenough studies in Italy and returns to work in marble and other materials in Italian neo-classic style. Others who follow are Hiram Powers, whose work is chiefly bust portraits in marble and who earns a reputation in Europe as well as in the U.S., and Thomas Crawford who executes many statues on government buildings.

Outstanding paintings of this period are landscapes in oils and water color by Thomas Doughty, Asher Brown Durand, and Thomas Cole, leaders of the Hudson River School of New York landscape painters. The early work of George Inness is also of this type. Samuel F. B. Morse paints portraits up to about 1837, when he abandons painting to experiment with early stages of development of the telegraph.

1831

Jan. 1. First number of the *Liberator*, militant Abolitionist newspaper founded and edited by William Lloyd Garrison, appears in Boston. Opening editorial concludes: "I am in earnest . . . I will not retreat a single inch, AND I WILL BE HEARD."

Feb. 15. Split between President Jackson and John C. Calhoun becomes open and complete when Calhoun arranges for publication of a pamphlet collection of correspondence between Jackson and the government during Seminole War; Jackson has already learned of Calhoun's unsuspected opposition, as secretary of war, to Jackson's conduct in 1818. Breach extends to supporters of Calhoun and those of Secretary of State Martin Van Buren, leader of the anti-Calhoun faction and a favorite of Jackson, when Peggy Eaton, former barmaid and wife of Secretary of War John H. Eaton, is ostracized as immoral by other Cabinet wives. **April 11.** Van Buren, like Jackson a widower, joins the President in supporting Mrs. Eaton, but resigns his post in the interest of harmony and with shrewd suspicion that the rest of the Cabinet will feel obliged to resign too.

May-August. Van Buren's maneuver is successful when a general Cabinet reshuffle follows, eliminating Calhoun supporters from the administration. Van Buren, sent temporarily abroad as minister to England (though his appointment is later formally rejected by Calhoun's deciding Senate vote), replaces Calhoun as President Jackson's heir-apparent.

Aug. 21. Nat Turner, crazed Negro preacher in Southampton County, Virginia, leads slave insurrection that takes lives of 60 whites, mostly women and children, before being put down. Twenty-eight Negroes, are convicted and 13, including Turner, executed after manhunt in which at least 100 others are killed.

Sept. 26. Anti-Masonic Party, first third party in U.S. history and first party to hold a national convention with an announced platform, meets at Baltimore to nominate William Wirt of Maryland for President. A vehicle for opponents of Jackson, party has

NAT TURNER
Confession, 1831
And on May 12, 1828, I heard a loud noise in the heavens, and the Spirit instantly appeared to me and said the Serpent was loosened, and Christ had laid down the yoke He had borne for the sins of men, and that I should take it on and fight against the Serpent, for the time was fast approaching, when the first should be last and the last should be first. . . .

And by signs in the heavens that it would make known to me when I should commence the great work, and until the first sign appeared, I should conceal it from the knowledge of men. And on the appearance of the sign (the eclipse of the sun last February), I should arise and prepare myself and slay my enemies with their own weapons. And immediately on the sign appearing in the heavens, the seal was removed from my lips, and I communicated the great work laid out for me to do, to four in whom I had the greatest confidence (Henry, Hark, Nelson, and Sam). It was intended by us to have begun the work of death on the 4th of July last. Many were the plans formed and rejected by us, and it affected my mind to such a degree that I fell sick, and the time passed without our coming to any determination how to commence; still forming new schemes and rejecting them, when the sign appeared again, which determined me not to wait longer.

ANDREW JACKSON
Message to Congress, 1830
It gives me pleasure to announce to Congress that the benevolent policy of the government, steadily pursued for nearly thirty years, in relation to the removal of the Indians beyond the white settlements is approaching to a happy consummation. Two important tribes have accepted the provision made for their removal at the last session of Congress, and it is believed that their example will induce the remaining tribes also to seek the same obvious advantages.

The consequences of a speedy removal will be important to the United States, to individual states, and to the Indians themselves. . . .

It will separate the Indians from immediate contact with settlements of whites; free them from the power of the states; enable them to pursue happiness in their own way and under their own rude institutions; will retard the progress of decay, which is lessening their numbers, and perhaps cause them gradually, under the protection of the government and through the influence of good counsels, to cast off their savage habits and become an interesting, civilized, and Christian community. . . .

Rightly considered, the policy of the general government toward the red man is not only liberal but generous. He is unwilling to submit to the laws of the states and mingle with their population. To save him from this alternative, or perhaps utter annihilation, the general government kindly offers him a new home, and proposes to pay the whole expense of his removal and settlement.

been formed by anti-Jacksonians in 1827 in New York State by exploiting popular feeling against secret societies, especially Freemasonry, following discovery that most New York office-holders, as well as Jackson himself, are members of that secret order. Party carries Vermont in election of 1832, but is absorbed by Whigs after 1836.

Supreme Court in *Cherokee Nation* v. *Georgia* refuses to act in case brought by the Cherokee to compel the state of Georgia to recognize territorial rights granted them by a series of treaties with the federal government since 1791. Court holds that Cherokee are not a "foreign nation" within meaning of the Constitution, but only a "dependent nation," therefore the Court cannot accept jurisdiction. Case is episode in removal of Indians to the West.

Extended debate on slavery in Virginia legislature during 1831-1832 ends with narrow defeat of emancipation proposals. Generally recognized as turning point in South's attitude toward slavery, decision is followed by enactment in all slave states of greatly strengthened slave codes restricting movements, education, and right to assembly; free Negroes are also restricted, and constitutional provisions against emancipation and manumission are passed.

Chloroform discovered by chemist Samuel Guthrie independently of Justus von Liebig of Germany and Eugene Soubeiran of France, who have discovered it in same year. It is first used as an anesthetic in 1847 in Scotland.

Legends of New England and Prose and Verse published by John Greenleaf Whittier, New England poet and Abolitionist.

Song, "America," written by the Reverend Samuel Francis Smith to the tune of "God Save the King," is first performed in Boston at Park Street Church.

1832

Although the Second Bank of the United States has, since 1823, helped business and stabilized the currency, it has been opposed persistently by various groups as a symbol of monopoly, aristocracy, and corporate power. **Feb. 10.** In an effort to force President Jackson's hand and create an issue for debate in the coming election campaign, director Nicholas Biddle, on advice of Henry Clay, moves for re-charter four years before old charter expires. **July 3.** Bank Bill narrowly passes Congress. **July 10.** Jackson vetoes bill, and thus in effect accepts Clay's challenge to make Bank the major issue in presidential campaign.

March 3. Supreme Court in *Worcester* v. *Georgia* disallows 1830 Georgia law that requires an oath of allegiance to the state of white residents of Cherokee country; Court rules that national government, not state, has jurisdiction over Indian territories. Opinion is defied by Georgia with support of President Jackson, who is supposed to have remarked: "John Marshall has made his decision, now let him enforce it!"

April 6-Aug. 2. Black Hawk War led by Chief Black Hawk in attempt to recover ceded lands in Wisconsin Territory and Illinois results in defeat of Sauk and Fox Indians.

May 21-22. In Democratic nominating convention, President Jackson is nominated for second term and Van Buren nominated for Vice-President; convention also adopts rule, in force till 1936, requiring two-thirds vote to choose candidates. In campaign, Clay, who has been nominated by National Republicans on December 12, 1831, finds that his advocacy of the Bank is disastrous, since antagonism of frontier, agrarian, and entrepreneurial interests outweighs sober support. **Dec. 5.** Jackson is reelected by 219 electoral votes to Clay's 49; popular vote is

ANDREW JACKSON
Veto of Bank Bill, 1832
The bank is professedly established as an agent of the executive branch of the government, and its constitutionality is maintained on that ground. Neither upon the propriety of present action nor upon the provisions of this act was the executive consulted. It has had no opportunity to say that it neither needs nor wants an agent clothed with such powers and favored by such exemptions. There is nothing in its legitimate functions which makes it necessary or proper. . . .

It is to be regretted that the rich and powerful too often bend the acts of government to their selfish purposes. . . .

Many of our rich men have not been content with equal protection and equal benefits but have besought us to make them richer by act of Congress. By attempting to gratify their desires, we have in the results of our legislation arrayed section against section, interest against interest, and man against man, in a fearful commotion which threatens to shake the foundations of our Union. . . .

If we cannot at once, in justice to interests vested under improvident legislation, make our government what it ought to be, we can at least take a stand against all new grants of monopolies and exclusive privileges, against any prostitution of our government to the advancement of the few at the expense of the many, and in favor of compromise and gradual reform in our code of laws and system of political economy.

Ordinance of Nullification, 1832
We, therefore, the people of the state of South Carolina, in Convention assembled, do declare and ordain . . . that *the several acts and parts of acts of the Congress of the United States purporting to be laws for the imposing of duties and imposts . . . are unauthorized by the Constitution of the United States and violate the true meaning and intent thereof, and are null, void, and no law, nor binding upon this state, its officers, or citizens.*

ANDREW JACKSON
Proclamation, 1832
I consider, then, the power to annul a law of the United States, assumed by one state, incompatible with the existence of the Union, contradicted expressly by the letter of the Constitution, unauthorized by its spirit, inconsistent with every principle on which it was founded, and destructive of the great object for which it was formed.

687,502 to 530,189. Van Buren is elected Vice-President with 189 electoral votes.

Nov. 24. Despite reduced tariff passed July 14, South Carolina Nullifiers call a state convention at Columbia that adopts an ordinance nullifying Tariffs of 1828 and 1832 and otherwise defies federal authority. **Nov. 27.** South Carolina legislature passes law enforcing ordinance and provides for armed resistance. Jackson orders alert of forts in Charleston harbor. **Dec. 4.** He recommends lowering of the tariff in Annual Message. **Dec. 10.** Jackson issues *Proclamation to the People of South Carolina*, drafted by Secretary of State Edward Livingston, which says that nullification is an "impractical absurdity" and warns that "disunion by armed force is treason." **Dec. 17.** South Carolina legislature replies with defiant resolutions. **Dec. 20.** New South Carolina Governor Robert Y. Hayne issues a counter-proclamation. **Dec. 28.** Calhoun, having been elected to the Senate, resigns the vice-presidency to take up the cause from Hayne's former Senate seat.

Testing the first reaping machine near Steeles Tavern, Va., 1831

Sketch of the Trollope family made in 1829, in Cincinnati

Successful demonstration of reaper invented by Cyrus Hall McCormick. Not manufactured commercially until about 1840.

Mrs. Frances M. Trollope, after traveling as far west as Cincinnati, returns to England and writes an Englishwoman's impressions of American life, *Domestic Manners of the Americans*. While not without praise or sympathy, the book includes sharp critical observations regarded as offensive and long afterward resented in the U.S.

Music school of Boston Academy of Music, established by Lowell Mason, is first such institution to offer advanced musical education in the U.S.

1832 - 1837

Principles of the electromagnetic recording telegraph established by Samuel F. B. Morse; in following few years, Morse devises dot-and-dash code and a system for relaying messages over long distances.

FRANCES TROLLOPE
Domestic Manners, 1832
And here again it may be observed that the theory of equality may be very daintily discussed by English gentlemen in a London dining room, when the servant, having placed a fresh bottle of cool wine on the table, respectfully shuts the door and leaves them to their walnuts and their wisdom; but it will be found less palatable when it presents itself in the shape of a hard, greasy paw and is claimed in accents that breathe less of freedom than of onions and whiskey. Strong, indeed, must be the love of equality in an English breast if it can survive a tour through the Union.

Daguerreotype view of Donald McKay's ship-yards in East Boston, 1855, by Southworth and Hawes

1833

The *Ann McKim* is built in Baltimore, first of the long, slim clipper ships that are designed for speed rather than bulky cargo in the California and Far East trade. Era reaches climax when *Flying Cloud*, built in Boston in 1851 by Donald McKay, in 1854 establishes record run for a sailing ship from New York around Cape Horn to San Francisco of 89 days, 8 hours. At least a dozen other ships are nearly as fast. These record runs are not equalled by steamships until long after the Civil War, when construction of clippers ends.

Jan. 16. To meet nullification threat, President Andrew Jackson requests authority from Congress to enforce revenue laws in South Carolina. So-called Force Bill is enacted on March 1 along with a compromise tariff formulated by Henry Clay. **Jan. 21.** In anticipation of compromise tariff, South Carolina suspends its nullification ordinance and then rescinds it on March 15, but in last gesture of defiance also nullifies the now superfluous federal Force Bill three days later.

March 19. President Jackson seeks removal of government deposits from the Bank of the United States as a result of his election triumph. **April 3.** Legality of removal is upheld by Attorney General Roger Brooke Taney, but two successive secretaries of the treasury refuse to take action. **Sept. 26.** Taney, whom Jackson has ap-

CHARLES A. DAVIS
"Major Jack Downing" on Jackson and the Bank, 1833
I have always been tellin the Gineral, as you know, that of all troubles there was none so tuff to git round as money troubles, and when such matters git in a snarl it was worse than tryin to straiten a melitia line arter dinner. I was always afraid that we was gittin too many folks to handle the money, and to be figerin at the 'counts. . . . And then agin I tell'd the Gineral, over and over agin, 'Don't meddle with the Bank,' says I; 'the money is safe enuff there, and one pocket,' says I, 'Gineral, is better than twenty.' . . .

Tother day, when we came to that part of the message where we have to speak of mony matters, we sent for Mr. Taney, our new Secretary of the Treasury, to bring in his accounts. He warn't quite ready, for he ain't as quick at siferin yet as he will be to rights; so we waited for him a spell, and left a place here and there in the message, jest big enuff to put in figers: and so last night the Gineral sent agin, and said he must have the 'counts, 'ready or not ready,' and up they came, sure enuff, and not more than half-cooked; but the Gineral won't wait for nothin when he's in a hurry.

148

pointed secretary of the treasury on September 23, issues necessary orders, and removal of public funds to state banks is begun; 23 such banks, called "pet" banks, are designated by the end of the year. **Dec. 26.** Clay introduces two resolutions of censure in the Senate, one critical of the treasury and the other of the President. These are passed by the Senate on March 28, 1834, but the House supports Jackson, and the Senate censure is expunged from the Senate journal on January 16, 1837.

May. Suppression of local antislavery society at Lane Theological Seminary in Cincinnati, Ohio, leads to withdrawal of most of the students under leadership of student Theodore Dwight Weld, who organizes a center of Abolitionist activity at Oberlin College in Oberlin, Ohio. Oberlin is first college to admit both men and women. In 1835, it also becomes first college to admit Negroes.

American Anti-Slavery Society formed from William Lloyd Garrison's New England Anti-Slavery Society (established in 1832) and a group led by Arthur and Lewis Tappan, New York merchant-philanthropist brothers.

Settlement of Iowa country begins with end of Black Hawk War and opening of Black Hawk Purchase, a 50-mile wide strip on west bank of the Mississippi River.

Village of Chicago, formerly Fort Dear-

Declaration of the American Anti-Slavery Society, 1834
More than fifty-seven years have elapsed since a band of patriots convened in this place to devise measures for the deliverance of this country from a foreign yoke. . . .

We have met together for the achievement of an enterprise, without which that of our fathers is incomplete; and which, for its magnitude, solemnity, and probable results upon the destiny of the world as far transcends theirs as moral truth does physical force. . . .

Their measures were physical resistance—the marshaling in arms, the hostile array, the mortal encounter. Ours shall be such as only the opposition of moral purity to moral corruption—the destruction of error by the potency of truth, the overthrow of prejudice by the power of love, and the abolition of slavery by the spirit of repentance. . . .

Our trust for victory is solely in God. We may be personally defeated, but our principles never. TRUTH, JUSTICE, REASON, HUMANITY must and will gloriously triumph. Already a host is coming up to the help of the Lord against the mighty, and the prospect before us is full of encouragement.

Masthead from "The Liberator," 1831

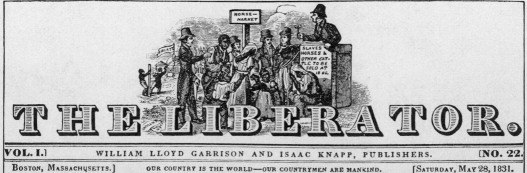

THE LIBERATOR.

VOL. I.]   WILLIAM LLOYD GARRISON AND ISAAC KNAPP, PUBLISHERS.   [NO. 22.

BOSTON, MASSACHUSETTS.]   OUR COUNTRY IS THE WORLD—OUR COUNTRYMEN ARE MANKIND.   [SATURDAY, MAY 28, 1831.

(Above) New Harmony, Indiana, a utopian community, founded in 1825 by Robert Owen, as it looked in 1832: watercolor by Karl Bodmer; (right) Andrew Jackson, seventh President of the United States: portrait by Thomas Sully; (below) race between Peter Cooper's "Tom Thumb," the first American railroad engine to carry passengers, and horse-drawn carriage, 1830

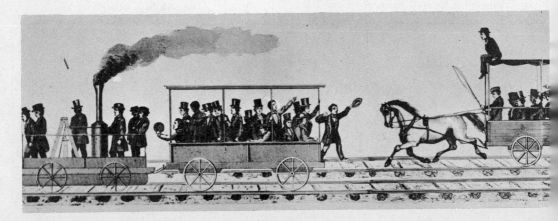

(Above) "Nat Turner and his Confederates": steel engraving, 1863,
after Felix Darley; (below) "Webster Speaking in Reply to Hayne,"
depicting Daniel Webster's defense of constitutional supremacy
during Senate debate in January 1830

Engraving of Ely Moore, 1837

ELY MOORE
Speech to New York General Trades'
Union, 1833
*What! Is it wrong for men to unite for
the purpose of resisting the encroachments of aristocracy? Wrong to restrict
the principle of selfishness to its proper
and legitimate bounds and objects?
Wrong to oppose monopoly and mercenary ambition? Wrong to consult the
interests and seek the welfare of the
producing classes? Wrong to attempt
the elevation of our moral and intellectual standing? Wrong to establish the
honor and safety of our respective vo-
cations upon a more secure and permanent basis? I ask—in the name of
Heaven I ask—can it be wrong for men
to attempt the melioration of their condition and the preservation of their natural
and political rights?*

born, organized on shore of Lake Michigan;
it is incorporated as a city in 1837.

Expedition led by Joseph R. Walker,
Rocky Mountain fur trader, climbs Sierra
Nevada from east, reaches Yosemite Valley
in Mexican Upper California. Crossing of
mountains is thought to be first made by
white men from the east.

Massachusetts separates the official Congregational church from the state by
amendment of state constitution, ratified by
popular vote of 32,000 to 3,000. This
marks end of church establishments in U.S.

Lewis Gaylord Clark founds *Knickerbocker
Magazine*, first successful popular monthly,
in New York; discontinued in 1865.

New York Sun, first successful penny daily, founded by Benjamin H. Day; it is published continuously under various manage-
ments until 1950, when it is absorbed by
the *New York World-Telegram*.

1833 - 1834

April 1-13, 1833. Convention of Texas
settlers at San Felipe, having been unsuccessful in persuading Mexican government
to recognize their "rights," votes to separate
from Mexico. **Jan. 3, 1834.** Presenting resolves to Mexican government headed by
President Antonio López de Santa Anna,
Stephen F. Austin is arrested and imprisoned for eight months. Rapid deterioration
of relations between settlers and Mexican
government follows.

August 1833. New York General Trades'
Union, convening with delegates from other
city centrals, forms the first national labor
federation, with a program of nonpolitical
objectives. Federation is headed by New
York printer Ely Moore, later a congress-

man. Various separate trades also create national organizations during 1834 to 1837, a period characterized by numerous strikes, but general labor movement collapses with financial Panic of 1837.

1834

Jan. 29. President Jackson orders War Department to intervene when Irish laborers working on Chesapeake and Ohio Canal in Maryland riot in protest against working conditions. This is first use of federal troops in a labor dispute.

April-June. Coalition of political factions is organized as the Whig Party, succeeding the National Republicans as the anti-Jackson party. Cooperative efforts to censure President Jackson for removal of bank deposits has resulted in union of National Republican and Southern states' rights forces — in effect, of Henry Clay and John C. Calhoun — which are further combined with representatives of Northern business interests, led by Daniel Webster.

June 28. Second Coinage Act establishes ratio of silver to gold at 16 to 1 instead of 15 to 1, and reduces content of U.S. dollar in the same proportion.

Rev. Jason Lee, Methodist missionary, leads expedition that explores Willamette Valley in Oregon and founds first mission and first American farming settlement in the Oregon country.

George Bancroft publishes first volume of his *History of the United States,* which covers time between the discovery of America and the end of the Revolution. The work reaches 10 volumes, the last published in 1874.

Southern Literary Messenger, leading Southern magazine, is founded in Rich-

GEORGE BANCROFT
Speech at Williams College, 1835
There is a spirit in man: not in the privileged few; not in those of us only who by the favor of Providence have been nursed in public schools. IT IS IN MAN. It is the attribute of the race. The spirit, which is the guide to truth, is the gracious gift to each member of the human family. . . .

If it be true that the gifts of mind and heart are universally diffused, if the sentiment of truth, justice, love, and beauty exists in everyone, then it follows, as a necessary consequence, that the common judgment in taste, politics, and religion is the highest authority on earth and the nearest possible approach to an infallible decision. . . .

If it be the duty of the individual to strive after a perfection like the perfection of God, how much more ought a nation to be the image of Deity. The common mind is the true Parian marble, fit to be wrought into likeness to a God. The duty of America is to secure the culture and the happiness of the masses by their reliance on themselves.

ABRAHAM LINCOLN
Sangamo Journal, 1836
To the Editor of the Journal:
In your paper of last Saturday, I see a communication over the signature of "Many Voters," in which the candidates who are announced in the Journal are called upon to "show their hands." Agreed. Here's mine!

I go for all sharing the privileges of the government who assist in bearing its burdens. Consequently, I go for admitting all whites to the right of suffrage who pay taxes or bear arms (by no means excluding females). . . .

While acting as their representative, I shall be governed by their will, on all subjects upon which I have the means of knowing what their will is; and upon all others, I shall do what my own judgment teaches me will best advance their interests. . . .

If alive on the 1st Monday in November, I shall vote for Hugh L. White for President. Very respectfully,

A. Lincoln

mond, Virginia. It publishes Edgar Allan Poe, William Gilmore Simms, and other Southern writers; it is discontinued in 1864.

1834 - 1839

Blacksmith Thomas Davenport invents first real electric motor with spinning armature. In 1835, he invents a commutator (device that reverses flow of electric current) and in 1839 an electric printing press.

1835

Jan. 30. President Jackson is unharmed after attempt on his life is made by Richard Lawrence, whose two pistols misfire; Lawrence is found to be insane and is placed in an asylum.

January-December. Whigs, unable to agree upon a candidate, allow nomination of various local favorites, among them Daniel Webster, Hugh L. White of Tennessee, and William Henry Harrison of Ohio (the latter actually run by the Anti-Masons), in hopes of preventing a majority and throwing the election into the House of Representatives. **May 20.** Martin Van Buren is nominated by the Democrats as successor to President Jackson; he promises to follow Jackson's policies. **Aug. 26.** Democratic address published in *Washington Globe* constitutes party's first platform.

June 30. Texans led by Colonel William B. Travis capture Mexican garrison at Anahuac; other armed clashes follow. **Oct.-Nov.** Texas conventions reject Mexican rule, favor self-government, and claim right of secession from Mexican republic.

July 6. Chief Justice John Marshall dies in Philadelphia. Roger B. Taney of Maryland is appointed his successor by President Jackson over strong Whig opposition. Taney continues in office until his death in 1864.

Oct. 21. William Lloyd Garrison, editor of Abolitionist newspaper, the *Liberator*, is dragged through the streets of Boston and nearly killed by a mob enraged at his tirades against slavery.

Oct. 29. Locofoco Party formed in New York as Equal Rights Party, taking over remnants of city's defunct labor party. A "radical" faction broken away from the Jacksonians, new party opposes monopoly rights and special privileges obtained for favored business interests by the entrenched Tammany organization; it advocates program of hard money, direct popular elections, free trade, and restraint of government powers. Name Locofoco derives from Tammany Hall meeting at which Tammany Democrats attempt to carry their ticket over Equal Rights protest by declaring adjournment and turning out the gas lights; Equal Rights faction goes on to nominate its own slate with aid of candles lit by newly invented friction matches, called locofocos. Support for the new party is provided by *New York Evening Post*, edited by William Cullen Bryant and William Leggett.

November. Beginning of Second Seminole War in Florida, when Seminole Indians refuse to be evacuated from their land to area beyond the Mississippi River. War ends only when removal of all but a few defiant groups is finally accomplished in 1842.

Louisville, Cincinnati, and Charleston Railroad chartered in attempt by Southern interests to draw off commerce from Ohio and Mississippi valleys, increasingly directed to Northern ports for distribution. Project is impeded by lack of cooperation of individual states and shortage of money, but com-

WILLIAM LEGGETT
New York Evening Post, 1834
Since the organization of the government of the United States, the people of this country have been divided into two great parties. One of these parties has undergone various changes of name; the other has continued steadfast, alike to its appellation and to its principles, and is now, as it was at first, the democracy. . . .

The one party is for a popular government; the other for an aristocracy. The one party is composed, in a great measure, of the farmers, mechanics, laborers and other producers of the middling and lower classes (according to the common gradation by the scale of wealth), and the other of the consumers—the rich, the proud, the privileged—of those who, if our government were converted into an aristocracy, would become our dukes, lords, marquises, and baronets. The question is still disputed between these two parties—it is ever a new question—and whether the democracy or the aristocracy shall succeed in the present struggle, the fight will be renewed whenever the defeated party shall be again able to muster strength enough to take the field.

GUSTAVE DE BEAUMONT
Religious Movements in the United States, 1835
It seems quite well established that Catholicism is gaining in the United States and that its ranks are continually growing, while other communions tend to split off from one another. Also, it is truthful to observe that although the Protestant sects are jealous of one another, all of them hate their common enemy, Catholicism. The Presbyterians are the ones whose enmity is deepest; they have stronger feelings than all of the other Protestants because they have a livelier faith; and furthermore, Catholic proselytizing annoys them, not because they find fault with it in principle, as the Quakers do, but because they practise it themselves.

SAMUEL F. B. MORSE
Imminent Dangers . . . [of] Immigration, 1835
1. It is a fact that in this age the subject of civil and religious liberty agitates in the most intense manner the various European governments.

2. It is a fact that the influence of American free institutions in subverting European despotic institutions is greater now than it has ever been, from the fact of the greater maturity and long-tried character of the American form of government.

3. It is a fact that popery is opposed in its very nature to democratic republicanism; and it is, therefore, as a political system, as well as religious, opposed to civil and religious liberty, and consequently to our form of government.

pleted portions serve as the basis of the Southern rail system constructed before the Civil War.

Legal discrimination against Roman Catholics in citizenship and public life ceases with repeal of last discriminatory law, surviving from colonial times, in North Carolina, in 1835.

Samuel Colt designs pistol with revolving cartridge cylinder. Cheaply mass-produced with interchangeable parts, the revolver's rapid fire and handy size make it especially useful for men on horseback. It becomes an important factor in U.S. victories in wars with the Plains Indians.

New York Herald, rival to the *Sun*, founded by James Gordon Bennett. Editorial policy is Democratic, in favor of secession, until attack on Fort Sumter, after which it backs the Union. It is the first newspaper to specialize in crime and society news, as well as personal editorials. Later, during the Civil War, it leads in rapid and comprehensive news coverage with more than 60 war correspondents.

William Gilmore Simms publishes *The Yemassee*, best-known of a series known as the Border Romances, all of which involve his native South Carolina and Southern frontier life. Also published is *Georgia Scenes, Characters and Incidents* by Augustus Baldwin Longstreet, which realistically depicts life in the Southern backwoods.

Charlotte Saunders Cushman, first American actress to achieve high rank in serious drama, appears in several cities; plays Lady Macbeth in New Orleans; her first New York performance is in 1837.

1835 - 1837

Elaborate transportation projects, chiefly canals, are undertaken by states north of the

Ohio River, many backed by British capital. Financial Panic of 1837 eventually halts most construction, leaving states with heavy debts.

1836

Feb. 23 - March 6. Siege of the Alamo in San Antonio, Texas, by more than 3,000 Mexicans under Santa Anna follows Texan capture of Anahuac in 1835. Force of about 180 Texans, including Davy Crockett, under Colonels William B. Travis and James Bowie holds out for almost two weeks, but is finally overcome and massacred. **March 27.** Another massacre by Santa Anna occurs at Goliad when after his victory there he kills 300 of its defenders under Colonel James Fannin. Additional American settlements are devastated during Santa Anna's march to Galveston Bay.

March 2-4. Convention of Texans in Washington, Texas, declares independence, establishes a provisional government. Samuel Houston has been appointed commander in chief of Texas army in Nov. 1835.

Increasing number of petitions to Congress for abolition of slavery causes Calhoun to propose that future petitions be barred in the Senate. **March 9.** Motion is defeated, 36 to 10. **March 11.** Subsequent motion by James Buchanan to consider and then reject petitions on hand is carried 34 to 6, establishing a pattern of consideration and rejection that temporarily satisfies both Abolitionists and Southerners.

April 21. At Battle of San Jacinto Houston's forces defeat about 1,600 Mexicans and capture Santa Anna. American battle cry is "Remember the Alamo!" **Oct. 22.** Although Mexican government has repudiated Santa Anna's promise of Texan independence, Houston, having been elected president of the Texas republic, takes the oath of office. **July 1 and 4.** Resolutions are

Message from the Alamo, 1836
Fellow Citizens and Compatriots:
I am besieged by a thousand or more of the Mexicans under Santa Anna. I have sustained a continued bombardment for twenty-four hours and have not lost a man. The enemy have demanded a surrender at discretion; otherwise the garrison is to be put to the sword if the place is taken. I have answered the summons with a cannon shot, and our flag still waves proudly from the walls.
I shall never surrender or retreat.
Then, I call on you in the name of liberty, of patriotism, and of everything dear to the American character to come to our aid with all dispatch. The enemy are receiving reinforcements daily and will no doubt increase to three or four thousand in four or five days. Though this call may be neglected, I am determined to sustain myself as long as possible and die like a soldier who never forgets what is due to his own honor and that of his country. Victory or death!

W. BARRET TRAVIS
LIEUTENANT COLONEL
COMMANDING

The Death of Davy Crockett
Thar's a great rejoicin' among the bears of Kaintuck, and the alligators of the Mississippi rolls up thar shiny ribs to the sun, and has grown so fat and lazy that they will hardly move out of the way for a steamboat. The rattlesnakes come up out of thar holes and frolic within ten foot of the clearings, and the foxes goes to sleep in the goose-pens. It is bekase the rifle of Crockett is silent forever, and the print of his moccasins is found no more in our woods.

JOHN C. CALHOUN
Speech in the Senate, 1837
We must meet the enemy on the frontier, with a fixed determination of maintaining our position at every hazard. Consent to receive these insulting petitions, and the next demand will be that they be referred to a committee in order that they may be deliberated and acted upon. . . .

As widely as this incendiary spirit has spread, it has not yet infected this body, or the great mass of the intelligent and business portion of the North; but unless it be speedily stopped, it will spread and work upward till it brings the two great sections of the Union into deadly conflict. . . .

Abolition and the Union cannot co-exist. As the friend of the Union, I openly proclaim it, and the sooner it is known the better. The former may now be controlled, but in a short time it will be beyond the power of man to arrest the course of events.

JAMES MADISON
"Advice to My Country," found after his death, 1836
The advice nearest my heart and deepest in my convictions is, that the Union of the states be cherished and perpetuated. Let the open enemy of it be regarded as a Pandora with her box opened, and the disguised one as the serpent creeping with his deadly wiles into paradise.

adopted by the House and Senate approving U.S. recognition of Texas, but President Jackson is determined to honor obligation to Mexico and avoid war.

May 26. House of Representatives, unwilling to accept formula similar to Senate's, passes "gag rule," tabling all antislavery petitions and motions over bitter objection of John Quincy Adams, who has been elected representative from Massachusetts following his defeat for re-election as President. Two other resolutions, besides prohibiting all discussion of slavery, state that Congress has no power over slavery in the states (adopted 182 to 9) and that interference with slavery in the District of Columbia is inexpedient (adopted 132 to 45). "Gag" provision must be reconsidered at every new session of Congress, which provides repeated occasions over eight years for protest by Adams, called "Old Man Eloquent" because of his persistence, and other Northern representatives, who insist that prevention of debate is a violation of Abolitionists' civil rights.

June 15. Arkansas, formerly part of Louisiana Purchase, is admitted to Union as twenty-fifth state and thirteenth slave state, in spite of protests of antislavery groups in Congress.

June 23. Deposit Act, also known as Surplus Revenue Act, requires secretary of the treasury to designate at least one bank in each state and territory for deposit of government funds; it provides also for distribution of surplus federal revenue in excess of $5 million among the states.

June 28. James Madison dies at his Virginia estate, Montpelier; he is buried near his home.

Acceptance by state banks of "land office money" (currency based on speculator's notes, secured usually by previous land purchases) causes rise in annual sales of public lands from $2,600,000 in 1832 to $24,900,000 in 1836. **July 11.** Resulting inflation leads President Jackson to issue Specie Circular, announcing that after August 15 government will accept only gold or silver in payment for public lands. Circular had been proposed originally by Senator Thomas Hart Benton of Missouri in the form of a resolution that was defeated in the Senate, but President Jackson orders it as an executive measure after Senate adjourns. Circular is successful in bringing about reduction of speculative land purchases, but it puts an intolerable strain on specie resources of state banks; "pet" banks are further weakened by having to pay on January 1, 1837, first installment due the states under the Surplus Revenue Act.

Wisconsin Territory is formed from the part of Territory of Michigan that lies west of present-day state of Michigan.

Starting from St. Louis, Dr. Marcus Whitman leads first expedition that includes women across the Rocky Mountains to Oregon, where Whitman establishes mission near present Walla Walla (Wash.). Expedition is sponsored by American Board of Commissioners for Foreign Missions.

Nature, first volume of essays by Ralph Waldo Emerson, is published in Boston; it sets forth tenets of Transcendentalism, a philosophical reaction against Unitarianism, which by this period has become orthodox rather than revolutionary.

New Orleans Picayune, leading Southern paper, founded by George W. Kendall and Francis Lumsden. It later becomes *Times-Picayune*.

Maria Monk publishes her *Awful Disclosures*, a best-selling account of her alleged experiences in a Montreal nunnery, which she had entered as a novice impostor.

RALPH WALDO EMERSON
Nature, 1836
Our age is retrospective. It builds the sepulchres of the fathers. It writes biographies, histories, and criticism. The foregoing generations beheld God and nature face to face; we, through their eyes. Why should not we also enjoy an original relation to the universe? . . .

To go into solitude, a man needs to retire as much from his chamber as from society. I am not solitary whilst I read and write, though nobody is with me. But if a man would be alone, let him look at the stars. . . .

Nature never wears a mean appearance. Neither does the wisest man extort her secret, and lose his curiosity by finding out all her perfection. Nature never became a toy to a wise spirit. The flowers, the animals, the mountains, reflected the wisdom of his best hour, as much as they had delighted the simplicity of his childhood. . . .

Standing on the bare gound,—my head bathed by the blithe air, and uplifted into infinite space,—all mean egotism vanishes. I become a transparent eye-ball; I am nothing; I see all; the currents of the Universal Being circulate through me; I am part or particle of God.

GEORGE TEMPLETON STRONG
Diary, 1837

April 19. . . . *State of things in Wall Street worse than ever. The whole city going to the devil in a pecuniary point of view. . . .*

May 2. . . . *Matters worse and worse in Wall Street as far as I can learn; everyone discouraged; prospect of universal ruin and general insolvency of the banks, which will be terrible indeed if it takes place. Workmen thrown out of employ by the hundred daily. Business at a stand; the coal mines in Pennsylvania stopped, and no fuel in prospect for next winter—delightful prospects, these. . . .*

May 5. . . . *Something like twenty failures yesterday! . . .*

May 10. . . . *Afternoon. The Bank of America, Merchants, and Manhattan, which has resolved to try and hold out a little longer, have closed. Immense crowd and excitement in Wall Street, but the military prevent any disturbance.*

Mary Lyon, pioneer educator, founds Mount Holyoke Female Seminary, later Mount Holyoke College, at South Hadley, Massachusetts; it is oldest surviving U.S. women's college.

1836 - 1837

Dec. 7, 1836. Martin Van Buren elected eighth President of the U.S. with 765,483 popular votes and 170 electoral votes; he carries 15 of 26 states. Combined Whig, including Anti-Mason, popular vote is 739,795; total Whig electoral vote is 113, of which William Henry Harrison receives 73, Hugh L. White 26, and Daniel Webster 14. South Carolina refuses, as in 1832, to vote for a major party candidate. **Feb. 8, 1837.** Richard M. Johnson, Democrat of Kentucky, is elected Vice-President by vote of the Senate, since no vice-presidential candidate has received an electoral majority.

1837

Jan. 26. Michigan becomes twenty-sixth state of the Union and thirteenth free state. Population is 175,000, largely emigrants from New York and New England who have come after opening of the Erie Canal.

March 4. President Jackson's *Farewell Address* is published; it shows concern for inflated economy by condemning paper currency and speculation, but damage is already done. Reversal of inflationary policy embodied in Specie Circular of July 11, 1836, has sharply reduced sale of public lands, the inflationary force on which all else depends.

March. Stock and commodity prices break, bringing on general economic collapse, known as Panic of 1837, beginning in May. Contributing causes are the distribution requirements of the Surplus Revenue

Act of 1836; contraction of credit by British bankers who are under pressure at home; crop failures; heavy state debts contracted for internal improvement programs; and the unfavorable trade balance with Europe, which causes a drain on specie. Among symptoms are soaring prices of food and other necessities; widespread unemployment; closed factories; wholesale bank failures, including "pet" banks with federal deposits; and drop to 10 percent of public land sales.

Sept. 5. In message to Congress, called into special session, President Van Buren urges adoption of specie currency, expresses opposition to state banks for deposit of public funds, and suggests the creation of independent federal depositories; suggestion is basis for later Independent Treasury Act of 1840.

Nov. 7. Elijah P. Lovejoy, antislavery editor, is attacked and killed by a mob in his newspaper office at Alton, Illinois.

In *Charles River Bridge* v. *Warren Bridge*, Chief Justice Taney, for the Supreme Court, upholds right of competing Warren Bridge against plea of Charles River Bridge Company that its erection is a violation of contract rights guaranteed by earlier Massachusetts charter to Charles River Bridge Company. Court holds that legislative grants must be narrowly construed, that implied rights may not be claimed, and that ambiguities must be decided in favor of the public rather than the corporation, which substantially modifies Justice Marshall's contract rulings. Case is a landmark in attack on monopoly privilege.

Blacksmith John Deere invents first plow with steel moldboard, necessary for plowing heavy, sticky prairie soil, by shaping blade of circular saw, which is smooth enough to

EDWARD BEECHER
The Riots at Alton, 1838
He came to this state, his paper was reestablished, and he at first supposed that he would not be called on to oppose slavery as he had, and so said, but made no pledge to be silent; nay, expressly stated that he would not be bound.

At length, by the progress of his own mind and of events, he is convinced that it is his duty to speak; and he does it. . . .

And here violence begins. He is first falsely accused of violating a pledge, and then told that it is the will of a majority that he forbear to print. . . .

The simple head and front of his offending is that he holds certain opinions which the majority of the community do not like; and which they proclaim to be subversive of the interests of the place!

And is a freeman to submit to such atrocious tyranny as this? Are the rights of conscience nothing? Is duty to God nothing? Are sacred chartered privileges nothing? . . .

It was not, then, a contest for abolition but for law and human society against anarchy and misrule. Now, if Brother Lovejoy was willing in such a contest to die; if with enlarged and far-reaching views he had calculated all these results—and that he had I well know—was it recklessness, was it obstinacy that urged him on, or a noble devotedness to the cause of God and man?

RALPH WALDO EMERSON
The American Scholar, 1837
I ask not for the great, the remote, the romantic; what is doing in Italy or Arabia; what is Greek art, or Provençal minstrelsy; I embrace the common, I explore and sit at the feet of the familiar, the low. Give me insight into today, and you may have the antique and future worlds. What would we really know the meaning of? The meal in the firkin; the milk in the pan; the ballad in the street; the news of the boat; the glance of the eye; the form and the gait of the body—show me the ultimate reason of these matters; show me the sublime presence of the highest spiritual cause lurking, as always it does lurk, in these suburbs and extremities of nature; let me see every trifle bristling with the polarity that ranges it instantly on an eternal law; and the shop, the plough, and the ledger referred to the like cause by which light undulates and poets sing; and the world lies no longer a dull miscellany and lumber room, but has form and order. There is no trifle, there is no puzzle, but one design unites and animates the farthest pinnacle and the lowest trench.

be self-polishing; this improvement on wooden and cast iron blades eventually revolutionizes prairie farming.

Hannah Farnham Lee publishes *Three Experiments in Living,* which describes living under, up to, and over one's means. It is enormously successful, with 30 editions in the U.S. and 10 in England, probably because of the Panic of 1837.

Ralph Waldo Emerson's Phi Beta Kappa address, "The American Scholar," delivered at Harvard, calls for a native American culture and describes functions of intellectuals in such terms that Oliver Wendell Holmes later calls it "our intellectual Declaration of Independence."

Horace Mann, president of Massachusetts senate, signs Education Bill of 1837 that establishes first state board of education in the U.S. On leaving senate in same year, Mann is appointed secretary of the board.

Early stories by Nathaniel Hawthorne published in book form as *Twice-Told Tales;* stories included are "Young Goodman Brown," "Roger Malvin's Burial," and others.

Mathew Carey, publisher and economist, publishes his *Principles of Political Economy.*

1837 - 1840

Lumber industry begins operations in Minnesota and northern Wisconsin; new market for crops induces farmers to move westward to timber country.

1837 - 1843

Distribution of $40 million surplus revenue in form of loans to states is halted after $28 million has been expended. By end of year, Treasury shows first deficit since 1822; deficit is extended and increased to $46,400,000 by 1843, which makes necessary an issue of $47 million in Treasury notes to pay for government expenditures.

1838

Jan. 5. President Van Buren forced to issue neutrality proclamation warning Americans against hostile acts toward Great Britain because of the *Caroline* affair. Americans along Canadian border who sympathize with Canadian rebellion against Britain have furnished insurgents with supplies and recruits, using a small steamboat, the *Caroline*, to transport them to Canada. Canadian militia has crossed to American side of the Niagara River, boarded and burned the boat, and killed one U.S. citizen. Anti-British feeling has become violent. British Foreign Office ignores State Department claim that American neutrality has been violated by burning of *Caroline*. Later incidents along Canadian border involve Americans sympathetic to the Canadian rebellion.

Aug. 18. Charles Wilkes, for the U.S. Navy, sails on six-vessel scientific expedition to the Pacific Ocean and the South Seas; during four-year voyage, he discovers that land known to be in the Antarctic Ocean is actually a continent.

New York Free Banking Act introduces competition among banks by removing requirement that special legislation is necessary to obtain a bank charter; control is provided by stipulating that banks must keep 12.5 percent specie reserve against note issues. Similar legislation is later enacted by Louisiana in 1842 and Massachusetts in 1858.

William Hickling Prescott publishes his three-volume *History of the Reign of Ferdi-*

JAMES FENIMORE COOPER
The American Democrat, 1838
They who have reasoned ignorantly, or who have aimed at effecting their personal ends by flattering the popular feeling, have boldly affirmed that "one man is as good as another"; a maxim that is true In neither nature, revealed morals, nor political theory. . . .

Some men fancy that a democrat can only be one who seeks the level—social, mental, and moral—of the majority, a rule that would at once exclude all men of refinement, education, and taste from the class. These persons are enemies of democracy as they at once render it impracticable. . . .

All that democracy means is as equal a participation in rights as is practicable; and to pretend that social equality is a condition of popular institutions is to assume that the latter are destructive of civilization; for, as nothing is more self-evident than the impossibility of raising all men to the highest standard of tastes and refinement, the alternative would be to reduce the entire community to the lowest. . . .

He is the purest democrat who best maintains his rights, and no rights can be dearer to a man of cultivation than exemptions from unseasonable invasions on his time by the coarse-minded and ignorant.

ALEXIS DE TOCQUEVILLE
Letter to Stoffels, 1835

I wished to show what in our days a democratic people really was; and by a rigorously accurate picture, to produce a double effect on the men of my day. To those who have fancied an ideal democracy, a brilliant and easily realized dream, I endeavored to show that they had clothed the picture in false colors; that the republican government which they extol, even though it may bestow substantial benefits on a people that can bear it, has none of the elevated features with which their imagination would endow it, and moreover, that such a government cannot be maintained without certain conditions of intelligence, of private morality, and of religious belief. . . .

To those for whom the word "democracy" is synonymous with destruction, anarchy, spoliation, and murder, I have tried to show that under a democratic government the fortunes and the rights of society may be respected, liberty preserved, and religion honored; that though a republic may develop less than other governments some of the noblest powers of the human mind, it yet has a nobility of its own; that after all it may be God's will to spread a moderate amount of happiness over all men, instead of heaping a large sum upon a few by allowing only a small minority to approach perfection. . . .

I have endeavored to abate the claims of the aristocrats, and to make them bend to an irresistible future; so that the impulse in one quarter and resistance in the other being less violent, society may march on peaceably toward the fulfillment of its destiny.

nand and Isabella. Also published is *Poems Written During the Progress of the Abolitionist Question*, by John Greenleaf Whittier, editor of the *Pennsylvania Freeman*, Abolitionist newspaper.

The first American edition of *Democracy in America* by Alexis de Tocqueville is published in New York; French edition (Part One) has been published in 1835, followed by English translation the same year. Part Two appears in 1840. *The American Democrat* by James Fenimore Cooper, as well as two of his novels published in same year, criticizes American lack of culture and alienates Cooper's audience, gained through his earlier pioneer novels.

1839

Anglo-American troubles continue with so-called Aroostook War. **Jan.** Maine legislature attempts to prevent British lumbering in Aroostook territory claimed by both New Brunswick, and Maine. **Feb. 12.** Maine land agent authorized to break up British camps is arrested by British authorities, leading to call-up of militia in both Maine and New Brunswick and war preparations by Nova Scotia legislature. Congress authorizes a force of 50,000 men and $10 million for possible conflict. **March.** Hostilities are averted when General Winfield Scott arranges truce, and British government agrees to refer dispute to a boundary commission.

Nov. 13. Liberty Party, organized by antislavery forces in Warsaw, New York, nominates former Kentucky slave-holder James G. Birney for President. Composed of moderate Abolitionists opposed to disunionist views of William Lloyd Garrison, party lasts long enough to be, though defeated, a decisive influence in election of 1844 by holding the balance of power. It later opposes Mexican War and extension of slave-holding territory.

Failure of Nicholas Biddle's Bank of the United States of Pennsylvania, operating as a state bank under Pennsylvania charter since 1836, reverses moderate economic recovery, contributes to deepening depression that lasts until 1843.

U.S. Supreme Court in *Bank of Augusta* v. *Earle*, a case arising from attempt by Alabama to exclude out-of-state corporations, declares that a corporation may do business in more than one state but denies that corporations are possessed of every legal right granted to natural persons by the Constitution and upholds right of a state to exclude a given corporation.

Charles Goodyear, after many experiments, accidentally discovers vulcanizing process for giving rubber strength and resistance to heat and cold when he drops a mixture of rubber and sulfur on a hot surface; he patents it in France in 1844.

Theodore Dwight Weld and his wife, Angelina Grimké, publish *Slavery As It Is*, presenting for the first time to a national audience documentary evidence of slave oppression and eye-witness accounts by Negroes, notably Frederick Douglass, an escaped slave.

Samuel D. Gross publishes *Elements of Pathological Anatomy*, first comprehensive work on pathology in English.

Henry Wadsworth Longfellow publishes *Voices of the Night*, his first book of poems; it is followed in 1841 by *Ballads and Other Poems*, which includes "The Village Blacksmith" and "The Wreck of the Hesperus."

1839 - 1840

Dec. 4, 1839. Whig convention meets. Guided by Thurlow Weed of New York, delegates bypass Henry Clay as vulnerable on various issues, nominate for President

THEODORE WELD
Slavery As It Is, 1839
We will prove that the slaves in the United States are treated with barbarous inhumanity; that they are overworked, underfed, wretchedly clad and lodged, and have insufficient sleep; that they are often made to wear round their necks iron collars armed with prongs, to drag heavy chains and weights at their feet while working in the field, and to wear yokes, and bells, and iron horns . . . that they are often hunted with bloodhounds and shot down like beasts, or torn in pieces by dogs; that they are often suspended by the arms and whipped and beaten till they faint, and, when revived by restoratives, beaten again till they faint, and sometimes till they die; that their ears are often cut off, their eyes knocked out, their bones broken, their flesh branded with red hot irons; that they are maimed, mutilated, and burned to death over slow fires. All these things, and more, and worse, we shall prove. Reader, we know wherof we affirm, we have weighed it well; more and worse WE WILL PROVE.

Massacre of the Whites by the Indians and Blacks in Florida.

The above is intended to represent the horrid Massacre of the Whites in Florida, in December 1835, and January, February, March and April 1836, when near Four Hundred (including women and children) fell victims to the barbarity of the Negroes and Indians.

(Above) Wood engraving from "An Authentic Narrative
of the Seminole War," 1836; (right) Martin Van
Buren, eighth President of the United States;
(below) daguerreotype of William Lloyd Garrison,
publisher of the *Liberator,* an Abolitionist
journal

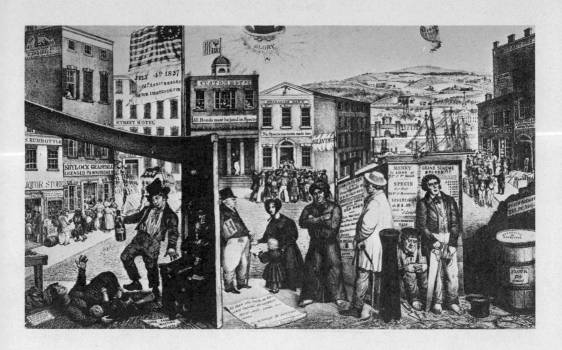

(Above) Cartoon containing bitter references to causes and effects
of financial panic of 1837

THE PRO-SLAVERY RIOT OF NOVEMBER 7, 1837, ALTON, ILL. DEATH OF
REV. E. P. LOVEJOY. FROM WOODCUT MADE IN 1838.

JOHN L. O'SULLIVAN
United States Magazine and Democratic
Review, 1839

*The far-reaching, the boundless future
will be the era of American greatness.
In its magnificent domain of space and
time, the nation of many nations is destined to manifest to mankind the excellence of divine principles; to establish
on earth the noblest temple ever dedicated to the worship of the Most High
— the Sacred and the True. Its floor shall
be a hemisphere; its roof the firmament
of the star-studded heavens; and its
congregation a union of many republics, comprising hundreds of happy millions, calling, owning no man master,
but governed by God's natural and
moral law of equality, the law of
brotherhood — of "peace and goodwill
among men." . . .*

*For this blessed mission to the nations
of the world which are shut out from
the life-giving light of truth has America
been chosen; and her high example
shall smite unto death the tyranny of
kings, hierarchs, and oligarchs, and carry
the glad tidings of peace and goodwill where myriads now endure an
existence scarcely more enviable than
that of beasts of the field. Who, then,
can doubt that our country is destined
to be the great nation of futurity?*

General William Henry Harrison, hero of
victory over Indians at Tippecanoe in 1811.
John Tyler of Virginia, an anti-Jackson
states' rights Democrat, is nominated for
Vice-President. **May 5, 1840.** Van Buren is
renominated by the Democrats.

1840

July 4. Independent Treasury Act, first
proposed by President Van Buren in 1837,
is enacted over bitter Whig opposition in
the Senate and the House. Passage is made
possible when Southern states' rights advocates combine their votes with those of
Northern hard-money Democrats, re-unit-
ing Calhoun men with rest of Democratic
Party. Act provides for establishment of
sub-treasuries for deposit of federal funds in
seven major cities, and for gradual change-
over to specie payment of all government
disbursements by June 1843.

First steamship line with scheduled transatlantic sailings established by Samuel Cu-
nard, a Canadian, with aid of British gov
ernment mail subsidy. First ship leaves Liverpool July 4; arrives at Boston on July 19.

The Dial, Transcendentalist magazine,
founded at Boston; discontinued April
1844; it is edited by Margaret Fuller and
Ralph Waldo Emerson.

"Log Cabin and Hard Cider" campaign
that follows nominating conventions shows
that Whig politicians have learned political
techniques of Jacksonians, which they elaborate and extend. Stimulating popular enthusiasm with rallies, placards, slogans, and
songs such as "Tippecanoe and Tyler too,"
"Van, Van is a used-up man," they estab-

lish the wealthy Harrison as a plain man of the people, as opposed to the image of an aristocratic and decadent Van Buren (actually a man of the people) who drinks wine at "The Palace" (the White House). **Dec. 2.** By means of unprecedented ridicule, irrelevance, and slander, Harrison, without a program or even a declared position on any public issue, is elected ninth President of the U.S. by electoral college, receiving 1,274,624 popular votes to Van Buren's 1,127,781; electoral vote is 234 to 60, with Harrison carrying 19 of 26 states. James G. Birney, candidate of Liberty Party, receives 7,059 votes scattered throughout every Northern state except Indiana. Tyler receives 234 electoral votes and becomes Vice-President.

Sixth National Census shows a population of 17,069,453, a gain of 33 percent since 1830; immigration since 1830 has been approximately 600,000.

William Cranch Bond named astronomical observer at Harvard; builds observatory in 1847.

College of Dental Surgery founded in Baltimore. American Society of Dental Surgeons is organized.

Richard Henry Dana, Jr., publishes *Two Years Before the Mast*, a revelation of brutal treatment on U.S. ships; best-selling work provides many Easterners with their first accurate knowledge of California, where Dana has spent a year. Edgar Allan Poe publishes his *Tales of the Grotesque and Arabesque*. James Fenimore Cooper's novel, *The Pathfinder*, is fourth in his Leatherstocking series.

RICHARD HENRY DANA
Two Years Before the Mast, 1840
Without any formal dedication of my narrative to that body of men of whose common life it is intended to be a picture, I have yet borne them constantly in mind during its preparation. I cannot but trust that those of them into whose hands it may chance to fall will find in it that which shall render any professions of sympathy and good wishes on my part unnecessary. And I will take the liberty, on parting with my reader, who has gone down with us to the ocean, and "laid his hand upon its mane," to commend to his kind wishes, and to the benefit of his efforts, that class of men with whom, for a time, my lot was cast. I wish the rather to do this, since I feel that whatever attention this book may gain, and whatever favor it may find, I shall owe almost entirely to that interest in the sea, and those who follow it, which is so easily excited in us all.

Press room of the New York "Tribune," 1861, when Horace Greeley was editor

1841

HORACE GREELEY

Letter to Paulina Davis, 1852

To my mind the bread problem lies at the base of all the desirable and practical reforms which our age meditates. Not that bread is intrinsically more important to man than temperance, intelligence, morality, and religion, but that it is essential to the just appreciation of all these. Vainly do we preach the blessings of temperance to human beings cradled in hunger and suffering at intervals the agonies of famine; idly do we commend intellectual culture to those whose minds are daily racked with the dark problem, "How shall we procure food for the morrow?" "Morality," "religion," are but words to him who fishes in the gutters for the means of sustaining life and crouches behind barrels in the street for shelter from the cutting blasts of a winter's night.

March 5-6. Whig Cabinet appointed by President William Henry Harrison consists largely of supporters of Henry Clay. Clay himself refuses to head the State Department, and post is given to Daniel Webster.

March 9. Supreme Court in Amistad Case sustains lower court decision that frees Negroes who had mutinied on a Spanish slaver, were subsequently captured by a U.S. warship off Long Island, and were taken to New London, Connecticut.

April 4. President Harrison dies of pneumonia and Vice-President John Tyler becomes tenth President of the U.S., the first Vice-President to succeed to the presidency. **April 9.** Address by Tyler, a Virginia states' rights Democrat opposed to the Jacksonians, threatens Whig program by advocating restrained fiscal policies.

April 10. Horace Greeley founds the *New York Tribune*, which becomes the most influential paper in the North and West until the Civil War. A liberal Whig until 1854, Greeley is afterward a founding and leading figure in the Republican Party.

July 7. Whig program is set forth by Clay in Senate resolutions that call for repeal of Independent Treasury Act, creation of a new national bank, higher tariffs, and distribution among the states of proceeds from sale of public lands.

Aug. 6. Bill to establish new bank is passed by Whig majorities in Congress. **Aug. 13.** As a necessary condition, Independent Treasury Act is repealed. **Aug. 16.** President Tyler accepts repeal but vetoes the bank bill as unconstitutional. **Sept. 9.** Second bank bill, incorporating changes supposed to be required by Tyler, is also vetoed for the same reasons. Since Whig majority is insufficient to pass bill over veto, stalemate lasting until 1846 develops, with Democrats determined to reestablish subtreasury system, but unable to, and with management of public funds meanwhile left to secretary of the treasury, who is obliged to use state banks for deposit.

Sept. 4. Distribution-Pre-emption Act ends long struggle between factions that disagree as to whether settlement or revenue should be the basic object of public land policy. Provisions of this act serve Western (pre-emption) interests by making permanent the allowance of squatters' rights granted temporarily and renewed at intervals since 1830. Proponents of distribution led by Henry Clay, who regard public lands as a national rather than a merely Western possession, are appeased by requirement that part of the proceeds of the sale of lands

GUSTAF UNONIUS
Memoirs, 1841
Many before us had taken possession of land in just this way. In their right of ownership they were protected by what he termed club law, the law, that is, which the people themselves in remote regions had established because of the peculiar conditions under which they were living. According to this law, Judge Lynch makes all judicial decisions. No one could prevent the canal company from selling the land, but it was quite possible effectively to prevent the land's being sold to anyone but its present occupant, who had spent time and money making it habitable.

All the settlers, whether on land held by Congress or by the canal company, had made a compact to stand by and protect one another against such trespassing. And woe betide anyone who sought to appropriate another man's land! He would do well before taking possession of his purchased ground to obtain the highest possible insurance on his house and life; otherwise neither would be worth much. I know of only one instance where such a thing was attempted.

Rev. Gustaf Unonius

Constitution of Brook Farm, 1841

In order more effectually to promote the great purposes of human culture; to establish the external relations of life on a basis of wisdom and purity; to apply the principles of justice and love to our social organization in accordance with the laws of Divine Providence; to substitute a system of brotherly cooperation for one of selfish competition; to secure to our children and those who may be entrusted to our care the benefits of the highest physical, intellectual, and moral education, which, in the progress of knowledge, the resources at our command will permit; to institute an attractive, efficient, and productive system of industry; to prevent the exercise of worldly anxiety by the competent supply of our necessary wants; to diminish the desire of excessive accumulation by making the acquisition of individual property subservient to upright and disinterested uses; to guarantee to each other forever the means of physical support and of spiritual progress; and thus to impart a greater freedom, simplicity, truthfulness, refinement, and moral dignity to our mode of life; we, the undersigned, do unite in a voluntary association.

be apportioned among the states. At insistence of Southerners, who fear that depletion of the federal treasury will be used as an excuse to raise the tariff rates, distribution of proceeds is to be repealed if tariffs reach 20 percent. Rise in rates passed in 1842 results in repeal of distribution requirement.

Overland migration to California is begun when John Bidwell, New York schoolteacher, and John Bartleson, land speculator and wagon master, lead party through South Pass in the Rocky Mountains and across Nevada to settle near Stockton.

Brook Farm, Transcendentalist experiment in communal living, established in Massachusetts by Unitarian minister George Ripley. The most famous of many cooperative, anti-capitalist communities that flourish from Massachusetts to Wisconsin between 1840 and 1852, it includes Nathaniel Hawthorne, Charles A. Dana, and other intellectuals among its members; it is destroyed by fire in 1846 and abandoned.

Letters and Notes on the Manners, Customs, and Condition of the North American Indians is published in two volumes with more than 300 engravings by George Catlin, pioneer American ethnologist who devotes most of his life to "rescuing from oblivion the looks and customs of the vanishing races of native man in America."

The Mercantile Agency, first commercial credit-rating agency, is established by Lewis Tappan, New York merchant; agency becomes R. G. Dun & Company in 1859, Dun & Bradstreet in 1933.

1841 - 1842

Dorr's Rebellion in Rhode Island. Rhode Island royal charter of 1663, which is state's constitution, allows suffrage only to property owners and their eldest sons; since population of state has grown increasingly urban, these obsolete requirements have disfranchised most city-dwellers — half the white male population. **Oct. 4, 1841.** Unauthorized convention led by Thomas W. Dorr meets at Providence to draw up new state constitution (the People's Constitution). **Dec.** It is ratified by large popular vote. **Feb. 1842.** Legislature, alarmed at prospect of people's rebellion, calls convention that draws up Freeman's Constitution that modifies charter. **March.** It is rejected in close vote. **April 18.** In separate elections, Dorr is chosen governor by People's Party and Governor Samuel W. King is reelected by Freeman's Party. State Supreme Court and federal government refuse to recognize People's Constitution, and Governor King calls out militia to put down Dorr's uprising. **May 18.** Dorr and followers fail in attempt to capture state arsenal, and rebellion collapses. **Nov. 21-23.** New Freeman's Constitution, modified in convention of September 12 to November 5, is adopted by popular vote; it allows for wider suffrage, but only for those born in United States.

Oct. 27, 1841. Slaveship *Creole* sails from Hampton Roads, Virginia, bound for New Orleans. During voyage, slaves mutiny and force officers to land at Nassau in the Bahamas, where British authorities free all except ringleaders. Secretary of State Daniel Webster attempts to recover the slaves as U.S. property, and is ignored by the British. **March 21-22, 1842.** Congressman Joshua R. Giddings of Ohio proposes resolutions against slavery and the coastal slave trade. **March 23.** He is censured by the Southern-dominated House and resigns. **April.** Giddings is reelected with a large majority by his district in a special election.

1841 - 1844

Sept. 11, 1841. Entire Cabinet except Daniel Webster resigns in protest against

THOMAS DORR
Address to Constitutional Assembly, 1842
When the Revolution severed the ties of allegiance which bound the colonies to the parent country, the sovereign power passed from its former possessors, not to the general government, which was the creation of the states; nor to the state governments; nor to a portion of the people; but to the whole people of the states, in whom it has ever since remained. This is the doctrine of our fathers and of the early days of the republic, and should be sacredly guarded as the only safe foundation of our political fabric.

The idea that government is in any proper sense the source of power in this country is of foreign origin, and at war with the letter and spirit of our institutions. The moment we admit the principle that no change in government can take place without permission of the existing authorities, we revert to the worn-out theory of the monarchies of Europe. . . .

If the people of Rhode Island are wrong in the course they have pursued, they will nevertheless have conferred one benefit upon their countrymen by the agitation of this question, in dissipating the notion that the people are the sovereigns of the country, and in consigning to the department of rhetorical declamation those solemn declarations of 1776, which are repeated in so many of the state constitutions, and which are so clearly and confidently asserted by the most eminent jurists and statesmen of our country.

HENRY DAVID THOREAU
United States Magazine and Democratic
Review, 1843

*In fact, no work can be shirked. It may
be postponed indefinitely, but not infinitely. Nor can any really important
work be made easier by cooperation or
machinery. Not one particle of labor
now threatening any man can be routed
without being performed. It cannot be
hunted out of the vicinity like jackals
and hyenas. It will not run. You may
begin by sawing the little sticks, or you
may saw the great sticks first, but sooner
or later you must saw them both.*

*We will not be imposed upon by this
vast application of forces. We believe
that most things will have to be accomplished still by the application called
"Industry." . . .*

*After all, the theories and specula-
tions of men concern us more than their
puny execution. It is with a certain
coldness and languor that we loiter
about the actual and so-called practical.
How little do the most wonderful inventions of modern times detain us. They
insult nature. Every machine or particular application seems a slight outrage
against universal laws. How many fine
inventions are there which do not clutter the ground? We think that those only
succeed which minister to our sensible
and animal wants, which bake or brew,
wash or warm, or the like. But are those
of no account which are patented by
fancy and imagination and succeed so
admirably in our dreams that they give
the tone still to our waking thoughts?*

President Tyler's second bank veto. **Sept.
13.** New Cabinet is appointed; replacements
are followed by frequent shifts, leaving
Webster, who remains in Cabinet until his
resignation on May 8, 1843, the dominant
figure in the administration. Webster's resignation paves way for eventual appointment a year later of John C. Calhoun as
secretary of state. Calhoun's appointment
indicates defeat of President Tyler's attempt
to organize independent political backing
and resurgence of the Democrats under
Southern leadership.

1841 - 1850

Iron industry makes rapid progress as a
result of improved production techniques,
use of anthracite coal instead of charcoal;
adoption of steam power and expansion of
railroads creates demands for iron products.
In addition, production of farm machinery,
pistols, sewing machines, clocks, and stoves
made with standard parts multiplies quantity and variety of iron production.

1842

Aug. 9. Lengthy negotiations culminate
in Webster-Ashburton Treaty between U.S.
and Britain, finally establishing Canadian
boundary from Maine to Lake of the
Woods. Settlement involves issues as old as
the Revolution, and concessions are mutual,
but American gains include area of northeastern Minnesota, the Mesabi Range, that
later is found to be one of the great iron-
ore regions of the world.

U.S. Supreme Court in *Prigg* v. *Pennsylvania* overturns Pennsylvania law that prohibits return of fugitive slaves, but also
holds that no state has responsibility of enforcing federal Fugitive Slave Law. Decision
leads to enactment of "personal liberty"
laws in many Northern states, forbidding
state authorities to assist federal agents seeking to return fugitive slaves.

In widely copied decision of *Common-wealth* v. *Hunt*, Chief Justice Lemuel Shaw for the Massachusetts Supreme Court rejects criminal conspiracy doctrine under which labor unions have been prosecuted since 1806. Doctrine had made social and economic pressure to persuade workmen to join unions a criminal offense; thus unions were unable to gain enough strength for effective strikes.

Phineas T. Barnum, former newspaper editor, opens Barnum's American Museum in New York, using collections from Scudder's American Museum and Peale's Museum, bought in previous year; he exhibits General Tom Thumb and other freaks as well as many hoaxes, drawing the public with extravagant advertising.

Rufus W. Griswold edits and publishes *Poets and Poetry of America*, unusually popular anthology.

1842 - 1843

"Oregon fever" starts migration to the Oregon Country, chiefly from the Ohio Valley states and Missouri. Main route is the Oregon Trail, from Independence, Missouri, to the mouth of the Columbia River.

1842 - 1846

Jan. 1842. Ether first used as an anesthetic by William E. Clarke, a medical student, in tooth extraction performed by Dr. Elijah Pope in Rochester, New York. **Oct. 16, 1846.** William T. G. Morton, another dentist, administers ether for the first time in general surgery during a public operation for a neck tumor performed by Dr. John C. Warren at Massachusetts General Hospital.

1843

January. *Memorial to the Legislature of Massachusetts*, indicting the treatment and

JESSE APPLEGATE
A Day with the Cow Column, 1843
It is within ten minutes of 7; the corral but now a strong barricade is every-where broken, the teams being attached to the wagons. The women and children have taken their places in them. The pilot (a borderer who has passed his life on the verge of civilization and has been chosen to the post of leader from his knowledge of the savage and his experience in travel through roadless wastes) stands ready, in the midst of his pioneers and aids, to mount and lead the way. Ten or fifteen young men, not today on duty, form another cluster. They are ready to start on a buffalo hunt, are well mounted, and well armed as they need be, for the unfriendly Sioux have driven the buffalo out of the Platte, and the hunters must ride fifteen or twenty miles to reach them. The cow drivers are hastening, as they get ready, to the rear of their charge to collect and prepare them for the day's march.

It is on the stroke of 7; the rushing to and fro, the cracking of the whips, the loud command to oxen, and what seems to be the inextricable confusion of the last ten minutes has ceased. . . . The clear notes of the trumpet sound in the front; the pilot and his guards mount their horses, the leading division of wagons moves out of the encampment, and takes up the line of march, the rest fall into their places with the precision of clockwork, until the spot so lately full of life sinks back into that solitude that seems to reign over the broad plain and rushing river as the caravan draws its lazy length toward the distant El Dorado.

DOROTHEA DIX
Memorial to the Legislature, 1843

Every new investigation has given depth to the conviction that it is only by decided, prompt, and vigorous legislation the evils to which I refer, and which I shall proceed more fully to illustrate, can be remedied. I shall be obliged to speak with great plainness, and to reveal many things revolting to the taste, and from which my woman's nature shrinks with peculiar sensitiveness.

But truth is the highest consideration. I tell what I have seen—painful and shocking as the details often are—that from them you may feel more deeply the imperative obligation which lies upon you to prevent the possibility of a repetition or continuance of such outrages upon humanity. . . .

I come to place before the legislature of Massachusetts the condition of the miserable, the desolate, the outcast. I come as the advocate of helpless, forgotten, insane, and idiotic men and women; of beings sunk to a condition from which the most unconcerned would start with real horror; of beings wretched in our prisons, and more wretched in our almshouses. . . .

If my pictures are displeasing, coarse, and severe, my subjects, it must be recollected, offer no tranquil, refined, or composing features. The condition of human beings, reduced to the extremest states of degradation and misery, cannot be exhibited in softened language, or adorn a polished page.

I proceed, gentlemen, briefly to call your attention to the present state of insane persons confined within this Commonwealth, in cages, closets, cellars, stalls, pens! Chained, naked, beaten with rods, and lashed into obedience.

care of the insane, is published by Dorothea Lynde Dix, pioneer in the reform of prisons, asylums, poorhouses, and hospitals; in previous two years she has visited hundreds of such institutions in Massachusetts and other states.

July 5. Settlers in Oregon Country, jurisdiction over part of which is disputed by Britain and the U.S., adopt constitution for a provisional government pending anticipated establishment of American authority. Disputed region is that between Columbia River and 49th parallel, claimed by both countries. **July.** Cincinnati convention on Oregon Country adopts resolution demanding land north to 54°40' for the U.S. Anglo-U.S. friction precipitates Oregon issue into campaign of 1844.

Texas question, dormant since the establishment of Texan independence in 1836, is revived when Mexico invades Texas in 1842. Britain and France, both anxious to encourage an independent buffer state against American expansion, arrange a truce between Texas and Mexico, after which Texas minister to Washington, Isaac Van Zandt, withdraws latest of several offers of U.S. annexation. Move arouses concern in the South, which has hoped annexed territory will become new slave state and is alarmed at reports that Britain will press for abolition of slavery in Texas if its independence is maintained. **Aug. 23.** Mexican President Santa Anna declares that annexation will mean war between Mexico and the U.S. **Oct. 16.** Negotiations for annexation are reopened with Van Zandt by the Tyler administration in the face of Northern opposition that makes Senate acceptance doubtful. Fearful that Texas will lose support of Great Britain if annexation is defeated in Senate, President Houston refuses U.S. offer.

Beginning of substantial immigration to U.S. of Scandinavians, who settle chiefly in

Wisconsin and Minnesota; an average of 2,100 arrive annually from 1843 to 1860.

Law of Cooling of Atmospheric Air, one of the most important American contributions to meteorology, is published by James P. Espy.

Oliver Wendell Holmes, author and physician, publishes "The Contagiousness of Puerperal Fever," a paper that shows by use of statistics that childbed fever, almost always fatal to mothers of newborn infants, is caused by contagion. Holmes is criticized for his opinion, but it is later confirmed by additional observations of other physicians.

Typewriter invented by Charles Thurber of Worcester, Massachusetts, but like other machines of the period, it is slower than writing by hand; first practical machine is not constructed until 1867.

Edgar Allan Poe, one of the originators of the detective story, wins $100 prize for his "The Gold Bug," published in the *Philadelphia Dollar Newspaper.* "The Murders in the Rue Morgue" has been published two years before.

History of the Conquest of Mexico published by William Hickling Prescott, known as first American scientific historian of U.S.; Prescott's dramatic writing style combined with untiring scholarship popularizes reading of history in the country.

Robert Sears, publisher and author, issues *The Wonders of the World, in Nature, Art, and Mind,* a best-selling illustrated volume that, with other heavily pictorial works, gains him a reputation as a patron of engraving.

1843 - 1845

Baptist church splits over slavery, with Southerners withdrawing to form Southern

OLE M. RAEDER
Letter to Norway, 1847
I cannot convince myself that all these countrymen of ours, as they leave our own country, are to be regarded as completely lost and as strangers to us. . . .

Let them become Americans, as is the duty of holders of American soil, but this need not prevent them from remaining Norwegian for a long time to come. The American character is not yet so fixed and established that it excludes all others.

The Americans are satisfied with demanding a few general traits of political rather than of really national significance. Under such lenient influences, the aliens are elevated and improved, rather than changed; they lose their sharp edges and adopt some of the good qualities of others. Even if America, fulfilling also in this respect a great and providential purpose, shall in the end absorb and mold together into a compact whole all the various nationalities which now are making their contributions in such rich measure, and shall not only blot out the many prejudices which now separate people in their home countries but also absorb some of the individual characteristics which now constitute the peculiar qualities of each nation; even if such be the case, then surely it will be for us, as well as for every other European nation, not merely a source of satisfaction as an historical fact, but perhaps also, in the course of events, a factor of real benefit that our Scandinavian North has become one of the parent nations for this nation to whose lot will undoubtedly some day fall the place of leadership in the affairs of the world.

JOSHUA GIDDINGS

Speech in the House, 1844

It is well known, Mr. Chairman, that since the formation of this confederacy there has long been a supposed conflict between the interests of free labor and of slave labor, between the Southern and Northern states. . . . This supposed conflict has given rise to difference of policy in our national councils. I refer to the tariff, in particular, as being a favorite measure of the North, while free trade is advocated by the South. . . .

By the fixed order of nature's law, our population at the north has increased so much faster than it has in the slave states that, under the late census, the North and West now hold the balance of political power. . . .

But let us admit Texas, and we shall place the balance of power in the hands of the Texans themselves. They, with the Southern states, will control the policy and the destiny of this nation; our tariff will then be held at the will of the Texan advocates of free trade. . . . Are the liberty-loving Democrats of Pennsylvania ready to give up our tariff? — to strike off all protection from the articles of iron and coal, and other productions of that state in order to purchase a slave market for their neighbors, who, in the words of Thomas Jefferson Randolph, "breed men for the market like oxen for the shambles"?

Baptist Convention at Atlanta in 1845. Methodist Church, South, is established separately from main body for same reason the year before.

Preaching of William Miller launches Millerite movement, based on belief in Second Coming of Christ in 1843-1844 period. Adventist Church is formed in 1845; Seventh-Day Adventists establish separate body in 1863.

1843 - 1847

Appearance of the Great Comet in 1843 stimulates astronomical observation; mathematician Benjamin Peirce, of Harvard University, does work on undiscovered but suspected celestial body simultaneously with others in Europe; concerted effort results in identification of planet Neptune in 1846. Maria Mitchell of Nantucket Island, Massachusetts, discovers comet in 1847.

1844

April 12. Treaty of annexation is negotiated with Texas government by Secretary of State John C. Calhoun. **April 18.** Calhoun sends note to British minister strongly defending slavery. **April 22.** President Tyler submits annexation treaty to Senate with message urging Southern states to act to guard their security and warning of the abolition risk in case of British interference in Texas. **June 8.** Calhoun's note arouses Northern suspicion, with the result that treaty is rejected in the Senate as a slaveholders' conspiracy. Tyler, realizing that he cannot hope for two-thirds support necessary to ratify treaty, moves that annexation be brought about by joint congressional resolution, but measure is still not acted on by June, when Congress adjourns.

Since President Tyler is without party support for renomination, leading candidates for President are Democrat Martin

Van Buren and Henry Clay, absent from the Senate since 1842 to seek Whig nomination. Crucial issue is Texas which places both men in a dilemma: neither can oppose annexation without alienating the South or support it without giving up Northern antislavery vote. **April 27.** Possibly after making an agreement, candidates publish letters expressing their opposition to immediate annexation; Clay's reason is that he cannot hope for Whig nomination without it; Van Buren's, that antislavery feeling is strong in key Democratic state of New York.

May 1. Henry Clay is unanimously nominated by Whig convention in Baltimore. **May 29.** At Democratic convention, James Knox Polk of Tennessee, an able but colorless congressional veteran, is nominated with Jackson's support after "two-thirds" rule proves insuperable obstacle to Van Buren, whose letter has offended not only the South but also Andrew Jackson, now an advocate of annexation. In effort to offset Polk's obscurity (Whigs in campaign ask "Who is James K. Polk?"), Democratic platform drawn up by Robert J. Walker of Mississippi takes an aggressive stand, demands acquisition of both Texas and all of Oregon Territory. From 1846 on demand is expressed by slogan "54°40′ or Fight!"

May 6-July 8. Several armed conflicts between Protestants and Catholics in Philadelphia leave 20 persons dead and about 100 injured. Clashes result from agitation by nativists, who are anti-Catholic and who resent naturalization of foreign immigrants, especially those from Catholic countries.

May 24. First successful telegraph is demonstrated by Samuel F. B. Morse, its developer, and his partner, Alfred Vail, who invent telegraphic printer in same year. Message "What Hath God Wrought!" is transmitted in Morse code on line from Washington, D. C., to Baltimore. Though construction of line has been financed by

ROBERT J. WALKER
Letter to Carroll Co., Kentucky, 1844
Such is our present boundary; and it can be exchanged for one that will give us perfect security, that will place our own people and our own settlements in rear of the Indian tribes, and that will cut them off from foreign influence; that will restore to us the uninterrupted navigation of the Red River and Arkansas, and of all their tributaries; that will place us at the north, upon a point to command the pass of Oregon, and, on the south, to secure New Orleans, and render certain the command of the Gulf of Mexico. . . .

This is no question of the purchase of new territory, but of the reannexation of that which once was all our own. It is not a question of the extension of our limits but of the restoration of former boundaries. It proposes no new addition to the valley of the Mississippi but of its reunion, and all its waters once more under our dominion. If the Creator had separated Texas from the Union by mountain barriers, the Alps or the Andes, these might be plausible objections; but he has planned down the whole valley, including Texas, and united every atom of the soil and every drop of the waters of the mighty whole. He has linked their rivers with the great Mississippi, and marked and united the whole for the dominion of one government and the residence of one people; and it is impious in man to attempt to dissolve this great and glorious Union.

JOHN NEAL

The Pioneer, 1843

The mightiest engine of our day is a newspaper. What are armies and treasuries, navies and forts, and magazines and foundries, or senate chambers and laws in comparison with newspapers, where newspapers are free? Of what avail are public meetings or combinations, or conspiracies, or revolutions, indeed, where newspapers are not free?

They are not so much the organs, or the expounders, or reservoirs, as they are the generators of public opinion.

We are a newspaper people. . . . People read newspapers who read nothing else. People read newspapers when and where they read nothing else. To the great body of our men, women and children, a newspaper is a drama of the universe. To call it the World, or the Times, or the Globe, or the Sun is by no means to overstate its value in their eyes. To them it is the only world they are acquainted with; a sun, without which they and their families would grope in darkness forever. Of the times, either in the Old World or the New, what know they but by the help of the newspapers? They have no books beyond the Bible, an almanac, or a stray Thomas-à-Kempis, or Josephus, or a tattered copy of Noah Webster's Third Part. And how would they be able to guess at the doings of the rest of the world; at the rise and fall of empire; the condition of Europe; or the progress of knowledge—ay, or of what their own rulers were doing for them—but for the newspapers?

the government, Morse fails to persuade it to buy rights to his invention and forms his own company instead.

July 1 and 27. Decisive turn in campaign occurs when Henry Clay tries to counter "patriotic" appeal of Democrats by changing his position on Texas, coming out with qualified support for annexation in "Alabama letters." **Dec. 4.** Clay's move proves fatal politically; Polk takes New York's 36 electoral votes with a bare 5,100 majority, made possible by 16,300 antislavery Whig votes that Clay has lost to James G. Birney of Liberty Party. Total electoral vote for Polk, who carries 15 states, is 170, with Clay having 105 and 11 states. Popular vote is Polk, 1,338,000; Clay, 1,300,000; Birney, 62,300. George M. Dallas of Pennsylvania is elected Vice-President.

American Journal of Psychiatry begins publication; it is first specialized medical journal. Association of Medical Superintendents of American Institutions for the Insane is founded; now known as American Psychiatric Association.

Springfield (Massachusetts) *Republican*, founded as a weekly in 1824, begins publication as a Whig daily under ownership of Samuel Bowles; it is noted for independent reporting.

1845

Jan. 23. Tuesday following first Monday in November established as national presidential election day by act of Congress.

March 2. Republic of Texas annexed by joint resolution of Congress as recommended by President Tyler in 1844; it is to become a state without first being a U.S. territory. Area thus acquired is arguably foreign territory, since Mexico has refused to recognize Texan independence; annexation measure therefore empowers the President to negotiate a treaty, but Mexican consent is not mentioned in the act.

March 3. Florida is admitted to the Union as twenty-seventh state and fourteenth slave state. A U.S. territory since 1822, population is 85,000.

March 3. For first time Congress overrides a presidential veto. Measure, which withholds payment for naval vessels ordered by President Tyler, had been vetoed by him on February 20.

March 4. President Polk's inaugural address asserts "clear and unquestionable" U.S. title to Oregon, maintains that annexation is exclusively a question between the U.S. and Texas since they are both "independent powers," does not acknowledge that Mexico has failed to recognize Texan independence.

March 28. Mexico breaks off diplomatic relations with U.S. **June.** It begins military preparations to prevent annexation of Texas. Other Mexican grievances are American boundary claims along Southwest border and influx of American settlers into California contrary to Mexican law. **May 28.** President Polk responds by ordering General Zachary Taylor, American commander in the Southwest, to maintain his troops as an "Army of Observation" ready to advance from Louisiana into Texas if Mexico invades Texas. **June 15.** Taylor is ordered to place himself "on or near the Rio Grande" for this purpose, though position is south of any border recognized by Mexico. **July 31.** Taylor actually marches only as far as the Nueces River where he stations himself near Corpus Christi with 3,500 men — about half the U.S. Army.

Upon news of Congress' action, Texas breaks off independence negotiations with

JAMES K. POLK
Inaugural Address, 1845
Perceiving no valid objection to the measure and many reasons for its adoption vitally affecting the peace, the safety, and the prosperity of both countries, I shall, on the broad principle which formed the basis and produced the adoption of our Constitution, and not in any narrow spirit of sectional policy, endeavor by all constitutional, honorable, and appropriate means to consummate the expressed will of the people and government of the United States by the reannexation of Texas to our Union at the earliest practicable period.

Nor will it become in a less degree my duty to assert and maintain by all constitutional means the right of the United States to that portion of our territory which lies beyond the Rocky Mountains. Our title to the country of the Oregon is "clear and unquestionable," and already are our people preparing to perfect that title by occupying it with their wives and children. But eighty years ago our population was confined on the west by the ridge of the Alleghenies. Within that period—within the lifetime, I might say, of some of my hearers—our people, increasing to many millions, have filled the eastern valley of the Mississippi, adventurously ascended the Missouri to its headsprings, and are already engaged in establishing the blessings of self-government in valleys of which the rivers flow to the Pacific.

WENDELL PHILLIPS
Can Abolitionists Vote. . . ?, 1845
The object of the American Anti-Slavery Society is the "entire abolition of slavery in the United States." Of course it is its duty to find out all the sources of pro-slavery influence in the land. It is its right, it is its duty to try every institution in the land, no matter how venerable or sacred, by the touchstone of anti-slavery principle; and if it finds anyone false, to proclaim that fact to the world, with more or less of energy according to its importance in society. It has tried the Constitution and pronounced it unsound. . . .

The history of our Union is lesson enough, for every candid mind, of the fatal effects of every, the least, compromise with evil. The experience of the fifty years passed under it shows us the slaves trebling in numbers, slaveholders monopolizing the offices and dictating the policy of the government, prostituting the strength and influence of the nation to the support of slavery here and elsewhere, trampling on the rights of the free states and making the courts of the country their tools. To continue this disastrous alliance longer is madness. The trial of fifty years only proves that it is impossible for free and slave states to unite on any terms without all becoming partners in the guilt and responsible for the sin of slavery. Why prolong the experiment? Let every honest man join in the outcry of the American Anti-Slavery Society.
NO UNION WITH SLAVEHOLDERS!

Mexico, which is about to grant recognition on condition that Texas refuse annexation. **June 23.** Texas Congress votes in favor of U.S. proposal. **July 4.** A special Texas convention is called to accept the terms. **Oct. 13.** Annexation as a state is ratified by popular vote. **Dec. 29.** Texas is admitted to the union as twenty-eighth state and fifteenth slave state. This is first time since 1802 that balance of slave and free states has not been observed, and only time a state has been admitted by joint resolution of Congress; action provokes Northern protest.

August. U.S. receives secret information that Mexican government is again willing to discuss Texas boundary. **Nov. 7.** President Polk and Secretary of State James Buchanan decide to send John Slidell of Louisiana on confidential mission to negotiate not only boundary but also the sale of New Mexico and Upper California as well, authorizing payment of $15 to $20 million and canceling of unpaid Mexican debt to U.S. **Dec. 16.** By the time Slidell reaches Mexico City, his mission is public knowledge, and Mexican government, faced with hostile public opinion, refuses to receive him on the ground that he does not officially represent the U.S.

Oct. 10. "Naval School" opens at Fort Severn, Annapolis, Maryland; it is called U.S. Naval Academy after 1850.

Dec. 2. President Polk's first annual message sets forth "Polk Doctrine" — an elaboration of Monroe Doctrine with respect to Texas and Oregon that asserts exclusive right of the people on "this continent" to decide "their own destiny." Message is aimed at British claims in Oregon as well as possible British and French support of Mexico.

Postal Act authorizes subsidies for steamers carrying mail to and from Europe and reduces postage rate to five cents per half ounce for 300 miles.

Narrative of the Life of Frederick Douglass, an American Slave is published by Frederick Douglass, Negro Abolitionist, writer, orator, and escaped slave, just before he goes to Europe to avoid danger of recapture.

George Lippard, reporter, author, lecturer, publishes *The Monks of Monk Hall,* later called *Quaker City,* an exposé of Philadelphia vice; it has an enormous sale in the U.S. and Europe. Scheduled to be shown in dramatized form in Philadelphia, it is canceled by the mayor, who fears that mobs will destroy the theater.

Leonora by William H. Fry, first grand opera composed by a native of the U.S., is performed in Philadelphia.

1845 - 1846

July 1845. Phrase "manifest destiny" appears in the *United States Magazine and Democratic Review* in an article by its editor, John L. O'Sullivan, that asserts the divine right of the American people to cover the continent. **Dec. 27.** Phrase becomes current with repetition by O'Sullivan in *New York Morning News* in an editorial on the annexation of Texas. **Jan. 3, 1846.** First use in Congress is by Representative Robert C. Winthrop of Massachusetts, who argues during Oregon debate that it is by right "our manifest destiny to spread over this whole continent."

Aug. 1845. Deputy sheriff murdered in upstate New York during Antirent War that has continued since 1839. Farmers, resentful of perpetual leases that have been in effect since colonial days, have formed secret societies and attacked law-enforcement agents. As a result of war, New York Governor Silas Wright recommends reform leg-

Resolutions of New York Antirent Convention, 1845

Whereas, the time has arrived when it becomes necessary for us, as citizens and tenants, residing on manors claimed and leased by landlords under grants from foreign governments, thus in a formal and public manner to correct false representations and misapplied constructions of the designs and purposes of the antirent associations in the various counties in this state. Public functionaries, and also the press, both powerful organs, have widely spread charges of combination of tenants for the secret purpose of hiring persons disguised as Indians to set law at defiance and obtaining right by might. When the public mind is abused, it is calculated to defeat the objects sought for, and tends to bring associations into disrepute; therefore, we publicly declare, before God and man, that no such combinations have been made within our knowledge or belief, and can exist in imagination.

The associations of tenants are for honorable and legal redress of grievances to be obtained from the proper tribunals. The only services employed are legal counsels; the only expenses those for publications, the attendance on courts and sessions of the legislature. Over the acts of individuals the associations have no control, and therefore disclaim any accountability.

(Above left) Joshua Giddings, a leader of House opposition to "gag rule" of 1836 tabling all antislavery petitions and motions; (above right) William Henry Harrison, ninth President of the United States; (below) lithograph of anti-Catholic rioting in Philadelphia in 1844 in which nine people were killed, scores injured, and two Catholic churches burned to the ground

(Left) John Tyler, tenth President of the United States, the first Vice President to succeed to the presidency; (below) Toussaint L'Ouverture, leader of the slave revolt of 1791, which led to the independence of Haiti; (bottom) Joseph Cinque, chief of captives who seized the Spanish slave-ship, "Amistad" in 1839

Toussaint Louverture

ROBERT C. WINTHROP
House Debate on Oregon, 1846
I spurn the notion that patriotism can only be manifested by plunging the nation into war, or that the love of one's own country can only be measured by one's hatred to any other country. Sir, the American spirit that is wanted at the present moment, wanted for our highest honor, wanted for our dearest interests, is that which dares to confront the mad impulses of a superficial popular sentiment even to such vulgar touches. . . . thoughts of moral and intelligent men. Every schoolboy can declaim about honor and war, the British lion and the American eagle; and it is a vice of our nature that the calmest of us have heartstrings which may vibrate for a moment even to such vulgar touches. . . .

I scorn the suggestion that the peace of my country is to be regarded as a mere pawn on the political chessboard, to be periled for any mere party triumph. . . .

I honor the administration, Mr. Speaker, for whatever spirit of conciliation, compromise, and peace it has hitherto manifested on this subject, and have no hesitation in saying so. If I have anything to reproach them with, or taunt them for, it is for what appears to me as an unreasonable and precipitate abandonment of that spirit. And if anybody desires on this account, or any other account, to brand me as a member of the peace party, I bare my bosom, I hold out both my hands to receive that brand. I am willing to take its first and deepest impression, while the iron is sharpest and hottest. If there be anything of shame in such a brand, I certainly glory in my shame.

islation that leads to writing of more liberal New York constitution of 1846.

1846

Jan. 4. New president of Mexico takes office after revolution overthrows government willing to negotiate Texas boundary with John Slidell. New government, believing that U.S. will soon be occupied in war with Britain over Oregon dispute, reasserts Mexican claim to most of Texas. **Feb. 6.** Slidell reports to Washington that Mexicans need to be "chastised," then leaves for home after his final request for an interview is refused on March 12.

Jan. 13. President Polk, apparently wishing either to force negotiations or to provoke an incident, orders General Zachary Taylor to proceed southward from the Nueces River to the Rio Grande.

April 23. President Polk's demand for the whole of Oregon leads to resolution by Congress calling for an end to joint Anglo-American occupation established by convention of 1818. **May 21.** Polk gives Britain required year's notice of termination of the agreement, although British have in previous December requested renewal of American proposal of 1827 for settlement on basis of 49th parallel and have been refused. **June 10.** President Polk, having received (at his insistence) a British treaty offering same terms as 1827 American proposal, lays it before the Senate for advice. **June 15.** Senate ratifies treaty, which provides for free navigation of Juan de Fuca Strait and Columbia River by both parties, as well as fixing Oregon's boundary at present-day line.

April 25. Mexican forces attack American scouting party north of the Rio Grande near Matamoros. **April 26.** General Taylor sends report to Washington saying that "hostilities may now be regarded as commenced" and calls upon governors of Texas and Louisiana for 5,000 volunteers. **May 1.** Mexicans cross the Rio Grande in force.

May 8-9. Early battles at Palo Alto and Resaca de la Palma near the Rio Grande result in defeat of numerically superior Mexican forces by Taylor, who becomes popular here ("Old Rough and Ready") by daring tactics. These engagements set the military pattern of a war won easily despite the vast distances involved, the lack of American preparations, and the strong opposition of the northeastern states. War proceeds in three main areas: the Rio Grande frontier, California, and central Mexico, invaded by sea-borne forces.

May 11. President Polk sends war message to Congress two days after news of skirmish at Matamoros reaches Washington. Message claims American right in disputed territory between Nueces and Rio Grande, asserts that "Mexico has invaded our territory . . . shed American blood on American soil." War with Mexico is formally recognized by House on same day, 174 to 14. Strength of opposition is indicated by 67 Whig votes against call for 50,000 volunteers and $10 million. **May 12.** In the Senate, Calhoun balks at resolution that assumes existence of a war Congress has never formally considered, but war declaration passes, 40 to 2. War is declared the next day.

June 14-July 5. Bear Flag revolt occurs in California, and Captain John C. Frémont at the head of a party of mountain men supposed to be "exploring" for the U.S., on his own initiative (or with secret instructions), supports the establishment by a few American settlers of the Republic of California (the Bear Flag Republic) at Sonoma. This maneuver antagonizes Spanish-speaking Californians on the verge of revolt from Mexico. **July 7.** Authority over California is

JAMES RUSSELL LOWELL
Biglow Letter, 1846
Ez fer war, I call it murder —
  There you hev it plain an' flat;
I don't want to go no furder
  Than my Testyment fer that;
God hez sed so plump an' fairly,
  It's ez long ez it is broad,
An' you've gut to git up airly
  Ef you want to take in God.

'Taint your eppyletts an' feathers
  Make the thing a grain more right;
'Taint afollerin' your bell-wethers
  Will excuse ye in His sight;
Ef you take a sword an' dror it,
  An' go stick a feller thru,
Guv'ment aint to answer for it,
  God 'll send the bill to you.

Wut's the use o' meetin -goin'
  Every Sabbath, wet or dry,
Ef it's right to go amowin'
  Feller-men like oats an' rye?
I dunno but wut it's pooty
  Trainin' round in bobtail coats —
But it 's curus Christian dooty
  This ere cuttin' folks's throats.

They may talk o' Freedom's airy
  Tell they're pupple in the face —
It 's a grand gret cemetary
  Fer the barthrights of our race;
They jest want this Californy
  So 's to lug new slave-states in
To abuse ye, an' to scorn ye,
  An' to plunder ye like sin.

Aint it cute to see a Yankee
  Take sech everlastin' pains,
All to git the Devil's thankee
  Helpin' on 'em weld their chains?
Wy, it 's jest ez clear ez figgers,
  Clear ez one an' one makes two,
Chaps thet make black slaves o' niggers
  Want to make wite slaves o' you.

American Review, 1846

Here, then, lies upon the Pacific coast, adjoining our western border, included between the parallels which embrace the southern sections of the United States and stretching northward to the southern boundary of Oregon, a region of country capable of sustaining a greater population than now inhabits the entire American Union. Traversed, through its entire length and from its most remote corners, by noble rivers all concentrating their waters, and forming at their common mouth, the finest harbor perhaps in the world; abounding in timber of the best quality for shipbuilding and all naval purposes, easily floated to a common point, and that the beautiful and capacious harbor of San Francisco, containing measureless waterpower, immense agricultural resources, and all the elements which nature can furnish of national wealth and national consequence—it is yet shut out from the influences of Christian civilization and abandoned to a people who neither know its capacities, nor feel the pressure of any obligation to develop and expand them. . . .

While California remains in possession of its present inhabitants and under control of its present government, there is no hope of its regeneration. This will demand a life, an impulse of energy, a fiery ambition of which no spark can ever be struck from the soft sluggishness of the American Spaniard.

proclaimed at Monterey with landing of naval expedition under Commodore John Sloat, whose forces also take San Francisco and occupy Sonoma. Frémont is made military commandant in the north. **Sept. 22-30.** Uprising of Mexican Californians under José Flores quickly reestablishes Mexican control in most of southern California.

July 6. General Taylor begins ascent of the Rio Grande and with 6,000 men advances on Monterrey, Mexico. **Sept. 21.** Monterrey is captured after a four-day siege. Taylor then grants an eight-week armistice, promising that American forces will not advance during that time. This is disapproved by President Polk, but Taylor does not receive word until November 2. **Nov. 19.** Feeling that Taylor, a Whig, does not fully support his policies, President Polk consents to another expedition urged by General Winfield Scott, also a Whig, against Veracruz and Mexico City.

Aug. 6. Independent Treasury system is reenacted by Congress. Passed by Democratic majority elected in 1844, bill is similar to the act of 1840, establishes fiscal system for the federal government that endures without substantial change until the Federal Reserve Act of 1913.

Dec. 12. Fearing that Great Britain or another foreign country might seize the Isthmus of Panama, the U.S. and New Granada (present-day Colombia and Panama) sign commercial treaty. Treaty gives the U.S. right of way across the isthmus as a route between the Atlantic and Pacific oceans in return for guarantee of Granadian sovereignty and a further guarantee that isthmus will remain neutral ground. Treaty is approved by the Senate on June 3, 1848.

Dec. 28. Iowa, originally part of Louisiana Purchase and until 1821 unsettled Indian territory, is admitted to the Union as the twenty-ninth state and fourteenth free state; population is 102,300.

Maine enacts first state-wide prohibition law. Similar laws have been passed in 12 more states by 1855, but by 1863 all except Maine's have been repealed or held invalid by state courts.

Smithsonian Institution is founded by act of Congress with bequest of £100,000 from James Smithson, English chemist. Physicist Joseph Henry is named first secretary-director.

Sewing machine invented by Elias Howe, who has experimented with it during previous two years while working in instrument maker's shop in Cambridge, Massachusetts.

Rotary press that can print 8,000 newspapers per hour is invented by Richard M. Hoe. First used by *Philadelphia Public Ledger* in 1847, it revolutionizes newspaper printing and circulation.

Commercial Review of the South and Southwest (later *De Bow's Review*) founded in New Orleans by James D. B. De Bow; at first moderate as to questions dividing North and South, it becomes the most important organ of extreme Southern views in the pre-Civil War period.

1846 - 1847

Congressman David Wilmot, a Pennsylvania Democrat, accelerates congressional debate on the merits of the Mexican War when he offers motion to exclude slavery from any territory acquired from Mexico. Attached as an amendment to a bill authorizing appropriation for territorial purchase, the so-called Wilmot Proviso, though never enacted, becomes the focus of national controversy for the next four years. **Aug. 8,**

JOSEPH HENRY
First Annual Report, 1847
The will makes no restriction in favor of any particular kind of knowledge; though propositions have been frequently made for devoting the funds exclusively to the promotion of certain branches of science having more immediate application to the practical arts of life, and the adoption of these propositions has been urged on the ground of the conformity of such objects to the pursuits of Smithson. But an examination of his writings will show that he excluded from his own studies no branch of general knowledge, and that he was fully impressed with the important philosophical fact that all subjects of human thought relate to one great system of truth. To restrict, therefore, the operations of the Institution to a single science or art would do injustice to the character of the donor, as well as to the cause of general knowledge.

If preference is to be given to any branches of research, it should be to the higher and apparently more abstract; to the discovery of new principles rather than of isolated facts. And this is true even in a practical point of view. Agriculture would have forever remained an empirical art had it not been for the light shed upon it by the atomic theory of chemistry; and incomparably more is to be expected as to its future advancement from the perfection of the microscope than from improvements in the ordinary instruments of husbandry.

HENRY CLAY

This is no war of defense, but one of unnecessary and of offensive aggression. It is Mexico that is defending her firesides, her castles and altars, not we.

ALBERT GALLATIN

Peace with Mexico, 1847

In their external relations, the United States, before this unfortunate war, had, while sustaining their just rights, ever acted in strict conformity with the dictates of justice and displayed the utmost moderation. They never had voluntarily injured any other nation. Every acquisition of territory from foreign powers was honestly made, the result of treaties not imposed but freely assented to by the other party. The preservation of peace was ever a primary object. The recourse to arms was always in self-defense. . . .

At present all these principles would seem to have been abandoned. The most just, a purely defensive war, and no other is justifiable, is necessarily attended with a train of great and unavoidable evils. What shall we say of one, iniquitous in its origin and provoked by ourselves, of a war of aggression, which is now publicly avowed to be one of intended conquest?

1846. Bill is passed by the House but defeated in the Senate two days later. **Feb. 15, 1847.** Amended bill, including Wilmot Proviso, is again passed in the House. **March 1.** Bill is passed in the Senate, but without Proviso. **March 3.** Senate bill is approved by House. By now, debate has hardened Whig opposition to the war as an unconstitutional thrust for territorial gain, while Democrats continue to defend it.

Oct. 1846-March 1847. Whig gains in state and congressional elections indicate unpopularity of Mexican War. Congressional attack on Polk unites Whigs and anti-slavery Democrats, but Congress continues to vote appropriations for war.

Dec. 6, 1846 - Jan. 13, 1847. Conquest of California is completed when General Stephen Watts Kearny, arriving with 120 dragoons after occupying Santa Fe, defeats Mexican forces at San Pasqual, then, with Commodore Robert F. Stockton's forces, proceeds to Los Angeles, which is captured on January 10. Frémont, having subdued remnants of Mexican resistance, signs Treaty of Cahuenga on January 13.

George Donner, elderly Illinois farmer, attempts to lead group of 87 settlers to California through pass in Sierra Nevada, now called Donner Pass. Ill-equipped and inexperienced group is caught by severe winter in the pass and 41 die of cold or starvation. Many of the survivors are sustained only by eating the bodies of their companions, including that of George Donner.

1847

Jan. 14. General Taylor learns that he has been ordered to remain in defensive position at Monterrey while 9,000 of his troops are assigned to attack on Veracruz; he decides that political intrigue inspired by mention of himself as a presidential possibility is responsible. **Feb. 5.** Taylor disobeys orders and advances with 5,000 men, mostly untried volunteers, farther into Mexico. **Feb. 22-23.** At Buena Vista, Taylor defeats Santa Anna's equally untrained and also exhausted 20,000 troops in a bloody battle, which ends war in north of Mexico. Reprimand sent January 27 from Secretary of War William L. Marcy for publishing complaints of the treatment he has received reaches Taylor shortly after battle; he is thereafter forced into idleness as commander in northern Mexico. **Nov. 26.** At his own request, he leaves for the U.S. and a hero's welcome.

Jan. 16. Conflict of authority between Kearny and Stockton, successor to Commodore Sloat, over right to organize a California government comes to a head when Stockton, opposed by Kearny, appoints Frémont territorial governor at Los Angeles. **Feb. 13.** Kearny receives orders to set up a government and establishes one at Monterey, but Frémont defies this move and continues as governor in Los Angeles. **May 31.** Frémont and Kearny leave for Washington where Frémont is eventually courtmartialed and dismissed from the service.

Feb. 19. Southern attitude toward newly acquired territory is stated by Calhoun in four resolutions aimed at keeping area involved in Mexican War open to slavery. He asserts that territories belong to all states and that the Union may not enact laws (against slavery) that will deprive any state of its rights. Argument set forth in four resolutions establishes Southern position that eventually becomes the basis of secession.

April 8. Having taken Veracruz on March 27, General Winfield Scott sets out for the interior of Mexico with 9,000 men. **April 18-Aug. 20.** Santa Anna withdraws

CHARLES SUMNER
Report on the War, 1847
A war of conquest is bad; but the present war has darker shadows. It is a war for the extension of slavery over a territory which has already been purged by Mexican authority from this stain and curse. Fresh markets of human beings are to be established; further opportunities for this hateful traffic are to be opened; the lash of the overseer is to be quickened in new regions; and the wretched slave is to be hurried to unaccustomed fields of toil. It can hardly be believed that now, more than eighteen hundred years since the dawn of the Christian era, a government, professing the law of charity and justice, should be employed in war to extend an institution which exists in defiance of these sacred principles.

It has already been shown that the annexation of Texas was consummated for this purpose. The Mexican War is a continuance, a prolongation, of the same efforts; and the success which crowned the first emboldens the partisans of the latter, who now, as before, profess to extend the area of freedom, while they are establishing a new sphere for slavery.

Volks Tribun (New York), 1846

Self-willed people, as you are, will you then never learn to comprehend that you have the means in your hands to help yourselves and all the unfortunate immigrants at the same time? Will you never learn to realize that you need not starve so long as you still have something to eat, and that you can get plenty to eat so long as you have uncultivated land and hands to cultivate it? Grow wise at last and use your sound sense to make yourselves happy. Hold fast what you have, and do not let the last remnant be stolen away before your eyes, for truly you have been robbed enough. Say to the speculators, "Hands off of our land; what is still ours shall be ours, and from now on we shall reserve it for honest labor and free use. We know now that we cannot satisfy our hunger with your bank notes; we need other means of sustenance and these must be produced; therefore we shall keep the soil so that we may be assured that we will not become your bondmen!"

If once the soil is free, then every honest workingman who leaves his old home in order to lead a happier life in the free air on this side of the ocean becomes a blessing to our republic, and we shall be able to welcome every immigrant ship with a thousand guns; for work gives abundance, and the more producing hands, the more wealth.

toward Mexico City with Scott's force engaging him several times until at Churubusco more than a third of Santa Anna's army is killed, wounded, or captured. With American troops only five miles from Mexico City, Santa Anna requests an armistice. **Aug. 24.** Armistice of Tacubaya is granted so that Mexico can consider peace proposals conveyed by President Polk through Nicholas Trist, chief clerk of the State Department. **Aug. 27-Sept. 6.** Terms discussed in negotiations include demand that Mexico cede area north of the Rio Grande. **Sept. 6.** Mexican government rejects peace offer, ending armistice.

July 21-24. Mormons under Brigham Young arrive in Great Salt Lake Valley after arduous journey from Kanesville (now Council Bluffs, Iowa). Salt Lake City (originally Great Salt Lake City) is founded as capital of the state of Deseret, of which Young is chosen governor.

Sept. 8 and 12. U.S. assault on Mexico City is begun as soon as armistice ends, with battles at gun foundry of Molino del Rey and at Chapultepec Hill. **Sept. 13-14.** City is finally captured by 6,000 American troops, who break through walls during the night. **Oct. 12.** Last effort at resistance by Santa Anna, who attempts to cut American supply line by besieging garrison at Puebla, fails when siege is raised by U.S. reinforcements. Santa Anna, having resigned the presidency and been dismissed as head of the army, flees. **Nov. 22.** New Mexican government proposes reopening of peace negotiations with Trist, who decides to ignore order of November 16 for his recall. **Dec. 4.** Trist consents to Mexican offer of negotiations.

Irish immigration of 105,500 is triple that of previous year because of potato famine of 1846. All-time peak year is 1851, when

221,200 arrive. Emigrants, who have arrived in substantial numbers since 1820, are mostly employed in canal and railroad construction.

Cyrus Hall McCormick begins manufacture of his reaper in Chicago factory after small-scale production in Virginia and elsewhere. Reaper revolutionizes not only U.S. but also European agriculture in following years.

Matthew Fontaine Maury, who has been appointed Superintendent of Depot of Charts and Instruments (later U.S. Naval Observatory and Hydrographical Office) in 1842, begins compiling his *Wind and Current Chart of the North Atlantic* that by 1855 materially reduces time of ocean travel.

Henry Wadsworth Longfellow's first long narrative poem, *Evangeline*, is published; it is a tragedy based on the 1755 exile of settlers from Acadia (Nova Scotia).

Ralph Waldo Emerson, essayist, publishes his first book of poems, including "Threnody," "Brahma," and "Concord Hymn"; *Poems* is dated 1847, but actually published in time for Christmas 1846.

Herman Melville's *Omoo*, novel based on his sea voyage to Tahiti, although largely comedy, contains opinions on the hypocrisy of missionaries and their degradation of native peoples that enrage reviewers when it is published.

Chicago Daily Tribune is founded; after struggle for existence, it is taken over by Joseph Medill and his partners in 1874.

1848

Jan. 24. James W. Marshall, a mechanic employed by John A. Sutter to supervise

RALPH WALDO EMERSON
Ode . . . to W. H. Channing, 1847
Though loathe to grieve
The evil time's sole patriot,
I cannot leave
My honied thought
For the priest's cant,
Or statesman's rant.

. . .

But who is he that prates
Of the culture of mankind,
Of better arts and life?
Go, blindworm, go,
Behold the famous States
Harrying Mexico
With rifle and with knife!

Or who, with accent bolder,
Dare praise the freedom-loving
*   mountaineer?*
I found by thee, O rushing Contoocook!
And in thy valleys, Agiochook!
The jackals of the negro holder.

The God who made New Hampshire
Taunted the lofty land
With little men;
Small bat and wren
House in the oak:
If earth fire cleave
The upheaved land, and bury the folk,
The southern crocodile would grieve.
Virtue palters; Right is hence;
Freedom praised, but hid;
Funeral eloquence
Rattles the coffin lid.

. . .

There are two laws discrete,
Not reconciled—
Law for man, and law for thing;
The last builds town and fleet,
But it runs wild,
And doth the man unking.

To Aspiring Young Men, 1846

The best business you can go into you will find on your father's farm or in his workshop. If you have no family or friends to aid you, and no prospect open to you there, turn your face to the great West and there build up your home and fortune.

Letter to Emerson

How beautiful to think of lean tough Yankee settlers, tough as guttapercha, with most occult *unsubduable fire in their belly, steering over the Western Mountains to annihilate the jungle, and bring bacon and corn out of it for the Posterity of Adam.—There is no Myth of Athene or Herakles equal to this fact.*

A Week on The Concord and Merrimac Rivers, 1849

The frontiers are not east or west, north or south but wherever a man fronts a fact.

building of a sawmill on the American River, discovers a gold nugget in the millrace on Sutter's property in the Sacramento Valley, California. **Dec. 5.** News, which has already spread locally, becomes national when President Polk announces gold discovery in annual message. Gold Rush that results brings 80,000 miners to California during 1849, about one quarter of them from foreign countries.

Need for territorial government for Oregon again raises issue of slavery in far Western territories. **Jan.-Aug.** Long debate covers extension of the principles of the Northwest Ordinance of 1787, which prohibited slavery in territories north of the Ohio River or extension of Missouri Compromise line of 1820 (latitude 36°30′) to the Pacific. Provisional Oregon law excludes slavery; Mexican laws have forbidden slavery in California and New Mexico regions. Various proposals covering all these points pass one house or the other of Congress. **June 27.** Calhoun objects that Mexican laws have been superseded, and that constitutional right to own slaves cannot be altered by Congress or territorial governments. **Aug. 13.** Oregon Bill is finally passed; it retains prohibition of slavery in Oregon, but leaves other questions unresolved. **Aug. 14.** President Polk signs bill despite Calhoun's plea for a veto.

Feb. 2. Negotiations between Nicholas Trist and the Mexican government, though unauthorized because of previous order for Trist's recall, result in signing of Treaty of Guadalupe Hidalgo that ends Mexican War. By its terms an area that encompasses present-day California, Nevada, Utah, western Colorado, western New Mexico, and most of Arizona, together with Texas (as of 1848), is relinquished to the U.S. by Mexico for the sum of $15 million and U.S. payment of its citizens' claims of $3,250,000. The southwest Texas border is fixed at the Rio Grande.

Feb. 23. President Polk submits treaty to Senate, though hesitantly because Trist lacked authority to negotiate it. **March 10.** Senate ratifies treaty 38 to 14; opponents are expansionists who want the annexation of all of Mexico. A proposal to append the Wilmot Proviso is defeated 38 to 15. **May 25.** Mexican congress ratifies, and treaty is declared in effect on July 4.

May 22-26. Slavery issue is brought into election campaign of 1848 when two separate New York delegations, the "Barnburners" (antislavery, anti-Polk, and pro-Wilmot Proviso) and the "Hunkers" (party regulars pledged to support the party candidate), arrive at Democratic National Convention in Baltimore. Neither delegation is seated by the convention, which nominates General Lewis Cass of Michigan for President, Polk having refused a second term. General William O. Butler is nominated for Vice-President. Cass is an advocate of "squatter sovereignty" (local right to allow or prohibit slavery), but Democratic platform fails to include this principle; it denies the power of Congress to interfere with slavery in the states, and is silent on slavery in the territories.

May 29. Wisconsin, which as a territory has included a third of present-day Minnesota, is admitted to the Union as thirtieth state and fifteenth free state, restoring balance of slave and free states. Population is about 150,000.

May. Six New York City newspapers join to pay costs of relaying by telegraph foreign news from Boston, where transatlantic ships make first stop. Association eventually becomes the Associated Press, largest and oldest of U.S. agencies.

June 7. At Whig National Convention in Philadelphia, Whigs reject Henry Clay, nominate General Zachary Taylor for President and Millard Fillmore of New York for

FREDERICK DOUGLASS
North Star, 1848
PEACE! PEACE! PEACE!

The shout is on every lip, and emblazoned on every paper. The joyful news is told in every quarter with enthusiastic delight. We are such an exception to the great mass of our fellow countrymen in respect to everything else, and have been so accustomed to hear them rejoice over the most barbarous outrages committed upon an unoffending people, that we find it difficult to unite with them in their general exultation at this time; and, for this reason, we believe that by peace they mean plunder.

In our judgment, those who have all along been loudly in favor of a vigorous prosecution of the war, and heralding its bloody triumphs with apparent rapture, and glorifying the atrocious deeds of barbarous heroism on the part of wicked men engaged in it, have no sincere love of peace, and are not now rejoicing over peace but plunder. They have succeeded in robbing Mexico of her territory, and are rejoicing over their success under the hypocritical pretense of a regard for peace. Had they not succeeded in robbing Mexico of the most important and most valuable part of her territory, many of those now loudest in their professions of favor for peace would be loudest and wildest for war —war to the knife.

Our soul is sick of such hypocrisy. . . . That an end is put to the wholesale murder in Mexico is truly just cause for rejoicing; but we are not the people to rejoice; we ought rather blush and hang our heads for shame, and, in the spirit of profound humility, crave pardon for our crimes at the hands of a God whose mercy endureth forever.

Seneca Falls Declaration, 1848

When, in the course of human events, it becomes necessary for one portion of the family of man to assume among the people of the earth a position different from that which they have hitherto occupied, but one to which the laws of nature and of nature's God entitle them, a decent respect to the opinions of mankind requires that they should declare the causes that impel them to such a course.

We hold these truths to be self-evident: that all men and women are created equal. . . .

The history of mankind is a history of repeated injuries and usurpations on the part of man toward woman, having in direct object the establishment of an absolute tyranny over her. To prove this, let facts be submitted to a candid world. . . .

Now, in view of this entire disfranchisement of one-half the people of this country, their social and religious degradation, in view of the unjust laws above mentioned, and because women do feel themselves aggrieved, oppressed, and fraudulently deprived of their most sacred rights, we insist that they have immediate admission to all the rights and privileges which belong to them as citizens of the United States. . . .

Resolved, therefore, that, being invested by the Creator with the same capabilities and the same consciousness of responsibility for their exercise . . . and this being a self-evident truth growing out of the divinely implanted principles of human nature, any custom or authority adverse to it, whether modern or wearing the hoary sanction of antiquity, is to be regarded as a self-evident falsehood, and at war with mankind.

Vice-President despite opposition of New England states and Ohio. Convention defeats attempt to affirm right of Congress to control slavery in the territories, confines Whig platform to a recitation of Taylor's military accomplishments.

June 22. New York Barnburners hold their own convention in Utica, New York, where they nominate Martin Van Buren for President. **Aug. 9.** Barnburners combine with other antislavery Democrats, Liberty Party adherents, and New England "Conscience Whigs," who are opposed to slavery, to form the Free-Soil Party at a national convention in Buffalo. Composed of delegates from 17 states, including 3 slave states (Maryland, Virginia, and Delaware), the Free-Soil Convention again chooses Van Buren for President and nominates Charles Francis Adams, son of John Quincy Adams of Massachusetts, for Vice-President. Antislavery platform supports Wilmot Proviso and free land for settlers; party adopts slogan "free soil, free speech, free labor, and free men."

July 19-20. Women's Rights Convention held in Wesleyan Methodist Church at Seneca Falls, New York, inaugurates modern feminist movement with resolutions on women's rights prepared under the leadership of Lucretia Mott and Elizabeth Cady Stanton.

Aug. 2. American forces evacuate Mexico. American casualties total 13,000 dead (11,000 from disease) and 4,000 wounded. Military and naval costs have been almost $100 million. Among young officers who have gained valuable experience are Lieutenants William T. Sherman, Ulysses S. Grant, John B. Sedgwick, George B. McClellan, Thomas J. Jackson, Pierre Beauregard, and Captain Robert E. Lee; except for Lee, they are all from 22 to 30 years old.

Although Oregon boundaries had been

settled by treaty of 1846 with British, Congress fails to consider Oregon's requests for territorial organization until the massacre by Indians of Marcus Whitman and 13 members of his mission. **August.** Bill to organize Oregon Territory is finally signed by President Polk.

Nov. 7. Taylor is elected twelfth President of the U.S. with vote of 1,361,000 to 1,222,000 for Cass. Each candidate carries 15 states, with 8 slave and 7 free states for Taylor and 8 free and 7 slave for Cass. Van Buren, with 291,000 Free-Soil votes, carries no states, but prevents New York from going Democratic by outpolling Cass there, which gives New York with its decisive 36 electoral votes to Taylor. Total electoral vote for Taylor and Fillmore is 163; Cass and Butler receive 127.

Rabbi Isaac Mayer Wise, having emigrated from Bohemia two years earlier, writes at the age of 29 years his "To the Ministers and Other Israelites," a document that outlines his planned program for the next 25 years. Wise advocates a reform of Judaism, plans union of Jewish congregations throughout the U.S., and founds Hebrew Union College in 1875.

James Russell Lowell publishes first series of his *Biglow Papers* in book form; they satirize the Mexican War as an effort to extend slavery. He also publishes *The Vision of Sir Launfal* and his witty *Fable for Critics*, which urges Americans to forget European writers and appreciate their own.

1848 - 1854

European revolutions of 1848 increase immigration, notably of Germans, to the U.S. German communities are established in New York, Baltimore, Cincinnati, St. Louis, and especially Milwaukee, which becomes virtually a German city. Peak years are 1852 to 1854, when 357,000 Germans

JAMES RUSSELL LOWELL
A Fable for Critics, 1848

*You steal Englishmen's books and think
    Englishmen's thought,
With their salt on her tail your wild
    eagle is caught;
Your literature suits its each whisper
    and motion
To what will be thought of it over the
    ocean;
The cast clothes of Europe your states-
    manship tries
And mumbles again the old blarneys
    and lies;
Forget Europe wholly, your veins throb
    with blood
To which the dull current in hers is but
    mud;
Let her sneer, let her say your experi-
    ment fails,
In her voice there's a tremble e'en now
    while she rails,
And your shore will soon be in the
    nature of things
Covered thick with gilt driftwood of
    runaway kings. . . .*

*O, my friends, thank your God, if you
    have one, that He
'Twixt the Old World and you set the
    gulf of a sea;
Be strong-backed, brown-handed,
    upright as your pines,
By the scale of a hemisphere shape
    your designs,
Be true to yourselves and this new
    nineteenth age.*

191

CHARLES SUMNER
Roberts v. Boston, 1849

The whole system of common schools suffers also. It is a narrow perception of their high aim which teaches that they are merely to furnish an equal amount of knowledge to all, and therefore, provided all be taught, it is of little consequence where and in what company. The law contemplates not only that all shall be taught, but that all shall be taught together. They are not only to receive equal quantities of knowledge, but all are to receive it in the same way. All are to approach the same common fountain together; nor can there by any exclusive source for individual or class.

The school is the little world where the child is trained for the larger world of life. It is the microcosm preparatory to the macrocosm, and therefore it must cherish and develop the virtues and the sympathies needed in the larger world. And since, according to our institutions, all classes, without distinction of color, meet in the performance of civil duties, so should they all, without distinction of color, meet in the school, beginning there those relations of equality which the constitution and laws promise to all.

EDWARD EVERETT
While president of Harvard; reply to a protest against the admission of a Negro student, 1848

If this boy passes the examination he will be admitted; and if the white students choose to withdraw, all the income of the college will be devoted to his education.

arrive. The German migration includes large numbers of well-educated liberals and many professional men.

1848 - 1862

"Oh! Susanna" by Stephen Foster is published and becomes popular in Gold Rush. Engaged to write songs for Christy's Minstrels, he writes over the next 15 years "Camptown Races," "Old Folks at Home" (also known as "Swanee River" and originally signed E. P. Christy), "Massa's in de Cold, Cold Ground," "My Old Kentucky Home," "Old Dog Tray," "Jeanie with the Light Brown Hair," "Old Black Joe," and "Beautiful Dreamer." Although most of Foster's songs are associated with the South, he visits the South only once, in 1852.

1849

Jan. 22. Sixty-nine Southern congressmen, having met on December 22, 1848, and again with a dozen more in January 1849, to consider ways of preventing legislation prohibiting slavery in the District of Columbia, present "Address" written by Calhoun listing Southern grievances against the North, but party discipline prevails over sectional alliances when Whig opposition induces all but two Southern Whigs to refuse their signatures.

March 3. Minnesota Territory is established by Congress. Population, which skyrockets within next 10 years, is about 4,000. At various times, parts of Minnesota have belonged to the territories of Wisconsin, Missouri, Iowa, Michigan, Indiana and Louisiana.

March 3. Department of the Interior (originally called Home Department) is created as sixth Cabinet post; it combines several departments, including Office of the Census, Office of Indian Affairs, General Land Office, and Pensions Office.

May 10. Astor Place riot in New York City takes place when partisans of American actor Edwin Forrest resent appearance of his competitor, British actor William Charles Macready, and angry mob stones Astor Place Opera House. When, in desperation, militia is called out, attacked by mob, and finally ordered to fire, 22 are killed and 36 injured.

Difficulty of resolving slavery question continues to prevent organization of New Mexico and California, with California particularly in need of a territorial government to control the waves of arriving gold-seekers. **Sept. 1 - Oct. 13.** At Monterey convention, California decides to wait no longer for a congressional decision and adopts a constitution that prohibits slavery. **Dec. 4.** President Taylor, in his annual message, recommends that Congress admit California on that basis, but Southern senators and representatives declare their opposition, since with 15 free and 15 slave states the admission of California will tip the balance against the South.

Dec. 3. New House of Representatives has slight Democratic majority, with 13 Free-Soil representatives holding balance of power. Deepening sectional conflict, foreshadowing doom of the split Whig Party, is indicated by bitter struggle to elect a speaker of the House. Southern Whigs oppose Whig candidate Robert C. Winthrop of Massachusetts because Northern Whigs have refused to declare themselves against the Wilmot Proviso; but Free-Soilers are equally strong against him because as speaker of previous House he has not given anti-slavery factions sufficient recognition. **Dec. 22.** After 63 ballots, Howell Cobb of Geor-

Account of the . . . Riot at . . . Astor Place, 1849

But law and order must be maintained; very true: it must be done at all hazards, but it should be done prudently and with the least possible sacrifice. Humanity has its claims as well as law; and it may not be necessary to the maintenance of public order that ignorant and misguided men, laboring under a temporary madness, should be shot down like dogs if they can be controlled by means more gentle. . . .

A zeal for the rights of Mr. Macready and his friends and for the cause of law and order is commendable, but it must not be forgotten that other rights must have been violated, or this riot could never have taken place. Those ignorant men had a right to education and to such conditions of cultivation as would have made them intelligent men and good citizens. They would never have raised their hands against society had society done its duty to them. Before they committed this wrong, they had been most deeply wronged themselves; and it would be better to provide 10,-000 schoolmasters to instruct people than 10,000 soldiers to prevent the result of their ignorance. . . .

This terrible tragedy is a lesson to us all. None can escape its warning. We are all responsible, all guilty; for we make a part of a society that has permitted thousands of its members to grow up in poverty and ignorance, and exposed to the temptations of vice and crime. This mob is but a symptom of our social condition, and it points out a disease to which we should lose no time in applying a proper remedy.

HENRY WADSWORTH LONGFELLOW
The Republic, 1849

Thou, too, sail on, O Ship of State!
Sail on, O Union, strong and great!
Humanity with all its fears,
With all the hopes of future years,
Is hanging breathless on thy fate! . . .

Fear not each sudden sound and shock,
'Tis of the wave and not the rock;
'Tis but the flapping of the sail,
And not a rent made by the gale!
In spite of rock and tempest's roar,
In spite of false lights on the shore,
Sail on, nor fear to breast the sea!
Our hearts, our hopes, are all with
*   thee,*
Our hearts, our hopes, our prayers,
*   our tears,*
Our faith triumphant o'er our fears,
Are all with thee—are all with thee!

gia is elected speaker, following a three-week debate in which disunion is frequently threatened.

Pacific Railroad Company (later the Missouri Pacific Railroad) chartered; built during 1851 to 1856 from St. Louis to Kansas City, it becomes the first railroad west of the Mississippi River.

To satisfy a $15 debt owed to J. R. Chapin, Walter Hunt of New York spends three hours bending wire into various forms and designs first modern safety pin. He sells rights to it to Chapin for $400.

Elizabeth Blackwell receives her medical degree from medical school in Geneva,

Baldwin locomotive, the type used by most of the major railroad companies of the 1800s: photographed in Philadelphia in the late 1850s

New York; she is first woman in the world to receive an M.D.

Henry David Thoreau, unable to find a publisher for his book of comments on life and literature, *A Week on the Concord and Merrimack Rivers*, publishes it at his own expense; it sells only 200 copies. Thoreau's essay, "Resistance to Civil Government" (later called "Civil Disobedience"), appears in *Aesthetic Papers*; it tells of his jailing for refusing to pay poll tax as a protest against slavery and the Mexican War.

Poems "Annabel Lee," "The Bells," and "Eldorado" by Edgar Allan Poe are published, "The Bells" a month after his death on October 7.

Henry David Thoreau

HENRY DAVID THOREAU
Resistance to Civil Government, 1849
Cast your whole vote, not a strip of paper merely but your whole influence. A minority is powerless while it conforms to the majority; it is not even a minority then; but it is irresistible when it clogs by Its whole weight. If the alternative is to keep all just men in prison or give up war and slavery, the state will not hesitate which to choose. If a thousand men were not to pay their tax bills this year, that would not be a violent and bloody measure, as it would be to pay them and enable the state to commit violence and shed innocent blood. . . .

I was put into a jail once on this account, for one night; and, as I stood considering the walls of solid stone two or three feet thick . . . I could not help being struck with the foolishness of that institution which treated me as if I were mere flesh and blood and bones to be locked up. . . . I saw that if there was a wall of stone between me and my townsmen, there was a still more difficult one to climb or break through before they could get to be as free as I was. . . .

I could not but smile to see how industriously they locked the door on my meditations, which followed them out again without let or hindrance, and they were really all that was dangerous. As they could not reach me, they had resolved to punish my body; just as boys, if they cannot come at some person against whom they have a spite, will abuse his dog. I saw that the state was half-witted, that it was timid as a lone woman with her silver spoons, and that it did not know its friends from its foes, and I lost all my remaining respect for it, and pitied it.

(Top) Fortified castle of Chapultepec, the last
major obstacle on General Winfield Scott's march to
Mexico City in 1847; (right) James K. Polk, eleventh
President of the United States; (below) battle of
Resaca de la Palma, May 9, 1846

"War News from Mexico": illustration by R. C. Woodville,
depicting public interest in the Mexican War; (below)
General Zachary Taylor's army nearing Monterrey, which was
captured on September 21, 1846

Read and Ponder
THE
FUGITIVE SLAVE LAW!

Which disregards all the ordinary securities of PERSONAL
LIBERTY, which tramples on the Constitution, by its denial
of the sacred rights of Trial by Jury, *Habeas Corpus*, and Appeal, and which enacts, that the Cardinal Virtues of
Christianity shall be considered, in the eye of the law, as CRIMES, punishable with the severest penalties,—
Fines and Imprisonment.
    Freemen of Massachusetts, REMEMBER, That Samuel A. Elliott of Boston, voted for this law, that Mil-
····· Filmore, our whig President *approved it and the Whig Journals of Massachusetts sustain them in this iniquity.*

Broadside announcing the enactment of the
Fugitive Slave Law, September 1850

1850

JOHN C. CALHOUN
Speech in Senate, March 4, 1850
*Unless something decisive is done, I
again ask what is to stop this agitation
before the great and final object at
which it aims—the abolition of slavery
in the South—is consummated? Is it,
then, not certain that if something decisive is not now done to arrest it, the
South will be forced to choose between
abolition and secession? Indeed, as
events are now moving, it will not require the South to secede to dissolve the
Union. Agitation will of itself effect it.*

WILLIAM H. SEWARD
Speech in Senate, March 11, 1850
*It is insisted that the admission of Cali-
fornia shall be attended by a compromise of questions which have arisen
out of slavery. I am opposed to any such
compromise, in any and all the forms in
which it has been proposed, because,
while admitting the purity and the patriotism of all from whom it is my misfortune to differ, I think all legislative
compromises radically wrong and essentially vicious. . . .*

*There is a higher law than the Consti-
tution which regulates our authority
over the domain and devotes it to . . .
noble purposes.*

California's writing in 1849 of constitution that prohibits slavery has aroused
Southern fears for balance of power in Senate between 15 slave and 15 free states.
This balance has been maintained with only
one exception since Missouri Compromise
of 1820. **Jan. 29.** Henry Clay, returned to
the Senate after a seven-year absence, introduces group of resolutions in an effort to
remove slavery issue from contention and
resolve national problems created by it.
Resolutions call for: admission of California
as a free state; recognition of right of territorial governments in rest of Mexican cession to permit or prohibit slavery as they
choose; relinquishment of Texan claims to
parts of Mexico in return for U.S. assumption of pre-annexation debt of Republic of
Texas; guarantee that federal government
will not interfere with slavery in District of
Columbia; abolition of slave trade in the
District; stricter fugitive slave law; and a
declaration stating that Congress has no
right to interfere with slave-trading among
slave states.

Feb. 5-Sept. 20. Ensuing debate is one
of bitterest and most extended in congressional history. Among Clay's supporters are
Lewis Cass of Michigan and Stephen A.
Douglas of Illinois. Opposed to Clay's resolutions are President Zachary Taylor, who
is stubbornly determined to have California

admitted without trading anything for it; extreme Southern sectionalists, such as Jefferson Davis of Mississippi, who demand removal of all restrictions on spread of slavery; and Antislavery and Free-Soil partisans led by William H. Seward of New York and Charles Sumner of Massachusetts, who stand on the Wilmot Proviso, as proposed in 1846.

March 7. Most dramatic moment of debate is provided by Daniel Webster, who breaks with his Free-Soil constituents to support Clay ("I speak today for the preservation of the Union. 'Hear me for my cause.' ").

March 12. California formally applies for admission to the Union.

March 31. Senator John C. Calhoun, exhausted and ill from his efforts on behalf of the South and the Union, dies at age 69.

April 19. Clayton-Bulwer Treaty, negotiated by Secretary of State John M. Clayton and British Minister to the U.S. Sir Henry Lytton Bulwer, promises that neither Britain nor the U.S. will attempt to secure exclusive control of ship canal routes across Central American isthmus.

June 10. Nashville, Tennessee convention of slave state representatives, having met on June 3, passes resolution calling for exten-

DANIEL WEBSTER
Speech in Senate, March 7, 1850
Secession! Peaceable secession! Sir, your eyes and mine are never destined to see that miracle. The dismemberment of this vast country without convulsion! The breaking up of the fountains of the great deep without ruffling the surface! Who is so foolish—I beg everybody's pardon—as to expect to see any such thing? . . .

Is the great Constitution under which we live here—covering this whole country—is it to be thawed and melted away by secession as the snows on the mountain melt under the influence of a vernal sun—disappear almost unobserved and die off? No, sir! No, sir! . . . I see it as plainly as I see the sun in heaven—I see that disruption must produce such a war as I will not describe, in its twofold characters.

Peaceable secession! Peaceable secession! The concurrent agreement of all the members of this great republic to separate! . . . Where is the line to be drawn? What states are to secede? What is to remain American? What am I to be? An American no longer? Where is the flag of the republic to remain? Where is the eagle still to tower? Or is he to cower, and shrink, and fall to the ground?

RALPH WALDO EMERSON
Speech in New York, 1854
I said I had never in my life up to this time suffered from the slave institution. Slavery in Virginia or Carolina was like slavery in Africa or the Fijis for me. There was an old Fugitive Law, but it had become, or was fast becoming, a dead letter, and, by the genius and laws of Massachusetts, inoperative. The new bill made it operative, required me to hunt slaves, and it found citizens in Massachusetts willing to act as judges and captors. Moreover, it discloses the secret of the new times, that slavery was no longer mendicant but was become aggressive and dangerous.

The way in which the country was dragged to consent to this, and the disastrous defection (on the miserable cry of Union) of the men of letters, of the colleges, of educated men, nay, of some preachers of religion, was the darkest passage in the history. It showed that our prosperity had hurt us and that we could not be shocked by crime. It showed that the old religion and the sense of the right had faded and gone out; that while we reckoned ourselves a highly cultivated nation, our bellies had run away with our brains, and the principles of culture and progress did not exist.

REV. J. H. THORNWELL
President of University of South Carolina, of the Compromise of 1850
The parties in this conflict are not merely abolitionists and slaveholders — they are atheists, socialists, communists, red republicans, jacobins on the one side, and the friends of order and regulated freedom on the other. In one word, the world is the battleground — Christianity and atheism the combatants; and the progress of humanity the stake.

July 9. President Taylor dies suddenly of acute intestinal infection, and Millard Fillmore becomes President. Fillmore's more conciliatory attitude toward a compromise and the indefatigable labor of Douglas, who battles for Clay's resolutions after Clay himself is forced by age and infirmity to retire from the fight, are more effective than Webster's March 7 speech.

What becomes known as the Compromise of 1850 is finally enacted as five separate measures, which are passed after an "Omnibus Bill" incorporating Clay's resolutions proves impossible to pass. **Sept. 9.** First and most important law passed is Texas-New Mexico Act, which makes New Mexico formally a territory and allows it to make its own decision on slavery question. On same day, California is admitted to the Union as the thirty-first state and sixteenth free state; its population has risen from 20,000 in 1848 to 100,000 because of the Gold Rush. Utah Act is also passed on September 9; it sets up a territorial government for Utah (the Mormon state of "Deseret") with same provisions as those for New Mexico. **Sept. 18.** New Fugitive Slave Act sets up stringent procedures, under federal control, for the apprehension and return of escaped slaves, with heavy penalties for those who interfere with law enforcement. **Sept. 20.** Last law of series abolishes slave trade in District of Columbia after January 1, 1851. Compromise is widely acclaimed throughout the country as a "final" solution of slavery question.

Northern radicals protest Fugitive Slave Act, which besides providing heavy fines for citizens who obstruct the act's operation, prejudges claims by slave owners against Negroes who are alleged to have escaped and makes it profitable for federal commissioners to dispose of such cases in owners' favor. Emerson calls it a "filthy enactment" and swears he will not obey it. Northern states defiantly pass stronger personal liberty laws, which inhibit, though seldom actually prevent, return of a relatively small number of runaways, estimated at 1,000 from 1850 to 1860.

Sept. 11. Jenny Lind, "the Swedish nightingale," having left the opera stage for "moral" reasons to sing in concerts only, makes her American debut at Castle Garden, New York City.

Nov. 11-18. Second Nashville convention, scantily attended, denounces compromise and claims Southern right to secede from the Union.

American sympathy with continuing European revolutions has led, in the case of Hungary's efforts to be free of Austria, to assurances of recognition by the Taylor administration while revolution is still in progress in 1849. Resulting protest by Austrian chargé d'affaires Chevalier Hülsemann draws sharp reply from Secretary of State Daniel Webster, appointed by Fillmore to replace Clayton. **Dec. 21.** Endorsed by both Whigs and Democrats, Webster defends American right to be concerned in European revolutionary movements. Popular sentiment is indicated later by warm reception accorded Hungarian patriot Lajos Kossuth on his visit to the U.S. after revolution has been crushed.

Seventh decennial census gives U.S. population as 23,191,876, including about 3,200,000 slaves. Increase over 1840 is 6 million, including approximately 1,700,000 immigrants. Urban population, in places of more than 2,500, is 15.3 percent, twice that of 1820; number of urban places has quadrupled.

Nathaniel Hawthorne publishes *The Scarlet Letter*, a novel whose theme is the moral

LEWIS CASS
Speech in Senate, 1852
While we disclaim any crusading spirit against the political institutions of other countries, we may well regard with deep interest the struggling efforts of the oppressed through the world, and deplore their defeat and rejoice in their success. And can anyone doubt that the evidences of sympathy which are borne to Europe from this great republic will cheer the hearts, even when they do not aid the purposes, of the downtrodden masses to raise themselves, if not to power at least to protection? . . .

I may add, what I distinctly stated to the martyr of the struggles of his own country, now the honored guest of ours, in the first conversation I had with him upon this subject—that the people of the United States were not prepared to maintain the rights of Hungary by war; that the only influence we could exert was a moral and not a physical one.

JAMES C. JONES
Speech in Senate, 1852
But have we a right to interfere at all, and is it proper and expedient that we should interfere? My doctrine is that our best interests would be subserved by having nothing to do with this matter. . . .

Are all our sympathies to be exhausted on Hungary? Weep over her wrongs to your heart's content; I will join you in the holy office; but I ask you to come back in the hours of quietude and look to your own country. Have you not enough here to engage your time, to enlist your talents, to enlist the talents of the loftiest intellect of the age?

FRITHJOF MEIDELL
Letter to Norway, 1855
How is the railroad getting along? Here in America it is the railroads that build up the whole country. Because of them the farmers get wider markets and higher prices for their products. They seem to put new life into everything. Even the old apple woman sets off at a dogtrot when she hears that whistle to sell her apples to the passengers. Every ten miles along the railways there are stations, which soon grow up into towns. "Soon," did I say? I should have said "immediately," because it is really remarkable how rapidly the stations are transformed into little towns. I can but compare it with the building of Aladdin's castle by means of his wonderful lamp, only that things move still faster here, where it is not necessary to sit and rub a rusty old oil lantern. Here you can buy houses all ready to be placed on the freight car, and in half a day's time they can be nailed together.

Since I have nothing else to write about this time, I shall attempt to describe how these towns spring up. First — that is, after the two old log houses that stand one on each side of the tracks — first, I say, the railroad company builds a depot. Next, a speculator buys the surrounding 100 acres and lays it out in lots, streets, and a marketplace. Then he graces the prospective town with the name of an early President or a famous general — or his own name — holds an auction, and realizes many hundred percent on his investment.

decadence of Puritans of New England in the seventeenth century. Also published this year: *Representative Men*, by Ralph Waldo Emerson, which is based on his earlier biographical lectures.

Harper's New Monthly Magazine (later *Harper's Magazine*) is founded in New York; it is heavily illustrated, publishes English serials, and contains an unusually large number of pages; it continues to the present day.

1850 - 1857

Sept. 20, 1850. Act of Congress authorizing grants of public land to Alabama, Mississippi, and Illinois for purposes of railroad construction between Mobile, Alabama, and Chicago allows states to grant railroad alternate sections along right of way with which to finance construction. **1856.** Illinois Central line is completed, connecting Chicago, Galena, and Cairo. The Central colonizes large areas of Illinois by sale of its lands, at enormous profit to itself. Other grants on similar terms are made to railroads by Mississippi and Alabama, creating a Mississippi Valley rail system that joins Chicago and Mobile by 1857. Total federal land-grant subsidy for these ventures is 21 million acres, but U.S. holds the alternate sections not granted to states; since these increase in value because of railroads, federal income from land sales increases.

Popular songs of the period include "Listen to the Mocking Bird," music by Septimus Winner, "Darling Nelly Gray" by Benjamin Russel Hanby, "Jingle Bells" by J. S. Pierpont, and "Frankie and Johnny," the original of which eventually proliferates in more than 100 other versions.

1850 - 1860

Large-scale adoption of steam power by American textile mills marks transition to steam as chief source of industrial power. Manufacture of machine tools becomes a separate industry; the vernier caliper and the turret lathe make possible precision production in mass quantities.

1851

Aug. 11-12. After failing in two earlier attempts, General Narciso Lopez leads an expedition of Spanish refugees and American Southerners from New Orleans to Cuba in attempt to inspire an uprising of Cubans against Spain. **Aug. 13.** Fifty-one Southerners are captured, tried, sentenced, and are executed three days later. **Aug. 21.** Riots occur in New Orleans upon news of executions, and Spanish consulate is demolished. **Sept. 1.** Lopez is executed in Havana and his followers, including about 75 Americans, sent to Spain. They are released when Congress agrees to pay for damage in New Orleans.

Herman Melville publishes his greatest novel, *Moby Dick*, using as background his own experiences aboard a whaling vessel. Also appearing this year are Nathaniel Hawthorne's novel on heredity, *The House of the Seven Gables*, and the first of Francis Parkman's works on the French in North America, *The Conspiracy of Pontiac*.

Massachusetts passes first law that permits towns to tax inhabitants for support of free libraries. Edward Everett and George Ticknor, with a combination of private donations, civic funds, and gifts of books, are largely instrumental in founding of Boston Public Library, 1852.

Whig-Republican newspaper, *New York Daily Times*, is founded by Henry J. Raymond; it becomes *The New York Times* in 1857.

Gleason's Pictorial Drawing-Room Companion, first U.S. pictorial magazine, is

HERMAN MELVILLE
Literary World, 1850
Believe me, my friends, that men, not very much inferior to Shakespeare, are this day being born on the banks of the Ohio. And the day will come when you shall say, "Who reads a book by an Englishman that is a modern?" The great mistake seems to be that even with those Americans who look forward to the coming of a great literary genius among us, they somehow fancy he will come in the costume of Queen Elizabeth's day; be a writer of dramas founded upon old English history or the tales of Boccaccio. Whereas great geniuses are parts of the times, they themselves are the times, and possess a corresponding coloring. . . .

Let America, then, prize and cherish her writers; yea, let her glorify them. They are not so many in number as to exhaust her goodwill. And while she has good kith and kin of her own to take to her bosom, let her not lavish her embraces upon the household of an alien; for, believe it or not, England, after all, is in many things an alien to us. . . .

Not that American genius needs patronage in order to expand; for that explosive sort of stuff will expand though screwed up in a vise, and burst it, though it were triple steel. It is for the nation's sake, and not for her authors' sake, that I would have America be heedful of the increasing greatness among her writers; for how great the shame if other nations should be before her in crowning her heroes of the pen! But this is almost the case now.

HARRIET BEECHER STOWE

Uncle Tom's Cabin, 1852

"I'm willin' to work night and day, and work while there's life and breath in me; but this yer thing I can't feel it right to do; and, Mas'r, I never shall do it — never!"

Tom had . . . a habitually respectful manner that had given Legree an idea that he would be cowardly and easily subdued. . . .

Legree looked stupefied and confounded; but at last burst forth —

"What! ye blasted black beast! tell me ye don't think it right to do what I tell ye! What have any of you cussed cattle to do with thinking what's right? I'll put a stop to it! Why, what do ye think ye are? May be ye think ye're a gentleman, master Tom, to be a telling your master what's right and what an't! So you pretend it's wrong to flog the gal!"

WILLIAM J. GRAYSON

The Hireling and the Slave, 1854

There Stowe, with prostituted pen,
  assails
One-half her country in malignant tales;
Careless, like Trollope, whether truth
  she tells,
And anxious only how the libel sells,
To slander's mart she furnishes supplies,
And feeds its morbid appetite for lies
On fictions fashioned with malicious art,
The venal pencil and malignant heart,
With fact distorted, inference unsound,
Creatures in fancy, not in nature found.

ABRAHAM LINCOLN

On meeting Mrs. Stowe, 1863

So you're the little woman who made the great book.

founded in Boston; it is discontinued in 1859.

1851 - 1856

Notorious adventuress Lola Montez, self-styled Spanish dancer (she is Irish), opens two-year American tour with performance of *Betty the Tyrolean* in New York. Laura Keene, London actress, makes her American debut in New York, and subsequently becomes first woman theatrical manager in the U.S. when in 1856 she forms her own company.

1852

March 20. *Uncle Tom's Cabin; or, Life Among the Lowly* by Harriet Beecher Stowe, having appeared originally as a serial in a Washington newspaper, is published in book form in two volumes. Within 16 months, 1,200,000 copies are sold, and a dramatization by George L. Aiken is produced, increasing antislavery sentiment throughout the North and creating great hostility in the South.

June 1. Democratic National Convention meets in Baltimore and nominates for President on the forty-ninth ballot Franklin Pierce of New Hampshire, one of the darkest horses in American political history; William R. King of Alabama is nominated for Vice-President. **June 16.** Whigs meet and nominate General Winfield Scott. Both party platforms accept Compromise of 1850, but Democrats add an endorsement of Virginia and Kentucky resolutions of 1798. Free Soil Party nominates John P. Hale of New Hampshire with platform opposing both the Compromise and slavery itself. **Nov. 2.** Pierce is elected fourteenth President of the U.S. with 1,601,000 votes to Scott's 1,386,000 and Hale's 156,000. Pierce carries 27 states with 254 electoral votes, Scott 4 states with 42 electoral votes. King is elected Vice-President. Results indicate both prevailing disposition in the country to have done with the slavery question and decline of Whig strength, particularly in the South.

June 29. Henry Clay, ill since 1850, dies of tuberculosis in Washington hotel; he is buried in Lexington, Kentucky.

Oct. 24. Daniel Webster, secretary of state until illness forces his retirement to his home at Marshfield, Massachusetts, dies murmuring, "I still live."

Elisha G. Otis invents passenger elevator, eventually making possible the skyscraper.

The Pro-Slavery Argument, a collection of essays by various authors, defends slavery because: it is responsible for the South's prosperity, it is advocated by the Scriptures, Negroes are "biologically inferior," and it makes possible education of barbarian people.

Sculptor Horatio Greenough publishes his book, *Structure and Organization*, which anticipates by 50 years Louis Sullivan's functional approach; Greenough attacks prevailing eclectic school of architecture that borrows from all styles and makes sense of none.

1852 - 1860

National labor unions are formed, among them typographers in 1852, hatters and cigar makers in 1856, and iron molders in 1859. Despite their efforts, money wages increase only 4 percent by 1860, as against a 12 percent rise in cost of living.

1853

Feb. 21. Amount of silver in all coins except the dollar is reduced by Coinage Act of 1853; act also authorizes minting of $3 gold pieces.

CHARLOTTE L. FORTEN
Journal, 1854
I wonder that every colored person is not a misanthrope. Surely we have everything to make us hate mankind. . . .

O! it is hard to go through life meeting contempt with contempt, hatred with hatred, fearing, with too good reason, to love and trust hardly anyone whose skin is white, however lovable, attractive, and congenial in seeming.

In the bitter, passionate feelings of my soul, again and again there rises the questions—"When, oh! when shall this cease?" "Is there no help?" "How long, oh! How long must we continue to suffer, to endure?" Conscience answers it is wrong, it is ignoble to despair; let us labor earnestly and faithfully to acquire knowledge, to break down the barriers of prejudice and oppression. Let us take courage; never ceasing to work, hoping and believing that if not for us, for another generation there is a better, brighter day in store, when slavery and prejudice shall vanish before the glorious light of liberty and truth; when the rights of every colored man shall everywhere be acknowledged and respected, and he shall be treated as a man and a brother!

ROBERT E. LEE
Letter to his wife, 1856
In this enlightened age there are few, I believe, but what will acknowledge that slavery as an institution is a moral and political evil in any country. It is useless to expatiate on its disadvantages. I think it, however, a greater evil to the white than to the black race, and while my feelings are strongly enlisted in behalf of the latter, my sympathies are more strong for the former.

CHARLES M. CONRAD
Letter to John P. Kennedy, 1852
As the squadron destined for Japan will shortly be prepared to sail, I am directed by the President to explain the objects of the expedition, and to give some general directions as to the mode by which those objects are to be accomplished. . . .

It is manifest from past experience that arguments or persuasion addressed to this people, unless they be seconded by some imposing manifestation of power, will be utterly unavailing. You will, therefore, be pleased to direct the commander of the squadron to proceed, with his whole force, to such point on the coast of Japan as he may deem most advisable, and there endeavor to open a communication with the government, and, if possible, to see the emperor in person, and deliver to him the letter of introduction from the President with which he is charged. . . .

If, after having exhausted every argument and every means of persuasion, the commodore should fail to obtain from the government any relaxation of their system of exclusion, or even any assurance of humane treatment of our shipwrecked seamen, he will then change his tone and inform them in the most unequivocal terms that it is the determination of this government to insist that hereafter all citizens or vessels of the United States that may be wrecked on their coasts or driven by stress of weather into their harbors shall, so long as they are compelled to remain there, be treated with humanity; and that if any acts of cruelty should hereafter be practised upon citizens of this country, whether by the government or by the inhabitants of Japan, they will be severely chastised.

March 4. President Pierce's inaugural address, which supports Compromise of 1850 and urges peaceful acquisition of new territory, is first to be spoken from memory.

May 19. Southern interests, anxious to have southern route available for a transcontinental railroad, secure appointment of railroad president James Gadsden of South Carolina to negotiate revision of southwestern border with Mexico. **Dec. 30.** Resulting cession by Mexican government of the 30,000-square-mile area containing southern portions of present-day Arizona and New Mexico becomes known as the Gadsden Purchase, for which the U.S. pays $10 million. This acquisition finally fixes borders of continental U.S. at present-day lines.

July 8. Expedition led by Commodore Matthew C. Perry arrives at Edo Bay (later Tokyo Bay); Perry is authorized by President Fillmore's administration to try to secure rights of shipwrecked American seamen in Japan and to explore commercial possibilities of that country, which has been almost completely closed to the Western world since the seventeenth century. **July 14.** Perry presents letters from President Fillmore, then withdraws in face of Japanese distrust to give time for reply. Washington Territory is organized; territory consists of present-day state, northern Idaho, and western Montana. Major task of first governor, Isaac Ingalls Stevens, is to negotiate treaties by which Indians will relinquish their lands.

New York Central Railroad Company is formed by consolidating 10 small railroads connecting New York City and Buffalo. Further mergers create first connection between Pittsburgh and Cincinnati.

1853 - 1856

Oct. 1853. New York Clearinghouse established to facilitate banking operations. Similar institutions set up in Boston in

1855 and Philadelphia, Baltimore, and Cleveland in 1856.

1854

Jan. 23. Senator Stephen A. Douglas introduces Kansas-Nebraska Act for the purpose of organizing these territories; act reopens slavery question by providing for exercise of "popular sovereignty" by territorial governments in deciding whether to permit or prohibit slavery; since both territories lie north of the 36°30′ parallel, this provision violates terms of Missouri Compromise (a measure explicitly repealed in the bill's final form).

Jan. 24. Act is immediately resisted by Northerners, who publish "Appeal of the Independent Democrats" condemning measure as a "slave-holders' plot." Signed by Senators Charles Sumner and Salmon P. Chase and others, "Appeal" becomes substantially the manifesto of a new political organization, the Republican Party.

Feb. 28. "Anti-Nebraska" forces meet at Ripon, Wisconsin, and urge formation of new political party to be called "Republican." **July 6.** Michigan citizens form first group organized under that name in Jackson, Michigan; their platform calls for repeal of Kansas-Nebraska Act and Fugitive Slave Law, as well as abolition of slavery in District of Columbia. **July 13.** Similar groups are formed at meetings in Ohio, Wisconsin, Indiana, and Vermont. By end of the year, Republican Party has spread throughout the North. Among its leaders are Sumner, Chase, Lyman Trumbull, and Orville H. Browning, who represent former affiliations as far apart as Abolitionists, Free Soilers, and conservative Whigs.

Feb. 28. Spanish authorities seize American merchant vessel *Black Warrior* at Havana because of error in her documents. U.S. Minister to Spain Pierre Soulé, who is

Appeal of the Independent Democrats, 1854

We appeal to the people. We warn you that the dearest interests of freedom and the Union are in imminent peril. . . . We tell you that the safety of the Union can only be insured by the full recognition of the just claims of freedom and man. The Union was formed to establish justice and secure the blessings of liberty. When it fails to accomplish these ends, it will be worthless; and when it becomes worthless, it cannot long endure.

We entreat you to be mindful of that fundamental maxim of democracy — equal rights and exact justice for all men. Do not submit to become agents in extending legalized oppression and systematized injustice over a vast territory yet exempt from these terrible evils. . . .

Whatever apologies may be offered for the toleration of slavery in the states, none can be urged for its extension into territories where it does not exist and where that extension involves the repeal of ancient law and the violation of solemn compact. Let all protest, earnestly and emphatically, by correspondence, through the press, by memorials, by resolutions of public meetings and legislative bodies, and in whatever other mode may seem expedient, against this enormous crime.

For ourselves, we shall resist it by speech and vote, and with all the abilities which God has given us. Even if overcome in the impending struggle, we shall not submit. We shall go home to our constituents, erect anew the standard of freedom, and call on the people to come to the rescue of the country from the domination of slavery. We will not despair; for the cause of human freedom is the cause of God.

JOHN GREENLEAF WHITTIER
The Kansas Emigrants, 1854

*We cross the prairie as of old
    The Pilgrims crossed the sea,
To make the West, as they the East,
    The homestead of the free!*

*We go to rear a wall of men
    On freedom's southern line,
And plant beside the cotton tree
    The rugged Northern pine!*

*We're flowing from our native hills
    As our free rivers flow;
The blessing of our motherland
    Is on us as we go.*

*We go to plant her common schools
    On distant prairie swells,
And give the Sabbaths of the wild
    The music of her bells.*

*Upbearing, like the Ark of old,
    The Bible in our van,
We go to test the truth of God
    Against the fraud of man.*

*No pause, nor rest, save where the
        streams
    That feed the Kansas run,
Save where our Pilgrim gonfalon
    Shall flout the setting sun!*

*We'll tread the prairie as of old
    Our fathers sailed the sea,
And make the West, as they the East,
    The homestead of the free!*

in Spain attempting to acquire Cuba for the U.S., tries to use *Black Warrior* incident to gain island by threat of war. **April-August.** Secretary of State William L. Marcy, with approval of President Pierce, instructs Soulé to meet with James Buchanan, minister to Great Britain, and James Mason, minister to France, at Ostend, Belgium, to work out plans to "detach" Cuba from Spain. **Oct. 18.** "Ostend Manifesto," the work of Soulé and Buchanan, declares Cuba indispensable for security of the Union and recommends purchase or, if necessary, seizure by the U.S. **Nov. 13.** Aggressive language of Manifesto leads Marcy to disavow it. **Dec. 17.** Soulé resigns. When Manifesto is published in following year, Republicans accuse administration of attempt to gain more slave territory.

April 26. Anticipating passage of Kansas-Nebraska Act, the Massachusetts Emigrant Aid Society (later New England Emigrant Aid Company) is organized for the purpose of colonizing Kansas with antislavery settlers; 2,000 have arrived by 1857, founding town of Lawrence and other free-state communities. Corresponding pro-slavery societies for establishing slave-state communities are organized secretly in Missouri.

May 30. Kansas-Nebraska Act is passed. Kansas Territory includes present-day Kansas and part of Colorado. Nebraska Territory includes present-day Nebraska as well as parts of Montana, South Dakota, North Dakota, Wyoming, and Colorado. Douglas, sponsor of the bill, believes genuinely in popular sovereignty and is convinced that a policy of vigorous national expansion is only solution to slavery problem; his other motives for sponsoring bill are said to be presidential ambitions and an interest in building of transcontinental railroad along central route from Chicago to the West Coast. Since railroad project conflicts with Southern desires for a southern route, Douglas can only retain Southern support for the railroad and himself by seeking repeal of Missouri Compromise, which he is willing to do because he believes conditions of climate will in any case exclude slavery from projected territories.

June 5. Reciprocity Treaty between Canada and the U.S. is signed; it provides for mutual exchange of offshore fishing rights from Cape Breton Island to the 36th parallel (approximately the latitude of Albemarle Sound, North Carolina) as well as duty-free entry of agricultural commodities. Treaty is abrogated by the U.S. on March 17, 1866, under provision for termination by either country after a period of 10 years.

Aug. 3. Graduation Act passed; it provides for disposal of unpurchased public lands that have been on the market but unsold for periods of from 10 to 30 years; price scale ranges from $1 per acre for 10-year land to 12½ cents per acre for 30-year land. Supporters are chiefly from North and West, in sectional alliance against South. Act is repealed in 1862 after about 26 million acres have been sold.

Oct. 16. Abraham Lincoln, local lawyer and politician, speaks in Peoria, Illinois; he condemns slavery, but denies that Kansas-Nebraska Act is slave-holders' conspiracy, favors gradual emancipation of slaves.

American, or Know-Nothing, Party, stemming from the anti-Catholic and anti-immigrant movement of the 1840s and organized on a national scale after 1852 election, reaches the height of its influence. Nickname derives from reply "I know nothing" which members of secret lodges are instructed to give when asked about party policies. The party gains a number of local offices, notably in New York, and a dozen congressional seats before it breaks up over slavery issue after election of 1856; at that time, many of its adherents join the Republicans.

ABRAHAM LINCOLN
Fragment, c. 1854
If A can prove, however conclusively, that he may of right enslave B, why may not B snatch the same argument and prove equally that he may enslave A?

You say A is white, and B is black. It is color, then; the lighter having the right to enslave the darker? Take care. By this rule, you are to be slave to the first man you meet with a fairer skin than your own.

You do not mean color exactly? You mean the whites are intellectually the superiors of the blacks, and therefore have the right to enslave them? Take care again. By this rule, you are to be slave to the first man you meet with an intellect superior to your own.

But, say you, it is a question of interest; and if you can make it your interest, you have the right to enslave another. Very well. And if he can make it his interest, he has the right to enslave you.

ABRAHAM LINCOLN
Letter to Speed, 1855
Our progress in degeneracy appears to me to be pretty rapid. As a nation, we began by declaring that "all men are created equal." We now practically read it "all men are created equal, except negroes." When the Know-Nothings get control, it will read "all men are created equal, except negroes, and foreigners and Catholics." When it comes to this I should prefer emigrating to some country where they make no pretense of loving liberty — to Russia, for instance, where despotism can be taken pure, and without the base alloy of hypocrisy.

HENRY DAVID THOREAU

Walden, 1854

I went to the woods because I wished to live deliberately, to front only the essential facts of life, and see if I could not learn what it had to teach, and not, when I came to die, discover that I had not lived. I did not wish to live what was not life, living is so dear; nor did I wish to practise resignation, unless it was quite necessary. I wanted to live deep and suck out all the marrow of life, to live so sturdily and Spartan-like as to put to rout all that was not life, to cut a broad swath and shave close, to drive life into a corner, and reduce it to its lowest terms, and, if it proved to be mean, why then to get the whole and genuine meanness of it, and publish its meanness to the world; or if it were sublime, to know it by experience and be able to give a true account of it in my next excursion. . . .

Our life is frittered away by detail. An honest man has hardly need to count more than his ten fingers, or in extreme cases he may add his ten toes, and lump the rest. Simplicity, simplicity, simplicity! I say, let your affairs be as two or three, and not a hundred or a thousand; instead of a million count half a dozen, and keep your accounts on your thumbnail.

I frequently tramped eight or ten miles through the deepest snow to keep an appointment with a beech tree, or a yellow birch, or an old acquaintance among the pines.

I would rather sit on a pumpkin, and have it all to myself, than to be crowded on a velvet cushion.

I have lived some thirty years on this planet, and I have yet to hear the first syllable of valuable or even earnest advice from my seniors.

Arrival of 13,000 Chinese marks beginning of large-scale Chinese immigration; highest number in any previous year has been 42. Chinese workers are employed largely in building of transcontinental railroad.

Walden, published by Henry David Thoreau after his two-year sojourn at Walden Pond expounds his philosophy: freedom is gained by man's rediscovery of himself; it is not widely read until after Thoreau's death.

Timothy Shay Arthur popularizes temperance crusade with his *Ten Nights in a Bar-Room and What I Saw There*, a lurid tale of the evils of drink that is outsold only by *Uncle Tom's Cabin* in this decade.

1854 - 1857

George Fitzhugh publishes his *Sociology for the South; or, the Failure of Free Society;* he is also author of *Cannibals All! or, Slaves Without Masters*, published in 1857. Both are widely read works that are approved in the South for their praise of its economy and their condemnation of Northern capitalist wage-labor system.

1854 - 1858

March 8, 1854. Having returned to Japan in February with seven warships, Commodore Perry presents gifts that, together with his display of naval force, persuade Japanese of the civilization and power of the West. **March 31.** Treaty of Kanagawa is signed; it declares peace and friendship between the U.S. and Japan, opens certain Japanese ports to American commerce, and makes provision for American nationals stranded by shipwreck. **June 18, 1857 and July 29, 1858.** Agreements negotiated by Townsend Harris, appointed consul to Japan in 1855, open additional ports, secure residence rights for Americans, and provide for exchange of diplomatic representatives.

1855

Walt Whitman publishes collection of his poems, *Leaves of Grass*, at his own expense; it goes almost unnoticed. Subsequent editions are equally unsuccessful, until poems are called "obscene," after which seventh edition has moderate sale. *The Song of Hiawatha* by Henry Wadsworth Longfellow, written in meter of Finnish epic, *Kalevala*, is immediately successful.

Frank Leslie's Illustrated Newspaper (later *Leslie's Weekly*), most successful of early illustrated papers, begins publication in New York; it is continued until 1922.

1855 - 1856

March 30, 1855. Struggle between pro- and antislavery factions for control of Kansas territorial government starts when 5,000 armed "Border Ruffians" from Missouri secure election of pro-slavery legislature by fraud and intimidation. **Oct. 23-Nov. 2.** Antislavery forces organize Free-State Party, and at Topeka draw up Free-State constitution that is adopted by popular vote along with ordinance prohibiting entry of Negroes into territory. **Jan. 15, 1856.** Election of Free-State legislature gives territory dual government.

1855 - 1860

June-Oct. 1855. Climax of American filibustering in Caribbean, carried on intermittently since 1850, is reached when military adventurer William Walker takes advantage of civil war in Nicaragua to set himself up as dictator, and later president, of that country. **Dec. 8.** Walker's action is formally condemned by Pierce administration. **May 14, 1856.** President Pierce receives Walker's representative, thus virtually recognizing his government. **July.** Walker proclaims opening of Nicaragua to slavery, which leads Northerners to condemn Walker as agent of

RALPH WALDO EMERSON
Letter to Walt Whitman, 1855
I greet you at the beginning of a great career.

WALT WHITMAN
Leaves of Grass, 2nd ed., 1856
Poets here, literates here, are to rest on organic different bases from other countries; not a class set apart, circling only in the circle themselves, modest and pretty, desperately scratching for rhymes, pallid with white paper, shut off, aware of the old pictures and traditions of the race, but unaware of the actual race around them—not breeding in and in among each other till they all have the scrofula. Lands of ensemble, bards of ensemble! Walking freely out from the old traditions, as our politics has walked out, American poets and literates recognize nothing behind them superior to what is present with them —recognize with joy the sturdy living forms of the men and women of These States, the divinity of sex, the perfect eligibility of the female with the male, all The States, liberty and equality, real articles, the different trades, mechanics, the young fellows of Manhattan Island, customs, instincts, slang, Wisconsin, Georgia, the noble Southern heart, the hot blood, the spirit that will be nothing less than master, the filibuster spirit, the Western man, native-born perceptions, the eye for forms, the perfect models of made things, the wild smack of freedom, California, money, electric telegraphs, free trade, iron and iron mines —recognize without demur those splendid resistless black poems, the steamships of the seaboard states, and those other resistless splendid poems, the locomotives, followed through the interior states by trains of railroad cars.

DeBow's Review, 1856

To the People of the South:

On the undersigned, managers of the "Lafayette Emigration Society," has devolved the important duty of calling the attention of the people of the slaveholding states to the absolute necessity of immediate action on their part in relation to the settlement of Kansas Territory. The crisis is at hand. Prompt and decisive measures must be adopted, or farewell to Southern rights and independence.

The Western counties of Missouri have, for the last two years, been heavily taxed, both in money and time, in fighting the battles of the South. Lafayette County alone has expended more than $100,000 in money, and as much, or more, in time. Up to this time, the border counties of Missouri have upheld and maintained the rights and interests of the South in this struggle, unassisted and unsuccessfully. But the Abolitionists, staking their all upon the Kansas issue, and hesitating at no means, fair or foul, are moving heaven and earth to render that beautiful territory not only a free state, so-called, but a den of Negro thieves and "higher law" incendiaries. . . .

How, then, shall these impending evils be avoided? The answer is obvious. Settle the territory with emigrants from the South. *The population of the territory at this time is about equal—as many pro-slavery settlers as Abolitionists; but the fanatics have emissaries in all the free states—in almost every village—and by misrepresentation and falsehood are engaged in collecting money and enlisting men to tyrannize over the South. Is it in the nature of Southern men to submit without resistance, to look to the North for their laws and institutions? We do not believe it!*

a slave-holders' conspiracy; but in fact he is sponsored throughout by the Accessory Transit Company, later under the leadership of Cornelius Vanderbilt. **May 1857.** Vanderbilt brings about Walker's downfall when Walker favors the wrong side in a two-faction fight for control of the company. **Aug. 1860.** Walker, after a long stay in the U.S., invades Honduras to the serious embarrassment of the American government. **Sept. 3-12.** U.S. does not intervene when he is captured by British Navy and tried and executed by Honduran authorities.

1856

Jan. 24. President Pierce indicates administration support for pro-slavery faction in Kansas when he condemns Topeka (Free-State) government as rebellious. Actually, Pierce has no choice if he is to uphold his appointed territorial governor, Wilson Shannon, who as pro-slavery man also condemns Topeka group. But appointment of Shannon reflects Pierce's stubborn and futile notion that harmony can be maintained if Nebraska becomes free state and Kansas a slave one.

Feb. 11. President Pierce issues order for both Border Ruffians and Free-State men to disperse, but both sides prepare for conflict. **May 21.** Incident known as "sack" of Lawrence by Ruffians results in one death and considerable property damage. **May 24-25.** In retaliation, Abolitionist John Brown, with four of his sons and three other followers, rides at night into settlement at Pottawatomie Creek and massacres five pro-slavery colonists. **June 4.** Governor Shannon orders armed groups to disband, but civil war breaks out. **Aug. 13.** Free-State men, armed with Sharps rifles ("Beecher's Bibles") shipped from antislavery groups in the East, attack town of Franklin. **Aug. 30.** Pro-slavery forces take Osawatomie, driving out Brown and 40 defenders. In all, these engagements and other guerrilla skirmishes in previous year have resulted in 200 deaths by December, along with the destruction of $2 million in property. Peace is restored only with aid of federal troops, summoned by new territorial governor, John W. Geary, appointed on September 11.

Feb. 22. American (Know-Nothing) Party nominates Millard Fillmore of New York for President and Andrew J. Donelson of Tennessee for Vice-President. **Sept. 17.** Whig convention nominates same candidates. **June 2.** Democrats, rejecting both Pierce and Douglas because of their connection with Kansas question, nominate James Buchanan of Pennsylvania for President and John C. Breckinridge of Kentucky for Vice-President; Democratic platform supports both Compromise of 1850 and Kansas-Nebraska Act. **June 17.** Republicans, in their first national convention, nominate Colonel John C. Frémont of California for President and William L. Dayton of New Jersey for Vice-President. Their platform upholds the right of Congress to regulate slavery in territories (as opposed to Douglas' "popular sovereignty"), strongly criticizes the Ostend Manifesto, advocates transcontinental railroad, and urges that Kansas be admitted as free state.

May 14. James King of William is assassinated in San Francisco by rival newspaper owner, one of many he has accused of dishonesty and corruption in his *San Francisco Daily Evening Bulletin.* A Vigilante Committee is formed immediately, and confidence in honesty of authorities is so low that Committee seizes assassin from sheriff, tries, convicts, and executes him. Similar committees grow up elsewhere in California, where lawlessness is rampant.

Partisan feeling in Congress prevents action on question of Kansas statehood. Democrats, led by Douglas, are unwilling to accept Topeka Free-State government; Re-

Constitution of the Vigilantes of San Francisco, 1856

Whereas, *it has become apparent to the citizens of San Francisco that there is no security for life and property, either under the regulations of society as it at present exists or under the laws as now administered; and that, by the association together of bad characters, our ballot boxes have been stolen and others substituted, or stuffed with votes that were never polled, and thereby our elections nullified, our dearest rights violated, and no other method left by which the will of the people can be manifested:*

Therefore, *the citizens whose names are hereunto attached do unite themselves into an association for the maintenance of the peace and good order of society, the prevention and punishment of crime, the preservation of our lives and property, and to insure that our ballot boxes shall hereafter express the actual and unforged will of the majority of our citizens.*

And we do bind ourselves, each unto the other, by a solemn oath, to do and perform every just and lawful act for the maintenance of law and order, and to sustain the law when faithfully and properly administered. But we are determined that no thief, burglar, incendiary, assassin, ballot-box stuffer, or other disturber of the peace shall escape punishment, either by the quibbles of the law, the insecurity of prisons, the carelessness or corruption of the police, or a laxity of those who pretend to administer justice.

OPPOSITE PAGE: (Top) "Conquering Prejudice": lithograph criticizing Daniel Webster's support of the Fugitive Slave Law; (bottom) collecting gold with a sluice box in Spanish Flat, California, 1852
THIS PAGE: (Above) Daguerreotype of Zachary Taylor, twelfth President of the United States; (below) "Democratic Funeral of 1848," a cartoon celebrating the Whig victory; (right) the thirteenth President of the United States, Millard Filmore

CHARLES SUMNER
Speech in Senate, 1856

It belongs to me now, in the first place, to expose the Crime Against Kansas in its origin and extent. . . . I say crime, and deliberately adopt this strongest term as better than any other denoting the consummate transgression. I would go further if language could further go. It is the crime of crimes — *surpassing far the* old *crimen majestatis [crime against a sovereign power], pursued with vengeance by the laws of Rome, and containing all other crimes, as the greater contains the less. I do not go too far when I call it the* crime against nature, *from which the soul recoils and which language refuses to describe. . . .*

Slavery now stands erect, clanking its chains on the territory of Kansas, surrounded by a code of death, and trampling upon all cherished liberties. . . .

And, sir, all this has been done, not merely to introduce a wrong which in itself is a denial of all rights . . . not merely, as has been sometimes said, to protect slavery in Missouri . . . but it has been done for the sake of political power, in order to bring two new slaveholding senators upon this floor and thus to fortify in the national government the desperate chances of a waning oligarchy. . . .

Sir, all this was done in the name of popular sovereignty. And this is the close of the tragedy. Popular sovereignty, which, when truly understood, is a fountain of just power, has ended in popular slavery; not merely in the subjection of the unhappy African race but of this proud Caucasian blood which you boast. The profession with which you began, of All by the People, *has been lost in the wretched reality of* Nothing for the People.

publicans are equally opposed to pro-slavery faction. **May 19-20.** In speech on Kansas, Senator Charles Sumner insults the absent Senator Andrew P. Butler of South Carolina during diatribe against the "harlot slavery" and "rape" of Kansas by "hirelings picked from the drunken spew and vomit of an uneasy civilization." **May 22.** Butler's nephew, Representative Preston Brooks, beats Sumner senseless with a cane while Sumner sits unable to rise from his Senate desk; resulting injuries force Sumner to remain away from his seat for three and a half years. **Aug. 30.** Congress adjourns without having resolved the underlying issue, which Republicans exploit in the approaching elections by frequent references to "Bleeding Kansas."

Nov. 4. In ensuing election, Republicans win Northeast despite attacks on them as a sectional threat to the Union by Whigs, Know-Nothings, and Democrats. James Buchanan is elected fifteenth President of the U.S. with 1,838,000 votes to Frémont's 1,335,000 and Fillmore's 874,000. Buchanan wins 14 slave and 5 free states, with electoral vote of 174; Frémont wins 11 free states with vote of 114; Fillmore wins Maryland with 8 votes. Result marks end of Whig Party and beginning of party divisions along sectional lines.

Gail Borden receives patent on process for condensing milk; he has earlier discovered a method of concentrating meat into a "meat biscuit," and in ensuing years he develops methods for concentrating fruit juices, tea, coffee, and cocoa. His work is beginning of commercial food processing.

The Physical Geography of the Sea, first comprehensive work on oceanography and a classic in its field, is published by Matthew Fontaine Maury; it is translated and published in many countries.

John Greenleaf Whittier, in addition to writing antislavery poems, writes ballads of New England life, such as "The Barefoot Boy" and "Maud Muller."

The Rise of the Dutch Republic, published by John Lothrop Motley, historian and diplomat, is a dramatically written history that, among other things, is a comparison of liberty and absolute power in government.

1857

March 4. Pro-slavery faction in Kansas, determined to enact a constitution guaranteeing slavery, forces Governor Geary to resign when he opposes its intention to adopt such a constitution without submitting it to popular vote. **May 26.** Geary's successor, Robert J. Walker of Mississippi, appointed by President Buchanan, demands such a vote. **June.** Pro-slavery forces hold rigged election of delegates to constitutional convention. **Oct. 5.** Free-State partisans, with help of strict supervision of Governor Walker, win decisive majority in election of a new territorial legislature.

Dred Scott, Negro slave, sues for his freedom in U.S. Supreme Court on ground that he has lived with his owner on free soil for four years. **March 6.** Court holds that, first, Scott is not a U.S. citizen and cannot sue; second, residence in free territory does not make him free; third, Missouri Compromise, which had made area north of 36°30′ free, was unconstitutional. Court hopes that decision will settle slavery question. As decision denies to Congress any right to exclude slavery from the territories, and as that right is the fundamental one on which Republican Party has been organized, Court's opinion is loudly denounced in the North. Even Stephen Douglas is disturbed, since if Congress cannot exclude slavery, then neither can any territorial legislatures

ROBERT PURVIS
Resolutions of Negro Protest, Philadelphia, 1857
Whereas, *the Supreme Court of the United States has decided in the case of Dred Scott that people of African descent are not and cannot be citizens of the United States, and cannot sue in any of the United States courts . . . and* Whereas, *this Supreme Court is the constitutionally approved tribunal to determine all such questions; therefore,*

Resolved, *that this atrocious decision furnishes final confirmation of the already well-known fact that, under the Constitution and government of the United States, the colored people are nothing and can be nothing but an alien, disfranchised, and degraded class. . . .*

Resolved, *that to persist in supporting a government which holds and exercises the power, as distinctly set forth by a tribunal from which there is no appeal, to trample a class underfoot as an inferior and degraded race, is on the part of the colored man at once the height of folly and the depth of pusillanimity.*

Resolved, *that no allegiance is due from any man, or any class of men, to a government founded and administered in iniquity, and that the only duty the colored man owes to a Constitution under which he is declared to be an inferior and degraded being, having no rights which white men are bound to respect, is to denounce and repudiate it, and to do what he can by all proper means to bring it into contempt.*

ROBERT J. WALKER
Inaugural Address, Kansas, 1857
If this principle can be carried into suc-
cessful operation in Kansas—that her
people shall determine what shall be
her social institutions—the slavery ques-
tion must be withdrawn from the halls
of Congress, and from our presidential
conflicts, and the safety of the Union
be placed beyond all peril. Whereas, if
the principle should be defeated here,
the slavery agitation must be renewed in
all elections throughout the country,
with increasing bitterness, until it
shall eventually overthrow the govern-
ment. . . .

And let me ask you, what possible
good has been accomplished by agitat-
ing in Congress and in presidential con-
flicts the slavery question? Has it eman-
cipated a single slave, or improved their
condition? Has it made a single state
free where slavery otherwise would
have existed? Has it accelerated the
disappearance of slavery from the more
northern of the slaveholding states, or
accomplished any practical good what-
ever? No, my fellow citizens, nothing
but unmitigated evil has already en-
sued, with disasters still more fearful
impending for the future, as a conse-
quence of this agitation.

There is a law more powerful than
the legislation of man—more potent
than passion or prejudice—that must
ultimately determine the location of
slavery in this country; it is the isother-
mal line; it is the law of the thermometer,
of latitude or altitude, regulating cli-
mate, labor, and productions, and, as a
consequence, profit and loss. Thus,
even upon the mountain heights of the
tropics, slavery can no more exist than
in northern latitudes, because it is
unprofitable, being unsuited to the con-
stitution of that sable race transplanted
here from the equatorial heats of Africa.

created by Congress, and their right to do
so is whole assumption in his doctrine of
popular sovereignty.

August. Panic of 1857 is set off by failure of Ohio Life Insurance and Trust Company; it is severe but short-lived, chiefly the
result of overspeculation in railroads and
real estate. Hundreds of banks and businesses are bankrupt, and banks throughout
the country suspend specie payments. Panic's political effect is to advantage of Republicans, who persuade manufacturers, notably in pivotal state of Pennsylvania, that a
higher tariff is needed and who court the
hard-hit farmers with promises of free
homesteads in the event of a Republican
victory in 1860.

Oct. 19-Nov. 8. Pro-slavery constitutional convention delegates meet at Lecompton,
Kansas, and draw up pro-slavery constitution of which only one article (guaranteeing
property rights as applied to slaves) is to be
submitted for popular approval. Vote is to
decide whether constitution will be adopted
"with slavery" (making Kansas a slave territory) or "without slavery," which means
that no new slaves will be brought in, but
those already in territory will not be freed.
Walker refuses to accept such a maneuver,
but President Buchanan, eager to please the
South, reneges on his promise to uphold
Walker and consents to it.

Dec. 17. Walker resigns. Buchanan's decision splits Democratic Party, since Douglas, too, refuses to accept Lecompton constitution ("I have not become the servile tool
of any President to receive and obey his instructions against my own judgment and
sense of right").

Publication of Hinton R. Helper's *The*
Impending Crisis of the South: How to Meet
It, work of a Southerner purporting to
show disastrous effect of slavery on the

Southern economy and on majority of Southern whites, who are not slave-holders, is to advantage of the Republicans, but book is banned in the South.

The *Atlantic Monthly* is founded in Boston; its first editor is James Russell Lowell, and initial issue contains an installment of Oliver Wendell Holmes' *The Autocrat of the Breakfast-Table*, previously published in 1831 and 1832. *Harper's Weekly*, a news magazine, is founded in New York; it is discontinued in 1916.

1857 - 1858

Dec. 21, 1857. Vote on Lecompton constitution, which Free-State advocates refuse to take part in, totals 6,226 for constitution with slavery, 569 for constitution without slavery. **Jan. 4, 1858.** Free-State legislature holds another election in which voters vote for entire constitution. Totals: with slavery, 138; without slavery, 24; against the constitution, 10,226. **May 4.** Compromise is reached when Kansas voters are given choice by Congress of accepting the Lecompton constitution and becoming a state, or rejecting it and remaining a territory. **Aug. 2.** Kansans reject constitution by vote of 11,300 to 1,800.

All men born free and equal?

OLIVER WENDELL HOLMES
Atlantic Monthly, 1860
There is nothing in New England corresponding to the feudal aristocracies of the Old World. Whether it be owing to the stock from which we were derived, or to the practical working of our institutions, or to the abrogation of the technical "law of honor," . . . we have no such aristocracy here as that which grew up out of the military systems of the Middle Ages. . . .

There is, however, in New England, an aristocracy, if you choose to call it so. . . . It has grown to be a caste, not in any odious sense, but, by the repetition of the same influences, generation after generation, it has acquired a distinct organization and physiognomy, which not to recognize is mere stupidity, and not to be willing to describe would show a distrust of the good nature and intelligence of our readers, who like to have us see all we can and tell all we see. . . .

[It is] the Brahmin caste of New England. This is the harmless, inoffensive, untitled aristocracy to which I have referred, and which I am sure you will at once acknowledge. There are races of scholars among us in which aptitude for learning, and all these marks of it I have spoken of, are congenital and hereditary. Their names are always on some college catalogue or other. They break out every generation or two in some learned labor which calls them up after they seem to have died out. At last some newer name takes their place, it may be; but you inquire a little and you find it is the blood of the Edwardses or the Chaunceys or the Ellerys or some of the old historic scholars disguised under the altered name of a female descendant.

FREE STATE
CONVENTION!

All persons who are favorable to a union of effort, and a permanent organization of all the Free State elements of Kansas Territory, and who wish to secure upon the broadest platform the co-operation of all who agree upon this point, are requested to meet at their several places of holding elections, in their respective districts on the 25th of August, instant, at one o'clock, P. M., and appoint five delegates to each representative to which they were entitled in the Legislative Assembly, who shall meet in general Convention at

Broadside calling for convention to organize
Kansas Territory as a free state, 1855

ABRAHAM LINCOLN
Address to Convention, 1858
If we could first know where we are and whither we are tending, we could better judge what to do and how to do it. We are now far into the fifth year since a policy was initiated with the avowed object and confident promise of putting an end to slavery agitation. Under the operation of that policy, that agitation has not only not ceased but has constantly augmented. In my opinion, it will not cease until a crisis shall have been reached and passed. "A house divided against itself cannot stand." I believe this government cannot endure, permanently, half slave and half free. I do not expect the Union to be dissolved; I do not expect the house to fall; but I do expect it will cease to be divided. It will become all one thing, or all the other. Either the opponents of slavery will arrest the further spread of it and place it where the public mind shall rest in the belief that it is in the course of ultimate extinction, or its advocates will push it forward till it shall become alike lawful in all the states, old as well as new, North as well as South.

1858

Feb. 2. President Buchanan supports the Lecompton constitution and recommends in submitting it to Congress that Kansas be admitted as a slave state. **Feb. 3.** Stephen A. Douglas leads revolt of Northern Democrats against Buchanan. **March 23.** In spite of Douglas, Senate votes to admit Kansas under constitution, but House does not. **April 23.** Compromise measure sponsored by the administration is submitted to Congress; it gives Kansas a choice of accepting the constitution and becoming a state or rejecting it and remaining a territory. **May 4.** The measure is passed over Douglas' opposition. Kansas argument has given Republicans a strong campaign issue and left the Democratic split unhealed; Buchanan has lost the support of the North, and Douglas has lost the South.

May 11. Minnesota is admitted to the Union as thirty-second state and seventeenth free state. Its population is about 150,000, many of these settlers having arrived since completion of railroads to Mississippi River.

June 16. Abraham Lincoln makes "House Divided" speech at Illinois Republican state convention that nominates him for U.S. senator; the "house divided" idea from St. Mark has already been used several times in connection with U.S. controversy over slavery.

July 24. Lincoln challenges Stephen A. Douglas. Democratic candidate, to public debates as part of campaign for election to U.S. Senate. **Aug. 21-Oct. 15.** Debates are held in seven Illinois cities; they are concerned with slavery and its moral, legal, political, and governmental aspects; although locally held, they draw attention of entire U.S. In the election, Lincoln wins a majority of the popular vote, but because of inequities of districting Douglas is reelected by the state legislature.

Oct. 25. Senator William H. Seward of New York, leading Republican presidential aspirant, pronounces the slavery issue an "irrepressible conflict" in speech at Rochester. The remark is ultimately fatal to Seward's presidential ambitions, since it marks him as an antislavery radical.

October-November. In autumn elections, Republicans carry all Northern states except Indiana and Illinois and gain 18 seats in Congress; new House of Representatives has a majority of Republicans and Democrats who are opposed to President Buchanan's Kansas policy.

Business depression that has continued since financial panic of 1857 is over by end of the year, when a period of prosperity begins.

Macy's department store is established in New York City. Its successful use on a

STEPHEN A. DOUGLAS
Speech in Alton, Illinois, 1858
Mr. Lincoln tries to avoid the main issue by attacking the truth of my proposition, that our fathers made this government divided into free and slave states, recognizing the right of each to decide all its local questions for itself. Did they not thus make it? It is true that they did not establish slavery in any of the states or abolish it in any of them; but, finding thirteen states, twelve of which were slave and one free, they agreed to form a government uniting them together as they stood, divided into free and slave states, and to guarantee forever to each state the right to do as it pleased on the slavery question. Having thus made the government and conferred this right upon each state forever, I assert that this government can exist as they made it, divided into free and slave states, if any one state chooses to retain slavery.

He says that he looks forward to a time when slavery shall be abolished everywhere. I look forward to a time when each state shall be allowed to do as it pleases. If it chooses to keep slavery forever, it is not my business, but its own; if it chooses to abolish slavery, it is its own business, not mine. I care more for the great principle of self-government, the right of the people to rule, than I do for all the Negroes in Christendom.

Constitutional Convention in Kansas Territory, December 1855: from "Leslie's Illustrated Newspaper"

OLIVER WENDELL HOLMES
Atlantic Monthly, 1858
*As to giving up because the almanac
or the family Bible says that it is about
time to do it, I have no intention of
doing any such thing. I grant you that I
burn less carbon than some years ago. I
see people of my standing really good
for nothing, decrepit, effete,* la lèvre in-
férieure déjà pendante [*the lower lip
already hanging*], *with what little life
they have left mainly concentrated in
their epigastrium. But as the disease of
old age is epidemic, endemic, and sporadic, and everybody that lives long
enough is sure to catch it, I am going to
say, for the encouragement of such as
need it, how I treat the malady in my
own case.*

*First, as I feel that, when I have any-
thing to do, there is less time for it than
when I was younger, I find that I give
my attention more thoroughly and use
my time more economically than ever
before; so that I can learn anything
twice as easily as in my earlier days. I
am not, therefore, afraid to attack a new
study. I took up a difficult language a
very few years ago with good success,
and think of mathematics and metaphysics by-and-by.*

*Second, I have opened my eyes to a
good many neglected privileges and
pleasures within my reach and requiring only a little courage to enjoy them.
You may well suppose it pleased me to
find that old Cato was thinking of learning to play the fiddle, when I had deliberately taken it up in my old age and
satisfied myself that I could get much
comfort, if not much music, out of it.*

*Third, I have found that some of
those active exercises, which are commonly thought to belong to young folks
only, may be enjoyed at a much later
period.*

large scale of a fixed-price policy, developed
in smaller New York stores since 1840, establishes an American retail sales custom.

Oliver Wendell Holmes publishes his
witty, conversational volume *The Autocrat
of the Breakfast-Table*, followed in later years
by *The Professor at the Breakfast-Table* and
The Poet at the Breakfast-Table; initially, all
appeared as serials. Henry Wadsworth
Longfellow publishes *The Courtship of Miles
Standish*, a long narrative poem in the same
meter as *Evangeline*; it is a love story based
on a traditional Pilgrim triangle.

1858 - 1859

1858. Rush of gold seekers to Colorado
starts when gold is discovered near present-
day Denver, although amount of gold is
small; slogan of the time is "Pikes Peak or
bust!" **May 6, 1859.** Rush increases when
first gold-bearing vein is found in Colorado.
June. Comstock Lode is discovered in Virginia City, Nevada; one of the world's richest deposits, it yields $300 million of gold
and silver in following 20 years.

1859

Feb. 14. Oregon is admitted to the
Union as the thirty-third state, and eighteenth free state; population is about
50,000.

May 9-19. Southern Commercial Convention at Vicksburg, Mississippi, advocates
repeal of U.S. laws prohibiting importation
of slaves.

Aug. 27. Edwin L. Drake, drilling with
steam-operated rig, finds oil near Titusville,
Pennsylvania, marking beginning of large-
scale petroleum industry. Petroleum rapidly
replaces whale oil as a lamp fuel.

Oct. 16. Abolitionist John Brown,

hoping to inspire a general slave insurrection and backed by six prominent Northerners, leads 18 of his 21 men, including 5 Negroes, in seizure of U.S. arsenal at Harpers Ferry, Virginia; he takes about 60 hostages and is able to hold off local militia, but no Negroes arrive to support him. **Oct. 18.** He surrenders to small force of U.S. Marines under Colonel Robert E. Lee; Brown is wounded, and 10 men, including 2 of his sons, are dead. **Dec. 2.** Brown is hanged after trial and conviction on charges of treason and conspiring with slaves to commit murder. Six of his men are hanged later. The raid spreads alarm throughout the South, and Ralph Waldo Emerson says: "He will make the gallows as glorious as the cross."

Dec. 19. President Buchanan's message to Congress affirms U.S. commitment to enforce slave importation laws, but administration also provides for protection of U.S. merchant ships from search, which allows foreign ships illegally flying U.S. flag to avoid British antislavery patrol of African coast.

Cooper Union, institute mainly for adult education, is established in New York City by Peter Cooper, pioneer industrialist and inventor, "for the advancement of science and art."

1860

Feb. 22. Strike of 20,000 New England shoe-industry workers, including many women, wins higher wages and demonstrates power of industry-wide protest.

Feb. 27. Abraham Lincoln speaks at Cooper Union in New York City, his first important appearance in the East; he appeals for understanding between North and South and criticizes extremists of both sections.

JOHN BROWN
Last Speech to the Court, 1859
I have, may it please the Court, a few words to say.

In the first place, I deny everything but what I have all along admitted, of a design on my part to free the slaves. . . . I never did intend murder, or treason, or the destruction of property, or to excite or incite the slaves to rebellion, or to make insurrection. . . .

This court acknowledges, too, as I suppose, the validity of the law of God. I see a book kissed here which I suppose to be the Bible, or at least the New Testament, which teaches me that all things whatsoever I would that men should do to me, I should do even so to them. It teaches me, further, to remember them that are in bonds as bound with them. I endeavored to act up to that instruction. I say I am yet too young to understand that God is any respecter of persons. I believe that to have interfered as I have done — as I have always freely admitted I have done — in behalf of His despised poor is no wrong but right.

Now, if it is deemed necessary that I should forfeit my life for the furtherance of the ends of justice and mingle my blood further with the blood of my children and with the blood of millions in this slave country whose rights are disregarded by wicked, cruel, and unjust enactments — I say, let it be done!

(Above) Franklin Pierce, fourteenth
President of the United States: portrait by
G.P.A. Healy; (right) Japanese watercolor
depicting Commodore Matthew C. Perry;
(below) cartoon criticizing James Buchanan
for declaring in the Ostend Manifesto of
1854 that the United States was justified in
using force to obtain Cuba from Spain

(Above) "The Great Republican Reform Party calling on their
candidate": lithograph pertaining to the Republicans in their
first national convention in 1856. John C. Fremont, candidate
for the presidency, is shown at right; (below) Buchanan,
fourth from left, and his Cabinet, 1856

Mississippi Senator Jefferson Davis, who in 1861 became President of the Confederate States of America

HERMAN MELVILLE

Misgivings, 1860

When ocean-clouds over inland hills
  Sweep storming in late autumn brown,
And horror the sodden valley fills,
  And the spire falls crashing in the town,

I muse upon my country's ills—
  The tempest bursting from the waste of Time
On the world's fairest hope linked with man's foulest crime.

Nature's dark side is heeded now—
  (Ah! optimist-cheer disheartened flown)—
A child may read the moody brow
  Of yon black mountain lone.
With shouts the torrents down the gorges go,
  And storms are formed behind the storm we feel:
The hemlock shakes in the rafter, the oak in the driving keel.

May 9. Constitutional Union Party, made up of combination of remnants of Whig and Know-Nothing parties, nominates John Bell of Tennessee for President and Edward Everett of Massachusetts for Vice-President; platform criticizes sectionalism and calls for "enforcement of the laws" of the Constitution. May 18. Abraham Lincoln of Illinois, regarded as a moderate on the slavery question, is nominated by the Republicans at Chicago convention; Hannibal Hamlin of Maine is nominated for Vice-President. Well-written platform is planned to win radicals as well as conservatives of West and East; it supports principles of Wilmot Proviso, domestic improvements, liberal immigration laws, and industrial development.

June 18. Democrats nominate Stephen A. Douglas for President on platform that supports territorial right to choose slavery without intervention by Congress. June 28. Radical delegates from eight Southern states bolt the party and nominate John C. Breckinridge of Kentucky; their platform supports territorial slavery.

Nov. 6. Abraham Lincoln is elected sixteenth President of the United States with 1,866,000 votes to 1,383,000 for Douglas, 848,000 for Breckinridge, and 593,000 for Bell. Vote is almost completely sectional: electoral vote is Lincoln, 180 (18 free states); Breckinridge, 72 (11 slave states); Bell, 39 (3 border slave states); and Douglas, 12 (Missouri and 3 New Jersey votes). Hannibal Hamlin is elected Vice-President.

Nov. 10. On receiving news of Lincoln's election, South Carolina legislature calls special state convention to meet at Columbia on December 20.

Dec. 3. President Buchanan in his State of the Union message decries disruption of the Union but declares, after consultation with the attorney general, that the federal government has no legal power to prevent it by force.

Dec. 18. Senator John J. Crittenden of Kentucky offers resolution in attempt to conciliate South; it calls for recognition of slavery everywhere south of 36°30' parallel. Dec. 31. Senate committee, urged by President-elect Lincoln, rejects resolution on the ground that its principle has been repudiated in the recent election.

Dec. 20. South Carolina secedes from the Union by unanimous vote at special convention. Dec. 24. Convention issues "Declaration of Immediate Causes," which affirms right of state sovereignty, condemns the North's attack on slavery, and refuses to be governed by a President who is hostile to slavery.

Oliver F. Winchester of New Haven, Connecticut, patents lever-action repeating rifle, first of many Winchesters; with superior manufacturing capacity of North, weapon gives important arms advantage in ensuing war.

1860 - 1861

April 3, 1860. Pony Express begins fast overland mail service from St. Joseph, Missouri, to Sacramento, California, a distance of more than 1,900 miles. Ten-day service to Sacramento is frequently achieved by riders changing horses at 157 stations 7 to 20 miles apart; fastest time under emergency circumstances is seven days, seven hours. Oct. 24, 1861. Pony Express is discontinued with completion of transcontinental telegraph. A financial failure, it has proved valuable at critical period in informing West Coast of news from Washington.

Dec. 30, 1860-Feb. 16, 1861. Federal arsenals and forts are seized by Southern state

MARK TWAIN
Roughing It, 1872
In a little while all interest was taken up in stretching our necks and watching for the "pony rider"—the fleet messenger who sped across the continent from St. Joe to Sacramento, carrying letters nineteen hundred miles in eight days! Think of that for perishable horse and human flesh and blood to do! . . .

Somehow or other all that passed us and all that met us managed to streak by in the night, and so we heard only a whiz and a hail, and the swift phantom of the desert was gone before we could get our heads out of the windows. But now we were expecting one along every moment and would see him in broad daylight. Presently the driver exclaims:

"Here he comes!"

Every neck is stretched farther and every eye strained wider. Away across the endless dead level of the prairie a black speck appears against the sky, and it is plain that it moves. Well, I should think so! In a second or two it becomes a horse and rider, rising and falling, rising and falling—sweeping toward us nearer and nearer—growing more and more distinct, more and more sharply defined—nearer and still nearer, and the flutter of the hoofs comes faintly to the ear—another instant a whoop and a hurrah from our upper deck, a wave of the rider's hand, but no reply, and man and horse burst past our excited faces and go swinging away like a belated fragment of a storm!

So sudden is it all and so like a flash of unreal fancy that, but for the flake of white foam left quivering and perishing on a mail sack after the vision had flashed by and disappeared, we might have doubted whether we had seen any actual horse and man at all, maybe.

GEN. WINFIELD SCOTT
Letter to William H. Seward, 1861
Say to the seceded states, "Wayward sisters, depart in peace."

JEFFERSON DAVIS
Inaugural Address, 1861
All we ask is to be left alone.

FERNANDO WOOD
Address to New York City Council, 1861
With our aggrieved brethren of the slave states we have friendly relations and a common sympathy. We have not participated in the warfare upon their constitutional rights or their domestic institutions. . . . Our ships have penetrated to every clime, and so have New York capital, energy, and enterprise found their way to every state, and, indeed, to almost every county and town of the American Union. . . . New York has a right to expect, and should endeavor to preserve, a continuance of uninterrupted intercourse with every section. . . .

If the confederacy is broken up, the government is dissolved; and it behooves every distinct community, as well as every individual, to take care of themselves.

When disunion has become a fixed and certain fact, why may not New York disrupt the bands which bind her to a venal and corrupt master — to a people and a party that have plundered her revenues, attempted to ruin her commerce, taken away the power of self-government, and destroyed the confederacy of which she was the proud Empire City? Amid the gloom which the present and prospective condition of things must cast over the country, New York, as a free city, may shed the only light and hope of a future reconstruction of our once blessed confederacy.

troops in South Carolina, Georgia, Alabama, Florida, Louisiana, Arkansas, and Texas. All these states eventually secede; most occupy federal property before formal secession occurs.

1861

Jan. 9. President Buchanan attempts to send reinforcements and provisions to federal garrison at Fort Sumter in Charleston Harbor, South Carolina. Unarmed supply vessel is repelled by cannonade from South Carolina batteries.

Jan. 9-Feb. 1. Six more Southern states secede from the Union: Mississippi, Florida, Alabama, Georgia, Louisiana, and Texas; all cite interference of North with their "institutions" as reason; secessionists are jubilant, but feeling in Alabama and Georgia is moderate and vote on measure almost fails to pass. Virginia, Arkansas, Tennessee, and North Carolina do not secede at this time but warn against federal interference with any state.

Jan. 29. Kansas is admitted to the Union as thirty-fourth state and nineteenth free state; its population is 107,000.

Feb. 4-23. Twenty-one Northern, Border, and Southern states send representatives to Washington, D.C., peace conference called by Virginia. Proposal agreed on is almost the same as Crittenden Compromise. President-elect Lincoln, still in Springfield, Illinois, advises against measure; Senate committee rejects it on eve of inauguration.

Feb. 4-March 11. Seven seceded states, aware of necessity for central government, send delegates to Montgomery, Alabama, to form new Southern union. **Feb. 8.** Provisional government is set up for Confederate States of America. **Feb. 9.** Jefferson Davis of Mississippi is elected President and Alexander H. Stephens of Georgia (who has three months earlier publicly opposed secession) Vice-President for six-year terms.

February. Henry Timrod of South Carolina publishes his ode "Ethnogenesis," which expresses hope for a Southern civilization and, with later passionate war poems, earns him the title of "the laureate of the Confederacy."

March 2. Congress reestablishes protection of U.S. industry by enacting Morrill Tariff, with duties on specific import items instead of on the value of imported goods, at the same time raising duties to 10 percent. Policy continues, with a gradual rise in duties to 47 percent average, until 1870.

March 4. Abraham Lincoln is inaugurated President of the U.S. His inaugural address asserts that the Union is indestructible, urges reconciliation of North and South, denies any intention of using force anywhere except to occupy government property, and reminds South that without an aggressor there can be no conflict.

March 5. President Lincoln discovers that garrison at Fort Sumter will be starved out if not provisioned. **April 6.** After long hesitation, and faced with the dilemma of risking civil war or conceding weakness of the federal government, Lincoln decides (after advising South Carolina governor that no arms are involved) to send an unsupported supply expedition. **April 12.** Without waiting for arrival of expedition, Confederates open fire on the fort, which is forced to surrender on April 14.

March 11. Permanent constitution of the Confederate States of America is adopted; it resembles U.S. Constitution but forbids enactment by Congress of a protective tariff or measures for internal improvements and requires a two-thirds vote of the House of

ABRAHAM LINCOLN
Inaugural Address, 1861
Apprehension seems to exist among the people of the Southern states that, by the accession of a Republican administration, their property and their peace and personal security are to be endangered. There has never been any reasonable cause for such apprehension. Indeed, the most ample evidence to the contrary has all the while existed and been open to their inspection. It is found in nearly all the published speeches of him who now addresses you. . . .

I hold that, in contemplation of universal law and of the Constitution, the Union of these states is perpetual. Perpetuity is implied, if not expressed, in the fundamental law of all national governments. It is safe to assert that no government proper ever had a provision in its organic law for its own termination. Continue to execute all the express provisions of our national Constitution, and the Union will endure forever — it being impossible to destroy it except by some action not provided for in the instrument itself. . . .

Plainly, the central idea of secession is the essence of anarchy. A majority, held in restraint by constitutional checks and limitations . . . is the only true sovereign of a free people. Whoever rejects it does of necessity fly to anarchy or to despotism. . . .

In your hands, my dissatisfied fellow countrymen, and not in mine is the momentous issue of civil war. The government will not assail you. You can have no conflict without being yourselves the aggressors. You have no oath registered in heaven to destroy the government, while I shall have the most solemn one to "preserve, protect, and defend" it.

MARY BOYKIN CHESNUT

Diary, 1861

Fort Sumter has been on fire. Anderson has not yet silenced any of our guns. So the aides, still with swords and red sashes by way of uniform, tell us. But the sound of those guns makes regular meals impossible. None of us go to table. Tea trays pervade the corridors going everywhere. Some of the anxious hearts lie on their beds and moan in solitary misery. Mrs. Wigfall and I solace ourselves with tea in my room. These women have all a satisfying faith. "God is on our side," they say. When we are shut in, Mrs. Wigfall and I ask "Why?" "Of course, He hates the Yankees," we are told. "You'll think that well of Him."

Not by one word or look can we detect any change in the demeanor of these Negro servants. Lawrence sits at our door, sleepy and respectful and profoundly indifferent. So are they all, but they carry it too far. You could not tell that they even heard the awful roar going on in the bay, though it has been dinning in their ears night and day. People talk before them as if they were chairs and tables. They make no sign. Are they stolidly stupid, or wiser than we are; silent and strong, biding their time?

ABRAHAM LINCOLN

We, on our side, are praying to Him to give us victory, because we believe we are right; but those on the other side pray to Him, look for victory, believing they are right. What must He think of us?

Representatives for any appropriation. African slave trade is prohibited (to appease France and Britain), but no "law denying or impairing the right of property in Negro slaves" is allowed.

April 15. President Lincoln, in effort to minimize Fort Sumter attack, calls for 75,000 militia to suppress "insurrection." **April 17-May 20.** Free states respond, but move provokes remaining Southern states — Virginia, Arkansas, Tennessee, and North Carolina — to secede and join the Confederacy. **May 21.** Richmond, Virginia, is chosen as capital of the Confederacy. Some of the ablest officers of the U.S. Army resign, including Robert E. Lee of Virginia, who previously has been offered the post of commander of the Union Army.

April 19. President Lincoln proclaims blockade of Southern ports; the Union has few effective naval ships but possesses the industrial capacity to build more, and the Confederacy has few major ports to be closed. Dependent on the North and Europe for manufactured goods, the Confederacy is gradually strangled by the increasingly effective blockade and eventual capture of its ports by Union armies. In the first year of the blockade, less than one-seventh as many ships reach Southern ports as in 1860.

May 3. The President calls for 42,000 volunteers to serve three-year enlistments and 40,000 additional men for regular Army and Navy.

May-July. Power of the President to suspend habeas corpus privilege or delegate this power to military commanders is challenged early in war. In the *Ex parte Merryman* case, a civilian Maryland secessionist protesting his arrest by Union military forces, Chief Justice Roger B. Taney, sitting as judge of a federal circuit court, holds that the power to suspend constitutional rights belongs only to Congress, even in wartime. **July.** President Lincoln justifies action of his administration in a message to Congress, which votes approval. Power of military agencies over civilians, both near the fighting and in the interior of the Union, is questioned throughout the war and Reconstruction era.

June 11. Western counties of Virginia, in bitter conflict with eastern areas from colonial times, form provisional state government loyal to the Union shortly after Virginia secedes. **Nov.-Feb. 1862.** Constitution is prepared, changing proposed state name Kanawha (place of white stone) to West Virginia.

July 21. First Battle of Bull Run, at Manassas Junction, Virginia, appears at first to be Union victory, but Confederate reinforcements beat back Union troops in a disorganized retreat to Washington. Confederate General Thomas J. Jackson makes a gallant stand, earning the nickname "Stonewall." As Confederate success exposes Washington to threat of capture, the North realizes that war effort must be serious and may be protracted. **July 24.** President Lincoln replaces General Irvin McDowell with Major General George B. McClellan, who is later made general in chief of the Union Army. Armies in the East on both sides are mostly inactive for months afterward, devoting themselves to organization, equipment, and training.

Aug. 5. First federal income tax of 3 percent on incomes over $800 is enacted; increased in following years, it supplies about one-fifth of federal government revenues by 1865, but the war is financed chiefly by loans and currency issues.

Oct. 24. First transcontinental telegraph begins operation. Continuation of existing

ROBERT E. LEE
Letter to Gen. Winfield Scott, 1861
General:

Since my interview with you on the 18th instant, I have felt that I ought no longer to retain my commission in the Army. I, therefore, tender my resignation, which I request you will recommend for acceptance. It would have been presented at once but for the struggle it has cost me to separate myself from a service to which I have devoted the best years of my life and all the ability I possessed.

During the whole of that time — more than a quarter of a century — I have experienced nothing but kindness from my superiors and the most cordial friendship from my comrades. To no one, General, have I been as much indebted as to yourself for uniform kindness and consideration; and it has always been my ardent desire to meet your approbation. I shall carry to the grave the most grateful recollections of your kind consideration, and your name and fame will always be dear to me.

Save in defense of my native state, I never desire again to draw my sword.

Be pleased to accept my most earnest wishes for the continuance of your happiness and prosperity.

GEN. BERNARD ELLIOTT BEE
At first Battle of Bull Run, 1861
Let us determine to die here, and we will conquer. There is Jackson standing like a stone wall. Rally behind the Virginians!

ETHEL LYNN BEERS

All Quiet Along the Potomac To-Night,
1861

"All quiet along the Potomac," they say,
 "Except here and there a stray picket
Is shot, as he walks on his beat, to and
 fro,
 By a rifleman hid in the thicket.
'Tis nothing—a private or two now
 and then
 Will not count in the news of the
 battle;
Not an officer lost, only one of the men
 Moaning out all alone the death
 rattle."

 . . .

There's only the sound of the lone
 sentry's tread,
 As he tramps from the rock to the
 fountain,
And thinks of the two on the low trundle
 bed,
 Far away in the cot on the moun-
 tain.

 . . .

Hark! was it the night wind that rustles
 the leaves?
 Was it the moonlight so wondrously
 flashing?
It looked like a rifle! "Ha! Mary, good-
 bye!"
 And his lifeblood is ebbing and
 splashing.
"All quiet along the Potomac to-night,"
 No sound save the rush of the river;
While soft falls the dew on the face of
 the dead,
 The picket's off duty forever.

line that reaches from East Coast to Missouri has been authorized by Congress in June 1860; in 16 months, with enormous difficulty, linemen have strung wire to San Francisco; making a total of 3,500 miles of telegraph line, open for use at both ends.

Nov. 8. Confederate agents James M. Mason and John Slidell, on the way to seek diplomatic recognition from England and France, are removed from British mail steamer *Trent* by order of U.S. naval vessel. Incident produces strong popular and official disapproval in Britain, where it is called a "violation of neutral right." War talk in Britain is calmed by the tactful joint efforts of Prince Consort Albert and President Lincoln. **Dec. 26.** Secretary of State Seward finally placates British by ordering release of the two Confederates.

Dec. 20. Congress appoints a Joint Committee on the Conduct of the War, dominated by radical Republicans who urge immediate emancipation of slaves, demand action by the almost idle Union armies, and protest Lincoln's assumption of extensive emergency powers.

At outset of the war, 11 Confederate states oppose 23 Union states (including California and Oregon, which are too far away to take part in hostilities). Population of the Confederacy is 9 million, including 3,500,000 slaves; population of the Union is 22 million. Small U.S. Army, except for one-third of the officers, is on the Union side, as is entire Navy. The South has been dependent on the North for virtually all products except food. But the Union must carry attack to the South, which is thinly populated and lacks roads and railroads, making long supply lines necessary. Both sides must build armies, and, in doing so, the Confederacy has advantage of a majority of the best officers from the U.S. Army who have resigned when their states seceded; Southern men, accustomed to outdoor life, are more easily trained as soldiers than Northerners (except for those from the West); Northerners are mostly city men and foreign immigrants. Equipping armies is a problem to both sides, but the Union is vastly superior in materials and manufacturing ability.

Dakota Territory is formed from parts of Minnesota and Nebraska territories; Colorado Territory from parts of territories of Utah, New Mexico, Kansas, and Nebraska; and Nevada Territory from part of Utah Territory.

U.S. mails begin for first time to carry merchandise as well as letters.

Yale University awards first Ph.D. degree in U.S.; graduate school has been established in 1847. Vassar Female College opens at Poughkeepsie, New York; it is nonsectarian and endowed by Matthew Vassar.

1861 - 1862

Jan. 3, 1861-March 8, 1862. Border slave states remain loyal to Union — Delaware unanimously, Maryland and Kentucky after failure of efforts to remain neutral, and Missouri only after a year-long intrastate civil war in which Union forces are victorious.

1861 - 1863

May 13, 1861. Great Britain declares neutrality; recognizes belligerent status but not independence of Confederacy; other European states soon do the same. British sentiment is divided, with the working class and most of the middle class favoring the free democratic North, while the upper classes, with some notable exceptions, tend to favor the "aristocratic" South. British

Scientific American, 1861
Although the vast insurrection has exerted a disorganizing influence upon many manufactures and other branches of business, it is really wonderful to witness the elasticity of our people and the facility with which they have adapted themselves to altered circumstances. Many old branches of industry have been destroyed, but new ones have sprung up, and there is now a great amount of industrial prosperity enjoyed in most of the manufacturing sections of our country.

The war has stimulated the genius of our people and directed it to the service of our country. Sixty-six new inventions relating to engines, implements, and articles of warfare have been illustrated in our columns. . . .

Other departments of industry have also been well represented. Our inventors have not devoted themselves exclusively to the invention of destructive implements; they have also cultivated the arts of peace. . . . In thus summing up our yearly progress in a general way, we can safely assert that for original and well-studied efforts of genius, they equal if they do not surpass the inventions of any former year. And as the number of patents issued is a very good exponent of the progress of our country, we can point to no less than 2,919, which is equal to the number (2,910) issued in 1857—four years ago. When the defection of eleven states and the distractions of our country are taken into consideration, it is not too much to assert that our inventors have done better last year than ever before, and that inventions are perhaps the most safe and profitable sources of investment in times of war as well as peace.

GEN. WILLIAM T. SHERMAN
Letter to John Sherman, 1863
We have reproached the South for arbitrary conduct in coercing their people; at last we find we must imitate their example. We have denounced their tyranny in filling their armies with conscripts, and now we must follow her example. We have denounced their tyranny in suppressing freedom of speech and the press, and here, too, in time, we must follow their example. The longer it is deferred the worse it becomes. Who gave notice of McDowell's movement on Manassas and enabled Johnston so to reinforce Beauregard that our army was defeated? The press. Who gave notice of the movement on Vicksburg? The press. Who has prevented all secret combinations and movements against our enemy? The press. . . .

In the South this powerful machine was at once scotched and used by the Rebel government, but in the North was allowed to go free. What are the results? After arousing the passions of the people till the two great sections hate each other with a hate hardly paralleled in history, it now begins to stir up sedition at home, and even to encourage mutiny in our armies. . . .

I say with the press unfettered as now we are defeated to the end of time. 'Tis folly to say the people must have news.

WILBUR F. STOREY
Statement of Aims of the Chicago Times, 1861
It is a newspaper's duty to print the news, and raise hell.

commercial interests, affected by U.S. tariffs and the prospect of free trade with an independent South, tend to favor the Confederacy; on the other hand, Britain is concerned about the prospect of a Union invasion of Canada if Britain offers any real aid. The South believes that Britain and France depend on Southern cotton exports, and that it will be only a short time before these countries are forced to both recognize and help the Confederacy. Actually, Britain has large surplus of cotton from previous year and need for Northern food grains affects British policy to a much greater extent. British government waits for decisive Confederate military successes before venturing beyond formal neutrality; such successes never come. Meanwhile, British sentiment favors Union increasingly, and decisively after Emancipation Proclamation of January 1, 1863.

Aug. 11. The *New York Daily News* loses postal privileges and is suspended for 18 months for such open hostility to the war effort that it is considered aid to the enemy. Five other Northern papers are seized or suspended for the same reason from 1861 to 1863, but President Lincoln is firm in prohibiting interference with publications unless "they are working palpable injury to the military."

1861 - 1865

Popular songs of the period are chiefly war songs. The North sings "John Brown's Body" and, later, Julia Ward Howe's "Battle Hymn of the Republic" to the same tune; "We Are Coming Father Abraham" is written in response to the President's appeal for 300,000 more soldiers; "Tramp! Tramp! Tramp!" and "Marching Through Georgia" are written near the end of the war. "Tenting on the Old Camp Ground" and "When Johnny Comes Marching Home" originate in the North but are soon taken up by the South as well. Most popular Southern songs are "Dixie" and "The Bonnie Blue Flag."

1862

In effort to secure the Mississippi River and thus split the Confederacy, Union forces in the West commanded by General Henry W. Halleck aim at Fort Henry on the Tennessee River and Fort Donelson on the Cumberland. **Feb. 6.** General Ulysses S. Grant takes Fort Henry with help of Union gunboats. **Feb. 16.** Grant takes Fort Donelson, defended by 15,000 Confederate troops. **Feb. 24.** General Don Carlos Buell occupies Nashville, Tennessee, which has been abandoned by Confederate troops on news of Fort Donelson defeat. General Albert S. Johnston, commander of Confederate forces in West, is forced to withdraw to railroad center of Corinth, Mississippi. South has lost Kentucky and half of Tennessee.

Feb. 25. Congress authorizes first U.S. legal tender bank notes; by 1865 more than $400 million in "greenbacks" has been issued. At first these stimulate business activity, but by end of the war they have depreciated to 39 cents gold equivalent per dollar.

March 6-8. Union forces defeat Confederates at Pea Ridge, Arkansas; this almost ends hostilities west of the Mississippi River and secures Missouri, to the north, for the Union.

March 8. Ironclad vessel *Virginia* (originally sunken federal ship *Merrimack* that has been raised by the Confederates and armored with iron plates) sinks two Northern ships at Hampton Roads. **March 9.** Northern ironclad *Monitor*, just arrived, engages *Virginia*; battle is inconclusive, but continued presence of *Virginia* at mouth of James

HORACE GREELEY
Open Letter to Lincoln, 1862
On the face of this wide earth, Mr. President, there is not one disinterested, determined, intelligent champion of the Union cause who does not feel that all attempts to put down the rebellion and at the same time uphold its inciting cause are preposterous and futile; that the rebellion, if crushed out tomorrow, would be renewed within a year if slavery were left in full vigor; that Army officers who remain to this day devoted to slavery can at best be but halfway loyal to the Union; and that every hour of deference to slavery is an hour of added and deepened peril to the Union.

ABRAHAM LINCOLN
Reply to Greeley, 1862
As to the policy I "seem to be pursuing," as you say, I have not meant to leave anyone in doubt.

I would save the Union. I would save it the shortest way under the Constitution. The sooner the national authority can be restored, the nearer the Union will be "the Union as it was." If there be those who would not save the Union unless they could at the same time save slavery, I do not agree with them. If there be those who would not save the Union unless they could at the same time destroy slavery, I do not agree with them. My paramount object in this struggle is to save the Union, and is not either to save or destroy slavery. If I could save the Union without freeing any slave, I would do it; and if I could save it by freeing all the slaves, I would do it; and If I could do it by freeing some and leaving others alone, I would also do that.

JOSEPH E. BROWN
Letter to Jefferson Davis, 1862
Georgia has promptly responded to every call made upon her by you for troops, and has always given more than you asked. She has now about 60,000 in the field. Had you called upon her executive for 20,000 more (if her just quota), they would have been furnished without delay. The plea of necessity, so far at least as this state is concerned, cannot be set up in defense of the Conscription Act. When the government of the United States disregarded and attempted to trample upon the rights of the states, Georgia set its power at defiance and seceded from the Union rather than submit to the consolidation of all power in the hands of the central or federal government. The Conscription Act not only put it in the power of the executive of the Confederacy to disorganize her troops, which she was compelled to call into the field for her own defense in addition to her just quota because of the neglect of the Confederacy to place sufficient troops upon her coast for her defense, which would have required less than half the number she has sent to the field, but also places it in his power to destroy her state government by disbanding her lawmaking power. . . .

While I shall throw no obstructions in the way of the general enrollment of persons embraced within the act, except as above stated, I do not feel that it is the duty of the executive of a state to employ actually the officers of the state in the execution of a law which virtually strips the state of her constitutional military powers, and, if fully executed, destroys the legislative department of her government, making even the sessions of her General Assembly dependent upon the will of the Confederate executive.

River prevents General George B. McClellan, commander of Army of the Potomac, from using river as a route for attack on Richmond, as planned.

March-April. General McClellan's forces land on Virginia peninsula. **April 5.** Yorktown is laid under siege lasting until May 5. McClellan has expected to take Yorktown quickly with help from Navy and from troops under General Irvin McDowell, but Navy is blocked by the *Virginia*, and President Lincoln has held McDowell to protect Washington, D.C.

April 6. Grant and his force reach Pittsburg Landing, Tennessee, 30 miles north of Corinth, where Buell is to join him; Confederate Generals Johnston and Pierre Beauregard attack before Buell arrives, nearly defeating Grant. **April 7.** Buell's troops having come during night, Grant forces Confederates back to Corinth with huge losses on both sides; 13,000 Union casualties and 11,000 Confederate, including General Johnston, killed on first day.

April 11. General Halleck joins Grant and Buell, and they proceed down Mississippi River. **May 30.** Beauregard evacuates Corinth. **June 3.** Memphis is taken.

April 16. No longer able to rely on enlistments, Confederacy passes Conscription Act, making all white males from 18 to 35 years old liable to three-year draft administered by central government. Exemptions because of occupation, privilege of paying substitutes, fraud, and evasions cause wide discontent, especially among the poor. Desertions during war amount to about 10 percent of army.

April 24-25. Flag Officer David G. Farragut with U.S. Gulf Squadron sails past forts guarding New Orleans at mouth of Mississippi River. Abandoned by its garrison, New Orleans surrenders. **May 1.** City is occupied by General Benjamin F. Butler; South's largest city is thereafter held by the North until end of the war.

April. Union spy James J. Andrews and 20 men capture railroad engine behind Confederate lines in Georgia, run it toward Chattanooga, Tennessee, destroying telegraph lines as they go. Chased and captured by Confederate troops in second engine, Andrews and seven of his men are hanged.

May 15. U.S. Department of Agriculture established; department has been agricultural branch of the Patent Office. Commissioner is not given Cabinet rank until 1889.

May 16. McClellan arrives within striking distance of Richmond, the Confederate capital, and awaits reinforcements, but Confederate command has sent General "Stonewall" Jackson along Shenandoah Valley toward Washington in effort to hold Union reinforcements back. **May 31.** Confederate General Joseph E. Johnston attacks McClellan. In two-day battle, Johnston is at first successful but then retires toward Richmond; he is wounded, and General Robert E. Lee takes over command.

May 20. Homestead Act grants free family-size parcels of public land to actual settlers after five years' residence. Encouragement of agricultural expansion results in crops able to meet Union demands as well as those of Europe, where harvests have been small. England requires Northern wheat as much as Southern cotton.

May. Thaddeus Lowe, balloonist, is first to make aerial photographs for military purposes when he records entire Richmond area for the Union in 64 overlapping photographs; Lowe is also first to carry telegraphic transmitter aloft to direct artillery fire and troop movements.

Homestead Act, 1862
Be it enacted . . . *that any person who is the head of a family, or who has arrived at the age of twenty-one years, and is a citizen of the United States, or who shall have filed his declaration of intention to become such, as required by the naturalization laws of the United States, and who has never borne arms against the United States government or given aid and comfort to its enemies, shall, from and after January 1, 1863, be entitled to enter one quarter section or a less quantity of unappropriated public lands, upon which said person may have filed a preemption claim . . . to be located in a body, in conformity to the legal subdivisions of the public lands, and after the same shall have been surveyed.*

Morrill Act, 1862
And be it further enacted, *that all moneys derived from the sale of the lands aforesaid by the state to which the lands are apportioned, and from the sales of land scrip hereinbefore provided for, shall be invested in stocks of the United States, or of the states, or some other safe stocks . . . the interest of which shall be inviolably appropriated, by each state which may take and claim the benefit of this act, to the endowment, support, and maintenance of at least one college where the leading object shall be, without excluding other scientific and classical studies, and including military tactics, to teach such branches of learning as are related to agriculture and the mechanic arts . . . in order to promote the liberal and practical education of the industrial classes in the several pursuits and professions in life.*

Liberator, 1862

We, the colored citizens of Queens County, N.Y., having met in mass meeting . . . to consider the speech of Abraham Lincoln . . . addressed to a committee of Free Colored Men, called at his request at the White House . . . on Thursday, August 14, 1862, and to express our views and opinions . . . on the subject of being colonized in Central America or some other foreign country . . . take the present opportunity to express our opinions most respectfully and freely. . . .

First, we rejoice that we are colored Americans, but deny that we are a "different race of people," as God has made of one blood all nations that dwell on the face of the earth. . . .

This is our native country; we have as strong attachment naturally to [it] . . . as any other people. Nor can we fail to feel a strong attachment to the whites with whom our blood has been commingling from the earliest days of this our country. . . .

We love this land and have contributed our share to its prosperity and wealth. . . .

We are called upon by the President of the United States to leave this land and go to another country, to carry out his favorite scheme of colonization. But at this crisis, we feel disposed to refuse the offers of the President, since the call of our suffering country is too loud and imperative to be unheeded. . . .

Why not declare slavery abolished and favor our peaceful colonization in the Rebel states, or some portion of them? . . . We would cheerfully return there and give our most willing aid to deliver our loyal colored brethren and other Unionists from the tyranny of rebels to our government.

June 12-15. Confederate General James E. B. ("Jeb") Stuart, called the "eyes" of Lee's army, leads daring cavalry raid, traveling around entire Union Army in three days with loss of only one man; raid briefly threatens Washington from North, gains information about Union troop movements, and improves Southern morale.

June 25. McClellan, four miles from Richmond, telegraphs President Lincoln that he is about to attack, but he is too late; Lee's army, reinforced by Jackson's, numbers 85,000. **June 26-July 1.** Lee attacks McClellan in first of series of battles called The Seven Days. Battles are inconclusive, but McClellan, feeling hopelessly outnumbered (although his forces are actually superior), retreats to the James River.

July 2. Morrill Land Grant Act authorizes sales of public land in each state loyal to the Union for endowment of state agricultural education. The act in effect creates the great state universities with income from sale of 17 million acres.

July 11. President Lincoln yields to political pressure and replaces McClellan with General Halleck, who has come to Washington from Western campaign. **July 25.** Halleck orders McClellan's army to northern Virginia to join with General John Pope's forces.

Aug. 25-27. General Lee, anxious to attack Pope before McClellan can reach him, sends Jackson on swing through Bull Run Mountains to attack from the rear at Manassas Junction. **Aug. 29-30.** Pope attacks Jackson but is unsuccessful and next day attacks Lee's newly arrived forces, which sweep his army back toward Washington. **Sept. 3.** Beaten Union Army retires to protection of Washington fortifications.

Sept. 7. Lee, hoping to convince Europe

of Confederate strength and win Maryland for the South by fighting on Union soil, invades Maryland, sending (Sept. 10) half his forces under Jackson to capture Harpers Ferry. On same day McClellan starts slow march toward Lee from Washington. **Sept. 13.** McClellan finds copy of Lee's orders and learns Confederate Army is split; Lee, discovering this, takes up position (Sept. 14) with his half of army at Sharpsburg, behind Antietam Creek. **Sept. 17.** McClellan, having waited too long before taking advantage of his knowledge, attacks Lee, who by this time has been reinforced. **Sept. 18.** Although Lee's army has remained firm through a bloody battle (12,000 Northern and 10,000 Southern casualties), his losses are so heavy that he is forced to retreat to Virginia. His stay in Maryland has not been long enough to impress either Europe or the citizens of Maryland.

Sept. 22. On the strength of the Antietam victory, President Lincoln issues preliminary Emancipation Proclamation, to take effect on January 1, 1863, in areas still in rebellion on that date. Previous acts of local military commanders have emancipated some slaves. Slavery has already been abolished, with compensation to owners, in District of Columbia on April 16, and, without compensation, in all territories on June 19. Act of Congress on August 6, 1861, has emancipated slaves used by the South against Union forces as labor or under arms; another act, on July 17, 1862, has freed slaves who are property of persons engaged in treason against the U.S. Proclamation actually frees no slaves, since it concerns only areas over which federal government has no jurisdiction.

Nov. 7. President Lincoln, impatient at McClellan's failure to press his advantage after Antietam, replaces him with General Ambrose E. Burnside, who plans to attack Lee at Fredericksburg, Virginia. **Dec. 13.** In

JOHN S. ROCK
Speech to Massachusetts Anti-Slavery Society, 1862
You are the only people, claiming to be civilized, who take away the rights of those whose color differs from your own. If you find that you cannot rob the Negro of his labor and of himself, you will banish him! What a sublime idea! You are certainly a great people! What is your plea? Why, that the slaveholders will not permit us to live among them as freemen, and that the air of northern latitudes is not good for us! Let me tell you, my friends, the slaveholders are not the men we dread! They do not desire to have us removed. The Northern pro-slavery men have done the free people of color tenfold more injury than the Southern slaveholders. In the South, it is simply a question of dollars and cents. The slaveholder cares no more for you than he does for me. . . .

This rebellion for slavery means something! Out of it emancipation must spring. I do not agree with those men who see no hope in this war. There is nothing in it but hope. Our cause is onward. As it is with the sun, the clouds often obstruct his vision, but in the end we find there has been no standing still. It is true the government is but little more antislavery now than it was at the commencement of the war; but while fighting for its own existence, it has been obliged to take slavery by the throat and, sooner or later, must choke her to death.

ABRAHAM LINCOLN
Unsent Letter, 1862
My dear McClellan: If you don't want to use the Army I should like to borrow it for a while. Yours respectfully, A. Lincoln.

DAVID R. LOCKE
"Petroleum V. Nasby" letter, 1862

Wareas, *when yoo giv a man a hoss, yoo air obleeged to also make him a present uv a silver-platid harnis and a $650 buggy, so ef we let the nigger live here, we are in dooty bound to marry him off-hand; and*

Wareas, *when this stait uv affares arrives our kentry will be no fit place for men uv educashen and refinement; and*

Wareas, *any man heving the intellek uv a brass-mounted jackass kin easily see that the two races want never intendid to live together; and*

Wareas, *bein in the magority, we kin do as we please, and ez the nigger aint no vote he kant help hisself; therefore be it*

Resolved, *that the crude, undeodorizd Afrikin is a disgustin obgik.*

Resolved, *that the Convenshun, when it hez its feet washed, smells sweeter than the Afrikin in his normal condishun, and is therefore his sooperior.*

Resolved, *that the niggers be druv out uv Wingert's Corners, and that sich property ez they may hev accumulatid be confiscatid, and the proceeds applide to the follerin purposes, to-wit:*

Payment uv the bills of the last Dimekratik Centrel Committee; payment uv the disintrestid patriots ez got up this meetin; the balance to remane in my hands.

Resolved, *that the Ablishnists who oppose these resolushens all want to marry a nigger.*

Battle of Fredericksburg Union forces attack Confederates at Marye's Heights, a line of well-fortified hills; 12,000 Union troops are killed or wounded, and Army retreats. Burnside is later relieved of his command at his own request.

Dec. 17. Radical Republicans in Senate fail in attempt to force President Lincoln to reorganize Cabinet by appointing radicals to all posts and replacing Secretary of State William H. Seward, the object of their wrath, with Secretary of the Treasury Salmon P. Chase, their favorite; Lincoln, supported by the entire Cabinet except Seward, persuades Republicans that no conflict exists in Cabinet and refuses to accept (though he pockets) resignations offered by both Seward and Chase.

Jay Cooke, Pennsylvania banker, is employed by U.S. Treasury Department to raise money by selling $500 million in bonds. By using 2,500 subagents and appealing to Northern patriotism, he raises $11 million more than authorized before he can stop machinery set in motion. Congress immediately authorizes extra amount.

Richard Jordan Gatling perfects machine gun he has worked on for past year; gun will fire 350 rounds per minute, but it is not adopted by Union authorities until war is almost over.

William Gannaway Brownlow, editor of the *Knoxville* (Tennessee) *Whig*, and Union sympathizer, publishes his *Sketches of the Rise, Progress, and Decline of Secession; with a Narrative of Personal Adventure Among the Rebels*; he has previously been arrested for treason in Tennessee because of pro-Union newspaper editorial and then released by Confederate authorities.

Photographer Mathew Brady receives official permission from President Lincoln and the Secret Service to establish complete photographic coverage of Civil War. Though he has photographed battles and events previously, he and his many photographic teams take more than 7,000 pictures of battles, individuals, camps, and devastated battlefields. Project ruins Brady financially; an enormously popular portrait photographer before the War, he spends $100,000, his entire fortune, on expenses.

Painter and illustrator Winslow Homer accompanies Union armies as artist-correspondent for *Harper's Weekly*.

1862 - 1863

Dec. 31, 1862-Jan. 2, 1863. General Braxton Bragg, who has replaced Beauregard and has dominated central Tennessee, is finally forced to withdraw after Battle of Murfreesboro (Stone River), in which each side sustains more than 9,000 casualties.

July 1, 1862. Pacific Railway Act authorizes Union Pacific Railroad to build line from Nebraska to Utah to meet Central Pacific, which is building eastward from California. **July 2, 1864.** Land grants of 10 alternate sections per mile given railroads to aid finances having proved inadequate, new act grants twice as much land. Union Pacific uses largely immigrant Irish labor; Central Pacific imports Chinese laborers.

1862 - 1864

Dislocation of foreign markets for cotton and efforts to become self-sufficient in food production result in drop in Southern cotton production from average of 4,500,000 bales per year to 1,600,000 in 1862 and a low of 300,000 in 1864.

1863

Jan. 1. President Lincoln issues Emancipation Proclamation, freeing "all slaves in areas still in rebellion," but actually most of

JAMES D. BURN
Three Years . . . in The United States, 1865
Many emigrants, after settling in America, feel disappointed as to the manners and habits of the people, and those who possess the means often return home. Afterward, when comparing the value of labor in their own country and their humble daily fare with the superior wages and excellent food they had in America, the original discontent . . . is revived, and they again cross the Atlantic. . . .

Three classes of people are most likely to better their condition by removing to the United States. In the first place, I would name unskilled laborers who have been accustomed to a low standard of wages, poor food, and miserable dwellings. The second class consists of those whose social and political rights and liberties are in the keeping of their lords and masters, as in several of the German states. The third class is made up of men from the various grades of society in the Old World who have managed their business of appropriation in such a bungling manner as to make them forfeit the good opinion of their neighbors and cause the administrators of the law to be solicitous for their personal safety!

All these will find a ready market for labor and enterprise in the United States, and with health, strength, and a willing mind, it is a man's own fault if he does not make himself a useful member of society and secure many of the comforts and conveniences of civilized life to which he was a stranger at home. One condition, perhaps, ought to be named as essential to the success of workingmen; they should bring with them youth and good health so that they may be enabled to battle with the seasons until they become acclimatized.

Letter to Norway, 1862

At this time life is not very pleasant in this so-called wonderful America. The country is full of danger, and at no time do we feel any security for our lives or property. A week ago in our county (Dodge County in southeastern Minnesota), the name of every citizen between eighteen and forty-five years of age was taken down, regardless of whether he, like myself, was married or not. Next month (October) there is to be a levy of soldiers for military service, and our county alone is to supply 118 men, in addition to those who have already enlisted as volunteers. . . .

To tempt people to enlist as volunteers, everybody who would volunteer was offered $225, out of which $125 is paid by the county and $100 by the state. Several men then enlisted, Yankees and Norwegians; and we others, who preferred to stay at home and work for our wives and children, were ordered to be ready at the next levy. Then who is to go will be decided by drawing lots. In the meantime, we were forbidden to leave the county without special permission, and we were also told that no one would get a passport to leave the country. Dejected, we went home, and now we are in a mood of uncertainty and tension, almost like prisoners of war in this formerly so free country. Our names have been taken down — perhaps I shall be a soldier next month and have to leave my home, my wife, child, and everything I have been working for over so many years.

these slaves continue to work productively for the South.

Feb. 3. French Emperor Napoleon III offers to mediate in American Civil War. **Feb. 6-March 3.** Secretary of State Seward and Congress, in resolution of both houses, promptly refuse offer, Congress criticizing it as "foreign intervention."

March 3. First Union conscription act makes all men 20 to 35, unmarried to 45 years old, liable to military service. Provisions are similar to those of Confederate draft act, making it easy to avoid actual service by paying $300 for a substitute to enlist for three years. This provision is especially objectionable to working-class men, for whom $300 is about two-thirds of annual income.

Confederate and Union armies spend most of winter facing each other across Rappahannock River in Virginia. By spring, Union Army, now commanded by General Joseph Hooker, numbers about 130,000 and Confederate Army, about 60,000. **April 30.** Hooker moves to hold Lee at Fredericksburg while sending force to attack his flank but hesitates and sets up position to the west at Chancellorsville. **May 2.** At Battle of Chancellorsville, Lee attacks Hooker from two directions. After a notable victory, General Jackson, riding around his lines, is shot accidentally by one of his men, and his left arm is amputated. Lee writes: "You are better off than I am, for while you have lost your left, I have lost my right arm." **May 5.** Hooker, badly beaten, although his forces are vastly superior, retreats across Rappahannock. **May 10.** Jackson dies of effects of amputation and pneumonia.

April. Having failed during winter to take key city of Vicksburg, Mississippi, from the north, Grant sends gunboats and supplies downriver at night to take positions south of the city, then sends army southward on west side of Mississippi River to cross to Union positions. **May 16-18.** Direct attacks having failed, Grant begins Siege of Vicksburg. **July 4.** Hopelessly cut off and having been under constant bombardment for seven weeks, Vicksburg surrenders. **July 9.** Port Hudson, Louisiana, is taken by Union forces, leaving North in control of Mississippi River. President Lincoln says, "The Father of Waters again goes unvexed to the sea."

June 3. Encouraged by Chancellorsville and hoping for further victories in order to win European recognition for the Confederacy, Lee starts up Shenandoah Valley toward Pennsylvania with Union General Hooker's Army of the Potomac following northward toward Gettysburg. Lee is unaware of Hooker's exact position as Jeb Stuart is away on a raid around Union Army. **June 15.** President Lincoln calls for 100,000 volunteers for six-month service; Confederate invasion of North stimulates response to this appeal. **June 28.** After numerous clashes between the Union command and the administration, President Lincoln accepts Hooker's resignation; General George G. Meade is appointed head of the Army of the Potomac in his stead. Meade realizes that a battle is probably imminent and works around the clock to prepare his forces. **June 30.** Confederate brigade searching for shoes in Gettysburg comes upon Union cavalry. Armies, now aware of each other's position, maneuver in attempt to gain advantage. **July 1.** Greatest battle of Civil War begins. Union forces are hard pressed by Confederates converging on Gettysburg from north and west, but by end of day have taken up position on Cemetery Ridge, southeast of town. **July 2.** Confederates attack flanks of Union position — Culp's Hill on north, Little Round Top on South — but Union line holds. Casualties on both sides are high. **July 3.** Lee, believing that Union center has been depleted in

General George E. Pickett

WILLIAM FAULKNER
For every Southern boy fourteen years old, not once but whenever he wants it, there is the instant when It's still not two o'clock on that July afternoon in 1863, the brigades are in position behind the rail fence, the guns are laid and ready in the woods and the furled flags are already loosened to break out and Pickett himself with his long oiled ringlets and his hat in one hand probably and his sword in the other looking up the hill waiting for Longstreet to give the word and it's all in the balance, it hasn't happened yet. . . .

THIS PAGE: (Left) Photograph of Lincoln by Mathew Brady, 1861; (below) cartoon from the 1860 election shows three of the candidates, Lincoln, Douglas, and Breckinridge, tearing the nation to shreds, while the Union candidate, Bell, applies glue from a tiny, useless pot OPPOSITE PAGE: (Top) As other states charge after the "secession humbug," Georgia takes a detour; (bottom) Colonel Burnside's Rhode Island brigade in action in First Battle of Bull Run, July 1861: drawing by Alfred R. Waud

THE "SECESSION MOVEMENT".

GEORGE E. PICKETT
Letter to LaSalle Corbell, 1863
On the Fourth—far from a glorious Fourth to us or to any with love for his fellowmen—I wrote you just a line of heartbreak. The sacrifice of life on that bloodsoaked field on the fatal 3rd was too awful for the heralding of victory, even for our victorious foe, who, I think, believe as we do, that it decided the fate of our cause. No words can picture the anguish of that roll call—the breathless waits between the responses. The "Here" of those who, by God's mercy, had miraculously escaped the awful rain of shot and shell was a sob—a gasp—a knell—for the unanswered name of his comrade called before his. There was no tone of thankfulness for having been spared to answer to their names, but rather a toll and an unvoiced wish that they, too, had been among the missing. . . .

Even now I can hear them cheering as I gave the order, "Forward!" I can feel their faith and trust in me and their love for our cause. I can feel the thrill of their joyous voices as they called out all along the line, "We'll follow you, Marse George. We'll follow you, we'll follow you." Oh, how faithfully they kept their word, following me on, on to their death, and I, believing in the promised support, led them on, on, on. Oh, God!

Slogan of the draft rioters in New York, July 1863
A Rich Man's War and a Poor Man's Fight.

order to meet flank attacks of previous day, orders artillery barrage to be followed by attack on Cemetery Ridge by Pickett's Virginia division —— 15,000 fresh men. Charge takes place at two o'clock in the afternoon; it is made in parade formation under withering artillery fire, and only a small number of Confederates reach the Union lines. Pickett withdraws after twenty minutes of fierce fighting within the Union position, his division destroyed. **July 4.** Having lost more than 20,000 men killed and wounded, Lee begins retreat into Virginia. Meade, his army exhausted — hardly anyone has slept for five days — does not follow up his advantage, and Confederates escape. However, battle is first major Union victory, and thereafter European recognition of the Confederacy is out of the question.

June 20. West Virginia, which has broken away from Virginia to support the Union, is admitted as the thirty-fifth state; its population is about 380,000, including 15,000 slaves.

June 20. Jay Cooke establishes first national bank in Philadelphia; it is chief agent for sale of U.S. bonds. By end of war, many state banks have become national banks, issuing national bank notes, which for the first time gives the country a uniform currency.

July 13-16. First draft drawings cause riots in New York City; rioters burn, loot, and kill, and Irish immigrant laborers, lowest paid of all, attack Negroes and lynch several of them. Rioting is put down by police, heavy rain, and arrival of regular Army troops brought from Gettysburg, Pennsylvania. Anti-Negro riots occur also in other Northern cities, notably Detroit.

Sept. 4. General William S. Rosecrans, with 55,000 men, advances on Chattanooga, Tennessee, occupied by General Braxton

Bragg. **Sept. 8.** Bragg retreats southward into Georgia to avoid being put out of action. Rosecrans, thinking he is in full retreat, pursues him, but Bragg has withdrawn only 25 miles and has received reinforcements from Virginia that increase his army to 70,000. **Sept. 19.** Bragg attacks fiercely. In two-day Battle of Chickamauga, Union forces are badly defeated and retreat to Chattanooga.

Although Britain favors the Union in Civil War, Confederate ships are still being built in Britain; British-built raiders have destroyed more than 250 Union ships. Charles Francis Adams, U.S. minister to Britain, warns British after Gettysburg and Vicksburg victories, that building of ironclads for Confederacy means war. **Oct.** British government takes over ships, and France follows suit, ordering vessels under construction in France to be sold to European governments. By end of year, the South has lost all hope of recognition from abroad.

Oct. 23. General Grant, now Western commander, reaches Chattanooga to join General Hooker, who has arrived from Virginia, and averts danger of starvation of besieged garrison by bringing in supplies. **Nov. 23.** Reinforced by General William T. Sherman and aware that Bragg's army has been weakened, Grant orders Sherman and Hooker to attack Confederate-held heights around Chattanooga. **Nov. 25.** Dramatic charge up heavily-fortified Missionary Ridge ends battle. Most of eastern Tennessee is now controlled by the Union, and from Chattanooga, Union armies can move into Georgia and Alabama.

Nov. 19. Statesman Edward Everett delivers oration as chief speaker at dedication of national cemetery at Gettysburg Battlefield; President Lincoln also makes brief 10-sentence address, after which Everett writes

ABRAHAM LINCOLN
Gettysburg Address, 1863
Four score and seven years ago our fathers brought forth on this continent a new nation, conceived in liberty and dedicated to the proposition that all men are created equal.

Now we are engaged in a great civil war, testing whether that nation or any nation so conceived and so dedicated can long endure. We are met on a great battlefield of that war. We have come to dedicate a portion of that field as a final resting place for those who here gave their lives that that nation might live. It is altogether fitting and proper that we should do this.

But, in a larger sense, we cannot dedicate—we cannot consecrate—we cannot hallow—this ground. The brave men, living and dead, who struggled here have consecrated it far above our poor power to add or detract. The world will little note nor long remember what we say here, but it can never forget what they did here. It is for us, the living, rather, to be dedicated here to the unfinished work which they who fought here have thus far so nobly advanced.

It is rather for us to be here dedicated to the great task remaining before us—that from these honored dead we take increased devotion to that cause for which they gave the last full measure of devotion; that we here highly resolve that these dead shall not have died in vain; that this nation, under God, shall have a new birth of freedom; and that government of the people, by the people, for the people shall not perish from the earth.

JAMES A. SEDDON
Letter to Jefferson Davis, 1863
The difficulty . . . with the consumer as with the government, is the redundancy of the currency and the consequent steady inflation of prices. This in its direct, and even more in its indirect, influences, not merely on the market and on the property of citizens but on their instincts of selfishness, on their sentiments, tastes, and aspirations, is a fearful evil, and more demoralizing to our people than the more dire calamities of war.

It pertains to another branch of the government and to an abler mind to portray this subject in its true colors and to propose correctives; but . . . I may be excused for saying that in my judgment the sole effective remedy is prompt reduction of the existing issues to the amount needed for currency by the people of the Confederacy, and the inflexible determination and pledge never to exceed it. No mode of utilizing the credit of the Confederacy can be so wasteful as the enhancement of all prices by a constantly increasing ratio, or so mischievous as the subversion of the standard of values, tempting all into the wild whirl of speculation, and corroding, by the vile greed of gain, all the nobler elements of character. If the present system be continued, prices, already many hundred percent above true values, must be indefinitely enhanced, the credit of the government must be wrecked utterly, and no alternative left for the continuance of our patriotic struggle and the preservation of our lives and liberties but grinding taxation and the systematized seizure, without present compensation, of all supplies needed for the employees as well as the armies of the Confederacy.

him, "I should be glad if I could flatter myself that I came as near to the central idea of the occasion in two hours as you did in two minutes."

Dec. 8. President Lincoln's plan of Reconstruction offers amnesty to Southerners taking loyalty oath and federal recognition of state governments in which 10 percent of 1860 voters have taken oath and state has agreed to free slaves.

Arizona Territory is formed from part of Territory of New Mexico; Territory of Idaho is formed from parts of Washington, Dakota, Utah, and Nebraska territories.

Congress grants 3 million acres of land to Atchison, Topeka and Santa Fe Railway in alternate sections in Kansas. Eventually line runs from Chicago to Los Angeles.

Congress authorizes, for the first time, free mail delivery service in certain cities for distribution of mail direct to destination.

1863 - 1865

Feb. 25. National Bank Act is passed; banks operating under this act must invest up to one-third of their reserves in U.S. securities, against which they may make extensive note issues to finance the war. Without a similar financial system, the Confederacy raises some money in taxes and foreign and domestic loans, but issue of more than $1 billion in paper money results in disastrous inflation.

1863 - 1867

Great Britain, Spain, and France have invaded Mexico in 1861 in effort to collect foreign debts after payments are suspended by nearly bankrupt country. Spain and Great Britain, learning that France, supported by Mexican conservatives, plans to set up Catholic empire under French support, have withdrawn in 1862. **June 7, 1863.** French troops, reinforced by Napoleon III, attack and after heavy fighting take Mexico City. President Benito Juárez, head of liberal Mexican government, flees to northern Mexico. **April 10, 1864.** Archduke Maximilian of Austria is established by Napoleon as emperor of Mexico; but Mexican people and government continue to fight French, while U.S. continues to recognize Juárez. **March 12, 1867.** Napoleon III, convinced by U.S. protests over past years that U.S. may provide military aid to Mexico, withdraws support from Maximilian. **May 15.** Emperor surrenders to Mexicans, who execute him in following month.

1864

March 9. General Grant is appointed commander in chief of all Union forces and moves to Eastern arena to oppose Lee. His policy, and President Lincoln's, is to use superior manpower and industrial strength of North to destroy Confederate armies; although Union casualties will be heavy, it is assumed that the South cannot support comparable losses of men and equipment.

May 4. General Sherman starts from Chattanooga into Georgia. He is opposed by Confederate General Joseph E. Johnston, who, as Sherman advances toward Atlanta, fights series of defensive actions as he retreats southeastward. **July 17.** Union Army reaches within eight miles of Atlanta, and President Jefferson Davis, impatient with Johnston's tactics, replaces him with General John B. Hood.

May 5-6. In desolate area of northern Virginia known as the Wilderness, Grant, with 100,000 men, meets Lee's army of 60,000 in tangled forest. Indecisive battle rages for two days, but Union casualties are far greater than Confederate.

FRANK WILKESON

Recollections of a Private Soldier, 1887

The next day, just before Longstreet's soldiers made their first charge on Corps II, I heard the peculiar cry a stricken man utters as the bullet tears through his flesh. I turned my head, as I loaded my rifle, to see who was hit. I saw a bearded Irishman pull up his shirt. He had been wounded in the left side just below the floating ribs. His face was gray with fear. The wound looked as though it were mortal. He looked at it for an instant, then poked it gently with his index finger. He flushed redly and smiled with satisfaction. He tucked his shirt into his trousers and was fighting in the ranks again before I had capped my rifle. The ball had cut a groove in his skin only. . . .

Wounded soldiers almost always tore their clothing away from their wounds so as to see them and to judge of their character. Many of them would smile and their faces would brighten as they realized that they were not hard hit and that they could go home for a few months. Others would give a quick glance at their wounds and then shrink back as from a blow, and turn pale as they realized the truth that they were mortally wounded. The enlisted men were exceedingly accurate judges of the probable result which would ensue from any wound they saw. They had seen hundreds of soldiers wounded, and they had noticed that certain wounds always resulted fatally. They knew when they were fatally wounded, and after the shock of discovery had passed, they generally braced themselves and died in a manly manner. It was seldom that an American or Irish volunteer flunked in the presence of death.

CLEMENT L. VALLANDIGHAM
Speech to Democratic Union Association, New York, 1863
I will not consent to put the entire purse of the country and the sword of the country into the hands of the executive, giving him despotic and dictatorial power to carry out an object which I avow before my countrymen is the destruction of their liberties and the overthrow of the Union of these states. I do not comprehend the honesty of such declarations or of the men who make them. I know that the charge is brought against myself, personally, and against many of us. I have not spent a moment in replying to it — the people will take care of all that.

The charge has been made against us — all who are opposed to the policy of this administration and opposed to this war — that we are for "peace on any terms." It is false. I am not, but I am for an immediate stopping of the war and for honorable peace. I am for peace for the sake of the Union of these states. More than that — I am for peace, and would be, even if the Union could not be restored, as I believe it can be; because without peace, permitting this administration for two years to exercise its tremendous powers, the war still existing, you will not have one remnant of civil liberty left among yourselves. The exercise of these tremendous powers, the apology for which is the existence of this war, is utterly incompatible with the stability of the Constitution and of constitutional liberty.

May 8-12. Ignoring his losses, Grant moves eastward toward Richmond and again meets Lee's army, at Spotsylvania Court House; in five days of bloody fighting in which neither side is victorious, Grant loses about 10,000 men. He doggedly wires Washington, "I propose to fight it out on this line if it takes all summer." War of attrition continues sporadically throughout April and May.

June 1-3. Having again moved to his left, Grant meets Lee at Cold Harbor, a few miles from Richmond. In another attempt to crush Lee's entrenched army, Grant loses about 7,000 men in only one hour of fighting. In a month, Grant has lost almost 60,000 men; finally realizing Lee's magnificent defensive skill, he is forced to change tactics.

June 7. Abraham Lincoln is nominated for reelection as President and Governor Andrew Johnson, Tennessee "War" Democrat, for Vice-President by Republican Party (using name "National Union Party"). **Aug. 29.** Democrats nominate General George B. McClellan for President and George H. Pendleton of Ohio for Vice-President. Democratic platform proposes immediate end of war, but McClellan repudiates it in campaign and demands preservation of the Union. Northern defeatist feeling and peace demands make Lincoln's chances for reelection seem slim.

June 12-18. Grant decides to try to capture railroad complex at Petersburg and cut supply lines to Richmond. He crosses the James River on a 2,000-foot pontoon bridge and almost achieves victory, but small Confederate force delays him until Lee's army arrives. Only alternative is to besiege Petersburg.

June 20. Union and Confederate armies start digging miles of trenches around Petersburg. They face each other for nine months, during which all Union attempts to break through Confederate lines fail.

July 2-13. Lee sends General Jubal A. Early through the Shenandoah Valley to raid Washington, D.C., hoping to divert some of Grant's troops from Petersburg. Traveling through Maryland, Early reaches within five miles of Washington by July 11. Two divisions of Union troops, hastily sent from Petersburg, drive Early back into Virginia.

July 4. Congress establishes Bureau of Immigration; contract labor law allows for admittance of immigrant laborers who agree to pay for their transportation out of wages earned for no more than one year after entry into U.S. Law is later repealed.

July 8. President Lincoln pocket-vetoes Wade-Davis Bill, congressional plan for postwar reconstruction of the South. Lincoln considers Bill's provisions too severe and issues statement of his reasons only after Congress adjourns; his leniency is heavily criticized by radical Republicans.

July 20 and 22. General Hood attacks Sherman near Atlanta but is forced to withdraw to the city and on September 1 to evacuate it; Sherman occupies it the next day. Capture of Atlanta lifts Union morale, which has sunk to new low over Grant's losses at Richmond, and improves President Lincoln's prospects for reelection.

Aug. 5. In effort to make blockade of South more effective, naval squadron commanded by Admiral Farragut sails into Mobile Bay, Alabama, although Farragut knows it bristles with mines, called torpedoes. ("Damn the torpedoes! Full steam ahead!") Mobile forts surrender by August 23, and port is closed to shipping, although Mobile is not occupied.

THOMAS SOUPER
Daily Missouri Democrat, 1865
I am about to enter upon the great enterprise of inducing labor and capital to Missouri. . . . The American Emigrant Company of New York have designated me their agent for Missouri.

This company . . . has been "chartered for the purpose of procuring and assisting emigrants from foreign countries to settle in the United States." . . . The direct advantages are these:

First, it secures a supply of diversified labor necessary to develop the varied resources of the country and to prosecute every branch of industry.

Second, it offers facilities to large corporations or special industrial interests to import in sufficient quantity the special kind of labor which they require.

Third, it gives each individual employer the opportunity of supplying himself with the exact number and description of operatives he needs.

Fourth, it will tend to equalize the value of labor in Europe and America, and thus, by raising the rate of wages in the Old World, undermine and finally destroy Its manufacturing supremacy.

Fifth, it opens, by its agencies, new sources of immigration and aims at the introduction in large numbers of a superior class of men from northern Europe, Belgium, France, Switzerland, as well as Germany, England, Scotland, and Wales. . . .

To railroad companies, mining companies, manufacturers of iron and steel, machinists, boilermakers, ship and house builders, manufacturers of all kinds, as well as to the farming interests generally, I now tender my best services and shall be happy to meet all my old friends in my new position.

First International, letter to Lincoln, 1864
We congratulate the American people upon your reelection by a large majority. If resistance to the slave power was the reserved watchword of your first election, the triumphant war cry of your reelection is "Death to slavery."

From the commencement of the titanic American strife, the workingmen of Europe felt instinctively that the star-spangled banner carried the destiny of their class. The contest for the territories which opened the dire epopee, was it not to decide whether the virgin soil of immense tracts should be wedded to the labor of the emigrant or prostituted by the tramp of the slave driver? . . .

While the workingmen, the true political power of the North, allowed slavery to defile their own republic; while before the Negro, mastered and sold without his concurrence, they boasted it the highest prerogative of the white-skinned laborer to sell himself and choose his own master. They were unable to attain the true freedom of labor or to support their European brethren in their struggle for emancipation, but this barrier to progress has been swept off by the red sea of civil war.

The workingmen of Europe feel sure that as the American War of Independence initiated a new era of ascendancy for the middle class, so the American antislavery war will do for the working classes. They consider it an earnest of the epoch to come that it fell to the lot of Abraham Lincoln, the single-minded son of the working class, to lead his country through the matchless struggle for the rescue of an enchained race and the reconstruction of a social world.

Sept. 19-Oct. 19. General Philip H. Sheridan, having become commander of the Army of the Shenandoah, defeats Early at Winchester, Fisher's Hill, and Cedar Creek, and devastates the Shenandoah Valley, which has become the grain-growing area supplying Richmond.

Oct. 31. Nevada is admitted to the Union as thirty-sixth state, although population does not meet requirements for state law. Action is hastened by Congress, anxious to acquire an additional free state to secure ratification of Thirteenth Amendment to the Constitution, prohibiting slavery; amendment is scheduled for submission to the states by next Congress, and ratification by 27 states is required.

Nov. 8. President Lincoln is reelected. National Union candidates carry all but three states, with electoral vote of 212 for Lincoln to 21 for McClellan (81 votes of Confederacy are not cast), but popular vote is only 2,200,000 for Lincoln to 1,800,000 for McClellan. Andrew Johnson is elected Vice-President.

Nov. 14. Leaving Atlanta in flames, Sherman begins march to Savannah, Georgia. His army of 60,000 men marches forward on 60-mile front, systematically destroying everything — buildings, roads, bridges, factories, cotton gins — that might be of use to the Confederacy. Sherman deliberately orders men to "forage," hoping total destruction will break will of the South. Looting soldiers strip everything in their path and destroy what they cannot use; Sherman later estimates that they have destroyed $100 million in Georgia property. **Dec. 10.** Army reaches Savannah, which surrenders on December 22.

Dec. 15-16. In two-day battle, Union Army takes Nashville after almost complete destruction of General Hood's army.

Montana Territory is formed from part of Idaho.

Although few strikes have been held during war, national labor groups have expanded; employers in Michigan and elsewhere set up associations of employers to counteract spread of labor unions.

First Bessemer-process steel plant starts operating at Wyandotte, Michigan; it produces chiefly steel railroad rails. Peter Cooper has previously used process experimentally in 1856 as first iron manufacturer in U.S. to use Bessemer converter. For some years more iron than steel rails are made.

First comfortable sleeping car is constructed by George Pullman; sleeping cars have been in use for almost 30 years, but builders have not been concerned with public comfort. Pullman's car has, in addition to well-constructed berths, more width, more height, and rubber-reinforced springs.

Clara Barton, who has organized nursing services for Union troops in Washington since beginning of war, works without payment or accreditation behind Union lines and on battlefields as superintendent of nurses. She later is responsible for establishment of American Red Cross.

George Perkins Marsh, lawyer, scholar, and minister to Italy, publishes *Man and Nature, or Physical Geography as Modified by Human Action*, a pioneer effort suggesting the importance of conservation, improvement of waste areas, and restoration of exhausted land.

GEORGE PERKINS MARSH
Man and Nature, 1864
It is rare that a middle-aged American dies in the house where he was born, or an old man even in that which he has built; and this is scarcely less true of the rural districts, where every man owns his habitation, than of the city, where the majority lived in hired houses. This life of incessant flitting is unfavorable for the execution of permanent improvements of every sort, and especially of those which, like the forest, are slow in repaying any part of the capital expended in them. It requires a very generous spirit in a landholder to plant a wood on a farm he expects to sell, or which he knows will pass out of the hands of his descendants at his death. . . .

We have now felled forest enough everywhere, in many districts far too much. Let us restore this one element of material life to its normal proportions, and devise means of maintaining the permanence of its relations to the fields, the meadows, and the pastures, to the rain and the dews of heaven, to the springs and rivulets with which it waters the earth.

GEN. WILLIAM T. SHERMAN
I am sick and tired of war. Its glory is all moonshine. It is only those who have never fired a shot nor heard the shrieks and groans of the wounded who cry aloud for blood, more vengeance, more desolation. War is hell.

1865

Jan.-April. General Sherman's army marches through South Carolina, then North Carolina, more destructively than

HORACE PORTER

The Meeting at Appomattox, 1865

At a little before 4 o'clock General Lee shook hands with General Grant, bowed to the other officers, and with Colonel Marshall left the room. . . . Lee signaled to his orderly to bring up his horse, and while the animal was being bridled, the general stood on the lowest step and gazed sadly in the direction of the valley beyond where his army lay — now an army of prisoners.

He smote his hands together a number of times in an absent sort of a way; seemed not to see the group of Union officers in the yard who rose respectfully at his approach; and appeared unconscious of everything about him. All appreciated the sadness that overwhelmed him, and he had the personal sympathy of everyone who beheld him at this supreme moment of trial. The approach of his horse seemed to recall him from his reverie, and he at once mounted.

General Grant now stepped down from the porch and, moving toward him, saluted him by raising his hat. He was followed in this act of courtesy by all our officers present; Lee raised his hat respectfully and rode off to break the sad news to the brave fellows whom he had so long commanded. . . .

The news of the surrender had reached the Union lines, and the firing of salutes began at several points, but the general sent orders at once to have them stopped, and used these words in referring to the occurrence: "The war is over, the Rebels are our countrymen again, and the best sign of rejoicing after the victory will be to abstain from all demonstrations in the field."

through Georgia; it is only slightly slowed by Johnston's forces.

Feb. 3. Hampton Roads, Virginia, peace conference between President Lincoln and Confederate Vice-President and others fails when Confederates insist on recognition of Confederate independence as condition.

March 3. Freedmen's Bureau is established by Congress to assist emancipated Southern Negroes and to care for deserted Southern land.

March 4. President Lincoln, in Second Inaugural Address, stresses again his conviction that when peace comes, it must be peace "with malice toward none" if it is to achieve a true reunion of the states.

March 25. General Lee's attempt to break out of Petersburg fails before Grant's superior forces. **April 1.** Lee makes his last attack of the war but is again unsuccessful. **April 2-3.** He evacuates Petersburg and Richmond in attempt to move south to join General Johnston, who is opposing Sherman in North Carolina.

April 7. Surrounded by Union forces, and with only 30,000 men remaining. Lee receives Grant's message requesting surrender. **April 9.** They meet at Appomattox Court House to discuss terms. All Confederate soldiers are released to return home; all may keep private horses and mules; officers may keep sidearms, but all other equipment is surrendered. Union Army gives hungry Confederates 25,000 rations.

April 14. President Lincoln is shot by John Wilkes Booth while watching *Our American Cousin* in Ford's Theater, Washington; he is taken, unconscious, to rooming house nearby. Simultaneously, Secretary Seward, ill at home, is attacked and severely wounded by Lewis Powell, confederate of Booth. Booth, having broken his leg in leap from theater box, escapes to Virginia. **April 15.** President Lincoln dies at 7:22 A.M., and Andrew Johnson becomes President. **April 26.** Booth, traced to barn near Bowling Green, Virginia, refuses to surrender; barn is set on fire, and Booth either shoots himself or is shot. **July 7.** Four of nine persons involved in assassination plot are hanged, including one woman; four are imprisoned; one is not convicted.

April 26. Johnston surrenders to Sherman, with final terms similar to those at Appomattox. **May 4.** All remaining Southern forces east of Mississippi surrender. **May 26.** Confederate forces west of Mississippi surrender near New Orleans in final capitulation of war.

May 29. President Johnson issues amnesty and reconstruction proclamation embodying principles of Lincoln's 1863 plan. During summer recess of Congress he recognizes provisional governments of Virginia, Louisiana, Arkansas, and Tennessee that Lincoln had set up and establishes such governments for other seven states. All states have abolished slavery, amended their constitutions, and repudiated their war debts by December, except Texas, which does so in following year.

July. *The Nation* is founded in New York; a weekly concerned with politics and the arts, it is edited by Edwin Lawrence Godkin and supported by Eastern intellectuals.

Nov. 18. *The Celebrated Jumping Frog of Calaveras County* by Mark Twain is published in *The Saturday Press*, New York; an immediate hit, it is reprinted in newspapers across the country.

Nov. 22-29. Mississippi enacts first "Black Code," attempting to control freed

GIDEON WELLES
Diary, 1865
April 15. A door which opened upon a porch or gallery and also the windows, were kept open for fresh air. The night was dark, cloudy, and damp, and about six it began to rain. . . .

Large groups of people were gathered every few rods, all anxious and solicitous. Some one or more from each group stepped forward as I passed to inquire into the condition of the President and to ask if there was no hope. Intense grief was on every countenance when I replied that the President could survive but a short time. . . .

A little before seven, I went into the room where the dying President was rapidly drawing near the closing moments. His wife soon after made her last visit to him. The death struggle had begun. Robert, his son, stood with several others at the head of the bed. He bore himself well, but on two occasions gave way to overpowering grief and sobbed aloud, turning his head and leaning on the shoulder of Senator Sumner. The respiration of the President became suspended at intervals and at last entirely ceased at twenty-two minutes past seven. . . .

April 19. . . . There were no truer mourners, when all were sad, than the poor colored people who crowded the streets, joined the procession, and exhibited their woe, bewailing the loss of him whom they regarded as a benefactor and father. Women, as well as men, with their little children, thronged the streets; sorrow, trouble, and distress depicted on their countenances and in their bearing.

JOHN GREENLEAF WHITTIER
Laus Deo!, 1866

It is done!
Clang of bell and roar of gun
Send the tidings up and down.
How the belfries rock and reel!
How the great guns, peal on peal,
Fling the joy from town to town!

Ring, O bells!
Every stroke exulting tells
Of the burial hour of crime.
Loud and long, that all may hear,
Ring for every listening ear
Of Eternity and Time!

Let us kneel:
God's own voice is in that peal,
And this spot is holy ground.
Lord, forgive us! What are we,
That our eyes this glory see,
That our ears have heard the sound!

For the Lord
On the whirlwind is abroad;
In the earthquake He has spoken;
He has smitten with His thunder
The iron walls asunder,
And the gates of brass are broken!

Loud and long
Lift the old exulting song;
Sing with Miriam by the sea;
He has cast the mighty down;
Horse and rider sink and drown;
"He hath triumphed gloriously!"

Did we dare,
In our agony of prayer,
Ask for more than He has done?
When was ever His right hand
Over any time or land
Stretched as now beneath the sun?

Negroes by such means as vagrancy laws and apprenticeship regulations that tie Negroes to land. Other Southern states soon pass similar laws; some are severe, others more liberal.

Dec. 4. New Congress convenes and forms 15-member Joint Committee on Reconstruction, controlled by radical Republicans. **Dec. 6.** President Johnson's first message to Congress announces that Union is restored, but Congress refuses to seat representatives and senators elected under provisional Southern governments that are recognized by Johnson. Joint Committee denies that these state governments exist legally until recognized by Congress under such conditions as Congress, and only Congress, may prescribe. Senator Charles Sumner contends that former states have committed suicide: Representative Thaddeus Stevens calls them a conquered province. Stevens first dominates Committee and, eventually, House and entire Republican Party.

Dec. 18. Thirteenth Amendment to Constitution declared in effect, having been ratified by 27 states, including 8 formerly Confederate states. Amendment prohibits slavery in all states and territories. Fearing obstruction in Southern states, Congress for first time assumes power to enforce provisions of an amendment.

About 4 million men have served in the war, but many of these have been for three-and six-months' enlistments, and figure includes repeaters who have enlisted for a fee, deserted, and enlisted again. Union Negro forces have numbered 180,000, half of them from the South. Total casualties: Union, 359,000 dead, 275,000 wounded; Confederacy, 258,000 dead, 100,000 wounded. War has cost Union $5 billion and Confederacy $3 billion. Most war costs having been financed by loans and paper money issues, the federal public debt reaches over $75 per capita, highest figure up to this time.

Union Stockyards open in Chicago; they become largest stockyards in the U.S., serving the cattle industry over a wide area.

Cornell University founded at Ithaca, New York, with endowments from private sources and with aid provided by the Morrill Act of 1862; Ezra Cornell, builder of telegraph system, is a major benefactor.

William Bullock develops first web press, using roll, or web, of paper instead of cut sheets; earliest models print 15,000 sheets per hour, both sides at once.

1865 - 1868

May 10, 1865. Jefferson Davis captured in Georgia; he spends two years in jail in Virginia, then is released on bond. **Dec. 25, 1868.** Treason charge against him is dropped.

Oct. 1865. Cheyenne and Arapaho Indians, at war with settlers and miners since 1861 in Colorado, are conquered following massacre of 450 Indians by militia in previous year. First Sioux War begins when U.S. starts building road from southern Wyoming to Montana; hostilities are intensified when miners and settlers invade Black Hills. War continues until 1868, when Indians consent to move to Dakota Territory reservation.

How they pale,
Ancient myth and song and tale,
In this wonder of our days,
When the cruel rod of war
Blossoms white with righteous law,
And the wrath of man is praise!

Blotted out!
All within and all about
Shall a fresher life begin;
Freer breathe the universe
As it rolls its heavy curse
On the dead and buried sin!

It is done!
In the circuit of the sun
Shall the sound thereof go forth.
It shall bid the sad rejoice,
It shall give the dumb a voice,
It shall belt with joy the earth!

Ring and swing,
Bells of joy! On morning's wing
Send the song of praise abroad!
With a sound of broken chains
Tell the nations that He reigns,
Who alone is Lord and God!

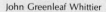

John Greenleaf Whittier

Freedman's Village in Arlington, Virginia

1866

Report of Joint Committee on Reconstruction, 1866

It is the opinion of your committee:

1. That the states lately in rebellion were, at the close of the war, disorganized communities, without civil government, and without constitutions or other forms, by virtue of which political relations could legally exist between them and the federal government.

2. That Congress cannot be expected to recognize as valid the election of representatives from disorganized communities. . . .

3. That Congress would not be justified in admitting such communities to a participation in the government of the country without first providing such constitutional or other guarantees as will tend to secure the civil rights of all citizens of the republic; a just equality of representation; protection against claims founded in rebellion and crime; a temporary restoration of the right of suffrage to those who have not actively participated in the efforts to destroy the Union and overthrow the government, and the exclusion from positions of public trust of, at least, a portion of those whose crimes have proved them to be enemies to the Union and unworthy of public confidence.

April 9. Congress passes Civil Rights Act over President Johnson's veto; Act grants same rights to all natural-born Americans (except Indians), including Negroes, who have been denied such rights by Dred Scott Decision. Veto called Act a violation of states' rights.

June 13. Congress, faced with doubts about constitutionality of Civil Rights Act, passes Fourteenth Amendment; Amendment spells out citizenship qualifications to include Negroes. It is not ratified, since all Southern states except Tennessee refuse to accept ratification as a condition of readmission to the Union; in this they are encouraged by President Johnson and Northern Democrats.

June 20. Joint Committee of Fifteen asserts that only Congress may control Reconstruction and recommends excluding senators and representatives of Southern states.

July 16. Congress passes extension of Freedman's Bureau Bill over President Johnson's veto of February 19. Strengthened Bill gives Bureau power of trial by the military of persons depriving freedmen of their civil rights. Johnson's veto has asserted that military trials violate the Fifth Amendment, and that with 11 states not represented, Congress cannot legislate in the matter.

July 19. Tennessee, controlled by Radicals, ratifies Fourteenth Amendment; it is readmitted to the Union on July 24.

Aug. 14. National Union Convention at Philadelphia hears President Johnson's unsuccessful attempt to gather all moderates into one party; much of the North believes that Johnson is supported by ex-Confederates and their Northern sympathizers. In congressional election campaign, Radicals emphasize Unionism of Republicans and point to race riots in Memphis and New Orleans on July ·30 as evidence that South is still rebellious. In November elections, Radicals gain control of Reconstruction when they win two-thirds of House and Senate seats.

Aug. 20. National Labor Union is organized in Baltimore; Ira Steward and George E. McNeill lead movement for eight-hour workday.

Southern states make unsuccessful efforts to attract European immigrants and even Chinese coolies to replace slave labor, and many farmers pay wages to former slaves; but lack of cash for wages shortly results in sharecropping system.

ANDREW JOHNSON
Speech at White House, February 1866
Whether the disunionists come from the South or the North, I stand now where I did then, to vindicate the Union of these states and the Constitution of the country. . . .

You have been struggling for four years to put down the rebellion. You denied in the beginning of the struggle that any state had the right to go out. You said that they had neither the right nor the power. The issue has been made, and it has been settled that a state has neither the right nor the power to go out of the Union. And when you have settled that by the executive and military power of the government and by the public judgment, you turn around and assume that they are out and shall not come in.

I am free to say to you, as your Executive, that I am not prepared to take any such position. . . . I say that when these states comply with the Constitution, when they have given sufficient evidence of their loyalty and that they can be trusted, when they yield obedience to the law, I say, extend to them the right hand of fellowship, and let peace and union be restored.

Shooting down blacks during riots in Memphis, Tenn., May 1866. Sketch from "Harper's Weekly"

GEN. THOMAS J. WOOD

Testimony before House Committee, 1867

During the time I was in command in Mississippi the commission of such crimes as are described in the question have been frequent. It might be well to add that the commission of crime generally has been frequent, but more particularly against persons of Union proclivities and of Northern men who have emigrated to Mississippi since the termination of the troubles and against freed people. Murder was quite a frequent affair against freedmen everywhere in that community, and the commission of crimes of a lesser grade was still more frequent than the commission of murder, such as beating and assaults. . . .

There was a great deal of variation; some months more cases were reported and others less. My impression is that the number of cases of killing was on the increase. . . .

The criminal laws of the state of Mississippi are, I think, very similar to the criminal laws of other states. The same grade of crimes is punishable by the statute in about the same way. The result of my observation was that great trouble grew out of the manner in which the executive and judicial officers performed their duties. . . . Justice cannot be administered with the public sentiment of the people of the state such as it remains, against the black people and against Union men.

Saying in Jackson, Mississippi, 1870s

If you shoot a Republican out of season, the fine will be ten dollars and costs.

First oil pipeline, laid in Pennsylvania fields, carries oil from pithole to railroad five miles distant; pipelines and railroads soon replace river barges and wagons for transportation of oil to refineries.

1866 - 1871

May 31, 1866. Six hundred members of U.S. branch of secret Irish society, the Fenians, organized with aim of freeing Ireland from Britain, cross Niagara River to Canada, attack and defeat Canadian militia, and escape; they are arrested by U.S. authorities but released. Raids and harassment continue until 1871. Canadian claims against U.S. for damages are unsuccessful.

1867

March 1. Nebraska is admitted to the Union as the thirty-seventh state, over veto of President Johnson, who fears that two recently elected Republican senators will join with large Republican majority in desire to impeach him; first attempt at impeachment, however, fails to materialize. Nebraska population, increased enormously through efforts of Western railroads to promote settlement, has risen to more than 120,000, quadruple that of 1860.

March 2. Congress passes first Reconstruction Act, over President Johnson's veto. Act divides the South into five military districts, or "conquered provinces" (in spite of Supreme Court decision of 1866 limiting military power over civilians where civil courts continue to function), declaring that no legal governments exist in any Southern state except Tennessee. It requires Southern acceptance of Negro suffrage and state conventions that include Negro delegates (but not Confederates disqualified under Fourteenth Amendment) to draft new constitutions; when satisfactory constitutions have been framed, states may submit them for federal approval.

March 2. Congress passes Tenure of Office Act to prevent President Johnson from controlling the military and to protect Secretary of War Edwin Stanton, who is in league with Radicals; Act prohibits removal of government officers without consent of the Senate. A further act requires that all military orders must be made through General Grant.

March 23. Southern states having failed to call conventions, Congress passes first supplementary Reconstruction Act, requiring federal military commanders to set up voter registration procedures. **July 19.** Second supplementary act gives military commanders power to pass on eligibility of voters.

May. Ku Klux Klan, formed originally on Christmas Eve, 1865, by Confederate officers as a social club, is formally organized at Nashville, Tennessee. Constitution is adopted and General Nathan B. Forrest is elected Grand Wizard. Its violent and illegal activities as it works to control Negroes and Northern Radicals' power cause Forrest to disband it in 1869, but it continues unofficially afterward.

Aug. 12. Aware that Secretary Stanton is conveying his plans to Radicals, President Johnson suspends him from office but does not actually remove him.

Aug. 28. Discovered in 1859, Midway Islands, west of Hawaii, are occupied for U.S. by Navy Captain William Reynolds.

Oct. 24. Secretary of State Seward's attempt to acquire Danish West Indies (Virgin Islands) for $7,500,000 fails when Senate does not ratify treaty.

Supreme Court voids federal and state loyalty-oath requirements that prevent ex-Confederates from practising certain professions.

Organization and Principles of the Ku Klux Klan, 1868
Creed
We, the Order of the_____, reverentially acknowledge the majesty and supremacy of the Divine Being and recognize the goodness and providence of the same. And we recognize our relation to the United States government, the supremacy of the Constitution, the constitutional laws thereof, and the Union of states thereunder.

Character and Objects of the Order
This is an institution of chivalry, humanity, mercy, and patriotism; embodying in its genius and its principles all that is chivalric in conduct, noble in sentiment, generous in manhood, and patriotic in purpose; its peculiar objects being:

First, to protect the weak, the innocent, and the defenseless from the indignities, wrongs, and outrages of the lawless, the violent, and the brutal; to relieve the injured and oppressed; to succor the suffering and unfortunate, and especially the widows and orphans of Confederate soldiers.

Second, to protect and defend the Constitution of the United States, and all laws passed in conformity thereto, and to protect the states and the people thereof from all invasion from any source whatever.

Third, to aid and assist in the execution of all constitutional laws, and to protect the people from unlawful seizure and from trial, except by their peers in conformity to the laws of the land.

253

THIS PAGE: (Above) Dead soldiers on the battlefield at Gettysburg
at the end of the first day's fighting, July 1863; (below) Wilmer
McLean's house in Appomattox, Virginia, where Lee met with Grant
on April 9, 1865 to agree on the terms of surrender
OPPOSITE PAGE: (top right) John Wilkes Booth, assassin of Abraham
Lincoln; (top left) Andrew Johnson, seventeenth President of the
United States: photograph by Mathew Brady; (bottom) funeral parade
for Lincoln in New York City

CHARLES LORING BRACE

Dangerous Classes of New York, 1872

The intensity of the American temperament is felt in every fiber of these children of poverty and vice. Their crimes have the unrestrained and sanguinary character of a race accustomed to overcome all obstacles. They rifle a bank, when English thieves pick a pocket; they murder, where European proletaires cudgel or fight with fists; in a riot, they begin what seems about to be the sacking of a city, where English rioters would merely batter policemen or smash lamps. . . . They are far more brutal than the peasantry from whom they descend, and they are much banded together in associations, such as "Dead Rabbit," "Plug-ugly," and various target companies. They are our enfants perdus, grown up to young manhood. . . .

We may say in brief that the young ruffians of New York are the products of accident, ignorance, and vice. Among a million people such as compose the population of this city and its suburbs, there will always be a great number of misfortunes; fathers die and leave their children unprovided for; parents drink and abuse their little ones, and they float away on the currents of the street; stepmothers or stepfathers drive out, by neglect and ill-treatment, their sons from home. Thousands are the children of poor foreigners who have permitted them to grow up without school, education, or religion.

All the neglect and bad education and evil example of a poor class tend to form others, who, as they mature, swell the ranks of ruffians and criminals. So, at length, a great multitude of ignorant, untrained, passionate, irreligious boys and young men are formed, who become the "dangerous class" of our city.

Congress establishes reservations in Oklahoma for Five Civilized Tribes (Cherokee, Creek, Chickasaw, Choctaw, and Seminole); they previously have been given most of Oklahoma in exchange for their southern lands but are held to have lost their rights by supporting the Confederacy.

Federal government founds Howard University for Negroes in Washington, D.C.; it is named for Union General O. O. Howard, commissioner of Freedmen's Bureau. Continuing to present day, it is supported by annual government appropriations.

Knights of the White Camelia organized in New Orleans; this and other secret societies, such as the White League, the Invisible Circle, and the Pale Faces, spread rapidly through the South to protect "white supremacy."

Horatio Alger publishes his first boys' rags-to-riches book, *Ragged Dick;* most popular author in the U.S., Alger writes in following 30 years about 100 similar books, which eventually sell 30 million copies.

1867 - 1868

March 30, 1867. Treaty for purchase of Alaska ("Seward's Folly"), negotiated by Russian minister to the U.S. Baron Edouard de Stoeckl and Secretary Seward, is submitted to Senate. **April 9.** Senate ratifies treaty after concentrated propaganda campaign. **July 14, 1868.** House appropriates $7,200,000 for payment after another campaign; some votes have been bought by Stoeckl, who is anxious to be rid of Russian "liability."

1867 - 1874

Dec. 4. Grangers, secret society of farmers and agriculturists, organizes in Washington, D.C.; it stresses need of farmers to decrease influence of middlemen, attacks monopolies, works for lower standard freight and passenger rates with fixed maximums, and urges founding of agricultural schools. By 1874, transportation rates have been fixed by "Granger laws" in Illinois, Wisconsin, and Iowa.

1867 - 1879

U.S. survey is completed west to the 100th meridian and north to the 40th parallel; in Nebraska and Wyoming on the north, and Utah, Nevada, and Arizona on the west. At latter date, U.S. Geological Survey is established, which proceeds to map rest of the country on this basis.

1867 - 1883

Western buffalo (bison) herds, main food resource of Plains Indians, are slaughtered for hides bringing $1 to $3 apiece. Buffalo population of some 13 million is reduced to a few hundred by 1883.

1868

Feb. 21. President Johnson, seeking a Supreme Court decision on the constitutionality of the Tenure of Office Act, dismisses Secretary Stanton (who has been reinstated since suspension) without approval of the Senate.

Feb. 24. House of Representatives passes resolution impeaching Johnson on 11 counts, the first nine alleging violation of Tenure of Office Act, the last two alleging attempt to defame Congress and failure to execute the Reconstruction Law.

February. Supreme Court agrees to consider case involving validity of military courts in Mississippi, although earlier it has

Declaration of Purpose of the Grange, 1874

We propose meeting together, talking together, working together, buying together, selling together, and generally acting together for our mutual protection and advancement, as occasion may require. We shall avoid litigation as much as possible by arbitration in the Grange. We shall constantly strive to secure entire harmony, goodwill, and vital brotherhood among ourselves, and to make order perpetual. We shall earnestly endeavor to suppress personal, local, sectional, and national prejudices, all unhealthy rivalry and all selfish ambition. . . .

For our business interests, we desire to bring producers and consumers, farmers and manufacturers into the most intimate relations possible. Hence, we must dispense with a surplus of middlemen: not that we are unfriendly to them, but we do not need them. Their surplus and their exactions diminish our profits. . . .

In our noble Order there is no communism, no agrarianism. We are opposed to such spirit and management of any corporation or enterprise as tends to oppress people and rob them of their just profits. We are not enemies to capital, but we oppose tyranny of monopolies. We long to see the antagonism between capital and labor removed by common consent and by an enlightened statesmanship worthy of the nineteenth century. . . .

We shall advance the cause of education among ourselves and for our children by all just means within our power. We especially advocate for our agricultural and industrial colleges that practical agriculture, domestic science, and all the arts which adorn the home be taught in their courses of study.

CHARLES SUMNER
Speech in Senate, 1868
This is one of the last great battles with slavery. Driven from these legislative chambers, driven from the field of war, this monstrous power has found a refuge in the executive mansion, where, in utter disregard of the Constitution and laws, it seeks to exercise its ancient, far-reaching sway. All this is very plain. Nobody can question it. Andrew Johnson is the impersonation of the tyrannical slave power. In him it lives again. . . .

I would not in this judgment depart from that moderation which belongs to the occasion; but God forbid that, when called to deal with so great an offender, I should affect a coldness which I cannot feel. . . .

Every sentiment, every conviction, every vow against slavery must now be directed against him. Pharaoh is at the bar of the Senate for judgment.

JAMES GRIMES
Speech in Senate, 1868
I cannot believe it to be our duty to convict the President of an infraction of a law when, in our consciences, we believe the law itself to be invalid, and therefore having no binding effect. If the law is unconstitutional, it is null and void, and the President has committed no offense and done no act deserving of impeachment. . . .

He is sworn to "preserve, protect, and defend the Constitution of the United States." He must defend it against all encroachments from whatever quarter. . . .

This government can only be preserved and the liberty of the people maintained by preserving intact the coordinate branches of it—legislative, executive, judicial—alike. I am no convert to any doctrine of the omnipotence of Congress.

denied its jurisdiction over presidential enforcement of Reconstruction acts. **March 27.** Congress, now completely controlled by Radicals who consider themselves the central power of the government, passes legislation depriving the Court of jurisdiction in order to prevent invalidation of Reconstruction procedures.

March 13. Senate impeachment trial begins before 42 Republicans and 12 Democrats, with two-thirds majority needed for conviction.

May 16. After long hearings, Senate managers, realizing case has proved weak, ask for test vote on eleventh count. At roll call, 7 Republicans have joined Johnson Democrats, making vote 19 for acquittal, 35 for conviction, 1 short of two-thirds majority. Managers ask for 10-day recess and try to rally support. **May 28.** Vote on two other charges is taken; result is the same. The President is acquitted, and proceedings are adjourned.

May 20-21. On first ballot of Chicago convention, Republicans nominate General Ulysses S. Grant for President; Schuyler Colfax of Indiana is nominated on fifth ballot as his running mate. Platform favors Radical Reconstruction and payment of national debt in gold but is ambiguous on Negro suffrage and the tariff. **July 9.** Democrats nominate Horatio Seymour of New York with Francis P. Blair, Jr., for Vice-President on twenty-second ballot; platform attacks Radical Reconstruction and advocates payment of national debt in greenbacks.

Southern conventions, dominated by Radicals and in all cases including Negroes, have met during winter and spring and adopted new state constitutions. **June 22-25.** Congress readmits seven Southern states to the Union after they have satisfied Reconstruction Act's requirements; states are Arkansas, South Carolina, North Carolina, Alabama, Florida, Louisiana, and Georgia. **Sept.** After military forces withdraw from Georgia, state legislature expels 27 Negro members. Congress again imposes military rule, declaring the state once more out of the Union.

July 28. Fourteenth Amendment is declared ratified, enough Southern states having been readmitted to the Union to make up the required three-fourths majority.

Nov. 3. General Grant wins 26 out of the 34 states voting (3 have not yet been readmitted), with 214 electoral votes to Seymour's 80; but popular vote is 3,000,000 to 2,700,000, only a 300,000 majority. Grant's great popularity in the North plus 700,000 Southern Negro votes account for his victory. Colfax is elected Vice-President.

Congress passes bill limiting work hours of federally employed laborers and mechanics to eight-hour day.

George Westinghouse, appalled by constant railroad accidents due to primitive braking systems, invents brake using compressed air; device is a great success. Westinghouse perfects his invention in 1872.

Open-hearth steel process first used in U.S. in Trenton, New Jersey; process makes possible use of more U.S. ore, as well as scrap iron, than can be utilized in Bessemer process.

As editor of newly founded California literary magazine, *Overland Monthly*, Bret Harte publishes his story "The Luck of Roaring Camp," the background of which is mining camps of the area; in following

Amendment XIII
Neither slavery nor involuntary servitude, except as a punishment for crime whereof the party shall have been duly convicted, shall exist within the United States or any place subject to their jurisdiction.

Amendment XIV
All persons born or naturalized in the United States and subject to the jurisdiction thereof are citizens of the United States and of the state wherein they reside. No state shall make or enforce any law which shall abridge the privileges or immunities of citizens of the United States; nor shall any state deprive any person of life, liberty, or property without due process of law; nor deny to any person within its jurisdiction the equal protection of the laws. . . .

No person shall be a senator or representative in Congress, or elector of President and Vice-President, or hold any office, civil or military, under the United States, or under any state, who, having previously taken an oath as a member of Congress, or as an officer of the United States, or as a member of any state legislature, or as an executive or judicial officer of any state to support the Constitution of the United States, shall have engaged in insurrection or rebellion against the same or given aid or comfort to the enemies thereof.

Amendment XV
The right of citizens of the United States to vote shall not be denied or abridged by the United States or by any state on account of race, color, or previous condition of servitude.

LOUISA MAY ALCOTT
Little Women, 1869

"You must take my place, Jo, and be everything to Father and Mother when I'm gone. They will turn to you, don't fail them; and if it's hard to work alone, remember that I don't forget you, and that you'll be happier in doing that than writing splendid books or seeing all the world; for love is the only thing that we can carry with us when we go, and it makes the end so easy. . . ."

So the spring days came and went, the sky grew clearer, the earth greener, the flowers were up fair and early, and the birds came back in time to say goodby to Beth, who, like a tired but trustful child, clung to the hands that had led her all her life, as Father and Mother guided her tenderly through the Valley of the Shadow, and gave her up to God.

Seldom except in books do the dying utter memorable words, see visions, or depart with beatified countenances, and those who have sped many parting souls know that to most the end comes as naturally and simply as sleep. As Beth had hoped, the "tide went out easily," and in the dark hour before the dawn, on the bosom where she had drawn her first breath, she quietly drew her last, with no farewell but one loving look, one little sigh.

With tears and prayers and tender hands, Mother and sisters made her ready for the long sleep that pain would never mar again, seeing with grateful eyes the beautiful serenity that soon replaced the pathetic patience that had wrung their hearts so long, and feeling with reverent joy that to their darling death was a benignant angel, not a phantom full of dread.

year he publishes "The Outcasts of Poker Flat." Louisa May Alcott publishes first volume of *Little Women*, based on life of her family; second volume is issued in following year. The book, immediately popular, is first enduring work of American children's literature.

State-supported University of California is chartered; first campus is at Oakland. University moves to Berkeley in 1873.

1868 - 1870

1868. Congress forms Wyoming Territory out of parts of territories of Dakota, Utah, and Idaho. Settlements have grown as a result of gold discoveries and railroad-building projects. **1869.** Territorial legislature grants suffrage to women for first time in U.S. history. **1870.** Mrs. Esther Morris becomes first woman justice of the peace.

1869

Feb. 27. Realizing that Negro vote in the South has won election for them, Republicans in Congress frame Fifteenth Amendment to the Constitution and propose it to the states. Amendment makes Negro suffrage mandatory not only in Southern but in Northern states, in which Fourteenth Amendment has been ineffective, by establishing right to vote of all (male) citizens regardless of "race, color, or previous condition of servitude."

March 18. Congress, supporting Grant administration hard money policy, passes Public Credit Act, which provides for payment of U.S. obligations in gold; long debate follows on question of whether $356 million in greenbacks should be redeemed.

May 10. Union Pacific Railroad building west from Nebraska joins Central Pacific building east from California at Promontory Point, Utah; junction completes first transcontinental railroad link. Regular runs from Boston to Oakland, California, begin the next year. Scandals involving railroad construction companies from 1867 (Crédit Mobilier, Crocker Corporation) slow down but do not stop further railroad expansion.

Sept. 24. Financial panic known as "Black Friday" occurs after Jay Gould and James ("Jubilee Jim") Fisk conspire to corner all gold in money market, hold it until price soars, then sell. To make sure government release of gold does not upset conspiracy, they have hired President Grant's brother-in-law to approach him. Grant has seemed to agree to persuasion, but he becomes aware of plot when gold prices reach peak and orders release of government gold, bringing about collapse of conspiracy, as well as ruin of hundreds of small investors. Though innocent, Grant appears to have been in league with conspirators.

In *Texas* v. *White*, Supreme Court rules that Confederate authorities have never actually had jurisdiction, since according to the Constitution the Union could not be dissolved; decision refrains from passing on legality of Reconstruction acts, but declares that it is the right of Congress, not the executive, to recognize state governments.

Noble Order of Knights of Labor is formed secretly in Philadelphia by disbanded union of garment cutters. Later a national organization, membership eventually includes almost all workers, skilled and unskilled, over 16 years old; lawyers, bankers, liquor dealers, and gamblers are excluded. By 1886 organization has 5,892 locals, with more than 700,000 members.

National Prohibition Party founded in Chicago. Oldest U.S. third political party, it

JIM FISK
During Congressional investigation of "Black Friday," 1869; referring to money he had lost trying to corner the market in gold.
Gone where the woodbine twineth.
[When asked what the phrase meant, he said, "Up the spout."]

JIM FISK
After Congressional investigation of "Black Friday," 1869
Nothing is lost save honor.

Preamble to Constitution of Knights of Labor, 1878
The recent alarming development and aggression of aggregated wealth, which, unless checked, will invariably lead to the pauperization and hopeless degradation of the toiling masses, render it imperative, if we desire to enjoy the blessings of life, that a check should be placed upon its power and upon unjust accumulation, and a system adopted which will secure to the laborer the fruits of his toil. And as this much-desired object can only be accomplished by the thorough unification of labor and the united efforts of those who obey the divine injunction that "In the sweat of thy brow shalt thou eat bread," we have formed the _____ with a view of securing the organization and direction, by cooperative effort, of the power of the industrial classes; and we submit to the world the objects sought to be accomplished by our organization, calling upon all who believe in securing "the greatest good to the greatest number" to aid and assist us.

CHARLES W. ELIOT
Inaugural Address, 1869

The very word "education" is a standing protest against dogmatic teaching. The notion that education consists in the authoritative inculcation of what the teacher deems true may be logical and appropriate in a convent or a seminary for priests, but it is intolerable in universities and public schools, from primary to professional. The worthy fruit of academic culture is an open mind, trained to careful thinking, instructed in the methods of philosophic investigation, acquainted in a general way with the accumulated thought of past generations, and penetrated with humility. . . .

As a people, we do not apply to mental activities the principle of division of labor; and we have but a halting faith in special training for high professional employments. The vulgar conceit that a Yankee can turn his hand to anything we insensibly carry into high places, where it is preposterous and criminal. We are accustomed to seeing men leap from farm or shop to courtroom or pulpit, and we half believe that common men can safely use the seven-league boots of genius. . . .

In education, the individual traits of different minds have not been sufficiently attended to. Through all the period of boyhood the school studies should be representative; all the main fields of knowledge should be entered upon. But the young man of nineteen or twenty ought to know what he likes best and is most fit for. If his previous training has been sufficiently wide, he will know by that time whether he is most apt at language or philosophy or natural science or mathematics. If he feels no loves, he will at least have his hates.

offers presidential and vice-presidential candidates in every national election to present day, but Party's chief influence is in local politics.

Massachusetts forms first state board of health in the U.S.

Thomas A. Edison patents first electric voting machine, but such machines are not officially authorized until 1890s.

Charles W. Eliot, author of *The New Education: Its Organization*, is appointed president of Harvard University; elective system of study and sabbatical years are introduced during his administration. Yale University establishes first school of fine arts in the U.S.

Mark Twain publishes *Innocents Abroad* after traveling in Europe; immediately popular, the book ridicules Old World manners and contrasts European with American democratic society.

Having organized his own stock company, playwright John Augustin Daly opens theater in New York and produces plays starring, among others, John Drew and Maurice Barrymore.

First all-professional U.S. baseball team, the Cincinnati Red Stockings, is founded; baseball has been played by amateurs since 1839, when Abner Doubleday laid out field with four bases and named the game baseball.

1870

Jan. 10. President Grant submits to Congress treaty of annexation of the Dominican Republic although his Cabinet has rejected it unanimously; Grant's pretext is that disorders must be controlled, but actually he wants island for a naval base. **March 15.** Senate committee on foreign relations advises against ratification, but treaty is submitted to Senate. **June 30.** Senate rejects treaty. Charles Sumner, who has opposed it, loses chairmanship of Foreign Relations Committee, and Attorney General E. R. Hoar, also strongly against it, is forced to resign from Cabinet.

January-July. Last four Southern states are readmitted to the Union after ratifying Fourteenth and Fifteenth amendments and framing constitutions satisfactory to Congress: Virginia in January, Mississippi in February, Texas in March, and Georgia in July (for the second time).

Feb. 7. Supreme Court holds that in cases of contracts made before passage, Legal Tender acts of 1862 and 1863 are unconstitutional; minority opinion is that war emergency at the time made them legitimate. President Grant appoints two new Supreme Court justices the same day, aware that they agree with minority in decision. In second legal tender case, they swing opinion, finding that legal tender is valid in any emergency, not necessarily war. On little evidence, Grant is thought to have packed the Court for his own purpose.

March 30. Fifteenth Amendment is declared ratified.

July 14. Tariff bill temporarily reverses trend toward higher duties, which by now average 47 percent, by putting many raw materials on free list and lowering duties slightly on other items.

U. S. Census shows total population of 39,818,000, of whom 4,900,900 are freed Negroes, and 2,315,000 immigrants who have arrived since 1860. Urban population (in places of over 2,500) has reached 25

FREDERICK LAW OLMSTED
Address in Boston, 1870

We have reason to believe, then, that towns which of late have been increasing rapidly on account of their commercial advantages are likely to be still more attractive to population in the future; that there will, in consequence, soon be larger towns than any the world has yet known; and that the further progress of civilization is to depend mainly upon the influences by which men's minds and characters will be affected while living in large towns.

Now, knowing that the average length of the life of mankind in towns has been much less than in the country, and that the average amount of disease and misery and of vice and crime has been much greater in towns, this would be a very dark prospect for civilization, if it were not that modern science has beyond all question determined many of the causes of the special evils by which men are afflicted in towns and placed means in our hands for guarding against them. It has shown, for example, that under ordinary circumstances, in the interior parts of large and closely built towns, a given quantity of air contains considerably less of the elements which we require to receive through the lungs than the air of the country or even of the outer and more open parts of a town; and that instead of them it carries into the lungs highly corrupt and irritating matters, the action of which tends strongly to vitiate all our sources of vigor —how strongly may perhaps be indicated in the shortest way by the statement that even metallic plates and statues corrode and wear away under the atmospheric influences which prevail in the midst of large towns more rapidly than in the country.

Petition to Congress, 1871

We the colored citizens of Frankfort and vicinity do this day memorialize your honorable bodies upon the condition of affairs now existing in this the state of Kentucky.

We would respectfully state that life, liberty, and property are unprotected among the colored race of this state. Organized bands of desperate and lawless men, mainly composed of soldiers of the late Rebel armies, armed, disciplined, and disguised, and bound by oath and secret obligations, have by force, terror, and violence subverted all civil society among colored people, thus utterly rendering insecure the safety of persons and property, overthrowing all those rights which are the primary basis and objects of the government which are expressly guaranteed to us by the Constitution of the United States as amended.

We believe you are not familiar with the description of the Ku Klux Klan's riding nightly over the country, going from county to county, and in the county towns spreading terror wherever they go by robbing, whipping, ravishing, and killing our people without provocation, compelling colored people to break the ice and bathe in the chilly waters of the Kentucky River.

The legislature has adjourned; they refused to enact any laws to suppress Ku Klux disorder. We regard them as now being licensed to continue their dark and bloody deeds under cover of the dark night. . . .

We appeal to you as law-abiding citizens to enact some laws that will protect us and that will enable us to exercise the rights of citizens.

percent, compared to 20 percent in 1860. About 2,032,000 more people have moved to the West than those moving eastward; about 622,000 more have moved to the North than to the South.

John D. Rockefeller, having merged several Cleveland refineries in 1867, forms Standard Oil Company of Ohio, with capitalization of $1 million; by concentrating on refining, making special low rate agreements with railroads, and gaining control of pipelines, company by 1879 controls about 95 percent of oil refining in the U.S.

Pennsylvania Railroad Company, a holding company, is organized; mergers of Eastern railroads occur throughout this period.

1870 - 1871

May 31, 1870 and April 20, 1871. In effort to control activities of secret societies working to drive Republicans out of the South, Congress passes Ku Klux Klan acts. Federal indictment of thousands of members and resulting 1,250 convictions effectively cripple such organizations politically, but authorities are not able to control others that work openly.

1870 - 1878

Beginning of motion-picture experiments. **1870.** Henry R. Heyl, applying French Zoëtrope that whirls pictures on drum to give effect of motion, projects whirling pictures with magic lantern. Oliver Wendell Holmes' studies of human motion to improve design of artificial legs lead to work of Eadweard Muybridge, who photographs running horses with series of cameras in 1877 and later projects transparencies. **1878.** Muybridge inquires of Thomas A. Edison whether pictures can be coordinated with sound of phonograph, but sound volume of phonograph is not great enough at this time.

1871

Oct. 8-9. Large portions of center of Chicago burn to the ground; 300 people are killed, 90,000 left homeless, and property damage is $196 million.

Oct. 26. William Marcy ("Boss") Tweed is indicted in New York City following exposé in *New York Times*. Enabled by new city charter to acquire control of the city treasury, Tweed and his henchmen have stolen between $30 and $200 million by falsifying contracts, bills, and vouchers and collecting from contractors. Tweed is convicted in 1873 and dies in jail. Members of his ring escape to Europe with their part of money.

November. Henry Morton Stanley, British-born naturalized American citizen, working as a reporter for *New York Herald*, finds David Livingstone, British explorer ("Dr. Livingstone, I presume"), at Ujiji in central Africa. Editor James Gordon Bennett has ordered Stanley to search for Livingstone, who has been unheard from since 1866, when he set out to discover the source of the Nile River.

Conservative, or "white supremacist," governments, called "Redeemers," replace Radical, or "Black Republican," governments in Virginia, North Carolina, and Georgia by end of year as Southerners use various political and economic pressures to keep Negroes from voting.

Federal government land grants to railroads are discontinued; grants to this time have totaled more than 131 million acres.

Walt Whitman publishes "Passage to India," his last great poem, and *Democratic Vistas*, prose work in which he discusses shortcomings of American democracy to date. Edward Eggleston publishes his novel of the Midwest, *The Hoosier Schoolmaster*.

Atlanta News, 1874
Radicalism has declared a war of extermination against the whites of the South. It proposes to punish rebels and make "treason odious" by the most vindictive measures its malignity can conceive. Our fate is to be less merciful than that of the Trojans, less sublime than that of the Carthaginians. We are not to perish by the sword as these people perished; we are to live, and live in degradation. Our helots and serfs of yesterday are to rule us politically and to sit beside us on terms of equality socially. All pride of race is to be crushed within us. We are to be the slave; the Negro is to be the master. . . .

Nor will it end in this civil rights bill. The next thing on the program will be to enact a compulsory education law, and compel us to send our children to public schools, there to herd with Negroes. This is not a gratuitous proposition. It has already been made and favorably received. . . .

Let there be White Leagues formed in every town, village, and hamlet of the South; and let us organize for the great struggle which seems to be inevitable. If the October elections which are to be held at the North are favorable to the Radicals, the time will have arrived for us to prepare for the very worst. The radicalism of the Republican Party must be met by the radicalism of white men. We have no war to make against the United States government, but against the Republican Party our hate must be unquenchable, our war interminable and merciless. . . .

We have submitted long enough to indignities, and it is time to meet brute force with brute force. Every Southern state should swarm with White Leagues, and we should stand ready to act.

RED CLOUD

Address at Cooper Union, 1870

You do not know who appears before you today to speak. I am a representative of the original American race, the first people of this continent. We are good and not bad. . . . We have given you nearly all our lands, and if we had any more land to give we would be very glad to give it. We have nothing more. We are driven into a very little land, and we want you now, as our dear friends, to help us with the government of the United States. . . .

I only want to do that which is peaceful, and the Great Fathers know it, and also the Great Father who made us both. I came to Washington to see the Great Father in order to have peace and in order to have peace continue. That is all we want, and that is the reason why we are here now. . . .

Look at me. I am poor and naked, but I am the Chief of the Nation. We do not want riches, we do not ask for riches, but we want our children properly trained and brought up. We look to you for your sympathy. Our riches will . . . do us no good; we cannot take away into the other world anything we have — we want to have love and peace. . . . We would like to know why commissioners are sent out there to do nothing but rob [us] and get the riches of this world away from us?

GEN. PHILIP H. SHERIDAN

The only good Indian is a dead Indian.

The Nick Carter Library
Another Redskin bit the dust!

Louisa May Alcott publishes *Little Men*, sequel to *Little Women*.

Phineas T. Barnum produces circus, "The Greatest Show on Earth," in Brooklyn after 15-year Connecticut retirement.

1871 - 1875

March 3, 1871. Protests against Spoils System and corruption in civil service lead to establishment by Congress of Commission on Civil Service Reform. **March 4.** President Grant appoints George W. Curtis as head of Commission. In next four years, Congress makes no appropriation and Curtis' recommendations are ignored. **1875.** Curtis resigns, and Commission ceases to function.

1871 - 1886

April 30, 1871. Campaign of "Apache extermination" ends when mob in Camp Grant, Arizona, massacres more than 100 Apaches who have put themselves under U.S. military protection; act produces great public indignation. Efforts to conciliate Apaches under new policy are partly successful, but hostilities in Arizona and New Mexico continue until 1886, when Chief Geronimo surrenders. Remnants of tribes are sent to reservations in Southwest.

1872

May 22. Congress passes Amnesty Act, which restores civil rights to all citizens of the South except for 500-700 former Confederate leaders.

Feb. 22. National Labor Union, having become Labor Reform Party, nominates Judge David Davis of Illinois for President. **May 1.** Liberal Republicans, in move against Radical Reconstruction policies and graft in government, nominate New York newspaper editor Horace Greeley for President, with Benjamin Gratz Brown of Missouri as his running mate; platform stresses civil service reform, public lands for settlers, and specie payments. Democrats and Liberal Colored Republicans pick same candidates. **June 5.** Republicans renominate President Grant, with Henry Wilson of New Hampshire for Vice-President. **Sept. 3.** "Straight" Democrats pick Charles O'Connor of New York and John Quincy Adams of Massachusetts.

Sept. 14. U.S. claims against Great Britain for damage done by the *Alabama* and other raiders built in England during the Civil War are finally settled by international tribunal, with representatives from Brazil, Italy, Switzerland, Britain, and the U.S. Tribunal awards the U.S. $15,500,000 for 100,000 tons of shipping destroyed and cargoes lost.

Nov. 5. President Grant is reelected by vote of 3,597,000 to 2,843,000 for Greeley; electoral vote is 286 to 66. **Nov. 29.** Greeley dies suddenly, before his electoral votes are cast. They are redistributed: Thomas A. Hendricks (courtesy vote for newly elected governor of Indiana), 42; Brown, 18; Charles J. Jenkins, 2; Davis, 1; and 3 votes for Greeley that are not counted.

First commercial production of Celluloid, invented by J. W. and I. S. Hyatt in 1870, marks beginning of era of synthetic materials.

Congress establishes Yellowstone National Park as "a pleasuring ground"; area has been described long before by Western explorers, but descriptions of geysers and hot springs are doubted and not verified until 1870. First national park is 3,471 square miles at junction of borders of Wyoming, Montana, and Idaho.

Mark Twain publishes *Roughing It*, an account of his experiences on Southwest and

MARK TWAIN
Roughing It, 1872
[You are as] ignorant as the unborn babe! ignorant as unborn twins!

Following the Equator, 1897
Everything human is pathetic. The secret source of Humor itself is not joy but sorrow. There is no humor in heaven.

There isn't a Parallel of Latitude but thinks it would have been the Equator if it had had its rights.

Man is the only animal that blushes. Or needs to.

Letters, 1917
I conceive that the right way to write a story for boys is to write so that it will not only interest boys but strongly interest any man who has ever been a boy. That immensely enlarges the audience.

More Maxims of Mark, 1927
You can straighten a worm, but the crook is in him and only waiting.

Notebook, 1935
Well enough for old folks to rise early, because they have done so many mean things all their lives they can't sleep anyhow.

Of the delights of this world man cares most for sexual intercourse. He will go any length for it—risk fortune, character, reputation, life itself. And what do you think he has done? In a thousand years you would never guess—He has left it out of his heaven! Prayer takes its place.

My books are water: those of the great geniuses are wine. Everybody drinks water.

JAMES McNEILL WHISTLER
Whistler v. Ruskin, 1878
Two and two continue to make four, in spite of the whine of the amateur for three, or the cry of the critic for five.

Ten O'Clock, 1888
Nature sings her exquisite song to the artist alone, her son and her master — her son in that he loves her, her master in that he knows her.

The Gentle Art of Making Enemies, 1890
To say of a picture, as is often said in its praise, that it shows great and earnest labour, is to say that it is incomplete and unfit for view.

Art should be independent of all clap-trap — should stand alone, and appeal to the artistic sense of eye and ear, without confounding this with emotions entirely foreign to it, as devotion, pity, love, patriotism, and the like. All these have no kind of concern with it.

The imitator is a poor kind of creature. If the man who paints only the tree, or flower, or other surface he sees before him were an artist, the king of artists would be the photographer. It is for the artist to do something beyond this: in portrait painting to put on canvas something more then the face the model wears for that one day; to paint the man, in short, as well as his features.

D. C. SEITZ
Whistler Stories, 1913
"I only know of two painters in the world," said a newly introduced feminine enthusiast to Whistler, "yourself and Velasquez." "Why," answered Whistler in dulcet tones, "why drag in Velasquez?"

Far West frontiers. Clergyman Edward Payson Roe publishes *Barriers Burned Away*, a novel based on the Chicago fire, written after he has visited the ruins. Book is his first work; he writes many others, all immediately popular.

James Abbott McNeill Whistler exhibits his "Arrangement in Grey and Black No. I" in London; it becomes famous later as "Whistler's Mother." Whistler, born in Massachusetts, lives and works almost entirely in Europe.

1872 - 1873

Sept. 4, 1872. *New York Sun* accuses several political figures, including Vice-President Schuyler Colfax, Representative James A. Garfield, and Henry Wilson (Republican candidate for Vice-President), of accepting bribes in form of stock gifts from Crédit Mobilier, construction company secretly owned by Union Pacific Railroad stockholders, as payment for political influence on behalf of railroad. **Feb. 18, 1873.** Resulting investigation ends in censure of two representatives. Although scandal has originated years before President Grant's administration, it adds to growing picture of mismanagement and graft.

1872 - 1877

European Marxian Socialists split with Anarcho-Communists in 1872 and transfer main organization of their First International to New York City; in 1876 they form Workingmen's Party, changed in following year to Socialist Labor Party, which works with trade-union movement.

1872 - 1895

New age of astronomical research opens when Henry Draper makes first successful photograph of the spectrum of a star in 1872, Asaph Hall discovers the moons of

Mars in 1877, Draper demonstrates photography of nebulae in 1880, and James E. Keeler discovers composition of Saturn's rings in 1895.

1873

Feb. 12. In spite of increased mining of silver in the West, Congress passes Fourth Coinage Act, which makes gold the U.S. monetary standard and eliminates the silver dollar. Called "the Crime of '73," the act is for two decades a basis of agitation by those who advocate unlimited coinage of silver.

March 3. Congressional legislation known as the "salary grab act" doubles salary of President and increases those of Supreme Court justices, congressmen, and other federal officials. Angry public reaction forces repeal in following year, except for salaries of President and justices.

March 3. Coal Lands Act allows purchase of public coal lands for $10 to $20 per acre depending upon distance from railroad; limit is 160 acres for individuals and 320 for groups. Timber Culture Act gives title to 160 acres of timberland to any person who keeps 40 acres of it in good condition.

June. Financial crisis, beginning in Vienna, spreads to other European countries, which withdraw investments from the U.S.

Sept. 18. Jay Cooke and Company, powerful banking house and financial agent for Northern Pacific Railway, fails, leading to Panic of 1873. U.S. financial structure has been weakened by wild speculation in railroads and their construction, as well as overexpansion in almost every other part of the economy. More than 100 banks fail, six times as many state chartered as nationally chartered, which eventually strengthens the national bank system. Resulting depression

HENRY ENO
Letter to his brother, 1869
I came here expecting to find a rich mineral country, also to find much such a population as California had in 1849 and '50. The great mineral wealth of eastern Nevada has not been exaggerated. In fact I did not expect to find so rich or so many silver mines. There is not so much wild reckless extravagance among the people of the towns and the miners as in the early days of California. There are not as many homicides according to the numbers, but there is perhaps more highway robberies committed. We have here, as twenty years ago, numbers too lazy to work but not too lazy to steal, and some too proud to work and not afraid to steal. The laws of Nevada license gambling, and here at Hamilton, in Treasure City, and Shermantown are some ten or twelve licensed gambling tables. The next session of the legislature may perhaps license highway robbery.

There are two banking establishments, two express offices, Wells Fargo and Union Express, some ten or twelve assay offices, and a small army of lawyers. The District Court has been in session ever since I arrived. A trial often occupies ten or twelve days. A very few lawyers are doing well. From what I can discover I believe that lawyers depend more upon perjury and subornation of perjury than upon principles of law or precedents. Experts in mining do a thriving business as witnesses.

SAMUEL F. MILLER

Slaughter-House Cases, 1873

Was it the purpose of the 14th Amendment, by the simple declaration that no state should make or enforce any law which shall abridge the privileges and immunities of citizens of the United States, to transfer the security and protection of all the civil rights which we have mentioned from the states to the federal government? And where it is declared that Congress shall have the power to enforce that article, was it intended to bring within the power of Congress the entire domain of civil rights heretofore belonging exclusively to the states?

All this and more must follow if the proposition of the plaintiffs in error be sound. For not only are these rights subject to the control of Congress whenever in its discretion any of them are supposed to be abridged by state legislation, but that body may also pass laws in advance limiting and restricting the exercise of legislative power by the states, in their most ordinary and usual functions, as in its judgment it may think proper on all such subjects. And still further, such a construction . . . would constitute this Court a perpetual censor upon all legislation of the states. . . .

The effect is to fetter and degrade the state governments by subjecting them to the control of Congress, in the exercise of powers heretofore universally conceded to them of the most ordinary and fundamental character. . . .

We are convinced that no such results were intended by the Congress which proposed these amendments, nor by the legislatures of the states which ratified them.

creates severe unemployment, lasting until 1878.

Oct. 31. Spanish officials in Cuba capture ship *Virginius*, which is running arms for Cuban revolutionary movement and illegally flying American flag; 53 members of crew, including Americans, are executed. Secretary of State Hamilton Fish demands and receives $80,000 from Spain for families of American crew members.

In Slaughter-House Cases, protest has been made against Louisiana legislative grant of monopoly in slaughtering industry on ground that such legislation violates the Fourteenth Amendment; U.S. Supreme Court holds that federal guarantees of Amendment apply only to Negroes, and that civil rights of most citizens are adequately protected by state laws.

More immigrants come to the U.S. than in any previous year; total is almost 460,000; one-third of these are from Germany and others chiefly from northwestern Europe, especially England and Ireland.

By this date, harvesting machinery is in common use, especially in the West, making farm labor about 12 times as effective as with hand methods and stimulating trend toward larger farms. Although harvesters have been used since the 1830s, production of more efficient machines in growing numbers has been stimulated by the Civil War and Europe's grain needs.

Bethlehem Steel Company, using Bessemer process, begins manufacturing in Pittsburgh, Pennsylvania; iron ore shipment from mines near Marquette, Michigan, have by now reached more than one million tons annually.

Bi-weekly *Home Companion* (later *Woman's Home Companion*, a monthly) starts publication in Cleveland; it continues until

1957. *St. Nicholas Magazine* for children, edited until 1905 by Mrs. Mary Mapes Dodge, begins publication in New York; it continues until 1940.

1873 - 1875

Rabbi Isaac Mayer Wise, advocate of Reform Judaism, organizes Union of American Hebrew Congregations in 1873 and Hebrew Union College in 1875, both in Cincinnati, Ohio.

1873 - 1895

Bellevue Hospital in New York opens first school of nursing in 1873, with instruction based on teachings of Florence Nightingale. One hundred and twelve medical schools are founded during this period, but 87 of them are concentrated in the Middle West; quality of instruction is so uneven that licensing control is established in almost all states by 1895.

1874

May. Federal troops restore order in Arkansas, where Carpetbaggers have seized control of government and stolen public funds; climax is reached in state election when both candidates for governor claim victory. Dispute ends with ascendancy of Democrat Elisha Baxter as governor, thus ending Northern (Republican) control of state.

Sept. 14. People of New Orleans battle unsuccessfully with federal officials in effort to take over Louisiana government, which has been more corrupt than that of any other Southern state under Reconstruction. Democrats claim to have elected Democratic governor, but federal forces reinstall Republican William Pitt Kellogg.

Rocky Mountain locusts devastate grain-growing areas of the Great Plains from

JAMES S. PIKE

The Prostrate State: South Carolina, 1874

Here sit 124 members. Of these, 23 are white men, representing the remains of the old civilization. These are good-looking, substantial citizens. They are men of weight and standing in the communities they represent. . . . There they sit, grim and silent. . . . They say little and do little as the days go by. . . . Grouped in a corner of the commodious and well-furnished chamber, they stolidly survey the noisy riot that goes on in the great black left and center, where the business and debates of the House are conducted, and where sit the strange and extraordinary guides of the fortunes of a once proud and haughty state. . . .

As things stand, the body is almost literally a Black Parliament, and it is the only one on the face of the earth which is the representative of a white constituency and the professed exponent of an advanced type of modern civilization. . . . The speaker is black, the clerk is black, the doorkeepers are black, the little pages are black, the chairman of the Ways and Means is black, and the chaplain is coal black. . . .

But underneath all this shocking burlesque upon legislative proceedings, we must not forget that there is something very real to this uncouth and untutored multitude. It is not all sham, nor all burlesque. They have a genuine interest and a genuine earnestness in the business of the assembly, which we are bound to recognize and respect, unless we would be accounted shallow critics. They have an earnest purpose, born of a conviction that their position and condition are not fully assured, which lends a sort of dignity to their proceedings.

(Above) House of Representatives committee appointed to draft
articles of impeachment against President Andrew Johnson: standing,
left to right—James F. Wilson, George S. Boutwell, John A. Logan;
seated, left to right—Benjamin Butler, Thaddeus Stevens, Thomas
Williams, John Bingham; (below) execution of Maximilian, Emperor of
Mexico, on June 9, 1867: the end of the Civil War had allowed the
United States to reassert the Monroe Doctrine and secure the withdrawal of French troops supporting Maximilian

(Above) Ulysses S. Grant, eighteenth President
of the United States; (right) another Nast cartoon,
"Great Expectations," a reaction to the Liberal
Republicans, and later the Democrats, nominating
Horace Greeley for President and Gratz Brown for
Vice President in 1872; (below) parade of Negroes
in honor of ratification of Fifteenth Amendment,
in 1870

The Old Chisholm Trail

*Well, come along, boys, and listen to
my tale;*
*I'll tell you of my troubles on the Old
Chisholm Trail.*

*Coma ti yi yippy, yippy yay, yippy
yay,*
Coma ti yi yippy, yippy yay.

*I woke up one morning on the Old
Chisholm Trail,*
Rope in my hand and a cow by the tail.

*I jumped in the saddle and grabbed holt
the horn,*
Best damn cowboy that ever was born.
. . .
*My seat's in the saddle and my saddle's
in the sky;*
*And I'll quit punchin' cows in the sweet
by and by.*

Good-Bye, Old Paint

*My foot in the stirrup, I'm a-leavin'
Cheyenne,*
*My pony won't stand, I'm off to
Montan'.*

*Good-bye, Old Paint, I'm a-leavin'
Cheyenne.*
*Good-bye, Old Paint, I'm a-leavin'
Cheyenne.*
*With my feet in the stirrup I'm off
to Montan',*
*Good-bye, Old Paint, I'm a-leavin'
Cheyenne.*

*I'm a-ridin' Old Paint, I'm a-leadin'
Old Fan,*
*Good-bye, little Annie, I'm off to
Cheyenne.*
. . .
*I'm a-ridin' Old Paint, I'm a-leadin'
Old Dan,*
*I'm off to Montana to throw the
hoolihan.*

Texas into Canada in worst occurrence of
this plague, which is a perennial discouragement to homesteaders.

Introduction of barbed wire begins limitation of cow country, which by now
stretches in completely open land from the
Rio Grande to Canada. Homesteaders
brought by railroads use wire to fence their
fields, which results in bitter battles with
cattle rangers, accustomed to free access to
water; but eventually legal rights of settlers
prevail, and cattle are confined to smaller
and smaller areas.

Open break between advocates of orthodox theism and those of liberal theism occurs with publication of John Fiske's *Outlines of Cosmic Philosophy*, which undertakes
to show that religion and hotly debated
Darwinian evolution theories are not incompatible. Ministers Henry Ward Beecher
and Lyman Abbott, among others, are supporters of Fiske's argument.

National Woman's Christian Temperance
Union (W.C.T.U.) is formed in Cleveland
to promote prohibition by educational, social, and political means. Frances Willard,
teacher and reformer, is influential in organization from 1879 and eventually forms international World's Woman's Christian
Temperance Union.

First streetcar to operate by electricity,
developed by Stephen Dudley Field, begins
running in New York City.

1874 - 1878

Aug. 4-18, 1874. First Chautauqua Assembly, organized by the Reverend John H.
Vincent and Lewis Miller of Ohio, meets at
Fair Point on Chautauqua Lake, New York.
Originally formed for training of church
workers and Sunday school teachers during
summer months, program eventually in-

cludes entertainment and general education. By 1878, correspondence study programs have been organized.

1875

Jan. 14. Congress passes Specie Resumption Act (twice before recommended by President Grant); Act provides for resumption of specie payments on January 1, 1879, and reduces limit of greenbacks in circulation from previous $382 million to $300 million, thus ending Civil War financing.

March 1. Congress passes Civil Rights Act, sponsored by Charles Sumner until his death in 1874, which guarantees equal rights to Negroes in public accommodations and jury duty. In 1883, Act is invalidated by Supreme Court, which holds that the federal government can protect only political, not social, rights.

March 18. Senate approves U.S.-Hawaii treaty that recognizes reciprocal commercial rights; independent Kingdom of Hawaii agrees to cede no territory to any other power.

March. John McCloskey, Roman Catholic archbishop of New York, becomes first American Cardinal.

May 1. *St. Louis Democrat* exposes widespread conspiracy of distillery owners and federal revenue officials (known as the "whisky ring") to withhold liquor taxes from the government. In ensuing investigation ordered by secretary of the treasury, a chief organizer is found to have been appointed by President Grant, and Grant's private secretary is indicted with 237 others. After indictment, President uses influence to save his secretary from conviction.

May. Churchill Downs at Louisville, Kentucky, is founded; first Kentucky Der-

BLANCHE K. BRUCE
Speech in Senate, 1876
We want peace and good order at the South; but it can only come by the fullest recognition of the rights of all classes. The opposition must concede the necessity of change, not only in the temper but in the philosophy of their party organization and management. The sober American judgment must obtain in the South as elsewhere in the republic, that the only distinctions upon which parties can be safely organized and in harmony with our institutions are differences of opinions relative to principles and policy of government, and that differences of religion, nationality, or race can neither with safety nor propriety be permitted for a moment to enter into the party contests of the day.

The unanimity with which the colored voters act with a party is not referable to any race prejudice on their part. On the contrary, they invite the political cooperation of their white brethren, and vote as a unit because proscribed as such. They deprecate the establishment of the color line by the opposition, not only because the act is unwise and wrong in principle but because it isolates them from the white men of the South, and forces them, in sheer self-protection and against their inclination, to act seemingly upon the basis of a race prejudice that they neither respect nor entertain. . . .

When we can entertain opinions and select party affiliations without proscription, and cast our ballots as other citizens and without jeopardy to person or privilege, we can safely afford to be governed by the considerations that ordinarily determine the political action of American citizens.

MARY BAKER EDDY
Miscellaneous Writings, 1896
My first plank in the platform of Christian Science is as follows: "There is no life, truth, intelligence, nor substance in matter. All is infinite Mind and its infinite manifestation, for God is All-in-all. Spirit is immortal Truth; matter is mortal error. Spirit is the real and eternal; matter is the unreal and temporal. Spirit is God, and man is His image and likeness. Therefore man is not material; he is spiritual." . . .

But, say you, is a stone spiritual? To erring material sense, No! but to unerring spiritual sense, it is a small manifestation of Mind, a type of spiritual substance, "the substance of things hoped for." Mortals can know a stone as substance only by first admitting that it is substantial. Take away the mortal sense of substance and the stone itself would disappear, only to reappear in the spiritual sense thereof. Matter can neither see, hear, feel, taste, nor smell having no sensation of its own. Perception by the five personal senses is mental and dependent on the beliefs that mortals entertain. . . . In dreams, things are only what mortal mind makes them; and the phenomena of mortal life are as dreams; and this so-called life is a dream soon told. In proportion as mortals turn from this mortal and material dream to the true sense of reality, everlasting Life will be found to be the only Life. That death does not destroy the beliefs of the flesh, our Master proved to His doubting disciple Thomas. Also, He demonstrated that divine Science alone can overbear materiality and mortality; and this great truth was shown by His ascension after death, whereby He arose above the illusion of matter.

by, one-and-one-quarter-mile race for three-year-olds, is run; it continues every May until present day.

Gold seekers begin to flood into Black Hills Indian reservation area of South Dakota, where gold has been discovered previous year. Within months, 15,000 prospectors have arrived. This and corruption among federal Indian affairs officials, as well as expansion of Northern Pacific Railway into the reservation area, result in beginning of the Second Sioux War.

By this year, refrigerator cars are used regularly for shipping meat from Midwest stockyards to the East. Previous shipping methods have been on the hoof (1,000 miles in 100 days); alive, by rail; and slaughtered in winter, frozen, and shipped by rail. Cars hold 50 percent more refrigerated dressed beef than live cattle, and railroads fight against method that brings less revenue, but demand for meat is too great. Various methods of cooling are used; first really efficient refrigerator car is patented by Joel Tiffany in 1877.

1875 - 1879

1875. Mary Baker Glover, a widow, publishes *Science and Health* (later adding *With Key to the Scriptures*), the basic text of Christian Science; she has developed the principles of the religion following her recovery from a serious injury she believed incurable, by means of "divine revelation, reason, and demonstration." After marrying Asa G. Eddy in 1877, she establishes the First Church of Christ, Scientist, in Boston in 1879.

An outgrowth of the Ancient Order of Hibernians of Ireland, an anti-landlord group, the "Molly Maguires" have since 1862 resorted to sabotage and even murder in fight against mine-owners.

1875 - 1880

Indictments and trial of "Molly Maguires," members of secret miners' union in Pennsylvania, in 1875-1877 leads to eventual hanging of 19 and imprisoning of others by 1880. Information about organization was collected by Pinkerton detective who joined it incognito.

1876

March 2. House of Representatives passes resolution impeaching Secretary of War William W. Belknap after investigation that indicates he has accepted bribes in connection with trading-post sales in Indian territory. Belknap resigns on same day. **Aug. 1.** He is acquitted by Senate; most of 25 senators who vote for acquittal do so because they think they cannot try an official who has resigned.

March 10. Educator of the deaf Alexander Graham Bell makes first demonstration of his magnetoelectric telephone; in following year he forms the Bell Telephone Company. In later years Bell invents the photophone, which sends sound by means of light, and an electric probe capable of locating metal in the human body; he also works on development of cylindrical wax phonograph records.

May 18. Greenback Party convention nominates Peter Cooper of New York for President and Samuel F. Carey of Ohio for Vice-President; platform demands repeal of Specie Resumption Act and legislation to create paper money. **June 16.** Republicans nominate Rutherford B. Hayes of Ohio, with William A. Wheeler of New York as his running mate. James G. Blaine, speaker of the House, has been leading Republican candidate, but just before convention he is accused of taking part in railroad graft; although he defends himself, publicity loses

JOHN T. MORSE, JR.
American Law Review, 1877
It was well known that the crimes . . . were conceived and executed by the members of a numerous and powerful association, commonly called by the familiar and dreaded sobriquet of Molly Maguires. The name and the organization were nothing new, both having come down by direct descent from the Ribbonmen of Ireland. . . .

The Association mustered strong at the polls, and played an audacious part in the distribution of public offices. Many a position of trust was filled by a Molly Maguire, elected by the suffrages of his abominable associates. Members of the order were county commissioners, high constables, chiefs of police. . . . Verily the jeopardy was extreme: with Molly Maguires to commit murders, with other Molly Maguires set to catch them, others to hold them in confinement, others to draw the juries to try them, others to act as witnesses to prove an alibi, and still others to preside at the trial—a condition of things was nearly consummated which would render it very reckless for any person, not belonging to the criminal Association, to live in that part of the country. Moreover, so soon as it became a political power, the order at once also became respected and courted by politicians; so that ere long the Mollies came to exercise a considerable influence in the State. No wise governor could be expected to make these well-organized wretches his enemies; and so it came to pass that in the rare and unusual event of a Molly actually being pursued successfully through all the protections which the Association threw around him, and being convicted and sentenced, he still had a last, and by no means a forlorn, hope in the gubernatorial power of pardon.

CARL SCHURZ
North American Review, 1881
The circumstances surrounding them place before the Indians this stern alternative—extermination or civilization. The thought of exterminating a race, once the only occupant of the soil upon which so many millions of our own people have grown prosperous and happy, must be revolting to every American who is not devoid of all sentiments of justice and humanity. To civilize them, which was once only a benevolent fancy, has now become an absolute necessity if we mean to save them. . . .

To fit the Indians for their ultimate absorption in the great body of American citizenship, three things are suggested by common sense as well as philanthropy: (1) that they be taught to work by making work profitable and attractive to them; (2) that they be educated, especially the youth of both sexes; (3) that they be individualized in the possession of property by settlement in severalty with a fee simple title, after which the lands they do not use may be disposed of for general settlement and enterprise without danger and with profit to the Indians. . . .

This progressive movement is, of course, different in degree with different tribes, but it is going on more or less everywhere. The failure of Sitting Bull's attempt to maintain himself and a large number of followers on our northern frontier in the old wild ways of Indian life will undoubtedly strengthen the tendency among the wild Indians of the Northwest to recognize the situation and to act accordingly. The general state of feeling among the red men is therefore now exceedingly favorable to the civilizing process.

him the nomination. Republican platform advocates "sound money." **June 27-29.** Democrats nominate Samuel J. Tilden, governor of New York, who has destroyed Tweed ring, with Thomas A. Hendricks of Indiana as his running mate; platform stresses economy, revenue tariff, and repeal of resumption clause of 1875 Act. Prohibition Party nominates General Green Clay Smith of Kentucky, with Gideon T. Stewart of Ohio.

June 25. General George A. Custer and a regiment of cavalry attack more than 1,000 Sioux, led by Chiefs Sitting Bull and Crazy Horse, camped on Little Bighorn River; cavalry is driven off, and Crazy Horse, shouting "Today is a good day to die!" leads Sioux in counterattack that cuts off Custer and 266 men. Surrounded by warriors in desperate half-hour battle, every cavalryman, including Custer, is killed. Attack leads to fearful reprisals as small groups of Indians are hunted down or driven into Canada until Second Sioux War ends, except for isolated incidents, with capture in October of the two chiefs.

Aug. 1. Colorado is admitted to the Union as thirty-eighth state after three unsuccessful attempts. Population by 1880 has increased to 194,000, five times that of 1870, because of railroad expansion and improvements in mining techniques.

Nov. 7. Tilden receives 4,284,000 popular votes to Hayes's 4,036,000; electoral vote is Tilden 184, to Hayes 163, but Republicans do not concede votes won by Tilden in Florida, Louisiana, South Carolina, and Oregon, without which he is one vote short of majority. **Dec. 6.** Four states in question each proffer two sets of electoral votes, the Southern states having disqualified enough Tilden votes to elect Hayes, and Democratic Oregon governor having illegally replaced one Republican elector with a Democrat. Since Constitution does not specify whether Senate (Republican-dominated) or House (Democratic) counts votes, and there are two sets for the four states, election results will depend on arm of Congress counting vote.

Centennial Exposition is held in Philadelphia to celebrate hundredth anniversary of the Declaration of Independence. Fifty nations send exhibits that are housed in 180 buildings on 236 acres of land. Technological progress is chief theme, and almost 10 million people come to see such machines as a self-binding reaper, web printing press, typewriter, refrigerator car, duplex telegraph, and Corliss engine, and Alexander Graham Bell's first telephone.

Johns Hopkins University in Baltimore is founded as first U.S. establishment primarily for graduate study. First president is Daniel Coit Gilman.

Felix Adler founds Society for Ethical Culture in New York City; movement, which eventually becomes international, emphasizes moral excellence as the goal man should seek.

Mark Twain publishes *The Adventures of Tom Sawyer*, novel based on experiences of his Mississippi River days; it becomes a best seller in same year.

National League, first major baseball league, is founded; teams represent Boston, Chicago, Cincinnati, Hartford, Louisville, New York, Philadelphia, and St. Louis.

1876 - 1878

Phase rule of thermodynamics is formulated by Josiah Willard Gibbs of Yale in his paper "On the Equilibrium of Heteroge-

ALEXANDER L. HOLLEY
Address to American Institute of Mining Engineers, 1876
The application of scientific methods to the investigation of natural laws and to the conduct of useful arts which are founded upon them is year by year mitigating the asperity and enlarging the outcome of human endeavor. . . .

The close and thoughtful observer must nevertheless conclude that neither the profession nor the craft of engineering may congratulate themselves too complacently, but that they should rather acknowledge to each other the embarrassing incompleteness of the union between engineering science and art. . . .

Thus, while the unschooled practician usually wastes his energies in unscientific methods and on impossible combinations, but generally carries into successful use his comparatively few well-founded attempts, the student merely of principles and abstract facts usually originates the ideas upon which progress is founded and rarely clothes them with practical bodies. In this chasm between science and art, how much effort and treasure, and even life, are swallowed up year by year! . . .

Some of us, I confess, are too fond of . . . perpetually repeating, in a manner more sentimental than efficient, that scientists should appreciate practice, and practicians should appreciate science, and capital should join the hands of science and practice, saying, "Bless you, my children," in the expectation that this will prove a fruitful union. Let us rather inquire if some new order of procedure in technical education, some revolutionary innovation, if need be, will not put the coming race of engineers on a plane which is lifted above the embarrassments from which we are slowly emerging.

SAMUEL TILDEN

I can retire to private life with the consciousness that I shall receive from posterity the credit of having been elected to the highest position in the gift of the people, without any of the cares and responsibilities of the office.

BRIGHAM YOUNG

Discourses, c. 1860

Talk about these rich valleys, why there is not another people on the earth that could have come here and lived. We prayed over the land and dedicated it and the water, air, and everything pertaining to them unto the Lord; and the smiles of Heaven rested on the land, and it became productive and today yields us the best of grain, fruit, and vegetables . . .

Until the Latter-day Saints came here, not a person among all the mountaineers and those who had traveled here, so far as we could learn, believed that an ear of corn would ripen in these valleys. We know that corn and wheat produce abundantly here, and we know that we have an excellent region wherein to raise cattle, horses, and every other kind of domestic animal that we need. We also knew this when we came here thirteen years ago this summer. Bridger said to me, "Mr. Young, I would give $1,000 if I knew that an ear of corn could be ripened in these mountains. I have been here twenty years and have tried it in vain, over and over again." I told him if he would wait a year or two we would show him what could be done.

neous Substances." Formulation is a basis of modern physical chemistry and chemical engineering.

1877

Jan. 29. To break Tilden-Hayes electoral vote deadlock, Congress sets up 15-member Electoral Commission: three Democrats and two Republicans from the House, three Republicans and two Democrats from the Senate, and two each Democratic and Republican members of the Supreme Court, with an additional justice who is independent, Justice David Davis. Davis, however, has been elected to the Senate and is replaced by Republican Justice Joseph P. Bradley. **Feb. 9.** Bradley, who has favored Tilden, is persuaded to change to Hayes, and commission votes 8 (Republicans) to 7 (Democrats) not to investigate disputed votes. Hayes is given Florida vote. **Feb. 16-23.** Three remaining states' votes are also given to Hayes. Republicans have won Southern Democratic support for commission's findings by consenting to three Southern demands: to appropriate large sums for Southern improvement, to appoint one Southerner to the Cabinet, and to withdraw federal troops from Southern states.

March 3. President Hayes, declared elected on previous day, takes oath of office as nineteenth President privately, since March 4 is a Sunday. **March 5.** Inauguration ceremony is held, and Hayes immediately appoints a Tennessean as postmaster general.

March 3. Desert Land Act allows individuals to buy 640 acres of public desert land at $1.25 an acre on agreement to irrigate within three years.

April 24. Last federal troops leave the

South. By this date Carpetbag rule has been eliminated in every Southern state. Period has been one of great corruption and extravagance, and Southern public debt has risen in some states to five times the 1865 level, with equivalent rises in state taxes, although property values are far below 1865 levels. Corruption and incompetence are not entirely responsible, however; much has been spent on reconstructing war-damaged areas, and many public services have been instituted that did not exist before, such as hospitals and free schools for both Negroes and whites.

July 17. Baltimore and Ohio Railroad workers strike in protest against wage reductions; move spreads quickly to other Eastern, and later Western, railroads, and riots occur in several cities. President Hayes sends federal troops when state militia is unable to control strikers. By end of strike, three dozen persons have been killed, and damage to railroad property has reached millions of dollars. Many states reenact conspiracy laws against labor groups as a result of violence.

In *Munn* v. *Illinois* (one of several cases called the "Granger Cases"), the Supreme Court upholds the right of a state to fix maximum rates and otherwise control businesses that concern "the public interest." It holds also that state control of commerce within the state does not conflict with federal control of interstate commerce.

Chief Joseph and Nez Percé Indians in Oregon find themselves, after 72 years of peace, at war with Americans, following theft of tribe's horses and subsequent revenge raid by a few young Indians. To avoid killing, Joseph sets out, hounded by troops, to take his 400 to 500 people — more than half of them women, children, and invalids — to Canada. With superb

MORRISON R. WAITE
Munn v. Illinois, 1877
When one becomes a member of society, he necessarily parts with some rights or privileges which, as an individual not affected by his relations to others, he might retain. "A body politic," as aptly defined in the preamble of the constitution of Massachusetts, "is a social compact by which the whole people covenants with each citizen, and each citizen with the whole people, that all shall be governed by certain laws for the common good." This does not confer power upon the whole people to control rights which are purely and exclusively private . . . but it does authorize the establishment of laws requiring each citizen to so conduct himself and so use his own property as not unnecessarily to injure another.

This is the very essence of government. . . . From this source come the police powers. . . . Under these powers the government regulates the conduct of its citizens one toward another and the manner in which each shall use his own property, when such regulation becomes necessary for the public good. . . .

So, too, in matters which do affect the public interest and as to which legislative control may be exercised, if there are no statutory regulations upon the subject, the courts must determine what is reasonable. The controlling fact is the power to regulate at all. If that exists, the right to establish the maximum of charge, as one of the means of regulation, is implied. In fact, the common-law rule which requires the charge to be reasonable is itself a regulation as to price. Without it the owner could make his rates at will and compel the public to yield to his terms or forgo the use.

Scientific American, 1909

The phonograph, for example, which, although not his greatest invention is probably the most marvelous in the eyes of the public, was suggested by experiments made with the telephone and automatic recording telegraph.

He was working on a machine provided with a disk of paper, similar to the present disk talking machine. On the traveling arm was a magnet which had an embossing point which embossed or indented dots and dashes on the paper, the platen having a grooved volute spiral on its surface. After recording Morse signals, a contact point swept over the record, and the indentations gave movement to the make and break and reproduced the signals on another line. When run at high speed, it would give a humming sound. He knew from the telephone about the movements of the diaphragm, and had caused his voice to work a ratchet wheel and toy figure. Then he conceived the idea of indenting by the voice and reproducing the sound by means of the indentations. The machine was made, but in cylinder form.

Then he decided to make a talking machine — with what success everyone knows. When the first operative machine was produced, he packed up the instrument and came to the office of the Scientific American. Without ceremony he placed the machine on the editor's desk and turned the crank. The machine literally spoke for itself. "Good morning," it said. "How do you do? How do you like the phonograph?" And thus the editors of the Scientific American constituted the first public audience that ever listened to the phonograph.

generalship, he escapes troops for four months over 1,000 miles of mountainous country but finally surrenders the starving remnants of his band on condition they be sent to reservation near their home. Government breaks agreement, sends them to malarial swamps in Oklahoma, where Joseph's six children and most of his band die.

Because of financial depression and legislation against violent activities of labor unions, number of national unions has decreased from 30 to 9 by this year, and membership from about 300,000 to 50,000.

Thomas A. Edison patents first practical phonograph; record is sheet of tin foil wrapped around a cylinder that can be turned. First sounds recorded are words of "Mary Had a Little Lamb."

Henry James, American author who has settled in England, publishes *The American*, a novel based on the conflict between American and European manners. Sidney Lanier publishes his *Poems*, a collection that is later enlarged.

Society of American Artists opens first American Salon des Refusés, based on original Paris group. Among first painters shown are Thomas Eakins, John La Farge, Albert P. Ryder, and George Inness.

1877 - 1880

First telephone communication between cities opens in 1877 between Salem, Massachusetts, and Boston, and Chicago and Milwaukee. By 1880 almost 150 separate telephone companies are operating 34,000 miles of lines.

1878

Jan. 17. U.S. signs treaty with Samoan chieftains giving U.S. rights to naval base at

Pago Pago Harbor of Tutuila Island; both parties to treaty are desirous of limiting German influence in Samoa.

Feb. 22. Greenback Labor Party meets in Toledo, Ohio, with 800 delegates from 28 states; platform advocates repeal of specie payments, free coinage of silver, recall of national bank notes, shorter workdays, and limitations on Chinese immigration.

Feb. 28. Pressures from Western silver-mining interests and farm and labor inflationists, who believe that increasing the amount of money in circulation will raise farm prices and wages, result in passage of Bland-Allison Act over President Hayes's veto. Act originally called for unlimited coinage of silver at ratio of 16 to 1 of gold, but modification has changed it to require Treasury to buy a minimum of $2 million and maximum of $4 million in silver each month, which is to be converted into silver dollars. Act does not entirely satisfy inflationists, but end of depression in this year quiets agitation.

June 3. Timber Cutting Act allows miners and settlers to cut timber for their own use free of charge on public land. Timber and Stone Act allows sale of otherwise useless timber and stone land in California, Washington, Oregon, and Nevada at $2.50 per acre for up to 160 acres.

July 11. President Hayes suspends Chester A. Arthur, New York port collector of customs, and Alonzo B. Cornell, port naval officer, who have been appointed by corrupt state machine headed by Republican Senator Roscoe Conkling. Previous efforts to separate civil service from Republican machine leaders have been blocked by Radicals in Senate, but move is made after Congress adjourns; Hayes's own appointments are later approved by new Democratic majority in Congress.

EDWIN R. MEADE
Address to Social Science Association of America, 1877
It does not simplify the question or render it less serious to know that the coolie comes to our shores voluntarily. As a slave, or one held under conditions of servitude, he would be subject to ordinary methods of legislation, and public sentiment would scarcely be divided respecting him; but, as now presented, he becomes a question of desirability, and the proper course at issue to prevent his further introduction becomes a very serious problem.

As suggested, he comes here as a laborer. He personifies the character in its absolutely menial aspect—what the operation of fifty centuries of paganism, poverty, and oppression have made him—a mere animal machine, performing the duties in his accepted sphere, punctually and patiently, but utterly incapable of any improvement; and in this aspect of the question the most serious phase of the problem is presented. . . .

Coolie labor means to white labor starvation, almshouses, prisons filled, and, lastly, capital wasting itself. Liberal wages and white labor mean prosperity for all classes and progress in the ways of Christian civilization. . . .

We boast that the Anglo-Saxon conquers or absorbs but never recognizes equality in other races; but we cannot overlook the fact that the Chinese nation has lasted from the dawn of centuries; that its government and people have witnessed the birth, decay, and dissolution of the greatest empires and republics that have existed; and that they now confront us upon the shores of the Pacific with a host which, by force of numbers alone, is able to convert this broad land into a Chinese colony, and the valley of the Mississippi a new battlefield of the races.

JOSEPH PULITZER
On his retirement from the St. Louis
Post-Dispatch, 1890
*I know that my retirement will make no
difference in its cardinal principles; that
it will always fight for progress and reform, never tolerate injustice or corruption, always fight demagogues of all
parties, never belong to any party, always oppose privileged classes and
public plunderers, never lack sympathy
with the poor, always remain devoted
to the public welfare; never be satisfied
with merely printing news; always be
drastically independent; never be afraid
to attack wrong, whether by predatory
plutocracy or predatory poverty.*

JOSEPH PULITZER
To editors of the New York World,
1895
*Always tell the truth, always the hu-
mane and moral side, always remember
that right feeling is the vital spark of
strong writing, and that publicity, publicity, PUBLICITY is the greatest moral
factor and force in our public life.*

CHARLES A. DANA
*Journalism consists in buying white
paper at two cents a pound and selling
it at ten cents a pound.*

November. In fall congressional elections,
14 Greenback candidates are sent to Congress. Republicans lose control of both
houses for first time since 1858.

Congress sets up District of Columbia
government that continues to present day:
three commissioners, two of whom are residents and are appointed by the President
and confirmed by the Senate, and one
member of Corps of Army Engineers. Since
1871 District has been a territorial government including Washington, Georgetown,
and County of Washington in Maryland.

Columbia grants franchise to French adventurer Lucien Napoleon Bonaparte Wyse
to build canal across Panama; he sells franchise to French company directed by Ferdinand Marie de Lesseps, who has directed
construction of the Suez Canal.

Joseph Pulitzer, Hungarian-born journalist and leader in St. Louis politics, purchases *St. Louis Dispatch* and merges it with
his *St. Louis Post*; *Post-Dispatch* eventually
becomes leading newspaper of the Middle
West.

1878 - 1880

Physicist Albert A. Michelson, using precise measuring apparatus of his own design,
is able to measure the speed of light accurate to 99.999 percent.

1879

Jan. 1. U.S. begins specie payments as
authorized by Act of 1875. Greenbacks are
now worth their face value in gold. Owing
to public's awareness that government has
acquired enough gold to back outstanding
currency, there is no rush to redeem them.

April 29. President Hayes vetoes rider

that forbids the President to use federal troops in congressional elections, attached by Democratic Congress to Army Appropriation Act; veto is on the ground that rider violates the constitutional guarantee of equality of branches of the government. Republicans support him in this, as well as in vetoes of five other attempts to pass the same measure.

May 8. George B. Selden applies for patent on first carriage to be run by an internal combustion engine; but realizing that American public is not ready for it, and wanting time to raise money to produce it, he continually amends patent (to keep application alive for his protection) until 1895, when he allows patent to be issued.

Dec. 31. Thomas Edison brings 3,000 spectators to his shop in special trains to see demonstration of hundreds of incandescent lamps. Although incandescent lamps have been invented years before, Edison's contributions are improvements in the bulb itself, and especially the precise working out of a system that makes electricity for home lighting able to compete with gas. By this time, Edison is so greatly respected that even before his patent is granted in following month, gas company stocks fall sharply.

Frank W. Woolworth and partner W. H. Moore open "five-cent" store in Utica, New York, based on experience of popularity of five-cent counter established by Woolworth while working in Moore's store. This first store is a failure, but another opened in same year with wider selection of merchandise and called a "five-and-ten-cent" store is successful. By the time of Woolworth's death in 1919 his company is operating more than 1,000 stores.

Henry George, reformer and economist, publishes *Progress and Poverty*, in which he advocates the single tax as the solution to

HENRY GEORGE
Progress and Poverty, 1879
The march of invention has clothed mankind with powers of which a century ago the boldest imagination could not have dreamed. But in factories where laborsaving machinery has reached its most wonderful development, little children are at work; wherever the new forces are anything like fully utilized, large classes are maintained by charity or live on the verge of recourse to it; amid the greatest accumulations of wealth, men die of starvation and puny infants suckle dry breasts; while everywhere the greed of gain, the worship of wealth shows the force of the fear of want. The promised land flies before us like the mirage. The fruits of the tree of knowledge turn, as we grasp them, to apples of Sodom that crumble at the touch. . . .

This association of poverty with progress is the great enigma of our times. It is the central fact from which spring industrial, social, and political difficulties that perplex the world, and with which statesmanship and philanthropy and education grapple in vain. From it come the clouds that overhang the future of the most progressive and self-reliant nations. It is the riddle which the Sphinx of Fate puts to our civilization, and which not to answer is to be destroyed. So long as all the increased wealth which modern progress brings goes but to build up great fortunes, to increase luxury, and make sharper the contrast between the House of Have and the House of Want, progress is not real and cannot be permanent. The reaction must come. The tower leans from its foundations, and every new story but hastens the final catastrophe.

JAMES B. WEAVER

Letter to Greenback Labor Party Convention, 1880

I am profoundly grateful for the honor conferred. . . . I accept the nomination as a solemn duty. The convention is to be congratulated upon the great work accomplished in the unification of the various Greenback and Labor elements into one compact organization. This was of first importance, and thoroughly prepares our forces to strike a decisive blow for industrial emancipation during the impending struggle. . . .

Our civilization demands a new party, dedicated to the pursuits of peace, and which will not allow the war issues ever to be reopened, and will render the military strictly subordinate to the civil power. The war is over, and the sweet voice of peace, long neglected, calls us to worship at her altars. Let us crowd her temples with willing votaries. Let us have a free ballot, a fair count, and equal rights for all classes—for the laboring man in Northern manufactories, mines, and workshops, and for the struggling poor, both white and black, in the cotton fields of the South.

I most earnestly and solemnly invoke united action of all industrial classes, irrespective of party, that we may make a manly struggle for the independence of labor, and to reestablish in the administration of public affairs the old-time Democracy of Jefferson and Jackson, and the pure Republicanism of Abraham Lincoln and Thaddeus Stevens. . . .

And, now, eschewing all violence and tumults as unworthy of the cause we represent, and relying upon Divine Providence and the justice of our cause, let us go forth in the great struggle for human rights.

all of the nation's economic ills. Albion W. Tourgée, carpetbagger judge, publishes his novel *A Fool's Errand,* first literary attempt to deal with Reconstruction.

Mary Cassatt, who does all her work in Europe, is first American painter to be invited to exhibit with French Impressionists.

1880

March. American branch of Salvation Army is established in Philadelphia; William Booth has started organization in England two years earlier in autocratic military pattern, with himself as general for life. Unorthodox missionary methods are at first resented in the U.S., but within a few years organization becomes accepted.

June 8. Republicans at Chicago nominate dark-horse candidate James A. Garfield of Ohio, on thirty-sixth ballot. President Hayes has declined to run for second term, and party is split into two factions — "Stalwarts," who favor Ulysses S. Grant, and "Half-Breeds," supporters of James G. Blaine who eventually back Garfield. To appease "Stalwarts," Chester A. Arthur is nominated for Vice-President. **June 9.** Greenback Labor Party nominates James B. Weaver of Iowa, with B. J. Chambers of Texas as his running mate. **June 17.** Prohibition Party nominates Neal Dow of Maine and H. A. Thompson of Ohio. **June 22.** Democrats nominate Winfield Scott Hancock of Pennsylvania, with William H. English of Indiana as his running mate; Hancock has no political experience and is chosen for his war record and personal popularity. Republican and Democratic platforms are almost identical: civil service reform, legislation for care of veterans, and restriction of Chinese immigration; but Republicans advocate protective tariff, while Democrats demand tariff only for revenue.

Nov. 2. Garfield wins by plurality of

about 9,000 with 4,453,000 votes to Hancock's 4,444,000; electoral vote is 214 to 155. Democratic and Republican vote is divided according to area of former slave states, except that Hancock also carries New Jersey, Nevada, and California. Republicans regain control of House of Representatives.

Nov. 17. U.S.-China treaty gives the U.S. the right to "regulate, limit, or suspend" (but not forbid) immigration of laborers from China. Cheap coolie labor and resulting racial conflict on West Coast have led for several years to pressure for abrogation of Burlingame Treaty of 1868, which allows unlimited Chinese immigration.

1880 census shows total population of 50,156,000; increase of 10,337,000 over 1870 includes 2,812,195 immigrants; about 42 percent of people live in places of more than 2,500 inhabitants.

Henry Adams, historian and biographer, publishes first of his two novels, *Democracy*, anonymously; his second, *Esther — a Novel*, is published in 1884 under name Frances Snow Compton. Lew Wallace, governor of New Mexico Territory, publishes *Ben Hur: a Tale of the Christ*, which sells 300,000 copies in 10 years, 2,000,000 by the 1960s. Joel Chandler Harris, one of the first American authors to deal with Negro folk literature, publishes *Uncle Remus: His Songs and His Sayings*, a collection of pieces written originally for the *Atlanta* (Georgia) *Constitution*.

1881

March 5. President Garfield appoints James G. Blaine secretary of state, a move that reopens split between "Stalwart" and "Half-Breed" factions of Republican Party.

March 23. President Garfield appoints opponent of Senator Conkling as collector of the port of New York; Conkling and

WILLIAM McELROY
Atlantic Monthly, 1880
And just here a word in reply to the familiar question, Would you vote for the devil if he received the party's regular nomination? I have no hesitation in affirming that I certainly would. Let's look at it. If the day ever comes when the devil is nominated, the other side will be pretty sure to run Gabriel against him. Of the two, my choice would be the devil. To be sure, it would not be an ideal nomination, but, then, neither is ours an ideal world. I am aware that the devil has split hoofs, pronounced horns, and a bifurcated tail. But do we choose candidates for their good looks? As to his moral character, I frankly admit it is not all I could desire; but after criticism has exhausted itself, the fact remains, conceded by both parties, that he is not as black as he is painted. . . .

Let me not be misunderstood. I yield to no one in my regard for Gabriel. But, as a practical man, I would feel called upon to vote against him, and do all I could for his opponent. . . .

Beware of those who take sentimental views of unsentimental matters. A man who would "rather be right than be president" by all means ought to decline a presidential nomination, and run for a position in a theological seminary, a Sunday school, or Vassar College; while he who holds that "one with God is a majority" antagonizes the system of reckoning which has come down to us from the fathers, and which has the approval of every practical inspector of American elections. Be practical in your politics, be practical, ever more be practical.

JAMES G. BLAINE
Letter to Thomas Osborn, 1881

For some years past a growing disposition has been manifested by certain states of Central and South America to refer disputes affecting grave questions of international relationship and boundaries to arbitration rather than to the sword. It has been on several such occasions a source of profound satisfaction to the government of the United States to see that this country is in a large measure looked to by all the American powers as their friend and mediator. The just and impartial counsel of the President in such cases has never been withheld, and his efforts have been rewarded by the prevention of sanguinary strife or angry contentions between peoples whom we regard as brethren.

The existence of this growing tendency convinces the President that the time is ripe for a proposal that shall enlist the goodwill and active cooperation of all the states of the Western Hemisphere, both north and south, in the interest of humanity and for the commonweal of nations. . . .

The President extends to all the independent countries of North and South America an earnest invitation to participate in a general congress to be held in the city of Washington on the 24th day of November, 1882, for the purpose of considering and discussing the methods of preventing war between the nations of America. . . .

The United States will enter into the deliberations of the congress on the same footing as the other powers represented, and with the loyal determination to approach any proposed solution, not merely in its own interest, or with a view to asserting its power, but as a single member among many coordinate and coequal states.

Senator Platt of New York block appointment temporarily, then resign in gesture of protest in May. Conkling's political career ends and "Stalwart" influence diminishes when New York legislature refuses to re-elect either senator.

July 2. An unbalanced, disappointed "Stalwart" office seeker, Charles J. Guiteau, who claims to be trying to secure presidency for Vice-President Chester A. Arthur, shoots President Garfield in Washington railroad station.

Sept. 19. After lingering on for two and a half months, Garfield dies at his home in Elberon, New Jersey. His assassination causes strong public resentment against "Stalwarts." **Sept. 20.** Vice-President Chester Alan Arthur takes oath of office as twenty-first President. Since Arthur has never before held elective office and has been closely associated with the "Stalwarts," there is great anxiety about what course he will follow, but he proves to be surprisingly independent of his faction of the party.

Nov. 14. Guiteau's trial for the murder of Garfield begins. He is convicted on Jan. 25, 1882, and executed the following June.

Nov. 22. Secretary of State Blaine invites Latin-American nations to Washington conference to be held in 1882 with the intention of establishing peace and confirming U.S. control of any canal dug across the Panamanian isthmus. Blaine's tendered resignation after Garfield's death has not yet been accepted, but President Arthur accepts it as of December 19, and although nine countries have already accepted, Blaine's successor revokes invitations.

December. President Arthur, in first annual message, approves removing federal civil service appointments from party control.

In *Springer* v. *United States*, the Supreme Court holds that income tax instituted during Civil War is constitutional, since it is not the type of direct tax prohibited in the Constitution.

Clara Barton, having worked with the International Red Cross in Geneva during the Franco-Prussian War, returns to the U.S. to establish the National Society of the Red Cross. She is its president until 1904, and in 1884 is responsible for adoption by the Geneva International Convention of amendment that allows the Red Cross to be of service in peacetime emergencies, as well as in war.

Chosen to establish Negro school of higher education at Tuskegee, Alabama, Booker T. Washington, teacher son of a white father and a former slave, organizes and becomes president of the Normal and Industrial Institute for Negroes (later Tuskegee Institute). Largely self-educated, Washington believes that Negro advancement depends on work efficiency, as well as education, and, therefore, teaches trades and professions in addition to academic subjects.

University of Pennsylvania establishes Wharton School of Finance and Commerce, first university business school.

Andrew Carnegie begins establishment of Carnegie libraries; eventually, he donates 2,500 library buildings at a cost of $60 million in many English-speaking countries; donations are given on condition that libraries be supplied and supported by communities in which they are built.

New York humor weekly *Judge* is founded by authors and artists who have left British *Puck*; it is discontinued in 1939.

1881 - 1887

Helen Hunt Jackson publishes *A Century*

FINLEY PETER DUNNE
Dissertations by Mr. Dooley, 1906
"Has Andhrew Carnaygie given ye a libry yet?" asked Mr. Dooley.

"Not that I know iv," said Mr. Hennessy.

"He will," said Mr. Dooley. "Ye'll not escape him. Befure he dies he hopes to crowd a libry on ivry man, woman, an' child in th' counthry. . . . Befure another year, ivry house in Pittsburg that ain't a blast-furnace will be a Carnaygie libry. In some places all th' buildin's is libries. If ye write him f'r an autygraft he sinds ye a libry. . . .

"Does he give th' books that go with it?" asked Mr. Hennessy.

"Books?" said Mr. Dooley. "What ar-re ye talkin' about? D'ye know what a libry is? I suppose ye think it's a place where a man can go, haul down wan iv his fav'rite authors fr'm th' shelf, an' take a nap in it. That's not a Carnaygie libry. A Carnaygie libry is a large, brown-stone, impenethrible buildin' with th' name iv th' maker blown on th' dure. Libry, fr'm th' Greek wurruds, libus, a book, an' ary, sildom,—sildom a book. A Carnaygie libry is archytechoor, not lithrachoor. Lithrachoor will be riprisinted. Th' most cillybrated dead authors will be honored be havin' their names painted on th' wall in distinguished comp'ny, as thus: Andhrew Carnaygie, Shakespeare; Andhrew Carnaygie, Byron; Andhrew Carnaygie, Bobby Burns; Andhrew Carnaygie, an' so on. Ivry author is guaranteed a place next to pure readin' matther like a bakin'-powdher advertisemint, so that whin a man comes along that niver heerd iv Shakespeare he'll know he was somebody, because there he is on th' wall. That's th' dead authors. Th' live authors will stand outside an' wish they were dead."

(Above) President of New York Stock Exchange announcing the
suspension of Jay Cooke and Company, precipitating the Panic
of 1873; (below) "If He Can't Respect Our Flag, Send Him Where He
Belongs": cartoon by Thomas Nast in *Harper's Weekly*, urging
support for the Cuban revolutionary movement of 1873

(Left) Samuel Tilden and (above) Rutherford
B. Hayes, candidates in the disputed
presidential election of 1876; (below) left
to right: Petroleum V. Nasby (D. R. Locke),
Mark Twain (S. L. Clemens), and Josh
Billings (H. W. Shaw)

HELEN HUNT JACKSON
A Century of Dishonor, 1881

The notion which seems to be growing more prevalent, that simply to make all Indians at once citizens of the United States would be a sovereign and instantaneous panacea for all their ills and all the government's perplexities, is a very inconsiderate one. To administer complete citizenship of a sudden, all round, to all Indians, barbarous and civilized alike, would be as grotesque a blunder as to dose them all round with any one medicine, irrespective of the symptoms and needs of their diseases. . . .

However great perplexity and difficulty there may be in the details of any and every plan possible for doing at this late day anything like justice to the Indian, however hard it may be for good statesmen and good men to agree upon the things that ought to be done, there certainly is, or ought to be, no perplexity whatever, no difficulty whatever, in agreeing upon certain things that ought not to be done and which must cease to be done before the first steps can be taken toward righting the wrongs, curing the ills, and wiping out the disgrace to us of the present condition of our Indians.

Cheating, robbing, breaking promises — these three are clearly things which must cease to be done. One more thing, also, and that is the refusal of the protection of the law to the Indian's rights of property, "of life, liberty, and the pursuit of happiness."

When these four things have ceased to be done, time, statesmanship, philanthropy, and Christianity can slowly and surely do the rest. Till these four things have ceased to be done, statesmanship and philanthropy alike must work in vain, and even Christianity can reap but small harvest.

of Dishonor in 1881 in effort to publicize desperate plight of American Indians that has resulted from U.S. Indian policy. In 1884 she publishes novel *Ramona*, whose theme is the injustice suffered by mission Indians. Books arouse public to need for reform and lead to passage of Dawes Severalty Act of 1887. Act dissolves tribes as legal units and distributes tribal lands among families and unmarried individuals — 160 acres to families and 80 acres to individuals; land cannot be disposed of for 25 years, but at end of that time, Indians become owners with no limitations.

1882

March 16. Senate approves Geneva Convention signed by the U.S. and almost all European countries, as well as some Asian and Latin-American nations, providing for care of the wounded in wartime.

May 6. Chinese Exclusion Act is passed; it suspends for 10 years all immigration of Chinese laborers, but immigration from China in this year reaches all-time peak of nearly 40,000, dropping in following year to about 8,000. Total during 1868-1882 period has been more than 200,000.

May 22. U.S. signs commerce and amity treaty with Korea, at the same time recognizing Korea's independence. Korea, in 1598 had driven off Japanese armies and Chinese allies and shut itself away from the world for nearly 300 years; as a result, it is called the "Hermit Kingdom," but in 1876 Japan has forced it to open several ports to foreign trade.

Aug. 3. Congress passes act prohibiting entry into the U.S. of "undesirables," such as the insane, criminals, and paupers, and fixes a head tax of 50 cents on all immigrants.

Sept. 4. Pearl Street electric power station, operated by steam and built by Thomas A. Edison, goes into operation in New York City; it supplies power for 400 incandescent lights in 59 buildings.

September. First Labor Day celebration is held in New York City; Peter J. McGuire, founder of United Brotherhood of Carpenters, has suggested a holiday honoring working people. After campaign by organized labor to create a national holiday, Colorado proclaims a legal holiday in 1887, and Labor Day becomes a national holiday in 1894.

March 3, 1883. Tariff of 1883 lowers duties an average of 5 percent, but retains protection.

German immigration reaches highest point of 250,630, largely owing to depressed conditions in Europe. Most immigrants settle in already established colonies in Middle West. Result is beginning of era of the German-language press, with almost 550 newspapers and periodicals published.

Knights of Columbus, fraternal organization of Catholic men, founded in New Haven, Connecticut, by nine men directed by Father Michael McGivney; order grows slowly at first, but by present day has thousands of branches, with more than a million members.

Dec. 4. Nine-man tariff commission appointed by the President recommends sharp reductions in duties.

1882 - 1896

Growing use of electricity stimulates invention of such appliances as the electric fan, electric iron, electric stove, and electric sewing machine.

CARROLL D. WRIGHT
The Factory System, 1882

The weal or woe of the operative population depends largely upon the temper in which the employers carry the responsibility entrusted to them. I know of no trust more sacred than that given into the hands of the captains of industry, for they deal with human beings in close relations; not through the media of speech or exhortation but of positive association, and by this they can make or mar. Granted that the material is often poor, the intellects often dull; then all the more sacred the trust and all the greater the responsibility. The rich and powerful manufacturer with the adjuncts of education and good business training holds in his hand something more than the means of subsistence for those he employs, he holds their moral well-being in his keeping, insofar as it is in his power to mold their morals. He is something more than a producer, he is an instrument of God for the upbuilding of the race. . . .

The factory system of the future will be run on this basis. The instances of such are multiplying rapidly now, and whenever it occurs, the system outstrips the pulpit in the actual work of the gospel, that is, in the work of humanity. It needs no gift of prophecy to foretell the future of a system which has in it more possibilities for good for the masses who must work for day wages than any scheme which has yet been devised by philanthropy alone.

To make the system what it will be, the factory itself must be rebuilt and so ordered in all its appointments that the great question for the labor reformer shall be how to get people out of their homes and into the factory.

MARK TWAIN
Life on the Mississippi, 1883

1883

We entered its deeper shadow, and so imminent seemed the peril that I was likely to suffocate; and I had the strongest impulse to do something, anything, to save the vessel. But still Mr. Bixby stood by his wheel, silent, intent as a cat, and all the pilots stood shoulder to shoulder at his back.

"She'll not make it!" somebody whispered.

The water grew shoaler and shoaler, by the leadsman's cries, till it was down to:

"Eight-and-a-half! E-i-g-h-t feet! E-i-g-h-t feet! Seven-and—"

Mr. Bixby said warningly through his speaking-tube to the engineer:

"Stand by, now!"

"Ay, ay, sir!"

"Seven-and-a-half! Seven feet! Six-and—"

We touched bottom! Mr. Bixby set a lot of bells ringing, shouted through the tube, "Now, let her have it—every ounce you've got!" then to his partner, "Put her hard down! snatch her! snatch her!" The boat rasped and ground her way through the sand, hung upon the apex of disaster a single tremendous instant, and then over she went! And such a shout as went up at Mr. Bixby's back never loosened the roof of a pilot-house before!

There was no more trouble after that. Mr. Bixby was a hero that night; and it was some little time, too, before his exploit ceased to be talked about by river-men. . . .

The last remark I heard that night was a compliment to Mr. Bixby, uttered in soliloquy and with unction by one of our guests. He said:

"By the Shadow of Death, but he's a lightning pilot!"

Jan. 16. Civil service corruption leads Congress to pass Pendleton Act as reform measure. Drafted by Dorman B. Eaton, secretary of National Civil Service Reform League, and sponsored by Senator George H. Pendleton, it sets up a three-man Civil Service Commission and establishes examinations as basis for choice of civil service appointees.

Oct. 22. Metropolitan Opera House opens in New York City; it burns in 1892 and is reopened in following year. Throughout this period numerous opera companies, symphony orchestras, and other music groups are established, but music and performers remain largely European.

Mark Twain publishes *Life on the Mississippi,* part of which has first been published as a serial in the *Atlantic Monthly* under the title of "Old Times on the Mississippi," enlarged after a revisit to the area.

Northern Pacific Railway, financed by Jay Cooke and reorganized in 1881 by Henry Villard, completes line from Lake Superior to Portland, Oregon. Atchison, Topeka and Santa Fe Railroad, having built line as far as Colorado by 1872, establishes route from Kansas City to Los Angeles by way of both Needles, California, and Yuma, Arizona, by leasing tracks of other companies, as well as using its own.

U.S. and Canadian railroads agree to adopt four standard time zones proposed by Charles F. Dowd of the U.S. and Sandford

Fleming of Canada. To this date long-line railroads have made local time adaptations individually, a method that has created great confusion, since railroad times often have overlapped.

Brooklyn Bridge, largest suspension bridge in the world at this date, is completed from lower Manhattan to Brooklyn, New York; it is 1,595 feet long and has cost $15 million. Designed by German-born John Augustus Roebling, who is also named chief engineer, it is completed by his son Washington Augustus Roebling when the father dies as a result of accident on bridge site just as construction begins.

Joseph Pulitzer, owner of *St. Louis Post-Dispatch*, buys the *New York World* from Jay Gould; sensational journalism: crime stories, large headlines, comic strips, strong editorials — as well as two-cent price — result in circulation increase in next four years from 20,000 to 250,000.

Ladies' Home Journal, a monthly, is founded by Cyrus H. K. Curtis; it continues to present day.

1883 - 1889

March 3, 1883. Congress authorizes building of three steel naval cruisers, first built since the Civil War; move is beginning of buildup of U.S. Navy, which has deteriorated to twelfth in rank among those of world powers. Secretary of the Navy William C. Whitney has by 1889, when he leaves office, modernized the Navy to such an extent that by 1900 it ranks third.

MONTGOMERY SCHUYLER
Harper's Weekly, 1883

It so happens that the work which is likely to be our most durable monument, and which is likely to convey some knowledge of us to the most remote posterity, is a work of bare utility; not a shrine, not a fortress, not a palace, but a bridge. This is of itself characteristic of our time. . . .

What monument of any architecture can speak its story more clearly and more forcibly than this gossamer architecture, through which its purpose, like the spider's touch,

"so exquisitely fine,
Feels at each thread, and lives
along the line"?

This aerial bow, as it hangs between the busy cities, "curving on a sky imbrued with color," is perfect as an organism of nature. It is an organism of nature. There was no question in the mind of its designer of "good taste" or of appearance. He learned the law that struck its curves, the law that fixed the strength and the relation of its parts, and he applied the law. His work is beautiful as the work of a ship-builder is unfailingly beautiful in the forms and outlines in which he is only studying "what the water likes," without a thought of beauty, and as it is almost unfailingly ugly when he does what he likes for the sake of beauty. The designer of the Brooklyn Bridge has made a beautiful structure out of an exquisite refinement of utility, in a work in which the lines of forces constitute the structure.

1884

E. S. BRAGG
Speech at Democratic National Convention, 1884
I stand today to voice the sentiment of the young men of my state when I speak for Grover Cleveland. His name is upon their lips. His name is in their hearts. They love him, gentlemen, and respect him, and they love him and respect him not only for himself, for his character, for his integrity, for his iron will, but they love him most for the enemies he has made.

Campaign slogan, 1884
A mugwump is a fellow with his mug on one side of the fence and his wump on the other.

WILLIAM TECUMSEH SHERMAN
Answer to telegram from the Republican Convention asking him to be the presidential candidate in 1884
If nominated, I will not accept. If elected, I will not serve.

Slogan of Cleveland's 1884 campaign
A Public Office Is a Public Trust.

May 17. Organic Act is passed; it applies the laws of Oregon to the "civil and judicial district" of Alaska, which has been governed in turn by the War and Treasury departments up to this time.

May 28. National Greenback-Labor Party meets and nominates Benjamin F. Butler of Massachusetts for President. Butler has also received (May 14) presidential nomination of Anti-Monopoly Party, with which the Greenback Party has joined to form the People's Party. **June 6.** Republicans at Chicago nominate James G. Blaine of Maine for President, with John A. Logan of Illinois as his running mate. Independent Republicans bolt convention, feeling Blaine is corrupt, and later back Democratic choice; group is sarcastically nicknamed "Mugwumps," Indian word meaning "chiefs." **July 11.** Democrats nominate Grover Cleveland, governor of New York, for President and Thomas A. Hendricks of Indiana for Vice-President. **July 23.** Prohibition Party nominates John P. St. John of Kansas.

Oct. 1-Nov. 1. World conference, meeting in Washington, D.C., recommends that meridian of Greenwich, England, be basis for counting mean time and longitude.

Anti-tariff cartoon argues that the "inevitable result" of industry protected from outside competition is over-production and in the end, a recession and unemployment

Benjamin F. Butler, National Greenback-Labor Party presidential candidate in the 1884 election

Oct. 6. Naval War College established at Newport, Rhode Island, to give naval officers postgraduate training.

Nov. 4. After campaign in which Democrats publicize Mulligan Letters, which expose Blaine's corrupt dealings as speaker of the House, and Republicans accuse Cleveland of having fathered an illegitimate child (he admits it immediately), Cleveland wins election. Blaine loses key state of New York by 1,100 votes when he fails to disavow statement of delegation of his supporters calling Democrats the party of "Rum, Romanism, and Rebellion"; silence loses him the Catholic vote. Popular vote is Cleveland, 4,880,000; Blaine, 4,850,000; Butler (partially supported by Republicans in hope he will reduce Cleveland vote), 175,000; St. John, 150,000. Electoral vote is Cleveland, 219; Blaine, 182. Although Republicans in the House gain 18 seats, it is not enough to alter Democratic control.

Dec. 6. Last part, the capstone, placed on Washington Monument in Washington, D.C. Monument is dedicated in February 1885 and opened in October 1888.

In Ku Klux Klan cases, Southern Negroes, kept from voting by the Klan, appeal to U.S. Supreme Court; Court holds that interference by private persons with a citi-

GEORGE TICKNOR CURTIS
Century Magazine, 1884
The staple of the argument that is openly pressed for this or that candidate for the nomination is his ability to "carry" this or that state which is supposed likely to be "the battleground" or one of the battlegrounds of the election. The "pivotal states," as they are denominated in the political jargon of these occasions, sometimes make the nomination turn upon considerations of the lowest kind.

Something in the past history of a public man is supposed to give him the best chance to capture the "soldier" vote, or the "Irish" vote, or the "German" vote, or the "Negro" vote, or the liquor or the antiliquor interest, or the workingman's interest, and so on through all the catalogue of diversified prejudices and passions which sway, or are supposed to sway, the popular impulses of different localities or classes at these times of the quadrennial ballot for a President. Very little is heard of the solid grounds on which the public character of a statesman ought to be able to challenge public confidence; very little of the qualities which should fit a man for the office. Nearly the whole effective force of a great party is expended in calculation of the elements of what is called the "strength" of the different prominent men of the party.

MARK TWAIN
Huckleberry Finn, 1884
Then I thought a minute, and says to myself, hold on, — s'pose you'd a done right and give Jim up; would you felt better than what you do now? No, says I, I'd feel bad — I'd feel just the same way I do now. Well, then, says I, what's the use you learning to do right, when it's troublesome to do right and ain't no trouble to do wrong, and the wages is just the same? I was stuck. I couldn't answer that. So I reckoned I wouldn't bother no more about it, but after this always do whichever come handiest at the time. . . .

Sometimes we'd have that whole river all to ourselves for the longest time. Yonder was the banks and the islands, across the water; and maybe a spark — which was a candle in a cabin window — and sometimes on the water you could see a spark or two — on a raft or a scow, you know; and maybe you could hear a fiddle or a song coming over from one of them crafts. It's lovely to live on a raft. We had the sky, up there, all speckled with stars, and we used to lay on our backs and look up at them, and discuss about whether they was made, or only just happened — Jim he allowed they was made, but I allowed they happened; I judged it would have took too long to make so many. Jim said the moon could a laid them; well, that looked kind of reasonable, so I didn't say nothing against it, because I've seen a frog lay most as many, so of course it could be done. . . .

But I reckon I got to light out for the Territory ahead of the rest, because Aunt Sally she's going to adopt me and sivilize me and I can't stand it; I been there before.

zen's right to vote in federal elections is a federal crime, since this right does not depend only on state law but also on the Constitution and U.S. laws.

Ottmar Mergenthaler patents his mechanical typesetter, which casts and sets type for printing. Called the Linotype machine, it revolutionizes mass-circulation newspaper production.

Lewis E. Waterman produces first practical fountain pens; unsuccessful attempts have been made since the seventeenth century.

Samuel Clemens ("Mark Twain") publishes *The Adventures of Huckleberry Finn*, epic novel of Mississippi River frontier, a criticism of social ills, such as slavery and feuding, as well as an entertainment. Joel Chandler Harris writes realistically of Georgia poor whites in *Mingoy, and Other Sketches in Black and White*, and later (1887) of Negroes under Reconstruction in *Free Joe and Other Georgian Sketches*.

1884 - 1885

Nov. 15-Feb. 26. International Berlin Conference on African Affairs, called by Germany and France, meets in Berlin. U.S. attends and agrees to work for the abolition of slavery and of the still-flourishing slave trade in Africa but does not ratify final agreements, which also involves acquisition of African territory.

1884 - 1889

Improved techniques in anesthesia include injection of cocaine into nerves to anesthetize surrounding areas, use of cocaine as a spinal anesthetic, and also as a local anesthetic. In surgery, technique for examining the stomach by means of endoscope inserted through the mouth is improved; appendicitis is identified as a specific infection, and first appendectomy after correct diagnosis is performed; first brain tumor operation in U.S. is performed; operations for hernia and breast removal are perfected. Emphasis on diagnosis, as well as technical excellence in surgery, begins with opening of St. Marys Hospital (later known as Mayo Clinic) in Rochester, Minnesota, by brothers William J. and Charles H. Mayo.

1884 - 1895

Edward L. Trudeau, pioneer in tuberculosis therapy, founds the Adirondack Cottage Sanatorium at Saranac Lake, New York, in 1884; in 1894 he establishes first research laboratory in the U.S. for study of tuberculosis. Early diagnosis of the disease is helped greatly by discovery of X rays by Wilhelm C. Röntgen in 1895.

1884 - 1899

Naturalist painter Winslow Homer, having settled permanently in Maine, where he remains in seclusion except for occasional painting trips, paints some of his finest oils and watercolors, such as "The Life Line," "Eight Bells," "The Gulf Stream," and "Rum Cay." His fresh style has at first been unpopular, but critics begin to appreciate him at about this time.

1885

Feb. 26. Congress passes Contract Labor Act. Immigration of laborers under contract to work for cost of passage is forbidden; exceptions are allowed for skilled, professional, and domestic workers.

April 3. Land Commissioner William A. J. Sparks suspends entries of all land titles suspected of being fraudulent; move makes available to actual settlers 2,750,000 acres of land hitherto controlled by speculators

ANDREW CARNEGIE
Triumphant Democracy, 1886
If side by side with progress in material things there was not found corresponding progress in the higher things of the spirit, there would be but little cause for congratulation among the citizens of the republic. If there was not spreading among the masses of the people along with their material blessings a love of the beautiful; if with their comforts there did not come the love of music; if, in short, "art," using the term in its broadest sense, did not shed everywhere around its elevating influence, we should have little reason to be proud or hopeful of our country, much less to extol it. To reach her proper position and play her part among the nations, she must not only be the wealthiest country in the world but richest in the diffusion of refinement and culture among the people.

It is not enough that the American workman should be in receipt of the highest wages and enjoy the best living. He should also be most appreciative of all the refinements of life, and his habits should be better than those of his fellows in other lands. His home must be more artistic, its interior in better taste, its furniture finer, its sanitary arrangements more perfect, and especially must it be to a greater degree than that of any corresponding class the home of music. There must be more and better books, engravings, and pictures, even in the humblest dwelling, compared with the workman's home in other lands. . . . The chromo on the wall, the flowerpot on the windowsill of the toiler's home mean much more for the republic than the picture gallery or the conservatory of the city home of the millionaire.

WILLIAM DEAN HOWELLS
Criticism and Fiction, 1891

For our novelists to try to write Americanly, from any motive, would be a dismal error; but being born Americans, I would have them use "Americanisms" whenever these serve their turn; and when their characters speak, I should like to hear them speak true American, with all the varying Tennesseean, Philadelphian, Bostonian, and New York accents. If we bother ourselves to write what the critics imagine to be "English," we shall be priggish and artificial, and still more so if we make our Americans talk "English." There is also this serious disadvantage about "English," that if we wrote the best "English" in the world, probably the English themselves would not know it, or, if they did, certainly would not own it. . . .

In fine, I would have our American novelists be as American as they unconsciously can. Matthew Arnold complained that he found no "distinction" in our life, and I would gladly persuade all artists intending greatness in any kind among us that the recognition of the fact pointed out by Mr. Arnold ought to be a source of inspiration to them, and not discouragement. . . .

The talent that is robust enough to front the everyday world and catch the charm of its workworn, careworn, brave, kindly face, need not fear the encounter, though it seems terrible to the sort nurtured in the superstition of the romantic, the bizarre, the heroic, the distinguished, as the things alone worthy of painting or carving or writing. The arts must become democratic, and then we shall have the expression of America in art; and the reproach which Mr. Arnold was half right in making us shall have no justice in it any longer; we shall be "distinguished."

and big business. In following two years Sparks advises many reforms of land laws, but in 1887 he resigns after dispute about a land-grant railroad case, and many of his reforms are revoked.

Nov. 25. Vice-President Thomas A. Hendricks dies at Indianapolis, Indiana, after less than a year in office.

Beginning of large immigration from eastern and southern Europe, known as "New Immigration." Many immigrants in following years are Jews from Russia, escaping persecution.

Largest lead source in the world, the Bunker Hill and Sullivan mines, discovered in Kellogg, Idaho. This, and Sunshine Silver Mine, in Shoshone County, found at the same time, eventually yield $250 million in silver and lead.

William Dean Howells, novelist and critic, publishes *The Rise of Silas Lapham*, landmark in realistic, sympathetic treatment of new industrial classes. Mark Twain publishes first volume of Ulysses S. Grant's *Personal Memoirs*. Grant, almost penniless, does not live to see great success of the two-volume work, written during his final illness, but his family receives about $500,000 from its sale.

First true skyscraper completed; Chicago's Home Life Insurance Building is made possible by the new use of all-iron frame construction.

Privately endowed Leland Stanford, Jr. University established near Palo Alto, California.

1885 - 1887

Overstocking of ranges during cattle boom of previous years causes beef price crash. Drought and severe cold follow during next two years.

1885 - 1900

Most architecture of the period is derived from classic sources; Charles F. McKim, Stanford White, Cass Gilbert, and George B. Post design such buildings as the Low Memorial Library at Columbia University, New York; Boston Public Library; Minnesota State Capitol; Supreme Court Building, Washington, D.C. During same period Louis H. Sullivan and Frank Lloyd Wright turn to functional design, as in the Chicago Auditorium and Chicago Stock Exchange Building; Wright also begins development of his "prairie style" homes.

1886

Jan. 19. Presidential Succession Act of 1792 is replaced by new law providing that if both President and Vice-President are unable to serve, they will be succeeded by Cabinet officers in order of creation of their departments.

Oct. 28. President Cleveland dedicates Statue of Liberty, erected on Bedloe's (present-day Liberty) Island in New York Harbor. A gift to the U.S. from the French people, it has been under construction since 1874 in France; 151 feet high and weighing 225 tons, it has been shipped in 214 packing cases in previous year. Raising of funds in the U.S. to build the pedestal has delayed its erection, but money is finally raised by Joseph Pulitzer, owner of *New York World*.

Dec. 8. American Federation of Labor founded at Columbus, Ohio, on nonpolitical craft union principles. Twenty-five trade unions participate, but unskilled workers are not represented. Samuel Gompers is elected president and, except for year 1895, contin-

LOUIS SULLIVAN
Address to Western Association of Architects, 1885
Many who have commented upon the practice of architecture in this country have regarded the absence of a style, distinctively American, as both strange and deplorable; and with a view to betterment they have advanced theories as to the nature, and immediate realization, of such a style that evidence a lack of insight equally strange and deplorable. These theories have been for the greater part suggested by the feelings awakened in contemplating the matured beauty of Old World art, and imply a grafting or transplanting process. They have been proved empirical by the sufficient logic of time; their advocates having ignored the complex fact that, like a new species of any class, a national style must be a growth, that slow and gradual assimilation of nutriment and a struggle against obstacles are necessary adjuncts to the purblind processes of growth, and that the resultant structure can bear only a chemical or metaphysical resemblance to the materials on which it has been nurtured. . . .

National sensitiveness and pride, conjoined with fertility of resource, will aid as active stimuli in the development of this instinct toward a more rational and organic mode of expression, leading through many reactions to a higher sphere of artistic development. . . .

We surely have in us the germ of artistic greatness, no people on earth possessing more of innate poetic feeling, more of ideality, greater capacity to adore the beautiful than our own people; but architects as a professional class have held it more expedient to maintain the traditions of their culture than to promulgate vitalizing thought.

HENRY CLEWS
North American Review, 1886
The Knights of Labor have undertaken to test, upon a large scale, the application of compulsion as a means of enforcing their demands. . . .

To the employer, it is a question whether his individual rights as to the control of his property shall be so far overborne as to not only deprive him of his freedom but also expose him to interferences seriously impairing the value of his capital. To the employees, it is a question whether, by the force of coercion, they can wrest, to their own profit, powers and control which, in every civilized community, are secured as the most sacred and inalienable rights of the employer. . . .

From the nature of the case, however, this labor disease must soon end one way or another; and there is not much difficulty in foreseeing what its termination will be. The demands of the Knights and their sympathizers, whether openly expressed or temporarily concealed, are so utterly revolutionary of the inalienable rights of the citizen and so completely subversive of social order that the whole community has come to a firm conclusion that these pretensions must be resisted to the last extremity of endurance and authority; and that the present is the best opportunity for meeting the issue firmly and upon its merits. . . .

The laboring man in this bounteous and hospitable country has no ground for complaint. His vote is potential and he is elevated thereby to the position of man. . . . Under the government of this nation, the effort is to elevate the standard of the human race and not to degrade it. In all other nations it is the reverse. What, therefore, has the laborer to complain of in America?

ues in office until 1924. Gompers has been instrumental in founding predecessor organization, Federation of Organized Trades and Labor Unions of U.S.A. and Canada, in 1881.

In *Wabash, St. Louis & Pacific Railroad Company* v. *Illinois*, Supreme Court invalidates a state railroad-regulating law, holding that only Congress can control interstate commerce; decision is in some aspects contrary to that in Granger cases of 1877, resulting in area where neither federal government nor states have control. In *Santa Clara County* v. *Southern Pacific Railroad*, Court establishes that the word "persons" in the Fourteenth Amendment applies not only to individuals but also to legal "persons," such as corporations.

Elihu Thomson patents electric welding machine, which is used in construction work to replace riveting, especially later in automobile industry.

Frances Hodgson Burnett's book about a model little gentleman, *Little Lord Fauntleroy*, becomes immediately popular and in next 20 years makes a generation of boys uncomfortable.

Painter and anatomy teacher Thomas Eakins, one of half dozen greatest American painters, is dismissed from Pennsylvania Academy of Fine Arts for employing undraped models in mixed life class; a master of anatomy, he earlier has painted a medical group, "The Gross Clinic," and later executes "The Agnew Clinic." He also paints portraits and sports subjects, notably "Max Schmitt in a Single Scull"; some of his portraits are so penetrating as to be offensive to their subjects.

Roman Catholic Archbishop James Gibbons of Baltimore, Maryland, becomes second U.S. Cardinal.

1886 - 1887

May 4, 1886. Bomb explodes in Haymarket Square, Chicago, after police break up anarchist meeting protesting treatment of strikers at McCormick Harvesting Machine Company on previous day; 7 policemen and 4 workmen die, and 70 policemen are wounded. **Aug. 20.** Eight agitators are convicted; 7 are sentenced to death, 1 to imprisonment. **Nov. 11, 1887.** Following commutations of sentences of 2 agitators and suicide of 1, remaining 4 are hanged. Identity of bomb thrower is never established. Public alarm at supposed radical control of labor movement, as well as failure in previous year of several strikes, is instrumental in lessening effectiveness of labor movements, especially the Knights of Labor, which expires within a few years.

1887

Jan. 20. Renewal of U.S.-Hawaii Treaty for reciprocal commerce is ratified by Congress after it is altered to include exclusive right of U.S. to build an armed naval base at Pearl Harbor, near Honolulu.

Feb. 3. Congress passes Electoral Count Act to avoid such disputes as that in 1876 election; law makes each state responsible for its electoral returns, which must be affirmed according to law of that state. Congress has no power over vote unless state cannot decide or fraud is committed.

Feb. 4. Congress passes Interstate Commerce Act. Granger laws principle of public regulation of railroads is embodied in powers of first federal regulatory agency, the Interstate Commerce Commission. Commission's rulings are rarely supported by the U.S. Supreme Court, and it is, therefore, not very effective, but passage of Act indicates public realization that changing economy requires changed methods of control.

AUGUST SPIES
Haymarket Riot Trial, 1886
The contemplated murder of eight men, whose only crime is that they have dared to speak the truth, may open the eyes of these suffering millions; may wake them up. . . . The class that clamors for our lives, the good, devout Christians, have attempted in every way, through their newspapers and otherwise, to conceal the true and only issue in this case. By simply designating the defendants as anarchists and picturing them as a newly discovered tribe or species of cannibals, and by inventing shocking and horrifying stories of dark conspiracies said to be planned by them, these good Christians zealously sought to keep the naked fact from the working people and other righteous parties, namely: that on the evening of May 4, 200 armed men, under the command of a notorious ruffian, attacked a meeting of peaceable citizens! . . .

But, "Anarchism is on trial!" foams Mr. Grinnell. If that is the case, your honor, very well; you may sentence me, for I am an anarchist. I believe . . . that the state of castes and classes—the state where one class dominates over and lives upon the labor of another class, and calls this order—yes, I believe that this barbaric form of social organization, with its legalized plunder and murder, is doomed to die and make room for a free society, voluntary association, or universal brotherhood, if you like. You may pronounce the sentence upon me, honorable judge, but let the world know that in A.D. 1886, in the state of Illinois, eight men were sentenced to death because they believed in a better future; because they had not lost their faith in the ultimate victory of liberty and justice!

GROVER CLEVELAND
Veto Message, June 1886

I am so thoroughly tired of disapproving gifts of public money to individuals who in my view have no right or claim to the same, notwithstanding apparent congressional sanction, that I interpose with a feeling of relief a veto in a case where I find it unnecessary to determine the merits of the application. In speaking of the promiscuous and ill-advised grants of pensions which have lately been presented to me for approval, I have spoken of their "apparent congressional sanction" in recognition of the fact that a large proportion of these bills have never been submitted to a majority of either branch of Congress, but are the result of nominal sessions held for the express purpose of their consideration and attended by a small minority of the members of the respective houses of the legislative branch of government. . . .

Heedlessness and a disregard of the principle which underlies the granting of pensions is unfair to the wounded, crippled soldier who is honored in the just recognition of his government. Such a man should never find himself side by side on the pension roll with those who have been tempted to attribute the natural ills to which humanity is heir to service in the Army. Every relaxation of principle in the granting of pensions invites applications without merit and encourages those who for gain urge honest men to become dishonest. Thus is the demoralizing lesson taught the people that as against the public Treasury the most questionable expedients are allowable.

Feb. 11. In move that antagonizes organized war veterans, President Cleveland vetoes Dependent Pension Bill, which provides pensions unrelated to war injuries. Pensions of Civil War veterans have by this time become a major drain on the U.S. Treasury in spite of policy of careful investigation of claims.

March 2. Hatch Act grants federal subsidies for agricultural experiment and education programs by states; legislation is an extension of Morrill Act of 1862.

March 5. Tenure of Office Act of 1867 is repealed. Independent presidential power to remove officials from office is restored after President Cleveland's insistence on constitutional right.

June 7. President Cleveland signs routine War Department order authorizing return to the South of captured Confederate battle flags. **June 15.** Protest from Union veterans and Republican politicians is so great that Cleveland cancels order. Flags are not finally returned for 18 years.

Dec. 6. Convinced that high protective tariffs have kept prices high and encouraged formation of trusts, President Cleveland, without consulting members of his party, concentrates his annual message on a plea for tariff reductions; Democratic high-tariff advocates are angered by move.

Physicists Albert A. Michelson and Edward W. Morley perform experiment that establishes that the velocity of the earth has no effect on the velocity of light; result is inspiration for Albert Einstein's Special Theory of Relativity.

Melvil Dewey founds State Library School in Albany, New York. He has earlier, in 1876, proposed his decimal system of library cataloging and is largely responsible for efficiency in library methods throughout the U.S.

1887 - 1888

June 25-July 26, 1887. Representatives of Britain, Germany, and the U.S. meet in Washington to discuss control of Samoa. British (having come to an agreement before meeting) support German claim to right of mandate over islands; meeting closes without decision. Germany then deports Samoan ruler and installs German-influenced government, which in following year discriminates against British and U.S. commerce. By end of 1888, tension has increased to point of all three countries' stationing warships in Samoa's Apia Harbor.

1888

Feb. 15. British and U.S. representatives in Washington work out Bayard-Chamberlain Treaty and practical arrangements to carry it out in effort to put an end to U.S.-Canadian conflict over Atlantic fisheries. **Aug. 21.** Republican Congress rejects treaty, partly because of reciprocal tariff clause, but practical arrangements remain basis for U.S.-Canadian fishing operations until 1923, when Canada rejects them.

March 12. Blizzard lasting 36 hours paralyzes New York City, 400 people die, and property damage is enormous, as transportation stoppage and cutoff of communications isolate city from the world. Messages from New York to Boston are sent by way of England.

May 16. Union Labor Party nominates Alson J. Streeter of Illinois for President. **May 17.** United Labor Party nominates Robert H. Cowdrey of Illinois for President. **May 31.** Prohibition Party nominates Clinton B. Fisk of New Jersey. **June 5.** Democrats, meeting in St. Louis, renomi-

THEODORE ROOSEVELT
Address to Union League Club, 1888
The Republican Party, and the Republican Party alone, has hitherto shown itself capable of grappling with the financial and business difficulties of the country, and I believe that its future will not belie its past. . . .

The Republican Party, and the country at large as well, is definitely committed to the policy of protection; and unquestionably any reversal of that policy at present would do harm and produce widespread suffering. . . .

The Republican Party stands for other things in addition to protection. It stands for the national idea, for honest money, and for any honest civil service.

FINLEY PETER DUNNE
Mr. Dooley Discusses Party Politics
Man an' boy I've seen the Dimmycratic party hangin' to th' ropes a score iv times. I've seen it dead an' burrid an' th' Raypublicans kindly buildin' a monymint f'r it an' preparin' to spind their declinin' days in th' custom house. I've gone to sleep nights wonderin' where I'd throw away me vote afther this an' whin I woke up there was that crazy-headed, ol' loon iv a party with its hair sthreamin' in its eyes, an' an axe in its hand, chasin' Raypublicans into th' tall grass, 'Tis niver so good as whin 'tis broke, whin rayspectable people speak iv it in whispers, an' whin it has no leaders an' only wan principel, to go in an' take it away fr'm th' other fellows. Something will turn up, ye bet, Hinnessey. Th' Raypublican party may die iv overfeedin' or all th' leaders pump out so much ile they won't feel like leadin'. An' annyhow they'se always wan ray iv light ahead. We're sure to have hard times.

EDWARD BELLAMY
Looking Backward, 1888

"The records of the period show that the outcry against the concentration of capital was furious. Men believed that it threatened society with a form of tyranny more abhorrent than it had ever endured. They believed that the great corporations were preparing for them the yoke of a baser servitude than had ever been imposed on the race, servitude not to men but to soulless machines, incapable of any motive but insatiable greed. Looking back, we cannot wonder at their desperation, for certainly humanity was never confronted with a fate more sordid and hideous than would have been the era of corporate tyranny which they anticipated. . . .

"The tendency toward monopolies, which had been so desperately and vainly resisted, was recognized at last, in its true significance, as a process which only needed to complete its logical evolution to open a golden future to humanity.

"Early in the last century the evolution was completed by the final consolidation of the entire capital of the nation. The industry and commerce of the country, ceasing to be conducted by a set of irresponsible corporations and syndicates of private persons at their caprice and for their profit, were entrusted to a single syndicate representing the people, to be conducted in the common interest for the common profit. . . . The epoch of trusts had ended in the great trust. In a word, the people of the United States concluded to assume the conduct of their own business, just as one hundred odd years before they had assumed the conduct of their own government, organizing now for industrial purposes on precisely the same grounds that they had then organized for political purposes."

nate President Cleveland, with Allen G. Thurman of Ohio as his running mate. **June 25.** Republicans at Chicago nominate Benjamin Harrison of Indiana for President and Levi P. Morton of New York for Vice-President. Democratic platform stresses revision of high protective tariff. Republican platform calls for continuation of tariff and high pensions for war veterans. Enormous campaign fund raised by Republicans makes possible widely publicized criticism of President Cleveland's low tariff policy, vetoes of pension bills, and consent to Confederate flag return. **Oct. 21.** Republicans publish falsified letter ostensibly from an uncertain naturalized citizen (but actually written by a Republican) asking British minister to U.S. how to vote in election and answer of minister that he should vote for Cleveland. Indignation over foreign interference in election loses many votes for Democrats.

June 13. U.S. Department of Labor is established by Congress; it is not given Cabinet rank until 1913.

Nov. 6. Benjamin Harrison carries all states except Solid South, Connecticut, and New Jersey. Popular vote is Harrison 5,447,000; Cleveland, 5,540,000; although Cleveland's popular plurality is almost 100,000, he receives only 168 electoral votes to Harrison's 233.

George Eastman perfects Kodak hand camera, making possible first amateur photography. Camera is preloaded with enough roll film for 100 two-inch diameter round photographs. When film has been exposed, camera with film is returned to factory. Prints and reloaded camera are then returned to owner.

Edward Bellamy publishes his utopian *Looking Backward, 2000-1887*, describing a society that provides for social and economic human needs. It eventually sells 1 million copies. Bellamy's later advocacy of nationalization of public services, especially in his magazine, the *Nationalist*, helps form platform of Populist Party in 1892 James Bryce, for six years British ambassador to the U.S., publishes *The American Commonwealth*, dealing with the structure and functions of the Constitution; the work, whose author is a friend and admirer of the U.S., is read throughout the country.

Composer Edward A. MacDowell settles in Boston after study and teaching in Europe; among compositions written there by first serious composer to be nationally recognized are *Woodland Sketches*, *Sonata Tragica*, and First and Second *(Indian)* Suites. After MacDowell's death in 1908, his widow establishes (1910) the MacDowell Colony for composers, writers, and artists at farm in Peterborough, New Hampshire.

By this year, trusts have grown so numerous that many important and minor U.S. industries are organized as combinations; among them are reaping, mowing, and threshing machines, plows, petroleum, copper, steel rails, steel and iron beams, wrought iron pipe, stoves, rubber, coal, beef, sugar, whiskey, glass, and even castor oil.

1889

March 2. Kansas passes first antitrust law, followed by North Carolina, Tennessee, and Michigan in the same year and 11 other Western and Southern states in following two years. But since state laws are unable to deal with interstate monopolies, demand develops for federal antitrust legislation. New Jersey establishes itself as home of giant corporations by authorizing incorporation of holding companies within the state.

March 16. Poised warships of Britain,

HENRY DEMAREST LLOYD
North American Review, 1884
The change from competition to combination is nothing less than one of those revolutions which march through history with giant strides. It is not likely that this revolution will go backward. Nothing goes backward in this country except reform. When Stephenson said of railroads that where combination was possible competition was impossible, he was unconsciously declaring the law of all industry. . . .

Literary theorists still repeat the cant of individualism in law, politics, and morals; but the world of affairs is gladly accepting, in lieu of the liberty of each to do as he will with his own, all it can get of the liberty given by laws that let no one do as he might with his own. The dream of the French Revolution, that man was good enough to be emancipated from the bonds of association and government by the simple proclamation of "Liberty, Fraternity and Equality," was but the frenzied expression of what was called freedom of self-interest in a quieter but not less bloody revolution, if the mortality of the factories, the mines, and the tenements be charged to its account. A rope cannot be made of sand; a society cannot be made of competitive units.

We have given competition its own way and have found that we are not good enough or wise enough to be trusted with this power of ruining ourselves in the attempt to ruin others. . . . We now need a renaissance of moral inventions, contrivances to tap the vast currents of moral magnetism flowing uncaught over the face of society. Morals and values rise and fall together. If our combinations have no morals, they can have no values. If the tendency to combination is irresistible, control of it is imperative.

(Above right) James A. Garfield, twentieth President of the United States; (above left) Chester A. Arthur, twenty-first President of the United States: photograph by Bell, 1882; (below) attack on President Garfield's life by Charles Guiteau, a disappointed office-seeker, July 1881

(Above) A view of the scene of the Haymarket
bombing in Chicago on May 4, 1886, published
in *Frank Leslie's Popular Monthly*; (right)
Grover Cleveland, twenty-second and twenty-
fourth President of the United States

ANDREW CARNEGIE
Wealth, 1889

Poor and restricted are our opportunities in this life; narrow our horizon; our best work most imperfect; but rich men should be thankful for one inestimable boon. They have it in their power during their lives to busy themselves in organizing benefactions from which the masses of their fellows will derive lasting advantage, and thus dignify their own lives. . . .

Thus is the problem of rich and poor to be solved. The laws of accumulation will be left free; the laws of distribution free. Individualism will continue, but the millionaire will be but a trustee for the poor; entrusted for a season with a great part of the increased wealth of the community, but administering it for the community far better than it could or would have done for itself. The best minds will thus have reached a stage in the development of the race in which it is clearly seen that there is no mode of disposing of surplus wealth creditable to thoughtful and earnest men into whose hands it flows save by using it year by year for the general good.

This day already dawns. But a little while, and although, without incurring the pity of their fellows, men may die sharers in great business enterprises from which their capital cannot be or has not been withdrawn, and is left chiefly at death for public uses, yet the man who dies leaving behind him millions of available wealth, which was his to administer during life, will pass away "unwept, unhonored, and unsung," no matter to what uses he leaves the dross which he cannot take with him. Of such as these the public verdict will then be: "The man who dies thus rich dies disgraced."

Germany, and the U.S. in Apia Harbor, Samoa, are wrecked by hurricane, thus averting naval battle. President Harrison in the meantime, on March 14, has sent three representatives to Berlin conference on Samoa. **June 14.** Samoan treaty (Treaty of Berlin), signed by three nations, provides for Samoan independence under protectorate of all three nations.

May 31. Dam above Johnstown, Pennsylvania, breaks when Conemaugh River is swelled by heavy rains; four towns are destroyed before river drowns Johnstown in 30 feet of water; about 2,300 people are killed.

June. Andrew Carnegie sets forth his theory of philanthropy in "The Gospel of Wealth" (originally titled "Wealth"), article that defends capitalism but urges businessmen to adjust its inequalities by donating their wealth to deserving causes.

Sept. 9. Producer Charles Frohman opens Bronson Howard's most popular play, *Shenandoah*, in New York City; theme is conflict between loyalty to the U.S. and the Confederacy caused by the Civil War.

Nov. 2. Dakota Territory is divided into states of North and South Dakota. President Harrison shuffles proclamations before signing to avoid conflict about order; thus, either is thirty-ninth or fortieth state. Two widely separated centers of population have led to division. Population of North Dakota is about 180,000, most settlers having arrived in last 20 years. South Dakota's population is about 350,000, having increased greatly since discovery of gold in Black Hills in 1874.

Nov. 8. Montana becomes forty-first state of the Union. It has previously been part of Oregon country, then part of Idaho Territory, and later Territory of Montana. First population boom in 1860s has been result of gold discovery; 1889 population is about 143,000.

Nov. 11. Washington becomes forty-second state. Until 1863 Washington Territory has included Idaho. Puget Sound area has developed earliest, but gold discoveries and railroads have brought settlers to interior. In 1878 Congress has refused statehood request because of small population, but by 1889 population has reached 357,000.

Nov. 14. Nellie Bly, reporter for *New York World*, starts on round-the-world trip. Attempt to better record of Jules Verne's fictional journey *Around the World in Eighty Days* is successful when she reaches home in 72 days, 6 hours, 11 minutes, and 14 seconds.

Dec. 6. Jefferson Davis, former President of the Confederate States of America, dies in New Orleans at age 81.

Mark Twain publishes his satire on literary treatment of the Age of Chivalry, *A Connecticut Yankee in King Arthur's Court.* Theodore Roosevelt publishes two volumes of his *The Winning of the West,* a history of early settlements west of the Alleghenies; final work is four volumes.

First classes begin at Barnard College for women, founded as part of New York City's Columbia University.

First safety bicycles are produced in quantity; result is greatly increased popularity of bicycling and severe traffic problems. Bicycle having two equal-sized wheels, with saddle between them, quickly replaces those with one large and one very small wheel. By 1893 more than a million bicycles are in use in the U.S.

WALTER B. HILL
Century Magazine, 1892
A few years ago, in a little country village, there was instituted a chapter of a certain benevolent insurance order. The Chancellor was subsequently elected Grand Chancellor of the State. Afterward, at a national convention, he was made Supreme Grand Chancellor of the United States. The next year he was elected Most Supreme Grand Chancellor of the World; and it became his duty, the order paying his expenses, to make an international visitation to the three chapters in Australia, New Zealand, and England that composed the aforesaid "world."

When that triumphal tour was completed, his return home was heralded, and the chapter of his village arranged for a reception of the honorable dignitary. Never shall I forget the feeling of solemn awe that settled down upon the little community as the evening approached when the Most Supreme Grand Chancellor of the World was to arrive. This favored American was a "bigger man than old Grant."

Not only are there offices enough to "go round" but the really capable and pushing American is generally honored with a score. I have heard a busy and overworked man decline to be at the head of an organization because he was at the head of twenty-five already.

Here then we have the great American safety valve—we are a nation of presidents.

1889 - 1890

Oct. 2-April 19. First International Con-

HAMILTON S. WICKS
Cosmopolitan, 1889

And now the hour of twelve was at hand, and everyone on the qui vive for the bugle blast that would dissolve the chain of enchantment hitherto girding about this coveted land. Many of the "boomers" were mounted on high-spirited and fleet-footed horses, and had ranged themselves along the territorial line, scarcely restrained even by the presence of the troop of cavalry from taking summary possession. The better class of wagons and carriages ranged themselves in line with the horsemen, and even here and there mule teams attached to canvas-covered vehicles stood in the front ranks, with the reins and whip grasped by the "boomers" wives. All was excitement and expectation. . . .

Suddenly the air was pierced with the blast of a bugle. Hundreds of throats echoed the sound with shouts of exultation. The quivering limbs of saddled steeds, no longer restrained by the hands that held their bridles, bounded forward simultaneously into the "beautiful land" of Oklahoma; and wagons and carriages and buggies and prairie schooners and a whole congregation of curious equipages joined in. . . .

The race was not over when you reached the particular lot you were content to select for your possession. The contest still was who should drive their stakes first, who would erect their little tents soonest, and then, who would quickest build a little wooden shanty. . . .

One did not know how far to go before stopping; it was hard to tell when it was best to stop; and it was a puzzle whether to turn to the right hand or the left. Everyone appeared dazed, and all for the most part acted like a flock of stray sheep.

ference of American States meets at Washington, D.C., with U.S. and 17 Latin-American countries (all except the Dominican Republic) attending. The U.S., which has called Conference, attempts to establish customs union, but other countries are unwilling. By adjournment on April 19, Conference has set up inter-American organization that is later called Pan American Union and has established basis for reciprocal tariffs as authorized by McKinley Tariff Act of following year.

1889 - 1893

April 22, 1889. Having yielded to pressure of boomers (homesteaders) to buy Indian lands and open Oklahoma (Indian Territory) to white settlement, U.S. declares land open. Wild rush into area starts at pistol shot, and within 24 hours claims covering about 2 million acres have been staked by' 50,000 settlers; in one day Guthrie is organized with nearly 15,000 inhabitants and Oklahoma City with 10,000. **May 2, 1890.** Congress forms Oklahoma Territory of lands not allotted to Indians. **1891 and 1892.** U.S. buys 4 million more acres of Indian land and opens them to settlement. **Sept. 16, 1893.** Second large rush to 6-million-acre Cherokee Outlet results in settlement of 100,000 people.

1890

June 27. Dependent Pension Act provides liberal pensions for needy or disabled Union Civil War veterans, whether war injured or not, and their families; within a few years number of pensioners has increased by one-third, and amount paid has jumped from about $90 million to $150 million.

July 2. Growing demand for federal control of monopolies results in passage of Sherman Antitrust Act, which empowers government and federal courts to prevent restraint of interstate and foreign commerce. Wording of Act fails to make clear what is considered a trust as well as what is considered restraint of trade, and whether railroads and labor unions are included in combinations. Thus, Act is ineffective and weakly enforced, and monopolies and combinations continue to grow.

July 3. Idaho becomes forty-third state of the Union, with a population of 88,500, largely gold seekers. Admission to Union follows long controversy over plan to divide Idaho Territory between Washington and Nevada, which has been rejected by Congress.

July 10. Wyoming is admitted to Union as forty-fourth state. Territory has been organized in 1869 to protect and govern settlements along railroads. Bunchgrass and buffalo grass of plains have attracted cattlemen, but winter of 1886-1887 has been so severe that one-sixth of cattle have died.

July 14. Congress passes Sherman Silver Purchase Act, a compromise between Western agrarian and silver states and pro-tariff interests of the East. U.S. Treasury is required to purchase monthly an amount of silver about equal to U.S. silver production (4,500,000 ounces), paying for it with notes redeemable in gold or silver. Measure tends to reduce U.S. gold reserve and weaken confidence in U.S. currency; it is repealed in 1893.

Oct. 1. McKinley Tariff raises duties to new highs, averaging about 50 percent, largely for protection of industry rather than revenue. Executive agreements for reciprocal raising of tariffs to equal duties of other countries are authorized for first time.

Oct. 1. Congress creates Weather Bureau as part of Department of Agriculture.

Nov. 1. Mississippi becomes first state to

EDWARD C. BILLINGS
U.S. v. Workingmen's Amalgamated Council of New Orleans, 1893
The defendants urge . . . that the right of the complainants depends upon an unsettled question of law. The theory of the defense is that this case does not fall within the purview of the statute; that the statute prohibited monopolies and combinations which, using words in a general sense, were of capitalists and not of laborers. I think the congressional debates show that the statute had its origin in the evils of massed capital; but, when the Congress came to formulating the prohibition which is the yardstick for measuring the complainant's right to the injunction, it expressed it in these words: "Every contract or combination in the form of trust, or otherwise in restraint of trade or commerce among the several states or with foreign nations, is hereby declared to be illegal."

The subject had so broadened in the minds of the legislators that the source of the evil was not regarded as material, and the evil in its entirety is dealt with. They made the interdiction Include combinations of labor as well as of capital; in fact, all combinations in restraint of commerce, without reference to the character of the persons who entered into them. It is true this statute has not been much expounded by judges, but, as it seems to me, its meaning, as far as relates to the sort of combinations to which it is to apply, is manifest and that it includes combinations which are composed of laborers acting in the interest of laborers.

JACOB RIIS

How the Other Half Lives, 1890

If the tenement is here continually dragged into the eye of public condemnation and scorn, it is because in one way or another it is found directly responsible for, or intimately associated with, three-fourths of the miseries of the poor. In the Bohemian quarter it is made the vehicle for enforcing upon a proud race a slavery as real as any that ever disgraced the South. Not content with simply robbing the tenant, the owner, in the dual capacity of landlord and employer, reduces him to virtual serfdom by making his becoming his tenant, on such terms as he sees fit to make, the condition of employment at wages likewise of his own making. . . .

Probably more than half of all the Bohemians in this city are cigar-makers, and it is the herding of these in great numbers in the so-called tenement factories . . . that constitutes at once their greatest hardship and the chief grudge of other workmen against them.

The manufacturer who owns, say, from three or four to a dozen or more tenements contiguous to his shop, fills them up with these people, charging them outrageous rents, and demanding often even a preliminary deposit of $5 "key money"; deals them out tobacco by the week, and devotes the rest of his energies to the paring down of wages to within a peg or two of the point where the tenant rebels in desperation. When he does rebel, he is given the alternative of submission, or eviction with entire loss of employment. . . .

Men, women, and children work together seven days in the week in these cheerless tenements to make a living for the family, from the break of day till far into the night.

restrict Negro civil rights by writing "understanding" clause into new constitution; clause requires voters to be able to read and understand state constitution.

Nov. 4. Democratic victories in congressional elections of 39 states result in shift to Democratic control of House of Representatives; reaction against McKinley Tariff is largely responsible.

Dec. 15. Sioux Chief Sitting Bull is killed by soldiers in South Dakota during U.S. Army effort to curb religious Ghost Dance, a rite dedicated to restoration of Indian lands taken by whites that is thought to be dangerous to white population of area. **Dec. 29.** Two hundred Sioux are massacred by cavalry at Battle of Wounded Knee Creek. Ghost Dance war ends in following month when sympathetic Indian agency government is set up.

1890 census shows population of 62,948,000; immigration since last census has been 5,247,000, largely from northern and western Europe, although substantial numbers have come from southern and eastern Europe during period. Settled areas are so widely distributed that census reports frontier no longer exists. Illiteracy is estimated at about 13 percent of population, about 4 percent less than in 1880.

How the Other Half Lives by Jacob A. Riis shocks many into awareness of city slum conditions and results in beginning of reforms. At this time, fortunes of about 1 percent of U.S. population total more than possessions of remaining 99 percent.

William Dean Howells publishes his novel *A Hazard of New Fortunes*, with background of New York City streetcar strike. William James publishes his *The Principles of Psychology*, the first important American treatment of experimental psychology.

Poems by Emily Dickinson, 114 selections from hundreds of poems, is issued reluctantly by publisher who fears that her original style will not be acceptable to the public; he, therefore, alters many poems. Writings have been found by her sister after her death four yours earlier. Though critics are hostile, public enthusiasm leads eventually to publication of all poems found.

Anna Sewell's *Black Beauty*, published years earlier in England, is first published in the U.S. by American Humane Education Society. Five Rudyard Kipling books are published in widely sold cheap editions made possible by pirating books just before International Copyright Agreement; among them are *Soldiers Three* and *Mine Own People*.

U.S. Post Office Department prohibits mailing of *The Kreutzer Sonata* by Leo Tolstoi; New York Governor Theodore Roosevelt calls Tolstoi a "sexual and moral pervert."

1891

March 3. Congress establishes Circuit Courts of Appeals to ease burden of U.S. Supreme Court.

March 3. Congress repeals Timber Culture Act of 1873 and passes Forest Reserve Act, by which the President is permitted to close public forest land to settlement for establishment of national parks. In following two years 13 million acres are closed.

March 4. International Copyright Act is passed; Act protects works of British, French, Belgian, and Swiss authors in U.S. Extensive pirating of foreign books by American publishers has resulted in loss of sales to U.S. authors and loss of royalties to foreign authors. Copyright protection is eventually extended to almost all nations.

HENRY JAMES
Letter to American Publishers' Copyright League, 1887
For it is through my observation of the case here, while you are observing it at home, that it is impressed upon me that Americans enjoy in another country a courtesy and an advantage which, among ourselves, we have so long and so ungenerously denied to the stranger, even when the stranger has given us some of the most precious enjoyment we know—has delighted and fortified and enriched us. I have all the material benefit of publishing my productions in England. I have only to put them forth shortly before their appearance in the United States to secure an effective copyright. The circumstance that the profit in question would be much more important if my writings were more so does not alter my sense of its being sadly out of keeping with the genius of our people to withhold reciprocity in a matter in which my own case is simply a small illustration.

It is out of keeping with the genius of our people to have to take lessons in liberality—in fair dealing—from other lands and to keep its citizens, in relation to those more hospitable countries, in a false, indefensible, intolerable position. . . .

To see vividly that we cannot hold up the American head about the world when the subject of copyright is broached is to number the days of a system which carries such detestable incidents in its bosom. . . .

Let it not be said—for then we may as well quit the field altogether—that we cannot afford the straight course. . . .

I know of no honorable thing that we cannot afford to do, least of all a thing that concerns our being as clever as other people.

HAMLIN GARLAND
Crumbling Idols, 1894
The American youth is continually called upon by such critics to take Addison or Scott or Dickens or Shakespeare as a model. Such instruction leads naturally to the creation of blank-verse tragedies on Columbus and Washington—a species of work which seems to the radical the crowning absurdity of misplaced effort. Thus, the American youth is everywhere turned away from the very material which he could best handle, which he knows most about, and which he really loves most—material which would make him individual and fill him with hope and energy. The Western poet and novelist is not taught to see the beauty and significance of life near at hand. He is rather blinded to it by his instruction.

He turns away from the marvelous changes which border life subtends in its mighty rush toward civilization. He does not see the wealth of material which lies at his hand, in the mixture of races going on with inconceivable celerity everywhere in America, but with special picturesqueness in the West. If he sees it, he has not the courage to write of it.

If, here and there, one has reached some such perception, he voices it timidly, with an apologetic look in his eye. . . .

Art, they think, is something far away, and literary subjects must be something select and very civilized. And yet for forty years an infinite drama has been going on in those wide spaces of the West—a drama that is as thrilling, as full of heart and hope and battle, as any that ever surrounded any man; a life that was unlike any ever seen on the earth and which should have produced its characteristic literature, its native art chronicle.

May 5. Carnegie Hall, endowed and built by Andrew Carnegie, opens in New York City.

July 31. Thomas A. Edison patents his kinetoscopic camera, which takes moving pictures on a strip of film; film, called a peep show, is seen by one person at a time when he looks into a lighted box and turns a crank. Later, pictures are projected onto a screen.

Nov. 9. Charles H. Hoyt's play *A Trip to Chinatown*, a farce about San Francisco, closes after 650 performances, longest consecutive run to this date.

Three federal prisons are authorized by Congress; they are to be built at McNeil's Island, off coast of Washington; Leavenworth, Kansas; and Atlanta, Georgia; they are first nonmilitary federal prisons.

George E. Hale, founder of Kenwood Observatory in Chicago, takes first successful sun photograph with spectroheliograph of his own invention. He later establishes Mount Wilson (California) Observatory as part of the Carnegie Institution of Washington (D.C.).

Hamlin Garland, advocate of literary realism, publishes his collection of stories of the hardships of farm life, *Main-Travelled Roads*.

Whitcomb L. Judson takes out patent on a slide fastener (zipper).

Endowed by John D. Rockefeller, University of Chicago is established, first classes begin in following year. Throop Polytechnic Institute is founded in Pasadena, California; classes begin in same year; name is changed in 1920 to California Institute of Technology. First correspondence school (now called International Correspondence School, Scranton, Pennsylvania) is opened;

purpose is to teach miners working methods that will add to safety of coal mines.

James A. Naismith, of Springfield, Massachusetts, invents basketball as an indoor substitute for baseball and football in YMCA Training College.

Sculptor Augustus Saint-Gaudens unveils Washington, D.C. memorial, commonly known as "Grief," a memorial to Mrs. Henry Adams; memorial to Colonel Robert Shaw in Boston, Massachusetts, is also by this artist. Other important sculptors of the period are Daniel Chester French, whose "Lincoln" for the Lincoln Memorial in Washington is not dedicated until 1922, and George Grey Barnard, whose work includes "The Struggle of the Two Natures in Man" and "The Prodigal Son."

1891 - 1892

March 14, 1891. Mob storms New Orleans jail and lynches 11 Italian immigrants, 3 of whom are Italian nationals, after freeing of Sicilians who have been accused and acquitted of murder of New Orleans sheriff. **March 31.** After Secretary of State Blaine refuses to take action on ground that crime is a state matter, Italy recalls its minister to the U.S., and the U.S. recalls its Italian minister. **April 12, 1892.** U.S. offers Italy $25,000 indemnity, and matter is settled when Italy accepts.

Oct. 16. Mob in Valparaiso, Chile, attacks U.S. sailors on shore leave, killing 2 and injuring 17, after U.S. Navy has seized Chilean ship transporting arms from San Diego, California, for rebels in Chilean civil war. Chile's assertion that no reparations or apology are due results in request for declaration of war by President Harrison in January 1892. Chile finally apologizes and pays $75,000 to injured sailors and relatives of dead.

CHARLES W. ELIOT
Forum, 1892
On taking a broad view of the changes in civilized society since 1830, do we not see that there has been great progress toward unity — not indeed toward uniformity, but toward a genuine unity? The different classes of society and the different nations are still far from realizing the literal truth of the New Testament saying, "We are members one of another," but they have lately made some approach to realizing that truth. Now, unity of spirit with diversity of gifts is the real end to be attained in social organization. It would not be just to contend that popular education has brought to pass all these improvements and ameliorations; but it has undoubtedly contributed to them all.

Moreover, we find on every hand evidences of increased intelligence in large masses of people. If war has not ceased, soldiers are certainly more intelligent than they used to be, else they could not use the arms of precision with which armies are now supplied. The same is true of all industry and trade — they require more intelligence than formerly in all the work people. While, therefore, we must admit that education has not accomplished all that might fairly have been expected of it, we may believe that it has had some share in bringing about many of the ameliorations of the social state in the past two generations.

MARK TWAIN
Pudd'nhead Wilson's Calendar, 1894
Training is everything. The peach was once a bitter almond; cauliflower is nothing but cabbage with a college education.

GEORGE B. GRINNELL
Scribner's, 1892

1892

As soon as railroads penetrated the buffalo country, a market was opened for their hides. Men too lazy to work were not too lazy to hunt, and a good hunter could kill in the early days from thirty to seventy-five buffalo a day, the hides of which were worth from $1.50 to $4 each. This seemed an easy way to make money, and the market for hides was unlimited. Up to this time the trade in robes had been mainly confined to those dressed by the Indians, and these were for the most part taken from cows. The coming of the railroad made hides of all sorts marketable, and even those taken from naked old bulls found a sale at some price. . . .

Thousands of hunters followed millions of buffalo and destroyed them wherever found and at all seasons of the year. They pursued them during the day, and at night camped at the watering places and built lines of fires along the streams to drive the buffalo back so that they could not drink. It took less than six years to destroy all the buffalo in Kansas, Nebraska, Indian Territory, and northern Texas. . . .

The extirpation of the northern herd was longer delayed. No very terrible slaughter occurred until the completion of the Northern Pacific Railroad; then, however, the same scenes of butchery were enacted. Buffalo were shot down by tens of thousands, their hides stripped off, and the meat left to the wolves. The result of the crusade was soon seen: the last buffalo were killed in the Northwest near the boundary line in 1883, and that year may be said to have finished up the species, though some few were killed in 1884 to 1885.

Jan. 11. The U.S. approves international agreement against African slave trade.

Feb. 22. Preliminary convention of the Populist Party is held at St. Louis, Missouri; Western and Southern farm organizations, labor, Granger, and Greenbackers have, since 1889, worked to form a third party believed necessary to end agricultural depression.

Feb. 29. England and the U.S. agree to international arbitration of disputes over ocean seal hunting in the Bering Sea. U.S. has leased sealing rights to a private company within the three-mile limit, and Canadians have hunted seals in waters beyond the limit. The U.S. has seized some Canadian vessels and called hunting in the area "piracy." In following year, international tribunal, with representatives of France, Italy, and Sweden, decides against the U.S., prohibits sealing for part of the year as a conservation measure, and eventually fixes an indemnity of $473,000, which the U.S. pays to Britain five years later.

May 5. Geary Chinese Exclusion Act extends exclusion for 10 years; it requires Chinese laborers to register and provides for deportation of those not specifically allowed to stay in the U.S.

June 10. Republican convention at Minneapolis, Minnesota, renominates President Benjamin Harrison, with Whitelaw Reid of New York as his running mate; platform supports McKinley high protective tariff and is ambiguous on currency. **June 21.** Democrats at Chicago nominate former President Grover Cleveland, with Adlai E. Stevenson of Illinois for Vice-President; platform stresses tariff for revenue only and attacks Silver Purchase Act of 1890. **June 29.** Prohibition Party meets at Cincinnati and nominates John Bidwell of California. **July 2.** Populist convention opens in Omaha, Nebraska, but few Southerners are represented because of fear of Negro control. Convention nominates General James B. Weaver, former Greenbacker of Iowa, for President and James G. Fleld of Virginia for Vice-President. Platform: free coinage of silver in ratio of 16 to 1 to gold; government ownership of railroads, telephone, and telegraph; graduated income tax; restrictions on immigration; eight-hour day; popular election of U.S. senators; and secret ballot. **Aug. 28.** Socialist Labor Party nominates Simon Wing of Massachusetts.

July 6. Strikers at Carnegie steel mill in Homestead, Pennsylvania, protesting wage cuts and demanding recognition of their union, fire on Pinkerton detectives hired by management to break strike; 10 are killed and many wounded in pitched battle. **July 9.** Governor of Pennsylvania sends state troops to restore and keep order; they remain at mill for three months until strike is declared over, and most workers return as nonunion men. Strike damages steel unions to such an extent that there is no important union for 40 years.

July 14. Federal troops are sent to Coeur d'Alene, Idaho, silver mines and martial law is declared when strikers clash with strikebreakers. Strikes also occur in Wyoming and Tennessee; Tennessee strike is in protest against use of convict labor. President Harrison resorts to use of federal troops to enforce court injunctions in several cases.

Oct. 15. President Harrison proclaims 1,800,000-acre Crow Indian reservation in Montana open to settlement.

Nov. 8. Grover Cleveland, who has firmly supported the gold standard and avoided taking a strong stand on the tariff, wins election by popular vote of 5,555,000 to

JOHN PETER ALTGELD
Labor Day Address, 1893
The lesson I wish to impress upon you is that in business, in the industries, in government, everywhere, only those interests and forces survive that can maintain themselves along legal lines; and if you permanently improve your condition it must be by intelligently and patriotically standing together all over the country. Every plan must fail unless you do this.

At present you are to a great extent yet a scattered force, sufficiently powerful, if collected, to make yourselves heard and felt; to secure not only a fair hearing but a fair decision of all questions. Unite this power and you will be independent; leave it scattered and you will fail. Organization is the result of education as well as an educator. Let all the men of America who toil with their hands once stand together and no more complaints will be heard about unfair treatment. The progress of labor in the future must be along the line of patriotic association, not simply in localities but everywhere. And let me caution you that every act of violence is a hindrance to your progress.

There will be men among you ready to commit it. They are your enemies. There will be sneaks and Judas Iscariots in your ranks, who will for a mere pittance act as spies and try to incite some of the more hotheaded of your number to deeds of violence in order that these reptiles may get the credit of exposing you. They are your enemies. Cast them out of your ranks. Remember that any permanent prosperity must be based upon intelligence and upon conditions which are permanent.

HENRY FORD

My Life and Work, 1922

My gasoline buggy was the first and for a long time the only automobile in Detroit. It was considered to be something of a nuisance, for it made a racket and it scared horses. Also it blocked traffic. For if I stopped my machine anywhere in town a crowd was around it before I could start up again. Finally, I had to carry a chain and chain it to a lamp post whenever I left it anywhere. And then there was trouble with the police. I do not know quite why, for my impression is that there were no speed limits in those days. Anyway, I had to get a special permit from the mayor and thus for a time enjoyed the distinction of being the only licensed chauffeur in America. I ran that machine about one thousand miles through 1895 and 1896 and then sold it to Charles Ainsley of Detroit for two hundred dollars. That was my first sale. I had built the car not to sell but only to experiment with. I wanted to start another car.

FRANK PHILLIPS

Founder of Phillips Oil Company, 1904

I think people are going to buy quite a passel of these gasoline buggies and they need gasoline to make 'em go. It may be the thing has a future.

HENRY FORD

Launching the Model T in 1909

I will build a motorcar for the great multitudes.

SAMUEL HOFFENSTEIN

What a lucky thing the wheel was invented before the automobile; otherwise, can you imagine the awful screeching?

Harrison's 5,183,000; Weaver receives 1,030,000 votes. Electoral vote is Cleveland, 277; Harrison, 145; and Weaver, 22. Public opposition to McKinley Tariff and alarm over year's labor disputes have contributed to Republican defeat. Democrats gain control of both Senate and House.

Dec. 27. Cathedral of St. John the Divine is begun in New York City; planned as largest church in the U.S., it is built on three-block site in Romanesque and, later, Gothic style; to present day, it is not completed.

The Adventures of Sherlock Holmes by Sir Arthur Conan Doyle is first Sherlock Holmes publication to be widely read in America. Eventually, books, theater, radio, movies, and television build popularity until detective becomes perhaps most popular fictional character in present-day U.S.

1892 - 1893

Sept. 1892. Tool and bicycle makers Frank and Charles Duryea of Massachusetts make first gasoline automobile in U.S., testing it indoors for fear of ridicule; motor is not powerful enough to make it successful, but they build one with more power in the following year. William Morrison of Iowa builds first successful electric automobile also in 1892. Curious crowds hamper its movement in Chicago streets so much that police have to clear the way. **1893.** Henry Ford road tests his first successful automobile.

Oct. 20, 1892. World's Columbian Exposition is dedicated at Chicago to celebrate anniversary of discovery of America. Vice-President Levi Morton delivers address, and John Philip Sousa's band provides music. Opening officially in May 1893, and running until November, fair and exposition cover 686 acres, cost about $28 million, and are visited by 21 million persons. Orderly grouping of buildings, lakes, and gardens, planned under leadership of Daniel Burnham, Richard Morris Hunt, and others, stimulates city planning movement throughout U.S. Classical style of most buildings ignores current original American trends, revives taste for Roman style, and hastens decline of taste for Gothic and Romanesque.

1892 - 1894

"Daisy Bell" ("A Bicycle Built for Two"), published in 1892, and "The Sidewalks of New York," published in 1894, are immediately popular and to present day are on list of all-time song hits.

1893

Jan. 4. President Harrison offers amnesty to all violators of federal antipolygamy laws, passed in 1862 and 1882, on condition that laws be observed from this time onward; laws have been aimed at Mormon multiple marriage practice. In 1890 Mormon Church has withdrawn its sanction of polygamy, but some elders who have acquired several wives before that time have had problem of what to do with them.

March 1. Congress passes Diplomatic Appropriations Act, creating post of ambassador to countries that send ambassadors to the U.S. Hitherto, highest rank has been minister. **April 3.** Thomas F. Bayard is appointed U.S. ambassador to Great Britain, first American in that office to hold that rank.

April 21. Financial Panic of 1893 begins when U.S. gold reserve falls below $100 million mark, considered safe minimum. U.S. Treasury has been drained of gold by sales of securities by foreign investors; in addition, revenues have decreased because of McKinley Tariff, and increased veterans'

JOHN JACOB ASTOR
A man who has a million dollars is as well off as if he were rich.

MRS. OLIVER HAZARD PERRY BELMONT
One of the leaders of Newport society
I know of no profession, art, or trade that women are working in today, as taxing on mental resource as being a leader of society.

WARD McALLISTER
To Charles Crandall, 1888
There are only about four hundred people in fashionable New York society. If you go outside that number you strike people who are either not at ease in a ballroom or else make other people not at ease.

WARD McALLISTER
Society As I Have Found It, 1890
I must here explain that behind what I call the "smart set" in society there always stood the old, solid, substantial, and respected people. Families who held great social power as far back as the birth of this country, who were looked up to by society, and who always could, when they so wished, come forward and exercise their power, when, for one reason or another, they would take no active part, joining in it quietly, but not conspicuously. Ordinarily, they preferred, like the gods, to sit upon Olympus.

FREDERICK JACKSON TURNER
Significance of the Frontier, 1893
In a recent bulletin of the superintendent of the census for 1890 appear these significant words:

Up to and including 1880 the country had a frontier of settlement, but at present the unsettled area has been so broken into by isolated bodies of settlement that there can hardly be said to be a frontier line. In the discussion of its extent, its westward movement, etc., it cannot, therefore, any longer have a place in the census reports.

This brief official statement marks the closing of a great historic movement. Up to our own day, American history has been in a large degree the history of the colonization of the Great West. The existence of an area of free land, its continuous recession, and the advance of American settlement westward explain American development. Behind institutions, behind constitutional forms and modifications lie the vital forces that call these organs into life and shape them to meet changing conditions. Now, the peculiarity of American institutions is the fact that they have been compelled to adapt themselves to the changes of an expanding people — to the changes involved in crossing a continent, in winning a wilderness, and in developing at each area of this progress out of the primitive economic and political conditions of the frontier into the complexity of city life.

BENJAMIN HARRISON
Have you not learned that not stocks or bonds or stately homes, or products of mill or field are our country? It is the splendid thought that is in our minds.

pensions have further depleted government funds. Amount of gold in Treasury is only one-fifth of paper money in circulation. **May 5.** Securities on New York Stock Exchange drop suddenly and reach a new low on June 27. By end of year, gold reserve has declined to $80 million, almost 600 banks and 15,000 businesses have failed, and one-third of U.S. railroads are bankrupt. Depression and widespread unemployment last until 1897.

June 30. President Cleveland calls special session of Congress for August 7 in attempt to deal with financial panic by requesting repeal of Sherman Silver Purchase Act.

July 12. Frederick Jackson Turner reads his essay "The Significance of the Frontier in American History," offering a theory that eventually changes American historical thought; hypothesis is that the presence of a frontier has been the significant impetus in the development of American democracy.

Aug. 1. Eight hundred and ten Populist and Republican delegates from 42 states attend National Bimetallic League Convention at Chicago. Convention agrees to repeal of Sherman Silver Purchase Act in exchange for legislation permitting free coinage of silver at ratio of 15½ or 16 to 1 to gold; delegates also recommend banking reforms.

Aug.-Oct. Special session of Congress struggles for two months over repeal of Sherman Silver Purchase Act; House passes measure in August but Senate not until October. Although President Cleveland finally wins, Democratic Party is split over issue.

Nov. 7. Colorado becomes second state to adopt women's suffrage.

Presbyterian Professor Charles A. Briggs is suspended from his post at Union Theological Seminary in New York after protest against his liberal views on religion and advocacy of higher criticism. Tried for heresy and acquitted, he is, nevertheless, suspended. He eventually becomes an Episcopal priest, and the Seminary, as a result of the trial, breaks connections with the Presbyterian Church and becomes nonsectarian.

Patent on Bell telephone expires, ending Bell Telephone Company monopoly; within a short time, many small companies begin telephone service in places not covered by Bell system.

1893 - 1894

Jan. 16. Revolution in Hawaii, abetted by U.S. Minister John L. Stevens and pro-annexation sugar interests and headed by Sanford B. Dole, overthrows regime of Queen Liliuokalani. **Jan. 17.** Stevens, without permission of State Department, recognizes new regime; in following month, treaty of annexation is submitted to Senate. **March 9.** President Cleveland withdraws treaty and sends James H. Blount to investigate circumstances. On discovering that Stevens' conduct has been improper, Cleveland condemns his actions and refuses to submit treaty of annexation. On August 7, 1894, Cleveland formally recognizes Hawaii, which has drawn up a very progressive constitution, as an independent republic.

1894

April 30. Coxey's Army, a group of 500 unemployed men led by Jacob S. Coxey of Ohio, reaches Washington, D.C., to urge public work programs for relief of unemployment and an issue of $500 million in legal tender notes to increase amount of money in circulation. **May 1.** Coxey and two other leaders are arrested on steps of the Capitol for trespassing, and army disbands. Coxey's Army is most famous of a number of groups of unemployed men who form themselves into protest armies during

WILLIAM GRAHAM SUMNER
Forum, 1894
Nine-tenths of the socialistic and semi-socialistic, and sentimental or ethical, suggestions by which we are overwhelmed come from failure to understand the phenomena of the industrial organization and its expansion. It controls us all because we are all in it. It creates the condition of our existence, sets the limits of our social activity, regulates the bonds of our social relations, determines our conceptions of good and evil, suggests our life philosophy, molds our inherited political institutions, and reforms the oldest and toughest customs. . . . I repeat that the turmoil of heterogeneous and antagonistic social whims and speculations in which we live is due to the failure to understand what the industrial organization is and its all-pervading control over human life, while the traditions of our schools of philosophy lead us always to approach the industrial organization, not from the side of objective study but from that of philosophical doctrine. Hence it is that we find that the method of measuring what we see happening by what are called ethical standards, and of proposing to attack the phenomena by methods thence deduced, is so popular. . . .

The great inventions both make the intension of the organization possible and make it inevitable, with all its consequences, whatever they may be. . . .

The first instinct of the modern man is to get a law passed to forbid or prevent what, in his wisdom, he disapproves. A thing which is inevitable, however, is one which we cannot control. We have to make up our minds to it, adjust ourselves to it, and sit down to live with it.

Pullman Workers to American Railway Union Convention, 1894

Mr. President and brothers of the American Railway Union: We struck at Pullman because we were without hope. We joined the American Railway Union because it gave us a glimmer of hope. Twenty thousand souls, men, women, and little ones, have their eyes turned toward this convention today, straining eagerly through dark despondency for a glimmer of the heaven-sent message you alone can give us on this earth. . . .

Five reductions in wages, in work, and in conditions of employment swept through the shops at Pullman between May and December 1893. The last was the most severe, amounting to nearly 30 percent, and our rents had not fallen. We owed Pullman $70,000 when we struck May 11. We owe him twice as much today. He does not evict us for two reasons: one, the force of popular sentiment and public opinion; the other, because he hopes to starve us out, to break through in the back of the American Railway Union, and to deduct from our miserable wages when we are forced to return to him the last dollar we owe him for the occupancy of his houses.

MARK HANNA

Go and live in Pullman and find out how much Pullman gets sellin' city water and gas ten percent higher to those poor fools! A man who won't meet his own men half-way is a Goddamn fool!

this time. Coxey later runs for many public offices and is finally elected mayor of Massillon, Ohio, 1931.

May 11. Workers at Pullman Palace Car Company strike in protest against wage reductions; amid violence and bloodshed, Chicago hoodlums loot and burn railroad cars. **June 26.** Eugene V. Debs, head of American Railway Union, calls out membership in sympathy with Pullman strikers; result is spread of railroad sympathy strikes that paralyze 50,000 miles of railroads in the Middle West. **July 2.** U.S. Court issues injunction against railroad strikers, and President Cleveland, over protest of Illinois governor John P. Altgeld, sends (July 3) federal troops to Chicago on grounds that strike involves U.S. mails and interstate commerce. **July 17.** Debs is indicted for criminal conspiracy and contempt of court and later sentenced to six months in prison. **July 20.** U.S. troops are withdrawn from Chicago, and two weeks later strike is officially ended without having accomplished its purpose.

June 21. Free-silver agitation increases with Democratic Silver Convention in Omaha, Nebraska; led by William Jennings Bryan, convention adopts platform plank of 16 to 1 silver-gold ratio. U.S. popular interest in coinage is reflected by enormous sales of publications dealing with the issue, notably William H. Harvey's *Coin's Financial School*, a book made up of dialogues and cartoons that largely interprets banking incorrectly but that nevertheless becomes the unquestioned guide of Bryan and the free-silver advocates.

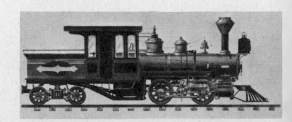

Aug. 18. Cause of conservation is furthered by Carey Act, which grants each public-land state a million acres of public land within the state for settlement and cultivation; funds received are to be used to reclaim other state lands.

Aug. 28. Democratic Congress, after long debate, passes first graduated income tax law as clause of Wilson-Gorman Tariff Act, which becomes law without President Cleveland's signature; Act lowers duties from average of almost 50 percent to about 40 percent. Income tax is called "socialism, communism, devilism" by one senator; it is declared a direct tax and, therefore, unconstitutional by the Supreme Court in following year.

Federal deficit is $61 million in first year since end of the Civil War that revenues have not exceeded expenditures. In January U.S. Treasury has issued bonds of $50 million in effort to supplement gold reserve, but effect is negligible, and in November another $50 million bond issue has been offered.

In year of unemployment and labor discontent, riot among striking miners in Pennsylvania leaves 11 dead; 136,000 coal miners strike in demand for higher wages in Ohio; a number of Negro miners are killed when attacked by strikers in Alabama; and 12,000 New York clothing workers strike against piecework and sweatshop systems.

Henry Demarest Lloyd publishes his widely read attack on trusts, *Wealth Against Commonwealth.*

HENRY DEMAREST LLOYD
Wealth Against Commonwealth, 1894
Nature is rich; but everywhere man, the heir of nature, is poor. Never in this happy country or elsewhere—except in the Land of Miracle, where "they did all eat and were filled"—has there been enough of anything for the people. Never since time began have all the sons and daughters of men been all warm, and all filled, and all shod and roofed. Never yet have all the virgins, wise or foolish, been able to fill their lamps with oil.

The world, enriched by thousands of generations of toilers and thinkers, has reached a fertility which can give every human being a plenty undreamed of even in the utopias. But between this plenty, ripening on the boughs of our civilization, and the people, hungering for it, step the "cornerers," the syndicates, trusts, combinations, with the cry of "overproduction"—too much of everything. Holding back the riches of earth, sea, and sky from their fellows who famish and freeze in the dark, they declare to them that there is too much light and warmth and food. They assert the right, for their private profit, to regulate the consumption by the people of the necessaries of life and to control production, not by the needs of humanity but by the desires of a few for dividends. The coal syndicate thinks there is too much coal. There is too much iron, too much lumber, too much flour—for this or that syndicate. The majority have never been able to buy enough of anything; but this minority have too much of everything to sell.

(Above) Andrew Carnegie, businessman and philanthropist: photo by Handy; (right) Benjamin Harrison, twenty-third President of the United States; (below) "The Bosses of the Senate": anti-trust cartoon by Keppler in *Puck*, 1889

(Above) Alexander Graham Bell demonstrating before a group of
scientists the telephone's ability to transmit sound by electricity
from Salem, Massachusetts to Boston, 1887; (below) land rush in the
Cherokee Strip, September 16, 1893

STEPHEN CRANE

1895

The Red Badge of Courage, 1895

The youth was in a little trance of astonishment. So they were at last going to fight. On the morrow, perhaps, there would be a battle, and he would be in it. For a time he was obliged to labor to make himself believe. He could not accept with assurance an omen that he was about to mingle in one of those great affairs of the earth. . . .

The only foes he had seen were some pickets along the river bank. They were a sun-tanned, philosophical lot, who sometimes shot reflectively at the blue pickets. When reproached for this afterward, they usually expressed sorrow, and swore by their gods that the guns had exploded without their permission. The youth, on guard duty one night, conversed across the stream with one of them. He was a slightly ragged man, who spat skillfully between his shoes and possessed a great fund of bland and infantile assurance. The youth liked him personally. . . .

However, he perceived now that it did not greatly matter what kind of soldiers he was going to fight, so long as they fought, which fact no one disputed. There was a more serious problem. He lay in his bunk pondering upon it. He tried to mathematically prove to himself that he would not run from a battle. . . .

He was forced to admit that as far as war was concerned he knew nothing of himself.

Jan. 22. National Association of Manufacturers holds its first meeting in Cincinnati; meeting is attended by hundreds of manufacturing companies.

March 5. A minority of House Democrats signs "Appeal of the Silver Democrats," framed by Richard P. Bland of Missouri and William Jennings Bryan of Nebraska. Appeal demands immediate return to free coinage of silver at a silver-to-gold ratio of 16 to 1 and increases split between silver and gold advocates in Democratic Party.

October. Stephen Crane at age 23 publishes his second novel, *The Red Badge of Courage*, which wins him international fame; based on one battle of the Civil War, it is an uncannily realistic account written by a man who has never known war. In a decade of popular romances, such as *When Knighthood Was in Flower*, *The Prisoner of Zenda*, and *Quo Vadis*, Crane's intense realism is especially notable.

First U.S. Supreme Court case involving Sherman Antitrust Act of 1890 is *U.S. v. E. C. Knight Company.* By distinguishing manufacturing from commerce and holding that the Sherman Act does not apply to manufacturing combinations within states, the Court greatly weakens enforcement of the law and removes federal control from all but interstate monopolies.

Dead rebel soldier at the foot of Little Round Top

Railroad cars burned during the Pullman strike, 1894

U.S. Supreme Court invalidates federal income tax in *Pollock* v. *Farmers' Loan and Trust Company* on ground that personal property taxes are direct taxes.

U.S. Supreme Court upholds use of federal troops and of labor injunctions to maintain movement of U.S. mails and interstate transportation in Pullman Strike of 1894, thus sanctioning the injunction as a strike-breaking device. Decision in effect removes protection of laws extended to labor unions since 1842.

George Westinghouse builds huge power generators at Niagara Falls. Although hydroelectric power has been manufactured there earlier, the Westinghouse generators are the first capable of producing hydroelectric power for a wide area.

Sears, Roebuck Company opens mail-order business; this company and Montgomery Ward and Company, which has been established in 1872 in response to farm, and especially Grange, resentment of profits taken by middlemen, as well as difficulty in reaching urban markets, soon revolutionize rural retailing. Rural free delivery postal service, established in the following year, helps end isolation of farm communities.

Republican editor William Allen White buys the *Emporia* (Kansas) *Daily and Weekly Gazette* and in the following year writes editorial "What's the Matter with Kansas?",

WILLIAM ALLEN WHITE
Emporia Gazette, 1896

Go East and you hear them laugh at Kansas; go West and they sneer at her; go South and they "cuss" her; go North and they have forgotten her. . . .The newspaper columns and magazine pages once devoted to praise of the state, to boastful facts and startling figures concerning her resources, now are filled with cartoons, jibes, and Pefferian speeches. Kansas just naturally isn't in the civilized world. She has traded places with Arkansas and Timbuctoo.

What is the matter with Kansas?

We all know; yet here we are at it again. We have an old mossback Jacksonian who snorts and howls because there is a bathtub in the state house; we are running that old jay for governor. We have another shabby, wild-eyed, rattle-brained fanatic who has said openly in a dozen speeches that "the rights of the user are paramount to the rights of the owner"; we are running him for chief justice so that capital will come tumbling over itself to get into the state. . . .Then, for fear some hint that the state had become respectable might percolate through the civilized portions of the nation, we have decided to send three or four harpies out lecturing, telling the people that Kansas is raising hell and letting the corn go to weeds.

GROVER CLEVELAND
Message to Congress, 1896

The insurrection in Cuba still continues with all its perplexities. It is difficult to perceive that any progress has thus far been made toward the pacification of the island or that the situation of affairs as depicted in my last annual message had in the least improved. . . .

The insurgents are undoubtedly encouraged and supported by the widespread sympathy the people of this country always and instinctively feel for every struggle for better and freer government and which, in the case of the more adventurous and restless elements of our population, leads in only too many instances to active and personal participation in the contest. . . .

These inevitable entanglements of the United States with the rebellion in Cuba, the large American property interests affected, and considerations of philanthropy and humanity in general, have led to a vehement demand in various quarters for some sort of positive intervention on the part of the United States. . . .

The United States has nevertheless a character to maintain as a nation, which plainly dictates that right and not might should be the rule of its conduct. Further, though the United States is not a nation to which peace is a necessity, it is in truth the most pacific of powers and desires nothing so much as to live in amity with all the world. Its own ample and diversified domains satisfy all possible longings for territory, preclude all dreams of conquest, and prevent any casting of covetous eyes upon neighboring regions, however attractive.

a strong criticism of Populism that makes him and his paper famous.

Woodville Latham demonstrates his moving-picture projector, the Pantoptikon, which combines Thomas Edison's Kinetoscope with the magic lantern. Other devices of this and the next few years are the Cinematograph, Phantascope, Vitascope, Kineoptican, Animatograph, Nickelodeon, and Biograph; none run films of more than a few minutes' duration.

Negro Baptist groups, meeting in Atlanta, Georgia, merge to form National Baptist Convention of the U.S.A.

1895 - 1896

Feb. 8, 1895. Since U.S. bond issues of 1894 have produced little public response, and gold reserve has continued to shrink as it is used not only for redeeming bonds but also for operational expenses of government, the secretary of the treasury is forced to buy with bonds $62 million in gold from banking syndicate of J. P. Morgan and August Belmont. Measure is strongly criticized by Populists and bimetallists. **Jan. 6, 1896.** In spite of loan, gold reserve declines to $79 million, and Treasury issues $100 million worth of bonds for purchase. It is quickly bought up, but since Treasury must continue to redeem bonds in gold, the reserve declines to below $90 million in July. By this time, financial depression is waning, but gold hoarding continues until fall election victory of gold-standard advocates.

Feb. 24. Oppressed by Spain and in midst of financial depression resulting from Panic of 1893 and U.S. high protective tariff on sugar, native Cubans begin fight for independence. **June 12.** President Cleveland calls upon sympathetic Americans to avoid giving help to rebels, but savage countermeasures undertaken by Spain and "yellow journalism" of William Randolph Hearst's *New York Morning Journal* and Joseph Pulitzer's *New York World* fan American sympathy for rebels almost to war pitch. **April 6, 1896.** Congress passes resolution granting belligerent rights to Cuba and offering Spain peace arbitration by President. **May 22.** Spain rejects offer.

1895 - 1899

Feb. 20, 1895. Congress approves President Cleveland's recommendation that the U.S. attempt to be named arbitrator of 56-year-old British-Venezuelan dispute over boundary between British Guiana and Venezuela that has continued since 1840. **Nov. 26.** Offer to Great Britain, which cites Monroe Doctrine as justification for U.S. intervention, is rejected by British foreign secretary. **Dec. 17.** President Cleveland presents British-U.S. correspondence to Congress with a statement so belligerent that Great Britain, considering dispute relatively unimportant, consents to appointment of boundary commission. **Feb. 2, 1897.** Great Britain and Venezuela agree to submit dispute to arbitration. **Oct. 3, 1899.** Settlement places boundary at line of first British claims but gives mouth of Orinoco River to Venezuela.

1896

Jan. 4. Utah becomes forty-fifth state of the United States after five unsuccessful attempts, starting in 1856; federal government has been unwilling to consider Utah constitutions until Mormon Church itself outlaws polygamy. Name of state is derived from that of Ute Indians.

April 6. American athlete James B. Connolly, winner of the hop, step, and jump, becomes first Olympic champion in 1,500 years at revival of Olympic Games in Athens, Greece; U.S. team, arriving on day of

RICHARD OLNEY
Letter to Ambassador Bayard, 1895
I am directed by the President to communicate to you his views upon a subject to which he has given much anxious thought and respecting which he has not reached a conclusion without a lively sense of its great importance as well as of the serious responsibility involved. . . .

[It is necessary] to decide to what extent, if any, the United States may and should intervene in a controversy between and primarily concerning only Great Britain and Venezuela, and to decide how far it is bound to see that the integrity of Venezuelan territory is not impaired by the pretensions of its powerful antagonist. . . .

There is . . . a doctrine of American public law, well founded in principle and abundantly sanctioned by precedent, which entitles and requires the United States to treat as an injury to itself the forcible assumption by a European power of political control over an American state. The application of the doctrine to the boundary dispute between Great Britain and Venezuela remains to be made and presents no real difficulty. Though the dispute relates to a boundary line, yet, as it is between states, it necessarily imports political control to be lost by one party and gained by the other. The political control at stake, too, is of no mean importance, but concerns a domain of great extent. . . .

In these circumstances, the duty of the President appears to him unmistakable and imperative. . . . Not to protest and give warning that the transaction will be regarded as injurious to the interests of the people of the United States as well as oppressive in itself would be to ignore an established policy with which the honor and welfare of this country are closely identified.

WILLIAM JENNINGS BRYAN
Speech to Democratic Convention, 1896

I come to speak to you in defense of a cause as holy as the cause of liberty — the cause of humanity. . . .

Those hardy pioneers who braved all the dangers of the wilderness, who have made the desert to blossom as the rose — those pioneers away out there, rearing their children near to nature's heart, where they can mingle their voices with the voices of the birds — out there where they have erected school-houses for the education of their children and churches where they praise their Creator, and the cemeteries where sleep the ashes of their dead — are as deserving of the consideration of this party as any people in this country.

It is for these that we speak. We do not come as aggressors. Our war is not a war of conquest. We are fighting in the defense of our homes, our families, and posterity. We have petitioned, and our petitions have been scorned. We have entreated, and our entreaties have been disregarded. We have begged, and they have mocked when our calamity came.

We beg no longer; we entreat no more; we petition no more. We defy them! . . .

If they dare to come out and in the open defend the gold standard as a good thing, we shall fight them to the uttermost, having behind us the producing masses of the nation and the world. Having behind us the commercial interests and the laboring interests and all the toiling masses, we shall answer their demands for a gold standard by saying to them, you shall not press down upon the brow of labor this crown of thorns. You shall not crucify mankind upon a cross of gold.

opening after long sea voyage, wins 9 of the 12 track and field events. Australian E. Flack's winning time in metric mile (1,500 meters), 4 min. 33.2 sec.

April 23. Koster and Bial's Music Hall in New York City holds first public exhibition of moving pictures, a series of short pieces ranging from blond dancers to surf on a beach. It is called "the crown and flower of nineteenth-century magic."

May 27. Prohibition Party meets and nominates Joshua Levering of Maryland for President. National Party (a minority of free-silverites) nominates Charles E. Bentley of Nebraska. **June 18.** Republicans, in convention maneuvered by Marcus A. Hanna, Cleveland industrialist, nominate William McKinley of Ohio for President, with Garret A. Hobart of New Jersey as his running mate. Platform backs gold standard but seeks to appease free-silver faction by promising international free-silver policy. **July 9.** Socialist Labor Party nominates Charles H. Matchett of New York. **July 11.** Free-silver-dominated Democrats, after hearing William Jennings Bryan's impassioned "cross of gold" speech, nominate him for President and Arthur Sewall of Maine for Vice-President. Platform backs free coinage of silver and attacks trusts, the high protective tariff, Supreme Court income tax ruling, and labor injunctions. **July 24.** National Silver Republicans, who have bolted Republicans on adoption of gold platform, back Democratic candidates. **July 25.** People's (Populist) Party also nominates Bryan. **Sept. 3.** National Democratic Party, consisting of gold advocates who have bolted Democratic convention because of free-silver issue, nominates John M. Palmer of Illinois. In campaign Bryan travels 18,000 miles and makes 600 speeches, earning name "the boy orator of the Platte." McKinley conducts "front-porch" campaign, addressing thousands of visitors who come to his Ohio home, while Hanna, as his campaign manager, distributes millions of leaflets and hires thousands of campaign speakers. Both candidates concentrate almost entirely on money issues.

Nov. 3. In election McKinley wins by popular vote of 7,102,000 to Bryan's 6,493,000; electoral vote is McKinley, 271; Bryan, 176; McKinley carries East and Middle West, and Bryan wins South and West. Republicans keep control of House and Senate.

U.S. Supreme Court in *Plessy* v. *Ferguson* accepts "separate but equal" doctrine of race relations. Distinguishing legal from social rights, Court rules that separate, equal treatment of Negroes under state laws is not discrimination as prohibited by Fourteenth Amendment to Constitution. Decision marks beginning of Jim Crow era.

Duryea brothers, whose automobiles have won most speed competitions in past two years, turn out 10 automobiles in their factory during the year.

Sarah Orne Jewett publishes the last of her revelations of problems in fading Maine settlements, *The Country of the Pointed Firs,* a collection of short stories. *The Damnation of Theron Ware* by Harold Frederic deals with religious hypocrisy of small-town Methodists and creates a sensation.

New York World publishes "The Yellow Kid," forerunner of modern comic strips; words are printed on bright yellow shirt of boy instead of outside of frame as in earlier cartoons.

Former baseball player William Ashley ("Billy") Sunday begins career of evangelism; he conducts 300 revivals in major cities and is heard by 100 million people before his death in 1935.

HENRY B. BROWN
Plessy v. Ferguson, 1896
We think the enforced separation of the races, as applied to the internal commerce of the state, neither abridges the privileges or immunities of the colored man, deprives him of his property without due process of law, nor denies him the equal protection of the laws, within the meaning of the Fourteenth Amendment. . . .

Every exercise of the police power must be reasonable and extend only to such laws as are enacted in good faith for the promotion for the public good and not for the annoyance or oppression of a particular class. . . .

So far, then, as a conflict with the Fourteenth Amendment is concerned, the case reduces itself to the question whether the statute of Louisiana is a reasonable regulation, and with respect to this there must necessarily be a large discretion on the part of the legislature. In determining the question of reasonableness, it is at liberty to act with reference to the established usages, customs, and traditions of the people, and with a view to the promotion of their comfort, and the preservation of the public peace and good order. . . .

Legislation is powerless to eradicate racial instincts or to abolish distinctions based upon physical differences, and the attempt to do so can only result in accentuating the difficulties of the present situation. If the civil and political rights of both races be equal, one cannot be inferior to the other civilly or politically. If one race be inferior to the other socially, the Constitution of the United States cannot put them upon the same plane.

JANE ADDAMS
Address to National Education Association, 1897

Italian parents count upon the fact that their children learn the English language and American customs before they themselves do, and act not only as interpreters of the language about them but as buffers between them and Chicago; and this results in a certain, almost pathetic, dependence of the family upon the child. When a member of the family, therefore, first goes to school, the event is fraught with much significance to all the others. The family has no social life in any structural form and can supply none to the child. If he receives it in the school and gives it to his family, the school would thus become the connector with the organized society about them. . . .

Too often the teacher's conception of her duty is to transform him into an American of a somewhat snug and comfortable type, and she insists that the boy's powers must at once be developed in an abstract direction, quite ignoring the fact that his parents have had to do only with tangible things. She has little idea of the development of Italian life. Her outlook is national and not racial; and she fails, therefore, not only in knowledge of but also in respect for the child and his parents. She quite honestly estimates the child upon an American basis. The contempt for the experiences and languages of their parents which foreign children sometimes exhibit, and which is most damaging to their moral as well as intellectual life, is doubtless due in part to the overestimation which the school places upon speaking and reading in English. This cutting into his family loyalty takes away one of the most conspicuous and valuable traits of the Italian child.

1896 - 1898

Aug. 6, 1896. Gold is discovered on Bonanza Creek in Yukon Territory, northwest Canada. **June 1897.** News reaches U.S., and thousands of gold seekers join rush to Canada. **July 14.** First large Klondike gold shipment, $750,000, arrives in San Francisco. By 1898 this inaccessible and hitherto almost unpopulated area contains 18,000 people. In spite of frozen ground and other difficult mining conditions, $22 million is mined in peak production year 1900.

1897

Jan. 12. National Monetary Conference, meeting at Indianapolis, endorses existing gold standard and appoints commission that later submits to Congress a plan for U.S. monetary system. U.S. begins period of prosperity with settlement of free-silver question in previous year's election.

March 2. Immigration bill that requires literacy tests for immigrants is vetoed by President Cleveland on the ground that it is a "radical departure from our national policy."

July 7. Dingley Tariff raises duties to new high levels, averaging almost 60 percent on the value of goods imported.

In *U.S.* v. *Trans-Missouri Freight Association*, the Supreme Court rules that association of 18 railroads formed to fix transportation rates is in violation of the Sherman Antitrust Act; railroads' argument that only combinations that restrain commerce unreasonably are illegal is rejected at this time, but it later becomes the policy of the Court.

First practical subway in the U.S. is completed in Boston. Plans for New York City subway have been rejected the year before as too great a financial burden on the city.

Congregational minister Charles M. Sheldon publishes *In His Steps,* a collection of his sermons in which he has shown young people what they would do if for a year they emulated Jesus Christ. To the present day, book has sold about 8 million copies in 20 languages.

Edwin Arlington Robinson publishes *The Children of the Night,* which includes poems from *The Torrent and the Night Before* of the previous year.

1897 - 1902

William James, leader of Pragmatist movement, publishes collections of his lectures and essays: *The Will to Believe and Other Essays in Popular Philosophy; Human Immortality; Talks to Teachers on Psychology and to Students on Some of Life's Ideals;* and *The Varieties of Religious Experience.*

1898

Jan. 12. Cubans loyal to Spain riot in Havana in protest against policy of new Spanish government, which has made extensive concessions to rebels in civil war. Policy is also disapproved by rebels, who want independence, and by interventionists in the U.S., who believe U.S. control of Cuba is vital to U.S. domination of the Caribbean.

Feb. 9. William Randolph Hearst's *New York Journal,* rabidly interventionist, publishes private letter from Spanish minister to the U.S., Dupuy de Lôme, that has been stolen by Cuban revolutionists; letter describes President McKinley as weak and further inflames U.S. anti-Spanish sentiment. De Lôme resigns his post immediately.

Feb. 15. U.S. battleship *Maine,* which has arrived at Havana in January to protect

WILLIAM JAMES
The Will to Believe, 1897
Objective evidence and certitude are doubtless very fine ideals to play with, but where on this moonlit and dream-visited planet are they found? I am, therefore, myself a complete empiricist so far as my theory of human knowledge goes. I live, to be sure, by the practical faith that we must go on experiencing and thinking over our experience, for only thus can our opinions grow more true; but to hold any one of them — I absolutely do not care which — as if it never could be reinterpretable or corrigible, I believe to be a tremendously mistaken attitude, and I think that the whole history of philosophy will bear me out. There is but one indefectibly certain truth, and that is the truth that pyrrhonistic scepticism itself leaves standing — the truth that the present phenomenon of consciousness exists. That, however, is the bare starting-point of knowledge, the mere admission of a stuff to be philosophized about. . . .

But please observe, now, that when as empiricists we give up the doctrine of objective certitude, we do not thereby give up the quest or hope of truth itself. . . .Our great difference from the scholastic lies in the way we face. The strength of his system lies in the principles, the origin, the terminus a quo of his thought; for us the strength is in the outcome, the upshot, the terminus ad quem. Not where it comes from but what it leads to is to decide. It matters not to an empiricist from what quarter an hypothesis may come to him: he may have acquired it by fair means or by foul; passion may have whispered or accident suggested it; but if the total drift of thinking continues to confirm it, that is what he means by its being true.

ALBERT SHAW
Review of Reviews, 1898
Modern warfare has become a matter of machinery, and . . . the most highly developed mechanical and industrial nation will by virtue of such development be most formidable in war.

This is a situation that the Spaniards in general are evidently quite unable to comprehend. Their ideas are altogether medieval. They believe themselves to be a highly chivalrous and militant people, and that the people of the United States are really in great terror of Spanish prowess. . . .

A country like ours, capable of supplying the whole world with electrical motors, mining machinery, locomotive engines, steel rails, and the structural material for modern steel bridges and "skyscrapers," not to mention bicycles and sewing machines, is equally capable of building, arming, and operating an unlimited number of ships of every type, and of employing every conceivable mechanical device for purposes of national defense. . . .

Quite regardless of the responsibilities for the Maine incident, it is apparently true that the great majority of the American people are hoping that President McKinley will promptly utilize the occasion to secure the complete pacification and independence of Cuba. . . .

The people of the United States do not intend to help Spain hold Cuba. On the contrary, they are now ready, in one way or in another, to help the Cubans drive Spain out of the Western Hemisphere. If the occasion goes past and we allow this Cuban struggle to run on indefinitely, the American people will have lost several degrees of self-respect and will certainly not have gained anything in the opinion of mankind.

American residents and property during revolution in Cuba, is blown up in the harbor, with a loss of 260 men. Perpetrator of explosion is never discovered, but American people are persuaded that Spain is responsible, and incident inflames U.S. anti-Spanish feeling, making intervention in revolution a certainty. "Remember the Maine!" becomes cry of interventionists.

Feb. 25. Pacific fleet, under Commodore George Dewey, is ordered to the Philippines by Assistant Secretary of the Navy Theodore Roosevelt, with instructions to engage the Spanish fleet there if war breaks out.

March 27. In spite of strong interventionist feeling in the U.S., President McKinley, in effort to maintain peace, orders minister to Spain, Stewart L. Woodford, to deny that U.S. desires annexation of Cuba but wants only cessation of brutalities, with armistice until October 1. **April 9.** Spain agrees to U.S. demands.

April 11. Yielding to public and political pressure, McKinley, in reversal of his anti-war policy, asks for congressional resolution authorizing use of U.S. Army and Navy to force Spain to leave Cuba and declares Cuba independent. **April 20.** McKinley signs resolution passed by Congress, but Spain breaks off diplomatic relations with the U.S. before Woodford can deliver ultimatum.

April 22. U.S. orders blockade of all Cuban ports, seizes one Spanish ship as first capture of war, and authorizes a volunteer force of 200,000 men to build up Army. One unit formed under Volunteer Army Act is "Rough Riders," commanded by Colonel Leonard Wood and Lieutenant Colonel Theodore Roosevelt, who has been a notably ardent advocate of annexation and has resigned his post as assistant secretary of the navy. At this time, U.S. Navy is relatively strong and well equipped, with both Atlantic and Pacific squadrons, but Army consists of only 28,000 men commanded by 2,100 officers and is inadequately equipped, especially for campaign in tropics.

April 24. Refusing to recognize Cuban independence as demanded by U.S. Congress, Spain declares war on U.S. **April 25.** U.S. declares war on Spain retroactively to April 21, when Spain has broken off diplomatic relations.

May 1. U.S. Pacific fleet destroys, captures, or cripples all 10 ships of the Spanish Pacific fleet at Manila in seven-hour battle that results in more than 300 Spanish deaths and 7 wounded for the U.S.

May 12. Louisiana continues Southern reaction against Reconstruction when it adopts new constitution that virtually disfranchises Negroes by property and literacy tests for voting; whites, however, are protected against restrictions by grandfather clause, which exempts descendants of men who voted before 1867.

May 19. Spanish Atlantic fleet, four cruisers and three destroyers, having sailed from Cape Verde Islands, arrives in harbor of Santiago de Cuba and anchors under protection of Cuban artillery. **May 29.** U.S. naval force from Key West, Florida, blocks entrance to harbor, bottling up Spanish ships.

May 24. U.S. battleship *Oregon* arrives at Key West after dramatic run from Pacific to join Atlantic fleet; 67-day journey, necessary for route around Cape Horn, arouses the U.S. to importance of a canal across the Isthmus of Panama.

June 1. Congress passes Erdman Arbitration Act, which authorizes federal mediation in disputes between interstate carriers and their employees and prohibits blacklisting of

HENRY WATTERSON
Louisville Courier-Journal, 1898
It is given out that the President will today sign the resolutions and transmit them along with his ultimatum, allowing Spain a short time — say twenty-four hours — to comply, or take the consequences.

All this, however, is a mere formality. It is the ceremonious preliminary to the duel. Spain's reply is already discounted. There is no probability — there is hardly a possibility — that it can be anything but a refusal of our demands. That reply received, the war will be on. Within an hour afterward the orders for the movement of our forces against Spain should be issued; by the opening of the coming week Havana should be invested, if not captured. . . .

Whether the war be long or short, it is a war into which this nation will go with a fervor, with a power, with a unanimity that would make it invincible if it were repelling not only the encroachments of Spain but the assaults of every monarch in Europe who profanes the name of divinity in the cause of kingcraft. We do not mean to say that there are not good people in this country . . . who are not earnestly and conscientiously opposed to this war. There are many others who believe it could have been averted, with the concession of all our demands, if a stronger hand had been at the helm of our diplomacy before the congressional crisis was reached. But all these will be as one with their countrymen in vigorously prosecuting the war, now that it is inevitable, to a splendid triumph for Americanism, for civilization, for humanity. . . .

That is the right of our might; that is the sign in which we conquer.

WALTER HINES PAGE
Atlantic Monthly, 1898
The problems that seem likely to follow the war are graver than those that have led up to it; and if it be too late to ask whether we entered into it without sufficient deliberation, it is not too soon to make sure of every step that we now take. The inspiring unanimity of the people in following their leaders proves to be as earnest and strong as it ever was under any form of government; and this popular acquiescence in war puts a new responsibility on those leaders, and may put our institutions and our people themselves to a new test. A change in our national policy may change our very character; and we are now playing with the great forces that may shape the future of the world — almost before we know it.

Yesterday we were going about the prosaic tasks of peace, content with our own problems of administration and finance, a nation to ourselves. . . . Today we are face to face with the sort of problems that have grown up in the management of world empires, and the policies of other nations are of intimate concern to us. Shall we still be content with peaceful industry, or does there yet lurk in us the adventurous spirit of our Anglo-Saxon forefathers? And have we come to a time when, no more great enterprises awaiting us at home, we shall be tempted to seek them abroad? . . .

Our greatest victory will not be over Spain but over ourselves — to show once more that even in its righteous wrath the republic has the virtue of self-restraint.

CAPT. JOHN W. PHILIP
At Battle of Santiago, 1898
Don't cheer, boys; the poor devils are dying.

union members by interstate transportation companies.

June 10. Congress passes War Revenue Bill that authorizes taxes on such items as tobacco, liquor, and flour and a government bond issue of $400 million; sale of bonds, however, reaches only half the authorized amount.

June 15. Six hundred U.S. Marines defeat Spanish forces in Battle of Guantanamo Bay, Cuba.

June 20. Island of Guam in the Pacific Ocean surrenders to commander of U.S.S. *Charleston*; on previous day, island has been shelled, but Spanish commander, unaware of war, has apologized to Captain Glass of the *Charleston* for not returning the salute, saying that there is no ammunition on the island.

June 22. Expeditionary force of 17,000 men under General William Shafter arrives in Cuba and begins landing operations east of Santiago. **July 1.** In attack on well-defended village of El Caney, about 7,000 U.S. troops battle 600 defenders for one day before capturing it. On same day, Theodore Roosevelt leads his "Rough Riders" (unmounted) in impetuous charge up Kettle Hill in attack on San Juan Hill that is successful, but casualties of two battles are nearly 1,600 men. Roosevelt becomes a national hero for attack but does not endear himself to his superiors. With capture of hills overlooking Santiago, U.S. can use artillery against city, as well as against Spanish fleet in the harbor.

July 3. Spanish fleet, ordered not to surrender, tries to run blockade of five U.S. battleships and two cruisers. In four-hour battle along coast, Spanish ships are destroyed, with more than 2,000 killed, wounded, and captured. American casualties are 1 killed and 1 wounded.

July 7. President McKinley signs annexation of Hawaii bill, passed by joint resolution in Congress; previously blocked by Cleveland and the Senate, annexation has been favored by President McKinley, especially after Japan has protested it. Joint resolution, which requires only a simple majority, is resorted to in order to avoid defeat by the Senate. Hawaii becomes a U.S. territory in 1900.

July 17. Santiago's 24,000 defenders surrender to U.S.

July 21. Four U.S. ships bombard and take Nipe, in last Cuban sea battle of the war.

July 25. General Wesley Merritt arrives with land reinforcements at Manila Bay to join U.S. fleet, which, lacking army support, has been blockading Manila since naval victory.

July 25-Aug. 12. U.S. forces take Puerto Rico, having met only minor resistance.

Aug. 4. U.S. War Department orders Cuban expeditionary force back to Long Island, New York, to escape further spread of food poisoning and disease, which has attacked 4,200 troops, 3,000 of whom have yellow fever.

Aug. 12. U.S. proposal, agreed to by Spain, calls for: Paris as place of treaty negotiations; end of hostilities; relinquishment of sovereignty by Spain over Cuba; cession by Spain of Puerto Rico and one of the Ladrone Islands to the U.S.; and U.S. occupation of Manila until control of the Philippines can be decided by treaty.

Aug. 13. U.S. forces and Filipino guerrillas, unaware that hostilities have ceased, fight battle for Manila. Surrender of the city on following day marks the end of 100 years of Filipino rebellion against Spain.

MORRISON I. SWIFT
Imperialism and Liberty, 1899

Every important thing that has happened, everything that is happening, goes to establish this proposition: That hard and selfish men and hard and selfish policies will control our imperialist relations; that the kind and well-meaning will be overruled. There is no intention of mildness, humanity, and justice in the forces that are now gaining ascendancy in American life. . . .

Wherever the basest of international principles of pilfering and freebooting are applied to gain markets, "along with these markets will go our beneficent institutions." The halo of our blessed institutions will pervade and rectify rapacity and wrong! But it will not. We shall not build beneficent institutions on ruffianism and rapacity. "We are after markets, the greatest markets in the world"; we do not care what we do to get them — we will cheerfully rob and kill, we will wrench their fatherland from the weak and call it ours — we admit it in cold blood, but, like the praying professional murderer, we piously declare that God and humanity will bless us in it. . . .

If this atrocious humbug found lodgment in the American spleen, every conceivable thing necessary for the world spread of American monopolies would be tolerated by the people, even down to the vivisection of whole savage races for trade experiments. This might be called a dull joke; it is still too early to say whether Americans, renowned among themselves for their biting perception of humor, will be able to see it. Our rulers have conducted their game very artfully, and the work now is to unravel the mesh in which that art has tangled us. How, from the essence of humanity, did the President extract the right to steal?

FINLEY PETER DUNNE

Mr. Dooley on the Philippines, 1898
"Whin we plant what Hogan calls th' starry banner iv Freedom in th' Ph'lippeens," said Mr. Dooley, "an' give th' sacred blessin' iv liberty to the poor, downtrodden people iv thim unfortunate isles, — dam thim! — we'll larn thim a lesson."

"Sure," said Mr. Hennessy, sadly, "we have a thing or two to larn ourselves."

"But it isn't f'r thim to larn us," said Mr. Dooley. " 'Tis not f'r thim wretched an' degraded crathers, without a mind or a shirt iv their own, f'r to give lessons in politeness an' liberty to a nation that manny-facthers more dhressed beef than anny other imperyal nation in th' wurruld. . . .

"I'm not much iv an expansionist mesilf. F'r th' las' tin years I've been thryin' to decide whether 'twud be good policy an' thrue to me thraditions to make this here bar two or three feet longer, an manny's th' night I've laid awake tryin' to puzzle it out. But I don't know what to do with th' Ph'lippeens anny more thin I did las' summer, befure I heerd tell iv thim. We can't give thim to anny wan without makin' th' wan that gets thim feel th' way Doherty felt to Clancy whin Clancy med a frindly call an' give Doherty's childher th' measles. We can't sell thim, we can't ate thim, an' we can't throw thim into th' alley whin no wan is lookin'. An' 'twud be a disgrace f'r to lave befure we've pounded these frindless an' ongrateful people into insinsibility. So I suppose, Hinnissy, we'll have to stay an' do th' best we can, an' lave Andhrew Carnegie secede fr'm th' Union. They'se wan consolation; an' that is, if th' American people can govern thimsilves, they can govern annything that walks."

Oct. 25. Although U.S. opinion on the Philippines has been divided at beginning of Paris meeting on October 1, President McKinley decides to demand that Spain cede the islands to the U.S. Dec. 10. Final terms of treaty, although Spain has strongly opposed Philippine demand, are: cession of the Philippines for payment of $20 million; surrender of all claims to Cuba, making it independent; Spanish assumption of the Cuban public debt of $400 million; and cession of Guam and Puerto Rico to the U.S. Treaty of Paris marks the end of Spanish rule in the Western Hemisphere.

Almost all important battles in Spanish-American War have been naval actions. Although the U.S. Army has been undermanned, poorly commanded, inadequately supplied, and insufficiently trained, the Navy has been vastly superior to Spain's. Of almost 5,500 U.S. deaths, fewer than 400 men have been killed in battle. More than 90 percent are victims of disease. Direct cost of war has been $250 million.

In *Holden* v. *Hardy*, a decision that becomes precedent for validity of state control of labor conditions, the U.S. Supreme Court upholds Utah law that sets maximum hours for miners, pointing out that mining is an especially dangerous industry.

The Supreme Court finds that a child born of Chinese parents in the U.S. may not be deported under the Chinese Exclusion Act, since native citizenship is not dependent on race or color.

Adolphus Busch builds the first Diesel engine in U.S., using foreign patents rights.

Observations of Finley Peter Dunne's Mr. Dooley, homely philosopher, for the first time attract national attention on publication of his comments on Dewey's victory at Manila, although observations have appeared regularly in Chicago papers for six years. Mr. Dooley's Irish-dialect comments on public affairs have enormous influence in following period. *David Harum*, novel of rural life, is published after death of its author, Edward Noyes Westcott; popular up to the present day, it is the beginning of so-called b'gosh school of fiction.

First group exhibit by American Impressionist painters, New York City. Group calling itself "Ten American Painters" includes some artists who have participated in 1877 exhibit of Society of American Artists.

1899

Jan. 15. Edwin Markham publishes social protest poem, "The Man with the Hoe," in the *San Francisco Examiner*; within one week it appears in newspapers throughout the U.S.; it becomes the most popular poem published up to this date in the U.S.

Feb. 6. Treaty of Paris is ratified by the Senate after heated debate between imperialists, who emphasize strategic advantage of U.S. control of the Philippines and fear that other nations will establish themselves on the islands, and anti-imperialists, who fight against acquiring territory peopled by alien races and believe that acquisition is contrary to self-government principles of the U.S. William Jennings Bryan is finally able to persuade opponents to vote for treaty, since by its terms resolution of Philippine question can be postponed.

Feb. 17. Anti-Imperialist League is founded; it unites liberal leaders of all U.S. parties to oppose expansion beyond the continental limits into foreign territories.

May 18-July 29. U.S. attends disarmament and arbitration conference at The Hague with 25 other nations invited by Czar Nicholas II of Russia. No agreement on arms results, but Permanent Court of Arbitration is established. Arbitration is not

EDWIN MARKHAM

The Man with the Hoe, 1899

*Bowed by the weight of centuries he
    leans
Upon his hoe and gazes on the ground,
The emptiness of ages in his face,
And on his back the burden of the
    world.
Who made him dead to rapture and
    despair,
A thing that grieves not and that never
    hopes,
Stolid and stunned, a brother to the ox?
Who loosened and let down this brutal
    jaw?
Whose was the hand that slanted back
    this brow?
Whose breath blew out the light within
    this brain?*

*Is this the thing the Lord God made and
    gave
To have dominion over sea and land;
To trace the stars and search the
    heavens for power;
To feel the passion of eternity? . . .
Down all the stretch of hell to its last
    gulf
There is no shape more terrible than
    this—
More tongued with censure of the
    world's blind greed—
More filled with signs and portents for
    the soul—
More fraught with menace to the
    universe.*
       . . .

*Through this dread shape the suffering
    ages look;
Time's tragedy is in that aching stoop;
Through this dread shape humanity
    betrayed,
Plundered, profaned, and disinherited,
Cries protest to the judges of the
    world,
A protest that is also prophecy.*

331

JOHN DEWEY
School and Society, 1899
All that society has accomplished for itself is put, through the agency of the school, at the disposal of its future members. All its better thoughts of itself it hopes to realize through the new possibilities thus opened to its future self. . . .

Our social life has undergone a thorough and radical change. If our education is to have any meaning for life, it must pass through an equally complete transformation. This transformation is not something to appear suddenly, to be executed in a day by conscious purpose. It is already in progress. . . . The introduction of active occupations, of nature study, of elementary science, of art, of history; the relegation of the merely symbolic and formal to a secondary position; the change in the moral school atmosphere, in the relation of pupils and teachers — of discipline; the introduction of more active, expressive, and self-directing factors — all these are not mere accidents. . . .

It remains but to organize all these factors, to appreciate them in their fullness of meaning, and to put the ideas and ideals involved into complete, uncompromising possession of our school system. To do this means to make each one of our schools an embryonic community life, active with types of occupations that reflect the life of the larger society and permeated throughout with the spirit of art, history, and science. When the school introduces and trains each child of society into membership within such a little community, saturating him with the spirit of service and providing him with the instruments of effective self-direction, we shall have the deepest and best guarantee of a larger society which is worthy, lovely, and harmonious.

made compulsory, however, and U.S. insists on its right to uphold the Monroe Doctrine when disputes involving the Western Hemisphere occur.

Dec. 2. Britain, Germany, and the U.S. sign Samoan treaty, dividing Samoa between Germany and the U.S., after Britain has withdrawn its claims in exchange for German territory in other Pacific areas and in West Africa. U.S. part of Samoa, governed by the Navy, becomes an important naval base.

The U.S. formally claims Wake Island, an atoll in the Central Pacific Ocean, for use as a cable station; it has been mapped in 1841 by a U.S. exploring expedition.

Educator John Dewey, head of University of Chicago's Laboratory School, begins revolution in American education with publication of *The School and Society*, which expresses, among other concepts, his belief that education must begin with actual experience rather than with the learning of traditional subjects.

Economist Thorstein Veblen publishes his first book, *The Theory of the Leisure Class*, while teaching at the University of Chicago.

Louis Sullivan designs Schlesinger & Mayer (now Carson, Pirie Scott & Company) department store in Chicago; it is the first major commercial modern-style building in the U.S.

1899 - 1902

Feb. 4. Filipinos, incensed at failure of the U.S. to grant them immediate independence, begin armed revolt against U.S. occupation forces; about 70,000 men on each side are engaged. Organized resistance ends by December, but guerrilla warfare continues until the spring of 1902 despite capture of Filipino leader in March 1901 and

American assurances that military occupation will cease and that independence will be granted after Filipinos have learned to govern themselves.

1900

March 6. Social Democrats meet in Indianapolis and nominate Eugene V. Debs of Indiana for President and Job Harriman of California for Vice-President. **May 10.** People's (Anti-Fusion) Party meets at Cincinnati and nominates Wharton Barker of Pennsylvania for President and Ignatius Donnelly of Minnesota for Vice-President. **May 10.** Fusion Populist Party nominates William Jennings Bryan for President and Charles A. Towne (who later withdraws in favor of Adlai E. Stevenson) for Vice-President. **June 2.** Socialist Laborites at New York nominate Joseph P. Maloney of Massachusetts for President, with Valentine Remmel of Pennsylvania as his running mate. **June 19.** Republicans at Philadelphia renominate President McKinley and, against his will, Theodore Roosevelt as his running mate. Roosevelt fears that he will be buried politically in the Vice-Presidency. Platform is pro-gold standard and pro-administration foreign policy and stresses need for canal across Panamanian isthmus. **June 27.** Prohibitionists nominate John G. Woolley of Illinois and Henry B. Metcalf of Rhode Island. **July 5.** Democrats also nominate William Jennings Bryan, but with Adlai E. Stevenson as his running mate. Platform is anti-imperialist and again demands free coinage of silver. McKinley repeats pattern of previous campaign, never leaving his home, but Roosevelt travels 21,000 miles, making 700 speeches, frequently wearing his "Rough Rider" hat.

March 14. Congress passes Gold Standard Act, making gold the only currency standard in the U.S. Act is made possible by increase in production of gold in the Klondike and South Africa. The U.S. dollar

THEODORE ROOSEVELT
Speech in Chicago, 1899
I wish to preach, not the doctrine of ignoble ease but the doctrine of the strenuous life.

EUGENE V. DEBS
While there is a lower class, I am in it.
While there is a criminal element, I am of it.
While there is a soul in jail, I am not free.

Republican campaign slogan, 1900
The Full Dinner Pail.

ADM. GEORGE DEWEY
Announcing his candidacy, 1900
If the American people want me for this high office, I shall be only too willing to serve them. . . . Since studying this subject I am convinced that the office of President is not such a very difficult one to fill.

"No Wonder He Was Ill," anti-McKinley cartoon

OPPOSITE PAGE: (Top left) William McKinley, twenty-fifth President
of the United States; (top right) the *Maine* in Havana harbor, 1900;
(bottom) landing of American troops at Daiquiri, Cuba, 1898
THIS PAGE: Burning the native district of Manila during the
insurrection in the Philippines, 1899-1902; (below) the United
States delegation to the First Hague Peace Conference in 1899
contained a mixture of peace advocates and imperialists, but was
dominated by Navy Captain Alfred T. Mahan, naval historian and strategist

JOHN HAY
Circular letter, 1899

Earnestly desirous to remove any cause of irritation and to insure at the same time to the commerce of all nations in China the undoubted benefits which should accrue from a formal recognition by the various powers claiming "spheres of interest" that they shall enjoy perfect equality of treatment for their commerce and navigation within such "spheres," the government of the United States would be pleased to see His German Majesty's government give formal assurances and lend its cooperation in securing like assurances from the other interested powers that each within its respective sphere of whatever influence:

First, will in no way interfere with any treaty port or any vested interest within any so-called sphere of interest or leased territory it may have in China.

Second, that the Chinese treaty tariff of the time being shall apply to all merchandise landed or shipped to all such ports as are within said "sphere of interest" (unless they be "free ports"), no matter to what nationality it may belong, and that duties so leviable shall be collected by the Chinese government.

Third, that it will levy no higher harbor dues on vessels of another nationality frequenting any port in such "sphere" than shall be levied on vessels of its own nationality, and no higher railroad charges over lines built, controlled, or operated within its "sphere" on merchandise belonging to citizens or subjects of other nationalities transported through such "sphere" than shall be levied on similar merchandise belonging to its own nationals transported over equal distances.

is valued at 25.8 grains of gold, and gold reserve of $150 million is to be held separately from other funds. Small-town national banks are authorized in order to appease farm interests.

March 20. Secretary of State John Hay announces that Germany, Russia, Britain, France, Italy, and Japan have accepted the Open Door Policy for China. Weakness of China has enabled foreign countries to force commercial and territorial concessions from it, and the U.S. has feared that they will discriminate against other powers in areas under their influence. In the previous year Hay has asked the powers to agree to protect Chinese independence and commercial equality for all powers in Chinese trade. Assurances have been vague, but Hay accepts them as approval.

April 12. Congress passes Foraker Act, which creates civil government for Puerto Rico, makes the island an unorganized territory, and extends the Dingley Tariff to include the island.

June. Peking, China, is occupied by Chinese groups known as Boxers, who are rebelling against foreign intrusion in China. Boxers besiege foreign legations of the city for several months and, with the encouragement of the empress dowager of China, kill scores of foreign missionaries, thousands of Chinese Christians ("secondary foreign devils"), and the German minister to China.

July 3. Secretary Hay, afraid that other powers will withdraw support of the Open Door Policy using the Boxer Rebellion as justification, sends circular letter stating that the U.S. desires a solution that will bring permanent safety and peace to China and safeguard equal and impartial world trade in all parts of the empire.

Aug. 14. International military expedition, including the U.S., occupies Peking, loots the city, rescues missionaries, and disperses remnants of Boxers.

September. Orville and Wilbur Wright fly their first full-scale glider at Kitty Hawk, North Carolina; its "warped wings" are first successful device built for lateral control in flying.

Nov. 6. President McKinley and Theodore Roosevelt win election with popular vote of 7,218,000 to Bryan's 6,357,000. Electoral vote is McKinley, 292; Bryan, 155; Republicans keep control of House and Senate.

Nov. 15. Andrew Carnegie founds the Carnegie Institute of Technology in Pittsburgh.

Dr. Walter Reed is named head of U.S. Army Yellow Fever Commission; he and his associates experiment with volunteers in Cuba and prove that yellow fever is transmitted by mosquitoes. Their findings make possible the virtual elimination of yellow fever from Cuba, the U.S., and, later, the Panama Canal Zone.

International Ladies' Garment Workers' Union is founded in New York City to fight a 70-hour workweek and a home-sewing system in which women earn a maximum of 30 cents per day.

Olds Company of Detroit begins first mass production of automobiles, turning out 400 cars in first year. Production in second year is 1,600 and in third, 4,000.

Doubleday and Company publishes first novel of Theodore Dreiser, *Sister Carrie*, realistic story of the deterioration of a man caused by an immoral girl. Probably because of disapproval of publisher's wife, Company prints only 1,000 copies and fails

THEODORE DREISER
Sister Carrie, 1900

Oh, the tangle of human life! How dimly as yet we see. Here was Carrie, in the beginning poor, unsophisticated, emotional; responding with desire to everything most lovely in life, yet finding herself turned as by a wall. Laws to say: "Be allured, if you will, by everything lovely, but draw not nigh unless by righteousness." Convention to say: "You shall not better your situation save by honest labour." If honest labour be unremunerative and difficult to endure; if it be the long, long road which never reaches beauty, but wearies the feet and the heart; if the drag to follow beauty be such that one abandons the admired way, taking rather the despised path leading to her dreams quickly, who shall cast the first stone? Not evil, but longing for that which is better, more often directs the steps of the erring. Not evil, but goodness more often allures the feeling mind unused to reason. . . .

Sitting alone, she was now an illustration of the devious ways by which one who feels, rather than reasons, may be led in the pursuit of beauty. . . .

Oh, Carrie, Carrie! Oh, blind strivings of the human heart! Onward, onward, it saith, and where beauty leads, there it follows. Whether it be the tinkle of a lone sheep bell o'er some quiet landscape, or the glimmer of beauty in sylvan places, or the show of soul in some passing eye, the heart knows and makes answer, following. It is when the feet weary and hope seems vain that the heartaches and the longings arise. Know, then, that for you is neither surfeit nor content. In your rocking-chair, by your window dreaming, shall you long, alone. In your rocking-chair, by your window, shall you dream such happiness as you may never feel.

335

Declaration of Woman's Christian Temperance Union, 1902

We therefore formulate and, for ourselves, adopt the following pledge, asking our sisters and brothers of a common danger and a common hope to make common cause with us in working its reasonable and helpful precepts into the practice of everyday life:

I hereby solemnly promise, God helping me, to abstain from all distilled, fermented, and malt liquors, including wine, beer, and cider, and to employ all proper means to discourage the use of and traffic in the same.

To conform and enforce the rationale of this pledge, we declare our purpose to educate the young; to form a better public sentiment; to reform so far as possible, by religious, ethical, and scientific means, the drinking classes; to seek the transforming power of Divine Grace for ourselves and all for whom we work, that they and we may willfully transcend no law of pure and wholesome living; and finally we pledge ourselves to labor and to pray that all of these principles, founded upon the Gospel of Christ, may be worked out into the customs of society and the laws of the land.

to promote book. Effect on Dreiser is a nervous breakdown and thoughts of suicide; he does not write another novel for 11 years.

First "little theater" in the U.S. is built in Chicago for the Hull House Players, a group sponsored by Jane Addams' social settlement, whose residents include actors, musicians, and artists, as well as social workers.

Carry Nation, prompted by her marriage to an alcoholic, begins her crusade of "hatchetation" of "joints"; singing hymns, praying, and smashing equipment with her hatchet, she wrecks many saloons in Kansas and moves on to San Francisco and the East. Arrested 30 times for disturbing the peace, she is an embarrassment to the temperance organizations, which do not support her, although she contributes to them.

At the turn of the century, census shows population of 75,995,000, an increase of almost 21 percent over 1890; figure includes 3,688,000 immigrants arrived since 1890. About 40 percent of population lives in places of 2,500 or more. New York is the largest city, with a population of 3,437,000; Chicago is second, with 1,699,000, followed by Philadelphia, with 1,294,000. Since 1890 almost 4 million more people have moved west of the Mississippi River than to the East. At this time life expectancy at birth is 48 years for males and 51 years for females.

Illiteracy of persons over 10 years old in the U.S. has decreased to 10.7 percent as compared with 20 percent in 1870. About 72 percent of children between 5 and 17 years old are enrolled in schools.

Immigration to the U.S. since 1820 has been 17,286,000 from Europe, 370,000 from Asia, 1,219,000 from Canada and Latin America, and 249,000 from all other places.

Since 1870, 430 million acres of land have been occupied by settlers, and 225 million acres have been improved and cultivated; this is more than in the entire period prior to 1870, beginning with settlement at Jamestown in 1607.

In period since the Civil War, railroad lines have increased from 37,000 miles to 193,000; three and a half times as much freight is carried by rail; tonnage of ships in coastal and internal trade has almost doubled, notably Great Lakes shipping, which now carries ores, as well as grains.

By this year the U.S. has about 150,000 miles of surfaced roads, and 8,000 passenger automobiles are registered.

Although electric power is produced by various means, its use is limited because of difficulty of transmission. By this year the longest electric power line in the U.S. is from Santa Ana, California, to Los Angeles, a distance of 35 miles.

Steel output is about 10 million tons, with steel for structural and other products exceeding steel for rails by two to one. More steel is produced by the open-hearth process than by the Bessemer process at this time. Hydraulic presses rather than steam hammers are in general use for forging.

Total value of farm machinery has tripled since 1870, with the invention of binders, specialized harrows, various plows, cream separators, and giant combines for harvesting and threshing. Almost nine times as much commercial fertilizer is used as in 1870.

Number of farms and farm acreage in the U.S. have doubled since 1870, and farm re-

HENRY A. ROWLAND
Address to American Physical Society, 1899
We meet together for mutual sympathy and the interchange of knowledge, and may we do so ever with appreciation of the benefits to ourselves and possibly to our science. Above all, let us cultivate the idea of the dignity of our pursuit so that this feeling may sustain us in the midst of a world which gives its highest praise, not to the investigation in the pure ethereal physics which our society is formed to cultivate but to the one who uses for satisfying the physical rather than the intellectual needs of mankind. He who makes two blades of grass grow where one grew before is the benefactor of mankind; but he who obscurely worked to find the laws of such growth is the intellectual superior as well as the greater benefactor of the two. . . .

The present generation suffers for the sins of the past and we die because our ancestors dissipated their wealth in armies and navies, in the foolish pomp and circumstance of society, and neglected to provide us with a knowledge of natural laws. In this sense they were the murderers and robbers of future generations of unborn millions, and have made the world a charnel house and a place of mourning where peace and happiness might have been. Only their ignorance of what they were doing can be their excuse, but this excuse puts them in the class of boors and savages who act according to selfish desire and not to reason and to the calls of duty. Let the present generation take warning that this reproach be not cast on it, for it cannot plead ignorance in this respect.

MARK TWAIN

To A. B. Paine, c. 1905

Nobody has heard of Davis; you may ask all around and you will see. You never see his name mentioned in print; these things are of no use to Davis, not any more than they are to the wind and the sea. You never see one of Davis's books floating on top of the United States, but put on you diving armor and get yourself lowered away down and down and down till you strike the dense region, the sunless region of eternal drudgery and starvation wages — there you will find them by the million. The man that gets that market, his fortune is made, his bread and butter are safe, for those people will never go back on him. An author may have a reputation which is confined to the surface, and lose it and become pitied, then despised, then forgotten, entirely forgotten — the frequent steps in a surface reputation. . . . But it is a different matter with the submerged reputation — down in the deep water; once a favorite there, always a favorite; once beloved, always beloved; once respected, always respected, honored, and believed in. For what the reviewer says never finds its way down into those placid deeps, nor the newspaper sneers, nor any breath of the winds of slander blowing above. Down there they never hear of these things. Their idol may be painted clay, up there at the surface, and fade and waste and crumple and blow away, there being much weather there; but down below he is gold and adamant and indestructible.

gions have become specialized. About half the wheat and barley, 40 percent of the corn, and almost all the flaxseed are grown in the west North Central states; most wool is produced in the Mountain states; a third of the oats is produced in the Middle West; three-quarters of the buckwheat is grown in New York and Pennsylvania; three-quarters of the peanuts in North Carolina and Virginia; three-quarters of the tobacco in the Southern border states; three-quarters of the rice in Louisiana; more than half the milk in Illinois, Wisconsin, Iowa, and New York. Meat-packing is concentrated in the Middle West, especially since the invention of refrigerator cars.

By 1900 the U.S. is exporting three times as much as at the end of the Civil War; major exports are cotton, meat, grain and grain products, petroleum products, and machinery; about three-quarters of U.S. exports go to Europe, and remainder is about evenly divided among the other continents. Imports, about half of which are from Europe, in 1900 are double those of 1866.

Dime novels have been enormously successful during this period; books such as those written under the pen name "Nick Carter" are turned out by many otherwise serious writers; publishers of these books have been inspired by the success of the penny dreadfuls in England.

1900 - 1901

April 7. President McKinley instructs the second (Taft) Philippine Commission to bear in mind that the government that is being established "is designed . . . for the happiness, peace, and prosperity of the people of the Philippine Islands." In following year government, staffed by Filipinos as well as the Commission, becomes well enough organized so that military government is withdrawn in July 1901, except in areas where guerrilla fighting continues.

1901

Jan. 10. First significant oil strike in Texas when Spindletop gusher blows in near Beaumont; discovery marks the beginning of change from domination of the state by cattle and railroad interests to control by oilmen.

Sept. 6. Although extraordinary precautions have been taken because an assassination attempt is suspected, President McKinley is shot by anarchist Leon Czolgosz while at the Pan-American Exposition in Buffalo, New York. **Sept. 14.** Although doctors have at first thought his condition not serious, gangrene affects two stomach wounds, and McKinley dies. Vice-President Theodore Roosevelt takes oath of office as twenty-sixth President.

Sept. 7. U.S. and other involved nations sign agreement placing Boxer Rebellion indemnity at $333 million. U.S. share is nearly $25 million, but the U.S. later cancels $18 million of debt. China spends this $18 million of U.S. share to send Chinese students to U.S. colleges and universities.

Oct. 16. President Roosevelt arouses wide resentment in the South by giving a luncheon for Negro educator Booker T. Washington.

October. Citizenship is granted to Indians of Five Civilized Tribes (Cherokees, Creeks, Choctaws, Chickasaws, and Seminoles), who have been moved to Oklahoma from the Southeast and later deprived of much of their land by unscrupulous practices of settlers and U.S. government agencies.

Nov. 18. U.S. and Britain sign second Hay-Pauncefote Treaty, which replaces Clayton-Bulwer Treaty of 1850 for joint rights in any canal across the Isthmus of Panama. Treaty of 1901 and related agree-

BOOKER T. WASHINGTON
Speech in Atlanta, 1895
As we have proved our loyalty to you in the past, in nursing your children, watching by the sickbed of your mothers and fathers, and often following them with tear-dimmed eyes to their graves, so in the future, in our humble way, we shall by you with a devotion that no foreigner can approach, ready to lay down our lives, if need be, in defense of yours; interlacing our industrial, commercial, civil, and religious life with yours in a way that shall make the interests of both races one. In all things that are purely social we can be as separate as the fingers, yet one as the hand in all things essential to mutual progress.

W. E. B. DU BOIS
On Booker T. Washington, 1903
Mr. Washington distinctly asks that black people give up, at least for the present, three things:

First, political power; second, insistence on civil rights; third, higher education of Negro youth; and concentrate all their energies on industrial education, the accumulation of wealth, and the conciliation of the South.

This policy has been courageously and insistently advocated for over fifteen years, and has been triumphant for perhaps ten years. As a result of this tender of the palm branch, what has been the return? . . .

1. The disfranchisement of the Negro.

2. The legal creation of a distinct status of civil inferiority for the Negro.

3. The steady withdrawal of aid from institutions for the higher training of the Negro. These movements are not, to be sure, direct results of Mr. Washington's teachings; but his propaganda has, without a shadow of doubt, helped their speedier accomplishment.

THEODORE ROOSEVELT
Message to Congress, 1901
There is a widespread conviction in the minds of the American people that the great corporations known as trusts are in certain of their features and tendencies hurtful to the general welfare. This springs from no spirit of envy or uncharitableness, nor lack of pride in the great industrial achievements that have placed this country at the head of the nations struggling for commercial supremacy. It does not rest . . . upon ignorance of the fact that combination of capital in the effort to accomplish great things is necessary when the world's progress demands that great things be done. It is based upon sincere conviction that combination and concentration should be, not prohibited but supervised and within reasonable limits controlled; and in my judgment this conviction is right.

It is no limitation upon property rights or freedom of contract to require that when men receive from government the privilege of doing business under corporate form, which frees them from individual responsibility and enables them to call into their enterprises the capital of the public, they shall do so upon absolutely truthful representations as to the value of the property in which the capital is to be invested. . . . Great corporations exist only because they are created and safeguarded by our institutions; and it is therefore our right and our duty to see that they work in harmony with these institutions.

MARK HANNA
Aboard funeral train carrying McKinley
I told William McKinley it was a mistake to nominate that wild man at Philadelphia . . . . Now look, that damned cowboy is President of the United States!

ments grant the U.S. the right to build, operate, and fortify canal, while providing equal access for peaceful purposes to all nations.

Nov. 27. Secretary of War Elihu Root, in reorganization of the Army because of shortcomings revealed by the Spanish-American War, establishes Army War College to provide advanced instruction and training for officers.

Dec. 3. First annual message of President Roosevelt announces campaign for regulation of large business combinations, proposing to retain combinations but prevent abuses by them.

In "Insular Cases" Supreme Court holds that territories gained by the U.S. in the Spanish-American War are neither parts of the U.S. nor foreign countries; that congressional authorization is necessary to impose duties on goods shipped to the U.S. from Puerto Rico; that goods shipped to Puerto Rico from the U.S. are duty free; and that citizens of such territories do not automatically have the rights of U.S. citizens, since such rights must be granted by Congress.

Social Democratic Party under Eugene V. Debs and reform arm of Socialist Labor Party merge to form Socialist Party.

U.S. Steel Corporation is organized by financiers headed by Elbert H. Gary and J. P. Morgan; it consolidates Carnegie Company and other properties, such as coal mines, iron ore mines, and railroads. Capitalized at over $1 billion, it is the world's largest industrial combination up to this time.

Reginald A. Fessenden patents radio transmitter in the U.S., although first wireless transmission has been achieved by Guglielmo Marconi six years earlier in Europe.

Fessenden's improvement is the beginning of radio communication across water, especially with ships.

John D. Rockefeller and his son, John D. Rockefeller, Jr., found, as one of many philanthropic organizations they create, the Rockefeller Institute for Medical Research.

King C. Gillette begins manufacture of modern safety razor with disposable blades.

1901 - 1903

March 2, 1901. Army Appropriation Bill, including provisions relating to Cuba known as the Platt Amendment, is passed by Congress. Cuban constitution drawn up in the same year, prior to planned evacuation by American troops, does not include provisions for future relations with the U.S. Cuba has been informed that the U.S. will not withdraw unless such provisions are included. **June 12.** Cuba adds provisions to constitution that make the island unofficially a protectorate of the U.S. **May 20, 1902.** U.S. withdraws from Cuba. **May 22, 1903.** Platt Amendment is added to U.S.-Cuban treaty to prevent its being dropped from Cuban constitution.

Frank Norris publishes *The Octopus*, which deals with struggle between wheat growers and the railroads; it is first novel of planned wheat trilogy. Second book, *The Pit*, is based on Chicago grain market. Norris dies before writing third novel, *The Wolf*, in which he has planned to picture a European famine relieved by wheat.

Jan. 24. U.S. signs treaty with Denmark for purchase of the Danish West Indies, but treaty fails in Danish Parliament. The transaction for the Virgin Islands (as they are known after purchase) is finally completed in 1917.

Feb. 19. Attorney General Philander C.

FRANK NORRIS
A Deal in Wheat, 1903
As Sam Lewiston backed the horse into the shafts of his buckboard and began hitching the tugs to the whiffletree, his wife came out from the kitchen door of the house and drew near. . . . For a long moment neither spoke. They had talked over the situation so long and so comprehensively the night before that there seemed to be nothing more to say.

The time was late in the summer, the place, a ranch in southwestern Kansas, and Lewiston and his wife were two of a vast population of farmers, wheat growers, who at that moment were passing through a crisis — a crisis that at any moment might culminate in tragedy. Wheat was down to sixty-six.

At length Emma Lewiston spoke.

"Well," she hazarded, looking vaguely out across the ranch toward the horizon, leagues distant; "well, Sam, there's always that offer of brother Joe's. We can quit — and go to Chicago — if the worst comes."

"And give up!" exclaimed Lewiston, running the lines through the torets. "Leave the ranch! Give up! After all these years!"

His wife made no reply for the moment. Lewiston climbed into the buckboard and gathered up the lines. "Well, here goes for the last try, Emmie," he said. "Good-by, girl. Maybe things will look better in town today."

"Maybe," she said gravely. She kissed her husband good-by and stood for some time looking after the buckboard traveling toward the town in a moving pillar of dust.

"I don't know," she murmured at length; "I don't know just how we're going to make out."

GEORGE F. BAER
Letter to W. F. Clark, 1902

I do not know who you are. I see that you are a religious man, but you are evidently biased in favor of the right of the workingman to control a business in which he has no other interest than to obtain fair wages for the work he does.

I beg of you not to be discouraged. The rights and interests of the laboring man will be protected and cared for, not by the labor agitators but by the Christian men to whom God in His infinite wisdom has given the control of the property interests of the country, and upon the successful management of which so much depends.

Do not be discouraged. Pray earnestly that right may triumph, always remembering that the Lord God Omnipotent still reigns, and that His reign is one of law and order and not of violence and crime.

THEODORE ROOSEVELT

The corporation has come to stay, just as the trade union has come to stay. Each can do and has done great good. Each should be favored as long as it does good, but each should be sharply checked where it acts against law and justice.

FINLEY PETER DUNNE

Mr. Dooley on Labor and Capital

It's too bad th' goolden days has passed. Capital still pats labor on th' back, but on'y with an axe. Labor rayfuses to be threated as a friend. It wants to be threated as an inimy. It thinks it gets more that way. They ar-re still a happy fam'ly, but it's more like an English fam'ly. They don't speak.

Knox announces that at the request of President Roosevelt the U.S. will prosecute the Northern Securities Company, a railroad holding company headed by J. P. Morgan, John D. Rockefeller, James J. Hill, and E. H. Harriman, for restraint of interstate commerce under the Sherman Antitrust Act. McKinley has failed to enforce the Act in spite of the extensive growth of holding companies during his administration.

1902

February. Dr. Charles W. Stiles, heavily supported by the Rockefeller Foundation, instigates antihookworm campaign throughout the South when he discovers that poor whites are not lazy but are weakened by the widespread invasion of the parasite.

March 6. Office of Permanent Bureau of the Census is established; it later becomes a part of the Department of Commerce.

May 12. Following refusal of mine operators to arbitrate when anthracite coal miners of Pennsylvania ask 20 percent wage increase and eight-hour day, about 150,000 United Mine Workers strike. **Oct. 16.** In first federal government action on behalf of labor, President Roosevelt appoints commission to settle strike. **Oct. 21.** Strike is discontinued, with miners, in March 1903, being awarded 10 percent wage increase but not recognition of union. Mine owners' stand against arbitration at beginning of strike arouses public opinion against large trusts.

June 2. Oregon becomes the first state in the U.S. to adopt general initiative and referendum, by which the people can override legislative rulings and initiate popular vote on legislation. Groups hostile to machine rule put through similar reforms, as well as reforms in primary elections, in other states in following few years.

June 17. Reclamation (Newlands) Act reserves funds from sale of public lands in 16 Southern and Western states to finance irrigation in dry areas; since Act also gives the President the right to retain public lands for the public, it is the beginning of systematic establishment of public parks.

June 28. Congress passes Spooner (Isthmian Canal) Act, which authorizes the financing and construction of the Panama Canal and appropriates $40 million for the purpose; in case the U.S. is unable to reach agreement for lease of Colombian area from New Panama Canal Company of France and negotiate treaty with Colombia (Panama being a province of Colombia), Act authorizes building of canal through Nicaragua.

July 1. Congress passes Philippine Government Act, which sets up a civil government under aid and supervision of the U.S.; islands become an unorganized territory. Taft Commission, appointed earlier by President McKinley, becomes supervisory agency.

Dec. 12. At the request of Venezuelan dictator Cipriano Castro, President Roosevelt intervenes in dispute between Venezuela and Britain, Germany, and Italy. During Castro's regime, Venezuela has become heavily indebted to the European nations, and they have finally sent warships to blockade Venezuelan ports. Bombardment of ports has led Castro to request that the U.S. propose arbitration. Settlement of dispute is achieved by the Hague Court in 1904.

Maryland passes the first workmen's compensation law, but it is invalidated later by the Supreme Court.

Arthur D. Little with his associates patents rayon (cellulose ester) and artificial

JOHN MUIR
Our National Parks, 1901
Any fool can destroy trees. They cannot run away; and if they could, they would still be destroyed—chased and hunted down as long as fun or a dollar could be got out of their bark hides, branching horns, or magnificent bole backbones. Few that fell trees plant them; nor would planting avail much toward getting anything like the noble primeval forests. During a man's life only saplings can be grown, in the place of the old trees—tens of centuries old—that have been destroyed. It took more than three thousand years to make some of the trees in these Western woods—trees that still stand in perfect strength and beauty, waving and singing in the mighty forests of the Sierra. Through all the wonderful, eventful centuries since Christ's time—and long before that—God has cared for these trees, saved them from drought, disease, avalanches, and a thousand straining, leveling tempests and floods; but He cannot save them from fools—only Uncle Sam can do that.

JOHN MUIR
In conversation, 1899
I am richer than Harriman. I have all the money I want and he hasn't.

JOHN BURROUGHS
Accepting the Universe, 1920
I see the Nature Providence going its impartial way. I see drought and flood, heat and cold, war and pestilence, defeat and death, besetting man at all times, in all lands. I see hostile germs in the air he breathes, in the water he drinks, in the soil he tills. I see the elemental forces as indifferent toward him as toward ants and fleas. I see pain and disease and defeat and failure dogging his footsteps. I see the righteous defeated and the ungodly triumphant—this and much more I see; and yet I behold through the immense biological vista behind us the race of man slowly, oh, so slowly! emerging from its brute or semi-human ancestry into the full estate of man, from blind instinct and savage passion into the light of reason and moral consciousness. I behold the great scheme of evolution unfolding despite all the delays and waste and failures, and the higher forms appearing upon the scene I see on an immense scale, and as clearly as in a demonstration in a laboratory, that good comes out of evil; that the impartiality of the Nature Providence is best; that we are made strong by what we overcome; that man is man because he is as free to do evil as to do good; that life is as free to develop hostile forms as to develop friendly; that power waits upon him who earns it; that disease, wars, the unloosened, devastating elemental forces have each and all played their part in developing and hardening man and giving him the heroic fiber.

silk; manufacture by the American Viscose Company in 1910 makes rayon the first commercially successful synthetic textile fiber.

Henry James, returning to his earlier theme, Americans abroad, after a period of portraying English society, publishes *The Wings of the Dove* and, in the next two years, *The Ambassadors* and *The Golden Bowl.*

Theodore Roosevelt publishes *Outdoor Pastimes of an American Hunter,* marking the beginning of an open-air-living vogue. He is joined by Stewart Edward White, John Muir, and John Burroughs, who publish many books and articles on outdoor living. Owen Wister publishes *The Virginian,* a novel of outdoor life in Wyoming; it becomes a best seller immediately.

1903

Jan. 24. Great Britain and the U.S. agree to form joint commission to settle dispute over ownership of Alaskan panhandle, claimed by both U.S. and Canada. During deliberations of commission, President Roosevelt hints at use of military force if U.S. is not satisfied with decision. **Oct.** Commission accepts U.S. claims, giving U.S. ocean outlets of panhandle.

Feb. 11. Expedition Act is passed to speed up action on federal antitrust suits; it gives antitrust cases precedence over others on Circuit Court schedules.

Feb. 14. Congress establishes U.S. Army General Staff Corps with the responsibility of preparing and carrying out military plans to eliminate conflict that has hitherto existed between commanding general and the secretary of war.

Feb. 14. Ninth Cabinet office is created

when President Roosevelt forms Department of Commerce and Labor; it includes Bureau of Corporations, authorized to investigate companies involved in interstate commerce. Department becomes two separate agencies ten years later.

Feb. 19. Elkins Act prohibits railroads from varying published rates and specifies punishment for shippers, agents, and railway personnel who accept or give rebates, a device that has been used to avoid prosecution for rate deviations in interstate commerce.

Feb. 23. For the first time a federal police power is ruled greater than that of the states when the Supreme Court upholds federal ruling that lottery tickets cannot be transported by mail from one state to another; up to this time, the federal government has regulated but not prohibited interstate commerce.

March 17. U.S. Senate ratifies Hay-Herran Treaty, which provides for a $10 million initial payment and renewable 99-year lease of land for the Panama Canal at rental of $250,000 per year. **Aug. 12.** Colombian Senate rejects Treaty because money is to be paid to New Panama Canal Company, and Senate wants delay until Company's charter expires, so that Colombia will receive payment.

May 23. Wisconsin enacts first direct primary election system in the U.S. Eventually system is adopted by almost all states, but procedures differ widely.

July 4. First service on Pacific cable is established when President Roosevelt sends around-the-world message that returns to him in 12 minutes.

Aug. 1. First transcontinental automobile journey is completed; Packard car arrives in New York 52 days after leaving San Fran-

AMOS P. WILDER
Outlook, 1902
Wisconsin people are not more Populistic than other well-fed, genial Americans who tolerate bathtubs in their homes and accept Carnegie libraries. But many of them believe that the unfolding life of the nation reveals new dangers to guard against; and it has not escaped attention that the nominating of candidates has become a confused and remote process, and that too often the men of power in political councils are the controlling forces in quasi-public corporations which desire favorable legislation. Wealth seeks to fortify itself with all the concomitants of ability, power, and secrecy. Personality is at work, both coercive and persuasive. There is intrigue, indecision, and the play of vice on weakness. The fighters are taking their posts. There is the cry of challenge and defiance. . . .

There are times when measures are above men. There are campaigns in which the issue is not the success or overthrow of men but approval or discrediting of a principle. The principle involved in Wisconsin is popular control. The opposition has sneered at primary elections and insists that it was a La Follette scheme to entrench himself, with the aid of typewriters, by sending his literature into the smallest hamlet; but the proposal that citizens get together and indicate on secret ballot whom they would have for mayor and whom they would send to the legislature and to Congress will not down. It commends itself over the present plan of voting for a lot of delegates, whom the citizen does not know, who are to go to some place, perhaps in another county, and vote for some person not specified. La Follette stands for the direct vote.

JACK LONDON

The Call of the Wild, 1903

All that stirring of old instincts which at stated periods drives men out from the sounding cities to forest and plain to kill things by chemically propelled leaden pellets, the blood lust, the joy to kill — all this was Buck's, only it was infinitely more intimate. He was ranging at the head of the pack, running the wild thing down, the living meat, to kill with his own teeth and wash his muzzle to the eyes in warm blood.

There is an ecstasy that marks the summit of life, and beyond which life cannot rise. And such is the paradox of living, this ecstasy comes when one is most alive, and it comes as a complete forgetfulness that one is alive. This ecstasy, this forgetfulness of living, comes to the artist, caught up and out of himself in a sheet of flame; it comes to the soldier, war-mad on a stricken field and refusing quarter; and it came to Buck, leading the pack, sounding the old wolf-cry, straining after the food that was alive and that fled swiftly before him through the moonlight. He was sounding the deeps of his nature, and of the parts of his nature that were deeper than he, going back into the womb of Time. He was mastered by the sheer surging of life, the tidal wave of being, the perfect joy of each separate muscle, joint, and sinew and that it was everything that was not death, that it was aglow and rampant, expressing itself in movement, flying exultantly under the stars and over the face of dead matter that did not move.

cisco, having traveled all the way under its own power.

Nov. 2. President Roosevelt orders warships to Panama to protect right of "free and uninterrupted transit" across the isthmus; Roosevelt has given tacit approval to revolution brewing in Colombia that has been instigated by members of New Panama Canal Company and native elements. **Nov. 3.** Province of Panama declares itself independent of Colombia. **Nov. 6.** The U.S. recognizes the Republic of Panama. **Nov. 13.** Minister from Panama, formerly an officer of New Panama Canal Company, is received in Washington.

Nov. 18. The U.S. signs Hay-Bunau-Varilla Treaty with Panama. Treaty gives the U.S. perpetual lease on 10-mile strip across the isthmus for payment of $10 million and $250,000 annually to begin nine years later. The U.S. is to guarantee Panamanian independence and neutrality of the Canal Zone.

Jack London publishes his most popular book, *The Call of the Wild*, and in the next year *The Sea-Wolf*. Kate Douglas Wiggin publishes *Rebecca of Sunnybrook Farm*; a sentimental book for girls, it eventually sells more than a million copies in the U.S. and is widely translated.

The Great Train Robbery, produced by Edwin Porter, is first movie to use motion of camera, as well as of actors, the first "Western," and the first film with a plot.

Alfred Stieglitz founds magazine *Camera Work* to advance photography as a fine art.

1903 - 1906

Dec. 17, 1903. Orville Wright is first man to fly a powered heavier-than-air machine when he stays aloft for 12 seconds in an airplane designed by himself and his brother Wilbur. Improved airplane flown in 1905 stays up for 38 minutes and travels 24 miles. Machine is patented in 1906.

Ida M. Tarbell, pioneer muckraker, begins publishing *The History of the Standard Oil Company* in *McClure's* magazine. Lincoln Steffens publishes *The Shame of the Cities*, also in *McClure's*, which, like other widely read magazines, publishes in this period exposures of graft and corruption in government and industry. Name "muckrakers" originates with Theodore Roosevelt, who, when pure sensationalism begins to replace efforts at reform, compares some authors with the man with the muckrake in *Pilgrim's Progress.*

1904

Jan. 4. U.S. Supreme Court holds that although citizens of Puerto Rico are not citizens of the U.S., neither are they aliens, and they may not be denied admission to the continental U.S.

Feb. 29. President Roosevelt appoints seven-man commission to take charge of construction of the Panama Canal. **May 4.** Canal strip is legally transferred to the U.S.

March 11. Morton Street Tunnel under the Hudson River nears completion when the shield from the New Jersey end touches that of the New York end, and William G. McAdoo becomes first man to cross the river below the surface.

March 14. In *Northern Securities* v. *United States*, first of more than 30 antitrust actions begun by Roosevelt administration, Supreme Court dissolves holding company formed by means of stock transaction to control four of the six railroad systems running from the Central states to the Pacific Coast; no criminal prosecutions follow. This

S. S. McCLURE
McClure's, 1903
How many of those who have read through this number of the magazine noticed that it contains three articles on one subject? We did not plan it so; it is a coincidence that the January McClure's is such an arraignment of American character as should make every one of us stop and think. How many noticed that?

The leading article, "The Shame of Minneapolis," might have been called "The American Contempt of Law." That title could well have served for the current chapter of Miss Tarbell's History of Standard Oil. And it would have fitted perfectly Mr. Baker's "The Right to Work." All together, these articles come pretty near showing how universal is this dangerous trait of ours. . . .

Capitalists, workingmen, politicians, citizens—all breaking the law, or letting it be broken. Who is left to uphold it? The lawyers? Some of the best lawyers in this country are hired, not to go into court to defend cases but to advise corporations and business firms how they can get around the law without too great a risk of punishment. The judges? Too many of them so respect the laws that for some "error" or quibble they restore to office and liberty men convicted on evidence overwhelmingly convincing to common sense. . . .

There is no one left; none but all of us. . . .

We forget that we all are the people; that while each of us in his group can shove off on the rest the bill of today, the debt is only postponed; the rest are passing it on back to us. We have to pay in the end, every one of us. And in the end the sum total of debt will be our liberty.

GEORGE WASHINGTON PLUNKITT
Plunkitt of Tammany Hall, 1905
Everybody is talkin' these days about Tammany men growin' rich on graft, but nobody thinks of drawin' the distinction between honest graft and dishonest graft. There's all the difference in the world between the two. Yes, many of our men have grown rich in politics. I have myself. I've made a big fortune out of the game, and I'm gettin' richer every day, but I've not gone in for dishonest graft—blackmailin' gamblers, saloonkeepers, disorderly people, etc.—and neither has any of the men who have made big fortunes in politics.

There's an honest graft, and I'm an example of how it works. I might sum up the whole thing by sayin': "I seen my opportunities and I took 'em."

Just let me explain by examples. My party's in power in the city, and it's goin' to undertake a lot of public improvements. Well, I'm tipped off, say, that they're going to lay out a new park at a certain place.

I see my opportunity and I take it. I go to that place and I buy up all the land I can in the neighborhood. Then the board of this or that makes its plan public, and there is a rush to get my land, which nobody cared particular for before.

Ain't it perfectly honest to charge a good price and make a profit on my investment and foresight? Of course, it is. Well, that's honest graft.

case and previous one against Trans-Missouri Freight Association in 1897 revive the Sherman Antitrust Act of 1890.

May 5. Socialist Party nominates Eugene V. Debs of Indiana for President at Chicago. **June 21.** Republicans meet at Chicago and nominate Theodore Roosevelt by acclaim, with Charles W. Fairbanks of Indiana as his running mate; platform is conservative Republican line. **June 29.** Prohibition Party meets at Indianapolis and nominates Dr. Silas C. Swallow of Pennsylvania. **July 2.** Socialist Labor Party meets and nominates Charles H. Corregan of New York. **July 5.** People's Party nominates Thomas E. Watson of Georgia. **July 9.** Democrats at St. Louis nominate Alton B. Parker of New York for President and Henry G. Davis of West Virginia for Vice-President; platform favors antitrust action and increased powers for Interstate Commerce Commission. **Aug. 31.** Continental Party meets at Chicago and nominates Austin Holcomb of Georgia.

Oct. 27. First section of New York City subway begins service from City Hall to 145th Street; line later becomes first subway in the world to run both underground and underwater.

Nov. 8. President Roosevelt and Fairbanks win election with popular vote of 7,628,000 to 5,084,000 for Parker and Davis. Five minor parties poll only 6 percent of vote. Electoral vote is Roosevelt, 336, Parker, 140; Parker wins only states of the Solid South, and Republicans are still in

Mobile, Alabama waterfront, 1905, with Alabama Iron Works at left

control of House and Senate. On election night, Roosevelt promises that he will consider his first partial term a first term and will not accept another nomination for the Presidency.

Unity Temple in Chicago, designed by Frank Lloyd Wright, is completed; it is first building designed entirely for poured concrete construction. Architect Bertram Goodhue's "Gothic" chapel, built for U.S. Military Academy at West Point, gives impetus to vogue for Gothic churches and academic buildings.

1904 - 1907

Dec. 6, 1904. President Roosevelt, when European powers threaten to intervene in Caribbean to collect debts owed by the Dominican Republic, asserts right of the U.S. to exercise international police powers in the Western Hemisphere when forced to do so by international conflicts. Statement, later called the Roosevelt Corollary to the Monroe Doctrine, changes Doctrine from prohibition of intervention by European powers to right of intervention by the U.S. **Jan. 20, 1905.** U.S. and the Dominican Republic sign agreement giving the U.S. charge of debt payments and customs finances of the Dominican Republic, which President Roosevelt carries out, although agreement is rejected by the U.S. Senate. **Feb. 25, 1907.** Permanent treaty is ratified between the U.S. and the Dominican Republic, which includes 1905 agreement, and U.S. withdraws from the island in following July.

THEODORE ROOSEVELT
Message to Congress, 1905
We must make it evident that we do not intend to permit the Monroe Doctrine to be used by any nation on this continent as a shield to protect it from the consequences of its own misdeeds against foreign nations. If a republic to the south of us commits a tort against a foreign nation, such as an outrage against a citizen of that nation, then the Monroe Doctrine does not force us to interfere to prevent punishment of the tort, save to see that the punishment does not assume the form of territorial occupation in any shape.

The case is more difficult when it refers to a contractual obligation. Our own government has always refused to enforce such contractual obligations on behalf of its citizens by an appeal to arms. It is much to be wished that all foreign governments would take the same view. But they do not; and in consequence we are liable at any time to be brought face to face with disagreeable alternatives. . . .

The only escape from these alternatives may at any time be that we must ourselves undertake to bring about some arrangement by which so much as possible of a just obligation shall be paid. It is far better that this country should put through such an arrangement, rather than allow any foreign country to undertake it.

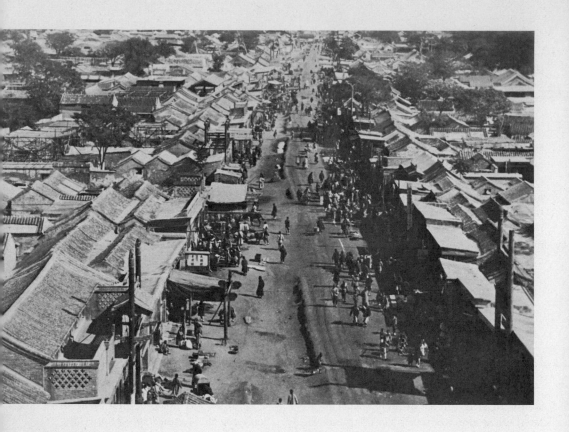

(Above) Peking, China, where, during
the Boxer Rebellion in 1900, members
of the European community were besieged in the diplomatic compound
until rescued by intervening troops;
(right) Theodore Roosevelt, twenty-
sixth President of the United States

(Left) W. E. Burghardt Du Bois, early advocate of civil rights for black Americans and one of the founders of the National Association for the Advancement of Colored People in 1910; (below) Executive Committee of the National Negro Business League, c. 1905: second from left, first row, Booker T. Washington

RUFUS W. PECKHAM
Lochner v. New York, 1905

It is not an act merely fixing the number of hours which shall constitute a legal day's work but an absolute prohibition upon the employer, permitting, under any circumstances, more than ten hours work to be done in his establishment. The employee may desire to earn the extra money which would arise from his working more than the prescribed time, but this statute forbids the employer from permitting the employee to earn it. . . .

The question whether this act is valid as a labor law, pure and simple, may be dismissed in a few words. There is no reasonable ground for interfering with the liberty of person or the right of free contract by determining the hours of labor in the occupation of a baker. There is no contention that bakers as a class are not equal in intelligence and capacity to men in other trades or manual occupations, or that they are not able to assert their rights and care for themselves without the protecting arm of the state, interfering with their independence of judgment and of action. They are in no sense wards of the state.

1905

April 17. In *Lochner* v. *New York*, the Supreme Court holds that New York State law regulating hours of bakery workers is unconstitutional; dissent by Justice Holmes protests that decision is based on an "economic theory which a large part of the country does not entertain."

May 31. After decisively defeating the Russian fleet, Japan asks President Roosevelt to mediate in Russo-Japanese War, which has continued since February 1904; conflict has endangered Open Door Policy in China when fighting involves Manchuria, a Chinese province. **June 8.** Roosevelt invites both powers to peace conference. **July 29.** Before conference convenes, Secretary of War Taft (with Roosevelt's sanction) makes agreement with Japanese foreign minister that the U.S. will not interfere with Japanese imperialist actions in Korea if Japan will cede all its claims in the Philippines. **Aug. 9-Sept. 5.** Peace conference held at Portsmouth, New Hampshire, gives Japan control of Korea and strengthens its position in Manchuria, but Japan receives no indemnity and only half (instead of all) of Sakhalin Island. In following year Roosevelt receives Nobel Peace Prize for his efforts as mediator.

(Below) Native carries the belongings of Japanese officers ashore at Chemulpo; (right) Japanese warship in action off the coast of Manchuria, 1904

Young boys at work
in a West Virginia
coal mine, 1908

June 27-July 8. Industrial Workers of the World is founded in Chicago by Eugene V. Debs, William D. ("Big Bill") Haywood, and others; organization seeks to unite all workers and establish control by unions over production. Its main success is among miners and migratory workers in Western states. By World War I, split over socialism and subjected to severe legal harassment, it suffers a sharp decline in membership.

June. Eighteen-hour train service begins between New York and Chicago with New York Central's "Twentieth Century Limited" and Pennsylvania Railroad's "fastest long-distance train in the world." Within a week both trains are wrecked, with a loss of 19 lives. **Nov. 8.** Chicago and North Western Railway runs first train equipped with electric lights, from Chicago to California.

Oct. 3. Theatrical producer David Belasco opens first of a series of Western plays, *The Girl of the Golden West*, in Pittsburgh, where it runs for three years. Play is later written as an opera by Giacomo Puccini and opens at New York's Metropolitan Opera House. It is first opera based on an American theme.

Dec. 30. Chairman Charles Evans Hughes, appointed by the governor of New

Industrial Workers of the World
Manifesto, 1905
Universal economic evils afflicting the working class can be eradicated only by a universal working-class movement. Such a movement of the working class is impossible while separate craft and wage agreements are made favoring the employer against other crafts in the same industry and while energies are wasted in fruitless jurisdiction struggles which serve only to further the personal aggrandizement of union officials.

A movement to fulfill these conditions must consist of one great industrial union embracing all industries, providing for craft autonomy locally, industrial autonomy internationally, and working-class unity generally. It must be founded on the class struggle, and its general administration must be conducted in harmony with the recognition of the irrepressible conflict between the capitalist class and the working class. It should be established as the economic organization of the working class, without affiliation with any political party.

GEORGE SANTAYANA
Address at University of California,
1911
A philosophy is not genuine unless it inspires and expresses the life of those who cherish it. I do not think the hereditary philosophy of America has done much to atrophy the natural activities of the inhabitants; the wise child has not missed the joys of youth or of manhood; but what has happened is that the hereditary philosophy has grown stale, and that the academic philosophy afterwards developed has caught the stale odor from it.

America is not simply, as I said a moment ago, a young country with an old mentality: it is a country with two mentalities — one, a survival of the beliefs and standards of the fathers, the other, an expression of the instincts, practice, and discoveries of the younger generations. In all the higher things of the mind — in religion, in literature, in the moral emotions — it is the hereditary spirit that still prevails, so much so that Mr. Bernard Shaw finds that America is a hundred years behind the times. The truth is that one-half of the American mind, that not occupied intensely in practical affairs, has remained, I will not say high-and-dry, but slightly becalmed; it has floated gently in the backwater, while, alongside, in invention and industry and social organization, the other half of the mind was leaping down a sort of Niagara Rapids.

This division may be found symbolized in American architecture: a neat reproduction of the colonial mansion — with some modern comforts introduced surreptitiously — stands beside the skyscraper. The American will inhabits the skyscraper; the American intellect inhabits the colonial mansion.

York, presides over last of 57 hearings of investigation into scandals in the life insurance business; hearings have involved many prominent financial figures and lead to wide reforms, as well as making Hughes nationally known.

In this and the following year, George Santayana, teacher of philosophy at Harvard University, publishes his five-volume *The Life of Reason*, which he calls a "biography of the human intellect." Work consists of *Reason in Common Sense, Reason in Society, Reason in Religion, Reason in Art*, and *Reason in Science.* Daniel de Leon publishes *Socialist Reconstruction of Society.*

Zane Grey, author of a series of often violent Western novels, publishes *The Spirit of the Border;* total sales of Grey's books is estimated at 15 million.

First Rotary Club is founded in Chicago, meeting at each member's office in rotation. Clubs, consisting of at least one member of each local business or profession, are spread widely in the U.S. by 1910 and later in foreign countries. In 1922 name becomes Rotary International.

Mount Wilson Observatory completed; it has been established by George Ellery Hale near Pasadena, California, as a department of the Carnegie Institution of Washington (D.C.).

1906

March 12. In *Hale* v. *Henkel*, the Supreme Court rules that witnesses in antitrust suits may be compelled to testify against their corporations and to produce corporation documents without a plea of immunity.

April 7. Act of Algeciras is signed by Italy, France, Spain, Germany, Great Britain, Austria-Hungary, and the U.S.; settlement of status of Morocco upholds independence and territorial integrity of the country. Germany has asked President Roosevelt to arrange international conference after France has sought to establish a protectorate; while Act appears to accede to Germany's viewpoint, it actually sets up French-Spanish police and an international bank to control Moroccan finances. Austria-Hungary has been the only country to back Germany in the conference.

April 18. Most severe earthquake in U.S. history, followed by fire, destroys most of San Francisco's central area; damage is estimated at about $400 million, and about 700 lives are lost. Rescue workers commandeer all available automobiles to transport injured and aged; this is first time automobiles (about one per 800 of population) have been thought of as anything but a useless toy.

June 30. Reports by muckrakers result in passage of Pure Food and Drug Act, which requires statement of contents of packages and prohibits manufacture and sale of adulterated foods and drugs. On the same day, Meat Inspection Act is passed, largely as a result of exposure of filthy conditions in Chicago meat-packing plants made in Upton Sinclair's *The Jungle*, published earlier in the year.

Nov. 9. President Roosevelt sails on a battleship to visit Panama Canal Zone in first trip ever made outside the U.S. by a President in office.

Dec. 4. Reverend Algernon S. Crapsey, former High Episcopal clergyman who has become a rationalist and denies the divinity of Christ, is convicted by an ecclesiastical court of heresy after a trial that has lasted since April and drawn the attention of the U.S. and England.

Dec. 24. Reginald A. Fessenden demon-

UPTON SINCLAIR
The Jungle, 1906
In the pickling of hams they had an ingenious apparatus, by which they saved time and increased the capacity of the plant—a machine consisting of a hollow needle attached to a pump; by plunging this needle into the meat and working with his foot, a man could fill a ham with pickle in a few seconds. And yet, in spite of this, there would be hams found spoiled, some of them with an odor so bad that a man could hardly bear to be in the room with them. To pump into these the packers had a second and much stronger pickle which destroyed the odor—a process known to the workers as "giving them thirty percent."

Also, after the hams had been smoked, there would be found some that had gone to the bad. Formerly these had been sold as "Number Three Grade," but later on some ingenious person had hit upon a new device, and now they would extract the bone, about which the bad part generally lay, and insert in the hole a white-hot iron. After this invention there was no longer Number One, Two, and Three Grade—there was only Number One Grade. The packers were always originating such schemes—they had what they called "boneless hams," which were all the odds and ends of pork stuffed into casings; and "California hams," which were the shoulders, with big knuckle joints, and nearly all the meat cut out; and fancy "skinned hams," which were made of the oldest hogs, whose skins were so heavy and coarse that no one would buy them—that is, until they had been cooked and chopped fine and labeled "headcheese!"

O. HENRY

The Four Million, 1906

*We must have a concrete idea of any-
thing, even if it be an imaginary idea,
before we can comprehend it. Now, I
have a mental picture of John Doe that
is as clear as a steel engraving. His eyes
are weak blue; he wears a brown vest
and a shiny black serge coat. He stands
always in the sunshine chewing something; and he keeps half-shutting his
pocket knife and opening it again with
his thumb. And, if the Man Higher Up is
ever found, take my assurance for it, he
will be a large, pale man with blue
wristlets showing under his cuffs, and
he will be sitting to have his shoes polished within sound of a bowling alley,
and there will be somewhere about him
turquoises.*

*Restless, shifting, fugacious as time
itself is a certain vast bulk of the population of the red brick district of the
lower West Side. They flit from furnished room to furnished room, transients forever—transients in abode,
transients in heart and mind. They sing
"Home, Sweet Home" in ragtime; they
carry their lares et penates in a band-
box; their vine is entwined about a picture hat; a rubber plant is their fig tree.*
*Hence the houses of this district, hav-
ing had a thousand dwellers, should
have a thousand tales to tell, mostly
dull ones no doubt; but it would be
strange if there could not be found a
ghost or two in the wake of all those
vagrant guests.*

*Well, little old Noisyville-on-the-
Subway is good enough for me.*

strates for the first time broadcasting of
voice and music by radio; operators aboard
many ships at sea report hearing the broadcast.

"O. Henry" (William Sidney Porter)
publishes his first collection of short stories
of New York City, *The Four Million.* Most
famous for his New York stories, O. Henry
writes more than 250 stories between 1899
and his death in 1910; many of the best of
these concern the South and the West.

"Typhoid Mary," who under a number
of assumed names has worked as a cook in
institutions and private homes, is finally
found eight years after it has become
known that, although well herself, she is a
carrier of typhoid fever. Because it is impossible to alter her carrier state, she is confined by health authorities for 23 years until
her death.

During New York theater season of this
year, six plays by George Bernard Shaw are
shown: *Caesar and Cleopatra, Arms and the
Man, Man and Superman, John Bull's Other
Island, Major Barbara*, and *Mrs. Warren's
Profession*; the last is raided by police as obscene and is closed after one performance.

1906 - 1909

Aug. 23. First president of Cuba asks
U.S. help in putting down revolt resulting
from election disputes. **Sept. 29.** After holding off for more than a month, President
Roosevelt appoints Secretary of War Taft
as provisional governor and sends troops to
the island. Insurrectionists are disbanded
within two weeks, but U.S. administration
does not cease until January 28, 1909.

1907

February. President Roosevelt confers
with San Francisco school board, which, on
reopening of schools after earthquake, has

ordered segregation of children of Oriental parentage in a separate school; Japan's protest against this discrimination has led to fear of an international crisis. San Francisco authorities agree to withdraw ruling on condition federal government act to exclude Japanese laborers. **Feb. 24.** Japan in "gentlemen's agreement" agrees to withhold passports of laborers who plan to travel to the U.S. and recognizes right of U.S. to refuse admission to those whose passports have originally been intended for travel to another country. **March 13.** School board rescinds segregation order. **March 14.** Authorized by Congress, Roosevelt excludes Japanese laborers from the continental U.S. **Dec. 16.** Most of U.S. Navy ("Great White Fleet") leaves on world cruise to exhibit U.S. naval strength. President Roosevelt has planned move partly to show Japan that U.S. concessions do not result from fear of Japanese power.

March 13. Financial Panic of 1907 begins with fall of stock market. **Oct. 21.** Run on Knickerbocker Trust Company of New York lasts until reserves are gone, and many other banks throughout the U.S. fail. Widespread unemployment and enormous increase in food prices lead to congressional inquiry into currency and banking systems, and finally to Federal Reserve Act of 1913.

March 21. U.S. Marines land in Honduras during revolution to protect American lives and large capital investments in banana plantations from dangers of war.

April 1. Panama Canal Commission is reorganized; Secretary of War Taft is to direct project, and Lieutenant Colonel George W. Goethals, of Army Corps of Engineers, is appointed to direct construction, which has been virtually at a standstill because of malaria and yellow fever in area and disagreement over whether canal shall be lock construction or sea level. When completed in 1914, canal runs 40 miles from Atlantic

Report of Department of Commerce and Labor, 1908
This legislation was the result of a growing alarm, particularly on the Pacific Coast and in states adjacent to Canada and Mexico, that labor conditions would be seriously affected by a continuation of the then existing rate of increase in admissions to this country of Japanese of the laboring classes. The Japanese government had always maintained a policy opposed to the emigration to continental United States of its subjects belonging to such classes; but it had been found that passports granted by said government to such subjects entitling them to proceed to Hawaii or to Canada or Mexico were being used to evade the said policy and gain entry to continental United States. . . .

In order that the best results might follow from an enforcement of the regulations, an understanding was reached with Japan that the existing policy of discouraging the emigration of its subjects of the laboring classes to continental United States should be continued and should, by cooperation of the governments, be made as effective as possible.

JAMES BRYCE
Of the Panama Canal
The greatest liberty that man has taken with nature.

THEODORE ROOSEVELT
New York Times, 1911
I took the Isthmus, started the Canal, and then left Congress — not to debate the Canal but to debate me.

AMOS BRONSON ALCOTT
Table Talk
Where there is a mother in the house,
matters speed well.

ABRAHAM LINCOLN
All that I am or hope to be, I owe to my
angel mother.

WILLIAM ROSS WALLACE
What Rules the World
They say that man is mighty,
  He governs land and sea,
He wields a mighty scepter
  O'er lesser powers that be;
But a mightier power and stronger
  Man from his throne has hurled,
For the hand that rocks the cradle
  Is the hand that rules the world.

HOWARD JOHNSON
Mother
Put them all together, they spell
  "Mother,"
A word that means the world to me.

JOHN G. NEIHARDT
Eight Hundred Rubles
One moment makes a father, but a
  mother
Is made by endless moments, load
  on load.

to Pacific oceans and costs about $365 million.

May 1907. First observance of Mother's Day is held in a church in Philadelphia; by 1911 every state celebrates Mother's Day on the second Sunday in May. Mother's Day is formalized by Congress on May 7, 1914, and two days later President Wilson asks for display of flag to express "our love and reverence for the mothers of our country."

June 15-Oct. 18. Second Hague Peace Conference meets; it has been called in 1904 but postponed because of Russo-Japanese War. The U.S. fails in attempt to establish a World Court, but Monroe Doctrine is reinforced when Conference agrees that armed force must not be used to collect debts owed by any American nation; agreement has been proposed by Argentina during Venezuelan crisis.

June 19. Western cattle grazing interests meet in Denver to protest President Roosevelt's land reservation policy. Repeal of the Forest Reserve Act of 1891, which allows closing of timber areas for creation of national parks, is effected by a rider to an appropriation bill. However, Roosevelt adds 21 reserves to bill before he signs it.

Nov. 14. Central American Peace Conference, arranged by U.S. Secretary of State Elihu Root with Mexico, meets in Washington as result of war in Central America. Five countries organize a Central American Court of Justice and sign treaty of peace.

Nov. 16. Oklahoma, formerly Oklahoma and Indian territories, is admitted to the U.S. as forty-sixth state. Citizens have voted to name the state Sequoya after Indian creator of Cherokee alphabet, but Congress has refused. Population is 1,414,000, more than five times that of 1890. Constitution includes prohibition of liquor.

Lee de Forest develops thermionic amplifier tube, an improvement of his Audion amplifier, which makes possible telephone transmission across the continent.

First Nobel Prize for Physics awarded to an American goes to Albert A. Michelson of the University of Chicago for his work in spectroscopy and metrology.

State prohibition laws are adopted in Georgia and Alabama.

Walter Rauschenbusch of Rochester (New York) Theological Seminary publishes *Christianity and the Social Crisis*, first of a series of books advocating application of principles of Christianity to social problems.

College of Agriculture and Mechanic Arts is established in Honolulu; first classes begin in following year. College becomes University of Hawaii in 1920.

Florenz Ziegfeld, former theatrical manager, presents his first revue, *The Follies of 1907*, in New York City; series of extravaganzas continues for 23 years.

First daily comic strip begins in the *San Francisco Chronicle*; drawn by H. C. ("Bud") Fisher, it is at first titled, "Mr. Mutt" and later "Mutt and Jeff."

1907 - 1915

Best sellers of the period, some of which continue to sell to the present day, are Harold Bell Wright's *The Shepherd of the Hills*, *The Calling of Dan Matthews*, *The Winning of Barbara Worth*, and *The Eyes of the World*; John Fox, Jr.'s *The Trail of the Lonesome Pine*; *The Circular Staircase* by Mary Roberts Rinehart; Gene Stratton Porter's *A Girl of the Limberlost*, *The Harvester*, *Laddie*, and *Michael O'Halloran*; *Mother* by Kathleen Norris; *Riders of the*

WALTER RAUSCHENBUSCH
Christianity and the Social Crisis, 1907
[Socialism] proposes to give to the whole body of workers the ownership of these vast instruments of production and to distribute among them all the entire proceeds of their common labor. There would then be no capitalistic class opposed to the working class; there would be a single class which would unite the qualities of both. Every workman would be both owner and worker, just as a farmer is who tills his own farm or a housewife who works in her own kitchen. This would be a permanent solution of the labor question. It would end the present insecurity, the constant antagonism, the social inferiority, the physical exploitation, the intellectual poverty to which the working class is now exposed even when its condition is most favorable.

If such a solution is even approximately feasible, it should be hailed with joy by every patriot and Christian, for it would put a stop to our industrial war, drain off the miasmatic swamp of undeserved poverty, save our political democracy, and lift the great working class to an altogether different footing of comfort, intelligence, security, and moral strength. . . .

Socialism is the ultimate and logical outcome of the labor movement. When the entire working class throughout the industrial nations is viewed in a large way, the progress of socialism gives an impression of resistless and elemental power. . . .

Christianity should enter into a working alliance with this rising class, and by its mediation secure the victory of these principles by a gradual equalization of social opportunity and power.

JAMES J. HILL
Address to White House Conservation Conference, 1908

The twofold significance of this meeting is found in the comparative novelty of its subject matter and of the method by which it has been approached. The subject is the conservation of our national wealth and a careful study of our national economic resources . . . It is this policy—the conservation of national resources, the best means of putting an end to the waste of the sources of wealth—which largely forms the subject matter of this conference. For the first time there is a formal national protest, under seal of the highest authority, against economic waste. . . .

In the movement of modern times, which has made the world commercially a small place and has produced a solidarity of the race such as never before existed, we have come to the point where we must to a certain extent regard the natural resources of this planet as a common asset, compare them with demands now made and likely to be made upon them, and study their judicious use. . . .

If we fail to consider what we possess of wealth available for the uses of mankind and to what extent we are wasting a national patrimony that can never be restored, we might be likened to the directors of a company who never examine a balance sheet.

The sum of resources is simple and fixed. From the sea, the mine, the forest, and the soil must be gathered everything that can sustain the life of man. Upon the wealth that these supply must be conditioned forever, as far as we can see, not only his progress but his continued existence on earth.

Purple Sage by Zane Grey; *Pollyanna* by Eleanor Hodgman Porter; *Tarzan of the Apes* by Edgar Rice Burroughs; and *Penrod* by Booth Tarkington.

1908

Feb. 3. In Danbury Hatters' case (*Loewe v. Lawlor*), the Supreme Court rules unanimously that boycott of industry by a labor union comes within the Sherman Antitrust Act as a conspiracy in restraint of trade and is, therefore, illegal. This is first time the Sherman Act has been applied to labor unions.

April 2. People's Party meets and nominates Thomas E. Watson of Georgia for President. **May 1.** United Christian Party nominates Daniel B. Turney of Illinois. **May 10.** Socialists meet and nominate Eugene V. Debs of Indiana. **June 16.** Republican Party at Chicago meets and nominates President Roosevelt's choice, William Howard Taft of Ohio, for President and James S. Sherman of New York for Vice-President; Roosevelt, having promised not to run again, feels that Taft will carry out his policies. Platform stresses need for stronger antitrust legislation, backs Roosevelt's conservation program, and promises tariff reduction. **July 2.** Socialist Labor Party meets and nominates August Gillhaus of New York. **July 10.** Democrats at Denver nominate William Jennings Bryan for President and John W. Kern as his running mate. Platform is antimonopoly, promises tariff reduction, and favors income tax. **July 15.** Prohibition Party meets and nominates Eugene W. Chafin of Illinois. **July 27.** Independence Party meets and nominates Thomas L. Hisgen of Massachusetts.

May 13. White House Conservation Conference, called by President Roosevelt, is attended by congressmen, Supreme Court justices, members of the Cabinet, and state governors; immediate reason for calling

Conference has been report of the Inland Waterways Commission that problem of crowded water routes cannot be separated from other problems of natural resources. **June 8.** National Conservation Commission is formed, with Gifford Pinchot as head. Commission's report on water, timber, soil, and mineral resources, submitted to Roosevelt in the following year, is first attempt to list them systematically.

May 28. Congress passes legislation regulating child labor in Washington, D.C., in hope that the states will follow suit.

May 30. National Monetary Commission established by the Aldrich-Vreeland Currency Act. Representing both houses of Congress, Commission is authorized to study U.S. and foreign banking and currency systems. Report made in 1912 is the basis of the Federal Reserve Act of 1913.

Oct. 1. Henry Ford introduces his Model T car; cost, $850. By 1909 his company is producing 19,000 automobiles annually, more than any other manufacturer. By turning out only one model (customers may have "any color, as long as it is black"), Ford is able to attain such efficiency that price has dropped to $310 by 1926.

Nov. 3. William Howard Taft and James S. Sherman defeat Bryan and Kern by popular vote of 7,675,000 to 6,412,000; electoral vote is Taft, 321; Bryan, 162. Republicans still dominate both House and Senate.

Nov. 30. U.S. and Japan sign Root-Takahira Agreement, which extends concessions made to Japan in 1905; it provides that both will uphold the Open Door Policy in China, support Chinese independence, and maintain the "existing status quo" in the Pacific, which Japan assumes to be U.S. recognition of its imperialistic aims in Korea and Manchuria.

FREDERICK DWIGHT
Independent, 1908
Every new and popular device exercises more or less tyranny. The mob spirit is generated and people hasten to chant the praises of the idol for fear of being called "reactionaries," a curious class who are supposed to be capable of all sorts of contemptible acts. . . .

At the moment I am thinking of automobiles. The advertising columns of the papers contain daily hymns to them. The proceedings of motor clubs are set forth at length. Our magazines teem with "motor flights" and astonishing tours and articles upon the romance of motoring. All is harmony and enthusiasm. . . .

Now it may be that a motor age, like a species of new Augustan Age, is about to dawn if aviation or some other novelty does not strangle it in its birth, and that it will be filled with blessings. But of course it does not follow that the period between the introduction and the complete development of automobiles is improved by them. . . .

I think the time when motor vehicles are desirable assets to society at large is yet to come, and that at present a certain excess must be charged to them in the debit column. They have engendered a reckless personal extravagance that must bring remorse and suffering to many some day. They have produced a new contempt for authority and an unusually lawless and irresponsible class. Finally, with little or no compensating advantage to the communities through which they hurry, they have caused the taxpayers heavy expense for roads, have almost driven the more leisurely from them, and have then proceeded to destroy the highways themselves. All of these things are doubtless curable and will be remedied in time. At present, however, they exist.

GEORGE E. WALSH
Independent, 1908

The moving picture drama furnishes entertainment for the millions, literally reproducing comic, tragic, and great events to some 16 million people a week at a nominal cost of a nickel or a dime. The effect of this new form of pictorial drama on the public is without parallel in modern history, for it more graphically illustrates the panorama of life than the photographs and texts of the daily newspaper and intrudes upon the legitimate theater through the actual dramatization of plays that have had a good run. The moving picture drama is for the multitude, attracting thousands who never go to the theater, and particularly appealing to the children. In the poorer sections of the cities where innumerable foreigners congregate, the so-called "nickelodeon" has held pre-eminent sway for the last year. . . .

In the last two years "nickelodeons" or moving picture theaters or exhibition halls have opened in nearly every town and village in the country, and every city from the Klondike to Florida and from Maine to California supports from two or three to several hundred. Millions of dollars have been invested in the shows, and it is estimated that on an average 2 million or 3 million people in this country attend the shows every day in the week. . . .

The demand for legitimate picture drama is growing, and within a short time most of our popular plays will be reproduced in the "nickelodeon" shortly after they have had a run on the road. More than this, the film companies are developing their own plays, paying experts in pantomime to invent plots and scenes which will show up well in moving pictures.

Dec. 2. Federal Council of the Churches of Christ in America is established in Philadelphia; it represents almost all Protestant churches.

In *Adair* v. *United States*, the Supreme Court invalidates a provision of the Erdman Act of 1898 that prohibits interstate railroads from requiring workers to agree not to join unions (yellow-dog contracts). Opinion is that union membership is not an interstate matter.

In *Muller* v. *Oregon*, the Supreme Court holds that an Oregon law limiting women's working hours is not unconstitutional.

The 47-story Singer Building in New York City is completed; but soon the Metropolitan Life Insurance Building (50 stories) is built, and in 1913 the Woolworth Building of 60 stories tops them both.

Gertrude Stein, expatriate American author, having settled in Paris in 1903 in a house that becomes a center for visiting artists and writers, publishes her first book, *Three Lives*.

"Ashcan School" of painting is established by a group of former newspaper illustrators when they begin painting unglamorous people and areas of New York City; group includes, among others, Robert Henri, John Sloan, and George Luks.

Movie houses called nickelodeons, first established in McKeesport, Pennsylvania, in 1905 by John P. Harris and Harry Davis, now number about 8,000 throughout the country. Usually set up in empty stores, they show continuous movies with piano accompaniment, and tickets cost five cents.

1909

Feb. 12. Sixty Negro and white leaders issue call for national conference on the Negro on the hundredth anniversary of Abraham Lincoln's birth. **May 30.** Conference convenes in New York; result is formation of the National Association for the Advancement of Colored People (N.A.A.C.P.) to fight for Negro rights by legal means.

April 6. Arctic explorer Robert Edwin Peary, his Negro aid, Matthew Henson, and four, Eskimos finish final dash from advance base to latitude 90 degrees north, first time in recorded history that men have reached the North Pole. **Sept. 1.** Dr. Frederick Cook of New York claims to have reached North Pole in previous year, but claim is discredited because of insufficient proof.

July 12. Congress submits Sixteenth (income tax) Amendment to the Constitution to the states for ratification; it is not finally ratified until 1913.

Payne-Aldrich Tariff is enacted by a special session of Congress to fulfill Republican campaign pledges, which have led public to expect reduced rates. Rates are revised downward to an average of about 38 percent on the value of goods imported, but tariff is actually increased on several hundred competitive items. In public controversy, President Taft defends this tariff as the best ever enacted by the Republican Party, but public disappointment helps Democrats win control of Congress 1910.

Leo H. Baekeland patents his thermosetting plastic, Bakelite; later it is used in many ways industrially, especially as an electric insulator. Invention is a major advance in U.S. plastics industry.

Herbert D. Croly publishes his first book on U.S. social and political problems, *The Promise of American Life.* Croly later founds weekly magazine, the *New Republic;* co-founder and associate editor is Walter Lippmann.

HERBERT D. CROLY
The Promise of American Life, 1909

The faith of Americans in their own country is religious, if not in its intensity, at any rate in its almost absolute and universal authority. It pervades the air we breathe. As children we hear it asserted or implied in the conversation of our elders. Every new stage of our educational training provides some additional testimony on its behalf. Newspapers and novelists, orators and playwrights, even if they are little else, are at least loyal preachers of the truth. The skeptic is not controverted; he is overlooked. It constitutes the kind of faith which is the implication rather than the object of thought, and consciously or unconsciously it enters largely into our personal lives as a formative influence. We may distrust and dislike much that is done in the name of our country by our fellow countrymen; but our country itself, its democratic system, and its prosperous future are above suspicion. . . .

The higher American patriotism, on the other hand, combines loyalty to historical tradition and precedent with the imaginative projection of an ideal national promise. The land of democracy has always appealed to its more enthusiastic children chiefly as a land of wonderful and more than national possibilities. . . .

Our American past compared to that of any European country has a character all its own. Its peculiarity consists, not merely in its brevity but in the fact that from the beginning it has been informed by an idea. From the beginning Americans have been anticipating and projecting a better future. From the beginning the land of democracy has been figured as the land of promise.

DANIEL BURNHAM, EDWARD BENNETT

Plan of Chicago, 1909

The plan of Chicago . . . is the result of a systematic and comprehensive study, carried on during a period of thirty months, with the sole purpose of mapping out an ideal project for the physical development of this city. Perfection of detail is not claimed, but the design as a whole is placed before the public in the confident belief that it points the way to realize civic conditions of unusual economy, convenience, and beauty. . . .

The education of a community inevitably brings about a higher appreciation of the value of systematic improvement and results in a strong desire on the part of the people to be surrounded by conditions in harmony with the growth of good taste; and as fast as the people can be brought to see the advantage to them of more orderly arrangement of the streets, transportation lines, and parks, it is well-nigh certain that they will bring about such desirable ends. Thus do the dreams of today become the commonplaces of tomorrow; and what we now deem fanciful will become mere matter-of-fact to the man of the future. . . .

If, therefore, the plan is a good one, its adoption and realization will produce for us conditions in which business enterprises can be carried on with the utmost economy, and with the certainty of successful issue, while we and our children can enjoy and improve life as we cannot now do. Then our own people will become homekeepers, and the stranger will seek our gates.

Daniel H. Burnham, architect and city planner, proposes his "city beautiful" plan for Chicago, which is 30 years ahead of its time in awareness of need for transportation, parks, and living space on a metropolitan area basis. Robie House in Chicago, designed by Frank Lloyd Wright, is completed; it is the most famous example of his "prairie" style.

First substantial animated cartoon in the United States is shown; it is entitled *Gertie the Dinosaur* and consists of 10,000 drawings by newspaper cartoonist Winsor McCay.

1909 - 1911

July 15, 1909. In effort to maintain balance of foreign control in China and safeguard American investment, President Taft seeks permission from Chinese regent for participation of U.S. private banks in international development of China. **July 4, 1911.** As a result of this "dollar diplomacy," Japan and Russia, urged by European nations, confirm each other's special interests in Manchuria, openly defying U.S.-sponsored Open Door Policy.

1910

Feb. 8. Boy Scouts of America is chartered; the U.S. is the twelfth country of the world to set up organized scouting after movement has been started in England by publication in 1908 of *Scouting for Boys* by Lieutenant General R. S. S. Baden-Powell; Baden-Powell has originally intended that his ideas be used by already existing boys' organizations. **March 17.** Camp Fire Girls is organized by Mr. and Mrs. Luther Halsey Gulick, Mrs. Ernest Thompson Seton, and other prominent educators.

March 19. Progressives led by George W. Norris, Nebraska Republican, revolt successfully against dictatorial powers of

House Speaker Joseph Cannon of Illinois ("Cannonism") when they pass amendment to House rules providing that Rules Committee be elected by House rather than appointed by the speaker, who, in addition, is made ineligible for membership on the Committee.

March 26. Immigration Act of 1907 is amended to exclude paupers, criminals, anarchists, and diseased persons from the U.S.

May. Halley's Comet passes the sun without the occurrence of disaster as predicted; many have believed that the earth will pass through the comet's tail and that everything on the earth will be destroyed.

June 18. Mann-Elkins Railroad Act is passed; law continues movement to strengthen powers of Interstate Commerce Commission over railroads and other carriers and communications systems provided for in Hepburn Act of 1906. Rulings of Commission are made binding pending appeals to courts, and corporations are to furnish proof of unreasonableness.

June 25. Congress establishes postal savings bank system recommended by President Taft; specific post offices are made depositories of funds on which 2 percent interest is paid; system continues until 1967.

June 25. In extension of corrupt practices acts passed by many states, Congress passes Publicity Act requiring U.S. representatives to file reports of campaign contributions received.

June 25. Congress passes Mann Act (White-Slave Traffic Act), which prohibits transportation of women across state lines for immoral purposes.

Aug. 31. Theodore Roosevelt, on return from Africa and Europe, makes New Na-

MARK TWAIN

Capt. Stormfield's Visit to Heaven, 1908
"Did you talk with those archangels and patriarchs, Sandy?"

"Who—I? Why, what can you be thinking about, Stormy? I ain't worthy to speak to such as they. . . ."

"You have got the same mixed-up idea about these things that everybody has down there. I had it once, but I got over it. Down there they talk of the heavenly King—and that is right— but then they go right on speaking as if this was a republic and everybody was on a dead level with everybody else, and privileged to fling his arms around anybody he comes across, and be hail-fellow-well-met with all the elect, from the highest down. How tangled up and absurd that is! How are you going to have a republic under a king? How are you going to have a republic at all, where the head of the government is absolute, holds his place forever, and has no parliament, no council to meddle or make in his affairs, nobody voted for, nobody elected, nobody in the whole universe with a voice in the government, nobody asked to take a hand in its matters, and nobody allowed to do it? Fine republic, ain't it?"

MARK TWAIN

In conversation, 1909; he died April 21, 1910
I came in with Halley's Comet in 1835. It is coming again next year, and I expect to go out with it. It will be the greatest disappointment of my life if I don't go out with Halley's Comet. The Almighty has said, no doubt: "Now here are these two unaccountable freaks; they came in together, they must go out together."

THEODORE ROOSEVELT
Speech in Kansas, 1910

I stand for the square deal. But when I say that I am for the square deal, I mean not merely that I stand for fair play under the present rules of the game but that I stand for having those rules changed so as to work for a more substantial equality of opportunity and of reward for equally good service. . . .

It has become entirely clear that we must have government supervision of the capitalization, not only of public service corporations, including, particularly, railways, but of all corporations doing an interstate business. . . .

The effort at prohibiting all combination has substantially failed. The way out lies, not in attempting to prevent such combinations but in completely controlling them in the interest of the public welfare. . . .

I do not ask for overcentralization; but I do ask that we work in a spirit of broad and far-reaching nationalism when we work for what concerns our people as a whole. . . .

The American people are right in demanding that New Nationalism, without which we cannot hope to deal with new problems. The New Nationalism puts the national need before sectional or personal advantage. It is impatient of the utter confusion that results from local legislatures attempting to treat national issues as local issues. It is still more impatient of the impotence which springs from overdivision of governmental powers, the impotence which makes it possible for local selfishness or for legal cunning, hired by wealthy special interests, to bring national activities to a deadlock. This New Nationalism regards the executive power as the steward of the public welfare.

tionalism speech in Kansas. He is increasingly estranged from Taft administration, convinced that Taft has been too cautious in continuing liberal Republican policies, and is angered by scandals in administration of conservation program. Actually, Taft administration begins more than twice as many antitrust actions as that of Roosevelt.

Sept. 7. Long dispute between Great Britain and the U.S. over Newfoundland fishing rights is settled by The Hague Court; commission is formed to settle disputes over fishing regulations, and the U.S. is allowed some concessions in Newfoundland waters. Award is confirmed by Great Britain and the U.S. in 1912.

Nov. 8. In fall elections, Democrats capture control of the House of Representatives; although Senate remains Republican, actually it is dominated by insurgents who have ties with Democrats. Victor Berger of Wisconsin is first Socialist ever elected to Congress. More than half the states elect Democratic governors, including Woodrow Wilson in New Jersey. Franklin Delano Roosevelt is elected to New York State Senate.

1910 census shows a population of 91,972,000, which includes 8,795,000 immigrants arrived since 1900; almost 46 percent of people live in places of 2,500 or more. Of people over 25 years old, less than half have completed grade-school education, and about 4 percent have graduated from college; but illiteracy has decreased since 1900 from 10.7 percent to 7.7 percent.

By this year prohibition laws have been enacted by Maine, Kansas, North Dakota, Georgia, Alabama, Oklahoma, Mississippi, North Carolina, Tennessee, and several hundred towns in Massachusetts.

Robert Millikan of the University of Chicago measures electric charge carried by an electron and later shows that the charge is constant. His work confirms much basic physical theory and inspires important advances in physics.

Educator Abraham Flexner publishes his report *Medical Education in the United States and Canada*; written for the Carnegie Foundation for the Advancement of Teaching, the report exposes inferior standards in the 155 U.S. medical schools and results in closing of many and reorganization of most others.

First U.S. air meet is held at Los Angeles, with audiences averaging 35,000 per day who watch all meet air speed records broken by Louis Paulhan of France and Glenn Curtiss of the U.S. Although many men want to fly, only five airplanes have been sold to individuals in the three years since first commercially made plane was produced.

1910 - 1911

First voluntary agreements for arbitration in labor disputes are set up in New York at instigation of Louis D. Brandeis and in Chicago after negotiation by Sidney Hillman of United Garment Workers. International Ladies' Garment Workers' Union achieves improvement in sweatshop system and garment industry in New York, especially after Triangle fire of 1911, which kills 146 workers and results in revision of New York building code and labor laws.

Andrew Carnegie, after giving funds to the Temple of Peace at The Hague, sets up the Carnegie Endowment for International Peace with a fund of $10 million; in 1911 he establishes the Carnegie Corporation of New York to support educational projects

ABRAHAM FLEXNER
Medical Education, 1910

We have still to deal with schools of our third division. They are most numerous in the South, but they exist in almost all medical "centers"—San Francisco, Chicago,—there plainly on the sufferance of the state board, for the law, if enforced, would stamp them out —St. Louis and Baltimore. Outside the South they usually make some pretense of requiring the "equivalent" of a high school education; but no examiner of any kind is employed, and the deans are extremely reluctant to be pinned down. Southern schools of this division, after specifying an impressive series of acceptable credentials ranging once more from university degrees downward, announce their satisfaction with a "grammar school followed by two years of a high school," or in default thereof a general assurance of adequate "scholastic attainments" by a state, city, or county superintendent, or some other person connected with education or purporting to be such; but the lack of such credentials is not very serious, for the student is admitted without them, with leave to procure them later.

Many of the schools accept students from the grammar schools. Credentials, if presented, are casually regarded and then usually returned, a few may be found, rolled up in a rubber band in a dusty pigeonhole. There is no protection against fraud or forgery. At the College of Medicine and Surgery, Chicago, a thorough search for credentials or some record of them was made by the secretary and several members of the faculty, through desk drawers, safe, etc., but without avail.

(Above) Steam dredges at work in the Culebra Cut over-mountain portion of the Panama Canal, during construction in 1907–1914; (below) cartoon depicting Roosevelt as Odysseus, tied to the mast of the ship of state in order to resist the sirens' call of Rockefeller, Morgan, and Carnegie, representing the trusts

(Above) William Howard Taft, twenty-seventh President of the
United States; (below) Eugene V. Debs, labor organizer and
perennial Socialist Party presidential candidate

WILLIAM JAMES
McClure's Magazine, 1910
The war against war is going to be no holiday excursion or camping party. The military feelings are too deeply grounded to abdicate their place among our ideals until better substitutes are offered than the glory and shame that come to nations as well as to individuals from the ups and downs of politics and the vicissitudes of trade. . . .

At the present day, civilized opinion is a curious mental mixture. The military instincts and ideals are as strong as ever, but are confronted by reflective criticisms which sorely curb their ancient freedom. Innumerable writers are showing up the bestial side of military service. Pure loot and mastery seem no longer morally avowable motives, and pretexts must be found for attributing them solely to the enemy. England and we, our Army and Navy authorities repeat without ceasing, arm solely for "peace"; Germany and Japan it is who are bent on loot and glory. "Peace" in military mouths today is a synonym for "war expected." The word has become a pure provocative, and no government wishing peace sincerely should allow it ever to be printed in a newspaper. Every up-to-date dictionary should say that "peace" and "war" mean the same thing, now in posse, now in actu. It may even reasonably be said that the intensely sharp competitive preparation for war by the nations is the real war, permanent, unceasing; and that the battles are only a sort of public verification of the mastery gained during the "peace" interval. . . .

When whole nations are the armies and the science of destruction vies in intellectual refinement with the sciences of production, I see that war becomes absurd and impossible from its own monstrosity.

with an endowment of $125 million. By this date he has already donated more than $60 million in accordance with his belief that wealth should be distributed for the good of the world.

1911

Jan. 21. National Progressive Republican League is formed by Senator Robert M. La Follette of Wisconsin and others. League urges general adoption of direct primaries; direct election of senators; and state constitution reforms to permit initiative, referendum, and recall.

Jan. 26. President Taft proposes reciprocal reduction of tariffs between the U.S. and Canada. **July 22.** U.S. Congress approves. Advanced to conciliate Canadian reaction to Payne-Aldrich Tariff of 1909, the proposals result in talk in the U.S. of annexing Canada, which arouses hostility of Canadian nationalists. **Sept. 21.** Made an issue in Canada, proposed agreement is repudiated when antireciprocity Conservatives win Canadian elections.

February. New automobile era begins when electric self-starter is demonstrated by General Motors; invented by Clyde J. Coleman in 1899, it has been perfected in this year by Charles F. Kettering. Invention makes it possible for women to drive without a male companion to crank the engine should it stop.

March 7. Twenty thousand U.S. troops are sent to Mexican border to protect interests of U.S. citizens during revolution led by liberal Francisco Madero against dictatorship; fighting has been so close to the border that crowds of U.S. citizens gather to watch. **April 14.** President Taft demands that Mexico cease fighting along the border. **May 25.** Madero's forces are victorious when Mexican President Díaz retires into exile after 34 years of control.

May 15. In *Standard Oil Company of New Jersey et al.* v. *United States*, Supreme Court orders Standard Oil Company dissolved on ground that it engages in "unreasonable" restraint of trade; thus, Court accepts "rule of reason" as principle for regulation of large corporations under Sherman Antitrust Act.

May 29. In *United States* v. *American Tobacco Company*, Supreme Court finds the "tobacco trust" to be in violation of the Sherman Antitrust Act in attempting to restrain commerce and effect a monopoly in the tobacco business.

July 7. Threat of complete extermination of fur seals in the North Pacific results in treaty signed by the U.S., Great Britain (for Canada), Russia, and Japan that outlaws pelagic sealing for 15 years north of the 30th parallel; the U.S. is given control of the area. Increase of seal herds has been prevented because seals killed are usually migrating pregnant females.

Oct. 16. Progressive Republicans meet in Chicago and nominate Robert M. La Follette for the Presidency.

Dec. 18. The U.S. abrogates 1832 treaty with Russia because Russia refuses to honor passports of Jewish U.S. citizens and those of various clergymen.

Socialist mayors are elected in 18 cities after campaigns advocating municipal ownership of public utilities and local transportation. Since 1900, era of municipal reform has been due in large part to muckrakers' exposures of graft and corruption.

Elmer Sperry patents the gyrocompass;

EDWARD D. WHITE
Standard Oil Co. v. U.S., 1911
It is certain that only one point of concord between the parties is discernible, which is, that the controversy in every aspect is controlled by a correct conception of the meaning of the first and second sections of the Antitrust Act. . . .

In view of the common law and the law in this country as to restraint of trade . . . and the illuminating effect which that history must have under the rule to which we have referred, we think it results . . . [that] as the contracts or acts embraced in the provision were not expressly defined, since the enumeration addressed itself simply to classes of acts, those classes being broad enough to embrace every conceivable contract or combination which could be made concerning trade or commerce or the subjects of such commerce, and thus caused any act done by any of the enumerated methods anywhere in the whole field of human activity to be illegal if in restraint of trade, it inevitably follows that the provision necessarily called for the exercise of judgment which required that some standard should be resorted to for the purpose of determining whether the prohibitions contained in the statute had or had not in any given case been violated. Thus not specifying but indubitably contemplating and requiring a standard, it follows that it was intended that the standard of reason which had been applied at the common law, and in this country in dealing with subjects of the character embraced by the statute, was intended to be the measure used for the purpose of determining whether in a given case a particular act had or had not brought about the wrong against which the statute provided.

JAMES OPPENHEIM
Bread and Roses, 1912

*As we come marching, marching, in
    the beauty of the day,
A million darkened kitchens, a
    thousand mill lofts gray,
Are touched with all the radiance that a
    sudden sun discloses,
For the people hear us singing: "Bread
    and roses! Bread and roses!"*

*As we come marching, marching, we
    battle too for men,
For they are women's children, and we
    mother them again.
Our lives shall not be sweated from
    birth until life closes;
Hearts starve as well as bodies; give
    us bread, but give us roses!*

*As we come marching, marching,
    unnumbered women dead
Go crying through our singing their
    ancient cry for bread.
Small art and love and beauty their
    drudging spirits knew.
Yes, it is bread we fight for — but we
    fight for roses, too!*

*As we come marching, marching, we
    bring the greater days.
The rising of the women means the
    rising of the race.
No more the drudge and idler — ten
    that toil where one reposes,
But a sharing of life's glories: Bread
    and roses! Bread and roses!*

he later perfects the gyroscope and invents the automatic pilot.

1911 - 1914

Naturalistic novelist Theodore Dreiser publishes first novel in 11 years, *Jennie Gerhardt*, and the next year publishes *The Financier*, first book of a trilogy based on the life of a millionaire streetcar manufacturer; second book, *The Titan*, is published in 1914, but the third, *The Stoic*, not until 1947, two years after Dreiser's death.

1911. The *Masses*, proletarian magazine, is founded in New York; it later becomes the *Liberator* and then the *New Masses*. **1912.** Harriet Monroe begins publishing *Poetry* magazine in Chicago. **1914.** The *New Republic* magazine begins publication; it is founded and edited by Herbert Croly along with other Progressives, most notably Walter Lippmann.

1911 - 1920

Novelist Edith Wharton publishes her best-known novel, *Ethan Frome*, New England tragedy; later she publishes *The Reef*, *The Custom of the Country*, *Summer*, and, in 1920, *The Age of Innocence*, which wins the Pulitzer Prize.

1912

Jan. 6. New Mexico becomes forty-seventh state of the U.S. after numerous efforts to attain statehood have failed until 1910, when Congress has passed enabling legislation.

Jan. 12. Lawrence, Massachusetts, textile workers begin strike to protest reduction of wages that follows enactment of minimum hours law; lasting for two months and characterized by violence, strike demonstrates the power of the Industrial Workers of the

World, which for the first time becomes influential in the East.

Feb. 14. Arizona, formerly part of New Mexico Territory, becomes forty-eighth state of the U.S. In previous August, President Taft has vetoed congressional resolution admitting it to statehood because of clause in state constitution providing for recall of judges by popular vote, which Taft feels will limit judicial independence. Arizona is admitted after removing clause but immediately reinserts it on becoming a state.

Feb. 25. Theodore Roosevelt, now alienated from Conservative Republicans and closer to Progressives who have backed Senator La Follette, consents to run against Taft for presidential nomination if asked.

March 7. U.S. Senate passes general arbitration agreement signed with France and Great Britain that provides for referral of international disputes to the Hague Court; but passage is not achieved until amendments proposed by Senator Henry Cabot Lodge of Massachusetts weaken it by adding reservations in cases that involve the Monroe Doctrine and Oriental exclusion from the U.S. and by requiring consent of the U.S. Senate before arbitration can be submitted to the Court.

April 7. Socialist Labor Party meets and nominates Arthur E. Reimer of Massachusetts for President. **May 12.** Socialists meet and again nominate Eugene V. Debs. **June 18.** Republicans meeting at Chicago are controlled by conservative elements, who exclude most Theodore Roosevelt backers by not seating contested delegations; President Taft and Vice-President Sherman are renominated, but Sherman dies on October 30. Platform advocates conservation, a corrupt practices act, financial reform, strict regulation of trusts, and a lower protective

THEODORE ROOSEVELT
February 1912
My hat is in the ring. The fight is on and I am stripped to the buff.

THEODORE ROOSEVELT
June 1912
We stand at Armageddon, and we battle for the Lord.

THEODORE ROOSEVELT
August 1912
I feel as fit as a bull moose.

WOODROW WILSON
A presidential campaign may easily degenerate into a mere personal contest and so lose its real dignity. There is no indispensable man.

VICTOR L. BERGER
American Magazine, 1912
As good a man as Eugene V. Debs is, I am not going to vote for him in the sense one is voting for Wilson, Taft, or Roosevelt—I simply vote the ticket of the Socialist Party. I have no hope that the Socialist Party will elect its candidate for President in this election. With us, the Socialist movement and its principles are paramount—not the candidate. . . .

Our sole object in state and nation for the next few years is to elect a respectable minority of Socialists.

We want a Socialist minority respected on account of its numbers—respected because it represents the most advanced economic and political intelligence of the day—respected because it contains the most sincere representatives of the proletariat, the class that has the most to gain and nothing to lose.

Given such a respectable minority in Congress and in the legislature of every state of the Union within the next few years, the future of our people, the future of this country will be safe.

Progressive Party Platform, 1912

The conscience of the people, in a time of grave national problems, has called into being a new party, born of the nation's awakened sense of injustice.

We of the Progressive Party here dedicate ourselves to the fulfillment of the duty laid upon us by our fathers to maintain that government of the people, by the people, and for the people whose foundations they laid.

We hold, with Thomas Jefferson and Abraham Lincoln, that the people are the masters of their Constitution to fulfill its purposes and to safeguard it from those who, by perversion of its intent, would convert it into an instrument of injustice. In accordance with the needs of each generation, the people must use their sovereign powers to establish and maintain equal opportunity and industrial justice, to secure which this government was founded and without which no republic can endure.

This country belongs to the people who inhabit it. Its resources, its business, its institutions, and its laws should be utilized, maintained, or altered in whatever manner will best promote the general interest. It is time to set the public welfare in the first place. . . .

Unhampered by tradition, uncorrupted by power, undismayed by the magnitude of the task, the new party offers itself as the instrument of the people to sweep away old abuses, to build a new and nobler commonwealth.

tariff. **June 22.** Roosevelt followers meet, declare Taft nomination fraudulent, and call upon Roosevelt to head third party. **July 2.** At Democratic convention in Baltimore, Woodrow Wilson of New Jersey is nominated for President on the forty-sixth ballot, after William Jennings Bryan swings support to him from Champ Clark of Missouri; Thomas R. Marshall of Indiana is nominated for Vice-President. Platform is like Republicans' on conservation, a corrupt practices act, and financial reform but stresses outlawing of monopolies, and tariff for revenue only. **Aug. 7.** Progressive ("Bull Moose") Party, meeting at Chicago, nominates Roosevelt for President and Hiram W. Johnson of California for Vice-President. Platform stresses tariff revision, changes in state and federal election laws, stricter control of combinations in industry, women suffrage, and reforms in labor laws for women and children.

April 14-15. "Unsinkable" steamship *Titanic* collides with iceberg and sinks with loss of more than 1,500 persons. Investigation shows that ship carried too few lifeboats and had been ordered to proceed at high speed through dangerous waters. **May 1.** Federal authorities order all steamships to provide enough lifeboats for all passengers.

Aug. 2. U.S. Senate passes resolution proposed by Senator Lodge expressing concern over possession by a non-American corporation of any strategic area in the Western Hemisphere; question has arisen when Japan is found to be negotiating with an American syndicate for an area of Lower California (Mexico). Known as the Lodge Corollary, resolution broadens scope of Monroe Doctrine to cover foreign corporations.

Aug. 14. U.S. Marines land in Nicaragua to prevent foreign occupation of possible canal route across the isthmus; foreign intervention has been threatened when Nicaragua has delayed payments of loans from European countries and U.S. banks that have been guaranteed by Nicaraguan customs revenues. Action is taken by authority of President Taft, although the U.S. Senate has failed to ratify various proposed U.S.-Nicaraguan agreements authorizing U.S. intervention.

Aug. 24. Domestic parcel post system is authorized; service begins in following year.

Nov. 5. Woodrow Wilson is elected President with a popular vote of 6,297,000 to 4,119,000 for Roosevelt and 3,487,000 for Taft; Socialist Debs receives 901,000 votes, twice as many as in any previous election. According to popular vote, Wilson is a minority President, but his electoral majority is greatest in U.S. election history to this time: Wilson, 435 (40 states); Roosevelt, 88 (6 states); Taft, 8 (2 states).

Alaska becomes an organized territory of the U.S. after 16 months of argument in Congress, but Alaskan legislature is restricted far more as to taxing and licensing powers than those of earlier territories.

By this year many states have passed laws controlling wages and hours, factory working conditions, and labor of women and children. Massachusetts passes first minimum wage law (invalidated by the Supreme Court in 1923); New York passes 54-hour-week labor law; and Congress passes eight-hour-day law for all federal workers.

Government-sponsored illustrations of engineering work on the Panama Canal are published; executed by etcher-lithographer Joseph Pennell, they are the first popularly successful artistic treatment of industrial or engineering themes.

WILLIAM HOWARD TAFT
Message to Congress, 1912
The diplomacy of the present administration has sought to respond to modern ideas of commercial intercourse. This policy has been characterized as substituting dollars for bullets. It is one that appeals alike to idealistic humanitarian sentiments, to the dictates of sound policy and strategy, and to legitimate commercial aims. It is an effort frankly directed to the increase of American trade upon the axiomatic principle that the government of the United States shall extend all proper support to every legitimate and beneficial American enterprise abroad. . . .

In Central America the aim has been to help such countries as Nicaragua and Honduras to help themselves. They are the immediate beneficiaries. The national benefit to the United States is twofold. First, it is obvious that the Monroe Doctrine is more vital in the neighborhood of the Panama Canal and the zone of the Caribbean than anywhere else. There, too, the maintenance of that doctrine falls most heavily upon the United States. It is therefore essential that the countries within that sphere shall be removed from the jeopardy involved by heavy foreign debt and chaotic national finances and from the ever present danger of international complications due to disorder at home. Hence, the United States has been glad to encourage and support American bankers who were willing to lend a helping hand to the financial rehabilitation of such countries because this financial rehabilitation and the protection of their customhouses from being the prey of would-be dictators would remove at one stroke the menace of foreign creditors and the menace of revolutionary disorder.

AMY LOWELL
Patterns, 1916
I shall go
Up and down,
In my gown.
Gorgeously arrayed,
Boned and stayed.
And the softness of my body will be
guarded from embrace
By each button, hook, and lace.
For the man who should loose me is
dead,
Fighting with the Duke in Flanders,
In a pattern called a war.
Christ! What are patterns for?

ROBERT FROST
Mending Wall, 1914
Before I built a wall I'd ask to know
What I was walling in or walling out,
And to whom I was like to give offense.
Something there is that doesn't love a
wall,
That wants it down.

CARL SANDBURG
Chicago, 1914
Hog Butcher for the World,
Tool Maker, Stacker of Wheat,
Player with Railroads and the Nation's
Freight Handler;
Stormy, husky, brawling,
City of the Big Shoulders.

Columbia University founds School of Journalism with bequest from newspaper publisher Joseph Pulitzer, who has died in the previous year.

Alexis Carrel, whose important work has been done at the University of Chicago and later at the Rockefeller Institute, receives Nobel Prize in Physiology and Medicine; award is for his work in transplanting organs and blood vessels and in suturing blood vessels. Two years later, Carrel performs first successful heart surgery on an animal by cutting off blood circulation for several minutes.

William Randolph Hearst begins to acquire control of a chain of newspapers. By 1934, chain consists of 30 newspapers, as well as 6 magazines, a Sunday supplement, a features syndicate, a newsreel, and 2 wire services.

1912 - 1914

Aug. 24, 1912. Congress passes Panama Canal Act, which provides toll-free passage of Canal for American vessels engaged in coastwise trade, although Hay-Pauncefote Treaty has provided entire equality for all nations. **March 5, 1914.** After British protest that Act shows bad faith on part of the U.S., President Wilson asks repeal of exemption, which Congress passes on June 11.

1912 - 1915

Amy Lowell publishes *A Dome of Many-Coloured Glass,* her first poetry collection, in 1912, and in 1914, *Sword Blades and Poppy Seed,* which contains her first free verse. Robert Frost publishes (in London) his first book of poetry, *A Boy's Will,* in 1913, and in the following year *North of Boston;* by 1915 he is recognized as a major poet. Vachel Lindsay's poem "General William Booth Enters into Heaven" appears in *Poetry* magazine in 1913, his *Congo and Other Poems* appearing a year later. Carl Sandburg's poetry is first recognized when he receives *Poetry* award in 1914 for poems about Chicago.

Liberal historian Charles Austin Beard reaches a wide audience with his analyses of major factors in the development of the U.S. government, *The Supreme Court and the Constitution* in 1912, *An Economic Interpretation of the Constitution of the United States* in 1913, and *The Economic Origins of Jeffersonian Democracy* in 1915.

1913

January-April. Garment workers' strike begins in New York City when 150,000 workers leave their jobs in protest against long hours, low wages, and refusal of employers to recognize union. Strike spreads to Boston and ends when workers win concessions on all three points.

Feb. 17. Armory Show opens at 69th Regiment Armory in New York City; organized by Association of Painters and Sculptors, it is the first full-scale presentation in the U.S. of contemporary European work, abstract, Cubist, Impressionist, and Postimpressionist. Show has revolutionary effects on public taste in the U.S., both for European art and for new departures and experiments by American artists.

Feb. 22. Liberal Mexican President Madero is assassinated by reactionaries under General Victoriano Huerta; Huerta is recognized by European nations but not by the U.S., which has supported Madero and has resisted pressures by U.S. business interests to support Huerta. **March 11.** President Wilson, in speech disapproving Huerta

THEODORE ROOSEVELT
Outlook, 1913
In this recent art exhibition the lunatic fringe was fully in evidence, especially in the rooms devoted to the Cubists and the Futurists, or Near-Impressionists. I am not entirely certain which of the two latter terms should be used in connection with some of the various pictures and representations of plastic art—and, frankly, it is not of the least consequence. The Cubists are entitled to the serious attention of all who find enjoyment in the colored puzzle pictures of the Sunday newspapers.

Of course there is no reason for choosing the cube as a symbol, except that it is probably less fitted than any other mathematical expression for any but the most formal decorative art. There is no reason why people should not call themselves Cubists, or Octagonists, Parallelopipedonists, or Knights of the Isosceles Triangle, or Brothers of the Cosine, if they so desire; as expressing anything serious and permanent, one term is as fatuous as another.

Take the picture which for some reason is called "A Naked Man Going Downstairs." There is in my bathroom a really good Navaho rug which, on any proper interpretation of the Cubist theory, is a far more satisfactory and decorative picture. Now if, for some inscrutable reason, it suited somebody to call this rug a picture of, say, "A Well-dressed Man Going Up a Ladder," the name would fit the facts just about as well as in the case of the Cubist picture of the "Naked Man Going Downstairs."

WOODROW WILSON
Message to the press, 1913
I think that the public ought to know the extraordinary exertions being made by the lobby in Washington to gain recognition for certain alterations of the tariff bill. Washington has seldom seen so numerous, so industrious, or so insidious a lobby. The newspapers are being filled with paid advertisements calculated to mislead the judgment of public men not only, but also the public opinion of the country itself. There is every evidence that money without limit is being spent to sustain this lobby and to create an appearance of a pressure of public opinion antagonistic to some of the chief items of the tariff bill.

It is of serious interest to the country that the people at large should have no lobby and be voiceless in these matters, while great bodies of astute men seek to create an artificial opinion and to overcome the interests of the public for their private profit. It is thoroughly worth the while of the people of this country to take knowledge of this matter. Only public opinion can check and destroy it.

The government in all its branches ought to be relieved from this intolerable burden and this constant interruption to the calm progress of debate. I know that I am speaking for the members of the two houses, who would rejoice as much as I would to be released from this unbearable situation.

WILLIAM JENNINGS BRYAN
Letter to W. W. Vick, 1913
Can you let me know what positions you have at your disposal with which to reward deserving Democrats?

regime, ends "dollar diplomacy," stating that the U.S. will no longer support special business interests in foreign countries.

Feb. 25. Sixteenth Amendment to the U.S. Constitution is declared ratified. It authorizes Congress to tax income from all sources without regard to a census and without apportionment among the states.

Feb. 28. Report by House committee headed by Representative Arsène Pujo that has inquired into a reported "money trust" states that concentration of money and financial power is increasing by means of business consolidations, interlocking directorates, questionable stock purchases, and other financial maneuvers; report lends impetus to moves for banking and currency reforms.

March 4. Congress separates U.S. Department of Commerce and Labor into two departments, both with Cabinet status, and sets up federal mediation board to settle labor disputes.

April 8. President Wilson appears before Congress to deliver his message on tariff revision; he is first President since John Adams to deliver a message to Congress in person; Thomas Jefferson has set precedent in 1801, when he has his address read by a clerk.

April 24. Secretary of State William Jennings Bryan achieves last of 21 ratifications of arbitration treaties with foreign countries; treaties provide that no signing country will resort to war until disputes have been submitted to arbitration by an international commission, which must be allowed one year to submit a report.

May 14. John D. Rockefeller, in greatest single philanthropic act in U.S. history up to this time, donates $100 million to establish the Rockefeller Foundation; it is chartered by the state of New York.

May 31. Seventeenth Amendment to the Constitution is declared ratified and in effect. It provides for election of U.S. senators directly by the people of each state, instead of by state legislatures.

Aug. 16. Mexican leader Huerta refuses President Wilson's proposal of an armistice when new revolution breaks out, leading to Wilson policy of "watchful waiting" and strict arms embargo. **Oct. 27.** In answer to demands of business that the U.S. intervene, Wilson declares that the U.S. never again will seek territory by conquest. **Nov. 7.** Wilson demands Huerta's resignation and upon Huerta's refusal announces U.S. policy of support of revolutionists. Early in following year, arms embargo is lifted to allow shipments to revolutionists, and Veracruz is blockaded by U.S. warships to prevent entry of arms sent to Huerta from Europe.

Oct. 3. Congress passes Underwood Tariff Act; average duties are reduced to 30 percent, and some important raw materials are admitted free. To compensate for anticipated losses of revenue, a tax of 1 percent is levied on corporate incomes of more than $4,000, under the new sixteenth constitutional amendment.

Dec. 23. President Wilson, after a long congressional debate and in defiance of banking interests, signs Federal Reserve Act, first basic overhaul of U.S. banking system since 1863. Act provides for division of U.S. into 8 to 12 reserve districts and for a Federal Reserve Board of 7 members authorized to regulate financial reserves, currency, and credit. National banks are required to become members of the system,

JOHN D. ROCKEFELLER
Random Reminiscences, 1909
We must always remember that there is not enough money for the work of human uplift and that there never can be. How vitally important it is, therefore, that the expenditure should go as far as possible and be used with the greatest intelligence!

I have been frank to say that I believe in the spirit of combination and cooperation when properly and fairly conducted in the world of commercial affairs on the principle that it helps to reduce waste; and waste is a dissipation of power. I sincerely hope and thoroughly believe that this same principle will eventually prevail in the art of giving as it does in business. It is not merely the tendency of the times developed by more exacting conditions in industry, but it should make its most effective appeal to the hearts of the people who are striving to do the most good to the largest number. . . .

I believe no really constructive effort can be made in philanthropic work without such a well-defined and consecutive purpose.

My own conversion to the feeling that an organized plan was an absolute necessity came about in this way.

About the year 1890 I was still following the haphazard fashion of giving here and there as appeals presented themselves. I investigated as I could, and worked myself almost to a nervous breakdown in groping my way, without sufficient guide or chart, through this ever widening field of philanthropic endeavor. There was then forced upon me the necessity to organize and plan this department of our daily tasks on as distinct lines of progress as we did our business affairs.

Detroit Journal, 1914

The Ford Motor Company will give to its employees during the year of 1914 the sum of $10 million in addition to their wages.

This will not be a wage increase but a distribution of profits. It will be added, however, semimonthly to the pay envelopes of the men. In 1915, the distribution might be more or less than $10 million dependent on business conditions.

A minimum wage of $5 a day will be established by the addition of the profit distribution to wages. The present minimum wage in the great motorcar factory is $2.34. From next Monday to the end of the year, even the lowliest laborer and the man who merely sweeps the floors will get at least $5 a day.

Further, the eight-hour day is instituted. At present the Ford factory has two nine-hour shifts. It now will install three eight-hour shifts. . . .

Between 25,000 and 30,000 men will benefit greatly by the profit distribution. Fifteen thousand of them now work in the huge factory out Woodward Avenue. Four thousand more men are to be hired there during the present month and will come under the profit-sharing plan. The others who will share in the rich division number 7,000 to 8,000 and are scattered all over the world, working in Ford branches in Canada, Mexico, South America, Europe, Asia, Africa, and the Antipodes, even the Fiji Islands being included. . . .

The plan of profit distribution is one of social justice, the Ford Company declares. The extra money to the employees will not come out of the public, as price of cars will not be raised but will be lowered when possible. The money will be diverted from the stockholders to the workingmen.

but membership of state banks is made voluntary.

In Minnesota rate cases, the Supreme Court upholds Minnesota law that regulates railroad rates within the state, finding that such laws are valid if they do not conflict with U.S. interstate laws.

Béla Schick devises Schick test for susceptibility to diphtheria. Large-scale testing and immunization of susceptible children sharply cut incidence of disease, which has been a major cause of death, especially in children.

Thomas Hunt Morgan of Columbia University publishes *Heredity and Sex* following research on the fruit fly to test the Mendelian law of inheritance. In previous years, Morgan has discovered that characteristics of flies are sex linked and has described characteristics of linkages.

Willa Cather, having resigned as editor of *McClure's* magazine in the previous year to write, publishes her novel *O Pioneers!*

1913 - 1914

Ford Motor Company sets up first moving assembly line, based on meat-packers' system of conveyor belts. Ford pays workers unheard-of minimum wage of $5 per day and shocks industry by establishing a 40-hour workweek. Assembly-line system results in lowering of prices of Model T Fords; more than 15 million are produced by 1927.

1913 - 1915

Feb. 14, 1913. President Taft vetoes immigration bill that requires a literacy test; a similar bill has been vetoed by President Cleveland in 1896; in 1915 President Wilson vetoes another such bill on ground that the people of the U.S. have not voted to reverse a policy that has been in effect since the beginning of U.S. history.

Hollywood becomes the center of the motion-picture industry, replacing New York City. Serial films are beginning to be popular. Music-hall performer Charles Spencer Chaplin begins (December 1913) his movie career in producer Mack Sennett's one-reel slapstick Keystone Comedies. *The Birth of a Nation*, 12-reel film masterpiece directed by David Wark Griffith, and based on *The Clansman* by Thomas Dixon, is first exhibited (February 1915) in Los Angeles under the title of the book; its public opening is at New York's Liberty Theater on March 3 with new title suggested by Dixon. A story of the Reconstruction era that establishes all essentials of film narrative technique, it becomes one of the greatest moneymakers in film history. Its apparent racist tone and sympathetic treatment of the Ku Klux Klan are strongly protested by Northern liberals and Negro leaders.

1914

Feb. 13. American Society of Composers, Authors and Publishers (ASCAP) is organized in New York City at a meeting of more than 100 persons involved in the music field; composer Victor Herbert is largely responsible for calling meeting.

April 9. Party of U.S. sailors is arrested in Tampico, Mexico, when they go ashore for supplies; they are released with apologies by authorities, but U.S. commander, Admiral Henry T. Mayo, on his own initiative demands hoisting of American flag on Mexican soil and special 21-gun salute by Mexicans. **April 14.** Feeling that he must support Mayo, President Wilson orders U.S. fleet to Tampico Bay, five days later requesting authorization from Congress to

WILLIAM DEAN HOWELLS
Harper's Monthly, 1912
The moving-picture show is in a mechanical way not only the latest of "the fairy dreams of science," but it is the most novel of all the forms of dramatic entertainment. Yet if pantomime is one of the oldest forms of drama, the moving-picture show is of an almost Saturnian antiquity, for pantomime is what the moving picture is, whether representing a veritable incident or a fanciful invention. As even the frequenter of it may not realize, its scenes have been photographically studied from the action of performers more rather than less skilled than the average, who have given the camera a dress rehearsal of the story thrown upon the white curtain for his pleasure or improvement. . . .

Of course, the stuff itself is crude enough, oftenest; yet sometimes it is not crude, and the pantomime has its fine moments, when one quite loses oneself in the artistic pleasure of the drama. Where a veritable incident is portrayed, one has the delight of perceiving how dramatic life is, and how full of tragedy and comedy.

It is a convention of the moving picture that life is mostly full of farce, but that is an error which it shares with the whole modern stage, and it is probable that when the moving-picture show is asked to be serious, as we propose it shall be, it will purge itself of this error.

ARTHUR BRISBANE
Chicago Record-Herald, 1913
Motion pictures are just a passing fancy and aren't worth comment in this newspaper.

WOODROW WILSON
Message to Senate, 1914
I suppose that every thoughtful man in America has asked himself, during these last troubled weeks, what influence the European war may exert upon the United States; and I take the liberty of addressing a few words to you in order to point out that it is entirely within our own choice what its effects upon us will be, and to urge very earnestly upon you the sort of speech and conduct which will best safeguard the nation against distress and disaster.

The effect of the war upon the United States will depend upon what American citizens say and do. Every man who really loves America will act and speak in the true spirit of neutrality, which is the spirit of impartiality and fairness and friendliness to all concerned. The spirit of the nation in this critical matter will be determined largely by what individuals and society and those gathered in public meetings do and say, upon what newspapers and magazines contain, upon what ministers utter in their pulpits and men proclaim as their opinions on the street. . . .

I venture, therefore, my fellow countrymen, to speak a solemn word of warning to you against that deepest, most subtle, most essential breach of neutrality which may spring out of partisanship, out of passionately taking sides. The United States must be neutral in fact as well as in name during these days that are to try men's souls. We must be impartial in thought as well as in action, must put a curb upon our sentiments as well as upon every transaction that might be construed as a preference of one party to the struggle before another.

use force to uphold U.S. rights. **April 21.** Before authorization is granted on April 22, U.S. forces shell and occupy Veracruz to forestall delivery of arms by approaching German ship. Incident causes anti-U.S. feeling in Mexico that brings two countries close to war.

April 25. Argentina, Brazil, and Chile (the ABC powers) offer to arbitrate U.S.-Mexican dispute is quickly accepted by President Wilson and Huerta. **May 20-June 30.** Commission, meeting in Ontario, Canada, rejects indemnity claims of U.S. but proposes resignation of Huerta. **June 24.** Plan is rejected by Mexico but has effect of forcing Huerta's resignation on July 15. **Nov. 23.** U.S. occupation forces withdraw from Veracruz, and in next year new anti-Huerta government is recognized by the U.S.

May 8. Congress passes Smith-Lever Act; Department of Agriculture and land-grant colleges of the states are to work together to establish system of education for farmers. Funds for program are to be provided equally by federal and state governments.

Aug. 1. Germany declares war on Russia. **Aug. 3.** Germany declares war on France and a day later invades Belgium. **Aug. 4.** Great Britain declares war on Germany. *President Wilson issues proclamation of U.S. neutrality in Russo-German conflict. **Aug. 5.** U.S. neutrality proclamation is broadened to include Anglo-German war, and President Wilson offers his good offices to belligerents to negotiate peace. **Aug. 19.** Wilson asks Americans to be neutral "in thought as well as in action." Controversy between U.S. and warring powers over rights of neutral shipping, seizure of contraband materials· (as well as classification of contraband), and effective blockade continues into following year.

Aug. 15. Panama Canal is officially opened to traffic.

Sept. 26. Congress passes Federal Trade Commission Act as part of President Wilson's program; Act seeks to eliminate unfair business practices in interstate commerce. Federal Trade Commission, which replaces Bureau of Corporations, is authorized to investigate and control activities of persons and corporations. Banks, common carriers, and communications enterprises are excluded, since other federal laws apply to these.

Oct. 15. Congress passes Clayton Antitrust Act, which refines and extends powers of federal government under Sherman Antitrust Act of 1890. Labor and farm organizations are exempted from regulations applying to "combinations in restraint of trade," and the use of court injunctions in labor disputes is severely limited, though these provisions are later weakened by rulings of the courts.

This year marks end of high tide of European immigration to the U.S. in the decade 1905-1914. During these years nearly 10.5 million people enter the U.S. Three-fourths of immigrants come from Slavic and southern regions of Europe, and less than 15 percent from western and northern Europe.

Robert H. Goddard patents his liquid-fuel rocket, which uses liquid ether and oxygen, although he does not fire this type of rocket until 1926. Known as the father of U.S. rocketry, Goddard later develops theory of rockets fired in stages as method for reaching the moon. His 1919 report "A Method of Reaching Extreme Altitudes" is a classic to the present day.

Theodore W. Richards receives Nobel Prize for Chemistry for his work in discovering the exact atomic weights of a large

MARY ANTIN
The Promised Land, 1912
Education was free. That subject my father had written about repeatedly, as comprising his chief hope for us children, the essence of American opportunity, the treasure that no thief could touch, not even misfortune or poverty. It was the one thing that he was able to promise us when he sent for us; surer, safer than bread or shelter. On our second day I was thrilled with the realization of what this freedom of education meant. A little girl from across the alley came and offered to conduct us to school. My father was out, but we five between us had a few words of English by this time.

We knew the word "school." We understood. This child, who had never seen us till yesterday, who could not pronounce our names, who was not much better dressed than we, was able to offer us the freedom of the schools of Boston! No application made, no questions asked, no examinations, rulings, exclusions; no machinations, no fees. The doors stood open for every one of us. The smallest child could show us the way.

This incident impressed me more than anything I had heard in advance of the freedom of education in America. It was a concrete proof—almost the thing itself. One had to experience it to understand it.

LEONARD WOOD

Military Obligation of Citizenship, 1915
The United States has been drifting for
years. No real military preparations of
an adequate character have been made.
Military preparedness means the or-
ganization of all the resources of a na-
tion—men, material, and money—so
that the full power of the nation may be
promptly applied and continued at maxi-
mum strength for a considerable period
of time. War today, when initiated by a
country prepared for war, comes with
great suddenness, because all prepara-
tions have been made in advance;
plans have been worked out to the last
detail, organization completed, and
reserve supplies purchased and assem-
bled long in advance, and the whole
force of the mighty machine can be
applied in a very brief period of time at
any designated point. . . .

Mere numbers of men and unde-
veloped military resources are of little
value. It has been well said that in the
sudden onrush of modern war undevel-
oped military resources are of no more
use than an undeveloped gold mine in
Alaska would be in a panic on Wall
Street. The comparison is not over-
drawn. You must remember, all of you,
that this country has never yet engaged
in war with a first-class power prepared
for war. . . .

I would say, briefly, have an army
sufficient for the peace needs of the na-
tion, a good militia, an adequate navy,
and behind them the largest possible
number of men trained to be efficient
soldiers if needed; but in time of peace
following their ordinary civil occupa-
tions—ready to come when wanted. A
country so prepared will have the larg-
est possible measure of peace.

number of elements; he is first American honored in chemistry.

1914 - 1915

German occupation of neutral (and unprepared) Belgium leads to movement advocating preparedness in the U.S. Such organizations as the National Security League, the League to Enforce Peace, the American Defense Society, and the American Rights Committee are formed, backed by such men as Theodore Roosevelt, Henry Cabot Lodge, and William Howard Taft.

1915

Jan. 25. Alexander Graham Bell in New York speaks to Dr. Thomas A. Watson in San Francisco in first transcontinental telephone call. They are the same two men who made first telephone call in 1876 from telephones in adjoining rooms; Bell's words are the same: "Mr. Watson, come here. I want you." **July 27.** First direct wireless service between the U.S. and Japan is established. **Oct. 21.** First transatlantic radio-telephone communication is made when message is completed between Arlington, Virginia, and the Eiffel Tower in Paris.

Jan. 28. Congress combines Revenue Cutter Service and Lifesaving Service to form U.S. Coast Guard.

Feb. 4. Germany announces that enemy merchant ships in British waters will be sunk on sight and that no effort will be made to rescue passengers and personnel; neutral vessels may enter war zone at their own risk. **Feb. 10.** U.S. reply states that loss of American vessels or lives will be considered a clear "violation of neutrality" for which Germany will be held strictly responsible. Germany attempts to persuade U.S. to warn citizens against travel on ships of belligerent nations, but State Department does nothing.

February. Founding of Washington Square Players (later the Theater Guild) in New York advances modern drama. In following summer, Provincetown Players is organized in Massachusetts by group of New Yorkers who produce early plays of Eugene O'Neill.

May 1. Germany warns that Americans traveling on ships in British waters do so at their own risk. **May 7.** British steamer *Lusitania* is sunk by German submarine off Ireland. Almost 1,200 people are drowned, including 128 Americans. **May 13.** Secretary of State Bryan reluctantly signs note drafted by President Wilson protesting sinking and demanding reparations for lost U.S. lives and an end to unrestricted submarine warfare. **May 28.** Germany replies that sinking is justified, since *Lusitania* was armed; although it was not armed, *Lusitania* carried munitions cargo. **June 7.** Secretary Bryan refuses to sign second Wilson *Lusitania* note demanding German promises, because he fears it will lead to U.S. involvement in war, but President Wilson, after accepting Bryan's resignation (June 8), sends it on June 9. **July 21.** Third *Lusitania* note warns Germany that future acts that violate U.S. rights will be considered "deliberately unfriendly."

July 28. President Wilson sends U.S. Marines to Haiti when internal disorders and revolution endanger lives and interests of foreign residents. **Sept. 16.** Haitian-U.S. treaty is signed, making Haiti virtually a U.S. protectorate.

Aug. 10. First military training camp for civilians ("Plattsburgh idea," which later spreads) is opened at Plattsburgh, New York.

WILLIAM JENNINGS BRYAN
Protest to Germany, 1915
American citizens act within their indisputable rights in taking their ships and in traveling wherever their legitimate business calls them upon the high seas, and exercise those rights in what should be the well-justified confidence that their lives will not be endangered by acts done in clear violation of universally acknowledged international obligations, and certainly in the confidence that their own government will sustain them in the exercise of their rights. . . .

The government of the United States cannot believe that the commanders of the vessels which committed these acts of lawlessness did so except under a misapprehension of the orders issued by the Imperial German naval authorities. It takes it for granted that, at least within the practical possibilities of every such case, the commanders even of submarines were expected to do nothing that would involve the lives of noncombatants or the safety of neutral ships, even at the cost of failing of their object of capture or destruction. It confidently expects, therefore, that the Imperial German government will disavow the acts of which the government of the United States complains, that they will make reparation so far as reparation is possible for injuries which are without measure, and that they will take immediate steps to prevent the recurrence of anything so obviously subversive of the principles of warfare for which the Imperial German government have in the past so wisely and so firmly contended.

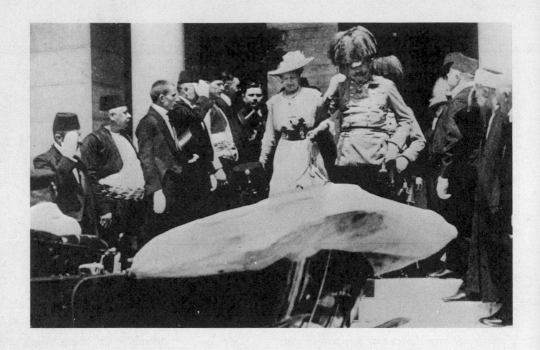

(Above) Archduke Ferdinand of Austria and his wife Sophie in Sarajevo, Bosnia, five minutes before they were killed; the assassination precipitated World War I; (below) English troops marching through London enroute to embarkation to the front

(Left) Woodrow Wilson, twenty-eighth President of the United States, photographed in 1912; (below) German forces advancing at Villiers Bretonneux move past a dead English soldier

FRANCIS G. WICKWARE
American Year Book, 1915
Failing to stop the export of munitions to the Allies by persuasion, legislation, or diplomacy, German effort turned as a last resort to direct action against the sources of supply and the means of transport to Europe. The last half of the year, in which this criminal campaign against American industries was chiefly operative, was ushered in by an attempt on the life of J. Pierpont Morgan by an insane instructor in German in Cornell University. . . .

So far as the destruction of munitions plants and the burning of ships and cargoes could be attributed with any shadow of probability to accident or natural causes, that allowance was made. But in the last quarter of the year the conviction has been forced home that disasters so numerous and widespread could be neither the result of coincidence nor the work of a few scattered fanatics, but must be the product of organized warfare on the munitions industry.

WOODROW WILSON
Speech in Philadelphia, 1915
There is such a thing as a man being too proud to fight.

HENRY FORD
Slogan of peace delegation, 1915
Out of the Trenches and Back to Their Homes by Christmas.

Aug. 15. *New York World* begins publication of papers acquired by U.S. Secret Service that expose plans for sabotage, espionage, and propaganda involving many German-Americans, Hamburg-American Steamship Line officials, and members of German Embassy staff, as well as consuls. German government officials are recalled.

Aug. 19. British steamer *Arabic* is sunk by Germans with loss of two American lives, although submarine commanders have been instructed not to sink liners without warning. **Sept. 1.** German ambassador to the U.S. promises that liners will not be sunk without warning and without safety for the lives of nonbelligerents, a policy that is continued throughout the year. **Oct. 5.** German apologies and assurances of an indemnity for loss of lives are considered a diplomatic triumph for the U.S.

September. President Wilson, against his judgment, consents to U.S. loans to warring nations; U.S. bankers immediately negotiate $500 million loan with Britain and France. During next year and a half, U.S. investors purchase about $2.3 billion in bonds of belligerent countries — about 100 times as many from the Allies as from Germany.

Dec. 4. Strongest effort of peace groups, which feel that U.S. interests are not affected by the war, is made by Henry Ford, when he sends peace ship *Oskar II* to Europe in unsuccessful attempt to achieve negotiated end to war.

Dec. 4. Georgia grants new charter to Ku Klux Klan, beginning revival that reaches height in early Twenties, not only in the South but in Northern and Midwestern states.

Dec. 7. President Wilson, his opposition to preparedness altered by *Lusitania* sinking, presents plan for defense measures to Congress; the next month he begins tour of country speaking in behalf of this program.

Eighty-acre tract in northwestern Colorado and northeastern Utah is set aside to establish Dinosaur National Monument; area has been found to be rich in fossils, including dinosaur remains. Monument is enlarged to about 200,000 acres in 1938.

Taxi industry begins when automobile owners discover that people will pay for a short automobile ride. Fare is a "jitney" (a nickel), and cars soon are called jitneys legally.

New York Society for the Suppression of Vice moves legally to suppress Margaret Sanger's *Family Limitation*, a work on birth control that court finds "contrary not only to the law of the state, but to the law of God."

Edgar Lee Masters publishes *Spoon River Anthology*, his collection of short poems that reveal dishonesty and brutality of lives of inhabitants of the small town. Van Wyck Brooks publishes *America's Coming-of-Age*.

EDGAR LEE MASTERS
Spoon River Anthology, 1915
ANNE RUTLEDGE
Out of me unworthy and unknown
The vibrations of deathless music;
"With malice toward none, with charity
for all."
Out of me the forgiveness of millions
toward millions,
And the beneficent face of a nation
Shining with justice and truth.
I am Anne Rutledge who sleep beneath
these weeds,
Beloved in life of Abraham Lincoln,
Wedded to him, not through union,
But through separation.
Bloom forever, O Republic,
From the dust of my bosom!

VAN WYCK BROOKS
America's Coming-of-Age, 1915
The very accent of the words "highbrow" and "lowbrow" implies an instinctive perception that this is a very unsatisfactory state of affairs. For both are used in a derogatory sense. The "highbrow" is the superior person whose virtue is admitted but felt to be an inept unpalatable virtue; while the "lowbrow" is a good fellow one readily takes to, but with a certain scorn for him and all his works. And what is true of them as personal types is true of what they stand for. They are equally undesirable, and they are incompatible; but they divide American life between them.

Marchers in a "Wake Up" parade, 1917

WILLIAM HOWARD TAFT
Our Chief Magistrate, 1916

The true view of the executive functions is, as I conceive it, that the President can exercise no power which cannot be fairly and reasonably traced to some specific grant of power or justly implied and included within such express grant as proper and necessary to its exercise. Such specific grant must be either in the federal Constitution or in an act of Congress passed in pursuance thereof. There is no undefined residuum of power which he can exercise because it seems to him to be in the public interest. . . . The grants of executive power are necessarily in general terms in order not to embarrass the executive within the field of action plainly marked for him, but his jurisdiction must be justified and vindicated by affirmative constitutional or statutory provision, or it does not exist.

There have not been wanting, however, eminent men in high public office holding a different view and who have insisted upon the necessity for an undefined residuum of executive power in the public interest.

1916

Feb. 10. Germany declares that all armed merchant ships of the Allies will be sunk without warning after March 1. **Feb. 17.** Fearful that the U.S. will be drawn into the war, Representative Jeff McLemore proposes resolution aimed at official limitation of travel by U.S. citizens on Allied ships. **Feb. 24.** President Wilson tells Senate committee that he refuses to approve "abridgment of the rights of American citizens." **Feb. 25.** Senator Thomas P. Gore introduces even stronger antitravel resolution in the Senate. **March 3 and 7.** At White House insistence, resolutions are tabled in both Senate and House.

Feb. 18. U.S. Senate ratifies Bryan-Chamorro Treaty between the U.S. and Nicaragua after delay of 18 months caused by efforts to insert Platt Amendment of 1901; Treaty grants the U.S. sole rights to canal route, as well as 99-year lease of two islands and the Gulf of Fonseca as naval bases. The U.S. and Nicaragua both ignore Central American Court of Justice decision against the Treaty.

Feb. 22. In House-Grey memorandum, the U.S. and Great Britain agree on peace negotiations and U.S. participation in war; Colonel Edward House, President Wilson's personal adviser and emissary, has agreed with British Foreign Secretary Sir Edward Grey that on indications from France and

Great Britain, the U.S. will call for negotiated peace. In case of refusal by Germany, memorandum states that the U.S. might well enter war against Germany.

March 7. Newton D. Baker is appointed secretary of war after forced resignation of Lindley M. Garrison in previous month. Garrison has resigned after President Wilson refused to accept his plan to transform state guard units into a continental army, because Wilson fears loss of congressional backing.

March 24. Following secret orders to sink any ship in the English Channel, German submarine torpedoes the unarmed French ship *Sussex*, injuring American passengers. **April 18.** President Wilson, resisting demands for a break with Germany, sends strong note stating that unless Germany discontinues such methods of warfare, the U.S. will break off relations. **May 4.** Germany agrees to ultimatum.

April 29. Socialist Labor Party meets and nominates Arthur E. Reimer of Massachusetts for President. **June 7.** Republican Party at Chicago meets and nominates Supreme Court Justice Charles Evans Hughes of New York for President and Charles W. Fairbanks of Indiana for Vice-President. On the same day, Progressive Party nominates Theodore Roosevelt for President, but Roosevelt refuses nomination and supports Hughes; this move eventually breaks up

JOHN M. WORK
The Gold Brick Twins, 1916
Did you ever buy a gold brick?

Now, don't get indignant. Maybe you have bought gold bricks a good many times without knowing it. If so, it will be well to get your eyes open so you will know a gold brick when you see it. . . .

Socialism is not hard to understand. Just consider a moment. It is easy to see, is it not, that the benefit of an industry goes to those who own and control it? Practically all the industries are now owned and controlled by capitalists. Therefore the capitalists get the benefit. Socialism will make these industries collectively owned and controlled. Owned by the public. Owned by all the people. Therefore, all the people will get the benefit. The billions of dollars which now go to the useless capitalists will then go to the useful masses.

That is clear, isn't it?

Then vote for it.

Vote the Socialist ticket.

The Republican and Democratic parties are each trying to put over a gold brick on you.

Are you going to fall for it?

Below and opposite page: German photographs of sinking Allied "armed" transports en route to England

CHARLES W. ELIOT
World's Work, 1916

There is endless talk in these days about "preparedness." Both political parties and both candidates for the presidency advocate a larger Navy and a larger Army. . . .

To undertake the maintenance of a great modern navy and a great modern army, always prepared for immediate action, involves the abandonment of a deeply rooted American policy—the ancient reliance for safety on the physical isolation of the country between two great oceans. . . .

Why should the American people make this formidable change in their national habits and their international policy? First, because the industrial and commercial interests of the nation have completely changed since the Civil War, and can no longer be preserved and promoted in isolation. . . .

The United States needs a navy modeled on the British Navy, and an army modeled on the Swiss Army; and in order to procure both it needs to adopt the principle of brief universal service in the Army or the Navy. The time lost by the young men from the productive industries and the service of the family will be a trifling loss compared with the gain from an increased feeling of devotion to the country in the hearts of multitudes and a quickened sense of responsibility for its welfare. The slight loss of individual liberty will be more than compensated by experience of a strict, cooperative discipline and by an enlarged sense of comradeship and community interest among the people.

Progressive Party, and its national committee supports Hughes, while a later conference at Indianapolis refuses to. **June 14.** Democrats meet at St. Louis and renominate President Wilson, with Vice-President Thomas R. Marshall as his running mate. **July 19.** Prohibition Party meets and nominates J. Frank Hanly of Indiana for President. Socialists hold no convention, but Allan L. Benson of New York is nominated for President in mail vote. Democrats campaign for Wilson with slogan "He Kept Us Out of War," which gains him many votes in states that have given women the suffrage. Hughes loses votes by failing to disclaim support of German-American and Irish-American groups that criticize President Wilson's foreign policy.

June. National Defense Act authorizes five-year expansion of Regular Army to about 220,000 men and establishes National Guard of more than 450,000 men and Officers Training Corps in colleges, as well as making some steps toward industrial mobilization. **Aug. 29.** Council of National Defense is established; six Cabinet members and expert civilian staff are to survey industrial, technical, social, and economic preparedness for possible war. Congress also passes "Big Navy" Act, largest naval appropriation up to this time, authorizing a construction program intended to make the U.S. fleet equal to any two others.

July 11. With automobile and truck production almost double that of the year before and 3,500,000 vehicles on the roads, President Wilson signs the Shackleford Good Roads Bill, which provides for $5 million in federal funds to be given to states that will supply equal amounts for road-building programs.

July 17. In Rural Credits Act, farmers and farmers' cooperatives are enabled to participate through Farm Loan Banks in financial reserve and credit facilities like those provided for banking and industry by Federal Reserve Act of 1913.

July 18. Britain denies commercial privileges to American companies and individuals whom it accuses of trading with the Central Powers. **Sept. 6 and 7.** President Wilson signs retaliatory Revenue Act and Shipping Board Act, both of which seek to control discrimination against blacklisted companies by foreign ships in U.S. ports. Acts are not put into effect, since Britain relaxes restrictions on listed companies.

Aug. 4. Denmark and the U.S. sign treaty providing for U.S. purchase of the Virgin Islands (Danish West Indies) for $25 million; the U.S. has feared that Germany wants the islands for a naval base. A governor is to be appointed by the President, and islanders are to have local home rule. U.S. citizenship is granted in 1927.

Aug. 11. Warehouse Act passed by Congress; law authorizes crop-financing loans to farmers, based on storage of certain major crops in authorized places, and begins a series of federal farm assistance programs that continues to the present day.

Aug. 29. Congress passes the Jones Act (Organic Act of the Philippine Islands), which restates the intention of the U.S. to establish Philippine independence when a stable government is formed and sets up machinery for self-government.

Sept. 2. Germany, after military successes, but fearing that the U.S. will enter the war, asks whether the U.S. will mediate. President Wilson declines to take any steps until after the fall elections. **Nov.** Wilson drafts peace mediation plan calling for a conference of nations involved, but the Allies will not consider any proposal.

Sept. 20. National Research Council is established to coordinate and stimulate war-

OSWALD GARRISON VILLARD
Annals of American Academy of Political and Social Science, 1916
The significance of preparedness, we are told, lies merely in the fact that Americans believe that our experiment in democracy is the most precious thing on earth; that it is of greater moment to all the world than any other experiment in human government, and that, for it, Americans are as ready and as willing to die as were their fathers in 1861 and their forefathers in the Revolution. . . .

And so we are counseled to take from our possible enemy the very things that have made him efficient and dangerous and become efficient and dangerous ourselves. Not that we shall ever make war — pace 1846 and 1898 — on anybody; merely that we shall follow in the footsteps of those who believe that the earth is ruled by fear, and that there is no other way to preserve peace than by being so armed that no one shall venture to attack us. And so we have gone about getting a "preparedness" which we are strenuously but falsely pretending will be ours when the legislation now before Congress passes, and so protect us at the close of the war in Europe, and even safeguard us should the present difficulties with Germany result in hostilities. . . .

Now, the real significance of this is that we have all at once, in the midst of a terrifying cataclysm, abjured our faith in many things American. We no longer believe, as for 140 years, in the moral power of an America unarmed and unafraid; we believe suddenly that the influence of the United States is to be measured only by the number of our soldiery and our dreadnoughts — our whole history to the contrary notwithstanding.

J. J. CARTY
Address to American Institute of Electrical Engineers, 1916

Because of the stupendous upheaval of the European war, with its startling agencies of destruction — the product of both science and the industries — and because of the deplorable unpreparedness of our own country to defend itself against attack, there has begun a great awakening of our people. . . . They are being aroused to the vital importance of the products of science in the national defense.

Arising out of this agitation comes a growing appreciation of the importance of industrial scientific research, not only as an aid to military defense but as an essential part of every industry in time of peace. . . .

Organizations and institutions of many kinds are engaged in pure scientific research and they should receive every encouragement, but the natural home of pure science and of pure scientific research is to be found in the university, from which it cannot pass. . . .

Instead of abdicating in their favor, may not our universities, stimulated by the wonderful achievements of these industrial laboratories, find a way to advance the conduct of their own pure scientific research, the grand responsibility for which rests upon them? This responsibility should now be felt more heavily than ever by our American universities, not only because the tragedy of the great war has caused the destruction of European institutions of learning but because even a worse thing has happened. So great have been the fatalities of the war that the universities of the Old World hardly dare to count their dead.

time scientific developments; Council is continued after war.

Nov. 7-9. For three days presidential election is in doubt until final California count shows the state to have gone Democratic by fewer than 4,000 votes. Final popular vote is Wilson, 9,130,000; Hughes, 8,538,000. Electoral vote is Wilson, 277; Hughes, 254. Democrats keep control of both House and Senate.

Nov. 29. U.S. establishes military government in the Dominican Republic to guarantee financial stability; U.S. forces and administrators have been in the Dominican Republic for a decade, but renewed disorders in public life and increase in the public debt through failure to collect revenues lead to full U.S. occupation, which is continued until 1924.

Dec. 12. Germany states to all neutrals that the Central Powers are willing to negotiate a peace. **Dec. 18.** President Wilson abandons his November plan and merely asks the Allies and the Central Powers to state their war aims. Germany makes no statement. **Dec. 30.** The Allies decline to consider Germany's December 12 offer.

Dec. 29. Congress passes Stock-Raising Homestead Act, which doubles maximum homestead allowance to 640 acres of grazing land; act excludes mineral and coal-mine land.

Michigan, Montana, Nebraska, South Dakota, and Utah establish state Prohibition. By this date, through political maneuvering and the influence of the clergy, the Anti-Saloon League has been largely responsible for dry laws in 24 states, with a combined population of about 32,500,000 people.

By this year U.S. commerce with the Allies is almost four times that of 1914, increased from about $800 million to about $3 billion; in the same period, trade with Germany and Austria-Hungary has dropped by about 70 percent.

John Dewey publishes *Democracy and Education*, in which he outlines ideas of late "progressive education" movement.

In this year there are 254,000 miles of railroads, more than at any time in U.S. history; since this peak, mileage has steadily declined to the present day.

1916 - 1917

March 15, 1916. General John J. Pershing begins pursuit of Francisco ("Pancho") Villa into Mexico. Villa's forces have shot 16 American engineers invited by President Carranza's government to run idle mines and have several times conducted raids into New Mexico and Texas, one of which has resulted in the death of 17 Americans. **Nov. 24.** Joint U.S.-Mexican commission signs agreement to withdraw U.S. troops from Mexico and set up U.S.-Mexican border guard system, but Carranza refuses to accept agreement. **Jan. 28, 1917.** Faced with prospect of war with Germany, President Wilson finally orders General Pershing to discontinue vain search for Villa and his guerrillas; search has resulted in frequent protests from Carranza government, although originally it had approved the move. Pershing withdraws on Febrary 5. After Carranza is reelected and new constitution adopted, the U.S. recognizes new Mexican government.

July 30, 1916. German saboteurs blow up munitions dump on Black Tom Island, New Jersey, causing $22 million damage. **Jan. 11, 1917.** Large foundry in New Jersey is blown up. Both acts of sabotage are later found by a claims commission to be the

JOHN DEWEY
Democracy and Education, 1916
Education is not infrequently defined as consisting in the acquisition of those habits that effect an adjustment of an individual and his environment. The definition expresses an essential phase of growth. But it is essential that adjustment be understood in its active sense of control of means for achieving ends. If we think of habit simply as a change wrought in the organism, ignoring the fact that this change consists in ability to effect subsequent changes in the environment, we shall be led to think of "adjustment" as a conformity to environment as wax conforms to the seal which impresses it. . . . Adaptation, in fine, is quite as much adaptation of the environment to our own activities as of our activities to the environment.

CHARLES A. BEARD
Summarizing the lessons of history
1. Whom the gods would destroy, they first make mad with power.
2. The mills of God grind slowly, but they grind exceeding small.
3. The bee fertilizes the flower it robs.
4. When it is dark enough, you can see the stars.

HENRY FORD
Newspaper interview, 1916
Records of old wars mean nothing to me. History is more or less bunk. It's tradition.

JAMES WELDON JOHNSON
Harper's, 1928

All of the Negro's folk-art creations have undergone a new evaluation. His sacred music—the spirituals; his secular music—ragtime, blues, jazz, and the work songs; his folklore—the Uncle Remus plantation tales; and his dances have received a new and higher appreciation. Indeed, I dare to say that it is now more or less generally acknowledged that the only things artistic that have sprung from American soil and out of American life, and been universally recognized as distinctively American products, are the folk creations of the Negro. . . .

But the story does not halt at this point. The Negro has done a great deal through his folk-art creations to change the national attitudes toward him; and now the efforts of the race have been reinforced and magnified by the individual Negro artist, the conscious artist. . . .

What, now, is the significance of this artistic activity on the part of the Negro and of its reactions on the American people? I think it is twofold. In the first place, the Negro is making some distinctive contributions to our common cultural store. I do not claim it is possible for these individual artists to produce anything comparable to the folk-art in distinctive values, but I do believe they are bringing something fresh and vital into American art, something from the store of their own racial genius —warmth, color, movement, rhythm, and abandon; depth and swiftness of emotion and the beauty of sensuousness. I believe American art will be richer because of these elements in fuller quantity.

work of Germany, and the U.S. is awarded $55 million damages in 1939, but Germany never pays.

1916 - 1927

Atomic research progresses during this period as the concentric-shell theory of atomic structure is developed by Gilbert N. Lewis and Irving Langmuir; William D. Harkins predicts that atomic nuclei contain neutrons, although they are not actually discovered until 1932; Arthur H. Compton demonstrates the corpuscular structure of radiation; and Clinton J. Davisson with Lester H. Germer discovers that electrons have wave characteristics similar to those of light.

1916 - 1928

Carl Sandburg publishes his *Chicago Poems* in 1916; collection is praised and criticized widely. In *Cornhuskers* (1918), *Smoke and Steel* (1920), and *Slabs of the Sunburnt West* (1922), Sandburg covers a wide range of subject matter. Edwin Arlington Robinson gains an immediate reputation when he publishes *The Man Against the Sky* in 1916. His Arthurian legend cycle, *Merlin* (1917), *Lancelot* (1920), and *Tristram* (1927), gains him further attention; between 1921 and 1928 he is awarded the Pulitzer Prize three times.

1916 - 1929

U.S. painters, influenced by French artists, such as Marcel Duchamp, who have moved to the U.S. at the beginning of World War I, experiment with Cubism and abstraction, although some change to a purist style. The work of many painters of the period, however, is an objective record of the local scene: examples are Eugene Speicher's portraits and Edward Hopper's and Reginald Marsh's city paintings. Most prominent painter of the period is John Marin, whose paintings — largely watercolor seascapes and landscapes — show influence of Expressionism, as well as Oriental style.

1917

Jan. 16. German Foreign Secretary Zimmermann sends coded note to German minister in Mexico instructing him to try to make an alliance between Germany and Mexico if the U.S. should enter the war in Europe. Mexico, supported by Germany, is to retake former Mexican areas of Arizona, Texas, and New Mexico; it is also to try to persuade Japan to transfer its allegiance to the Central Powers. **Feb. 24.** The British Navy, having intercepted and decoded Zimmermann's message, gives it to the U.S. ambassador to Great Britain, who sends it to the State Department. **March 1.** State Department authorizes newspaper publication.

Jan. 29. President Wilson vetoes literacy test for immigrants, stating that literacy is not a criterion of fitness to become a citizen. Act is passed over the veto; it requires all immigrants older than 16 to be able to read between 30 and 80 ordinary words in English or some other language.

Jan. 31. Germany informs the U.S. that unrestricted submarine warfare will be resumed on the following day; submarines will attack all Allied and neutral ships except for one U.S. ship per week that will be allowed to go to and from England under specific conditions.

January. The Allies send outline of peace demands to the U.S.; plan includes not only payment of indemnities and evacuation of occupied territories but also requires the reorganization of all Europe after the expulsion of the Ottoman Empire. **Jan. 22.** Pres-

ISRAEL ZANGWILL
The Melting Pot, 1908
America is God's crucible, the Great Melting Pot, where all the races of Europe are reforming. Here you stand, goodfolk, think I, when I see them at Ellis Island, here you stand in your fifty groups with your fifty languages and histories and your fifty blood-hatreds and rivalries. But you won't long be like that, brothers, for these are the fires of God you've come to—these are the fires of God. A fig for your feuds and vendettas. Germans and Frenchmen, Irishmen and Englishmen, Jews and Russians, into the crucible with you all. God is making the American.

JOHN J. MAHONEY
U.S. Bureau of Education Bulletin, 1920
Americanization—to give the term its most comprehensive meaning—is the business of making good American citizens, the business of acquainting everyone who inhabits American soil with both physical and spiritual America to the end that this acquaintance may result in a sturdy loyalty to American institutions and American ideals and the habit of living the life of the good American citizen. Really to Americanize America, we must reach the native-born and the immigrant, the adult and the child in school; and, incidentally, our task of Americanizing the newcomer will be rendered comparatively easy if we can but succeed first in Americanizing ourselves. . . .

Americanization does not imply that the immigrant must give up his cherished spiritual heritages. His language, his religion, his social customs he may retain and yet become a good American. Americanization is a giving, not a taking away. The wise worker in Americanization will adhere to the policy "Hands off."

WOODROW WILSON
Address to Senate, January 1917

The present war must . . . be ended; but we owe it to candor and to a just regard for the opinion of mankind to say that, so far as our participation in guarantees of future peace is concerned, it makes a great deal of difference in what way and upon what terms it is ended. The treaties and agreements which bring it to an end must embody terms which will create a peace that is worth guaranteeing and preserving, a peace that will win the approval of mankind, not merely a peace that will serve the several interests and immediate aims of the nations engaged. . . .

The question upon which the whole future peace and policy of the world depends is this: Is the present war a struggle for a just and secure peace, or only for a new balance of power? If it be only a struggle for a new balance of power, who will guarantee, who can guarantee the stable equilibrium of the new arrangement? Only a tranquil Europe can be a stable Europe. There must be, not a balance of power but a community of power; not organized rivalries but an organized, common peace. . . .

It must be a peace without victory. . . . Victory would mean peace forced upon the loser, a victor's terms imposed upon the vanquished. It would be accepted in humiliation, under duress, at an intolerable sacrifice, and would leave a sting, a resentment, a bitter memory upon which terms of peace would rest, not permanently but only as upon quicksand. Only a peace between equals can last.

ident Wilson, after receiving Allied terms, speaks to the Senate, outlining his own program and emphasizing the necessity of an international organization to establish and maintain lasting peace; he also stresses that peace achieved now cannot endure unless it is a "peace without victory."

Feb. 3. The U.S.S. *Housatonic* is sunk after warning by a German submarine. On the same day, President Wilson announces to Congress that the U.S. has broken off diplomatic relations with Germany. **Feb. 7.** The Senate approves Wilson's decision.

Feb. 23. Smith-Hughes Act provides federal funds for states to aid state vocational education programs; states are to match amounts contributed by the federal government.

March 1. House of Representatives, spurred by news of Germany's Mexican note, passes Armed Ship Bill at request of President Wilson, who feels that arming U.S. merchant ships will cut down submarine attacks and thus avert war; but a handful of senators, led by Robert M. La Follette, filibuster until close of Senate session, and Senate is unable to vote on bill. **March 8.** Secretary of State Robert Lansing advises Wilson that he can legally arm ships without approval of Congress. **March 12 and 13.** State Department announces that ships in war zones will be armed, and the Navy instructs armed ships to fire on submarines. By March 21, four more U.S. merchant ships have been sunk in European waters.

March 2. Organic Act for Puerto Rico makes Puerto Rico a U.S. territory and its inhabitants U.S. citizens and sets up a U.S.-style government with a governor appointed by the President.

March 15. Czar Nicholas II of Russia is forced to abdicate in revolution; temporary moderate government is formed. Errors of incompetent supreme command under Kerensky who becomes minister of war in May and prime minister in July result in continuing defeats of Russian Army by Germans, and by end of summer, Russians are crushed. **Nov. 6-7.** Lenin leads October (November, new-style date) Revolution, overthrowing Kerensky and setting up Communist organization. **Dec.** Russia signs armistice agreement with Germany and in March 1918 signs separate peace, the Treaty of Brest-Litovsk. Russia's withdrawal from the war frees great numbers of German troops for service on the Western Front.

March 21. Urged to declare war on Germany by all members of his Cabinet on the previous day, President Wilson calls for a special session of Congress. **April 2.** Wilson asks Congress for a declaration of war against Germany, saying that the war is for world peace, and that "the world must be made safe for democracy." **April 4.** War resolution passes the Senate. **April 6.** The House passes the resolution, and President Wilson signs it. (War against Austria-Hungary is not declared until December 7.)

March 31. General Munitions Board is established to coordinate war industry, but lack of organization and weak enforcement powers make it relatively ineffectual.

April 16. Congress charters Emergency Fleet Corporation, capitalized at $50 million, to purchase, lease, and build merchant vessels.

April. By this time, U.S. private loans to the Allies have reached more than $2 billion since first permitted by the U.S. government in September 1915. Most of these sums are spent in the U.S. for food and munitions, helping stimulate war prosperity boom.

April-December. The U.S. mobilizes for

WOODROW WILSON
Address to Congress, April 1917
With a profound sense of the solemn and even tragical character of the step I am taking and of the grave responsibilities which it involves, but in unhesitating obedience to what I deem my constitutional duty, I advise that the Congress declare the recent course of the Imperial German government to be in fact nothing less than war against the government and people of the United States; that it formally accept the status of belligerent which has thus been thrust upon it; and that it take immediate steps, not only to put the country in a more thorough state of defense but also to exert all its power and employ all its resources to bring the government of the German Empire to terms and end the war. . . .

The world must be made safe for democracy. Its peace must be planted upon the tested foundations of political liberty. We have no selfish ends to serve. We desire no conquest, no dominion. We seek no indemnities for ourselves, no material compensation for the sacrifices we shall freely make. We are but one of the champions of the rights of mankind. We shall be satisfied when those rights have been made as secure as the faith and the freedom of nations can make them.

Just because we fight without rancor and without selfish object, seeking nothing for ourselves but what we shall wish to share with all free peoples, we shall, I feel confident, conduct our operations as belligerents without passion and ourselves observe with proud punctilio the principles of right and of fair play we profess to be fighting for.

NORMAN THOMAS
Letter to the New Republic, 1917
As conscientious objectors we turn to your journal because, more powerfully than any other, it has expressed in subtle analyses our abiding faith in humane wisdom. . . .

The complexity and richness of life have permitted, and increasingly so, the more or less free play of all modes of energy. There are many men best adapted by training and temperament to the performance of physical acts of heroism; there are some men more naturally suited to the performance of intellectual deeds of courage, while yet some others shine in deeds of moral bravery. Why sanction the inhuman device of forcing all manner of men into the narrowly specific kind of devotion for which so many of them are hopelessly unfit? . . .

The one ineradicable fact which no amount of official intimidation can pulverize out of existence is that there is a type of man to whom (military) participation in war is tantamount to committing murder. He cannot, he will not commit murder. There is no human power on God's earth that can coerce him into committing (what he knows to be) the act of murder. You may call him sentimentalist, fool, slacker, mollycoddle, woman—anything "disreputable" you please. But there he is, a tremendous fact. Shall he be maltreated for his scruples? Or shall he be respected (as his deriders are) for his conscientiousness? We cannot leave so momentous an issue to chance or to the cold machinery of administration. Men of sensitive insight must help prepare a social setting within America sufficiently hospitable to all conscientious objectors.

war. **April 14.** Committee on Public Information is established; it is the most vigorous and comprehensive propaganda agency of the U.S. government up to this time. **April 24.** Liberty Loan Act is passed; sale of bonds to the public provides financing for U.S. war effort and war supplies for the Allies. Five loan drives from June 1917 to April 1919 raise more than $20 billion. **May 18.** Congress passes Selective Service Act; under this and later supplementary acts, 24,200,000 men aged 18 to 45 register, and almost 3 million are drafted; more than 2 million men serve overseas. Many individuals serve in Allied units, especially before U.S. war declaration. **June 15.** Espionage Act is passed; it provides severe penalties for activity that hinders the war effort or aids the enemy, and includes post-office censorship measures to control circulation of seditious publications. **July 28.** General Munitions Board is replaced by War Industries Board; under financier Bernard Baruch after March 4, 1918, the Board has effective power in economic aspects of war, aids technological step-up, rationing, standardization of industry, and purchasing. **Aug. 10.** In Lever Food and Fuel Control Act, Congress authorizes price-fixing and other measures to control domestic industry and domestic consumption; Act prohibits use of grains and sugars for the manufacture of liquor. Administrator Herbert Hoover, in charge of food, achieves self-control by consumers and much extra effort in war production. **Oct. 3.** Congress passes War Revenue Act, providing for increased corporation and personal income taxes, excess profits taxes, and luxury taxes. Act makes these taxes the major source of federal revenue during the war. **Oct. 6.** Trading with the Enemy Act is passed; the government is given control over all foreign trade, the power to censor foreign mail, and the right to seize and dispose of U.S. property of enemy citizens. **Dec. 26.** U.S. Railroad Administration is established; government takes over control of most available track on behalf of the war effort and, later, waterways and express systems. Control continues until March 1, 1920.

May 4. U.S. Navy begins convoy duty in the North Atlantic for troop transports and merchant ships; later the Navy pursues submarines and joins the British Navy in attempt to keep the German fleet out of the North Sea.

June 14. General Pershing arrives in Paris to direct U.S. overseas army. **June 26.** First U.S. troops reach France at Saint-Nazaire. **July 4.** Colonel Charles E. Stanton, for General Pershing, says, "Lafayette, we are here," at the tomb of the French general.

August. Two-way communication by radio telephone from an airplane to the ground is made. In same month two airborne planes communicate with each other over Langley Field, Virginia.

Nov. 2. U.S. and Japan sign Lansing-Ishii Agreement. Japan, having joined the Allies in 1914, has tried to increase her powers in China over protest of the U.S., which seeks to maintain its Open Door Policy. Japan has signed secret agreements that confirm its aims in China with many of the Allies and tries also to persuade the U.S. to agree. The resulting Lansing-Ishii Agreement grants Japan "special interests" in China owing to contiguity; Japan interprets this as meaning it has political rights despite its avowal to respect the Open Door Policy and territorial integrity of China.

In *Wilson* v. *New*, the U.S. Supreme Court upholds the Adamson Act, which sets eight-hour day for railroad workers in interstate commerce. Act has been passed hastily in 1916 to avoid national railroad strike. Court holds that although Act fixes wages, Congress has the power to set standards in emergencies.

CHARLES E. STANTON
Address at the tomb of Lafayette, Paris, 1917
America has joined forces with the Allied Powers, and what we have of blood and treasure are yours. Therefore it is that with loving pride we drape the colors in tribute of respect to this citizen of your great republic. And here and now in the presence of the illustrious dead we pledge our hearts and our honor in carrying this war to a successful issue. Lafayette, we are here.

GEORGE M. COHAN
Over There, 1917
Over there, over there,
Send the word, send the word over there,
That the Yanks are coming, the Yanks are coming,
The drums rum-tumming everywhere.
So prepare, say a prayer,
Send the word, send the word to beware,
We'll be over, we're coming over,
And we won't come back till it's over over there.

Suffragette Letter to the Commissioners of the District of Columbia, 1917
As political prisoners, we, the undersigned, refuse to work while in prison. We have taken this stand as a matter of principle after careful consideration, and from it we shall not recede.

This action is a necessary protest against an unjust sentence: In reminding President Wilson of his preelection promises toward woman suffrage, we were exercising the right of peaceful petition, guaranteed by the Constitution of the United States, which declares peaceful picketing is legal in the District of Columbia. That we are unjustly sentenced has been well recognized — when President Wilson pardoned the first group of suffragists who had been given sixty days in the workhouse, and again when Judge Mullowny suspended sentence for the last group of picketers. We wish to point out the inconsistency and injustice of our sentences — some of us have been given sixty days, a later group, thirty days, and another group given a suspended sentence for exactly the same action.

Conscious, therefore, of having acted in accordance with the highest standards of citizenship, we ask the commissioners of the District to grant us the rights due political prisoners.

Three experimental plants in Texas produce first helium in quantity; but production is not fast enough to be useful for military balloons in France, and most helium produced has not been shipped from the U.S. at end of the war.

First Pulitzer Prizes for biography and history are awarded; fund has been set up by bequest from publisher Joseph Pulitzer of *St. Louis Post-Dispatch* and *New York World.*

Hamlin Garland publishes *A Son of the Middle Border,* stimulating Middle Western regional literature; it is the first of 15 semihistorical works. Garland wins the Pulitzer Prize for biography in 1922 for *A Daughter of the Middle Border.*

Expatriate American poet T. S. Eliot publishes in England his first book of poems, *Prufrock and Other Observations,* which, with his *The Waste Land,* published in 1922, sets an entirely new style of poetry. During this same period, Eliot gains a firm reputation as a critic.

Julius Rosenwald Fund is chartered to serve "the well-being of mankind"; its funds ($30 million in 1929) aid Southern rural education, race relations, and the health and education of Negroes; it is dissolved in 1948.

1917 - 1918

Oct. 16, 1917. Four women who have been arrested for picketing for women's suffrage before the White House are given six-month prison sentences. Others are arrested in the following month. **Jan. 10, 1918.** House of Representatives adopts (Susan B. Anthony) resolution to submit a women's suffrage amendment to the states for ratification. **Sept. 30.** President Wilson, citing the increase of 1 million in women workers since 1915, urges women's suffrage on the

Senate as a "necessary war measure"; proposal is not carried, although New York State has passed a suffrage amendment in the previous year, and there are strong movements in other states.

1917 - 1920

Dec. 18. Eighteenth Amendment to the Constitution is adopted by Congress and sent to the states for ratification; by this time 29 states have enacted Prohibition laws of one kind or another. The Amendment is ratified by January 29, 1919, and goes into effect on January 29, 1920.

1918

Jan. 8. In speech to Congress, President Wilson outlines the Fourteen Points, which he feels must be basis of peace. **Feb. 11.** Wilson supplements the Fourteen Points by the "Four Principles." "Five Particulars" for peace with Austria-Hungary are announced on September 27.

March 21. Weakened by British naval blockade and deterioration of its submarine campaign, Germany tries to defeat the Allies on the Western Front before large numbers of troops can arrive from the U.S. **April 5.** By this date, Germany has split the British and French armies by penetrating British 5th Army lines and has reached within 10 miles of British war supply dump at Amiens. Only 2,200 U.S. troops have taken part in the action. **April 9.** As Amiens drive is slowed, Germans launch attack to the north near Armentières and achieve a significant advance but cannot take advantage of gap in British lines.

March. Daylight saving time goes into effect.

April 14. With President Wilson's consent, General Ferdinand Foch of France is made supreme commander of the Allied ar-

Away With Rum, c. 1924
*We're coming, we're coming, our brave
    little band;
On the right side of temp'rance we now
    take our stand.
We don't use tobacco because we all
    think,
That the people who do so are likely to
    drink!*

*Away, away with rum, by gum,
With rum by gum; with rum by gum.
Away, away with rum by gum;
The song of the Salvation Army.*

RING LARDNER
What of It?, 1925
For the benefit of the majority of my readers who probably have not heard of same, I may as well exclaim the meaning of the verb Prohibition. Well the dictionary says it is the forbidding by law of the manufacture or sale of intoxicating liquors as beverages. Well they was a lot of people in the U.S. that was in flavor of such a forbidding and finely congress passed a law making the country dry and the law went into effect about the 20 of Jan. 1920 and the night before it went into effect everybody had a big party on acct. of it being the last chance to get boiled. As these wds. is written the party is just beginning to get good.

Now they's a little group of wilful men that keeps hollering that the law ain't no good and please modify it so as to give us light wines and beer but the gen. attitude in regards to this plea as revealed by a personal souse to souse canvas is who and the hell would drink them.

GEORGES CLEMENCEAU
On hearing that President Wilson had Fourteen Points, 1918
Le bon Dieu n'avait que dix! (The good Lord had only ten!)

Columbia University Appeal to the Press, 1917

Do not use the phrases "The Allies," "the Entente Powers," etc. Say: "our Allies," "our gallant Allies," "the French," etc. Say "we" whenever possible. Write of "our Allies' advance upon St. Quentin," "our Allies take Le Fer." Speak of "the enemy" in alluding to Germany. Germany is our enemy. . . .

Keep the news of our battles, our advances, our triumphs, or our reverses on the front page. The troops in the trenches are our troops. They are ours in a double sense. Thousands of them are our fellow citizens; the rest are fighting in our cause.

RANDOLPH BOURNE

Untimely Papers, 1919

Every individual citizen who in peacetimes had no function to perform by which he could imagine himself an expression or living fragment of the State becomes an active amateur agent of the Government in reporting spies and disloyalists, in raising Government funds, or in propagating such measures as are considered necessary by officialdom. Minority opinion, which in times of peace, was only irritating and could not be dealt with by law unless it was conjoined with actual crime, becomes, with the outbreak of war, a case for outlawry. Criticism of the State, objections to war, lukewarm opinions concerning the necessity or the beauty of conscription are made subject to ferocious penalties, far exceeding in severity those affixed to actual pragmatic crimes. Public opinion, as expressed in the newspapers and the pulpits and the schools becomes one solid block.

mies. General Pershing puts U.S. troops at Foch's disposal, although he is determined to keep U.S. Army a separate unit.

April-June. The U.S. enacts further war mobilization measures. **April 5.** War Finance Corporation is formed to support war industries through loans and bond sales; authorized financing is set at $3,500,000,000. **April 8.** National War Labor Board is created to mediate labor disputes. **May 16.** Sedition Act is passed; aimed at Socialists and pacifists, Act broadens Espionage Act of 1917. It provides severe penalties for any verbal or other form of criticism of virtually any phase of the war effort. Under Sedition Act, Representative Victor L. Berger, Socialist elected in 1910, is indicted for pacifist activities and is refused seat in the House when elected again this year, and Socialist labor leader Eugene V. Debs is sentenced to 10 years in prison. **June 8.** War Labor Policies Board is formed; function is to prevent interference with the war effort by equalizing labor conditions.

May 28. American troops, in first U.S. offensive, capture Cantigny.

May 30. Having beaten back the Allies from Reims to Noyon and having taken Soissons, the Germans reach the Marne River on a 40-mile front, about 50 miles from Paris. **June 3-4.** A full division of U.S. troops with parts of other divisions, added to the Allied forces at Château-Thierry, help French stop the German drive at that point.

June 3. In *Hammer* v. *Dagenhart*, Supreme Court finds federal law that forbids interstate shipping of products made by child labor unconstitutional, holding that law violates rights of the states; Justice Holmes dissents, asserting that Congress may control interstate commerce in any way. Similar decision in 1922 finds 1919 Child Labor Act invalid.

June 6. In first large-scale participation of American troops, about 27,500 infantry and marines attack German lines and recapture Vaux, Bouresches, and Belleau Wood by July 1.

June 9. Germans, having advanced far enough to threaten Paris, launch a great attack along a front between Noyon and Montdidier. French troops and 27,000 Americans, briefly forced back for about six miles, by June 15 are able to hold the Germans at that point.

July 15. Germans attack from both east and west of Reims, making almost no progress to the east but crossing the Marne River on the west. Once across the river, however, they are held by Allied troops, including 85,000 Americans. By this month, more than 1 million U.S. troops have arrived in France, and Marshal Foch is able to take the offensive for the first time. **July 18.** French units with 270,000 U.S. troops attack eastward between the Aisne and Marne rivers to eliminate the German pocket that threatens Paris. **Aug. 6.** By this date the pocket has been crushed, and the Allies have swung northeastward to a line between Soissons and Reims.

Aug. 8. British troops, supported by about 54,000 Americans, strike eastward along the Somme River. Offensive in this area continues for three months.

Aug. 10. General Pershing, who, since first put in command of U.S. forces, has insisted on a separate U.S. Army, organizes the 1st U.S. Army under his own command, although he remains commander of the American Expeditionary Force. Marshal Foch, convinced of the competence of American troops, agrees.

Aug. 17. French troops, accompanied by about 85,000 Americans, attack northward along Soissons-Reims line toward the Bel-

SGT. DANIEL DALY, U.S.M.C.
Near Belleau Wood, 1918
Come on, you sons of bitches! Do you want to live forever?

GEN. JOHN J. PERSHING
Attributed, 1918
Hell, Heaven or Hoboken by Christmas.

Saying of American soldiers, 1917-18
The first hundred years are the hardest.

Hinky Dinky Parlay-Voo, c. 1918
Mademoiselle from Armentiers,
  parlay-voo,
Mademoiselle from Armentiers,
  parlay-voo,
Mademoiselle from Armentiers,
She hasn't been kissed in forty years.
  Hinky dinky parlay-voo.
      . . .
Officers came across the Rhine,
  parlay-voo,
Officers came across the Rhine,
  parlay-voo,
Officers came across the Rhine
To kiss all the girls and drink the wine.
  Hinky dinky parlay-voo.
      . . .
You may forget the gas and shells,
  parlay-voo,
You may forget the gas and shells,
  parlay-voo,
You may forget the gas and shells—
You'll never forget the mad'moiselles.
  Hinky dinky parlay-voo.

LENIN
Letter to American workers, 1918
The history of modern, civilized America opened with one of those great, really liberating, really revolutionary wars of which there have been so few compared to the vast numbers of wars of conquest which, like the present imperialist war, were caused by squabbles among kings, landowners, or capitalists over the division of usurped lands or ill-gotten gains. . . .

About 150 years have passed since then. Bourgeois civilization has borne all its luxurious fruits. America has taken first place among the free and educated nations in level of development of the productive forces of collective human endeavor, in the utilization of machinery and of all the wonders of modern engineering. . . .

The American people, who set the world an example in waging a revolutionary war against feudal slavery, now find themselves in the latest, capitalist stage of wage slavery to a handful of multimillionaires, and find themselves playing the role of hired thugs. . . .

The American people have a revolutionary tradition which has been adopted by the best representatives of the American proletariat, who have repeatedly expressed their complete solidarity with us Bolsheviks. . . .

I am not surprised that Wilson, the head of the American multimillionaires and servant of the capitalist sharks, has thrown Debs into prison. Let the bourgeoisie be brutal to the true internationalists, to the true representatives of the revolutionary proletariat! The more fierce and brutal they are, the nearer the day of the victorious proletarian revolution.

gian border, which they near by November 11. U.S. troops, however, have been withdrawn by mid-September to take part in planned Meuse-Argonne offensive to the east.

Aug. 21. British, aided by 108,000 American troops, attack in Belgium from Ypres; battle continues until the Armistice.

Sept. 12. In preparation for future attack on German supply lines (Meuse-Argonne offensive), more than a half million American troops, aided by some Allied air units, all under General Pershing, attack bulge in German lines at Saint-Mihiel; within a day, the bulge has been cut off. At the cost of 7,000 U.S. casualties, 16,000 German prisoners and more than 400 pieces of artillery are taken.

Sept. 26. Huge pincer offensive, planned as a joint effort by Marshal Foch with Allied leaders, begins with U.S. troops concentrated between the Meuse River and the Argonne Forest. U.S. objective is main supply railroad and iron mines being used by Germans. Germans are gradually worn down until end of October, when they suddenly give ground and retreat eastward and northward until November 11, when the Armistice is declared. Prolonged battle costs about 120,000 American casualties.

Sept. 29. General Erich von Ludendorff, aware that the German Army is near collapse and alarmed by the surrender of Bulgaria, urges the German government to request an armistice. **Oct. 3.** Prince Maximilian of Baden becomes chancellor of Germany and immediately sends peace note to President Wilson, saying that Germany will accept Wilson's Fourteen Points as a basis for peace. **Oct. 30.** Austria also requests an armistice.

Oct. 16. Congress passes wartime measure that prohibits entry into the country of aliens who advocate overthrowing the government by force. In 1920 an additional act is passed that allows deportation of alien anarchists and enemies of the U.S.

Oct. 24-Nov. 4. Italians, with a small contingent of U.S. troops, achieve final defeat of the Austrian Army in a ten-day offensive at Vittorio Veneto.

Oct. 25. President Wilson appeals to the people to retain a Democratic Congress as a demonstration of confidence in his policies. Appeal is widely disapproved, since Wilson had declared a moratorium on politics during the war; 26 Democratic seats are lost in the House and 6 in the Senate, resulting in Republican majorities in House and Senate.

Nov. 5. President Wilson, having spent almost a month in armistice negotiations, finally transmits Allied peace terms to Germany. Delay has been caused by refusal of the Allies to accept Wilson's Fourteen Points and by Wilson's reluctance to deal with the German government, which he feels does not represent the German people. Suggestion that the U.S. will negotiate separately with Germany finally has persuaded the Allies to accept the Fourteen Points but with some reservations.

Nov. 6. German representatives start for France to negotiate an armistice. Three days earlier, revolution has broken out and is sweeping the country. The German fleet has mutinied when ordered on a hopeless mission against the British Navy. Turkey and Austria have surrendered. The Allied offensive continues on all fronts. **Nov. 9.** Kaiser William abdicates, and Prince Maximilian resigns in favor of Socialist Friedrich Ebert; Germany becomes a republic.

Nov. 11. With home and military situations as they are, Germany has no choice

WOODROW WILSON
Appeal to voters, 1918
The congressional elections are at hand. They occur in the most critical period our country has ever faced or is likely to face in our time. If you have approved of my leadership and wish me to continue to be your unembarrassed spokesman in affairs at home and abroad, I earnestly beg that you will express yourselves unmistakably to that effect by returning a Democratic majority to both the Senate and the House of Representatives.

I am your servant and will accept your judgment without cavil. But my power to administer the great trust assigned me by the Constitution would be seriously impaired should your judgment be adverse, and I must frankly tell you so because so many critical issues depend upon your verdict. No scruple or taste must in grim times like these be allowed to stand in the way of speaking the plain truth. . . .

I need not tell you, my fellow countrymen, that I am asking your support, not for my own sake or for the sake of a political party but for the sake of the nation itself in order that its inward unity of purpose may be evident to all the world. In ordinary times I would not feel at liberty to make such an appeal to you. In ordinary times divided counsels can be endured without permanent hurt to the country. But these are not ordinary times.

If in these critical days it is your wish to sustain me with undivided minds, I beg that you will say so in the way which it will not be possible to misunderstand, either here at home or among our associates on the other side of the sea. I submit my difficulties and my hopes to you.

H. L. MENCKEN
Book of Prefaces, 1917
Save where Continental influences have measurably corrupted the Puritan idea — e.g., in such cities as New York, San Francisco, and New Orleans — the prevailing American view of the world and its mysteries is still a moral one, and no other human concern gets half the attention that is endlessly lavished upon the problem of conduct, particularly of the other fellow. . . .

Naturally enough, this moral obsession has given a strong color to American literature. In truth, it has colored it so brilliantly that American literature is set off sharply from all other literatures. In none other will you find so wholesale and ecstatic a sacrifice of aesthetic ideas, of all the fine gusto of passion and beauty, to notions of what is meet, proper, and nice. From the books of grisly sermons that were the first American contribution to letters down to that amazing literature of "inspiration" which now flowers so prodigiously, with two literary ex-presidents among its chief virtuosi, one observes no relaxation of the moral pressure. . . .

The literature of the nation, even the literature of the enlightened minority, has been under harsh Puritan restraints from the beginning, and despite a few stealthy efforts at revolt — usually quite without artistic value or even common honesty, as in the case of the cheap fiction magazines and that of smutty plays on Broadway, and always very short-lived — it shows not the slightest sign of emancipating itself today. The American, try as he will, can never imagine any work of the imagination as wholly devoid of moral content. It must either tend toward the promotion of virtue, or be suspect and abominable.

but to accept drastic terms of Armistice, which is signed at 5 A.M. in Marshal Foch's railroad car in the Forest of Compiègne. Hostilities cease at 11 A.M. In the U.S., where the news is received at 3 A.M. New York time, the wildest demonstrations in U.S. history take place.

Nov. 18. President Wilson announces that he will attend the peace conference, incurring wide criticism in the U.S., where he is called "egotistic." Republican criticism is strongest when it is announced that Wilson's peace commission lacks a member of the Senate and contains only one Republican.

Estimated casualties of World War I: Total Allies: of 42,189,000 who have served, 5,152,000 dead, 12,831,000 wounded, 4,121,000 prisoners or missing. Central Powers: of 65,039,000 who have served, 8,538,000 dead, 21,219,000 wounded, 7,751,000 prisoners or missing. U.S.: of 4,355,000 who have served, 1·26,000 dead (about 50,000 in battle and the rest of disease, especially influenza, which has devastated U.S. military camps), 234,000 wounded, 4,500 prisoners or missing.

The Education of Henry Adams, first published privately in 1907, is published after the author's death and becomes a best seller. Booth Tarkington publishes his study of three generations, *The Magnificent Ambersons.* Both receive the Pulitzer Prize in the following year. Willa Cather publishes her novel of prairie life, *My Antonia.* First installments of *Ulysses*, by James Joyce, appear in the *Little Review* and are burned by the U.S. Post Office Department as obscene. Book is banned from the U.S. until 1933.

The United Lutheran Church in America is formed from 45 divided synods when members reach an agreement on a common doctrine.

1918 - 1919

In several cases the Supreme Court upholds war power of the U.S. government. In *Arver* v. *U.S.*, the Court finds that conscription is authorized by the Constitution in Article I ("to declare war . . . to raise and support armies"); a temporary Prohibition measure, passed to conserve grain and sugar, is called a valid exercise of government wartime powers; and in *Northern Pacific Railway* v. *North Dakota*, the Court finds that the seizure and operation of railroads comes within granted war powers.

September. Influenza epidemic, traveling westward from Europe, begins in eastern U.S. and spreads to 46 states. Before it subsides in 1919, it kills about 500,000 people, disrupts services, shuts down war plants, suspends the draft in some places, and causes panic throughout the U.S. Throughout the world at least 20,000,000 people die, and one billion are sick.

1918 - 1927

May 15, 1918. New York City to Washington, D.C., flight is beginning of first scheduled airmail service in the U.S. Stamps cost 24 cents (reduced to 6 cents by November). **Sept. 10.** In first one-day Chicago to New York City airmail flight, overall time for delivery of mail is less than 13 hours. Daily service is begun in following year. **July-Aug. 1920.** First airmail flight between New York City and San Francisco. Air transport grows rapidly as private bidders are given airmail contracts. Regular night flights begin in 1924. Aerial navigation is aided by installation of radio beacons in 1925, and Air Commerce Act is passed in 1926; Act provides for government backing of civil airlines and building of airports. **Sept. 1, 1927.** Airlines and American Railway Express Agency cooperate to establish air express.

ORVILLE WRIGHT
Interview, 1917
When my brother and I built and flew the first man-carrying flying machine, we thought that we were introducing into the world an invention which would make further wars practically impossible. That we were not alone in this thought is evidenced by the fact that the French Peace Society presented us with medals on account of our invention. We thought governments would realize the impossibility of winning by surprise attacks, and that no country would enter into war with another when it knew it would have to win by simply wearing out the enemy.

Photograph of the instant of take-off on the first flight of the Wright brothers' plane on the beach at Kitty Hawk, North Carolina, December 17, 1903

WILBUR WRIGHT
Interview, 1906
I do not believe [the airplane] will supplant surface transportation. I believe it will always be limited to special purposes. It will be a factor in war. It may have a future as a carrier of mail.

(Above) Outbreak of hostilities on the streets of Moscow following
Leninist siege of the Duma, 1917; (below) peace parade in New York
City, 1914

(Above) British officer moving his men
out of the sap with shells bursting
around them; (right) bomb damage in Paris

New Republic, 1919

In our opinion the Treaty of Versailles subjects all liberalism, and particularly that kind of liberalism which breathes the Christian spirit, to a decisive test. . . .

If a war which was supposed to put an end to war culminates without strenuous protest by humane men and women in a treaty of peace which renders peace impossible, the liberalism which preached this meaning for the war will have committed suicide. That such a protest on the part of national liberals may not have much immediate success in defeating the ratification of the Treaty is not essential. The Treaty of Versailles, no matter under what kind of compulsion it is ratified by the nations, is impossible of execution and will defeat itself.

WILLIAM E. BORAH
Speech in Senate, 1919

We have joined in alliance with all the European nations which have thus far joined the League and all nations which may be admitted to the League. We are sitting there dabbling in their affairs and intermeddling in their concerns. In other words, Mr. President—and this comes to the question which is fundamental with me—we have forfeited and surrendered, once and for all, the great policy of "no entangling alliances" upon which the strength of this republic has been founded for 150 years. . . .

Sir, we are told that this treaty means peace. Even so, I would not pay the price. Would you purchase peace at the cost of any part of our independence?

1919

Jan. 18. Paris peace conference opens without Germany or its associates. All major matters are discussed privately by President Wilson of the U.S., Prime Minister David Lloyd George of Great Britain, Premier Georges Clemenceau of France, and Premier Vittorio Orlando of Italy.

Jan. 25. Peace conference agrees, after urging by President Wilson, that a League of Nations must be an integral part of the peace treaty. **Feb. 3.** Commission, headed by Wilson, starts writing draft of League of Nations Covenant. **Feb. 14.** Draft is submitted to conference, and on the following day, Wilson leaves for the U.S.

Feb. 26. Opposition to the League already having grown in the U.S., President Wilson finds that Senate and House committees on foreign relations and many senators are unwilling to consider peace treaty that contains Covenant. They insist on first considering treaty alone. Wilson resists this proposal.

March 14. President Wilson arrives in Paris for negotiations on peace treaty. Although the Allies generally have agreed to Wilson's Fourteen Points, every Ally has an exception to propose in its own favor. Wilson's peace of conciliation becomes impossible in view of concessions he must make to every nation's territorial and economic demands. In addition to compromises on the peace treaty, Wilson, on the advice of senators in favor of the League, proposes amendments to the League Covenant that specifically exempt the U.S. from some of its measures; pro-League senators hope that these amendments will gain support of anti-League forces.

March 15-17. American Legion is formed in Paris when delegates from 1,000 units of the American Expeditionary Force meet.

April 19. Theater Guild, New York City, opens first play of many successes; Guild has been organized to improve and encourage American drama.

May 7. The completed peace treaty with League Covenant attached is submitted to Germany. **June 28.** Germany signs treaty. **July 10.** President Wilson presents treaty to the Senate for ratification. Senate opinion is divided three ways: Democrats for immediate ratification; moderates who want the U.S. to join the League of Nations with reservations to protect U.S. interests; and anti-League senators who refuse to accept the Covenant under any circumstances; 6 of the latter are on the 17-man Senate Foreign Relations Committee. Senate hearings and vigorous public debate continue until September 10, when Senate Committee submits 49 changes.

August. Communist Labor Party of America (present-day American Communist Party) is formed in Chicago after split from Socialist Party; Communists adopt platform and symbol of the Third International.

Sept. 3. President Wilson starts tour of country, convinced that if he takes his case for the League and the treaty to the people, popular pressure will force its ratification. He is opposed by a large national propaganda campaign and by two senators who make their own tour at the same time. Wilson makes about 37 speeches, traveling to 29 Middle Western and Western cities by September 25. **Oct. 2.** Having become ill in Colorado and returning to Washington, Wilson has a stroke, which eliminates him from treaty discussions.

Sept. 9. About three-quarters of 1,500-man Boston police force goes on strike.

WOODROW WILSON
Speech in Omaha, 1919
I wish I could do what is impossible in a great company like this. I wish I could read that Covenant to you, because I do not believe, if you have not read it yourself and have only listened to certain speeches that I have read, that you know anything that is in it. Why, my fellow citizens, the heart of the Covenant is that there shall be no war. To listen to some of the speeches that you may have listened to or read, you would think that the heart of it was that it was an arrangement for war. On the contrary, this is the heart of that treaty. . . .

This is the Covenant of the League of Nations that you hear objected to, the only possible guarantee against war. I would consider myself recreant to every mother and father, every wife and sweetheart in this country, if I consented to the ending of this war without a guarantee that there would be no other. You say, "Is it an absolute guarantee?" No; there is no absolute guarantee against human passion; but even if it were only 10 percent of a guarantee, would not you rather have 10 percent guarantee against war than none? If it only creates a presumption that there will not be war, would you not rather have that presumption than live under the certainty that there will be war? For, I tell you, my fellow citizens, I can predict with absolute certainty that within another generation there will be another world war if the nations of the world do not concert the method by which to prevent it.

CALVIN COOLIDGE
Message to Samuel Gompers, 1919
There is no right to strike against the public peace by anybody, anywhere, any time.

WOODROW WILSON
Letter to Senator Hitchcock, 1919
My Dear Senator: You were good enough to bring me word that the Democratic senators supporting the treaty expected to hold a conference before the final vote on the Lodge resolution of ratification and that they would be glad to receive a word of counsel from me.

I should hesitate to offer it in any detail, but I assume that the senators only desire my judgment upon the all-important question of the final vote on the resolution containing the many reservations by Senator Lodge. On that I cannot hesitate, for, in my opinion, the resolution in that form does not provide for ratification but, rather, for the nullification of the treaty. I sincerely hope that the friends and supporters of the treaty will vote against the Lodge resolution of ratification.

I understand that the door will probably then be open for a genuine resolution of ratification.

I trust that all true friends of the treaty will refuse to support the Lodge resolution.

Widespread looting occurs. Governor Calvin Coolidge calls out entire State Guard and breaks strike, saying that no one has a right to strike against the public safety.

Sept. 22. U.S. Steel Corporation workers strike when management refuses to discuss issues, mainly union status questions. Strike lasts for almost four months. Steel and coal industry unions have not been so successful as others in membership gains and in dealing with employers since the war.

Oct. 28. Volstead Act is passed over President Wilson's veto; Act provides enforcement power for Prohibition amendment. Almost immediately, after distillers and liquor distributors go out of business, criminal elements (bootleggers) take over, their operations growing steadily through the 1920s.

Nov. 6. Senator Lodge presents a resolution of ratification of the peace treaty after the 49 changes of the anti-League senators have been defeated; resolution contains only 14 reservations. **Nov. 18.** President Wilson, unwilling to make even this more moderate compromise, writes to pro-League Democrats, urging them to vote down the new resolution, since it provides "for the nullification of the treaty."

Nov. 19. Wilson supporters accede to his request and, with anti-League Republicans, block ratification, since their votes make a two-thirds majority impossible. Although a compromise is worked out in the following weeks, the final ratifying resolution still contains reservations that Wilson will not accept, and he again asks his followers to vote against it. The final vote once more fails of a two-thirds majority, and the U.S. never joins the League of Nations.

Financial cost of World War I to the U.S., including loans to the Allies, is about

$41,500,000,000, more than half of which has been raised by borrowing; 1917 public debt of $1,300,000,000 has risen to $26 billion by 1919, a per capita debt of $246.

In *Schenck* v. *United States*, the Supreme Court unanimously upholds the Espionage Act, finding that free speech does not include the right to encourage resistance to conscription and that it must always be under control, especially in wartime.

Sherwood Anderson publishes *Winesburg, Ohio*, short stories of "average" people. James Branch Cabell publishes his version of the Faust story, *Jurgen: a Comedy of Justice*. Henry L. Mencken publishes the first edition of *The American Language*, which appears in various editions and with various supplements until 1948.

1919 - 1920

Dec. 22, 1919. About 250 alien "anarchists," Communists, and labor agitators are deported and sail for Russia. Fear generated by wartime hysteria and by Russian agitation against Western nations and in behalf of the Bolshevik Revolution in Russia leads to "Red scare." **Jan. 2, 1920.** Federal agents in nationwide raids arrest 2,700 persons; mass arrests, police espionage, and raids continue into May.

1920

Feb. 13. Secretary of State Robert Lansing leaves office; President Wilson has accused him of conducting unauthorized Cabinet meetings during Wilson's incapacity and has requested his resignation.

Feb. 28. Congress passes Esch-Cummins (Transportation) Act, which releases the railroads from government wartime control on March 1, greatly extends the powers of the Interstate Commerce Commission as

OLIVER WENDELL HOLMES, JR.
Schenck v. U.S., 1919
The most stringent protection of free speech would not protect a man in falsely shouting fire in a theater and causing a panic.

ROBERT BENCHLEY
The Making of a Red, 1919
Shortly before the United States entered the war, Peters made a speech at a meeting of the Civic League in his home town. His subject was: "Interurban Highways: Their Development in the Past and Their Possibilities for the Future." So far, 100 percent American. But, in the course of his talk, he happened to mention the fact that war, as an institution, has almost always had an injurious effect on public improvements of all kinds. In fact (and note this well — the government's sleuth in the audience did) he said that, all other things being equal, if he were given his choice of war or peace in the abstract, he would choose peace as a condition under which to live. Then he went on to discuss the comparative values of macadam and wood blocks for paving.

In the audience was a civilian representative of the Military Intelligence Service. He had a premonition that some sort of attempt was going to be made at this meeting of the Civic League to discredit the war and America's imminent participation therein. And he was not disappointed (no Military Intelligence sleuth ever is), for in the remark of Peters, derogatory to war as an institution, his sharp ear detected the accent of the Wilhelmstrasse.

H. L. MENCKEN
Prejudices: Third Series, 1922
In more than one direction, indeed, I probably go a great deal further than even the Young Intellectuals. It is, for example, one of my firmest and most sacred beliefs, reached after an inquiry extending over a score of years and supported by incessant prayer and meditation, that the government of the United States, in both its legislative arm and its executive arm, is ignorant, incompetent, corrupt, and disgusting—and from this judgment I except no more than twenty living lawmakers and no more than twenty executioners of their laws. It is a belief no less piously cherished that the administration of justice in the Republic is stupid, dishonest, and against all reason and equity—and from this judgment I except no more than thirty judges, including two upon the bench of the Supreme Court of the United States.

It is another that the foreign policy of the United States—its habitual manner of dealing with other nations, whether friend or foe—is hypocritical, disingenuous, knavish, and dishonorable—and from this judgment I consent to no exceptions whatever, either recent or long past. And it is my fourth (and, to avoid too depressing a bill, final) conviction that the American people, taking one with another, constitute the most timorous, sniveling, poltroonish, ignominious mob of serfs and goose-steppers ever gathered under one flag in Christendom since the end of the Middle Ages, and that they grow more timorous, more sniveling, more poltroonish, more ignominious every day.

concerns the railroads, and establishes a Railroad Labor Board to handle labor disputes.

March 19. Although Versailles Treaty ratification and Covenant of the League of Nations are finally defeated by the Senate for second time on this date, the U.S. takes part in work of many League technical commissions until the League is terminated in 1946 in favor of the United Nations.

May 5. Socialist Labor Party meets and nominates W. W. Cox of Missouri for President. **May 8.** Socialist Party meets and nominates Eugene V. Debs of Indiana for President, although he is serving a 10-year sentence for sedition. **June 8.** Republicans meet at Chicago and nominate Warren G. Harding of Ohio for President; nomination is engineered by party bosses, who are unable to engineer vice-presidential nomination; this goes on first ballot to Calvin Coolidge, governor of Massachusetts. **June 28.** Democrats meet at San Francisco and nominate Governor James M. Cox of Ohio for President on the forty-fourth ballot; Assistant Secretary of the Navy Franklin D. Roosevelt of New York is named Cox's running mate. **July 11.** Farmer-Labor Party (formed on June 12) meets and nominates Parley P. Christensen of Utah for President. **July 12.** Single Tax Party meets and nominates Robert C. Macauley of Pennsylvania. **July 21.** Prohibition Party meets and nominates Aaron S. Watkins. Republican platform vaguely advocates an "agreement among nations" to preserve peace but is against the Covenant of the League of Nations; Harding campaigns from his home, stressing a "return to normalcy." Democratic platform is in favor of the Covenant, as well as the Versailles Treaty, but leaves the door open for reservations to the Covenant to protect U.S. interests.

May 20. In a joint resolution, Congress

declares war with Germany and Austria-Hungary ended, but President Wilson vetoes the resolution.

June 5. Congress passes Jones (Merchant Marine) Act, which, in addition to repealing measures passed during the war to regulate shipping, seeks to build up the U.S. Merchant Marine by various procedures.

June 10. Congress passes Water Power Act, which sets up the Federal Power Commission to regulate generation of electric power from navigable streams and waters of public lands and transportation on these waters.

Aug. 26. Women finally get the vote when the Nineteenth Amendment to the Constitution is declared ratified. By this time, 15 states have passed women's suffrage laws.

Nov. 2. In election, Harding wins decisively with a popular vote of 16,152,000 to Cox's 9,147,000; Debs polls almost 1 million votes in spite of being a federal prisoner. Electoral vote is Harding, 404; Cox, 127. Harding's victory dashes President Wilson's hope that the election will result in a national referendum in favor of the Versailles Treaty and the League Covenant.

Dec. 10. President Wilson's disappointment over his failure to get popular backing for the League of Nations is partially softened when he is awarded the 1919 Nobel Peace Prize.

U.S. census of this year shows a population of 105,711,000, almost a 15 percent increase over 1910; this includes 5,736,000 immigrants, fewer than in previous decade; to the present day, immigration has never again been so large. Movement of population shows 4,189,000 more people moving westward than eastward and 430,000 more

WARREN G. HARDING
Address to Congress, 1921

Nearly two and a half years ago the World War came to an end, and yet we find ourselves today in the technical state of war, though actually at peace, while Europe is at technical peace, far from tranquillity and little progressed toward the hoped-for restoration. It ill becomes us to express impatience that the European belligerents are not yet in full agreement, when we ourselves have been unable to bring constituted authority into accord in our own relations to the formally proclaimed peace.

Little avails in reciting the causes of delay in Europe or our own failure to agree. But there is no longer excuse for uncertainties respecting some phases of our foreign relationship. In the existing League of Nations, world-governing with its superpowers, this republic will have no part. There can be no misinterpretation, and there will be no betrayal of the deliberate expression of the American people in the recent election; and, settled in our decision for ourselves, it is only fair to say to the world in general, and to our associates in war in particular, that the League Covenant can have no sanction by us. The aim to associate nations to prevent war, preserve peace, and promote civilization our people most cordially applauded. We yearned for this new instrument of justice, but we can have no part in a committal to an agency of force in unknown contingencies; we can recognize no super-authority.

American Review of Reviews, 1923
It would be a commonplace remark to say that when wireless telephoning became practical, about the year 1914, no one dreamed that its use would ever be general or popular. Even two years ago few enthusiasts would have dared to assert that they would live to see hundreds of thousands of persons interested in radio-telephony. The rapidity with which the thing has spread has possibly not been equaled in all the centuries of human progress. . . .

These broadcasting stations are operated by manufacturers of radio supplies, who are repaid by the creation of a boom market for sets and parts; by newspapers and department stores, which see an advertising value in the new fad; and by amateur enthusiasts or experimenters. No one knows how many thousand persons each night are informed, before and after a musical selection or a talk, that "This is WSB, the Atlanta Journal"; or "This is WHB, the Sweeney Automobile School, Kansas City"; or "This is WOO, John Wanamaker, Philadelphia"; or "This is WDAP, the Drake Hotel, Chicago." . . .

Last month General Pershing spoke one evening to a radio audience from St. Louis; it is entirely probable that his voice carried to every state in the Union. The musical selections of WJZ, from Newark, N.J., have been heard in England.

There are now more than 500 broadcasting stations scattered all over this country. The amateur listener is unfortunate, indeed, who cannot hear any one that he chooses among half a dozen, while the more patient or skillful person can pick up one after another a score of stations.

moving northward than southward. For first time, rural population is smaller than urban. Only 6 percent of the population is illiterate, almost 2 percent less than in 1910. Bureau of Public Health finds average life expectancy at birth is 54.1 years.

In *Missouri* v. *Holland*, the Supreme Court finds that Congress may gain from treaties powers that it is not given in the U.S. Constitution; acts of Congress are controlled by the restrictions of the 10th Amendment, but treaties are not; therefore, powers not enumerated in the Constitution may be assumed by means of treaty.

1920 - 1922

Aug. 20, 1920. First regular licensed radio broadcasting is started by Station WWJ in Detroit. **Nov. 2.** First national service begins when Station KDKA in East Pittsburgh broadcasts Harding-Cox election returns; KDKA has been operated experimentally by Westinghouse Electric and Manufacturing Company. **1922.** WEAF, New York, broadcasts first-known commercially sponsored program.

Eugene O'Neill's first full-length play, *Beyond the Horizon,* opens, and in the same year, *The Emperor Jones;* in 1921 *Anna Christie* is produced, and in 1922, *The Hairy Ape.*

1920 - 1925

Sinclair Lewis' novel *Main Street,* a satire of small-town life, receives national attention in 1920; he continues the theme with *Babbitt* in 1922. F. Scott Fitzgerald publishes his enormously successful novel *This Side of Paradise,* as well as a volume of short stories, *Flappers and Philosophers,* in 1920; *The Beautiful and the Damned* (1922) and *Tales of the Jazz Age* (1922) are followed by his major work, *The Great Gatsby,* in 1925.

Edith Wharton publishes her novel of 1870 New York society, *The Age of Innocence*, Pulitzer Prize novel of 1921. John Dos Passos publishes *Three Soldiers*, novel reflecting postwar disillusionment, in 1921; *Manhattan Transfer*, dealing with city life, is published in 1925.

1920 - 1927

April 15, 1920. Paymaster and guard for Massachusetts shoe factory are killed during payroll robbery. Three weeks later, Nicola Sacco and Bartolomeo Vanzetti, Brockton, Massachusetts, workmen, are arrested and charged with the murder. **July 14, 1921.** Nicola Sacco and Bartolomeo Vanzetti are convicted of murder. Worldwide protest results, since many people believe the immigrant laborers have been convicted for their anarchist beliefs rather than for murder. Many attempts are made for retrial on ground of false identification, but all fail, even when, in 1925, a convict confesses that he and others were responsible. **April 9, 1927.** The men are sentenced to die, the Massachusetts Supreme Court having refused to reverse the decision. Bowing to protest throughout the world, Massachusetts governor appoints investigating committee, which later advises him not to exercise clemency. **Aug. 23.** Sacco and Vanzetti, still protesting innocence, are executed.

1921

March 4. President Harding, referring to the League of Nations in his inaugural address, says, "We seek no part in directing the destinies of the world."

May 19. Congress passes law to limit immigration; called the Quota Act, it allows only 3 percent of 1910 immigration from any country in one year and puts an overall limit of 357,000 on annual immigration.

BARTOLOMEO VANZETTI
Final statement in court, 1927
Now, I should say that I am not only innocent of all these things, not only have I never committed a real crime in my life—though some sins but not crimes—not only have I struggled all my life to eliminate crimes, the crimes that the official law and the official moral condemns, but also the crime that the official moral and the official law sanctions and sanctifies—the exploitation and the oppression of the man by the man, and if there is a reason why I am here as a guilty man, if there is a reason why you in a few minutes can doom me, it is this reason and none else. . . .

Well, I have already say that I not only am not guilty . . . but I never commit a crime in my life—I have never steal and I have never kill and I have never spilt blood, and I have fought against the crime, and I have fought and I have sacrificed myself even to eliminate the crimes that the law and the church legitimate and sanctify.

This is what I say: I would not wish to a dog or to a snake, to the most low and misfortunate creature of the earth—I would not wish to any of them what I have had to suffer for things that I am not guilty of. But my conviction is that I have suffered for things that I am guilty of. I am suffering because I am a radical and indeed I am a radical; I have suffered because I was an Italian, and indeed I am an Italian; I have suffered more for my family and for my beloved than for myself; but I am so convinced to be right that if you could execute me two times, and if I could be reborn two other times, I would live again to do what I have done already.

I have finished. Thank you.

EDWARD E. PURINTON
Independent, 1921

Among the nations of the earth today America stands for one idea: Business. National opprobrium? National opportunity. For in this fact lies, potentially, the salvation of the world.

Through business, properly conceived, managed, and conducted, the human race is finally to be redeemed. How and why a man works foretells what he will do, think, have, give, and be. And real salvation is in doing, thinking, having, giving, and being—not in sermonizing and theorizing. . . .

What is the finest game? Business. The soundest science? Business. The truest art? Business. The fullest education? Business. The fairest opportunity? Business. The cleanest philanthropy? Business. The sanest religion? Business. . . .

I am aware that some of the preceding statements will be challenged by many readers. I should not myself have made them, or believed them, twenty years ago, when I was a pitiful specimen of a callow youth and cocksure professional man combined. A thorough knowledge of business has implanted a deep respect for business and real businessmen.

The future work of the businessman is to teach the teacher, preach to the preacher, admonish the parent, advise the doctor, justify the lawyer, superintend the statesman, fructify the farmer, stabilize the banker, harness the dreamer, and reform the reformer. Do all these needy persons wish to have these many kind things done to them by the businessman? Alas, no. They rather look down upon him, or askance at him, regarding him as a mental and social inferior—unless he has money or fame enough to tilt their glance upward.

June 10. Congress passes Budget and Accounting Act in effort to reform U.S. budget practices. Act creates Bureau of Budget and provides for annual submission to Congress of a budget for the coming year, accounting of the past year's expenses, and recommendations on financial measures. **June 21.** Charles G. Dawes is appointed director of the budget.

July 2. Congress, in joint resolution, declares World War I ended. **August.** Separate treaties with Germany, Austria, and Hungary are signed and ratified shortly thereafter.

July 21. General William ("Billy") Mitchell, assistant chief of the air service, demonstrates the superiority of aircraft over ships and the military value of concentrated bombing when massed planes sink a former German battleship in test off Virginia coast. Mitchell, outstanding U.S. air combat commander of World War I, is a strong advocate of a separate air force.

Aug. 9. Veterans Bureau is established; directly under the President, the Bureau is to coordinate all veterans' welfare action.

Aug. 15. Congress passes Packers and Stockyards Act to eliminate manipulation of prices and monopolies in meat-packing industries; regulations are to be enforced by the Department of Agriculture. **Aug. 24.** Similar legislation, the Future Trading Act, is designed to control speculation in grain; Act is voided by the Supreme Court in 1922 and another passed, to be enforced under the interstate commerce power.

Aug. 16. Department of Labor estimates that unemployment throughout the country has risen to more than 5 million. End of wartime boom has brought business depression. Many industries have announced drastic wage cuts, in some cases up to 22 percent. **Sept. 30.** National conference on unemployment proposes a program to provide jobs and advises manufacturers and retailers to reduce prices. Agricultural depression is most severe and long lasting, with forced sales of farms, foreclosures, and bankruptcies increasing steadily into the middle Thirties.

Nov. 2. National Birth Control League and Voluntary Parenthood League are combined to form American Birth Control League in New York City; League is headed by Mrs. Margaret Sanger. In the same year a New York physician is convicted of disseminating birth control information for selling *Married Love* by Marie C. Stopes.

Nov. 5. President Harding proclaims November 11, Armistice Day, a national holiday. **Nov. 11.** First burial ceremony is held at the Tomb of the Unknown Soldier (present-day Tomb of the Unknowns) at Arlington (Virginia) National Cemetery.

Nov. 23. Congress passes the Sheppard-Towner Act, which provides funds to states for maternal and infant welfare. Act is widely criticized as interference with states' rights.

Clayton Antitrust Act of 1914 is considerably weakened as to labor union protection when the Supreme Court finds in *Duplex Printing Press Company* v. *Deering* that anti-injunction clauses of the act do not apply to secondary boycotts by labor unions.

1921 - 1922

May 27, 1921. Congress passes Emergency Tariff Act, which raises tariffs on most agricultural products, a reversal of the reductions achieved by the Wilson administration. **Sept. 21, 1922.** Protective Fordney-McCumber Tariff Act is passed; it raises duties on manufactured goods and, in an attempt to protect farmers, places even higher tariffs on farm products than those of the previous year.

HENRI HAUSER
L'Amérique vivante, 1924
The industrial wealth of the United States must not deceive us. Agriculture is still the greatest American industry. That is why the farmer is the prime element, one might say the backbone of the nation. This is still the first agricultural country of the world. . . .

What are the complaints of the farmers who still make up 30 percent of the active population and who produce about 18 percent of the national income? They charge that they cannot get a sufficiently remunerative return for their products. That is difficult to believe when one sees the prodigious movements of agricultural goods, fruits, vegetables, and bacon in the ports and markets of the great cities. The American stomach is blessed with an enormous capacity. . . .

The United States could, if need be, absorb all the Fords but not all the lard of Chicago, nor the wheat, the corn, the grains of the Mississippi Valley. The question of exports is central here.

If the high tariffs lead, by retaliation, to the closing of certain outlets, if the rise in the value of the dollar loses customers for American products, that does not halt a spindle in the immense cotton factories of New England or Carolina. But the farmer cannot regard these developments with the same tranquillity. The result is that, farther away from Europe, more ignorant of European affairs, he is nevertheless more sensitive to fluctuations in the European markets. Politically, he will be more moved by descriptions of the troubled state of European economy. That explains many of the characteristics of the politics of the Western senators.

WILLIAM ALLEN WHITE
Letter to Herbert B. Swope, 1921
An organizer of the Ku Klux Klan was in Emporia the other day, and the men whom he invited to join his band at $10 per join turned him down. . . . The proposition seems to be:

> *Anti-foreigners*
> *Anti-Catholics*
> *Anti-Negroes.*

There are, of course, bad foreigners and good ones, good Catholics and bad ones, and all kinds of Negroes. To make a case against a birthplace, a religion, or a race is wickedly un-American and cowardly. The whole trouble with the Ku Klux Klan is that it is based upon such deep foolishness that it is bound to be a menace to good government in any community. Any man fool enough to be Imperial Wizard would have power without responsibility and both without any sense. That is social dynamite.

American institutions, our courts, our legislators, our executive officers are strong enough to keep the peace and promote justice and goodwill in the community. If they are not, then the thing to do is to change these institutions and do it quickly, but always legally. For a self-constituted body of moral idiots, who would substitute the findings of the Ku Klux Klan for the processes of law to try to better conditions, would be a most un-American outrage which every good citizen should resent. . . .

The picayunish cowardice of a man who would substitute Klan rule and mob law for what our American fathers have died to establish and maintain should prove what a cheap screw outfit the Klan is.

Nov. 12, 1921. Washington (D.C.) Conference convenes, with all major powers represented except Russia, which has not been invited. Seven treaties are made among Great Britain, France, Japan, Italy, the U.S., and four other nations, involving limitation of warships, restrictions on use of submarines, outlawing of poison gas, rights to Pacific island territories, joint consultation in case of aggression in the Pacific, guarantee of the Open Door Policy in China, and various other Pacific area questions. Conference adjourns in February 1922.

1921 - 1924

1921. The South is swept by whippings, tarrings, brandings, and destruction of property of Negroes and white sympathizers; most activity involves the Ku Klux Klan, and many incidents seem to be unmotivated. **1922.** Klan activity has become so violent in the Middle West that Oklahoma is placed under martial law to control terrorists. **1923.** *Baltimore Sun* and *New York World* expose activities of the Ku Klux Klan in the South, North, and Middle West. Louisiana refuses to indict offenders, even though evidence of torture and murder is given, but Indiana Grand Dragon is convicted of second degree murder. **1924.** Klan has an estimated 4 million members, but by 1930 the number has decreased to about 30,000.

1922

Feb. 18. Congress passes Capper-Volstead Act, which encourages consumer and producer cooperatives and exempts various agricultural associations from the antitrust laws.

April 15. Senator John B. Kendrick of Wyoming calls upon Secretary of the Interior Albert B. Fall to explain information received from Wyoming that the Teapot Dome oil fields are in fact leased to Harry

F. Sinclair's Mammoth Oil Company when the Senate has set them aside for the U.S. Navy.

May 23. Anne Nichols' play *Abie's Irish Rose*, whose underlying theme is religious prejudice, opens in New York City and runs for more than five years, the longest run of any U.S. play to this date.

May 30. Lincoln Memorial is dedicated in Washington, D.C. It has been designed by Henry Bacon in Greco-Roman style, with 36 columns to represent the states of the Union at the time of Abraham Lincoln's death, and contains a colossal seated statue of Lincoln by Daniel Chester French.

June 22. Bitter antiemployer feeling in railroad and coal strikes culminates in murder of strikebreakers by union miners in Herrin, Illinois. Labor union membership declines by almost one-third in this decade because of 1921-1922 depression, federal court attacks, and employer opposition.

Nov. 7. In fall elections Republicans lose 76 House seats and 8 Senate seats but retain majorities in both houses of Congress.

Explorer and film maker Robert J. Flaherty opens his pioneer film *Nanook of the North*, made during a 16-month stay with the Eskimos; later termed "documentary," the film sets a standard for such works.

Winner of international competition for an architectural design for the Chicago Tribune Tower is a Gothic-style building, but the massed modern tower of Finnish second prize winner Eliel Saarinen has far greater influence on future building design. Saarinen moves to the U.S. in the following year.

1922 - 1925

Feb. 9, 1922. Congress authorizes World

LOUIS SULLIVAN
Architectural Record, 1923

In its preliminary advertising, the Tribune broadcasted the inspiring idea of a new and great adventure, in which pride, magnanimity, and its honor were to be inseparably unified and voiced in "the most beautiful office building in the world." . . .

Viewed in this light, the second and the first prize stand before us side by side. One glance of the trained eye, and instant judgment comes; that judgment which flashes from inner experience in recognition of a masterpiece. The verdict of the Jury of Award is at once reversed, and the second prize is placed first, where it belongs by virtue of its beautifully controlled and virile power. The first prize is demoted to the level of those works evolved of dying ideas, even as it sends forth a frantic cry to escape from the common bondage of those governed by ideas. . . .

The Finnish master-edifice is not a lonely cry in the wilderness, it is a voice, resonant and rich, ringing amidst the wealth and joy of life. In utterance sublime and melodious, it prophesies a time to come, and not so far away, when the wretched and the yearning, the sordid and the fierce shall escape the bondage and the mania of fixed ideas. . . .

Why did the men behind the Tribune throw this priceless pearl away? . . .

Confronted by the limpid eye of analysis, the first prize trembles and falls, self-confessed, crumbling to the ground. . . .

This design, this imaginary building, this simulacrum, is so helpless, so defenseless when brought face to face with mastery of ideas and validity of grounds, that it is cruel to go on, for analysis is now becoming vivisection, unless we recognize the palpable effect of self-hypnotism.

GEORGE JEAN NATHAN
Civilization in the United States, Harold
Stearns, ed., 1922
*No, the fault is not with the managers
and producers but with the playwrights.
The latter, where they are not mere par-
rots, are cowards. Young and old, new
and experienced, talented and talentless
alike, they are in the mass so many Saturday Evening Post souls, alone dreaming of and intent upon achieving a sufficient financial gain to transmute the
Ford into a Rolls-Royce and the Hudson
Bay seal collar into Russian sable. A
baby cannot be nourished and developed physically upon water; a theatrical public, for all its potential willingness, cannot be developed aesthetically
upon a diet of snide writing. . . .*

*In no civilized country in the world
today is there among playwrights so little fervor for sound drama as in the
United States. . . .*

*In the United States, with hardly
more than two exceptions, there is at
the moment not a playwright who isn't
thinking of "success" above honest
work. Good and bad craftsmen alike,
they all think the same. Gold, silver,
copper. And the result is an endless
procession of revamped crook plays,
detective plays, Cinderella plays, bou-
doir plays, bucolic plays: fodder for
doodles. The cowardice before the
golden snake's eye spreads to the highest as well as to the lowest. Integrity
is thrown overboard as the ship is
steered unswervingly into the Golden
Gate. . . .*

*The American professional theater is
today at once the richest theater in the
world, and the poorest. Financially, it
reaches to the stars; culturally, with
exception so small as to be negligible, it
reaches to the drains.*

War Foreign Debt Commission to renegotiate international war debts — postwar relief
loans as well as war loans — which amount
to more than $10 billion. Britain and
France, especially, with debts to the U.S.
totaling about $7,682,000,000, have argued
for cancellation of debts by all countries,
but President Wilson has been adamant.
When arguments are advanced in 1922 for
reduction of the debts, President Harding
also refuses, as President Coolidge does
later. **Nov. 14, 1925.** Because of severe financial depression in Europe, the U.S. finally agrees on drastic reduction of debts, as
well as of interest rate, but still insists on
partial payment. This stand creates anti-
U.S. sentiment in Europe, which in turn results in isolationist feeling in the U.S.

The *Reader's Digest,* publishing condensa-
tions of material from other publications, is
founded by De Witt Wallace in 1922 in
New York. In 1923 Henry R. Luce and
Briton Hadden found *Time,* a weekly news
magazine. H. L. Mencken and George Jean
Nathan begin publishing the *American Mercury,* containing literary and critical pieces,
in 1924. Henry Siedel Canby begins publishing the *Saturday Review of Literature* in
the same year. Harold W. Ross founds sophisticated weekly magazine, *The New
Yorker,* in 1925; James Thurber becomes
editor for a short time in 1927.

1922. Albert H. Taylor and Leo C.
Young demonstrate results of research into
radio detection, the forerunner of radar.
1925. Pulse-ranging radar similar to
present-day technique is first used for investigation of the ionosphere by Gregory Breit
and Merle A. Tuve.

1922-1927

1922. Technicolor process for moving
pictures makes commercial debut, but it is
not used widely until about 20 years later.
1923. Lee De Forest demonstrates sound

on movie film; the first full-length movie using sound (*The Jazz Singer*, starring Al Jolson) is shown in 1927.

1923

March 4. Congress passes Intermediate Credits Act, which expands and strengthens agricultural credit system and encourages farm cooperatives in an effort to counter agricultural depression.

March. Emphatic protest by Indians results in defeat of Bursum Bill, which would have transferred Pueblo lands to white settlers without compensation. In the following year, Pueblo Land Board is established to set amount of compensation, which is not paid until 1933.

May 4. In spite of President Harding's warning that federal authorities will have to take over Prohibition enforcement, Governor Alfred E. Smith of New York signs legislation repealing New York's Prohibition enforcement act.

July 28. President Harding becomes ill suddenly on return trip from Alaska and is rushed to San Francisco, where he dies on August 2. **Aug. 3.** Calvin Coolidge is sworn in as President by his father in Vermont at 2:30 A.M., when the news reaches him.

Dec. 6. In President Coolidge's first annual message to Congress, he supports a World Court, enforcement of Prohibition, lower taxes, and government economy. This is the first time an official presidential message has been broadcast.

In *Adkins* v. *Children's Hospital*, the Supreme Court calls unconstitutional a 1918 District of Columbia act that seeks to set minimum wages for women.

In *Wolff Packing Company* v. *Court of Industrial Relations*, Supreme Court finds that

CALVIN COOLIDGE
Memorial Day Address, 1923
There are two fundamental motives which inspire human action. The first and most important, to which all else is subordinate, is that of righteousness. There is that in mankind, stronger than all else, which requires them to do right. When that requirement is satisfied, the next motive is that of gain. These are the moral motive and the material motive. While in some particular instance they might seem to be antagonistic, yet always, when broadly considered or applied to society as a whole, they are in harmony. American institutions meet the test of these two standards. They are founded on righteousness, they are productive of material prosperity. They compel the loyalty and support of the people because such action is right and because it is profitable.

These are the main reasons for the formation of patriotic societies. Desiring to promote the highest welfare of civilization, their chief purpose is to preserve and extend American ideals. No matter what others may do, they are determined to serve themselves and their fellowmen by thinking America, believing America, and living America. That faith they are proud to proclaim to all the world.

GEORGE SUTHERLAND
Adkins v. Children's Hospital, 1923
We cannot accept the doctrine that women of mature age, sui juris, require or may be subjected to restrictions upon their liberty of contract which could not lawfully be imposed in the case of men under similar circumstances.

E. E. CUMMINGS

The Cambridge ladies, 1923

the Cambridge ladies who live in
*   furnished souls*
are unbeautiful and have comfortable
*   minds*
(also, with the church's protestant
*   blessings*
daughters, unscented shapeless spirited)
they believe in Christ and Longfellow,
*   both dead,*
are invariably interested in so many
*   things—*
at the present writing one still finds
delighted fingers knitting for the is it
*   Poles? . . .*
. . . . the Cambridge ladies do not
*   care, above*
Cambridge if sometimes in its box of
sky lavender and cornerless, the
moon rattles like a fragment of angry
*   candy*

E. E. CUMMINGS

next to of course god, 1926

"next to of course god america i
love you land of the pilgrims' and so
*   forth oh*
say can you see by the dawn's early my
country 'tis of centuries come and go
and are no more what of it we should
*   worry*
in every language even deafanddumb
thy sons acclaim your glorious name
*   by gorry*
by jingo by gee by gosh by gum
why talk of beauty what could be more
*   beaut-*
iful than these heroic happy dead
who rushed like lions to the roaring
*   slaughter*
they did not stop to think they died
*   instead*
then shall the voice of liberty be mute?"

He spoke. And drank rapidly a glass of
*   water*

a state legislature cannot control an industry on the ground that it is involved in the public interest merely by stating that it is in this category. In a later similar decision, Justice Holmes dissents, holding that states have the right to enact any legislation not specifically prohibited by the federal Constitution. By 1934 Court has come to agree with Holmes's opinion that any industry may be in the public interest and thus liable to state control.

By this year, about 13,300,000 automobiles are registered in the U.S., slightly less than triple the number in 1917; this number is two million less than the number of telephones being used in the same year.

Du Pont Company acquires rights to manufacture cellophane from a French company; first U.S.-made cellophane is produced in Buffalo in 1924. It has been produced in Switzerland since 1912.

The Covered Wagon, voted one of 10 best movies of the year by *Film Daily*, sets the style for Western spectacles and is the beginning of popularity of Westerns which continues to the present day; production costs have been $350,000, and it nets $1,500,000 on the road.

E. E. Cummings publishes his first book of poems, *Tulips and Chimneys*, written in original poetic and typographic style; this is followed by *XLI Poems* in 1925 and *&* and *is 5* in 1926.

1924

Feb. 8. Commonwealth Land Party (Single Tax Party of 1920) meets and nominates W. J. Wallace of New Jersey for President. **May 11.** Socialist Labor Party meets and nominates Frank T. Johns of Oregon. **June 3.** American Party meets and nominates Judge Gilbert O. Nations of Washington, D.C. **June 5.** Prohibition Party meets and nominates Herman P. Faris for President and Marie C. Brehm for Vice-President. **June 10.** Republicans meet at Cleveland and nominate President Calvin Coolidge for reelection and General Charles G. Dawes of Illinois for Vice-President. **June 24.** Democrats meet at New York and nominate John W. Davis of West Virginia for President and Governor Charles W. Bryan of Nebraska for Vice-President; nomination of Davis follows 16-day battle between supporters of Alfred E. Smith and William G. McAdoo; and Davis is not nominated until the 103rd ballot. **July 4.** Progressive Party is formed in Cleveland by Conference for Progressive Political Action, representing farmers and workers; new party is backed by the American Federation of Labor, Farmer Labor Party, and Socialist Party. Convention nominates Senator Robert M. La Follette of Wisconsin for President and Senator Burton K. Wheeler of Montana for Vice-President. **July 11.** Workers' (Communist) Party meets and nominates William Z. Foster for President. Republican platform supports lower taxes, higher tariffs, economy, arms limitation, and international cooperation to keep peace. Democratic platform advocates competitive tariff, disarmament, and the League of Nations, and strikes at Harding administration graft. Progressives favor freedom of labor union action, government ownership of water resources and railroads, and child labor limitation, and denounce corruption, monopolies, and administration finance program.

Feb. 12. George Gershwin's *Rhapsody in Blue*, a new kind of symphonic jazz, is performed for the first time, with Gershwin as piano soloist accompanied by Paul Whiteman's orchestra. In the following year, Gershwin produces a sequel, *Concerto in F*, commissioned by Walter Damrosch, and in 1928, his symphonic poem, *An American in Paris*, which includes French taxi horns among its instruments.

WILL ROGERS
Newspaper column, 1925
To stop this Country now would be like spitting on a Railroad track to stop a Train. . . . That's why I can never take a Politician seriously. They are always shouting that "such and such a thing will ruin us, and that this is the eventful year in our Country's life."

Say, all the years are the same. Each one has its little temporary setbacks, but they don't mean a thing in the general result. Nobody is making History. Everybody is just drifting along with the tide. If any office holder feels he is carrying a burden of responsibility, some Fly will light on his back and scratch it off for him some day. Congress can pass a bad law and as soon as the old Normal Majority find it out they have it scratched off the books.

We lost Roosevelt TR, a tough blow. But here we are still kicking. So, if we can spare men like Roosevelt and Wilson there is no use in any other Politician ever taking himself serious.

Henry Ford has been a big factor in the Industrial development of the Country. Yet if he was gone there would still be enough of those things left to clutter up the Highways for Years. John D. Rockefeller who has done a lot for humanity with his Gifts; yet when he is gone and Gasoline raises 2 Cents, and all expenses and the Estate is settled we will kick along. . . .

So I can find nothing for alarm in our immediate future. The next time a Politician gets spouting off about what this Country needs, either hit him with a tubercular Tomato or lay right back in your seat and go to sleep. Because THIS COUNTRY HAS GOT TOO BIG TO NEED A DAMN THING.

THIS PAGE: (Above) Warren G. Harding, twenty-ninth
President of the United States, in Kansas; (below)
Czech troops, who fought with Russia against
Austria, joined with the White Russians in the
civil war and were supported by troops from Britain
and the United States
OPPOSITE PAGE: (Top) Woman's suffrage parade on
Fifth Avenue in New York, 1915; (bottom) govern-
ment agents disposing of captured liquor by the
easiest means

LOUIS MARSHALL
Letter to President Coolidge, 1924

This is the first time in the history of American legislation that there has been an attempt to discriminate in respect to European immigration between those who come from different parts of the continent. It is not only a differentiation as to countries of origin, but also of racial stocks and of religious beliefs. Those coming from Northern and Western Europe are supposed to be Anglo-Saxon or mythical Nordics, and to a large extent Protestant. Those coming from Southern and Eastern Europe are of different racial stocks and of a different faith. There are today in this country millions of citizens, both native-born and naturalized, descended from those racial stocks and entertaining those religious beliefs against which this bill deliberately discriminates. There is no mincing of the matter. . . .

What we regard as the danger lurking in this legislation is, that it stimulates racial, national and religious hatreds and jealousies, that it encourages one part of our population to arrogate to itself a sense of superiority, and to classify another as one of inferiority. At a time when the welfare of the human race as an entirety depends upon the creation of a brotherly spirit, the restoration of peace, harmony and unity, and the termination of past animosities engendered by the insanity and brutality of war, it should be our purpose, as a nation which has demonstrated that those of diverse racial, national and religious origins can live together and prosper as a united people, to serve as the world's conciliator. Instead of that this bill, if it becomes a law, is destined to become the very Apple of Discord.

Feb. 27. A treaty is signed with the Dominican Republic that supersedes that of 1907; an election is held, and in July, when a president is inaugurated, U.S. Marines are withdrawn.

April 9. Dawes Plan on German reparations is reported. Reparations due from Germany have been fixed at 132 billion gold marks in 1921, a figure that has been accepted by Germany after an Allied threat to occupy the Ruhr, with its great coal and iron industries; but the mark has collapsed, becoming worthless by 1923, and Germany has defaulted on payments; France and Belgium, angry at Germany's failure, have occupied Ruhr. A committee, headed by Charles G. Dawes, has been appointed to investigate German finances. Dawes Plan calls for Allied supervision of the Reichsbank; total reparations are left undetermined, with a graduated plan of payment and a loan to Germany of 800 million gold marks. Total reparations are finally set by Young Plan, which becomes effective in 1930.

May 19. Soldiers Bonus Bill is passed over President Coolidge's veto. President Harding has vetoed a similar bill in 1922, but veterans' organizations persistently have put pressure on Congress. All veterans under the rank of major are given 20-year annuities, based on $1.25 per day for overseas service and $1 per day for service in the U.S., on which they may borrow from the government.

May 26. Congress passes second quota law, which cuts immigration to half of 1921 quota; new annual quota is based on 2 percent of nationals from each country present in U.S. in 1890; change of date from 1910 to 1890 is made to reduce number of immigrants from southern and eastern Europe, about 70 percent of 1910 entries. Act is to control immigration until 1927, at which time a survey of national origins will be the basis for an immigration limit of 150,000. Strongly opposed, second quota law is not put into effect until 1929. Neither 1921 nor 1924 quota law applies to citizens of countries in the Americas and Canada.

June 2. Congress submits proposed constitutional Child Labor Amendment to the states for ratification, but opinion that the issue is a matter for state legislation is so strong that only 26 of the necessary 36 states have ratified it 26 years later.

June 15. Congress passes act making all native-born Indians full U.S. citizens.

July 1. "Hate America" meetings are held in Tokyo on this date, officially called "Humiliation Day," because of U.S. Immigration Act of 1924 that prohibits all immigration of Japanese persons, who are considered "ineligible to citizenship." Act follows earlier California and other state laws that restrict ownership and right to rent agricultural land.

Aug. 24. Congress passes Agricultural Credits Act in effort to forestall bankruptcies and dumping of surplus farm goods by dealers; dealers and cooperatives are granted loans to allow them to hold goods.

Nov. 4. President Coolidge is elected by popular vote of 15,718,000 to Davis' 8,385,000. Electoral vote is Coolidge, 382; Davis, 136. La Follette receives almost 5 million votes but carries only Wisconsin, with 13 electoral votes.

Nov. 30. Radio Corporation of America demonstrates wireless telegraph transmission of photographs from New York to London; process takes about 25 minutes per photograph.

J. Edgar Hoover is appointed head of Bureau of Investigation (established in 1908 and renamed Federal Bureau of Investiga-

Manufacturers Record, 1924
Because the Child Labor Amendment in reality is not legislation in the interest of children but legislation which would mean the destruction of manhood and womanhood through the destruction of the boys and girls of the country, the Manufacturers Record *has been giving much attention to the discussion of the subject, and will continue to do so. . . .*

This proposed amendment is fathered by Socialists, Communists, and Bolshevists. They are the active workers in its favor. They look forward to its adoption as giving them the power to nationalize the children of the land and bring about in this country the exact conditions which prevail in Russia. These people are the active workers back of this undertaking, but many patriotic men and women, without at all realizing the seriousness of this proposition, thinking only of it as an effort to lessen child labor in factories, are giving countenance to it.

If adopted, this amendment would be the greatest thing ever done in America in behalf of the activities of hell. It would make millions of young people under eighteen years of age idlers in brain and body, and thus make them the devil's best workshop. It would destroy the initiative and self-reliance and manhood and womanhood of all the coming generations. . . .

The only thing that can prevent its adoption will be active, untiring work on the part of every man and woman who appreciates its destructive power and who wants to save the young people of all future generations from moral and physical decay under the domination of the devil himself.

LEWIS MUMFORD
Sticks and Stones, 1924

It would be a piece of brash aesthetic bigotry to deny the aesthetic values that derive from machinery: the clean surfaces, the hard lines, the calibrated perfection that the machine has made possible carry with them a beauty quite different from that of handicraft—but often it is a beauty. . . . Many of our power plants are majestic; many of our modern factories are clean and lithe and smart, designed with unerring logic and skill. Put alongside buildings in which the architect has glorified his own idiosyncrasy or pandered to the ritual of conspicuous waste, our industrial plants at least have honesty and sincerity and an inner harmony of form and function. . . .

The error with regard to these new forms of building is the attempt to universalize the mere process or form, instead of attempting to universalize the scientific spirit in which they have been conceived. The design for a dwelling house which ignores everything but the physical necessities of the occupants is the product of a limited conception of science which stops short at physics and mechanics and neglects biology, psychology, and sociology. . . .

The end of a civilization that considers buildings as mere machines is that it considers human beings as mere machine tenders; it therefore frustrates or diverts the more vital impulses which would lead to the culture of the earth or the intelligent care of the young. . . .

The architecture of other civilizations has sometimes been the brutal emblem of the warrior, like that of the Assyrians. It has remained for the architecture of our own day in America to be fixed and stereotyped and blank, like the mind of a robot.

tion in 1935), and Bureau is immediately reorganized to eliminate political considerations.

Lewis Mumford publishes his social history of architecture, *Sticks and Stones.* In Paris newspaper reporter Ernest Hemingway publishes *In Our Time*, a collection of short stories that sets a new terse style in prose. Columnist Ring (Ringgold Wilmer) Lardner publishes his collection *How To Write Short Stories*, which, with earlier stories, revives an American tradition of vernacular satire; *The Love Nest* and *Round Up* are published in 1926 and 1929, respectively.

By this year, there are 2,500,000 radios in the U.S., as opposed to 5,000 sets in 1920, used mostly by professionals.

Name of Trinity College in Durham, North Carolina, is changed by the trustees to Duke University to comply with conditions of multimillion-dollar trust fund established by tobacco millionaire James B. Duke.

1924-1927

Congressional committees investigating rumors that have started in 1922 find that graft and corruption have been rife during the Harding administration. Officials appointed innocently by Harding have used their offices for personal gain; departments involved are Interior, Navy, Justice, the Veterans Bureau, and the Office of the Alien Property Custodian. Secretary of the Interior Albert B. Fall is found to have accepted a bribe and leased naval oil reserves at Teapot Dome, Wyoming, and in California to a private oil company; eventually, he is sent to prison, and Secretary of the Navy Edwin N. Denby, who has been innocently involved, is forced to resign. Attorney General Harry M. Daugherty, in conjunction with members of the "Ohio Gang," a group of grasping politicians, is found to have accepted bribes from Prohibition law violators, as well as failing to act on graft he knew existed in the Veterans Bureau; Daugherty, although not convicted, is forced to resign by President Coolidge. Colonel Charles R. Forbes, head of the Veterans Bureau until his resignation in 1923, is convicted of fraud, bribery, and conspiracy. Colonel Thomas W. Miller, Alien Property Custodian, is convicted when it is found that he has been taking part in wholesale looting of alien properties. Harry F. Sinclair and Edward L. Doheny, to whom the Wyoming and California oil fields have been leased, are acquitted of bribery and conspiracy, although more than $300,000 has passed between them and Secretary Fall. President Harding's sudden illness is thought to be the result of receiving a long coded message from Washington during the congressional investigations.

1925

Jan. 5. Mrs. Nellie Tayloe Ross takes office as governor of Wyoming; she is the first woman governor in the U.S.

May 5. Tennessee schoolteacher John T. Scopes is arrested for teaching the theory of evolution, forbidden by state law. **July 10-21.** In "monkey trial," which attracts enormous public attention, Scopes is defended by Clarence Darrow and Dudley Field Malone; William Jennings Bryan is one of the prosecuting attorneys. Scopes is convicted and fined $100 (later reversed on a technicality by the Tennessee Supreme Court). **July 26.** Bryan dies, supposedly as a result of the strain of the fundamentalist versus modernist trial, in which he has been subjected to a withering examination by Darrow of the fundamentalist literal interpretation of the Bible.

September. Colonel William ("Billy") Mitchell, outspoken advocate of a strong,

WARREN G. HARDING
Quoted by William Allen White, Autobiography, 1946
My God, this is a hell of a job! I have no trouble with my enemies. I can take care of my enemies all right. But my damn friends, my God-damn friends, White, they're the ones that keep me walking the floor nights!

WILLIAM JENNINGS BRYAN
In cross examination by Clarence Darrow, 1925
Q. Do you claim that everything in the Bible should be literally interpreted?
A. I believe that everything in the Bible should be accepted as it is given there.
Q. But when you read that Jonah swallowed the whale—or that the whale swallowed Jonah—excuse me, please, how do you literally interpret it? . . . You believe that God made such a fish, and that is was big enough to swallow Jonah?
A. Yes, sir.
Q. Perfectly easy to believe that Jonah swallowed the whale?
A. If the Bible said so.

BILLY SUNDAY
Interview, 1925
If a minister believes and teaches evolution, he is a stinking skunk, a hypocrite, and a liar.

GEN. WILLIAM MITCHELL
Aviation, 1925
*I have been asked from all parts of the
country to give my opinion about the
reasons for the frightful aeronautical
accidents and loss of life, equipment,
and treasure that have occurred during
the last few days. . . .*

*About what happened, my opinion is
as follows: These accidents are the direct result of the incompetency, criminal negligence, and almost treasonable
administration of the national defense
by the Navy and War departments. In
their attempts to keep down the development of aviation into an independent department, separate from the
Army and Navy and handled by aeronautical experts, and to maintain the existing systems, they have gone to the
utmost lengths to carry their point. All
aviation policies, schemes, and systems
are dictated by the nonflying officers of
the Army or Navy, who know practically
nothing about it. The lives of the air-
men are being used merely as pawns in
their hands. . . .*

*Our pilots know they are going to be
killed if they stay in the service, on account of the methods employed in the
old floating coffins that we are still
flying. Those pilots that still remain
have held on so long that if they got out
they would starve. They don't dare
open their mouths and tell the truth
because they and their families might
be booted out to some obscure
place. . . .*

*As a patriotic American citizen, I can
stand by no longer and see these disgusting performances by the Navy and
War departments at the expense of the
lives of our people and the delusion of
the American public.*

independent air force, who has proved in
1921 that capital ships can be sunk by airplanes, accuses the War and Navy departments of "incompetency, criminal negligence, and almost treasonable administration of the National Defense." **Dec. 17.**
Court-martial finds Mitchell guilty of insubordination, suspending him from the service
for five years. Mitchell resigns as of February 1926. During World War II, he is posthumously restored to the rank of major
general, and in 1946 Congress has a special
medal struck in his honor.

October. Florida land boom reaches peak
just before its collapse; period of speculation
in Florida real estate is said to be greatest
business stampede in U.S. history.

By this year, personal and corporate income and estate and gift taxes make up almost half of U.S. government revenue; customs duties have dropped to 14.4 percent
of revenue, as opposed to about 57 percent
in 1890.

Simon Guggenheim and his wife establish the John Simon Guggenheim Memorial
Foundation in memory of their son; function is to "further the development of
scholars and artists by assisting them to engage in research . . . under the freest possible conditions."

Theodore Dreiser publishes his novel *An
American Tragedy*, based on the Grace
Brown murder case; it brings him greater
acclaim as a novelist than he has yet
known.

1925 - 1927

C. Francis Jenkins demonstrates television; his work has been based on that of
European scientists. First actual transmission
of television signals occurs when the president of American Telephone and Telegraph
Company in New York sees and speaks to

Secretary of Commerce Herbert Hoover in Washington, D.C.

1926

Jan. 27. U.S. Senate approves American participation in Permanent Court of International Justice at The Hague, with certain reservations to protect U.S. interests; when one reservation proves to be unacceptable to the Court, the U.S. does not actually join. The U.S. has urged establishment of the Court in 1899 and 1907 at two Hague conferences, and Court has been formed by the League of Nations in 1920. Continuing efforts are made by Presidents Coolidge, Hoover, and Franklin Roosevelt to enroll the U.S. in the Court, but, largely because of the isolationist propaganda of the Hearst newspapers and "Radio Priest" Father Charles E. Coughlin, all efforts finally fail in 1935.

Feb. 26. Congress passes Revenue Act, which reduces income and inheritance taxes and removes many excise and nuisance taxes.

March 7. Radio Corporation of America, American Telephone and Telegraph Company, and British General Post Office hold first successful transatlantic radiotelephone conversation between New York and London.

April. Book-of-the-Month-Club begins enrolling members, acquiring 40,000 in the first year; new form of book distribution revolutionizes book publishing.

May 5. Sinclair Lewis rejects the Pulitzer Prize for his novel *Arrowsmith*, saying that such prizes make writers, "safe, polite, obedient, and sterile."

July 2. Congress establishes the Army Air Corps, in the same year that Colonel "Billy" Mitchell, who has advocated a separate

SINCLAIR LEWIS
Martin Arrowsmith's prayer, 1925
God give me unclouded eyes and freedom from haste. God give me a quiet and relentless anger against all pretense and all pretentious work and all work left slack and unfinished. God give me a restlessness whereby I may neither sleep nor accept praise till my observed results equal my calculated results or in pious glee I discover and assault my error. God give me strength not to trust in God!

SINCLAIR LEWIS
American People's Encyclopedia, 1948
In a democracy like this, while we stimulate a young man with belief that he may some day be president — at least of a motor agency — we also fail to inform him that in his competition with other equally fortunate freemen it will be well for him to have more talent and industry than the others. This is especially the case with writing fiction. Thanks to sentimental schoolteachers and the advertisements of firms which are not without guile in screaming that they can teach you to write, there is a general belief that anybody, man or woman, who has failed at plumbing, farming or housewifery, has only to take a couple of easy lessons — dealing with such trade secrets as: should you write with a pen or typewriter; and are blonde airplane stewardesses or red-haired girls from Iceland the snappier heroines just now — to be able to compose a novel which will win the Pulitzer Prize and be sold to the movies for a million dollars.

RICHARD E. BYRD
Alone, 1928

The day was dying, the night being born—but with great peace. Here were the imponderable processes and forces of the cosmos, harmonious and soundless. Harmony, that was it! That was what came out of the silence—a gentle rhythm, the strain of a perfect chord, the music of the spheres, perhaps.

It was enough to catch that rhythm, momentarily to be myself a part of it. In that instant I could feel no doubt of man's oneness with the universe. The conviction came that that rhythm was too orderly, too harmonious, too perfect to be a product of blind chance—that, therefore, there must be purpose in the whole and that man was part of that whole and not an accidental offshoot. It was a feeling that transcended reason; that went to the heart of man's despair and found it groundless. The universe was a cosmos, not a chaos; man was as rightfully a part of that cosmos as were the day and night.

air force, resigns from the Army after being court-martialed.

Oct. 25. The Supreme Court holds that the President has power to remove executive officers, thus voiding the Tenure of Office Act of 1867 requiring the consent of the Senate. The Act had been passed to tie President Johnson's hands, and his defiance of it was the cause of his near impeachment.

Nov. 2. In fall elections, Republicans lose seats in both Senate and House, and Progressives gain.

Congress passes Air Commerce Act, which, through Bureau of Air Commerce, provides for federal aid to development of the aviation industry, establishment of navigation guides and airports, and licensing of pilots and aircraft.

Drs. George R. Minot and William P. Murphy discover first successful treatment of formerly fatal pernicious anemia when they use liver diet; in 1934 they share the Nobel Prize for Medicine with George Hoyt Whipple for their work.

1926-1927

Historian, poet, folklorist Carl Sandburg publishes the first two volumes of his biography of Abraham Lincoln, *The Prairie Years* (the four-volume *The War Years* is published in 1939); in the following year he publishes his collection of folksongs, *The American Songbag*.

National Broadcasting Company is organized as first nationwide radio broadcasting network in 1926; Columbia Broadcasting System is organized in 1927.

1926-1929

May 9, 1926. Richard E. Byrd, with

Floyd Bennett, makes first flight over the North Pole and is awarded the Congressional Medal of Honor. In 1927 he and three others fly from New York to France with first official mail service, and in 1929, on his first expedition to the Antarctic, he flies over the South Pole.

1927

Jan. 27. U.S. Senate unanimously resolves that Mexican-U.S. conflicts be settled by negotiation or arbitration. Formerly permanent oil land concessions of U.S. oil companies have been limited to 50 years by the Mexican government, and a law has been passed limiting the amount of land that can be owned by aliens. **Sept.** President Coolidge appoints Dwight W. Morrow ambassador to Mexico. **Nov. 17.** Morrow's efforts are so successful that the Mexican Supreme Court voids limitation clauses in oil land law, and in the next month Mexican Congress grants unlimited concessions on lands used before 1917.

Feb. 10. President Coolidge calls for naval-limitation conference of five major powers at Geneva, but France and Italy do not attend. **June 20-Aug. 4.** Conference, attended by Britain, Japan, and the U.S., accomplishes nothing, since Britain and the U.S. are unable to come to terms on restriction of cruisers. Eighteen months later the U.S. starts building fifteen 10,000-ton cruisers.

April 17. To an open letter of inquiry about his affiliation with the Roman Catholic Church, Governor Alfred E. Smith of New York, who is being considered as a Democratic presidential nominee, answers, "I recognize no power in the institution of my Church to interfere with the operations of the Constitution of the United States."

May 21. Charles A. Lindbergh is greeted by 100,000 anxiously waiting people in Paris when he arrives in his monoplane, the

ALFRED E. SMITH
Atlantic Monthly, 1927

I summarize my creed as an American Catholic. I believe in the worship of God according to the faith and practice of the Roman Catholic Church. I recognize no power in the institutions of my church to interfere with the operations of the Constitution of the United States or the enforcement of the law of the land. I believe in absolute freedom of conscience for all men and in equality of all churches, all sects, and all beliefs before the law as a matter of right and not as a matter of favor. I believe in the absolute separation of church and state and in the strict enforcement of the provisions of the Constitution, that Congress shall make no law respecting an establishment of religion or prohibiting the free exercise thereof. I believe that no tribunal of any church has any power to make any decree of any force in the law of the land, other than to establish the status of its own communicants within its own church.

I believe in the support of the public school as one of the cornerstones of American liberty. I believe in the right of every parent to choose whether his child shall be educated in the public school or in a religious school supported by those of his own faith. I believe in the principle of noninterference by this country in the internal affairs of other nations and that we should stand steadfastly against any such interference by whomsoever it may be urged. And I believe in the common brotherhood of man under the common fatherhood of God.

In this spirit I join with fellow Americans of all creeds in a fervent prayer that never again in this land will any public servant be challenged because of the faith in which he has tried to walk humbly with his God.

CHARLES A. LINDBERGH
New York Times, 1927
The engine was working perfectly and that cheered me. I was going along a hundred miles an hour and I knew that if the motor kept on turning I would get there. After that I thought only about navigating, and then I thought that I wasn't so badly off after all. . . .

Fairly early in the afternoon I saw a fleet of fishing boats. On some of them I could see no one, but on one of them I saw some men and flew down, almost touching the craft and yelled at them, asking if I was on the right road to Ireland.

They just stared. Maybe they didn't hear me. Maybe I didn't hear them. Or maybe they thought I was just a crazy fool.

An hour later I saw land. I have forgotten just what time it was. It must have been shortly before 4 o'clock. It was rocky land and all my study told me it was Ireland. And it was Ireland!

F. SCOTT FITZGERALD
Of Lindbergh
In the spring of '27, something bright and alien flashed across the sky. A young Minnesotan who seemed to have had nothing to do with his generation did a heroic thing, and for a moment people set down their glasses in country clubs and speakeasies and thought of their old best dreams.

JAMES J. WALKER
Welcoming Lindbergh, after the ticker-tape parade up Broadway, 1927
Charles Lindbergh, New York is yours. I don't give it to you. You won it. And one other thing. Before you go, you will have to provide us with a new street-cleaning department to clean up the mess.

Spirit of St. Louis, after a 3,600-mile, 33½-hour solo flight from New York. Lindbergh, 25 years old, has been competing for a $25,000 prize offered for the first nonstop flight from New York to Paris.

July 29. Bellevue Hospital in New York City installs first electric respirator (later called iron lung), originally designed for use in almost any kind of respiratory failure.

Nov. 13. Holland Tunnel, first underwater tunnel for vehicles built under Hudson River, opens; running from New York City to Jersey City, it is a double tunnel with two lanes in each direction.

Dec. 27. *Show Boat,* a new kind of musical comedy, opens in New York City; by Oscar Hammerstein II and Jerome Kern, it is adapted from Edna Ferber's novel.

Vernon L. Parrington publishes first two volumes of his *Main Currents in American Thought;* third volume is issued in 1930. Charles and Mary Beard publish first two volumes of their history *The Rise of American Civilization;* third volume, *America in Midpassage,* is published in 1939.

Ole Edvart Rölvaag publishes his finest novel, *Giants in the Earth,* which, like others, deals with immigrant pioneers.

1927 - 1928

April 6, 1927. French Foreign Minister Aristide Briand unofficially proposes an agreement between the U.S. and France to outlaw war. **June 11.** Secretary of State Frank B. Kellogg formally acknowledges the proposal, and Briand submits a draft about a week later. **Dec. 28.** Kellogg, having consulted the Senate Foreign Relations Committee, changes the draft to include all nations. Pact outlaws war as an instrument of national policy but does not reject defensive war. No sanctions are provided except force of world opinion. **April 13, 1928.** Draft of the Kellogg-Briand Pact is sent to other nations; eventually 63 countries sign it.

Aug. 2, 1927. It has been assumed that President Coolidge will run for office again, but he announces from South Dakota, "I do not choose to run for President in 1928." Near the end of his term, in December 1928, although he has encouraged financial speculation and ignored economic problems, Coolidge tells Congress, "The country can . . . anticipate the future with optimism."

1927 - 1933

April 1927. President Coolidge sends Henry L. Stimson, preceded by U.S. Marines, to Nicaragua to settle differences between President Adolfo Díaz, U.S.-supported Conservative, and revolutionist General César Sandino, one of several who support Juan Sacasa over Díaz. Withdrawal of Marines in 1925 has led to renewal of civil war. In spite of U.S. supervision of elections, internal warfare continues until 1933.

1928

Jan. 16. Pan-American conference at Havana is opened by President Coolidge. Latin-American nations attack U.S. claim to the right of intervention in internal affairs of Western Hemisphere nations under 1904 Roosevelt Corollary to the Monroe Doctrine. The U.S. gradually modifies the Corollary; in a series of hemispheric conferences, the Monroe Doctrine is transformed into one of hemispheric solidarity and mutual responsibility.

April 13. Socialist Party convention meets and nominates Norman Thomas of New York for President. **May 12.** Socialist

CALVIN COOLIDGE
Message to Congress, 1927
For many years numerous Americans have been living in Nicaragua, developing its industries and carrying on business. At the present time there are large investments in lumbering, mining, coffee growing, banana culture, shipping, and also in general mercantile and other collateral business. All these people and these industries have been encouraged by the Nicaraguan government. That government has at all times owed them protection, but the United States has occasionally been obliged to send naval forces for their proper protection. In the present crisis such forces are requested by the Nicaraguan government, which protests to the United States its inability to protect these interests and states that any measures which the United States deems appropriate for their protection will be satisfactory to the Nicaraguan government. . . .

There is no question that if the revolution continues, American investments and business interests in Nicaragua will be very seriously affected, if not destroyed. The currency, which is now at par, will be inflated. American as well as foreign bondholders will undoubtedly look to the United States for the protection of their interests. . . .

I am sure it is not the desire of the United States to intervene in the internal affairs of Nicaragua or of any other Central American republic. Nevertheless, it must be said that we have a very definite and special interest in the maintenance of order and good government in Nicaragua at the present time, and that the stability, prosperity, and independence of all Central American countries can never be a matter of indifference to us.

FRANKLIN D. ROOSEVELT
Nominating speech, Democratic National Convention, 1928
We offer one who has the will to win —who not only deserves success but commands it. Victory is his habit—the happy warrior, Alfred Smith.

ALFRED E. SMITH
Campaign catch phrase, 1928
Let's look at the record.

When asked to permit a moving picture of him laying the cornerstone of the New York State Office Building
Nothing doing. That's just baloney. Everybody knows I can't lay bricks.

Republican National Committee advertisement, 1928
A Chicken in Every Pot, a Car in Every Garage.

GEORGE HIGGINS MOSES
Of Western and Southern "radical" Republicans, 1928
Sons of the Wild Jackass.

Labor Party meets and nominates Frank T. Johns, who is later killed and replaced by Verne L. Reynolds. **May 25.** Workers' Party meets and nominates William Z. Foster. **June 12.** Republicans meet at Kansas City and nominate Secretary of Commerce Herbert C. Hoover of California for President and Senator Charles Curtis of Kansas as his running mate. **June 26.** Democrats meet at Houston and nominate Governor Alfred E. Smith of New York for President and Senator Joseph T. Robinson of Arkansas for Vice-President. **July 12.** Prohibition Party meets and nominates William F. Varney of New York. Republican platform supports a federal farm board to stabilize agriculture, a protective tariff, and current foreign policy. Democrats also favor a farm board, promise enforcement of Prohibition (although Smith calls for repeal of the Eighteenth Amendment), call for more freedom for labor in disputes, and demand changes in foreign policy.

May 3. For the second time, Congress passes the McNary-Haugen Bill for relief of farmers who are still caught in an agricultural depression. Bill has come up four other times since 1924. President Coolidge vetoes bill for the second time on the grounds that it would tend to fix prices and encourage overproduction.

May 15. Congress appropriates $325 million for Mississippi Valley flood control over a 10-year period.

May 22. Congress passes Merchant Marine (Jones-White) Act, providing federal aid to U.S. private shipping by subsidized mail contracts, and doubling sums available — up to $250 million — for loans for new ship construction. Act also allows sale of U.S.-owned ships to private companies at low prices.

July 30. George Eastman at Rochester, New York, shows a group of viewers the first color motion pictures ever exhibited; original films show colorful subjects, from flowers, goldfish, peacocks, and butterflies to pretty girls.

Nov. 6. Herbert Hoover wins election by a landslide, with 21,392,000 votes to Smith's 15,016,000. Electoral vote is Hoover, 444; Smith, 87. Hoover takes 40 of the 48 states, including 5 states of the Solid South; against Smith are his unpolished background and his Roman Catholic religion.

Vesto M. Slipher, after observations of 43 spiral nebulae, demonstrates at Lowell Observatory, Arizona, that the nebulae are steadily moving away from the earth at increasing speeds.

Franz Boas, professor of anthropology at Columbia University, publishes his attack on the master race theory, *Anthropology and Modern Life*.

Stephen Vincent Benét publishes his epic poem of the Civil War, *John Brown's Body*. Edna St. Vincent Millay publishes famous sonnets in the volume *The Buck in the Snow and Other Poems*.

Italian conductor Arturo Toscanini becomes conductor of the New York Philharmonic-Symphony Orchestra; he has formerly conducted the orchestra of the Metropolitan Opera. Continuing with the Philharmonic until 1936, he then joins the NBC Symphony, remaining for 17 years.

Walt Disney released first Mickey Mouse cartoon, *Plane Crazy;* in the same year he produces *Steamboat Willie,* the first animated cartoon to use sound.

HERBERT HOOVER
Speech in New York, 1928
When the war closed, the most vital of all issues both in our own country and throughout the world was whether governments should continue their wartime ownership and operation of many instrumentalities of production and distribution. We were challenged with a peacetime choice between the American system of rugged individualism and a European philosophy of diametrically opposed doctrines — doctrines of paternalism and state socialism. The acceptance of these ideas would have meant the destruction of self-government through centralization of government. It would have meant the undermining of the individual initiative and enterprise through which our people have grown to unparalleled greatness.

The Republican Party from the beginning resolutely turned its face away from these ideas and these war practices. . . .

By adherence to the principles of decentralized self-government, ordered liberty, equal opportunity, and freedom to the individual, our American experiment in human welfare has yielded a degree of well-being unparalleled in all the world. It has come nearer to the abolition of poverty, to the abolition of fear of want than humanity has ever reached before. Progress of the past seven years is the proof of it. This alone furnishes the answer to our opponents, who ask us to introduce destructive elements into the system by which this has been accomplished.

WILLIAM E. BORAH
Speech in Senate, September 1929

Senators of the West, this is the only body left in the government where we have anything like an equality. This is the only body left where there is anything like an equality in shaping the economic policies of the country as between the industrial interests and agriculture. We cannot conceal the fact that there is an economic conflict in that situation. The industrial interests are naturally indisposed toward duties upon farm products, or upon raw materials, as was so well illustrated in this bill with reference to manganese. They are naturally desirous — it is human nature to desire — that their raw materials be free, and that their food products be free. . . .

We in the West are now a developing country, a growing country. We are like this country was when Clay was speaking and when the men of his time were making the fight. Protection is more applicable to us than to any other part of the country, and more necessary in order that we may develop; and it is because of that fact that we must necessarily guard the power that we have and the rights we have upon this floor.

Feb. 11. Owen D. Young and J. P. Morgan as U.S. representatives meet in Paris with Committee on German Reparations to revise Dawes Plan of 1924. Young Plan lowers amount due from Germany and extends time for payment. It also lowers debts among Allies and sets up Bank for International Settlements.

May 27. Supreme Court confirms right of the President to prevent passage of legislation by the pocket veto (holding of a bill presented for signature for 10 days when Congress adjourns within the period limit so that the bill cannot become law).

June 15. In Agricultural Marketing Act, Congress seeks to stabilize farm prices by means of a Federal Farm Board that aids financing of agricultural markets. Act does not contain price-fixing measures that had resulted in President Coolidge's veto of McNary-Haugen Bill of 1927.

July 1. National origins immigration quota law goes into effect. In same year, consuls are authorized to refuse admission to any applicant who might become a "public charge."

Sept. 24. In first instrument flight, Lieu-

Wall Street the day of the Crash, 1929

Homes of the unemployed on Riverside Drive in New York City, 1934

tenant James Doolittle flies entirely by radio signals received in his airplane.

Oct. 24. Several weeks' decline in stock prices becomes panic, and 13 million shares are sold. House of Morgan tries to halt drop by buying but, except for a momentary lull, is unsuccessful. **Oct. 29.** Selling begins again, and more than 16 million shares change hands. By mid-November, loss in stock paper values is about $26 billion. End of unprecedented speculation is not directly related to decline in earning power of industry or expansion of consumer debt, but it marks the beginning of 10 years of depression.

In this year, manufacture of nearly 3 million cars for the first time puts the automobile industry ahead of all others in value produced.

Robert S. and Helen Lynd of Columbia University publish *Middletown*, classic sociological study of Muncie, Indiana.

Thomas Wolfe publishes *Look Homeward, Angel*, his first novel; *Of Time and the River* is published in 1935 and *The Web and the Rock* in 1939. All are to some extent autobiographical. William Faulkner publishes *Sartoris*, first novel in cycle on the fate of the South; others are *The Sound and the*

Minneapolis Star, October 1929
Wave after wave of selling again moved down prices on the Stock Exchange today and billions of dollars were clipped from values.

Traders surged about the brokerage offices watching their holdings wiped out, and scenes on the floor of the Exchange were of the kind never before witnessed. It was one of the worst breaks in history, with all leaders crashing down through resistance barriers. . . .

The reaction came with the same abruptness as the one yesterday in which billions of dollars in value were lost.

For a time, in the morning, the market was showing signs of rallying power. Banking support was given the leaders, and U.S. Steel staged a substantial recovery that was carried over to the other pivotal shares.

Then new waves of selling out of poorly margined accounts started another reaction.

Tickers at 12:20 were 68 minutes behind. All records for volume were being broken.

Headline, Variety, October 1929
Wall Street Lays An Egg.

WILLIAM FAULKNER
The Sound and the Fury, 1929
It was a while before the last stroke ceased vibrating. It stayed in the air, more felt than heard, for a long time. Like all the bells that ever rang still ringing in the long dying light-rays and Jesus and Saint Francis talking about his sister. Because if it were just to hell; if that were all of it. Finished. If things just finished themselves. Nobody else there but her and me. If we could just have done something so dreadful that they would have fled hell except us. I have committed incest I said Father it was I it was not Dalton Ames. And when he put Dalton Ames. Dalton Ames. Dalton Ames. When he put the pistol in my hand I didn't. That's why I didn't. He would be there and she would and I would. Dalton Ames. Dalton Ames. Dalton Ames. If we could have just done something so dreadful and Father said That's sad too, people cannot do anything that dreadful they cannot do anything very dreadful at all they cannot even remember tomorrow what seemed dreadful today and I said, You can shirk all things and he said, Ah can you. And I will look down and see my murmuring bones and the deep water like wind, like a roof of wind, and after a long time they cannot distinguish even bones upon the lonely and inviolate sand. Until on the Day when He says Rise only the flatiron would come floating up. It's not when you realise that nothing can help you —religion, pride, anything—it's when you realise that you dont need any aid.

Fury in the same year, *As I Lay Dying* in 1930, *Sanctuary* in 1931, and *Absalom, Absalom!* in 1936. Ernest Hemingway publishes *A Farewell to Arms.*

Museum of Modern Art is founded in New York City; collection consists of international art of late nineteenth and twentieth centuries.

1930

Jan. 21-April 22. At London Naval Conference, five major naval powers continue principles of 1921 agreements without major changes; they do not discuss limitation of air or land armaments. The U.S., Britain, and Japan agree to limit cruiser construction; France and Italy do not. The U.S. Senate ratifies treaty in July.

Feb. 10. Almost 190 corporations and persons are arrested in Chicago on charges of violating the Prohibition amendment. They have done $50 million national business in liquor, selling more than 7 million gallons of whisky.

March 30. Captain Frank M. Hawks succeeds in first transcontinental glider flight. Departing San Diego, California, he reaches New York City in one week.

May 26. The Supreme Court holds unanimously that buying liquor is not a violation of the Prohibition amendment.

June 17. President Hoover signs Smoot-Hawley Tariff, although in May a petition signed by more than 1,000 economists has protested it and urged him to veto it if passed. Tariff raises duties so drastically on almost 900 articles that it results in sharp decline in international trade, and a deepening depression.

July 3. Congress creates Veterans Administration, which combines all federal agencies for aid to former servicemen under one department.

Sept. 9. U.S. State Department, fearing further unemployment, orders restrictions on immigration that prohibit almost any laborer from entering the country.

Nov. 4. In first defeat since 1916, Republicans lose majority in the House of Representatives and eight seats in the Senate.

Dec. 2. Unsuccessful in his attempts to establish self-help relief for unemployment through states and local organizations, President Hoover finally asks Congress for $100 to $150 million for public works, announcing that unemployment has reached about 4,500,000. Message also blames Depression on world conditions beyond control of the U.S.

Dec. 11. New York City's Bank of the United States closes as result of stock market crash. Bank has 60 branches and almost half a million depositors. During this year, more than 1,300 banks in the U.S. are forced to close.

State Department publishes 1928 J. Reuben Clark interpretation of Monroe Doctrine as relating only to European powers vis-à-vis Western Hemisphere states and not primarily to U.S. relations with Hemisphere nations. Memorandum repudiates Roosevelt Corollary of 1904 and improves hemispheric relations.

Lowell Observatory, Arizona, photographically identifies planet Pluto; discovery confirms mathematical prediction of Percival Lowell 16 years earlier and is significant advance in mathematical astronomy.

1930 census shows population of 122,775,000, which includes 4,107,000 immigrants arrived since 1920. Illiteracy is lower than ever before, at 4.3 percent. Av-

CHARLES A. BEARD
Harper's, 1931
There is another side to this stalwart individualism that also deserves consideration. Great things have been done in its name, no doubt, and it will always have its place in any reasoned scheme of thinking. Individual initiative and energy are absolutely indispensable to the successful conduct of any enterprise, and there is ample ground for fearing the tyranny and ineptitude of governments. . . . But on other pages of the doom book other entries must be made. In the minds of most people who shout for individualism vociferously, the creed, stripped of all flashy rhetoric, means getting money, simply that and nothing more. And to this creed may be laid most of the shame that has cursed our cities and most of the scandals that have smirched our federal government. . . .

The cold truth is that the individualist creed of everybody for himself and the devil take the hindmost is principally responsible for the distress in which Western civilization finds itself—with investment racketeering at one end and labor racketeering at the other. Whatever merits the creed may have had in days of primitive agriculture and industry, it is not applicable in an age of technology, science, and rationalized economy. Once useful, it has become a danger to society. Every thoughtful businessman who is engaged in management as distinguished from stock speculation knows that stabilization, planning, orderly procedure, prudence, and the adjustment of production to demand are necessary to keep the economic machine running steadily and efficiently.

(Above) "It's Washday Every Day in Washington":
cartoon by McCutcheon in the Chicago *Tribune*
pertaining to the Senate's investigation into the
Teapot Dome Oil reserve scandal and related
corruption in Harding's administration; (right)
Ku Klux Klan parade in Washington, 1926; (below)
Calvin Coolidge, thirtieth President of the United
States, photographed at the White House with his
wife and sons, 1923

(Above) Herbert Hoover, thirty-first President of the United States,
shopping at a dime store during the Depression; (below) Clarence
Darrow and William Jennings Bryan, the opposing lawyers at the
celebrated Scopes "Monkey Trial" in Dayton, Tennessee, 1925

I'll Take My Stand, 1930

All the articles bear in the same sense upon the book's title subject: all tend to support a Southern way of life against what may be called the American or prevailing way; and all as much as agree that the best terms in which to represent the distinction are contained in the phrase, "Agrarian versus Industrial.". . .

The South is a minority section that has hitherto been jealous of its minority right to live its own kind of life. The South scarcely hopes to determine the other sections, but it does propose to determine itself, within the utmost limits of legal action. Of late, however, there is the melancholy fact that the South itself has wavered a little and shown signs of wanting to join up behind the common or American industrial ideal. It is against that tendency that this book is written. The younger Southerners, who are being converted frequently to the industrial gospel, must come back to the support of the Southern tradition. They must be persuaded to look very critically at the advantages of becoming a "new South" which will be only an undistinguished replica of the usual industrial community. . . .

For, in conclusion, this much is clear: If a community, or a section, or a race, or an age, is groaning under industrialism, and well aware that it is an evil dispensation, it must find the way to throw it off. To think that this cannot be done is pusillanimous. And if the whole community, section, race, or age thinks it cannot be done, then it has simply lost its political genius and doomed itself to impotence.

erage life expectancy at birth is 61 years, an increase of 11 years since 1900. In a survey made this year, it is found that one of every five Americans owns an automobile.

Federal Bureau of Narcotics is formed as a unit of the Treasury Department to handle licensing of narcotics handlers, import permits, and law enforcement in cooperation with states.

Dr. Karl Landsteiner receives Nobel Prize for Medicine for his work on human blood groups. Born in Austria, Landsteiner has become an American citizen.

Louis Bamberger and his sister, Mrs. Felix Fuld, found the Institute for Advanced Study at Princeton University; Albert Einstein joins Institute in 1933.

I'll Take My Stand, cooperative book by 12 Southern writers, defends concrete, regional forms of writing.

Sinclair Lewis is first American to be awarded the Nobel Prize for Literature.

Hart Crane publishes *The Bridge*, a series of poems based on the Brooklyn Bridge as a symbol of American art and engineering.

Marc Connelly receives the Pulitzer Prize for *Green Pastures*, a play about Negro religion based on Roark Bradford's novel *Ol' Man Adam an' His Chillun.*

Grant Wood exhibits "American Gothic" in Chicago; painting is one of his first after change from pseudo-Impressionist style to technique influenced by Flemish primitives.

1930 - 1935

Ernest O. Lawrence builds first cyclotron, making possible atomic fission, in 1930. Harold C. Urey discovers isotope of hydrogen with atomic weight of 2 (deuterium, or heavy hydrogen) in 1931. In 1935 Arthur J. Dempster discovers uranium-235, sole natural element that is fissionable and plentiful.

1931

Jan. 19. Wickersham Commission, appointed by President Hoover to recommend means of enforcing Prohibition amendment, reports that enforcement is almost impossible because profits from illegal sale of liquor are great and the public, in general, does not favor the law. Commission recommends changes in the amendment and federal enforcement only instead of state-federal measures.

January. Unemployment is estimated at between 4 and 5 million. **Sept.-Oct.** In spreading bank panic, more than 800 U.S. banks close. Americans start hoarding gold for fear the U.S. will go off the gold standard.

Feb. 26. President Hoover vetoes Veterans Compensation Act, which authorizes loans equal to half the value of 1924 bonus allowances; Act is passed over his veto on following day.

March 3. "Star-Spangled Banner," words of which have been written by Francis Scott Key in 1814, is officially made U.S. national anthem.

May 1. The 102-story Empire State Building, tallest in the world, is dedicated and opened in New York City.

Oct. 5. Clyde Pangborn and Hugh Herndon complete first nonstop transpacific flight; trip from Japan to Washington State takes about 41 hours.

Dec. 26. Musical political satire *Of Thee I Sing,* by George S. Kaufman, Ira and George Gershwin, and Morrie Ryskind, opens in New York City. Enormously pop-

ROBERT M. LA FOLLETTE, JR.
Nation, 1931

For eighteen months, unemployment has been spreading poverty and acute suffering through industrial and agricultural areas alike. No one yet knows when the present economic disaster will be brought to an end. The illusory prosperity and feverish optimism which marked preceding years have given way to fearful economic insecurity and to widespread despair. . . . The administration's efforts to attain economic security have consisted of attempts to minimize the seriousness of the Depression, of bold assurances that steps which would restore prosperity were about to be taken, and of a woefully unsuccessful program to stimulate private or local agencies to undertake tasks which the administration was determined to shirk. . . .

Timidity and disingenuousness have marked the course of the administration at a time when heroic courage and bold frankness were necessary. Vigor and firm leadership have been displayed by the President at times, but only to resist proposals which would have mitigated suffering but which necessarily involved an additional levy upon wealthy income taxpayers. . . .

The third winter of unemployment is approaching. Responsibility for the failure of the federal government to provide a program for the relief of distress among millions of our people rests squarely upon President Hoover. The bankruptcy of his leadership in the worst economic crisis in our history reveals the tragic failure of rugged individualism and places the major cost of deflation upon those least able to bear it—the unemployed.

FREDERICK LEWIS ALLEN
Only Yesterday, 1931

In 1920, when prohibition was very young, Johnny Torrio of Chicago had an inspiration. Torrio was a formidable figure in the Chicago underworld. He had discovered that there was big money in the newly outlawed liquor business. He was fired with the hope of getting control of the dispensation of booze to the whole city of Chicago. At the moment there was a great deal too much competition; but possibly a well-disciplined gang of men handy with their fists and their guns could take care of that, by intimidating rival bootleggers and persuading speakeasy proprietors that life might not be wholly comfortable for them unless they bought Torrio liquor. . . .

The profits of bootlegging in Chicago proved to be prodigious, allowing an ample margin for the mollification of the forces of the law. The competition proved to be exacting. . . . But Al Capone had been an excellent choice as leader of the Torrio offensives. . . . As the profits from beer and "alky-cooking" (illicit distilling) rolled in, young Capone acquired more finesse—particularly finesse in the management of politics and politicians. By the middle of the decade he had gained complete control of the suburb of Cicero, had installed his own mayor in office, had posted his agents in the wide-open gambling-resorts and in each of the 161 bars, and had established his personal headquarters in the Hawthorne Hotel. He was taking in millions now. Torrio was fading into the background; Capone was becoming the Big Shot.

ular, it becomes first musical comedy to win the Pulitzer Prize.

Alphonse ("Scarface Al") Capone, Chicago gangster who has an annual income of at least $20 million, is imprisoned for income tax evasion.

J. G. Lansky first detects radio wave interference from the Milky Way after noticing a steady hissing sound when his radio aerial is turned in that direction.

Lincoln Steffens, foremost muckraker at turn of the century, publishes his *Autobiography*, in which he favors a more revolutionary approach to reform than his earlier efforts.

Pearl Buck publishes *The Good Earth*, which tops best seller lists for two years; in 1938 she wins the Nobel Prize for Literature.

International Bible Students Association becomes Jehovah's Witnesses; in 1939 organization is incorporated under the name Watch Tower Bible and Tract Society of Pennsylvania.

1931 - 1933

June 20, 1931. President Hoover proposes an international moratorium on war debts and reparations because of worldwide depression. Moratorium is initially set at one year; token payments are made in 1933, after which all nations except Finland suspend payments entirely.

1932

Jan. 22. Reconstruction Finance Corporation (RFC) is established with Charles G. Dawes as head, and U.S. government becomes major source of business capital.

Measure provides that credit of federal government be used to support railroads and financial institutions and to revive the economy by aiding business corporations. New government corporation is capitalized at $500 million, with $2 billion borrowing power. By end of year, RFC has loaned about $1,500,000,000 to U.S. financial institutions.

Feb. 2. The U.S. attends disarmament conference at Geneva, Switzerland, called by League of Nations. President Hoover's proposals for scrapping of all offensive weapons and reduction of land armaments by one-third are rejected. Meeting produces no important results.

Feb. 27. In effort to bolster U.S. foreign credit and counteract gold hoarding, Congress passes Glass-Steagall Act, which releases about $750 million of U.S. gold to industry and business. Gold has been part of that used to support U.S. currency.

March 3. Twentieth ("Lame Duck") Amendment is submitted to the states for ratification. It provides that Congress shall convene on January 3 after fall elections, that terms of President and Vice-President shall start on January 20 rather than March 4, and that in the event of the death of the President-elect before inauguration, the Vice-President-elect shall succeed to the office. Amendment is declared ratified on February 6, 1933.

March 23. Passage of Norris-LaGuardia Anti-Injunction Act is a distinct gain for labor, since it prohibits injunctions in most labor disputes. Use of injunctions has been challenged since Sherman Antitrust Act of 1890.

April 30. Convention of Socialist Labor Party meets and nominates Verne L. Reyn-

HERBERT HOOVER
Veto of the Muscle Shoals Bill, 1931
I am firmly opposed to the government entering into any business the major purpose of which is competition with our citizens. There are national emergencies which require that the government should temporarily enter the field of business, but they must be emergency actions and in matters where the cost of the project is secondary to much higher considerations. There are many localities where the federal government is justified in the construction of great dams and reservoirs, where navigation, flood control, reclamation, or stream regulation are of dominant importance, and where they are beyond the capacity or purpose of private or local government capital to construct. In these cases power is often a by-product and should be disposed of by contract or lease. But for the federal government deliberately to go out to build up and expand such an occasion to the major purpose of a power and manufacturing business is to break down the initiative and enterprise of the American people; it is destruction of equality of opportunity among our people; it is the negation of the ideals upon which our civilization has been based. . . .

I hesitate to contemplate the future of our institutions, of our government, and of our country if the preoccupation of its officials is to be no longer the promotion of justice and equal opportunity but is to be devoted to barter in the markets. That is not liberalism, it is degeneration.

GEORGE SOULE
Harper's, 1932

If you want to hear discussions of the future revolution in the United States, do not go to the breadlines and the mill towns, but to Park Avenue and Wall Street, or to the gatherings of young literary men. Well-fed people will anxiously inquire when you think the revolution is coming. They will admit in a large way that profits must be abolished and that some form of Communism might be desirable. In the next breath they may express doubt whether the Democrats can muster enough votes to defeat Mr. Hoover for reelection, or they may oppose moderate reforms like unemployment insurance, or may support the sales tax, which transfers burdens from the rich to the poor. Nevertheless, they vaguely expect profound changes.

But you will find that searching for actual flesh-and-blood revolutionary proletarians is a thankless task. Most of those who really suffer from the depression are, according to the best-informed reports, simply stricken dumb by it. Like the Republican administration, they are awaiting nothing more drastic than the return of prosperity. . . .

As long as people wait for the downtrodden and the hopeless to produce a revolution, the revolution is far away. Revolutions are made, not by the weak, the unsuccessful, or the ignorant, but by the strong and the informed. They are processes, not merely of decay and destruction but of advance and building. An old order does not disappear until a new order is ready to take its place.

olds of New York for President. **May 21.** Socialist Party nominates Norman Thomas of New York. **May 28.** Communist Party nominates William Z. Foster of New York; his running mate is a Negro, James W. Ford of Alabama. **June 14.** Republicans meet at Chicago and renominate President Hoover and Vice-President Curtis. **June 27.** Democrats meet at Chicago and nominate Governor Franklin Delano Roosevelt of New York for President on the fourth ballot, with John Nance Garner of Texas as his running mate. **July 5.** Prohibition Party meets and nominates William D. Upshaw of Georgia. **July 10.** Farmer-Labor Party nominates Jacob S. Coxey of Ohio. Republican platform calls for government economy; a protective tariff; participation in international monetary conference; further limits on immigration; the gold standard; veterans' pensions; and revision of the Prohibition amendment. Democratic platform calls for government economy; tariff for revenue; state unemployment and old-age insurance; participation in international monetary conference; banking and financial reform, largely to be achieved by federal regulation; every possible aid to farmers; veterans' pensions for men with service-connected disabilities; and repeal of Prohibition.

May 21. Amelia Earhart lands in Ireland after 13½-hour, 2,026-mile flight from Newfoundland, becoming first woman to fly alone across the Atlantic. Four years earlier she has been first woman passenger to fly the Atlantic.

May 29. One thousand veterans of World War I arrive in Washington, D.C., to urge full cash payment of veterans' bonuses. During June they are joined by about 14,000 more. **June 15.** House of Representatives passes bill to provide full payment of bonuses, but Senate defeats it two days later. Most veterans then leave for home with funds provided by the government, but many stay in Washington despite efforts of Washington police to evict them. **July 28-29.** After two deaths have occurred, President Hoover sends federal troops and tanks, commanded by General Douglas MacArthur, to disperse the veterans.

July 21. Faced with rapidly increasing unemployment, President Hoover approves Emergency Relief Act, which broadens scope of RFC, including help to agriculture; raises amount of authorized financing of business and industry; and provides for financing of state and local public works.

July 22. Congress passes Federal Home Loan Bank Act, recommended by President Hoover in 1931. Act authorizes 12 federal regional banks to protect homeowners by granting loans and to encourage new construction for relief of unemployment. Land banks to aid farmers, authorized by Congress in 1916, are also strengthened.

July. Depression reaches low point. Farm purchasing power is almost one-half that of 1929; monthly wages are 60 percent of 1929; dividends are about 57 percent; industry operates at half 1929 volume; more than 5,000 banks, especially rural ones, have closed since 1930; average monthly unemployment is 12 million. President Hoover and Vice-President Curtis, as well as Cabinet members, cut their own salaries and plan federal public works to ease unemployment.

July-October. During election campaign, Roosevelt promises program of social reconstruction and federal support of the economy aimed at the "forgotten man." He stresses distribution of the wealth with least possible federal interference. Hoover stresses private enterprise, calling Roosevelt's pro-

MALCOLM COWLEY
The New Republic, 1932
When the veterans of the Bonus Army first tried to escape, they found that the bridges into Virginia were barred by soldiers and the Maryland roads blocked against them by state troopers. They wandered from street to street or sat in ragged groups, the men exhausted, the women with wet handkerchiefs laid over their smarting eyes, the children waking from sleep to cough and whimper from the tear gas in their lungs. The flames behind them were climbing into the night sky. About four in the morning, as rain began to fall, they were allowed to cross the border into Maryland, on condition that they move as rapidly as possible into another state. . . .

Their shanties and tents had been burned, their personal property destroyed, except for the few belongings they could carry on their backs; many of their families were separated, wives from husbands, children from parents. Knowing all this, they still did not appreciate the extent of their losses. Two days before, they had regarded themselves, and thought the country regarded them, as heroes trying to collect a debt long overdue. . . . When threatened with forcible eviction, they answered that no American soldier would touch them: hadn't a detachment of Marines . . . thrown down its arms and refused to march against them? . . .

But 1,000 homeless veterans, or 50,000, don't make a revolution. . . . No, if any revolution results from the flight of the Bonus Army, it will come from a different source, from the government itself. The army in time of peace, at the national capital, has been used against unarmed citizens — and this, with all it threatens for the future, is a revolution in itself.

FRANKLIN D. ROOSEVELT
Speech accepting Democratic nomination, 1932
I pledge you, I pledge myself, to a new deal for the American people. Let us all here assembled constitute ourselves prophets of a new order of competence and courage. This is more than a political campaign; it is a call to arms.

DAVID LAWRENCE
Advising the readers of his column to vote for Hoover, 1932
[It is] dangerous to change parties in mid-Depression.

Slogan ascribed ironically to the Republicans, 1932
Don't Swap Barrels Going Over Niagara.

DWIGHT MORROW
Any party which takes credit for the rain must not be surprised if its opponents blame it for the drought.

FRANKLIN D. ROOSEVELT
Speech during campaign, 1932
It is common sense to take a method and try it. If it fails, admit it frankly and try another. But above all, try something.

gram socialistic; he warns that if the "new deal" (a phrase used by Roosevelt in his acceptance speech) is adopted, "the grass will grow in the streets . . . the weeds will overrun the fields."

Nov. 8. Roosevelt is elected by popular vote of 22,810,000 to Hoover's 15,759,000. Electoral vote is Roosevelt, 472; Hoover, 59. Roosevelt wins in all states except Delaware, Pennsylvania, Connecticut, New Hampshire, Vermont, and Maine. Democrats win control in Congress amounting to almost two-thirds of the Senate and almost three-quarters of the House.

November. Government-appointed Committee on the Costs of Medical Care recommends state-sponsored medical care supported by taxes or insurance for the medically indigent. American Medical Association calls idea idealistic, cumbersome, impersonal, and bureaucratic.

December. Enthusiasm for technocracy reaches height; idea of Howard Scott of New York City, scheme involves regulation of national affairs by experts in place of elected officials, and price controls based on units of energy.

Wisconsin enacts first unemployment insurance law in the U.S.

American Federation of Labor adopts new constitution, confirming traditional "craft union" structure; membership by this year is about 2,500,000.

James T. Farrell publishes first volume of his Studs Lonigan trilogy, *Young Lonigan*; trilogy deals with life in deteriorating middle-class section of Chicago. Remaining volumes are *The Young Manhood of Studs Lonigan* in 1934 and *Judgment Day* in 1935. Erskine Caldwell publishes *Tobacco Road*, a realistic examination of Southern poor whites.

Ferde Grofé completes his *Grand Canyon Suite*, which becomes one of the best-known American musical compositions throughout the world. One of most popular songs of this year is "Brother, Can You Spare a Dime?"

Nebraska capitol at Lincoln is completed. Designed by Bertram Goodhue, it is first important public building that attempts use of modern or original style in architecture and sculpture.

1932 - 1933

Jan. 7, 1932. The U.S. protests Japanese occupation of Manchuria, which has started in 1931. Secretary of State Henry Stimson announces that the U.S. will not recognize any arrangement violating the Open Door in China or imposed on China by force in violation of treaties. **March 3.** Japan expels Chinese forces from Shanghai. **March 11.** League of Nations adopts Stimson nonrecognition policy, and Japan withdraws from China but not from Manchuria. **Oct.** Special commission appointed by League to investigate Japanese activity in Manchuria decries Japan's actions and recommends making Manchuria an autonomous state of China with safeguards for Japanese interests. **March 1933.** Japan withdraws from the League of Nations.

1933

Feb. 25. First U.S. aircraft carrier is christened *Ranger*, after John Paul Jones's ship, by Mrs. Herbert Hoover.

March 4. Franklin D. Roosevelt is inaugurated as President; inaugural address inspires public confidence, attacks Hoover administration measures for failure of economic recovery, and sets the stage for the vigorous economic and social experiments of the New Deal. Inaugural also proclaims U.S. "good neighbor" policy, at first toward the

NATHANIEL PEFFER
Harper's, 1933
A year has passed since Japan's absorption of Manchuria presented the most serious threat to world peace since 1918, and the first concrete test of all the hopes, plans, and devices contrived for the prevention of war. It is time to take a reckoning.

Two items stand out in such a reckoning.

First, America, while clinging to the fiction of isolation from Europe, has become definitely, alarmingly, and perhaps inextricably involved in Asia.

Second, the promise of control of war by international machinery has proved illusive. . . .

When the balance of all the forces working on history in the Far East is taken, the resultant will be found to be the definitive entry of the United States into the East. The United States has not only intervened but made unequivocal commitments and thereby, with or without deliberate intent, moved to a new position in world affairs. The pronouncements of the American government with reference to Manchuria, so glibly hailed by liberals, will constitute, unless revoked, a pledge and policy no less binding than the Monroe Doctrine but infinitely harder to effectuate. They will embroil us in the most inflammable area in the world; make us the protagonist of the status quo in a region where the status quo is inherently unstable; enroll us as a partisan in a congeries of crusty international feuds, and, unless revoked, will have a more positive influence on the course of our history than the Monroe Doctrine, since they concern a part of the world more contested than South America and state a position less easy to defend. And of this fact the American people remain singularly unaware and wholly uncritical.

FRANKLIN D. ROOSEVELT
First Inaugural Address, 1933
*I am certain that my fellow Americans
expect that on my induction into the
presidency I will address them with a
candor and a decision which the present situation of our nation impels. This
is preeminently the time to speak the
truth, the whole truth, frankly and boldly.
Nor need we shrink from honestly facing
conditions in our country today. This
great nation will endure as it has endured, will revive and will prosper.*

*So, first of all, let me assert my firm
belief that the only thing we have to
fear is fear itself — nameless, unreason-
ing, unjustified terror which paralyzes
needed efforts to convert retreat into
advance. In every dark hour of our national life a leadership of frankness and
vigor has met with that understanding
and support of the people themselves
which is essential to victory. I am convinced that you will again give that
support to leadership in these critical
days. . . .*

*Compared with the perils which our
forefathers conquered because they believed and were not afraid, we have still
much to be thankful for. Nature still offers her bounty, and human efforts have
multiplied it. Plenty is at our doorstep,
but a generous use of it languishes in
the very sight of the supply. Primarily
this is because the rulers of the exchange of mankind's goods have failed,
through their own stubbornness and
their own incompetence, have admitted
their failure, and abdicated. . . .*

*The money changers have fled from
their high seats in the temple of our civilization. We may now restore that temple to the ancient truths.*

world, and later applied especially to the
Western Hemisphere.

March 5. On Sunday after inauguration,
President Roosevelt proclaims a national
bank holiday from March 6 through March
9. By this time, about one-half of all U.S.
banks have failed or suspended payments,
especially in small cities and rural areas, and
almost all states have closed or placed restrictions on banks. National holiday suspends activity of the Federal Reserve System and all financial institutions and bans
transactions in bullion or currency. **March
13.** Banks begin to reopen, and by end of
the month about three-quarters of banks are
operating, confidence in banks and currency
is restored, large-scale runs and failures
cease, stocks go up, and hoarded gold begins to return to the Treasury. Roosevelt
has acted under authority of a 1917 wartime measure, but Congress has approved
action by passing the Emergency Banking
Relief Act on March 9.

March 9. Congress meets in special
session called by President Roosevelt to
deal with financial crisis, but Roosevelt continues session until June 16 to handle farm
relief and unemployment; session is later
called the "Hundred Days" of the New
Deal. By June 16 Congress has enacted a
wide program of social and economic experiments that goes far beyond economic recovery goals. Many laws passed are later
changed or extended by supplementary laws
and by interpretation by the courts.

March 12. President Roosevelt begins
new policy of speaking directly to the
people by means of radio in fireside chats;
in first talk, he explains the emergency measures he has taken to stem the financial
panic.

March 20. President Roosevelt signs
Economy Act. It aims at saving about $500
million by cutting government salaries, de-

partmental budgets, and veterans' pensions, especially those paid to ex-servicemen without service-connected disabilities. Act actually saves about half of amount desired.

March 22. President Roosevelt signs act that legalizes sale of beers and wines of 3.2 percent or less alcohol volume and places revenues on sales.

March 31. Civilian Conservation Corps (CCC) is formed to employ young men of 18 to 25 years of age in such projects as reforestation, flood control, soil erosion control, and road construction. Program is run by War, Interior, Labor, and Agriculture departments, with army officers directing work and camps. At point of maximum enrollment, CCC has 500,000 members, and by 1942 it has employed about 3 million men.

April 19. The U.S. goes off the gold standard, and prices in the U.S. go up. Emergency Banking Relief Act of March 9 has authorized withdrawal by the Treasury of all gold and gold certificates and prohibited exporting and hoarding of gold.

May 12. Congress creates Federal Emergency Relief Administration (FERA) under Harry L. Hopkins to contribute $500 million of federal funds to state relief agencies. Contributions are outright grants, not loans as in Hoover administration relief measures.

May 12. Creation of Agricultural Adjustment Administration (AAA) provides financial aid to farmers, attempts to reduce crop surpluses by making direct payments to farmers who cut down acreage planted in surplus commodities, and raises farm income by controlling prices of basic crops. Some of these features are held unconstitutional by the Supreme Court in 1936.

May 18. Tennessee Valley Authority (TVA) is established as a government cor-

HENRY A. WALLACE
Radio address, 1933

It should be made plain at the outset that the new Farm Act initiates a program for a general advance in buying power, an advance that must extend throughout America, lightening the way of the people in city and country alike. We must lift urban buying power as we lift farm prices. The Farm Act must not be considered an isolated advance in a restricted sector; it is an important part of a large-scale, coordinated attack on the whole problem of depression. . . .

To reorganize agriculture, cooperatively, democratically, so that the surplus lands on which men and women now are toiling, wasting their time, wearing out their lives to no good end shall be taken out of production—that is a tremendous task. The adjustment we seek calls, first of all, for a mental adjustment, a willing reversal of driving, pioneer opportunism and ungoverned laissez-faire. The ungoverned push of rugged individualism perhaps had an economic justification in the days when we had all the West to surge upon and conquer; but this country has filled up now and grown up. There are no more Indians to fight. No more land worth taking may be had for the grabbing. We must experience a change of mind and heart. . . .

I hope that you will come to feel in time, as I do now, that the rampageous individualist who signs up for adjustment and then tries to cheat is cheating not only the government but his neighbors. I hope that you will come to see in this act, as I do now, a Declaration of Interdependence; a recognition of our essential unity and of our absolute reliance one upon another.

ROBERT MORSS LOVETT
Current History, 1934

Life is more than meat and the body more than that which sustains it.

The chief disappointment in connection with the fair as a record of progress lay in the obscuring of this cardinal truth. Fundamental to civilization, the most important exhibit was a huge diorama which portrayed the gathering of water into reservoirs, whence streams issued to spin turbines and set a current racing across the country to light farms, mines, and quarries, to move trains, and awaken to life cities with their homes, skyscrapers, stores, and factories. It exemplified the enormous difference between the machine age and the power age, between the industrial revolution and the technological. It reminded one that the machine by itself is a tool, an extension of the human hand, and that the possession of power in cheap and accessible form makes possible the unlimited exercise of human ingenuity to convert this machine into a thing of independent life, automatic, self-regulating, self-renewing. One wondered how many of the spectators who gazed on this exhibit saw its anticipation of a time when the functional need for man would be as limited as that for the horse, and their present lives as meaningless. The basic theme of the fair as expressed officially was "the achievements of science and their application through industry to the creation of a larger life for mankind." The achievements of science were there in abundance, and their applications; but where, one was moved to ask, was the evidence of the larger life for mankind, or even the promise of it?

poration set up to coordinate and develop all aspects of resources of the Tennessee River Valley, which covers parts of seven states. Plan includes social and economic improvement of people, as well as conservation, flood control, and rural electrification. These principles of regional planning have long been urged by conservationists and by Senator George Norris of Nebraska, who has sponsored similar measures that have been vetoed in 1928 and 1931 by Presidents Coolidge and Hoover as government interference with private enterprise.

May 27. Federal Securities "Truth in Securities" Act requires that reliable information on all new securities offered for sale be given to investors by means of public sworn statements to the Federal Trade Commission (FTC).

May 27. A Century of Progress International Exposition opens in Chicago; it celebrates Chicago's centennial and marks public acceptance of modern architectural technique and design.

June 6. Congress establishes the U.S. Employment Service, which, jointly with states, establishes and maintains employment agencies.

June 12-July 27. At London conference on tariffs and currency stabilization, the U.S. declines to cooperate in international currency stabilization program with gold standard nations; proposal for bilateral tariff agreements without such stabilization is rejected by European nations. Conference fails.

June 13. Home Owners' Loan Corporation (HOLC) is created to give financial help to nonfarm homeowners by refinancing mortgages and providing advances for taxes, repairs, and maintenance. Eventually, Corporation makes loans involving more than 1 million mortgages.

June 13. Congress passes National Industrial Recovery Act (NIRA), which embodies three programs. First, to be handled by National Recovery Administration (NRA), attempts to reduce unemployment and stimulate business by setting up system of self-regulation in industry, with agreed-on fair trade codes, under government supervision; cooperating industries are to be exempt from antitrust laws, and courts may issue injunctions against code violators; the President may approve proposed codes and prescribe them; General Hugh S. Johnson is appointed head of the NRA. Second, National Labor Board (later National Labor Relations Board, NLRB), headed by Senator Robert F. Wagner of New York, is created to guarantee the right of labor to bargain collectively through its own representatives; Act also sets up enforcement machinery. Third, Public Works Administration (PWA), under leadership of Secretary of the Interior Harold L. Ickes, is established to provide employment and stimulate business by providing purchasing power; PWA is to provide funds of $3,300,000,000 for construction of public projects. NIRA is invalidated by the Supreme Court in 1935 on the grounds that it gives the Executive excessive power, that the Constitution does not provide for such legislation, and that the Act regulates businesses not engaged in interstate commerce.

June 15. National Guard (state forces partially supported by the federal government) is made part of the Army of the United States in wartime and in national emergencies declared by Congress.

June 16. Farm Credit Act is passed to help in refinancing farm mortgages and financing crops. These functions and other farm credit operations of the federal government are combined in a single agency, the Farm Credit Administration (FCA).

June 16. Banking (Glass-Steagall) Act es-

HUGH S. JOHNSON
On his appointment as head of NRA, 1933
It will be red fire at first and dead cats afterwards. This is just like mounting the guillotine on the infinitesimal gamble that the ax won't work.

HUGH S. JOHNSON
The Blue Eagle from Egg to Earth, 1935
The Apostles of Plenty must temper their doctrine. The answer is not to produce as much as you can at the lowest cost you can get, especially if that low cost comes out of wages or too abruptly out of employment. . . .

Always the answer is "balance" — balance of supply to demand, balance of prices at fair exchange parity throughout the whole economic structure, and balance of benefits among great economic areas. You cannot even move toward this balance in this modern muddle without some direction. NRA offers one way to get that supervision in industry just as AAA offers it in agriculture and the various securities and fiscal acts in investment and banking. These statutory makeshifts are not the final answer. Everybody knows that. They are hasty and imperfect. But the very heart of the New Deal is the principle of concerted action in industry and agriculture under government supervision looking to a balanced economy as opposed to the murderous doctrine of savage and wolfish competition and rugged individualism, looking to dog-eat-dog and devil take the hindmost. This Utopian balance will never be achieved — there will never be perfection. But every plan should try to achieve it instead of trying to prevent it.

FRANKLIN D. ROOSEVELT
Letter to Maxim Litvinov, 1933
I am glad to have received the assurance expressed in your note to me of this date that it will be the fixed policy of the government of the Union of Soviet Socialist Republics:

1. To respect scrupulously the indisputable right of the United States to order its own life within its own jurisdiction in its own way and to refrain from interfering in any manner in the internal affairs of the United States, its territories, or possessions.

2. To refrain and to restrain all persons in government service and all organizations of the government or under its direct or indirect control, including organizations in receipt of any financial assistance from it, from any act overt or covert liable in any way whatsoever to injure the tranquillity, prosperity, order, or security of the whole or any part of the United States, its territories, or possessions, and, in particular, from any act tending to incite or encourage armed intervention, or any agitation or propaganda having as an aim the violation of the territorial integrity of the United States, its territories, or possessions, or the bringing about by force of a change in the political or social order of the whole or any part of the United States, its territories, or possessions. . . .

It will be the fixed policy of the Executive of the United States within the limits of the powers conferred by the Constitution and the laws of the United States to adhere reciprocally to the engagements above expressed.

tablishes Federal Deposit Insurance Corporation (FDIC), guaranteeing individual bank deposits up to $5,000 against bank failures.

June. Emergency Housing Division, a branch of the PWA, is organized to finance slum clearance and private housing projects.

October. Commodity Credit Corporation is organized to keep farm prices up by lending money to farmers so that they can hold their produce instead of selling on a low market.

Nov. 8. Civil Works Administration is set up under the leadership of Harry L. Hopkins; a further unemployment relief program, it aims to make jobs for 4 million people on new federal, state, and local projects. Eventually about $1 billion is spent on nearly 400,000 work projects.

Nov. 16. President Roosevelt, hoping for increased foreign trade, establishes diplomatic relations with the Soviet Union, which has not been recognized by the U.S. since 1917. Soviet Union promises to discontinue propaganda against U.S. government and to recognize rights of U.S. citizens in Russia.

Dec. 5. Twenty-first Amendment to the Constitution, which repeals the Prohibition amendment, is declared ratified.

Dec. 26. At Montevideo Conference of U.S. and Latin-American nations, Secretary of State Cordell Hull for the U.S. and representatives of all other nations declare that no state has the right to intervene in the internal or external affairs of another. President Roosevelt echoes this for the U.S. two days later in saying that the U.S. is "from now on . . . opposed to armed intervention."

Fiorello La Guardia is elected mayor of New York City on liberal fusion ticket, ending 16-year rule of Tammany Hall, characterized by corruption; La Guardia is reelected in 1937 and 1941.

Affected seriously by the Depression, 2,000 rural schools do not open for the fall semester; 200,000 teachers are out of work; and about 2,300,000 eligible children are not in school; in addition, a number of colleges and universities are forced to close.

Thomas Hunt Morgan of California Institute of Technology receives the Nobel Prize for Medicine for his investigations and discoveries concerning the chromosome in the transmission of heredity. Morgan has written *The Theory of the Gene.*

U.S. District Court voids ban on James Joyce's novel *Ulysses,* which has repeatedly been burned and confiscated as obscene by U.S. Post Office. Judge John M. Woolsey, in his decision, calls it "a sincere and honest book" and says, "I do not detect anywhere the leer of a sensualist." Ruling helps establish new legal criteria of obscenity in literature and art. Erskine Caldwell's *God's Little Acre* is similarly cleared in case brought by New York Society for the Prevention of Vice.

Gertrude Stein's *Autobiography of Alice B. Toklas,* actually her own rather than her secretary's, sells widely, although her other books have had small audiences.

The Great Lakes are linked with the Gulf of Mexico when the Illinois Waterway is opened.

1934

Jan. 1. Dr. Francis E. Townsend of Long Beach, California, proposes his old-age pension plan, providing that all U.S. citizens more than 60 years old receive $200 per month; funds are to be raised by taxes on business transactions. Townsend feels that

JOHN M. WOOLSEY
U.S. v. One Book Called Ulysses, 1933
I have read Ulysses once in its entirety and I have read those passages of which the government particularly complains several times. In fact, for many weeks, my spare time has been devoted to the consideration of the decision which my duty would require me to make in this matter. . . .

The words which are criticized as dirty are old Saxon words known to almost all men and, I venture, to many women, and are such words as would be naturally and habitually used, I believe, by the types of folk whose life, physical and mental, Joyce is seeking to describe. In respect of the recurrent emergence of the theme of sex in the minds of his characters, it must always be remembered that his locale was Celtic and his season spring.

Whether or not one enjoys such a technique as Joyce uses is a matter of taste on which disagreement or argument is futile, but to subject that technique to the standards of some other technique seems to me to be little short of absurd. Accordingly, I hold that Ulysses is a sincere and honest book, and I think that the criticisms of it are entirely disposed of by its rationale. . . .

I am quite aware that owing to some of its scenes Ulysses is a rather strong draft to ask some sensitive, though normal, persons to take. But my considered opinion, after long reflection, is that, while in many places the effect of Ulysses on the reader undoubtedly is somewhat emetic, nowhere does it tend to be an aphrodisiac.

Ulysses may, therefore, be admitted into the United States.

HARRY L. HOPKINS
Radio address, 1934

It is a curious thing what a quantity of sickness, coldness, hunger, and bare-footedness we are willing to let other men suffer. It literally has no limit. You can hear it in the cautious tone of voice of a man who says, "We'd better be careful or we will have a major disaster." What, might we ask him, would he consider to be a major disaster? Obviously it has nothing to do with numbers. For 18 million persons is a large enough number used in any connection to satisfy most men. . . . For most people large figures are as unusable to their reasoning processes as the astronomer's light-years are to a man with a piece of smoked glass. Yet we can easily roll across our tongues, without a reaction setting up in the heart or mind, the simple statement that 18 million Americans are so poor of this world's goods that they are on relief. . . .

Many of you will say to me that these people like being on relief and that they are better off on relief than they have ever been before. We have heard that one very often. We are told they will not work any more. May I ask you one thing? When you know that a relief budget, for lack of funds, is placed at the very minimum of a family's needs and that in very few places it can take care of rent and that it can hope to do little more than keep body and soul together; and when you realize that this is a nominal budget only, and because we lack funds sometimes families are permitted to receive less than 50 percent of that so-called ideal budget, which is in itself inadequate to life, may I ask you if this is an indictment of relief, that it is said to offer more than life offered before, or is it an indictment of something else?

plan will stabilize the U.S. economy, since pensioners must spend each month's pension within one month.

Jan. 30. Gold Reserve Act of this year gives the President flexible but limited powers to regulate the value of the dollar in order to give government control of dollar devaluation and to increase prices of goods. On the following day, the President proclaims value of the dollar is 59.06 cents in relation to its gold content.

Jan. 31. Congress creates Federal Farm Mortgage Corporation to provide further aid for debt-ridden farmers through easier credit terms.

Feb. 2. President Roosevelt establishes Export-Import Bank of Washington to provide financial help through various credit devices in an attempt to encourage foreign trade.

Feb. 23. Crop Loan Act sets up a fund of $40 million to extend crop financing measure of previous year.

February. Civil Works Administration (CWA) is dismantled. Federal Emergency Relief Administration (FERA) takes over relief burdens and continues operation until 1935.

February. U.S. postmaster general cancels all domestic airmail contracts on ground of collusion among airlines in fixing prices. Army Air Corps takes over delivery of airmail until May, when private lines resume service under supervision of Interstate Commerce Commission.

March 24. After rejection by the Philippines of an independence act passed in 1933, Tydings-McDuffie Act establishes the Commonwealth of the Philippines and provides for complete independence in 1946.

Under the Commonwealth, U.S. supervision is decreased and includes only controls over such matters as defense and foreign affairs. Manuel Quezon is elected first president in 1935 after ratification of new constitution.

March 27. Vinson Naval Parity Act authorizes construction of airplanes and ships up to limits of naval treaties of 1922 and 1930, providing for building of 100 ships and 1,000 planes over five years. Construction is held up until 1938, however, since Congress does not appropriate enough money for program.

March 28. For the first time, President Roosevelt is defied by Congress when his veto of bill increasing government salaries and veterans' pensions is overridden.

April 7-June 28. Jones-Connally Farm Relief Act, Bankhead Cotton Control Act, Jones-Costigan Sugar Act, and Kerr-Smith Tobacco Control Act are passed in effort to cut production of surplus agricultural commodities. In some cases, reduction of acreage is voluntary as specified by the AAA; but in others it is compulsory, and violators are subject to taxes on excess production. Tax aspect of acts is invalidated by the Supreme Court in 1936.

April 13. Congress passes Johnson Debt Default Act, which prohibits U.S. loans to any nation that is in default on war debt payments.

April 23. Senator Gerald P. Nye of North Dakota is appointed to head committee investigating role of munitions manufacturers and financiers in involving the U.S. in World War I for profit to be gained from sale of arms and from loans. Although evidence gathered is not conclusive, publicity increases isolationist feeling in the U.S.

BENNETT CHAMP CLARK
Harper's Monthly, 1935
Some of us in the Senate, particularly the members of the Munitions Investigation Committee, have delved rather deeply into the matter of how the United States has been drawn into past wars and what forces are at work to frighten us again into the traps set by Mars. . . .

Just who profited from the last war? Labor got some of the crumbs in the form of high wages and steady jobs. But where is labor today, with its 14 million unemployed? Agriculture received high prices for its products during the period of the war and has been paying the price of that brief inflation in the worst and longest agricultural depression in all history. Industry made billions in furnishing the necessities of war to the belligerents and then suffered terrific reaction like the dope addict's morning after. War and depression—ugly, misshapen, inseparable twins—must be considered together. Each is a catapult for the other. The present worldwide depression is a direct result of the World War. Every war in modern history has been followed by a major depression.

Therefore, I say, let the man seeking profits from war or the war-torn countries do so at his own risk. . . .

I deny with every fiber of my being that our national honor demands that we must sacrifice the flower of our youth to safeguard the profits of a privileged few. I deny that it is necessary to turn back the hands of civilization to maintain our national honor. I repudiate any such definition of honor. Is it not time for every lover of our country to do the same thing?

(Above) Eviction in Chicago during the Depression; (below) parade of jobless workers in Chicago in 1932; some 13,000 persons participated.

(Above left) John T. McCutcheon's Pulitzer Prize cartoon of 1932; (above right) South Dakota farmers working on an irrigation project sponsored by WPA, 1936; (below) street scene in New Orleans, recorded by Ben Shahn for the FSA nationwide study of the Depression

FRANKLIN D. ROOSEVELT
Fireside Chat, June 1934

I could cite statistics to you as unanswerable measures of our national progress. . . .

But the simplest way for each of you to judge recovery lies in the plain facts of your own individual situation. Are you better off than you were last year? Are you debts less burdensome? Is your bank account more secure? Are your working conditions better? Is your faith in your own individual future more firmly grounded?

Also, let me put to you another simple question: Have you as an individual paid too high a price for these gains? Plausible self-seekers and theoretical diehards will tell you of the loss of individual liberty. Answer this question also out of the facts of your own life. Have you lost any of your rights or liberty or constitutional freedom of action and choice? Turn to the Bill of Rights of the Constitution, which I have solemnly sworn to maintain and under which your freedom rests secure. Read each provision of that Bill of Rights and ask yourself whether you personally have suffered the impairment of a single jot of these great assurances. I have no question in my mind as to what your answer will be. The record is written in the experiences of your own personal lives. . . .

In the working out of a great national program which seeks the primary good of the greater number, it is true that the toes of some people are being stepped on and are going to be stepped on. But these toes belong to the comparative few who seek to retain or to gain position or riches or both by some shortcut which is harmful to the greater good.

April 27. Home Owners' Loan Act extends funds of act of 1933 to encourage home building and maintenance.

May 18. In effort to control widespread crime, Congress enacts several laws that authorize use of federal powers against crimes involving more than one state and against federal agents; in addition, the death penalty is established for kidnapping across state lines, a result of kidnap-murder of son of Charles A. Lindbergh.

May 23. Du Pont laboratories researcher Dr. Wallace H. Carothers produces an immensely strong synthetic fiber that he calls polymer 66. It is patented later under the name nylon, and first use is bristles for toothbrushes.

May 29. New treaty with Cuba abrogates Platt Amendment of 1901, which has made Cuba virtually a U.S. protectorate. Ambassador to Cuba Sumner Welles has negotiated treaty with conservative Cuban government and dictator Fulgencio Batista.

June 6. Securities and Exchange Commission (SEC) is formed to license stock exchanges, control trading in securities, and correct dishonest practices in the markets.

June 7. Corporate Bankruptcy Act provides for reorganization of bankrupt corporations on formal request or consent of two-thirds of their creditors.

June 12. Reciprocal Trade Agreements Act gives the President power to raise or lower tariffs 50 percent by agreement with other governments. By 1938, agreements have been reached with 18 nations, with which trade is increased about 40 percent but with little effect on total foreign trade. However, gesture of reciprocal adjustment eases foreign resentment of generally high U.S. tariffs.

June 18. Wheeler-Howard Indian Reorganization Act reverses trend toward decline of tribal societies by returning lands open to sale to tribal ownership; Dawes Severalty (General Allotment) Act of 1887 has divided tribal lands for sale to individuals and has been a conspicuous failure.

June 28. Federal Housing Administration is established to insure housing loans made by private financial organizations. In 1937 establishment of the U.S. Housing Authority extends loans to local governments for public housing.

Aug. 6. U.S. troops and administrators are withdrawn from Haiti after 19 years; U.S. financial aid has stabilized Haitian economy, and political order has been restored. U.S. financial control continues until 1947.

Nov. 6. In fall elections Democrats gain nine seats in the Senate and nine in the House of Representatives.

Nov. 6. Nebraska adopts constitutional amendment written by Senator George Norris and becomes the first state in the U.S. with a unicameral legislature.

November. Author Upton Sinclair is Democratic candidate for governor of California on EPIC ("end poverty in California") program; he is defeated by a massive coalition of regular parties and business interests.

Censorship of moving pictures is begun by the Catholic Legion of Decency; program meets little resistance.

Federal Communications Commission (FCC) replaces Federal Radio Commission; it is authorized to control all foreign and interstate radio, telegraph, and cable communications.

New York Times, 1934
The full force of the motion-picture industry, overwhelming in this fabulous city, has been thrown into the crusade to keep Upton Sinclair out of the governor's chair at Sacramento. . . .

The city of Los Angeles has turned into a huge movie set, where many newsreel pictures are made every day depicting the feelings of the people against Mr. Sinclair. Equipment from one of the major studios, as well as some of its second-rate players, may be seen at various street intersections or out in the residential neighborhood, "shooting" the melodrama and unconscious comedy of the campaign. Their product can be seen in leading motion-picture houses in practically every city or town of the State.

In one of the "melodramas" recently filmed and shown here in Los Angeles, an interviewer approaches a demure old lady, sitting on her front porch and rocking away in her rocking chair.

"For whom are you voting, Mother?" asked the interviewer.

"I am voting for Governor Merriam," the old lady answers in a faltering voice.

"Why, Mother?"

"Because I want to save my little home. It is all I have left in this world."

In another recent newsreel there is shown a shaggy man with bristling Russian whiskers and a menacing look in his eye.

"For whom are you voting?" asks the interviewer.

"Vy, I am foting for Seenclair."

"Why are you voting for Mr. Sinclair?"

"Vell, his system worked vell in Russia, vy can't it vork here?" . . .

Low paid "bit" players are said to take the leading roles in most of these "newsreels," particularly where dialogue is required.

LAWRENCE DENNIS
American Mercury, 1935

In the conflicts of minority groups acting under the prevailing degree of national or social discipline, kept at a minimum by our constitutional and juridical system, there is likely to result eventually an intolerable degree of chaos, from which a formula like fascism may seem to offer the only remedy. The relevancy of fascism to such a clash would consist chiefly in its bid to make explicit and effective a unique concept of national interest and, of course, to provide the necessary personnel and machinery for realization. It is conceivable that many of our conservatives who are now worried over the dangers of losing liberty under a possible fascism might some day welcome a fascist dictator and a disciplined political party to curb the abuses of constitutional liberties and legal powers now commonly committed by irresponsible minorities. Nor is it unthinkable that many recent Wall Street and Park Avenue converts to states' rights, if given a stiff dose of economic sabotage and antinationalism by some plausible demagogue under the label of states' rights, might make a hasty return to their first love — a strong central government.

The breakdown of the social mechanics of liberal capitalism is too obvious a reason for the triumph of fascism to need much explanation. In this connection it must be remembered that those who have been driven by defeat and frustration to challenge the present system and to follow a leader offering a substitute are not likely to assist in improving a system which they now are attacking.

1934 - 1935

Roosevelt administration measures, while creating employment, raising incomes, improving labor conditions, stemming tide of bank and business failures, and inspiring a sense of hopefulness, are violently opposed by a number of factions. The American Liberty League, formed by conservatives, opposes prolabor legislation and increase of tax rate on high incomes. Old-age pension plans and Share-the-Wealth plans advocated by Francis E. Townsend, Senator Huey P. Long of Louisiana, and Reverend Gerald L. K. Smith call for direct payments to U.S. citizens. Father Charles E. Coughlin (the "Radio Priest") of Michigan organizes the National Union for Social Justice, favoring inflation and isolationism, and speaks to a wide audience, condemning labor, Communists, international financiers, Jews, and President Roosevelt. The New Deal is called Communist, Socialist, Bolshevik, and un-American, and work projects are called boondoggling, but most Americans are heartened by obvious lifting of the Depression.

1934 - 1936

F. Scott Fitzgerald publishes his novel of character disintegration *Tender Is the Night;* his last volume of short stories, *Taps at Reveille,* appears in 1935 and a series of essays, "The Crack-Up," in 1936.

1935

Jan. 4. President Roosevelt in his message to Congress sets goal of economic security for the ordinary man through social reform, rather than emphasizing revival of the national economy and business; he also recommends further solutions to unemployment.

Jan. 29. Senate fails to ratify agreement providing for U.S. participation in the Permanent Court of International Justice, although it has been authorized by President Hoover in 1929 and is approved by President Roosevelt. Vote is barely short of necessary two-thirds majority.

April 8. Passage of Emergency Relief Appropriation Act establishes the Works Progress Administration (WPA), which continues until 1943. Act ends direct federal relief payments but continues to provide relief by employing workers on public projects. By 1943, nearly 15 million people have been employed at various times. Important specialized projects are National Youth Administration, which employs needy students and other youths; Federal Arts Project, in which artists decorate public buildings, index works of art, and teach in first federal project involving the fine arts; Federal Theater Project, which helps experimental theater and brings live theater to many towns for the first time since the advent of radio and movies; Federal Writers' Project, which compiles many local histories and publishes historic archives.

April 27. Soil Conservation Service is established to try to halt soil erosion in the Great Plains, where the most destructive drought ever known in the Middle West has turned the land into a dust bowl. Many have left their farms and become "Okies," moving to other areas in hope of finding work.

May 1. Resettlement Administration (RA) is established to help or resettle farm families living on marginal or submarginal land. Under the program, unproductive farmland is shifted to soil conservation and reforestation programs, model towns are built, and family ownership of small farms is supported.

May 11. Rural Electrification Administration (REA) is established by President Roosevelt to build power lines and provide elec-

STUART CHASE
Rich Land, Poor Land, 1936
The continental soil, the center of vitality, is visibly and rapidly declining. The forest cover has been stripped and burned and steadily shrinks. The natural grass cover has been torn to ribbons by steel plows and the hooves of cattle and sheep. The skin of America has been laid open. Streams have lost their measured balance, and, heavy with silt, run wild in flood to the sea at certain seasons, to fall to miserable trickles in the drier months. This land may be bristling with tall chimneys and other evidences of progress, but it has lost its old stability. . . .

Kansas farms are blowing through Nebraska at an accelerating rate. In the spring of 1934, the farms of the Dust Bowl—which includes western Oklahoma, western Kansas, eastern Colorado, the panhandle of Texas, and parts of Wyoming—blew clear out to the Atlantic Ocean, 2,000 miles away. On a single day 300 million tons of rich top soil was lifted from the Great Plains, never to return, and planted in places where it would spread the maximum of damage and discomfort. Authentic desert sand dunes were laid down. People began to die of dust pneumonia. More than 9 million acres of good land has been virtually destroyed by wind erosion, and serious damage is reported on nearly 80 million acres.

Taking the continent as a whole, it is reliably estimated that half of its original fertility has been dissipated by these various agents. The rate of loss tends to follow the laws of compound interest. The stricken areas grow cumulatively larger.

FRANKLIN D. ROOSEVELT
Message to Congress, 1935
In the important field of security for our old people, it seems necessary to adopt three principles — first, noncontributory old-age pensions for those who are now too old to build up their own insurance; it is, of course, clear that for perhaps thirty years to come funds will have to be provided by the states and the federal government to meet these pensions. Second, compulsory contributory annuities, which in time will establish a self-supporting system for those now young and for future generations. Third, voluntary contributory annuities by which individual initiative can increase the annual amounts received in old age. . . .

The establishment of sound means toward a greater future economic security of the American people is dictated by a prudent consideration of the hazards involved in our national life. No one can guarantee this country against the dangers of future depressions, but we can reduce these dangers. We can eliminate many of the factors that cause economic depressions and we can provide the means of mitigating their results. This plan for economic security is at once a measure of prevention and a method of alleviation.

We pay now for the dreadful consequence of economic insecurity — and dearly. This plan presents a more equitable and infinitely less expensive means of meeting these costs. We cannot afford to neglect the plain duty before us. I strongly recommend action to attain the objectives sought in this report.

Uncomplimentary remark applied to F.D.R. after 1935
That Man in the White House.

tricity to areas not served by private companies; measure encourages rural power cooperatives and municipally owned power systems. By 1940, number of farms receiving electricity has almost tripled from 1935 figure (12.6 percent).

June 7. National Resources Committee is formed to collect information, make estimates, and plan development of such natural resources as water, land, and mining areas, as well as human resources.

July 5. Because of Supreme Court invalidation of the NRA, a new National Labor Relations Board is established by the Wagner Act. Board is to supervise labor negotiations, guaranteeing collective bargaining rights of employees and controlling unfair labor practices of employers. Many states also enact similar legislation. Board is upheld by the Supreme Court in 1937.

Aug. 14. Social Security Act establishes federal payroll tax to finance a cooperative federal-state system of unemployment insurance, as well as grants to states to support and encourage state systems of relief to the blind, to dependent children, and for maternity and infant care. Old-age and, later, survivors' pensions are to be paid directly by the federal government.

Aug. 24. Banking Act of 1935 refines and strengthens operation of the Federal Reserve System.

Aug. 28. Public Utility Holding Company Act places various aspects of public utility industry under authority of the Federal Trade Commission, the Federal Power Commission, and the Securities and Exchange Commission and counteracts monopolies by forbidding financial consolidation of public utility systems that is not necessary for efficient operation.

Aug. 28. After the Supreme Court invalidates an earlier measure designed to allow farmers to hold bankrupt farms, Congress passes Frazier-Lemke Amendment to Federal Bankruptcy Act, which provides a three-year grace period for farmers whose mortgages are foreclosed; during period they may retain their properties by payment of a reasonable rent to be determined by the courts.

Aug. 30. Revenue Act of 1935 (Wealth Tax Act) increases income tax rates in high income brackets, individual as well as corporate, and raises gift and estate taxes. Act affects individuals with incomes of more than $50,000 and taxes incomes of more than $1 million up to 75 percent.

Aug. 31. Neutrality Act of 1935 is passed; it gives the President power to declare an embargo on arms, but not raw materials, to belligerents in case of European war and to allow U.S. citizens to travel on belligerent vessels only at their own risk. Desire to separate U.S. financial interests from foreign wars, as well as Italy's apparent designs on Ethiopia, is responsible for proposal.

Sept. 8. Dr. Carl A. Weiss shoots Senator Huey P. Long in the capitol of Louisiana. Long has become virtually a dictator of Louisiana and has become powerful in national politics. Before his death (two days later), he has been planning to form a third political party.

Sept. 25. Maxwell Anderson's verse drama *Winterset* opens; it is inspired by the Sacco-Vanzetti case. **Oct. 10.** *Porgy and Bess* opens in New York City; folk opera by George Gershwin based on *Porgy*, a play by Dorothy and DuBose Heyward, it runs for only four months but eventually is revived many times and is shown in U.S. road shows, as well as in Europe, Latin America, and the Soviet Union. Clifford Odets' *Awake and Sing*, play about life in

HUEY LONG
Radio address, 1935

But, my friends, unless we do share our wealth, unless we limit the size of the big man so as to give something to the little man, we can never have a happy or free people.

I wonder if any of you people who are listening to me were ever at a barbecue! We used to go there — sometimes 1,000 people or more. If there were 1,000 people, we would put enough meat and bread and everything else on the table for 1,000 people. Then everybody would be called and everyone would eat all they wanted. But suppose at one of these barbecues for 1,000 people that one man took 90 percent of the food and ran off with it and ate until he got sick and let the balance rot. Then 999 people would have only enough for 100 to eat and there would be many to starve because of the greed of just one person for something he couldn't eat himself.

Well, ladies and gentlemen, America, all the people of America, have been invited to a barbecue. God invited us all to come and eat and drink all we wanted. He smiled on our land and we grew crops of plenty to eat and wear. He showed us in the earth the iron and other things to make everything we wanted. He unfolded to us the secrets of science so that our work might be easy. God called: "Come to my feast."

Then what happened? Rockefeller, Morgan, and their crowd stepped up and took enough for 120 million people and left only enough for 5 million for all the other 125 million to eat. And so many millions must go hungry and without these good things God gave us unless we call on them to put some of it back.

"What Helps Business Helps You"

ANDRE MAUROIS
Etats-Unis 39, 1939
The Daughters of the American Revolution are the women or girls whose ancestors took part a hundred and fifty years ago in the war for independence. In France we lack this type of aristocracy. The Sons of the Regicides do not hold conventions in Bourges nor the Daughters of the Victims of the Terror at Nantes. That's because our regimes followed each other so rapidly that each wiped out the loyalties of its predecessors; the conquerors of the Bastille ceased to hold reunions as soon as Bonaparte came upon the scene. In America the continuity of the regime permitted the Revolution to become hereditary and conservative.

the Bronx, is immediately popular; in the same year three other plays by Odets, *Till the Day I Die, Paradise Lost,* and *Waiting for Lefty,* are shown in New York City.

Nov. 9. Committee for Industrial Organization is founded by the heads of eight unions within the American Federation of Labor to develop industry-wide unions that include clerical and unskilled workers, as well as skilled workers who are eligible for the A.F.L.

President Roosevelt places all remaining public lands in the U.S. under conservation program.

Fear of radicals results in pressure by the American Legion and Daughters of the American Revolution on state governments to require loyalty oaths of teachers; eventually they are successful in 19 states.

Pan American Airways begins transpacific air service from San Francisco to Manila.

1936

Jan. 15. Japan, which has denounced the Washington Naval Treaty of 1922 dealing with reduction of navies and maintenance of the Open Door in China, withdraws from the London Naval Conference. **March 25.** Britain, France, and the U.S. agree to minor and fairly ineffectual limitations on naval armaments.

Jan. 24. Congress passes Adjusted Compensation Act over President Roosevelt's veto; Act provides for immediate payment, if requested, of veterans' bonus certificates. More than $1,500,000,000 in benefits is paid out to about 3 million veterans by the middle of the year.

Feb. 29. Neutrality Act of 1936 extends 1935 act to May 1937 and adds prohibition of credit or loans to belligerent nations.

Feb. 29. Since Agricultural Adjustment Act of 1933 has been invalidated by the Supreme Court in January, Congress passes Soil Conservation and Domestic Allotment Act; law aims to continue policies of restriction of surplus crops, as well as to conserve soil by compensation for cutting acreage of soil-depleting crops and planting soil-improving and -conserving crops.

April 26. Socialist Labor Party nominates John W. Aiken of Massachusetts for President. **May 5.** Prohibition Party meets and nominates Dr. D. Leigh Colvin of New York. **May 22.** Socialist Party meets and nominates Norman Thomas of New York. **June 11.** Republicans at Cleveland nominate Governor Alfred M. Landon of Kansas for President and Colonel Frank Knox of Illinois for Vice-President. **June 19.** Representative William Lemke of North Dakota announces that he is the presidential candidate on the Union Party ticket; Union Party is backed by Father Coughlin's National Union for Social Justice. **June 23.** Democrats meet at Philadelphia and renominate President Roosevelt and Vice-President Garner. Roosevelt is endorsed by several progressive and labor organizations. **June 24.** Communists meet and nominate Earl Browder of Kansas. Republican platform criticizes "unconstitutionality" of the New Deal and usurping of congressional power by the executive but proposes no alternatives to major New Deal measures. Democratic platform stands on New Deal record. Roosevelt criticizes despotism of "economic royalists."

June 19. Robinson-Patman Act is passed; it prohibits prices so low that competition is destroyed and pricing that encourages monopolies or reduces competition. Its greatest effect is on chain stores involved in interstate commerce.

June 22. Revenue Act of 1936 provides, among other things, for taxation of undis-

CHARLES E. COUGHLIN
Radio address, 1936
In 1936, when our disillusionment is complete, we pause to take inventory of our predicament. You citizens have shackled about your limbs a tax bill of $35 billion, most of which . . . was created by a flourish of a fountain pen. Your erstwhile savior, whose golden promises ring upon the counter of performance with the cheapness of tin, bargained with the money changers that, with 70 billion laboring hours in the ditch, or in the factory, or behind the plow, you and your children shall repay the debt which was created with a drop of ink in less than ten seconds.

Is that driving the money changers out of the temple? . . .

My friends, I come before you tonight not to ask you to return to the Landons, to the Hoovers, to the Old Deal exploiters who honestly defended the dishonest system of gold standardism and rugged individualism. Their sun has set never to rise again. . . .

Alas! The temple still remains the private property of the money changers. The golden key has been handed over to them for safekeeping—the key which now is fashioned in the shape of a double cross. . . .

Neither Old Dealer nor New Dealer, it appears, has courage to assail the international bankers, the Federal Reserve bankers. In common, both the leaders of the Republicans and the Democrats uphold the old money philosophy. Today in America there is only one political party—the banker's party. In common, both old parties are determined to sham-battle their way through this November election with the hope that millions of American citizens will be driven into the no-man's-land of financial bondage.

Literary Digest, October 1936
LANDON, 1,293,669
ROOSEVELT, 972,897

*FINAL RETURNS IN THE DIGEST'S POLL
OF TEN MILLION VOTERS*

*Well, the great battle of the ballots in
the poll of 10 million voters, scattered
throughout the forty-eight states of the
Union, is now finished, and in the table
below we record the figures received
up to the hour of going to press.*

*These figures are exactly as received
from more than one in every five voters
polled in our country—they are neither
weighted, adjusted, nor interpreted.*

*Never before in an experience cover-
ing more than a quarter of a century in
taking polls have we received so many
different varieties of criticism—praise
from many; condemnation from many
others—and yet it has been just of the
same type that has come to us every
time a Poll has been taken in all these
years. . . .*

*The Poll represents the most exten-
sive straw ballot in the field—the most
experienced in view of its twenty-five
years of perfecting—the most unbiased
in view of its prestige—a Poll that has
always previously been correct.*

JAMES A. FARLEY
After Roosevelt's landslide victory,
1936
As Maine goes, so goes Vermont.

tributed profits of corporations, in addition
to already existing corporation income tax.
Act is widely attacked by industry as hampering the practice of setting aside funds for
expansion and as a cushion of support for
slow periods.

June 26. Merchant Marine Act attempts
to strengthen U.S. merchant fleet by direct
subsidy instead of by existing ocean mail
contracts; Act also creates U.S. Maritime
Commission.

June 30. Congress passes Walsh-Healey
Public Contracts Act, specifying labor conditions for employees of firms having government contracts; established minimum
wages are to be paid, 8-hour day and 40-
hour week are to be maintained, and child
labor is prohibited.

Nov. 3. After bitterly fought campaign, in
which about 80 percent of U.S. newspapers
support Governor Landon, President Roosevelt wins election by a popular vote of
27,753,000 to Landon's 16,675,000. Electoral vote is Roosevelt, 523; Landon, 8;
Roosevelt carries every state but Maine and
Vermont; this is greatest electoral majority
in any election involving two or more candidates. Election results in about 80 percent
Democratic membership in both House and
Senate.

Dec. 1. President Roosevelt opens Inter-
American Conference for Maintenance of
Peace at Buenos Aires, Argentina; Conference adopts agreement pledging consultation among Western Hemisphere nations
whenever any of them is threatened by foreign aggression.

Dec. 11. King Edward VIII of England
abdicates his throne after British government refuses to accept as queen American
divorcée Wallis Warfield Simpson. Succeeded by his brother George VI, Edward
is given the title duke of Windsor.

By this year, the gross national debt has risen to about $34 billion, as opposed to more than $22 billion at beginning of Roosevelt administration. Income of government has risen, but its expenditures have gone up at a greater rate, largely because of relief measures.

Boulder (Hoover) Dam on the Colorado River is completed; reservoir (Lake Mead) back of dam has total capacity of more than 10 trillion gallons of water, the largest man-made lake in the world. Dam is the highest in the world to this time.

Robert M. Hutchins, president of the University of Chicago, publishes *The Higher Learning in America*, a manifesto of the movement against progressive education and the elective system in colleges.

Margaret Mitchell publishes her Pulitzer Prize novel, *Gone with the Wind*; before her death in 1949, the Civil War and Reconstruction novel sells about 8 million copies in 40 countries, almost certainly the greatest sale of any novel published in the U.S. Movie made from book wins Academy award for 1939.

Dramatist Eugene O'Neill receives the Nobel Prize for Literature.

Henry R. Luce begins publication of *Life*, weekly photographic news and feature magazine, inaugurating an era of photojournalism; he has bought title of satire magazine discontinued in this year.

1936 - 1939

Although the U.S. remains officially neutral in the Spanish Civil War, American opinion favors the Loyalists. Hundreds go to Spain to fight the Fascist insurgents, just as men from many European countries join in a conflict that becomes a World War II proving ground.

ROBERT M. HUTCHINS
The Higher Learning in America, 1936
The most striking fact about the higher learning in America is the confusion that besets it. This confusion begins in the high school and continues to the loftiest levels of the university. . . .

The college of liberal arts is partly high school, partly university, partly general, partly special. Frequently it looks like a teacher-training institution. Frequently it looks like nothing at all. . . .

For the sake of abbreviation I have of course exaggerated the plight of the higher learning. It has, in fact, many admirable qualities, not the least of which is its friendly reception of anybody who would like to avail himself of it. But we who are devoting our lives to it should learn something from the experience of recent years. Up to the onset of the present depression it was fashionable to call for more and more education. Anything that went by the name of education was a good thing just because it went by that name. I believe that the magic of the name is gone and that we must now present a defensible program if we wish to preserve whatever we have that is of value. . . .

We may get order in the higher learning by removing from it the elements which disorder it today, and these are vocationalism and unqualified empiricism. If when these elements are removed we pursue the truth for its own sake in the light of some principle of order, such as metaphysics, we shall have a rational plan for a university. We shall be able to make a university a true center of learning; we shall be able to make it the home of creative thought.

JOEL SEIDMAN
New Frontiers, 1937

1937

In the warfare between nonunion mass production industry and the CIO, the General Motors strike* was the first major battle. Realizing that much might depend upon the outcome, both sides unstintingly threw their resources into the struggle. . . .

Behind the General Motors strike there was a long record of efforts by the United Automobile Workers of America to bargain collectively, with delays and evasions on the part of the corporation. Especially did the workers rebel against the speeding up of production and the spy system employed by the company. Repeated efforts of the union to win recognition and obtain a union contract came to naught, and in the meantime discrimination against union members continued. . . .

From the first the corporation officials insisted that they would not negotiate so long as the strikers held the plants. The men suspected a ruse, knowing that if they left the plants they would lose their power to prevent production. . . .

Finally, on February 11, an agreement was reached and the strike ended. . . .

The strikers hailed the settlement as a signal victory for them. For the first time the giant General Motors Corporation had been fought to a standstill by its workers and forced to engage in collective bargaining with them. After forty-four days the sit-downers marched out of the plant, heads and spirits high, singing "Solidarity Forever." Out they came, two by two, with a large American flag at the head of the procession, to the cheers of 2,000 sympathizers assembled at the plants.

Jan. 6. Because of Spanish Civil War, started in previous year, Congress passes joint resolution forbidding export of munitions to either side in Spain; resolution is necessary because previous neutrality acts apply only to wars between nations; it hampers mainly Loyalists, however, since Insurgents are supplied by Germany and Italy. **May 1.** Neutrality Act of 1937 is passed in effort to remedy shortcomings of previous ones. In addition to prohibiting shipment of arms on U.S. vessels, travel on belligerent vessels is made unlawful, and belligerents who purchase nonmilitary goods in the U.S. are required to pay for them immediately and transport them in their own ships. The latter is called the "cash and carry" clause. **Sept. 14.** Executive order restrains U.S. munitions trade arising from Japanese attack on China; because of Japan's large merchant fleet, this is largely to China's disadvantage.

Jan. 20. President Roosevelt is inaugurated at first January 20 inauguration, as provided by the Twentieth Amendment; he promises further measures against continuing economic depression that leaves "one-third of a nation ill-housed, ill-clad, ill-nourished."

January. Auto workers at General Motors' Fisher body plants in Flint, Michigan, stage first major sit-down strike in the U.S.; strikers entrench themselves in factories and, despite Michigan court ruling that they are in violation of property rights, are highly successful. Strikes and sit-downs continue, especially in the automobile and steel industries. General Motors recognizes the United Auto Workers in February, and U.S. Steel signs contract in the spring rather than risk a strike.

Feb. 5. In an effort to win Supreme

Court approval of New Deal legislation, President Roosevelt proposes reorganization of the federal judiciary. Plan to increase the number of Supreme Court justices from 9 to 15 is resisted by Congress and the press as an attempt to "pack" the Court and leads to first serious political defeat for Roosevelt, but practical success is gained when the Court, in a series of decisions between March and May, upholds the Social Security Act, the Wagner Labor Relations Act, and other important New Deal measures. In addition, Roosevelt is able to appoint seven new justices within the next four years because of death or retirement of elderly incumbents.

March 1. Important gains by organized labor are achieved when United States Steel Corporation accepts first union contract with United Steel Workers-CIO; contract raises wages, lowers hours, and provides for overtime pay. **April 26.** A further gain is the Guffey-Vinson Bituminous Coal Act, which reenacts valid parts of earlier New Deal laws that seek to regulate production and labor conditions in the soft coal industry; the Supreme Court has held parts of original law unconstitutional.

May 30. "Little Steel" companies, led by Republic Steel, refuse to recognize steel union; union demonstrators outside of Republic plant in South Chicago are fired on by police, who kill 4 and injure 84; incident is known as "Memorial Day Massacre." Recognition by independent steel companies is not achieved until 1941.

July 22. Congress passes Bankhead-Jones Farm Tenant Act, which seeks to promote family farm ownership, discourage tenant farming and sharecropping, and improve labor conditions of migrant workers. Act establishes the Farm Security Administration (FSA), which takes over work of the Resettlement Administration.

WILLIAM ALLEN WHITE
Atlantic Monthly, 1937
In no other land is the middle class so solidly fortified as it is in America. The constitutional prohibition against titles of nobility has done something, but not everything, and perhaps not much to strengthen the foundations of the middle-class fortification. . . .

But the swift subsidence of wealth after October 1929 reacted like an earthquake shock upon the American bourgeoisie. The appearance of the unemployed not merely in millions, but in tens of millions, produced a caste with broken morale. That gave the American burghers something to think about.

For the first time in American history, labor is becoming class-conscious in a considerable area. . . . The appearance of the vertical union, Mr. Lewis's CIO, is a new thing, a labor orgainzation with a class-conscious background.

Moreover, the labor vote in the election of 1936 for the first time was cast solidly for a President and a Congress. Labor claimed naturally to have captured Washington. . . . The labor that was one of the six powerful and more or less antagonistic minorities which produced the Democratic vote in 1936 was for the moment class-conscious to the core so far as leadership is concerned. It has revived the public-be-damned attitude of the elder Vanderbilt. The middle class has been able to tolerate the public-be-damned attitude from its plutocrats who were merely spoiled children. But the middle class is batting surprised and even troubled eyes when it is damned nonchalantly by the proletariat.

FRANKLIN D. ROOSEVELT
Speech in Chicago, 1937
The political situation in the world, which of late has been growing progressively worse, is such as to cause grave concern and anxiety to all the peoples and nations who wish to live in peace and amity with their neighbors. . . .

It began through unjustified interference in the internal affairs of other nations or the invasion of alien territory in violation of treaties and has now reached a stage where the very foundations of civilization are seriously threatened. The landmarks and traditions which have marked the progress of civilization toward a condition of law, order, and justice are being wiped away . . . .

It seems to be unfortunately true that the epidemic of world lawlessness is spreading. When an epidemic of physical disease starts to spread, the community approves and joins in a quarantine of the patients in order to protect the health of the community against the spread of the disease.

It is my determination to pursue a policy of peace and to adopt every practicable measure to avoid involvement in war. It ought to be inconceivable that in this modern era, and in the face of experience, any nation could be so foolish and ruthless as to run the risk of plunging the whole world into war by invading and violating, in contravention of solemn treaties, the territory of other nations that have done them no real harm and which are too weak to protect themselves adequately. Yet the peace of the world and the welfare and security of every nation is today being threatened by that very thing.

Aug. 26. Judicial Procedure Reform Act is signed; it allows federal judges, including those of the Supreme Court, to retire at 70 with full pensions after 10 or more years of service.

Sept. 1. U.S. Housing Authority is established by the U.S. Housing Act to provide loans to local authorities for low-cost housing and rent subsidies.

Oct. 5. President Roosevelt, convinced that international measures are necessary to preserve world peace, urges a quarantine of aggressors by all peace-loving nations; U.S. opinion, however, is still predominantly isolationist, and move is not popular among some groups.

Nov. 10. Brazil adopts new constitution, which gives President Getúlio Vargas far-reaching powers to stem disturbances by radicals. Although Vargas government is considered Fascist by many, the U.S. does not acknowledge this and acts immediately to diminish German influence in Brazil. By March 1939 the U.S. and Brazil have signed several agreements guaranteeing to Brazil funds for improving its economy.

Nov. 15-Dec. 21. Congress meets in special session called by President Roosevelt, who recommends legislation involving farmers, labor, conservation, and government reorganization. Congress fails to act largely because Southern Democrats have by now joined Republicans in opposing most administration policies.

Dec. 12. U.S. gunboat *Panay* is attacked by Japanese planes in Chinese waters and sunk; 2 of crew are killed and 30 injured. **Dec. 14.** The U.S. demands that Japan apologize, pay reparations, and guarantee that such incidents will not recur. Japan sends formal apologies and guarantees on the same day.

December. Senator Robert M. La Follette's committee reports, after investigation of means of suppressing labor unions, that various companies use espionage, strikebreakers, vigilantes against organizers, blacklisting of union members, and even private armies supplied from private arsenals.

Musical comedy *I'd Rather Be Right*, by George S. Kaufman and Moss Hart, with songs by Richard Rodgers and Lorenz Hart, is a satire on President Roosevelt. International Ladies' Garment Workers' Union produces *Pins and Needles*, a musical comedy that becomes enormously successful; one of its most popular songs is "Sing Me a Song with Social Significance."

1937 - 1940

Supreme Court invalidates Oregon conviction of labor organizer on the ground that a speech given at an orderly meeting is not a public danger. In the same year, Georgia conviction of a Communist organizer is reversed. In following years, Supreme Court rules that the states may not infringe on liberties specified in the Fourteenth Amendment, upholding, in 1938, the right to distribute religious tracts without a license; in 1939, the right of peaceful assemblage; in 1940, the right to collect funds for religious organizations and the right of peaceful picketing.

1938

Jan. 3. President Roosevelt in his annual message points out that world unrest makes it vital for the U.S. to keep itself defensively strong. Later in January, he proposes to Congress increased appropriations for defense tools and naval construction.

Jan. 6. President Roosevelt sends message to House of Representatives warning against passage of Ludlow Resolution,

ALFRED HAYES

Joe Hill, 1938

I dreamed I saw Joe Hill last night
  Alive as you and me.
Says I, "But Joe, you're ten years
    dead."
  "I never died," says he,
  "I never died," says he.

"In Salt Lake, Joe," says I to him,
  Him standing by my bed,
"They framed you on a murder charge."
  Says Joe, "But I ain't dead,"
  Says Joe, "But I ain't dead."

"The copper bosses killed you, Joe,
  They shot you, Joe," says I.
"Takes more than guns to kill a man,"
  Says Joe, "I didn't die,"
  Says Joe, "I didn't die."

And standing there as big as life
  And smiling with his eyes,
Joe says, "What they forgot to kill
  Went on to organize,
  Went on to organize."

"Joe Hill ain't dead," he says to me,
  "Joe Hill ain't never died.
Where working men are out on strike
  Joe Hill is at their side,
  Joe Hill is at their side."

"From San Diego up to Maine
  In every mine and mill,
Where workers strike and organize,"
  Says he, "You'll find Joe Hill,"
  Says he, "You'll find Joe Hill."

I dreamed I saw Joe Hill last night
  Alive as you and me.
Says I, "But Joe, you're ten years
    dead."
  "I never died," says he,
  "I never died," says he.

HENRY A. WALLACE
Report, 1938

Agriculture needs crop adjustment to prevent these . . . recurring cycles of underproduction and overproduction. Consumers need it, too, because widely fluctuating production, with its inevitable addition to the farmers' costs, means higher consumer prices in the end. . . . Consumers need protection against excessively high prices, while producers need it against excessively low prices. The groups have a common interest. . . .

The ever-normal-granary features of the AAA aim at permanent abundance. They provide, with normal yields, for supply levels of cotton, wheat, corn, tobacco, and rice at above-normal percentages sufficient to cover the usual domestic and export requirements and to build up enlarged carry-overs. In wheat and corn the carry-overs on the average will be much larger. Shifts to soil-conserving crops will improve the land and develop a production-power reserve for emergencies. Crop insurance for wheat will give farmers better protection against crop failure and consumers better protection against high prices; for the premiums will be wheat, which will add to the ever-normal-granary supply. Moreover, the community has protection against artificial shortage. Marketing quotas can be proclaimed only when supplies reach high levels, and commodity loans will be available to the farmers only when accumulating stocks threaten them with price collapse. There is no loophole for improper storage as a means of extortion. All phases of the act look toward stable, abundant production and fair prices.

which would make a national referendum necessary for a declaration of war except in a case of invasion. Roosevelt asserts that such a measure would encourage violation of American rights by foreign nations and leave the President helpless to deal with foreign affairs. Resolution is returned to committee and shelved in the House.

Feb. 16. Second Agricultural Adjustment Act (AAA) extends acreage and crop quotas financed from government revenue, authorizes wheat crop insurance, and attempts to establish an "ever normal granary" by crop carry-over in government storage to stabilize supplies and prices.

March 18. Mexican government expropriates foreign oil concessions; the U.S. accepts negotiated cash compensation in 1941.

May 17. Naval Expansion (Vinson Naval) Act authorizes building of a "two-ocean navy" over the next 10 years. Earlier treaties on naval limitation lapse during this year.

May 26. House Committee on Un-American Activities is established by Congress; Committee is to investigate organizations of Communist, Fascist, Nazi, and other "un-American" character. Martin Dies of Texas is made chairman.

May 27. Congress passes Revenue Act of 1938 without President Roosevelt's approval. Act nominally reduces corporation taxes; its effect, however, is to reduce taxes of large corporations while increasing those of small firms.

June 16. Temporary National Economic Committee (TNEC) is established after President Roosevelt has proposed measures to counteract monopolies and increasing centralization of economic power in industry. Committee is to investigate monopolies, price-fixing, and restraint of competition and trade. Committee makes its recommendations in 1941 after one and a half years of public hearings.

June 21. Emergency Relief Appropriation is signed; President Roosevelt has addressed the Congress and the nation in April asking for expansion of relief and business aid programs to combat new business recession that has begun in the previous summer.

June 23. Civil Aeronautics Authority is formed as an independent agency of the federal government to supervise most aspects of nonmilitary flying.

June 24. Federal Food, Drug, and Cosmetic Act controls misbranding and false advertising claims by manufacturers; misbranding is to be handled by Food and Drug Administration and advertising by Federal Trade Commission.

June 25. Fair Labor Standards Act (Wages and Hours Law), enacted by Congress using interstate commerce power, is signed. It sets an increasing scale of minimum wages and descending scale of maximum hours, as well as prohibiting child labor in industries engaged in, or affected by, interstate commerce. In 1941 Supreme Court holds Act constitutional, overruling 1918 and 1922 decisions against such legislation.

July 5. President Roosevelt calls the lagging economic conditions in the South the "nation's number one economic problem" in message to conference meeting to investigate Southern conditions. Report, issued publicly in August, confirms that low living standards in Southern states hamper development.

Sept. 27. President Roosevelt appeals personally to Chancellor Adolf Hitler of Germany and Premier Benito Mussolini of Italy for cooperation in the peaceful solu-

National Emergency Council report on the South, 1938

The rapidly growing population of the South is faced with the problem of finding work that will provide a decent living. Neither on the farm nor in the factory is there the certainty of a continuing livelihood, and thousands of Southerners shift each year from farm to mill or mine and back again to farm.

The insecurity of work in Southern agriculture, its changes in method and its changes in location make the labor problem of the South not simply an industrial labor problem. Neither the farm population nor the industrial workers can be treated separately, because both groups, as a whole, receive too little income to enable their members to accumulate the property that tends to keep people stable. Industrial labor in the South is to a great extent unskilled and, therefore, subject to the competition of recurring migrations from the farm — people who have lost in the gamble of one-crop share farming. On the other hand, the industrial workers, with low wages and long hours, are constantly tempted to return to the farm for another try. . . .

Low wages and poverty are in great measure self-perpetuating. Labor organization has made slow and difficult progress among the low-paid workers, and they have had little collective bargaining power or organized influence on social legislation. Tax resources have been low because of low incomes in the communities, and they have been inadequate to provide for the type of education modern industry requires. Malnutrition has had its influence on the efficiency of workers.

(Above) Chicago police battle strikers in 1937; (below) Japanese
machine-gunners set up their guns on the top of a building in a
Chinese city, 1937

(Right) Nazi troops reoccupy
Dusseldorf in the Rhineland in
1936; (below) American Inquiry
Commission, headed by Clarence
Darrow, hears testimony about the
building of concentration
camps in Nazi Germany in 1934

Mercury Theatre on the Air, 1938
*Good evening, ladies and gentlemen.
From the Meridian Room in the Park
Plaza in New York City, we bring you
the music of Ramon Raquello and his
orchestra. With a touch of the Spanish,
Ramon Raquello leads off with "La
Cumparsita." (Piece starts playing)*

*Announcer: Ladies and gentlemen,
we interrupt our program of dance music to bring you a special bulletin from
the Intercontinental Radio News. At
twenty minutes before eight, central
time, Professor Farrell of the Mount
Jennings Observatory, Chicago, Illinois,
reports observing several explosions of
incandescent gas, occurring at regular
intervals on the planet Mars. . . .*

*Now, nearer home, comes a special
announcement from Trenton, New Jersey. It is reported that at 8:50 p.m. a
huge, flaming object, believed to be a
meteorite, fell on a farm in the neighborhood of Grovers Mill, New Jersey,
twenty-two miles from Trenton. . . .*

*We take you now to Grovers Mill,
New Jersey. (Crowd noises . . . police
sirens)*

*Reporter: I wish I could convey the
atmosphere . . . the background of
this . . . fantastic scene. Hundreds of
cars are parked in a field in back of us.
Police are trying to rope off the roadway leading into the farm. But it's no
use. They're breaking right through.
Their headlights throw an enormous
spot on the pit where the object's half-
buried. . . .*

*Just a minute! Something's happen-
ing! Ladies and gentlemen, this is terrific! This end of the thing is beginning to
flake off! The top is beginning to ro-
tate like a screw! The thing must be
hollow! . . .*

Wait a minute! Someone's crawling
out of the hollow top. *Some one
or . . . something. . . .*

tion of unsettled European problems. By
this time Germany has reoccupied the
Rhineland, signed Anti-Comintern Pact
with Italy and Japan, annexed Austria, and
is ready to take over the Sudetenland of
Czechoslovakia either by agreement or
force.

Oct. 6. U.S. Ambassador Joseph C.
Grew protests to Japan its violations of the
Open Door in China. Japan replies that
present and future world conditions make
the Open Door obsolete. U.S. State Department refuses to recognize Japan's "new
order."

Oct. 30. "Invasion from Mars," radio
play produced by Orson Welles based on
H. G. Wells's *War of the Worlds*, causes
widespread panic when listeners (in spite of
frequent disclaimers during play) think vivid
account of attack from Mars is a bona fide
news broadcast.

October. Gallup Poll shows that most
Americans approve Munich Agreement,
signed by Germany, Italy, Britain, and
France on September 30, which gives all
Sudetenland and Czech military fortifica-
tions to Germany in order to keep peace in
Europe.

Nov. 8. Although President Roosevelt has
intervened in primaries in effort to help liberal Democrats, Republicans gain 81 House
seats and 8 Senate seats in fall elections.
Democrats retain majorities, but this is first
gain for Republicans since 1928.

November. Committee for Industrial Organization, expelled from the American
Federation of Labor, which refuses to recognize industrial unions, holds convention
and creates independent body with name
changed to Congress of Industrial Organizations (CIO); leading unions are steel, auto,
garment, and mine workers. John L. Lewis
is elected first president.

December. At International Conference of American States in Lima, Roosevelt Corollary of the Monroe Doctrine becomes one of joint responsibility in Western Hemisphere affairs; American nations proclaim mutual solidarity in case of any threat to the peace, security, or territorial integrity of an American state.

December. In first case challenging inequality of education in the South, the Supreme Court holds that a Negro must be admitted to University of Missouri Law School, since no other facilities for legal education exist in the area.

1939

Jan. 4. President Roosevelt devotes most of his annual message to warning of danger to international peace and democracy by aggressors in Europe. **Jan. 5.** Roosevelt's 1940 budget, submitted to Congress, includes about $1,320,000,000 for national defense. **Jan. 12.** The President asks further defense appropriations of $525 million, including air defense program.

Feb. 27. Supreme Court finds sit-down strikes illegal; in past few years, sit-down strikes have involved about 500,000 workers in textile, steel, rubber, oil, and shipbuilding industries and have proved one of labor's most effective weapons.

March 4-April 29. President Roosevelt asks Congress for still further defense appropriations.

March 15. Germany invades Czechoslovakia. **March 22.** Germany annexes Lithuanian Baltic port of Memel and, two days later, demands from Poland passage through the Polish Corridor to Danzig. **March 31.** England and France promise help to Poles if they are threatened. **April 7.** Italy invades Albania. **April 13.** England and France offer help to Greece and Ruma-

There, I can see the thing's body. It's large as a bear and it glistens like wet leather. But that face. It . . . it's indescribable. I can hardly force myself to keep looking at it. The eyes are black and gleam like a serpent. The mouth is V-shaped with saliva dripping from its rimless lips that seem to quiver and pulsate. . . .

A humped shape is rising out of the pit. I can make out a small beam of light against a mirror. What's that? There's a jet of flame springing from that mirror, and it leaps right at the advancing men. It strikes them head on! Good Lord, they're turning into flame! (Screams and unearthly shrieks)

Now the whole field's caught fire. (Explosion) *The woods . . . the barns . . . the gas tanks of automobiles . . . it's spreading everywhere. It's coming this way. About twenty yards to my right. . . .* (Crash of microphone . . . then dead silence . . .)

Announcer: Ladies and gentlemen, due to circumstances beyond our control, we are unable to continue the broadcast from Grovers Mill. Evidently there's some difficulty with our field transmission. . . .

Ladies and gentlemen, I have a grave announcement to make. Incredible as it may seem, both the observations of science and the evidence of our eyes lead to the inescapable assumption that those strange beings who landed in the Jersey farmlands tonight are the vanguard of an invading army from the planet Mars. The battle which took place tonight at Grovers Mill has ended in one of the most startling defeats ever suffered by an army in modern times; seven thousand men armed with rifles and machine guns pitted against a single fighting machine of the invaders from Mars. One hundred and twenty known survivors.

GRACE OVERMYER
Report on WPA Federal Arts Projects, 1939

Pledged to avoid interference with "normal private employment," the workers on the Arts Projects have been obliged to take art into places where little, if any, art had ever gone before. . . . Through the Arts Projects, free and popular-priced dramatic and musical entertainment—most of it of good, and some of excellent, quality—and free class instruction in scores of cultural branches incidental to the musical, dramatic, and graphic arts, have been brought to millions of American citizens of the economic stratum generally described as "underprivileged." . . .

Of the 4 million persons who, within two years, participated in activities of the new federally sponsored Community Art Centers—combined art schools and galleries operating in eighteen states—more than half live in sections of the West, Middle West, and South in which art activities had previously been lacking; and the other half, mostly in the poorer parts of cities. Of the 25 million to 30 million persons who attended 1,700 performances by the Federal Theatre between February 1936—the date of its first play—and the beginning of 1938, fully half were youthful products of the motion-picture era who had never before seen a performance by actors on a stage. Of the stupendous audience total of 92 million, to whom, it is estimated, the Federal Music Project, through more than 100,000 programs, brought "living music" between October 1935 and January 1938, there is reason to reckon that at least nine-tenths lacked the means to attend the high-priced performances in opera houses and concert halls.

nia in case of aggression. The U.S., maintaining a policy of strict neutrality in spite of strong anti-German and anti-Italian feeling, observes events in Europe while Germany and Italy continue aggression.

April 3. Administrative Reorganization Act of 1939 is signed; Act consolidates and coordinates many specialized agencies formed since turn of the century, many of them by the New Deal. President Roosevelt has for two years recommended simplifying government setup, but measures have been defeated by Republicans and conservative Democrats who feel that passage will give President dictatorial powers.

April 15. President Roosevelt asks Hitler and Mussolini to guarantee that they will not attack 31 European and Near Eastern nations. Hitler replies that Germany is only righting the wrongs of Versailles.

May 10. Three branches of the Methodist Church, with about 7,500,000 members, are reunited after splits of main body in 1830 and 1844.

May 22. Germany and Italy sign a military alliance.

June 28. Pan American World Airways institutes regular transatlantic passenger flights with *Dixie Clipper*, a "flying boat" carrying 22 passengers from New York to Lisbon, Portugal; flight takes about 24 hours.

June. WPA rolls are reduced when Congress refuses to appropriate amounts asked for by President Roosevelt to handle further unemployment following 1937 business recession. Emergency Relief Appropriations Act of 1939 limits time of employment on government projects, reduces wages, and abolishes Federal Theater Project. As a result, WPA workers hold nationwide strike, and many lose their jobs.

July 13. Congress passes amendments to Social Security Act that broaden it as to age, payments, and categories of persons covered.

July 25. U.S. Senate ratifies U.S.-Panama treaty worked out in 1936 by President Roosevelt and President Harmodio Arias of Panama; treaty gives Panama most commercial rights of an independent state and puts it on more equal basis with the U.S. in management of Panamanian affairs. Delay in ratification has been caused by opposition of U.S. naval and military authorities.

Aug. 2. Albert Einstein writes to President Roosevelt to tell him that atomic fission can be used to make bombs and that two German physicists have achieved fission of uranium. Einstein has been asked by a number of prominent physicists to inform Roosevelt of the danger if Germany succeeds in using atomic fission explosives. Einstein has come to the U.S. in 1933 after the Nazi ascendancy in Germany.

Aug. 23. Germany and the Soviet Union sign agreement that neither will attack the other, nor remain neutral in case of attack by another nation.

Aug. 24. President Roosevelt appeals to Poland, Germany, and Italy, urging arbitration, conciliation, or negotiation of German-Polish conflict to avoid war. Poland accepts offer, choosing conciliation.

Sept. 1. Germany invades Poland without declaration of war. **Sept. 3.** Britain and France declare war on Germany, and Belgium declares itself neutral.

Sept. 4. After sinking the day before of

ALBERT EINSTEIN
Letter to Roosevelt, 1939
Some recent work by E. Fermi and L. Szilard, which has been communicated to me in manuscript, leads me to expect that the element uranium may be turned into a new and important source of energy in the immediate future. Certain aspects of the situation which has arisen seem to call for watchfulness and, if necessary, quick action on the part of the administration. I believe, therefore, that it is my duty to bring to your attention the following facts and recommendations.

In the course of the last four months it has been made probable—through the work of Joliot in France as well as Fermi and Szilard in America—that it may become possible to set up a nuclear chain reaction in a large mass of uranium, by which vast amounts of power and large quantities of new radium-like elements would be generated. Now it appears almost certain that this could be achieved in the immediate future.

This new phenomenon would also lead to the construction of bombs, and it is conceivable—though much less certain—that extremely powerful bombs of a new type may thus be constructed. A single bomb of this type, carried by boat and exploded in a port, might very well destroy the whole port together with some of the surrounding territory. However, such bombs might very well prove to be too heavy for transportation by air. . . .

In view of this situation you may think it desirable to have some permanent contact maintained between the administration and the group of physicists working on chain reactions in America.

JOHN STEINBECK

The Grapes of Wrath, 1939

One man, one family driven from the land; this rusty car creaking along the highway to the west. I lost my land, a single tractor took my land. I am alone and I am bewildered. And in the night one family camps in a ditch and another family pulls in and the tents come out. The two men squat on their hams and the women and children listen. Here is the node, you who hate change and fear revolution. Keep these two squatting men apart; make them hate, fear, suspect each other. Here is the anlage of the thing you fear. This is the zygote. For here "I lost my land" is changed; a cell is split and from its splitting grows the thing you hate—"We lost our land." The danger is here, for two men are not as lonely and perplexed as one. And from this first "we" there grows a still more dangerous thing: "I have a little food" plus "I have none." If from this problem the sum is "We

British passenger ship *Athenia* by a submarine, killing 30 American passengers, Secretary of State Cordell Hull advises Americans to travel to Europe only under most extreme necessity.

Sept. 5. The U.S. declares neutrality; on September 3, President Roosevelt has said in radio talk that, although he is aware the nation is not neutral in thought, it must remain neutral in policy. **Sept. 8.** In order to facilitate action, Roosevelt declares a limited emergency.

Sept. 17. German forces demand Polish surrender after reaching Warsaw. On the same day, the Soviet Union invades Poland, and most resistance stops. **Sept. 28.** Germany and Soviet Union divide Poland into German and Soviet areas, and a week later the last Polish forces surrender.

Oct. 2. Declaration of Panama specifies certain Western Hemisphere ocean safety zones south of Canada, in which naval action by belligerents is forbidden.

Nov. 2. Congress, meeting in special session called by President Roosevelt, re-

A migratory Mexican farm worker standing outside his home located near a pea field in Imperial Valley, California, 1937. This and photo on opposite page by Dorothea Lange for the FSA

Living conditions of less fortunate in Marysville, Calif., 1935

peals arms embargo clauses of Neutrality Act of 1937 and authorizes trade with belligerents on a cash-and-carry basis.

Nov. 30. Soviet Union invades Finland. Four months later, after a winter campaign in which Soviet armor is often at a disadvantage, Finno-Russian peace treaty is signed.

John Steinbeck publishes *The Grapes of Wrath*, Pulitzer Prize novel of displaced Oklahoma farm family migrating to California. In previous years, he has published *Tortilla Flat, In Dubious Battle,* and *Of Mice and Men.*

1939 - 1940

Aug. 2, 1939. President Roosevelt signs Hatch Act limiting political activity of government personnel; Act prohibits most federal employees from taking part in campaigns, accepting money from persons on relief, and using offices to influence federal elections. **July 20, 1940.** Amendment to Hatch Act limits annual national political expenses of parties to $3 million and individual campaign contributions to $5,000.

have a little food," the thing is on its way, the movement has direction. Only a little multiplication now, and this land, this tractor are ours. The two men squatting in a ditch, the little fire, the side-meat stewing in a single pot, the silent, stone-eyed women; behind, the children listening with their souls to words their minds do not understand. The night draws down. The baby has a cold. Here, take this blanket. It's wool. It was my mother's blanket — take it for the baby. This is the thing to bomb. This is the beginning — from "I" to "we."

If you who own the things people must have could understand this, you might preserve yourself. If you could separate causes from results, if you could know that Paine, Marx, Jefferson, Lenin, were results, not causes, you might survive. But that you cannot know. For the quality of owning freezes you forever into "I," and cuts you off forever from the "we."

German troops storm a Polish city in September 1939

WENDELL L. WILLKIE

Campaign speech, 1940

I say this in dead earnest—if, because of some fine speeches about humanity, you return this Administration to office, you will be serving under an American totalitarian government before the long third term is finished.

FRANKLIN D. ROOSEVELT

Campaign speech, 1940

I consider it a public duty to answer falsifications with facts. I will not pretend that I find this an unpleasant duty. I am an old campaigner, and I love a good fight.

OSCAR AMERINGER

If You Don't Weaken, 1940

Politics is the art by which politicians obtain campaign contributions from the rich and votes from the poor on the pretext of protecting each from the other.

1940

Jan. 26. Japan's commercial treaty with the U.S. expires, and Secretary of State Cordell Hull tells Japan that the U.S. is not going to renew it. By end of March, Japan has established a puppet government in China.

April 7. Socialist Party convention nominates Norman Thomas of New York for President. **April 28.** Socialist Labor Party nominates John W. Aiken of Massachusetts. **May 10.** Prohibition Party nominates Roger W. Babson of Massachusetts. **June 2.** Communist Party nominates Earl Browder of Kansas. **June 28.** Republicans at Philadelphia nominate dark-horse candidate Wendell L. Willkie of New York for President and Senator Charles L. McNary of Oregon for his running mate. **July 18.** Democrats renominate President Roosevelt, although he has told the convention that he does not want a third term; Secretary of Agriculture Henry A. Wallace of Iowa is chosen for his running mate. Republican and Democratic platforms both support current foreign and defense policies and oppose involvement in foreign wars. Republicans approve most New Deal reforms but attack methods.

April 9. German troops invade Norway and Denmark; French and British forces sent to help resistance in Norway are unsuccessful and withdraw in June, but British troops occupy Iceland to prevent Germany from using it as a base.

April 20. Radio Corporation of America laboratories demonstrate first electron microscope; instrument is 10 feet high, weighs 700 pounds, and has magnification power of 20,000 to 25,000 diameters.

May 10. Germany invades Belgium, the Netherlands, and Luxembourg. Prime Minister Neville Chamberlain of England resigns and is replaced by Winston Churchill, heading a coalition government.

May 28. Belgian Army surrenders on orders from King Leopold; this strands English and French troops in Belgium, and more than 340,000 men are forced to withdraw across English Channel from Dunkirk, France. Operation takes a week; more than 850 vessels, from warships to private power boats, carry troops to England. **June 3.** During evacuation, the U.S. agrees, in answer to Prime Minister Churchill's appeal, to send Britain outdated and surplus war supplies, including aircraft.

Committee to Defend America, newspaper advertisement, 1940

Hitler is striking with all the terrible force at his command. His is a desperate gamble, and the stakes are nothing less than domination of the whole human race.

If Hitler wins in Europe—if the strength of the British and French armies and navies is forever broken—the United States will find itself alone in a barbaric world—a world ruled by Nazis, with "spheres of influence" assigned to their totalitarian allies. However different the dictatorships may be, racially, they all agree on one primary objective: "Democracy must be wiped from the face of the earth." . . .

There is nothing shameful in our desire to stay out of war, to save our youth from the dive bombers and the flame throwing tanks in the unutterable hell of modern warfare.

But is there not an evidence of suicidal insanity in our failure to help those who now stand between us and the creators of this hell?

Homeless citizens after 1940 bombing of Rotterdam by German Air Force

FRANKLIN D. ROOSEVELT
Speech at University of Virginia, 1940
The government of Italy has now chosen to preserve what it terms its "freedom of action" and to fulfill what it states are its promises to Germany. In so doing it has manifested disregard for the rights and security of other nations, disregard for the lives of the peoples of those nations which are directly threatened by this spread of the war, and has evidenced its unwillingness to find the means through pacific negotiations for the satisfaction of what it believes are its legitimate aspirations.

On this 10th day of June, 1940, the hand that held the dagger has struck it into the back of its neighbor.

On this 10th day of June, 1940, in this university, founded by the first great American teacher of democracy, we send forth our prayers and our hopes to those beyond the seas who are maintaining with magnificent valor their battle for freedom.

In our unity—in our American unity—we will pursue two obvious and simultaneous courses; we will extend to the opponents of force the material resources of this nation, and at the same time we will harness and speed up the use of these resources in order that we ouselves in the Americas may have equipment and training equal to the task of any emergency and every defense.

All roads leading to the accomplishment of these objectives must be kept clear of obstructions. We will not slow down or detour. Signs and signals call for speed—full speed ahead.

May 31. By this date, President Roosevelt has requested defense appropriations amounting to $4,260,000,000 and has proposed production of 50,000 airplanes per year.

June 5. Battle of France begins when German Army crosses the Somme River, reaching Paris by June 14. Italy has declared war on Britain and France and attacked France from the south on June 10. **June 13.** Premier Paul Reynaud of France asks the U.S. for aid, but Marshal Henri Philippe Pétain succeeds Reynaud as head of government; Pétain negotiates peace with Germany on June 22 and with Italy two days later. Free French government moves to London, and Marshal Pétain sets up government of occupation at Vichy on July 2.

June 15. U.S. National Defense Research Committee is established; it is headed by Dr. Vannevar Bush.

June 15-17. Soviet Army occupies Lithuania, Latvia, and Estonia, which become part of the Soviet Union in August.

June 16. Pittman Resolution provides for sale of armaments to Latin-American countries; Germany and Italy are informed that the U.S. will not recognize transfer from one non-American country to another of any geographic region of the Western Hemisphere.

June 22. Congress passes tax measures that will raise $3-4 billion per year. National debt limit is increased from $45 billion to $49 billion.

June 26. Reconstruction Finance Corporation, established in 1932, is authorized to make loans to plants producing war materials.

June 29. Alien Registration (Smith) Act requires registration and fingerprinting of about 5 million aliens; Act also makes unlawful influences designed to overthrow any government in the U.S. by force.

July 20. President Roosevelt signs act providing for a $4 billion two-ocean Navy of 200 ships.

July 30. In order to forestall take-over by Germany of European possessions in the Western Hemisphere, 21 American nations sign Act of Havana. Agreement provides that as a measure of defense, any or all of American republics may assume protection of any European possession that seems to threaten aggression against it.

Aug. 8. Battle of Britain begins when Germany launches huge air offensive against coasts, cities, and installations of British Isles in effort to soften them up for planned invasion; British lack planes but secretly have developed radar. By October 12, after sustaining very heavy losses in aircraft, Germany is forced to give up idea of invasion, although extensive bombing continues.

Aug. 18. President Roosevelt and Canada's Prime Minister MacKenzie King establish Permanent Joint Board of Defense.

Aug. 27. President Roosevelt signs bill authorizing him to call out the National Guard and the organized reserves for a year's service.

Sept. 3. The U.S. announces transfer of 50 overage destroyers to Britain in exchange for 99-year leases of air and naval bases on Newfoundland, British Guiana, Bermuda, and islands of the West Indies.

Sept. 4. Secretary Hull notifies Japan that the U.S. will oppose Japanese aggres-

WENDELL WILLKIE
Speech in Indiana, 1940
But I cannot follow the President in his conduct of foreign affairs in this critical time. There have been occasions when many of us have wondered if he is deliberately inciting us to war. I trust that I have made it plain that in the defense of America, and of our liberties, I should not hesitate to stand for war. But like a great many other Americans I saw what war was like at first hand in 1917. I know what war can do to demoralize civil liberties at home. And I believe it to be the first duty of a President to try to maintain peace.

But Mr. Roosevelt has not done this. He has dabbled in inflammatory statements and manufactured panics. Of course, we in America like to speak our minds freely, but this does not mean that at a critical period in history our President should cause bitterness and confusion for the sake of a little political oratory. The President's attacks on foreign powers have been useless and dangerous. He has courted a war for which the country is hopelessly unprepared—and which it emphatically does not want. He has secretly meddled in the affairs of Europe, and he has even unscrupulously encouraged other countries to hope for more help than we are able to give.

"Walk softly and carry a big stick" was the motto of Theodore Roosevelt. It is still good American doctrine for 1940. Under the present administration the country has been placed in the false position of shouting insults and not even beginning to prepare to take the consequences.

DONALD BENEDICT ET AL.
Statement to court, 1941

We have also been led to our conclusion on the Conscription Law in the light of its totalitarian nature. It is a totalitarian move when our government insists that the manpower of the nation take a year of military training. It is a totalitarian move for the President of the nation to be able to conscript industry to produce certain materials which are deemed necessary for national defense without considering the actual physical needs of the people. We believe, therefore, that by opposing the Selective Service Law, we will be striking at the heart of totalitarianism as well as war. . . .

If we register under the act, even as conscientious objectors, we are becoming part of the act. The fact that we as conscientious objectors may gain personal exemption from the most crassly un-Christian requirements of the act does not compensate for the fact that we are complying with it and accepting its protection. If a policeman (or a group of vigilantes) stops us on the street, our possession of the government's card shows that we are "all right" — we have complied with the act for the militarization of America. If that does not hurt our Christian consciences, what will? . . .

For these reasons we hereby register our refusal to comply in any way with the Selective Training and Service Act. We do not expect to stem the war forces today; but we are helping to build the movement that will conquer in the future.

sion in French Indochina, but three weeks later Japan signs treaty with governor general of Indochina, who is loyal to French Vichy government, and gains air and troop bases there.

Sept. 14. Congress passes Selective Training and Service Act, first U.S. compulsory military training in peacetime; Act calls for registration of men between 21 and 35 years and training of a limit of 900,000 in first year. First draft numbers are chosen on October 29.

Sept. 26. President Roosevelt proclaims an embargo on export of scrap iron and steel to all countries except Britain and those in the Western Hemisphere. **Oct. 8.** Japanese ambassador terms measure an "unfriendly act."

Sept. 27. Japan signs military and economic pact with Germany and Italy, pledging mutual assistance.

Oct. 25. Strongly anti-Roosevelt labor leader John L. Lewis urges all members of Congress of Industrial Organizations (CIO) to vote for Willkie, saying he will resign the presidency of the CIO if Roosevelt wins election.

October. Germans occupy Rumania, and Italy invades Greece. British land forces on Greek islands, including Crete.

Nov. 5. President Roosevelt wins election by popular vote of 27,308,000 to Willkie's 22,321,000. Electoral vote is Roosevelt, 449; Willkie, 82. Democrats retain control of Congress.

Nov. 21. Lewis resigns as head of CIO; Philip Murray becomes president on following day.

Dec. 9. British forces attack Italians in

North Africa and within two months have destroyed Rodolfo Graziani's army, taking about 130,000 prisoners.

Dec. 20. U.S. Office of Production Management for Defense (later OPM) is set up, headed by William S. Knudsen; Office is coordinating agency for defense plants and is to send all possible aid to nations fighting the Axis. On the next day, Germany calls U.S. help to Britain "moral aggression."

1940 census shows U.S. population of 131,669,000, including 528,000 immigrants arrived since 1930; this is lowest immigration in more than a century, the result of 1927 quota law and world conditions. More than 56 percent of people live in places of 2,500 or more population. Average life expectancy has increased to about 63 years. Illiteracy is 2.9 percent, 1.4 percent less than in 1930.

Research on radar is intensified by National Defense Research Committee.

Richard Wright publishes *Native Son*, novel of a young Negro in an antagonistic society. *You Can't Go Home Again* by Thomas Wolfe is published, two years after his death.

1940 - 1941

Edwin M. McMillan and Philip H. Abelson discover first transuranium element, atomic number 93, which they call neptunium; early in 1941, McMillan, Glenn T. Seaborg, and others discover plutonium; both elements are radioactive.

1941

Jan. 6. In annual message that asks for further aid to anti-Axis nations, President Roosevelt enumerates "four freedoms" that he feels are necessary to postwar world:

RICHARD WRIGHT
Native Son, 1940
"You know where the white folks live?"

"Yeah," Gus said, pointing eastward. "Over across the 'line'; over there on Cottage Grove Avenue."

"Naw; they don't," Bigger said.

"What you mean?" Gus asked, puzzled. "Then, where do they live?"

Bigger doubled his fist and struck his solar plexus.

"Right down here in my stomach," he said.

Gus looked at Bigger searchingly, then away, as though ashamed.

"Yeah; I know what you mean," he whispered.

"Every time I think of 'em, I feel 'em," Bigger said.

"Yeah; and in your chest and throat, too," Gus said.

"It's like fire."

"And sometimes you can't hardly breathe. . . ."

Bigger's eyes were wide and placid, gazing into space.

"That's when I feel like something awful's going to happen to me. . . ." Bigger paused, narrowed his eyes. "Naw; it ain't like something going to happen to me. It's . . . It's like I was going to do something I can't help. . . ."

"Yeah!" Gus said with uneasy eagerness. His eyes were full of a look compounded of fear and admiration for Bigger. "Yeah; I know what you mean. It's like you going to fall and don't know where you going to land. . . ."

BURTON K. WHEELER
Speech, 1941

The Lend-Lease policy, translated into legislative form, stunned a Congress and a nation wholly sympathetic to the cause of Great Britain. The Kaiser's blank check to Austria-Hungary in the First World War was a piker compared to the Roosevelt blank check of World War II. It warranted my worst fears for the future of America, and it definitely stamps the President as war-minded.

The lend-lease-give program is the New Deal's triple-A foreign policy; it will plow under every fourth American boy.

Never before have the American people been asked or compelled to give so bounteously and so completely of their tax dollars to any foreign nation. Never before has the Congress of the United States been asked by any President to violate international law. Never before has this nation resorted to duplicity in the conduct of its foreign affairs. Never before has the United States given to one man the power to strip this nation of its defenses. Never before has a Congress coldly and flatly been asked to abdicate.

If the American people want a dictatorship—if they want a totalitarian form of government and if they want war—this bill should be steam-rollered through Congress, as is the wont of President Roosevelt.

Approval of this legislation means war, open and complete warfare. I, therefore, ask the American people before they supinely accept it—Was the last World War worthwhile?

freedom of speech and expression, freedom of worship, freedom from want, and freedom from fear.

January-March. U.S. and British military leaders hold secret talks in Washington; plan arrived at is for both countries to concentrate on conquering Germany first in the event that the U.S. should become involved in war against Japan.

March 3. Panama agrees for the duration of the war to allow the U.S. to maintain air defense installations beyond the limit of the Canal Zone.

March 11. Lend-Lease Act is signed by President Roosevelt. Congress authorizes the President to lend an initial $7 billion worth of war matériel to any nations whose defense he considers vital to that of the U.S. Measure is primarily intended to aid Great Britain, whose credit is rapidly becoming exhausted.

March 24. Axis forces begin counteroffensive against British troops in North Africa, forcing their withdrawal to Egypt.

April 6. Germany invades Yugoslavia and Greece; by April 23, both have surrendered, and British troops have withdrawn to Crete, which Germany, using airborne troops, subdues by June 1 after 11 days of fighting.

April 9. Feeling that defense of Greenland is necessary to that of the Western Hemisphere, U.S. Secretary of State Cordell Hull and Danish Minister Henrik de Kauffmann sign agreement that U.S. will defend Greenland against aggressors in return for right to build and maintain military installations there.

April 11. President Roosevelt tells Prime Minister Churchill that henceforth U.S.

ocean security zone to be patrolled will be extended to longitude 26° west, a line about halfway between England and U.S. East Coast. German submarines, working in packs, have done enormous damage to Allied and neutral shipping, especially in the North Atlantic.

April 11. Office of Price Administration and Civilian Supply (later OPA) is established to recommend price controls for prevention of wartime inflation. First act is to freeze steel prices. In September, secretary of the treasury says that price controls must be more stringent to ward off inflation. **Dec. 26.** OPA announces tire rationing, which eventually cuts down civilian consumption by 80 percent.

April 13. The Soviet Union and Japan sign nonaggression pact at Moscow.

May 27. President Roosevelt declares an unlimited national emergency; three weeks later the U.S. suspends diplomatic relations with Germany and Italy and freezes all their assets in the U.S. Germany and Italy immediately order closing of U.S. consulates in all countries controlled by the Axis.

June 22. Germany (and later Rumanian and Finnish troops) invades the Soviet Union along an 1,800-mile front from Finland to the Black Sea. **June 24.** President Roosevelt pledges U.S. assistance to the Soviet Union. **July 13.** Britain and the Soviet Union sign pact at Moscow agreeing that neither will make a separate peace with Germany.

June 25. Fair Employment Practices Committee is established to promote Negro equality in defense industries and government employment. The measure is a forerunner of later laws designed to establish economic opportunity and effective equality for Negroes.

CHARLES A. LINDBERGH
Speech in New York, 1941
I know I will be severely criticized by the interventionists in America when I say we should not enter a war unless we have a reasonable chance of winning. That, they will claim, is far too materialistic a viewpoint. They will advance again the same arguments that were used to persuade France to declare war against Germany in 1939. But I do not believe that our American ideals and our way of life will gain through an unsuccessful war. And I know that the United States is not prepared to wage war in Europe successfully at this time. We are no better prepared today than France was when the interventionists in Europe persuaded her to attack the Siegfried Line. . . .

In time of war, truth is always replaced by propaganda. . . . But we in this country have a right to think of the welfare of America first, just as the people in England thought first of their own country when they encouraged the smaller nations of Europe to fight against hopeless odds. When England asks us to enter this war, she is considering her own future and that of her Empire. In making our reply, I believe we should consider the future of the United States and that of the Western Hemisphere.

It is not only our right but it is our obligation as American citizens to look at this war objectively and to weigh our chances for success if we should enter it. I have attempted to do this, especially from the standpoint of aviation; and I have been forced to the conclusion that we cannot win this war for England, regardless of how much assistance we extend.

Atlantic Charter, 1941

Joint declaration of the President of the United States of America and the Prime Minister, Mr. Churchill, representing His Majesty's government in the United Kingdom. . . .

First, their countries seek no aggrandizement, territorial or other.

Second, they desire to see no territorial changes that do not accord with the freely expressed wishes of the peoples concerned.

Third, they respect the right of all peoples to choose the form of government under which they will live. . . .

Fourth, they will endeavor, with due respect for their existing obligations, to further the enjoyment by all states, great or small, victor or vanquished, of access, on equal terms, to the trade and to the raw materials of the world. . . .

Fifth, they desire to bring about the fullest collaboration between all nations in the economic field. . . .

Sixth, after the final destruction of the Nazi tyranny, they hope to see established a peace which will afford to all nations the means of dwelling in safety within their own boundaries. . . .

Seventh, such a peace should enable all men to traverse the high seas and oceans without hindrance.

Eighth, they believe that all of the nations of the world, for realistic as well as spiritual reasons, must come to the abandonment of the use of force. . . . They believe, pending the establishment of a wider and permanent system of general security, that the disarmament of such nations is essential.

July 7. The U.S., by agreement with the Icelandic government, occupies Iceland for the duration of the war to prevent its use by Germany for military bases; this move frees the large majority of British troops already there.

July 23-26. Japan occupies French Indochina. **July 25.** The U.S. and Britain halt all trade with Japan by freezing Japan's credits. On the following day, President Roosevelt calls Philippine armed forces into the service of the U.S under Lieutenant General Douglas MacArthur and names MacArthur commander of all U.S. and Philippine forces. Japanese ambassador to the U.S. is warned that further aggression by Japan in the Far East will lead to U.S. move to protect American rights.

Aug. 14. President Roosevelt and Prime Minister Churchill, having met off Newfoundland in two warships a few days earlier, issue joint statement of eight war and peace aims their governments wish to pursue; they pledge themselves to a common goal of destroying Nazi tyranny. By September 24, 11 anti-Axis countries have endorsed the Atlantic Charter.

Aug. 18. Term of service of U.S. Army draftees is extended for 18 months.

Sept. 4. U.S. destroyer *Greer*, in defensive waters off Iceland, is attacked by German submarine. A week later, President Roosevelt warns that German and Italian ships will cross American defense zones at their own risk and issues orders to U.S. Navy vessels to shoot on sight any Axis ships encountered in these zones.

Sept. 29. Missions from Britain and the U.S. consult in Moscow on war needs of the Soviet Union. By this time Germany has conquered most of the Ukraine and reached Leningrad. **Oct. 1.** The U.S. and

Britain agree to give Soviet Union war matériel, and U.S. about a month later extends $1 billion of lend-lease credit. Russians suffer food shortage during ensuing winter.

Oct. 11. President Roosevelt secretly suggests to Britain that the two countries make joint effort to develop an atomic bomb.

Oct. 17. German submarine torpedoes U.S. destroyer *Kearny* near Iceland, with loss of 11 lives. At the end of October, U.S. destroyer *Reuben James,* convoying merchant ships between U.S. and Iceland, is sunk by German submarine; only 44 of the 120-man crew are rescued.

Nov. 13. Following President Roosevelt's request of October 9, Congress amends Neutrality Act of 1939 to permit arming of U.S. merchant ships and authorizes them to go to belligerent ports.

Nov. 17. Joseph C. Grew, U.S. ambassador to Japan, warns President Roosevelt that Japan may attack the U.S.

Nov. 20. Secretary Hull talks with Japanese representatives in Washington, who demand that the U.S. reestablish normal trade relations with Japan, give up interests in China, and stop naval expansion in the Pacific. **Nov. 26.** Secretary Hull proposes Japanese withdrawal from China and Indochina and a nonaggression pact in return for reestablishment of commercial relations. **Nov. 27.** Commanders of U.S. Pacific forces are warned that a Japanese carrier force has left Japan and that an attack may be imminent.

Nov. 22. Germans take Rostov-on-Don. **Nov. 29.** Soviet troops retake Rostov and in next two weeks start counteroffensive.

Dec. 6. President Roosevelt appeals to Japanese emperor to keep peace.

ROBERT A. TAFT
Speech in Senate, 1941
Mr. President, the adoption of the joint resolution now before the Senate would be direct authority from the Congress to the President to carry on an undeclared war against Germany, Italy, and Japan on all the oceans of the world and in all the ports into which seagoing ships may sail. . . .

The repeal of Sections 2 and 3 of the Neutrality Act would mean the dispatch of American ships into British ports through the submarine blockade of the Germans. It cannot be doubted that many of those ships would be sunk and that many Americans would be drowned. It cannot be doubted that that would be the first result of our vote here to repeal the Neutrality Act and authorize Americans and American ships, not only authorize them but perhaps order them, to proceed into the battlefields of Europe.

It was just such sinkings and such deaths which took us into the World War. It is an almost inevitable cause of complete war. It is probably more likely to be so now than it was in the World War, because now these ships would be invariably carrying contraband manufactured by the United States and shipped by us to the British in order to enable them to carry on war against Germany. There could hardly be any doubt in the mind of any German commander as to any such ship that it would be carrying contraband.

It is only because of the provisions of the Neutrality Act which we are asked to repeal that we are not at war today.

FRANKLIN D. ROOSEVELT
Address to Congress, 1941
Yesterday, December 7, 1941 — a date which will live in infamy — the United States of America was suddenly and deliberately attacked by naval and air forces of the Empire of Japan. . . .

The attack yesterday on the Hawaiian Islands has caused severe damage to American naval and military forces. Very many American lives have been lost. In addition, American ships have been reported torpedoed on the high seas between San Francisco and Honolulu. . . .

As commander in chief of the Army and Navy I have directed that all measures be taken for our defense.

Always will we remember the character of the onslaught against us. No matter how long it may take us to overcome this premeditated invasion, the American people, in their righteous might, will win through to absolute victory. I believe I interpret the will of the Congress and of the people when I assert that we will not only defend ourselves to the uttermost but will make very certain that this form of treachery shall never endanger us again.

Hostilities exist. There is no blinking at the fact that our people, our territory, and our interests are in grave danger.

With confidence in our armed forces — with the unbounded determination of our people — we will gain the inevitable triumph — so help us God.

I ask that the Congress declare that since the unprovoked and dastardly attack by Japan on Sunday, December 7, a state of war has existed between the United States and the Japanese Empire.

Dec. 7. Japanese carrier-based planes attack U.S. naval base at Pearl Harbor (at same time in Washington that Japanese representatives are delivering to Secretary Hull Japan's rejection of November 26 proposals); also attacked are Guam, the Philippines, Midway Island, Hong Kong, and the Malay Peninsula. Surprise attack on Pearl Harbor at 7:55 A.M. Sunday finds most U.S. warships docked or at anchor and planes on the ground; 19 ships are sunk or disabled, including 8 battleships and 3 destroyers; about 140 U.S. planes are destroyed; about 2,300 people, mostly sailors and soldiers, are killed, and 1,200 are wounded. Japanese lose 29 planes and 5 midget submarines.

Dec. 8. Congress declares war on Japan with only one dissenting vote. **Dec. 11.** Germany and Italy declare war on the U.S., and Congress adopts resolution recognizing a state of war with them.

Dec. 8-25. Japan, having crippled U.S. Pacific fleet and begun invasion of Malaya and Thailand, invades the Philippines and captures Guam, Wake Island, and Hong Kong.

Dec. 17-23. Conference attended by representatives of industry and labor votes no-strike and no-lockout policy for war industries and recommends a board to settle differences. National War Labor Board (WLB) is established in the following month, supplanting the National Defense Mediation Board.

Dec. 19. Congress extends Selective Service ages to 20 to 44 years.

In *United States* v. *Classic*, the Supreme Court upholds federal power to regulate state primary elections involving candidates for federal office; decision tends to increase Negro vote in Southern states.

The Supreme Court upholds Fair Labor Standards Act of 1938 on the ground that commerce is a national function and cannot be regulated in part by the states and in part by the federal government. Decision follows opinion in dissent of Justice Oliver Wendell Holmes, Jr., in 1918.

Sir Howard Florey, who has been working on large-scale manufacture of penicillin in England, comes to the U.S. to persuade drug manufacturers of its great value in saving lives; penicillin is soon turned out in large quantities, though not for unlimited civilian use until after the war.

1941 - 1946

The Supreme Court calls unconstitutional a California law that excludes "Okies," calling it a barrier to interstate commerce. In 1946 the Court makes a similar ruling in the case of a Jim Crow law involving interstate travel of Negroes.

1942

Jan. 1. Declaration of the United Nations is signed in Washington, D.C., by 26 countries, including the U.S., Great Britain, the Soviet Union, and China; each country pledges maximum war effort against the Axis and agrees not to sign a separate armistice or peace treaty.

Jan. 2. The Japanese occupy Manila, the Philippines; General MacArthur's troops retreat to Bataan Peninsula, with headquarters on Corregidor.

Jan. 11. Japan invades the Dutch East Indies, completing, except for a portion of New Guinea, occupation by the following summer.

Jan. 12. The U.S. and Mexico form mutual defense commission. In the following

Hallelujah I'm A-Travelin', c. 1946
Stand up and rejoice! A great day is
here!
We are fighting Jim Crow, and the
vict'ry is near!

Hallelujah, I'm a-travelin'
Hallelujah, ain't it fine?
Hallelujah, I'm a travelin'
Down freedom's main line!

I read in the news, the Supreme Court
has said,
"Listen here, mister Jim Crow, it's
time you was dead."

The judges declared in Washington town,
"You white folks must take that old
Jim Crow sign down."

I'm paying my fare on the Greyhound
Bus line,
I'm riding the front seat to Nashville
this time.

Columbia's the gem of the ocean, they
say,
We're fighting Jim Crow in Columbia
today.

I hate Jim Crow and Jim Crow hates me,
And that's why I'm fighting for my
liberty.

(Above) Mussolini welcomes Hitler to Florence in 1940 to discuss
their plans for Europe; (below) "Wake Up, You're On Next!": cartoon
by Herb Kruckman

Explosions rock American naval base at Pearl Harbor following surprise
Japanese attack, December 7, 1941

MICHAEL DARROCK
Harper's, 1943

When the Japanese bombed Pearl Harbor the reverberations cracked open the price-control machinery in Washington. Supplies of important raw materials — rubber, tin, chemicals — suddenly were cut off, and all hell was ready to tear loose on prices. What would happen when business opened on that Monday after the first news anybody could guess. . . .

Within a month after the attack the President presented his "blueprint for victory" to the Congress. His message made it abundantly clear that we were in war up to our ears. One-half of our entire national production was to be devoted to the war effort. Among other things, the program outlined meant the end of selective price control. The turning point had arrived; every part of the national economy would now feel the effects of overwhelming demand and scant supply.

Spurred by war, Congress passed the Emergency Price Control Act and the President signed it at the end of January. For the first time the Office of Price Administration, as the price-control agency was named, had full powers to control prices and rents, and to punish violators. The very existence of price-control legislation was a major victory. In the First World War we had been suckers; in the Second World War we took the lesson of twenty-five years before and put it to work. We caught the danger early and kept our levees just a little higher than the floodwaters, at least during the opening stages. The question was, could we check the much greater pressures that actual all-out war would produce?

two weeks at Rio de Janeiro conference of American nations, all 21 delegates approve discontinuing diplomatic relations with the Axis; 19 governments follow delegates' recommendations at once, Chile one year later, and Argentina two years later.

Jan. 16. President Roosevelt establishes War Production Board (WPB), which is to be in charge of all war production and supply; this board supplants OPM.

Jan. 24. Three-day naval battle begins in Makasar Strait between Celebes and Borneo; Japanese invasion ships sustain major damage inflicted by Allied air and sea forces.

Jan. 30. President Roosevelt signs Emergency Price Control Act to curb rising prices and to put ceilings on rents in war industry areas. During World War II, retail price increases are considerably less than in World War I.

Jan. 31. U.S. carrier-based planes bombard Gilbert and Marshall islands. On the same day, British forces retreat from Malaya to Singapore but are forced to surrender that island to Japan on February 15.

January. Battle for North Africa between Germany and Britain continues, with Axis forces halted 60 miles west of Alexandria, Egypt, by the end of June.

Soviet forces continue counter-offensive begun at end of previous year toward the Ukraine; Red Army advances cease by March 15, but not before German forces are turned back from Moscow, Leningrad, and the Caucasus.

January-June. U.S. and Great Britain form special joint agencies to deal with raw materials, armaments, and foods. Most conferences are held in Washington.

Feb. 7-Nov. 21. Special wartime agencies are established to direct and control almost all aspects of national life; among others are strategic intelligence, housing, alien property, shipping, public information, and foreign relief. Among agencies formed in previous year are those that direct Western Hemisphere affairs, civilian defense, scientific research, lend-lease to Allies, censorship, and transportation.

Feb. 25. British are forced to withdraw from Rangoon, Burma, which makes it possible for Japan to cut off the Burma Road, main supply route between Allies and China. Japanese have attacked through forests from Thailand instead of by sea as expected.

Feb. 27. U.S. fleet starts three-day battle of the Java Sea in effort to delay Japanese invasion of Java; Allied losses are enormous at little cost to Japan.

March 5-9. Japan takes Batavia (present-day Jakarta), capital of Dutch East Indies, lands on island of New Guinea, and takes all of Java.

March 17. General Douglas MacArthur, on presidential orders, arrives in Australia from the Philippines to take command of Southwest Pacific Allied forces. In April, when Bataan falls, American forces on Bataan withdraw to Corregidor.

March. Federal government moves more than 110,000 Japanese from the West Coast to inland relocation camps; about 75,000 of these are American-born citizens of Japanese ancestry. Exclusion lasts until January 1945, is later called "our worst wartime mistake."

April 18. In surprise raid, U.S. carrier-based bombers reach and damage Tokyo and other Japanese cities; some crews are downed for lack of fuel to reach bases in China; others land in Japanese-occupied

EUGENE V. ROSTOW
Harper's, 1945
During the bleak spring of 1942, the Japanese and the Japanese-Americans who lived on the West Coast of the United States were taken into custody and removed to camps in the interior. More than 100,000 men, women, and children were thus exiled and imprisoned. More than two-thirds of them were American citizens.

These people were taken into custody as a military measure on the ground that espionage and sabotage were especially to be feared from persons of Japanese blood. The whole group was removed from the West Coast because the military authorities thought it would take too long to conduct individual investigations on the spot. They were arrested without warrants and were held without indictment or a statement of charges, although the courts were open and freely functioning. They were transported to camps far from their homes, and kept there under prison conditions, pending investigations of their "loyalty." Despite the good intentions of the chief relocation officers, the centers were little better than concentration camps.

If the evacuees were found "loyal," they were released only if they could find a job and a place to live, in a community where no hoodlums would come out at night to chalk up anti-Japanese slogans, break windows, or threaten riot. If found "disloyal" in their attitude to the war, they were kept in the camps indefinitely—although sympathy with the enemy is no crime in the United States (for white people at least) so long as it is not translated into deeds or the visible threat of deeds.

Song sung during siege of Bataan, 1942
We're the battling bastards of Bataan;
No mama, no papa, no Uncle Sam;
No aunts, no uncles, no cousins, no
nieces;
No pills, no planes, no artillery pieces.
. . . And nobody gives a damn.

WILLIAM T. CUMMINGS
Attributed, field sermon on Bataan,
1942
There are no atheists in the foxholes.

LT. NORMAN REYES
Radio report from Corregidor, April 9,
1942
Bataan has fallen, but the spirit that
made it stand—a beacon to all the
liberty-loving people of the world—
cannot fall!

Message from the hopelessly outnumbered defenders of Wake Island, answering a Navy request to report if anything was needed.
Send us more Japs!

DAVID F. MASON
Report to base, 1942
Sighted sub. Sank same.

China but are helped to escape by Chinese
underground.

April 18. President Roosevelt establishes
War Manpower Commission to supervise
war training and recruiting, the draft, and
industrial and agricultural war efforts.

May 4-7. U.S. forces frustrate Japan's
plan to capture Port Moresby, New Guinea, in Battle of the Coral Sea, first naval
engagement in which there is no contact of
ships, all fighting being done by planes.

May 6. At end of month-long siege,
11,500 American and Filipino forces and
refugees on Corregidor surrender to Japanese when lack of food and supplies makes
further resistance impossible.

May 14. Congress passes measure provid-
ing for formation of the Women's Army
Auxiliary Corps (WAAC, later WAC),
which is soon followed by Women Accept-
ed for Volunteer Emergency Service
(WAVES, Navy); Women's Auxiliary Fer-
rying Squadron (WAFS, Air Force); Wom-
en's Reserve of the Coast Guard Reserve
(SPARS, derived from Coast Guard motto,
Semper Paratus [Always Ready]); and the
Women's Reserve of the U.S. Marine
Corps (WM).

May 30. British Royal Air Force, which
advocates night saturation bombing, attacks
Cologne, Germany, in 1,000-bomber raid
and in June makes equally large raids on
Essen and Bremen.

June 3-6. In most decisive naval battle of
the war, Japanese lose 4 carriers and about
275 planes when they attempt to seize the
Midway Islands, as a base for attack on
Hawaii and the U.S. West Coast. This is
first major defeat of modern Japanese Navy,
and losses equalize Allied and Japanese naval power.

June 3-21. Japanese planes twice bomb Alaskan coastal town, two western islands of the Aleutians are occupied, and the coast of Oregon is shelled by a Japanese ship.

June 10. To avenge killing of Gestapo official, Germans destroy entire town of Lidice, Czechoslovakia, killing all men and removing all women and children to camps.

June 27. Federal Bureau of Investigation (FBI) announces capture of eight German saboteurs brought by submarines to Florida coast and Long Island, New York. Six are executed and two imprisoned.

June. By this month, shipyards of Henry J. Kaiser on the West Coast have been assigned one-third of U.S. wartime shipbuilding. Assembly-line methods, in which ships are made in parts that are welded together instead of built from the keel up, make it possible for a ship to be completed in less than a week; Kaiser's record is four days from start to finish.

July 21. Japanese land troops near Gona, New Guinea, with intent to launch an overland attack on Port Moresby, crossing mountains toward the south coast, but by mid-November Allied forces have forced them back across the mountains to Buna and Gona and taken several other New Guinea positions.

July 22. German Army crosses Don in two-pronged drive toward the Caucasus and Stalingrad (present-day Volgograd), which they enter in mid-September.

July. Joint Chiefs of Staff, meeting in London, plan invasion of Axis-held North Africa and increased activity against Japan in the Pacific, postponing second front in Europe (attack from French coast). **Aug. 12.** Soviet Premier Joseph Stalin, Prime Minister Winston Churchill, and W. Averill

WILLIAM L. WHITE
They Were Expendable, 1942
Suppose you're a sergeant machine-gunner, and your army is retreating and the enemy advancing. The captain takes you to a machine gun covering the road. "You're to stay here and hold this position," he tells you. "For how long?" you ask. "Never mind," he answers, "just hold it." Then you know you're expendable. In a way anything can be expendable — money or gasoline or equipment or most usually men. They are expending you and that machine gun to get time.

FRANKLIN D. ROOSEVELT
Message to the American Booksellers Association, 1942
We all know that books burn — yet we have the greater knowledge that books cannot be killed by fire. People die, but books never die. No man and no force can abolish memory. In this war, we know, books are weapons.

HENRY A. WALLACE
Address, 1942
The object of this war is to make sure that everybody in the world has the privilege of drinking a quart of milk a day.

Japanese war cry, Pacific, 1942
Go to Hell, Babe Ruth — American, you die.

JOHN HERSEY
Into the Valley, 1943

Individually the Marines in that outfit were as brave as any fighters in any army in the world, I am positive; but when fear began to be epidemic in that closed-in place, no one was immune. No one could resist it. . . .

The Marines had been deeply enough indoctrinated so that even flight did not wipe out the formulas, and soon the word came whispering back along the line:

"Withdraw."

"Withdraw . . ."

Then they started moving back, slowly at first, then running wildly, scrambling from place of cover to momentary cover. . . .

It was at this moment that Charles Alfred Rigaud, the boy with tired circles under his eyes, showed himself to be a good officer and a grown man.

Despite snipers all around us, despite the machine guns and the mortar fire, he stood right up on his feet and shouted out: "Who in Christ's name gave that order?"

This was enough to freeze the men in their tracks. They threw themselves on the ground, in attitudes of defense; they took cover behind trees from both the enemy and the anger of their captain.

Next, by a combination of blistering sarcasm, orders and cajolery, he not only got the men back into positions: he got them into a mood to fight again.

"Where do you guys think you're going?" he shouted. And: "Get back in there. . . . Take cover, you. . . . What do you guys do, just invent orders? . . . Listen, it's going to get dark and we got a job to do. . . . You guys make me ashamed. . . ."

But the most telling thing he said was: "Gosh, and they call you Marines."

Harriman (representing President Roosevelt) meet in Moscow. Stalin is told that the Allies cannot relieve hard-pressed Soviet forces by opening a second front in 1942.

Aug. 7. In first major offensive against Japan, U.S. Marines land on Guadalcanal in Solomon Islands and take airport. Sea, air, and land battles for the island seesaw back and forth for six months; losses are heavy on both sides. By February 9, 1943, all Japanese are cleared from the island.

Aug. 17. U.S. 8th Air Force makes first independent U.S. bombing attack in Europe when B-17s raid railroad yards near Rouen, France. U.S. advocates pinpoint bombing by daylight.

Aug. 19. British and Canadian troops, with a few U.S. Rangers, raid Dieppe on coast of France; about half of force is killed, wounded, or taken prisoner. In previous months, commando raids have been made on other parts of French coast.

September. Brigadier General Leslie R. Groves is appointed military head of Manhattan District for development of atomic bomb. Major construction on three plants — at Oak Ridge, Tennessee; Los Alamos, New Mexico; and Richland, Washington — does not begin until following year.

Oct. 1. Test pilot for Bell Aircraft Corporation flies first American jet airplane in California.

Oct. 9. Britain and the U.S. declare that they will give up extraterritorial rights in China and in January of the following year sign treaties with China to this effect; treaties give China equal status among world powers.

Nov. 3. In fall elections Democrats keep

majorities in House and Senate, although Republicans gain 9 Senate seats and 46 in the House.

Nov. 8. U.S. and British amphibious operation begins in North Africa under Lieutenant General Dwight D. Eisenhower and Admiral Sir Andrew Cunningham. Landings are made at Casablanca, Oran, and Algiers; Oran is taken on November 10. **Nov. 11.** In effort to minimize casualties, Allies make treaty with Admiral Jean Darlan, representative of French Vichy government, that involves his becoming high commissioner of French North Africa. Immediately German forces are sent into unoccupied France. **Nov. 27.** French fleet at Toulon is sunk by its crews to prevent take-over by Germans.

Nov. 13. Draft age is lowered to 18 years, and all men between 18 and 38 become eligible; at the same time, voluntary enlistments are ended. Some industrial and agricultural workers, as well as clergymen, are deferred.

Dec. 2. First controlled self-sustaining nuclear chain reaction, set off by Enrico Fermi and associates at the University of Chicago, demonstrates feasibility of atomic bomb and potentiality of nuclear power for peacetime uses.

December. By end of 1942, Japan has taken control of an area that reaches from Burma on the west to the Marshall and Gilbert islands on the east, from the western Aleutian Islands on the north to the Dutch East Indies on the south, and includes Korea, Manchuria, Thailand, French Indochina, and much of mainland China.

1942 - 1945

Rationing of foods and materials essential to the war effort begins generally in 1942

Could you tell him you're tired of buying WAR BONDS?

Ad designed to stimulate support for war

HENRY ADAMS
The Education of Henry Adams, 1907
At the rate of progress since 1800, every American who lived into the year 2000 would know how to control unlimited power. . . . To him the nineteenth century would stand on the same plane as the fourth — equally childlike — and he would only wonder how both of them, knowing so little, and so weak in force, should have done so much.

Code message indicating success of chain reaction experiment, 1942
The Italian navigator has landed; the natives are friendly.

FRANKLIN D. ROOSEVELT
Radio message, 1943
The decisions reached and the actual plans made at Casablanca were not confined to any one theater of war or to any one continent or ocean or sea. Before this year is out, it will be made known to the world—in actions rather than in words—that the Casablanca Conference produced plenty of news; and it will be bad news for the Germans and Italians—and the Japanese. . . .

In an attempt to ward off the inevitable disaster, the Axis propagandists are trying all of their old tricks in order to divide the United Nations. They seek to create the idea that if we win this war, Russia, England, China, and the United States are going to get into a cat-and-dog fight. This is their final effort to turn one nation against another in the vain hope that they may settle with one or two at a time—that any of us may be so gullible and so forgetful as to be duped into making "deals" at the expense of our allies.

To these panicky attempts to escape the consequences of their crimes we say—all the United Nations say—that the only terms on which we shall deal with any Axis government or any Axis factions are the terms proclaimed at Casablanca: "Unconditional surrender." In our uncompromising policy we mean no harm to the common people of the Axis nations. But we do mean to impose punishment and retribution in full upon their guilty, barbaric leaders.

(although auto tire rationing has begun almost immediately after Pearl Harbor); sugar, coffee, fuel oil, gasoline, fats, oils, butter, meats, cheese, canned and processed foods, and, finally, shoes are rationed. Except for sugar, all products are off rationing lists by end of 1945; sugar rationing is discontinued 18 months later.

1943

January. President Roosevelt and Prime Minister Churchill meet at Casablanca, Morocco; decisions made are that unconditional surrender of Axis powers will be the only acceptable basis for ending the war; a second front must be launched (although no date or place is fixed); Sicily and Italy will be invaded as a separate operation from second front; General Dwight D. Eisenhower is to command all of North African campaign.

March-September. Battle of the Bismarck Sea results in the sinking of 12 Japanese transports and 10 warships; by September 16, Allied forces have retaken Lae in New Guinea.

April 7. British and U.S. forces under command of General Eisenhower join lines in Tunisia in campaign to drive Axis forces out of Africa. With U.S. forces attacking from the west and British from the east, Axis are encircled and a month later retreat to Cap Bon Peninsula, where on May 12, more than 200,000 surrender in end of North African phase of war.

April 8. Because of threatened inflation, President Roosevelt freezes wages, salaries, and prices. **April 17.** War Manpower Commission freezes 27 million workers in essential industries in their jobs.

April 26. Soviet Union breaks off diplomatic relations with Polish government-in-exile.

May 27. President Roosevelt directs that all war contracts must include clauses prohibiting racial discrimination in war industries. Upgrading of Negroes results in riots; rioters controlled by federal troops.

May. President Roosevelt, Prime Minister Churchill, and many British and U.S. officials, meeting in Washington, D.C., settle May 1, 1944, as date for invasion of northwestern Europe.

May. After three weeks of fighting, U.S. forces retake Attu Island in the western Aleutians; three months later U.S. and Canadian forces attack Kiska but find that Japanese have abandoned it.

June 3. Generals Henri Giraud and Charles de Gaulle, after meeting in French Algiers, announce establishment of French Committee of National Liberation (later French Provisional Government-in-Exile); the two generals are to be co-presidents. Committee pledges maximum support of the Allies against the Axis.

June 14. Supreme Court reverses 1940 decision and holds that children cannot be required to salute the flag in school if their religion prohibits it; case has been brought by Jehovah's Witnesses.

June 25. War Labor Disputes (Smith-Connally) Act is passed over President Roosevelt's veto. Act authorizes the President to prevent labor disputes from interfering with war production by having government operate industry. This authority is later used in mine and railroad disputes.

June 30-December. U.S. naval and amphibious forces begin "island hopping"

ROBERT L. JACKSON
West Virginia Board of Education v. Barnette, 1943

The Fourteenth Amendment, as now applied to the states, protects the citizen against the state itself and all of its creatures—boards of education not excepted. These have, of course, important, delicate, and highly discretionary functions, but none that they may not perform within the limits of the Bill of Rights. That they are educating the young for citizenship is reason for scrupulous protection of constitutional freedoms of the individual if we are not to strangle the free mind at its source and teach youth to discount important principles of our government as mere platitudes.

Such boards are numerous and their territorial jurisdiction often small. But small and local authority may feel less sense of responsibility to the Constitution, and agencies of publicity may be less vigilant in calling it to account. The action of Congress in making flag observance voluntary and respecting the conscience of the objector in a matter so vital as raising the Army contrasts sharply with these local regulations in matters relatively trivial to the welfare of the nation. There are village tyrants as well as village Hampdens, but none who acts under color of law is beyond reach of the Constitution. . . .

We think the action of the local authorities in compelling the flag salute and pledge transcends constitutional limitations on their power and invades the sphere of intellect and spirit which it is the purpose of the First Amendment to our Constitution to reserve from all official control.

PVT. BILL STEELE
Yank, 1943

As soon as they land down here, nine out of 10 GIs say, "I wish to hell I could get back to the States — long enough to buy a knife." Nor is it only knives we need — every Johnny Jeep among us could make out a long list of items he wishes he had thought to remember to ship into his barracks bag when he left that port of embarkation. The moral is: Whatever you're going to need, you'd better bring with you.

Chances are that down here there won't be any civilian outlets where you can get a shaving mirror or a flashlight. And though the PXs — if you are lucky enough to be near one — try hard to supply such items, they're usually just out when you get there. . . .

Swim trunks — don't forget 'em! It's awkward to want a swim at a convenient seashore and not be able to for fear some nurse with a lieutenant's commission or a local maid might make a visit to the beach. You'll wear the trunks en route too — for a sun bath on deck. . . .

There's many a man who'd hock his PFC stripe for a bottle of anti-mosquito dope. The numerous mosquitoes here are active little fellows. They'll drain a fellow of his last corpuscles at night and appear at the Red Cross station as blood donors the next morning. Oil of citronella is effective in repelling them. . . .

Here's a final tip to act on when the time comes for you to trade your mainland address for an APO in the Pacific. Have plenty of pictures of the girl back home with you. You'll understand the reason the first day after you arrive.

campaign in Solomon Islands; strategy is to take key islands as bases for attacking next target and bypassing others, since seizure of every Japanese-occupied island will be too costly. By end of the year, the U.S. has gained control of the Solomons (except Bougainville) and landed at two points on New Britain.

July 10. U.S., British, and Canadian forces begin sea and air invasion of Sicily from bases in Tunisia. By August 17, Sicily has been captured, to be used as takeoff point for invasion of the Italian mainland.

July 19. "Big Inch," world's longest oil pipeline, is dedicated. It has been laid over about 1,300 miles from Texas to Pennsylvania, crossing about 230 rivers and streams.

July 25. Italy's Premier Mussolini and his Cabinet resign; new government is headed by Marshal Pietro Badoglio. **July 28.** Italian Fascist Party is dissolved.

August. Russians battle fiercely against German offensive begun on July 5 and by November 6 have retaken Orel, Belgorod, Smolensk, Dnepropetrovsk, and Kiev. By beginning of 1944 they have pushed Germans back west of Kiev and entered Poland.

Quebec Conference meets, attended by President Roosevelt, Prime Minister Churchill, chiefs of staff, and other advisers. May 1, 1944, date for invasion of Europe is discussed, as well as supplementary invasion of southern France. Plans are made for increased military operations in the Far East, especially Burma.

Sept. 3. British and Canadians invade Italy from Sicily. **Sept. 8.** Italy surrenders unconditionally. **Sept. 9.** U.S. forces land south of Naples and meet determined German resistance, which ends by September

15. By this time, Germany has taken Rome, and the Italian fleet has surrendered to the Allies. **Sept. 12.** Mussolini, who has been arrested by new Italian government, escapes and sets up Fascist government in German-occupied parts of Italy, where German armies continue to fight until end of war.

Sept. 21. House of Representatives adopts Fulbright Resolution, which advocates formation of "international machinery" to achieve and keep a "just and lasting peace." **Nov. 5.** Senate adopts resolution introduced by Senator Tom Connally of Texas that is similar but requires Senate ratification of any international agreement made to this end.

Oct. 13. Italy declares war on Germany.

October. Representatives of Britain, the U.S., and the Soviet Union meet in Moscow; the U.S. and Britain tell Russians of second front preparations; Soviets pledge declaration of war on Japan once Germany is beaten and refuse to recognize Polish government-in-exile. Allies set up European Advisory Commission to work out basic principles for postwar treatment of Germany and Italy. All three powers declare that they recognize the necessity of an international organization to maintain world peace.

Nov. 9. Assistance for victims of war is planned when 44 nations meeting in Washington establish United Nations Relief and Rehabilitation Administration (UNRRA). In next two years, member nations agree to contribute $4 billion for relief.

Nov. 22. Generalissimo and Madame Chiang Kai-shek of China meet in Cairo, Egypt, with President Roosevelt and Prime Minister Churchill; in Declaration of Cairo they agree to demand unconditional surrender of Japan, declare that their countries do not aim for territorial expansion, state that

ERNIE PYLE
Here Is Your War, 1943

On the day of final peace, the last stroke of what we call the "Big Picture" will be drawn. I haven't written anything about the "Big Picture," because I don't know anything about it. I only know what we see from our worm's-eye view, and our segment of the picture consists only of tired and dirty soldiers who are alive and don't want to die; of long darkened convoys in the middle of the night; of shocked silent men wandering back down the hill from battle; of chow lines and Atabrine tablets and foxholes and burning tanks and Arabs holding up eggs and the rustle of high-flown shells; of jeeps and petrol dumps and smelly bedding rolls and C rations and cactus patches and blown bridges and dead mules and hospital tents and shirt collars greasy-black from months of wearing; and of laughter too, and anger and wine and lovely flowers and constant cussing. All these it is composed of; and of graves and graves and graves.

That is our war, and we will carry it with us as we go on from one battleground to another until it is all over, leaving some of us behind on every beach, in every field. . . . Medals and speeches and victories are nothing to them any more. They died and others lived and nobody knows why it is so. They died and thereby the rest of us can go on and on. When we leave here for the next shore, there is nothing we can do for the ones beneath the wooden crosses, except perhaps to pause and murmur, "Thanks, pal."

WENDELL L. WILLKIE
One World, 1943
America must choose one of three courses after this war: narrow nationalism, which inevitably means the ultimate loss of our own liberty; international imperialism, which means the sacrifice of some other nation's liberty; or the creation of a world in which there shall be an equality of opportunity for every race and every nation. I am convinced the American people will choose, by overwhelming majority, the last of these courses. To make this choice effective, we must win not only the war but also the peace, and we must start winning it now.

To win this peace three things seem to me necessary—first, we must plan now for peace on a world basis; second, the world must be free, politically and economically, for nations and for men, that peace may exist in it; third, America must play an active, constructive part in freeing it and keeping its peace.

When I say that peace must be planned on a world basis, I mean quite literally that it must embrace the earth. Continents and oceans are plainly only parts of a whole, seen, as I have seen them, from the air. . . . And it is inescapable that there can be no peace for any part of the world unless the foundations of peace are made secure throughout all parts of the world.

This cannot be accomplished by mere declarations of our leaders, as in an Atlantic Charter. Its accomplishment depends primarily upon acceptance by the peoples of the world. . . . The Four Freedoms will not be accomplished by the declarations of those momentarily in power. They will become real only if the people of the world forge them into actuality.

Japan must be deprived of all Pacific islands gained since 1914 and must return Chinese territories to China, and agree that Korea must become independent as soon as possible. Soviet Union does not attend, not being at war with Japan.

Nov. 23. After three days of bloody fighting, U.S. Marines take Tarawa and Makin islands in the Gilberts in second step toward Japan via Solomon, Gilbert, Marshall, Mariana, and Bonin islands.

Nov. 28. President Roosevelt, Prime Minister Churchill, and Premier Stalin meet at Teheran, Iran, and plan second front in Western Europe; Stalin again promises to enter war against Japan. General Eisenhower is named commander of the invasion of Western Europe on Dec. 24.

Dec. 17. President Roosevelt signs bill repealing Chinese Exclusion Acts and setting annual Chinese immigration quota at 105.

Dec. 31. By this date, Allied forces have control of southern Italy to a line across the peninsula about halfway between Naples and Rome.

By end of 1943, Allies have taken the initiative in all theaters of war: Pacific, Mediterranean, Eastern Europe, and Southeast Asia; air attacks on Germany are constant from Allied bases in England.

Wendell Willkie publishes his *One World*, following his 31,000-mile, 49-day journey around the world; a strong plea for international cooperation, it sells 1 million copies within two months and eventually more than 2 million. Other best sellers of this year are *A Tree Grows in Brooklyn* by Betty Smith and *Here Is Your War* by Ernie Pyle; the latter is one of many war books, mostly by correspondents. Pyle is killed on island near Okinawa in April 1945.

Regional painting thrives in this period, especially Middle Western subjects, such as those by Grant Wood, Thomas Hart Benton, and John Steuart Curry. At the same time, many refugee artists work in the U.S., among them Piet Mondrian, Marc Chagall, and Fernand Léger. Most original painting is by Jackson Pollock, who gives his first one-man show in this year.

1943 - 1944

1943. The Supreme Court declines to consider case involving exclusion of Japanese from the West Coast but upholds military curfew in that area. **1944.** Court upholds Japanese exclusion (*Korematsu* v. *U.S.*), although dissent calls relocation unconstitutional; however, in another case, the Court finds that no person whose loyalty to the U.S. has been established may be relocated.

1943 - 1945

May 15, 1943. The Soviet Union dissolves the Third International (Comintern). A year later, U.S. Communist Party is dissolved but reformed as the Communist Political Association. This group is discontinued in 1945 and again becomes the Communist Party.

1943 - 1948

U.S. scientists begin research on antihistamines for use in treatment of allergies. Several have been discovered by 1948, including Dramamine, which is found to be effective in controlling motion sickness.

1944

Jan. 11. Allies begin air attacks against Germany from Britain in preparation for invasion of France. **March 4.** Berlin is bombed for first time by U.S. planes;

JACKSON POLLOCK
Arts and Architecture, 1944
    Where did you study?
At the Art Student's League, here in New York. I began when I was seventeen. Studied with Benton, at the League, for two years.

    How did your study with Thomas Benton affect your work, which differs so radically from his?
My work with Benton was important as something against which to react very strongly, later on; in this, it was better to have worked with him than with a less resistant personality who would have provided a much less strong opposition. At the same time, Benton introduced me to Renaissance art. . . .

    Do you find it important that many famous modern European artists are living in this country?
Yes. I accept the fact that the important painting of the last hundred years was done in France. American painters have generally missed the point of modern painting from beginning to end. (The only American master who interests me is Ryder.) Thus the fact that good European Moderns are now here is very important, for they bring with them an understanding of the problems of Modern painting. . . .

    Do you think there can be a purely American art?
The idea of an isolated American painting, so popular in this country during the 'thirties, seems absurd to me, just as the idea of creating a purely American mathematics or physics would seem absurd. . . . And in another sense, the problem doesn't exist at all; or, if it did, would solve itself: An American is an American and his painting would naturally be qualified by that fact, whether he wills it or not. But the basic problems of contemporary painting are independent of any one country.

Newspaper headline in most U.S. papers when Italy surrendered, 1943
One Down, Two to Go.

ERNIE PYLE
Brave Men, 1944
Then darkness enveloped the whole American armada. Not a pinpoint of light showed from those hundreds of ships as they surged on through the night toward their destiny, carrying across the ageless and indifferent sea tens of thousands of young men, fighting for . . . for . . . well, at least for each other.

GEN. DWIGHT D. EISENHOWER
Radio broadcast, June 6, 1944
People of Western Europe: A landing was made this morning on the coast of France by troops of the Allied Expeditionary Force. This landing is part of the concerted United Nations plan for the liberation of Europe, made in conjunction with our great Russian allies. . . . I call upon all who love freedom to stand with us now. Together we shall achieve victory.

GEN. GEORGE S. PATTON, JR.
Speech to troops of Third Army, before invasion of France, July 1944
Sure, we all want to get home. We want to get this thing over with. But the quickest way to get it over with is to go get the bastards. The quicker they're whipped, the quicker we go home. The shortest way home is through Berlin..

And there's one thing you'll be able to say when you do go home. When you're sitting around your fireside, with your brat on your knee, and he asks you what you did in the great World War II, you won't have to say you shovelled . . . in Louisiana.

bombing reaches height in April and in May just before invasion begins. General Eisenhower establishes Supreme Headquarters, Allied Expeditionary Force (SHAEF), in Britain immediately after start of air attacks.

Jan. 18-March 3. Having begun counter-offensive on three fronts late in previous year, Russians relieve Leningrad defenders, who have been besieged for 17 months, and retake Stalingrad, Rostov-on-Don, Kharkov, and Rzhev.

January. General Joseph ("Vinegar Joe") Stilwell, U.S. commander in Southeast Asia, launches campaign in northern Burma aimed at capturing airfield at Myitkyina to gain Allied access to China. By May 17, 1944, airfield is taken.

March 19. U.S. forces conquer essential parts of Admiralty Islands and one month later capture Japanese airfields at Hollandia, on north coast of Netherlands (present-day West) New Guinea.

March 20. German forces occupy Hungary. **April 10.** Soviet forces retake Odessa and, a month later, Sevastopol; at beginning of year, German invaders have been cleared from the area between Moscow and Leningrad.

June 4. U.S. 5th Army liberates Rome, having landed to the south with other Allied units in January.

June 6. D-Day invasion of Europe begins; date in early May has been changed because of necessity of shipping landing craft from Mediterranean theater, and because tides, the moon, daylight, and weather conditions must be favorable to amphibious landings, as well as paratroop landings inland. Invasion, along 50-mile Normandy coastline, is spearheaded by about 175,000 troops carried in 4,000 landing craft and supported by 600 warships and about 11,000 planes. **June 13.** Germans counterattack by bombarding England, especially London, with V-1 rockets, pilotless and jet propelled.

June 15. B-29 long-range Superfortresses bomb Kyushu from bases in China and India in first raid of campaign against Japanese home islands. In November, raids are carried out from rebuilt airfields on captured Saipan Island, in the Marianas.

June 21. Three-day air and naval battle of Philippine Sea costs Japan 450 planes and 3 carriers, as well as crippling 4 carriers, a battleship, and a cruiser. The U.S. losses include 20 aircraft and negligible ship damage.

June 22. President Roosevelt signs Servicemen's Readjustment Act ("G.I. Bill of Rights"); it establishes educational and other benefits for veterans after demobilization. By end of 1946, two million veterans are beneficiaries of this law, mostly in colleges and universities.

June 23. Soviet forces launch offensive south of Leningrad along 300-mile line.

June 26. Republicans meet at Chicago and nominate Governor Thomas E. Dewey of New York for President and Governor John W. Bricker of Ohio for Vice-President. **July 20.** Democrats at Chicago renominate President Roosevelt but choose Senator Harry S. Truman of Missouri for Vice-President instead of Vice-President Wallace. Minor party candidates are: Norman Thomas of New York, Socialist; Claude A. Watson of California, Prohibition; and Edward A. Teichert of Pennsylvania, Socialist Labor. Platforms of both Democrats and Republicans advocate membership in an international organization to

JOHN DESMOND
New York Times Magazine, 1944
The stage is a rough board affair, supported by freshly hewn logs. On it a girl, dressed in a simple cotton dress like those you see on the boardwalk at Jones Beach on a summer afternoon, is singing. Behind her two other entertainers are sitting on camp stools and to the right an accordionist pumps his arms. His instrument pours out a volume of sound that somehow manages to approximate the tune of "Shoo-Shoo Baby.". . .

It is hot—115 degrees in back of the stage, 130 plus under the arc lights that are powered by a mobile Army generator standing nearby. . . .

The singer and the performers with her on New Guinea make up an overseas company of the Camp Shows branch of the United Service Organizations. At the present time, eighty such companies are out of the country, giving shows in bomb-damaged opera houses it Italy, in rickety Nissen huts in North Africa, in storage barns in Alaska and the Aleutians, in jungles, deserts, mountain hideouts—in fact, wherever American boys are stationed.

In the simplest terms, Camp Shows' job is to bring Hollywood and Broadway to the serviceman. . . .

The spontaneous response of the servicemen is so swift and heartfelt that there is scarcely an actor who has been overseas who does not fear the day when he will again face a city audience. . . .

Letters from all theaters flood into the USO-Camp Shows from soldiers and sailors in the fighting zones and from their parents at home attesting the gratitude of the servicemen for the "live shows."

The Sad Sack's Catechism, World War II
If it moves, salute it.
If it doesn't move, pick it up.
If you can't pick it up, paint it.

Army saying, World War II
Kilroy was here.

BILL MAULDIN
Cartoon captions, Up Front, 1944
He's right, Joe, when we ain't fightin'
we should ack like sojers.

I feel like a fugitive from th' law of
averages.

GEN. GEORGE S. PATTON, JR.
Instructions to Third Army, 1944
Any commander who fails to obtain his
objective, and who is not dead or se-
verely wounded, has not done his full
duty.

ADM. WILLIAM F. HALSEY, JR.
Radio message, 1944, after Japanese
claims that most of the U.S. Third Fleet
had been sunk or was retiring
Our ships have been salvaged and are
retiring at high speed toward the Japa-
nese fleet.

ADM. WILLIAM F. HALSEY, JR.
Suggested reply to Japanese question:
"Where is the American fleet?" 1944
Send them our latitude and longitude.

maintain world peace. CIO Political Action Committee supports Democrats.

July 1-22. United Nations Monetary and Financial Conference is held at Bretton Woods, New Hampshire, with 44 nations attending. Policies and plans are developed for mutual assistance in economic recovery and restoration of trade; International Monetary Fund is established for currency stabilization, along with International Bank for Reconstruction and Development. The Soviet Union takes part in Conference but does not join new financial institutions.

July 2. By this date Allies have taken Cherbourg, France, and landed about 1 million troops in Normandy, with vehicles and supplies to support them. **July 18.** British have taken Caen, and U.S. forces take Saint-Lô. Advancing from Saint-Lô a week later, armored forces penetrate Brittany and by August 9, Americans have laid siege to ports of Brest, Lorient, and Saint-Nazaire.

July 18. Premier Hideki Tojo, disgraced by loss of Saipan, resigns as head of Japanese government; his Cabinet follows suit.

July 19. U.S. forces capture Leghorn, on west coast of Italy. **Aug. 12.** Allies take Florence, forcing Germans to line north of the Arno River.

July 20. German Army factions attempt bomb assassination of Adolf Hitler; following its failure, many high-ranking officers, including Field Marshall Rommel, are executed or commit suicide.

July 27. The Soviet Union, opposed strongly by the U.S. and Britain, recognizes as government of Russian-occupied Poland the Polish Committee of National Liberation, which is later seated in Lublin.

Aug. 9. By this date, Pacific island-hopping campaign has resulted in establishment of U.S. footholds in the Marshalls and the Marianas.

Aug. 14. War Production Board authorizes partial conversion of war industries to civilian output. Office of War Mobilization and Reconversion is established in October in anticipation of economic and social problems in transition from war to peace.

Aug. 15. Southern France is invaded by Allied forces, which land between Marseilles and Nice and fight up the Rhône River Valley toward armies in northern France. **Aug. 25.** French 2nd Armored Division enters Paris, and three days later U.S. 3rd Army reaches the Marne River. **Sept. 4.** British and Canadian troops capture Brussels and badly needed port of Antwerp, which is also German V-2 rocket launching site. By this time the Allies have landed more than 2 million men and their supplies on the Continent.

Aug. 21-Oct. 7. Representatives of the U.S., Britain, China, and the Soviet Union meet at Dumbarton Oaks, Washington, D.C., to discuss postwar world organization. Proposals agreed on later serve as basis for United Nations Charter. Security Council is planned as executive branch, but the Soviet Union does not agree on voting plan, refusing to consent to the rule that a Security Council nation may not vote in an issue involving itself.

Aug. 22. Allied forces, having circled Germans and attacking from north and south, close German escape gap between Falaise and Argentan, killing or capturing about 500,000 German troops.

Sept. 11. U.S. forces enter Germany through Luxembourg. In next two weeks, in largest airborne operation ever attempted, Allies land more than 20,000 paratroops

PFC. VERNER ODEGARD
Yank, 1944

We didn't have a damn thing to do with the taking of Paris. We just came in a couple of days later when somebody got the bright idea of having the parade and we just happened to be there and that's all there is to it. What can you do, though — that's just the way it goes. And after all, we did a helluva lot of things that we didn't get credit for.

As long as I live I don't guess I'll ever see a parade like that. Most of us slept in pup tents in the Bois de Boulogne the night before, and it rained like hell and we were pretty dirty, so they picked out the cleanest guys to stand up in front and on the outside. I had a bright new shiny patch, so they put me on the outside. It was a good place to be, too, because every guy marching on the outside had at least one girl on his arm kissing him and hugging him.

We were marching 24 abreast down the Champs Elysees and we had a helluva time trying to march, because the whole street was jammed with people laughing and yelling and crying and singing. They were throwing flowers at us and bringing us big bottles of wine.

The first regiment never did get through. They just broke in and grabbed the guys and lifted some of them on their shoulders and carried them into cafes and bars and their homes and wouldn't let them go. I hear it was a helluva job trying to round them all up later.

T/SGT. DONALD HAGUALL

Yank, 1944

Sure, there were lots of bodies we never identified. You know what a direct hit by a shell does to a guy. Or a mine, or a solid hit with a grenade, even. Sometimes all we have is a leg or a hunk of arm.

The ones that stink the worst are the guys who got internal wounds and are dead about three weeks with the blood staying inside and rotting, and when you move the body the blood comes out of the nose and mouth. Then some of them bloat up in the sun, they bloat up so big that they bust the buttons and then they get blue and the skin peels. They don't all get blue, some of them get black.

But they all stink. There's only one stink and that's it. You never get used to it, either. As long as you live, you never get used to it. And after a while, the stink gets in your clothes and you can taste it in your mouth.

You know what I think? I think maybe if every civilian in the world could smell that stink, then maybe we wouldn't have any more wars.

FRANKLIN D. ROOSEVELT

Speech to Teamsters Union, 1944

These Republican leaders have not been content with attacks upon me, or on my wife, or on my sons—no, not content with that, they now include my little dog Fala. Unlike the members of my family, he resents this.

and their equipment in the Netherlands to secure bridgeheads for advancing ground troops. **Oct. 21.** U.S. forces take Aachen, Germany, after three-week battle, and one month later Metz and Strasbourg are captured.

Sept. 11-16. President Roosevelt and Prime Minister Churchill meet in Quebec to discuss European and Pacific battle plans, occupation zones after defeat of Germany, and treatment of Germany after the war.

Sept. 15. Invasion of Palau Islands begins; about two weeks later, marines take Peleliu, about 500 miles from the Philippines.

Sept. 29. President Roosevelt, concerned over increase of Nazi and Fascist influence in Argentina and lack of cooperation against Axis, accuses Argentina of reneging on inter-American obligations.

Oct. 20. U.S. forces headed by General MacArthur return to Philippines, landing on Leyte. Six-day naval battle in Leyte Gulf (actually four separate operations), with loss of 24 Japanese carriers, battleships, cruisers, and destroyers, marks end of Japanese fleet as an effective force.

October. Prime Minister Churchill and Premier Stalin, meeting in Moscow, plan division of postwar influence in southeastern Europe; the Soviet Union is to control Hungary, Bulgaria, and Rumania; Britain is to predominate in Greece; and Yugoslavia is to be divided between Great Britain and Soviet Union. President Roosevelt, not present at the conference, announces that he will not be obligated by British-Soviet decisions.

Nov. 7. President Roosevelt is elected for a fourth term with popular vote of 25,607,000 to Dewey's 22,015,000; vote includes several million absentee ballots sent by members of the armed forces. Minor candidates receive less than 1 percent of vote. Electoral vote is Roosevelt, 36 states with 432 votes; Dewey, 12 states with 99 votes. About 70 percent of U.S. press has supported Dewey. CIO Political Action Committee claims that its support has helped elect 120 Democratic representatives and 17 senators.

Dec. 15. Congress creates new rank, General of the Army ("five-star general"), for Generals Eisenhower, Henry Arnold, MacArthur, and George C. Marshall.

Dec. 16-27. In Battle of the Bulge, last major Axis counteroffensive of the war, German armored forces drive toward Antwerp, attacking thinly defended Allied line, in hope of splitting British-U.S. armies. Delayed by defenders of Bastogne, which is almost surrounded, Germans are finally defeated with heavy losses on both sides. By January 31, 1945, Allied forces have regained former line in the Ardennes.

Dec. 26. Russians, driving westward on all fronts, have by this date taken Estonian port of Tallinn, entered East Prussia, with Yugoslav forces taken Belgrade, and laid siege to Budapest. In addition, British and Greek forces have driven Germans out of Greece.

U.S. Supreme Court, in Texas case involving exclusion of Negroes from Democratic Party, and consequently from participating in primaries, holds that exclusion from a political party on ground of race is tantamount to a denial of suffrage and hence a violation of the Fifteenth Amendment.

1944 - 1945

By 1944, military goods are about 65 percent of total U.S. production as opposed to 2 percent in 1939. Aluminum produc-

E. B. WHITE

The New Yorker, December 23, 1944

They are not wrapped as gifts (there was no time to wrap them), but you will find them under the lighted tree with the other presents. They are the extra gifts, the ones with the hard names. Certain towns and villages. Certain docks and installations. Atolls in a sea. Assorted airstrips, beachheads, supply dumps, rail junctions. Here is a gift to hold in your hand—Hill 660. Vital from a strategic standpoint. "From the Marines," the card says. Here is a small strip of the Italian coast. Merry Christmas from the members of the American Fifth (who waded ashore). This is Kwajalein, Maloelap, Wotje. This is Eniwetok. . . .

Who wouldn't love the Norman coast for Christmas? Who hasn't hoped for the Atlantic Wall, the impregnable? Here is the whole thing under the lighted tree. First the beaches (greetings from the Navy and the Coast Guard), then the cliffs, the fields behind the cliffs, the inland villages and towns, the key places, the hedgerows, the lanes, the houses, and the barns. Ste. Mère Eglise (with greetings from Omar Bradley and foot soldiers). This Norman cliff (best from the Rangers). St. Jacques de Nehou (from the 82nd Airborne Division, with its best). . . .

Still the gifts come. You haven't even noticed the gift of the rivers Marne and Aisne: Château-Thierry, Soissons (this is where you came in). Verdun, Sedan (greetings from the American First Army, greetings from the sons of the fathers). Here is a most unusual gift, a bit of German soil. Priceless. A German village, Roetgen. . . . there isn't time to look at them all. It will take years. This is a Christmas you will never forget, people have been so generous.

State Department report on Yalta Conference, 1945

The Premier of the Union of Soviet Socialist Republics, the Prime Minister of the United Kingdom, and the President of the United States of America have consulted with each other in the common interests of the peoples of their countries and those of liberated Europe. They jointly declare their mutual agreement to concert during the temporary period of instability in liberated Europe the policies of their three governments in assisting the peoples liberated from the domination of Nazi Germany and the peoples of the former Axis satellite states of Europe to solve by democratic means their pressing political and economic problems.

The establishment of order in Europe and the rebuilding of national economic life must be achieved by processes which will enable the liberated peoples to destroy the last vestiges of Nazism and Fascism and to create democratic institutions of their own choice. . . .

To foster the conditions in which the liberated peoples may exercise these rights, the three governments will jointly assist the people in any European liberated state or former Axis satellite state in Europe where in their judgment conditions require (a) to establish conditions of internal peace; (b) to carry out emergency measures for the relief of distressed peoples; (c) to form interim governmental authorities broadly representative of all democratic elements in the population and pledged to the earliest possible establishment through free elections of governments responsive to the will of the people; and (d) to facilitate where necessary the holding of such elections.

tion, mainly for aircraft, has increased 500 percent; synthetic rubber production has risen from 2,000 tons in 1939 to more than 900,000 tons in 1945.

1944 - 1950

Glenn Seaborg and associates produce four man-made elements, americium, curium, berkelium, and californium, element numbers 95 through 98.

1945

Jan. 23. Soviet troops reach Oder River on border of Germany after offensive that has begun in Poland on January 12.

Feb. 4-11. President Roosevelt, Prime Minister Churchill, and Premier Stalin meet in the Crimea at Yalta. Their agreements (many of which are not made public until after the war) give the Soviet Union extensive territorial and other rights in the Far East in return for promise to enter war against Japan; they also work out plans for treatment of Germany and liberated nations, and reparations are discussed. Voting in United Nations Security Council is agreed on, and date is set for San Francisco Conference on Charter.

Feb. 8. Allied drive across Germany begins with attacks in northern, central, and southern Germany. **March 2.** U.S. troops have crossed the Saar River, entered the Ruhr Valley, and are approaching Düsseldorf. **March 23.** Allies cross Rhine near Wesel. **March 26.** U.S. forces cross Rhine at Worms and push northward into the Ruhr. **March 29.** Mannheim and Frankfurt am Main captured. **April 11.** U.S. forces reach Elbe River. **April 17.** Düsseldorf surrenders, and on following day Ruhr pocket is liquidated; German prisoners total 325,000, including 30 generals.

Feb. 10. B-29s raid Tokyo nine days before U.S. marines land 750 miles from Japan on Iwo Jima; island is taken only after major struggle lasting for almost a month; casualties are heavy. **March 24-27.** Carrier-based planes pound Japanese in Okinawa, 350 miles from Japan, in preparation for invasion that begins on April 1. Japanese air attacks on invasion forces, continuing into June, result in heaviest losses of war, about 45,000 killed or wounded. Okinawa is taken by June 21.

Feb. 24. After battle of almost three weeks, U.S. forces take Manila, capital of the Philippines; this marks end of campaign in these islands.

March 3. Finland, out of the war since end of 1941, declares war on Germany.

March 3. In Act of Chapultepec, all American nations except Argentina sign mutual security pact that permits "use of armed force to prevent or repel aggression" by one state against another. **March 12.** Argentina is admitted to Pan American Union and 15 days later declares war on the Axis.

April 5. Soviet Union abrogates nonaggression pact with Japan but does not declare war. On same day, Japanese premier and his Cabinet resign.

April 12. President Roosevelt dies of a cerebral hemorrhage at Warm Springs, Georgia, after less than three months of his fourth term. Vice-President Harry S. Truman becomes thirty-third President.

April 20. U.S. forces take Nürnberg, and three days later Russians enter Berlin. **April 25.** Soviet troops from the east and U.S. forces from the west meet on the Elbe River at Torgau. On the next day, British take Bremen.

April 25-June 26. United Nations Charter is drafted at San Francisco. Fifty nations

ARTHUR H. VANDENBERG
Speech in Senate, 1945
In this hour of anxious tragedy, when the bowed hearts of all the civilized earth join ours this fateful morning in humble poignant sorrow that Franklin Delano Roosevelt, the thirty-first President of the United States, has been gathered to his fathers, nothing that we say here can add to the glory of his stature or to the measure of our grief. He belongs now to history, where he leaves a mark which not even rushing centuries can erase.

Those who were his loyal opposition, no less than those who were his intimate associates, have always recognized in him a rare crusader for his human faiths, an amazing genius in behalf of his always vigorous ideals, a valiant knight in the armor of his commandership as he waged global war. . . .

He bravely mastered his own physical handicap with a courage which never lapsed as he fought his way to an unprecedented pinnacle at home and to dominant influence around the world. His untimely death will be mourned at every hearthstone, and on every battle front where freedom wins the victory to which he literally gave his life. A successful peace must be his monument.

FRANKLIN D. ROOSEVELT
Undelivered speech, 1945
Today we are faced with the preeminent fact that, if civilization is to survive, we must cultivate the science of human relationships — the ability of all peoples, of all kinds, to live together and work together in the same world, at peace.

United Nations Charter, 1945
*WE THE PEOPLES OF THE UNITED
NATIONS DETERMINED*

*to save succeeding generations from
the scourge of war, which twice in our
lifetime has brought untold sorrow to
mankind, and*

*to reaffirm faith in fundamental hu-
man rights, in the dignity and worth of
the human person, in the equal rights
of men and women and of nations large
and small, and*

*to establish conditions under which
justice and respect for the obligations
arising from treaties and other sources
of international law can be maintained,
and*

*to promote social progress and better
standards of life in larger freedom, . . .
HAVE RESOLVED TO COMBINE OUR
EFFORTS TO ACCOMPLISH THESE
AIMS.*

*Accordingly, our respective Govern-
ments, through representatives assembled in the city of San Francisco, who
have exhibited their full powers found
to be in good and due form, have
agreed to the present Charter of the
United Nations and do hereby establish
an international organization to be
known as the United Nations.*

GEN. DWIGHT D. EISENHOWER
Telegram to the Combined Chiefs of
Staff
*The mission of this Allied Force was ful-
filled at 3 a.m., local time, May 7,
1945. Eisenhower.*

Inscription discovered by a Yank report-
er at Verdun, 1945
*Austin White—Chicago, Ill.—1918
Austin White—Chicago, Ill.—1945
This is the last time I want to write my
name here.*

take part in meeting; Charter is signed by
all and becomes effective October 24.

April 28. As Allied armies invade Po
Valley in Italy, Italian partisans capture and
kill Benito Mussolini and his mistress as
they are trying to escape to Switzerland.

May 2. Berlin is taken a day after announcement by provisional German government that Hitler has committed suicide.
Germans in Italy surrender on the same
day, and two days later German forces in
Denmark, the Netherlands, and northwest
Germany follow suit. **May 7.** Unconditional German surrender is signed at Allied
Reims headquarters; it becomes effective at
midnight May 8-9. A month later, Germany is divided into four sectors by European
Advisory Commission; northwestern area is
to be controlled by Britain, the Rhineland
and the Saar by France, southwestern area
by the U.S., and eastern area by the Soviet
Union; Berlin, within Soviet area, is divided into four similar sectors.

May 3. Rangoon captured by Allies. This
virtually closes Burma campaign.

May-December. Immediately after end
of war in Europe, the U.S. begins to convert to peacetime economy. Rationing on
all items but sugar is ended; War Production Board lifts ban on manufacture of consumer goods, removing 210 controls on August 20 and, except for shortage materials,
ending Controlled Materials Plan on September 30; production of military aircraft
by December is one-half that of previous
year, manpower controls are ended in August; and by end of the year, National War
Labor Board is replaced by National Wage
Stabilization Board.

July 16. First atomic bomb is exploded in
the desert at Alamogordo, New Mexico.
President Truman informs Churchill and

Stalin at Potsdam Conference of successful test, but public announcement is not made until August 6.

July 17-Aug. 2. U.S., Great Britain, and Soviet Union hold Potsdam Conference. Unconditional surrender of Japan is reaffirmed as war aim, and ultimatum is sent to Japanese government; treaties with Germany and her allies are discussed; war crimes trials are planned.

July 28. U.S. Senate ratifies United Nations Charter, with two dissenting votes.

July 29. Japan rejects unconditional surrender demand sent from Potsdam Conference, although mainland of Japan has been heavily bombed by U.S. forces since beginning of May.

Aug. 6. Atomic bomb is dropped on Hiroshima, Japan; about four square miles of the city are devastated by explosion equal to 20,000 tons of TNT; more than 135,000 people are killed or injured.

Aug. 8. The Soviet Union declares war on Japan and invades Manchuria; declaration comes three months after Germany's surrender as promised.

Aug. 9. The U.S. drops second atomic bomb, this time on Nagasaki, a provincial capital and naval base in southern Japan.

Aug. 15. V-J Day ending war in Pacific is proclaimed after Potsdam ultimatum has been accepted by Japanese on August 10 and unconditional surrender has been agreed to on August 14; Emperor Hirohito is allowed to retain his throne. Occupation of Japan begins two weeks later, and formal surrender is signed aboard battleship *Missouri* in Tokyo Bay on September 2. **Sept. 9.** At Nanking, Japanese sign formal surrender of forces in China.

HARRY S. TRUMAN
Address to the nation, 1945
Sixteen hours ago an American airplane dropped one bomb on Hiroshima, an important Japanese Army base. That bomb had more power than 20,000 tons of TNT. . . .

With this bomb we have now added a new and revolutionary increase in destruction to supplement the growing power of our armed forces. In their present form these bombs are now in production, and even more powerful forms are in development.

It is an atomic bomb. It is a harnessing of the basic power of the universe. The force from which the sun draws its power has been loosed against those who brought war to the Far East.

Before 1939, it was the accepted belief of scientists that it was theoretically possible to release atomic energy. But no one knew any practical method of doing it. . . .

We have spent $2 billion on the greatest scientific gamble in history—and won.

But the greatest marvel is not the size of the enterprise, its secrecy, nor its cost, but the achievement of scientific brains in putting together infinitely complex pieces of knowledge held by many men in different fields of science into a workable plan. And hardly less marvelous has been the capacity of industry to design, and of labor to operate, the machines and methods to do things never done before so that the brainchild of many minds came forth in physical shape and performed as it was supposed to do. . . .

Under present circumstances it is not intended to divulge the technical processes of production or all the military applications, pending further examination of possible methods of protecting us and the rest of the world from the danger of sudden destruction.

GEN. DOUGLAS MacARTHUR

Address to the nation, Sept. 2, 1945

Today the guns are silent. A great tragedy has ended. A great victory has been won. The skies no longer rain death — the seas bear only commerce — men everywhere walk upright in the sunlight. The entire world lies quietly at peace. The holy mission has been completed. And in reporting this to you, the people, I speak for the thousands of silent lips, forever stilled among the jungles and the beaches and in the deep waters of the Pacific which marked the way. I speak for the unnamed brave millions homeward bound to take up the challenge of that future which they did so much to salvage from the brink of disaster.

As I look back on the long, tortuous trail from those grim days of Bataan and Corregidor, when an entire world lived in fear, when democracy was on the defensive everywhere, when modern civilization trembled in the balance, I thank a merciful God that He has given us the faith, the courage, and the power from which to mold victory. We have known the bitterness of defeat and the exultation of triumph, and from both we have learned there can be no turning back. We must go forward to preserve in peace what we won in war.

A new era is upon us. Even the lesson of victory itself brings with it profound concern, both for our future security and the survival of civilization. The destructiveness of the war potential, through progressive advances in scientific discovery, has in fact now reached a point which revises the traditional concept of war.

Aug. 21. Lend-lease program ends. Total U.S. receipts during the war have been about $8 billion; outlay has been almost $50 billion. U.S. aid for recovery of wartorn nations is continued by UNRRA and, later, the Marshall Plan (European Recovery Program).

Sept. 11-Oct. 2. Council of Foreign Ministers of principal Allies meets at London to draft treaties with former Axis powers. Failure to agree on proposed treaty with Germany is first serious breach between the Soviet Union and the other major Allies. A second conference, held at Moscow from December 16 to 26, considers Far East questions also, as well as eventual international atomic energy control.

Dec. 22. President Truman orders special arrangement for admission of displaced persons to U.S. Forty thousand are admitted under this order before legislation in 1948 authorizes increases in immigration quotas for war victims. At end of World War II, fought by 57 Allied and Axis countries, military personnel killed and missing are: Allies, 10,650,000; Axis, 4,650,000. This does not include estimated equal number of civilian deaths resulting from starvation, bombing of cities, and mass murders by Axis powers. The U.S., Britain, the Soviet Union, China, France, Germany, Italy, and Japan have borne major cost in dollars and lives. In proportion to population, the U.S. killed and missing figures are lightest: 292,000, or 1 per 450 of population; U.S.S.R. figures are heaviest: 7,500,000, or 1 per 22 of population. Proportion of deaths to total casualties in World War II (less than 1 to 4) is less than half that of World War I because of more efficient and rapid methods of evacuation of wounded, use of blood plasma, and control of disease and infection with penicillin and sulfa drugs. Cost to the U.S. in loans and matériel supplied is about $350 billion. About 16 million U.S. citizens have served in military units. At end of the war, about 10 million European civilians are out of their own countries as refugees, prisoners, or slave laborers.

Although U.S. citizens and corporations have been taxed more than ever before, revenue from all taxes has amounted to less than half of wartime expenditures. Government borrowing to raise the remainder increases the national debt from 1940 level of per capita $325 to $1,849.

During the war, the U.S. government has, through the Defense Plant Corporation, financed about 85 percent of new war plants; by 1945 it owns about nine-tenths of aircraft, shipbuilding, magnesium, and synthetic rubber plants; about three-quarters of aluminum producers; and about half of machine-tool manufacturers.

Arthur M. Schlesinger, Jr., publishes his Pulitzer Prize history *The Age of Jackson.*

1946

Jan. 10. First meeting of the General Assembly of the United Nations is held in London; 51 nations take part. Security Council meets in the same month.

Jan. 19. Iran protests to the United Nations Security Council against presence of Soviet troops in Iran after agreed-on date for Allied withdrawal. U.S. supports Iran. In April the Soviet Union states that troops will withdraw on May 6.

Feb. 21. Office of Economic Stabilization is reestablished within Office for Emergency Management. **June 30.** Price control expires, but some controls are reestablished on July 25 and continue until following June; however, most wage and price controls are terminated in this year.

House of Representatives report, 1950
The Second World War and events taking place in its aftermath resulted in the greatest dislocation of population ever recorded in history. According to various estimates, from September 1, 1939, to the end of 1947, between 30 and 40 million people were moved from their homelands to other areas of Europe and Asia. Great numbers of these people were forced to move as a part of the Nazi program of slave labor; others were moved by the Soviet government and its satellites; others fled to escape approaching hostile military forces; still others were exiles and fugitives from political and religious persecution. . . .

According to best available estimates, there were more than 8,000,000 displaced persons in western Europe on VE-day, the end of hostilities in that theater of operation. After a long nightmare of despair, millions of people, liberated at war's end from prisoner-of-war stockades, slave-labor enclosures, and concentration camps, became the responsibility of the Allied armies. . . .

The vast majority of these people had but one common goal—to return to their homelands. Within a matter of days after liberation, the Allied armies organized transportation by truck, train, air, and boat. . . .

However . . . the war had caused far-reaching changes in the political and social structure of many of the countries of origin of the displaced persons. Regimes had been changed, boundaries had been redrawn, and unilateral annexations of territories had occurred. As a result, many displaced persons had to face the prospect of changed citizenship; many more had to face political and religious persecution if they returned to their homes. Many would not accept the change of their personal status imposed upon them without their consent.

WINSTON CHURCHILL
Speech in Fulton, Missouri, 1946
A shadow has fallen upon the scenes so lately lighted by the Allied victory. Nobody knows what Soviet Russia and its Communist international organization intends to do in the immediate future, or what are the limits, if any, to their expansive and proselytizing tendencies. . . .

We understand the Russians need to be secure on her western frontiers from all renewal of German aggression. We welcome her to her rightful place among the leading nations of the world. Above all we welcome constant, frequent, and growing contacts between the Russian people and our own people on both sides of the Atlantic. It is my duty, however, to place before you certain facts about the present position in Europe. . . .

From Stettin in the Baltic to Trieste in the Adriatic, an iron curtain has descended across the Continent. Behind that line lie all the capitals of the ancient states of central and eastern Europe. Warsaw, Berlin, Prague, Vienna, Budapest, Belgrade, Bucharest, and Sofia, all these famous cities and the populations around them lie in the Soviet sphere and all are subject in one form or another, not only to Soviet influence but to a very high and increasing measure of control from Moscow. Athens alone, with its immortal glories, is free to decide its future at an election under British, American, and French observation. The Russian-dominated Polish government has been encouraged to make enormous and wrongful inroads upon Germany, and mass expulsions of millions of Germans on a scale grievous and undreamed of are now taking place.

March 5. Winston Churchill, in speech at Fulton, Missouri, asserts that an "iron curtain" has come down across Europe "from Stettin in the Baltic to Trieste in the Adriatic," ending an era of hopeful wartime collaboration between Western Allies and the Soviet Union. President Truman is in the audience.

April 1. Strike of 400,000 United Mine Workers begins; workers, whose wages have been fixed for several years, demand more money and fringe benefits. President Truman seizes mines and threatens to continue operating them under government authority when employers refuse government-negotiated contract. Second strike in November, defying an injunction, leads to contempt citation against John L. Lewis, who is fined $10,000, and union, which is fined $3,500,000. Almost all the largest labor unions call strikes this year after lifting of wartime restrictions.

April 18. League of Nations dissolves itself, transferring its properties to the United Nations.

April 25. Council of Foreign Ministers meets at Paris to discuss peace treaties for satellites of the Axis and arrives at terms by July 4. Council calls a meeting of 21 nations to consider treaty drafts, but there are persistent disagreements between Western countries and the Soviet Union, which finally objects to participation of smaller nations. Conference breaks up in October with agreement on only minor issues.

May 20. General George C. Marshall, special envoy to China with rank of ambassador, accuses both sides in Chinese civil war of generating hate campaigns. **June 24.** Head of Communist Chinese, Mao Tse-tung, insists that the U.S. cease supplying arms to Nationalist Chinese and evacuate its forces from China. Seven months later,

Communists and Nationalists are informed that the U.S. has given up efforts at mediation of the conflict. In 1949, Nationalists, under Chiang Kai-shek, withdraw to island of Formosa, leaving mainland to Communists.

June 14. Bernard Baruch, U.S. delegate to UN Atomic Energy Commission, proposes plan to outlaw manufacture of atomic bombs, dismantle those already existing, and share atomic energy secrets with other nations. Plan includes right of international inspection of manufacturing facilities, but the Soviet Union, which has a similar plan, does not accept international inspection.

July 4. The U.S. grants full independence to the Philippines as provided in the Philippine Commonwealth and Independence (Tydings-McDuffie) Act of 1934. Republic of the Philippines remains allied to the U.S. and leases military bases to U.S. forces.

July 7. Mother Frances Xavier Cabrini is canonized; she is first U.S. citizen to become a saint.

July. U.S. explodes two atomic bombs off Bikini Atoll in Pacific in first test of effect on military equipment, especially warships.

Aug. 1. U.S. Atomic Energy Commission is established. Five-man civilian board headed by David E. Lilienthal is authorized to develop and control all military and peaceful aspects of atomic energy.

Aug. 1. President Truman signs bill implementing proposal of Senator J. William Fulbright of Arkansas to use funds from postwar sale of wartime surplus goods to Allies to pay for international exchange of students and teachers, on model of educational use of Boxer Rebellion indemnity funds in 1901. Action creates world's larg-

BERNARD M. BARUCH
Address to UN Atomic Energy Commission, 1946
My fellow members of the United Nations Atomic Energy Commission and My Fellow Citizens of the World:

We are here to make a choice between the quick and the dead. That is our business.

Behind the black portent of the new atomic age lies a hope which, seized upon with faith, can work our salvation. If we fail, then we have damned every man to be the slave of fear. Let us not deceive ourselves: We must elect world peace or world destruction.

Science has torn from nature a secret so vast in its potentialities that our minds cower from the terror it creates. Yet terror is not enough to inhibit the use of the atomic bomb. The terror created by weapons has never stopped man from employing them, for each new weapon a defense has been produced, in time. But now we face a condition in which adequate defense does not exist.

Science, which gave us this dread power, shows that it can be made a giant help to humanity, but science does not show us how to prevent its baleful use. So we have been appointed to obviate that peril by finding a meeting of the minds and the hearts of our peoples. Only in the will of mankind lies the answer. . . .

In this crisis, we represent not only our governments but, in a larger way, we represent the peoples of the world. We must remember that the peoples do not belong to the governments but that the governments belong to the peoples. We must answer their demands; we must answer the world's longing for peace and security.

HENRY A. WALLACE
The Fight for Peace, 1946

Make no mistake about it — another war would hurt the United States many times as much as the last war. We cannot rest in the assurance that we invented the atom bomb — and therefore that this agent of destruction will work best for us. He who trusts in the atom bomb will sooner or later perish by the atom bomb — or something worse. . . .

The real peace treaty we now need is between the United States and Russia. On our part, we should recognize that we have no more business in the political affairs of Eastern Europe than Russia has in the political affairs of Latin America, Western Europe, and the United States. . . .

Russian ideas of social-economic justice are going to govern nearly a third of the world. Our ideas of free-enterprise democracy will govern much of the rest. The two ideas will endeavor to prove which can deliver the most satisfaction to the common man in their respective areas of political dominance. But by mutual agreement, this competition should be put on a friendly basis and the Russians should stop conniving against us in certain areas of the world just as we should stop scheming against them in other parts of the world. Let the results of the two systems speak for themselves. . . .

Under friendly, peaceful competition the Russian world and the American world will gradually become more alike. The Russians will be forced to grant more and more of the personal freedoms; and we shall become more and more absorbed with the problems of social-economic justice.

est international fund for such purposes; program continues to the present day.

Aug. 2. U.S. Senate resolution accepts compulsory jurisdiction of new International Court of Justice under United Nations Charter.

Sept. 20. President Truman dismisses Henry Wallace, secretary of commerce, following Wallace's advocacy of continued cooperation with the Soviet Union. Dismissal ends debate in U.S. government on "hard" or "soft" policy toward Soviets.

Oct. 1. After ten-month trial at Nürnberg, Germany, of 24 major Nazis for crimes against peace, humanity, and the laws of war, 12 are sentenced to death. In U.S. zone of occupation, 12 other trials of major war criminals are subsequently held at Nürnberg under international authority.

Oct. 1. Acting Secretary of State Dean Acheson states that the U.S. will keep occupation forces in South Korea until North Korea is evacuated by Soviet troops and a free government is formed for the unified country.

Nov. 5. In fall elections, Republicans win enough seats to control both House and Senate for first time in 16 years.

Dec. 2. Britain and the U.S. sign agreement for economic merger of their occupation sectors of Germany. Previously in this year, the U.S. has slowed down dismantling of West German industrial equipment for reparations payments.

Dec. 14. The UN accepts John D. Rockefeller's $8,500,000 gift site in New York City for its headquarters.

Robert Penn Warren publishes *All the King's Men,* his novel of Southern politics;

it wins the Pulitzer Prize in the following year.

1946 - 1949

June 4, 1946-Oct. 19, 1949. Trial of high-ranking Japanese leaders results in sentences of hanging for 7 (after U.S. Supreme Court has denied its right to hear appeal), life imprisonment for 16, and shorter terms for 2 by November 12, 1948. Local trials held at sites of Japanese wartime military activity result in 4,200 convictions and 720 executions by the time they are officially announced closed on October 19, 1949.

1947

Feb. 10. The U.S. Supreme Court upholds a state law permitting parochial school children to ride on public school buses. This is the first of many cases in this period on separation of church and state in relation to schools.

March 10-April 24. Secretary of State George C. Marshall and British Foreign Minister Ernest Bevin meet in Moscow with Soviet officials; they are unable to agree on type of government for Germany, Britain and the U.S. advocating a federal form and the Soviet Union a centralized form. Britain and the U.S. refuse the Soviet demand for $10 billion in reparations from Germany.

March 12. President Truman asks economic and military aid for Greece and Turkey to strengthen them against "attempted subjugation by armed minorities or by outside pressures", and announces the principle of containment of Soviet expansion (the Truman Doctrine). Congress later approves and allocates an initial $400 million to immediate aid of Greece and Turkey. **Sept. 18.** The Soviet Union attacks the U.S. as "warmongers" in UN General Assembly.

HARRY S. TRUMAN
Address to Congress, 1947
At the present moment in world history nearly every nation must choose between alternative ways of life. The choice is too often not a free one.

One way of life is based upon the will of the majority, and is distinguished by free institutions, representative government, free elections, guarantees of individual liberty, freedom of speech and religion, and freedom from political oppression. The second way of life is based upon the will of a minority forcibly imposed upon the majority. It relies upon terror and oppression, a controlled press and radio, fixed elections, and the suppression of personal freedoms.

I believe that it must be the policy of the United States to support free peoples who are resisting attempted subjugation by armed minorities or by outside pressures. I believe that we must assist free peoples to work out their own destinies in their own way. I believe that our help should be primarily through economic and financial aid, which is essential to economic stability and orderly political processes.

The world is not static and the status quo is not sacred. But we cannot allow changes in the status quo in violation of the Charter of the United Nations by such methods as coercion or by such subterfuges as political infiltration. In helping free and independent nations to maintain their freedom, the United States will be giving effect to the principles of the Charter of the United Nations.

It is necessary only to glance at a map to realize that the survival and integrity of the Greek nation are of grave importance in a much wider situation.

JACKIE ROBINSON
Interview, 1948
At the beginning of the World Series of 1947, I experienced a completely new emotion, when the National Anthem was played. This time, I thought, it is being played for me, as much as for anyone else. This is organized major league baseball, and I am standing here with all the others; and everything that takes place includes me.

GEORGE C. MARSHALL
Speech at Harvard, 1947
It is logical that the United States should do whatever it is able to do to assist in the return of normal economic health in the world, without which there can be no political stability and no assured peace. Our policy is directed not against any country or doctrine but against hunger, poverty, desperation, and chaos. Its purpose should be the revival of a working economy in the world so as to permit the emergence of political and social conditions in which free institutions can exist.

Such assistance, I am convinced, must not be on a piecemeal basis as various crises develop. Any assistance that this government may render in the future should provide a cure rather than a mere palliative.

JOHN L. LEWIS
Of the Taft-Hartley Law, 1953
Every day, I have a matutinal indisposition that emanates from the nauseous effluvia of that oppressive slave statute.

March 31. Wartime draft ends. Because of political pressures to return everyone to civilian life, demobilization proceeds faster than at first planned, but enough men are available to maintain armies of occupation.

April 11. Jack Roosevelt ("Jackie") Robinson becomes first Negro major-league baseball player in this century when he signs contract with the Brooklyn Dodgers.

June 5. The U.S. ratifies peace treaties with minor Axis nations — Italy, Hungary, Bulgaria, and Rumania. All agree to pay reparations and to return land occupied; some cede to the Soviet Union and its satellites land within their prewar boundaries; Italy also cedes land to France and Greece.

June 5. Secretary of State Marshall proposes that the U.S. contribute to economic recovery of those European countries that will determine their needs and cooperate economically. Although Great Britain and France invite 22 nations to meet in Paris to draft plans, only 16 participate, since the Soviet Union and its satellites denounce plan as one to enslave Europe and withdraw to form their own mutual assistance system. **July 12.** Marshall Plan Conference creates Committee of European Economic Cooperation, which two months later reports that Europe's needs over the next four years will require aid of between $19 billion and $22 billion. In April 1948 Congress votes funds for four-year plan; aid eventually amounts to $12 billion.

June 23. Labor Management Relations (Taft-Hartley) Act is passed over President Truman's veto. Act, which seeks to swing balance of power in management-union relationships away from "excess" privileges unions have gained during New Deal, is bitterly opposed by unions, especially because of strike and closed shop restrictions; Act also provides for supervision of finances and limitation of political activities.

July 7. Hoover Commission is created to investigate inefficiency and to recommend reorganization of the executive branch of the government. Former President Hoover is chairman.

July 11. General Albert C. Wedemeyer is appointed to analyze and report on situation in China and Korea. In August he attacks use of force by Communists, as well as economic policies and corruption of Nationalists.

July 18. President Truman signs Presidential Succession Act, which changes line of succession after the Vice-President to speaker of the House, president pro tempore of the Senate, and Cabinet members according to rank.

July 26. President Truman signs National Security Act, which unifies all branches of the armed services as the National Military Establishment under a secretary of defense. Department is reorganized and renamed Department of Defense in 1949.

Oct. 30. At Geneva Trade Conference, 23 nations (comprising three-fourths of world's commerce) agree on tariff reductions for about two-thirds of their international trade items.

October. U.S. Air Force pilot tests first airplane that exceeds the speed of sound, X-1 research model made by Bell Aircraft Corporation.

The U.S. accepts UN trusteeship over the Carolines, the Marshalls, and the Marianas; all are in the Pacific and are former Japanese possessions or League of Nations mandates.

Transistor, which, substantially smaller, replaces the vacuum tube in electronic communications equipment, is invented at Bell Telephone Laboratories by three scientists,

HARRY S. TRUMAN
Memorandum, 1947
I have just made some additions to my Kitchen Cabinet, which I will pass on to my successor in case the Cow should fall down when she goes over the moon.

I appointed a Secretary for Inflation. I have given him the worry of convincing the people that no matter how high the prices go, nor how low wages become, there just is not any danger to things temporal or eternal. I am of the opinion that he will take a real load off my mind — if Congress does not.

Then I have appointed a Secretary of Reaction. I want him to abolish flying machines and tell me how to restore oxcarts, oar boats and sailing ships. What a load he can take off my mind if he will put the atom back together so it cannot be broken up. . . .

I have appointed a Secretary for Columnists. His duties are to listen to all radio commentators, read all columnists in the newspapers from ivory tower to lowest gossip, coordinate them and give me the result so I can run the United States and World as it should be. . . .

I have appointed a Secretary of Semantics — a most important post. He is to furnish me with 40 to 50 dollar words. Tell me how to say yes and no in the same sentence without a contradiction. He is to tell me the combination of words that will put me against inflation in San Francisco and for it in New York. He is to show me how to keep silent — and say everything. You can very well see how he can save me an immense amount of worry.

BERNARD DE VOTO
Harper's, 1949

This feeling that the interrogation of private citizens about other citizens is natural and justified is something new to American life. As little as ten years ago we would have considered it about on a par with prohibition snooping, night-riding, and blackmail. A single decade has come close to making us a nation of common informers. . . .

True, we have occasional qualms. The Committee on Un-American Activities blasts several score reputations by releasing a new batch of gossip. Or a senator emits some hearsay and officially unaccused persons lose their jobs without recourse. Or another senator blackens the name of a dead man and then rejoices in his good deed, though the people he claimed to be quoting announce that they didn't say what he said they did. . . . Or we find out that the FBI has put at the disposal of this or that body a hash of gossip, rumor, slander, backbiting, malice, and drunken invention which, when it makes the headlines, shatters the reputations of innocent and harmless people and of people who our laws say are innocent until someone proves them guilty in court. We are shocked. Sometimes we are scared. Sometimes we are sickened. We know that the thing stinks to heaven, that it is an avalanching danger to our society. But we don't do anything about it. . . .

I say it has gone too far. We are dividing into the hunted and the hunters. There is loose in the United States today the same evil that once split Salem Village between the bewitched and the accused and stole men's reason quite away.

who in 1956 receive Nobel Prize for their work.

1947 - 1951

March 22, 1947. President Truman orders investigation into loyalty of all employees of the Executive branch of the government; check begins in August and continues until April 1951. The vast majority of those investigated (more than 3 million) are cleared; at least 3,000 others resign, while only 212 are dismissed.

1948

Jan. 23. Split between Soviet-held North Korea and U.S.-occupied South Korea broadens when the Soviet Union announces that UN Temporary Commission on Korea will not be allowed to enter North Korea. **May 10.** Korean elections are held, but they are boycotted by the North. **Aug. 15.** Republic of Korea is formed at Seoul, South Korea. **Sept. 9.** North Korea proclaims Democratic People's Republic of Korea, which claims to be government of entire country.

March 8. The Supreme Court holds that released-time religious education given on public school property, even though by private teachers, is a violation of the First Amendment of the Constitution.

April 30. Organization of American States (OAS) is formed at Bogotá, Colombia, by the U.S. and 20 Latin-American nations; OAS is a regional group for mutual defense and general cooperation. Organization becomes legally effective in 1951, when two-thirds of nations have ratified charter.

May 14. The U.S. recognizes the new state of Israel, but surrounding Arab countries do not, vigorously protesting existence of new nation. **Sept. 17.** Ralph J. Bunche of the U.S. succeeds Swedish Count Folke Bernadotte as UN mediator of Israel-Arab conflicts after Bernadotte's assassination in Jerusalem. Bunche is successful in working out armistice agreements.

May 25. General Motors Corporation signs first sliding wage scale union contract with United Automobile Workers; it includes clause that adjusts wages to cost of living index.

May 30. U.S. Supreme Court holds that enforcing a private contract restricting sale or rental of property because of race is a violation of the Fourteenth Amendment.

June 11. U.S. Senate approves Vandenberg Resolution, which favors U.S. participation in regional security agreements within the UN framework; principle is widely applied in succeeding years.

June 21. Republican Party meets at Philadelphia and nominates Governor Thomas E. Dewey of New York for President and Governor Earl Warren of California for Vice-President. **July 15.** Democrats at Philadelphia renominate President Truman, with Senator Alben W. Barkley of Kentucky as his running mate. Southern Democrats walk out of convention, refusing to support strong civil rights platform; they meet in the same month in Alabama, where they nominate Governor J. Strom Thurmond of South Carolina to run on a States' Rights ticket. **July 24.** Newly formed Progressive Party, partly made up of Democrats who oppose Truman's foreign policy and others who feel he cannot win election, nominates former Vice-President Henry A. Wallace for President. Minor party candidates are: Socialist, Norman Thomas of New York; Prohibition, Claude A. Watson of California; and Socialist Labor, Edward A. Teichert of Pennsylvania. Republican platform is dedicated to maintenance of peace and the principles of Taft-Hartley

ARTHUR H. VANDENBERG
Senate Resolution, 1948
Resolved, *that the Senate reaffirm the policy of the United States to achieve international peace and security through the United Nations, so that armed force shall not be used except in the common interest, and that the President be advised of the sense of the Senate that this government, by constitutional process, should particularly pursue the following objectives within the United Nations Charter:*

1. Voluntary agreement to remove the veto from all questions involving pacific settlements of international disputes and situations, and from the admission of new members.

2. Progressive development of regional and other collective arrangements for individual and collective self-defense in accordance with the purposes, principles, and provisions of the Charter.

3. Association of the United States, by constitutional process, with such regional and other collective arrangements as are based on continuous and effective self-help and mutual aid, and as affect its national security.

4. Contributing to the maintenance of peace by making clear its determination to exercise the right of individual or collective self-defense under Article 51 should any armed attack occur affecting its national security.

5. Maximum efforts to obtain agreements to provide the United Nations with armed forces as provided by the Charter, and to obtain agreement among member nations upon universal regulation and reduction of armaments under adequate and dependable guarantee against violation.

HARRY S. TRUMAN
Message to Congress, 1948

Today the American people enjoy more freedom and opportunity than ever before. Never in our history has there been better reason to hope for the complete realization of the ideals of liberty and equality.

We shall not, however, finally achieve the ideals for which this nation was founded so long as any American suffers discrimination as a result of his race, or religion, or color, or the land of origin of his forefathers.

Unfortunately there still are examples — flagrant examples — of discrimination which are utterly contrary to our ideals. Not all groups of our population are free from the fear of violence. Not all groups are free to live and work where they please or to improve their conditions of life by their own efforts. Not all groups enjoy the full privileges of citizenship and participation in the government under which they live.

We cannot be satisfied until all our people have equal opportunities for jobs, for homes, for education, for health, and for political expression, and until all our people have equal protection under the law. . . .

The peoples of the world are faced with the choice of freedom or enslavement, a choice between a form of government which harnesses the state in the service of the individual and a form of government which chains the individual to the needs of the state. . . .

If we wish to inspire the peoples of the world whose freedom is in jeopardy, if we wish to restore hope to those who have already lost their civil liberties, if we wish to fulfill the promise that is ours, we must correct the remaining imperfections in our practice of democracy.

Act. Democrats demand repeal of the Taft-Hartley Act, as well as civil rights legislation.

June 24. New Selective Service Act is signed to provide manpower for occupation of Germany and Italy and expanding military aid programs. Men of 19 to 25 are inducted for 21 months' service; 18-year-olds are permitted to volunteer for one year in any of the regular services.

June 25. Displaced Persons Act is signed, providing for admission to the U.S. of displaced persons from Europe; about 400,000 persons enter the U.S. under Act and later amendments.

Nov. 2. President Truman unexpectedly wins election in spite of States Rights' Party split-off. *Chicago Tribune* has been so sure of his defeat that it has gone to press with headline announcing it. Popular vote is Truman, 24,106,000; Dewey, 21,970,000; Thurmond, 1,169,000. Electoral vote is Truman, 303; Dewey, 189; Thurmond, 39. Democrats regain control of Congress, with majorities in both houses.

Atomic particle (pi-meson) is created synthetically (a possibility implicit in Einstein formula $E = mc^2$) by University of California scientists in synchrocyclotron.

Zoologist Alfred C. Kinsey and associates publish *Sexual Behavior in the Human Male*, a study based on thousands of personal interviews; report shows, among other things, wide differences between actual sex practices and conventional beliefs about them. *Sexual Behavior in the Human Female* is published in 1953.

Norman Mailer publishes *The Naked and the Dead*, his best-selling war novel.

1948 - 1949

Jan. 17, 1948. As a result of UN mediation (participated in by U.S.), truce is signed between the Republic of Indonesia, which has proclaimed its independence in 1945, and the Netherlands, which still considers Indonesia a group of Dutch colonies; in December, however, the UN condemns the Netherlands for violating truce by military action. **Dec. 27, 1949.** The Netherlands formally transfers its sovereignty to the United States of Indonesia.

May 1948. The U.S. announces testing of three new atomic weapons at Eniwetok Atoll in the Pacific. **Nov. 4.** U.S. proposal for international control of atomic energy is approved by UN General Assembly. **Sept. 1949.** The U.S. announces that the Soviet Union has exploded an atomic bomb.

June 1948. The Soviet Union begins blockade of ground and water transportation routes into Berlin from the West in effort to force Western Allies to give up control of western part of the city, which is in the center of the Soviet occupation zone. U.S. and British air forces ship food and other vital supplies into West Berlin for almost 16 months by air transport. By the time the Soviet Union has canceled the blockade in May 1949, about 1,600,000 tons of supplies have been airlifted to 2,500,000 Berliners. Airlift continues until September 30, increasing total tonnage to more than 2,300,000.

1949

Jan. 20. President Truman's Inaugural Address stresses international cooperation through the UN, the Marshall Plan, and regional security pacts and adds "Point Four"

ALBERT EINSTEIN
Atlantic Monthly, 1947
The bomb has been made more effective. . . . Unless another war is prevented it is likely to bring destruction on a scale never before held possible and even now hardly conceived, and . . . little civilization would survive it.

ALBERT EINSTEIN
Speech at Princeton, 1950
The armament race between the U.S.A. and the U.S.S.R., originally supposed to be a preventive measure, assumes hysterical character. On both sides, the means to mass destruction are perfected with feverish haste — behind the respective walls of secrecy. The H-bomb appears on the public horizon as a probably attainable goal. Its accelerated development has been solemnly proclaimed by the President.

If successful, radioactive poisoning of the atmosphere and hence annihilation of any life on earth has been brought within the range of technical possibilities. The ghostlike character of this development lies in its apparently compulsory trend. Every step appears as the unavoidable consequence of the preceding one. In the end, there beckons more and more clearly general annihilation.

DEAN ACHESON
Speech, 1949
It is clear that the North Atlantic Pact is not an improvisation. It is the statement of the facts and lessons of history. We have learned our history lesson from two world wars in less than half a century. That experience has taught us that the control of Europe by a single aggressive, unfriendly power would constitute an intolerable threat to the national security of the United States.

We participated in those two great wars to preserve the integrity and independence of the European half of the Atlantic community in order to preserve the integrity and independence of the American half. It is a simple fact, proved by experience, that an outside attack on one member of this community is an attack upon all members.

proposal for U.S. technical assistance to economically underdeveloped countries. By 1952, 37 nations outside the Communist bloc have benefited by this program.

Feb. 24. Highest altitude ever reached by a man-made projectile is achieved by guided missile Wac-Corporal when it travels to a height of 250 miles.

April 4. North Atlantic Treaty Organization (NATO) is formed by the U.S., Canada, Great Britain, Denmark, Norway, Iceland, France, Belgium, the Netherlands, Luxembourg, Italy, and Portugal when they sign mutual security pact; U.S. Senate ratifies agreement in July. Greece and Turkey join NATO in 1952.

May 8. West Germany adopts federal system of government at Bonn. **June 20.** Paris Conference of Council of Foreign Ministers again fails to agree on question of German unity. **Sept. 21.** U.S. replaces West German military occupation forces by

OPPOSITE PAGE: 1948
election winner Truman
holds edition of the
"Chicago Tribune" which
called the election too
early
THIS PAGE: Scene outside
an employment agency as
returning veterans swelled
the numbers of unemployed
in the late 1940s

civilian commission. **Oct. 7.** East Germany
becomes German Democratic Republic.

June 20. President Truman signs Reorganization Act of 1949, which permits the
President to reorganize the executive branch
of the government; Act follows recommendations by the Hoover Commission.

June 29. U.S. troops are withdrawn from
Korea, leaving only military advisers. **Sept.
8.** UN Korean commission announces that
it has not been able to settle conflict between North and South Korea, and that it
fears country is close to civil war.

Oct. 14. Under the Smith Act of 1940,
11 leaders of U.S. Communist Party are
sentenced to fines and prison terms for conspiracy to overthrow the government of the
U.S. by force.

Death of a Salesman, tragedy by Arthur
Miller, opens on Broadway and wins Pulitzer Prize.

ARTHUR MILLER
Death of a Salesman, 1949
*Nobody dast blame this man. You
don't understand: Willy was a salesman. And for a salesman, there is no
rock bottom to the life. He don't put a
bolt to the nut, he don't tell you the law
or give you medicine. He's a man way
out there in the blue, riding on a smile
and a shoeshine. And when they start
not smiling back — that's an earthquake.
And then you get yourself a couple of
spots on your hat, and you're finished.
Nobody dast blame this man. A salesman is got to dream, boy. It comes with
the territory.*

Marines begin the invasion of Inch'on, September 1950

JOSEPH R. McCARTHY
Speech in Wheeling, West Virginia, 1950

At war's end we were physically the strongest nation on earth and, at least potentially, the most powerful intellectually and morally. . . .

The reason why we find ourselves in a position of impotency is not because our only powerful, potential enemy has sent men to invade our shores, but rather because of the traitorous actions of those who have been treated so well by this nation. It has not been the less fortunate or members of minority groups who have been selling this nation out, but rather those who have had all the benefits that the wealthiest nation on earth has had to offer — the finest homes, the finest college education, and the finest jobs in government we can give.

This is glaringly true in the State Department. . . .

In my opinion the State Department . . . is thoroughly infested with Communists.

I have in my hand fifty-seven cases of individuals who would appear to be either card-carrying members or certainly loyal to the Communist Party, but who nevertheless are still helping to shape our foreign policy.

1950

Jan. 13-Aug. 1. The Soviet Union boycotts meetings of the UN Security Council because of the latter's refusal to oust Nationalist Chinese representatives.

Jan. 31. President Truman announces U.S. program to develop a hydrogen bomb.

Feb. 7. The U.S. recognizes newly formed anti-Communist state of Vietnam, with capital at Saigon. **June 27.** President Truman announces dispatch of 35-man military mission to Vietnam to teach use of U.S. weapons. **Dec. 23.** The U.S. signs agreement with France, Vietnam, Cambodia, and Laos to provide military assistance. In the following year U.S. also agrees to provide financial assistance to Saigon government.

Feb. 11. Wisconsin Senator Joseph R. McCarthy's letter to President Truman charging that the State Department is heavily infiltrated by Communists and Communist sympathizers is made public.

May 14. Meeting of foreign ministers of U.S., Great Britain, and France, acting without the Soviet Union, announces the admission of West Germany to system of international cooperation and mutual defense.

June 25. After North Koreans invade South Korea, UN Security Council orders cease-fire in Korea and calls for UN members to supply armed forces to restore peace in the area. Resolution is not vetoed by the Soviet Union because Soviet delegate is boycotting Security Council and is not present. **June 27.** President Truman orders U.S. Air Force and Navy to Korea. **June 30.** After North Koreans have taken Seoul, capital of South Korea, President Truman authorizes the use of U.S. ground forces against the invasion in South Korea and the use of U.S. military aircraft against targets north of the 38th parallel.

July 7. U.S. government orders increased draft to supply forces for UN Korean command. **July 8.** General Douglas MacArthur is chosen head of UN forces in Korea. **July 19.** President Truman urges partial U.S. mobilization.

Aug. 1. Island of Guam in Pacific becomes an unincorporated territory of the U.S. and is granted civil rule under administration of U.S. Department of Interior. Guamanians are U.S. citizens but are not represented in Congress and do not vote in national elections.

Sept. 6. North Koreans, advancing deep into South Korea, capture P'ohangdong on east coast but are unable to drive UN forces

HARRY S. TRUMAN
Message, June 27, 1950

The attack upon Korea makes it plain beyond all doubt that Communism has passed beyond the use of subversion to conquer independent nations and will now use armed invasion and war. It has defied the orders of the Security Council of the United Nations. . . .

Accordingly, I have ordered the Seventh Fleet to prevent any attack on Formosa. . . .

I have also directed that United States forces in the Philippines be strengthened and that military assistance to the Philippine government be accelerated.

I have similarly directed acceleration in the furnishing of military assistance to the forces of France and the Associated States in Indochina and the dispatch of a military mission to provide close working relations with those forces.

I know that all members of the United Nations will consider carefully the consequences of this latest aggression in Korea in defiance of the Charter of the United Nations. A return to the rule of force in international affairs would have far-reaching effects. The United States will continue to uphold the rule of law.

Woman nurses her injured husband amid ruins of Seoul, 1950

HARRY S. TRUMAN

Veto of McCarran Act, 1950

Specifically, some of the principal objections to the bill are as follows:

1. It would aid potential enemies by requiring the publication of a complete list of vital defense plants, laboratories, and other installations.

2. It would require the Department of Justice and its Federal Bureau of Investigation to waste immense amounts of time and energy attempting to carry out its unworkable registration provisions.

3. It would deprive us of the great assistance of many aliens in intelligence matters.

4. It would antagonize friendly governments.

5. It would put the government of the United States in the thought-control business.

6. It would make it easier for subversive aliens to become naturalized as United States citizens.

7. It would give government officials vast powers to harass all of our citizens in the exercise of their right of free speech.

Legislation with these consequences is not necessary to meet the real dangers which Communism presents to our free society. Those dangers are serious, and must be met. But this bill would hinder us, not help us, in meeting them. Fortunately, we already have on the books strong laws which give us most of the protection we need from the real dangers of treason, espionage, sabotage, and actions looking to the overthrow of our government by force and violence. Most of the provisions of this bill have no relation to these real dangers.

off peninsula at Pusan beachhead. **Sept. 15.** UN counteroffensive begins when troops are landed at Inch'on on west coast; at the same time, UN forces break through surrounding lines at Pusan. **Sept. 26.** Seoul is recaptured, and Inch'on forces advance across peninsula, meeting defenders of Pusan.

Sept. 8. President Truman signs Defense Production Act, giving him extensive powers to stabilize wages and prices.

Sept. 23. Congress passes McCarran (Internal Security) Act over President Truman's veto. Act provides for stringent measures to control Communists during national emergencies and registration of Communist organizations and individuals; it also forbids entry into the U.S. of those who have belonged to totalitarian organizations. Six months later, Act is amended to allow entry of those who have been forced into these organizations when under 14 years of age.

Oct. 1. Chinese Communists declare that they cannot allow crossing of 38th parallel by UN troops. **Oct. 20.** After meeting of President Truman and General MacArthur, UN forces take P'yongyang, capital of North Korea, and head toward the Yalu River. **Nov. 26.** Chinese "volunteers" cross the Yalu in force and enter North Korea.

Nov. 1. Two Puerto Rican nationalists attempt to kill President Truman. One is shot and killed by guards; the other is wounded and later sentenced to death, but in 1952 Truman commutes sentence to life imprisonment.

Nov. 3. UN General Assembly adopts resolution asserting its power to act on "threats to peace" if UN Security Council is deadlocked or its proposed action is vetoed by any power.

Nov. 7. Fall elections show Republican gains in many states and in both House and Senate, but Democrats retain control of Congress.

Nov. 24. UN forces begin all-out offensive but are forced back by Chinese and North Korean counteroffensive. **Dec. 4-5.** UN forces, in retreat southward, abandon P'yongyang.

Nov. 29. National Council of the Churches of Christ in the United States of America is formed; organization unites 25 Protestant and 4 Eastern Orthodox groups, marking first stage of postwar movement toward Christian unity. Membership is 32 million.

Nov. 30. UN Security Council proposes resolution appealing to Chinese to withdraw from Korea and offers safeguard of Yalu River border. The Soviet Union vetoes resolution.

Dec. 6. France, which six months previously has refused to agree to rearming West Germany for service in NATO, accepts a plan for German rearmament as part of a Western Europe defense force under a supreme commander. **Dec. 18.** Foreign ministers of North Atlantic pact nations meeting in Brussels agree on plans for rearmament and defense of Western Europe, including West Germany, with U.S. participation. **Dec. 19.** General Dwight D. Eisenhower is chosen as supreme commander and in the following spring assumes command of SHAPE (Supreme Headquarters, Allied Powers in Europe), which is set up in Paris.

Dec. 24. Evacuation of about 200,000 UN troops and civilian refugees who have been pushed back by Communist counteroffensive to port of Hungnam on the east coast of North Korea is completed; it is ac-

HERBERT HOOVER
Radio address, 1950
The foundation of our national policies must be to preserve for the world this Western Hemisphere Gibraltar of Western civilization. . . .

We can, without any measure of doubt, with our own air and naval forces, hold the Atlantic and Pacific Oceans with one frontier on Britain . . . the other, on Japan, Formosa, and the Philippines. . . .

To do this we should arm our air and naval forces to the teeth. We have little need for large armies unless we are going to Europe or China. . . .

We should have none of appeasement. Morally there is no appeasement of Communism. Appeasement contains more dangers than Dunkirks. We want no more Teherans and no more Yaltas. We can retrieve a battle but we cannot retrieve an appeasement. . . .

We are not blind to the need to preserve Western civilization on the continent of Europe or to our cultural and religious ties to it. But the prime obligation of defense of Western Continental Europe rests upon the nations of Europe. The test is whether they have the spiritual force, the will, and acceptance of unity among them by their own volition. . . .

To warrant our further aid they should show they have spiritual strength and unity to avail themselves of their own resources. But it must be far more than pacts, conferences, paper promises, and declarations. Today it must express itself in organized and equipped combat divisions of such huge numbers as would erect a sure dam against the red flood. And that before we land another man or another dollar on their shores. Otherwise we shall be inviting another Korea.

GILBERT SELDES

The Great Audience, 1950

Television will be used as the primary force in the creation of a unified entertainment industry which will include sports, the theater and the movies, newsreels, radio, night clubs, vaudeville, as well as any minor activities, and will profoundly affect newspapers, magazines, books, the fine arts, and ultimately education. Coexisting within this pyramid of entertainment there will be a highly unified communications industry affecting political life. . . .

The audience that television will create if it excites and feeds only one group of appetites will be lower in the scale of human values simply because so many natural human wants will go unsatisfied and so many capacities will atrophy from disuse.

For if the television audience is conceived and created in the image of the robot man, all the other entertainments absorbed into television will be squeezed into the same zone of interest. . . . The area of effect will depend on what is popular at any moment. Night clubs and resurgent vaudeville will come under the influence of television at once, since they depend on personalities, on flash popularity, which television can build; from there the effects will radiate to musical shows. If television goes in for a series of short dramatizations, the writers of short stories will be touched; if methods are found to visualize fantasy, Superman and Batman and the rest will be written with television in mind.

complished under protection of UN aerial and naval bombardment.

1950 census shows U.S. population has increased more than 14 percent in past decade, to 150,697,000, which includes immigration of 1,035,000 since 1940. Compared with previous decade, immigration from the Americas and Asia has doubled, and that from Europe has almost doubled. People living in cities make up 64 percent of the population. Illiteracy is 3.2 percent. Since 1940 many Southern Negroes have moved northward, and many Northern cities, especially in their central areas, have doubled their Negro populations.

1950-1951

Federal Communications Commission authorizes color television broadcasting. Regular programs begin in June 1951, but limitation on manufacture because of the war and the fact that black and white sets cannot receive this type of picture force abandonment of broadcasting in October.

1950-1953

Jan. 25, 1950. As a result of second trial (the first one having ended in deadlock the previous July), Alger Hiss, former State Department official, is sentenced to five years in prison for perjury after having denied that he has engaged in espionage for the Soviet Union. **March 7.** Judith Coplon, employee of the Department of Justice, is convicted for the second time of attempted espionage for the Soviet Union. Seventeen years later she is finally freed on the ground that the Federal Bureau of Investigation (FBI) has used wiretap evidence against her. Valentin Gubitchev, her conspirator and a member of the Soviet UN staff, is also convicted at this time but agrees to return to the Soviet Union. **Dec. 9.** Harry

Gold, U.S. confederate of a British spy, is sentenced to 30 years in prison for atomic espionage. **April 5, 1951.** Ethel and Julius Rosenberg are sentenced to death for atomic espionage, and Morton Sobell, who has worked with them, to 30 years in prison. **June 19, 1953.** The Rosenbergs are executed.

1950-1954

Tranquilizer Miltown is first developed in 1950 and becomes widely used. Treatment of mental illness is advanced when, in 1952, drug reserpine is isolated from an Indian shrub and when, in 1954, tranquilizer chlorpromazine is put to use for mental disorders.

1951

Jan. 4. Huge Communist offensive forces UN troops to abandon Seoul and retreat southward.

Jan. 5-April 4. Senate holds "Great Debate" on U.S. military commitments in Europe and the relative authority of the President and Congress in fulfilling these obligations. Debate ends in triumph for collective security concept when Senate adopts substitute resolution endorsing dispatch of U.S. troops to defend Europe.

Feb. 1. The UN adopts U.S. resolution accusing Communist China of aggression in Korea.

Feb. 26. Twenty-second Amendment to the U.S. Constitution is declared ratified. Proposed in 1947, it limits the U.S. presidency to two terms; if an acting President has been in office for more than two years, the period is considered a complete first term. President Truman, however, is exempt from limitation.

New York Times, May 1951
The pending Durham-Humphrey bill to give the Federal Food and Drug Administration authority to name the drugs that may be sold only on a physician's prescription was condemned as "a handmaid of socialized medicine" yesterday at the opening of the Proprietary Association's sixty-ninth annual meeting. . . .

James F. Hoge, general counsel of the group, called the measure "the most dangerous threat to freedom of medical care in America . . ." and asserted that "it jeopardizes the traditional right of self-medication and choice of remedies."

Newsweek, November 1951
When is a prescription drug not a prescription drug?

Except for narcotics and the obviously lethal drugs, the more cautious of the 80,000 pharmacists working in 47,000 drugstores in the United States have always felt some uncertainty about prescription-counter procedures under the Federal Food, Drug, and Cosmetics Act of 1938. Under the law, primary responsibility for designating restricted drugs lay with the manufacturer. But some drug makers stamped for prescription use only a product which others dispensed for over-counter sales.

By next spring, much of the perplexity of these pharmacists should be resolved. On Oct. 26, President Truman signed an amendment to the 1938 act . . . making refilling of prescriptions for dangerous drugs without specific authorization of the prescribing physician a Federal-law violation. After April 26, 1952, drug manufacturers must label all dangerous drugs: "Caution: Federal law prohibits dispensing without prescription."

GEN. DOUGLAS MacARTHUR
Address to Congress, 1951

It has been said, in effect, that I am a warmonger. Nothing could be further from the truth. I know war as few other men now living know it, and nothing to me is more revolting. I have long advocated its complete abolition as its very destructiveness on both friend and foe has rendered it useless as a means of settling international disputes. . . .

But once war is forced upon us, there is no other alternative than to apply every available means to bring it to a swift end. War's very object is victory — not prolonged indecision. In war, indeed, there can be no substitute for victory. . . .

I am closing my fifty-two years of military service. When I joined the Army, even before the turn of the century, it was the fulfillment of all my boyish hopes and dreams. The world has turned over many times since I took the oath on the plain at West Point, and the hopes and dreams have long since vanished. But I still remember the refrain of one of the most popular barrack ballads of that day which proclaimed most proudly that—

> *Old soldiers never die;*
> *they just fade away.*

And like the old soldier of that ballad, I now close my military career and just fade away — an old soldier who tried to do his duty as God gave him the light to see that duty.

Good-by.

March 24. General MacArthur, convinced that Chinese troops on Manchurian border must be attacked in order to win the war, threatens China with bombing and naval bombardment. **April 11.** President Truman relieves MacArthur of all his Far Eastern commands. MacArthur is replaced by General Matthew B. Ridgway. **April 19.** General MacArthur speaks at joint session of Congress, urging military action against China. **May 3-June 25.** Senate investigation of MacArthur's dismissal ends with adoption (June 27) by the two investigative committees of a "declaration of faith," affirming U.S. unity and warning Soviet Union of ultimate ruin if it attacks U.S.

May 18. UN General Assembly adopts resolution proposed by U.S. Congress to stop shipment of arms to Communist China and North Korea.

June 4. In decision involving 11 leaders of the U.S. Communist Party convicted in 1949 of conspiracy to overthrow the U.S. government by force, the Supreme Court upholds the Smith Act, under which they have been convicted. Dissent declares that Smith Act violates the First Amendment and that there is a difference between the teaching of Marx-Lenin principles and "conspiracy to overthrow."

June 23. Soviet UN delegate proposes Korean truce. **June 29.** In a broadcast to commander in chief of Communist forces in Korea, General Ridgway suggests meeting to discuss armistice. **July 10.** Truce talks begin in Kaesong, moving to Panmunjom in October. Sporadic battles continue during talks.

July 11. New York City's policy of allowing "released time" to children for religious study outside of schools is upheld by the New York State Court of Appeals; decision is confirmed by the U.S. Supreme Court the following year.

Aug. 17. First U.S. microwave radio-relay system begins operation when call is placed and relayed 3,000 miles between New York and San Francisco by system of 107 receiving and transmitting towers built 30 miles apart. **Sept. 4.** The first transcontinental television broadcast by this system is President Truman's opening address at the Japanese Peace Conference in San Francisco, which is telecast over 94 stations.

Sept. 1. The U.S., Australia, and New Zealand (ANZUS Powers) sign a mutual security pact, and in the following year the first meeting of the council established by the pact is held in Honolulu to discuss defense matters of common interest.

Sept. 8. Treaty of Peace with Japan is signed in San Francisco by 48 nations but not the Soviet Union; Treaty restores Japanese sovereignty and independence, strips away all territories outside Japanese islands, and ends occupation. The U.S. is to continue occupation of the Ryukyu and Bonin islands, with the understanding that they might be placed under UN trusteeship with the U.S. as sole administrator. Separate U.S.-Japanese treaty permits the U.S. to maintain military bases in Japan.

Oct. 24. President Truman declares that the state of war with Germany is officially ended.

Dec. 21-22. At reactor testing station at Arco, Idaho, the use of atomic energy to produce electric power is demonstrated for first time.

Dec. 24. National Broadcasting Company broadcasts Gian Carlo Menotti's *Amahl and the Night Visitors*, suggested by Hiero-

WILLIAM O. DOUGLAS
The Nation, 1952
There is much talk these days of war. I, of course, am not in a position to know, but I have a feeling that the fears of America are often misplaced. I have a feeling that we have misinterpreted and misjudged some of the forces in the world. . . .

I don't think there is going to be war with Russia at this time. And why?

I think the stakes involved, the immediate stakes are the stakes of Asia and the Middle East. I think that Soviet Russia will not move in a military way until it has on its side the balance of the people of the world. Freedom and justice and equality are the bulwark against any form of totalitarianism, the most virulent of which is communism. . . .

The great struggles for the world today are at the political level. The battle for Asia is at the political level, and in that sense, I think we in America have misinterpreted the signs of the times. It is my deep conviction that the peoples of Asia cannot be won by guns or by dollars. The peoples of Asia must be won, if they are to be won, with ideas. . . .

If you are suspicious that every one who has a new idea may be a secret Communist agent representing the Kremlin, of course, you will be suspicious of the peoples of the Middle East who are speaking and working and striving for a higher standard of living for themselves. And, if you practice racial discrimination, if you do not believe that a man is entitled to the same opportunities, whatever his religion, whatever his race, whatever his creed, when you turn to the colored people of Asia, you will be confused and in trouble, because you who are not able to recognize equality at home will not be able to recognize equality abroad.

(Above) President Truman confers with General MacArthur on Wake Island, October 1950; (below) East Berliners view fires of protest during the Berlin uprising, 1953

"It's Okay—We're Hunting Communists"

(Above) Dwight D. Eisenhower, thirty-fourth President of the United States, speaking before the United Nations in October 1960; (right) Herblock cartoon drawn during the House Un-American Activities Committee's investigations of 1947

J. D. SALINGER

The Catcher in the Rye, 1951

If you really want to hear about it, the first thing you'll probably want to know is where I was born, and what my lousy childhood was like, and how my parents were occupied and all before they had me, and all that David Copperfield kind of crap, but I don't feel like going into it, if you want to know the truth. In the first place, that stuff bores me, and in the second place, my parents would have about two hemorrhages apiece if I told anything pretty personal about them. They're quite touchy about anything like that, especially my father. They're nice and all—I'm not saying that—but they're also touchy as hell. Besides, I'm not going to tell you my whole goddam autobiography or anything. I'll just tell you about this madman stuff that happened to me around last Christmas just before I got pretty run-down and had to come out here and take it easy. I mean that's all I told D. B. about, and he's my brother and all. He's in Hollywood. That isn't too far from this crumby place, and he comes over and visits me practically every week end. He's going to drive me home when I go home next month maybe. He just got a Jaguar. One of those little English jobs that can do around two hundred miles an hour. It cost him damn near four thousand bucks. He's got a lot of dough, now. He didn't use to. He used to be just a regular writer, when he was home. He wrote this terrific book of short stories, The Secret Goldfish, in case you never heard of him. The best one in it was "The Secret Goldfish." It was about this little kid that wouldn't let anybody look at his goldfish because he'd bought it with his own money. It killed me.

nymus Bosch's painting "Adoration of the Magi." It becomes an annual Christmas tradition and in 1953 is first commercial color telecast. Menotti's opera *The Consul*, produced in the previous year, and *The Saint of Bleecker Street*, 1954, both win Pulitzer Prizes.

Jerome David Salinger publishes his novel *Catcher in the Rye*, told in the first person by a teen-age boy in conflict with the adult world.

1951-1953

June 1951. By this month UN forces have fought back to a line a few miles north of the 38th parallel. For two years, there are no important developments in ground fighting; however, air action, with use of jet planes, is carried out between the Yalu River and the 38th parallel, and UN warships range up and down North Korean coasts bombarding installations and ports.

Investigation by House Ways and Means Subcommittee uncovers widespread corruption in the Bureau of Internal Revenue and results in hundreds of resignations and removals, including the commissioner and an assistant attorney general.

1951-1959

Lever House in New York City, completed in 1952 and designed by Skidmore, Owings & Merrill, and works of Ludwig Mies van der Rohe, especially steel and glass apartment towers in Chicago and the Seagram Building in New York City, establish functionalism coupled with refined engineering as the dominant urban architectural style. Nonconformist work of Eero Saarinen, who designs General Motors Technical Center in Warren, Michigan, and emphasis on texture in buildings by Edward Durell Stone, such as U.S. Embassy in New Delhi, India, also establish trends.

1952

Jan. 9. President Truman and British Prime Minister Winston Churchill issue communiqué reaffirming that joint bomber bases in Britain will not be used in an emergency without consent of both countries.

Jan. 12. The Soviet Union submits proposal to the UN embodying Western demand for an atomic control plan that provides for inspection on a continuing basis and for prohibition and controls to be put into operation simultaneously. West, however, is cool to the proposal because, among other things, it applies only to atomic weapons and, in addition, expresses strong opposition to international operation of atomic plants.

April 6. It is announced that U.S. is developing a hydrogen bomb. **Nov. 1.** The U.S. explodes hydrogen bomb on Eniwetok Atoll; it is the most powerful bomb yet made.

April 8. President Truman seizes steel mills to avoid strike by 600,000 steelworkers in wage-price dispute. **June 2.** The Supreme Court rules that seizure is unconstitutional in that the President has had authority of neither the Constitution nor Congress. **July 24.** Further steel strike is settled by Truman's intervention; steelworkers gain wage increase, and management gains price increase.

April 13. Federal Communications Commission ends ban on building of new television broadcasting stations and allows more than 2,000 new stations to open by allocating 70 new ultrahigh frequency (UHF) channels to augment the 12 very high frequency (VHF) channels already in existence. About 65 million persons watch the presidential nominating conventions this year.

Sign on the outskirts of Ellenton, South Carolina, evacuated when the Atomic Energy Commission built the first H-bomb plant near the town.
It is hard to understand why our town must be destroyed to make a bomb that will destroy someone else's town that they love as much as we love ours.

HARRY S. TRUMAN
Message to Congress, January 1953
Recently in the thermonuclear tests at Eniwetok, we have entered another stage in the world-shaking development of atomic energy. From now on man moves into a new era of destructive power, capable of creating explosions of a new order of magnitude, dwarfing the mushroom clouds of Hiroshima and Nagasaki.

KENNETH HEUER
The End of the World, 1953
Whereas the end of the world is approaching . . .

This characteristic phrase, which opened the royal proclamations during the tenth century, might have been written today. At present, there is a general and universal physical fear, with only one question: "When will I be blown up?"

The idea of the end of the world had recurred again and again in the past, and yet the earth has not ceased to exist. However, prophecies in the near and distant past were based upon revelations in the Bible, the superstitions of astrology, or bad scientific theory. Today the warnings come from absolute and irrefutable scientific fact: the basic power of the universe has been released, and man is rapidly attaining the position where he can end the earth as an inhabited world.

ADLAI E. STEVENSON

Acceptance speech, 1952

And, my friends, more important than winning the election is governing the nation. That is the test of a political party —the acid, final test. When the tumult and the shouting die, when the bands are gone and the lights are dimmed, there is the stark reality of responsibility in an hour of history haunted with those gaunt, grim specters of strife, dissension, and materialism at home, and ruthless, inscrutable, and hostile power abroad.

The ordeal of the 20th century—the bloodiest, most turbulent era of the Christian age—is far from over. Sacrifice, patience, understanding, and implacable purpose may be our lot for years to come. Let's face it. Let's talk sense to the American people. Let's tell them the truth, that there are no gains without pains, that we are now on the eve of great decisions, not easy decisions, like resistance when you're attacked, but a long, patient, costly struggle which alone can assure triumph over the great enemies of man—war, poverty, and tyranny—and the assaults upon human dignity which are the most grievous consequences of each.

Let's tell them that the victory to be won in the 20th century, this portal to the Golden Age, mocks the pretensions of individual acumen and ingenuity. For it is a citadel guarded by thick walls of ignorance and of mistrust which do not fall before the trumpets' blast or the politicians' imprecations or even a general's baton. They are, my friends, walls that must be directly stormed by the hosts of courage, of morality and of vision, standing shoulder to shoulder, unafraid of ugly truth, contemptuous of lies, half truths, circuses, and demagoguery.

May 27. The U.S., Britain, and five other European nations sign agreement to form European Defense Community (EDC) with joint armed forces; in August, President Truman signs protocol to North Atlantic Treaty extending its defense guarantees to include EDC; French National Assembly, however, rejects EDC.

June 27. Congress passes the Immigration and Nationality (McCarran-Walter) Act over President Truman's veto. Act removes former bans on Asiatic and Pacific immigration, retains quota principle established in 1924, stiffens law on admittance, exclusion, and deportation of aliens dangerous to national security of U.S., and gives top priority to immigrants with superior education and needed skills. Truman has called the Act inhumane and discriminatory.

July 11. Republican Convention at Chicago nominates General Dwight D. Eisenhower of Pennsylvania, who has been opposed by Senator Robert A. Taft of Ohio; Eastern internationalist Republicans, who back Eisenhower, win out over Western isolationists after dispute over credentials of Southern delegates. Senator Richard M. Nixon of California is nominated for Vice-President. **July 26.** Democrats, meeting at Chicago, nominate Governor Adlai E. Stevenson of Illinois after President Truman has announced that he will not run for a second term. (Two-term constitutional amendment does not apply to Truman, who otherwise would have been ineligible under this law.) Senator John J. Sparkman of Alabama is nominated for Vice-President. Minor party candidates are: Vincent W. Hallinan, Progressive and American Labor; Farrell Dobbs, Socialist Workers; General Douglas MacArthur, America First, Christian Nationalist, and Constitution (seven states only); Darlington Hoopes, Socialist; and Stuart Hamblen, Prohibition. Republican platform stresses government economy, criticizes Truman administration's

Asian policies, and advocates retaining the Taft-Hartley Act. Democrats advocate continuance of New Deal and Fair Deal policies, repeal of Taft-Hartley Act, and federal civil rights legislation.

July 16. President Truman signs "G.I. Bill of Rights" for Korean veterans; it provides benefits similar to those granted to World War II veterans.

Oct. 8. Korean truce talks, which are deadlocked on question of repatriation of prisoners, are recessed indefinitely by UN negotiations. Communists insist on mandatory return of North Koreans and Chinese, and the UN, believing that some have been forced into service, holds out for voluntary repatriation.

Nov. 4. General Eisenhower wins overwhelmingly in election, which gives both candidates the largest popular vote in history: Eisenhower, 33,936,000; Stevenson, 27,315,000. Electoral vote is Eisenhower, 442 (including 4 normally Democratic Southern states); Stevenson, 89. Republicans win majorities in both houses of Congress, but Senate majority is only 48 Republicans to 47 Democrats and 1 independent.

Nov. 29. In accordance with campaign promise made in October, President-elect Eisenhower leaves for Korea to inspect UN war situation. Three-day visit, in which he visits front lines, is kept secret until after he has left danger areas.

Continuing concentration of economic power is shown in report that 59 corporations, 35 of them financial rather than industrial, are in billion-dollar assets class.

By this year, various trade agreements have reduced tariffs to an average of 13 percent as opposed to the 53 percent of the early Thirties.

DWIGHT D. EISENHOWER
Speech in Detroit, 1952
The first task of a new administration will be to review and reexamine every course of action open to us with one goal in view — to bring the Korean War to an early and honorable end. That is my pledge to the American people.

For this task a wholly new administration is necessary. The reason for this is simple. The old administration cannot be expected to repair what it failed to prevent.

Where will a new administration begin? It will begin with its President taking a simple, firm resolution. That resolution will be: To forgo the diversions of politics and to concentrate on the job of ending the Korean War — until that job is honorably done.

That job requires a personal trip to Korea. I shall make that trip. Only in that way could I learn how best to serve the American people in the cause of peace.

I shall go to Korea.

That is my second pledge to the American people. . . .

We will, of course, constantly confer with associated free nations of Asia and with the cooperating members of the United Nations. Thus we could bring into being a practical plan for world peace.

That is my third pledge to you.

As the next administration goes to work for peace, we must be guided at every instant by that lesson I spoke of earlier. The vital lesson is this: To vacillate, to appease, to placate is only to invite war — vaster war, bloodier war. In the words of the late Senator Vandenberg, appeasement is not the road to peace; it is only surrender on the installment plan.

I will always reject appeasement.

And that is my fourth pledge to you.

DWIGHT MACDONALD
Diogenes, 1953

For about a century, Western culture has really been two cultures: the traditional kind—let us call it "High Culture"—that is chronicled in the textbooks, and a "Mass Culture" manufactured wholesale for the market. In the old art forms, the artisans of Mass Culture have long been at work: in the novel, the line stretches from Eugène Süe to Lloyd C. Douglas; in music, from Offenbach to Tin-Pan Alley; in art, from the chromo to Maxfield Parrish and Norman Rockwell; in architecture, from Victorian Gothic to suburban Tudor. Mass Culture has also developed new media of its own, into which the serious artist rarely ventures; radio, the movies, comic books, detective stories, science-fiction, television. . . .

The problem is acute in the United States and not just because a prolific Mass Culture exists here. If there were a clearly defined cultural élite, then the masses could have their kitsch and the élite could have its High Culture, with everybody happy. But the boundary is blurred. A statistically significant part of the population, I venture to guess, is chronically confronted with a choice between going to the movies or to a concert, between reading Tolstoy or a detective story, between looking at old masters or at a TV show; i.e., the pattern of their cultural lives is "open" to the point of being porous. Good art competes with kitsch, serious ideas compete with commercialized formulae—and the advantage lies all on one side.

There seems to be a Gresham's Law in cultural as well as monetary circulation: bad stuff drives out the good, since it is more easily understood and enjoyed.

The *Revised Standard Version* of the Bible for Protestants is published; it has been edited by 32 scholars, who have worked since 1937, directed by Luther A. Weigle, dean emeritus of Yale Divinity School. In this same year, the Confraternity of Christian Doctrine publishes first eight books (volume 1) of the Old Testament for Roman Catholics.

1952-1953

To compete with television, Hollywood develops three-dimensional movie techniques in 1952. Natural Vision (3-D) films must be viewed through special eyeglasses and are not lastingly popular. Cinerama, made with three separate film strips and seven-channel stereophonic sound, succeeds but is prohibitively expensive. In 1953, CinemaScope, a less expensive, wide-screen system with stereophonic sound, is developed; this proves to be so successful that within a few years almost every movie theater in the U.S. has converted to Cinema-Scope projection installations.

1952-1962

Off-Broadway theater begins to grow with revival of Tennessee Williams' *Summer and Smoke*. It gains momentum, reaching its peak in 1961-1962, when there are 100 off-Broadway productions, 34 more than on Broadway.

1953

January-December. Each side in the Korean War accuses the other of atrocities. The U.S. continues to be accused of germ warfare, which it denies, appealing to the UN to investigate. UN adopts resolution accusing Communists of massacring or torturing 38,000 persons, of whom 35,000 are believed to be dead.

Feb. 2. President Eisenhower lifts U.S. fleet blockade of Chinese Nationalists on Formosa; move opens way for attacks by Nationalists on Red Chinese mainland.

March 10. Five days after death of Joseph Stalin, Senate Foreign Relations Committee shelves resolution condemning the Soviet Union for its forcible absorption of free European peoples. In January, Secretary of State John Foster Dulles has promised U.S. support to peoples behind the iron curtain. In April President Eisenhower asks that Eastern European nations be allowed their independence.

March 30. Dr. Albert Einstein announces formulas revising the unified field theory developed by him in 1945; theory aims to combine electromagnetic and gravitational equations in a single universal law. Although Einstein feels that this revision is a step forward, he is not satisfied that he has achieved his goal at the time of his death in 1955.

March 30. In a joint resolution, Congress authorizes new Cabinet-level Department of Health, Education, and Welfare, which replaces Federal Security Agency. Mrs. Oveta Culp Hobby is appointed first secretary.

April 11. UN truce team and Communists in Korea agree to exchange sick and wounded prisoners, although armistice has not yet been signed. **April 26.** Truce talks are resumed, while fighting continues. **June 8.** Agreement is reached on repatriation of prisoners of war; those who do not wish to return are to be held for up to 120 days, 90 days of which they are to be available to political persuasion. If they still refuse repatriation, they are to be freed as civilians.

April 20. U.S. government orders Communist Party to register with the Depart-

JOHN FOSTER DULLES
Testimony before Senate Foreign Relations Committee, 1953
We shall never have a secure peace or a happy world so long as Soviet Communism dominates one-third of all of the peoples that there are, and is in the process of trying at least to extend its rule to many others.

These people who are enslaved are people who deserve to be free, and who, from our own selfish standpoint, ought to be free; because if they are the servile instruments of aggressive despotism, they will eventually be welded into a force which will be highly dangerous to ourselves and to all of the free world. Therefore, we must always have in mind the liberation of these captive peoples.

Now, liberation does not mean a war of liberation. Liberation can be accomplished by processes short of war. We have, as one example—not an ideal example, but it illustrates my point—the defection of Yugoslavia under Tito from the domination of Soviet Communism. . . . It illustrates that it is possible to disintegrate this present monolithic structure which, as I say, represents approximately one-third of all the people that there are in the world. . . .

A policy which only aims at containing Russia where it now is, is, in itself, an unsound policy; but it is a policy which is bound to fail because a purely defensive policy never wins against an aggressive policy. If our only policy is to stay where we are, we will be driven back. It is only by keeping alive the hope of liberation, by taking advantage of that wherever opportunity arises, that we will end this terrible peril which dominates the world, which imposes upon us such terrible sacrifices and so-great fears for the future.

MIKE MANSFIELD
Congressional Record, 1953
The Supreme Court of the United States on June 23, 1947, rendered an opinion in the case of United States against California and on June 5, 1950, rendered opinion in the cases of United States against Texas, holding that the United States has paramount rights in, and full dominion and power over, the submerged lands of the Continental Shelf. . . .

It is not my purpose to join in the complicated and technical controversy revolving around the ownership of these offshore lands. The Supreme Court of the United States has twice determined the question in unmistakable language. The high court has ruled that this oil, which the Geological Survey has estimated to be worth at least $40 billion—others up to $300 billion at present prices—belongs to all the people of all the states. In my view the issue of ownership has been settled.

BEN HECHT
A Child of the Century, 1954
Politics is the only profession in which a man improves with age. This is not because he grows wiser but because a man with one foot in the grave has the ideal political attitude of "to hell with tomorrow."

The crowd has a giddy faith in the aged politico. It knows that a dying man is least worried about disasters and will, therefore, shy less at them. But it is not only insensitivity that makes the venerable beloved. Power is the only immorality possible to old men. History-making is the only spree on which the doddering may embark. And history is the great diversion of the crowd.

ment of Justice as an organization that is controlled by the Soviet Union.

May 8. The Senate Foreign Relations Committee is told by President Eisenhower that he has granted France $60 million of aid in France's war against Vietminh (Communist) rebels in Indochina; additional financial aid to France is announced in September.

May 22. President Eisenhower signs Tidelands Oil Bill; action reverses policy of President Truman, who in January has set aside underwater oil lands as a naval petroleum reserve. Bill gives coastal states offshore oil lands within the 3-mile limit (10½-mile limit for Texas and Florida), opening the way for immediate exploitation, and reserves to the federal government only oil lands beyond these limits (the outer Continental Shelf).

July 1. Following riots and strikes in East Germany, which are ended only by Soviet and East German military force, President Eisenhower announces that the U.S. will not intervene physically in the affairs of the iron curtain countries; he believes that people will seek their own freedom and revolt against repression. In November Secretary of State Dulles reiterates this belief, but declares that the U.S. does not morally approve of Soviet subjugation of nations.

July 27. Korean armistice is signed, and hostilities cease. Terms set up neutral zone two and a half miles wide and commissions to handle prisoners and administer the truce. The Korean War has been fought by UN forces from 16 countries, with the U.S. supplying the major number of men; in addition, medical units have been sent from 5 other countries. Communist Chinese have aided the North Koreans, and much matériel has been supplied to the North by the

Soviet Union. Casualty figures are: U.S. and other UN forces, about 39,000 killed or died while prisoners; South Korean, 70,000 military personnel killed or died, and 500,000 South Korean civilians died from disease, starvation, or as war casualties. Estimated Communist military casualties of all kinds (60 percent Chinese) are 1,600,000; in addition, about 400,000 of Communist forces have died of disease. The Korean War is the first in which helicopters have been used extensively to fly in supplies, transport the wounded, and carry troops.

Aug. 7. President Eisenhower signs Refugee Relief Act, which provides for admission to the U.S. in next three years of 214,000 victims of Communist persecution in addition to the regular quotas.

Aug. 8. Georgi Malenkov, head of Soviet government, announces that the Soviet Union has mastered production of the hydrogen bomb but declares that the Soviet Union is willing to settle all disputes by peaceful means. **Aug. 20.** The Soviet Union reveals testing of a hydrogen bomb; U.S. Atomic Energy Commission announces that the Soviet Union has conducted an atomic test on August 12 involving both fission and thermonuclear reactions.

Sept. 26. The U.S. agrees to give Spain $226 million in military and financial aid in return for the right to establish military bases in that country, although Spain does not join NATO defense organization.

September. About 90,000 Korean War prisoners have been exchanged by this month, but after talks with delegates from their home countries, many prisoners have elected to remain; these include 15,000 Chinese, almost 8,000 North Koreans, 335 South Koreans, 23 Americans, and 1 Brit-

J. ROBERT OPPENHEIMER
Foreign Affairs, 1953
We have greatly developed and greatly increased our atomic activities. This growth, though natural technically, is not inevitable. . . . We have from the first maintained that we should be free to use these weapons; and it is generally known we plan to use them. It is also generally known that one ingredient of this plan is a rather rigid commitment to their use in a very massive, initial, unremitting strategic assault on the enemy. . . .

There are two things that everyone would like to see happen; but few people, if any, confidently believe that they will happen soon. One is a prompt, a happily prompt, reform or collapse of the enemy. One is a regulation of armaments as part of a general political settlement—an acceptable, hopeful, honorable, and humane settlement to which we could be a party.

There is nothing repugnant in these prospects; but they may not appear to be very likely in the near future. Most of us, and almost all Europeans, appear to regard the outbreak of war in this near future as a disaster. Thus the prevailing view is that we are probably faced with a long period of cold war in which conflict, tension, and armaments are to be with us. The trouble then is just this —during this period the atomic clock ticks faster and faster. We may anticipate a state of affairs in which two Great Powers will each be in a position to put an end to the civilization and life of the other, though not without risking its own. We may be likened to two scorpions in a bottle, each capable of killing the other, but only at the risk of his own life.

EUGENE KINKEAD
New Yorker, 1957

In every war but one that the United States has fought, the conduct of those of its servicemen who were held in enemy prison camps presented no unforeseen problems to the armed forces and gave rise to no particular concern in the country as a whole. In some of those camps . . . our men were grievously treated and fell victim to starvation and disease, yet there was no wholesale breakdown of morale or wholesale collaboration with the captors. Moreover, whatever the rigors of the camps, in every but that one a respectable number of prisoners managed, through ingenuity, daring, and plain good luck, to escape.

The exception was the Korean War. . . . Roughly one out of every three American prisoners in Korea was guilty of some sort of collaboration with the enemy, ranging from such serious offenses as writing anti-American propaganda and informing on comrades to the relatively innocuous ones of broadcasting Christmas greetings home. . . .

Then, when the war ended and the prisoners began to return, it became clear that some of them had behaved brutally to their fellow prisoners, and for a time the newspapers carried reports of grisly incidents in the prison camps, including the murder of Americans by other Americans. . . .

All in all, regrettable things happened in the prison camps of North Korea, and the public has been inclined to attribute them solely to the cruelty of the Communists and, in particular, to the mysterious technique known as brainwashing.

E. B. WHITE
The Second Tree from the Corner, 1953
The time not to become a father is eighteen years before a world war.

on. Earlier, South Korean guards on orders from President Syngman Rhee have sanctioned the escape of about 27,000 North Koreans who wish to remain in South Korea.

Oct. 20. Secretary of State Dulles confirms that the U.S. has canceled financial aid to Israel because Israel has failed to obey UN order to discontinue work on Jordan River hydroelectric project that is strongly opposed by Syria. The U.S. resumes aid after Israel agrees a week later to halt work.

Nov. 27. UN General Assembly declares Puerto Rico a self-governing political unit; although voluntarily associated with the U.S., it is no longer considered a colonial territory.

Dec. 16. It is announced that Major Charles E. Yeager has achieved air speed record of more than 1,600 miles per hour in a Bell Aircraft X-1A rocket-powered plane.

In a joint resolution, Congress proposes ending of all limitations that apply to Indian tribes of the U.S., giving individual Indians the same civil status as other citizens.

First educational television station, KUHT, operated by the University of Houston, Texas, broadcasts. Educational television, aided by public contributions and foundation grants, develops rapidly, with 52 stations by 1960.

1953-1954

June 14, 1953. At Dartmouth College commencement exercises, President Eisenhower admonishes his listeners not to join the book burners, a term applied to Republican Senator Joseph R. McCarthy, chairman of the Senate Permanent Subcommittee on Investigations, because of his campaign to remove from State Department libraries books alleged to be by Communists or their fellow travelers. **Feb. 4, 1954.** McCarthy embarks on national tour to expose "twenty years of treason" of the Democratic Party. **April 22-June 17.** Televised Army-McCarthy Senate hearings are a national sensation; McCarthy's claims of Communism in the U.S. Army, presented with clever showmanship but no substantiation, are further examples of McCarthyism, which has come to mean accusation without proof. **May 31.** Although not referring to McCarthy by name, President Eisenhower warns that thought control is endangering freedom.

Aug. 3, 1953. Congress approves Korean relief measure with appropriation of $200 million. **Jan. 26, 1954.** Senate approves U.S.-South Korea Mutual Defense Treaty; it becomes effective on November 17.

1953-1955

Dec. 8, 1953. Dr. Alton Ochsner reports that increase in lung cancer in the U.S. is caused by cigarette smoking. His findings are confirmed in the following year by the American Cancer Society. Cigarette sales decline at the time but by 1955 have begun rising again, especially sales of filter cigarettes.

1953-1957

Dec. 8, 1953. President Eisenhower makes "Atoms for Peace" proposal to the UN, urging that atomic resources and research into peaceful uses of atomic energy be turned over to an international body. **Sept. 6, 1954.** Unable to deal with the Soviet Union on "Atoms for Peace" program, President Eisenhower announces that the U.S., Great Britain, Canada, Australia, South Africa, and France are planning to form an agency to develop peaceful uses of nuclear power. **Oct. 23, 1956.** Eighty-two

JOSEPH R. McCARTHY
Speech in Madison, Wisconsin, 1954
The Democratic label is now the property of men and women who have been unwilling to recognise evil or who bent to whispered pleas from the lips of traitors . . . men and women who wear the political label stitched with the idiocy of a Truman, rotted by the deceit of an Acheson, corrupted by the Red slime of a White.

EDWARD R. MURROW
See It Now, March 10, 1954
This is no time for men who oppose Senator McCarthy's methods to keep silent. Or for those who approve. We can deny our heritage and our history —but we cannot escape responsibility for the result. There is no way for a citizen of the republic to abdicate his responsibilities. As a nation we have come into our full inheritance at an early age. We proclaim ourselves—as indeed we are—the defenders of the free world, what's left of it.

We cannot defend freedom abroad by deserting it at home. The actions of the junior Senator from Wisconsin have caused alarm and discomfort among our allies abroad and given comfort to our enemies. And whose fault is that? Not really his. He didn't create the situation of fear, merely exploited it, and skillfully. Cassius was right. "The fault, dear Brutus, is not in our stars but in ourselves."

JOSEPH R. McCARTHY
At St. Patrick's Day dinner, 1954
The snakes didn't like St. Patrick's methods, and the Communists don't like mine.

JOHN FOSTER DULLES
Speech to Council on Foreign Relations, 1954

We need allies and collective security. Our purpose is to make these relations more effective, less costly. This can be done by placing more reliance on deterrent power and less dependence on local defensive power. This is accepted practice so far as local communities are concerned. We keep locks on our doors, but we do not have an armed guard in every home. We rely principally on a community security system so well equipped to punish any who break in and steal that, in fact, would-be aggressors are generally deterred. That is the modern way of getting maximum protection at a bearable cost. . . .

We want, for ourselves and the other free nations, a maximum deterrent at a bearable cost. . . .

The way to deter aggression is for the free community to be willing and able to respond vigorously at places and with means of its own choosing. . . .

The President and his advisers, as represented by the National Security Council, had to take some basic policy decisions. This has been done. The basic decision was to depend primarily upon a great capacity to retaliate, instantly, by means and at places of our choosing. Now the Department of Defense and the Joint Chiefs of Staff can shape our military establishment to fit what is our policy instead of having to try to be ready to meet the enemy's many choices. That permits of a selection of military means instead of a multiplication of means. As a result, it is now possible to get and share more basic security at less cost.

ADLAI STEVENSON
Of the Eisenhower-Dulles foreign policy
The power of positive brinking.

member states of the UN vote to establish an international agency to promote peaceful uses of atomic energy. **July 29, 1957.** International Atomic Energy Agency comes into existence officially when President Eisenhower signs ratification papers of U.S. membership.

1954

Jan. 2. Under a grant from the Rockefeller Foundation, Louisville (Kentucky) Orchestra begins series of 46 concerts featuring specially commissioned works of 19 living composers. **July 17.** Annual jazz festival is initiated at Newport, Rhode Island.

Jan. 12. Secretary of State Dulles announces shift of U.S. foreign policy from containment of the Soviet Union, as announced in the Truman Doctrine of 1947, to a plan of massive retaliation by means of its own choosing. **Jan. 21.** A reduction of military manpower and a cut of $4 billion in U.S. military budget is recommended by President Eisenhower.

Jan. 25-Feb. 18. Council of Foreign Ministers meets in Berlin, but no agreement is achieved on problem of reunification of Germany. Proposal by the Soviet Union of a security treaty covering all European nations with the U.S. and Communist China in the role of observers is turned down by the U.S., France, and Great Britain.

March 1. U.S. Atomic Energy Commission announces first of a new series of test explosions at its Pacific proving grounds in the Marshall Islands; danger of fallout is subsequently revealed. Soviet nuclear testing in the autumn also creates broad areas of fallout.

March 8. The U.S. and Japan sign mutual defense agreement guaranteeing U.S. assistance in building up Japan's defense forces.

March 16. It is reported in the French National Assembly that the U.S. has contributed more than three-fourths of France's cost of fighting Communists in Indochina. **May 7.** Although the U.S. has expected the French to win the war, Vietminh rebels take vital French fort at Dien Bien Phu during 19-nation Geneva Conference that is attempting to work out truce. **July 21.** Signing of armistice ends war of more than seven years; agreement divides Vietnam at about the 17th parallel into northern and southern parts, the north going to the Vietminh rebels and the south to the Vietnam government supported by France.

April 1. U.S. Air Force Academy is authorized. First class convenes in Denver in the following year, and the Academy moves to its permanent establishment near Colorado Springs three years later.

May 13. UN Subcommittee on Disarmament meets in London. After more than a month of discussion, the five powers are unable to agree on the banning and inspection of atomic weapons and reduction in conventional forces and armaments.

June 1. Investigating panel of U.S. Atomic Energy Commission (AEC) withdraws security clearance of J. Robert Oppenheimer, ending his work as AEC consultant, against advice of many leading scientists. Oppenheimer, who has led wartime atomic bomb effort, has been accused of being, among other things, pro-Communist; although the panel finds him loyal, it recommends that he be dismissed as lacking "enthusiasm" for the hydrogen-bomb project. In 1963 Oppenheimer receives AEC's highest honor, the Fermi Prize.

June 27. Pro-Communist regime in Guatemala is overthrown and replaced by an anti-Communist military junta. On the previous day, the U.S. and nine Latin-American nations have requested a meeting of the

Atomic Energy Commission report, 1954
On the basis of the record before the Commission, comprising the transcript of the hearing before the Gray Board, as well as reports of Military Intelligence and the Federal Bureau of Investigation, we find Dr. Oppenheimer is not entitled to the continued confidence of the government and of this Commission because of the proof of fundamental defects in his "character."

In respect to the criterion of "associations," we find that his associations with persons known to him to be Communists have extended far beyond the tolerable limits of prudence and self-restraint which are to be expected of one holding the high positions that the government has continuously entrusted to him since 1942. These associations have lasted too long to be justified as merely the intermittent and accidental revival of earlier friendships.

J. ROBERT OPPENHEIMER
On AEC decision, 1954
Without commenting on the security system which has brought all this about, I do have a . . . word to say. Our country is fortunate in its scientists — in their high skill and their devotion. I know that they will work faithfully to preserve and strengthen this country. I hope that the fruit of their work will be used with humanity, with wisdom and with courage. I know that their counsel, when sought, will be given honestly and freely. I hope that it will be heard.

GEORGE F. KENNAN

Seek the Finer Flavor, 1954

There are forces at large in our society today that are too diffuse to be described by their association with the name of any one man or any one political concept.

They have no distinct organizational forms. They are as yet largely matters of the mind and the emotion in large masses of individuals. But they all march, in one way or another, under the banner of an alarmed and exercised anti-communism. . . .

It is no wonder that these people constantly find the wrong answers. They tell us to remove our eyes from the constructive and positive purposes and to pursue with fanaticism the negative and vindictive ones. They sow timidity where there should be boldness; fear where there should be serenity; suspicion where there should be confidence and generosity. In this way they impel us — in the name of our salvation from the dangers of communism — to many of the habits of thought and action which our Soviet adversaries, I am sure, would most like to see us adopt and which they have tried unsuccessfully over a period of some thirty-five years to graft upon us through the operations of the Communist Party.

These forces are narrowly exclusive in their approach to our world position, and carry this exclusiveness vigorously into the field of international cultural exchanges. They tend to stifle the interchange of cultural impulses that is vital to the progress of the intellectual and artistic life of our people. The people in question seem to feel either that cultural values are not important at all or that America has reached the apex of cultural achievement and no longer needs in any serious way the stimulus of normal contact with other peoples in the

foreign ministers of the American states to discuss the Communist menace in Guatemala and its threat to the entire Western Hemisphere. **Sept. 1.** U.S. and Guatemala sign technical assistance agreement, which brings Point Four program in full to Guatemala.

July 22. Revised Organic Act of the Virgin Islands creates executive governorship, the governor to be appointed by U.S. President. In 1958 President Eisenhower appoints first native governor.

Aug. 2. Housing Redevelopment Act establishes policy of federal aid to urban renewal projects, with assistance in mortgage financing of new construction, rehabilitation of existing structures, and program of home building to accommodate families losing their homes as a result of slum clearance.

Aug. 5. In oil dispute between Great Britain and Iran, agreement is reached that gives right to oil production and sale to eight companies, five of which are American, with Iran to receive 50 percent of net profit.

Aug. 11. Chinese Communist leader Chou En-lai announces policy of liberation of Formosa, Nationalist Chinese island 121 miles off Chinese coast. **Aug. 17.** President Eisenhower replies that the U.S. Seventh Fleet will repel any invasion attempt. **Sept. 3-10.** Communists bombard Quemoy and Little Quemoy, Nationalist islands immediately off the Chinese coast, and Nationalists in return bombard nearby Communist island of Amoy. **Dec. 2.** Chinese Nationalists and the U.S. sign mutual defense treaty, but it does not include U.S. protection of small Nationalist islands along the Chinese coast.

Aug. 24. President Eisenhower signs Communist Control Act, which deprives individual Communists, the Communist Party, and other Communist organizations of many rights and privileges enjoyed by ordinary citizens and groups; Act also denies rights under National Labor Relations Act of 1935 to Communist-infiltrated labor unions.

Aug. 30. Atomic Energy Act allows development of peaceful atomic energy projects by private companies, which are also permitted to own nuclear materials; patents taken out must be shared for five years with other companies. Act also allows the U.S. to share information on atomic weapons and industrial uses with friendly nations. In November the U.S. and Great Britain pledge fissionable materials to international agency for research.

Sept. 1. Social Security amendments increase benefits and liberalize qualifications for receiving them, as well as adding new categories of beneficiaries, which increase rolls by 10 million people, including farm and domestic workers.

Sept. 8. South East Asia Treaty Organization (SEATO) is established by the U.S. and seven other nations, only three (Pakistan, Thailand, and the Philippines) of which are Asian; mutual security pact pledging joint military defense and promotion of political rights and economic development of area is signed. Formosa is not included in treaty.

Sept. 27. The U.S. and Canada agree to establish a line of radar stations (Distant Early Warning, or DEW, Line) across northern Canada from Greenland to Alaska. Earlier, work has been started on two other lines north of the U.S.-Canadian border — Pinetree Chain, which is already in operation, and Mid-Canada Line, which is still under construction. DEW Line begins functioning in 1957.

field of arts and letters.

They look with suspicion both on the sources of intellectual and artistic activity in this country and on impulses of this nature coming to us from abroad. . . .

In this way, we begin to draw about ourselves a cultural curtain similar in some respects to the Iron Curtain of our adversaries. In doing so, we tend to inflict upon ourselves a species of cultural isolation and provincialism wholly out of accord with the traditions of our nation and destined, if unchecked, to bring to our intellectual and artistic life the same sort of sterility from which the cultural world of our Communist adversaries is already suffering.

Within the framework of our society, as in its relations to external environment, the tendency of these forces is exclusive and intolerant—quick to reject, slow to receive, intent on discovering what ought not to be rather than what ought to be. They claim the right to define a certain area of our national life and cultural output as beyond the bounds of righteous approval. This definition is never effected by law or by constituted authority; it is effected by vague insinuation and suggestion. And the circle, as I say, tends to grow constantly narrower. One has the impression that, if uncountered, these people would eventually narrow the area of political and cultural respectability to a point where it included only themselves, the excited accusers, and excluded everything and everybody not embraced in the profession of denunciation.

Senate resolution, 1954

The senator from Wisconsin, Mr. Mc-Carthy, in . . . charging three members of the Select Committee with "deliberate deception" and "fraud" . . . in repeatedly describing this special Senate session as a "lynch bee" in a nationwide television and radio show . . . and in characterizing the said committee as the "unwitting handmaiden," "involuntary agent," and "attorneys in fact" of the Communist Party, and in charging that the said committee in writing its report "imitated Communist methods" . . . acted contrary to senatorial ethics and tended to bring the Senate into dishonor and disrepute, to obstruct the constitutional processes of the Senate, and to impair its dignity; and such conduct is hereby condemned.

JOSEPH R. McCARTHY

Asked to explain his condemnation, 1954

Well, I wouldn't call it a vote of confidence.

EARL WARREN

Brown v. Board of Education of Topeka, 1954

Today, education is perhaps the most important function of state and local governments. Compulsory school-attendance laws and the great expenditures for education both demonstrate our recognition of the importance of education to our democratic society. It is required in the performance of our most basic public responsibilities, even service in the armed forces. It is the very foundation of good citizenship.

Oct. 27. Twenty-six comic-book publishers adopt voluntary code to eliminate from their lists obscene, vulgar, and horror comics. Protest against quality of comics is so strong that by 1955 13 states have enacted laws to control their content; although dropping from 422 to 335 titles, they still make up 35 percent of newsstand sales.

Oct. 28. Ernest Hemingway wins Nobel Prize for Literature, mainly for his latest work, *The Old Man and the Sea,* published in 1952.

Nov. 2. In close fall elections, Democrats win majority in both houses of Congress, the Senate by only one seat.

Dec. 2. Senator Joseph R. McCarthy, who has broken with Republican leaders and lost his position as head of the Senate Permanent Subcommittee on Investigations when Republicans are defeated in the fall elections, is formally condemned by a 67 to 22 Senate vote for acting contrary to Senate traditions during his investigation of Communism in government and the U.S. Army.

1954-1955

May 17, 1954. The Supreme Court, in *Brown* v. *Board of Education of Topeka,* reverses 1896 ruling allowing "separate but equal" educational facilities for Negroes. Court holds unanimously in case involving public schools that segregation is a violation of the Fourteenth Amendment, since it denies Negroes equal protection of the laws. **May 31, 1955.** The Supreme Court orders lower courts to use "all deliberate speed" in admitting Negro children to public schools. In some border states, compliance is almost immediate; in the deep South, decision meets with great hostility, and such groups as White Citizens' Committees are formed to fight it.

Government contract is awarded to private Dixon-Yates utility combine to build plant in West Memphis, Tennessee, to supplement electric power lost by Tennessee Valley Authority (TVA) to U.S. Atomic Energy Commission, thus enabling TVA to meet growing power needs of Memphis. Democrats accuse the Eisenhower administration of trying to dismember TVA. In the following year, Memphis announces plans to build municipal generating plant, and President Eisenhower cancels Dixon-Yates contract.

1954-1956

Feb. 23, 1954. Largest immunization test in history begins when Dr. Jonas E. Salk begins vaccinating elementary school pupils with his newly developed inactivated virus antipoliomyelitis vaccine; 2,480,000 children take part in the test. **Oct. 21.** Nobel Prize for Medicine and Physiology is awarded to three U.S. scientists who have discovered method of growing polio virus in quantities large enough to produce vaccine. **April 12, 1955.** Report on results of Salk test states that vaccine is believed to be 60 to 90 percent effective. **Aug. 12.** President Eisenhower signs Poliomyelitis Vaccination Assistance Act, which authorizes the U.S. Public Health Service to give $30 million to the states for purchase of poliomyelitis vaccine. By this year polio cases, which had been rising for almost a generation, have dropped sharply to about half the 1952 figure as a result of vaccination of children. In 1956 an oral (live virus) vaccine is developed; it eventually proves to be faster acting and easier to administer and is found to give protection to a community, as well as to individuals vaccinated.

Sept. 30, 1954. First atomic-powered submarine, U.S.S. *Nautilus,* is commissioned at Groton, Connecticut. In 1957, two more, the *Seawolf* and the *Skate,* are

Today it is a principal instrument in awakening the child to cultural values, in preparing him for later professional training, and in helping him to adjust normally to his environment. In these days, it is doubtful that any child may reasonably be expected to succeed in life if he is denied the opportunity of an education. Such an opportunity, where the state has undertaken to provide it, is a right which must be made available to all on equal terms.

We come then to the question presented: Does segregation of children in public schools solely on the basis of race, even though the physical facilities and other "tangible" factors may be equal, deprive the children of the minority group of equal educational opportunities? We believe that it does. . . .

To separate them from others of similar age and qualifications solely because of their race generates a feeling of inferiority as to their status in the community that may affect their hearts and minds in a way unlikely ever to be undone. . . .

Whatever may have been the extent of psychological knowledge at the time of Plessy v. Ferguson, this finding is amply supported by modern authority. Any language in Plessy v. Ferguson contrary to this finding is rejected.

We conclude that in the field of public education the doctrine of "separate but equal" has no place. Separate educational facilities are inherently unequal. Therefore, we hold that the plaintiffs and others similarly situated for whom the actions have been brought are, by reason of the segregation complained of, deprived of the equal protection of the laws guaranteed by the Fourteenth Amendment.

JAMES H. GRAY
Atlantic Monthly, 1957

As all the Seaway advocates have been saying for thirty years, the purpose of the St. Lawrence Canal is to give the whole Great Lakes industrial area and the consumers of the mid-continent the benefit of lower costs that come with ocean transportation. . . .

The Canadian view has always been that the ships of the world will ply the waterway with freedom of call. . . . But when Canadians sat down to discuss canal tolls, they discovered that the United States has no great burning ambition to permit that to happen.

American taxpayers subsidize their shipping to the extent of about $100 million a year. Whenever it is decided that a sea route is "essential to the trade and economy of the nation," ships using the route are entitled to a subsidy which will amount to about $750 per day. . . . When the United States, early in 1956, promulgated the Great Lakes-Northern Europe and Western Europe route as "essential to the trade and economy of the nation," Canada regarded it as an unfair act, one that violated the spirit of the St. Lawrence agreement. . . .

In applying the subsidy regulation to the St. Lawrence Seaway, the United States sowed seeds of doubt as to its good faith in future operation of the Seaway. . . .

Canada expects that ships will use the waterway right up to Fort William. . . . But if they are discouraged from entering the waterway by high tolls or competition from subsidized American bottoms, they will not be able to move out Canadian grain, which was one of Canada's main reasons for building the Canal.

The shipping subsidy is an almost perfect example of how domestically motivated legislation can fog up international relations.

completed; the *Skate* is the first planned for assembly line production.

1954-1958

Four new man-made radioactive elements are produced: number 99, einsteinium, and number 100, fermium, in 1954; number 101, mendelevium, in 1955; and number 102, nobelium, in 1958. All are developed in the U.S. In 1955 a new atomic particle, the antiproton, is discovered, and in the following year the existence of the antineutron is confirmed; both discoveries are made at the University of California.

1954-1959

May 13, 1954. The U.S. authorizes building of the St. Lawrence Seaway in co-operation with Canada. **April 25, 1959.** The world's largest inland waterway, it opens to traffic, allowing oceangoing ships to travel 135 miles from Montreal to Lake Ontario and, through other lakes, 2,300 miles inland from the Atlantic Ocean. Related hydroelectric project has started operating in 1958.

1955

Jan. 1. The U.S., through the Foreign Operations Administration, begins giving economic assistance to Laos, Cambodia, and South Vietnam.

Jan. 28. Congress authorizes the President to use force to protect Formosa and the Pescadores from attack. **March 3.** Although Chinese Communists have been attacking smaller coastal islands, they decide risk of general war is too great when Secretary Dulles announces that U.S. protection will be extended.

Feb. 26. British physicist Cecil F. Powell estimates unofficially that by this time the U.S. has 4,000 atomic bombs stockpiled, and that the Soviet Union has 1,000, enough to kill everyone on earth several times over.

Feb. 28. Israelis and Egyptians clash on the Gaza Strip. **March 29.** The UN Security Council condemns Israel as the aggressor. **Sept. 4.** A cease-fire is worked out. **Nov. 16.** Israel asks the U.S. to sell it arms; however, no agreement is reached.

April 1. U.S. Senate ratifies treaties ending occupation of West Germany, which becomes independent, while Western occupation forces still there become security troops. One month later, West Germany formally becomes a member of NATO.

June 6. United Automobile Workers sign contract with Ford Motor Company and six days later with General Motors Corporation providing for pay during layoffs.

June 25. President Eisenhower signs peace treaty with Austria. After prolonged negotiations, treaty has been agreed to by all major powers. Pact establishes Austria's borders at 1938 pre-Hitler lines and guarantees Austria's independence.

July 21. At summit meeting of United States, Soviet Union, Great Britain, and France in Geneva, Switzerland, President Eisenhower proposes "Open Skies" policy of mutual aerial inspection by the major powers to forestall threats of war or surprise attacks. Besides disarmament, Eisenhower, British Prime Minister Anthony Eden, Soviet Premier Nikolai Bulganin, and French Premier Edgar Faure discuss unification of Germany and European security. Because of remilitarization of West Germany, the Soviet Union is opposed to its unification and rejects the West's proposals for ensuring European security, insisting instead on a European mutual defense alliance, including Germany but not the U.S. No significant agreements result.

DWIGHT D. EISENHOWER
Address at summit meeting, 1955
Gentlemen, since I have been working on this memorandum to present to this conference, I have been searching my heart and mind for something that I could say here that could convince everyone of the great sincerity of the United States in approaching this problem of disarmament. I should address myself for a moment principally to the delegates from the Soviet Union, because our two great countries admittedly possess new and terrible weapons in quantities which do give rise in other parts of the world, or reciprocally, to the fears and dangers of surprise attack.

I propose, therefore, that we take a practical step, that we begin an arrangement, very quickly, as between ourselves — immediately. These steps would include:

To give to each other a complete blueprint of our military establishments, from beginning to end, from one end of our countries to the other; lay out the establishments and provide the blueprints to each other.

Next, to provide within our countries facilities for aerial photography to the other country — we to provide you the facilities within our country, ample facilities for aerial reconnaissance, where you can make all the pictures you choose and take them to your own country to study; you to provide exactly the same facilities for us and we to make these examinations — and by this step to convince the world that we are providing as between ourselves against the possibility of great surprise attack, thus lessening danger and relaxing tension. Likewise, we will make more easily attainable a comprehensive and effective system of inspection and disarmament, because what I propose, I assure you, would be but a beginning.

Nation, 1955

When John W. Livingston, director of organizing for the merging A.F. of L.-C.I.O., surveys his job, he will be looking beyond heavy industry, public utilities, and transportation. These, already fairly well organized, compose the bulk of the 16 million members to whom President George Meany will be pointing with pride. Livingston, the husky auto worker from the Ozarks, will be concerned rather with the 45 million wage earners outside the union fold. They include most women workers, most white-collar employees, and most of the men and women, white and Negro, employed in the South. If within the next ten years he could double the membership of the A.F. of L.-C.I.O., his name would go down in labor history alongside that of John L. Lewis. . . .

Any serious proposal to add millions to the labor movement must take into account the South, where industry is burgeoning, wages are low, and security generally nonexistent. The emancipation of Southern labor is the key, not only to the creation of a truly national labor movement but to the refreshment of American political life. A South brought up to national wage standards, liberated from industrial-plantation feudalists, and freed from bondage to the race issue would give a new turn to the national life. . . .

Nevertheless, repeated "Southern drives" have petered out. A good bit of the blame must be placed at labor's door because of its hesitant attitude toward Negroes. A firm stand has been diluted out of concern for the prejudices of the white worker; as a result neither white nor Negro is organized.

Sept. 24. President Eisenhower suffers heart attack while in Colorado. Debate follows on how to handle possible incapacity (not death) of a President, since Eisenhower is unable to return to Washington until November.

Sept. 26. Two days after news of President Eisenhower's heart attack, stocks show sharpest drop since 1929. Dollar loss is $14 billion, greatest in U.S. history; more than 7,700,000 shares are traded in a single day.

Sept. 29. *A View from the Bridge* and *A Memory of Two Mondays,* two short plays by Pulitzer Prize playwright Arthur Miller, open in New York City; Miller's play *The Crucible,* based on the Salem witch trials and interpreted by some to refer to the McCarthy Senate hearings, has been produced the previous year.

Nov. 28-Dec. 1. White House Conference on Education recommends expanded federal aid to all levels of public education despite controversy over federal control.

Dec. 5. American Federation of Labor and Congress of Industrial Organizations merge with strong central government, equal recognition for craft and industrial unions, and an agreement to avoid competitive organizing drives. Combined AFL-CIO membership is about 16 million workers in this year.

By the end of this year, the U.S. has admitted more than 406,000 displaced persons since special admission act, passed in 1948.

By this year, electronic computers are beginning to be used widely in commerce, industry, transportation, and education.

1955-1956

Dec. 5, 1955. Negro boycott of segregated city bus lines in Montgomery, Alabama, begins. Lasting through 1956, when a Supreme Court decision forces desegregation of local transportation facilities, boycott results in loss to bus lines of much of their business. The Interstate Commerce Commission has earlier banned segregation on interstate transportation. Dr. Martin Luther King, Jr., leads movement and, with the National Association for the Advancement of Colored People (NAACP), spearheads further activity against segregation in stores, theaters, and other public places. Desegregation movement continues in spite of segregationist reprisals, such as job dismissals, mortgage foreclosures, and boycott of Negro businesses.

In these two years, private colleges, universities, and medical schools benefit from Ford Foundation education grants totaling more than $360 million; gifts are mainly for increases in faculty salaries, but more than $6 million benefits educational television.

1956

Jan. 19. Alabama Senate approves nullification of the Supreme Court decision integrating public schools. **Feb. 1.** Legislature of Virginia adopts resolution of interposition, challenging Supreme Court's outlawing of segregated public schools.

Feb. 6. Autherine Lucy, first Negro student to attempt to enter the University of Alabama, is suspended after three days of riots due to her presence. In March she is expelled because of lawsuit she has brought against the University. In this year, violence erupts in several places in the South when Negro students attempt to enroll in all-white schools and colleges.

Feb. 15. U.S. District Court in Louisiana voids all state laws that do not conform to Supreme Court's 1954 ruling on segregation.

HERBERT RAVENEL SASS
Atlantic Monthly, 1956
The fact that the United States is overwhelmingly pure white is not only important; it is also the most distinctive fact about this country when considered in relation to the rest of the New World. . . . In general the pure-blooded white nations have outstripped the far more numerous American mixed-blood nations in most of the achievements which constitute progress as commonly defined.

These facts are well known. But now there lurks in ambush, as it were, another fact: we have suddenly begun to move toward abandonment of our 350-year-old system of keeping our races pure and are preparing to adopt instead a method of racial amalgamation similar to that which has created the mixed-blood nations of this hemisphere; except that the amalgamation being prepared for this country is not Indian and white but Negro and white. It is the deep conviction of nearly all white Southerners in the states which have large Negro populations that the mingling or integration of white and Negro children in the South's primary schools would open the gates to miscegenation and widespread racial amalgamation. . . .

It must be realized too that the Negroes of the U.S.A. are today by far the most fortunate members of their race to be found anywhere on earth. Instead of being the hapless victim of unprecedented oppression, it is nearer the truth that the Negro in the United States is by and large the product of friendliness and helpfulness unequaled in any comparable instance in all history. Nowhere else in the world, at any time of which there is record, has a helpless, backward people of another color been so swiftly uplifted and so greatly benefited by a dominant race.

Declaration of Constitutional Principles, 1956

The unwarranted decision of the Supreme Court in the public-school cases is now bearing the fruit always produced when men substitute naked power for established law. . . .

This unwarranted exercise of power by the Court, contrary to the Constitution, is creating chaos and confusion in the states principally affected. It is destroying the amicable relations between the white and Negro races that have been created through ninety years of patient effort by the good people of both races. It has planted hatred and suspicion where there has been heretofore friendship and understanding.

Without regard to the consent of the governed, outside agitators are threatening immediate and revolutionary changes in our public-school systems. If done, this is certain to destroy the system of public education in some of the states.

With the gravest concern for the explosive and dangerous condition created by this decision and inflamed by outside meddlers:

We reaffirm our reliance on the Constitution as the fundamental law of the land.

We decry the Supreme Court's encroachments on rights reserved to the states and to the people, contrary to established law and to the Constitution.

We commend the motives of those states which have declared the intention to resist forced integration by any lawful means. . . .

In this trying period, as we all seek to right this wrong, we appeal to our people not to be provoked by the agitators and troublemakers invading our states and to scrupulously refrain from disorders and lawless acts.

Feb. 17. After he receives evidence of corrupt lobbying, President Eisenhower vetoes Natural Gas Bill, which provides exemption for independent producers from control by the Federal Power Commission.

March 7. The State of Virginia, which has closed its public schools after desegregation ruling of the Supreme Court, amends law to permit use of state money for private schools in attempt to defy Court's decision.

March 12. One hundred and one Southern senators and representatives publish manifesto against school integration, calling on states to disobey and resist "by all lawful means" the Supreme Court's rulings on desegregation of public schools.

March 28. Iceland demands removal of all NATO forces from the island. The U.S., unwilling to evacuate air base important to world network, is successful by November in persuading the Icelandic government to allow the U.S. to continue operating the Keflavik Air Base.

April 9. In *Slochower* v. *New York City Higher Education Board*, the Supreme Court finds that public servants may not be excluded from the protection of the Fifth Amendment of the U.S. Constitution, and that exercising the privilege against self-incrimination is not equivalent either to a confession of guilt or a conclusive presumption of perjury.

May 2. Methodist Church conference in Minneapolis demands end to racial segregation in Methodist churches.

May 28. Agricultural (Soil Bank) Act provides for paying farmers for taking cropland out of production and placing land into soil-building cover crops or trees to cut surpluses and improve land without impairing farm income.

June 29. Federal-Aid Highway Act is signed; it authorizes a 13-year program of highway construction, to be financed by various taxes on motorists. Federal funds are to cover 90 percent of the cost of a 41,000-mile interstate system and up to 50 percent of road construction within states.

July 19. After Egypt has accepted offer of financial aid for building of Aswan Dam, the U.S. retracts offer. July 26. Egyptian President Gamal Abd-al-Nasser announces nationalization of the Suez Canal, saying that revenue from Canal will be used to finance the Dam.

Aug. 16. At Democratic National Convention in Chicago, Adlai E. Stevenson of Illinois is nominated for President, although former President Harry S. Truman has backed Averell Harriman; the next day Senator Estes Kefauver of Tennessee is chosen for Vice-President, winning nomination over Senator John F. Kennedy of Massachusetts. Aug. 22. Republicans, meeting in San Francisco, renominate President Eisenhower and Vice-President Nixon. Minor party candidates are: T. Coleman Andrews, States' Rights; Enoch A. Holtwick, Prohibition; Eric Hass, Socialist Labor; and Darlington Hoopes, Socialist. Democratic and Republican platforms differ very little: both support desegregation; Democrats favor public water power, while Republicans advocate combinations of private and government organizations; both support parity payments to farmers, the Democrats fixed payments and the Republicans flexible ones.

Sept. 25. First transatlantic telephone cable begins operation; two cables, each 2,250 miles long, stretching from Newfoundland to Scotland, have three times the capacity of radio telephone circuits.

Oct. 20. Soviet Premier Bulganin's letter to President Eisenhower endorsing proposal

JAMES MacGREGOR BURNS
New York Times Magazine, 1955
Not long ago a London editor was trying to guide his readers through the wilderness of the American party system. There are four parties, he explained—liberal Republicans, conservative Republicans, conservative Democrats, and liberal Democrats. The first three parties, he went on, combined to elect Mr. Eisenhower President, and the last three now combine to oppose him in Congress.

The story is pertinent to the news out of Washington: McCarthy breaks with President; Knowland attacks administration foreign policy; Democrats unite in censuring McCarthy but divide over attacking President; Eisenhower solicits bipartisan support for his program of "progressive moderation.". . .

This raises the question of what we mean by "Republican" and by "Democrat." It is fashionable to say that the terms are utterly meaningless. But this is not so. Party platforms and presidential statements show that most Democrats stand for the increased use of government for the broader distribution of social welfare, even if it means unbalanced budgets, big government, and higher taxes, especially on the rich. They show that most Republicans would restrict government in order to give more scope to private initiative and investment, even if this means considerable inequality of income and even some temporary hardship for the mass of people.

This, of course, is a generalization, but a generalization that focuses on the crucial issue separating Democrats from Republicans—the extent to which government should be used to distribute social welfare.

DWIGHT D. EISENHOWER
Address to the nation, 1957
The Middle East is a land bridge between the Eurasian and African continents. Millions of tons of commerce are transmitted through it annually. Its own products, especially petroleum, are essential to Europe and the Western world.

The United States has no ambitions or desires in this region other than that each country there may maintain its independence and live peacefully within itself and with its neighbors, and, by peaceful cooperation with others, develop its own spiritual and material resources. But that much is vital to the peace and well-being of us all. This is our concern today. So tonight I report to you on the matters in controversy and on what I believe the position of the United States must be. . . .

The United States and other free nations are making clear by every means at their command the evil of Soviet conduct in Hungary. It would indeed be a sad day if the United States ever felt that it had to subject Israel to the same type of moral pressure as is being applied to the Soviet Union.

There can, of course, be no equating of a nation like Israel with that of the Soviet Union. The peoples of Israel, like those of the United States, are imbued with a religious faith and a sense of moral values. We are entitled to expect, and do expect, from such peoples of the free world a contribution to world order which unhappily we cannot expect from a nation controlled by atheistic despots.

of presidential candidate Adlai E. Stevenson that all nations stop nuclear testing is made public. Bulganin is accused by some U.S. officials of interfering in U.S. elections.

Oct. 23. Police in Budapest, Hungary, fire upon demonstrators who demand that the government form a democracy and free the country from domination by the Soviet Union. **Oct. 30.** Free elections and a policy of neutrality are promised, and Soviet troops begin leaving Budapest and apparently also Hungary. **Nov. 4.** Soviet tanks and troops sweep through Budapest, brutally crushing opposition. All resistance ends three days later. Premier Imre Nagy has appealed to the UN for help, but too late. A new Communist dictatorship is set up; about 160,000 democratic-minded students and workers flee across the borders, mostly into Austria. Two years later it is announced that Nagy and other leaders of the uprising have been executed.

Oct. 29-Nov. 1. When August international conference fails to settle Suez Canal issues, Israel, Britain, and France attack Egypt. **Nov. 6.** Pressure by the U.S. and the Soviet Union brings about cease-fire.

Nov. 6. President Eisenhower wins election by a landslide, with Stevenson taking only seven Southern states. Popular vote is Eisenhower, 35,590,000; Stevenson, 26,023,000. Electoral vote is 457 to 73 (with one Alabama elector refusing to vote for Stevenson). Election is a personal victory for Eisenhower, who runs far ahead of other Republican candidates. Congress becomes Democratic in both houses, the first time in 108 years that the party of an incoming President has not had control of at least one house of Congress.

Dec. 2. Released from prison in 1955 after serving sentence for revolutionary activities, Cuban leader Fidel Castro lands with a small group of guerrillas in Oriente Province, determined to overthrow government of dictator Fulgencio Batista.

Dec. 6. President Eisenhower orders Defense Department to set up system of emergency air and sea transportation to bring to the U.S. 15,000 Hungarian refugees.

1956-1957

Nov. 17, 1956. The Soviet Union declares that it will accept a modified form of the "Open Skies" policy proposed by the U.S. in the previous year, but in 1957, after extended discussion between U.S. and Soviet disarmament representatives, the Soviet Union withdraws acceptance.

1956-1958

March 27, 1956. Internal Revenue officers close down Communist newspaper the *Daily Worker* for nonpayment of taxes. A week later, $4,500 partial tax payment is made, and paper resumes publication. **Jan. 13, 1958.** Because of lack of funds, it is forced to become a weekly *(The Worker)* rather than a daily.

1957

Feb. 25. On the ground that enforcement of such a law would leave nothing for adults to read except that suitable for children, the Supreme Court voids Michigan law against selling publications that might corrupt children.

March 7. Congress approves the so-called Eisenhower Doctrine, which seeks to prevent subversion or conquest of Middle Eastern countries by supplying economic and military assistance (including the use of U.S. armed forces) upon request to those countries threatened by Communist aggression. In the same year, disturbances in Jor-

Michigan Penal Code, Sec. 343, 1954
Any person who shall import, print, publish, sell, possess with the intent to sell, design, prepare, loan, give away, distribute or offer for sale, any book, magazine, newspaper, writing, pamphlet, ballad, printed paper, print, picture, drawing, photograph, publication or other thing, including any recordings, containing obscene, immoral, lewd or lascivious language, or obscene, immoral, lewd or lascivious prints, pictures, figures or descriptions, tending to incite minors to violent or depraved or immoral acts, manifestly tending to the corruption of the morals of youth, or shall introduce into any family, school or place of education or shall buy, procure, receive or have in his possession, any such book, pamphlet, magazine, newspaper, writing, ballad, printed paper, print, picture, drawing, photograph, publication or other thing, either for the purpose of sale, exhibition, loan or circulation, or with intent to introduce the same into family, school or place of education, shall be guilty of a misdemeanor.

FELIX FRANKFURTER
Butler v. Michigan, 1957
Surely, this is to burn the house to roast the pig.

EDWARD TELLER, ALBERT L. LATTER
Our Nuclear Future, 1958

In a limited nuclear war the radioactive fallout will probably kill many of the innocent bystanders. We have seen that the testing program gives rise to a danger which is much smaller than many risks which we take in our stride without any worry. In a nuclear war, even in a limited one, the situation will probably be quite different. That noncombatants suffer in wars is not new. In a nuclear war, this suffering may well be increased further due to the radioactive poisons which kill friend and foe, soldier and civilian alike.

Fortunately there exists a way out. Our early nuclear explosives have used fission. In the fission process a great array of radioactive products are formed, some of them intensely poisonous. More recently we have learned how to produce energy by fusion. Fusion produces fewer and very much less dangerous radioactivities. Actually the neutrons which are a by-product of the fusion reaction may be absorbed in almost any material and may again produce an assortment of radioactive nuclei. However, by placing only certain materials near the thermonuclear explosion, one may obtain a weapon in which the radioactivity is harmless. Thus the possibility of clean nuclear explosions lies before us.

Clean, flexible, and easily delivered weapons of all sizes would make it possible to use these bombs as we want to use them: as tools of defense. When stopping an aggressor we would not let loose great quantities of radioactive atoms which would spread death where we wanted to defend freedom. Clean nuclear weapons would be the same as conveniently packaged high explosives. They would be nothing more.

dan and Syria lead to sending of U.S. Sixth Fleet, but no intervention is necessary.

April 10. The Suez Canal reopens after UN engineering team removes sunken ships and other barriers placed in it by Egypt to render it unnavigable during the nationalization crisis.

May 2. Dave Beck, president of the Teamsters Union, is indicted for income tax evasion and 18 days later is removed from executive positions within the AFL-CIO when it is discovered that he has used union funds for his own personal gain and profit. Beck is convicted of embezzlement in December. **Dec. 6.** The AFL-CIO expels the Teamsters Union for domination by corrupt leaders, especially James Hoffa.

June 17. In *Watkins* v. *United States*, the Supreme Court voids a conviction for contempt of Congress, ruling that the freedoms of the First Amendment of the U.S. Constitution cannot be abridged in legislative inquiries and that unless a particular inquiry is justified by a specific legislative need, protected freedoms should not be jeopardized.

June 24. Three leading atomic scientists report on the possibility of producing a smaller hydrogen bomb with essentially no radioactive fallout, revealing that they have already reduced radioactive fallout from a hydrogen bomb explosion by 95 percent and that with further development the fallout will become essentially negligible.

July 1. International Geophysical Year begins; scientists of about 70 nations (including the U.S.) take part in an 18-month study of the earth, atmosphere and space, oceans and glaciers, and the sun.

July 2. To the UN Disarmament Subcommittee meeting in London, the U.S. proposes a 10-month halt in nuclear testing as a first step toward disarmament; this time could be used for setting up an inspection system. **Aug. 21.** As a concession to Soviet demands for a longer suspension, President Eisenhower announces that the U.S. has offered to suspend nuclear testing for two years on condition that the Soviet Union agree to inspection and to a halt in the production of fissionable materials for weapons purposes; the Soviet Union does not concur, and talks in London are suspended indefinitely the following month.

Aug. 29. In spite of filibuster of more than 24 hours by Senator Strom Thurmond of South Carolina, Congress passes a bill that for the first time since 1875 seeks to protect the civil rights of Negroes. Act creates a commission to investigate denial of voting rights because of race or religion and makes interference with the right to vote in national elections a federal offense. Although the number of Negroes who have registered to vote has increased, it is still much less than those eligible.

Oct. 4. Soviet scientists, investigating upper atmosphere conditions as part of International Geophysical Year program, send "Sputnik," first rocket-powered artificial earth satellite, into orbit. Second Soviet satellite, carrying a dog, is orbited on November 3. The world and the U.S., long accustomed to thinking of the U.S. as superior in all branches of advanced technology, are astonished. Critics of U.S. educational system decry lack of discipline in study of scientific fundamentals in U.S. schools, as well as failure to recruit and train bright students.

Oct. 16. Two aluminum pellets, fired into space by the U.S. Air Force, escape the earth's gravity and go into outer space.

Nov. 25. Eisenhower has a slight stroke. This illness, as well as previous heart attack and intestinal operation, causes renewed dis-

WALTER LIPPMANN
New York Herald Tribune, 1957
The few who are allowed to know about such things, and are able to understand them, are saying that the launching of so big a satellite signifies that the Soviets are much ahead of this country in the development of rocket missiles. Their being so much ahead cannot be the result of some kind of lucky guess in inventing a gadget. It must be that there is a large body of Soviet scientists, engineers, and production men, plus many highly developed subsidiary industries, all successfully directed and coordinated, and bountifully financed.

In short, the fact that we have lost the race to launch the satellite means that we are losing the race to produce ballistic missiles. This in turn means that the United States and the Western world may be falling behind in the progress of science and technology.

This is a grim business. . . .

It is a grim business because a society cannot stand still. If it loses the momentum of its own progress, it will deteriorate and decline, lacking purpose and losing confidence in itself.

The critical question is how we as a people, from the President down, will respond to what is a profound challenge to our cultural values — not to the ideal of the American way of life but to the way in fact we have been living our life. One response could be to think of it all in terms of propaganda, and to look around for some device for doing something spectacular to outmatch what the Russians have done. The other response would be to look inward upon ourselves, and to concern ourselves primarily with our own failings, and to be determined not so much to beat the Russians as to cure ourselves.

JACK KEROUAC

On The Road, 1957

And in fact that was the point, and they all sat around looking at Dean with lowered and hating eyes, and he stood on the carpet in the middle of them and giggled—he just giggled. He made a little dance. His bandage was getting dirtier all the time; it began to flop and unroll. I suddenly realized that Dean, by virtue of his enormous series of sins, was becoming the Idiot, the Imbecile, the Saint of the lot.

"You have absolutely no regard for anybody but yourself and your damned kicks. All you think about is what's hanging between your legs and how much money or fun you can get out of people and then you just throw them aside. Not only that but you're silly about it. It never occurs to you that life is serious and there are people trying to make something decent out of it instead of just goofing all the time."

That's what Dean was, the HOLY GOOF. . . .

Then a complete silence fell over everybody; where once Dean would have talked his way out, he now fell silent himself, but standing in front of everybody, ragged and broken and idiotic, right under the lightbulbs, his bony mad face covered with sweat and throbbing veins, saying, "Yes, yes, yes," as though tremendous revelations were pouring into him all the time now, and I am convinced they were, and the others suspected as much and were frightened. He was BEAT—the root, the soul of Beatific. What was he knowing?

cussion of methods for dealing with incapacity of the President.

Nov. 25. In *Yates* v. *United States,* the Supreme Court holds that, under Smith Act, teaching the violent overthrow of the government in principle may not be equated with actually inciting to overthrow.

John Kerouac publishes his novel *On the Road,* a testament of the beat generation, which rejects modern society. Allen Ginsberg's book of poetry *Howl,* published in 1956, has dealt with the same theme.

1957-1958

Nov. 10, 1957. U.S. Office of Education publishes two-year survey of education in the Soviet Union, which shows that emphasis on scientific and technical education in the U.S.S.R. is far ahead of that in the U.S. **June 1958.** U.S. educators who have made a government-sponsored trip to the Soviet Union confirm these findings.

1957-1959

Sept. 24, 1957. To ensure enforcement of U.S. District Court order requiring enrollment of Negroes at the Central High School in Little Rock, Arkansas, President Eisenhower calls the Arkansas National Guard into federal service and dispatches 1,000 paratroopers to Little Rock. Nine Negro students enter guarded school on the following day. Troops remain in service until November 27. Other Southern and border states resist integration or register only token numbers of Negroes in previously all-white schools. **Sept. 1958.** The Supreme Court rejects any delay of integration in Little Rock, ruling it the duty of state and local officials to end school segregation as promptly as possible. **Aug. 12, 1959.** Following failure of a maneuver by Arkansas Governor Orval E. Faubus to segregate city schools by changing their category to private schools, high schools in Little Rock reopen with Negro students attending under police protection.

1958

Jan. 31. In the space exploration race with the Soviet Union, the U.S. begins to close the gap by putting into orbit by a Jupiter-C rocket the artificial satellite Explorer I, weighing 31 pounds. **March 17.** The U.S. Navy launches a three-pound satellite, Vanguard I. **May 15.** The Soviet Union sends Sputnik III, a 3,000-pound capsule, into orbit. **Dec. 18.** Score, 8,800-pound Atlas missile, is orbited by the U.S. All ventures achieve firsts in space exploration: Explorer I discovers inner (Van Allen) radiation belt; Vanguard I provides first proof that the earth is (slightly) pear shaped; Sputnik III contains first space laboratory for measuring aspects of the atmosphere; and Score transmits a voice from space for the first time.

Feb. 16. In Indonesian civil war, anti-Communist rebels in Padang order American-owned oil companies to cease all shipments to Java. The U.S. adopts policy of neutrality. **Aug. 18.** After rebels are repulsed, the U.S. is reported to be shipping light military equipment to pro-Communist government.

March 6. It is revealed that President Eisenhower has rejected proposal to make the U.S. the first nation to produce planes powered by nuclear energy; he holds that such a prestige effort is wasteful of scarce materials and talent.

April 14. It is formally announced that American pianist Harvey L. ("Van") Cliburn has won the international Tchaikovsky piano competition in Moscow, playing Rachmaninoff's Third Piano Concerto;

DWIGHT D. EISENHOWER
Address to the nation, 1957
To make this talk I have come to the President's office in the White House. I could have spoken from Rhode Island, where I have been staying recently; but I felt that, in speaking from the house of Lincoln, of Jackson, and of Wilson, my words would better convey both the sadness I feel in the action I was compelled today to take and the firmness with which I intend to pursue this course until the orders of the federal court at Little Rock can be executed without unlawful interference.

In that city, under the leadership of demagogic extremists, disorderly mobs have deliberately prevented the carrying out of proper orders from a federal court. Local authorities have not eliminated that violent opposition, and, under the law, I yesterday issued a proclamation calling upon the mob to disperse. This morning the mob again gathered in front of the Central High School of Little Rock, obviously for the purpose of again preventing the carrying out of the court's order relating to the admission of Negro children to that school.

Whenever normal agencies prove inadequate to the task and it becomes necessary for the executive branch of the federal government to use its powers and authority to uphold federal courts, the President's responsibility is inescapable. In accordance with that responsibility, I have today issued an executive order directing the use of troops under federal authority to aid in the execution of federal law at Little Rock, Arkansas. This became necessary when my proclamation of yesterday was not observed, and the obstruction of justice still continues.

(Above) British soldiers fighting in the town of
Ismailia, following Egyptian seizure of the Suez
Canal; (left) cartoon in the Cleveland *Plain Dealer*
commenting on Russia's space successes

Let 'em eat cake

'The Civil Rights Bill Would Destroy Our Southern Way of Life, Suh!'

(Above) Cartoon by Ross Lewis for *The Milwaukee Journal*, 1948;
(below) restless youths of Little Rock, Arkansas, at the beginning
of school integration, 1957

NORMAN COUSINS
Saturday Review, 1958

It is wrong to say that nuclear explosives are being tested; they are being used. Every time one of the explosives is fired human beings are hurt. Just in the act of exploding a test nuclear bomb, life-destroying materials are put into the air. These explosions form no ordinary clouds; they are not dispersed by the winds; they retain their ability to poison and kill for more than two dozen years. With each bomb the canopy of poison above the earth grows heavier. Not long ago only one nation was involved in this kind of experimentation. Today, three nations are contributing to the general poisoning. Tomorrow, perhaps a half-dozen or more national sovereignties will insist on their right to add their own portions of poison to the sky. . . .

Meanwhile, what the world needs today are two billion angry men who will make it clear to their national leaders that the earth does not exist for the purpose of being a stage for the total destruction of man. Two billion angry men can insist that the world's resources be utilized for human good. They can demand that the nations stop using the sky as an open sewer for radioactive poisons, and that an end be put to the uncontrolled devices that pursue future generations by way of damaged genes. They can compel the nations to end the long age of the cave and begin a real civilization. A war is now being waged against the world's peoples and they have the need and duty to defend themselves.

award highlights increase in cultural exchange between the U.S. and the Soviet Union in this period.

April 16. Dr. Edward Teller says that suspension of nuclear testing may sacrifice millions of lives in case of nuclear war. **April 28.** Disagreeing with report by U.S. Atomic Energy Commission that radioactive fallout has not reached dangerous levels, Dr. Linus Pauling states that radiation from carbon 14 already released by testing will cause defects in 5 million children and millions of cancer and leukemia cases in the next 300 generations. **Aug. 10.** A UN committee reports that radiation, even in very small amounts, can cause damage to health and to the children of future generations; report states, however, that dosage varies with area, and that the situation needs further study.

April 27. Vice-President Richard M. Nixon leaves on a goodwill tour of South America. He is so hostilely received by demonstrators, especially in Venezuela and Peru, that President Eisenhower sends troops to Caribbean in case of further trouble. Nixon arrives back in U.S. on May 15.

April 29. The U.S. offers resolution to the UN Security Council that an Arctic armament inspection zone be set up, with agreements on other areas to follow. **May 2.** The proposal is vetoed by the Soviet Union.

May 3. To 11 nations conducting scientific work the U.S. proposes in the Antarctic, a treaty providing for demilitarization of the continent and international cooperation in research there. The treaty is signed in the following year by all 12 nations.

May 3. The U.S. rejects Polish proposal to denuclearize central Europe, because it could not be controlled by inspection and would leave Western forces in Germany exposed to numerically stronger Soviet forces.

July 15. In response to an appeal by President Camille Chamoun of Lebanon, made following an uprising against his own government and the overthrow of the government of neighboring Iraq, both inspired by Arab nationalism, the U.S. sends more than 5,000 marines to restore order under the Eisenhower Doctrine. British troops enter Jordan shortly afterward when rebels threaten attack on King Hussein's government. U.S. and British troops are withdrawn in October.

July 29. National Aeronautics and Space Administration is formed to handle space research; military space investigation and activity are to be handled by the Department of Defense.

Aug. 3. U.S.S. *Nautilus,* nuclear-powered submarine, makes first submerged under-ice crossing of the North Pole on voyage from Hawaii to Iceland. **Aug. 11.** The U.S.S. *Skate* follows suit on round trip from Connecticut to North Pole. **Oct. 6.** U.S.S. *Seawolf* completes 60-day submersion.

Aug. 6. President Eisenhower signs the Defense Reorganization Act, which makes important changes in the organization of the Department of Defense, including eliminating ambiguities about command authority, centralizing research and engineering within the Department, and making each service secretary responsible to secretary of defense.

Aug. 23. Chinese Communists resume bombardment of offshore Quemoy Islands. **Sept. 3.** The U.S. fleet begins escorting supply vessels from Formosa to Quemoy, up to the three-mile territorial limit of Chinese waters. **Sept. 30.** Secretary of State Dulles suggests a cease-fire to break dead-

DWIGHT D. EISENHOWER
Address to the nation, 1958
In response to this appeal from the government of Lebanon, the United States has dispatched a contingent of United States forces to Lebanon to protect American lives and by their presence there to encourage the Lebanese government in defense of Lebanese sovereignty and integrity. These forces have not been sent as any act of war. They will demonstrate the concern of the United States for the independence and integrity of Lebanon, which we deem vital to the ntaional interest and world peace. Our concern will also be shown by economic assistance. We shall act in accordance with these legitimate concerns.

The United States, this morning, will report its action to an emergency meeting of the United Nations Security Council. As the United Nations charter recognizes, there is an inherent right of collective self-defense. In conformity with the spirit of the charter, the United States is reporting the measures taken by it to the Security Council of the United Nations, making clear that these measures will be terminated as soon as the Security Council has itself taken the measures necessary to maintain international peace and security. . . .

Lebanon is a small peace-loving state with which the United States has traditionally had the most friendly relations. There are in Lebanon about 2500 Americans and we cannot, consistently with our historic relations and with the principles of the United Nations, stand idly by when Lebanon appeals itself for evidence of our concern and when Lebanon may not be able to preserve internal order and to defend itself against indirect aggression.

New Republic, 1958

We watched Sherman Adams last week sit ramrod-stiff for his public humiliation in the great cream-yellow barn of a House caucus room as big as an airplane hangar. Here was the mysterious, rarely seen Adams—small, white-haired, ascetic; muscular, proud face, a gnomelike man with a square jaw. He came prepared to admit that he had been "a little imprudent," and he was prepared to die, apparently, before he would go an inch beyond that. We are inclined to believe he is sincere in this attitude, too, for it is his extraordinary insensitivity rather than his deeds that tell the story. . . .

The scene shifts to the Eisenhower press conference and the heartfelt comment, "I need him." When all else is forgotten of this Administration that poignant cry may be remembered. It summarizes all the desolate story of delegated powers, lack of leadership, and inadequacy.

Administration defenders are raising the tu quoque red herring that Congressmen also exert pressure and take junkets. Obviously Congressmen should mend their ways, but the analogy falls on its face. Congressmen are elected; Adams is not. They don't appoint regulatory commissioners; Adams does. They don't throw moral thunderbolts from Eisenhower's elbow; Adams does. They don't take sanctuary from the press in the White House; Adams does.

lock in negotiations with Communist China. **Oct. 6.** The Chinese Communists order the cease-fire, but on October 25 it becomes effective only on alternate days.

Aug. 25. Presidential pension law goes into effect. This is the first law ever enacted to provide an income for former U.S. Presidents.

Aug. 29. President Eisenhower signs Welfare and Pension Plans Disclosure Act, which requires reporting of management and resources of all except very small labor welfare and pension plans. Since World War II, such funds have become a major source of investment capital, but they have not been regulated to protect either the beneficiaries or the public.

Sept. 2. President Eisenhower signs National Defense Education Act which authorizes low-interest, long-term tuition loans to college and graduate students, with inducements to enter the teaching profession and special encouragements for study of mathematics, languages, and sciences. Aid to educational television is also authorized. Part of startled U.S. response to Soviet space-satellite successes, the Act is based largely on 1957 U.S. Office of Education report on education in the Soviet Union.

Sept. 22. Assistant to the President Sherman Adams resigns because of charges of improper use of official influence. During this year several cases of "conflict of interest" by corporation executives serving in federal government have been disclosed.

Oct. 4. The U.S. and Japan begin negotiations in Tokyo to revise the security treaty of 1951 in order to allow Japan greater power over its arms and military forces. U.S. occupation forces have been withdrawn from Japan in the previous year, but the Japanese (encouraged by the Soviet

Union) are strongly opposed to the 1951 treaty and to occupation of former Japanese islands by the U.S.

Oct. 11. Pioneer moon rocket is launched by the U.S.; it fails to reach the moon but reaches an altitude of more than 79,000 miles, 30 times as high as any earlier man-made object.

Oct. 25. Communist China completes withdrawal of its troops from North Korea. In the following year North Korea is accused of 218 violations of the armistice by the Military Armistice Commission of the UN.

Oct. 26. Pan American World Airways begins transatlantic jet service. **Dec. 10.** Regular commercial jet flights begin within the U.S.

Nov. 4. As a result of dissatisfaction with Republican farm, labor, and foreign affairs policies, Democrats gain seats in both houses of Congress in the fall elections, acquiring 50 more seats in the House and 15 more in the Senate. Senator John F. Kennedy of Massachusetts polls the greatest plurality in the state's history.

Nov. 8. The U.S. signs agreement with the European Atomic Energy Community (Euratom) to cooperate in exchange of atomic materials and information for research.

Nov. 10. Soviet Premier Khrushchev announces that the Soviet Union is planning to turn over East Berlin to the East German government. **Nov. 21.** The U.S., alarmed at the prospect of a blockade of West Berlin by the East Germans, states that it will protect its sector of the city. **Nov. 27.** The Soviet Union proposes that West Berlin become a free, independent city and announces that it will turn over

LYNDON B. JOHNSON
Texas Quarterly, 1958
Texans are independent and individual, but not the monopolists of these virtues that we sometimes suppose ourselves to be. The traits are American in origin and, fortunately for the republic, are deposited quite widely, not part of certain regional hoards. . . .

I realize, as I say this, that others might point to the Senate where I serve — and where I am, in fact, a designated leader of the majority party — and suggest that the example there of a two-party, two-philosophy system contradicts or is in conflict with this thesis. The opposite is so. Had I not been privileged to serve in Congress, I might never have come to hold the respect for individuality of philosophy that I do. . . .

This leads to a listing of the tenets of my own beliefs, the specific tenets of my own philosophy. I would set them down this way:

First, I believe every American has something to say and, under our system, a right to an audience.

Second, I believe there is always a national answer to each national problem, and, believing this, I do not believe that there are necessarily two sides to every question.

Third, I regard achievement of the full potential of our resources — physical, human, and otherwise — to be the highest purpose of governmental policies next to the protection of those rights we regard as inalienable.

Fourth, I regard waste as the continuing enemy of our society and the prevention of waste — waste of resources, waste of lives, or waste of opportunity — to be the most dynamic of the responsibilities of our government.

JOHN KENNETH GALBRAITH
The Affluent Society, 1958

Wealth is not without its advantages and the case to the contrary, although it has often been made, has never proved widely persuasive. But, beyond doubt, wealth is the relentless enemy of understanding. The poor man has always a precise view of his problem and its remedy: he hasn't enough and he needs more. The rich man can assume or imagine a much greater variety of ills and he will be correspondingly less certain of their remedy. Also, until he learns to live with his wealth, he will have a well-observed tendency to put it to the wrong purposes or otherwise to make himself foolish.

As with individuals so with nations. And the experience of nations with well-being is exceedingly brief. Nearly all throughout all history have been very poor. The exception, almost insignificant in the whole span of human existence, has been the last few generations in the comparatively small corner of the world populated by Europeans. Here, and especially in the United States, there has been great and quite unprecedented affluence.

The ideas by which the people of this favored part of the world interpret their existence, and in measure guide their behavior, were not forged in a world of wealth. These ideas were the product of a world in which poverty had always been man's normal lot, and any other state was in degree unimaginable. . . .

No one would wish to argue that the ideas which interpreted this world of grim scarcity would serve equally well for the contemporary United States. Poverty was the all-pervasive fact of that world. Obviously it is not of ours. One would not expect that the preoccupations of a poverty-ridden world would be relevant in one where the

East Berlin to East Germany by the following June.

Nov. 24. UN approves setting up a Committee on the Peaceful Uses of Outer Space in an effort to keep this field clear of political rivalries. A permanent committee is established in the following year, its members being representatives of 5 neutral, 12 Western and pro-Western, and 7 Communist nations.

Nov. 28. The U.S. fires Atlas intercontinental ballistic missile a distance of more than 6,000 miles in Atlantic Ocean testing zone.

Dec. 20. Military-civilian regime that has overthrown Venezuelan dictatorship in January alters tax laws to provide Venezuela with 60, instead of 50, percent of profits of oil companies (including U.S.).

Slowdown of business activity, with unemployment of 4,681,000, continues from last months of the previous year. Rate of national economic growth lags markedly behind growth rate of the Soviet Union.

This year, for the first time, airlines carry more transatlantic passengers than ships do.

John Kenneth Galbraith publishes *The Affluent Society,* arguing that the abundance made possible by modern technology cannot all be used up in private consumption or in investment but must be devoted to expanded public services.

The Solomon R. Guggenheim Museum, designed by Frank Lloyd Wright, is completed; it is the first and only structure of Wright's to be built in New York City. Wright dies in the following year.

U.S. churches report large increases in membership since 1950; those with greatest percentages of gain are the Roman Catholic Church, the Southern Baptist Convention, the Churches of Christ, and the Methodists, which all together total more than 13 million new members.

1958-1959

March 31, 1958. The Soviet Union announces that it is discontinuing nuclear testing independent of Western nations but resumes testing six months later because the U.S. and Great Britain have not stopped doing so. **Oct. 31.** Representatives of the U.S., Great Britain, and the Soviet Union meet in Geneva, Switzerland, to discuss suspension of nuclear tests under international control. **Nov. 1.** UN approves U.S. resolution to suspend nuclear testing during the Geneva negotiations; the Soviet Union votes against it. **Aug. 1959.** When the U.S. announces that it is extending its nuclear test ban, Great Britain and the Soviet Union follow suit; however, everyone resumes testing two years later.

1959

Jan. 3. Alaska, with Juneau as capital, is declared the forty-ninth state of the Union. Its area is 586,400 square miles, making it the largest state, and its population is about 191,000, smallest of any state. First requested in 1916, statehood has not been approved until 1958, partly because private interests, such as canning companies, fear higher taxes and loss of federal subsidies. Addition of forty-ninth state requires change in U.S. flag, which is redesigned with a field of seven rows of seven stars each.

Jan. 19. Virginia state laws aimed at preventing school integration are ruled invalid by the Virginia Supreme Court. Two weeks later, schools in Norfolk and Arlington are desegregated with no disorders.

ordinary individual has access to amenities — foods, entertainment, personal transportation, and plumbing — in which not even the rich rejoiced a century ago. So great has been the change that many of the desires of the individual are no longer even evident to him. They become so only as they are synthesized, elaborated, and nurtured by advertising and salesmanship, and these, in turn, have become among our most important and talented professions. Few people at the beginning of the nineteenth century needed an adman to tell them what they wanted.

It would be wrong to suggest that the economic ideas which once interpreted the world of mass poverty have made no adjustment to the world of affluence. There have been many adjustments, including some that have gone unrecognized or have been poorly understood. But there has also been a remarkable resistance. And the total alteration in underlying circumstances has not been squarely faced. As a result we are guided, in part, by ideas that are relevant to another world; and as a further result we do many things that are unnecessary, some that are unwise, and a few that are insane. We enhance substantially the risk of depression and thereby the threat to our affluence itself.

Time, May 4, 1959

Prime Minister Fidel Castro thumbed through his press clippings one morning last week and danced a little jig in his suite at Manhattan's Statler Hilton Hotel. "You see," he cried, "they are beginning to understand us better." On his two-week U.S. tour, Cuba's gregarious boss drew bales of friendly notices and crushing crowds wherever he showed his beard. "I come to speak to the public opinion," said Castro somewhere in every speech. "I speak the truth.". . .

Castro dropped in unannounced on the Bronx Zoo ("the best thing New York City has"). "I heard there was a riot at the gate," said Zoo Director James Oliver. "I rushed right out and there he was." Castro fed elephants, gorillas and orangutans, ate a hot dog and an ice-cream cone, vaulted a rail, and to the horror of the guards, reached into a cage and patted a Bengal tiger. "They don't do anything," he said. . . .

He told the rally of 20,000 Spanish-speaking New Yorkers that "I came for a suffering, backward and hungry Latin America." His aim: "Humanism — liberty with bread." The crowd took up the chant, "Fi-del Cas-tro! Fi-del Cas-tro!". . .

Moderate Cubans hoped that Castro had learned as well as talked on his U.S. trip. One ranking member of the Castro party declared that "Fidel was astonished at his warm reception. It profoundly changed his thinking about the U.S."

March 30. The Supreme Court holds that separate trials by a state and by the federal government for the same crime do not constitute double jeopardy.

April 5. The U.S. Naval Research Laboratory reports that Soviet nuclear tests made in the fall of 1958 have increased atmospheric radioactivity in the eastern U.S. by 300 percent.

April 7. Twenty-eight-year-old Negro playwright Lorraine V. Hansberry receives New York Drama Critics Circle Award for her play *A Raisin in the Sun*, the story of a Chicago Negro family struggling for a better life. Miss Hansberry dies six years later of cancer.

April 9. Seven astronauts are chosen by National Aeronautics and Space Administration to embark on a training program that will equip each of them to be ready to ride a manned space capsule in 1961.

April 15-28. Fidel Castro, head of revolutionary government in Cuba since defeat of dictator Batista, visits the U.S., where he has much support in spite of wholesale executions of Batista supporters.

May 1. Organization of American States observation group in Panama obtains surrender of small invasion force of revolutionaries, most of whom are Cuban.

May. The U.S. signs agreements with Canada, the Netherlands, Turkey, and West Germany to supply information and equipment needed to train their forces in the use of atomic weapons; agreements are the beginning of move to enable forces of these countries to take part in atomic conflicts if necessary.

July 1. It is announced that the U.S. will resume economic and technical aid to

Egypt, which has joined with Syria as the United Arab Republic (U.A.R.) in the previous year. In December the U.A.R. receives from the International Bank more than $56 million for work on the Suez Canal.

July 15. Nationwide steel strike begins after two-week delay requested by President Eisenhower. **Oct. 21.** When virtually no progress is made in negotiations, U.S. District Court in Pittsburgh, at request of Eisenhower, orders 80-day injunction under the Taft-Hartley Act. **Nov. 7.** Strike ends after Supreme Court decision upholds injunction, which has been held up until now by legal argument; strike has lasted for 116 days, the longest steel strike in U.S. history. Settlement is reached the following January, the steelworkers winning major demands.

Aug. 1. Vice-President Nixon, during a visit to Moscow, tells the Soviet people over television and radio that any attempt by Premier Khrushchev to spread Communism outside the Soviet Union will result in fear and tension for them.

Aug. 21. Hawaii is proclaimed fiftieth state of the Union, after failing since 1903 to attain statehood. Population is about 656,000, half of whom live in the capital, Honolulu, on the island of Oahu. Land area is 6,424 square miles and consists of eight major islands, of which seven are inhabited, and several minor islands. Population is Japanese, Caucasian, Hawaiian, Filipino, and Chinese. Second new U.S. flag within a year is designed, with a field of five six-star rows alternating with four five-star rows, to become official on July 4, 1960.

Aug. 24. Seating of two Hawaiian senators and one representative increases number of U.S. senators to 100 and number of representatives to 437, but after the 1960 census, and becoming effective with the

Time, August 3, 1959

Usually self-confident, Nikita Khrushchev had plainly shown that he was bothered by the challenges of the Nixon visit and the U.S. exhibition. For days the official Soviet press had sniped at the exhibition in a campaign to convince Russians that what they would see would not really be representative of U.S. life. . . .

After a stop at a booth where Khrushchev took a skeptical sip at a Pepsi-Cola, Nixon and Khrushchev went on to the exhibitions most publicized display: a six-room, model ranch house with a central viewing corridor so that visitors can see the shiny new furnishings. Soviet propaganda had been telling Russians in advance that the ranch house they would see at the U.S. exhibition was no more typical of workers' homes in the U.S. than the Taj Mahal was typical in India or Buckingham Palace in Britain.

Nixon made a point of telling Khrushchev that the house was well within the means of U.S. working-class families. The house cost $14,000, Nixon said, and could be paid off over the course of 25 or 30 years. "You know we are having a steel strike," said he, finessing a certain Russian high card. "Well, any steelworker can afford this house." Then the conversation drifted to kitchen equipment and exploded into a cold-war debate that newsmen dubbed the "kitchen conference" and the "Sokolniki summit."

The New Republic, 1959

To be candid about it, traveling with Nikita Khrushchev produces a galling sense of irritation. He is a fascinating figure, compounded of such bizarre contrasts as Mayor Fiorello La Guardia, W. C. Fields, Jimmy Hoffa and—oddly enough—Winston Churchill. He is comical as a clown and tough as nails. The unspoken source of his confidence is the very fact of his being here. Six months ago the administration said, "Put down your gun or we won't play!" Well, the gun is still pointed—and Mr. Khrushchev is here. . . .

Mr. K's proposal to end armaments was as simple as a minister's proposal to end sin. Just end it. Two thirds of his speech at the UN could have been given by Eisenhower. He told of the horrors of war and the joys of turning arms expenses to peaceful pursuits. But Mr. K assigned every virtue to Communists, every vice to the West.

It was a tremendous scene in the great modernistic hall of the UN as he presented his hour-and-a-half speech under spotlights, with spectators all wearing earphones, in a building that rises to a soaring dome and looks like part conservatory, part cathedral, and part wigwam. . . .

A nation which has Eisenhowers gets Khrushchevs. Mr. K gives to this reporter the impression of contemptuous self-confidence. Repeatedly he mentions that the Soviet is turning out three engineers to one in America. He arrived in Washington with the moon in his pocket. Mr. K emphasizes that the Soviet has a sense of mission, of knowing where it is going. Under the tranquilizers of Washington, America lacks what Lippmann calls a sense of national purpose. Perhaps even Khrushchev cannot arouse the country.

1962 elections, the latter number is reduced to the 435 fixed by Congress in 1929.

Sept. 14. President Eisenhower signs Labor-Management Reporting and Disclosure Act, which seeks to control internal administration of labor unions and to protect rights of individual union members against corruption of union officials. Secondary boycott provisions of Taft-Hartley Act are also amended. Passage of the law is in part owing to disclosures before congressional committees of racketeering influences in unions.

Sept. 15-27. Soviet Premier Khrushchev visits the U.S. for informal talks with President Eisenhower and tours the U.S. After he leaves the U.S. is told that among other understandings to relieve world tension, Khrushchev has withdrawn the Soviet ultimatum on Berlin.

Dec. 30. The U.S. commissions first nuclear submarine that is able to carry and launch missiles, the *George Washington*.

During this year the U.S. and the Soviet Union continue to make advances in space exploration. Of three Soviet spacecraft, one goes into orbit around the sun, becoming the first artificial planet; one lands on the moon; and one passes around the moon, sending photographs of the hitherto unseen opposite side. Four U.S. space probes, much smaller, transmit photographs and first television pictures of the earth and information on various aspects of the atmosphere.

1959-1960

June 11, 1959. *Lady Chatterley's Lover* by D. H. Lawrence is banned from the U.S. mails by Postmaster General Arthur E. Summerfield as pornographic, smutty, obscene, and filthy. **March 25, 1960.** U.S.

Court of Appeals rules that novel is not obscene and may be sent through the mails.

Nov. 30, 1959. Citizens of Panama, resentful of any equalities between Canal Zone Americans and native Panamanians, focus on question of flying Panamanian flag in the Canal Zone. Mobs attack U.S. Embassy and try unsuccessfully to invade the area. **Sept. 17, 1960.** It is announced that President Eisenhower has ordered that both flags be flown.

1960

Jan. 23. Lieutenant Don Walsh of the U.S. Navy and Jacques Piccard set new ocean diving record in the bathyscaphe *Trieste* when they descend to a depth of 35,800 feet in the Marianas Trench, near the island of Guam in the Pacific Ocean.

Feb. 2. Four Negro college students who stage sit-in to force desegregation of a lunch counter in Greensboro, North Carolina, set off series of such demonstrations throughout the South; hundreds of Negroes and whites, mostly students, take part. The following year, the first sit-in convictions to reach the Supreme Court are set aside when Court voids conviction of 16 Negroes for breach of peace; however, decision does not outlaw all restaurant segregation, nor does it cover sit-in convictions for trespassing.

April 21. Because of subterfuge practised by Southern states to keep Negroes from registering to vote, Congress passes Civil Rights Act of 1960 in spite of continuous Senate filibuster lasting more than 125 hours. Act allows federal authorities to step in when state registration practices are questionable.

May 5. Just before Paris summit meeting of President Eisenhower and Premier Khrushchev, the Soviet Union announces that a U.S. photographic reconnaissance plane (U-

LOUIS E. LOMAX
Harper's Magazine, 1960
The demonstrators have shifted the desegregation battle from the courtroom to the market place, and have shifted the main issue to one of individual dignity, rather than civil rights. Not that civil rights are unimportant—but, as these students believe, once the dignity of the Negro individual is admitted, the debate over his right to vote, attend public schools, or hold a job for which he is qualified becomes academic. . . .

In March five Southern cities had already yielded to the demands of the demonstrators and were serving Negroes at lunch counters without incident. Eighteen other cities had interracial committees working to resolve the matter. In each case the students have made it plain that they will not accept segregation in any form.

But neither the students nor their real supporters dwelt unduly on such practical results. For them, individually and as a group, the victory came when they mustered the courage to look the segregationists in the face and say, "I'm no longer afraid!"

The genius of the demonstrations lies in their spirituality; in their ability to enlist every Negro, from the laborer to the leader, and inspire him to seek suffering as a badge of honor. By employing such valid symbols as singing, praying, reading Gandhi, quoting Thoreau, remembering Martin Luther King, preaching Christ, but most of all by suffering themselves—being hit by baseball bats, kicked, and sent to jail—the students set off an old-fashioned revival that has made integration an article of faith with the Negro masses who, like other masses, are apathetic toward voting and education.

State Department statement on U-2 incident, May 7, 1960

The Department has received the text of Mr. Khrushchev's further remarks about the unarmed plane which is reported to have been shot down in the Soviet Union. As previously announced, it was known that a U-2 plane was missing. As a result of the inquiry ordered by the President it has been established that insofar as the authorities in Washington are concerned there was no authorization for any such flight as described by Mr. Khrushchev.

Nevertheless it appears that in endeavoring to obtain information now concealed behind the Iron Curtain a flight over Soviet territory was probably undertaken by an unarmed civilian U-2 plane.

DWIGHT D. EISENHOWER

Address to the nation, May 25, 1960

Our first information about the failure of this mission did not disclose whether the pilot was still alive, was trying to escape, was avoiding interrogation, or whether both plane and pilot had been destroyed. Protection of our intelligence system and the pilot, and concealment of the plane's mission, seemed imperative. It must be remembered that over a long period these flights had given us information of the greatest importance to the nation's security. In fact, their success has been nothing short of remarkable.

For these reasons, what is known in intelligence circles as a "covering statement" was issued. It was issued on assumptions that were later proved incorrect. Consequently, when later the status of the pilot was definitely established and there was no further possibility of avoiding exposure of the project, the factual details were set forth.

2) has been shot down over Soviet territory on May 1. **May 7.** Premier Khrushchev announces that the plane's pilot, Francis Gary Powers, is alive and has confessed to having been on a spying mission. **May 9.** U.S. Secretary of State Christian Herter admits such flights have existed for several years in order to gather information to protect the West from surprise attack and asserts that flights will be continued unless the Soviet Union lessens the danger of aggression. **May 11.** Eisenhower admits that he personally has authorized the U-2 flights. **May 16.** At opening of summit conference, Eisenhower announces that U-2 flights have been suspended and are not to be resumed; Khrushchev withdraws invitation to Eisenhower to visit the Soviet Union. **May 17.** Summit conference breaks up amid charges and countercharges between East and West. **Aug. 17-19.** At trial in Moscow, Powers is found guilty of espionage for the U.S. and sentenced to 10 years' loss of liberty, 3 of which are to be spent in prison and the remainder at labor in a restricted area. The following January, Khrushchev says that he will stop making an issue out of the U-2 incident in hopes of bettering relations with Eisenhower's successor. Powers is released and flown back to the U.S. a year later in exchange for the Soviet spy Rudolf Abel.

June 16. President Eisenhower's proposed visit to Japan is canceled because of anti-U.S. riots in that country; riots are directed against new U.S.-Japanese mutual security treaty that provides for possible wartime uses of U.S. bases in Japan and equipping of Japanese forces with atomic weapons. Results of election in autumn in effect indicate approval of Japanese ratification of the treaty in June.

June 27. Disarmament conference with 10 countries represented breaks up with no agreement after long deadlock over international inspection, disarmament procedure, and Soviet demand that the U.S. withdraw from foreign military bases.

June 29. Following strong Cuban criticism of the U.S. and deterioration of relations between the two countries, during which Cuba draws closer to the Soviet Union, the U.S. protests to the Organization of American States that Cuba is causing trouble in the Caribbean. On same day, Cuba seizes U.S.-owned oil refinery. **July 6.** The U.S. cuts, and later suspends entirely, the quota of sugar sold by Cuba to the U.S. **Aug. 7.** Premier Castro announces "forcible expropriation" of all U.S.-owned companies. **Oct. 19.** U.S. blocks shipment to Cuba of all goods except medical supplies and food.

July 1. A second U.S. reconnaissance plane is shot down over Soviet territory. Two survivors are imprisoned but released in the following year.

July 13. Democratic convention at Los Angeles nominates Senator John F. Kennedy of Massachusetts on the first ballot. Senator Lyndon B. Johnson of Texas, who has rivaled Kennedy for the nomination, is chosen for Vice-President the next day. **July 27.** Republicans at Chicago nominate Vice-President Richard M. Nixon of California for President; on following day Henry Cabot Lodge of Massachusetts is chosen as his running mate. Minor party candidates are: Eric Hass, Socialist Labor; Farrell Dobbs, Socialist Workers; Rutherford L. Decker, Prohibition; and Arkansas Governor Orval Faubus, National States' Rights. Democratic platform stresses stronger civil rights legislation and federal medical care for the aged through the Social Security system, as well as denouncing the Eisenhower fiscal policy. Republicans support the Eisenhower foreign policy, a health program, increase in national defense, and a strong civil rights act.

JOHN F. KENNEDY
Speech to Greater Houston Ministerial Association, 1960
Because I am a Catholic, and no Catholic has ever been elected President, the real issues in this campaign have been obscured, perhaps deliberately, in some quarters less responsible than this. So it is apparently necessary for me to state once again, not what kind of church I believe in, for that should be important only to me, but what kind of America I believe in. . . .

For, while this year it may be a Catholic against whom the finger of suspicion is pointed, in other years it has been, and may someday be again, a Jew — or a Quaker — or a Unitarian — or a Baptist. . . . Today I may be the victim, but tomorrow it may be you. . . .

Contrary to common newspaper usage, I am not the Catholic candidate for President. I am the Democratic Party's candidate for President who happens also to be a Catholic. I do not speak for my church on public matters — and the church does not speak for me.

Whatever issue may come before me as President if I should be elected — on birth control, divorce, censorship, gambling, or any other subject — I will make my decision in accordance with these views, in accordance with what my conscience tells me to be in the national interest, and without regard to outside religious pressure or dictates.

And no power or threat of punishment could cause me to decide otherwise.

But if the time should ever come — and I do not concede any conflict to be remotely possible — when my office would require me to either violate my conscience or violate the national interest, then I would resign the office. And I hope any other conscientious public servant would do likewise.

State Department memo to Dag Hammarskjold, 1960
On Sept. 26, 1960, the Prime Minister of Cuba, Mr. Fidel Castro, addressed the General Assembly at considerable length on the relations between the present Cuban regime and the United States. His speech contained many unfounded accusations, half-truths, malicious innuendos and distortions of history—all aimed against the historic friendship between Cuba and the United States, a friendship which he seems anxious to destroy. . . .

When Prime Minister Castro came to power in January, 1959, with promises to his people seemingly made in all sincerity, the United States hoped he would perfect their evolution by needed internal reforms. . . .

The present Government of Cuba has deliberately and consciously sought to exacerbate relations with the United States. For openly announced political reasons Cuba's imports from the United States have been reduced to less than one-half of the level of two years ago. Property is not expropriated, but confiscated without payment, to serve political rather than social ends.

Growing intervention in Cuban affairs by the Soviet Union and Communist China is welcomed by the Government of Cuba. The present Cuban Government seeks to intervene in internal affairs of other American states and to undermine the inter-American system.

The present Cuban Government claims to speak for the Cuban people but denies them the right to choose their own spokesmen in free elections. It claims to believe in democracy, yet only the Communist party is permitted to function. It speaks of the rights of man, but Cuban jails are crowded with thousands of political prisoners.

July 20. First successful underwater launching of Polaris missiles is accomplished when they are fired from a submerged atomic submarine at targets more than 1,100 miles away.

Sept. 13. President Eisenhower signs Social Security amendments, which grant federal aid to states for medical programs for the needy aged and eventually for other needy persons; but they do not form the all-inclusive plan urged by many at this time.

Sept. 20-Dec. 21. Attended at various times by many heads of state, including Eisenhower, Khrushchev, Castro, Nasser, Macmillan, Nehru, and Tito, the opening of the fifteenth session of the UN General Assembly in New York City is probably the greatest diplomatic gathering in history. Khrushchev uses the forum to denounce Eisenhower's policies but leaves opening for a conference with a new President.

Sept. 26. In the first of four television debates Vice-President Nixon and Senator Kennedy exchange views on domestic policy. This and the subsequent debates bring contrasting personalities of the candidates before the electorate more immediately than in any previous election. To permit the debates, Congress suspends a Federal Communications Commission rule requiring that all candidates be allowed equal broadcast time.

Oct. 26. In response to Cuban government threats against U.S. military occupation of naval base at Guantánamo, Cuba (agreed to in treaty of 1903), it is announced that if necessary the U.S. will defend the base by force of arms.

Nov. 3. Dr. Willard Frank Libby of the University of California (formerly of the University of Chicago) wins Nobel Prize for Chemistry for technique of dating geological and archeological material by measuring disintegration of its radioactive carbon 14 content.

Nov. 8. Senator Kennedy wins election, in which a record number of citizens vote, taking 50.1 percent of the major party vote. Popular vote is Kennedy, 34,227,000; Nixon, 34,108,000. Electoral vote is in question for a time because of recounts demanded by some states and votes of unpledged electors from Mississippi; final electoral vote (not official until January 1961) is Kennedy, 303, with 23 states; Nixon, 219, with 26 states; and 15 electoral votes going to Senator Harry F. Byrd of Virginia. Both houses of Congress remain under Democratic control.

Nov. 8. It is announced that the U.S. will relinquish most bases in the British West Indies leased for 99 years during World War II in exchange for U.S. destroyers sent to Britain.

Nov. 14. Two elementary schools in New Orleans begin school desegregation in the Deep South amid riots and extensive absences among white children.

Nov. 16. Concerned about U.S. balance of payments deficit and drain of gold from the country, President Eisenhower orders all U.S. agencies to limit spending in foreign countries.

Nov. 17. Because of increase of tension in the Caribbean and major buildup of Cuban armed forces, it is revealed that President Eisenhower has sent U.S. naval units to the Caribbean with orders to prevent possible Cuban Communist attacks on Nicaragua and Guatemala.

Dec. 2. President Eisenhower announces appropriation of $1 million for care of those

WILLIAM D. WORKMAN, JR.
The Case of the South, 1960
Much of the legislation enacted in the Southern states in both the immediate and the distant past has been aimed basically at preserving domestic tranquillity as well as racial integrity. This is especially true in the fields of education and recreation, where indiscriminate mingling of the races is bound to bring discord and strife. Whatever the future may bring, and whatever may be the judgment of non-Southerners, the governmental agencies of the South are acting wisely when they seek to prevent mass mingling of the races in schools, pools, and parks. And distressing though it may be, the closing of such institutions in many cases would be the sensible alternative to the emotional, social, and physical upheaval which would follow on the heels of forced race mixing. . . .

If an area of biracial activity can be carved out of the no-man's-land which now separates the two races by law in most Southern communities, there seems no cause for undue alarm. If the South is to protect the right of some (most) white people to move within segregated circles, then in all fairness it should permit other white people to move within integrated circles if that be their wish. For many years to come, the impetus of such movement will have to be from the whites to the Negroes, but the Southern argument against compulsory integration should apply with equal validity against compulsory segregation of those inclined, however mistakenly, toward racial commingling, so long as the rights of all are protected with respect to preference of association.

Children of an unemployed coal miner from Appalachia who came to Chicago to search for work

The American City; report of Committee for Economic Development, 1960

Within the span of a century America has gone through two great changes in its living patterns. In the last quarter of the nineteenth century and the first quarter of the twentieth century we shifted from a predominantly rural to urban society.

The second change in American life during the twentieth century is from a basically urban to metropolitan condition. Prior to the metropolitan era, cities were centers of industrial and commercial activity. . . . There was little question where the city ended and the country began. Outside of city boundaries there were no large population concentrations, and government structure outside these boundaries was designed for a basically rural condition.

The metropolitan area is in effect a new community. Its boundaries often are hard to define. In some instances they change and expand frequently. The area ignores old geographic boundaries, jumping over and around rivers and

emigrating to the U.S. to escape Fidel Castro's regime in Cuba.

Dec. 15. The U.S. announces its support of rightist rebels in Laos one day before they gain control from pro-Communist coalition government. Ten days earlier, coalition government has demanded that the U.S. stop sending arms to the rebels and has agreed to a cease-fire. **Dec. 30.** New rightist government appeals to the UN, citing reported troop movements from North Vietnam. On the following day, the U.S. warns North Vietnam and Communist China to refrain from military action in Laos.

1960 census shows a U.S. population of 179,323,000 of which nearly 70 percent live in places of 2,500 or more. Immigration since the previous census has been 2,515,000. Shifts in population make it necessary to change the number of seats in the House of Representatives for 25 states; trend is mainly westward, with California gaining eight seats since 1950.

The U.S. achieves three firsts in space exploration in this year: Discoverer 13 is first capsule recovered from orbit; Discoverer 14 is first to be recovered in mid-air (at 8,500 feet); and Tiros 1 is first weather satellite, sending back to earth about 23,000 television pictures of global cloud cover. The Soviet Union succeeds in a controlled landing of animals (insects, mice, and dogs) in Sputnik 5.

The U.S. automobile industry begins shift to compact economy cars to meet falling sales and increased imports of foreign economy and sports models.

First report on a working laser is published; the laser is a nondiffusing intensified light beam that can be focused on a fine point. Its development opens new possibilities in communications, surgery, range finding, and welding.

Edmund Wilson publishes his *Apologies to the Iroquois*, which is concerned especially with injustices suffered by the people of the Iroquois Six Nations at the hands of the U.S.

land masses. It ignores the political lines of districts, villages, towns, cities, counties, and states.

The metropolitan area reflects a new kind of society resulting from higher average incomes, the development of new tastes in living standards, and technological means for releasing people from the old patterns. . . .

These tendencies have increased rather than decreased the problems of government. As our population grows and our technology advances, the decisions about the use of land and of public revenue become increasingly complex. The governmental machinery to make these decisions and the governmental influences on private market decisions have not kept pace with this complexity. As a result, we are faced with increasing traffic congestion, blight in our central cities, unequal public burdens of suburban expansion, duplication of public facilities, and an inefficient use of public and private resources.

Wyoming sheep farmer and his family at supper

DWIGHT D. EISENHOWER
Farewell Address, 1961

This conjunction of an immense military establishment and a large arms industry is new in the American experience. The total influence—economic, political, even spiritual—is felt in every city, every statehouse, every office of the federal government. We recognize the imperative need for this development. Yet we must not fail to comprehend its grave implications. Our toil, resources, and livelihood are all involved; so is the very structure of our society.

In the councils of government we must guard against the acquisition of unwarranted influence, whether sought or unsought, by the military-industrial complex. The potential for the disastrous rise of misplaced power exists and will persist.

JOHN F. KENNEDY
Inaugural Address, 1961

I have sworn before you and Almighty God the same solemn oath our forebears prescribed nearly a century and three-quarters ago.

The world is very different now. For man holds in his mortal hands the power to abolish all forms of human poverty and all forms of human life. And yet the same revolutionary beliefs for which

1961

Jan. 3. The U.S. breaks off diplomatic relations with Cuba after Cuba accuses the government of planning an invasion and demands that personnel of U.S. embassy be reduced to 11 members. **April 3.** The U.S. urges Cuba to give up communism, calling the country a "Soviet satellite."

Jan. 19. Federal Communications Commission authorizes first communications satellite with a solar-powered receiver and transmitter; it is to be developed and owned by American Telephone and Telegraph Company and Bell Laboratories. Authorization follows heated debate in Congress over use by private industry of fruits of government research. Telstar is launched from Cape Canaveral in July 1962 and transmits television broadcasts from the U.S. to Europe.

Jan. 20. President Kennedy is inaugurated. His eloquent address, which calls for vigorous action on domestic issues, an international alliance to combat the world's problems, the "success of liberty," and negotiation to ease international tensions, evokes widespread enthusiasm and optimism.

Jan. 30. President Kennedy says in his first State of the Union message that U.S.

Toast to peace at the Belgrade Conference, 1961: Center figures are Sihanouk, Cambodia; Nasser, U.A.R.; Selassie, Ethiopia; Tito, Yugoslavia; Sukarno, Indonesia; Nehru, India

educational institutions are inadequate, and that 2 million more children than can be properly accommodated are being taught by 90,000 improperly qualified teachers. Congress makes no move in this year or the next to provide aid to schools.

Jan. 31. In a close vote, liberal Democrats in the U.S. House of Representatives force increase of membership of House Rules Committee from 12 to 15. Result is to break Republican and conservative Southern Democrat control, which has held up civil rights and other legislation.

January. Federal court finds 29 electric companies guilty of conspiracy to fix prices. In April, companies and their executives are fined $2 million, and some executives are sentenced to prison.

Feb. 15. President Kennedy says that the U.S. will uphold the UN charter by opposing any intervention by a single country in affairs of the Congo, now independent but in a state of civil war since the end of Belgian control in June 1960. **Feb. 21.** The UN Security Council authorizes international police action to terminate civil war.

March 1. President Kennedy establishes Peace Corps for service abroad by American volunteers, who will aid general education, technical instruction, and social develop-

our forebears fought are still at issue around the globe — the belief that the rights of man come not from the generosity of the state but from the hand of God.

We dare not forget today that we are the heirs of that first revolution. Let the word go forth from this time and place, to friend and foe alike, that the torch has been passed to a new generation of Americans — born in this century, tempered by war, disciplined by a hard and bitter peace, proud of our ancient heritage — and unwilling to witness or permit the slow undoing of those human rights to which this nation has always been committed, and to which we are committed today at home and around the world.

Let every nation know, whether it wishes us well or ill, that we shall pay any price, bear any burden, meet any hardship, support any friend, oppose any foe to assure the survival and the success of liberty. . . .

And so, my fellow Americans — ask not what your country can do for you — ask what you can do for your country.

My fellow citizens of the world — ask not what America will do for you but what together we can do for the freedom of man.

Principles of John Birch Society, 1962
*We believe that the Communists seek to
drive their slaves and themselves along
exactly the opposite and downward
direction, to the Satanic debasement of
both man and his universe. We believe
that communism is as utterly incompatible with all religion as it is contemptuous of all morality and destructive of
all freedom. It. is intrinsically evil. It
must be opposed, therefore, with equal
firmness, on religious grounds, moral
grounds, and political grounds. We believe that the continued coexistence of
communism and a Christian-style civilization on one planet is impossible. The
struggle between them must end with
one completely triumphant and the
other completely destroyed. We intend
to do our part, therefore, to halt, weak-
en, rout, and eventually to bury, the
whole international Communist conspiracy.*

*One of our most immediate objec-
tives . . . is to get the United States out
of the United Nations, and the United
Nations out of the United States. We
seek thus to save our own country from
the gradual and piecemeal surrender of
its sovereignty to this Communist-con-
trolled supergovernment, and to stop
giving our support to the steady enslavement of other people through the machinations of this Communist agency.*

*We believe that a constitutional re-
public, such as our founding fathers
gave us, is probably the best of all forms
of government. We believe that a democracy, which they tried hard to obviate, and into which the liberals have
been trying for fifty years to convert our
republic, is one of the worst of all forms
of government.*

ment in underdeveloped countries on all
continents. At first temporary, the Peace
Corps is approved by Congress on September 21 and allotted an initial appropriation
of $30 million.

March 8. The U.S. Senate becomes concerned over spread of the John Birch Society after many leading figures, including
former Presidents Roosevelt, Truman, and
Eisenhower, are accused of being "Com-
symps" (Communists or sympathizers). The
society is semisecret, has been organized by
Robert H. W. Welch, Jr. in 1958, and is an
extreme right-wing organization dedicated
to fighting communism, which it claims is
more of a danger to the U.S. from within
than from without the country.

March 13. President Kennedy proposes
the Alliance for Progress, involving wide
U.S. support for joint social and economic
development efforts in the Western Hemisphere. **Aug. 17.** Latin-American nations
rally to this program in conference at Punta
del Este, Uruguay.

March 29. The Twenty-third Amendment to the U.S. Constitution is ratified; it
for the first time allows residents of the
District of Columbia to vote in presidential
elections.

April 12. The Soviet Union announces
that it has put the world's first space man
in orbit — Yuri Gagarin, who makes one
orbit of the earth and lands his spacecraft
safely. **May 5 and July 21.** First U.S.
spacemen, Alan B. Shepard, Jr., and Virgil
Grissom, are launched from Cape Canaveral
in suborbital flights that reach an altitude of
more than 116 miles; both are recovered
safely. **Aug. 6.** The Soviet Union sends up
another manned spacecraft, which orbits the
earth 17 times; the pilot lands the next day
by parachute, with no ill effects, although
he has been "seasick" during the 25-hour
flight.

April 17. Cuban rebels, trained by the U.S. and using U.S. equipment (though not manpower), attempt an invasion of Cuba; they meet disaster in three-day battle at Bay of Pigs. The U.S. role in the abortive invasion is an international embarrassment; defeat of the attack, which has been planned to coincide with a popular uprising against Fidel Castro, only enhances Castro's prestige. **April 24.** President Kennedy accepts full responsibility for the invasion. Cuba indicates that 1,200 rebel prisoners can be ransomed by the U.S.

April 26. Congress passes depressed areas bill, which establishes program of federal aid to areas of permanent unemployment or exhausted resources; appropriation is almost $400 million.

May 5. President Kennedy signs legislation that increases minimum wages from $1 to $1.15 per hour for two years and then to $1.25 per hour; bill includes categories that add more than 3,600,000 workers to those covered up to this time.

May 9. Newton N. Minow, chairman of Federal Communications Commission, attacks the content of television broadcasts, calling television a "vast wasteland." He demands an increase of educational and public service programs, decrying excess of violence.

May 14. Mobs in Anniston and Birmingham, Alabama, attack busloads of "Freedom Riders," interracial groups riding southward to force integration in interstate transportation facilities; groups are backed by the Congress of Racial Equality (CORE). Several riders are severely beaten and one bus is set on fire. Picketing, boycotts, and sit-ins continue in the South, although desegregation of schools proceeds more peacefully than in previous years. In the North, protests are made against *de facto* segregation in schools, and growing bitterness among Ne-

STUART H. LOORY
New York Herald Tribune, 1961
A wild mob of men and women, uncontrolled by police, pounced on newsmen and then on a group of nineteen Negro and white students . . . at the Greyhound bus terminal here after a ride from Birmingham to test segregated intrastate bus practices. . . .

The mob had first pummeled three National Broadcasting Co. newsmen and several other photographers, smashing their equipment. Then it turned to vent its unsatisfied fury on the band of students who stood quietly on the bus platform, apparently not knowing what to do after completing the ride from Birmingham.

Using metal pipes, baseball bats, sticks and fists, the mob surged on the small group of Freedom Riders, clubbing, punching, chasing and beating both whites and Negroes. When some of the bus riders began to run, the mob went after them, caught them and threw them to the ground. The attackers stomped on at least two of them. One of the mobsters carried an open knife but didn't use it.

In two hours it was over, after the police used tear gas. The toll was twenty-two injured with five of them in the hospital. . . .

One woman was among the nine persons arrested—all of them white. Some were booked on charges of disorderly conduct and refusing to obey an officer. Two were held on drunk charges.

(Above left) John F. Kennedy, thirty-fifth President of the United
States, photographed in Seattle, September 1960; (above left) Dean
Rusk, appointed secretary of state by Kennedy; (below) Ambassador
Adlai E. Stevenson, photographed at the United Nations during the
Bay of Pigs incident, 1961

(Above) West Berlin woman
attempts to ask favor of
an East German soldier
patrolling the wall: (right)
cartoonist's view of the
1961 Vienna meeting between
John F. Kennedy and Nikita
Khrushchev

JOHN F. KENNEDY
Address, July 1961

Seven weeks ago tonight I returned from Europe to report on my meeting with Premier Khrushchev and the others. His grim warnings about the future of the world, his aide-memoire on Berlin, his subsequent speeches and threats which he and his agents have launched, and the increase in the Soviet military budget that he has announced have all prompted a series of decisions by the administration and a series of consultations with the members of the NATO organization. In Berlin, as you recall, he intends to bring to an end, through a stroke of the pen, first, our legal rights to be in West Berlin and, secondly, our ability to make good on our commitment to the two million free people of that city. That we cannot permit. . . .

But that isolated outpost is not an isolated problem. The threat is worldwide. Our effort must be equally wide and strong and not be obsessed by any single manufactured crisis. We face a challenge in Berlin, but there is also a challenge in southeast Asia, where the borders are less guarded, the enemy harder to find, and the danger of communism less apparent to those who have so little. We face a challenge in our own hemisphere and indeed wherever else the freedom of human beings is at stake. . . .

Today the endangered frontier of freedom runs through divided Berlin. We want it to remain a frontier of peace. . . . I cannot believe that the Russian people, who bravely suffered enormous losses in the Second World War, would now wish to see the peace upset once more in Germany. The Soviet Government alone can convert Berlin's frontier of peace into a pretext for war.

groes results in growth of such organizations as Black Muslims, who advocate separation of the races.

May 17. The U.S. proposes a revised international neutrality program for Laos at Geneva Conference; efforts to guarantee neutrality have begun in 1954 and have been suspended during Laotian political crisis and Communist uprising of 1958.

June 4. In Vienna, President Kennedy concludes unsatisfactory meetings with Premier Khrushchev on Berlin, Laos, and disarmament; Khrushchev insists that the Soviet Union will sign a separate peace treaty with East Germany.

June 21. The world's first large-scale plant for desalinating sea water goes into operation at Freeport, Texas; capacity is 1 million gallons daily.

July 25. President Kennedy asks Congress for a $3,500,000,000 increase in defense funds to meet the increasing threat to peace in Europe and the East by the Soviet Union. Appropriation is quickly approved by Congress. **July 31.** Congress authorizes the President to call 250,000 reservists to active duty for up to one year and to increase length of duty of regular forces. Authorization is extended in 1962.

Aug. 2. President Kennedy assures Nationalist China that the U.S. will oppose Communist Chinese membership in the UN and will back Nationalist China's right to membership.

Aug. 13. The Soviet Union and East Germany begin construction of the Berlin Wall, sealing off East Berlin and East Germany from free access to the West as guaranteed by Four-Power agreements on the status of Germany. The U.S., Britain, and France make joint protest on August 15, but by August 18 wall is completed, with only six crossing points, all heavily guarded. Barrier almost completely stops exodus from East to West, estimated by Western authorities as 2,700,000 persons since 1949.

Sept. 5. President Kennedy orders resumption of limited nuclear testing (with no fallout) following renewed atmospheric tests by the Soviet Union four days earlier. **Oct. 23 and 30.** In spite of appeal by the UN, the Soviet Union tests bombs of about 30 and 50 megatons. **November.** Kennedy announces that the U.S. may have to resume atmospheric testing in 1962.

Jane Jacobs publishes *The Death and Life of American Cities*, in which she attacks large-scale urban renewal programs and argues for maintenance of traditional neighborhoods.

Henry Miller publishes *Tropic of Cancer*, widely known since its 1934 publication in Paris, but barred from the U.S. until this time by censors, who have branded it "obscene."

1961 - 1964

Sept. 6, 1961. National Wilderness Preservation System, which would set aside permanently 9.1 million acres of forest as public lands, is approved by the Senate but shelved in the House because of opposition by mining and other commercial interests. It is not passed until September 1964.

1961 - 1965

Feb. 1, 1961. First U.S. intercontinental ballistic missile (ICBM) is fired, traveling 4,200 miles. Minuteman 1 defense program

JANE JACOBS
The Death and Life of Great American Cities, 1961
There is a wistful myth that if only we had enough money to spend — the figure is usually put at a hundred billion dollars — we could wipe out all our slums in ten years, reverse decay in the great, dull, gray belts that were yesterday's and day-before-yesterday's suburbs, anchor the wandering middle class and its wandering tax money, and perhaps even solve the traffic problem.

But look what we have built with the first several billions: Low-income projects that become worse centers of delinquency, vandalism and general social hopelessness than the slums they were supposed to replace. Middle-income housing projects which are truly marvels of dullness and regimentation, sealed against any buoyancy or vitality of city life. Luxury housing projects that mitigate their inanity, or try to, with a vapid vulgarity. Cultural centers that are unable to support a good bookstore. Civic centers that are avoided by everyone but bums, who have fewer choices of loitering place than others. Commercial centers that are lackluster imitations of standardized suburban chain-store shopping. Promenades that go from no place to nowhere and have no promenaders. Expressways that eviscerate great cities. This is not the rebuilding of cities. This is the sacking of cities.

JEROME B. WIESNER

Address to National Academy of Sciences, 1963

Science has contributed steadily to the development of the nation, and, at every step, the needs of the federal government and federal funds have been a major incentive in its achievements. At some point in every historical period, the question of the role of the federal government in science and the search for the proper form of science organization within the federal establishment have been a burning issue. Though the research efforts involved may appear minuscule by our standards, they were as important to their times as our much bigger programs are to ours. . . .

There is obviously no simple, or even single, answer to the question of how to make the best use of our available resources. Public support of science has, until now, largely been exempted from this debate because funds for it were a small part of the very large sums of money provided to insure military security. The only substantial sums provided for any other purpose in recent times were those related to health needs. The existence of unfulfilled social and economic needs, coupled with a significant fact — the leveling off of research and development in relation to gross national product — suggest that the country faces an era of reevaluation. This process of leveling off is the reason for many of the current questions. It indicates that confusions which were of no consequence ten years ago must be gotten straight today. To the extent that federally supported research and development is justified for social purposes other than national security, it will be judged by different standards, less well-defined, and more controversial as well.

begins to function in December 1962 and is completed in June 1965, when the U.S. has 800 such missiles, capable of traveling 6,300 miles at 15,000 miles per hour. Individual underground launch sites are established in five areas in the western U.S.

1962

Jan. 4. President Kennedy announces program of increased economic aid to South Vietnam. **Feb. 8.** South Vietnam Military Assistance Command (MAC) is established by the U.S. Defense Department. A week later, President Kennedy announces that U.S. training troops (advisers) in Vietnam have orders to fire if fired upon but that they are not actually combat troops.

Jan. 15. In effort to ease tension over Berlin, the U.S. removes its tanks from duty at the Berlin Wall. Two days later, Soviet tanks are also removed. It is estimated that by October 13,000 East Germans have escaped to the West in spite of shoot-to-kill policy of Eastern regime; in addition, 52,000 East Germans who visit the West legally do not return home.

Jan. 29. After more than three years of negotiations to suspend nuclear tests under international control, the Geneva (Switzerland) talks end in failure.

Feb. 14. The Organization of American States excludes Cuba from participating in its activities because of Communist form of government; Cuba remains a member, however. Decision is approved by only 14 of 21 states, since the OAS charter does not provide for suspension of a state for any reason.

Feb. 20. John H. Glenn, Jr., first U.S. astronaut to achieve orbit, circles the earth three times. **May 24.** M. Scott Carpenter makes three-orbit space flight, and in October, Walter M. Schirra, Jr., completes six orbits. During this year, two Soviet astronauts complete flights in which they are both in space at the same time and come within about three miles of each other during their 64- and 48-orbit trips.

March 27. Archbishop Joseph Francis Rummel orders all Catholic schools in New Orleans diocese to integrate their students. In April, he excommunicates three persons who have tried to organize opposition to desegregation. **Oct. 1.** Protected by federal officers, Negro Air Force veteran James Meredith begins classes at the University of Mississippi after he has been personally forbidden access to the campus by Mississippi Governor Ross R. Barnett. Riots on the previous day have resulted in two deaths and hundreds of injuries and have required 3,000 troops to quell.

April 10. In spite of recently written union-management contract that has sought to head off steel price rises, United States Steel Corporation and five other companies raise prices. President Kennedy, stating that they defy the public interest, uses strong official measures that result in rescinding of price rise, especially after Inland Steel has announced on April 13 that it will not raise its prices.

April 24. President Kennedy authorizes renewed atmospheric testing of nuclear weapons. **Nov. 4.** Kennedy announces that present series of atmospheric tests is finished, but that underground testing will continue.

Aug. 22. President Kennedy confirms reports that Soviet supplies and technicians are pouring into Cuba, but for two months the U.S. believes that activity is wholly for Cuban defense. **Oct. 22.** Kennedy announces that the Soviet Union has been building missile and bomber bases in Cuba

JAMES H. MEREDITH
Saturday Evening Post, 1962
Through all that has happened I have tried to remain detached and objective. I have had all sorts of reactions to things that have happened, but mostly they have been personal reactions and realistic reactions, both at the same time. When I was in the middle of the force of marshals being gathered to take me to Oxford I thought, personally, how utterly ridiculous this was, what a terrible waste of time and money and energy, to iron out some rough spots in our civilization. But realistically I knew that these changes were necessary. I knew change was a threat to people and that they would fight it and that this was the only way it could be accomplished. . . .

When I hear the jeers and the catcalls—"We'll get you, nigger" and all that—I don't consider it personal. I get the idea people are just having a little fun. I think it's tragic that they have to have this kind of fun about me, but many of them are children of the men who lead Mississippi today, and I wouldn't expect them to act any other way. . . .

It hasn't been all bad. Many students have spoken to me very pleasantly. They have stopped banging doors and throwing bottles into my dormitory now.

One day a fellow from my home town sat down at my table in the cafeteria. "If you're here to get an education, I'm for you," he said. "If you're here to cause trouble, I'm against you." That seemed fair enough to me.

JOHN F. KENNEDY

Address to the nation, 1962

This government, as promised, has maintained the closest surveillance of the Soviet military buildup on the island of Cuba. Within the past week unmistakable evidence has established the fact that a series of offensive missile sites is now in preparation on that imprisoned island. The purpose of these bases can be none other than to provide a nuclear strike capability against the Western Hemisphere. . . .

Acting, therefore, in the defense of our own security and of the entire Western Hemisphere, and under the authority entrusted to me by the Constitution as endorsed by the resolution of the Congress, I have directed that the following initial *steps be taken immediately:*

First, to halt this offensive buildup, a strict quarantine on all offensive military equipment under shipment to Cuba is being initiated. All ships of any kind bound for Cuba from whatever nation or port will, if found to contain cargoes of offensive weapons, be turned back. This quarantine will be extended, if needed, to other types of cargo and carriers. . . .

Second, I have directed the continued and increased close surveillance of Cuba and its military buildup. . . . I have directed the Armed Forces to prepare for any eventualities; and I trust that, in the interest of both the Cuban people and the Soviet technicians at the sites, the hazards to all concerned of continuing this threat will be recognized.

Third, it shall be the policy of this nation to regard any nuclear missile launched from Cuba against any nation in the Western Hemisphere as an attack by the Soviet Union on the United States, requiring a full retaliatory response upon the Soviet Union.

and that the U.S. will quarantine the island as of October 24 to prevent shipment of offensive weapons. He threatens "further action" unless offensive weapons are removed. **Oct. 25.** UN Ambassador Adlai E. Stevenson exhibits aerial photographs of Cuba missile bases. **Oct. 27.** Kennedy refuses Premier Khrushchev's offer to remove weapons if the U.S. removes its weapons from Turkey. The following day, Khrushchev agrees to dismantle bases and return missiles to the U.S.S.R. under UN inspection on condition that the U.S. agrees not to invade Cuba. **Oct. 30.** UN Secretary-General U Thant flies to Cuba to confer with Prime Minister Castro on international inspection of dismantling, but Castro will not allow it. **Nov. 2.** Kennedy announces that bases are being dismantled, saying that the U.S. will continue surveillance by air and sea until UN observation can be arranged. **Nov. 20.** Kennedy announces that blockade of Cuba has been lifted; all missiles have been embarked, and Premier Khrushchev has agreed to remove, within 30 days, 42 U.S.S.R. bombers capable of carrying nuclear warheads. In January 1963 Secretary U Thant receives Soviet-U.S. note stating that missile crisis has ended.

Oct. 4. In move to increase world markets for U.S. goods, Congress passes Trade Expansion Act, which gives the President more authority than ever before to reduce tariffs; it also allows him to provide aid to companies and individuals who are adversely affected by lowered duties.

Oct. 4. Congress passes stricter drug bill to control release of new drugs. Action follows European epidemic of births of deformed infants, traced to use of sedative thalidomide. U.S. Food and Drug Administration physician Frances O. Kelsey is hailed for her firmness in withholding drug from the U.S. market under considerable pressure from manufacturers on grounds that its safety has not been proved. Trials of thalidomide producers and sellers do not begin until 1968.

Oct. 23. Stamp collectors rush to buy commemorative stamp issued in honor of late UN Secretary-General Dag Hammarskjöld when printing error is discovered. To avoid speculation in rarities, U.S. postmaster general orders printing of 10 million defective stamps, but, as only one printed unintentionally, the Post Office Department authenticates 50-stamp pane of collector who first observed error.

Nov. 6. In fall elections, Democrats lose a few seats in the House but gain four in the Senate, retaining control of both houses. Negro candidates gain in both parties.

Nov. 20. President Kennedy bans racial and religious restrictions in all housing purchased or constructed through federal loan and insurance programs.

Dec. 14. U.S. space probe Mariner 2 transmits world's first "close-up" information about planet Venus and its atmosphere after 109-day, 180-million-mile flight. Probe's course has been altered on eighth day of journey when it is calculated that it will pass Venus at a distance of 233,000 miles; change brings it within 21,600 miles.

Dec. 23. Cuba begins releasing prisoners captured in the Bay of Pigs invasion. A private committee has raised $50 million with which to provide medicines, food, and cash in exchange for the prisoners. Sixty ill prisoners have been ransomed earlier in the year.

During this year, President Kennedy has made almost 300 requests for legislation, and Congress has approved only 44 percent of them. Especially neglected are medical care for the aged under Social Security, aid

J. N. JAMES
Scientific American, 1963
The voyage of Mariner II was a technological feat of the first magnitude. The craft had in effect been launched three times: first from the surface of the earth, then from a "parking" orbit of the earth and finally from an orbit of the sun, nine days and 1.5 million miles from the earth, where it was put through a maneuver to place it in a new solar orbit. Throughout most of the flight it maintained a rigid orientation in space with respect to the sun and also with respect to the earth. It even recovered its proper orientation after being struck by an object in space. . . .

Scientific instruments accounted for less than 10 per cent of the total weight of the craft. All across the void between the two planets, however, they produced unprecedented quantities of data about the magnetic fields of the solar system, cosmic rays and the solar wind—the streams of protons and electrons that issue from the sun. At the rendezvous with Venus the instruments observed the planet with a resolution impossible at this time from the earth. . . .

After making its nearest approach to Venus at 32 seconds before noon Pacific Standard Time on December 14, Mariner II continued in its now eternal orbit around the sun. . . . On the 129th day, January 2, 1963, [it] ceased to transmit information to the earth. It gave no clue as to why it stopped sending. . . . Scientists and engineers will spend years studying the 11 million measurements it sent back, all now recorded on magnetic tapes and stored in vaults.

RACHEL CARSON
Silent Spring, 1962
There was once a town in the heart of America where all life seemed to live in harmony with its surroundings. The town lay in the midst of a checkerboard of prosperous farms, with fields of grain and hillsides of orchards where, in spring, white clouds of bloom drifted above the green fields. In autumn, oak and maple and birch set up a blaze of color that flamed and flickered across a backdrop of pines. Then foxes barked in the hills and deer silently crossed the fields, half hidden in the mists of the fall mornings . . . .

Then a strange blight crept over the area and everything began to change. Some evil spell had settled on the community: mysterious maladies swept the flocks of chickens; the cattle and sheep sickened and died. Everywhere was a shadow of death. The farmers spoke of much illness among their families. In the town the doctors had become more and more puzzled by new kinds of sickness appearing among their patients. There had been several sudden and unexplained deaths, not only among adults but even among children, who would be stricken suddenly while at play and die within a few hours.

There was a strange stillness. The birds, for example—where had they gone? Many people spoke of them, puzzled and disturbed. The feeding stations in the backyards were deserted. The few birds seen anywhere were moribund; they trembled violently and could not fly. It was a spring without voices. . . .

No witchcraft, no enemy action had silenced the rebirth of new life in this stricken world. The people had done it themselves.

to education, welfare programs, and help to cities; foreign aid has been cut by 20 percent.

In her best-selling book *Silent Spring*, Rachel Carson presents the argument that use of pesticides is seriously upsetting the balance of nature and could eventually make the world uninhabitable. Book excites great public interest, although some scientists call it one-sided. In 1963 a federal advisory committee issues cautions on the use of pesticides.

John Steinbeck is awarded the Nobel Prize for Literature, primarily for his novel *The Winter of Our Discontent*, published in 1961. In this year, he publishes *Travels with Charley: In Search of America*.

1962 - 1963

June 25, 1962. The Supreme Court rules that reciting of official school prayer written by state officials of New York is unconstitutional, saying that it is not the business of government to compose prayers or to carry on religious programs. Although this decision covers only the official prayer, the Court holds in 1963 that requirement of any prayer, as well as Bible reading, is unconstitutional.

1962 - 1964

March 26, 1962. In *Baker* v. *Carr,* the Supreme Court holds that apportionment of seats in state legislatures may be reviewed by the federal courts. Decision results in many similar suits; by 1964, 39 states have become involved in reapportionment litigation.

1962 - 1968

Sept. 23, 1962. New York City's cultural complex, Lincoln Center for the Performing

Arts, is inaugurated with a concert at Philharmonic Hall, the first of seven buildings to be completed. Last of organizations to be opened is the Juilliard School of Music, in 1968. Fourteen-acre complex is to cost about $160 million, most of which has been contributed privately.

1963

Jan. 28. South Carolina, the last state to hold out against school integration, finally bows to federal law and opens colleges to Negroes; the first Negro enrollment is at Clemson College.

Feb. 21. President Kennedy submits his plan for hospital and medical care of the aged as part of the Social Security System to Congress; it is not passed until 1965, under the name Medicare.

March 18. The Supreme Court rules that defendants must have counsel in all criminal cases, and that it must be provided by the state if necessary. The Court also finds that illegally acquired evidence is inadmissable in state, as well as in federal courts.

March 20. First large "Pop art" exhibition opens at the Solomon R. Guggenheim Museum in New York City; such artists as Andy Warhol, Robert Rauschenberg, and Jasper Johns exhibit works representing (and sometimes actually made of) such ordinary objects as soup cans, advertisements, and comic strips.

April 3. Civil rights demonstrations begin in Birmingham, Alabama; over a five-week period, they swell in intensity as demonstrators are brutally treated by police and white citizens. Public indignation increases steadily as demonstrators, including children, are beaten, attacked by police dogs, and otherwise mistreated. **April 12.** Dr. Martin Luther King, Jr., and other leaders are arrest-

HUGO L. BLACK
Gideon v. Wainwright, 1963
Reason and reflection require us to recognize that in our adversary system of criminal justice, any person haled into court, who is too poor to hire a lawyer, cannot be assured a fair trial unless counsel is provided for him. This seems to us to be an obvious truth. Governments, both state and federal, quite properly spend vast sums of money to establish machinery to try defendants accused of crime. Lawyers to prosecute are everywhere deemed essential to protect the public's interest in an orderly society. Similarly, there are few defendants charged with crime, few indeed, who fail to hire the best lawyers they can get to prepare and present their defense. That government hires lawyers to prosecute and defendants who have the money hire lawyers to defend are the strongest indications of the widespread belief that lawyers in criminal courts are necessities, not luxuries. The right of one charged with crime to counsel may not be deemed fundamental and essential to fair trials in some countries, but it is in ours. From the very beginning, our state and national constitutions and laws laid great emphasis on procedural and substantive safeguards designed to assure fair trials before impartial tribunals in which every defendant stands equal before the law. This noble ideal cannot be realized if the poor man charged with crime has to face his accusers without a lawyer to assist him.

MARTIN LUTHER KING, JR.

Letter from Birmingham City Jail, 1963

I must confess that over the past few years I have been gravely disappointed with the white moderate. I have almost reached the regrettable conclusion that the Negro's great stumbling block in his stride toward freedom is not the White Citizen's Counciler or the Ku Klux Klanner but the white moderate who is more devoted to "order" than to justice; who prefers a negative peace which is the absence of tension to a positive peace which is the presence of justice; who constantly says "I agree with you in the goal you seek, but I cannot agree with your methods"; who paternalistically believes he can set the timetable for another man's freedom; who lives by a mythical concept of time and who constantly advises the Negro to wait for a "more convenient season." Shallow understanding from people of goodwill is more frustrating than absolute misunderstanding from people of ill will. Lukewarm acceptance is much more bewildering than outright rejection.

I had hoped that the white moderate would understand that law and order exist for the purpose of establishing justice and that when they fail in this purpose they block social progress. I had hoped that the white moderate would understand that the present tension in the South is a necessary phase of the transition from an obnoxious negative peace, in which the Negro passively accepted his unjust plight, to a substantive and positive peace, in which all men will respect the dignity and worth of human personality.

ed. **May 8.** President Kennedy announces that the Justice Department has achieved a truce between demonstrators and business leaders; but three days later, two bombings cause a furious riot in which 50 persons are injured. President Kennedy stations 3,000 riot-control troops near Birmingham to keep peace and protect demonstrators.

April 5. After experiencing six-hour delays in communication during the Cuban crisis, the U.S. and the Soviet Union agree to setting up of a "hot line," direct teletypewriter contact between Washington and Moscow, to avoid risk of accidental war. Cable, leased from commercial companies, goes via England, Denmark, Sweden, and Finland.

April 26. The U.S. joins with the Soviet Union in urging renewed neutrality of Laos, but throughout the year the Laos government remains split into three military factions — royalist, neutralist, and pro-Communist — which control three separate zones of the country.

April-September. During the summer, demonstrations are held throughout the U.S., in the North as well as the South. In 75 Southern cities, almost 14,000 arrests are made, but about 200 public accommodations are desegregated. Many Northern and Western civil rights demonstrations are held in sympathy, but others are held to protest discrimination in schools, employment, and housing outside the South.

May 9. Experimental satellite West Ford II is launched from California; it releases 400 million copper needles in a polar orbit to reflect radio signals over long distances on earth.

May 21. In national referendum, wheat farmers reject federal production control aimed at reducing the wheat surplus and supporting the price of wheat. Food and Agriculture Act of 1962 requires two-thirds majority, and only 48 percent vote in favor of controls.

June 12. NAACP Mississippi field secretary Medgar W. Evers is shot in the back as he enters his home in Jackson, and civil rights demonstrations there become riots in protest against murder. A white man is later arrested for the killing; two trials end with juries unable to reach a verdict.

June 19. Following Birmingham riots, President Kennedy appeals for even stronger civil rights legislation than he has requested of Congress in February. During his first two years in office, Kennedy has relied on executive action rather than legislation; these are his first attempts to put through a civil rights law.

July. The U.S. attempts to persuade South Vietnamese government to cease repression of Buddhists, whom it has accused of antigovernment activities; several Buddhists have burned themselves alive in protest. When U.S. efforts fail, financial aid is partially withdrawn. **Nov. 1-2.** Military coup overthrows government; President Ngo Dinh Diem and his brother Ngo Dinh Nhu are killed. The U.S. restores aid to Buddhist-led regime, about $500 million per year. By the end of the year, 16,000 U.S. advisers are in South Vietnam.

Aug. 5. The U.S., Great Britain, and the Soviet Union sign long-discussed treaty banning nuclear tests in the oceans, the atmosphere, and outer space, inviting other nations to join. **Sept. 24.** U.S. Senate ratifies treaty, which goes into effect on October 10 and by the end of the year is signed by 113 nations; it is rejected by France and Communist China. **Oct. 16.** The U.S. sends up two satellites equipped to detect violations of the treaty.

JOHN F. KENNEDY
Address to the nation, 1963
I speak to you tonight in a spirit of hope. Eighteen years ago the advent of nuclear weapons changed the course of the world as well as the war. Since that time, all mankind has been struggling to escape from the darkening prospects of mass destruction on earth. In an age when both sides have come to possess enough nuclear power to destroy the human race several times over, the world of communism and the world of free choice have been caught up in a vicious circle of conflicting ideology and interests. Each increase of tension has produced an increase in arms; each increase in arms has produced an increase in tension.

In these years, the United States and the Soviet Union have frequently communicated suspicions and warnings to each other, but very rarely hope. Our representatives have met at the summit and at the brink; they have met in Washington and in Moscow, at the United Nations and in Geneva. But too often these meetings have produced only darkness, discord, or disillusion.

Yesterday a shaft of light cut into the darkness. Negotiations were concluded in Moscow on a treaty to ban all nuclear tests in the atmosphere, in outer space and underwater. For the first time, an agreement has been reached on bringing the forces of nuclear destruction under international control. . . .

This treaty is not the millennium. It will not resolve all conflicts, or cause the Communists to forgo their ambitions, or eliminate the dangers of war. . . . But it is an important first step — a step toward peace — a step toward reason — a step away from war.

MARTIN LUTHER KING, JR.
Speech at Lincoln Memorial, 1963

I say to you today, my friends, that in spite of the difficulties and frustrations of the moment I still have a dream. It is a dream deeply rooted in the American dream.

I have a dream that one day this nation will rise up and live out the true meaning of its creed: "We hold these truths to be self-evident; that all men are created equal."

I have a dream that one day on the red hills of Georgia the sons of former slaves and the sons of former slaveowners will be able to sit down together at the table of brotherhood.

I have a dream that one day even the state of Mississippi, a desert state sweltering with the heat of injustice and oppression, will be transformed into an oasis of freedom and justice.

I have a dream that my four little children will one day live in a nation where they will not be judged by the color of their skin but by the content of their character.

I have a dream today. . . .

I have a dream that one day every valley shall be exalted, every hill and mountain shall be made low, the rough places will be made plain, and the crooked places will be made straight, and the glory of the Lord shall be revealed, and all flesh shall see it together. . . .

When we let freedom ring, when we let it ring from every village and every hamlet, from every state and every city, we will be able to speed up that day when all of God's children, black men and white men, Jews and Gentiles, Protestants and Catholics, will be able to join hands and sing in the words of the old Negro spiritual, "Free at last! Free at last! Thank God Almighty, we are free at last!"

Aug. 16. Railroad management and five operating unions of railroad workers agree to submit long-standing disagreements on work rules and employment to binding arbitration by a special board. Bargaining disputes have continued since 1959. Sporadic strike threats continue until April 1964 when, after presidential intervention, agreement is arrived at in which workers receive substantial benefits.

Aug. 28. Two hundred thousand civil rights and desegregation advocates (mostly Negro) from the entire country gather for a massive peaceful "March on Washington for Jobs and Freedom." Although some violence is expected, none occurs.

Sept. 15. Negro church in Birmingham, Alabama, is bombed, killing four little girls and wounding other children. On the same day, two Negro boys are killed, one by police and one by other (white) boys. Although three men are arrested on the bombing charge, their guilt is never proved.

Oct. 9. President Kennedy approves sale through private sources of 4 million metric tons of wheat to the Soviet Union at world price for wheat. Soviet wheat production has declined in a poor agricultural year.

Oct. 16. American Telephone and Telegraph Company completes third and longest transatlantic telephone cable; company announces that future expansion of service will be by use of satellites.

Nov. 19. Cambodia severs economic and military relations with the U.S., saying that the U.S. is attempting to undermine its regime and is sponsoring subversive activities against Cambodia from bases in South Vietnam. All during the year Cambodia's sympathies have been turning toward Communist China.

Nov. 22. President Kennedy is assassinated in Dallas, Texas, while riding in a motorcade. Official time of death is 1:00 P.M., C.S.T. At 2:39 P.M., Lyndon Baines Johnson is sworn in as President. In speech on arrival Washington, D.C., he declares that he will follow Kennedy's policies. **Nov. 25.** Kennedy is buried in state funeral, modeled after Abraham Lincoln's, at Arlington National Cemetery; ceremony is attended by kings, presidents, and other leaders of 92 nations.

Nov. 24. Lee Harvey Oswald, accused assassin of President Kennedy, is shot by Jack Ruby (Rubenstein) in basement of Dallas Municipal Building while in custody of the police. Millions see assassination on television while watching news broadcast. Ruby is found guilty of murder and sentenced to death in March 1964. Granted a new trial in 1966, he dies in January 1967 of a blood clot and cancer.

Nov. 26. President Johnson tells 100 representatives of Latin-American countries that he will push forward efforts of the Alliance for Progress. The Alliance has succeeded in instituting land, government, and social reforms in many countries, but has been weakened when military coups have taken over democratic governments of Guatemala, Ecuador, the Dominican Republic, and Honduras.

Nov. 29. Special commission is named by President Johnson to investigate all aspects of assassination of President Kennedy. Chief Justice Earl Warren is named chairman.

An effective measles vaccine, first tested by John F. Enders and T. C. Peebles in 1958, is licensed for U.S. manufacture.

During this year, newsmen continue to criticize the government for its "management" of news, which has become evident during the Cuban crisis of 1962 when much news has been suppressed or delayed in the

LYNDON B. JOHNSON
Address to Congress, 1963

All I have I would have given gladly not to be standing here today.

The greatest leader of our time has been struck down by the foulest deed of our time. Today John Fitzgerald Kennedy lives on in the immortal words and works that he left behind. He lives on in the mind and memories of mankind. He lives on in the hearts of his countrymen.

No words are sad enough to express our sense of loss. No words are strong enough to express our determination to continue the forward thrust of America that he began.

The dream of conquering the vastness of space—the dream of partnership across the Atlantic, and across the Pacific as well—the dream of a Peace Corps in less developed nations—the dream of education for all of our children—the dream of jobs for all who seek them and need them—the dream of care for our elderly—the dream of an all-out attack on mental illness—and, above all, the dream of equal rights for all Americans, whatever their race or color—these and other American dreams have been vitalized by his drive and by his dedication.

Now the ideas and the ideals which he so nobly represented must and will be translated into effective action. . . .

On the 20th day of January, in 1961, John F. Kennedy told his countrymen that our national work would not be finished "in the first thousand days, nor in the life of this administration, nor even perhaps in our lifetime on this planet. But"—he said—"let us begin." Today in this moment of new resolve, I would say to my fellow Americans, let us continue.

JAMES BALDWIN

The Fire Next Time, 1963

There is no reason for you to try to become like white people and there is no basis whatever for their impertinent assumption that they must accept you. The really terrible thing, old buddy, is that you must accept them. And I mean that very seriously. You must accept them and accept them with love. For these innocent people have no other hope. They are, in effect, still trapped in a history which they do not understand; and until they understand it, they cannot be released from it. They have had to believe for many years, and for innumerable reasons, that black men are inferior to white men. Many of them, indeed, know better, but, as you will discover, people find it very difficult to act on what they know. To act is to be committed, and to be committed is to be in danger. In this case, the danger, in the minds of most white Americans, is the loss of their identity. . . .

But these men are your brothers — your lost, younger brothers. And if the word integration *means anything, this is what it means: that we, with love, shall force our brothers to see themselves as they are, to cease fleeing from reality and begin to change it. For this is your home, my friend, do not be driven from it; great men have done great things here, and will again, and we can make America what America must become. . . .*

You know, and I know, that the country is celebrating one hundred years of freedom one hundred years too soon. We cannot be free until they are free.

"national interest." Controversy tends to undermine confidence of the public in the truth of news from trouble spots such as Vietnam.

The U.S. progresses in development of communications satellites and ends its first man-in-space program, Mercury, with 22-orbit flight of L. Gordon Cooper, Jr. The Soviet Union sends into orbit the first space woman, Valentina V. Tereshkova, who orbits the earth 48 times, while her fellow astronaut, whose vehicle has been launched two days earlier, makes 81 orbits.

James Baldwin, Negro author, playwright, and prominent civil rights spokesman, publishes *The Fire Next Time*. In 1961 and 1962, he has published *Nobody Knows My Name* and *Another Country*; all are widely read.

1964

Jan. 9. Republic of Panama suspends relations with the U.S. after riots over status of the Canal Zone. **Jan. 11.** The UN refers dispute to the Organization of American States, and temporary agreement is reached on April 3. **Dec. 18.** The U.S. offers to renegotiate present canal treaty, at the same time announcing plans to build a new, sea-level, canal across Colombia or the isthmus.

Jan. 11. Report by surgeon general's special committee, *Smoking and Health*, strongly links cigarette smoking with cancer (as well as with other diseases) and calls for federal regulation. **June 24.** Federal Trade Commission announces that, starting in 1965, cigarette packages must carry health warnings.

Jan. 23. Twenty-fourth Amendment to the Constitution is ratified, to go into effect on February 4, 1964; Amendment forbids use of poll or other taxes to qualify voters in federal elections.

Feb. 17. The Supreme Court finds that each congressional district within a given state must have approximately the same population, so that each representative in Congress from that state will represent an equal number of people.

March 4. President James R. Hoffa of the Teamsters' Union is convicted of tampering with a federal jury in 1962; he is fined $10,000 and sentenced to eight years in prison. In July, he and six others are found guilty of fraudulent use of union funds; he is fined an additional $10,000 and sentenced to five years in prison.

March 16. President Johnson calls on Congress for a full-scale war on poverty. Plan for attack on long-standing and growing impoverishment of 11-state Appalachian area is proposed on April 28. **Aug. 11.** Congress passes Economic Opportunity Act, which provides for Job Corps, Domestic Peace Corps, work-training and work-study programs for youths, and help to local aid programs; Appalachia appropriation is not passed until 1965.

May 19. The U.S. warns that it will use every means short of military action to halt fighting in Laos and to preserve that country's independence. **May 27.** The State Department announces that light military planes have been sent to Laos for use of anti-Communist forces.

May 21. For the first time, a Negro is named moderator of the General Assembly of the United Presbyterian Church of the U.S.A. Meeting also adopts strong antidiscrimination amendments to the church's Form of Government.

May 25. The Supreme Court orders public schools of Prince Edward County, Virginia, to reopen without segregation; they have been closed since 1959 to avoid compliance with court's integration order.

J. WILLIAM FULBRIGHT
Speech in Senate, 1964
We are a people used to looking at the world, and indeed at ourselves, in moralistic rather than empirical terms. We are predisposed to regard any conflict as a clash between good and evil rather than as simply a clash between conflicting interests. We are inclined to confuse freedom and democracy, which we regard as moral principles, with the way in which they are practised in America—with capitalism, federalism, and the two-party system, which are not moral principles but simply the preferred and accepted practices of the American people. . . .

Our national vocabulary is full of "self-evident truths," not only about "life, liberty, and happiness" but about a vast number of personal and public issues, including the cold war. It has become one of the "self-evident truths" of the postwar era that just as the President resides in Washington and the Pope in Rome, the devil resides immutably in Moscow. We have come to regard the Kremlin as the permanent seat of his power and we have grown almost comfortable with a menace which, though unspeakably evil, has had the redeeming virtues of constancy, predictability, and familiarity. Now the devil has betrayed us by traveling abroad and, worse still, by dispersing himself, turning up now here, now there, and in many places at once, with a devilish disregard for the laboriously constructed frontiers of ideology. . . .

The master myth of the cold war is that the Communist bloc is a monolith composed of governments which are not really governments at all but organized conspiracies . . . resolute and implacable in their determination to destroy the free world.

WILLIAM BRADFORD HUIE
Three Lives for Mississippi, 1965
Momentarily, I comforted one of the murderers, then left him confused.

I said: "Well, you were correct on one point. You killed Schwerner because you said he was an 'agitating, trouble-making, nigger-loving, Communist, atheistic, Jew outsider.' It's true that he called himself an atheist."

"He did, huh? He didn't believe in nothing?"

"Oh, yes," I said, "He believed in something. He believed devoutly."

"What'd he believe in?"

"He believed in you!"

"In me! What the hell!"

"Yeah," I said. "He believed in you. He believed love could conquer hate. He believed love could change even you. He didn't think you were hopeless. That's what got him killed."

As I say, that left him somewhat confused.

One of the murderers said: "We couldn't get at them South-haters in Washington. But we could get at them three we had. So we showed 'em." Every one of the murderers seems to believe that "we showed" somebody something.

I think it can be said truly that the white-supremacy society of Mississippi has been shaken. Murder helped to shake it. And since most men will call this shaking process good, I believe most men of good will will agree that James Chaney, Andrew Goodman, and Michael Schwerner did not die in vain. Their deaths served the cause of freedom for all people, white and Negro, in Mississippi, in the United States, and, hopefully, throughout the world.

June 10. Filibuster by Southern senators is cut off after 75 days by majority vote; this is the first time cloture has been invoked on a civil rights issue in the Senate. The bill is finally approved on June 19. It bans racial discrimination in voting, in education, in public places, in employment, and in all federally aided programs — an even stronger bill than that proposed by President Kennedy.

June 14. The United Steelworkers and 11 steel companies sign pact to encourage equal job opportunities in the steel industry for all races. **July 2.** National Labor Relations Board bans racial discrimination in labor union membership, calling it unfair labor practice.

June 15. The Supreme Court finds in a series of decisions that in states with bicameral legislatures, seats in both houses must be apportioned by population rather than by using the "little federal system," and that populations of districts must be approximately equal. Decision follows long fight by urban and suburban areas that are underrepresented because of both the "little federal system" and obsolete apportionment; example of the latter is Connecticut, in which one member of the lower house represents 190 citizens of a small town, while another represents 81,000 citizens of Hartford.

June 21. Three young civil rights workers (two white youths from New York and one Negro Mississippian) are, allegedly, arrested for speeding in Mississippi, held for six hours, and then released; their station wagon is later found burned. **Aug. 4.** After extensive search, FBI agents find their bodies buried in a dam; they have been shot. **Dec. 4.** The FBI arrests 21 white Mississippians on conspiracy charges, but a week later the charges are dismissed on a technicality. The Department of Justice starts plans to bring the case before a federal grand jury.

June-September. An affiliation of civil rights groups, in a massive attack on stubbornly segregated Mississippi, trains and sends to the South hundreds of young workers, many of them college students. Mississippi, to fight the "invasion," enacts laws and Ku Klux Klan groups gather. The summer is marked by burnings, floggings, and shootings. Results of the campaign are discouraging, as only about 1,000 Negroes are registered to vote, many who try being turned down on newly enacted legal technicalities.

July 13. Republican National Convention meets at San Francisco and nominates militantly conservative Arizona Senator Barry M. Goldwater for President, with Representative William E. Miller of New York for Vice-President. **Aug. 24.** Democrats meet at Atlantic City and by acclamation nominate President Johnson; he chooses Senator Hubert H. Humphrey of Minnesota as his running mate. Minor party candidates are: Eric Haas, Socialist Labor; Earle H. Munn, Prohibition; Clifton DeBerry, Socialist Worker; and John Kasper, National States Rights. Republicans refuse to repudiate the support of the John Birch Society; their platform supports the Civil Rights Act, although Goldwater has voted against it as senator, and economy in government. Democrats support policies of the Johnson administration.

July 16. Rioting begins in New York City when a police officer shoots and kills a teen-age Negro boy during a disturbance. Anger at slum conditions and resentment of police treatment cause riots in many Northern cities, especially in New York and New Jersey, and in Philadelphia and Chicago. Civil rights groups accuse the police of brutality and emphasize a need for investigation into community relations.

Aug. 31. The U.S. Census Bureau announces that as of July 1, California has be-

BARRY M. GOLDWATER
Acceptance speech, 1964
The Good Lord raised this mighty . . . Republic to be a home for the brave and to flourish as the land of the free—not to stagnate in the swampland of collectivism, not to cringe before the bully of Communism.

Now my fellow Americans, the tide has been running against freedom. Our people have followed false prophets. We must, and we shall return to proven ways—not because they are old, but because they are true. . . .

We are at war in Vietnam. And yet the President, who is the Commander in Chief of our forces, refuses to say, refuses to say mind you, whether or not the objective over there is victory, and his Secretary of Defense continues to mislead and misinform the American people and enough of it has gone by. . . .

Today—today in our beloved country we have an Administration which seems eager to deal with Communism in every coin known—from gold to wheat; from consulates to confidence, and even human freedom itself. . . .

The task of preserving and enlarging freedom at home and of safeguarding it from the forces of tyranny abroad is great enough to challenge all our resources and to require all our strength.

Anyone who joins us in all sincerity we welcome. Those, those who do not care for our cause, we don't expect to enter our ranks in any case. And let our Republicanism so focused and so dedicated not be made fuzzy and futile by unthinking and stupid labels.

I would remind you that extremism in the defense of liberty is no vice.

And let me remind you also that moderation in the pursuit of justice is no virtue!

(Above) Stokely Carmichael of the Student Nonviolent Coordinating Committee, speaking in Minneapolis, Minnesota; (right) state trooper seizes an American flag being carried by a five-year-old boy at a civil rights demonstration in Mississippi; (below) James Meredith attends classes at the University of Mississippi escorted by U.S. marshals, 1962

(Right) Dr. Martin Luther King, Jr. arrested in Montgomery, Alabama, during the bus boycott of 1955; (below) Lyndon B. Johnson is sworn in as President aboard the presidential plane, November 22, 1963

Warren Commission report, 1964
This Commission was created to ascertain the facts relating to the preceding summary of events and to consider the important questions which they raised. The Commission has addressed itself to this task and has reached certain conclusions based on all the available evidence. No limitations have been placed on the Commission's inquiry; it has conducted its own investigation, and all government agencies have fully discharged their responsibility to cooperate with the Commission in its investigation. These conclusions represent the reasoned judgment of all members of the Commission and are presented after an investigation which has satisfied the Commission that it has ascertained the truth concerning the assassination of President Kennedy. . . .

The shots which killed President Kennedy and wounded Governor Connally were fired from the sixth-floor window at the southeast corner of the Texas School Book Depository. . . .

The shots which killed President Kennedy and wounded Governor Connally were fired by Lee Harvey Oswald. . . .

The Commission has found no evidence that Oswald was involved with any person or group in a conspiracy to assassinate the President. . . .

Because of the difficulty of proving negatives to a certainty, the possibility of others being involved with either Oswald or Ruby cannot be established categorically, but if there is any such evidence it has been beyond the reach of all the investigative agencies and resources of the United States and has not come to the attention of this Commission.

come the most populous state of the Union. In 1960 census, New York's population had exceeded California's by 1 million.

Sept. 9. United Automobile Workers reach agreement with Chrysler Corporation providing for more extensive benefits than ever before. Similar contracts with Ford Motor Company and General Motors Corporation follow by October. Settlements are criticized by the Administration as exceeding the 3.2 percent wage increase limit suggested for "noninflationary" raises.

Sept. 27. Special commission headed by Chief Justice Warren of the Supreme Court publishes its extensive report on the assassination of President Kennedy; report concludes that Lee Harvey Oswald has been the lone assassin and has not been involved in any conspiracy.

Oct. 14. Nobel Peace Prize is awarded to civil rights leader Martin Luther King, Jr.; prize is for the "furtherance of brotherhood among men."

Nov. 3. President Johnson wins election by greatest popular-vote landslide in U.S. history: Johnson, 43,126,000; Goldwater, 27,175,000. Johnson takes 44 states and the District of Columbia (voting for the first time in a presidential election), with 486 electoral votes; Goldwater holds only Arizona and five Deep South states, with 52 electoral votes. Democrats gain two seats in the Senate and 38 in the House, and win 17 out of 25 governorship contests.

1964 - 1965

July 31, 1964. U.S. lunar probe, Ranger 7, crash-lands on the moon after transmitting more than 4,300 "close-up" pictures of the moon's surface. Moon shot in January has failed when television system does not respond to signals and no photographs are sent, although probe does land on the moon. **Nov. 28.** Mariner 4 is launched toward Mars to transmit photographs when it passes the planet. **July 15, 1965.** Mariner sends 21 close-up photographs taken from 10,500 to 7,000 miles above surface of Mars.

1964 - 1968

Tonkin Gulf attack and resolution. **Aug. 2, 1964.** U.S. reports that North Vietnamese PT boats have attacked a U.S. destroyer in international waters in the Gulf of Tonkin; no damage is said to have resulted, and PT boats are said to have been driven off by carrier-based planes. **Aug. 5, 1964.** Charging a second attack, U.S. sends jets to bomb PT boat bases in North Vietnam, as well as an oil supply depot; in 64-sortie raid, 25 boats and the oil depot are destroyed. **Aug. 7, 1964.** Congress approves President's retaliatory action in Vietnam almost unanimously and gives administration broad power to continue war by executive action. **1967.** By this year, many doubts have been expressed about reality of North Vietnamese attacks in Tonkin Gulf, which, with consequent retaliation, are seen in retrospect as major step in escalation of war. **February 1968.** Hearings by Senate Foreign Relations Committee on Tonkin affair end inconclusively, with certain senators charging Johnson administration with having manufactured incident, while Secretary of State Dean Rusk defends government policy in Vietnam.

1965

Jan. 4. President Johnson's state of the union address promises a "Great Society," in which the quality of life will be improved for all. He has first used the term on May 22, 1964, in a speech at Ann Arbor, Michigan, and has stressed the concept during the election campaign.

Feb. 7. President Johnson orders first air

Senior Scholastic, 1968
On the order of Senator Fulbright, the Senate Foreign Relations staff recently began probing the background of the Tonkin incidents and prepared a report. The findings have not been released, but aides of the Senator say they question the Presidential decision that led to the U.S. bombing of North Vietnam. . . .

Secretary McNamara acknowledges that "ambiguous" and "conflicting" reports were received from the destroyers. But he has maintained that there was no doubt then or now that the North Vietnamese had attacked the destroyers. He has declared that the U.S. had "incontrovertible" evidence of the attacks before the President ordered air retaliation. . . .

A few Senators question some exaggerations of U.S. wounded in the North Vietnamese messages, although Senator Fulbright admits that it is only natural for the patrol boat commanders to engage in a little "puffery." . . .

When retiring Defense Secretary McNamara testified before the Senate Foreign Relations Committee last month, he displayed a bullet allegedly fired at the Maddox. "You have one bullet," Senator Albert Gore (D., Tenn.) retorted, "and we sent 64 sorties in retaliation!"

The strongest criticism, however, has been directed at President Johnson's using the Gulf of Tonkin resolution as a "blank check" to justify each succeeding escalation of the Vietnam war. By doing so, his critics argue, the U.S. effort has been made a "hostage" to an incident that is shrouded in doubt and controversy.

New York Times, 1965

The past week in Alabama has been a time of dangerous competition between the forces of racism and reason, of violence and law, of the defeated past and the struggling future. . . .

Gov. George C. Wallace and Sheriff James Clark symbolize a reactionary, racist cause that is already defeated and dying. In its final stage it has nothing to fall back upon except the desperate tactic of brutal force. The Rev. Martin Luther King symbolizes the cause of the Southern Negro who at the beginning of this second century of emancipation, is struggling to achieve his rights by legal, peaceful means. By law and by moral commitment, the overwhelming majority of Americans have taken their stand in this contest. There can be no doubt about the outcome.

The nation has thus far been fortunate in averting a catastrophic confrontation between these contending forces, but there have been losses, most recently the brutal killing of the Rev. James J. Reeb, a young white minister. The task now before the nation is to make sure that confrontation never occurs. . . .

The United States has been extremely fortunate that the struggle for Negro rights has remained up to now under mature responsible leadership which always seeks peaceful solutions by legal and political means. If that leadership is to be vindicated, then those means must be seen to be working. Otherwise the young Negro hotheads thirsting for a dramatic showdown for its own sake will be encouraged, and the white demagogues and their police henchmen will be emboldened to new acts of violence and repression.

raid of North Vietnam since 1964 in reprisal for Viet Cong attack on U.S. military compound in South Vietnam; with further Viet Cong attacks, additional bombing raids are made.

March 6. Two battalions of U.S. Marines ready for combat are sent to South Vietnam. **April.** Marine antiaircraft battalion goes to Vietnam, followed in the next month by an entire Marine division. **June 5.** State Department announces that U.S. troops are no longer being used as advisers but are participating directly in the fighting.

March 21. Martin Luther King, Jr., leads march from Selma, Alabama, to capital at Montgomery to protest discrimination against Negroes in voting registration. Marchers at first number 3,200 from all over the United States; joined by others and finally met by groups assembled at Montgomery, they total 25,000 by end of the march five days later. Marchers are protected by nationalized Alabama Guard. Although march is remarkably free of physical violence, Mrs. Viola Liuzzo is shot after it is over while transporting marchers, and a Boston minister has been clubbed to death while making preparations. Local juries fail to convict accused killers in either case. **Dec. 3.** Federal court in Alabama finds three Ku Klux Klansmen guilty of conspiracy in the murder of Mrs. Liuzzo. They receive maximum sentence, 10 years in prison.

April 7. President Johnson proposes to North Vietnam "unconditional discussions" to end the Vietnam war, but Hanoi ignores offer. In May, U.S. bombing is halted for several days in hope that discussion offer will be considered, but Hanoi, which demands that U.S. stop bombing altogether, states that U.S. insistence on discussions without prior conditions is an attempt to force Vietnam to accept U.S. terms.

April 9. Congress passes Elementary and

Secondary Education Act, which provides $1.3 billion for federal aid to public schools.

June 7. The Supreme Court invalidates a nineteenth-century Connecticut law forbidding the use of contraceptives, even for married couples, on the ground that the law violates the "right of privacy" guarantee in the Constitution.

July 20. Secretary of Defense Robert S. McNamara states that the military situation in Vietnam has grown worse in spite of active U.S. intervention in the fighting. **July 28.** President Johnson announces that the number of troops in South Vietnam will be increased to 125,000 and that draft calls will be doubled.

July 30. President Johnson signs long awaited Medicare bill, providing doctor's care and hospitalization for the aged through the Social Security System; bill becomes effective in July 1966.

Aug. 12-17. Negroes in Watts ghetto area of Los Angeles riot for six days; disorders, which start when a white police officer stops a Negro driver for drunkenness, lead to 35 deaths, an estimated $40 million property damage, and 4,000 arrests. National Guard troops are used to restore order in what investigators later call "an explosion . . . an all but hopeless violent protest."

Aug. 31. Congress establishes Cabinet-level Department of Housing and Urban Affairs to strengthen and coordinate federal action on problems of cities. The Housing and Urban Development Act aims to supplement rents of low-income tenants in federally supported housing projects; although Congress passes the bill, it deletes entire appropriation. In January 1966 President appoints Dr. Robert C. Weaver as secretary; he is first Negro Cabinet member.

Oct. 3. President Johnson signs U.S. Im-

FRANK CHURCH
Speech in Senate, 1965
The world is not a big Red sea in which this country is being scuttled, but a vast arena of political upheaval, in which the quest for freedom, ever stronger, has overthrown the colonial empires of the past. It isn't a tidy world, nor is it a secure one. But it is one for which the United States set the revolutionary example.

ROBERT F. KENNEDY
Speech at International Police Academy, 1965
In the 1960s, it should not be necessary to repeat that the great struggle of the coming decades is one for the hearts and minds of men. But too often, of late, we have heard instead of the language of gadgets — of force-ratios and oil-blots, techniques and technology, of bombs and grenades which explode with special violence, of guns which shoot around corners, of new uses for helicopters and special vehicles.

Men's allegiance, however, and this kind of war, are not won by superior force, by the might of numbers or by the sophistication of technology. . . .

Conventional military force — and all our advanced weapons technology — is useful only to destroy. . . .

Guns and bombs cannot build, cannot fill empty stomachs or educate children, cannot build homes or heal the sick. But these are the ends for which men establish and obey governments; they will give their allegiance only to governments which meet these needs.

Chronology 1965

LOUDON WAINWRIGHT
Life, 1965

It shouldn't happen every evening, but a crisis like the lights going out has its good points. In the first place it deflates human smugness about our miraculous technology. . . .

It seemed to me that the blackout quite literally transformed the people of New York. Ordinarily smug and comfortable in the high hives of the city where they live and work, they are largely strangers to one another when the lights are on. In the darkness they emerged, not as shadows, but far warmer and more substantial than usual. Stripped of the anonymity that goes with full illumination, they became humans conscious of and concerned about the other humans around them. In the crowded streets businessmen, coats removed so that their light-colored shirts could be seen, became volunteer cops and directed traffic. Though the sidewalks were jammed, there was little of the rude jostling that is a part of normal, midday walking in New York. In the theatrically silver light of a perfect full moon (a must for all future power failures) people peered into the faces of passersby like children at a Halloween party trying to guess which friends hide behind which masks. In fact, the darkness made everyone more childlike. There was much laughter, and as they came down the stairs of the great office buildings in little night processions led by men with flashlights and candles, people held hands with those they could not see.

Perhaps the best thing about such an event is that it gives all of us a story to tell. . . . We will be listening to versions of "The Night the Lights Went Out" long after a federal commission discovers that it all started when a little boy in upstate New York dropped his electric toothbrush in the toilet.

migration and Nationality amendments, which abolish the 1921 national origins quota system, designed to control and limit immigration from specific areas. New law allows, by 1968, 20,000 immigrants annually from each independent country outside the Western Hemisphere (up to 170,000 total) and 120,000 immigrants from Western Hemisphere countries. Persons to be accepted are classified only by categories such as family relationships, skills, and refugee status.

Nov. 9-10. Starting at about 5:15 P.M. on Nov. 9, massive power failure in northeastern U.S. blacks out New York State, most of New England, and parts of New Jersey and Pennsylvania, as well as Quebec and Ontario, Canada, an area affecting 30 million people; most power is not restored until the following morning. Although citizens of paralyzed areas — even those trapped in stalled subways and elevators — take inconvenience in good spirit, event points up necessity for auxiliary power for vital services. Investigation shows that blackout has been caused by malfunction of a relay device in Queenston, Ontario.

U.S. bombing raids of North Vietnam, first aimed at strictly military targets in the southern part, gradually spread farther north, covering most of the country and approaching heavily populated city of Hanoi. The U.S. feels by the end of the year that Communists in South Vietnam have been stopped, but the Viet Cong nevertheless holds as much territory and controls as many South Vietnamese people as in January. By August, Congress has appropriated $2,400,000,000 specifically for the war, and anticipates the need for $12 billion in 1966. Protests against the war, especially among students and teachers, have grown numerous by the end of the year.

In the U.S. Gemini space program, five manned launches are made, each with two astronauts; rendezvous is effected between two Gemini spacecraft. Astronauts carry out complicated navigational and docking maneuvers, leave the spacecraft to "walk" and to work in space, and achieve one flight lasting two weeks. Soviet astronaut has been first man to make space walk. Also in this year, the Soviet Union sends two unmanned spacecraft to Venus, one of which lands on the planet on March 1, 1966, and the U.S. improves moon photography, one series of photographs being broadcast directly on commercial television.

Arthur Schlesinger, Jr., is criticized after the publication of his book on President Kennedy, *A Thousand Days*, because he reveals in it that Kennedy had planned to replace Secretary of State Dean Rusk in 1965. Critics feel that it will hamper Rusk, who has been retained in the post by President Johnson.

"Op art" (optical, or kinetic, art), new style of nonobjective painting depending for effect on color dynamics and devices to create optical illusions of motion and perspective, overshadows Pop art of the previous year.

By the end of this year, there are more than 5 million color television sets in the U.S.; networks predict that by the end of 1966, all nighttime programs will be broadcast in color and color broadcasts of daytime shows will increase rapidly.

1965 - 1966

April 28, 1965. President Johnson announces that he has sent 405 U.S. Marines to the Dominican Republic to evacuate Americans and protect their property in civil war. **May 2.** Johnson tells the U.S. that there are 14,000 U.S. troops in the Dominican Republic to prevent formation of another Communist government in the Western Hemisphere, although many persons are

HARRY S. ASHMORE
Mass Communications, 1966
The continuing loss of excellence is agreed to by almost all of those who are concerned with the quality of television programming, and is not seriously disputed even by the industry spokesmen who measure progress in dollars. Each television season in recent years has ended with the critics denouncing the new low in the general level of programming while the trade journals announced that the broadcasters' income and profits have reached a new high. I have no doubt that the proprietors of TV still prefer a good program to a bad one, all things being equal, and I know that some of them, at least, know the difference. But the things that count are anything but equal. The determining fact seems to be that an audience of multiple millions is necessary to market the commercials that pay the freight, and this requires — or at least can only be maintained by — a common denominator of bland mediocrity. . . .

An occasional brilliant program still reaches the air. But these breakthroughs grow fewer as the broadcasters improve their ability to extract profits from every moment of the broadcast day. . . .

There can be no doubt that great financial resources, plus the celebrity-making power of the medium, contribute to the broadcasters' ability to checkmate every Washington effort to correct their most evident abuses. But, unlike the other special interests that seek support and/or immunity from Washington, broadcasting enjoys another overwhelming advantage that so far has made it impossible to muster any effective force for governmental reform — the stubborn, democratic fact that the great majority of viewers like their television the way it is.

EDMUND K. FALTERMAYER
Fortune, 1965
The American Dream is now largely ful-
filled. But [it] . . . was never really a
blueprint for a mature society. . . .

The society we have built fulfills the
lopsided American Dream with a
vengeance. Our immaculate homes are
crowded with gleaming appliances and
our refrigerators are piled high with
convenience foods. But beyond our
doorsteps lies a shamefully neglected
social and physical environment. For-
eigners who come to these shores ex-
pecting to find splendid countryside
and magnificent cities discover other
things instead: noise, vandalism, pollut-
ed air, befouled streams, filthy streets,
forests of ugly telegraph poles and
wires, decrepit mass-transit systems,
and parks that are unkempt and unsafe.
They also see: a countryside being de-
voured by housing subdivisions and by
shopping centers whose graceless
buildings are little more than merchan-
dise barns; highways splattered with
enormous billboards and hideous drive-
ins that shriek for the passing motorist's
attention; central cities that, except for a
rather insignificant amount of recon-
struction at the core, are sprawling
wastelands of decayed speculative con-
struction left over from yesteryear. The
only places where Americans have ex-
tensively beautified their country, visi-
tors soon discover, are certain upper-
middle-class suburbs—fine for those
who can afford them—and some col-
lege campuses. Otherwise, there is little
relief from what the English magazine
Architectural Review a decade ago
called "the mess that is man-made
America."

doubtful that Dominican rebels are Communist. **May 5.** Mission from the OAS
achieves a truce to be guaranteed by an
OAS peace-keeping force. **June 24, 1966.**
Council of the OAS votes to withdraw Inter-American peace-keeping force after election in which all three candidates have
asked for their removal. **June 28.** First U.S.
troops leave for home.

Aug. 10, 1965. Under Voting Rights Act
of 1965, federal authorities begin check of
registration and voting procedures to protect rights of Negro voters in parts of Alabama, Mississippi, and Louisiana. In some
districts, less than 50 percent of eligible voters have voted in 1964 because they have
been prevented from registering or, in some
cases, from voting even though registered.
April 10, 1966. The Department of Justice
announces that the number of Negroes registered to vote in five Deep South states has
increased by almost 50 percent since passage of Voting Rights Act.

Aug. 12, 1965. Federal agencies and
states and cities adjacent to Lake Erie agree
on program to end pollution of the lake.
This is the first important federal action under the Water Quality Act of 1965 to solve
the national problem of pollution and potential shortage of usable water, a problem
that receives increasing attention. In 1966,
Congress passes Clean Waters Restoration
Act, which provides help for keeping river
water pure, and an air pollution act, with a
3-year appropriation of $186 million for
federal and local programs to cut down air
pollution.

Dec. 24, 1965. Christmas truce in Vietnam begins, after offers by the Viet Cong
and the U.S. and the urging of Pope Paul
VI. **Dec. 29.** President Johnson sends highly placed U.S. officials to Rome, Paris,
Warsaw, Ottawa, Moscow, and Yugoslavia
to confer with heads of state on peace. **Jan.**

31, 1966. On last day of truce, Johnson announces that since U.S. peace efforts over 37 days have been rejected by North Vietnam, bombing raids will be resumed.

1966

Jan. 1. The U.S. publishes Vietnam casualty figures for 1965: U.S., 1,350 dead, 5,300 wounded, almost 150 missing or captured; South Vietnam, 11,100 dead, 22,600 wounded, 7,400 missing; Viet Cong, 34,600 dead (est.), 5,750 captured.

Jan. 17. In air crash over the coast of Spain, a U.S. B-52 bomber drops four unarmed hydrogen bombs, three on land and one into the sea. Search for sunken bomb takes three months and thousands of members of U.S. forces; it is found and raised intact. Land operation, because two bombs have ruptured and scattered radioactive particles, involves removing 1500 tons of topsoil and plant matter to the U.S. for safe disposal.

Jan. 24. In proposing record budget to Congress, President Johnson admits that the necessity of appropriating funds for "our increased commitments in Vietnam" has hindered advancement of the Great Society.

Feb. 5. The U.S. announces that it will sell 200 tanks to Israel to maintain the balance of armaments in the Middle East. It has previously supplied similar tanks to Jordan. **May 20.** The U.S. confirms that because the Soviet Union has sold planes to Arab nations, the U.S. is selling light bombers to Israel.

Feb. 8. After conference in Honolulu with Premier Nguyen Cao Ky of South Vietnam, President Johnson, with Ky, issues "Declaration of Honolulu" stating that the two countries will fight aggression and also fight for social and economic reforms

ROBERT S. McNAMARA
Speech to American Society of Newspaper Editors, 1966
First, we have to help protect those developing countries which genuinely need and request our help, and which—as an essential precondition—are willing and able to help themselves.

Second, we have to encourage and achieve a more effective partnership with those nations who can and should share international peacekeeping responsibilities.

Third, we must do all we realistically can to reduce the risk of conflict with those who might be tempted to take up arms against us. . . .

In the last eight years alone there have been no less than 164 internationally significant outbreaks of violence —each of them specifically designed as a serious challenge to the authority, or the very existence, of the government in question. . . .

Whether Communists are involved or not, violence anywhere in a taut world transmits sharp signals through the complex ganglia of international relations; and the security of the United States is related to the security and stability of nations half a globe away.

But neither conscience nor sanity itself suggests that the United States is, should, or could be the global gendarme. . . . The United States has no mandate from on high to police the world, and no inclination to do so. There have been classic cases in which our deliberate nonaction was the wisest action of all. Where our help is not sought, it is seldom prudent to volunteer.

Consumer Reports, 1967
On April 11, 1967, the U.S. Supreme Court struck perhaps its biggest blow in years in the cause of the consumer. It did so by concurring, 7 to 0, with a Federal Trade Commission finding that the nation's largest advertiser, Procter & Gamble Co., violated the antitrust laws ten years ago when it acquired the Clorox Chemical Co. The FTC, in ordering the annulment of that corporate marriage, was largely persuaded in its course by the formidable television advertising power gained for Clorox household liquid bleach as a result of the merger. Television, the FTC said, can be a monopoly tool in the hands of a very large advertiser, who can get special discounts and other privileges unavailable to a small advertiser. . . .

The Procter & Gamble-Clorox wedding took place in August 1957. . . .

Although some 200 firms were producing household liquid bleach, Clorox dominated the field. It was the only truly national brand and commanded 48.8 percent of total sales. . . . Clorox owed its success to classic "creation" of product differentiation. Its household liquid bleach is essentially the same as any other brand. . . .

But if Clorox was already big enough to dominate the bleach market, what difference would it make, one might ask, if an even bigger company marketed the brand? The fact is, if effective national competition with Clorox was difficult before the merger, it became well-nigh impossible afterward. The power to preempt commercial time on network television presents a virtually impregnable barrier to other companies that might want to compete on a national scale.

in South Vietnam. In later statement, Ky urges escalation of bombing and refuses to negotiate with the Viet Cong.

Feb. 15. Federal Civil Rights Commission reports that fewer than 8 percent of Southern Negro children attend integrated schools; commission blames Southern school boards using "free choice" system, which allows Negroes to pick their schools and also allows intimidation by whites.

March 2. President Johnson proposes that Congress establish a Cabinet-level Department of Transportation. **Oct. 13.** Congress creates department that consists of 34 federal air, rail, and highway agencies and includes the Coast Guard and the safety functions of the Civil Aeronautics Board and Interstate Commerce Commission.

March 9. Defense Department concedes to critics that more than 21 percent of U.S. Army enlisted men killed in combat in Vietnam are Negroes, but it denies that Negroes (who make up 11 percent of U.S. male population aged 18-29) are given more combat assignments than whites.

March 20. Almost 200 U.S. Asian scholars ask membership in the UN for Communist China, and recognition of the regime by the U.S., as well as an end to the U.S. trade embargo against the Communists. **May 20.** House Foreign Affairs Committee urges attempt to increase peaceful contacts with Communist China and warns against violence of Chinese response if the U.S. tries to overthrow North Vietnamese government.

March 21. President Johnson proposes truth in packaging law, covering about 8,000 drug, cosmetic, and food products; law, which is passed by Congress in this year, requires clear and accurate statement of ingredients and amounts, and bans the use of confusing phrases such as "giant half quart."

March 31. France announces that all its troops will be withdrawn from the NATO integrated command by July 1, 1966, and that all foreign bases (U.S., Canadian, and West German) and two NATO headquarters must be removed from France by April 1, 1967. President de Gaulle declares, however, that France intends to remain a member of NATO.

March 31. Decrying inflationary trend, President Johnson asks housewives to boycott products whose prices keep rising and businessmen to cut down spending on capital improvements; he says a raise in taxes may be necessary if inflation continues. **May 4.** Federal Reserve Board chairman William McChesney Martin, Jr. implies that if taxes are not raised, the board will tighten money by raising interest rates.

April 9. After almost a month of antigovernment demonstrations against "rotten" military regime of Premier Ky, Buddhists announce plans to overthrow U.S.-supported Ky regime in South Vietnam. **April 14.** South Vietnam's Premier Ky approves plan for national elections, a new constitution, and a civilian government; Buddhist protests have become increasingly violent.

April 14. Sole manufacturer of psychedelic drug LSD (lysergic acid diethylamide) withdraws all supplies from the market because of public controversy over its widespread use and damaging effects; value of move is doubtful, however, since drug is easily made by amateurs and only minute doses are needed.

April 27. After four years of hearings, the Interstate Commerce Commission approves merger of the New York Central and Pennsylvania railroads; merger is the biggest in

DANIEL X. FREEDMAN
Bulletin of the Atomic Scientists, 1968
My current opinion is that the chief abuse of LSD is irresponsible, alluring, and provocative advertising by the bored mass media. Couched in the language of drugs, an ideology has been insinuated into youth culture by a band of articulate writers and vagrant professionals. These have replaced the old medicine show with an updated campus version complete with readings and tempting arguments, if not pills, to sell: "Tune in, turn one, drop out." A drug mystique has been welded to the serious shifts and strains inherent in the experience of the potentially most unstable group of any society—the adolescent and young adult.

We need not determine whether this is indeed a "now" generation valuing honesty, love, direct confrontation, uncomplicated action, and avoiding ideologies in favor of simple justice. These values, however germane to the LSD experience, were not born from the drugged mind. The Pied Pipers of LSD—peddling a drug which can enhance poor judgment—would lure youth from the acquisition of competence, or even from the serious study of man's attempts to deal with the two orders of reality in his personal development and in his religious, artistic, philosophical, and scientific endeavors. . . .

We should not forget to assess the cost of sustained euphoria or pleasure states; we have to wonder whether the mind of man is built to accommodate an excess of either pleasure or rationality. We do not know whether or not there are individuals with sufficient strength to take these drugs for growth or pleasure within the social order without increased and credulous alienation from it.

J. WILLIAM FULBRIGHT

Speech at Johns Hopkins University, 1966

The question that I find intriguing is whether a nation so extraordinarily endowed as the United States can overcome that arrogance of power which has afflicted, weakened, and, in some cases, destroyed great nations in the past.

The causes of the malady are a mystery but its recurrence is one of the uniformities of history: Power tends to confuse itself with virtue and a great nation is peculiarly susceptible to the idea that its power is a sign of God's favor, conferring upon it a special responsibility for other nations — to make them richer and happier and wiser, to remake them, that is, in its own shining image. . . .

There is a kind of voodoo about American foreign policy. Certain drums have to be beaten regularly to ward off evil spirits; for example, the maledictions which are regularly uttered against North Vietnamese aggression, the "wild men" in Peking, communism in general, and President de Gaulle. Certain pledges must be repeated every day lest the whole free world go to rack and ruin — for example, we will never go back on a commitment no matter how unwise; we regard this alliance or that as absolutely "vital" to the free world; and, of course, we will stand stalwart in Berlin from now until Judgment Day. . . .

Some of our superpatriots assume that any war the United States fights is a just war, if not indeed a holy crusade, but history does not sustain their view. . . . In a historical frame of reference it seems to me logical and proper to question the wisdom of our present military involvement in Asia.

U.S. history, creating the new Pennsylvania New York Central Transportation Company, with $4 billion in assets and 19,000 miles of track on which it hauls one-eighth of U.S. rail freight. Merger is not to go into effect until 1968.

April 28. President Johnson proposes to Congress his civil rights bill, which broadens present laws, especially in that it provides for nationwide open housing. This part of the bill leads to its defeat because of strong opposition by real estate interests and many congressmen.

May 1. U.S. forces for the first time fire on targets in Cambodia after being attacked from over the Vietnam-Cambodia border.

May 12. Senator Robert F. Kennedy criticizes U.S. refusal to agree with China not to use nuclear weapons against each other; the State Department has revealed China's offer on the previous day.

May 15. Military government of South Vietnam acts against Buddhist rebels in Da Nang who oppose Premier Ky's government, especially since his announcement of the previous week that he does not intend to resign after elections to set up a civilian government. **May 16.** Buddhist leader appeals to the U.S. for support but is told that the U.S. is trying to use diplomacy to bring the two factions together. Battle in Da Nang lasts for a week; 75 are killed and 500 wounded. **June 23.** Buddhist opposition is finally crushed by Ky's forces when last stronghold in Saigon is taken.

May. Vietnam debate continues in this month among government officials, including Senator J. William Fulbright who says that the U.S. is confusing power with virtue; Senator Wayne Morse of Oregon, who wants a peaceful settlement; Vice-President Humphrey, who cites U.S. pledges to maintain law and order; former presidential candidate Barry M. Goldwater, who calls for removal of Senator Fulbright as chairman of Senate Foreign Relations Committee, and President Johnson, who terms those who oppose the war "Nervous Nellies"; as well as 10,000 persons who picket the White House and 63,000 who pledge not to vote for any pro-Vietnam war candidate.

June 6. Negro law student James Meredith, who has been first to integrate University of Mississippi in 1962, is shot during "pilgrimage" from Tennessee border to capital of Mississippi; he has started his walk to show Mississippi Negroes that there is nothing to fear. SCLC, CORE, and SNCC take up march where wounded Meredith has stopped, and more than 1,000 people join to meet with 15,000 demonstrators at capital; but relations between marchers are strained as SCLC followers advocate racial cooperation and SNCC followers emphasize their "Black Power" slogan. In July, CORE also adopts black power, but the NAACP rejects the concept as "racist," "a reverse Mississippi."

June 11. Secretary McNamara announces that military strength in Vietnam will be increased to 285,000; he says that U.S. troops will be able to slow down guerrilla action, although civil unrest in South Vietnam is hampering operations. He also announces that although 21,000 Viet Cong have been killed since January, recruitment of North Vietnam troops has resulted in larger than ever Communist opposition.
June 18. President Johnson indicates that bombing of North Vietnam will be intensified in order to "raise the cost of aggression at its source."

June 14. The Supreme Court upholds the right of Puerto Ricans to vote if they do not speak English but are literate in Spanish, even if there is a state law requiring literacy in English.

LYNDON B. JOHNSON
Speech at Princeton University, 1966
The exercise of power in this century has meant for all of us in the United States not arrogance but agony. We have used our power not willingly and recklessly ever but always reluctantly and with restraint. Unlike nations in the past with vast power at their disposal, the United States of America has never sought to crush the autonomy of her neighbors. We have not been driven by blind militarism down courses of devastating aggression. . . .

Surely it is not a paranoiac vision of America's place in the world to recognize that freedom is still indivisible, still has adversaries whose challenge must be answered. Today, of course, as we meet here, that challenge is sternest at the moment in Southeast Asia. Yet there, as elsewhere, our great power is also tempered by great restraint.

What nation has announced such limited objectives or such willingness to remove its military presence once those objectives are secured and achieved? What nation has spent the lives of its sons and vast sums of its fortune to provide the people of a small thriving country the chance to elect the course that we might not ourselves choose?

The aims for which we struggle are aims which in the ordinary course of affairs men of the intellectual world applaud and serve—the principle of choice over coercion, the defense of the weak against the strong and the aggressive, the right—the right—of a young and frail nation to develop free from the interference of her neighbors, the ability of a people however inexperienced and however different and however diverse to fashion a society consistent with their own traditions and values and aspirations.

RALPH NADER
Unsafe at Any Speed, 1965

For over half a century the automobile has brought death, injury, and the most inestimable sorrow and deprivation to millions of people. With Medea-like intensity, this mass trauma began rising sharply four years ago, reflecting new and unexpected ravages by the motor vehicle. A 1959 Department of Commerce report projected that 51,000 persons would be killed by automobiles in 1975. That figure will probably be reached in 1965, a decade ahead of schedule.

A transportation specialist, Wilfred Owen, wrote in 1946, "There is little question that the public will not tolerate for long an annual traffic toll of 40,000 to 50,000 fatalities." Time has shown Owen to be wrong. Unlike aviation, marine, or rail transportation, the highway-transport system can inflict tremendous casualties and property damage without in the least affecting the viability of the system. Plane crashes, for example, jeopardize the attraction of flying for potential passengers and therefore strike at the heart of the air-transport economy. They motivate preventative efforts. The situation is different on the roads. . . .

A principal reason why the automobile has remained the only transportation vehicle to escape being called to meaningful public account is that the public has never been supplied the information nor offered the quality of competition to enable it to make effective demands through the marketplace and through government for a safe, nonpolluting, and efficient automobile that can be produced economically. The consumer's expectations regarding automotive innovations have been deliberately held low and mostly oriented to very gradual annual style changes.

June 30. Report of House Armed Services Committee after an investigation of the draft finds it basically sound but recommends drafting at an earlier age (19 or 20 instead of 22 or 23) and making those deferred for college eligible until age 35. Selective Service Director Lewis B. Hershey has testified that he opposes the lottery system that many feel is the fairest possible way to choose draftees. **Nov. 29.** Mental Standards for armed forces are lowered from score of 16 to score of 10 (out of 100). Defense Department announces that 2,400,000 men who have been rejected will be reexamined.

July. Violence erupts in slum areas of 16 cities throughout the U.S. Whites battle Negroes in a month of shootings, robberies, burning, and looting. Vice-President Humphrey calls for nationwide campaign to aid slum-dwellers, saying it is time "to recognize the National Guard is no answer to the problem of the slums."

Sept. 9. Congress passes two bills, the Traffic Safety Act and the Highway Safety Act. The first, an almost direct result of Ralph Nader's book *Unsafe at Any Speed,* sets automobile production safety standards that will be required in 1968 models; it also provides for federal tire safety standards and requires auto manufacturers to call back after sale all models in which mechanical defects have been discovered. The highway bill provides federal funds for state and local traffic and road safety programs. By this time, there are 78 million passenger cars and 16 million trucks and buses registered in the U.S.; they travel a total of 910 billion miles per year; the number of deaths attributable to automobiles so far in the century is three times as great as military deaths in all U.S. wars.

Sept. 11. In spite of bloody anti-election campaign by the Viet Cong, South Vietnam voters elect assembly to form new constitution in preparation for civilian government in 1967. On election day, 19 persons are killed and 120 wounded in shootings and bombings of polling places and transportation facilities.

Oct. 4. France explodes last in a series of nuclear devices being tested, explaining that tests are necessary for "world equilibrium." This and China's explosion of a nuclear missile bomb three weeks later draw protests from many countries against contamination of the atmosphere.

Oct. 7. Congress approves nearly $3 billion for foreign aid, 28 percent of which is for military aid. Defense appropriation of $58 billion also passed by Congress on October 11, is over $400 million more than has been asked for by the President. Bill authorizes the President to call up as many as 789,000 reserve forces without declaration of a national emergency or approval by Congress.

Oct. 20. Congress authorizes $1,200,-000,000 for federally assisted slum rebuilding programs. Bill provides for about 60 "demonstration cities" and mortgage insurance for construction of new towns and villages.

Nov. 8. Republicans gain at all levels in fall election: 3 Senate seats, 47 seats in the House, 8 governorships, and 540 seats in state legislatures. Edward Brooke of Massachusetts is elected to the Senate by a large margin — the first Negro senator since Reconstruction.

Dec. 14. Mrs. John F. Kennedy notifies publishers Harper & Row and *Look* magazine that she plans court action to prevent publication of William R. Manchester's *The Death of a President*, written at the request of the Kennedy family. She feels that its sensationalism will injure her and her children. **Dec. 21.** *Look* agrees to delete parts

FRANK L. WHITNEY
Speech in Cleveland, 1966
How are we going to save our cities? Let's face it, gentlemen, we are not, at least not in the sense of returning them to their exalted status of a generation or more past.

Megalopolis is here to stay. Call it what you will — urban sprawl, slums of tomorrow, ticky-tack houses. It is here and it will be expanded. It will not change the texture of our communities. Certainly it is the ware of the future.

This will make many politicians unhappy — those who like a large but neatly packaged constituency. It will make many planners and architects unhappy — those who can relate only to the structure that is tall and thin or to the glory that was Rome. . . .

But this is what's happening and it will continue at flood. We live in an electronic age — an age of automation and instant communication. Electronics and automation have fractured our existing industrial patterns. They disperse industries to every corner of our country. Like it or not, this permits each of us to dictate our environment — and the exodus from the city is well underway.

This is not because of poor city government, although in many cases it has been profoundly inept. It is not because of high city taxes, although taxes within the city area will continue to increase. It is not because of crime or poor educational facilities. These only accelerate the move. The basic cause is simply that more and more people are permitted a choice and their choice is based on two fundamental factors — living near their work and, increasingly important, expanded opportunities and time for recreation.

RICHARD S. LEWIS

Bulletin of the Atomic Scientists, 1968

The thundering success of the 364-foot Saturn 5 launch vehicle on its maiden test flight last November marked a dramatic upturn in the fortunes of the U.S. space program, which had been sliding downhill since the Apollo fire in January 1967. It has revived the possibility that a manned lunar landing can be made in this decade. While the deadline has lost much of the urgency which impelled President Kennedy to set it, in 1961, it is still considered important by the Johnson administration. The principal reason is that it would demonstrate a technological capability of meeting the most ambitious commitment in the history of technology within a predictable time frame. . . .

In retrospect, Mr. Kennedy's request to Congress in May 1961 that "this nation should commit itself to achieving the goal before this decade is out of landing a man on the moon and returning him safely to Earth" appears to be one of the most important acts of his administration. He, himself, came to regard it so, and his technical advisers believed it would become as monumental in history as the Louisiana Purchase or the Panama Canal. . . .

However, the impact of the mandate was not confined to providing the fledgling manned space flight program with a destination. . . .

In the long range, it has determined the priorities, the engineering designs, and the scientific objectives of the space program in this decade, and it is quite likely to control future space work for the remainder of this century. This unforeseen result might be called the Kennedy Effect. While its intent in the beginning was to enlarge American competence in space, its implementation has built a Procrustean bed and the

offensive to Mrs. Kennedy and Harper & Row soon also agrees. Some observers feel that the book's exposure of tensions between aides of President Kennedy and President Johnson plays a large part in the dispute.

During 1966, the U.S. makes 62 successful launches of various kinds of spacecraft, five of them manned; this makes a total of 267 since the beginning of 1962. Four weather satellites are launched, one of which photographs weather of the whole world every 24 hours. The U.S.S.R. and the U.S. both make soft landings on the moon, and both send satellites into orbit around the moon. Last flight of the U.S. Gemini series lasts for about 100 hours. The U.S.S.R. announces no manned flights, renewing speculation that they have encountered medical problems with their astronauts. They do launch for biomedical research a space ship containing two dogs; the capsule is recovered after 22 days.

1967

Jan. 6. About 4,000 U.S. and South Vietnamese forces attack Viet Cong in Mekong River Delta, first U.S. involvement in this area. **Jan. 8.** Largest offensive of the war begins when 30,000 U.S. and South Vietnamese troops attack in "Iron Triangle," northwest of Saigon. In 19-day campaign, 6,000 civilians are sent to refugee centers and area is cleared by burning homes or flattening them with bulldozers, and defoliating thousands of acres.

Jan. 10. The Supreme Court finds that a U.S. citizen with a valid passport may visit a country designated off limits by the State Department without committing a crime. **December 20.** U.S. Court of Appeals forbids the State Department to deny passports as a means of restricting travel to such countries.

Jan. 27. Trapped on top of Saturn 1-B rocket on the ground, three astronauts die in capsule of their spacecraft when fire sweeps through it during full-scale simulation of launching scheduled for February 27. Taped record of voices shows that intensity of fire in oxygen-laden atmosphere has killed them in about 13 seconds, during which time they have had no chance to unscrew exit hatch. **April 9.** Investigating board decries "deficiencies in design and engineering, manufacture and quality control" of whole Apollo project.

January-February. Defense Department announces that 1966 deaths in Vietnam are: U.S., 5,000 (6,700 since 1961); South Vietnam, 10,100; Viet Cong and North Vietnam, 61,600. A reported 20,200 Viet Cong have defected to the South, and 117,000 South Vietnamese soldiers have deserted. As of January, 380,000 U.S. troops are in Vietnam; Communist troops in South Vietnam have increased to an estimated 275,000 men, 25,000 more than in 1965.

Feb. 4. In response to protests by 40 congressmen and Negro leaders, Defense Department cancels shore leave of 3,800 sailors of the aircraft carrier *Franklin D. Roosevelt* in Cape Town, South Africa. Protests warn that stopover will appear to approve South Africa's apartheid policy and that Negro sailors will be discriminated against while ashore.

Feb. 9. President Johnson proposes foreign aid appropriation of $3,100,000,000; cut first by the Senate and again by the House, final amount is $2,300,000,000, lowest in 20 years.

Feb. 10. Twenty-fifth Amendment to the U.S. Constitution is ratified by the states. Amendment gives the President power (subject to congressional approval) to

American space program has been severely mutilated to fit it. . . .

In the context of budget stresses imposed by the war overseas, and by poverty at home, the Kennedy Effect has sustained Apollo by reducing the space program essentially to a single priority. Projects of lesser priority have been shelved into the next decade or into limbo.

No new programs can be started under these conditions. That implies little progress in space technology or science in the next decade, for new programs require years of lead-time. . . .

By its stringent singularity of purpose, the Kennedy Effect has tended to confine rather than extend the national potential in space. It will realize its objective of putting astronauts on the moon, but for a long time after that they will not be able to do anything else.

ROBERT F. KENNEDY
Speech in South Africa, 1966
The answer is to rely on youth — not a time of life but a state of mind, a temper of the will, a quality of imagination, a predominance of courage over timidity, of the appetite for adventure over the love of ease. The cruelties and obstacles of this swiftly changing planet will not yield to obsolete dogmas and outworn slogans. They cannot be moved by those who cling to a present that is already dying, who prefer the illusion of security to the excitement and danger that comes with even the most peaceful progress.

It is a revolutionary world we live in; and this generation, at home and around the world, has had thrust upon it a greater burden of responsibility than any generation that has ever lived.

SOL STERN
Ramparts, 1967

If older Americans have been a little put off by the style of the draft card burners or the Mario Savios, there has always been somewhat of a consensus about the good works of the young men and women of the United States National Student Association. . . .

The quality which rank and file NSA-ers have cherished most about themselves is independence, especially independence from government controls. It was this quality that was supposed to distinguish their organization from national unions of students in the communist world. The quality for the most part was genuine, for the rank and file never knew of the CIA connection.

There were many arguments put forward by NSA's current officers as to why the CIA-NSA relationship should be kept secret. . . . The most pathetic, which appeared again and again, was this: exposing the story would not only hurt NSA, it would hurt the CIA. Covert Action Division No. Five, after all, was not in the business of assassinating Latin American leftists, it was supporting liberal groups like NSA. . . . NSA might be anti-communist, but certainly no one could ever argue that its anti-communism was more militant or more narrow-minded than that of the average American. Rather, it was less so. Thus the exposure of the NSA-CIA tie would deeply hurt the enlightened, liberal, internationalist wing of the CIA. . . .

The twisted sickness of this Orwellian argument should speak for itself. Yet it is extraordinary, and frightening, that it could be so easily made by the talented young liberals at the head of NSA. One would think the idea of "an enlightened wing of the CIA" would be an obvious contradiction in terms.

choose a Vice-President when that office is vacant; it also covers inability of the President to discharge his duties, providing for notification of this event by the President himself or by such a body of government officers as the Congress may appoint.

Feb. 13. The National Student Association (NSA) reveals that since 1952, it has secretly received more than $3 million from the U.S. Central Intelligence Agency (CIA) for use in student exchange programs. **Feb. 14.** CIA admits financing programs, but says that secretiveness has been to avoid labeling of NSA as a government agency, not because students are spies.

Feb. 17. It is revealed that New Orleans District Attorney James Garrison is seeking to prove that President Kennedy's assassination is the result of a conspiracy originating in New Orleans, and that Lee Harvey Oswald is not the killer. **Sept. 4.** After a number of arrests, charges, and countercharges, Chief Justice Earl Warren says he has not seen any evidence to change conclusion of Warren Report. **Sept. 6.** Garrison accuses Warren of trying to subvert his investigation.

March 1. House of Representatives denies his seat to Adam Clayton Powell, Jr., New York Negro, on ground that he has used government funds for private purposes; most Negro leaders condemn action, which Powell calls "lynching, Northern style." **April 7.** Court dismisses suit by Powell to regain seat, saying it has no power over actions of Congress. **April 11.** In special New York election to fill vacancy, Powell is overwhelmingly reelected over two opponents, but his congressional status remains the same.

March 14. UN Secretary-General U Thant proposes peace plan to Vietnam combatants involving initial talks during a truce and reconvening of the Geneva conference. South Vietnam and the U.S. accept (although with reservations); North Vietnam refuses plan. **April 21.** U Thant, on return from tour of the Middle East and East, states that U.S. bombing of Haiphong that has occurred on the previous day was ill-considered at "this time of delicate negotiations."

April 15. Sponsored by Spring Mobilization Committee, huge anti-Vietnam war parades are held in New York and San Francisco. San Francisco marchers number about 50,000; estimates of number of New York marchers vary from 100,000-125,000 police estimate to about 350,000 estimated by Dr. Martin Luther King, Jr., who leads the march.

April 16. Riots break out in Negro ghetto area of Cleveland, beginning several months of widespread violence during which 159 riots occur. Especially damaging are six-day riot in Newark, New Jersey, in which 26 persons die and 1,500 are injured, and week-long riot in Detroit, with 40 deaths, 2,000 injuries, and 5,000 people left homeless; the Detroit disturbance takes 4,700 U.S. paratroopers and 8,000 National Guardsmen to quell.

April 21. Joseph Stalin's daughter, Svetlana Alliluyeva, arrives in the U.S., having requested political asylum at the U.S. embassy in New Delhi, India, in March. Her statement says that she has come because she has been denied the opportunity of self-expression in Russia. Her book, *Twenty Letters to a Friend,* is published later in year.

April 24. Soviet Cosmonaut Vladimir Komarov, after 18 orbits, is killed on reentry when his spacecraft's parachute fails to open. This is only manned flight of the year by any nation; U.S. manned flights are suspended after Apollo disaster.

TOM HAYDEN
New York Review of Books, 1967
After three years of wondering when "the riot" would come to Newark, people knew that this could be it. While city officials pointed with pride to Newark's record of peace, most of the community knew it was only a matter of time until the explosion: "And when Newark goes," according to street wisdom, "it's going to really go." Despite millions in antipoverty and job-training funds during the last three summers, the ailments which afflict every black community had become no better. According to the city officials themselves, Newark has the highest percentage of bad housing of any city in the nation, the highest maternal mortality rate, and the second highest infant mortality rate; the unemployment rate in the ghetto is higher than 15 percent. Every effort to create an organized movement for change has been discredited, absorbed, or met with implacable hostility by politicians. The city's 250,000 Negroes — a majority of the population — felt with good reason excluded from the institutions of business and government. . . .

Regardless of what the mayor did, regardless of what civil rights leaders did, regardless of what planners of the demonstration did, the riot was going to happen. The authorities had been indifferent to the community's demand for justice; now the community was going to be indifferent to the authorities' demand for order. This was apparent to community organizers who walked around the projects Thursday afternoon talking to young people. All the organizers urged was that burning of buildings be minimized so as to spare lives.

THIS PAGE: (Above left) Robert McNamara, secretary of defense, 1961–1968; (above right) "Start by lifting a calf—": cartoon by Reg Manning in the *Arizona Republic*, 1966; (below) result of pollution of a river in Louisiana
OPPOSITE PAGE: (Top) Crowds take over the streets in Detroit, Michigan, following outbreak of riots, 1967; (bottom) military police confront protesters during a peace march in Washington, D.C., October, 1967

DANIEL P. MOYNIHAN
New Leader, 1967

Certainly things have not turned out as we had every reason to think they would. . . .

The violence abroad and the violence at home — regardless of political persuasion, all agree that these are the problems, that they are somehow interconnected, and that in combination they have the potential for polarizing, then fracturing, American society. But the situation is especially embarrassing for American liberals, because it is largely they who have been in office and presided over the onset both of the war in Vietnam and the violence in American cities. Neither may be our fault, yet in a world not overmuch given to nice distinctions in such matters, they most surely must be judged our doing.

The Vietnam war was thought up and is being managed by the men John F. Kennedy brought to Washington to conduct American foreign and defense policy. They are persons of immutable conviction on almost all matters we would consider central to liberal belief, as well as men of personal honor and the highest intellectual attainment. Other liberals also helped to persuade the American public that it was entirely right to be setting out on the course which has led us to the present point of being waist deep in the big muddy. It is this knowledge, this complicity if you will, that requires many of us to practise restraint where others may exercise all their powers of invective and contempt. The plain fact is that if these men got us into the current predicament, who are we to say we would have done better?

This is more the case with respect to the violence at home. The summer of 1967 came in the aftermath of one of the most extraordinary periods of liberal

April 24-28. General William C. Westmoreland, commander of U.S. forces in Vietnam, criticizes antiwar factions as "unpatriotic." Senator J. William Fulbright accuses the administration of having Westmoreland speak in order to prepare the country for escalation of the war.

May 1. Public Health Service survey shows that 72 percent of men who smoke more than two packs of cigarettes per day have at least one chronic ailment, while only 53 percent of those nonsmokers do; conditions listed are bronchitis, sinusitis, peptic ulcers, emphysema, and heart disease. Survey does not find, however, that these conditions are actually caused by smoking.

May 2-9. "International Tribunal on War Crimes" meets in Stockholm. Formed by 94-year-old British philosopher Bertrand Russell, tribunal finds the U.S. guilty of committing atrocities in Vietnam, especially "widespread, systematic and deliberate" bombing of civilians, and names as accessories South Korea, Australia, and New Zealand.

May 11. Israel warns Syria in UN Security Council that it feels justified in defending itself against intensified terrorist raids. Sporadic fighting has continued along Israel's Egyptian, Jordanian, and Syrian borders for 12 years. **May 18.** United Arab Republic President Gamal Abd-al-Nasser, annoyed by statements from Jordan and Saudi Arabia that he leans on UN peace-keeping forces for protection, demands that forces be removed immediately from armistice line between Egypt and Israel. UN Secretary-General U Thant reluctantly discontinues UN Emergency Force mission on May 19. **May 22.** Nasser declares Strait of Tiran closed, thus blocking shipping to Elath, Israel's only outlet to the South and East. **May 23-June 4.** All efforts at mediation by other nations and the UN are blocked by the Soviet Union on the ground that Israel is at fault in the dispute. **June 5.** Deciding that further negotiation is useless, and following shelling by Jordan and Syria, Israel attacks in force on all fronts. **June 6.** UN Security Council passes cease-fire resolution and the U.A.R. breaks off relations with the U.S. and denounces Britain on the ground that they have taken part in air war on Israel's side; both deny this. **June 10.** The Soviet Union breaks off relations with Israel on day that both sides accept cease-fire. In six days, Israel has captured territory quadruple its size — including the Sinai Peninsula, the old city of Jerusalem, all Jordanian territory west of the Jordan River, and heights in Syria from which it has been shelled for years. Hundreds of Arab planes and Soviet-built tanks are destroyed, and 35,000 Arabs are killed; Israeli casualties are 679 dead and 2,600 wounded.

May 15. So-called Kennedy Round (talks on lowering of world tariff barriers) succeeds at Geneva when, after four years of negotiation, 53 countries agree to wide tariff cuts affecting more than $40 billion in world commerce. Agreement is formally signed on June 30.

May 29. The Supreme Court finds California's constitutional amendment that allows property owners to discriminate in rentals or sales of housing is unconstitutional; amendment has been approved by California voters.

June 12. The Supreme Court holds unanimously that 1924 Virginia law which forbids marriage between Negroes and whites is unconstitutional; decision also affects 15 other states with similar laws.

June 16. Unauthorized wiretapping and electronic eavesdropping by federal agencies

legislation, liberal electoral victories, and the liberal dominance of the media of public opinion that we have ever experienced. The period was, moreover, accompanied by the greatest economic expansion in human history. And, to top it all, some of the worst violence occurred in Detroit, a city with one of the most liberal and successful administrations in the nation; a city in which the social and economic position of the Negro was generally agreed to be far and away the best in the nation. Who are we, then, to be pointing fingers?

The question is addressed as much to the future as to the past, for the probabilities are that the present situation will persist for some time. By this I mean that President Johnson will almost certainly be reelected in 1968 and that, with some modifications, the national government will remain in the hands of the same kinds of liberals who have been much in evidence for the last seven years. The war in Asia is likely to go on many years, too, although possibly in different forms. Most importantly, the violence in our cities, tensions between racial and ethnic groups, is just as likely to continue and, if anything, get worse (as indeed the war could get worse). But our responses will have to be sufficiently different from those of the immediate past to suggest that we are aware of some of our apparent shortcomings.

ROBERT YOAKUM

New Republic, 1967

Dodd was the sixth senator to be censured, the second from the state of Connecticut to be so rebuked, the first senator to be censured for personal financial misconduct, the first such defendant to vote at his own trial, although, even so, he was condemned by the largest vote in the history of such proceedings. . . .

One of Dodd's defense speeches was almost identical to a television speech he had delivered earlier to constituents in Connecticut—with an interesting exception. In the Senate he didn't use the theme that ran all the way through his address back home: he was in all this bad trouble because he was an anti-communist. . . .

"The campaign against me," he told his constituents, "has its origin in a strange coming together of hateful and vengeful interest. . . . There was a minor press wolfpack . . . which has been after my scalp for many years because of my position on communism and communist aggression, and because of my repeated criticism of the blindness and softness and insistence on appeasement to which they are all addicted. . . . The communists have always regarded me as a prime enemy. In fact, the communist propaganda apparatus has been having a field day. . . . In a sense, I am technically responsible for the incredibly sloppy bookkeeping that went on in my office. . . . I'm responsible because I was on the Senate floor making speeches, or conducting hearings, or gathering the facts about communism, subversion and terrorism, so that I could present them to the Congress and the people."

are forbidden by U.S. Attorney General except in case of national security or emergency; in all other cases federal agents must have advance written approval of the Attorney General.

June 17. Communist China explodes a hydrogen bomb with power of "several megatons."

June 20. Congress extends draft law to June 30, 1971; the President is given power to cancel deferments of most graduate students, but not undergraduates unless it is necessary because of military manpower shortage.

June 23. Senator Thomas J. Dodd of Connecticut is censured by the Senate for "conduct contrary to accepted morals" (using campaign funds for his personal benefit). The fact that Dodd does not lose his seat inevitably leads to comparisons between treatment of the white Connecticut Senator and Negro Representative Adam Clayton Powell, Jr., of New York.

June 23 and 25. President Johnson and Soviet Premier Aleksei N. Kosygin hold talks in Glassboro, New Jersey. (Site has been chosen as a halfway point compromise when Kosygin declines to go to Washington and Johnson declines to go to New York.) After two days of apparently cordial talks, neither man has changed his position on any important question, but many are encouraged that the meeting has taken place at all.

July 23. In plebiscite to decide status of Puerto Rico, 60 percent vote to remain a commonwealth associated with the U.S., 38 percent for statehood, and 1 percent for becoming an independent country.

Aug. 11. U.S. planes begin attacks on

North Vietnamese targets near the Chinese border that have in the past been off limits; the Soviet Union calls escalation "a new and extremely serious step."

Sept. 3. Almost 5 million South Vietnamese voters elect Nguyen Van Thieu president, with Nguyen Cao Ky vice-president; they have been opposed by 10 nonmilitary candidates in election called fraudulent by some but "reasonably honest" by 22 American observers sent by President Johnson.

Sept. 15. President Johnson again urges Congress to pass legislation controlling sale of guns, pointing out that criminals who are kept from voting or driving an automobile by state laws can legally buy rifles and shotguns without a permit. Legislation fails to pass during this year.

Sept. 18. Defense Secretary McNamara announces that over the next five years, the U.S. will construct a "light" antimissile system because Communist China is developing nuclear warheads and missile systems, not because of any intention to increase pace of arms race with the Soviet Union. McNamara also says that appeals for a "heavy" missile system have been rejected because even with such a system, the U.S. and the Soviet Union could destroy each other.

Oct. 2. Thurgood Marshall, first Negro to become a member of the U.S. Supreme Court, takes oath of office at the Supreme Court building.

Oct. 10. It is revealed that Secretary McNamara, testifying before a Senate subcommittee in August, has said that in his opinion U.S. casualties will not be increased if bombing of North Vietnam is reduced. Military and civilian leaders have, since be-

ROBERT S. McNAMARA
Speech in San Francisco, 1967
The cornerstone of our strategic policy continues to be to deter deliberate nuclear attack upon the United States, or its allies, by maintaining a highly reliable ability to inflict an unacceptable degree of damage upon any single aggressor, or combination of aggressors, at any time during the course of a strategic nuclear exchange—even after our absorbing a surprise first strike. This can be defined as our "assured destruction capability."

Now it is imperative to understand that assured destruction is the very essence of the whole deterrence concept. We must possess an actual, assured destruction capability. And that actual assured destruction capability must also be credible. . . . A potential aggressor must himself believe that our assured destruction capability is in fact actual and that our will to use it in retaliation to an attack is in fact unwavering. . . .

When calculating the force we require, we must be "conservative" in all our estimates of both a potential aggressor's capabilities and his intentions. Security depends upon taking a "worst plausible case"—and having the ability to cope with that eventuality. In that eventuality, we must be able to absorb the total weight of nuclear attack on our country—on our strike-back forces; on our command and control apparatus; on our industrial capacity; on our cities and on our population—and still be fully capable of destroying the aggressor to the point that his society is simply no longer viable in any meaningful, twentieth-century sense. That is what deterrence to nuclear aggression means. It means the certainty of suicide to the aggressor—not merely to his military forces, but to his society as a whole.

U.S. News & World Report, 1967 ©
*"Whether or not marijuana is a more
dangerous drug than alcohol is debat-
able. I don't happen to think it is."*

*Exactly what Dr. James L. Goddard
meant by that statement on October 17
quickly became an issue—since, in
general, the medical profession feels it
is too early to establish for certain the
effects of marijuana smoking. . . .*

*Psychological dependence on mari-
juana is possible, Dr. Goddard conceded, but he added that a person can
become psychologically dependent on
any drug, including aspirin. And he was
reported to have added that society
should be able to accept both alcohol
and marijuana. . . .*

*On Capitol Hill, Representative Dan
Kuykendall (Rep.), of Tennessee, termed
Dr. Goddard's remarks "absolutely inex-
cusable" and urged Congress to demand his resignation. . . .*

*Dr. Goddard himself, in the center of
the controversy, amplified his earlier
remarks to say that it was "false" that
he sees no difference between smoking
marijuana and having a cocktail. . . .*

*"The possession and use of mari-
juana carries a very severe legal penalty, while the use of alcohol has no such
severe penalties attached. But we do
know the physical and mental penalties
that the alcoholic must pay—that is
well documented. For the user of marijuana, the threat is of the unknown effects, which science has yet to determine. Smoking marijuana and drinking
both present dangers to the individual."*

ginning of the bombing, disagreed on its effectiveness; with many of the military
claiming it is necessary and many civilians
doubting that it is effective at all.

Oct. 17. Dr. James L. Goddard, Food
and Drug Administration chief, says that in
his opinion marijuana is not a more dangerous drug than alcohol, but that both can be
dangerous to users if abused.

Oct. 18. At international conference of
Roman Catholic laymen, delegates endorse
by a vote of greater than three to one a
resolution requesting the church to allow
parents to be responsible for use of birth
control devices and medication.

Oct. 18. President Johnson's efforts to
persuade Congress to pass an anti-inflationary 10 percent surcharge on income tax receives a blow when the House demands
that instead, Johnson cut his nonmilitary
spending bill by about $6 billion.

Oct. 20. All-white Mississippi federal
jury convicts seven men in conspiracy to
murder three young civil rights workers in
1964; one of the defendants, who receive
varying sentences of 3 to 10 years, is an
imperial wizard of the White Knights of the
Ku Klux Klan; another is a chief deputy
sheriff.

Oct. 21-22. About 35,000 antiwar protesters gather in Washington, D.C., for
march from the Lincoln Memorial to the
Pentagon, where they are met by solid lines
of troops with fixed bayonets. About 650
marchers are arrested after sporadic incidents of violence. On October 21, thousands of New Yorkers, to show support of
U.S. troops serving in Vietnam, drive with
their automobile headlights on.

Oct. 26. Following incidents in which
college students have interfered with mili-

tary recruitment on campuses, General Lewis B. Hershey, head of Selective Service, instructs draft boards to cancel deferments of those who have taken part. Many draft boards do not follow order, however, since it meets with strong disapproval on virtually all sides, as using the draft for punishment violates the Selective Service Act.

Oct. 28. The U.S. turns over to Mexico 437 acres of formerly Mexican land that have been in dispute since the 1850s, when the Rio Grande changed its course, thus altering the Texas-Mexican border by leaving the land on the Texas side.

Nov. 7. Both Democrats and Republicans claim victory in fall elections, but major feature is election of Negro mayors in Gary, Indiana, and Cleveland, as well as rejection of segregationist woman candidate for mayor of Boston.

Nov. 18. British pound is devalued from $2.80 to $2.40, after financial crisis following report that a $300 million gap exists between Britain's exports and imports. Within four days, 18 small nations also devalue their currency, but major powers state that they will not follow suit. To protect the pound from further pressure, Britain is to receive $3 billion international credits. **Nov. 23.** London market is overwhelmed by gold buying, putting pressure on the U.S. dollar.

Nov. 20. Census Clock in the Department of Commerce registers U.S. population of 200 million; number is based on balanced statistics that average out to an increase of one U.S. citizen every 14½ seconds. Projected date for a population of 500 million is — barring catastrophes — the year 2015.

Dec. 14. Stanford University scientists announce that they have succeeded in pro-

ROBERT McAFEE BROWN
Look, 1967
The war is so wrong, and ways of registering concern about it have become so limited, that civil disobedience seems to me the only honorable route left. . . .

For myself, it is clear what civil disobedience will involve. I teach. I spend my professional life with American youth of draft age. And while I will not use the classroom for such purposes, I will make clear that from now on my concerns about Vietnam will be explicitly focused on counseling, aiding and abetting all students who declare that out of moral conviction they will not fight in Vietnam. I will "counsel, aid and abet" such students to find whatever level of moral protest is consonant with their consciences, and when for them this means refusing service in the armed forces, I will support them in that stand. . . .

I will continue to do this until I am arrested. As long as I am not arrested, I will do it with increasing intensity, for I am no longer willing that 18- or 19-year old boys should pay with their lives for the initially bumbling but now deliberate folly of our national leaders. Nor am I willing to support them in action that may lead them to jail, from a safe preserve of legal inviolability for myself. I must run the same risks as they, and therefore I break the law on their behalf, so that if they are arrested, I too must be arrested. If this means jail, I am willing to go with them, and perhaps we can continue there to think and learn and teach and reflect and emerge with a new set of priorities for American life. . . .

Our country is committing crimes so monstrous that the only thing more monstrous would be continuing silence or inaction in the face of them.

RICHARD H. ROVERE
New Yorker, 1967

I pick up an antiwar manifesto signed by many people who to my certain knowledge favored the Korean intervention and find them saying that because "Congress has not declared a war, as required by the Constitution," the war in Vietnam is "unconstitutional and illegal." For my part, I would be happy if the Supreme Court ruled the war unconstitutional next Monday morning. But I cannot imagine a theory of the war or of the Constitution that would hold our presence in Vietnam to be in violation of our fundamental law and would not require the same judgment on our earlier presence in Korea.

Nor can I see that it would make much difference if Congress did declare the existence of a state of war or if the Supreme Court certified the carnage as constitutional. Can any legislature turn an unjust cause into a just one by an observance of due process? . . .

The signers of this antiwar manifesto were brought together by, they say, a common desire to assist young men in avoiding conscription. A worthy purpose it may well be, but the draft is legal; the Selective Service Act has been in force for twenty-seven years, and the Supreme Court has yet to strike it down. Such sticklers for law might consider turning themselves in for sedition and conspiracy. I find the names of some of them also attached to an appeal calling upon other citizens to join them and Henry David Thoreau — part of whose Civil Disobedience *is used as the manifesto for this particular group — in withholding from the Internal Revenue Service that part of their taxes which, by their calculations, "is being used to finance the war." The income-tax laws are at least as legal and constitutional as Selective Service. Thoreau didn't want*

ducing the active, inner core of a virus, a feat that approaches production of life itself.

Dec. 15. President Johnson signs Wholesome Meat Act in presence of Upton Sinclair, whose novel, *The Jungle,* published in 1906, had originally been responsible for public awareness of filthy conditions in the meat-packing industry.

Although Congress cooperates with President Johnson in this year in passing many measures he has requested, he has been unable to put over much of his antipoverty program, an open housing act, a law against gaining evidence by wiretapping, a bill controlling gun sales and ownership, a measure providing for payment of most presidential campaign expenses by the government, as well as his anti-inflationary 10 percent surtax on income.

The Supreme Court declines to hear two cases involving refusal by young men to participate in the Vietnam war on the ground that the war is illegal.

U.S. Bureau of Narcotics reports that drug addiction is increasing, the number of known addicts being almost 60,000 in 1966. More than 80 percent of these are in New York, California, Illinois, New Jersey, and Michigan, and about half are between the ages of 21 and 30.

At the end of this year, U.S. troops in Vietnam have increased by over 100,000 to a total of 486,000. U.S. deaths in this year are 9,350 — almost 3,000 more than the total of the previous six years.

During this year, the U.S. gathers enough information about the moon (through photographs and chemical analyses of the surface) to complete project of selecting landing sites. The Soviet Union succeeds in docking two unmanned orbiting satellites as a start toward program of construction of scientific space stations. The U.S. and the Soviet Union both send probes to Venus, and both send up a number of weather and communications satellites. Satellites are launched also by France, Italy, and Britain.

German citizen Hermann Winter builds a catapult and fires 120 dumplings at noisy, low-flying U.S. helicopters; his campaign succeeds when the Army agrees to fly over his town at a higher altitude.

1967 - 1968

Nov. 16, 1967. Senate Foreign Relations Committee votes unanimously to require approval of Congress in the future for sending any troops abroad except to repel an attack on the U.S. or to protect U.S. citizens; move (which does not include Vietnam war) is the result of embarrassment of a number of U.S. congressmen over having given President Johnson blanket endorsement of his retaliatory action after Gulf of Tonkin attack in 1964. **Jan. 30, 1968.** Foreign Relations Committee decides to reexamine Gulf of Tonkin incident, feeling that Johnson may have "overreacted" on basis of too little information.

Nov. 29, 1967. It is announced that Secretary of Defense Robert S. McNamara will become president of the World Bank. **Jan. 19, 1968.** Clark M. Clifford is chosen to replace McNamara.

Dec. 3, 1967. Surgeons in Cape Town, South Africa, perform world's first transplant of a human heart. Within five weeks, four more such operations are performed in Cape Town and the U.S.; four patients (including the first) have died by late January 1968. Although all deaths have been from causes other than rejection of foreign tissue, many medical sources feel that transplants have been made after too little research; op-

to help pay for the Mexican War, which may have been, as he passionately believed it was, immoral, but it was certainly not illegal or unconstitutional. Anyway, a "legal" war is a legal fiction.

New York Times, March 1, 1967
[Hermann] Winter announced today that he had signed an armistice with the Luftwaffe after having forced the West German Air Force's noisy jet planes to keep a proper altitude above his Bavarian home by firing dumplings at them. . . .

"I have a truce with our Luftwaffe," he added "but I am still on a war footing with the United States Air Force and the NATO planes that come overhead." . . .

He said the American aircraft included jet-powered helicopters, which flew as low as 150 feet over his house. . . .

His . . . missiles make a dull splat when they strike their targets, he added.

New York Times, March 3, 1967
United States military officials, faced with the threat of antiaircraft dumplings, agreed today to negotiate.

New York Times, March 4, 1967
Hermann Winter claimed victory today in his dumpling war against low-flying aircraft. He said the offending United States Army helicopter unit had surrendered unconditionally. . . .

At the helicopter base ceremony he was received with full military honors and was assured that from now on the helicopters would maintain an altitude of at least 1,600 feet.

EUGENE RABINOWITCH

Bulletin of the Atomic Scientists, 1968
The great failure, the crime before the future generations of mankind, has been not a sin of commission, but a sin of omission: a failure to stem the worldwide trend toward pre-atomic "normalcy" by an imaginative, large-scale use of American power and wealth, to lead in a worldwide mobilization of technical, economic, and intellectual resources for the building of a viable world community.

The day of reckoning may be approaching, not in the form of American withdrawal and communist takeover in the Far East but in a wave of world hunger and the accompanying surge of world anarchy predicted by many thoughtful analysts for the next decade. . . .

There is little reason to feel sanguine about the future of our (and the whole Western) society on the world scale. There is a mass revulsion against war, yes; but no sign of conscious intellectual leadership in a rebellion against the deadly heritage of international anarchy. There is no broad recognition of the breathtaking perspectives of the scientific revolution—from all-destroying nuclear and biological war, likely if the international anarchy continues; from unprecedented world hunger, inevitable if man's procreation and food production are not brought into harmony by rational effort, to practically unlimited supply of energy, fresh water, food, shelter, and clothing for all—if stable peace is maintained and worldwide constructive cooperation is established.

In sad recognition that the past six years have brought mankind no closer to choosing the creative path, but have brought it farther down the road to disaster, the Bulletin clock is moved, on this sad New Year's Day, closer to midnight.

erations lead to discussion of moral and legal problems of substitutions of human organs. One South African patient recovers from operation and appears to be in good health.

1968

Jan. 2. New Year's truce, described as the "worst ever" by U.S. authorities, ends in Vietnam.

Jan. 5. Author and pediatrician Benjamin Spock and four others are indicted on charges of conspiring to counsel young men to violate U.S. draft laws. **June 14.** Four, including Dr. Spock, are convicted; they appeal.

Jan. 9. U.S. spacecraft Surveyor 7 makes successful landing on moon and begins transmitting pictures to earth.

Jan. 15. Supreme Court gives final approval to merger of New York Central and Pennsylvania lines to form largest railroad in the U.S.

Jan. 21. Communist forces begin siege of U.S. stronghold of Khe Sanh, 14 miles south of Vietnam demilitarized zone (DMZ). Savage fighting continues until April 5, when the U.S. announces that siege has been lifted. Fortress is evacuated soon afterward.

Jan. 22. U.S. B-52 bomber carrying four unarmed hydrogen bombs crashes near Thule, Greenland, scattering bomb fragments, some radioactive, over ice.

Jan. 23. U.S.S. *Pueblo*, Navy intelligence ship, is seized off Korean coast by North Korean patrol boats and taken into port of Wonsan; justification for action is charge that *Pueblo* has violated North Korean waters. U.S. denies charge. **Jan. 26.** The U.S.

appeals to UN Security Council to obtain safe return of ship. Negotiations continue for months, but *Pueblo* remains in North Korean hands.

Feb. 16. National Security Council abolishes most draft deferments for graduate students and also suspends most occupational deferments. Several universities warn that action will seriously harm U.S. graduate programs.

Feb. 28. Governor George Romney of Michigan withdraws from race for Republican presidential nomination; two leading candidates remaining are Richard M. Nixon and Governor Nelson Rockefeller of New York. **March 21.** Rockefeller also withdraws. **April 30.** Rockefeller reverses stand, saying that he will seek nomination.

March 11. The U.S. and South Vietnamese troops launch largest offensive of war thus far against enemy forces in Saigon area. **March 14.** The U.S. reports that number of American casualties in Vietnam now exceeds total in Korean War.

March 12. Senator Eugene McCarthy of Minnesota makes surprisingly good showing in New Hampshire Democratic presidential primary. **March 16.** Senator Robert F. Kennedy of New York announces his intention to seek Democratic presidential nomination.

March 19. President Johnson signs into law bill eliminating requirement that at least 25 percent of U.S. currency must be backed by gold. Action follows soon after London gold market is closed at request of the U.S. to halt heavy selling of gold.

March 31. In action that takes even his advisors by surprise, President Johnson states in nationwide TV address that he will neither seek nor accept nomination for an-

LYNDON B. JOHNSON
Address to the nation, 1968
There is divisiveness in the American house now. There is divisiveness among us all tonight. Holding the trust that is mine—as President of all the people—I cannot disregard the peril to the progress of the American people and the hope and the prospects of peace for all peoples. . . .

Through all time to come, America will be a stronger nation, a more just society, a land of greater opportunity and fulfillment because of what we have done together in these years of unparalleled achievement. Our reward will come in the life of freedom and peace and hope that our children will enjoy through ages ahead. What we won when all our people united must not now be lost in suspicion, distrust, and selfishness or politics among any of our people.

Believing this as I do, I have concluded that I should not permit the presidency to become involved in the partisan divisions that are developing in this political year. With America's sons in the field far away, with America's future under challenge here at home, with our hopes and the world's hopes for peace in the balance every day, I do not believe that I should devote an hour or a day of my time to any duties other than the awesome duties of this office, the presidency of your country.

Accordingly, I shall not seek and I will not accept the nomination of my party for another term as your President. But, let men everywhere know, however, that a strong and a confident, a vigilant America stands ready to seek an honorable peace and stands ready tonight to defend an honored cause, whatever the price, whatever the burden, whatever the sacrifice that duty may require.

MARTIN LUTHER KING, JR.

Speech in Memphis, April 3, 1968

And then I got into Memphis. And some began to say the threats — or talk about the threats that were out. Or what would happen to me from some of our sick white brothers.

Well, I don't know what will happen now. We've got some difficult days ahead. But it really doesn't matter with me now. Because I've been to the mountain top. I won't mind.

Like anybody, I would like to live a long life. Longevity has its place. But I'm not concerned about that now. I just want to do God's will.

And He's allowed me to go up to the mountain. And I've looked over, and I've seen the Promised Land.

I may not get there with you, but I want you to know tonight that we as a people will get to the Promised Land.

So I'm happy tonight. I'm not worried about anything. I'm not fearing any man. Mine eyes have seen the glory of the coming of the Lord.

Mrs. Martin Luther King, Jr., with daughter Bernice at funeral services for her husband

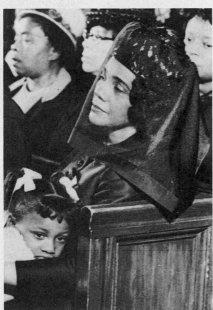

other term and simultaneously announces that he has ordered limitation on bombing of North Vietnam. **April 27.** Vice President Hubert H. Humphrey of Minnesota announces that he will seek Democratic presidential nomination.

April 3. The U.S. and North Vietnam agree to establish direct contact between their representatives as first step toward ending fighting in Vietnam. After weeks of charges and countercharges, Paris is agreed on as site of talks. **May 10.** Talks begin, but little progress toward cessation of hostilities is apparent for months.

April 4. Martin Luther King, Jr., leading Negro proponent of nonviolent protest against injustice, is shot to death by assailant while staying in Memphis, Tennessee, motel. King is in city to support strike of Negro garbage collectors for higher wages. Murder is followed by racial violence in many U.S. cities. **June 8.** James Earl Ray is arrested by Scotland Yard detectives at London Airport and charged with the crime.

April 11. President Johnson signs civil rights bill that includes prohibition against racial discrimination in sale or rental of about 80 percent of U.S. housing. Passage of bill, which has been often proposed in past, is speeded in House of Representatives following King assassination.

April 23. Methodist and Evangelical United Brethren churches merge to form United Methodist Church, second largest Protestant body in the U.S. with over 11 million members.

April 24. Campus of Columbia University is closed after two days of tumultuous student demonstrations. **April 30.** New York City police forcibly remove students and non-student supporters from five university buildings that they have held for several days.

April 26. Atomic Energy Commission explodes experimental hydrogen bomb, largest yet tested in the U.S., 3,800 feet below Nevada desert. Man-made "earthquake" is felt in California coastal cities.

May 29. President Johnson signs "Truth-in-Lending" bill that, among other provisions, requires that consumers be informed of actual cost of credit in on-time purchases.

June 5. Robert F. Kennedy is shot in Los Angeles shortly after he has claimed victory over McCarthy in California primary. Sirhan B. Sirhan, a Jordanian Arab, is seized by Kennedy aides at the scene of the shooting. Kennedy dies the next morning. President Johnson names June 9 national day of mourning and appoints commission of distinguished citizens to investigate phenomenon of physical violence in the U.S. Memorial services are led by last surviving brother, Senator Edward M. Kennedy of Massachusetts.

June 10. General William C. Westmoreland turns over command of U.S. forces in Vietnam to General Creighton W. Abrams. Westmoreland is named Army chief-of-staff.

June 19. Climax of Poor People's Campaign, planned by Martin Luther King before his death and carried through partly as a memorial to him, occurs in Washington, D.C., when more than 50,000 people, about half of them white, take part in Solidarity Day March.

June 26. Earl Warren resigns as chief justice of Supreme Court, resignation to take effect when new chief justice is confirmed by Senate. President Johnson names Associate Justice Abe Fortas to post and nomi-

WILL HERBERG
National Review, 1968
There is a second type of political assassination that is of a very different kind. It might be called the American, or frontier, type. Here it is not a cause or ideology that animates the assassin, but the frontier vigilante notion of taking the law into your own hands. There is a deep contempt for the slow and uncertain processes of official law; that can be rectified only by taking your "trusty old gun" off the wall, and executing rough and ready justice at the end of the muzzle. This was once the only "justice" available on the frontier; it has remained over, in much corrupted form, in the lynch mob and in such assassinations as that perpetrated by Jack Ruby a few years ago. . . .

The United States, in this century, has become an imperial nation. Nothing that happens anywhere on the surface of the globe can leave American national interests unaffected. . . .

So, the prospects are that what I have been calling the European, or Continental, type of political assassination is not going to fade away by itself. In fact, European, or Continental, is no longer the appropriate name for it. Deep ethnic heterogeneity has made what is European into essentially American; and America's new imperial role makes what is essentially American into European, Asiatic, global. . . . We need not have any more political assassinations (although we not unprobably will); we will have to look to our security and police arrangements for that. But the tensions out of which political assassinations come are bound to grow and multiply.

Chicago Daily News, Aug. 25, 1968
We can look forward to an orderly and productive session, in which the biggest surprise may turn out to be the fact that there are no surprises at all. For Chicago is, after all, an old pro at the convention business, just as Mayor Daley—when he hangs onto his cool—is an old pro at making things go the way he wants them to go.

JIMMY BRESLIN
Chicago Sun-Times, Aug. 29, 1968
In 20 years of being with the police, having police in the family, riding with police in cars, drinking with them, watching them work in demonstrations . . . all over the world, this performance of the police of Chicago . . . last night was the worst act I have ever seen perpetrated by policemen.

JACK MABLEY
Chicago's American, Aug. 29, 1968
I have heard Rubin speak and he was obscene and revolting. In America a man may be arrested for obscenity or revolution. But Rubin was grabbed off the street and rushed to jail because of what he thinks. This is the way it is done in Prague. This is what happens to candidates who finish second in Vietnam. This is not the beginning of the police state, it is the police state.

Newsweek, Sept. 6, 1968
All the unmuzzled passions, inconsolable frustrations and polarizing hatreds plaguing the republic surged to the surface in the guarded streets, chaotic hotels and security-taut International Amphitheatre of Chicago, a city transformed by fear and force . . . [where] beefy cops . . . went on a sustained

nates Judge Homer Thornberry as new associate justice. **July 19.** Senate Judiciary Committee finishes hearing four days of testimony by Fortas on his fitness to be chief justice. **Oct. 1.** In key vote, Democratic Senate leaders fail to end Southern filibuster on Fortas nomination, after which Fortas withdraws name and President rescinds nomination of Thornberry.

June 28. President Johnson signs into law bill combining 10 percent income tax surcharge with $6 billion cut in government expenditures.

July 1. Sixty-two nations, including the U.S., the U.K., and the U.S.S.R., sign nuclear nonproliferation treaty when it is opened for signature in Washington, London, and Moscow. Doubts are raised about U.S. Senate's willingness to ratify treaty, and action is postponed until after presidential election.

July 15. Direct airline service between the U.S. and the U.S.S.R. is inaugurated by Aeroflot, the Soviet airline, and Pan American World Airways.

July 19. House of Representatives kills proposals for federal registration of guns. **July 23.** House refuses to require state licensing of gun owners. **Oct. 10.** Congress passes watered-down gun control law that bans interstate sale of rifles, shotguns, and ammunition.

July 26. Truong Dinh Dzu, runner-up in South Vietnamese presidential elections of 1967, is sentenced to five years' imprisonment for conduct detrimental to the people and the armed forces.

Aug. 1. President Johnson signs into law most comprehensive housing bill in 19 years, authorizing $5.3 billion to provide more than 1.7 million new or renovated low-cost housing units in three-year period.

Aug. 8. Republican Party convention at Miami Beach nominates Richard M. Nixon of California for the presidency; he names Governor Spiro T. Agnew of Maryland as his running mate. Platform stresses need for change. **Aug. 28.** Democrats at Chicago, against backdrop of violence in the streets and bitter disaffection of McCarthy supporters, nominate Hubert H. Humphrey of Minnesota for President, and, the next day, choose Edmund S. Muskie of Maine for Vice-President. Charges of police brutality and countercharges of student provocation reveal deep division in party and bode ill for Democrats in election. Platform stresses achievements of past eight years. **Sept. 17.** George C. Wallace of Alabama is nominated at Dallas convention of his American Independence Party; he names Curtis LeMay as his running mate on October 3. Wallace campaign emphasizes alleged welfare statism of two major parties and appeals to racist feelings of many Americans.

Aug. 20. Armed forces of the Soviet Union, Poland, East Germany, Hungary, and Bulgaria invade Czechoslovakia after weeks of rumors that Czech liberalization program, under way for a year, would arouse open opposition by Russians. **Aug. 21.** President Johnson and other world leaders condemn Soviet action.

Sept. 9. Arthur Ashe wins U.S. tennis title at Forest Hills, New York. Tournament is open for first time to both amateurs and professionals, and Ashe is first Negro to win men's crown.

Sept. 26. Walt Disney's Mickey Mouse celebrates his 40th "birthday."

Sept. 30. One million New York City

rampage unprecedented outside the most unreconstructed boondocks of Dixie. 'Kill 'em! Kill 'em!' they shouted as they charged the harum-scarum mobs. . . . Time and again, the police singled out reporters and photographers for clubbing. . . . 'You're murderers,' screamed a youth — until a cop silenced him with a rap across the face.

New Statesman, Aug. 29, 1968
The Democratic Party, having realized most of the domestic reforms proposed by the New Deal in the 1930s, and being unable to resolve the Southeast Asian freak-out to which its present president has committed the country, is empty of ideological and moral content, expects defeat and, on some guilt-ridden substratum of the conglomerate psyche, cherishes that apocalyptic prospect. . . .They will nominate Humphrey . . . because they are no longer fit to govern. . . . So let the rough beast slouch in 1968 even if his name is Nixon.

Chicago Tribune, Aug. 30, 1968
The bearded, dirty, lawless rabble . . . used every sort of provocation against police and National Guardsmen — vile taunts, lye solutions, bricks, and rubble. The police and Guardsmen used such force as was necessary. For enforcing law and order, Mayor Daley and the police deserve congratulations rather than criticism.

Shortly calm will return to the city, and the orderly life we have known will be resumed. That would be an optimum time for our visitors to see Chicago in its normal character. We should love to see them come back again and to appreciate our city and its people as they really are.

JEREMY LARNER, DAVID WOLF
Life, 1968

When you stop to think about it, the small group of black track stars who organized the "Olympic Project for Human Rights" have got quite a lot done in less than a year. Led by Harry Edwards, a professor at San Jose State, they helped keep South Africa out of the Games. . . .

The most prominent spokesmen of the original group were Tommie Smith, Lee Evans and John Carlos, all of San Jose State. They are not separatists. They do not believe in violence. They are dedicated to ending what they see as exploitation of black athletes and, in the process, gaining dignity and equality for all black people. . . .

After Smith overcomes a badly pulled muscle to set a world record and win the gold medal in the 200 meters, he and bronze medalist John Carlos hurriedly assemble the symbols of a protest. They borrow a black scarf for Smith and a black shirt and African beads for Carlos. They pull up their sweatpants and take off their shoes to show their black knee socks. Sharing Smith's pair of gloves, Tommie raises his right fist and John his left and both bow their heads as the band plays The Star-Spangled Banner. *In the grandstand, Lee Evans puts on the other pair of gloves, raises his right fist and stands in the same pose—but no one sees him. Later, on TV, Smith solemnly explains that the shoes off symbolized black poverty and the raised fists black unity.*

Carlos, walking down the Avenida Revolución that afternoon, says, "We wanted all the black people in the world—the little grocer, the man with the shoe repair store—to know that when that medal hangs on my chest or Tommie's, it hangs on his also."

schoolchildren return to school after three-week teachers' strike. **Oct. 14.** Bitter new strike begins; it is not settled until middle of November.

Oct. 7. Report is released indicating that about one-half of U.S. Catholic priests reject anti-birth control position of Pope Paul VI, as revealed in encyclical of July 29 and defended in later pronouncements.

Oct. 10. Senate Democrats give up fight to clear television debates between major presidential candidates. Humphrey urges debates, but Nixon opposes them.

Oct. 11. Apollo 7, main U.S. hope for moon landing in 1969 or 1970, lifts off on successful 11-day, 163-orbit flight, which is marred only by minor technical difficulties and fact that three astronauts all catch bad colds.

Oct. 12. After assurances by the Mexican government that it can keep peace in the aftermath of widespread and bloody rioting, Olympic Games begin in Mexico City. The U.S. wins record number of medals, but games are marred by black power demonstrations that result in dismissal of two members of U.S. team, both medal winners.

Oct. 16. Robert W. Holley, of the Salk Institute, La Jolla, California; H. Gobind Khorana, of the University of Wisconsin; and Marshall W. Nirenberg, of the National Institutes of Health, are jointly awarded 1968 Nobel Prize in Physiology or Medicine. **Oct. 30.** Luis W. Alvarez, of the University of California at Berkeley, is awarded 1968 Nobel Prize in Physics, and Lars Onsager, of Yale University, is awarded 1968 Nobel Prize in Chemistry. Awards give the U.S. sweep in all three science categories for first time since 1946 and raise to 79 the total number of scientists working in this country who have won science prizes since establishment of awards in 1901.

Oct. 17. Mrs. Jacqueline Kennedy, widow of slain president, announces that she will marry Greek ship-owner and billionaire Aristotle S. Onassis. They are married on Onassis' private Aegean island three days later, amid near-universal press condemnation.

Oct. 31. President Johnson announces end of all bombing of North Vietnam. Hanoi agrees to widen Paris talks to include South Vietnamese government and National Liberation Front (Viet Cong) representatives the next day. South Vietnamese government at first refuses to participate, causing delay.

Nov. 5. In one of the closest elections in U.S. history, Richard M. Nixon is chosen 37th President. Nixon-Agnew ticket wins 302 electoral votes, with 43.4 percent of major party vote; Humphrey-Muskie wins 191 electoral votes with 43.1 percent; and Wallace-LeMay wins 45 electoral votes with 13.5 percent. Popular vote figures are not final until January 1969 but are about 31,375,000 for Nixon, 31,125,000 for Humphrey, and 9,775,000 for Wallace. For first time since Reconstruction, Democratic candidate wins no states in Solid South, although he takes Texas. Democrats retain control of both houses of Congress, but election on the whole indicates national conservative trend.

RICHARD M. NIXON
Speech to the nation, 1968
We stand at a great turning point — when the nation is groping for a new direction, unsure of its role and its purposes, caught in a tumult of change. And for the first time, we face serious, simultaneous threats to the peace both at home and abroad. . . .

The next President must unite America. He must calm its angers, ease its terrible frictions, and bring its people together once again in peace and mutual respect. He has to take hold of America before he can move it forward.

This requires leadership that believes in law, and has the courage to enforce it; leadership that believes in justice, and is determined to promote it; leadership that believes in progress, and knows how to inspire it. . . .

The President is the one official who represents every American — rich and poor, privileged and underprivileged. He represents those whose misfortunes stand in dramatic focus, and also the great, quiet forgotten majority — the non-shouters and the non-demonstrators, the millions who ask principally to go their own way in decency and dignity, and to have their own rights accorded the same respect they accord the rights of others. Only if he listens to the quiet voices can he be true to this trust.

This I pledge, that in a Nixon Administration, America's citizens will not have to break the law to be heard, they will not have to shout or resort to violence. We can restore peace only if we make government attentive to the quiet as well as the strident, and this I intend to do.

"The Train Robbery"; cartoon from "Punch" giving English view of the effect of the Vietnam war on the United States economy

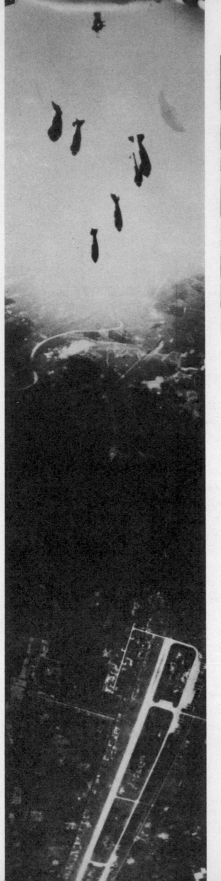

THIS PAGE: (Above) U.S. trooper puts rifle to the head of a woman Viet Cong suspect; (left) U.S. bombing of Phuc Yen airfield in North Vietnam; (below) cartoon by Hugh Haynie in the *Courier-Journal*, Louisville, Kentucky, 1968
OPPOSITE PAGE: (Top) President Richard M. Nixon (right) with Vice President Spiro Agnew; (bottom) Apollo 12 astronaut photographed with container of lunar soil collected during extra-vehicular activity, July 1969. Astronaut who took photo is reflected in the face shield.

Suspended here in Asia . . .
We think back
with chagrin . . .

How difficult
the getting out . . .
How easy getting in . . .

HUGH HAYNIE
The Courier-Journal

DEAN RUSK
Statement on Pueblo, 1968

The United States representative at Panmunjom has just obtained the release of the 82 officers and men of the U.S.S. Pueblo *who last January were illegally seized with their ship on the high seas. . . .*

After ten months of negotiations, during which we made every sort of reasonable offer, all of which were harshly rejected, we had come squarely up against a painful problem: how to obtain the release of the crew without having this government seem to attest to statements which simply are not true. Then, within the past week, a way which does just that was found, and a strange procedure was accepted by the North Koreans. Apparently the North Koreans believe there is propaganda value even in a worthless document which General Woodward publicly labeled false before he signed it. General Woodward said:

"The position of the United States government with regard to the Pueblo, *as consistently expressed in the negotiations at Panmunjom and in public, has been that the ship was not engaged in illegal activity, that there is no convincing evidence that the ship at any time intruded into the territorial waters claimed by North Korea, and that we could not apologize for actions which we did not believe took place. The document which I am going to sign was prepared by the North Koreans and is at variance with the above position, but my signature will not and cannot alter the facts. I will sign the document to free the crew and only to free the crew."*

Dec. 1. President's National Commission on the Causes and Prevention of Violence, established following the assassination of Sen. Robert F. Kennedy, publishes its report on the disorders accompanying the Democratic National Convention in Chicago in August. The report is strongly critical of the city's administration and police.

Dec. 21. Apollo 8 spacecraft lifts off from Cape Kennedy carrying three U.S. astronauts. Lunar orbit is achieved three days later and while circling the moon 10 times the astronauts make several live voice and television broadcasts to Earth, including a Christmas Day reading from the Book of Genesis. **Dec. 27.** The mission ends successfully with a splashdown in the Pacific Ocean 1,200 miles southwest of Hawaii.

Dec. 23. North Korea releases the crew of the U.S.S. *Pueblo*, Navy intelligence ship captured in January. Ten months of negotiation have resulted in a bizarre agreement whereby the U.S. formally admits and apologizes for intruding into North Korean waters while simultaneously repudiating the admission. Subsequent investigations reveal that the crew members have been subjected to torture while in captivity. **April 15, 1969.** North Korean MiG jets shoot down U.S. Navy intelligence airplane over the Sea of Japan, claiming it has violated North Korean airspace. All 31 crewmen are presumed dead. President Nixon orders a naval task force into the area and announces that reconnaissance flights will continue with added air and sea protection.

1969

Jan. 3. Congress convenes and the House votes to reseat New York Representative Adam Clayton Powell, Jr., though it strips him of seniority and levies a heavy fine.

Jan. 6. In an unprecedented action, a challenge is lodged against the vote of a North

Carolina presidential elector during the formal congressional count of the electoral vote. The elector had been pledged to Nixon but has voted for Wallace. The challenge and its rejection mark the beginning of a debate on reform of the electoral system that continues through the year.

Jan. 7. Sirhan B. Sirhan, charged with the murder of Sen. Robert F. Kennedy, goes on trial in Los Angeles. **April 17.** He is found guilty and on May 21, despite a plea from Sen. Edward Kennedy, is sentenced to death. He remains in jail pending appeal.

Jan. 20. President Nixon is inaugurated amid heavy security precautions because of threats of disruption by various radical and antiwar groups.

January-February. Massive leakage from offshore oil-drilling installations near Santa Barbara, California, causes widespread property damage, water pollution, and wildlife destruction. Leaks recur throughout the year here and elsewhere, adding fuel to a growing debate on pollution and conservation.

Feb. 8. After 148 years the *Saturday Evening Post* publishes its last issue.

Feb. 24. Mariner 6 unmanned space probe is launched toward Mars equipped with television camera for close photographic study of the planet. An identical Mariner 7 is launched a month later. Each passes about 2,130 miles above Mars, Mariner 6 on July 31 and Mariner 7 on August 5, and together they transmit 198 pictures of the Martian surface. **May 15-16.** Soviet space probes Venera 5 and 6 reach Venus and enter its atmosphere. Before the instruments fail they report temperatures of about 800° F. and an extremely dense atmosphere of carbon dioxide.

March 10. James Earl Ray pleads guilty to the murder of Rev. Martin Luther King, Jr.,

RICHARD M. NIXON
Inaugural address, 1969
Standing in this same place a third of a century ago, Franklin Delano Roosevelt addressed the nation ravaged by depression, gripped in fear. He could say in surveying the nation's troubles: "They concern, thank God, only material things."

Our crisis today is in reverse.

We find ourselves rich in goods, but ragged in spirit; reaching with magnificent precision for the moon, but falling into raucous discord on earth. . . .

In these difficult years, America has suffered from a fever of words; from inflated rhetoric that promises more than it can deliver; from angry rhetoric that fans discontents into hatreds; from bombastic rhetoric that postures instead of persuading.

We cannot learn from one another until we stop shouting at one another—until we speak quietly enough so that our words can be heard as well as our voices. . . .

Only a few short weeks ago, we shared the glory of man's first sight of the world as God sees it, as a single sphere reflecting light in the darkness. . . .

In that moment of surpassing technological triumph, men turned their thoughts toward home and humanity—seeing in that far perspective that man's destiny on earth is not divisible; telling us that however far we reach into the cosmos our destiny lies not in the stars but on earth itself, in our own hands, in our own hearts.

We have endured a long night of the American spirit. But as our eyes catch the dimness of the first rays of dawn, let us not curse the remaining dark. Let us gather the light.

BARRY GOLDWATER
Speech in Senate, 1969

Now we are being asked to adopt a nuclear nonproliferation treaty with the Soviet Union and other nations. The arguments are familiar. They are all lofty and noble. . . . I ask you who, on the surface, could oppose such an appeal? . . .

But my objection to the nonproliferation treaty at this time has to do more with the effect it might have on foreign affairs generally. Look at what has happened in the struggle between East and West since we ratified the test ban treaty and presumably took a giant step toward resolving our differences. The Soviet Union has repeatedly demonstrated that, far from reducing or being interested in a reduction of world tensions, it has actively and aggressively promoted such tensions on a worldwide basis. Vietnam is a case in point. The Vietcong and Hanoi couldn't have kept up the pace at which they are killing American soldiers for six months without the supplies and support sent to them by our partner in the test ban treaty. The Middle East would not today be the tinder box threatening the peace of three continents if it were not for an aggressive policy of Soviet arming of the Arab nations. The Mediterranean would not today be bristling with Soviet naval power. Czechoslovakia would not have been invaded, nor would Rumania and West Germany be threatened.

No, I tell you there can be no case made in fact for the argument that the Soviet Union is mellowing and that we must further that softening process through the ratification of a nuclear nonproliferation treaty. . . . Do we, in ratifying this treaty, announce to the world that we are ready to forget that the Soviet Union has a long, dishonorable history of broken treaties?

and is sentenced to 99 years in prison.

March 13. Nuclear nonproliferation treaty, designed to prevent the spread of nuclear weapons to nations other than those already possessing them, is ratified by the Senate.

March 20. Federal grand jury in Chicago indicts 8 persons for violating the anti-riot provision of the 1968 Civil Rights Bill, which prohibits crossing a state line with the intent to incite or participate in a riot. They are also charged with conspiring to violate the law. Charges stem from the disturbances at the Democratic National convention in 1968. **Sept. 24.** The trial of the "Chicago 8" (later 7) begins and is marked throughout by noisy demonstrations inside and outside the courtroom.

March 28. Former President and General of the Army Dwight D. Eisenhower dies at Walter Reed Hospital in Washington, D.C. After a state funeral attended by high-ranking dignitaries from around the world, he is buried in his boyhood home, Abilene, Kansas.

April 3. Latest figures show that the American combat death toll in the Vietnam war has passed that of the Korean War. By the end of the year more than 40,000 American troops have died in South Vietnam since 1961.

April 4. Houston surgeons implant an artificial heart in a patient. It functions for three days, until replaced by a transplanted human heart.

April 16. Michigan legislature bans the sale of DDT. As public awareness of the dangers of unrestricted use of pesticides grows, several states follow suit. **Nov. 20.** Department of Agriculture announces a step-by-step phaseout that by 1971 would reduce DDT use by about 90 percent.

April 29. Congressional hearing discloses a

$2.1 billion cost overrun on the C-5A jet transport being built for the Air Force by Lockheed Aircraft Corporation. Investigation soon widens to include many other defense projects with similar huge deficits.

May 4. *Life* magazine discloses financial transactions between Supreme Court Justice Abe Fortas and a financier recently convicted of violating securities laws. **May 15.** After widespread criticism Fortas resigns, the first justice to do so under fire.

May 10. U.S. and South Vietnamese forces launch ten-day assault on "Hamburger Hill" in the A Shau Valley. One of the bloodiest battles of the war, it draws heavy criticism at home, since the hill has little strategic value. **May 28.** U.S. forces abandon the hill.

May 21. President Nixon names District of Columbia Court of Appeals Judge Warren Burger as chief justice of the Supreme Court. He is confirmed by the Senate on June 9.

May-July. At the President's request New York Gov. Nelson Rockefeller undertakes a series of fact-finding tours of Central and South America. His visits are marked by violent anti-American demonstrations and harsh repressive measures in several countries.

June 2. Talks begin between the U.S. and Japan on the status of the Ryukyu Islands, including Okinawa, held by the U.S. since World War II. **Nov. 21.** President Nixon and Premier Sato announce jointly that the islands will be returned to Japan in 1972.

June 6. District of Columbia Court of Appeals rules illegal a 1967 order from Gen. Lewis B. Hershey, head of Selective Service, instructing local draft boards to reclassify antiwar and antidraft demonstrators. **June 14.** Hershey announces that he will not notify local boards of the ruling. **Oct. 10.** It is announced that Hershey will be replaced as head of Selective Service in 1970.

EDWARD KENNEDY
Speech in Senate, 1969

After the cessation of bombing last November, the President issued an order to the field that American military forces were to maintain a constant and steady pressure upon the enemy. As a result, the levels of combat and casualties did not remain the same, but actually increased. The number of U.S. offensive actions making contact with the enemy grew significantly; the total number of U.S. battalion-size operations was raised; the amount of bomb tonnage dropped in the South rose to a total greater than the amount of bomb tonnage previously dropped on the North and South. . . .

In his April 18 press conference, President Nixon reaffirmed President Johnson's earlier directive by stating that he has not ordered, nor did he intend to order, any reduction of our activity in Vietnam. He explained that this was in the interest of maintaining the strength of our bargaining position in Paris.

I am compelled to speak on this question today, for I believe that the level of our military activity in Vietnam runs opposite to our stated intentions and goals in Paris. But, more important, I feel it is both senseless and irresponsible to continue to send our young men to their deaths to capture hills and positions that have no relation to ending this conflict.

President Nixon has told us, without question, that we seek no military victory, that we seek only peace. How then can we justify sending our boys against a hill a dozen times or more, until soldiers themselves question the madness of the action? The assault on "Hamburger Hill" is only symptomatic of a mentality and a policy that requires immediate attention. American boys are too valuable to be sacrificed for a false sense of military pride.

NEIL ARMSTRONG
July 20, 1969
That's one small step for a man, one giant leap for mankind.

NEIL ARMSTRONG
Speech to Congress, 1969
The plaque on the "Eagle" which summarized our hopes bears this message:

"Here men from the planet earth first set foot upon the moon, July 1969 A.D. We came in peace for all mankind."

Those nineteen hundred and sixty-nine years had constituted the majority of the age of Pisces — a twelfth of the great year that is measured by the thousand generations the precession of the earth's axis requires to scribe a giant circle in the heavens.

In the next twenty centuries, the age of Aquarius of the great year, the age for which our young people have such high hopes, humanity may begin to understand its most baffling mystery — where are we going? The earth is, in fact, traveling many thousands of miles per hour in the direction of the constellation Hercules — to some unknown destination in the cosmos. Man must understand his universe in order to understand his destiny. . . .

Who knows what mysteries will be solved in our lifetime, and what new riddles will become the challenge of the new generations? Science has not mastered prophesy. We predict too much for next year yet far too little for the next ten. Responding to challenge is one of democracy's great strengths. Our successes in space lead us to hope that this strength can be used in the next decade in the solution of many of our planet's problems.

June 8. President Nixon announces the withdrawal of 25,000 troops from Vietnam, to be completed by August 31. Calling the move a first step, he promises further reductions if the other side scales down combat operations. Subsequent withdrawals are announced on September 16 (35,000) and December 15 (50,000).

June 14. Physicist at the University of Maryland reports detecting gravity waves, a phenomenon predicted by Einstein's general theory of relativity.

June 17. New York Mayor John V. Lindsay loses to conservative "law and order" candidate in Republican primary. **Nov. 4.** As the nominee of the Liberal Party and his own Independent Party, he wins reelection over the major party candidates.

July 1. The Army and the Air Force announce that Social Security numbers will replace the serial numbers used for identification since 1918. The Navy and the Marine Corps plan to follow suit in 1972.

July 8. Charles Evers, brother of slain civil rights worker Medgar Evers, becomes mayor of Fayette, Mississippi. He is the first Negro to be elected mayor of a biracial Mississippi city since Reconstruction.

July 11. The 1968 conviction of Dr. Benjamin Spock for conspiracy to counsel draft evasion is overturned by the Boston Court of Appeals. The conviction of one of his codefendants is also overturned, and the others are granted retrial.

July 20. Four days after liftoff from Cape Kennedy in the Apollo 11 spacecraft, astronaut Neil Armstrong becomes the first man to set foot on a celestial body. Near the lunar landing module *Eagle*'s landing site on the moon's Mare Tranquilitatis Armstrong and Edwin Aldrin set up scientific experiments and collect samples of moon material and then rejoin Michael Collins in the orbiting command ship. **July 24.** Apollo 11 splashes down in the Pacific 950 miles southwest of Hawaii. The astronauts are greeted by President Nixon aboard the carrier *Hornet* and begin an 18-day quarantine period to guard against the possibility of harmful microorganisms from the moon. **Nov. 14-24.** Apollo 12 astronauts successfully complete second lunar landing mission. The landing module *Intrepid* is piloted to the surface about 600 feet from the 1967 Surveyor 3 moon probe.

Aug. 6. After months of congressional and public debate the Senate narrowly votes down military appropriations bill amendments that would block construction of an antiballistic missile system requested by the President. Bill with ABM provision passes the Senate in September and the House in November.

Aug. 8. President Nixon proposes a reorganization of the nation's welfare system. His "family assistance system" would guarantee a minimum income of $1,600 yearly for a family of four and would provide employment and job-training incentives.

Aug. 15-17. Woodstock Music and Art Fair, a three-day rock concert, is held near Bethel, New York. An estimated 400,000 people attend and despite crowded conditions, lack of facilities, and heavy rains, there is no violence and only a small number of arrests, mostly for drug possession. Marijuana is so widespread that no attempt is made to stem its use.

Aug. 17. Dr. Philip Blaiberg of Capetown, South Africa, who has been the longest surviving of the more than 100 heart-transplant patients since 1967, dies after living more than 19 months with a donated heart.

Aug. 18. President Nixon names Clement Haynsworth to the Supreme Court. Opposition to the appointment grows steadily, first because of Haynsworth's record on civil

BARBARA A. GUNN
Speech to California 4-H conference
In 1961, only 8 years ago, we knew what was wrong with our young people. Remember? (Eight years ago means that those who were 14-year-olds in the survey in 1961 are now — 8 years later — 22 — and they may have been listening to us back in 1961.)

The 1961 Gallup poll . . . concluded:

"In general, the typical American youth shows few symptoms of frustration, and is most unlikely to rebel or involve himself in crusades of any kind. . . .

"The United States has bred a generation of nice little boys and girls who are just what we have asked them to be. . . . We see well scrubbed faces politely and shamelessly revealing compromise, conformity and intellectual poverty. We see them in their cotton-batting world of gossip, television and thrillers. These are the majority. . . . How did youth become so bland? So cautious? So self-satisfied, secure, and unambitious? . . .

"We've got to teach our children to think. . . . We have to make them excited about ideas. And we've got to convince them that there's nothing shameful in being different. . . ."

You know — I think they were listening to us in 1961. . . .

And I wonder if it wouldn't be well to pause before we start in again with our advice, to pause and to listen to what they seem to be saying to us. . . .

When we listen, we hear: (1) Enjoy, enjoy. (2) Do your own thing. (3) Don't put people down. (4) Be comfortable. (5) Love.

Theirs is a tough morality. It's strong. It takes courage. They're coming out of their cotton-batting world. Maybe we should join them.

EDMUND S. MUSKIE
Speech at Bates College, 1969

Today's protest is a sign of concern and frustration. It is a sign of broken communications.

There are those who say there is nothing to learn from the moratorium. There are those who downgrade the right to petition.

I say that on the issues of Vietnam we have much to learn from each other, and we can only learn if we are willing to listen to each other and to reason with each other.

This applies to the President and to those who protest. Only in this way can we develop policies on Vietnam which can meet our national interests and end the ugly divisions caused by our involvement there. I regret that the President has not seen this day as an opportunity to unite rather than divide the country. His participation, in a forum of his choosing, could have added a constructive dimension to this national dialogue.

We are engaged in a unique and somewhat awkward experiment. We are engaged in an effort to change a major aspect of our foreign policy in public view, while our country is involved in a war and in diplomatic negotiations to end that war.

Our national debate over the wisdom of past policies, the validity of present policies, and our alternatives for future policies is open for worldwide inspection. The magnitude of today's moratorium, for example, transmitted almost instantaneously by radio and television, will have a significant impact in Washington, in Paris, in Moscow, in Hanoi, and in Saigon.

We cannot predict either the nature or the precise direction of the changes we shall cause. We may never be able to measure our impact, but we can be sure our voices will be heard.

rights and later because of his failure to disqualify himself in several cases heard by his Court of Appeals in which he had a financial interest. **Nov. 21.** The appointment is voted down by the Senate.

Sept. 3. Ho Chi Minh, president of North Vietnam, dies in Hanoi.

Sept. 10. State of Alaska receives bids totaling more than $900 million for leases to oil lands on its North Slope. **Sept. 14.** Oil tanker S.S. *Manhattan* completes Northwest Passage, becoming the first commercial ship to do so and proving the feasibility of using the route for transporting oil from the North Slope field to eastern Canada and U.S.

Sept. 16. Bikini atoll in the Pacific Ocean, site of 23 nuclear test explosions during 1946-1958, is declared safe for habitation by the Atomic Energy Commission.

Sept. 27. In a game marking the centennial of collegiate football Rutgers defeats Princeton 27-0. Rutgers had also won the 1869 game, 6 goals to 4.

Oct. 15. First National Moratorium Day observances draw large crowds to antiwar demonstrations across the country. Many Senators and congressmen participate and in Washington Mrs. Martin Luther King, Jr., leads 45,000 people in a march from the Washington Monument to the White House. **Nov. 15.** More than 250,000 people gather in Washington for the second Moratorium Day, eclipsing the figure for the 1963 March on Washington. In San Francisco the largest crowd in the city's history protests the Vietnam War, and similar demonstrations take place in most other cities. President Nixon pointedly ignores the day's activities, which despite official warnings, are relatively free of violence.

Oct. 16. New York Mets, perennially of the National League cellar, top an almost incredible late season pennant rush by winning the World Series in 5 games.

Oct. 18. Secretary of Health, Education, and Welfare Robert H. Finch orders the removal of cyclamate artificial sweeteners from the market by early 1970. Experimental evidence has linked cyclamates to cancer in animals. **Oct. 22.** Food and Drug Administration announces plans to review several other food additives, including the widely used monosodium glutamate, which has produced brain damage in experimental mice.

Oct. 29. Supreme Court rules unanimously that school segregation must end immediately, thus rejecting the 1955 "all deliberate speed" formula. The ruling follows months of controversy over the administration's ambiguous position on enforcing desegregation in the South.

Nov. 13. Speaking in Des Moines, Iowa, Vice President Agnew delivers scathing attack on network television news coverage and commentary, calling it biased, provincial, and unrepresentative. **Nov. 20.** In Montgomery, Alabama, Agnew broadens his criticisms to include the press, particularly the *New York Times* and the *Washington Post*.

Nov. 16. Report is published charging a U.S. infantry unit with killing from 450 to 567 unarmed men, women, and children in the South Vietnamese village of Songmy in March 1968. A sergeant and a lieutenant face court-martial charges of assault and murder. Army investigation into the incident continues.

Nov. 17. Preliminary meetings for the strategic arms limitation talks (SALT) between the U.S. and U.S.S.R. open in Helsinki, Finland.

Nov. 20. Group of American Indians representing more than 20 tribes occupies and claims Alcatraz Island in San Francisco Bay.

SPIRO T. AGNEW
Speech in Des Moines, 1969
A small group of men, numbering perhaps no more than a dozen anchormen, commentators, and executive producers, settle upon the 20 minutes or so of film and commentary that's to reach the public. . .

They decide what 40 to 50 million Americans will learn of the day's events in the nation and in the world. . . .

They can make or break by their coverage and commentary a moratorium on the war.

They can elevate men from obscurity to national prominence within a week. They can reward some politicians with national exposure and ignore others. . . .

Nor is their power confined to the substantive. A raised eyebrow, an inflection of the voice, a caustic remark dropped in the middle of a broadcast can raise doubts in a million minds about the veracity of a public official or the wisdom of a government policy. . . .

The American people would rightly not tolerate this concentration of power in government.

Is it not fair and relevant to question its concentration in the hands of a tiny, enclosed fraternity of privileged men elected by no one and enjoying a monopoly sanctioned and licensed by government?

The views of the majority of this fraternity do not—and I repeat, not—represent the views of America. . . .

I'm not asking for government censorship or any other kind of censorship. I'm asking whether a form of censorship already exists when the news that 40 million Americans receive each night is determined by a handful of men responsible only to their corporate employers and is filtered through a handful of commentators who admit to their own set of biases.

Indian statement from Alcatraz, 1970

Indians of All Tribes greet our brothers and sisters of all races and tongues upon our Earth Mother. We here on Indian land, Alcatraz, represent many tribes of Indians.

We are still holding the island of Alcatraz in the true names of Freedom, Justice and Equality, because our brothers and sisters of this earth have lent support to our just cause. We reach out our hands and hearts and send spirit messages to all Indians.

Our anger at the many injustices forced upon us since the first white men landed on these sacred shores has been transformed into a hope that we be allowed the long-suppressed right of all men to plan and to live their own lives in harmony and cooperation with all fellow creatures and with nature. . . .

We are quite serious in our demand to be given ownership of this island in the name of Indians of All Tribes. We are here to stay, men, women, and children. We feel that this request is but little to ask from a government which has systematically stolen our lands, destroyed a once beautiful landscape, killed off the creatures of nature, polluted air and water, ripped open the very bowels of our earth in senseless greed, and instituted a program to annihilate the many Indian tribes of this land by theft, suppression, prejudice, termination, and so-called relocation and assimilation.

We are a proud people! We are Indians! We have observed and rejected much of what so-called civilization offers. We are Indians! We will preserve our traditions and ways of life by educating our own children. We are Indians! We will join hands in a unity never before put into practice. Our Earth Mother awaits our voices. We are Indians of All Tribes!!!

Former prison site has been abandoned by the government and the Indians demand title to it under an old Sioux treaty. They plan to erect an Indian cultural and educational center.

Nov. 25. President Nixon renounces use of bacteriological agents in warfare and orders the destruction of stocks of such weapons. First strike use of certain chemical agents is also renounced, though others, including tear gas and chemical defoliants widely used in Vietnam, are retained.

Nov. 26. Following passage by Congress of enabling legislation, President Nixon issues executive order establishing a lottery system for choosing men to be drafted into the armed forces. First lottery drawing since 1942 is held on December 1.

Dec. 17. Secretary of the Air Force announces the closing of "Project Bluebook," a 21-year investigation into unidentified flying objects. Study of more than 12,000 UFO sightings has revealed no evidence that they are "flying saucers" of extraterrestial origin, although a small number of the sightings remain unexplained.

During the year several traditionally all-male colleges, including Yale, Bowdoin, and Colgate, have begun admitting small numbers of women students.

Census Bureau estimates the population of the country at the end of the year to be 204,334,344.

PART II
Maps and Tables

1. EXPLORATION OF THE NEW WORLD

The age of exploration opened in 1420 when Portugal's Prince Henry the Navigator attempted to discover a sea route to the East around Africa. Portugal's preemption of the African route prompted Spain to seek, toward the end of the 15th century, another and preferably a shorter way. It was this that drove Columbus westward to the New World in 1492. Others soon followed, Spanish, Portuguese, English, and Italian adventurers who set out to investigate the newly discovered lands and to determine if there was a way to the Orient around or through them. Amerigo Vespucci was the first to show that it was indeed a new hemisphere that had been discovered.

Pedro Alvares Cabral found Brazil for Portugal. Spain's attention was first centered on North America because of the discovery of Florida by Ponce de León, but the finding of vast wealth by Cortés and Pizarro in Central and South America diverted its activities southward for a time. Eventually Spain sought riches in the Southwest, but it was never able to locate El Dorado there. French exploration and settlement focused on Canada and what is today the midwestern United States. The early voyages of Jacques Cartier became the basis for later French claims. But it was Samuel de Champlain, and those who followed him into the interior of the continent, who established France's colonial empire.

England came relatively late to North America, but of course its empire became ultimately the dominant one in the region. France retained a strong foothold until the 1760s; Spain endured longer, but with diminishing power and influence after 1800.

John Smith's map of New England drawn in 1614. Engraving by De Passe reprinted in "Mercantor's Atlas," 1637

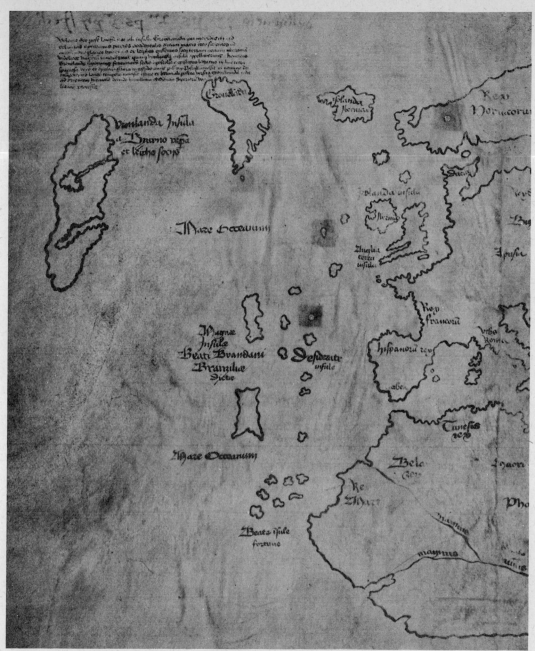

THE VINLAND MAP, only half of which is shown here, was probably drawn by a church scholar during an extended church council held in Basel from 1431 to 1449. The map is striking because it contains the earliest known representation of North America and because it indicates that this knowledge was available to some as early (or late) as about 1440. The Norse sagas describe the settlement of Greenland in 986 by Eric the Red. In the same year, as related in the sagas, Bjarni Herjolfson was blown off course and came upon mainland North America. About four years later Lief, Eric's son, explored this land southward. Other expeditions were undertaken by Leif's brothers, by Thorfinn Karlsefni, and finally, by Leif's sister, Freydis (1024-25). In each case the parties wintered on shore and a colony may have been started. Examining the map, Norway appears at the top right. Just to the left is Iceland, a Norse colony since 874, and then Greenland. On the left is an oddly shaped body labeled: "Island of Vinland, discovered by Bjarni and Leif in company." The map clearly reflects the Norse sagas, but how general this knowledge was remains unclear. Other maps of the period show nothing similar and if Columbus or John Cabot knew anything of Vinland, it would only have fortified an already compelling impulse to seek the far side of the ocean

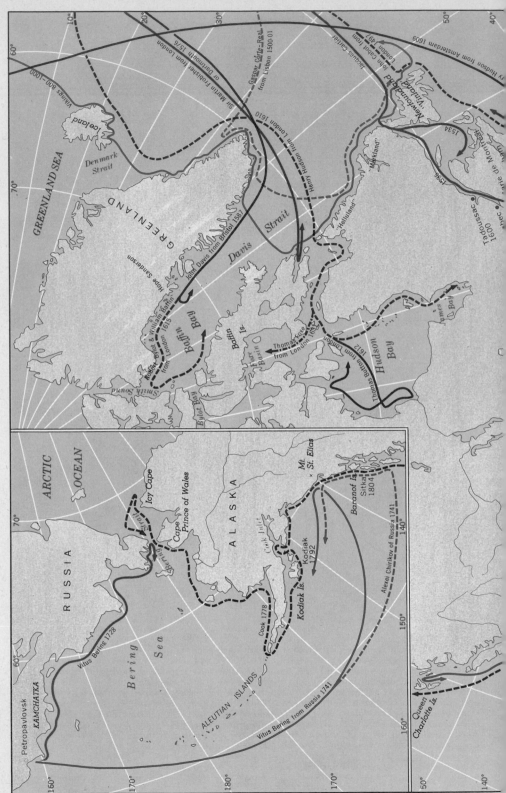

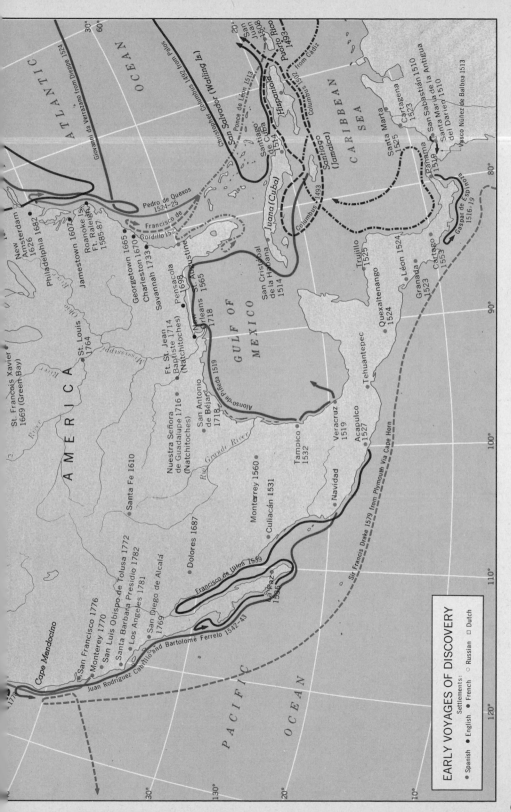

HAVANA.   Portus.   St. DOMINGO.   CARTAGENA.   MEXICO.

Septentrionalissimas Americæ partes, Grœnlandiam puta, Islandiā et adjacentes, quod Americæ tabulæ commodè comprehendi non potuerint, peculiari hac tabella Spectatoribus exhibendas duximus.

AMERICA SEPTENTRIONAL

Tropicus Cancri

MAR DEL ZU

CIRCULUS ÆQUINOCTIALIS

OCEANU

Tropicus Capricorni

PERUV.

MARE PACI CUM

AMERICÆ nova Tabula.
Auct. Guilielmo Blaeuw.

Cum privilegio decem annorum.

TERRA AUSTRALIS INCOG

Grœnlandi.

Virginiani.

Rex et Regina Floridæ.

Rex et Regina Virginiæ.

Mexicani.

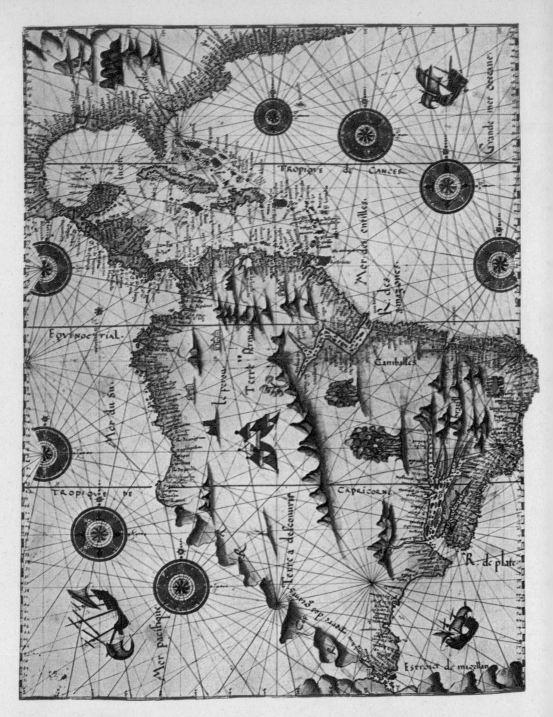

(Overleaf) **AMERICAE NOVA TABULA** by Willem Blaeu, from his "Novus Atlas," 1635. The first modern world atlases had been published in Antwerp by Abraham Ortelius (1570) and in Amsterdam by Gerardus Mercator (in stages, 1585-1595). Blaeu and his son Johann operated in Amsterdam the largest map-making establishment of the time. The Blaeus were heir to a great tradition of cartography in the Netherlands. This map accurately represents the state of knowledge about the New World

(Above) **MARINER'S GUIDE TO THE NEW WORLD,** manuscript map by Pierre Desceliers, c. 1546 (like many maps of the period drawn with North at the right and turned for this reproduction). Desceliers, one of the "Dieppe school" of map-makers, presumably got much information from mariners putting into that port and from fishermen working the Grand Bank. He apparently also had access to Spanish sources, even though Spain responded to competition by trying to keep discoveries secret

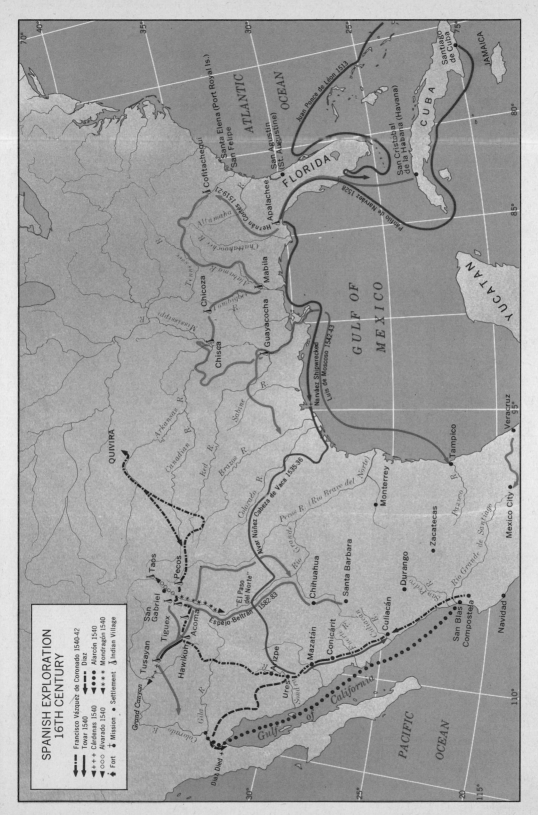

SPANISH EXPLORATION
16TH CENTURY

Francisco Vázquez de Coronado 1540-42
Tovar 1540
Cárdenas 1540
Alvarado 1540
Diaz
Alarcón 1540
Mondragón 1540

♦ Fort   ♁ Mission   • Settlement   ⌂ Indian Village

Juan Ponce de Léon 1513

ATLANTIC OCEAN

Santa Elena (Port Royal Is.)
San Felipe
San Agustin (St. Augustine)
Apalachee
FLORIDA

San Cristobal de la Habana (Havana)
CUBA
Santiago de Cuba
JAMAICA

Pánfilo de Narváez 1528

Cofitachequi
Altamaha R.
Hernan Cortés 1519-21
Chattahoochee R.
Mabila
Chicoza
Alabama R.
Tombigbee R.
Guayacocha
Chisca
Narváez Shipwrecked
Luis de Moscoso 1542-43
GULF OF MEXICO

YUCATAN

Mississippi R.
Arkansas R.
Canadian R.
Red R.
Brazos R.
Colorado R.
Sabine R.

QUIVIRA

Alvar Nuñez Cabeza de Vaca 1535-36

Pecos R. (Rio Bravo del Norte)

Rio Grande

Tampico
Veracruz

Monterrey
Zacatecas
Durango
Santa Barbara
Chihuahua
Mexico City

Taos
Pecos
San Gabriel
Tiguex
Acoma
"El Paso del Norte"
Espejo-Beltrán
1582-83
Tusayan
Hawikuh
Grand Canyon
Gila R.
Colorado R.

Culiacán
Mazatán
Conicárit
Arizpe
Ures
San Blas
Compostela
Navidad

Rio Grande de Santiago

PACIFIC OCEAN

Gulf of California

Diaz Died

645

Map of Baja California and northwest Mexico drawn by Father Kino, 1701

Upper St. Lawrence River on a 1609 map in "Histoire de la Nouvelle France" by Lescarbot

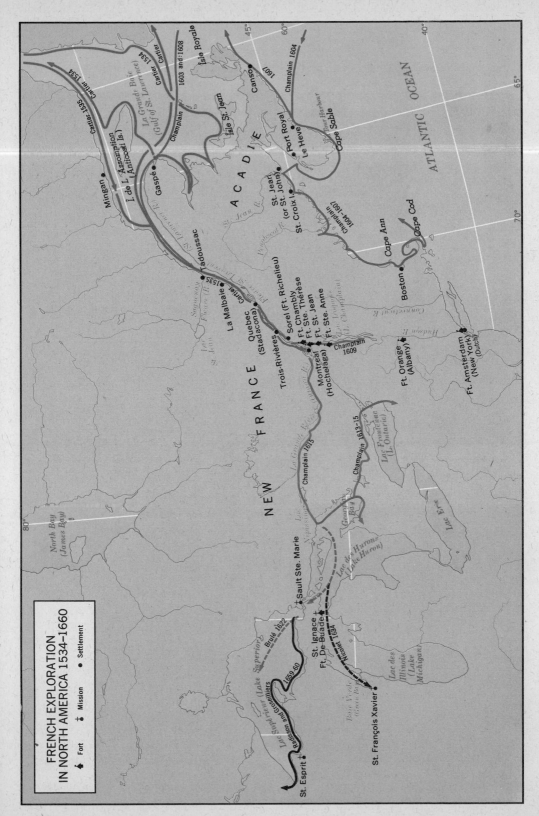

FRENCH EXPLORATION
IN NORTH AMERICA 1534–1660

† Fort † Mission • Settlement

North Bay
(James Bay)

NEW FRANCE

ACADIE

ATLANTIC OCEAN

Cartier 1534
Cartier 1534
Cartier 1535
Cartier
Cartier
1603 and 1608
La Grande Baie
(Gulf of St. Lawrence)
Champlain
Isle Royale
Champlain 1604
Canso
1607
Isle St. Jean
Tour Harbour
Port Royal
Le Heve
Cape Sable
Mingan
I. de L'Assomption
(Anticosti Is.)
Gaspé
Cap St. Jean R.
St. Jean
(or St. John)
St. Croix I.
Champlain
1604–1607
Tadoussac
Cartier 1535
La Malbaie
Penobscot R.
Cape Ann
Cape Cod
Quebec
(Stadacona)
Sorel (Ft. Richelieu)
Ft. Chambly
Ft. Ste. Thérèse
Ft. St. Jean
Ft. Ste. Anne
Trois-Rivières
Champlain 1609
Boston
Connecticut R.
Hudson R.
Montréal
(Hochelaga)
Ft. Orange
(Albany)
Ft. Amsterdam
(New York)
(New Dutch)
Champlain 1613
Champlain 1613–15
Lac Frontenac
(L. Ontario)
Georgian Bay
Lac des Hurons
(Lake Huron)
Lac Erie
Sault Ste. Marie
Brulé 1622
1659–60
Lac Supérieur (Lake Superior)
Radisson and Groseilliers
St. Ignace
Ft. De-Buade
Nicolet 1634
Lac des
Illinois
(Lake
Michigan)
Baie Verte
(Green Ba...)
St. François Xavier
St. Esprit

80° 70° 65° 45° 60° 40°

647

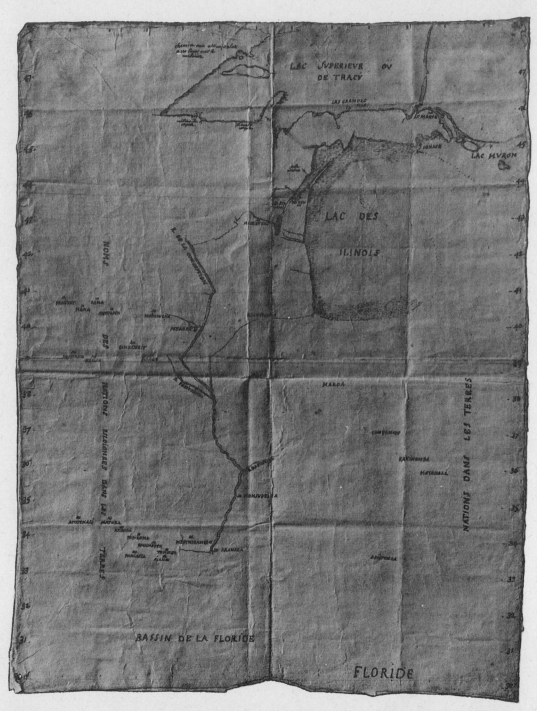

Father Jacques Marquette's map of his voyage with Louis Jolliet from Mackinac down Lake Michigan ("Lac des Ilinois"), the Illinois River and the Mississippi as far as Arkansas in 1673

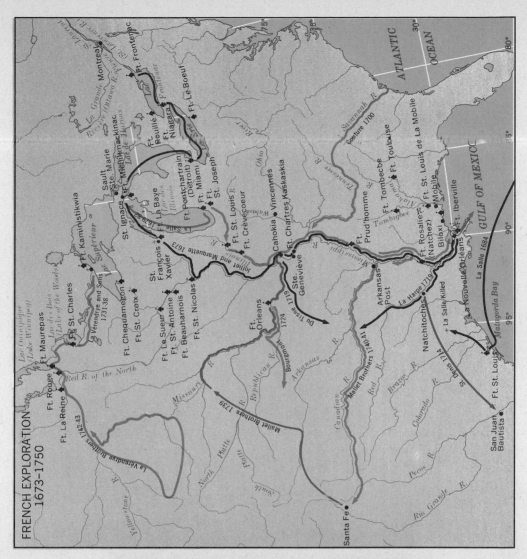

FRENCH EXPLORATION 1673-1750

St. Laurent R.

Le Grand Montréal Lac St. Pierre (Ottawa R.) Ft. Frontenac

Lac St. Louis

Ft. Frontenac Ft. Le Boeuf

ATLANTIC OCEAN

Lac Rivière (Ottawa R.)

Lac Huronus Ft. Rouillé Niagara

Sault Ste. Marie St. Ignace Ft. Michilimackinac Ft. Pontchartrain (Detroit) Ft. Miami Ft. St. Joseph

Genesee 1700

Ft. St. Louis de La Mobile

Ft. Kaministikwia

Lac Supérieur La Baye Ohio Ft. St. Louis Ft. Crèvecoeur

Tennessee R. Ft. Toulouse

Ft. Tombecbe

Sault Ste. Marie

St. François Xavier Joliet and Marquette 1673 Illinois R. Cahokia Vincennes Ft. Chartres Kaskaskia

Ft. Prud'homme Ft. St. Louis de La Mobile Mobile Ft. Iberville

Ft. Chequamegon Ft. St. Croix Ft. Le Sueur Ft. St. Antoine Ft. Beauharnois Ft. St. Nicolas

Ft. Rosalie (Natchez) Tombigbee Biloxi

GULF OF MEXICO

La Vérendrye and Sons 1731-38

St. Charles

Red R. of the North

Ste. Geneviève Du Tisné 1719

Arkansas Post La Harpe 1719 Natchitoches La Nouvelle Orléans

La Salle 1684

Ft. Rouge Ft. Maurepas Lac des Bois (Lake of the Woods) Ft. Orleans Bourgmont 1724 Arkansas R.

St. Denis 1714 + La Salle/Killed Matagorda Bay

Ft. La Reine

Mallet Brothers 1739 Republican R. Mallet Brothers 1740-41 Red R.

Ft. St. Louis

Lac Ouinipigue (Lake Winnipeg)

Missouri R. Canadian R. Brazos R. Colorado R.

La Vérendrye Brothers 1742-43

Platte R. North Platte R. South Platte R. Pecos R. Rio Grande R.

San Juan Bautista

Santa Fe

2. THE REVOLUTION

When French sovereignty was ended in North America by the Treaty of 1763 at the close of the French and Indian War, England asserted its rule over the newly won areas; and by the Proclamation of 1763 westward expansion was precluded, the land west of the Appalachians being reserved for the Indians. Yet it was largely the Indian tribes themselves, by dealing directly with the colonists, that encouraged westward migration and land speculation; and in any event the movement was not to be stopped by words.

Partly as a result of the attempt, the American Revolution began in Massachusetts in 1775. It ended in Virginia in 1781, a fact that illustrates the general movement of the war from north to south. Fighting began at Lexington and Concord in April 1775; the neighboring New England colonies were aroused, but after the Battle of Bunker Hill the theater of operations moved elsewhere.

The British focused on New York in 1776 and 1777, attaining some successes there; but their efforts in the North had generally failed by 1778. The British then concentrated on the South, hoping to secure a strong base from which to retake the northern colonies. American forces led by Washington, Gates, Greene, and La Fayette set out to defeat British General Cornwallis, but victory came slowly. The penultimate battle of the war occurred on September 8, 1781, at Eutaw Springs, S.C. Cornwallis thereupon retired to Yorktown, Va., where a combination of American military and French naval might forced him to surrender on October 19th.

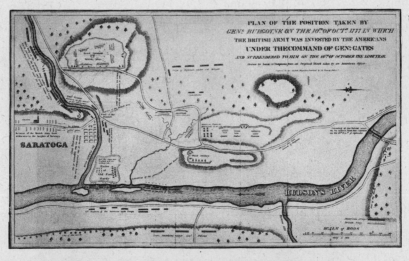

Plan showing positions of the two armies during the battle at Saratoga

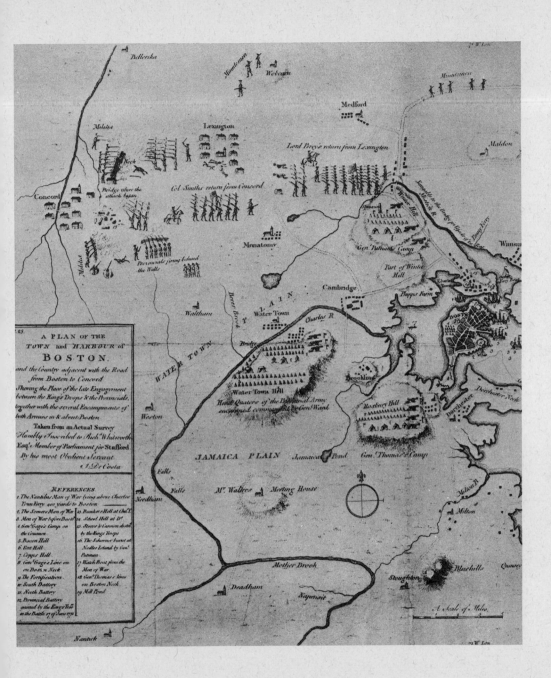

A PLAN OF THE
TOWN and HARBOUR of
BOSTON.
and the Country adjacent with the Road
from Boston to Concord
Shewing the Place of the late Engagement
between the Kings Troops & the Provincials,
together with the several Encampments of
both Armies in & about Boston

Taken from an Actual Survey

Humbly Inscribed to Rich.ᵈ Whitworth
Esq.ᵉ Member of Parliament for Stafford
By his most Obedient Servant
J. De Costa

REFERENCES
1. The Nautalas Man of War lying above Charles
   Town Ferry 900 yards to Boston
2. The Somers Man of War
3. Men of War before Boston
4. Gen.ˡ Gage's Camp on
   the Common
5. Bacon Hill
6. Fort Hill
7. Copps Hill
8. Gen.ˡ Gage's Line on
   on Bost.ⁿ Neck
9. The Fortification
10. South Battery
11. North Battery
12. Provincial Battery
    gained by the Kings Troops
    in the Battle 17 of June 1775

13. Bunkers Hill at Ch.ˡ T.
14. School Hill at D.ᵒ
15. Stores & Cannon destroy
    by the Kings Troops
16. The Schooner burnt at
    Noddle Island by Gen.ˡ
    Putnam
17. Wash.Boats from the
    Men of War
18. Gen.ˡ Thomas's lines
    on Boston Neck
19. Mill Pond

A Scale of Miles.

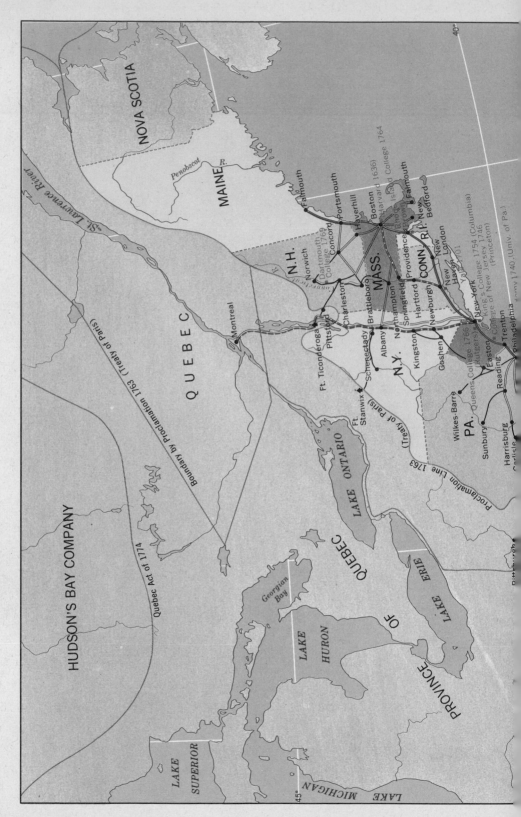

HUDSON'S BAY COMPANY

NOVA SCOTIA

MAINE

Penobscot R.

QUEBEC

St. Lawrence River

Quebec Act of 1774

Boundary by Proclamation 1763 (Treaty of Paris)

Montreal

N.H.

Norwich
Dartmouth College 1769
Concord
Charleston
Brattleboro
Northampton
Springfield
Hartford

Ft. Ticonderoga
Pittsfield
Schenectady
Albany
N.Y.
Kingston
Newburgh
Goshen

Ft. Stanwix

(Treaty of Paris)

LAKE ONTARIO

Proclamation Line 1763

Falmouth
Haverhill
Portsmouth
Boston 1636
Harvard College 1764
Brown
Rhode Island College 1764
Providence
New Bedford
New London
New Haven
Yale 1701
MASS.
CONN.
R.I.

Falmouth

New York
King's College 1754 (Columbia)
College of New Jersey 1746 (Princeton)
Trenton
Easton
Philadelphia University of Pa.
Reading
Wilkes-Barre
PA.
Queens College 1766 (Rutgers)
Sunbury
Harrisburg
Carlisle

Pittsburgh

Georgian Bay

LAKE HURON

LAKE SUPERIOR

LAKE MICHIGAN

QUEBEC

OF

PROVINCE

LAKE ERIE

45°

40°

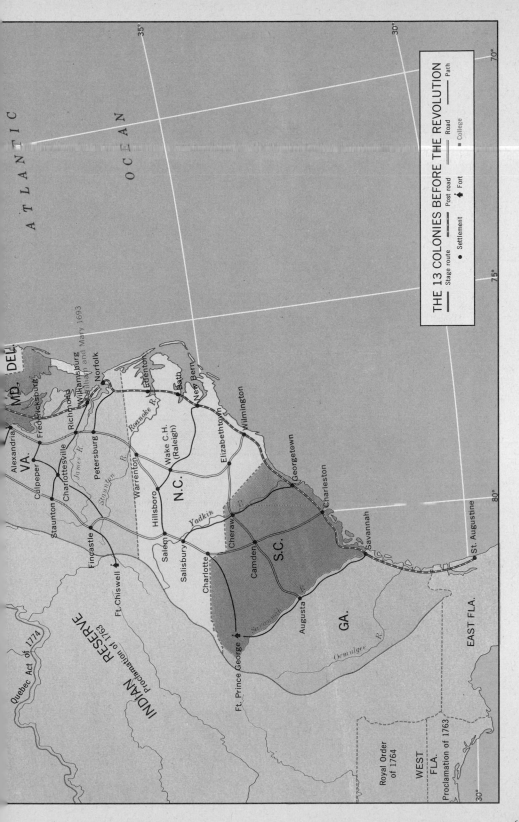

THE 13 COLONIES BEFORE THE REVOLUTION

Stage route — — Post road ═══ — Road ═══ — Path ───

● Settlement — ⚓ Fort — ■ College

653

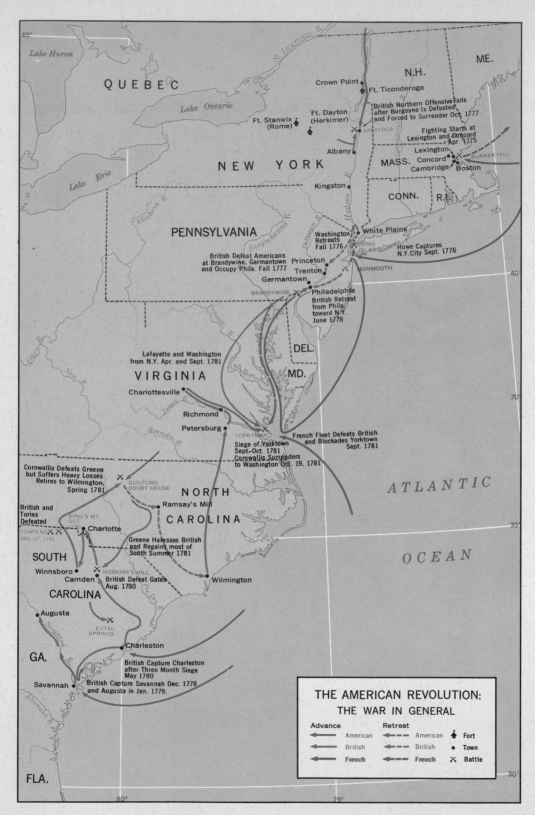

Lake Huron

QUEBEC

Lake Ontario

St. Lawrence R.

Crown Point
Ft. Ticonderoga

N.H.

ME.

British Northern Offensive Fails
after Burgoyne Is Defeated
and Forced to Surrender Oct. 1777

Fighting Starts at
Lexington and Concord
Apr. 1775

Ft. Stanwix
(Rome)

Ft. Dayton
(Herkimer)

SARATOGA

BUNKER HILL

Albany

Lake Erie

Allegheny R.

NEW YORK

Lexington
Concord
Cambridge Boston

MASS.

Kingston

CONN.

R.I.

PENNSYLVANIA

Susquehanna R.

White Plains

Washington
Retreats
Fall 1776

Howe Captures
N.Y.City Sept. 1776

British Defeat Americans
at Brandywine, Germantown
and Occupy Phila. Fall 1777

Princeton
Trenton
Germantown

LONG ISLAND

MONMOUTH

BRANDYWINE

DEL.

Philadelphia
British Retreat
from Phila.
toward N.Y.
June 1778

Hudson R.

Delaware R.

Lafayette and Washington
from N.Y. Apr. and Sept. 1781

MD.

Potomac R.

VIRGINIA

James R.

Charlottesville

Richmond
Petersburg

YORKTOWN

Siege of Yorktown
Sept.-Oct. 1781
Cornwallis Surrenders
to Washington Oct. 19, 1781

French Fleet Defeats British
and Blockades Yorktown
Sept. 1781

ATLANTIC

Roanoke R.

Cornwallis Defeats Greene
but Suffers Heavy Losses
Retires to Wilmington,
Spring 1781

GUILFORD
COURT HOUSE

NORTH

Ramsay's Mill

CAROLINA

British and
Tories
Defeated

KING'S MT.
OCT.

COWPENS
JAN. 17, 1781

Charlotte

Greene Harasses British
and Regains most of
South Summer 1781

OCEAN

SOUTH

Winnsboro
Camden

HOBKIRK'S HILL

British Defeat Gates
Aug. 1780

Wilmington

Pee Dee R.

CAROLINA

Augusta

Savannah R.

EUTAU
SPRINGS

Charleston

GA.

Savannah

Altamaha R.

British Capture Charleston
after Three Month Siege
May 1780

British Capture Savannah Dec. 1778
and Augusta in Jan. 1779.

FLA.

THE AMERICAN REVOLUTION:
THE WAR IN GENERAL

Advance		Retreat		
American		American		Fort
British		British		Town
French		French		Battle

45°

40°

35°

30°

70°

75°

80°

CAMPAIGNS IN NEW YORK 1776

Peekskill
Stony Point
NEW YORK
CONN.
WHITE PLAINS
OCT. 28
NEW JERSEY
New Rochelle
Hackensack
Ft. Lee
Ft. Washington
Newark
HARLEM HTS.
SEPT. 16
KIP'S BAY
BROOKLYN HTS.
AUG. 27
LONG ISLAND
STATEN
ISLAND
Flatbush
Gravesend
Sir William Howe July
Admiral Howe Aug.

UPSTATE NEW YORK 1777

Montreal
Ft. St. John
Burgoyne's Campaign Opens June 13
CANADA
Lake Champlain
Plattsburgh
Crown Point
N.H.
Ft. Ticonderoga July 5
Oswego
Ft. Stanwix (Rome)
Siege Aug. 3-22
L. George
Skenesborough
Ft. Anne
Ft. Dayton (Herkimer)
Ft. Edward
Manchester
ORISKANY AUG. 6
Saratoga
Burgoyne Surrenders Oct. 17
Lake Ontario
BENNINGTON AUG. 16
NEW YORK
FREEMAN'S FARM SEPT. 19
BEMIS HTS. OCT. 7
Stillwater
Albany
MASS.
Kingston
Oct. 15
PA.
CONN.

655

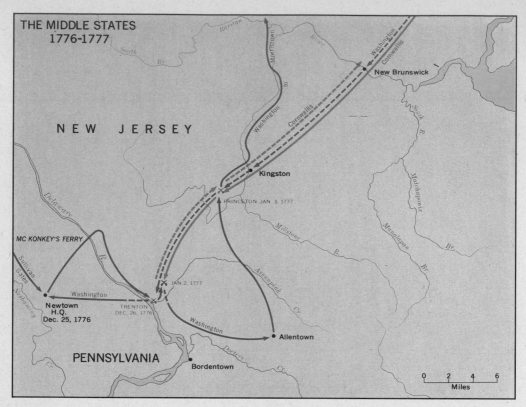

THE MIDDLE STATES
1776-1777

NEW JERSEY

New Brunswick

Kingston

PRINCETON JAN. 3, 1777

MC KONKEY'S FERRY

JAN. 2, 1777

Newtown
H.Q.
Dec. 25, 1776

TRENTON
DEC. 26, 1776

Washington

Allentown

PENNSYLVANIA

Bordentown

0   2   4   6
Miles

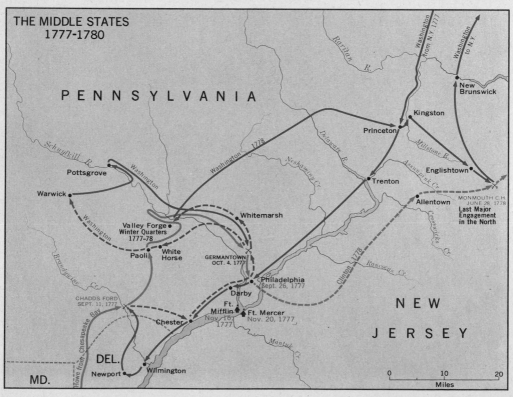

THE MIDDLE STATES
1777-1780

PENNSYLVANIA

New
Brunswick

Kingston

Princeton

Washington 1778

Englishtown

Pottsgrove

Trenton

Warwick

MONMOUTH C.H.
JUNE 28, 1778
Last Major
Engagement
in the North

Allentown

Valley Forge
Winter Quarters
1777-78

Whitemarsh

Paoli

White
Horse

GERMANTOWN
OCT. 4, 1777

NEW

CHADDS FORD
SEPT. 11, 1777

Philadelphia
Sept. 26, 1777

Darby

JERSEY

Chester

Ft.
Mifflin

Ft. Mercer
Nov. 20, 1777

Nov. 16,
1777

DEL.

MD.

Newport

Wilmington

0   10   20
Miles

656

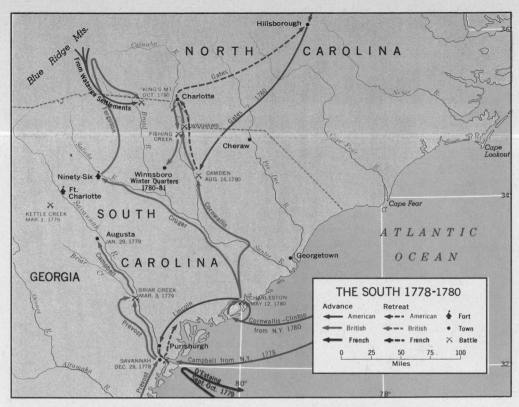

THE SOUTH 1778-1780

Advance
← American
← British
← French

Retreat
⇠ American
⇠ British
⇠ French

♠ Fort
● Town
✕ Battle

0 25 50 75 100
Miles

Labels on map: Hillsborough, NORTH CAROLINA, Blue Ridge Mts., Catawba, From Watauga Settlements, Gates, Neuse R., KING'S MT. OCT. 1780, Ferguson, Charlotte, Broad, Fishing Creek, WAXHAWS, Cheraw, Cape Fear, Cape Lookout, Ninety-Six, Saluda R., Winnsboro Winter Quarters 1780-81, CAMDEN AUG. 16, 1780, Gates, Ft. Charlotte, Pee Dee, Cornwallis, KETTLE CREEK MAR. 3, 1779, SOUTH, Cruger, Santee R., ATLANTIC OCEAN, Cape Fear, Augusta JAN. 29, 1779, CAROLINA, Campbell Cr., Georgetown, GEORGIA, Briar Cr., BRIAR CREEK MAR. 3, 1779, Ocmulgee, Campbell, Lincoln, CHARLESTON MAY 12, 1780, Prevost, Purisburgh, Cornwallis-Clinton from N.Y. 1780, SAVANNAH DEC. 29, 1778, Campbell from N.Y. 1778, Altamaha R., Prevost, D'Estaing Sept.-Oct. 1779, 80°, 78°

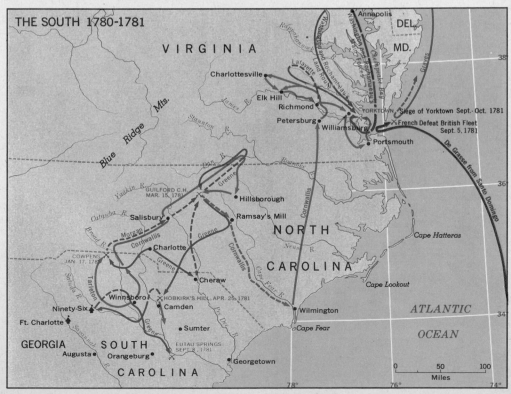

THE SOUTH 1780-1781

Labels on map: Annapolis, DEL., MD., VIRGINIA, Rappahannock, Washington and Rochambeau's, Washington and Rochambeau's French Fleet, Chesapeake Bay, Charlottesville, James R., Lafayette, Lafayette and Rochambeau Road, Elk Hill, Richmond, YORKTOWN, Siege of Yorktown Sept.-Oct. 1781, Graves, Petersburg, Williamsburg, French Defeat British Fleet Sept. 5, 1781, Portsmouth, Blue Ridge Mts., Staunton R., Dan R., Roanoke R., De Grasse from Santo Domingo, Yadkin R., GUILFORD C.H. MAR. 15, 1781, Greene, Hillsborough, Catawba R., Salisbury, Ramsay's Mill, Cape Hatteras, Morgan, Cornwallis, Greene, Charlotte, NORTH, Neuse R., COWPENS JAN. 17, 1781, Broad R., Cornwallis, Cornwallis, Cape Lookout, Tarleton, Cheraw, HOBKIRK'S HILL APR. 25, 1781, Cape Fear R., Winnsboro, CAROLINA, Cape Hatteras, ATLANTIC, Ninety-Six, Saluda R., Camden, Wilmington, Ft. Charlotte, Greene, Sumter, Cape Fear, OCEAN, GEORGIA, SOUTH, EUTAW SPRINGS SEPT. 8, 1781, Augusta, Orangeburg, Georgetown, CAROLINA, 78°, 76°, 74°

0 50 100
Miles

3. THE FRONTIER 1750–1890

The existence of a vast, unknown territory beyond the Appalachians invited explorers and adventurers, no matter what the barriers. Beginning about 1750, individual parties went west; Cumberland Gap was discovered in April of that year. In subsequent decades hunters, traders, and finally farmers moved into the Ohio Valley. By the end of the century, all hindrances to westward expansion were gone. Three new states were admitted—Vermont, Kentucky, and Tennessee—and congressional land policy set aside the Northwest Territory from which other states would be carved.

Apart from the patchwork of Indian land cessions, territorial additions were normally very large—the Louisiana Purchase, the Mexican cession, and the Oregon Territory. In each case this was far more land than could be readily settled or even explored. But as early as 1800 Americans had begun to believe that it was their destiny to occupy all of the territory west to the Pacific between Canada and Mexico, and the new acquisitions were absorbed sooner than anyone might have expected. Besides the addition of territory, westward expansion also involved land speculation, the search for new resources and farmland, and the ever present quest for opportunity. It also involved the continuing and merciless displacement of the Indian proprietors, or at least inhabitants, of the various acquired territories.

Westward expansion was not contiguous. The large area beyond the Mississippi Valley, consisting of the Great Plains and mountainous regions, was at first bypassed in favor of the West Coast. It was not until after the Civil War that agriculture and permanent settlements came to the arid lands beyond the Mississippi Valley farm belt.

Centers of population from 1790 to 1960 (Unshaded star indicates revised 1950 center after admission of Alaska and Hawaii in 1959)

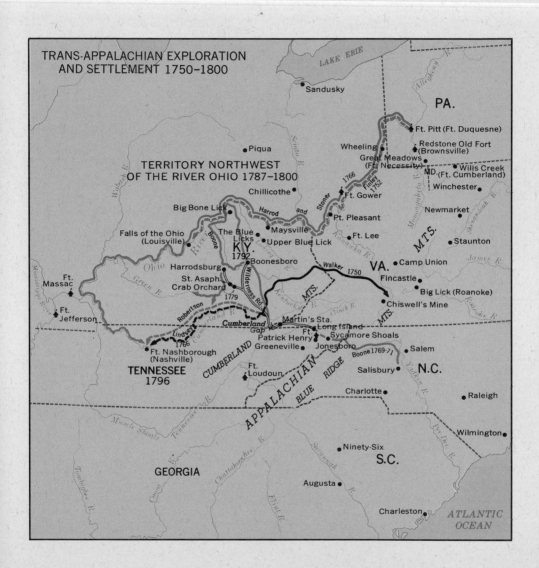

TRANS-APPALACHIAN EXPLORATION AND SETTLEMENT 1750–1800

LAKE ERIE

Sandusky

PA.

Piqua

Ft. Pitt (Ft. Duquesne)

Wheeling

Redstone Old Fort (Brownsville)

Great Meadows (Ft. Necessity)

TERRITORY NORTHWEST OF THE RIVER OHIO 1787–1800

Wills Creek

MD. (Ft. Cumberland)

Chillicothe

1766

Finley

1752

Stoner

Ft. Gower

Winchester

Big Bone Lick

Harrod

and

Newmark

Falls of the Ohio (Louisville)

The Blue Licks

Maysville

Pt. Pleasant

Ft. Lee

Staunton

Boone

Upper Blue Lick

KY. 1792

Boonesboro

Camp Union

Ohio River

Harrodsburg

Walker 1750

Fincastle

VA.

MTS.

Ft. Massac

St. Asaph.

Crab Orchard

Big Lick (Roanoke)

Ft. Jefferson

Robertson

1779

Chiswell's Mine

Martin's Sta.

Cumberland Gap

Ft. Long Island

Lindsey

1766

Patrick Henry

Sycamore Shoals

Greeneville

Jonesboro

Boone 1769-71

Salem

Ft. Nashborough (Nashville)

CUMBERLAND

Salisbury

N.C.

TENNESSEE 1796

Ft. Loudoun

APPALACHIAN

BLUE RIDGE

Charlotte

Raleigh

Wilmington

Ninety-Six

S.C.

GEORGIA

Augusta

Charleston

ATLANTIC OCEAN

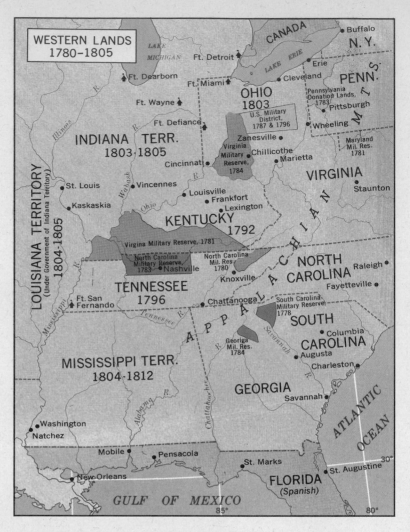

WESTERN LANDS 1780-1805

CANADA

LAKE MICHIGAN

Buffalo
N.Y.

LAKE ERIE

Ft. Dearborn

Ft. Detroit

Ft. Miami

Erie
Cleveland

PENN.

Ft. Wayne

OHIO
1803

Pennsylvania
Donation Lands,
1783
Pittsburgh

INDIANA TERR.
1803-1805

Ft. Defiance

U.S. Military
District,
1787 & 1796

Wheeling

Zanesville

Virginia
Military
Reserve,
1784

Chillicothe
Marietta

Maryland
Mil. Res.
1781

Cincinnati

VIRGINIA

St. Louis

Vincennes

Staunton

Kaskaskia

Louisville
Frankfort
Lexington

KENTUCKY
1792

LOUISIANA TERRITORY
(Under Government of Indiana Territory)
1804-1805

Virginia Military Reserve, 1781

North Carolina
Military Reserve,
1783
Nashville

North Carolina
Mil. Res.
1780

NORTH
CAROLINA

Raleigh

Knoxville

Fayetteville

TENNESSEE
1796

Ft. San
Fernando

Chattanooga

APPALACHIAN MTS.

South Carolina
Military Reserve,
1778

SOUTH

Georiga
Mil. Res.
1784

CAROLINA

Columbia

Augusta

MISSISSIPPI TERR.
1804-1812

Charleston

GEORGIA

Washington
Natchez

Savannah

ATLANTIC
OCEAN

Mobile
Pensacola

St. Marks

30°

New Orleans

St. Augustine

FLORIDA
(Spanish)

GULF OF MEXICO
85°

80°

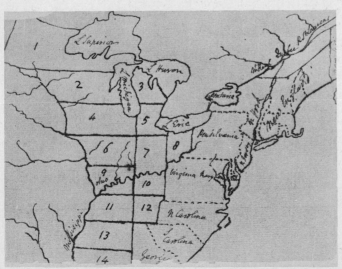

Sketch map showing Jefferson's proposal for division of the western
lands ceded to America in 1784.
OPPOSITE PAGE: (Top) Map of Kentucky by John Filson, 1784; (bottom)
map of the Great Lakes region in
1816 by John Eddy

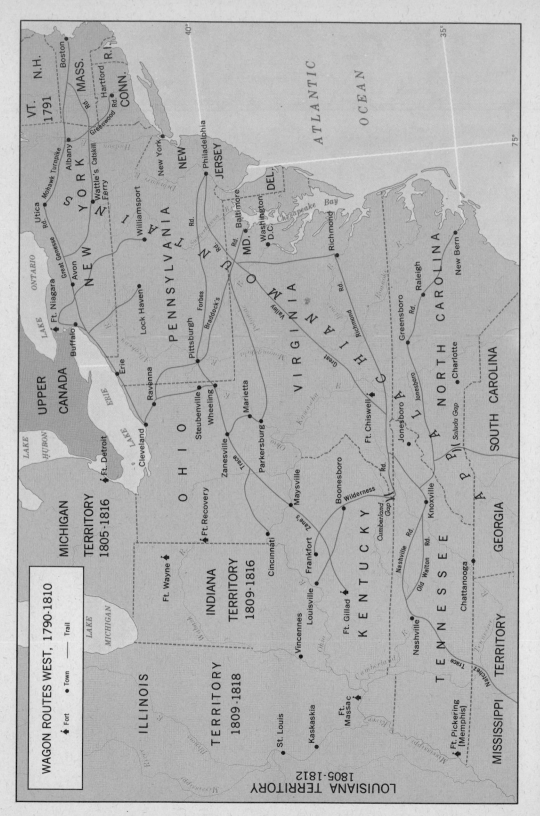

WAGON ROUTES WEST, 1790-1810

⚓ Fort   ● Town   —— Trail

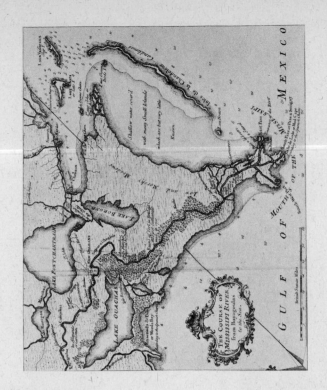

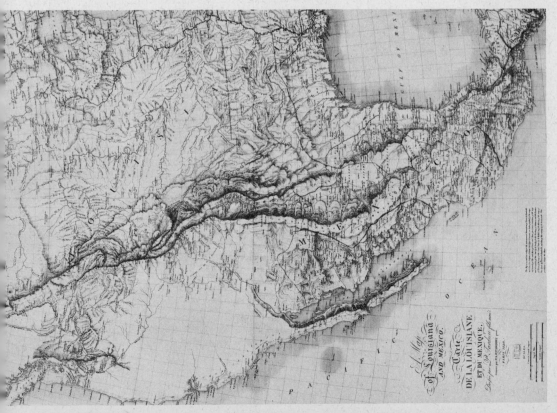

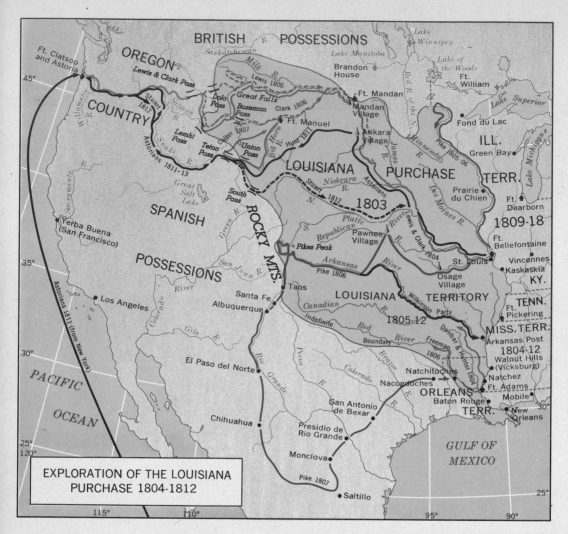

EXPLORATION OF THE LOUISIANA
PURCHASE 1804-1812

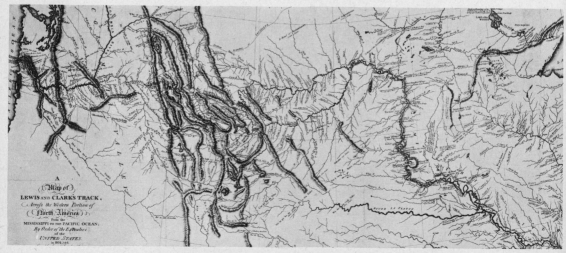

Printed map copied from one drawn by Clark showing the area explored

664

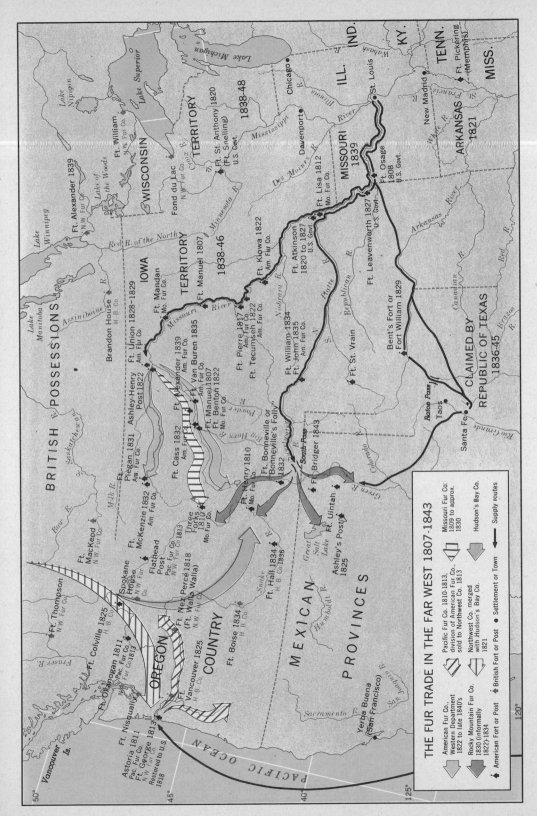

THE FUR TRADE IN THE FAR WEST 1807-1843

IND.

KY.

TENN.

MISS.

ARKANSAS
1821

Ft. Pickering
(Memphis)

St. Francis R.

New Madrid

White R.

St. Louis

Chicago

ILL.

MISSOURI
1839

Ft. Osage
1808
U.S. Govt.

Ft. Lisa 1812
Mo. Fur Co.

Ft. Leavenworth 1827
U.S. Govt.

Davenport

Des Moines R.

Mississippi River

Illinois River

Wabash R.

Arkansas River

Canadian R.

Red R.

CLAIMED BY
REPUBLIC OF TEXAS
1835-45

Brazos R.

Rio Grande

Santa Fe

Taos

Raton Pass

Bent's Fort or
Fort William 1829

Ft. St. Vrain

Colorado R.

Republican R.

Platte R.

N. Platte R.

S. Platte R.

Ft. Atkinson
1820 to 1827
U.S. Govt.

Ft. Kiowa 1822
Am. Fur Co.

Ft. Pierre 1817
Am. Fur Co.

Ft. Tecumseh 1822
Am. Fur Co.

Ft. William 1834
Ft. John 1835
Am. Fur Co.

Niobrara R.

Ft. Mandan
Mo. Fur Co.

Ft. Manuel 1807

Missouri River

Ft. Union 1828-1829
Am. Fur Co.

Brandon House
H. B. Co.

IOWA
TERRITORY
1838-46

WISCONSIN
TERRITORY
1838-48

Ft. St. Anthony 1820
(Ft. Snelling)
U.S. Govt.

Fond du Lac

Minnesota R.

Crow Wing R.

Red R. of the North

Assiniboine R.

Saskatchewan R.

Lake Winnipeg

Lake Manitoba

Lake Nipigon

Lake Superior

Lake Michigan

Ft. William
N.W. Fur Co.

Ft. Alexander 1839
N.W. Fur Co.

Lake of the Woods

BRITISH POSSESSIONS

Ft. Henry 1810
Mo. Fur Co.

South Pass

Ft. Bridger 1843

Ft. Bonneville or
Bonneville's Folly
1832

Green R.

Ft. Uintah

Ashley's Post
1825

Great Salt Lake

Humboldt R.

Ft. Hall 1834
H. B. Co. 1836

Snake R.

Ft. Boise 1834
H. B. Co.

Ft. Nez Percé 1818
(Ft. Walla Walla)
N.W. Fur Co.

Flathead Post

Ft. McKenzie 1832
Am. Fur Co.

Piegan 1831
Am. Fur Co.

Milk R.

Ft. Benton 1822
Mo. Fur Co.

Ft. Manuel 1807

Ft. Van Buren 1835
Am. Fur Co.

Ft. Alexander 1839
Am. Fur Co.

Ft. Cass 1832
Am. Fur Co.

Ashley-Henry
Post 1822

Powder R.

Big Horn R.

Bow R.

Three Forks
1810
Mo. Fur Co.

Spokane House
N.W. Fur Co.

Ft. Okanogan 1811
N.W. Fur Co. 1813

Ft. Colville 1825
H. B. Co.

Ft. Thompson
N.W. Fur Co.

Fraser R.

Ft. MacLeod
N.W. Fur Co.

OREGON
COUNTRY

Ft. Vancouver 1825
H. B. Co.

Ft. Nisqually
H. B. Co.

Astoria 1811
Pac. Fur Co.
Ft. George 1813
N.W. Fur Co.
Restored to U.S.
1818

Vancouver Is.

MEXICAN PROVINCES

Sacramento R.

San Joaquin R.

Yerba Buena
(San Francisco)

PACIFIC OCEAN

50°

45°

40°

125°

120°

THE FUR TRADE IN THE FAR WEST 1807-1843

American Fur Co.
Western Department
1822 to late 1840's

Rocky Mountain Fur Co.
1830 (informally
1822)-1834

Pacific Fur Co. 1810-1813,
division of American Fur Co.
sold to Northwest Co. 1813

Northwest Co. merged
with Hudson's Bay Co.
1821

Missouri Fur Co.
1809 to approx.
1830

Hudson's Bay Co.

Supply routes

American Fort or Post   Settlement or Town

British Fort or Post

665

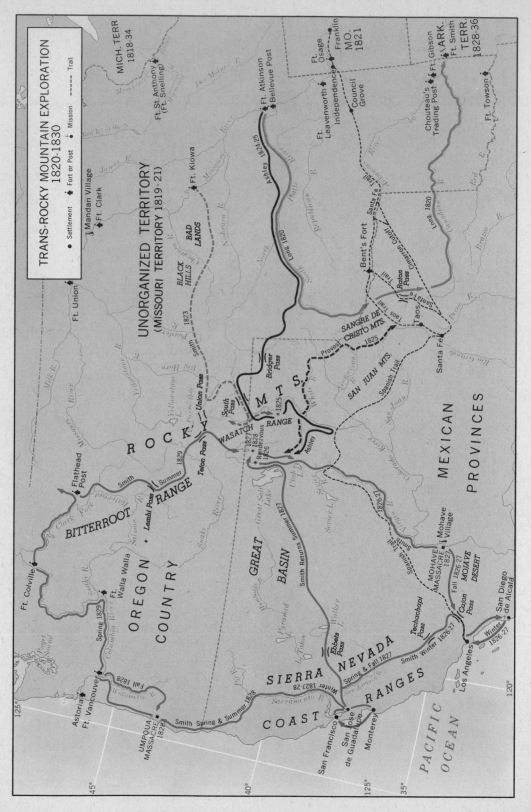

TRANS-ROCKY MOUNTAIN EXPLORATION
1820-1830

● Settlement   ◆ Fort or Post   ✝ Mission   --- Trail

MICH. TERR.
1818-34

Ft. St. Anthony
(Ft. Snelling)

‖ Mandan Village
● Ft. Clark

UNORGANIZED TERRITORY
(MISSOURI TERRITORY 1819-21)

BLACK
HILLS

BAD
LANDS

Ft. Kiowa

Ft. Union

Ft. Atkinson
Bellevue Post

Ashley 1824-25

Long 1820

Ft. Osage
Franklin
MO. 1821

Ft. Leavenworth
Independence
Council
Grove

Chouteau's
Trading Post
Ft. Gibson
Ft. Smith
ARK.
TERR.
1828-36

Ft. Towson

Santa Fe Trail
Long 1820

Bent's Fort

Cimarron Cutoff

Raton
Pass

Taos

Taos Trail

Santa Fe

SANGRE DE
CRISTO MTS.
1825

SAN JUAN MTS.

Spanish Trail

Smith 1823

Provost

Bridger
Pass

ROCKY

MTS.

South
Pass

1825

Ashley

WASATCH RANGE

RENDEZVOUS
1826
1827
1828

MEXICAN

PROVINCES

Ft. Union

Flathead
Post

Smith
Summer 1829

Teton Pass

BITTERROOT
RANGE

Lerhi Pass

Ft. Colville

Spring 1829

Ft.
Walla Walla

OREGON
COUNTRY

GREAT

BASIN

Great Salt
Lake

Utah L.

Sevier L.

1826-2
Smith

Spanish Trail

Smith Returns Summer 1827

MOHAVE
MASSACRE
1827

Mohave
Village

MOJAVE
DESERT

Cajon
Pass

Astoria
Ft. Vancouver

Fall 1828

UMPQUA
MASSACRE
1828

Smith Spring & Summer 1828

SIERRA

NEVADA

Ebbets
Pass

Tehachapi
Pass

Los Angeles

Smith Winter 1826-27

Winter
1826-27

San Diego
de Alcala

Winter 1827-28

COAST

RANGES

San Francisco

San Jose
de Guadalupe
Monterey

Spring & Fall 1827

PACIFIC

OCEAN

666

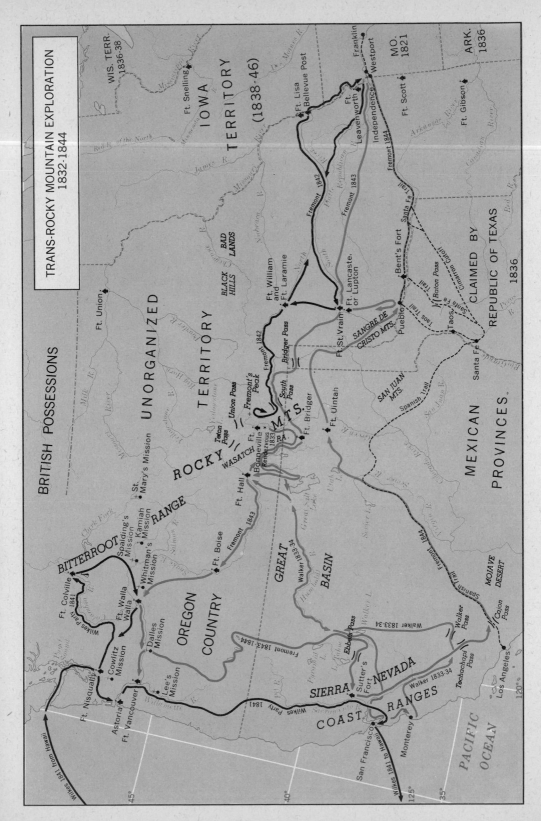

TRANS-ROCKY MOUNTAIN EXPLORATION
1832-1844

BRITISH POSSESSIONS

WIS. TERR.
1836-38

IOWA

TERRITORY

(1838-46)

MO.
1821

ARK.
1836

Ft. Snelling

Ft. Lisa
Bellevue Post

Franklin
Westport
Independence
Ft. Leavenworth

Ft. Scott

Ft. Gibson

Red R. of the North

James R.

Fremont 1842

Fremont 1843

Fremont 1844

Santa Fe Trail

Ft. Union

BAD
LANDS

BLACK
HILLS

Ft. William
Ft. Laramie

Ft. Lancaster,
or Lupton

Bent's Fort

CLAIMED BY

REPUBLIC OF TEXAS

1836

Raton Pass

Cimarron Cutoff

Taos Trail

Santa Fe Trail

Ft. St. Vrain

Pueblo

Taos

Santa Fe

SANGRE DE
CRISTO MTS.

UNORGANIZED

TERRITORY

Union Pass

Fremont's
Peak

South
Pass

Bridger Pass

Fremont 1842

ROCKY

MTS.

Ft. Bridger

Ft. Uintah

SAN JUAN
MTS.

Spanish Trail

MEXICAN

PROVINCES.

Teton
Pass

Ft.
Bonneville
Rendezvous
1833

WASATCH

RANGE

St.
Mary's Mission

Spalding's
Mission

Kamiah
Mission

Whitman's
Mission

Ft. Hall

Ft. Boise

Fremont 1843

GREAT

BASIN

Walker 1833-34

Great Salt L.

BITTERROOT

Ft. Colville
1841

Ft. Walla
Walla

Wilkes Party 1841

Dalles Mission

OREGON

COUNTRY

Fremont 1843-1844

Walker 1833-34

Walker
Pass

MOJAVE
DESERT

Cajon
Pass

Spanish Trail

Fremont 1844

Ft. Nisqually

Cowlitz
Mission

Lee's Mission

Astoria
Ft. Vancouver

Wilkes Party 1841

SIERRA

NEVADA

COAST

RANGES

Ebbets Pass

Sutter's
Fort

Tehachapi
Pass

Walker 1833-34

Los Angeles

Monterey

San Francisco

Wilkes 1841 to Hawaii

Wilkes 1841 from Hawaii

PACIFIC

OCEAN

45°

40°

35°

120°

125°

667

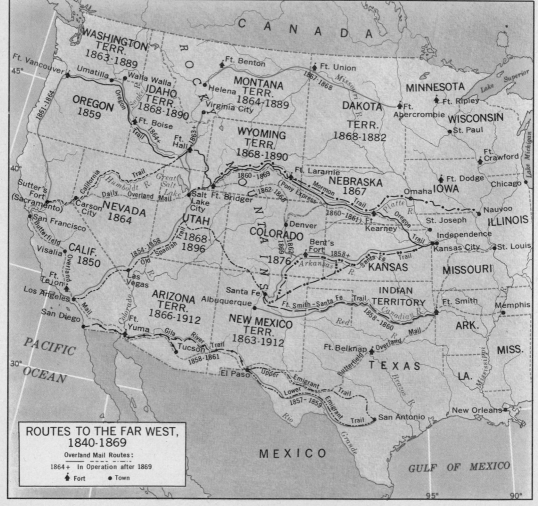

ROUTES TO THE FAR WEST,
1840-1869

Overland Mail Routes:

1864+ In Operation after 1869

⚑ Fort   ● Town

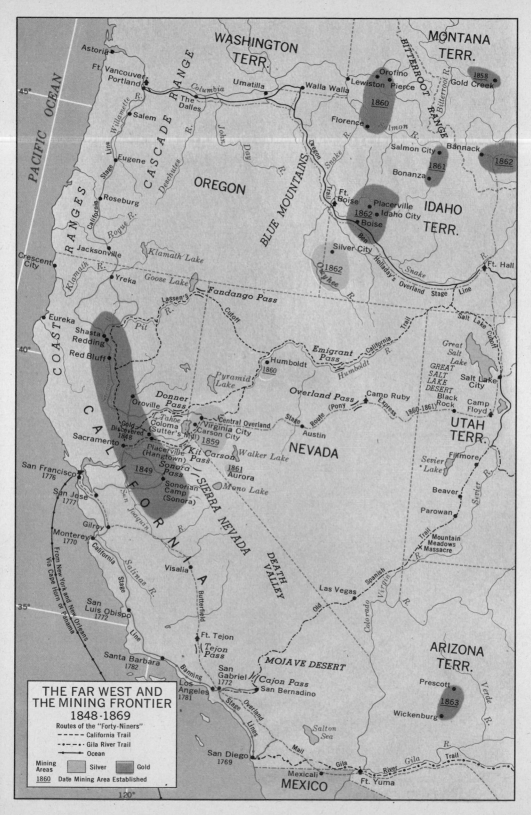

PACIFIC OCEAN

WASHINGTON TERR.

MONTANA TERR.

Astoria
Ft. Vancouver
Portland
The Dalles
Umatilla
Walla Walla
Salem
Eugene
Roseburg
Jacksonville
Crescent City
Yreka

OREGON

CASCADE RANGE

Columbia R.

John Day R.

Deschutes R.

Willamette R.

Rogue R.

Klamath R.

Klamath Lake

Goose Lake

BLUE MOUNTAINS

Lewiston
Orofino
Pierce
1860
Florence
Salmon R.
Salmon City
Bonanza
1861
Bannack
1862
Gold Creek
1858

BITTERROOT RANGE

Ft. Boise
Placerville
Idaho City
1862
Boise
Silver City
Owyhee
1862

IDAHO TERR.

Ft. Hall

Snake R.

Oregon Trail

Holladay's Overland Stage Line

Salt Lake Cutoff

COAST RANGES

Eureka
Shasta
Redding
Red Bluff

California Stage Line

Pit R.

Lassen's

Fandango Pass

Cutoff

Sacramento R.

Pyramid Lake

Humboldt
1860

Emigrant Pass

California Trail

Humboldt R.

Great Salt Lake

GREAT SALT LAKE DESERT

Salt Lake City

UTAH TERR.

CALIFORNIA

Oroville
Donner Pass
L. Tahoe
Coloma (Sutter's Mill)
Gold Discovered 1848
Central City
Virginia City
Carson City
1859
Sacramento
Placerville (Hangtown)
1849
Kit Carson Pass
Sonora Pass
Sonorian Camp (Sonora)
San Francisco 1776
San Jose 1777
Gilroy
Monterey 1770

SIERRA NEVADA

Walker Lake
Aurora
1861
Mono Lake

NEVADA

Austin

Overland Pass (Pony)

Camp Ruby

Stage Route

Express 1860-1861

Black Rock

Camp Floyd

Sevier Lake

Fillmore

Beaver

Parowan

Sevier R.

San Joaquin R.

Salinas R.

California Stage Line

Visalia

DEATH VALLEY

MOJAVE DESERT

Mountain Meadows Massacre

San Luis Obispo 1772

Ft. Tejon
Tejon Pass

Las Vegas

Spanish Trail

Virgin R.

Colorado R.

Old

ARIZONA TERR.

Santa Barbara 1782

Banning
San Gabriel 1772
Cajon Pass
San Bernardino
Los Angeles 1781

Salton Sea

Prescott
1863
Wickenburg

Verde R.

THE FAR WEST AND
THE MINING FRONTIER
1848-1869

Routes of the "Forty-Niners"
- - - - California Trail
-·-·- Gila River Trail
——— Ocean

Mining Areas   ☐ Silver   ☐ Gold
1860   Date Mining Area Established

San Diego 1769

Mexicali
Ft. Yuma

Gila River
Gila R.

Mail

Trail

MEXICO

669

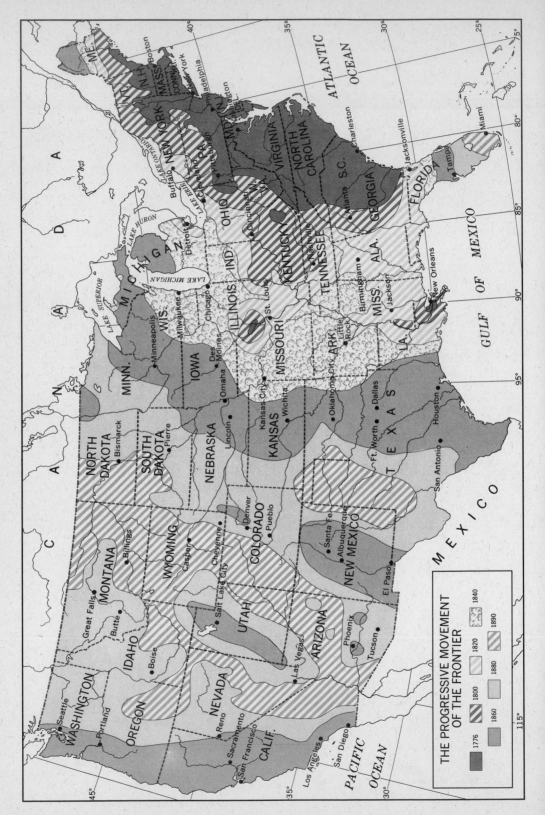

THE PROGRESSIVE MOVEMENT
OF THE FRONTIER

1776	1800	1840
	1820	1890
	1860	1880

Territorial Acquisitions 1783—1968

year	acquisition	area
1783	Original territory of 13 colonies and claims	888,685 sq. mi.
1803	Louisiana Purchase from France	827,192 sq. mi.
1819	Florida and adjacent areas purchased from Spain	72,003 sq. mi.
1845	Independent Republic of Texas annexed	390,144 sq. mi.
1846	Oregon Territory acquired from Great Britain	285,580 sq. mi.
1848	Mexican Cession from Mexican War	529,017 sq. mi.
1853	Gadsden Purchase from Mexico	29,640 sq. mi.
1858	Johnston and Sand Islands in the Pacific, under Guano Island Act (1856)	less than 1 sq. mi.
1862	Palmyra Island annexed by Hawaii	4 sq. mi.
1863	Swan Islands in Caribbean, under Guano Island Act	1 sq. mi.
1865	Navassa in Caribbean, under Guano Island Act	2 sq. mi.
1867	Alaska purchased from Russia	586,412 sq. mi.
1867	Midway Islands annexed	2 sq. mi.
1898	Independent Republic of Hawaii annexed	6,450 sq. mi.
1898	Guam annexed	212 sq. mi.
1898	Philippines annexed (granted independence July 4, 1946)	115,600 sq. mi.
1898	Puerto Rico annexed (granted commonwealth status, July 25, 1952)	3,435 sq. mi.
1898	Wake Island claimed	2.5 sq. mi.
1899	American Samoa, by treaty with Great Britain and Germany	76 sq. mi.
1903	Canal Zone leased from Panama	553 sq. mi.
1903	Guantanamo (naval base) leased from Cuba	30 sq. mi.
1914	Corn Islands leased from Nicaragua	4 sq. mi.
1916	Virgin Islands purchased from Denmark	133 sq. mi.
1919	Quita Sueno Bank, Roncador Cay, and Serrana Bank in Caribbean, under Guano Island Act	less than 0.5 sq. mi.
1922	Kingman Reef in Pacific annexed	less than 0.5 sq. mi.
1925	Swains Island in Pacific annexed, included in American Samoa	1.75 sq. mi.
1934	Howland, Baker, and Jarvis islands in Pacific, under Guano Island Act	3 sq. mi.
1939	Canton and Enderbury islands, jointly with Great Britain	27 sq. mi.
1947	United Nations Trust Territory of the Pacific Islands (Micronesia), including Caroline, Marshall, and Mariana groups	687 sq. mi.
1952	Ryukyu Islands, including Okinawa, by treaty with Japan. Other islands in treaty later returned to Japan (Volcano Islands, including Iwo Jima, Bonin Islands, Marcus Island, Rosario Island, Parece Vela — 52.5 sq. mi.)	848 sq. mi.
1968	Northern half of Cordova Island in Rio Grande, ceded by Mexico in return for the Chamizol (630 ac.)	193 ac.
	Total; U.S., possessions, territories, and trusts	3,628,062 sq. mi.

4. CANADA AND MEXICO

In many ways the United States was unique among nations, and this fact had a decided influence on public attitudes and official policy. Separation from Europe by 3,000 miles of ocean, the existence of a vast continent available for exploitation and settlement, and particularly the lack of powerful neighbors combined to shape the course of 19th-century history.

Goaded onward by Manifest Destiny and a limited imperialism, the United States was able, in the course of a century, to settle the continent. Large land cessions were acquired from Mexico by war, filling out the present boundaries of the Southwest. Various boundary disputes with Canada were settled short of war, though not without much irritation on both sides.

Conflicting territorial claims with Mexico continued to exist past the middle of the 20th century. The undefended boundary with Canada was held up as a model for other nations to emulate; yet there was also intermittent talk of adding Canada and Mexico to the national domain. Such proposals did not materialize, however, and seemed unlikely to do so in the future.

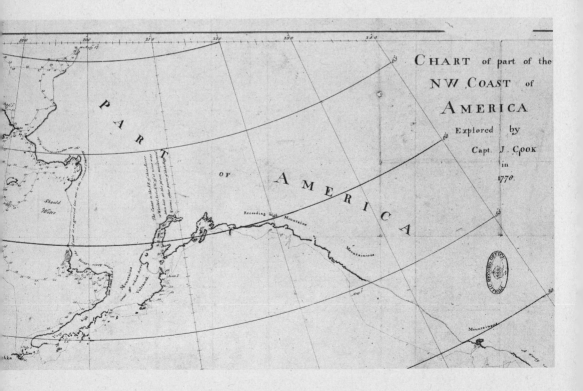

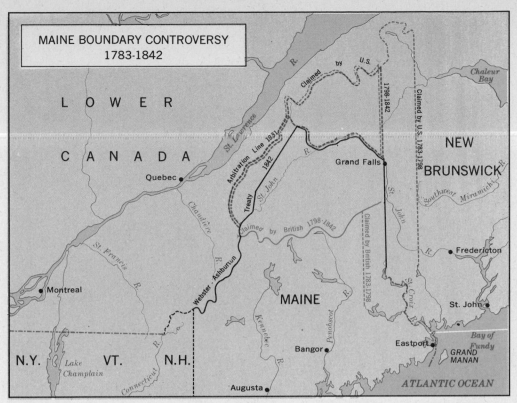

**MAINE BOUNDARY CONTROVERSY
1783-1842**

Claimed by U.S.

Chaleur Bay

St. Lawrence R.

L O W E R

C A N A D A

1798-1842

Claimed by U.S. 1783-1798

NEW
BRUNSWICK

St. Lawrence

Arbitration Line 1831

1842

Quebec

Treaty

Grand Falls

St. John

Southwest Miramichi R.

Chaudière R.

St. John R.

Claimed by British 1798-1842

Claimed by British 1783-1798

St. Croix R.

Fredericton

St. Francis R.

Webster - Ashburton

MAINE

Kennebec R.

Penobscot R.

St. John

Montreal

R.

Eastport

Bay of Fundy

GRAND MANAN

N.Y.

Lake Champlain

VT.

N.H.

Bangor

Connecticut R.

Augusta

ATLANTIC OCEAN

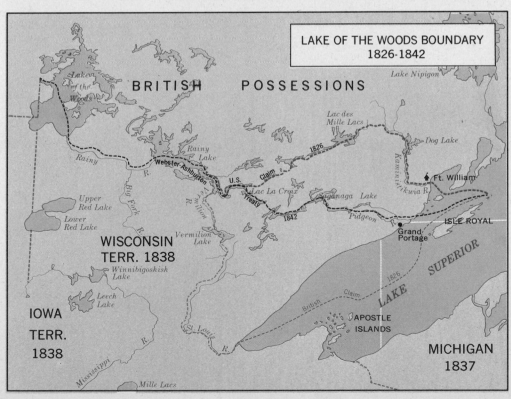

**LAKE OF THE WOODS BOUNDARY
1826-1842**

Lake Nipigon

Lake of the Woods

B R I T I S H   P O S S E S S I O N S

Lac des Mille Lacs

Dog Lake

Rainy

Rainy Lake

Webster-Ashburton

1826

Kaministikwia R.

Ft. William

Rainy R.

U.S. Claim

Lac La Croix

Saganaga Lake

Big Fork R.

Treaty

1842

Pidgeon

Grand Portage

ISLE ROYAL

Upper Red Lake

Lower Red Lake

Vermilion R.

Vermilion Lake

WISCONSIN
TERR. 1838

Winnibigoshish Lake

1826

British Claim

APOSTLE ISLANDS

LAKE SUPERIOR

Leech Lake

IOWA

TERR.

1838

St. Louis R.

Mississippi R.

MICHIGAN
1837

Mille Lacs

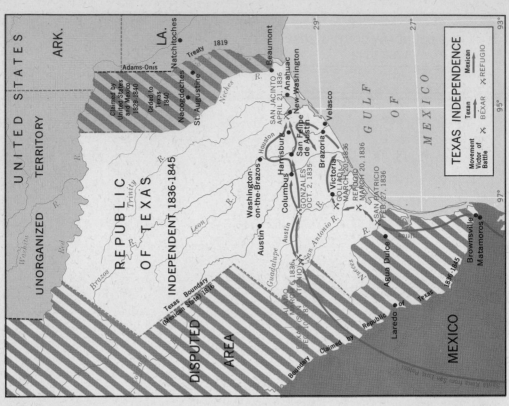

TEXAS INDEPENDENCE

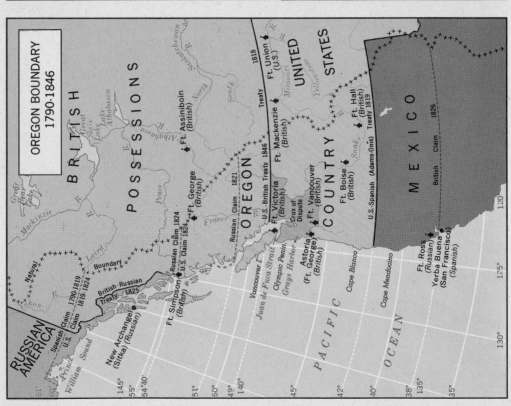

OREGON BOUNDARY 1790-1846

674

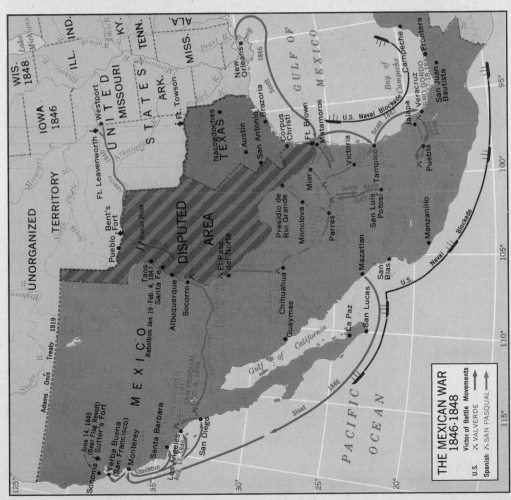

THE MEXICAN WAR
1846-1848

Victor of Battle

U.S. ✕ VALVERDE Movements

Spanish ✕ SAN PASQUAL

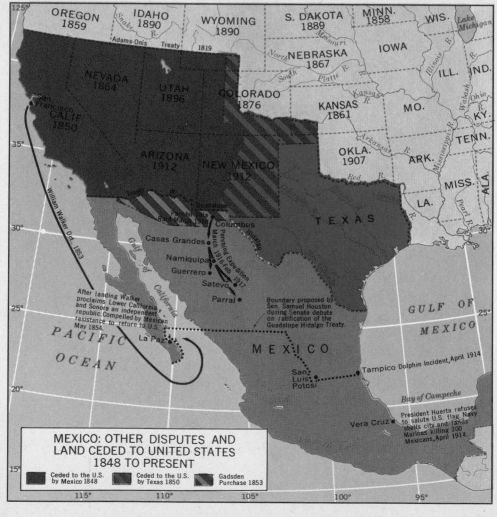

MEXICO: OTHER DISPUTES AND LAND CEDED TO UNITED STATES 1848 TO PRESENT

OREGON 1859

IDAHO 1890

WYOMING 1890

S. DAKOTA 1889

MINN. 1858

WIS.

Lake Michigan

'Adams-Onis' Treaty   1819

NEVADA 1864

UTAH 1896

COLORADO 1876

NEBRASKA 1867

IOWA

ILL.   IND.

San Francisco

CALIF. 1850

ARIZONA 1912

NEW MEXICO 1912

KANSAS 1861

MO.

KY.

OKLA. 1907

ARK.

TENN.

Treaty at Guadalupe

Pancho Villa Raid March 1916

Columbus

T E X A S

MISS.   ALA.

LA.

William Walker Oct. 1853

Casas Grandes

Namiquipa

Guerrero

Satevo

Parral

Pershing Expedition March 1916 Feb. 1917

Boundary proposed by Sen. Samuel Houston during Senate debate on ratification of the Guadalupe Hidalgo Treaty.

GULF OF MEXICO

After landing Walker proclaims Lower California and Sonora an independent republic. Compelled by Mexican resistance to return to U.S. May 1854.

La Paz

M E X I C O

PACIFIC OCEAN

San Luis Potosí

Tampico Dolphin Incident, April 1914

Bay of Campeche

Vera Cruz

President Huerta refuses to salute U.S. flag. Navy shells city and lands Marines, killing 300 Mexicans, April 1914.

MEXICO: OTHER DISPUTES AND LAND CEDED TO UNITED STATES 1848 TO PRESENT

Ceded to the U.S. by Mexico 1848

Ceded to the U.S. by Texas 1850

Gadsden Purchase 1853

The States of the Union

state	date of admission	order of admission	capital	area, 1960 total	area, 1960 rank order
Alabama	Dec. 14, 1819	22	Montgomery	51,609	29
Alaska	Jan. 3, 1959	49	Juneau	586,412	1
Arizona	Feb. 14, 1912	48	Phoenix	113,909	6
Arkansas	June 15, 1836	25	Little Rock	53,104	27
California	Sept. 9, 1850	31	Sacramento	158,693	3
Colorado	Aug. 1, 1876	38	Denver	104,247	8
Connecticut	Jan. 9, 1788*	5	Hartford	5,009	48
Delaware	Dec. 7, 1787*	1	Dover	2,057	49
Florida	Mar. 3, 1845	27	Tallahassee	58,560	22
Georgia	Jan. 2, 1788*	4	Atlanta	58,876	21
Hawaii	Aug. 21, 1959	50	Honolulu	6,450	47
Idaho	July 3, 1890	43	Boise	83,557	13
Illinois	Dec. 3, 1818	21	Springfield	56,400	24
Indiana	Dec. 11, 1816	19	Indianapolis	36,291	38
Iowa	Dec. 28, 1846	29	Des Moines	56,290	25
Kansas	Jan. 29, 1861	34	Topeka	82,264	14
Kentucky	June 1, 1792	15	Frankfort	40,395	37
Louisiana	Apr. 30, 1812	18	Baton Rouge	48,523	31
Maine	Mar. 15, 1820	23	Augusta	33,215	39
Maryland	Apr. 28, 1788*	7	Annapolis	10,577	42
Massachusetts	Feb. 6, 1788*	6	Boston	8,257	45
Michigan	Jan. 26, 1837	26	Lansing	58,216	23
Minnesota	May 11, 1858	32	St. Paul	84,068	12
Mississippi	Dec. 10, 1817	20	Jackson	47,716	32
Missouri	Aug. 10, 1821	24	Jefferson City	69,686	19
Montana	Nov. 8, 1889	41	Helena	147,138	4
Nebraska	Mar. 1, 1867	37	Lincoln	77,227	15
Nevada	Oct. 31, 1864	36	Carson City	110,540	7
New Hampshire	June 21, 1788*	9	Concord	9,304	44
New Jersey	Dec. 18, 1787*	3	Trenton	7,836	46
New Mexico	Jan. 6, 1912	47	Santa Fe	121,666	5
New York	July 26, 1788*	11	Albany	49,576	30
North Carolina	Nov. 21, 1789*	12	Raleigh	52,586	28
North Dakota	Nov. 2, 1889	39	Bismarck	70,665	17
Ohio	Mar. 1, 1803	17	Columbus	41,222	35
Oklahoma	Nov. 16, 1907	46	Oklahoma City	69,919	18
Oregon	Feb. 14, 1859	33	Salem	96,981	10
Pennsylvania	Dec. 12, 1787*	2	Harrisburg	45,333	33
Rhode Island	May 29, 1790*	13	Providence	1,214	50
South Carolina	May 23, 1788*	8	Columbia	31,055	40
South Dakota	Nov. 2, 1889	40	Pierre	77,047	16
Tennessee	June 1, 1796	16	Nashville	42,244	34
Texas	Dec. 29, 1845	28	Austin	267,339	2
Utah	Jan. 4, 1896	45	Salt Lake City	84,916	11
Vermont	Mar. 4, 1791	14	Montpelier	9,609	43
Virginia	June 25, 1788*	10	Richmond	40,817	36
Washington	Nov. 11, 1889	42	Olympia	68,192	20
West Virginia	June 20, 1863	35	Charleston	24,181	41
Wisconsin	May 29, 1848	30	Madison	56,154	26
Wyoming	July 10, 1890	44	Cheyenne	97,914	9

*Original state; date shown is that of ratification of Constitution.

5. THE CIVIL WAR

The Civil War has been called the first modern war, and its battles and campaigns were avidly studied by French and German commanders in the years before World War I. It was fought on several fronts, simultaneously on both land and sea, and with an unprecedented involvement of men, money, and material.

The war began in the East but soon developed into a series of engagements in three theaters: eastern, middle (Tennessee), and western (along the Mississippi River). Victory for the North moved from west to east. After the battle of Vicksburg opened the Mississippi and split the Confederacy, in 1863, the North was gradually able to move into the Southern states and destroy their war making capacity, while increasing its own supplies of men and material. Grant's campaigns in Virginia and Sherman's "March to the Sea" in 1864 effectively ended the South's ability to continue the war.

Citizens of Charleston watch the bombardment of Ft. Sumter from waterfront rooftops

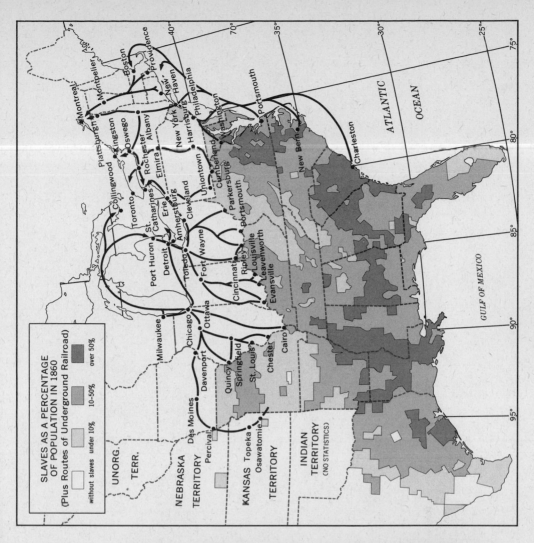

SLAVES AS A PERCENTAGE
OF POPULATION IN 1860
(Plus Routes of Underground Railroad)

over 50%

10-50%

under 10%

without slaves

"STAND UP A MAN!"

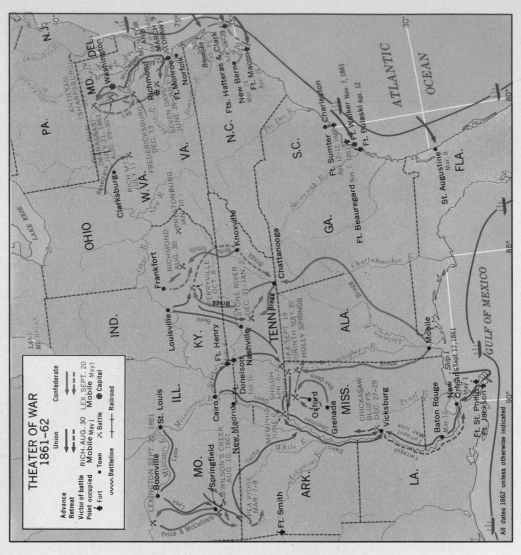

THEATER OF WAR
1861-62

Advance   Union   Confederate

Advance

Retreat

Victor of battle   RICH. AUG. 30   LEX. SEPT. 20

Point occupied   Mobile May 1   Mobile May 1

↟ Fort   ● Town   ✕ Battle   ⊕ Capital

ᴠᴠᴠ Battleline   +--+ Railroad

All dates 1862 unless otherwise indicated

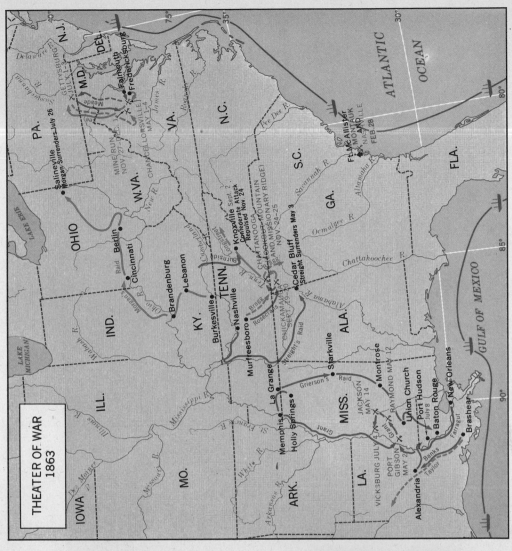

THEATER OF WAR
1863

IOWA

ILL.

MO.

IND.

OHIO

PA.

N.J.

DEL.

M.D.

W.VA.

VA.

N.C.

S.C.

GA.

ALA.

MISS.

ARK.

LA.

FLA.

TENN.

KY.

ATLANTIC OCEAN

GULF OF MEXICO

LAKE MICHIGAN

LAKE ERIE

Delaware R.

Susquehanna R.

James R.

Pee Dee R.

Savannah R.

Ocmulgee R.

Chattahoochee R.

Alabama R.

Altamaha R.

Mississippi R.

St. Francis R.

Arkansas R.

White R.

Wabash R.

Illinois R.

Des Moines R.

Missouri R.

New R.

Ohio R.

Tennessee R.

Cumberland R.

GETTYSBURG JULY 1-3
Lee
Meade
Fairmouth
Fredericksburg
CHANCELLORSVILLE MAY 1-4
MINE RUN NOV. 27-DEC. 1
Salineville Morgan Surrenders July 26
Berlin
Raid
Cincinnati
Brandenburg
Lebanon
Burkesville
Nashville
Murfreesboro
La Grange
Memphis
Holly Springs
Knoxville Sept. 2
Confederate Attack Repulsed Nov. 24
CHATTANOOGA
LOOKOUT MOUNTAIN AND MISSIONARY RIDGE
NOV. 24-25
CHICKAMAUGA SEPT. 19-20
Bragg
Rosecrans
Cedar Bluff Streight Surrenders May 3
Streight's Raid
Starkville
Montrose
Grierson's Raid
JACKSON MAY 14
RAYMOND MAY 12
Union Church
Port Hudson July 8
Baton Rouge
New Orleans
Brashear
Farragut
Banks
Taylor
Alexandria
VICKSBURG JULY 4
PORT GIBSON MAY 1
Grant
Ft. McAllister MONTAUK AND NASHVILLE FEB. 28

681

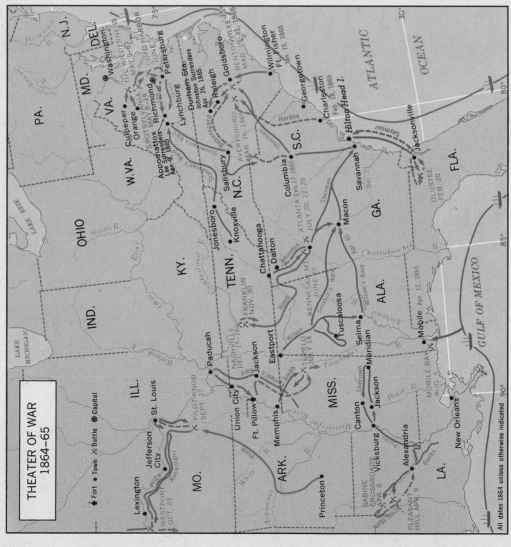

THEATER OF WAR
1864–65

⚓ Fort • Town ✕ Battle ⊕ Capital

All dates 1864 unless otherwise indicated

N.J.

DEL.

MD.

PA.

W. VA.

VA.

OHIO

Washington

Culpeper
Orange
THE WILDERNESS
MAY 5-6
SPOTSYLVANIA
MAY 8-19
Richmond
Appomattox
Lee Surrenders
Apr. 9, 1865
COLD HARBOR
JUNE 3
Petersburg
Lynchburg

Durham's Sta.
Johnston Surrenders
Apr. 26, 1865
Raleigh
Goldsboro
BENTONVILLE
MAR. 19-21, 1865

Wilmington
Ft. Fisher
Jan. 15, 1865

Georgetown

ATLANTIC
OCEAN

KY.

IND.

LAKE
MICHIGAN

LAKE ERIE

Scioto R.

Jonesboro
Salisbury
Knoxville
N.C.

AVERYSBORO
MAR. 16, 1865
Columbia
Feb. 17, 1865

S.C.

Charleston
Feb. 18, 1865

Hardee

Hilton Head I.

Jacksonville

FLA.

OLUSTEE
FEB. 20

Seymour

Chattanooga
Dalton
TENN.
FRANKLIN
NOV. 30
KENNESAW MTN.
JUNE 27
ATLANTA
JULY 20, 22, 28
Macon

GA.

Savannah
Dec. 21

Chattahoochee R.

Sherman

Johnston

Hood

Croxton's Raid

Wilson's Raid

ILL.

Paducah
Union City
NASHVILLE
DEC. 15-16
Jackson
A.J. Smith
Eastport
Tupelo
TUPELO
JULY 14
Wilson
Tuscaloosa
Selma
ALA.

Mobile Apr. 12, 1865

Mobile Bay
AUG. 5

GULF OF MEXICO

St. Louis
PILOTKNOB
SEPT. 27
Price
Ft. Pillow
Memphis

ARK.

MISS.

Canton
Sherman
Jackson
Meridian
Pearl R.

Tombigbee R.

Alabama R.

Jefferson City
Rosecrans

MO.

Lexington
WESTPORT
OCT. 23

Price

Princeton

White R.

Arkansas R.

Mississippi R.

Vicksburg
Porter
Alexandria
Banks
SABINE
CROSSROADS
APR. 8
PLEASANT
HILL APR. 9
Kirby Smith

LA.

New Orleans

682

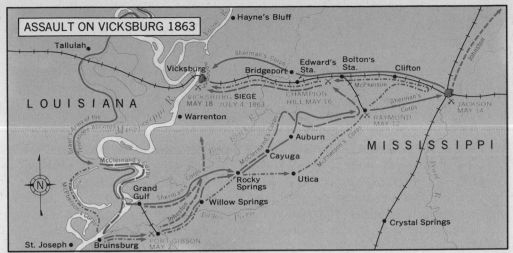

ASSAULT ON VICKSBURG 1863

Hayne's Bluff

Tallulah

Vicksburg

Sherman's Corps

Bridgeport · Edward's Sta. · Bolton's Sta. · Clifton

Johnston

LOUISIANA

VICKSBURG SIEGE MAY 18 JULY 4 1863 · CHAMPION HILL MAY 16

McPherson

Sherman's Corps

JACKSON MAY 14

Warrenton

RAYMOND MAY 12

MISSISSIPPI

Grant's Army of the Tennessee Auburn's Corps

Auburn

McClernand's Corps

Cayuga

McPherson's Corps

McClernand's Corps

Rocky Springs

Utica

Grand Gulf

Sherman's Corps

Willow Springs

Johnston

Crystal Springs

St. Joseph · Bruinsburg

PORT GIBSON MAY 2

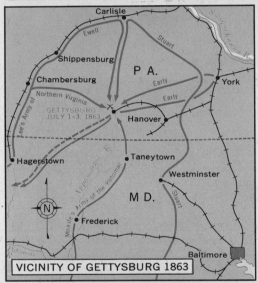

Carlisle

Ewell · Stuart

Shippensburg

P. A.

Chambersburg

Lee's Army of Northern Virginia

York

GETTYSBURG JULY 1-3, 1863

Early

Early

Hanover

Hagerstown

Meade's Army of the Potomac

Taneytown

Westminster

M D.

Stuart

Frederick

Baltimore

VICINITY OF GETTYSBURG 1863

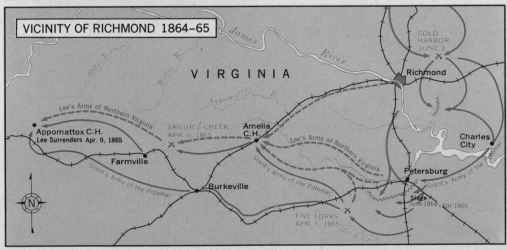

VICINITY OF RICHMOND 1864–65

James River

COLD HARBOR JUNE 3

VIRGINIA

Richmond

Lee's Army of Northern Virginia

Appomattox R.

SAILOR'S CREEK APR. 6, 1865

Amelia C.H.

Charles City

Appomattox C.H.
Lee Surrenders Apr. 9, 1865

Lee's Army of Northern Virginia

Farmville

Grant's Army of the Potomac

Petersburg

Grant's Army of the Potomac

Burkeville

Grant's Army of the Potomac

Siege
June 1864 - Apr. 1865

FIVE FORKS APR. 1, 1865

6. THE SPANISH-AMERICAN WAR AND WORLD WAR I

Under the Monroe Doctrine the United States became the policeman of the Western Hemisphere. Frequent intervention, from the Civil War on, in the political life of South and Central American countries was prompted by the desire to stabilize their governments, secure their economic development, and protect American interests. The Spanish-American war was also imbued with a crusading zeal to free the Caribbean (and the Pacific) from Spanish tyranny. In the process, of course, the United States gained some valuable and coveted territory.

America's traditional dislike of European embroilments might have kept the country out of World War I if that conflict had been confined to the land mass of Europe. But the Great War had an important ocean counterpart and Atlantic commerce was severely disrupted, especially by German submarine attacks. President Wilson was forced early in 1917 to call for a declaration of war. Effective deployment of American strength did not occur until the spring of 1918. The Allied onslaughts of that year finally broke stubborn German resistance, and the war ended in November.

"Spanish 'Justice and Honor' be darned!"—Uncle Sam's image in the Hearst press, 1898

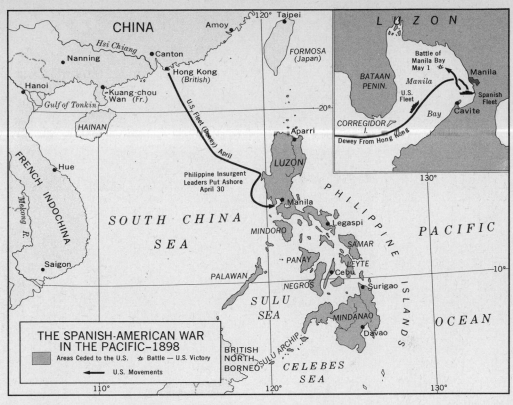

THE SPANISH-AMERICAN WAR IN THE PACIFIC—1898

Areas Ceded to the U.S. ⚹ Battle — U.S. Victory

← U.S. Movements

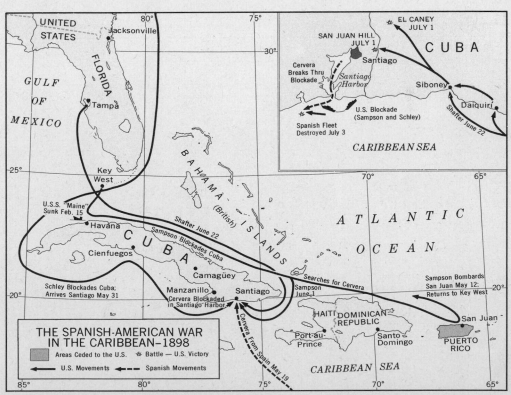

THE SPANISH-AMERICAN WAR IN THE CARIBBEAN—1898

Areas Ceded to the U.S. ⚹ Battle — U.S. Victory

← U.S. Movements ⬸⬸⬸ Spanish Movements

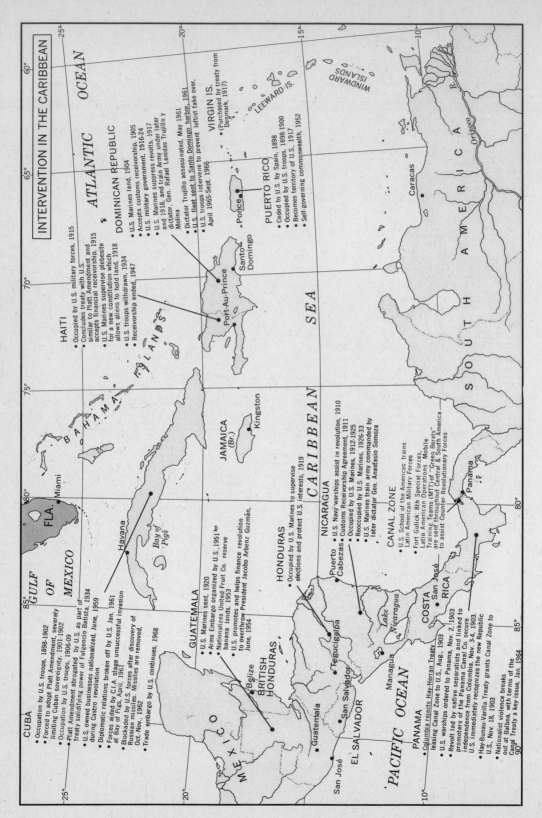

INTERVENTION IN THE CARIBBEAN

ATLANTIC OCEAN

DOMINICAN REPUBLIC
• U.S. Marines land, 1904
• Accepts customs receivership, 1905
• U.S. military government, 1916-24
• U.S. Marines suppress revolts, 1917
• Dictator Trujillo assassinated, May 1961
• U.S. fleet sent to Santo Domingo harbor, 1961 to prevent leftist take over.
• U.S. troops intervene April 1965-Sept. 1966

HAITI
• Occupied by U.S. military forces, 1915
• Concludes treaty with U.S. similar to Platt amendment and accepts financial receivership, 1915
• U.S. Marines supervise plebesite for a new constitution which allows aliens to hold land, 1918
• U.S. troops withdrawn, 1934
• Receivership ended, 1947

VIRGIN IS.
(Purchased by treaty from Denmark, 1917)

LEEWARD IS.

WINDWARD ISLANDS

PUERTO RICO
• Ceded to U.S. by Spain, 1898
• Occupied by U.S. troops, 1898-1900
• Becomes territory of U.S. 1917
• Self-governing commonwealth, 1952

Ponce

Santo Domingo

Port-Au-Prince

ISLANDS

CARIBBEAN SEA

SOUTH AMERICA

Orinoco

Caracas

JAMAICA (Br.)
Kingston

BAHAMA

GULF OF MEXICO

FLA.
Miami

CUBA
• Occupation by U.S. troops, 1898-1902
• Forced to adopt Platt Amendment, severely limiting Cuban sovereignty, 1901-1902
• Occupation by U.S. troops, 1906-09
• Platt Amendment abrogated by U.S. as part of treaty solidifying power of Fulgencio Batista, 1934
• U.S. owned businesses nationalized, June, 1959 during Castro revolution
• Diplomatic relations broken off by U.S. Jan. 1961
• Forces aided by C.I.A. stage unsuccessful invasion at Bay of Pigs, April, 1961
• Blockaded by U.S. forces after discovery of Russian missiles. Missiles are removed, Oct.-Nov. 1962
• Trade embargo by U.S. continues, 1968

Havana

Bay of Pigs

GUATEMALA
• U.S. Marines sent, 1920
• Arms Embargo organized by U.S. 1951
• Nationalizes United Fruit Co. reserve banana lands, 1953
• U.S. promotes and helps finance revolution to overthrow President Jacobo Arbenz Guzmán, June, 1954

HONDURAS
• Occupied by U.S. Marines to supervise elections and protect U.S. interests, 1919

NICARAGUA
• U.S. Navy warships assist in revolution, 1910
• Customs Receivership Agreement, 1911
• Occupied by U.S. Marines, 1912-1925
• Reoccupied by U.S. Marines, 1926-33
• U.S. Marines train army commanded by later dictator Gen. Anastasio Somoza

Puerto Cabezas

CANAL ZONE
• U.S. School of the Americas; trains Latin American Military Forces
• Fort Gulick; 8th Special Forces, Mobile Training Teams (MTT) of "Green Berets" are sent throughout Central & South America to assist Counter-Revolutionary Forces

Managua
Lake Nicaragua

COSTA RICA
San José

Tegucigalpa

Belize
BRITISH HONDURAS

MEXICO

San Salvador
EL SALVADOR

Guatemala

San José

PACIFIC OCEAN

PANAMA
• Columbia rejects Hay-Herran Treaty leasing Canal Zone to U.S., Aug., 1903
• U.S. warships ordered to Panama, Nov. 2, 1903
• Revolt led by native separatists and linked to promoters of the Panama Canal Co. secure independence from Colombia, Nov. 3-4, 1903.
• U.S. immediately recognizes the new Republic of Panama, Nov. 18, 1903
• Hay-Bunau-Varilla Treaty grants Canal Zone to U.S., Nov. 18, 1903
• Nationalist violence breaks out at Balboa, with terms of the Canal Treaty a key issue, Jan. 1964

Panama

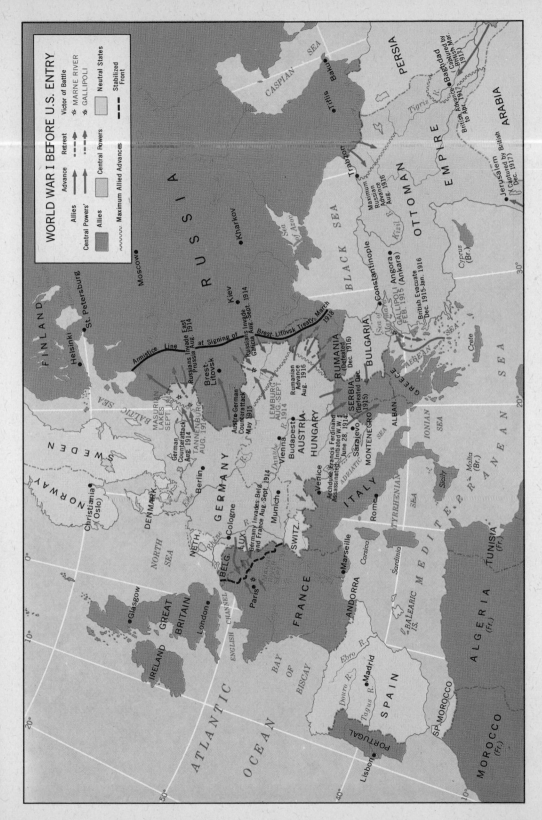

WORLD WAR I BEFORE U.S. ENTRY

Victor of Battle
✶ MARNE RIVER
✱ GALLIPOLI

Neutral States

Stabilized Front

	Advance	Retreat
Allies	→	⇢
Central Powers'	→	

Allies

Central Powers

Maximum Allied Advances

NORWAY

SWEDEN

FINLAND

Helsinki

St. Petersburg

Moscow

RUSSIA

Christiania (Oslo)

DENMARK

NORTH SEA

GREAT BRITAIN

Glasgow

London

IRELAND

ENGLISH CHANNEL

BALTIC SEA

German Counterattack Aug. 1914

Berlin

GERMANY

Cologne

Munich

NETH.

BELG.

LUX.

Germany Invades Belg. and France Aug.-Sept. 1914

Paris

FRANCE

SWITZ.

Marseille

Corsica

Sardinia

BAY OF BISCAY

SPAIN

Madrid

Ebro R.

Douro R.

Tagus R.

PORTUGAL

Lisbon

ATLANTIC OCEAN

ANDORRA

BALEARIC IS.

SP. MOROCCO

MOROCCO (Fr.)

ALGERIA (Fr.)

TUNISIA (Fr.)

MEDITERRANEAN SEA

Sicily

Malta (Br.)

TYRRHENIAN SEA

ITALY

Rome

Venice

Vienna

AUSTRIA-HUNGARY

Budapest

Danube R.

MASURIAN LAKES SEPT.

TANNENBURG AUG. 1914

Russians Invade East Prussia Aug. 1914

Brest-Litovsk

Austro-German Counterattack May 1915

Kiev

Russians Invade Galicia Aug.-Sept. 1914

LEMBURG AUG.-SEPT. 1914

Kharkov

Armistice Line at Signing of Brest-Litovsk Treaty, March 1918

Archduke Francis Ferdinand Assassinated, Initiated W.W.I June 28, 1914

Sarajevo

MONTENEGRO

SERBIA (Defeated Dec. 1915)

ALBAN.

RUMANIA (Defeated Dec. 1916)

Rumanian Advance Aug. 1916

BULGARIA (Defeated Dec. 1916)

GREECE

IONIAN SEA

ADRIATIC SEA

AEGEAN SEA

Crete

BLACK SEA

Sea of Azov

CASPIAN SEA

Bakú

Tiflis

Trebizond

Maximum Russian Advance Aug. 1916

OTTOMAN EMPIRE

PERSIA

ARABIA

Baghdad (Captured by British Mar. 1917)

British Advance 1917 to Apr. 1917

Tigris R.

Kizil R.

Jerusalem (Captured by British Dec. 1917)

Constantinople

Angora (Ankara)

Sea of Marmora

GALLIPOLI 1915 FEB. 1915

British Evacuate Dec. 1915-Jan. 1916

Cyprus (Br.)

Rhine R.

Elbe R.

MARNE RIVER

LOIRE R.

687

WORLD WAR I — SUBMARINE WARFARE

German Submarine Zone

Ship Sunk

British Antisubmarine Minefields

688

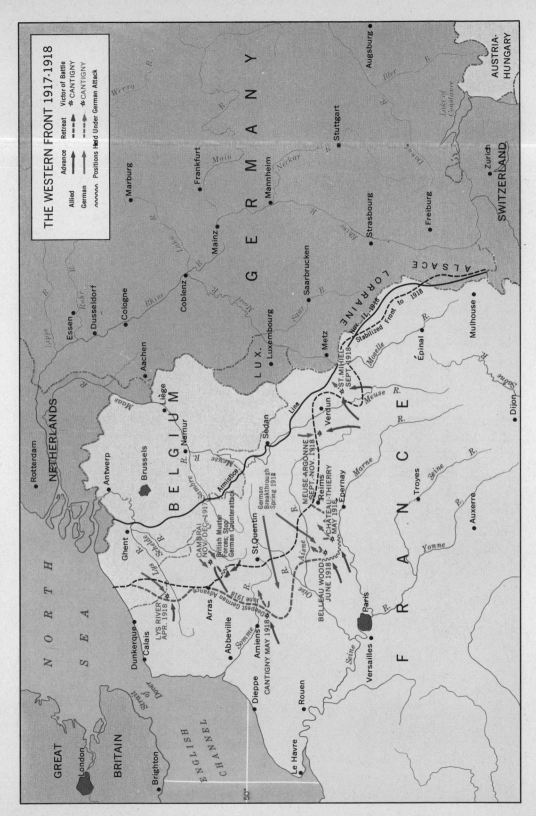

THE WESTERN FRONT 1917-1918

	Advance	Retreat	Victor of Battle
Allied	↑↑	┅┅	✳ CANTIGNY
German	↑↑	┅┅	✳ CANTIGNY
		⌇⌇	Positions Held Under German Attack

GREAT BRITAIN

London

Brighton

NORTH SEA

Strait of Dover

ENGLISH CHANNEL

NETHERLANDS

Rotterdam

Maas R.

Antwerp

Ghent

Dunkerque

Calais

Dieppe

Le Havre

Rouen

Abbeville

Amiens

CANTIGNY MAY 1918

Somme

Arras

LYS RIVER APR. 1918

Lys R.

Scheldt R.

BELGIUM

Brussels

Liège

Namur

Sambre R.

Meuse R.

Maas R.

Sedan

CAMBRAI NOV./DEC. 1917

British Muster Forces; Stop German Counterattack

Armistice Line

St. Quentin

German Breakthrough Spring 1918

Deepest German Advance June 1918

Oise R.

Aisne R.

BELLEAU WOOD JUNE 1918

CHÂTEAU-THIERRY MAY 1918

Reims

MEUSE-ARGONNE SEPT.–NOV. 1918

Epernay

Marne R.

Verdun

ST. MIHIEL SEPT. 1918

Meuse R.

Nov. 11, 1918 Line

Stabilized Front to 1918

Moselle R.

Metz

LUX.

Luxembourg

Saar R.

Saarbrucken

LORRAINE

ALSACE

Strasbourg

Freiburg

Rhine R.

Mulhouse

SWITZERLAND

Zurich

Lake of Constance

AUSTRIA-HUNGARY

Augsburg

Iller R.

Stuttgart

Neckar R.

Mannheim

Main R.

Frankfurt

Marburg

Werra R.

GERMANY

Aachen

Cologne

Dusseldorf

Essen

Ruhr R.

Lippe R.

Coblenz

Mainz

Lahn R.

Mosel R.

Epinal

Dijon

Saône R.

Troyes

Auxerre

Seine R.

Yonne R.

FRANCE

Versailles

Paris

Seine R.

689

The Treaty of Versailles brought no enduring peace, but it did redraw the map of Europe and set up the League of Nations, the first worldwide organization for settling international disputes and ending wars. The failure of the United States to participate in the League and the harsh terms of the Treaty left European conditions very unsettled until the resurgence of Germany in 1933. A second war—perhaps only another phase of the first—broke out in 1939.

For the United States, World War II was its first two-ocean war; in fact, it seemed to be two wars fought at the same time. The conflict with Germany focused on the Mediterranean. The main assault on the Third Reich began on June 6, 1944, with the invasion of the heavily fortified French coast by an Allied armada of 5,000 ships. The European war ended in May 1945. The war with Japan began at Pearl Harbor, in an attack that had been feared and warned of by prescient observers for nearly half a century. It ended after the atomic bombing of two Japanese cities in August 1945.

Even before the war was over plans were well under way to establish a new and stronger international organization, and the United Nations came into existence in 1945. This time the United States was an active if not always very willing participant. But other organizations for mutual and regional security also sprang up during the difficult postwar years: NATO, SEATO, CENTO, and so forth. They did not produce a quiet world; but things might have been a great deal worse without them.

New York Preparedness Parade

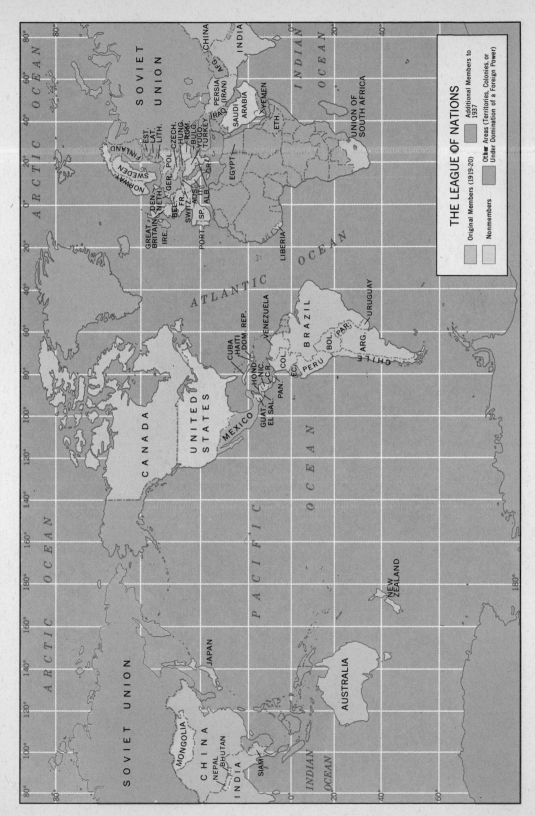

THE LEAGUE OF NATIONS

Original Members (1919-20)

Additional Members to 1937

Nonmembers

Other Areas (Territories, Colonies, or Under Domination of a Foreign Power)

WORLD WAR II IN EUROPE TO MAY 1943

Allies and Allied Controlled Areas

Vichy France and Vichy Controlled Areas

Axis Occupied Areas

Axis Powers

Axis Allied States

Neutral States

Thrusts — Allied ➞ Axis ➞ — Victor of Battle — Allied ✷ Axis ✷ — ANZIO DUNKIRK

ARCTIC OCEAN

ATLANTIC OCEAN

Murmansk

Narvik
British Landings April-May 1940

Archangel

Namsos
Trondheim

Russo-Finnish War Nov. 1939-March 1940

Bergen

FINLAND

Leningrad

UNION OF SOVIET

Gorki

SWEDEN

Helsinki

Oslo

Stockholm

Moscow

NORWAY

BALTIC SEA

EST.
Invaded by Russia June 1940

Voronezh

Glasgow

NORTH SEA

DEN.
Copenhagen

Riga
LAT.
LITH.

Smolensk
July 1941

SOCIALIST

REPUBLICS

STALINGRAD, NOV. 1942-FEB. 1943

IRELAND

GREAT BRITAIN

NETH.

Danzig
Minsk

Russia Attacks Poland Sept. 1939

Kursk

Kharkov

London

BELG.

Berlin

POLAND

Warsaw

Kiev

Rostov

DUNKIRK MAY JUNE 1940

GERMANY

Prague

LUX.

CZECH.

Germany Invades Poland and Initiates W.W. II Sept. 1, 1939

Germany Invades Russia June 1941

Paris

FRANCE

Munich

AUSTRIA

Vienna

HUNGARY

RUMANIA

Odessa

Sevastopol

Bordeaux

SWITZ.

Milan

YUGO.

Belgrade

Bucharest

BLACK SEA

VICHY
German Occupied Nov. 1942

Marseilles

CORSICA

ADRIATIC SEA

Sofia

BULGARIA

Istanbul

Ankara

PORT.

SPAIN

Barcelona

Rome

ITALY

ALB.

GREECE

TURKEY

Lisbon

Madrid

SARDINIA

Athens

CYPRUS (Br.)

SYRIA (Fr.)

Gibralter (Br.)

Allied Landings Nov. 1942

MEDITERRANEAN SEA

SICILY

CRETE
British Evacuate Crete May 1941

SP. MOROCCO

Oran

Algiers

Tunis
Axis Forces in North Africa Surrender May 1943

EL ALAMEIN, OCT.-NOV. 1942

PAL. (Br.)

MOROCCO
Joined Allies Nov. 1942

Mareth Line March 1943

Arrival of German Afrika Korps Feb. 1941

Tripoli

Bengasi

Cairo

TUNISIA
Joined Allies Nov. 1942

ALGERIA
Joined Allies Nov. 1942

Line Feb. 1941

Italians invade Egypt Sept. 1940 Repulsed by British Dec. 1940-Feb. 1941

LIBYA

EGYPT

692

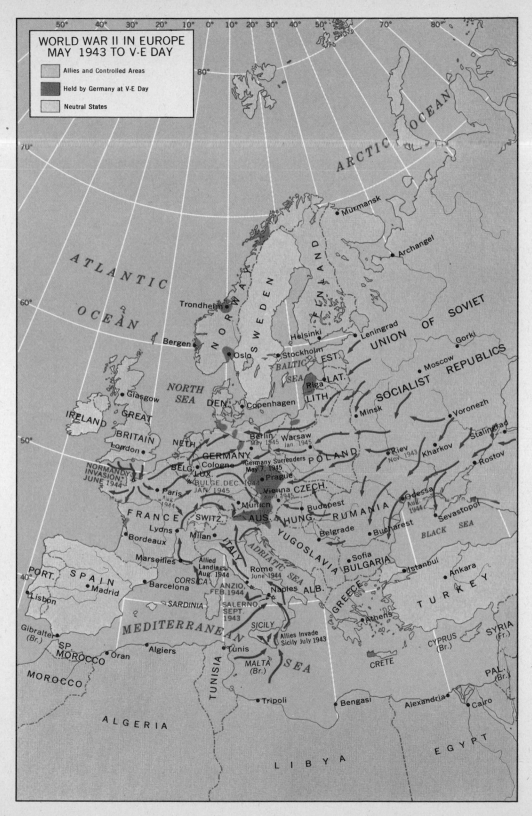

WORLD WAR II IN EUROPE
MAY 1943 TO V-E DAY

Allies and Controlled Areas

Held by Germany at V-E Day

Neutral States

ARCTIC OCEAN

ATLANTIC OCEAN

• Murmansk

• Archangel

NORWAY

SWEDEN

FINLAND

UNION OF SOVIET

Trondheim •

Bergen •

Oslo •

Helsinki •

Stockholm •

Leningrad •

• Gorki

BALTIC SEA

EST.

Moscow •

REPUBLICS

SOCIALIST

NORTH SEA

• Glasgow

GREAT BRITAIN

IRELAND

DEN.

• Copenhagen

Riga •

LAT.

LITH.

Minsk •

• Voronezh

• Stalingrad

London •

NETH.

Berlin
May 1945

Warsaw
Jan. 1945

POLAND

Kiev
Nov. 1943

Kharkov •

• Rostov

GERMANY

NORMANDY
INVASION
JUNE 1944

BELG.

Cologne •

Germany Surrenders
May 7, 1945

LUX.

BULGE, DEC. 1944
JAN. 1945

Paris •

Aug. 1944

Prague •

CZECH.

Vienna
1945

Odessa
Aug.
1944

FRANCE

Munich
April 1945

AUS.

HUNG.

Budapest •

RUMANIA

• Sevastopol

Lyons •

SWITZ.

Milan •

Belgrade •

Bucharest •

BLACK SEA

Bordeaux •

YUGOSLAVIA

Marseilles •

Allied
Landings
Aug. 1944

Rome
June 1944

ITALY

ADRIATIC SEA

Sofia •

BULGARIA

• Istanbul

Ankara •

TURKEY

PORT.

SPAIN

CORSICA

ANZIO
FEB. 1944

Naples

ALB.

GREECE

CYPRUS
(Br.)

SYRIA
(Fr.)

Lisbon •

Madrid •

Barcelona •

SARDINIA

SALERNO
SEPT.
1943

Athens •

MEDITERRANEAN SEA

SICILY

Allies Invade
Sicily July 1943

Gibraltar
(Br.)

SP.
MOROCCO

Oran •

Algiers •

Tunis •

MALTA
(Br.)

CRETE

PAL.
(Br.)

MOROCCO

ALGERIA

TUNISIA

• Tripoli

• Bengasi

Alexandria •

• Cairo

LIBYA

EGYPT

693

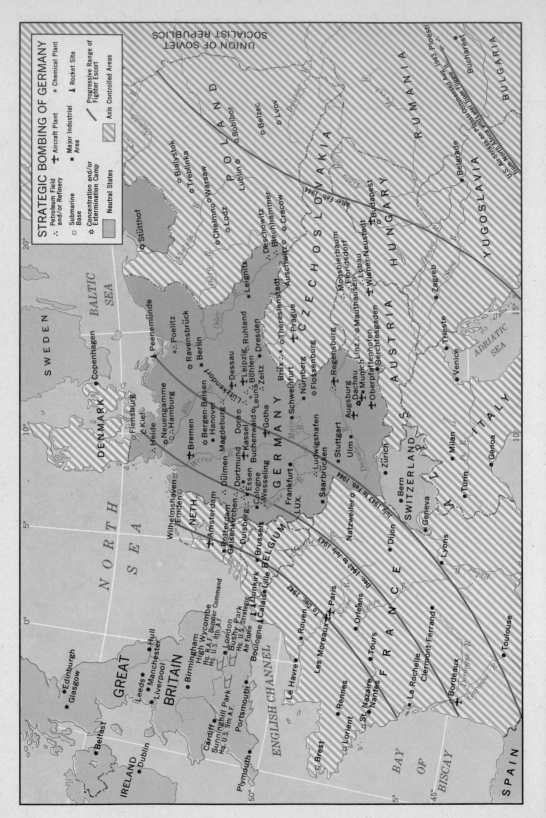

STRATEGIC BOMBING OF GERMANY

- ∴ Petroleum Field and/or Refinery
- ✚ Aircraft Plant
- ✱ Chemical Plant
- ☐ Submarine Base
- ■ Major Industrial Area
- ▲ Rocket Site
- ✿ Concentration and/or Extermination Camp
- — Progressive Range of Fighter Escort
- ▨ Axis Controlled Areas
- ▨ Neutral States

UNION OF SOVIET SOCIALIST REPUBLICS

SWEDEN

BALTIC SEA

DENMARK

Copenhagen

NORTH SEA

GREAT BRITAIN

IRELAND

Dublin
Belfast

Edinburgh
Glasgow

Leeds
Manchester
Liverpool
Birmingham

Hull

Cardiff
High Wycombe
Hq. R.A.F. Bomber Command
Hq. U.S. 8th A.F.
Bushy Park
Hq. U.S. Strategic Air Force
London
Sunninghill Park
Hq. U.S. 9th A.F.
Portsmouth
Bodleigh
Plymouth

ENGLISH CHANNEL

Brest
Lorient
St. Nazaire
Nantes
Rennes
Le Havre
Rouen
Les Moreaux
Paris
Orléans
Tours
La Rochelle
Clermont-Ferrand
Bordeaux
Toulouse

BAY OF BISCAY

SPAIN

FRANCE

Dijon
Lyons
Geneva
Bern
SWITZERLAND
Zürich

Dec. 1942 to July 1943
To Dec. 1942
July 1943 to Feb. 1944
After Feb. 1944

Calais Lille
Dunkirk
Boulogne
BELGIUM
Brussels

NETH.
Amsterdam
Rotterdam
Wilhelmshaven
Emden

Flensburg
Kiel
Helde
Neuengamme
Hamburg
Bremen
Bergen-Belsen
Hanover
Dülmen
Dortmund
Gelsenkirchen
Duisberg
Essen
Cologne
Wesseling
LUX.
Frankfurt
Saarbrücken
Natzweiler

Magdeburg
Dora
Kassel
Buchenwald
Gotha
Ludwigshafen

Peenemünde
Poelitz
Ravensbrück
Berlin
Dessau
Leipzig, Ruhland
Leuna
Böhlen
Zeitz
Dresden
Theresienstadt
Prague
Brüx
Schwelnfurt
Nürnberg
Flossenburg
Regensburg
Augsburg
Dachau
Stuttgart
Ulm
Munich
Linz
Mauthausen
Oberpfaffenhofen
Berchtesgaden

Stütthof
Białystok
Treblinka
Chełmno
Warsaw
Łódź
Lublin
Sobibor
Belzec
Lvov

POLAND
Deschowitz
Blechhammer
Leignitz
Auschwitz
Cracow

GERMANY

CZECHOSLOVAKIA

Moosierbaum
Floridsdorf
Lobau
Wiener-Neustadt
Budapest

AUSTRIA
Zagreb

HUNGARY

Trieste
Venice
Milan
Turin
Genoa

ITALY

ADRIATIC SEA

YUGOSLAVIA

Belgrade

RUMANIA

1943 Ploesti

Bucharest

BULGARIA

U.S. Air strikes on Ploesti Allied and other commenced from North Africa early in

694

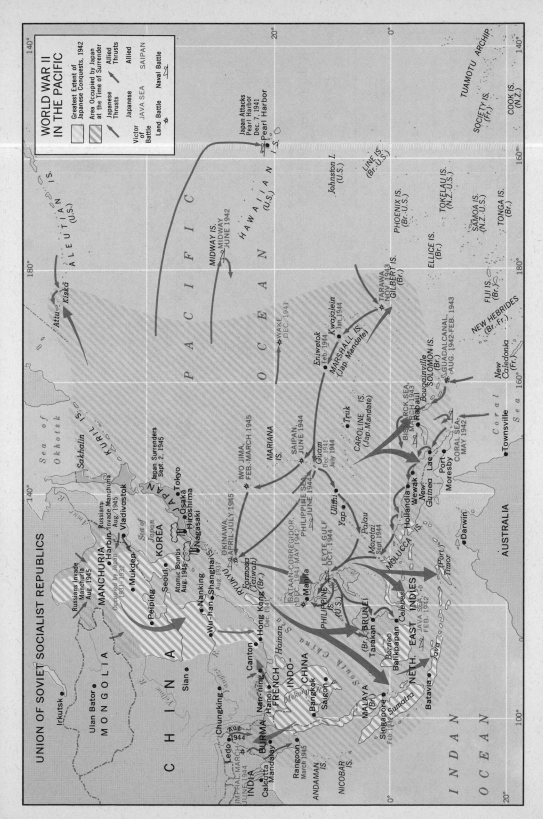

WORLD WAR II
IN THE PACIFIC

Greatest Extent of
Japanese Conquests, 1942

Area Occupied by Japan
at the Time of Surrender

Japanese
Thrusts

Allied
Thrusts

Japanese
Thrusts

Allied
Thrusts

Victor
of
Battle

JAVA SEA

SAIPAN

Land Battle

Naval Battle

UNION OF SOVIET SOCIALIST REPUBLICS

Irkutsk

MONGOLIA

Ulan Bator

Sian

CHINA

Chungking

Yangtze R.

Nan-ning

Canton

Hong Kong (Br.)

Hainan

South China Sea

FRENCH
INDO-
CHINA

Hanoi

Saigon

Bangkok

BURMA

Mandalay

Rangoon
March 1945

Ledo

Calcutta

INDIA

IMPHAL MARCH-
JUNE 1944

Aug.
1944

ANDAMAN
IS.

NICOBAR
IS.

Amur R.

Sea of
Okhotsk

Sakhalin

Russians Invade
Manchuria
Aug. 1945

MANCHURIA
Occupied by Japan
(1931-1932)

Harbin Invade Manchuria
Aug. 1945

Russians
Aug. 1945

Mukden

Peiping

Nanking

Shanghai
Aug. 1937

Wu-han

Vladivostok

KURIL IS.

Sea of
Japan

KOREA

Seoul

Russians Invade Manchuria
Aug. 1945

JAPAN

Osaka

Tokyo

Hiroshima

Nagasaki

Atomic Bombs
Aug. 1945

Japan Surrenders
Sept. 2, 1945

RYUKYU IS.

Formosa
(Taiwan)

OKINAWA
APRIL-JULY 1945

IWO JIMA,
FEB.-MARCH 1945

PACIFIC

OCEAN

ALEUTIAN (U.S.)

Attu

Kiska

180°

140°

140°

160°

180°

160°

140°

MIDWAY IS.
MIDWAY
JUNE 1942

HAWAIIAN IS.
(U.S.)

Japan Attacks
Pearl Harbor
Dec. 7, 1941

Pearl Harbor

Johnston I.
(U.S.)

LINE IS.
(Br.-U.S.)

WAKE
DEC. 1941

MARIANA
IS.

SAIPAN,
JUNE 1944

Guam
Dec. 1941
July 1944

Truk

CAROLINE IS.
(Jap. Mandate)

Eniwetok
Feb. 1944

Kwajalein
Jan. 1944

MARSHALL IS.
(Jap. Mandate)

TARAWA
NOV. 1943
GILBERT IS.
(Br.)

PHOENIX IS.
(Br.-U.S.)

TOKELAU IS.
(N.Z.-U.S.)

ELLICE IS.
(Br.)

SAMOA
(N.Z.-U.S.)

TONGA IS.
(Br.)

TUAMOTU ARCHIP.

SOCIETY IS.
(Fr.)

COOK IS.
(N.Z.)

FIJI IS.
(Br.)

NEW HEBRIDES
(Br.-Fr.)

New
Caledonia
(Fr.)

GUADALCANAL,
AUG. 1942-FEB. 1943

SOLOMON IS.

Bougainville
1943

Rabaul
BISMARCK SEA,
MARCH 1943

Lae

New
Guinea

Wewak

Hollandia

MOLUCCA IS.

Morotai
Sept. 1944

Palau

Yap

Ulithi

PHILIPPINE SEA,
JUNE 1944

LEYTE GULF
OCT. 1944

PHILIPPINE
IS.
(U.S.)

BATAAN-CORREGIDOR,
DEC. 1941-MAY 1942

Manila

BRUNEI
(Br.)

Tarakan

Borneo

Balikpapan

Celebes

NETH.
EAST INDIES

Java

JAVA SEA,
FEB. 1942

Batavia

Sumatra

MALAYA
(Br.)

Singapore
Feb. 1942

MELAKA

Coral Sea

CORAL SEA,
MAY 1942

Port
Moresby

Port

Darwin

AUSTRALIA

Townsville

Timor
(Port.)

INDIAN

OCEAN

140°

100°

20°

0°

20°

695

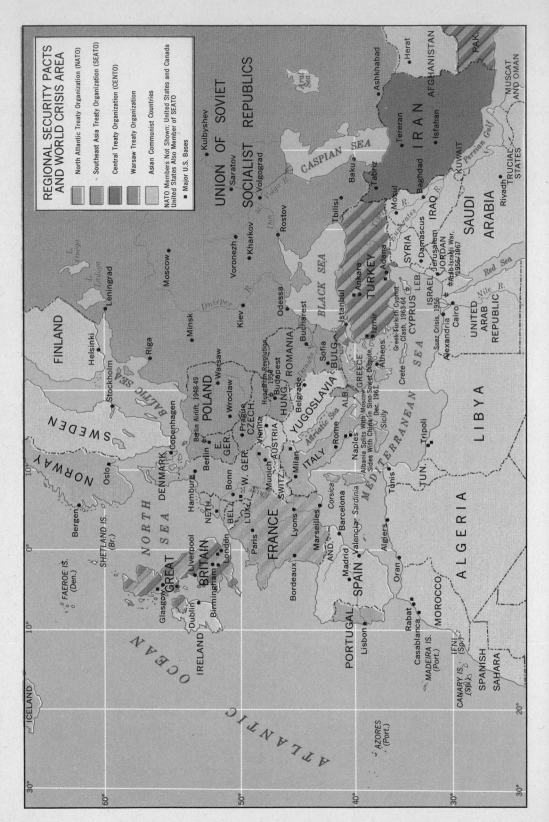

REGIONAL SECURITY PACTS AND WORLD CRISIS AREA

North Atlantic Treaty Organization (NATO)

Southeast Asia Treaty Organization (SEATO)

Central Treaty Organization (CENTO)

Warsaw Treaty Organization

Asian Communist Countries

NATO Members Not Shown: United States and Canada
United States Also Member of SEATO
■ Major U.S. Bases

UNION OF SOVIET SOCIALIST REPUBLICS

FINLAND

SWEDEN

NORWAY

NORTH SEA

GREAT BRITAIN

IRELAND

ATLANTIC OCEAN

ICELAND

FAEROE IS. (Den.)

SHETLAND IS. (Br.)

Bergen

Oslo

Stockholm

Helsinki

Leningrad

Moscow

Kuibyshev

Saratov

Volgograd

Voronezh

Kharkov

Rostov

Tbilisi

Minsk

Riga

Kiev

Odessa

DENMARK

Copenhagen

Hamburg

NETH.

BEL.

LUX.

POLAND

Berlin Airlift, 1948-49

Warsaw

Wrocław

E. GER.

Berlin

Bonn

W. GER.

Prague

CZECH.

Vienna

AUSTRIA

SWITZ.

Munich

Milan

Hungarian Revolution, 1956

Budapest

HUNG.

ROMANIA

Bucharest

Sofia

BULG.

BLACK SEA

Belgrade

YUGOSLAVIA

Danube

ALB.

Rome

ITALY

Naples

Adriatic Sea

Sicily

Albania Splits With Moscow, Sides With China in Sino-Soviet Dispute, Dec. 1961

GREECE

Athens

Crete

MEDITERRANEAN SEA

Istanbul

Izmir

Ankara

TURKEY

Adana

CYPRUS

Greek-Turkish Cypriot Clash, 1963-64

LEB.

SYRIA

Damascus

Tbilisi

Baku

Tabriz

Mosul

Baghdad

IRAQ

Tehran

IRAN

Isfahan

Herat

Ashkhabad

AFGHANISTAN

PAK.

Aral Sea

CASPIAN SEA

Volga R.

Persian Gulf

KUWAIT

SAUDI ARABIA

Riyadh

MUSCAT AND OMAN

TRUCIAL STATES

Red Sea

JORDAN

ISRAEL

Jerusalem

Arab-Israeli War, 1956-1967

Suez Crisis, 1956

Alexandria

Cairo

UNITED ARAB REPUBLIC

Nile R.

LIBYA

Tripoli

TUN.

Tunis

Algiers

ALGERIA

Oran

SPAIN

Madrid

Valencia

Barcelona

Sardinia

Corsica

AND.

FRANCE

Marseilles

Lyons

Bordeaux

Paris

London

Liverpool

Birmingham

Glasgow

Dublin

PORTUGAL

Lisbon

Rabat

Casablanca

MOROCCO

IFNI (Sp.)

SPANISH SAHARA

CANARY IS. (Sp.)

MADEIRA IS. (Port.)

AZORES (Port.)

BALTIC SEA

L. Onega

L. Ladoga

Dnieper R.

Dniester R.

Don R.

Volga R.

Euphrates R.

Tigris R.

696

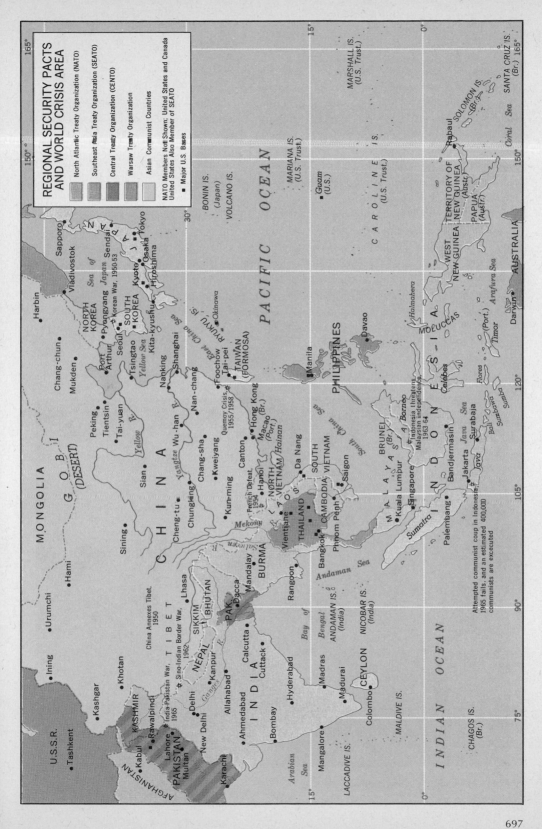

REGIONAL SECURITY PACTS AND WORLD CRISIS AREA

North Atlantic Treaty Organization (NATO)

Southeast Asia Treaty Organization (SEATO)

Central Treaty Organization (CENTO)

Warsaw Treaty Organization

Asian Communist Countries

NATO Members Not Shown; United States and Canada
United States Also Member of SEATO

■ Major U.S. Bases

U.S.S.R.

Tashkent

MONGOLIA

G O B I (DESERT)

Ining

Urumchi

Hami

Kashgar

Khotan

Kashgar

Sining

Chang-chun

Mukden

Harbin

Vladivostok

Sapporo

Sendai

Tokyo

Osaka Kyoto

Hiroshima

J A P A N

Kita-kyushu

Korean War, 1950-53

Sea of Japan

NORTH KOREA

Pyongyang

Seoul

SOUTH KOREA

Port Arthur

Tsingtao

Yellow Sea

Peking

Tientsin

Tai-yuan

Yellow R.

Nanking

Shanghai

C H I N A

Cheng-tu

Chungking

Chang-sha

Nan-chang

Wu-han

Yangtze R.

Kweiyang

Kunming

Canton

Quemoy Crisis, 1955/1958

Foochow

Tai-pei

TAIWAN (FORMOSA)

Hong Kong (Br.)

Macao (Port.)

Hainan

East China Sea

RYUKYU IS.

Okinawa

China Annexes Tibet, 1950

T I B E T

Lhasa

Sino-Indian Border War, 1962

BHUTAN

SIKKIM

NEPAL

India-Pakistan War, 1965

Rawalpindi

Lahore

Multan

PAKISTAN

AFGHANISTAN

Kabul

KASHMIR

Delhi

New Delhi

Kanpur

Allahabad

Ahmedabad

Bombay

I N D I A

Hyderabad

Madras

Madurai

Mangalore

Colombo

CEYLON

MALDIVE IS.

LACCADIVE IS.

Ganges R.

Calcutta

Cuttack

Bay of Bengal

ANDAMAN IS. (India)

NICOBAR IS. (India)

Karachi

Arabian Sea

Dacca

PAK.

Mandalay

BURMA

Rangoon

Andaman Sea

Salween R.

Mekong R.

French Defeat, 1954

Hanoi

NORTH VIETNAM

Vientiane

THAILAND

Bangkok

CAMBODIA

Phnom Penh

Da Nang

SOUTH VIETNAM

Saigon

South China Sea

M A L A Y A

Kuala Lumpur

Singapore

BRUNEI

Borneo

Sumatra

Palembang

Bandjermasin

Jakarta

Java

Surabaja

Bali

Sumbawa

Flores

Sumba

Java Sea

I N D O N E S I A

Indonesia Threatens Malaysian Independence, 1963-64

Celebes

MOLUCCAS

Halmahera

Timor (Port.)

Attempted communist coup in Indonesia,
1965 fails, and an estimated 400,000
communists are executed

PHILIPPINES

Manila

Davao

P A C I F I C   O C E A N

BONIN IS. (Japan)

VOLCANO IS.

MARIANA IS. (U.S. Trust.)

Guam (U.S.)

C A R O L I N E   IS.

CAROLINE IS. (U.S. Trust.)

MARSHALL IS. (U.S. Trust.)

WEST NEW GUINEA

TERRITORY OF NEW GUINEA (Austr.)

PAPUA (Austr.)

Rabaul

SOLOMON IS. (Br.)

SANTA CRUZ IS. (Br.)

Coral Sea

Darwin

AUSTRALIA

Arafura Sea

I N D I A N   O C E A N

CHAGOS IS. (Br.)

15°

165°

150°

0°

75°

90°

105°

120°

135°

15°

30°

15°

0°

Following World War II there was no "return to normalcy" for the United States, but instead almost unceasing involvement in foreign affairs in an era of world revolution. The globe, which was in the process (as some saw it) of becoming One World, was nevertheless divided into spheres of influence between Communist and non-Communist nations. Russia dominated Eastern Europe, and Red China, after 1949, was the primary influence in the Far East. Old forms of colonialism were discredited, and scores of new nations, particularly in Africa, gained their independence. The United States made financial and military commitments in all parts of the world, to reconstruct war-torn Europe and Asia, to aid developing countries, and to stave off the growing menace of Communism.

For the first time the country moved into the bewildering realm of "limited warfare," in which no conflict ever arrived at an unambiguous solution. The Korean War ended in 1953 in an uneasy stalemate. The Middle East was constantly in turmoil, with serious crises erupting in 1956, 1967, and 1970; Arab-Israeli hostility in the region posed almost continuous threats to the peace of the world. In the Far East, the Geneva Conference of 1954 tried to solve the problem of Indochina by arranging for a French withdrawal and by partitioning the area. But the United States committed itself to resist a Communist take-over there by either China or North Vietnam, and found itself embroiled in a long-drawn out conflict not only in Vietnam but also, as the 1970s opened, in neighboring Laos.

Atom bomb explodes in test in New Mexico, July 16, 1945

699

POST-WAR EUROPE

→ Air Corridors to Berlin

Occupation Zones of Germany
and Austria 1945-1950

	U.S.		French
	British		Russian

ATLANTIC OCEAN

30°   20°   10°   0°   10°   20°   30°   40°   50°

70°

60°

50°

Murmansk

Archangel

N O R W A Y

S W E D E N

F I N L A N D

FAEROE IS.
(Den.)

SHETLAND IS.
(Br.)

Trondheim

L. Omega

L. Ladoga

Bergen

Oslo

Helsinki

Leningrad

Göteborg

Stockholm

Baltic Sea

Riga

UNION   OF

Moscow

Dvina R.

SOCIALIST

SOVIET

Minsk

REPUBLICS

Dnieper R.

NORTH
SEA

GREAT

Glasgow

IRELAND

Dublin

BRITAIN

Leeds

Liverpool

Birmingham

London

Amsterdam

NETH.

Brussels

BEL.

LUX.

Le Havre

Paris

Nantes   Loire R.

DEN.

Copenhagen

Kaliningrad

Hamburg

Hannover

G E R M A N Y

Bonn

Frankfurt

Berlin

POLAND

Warsaw

Kiev

Russians blockade Berlin
June 1948
Airlift till May 1949

Merger of Communist and
nationalist parties win elections
1948

Prague

CZECHOSLOVAKIA

Cracow

Dniester R.

Vienna

Budapest

Odessa

F R A N C E

Bay of
Biscay

Bordeaux

Lyons

Rhône R.

Garonne R.

Rhine R.

SWITZ.

Munich

AUSTRIA

Austria ind. neutral
state; occupation
ended July 1955

HUNGARY

RUMANIA

Belgrade

Bucharest

Danube

Black
Sea

Milan

Po R.

Genoa

Trieste

YUGOSLAVIA

Tito becomes premier March 1945
breaks from Kremlin summer 1948

Sofia

BULGARIA

Istanbul

Marseilles

I T A L Y

Adriatic
Sea

Tirane

Salonika

TURKEY

Corsica

Rome

ALB.

GREECE

Izmir

Madrid

Barcelona

Valencia

AND.

Naples

Athens

PORTUGAL

Lisbon

S P A I N

Seville

Douro R.

Tagus R.

Ebro R.

BALEARIC IS.

M E D I T E R R A N E A N

Sardinia

Palermo

Sicily

Civil War
Dec. 1944
to Oct. 1949

Crete

Gibraltar
(Br.)

Sp. MOROCCO

Casablanca

MOROCCO
(Fr.)

Oran

Algiers

Tunis

T U N I S I A
(Fr.)

A L G E R I A
(Fr.)

Malta
(Br.)

S E A

Tripoli

Bengasi

L I B Y A

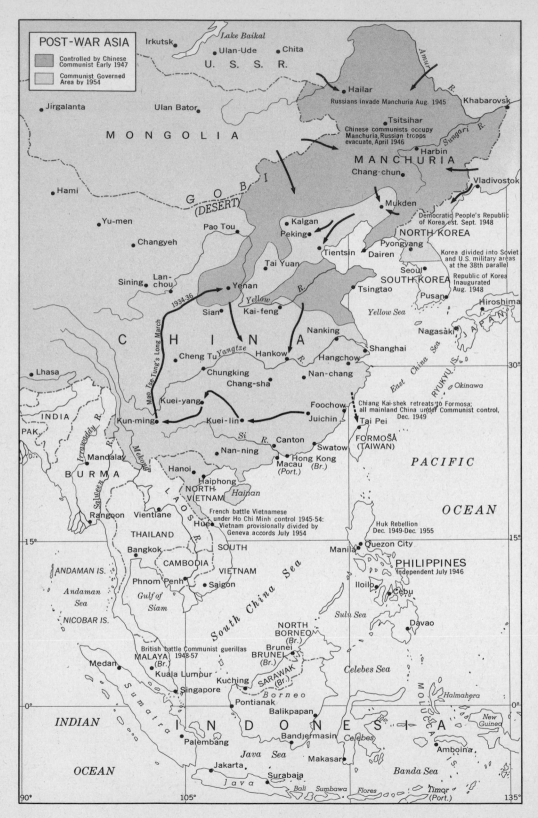

POST-WAR ASIA

Controlled by Chinese Communist Early 1947

Communist Governed Area by 1954

Irkutsk • Lake Baikal

• Ulan-Ude • Chita

U. S. S. R.

• Jirgalanta • Ulan Bator

Amur R.

Hailar
Russians invade Manchuria Aug. 1945

• Khabarovsk

M O N G O L I A

Tsitsihar
Chinese communists occupy Manchuria, Russian troops evacuate, April 1946

Sungari R.

• Harbin

• Hami

G O B I

(DESERT)

MANCHURIA

Chang-chun •

• Vladivostok

• Yu-men

Pao Tou

Kalgan •

Mukden •

Democratic People's Republic of Korea est. Sept. 1948

NORTH KOREA

• Changyeh

Peking •

Tientsin •

Pyongyang •

Dairen •

Korea divided into Soviet and U.S. military areas at the 38th parallel

Sining • Lan-chou

Tai Yuan •

Seoul •

SOUTH KOREA

Republic of Korea inaugurated Aug. 1948

1934-36

Yenan •

Yellow R.

Tsingtao •

Pusan •

• Hiroshima

• Lhasa

Mao Tse Tung's Long March

Sian •

Kai-feng •

Nanking •

Yellow Sea

• Nagasaki

JAPAN

C H I N A

Cheng Tu • Yangtze

Hankow •

Nan-chang •

Hangchow •

Shanghai •

East China Sea

RYUKYU IS.

• Okinawa

30°

INDIA

Chungking •

Chang-sha •

PAK.

Mao Tse Tung's Long March

Kuei-yang •

Foochow •

Kun-ming •

Kuei-lin •

Juichin •

Tai Pei •

Chiang Kai-shek retreats to Formosa; all mainland China under Communist control, Dec. 1949

FORMOSA (TAIWAN)

PACIFIC

Irrawaddy R.

Salween R.

Mekong R.

• Mandalay

Nan-ning •

Si R.

Canton •

Swatow •

Macau (Port.)

Hong Kong (Br.)

BURMA

Hanoi •

NORTH VIETNAM

Haiphong •

Hainan

OCEAN

• Rangoon

• Vientiane

Hué •

French battle Vietnamese under Ho Chi Minh control 1945-54; Vietnam provisionally divided by Geneva accords July 1954

Huk Rebellion Dec. 1949-Dec. 1955

15°

THAILAND

Bangkok •

LAOS

SOUTH

CAMBODIA

VIETNAM

Manila •

Quezon City •

PHILIPPINES

independent July 1946

15°

ANDAMAN IS.

Phnom Penh •

Saigon •

Iloilo •

Cebu •

Andaman Sea

Gulf of Siam

South China Sea

NICOBAR IS.

NORTH BORNEO (Br.)

Sulu Sea

• Davao

British battle Communist guerillas 1948-57

Brunei •

BRUNEI (Br.)

MALAYA (Br.)

• Medan

Kuala Lumpur •

Kuching •

SARAWAK (Br.)

Celebes Sea

Halmahera

Singapore •

B o r n e o

Pontianak •

0°

New Guinea

0°

INDIAN

I N D O N E S I A

Balikpapan •

• Palembang

Bandjermasin •

MOLUCCA IS.

OCEAN

Jakarta •

Java Sea

Makasar •

• Amboina

Surabaja •

Banda Sea

Java

Bali

Sumbawa

Flores

Timor (Port.)

90° 105° 135°

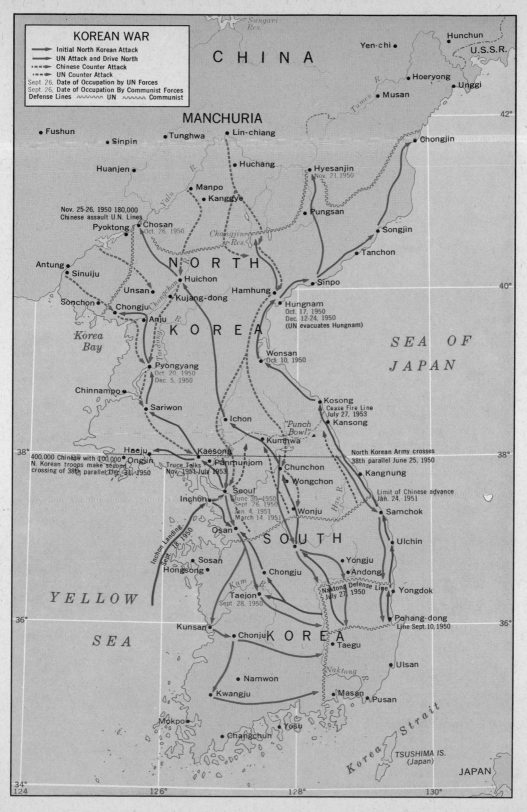

KOREAN WAR

→ Initial North Korean Attack
→ UN Attack and Drive North
--→ Chinese Counter Attack
--→ UN Counter Attack
Sept. 26, Date of Occupation by UN Forces
Sept. 26, Date of Occupation By Communist Forces
Defense Lines ∿∿∿ UN ∿∿∿ Communist

CHINA

MANCHURIA

U.S.S.R.

Hunchun

Yen-chi

Hoeryong

Musan

Unggi

Fushun
Sinpin
Tunghwa
Lin-chiang
Chongjin
Huanjen
Huchang
Hyesanjin
Nov. 21, 1950
Manpo
Kanggye
Pungsan
Songjin
Nov. 25-26, 1950 180,000
Chinese assault U.N. Lines
Pyoktong
Chosan
Oct. 26, 1950
Changjin
Res.
Tanchon
Antung
Sinuiju
N O R T H
Sinpo
Unsan
Huichon
Chongju
Kujang-dong
Hamhung
Sonchon
Anju
Hungnam
Oct. 17, 1950
Dec. 12-24, 1950
(UN evacuates Hungnam)
Korea
Bay
K O R E A
Pyongyang
Oct. 20, 1950
Dec. 5, 1950
Wonsan
Oct. 10, 1950
SEA OF
JAPAN
Chinnampo
Sariwon
Kosong
Cease Fire Line
July 27, 1953
Kansong
Ichon
"Punch
Bowl"
Kumhwa
Haeju
Kaesong
Ongjin
Panmunjom
North Korean Army crosses
38th parallel June 25, 1950
400,000 Chinese with 100,000
N. Korean troops make second
crossing of 38th parallel Dec. 31, 1950
Truce Talks
Nov. 1951-July 1953
Chunchon
Wongchon
Kangnung
Seoul
June 30, 1950
Sept. 26, 1950
Jan. 4, 1951
March 14, 1951
Inchon
Limit of Chinese advance
Jan. 24, 1951
Wonju
Samchok
Osan
S O U T H
Ulchin
Inchon Landing
Sept. 18, 1950
Sosan
Yongju
Andong
Hongsong
Chongju
Yongdok
YELLOW
Taejon
Sept. 28, 1950
Kunsan
Naktong Defense Line
July 27, 1950
Pohang-dong
Line Sept. 10, 1950
SEA
Chonju
K O R E A
Taegu
Namwon
Ulsan
Kwangju
Masan
Pusan
Mokpo
Yosu
Changchun
Korea
Strait
TSUSHIMA IS.
(Japan)
JAPAN

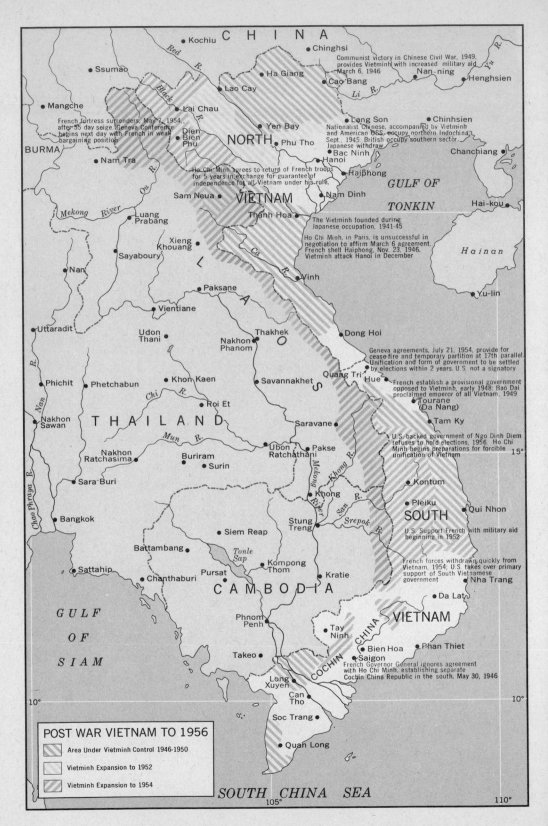

CHINA

• Kochiu

• Chinghsi

Communist victory in Chinese Civil War, 1949, provides Vietminh with increased military aid March 6, 1946.

• Ssumao

• Ha Giang

• Cao Bang

• Nan-ning

• Henghsien

Red R.

• Lao Cay

• Li R.

• Yu R.

• Mangche

Black R.

• Lai Chau

French fortress surrenders, May 7, 1954, after 55 day seige. Geneva Conference begins next day with French in weak bargaining position.

• Dien Bien Phu

• Yen Bay

NORTH • Phu Tho

• Long Son

Nationalist Chinese, accompanied by Vietminh and American OSS, occupy northern Indochina, Sept., 1945. British occupy southern sector. Japanese withdraw.

• Chinhsien

BURMA

• Nam Tra

• Bac Ninh

• Hanoi

• Chanchiang

Ho Chi Minh agrees to return of French troops for 5 years in exchange for guarantee of independence for all Vietnam under his rule.

• Haiphong

GULF OF TONKIN

• Sam Neua

VIETNAM

• Nam Dinh

• Hai-kou

Ou R.

• Thanh Hoa

The Vietminh founded during Japanese occupation, 1941-45.

Hainan

Mekong River

• Luang Prabang

• Xieng Khouang

Ca R.

Ho Chi Minh, in Paris, is unsuccessful in negotiation to affirm March 6 agreement. French shell Haiphong, Nov. 23, 1946. Vietminh attack Hanoi in December

• Sayaboury

L

• Vinh

• Nan

• Yu-lin

• Paksane

A

• Uttaradit

• Vientiane

Nam R.

• Udon Thani

• Thakhek

• Dong Hoi

Geneva agreements, July 21, 1954, provide for cease-fire and temporary partition at 17th parallel. Unification and form of government to be settled by elections within 2 years. U S not a signatory

• Nakhon Phanom

O

• Phichit

• Phetchabun

• Khon Kaen

• Savannakhet

• Quang Tri

• Hue

French establish a provisional government opposed to Vietminh, early 1948. Bao Dai proclaimed emperor of all Vietnam, 1949

Chi R.

S

• Tourane (Da Nang)

• Nakhon Sawan

• Roi Et

THAILAND

• Saravane

• Tam Ky

Mun R.

• Nakhon Ratchasima

• Buriram

• Surin

• Ubon Ratchathani

• Pakse

Khong R.

U.S. backed government of Ngo Dinh Diem refuses to hold elections, 1956. Ho Chi Minh begins preparations for forcible unification of Vietnam

15°

• Sara Buri

• Kontum

• Pleiku

SOUTH

• Qui Nhon

• Bangkok

Chao Phraya R.

• Khong

Mekong River

San R.

Srepok R.

• Stung Treng

U.S. support French with military aid beginning in 1952

• Siem Reap

• Battambang

Tonle Sap

• Kompong Thom

• Kratie

French forces withdrawn quickly from Vietnam, 1954; U.S. takes over primary support of South Vietnamese government

• Nha Trang

• Pursat

CAMBODIA

• Da Lat

• Chanthaburi

• Sattahip

• Phnom Penh

• Tay Ninh

COCHIN CHINA

VIETNAM

GULF

OF

SIAM

• Takeo

• Bien Hoa

• Saigon

• Phan Thiet

French Governor General ignores agreement with Ho Chi Minh, establishing separate Cochin China Republic in the south, May 30, 1946

• Long Xuyen

• Can Tho

10°

10°

• Soc Trang

POST WAR VIETNAM TO 1956

Area Under Vietminh Control 1946-1950

Vietminh Expansion to 1952

Vietminh Expansion to 1954

• Quan Long

SOUTH CHINA SEA

105°

110°

702

VIETNAM CONFLICT

C H I N A

Mengtzu

Ching-hsi

Ssu-mao

Ha Giang
Cao Bang

Nan-ning

Hengsien

Lao Cai

Panhuo

Chin-hsien

Meng-che
Yun Ching-hung

Lai
Chau

NORTH

Lang Son

Peihai

French Defeat
May 7, 1954

Dien Bien Phu

Yen Bai

Thai Nguyen
Kep

Chanchiang

BURMA

Nam Tra

Phu Tho
Hanoi

Campha

Hai-kou

Hoa
Binh

VIETNAM

Haiphong

Sam Neua

Ma R.

Nam Dinh

GULF OF

Luang
Prabang

Thanh
Hoa

TONKIN

PLAIN OF
JARS

Xieng
Khouang

Ca R.

Hainan

Sayaboury

L

Nan

Vinh

N. Viet. torpedo boats skirmish
with U.S. destroyers Aug. 2-4, 1964
U.S. responds with first air attacks
on North. Congress follows with
Tonkin Bay resolution

7th Fleet

Yu-lin

Pak Sane

Ha Tinh

Vientiane
Nong Khai

Mu Gia
Pass

Dong Hoi

Uttaradit

Udon

Nakhon
Phanom

Thakhek

A

O

S

Demilitarized Zone
Quang Tri

Sakon
Nakhon

Hue

Buddhist uprisings
April-June 1966 crushed by
Central Government

Phichit

Khon
Kaen

Savannakhet

Da Nang

Phetchabun

Roi Et

An Hoa

Tam Ky
Chu Lai

Nakhon
Sawan

T H A I L A N D

Air strikes on
Ho Chi Minh Trail

Saravane

Van Tuong Aug. 29, 1965
first major involvement of
U.S. ground forces   15°

Ta Khli

Mun R.

Ubon

Pakse

Quang Ngai

Korat AB

Buriram

Nakhon
Ratchasima

Khong

Kontum

Sara Buri

Pleiku
An Khe

Qui Nhon

Don Muang AB

Bangkok

Stung
Treng

V.C. raid U.S. base,
U.S. responds with
air raids on N. Viet.
Feb. 7, 1965

SOUTH

Tuy Hoa

Siem Reap

Tonle
Sap

CENTRAL
HIGHLANDS

Battambang

U-Tapao AB
Sattahip

Chanthaburi

Pursat

Kompong
Thom

Kratie

Nha Trang

Cam Ranh

C A M B O D I A

Phuoc
Binh

Da Lat

Phnom
Penh

Zone
C

Tay Ninh
Zone
D

VIETNAM

GULF
OF
SIAM

Takeo

Tan Son
Nhut AB

Bien Hoa
Saigon

Phan Thiet

Sihanoukville

PLAIN OF
REEDS

My
Tho

Buddhist uprisings May-Sept. 1963
Military coup overthrows Ngo Dinh Diem
regime, Nov. 1, 1963
V.C. bomb U.S. embassy Mar. 30, 1965

Rach Gia

Can
Tho

Vung
Tau

Mekong
River
Delta

10°

Khanh
Hung

10°

Quan
Long

U.S. Forces In South Vietnam in 1964-16,500
By June 1965-125,000
By June 1967- 440,000

VIETNAM CONFLICT

(U.S.)   Communist

Principal Naval Bases

Principal Air Bases

☐ Principal U.S. Bases (Ground Forces)

★ Battle Site   Special Forces Camps

SOUTH CHINA SEA

105°

110°

Labels along arrows: U.S. air strikes against North Vietnam · Ho Chi Minh Trail chief supply route from North to South

703

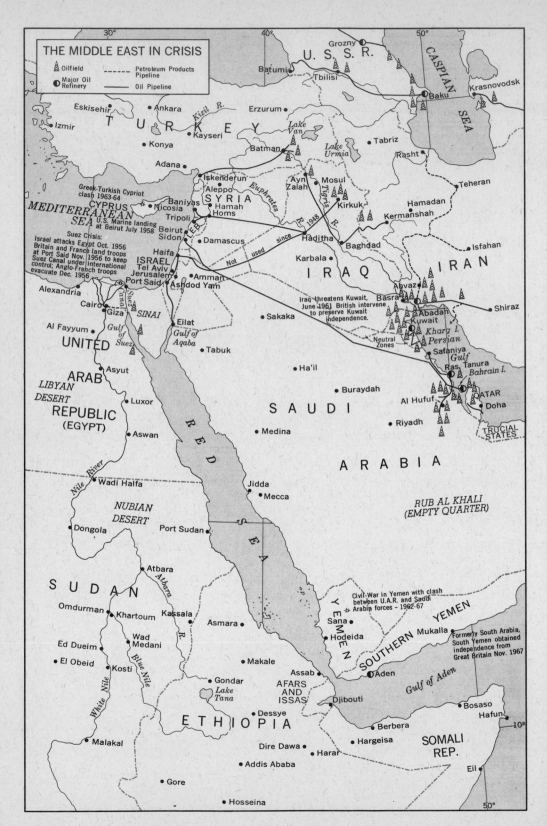

THE MIDDLE EAST IN CRISIS

⛽ Oilfield - - - Petroleum Products Pipeline

◖ Major Oil Refinery —— Oil Pipeline

U.S.S.R.

Grozny

Batumi   CASPIAN

Tbilisi   SEA

Baku Krasnovodsk

Eskisehir Ankara Erzurum

Izmir T U R K E Y *Kizil R.*

  Kayseri *Lake Van* Tabriz Rasht

Konya Batman *Lake Urmia*

Adana   Teheran

Greek-Turkish Cypriot clash 1963-64

Iskenderun Ayn Zalah Mosul

Aleppo   Hamadan

C Y P R U S Baniyas **SYRIA** Kirkuk Kermanshah

MEDITERRANEAN Nicosia Hamah

SEA Tripoli Homs *Euphrates* Isfahan

U.S. Marine landing at Beirut July 1958 Beirut Haditha Baghdad

  Sidon Damascus Karbala

Suez Crisis: Israel attacks Egypt Oct. 1956 Britain and France land troops at Port Said Nov. 1956 to keep Suez Canal under international control; Anglo-French troops evacuate Dec. 1956

Haifa **I R A Q** **I R A N**

ISRAEL Tel Aviv Ahvaz Shiraz

Jerusalem Amman Basra

Port Said Ashdod Yam Abadan

Alexandria   Kuwait

Iraq threatens Kuwait, June 1961 British intervene to preserve Kuwait independence.

Cairo Giza *SINAI* Sakaka Neutral Zones

Al Fayyum *Gulf of Suez* Eilat Safaniya *Persian*

UNITED *Gulf of Aqaba* Ras Tanura *Gulf*

 Asyut Tabuk Bahrain I.

LIBYAN DESERT **ARAB** Ha'il Al Hufuf **QATAR**

REPUBLIC Luxor Buraydah Doha

(EGYPT) Aswan **S A U D I** **TRUCIAL STATES**

Nile River Wadi Halfa Medina Riyadh

    A R A B I A

RED Jidda *RUB AL KHALI (EMPTY QUARTER)*

NUBIAN DESERT Mecca

Dongola Port Sudan

Atbara

S U D A N *Athara R.* Civil War in Yemen with clash between U.A.R. and Saudi Arabia forces - 1962-67

Omdurman Khartoum Kassala Asmara Sana **SOUTHERN** **YEMEN**

Ed Dueim Wad Medani   Hodeida Mukalla Formerly South Arabia, South Yemen obtained independence from Great Britain Nov. 1967

El Obeid Kosti *Blue Nile* Makale

White Nile Gondar *Lake Tana* **Y E M E N** Assab Aden *Gulf of Aden* Bosaso

Malakal **AFARS AND ISSAS** Djibouti Hafun

Dessye Berbera

E T H I O P I A Hargeisa **SOMALI REP.**

Dire Dawa Harar

Addis Ababa Eil

Gore

Hosseina

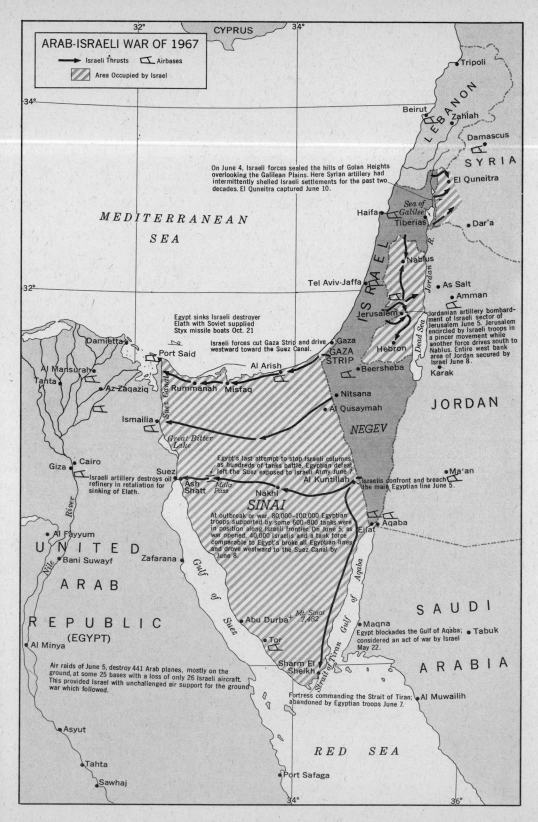

ARAB-ISRAELI WAR OF 1967

→ Israeli Thrusts   ⌐ Airbases

▨ Area Occupied by Israel

CYPRUS

32°   34°

MEDITERRANEAN SEA

LEBANON

● Tripoli

Beirut ● Zahlah

● Damascus

SYRIA

El Quneitra ●

On June 4, Israeli forces sealed the hills of Golan Heights overlooking the Galilean Plains. Here Syrian artillery had intermittently shelled Israeli settlements for the past two decades. El Quneitra captured June 10.

Sea of Galilee

Haifa   Tiberias   ● Dar'a

Nablus ●

Tel Aviv-Jaffa   ● As Salt

● Amman

Jerusalem   Jordanian artillery bombardment of Israeli sector of
Jerusalem June 5. Jerusalem
encircled by Israeli troops in
a pincer movement while
another force drives south to
Nablus. Entire west bank
area of Jordan secured by
Israel June 8.

Egypt sinks Israeli destroyer
Elath with Soviet supplied
Styx missile boats Oct. 21

Israeli forces cut Gaza Strip and drive
westward toward the Suez Canal.

Gaza

GAZA
STRIP

Hebron ●

Damietta ●

Port Said

● Beersheba

Karak ●

Al Mansurah ●

Al Arish

● Nitsana

JORDAN

Tanta ●

Az Zaqaziq ●   Rummanah   Misfaq

● Al Qusaymah

Ismailia ●

NEGEV

Great Bitter
Lake

Egypt's last attempt to stop Israeli columns
as hundreds of tanks battle. Egyptian defeat
left the Suez exposed to Israeli Army June 7.

● Ma'an

Giza ●   ● Cairo

Suez   Ash   Milla
Shatt   Pass   Al Kuntillah

Israelis confront and breach
the main Egyptian line June 5.

Israeli artillery destroys oil
refinery in retaliation for
sinking of Elath.

Nakhl

● Al Fayyum

SINAI

Eilat   ● Aqaba

Bani Suwayf ●

UNITED

Zafarana ●

At outbreak of war, 80,000-100,000 Egyptian
troops supported by some 600-800 tanks were
in position along Israeli frontier. On June 5, as
war opened, 40,000 Israelis and a tank force
comparable to Egypt's broke all Egyptian lines
and drove westward to the Suez Canal by
June 8.

ARAB

REPUBLIC

(EGYPT)

Abu Durba   Mt. Sinai
7,482

● Al Minya

SAUDI

● Magna   ● Tabuk

Egypt blockades the Gulf of Aqaba;
considered an act of war by Israel
May 22.

● Tor

ARABIA

Air raids of June 5, destroy 441 Arab planes, mostly on the
ground, at some 25 bases with a loss of only 26 Israeli aircraft.
This provided Israel with unchallenged air support for the ground
war which followed.

Sharm El
Sheikh

● Al Muwailih

Fortress commanding the Strait of Tiran;
abandoned by Egyptian troops June 7.

● Asyut

RED SEA

● Tahta

● Port Safaga

● Sawhaj

34°   36°

9. POPULATION

The shift of population in the United States has not been only a westward movement. Moves from rural to urban areas (and vice versa), from one section to another, from west to east, from city to city, and from city to suburb and exurb have all played significant roles in the growth and distribution of population.

Between 1790 and 1930 more than 36 million foreign-born persons came to the United States. By far the largest numbers arrived between 1880 and 1930. Early waves of immigration (1830–1870) came largely from England, Ireland, Germany, and Scandanavia, while the post-1880, or "New Immigration," was mostly from eastern and southern Europe—Russia, Poland, Italy, and the Balkans. The early immigrants usually went west to city or farm, except for the Irish, who remained in the East near industrial centers. The new immigrants gathered in the cities, near the factories that employed them. Avoidance of the South was almost unanimous among immigrants.

After 1924, with the passage of the National Origins Quota Act, immigration was severely restricted. For a number of years after 1930, more people left the country than entered (although of course the population continued to grow). By 1960 only 5 percent of the population was foreign-born.

Not all immigrants were willing ones. The most notable example was the African blacks, millions of whom were captured and brought to the United States as slaves. Their descendants now constitute more than 10 percent of the population.

Main building on Ellis Island, center for processing immigrants, in 1905

706

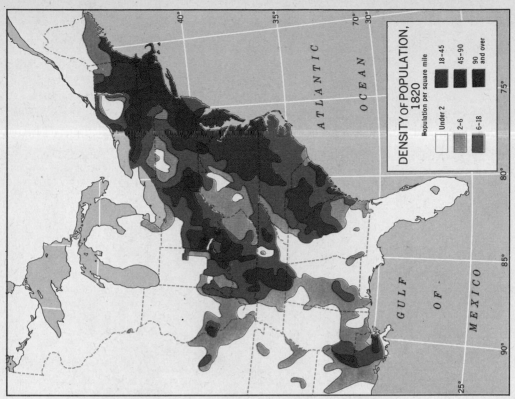

DENSITY OF POPULATION, 1820
Population per square mile

Under 2 | 2-6 | 6-18 | 18-45 | 45-90 | 90 and over

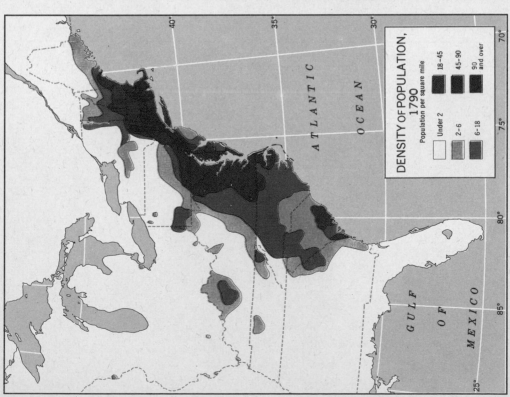

DENSITY OF POPULATION, 1790
Population per square mile

Under 2 | 2-6 | 6-18 | 18-45 | 45-90 | 90 and over

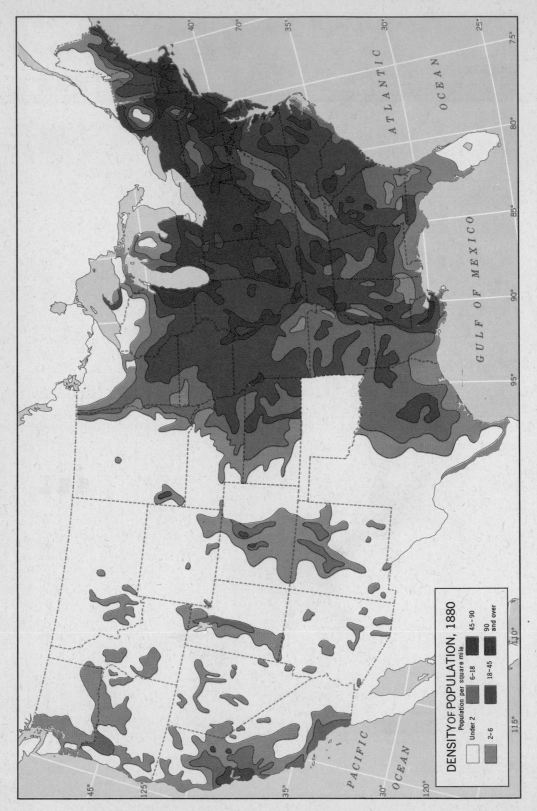

DENSITY OF POPULATION, 1880

Population per square mile

Under 2
2–6
6–18
18–45
45–90
90 and over

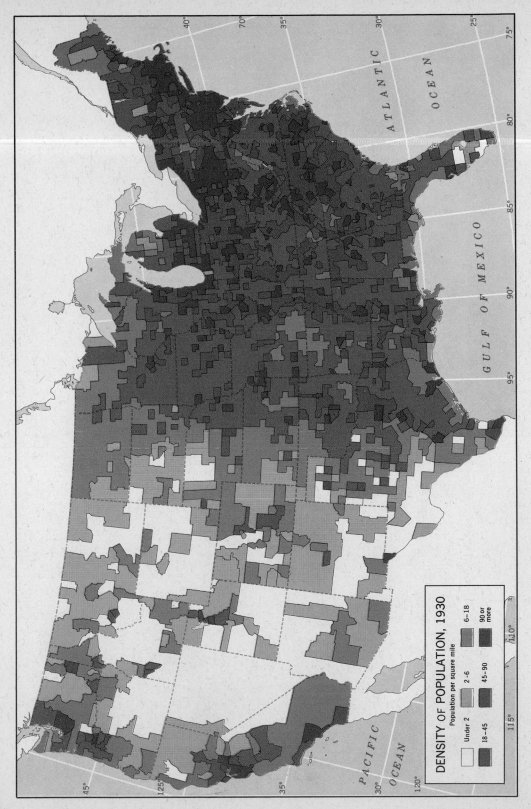

DENSITY OF POPULATION, 1930
Population per square mile

Under 2   2-6   6-18
18-45   45-90   90 or more

ATLANTIC OCEAN

GULF OF MEXICO

PACIFIC OCEAN

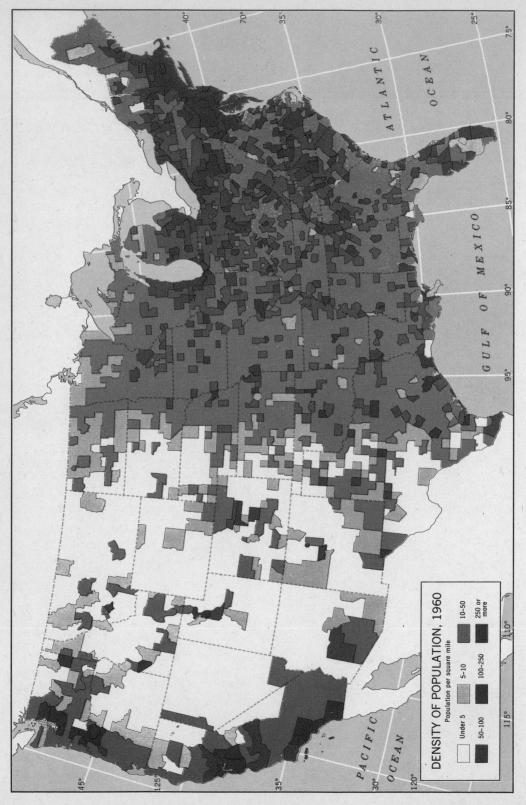

DENSITY OF POPULATION, 1960
Population per square mile

Under 5
5-10
10-50
50-100
100-250
250 or more

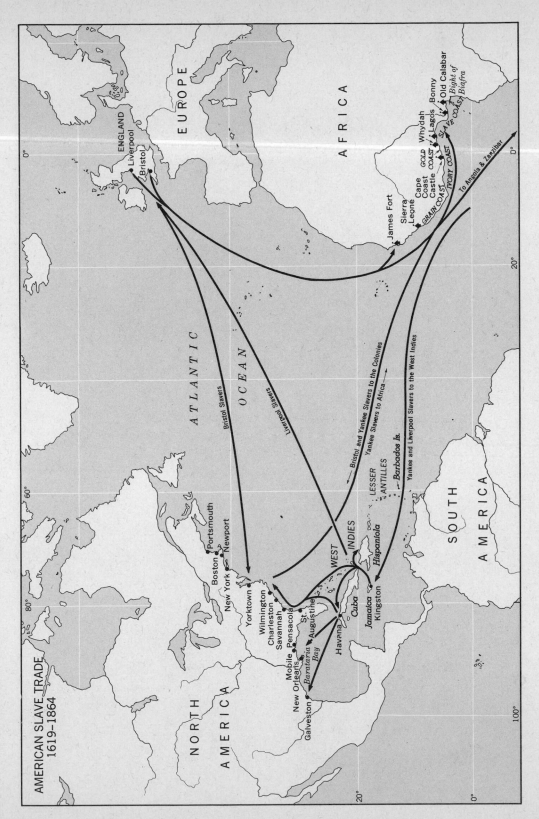

AMERICAN SLAVE TRADE
1619-1864

EUROPE

AFRICA

ENGLAND
Liverpool
Bristol

ATLANTIC

OCEAN

Bristol Slavers

Liverpool Slavers

Bristol and Yankee Slavers to the Colonies

Yankee Slavers to Africa

Yankee and Liverpool Slavers to the West Indies

James Fort
Sierra
Leone
Cape
Coast
GRAIN COAST
Castle
GOLD
COAST
Whydah
Lagos
IVORY COAST
SLAVE COAST
Bonny
Old Calabar
Bight of
Biafra

To Angola & Zanzibar

NORTH
AMERICA

Boston
Portsmouth
New York
Newport
Yorktown
Wilmington
Charleston
Savannah
St.
Augustine
Mobile
Pensacola
New Orleans
Barataria
Bay
Galveston
Havana

WEST
INDIES

Cuba

Hispaniola

Jamaica
Kingston

LESSER
ANTILLES

Barbados Is.

SOUTH
AMERICA

711

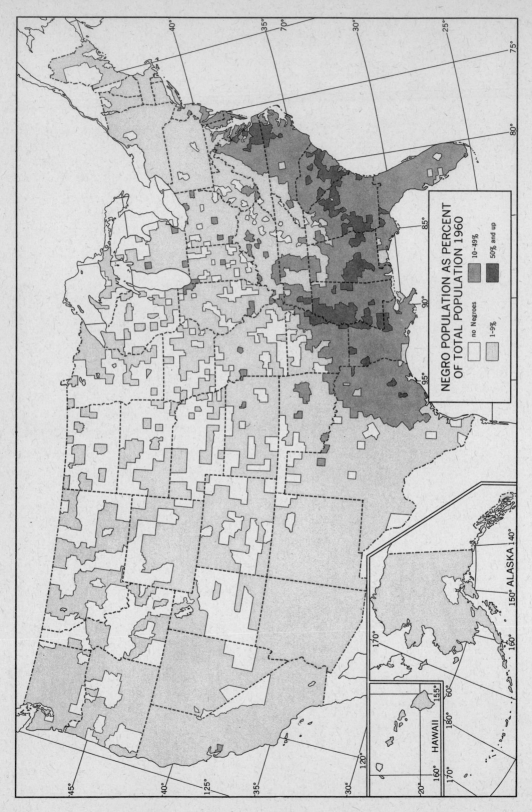

NEGRO POPULATION AS PERCENT
OF TOTAL POPULATION 1960

no Negroes

1-9%

10-49%

50% and up

ALASKA

HAWAII

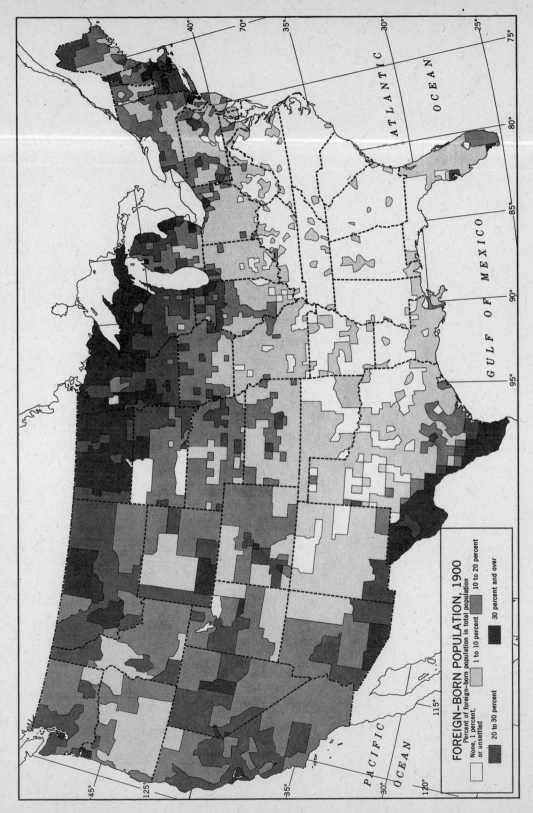

FOREIGN–BORN POPULATION, 1900
Percent of foreign-born population in total population

None, 1 percent, or unsettled
1 to 10 percent
10 to 20 percent
20 to 30 percent
30 percent and over

Immigration by Country of Origin, 1820–1968

decade	total all countries[1]	Northwestern Europe				Central Europe			Eastern Europe		Southern Europe	
		Great Britain	Ireland[2]	Scandinavia[3]	other north-western[4]	Germany[5]	Poland[6]	other central[7]	U.S.S.R. and Baltic States[8]	other eastern[9]	Italy	other southern[10]
1820–1830	151,824	27,489	54,338	283	13,280	7,729	21	—	89	21	439	2,819
1831–1840	599,125	75,810	207,381	2,264	51,830	152,454	369	—	277	7	2,253	3,043
1841–1850	1,713,251	267,044	780,719	14,442	95,231	434,626	105	—	551	59	1,870	2,854
1851–1860	2,598,214	423,974	914,119	24,680	116,896	951,667	1,164	—	457	83	9,231	10,389
1861–1870	2,314,824	606,896	435,778	126,392	75,108	787,468	2,027	7,800	2,512	129	11,725	9,435
1871–1880	2,812,191	548,043	436,871	243,016	124,261	718,182	12,970	72,969	39,284	348	55,759	20,559
1881–1890	5,246,613	807,357	655,482	656,494	206,330	1,452,970	51,806	353,719	213,282	7,910	307,309	24,387
1891–1900	3,687,564	271,538	388,416	371,512	106,874	505,152	96,720	592,707	505,290	16,536	651,893	52,340
1901–1910	8,762,489	525,950	339,065	505,324	198,198	341,498	—	2,145,266	1,597,306	172,264	2,045,877	265,268
1911–1920	5,735,811	341,408	146,181	203,452	162,452	143,945	4,813	901,656	921,957	90,521	1,109,524	350,655
1921–1930	4,107,209	330,213	220,591	198,210	122,807	412,202	227,734	214,806	89,423	85,250	455,315	121,302
1931–1940	528,431	29,378	13,167	11,286	30,667	114,058	17,026	31,652	7,401	5,546	68,028	20,080
1941–1950	1,034,503	131,592	26,967	26,901	77,225	226,578	7,571	38,252	4,307	2,031	57,661	22,083
1951–1960	2,519,363	195,498[19]	57,332	57,101	140,332	477,765	9,985	112,886	6,288	3,796	185,491	85,703
1961–1968	2,586,626	180,051	34,705	37,984[21]	91,126	169,791	49,391	30,374	6,372	6,941	159,711	135,373
Total 1820–1968	44,398,038	4,762,241	4,711,112	2,479,341	1,612,617	6,896,085	481,702	4,502,087	3,394,796	391,442	5,122,086	1,126,290

[1]For 1820–1867 excludes returning citizens.
[2]Comprises Eire and Northern Ireland.
[3]Comprises Norway, Sweden, Denmark, and Iceland.
[4]Comprises Netherlands, Belgium, Luxembourg, Switzerland, and France.
[5]Includes Austria 1938 to 1945.
[6]Between 1899 and 1919, included with Austria-Hungary, Germany, and Russia.
[7]Comprises Czechoslovakia (since 1920), Yugoslavia (since 1920), Hungary (since 1861), and Austria (since 1861, except for the years 1938–1945, when Austria was included with Germany).
[8]Comprises U.S.S.R. in Europe, Latvia, Estonia, Lithuania, and Finland.
[9]Comprises Rumania, Bulgaria, and Turkey in Europe.
[10]Comprises Spain, Portugal, Greece, and other Europe, not elsewhere classified.

714

decade	Asia				America			Africa	Australasia		all other countries[13]
	Turkey in Asia[11]	China	Japan[12]	other Asia[13]	Canada and Newfoundland[14]	Mexico	other America		Australia and New Zealand	other Pacific Islands[13]	
1820–1830	—	3	—	12	2,486	4,818	4,647	17	—	—	33,333
1831–1840	—	8	—	40	13,624	6,599	13,201	54	—	—	69,911
1841–1850	—	35	—	47	41,723	3,271	17,475	55	—	—	53,144
1851–1860	—	41,397	—	58	59,309	3,078	12,333	210	—	—	29,169
1861–1870	2	64,301	186	141	153,878	2,191	10,538	312	36	—	17,969
1871–1880	67	123,201	149	406	383,640	5,162	15,242	358	9,886	1,028	790
1881–1890	2,220	61,711	2,270	2,179	393,304	1,913[18]	31,750	857	7,017	5,557	789
1891–1900	26,799	14,799	25,942	3,696	3,311[16]	971[18]	34,690[17]	350[16]	2,740	1,225[16]	14,063
1901–1910	77,393	20,605	129,797	15,772	179,226	49,642	133,020	7,368	11,975	1,049	626[15]
1911–1920	79,389	21,278	83,837	8,055	742,185	219,004	182,482	3,443	12,348	1,079	1,147
1921–1930	19,165	29,907	33,462	14,866	924,515	459,287	132,914	6,286	8,299	427	228
1931–1940	328	4,928	1,948	8,140	108,527	22,319	29,191	1,750	2,231	186	4,594
1941–1950	218	16,709	1,555	13,298	171,718	60,589	122,497	7,367	13,805	746	4,833
1951–1960	866	9,657[20]	46,250	90,680	377,952	299,811	319,181	14,092	11,506	1,470	15,721
1961–1968	2,784	23,073	31,162	201,270	357,157	363,368	670,078	17,395	14,587	1,313	2,620
Total 1820–1968	209,231	431,612	356,558	358,660	3,912,555	1,502,023	1,729,239	64,914	94,430	14,080	244,937

[11]No record of immigration from Turkey in Asia until 1869.
[12]No record of immigration from Japan until 1861.
[13]Philippine Islands are included in "Other Asia" in 1952 (1,179), 1953 (1,074), 1954 (1,234), 1955 (1,598), 1956 (1,792), and 1957 (1,874). From 1934 to 1951, inclusive, they are included in "All other countries."
[14]Prior to 1920 Canada and Newfoundland were recorded as British North America. From 1820 to 1898 the figures include all British North American possessions.
[15]Excludes 32,897 persons returning to their homes in the United States.
[16]Included in "All other countries", 1892 and 1893.
[17]Included in "All other countries", 1892.
[18]No record of immigration from Mexico for 1886 to 1893.
[19]Beginning 1952, includes data for United Kingdom not specified, formerly included with "Other Southern."
[20]Beginning 1957, includes Taiwan.
[21]Excludes, Iceland.

715

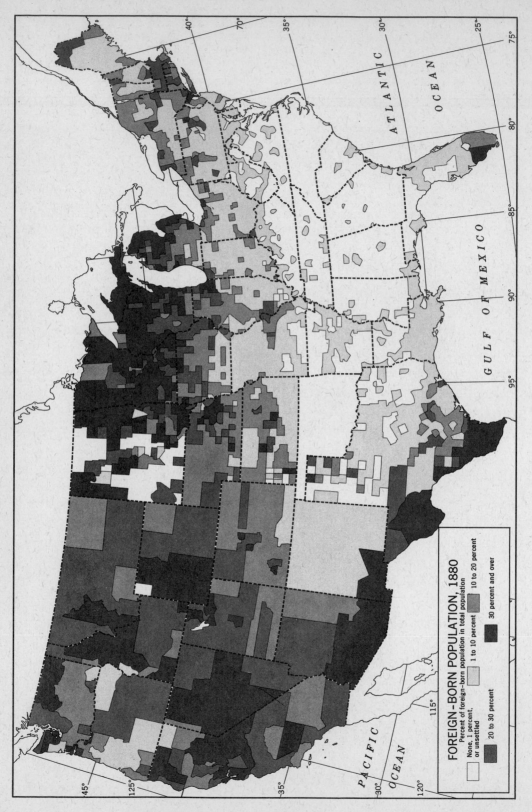

FOREIGN-BORN POPULATION, 1880

Percent of foreign-born population in total population

None, 1 percent, or unsettled

1 to 10 percent

10 to 20 percent

20 to 30 percent

30 percent and over

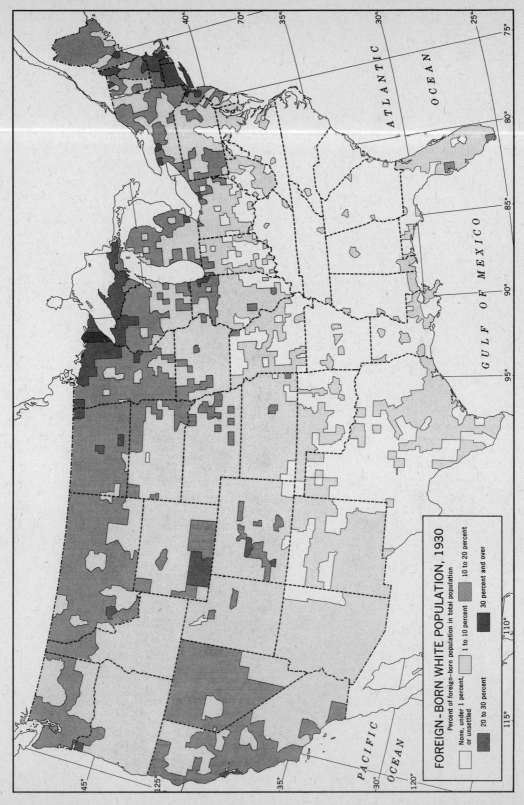

FOREIGN-BORN WHITE POPULATION, 1930

Percent of foreign-born population in total population

None, under 1 percent, or unsettled

1 to 10 percent

10 to 20 percent

20 to 30 percent

30 percent and over

ATLANTIC OCEAN

GULF OF MEXICO

PACIFIC OCEAN

Population of the United States 1790–1969

year	total population (1,000s)	% increase in decade	white population total (1,000s)	white population % of total	nonwhite population total (1,000s)	nonwhite population % of total	urban population[1] total (1,000s)	urban population[1] % of total	rural population total (1,000s)	rural population % of total
1790	3,929	—	3,172	80.7	757	19.3	202	5.1	3,728	94.9
1800	5,297	34.8	4,306	81.1	1,002	18.9	322	6.1	4,986	93.9
1810	7,224	36.4	5,862	81.0	1,378	19.0	525	7.3	6,714	92.7
1820	9,618	33.1	7,867	81.6	1,772	18.4	693	7.2	8,945	92.8
1830	12,901	34.1	10,537	81.9	2,329	18.1	1,127	8.8	11,739	91.2
1840	17,120	32.7	14,196	83.2	2,874	16.8	1,845	10.8	15,224	89.2
1850	23,261	35.9	19,553	84.3	3,639	15.7	3,544	15.3	19,648	84.7
1860	31,513	35.5	26,923	85.6	4,521	14.4	6,217	19.8	25,227	80.2
1870	39,905	26.6	33,589	87.1	4,969	12.9	9,902	25.7	28,656	74.3
1880	50,262	26.0	43,403	86.5	6,753	13.5	14,130	28.2	36,026	71.8
1890	63,056	25.5	55,101	87.5	7,846	12.5	22,106	35.1	40,841	64.9
1900	76,094	20.7	66,809	87.9	9,185	12.1	30,160	39.7	45,835	60.3
1910	92,407	21.4	81,732	88.9	10,240	11.1	41,999	45.7	49,973	54.3
1920	106,466	15.2	94,821	89.7	10,890	10.3	54,158	51.2	51,552	48.8
1930[2]	123,188	15.7	110,287	89.8	12,488	10.2	68,955	56.2	53,821	43.8
1940	132,122	7.3	118,215	89.8	13,454	10.2	74,424	56.5	57,245	43.5
1950	151,683	14.8	134,942	89.5	15,755	10.5	96,468	64.0	54,229	36.0
1960[3]	180,684	19.1	158,832	88.6	20,491	11.4	125,269	69.9	54,042	30.1
1969[4]	202,253	11.9	177,482	87.8	24,771	12.2	NA	NA	NA	NA

[1]Urban areas defined as incorporated places of 2,500 or more inhabitants, 1790–1940; 1950 definition includes all places of 2,500 or more inhabitants.

[2]1930 census includes persons of Mexican birth or ancestry in white population.

[3]Includes Alaska and Hawaii as of 1959.

[4]Estimate

NA—Not available

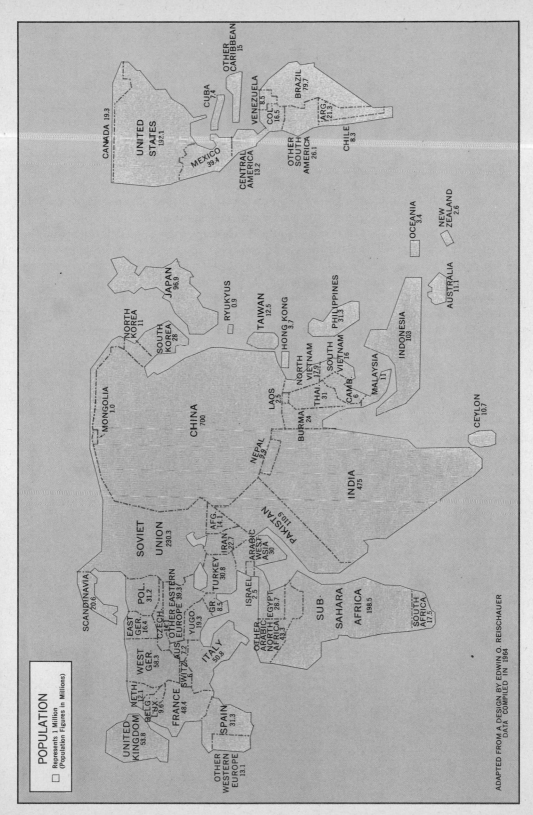

POPULATION

□ Represents 1 Million
(Population Figures in Millions)

CANADA 19.3

UNITED STATES 192.1

MEXICO 39.4

CUBA 7.4

OTHER CARIBBEAN 15

VENEZUELA 8.5

COL. 16.5

CENTRAL AMERICA 13.2

OTHER SOUTH AMERICA 26.1

BRAZIL 79.7

ARG. 21.3

CHILE 8.3

JAPAN 96.9

NORTH KOREA 11

SOUTH KOREA 28

RYUKYUS 0.9

TAIWAN 12.5

HONG KONG 3.7

PHILIPPINES 31.3

MONGOLIA 1.0

CHINA 700

NORTH VIETNAM 17.9

SOUTH VIETNAM 16

THAI. 31

CAMB. 6

MALAYSIA 11

INDONESIA 103

LAOS 2.5

BURMA 24

NEPAL 9.9

INDIA 475

CEYLON 10.7

OCEANIA 3.4

NEW ZEALAND 2.6

AUSTRALIA 11.1

SCANDINAVIA 20.6

SOVIET UNION 230.3

AFG. 14.1

IRAN 22.7

ARABIC WEST ASIA 30

PAKISTAN 110.9

EAST GER. 16.4

POL. 31.2

CZECH. 14.1

OTHER EASTERN EUROPE 39.3

AUS. 7.2

YUGO. 19.3

GR. 8.5

TURKEY 30.8

ISRAEL 2.5

EGYPT 28.7

OTHER ARABIC NORTH AFRICA 13.3

SUB-SAHARA AFRICA 198.5

SOUTH AFRICA 17.5

UNITED KINGDOM 53.8

NETH. 12.1

BELG. LUX. 9.6

WEST GER. 58.3

SWITZ. 6

FRANCE 48.4

ITALY 50.8

SPAIN 31.3

OTHER WESTERN EUROPE 13.1

ADAPTED FROM A DESIGN BY EDWIN O. REISCHAUER
DATA COMPILED IN 1964

For nearly three centuries, from 1620 to about 1900, the story of the American Indian is the other face of the coin of westward expansion. When the first settlers came to North America there was a native population numbering somewhat less than a million and distributed over the whole continent. By 1960, there were a little more than half a million Indians, located mostly on government reservations west of the Mississippi.

Between colonial times and the present stretches a long series of dealings with and betrayals of the Indian that have been condemned by many, apologized for by some, and defended only by a few. The pressure of the westward movement doubtless made it inevitable that the native Americans would be dispossessed of their vast domain and crowded onto reservations. But as the 20th century showed, even the reservation was no certain protection.

Setting apart all of the Far West for the Indians proved early to be unrealistic. The westward movement was diverted for a time to Texas and the Pacific Coast, but by 1850 the desire to open up the whole West was too great to be resisted. The closest thing to a real Indian country was Oklahoma, but even this became a state, in 1907.

The Alaskan Indians and the Eskimos remained undisturbed the longest, but they too proved to be not immune to "progress." The discovery of vast oil reserves in Alaska in the 1960s led to a new "Gold Rush," and the melancholy story gave promise of being retold once more.

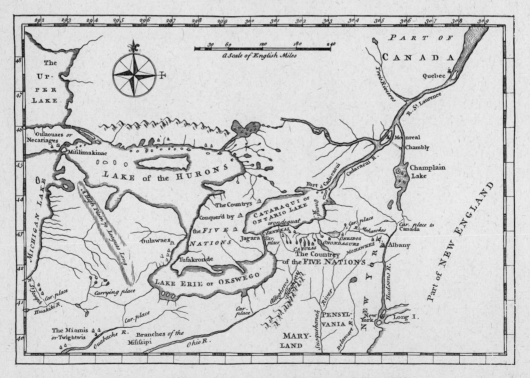

Map of the five Iroquois nations from "History of the Five Indian Nations" by Colden, 1755

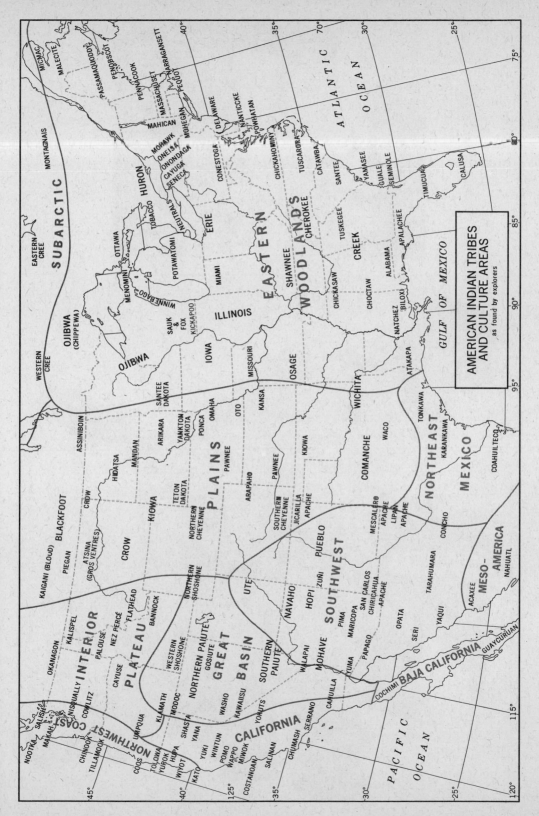

AMERICAN INDIAN TRIBES
AND CULTURE AREAS
as found by explorers

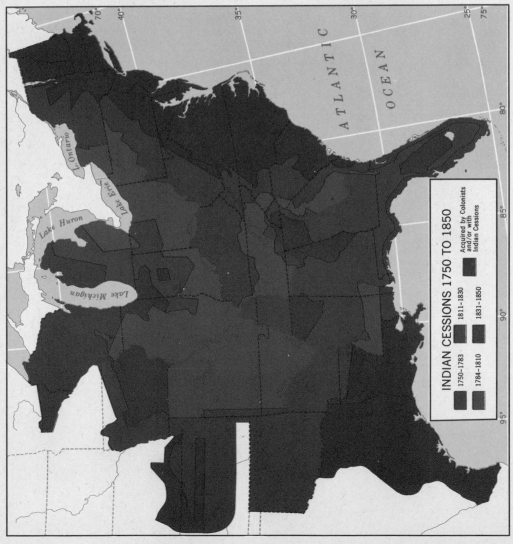

INDIAN CESSIONS 1750 TO 1850

1750–1783

1784–1810

1811–1830

1831–1850

Acquired by Colonists
and/or with
Indian Cessions

L. Ontario

Lake Erie

Lake Huron

Lake Michigan

A T L A N T I C

O C E A N

INDIAN CESSIONS 1850 TO 1900

Land ceded prior to 1850

Ceded by Indians 1850–1870

Ceded by Indians 1871–1890

Land to which Indians possessed original title 1890

Land taken by U.S. Govt. without Indian Cession

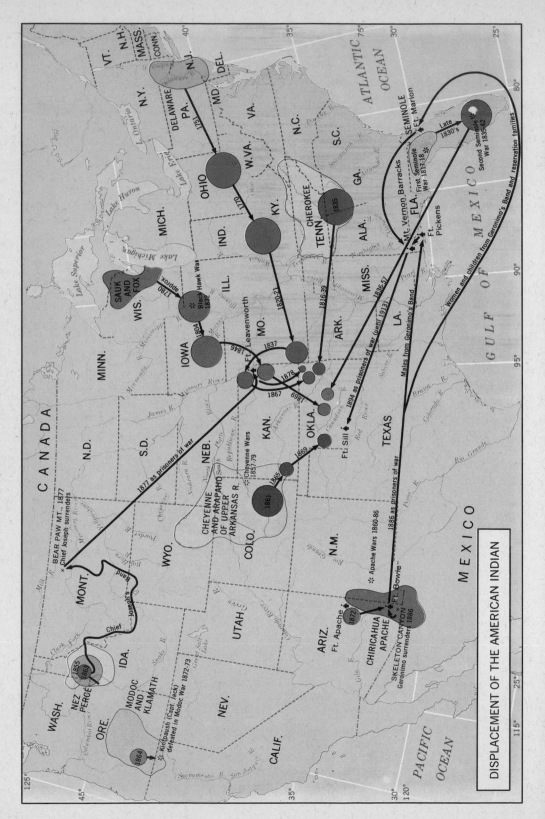

DISPLACEMENT OF THE AMERICAN INDIAN

724

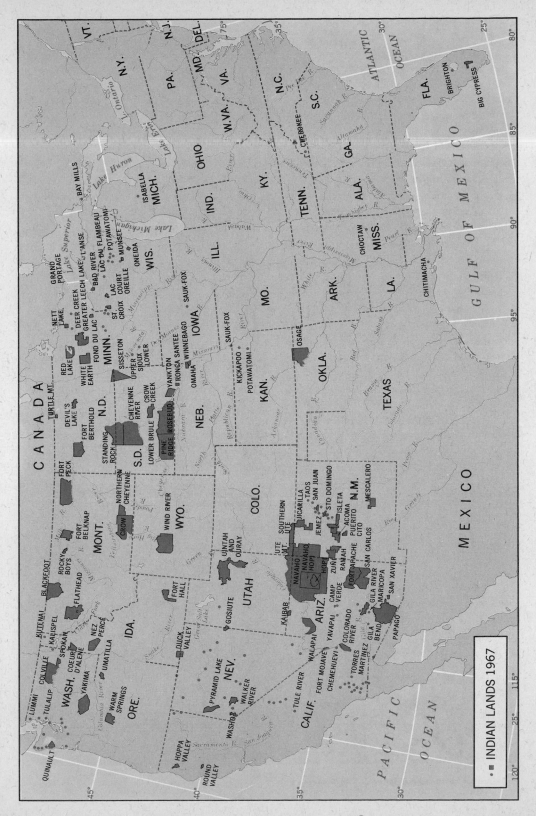

INDIAN LANDS 1967

In the century between the War of 1812 and World War I the United States changed from a predominantly rural and agricultural society into the leading industrial and urban nation of the world. Until the last third of the 19th century most native industries — except for iron and machinery manufacture — depended on agriculture: textiles, lumber, flour, clothing, distilling. Lumber, mining, and ironworks generally were located near their source of supplies, but other industries tended to locate on the basis of capital and labor supply. The South remained relatively underdeveloped industrially until after World War II.

The rapid industrialization of the North following the Civil War was prompted by advances in technology and economic concentration, by the increasing availability of resources as the frontier moved westward, and by the constant flow of immigrants, insuring a steady supply of both skilled and unskilled labor. Better transportation also facilitated the development of both domestic and foreign markets. The nation's greatest industrial strides occurred after World War II, when a period of unparalleled affluence astounded even the most optimistic prophets.

The country has been involved in foreign trade since the colonies were part of the British mercantile system. But independence, combined with the advance of technology and industrialization, changed the character of foreign commerce. In recent times, the 19th-century balance of imports over exports has been reversed, as American business has invested heavily in other countries. At present, American commerce spreads over much of the world, and a relaxation of world tensions would permit and probably necessitate the Americanization of the entire global economy.

Cake batter being readied for baking in a modern bakery

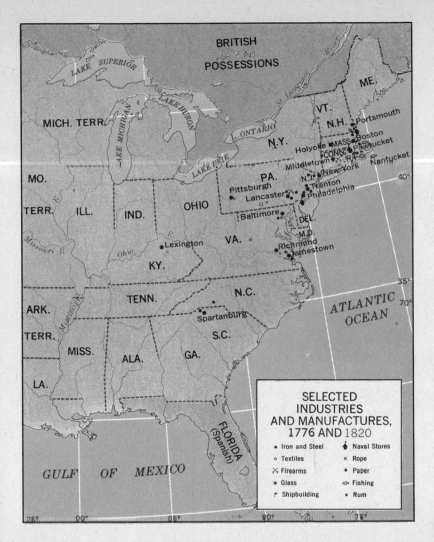

SELECTED INDUSTRIES AND MANUFACTURES, 1776 AND 1820

- ■ Iron and Steel
- ◇ Textiles
- ✕ Firearms
- ✱ Glass
- ⌐ Shipbuilding
- ⚓ Naval Stores
- ✕ Rope
- ◆ Paper
- ⌐ Fishing
- ● Rum

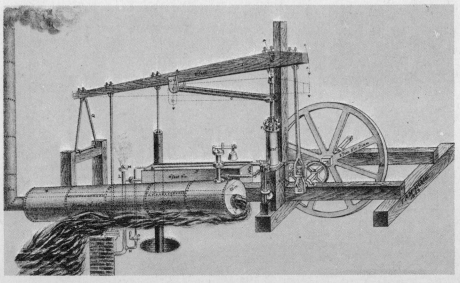

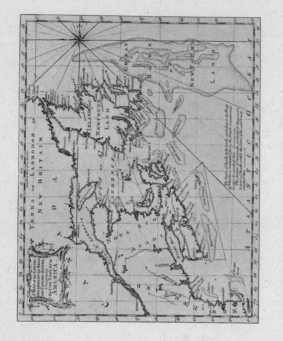

(Above) Map of the Atlantic Ocean, showing the route of the annual passage of herring and the location of major fisheries; (above right) map of North Atlantic fisheries in the 18th century; (right) map of the Gulf Stream drawn by Benjamin Franklin

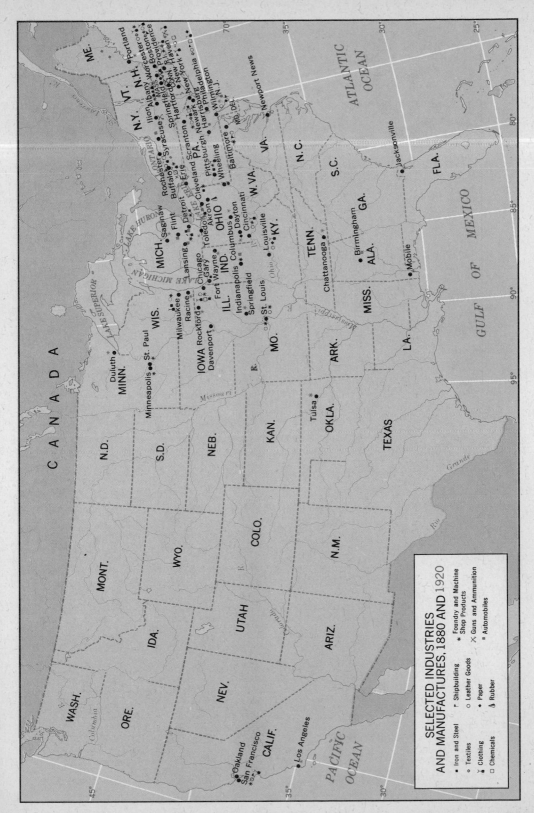

SELECTED INDUSTRIES
AND MANUFACTURES, 1880 AND 1920

- Iron and Steel   ⊢ Shipbuilding   ✱ Foundry and Machine Shop Products
- ◇ Textiles   ○ Leather Goods   ✕ Guns and Ammunition
- ⅄ Clothing   ◆ Paper   ■ Automobiles
- □ Chemicals   ⅄ Rubber

729

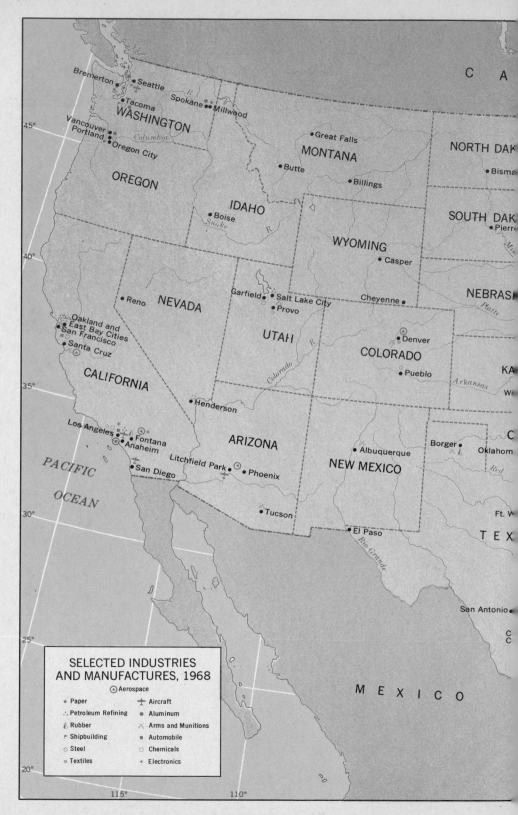

SELECTED INDUSTRIES
AND MANUFACTURES, 1968

Ⓐ Aerospace

- Paper
- Petroleum Refining
- Rubber
- Shipbuilding
- Steel
- Textiles

- Aircraft
- Aluminum
- Arms and Munitions
- Automobile
- Chemicals
- Electronics

D A

Duluth

NESOTA

eapolis

alls

IOWA

Moines   Davenport

aha

n

MISSOURI

sa

ARKANSAS

Little Rock

Jones Mills

LOUISIANA

umont

Port Arthur

Texas City

Freeport

avaca

LAKE   SUPERIOR

WISCONSIN

Milwaukee

Belvidere

Chicago   Gary

Peoria

ILLINOIS   INDIANA

Indianapolis

Terre Haute

St. Louis

Henderson

MICHIGAN

LAKE   HURON

LAKE MICHIGAN

Lansing   Flint

Kalamazoo   Detroit

Toledo   Akron

LAKE ERIE

Cleveland

OHIO

Columbus   Morgantown

Parkersburg

Cincinnati   W.VA.

Charleston

Portsmouth   Ashland

Ohio   Louisville

KENTUCKY

Nashville

TENNESSEE   Alcoa

Memphis   Chattanooga

Sheffield   Calhoun

Gadsden

Birmingham   Atlanta

Childersburg

Thomaston   Macon

MISS.   ALABAMA

Jackson   GEORGIA

Mobile

Lake Charles   New Orleans

LAKE ONTARIO

Niagara Falls   Syracuse

Buffalo   NEW YORK

PENNSYLVANIA

Youngstown   Bethlehem

Pittsburgh

Wilmington

MD.   Baltimore

Washington

Richmond

VIRGINIA   Newport News

Greensboro

Kannopolis

Badin   NORTH

Gastonia   CAROLINA

Spartanburg

SOUTH

CAROLINA   McCormick

Charleston

Massena

Watertown   VT.   N.H.

Holyoke   MASS.

New Haven   CONN.

N. J.   New York

DEL.

Richmond

ATLANTIC

OCEAN

MAINE

Waterville

Portland

Boston

Quincy

R.I.   Fall River

Providence

Farmingdale

40°

35°

30°

GULF   OF   MEXICO

FLA.

Jacksonville

Tampa

Miami

BAHAMA

ISLANDS

25°

CUBA

75°

95°   90°   85°   80°

731

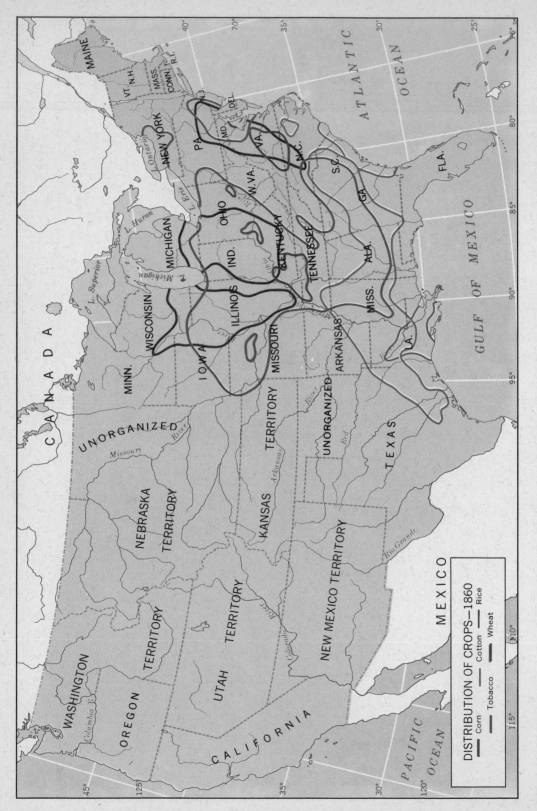

DISTRIBUTION OF CROPS—1860

Corn ▬▬ Rice

Tobacco ▬▬ Wheat

Cotton ▬▬

732

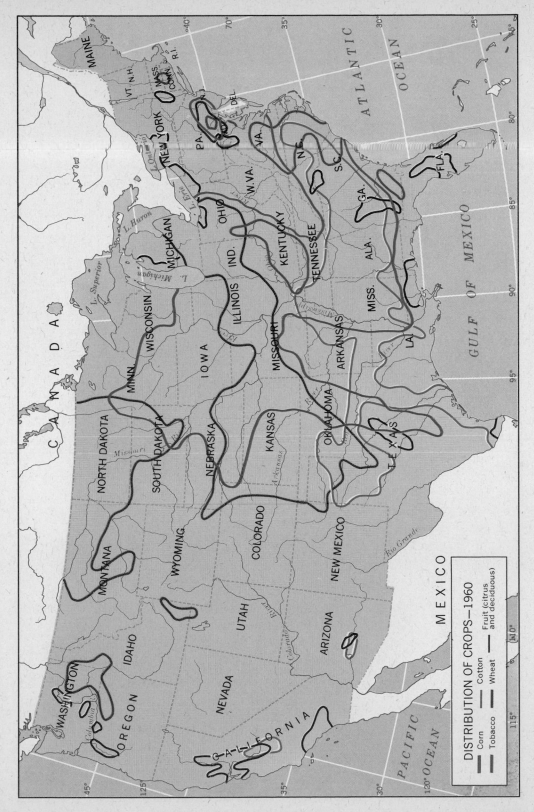

MAINE
VT. N.H.
MASS.
CONN. R.I.
NEW YORK
PA. N.J.
DEL.
W.VA.
VA.
OHIO
IND.
KENTUCKY
N.C.
S.C.
TENNESSEE
GA.
ALA.
MISS.
FLA.
MICHIGAN
WISCONSIN
MINN.
IOWA
ILLINOIS
MISSOURI
ARKANSAS
LA.
OKLAHOMA
KANSAS
TEXAS
NEBRASKA
NORTH DAKOTA
SOUTH DAKOTA
WYOMING
COLORADO
NEW MEXICO
MONTANA
IDAHO
UTAH
ARIZONA
NEVADA
OREGON
WASHINGTON
CALIFORNIA

CANADA

MEXICO

ATLANTIC OCEAN

GULF OF MEXICO

PACIFIC OCEAN

L. Superior
L. Michigan
L. Huron
L. Erie
L. Ontario

Missouri
Mississippi
Arkansas
Rio Grande
Columbia
Colorado

DISTRIBUTION OF CROPS—1960

Corn
Tobacco
Cotton
Wheat
Fruit (citrus and deciduous)

40°
70°
35°
30°
25°
45°
80°
85°
90°
95°
110°
115°
120°
35°
30°
125°
45°

733

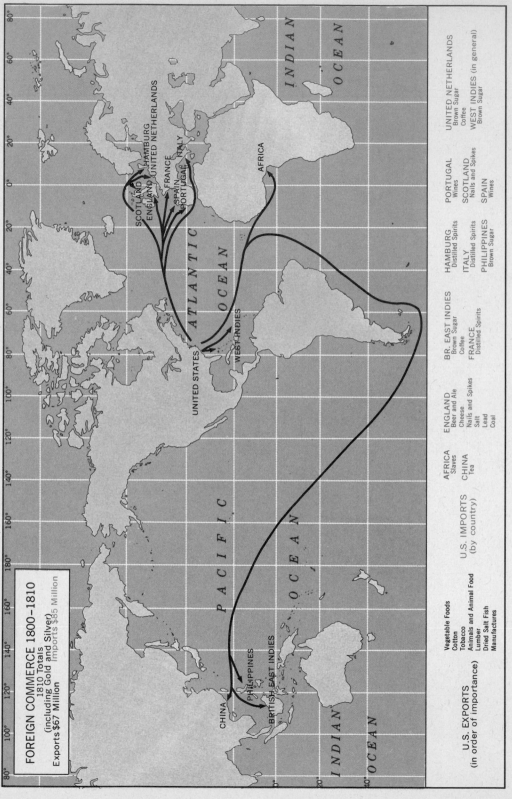

FOREIGN COMMERCE 1800–1810
1810 Totals
(including Gold and Silver)
Exports $67 Million   Imports $85 Million

INDIAN OCEAN

INDIAN OCEAN

ATLANTIC OCEAN

PACIFIC OCEAN

INDIAN OCEAN

SCOTLAND
ENGLAND
HAMBURG
UNITED NETHERLANDS
FRANCE
SPAIN
PORTUGAL
ITALY
AFRICA

UNITED STATES

WEST INDIES

CHINA
PHILIPPINES
BRITISH EAST INDIES

U.S. EXPORTS
(in order of importance)

Vegetable Foods
Cotton
Tobacco
Animals and Animal Food
Lumber
Dried Salt Fish
Manufactures

U.S. IMPORTS
(by country)

AFRICA
Slaves
CHINA
Tea

ENGLAND
Beer and Ale
Cheese
Nails and Spikes
Salt
Lead
Coal

BR. EAST INDIES
Brown Sugar
Coffee
FRANCE
Distilled Spirits

HAMBURG
Distilled Spirits
ITALY
Distilled Spirits
PHILIPPINES
Brown Sugar

PORTUGAL
Wines
SCOTLAND
Nails and Spikes
SPAIN
Wines

UNITED NETHERLANDS
Brown Sugar
Coffee
WEST INDIES (in general)
Brown Sugar

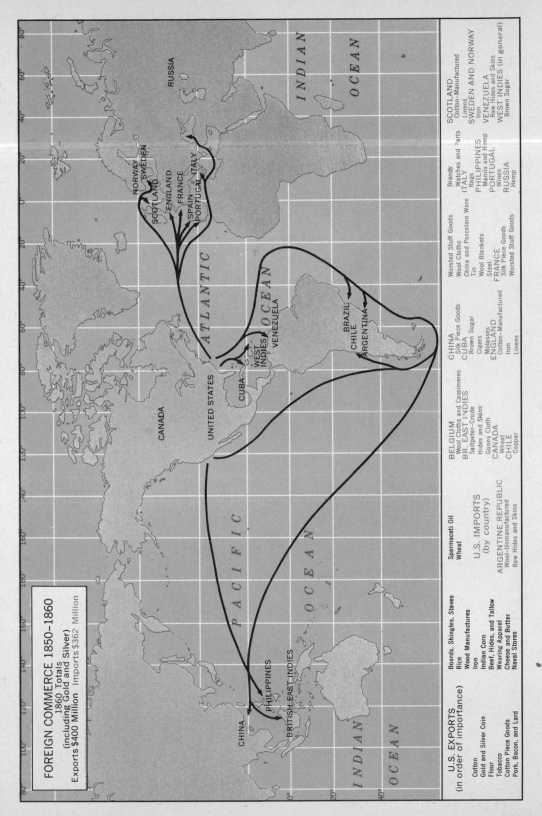

FOREIGN COMMERCE 1850–1860
1860 Totals
(including Gold and Silver)
Exports $400 Million   Imports $362 Million

U.S. EXPORTS
(in order of importance)

Cotton
Gold and Silver Coin
Flour
Tobacco
Cotton Piece Goods
Pork, Bacon, and Lard

Boards, Shingles, Staves
Rice
Wood Manufactures
Iron
Indian Corn
Beef, Hides, and Tallow
Wearing Apparel
Cheese and Butter
Naval Stores

Spermaceti Oil
Wheat

U.S. IMPORTS
(by country)

ARGENTINE REPUBLIC
Wool–Unmanufactured
Raw Hides and Skins

BELGIUM
Wool Cloths and Cassimeres
BR. EAST INDIES
Saltpeter–Crude
Hides and Skins
Gunny Cloth
CANADA
Wheat
CHILE
Copper

CHINA
Silk Piece Goods
CUBA
Brown Sugar
Cigars
Molasses
ENGLAND
Cotton–Manufactured
Iron
Linens

Worsted Stuff Goods
Wool Cloths
China and Porcelain Ware
Tin
Wool Blankets
Steel
FRANCE
Silk Piece Goods
Worsted Stuff Goods

Brandy
Watches and Parts
ITALY
Rags
PHILIPPINES
Manila and Hemp
PORTUGAL
Wines
RUSSIA
Hemp

SCOTLAND
Cotton–Manufactured
Linens
SWEDEN AND NORWAY
Iron
VENEZUELA
Raw Hides and Skins
WEST INDIES (in general)
Brown Sugar

735

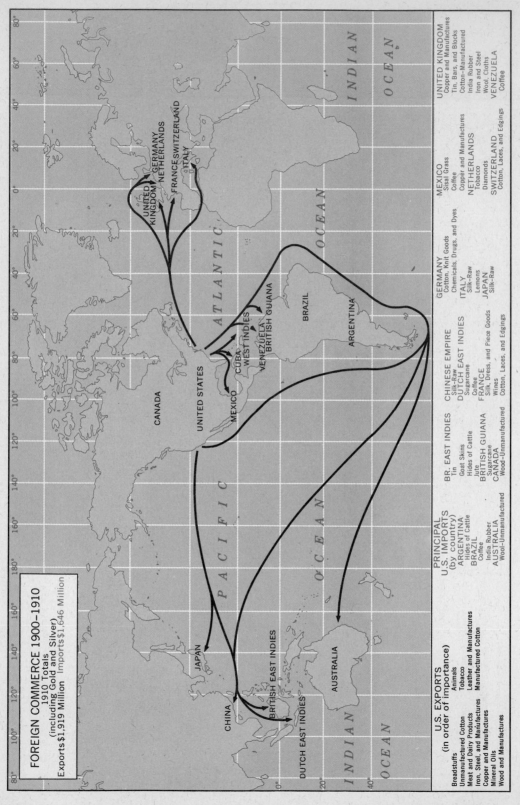

FOREIGN COMMERCE 1900–1910
1910 Totals
(including Gold and Silver)
Exports $1,919 Million Imports $1,646 Million

U.S. EXPORTS
(in order of importance)

Breadstuffs
Unmanufactured Cotton
Meat and Dairy Products
Iron, Steel, and Manufactures
Copper and Manufactures
Mineral Oils
Wood and Manufactures

Animals
Tobacco
Leather and Manufactures
Manufactured Cotton

PRINCIPAL
U.S. IMPORTS
(by country)

ARGENTINA
Hides of Cattle
BRAZIL
Coffee
India Rubber
AUSTRALIA
Wool—Unmanufactured

BR. EAST INDIES
Tin
Goat Skins
Hides of Cattle
Jute
BRITISH GUIANA
Sugarcane
CANADA
Wood—Unmanufactured

CHINESE EMPIRE
Silk—Raw
DUTCH EAST INDIES
Coffee
FRANCE
Silk, Dress, and Piece Goods
Wines
Cotton, Laces, and Edgings

GERMANY
Cotton, Knit Goods
Chemicals, Drugs, and Dyes
ITALY
Silk—Raw
Lemons
JAPAN
Silk—Raw

MEXICO
Sisal Grass
Coffee
Copper and Manufactures
NETHERLANDS
Tobacco
Diamonds
SWITZERLAND
Cotton, Laces, and Edgings

UNITED KINGDOM
Copper and Manufactures
Tin, Bars, and Blocks
Cotton—Manufactured
India Rubber
Iron and Steel
Wool, Cloths
VENEZUELA
Coffee

UNITED KINGDOM
FRANCE SWITZERLAND
GERMANY
NETHERLANDS
ITALY

INDIAN OCEAN

ATLANTIC OCEAN

PACIFIC OCEAN

INDIAN OCEAN

CANADA
UNITED STATES
MEXICO
CUBA
WEST INDIES
VENEZUELA
BRITISH GUIANA
BRAZIL
ARGENTINA

JAPAN
CHINA
BRITISH EAST INDIES
DUTCH EAST INDIES
AUSTRALIA

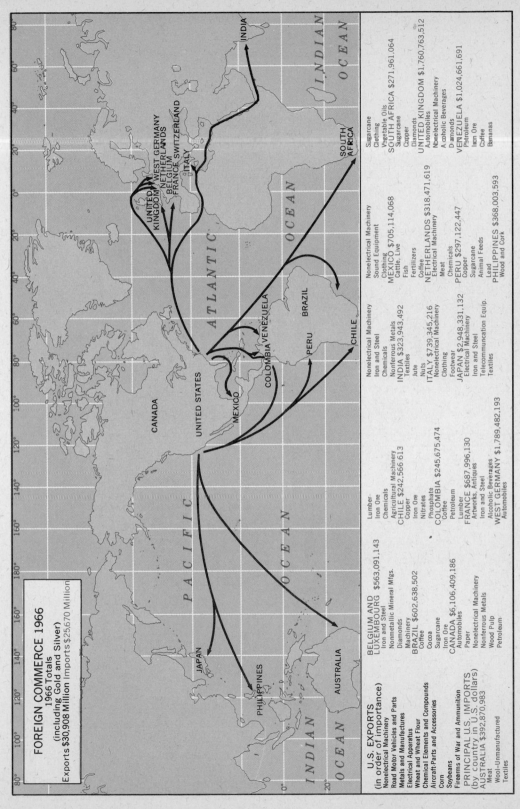

FOREIGN COMMERCE 1966
1966 Totals
(including Gold and Silver)
Exports $30,908 Million Imports $25,670 Million

U.S. EXPORTS
(in order of importance)
Nonelectrical Machinery
Road Motor Vehicles and Parts
Metals and Manufactures
Electrical Apparatus
Wheat and Wheat Flour
Chemical Elements and Compounds
Aircraft-Parts and Accessories
Corn
Soybeans
Firearms of War and Ammunition

PRINCIPAL U.S. IMPORTS
(by country in U.S. dollars)
AUSTRALIA $392,870,983
Meat
Wool—Unmanufactured
Textiles

BELGIUM AND
LUXEMBOURG $563,091,143
Iron and Steel
Nonelectrical Machinery
Nonmetallic Mineral Mfgs.
Diamonds
Machinery
BRAZIL $602,638,502
Coffee
Cocoa
Sugarcane
Iron Ore
CANADA $6,106,409,186
Automobiles
Paper
Nonelectrical Machinery
Nonferrous Metals
Wood Pulp
Petroleum

Lumber
Iron Ore
Chemicals
Agricultural Machinery
CHILE $242,566,613
Copper
Iron Ore
Nitrates
Phosphate
COLOMBIA $245,675,474
Coffee
Petroleum
Lumber
FRANCE $687,996,130
Artworks, Antiques
Iron and Steel
Alcoholic Beverages
WEST GERMANY $1,789,482,193
Automobiles

Nonelectrical Machinery
Iron and Steel
Chemicals
Nonferrous Metals
INDIA $323,943,492
Textiles
Jute
Nuts
ITALY $739,345,216
Nonelectrical Machinery
Clothing
Footwear
Electrical Machinery
Iron and Steel
Telecommunication Equip.
Textiles

Nonelectrical Machinery
Sound Equipment
Clothing
MEXICO $705,114,068
Cattle, Live
Fish
Fertilizers
Coffee
NETHERLANDS $318,471,619
Electrical Machinery
Meat
Chemicals
PERU $297,122,447
Copper
Sugarcane
Animal Feeds
Lead
PHILIPPINES $368,003,593
Wood and Cork

Sugarcane
Clothing
Vegetable Oils
SOUTH AFRICA $271,961,064
Sugarcane
Copper
Diamonds
UNITED KINGDOM $1,760,763,512
Automobiles
Nonelectrical Machinery
Alcoholic Beverages
Diamonds
VENEZUELA $1,024,661,691
Petroleum
Iron Ore
Coffee
Bananas

JAPAN $2,948,331,132
Electrical Machinery

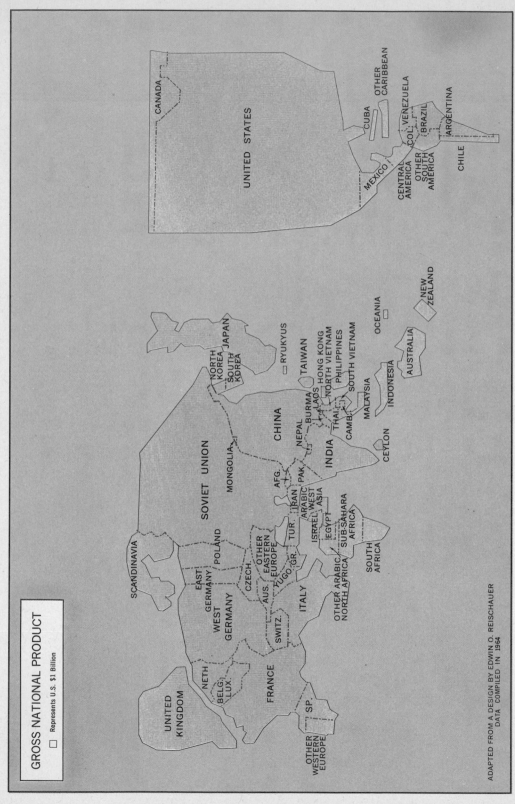

GROSS NATIONAL PRODUCT

☐ Represents U.S. $1 Billion

ADAPTED FROM A DESIGN BY EDWIN O. REISCHAUER
DATA COMPILED IN 1964

738

U.S. Gross National Product, 1919–1968
(Billions of dollars, current prices)

year	total
1919	78.9
1920	88.9
1921	74.0
1922	74.0
1923	86.1
1924	87.6
1925	91.3
1926	97.7
1927	96.3
1928	98.2
1929	104.4
1930	91.1
1931	76.3
1932	58.5
1933	56.0
1934	65.0
1935	72.5
1936	82.7
1937	90.8
1938	85.2
1939	91.1
1940	100.6
1941	125.8
1942	159.1
1943	192.5
1944	211.4
1945	213.6
1946	210.7
1947	234.3
1948	259.4
1949	258.1
1950	284.6
1951	329.0
1952	347.0
1953	365.4
1954	363.1
1955	397.5
1956	419.2
1957	442.8
1958	444.5
1959	482.7
1960*	502.6
1961	518.2
1962	554.9
1963	583.9
1964	632.4
1965	684.9
1966	747.6
1967	789.7
1968[1]	860.6

*First year for which figures include Alaska and Hawaii.
[1]Preliminary

Total Horsepower of All Prime Movers
(1,000s)

year	total
1850	8,495
1860	13,763
1870	16,931
1880	26,314
1890	44,086
1900	63,952
1910	138,810
1920	453,450
1930	1,663,944
1940	2,758,332
1950	4,760,262
1960*	10,972,625
1968	17,912,944

*First year for which figures include Alaska and Hawaii.

Indexes of National Productivity
Real gross private domestic product[1]

year	total economy	by input		
		Per unit of labor	Per unit of capital	Per unit total input
1890	45.7	52.4	77.8	58.6
1900	55.6	61.7	77.0	65.7
1910	64.4	67.7	82.4	71.6
1920	78.3	79.6	85.4	81.2
1930	97.5	98.8	89.0	96.3
1940	124.0	124.4	114.9	122.0
1950	175.4	162.8	145.5	158.7
1960*	227.6	205.9	143.8	189.0
1968	137.9[2]			

[1]Base year, 1929 = 100.
[2]Based on redefinition of index, 1957–1959 = 100. On 1929 base, figure is approximately equal to 300.
*First year for which figures include Alaska and Hawaii.

12. TRANSPORTATION

The movement of population across the continent after the Revolution necessitated efficient surface transportation, in part to facilitate travel, but mainly to haul freight. The subsequent development of the United States into a commercial and industrial nation prompted the growth of a transportation network unequalled anywhere in the world. Most early public works were undertaken by private companies and by local government bodies. In the 19th century only the Cumberland Road was constructed by the national government. Not until the heavy increase in automotive traffic in the 20th century did the federal government undertake a program of highway construction. Ninety percent of the cost of the interstate highway system projected for 1975 will have been paid for by federal funds.

The geography of the area between the Atlantic and the Mississippi made the use of natural inland waterways and canals desirable for the transport of larger amounts of freight than could be hauled by road. By 1860 more than 3,000 miles of canals had been built, of which the most famous was the Erie. The most recent and ambitious addition to the inland waterway system is the St. Lawrence Seaway, connecting the Great Lakes cities with the oceans of the world.

Canal-building was hardly under way when the railroad came on the scene. Between 1830 and 1865 more than 30,000 miles of track were laid, and in the decades after the Civil War railroad networks covered the nation. The railroads still maintain an advantage in the hauling of freight, but passenger traffic has more and more in recent years become the province of the airlines and of automobiles.

Early railroad scene, Little Falls, New York

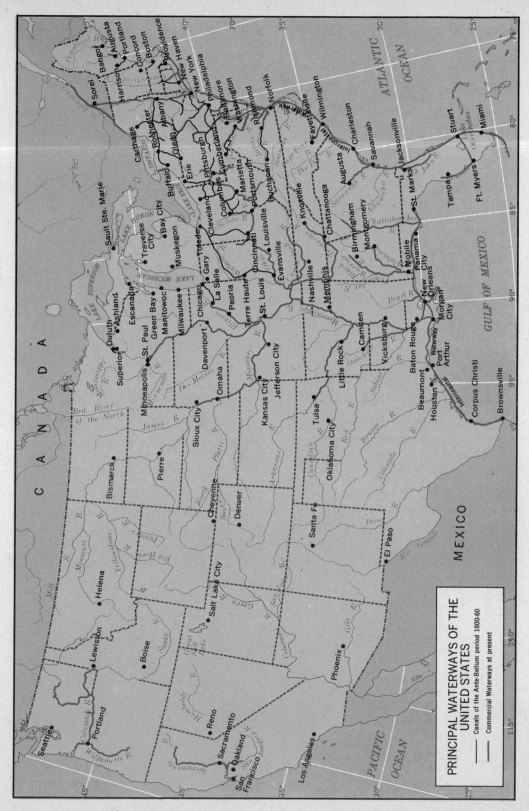

PRINCIPAL WATERWAYS OF THE
UNITED STATES

Canals of the Ante-Bellum period 1800-60
Commercial Waterways at present

741

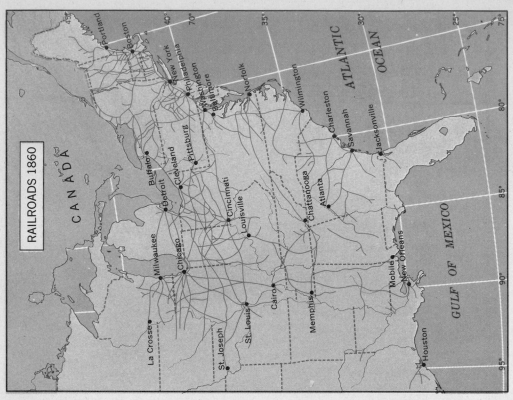

RAILROADS 1860

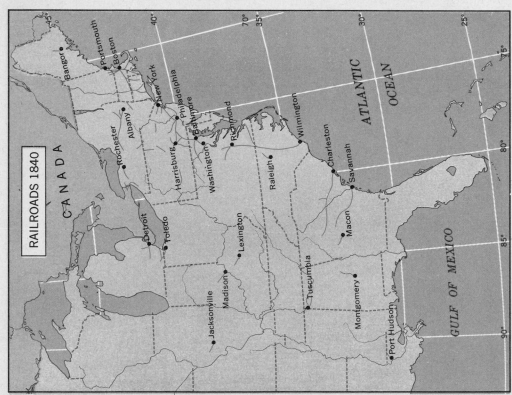

RAILROADS 1840

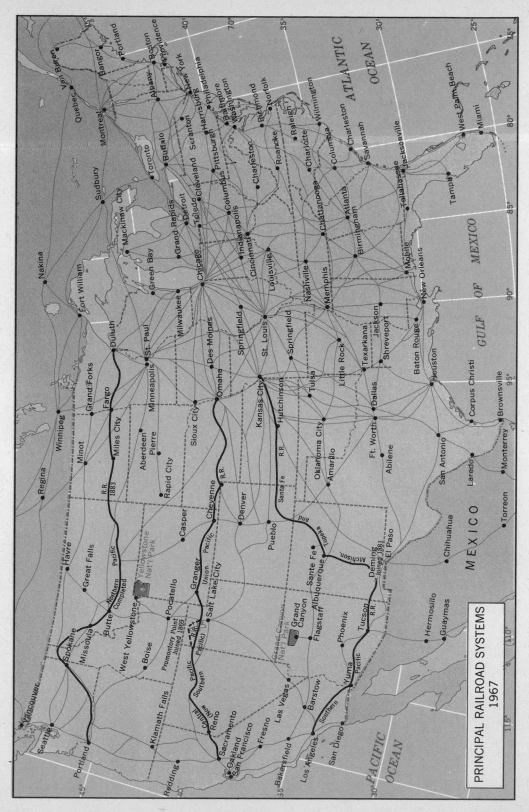

PRINCIPAL RAILROAD SYSTEMS
1967

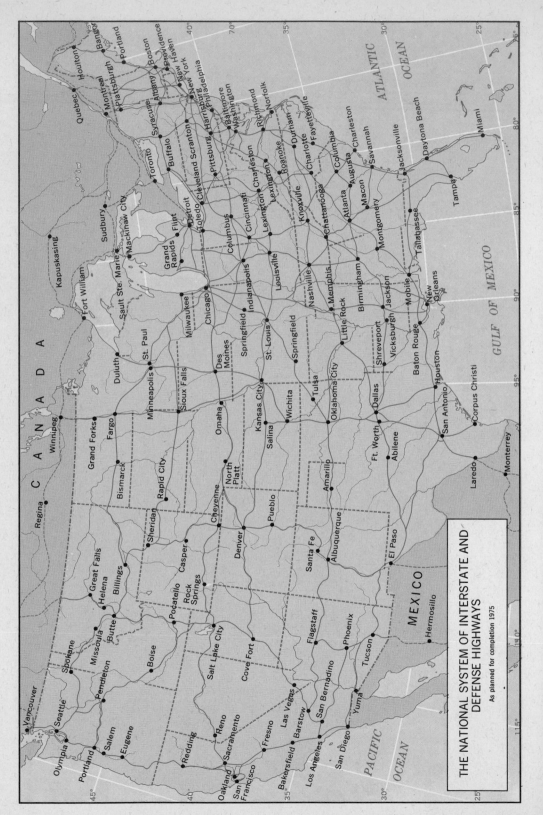

THE NATIONAL SYSTEM OF INTERSTATE AND
DEFENSE HIGHWAYS

As planned for completion 1975

744

Highway Mileage 1905–1967

year	existing surfaced (1,000 mi.)	federal[1]
1905	161	—
1910	204	—
1915	276	—
1920	369	—
1925	521	179,501
1930	694	193,652
1935	1,080	219,869
1940	1,367	235,482
1945	1,721	308,741
1950	1,939	643,939
1955	2,273	749,166
1960*	2,557	837,942
1965	2,809	909,000
1967	2,857	911,000

[1]Includes estimates on federal-aid primary system throughout, Federal aid on secondary systems beginning in 1942, and national system of interstate and defense highways beginning in 1951. Estimates as of end of calendar year.

*First year for which figures include Alaska and Hawaii.

View of the Kennedy Expressway, the main route into Chicago for the daily commuters from the northwestern suburbs.

Rail Transportation, 1882–1920[1]

year	passenger miles[2]	freight ton-miles[2]
1882	7,688	39,302
1883	8,541	44,065
1884	8,779	44,725
1885	9,134	49,152
1886	9,660	52,802
1887	10,570	61,561
1888	11,191	65,423
1889	11,965	68,677
1890	12,522	79,193
1891	12,844	81,074
1892	13,363	88,241
1893	14,229	93,588
1894	14,289	80,335
1895	12,188	85,228
1896	13,049	95,328
1897	12,257	95,139
1898	13,380	114,078
1899	14,591	123,667
1900	16,038	141,597
1901	17,354	147,077
1902	19,690	157,289
1903	20,916	173,221
1904	21,923	174,522
1905	23,800	186,463
1906	25,167	215,878
1907	27,719	236,601
1908	29,083	218,382
1909	29,109	218,803
1910	32,338	255,017
1911	33,202	253,784
1912	33,132	264,081
1913	34,673	301,730
1914	35,357	288,637
1915	32,475	277,135
1916	35,220	366,173
1917	40,100	398,263
1918	43,212	408,778
1919	46,838	367,161
1920	47,370	413,699

[1]Figures from 1891 to 1915 are for year ending June 30; figures from 1916 to 1920 are for year ending December 31.

[2]Millions

An automobile graveyard outside Detroit, Michigan

Transportation in the United States, 1921—1968

year	miles of travel motor vehicles[1]	rail transportation[2]		scheduled commercial air transportation* miles flown			
		passenger miles	freight ton-miles	passenger (1,000s)		revenue[3]	
				domestic	international	domestic	international
1921	55,027	37,706	309,533	—	—	—	—
1922	67,697	35,811	342,188	—	—	—	—
1923	84,995	38,294	416,256	—	—	—	—
1924	104,838	36,368	391,945	—	—	—	—
1925	122,346	36,167	417,418	—	—	—	—
1926	140,735	35,673	447,444	—	—	4,318,087	—
1927	158,453	33,798	432,014	—	—	5,856,189	14,300
1928	172,856	31,718	436,087	—	—	10,527,870	145,580
1929	197,720	31,165	450,189	—	—	22,728,869	2,412,630
1930	206,320	26,876	385,815	85,125[6]	18,622[6]	32,644,703	4,300,500
1931	216,151	21,933	311,073	106,952[6]	14,171[6]	43,109,166	4,537,241
1932	200,517	16,997	235,309	127,433[6]	20,754[6]	45,893,522	5,278,365
1933	200,642	16,368	250,651	174,820[6]	24,956[6]	49,256,320	5,857,163
1934	215,563	18,069	270,292	189,806[6]	36,844[6]	41,525,667	7,539,106
1935	228,568	18,509	283,637	316,336[6]	46,035[6]	55,918,151	7,949,547
1936	252,128	22,460	341,182	438,989[6]	41,829[6]	64,307,480	6,904,246
1937	270,110	24,695	362,815	411,545	53,742[6]	66,791,079	7,909,158
1938	271,177	21,657	291,866	479,844	53,208	68,610,143	7,042,503
1939	285,402	22,713	335,375	682,904	71,845	82,924,922	7,607,474
1940	302,188	23,816	375,369	1,052,156	99,795	110,101,039	9,651,733
1941	333,612	29,406	477,576	1,384,733	162,824	134,405,836	14,410,358
1942	268,224	53,747	640,992	1,418,042	236,956	111,340,622	18,681,059
1943	208,192	87,925	730,132	1,634,135	244,229	105,354,810	18,457,864
1944	212,713	95,663	740,586	2,178,207	310,574	138,732,219	22,272,638
1945	250,173	91,826	684,148	3,362,455	447,968	208,969,279	32,608,704
1946	340,880	64,754	594,943	5,947,956	1,100,741	309,888,684	59,375,572
1947	370,894	45,972	657,878	6,109,508	1,810,045	325,054,389	86,481,082
1948	397,957	41,224	641,104	5,980,993	1,888,997	338,216,783	98,053,441
1949	424,461	35,133	529,111	6,752,622	2,053,998	351,645,414	104,525,884
1950	458,246	31,790	591,550	8,002,825	2,206,396	364,256,468	93,830,809
1951	491,093	34,640	649,831	10,566,182	2,599,847	406,105,269	97,654,162
1952	513,581	34,033	617,942	12,528,318	3,021,001	458,568,848	103,500,435
1953	544,433	31,679	608,954	14,760,309	3,385,563	518,532,000	110,052,000
1954	560,857	29,310	552,197	16,768,706	3,749,634	550,648,000	116,668,000
1955	603,434	28,548	626,893	19,819,221	4,420,166	620,720,000	131,535,000
1956	627,843	28,216	651,188	22,361,824	5,126,052	687,617,000	146,903,000
1957	647,004	25,914	621,907	25,339,560	5,769,472	784,752,000	156,592,000
1958	664,653	23,295	554,534	25,343,387	6,123,948	778,927,000	172,713,000
1959	700,478	22,075	578,637	29,307,600	7,064,211	841,925,000	172,143,000
1960	718,845	21,284[5]	575,360[5]	30,556,616	8,306,348	820,756,000	162,634,000
1961	737,535	20,308	566,295	31,062,345	8,768,501	795,169,000	161,297,000
1962	767,774	19,926	595,774	33,622,638	10,137,777	827,694,000	171,500,000
1963	805,423	18,519	625,170	38,457,000	11,905,000	888,793,000	192,140,000
1964	846,500	18,271	662,089	44,141,000	14,352,000	957,575,000	214,375,000
1965	887,812	17,454	705,705	51,888,000	16,789,000	1,088,112,000	247,766,000
1966	930,497	17,162	746,699	60,591,000	19,298,000	1,178,458,000	285,711,000
1967	965,132[4]	15,264	727,075	75,487,000	23,259,000	1,462,240,000	350,719,000
1968	NA	NA	NA	87,508,000	26,451,000	1,715,857,000	408,136,000

*Domestic includes Hawaii carriers for all years and, beginning 1959, intra-Alaska. International includes carriers of Mainland-Alaska and outlying areas.

[1] In million vehicle-miles; includes all automobiles, buses, trucks, and motorcycles.
[2] Millions
[3] Includes passenger, express, freight, and mail flights.
[4] Estimate
[5] First year for which figures include Alaska and Hawaii.
[6] Includes nonrevenue passenger-miles flown.
NA—Not available

13. NATURAL RESOURCES

Farming came to North America with colonization, and until well into the period of industrialization agriculture was recognized as the greatest single economic resource of the United States. The grain of the Northeast and Midwest and the tobacco and cotton of the South dominated both foreign and domestic commerce. The nation's other resources—coal, iron, copper, petroleum, silver, gold, and other metals—were discovered and put to use as the frontier moved west and as industrialization proceeded. It was the wide availability of resources as well as the willingness to use them that made the United States the land of opportunity.

The continent seemed so vast, however, and its contents so unlimited, that the population tended to exploit thoughtlessly what was available. Land was often farmed until it was exhausted. Vast stands of timber were destroyed and not replaced. Wildlife was killed off with no thought of its eventual extinction. It was only gradually that conservation measures were adopted, and then often against powerful opposition. Since World War II the manifold threats to the environment have been more widely recognized and steps have been taken to rehabilitate the surroundings to ensure long-term use of a still-abundant supply of natural and agricultural resources. But there is fear that these steps are, if not too late, then too little. Whether the country can control and save its natural environment is perhaps the most serious question of the coming decade.

"The Peaceable Kingdom" by Edward Hicks

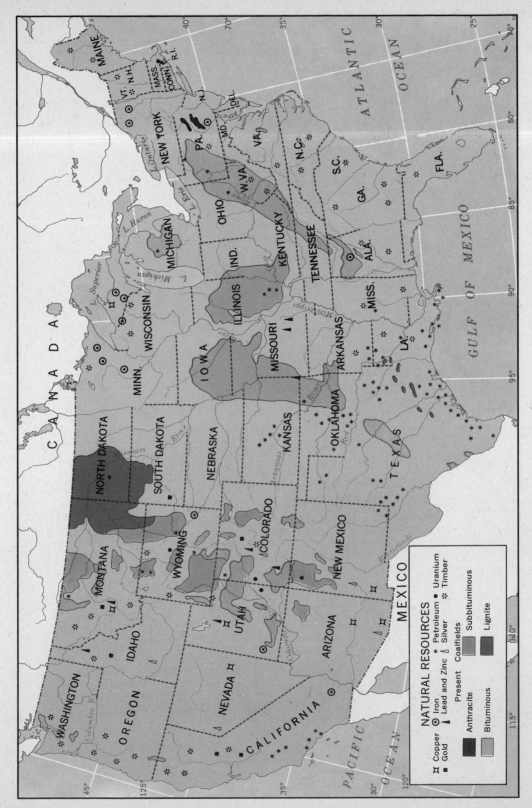

NATURAL RESOURCES

⌗ Copper   ⊙ Iron   * Petroleum   ● Uranium

■ Gold   ⊿ Lead and Zinc   ∧ Silver   ✱ Timber

Present   Coalfields

Anthracite   Subbituminous

Bituminous   Lignite

749

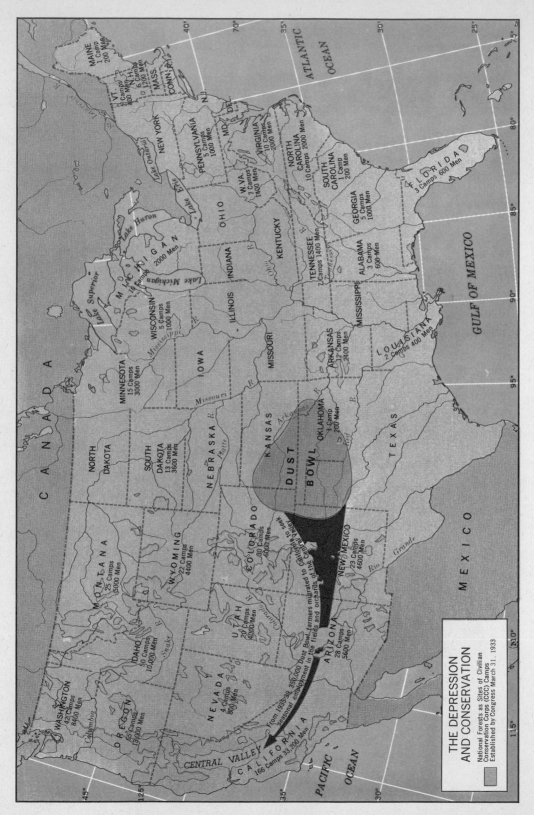

THE DEPRESSION
AND CONSERVATION

National Forests as Sites of Civilian
Conservation Corps (CCC) Camps
Established by Congress March 31, 1933

ATLANTIC
OCEAN

GULF OF MEXICO

PACIFIC
OCEAN

MEXICO

CANADA

MAINE 1 Camp 200 Men

VT. 4 Camps 800 Men

N.H. 6 Camps 1200 Men

MASS.

CONN.

N.J.

DEL.

MD.

NEW YORK

PENNSYLVANIA 5 Camps 1000 Men

VIRGINIA 10 Camps 2000 Men

W.VA. 7 Camps 1400 Men

NORTH CAROLINA 10 Camps 2000 Men

SOUTH CAROLINA 1 Camp 200 Men

GEORGIA 5 Camps 1000 Men

F L O R I D A 3 Camps 600 Men

OHIO

INDIANA

KENTUCKY

TENNESSEE 7 Camps 1400 Men

ALABAMA 3 Camps 600 Men

MISSISSIPPI

LOUISIANA 2 Camps 400 Men

M I C H I G A N 10 Camps 2000 Men

WISCONSIN 5 Camps 1000 Men

ILLINOIS

IOWA

MISSOURI

ARKANSAS 12 Camps 2400 Men

MINNESOTA 15 Camps 3000 Men

NORTH DAKOTA

SOUTH DAKOTA 13 Camps 3600 Men

NEBRASKA

KANSAS

D U S T B O W L

OKLAHOMA 1 Camp 200 Men

T E X A S

MONTANA 25 Camps 5000 Men

WYOMING 22 Camps 4400 Men

COLORADO 30 Camps 6000 Men

NEW MEXICO 23 Camps 4600 Men

IDAHO 50 Camps 10,400 Men

U T A H 20 Camps 4000 Men

ARIZONA 28 Camps 5600 Men

NEVADA 4 Camps 800 Men

WASHINGTON 42 Camps 8400 Men

O R E G O N 55 Camps 13,000 Men

From 1935-39 350,000 Dust Bowl farmers migrated to California
to seek seasonal employment in the fields and orchards of the Central Valley

CENTRAL VALLEY

C A L I F O R N I A 166 Camps 33,200 Men

Lake Ontario

Lake Erie

Lake Huron

Lake Michigan

Lake Superior

Mississippi R.

Missouri R.

Arkansas R.

Red R.

Rio Grande

Columbia R.

Snake R.

Ohio R.

Platte R.

Tennessee R.

750

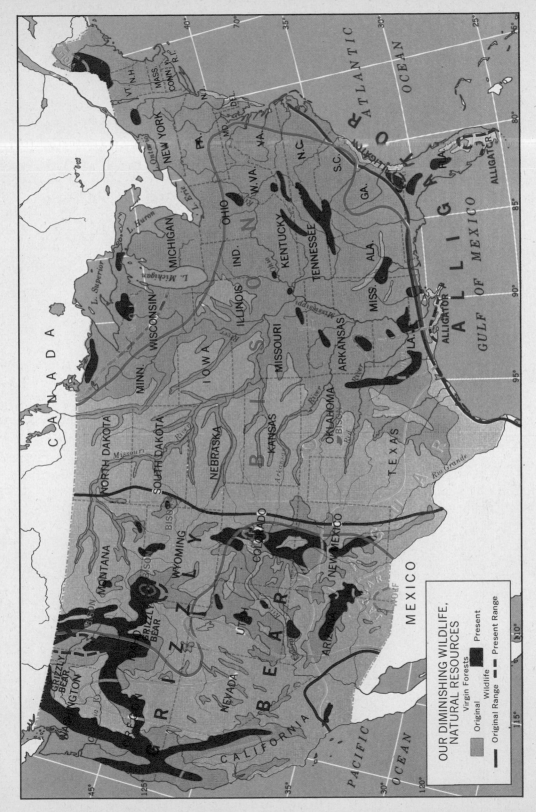

OUR DIMINISHING WILDLIFE,
NATURAL RESOURCES

Virgin Forests

Original | Present

Wildlife

Original Range | Present Range

ATLANTIC OCEAN

GULF OF MEXICO

PACIFIC OCEAN

CANADA

MEXICO

ALLIGATOR

GRIZZLY BEAR

BISON

WOLF

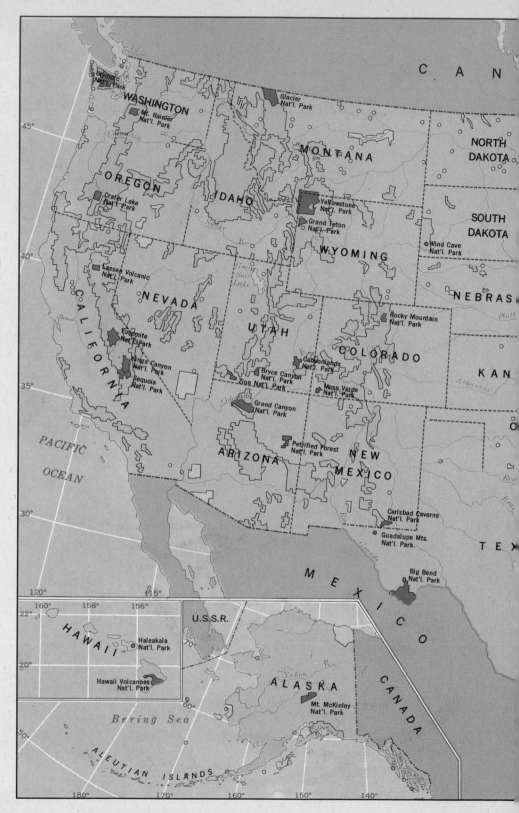

CANADA

WASHINGTON

Olympic
Nat'l. Park

Glacier
Nat'l. Park

Mt. Rainier
Nat'l. Park

MONTANA

NORTH
DAKOTA

OREGON

IDAHO

Crater Lake
Nat'l. Park

Yellowstone
Nat'l. Park

Grand Teton
Nat'l. Park

WYOMING

SOUTH
DAKOTA

Wind Cave
Nat'l. Park

Lassen Volcanic
Nat'l. Park

NEVADA

Great
Salt
Lake

UTAH

Rocky Mountain
Nat'l. Park

COLORADO

NEBRAS

KAN

CALIFORNIA

Yosemite
Nat'l. Park

Kings' Canyon
Nat'l. Park

Sequoia
Nat'l. Park

Bryce Canyon
Nat'l. Park

Zion Nat'l. Park

Canyonlands
Nat'l. Park

Mesa Verde
Nat'l. Park

Colorado

Grand Canyon
Nat'l. Park

PACIFIC

OCEAN

ARIZONA

Petrified Forest
Nat'l. Park

NEW
MEXICO

Carlsbad Caverns
Nat'l. Park

Guadalupe Mts.
Nat'l. Park

TEX

Big Bend
Nat'l. Park

MEXICO

CANADA

HAWAII

U.S.S.R.

Haleakala
Nat'l. Park

Hawaii Volcanoes
Nat'l. Park

ALASKA

Mt. McKinley
Nat'l. Park

Bering Sea

ALEUTIAN ISLANDS

NATIONAL PARKS, FORESTS AND WILDLIFE REFUGES

National Park

National Forest

National Wildlife Refuge

A

Isle Royale Nat'l. Park

Lake Superior

MICHIGAN

MINNESOTA

WISCONSIN

Lake Michigan

Lake Huron

IOWA

ILLINOIS

INDIANA

OHIO

Lake Erie

Lake Ontario

NEW YORK

PENNSYLVANIA

MAINE

Acadia Nat'l. Park

VT.

N.H.

MASS.

CONN. R.I.

NEW JERSEY

MARYLAND

DEL.

WEST VIRGINIA

Shenandoah Nat'l. Park

MISSOURI

KENTUCKY

Mammoth Cave Nat'l. Park

VIRGINIA

TENNESSEE

Great Smoky Mts. Nat'l. Park

NORTH CAROLINA

ARKANSAS

Hot Springs Nat'l. Park

MISS.

ALABAMA

SOUTH CAROLINA

GEORGIA

ATLANTIC OCEAN

LOUISIANA

FLORIDA

GULF   OF   MEXICO

Everglades Nat'l. Park

BAHAMA ISLANDS

CUBA

40°

35°

30°

25°

95°   90°   85°   80°

753

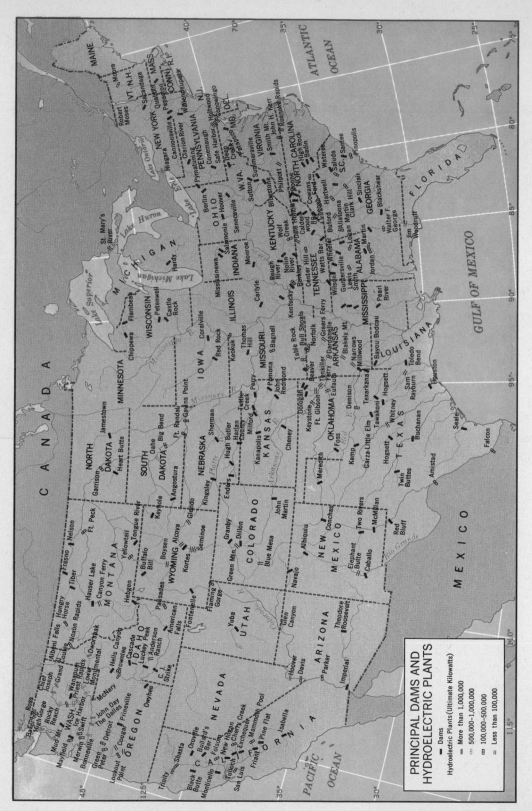

PRINCIPAL DAMS AND
HYDROELECTRIC PLANTS

	Dams
	Hydroelectric Plants (Ultimate Kilowatts)
▮	More than 1,000,000
▯	500,000–1,000,000
⊟	100,000–500,000
=	Less than 100,000

Land Utilization 1850–1964

year	total land area	land in farms (in millions of acres)						land not in farms			
		total	cropland[1]	grassland pasture	woodland pasture	woodland not pastured	other[2]	total	grazing land	forest land not grazed	other[3]
1850	1,884	294 (15.6%)	113	NA	NA	NA	NA	1,590 (84.4%)	NA	NA	NA
1860	1,903	407 (21.4%)	163	NA	NA	NA	NA	1,496 (78.6%)	NA	NA	NA
1870	1,903	408 (21.4%)	189	NA	NA	NA	NA	1,495 (78.6%)	NA	NA	NA
1880	1,903	536 (28.2%)	188	122	NA	NA	36	1,367 (71.8%)	883	368	116 (6.1%)
1890	1,903	623 (32.7%)	248	144	NA	NA	41	1,280 (67.3%)	818	344	118 (6.2%)
1900	1,903	839 (44.1%)	319	276	87	103	54	1,064 (55.9%)	768	175	121 (6.4%)
1910	1,903	879 (46.2%)	347	284	98	93	57	1,024 (53.8%)	739	162	123 (6.5%)
1920	1,903	956 (50.2%)	402	328	77	91	58	947 (49.8%)	661	160	126 (6.6%)
1925	1,903	924 (48.6%)	391	331	77	67	58	979 (51.4%)	646	203	130 (6.8%)
1930	1,903	987 (51.9%)	413	379	85	65	45	916 (48.1%)	578	208	130 (6.8%)
1935	1,903	1,055 (55.4%)	416	410	108	77	44	848 (44.6%)	533	184	131 (6.9%)
1940	1,905	1,061 (55.7%)	399	461	100	57	44	844 (44.3%)	504	203	137 (7.2%)
1945	1,905	1,142 (59.9%)	403	529	95	71	44	763 (40.1%)	428	186	149 (7.8%)
1950	1,904	1,159 (60.9%)	409	485	135	85	45	745 (39.1%)	400	201	144 (7.6%)
1954	1,904	1,158 (60.8%)	399	526	121	76	36	746 (39.2%)	353	238	155 (8.1%)
1959[4]	2,271	1,124 (49.5%)	392	532	93	70	37	1,147 (50.5%)	319	431	397 (17.5%)
1964[4]	2,266	1,110 (49.0%)	387	547	82	64	30	1,156 (51.0%)	293	443	420 (18.5%)

[1]Comprises cropland used for crops, soil improvement crops, and idle cropland.
[2]Farmsteads, roads, and other land.
[3]Comprises urban, industrial, and residential areas; rural parks; wildlife refuges; highway, road, and railroad rights-of-way; ungrazed desert; rocky, barren, swamp, tundra, and other land not otherwise counted.
[4]Figures include Alaska and Hawaii.
NA – Not available

Apart from the frontier, the most noticeable fact in American population trends has been the change from a rural to an urban society. In 1790, 95 percent of the population was rural; in 1860 the figure was still 80 percent; but in 1960 it was only 30 percent.

As cities grew in size, they also changed. The tendency of dwellers in the central city to move to suburbs began before the Civil War. Their places were taken by newly arrived immigrants, who came by the millions, especially after 1880. With the near halt of immigration after 1930, the continuing flight of whites to the suburbs and beyond was made up for by incoming blacks, who began to migrate from the rural South to the northern and western cities around the time of World War I. By 1970, Washington and perhaps Detroit were more than half black, and another decade would probably see blacks outnumbering whites in half a dozen U.S. cities.

As the 20th century wore on, the United States, the world's most affluent nation, was nevertheless forced to recognize that millions of Americans lived in poverty. Within the confines of a single city it was possible to demonstrate the extremes of wealth and poverty that were, for all practical purposes, nationwide. When depicted on an international scale, the contrasts were even more striking. On a map designed to represent relative population distribution and allocation of wealth, two-thirds of the world's people are found in the poor half of the globe and nearly four-fifths of the wealth in the other half.

The present problem of the cities, like that of the environment, is vexing and difficult. But cities are coextensive with civilization; they are perhaps man's greatest invention. It seems the better part of wisdom to try to save them.

The earliest known view of Manhattan

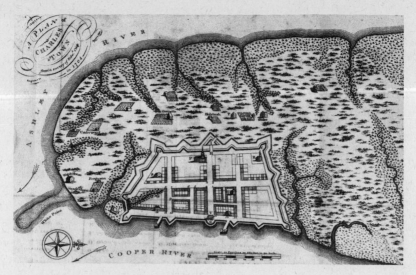

Plan of Charleston and nearby plantations

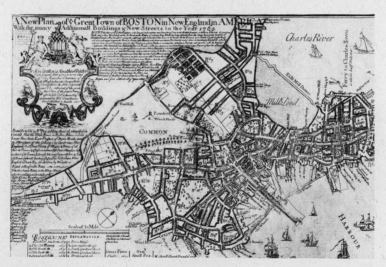

Plan of Boston

(Top) Redraft of L'Enfant's plan for the city of Washington showing location for the president's house, Mall, and Capitol, original drawn in 1791; (bottom) Philadelphia and environs in 1706, showing the plan for the city and the public lands

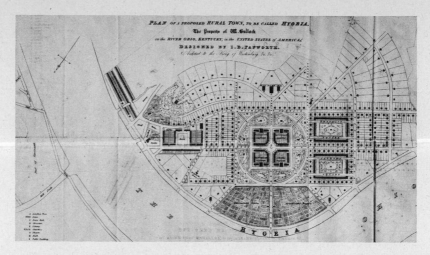

Plan of the proposed town of Hygeia

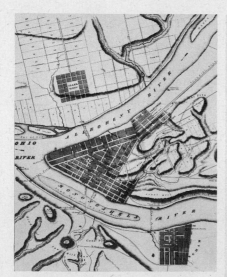

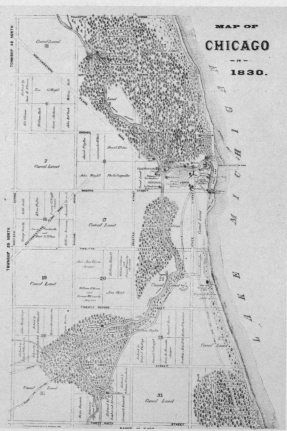

(Above) Plan for the development of Pittsburgh and the adjacent country; (right) map showing Chicago in 1830, with later streets and some of the early property lines superimposed

Population of 25 Largest U.S. Cities

city[1]	1910	1920	1930	1940	1950	1960	1969 (estimate)	standard metropolitan statistical areas 1968 (estimate)	rank by 1968 SMSA population
New York	4,766,883	5,620,048	6,930,446	7,454,995	7,891,957	7,781,984	7,975,000	11,679,858	1
Chicago	2,185,283	2,701,705	3,376,438	3,396,808	3,620,962	3,550,404	3,460,000	6,810,000	3
Los Angeles	319,198	576,673	1,238,048	1,504,277	1,970,358	2,481,595	2,810,000	7,120,000	2
Philadelphia	1,549,008	1,823,779	1,950,961	1,931,334	2,071,605	2,002,512	2,015,000	4,800,000[2]	4
Detroit	465,766	993,678	1,568,662	1,623,452	1,849,568	1,670,144	1,570,000	4,214,000[2]	5
Houston	78,800	138,276	292,352	384,514	596,163	938,219	1,165,000	1,850,000	13
Baltimore	558,485	733,826	804,874	859,100	949,708	939,024	905,000	1,992,210	12
Dallas	92,104	158,976	260,475	294,734	434,462	679,684	815,000	1,453,000	15
Washington, D.C.	331,069	437,571	486,869	663,091	802,178	763,956	815,000	2,663,000[3]	7
Cleveland	560,663	796,841	900,429	878,336	914,808	876,050	770,000	2,175,000[4]	11
Milwaukee	373,857	457,147	578,249	587,472	637,392	741,324	750,000	1,460,000	14
San Francisco	416,912	506,676	634,394	634,536	775,357	740,316	705,000	3,130,500	6
San Antonio	96,614	161,379	231,542	253,854	408,442	587,718	695,000	834,000[2]	24
St. Louis	687,029	772,897	821,960	816,048	856,796	750,026	665,000	2,345,000	10
New Orleans	339,075	387,219	458,762	494,537	570,445	627,525	660,000	1,095,500	21
San Diego	39,578	74,361	147,995	203,341	334,387	573,224	680,000	1,320,500	17
Boston	670,585	748,060	781,188	770,816	801,444	698,080	570,000	2,600,000	8
Kansas City, Mo.	248,381	324,410	399,746	399,178	456,622	475,539	555,000	1,347,000	16
Seattle	237,194	315,312	365,583	368,302	467,591	557,087	550,000	1,317,947[4]	18
Memphis	131,105	162,351	253,143	292,942	396,000	497,524	545,000	761,000[2]	25
Columbus	181,511	237,031	290,564	306,087	375,901	471,316	535,000	860,000[2]	22
Pittsburgh	533,905	588,343	669,817	671,659	676,806	604,000	530,000	2,500,000	9
Phoenix	11,134	29,053	48,118	65,414	106,818	439,170	515,000	859,000[2]	23
Indianapolis	233,650	314,194	364,161	386,972	427,173	476,258	510,000	1,100,000	20
Denver	213,381	256,491	287,861	322,412	415,786	493,887	480,000	1,157,000	19

[1] In order of population, 1969
[2] July 1, 1967
[3] July 1, 1966
[4] April 1, 1968

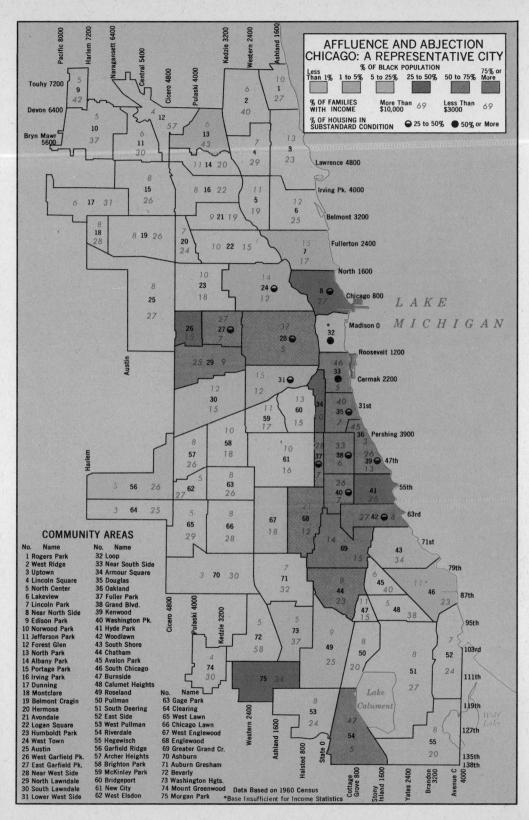

AFFLUENCE AND ABJECTION
CHICAGO: A REPRESENTATIVE CITY

Data Based on 1960 Census
*Base Insufficient for Income Statistics

Population—Metropolitan and Nonmetropolitan Residence, by Color: 1950 to 1968
[In thousands, except percent. As of April. Minus sign (−) denotes decrease]

residence and color	population		1968		average annual percent change	
	1950	1960	total	percent	1950–1960	1960–1968
Total	150,527	178,458	198,234	100.0	1.7	1.3
Standard metropolitan statistical areas	89,162	112,900	127,477	64.3	2.4	1.5
Central cities	52,190	57,790	58,373	29.4	1.0	0.1
Outside central cities	36,972	55,111	69,104	34.9	4.0	2.8
Nonmetropolitan areas	61,365	65,558	70,754	35.7	0.7	1.0
White	134,429	158,051	174,097	100.0	1.6	1.2
Standard metropolitan statistical areas	80,228	99,739	110,891	63.7	2.2	1.3
Central cities	45,322	47,463	45,622	26.2	0.5	−0.5
Outside central cities	34,906	52,276	65,269	37.5	4.0	2.8
Nonmetropolitan areas	54,201	58,312	63,206	36.3	0.7	1.0
Nonwhite	16,098	20,407	24,137	100.0	2.4	2.1
Standard metropolitan statistical areas	8,934	13,161	16,586	68.7	3.9	2.9
Central cities	6,868	10,327	12,752	52.8	4.1	2.6
Outside central cities	2,066	2,834	3,835	15.9	3.2	3.8
Nonmetropolitan areas	7,164	7,246	7,550	31.3	0.1	0.5
Negro	14,972	18,793	22,056	100.0	2.3	2.0
Standard metropolitan statistical areas	8,325	12,168	15,128	68.6	3.8	2.7
Central cities	6,440	9,687	11,907	54.0	4.1	2.6
Outside central cities	1,885	2,481	3,221	14.6	2.7	3.3
Nonmetropolitan areas	6,647	6,625	6,928	31.4	(Z)	0.6

Z Less than 0.05 percent.

Negro Population

year	number (1,000s)	percent	city[3]	1970 projections number	percent
1790	757	19.3	New York	1,500,000	19
1800	1,002	18.9	Chicago	1,150,000	32
1810	1,378	19.0	Los Angeles	700,000	23
1820	1,772	18.4	Philadelphia	700,000	32
1830	2,329	18.1	Detroit	800,000	47
1840	2,874	16.8	Houston	310,000	27
1850	3,639	15.7	Baltimore	432,000	47
1860	4,442	14.1	Dallas	200,000	25
1870	4,880	12.7	Washington, D.C.	574,000	68
1880	6,581	13.1	Cleveland	305,000	38
1890	7,489	11.9	Milwaukee	146,000	18
1900	8,834	11.6	San Francisco	126,000	17
1910	9,828	10.7	San Antonio	72,000	10
1920	10,463	9.9	St. Louis	320,000	46
1930	11,891	9.7	New Orleans	303,000	45
1940	12,866	9.8	San Diego	72,000	10
1950[1]	15,045	9.9	Boston	85,000	13
1960	18,872	10.5	Kansas City, Mo.	120,000	24
1968[2]	22,229	11.1	Seattle	56,000	9
			Memphis	226,000	39
			Columbus	167,000	32
			Pittsburgh	126,000	21
			Phoenix	60,000	10
			Indianapolis	145,000	29
			Denver	51,000	10

[1]Includes Alaska and Hawaii after 1950.
[2]Estimate as of July 1.
[3]In order of metropolitan area population, 1969.

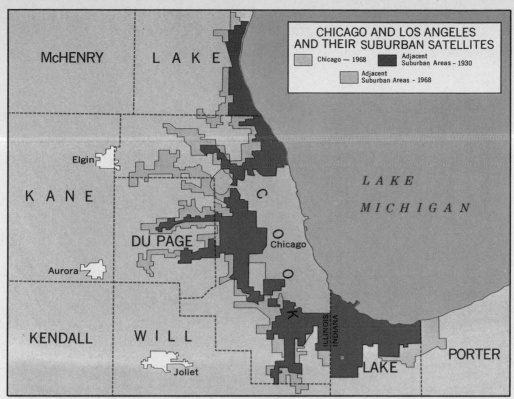

CHICAGO AND LOS ANGELES AND THEIR SUBURBAN SATELLITES

- Chicago — 1968
- Adjacent Suburban Areas - 1968
- Adjacent Suburban Areas - 1930

McHENRY

L A K E

Elgin

K A N E

DU PAGE

Aurora

Chicago

KENDALL

W I L L

Joliet

ILLINOIS
INDIANA

LAKE

PORTER

LAKE MICHIGAN

C O O K

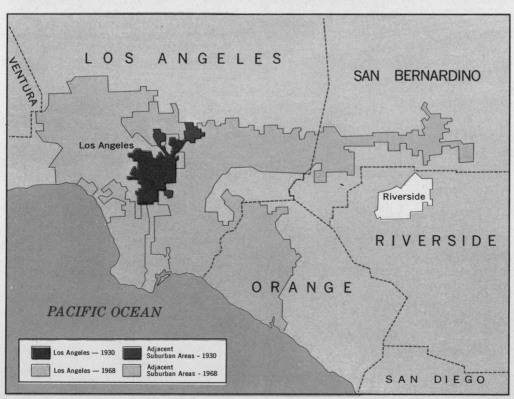

VENTURA

L O S   A N G E L E S

SAN   BERNARDINO

Los Angeles

Riverside

R I V E R S I D E

O R A N G E

PACIFIC OCEAN

- Los Angeles — 1930
- Los Angeles — 1968
- Adjacent Suburban Areas - 1930
- Adjacent Suburban Areas - 1968

SAN   DIEGO

763

Largest Cities by Area

city	area in sq. mi.
Jacksonville*	827
Oklahoma City	648
Los Angeles	463
Houston	453
New York	320
Kansas City, Mo.	316
San Diego	310
Dallas	295
Phoenix	248
Chicago	224
Fort Worth	200
New Orleans	200
San Antonio	183
Memphis	180
Detroit	139
Atlanta	131
Philadelphia	129
Columbus	116
Seattle	99
Denver	98
Milwaukee	97

*On October 1, 1968, Jacksonville, Fla., city proper became coextensive with Duval County (827 sq. mi.).

Housing development adjacent to a superhighway

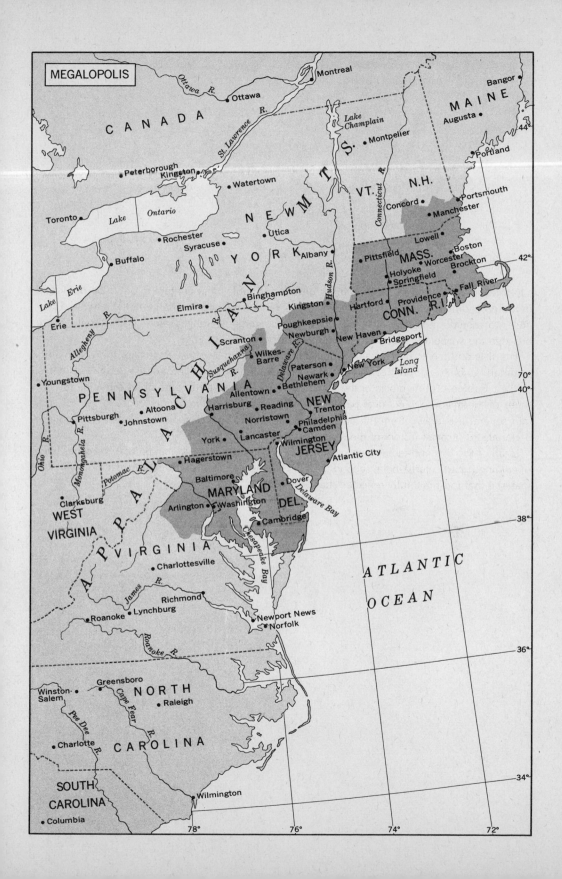

MEGALOPOLIS

15. ADDITIONAL INFORMATION

On the following pages are a number of lists and tables that contain information not found in the preceding sections of Part II. The various items have been chosen to fulfill a twofold purpose: to provide in readily available form much commonly sought reference material, and to broaden the scope and usefulness of the work as a whole.

The lists and tables may be said to fall into two main categories. Pages 767 – 778 contain a summary guide to the political history of the United States, in the form of lists of the Presidents, of their Cabinets, of members of the Supreme Court, and so forth; and tables outlining the fortunes of the major U.S. political parties since the founding of the nation. Pages 779 – 792 contain several lists drawn from the area of popular culture, which together provide some of the materials for a social history of the country.

In all of the lists and tables here presented, a fundamentally historical point of view has been maintained; particularly in the second category, items were chosen from the wealth of available material that most faithfully reflected that principle.

Presidential Elections 1789–1968[1]

Year	Presidential candidates	Political parties	Electoral votes	Popular votes[2]
1789	**George Washington**	(No formally	69[3]	
	John Adams	organized	34	
	John Jay	parties)	9	
	R. H. Harrison		6	
	John Rutledge		6	
	John Hancock		4	
	George Clinton		3	
	Samuel Huntington		2	
	John Milton		2	
	James Armstrong		1	
	Benjamin Lincoln		1	
	Edward Telfair		1	
	(Not voted)		12	
1792	**George Washington**	Federalist	132	
	John Adams	Federalist	77	
	George Clinton	Democratic-Republican	50	
	Thomas Jefferson		4	
	Aaron Burr		1	
1796	**John Adams**	Federalist	71	
	Thomas Jefferson	Democratic-Republican	68	
	Thomas Pinckney	Federalist	59	
	Aaron Burr	Antifederalist	30	
	Samuel Adams	Democratic-Republican	15	
	Oliver Ellsworth	Federalist	11	
	George Clinton	Democratic-Republican	7	
	John Jay	Independent-Federalist	5	
	James Iredell	Federalist	3	
	George Washington	Federalist	2	
	John Henry	Independent	2	
	S. Johnston	Independent-Federalist	2	
	C. C. Pinckney	Independent-Federalist	1	
1800	**Thomas Jefferson**	Democratic-Republican	73[4]	
	Aaron Burr	Democratic-Republican	73	
	John Adams	Federalist	65	
	C. C. Pinckney	Federalist	64	
	John Jay	Federalist	1	
1804	**Thomas Jefferson**	Democratic-Republican	162	
	C. C. Pinckney	Federalist	14	
1808	**James Madison**	Democratic-Republican	122	
	C. C. Pinckney	Federalist	47	
	George Clinton	Independent-Republican	6	
	(Not voted)		1	
1812	**James Madison**	Democratic-Republican	128	
	De Witt Clinton	Fusion	89	
	(Not voted)		1	
1816	**James Monroe**	Republican	183	
	Rufus King	Federalist	34	
	(Not voted)		4	
1820	**James Monroe**	Republican	231	
	John Q. Adams	Independent-Republican	1	
	(Not voted)		3	
1824	**John Q. Adams**	No distinct	84[5]	108,740
	Andrew Jackson	party	99	153,544
	Henry Clay	designations	37	47,136
	W. H. Crawford		41	46,618

[1]Minor candidates polling less than 10,000 popular votes are excluded.
[2]Electors were chosen by legislatures in many states, not by popular vote, in early elections.
[3]In this election, and in others until 1804, each elector voted for two men without indicating which was to be President and which Vice President. Because the two houses of the New York legislature could not agree on electors the state did not cast its electoral vote. North Carolina and Rhode Island had not yet ratified the Constitution.
[4]As both Jefferson and Burr received the same number of electoral votes the decision was refered to the House of Representatives. The 12th Amendment (1804) provided that electors cast separate ballots for President and Vice President.
[5]As no candidate received a majority of the electoral votes the decision was made by the House of Representatives.

Year	Presidential candidates	Political parties	Electoral votes	Popular votes
1828	**Andrew Jackson**	Democratic	178	647,286
	John Q. Adams	National Republican	83	508,064
1832	**Andrew Jackson**	Democratic	219	687,502
	Henry Clay	National Republican	49	530,189
	William Wirt	Anti-Masonic	7	
	John Floyd	Nullifiers	11	
	(Not voted)		2	
1836	**Martin Van Buren**	Democratic	170	765,483
	William H. Harrison	Whig	73	
	Hugh L. White	Whig	26	739,795[6]
	Daniel Webster	Whig	14	
	W. P. Mangum	Anti-Jackson	11	
1840	**William H. Harrison**	Whig	234	1,274,624
	Martin Van Buren	Democratic	60	1,127,781
1844	**James K. Polk**	Democratic	170	1,338,464
	Henry Clay	Whig	105	1,300,097
	James G. Birney	Liberty		62,300
1848	**Zachary Taylor**	Whig	163	1,360,967
	Lewis Cass	Democratic	127	1,222,342
	Martin Van Buren	Free Soil		291,263
1852	**Franklin Pierce**	Democratic	254	1,601,117
	Winfield Scott	Whig	42	1,385,453
	John P. Hale	Free Soil		155,825
1856	**James Buchanan**	Democratic	174	1,832,955
	John C. Frémont	Republican	114	1,339,932
	Millard Fillmore	American	8	871,731
1860	**Abraham Lincoln**	Republican	180	1,865,593
	J. C. Breckinridge	Democratic(S)	72	848,356
	Stephen A. Douglas	Democratic	12	1,382,713
	John Bell	Constitutional Union	39	592,906
1864	**Abraham Lincoln**	Unionist	212	2,206,938
	George B. McClellan	Democratic	21	1,803,787
	(Not voted)		81	
1868	**Ulysses S. Grant**	Republican	214	3,013,421
	Horatio Seymour	Democratic	80	2,706,829
	(Not voted)		23	
1872	**Ulysses S. Grant**	Republican	286	3,596,745
	Horace Greeley[7]	Democratic		2,843,446
	Charles O'Connor	Straight Democratic		29,489
	Thomas A. Hendricks	Independent-Democratic	42	
	B. Gratz Brown	Democratic	18	
	Charles J. Jenkins	Democratic	2	
	David Davis	Democratic	1	
	(Not voted)		17	
1876	**Rutherford B. Hayes**	Republican	185	4,036,572
	Samuel J. Tilden	Democratic	184	4,284,020
	Peter Cooper	Greenback		81,737
1880	**James A. Garfield**	Republican	214	4,453,295
	Winfield S. Hancock	Democratic	155	4,414,082
	James B. Weaver	Greenback-Labor		308,578
	Neal Dow	Prohibition		10,305
1884	**Grover Cleveland**	Democratic	219	4,879,507
	James G. Blaine	Republican	182	4,850,293
	Benjamin F. Butler	Greenback-Labor		175,370
	John P. St. John	Prohibition		150,369
1888	**Benjamin Harrison**	Republican	233	5,447,129
	Grover Cleveland	Democratic	168	5,537,857
	Clinton B. Fisk	Prohibition		249,506
	Anson J. Streeter	Union Labor		146,935
1892	**Grover Cleveland**	Democratic	277	5,555,426
	Benjamin Harrison	Republican	145	5,182,690
	James B. Weaver	People's	22	1,029,846
	John Bidwell	Prohibition		264,133
	Simon Wing	Socialist Labor		21,164

[6]Whig tickets were pledged to various candidates in various states.
[7]Greeley died shortly after the election in November. Three electors pledged to him cast their votes for him, but they were not counted; the others cast their votes for the other candidates listed.

Year	Presidential candidates	Political parties	Electoral votes	Popular votes
1896	**William McKinley**	Republican	271	7,102,246
	William J. Bryan	Democratic[8]	176	6,492,559
	John M. Palmer	National Democratic		133,148
	Joshua Levering	Prohibition		132,007
	Charles H. Matchett	Socialist Labor		36,274
	Charles E. Bentley	Nationalist		13,969
1900	**William McKinley**	Republican	292	7,218,491
	William J. Bryan	Democratic[8]	155	6,356,734
	John C. Wooley	Prohibition		208,914
	Eugene V. Debs	Socialist		87,814
	Wharton Barker	People's		50,373
	J. F. Malloney	Socialist Labor		39,739
1904	**Theodore Roosevelt**	Republican	336	7,628,461
	Alton B. Parker	Democratic	140	5,084,223
	Eugene V. Debs	Socialist		402,283
	Silas C. Swallow	Prohibition		258,536
	Thomas E. Watson	People's		117,183
	Charles H. Corregan	Socialist Labor		31,249
1908	**William H. Taft**	Republican	321	7,675,320
	William J. Bryan	Democratic	162	6,412,294
	Eugene V. Debs	Socialist		420,793
	Eugene W. Chafin	Prohibition		253,840
	Thomas L. Hisgen	Independence		82,872
	Thomas E. Watson	People's		29,100
	August Gillhaus	Socialist Labor		14,021
1912	**Woodrow Wilson**	Democratic	435	6,296,547
	Theodore Roosevelt	Progressive	88	4,118,571
	William H. Taft	Republican	8	3,486,720
	Eugene V. Debs	Socialist		900,672
	Eugene W. Chafin	Prohibition		206,275
	Arthur E. Reimer	Socialist Labor		28,750
1916	**Woodrow Wilson**	Democratic	277	9,127,695
	Charles E. Hughes	Republican	254	8,533,507
	A. L. Benson	Socialist		585,113
	J. Frank Hanly	Prohibition		220,506
	Arthur E. Reimer	Socialist Labor		13,403
1920	**Warren G. Harding**	Republican	404	16,143,407
	James M. Cox	Democratic	127	9,130,328
	Eugene V. Debs	Socialist		919,799
	P. P. Christensen	Farmer-Labor		265,411
	Aaron S. Watkins	Prohibition		189,408
	James E. Ferguson	American		48,000
	W. W. Cox	Socialist Labor		31,715
1924	**Calvin Coolidge**	Republican	382	15,718,211
	John W. Davis	Democratic	136	8,385,283
	Robert M. LaFollette	Progressive	13	4,831,289
	Herman P. Faris	Prohibition		57,520
	Frank T. Johns	Socialist Labor		36,428
	William Z. Foster	Workers		36,386
	Gilbert O. Nations	American		23,967
1928	**Herbert C. Hoover**	Republican	444	21,391,993
	Alfred E. Smith	Democratic	87	15,016,169
	Norman Thomas	Socialist		267,835
	Verne L. Reynolds	Socialist Labor		21,603
	William Z. Foster	Workers		21,181
	William F. Varney	Prohibition		20,106
1932	**Franklin D. Roosevelt**	Democratic	472	22,809,638
	Herbert C. Hoover	Republican	59	15,758,901
	Norman Thomas	Socialist		881,951
	William Z. Foster	Communist		102,785
	William D. Upshaw	Prohibition		81,869
	Verne L. Reynolds	Socialist Labor		33,276
	William H. Harvey	Liberty		53,425

[8]Includes a variety of joint tickets with People's Party electors committed to Bryan.

Year	Presidential candidates	Political parties	Electoral votes	Popular votes
1936	**Franklin D. Roosevelt**	Democratic	523	27,752,869
	Alfred M. Landon	Republican	8	16,674,665
	William Lemke	Union		882,479
	Norman Thomas	Socialist		187,720
	Earl Browder	Communist		80,159
	D. Leigh Colvin	Prohibition		37,847
	John W. Aiken	Socialist Labor		12,777
1940	**Franklin D. Roosevelt**	Democratic	449	27,307,819
	Wendell L. Willkie	Republican	82	22,321,018
	Norman Thomas	Socialist		99,557
	Roger Q. Babson	Prohibition		57,812
	Earl Browder	Communist		46,251
	John W. Aiken	Socialist Labor		14,892
1944	**Franklin D. Roosevelt**	Democratic	432	25,606,585
	Thomas E. Dewey	Republican	99	22,014,745
	Norman Thomas	Socialist		80,518
	Claude A. Watson	Prohibition		74,758
	Edward A. Teichert	Socialist Labor		45,336
1948	**Harry S. Truman**	Democratic	303	24,105,812
	Thomas E. Dewey	Republican	189	21,970,065
	Strom Thurmond	States' Rights	39	1,169,063
	Henry Wallace	Progressive		1,157,172
	Norman Thomas	Socialist		139,414
	Claude A. Watson	Prohibition		103,224
	Edward A. Teichert	Socialist Labor		29,244
	Farrell Dobbs	Socialist Workers		13,613
1952	**Dwight D. Eisenhower**	Republican	442	33,936,234
	Adlai E. Stevenson	Democratic	89	27,314,992
	Vincent Hallinan	Progressive		140,023
	Stuart Hamblen	Prohibition		72,949
	Eric Hass	Socialist Labor		30,267
	Darlington Hoopes	Socialist		20,203
	Douglas MacArthur	Constitution		17,205
	Farrell Dobbs	Socialist Workers		10,312
1956	**Dwight D. Eisenhower**	Republican	457	35,590,472
	Adlai E. Stevenson	Democratic	73	26,022,752
	Walter Jones	(not a candidate)	1	
	T. Coleman Andrews	States' Rights		107,929
	Eric Hass	Socialist Labor		44,300
	Enoch A. Holtwick	Prohibition		41,937
1960	**John F. Kennedy**	Democratic	303	34,226,731
	Richard M. Nixon	Republican	· 219	34,108,157
	Harry F. Byrd	(not a candidate)	15	
	Eric Hass	Socialist Labor		47,522
	R. L. Decker	Prohibition		46,203
	Orval Faubus	National States' Rights		44,977
	Farrell Dobbs	Socialist Workers		40,165
	Charles L. Sullivan	Constitution		18,162
1964	**Lyndon B. Johnson**	Democratic	486	43,130,000
	Barry M. Goldwater	Republican	52	27,178,000
	Eric Hass	Socialist Labor		44,697
	Clifton DeBerry	Socialist Workers		32,327
	E. Harold Munn	Prohibition		22,962
1968	**Richard M. Nixon**	Republican	301	31,770,237
	Hubert H. Humphrey	Democratic	191	31,270,533
	George C. Wallace	Amer. Independent	46	9,897,141
	Henning Blomen	Socialist Labor		52,588
	Dick Gregory	New Party		47,097
	Fred Halstead	Socialist Workers		41,300
	Eldridge Cleaver	Peace and Freedom		36,385
	Eugene J. McCarthy			25,858
	E. Harold Munn	Prohibition		14,519

Cabinet Officers 1789–1970

Secretaries of State

President	Secretary	Year
Washington	John Jay[1]	
	Thomas Jefferson	1789
	Edmund Randolph	1794
	Timothy Pickering	1795
J. Adams	Timothy Pickering	
	John Marshall	1800
Jefferson	James Madison	1801
Madison	Robert Smith	1809
	James Monroe	1811
Monroe	John Q. Adams	1817
J. Q. Adams	Henry Clay	1825
Jackson	Martin Van Buren	1829
	Edward Livingston	1831
	Louis McLane	1833
	John Forsyth	1834
Van Buren	John Forsyth	
W. H. Harrison	Daniel Webster	1841
Tyler	Daniel Webster	
	Hugh S. Legaré	1843
	Abel P. Upshur	1843
	John C. Calhoun	1844
Polk	James Buchanan	1845
Taylor	John M. Clayton	1849
Fillmore	Daniel Webster	1850
	Edward Everett	1852
Pierce	William L. Marcy	1853
Buchanan	Lewis Cass	1857
	Jeremiah S. Black	1860
Lincoln	William H. Seward	1861
A. Johnson	William H. Seward	
Grant	Elihu B. Washburne	1869
	Hamilton Fish	1869
Hayes	William M. Evarts	1877
Garfield	James G. Blaine	1881
Arthur	James G. Blaine	
	F. T. Frelinghuysen	1881
Cleveland	Thomas F. Bayard	1885
B. Harrison	James G. Blaine	1889
	John W. Foster	1892
Cleveland	Walter Q. Gresham	1893
	Richard Olney	1895
McKinley	John Sherman	1897
	William R. Day	1898
	John Hay	1898
T. Roosevelt	John Hay	
	Elihu Root	1905
	Robert Bacon	1909
Taft	Philander C. Knox	1909
Wilson	William J. Bryan	1913
	Robert Lansing	1915
	Bainbridge Colby	1920
Harding	Charles E. Hughes	1921
Coolidge	Charles E. Hughes	
	Frank B. Kellogg	1925
Hoover	Henry L. Stimson	1929
F. D. Roosevelt	Cordell Hull	1933
	E. R. Stettinius, Jr.	1944
Truman	E. R. Stettinius, Jr.	
	James F. Byrnes	1945
	George C. Marshall	1947
	Dean G. Acheson	1949
Eisenhower	John Foster Dulles	1953
	Christian A. Herter	1959
Kennedy	Dean Rusk	1961
L. B. Johnson	Dean Rusk	
Nixon	William P. Rogers	1969

Secretaries of War

President	Secretary	Year
Washington	Henry Knox	1789
	Timothy Pickering	1795
	James McHenry	1796
J. Adams	James McHenry	
	Samuel Dexter	1800
Jefferson	Henry Dearborn	1801
Madison	William Eustis	1809
	John Armstrong	1813
	James Monroe	1814
	W. H. Crawford	1815
Monroe	J. Graham (ad int.)	1817
	John C. Calhoun	1817
J. Q. Adams	James Barbour	1825
	Peter B. Porter	1828
Jackson	John H. Eaton	1829
	Lewis Cass	1831
	Benjamin F. Butler	1837
Van Buren	Joel R. Poinsett	1837
W. H. Harrison	John Bell	1841
Tyler	John C. Spencer	1841
	James M. Porter	1843
	William Wilkins	1844
Polk	William L. Marcy	1845
Taylor	G. W. Crawford	1849
Fillmore	Charles M. Conrad	1850
Pierce	Jefferson Davis	1853
Buchanan	John B. Floyd	1857
	Joseph Holt	1861
Lincoln	Simon Cameron	1861
	Edwin M. Stanton	1862
A. Johnson	U. S. Grant (ad int.)	1867
	John M. Schofield	1868
Grant	John A. Rawlins	1869
	William T. Sherman	1869
	William W. Belknap	1869
	Alphonso Taft	1876
	James D. Cameron	1876
Hayes	George W. McCrary	1877
	Alexander Ramsey	1879
Garfield	Robert T. Lincoln	1881
Arthur	Robert T. Lincoln	
Cleveland	William C. Endicott	1885
B. Harrison	Redfield Proctor	1889
	Stephen B. Elkins	1891
Cleveland	Daniel S. Lamont	1893
McKinley	Russell A. Alger	1897
	Elihu Root	1899
T. Roosevelt	Elihu Root	
	William H. Taft	1904
	Luke E. Wright	1908
Taft	Jacob M. Dickinson	1909
	Henry L. Stimson	1911
Wilson	Lindley K. Garrison	1913
	Newton D. Baker	1916
Harding	John W. Weeks	1921
Coolidge	John W. Weeks	
	Dwight F. Davis	1925
Hoover	James W. Good	1929
	Patrick J. Hurley	1929
F. D. Roosevelt	George H. Dern	1933
	Harry H. Woodring	1936
	Henry L. Stimson	1940
Truman	Henry L. Stimson	
	Robert P. Patterson	1945
	Kenneth C. Royall[2]	1947

[1.]John Jay was secretary for foreign affairs under the confederation, and continued to act, at the President's request, until Jefferson returned from Europe March 21, 1970.

[2.]After Sept. 1947 the secretary of defense represented the national military establishment.

Secretaries of the Treasury

President	Secretary	Year
Washington	Alexander Hamilton	1789
	Oliver Wolcott, Jr.	1795
J. Adams	Oliver Wolcott, Jr.	
	Samuel Dexter	1801
Jefferson	Samuel Dexter	
	Albert Gallatin	1801
Madison	Albert Gallatin	
	George W. Campbell	1814
	Alexander J. Dallas	1814
	W. H. Crawford	1816
Monroe	W. H. Crawford	
J. Q. Adams	Richard Rush	1825
Jackson	Samuel D. Ingham	1829
	Louis McLane	1831
	William J. Duane	1833
	Roger B. Taney	1833
	Levi Woodbury	1834
Van Buren	Levi Woodbury	
W. H. Harrison	Thomas Ewing	1841
Tyler	Thomas Ewing	
	Walter Forward	1841
	John C. Spencer	1843
	George M. Bibb	1844
Polk	Robert J. Walker	1845
Taylor	W. M. Meredith	1849
Fillmore	Thomas Corwin	1850
Pierce	James Guthrie	1853
Buchanan	Howell Cobb	1857
	Phillip F. Thomas	1860
	John A. Dix	1861
Lincoln	Salmon P. Chase	1861
	W. P. Fessenden	1864
	Hugh McCulloch	1865
A. Johnson	Hugh McCulloch	
Grant	George S. Boutwell	1869
	Wm. A. Richardson	1873
	B. H. Bristow	1874
	Lot M. Morrill	1876
Hayes	John Sherman	1877
Garfield	William Windom	1881
Arthur	William Windom	
	Charles J. Folger	1881
	Walter Q. Gresham	1884
	Hugh McCulloch	1884
Cleveland	Daniel Manning	1885
	Charles S. Fairchild	1887
B. Harrison	William Windom	1889
	Charles Foster	1891
Cleveland	John G. Carlisle	1893
McKinley	Lyman J. Gage	1897
T. Roosevelt	Lyman J. Gage	
	Leslie M. Shaw	1902
	George B. Cortelyou	1907
Taft	Franklin MacVeagh	1909
Wilson	William G. McAdoo	1913
	Carter Glass	1919
	David F. Houston	1920
Harding	Andrew W. Mellon	1921
Coolidge	Andrew W. Mellon	
Hoover	Andrew W. Mellon	
	Ogden L. Mills	1932
F. D. Roosevelt	W. H. Woodin	1933
	H. Morgenthau, Jr.	1934
Truman	H. Morgenthau, Jr.	
	F. M. Vinson	1945
	John W. Snyder	1946
Eisenhower	G. M. Humphrey	1953
	Robt. B. Anderson	1957
Kennedy	C. Douglas Dillon	1961
L. B. Johnson	C. Douglas Dillon	
	Henry H. Fowler	1965
Nixon	David M. Kennedy	1969

Postmasters General

President	Postmaster	Year
Washington	Samuel Osgood	1789
	Timothy Pickering	1791
	Joseph Habersham	1795
J. Adams	Joseph Habersham	
Jefferson	Joseph Habersham	
	Joseph Habersham	1801
Madison	Gideon Granger	
	Return J. Meigs, Jr.	1814
Monroe	Return J. Meigs, Jr.	
	John McLean	1823
J. Q. Adams	John McLean	
Jackson	William T. Barry	1829
	Amos Kendall	1835
Van Buren	Amos Kendall	
	John M. Niles	1840
W. H. Harrison	Francis Granger	1841
Tyler	Francis Granger	
	Charles A. Wickliffe	1841
Polk	Cave Johnson	1845
Taylor	Jacob Collamer	1849
Fillmore	Nathan K. Hall	1850
	Samuel D. Hubbard	1852
Pierce	James Campbell	1853
Buchanan	Aaron V. Brown	1857
	Joseph Holt	1859
	Horatio King	1861
Lincoln	Montgomery Blair	1861
	William Dennison	1864
A. Johnson	William Dennison	
	Alex. W. Randall	1866
Grant	John A. J. Creswell	1869
	James W. Marshall	1874
	Marshall Jewell	1874
	James N. Tyner	1876
Hayes	David McK. Key	1877
	Horace Maynard	1880
Garfield	Thomas L. James	1881
Arthur	Thomas L. James	
	Timothy O. Howe	1881
	Walter Q. Gresham	1883
	Frank Hatton	1884
Cleveland	William F. Vilas	1885
	Don M. Dickinson	1888
B. Harrison	John Wanamaker	1889
Cleveland	Wilson S. Bissel	1893
	William L. Wilson	1895
McKinley	James A. Gary	1897
	Charles E. Smith	1898
T. Roosevelt	Charles E. Smith	
	Henry C. Payne	1902
	Robert J. Wynne	1904
	George B. Cortelyou	1905
	G. von L. Meyer	1907
Taft	Frank H. Hitchcock	1909
Wilson	Albert S. Burleson	1913
Harding	Will H. Hays	1921
	Hubert Work	1922
	Harry S. New	1923
Coolidge	Harry S. New	
Hoover	Walter F. Brown	1929
F. D. Roosevelt	James A. Farley	1933
	Frank C. Walker	1940
Truman	Frank C. Walker	
	Robert E. Hannegan	1945
	Jesse M. Donaldson	1947
Eisenhower	A. E. Summerfield	1953
Kennedy	J. Edward Day	1961
	J. A. Gronouski	1963
L. B. Johnson	J. A. Gronouski	
	L. F. O'Brien	1965
	W. Marvin Watson	1968
Nixon	Winton M. Blount	1969

Attorneys General

President	Attorney General	Year
Washington	Edmund Randolph	1789
	William Bradford	1794
	Charles Lee	1795
J. Adams	Charles Lee	
Jefferson	Levi Lincoln	1801
	John Breckinridge	1805
	Caesar A. Rodney	1807
Madison	Caesar A. Rodney	
	William Pinkney	1811
	Richard Rush	1814
Monroe	Richard Rush	
	William Wirt	1817
J. Q. Adams	William Wirt	
Jackson	John McP. Berrien	1829
	Roger B. Taney	1831
	Benjamin F. Butler	1833
Van Buren	Benjamin F. Butler	
	Felix Grundy	1838
	Henry D. Gilpin	1840
W. H. Harrison	John J. Crittenden	1841
Tyler	John J. Crittenden	
	Hugh S. Legaré	1841
	John Nelson	1843
Polk	John Y. Mason	1845
	Nathan Clifford	1846
	Isaac Toucey	1848
Taylor	Reverdy Johnson	1849
Fillmore	John J. Crittenden	1850
Pierce	Caleb Cushing	1853
Buchanan	Jeremiah S. Black	1857
	Edwin M. Stanton	1860
Lincoln	Edward Bates	1861
	James Speed	1864
A. Johnson	James Speed	
	Henry Stanbery	1866
	William M. Evarts	1868
Grant	Ebenezer R. Hoar	1869
	Amos T. Akerman	1870
	George H. Williams	1871
	Edwards Pierrepont	1875
	Alphonso Taft	1876
Hayes	Charles Devens	1877
Garfield	Wayne MacVeagh	1881
Arthur	Wayne MacVeagh	
	Ben. H. Brewster	1881
Cleveland	A. H. Garland	1885
B. Harrison	William H. H. Miller	1889
Cleveland	Richard Olney	1893
	Judson Harmon	1895
McKinley	Joseph McKenna	1897
	John W. Griggs	1898
	Philander C. Knox	1901
T. Roosevelt	Philander C. Knox	
	William H. Moody	1904
	C. J. Bonaparte	1906
Taft	G. W. Wickersham	1909
Wilson	J. C. McReynolds	1913
	Thomas W. Gregory	1914
	A. M. Palmer	1919
Harding	H. M. Daugherty	1921
Coolidge	H. M. Daugherty	
	Harlan F. Stone	1924
	John G. Sargent	1925
Hoover	William D. Mitchell	1929
F. D. Roosevelt	Homer S. Cummings	1933
	Frank Murphy	1939
	Robert H. Jackson	1940
	Francis Biddle	1941
Truman	Francis Biddle	
	Thomas C. Clark	1945
	J. Howard McGrath	1949
	J. P. McGranery	1952
Eisenhower	H. Brownell, Jr.	1953
	William P. Rogers	1957
Kennedy	Robert Kennedy	1961
L. B. Johnson	Robert Kennedy	
	N. Katzenbach	1965
	Ramsey Clark	1967
Nixon	John N. Mitchell	1969

Secretaries of the Navy

President	Secretary of the Navy	Year
J. Adams	Benjamin Stoddert	1798
Jefferson	Benjamin Stoddert	
	Robert Smith	1802
Madison	Paul Hamilton	1809
	William Jones	1813
	B. W. Crowninshield	1815
Monroe	B. W. Crowninshield	
	Smith Thompson	1819
	Samuel L. Southard	1823
J. Q. Adams	Samuel L. Southard	
Jackson	John Branch	1829
	Levi Woodbury	1831
	Mahlon Dickerson	1834
Van Buren	Mahlon Dickerson	
	James K. Paulding	1838
W. H. Harrison	George E. Badger	1841
Tyler	George E. Badger	
	Abel P. Upshur	1841
	David Henshaw	1843
	Thomas W. Gilmer	1844
	John Y. Mason	1844
Polk	George Bancroft	1845
	John Y. Mason	1846
Taylor	William B. Preston	1849
Fillmore	William A. Graham	1850
	John P. Kennedy	1852
Pierce	James C. Dobbin	1853
Buchanan	Issac Toucey	1857
Lincoln	Gideon Welles	1861
A. Johnson	Gideon Welles	
Grant	Adolph E. Borie	1869
	George M. Robeson	1869
Hayes	R. W. Thompson	1877
	Nathan Goff, Jr.	1881
Garfield	William H. Hunt	1881
Arthur	William H. Hunt	
	William E. Chandler	1882
Cleveland	William C. Whitney	1885
B. Harrison	Benjamin F. Tracy	1889
Cleveland	Hilary A. Herbert	1893
McKinley	John D. Long	1897
T. Roosevelt	John D. Long	
	William H. Moody	1902
	Paul Morton	1904
	C. J. Bonaparte	1905
	Victor H. Metcalf	1906
	T. H. Newberry	1908
Taft	G. von L. Meyer	1909
Wilson	Josephus Daniels	1913
Harding	Edwin Denby	1921
Coolidge	Edwin Denby	
	Curtis D. Wilbur	1924
Hoover	Charles F. Adams	1929
F. D. Roosevelt	Claude A. Swanson	1933
	Charles Edison	1940
	Frank Knox	1940
	James V. Forrestal	1944
Truman	James V. Forrestal[2]	

2. After Sept. 1947 the secretary of defense represented the national military establishment.

Secretaries of the Interior

Taylor	Thomas Ewing	1849
Fillmore	T. M. T. McKennan	1850
	Alex. H. H. Stuart	1850
Pierce	Robert McClelland	1853
Buchanan	Jacob Thompson	1857
Lincoln	Caleb B. Smith	1861
	John P. Usher	1863
A. Johnson	John P. Usher	
	James Harlan	1865
	Orville H. Browning	1866
Grant	Jacob D. Cox	1869
	Columbus Delano	1870
	Zachariah Chandler	1875
Hayes	Carl Schurz	1877
Garfield	Samuel J. Kirkwood	1881
Arthur	Samuel J. Kirkwood	
	Henry M. Teller	1882
Cleveland	Lucius Q. C. Lamar	1885
	William F. Vilas	1888
B. Harrison	John W. Noble	1889
Cleveland	Hoke Smith	1893
	David R. Francis	1896
McKinley	Cornelius N. Bliss	1897
	Ethan A. Hitchcock	1898
T. Roosevelt	Ethan A. Hitchcock	
	James R. Garfield	1907
Taft	Richard A. Ballinger	1909
	Walter L. Fisher	1911
Wilson	Franklin K. Lane	1913
	John B. Payne	1920
Harding	Albert B. Fall	1921
	Hubert Work	1923
Coolidge	Hubert Work	
	Roy O. West	1928
Hoover	Ray Lyman Wilbur	1929
F. D. Roosevelt	Harold L. Ickes	1933
Truman	Harold L. Ickes	
	Julius A. Krug	1946
	Oscar L. Chapman	1949
Eisenhower	Douglas McKay	1953
	Fred A. Seaton	1956
Kennedy	Stewart L. Udall	1961
L. B. Johnson	Stewart L. Udall	
Nixon	Walter J. Hickel	1969

Secretaries of Agriculture

Cleveland	Norman J. Colman	1889
B. Harrison	Jeremiah M. Rusk	1889
Cleveland	J. Sterling Morton	1893
McKinley	James Wilson	1897
T. Roosevelt	James Wilson	
Taft	James Wilson	
Wilson	David F. Houston	1913
	Edw. T. Meredith	1920
Harding	Henry C. Wallace	1921
Coolidge	Howard M. Gore	1924
	W. M. Jardine	1925
Hoover	Arthur M. Hyde	1929
F. D. Roosevelt	Henry A. Wallace	1933
	Claude R. Wickard	1940
Truman	Claude R. Wickard	
	Clinton P. Anderson	1945
	Charles F. Brannan	1948
Eisenhower	Ezra Taft Benson	1953
Kennedy	Orville Freeman	1961
L. B. Johnson	Orville Freeman	
Nixon	Clifford M. Hardin	1969

Secretaries of Commerce and Labor

T. Roosevelt	George B. Cortelyou	1903
	Victor H. Metcalf	1904
	Oscar S. Straus	1906
Taft	Charles Nagel	1909

Secretaries of Commerce

Wilson	William C. Redfield	1913
	Josh. W. Alexander	1919
Harding	Herbert C. Hoover	1921
Coolidge	Herbert C. Hoover	
	William F. Whiting	1928
Hoover	Robert P. Lamont	1929
	Roy D. Chapin	1932
F. D. Roosevelt	Daniel C. Roper	1933
	Harry L. Hopkins	1938
	Jesse H. Jones	1940
	Henry A. Wallace	1945
Truman	Henry A. Wallace	
	W. A. Harriman	1946
	Charles Sawyer	1948
Eisenhower	Sinclair Weeks	1953
	Lewis L. Strauss[3]	1958
	F. H. Mueller	1959
Kennedy	Luther Hodges	1961
L. B. Johnson	Luther Hodges	
	John T. Connor	1964
	Alexander Trowbridge	1967
	Cyrus R. Smith	1968
Nixon	Maurice H. Stans	1969

Secretaries of Labor

Wilson	William B. Wilson	1913
Harding	James J. Davis	1921
Coolidge	James J. Davis	
Hoover	James J. Davis	
	William N. Doak	1930
F. D. Roosevelt	Frances Perkins	1933
Truman	Frances Perkins	
	L. B. Schwellenbach	1945
	Maurice J. Tobin	1948
Eisenhower	Martin P. Durkin	1953
	James P. Mitchell	1953
Kennedy	Arthur Goldberg	1961
	W. W. Wirtz	1962
L. B. Johnson	W. W. Wirtz	
Nixon	George P. Shultz	1969
	James Hodgson	1970

Secretaries of Defense

Truman	James V. Forrestal	1947
	Louis A. Johnson	1949
	George C. Marshall	1950
	Robert A. Lovett	1951
Eisenhower	Charles E. Wilson	1953
	Neil H. McElroy	1957
	T. S. Gates, Jr.	1959
Kennedy	R. S. McNamara	1961
L. B. Johnson	R. S. McNamara	
	Clark M. Clifford	1968
Nixon	Melvin R. Laird	1969

[3.]Recess appointment, Oct. 1958 to June 1959. Senate failed to confirm appointment.

Secretaries of Health, Education, and Welfare

Eisenhower	Oveta Culp Hobby	1953
	Marion B. Folsom	1955
	Arthur S. Flemming	1958
Kennedy	Abraham Ribicoff	1961
	A. J. Celebrezze	1962
L. B. Johnson	A. J. Celebrezze	
	John W. Gardner	1965
	Wilbur J. Cohen	1968
Nixon	Robert H. Finch	1969
	Elliot Richardson	1970

Secretaries of Housing and Urban Development

L. B. Johnson	Robert C. Weaver	1966
Nixon	George Romney	1969

Secretaries of Transportation

L. B. Johnson	Allen Boyd	1967
Nixon	John A. Volpe	1969

Composition of Congress 1789–1971

(Ad—administration; AM—Anti-Masonic; C—coalition; D—Democratic; DR—Democratic-Republican; Fed—Federalist; J—Jacksonian; NR—National Republican; Op—opposition; R—Republican; U—Unionist; W—Whig)   *Composition at opening of first session.

Congress	Term	Speaker of the House	House* Major party	House* Principal minority party	House* Other (exc. vac.)	Senate* Major party	Senate* Principal minority party	Senate* Other (exc. vac.)
1st	1789–91	F. A. Muhlenberg	Ad-38	Op-26		Ad-17	Op-9	
2nd	1791–93	Jonathan Trumbull	Fed-37	DR-33		Fed-16	DR-13	
3rd	1793–95	F. A. Muhlenberg	DR-57	Fed-48		Fed-17	DR-13	
4th	1795–97	Jonathan Dayton	Fed-54	DR-52		Fed-19	DR-13	
5th	1797–99	Jonathan Dayton	Fed-58	DR-48		Fed-20	DR-12	
6th	1799–1801	Theodore Sedgwick	Fed-64	DR-42		Fed-19	DR-13	
7th	1801–03	Nathaniel Macon	DR-69	Fed-36		DR-18	Fed-13	
8th	1803–05	Nathaniel Macon	DR-102	Fed-39		DR-25	Fed-9	
9th	1805–07	Nathaniel Macon	DR-116	Fed-25		DR-27	Fed-7	
10th	1807–09	Joseph B. Varnum	DR-118	Fed-24		DR-28	Fed-6	
11th	1809–11	Joseph B. Varnum	DR-94	Fed-48		DR-28	Fed-6	
12th	1811–13	Henry Clay	DR-108	Fed-36		DR-30	Fed-6	
13th	1813–15	H. Clay and Langdon Cheves	DR-112	Fed-68		DR-27	Fed-9	
14th	1815–17	Henry Clay	DR-117	Fed-65		DR-25	Fed-11	
15th	1817–19	Henry Clay	DR-141	Fed-42		DR-34	Fed-10	
16th	1819–21	H. Clay and John W. Taylor	DR-156	Fed-27		DR-35	Fed-7	
17th	1821–23	Philip P. Barbour	DR-158	Fed-25		DR-44	Fed-4	
18th	1823–25	Henry Clay	DR-187	Fed-26		DR-44	Fed-4	
19th	1825–27	John W. Taylor	Ad-105	J-97		Ad-26	J-20	
20th	1827–29	Andrew Stevenson	J-119	Ad-94		J-28	Ad-20	
21st	1829–31	Andrew Stevenson	D-139	NR-74		D-26	NR-22	
22nd	1831–33	Andrew Stevenson	D-141	NR-58	14	D-25	NR-21	2
23rd	1833–35	A. Stevenson and John Bell	D-147	AM-53	60	D-20	NR-20	8
24th	1835–37	James K. Polk	D-145	W-98		D-27	W-25	
25th	1837–39	James K. Polk	D-108	W-107	24	D-30	W-18	4
26th	1839–41	R. M. T. Hunter	D-124	W-118		D-28	W-22	
27th	1841–43	John White	W-133	D-102	6	W-28	D-22	2
28th	1843–45	John W. Jones	D-142	W-79	1	W-28	D-25	1
29th	1845–47	John W. Davis	D-143	W-77	6	D-31	W-25	
30th	1847–49	Robert C. Winthrop	W-115	D-108	4	D-36	W-21	1
31st	1849–51	Howell Cobb	D-112	W-109	9	D-35	W-25	2
32nd	1851–53	Linn Boyd	D-140	W-88	5	D-35	W-24	3
33rd	1853–55	Linn Boyd	D-159	W-71	4	D-38	W-22	2
34th	1855–57	Nathaniel P. Banks	R-108	D-83	43	D-40	R-15	5
35th	1857–59	James L. Orr	D-118	R-92	26	D-36	R-20	8
36th	1859–61	William Pennington	R-114	D-92	31	D-36	R-26	4
37th	1861–63	Galusha A. Grow	R-105	D-43	30	R-31	D-10	8
38th	1863–65	Schuyler Colfax	R-102	D-75	9	R-36	D-9	5
39th	1865–67	Schuyler Colfax	U-149	D-42		U-42	D-10	
40th	1867–69	Schuyler Colfax	R-143	D-49		R-42	D-11	
41st	1869–71	James G. Blaine	R-149	D-63		R-56	D-11	
42nd	1871–73	James G. Blaine	R-134	D-104	5	R-52	D-17	5
43rd	1873–75	James G. Blaine	R-194	D-92	14	R-49	D-19	5

Congress	Term	Speaker of the House	House*			Senate*		
			Major party	Principal minority party	Other (exc. vac.)	Major party	Principal minority party	Other (exc. vac.)
44th	1875–77	M. C. Kerr & S. J. Randall	D-169	R-109	14	R-45	D-29	2
45th	1877–79	Samuel J. Randall	D-153	R-140		R-39	D-36	1
46th	1879–81	Samuel J. Randall	D-149	R-130	14	D-42	R-33	1
47th	1881–83	Joseph W. Keifer	R-147	D-135	11	R-37	D-37	1
48th	1883–85	John G. Carlisle	D-197	R-118	10	R-38	D-36	2
49th	1885–87	John G. Carlisle	D-183	R-140	2	R-43	D-34	
50th	1887–89	John G. Carlisle	D-169	R-152	4	R-39	D-37	
51st	1889–91	Thomas B. Reed	R-166	D-159		R-39	D-37	
52nd	1891–93	Charles F. Crisp	D-235	R-88	9	R-47	D-39	2
53rd	1893–95	Charles F. Crisp	D-218	R-127	11	D-44	R-38	3
54th	1895–97	Thomas B. Reed	R-244	D-105	7	R-43	D-39	6
55th	1897–99	Thomas B. Reed	R-204	D-113	40	R-47	D-34	7
56th	1899–1901	David B. Henderson	R-185	D-163	9	R-53	D-26	8
57th	1901–03	David B. Henderson	R-197	D-151	9	R-55	D-31	4
58th	1903–05	Joseph G. Cannon	R-208	D-178		R-57	D-33	
59th	1905–07	Joseph G. Cannon	R-250	D-136		R-57	D-33	
60th	1907–09	Joseph G. Cannon	R-222	D-164		R-61	D-31	
61st	1909–11	Joseph G. Cannon	R-219	D-172		R-61	D-32	
62nd	1911–13	Champ Clark	D-228	R-161	1	R-51	D-41	
63rd	1913–15	Champ Clark	D-291	R-127	17	D-51	R-44	1
64th	1915–17	Champ Clark	D-230	R-196	9	D-56	R-40	
65th	1917–19	Champ Clark	D-216	R-210	6	D-53	R-42	
66th	1919–21	Frederick H. Gillett	R-240	D-190	3	R-49	D-47	
67th	1921–23	Frederick H. Gillett	R-301	D-131	1	R-59	D-37	
68th	1923–25	Frederick H. Gillett	R-225	D-205	5	R-51	D-43	2
69th	1925–27	Nicholas Longworth	R-247	D-183	4	R-56	D-39	1
70th	1927–29	Nicholas Longworth	R-237	D-195	3	R-49	D-46	1
71st	1929–31	Nicholas Longworth	R-267	D-167	1	R-56	D-39	1
72nd	1931–33	John N. Garner	D-220	R-214	1	R-48	D-47	1
73rd	1933–35	H. T. Rainey & J. W. Byrns	D-310	R-117	5	D-60	R-35	1
74th	1935–37	J. W. Byrns and William B. Bankhead	D-319	R-103	10	D-69	R-25	2
75th	1937–39	William B. Bankhead	D-331	R-89	13	D-76	R-16	4
76th	1939–41	W. B. Bankhead and Sam Rayburn	D-261	R-164	4	D-69	R-23	4
77th	1941–43	Sam Rayburn	D-268	R-162	5	D-66	R-28	2
78th	1943–45	Sam Rayburn	D-218	R-208	4	D-58	R-37	1
79th	1945–47	Sam Rayburn	D-242	R-190	2	D-56	R-38	1
80th	1947–49	Joseph W. Martin, Jr.	R-245	D-188	1	R-51	D-45	
81st	1949–51	Sam Rayburn	D-263	R-171	1	D-54	R-42	
82nd	1951–53	Sam Rayburn	D-234	R-199	1	D-49	R-47	
83rd	1953–55	Joseph W. Martin, Jr.	R-221	D-211	1	R-48	D-47	1
84th	1955–57	Sam Rayburn	D-232	R-203		D-48	R-47	1
85th	1957–59	Sam Rayburn	D-233	R-200		D-49	R-47	
86th	1959–61	Sam Rayburn	D-283	R-153		D-64	R-34	
87th	1961–63	S. Rayburn & J. McCormack	D-263	R-174		D-64	R-36	
88th	1963–65	John McCormack	D-259	R-176		D-67	R-33	
89th	1965–67	John McCormack	D-295	R-140		D-68	R-32	
90th	1967–69	John McCormack	D-248	R-187		D-64	R-36	
91st	1969–71	John McCormack	D-243	R-192		D-57	R-43	

Members of the Supreme Court 1789–1970

Name	Appointment From	President	Service
Chief Justices			
John Jay (1745–1829)	N. Y.	Washington	1790–1795[1]
John Rutledge (1739–1800)	S. C.	Washington	1795–1795[2]
Oliver Ellsworth (1745–1807)	Conn.	Washington	1796–1800[1]
John Marshall (1755–1835)	Va.	J. Adams	1801–1835[3]
Roger B. Taney (1777–1864)	Md.	Jackson	1836–1864[3]
Salmon P. Chase (1808–1873)	Ohio	Lincoln	1864–1873[3]
Morrison R. Waite (1816–1888)	Ohio	Grant	1874–1888[3]
Melville W. Fuller (1833–1910)	Ill.	Cleveland	1888–1910[3]
Edward D. White (1845–1921)	La.	Taft	1910–1921[3]
William H. Taft (1857–1930)	Conn.	Harding	1921–1930[4]
Charles E. Hughes (1862–1948)	N. Y.	Hoover	1930–1941[4]
Harlan F. Stone (1872–1946)	N. Y.	F. Roosevelt	1941–1946[3]
Frederick M. Vinson (1890–1953)	Ky.	Truman	1946–1953[3]
Earl Warren (1891–)	Calif.	Eisenhower	1953–1969[4]
Warren E. Burger (1907–)	Va.	Nixon	1969–
Associate Justices			
James Wilson (1742–1798)	Pa.	Washington	1789–1798[3]
John Rutledge (1739–1800)	S. C.	Washington	1790–1791[1]
William Cushing (1732–1810)	Mass.	Washington	1790–1810[3]
John Blair (1732–1800)	Va.	Washington	1790–1796[1]
James Iredell (1751–1799)	N. C.	Washington	1790–1799[3]
Thomas Johnson (1732–1819)	Md.	Washington	1792–1793[1]
William Paterson (1745–1806)	N. J.	Washington	1793–1806[3]
Samuel Chase (1741–1811)	Md.	Washington	1796–1811[3]
Bushrod Washington (1762–1829)	Va.	J. Adams	1799–1829[3]
Alfred Moore (1755–1810)	N. C.	J. Adams	1800–1804[1]
William Johnson (1771–1834)	S. C.	Jefferson	1804–1834[3]
Brockholst Livingston (1757–1823)	N. Y.	Jefferson	1807–1823[3]
Thomas Todd (1765–1826)	Ky.	Jefferson	1807–1826[3]
Gabriel Duval (1752–1844)	Md.	Madison	1811–1835[1]
Joseph Story (1779–1845)	Mass.	Madison	1812–1845[3]
Smith Thompson (1768–1843)	N. Y.	Monroe	1823–1843[3]
Robert Trimble (1777–1828)	Ky.	J. Q. Adams	1826–1828[3]
John McLean (1785–1861)	Ohio	Jackson	1830–1861[3]
Henry Baldwin (1780–1844)	Pa.	Jackson	1830–1844[3]
James M. Wayne (1790–1867)	Ga.	Jackson	1835–1867[3]
Philip P. Barbour (1783–1841)	Va.	Jackson	1836–1841[3]
John Catron (1786–1865)	Tenn.	Van Buren	1837–1865[3]
John McKinley (1780–1852)	Ala.	Van Buren	1838–1852[3]
Peter V. Daniel (1784–1860)	Va.	Van Buren	1841–1860[3]
Samuel Nelson (1792–1873)	N. Y.	Tyler	1845–1872[4]
Levi Woodbury (1789–1851)	N. H.	Polk	1845–1851[3]
Robert C. Grier (1794–1870)	Pa.	Polk	1846–1870[4]
Benjamin R. Curtis (1809–1874)	Mass.	Fillmore	1851–1857[1]
John A. Campbell (1811–1889)	Ala.	Pierce	1853–1861[1]
Nathan Clifford (1803–1881)	Maine	Buchanan	1858–1881[3]
Noah H. Swayne (1804–1884)	Ohio	Lincoln	1862–1881[4]
Samuel F. Miller (1816–1890)	Iowa	Lincoln	1862–1890[3]
David Davis (1815–1886)	Ill.	Lincoln	1862–1877[1]
Stephen J. Field (1816–1899)	Calif.	Lincoln	1863–1897[4]
William Strong (1808–1895)	Pa.	Grant	1870–1880[4]
Joseph P. Bradley (1813–1892)	N. J.	Grant	1870–1892[3]
Ward Hunt (1810–1886)	N. Y.	Grant	1873–1882[6]
John M. Harlan (1833–1911)	Ky.	Hayes	1877–1911[3]
William B. Woods (1824–1887)	Ga.	Hayes	1881–1887[3]
Stanley Matthews (1824–1889)	Ohio	Garfield	1881–1889[3]
Horace Gray (1828–1902)	Mass.	Arthur	1882–1902[3]
Samuel Blatchford (1820–1893)	N. Y.	Arthur	1882–1893[3]
Lucius Q. C. Lamar (1825–1893)	Miss.	Cleveland	1888–1893[3]
David J. Brewer (1837–1910)	Kans.	Harrison	1890–1910[3]
Henry B. Brown (1836–1913)	Mich.	Harrison	1891–1906[4]
George Shiras, Jr. (1832–1924)	Pa.	Harrison	1892–1903[4]

[1]Resigned
[2]Rejected
[3]Died in office
[4]Retired
[5]Promoted to Chief Justice
[6]Disabled

Name	Appointment From	President	Service
Howell E. Jackson (1832 – 1895)	Tenn.	Harrison	1893 – 1895[3]
Edward D. White (1845 – 1921)	La.	Cleveland	1894 – 1910[5]
Rufus W. Peckham (1838 – 1909)	N. Y.	Cleveland	1896 – 1909[3]
Joseph McKenna (1843 – 1926)	Calif.	McKinley	1898 – 1925[4]
Oliver W. Holmes (1841 – 1935)	Mass.	T. Roosevelt	1902 – 1932[4]
William R. Day (1849 – 1923)	Ohio	T. Roosevelt	1903 – 1922[4]
William H. Moody (1853 – 1917)	Mass.	T. Roosevelt	1906 – 1910[6]
Horace H. Lurton (1844 – 1914)	Tenn.	Taft	1910 – 1914[3]
Charles E. Hughes (1862 – 1948)	N. Y.	Taft	1910 – 1916[1]
Willis Van Devanter (1859 – 1941)	Wyo.	Taft	1911 – 1937[4]
Joseph R. Lamar (1857 – 1916)	Ga.	Taft	1911 – 1916[3]
Mahlon Pitney (1858 – 1924)	N. J.	Taft	1912 – 1922[6]
James C. McReynolds (1862 – 1946)	Tenn.	Wilson	1914 – 1941[4]
Louis D. Brandeis (1856 – 1941)	Mass.	Wilson	1916 – 1939[4]
John H. Clarke (1857 – 1945)	Ohio	Wilson	1916 – 1922[1]
George Sutherland (1862 – 1942)	Utah	Harding	1922 – 1938[4]
Pierce Butler (1866 – 1939)	Minn.	Harding	1923 – 1939[3]
Edward T. Sanford (1865 – 1930)	Tenn.	Harding	1923 – 1930[3]
Harlan F. Stone (1872 – 1946)	N. Y.	Coolidge	1925 – 1941[5]
Owen J. Roberts (1875 – 1955)	Pa.	Hoover	1930 – 1945[1]
Benjamin N. Cardozo (1870 – 1938)	N. Y.	Hoover	1932 – 1938[3]
Hugo L. Black (1886 –)	Ala.	F. Roosevelt	1937 –
Stanley F. Reed (1884 –)	Ky.	F. Roosevelt	1938 – 1957[4]
Felix Frankfurter (1882 – 1965)	Mass.	F. Roosevelt	1939 – 1962[4]
William O. Douglas (1898 –)	Conn.	F. Roosevelt	1939 –
Frank Murphy (1890 – 1949)	Mich.	F. Roosevelt	1940 – 1949[3]
James F. Byrnes (1879 –)	S. C.	F. Roosevelt	1941 – 1942[1]
Robert H. Jackson (1892 – 1954)	N. Y.	F. Roosevelt	1941 – 1954[3]
Wiley B. Rutledge (1894 – 1949)	Iowa	F. Roosevelt	1943 – 1949[3]
Harold H. Burton (1888 – 1964)	Ohio	Truman	1945 – 1958[4]
Tom C. Clark (1899 –)	Tex.	Truman	1949 – 1967[4]
Sherman Minton (1890 – 1965)	Ind.	Truman	1949 – 1956[4]
John M. Harlan (1899 –)	N. Y.	Eisenhower	1955 –
William J. Brennan, Jr. (1906 –)	N. J.	Eisenhower	1956 –
Charles E. Whittaker (1901 –)	Mo.	Eisenhower	1957 – 1962[4]
Potter Stewart (1915 –)	Ohio	Eisenhower	1959 –
Byron R. White (1917 –)	Colo.	Kennedy	1962 –
Arthur J. Goldberg (1908 –)	Ill.	Kennedy	1962 – 1965[1]
Abe Fortas (1910 –)	D. C.	Johnson	1965 – 1969[1]
Thurgood Marshall (1908 –)	N. Y.	Johnson	1967 –
Harry A. Blackmun (1908 –)	Minn.	Nixon	1970 –

[1]Resigned
[2]Rejected
[3]Died in office
[4]Retired
[5]Promoted to Chief Justice
[6]Disabled

New York Drama Critics' Circle Awards 1935–1969

year	winner
1935–36	*Winterset*, Maxwell Anderson
1936–37	*High Tor*, Maxwell Anderson
1937–38	*Of Mice and Men*, John Steinbeck
	Shadow and Substance, Paul Vincent Carroll[1]
1938–39	(no award)
	The White Steed, Paul Vincent Carroll[1]
1939–40	*The Time of Your Life*, William Saroyan
1940–41	*Watch on the Rhine*, Lillian Hellman
	The Corn Is Green, Emlyn Williams[1]
1941–42	(No award)
	Blithe Spirit, Noel Coward[1]
1942–43	*The Patriots*, Sidney Kingsley
1943–44	(No award)
	Jacobowsky and the Colonel, Franz Werfel–S. N. Behrman[1]
1944–45	*The Glass Menagerie*, Tennessee Williams
1945–46	(No award)
	Carousel, Richard Rodgers & Oscar Hammerstein II[2]
1946–47	*All My Sons*, Arthur Miller
	No Exit, Jean-Paul Sartre[1]
	Brigadoon, Alan Jay Lerner and Frederick Loewe[2]
1947–48	*A Streetcar Named Desire*, Tennessee Williams
	The Winslow Boy, Terence Rattigan[1]
1948–49	*Death of a Salesman*, Arthur Miller
	The Madwoman of Chaillot, Jean Giraudoux–Maurice Valency[1]
	South Pacific, Richard Rodgers, Oscar Hammerstein II & Joshua Logan[2]
1949–50	*The Member of the Wedding*, Carson McCullers
	The Cocktail Party, T. S. Eliot[1]
	The Consul, Gian-Carlo Menotti[2]
1950–51	*Darkness at Noon*, Sidney Kingsley
	The Lady's Not for Burning, Christopher Fry[1]
	Guys and Dolls, Abe Burrows, Jo Swerling & Frank Loesser[2]
1951–52	*I Am a Camera*, John Van Druten
	Venus Observed, Christopher Fry[1]
	Pal Joey, Richard Rodgers, Lorenz Hart & John O'Hara[2]
	Don Juan in Hell, George B. Shaw
1952–53	*Picnic*, William Inge
	The Love of Four Colonels, Peter Ustinov[1]
	Wonderful Town, Joseph Fields, Jerome Chodorov, Betty Comden, Adolph Green & Leonard Bernstein[2]
1953–54	*The Teahous of the August Moon*, John Patrick
	Ondine, Jean Giraudoux[1]
	The Golden Apple, John Latouche & Jerome Moross[2]
1954–55	*Cat on a Hot Tin Roof*, Tennessee Williams
	Witness for the Proscution, Agatha Christie[1]
	The Saint of Bleecker Street, Gian-Carlo Menotti[2]

year	winner
1955–56	*The Diary of Anne Frank*, Frances Goodrich & Albert Hackett
	Tiger at the Gates, Jean Giraudoux-Christopher Fry[1]
	My Fair Lady, Frederick Loewe & Alan Jay Lerner[3]
1956–57	*Long Day's Journay Into Night*, Eugene O'Neill
	Waltz of the Toreadors, Jean Anouilh[1]
	The Most Happy Fella, Frank Loesser[2]
1957–58	*Look Homeward, Angel*, Ketti Frings
	Look Back in Anger, John Osborne[1]
	The Music Man, Meredith Willson[3]
1958–59	*A Raisin in the Sun*, Lorraine Hansberry
	The Visit, Friedrich Duerrenmatt–Maurice Valency[1]
	La Plume de ma Tante, Robert Dhery & Gerard Calvi[2]
1959–60	*Toys in the Attic*, Lillian Hellman
	Five Finger Exercise, Peter Shaffer[1]
	Fiorello!, Jerome Weidman, George Abbott, Jerry Bock, Sheldon Harnick[2]
1960–61	*All the Way Home*, Tad Mosel
	A Taste of Honey, Shelagh Delaney[1]
	Carnival, Michael Stewart[2]
1961–62	*The Night of the Iguana*, Tennessee Williams
	A Man for All Seasons, Robert Bolt[1]
	How to Succeed in Business Without Really Trying, Abe Burrows, Jack Weinstock, Willie Gilbert & Frank Loesser[2]
1962–63	*Who's Afraid of Virginia Woolf?*, Edward Albee
	Beyond the Fringe, Alan Bennett, Peter Cook, Jonathan Miller, and Dudley Moore[4]
1963–64	*Luther*, John Osborne
	Hello, Dolly!, Michael Stewart and Jerry Herman[2]
	The Trohan Women, Euripides[4]
1964–65	*The Subject Was Roses*, Frank D. Gilroy
	Fiddler on the Roof, Joseph Stein, Jerry Bock, and Sheldon Harnick[2]
1965–66	*The Persecution and Assassination of Marat as Performed by the Inmates of the Asylum of Charenton under the Direction of the Marquis de Sade*, Peter Weiss
	The Man of La Mancha, Dale Wasserman, Mitch Leigh & Joe Darion
1966–67	*The Homecoming*, Harold Pinter
	Cabaret, Joe Masteroff, John Kander, and Fred Ebb[2]
1967–68	*Rosencrantz and Guildenstern Are Dead*, Tom Stoppard
	Your Own Thing, Donal Driver, Hal Hester, and Danny Apolinar[2]
1968–69	*The Great White Hope*, Howard Sackler
	1776, Sherman Edwards and Peter Stone[2]

[1]·Citation for best foreign play   [2]·Citation for best musical   [3]·For "distinguished and original contribution to the theater."   [4]·Special citation

1765	The Girl I Left Behind Me	
	Yankee Doodle	
1767	The Banks of the Dee	
1768	The Liberty Song	
1774	Free America	
1775	The American Hero	
1778	The Battle of the Kegs (Chester)	
1798	Adams and Liberty	
	Hail Columbia	
	The President's March	
1800	The American Star	
1803	Jefferson and Liberty	
1814	The Star-Spangled Banner	
1823	Home, Sweet Home	
1825	The Meeting of the Waters of Hudson and Erie	
1826	The Hunters of Kentucky	
	The Old Oaken Bucket	
1827	The Coal Black Rose	
	The Minstrel's Return from the War	
	My Long Blue Tail	
1830	Jim Crow	
1832	America	
1833	Long Time Ago	
1834	Zip Coon	
1835	Old Rosin the Beau	
1837	Woodman, Spare That Tree	
1838	A Life on the Ocean Wave	
1840	The Old Arm Chair	
	Rocked in the Cradle of the Deep	
	Tippecanoe and Tyler Too	
1841	Niagara Falls	
1843	Columbia, the Gem of the Ocean	
	Excelsior	
	My Old Aunt Sally	
	Old Dan Tucker	
	The Old Granite State	
1844	The Blue Juniata	
	Vive La Compagnie	
1846	The Bridge of Sighs	
	The Rose of Alabama	
1848	Oh, Susanna	
	Old Uncle Ned	
1849	Nelly Bly	
1850	De Camptown Races	
1851	Old Folks at Home	
	Wait for the Wagon	
1852	Lily Dale	
	Massa's in de Cold Cold Ground	
1853	The Hazel Dell	
	My Old Kentucky Home	
	Old Dog Tray	
1854	Jeanie with the Light Brown Hair	
	What Is Home Without a Mother?	
1855	Come Where My Love Lies Dreaming	
	Listen to the Mocking Bird	
	Rosalie, the Prairie Flower	
1856	Darling Nellie Gray	
	Root, Hog or Die	
1857	Jingle Bells	
	Mrs. Lofty and I	

1860	Dixie	
	Old Black Joe	
	'Tis But a Little Faded Flower	
1861	John Brown's Body	
	Maryland, My Maryland	
	The Vacant Chair	
1862	Battle Hymn of the Republic	
	The Bonnie Blue Flag	
	Grafted into the Army	
	We Are Coming, Father Abraham, 300,000 More	
1863	Babylon Is Fallen	
	The Battle Cry of Freedom	
	Just Before the Battle, Mother	
	When Johnny Comes Marching Home	
1864	All Quiet Along the Potomac Tonight	
	Beautiful Dreamer	
	Come Home, Father	
	Sherman's March to the Sea	
	Tenting on the Old Camp Ground	
	Where, Oh Where, Has My Little Dog Gone?	
1865	Ellie Rhee	
	Marching Through Georgia	
1866	We Parted by the River	
	When You and I Were Young, Maggie	
1868	The Flying Trapeze	
1869	The Little Brown Jug	
	Shew, Fly, Don't Bother Me	
	Sweet Genevieve	
1871	Goodbye, Liza Jane	
	Mollie Darling	
	Susan Jane	
1873	The Mulligan Guard	
	Silver Threads Among the Gold	
1874	The Skidmore Guard	
1876	Grandfather's Clock	
	I'll Take You Home Again, Kathleen	
	Rose of Killarney	
1877	Early in de Mornin'	
	Roll Out! Heave Dat Cotton	
1878	Carry Me Back to Old Virginny	
	A Flower from Mother's Grave	
	Lullaby	
1879	In the Morning by the Bright Light	
	Oh, Dem Golden Slippers	
1880	Cradle's Empty, Baby's Gone	
	De Golden Wedding	
	Why Did They Dig Ma's Grave So Deep?	
1881	Paddy Duffy's Cart	
1883	My Dad's Dinner Pail	
	Strolling on the Brooklyn Bridge	
	There Is a Tavern in the Town	
	When the Robins Nest Again	
1884	Always Take Mother's Advice	
	White Wings	
1885	Poverty's Tears Ebb and Flow	
	Remember, Boy, You're Irish	
1886	The Letter That Never Came	
1887	If the Waters Could Speak As They Flow	

	The Outcast Unknown	
1888	Drill, Ye Tarriers, Drill	
	The Whistling Coon	
	With All Her Faults I Love Her Still	
1889	Down Went McGinty	
	Oh, Promise Me	
1890	The Irish Jubilee	
	Maggie Murphy's Home	
	Throw Him Down, McCloskey	
1891	Molly O!	
	The Pardon Came Too Late	
	The Picture That Is Turned Toward the Wall	
	Ta-ra-ra boom-de-ré	
1892	After the Ball	
	The Bowery	
	Daddy Wouldn't Buy Me a Bow Wow	
	Daisy Bell	
1893	The Fatal Wedding	
	Little Alabama Coon	
	Two Little Girls in Blue	
1894	And Her Golden Hair Was Hanging Down Her Back	
	The Little Lost Child	
	She May Have Seen Better Days	
	The Sidewalks of New York	
1895	America, the Beautiful	
	The Band Played On	
	Down in Poverty Row	
	My Best Girl's a New Yorker	
1896	All Coons Look Alike to Me	
	A Hot Time in the Old Town	
	In the Baggage Coach Ahead	
	Sweet Rosie O'Grady	
	You're Not the Only Pebble on the Beach	
1897	At a Georgia Camp Meeting	
	Break the News to Mother	
	On the Banks of the Wabash Far Away	
1898	Gold Will Buy Most Anything But a True Girl's Heart	
	Gypsy Love Song	
	I Guess I'll Have to Telegraph My Baby	
	When You Ain't Got No More Money, Well, You Needn't Come Around	
	When You Were Sweet Sixteen	
1899	Hello, Ma Baby	
	I'd Leave My Happy Home for You	
	My Wild Irish Rose	
	When Chloe Sings a Song	
1900	A Bird in a Gilded Cage	
	The Bridge of Sighs	
	Goodbye, Dolly Gray	
1901	Just A-Wearyin' for You	
	Mighty Lak a Rose	
	Way Down in Old Indiana	
1902	Bill Bailey, Won't You Please Come Home?	
	Down Where the Wurzburger Flows	
	In the Good Old Summer Time	
	The Mansion of Aching Hearts	

1903 Bedelia
Ida, Sweet As Apple Cider
Navajo
Sweet Adeline
Toyland
1904 Blue Bell
Give My Regards to Broadway
Meet Me in St. Louis
The Yankee Doodle Boy
1905 Dearie
In My Merry Oldsmobile
In the Shade of the Old Apple
Tree
Mary's a Grand Old Name
My Gal Sal
Wait Till the Sun Shines Nellie
1906 Anchors Aweigh
Chinatown, My Chinatown
I Love You Truly
Waiting at the Church
You're a Grand Old Flag
1907 Harrigan
It's Delightful to Be Married
On the Road to Mandalay
School Days
1908 Cuddle Up a Little Closer
Shine On, Harvest Moon
Take Me Out to the Ball Game
You're in the Right Church But
the Wrong Pew
1909 By the Light of the Silvery
Moon
Casey Jones
Has Anybody Here Seen Kelly?
I Wonder Who's Kissing Her
Now
Put On Your Old Gray Bonnet
1910 Ah, Sweet Mystery of Life
Come, Josephine, in My Flying
Machine
Down by the Old Mill Stream
Let Me Call You Sweetheart
Mother Machree
Some of These Days
1911 Alexander's Ragtime Band
Good Night, Ladies
I Want a Girl Just Like the Girl
That Married Dear Old Dad
Oh, You Beautiful Doll
Till the Sands of the Desert
Grow Cold
1912 The Memphis Blues
Moonlight Bay
My Melancholy Baby
Row, Row, Row
The Sweetheart of Sigma Chi
When Irish Eyes Are Smiling
1913 Ballin' the Jack
The Curse of an Aching Heart
He'd Have to Get Under
Peg o' My Heart
The Trail of the Lonesome Pine
You Made Me Love You
1914 The Aba Daba Honeymoon
By the Beautiful Sea
Play a Simple Melody
St. Louis Blues
Too-ra-loo-ra-loo-ral
When You Wore a Tulip
1915 Auf Wiedersehen
Babes in the Wood
Hello, Frisco

Hello, Hawaii, How Are You?
How'd You Like to Spoon with
Me?
I Didn't Raise My Boy to Be a
Soldier
1916 Ireland Must Be Heaven, For
My Mother Came from There
Poor Butterfly
Pretty Baby
Turn Back the Universe and
Give Me Yesterday
Yacka Hula Hickey Dula
1917 Beale Street Blues
The Darktown Strutters' Ball
For Me and My Gal
Goodbye, Broadway, Hello,
France
Hail, Hail, the Gang's All Here
Lily of the Valley
Oh, Johnny, Oh, Johnny, Oh!
Over There
1918 After You've Gone
Hello, Central, Give Me No
Man's Land
Ja Da
K-K-K-Katy
Oh, How I Hate to Get Up in
the Morning
Rock-a-bye Your Baby with a
Dixie Melody
1919 How Ya Gonna Keep 'Em
Down on the Farm?
I'm Forever Blowing Bubbles
Let the Rest of the World Go
By
A Pretty Girl Is Like a Melody
Smilin' Through
Swanee
1920 Avalon
I'll Be with You in Apple
Blossom Time
The Japanese Sandman
Look for the Silver Lining
My Mammy
When My Baby Smiles at Me
1921 Ain't We Got Fun?
April Showers
I'm Just Wild About Harry
Ma, He's Making Eyes at Me
My Man
The Sheik of Araby
Wabash Blues
1922 Carolina in the Morning
Chicago
Mister Gallagher and Mister
Shean
My Buddy
Three O'Clock in the Morning
Toot, Toot, Tootsie
1923 Barney Google
Charleston
Oh, Gee, Oh, Gosh, Oh Golly,
I'm in Love
That Old Gang of Mine
Who's Sorry Now?
Yes, We Have No Bananas
1924 California, Here I Come
Fascinating Rhythm
Indian Love Call
I'll See You in My Dreams
The Man I Love
Somebody Loves Me

Tea for Two
1925 Five Feet Two, Eyes of Blue
I'm Sitting on Top of the World
If You Knew Susie, Like I Know
Susie
Manhattan
Moonlight and Roses
Sweet Georgia Brown
Yes, Sir, That's My Baby
1926 Baby Face
Black Bottom
Blue Heaven
Breezin' Along with the Breeze
Bye, Bye, Blackbird
Charmaine
Do, Do, Do
When the Red, Red Robin
Comes Bob, Bob, Bobbin'
Along
1927 The Best Things in Life Are
Free
Blue Skies
Can't Help Lovin' Dat Man
I'm Looking Over a Four Leaf
Clover
Let a Smile Be Your Umbrella
on a Rainy Day
Me and My Shadow
Ol' Man River
The Varsity Drag
1928 Button Up Your Overcoat
Carolina Moon
I Can't Give You Anything But
Love
I Wanna Be Loved by You
Let's Do It
Makin' Whoopee
Short'nin' Bread
Sonny Boy
Stout Hearted Men
Sweet Sue, Just You
You're the Cream in My Coffee
1929 Ain't Misbehavin'
Am I Blue?
Happy Days Are Here Again
Moanin' Low
Singin' in the Rain
Stardust
Tip Toe Thru the Tulips with
Me
With a Song in My Heart
1930 Betty Co-Ed
Beyond the Blue Horizon
Body and Soul
Georgia on My Mind
Get Happy
I Got Rhythm
On the Sunny Side of the Street
Ten Cents a Dance
Three Little Words
Time on My Hands
Walkin' My Baby Back Home
1931 Between the Devil and the
Deep Blue Sea
Goodnight, Sweetheart
I Found a Million Dollar Baby
I Love a Parade
I've Got Five Dollars
Life Is Just a Bowl of Cherries
Love Letters in the Sand
Minnie the Moocher
Mood Indigo

781

When the Moon Comes Over
the Mountain
Where the Blue of the Night
Meets the Gold of the Day
1932 April in Paris
Brother, Can You Spare a
Dime?
I'm Gettin' Sentimental Over
You
Let's Have Another Cup of
Coffee
Night and Day
Shuffle Off to Buffalo
You're an Old Smoothie
You're Getting to Be a Habit
with Me
1933 The Boulevard of Broken
Dreams
Carioca
Easter Parade
Heat Wave
It's Only a Paper Moon
Smoke Gets in Your Eyes
Stormy Weather
Who's Afraid of the Big Bad
Wolf?
1934 All Through the Night
Blue Moon
Carry Me Back to the Lone
Prairie
The Continental
Stars Fell on Alabama
Stay As Sweet As You Are
Tumbling Tumbleweeds
Wagon Wheels
1935 Begin the Beguine
Cheek to Cheek
I Got Plenty o' Nuthin
I'm in the Mood for Love
It Ain't Necessarily So
Just One of Those Things
Lullaby of Broadway
The Music Goes 'Round and
'Round
Summertime
1936 I Can't Get Started with You
I'm an Old Cowhand
Is It True What They Say About
Dixie?
It's De-Lovely
I've Got you Under My Skin
Pennies from Heaven
The Whiffenpoof Song
1937 Bei Mir Bist Du Schoen
The Dipsy Doodle
A Foggy Day
Harbor Lights
In the Still of the Night
I've Got My Love to Keep Me
Warm
The Lady Is a Tramp
My Funny Valentine
Nice Work If You Can Get It
Sweet Leilani
Whistle While You Work
1938 A-Tisket, A-Tasket
Falling in Love with Love
The Flat Foot Floogie
I'll Be Seeing You
Jeepers Creepers
September Song
You Must Have Been a
Beautiful Baby

1939 Beer Barrel Polka
God Bless America
I Didn't Know What Time It
Was
I'll Never Smile Again
Over the Rainbow
Three Little Fishes
1940 How High the Moon
It's a Big Wonderful World
The Last Time I Saw Paris
When You Wish Upon a Star
You Are My Sunshine
1941 Bewitched, Bothered and
Bewildered
Chattanooga Choo Choo
Deep in the Heart of Texas
I Don't Want to Set the World
on Fire
I Got It Bad and That Ain't
Good
I'll Remember April
1942 Dearly Beloved
Paper Doll
Praise the Lord and Pass the
Ammunition
That Old Black Magic
White Christmas
1943 Comin' in on a Wing and a
Prayer
I'll Be Seeing you
A Lovely Way to Spend an
Evening
Mairzy Doats
Oh, What a Beautiful Mornin'
People Will Say We're in Love
Tico Tico
1944 Ac-cent-tchu-ate the Positive
Don't Fence Me In
Rum and Coca-Rola
Sentimental Journey
Spring Will Be a Little Late This
Year
Swinging on a Star
1945 It Might as Well Be Spring
It's a Grand Night for Singing
June Is Bustin' Out All Over
Laura
Let It Snow, Let It Snow, Let It
Snow
On the Atchison, Topeka and
the Santa Fe
1946 Come Rain or Come Shine
How Are Things in Glocca
Morra?
Ole Buttermilk Sky
South America, Take It Away
Tenderly
They Say It's Wonderful
Zip-a-Dee-Doo-Dah
1947 Almost Like Being in Love
I'll Dance at Your Wedding
Papa, Won't You Dance with
Me?
The Stanley Steamer
Too Fat Polka
1948 "A" You're Adorable
Baby, It's Cold Outside
Buttons and Bows
Mañana Is Soon Enough for Me
On a Slow Boat to China
Once in Love with Amy
Tennessee Waltz

1949 Bali Ha'i
Bibbidi-Bobbidi-Boo
Dear Hearts and Gentle People
Diamonds Are a Girl's Best
Friend
Riders in the Sky
Mockin' Bird Hill
Mule Train
Rudolph, the Red Nosed
Reindeer
Some Enchanted Evening
1950 A Bushel and a Peck
C'est Si Bon
If I Knew You Were Comin' I'd
'Ave Baked a Cake
My Heart Cries for You
Rag Mop
Sam's Song
The Thing
1951 Come On-a My House
Cry
Hello, Young Lovers
In the Cool, Cool, Cool of the
Evening
Kisses Sweeter Than Wine
The Little White Cloud That
Cried
My Truly, Truly Fair
Shrimp Boats
1952 Botch-a-Me
High Noon
I Saw Mommy Kissing Santa
Claus
Jambalaya
Takes Two to Tango
Wheel of Fortune
Your Cheatin' Heart
1953 Baubles, Bangles and Beads
Ebb Tide
I Believe
I Love Paris
Oh, My Papa
Stranger in Paradise
That Doggie in the Window
1954 The Happy Wanderer
Hernando's Hideaway
Hey, There
The High and the Mighty
Let Me Go, Lover
Mister Sandman
The Naughty Lady of Shady
Lane
Papa Loves Mambo
Shake, Rattle and Roll
Sh-Boom
Three Coins in the Fountain
Young at Heart
1955 The Ballad of Davy Crockett
Cherry Pink and Apple
Blossom White
Dance with Me, Henry
Love Is a Many Splendored
Thing
Rock Around the Clock
Sixteen Tons
Unchained Melody
Whatever Lola Wants
The Yellow Rose of Texas
1956 Around the World
Blue Suede Shoes
Don't Be Cruel
The Great Pretender

782

The Green Door
Heartbreak Hotel
Hound Dog
I Could Have Danced All
  Night
Memories Are Made of This
On the Street Where You Live
See You Later, Alligator
Teen Age Crush
Whatever Will Be, Will Be

1957 All Shook Up
April Love
Maria
A Rose and a Baby Ruth
Seventy-Six Trombones
Tammy
Tonight

1958 At the Hop
Catch a Falling Star
Chanson d'Amour
The Chipmunk Song
Everybody Loves a Lover
The Purple People Eater
Tom Dooley
Volare

1959 The Battle of New Orleans
Climb Every Mountain
Everything's Coming Up Roses
High Hopes
Kookie Kookie
Mack the Knife
Personality
The Sound of Music

1960 Calcutta
Cathy's Clown
Dolce Far Niente
If Ever I Would Leave You
Itsy Bitsy Teenie Bikini
Never on Sunday
The Twist

1961 Big Bad John
Exodus
The Lion Sleeps Tonight
Love Makes the World Go
  Round
Moon River
Where the Boys Are
Wonderland By Night

1962 Blowin' in the Wind
Can't Help Falling in Love
Days of Wine and Roses
Do You Love Me?
Go Away, Little Girl

Roses Are Red, My Love

1963 Call Me Irresponsible
Danke Schoen
Eighteen Yellow Roses
Fingertips
Hey, Paula
Sugar Shack
Those Lazy, Hazy, Crazy Days
  of Summer

1964 Chim Chim Cheree
Fiddler on the Roof
From Russia with Love
Hello, Dolly!
I Get Around
I Want to Hold Your Hand
Oh, Pretty Woman
Send Me the Pillow You
  Dream On

1965 Downtown
Hard Day's Night
It Was a Very Good Year
King of the Road
Satisfaction
Sounds of Silence
Turn! Turn! Turn!

1966 Ballad of the Green Berets
Batman Theme
Born Free
Eleanor Rigby
Rainy Day Woman #12 & 35
Strangers in the Night
Sunshine Superman

1967 Ode to Billy Joe
Penny Lane
Respect
Ruby Tuesday
Snoopy vs. The Red Baron
Strawberry Fields Forever
White Rabbit

1968 Harper Valley P.T.A.
Hey Jude
Love Is Blue
Mrs. Robinson
Stoned Soul Picnic
The Dock of the Bay
Tip-Toe Thru the Tulips

1969 A Boy Named Sue
Aquarius
Get Back
Honky Tonk Women
Hair
In the Year 2525
Lay Lady Lay

Leading Magazines 1950–1968

June 30, 1950	circulation	Dec. 31, 1960	circulation	Dec. 31, 1968	circulation
Reader's Digest	over 8,500,000	Reader's Digest	12,592,912	Reader's Digest	17,602,526
Life	5,364,567	TV Guide	7,079,511	TV Guide	13,729,289
Ladies' Home Journal	4,564,101	Life	6,764,686	McCall's	8,532,497
Saturday Evening Post	4,069,220	McCall's	6,560,452	Life	7,802,820
Woman's Home Companion	4,059,383	Ladies' Home Journal	6,550,415	Look	7,797,521
McCall's Magazine	3,807,101	Saturday Evening Post	6,377,367	Better Homes & Gardens	7,571,606
Woman's Day	3,756,938	Look	6,322,417	Woman's Day	7,201,775
Better Homes & Gardens	3,460,401	Everywoman's Family Circle	5,616,029	Ladies' Home Journal	6,964,719
Look	3,200,145	Woman's Day	5,051,066	Family Circle	6,503,415
Collier's	3,161,048	Better Homes & Gardens	5,037,498	National Geographic	6,077,806
American Legion	3,027,896	Good Housekeeping	4,961,039	Good Housekeeping	5,678,017
Good Housekeeping	3,010,883	American Home	3,675,676	Playboy	5,379,003
American Home	2,813,804	Redbook Magazine	3,220,354	Redbook	4,566,264
Coronet	2,662,613	Coronet	3,122,628	Time	3,904,462
American Magazine	2,549,874	American Legion	2,748,419*	American Home	3,696,940
Household	2,086,029	Time	2,541,977	American Legion	2,593,963
True Story	2,075,781	National 'Geographic Magazine	2,517,846	Boys' Life	2,534,946
Family Circle	2,028,662	True	2,408,348	True	2,393,066
Cosmopolitan	1,972,631	True Story	2,328,287	Newsweek	2,307,921
Redbook Magazine	1,963,316	Boys' Life	2,047,313	True Story	2,247,537

* As of September 15, 1960

Popular Books 1640–1969

The following list of popular books in America is arranged chronologically by date of first publication, starting with the first book published in America, *The Bay Psalm Book*, 1640. But at least six other books, published earlier in England, were enormously popular in this country, in the 17th and 18th centuries and in the 20th. These six are Calvin's *Institutes of the Christian Religion* (first American printing 1813), John Foxe's *Book of Martyrs* (first American printing 1793), the King James Bible (first American printing 1781–2), Lewis Bayly's *The Practice of Piety* (first American printing 1665), Shakespeare's *Plays* (first American collected edition 1796), and Bacon's *Essays* (first American printing 1688).

Many of the books in the list, of course, were popular in other years than the one in which they appear, but they nevertheless appear only once, according to the date of publication. Thus, for example, *Peyton Place* was the number two bestseller of 1957, the year *after* it was published—but it is listed only for 1956.

1640	Bay Psalm Book, Richard Mather, John Eliot, and Thomas Weld
1643	New England's First Fruits
1644	Bloudy Tenent of Persecution, Roger Williams
1646	Milk for Babes, John Cotton
1647	The Simple Cobler of Aggawam, Nathaniel Ward
1650	The Tenth Muse, Anne Bradstreet
1662	The Day of Doom, Michael Wigglesworth
1665	The Great Assize, Samuel Smith
1669	The Indian Primer, John Eliot
	No Cross, No Crown, William Penn
1672	An Alarm to Unconverted Sinners, Joseph Alleine
1676	New England's Crisis, Benjamin Tompson
1678	Pilgrim's Progress, John Bunyan
1682	. . . Narrative of the Captivity and Restauration of Mrs. Mary Rowlandson, Mrs. Mary Rowlandson
1683	The New England Primer, Benjamin Harris
1690	Treatises of Civil Government, John Locke
1693	Wonders of the Invisible World, Cotton Mather
1702	Magnalia Christi Americana, Cotton Mather
1706	Horae Lyricae, Isaac Watts
1707	The Redeemed Captive Returned to Zion, John Williams
1715–20	Iliad, Alexander Pope
1715	Divine Songs for Children, Isaac Watts
1719	Robinson Crusoe, Daniel Defoe
1725–64	Astronomical Diary and Almanack, Nathaniel Ames
1726	Gulliver's Travels, Jonathan Swift
1726–30	The Seasons, James Thomson
1727	History of the Five Indian Nations, Cadwallader Colden
1733–47	Poor Richard's Almanack, Benjamin Franklin (1748–58, Poor Richard Improved)
1733–34	An Essay on Man, Alexander Pope
1740–41	Pamela, Samuel Richardson
1742	Joseph Andrews, Henry Fielding
1742–45	The Complaint, or Night Thoughts on Life, Death, and Immortality, Edward Young
1743	The Grave, Robert Blair
1747–48	Clarissa Harlowe, Samuel Richardson
1749	Tom Jones, Henry Fielding
1751	Family Companion; or the Oeconomy of Human Life, Robert Dodsley (?)
1754	Freedom of Will, Jonathan Edwards
1757	History of England, Tobias George Smollett

1760	Tristram Shandy, Laurence Sterne
1761	New Eloisa, Jean Jacques Rousseau
1764	Castle of Otranto, Horace Walpole
	Rights of British Colonies, James Otis
1765–69	Commentaries of the Laws of England, Sir William Blackstone
1766	The Vicar of Wakefield, Oliver Goldsmith
1768	Letters from a Farmer in Pennsylvania, John Dickinson
	A Sentimental Journey, Laurence Sterne
1769	History of the Reign of Charles V, William Robertson
1770	The Deserted Village, Oliver Goldsmith
1772	Rising Glory of America, Philip Freneau and Hugh H. Brackenridge
1774	Letters, Philip D. Stanhope, Earl of Chesterfield
1775	M'Fingal, John Trumbull
1776	The American Crisis, Thomas Paine
	Apology for the Bible, Richard Watson
	Common Sense, Thomas Paine
1779	The Sorrows of Young Werther, Johann Wolfgang Goethe
1782	Letters from an American Farmer, Crèvecoeur
1783	American Spelling Book, Noah Webster
1784	Reason the Only Oracle of Man, Ethan Allen
1787–88	The Federalist papers, Alexander Hamilton, James Madison, and John Jay
1787	Notes on Virginia, Thomas Jefferson
1791–92	The Rights of Man, Thomas Paine
1791	Charlotte Temple: A Tale of Truth, Susanna Haswell Rowson
1792	Advice to the Privileged Orders, Joel Barlow
	Modern Chivalry, Hugh H. Brackenridge
1794	Autobiography, Benjamin Franklin
	Mysteries of Udolpho, Mrs. Ann Radcliffe
1796	Hasty Pudding, Joel Barlow
	The Monk, Matthew Gregory Lewis
1797	The Coquette, Mrs. Hannah Foster
1799	Arthur Mervyn, Charles Brockden Brown
	Ormond, Charles Brockden Brown
	Pleasures of Hope, Thomas Campbell
c. 1800	The Life and Memorable Actions of George Washington, Mason Locke Weems
1803	Thaddeus of Warsaw, Jane Porter
1805	The Lay of the Last Minstrel, Sir Walter Scott

1807	Hours of Idleness, George Gordon, Lord Byron	1837	Life of Washington, Jared Sparks
1808	Marmion, Sir Walter Scott		Nick of the Woods, Robert Montgomery Bird
1809	Gertrude of Wyoming, Thomas Campbell		Pickwick Papers, Charles Dickens
	History of New York, Washington Irving		Twice-Told Tales, Nathaniel Hawthorne
1810	The Lady of the Lake, Sir Walter Scott		Zenobia, William Ware
	The Scottish Chiefs, Jane Porter	1838	The American Democrat, James Fenimore Cooper
1811	The Asylum, or Alonzo and Melissa, Isaac Mitchell		Oliver Twist, Charles Dickens
1812–18	Childe Harold, George Gordon, Lord Byron		The Robber, George P. R. James
1813	Bride of Abydos, George Gordon, Lord Byron	1839	The Green Mountain Boys, Daniel P. Thompson
1814	Waverley, Sir Walter Scott		Hyperion, Henry Wadsworth Longfellow
1815	Guy Mannering, Sir Walter Scott		Selections from the American Poets, William Cullen Bryant
	Moral Pieces in Prose and Verse, Lydia Huntley Sigourney		Tales of the Grotesque and Arabesque, Edgar Allan Poe
1817	Lalla Rookh, Thomas Moore	1840	Two Years Before the Mast, Richard Henry Dana
1818	The Heart of Midlothian, Sir Walter Scott	1841	The Ancient Regime, George P. R. James
1819–24	Don Juan, George Gordon, Lord Byron		The Deerslayer, James Fenimore Cooper
1819–20	The Sketch Book, Washington Irving		The Old Curiosity Shop, Charles Dickens
1819	Ivanhoe, Sir Walter Scott	1842	American Notes, Charles Dickens
1821	Kenilworth, Sir Walter Scott		The Poets and Poetry of America, Rufus Wilmot Griswold
	The Spy, James Fenimore Cooper	1843	A Christmas Carol, Charles Dickens
1822	Bracebridge Hall, Washington Irving	1844	The Monks of Monk Hall (reprinted 1845 as The Quaker City), George Lippard
1823	The Pilot, James Fenimore Cooper		
	The Pioneers, James Fenimore Cooper		The Three Musketeers, Alexandre Dumas
	Quentin Durward, Sir Walter Scott	1845	The Count of Monte Cristo, Alexandre Dumas
1824	A Narrative of the Life of Mrs. Mary Jemison, James E. Seaver		Festus, Philip James Bailey
1826	Commentaries, James Kent		Narrative of the Life of Frederick Douglass, Frederick Douglass
	The Last of the Mohicans, James Fenimore Cooper		The Raven and Other Poems, Edgar Allan Poe
1827	The Prairie, James Fenimore Cooper		Satanstoe, James Fenimore Cooper
	Tamerlane and Other Poems, Edgar Allan Poe	1846	Mosses from an Old Manse, Nathaniel Hawthorne
1828	American Dictionary of the English Language, Noah Webster		Napoleon and His Marshals, Joel Tyler Headley
	Lucy Temple, Susanna Haswell Rowson		Typee, Herman Melville
1829	The Conquest of Granada, Washington Irving Richelieu, George P. R. James	1847	Evangeline, Henry Wadsworth Longfellow
1830	The Book of Mormon, Joseph Smith		Home Influence: A Tale for Mothers and Daughters, Grace Aguilar
1831	The Dutchman's Fireside, James Kirke Paulding		Jane Eyre, Charlotte Brontë
1832	The Alhambra, Washington Irving	1848	The Biglow Papers, James Russell Lowell
	An Essay on Calcareous Manures, Edmund Ruffin		Vanity Fair, William Makepeace Thackeray
1833	The Life and Writings of Major Jack Downing, Seba Smith		The Vision of Sir Launfal, James Russell Lowell
	My Mother's Gold Ring, Lucius Manlius Sargent	1849	The Female Poets of America, Rufus Wilmot Griswold
1834	The Hunchback of Notre Dame, Victor Hugo		The Oregon Trail, Francis Parkman
	The Last Days of Pompeii, Edward Bulwer Lytton		Redburn, Herman Melville
1834–35	Outre-Mer, Henry Wadsworth Longfellow	1850	David Copperfield, Charles Dickens
1835	Georgia Scenes, Characters, and Incidents, Augustus B. Longstreet		Representative Men, Ralph Waldo Emerson
	The Yemassee, William Gilmore Simms		Reveries of a Bachelor, Ik. Marvel
1836	Astoria, Washington Irving		The Scarlet Letter, Nathaniel Hawthorne
	Awful Disclosures, Maria Monk	1851	The Golden Legend, Henry Wadsworth Longfellow
	Eclectic Reader, William McGuffey		
	Nature, Ralph Waldo Emerson		
	The Slave; or, Memoirs of Archy Moore, Richard Hildreth		

The House of the Seven Gables, Nathaniel Hawthorne
Moby Dick, Herman Melville
The Sunny Side; or The Country Minister's Wife, Elizabeth Stuart Phelps

1852 The Blithedale Romance, Nathaniel Hawthorne
The Curse of Clifton, Mrs. E. D. E. N. Southworth
Uncle Tom's Cabin, Harriet Beecher Stowe

1853 Fern Leaves from Fanny's Portfolio, Fanny Fern
Heir of Redclyffe, Charlotte Mary Yonge
A Key to Uncle Tom's Cabin, Harriet Beecher Stowe

1854 Hot Corn, Solon Robinson
The Lamplighter, Maria Susanna Cummins
The Panorama and Other Poems, John Greenleaf Whittier
Ten Nights in a Bar-Room, Timothy Shay Arthur
Walden, Henry David Thoreau

1855 Leaves of Grass, Walt Whitman
The Prince of the House of David, Joseph Holt Ingraham
The Song of Hiawatha, Henry Wadsworth Longfellow

1856 John Halifax, Gentleman, Dinah Maria Mulock
Widow Bedott Papers, Frances Miriam Whitcher

1857 Barchester Towers, Anthony Trollope
Impending Crisis of the South, Hinton R. Helper
Nothing to Wear, William Allen Butler

1858 Autocrat of the Breakfast-Table, Oliver Wendell Holmes
The Courtship of Miles Standish, Henry Wadsworth Longfellow

1859 Beulah, Augusta Jane Evans
A Tale of Two Cities, Charles Dickens
The Virginians, William Makepeace Thackeray

1860 The Conduct of Life, Ralph Waldo Emerson
Malaeska, or the Indian Wife of the White Hunter, Ann Sophia Stephens
The Marble Faun, Nathaniel Hawthorne
Seth Jones; or, The Captives of the Frontier, Edward S. Ellis
The Woman in White, William Wilkie Collins

1861 East Lynne, Mrs. Henry Wood
Elsie Venner, Oliver Wendell Holmes
Great Expectations, Charles Dickens
Silas Marner, George Eliot

1862 Artemus Ward: His Book, Artemus Ward
History of the Great Rebellion, T. P. Kettell
Maum Guinea and Her Plantation Children, Metta Victoria Victor

1863 The Fatal Marriage, Mrs. E. D. E. N. Southworth
Our Old Home, Nathaniel Hawthorne
The Tales of a Wayside Inn, Henry Wadsworth Longfellow

1864 Cudjo's Cave, John T. Trowbridge

In War Time and Other Poems, John Greenleaf Whittier

1864–66 The American Conflict, Horace Greeley

1865 Hans Brinker, Mary Elizabeth Dodge
The Man Without a Country, Edward Everett Hale
The Secret Service, Albert D. Richardson

1866 Snow-Bound, John Greenleaf Whittier

1867 Beyond the Mississippi, Albert D. Richardson
Under Two Flags, Ouida

1867ff. Ragged Dick series, Horatio Alger

1868 The Moonstone, William Wilkie Collins

1868–69 Little Women, Louisa May Alcott

1869 Innocents Abroad, Mark Twain

1869–80 Farmer's Allminax, Josh Billings

1869ff. Luck and Pluck series, Horatio Alger

1870 'The Heathen Chinee' ('Plain Language from Truthful James'), Bret Harte
Rubáiyat of Omar Khayyám, Edward FitzGerald
Society and Solitude, Ralph Waldo Emerson

1871 Democratic Vistas, Walt Whitman
The Hoosier Schoolmaster, Edward Eggleston

1871ff. Tattered Tom Series, Horatio Alger

1872 Barriers Burned Away, Edward Payson Roe
Roughing It, Mark Twain

1873 Farm Ballads, Will Carleton
The Gilded Age, Mark Twain and Charles Dudley Warner

1874 Opening a Chestnut Burr, Edward Payson Roe

1875 Science and Health, Mary Baker Eddy

1876 Tom Sawyer, Mark Twain

1877 The American, Henry James

1878 The Leavenworth Case, Anna Katharine Green

1879 Progress and Poverty, Henry George

1880 Ben-Hur, Lew Wallace
Manliness of Christ, Thomas Hughes
A Tramp Abroad, Mark Twain

1881 Portrait of a Lady, Henry James
Uncle Remus, Joel Chandler Harris
Washington Square, Henry James

1882 Atlantis: The Antediluvian World, Ignatius Donnelly
A Modern Instance, William Dean Howells
The Prince and the Pauper, Mark Twain

1883 Life on the Mississippi, Mark Twain
The Old Swimmin'-Hole and 'Leven More Poems, James Whitcomb Riley
Peck's Bad Boy and His Pa, George Wilbur Peck
Treasure Island, Robert Louis Stevenson

1884 The Adventures of Huckleberry Finn, Mark Twain
Ramona, Helen Hunt Jackson
A Roman Singer, Francis Marion Crawford

1885 King Solomon's Mines, H. Rider Haggard
The Rise of Silas Lapham, William Dean Howells

1885–86	Personal Memoirs, Ulysses S. Grant
1886	The Bostonians, Henry James
	Kidnapped, Robert Louis Stevenson
	Little Lord Fauntleroy, Frances Hodgson Burnett
1887	Mr. Barnes of New York, Archibald Clavering Gunter
	She, H. Rider Haggard
	A Study in Scarlet, Sir Arthur Conan Doyle
1888	Acres of Diamonds, Russell Conwell
	Looking Backward, Edward Bellamy
1889	A Connecticut Yankee in King Arthur's Court, Mark Twain
	The Gospel of Wealth, Andrew Carnegie
	Mr. Potter of Texas, Archibald Clavering Gunter
1890	A Cigarette-Maker's Romance, Francis Marion Crawford
	A Hazard of New Fortunes, William Dean Howells
	How the Other Half Lives, Jacob A. Riis
	The Light That Failed, Rudyard Kipling
	The Principles of Psychology, William James
1891	Caesar's Column, Ignatius Donnelly
	Colonel Carter of Cartersville, Francis Hopkinson Smith
	Main-Travelled Roads, Hamlin Garland
	Tales of Soldiers and Civilians, Ambrose G. Bierce
1892	Don Orsino, Francis Marion Crawford
1893	The Heavenly Twins, Sarah Grand
	Maggie, Stephen Crane
1894	Coin's Financial School, William Hope Harvey
	If Christ Came to Chicago, William T. Stead
	The Memoirs of Sherlock Holmes, Sir Arthur Conan Doyle
	Prisoner of Zenda, Anthony Hope
	The Tragedy of Pudd'nhead Wilson, Mark Twain
	Trilby, George Du Maurier
1895	The Jucklins, Opie Read
	The Red Badge of Courage, Stephen Crane
1896	The Boston Cooking School Cook Book, Fannie Farmer
	The Damnation of Theron Ware, Harold Frederic
	The Honorable Peter Stirling, Paul Leicester Ford
	In His Steps, Charles M. Sheldon
	Quo Vadis?, Henryk Sienkiewicz
1897	Captains Courageous, Rudyard Kipling
	The Choir Invisible, James Lane Allen
	Hugh Wynne, S. Weir Mitchell
	The Will to Believe, William James
1898	Bob, Son of Battle, Alfred Ollivant
	David Harum, Edward Noyes Westcott
	Mr. Dooley in Peace and War, Finley Peter Dunne
	When Knighthood Was in Flower, Charles Major
1899	Fables in Slang, George Ade
	Janice Meredith, Paul Leicester Ford
	'The Man with the Hoe', Edwin Markham

	A Message to Garcia, Elbert Hubbard
	The Sky Pilot, Ralph Connor
1900	Alice of Old Vincennes, Maurice Thompson
	Eben Holden, Irving Bacheller
	Sister Carrie, Theodore Dreiser
	To Have and To Hold, Mary Johnston
	Wonderful Wizard of Oz, Lyman F. Baum
1901	The Crisis, Winston Churchill
	Graustark, George Barr McCutcheon
	Mrs. Wiggs of the Cabbage Patch, Alice Hegan Rice
	The Octopus, Frank Norris
	Up from Slavery, Booker T. Washington
1902	The Mississippi Bubble, Emerson Hough
	The Varieties of Religious Experience, William James
	The Virginian, Owen Wister
1903	The Ambassador, Henry James
	The Call of the Wild, Jack London
	The Little Shepherd of Kingdom Come, John Fox
	The Pit, Frank Norris
	Rebecca of Sunnybrook Farm, Kate Douglas Wiggin
	Souls of Black Folk, W. E. B. Du Bois
1904	The Crossing, Winston Churchill
	Freckles, Gene Stratton-Porter
	The Sea-Wolf, Jack London
	The Shame of the Cities, Lincoln Steffens
1905	The Clansman, Thomas Dixon
	The Garden of Allah, Alfred Hichens
	The House of Mirth, Edith Wharton
1906	The Fighting Chance, Robert W. Chambers
	The Four Million, O. Henry
	The Jungle, Upton Sinclair
	The Spoilers, Rex Beach
1907	Songs of a Sourdough, Robert W. Service
1908	The Circular Staircase, Mary Roberts Rinehart
	The Trail of the Lonesome Pine, John W. Fox
	The Voice of the City, O. Henry
1909	A Girl of the Limberlost, Gene Stratton-Porter
	The Rosary, Florence Louisa Barclay
	The Silver Horde, Rex Beach
1910	Molly Make-Believe, Eleanor Abbott
	Twenty Years at Hull House, Jane Addams
1911	Ethan Frome, Edith Wharton
	The Winning of Barbara Worth, Harold Bell Wright
1912	Autobiography of an Ex-Colored Man, James Weldon Johnson
	The Promised Land, Mary Antin
	Riders of the Purple Sage, Zane Grey
1913	A Boy's Will, Robert Frost
	The New Freedom, Woodrow Wilson
	O Pioneers!, Willa Cather
	Pollyanna, Eleanor Hodgman Porter
1914	Penrod, Booth Tarkington
	Tarzan of the Apes, Edgar Rice Burroughs
	Trees and Other Poems, Joyce Kilmer

1915	Michael O'Halloran, Gene Stratton-Porter
	Spoon River Anthology, Edgar Lee Masters
	The Turmoil, Booth Tarkington
1916	Chicago Poems, Carl Sandburg
	Democracy and Education, John Dewey
	A Heap o' Livin', Edgar A. Guest
	Seventeen, Booth Tarkington
1917	The Light in the Clearing, Irving Bacheller
	Over the Top, Arthur Guy Empey
	Son of the Middle Border, Hamlin Garland
1918	Dere Mable, Edward Streeter
	The Education of Henry Adams, Henry Adams
	The Four Horsemen of the Apocalypse, V. Blasco Ibáñez
	The Magnificent Ambersons, Booth Tarkington
	My Antonia, Willa Cather
	The U. P. Trail, Zane Grey
1919	In Flanders Field and Other Poems, John D. McCrae
	Jurgen, James Branch Cabell
	Winesburg, Ohio, Sherwood Anderson
1920	The Age of Innocence, Edith Wharton
	The Americanization of Edward Bok, Edward Bok
	The Economic Consequences of the Peace, John M. Keynes
	Main Street, Sinclair Lewis
	Outline of History, Herbert George Wells
	This Side of Paradise, F. Scott Fitzgerald
1921	If Winter Comes, Arthur Stuart-Menteth Hutchinson
	The Mind in the Making, James Harvey Robinson
	The Sheik, Edith M. Hull
	Story of Mankind, Hendrik W. Van Loon
1922	Babbitt, Sinclair Lewis
	Etiquette: The Blue Book of Social Usage, Emily Post
	Forsyte Saga, John Galsworthy
	Self-Mastery Through Conscious Autosuggestion, Emile Coué
	The Waste Land, T. S. Eliot
1923	Black Oxen, Gertrude Atherton
	Flaming Youth, Warner Fabian
	Life of Christ, Giovanni Papini
	The Prophet, Kahlil Gibran
1924	The Green Hat, Michael Arlen
	The Plastic Age, Percy Marks
	So Big, Edna Ferber
1925	An American Tragedy, Theodore Dreiser
	Arrowsmith, Sinclair Lewis
	Gentlemen Prefer Blondes, Anita Loos
	The Great Gatsby, F. Scott Fitzgerald
	The Man Nobody Knows, Bruce Barton
	The Private Life of Helen of Troy, John Erskine
1926	Abraham Lincoln: The Prairie Years, Carl Sandburg
	The Benson Murder Case, S. S. Van Dine
	Microbe Hunters, Paul De Kruif
	The Murder of Roger Ackroyd, Agatha Christie
	The Story of Philosophy, Will Durant
	The Sun Also Rises, Ernest Hemingway
1927	archy and mehitabel, Don Marquis
	The Bridge of San Luis Rey, Thornton Wilder
	Elmer Gantry, Sinclair Lewis
	Giants in the Earth, Ole Rölvaag
	Rise of American Civilization, Charles and Mary Beard
	We, Charles Augustus Lindbergh
1928	Art of Thinking, Abbé Ernest Dimnet
	John Brown's Body, Stephen Vincent Benét
1929	All Quiet on the Western Front, Erich Maria Remarque
	Dodsworth, Sinclair Lewis
	A Farewell to Arms, Ernest Hemingway
	The Little Engine That Could, Watty Piper
	Look Homeward, Angel, Thomas Wolfe
	Magnificent Obsession, Lloyd C. Douglas
	The Sound and the Fury, William Faulkner
1930	Charlie Chan Carries On, Earl Derr Biggers
	Cimarron, Edna Ferber
	42nd Parallel, John Hersey
	The Maltese Falcon, Dashiell Hammett
1931	The Dutch Shoe Mystery, Ellery Queen
	The Epic of America, James Truslow Adams
	The Good Earth, Pearl Buck
	Only Yesterday, Frederick Lewis Allen
1932	Life Begins at Forty, Walter B. Pitkin
	Light in August, William Faulkner
	The Thin Man, Dashiell Hammett
	Tobacco Road, Erskine Caldwell
	Young Lonigan, James T. Farrell
1933	Anthony Adverse, Hervey Allen
	Autobiography of Alice B. Toklas, Gertrude Stein
	The Case of the Velvet Claws, Erle Stanley Gardner
	God's Little Acre, Erskine Caldwell
	Lost Horizon, James Hilton
1934	Good-Bye, Mr. Chips, James Hilton
	So Red the Rose, Stark Young
	Tender is the Night, F. Scott Fitzgerald
	While Rome Burns, Alexander Woollcott
1934–35	R. E. Lee, Douglas Southall Freeman
1935	It Can't Happen Here, Sinclair Lewis
	Life with Father, Clarence Day
	Man the Unknown, Alexis Carrel
	Of Time and the River, Thomas Wolfe
	Vein of Iron, Ellen Glasgow
1936	Drums Along the Mohawk, Walter D. Edmonds
	Gone with the Wind, Margaret Mitchell
	How to Win Friends and Influence People, Dale Carnegie
	Inside Europe, John Gunther
	The Last Puritan, George Santayana
	Wake Up and Live!, Dorothea Brande
1937	The Citadel, Archibald Joseph Cronin
	The Late George Apley, J. P. Marquand
	Northwest Passage, Kenneth Roberts

	Of Mice and Men, John Steinbeck		A Rage to Live, John O'Hara
1938	All This, and Heaven Too, Rachel Field		This I Remember, Eleanor Roosevelt
	The Importance of Living, Lin Yutang	1950	Betty Crocker's Picture Cook Book
	Rebecca, Daphne du Maurier		The Cardinal, Henry Morton Robinson
	The Yearling, Marjorie Kinnan Rawlings		The Disenchanted, Budd Schulberg
			Joy Street, Francis Parkinson Keyes
1939	Inside Asia, John Gunther		Kon-Tiki, Thor Heyerdahl
	Grapes of Wrath, John Steinbeck		Look Younger, Live Longer, Gayelord Hauser
	Mein Kampf, Adolf Hitler		The Martian Chronicles, Ray Bradbury
	Mrs. Miniver, Jan Struther		My Gun is Quick, Mickey Spillane
1940	For Whom the Bell Tolls, Ernest Hemingway	1951	The Caine Mutiny, Herman Wouk
	How to Read a Book, Mortimer Adler		Catcher in the Rye, J. D. Salinger
	Native Son, Richard Wright		From Here to Eternity, James Jones
	Oliver Wiswell, Kenneth Roberts		Lie Down in Darkness, William Styron
1941	Berlin Diary, William L. Shirer		A Man Called Peter, Catherine Marshall
	Blood, Sweat and Tears, Winston Churchill		Requiem for a Nun, William Faulkner
	The Keys of the Kingdom, Archibald Joseph Cronin		The Sea Around Us, Rachel Carson
		1952	East of Eden, John Steinbeck
	Mission to Moscow, Joseph Edward Davies		Grant, Edna Ferber
1942	Go Down, Moses, William Faulkner		The Old Man and the Sea, Ernest Hemingway
	The Last Time I Saw Paris, Elliot Paul		The Power of Positive Thinking, Norman Vincent Peale
	The Robe, Lloyd Douglas		The Silver Chalice, Thomas B. Costain
	See Here, Private Hargrove, Marion Hargrove	1953	The Adventures of Augie March, Saul Bellow
	They Were Expendable, William Lindsay White		Battle Cry, Leon M. Uris
1943	Guadalcanal Diary, Richard Tregaskis		Desirée, Annemarie Selinko
	Here Is Your War, Ernie Pyle		A House Is Not a Home, Polly Adler
	Men, Women, and Dogs, James Thurber		Sexual Behavior in the Human Female, Alfred C. Kinsey et al.
	One World, Wendell Willkie	1954	Benton's Row, Frank Yerby
	A Tree Grows in Brooklyn, Betty Smith		The Mad Reader
1944	A Bell for Adano, John Hersey		No Time for Sergeants, Mac Hyman
	Brave Men, Ernie Pyle		Shane, Jack Schaefer
	Forever Amber, Kathleen Winsor		Sweet Thursday, John Steinbeck
	I Never Left Home, Bob Hope	1955	Andersonville, Mackinlay Kantor
	Strange Fruit, Lillian Smith		Auntie Mame, Patrick Dennis
	Yankee from Olympus, Catherine Bowen		Eloise, Kay Thompson
1945	Black Boy, Richard Wright		The Man in the Gray Flannel Suit, Sloan Wilson
	The Black Rose, Thomas B. Costain		Marjorie Morningstar, Herman Wouk
	The Egg and I, Betty MacDonald		Ten North Frederick, John O'Hara
	Up Front, Bill Mauldin		Why Johnny Can't Read, Rudolf Flesch
1946	All the King's Men, Robert Penn Warren	1956	Don't Go Near the Water, William Brinkley
	The Common Sense Book of Baby and Child Care, Benjamin Spock, M.D.		Howl, Allen Ginsberg
	Foxes of Harrow, Frank Yerby		The Last Hurrah, Edwin O'Connor
	Hiroshima, John Hersey		Peyton Place, Grace Metalious
	The Miracle of the Bells, Russell Janney		Profiles in Courage, John F. Kennedy
			A Walk on the Wild Side, Nelson Algren
	Peace of Mind, Joshua Loth Liebman	1957	The Assistant, Bernard Malamud
1947	Inside U.S.A., John Gunther		Atlas Shrugged, Ayn Rand
	I, the Jury, Mickey Spillane		By Love Possessed, James Gould Couzzens
	Kingsblood Royal, Sinclair Lewis		The Cat in the Hat, Dr. Seuss
	The Wayward Bus, John Steinbeck		A Death in the Family, James Agee
1948	The Big Fisherman, Lloyd C. Douglas		On the Road, Jack Kerouac
	Crusade in Europe, Dwight D. Eisenhower		Where Did You Go? Out. What Did You Do? Nothing., Robert Paul Smith
	The Naked and the Dead, Norman Mailer	1958	Doctor Zhivago, Boris Pasternak
	The Seven Storey Mountain, Thomas Merton		Exodus, Leon Uris
	Sexual Behavior in the Human Male, Alfred Charles Kinsey		Lolita, Vladimir Nabokov
			Masters of Deceit, J. Edgar Hoover
	The Young Lions, Irwin Shaw		Only in America, Harry Golden
1949	Father of the Bride, Edward Streeter		'Twixt Twelve and Twenty, Pat Boone
	Point of No Return, John P. Marquand	1959	Act One, Moss Hart
			Advise and Consent, Allen Drury

1960
Goldfinger, Ian Fleming
Goodbye, Columbus, Phillip Roth
Hawaii, James Michener
The Status Seekers, Vance Packard
Ceremony in Lone Tree, Wright Morris
The Conscience of a Conservative, Barry Goldwater
Rabbit, Run, John Updike
The Rise and Fall of the Third Reich, William L. Shirer
To Kill a Mockingbird, Harper Lee

1961
The Agony and the Ecstasy, Irving Stone
The Carpetbaggers, Harold Robbins
Catch-22, Joseph Heller
Franny and Zooey, J. D. Salinger
The Making of the President, 1960, Theodore H. White
Nobody Knows My Name, James Baldwin
Stranger in a Strange Land, Robert Heinlein

1962
Fail-Safe, Eugene Burdick and Harvey Wheeler
Happiness Is a Warm Puppy, Charles M. Schulz
One Flew Over the Cuckoo's Nest, Ken Kesey
The Reivers, William Faulkner
Ship of Fools, Katherine Anne Porter
Silent Spring, Rachel Carson

1963
The Fire Next Time, James Baldwin
The Group, Mary McCarthy
Raise High the Roof Beam, Carpenters, and Seymour—An Introduction, J. D. Salinger
The Shoes of the Fisherman, Morris L. West
The Spy Who Came in From the Cold, John Le Carré
V, Thomas Pynchon

1964
Candy, Terry Southern and Mason Hoffenberg
Games People Play, Eric Berne, M.D.
Herzog, Saul Bellow

In His Own Write, John Lennon
A Moveable Feast, Ernest Hemingway
Sometimes a Great Notion, Ken Kesey
Why We Can't Wait, Martin Luther King, Jr.

1965
American Dream, Norman Mailer
Everything That Rises Must Converge, Flannery O'Connor
The Green Berets, Robin Moore
Manchild in the Promised Land, Claude Brown
A Thousand Days, Arthur Schlesinger, Jr.
Thunderball, Ian Fleming
Unsafe at Any Speed, Ralph Nader

1966
The Fixer, Bernard Malamud
Giles Goat-Boy, John Barth
In Cold Blood, Truman Capote
The Moon is a Harsh Mistress, Robert Heinlein
Quotations of Mao Tse-tung
Valley of the Dolls, Jacqueline Susann

1967
The Chosen, Chaim Potok
Division Street: America, Studs Terkel
The Naked Ape, Desmond Morris
The New Industrial State, John Kenneth Galbraith
Our Crowd, Stephen Birmingham
Rosemary's Baby, Ira Levin

1968
The Algiers Motel Incident, John Hersey
The American Challenge, J. J. Servan-Schreiber
The Double Helix, James D. Watson
The Electric Kool-Aid Acid Test, Tom Wolfe
Myra Breckinridge, Gore Vidal
The Rich and the Super-Rich, Ferdinand Lundberg

1969
The Andromeda Strain, Michael Crichton
The Peter Principle, Dr. Laurence Peter and Raymond Hall
Portnoy's Complaint, Philip Roth
Slaughterhouse-Five, Kurt Vonnegut

Academy Award Winners 1927–1968

year	best picture	best actor	best actress
1927–28	Wings	Emil Jannings (The Last Command, The Way of All Flesh)	Janet Gaynor (Seventh Heaven, Street Angel, Sunrise)
1928–29	Broadway Melody	Warner Baxter (In Old Arizona)	Mary Pickford (Coquette)
1929–30	All Quiet on the Western Front	George Arliss (Disraeli)	Norma Shearer (The Divorcee)
1930–31	Cimarron	Lionel Barrymore (A Free Soul)	Marie Dressler (Min and Bill)
1931–32	Grand Hotel	Wallace Beery (The Champ) Fredric March (Dr. Jekyll and Mr. Hyde)	Helen Hayes (The Sin of Madelon Claudet)
1932–33	Cavalcade	Charles Laughton (The Private Life of Henry VIII)	Katharine Hepburn (Morning Glory)
1934	It Happened One Night	Clark Gable (It Happened One Night)	Claudette Colbert (It Happened One Night)

year	best picture	best actor	best actress
1935	Mutiny on the Bounty	Victor McLaglen (The Informer)	Bette Davis (Dangerous)
1936	The Great Ziegfeld	Paul Muni (The Story of Louis Pasteur)	Luise Rainer (The Great Ziegfeld)
1937	The Life of Emile Zola	Spencer Tracy (Captains Courageous)	Luise Rainer (The Good Earth)
1938	You Can't Take It with You	Spencer Tracy (Boys Town)	Bette Davis (Jezebel)
1939	Gone with the Wind	Robert Donat (Goodbye, Mr. Chips)	Vivien Leigh (Gone with the Wind)
1940	Rebecca	James Stewart (The Philadelphia Story)	Ginger Rogers (Kitty Foyle)
1941	How Green Was My Valley	Gary Cooper (Sergeant York)	Joan Fontaine (Suspicion)
1942	Mrs. Miniver	James Cagney (Yankee Doodle Dandy)	Greer Garson (Mrs. Miniver)
1943	Casablanca	Paul Lukas (Watch on the Rhine)	Jennifer Jones (The Song of Bernadette)
1944	Going My Way	Bing Crosby (Going My Way)	Ingrid Bergman (Gaslight)
1945	The Lost Weekend	Ray Milland (The Lost Weekend)	Joan Crawford (Mildred Pierce)
1946	The Best Years of Our Lives	Fredric March (The Best Years of Our Lives)	Olivia de Havilland (To Each His Own)
1947	Gentleman's Agreement	Ronald Colman (A Double Life)	Loretta Young (The Farmer's Daughter)
1948	Hamlet	Laurence Olivier (Hamlet)	Jane Wyman (Johnny Belinda)
1949	All the King's Men	Broderick Crawford (All the King's Men)	Olivia de Havilland (The Heiress)
1950	All About Eve	Jose Ferrer (Cyrano de Bergerac)	Judy Holliday (Born Yesterday)
1951	An American in Paris	Humphrey Bogart (The African Queen)	Vivian Leigh (A Streetcar Named Desire)
1952	The Greatest Show on Earth	Gary Cooper (High Noon)	Shirley Booth (Come Back, Little Sheba)
1953	From Here to Eternity	William Holden (Stalag 17)	Audrey Hepburn (Roman Holiday)
1954	On the Waterfront	Marlon Brando (On the Waterfront)	Grace Kelly (The Country Girl)
1955	Marty	Ernest Borgnine (Marty)	Anna Magnani (The Rose Tattoo)
1956	Around the World in 80 Days	Yul Brynner (The King and I)	Ingrid Bergman (Anastasia)
1957	The Bridge on the River Kwai	Alec Guinness (The Bridge on the River Kwai)	Joanne Woodward (The Three Faces of Eve)
1958	Gigi	David Niven (Separate Tables)	Susan Hayward (I Want to Live)
1959	Ben-Hur	Charlton Heston (Ben-Hur)	Simone Signoret (Room at the Top)
1960	The Apartment	Burt Lancaster (Elmer Gantry)	Elizabeth Taylor (Butterfield 8)
1961	West Side Story	Maximilian Schell (Judgment at Nuremberg)	Sophia Loren (Two Women)
1962	Lawrence of Arabia	Gregory Peck (To Kill a Mockingbird)	Anne Bancroft (The Miracle Worker)
1963	Tom Jones	Sidney Poitier (Lilies of the Field)	Patricia Neal (Hud)
1964	My Fair Lady	Rex Harrison (My Fair Lady)	Julie Andrews (Mary Poppins)
1965	The Sound of Music	Lee Marvin (Cat Ballou)	Julie Christie (Darling)
1966	A Man for All Seasons	Paul Scofield (A Man for All Seasons)	Elizabeth Taylor (Who's Afraid of Virginia Woolf?)
1967	In the Heat of the Night	Rod Steiger (In the Heat of the Night)	Katharine Hepburn (Guess Who's Coming to Dinner?)
1968	Oliver!	Cliff Robertson (Charly)	Katharine Hepburn (The Lion in Winter)
1969	Midnight Cowboy	John Wayne (True Grit)	Maggie Smith (The Prime of Miss Jean Brodie)

PART III
Biographies

ABBOT, FRANCIS ELLINGWOOD (1836–1903), religious leader and philosopher. Born in Boston on November 6, 1836, Abbot graduated from Harvard in 1859 and attended its divinity school for a year before going to Meadville, Pennsylvania, to take charge of a girls' school and to conclude his studies at Meadville Theological Seminary. He graduated in 1863 and became pastor of the Unitarian Church in Dover, New Hampshire. He wrote philosophical articles for the *North American Review* that were greatly admired. His radical religious views, however, led him to form a Free Religious Association—based on the view that "God in Christ" must be replaced by "God in Humanity"—that caused a split in his Dover congregation in 1869. Philosophical chairs at Cornell and Harvard were denied him, despite strong recommendations, by theological opposition. He finally accepted the Unitarian pastorate in Toledo, Ohio; the congregation changed its name to the Independent Church and offered funds for the publication of a weekly journal of Free Religion. He edited the *Index* for ten years and also organized the National Liberal League (1876) to support religious freedom. Returning to Harvard, he took his doctorate in 1881; a version of his thesis, *Scientific Theism*, soon ran through three editions and a German translation, winning him European attention. In 1888 he substituted for Josiah Royce at Harvard, but his lectures (*The Way Out of Agnosticism*, 1890) were publicly attacked by the returning Royce on personal grounds. Abbot, whose belief in the unity of reason and experience was to become acceptable 20 years later, was embittered by the controversy and withdrew into solitude to prepare his major work, *The Syllogistic Philosophy*, 1906. When it was completed, just ten years after his wife's death, he committed suicide by poison over her grave, on October 23, 1903.

ABBOTT, LYMAN (1835–1922), Congregationalist clergyman, editor, and author. Born in Roxbury, Massachusetts, on December 18, 1835, Abbott was raised in Farmington, Maine, and in New York City. After attending his uncle Charles's school for boys in Norwich, Connecticut, he entered New York University at 14. Upon graduation, he joined his brothers' law firm in New York. By 1859 he was earning a good income in the law, but he decided to satisfy his boyhood aspirations to the ministry. He returned to Farmington where he was ordained in 1860. He took over the Congregational Church in Terre Haute, Indiana, during the Civil War, and in 1865 returned to New York to serve as corresponding secretary of the American Union Commission, a group of ministers and laymen formed to cooperate with the government in the task of Southern reconstruction. He held this post for four years, and was simultaneously pastor of the New England Congregational Church in New York. His book reviews for *Harper's Magazine* led the American Tract Society to appoint him editor of the *Illustrated Christian Weekly* in 1870. He joined Henry Ward Beecher in the editorship of the *Christian Union* in 1876, and became editor-in-chief in 1881. He also succeeded Beecher as pastor of the Plymouth Congregation in Brooklyn, but he resigned in 1899 to devote himself entirely to editing. He had renamed the *Christian Union* the *Outlook* in 1893, and it became a powerful exponent of progressive and practical Christianity. Although his books ranged from sympathetic interpretations of modern science to widely read works of devotion, the bulk of his writings, from *Christianity and Social Problems*, 1897, to *America in the Making*, 1911, made him a major proponent of the Social Gospel, the attempt to apply Christianity to the problems of the industrial world. His views were middle-of-the-road, opposed both to socialism and to laissez faire economics. He died in New York City on October 22, 1922.

ACHESON, DEAN GOODERHAM (1893–), lawyer, public official, and author. Born in Middletown, Connecticut, on April 11, 1893, Acheson received his B.A. from Yale in 1916 and his LL.B. from Harvard in 1918. He was private secretary to U.S. Supreme Court Justice Louis D. Brandeis from 1919 to 1921, and practised with a Washington law firm until 1933, when President Franklin Roosevelt appointed him undersecretary of the treasury. As a Depression measure, the administration sought to depart from the international gold standard through the gold-purchase plan, but Acheson considered the plan illegal and was emphatic in his view. After six months in the Treasury, Roosevelt asked for his resignation. Acheson resumed his successful Washington law practice until the attorney general named him to direct a study of administrative tribunals in 1939. The report (1941) on "judicial fair play" was considered a landmark in administrative reform. Long active in promoting aid to Great Britain, Acheson was then appointed assistant secretary of state by Roosevelt. He served as undersecretary from 1945 to 1947 before becoming secretary of state in 1949. Never outspoken in his hostility to the Russians, he was accused during the second Truman administration of being "soft on Communism." During his four years in the Cabinet he oversaw the development of the International Bank for Reconstruction and Development, the United Nations Relief and Rehabilitation Agency, the Baruch Plan for the international control of atomic energy, and the Marshall Plan for European economic recovery. He resumed his Washington law practice in 1953, and also served as chief advisor on foreign policy to the Democratic National Committee. His books include *Power and Diplomacy*, 1958, the autobiographical *Morning and Noon*, 1965, and *Present at the Creation*, 1969.

ADAMS, ABIGAIL (1744–1818), letter writer. Born in Weymouth, Massachusetts, on November 11(O.S.), 1744, Abigail Smith was a delicate child who spent much of her time in seclusion with her grandparents in Mount Wollaston. Though she received no formal schooling, her broadmindedness and intelligence found scope in letter writing. In 1764 she married John Adams, a practising lawyer in Boston. Their four children were born in

the next ten years: John Quincy, Thomas, Charles, and Abby. She resolutely supported her husband in his insistence on colonial independence and brought to his cause a loyal zeal. During the early days of the Revolution her husband was much in Philadelphia and she had entire care of the family. Her letters, written during her husband's long absences, conveyed a vivid picture of the times. With the signing of the peace treaty in 1783, she joined her husband in Paris; after eight months they moved to London, where he served as the first American minister to George III's court. Despite the social discourtesies she suffered, "England," she wrote later, "is the country of my greatest partiality." In 1789 her husband was elected Vice President and in 1796 President. One of the most distinguished and influential of First Ladies, Mrs. Adams returned to Quincy in 1801 to live as tranquilly "as that bald old fellow, called Time" would permit. Shortly before her death from typhoid fever on October 28, 1818, she had laughed at proposals to publish her letters. A vital source of social history, they have been often republished.

ADAMS, BROOKS (1848–1927), historian. Born at Quincy, Massachusetts, on June 24, 1848, Brooks was a grandson of John Quincy Adams and a brother of Charles Francis Adams, Jr., and Henry Adams. He graduated from Harvard in 1870 and after a year at the Law School served as secretary to his diplomat father during the *Alabama* claims arbitration in Geneva. He then returned to Boston and practised law until 1881. He traveled extensively in Europe, the Middle East, and India, and began an exchange of letters with his brother Henry, also an historian, in which they developed the then-revolutionary idea that American democracy was foreordained to degradation and decay. His first work, *The Emancipation of Massachusetts*, 1887, was a protest against the ancestor-worship common in previous New England historiography. *The Law of Civilization and Decay*, 1895, developed his theory that civilizations rise and fall according to a pre-determined pattern of commercial growth and decline. *America's Economic Supremacy*, 1900, and *New Empire*, 1902, developed the theory further and predicted that in 50 years there would be only two powers in the world, Russia and the United States, the latter having economic supremacy. His study of the defects of the American form of government, *The Theory of Social Revolutions*, 1913, concluded that the immediate danger lay in the fact that great wealth exerted tremendous private power, but shirked public responsibility. In 1920 he saw his late brother Henry's book, *The Degradation of Democratic Dogma*, through the press, prefacing it with a family chronicle going back to President John Adams and ending with a renunciation of "democratic dogma" by his two grandsons. Although he never held public office, he was elected to the Massachusetts constitutional convention in 1917. World War I was, for him, the fulfillment of his prediction of the collapse of modern Western civilization. He died in Boston on February 13, 1927.

ADAMS, CHARLES FRANCIS (1807–1886), diplomat and statesman. Born in Boston on August 18, 1807, Adams was the grandson of John Adams and son of John Quincy Adams. At the age of two, he went with his father to Russia and lived in St. Petersburg for six years. His regular schooling began in England, where he attended a boarding school for two years, and continued at the Latin School in Boston. He graduated from Harvard in 1825 and went to live in the White House during the last two years of his father's term, studying law and moving among the statesmen of the Capitol. Returning to Boston, he concluded his studies under Daniel Webster and was admitted to the bar in 1829. He took over the management of his father's financial affairs so that the former President could return to Washington as a congressman. Although he disapproved of his father's second career and did not yet agree with his measures to support the antislavery cause, he campaigned for him and supported his pro-Abolitionist policies.

He also practised law and wrote articles on American history for the *North American Review*. In 1835 his series of newspaper articles was reprinted as the widely read pamphlet, *An Appeal from the New to the Old Whigs, by a Whig of the Old School*. By 1837 the attacks against the Abolitionists had converted him fully to their cause. During his five years in the state legislature, 1840–1845, he put Massachusetts on record as being Abolitionist despite a lack of party support. He founded the *Boston Whig* in 1846 and edited it until 1848, when he became vice-presidential candidate of the Free Soil Party. With the formation of the Republican Party, he represented his father's old district in Washington, 1858–1861, and became a party leader. Lincoln's election brought demands that Adams be given a Cabinet post, but the grave delicacy of diplomatic relations with Great Britain led to his appointment as minister to the Court of St. James. Before Adams could disembark, the English had acknowledged the belligerence of the Southern states and threatened, for the next few years, to recognize the Confederacy, an action implying defeat of the Union. His wisdom and dignity in the face of aristocratic sympathy for the South and of the British need for cotton were instrumental in maintaining the continued neutrality of Great Britain. In 1868, he returned to America, where he found a changed political scene and declined the only post he was offered — the presidency of Harvard — and resettled in Quincy. His last public service was as the American member of the five-man tribunal held in Geneva, 1871–1872, to adjudicate the *Alabama* claims. American success in the case was wholly attributed to his skillful diplomacy. Adams received support for the presidential nomination at the 1872 Liberal Republican convention, but lost to Horace Greeley. He published numerous political pamphlets and addresses, and edited many family papers. He died in Boston on November 21, 1886.

ADAMS, CHARLES FRANCIS, JR. (1835–1915), historian, civic leader, and railroad expert. Born in Boston on May 27, 1835, Adams was a grandson of John Quincy Adams and older brother of Henry and Brooks Adams. He graduated from Harvard in 1856, entered a leading Boston law firm, and was admitted to the bar in 1858 but, not caring for the law, he was glad when family circumstances allowed him to join the Union Army. He served for three and a half years, fighting in the battles of Antietam and Gettysburg, and rising from first lieutenant to colonel. He declined a high staff position so that he could stay with his Negro regiment, the 5th Massachusetts Cavalry. In June 1865 he was mustered out as a brigadier general and for a year toured Europe to regain his health. Again avoiding law, he turned to the study of the American railroads, which were at the time overbuilt, corruptly financed, and the object of uncontrolled stock speculation and manipulation. Parts of his *Chapters of Erie and Other Essays*, 1871, *Railroads: Their Origin and Problems*, 1878, and *Notes on American Railroad Accidents*, 1879, appeared first in periodicals. His exposés led to the formation of the Massachusetts Board of Railroad Commissioners; Adams was appointed its youngest member in 1869 and served as chairman from 1872 to 1879. He also became chairman of the Union Pacific in 1878 and was named the railroad's president in 1884, a position from which he was ousted in 1890 by Jay Gould. He devoted himself to civic affairs in his home town of Quincy, putting its budget in the black, arranging for its first public library, and reorganizing its antiquated school system. His *New Departure in the Common Schools of Quincy*, 1879, went through six editions, and the "Quincy system," substituting a problems approach for rote memorization, was widely adopted. He served on the Harvard Board of Overseers for 24 years, and was president of the Massachusetts Historical Society from 1895 until his death on May 20, 1915, in Washington.

ADAMS, FRANKLIN PIERCE (1881–1960), journalist and humorist. Born in Chicago on November 15, 1881, Adams graduated from Armour Institute of Technology in 1899, went to the University of Michigan, and "almost completed my freshman year." He then worked for an insurance company as a supply clerk and salesman until, in 1903, he joined the staff of the *Chicago Journal*. He conducted a column, "A Little About Everything," and wrote a daily weather story. The following year he went to New York to do a column for the *Evening Mail*, "Always in Good Humor." In 1913 he moved to the *New York Tribune* with the column "The Conning Tower." He served in Army Intelligence during World War I: "I didn't fight and I didn't shoot/But, General, how I did salute!" He also wrote an occasional column, "The Listening Post," for *Stars and Stripes*. After the armistice, he returned to the *Tribune* until 1923 when he set up his "Conning Tower" at the *New York World*. He returned to the *Tribune*—by now the *Herald Tribune*—in 1931, and the column, signed, as were most of his writings, with his initials "F.P.A.," was syndicated in six newspapers. His trenchant comments on the American scene were supplemented by his "mocking and impudent" poems, and the column often included contributions from people he knew: Groucho Marx, Edna St. Vincent Millay, Deems Taylor, Heywood Broun, Sinclair Lewis, Dorothy Parker, John Erskine, and other notables. His wit received national recognition in 1938, when he became a regular panelist on the radio program, *Information Please*. After moving "The Conning Tower" to the *New York Post*, F.P.A. stopped writing it in 1941. In *The Melancholy Lute*, 1936, he collected ten books of verse going back to *Tobogganing on Parnassus*, 1911. A two-volume collection of his columns and other writings, *The Diary of Our Own Samuel Pepys*, appeared in 1936. Adams died in New York on March 23, 1960.

ADAMS, HENRY BROOKS (1838–1918), historian. Born in Boston on February 16, 1838, the grandson of John Quincy Adams and the brother of Charles Francis Adams, Jr., and

Brooks Adams, Henry graduated from Harvard in 1858. He went to Berlin to study civil law, but after one lecture he decided instead to tour Germany and Italy, where he secured an interview with Garabaldi that was published in the *Boston Courier*. A few months later he returned to Boston and became secretary to his father, then a congressman and later, during the Civil War, minister to Great Britain. His first historical articles began appearing in the *North American Review* before his return to America in 1868. He took up residence in Washington, but the quality of Grant's Cabinet appointments soon dashed his hopes for political reform, and he accepted Harvard's offer to teach history in 1870, becoming at the same time editor of the *Review*. In his medieval history course, he introduced seminar teaching for the first time in America; his joint researches with students resulted in his first book, *Essays in Anglo-Saxon Law*, 1876. After seven years of teaching, he left the "laborious banishment" and returned to Washington in order to write and be with old friends, including Secretary of State William M. Evarts and John Hay. He produced *Documents Relating to New England Federalism, 1800–1815*, 1877, biographies of *Albert Gallatin*, 1879, and *John Randolph*, 1882, as well as two novels, *Democracy*, 1880, and *Esther*, 1884. He also began his nine-volume *History of the United States from 1801–1817*, 1889–1891, a monumental work interrupted by the death of his wife and subsequent travels to Mexico and the Caribbean, the South Seas and the Orient, Russia, and Europe. Adams was chosen president of the American Historical Association in 1894. He privately printed his *Mont Saint Michel and Chartres*, 1904, but the wide appeal of this study of medieval life, art, and philosophy required a public reprint in 1913. The same was true of its sequel, the autobiographical *Education of Henry Adams*, 1906, 1918, in which, among other subjects, he developed his dynamic theory of history. His other writings include *A Letter to American Teachers of History*, 1910, and *The Degradation of Demo-*

cratic Dogma, 1919. He died in Washington on March 27, 1918.

ADAMS, JOHN (1735–1826), lawyer, public official, and 2nd U.S. President. Born in Braintree (later Quincy), Massachusetts, on October 19 (O.S.), 1735, Adams graduated from Harvard in 1755 and three years later, having taught school for a time before taking up the study of law, was admitted to the bar. As his practice grew he became involved in public affairs. Real prominence came first in 1765 when, in protest against the Stamp Act, he drafted the instructions to Braintree's representatives in the legislature; these were used as models by many other Massachusetts towns. Later that year he published a series of articles in the *Boston Gazette* that were issued in book form in 1768 as *A Dissertation on the Canon and Feudal Law*. Moving to Boston in 1768, he continued his practice and included among his cases a defense of John Hancock against a charge of smuggling; but his most famous appearance before the bar came in 1770 when he displayed the depth of his integrity and courage by defending the British soldiers accused of murder in the Boston Massacre. The following year he was elected to the legislature. He consistently opposed the harsh measures imposed by England on the colonies and in 1774 was elected to the Continental Congress. He gradually became convinced of the necessity of American independence and in June 1776 seconded Richard Henry Lee's motion to that effect. He served on the committee charged with drafting the Declaration of Independence and, though Jefferson wrote the document, was its leading advocate in debate. He continued in Congress, serving on several major committees, until 1778 when he sailed for France to join Benjamin Franklin and Arthur Lee in a mission to the French government. On his recommendation Congress soon named Franklin the sole representative; Adams returned to America in June 1779 and was immediately elected to the Massachusetts constitutional convention, for which he wrote most of the first draft of the new instrument. In November he sailed again for Paris, this time secretly empowered to negotiate peace with Great Britain. He was extremely distrustful of the French government and at length persuaded his colleagues John Jay and Franklin to disregard their instructions from Congress and to initiate direct talks with the British without first consulting the French. The preliminary treaty was signed in November 1782; in the meanwhile Adams, appointed minister to Holland in 1780, had secured from that country diplomatic recognition, a loan, and a commercial treaty. He remained in Holland until his appointment as minister to Great Britain in 1785. Returning to America in 1788, he was elected the first Vice President under the new Constitution the next year. His eight years in the office were unpleasant: "My country has in its wisdom contrived for me the most insignificant office that ever the invention of man contrived or his imagination conceived." Nonetheless he emerged one of the principal leaders of the Federalists and in 1796 was elected President. He took office at a time of serious problems in foreign affairs; Jay's Treaty had antagonized France and a conciliatory commission sent by Adams was refused a hearing until a bribe were paid to agents known only as X, Y, and Z. The affair inflamed Congress and the American public and the Federalists began calling for war; Adams endorsed defensive military preparations but ignored party pressure by continuing to seek a peaceful solution to the diplomatic impasse. He assented to the passage of the Alien and Sedition Acts in 1798 and appointed George Washington to command the newly mobilized army. France finally relented and indicated a willingness to receive a minister; Adams enraged Hamilton and other Federalists by sending one and averting war. Hamilton's opposition, combined with popular dislike of the Alien and Sedition laws, swung support away from Adams, and in the election of 1800 he was defeated by Thomas Jefferson. Among his final official acts were a number of last-minute, or "midnight," appointments to the federal judiciary, including that of John Marshall as chief justice of the Supreme Court. Retiring to Quincy, Adams lived out his life quietly; he removed himself from public affairs and devoted much time to correspondence. Through the agency of Benjamin Rush, he and Jefferson were eventually reconciled and between them passed a series of remarkable epistolary observations and speculations on man and government. Adams died at home on the 50th anniversary of the Declaration of Independence, July 4, 1826, uttering with his last breath the words "Thomas Jefferson still lives"; but Jefferson had died a few hours earlier.

ADAMS, JOHN QUINCY (1767–1848), diplomat, public official, and 6th U.S. President. Born in Braintree (later Quincy), Massachusetts, on July 11, 1767, the oldest son of John and Abigail Adams, John Quincy received most of his early schooling in Europe, where he accompanied his father on diplomatic missions. In 1781 he traveled to Russia as private secretary to the American representative there, and a year later joined his father in Paris. When the elder Adams was named minister to Great Britain in 1784, he returned to Massachusetts and entered Harvard, from which he graduated in 1787. Three years later he was admitted to the bar. A series of newspaper articles supporting Washington's neutrality policy led to his appointment as minister to the Netherlands in 1794; after two years of valuable service there he was named minister to Portugal, but before he was able to assume the post his father was elected President and changed his assignment to Berlin. He returned to America in 1801; in 1802 he was elected to the Massachusetts legislature, which in turn sent him to the U.S. Senate the next year. Though nominally a Federalist, he steered a completely independent course during his five years in the Senate, particularly in supporting the Louisiana Purchase appropriations and, in 1807, Jefferson's embargo proposal. His resignation was finally forced in 1808 by angered New England Federalists. Retaining his independence, he formed connections with the Republicans and in 1809 was named minister to Russia by President Madison. In 1811, while in Russia, he declined an appointment to the Supreme Court. Adams was the chief American negotiator at the talks that resulted in the Treaty of Ghent in 1814, and soon afterwards was made minister to Great Britain. There he remained until 1817, when he became President Monroe's secretary of state. During his eight years in that office he brought his considerable skill and experience to bear on a number of problems and scored brilliant successes, notably in a treaty with Great Britain in 1818 extending the American-Canadian border westward to the Rockies along the 49th parallel and arranging for future arbitration of the Oregon question, and in a treaty with Spain in 1819 ceding Florida to the U.S. in return for a renunciation of American claims to Texas. The Monroe Doctrine, announced by the President in 1823, was largely the work of Adams. In the election of 1824 he was a leading contender; the electoral vote failed to show a majority for any of the candidates, however, and the choice went to the House of Representatives. Henry Clay, who had run fourth, controlled the deciding block of votes, and he favored Adams over Andrew Jackson as the lesser of two evils. Jackson's followers quickly raised the charge of "corrupt bargain" that, while unfounded, seemed even more credible when Adams named Clay secretary of state. The next four years were notable primarily for the growth of a new party alignment and the unrestrained antagonism between the Jacksonians and the National Republicans. Adams himself commanded little personal following and could accomplish nothing of importance. Defeated by Jackson in 1828, he retired to Quincy upon leaving office in March 1829, but the next year inaugurated the final phase of his career with his election to Congress, where he served until his death. His independence of party policy became more pronounced than ever and was an endless source of confusion to those of less spirit and breadth of view. His principal efforts centered on the increasing flow of antislavery petitions from individuals, groups, and even state legislatures. Adams himself was strongly antislavery in sentiment, though not a political Abolitionist, and he presented the petitions to the House for discussion. Their numbers increased to the point that in 1836 the pro-slavery element in the House invoked a "gag rule," prohibiting discussion of the matter. Despite Adams' ardent exertions the rule was retained until 1844. In 1839 he defied the rule by offering resolutions for a scheme of gradual elimination of slavery, and on many occasions he was threatened with censure for his insistence on the right to petition the Congress; his defense of the cause and of himself earned him the nickname "Old Man Eloquent." In 1841 he appeared before the Supreme Court and successfully defended the African mutineers of the slave ship Amistad. He fervently opposed the annexation of Texas and the Mexican War as unconstitutional and unjustifiable means of extending the domain of slavery and was still protesting when he suffered a stroke and collapsed in the House. He died two days later on February 23, 1848.

ADAMS, SAMUEL (1722–1803), political leader and Revolutionary statesman. Born in Boston on September 27, 1722, Adams came of a prominent family and was a second cousin to John Adams. He graduated from Harvard College in 1740 and devoted some time to the study of law. His life from 1740 to 1756 was marked by a series of financial difficulties attributable mainly to his own incompetent management; a stint as Boston's tax collector, from 1756 to 1764, was a similar failure, leaving him heavily in debt. He had dabbled in politics before 1764, but that year, with the passage of the Sugar Act, marked the beginning of his rise to power and influence. Adams led the condemnation of the Act and the following year was elected to the Massachusetts General Court. The Stamp Act of 1765 roused the public to elect a controlling number of popular-radical members to the Court, and

Adams quickly became a central figure. He was important in instigating the Stamp Act riots in Boston. In reaction to the Townshend duties he organized the Non-Importation Association in 1768. He stirred up antagonism between Boston and the troops sent there in 1768 and after the Boston Massacre of 1770 led the agitation for their removal. When the duties were repealed in 1770, except for a largely symbolic one on tea, Adams continued to condemn the tax despite the cooling of public sentiment and the dwindling power of the radicals. There is evidence that by this time he had already fixed upon American independence as his goal. His fierce polemics were constantly in the newspapers during the lull from 1770 to 1773 as he hounded the British on issue after issue. He was responsible for the formation of Boston's Committee of Correspondence in 1772 and for the spread of this institution throughout the colony. The declaration of rights published by the Boston committee was his work and in many ways anticipated the Declaration of Independence; he continued to articulate the philosophical arguments for independence and in doing so filled a sorely felt need among radicals. The Tea Act of 1773 reawakened popular resentment of the British government, and Adams was ready at hand as a leader; a series of mass meetings in Boston culminated in the Boston Tea Party which he apparently had arranged beforehand. He led the resistance to the Coercive Acts that followed, and was active in the adoption by Massachusetts of the Suffolk Resolves. He was sent to the first and second Continental Congresses and, with John Hancock, was excepted from the pardon to rebels offered by General Gage. With the signing of the Declaration of Independence, which he had strongly supported, Adams began slowly to recede from prominence. His great abilities had been primarily as a tireless propagandist and agitator and as a powerful polemicist. He continued a member of Congress until 1781, and was thereafter engaged in state politics. He retired from public life in 1796 and died on October 2, 1803.

ADDAMS, JANE (1860–1935), social reformer. Born on September 6, 1860, of a prosperous and prominent family in Cedarville, Illinois, Miss Addams was destined to become a leading figure of the Progressive era of reform. She graduated from Rockford College in 1881 and for several years traveled and studied in search of a vocation. In London in 1888 she visited Toynbee Hall, a pioneer settlement house. She determined to devote herself to the reform and betterment of life among the urban poor. Returning to Chicago in 1889 she established Hull House in an industrial slum neighborhood. She attracted a number of socially minded artists and educators to Hull House and together they instituted a number of pioneer programs for the people of the community. Through personal contacts and her extensive writings she was able to maintain the settlement on a firm financial basis. Her deep interest in reform led her into the labor, woman suffrage, and pacifist movements. She worked for the reform of social and welfare services and participated in Theodore Roosevelt's Progressive campaign in 1912. She was chairman of the 1915 International Congress of Women and president of the subsequent Women's International League for Peace and Freedom. In 1931 she was jointly awarded the Nobel Prize for Peace. Her major written work, *Twenty Years at Hull House*, is a classic in social reform literature. After several years of ill health, she died on May 21, 1935.

ADE, GEORGE (1866–1944), humorist and playwright. Born in Kentland, Indiana, on February 9, 1866, Ade completed his education at Purdue University before taking a position in 1890 on the staff of the *Chicago Record*. His humorous column, produced in collaboration with the artist John T. McCutcheon, evolved finally into the popular *Fables in Slang*, published in 1899. The book, a bestseller, was followed by 11 subsequent volumes of short, humorous fables in which he gently, though often satirically, lampooned the follies and foibles of his fellow countrymen. Ade's work was particularly notable for its facile use of the vernacular, and he created what many thought to be masterful portraits of the common man. He turned to the theater with equal success and at one point in his career had three plays running simultaneously in New York. He wrote a number of early movie scripts and, in the midst of Prohibition, another popular book, *The Old Time Saloon*. He died at his Indiana estate on May 16, 1944.

ADLER, CYRUS (1863–1940), educational administrator and religious leader. Born on September 13, 1863, in Van Buren, Arkansas, Adler was raised from the age of three by an uncle in Philadelphia who was extremely religious and oversaw the boy's education in a Jewish parochial school and under several noted rabbis. He earned his B.A. and M.A. degrees from the University of Pennsylvania in 1883 and 1886 and his Ph.D. in Semitics from Johns Hopkins University in 1887. He remained there, teaching Semitic languages until 1893. In 1889 he became a curator at the United States National Museum, supervising oriental antiquity, historical archeology, and historical religion collections until 1908. He also became librarian at the Smithsonian Institution in 1892 and was assistant secretary from 1905 to 1908. He resigned in the latter year to become president of the new Dropsie College for Hebrew and Cognate Learning in Philadelphia, a post he held until his death, and which made him an important lay leader of American Jews. He established the United Synagogue of America in 1913, but resigned in 1917 because of the Zionist principles it was adopting. He was anti-Zionist and opposed the influence of Rabbi Stephen Wise and his group, the American Jewish Congress. Despite the fact that he was not a rabbi, he was named acting president of the Jewish Theological Seminary in New York City, becoming its president in 1924. He largely planned and directed the publication of the *Jewish Encyclopedia*, the *American Jewish Year Book*, the *Jewish Quarterly Review*, the *Jewish Classics*, and an English translation of the Hebrew Scriptures. He was a member of the Jewish Agency for Palestine, the Hebrew University in Jerusalem, and the Jewish Welfare Board. He attended the Peace Conference at Versailles in 1919 and made a plea for the social and economic rights of all minority groups, which was incorporated in the final draft of the peace treaty. A major force in conservative Judaism, he died in Philadelphia on April 7, 1940.

ADLER, MORTIMER JEROME (1902–), philosopher, educator, and author. Born on December 28, 1902, in New York City, Adler attended the city's public schools and after leaving high school went to Columbia University, where he studied philosophy and psychology. He left the college without a degree in 1923, whereupon he began to teach at Columbia and at the People's Institute. His first book, *Dialectic,* appeared in 1927 and gained him an immediate reputation as an important, though somewhat controversial, young philosopher. He received his Ph.D. from Columbia in 1928, but left it two years later to go to the University of Chicago, as professor of the philosophy of law and as an associate of and advisor to the president, Robert M. Hutchins. While at Chicago he and Hutchins instituted important changes at the university, reorganizing the curriculum and emphasizing reading and discussion of the classics of the Western tradition. Out of these activities came the 54-volume *Great Books of the Western World,* which was published in 1952, and of which Hutchins was editor-in-chief and Adler associate editor. The set included a massive and detailed index, the *Syntopicon,* of which Adler was editor and on which he worked for eight years. He surrendered his professorship at the University of Chicago in 1952 to found in San Francisco the Institute for Philosophical Research, which undertook to take stock of Western thought on subjects that have been of continuing philosophical interest from the advent of philosophy in ancient Greece to the present day. The first "great idea" to be treated was that of freedom; the results of extensive researches by a large staff were written up by Adler as *The Idea of Freedom*, Volume I, 1958, and Volume II, 1961. Among other subjects subsequently investigated by the institute were progress, love, justice, happiness, equality, language and thought, rhetoric, and revolution. Adler returned to Chicago in 1964, and thereupon served as editor of or editorial consultant to a series of works published by Encyclopaedia Britannica, including the 10-volume *Gateway to the Great Books*, 1963, the 20-volume *Annals of America*, 1969, and the 3-volume *Negro in American History*, also 1969. At the same time he delivered several series of lectures at the University of Chicago, each of which was developed into a book: *The Conditions of Philosophy*, 1965, *The Difference of Man and the Difference It Makes*, 1969, and *The Time of Our Lives*, 1970. Among his other works are *Art and Prudence*, 1937, *What Man Has Made of Man*, 1938, *A Dialectic of Morals*, 1941, and *The Capitalist Manifesto*, 1958 (with Louis O. Kelso). He was also the author of the best-seller *How to Read a Book*, which appeared in 1940.

AGASSIZ, JEAN LOUIS RODOLPHE (1807–1873), naturalist, geologist, educator. Born in Switzerland on May 28, 1807, Agassiz was early inclined to the study of nature. He studied at a number of European universities, taking a Ph.D. at Erlangen and an M.D. at Munich. His first major work, on the fishes of Brazil, was published in 1829. Moving to Paris, then the center of zoological research, in 1832, he published a monumental work on fossil fish. He met the great naturalist and explorer Baron von Humboldt, whose influence won Agassiz a professorship at Neuchatel, a post he held until 1846. During this time he continued his researches in zoology, publishing a number of major works, and in 1836 he began a series of pioneer studies on glaciation that were to establish definitely the occurrence of an "Ice Age" in geological history. In 1846 he jour-neyed to the United States for study and lecturing. He accepted the chair of natural history at the newly established Lawrence Scientific School at Harvard in 1848. His many expeditions led him to publish *Contributions to the Natural History of the United States* from 1857 to 1862, and in 1859 he founded Harvard's comprehensive Museum of Comparative Zoology. His naturalization as an American citizen ended the chance that belated recognition in Europe might draw him back there; he remained in the United States for the rest of his life. His major accomplishment in this country was not in basic research; rather it was the wide interest in natural history that he stimulated and the vivid and effective teaching methods he employed that left their lasting impression on American education. To this end, and with a generous gift from an admirer in New York, he established the Anderson School of Natural History in 1873 to train teachers and spread his methods. His achievements as an educator stand unchallenged, while much of his later scientific work was marred by his opposition to Darwin's natural selection hypothesis and his own tendency towards a teleological interpretation of evolution. He died on December 12, 1873.

AGEE, JAMES (1909–1955), author, playwright, and critic. Born on November 27, 1909, in Knoxville, Tennessee, Agee attended Phillips Exeter Academy and graduated from Harvard in 1932. His first work was published two years later, a book of verse called *Permit Me Voyage*. He joined the editorial staff of *Fortune* magazine in 1932, wrote for *Time* magazine from 1939 to 1943, and contributed film criticism to *The Nation, Partisan Review, Harper's*, and the *Forum*. His reporting was perceptive, illuminating social issues with warmth and concern. Sent with photographer Walker Evans by *Fortune* magazine to investigate sharecroppers in Alabama, he became deeply concerned about their poor living conditions and went beyond his assignment to produce *Let Us Now Praise Famous Men*, 1941, a moving text and picture book. After 1948 he worked mainly in the film medium. He wrote and narrated *The Quiet One*, about an underprivileged Harlem boy, and wrote scripts for *The African Queen, Night of the Hunter, Mr. Lincoln*, and *The Bride Comes to Yellow Sky*, a story by Stephen Crane. In 1951 he published a novella, *The Morning Watch*, a sensitive study of a schoolboy; a novel, *A Death in the Family*, a young boy's view of his family after the death of his father, was published posthumously and awarded a Pulitzer Prize in 1958. He died on May 16, 1955. A collection of his film criticism and screenplays was published in two volumes as *Agee on Film*, 1958–1960.

AGNEW, SPIRO THEODORE (1918–   ), public official. Born in Baltimore on November 9, 1918, Agnew studied for three years at Johns Hopkins University and then, while working for several insurance companies, attended night classes at the Baltimore Law School. After serving in France and Germany during World War II he returned to take his law degree in 1947. He gained a local reputation as a lawyer specializing in labor cases and in 1957 was appointed as a Republican to the Zoning Board of Appeals of Baltimore County. In 1962 he became the first Republican to serve as county executive of Baltimore County since 1895. In 1966 he ran for governor of Maryland; attracting the support of blacks and liberals, mainly because his opponent was an outspoken segregationist, he was elected by a large margin and during his first year in office conducted a vigorous though only mildly reformist administration that further secured him with such groups. Later, particularly after Baltimore suffered a violent racial disturbance in April 1968, he began moving to a more conservative position and strongly denounced student protesters and militant civil rights leaders. He criticized the Poor People's Campaign in Washington and took up the "law and order" cry. A supporter of New York's Gov. Nelson Rockefeller for the 1968 Republican presidential nomination until Rockefeller

withdrew from the race, he switched to Richard Nixon and at the party's convention placed him in nomination. Shortly afterwards Agnew, though little known outside Maryland, was chosen as Nixon's running mate. After a campaign marked by a number of perhaps ill considered and in any case widely publicized remarks—and the Democrats' question, "Who is Spiro Agnew?"—he was elected along with Nixon by a narrow popular margin. Continuing his swing to the right, he soon became the administration's principal traveling representative and political phrasemaker.

AIKEN, CONRAD POTTER (1889–   ), poet and author. Born on August 5, 1889, in Savannah, Georgia, Aiken suffered a severe shock at the age of 11 when his father killed his mother Georgia, Aiken suffered a severe shock at the age of 11 when his father killed his mother enrolled in the Middlesex School in Concord, and graduated from Harvard, where he was a friend of T. S. Eliot, in 1911. Always interested in writing, he was contributing editor of the *Dial* during 1917–1919, and London correspondent for the *New Yorker* during the 1930s. Most of his life was spent in Massachusetts, though before 1947 he divided his time about equally between the United States and England. During 1915–1920, he produced five poetic "symphonies" in which he sought to develop a form of poetry that resembled music. His later verse was by turns narrative, lyrical, or reflective. *The Great Circle*, 1933, one of his five novels, was so admired by Freud that he offered Aiken free treatment as an experiment, but the two men never met. His short stories, similarly psychoanalytical in nature, were highly regarded. He also edited poetical anthologies, and wrote critical essays and an autobiography, *Ushant*, 1952. His *Selected Poems*, 1929, won a Pulitzer Prize, but his reputation as a major author rests on *Collected Poems*, 1953, a selection from 18 previous volumes of poetry, which won the National Book Award.

ALBEE, EDWARD FRANKLIN (1928–), playwright. Born on March 12, 1928, in Washington, D.C., Albee was adopted as an infant by Reed A. Albee, the son of an owner of vaudeville houses. Raised in New York, he attended Rye Country Day School and several boarding schools, graduating from Choate Preparatory School in Wallingford, Connecticut. He decided to be a writer after two years at Trinity College in Hartford, Connecticut, and supported himself with jobs ranging from minor writing on radio to being a Western Union delivery man. His work was unpublished until his first play, *The Zoo Story*, appeared in 1958. About two men who meet on a park bench in New York City, it focused on the lack of communication among men who consider themselves different from one another for reasons of wealth or social distinction. *The Death of Bessie Smith*, written in 1959, concerned the characters of a nurse and members of the staff of a Southern hospital where blues singer Bessie Smith was brought in critical condition before her death and refused treatment because of her color. Both of these plays were first performed in German in Berlin. *The American Dream*, 1960, used cliché characters and dialogue to reveal the fact that a couple have mutilated their foster son in an attempt to mold him to their standards of acceptability. Albee became known as a brilliant playwright able to sustain incredible tension and to invoke scathing social commentary. His major work, *Who's Afraid of Virginia Woolf?*, produced on Broadway in 1962, is about the life of a New England college professor and his wife who are terrified of themselves and of being together, and who use a fantasy child they have created to torment one another psychologically; in an all-night drinking party they expose and "kill" the child before two equally deluded guests. Albee's work, satirical and often savage in intensity, was a mainstay of the "theater of the absurd" movement. Others among his plays were *The Sandbox*, 1959, *Tiny Alice*, 1965, and *A Delicate Balance*, 1966.

ALCOTT, AMOS BRONSON (1799–1888), educator, philosopher, and reformer. Born near Wolcott, Connecticut, on November 29, 1799, Alcott (he changed the name from the original Alcox) received little education and, barred from Yale by the need to help support his family, spent the years 1818–1823 as an itinerant peddler in Virginia and the Carolinas. For the next ten years he taught in a number of schools in the Northeast, but his educational theories, when put to practice, usually roused public opposition and led to his dismissal. His manner of teaching, based on the methods and examples of Jesus, Socrates, and Pestalozzi, aimed at the development of the whole child and combined gymnastics, conversation, and an emphasis on learning as a pleasant end in itself. Alcott attempted to stimulate the child's capacity for independent thought and, while firm, he was consistently gentle with his charges, dispensing with corporal punishment and referring disciplinary judgments to the class as a whole. In 1834 he opened his own school, the Temple School, in Boston; again, public opposition, bolstered by suspicions of his unorthodox religious beliefs and his acceptance of a Negro pupil, forced him to close it in 1839. He moved to Concord in 1840 and became an intimate of Emerson and the Transcendentalist circle; more loftily spiritual and mystical even than they, he won their love and admiration and often their financial aid as his complete impracticality made the support of his wife and children difficult. To the *Dial* he contributed a great number of "Orphic Sayings." Following a visit, at Emerson's expense, to England in 1842 to observe the Alcott House school named in his honor, he established in northern Massachusetts a utopian community, "Fruitlands," in 1844 to practise communally his ideas on spiritual living. As usual, practical necessities yielded to opportunities for talk and for work with various reform movements—primarily Abolitionism and women's rights—and "Fruitlands" was deserted by its nearly starved remaining members within a few months. After moving from town to town around New England, Alcott and his family returned to Concord in 1857. For several years after 1853 he made numerous lecture tours during which, rather than actually lecturing, he conversed on stage, often vaguely, sometimes completely obscurely, but always brilliantly. In 1859 he became superintendent of the Concord schools and successfully introduced many of his educational ideas. He remained cheerfully improvident, aided by his adoring family and friends who included most of the notable intellectual figures of the day, until financial security came at last with the publication in 1868 of *Little Women* by his daughter, Louisa May Alcott. In 1879 he founded the Summer School of Philosophy in Concord which continued until his death in Boston on March 4, 1888.

ALCOTT, LOUISA MAY (1832–1888), author. Born on November 29, 1832, in Germantown, Pennsylvania, the daughter of educator and philosopher Amos Bronson Alcott, Louisa was raised in Boston and Concord and was educated primarily by her father, with tutoring from her neighbor, Thoreau, and guidance from Emerson and Theodore Parker. Her first book, a collection of fairy tales, *Flower Fables*, was not published until 1855, six years after she wrote it; so she attempted to earn money for her family by sewing and teaching until, at 17, she was attracted by the theater and wrote several plays, one of which was sold to the Boston Theater, but never performed. Continuing to write poems and short stories, she contributed regularly to magazines and in 1860 was finally published in the *Atlantic Monthly*. As a nurse during the Civil War, she wrote letters to her family, compiled in *Hospital Sketches*, 1863. Public notice followed and she published her first novel, *Moods*, in 1864. After traveling to Europe she edited the children's magazine, *Merry's Museum*. She published *Little Women* in 1868; based on her own family life, its warmth and sensibility had a universal appeal. The book was translated into several languages and was

successful enough to make her family comfortable. Thereafter, she participated in women's rights and temperance movements, settled in Boston, and wrote other enormously successful autobiographical novels, among them *An Old Fashioned Girl*, 1870, *Little Men*, 1871, and *Jo's Boys*, 1886. She died two days after her father's death in Boston, on March 6, 1888.

ALDRIDGE, IRA FREDERICK (1804?–1867), actor. Born around 1804, probably in New York City, Aldridge may have grown up there but in any event apparently got his start in acting at the African Theater in New York. Finding, doubtless, that the opportunities for black actors in America were rather limited, he went to England around 1824 and made his English debut the next year. A protegé of Edmund Kean, he soon became one of the leading tragedians of his time, appearing notably in such roles as Othello, Lear, and Macbeth. It is not known whether he ever returned to the United States, but if he did, it was during the 1830s, and the engagement, in Baltimore, was unsuccessful. After 1853 he played primarily on the Continent, where he was enormously popular, amassed a fortune, and received numerous honors, including tributes from the Austrian emperor and the king of Prussia. He became a British subject in 1863. Known as the "African Roscius," he died while on his way to fulfill an engagement in Russia, at Lodz, Poland, on August 7, 1867.

ALGER, HORATIO (1832–1899), author. Born in Revere, Massachusetts, on January 13, 1832, Alger was the son of a stern Unitarian minister who intended that his son should follow his footsteps. "Holy Horatio," as his schoolmates called him, graduated from Harvard in 1852 and after a few years with a Boston newspaper and as a tutor entered Harvard Divinity School. Graduating in 1860, he used an unexpected but timely legacy to finance a year in Paris where he pursued, subject to painful conflicts with his Puritan conscience, the bohemian goals of art and the pleasures of the flesh. After his return to the United States he tried unsuccessfully to enlist in the Union Army for Civil War service and finally, in 1864, gave himself over to conscience and his father by assuming the ministry of the Unitarian church in Brewster, Massachusetts. Determined still, however, that literature was to be his life, he submitted several stories and plot outlines to William T. Adams ("Oliver Optic," an author and publisher of juvenile fiction), received encouragement, and in 1866 resigned his pulpit and went to New York City. The next year Alger's first successful novel, *Ragged Dick, or Street Life in New York*, was serialized in Adams' *Student and Schoolmate*. The hero, Dick Hunter, is a New York bootblack, a boy of the streets who, by pluck, honesty, hard work, and a little luck, rises from his lowly station to become, in the course of several sequels, a rich man. The pattern set in *Ragged Dick* was followed without variation in well over 100 books during the next thirty years. Alger's books were from the outset enormously popular; capturing the already stimulated imagination of American youth in the period of great industrial growth and huge new personal fortunes, Alger communicated something of Herbert Spencer's philosophy of laissez faire while entertaining, rather than exercising, his readers. The appeal of his single story idea is indicated in the fact that he became the most popular author of his generation with a series of books whose literary quality was consistently and outrageously bad. For many years he was associated with the Newsboys' Lodging House in New York as its chief benefactor, advisor, and hero. Except for two Western trips to gather material for more books, he remained in New York City until 1895 when he moved to Peekskill, New York; after a brief and fruitless romance that led him to Paris and a nervous breakdown, he returned to America and lived with his sister in Natick, Massachusetts, until his death on July 18, 1899.

ALI, MUHAMMAD (1942–   ), boxer. Born Cassius Marcellus Clay, Jr., on January 18, 1942, in Louisville, Kentucky, Ali attended DuValle Junior High School and Central High School in Louisville. At 12 a local policeman encouraged him to learn boxing; he trained for six weeks and boxed on the television program *Champions of Tomorrow* and won. He continued fighting as an amateur for 6 years, winning 100 of 108 matches and 6 Golden Gloves titles in Kentucky. Accepted for the American Olympic team in 1960, he won the light heavyweight gold medal. He turned professional, and was trained by Archie Moore and Angelo Dundee. He won his first professional fight on October 29, 1960, and began attracting nationwide attention. He granted interviews to newspapermen and television broadcasters, in which he would boast of his prowess and recite his own doggerel. He claimed, sometimes correctly, to predict the round in which he would knock out his opponent. By 1963 he had fought 19 professional fights and won all of them, including matches with Archie Moore, Charlie Powell, Doug Jones, and Henry Cooper. In August 1963 he made a record album called *I Am the Greatest!*, in which he claimed he would beat heavyweight champion Sonny Liston in the eighth round. This and other bold publicity stunts led to record-breaking attendance and nationwide closed circuit television coverage of the match on February 25, 1964. He scored a technical knockout against the heavily favored Liston in the seventh round. At a press conference the next day, he announced that his name was Muhammad Ali and his religion was Islam as practised by the "Black Muslims." The World Boxing Association withdrew its recognition of him in March 1964, because of his behavior before the Liston fight, which included an arrangement for promotion of future fights with International Sports, Inc. The Association also banned a rematch. A rematch was nonetheless set for May 25, 1965. Liston was knocked out in one minute of the first round, the shortest bout in championship history. Muhammad Ali was hailed as one of the finest boxers of the 20th century, and was particularly noted for his speed and agility. He refused induction into the Army in 1967 because of his Muslim beliefs and was denied reclassification as a conscientious objector. He was convicted of draft evasion in June 1967. With much attendant controversy he was stripped of his world boxing championship title by the W.B.A. and the New York State Athletic Commission, by whom he was said to have exhibited behavior "detrimental to boxing."

ALLEN, ETHAN (1738–1789), Revolutionary soldier. Born on January 21, 1738, in Litchfield, Connecticut, of modest parentage, Allen was hindered from completing his education by the death of his father in 1755, after which he assumed the financial responsibility for his family. During his youth, he became intrigued by the ideas of a young rationalist, Thomas Young, and later wrote a book based on them, *Reason, the Only Oracle of Man*, 1784. After serving in the French and Indian War in 1757, he acquired, along with his brothers, large land holdings in an area known as the New Hampshire Grants, jurisdiction over which was being disputed by New York and New Hampshire. Eager to control the land themselves, the Allens formed the Green Mountain Boys, a group that harassed New Yorkers in the area and eventually grew so notorious that the governor of New York offered a £100 reward for Ethan's capture. He intended to petition the King to confer separate status on the area, now called Vermont, but the Battles of Lexington and Concord interrupted his mission. He was instructed by the Connecticut Assembly to capture Fort Ticonderoga and, with the able assistance of Col. Benedict Arnold, succeeded triumphantly. Assured by this success, he attempted to take Montreal, but was promptly captured and imprisoned by the British for three years. In 1778 an arrangement was made for his release in exchange for a British prisoner. His *Narrative of Colonel Ethan Allen's Captivity*, 1779, neglected mention of Arnold's aid in capturing Fort Ticonderoga and berated the British. The honorary

rank of colonel was conferred on him when he was released from prison, but he returned to his own affairs in Vermont. With his brothers, he resumed the activities of the Green Mountain Boys and appealed to his former captors, the British in Canada, to grant separatism to Vermont. He died in Burlington on February 11, 1789. Two years later Vermont achieved statehood and under her tax laws, the Allens lost all of their property.

ALLEN, FRED (1894–1956), humorist. Born on May 31, 1894, in Cambridge, Massachusetts, John Florence Sullivan started a career on the vaudeville stage as a juggler. One evening when the audience was decidedly unappreciative, the theater manager stepped on the stage and asked him, yet a boy, just where he had learned to juggle. He quipped, "I took a correspondence course in baggage smashing," and his career as a humorist was on its way. He toured vaudeville theaters for ten years, at $25 a week. During World War I he was in the Army and returned to the stage as "Freddie James, world's worst juggler." An agent named Allen suggested his final professional name. He began to rely on the dry humor and the sing-song, nasal delivery that became his trademarks. For his material, which was frequently topical, he studied newspapers and magazines. In 1932, he began the radio program *Allen's Alley*, with his wife Portland Hoffa. The show continued until 1949, and at its peak had 20,000,000 listeners. Characters populating the *Alley* included Senator Claghorn, Titus Moody, Mrs. Nussbaum, and Ajax Cassidy. Withering criticisms of Hollywood, Madison Avenue, and the banal world of broadcasting did not exclude his own sponsors and network executives—such as the "vice president in charge of waving fingers at comedians." Allen philosophized that "a conference of radio executives is a meeting at which a group of men who, singly, can do nothing, agree collectively that nothing can be done." He wrote nearly all the material for his show and frequent guest appearances. In 1954 appeared *Treadmill to Oblivion*, a book about his years in radio. He appeared in movies, twice with Jack Benny (*Love Thy Neighbor* and *It's in the Bag*), with whom he conducted a comic "feud" for many years. In 1955, he became a regular panel member on the television quiz show *What's My Line?* He was writing his autobiography at the time of his death in New York City on March 17, 1956.

ALTGELD, JOHN PETER (1847–1902), jurist, public official, and political leader. Born in Prussia on December 30, 1847, the young Altgeld moved with his family to a farm in Ohio where he remained until he was 21. Growing up in poverty, he received little formal education, and his years in Ohio were interrupted only by a brief service in the Civil War. In 1869 he left Ohio and for five years labored, taught school, and studied law. In 1874, living in Savannah, Missouri, he was elected prosecuting attorney for Andrew County. He resigned the following year and moved to Chicago. He lost a bid for Congress in 1884, but in 1886 he was elected superior court judge in Cook County. He resigned from the post in 1891, having become chief judge of the court. In 1892 he was elected as the first Democratic governor of Illinois since the Civil War; within a short time after assuming office he became a center of great controversy when, upon the urging of Clarence Darrow and other reform leaders, he pardoned three of the convicted "conspirators" of the Haymarket riot of 1886. Though his decision now seems to have been fully justifiable, he drew the immediate and bitter condemnation of Republicans, of the great capitalists, and of the press. The furor was revived in July 1894 when, during the Pullman strike, he protested to President Cleveland the sending of regular army troops to Illinois, basing his dissent on the unconstitutionality of the action and on the fact that, despite their exaggeration by the press, the disorders were of small scale and entirely within the ability of local government to con-

trol. Altgeld was defeated for reelection in 1896. He died on March 12, 1902.

AMES, FISHER (1758–1808), publicist, orator, and statesman. Born in Dedham, Massachusetts, on April 9, 1758, the third son of Nathaniel Ames, Ames's intellectual precocity enabled him to graduate from Harvard College at the age of 16. From that year, 1774, until 1781 he studied on his own; in 1779 he turned from the classics to law and in 1781 was admitted to the bar. His published essays on Shays's Rebellion and in support of a federal convention brought him to public notice. He was elected to the Massachusetts ratifying convention in 1787 and to Congress in 1789. He remained a member of the House until 1797 and, a brilliant Federalist theoretician and speaker, was a staunch supporter of Hamilton. Beset by ill health, he roused himself to deliver in April 1796 his greatest speech, favoring the enabling appropriation bill for Jay's Treaty. He declined reelection in 1796 and the presidency of Harvard in 1805. His last years were spent at home where he continued to write in support of the Federalist view of government. He died on July 4, 1808.

ANDERSON, MARIAN (1902–), singer. Born on February 17, 1902, in Philadelphia, Marian Anderson displayed vocal talent as a child, but her family could not afford to give her formal training. From the age of six, she was tutored in the choir of the Union Baptist Church, where she sang bass, alto, tenor, and soprano parts. Members of the congregation raised funds for her to go to music school for a year. At 19 she became a pupil of Giuseppe Boghetti, who was so impressed that he gave her free lessons for another year. In 1925 she won first prize in a contest with 300 entrants, the prize being a series of recitals, including one in New York City with the New York Philharmonic Orchestra. Although many concert opportunities were closed to her because of her color, she toured Southern college campuses and appeared at New York City's

Town Hall. In 1933 she made a successful European tour. Still relatively unknown in America, she received scholarships to study abroad and appeared before the crowned heads of Sweden, Norway, Denmark, and England, and at the Salzburg music festival in 1935. On hearing her sing, the Scandinavian composer Sibelius wrote *Solitude* for her. Her pure vocal quality and tremendous range made her the "world's greatest contralto" in the opinion of many listeners. In 1939 she attempted to rent concert facilities in Washington's Constitution Hall, owned by the Daughters of the American Revolution, but was refused because of her race. This produced widespread protest from musical people and by public figures, including Mrs. Eleanor Roosevelt, who resigned from the D.A.R. Substitute facilities were provided at the Lincoln Memorial on Easter Sunday, and Miss Anderson drew an audience of 75,000. She was awarded the Spingarn medal for high achievement among members of her race in that year and the $10,000 Bok Award in 1940. By 1941 she and Paul Robeson were the highest paid Negro concert artists in the country. On January 7, 1955, she became the first Negro to perform at the Metropolitan Opera. Before she began to sing her role of Ulrica in Verdi's *The Masked Ball*, she was given a standing ovation by the audience. In 1957 she made a 12-nation, 35,000 mile tour of European countries sponsored by the Department of State, the American National Theatre and Academy, and Edward R. Murrow's *See It Now*. Her role as a goodwill ambassador for America was formalized in September 1958, when she was made a delegate to the United Nations.

ANDERSON, MAXWELL (1888 – 1959), playwright. Born on December 15, 1888, in Atlantic, Pennsylvania, Anderson received his B.A. degree from the University of North Dakota in 1911 and his M.A. degree from Stanford in 1914. He taught school in North Dakota and California and began a career in journalism in those states, continuing in New York until

the success of his first play, *White Desert*, in 1923. Then he devoted himself to the drama. His themes were philosophical, portraying the dual existence of both good and evil in men. His dramas were consistently provocative and outstanding. With Laurence Stallings he wrote *What Price Glory?*, 1924, a war drama, *First Flight*, 1925, about the youth of Andrew Jackson, and *The Buccaneer*, 1925, about the pirate Sir Henry Morgan. Turning to verse, he drew upon history for *Elizabeth the Queen*, 1930. *Both Your Houses*, a political satire in prose, won a Pulitzer Prize in 1933, but Anderson resumed the use of verse in a series of notable dramas, including *Mary of Scotland*, 1933, *Valley Forge*, 1934, *Winterset*, 1935, and *High Tor*, 1936, the latter two winning New York Drama Critics' Circle Awards. He was generally acclaimed by critics, but shared with other playwrights a dislike for the traditional role of the critic in determining the fate of a play. He was one of the founders of the Playwrights Company in 1938. One of his last works was the stage adaptation of William March's novel *The Bad Seed*, in 1954, the basis of the academy award winning movie of 1957. Anderson died on February 28, 1959, in Stamford, Connecticut.

ANDERSON, SHERWOOD (1876 – 1941), author. Born in Camden, Ohio, on September 13, 1876, Anderson grew up in poverty and at 14 left school for a succession of petty jobs that eventually took him to Chicago. In 1898 he joined the National Guard and served for a while in Cuba; in 1899 he returned and spent a year in a preparatory school. He became an advertising copywriter and in 1907 organized his own business, a small paint factory in Elyria, Ohio. After five years as a businessman, he left suddenly, moving back to Chicago and seeking a literary life. He became a member of the Chicago circle of Sandburg, Dreiser, Masters, Hecht, and others, contributed to several little magazines, and published his first two novels. In 1919 he published his most famous book, a collection of interrelated short stories and sketches entitled *Winesburg,*

Ohio. This was followed by two similar volumes, and the three books constitute his best work and his claim to lasting reputation. He returned to the novel form, producing a number of social and autobiographical works, but these were distinctly minor efforts. His short stories were primarily concerned with the frustrations and narrowness of life in the small towns of the Midwest and their deforming effects on human beings. In 1925 he moved to Marion, Virginia, and published two country newspapers. He died while visiting Panama on March 8, 1941.

ANGELL, JAMES BURRILL (1829 – 1916), journalist, educator, and diplomat. Born on January 7, 1829, near Scituate, Rhode Island, Angell was educated at Brown University, then under the progressive administration of Francis Wayland. After graduation in 1849, he journeyed through the South, coming into intimate contact with the workings of slavery, and then worked briefly for a civil engineer. He spent nearly two years in Europe, studying modern languages and literature, and in 1852 was invited by Wayland to join the faculty of Brown. In 1853 he began a course in modern languages, but after Wayland's resignation in 1855 and the university's return to a conservative curriculum, he sought other channels for his energy and intellect. He contributed to the *North American Review*, revised and edited Chambers' *Handbook of French Literature* in 1857, and wrote editorials for the *Providence Journal*, of which he became editor in 1860. With the *Journal* until 1866, he was an unwavering Unionist and a strong supporter of President Lincoln during the Civil War, and exhibited a flair for understanding and writing about world politics and matters involving international law. He was unsuccessful in attempts to buy the paper, however, and consequently accepted, in 1866, the presidency of the University of Vermont. There his leadership created unprecedented enthusiasm for the school among the citizens of Vermont, and the impoverished institution was substantially improved. In 1871 he was elected president of the University of Michigan, where he developed further his concepts of the duties of the state university to the state and its relationship to the larger academic world. He believed that the central aspect of an educational institution was the men — teachers and students — who constituted it. While president, he also taught international law and the history of treaties, was dean of the College, and was the school registrar. He instituted lasting changes in the curriculum, simultaneously raised academic standards while broadening the accessibility of the university to prospective students, and effectively promoted improved secondary education in the state. His attempts to separate a basic first two-year junior university and a more advanced final two-year university, and to broaden the graduate program, were too advanced to be accepted at the time. He was named by President Hayes U. S. minister to China in 1880 and charged with negotiating a new immigration treaty; he retained the post until 1881 and then returned to Ann Arbor. President McKinley appointed him minister to Turkey in 1897 and he served for a year. A founder of the American Historical Association in 1884, he served as its president in 1893 – 1894. He retired from the presidency of the university in 1909 and died in Ann Arbor on April 1, 1916.

ANTHONY, SUSAN BROWNELL (1820 – 1906), social reformer. Born of a well-to-do Quaker family in Adams, Massachusetts, on February 15, 1820, Miss Anthony grew up independent, strong-willed, and not a little prudish in her moral outlook. She received an unusually good education for a woman of her time, and from 1835 to 1849 she taught school. Returning home in 1850, she became acquainted with the leading circle of Abolitionists who met regularly in her father's home; she also met the women who were to be her companions in the suffrage movement — Elizabeth Cady Stanton, Lucretia Mott, Amelia Bloomer, and Lucy Stone. In 1852 her first efforts at active work for temperance were rebuffed because of her sex; organizing a separate temperance group for women, she continued her campaigning. From 1856 until the Civil War she was an agent for the American Anti-Slavery Society. She was an early advocate of Negro suffrage and attempted to have the Fourteenth Amendment extended to include women. From 1868 to 1870 she helped publish a radical New York weekly, *The Revolution*. In November 1872 she challenged the law by voting; before she was brought to trial she voted again the following March. Though she was convicted, she steadfastly refused to pay the imposed fine. As an officer of the National Woman Suffrage Association from its founding in 1869 and as vice-president and president of the National American Woman Suffrage Association from 1890 until 1900, Miss Anthony wrote and lectured ceaselessly, against constant opposition, ridicule, and vituperation, for her cause; and she organized international associations to promote it throughout the world. She died in Rochester, New York, on March 13, 1906.

ANTIN, MARY (1881–1949), author. Born in Russia in 1881, Miss Antin emigrated to the United States with her parents in 1894. She attended school in Boston and later, from 1901 to 1904, studied at Columbia University and Barnard College. Her first book about her immigrant experiences, *From Polotzk to Boston*, was written in Yiddish; it was published in an English translation in 1899. Her subsequent books, *The Promised Land* and *They Who Knock at Our Gates*, published in 1912 and 1914, dealt also with immigrants, their hopes, character, and experiences. In 1901 she married Anton Grabau, a paleontologist and professor at Columbia University. She lectured for a number of years on the subject of immigration and campaigned against proposals in Congress to adopt restrictive immigration legislation. She was widely acclaimed for her efforts to secure understanding for the immigrant and the realization of the American promise. She died at Suffolk, New York, on May 15, 1949.

APPLEGATE, JESSE (1811–1888), surveyor, publicist, and public official. Born in Kentucky on July 5, 1811, Applegate grew up in Missouri where his family had moved during his childhood. Following a period of study at Rock Spring Seminary in Illinois, he taught school and then, being proficient in mathematics and surveying, became a clerk in the surveyor general's office in St. Louis. He advanced to deputy surveyor general and until 1843 farmed and did field work in Missouri. In 1843 he joined the movement westward, leading the cattle column of an Oregon-bound wagon train. His book recording the experience, *A Day with the Cow-Column in 1843*, became a classic in the literature of Western settlement. In 1845 he led the party that opened the southern passage into Oregon. A capable and persuasive writer and a powerful personality, Applegate became a political leader in Oregon. He reorganized the pre-territorial provisional government and succeeded in unifying the English and American settlements in the region. He was successful in his cattle business on his Yoncalla ranch and there he remained, writing occasional newspaper essays on public issues. Politically a Whig and then, with the dissolution of that party, a Republican, Applegate was an influential supporter of Lincoln and the Union. He died on April 22, 1888.

APPLESEED, JOHNNY see CHAPMAN, JOHN

ARDEN, ELIZABETH (1884–1966), business leader. Born on December 31, 1884, in Woodbridge, Ontario, Canada, Florence Nightengale Graham attended school locally until she was 18, briefly pursued a nurse's training, was a secretary, and held various other jobs until moving to New York City about 1908. She became an assistant to beauty specialist Eleanor Adair and in 1910 with about $1000 went into partnership with Elizabeth Hubbard in a beauty salon on Fifth Avenue. The partnership split up, and she decided upon the corporate name of Elizabeth Arden.

In 1914 she hired chemists to produce a fluffy face cream and a sparkling astringent lotion, the forerunners of her line, which eventually included about 300 items. A pioneer in advertising beauty aids, she popularized the products in newspapers and fashion magazines by stressing their acceptable, "ladylike" qualities, in an age when makeup and beauty aids were thought of only in connection with "low" women. In 1915 she opened a wholesale department, marketing the items internationally in pharmacies and department stores. As scrupulous as she was ambitious, she ruled on all aspects of her business, from the tone of advertisements to the names of products. By the time of her death she had 50 establishments throughout the world for hairdressing and facial treatments, and 50 sumptuous salons in major U.S. cities and resorts, Canada, Mexico, Peru, Europe, and Australia, providing exercise, steam bath, massage, facial, shampoo, hair setting and restyling, manicure, pedicure, and lunch — at about $50 a day. She operated Maine Chance beauty spas in Mount Vernon, Maine, from June through September, and in Scottsdale, Arizona, near Phoenix, in the winters, where a one-week beauty restoration cost about $750. Her clientele included socialites, politicians, European royalty, and movie stars. Also one of the nation's foremost race horse owners, she operated the Main Chance stable near Lexington, Kentucky; among her horses was Jet Pilot, winner of the 1947 Kentucky Derby. She bolstered her own image of "ageless" beauty by concealing her age, which was not divulged until her death on October 18, 1966, in New York City.

ARMOUR, PHILIP DANFORTH (1832–1901), meat packer. Born on May 16, 1832, in Stockbridge, New York, Armour was a miner, a farmer, and a wholesale grocer before entering the meat packing and grain industry with John Plankinton in 1863. During the last months of the Civil War, confident that the price of pork would fall as the Union approached victory, Armour went to New York from the Milwaukee-based Plankinton, Armour and Company, and offered barrels of pork at $30 to $40 for future delivery. When the price dropped, as expected, he purchased for $18 what he had already sold at the higher prices, and netted nearly $2 million. Returning to Milwaukee, he invested in a grain commission house opened in Chicago by his brother Herman. With the addition of a meat-packing house, the firm was reorganized as a partnership of Philip, Herman, and another brother, Andrew, in 1870; in 1875 Philip moved to Chicago to assume control of the business. Among his pioneer ventures, soon to be copied by competitors, were shipping live hogs to the Chicago stock yards for slaughtering, and using waste materials for innumerable by-products. With little competition, he made Chicago the major pork-packing city in the nation. He began to can meat and exported it to England, France, and Germany. With the development of refrigeration, he purchased his own cars and shipped meat to the eastern cities, where he established distribution plants. Armour became known for his spectacular trades and winnings on the stock exchange. During 1898–1899 he became involved, along with other meat packers, in the "embalmed beef" scandals. Protesting that graft, if it existed elsewhere, had never touched Armour and Company, he nevertheless did not recover from the shock of this and subsequent inquiries and died on January 29, 1901, in Pasadena, California. His wealth was estimated at $50 million at the time of his death. His son, J. Ogden, became president of the company upon his death. When J. Ogden retired in 1923, Armour and Company were the world's largest meat packers.

ARMSTRONG, LOUIS DANIEL (1900–), trumpeter and band leader. Born on July 4, 1900, in New Orleans, Armstrong admired the cornet of Buck Jones as a child, but could not afford an instrument. At 13 he was sent to the Colored Waifs' Home for Boys, a reform school in "back-o-town" New Orleans, for firing a shot into a New Year's parade. There he found a trumpet and taught himself to play it. He was leader of the reform school band until his release 18 months later. Then he worked as a coalman, a milkman, and a rag-and-bones man, having convinced his idol, Joe "King" Oliver, to give him trumpet lessons in the evenings. When Oliver left for Chicago in 1917, Armstrong replaced him in Kid Ory's band. He joined Oliver in Chicago in 1922, and Fletcher Henderson's orchestra in New York in 1924. Nicknamed "Satchmo," short for "Satchelmouth," he introduced "scat" singing, using his voice as a musical instrument and singing nonsense syllables instead of words. He became famous for his solo improvisational performances. In Chicago in 1925 with Erskine Tate's orchestra, he was billed as the "World's Greatest Trumpeter." He formed his own band, the "Hot Five," in 1926, and later the "Hot Seven." Their records, now considered collector's items, were made with the finest jazz performers and blues singers of the time. Through the years, "Satchmo" changed his style very little. His sure tone, endless capacity for creating new melodies, and lively, joyous quality brought an appreciation for jazz from New Orleans to audiences across America and abroad. He was well known as a comedian and as a movie performer after 1930. A jovial good will ambassador, he toured the United States and Europe in the 1930s and played command performances in 1934 before King George VI, dedicating a number to the king with the words, "This one's for you, Rex!" Highlights of his tour of Europe and Africa in 1956 were filmed by newscasters and released under the title *Satchmo, the Great.* His more famous recordings include "Shine," "Chinatown," "Tiger Rag," "I Can't Give You Anything But Love," "Ain't Misbehavin'," "C'est si bon," and "I'll Walk Alone." He wrote, among others, "Sister Kate," "If We Never Meet Again," and "Don't Jive Me Some Day."

ARMSTRONG, NEIL ALDEN (1930–), astronaut. Born on August 5, 1930, near Wapako-

neta, Ohio, Armstrong early developed a deep interest in aviation and received his pilot's license on his sixteenth birthday. In 1947 he entered Purdue University as a naval air cadet. Two years later he was called to active duty; during his service in Korea he flew 78 combat missions and was awarded the Air Medal three times. Returning to Purdue, he graduated in 1955 and joined the staff of the National Advisory Committee for Aeronautics as a civilian test pilot. During the next seven years he tested several new types of aircraft, including the X-15 rocket plane, and in 1962 was accepted into the astronaut training program of the National Aeronautics and Space Administration. His first space flight came in March 1966 when he commanded Gemini 8 and performed the first manual docking maneuver in space. Trouble developed in the thruster control system a short time later and for half an hour Armstrong fought to control a wild spin of the capsule that threatened to wreck the mission. Upon his return to Cape Kennedy he began training for the upcoming Apollo flights. On July 16, 1969, in command of Apollo XI, Armstrong again entered space and, with astronauts Edwin Aldrin and Michael Collins, headed for the moon. Four days later he piloted the lunar landing module *Eagle* to the moon's surface, landing at the edge of the Mare Tranquillitatis. After several hours of preparation he descended a ladder and, as an automatic television camera beamed the event back to Earth, set foot on the moon with the words, "That's one small step for a man, one giant leap for mankind." (Four months later Charles Conrad of the Apollo XII mission wryly observed "That may have been a small step for Neil, but that's a long one for me.") Armstrong and Aldrin set up several scientific experiments on the lunar surface before returning to the *Eagle* with a quantity of moon material for study on Earth. The next day they rocketed back to the command ship in lunar orbit and began the return trip to Earth. After splashdown in the Pacific on July 24th they were met by President Nixon on board the carrier *Hornet* before beginning an 18-day period of quarantine to guard against the scant possibility of dangerous microorganisms from the moon. Upon their release they were given warm receptions in many cities and foreign countries and then returned to their duties at the NASA Manned Spacecraft Center in Houston.

ARNOLD, BENEDICT (1741–1801), Revolutionary soldier and traitor. Born on January 14, 1741, in Norwich, Connecticut, of an eminent Rhode Island family, Arnold served briefly in the French and Indian War and returned home to complete an apprenticeship as a druggist, opened his own store and a book shop, and began to invest in ships and trade with Canada and the West Indies. At the outbreak of the Revolutionary War, he was made a colonel by Massachusetts, consenting to serve in 1775 under the command of Ethan Allen in the expedition to capture Fort Ticonderoga. The rank of major general was conferred on him by General Washington after he served in the Canadian invasion and fought courageously, if not spectacularly, against the British at Ridgefield, Connecticut, in April 1777. He served with Gen. Horatio Gates in the Saratoga campaign, which forced 5,700 British soldiers under the command of Gen. John Burgoyne to surrender, but he received a paralyzing wound in the leg and was consequently placed in command of Philadelphia, from which British troops were withdrawing. A controversy involving his participation in the city's social life prompted authorities to court-martial him. Although he was only reprimanded, he was extremely sensitive to criticism and his humiliation, compounded with the feeling that Congress did not appreciate him as a soldier, having promoted five generals over him in 1777, prompted him to correspond with Sir Henry Clinton, proposing his defection to the British. At his petition, he was granted control of the key station in the Hudson River Valley, West Point, and secretly connived with Clinton's emmissary, John André, to surrender it to the enemy for the sum of £20,000. But André was captured with papers disclosing the plot, and Arnold fled on a British warship, while André was hanged. He aided the British further in Virginia and Connecticut, then attempted to reestablish his business in England, Canada, and the West Indies. He met only with failure and ostracism at every turn, however, until his death in London on June 14, 1801.

ARNOLD, HENRY HARLEY (1886–1950), soldier. Born on June 25, 1886, in Gladwyne, Pennsylvania, "Hap" Arnold graduated from West Point in 1907 and was assigned to the infantry. He later transferred to the aviation corps, then part of the Army Signal Corps, and in 1911 received his pilot's license after taking instruction from Orville Wright. During World War I he served in Panama organizing the air defenses and for several years thereafter was commanding officer at various air fields. He studied at the Army Industrial College and in 1929 graduated from the Command and General Staff School. In 1936 he became assistant chief and two years later chief of the Army Air Corps. Throughout the 1920s and 1930s he was a leading advocate of military air power and supported Gen. William Mitchell in pressing for increased appropriations, better equipment and training, and more independence for the service. With the approach of World War II he arranged for the training of more military pilots at private flying schools, leaving it to Congress later to approve and pay for the program. In 1941 he was promoted to major general and named deputy chief of staff of the Army, becoming the first air officer to serve on the general staff, and in 1942 he became commanding general of the Army Air Forces. Serving also on the Allied combined chiefs of staff, he was instrumental in planning overall Allied strategy. His major achievement, however, was in developing, refining, and successfully applying air power as both a strategic and tactical weapon. He planned the massive air strikes against Germany and later Japan, and in 1944 took a major step toward the eventual creation of an independent Air Force in forming the 20th Air

Force, which, unlike other such groups, was retained under his immediate command instead of being assigned to a theater or group commander, and which was used as an independent mobile strike force. In December of that year he was promoted to general of the army; the commission was changed in 1949 to general of the air force, the first and only such rank ever held. In 1946 he retired to a farm near Sonoma, California, where he died on January 15, 1950.

ARP, BILL see **SMITH, CHARLES HENRY**

ARTHUR, CHESTER ALAN (1830–1886), public official and 21st U.S. President. Born on October 5, 1830, in Fairfield, Vermont, the son of an Irish immigrant who became a Baptist minister, Arthur lived intermittently in the United States and in Canada during his childhood. He graduated from Union College in Schenectady, New York, in 1848, and while teaching school, he studied law, winning admission to the bar in 1854. His legal career was noted for two cases, one in which he secured the freedom of Negro slaves in New York who were traveling between two slave states, and another in which he secured equal rights for Negroes in seating and in service on city transportation. He threw himself into Republican politics, participating in the anti-Nebraska Convention of 1854, involving himself locally in partisan affairs, and serving under Gov. Edwin P. Morgan as engineer-in-chief during the Civil War. Upon Morgan's retirement, he returned to his law practice, having distinguished himself as a competent, efficient executive. In 1871 he was appointed by President Grant as collector of customs for the port of New York. His service did not meet President Hayes's standards of reform in this previously notorious patronage position, and although he had exercised prudence in hiring on the basis of the results of civil service examinations, he was removed by Hayes in 1878, with Senate approval in 1879. At the 1880 Republican convention he worked along with other staunch partisans for the

nomination of Grant for a third term. When Grant was defeated by James A. Garfield, Arthur was chosen as the vice-presidential nominee to placate the Republican "Stalwart" faction. He openly opposed President Garfield, after winning the election, on the issue of New York patronage. When Garfield was assassinated in 1881, there was much consternation over his accession, in view of his reputation as a spoilsman. But in his inaugural address he assured the public that he would avoid party prejudice in his administration. To the amazement of his critics, he was true to his word. His selections for government office were irreproachable. He proceeded against post office officials involved in the $4 million postal star route frauds, vetoed the 1882 Chinese exclusion act, strongly supported the Pendleton Act of 1883, which created a civil service commission to regulate patronage hiring, and secured increased funds for national defense. In 1884 he lost the nomination to James G. Blaine, who was defeated by Grover Cleveland despite Arthur's loyal support. Retiring to New York City, he died on November 18, 1886.

ASBURY, FRANCIS (1745–1816), Methodist preacher and bishop. Born on August 20, 1745, near Birmingham, England, Asbury became a Methodist preacher after brief schooling. He traveled for four years as a preacher for the Wesleyan conference. In August 1771, he and other English preachers volunteered to become missionaries in America. Arriving in Philadelphia that October, he embarked the next month on trips through the colonies and eventually to the Mississippi territory. He was made superintendent of the American Methodists in 1772; succeeded in 1773 by Thomas Rankin, he wrangled with his new superior and was summoned back to England in 1775. But he stayed in America, convinced of the inevitability of independence, and was left as the only English missionary in New England at the outbreak of the American Revolution. He united lay preachers under Wesley's code and formed the "circuit riders," who traveled on horseback preaching to settlers on the Western frontier. As a citizen of Delaware, he conferred with Northern and Southern Methodists and established himself as leader of the organization in 1782. When the Methodist Episcopal Church was consecrated in America in 1784, Wesley sent Thomas Coke to act as joint superintendent with him, but Asbury refused to accept the appointment without the assent of the preachers. Voted joint superintendent, he called himself bishop and subordinated Coke to his rule. He traveled nearly 27,000 miles, developing three Methodist meeting halls into a league of 412 societies and 214,235 adherents. He ordained more than 4,000 ministers and established Methodism as one of the three predominent religions in the South. In later years he traveled and preached in a sulky. His *Journals*, published in three volumes in 1821, contain valuable documentation of the social history of the early frontier. He died in Virginia after a long illness on March 31, 1816.

ASTOR, JOHN JACOB (1763–1848), fur trader and real estate developer. Born on July 17, 1763, near Heidelberg, Germany, the son of a butcher, Astor left home at the age of 17, following the death of his mother and his father's remarriage. He knew how to read and write and had resolved, according to a story about him, never to cheat, gamble, or be idle. He earned money working on a timber raft and sailed to England. There he joined a brother, saved money, and learned the English language in preparation for his intended journey to America. On his way in 1783, he befriended a German immigrant who was well versed in American fur trading with the Indians. By the time he reached New York City in 1784, he had settled on fur trading as his occupation. He owned his own shop by 1786. He traveled constantly to the nearby frontiers, made an arrangement with Montreal for importing furs after the Jay Treaty, and through his shrewd business sense was a prominent man in the industry by 1800, having amassed

a fortune of $250,000. Subsequently, he gained entry to the ports controlled by the East India Company and netted $50,000 in Canton alone. He began also to invest in real estate in the city. Following the Louisiana Purchase, he extended his trade into the West and in 1808 combined all of his holdings in the American Fur Company. His plans to control the fur trade in the Far West suffered unforeseen disasters and were halted by the War of 1812. But his real estate soared in value and during the war, especially after 1813, he loaned money to the government at enormous rates of interest. After the war, he again maneuvered to dominate trade west of the Mississippi, but his ambitious plans were undermined by Indian raids and a decline in the fur market. He sold his interests in June 1834 and retired, the richest man in America, to administer his fortune. He died on March 29, 1848, leaving funds to establish a public library, now incorporated into the New York Public Library. The Astor family continued to gain property and wealth. Of the branch of the family that emigrated to England, American-born Lady Astor, who had married Waldorf, great-great grandson of John Jacob, became the first woman to enter the British House of Commons.

AUDEN, WYSTAN HUGH (1907–   ), poet. Born in York, England, on February 21, 1907, Auden took a degree at Christ Church, Oxford, in 1928 and for a time taught school. His first book of poems was published privately in 1928. During the next several years he continued to write and publish poetry—including *Poems*, 1930, and *Look, Stranger!*, 1936—and, with Christopher Isherwood and the composer Benjamin Britten, poetic plays. He was awarded King George's Gold Medal for poetry in 1937. His poetry of the 1930s was greatly concerned with social issues and influenced by Freud and the "psychological" aspects of Marxism. He married Erika Mann, daughter of German novelist Thomas Mann, in 1936; in 1939 he came to the United States where he remained, becoming a citizen in

1946. His poetry became less directly social and turned, largely under the influence of Kierkegaard, to religious and existentialist themes. He published, among others, *The Age of Anxiety*, 1947, and *Nones*, 1951. In 1948 he was awarded the Pulitzer Prize for poetry. He continued to work occasionally with music, and in 1951 he collaborated on the libretto for Stravinsky's *The Rake's Progress*. His later publications include *The Shield of Achilles*, 1955, and the prose works *The Enchafèd Flood: the Romantic Iconography of the Sea*, 1950, and *The Dyer's Hand and Other Essays*, 1962. From 1956 to 1961 he was professor of poetry at Oxford. His official residence continued to be the United States.

AUDUBON, JOHN JAMES (1785 – 1851), artist and naturalist. Born on April 26, 1785, in what is now Haiti, on a plantation owned by his father, a French naval officer, Audubon was taken to France in 1789 and was cared for until he was 18 by an indulgent foster mother. His formal education was somewhat indifferently attended to, but he early developed an abiding interest in nature and in drawing. He came to America in 1803 and for a while lived the life of a dandyish aristocrat. He left, spent a year in France, and returned in 1806, this time to enter business. He tried a number of jobs and finally, in partnership with a friend, operated a series of general stores in Kentucky. In 1808 he married, bringing his wife to Kentucky with him where, careless of business, he spent a great deal of his time exploring the woods and making drawings of birds. His business venture ended in bankruptcy and from 1820, with his wife's financial support, he devoted himself to his amateur ornithology. In 1826 he took his collection of drawings to Europe to seek a publisher; he was immediately recognized and in 1827 was elected to the Royal Society of Edinburgh. His drawings, though occasionally falling short of complete scientific accuracy, were hailed as a collective masterwork. Financed by subscription, *The Birds of America* began to appear in London in 1827 and

was completed 11 years later. The text, issued separately as *Ornithological Biography*, occupied Audubon from 1831 to 1839; in the latter year he also published an index to the work. These years were spent shuttling back and forth between America and Europe; in 1839 he returned to the United States permanently, issued a "miniature edition" of *Birds*, and began his next work, *Viviparous Quadrupeds of North America*, which was completed by his sons and his collaborator, John Bachman, and published, plates and text, between 1842 and 1854. Audubon died on January 27, 1851.

AUSTIN, STEPHEN FULLER (1793 – 1836), frontier colonizer and political leader. Born in Austinville, Virginia, on November 3, 1793, Austin grew up on the Missouri frontier, where his father, Moses, took the family in 1798. Stephen received a remarkably good education for one of his means and background, and from 1810 to 1820 he served in various private and public capacities in Missouri, including five years in the territorial legislature. The financial panic of 1819 sent his father to colonize in Texas where he died a short time later; Austin himself hesitated in Arkansas until July 1821 before succumbing to his father's enthusiasm for Texas settlement. Giving himself loyally to Mexican citizenship, he confirmed his father's land grant and in 1822 founded a colony. Revolution in Mexico required him to go to Mexico City to reconfirm the grant; when he returned he was armed with effectively dictatorial powers. Under a state colonization law passed by the Coahuila legislature in 1825, colonization of Texas expanded rapidly. Austin remained the major power and leader; his connections in Mexico City, combined with his considerable diplomatic skill and his membership in the state legislature, enabled him to fend off an Anglo-Mexican attempt to bar slavery from Texas. His major accomplishment during these years was the extremely difficult double task of holding in check the growing American colonies while allaying Mexican suspicions that colonization might be a subtle prelude to annexation. In 1833 his efforts to have Texas separated from Coahuila and made a state of the Mexican confederation caused his imprisonment; when he was released in July 1835 revolution was too close to halt, and fighting actually broke out in October. He was sent to secure help from the United States; he returned in June 1836, shortly after the revolution ended, and, losing the presidency of the new republic to Sam Houston, served as secretary of state. He died on December 27, 1836.

AYER, FRANCIS WAYLAND (1848–1923), advertising agent. Born in Lee, Massachusetts, on February 4, 1848, Ayer was the son of an itinerant schoolteacher. He taught school himself for a few years in his youth, studied for a year at the University of Rochester, and in 1869 moved to Philadelphia. There, after a few months working as an advertising solicitor for the *National Baptist*, he opened his own advertising firm, naming it N. W. Ayer & Son, after his father. At a time when advertising was considered at best a calling of doubtful respectability, Ayer brought to the business an ethical approach that worked a revolution in methods and standards. He changed the role of the agent from that of middleman between advertiser and publisher to one of advisor to the advertiser; he developed an "open contract" that promised the client optimal use of his advertising budget, supported his claims with an itemized account of expenses, and charged a flat commission fee for the service, thus initiating the system that has since become customary. The firm was the first to provide the client with advertising copy, the first to conduct market research, and as an additional service issued the *American Newspaper Annual and Directory*. He pioneered in the use of trademarks, slogans, and other now common advertising devices, and the great reputation for integrity that he enjoyed—he refused, for example, to represent useless or fraudulent products—did much to establish advertising as a necessary and reputable adjunct to business. From 1895 to 1910 he served as president of the Merchants' National Bank of Philadelphia, and during his later years devoted much time to the Baptist Church, the Y.M.C.A., and his New York dairy farm. He died on March 5, 1923.

BABBITT, IRVING (1865–1933), educator and author. Born on August 2, 1865, in Dayton, Ohio, Babbitt held various jobs as a boy, from selling newspapers in New York to working on a ranch in Wyoming. He attended high school in Cincinnati and graduated from Harvard in 1889. As an instructor at the University of Montana for two years, he earned tuition for a year of study at the Sorbonne, then entered the Harvard graduate school and earned his master's degree in Oriental studies in 1893. A fellow student was Paul Elmer More, who later became his close friend and associate in the neo-humanist movement. In 1894, Babbitt became a teacher of French and comparative literature at Harvard; he was made an assistant professor in 1902 and professor in 1912. At Harvard and as a guest lecturer at universities and colleges in America and abroad, his lectures on the romantic movement, especially in English, French, and German literature, won wide publicity. He urged a return to the rational values of the classics, away from the emotionalism of his time, advocating the development of a "new humanism" consistent with the modern spirit. A widely publicized controversy developed in 1929–1930 between the humanists and the anti-humanists led by H. L. Mencken, who argued that the artist should present an unembellished, natural picture of life. His books on literature and various social and political phenomena included *Literature and the American College*, 1908, *The New Laokoön*, 1910, *The Masters of Modern French Criticism*, 1912, *Rousseau and Romanticism*, 1919, and *On Being Creative and Other Essays*, 1932. He died in Cambridge on July 15, 1933.

BACON, NATHANIEL (1647–1676), colonial leader. Born on January 2, 1647, in the county of Suffolk, England, Bacon was of a prominent and wealthy family and a cousin of Francis Bacon. He studied at Cambridge and at Gray's Inn. In 1674 he emigrated to Virginia, established two plantations, and within a year was appointed to the governor's council. He was soon at odds with Governor William Berkeley; the latter was reluctant to authorize reprisals against the Indians who were raiding frontier settlements, possibly because he feared the expense and consequences of a general Indian war, and Bacon was strongly in sympathy with the frontier inhabitants who demanded action. In 1676 an expeditionary force was organized in defiance of Berkeley and Bacon was chosen to lead it. Raids were launched against the Pamunkey, Susquehannock, and Occaneechee tribes, while Berkeley denounced Bacon and his followers as rebels. Public opinion, which by this time was demanding governmental reforms as well as protection from the Indians, forced the governor to back down, however, and Bacon returned to the council. He soon organized another raiding party and was again denounced by Berkeley. Bacon then occupied Jamestown, the capital, and Berkeley fled. When Bacon left the town to move again against the Pamunkey villages, the governor returned. Bacon led his force back to Jamestown and, after a sharp battle, burned it while the governor once again fled. By this time Bacon was in control of virtually all of Virginia; he withdrew to Green Spring to consolidate his power, but in October 1676 he died suddenly, and the rebellion quickly collapsed.

BAKER, GEORGE FISHER (1840–1931), financier and philanthropist. Born on March 27, 1840, in Troy, New York, Baker became a clerk in the state banking department at the age of 16. He quickly demonstrated considerable ability in this work and in 1863 was invited to help found the First National Bank of New York City. Buying a small number of shares in the bank, he began as teller and bookkeeper and within two years was cashier and active head of the institution. He was frequently consulted by the secretary of the treasury. He convinced the bank's president to remain in business during the financial panic of 1873 and four years later himself became president. Under his direction the bank developed firm connections with other major financial and commercial establishments and, though it remained a rather small bank, it and Baker became central figures in American finance, ranking in power with J. P. Morgan. In 1908 he founded the First Security Corporation to deal, as the bank legally could not, in the securities market. From 1909 until his death Baker was chairman of the board of First National and served additionally as director of over 80 other business corporations. After 1912 he devoted much time to philanthropy; among his major benefactions were a $6 million gift to Harvard for the establishment of the Graduate School of Business Administration, large grants to the Metropolitan Museum of Art and the American Red Cross, and others to many colleges, hospitals, libraries, museums, and other institutions, to a total of over $19 million. Enormously wealthy, he made money even during the Depression. He died on May 2, 1931.

BAKER, NEWTON DIEHL (1871–1937), lawyer, public official, and statesman. Born on December 3, 1871, in Martinsburg, West Virginia, Baker attended Johns Hopkins University, where one of his instructors was Woodrow Wilson. He graduated in 1892 and entered Washington and Lee University, earning his law degree in 1894. He returned to Martinsburg to practise, spending his evenings studying five foreign languages. In 1896 he was called to Washington to become secretary to the postmaster general. The following year he went to Europe and met a Cleveland politician, who was impressed with his learning and invited him there to practise. In Cleveland, Baker became assistant director of the city's law department, city soliciter, and the principal advisor to the municipal administration under reform mayor Tom L. Johnson. In 1911 he was elected mayor of Cleveland, winning reelection in 1913. An ardent supporter of Wilson in the presidential campaign in 1912, he became a prominent national figure. In 1916 President Wilson appointed him secretary of war. During his first year of service, faced with the Mexican situation and the World War in Europe, he did surprisingly little to reinforce the military, but when the United States entered the war he presented a plan for conscription that enlarged the Army from 95,000 to 4,000,000 men. He supported General Pershing's policy of keeping American troops apart from the Allied forces, and he shared President Wilson's liberal, intellectual outlook. He was, however, sharply criticized by some of his contemporaries. Shortages of equipment and food were blamed on his administration; he was called a pacifist, willing to let the military bear the conduct of the war; and a Senate probe begun in 1917 forced him to remove inexperienced, bureaucratic generals from the War Department. After the war, he returned to practice in Cleveland. He supported American entry into the League of Nations in the 1920s and was appointed to the Permanent Court of Arbitration at The Hague in 1928. His views became more conservative as he grew older, and in 1936 he was considered for the vice-presidential nomination of a new coalition party of Republicans and conservative Democrats. But poor health forced his retirement, and he died in Shaker Heights, Ohio, on December 25, 1937.

BAKER, RAY STANNARD (1870–1946), journalist and author. Born on April 17, 1870, in Lansing, Michigan, Baker was raised from the age of five in northwestern Wisconsin, then frontier territory. He graduated from Michigan State Agricultural College in 1889 and entered law school at the University of Michigan, but switched to literature. At 22 he became a reporter for the *Chicago Record*; his first major story concerned a Chicago restaurant strike and earned him a regular staff job. On an assignment to report on coal thefts, he demonstrated an ability to probe below the surface of news events; he discovered that the culprits lived in run-down, unheated shacks and earned such low wages that they could not afford heat. His coverage of the march of "Coxey's army" in 1894 earned him an editorship on the *Record*, but McClure's Syndicate hired him away as an editor in 1897. From 1899 to 1905 he was associate editor of *McClure's Magazine*, working with other noted journalists in the "muckraking" movement, including Ida M. Tarbell, Lincoln Steffens, and William Allen White. Together they founded *The American Magazine*, which Baker co-edited from 1906 to 1915. He met Woodrow Wilson in Paris in 1919 while serving as director of the Press Bureau of the American Commission to Negotiate Peace. They developed a close friendship, from which emerged 18 books by Baker, including an eight-volume biography, *Woodrow Wilson—Life and Letters*, 1927–1939, which won a Pulitzer Prize. He wrote other books on a wide range of subjects, including *Seen in Germany*, 1901, *Following the Color Line*, 1908, *The Spiritual Unrest*, 1910, and *The New Industrial Unrest*, 1920. Under the pseudonym David Grayson, he wrote collections of immensely popular philosophical essays; his autobiography, in three volumes, appeared in 1941–1945. He died on July 12, 1946, at his home in Amherst, Massachusetts.

BALANCHINE, GEORGE (1904–   ), choreographer. Born Georgi Melitonovitch Balanchivadze on January 9, 1904, in St. Petersburg, Russia, Balanchine, the son of composer Meliton Balanchivadze, was trained at the Imperial ballet school from the age of ten and graduated in 1921 after it had become the Soviet State Ballet School. He continued his studies at the Conservatory of Music and joined the Soviet State Dancers. He toured with them to Paris in 1924 and decided to remain, joining the Ballet Russe of ballet master Sergei Diaghilev, who suggested his new name. Balanchine worked more frequently as a choreographer than a dancer because of his slight build. By 1929, when Diaghilev died and the troupe disbanded, he had choreographed *Enigma, La*

Chatte, and *Apollo.* He went to London and arranged the dance for Cole Porter's *Wake Up and Dream,* then became ballet master of the Royal Danish Ballet in Copenhagen. In 1932 he organized the Ballet Russe de Monte Carlo, and the next year in Paris formed his own company, Les Ballets. During this period he composed *Cotillon* and *La Concurrence.* Stressing visual pattern and movement rather than an intricate plot, his dances were precise improvisations on themes of classic ballet. In 1933 Lincoln Kirstein, a Boston philanthropist, invited him to America to establish a school for American dancers. Together they founded in 1934 the School of American Ballet, which produced a throng of good American dancers to dance in the companies they subsequently formed: the American Ballet Company, Ballet Caravan, Ballet Society, and the New York City Ballet. Balanchine choreographed nearly 100 ballets, among them *Concerto Barocco, Le Bourgeois Gentilhomme, Danses Concertantes, Symphonies Concertante, Waltz Academy, The Four Temperaments, The Triumph of Bacchus, Orpheus, Serenade, Le Baiser de la Fee, Agon, Firebird, Swan Lake,* and the *Nutcracker.* For the musical comedy stage he arranged the dances for *Babes in Arms,* 1937, *I Married an Angel,* 1938, *Cabin in the Sky,* 1940, *Louisiana Purchase,* 1940, *Song of Norway,* 1944, and *Courtin' Time,* 1951.

BALDWIN, JAMES (1924–), author. Born in New York City on August 2, 1924, Baldwin grew up under the strict guidance of his strongly religious father. At the age of 14 he was a Youth Minister preaching in storefront churches in Harlem. In high school his interest turned to writing, and, leaving home at 17, he spent several years alternating between holding menial jobs and writing with the support of a series of fellowships. None of this early work was successful. In 1948 he left America for Paris where, in an atmosphere relatively free of racial prejudice and tension, he remained expatriated for nearly ten years. In Paris he lived in poverty but continued to write, receiving encouragement from Richard Wright. His first published novel, *Go Tell It on the Mountain,* appeared in 1953; in 1955 came a volume of essays, *Notes of a Native Son.* Both received good critical notices but little public acceptance. Popular success began after his return to the United States in 1957; *Nobody Knows My Name,* another collection of essays published in 1961, and *Another Country,* 1962, established him not only as a leading black spokesman but as a major force in contemporary American literature. He followed with *The Fire Next Time* in 1963 and two successful plays, *Blues for Mister Charlie* and *The Amen Corner.* In 1965 he published a volume of short stories, *Going to Meet the Man,* and in 1968 another novel, *Tell Me How Long the Train's Been Gone.*

BALLOU, ADIN (1803–1890), clergyman and social reformer. Born in Cumberland, Rhode Island, on April 23, 1803, Ballou developed early interests in both scholarship and religion. Discouraged from a formal pursuit of the former, he began to preach locally at the age of 18. Reversing his original opinion of Universalism, he joined that sect and began active work in its behalf in 1823. He withdrew because of a theological dispute and in 1831 formed his own splinter Universalist group, which lasted for ten years. He was active in a number of reform movements, particularly those directed toward peace, temperance, and the abolition of slavery. In 1840, in order to expound his views on society and the imperative call to establish the Kingdom of God on earth, he began to publish *The Practical Christian,* a biweekly newspaper that continued for 20 years. His ideas came to fruition almost immediately when, with 31 associates, he founded the Hopedale Community, a self-contained religious society based on "Fraternal Communism." Actually a joint-stock company, the group purchased 250 acres of land near Milford, Massachusetts, and prospered for several years. Presiding over the community until 1856, Ballou retired with full confidence in the success of his experiment;

three years later, when the community was dissolved by two brothers who had acquired a controlling interest in the stock, he blamed the failure on a lack of whole-hearted moral dedication among the members. He remained as pastor of the Hopedale parish which succeeded the community until 1880. He died on August 5, 1890.

BANCROFT, GEORGE (1800–1891), historian, public official, and diplomat. Born in Worcester, Massachusetts, on October 3, 1800, Bancroft quickly demonstrated his intellectual capacity. Graduating from Harvard in 1817, he studied divinity for a year and then, in 1818, with financial support arranged by President Norton of Harvard, he continued his studies in Germany. With four years of European scholarship and a Ph.D. from Göttingen, he returned to Harvard to teach for a year. Dissatisfied, he established, with Joseph Cogswell, the Round Hill School in Northampton, Massachusetts. He remained with the school for eight years, during which time he began, through articles and pamphlets, to enter political affairs. He also began his great work, the *History of the United States*, publishing the first three volumes in 1834, 1837, and 1840. Written in florid prose and with a marked democratic and nationalist bias, the work confirmed Bancroft as the nation's foremost historian. He gained influence in the Democratic Party and upon Van Buren's election in 1836 was appointed collector of the port of Boston, where Nathaniel Hawthorne was given a patronage post. In 1845 he became Polk's secretary of the navy and promoted the establishment of the Naval Academy; he directed the occupation of California and, as acting secretary of war, issued the order that sent Gen. Zachary Taylor across the Texas frontier and led directly to the Mexican War. In 1846 he became minister to England where he continued research for his *History*; he returned in 1849 and devoted the next 18 years to his massive project, ultimately publishing six more volumes. In 1867 he became minister to Prussia and in 1871 minister to the

German empire, in which position he represented the United States in the arbitration of the Oregon boundary dispute with Great Britain. He returned again to the United States in 1874, published the tenth volume of the *History* shortly thereafter, and prepared a revised six-volume Centenary Edition. In 1882 he published a two-volume work on the establishment of the Constitution; four years later it was included in the final revised edition of the *History*. He continued to publish books and articles until his death on January 17, 1891.

BANNEKER, BENJAMIN (1731–1806), mathematician. Born on November 9, 1731, in Ellicott, Maryland, Banneker was the son of a slave father and a free mother. Free himself, he was educated in a local school, where he early displayed a particular talent for mathematics, and afterwards continued to study a wide range of subjects with books borrowed from a friendly white neighbor. In his youth he constructed a wooden clock, apparently the first to be made in America, which struck the hours and kept remarkably accurate time for many years. His interests ranged from the habits of bees and 17-year locusts to astronomy, and it was in the latter field that he did his most notable work. As his reputation grew he came to the attention of Thomas Jefferson, who in 1790 secured him a position with the surveying team appointed to lay out the District of Columbia and the site of the city of Washington. When the chief architect, Pierre L'Enfant, refused to cooperate fully and departed, taking with him his detailed maps, Banneker was able to reproduce the plans from memory. In 1791 he published an almanac containing the results of his astronomical observations and calculations. He sent a copy to Jefferson, who was sufficiently impressed by the work, and by Banneker's accompanying letter defending the intellectual equality of the Negro, to forward it to the French Academy of Sciences. Editions of the almanac continued to appear regularly until 1802. He died in 1806.

BARBER, SAMUEL (1910–), composer. Born on March 9, 1910, in West Chester, Pennsylvania, Barber had decided on a musical career as early as the age of eight. He had composed an opera a year earlier. He was one of the first students at the Curtis Institute in Philadelphia, studying piano, voice, and conducting, from 1924 to 1934. Before graduation he wrote *Dover Beach*, for voice and string quartet, the *Overture to "The School for Scandal,"* and *Music for a Scene from Shelley*. The latter two compositions established his reputation. Thereafter his work became popular in Europe as well as America, where he ranked as a leading composer of serious music. His *Symphony in One Movement*, 1936, was the first piece by an American to be played at the Salzburg music festival in Austria. From his *String Quartet*, 1936, the second movement, called *Adagio for Strings*, became his most popular lyrical work. During World War II, while serving in the Army, he wrote the *Second Symphony*, commissioned by and dedicated to the Army Air Force. It was premiered in 1944. His other compositions include the *Essays for Orchestra*, 1937 and 1942, *Violin Concerto*, 1939, *Cello Concerto*, 1945, *Piano Sonata*, 1948, the ballet *Medea*, 1946, and the opera *Vanessa*, 1958, which won a Pulitzer Prize. Although Barber's later works, such as the *Pianoforte Sonata*, 1951, are marked by dissonance and the use of the 12-tone scale, his work is eminently melodic and listenable. The harmonies are pure and strong, as in the popular *Adagio*, and often reach thrilling climaxes, as in the *Violin Concerto*. In 1963 his *First Piano Concerto* was awarded a Pulitzer Prize, making Barber the first composer to win two.

BARLOW, JOEL (1754–1812), poet, political theorist, and diplomat. Born in Redding, Connecticut, on March 24, 1754, Barlow graduated from Yale in 1778 firmly determined to win literary fame in the new nation. He served three years as a chaplain in the Revolutionary Army; in 1786, after several years of sundry short-lived activities, he was admitted to the bar. He was a leading member of the circle known as the Connecticut Wits and was all the while hard at work on his projected philosophical epic of America. This he finally published as *The Vision of Columbus* in 1787; though of less than epic merit, the work won recognition by its energy and optimistic nationalism. In 1788 Barlow sailed to France as a land company agent, then to London for a lengthy stay. Exposed to European Enlightenment thinking, he became more and more radical in his political views. He was associated with Thomas Paine and in 1792, in reply to Burke's tract on the French Revolution, he wrote *Advice to the Privileged Orders*, a radically democratic document that won him citizenship in France and proscription in England. The following year, while living in France, he wrote his best-remembered poetical work, *Hasty Pudding*, a humorous pastoral evocation of New England. From 1795 to 1797 he was in Algiers securing the release of American prisoners and negotiating treaties. He returned to the United States in 1805 and two years later published a revised and expanded version of his epic poem, now entitled *The Columbiad*. In 1811 he was sent to negotiate a commercial treaty with France; his scheduled meeting with Napoleon was prevented by the French defeat in Russia. Barlow was caught up in the disastrous retreat from Moscow and died of exposure in Zarnowiec, Poland, on December 24, 1812.

BARNARD, HENRY (1811–1900), educator. Born on January 24, 1811, in Hartford, Connecticut, Barnard received his initial education in a district school. He and a friend found the conditions so intolerable there that they plotted to run away to sea, but his father offered to enroll him in a private academy. At the Monson Academy in Massachusetts, and the Hopkins Grammar School, Henry prepared for college, entering Yale in 1826. While participating in the "Bread and Butter Rebellion," a student strike for better food in 1828 and 1829, he visited schools in several cities and wrote about them in the *New England Re-*

view. Graduating from Yale in 1830, he taught school, read law, and attended Yale Law School, gaining admission to the bar in 1835. Still interested in education, he toured Europe during 1835–1836, speaking to prominent men and learning the most advanced theories of the subject. In 1837 he was elected to the Connecticut state legislature. He conducted a successful campaign in 1838 for a bill providing better administration of common schools. The bill provided for a board of commissioners for the school system, of which Barnard, despite his law background, was chosen secretary. Aiming to stimulate citizens and the legislature to reform deplorable schoolhouse conditions, he personally visited schools, wrote letters and sent questionnaires to parents, made extensive reports to the legislature, and founded a teacher training institute and the *Connecticut Common School Journal*. In 1843 he moved to Rhode Island as the first commissioner of public schools, and implemented a similar program. He returned to Connecticut in 1851 as the state superintendent of schools. In 1855 he founded the *American Journal of Education*. From 1858 to 1861 he was chancellor of the University of Wisconsin, In 1866 president of St. John's College, Annapolis, Maryland, and from 1867 to 1870, first U.S. commissioner of education. His reports, which created a new literature of education, were surveys of the history of educational legislation or scientific investigations of actual conditions. He relied on public willingness to correct a fault after he demonstrated it. He died in Hartford on July 5, 1900.

BARNUM, PHINEAS TAYLOR (1810–1891), showman. Born on July 5, 1810, in Bethel, Connecticut, Barnum never cared for manual labor. He preferred mental exercise and held various jobs, from editing an Abolitionist newspaper to selling tickets for a Philadelphia theater. In Philadelphia in 1835 he saw Joice Heth, an old Negress, being exhibited as the 160-year-old nurse of George Washington. The show was obviously phony, but she was well schooled in the customs and predilections of

the former President, and her performance caught Barnum's fancy. Wondering just how far he could stretch the public imagination, he bought Joice Heth and displayed her in the role of Washington's nurse against a background of patriotic notices, billboards proclaiming her 100-year association with the Baptist Church, and antiquated purchase sheets signed by Washington's father. When she died, he buried her amid publicized mourning in his own family plot, then ran anonymous newspaper articles attacking her authenticity, and other articles defending his patriotic intentions. Convinced by now that there was no limit to the public's gullibility, he purchased Scudder's American Museum in New York City in 1841 and renamed it Barnum's American Museum. It became a house of curiosities; wooly horses, bearded ladies, Feejee mermaids, and the dwarf General Tom Thumb roamed about the place. Not the least of the attractions was a door marked "Egress," which many patrons flocked to see, only to find themselves outside. In a serious gesture, he brought Swedish singer Jenny Lind to the United States in 1850 and made a celebrity of her and a wealthier man of himself. To offset the solemnity of Miss Lind's tour, he presented New York City with its first live hippopotamus. In a break from amusements, he served in the Connecticut legislature, 1867–1869, and in 1875 was mayor of Bridgeport, where he developed the industrial section of the city into an exemplary workers' community and where he had built his grotesque mansion "Iranistan." In 1871 he proclaimed with extravagant publicity the opening of the "Greatest Show on Earth," a circus that he quickly developed into a three-ring extravaganza. He combined forces with his chief competitor, James A. Bailey, in 1881 to form the great Barnum and Bailey Circus, and the next year he purchased Jumbo, a huge African elephant, from the Royal Zoological Society in London, and proceeded to advertise it as the world's only surviving mastodon. Although his publicity was usually deceptive, he openly professed his belief, apparently correct, that Americans wanted to be "humbugged," or diverted from reality, and he always presented a show that was worth more than the price of admission. Reputedly the author of the claim "There's a sucker born every minute," he possessed a genius for showmanship that reaped him a fortune and brought entertainment to millions of people. Among his candid writings were an autobiography in 1855 and *Humbugs of the World*, 1865. He died in Philadelphia on April 7, 1891.

BARRYMORE, MAURICE (1847–1905), actor. Born in 1847 in Fort Agra, India, where his father was employed by the East India Company, Herbert Blythe, who later changed his name to Barrymore, was educated at Harrow School and Oxford University in England. He abandoned a prospective law career to be an actor, first appearing in 1872 in London in a revival of *London Assurance* and in Bulwer-Lytton's *Money*. In 1875 he went to America and made a Boston debut in *Under the Gaslight*. Subsequently he joined Augustin Daly's summer stock company and met Georgiana Emma Drew, the daughter of distinguished actors John and Louisa Drew, and married her on December 31, 1876. The couple were both prominent in Daly's company, appearing with such actors as Fanny Davenport and Joseph Jefferson. They formed their own road company with her brother, John Drew, which toured in 1878 and 1879, and they appeared individually or together in A. M. Palmer's company (she at various times with Edwin Booth, Lawrence Barrett, and John McCullough). He also joined Lester Wallach's company and made a notable appearance as Captain Absolute in *The Rivals*. After 1881 he appeared in London opposite Madame Modjeska, for whom he wrote the play *Nadjeska*. They starred together in *Romeo and Juliet* in New York in the last performance given at the Booth Theatre (1883). Mrs. Barrymore gave her final performances in Boston in *Settled Out of Court* and *The Sportsman*, both in 1892, and died in Santa Barbara, California, on July 2, 1898. Maurice played in Belasco's

Heart of Maryland in New York in 1895 and London in 1898, and was featured in Palmer's company and in various vaudeville theaters. He died on March 26, 1905. Their three children, raised in the tradition of the theater, became known as the "royal family" of the American stage. LIONEL BARRYMORE (1878–1954) was born on April 28, 1878, in Philadelphia, and was first interested in painting as a career. He first appeared on the stage at the age of 6 and returned at 15 in *The Rivals* with his grandmother, Louisa Drew, but then went to Paris and studied painting for three years. He appeared with his uncle, John Drew, in *Second in Command*, and after another visit to Paris turned finally to acting. He made a few motion pictures at the Biograph studios under D. W. Griffith, including *The New York Hat* with Mary Pickford. His greatest stage roles were in *Peter Ibbetson* in 1917, *The Copperhead* in 1918, and in *The Jest* in 1919, with his brother John. After 1925 he starred in numerous motion pictures, including *Grand Hotel, Reunion in Vienna, Dinner at Eight, Treasure Island, David Copperfield, Rasputin and the Empress*, with his brother and his sister, Ethel, and *Free Soul*, for which he won an Academy Award in 1931. Subsequently he played Mr. Scrooge in an annual radio broadcast of Dickens' *A Christmas Carol* and starred in the *Dr. Kildare* movie and radio series. He published *We Barrymores* in 1951 and *Mr. Cantonwine: A Moral Tale*, 1953. He died in Van Nuys, California, on November 15, 1954. ETHEL BARRYMORE (1879–1959) was born in Philadelphia on August 15, 1879. She attended the Convent of the Sacred Heart in her native city and made her stage debut at 14 in a New York production of *The Rivals*, which also featured her brother Lionel and Louisa Drew. She next appeared with John Drew in *The Bauble Shop* and then went to London, playing in *Secret Service, The Bells*, and *Peter the Great*, 1897–1898. Returning to Broadway, she starred in *Captain Jinks of the Horse Marines* in 1901. Subsequent roles in *A Doll's House* and *Alice-Sit-by-the-Fire*, both 1905, *Sunday*,

1906, *Mid-Channel*, 1910, *Trelawney of the Wells*, 1911, *Declassee*, 1919, *The Second Mrs. Tanqueray*, 1924, *The Constant Wife*, 1928, *Scarlet Sister Mary*, 1931, *Whiteoaks*, 1938, and *The Corn is Green*, 1942, won her the lasting tributes of the theater. She also played in vaudeville, on radio, television, and in motion pictures, with her brothers in *Rasputin and the Empress*, 1932, and in *None but the Lonely Heart*, 1944, for which she won an Academy Award. She died in Hollywood on June 18, 1959. **JOHN BARRYMORE** (1882 – 1942) was born in Philadelphia on February 15, 1882. He first appeared in 1903 in *Magda*, in Chicago, and in *Glad of It* in New York. In London in 1905 he played in *The Dictator*, and in Australia that year appeared with William Collier's company. He toured in *The Boys of Company B* and returned to Chicago in 1908 to play in *A Stubborn Cinderella*. He appeared on the Broadway stage in *Thief in the Night*, *My Dear Children*, and *The Jest*, with his brother Lionel, and starred in 1920 as Richard III, and in New York and London in 1923 and 1924 as Hamlet. Dubbed the "great profile," he starred in movies such as *Rasputin and the Empress*, with his brother and sister, *The Dictator*, *Sherlock Holmes*, *The Test of Honor*, *Beau Brummel*, *Don Juan*, *Dinner at 8*, *Grand Hotel*, and *Counsellor-at-Law*. He died in Hollywood on May 29, 1942.

BARTON, CLARISSA HARLOWE (1821 – 1912), public health administrator. Born on December 25, 1821, in Oxford, Massachusetts, Clara Barton was the youngest of five children. Her family educated her and she grew up willful and independent, with a love for outdoor sports and the courage of a man. She began an 18-year career of teaching at the age of 15. In 1851 she attended the Liberal Institute in Clinton, New York, then established a free school in New Jersey, which became so large that the townsmen would not allow a woman to run it. Rather than subordinate herself to a male principal, she resigned. She was employed by the U.S. Patent Office in 1854. In 1861, she showed characteristic initiative in organizing facilities to recover soldiers' lost baggage and securing medicine and supplies for soldiers wounded in the first Battle of Bull Run, and gained permission to move personally through the battle lines to distribute provisions and minister to the wounded. She carried on this work through the remainder of the Civil War, traveling with the Army as far south as Charleston. In 1869 she went abroad and became involved with relief in the Franco-Prussian War. Learning of the activities of the European Red Cross in Geneva, she promoted U.S. participation in the Geneva Convention, published a pamphlet on the benefits of the Red Cross, and lobbied for it among state officials and congressman in Washington. Not until President Arthur took office was U.S. entry into the Geneva Convention secured in 1882, and the American Red Cross was organized with Clara Barton as president. For 23 years she closely supervised all of the organization's activities until charges of authoritarianism were brought against her by members of her executive council. Public contributions to the organization diminished, and only congressional intercession, in 1904, kept it from dissolving. It was agreed that she was a poor business manager; this did not, however, negate the scope and value of her contributions, which encompassed relief work in the United States, in Armenia, and Cuba during war times, and which included adoption of the "American amendment" to the Geneva Convention allowing the Red Cross to provide relief in times of natural disasters and calamities, as well as during war. Shortly before her death, she planned to establish a Red Cross in Mexico. But, her nerves exhausted, she died in Glen Echo, Maryland, on April 12, 1912.

BARTRAM, JOHN (1699 – 1777), botanist. Born on May 23, 1699, near Philadelphia, Bartram was briefly educated and planned to be a farmer. He was interested in botany from the age of 10, and he purchased some land in 1728 near the Schuylkill River in Philadelphia to conduct experiments in hybridization.

Stimulated by this work, he began a correspondence with Peter Collinson, an English naturalist, around 1733, and the two exchanged notes and specimens. His circle of admirers grew, and soon he was writing to Linnaeus, who considered him a great natural botanist. In Philadelphia, his garden became a favorite spot for Franklin and Washington, and other noted men. Through Collinson's influence, Bartram became botanist in the American colonies for King George III in 1765. He traveled to the frontiers to collect bulbs and seeds and new specimens. His experiences were recorded in journals, the best known of which was *Observations on the Inhabitants, Climate, Soil, etc. . . . from Pennsylvania to . . . Lake Ontario*, 1751. Among the varieties he located was the shrub *Franklinia alatamaha*; the moss *Bartramia* was named for him. America's first botanist, he died on September 22, 1777. His son WILLIAM BARTRAM, born on February 9, 1739, in Philadelphia, also became a botanist. He earned praise in his youth for drawings of specimens gathered by his father. He tended the garden and increased its varieties. Most famous for his journal, *Travels through North and South Carolina, Georgia, East and West Florida, the Cherokee Country, etc.*, 1791, which made significant contributions to English romantic literature as well as to science, he died on July 22, 1823, in Philadelphia.

BARUCH, BERNARD MANNES (1870–1965), financier, public official, and presidential confidant. Born in Camden, South Carolina, on August 19, 1870, Baruch attended City College in New York City. After graduating in 1889 he entered business and was a highly successful speculator on Wall Street. In 1916 he was appointed to the advisory commission of the Council of National Defense by President Wilson; responsible positions in the regulation of vital raw materials led to his appointment as chairman of the War Industries Board in March 1918. After the war he was on a number of economic councils and an advisor to Wilson at the Versailles peace conference. He continued to serve on governmental commissions, acting as an advisor and consultant on industrial mobilization during World War II. In 1946 he represented the United States in the United Nations Atomic Energy Commission, where he presented the first proposal for the international development and control of atomic energy. He was probably best known as a popular sage and an advisor to every U.S. President from Wilson to Kennedy. He died on June 20, 1965.

BAUM, LYMAN FRANK (1856–1919), author. Born on May 15, 1856, in Chittenango, New York, Baum attended an academy in Syracuse. He was editor of the *Dakota Pioneer* at Aberdeen, South Dakota, from 1888 to 1890, and of *Chicago Show Window*, a trade magazine for window decorators, from 1897 to 1902. His first book was an instantly successful children's story, *Father Goose: His Book*, 1899. He thereupon presented a draft of a book called *Wizard of Oz* to his publisher. It appeared in 1900, as *The Wonderful Wizard of Oz*; and the potential for a stage production being obvious, it was produced in Chicago in 1901 as a musical extravaganza. (Later the story became a motion picture, with Bert Lahr and Ray Bolger, and with Judy Garland, as Dorothy, singing "Over the Rainbow.") After this enormous success, Baum traveled in Europe, and spent time writing in Italy and Sicily. He moved to Pasadena, California, into a large house with a flower garden, in which he kept a cage full of rare songbirds. He continued to write "Wizard of Oz" stories including the *Woggle Bug Book*, 1905, and *The Tik-Tok Man of Oz*, 1914. Fourteen Oz books flowed from his pen; singly and together, they have become classics in children's literature. Other stories included *The Life and Adventures of Santa Claus*, 1902, *Enchanted Isle of Yew*, 1903, *The Magical Monarch of Mo*, 1903, *The Daring Twins*, 1910, and *Sky Island*, 1912. Besides his own, he wrote under other names:

Schuyler Staunton, Floyd Akers, Edith Van Dyne. Eight of his tales were adapted for the stage. He died on May 6, 1919, in Hollywood.

BEARD, CHARLES AUSTIN (1874–1948), political scientist, historian, and educator. Born near Knightstown, Indiana, on November 27, 1874, Beard graduated from DePauw University in 1898 and spent the next four years abroad. He studied for a while at Oxford and then returned to the United States to continue his studies at Columbia University. He taught history and politics at Columbia from 1907; during his tenure his interest shifted from European history to American. His early and influential works, *An Economic Interpretation of the Constitution of the United States*, 1913, and *The Economic Origins of Jeffersonian Democracy*, 1915, while not explicitly embodying economic determinism, did much to foster that approach to history among other historians. Beard was an influential leader of the Progressive movement and one of its intellectual mainstays. In 1917 he resigned from Columbia in protest against the administration's policy concerning academic freedom. He helped found the New School for Social Research in 1919, and thereafter was from time to time an advisor to the governments of Japan and Yugoslavia. With his wife Mary, a distinguished historian in her own right, he produced *The Rise of American Civilization*, in four parts, beginning in 1927 and concluding with *America in Midpassage*, 1939, and *The American Spirit*, 1942. During the 1930s and 1940s Beard was deeply concerned with American foreign policy; his outlook tended toward isolationism, and he severely criticized Roosevelt's policies in the period leading to World War II. He died on September 1, 1948.

BEARD, DANIEL CARTER (1850–1941), artist, author, and woodsman. Born on June 21, 1850, in Cincinnati, Dan Beard attended school in Covington, Kentucky, and from 1880 to 1884 studied at the Art Students League in New York. He was a successful illustrator, his work appearing in leading magazines and in many books. His interest in woodcraft and outdoor life led him to write numerous books on the subject, including *American Boys' Handy Book*, 1882, *Outdoor Handy Book*, 1900, *Boy Pioneers and Sons of Daniel Boone*, 1909, *The Buckskin Book*, 1911, *Shelters, Shacks, and Shanties*, 1914, *American Boys' Book of Wild Animals*, 1921, and *Wisdom of the Woods*, 1927. From 1893 to 1900 he taught at the Woman's School of Applied Design, inaugurating the first class in animal drawing. He edited *Recreation* from 1905 to 1906. In 1905 he founded the Sons of Daniel Boone; in 1910 the society was merged with the newly chartered Boy Scouts of America, patterned after the movement begun in England by Robert Baden-Powell. Beard became national commissioner of the scouts and, in recognition of his leadership in promoting and establishing scouting in the United States, was given the only golden eagle medal ever awarded. From 1911 to 1914 he organized and headed the department of woodcraft at Culver Military Academy in Indiana. For many years he served as associate editor of the Boy Scout magazine, *Boy's Life*. He died in Suffern, New York, on June 11, 1941; Mt. Beard, adjoining Mt. McKinley in Alaska, is named for him.

BEAUMONT, WILLIAM (1785–1853), surgeon. Born on November 21, 1785, in Lebanon, Connecticut, Beaumont received a rudimentary public school education, was apprenticed in 1810 to a Vermont surgeon, and was licensed to practise medicine two years later. He served in the Army during the War of 1812, and after four years of private practice in Plattsburg, New York, he enlisted for a second time in 1819 and was sent to Fort Mackinac as post surgeon. In 1822 he found a young Canadian trapper, Alexis St. Martin, with a gunshot wound in his abdomen that had left a permanent opening into his stomach. He restored the man to health but was unable to close the wound; at one point, to save St. Martin from being deported back to Canada as a pauper, he took him into his own home. About 1825 it occurred to Beaumont to take advantage of St. Martin's condition and to study the action of the stomach in a living man. Soon after he began his observations, however, St. Martin ran away, and it was not until 1829 that Beaumont, then at Fort Crawford, located him and persuaded him to return. There, and later in Washington, D.C., he pursued his investigations. To his earlier findings on the movements of the stomach during digestion, the relative digestibility of various foods, and the ability of gastric juice to digest food even outside the body, he added further observations on the nature of the gastric juice itself. A collaborator, Professor Robley Dunglison of the University of Virginia, determined that the principal constituent was free hydrochloric acid and suggested the presence of another chemical (later shown to be pepsin) that defied analysis. Beaumont's work was summed up in his classic *Experiments and Observations on the Gastric Juice and the Physiology of Digestion*, 1833. In 1834 St. Martin returned to Canada and thereafter refused to participate in further experiments; in the same year Beaumont was transferred to St. Louis. He resigned from the Army in 1840 and carried on a private practice until his death on April 25, 1853.

BECKER, CARL LOTUS (1873–1945), historian. Born on September 7, 1873, near Waterloo, Iowa, Becker attended Cornell College in Mt. Vernon, Iowa, and graduated from the University of Wisconsin in 1896, where he remained as a graduate student, a fellow, and a doctoral candidate until taking his Ph.D. in 1907. He was a fellow in constitutional law at Columbia during 1898–1899. Before settling into his position as professor of European history at Cornell University, he was an instructor in history and political science at Pennsylvania State College from 1899 to 1901, in history at Dartmouth until 1902, at the University of Kansas until 1916, and at the University of Minnesota until 1917. At Cornell, he was a popular lecturer and found time to write essays on aspects of American, French, colonial, and modern European history. The style for which he became known blended great learning with a masterly literary style. His broad analyses of historical institutions reflected his apprenticeship under Frederick Jackson Turner at the University of Wisconsin; his views on subjective historical interpretation were the subject of his famous presidential address "Every Man His Own Historian," to the American Historical Association in 1931. He wrote many books including *The Declaration of Independence*, 1922, *Our Great Experiment in Democracy*, 1924, *Modern History*, 1931, *The Heavenly City of the Eighteenth Century Philosophers*, 1932, and *Progress and Power*, 1936. He died in Ithaca, New York, on April 10, 1945.

BEECHER, CATHARINE ESTHER (1800–1878), educator and reformer. Born in East Hampton on Long Island, New York, on September 6, 1800, Miss Beecher was the oldest daughter in one of the 19th century's most remarkable families. Daughter of Lyman Beecher and sister of Edward and Henry Ward Beecher and Harriet Beecher Stowe, to name only the three most prominent, she grew up in an atmosphere of learning but was kept by her sex from receiving much formal education. She attended schools for young ladies conducted in the fashion of the day while independently studying Latin, philosophy, and mathematics. In 1828 she established the Hartford Female Seminary in Hartford, Connecticut, an advanced school for girls in which she introduced calisthenics in a course of physical education. Moving with her father to Cincinnati, Ohio, in 1832, she opened the Western Female Institute; financial difficulties closed the school five years later. The rest of her life was devoted to the promotion of equal educational opportunities for women. She inspired the founding of several women's colleges in the Midwest, and her writings did much to introduce domestic science into the American curriculum. Though in sympathy with much of the 19th-century reform spirit, she stoutly opposed woman suffrage. She died on May 12, 1878.

BEECHER, EDWARD (1803–1895), clergyman and educator. Born in East Hampton, Long Island, New York, on August 27, 1803, Beecher was the third child of Lyman Beecher and a member of the illustrious family that included also Henry Ward and Catharine Beecher, and Harriet Beecher Stowe. Graduating at the head of his Yale class of 1822, he alternately taught and studied until 1826 when he became pastor of the prominent Park Street Church in Boston. In 1830 he was invited to become the first president of Illinois College, at Jacksonville—the state's first institution of higher learning. While leading the college to distinction in spite of deep financial trouble, Beecher gradually became involved in the Abolitionist movement. He was a close associate of Elijah Lovejoy, the victim of the Alton riots in 1837; the event created a furor in the North, and Beecher's *Narrative of Riots at Alton*, appearing the next year, became an important document of the period. He continued his connection with the college until 1844; in that year he resigned and returned to the ministry in Boston, where he was a founder and, from 1849 to 1853, editor of the *Congregationalist*. From 1855 to 1871 he was again in Illinois as pastor of a church in Galesburg. In 1871 he moved to Brooklyn where his brother, Henry Ward, was an immensely popular preacher; there he remained until his death on July 28, 1895.

BEECHER, HENRY WARD (1813–1887), clergyman. Born on June 24, 1813, in Litchfield, Connecticut, one of 13 children of clergyman Lyman Beecher, he graduated from Amherst in 1834 after an undistinguished career in various schools. He studied for three years at Lane Theological Seminary while his father was its president and in 1837 became pastor of a small church at Lawrenceburg, Indiana. Two years later, he transferred to the Second Presbyterian Church of Indianapolis. He developed a forceful, imaginative style of delivering his sermons, intending to affect his parishioners emotionally and thereby to improve their characters. His own manner and dress were noticeably independent and unorthodox and his large congregation became as interested in his personality and conduct as in his gospel. By 1847, his reputation as an orator and a writer won him the pastorate of the Plymouth (Congregational) Church in Brooklyn. There he involved himself in social and political issues, adhering to antislavery doctrines, campaigning for political candidates, and supporting the Civil War and moderate Reconstruction policies, in general using his ebullient oratory to espouse the opinions of other men rather than to offer ideas of his own. He edited the Congregationalist *Independent* in the 1860s, and later the *Christian Union*. In a sensational scandal in 1874, he was brought to trial on charges of adultery. The jury could not agree on a verdict and he was acquitted, returning to lecture and to preach at the Plymouth Church. His writings include *Seven Lectures to Young Men*, 1844, *Evolution and Religion*, 1885, and *Life of Jesus the Christ*, 1871–1891. He died in Brooklyn on March 8, 1887.

BEECHER, LYMAN (1775–1863), clergyman. Born on October 12, 1775, in New Haven, Connecticut, the son and grandson of blacksmiths, Beecher attended Yale, where he was profoundly influenced by its president, theologian Timothy Dwight. He graduated in 1797 and entered the divinity school, being ordained by Dwight in 1799. He established himself at the Presbyterian Church in East Hampton, New York, during 1799–1810. His reputation for fiery preaching reached Litchfield, Connecticut, a center of wealth in New England, and he was called in 1810 to become pastor of its church. He conducted "continuous revivals," railing at intemperance, Roman Catholicism, and religious tolerance. He brought about the passage of blue laws, formed a society to educate men for the ministry, and published sermons in the *Connecticut Observer*, some of which were translated into foreign languages. When the new Hanover Street Church was founded in Boston in 1826, he was asked to organize it. His influence on the town was profound; unfortunately his denunciations of Catholicism became an incentive for townsmen to plunder the Ursuline Convent in 1831. He accepted an offer from Cincinnati to become president of its new Lane Theological Seminary and moved in 1832. There, his Calvinist doctrines were violently attacked for being too "moderate" and he was tried for heresy. Eager to affect the religious development of the West, he was stunned by this response, and when acquitted, faced yet another battle at the Seminary where rules had been passed during his absence forbidding students to discuss the slavery issue. An Abolitionist, he fought for revision of the rules, but nevertheless lost most of his students to Oberlin College. He resigned in 1850 and lived with his son Henry in Brooklyn, where he died on January 10, 1863. He raised 13 extremely gifted children, the majority of whom attained either contemporary or lasting fame, notably Harriet Beecher (Stowe) and Henry Ward Beecher.

BELASCO, DAVID (1853–1931), actor, playwright, and producer. Born on July 25, 1853, in San Francisco, California, Belasco attracted audiences as a child by reciting ballads in the street. He attended Lincoln College in California and subsequently managed, acted in, and adapted plays for several theaters in San Francisco. He toured in *Hearts of Oak*, which he wrote with James A. Herne in 1879. From 1880 he lived in New York City, managing the Madison Square Theatre until 1886, then the Lyceum, and became an independent producer in 1890 in a theater rented from Oscar Hammerstein. There his most popular productions were *The Heart of Maryland*, 1895, and *Madame Butterfly*, 1900, later made into an opera by Puccini. He concentrated on his own material and later was harshly criticized for ignoring eminent drama-

tists and actors alike. But he raised obscure actors and playwrights to stardom. In 1906 he built the Belasco Theatre in New York City. He attained a popularity unprecedented by any U.S. producer, with an ability to draw crowds on the strength of his name alone. Fanatical about technical precision, he achieved amazingly realistic effects through innovative stage lighting and various mechanical devices. He unfortunately lacked perspective and frequently was criticized for poor taste and sensationalism. Associated with the production of more than 300 plays, he was dubbed the "bishop of Broadway." He died on May 14, 1931.

BELCHER, JONATHAN (1682–1757), merchant and colonial governor. Born in Cambridge, Massachusetts, on January 8, 1682 (N.S.), the son of a prosperous merchant and colonial politician, Belcher graduated from Harvard in 1699 and spent several years in Europe. Upon his return to Boston he set about amassing a fortune as a merchant and from 1718 became active in politics. Elected several times to the Massachusetts Council, he was sent by the Council to England in 1728 to represent it in a dispute with Governor Burnet, who died shortly after Belcher's arrival in London. Belcher was able to secure a commission as the new governor of Massachusetts and New Hampshire. He held the post from 1730 until he was dismissed in 1741 after many conflicts with royal authority. In July 1746, having cleared his tarnished reputation, he was commissioned governor of New Jersey. Here his most notable work was his patronage of the College of New Jersey (now Princeton), which he rechartered in 1747 and saw moved to Newark. He died on August 31, 1757.

BELL, ALEXANDER GRAHAM (1847–1922), inventor and teacher of the deaf. Born on March 3, 1847, in Edinburgh, Scotland, Bell was the son of Alexander Melville Bell and grandson of the educator Alexander Bell, both of whom were avid students of elocution. His father had developed a system of symbolizing the various positions of the vocal chords during speech, and he applied this system in 1870 to a method for training deaf persons to speak. He worked with his father in London until 1870, taking courses in anatomy and physiology at University College. After two years in Canada he traveled to Boston in 1872 to train teachers for the pioneer educational institution for the deaf established by the Boston School Board. He joined the faculty of Boston University in 1873 and trained teachers in vocal physiology, while independently tutoring deaf students. In 1865 he began studying the production of vocal pitch. He developed a "phonautograph" between 1873 and 1876, a combination of several telegraphs with an electrical speaking device. His idea for the telephone came in 1874. He was encouraged by Prof. Joseph Henry, a developer of the telegraph, and by 1876 had perfected a device capable of reproducing intelligible human speech, which he exhibited with great success at the Centennial Exhibition in Philadelphia that year. In 1877 he supervised a telephone conversation between Boston and New York. For several years, he was involved in litigation involving patents, but ultimately was awarded all rights to the telephone. The first Bell Telephone Company was formed in 1877 to produce the device for a mass market. In 1882 he became a U.S. citizen and the same year founded the Volta Laboratory, where developments were made on his photophone, a device for transmitting speech by beams of light, and on Thomas Edison's phonograph. He presided over the National Geographic Society from 1896 to 1904, from 1898 was a regent of the Smithsonian Institution, and in 1907 founded the Aerial Experiment Association. He died in his summer home in Nova Scotia on August 2, 1922.

BELLAMY, EDWARD (1850 – 1898), author and reformer. Born in Chicopee Falls, Massachusetts, on March 26, 1850, Bellamy studied for a short while at Union College and, at the age of 18, left for a year of study in Germany. While there he developed his interest in the plight of the poor in an urban, industrialized society. For several years after his return he worked with little real interest as a journalist. He wrote a number of short stories and two novels, one unfinished, and was briefly hailed as a new Hawthorne. In 1888 his long concern with social problems found expression in *Looking Backward*, a utopian novel which pictured the United States in the year 2000 as a happy, peaceful society in which all industry had been nationalized and wealth was equitably distributed among all. An immediate success, the book sold a million copies and Nationalist clubs, devoted to the realization of Bellamy's scheme, sprang up all over the nation. In response he established the *Nationalist* in 1889 and its successor, the *New Nation*, in 1891 to promote the cause. His program influenced the Populist Party platform in 1892. A sequel to *Looking Backward*, *Equality*, was published in 1897 but failed to match the earlier book's success. Long in poor health, Bellamy died on May 22, 1898.

BELLOW, SAUL (1915 –), author. Born on July 10, 1915, in Lachine, Quebec, Bellow lived in a poor section of Montreal before moving to Chicago in 1924. He attended the University of Chicago for a time and graduated from Northwestern University in 1937. He became a biographer in a W.P.A. writers' project and taught school for nearly four years at Pestalozzi-Froebel Teachers College in Chicago. He also worked on Mortimer Adler's "Great Books" project at Encyclopaedia Britannica during 1943. During World War II he served briefly in the merchant marine. His first novel, *Dangling Man*, 1944, concerned the life of a man in Chicago awaiting his call to military duty. His next, *The Victim*, 1947, probed a conflict that figured prominently in all his later works – the self-sacrifice required by society versus the need to be an individual. In *The Adventures of Augie March*, 1953, he treated this problem more deeply and experimented with a rambling, inductive literary form. *Henderson the Rain King*, 1959, his next major work, told of a millionaire's adventures in Africa in a symbolic search for the meaning of life and the answer to his destiny. The all-encompassing tragicomic qualities of Henderson were expanded in *Herzog*, 1964, Bellow's most autobiographical work, about a university professor who comes to grips with his own alienation from society. Through a series of episodes that are both hilarious and poignant, Herzog arrives at acceptance of his own condition and a consequent relaxation of his need for self-justification. Among Bellow's later works were a play, *The Last Analysis*, 1965, and *Mr. Sammler's Planet*, 1969. He taught English at the universities of Minnesota and Puerto Rico and was a professor in the Committee on Social Thought at the University of Chicago from 1962.

BELLOWS, GEORGE WESLEY (1882 – 1925), painter and lithographer. Born on August 12, 1882, in Columbus, Ohio, Bellows went to Ohio State University, but he was anxious to pursue his art career and consequently left school before graduation. He went in 1904 to New York City and studied with Robert Henri, quickly developing a mastery of the palette and a highly individual style. An excellent athlete, he was moved by action and tense movement and transmitted this feeling onto canvas by using vigorous, thick brush strokes, stark contrasts between light and shadow and solid mass and texture. His first successful painting of "Forty-Two Kids," 1907, tumbling about a dock area, swimming, diving, and playing in groups, was followed by a series that was inspired by Tom Sharkey's famous boxing arena. The series was revolutionary in its bold interpretation of physical conflict, previously shown statically by other American artists. "Stag at Sharkey's," 1907, was the most celebrated of the group. He was active in organizing the Armory Show of 1913 that introduced modern art to America. In 1915 he began a series of vigorous war paintings, again producing some of the finest American renderings of the subject. He turned to lithography in 1916 and became as skillful and creative in this medium as in paint. An ex-cellent draftsman, he illustrated books and produced memorable drawings. He taught sporadically at the Art Students' League in New York and at the Art Institute of Chicago. He died in New York City on January 8, 1925.

BENCHLEY, ROBERT CHARLES (1889 – 1945), critic and humorist. Born on September 15, 1889, in Worcester, Massachusetts, Benchley graduated from Harvard in 1912 and after holding a number of small jobs joined the staff of *Life* magazine in 1920 as drama critic. In an amateur revue in 1922 he delivered his classic comedy monologue, "The Treasurer's Report," which launched his career as a humorist. The piece was made into a movie short, the first of more than 40; another short, "How to Sleep," won an award in 1935 from the Motion Picture Academy of Arts and Sciences. In 1929 he left *Life* to join the *New Yorker* where, until 1940, he wrote drama criticism and conducted "The Wayward Press," a humorous column published under the byline of the pseudonymous Guy Fawkes. Benchley's quiet, whimsical humor was directed mainly to depicting the struggles of an ordinary man — himself — completely befuddled by the world; often it ascended, or descended, by hardly noticeable steps into pure nonsense. His pieces were collected in several volumes, among them *My Ten Years in a Quandary and How They Grew*, 1936, *After 1903 — What?*, 1938, and *Benchley Beside Himself*, 1943. He appeared in a large number of feature films, often as a confused, annoyed, and mildly sarcastic drunk. He died in New York on November 21, 1945.

BENEDICT, RUTH FULTON (1887 – 1948), anthropologist. Born on June 5, 1887, in New York City, Ruth Fulton attended Vassar College and graduated in 1909. She lived in Europe for a year, residing successively with Swiss, German, Italian, and English families. Returning to the United States she settled in California and taught high school. She married in 1914. Beginning in 1919 she studied anthropology under Franz Boas at Columbia University.

Taking her doctorate in 1923, she became an instructor, an associate professor in 1930, and a full professor in 1948, only a few months before her death. The first 11 years of her research centered on the religion and folklore of the American Indians—predominantly the Pueblo Mission, Apache, Blackfoot, and Serrano tribes. Her two-volume *Zuni Mythology*, 1935, was based on this work. *Patterns of Culture*, 1934, was her major contribution to anthropology. Translated into 14 languages, it brought knowledge of the subject to a wide audience. The book presented a comparison of three primitive societies, showing that each culture was but a small expression of the whole of the human personality, and suggesting that limitless combinations of human behavior would continually produce new cultures. Five years later, with the publication of *Race: Science and Politics*, she showed that the unity of man is a simple fact, despite the arrogance of racists everywhere. The phrase "the human race" was given new meaning in her work. During World War II she was a special advisor to the U.S. Office of War Information on dealing with peoples of occupied territories and enemy lands. Her longstanding interest in Japanese culture bore fruit in *Chrysanthemum and the Sword*, 1946. In the summer of 1948 she began the most comprehensive research undertaking of her career as director of a research project on contemporary European and Asian cultures sponsored by the Medical Services Branch of the Office of Naval Research and Columbia. Returning from Europe she became ill and died in New York City on September 17, 1948.

BENÉT, STEPHEN VINCENT (1898–1943), author. Born in Bethlehem, Pennsylvania, on July 22, 1898, into a family with both military and literary traditions, Benét published his first book when he was 17. Graduating from Yale in 1919, he continued to write novels, short stories, and poetry. In France on a Guggenheim fellowship, he published his best-known work, *John Brown's Body*, in 1928. A poetic

treatment of the Civil War, the work won Benét a Pulitzer Prize in 1929. Much of his subsequent work was similarly on historical themes. He wrote a number of deft short stories, among them the celebrated tale, "The Devil and Daniel Webster." A long poem, *Western Star*, unfinished at his death, was also awarded a Pulitzer Prize. Benét died in New York City on March 13, 1943.

BENJAMIN, JUDAH PHILIP (1811–1884), lawyer and statesman. Born on August 6, 1811, in the island of St. Thomas, British West Indies, Benjamin was raised in Charleston, South Carolina, from his early boyhood. He attended Fayetteville Academy in North Carolina, and Yale during 1825–1827, but did not earn a degree. To prepare for a career in law, he was a clerk in a notary's office. Subsequent work in international law and his compilation of a review of Louisiana law, published in 1834, enhanced his reputation. He joined the Whig Party, and in 1842 was elected to the Louisiana state legislature; in 1852 he was elected to the Senate. One of the first Southerners to advocate secession, he resigned from the Senate in 1861. Three weeks later, Jefferson Davis appointed him attorney general of the Confederacy; shortly thereafter, he became secretary of war. Although the condition of the war department was deplorable when he took it over, the shocking shortages of equipment and supplies were blamed on Benjamin. Investigations into his responsibility for the severe Confederate losses at Roanoke Island were being conducted when Davis, presumably as a gesture of confidence, named Benjamin secretary of state. The outcry against him increased, but he ignored it. Eminently rational, he realized earlier than most Southerners that states' rights and slavery could not be maintained. Near the end of 1864, his plan to arm slaves was a source of major alarm. In an address, he conceded that the plan would allow slaves to fight for their freedom, and he was censured by the Confederate House in 1865. Nevertheless, a bill was passed for enrollment of blacks into the Confederate army. After the fall of Richmond he escaped to the West Indies, whence he sailed to England. There he was admitted to the bar in 1866, and in 1869 became a Queen's Counsel. He was successful in many fields of law but specialized in appeals, appearing primarily before the House of Lords and the Judicial Committee of the Privy Council. He died in Paris on May 6, 1884.

BENNETT, JAMES GORDON (1795 – 1872), editor. Born in 1795 near Keith, Banffshire, Scotland, Bennett studied for the Roman Catholic priesthood in Aberdeen, but emigrated to Nova Scotia in 1819 and on to the United States, working in Charleston, South Carolina, and in Boston, variously as a teacher, an office clerk, a proofreader, and a translator, before settling in New York City in 1823. There he planned a vocational school, which did not open owing to a lack of funds, did minor newspaper writing, and gave church lectures on political economy. In 1827 he became editor and Washington correspondent for the *New York Enquirer*, writing bold sketches of national political figures and diverting accounts of social and political activities in the capital, and becoming well known as a controversial reporter. He encouraged James Watson Webb, the main proprietor of the *New York Courier*, to effect a combination with the *Enquirer*, and became virtual director of the organ in 1829, although he was nominally only associate editor until 1832. Under his leadership the paper gave support to Jackson and to Democratic policies until Webb suddenly took control, made the paper a Whig organ, and Bennett resigned. He founded the short-lived *New York Globe* and during 1833 – 1834 was the chief editor and proprietor of the Philadelphia *Pennsylvanian*. Having marked the success of Benjamin H. Day's penny newspaper, the *New York Sun*, he returned to New York and sought employment with the *Sun* but was refused. He set up editing, reporting, printing, and sales headquarters with $500 capital in a cellar and began issuing his own paper, the *New York Herald*, which had four four-column

pages and sold for a penny. He declared political independence and vowed to present "a picture of the world." He was unique in printing financial and society news, an account of the New York fire of 1835, and the Helm-Jewett love-nest murder story. He stationed six correspondents in Europe, used the telegraph, hired a police reporter, and during the Civil War had 63 correspondents relaying news from various battlefronts. He was frequently severely censured for sensationalism and the irreverence of his editorials, but the *Herald* was a commercial success. At the time of his resignation in 1866, the daily circulation was 90,000. He died in New York City on June 1, 1872. His son JAMES GORDON BENNETT (1841 – 1918), born on May 10, 1841, was educated in Europe and returned to New York to manage the *Herald* in 1866. At his father's death, he moved to Paris and actively controlled the paper by cable. He published a daily edition in London and Paris, and printed storm warnings transmitted from the United States in the London edition. He sponsored Henry M. Stanley's expedition of 1869 – 1872 to central Africa to find David Livingston and financed the *Jeanette* Polar expedition of 1879. With John W. Mackey he organized the Commercial Cable Company in 1883. He died in Paris on May 14, 1918.

BENTON, THOMAS HART (1782 – 1858), public official and political leader. Born near Hillsborough, North Carolina, on March 14, 1782, Benton moved with his widowed mother to a frontier area south of Nashville, Tennessee, shortly after his brief attendance at the University of North Carolina in 1799. In 1806 he was admitted to the bar, and three years later entered the state senate. After serving under Jackson in the War of 1812, he moved to the frontier town of St. Louis in 1815, where he carried on his law practice and edited the *St. Louis Enquirer*. In 1820 he was elected to the Senate to begin his thirty years of service in that body. A Westerner, ardent expansionist, Democrat, and hard-money advocate, Benton rose to preeminence in the Senate. He led the battles against the National Bank and in favor of a separate treasury and was primarily responsible for what fiscal stability was achieved in this period; he opposed the annexation of Texas as contrary to treaty, but strongly favored the occupation of the Pacific regions. One of his proposals anticipated the later homestead system of land distribution. A stout believer in the Union, he moderated his early views on slavery when it appeared that this issue was both hindering westward expansion and threatening disunion. His growing dislike of slavery, capped by his opposition to the Compromise of 1850, led to his defeat for reelection in that year. Still popular on other issues, however, he was sent to the House of Representatives; but his continued apostasy on slavery soon lost him that seat as well as the governor's race in 1856. During his last years he wrote an important political autobiography, *Thirty Years' View*. He died on April 10, 1858.

BENTON, THOMAS HART (1889 –   ), painter, lithographer, and writer. Born on April 15, 1889, in Neosho, Missouri, grandnephew of Missouri Sen. Thomas Hart Benton (1782 – 1858), he traveled throughout the Midwest with his father, who was also active in Missouri politics. While traveling, he became curious about the origins of American tradition; his study was brief but intense. He commenced his formal art education in Chicago at the School of the Art Institute in 1906, and, after several years of study in Paris, began a professional career as an artist in 1912. After naval service in World War I, he turned to teaching at Bryn Mawr College, Dartmouth College, and the Art Students League of New York. He traveled for ten years through the southern and western United States and settled finally in Kansas. In 1937 he recorded his travels in *An Artist in America*. During the 1920s and 1930s increasing attention was given to Benton's style, dubbed Regionalism, which portrayed life in the midwestern and southern states as he had seen it. His depictions were not always flattering. Nevertheless,

Regionalism, with its linear design and flat, cartoonish figures, was welcomed as a truly American style of painting. The colors were appealing, and pictures such as "Louisiana Rice Field" and "Threshing Wheat" touched the American sentiment. Benton also exalted American folk themes and legends in works such as "Huck Finn and Nigger Jim" and "The Jealous Lover of Lone Green Valley." Controversial mural paintings of the 1930s earned him the Gold Medal Award from the Architectural League of New York. Later murals were executed for the Missouri state capitol at Jefferson City, and for the Truman Library in Independence, Missouri. His paintings are included in the collections of the Museum of Modern Art and the Metropolitan Museum of Art in New York City.

BENTON, WILLIAM (1900 –   ), businessman, educator, and statesman. Born in Minneapolis on April 1, 1900, Benton grew up there and on a ranch in Montana. He was educated at Carleton College and at Yale, graduating from the latter in 1921. He entered the advertising business and in 1929, with Chester Bowles, founded the agency of Benton and Bowles, which by 1935 had become one of the leading companies of its kind in the world. In that year he left the firm, having promised himself to do so when he had made a million dollars, and two years later became vice president of the University of Chicago, of which his classmate Robert M. Hutchins was president. There he initiated and led a program of extending and diversifying the activities of the university, organized the Chicago Round Table, a distinguished and popular radio forum, and sought to acquire the Encyclopaedia Britannica company as a source of income for the institution. The trustees hesitated, whereupon Benton put up his own money as working capital. The university then accepted the gift, committing the management and the common stock to Benton, and retaining the preferred stock and a royalty contract. He was chairman of the board and publisher of Britannica from 1943 on. In 1945 he resigned from the university to become assistant secretary of state. In this position he initiated and organized many reforms and innovations. He began the Voice of America broadcasts, including broadcasting in Russian to the U.S.S.R., established the United States information offices, promoted international visits of professors and students, and led U.S. participation in the United Nations Educational, Scientific, and Cultural Organization (UNESCO). He resigned in 1947 and in 1949 was appointed U.S. senator from Connecticut; in 1950 he was elected to serve two years of an unexpired term. In the Senate he was a champion of freedom and civil rights; before leaving it in 1952 he led a revolt against the activities of Sen. Joseph R. McCarthy that culminated, several years later, in McCarthy's condemnation by his peers. Benton then turned his attention to various public and educational pursuits while continuing to oversee the growth of Britannica, which by the early 1970s had become one of the largest publishers in the world. In 1963 he was appointed by President Kennedy U.S. representative to UNESCO, with the rank of ambassador, a post he retained under President Johnson. He was the author of several books, among them *This Is the Challenge*, 1958, and *The Voice of Latin America*, 1961, and of scores of articles in major magazines.

BERENSON, BERNARD (1865–1959), art critic and historian. Born on June 26, 1865, in Vilna, Lithuania, Berenson was brought to America at the age of 10. Of a family of modest means, he received the patronage of a Boston art collector who financed his education at Harvard. Graduating in 1887, he went to Europe, studied at Oxford and Berlin, and in the galleries and museums of Italy trained himself to recognize the masters of ancient art by their various styles and techniques. Settling in Settignano, near Florence, he acquired I Tatti, an 18th-century mansion, which he furnished with antiques of the Tuscan Renaissance, and lived there the rest of his life. By 1900 he had written several major books on Italian art, in-

cluding *The Venetian Painters of the Renaissance, Drawings of the Florentine Painters,* and *The Italian Painters of the Renaissance,* and was considered a leading art historian. He was called to verify or authenticate nearly every significant art collection gathered by museums or private collectors in the United States during his time. His method for identifying works relied on isolating certain characteristics that appeared in everything produced by an artist, and in the works of no other artist. Berenson "discovered" two unknown Renaissance painters by this method, whom he named Alunno di Domenico and Amico di Sandro. During World War II he remained secluded in Tuscany and afterward directed the restoration of masterpieces. His autobiographical trilogy published in the 1950s, comprising *Sketch for a Self-Portrait, Aesthetics and History,* and *Rumor and Reflection,* brought him to the attention of the general public. At his death on October 6, 1959, his bequest of I Tatti to Harvard University became known.

BERGER, VICTOR LOUIS (1860–1929), journalist and Socialist leader. Born in Austria on February 28, 1860, Berger moved as a child to Hungary and was educated in private schools. After studying at universities in Vienna and Budapest, he emigrated to the United States in 1878. In 1881 he became a public school teacher in Milwaukee. Active from the start in local politics, he founded in 1892 the *Wisconsin Vorwärts*. In association with Eugene V. Debs of the defunct American Railway Union, he helped establish the Social Democratic Party to advocate the national adoption of socialism through orderly means. In March 1900 the group merged with the Socialist Labor Party and began a rapid rise in popularity. The following year Berger became editor of the *Social Democratic Herald* which in 1911 became *The Milwaukee Leader*. He remained at the head of this daily until his death. He continued to write and campaign for the Socialist Party; in 1910 the party captured the mayoralty of Milwaukee and Berger was elected to Congress for one term. His opposition to American entry into World War I led to sanctions against his newspaper and his own indictment under the Espionage Act in 1918. In that year he was again elected to Congress but was denied his seat because of his antiwar views. In a special election to fill the seat he was reelected and again barred. The seat remained vacant for the remainder of the term. He was convicted of the 1918 charge but three years later the decision was reversed by the Supreme Court. In 1923 he was finally admitted to Congress where he served three terms. He died in Milwaukee on August 7, 1929.

BERLE, ADOLF AUGUSTUS (1895 –   ), lawyer, public official, and diplomat. Born in Boston on January 29, 1895, Berle graduated from Harvard in 1913 and three years later began the practice of law in Boston and then in New York. He served in World War I and was a consultant with the Paris Peace Commission in 1918–19. In 1927 he became a professor of corporation law at the Columbia Law School. In 1932 he published, with Gardiner C. Means, *The Modern Corporation and Private Property,* a pioneer study of the concentration of wealth in industry and the changed meaning of corporate ownership. Largely as a result of this book, which outlined the need for industrial integration and control, Berle was a natural choice for Roosevelt's "brains trust" advisory staff in the 1932 presidential campaign. From 1938 to 1944 he was assistant secretary of state and during 1945–1946, after representing the United States in a number of conferences of American nations, was ambassador to Brazil. He continued to teach and write on subjects pertaining to business organization and law and the social context and significance of industry.

BERLE, MILTON (1908–   ), comedian. Born in New York City on July 12, 1908, Berle was originally named Milton Berlinger. As a child he appeared in several local amateur shows, sometimes impersonating Charlie Chaplin, and was signed to tour with a vaudeville company. With his younger sister Rosalind also in the act, and, after a time, with his mother managing the company, he was successful enough to win a role in the Broadway musical *Floradora* in 1920. He appeared in a number of silent movies for Biograph Studios and other companies, including *The Perils of Pauline* and *Humoresque,* and by 1932, after an engagement at New York's Palace Theater during which a new attendance record was set, he was a national headliner. His unique style of comedy—relying chiefly on his energetic delivery, zany antics, a marked proclivity for mugging, and his much-publicized belief that all jokes and gags, from whatever source, were in the public domain—won him great popularity in vaudeville and night clubs around the country. He starred in the 1936 *Ziegfeld Follies* and appeared in numerous other Broadway productions, including *Life Begins at 8:40* and *See My Lawyer,* and from 1937 was featured in many motion pictures, among them *New Faces of 1937, Radio City Revels,* 1938, *Tall, Dark and Handsome,* 1941, *Over My Dead Body,* 1943, and *Always Leave Them Laughing,* 1949. At the same time he was a regular performer on several radio programs. In September 1948 he entered the new field of commercial television as star and master of ceremonies of the *Texaco Star Theater.* During the next eight years "Tuesday night with Uncle Miltie" became something of an institution and was such a success that Berle was nicknamed "Mr. Television" for having done more than any other person to establish the popularity of the new medium. After a two-year absence he returned to television in 1958–1959 with the *Kraft Music Hall.* In later years he continued to appear occasionally in movies and as a guest star on television.

BERLIN, IRVING (1888–   ), composer and lyricist. Born in Russia on May 11, 1888, Israel Baline was brought to the United States at the age of five and thereafter changed his name to Irving Berlin. He grew up in poverty and received only two years of formal schooling. From a singing waiter in the Bowery and Chinatown he emerged as one of the leading songwriters of the 20th century and a major force in the shaping of the modern popular song. His first musical comedy, *Watch Your Step*, was written in 1914; five years later he began his own publishing company. Through the years he wrote a number of musical comedies and such songs as "Alexander's Ragtime Band," "Oh, How I Hate to Get Up in the Morning," "All Alone," "Remember," and "White Christmas." "God Bless America," which was written in 1918 but first performed in 1938, became vastly popular before and during World War II; the income from the song was assigned to the Boy and Girl Scouts. For the song, which has come to be considered as almost a second national anthem, Berlin was awarded a special Congressional gold medal in 1955.

BERNSTEIN, LEONARD (1918–), conductor and composer. Born on August 25, 1918, in Lawrence, Massachusetts, the son of a Russian immigrant, Bernstein began to take piano lessons as a child and by the age of 14 had learned all that local instructors could teach him. He went to Boston to study further and graduated from Harvard in 1939, having earned his tuition by giving piano lessons. With the intent of becoming a conductor, he entered the Curtis Institute in Philadelphia, and in 1940 and 1941 received scholarships in conducting from the Berkshire Music Center in Tanglewood, Massachusetts. By 1942 he was assistant conductor of the Tanglewood orchestra. His first work, the *Sonata for Clarinet and Piano*, received its premiere in 1942. His *Jeremiah* symphony, based on Jewish religious music, was completed the same year. In 1943 he became assistant conductor of the New York Philharmonic. Substituting for a guest conductor in November of that year he was enthusiastically received, and his career was under way. In 1944 he led the Pittsburgh Symphony in the first performance of his *Jere-*

miah. Later that year, he conducted the premiere of his first ballet, *Fancy Free*, and its musical comedy derivative, *On the Town*, made into a motion picture in 1949. He conducted the Czech Philharmonic at the Prague International Festival as the representative of the U.S. government in 1946. His second ballet, *Facsimile*, was performed that year. Inspired by the poem by W. H. Auden, in 1949 he completed his second symphony, *The Age of Anxiety*. He became the first American composer to conduct at La Scala in Milan in 1953, and was made permanent conductor of the New York Philharmonic in 1958; he resigned from this post in 1969 to devote more time to composition. Gregarious and personable, he gained national fame as a lecturer on music and as the conductor of Young People's Concerts on network television. His lectures were compiled in *The Joy of Music*, 1959. His other compositions include the one-act opera *Trouble in Tahiti*, 1952; the scores for the 1954 motion picture *On the Waterfront*, and the musicals *Wonderful Town*, 1953, *Candide*, 1956, and *West Side Story*, also made into a motion picture, 1957.

BETHE, HANS ALBRECHT (1906–), physicist. Born in Strasbourg, then a part of Germany, on July 2, 1906, Bethe was educated at the universities of Frankfurt and Munich, taking his Ph.D. in physics at the latter in 1928. For five years he taught in various German universities; in 1933 he fled the Nazi regime, going first to England and in 1935 to the United States, where he joined the faculty of Cornell University. He had already established a reputation with his investigations of particle behavior from a quantum-mechanical standpoint when he turned his attention to the problem of stellar energy. The apparent paradox posed by the extremely long lifespans of stars despite their enormous energy production led him to consider various nuclear reactions as possible sources; by 1939 he had worked out a likely solution involving the fusion of hydrogen nuclei into helium nuclei by means of a carbon catalyst. This "carbon cycle" has become universally accepted as the primary mechanism of energy production in normal stars. He became a U.S. citizen in 1941 and was soon involved in wartime research, first at the Massachusetts Institute of Technology, where he developed a wave guide device for radar, and from 1943 to 1946 at Los Alamos, New Mexico, where he headed the Theoretical Physics Division of the atomic bomb project. He was given the Presidential Medal of Merit in the latter year. The success of the project and the continuation of nuclear testing led him to warn publicly against the dangers of radioactive fallout. In 1948 he refused to return to Los Alamos to join the H-bomb project under Edward Teller, but by 1951 the Korean War and hints of Soviet progress in the field induced him to change his mind. He continued, however, to speak and write against nuclear warfare, excessive stockpiling of nuclear weapons, and atmospheric testing. In 1961 he was awarded the Atomic Energy Commission's Fermi Award. From 1956 to 1964 he served on the President's Science Advisory Committee and in 1958 headed the President's Study of Disarmament. He was an informal advisor to presidents Eisenhower, Kennedy, and Johnson on nuclear weaponry and disarmament and in 1963 helped negotiate the partial test ban treaty with the Soviet Union. In 1967, for his contributions to basic nuclear theory and to the understanding of nuclear processes in stars, he was awarded the Nobel Prize for Physics.

BETTELHEIM, BRUNO (1903–), psychologist and educator. Born on August 28, 1903, in Vienna, Bettelheim graduated in 1921 from the Reform Realgymnasium and took his doctorate from the University of Vienna in 1938. During 1938–1939 he was incarcerated in the Nazi concentration camps at Dachau and Buchenwald; his activities in interrogating other prisoners to determine the effect of the camps and Nazi methods stimulated and en-

lightened much of his later work. Upon his release, he came to the United States and was first associated with the University of Chicago as a researcher in progressive education until 1942, when he went to Rockford College in Illinois as an associate professor of psychology until 1944. He first gained international recognition in 1943 with the now classic article "Individual and Mass Behavior in Extreme Situations," which appeared in the *Journal of Abnormal and Social Psychology*. Focusing on methods of tyranny and totalitarian terrorism to produce complacency or submissiveness, he recounted his experiences and observations in the concentration camps. General Eisenhower required that all military government officers serving in Europe during World War II and in the subsequent occupation read the article to better equip themselves to handle survivors from the camps. He returned to the University of Chicago in 1944, becoming a full professor in 1952. Upon his return, he accepted the directorship of the Sonia Shankman Orthogenic School, a residential institution for the education and treatment of severely disturbed children who had failed to respond to other therapeutic attempts. With the school and his experiences with disturbed children as examples, he advised parents, teachers, and social workers in the smaller problems of raising normal children. His "preventive psychiatry" was equally understanding of the problems of being a parent and a child. He stressed the need for tolerance; in a family situation this meant viewing children as well as parents as individuals with needs to be satisfied—an emphasis not so much on "molding" a person as on understanding what makes him different from other people. His works on race similarly viewed tolerance as a moral imperative, and one that does not need scientific backing for validity. Bettelheim achieved his greatest renown for his remarkable success in treating previously unreachable autistic children. Notable among his books were *Love Is Not Enough*, 1950, *Truants From Life*, 1954, *Symbolic Wounds; Puberty Rites and the Envious Male,* 1954, *The Informed Heart,* 1960, *Children of the Dream,* 1962, and *The Empty Fortress,* 1967.

BEVERIDGE, ALBERT JEREMIAH (1862 – 1927), public official and historian. Born in Highland County, Ohio, on October 6, 1862, Beveridge graduated from DePauw University, then Asbury College, in 1885 and two years later was admitted to the bar and began practice in Indianapolis. His considerable reputation as a political orator won him election to the Senate in 1899 as a Republican. One of the original Progressive Republicans, Beveridge supported Theodore Roosevelt's program of industrial reform and regulation and, like many Progressives, was a proponent of "Anglo-Saxon supremacy." When he was defeated for reelection in 1911 he became active in the new Progressive Party, but he never again held public office. His four-volume *Life of John Marshall* appeared from 1916 to 1919 and was widely acclaimed as a major work of historical biography. When he died, on April 27, 1927, he had completed two volumes of a biography of Abraham Lincoln, which were published posthumously.

BIDDLE, NICHOLAS (1786 – 1844), author and financier. Born in Philadelphia on January 8, 1786, of a leading Quaker family, Biddle was a precocious youth and entered the University of Pennsylvania at the age of ten. He completed his studies in three years and went on to the College of New Jersey (now Princeton) for an additional two years. After devoting some time to the study of law he became, in 1804, secretary to the U.S. minister to France; two years later he moved to London to be secretary to the legation under James Monroe. Upon his return to America in 1807 Biddle resumed his legal studies and in 1809 was admitted to the bar. From 1806 he had been a regular contributor to *Port Folio,* the first American literary journal, and as the years passed he assumed considerable editorial influence, becoming editor officially in 1812. In 1810 he had begun work on the *History of the Expedition of Captains Lewis and Clark* at Clark's request, making use of his notes, journals, and oral reports; but Biddle's election to the state senate in 1814 forced him to leave both *Port Folio* and the nearly complete *History* to others. He strongly supported the policies of Madison and Monroe, wrote Pennsylvania's negative reply to the Hartford Convention's call for extensive constitutional amendments, and, at Monroe's request, compiled *Commercial Regulations,* a digest of international trade laws. In 1819 Monroe appointed him a director of the Bank of the United States and in 1822 he became its president. Under his conservative guidance the bank maintained a sound and stable currency, discouraged inflation in the money and credit markets, safeguarded against speculative and unsound financial practices by other banks and institutions, and incurred the abiding enmity of inflationists, particularly Western farmers. When the various anti-bank groups rallied behind Andrew Jackson in 1828, Biddle was drawn into politics. With or without his knowledge, bank money was used to finance anti-Jackson campaigns and publications. In 1832 Biddle overstepped himself by seeking an early renewal of the bank's charter and pushing the issue into that year's presidential election. Jackson's victory doomed the bank. Biddle continued as president through the expiration of the charter in 1836 and for three years more under a state charter for the Bank of the United States of Pennsylvania. He retired to his country estate in 1839 and remained there until his death on February 27, 1844.

BIERCE, AMBROSE GWINNETT (1842 – 1914?), journalist and author. Born on June 24, 1842, in Meigs County, Ohio, Bierce ended his education early and entered the printer's trade. In 1861 he enlisted in an Indiana volunteer infantry regiment and during the Civil War saw action at Shiloh, Corinth, Chickamauga, and other major battles in the West; in 1864 he was seriously wounded at Kenesaw Mountain. On leaving the Army in 1866 he journeyed west to San Francisco and while employed at the U.S. Mint began to contribute to various periodicals, particularly the *News Letter* and the *Argonaut*. He became editor of the former in 1868 and held the position until 1872, when he left for a three-year stay in England. While writing for *Fun* and *Figaro* and editing the *Lantern* for the Empress Eugenie, he collected much of his earlier work and published it in book form as *The Fiend's Delight*, 1872, *Nuggets and Dust Panned Out in California*, 1872, and *Cobwebs from an Empty Skull*, 1874. Bierce's mordant and often vitriolic wit, his fascination with the supernatural, and his precise craftsmanship with language were well exhibited in these books, which also earned him the nickname "Bitter Bierce." Returning to San Francisco, he became associate editor of the *Argonaut* in 1877 and editor of the *Wasp* in 1880. In 1887 he joined William Randolph Hearst's *San Francisco Examiner*. Bierce came to be the acknowledged literary arbiter of the West, holding a position comparable to that of William Dean Howells in the East. In 1891 he published *Tales of Soldiers and Civilians*, based on his Civil War experiences and containing the masterful "Occurrence at Owl Creek Bridge"; two years later appeared *Can Such Things Be?*, a collection of tales of the supernatural. Influenced by Poe and others, Bierce was in turn a strong influence on O. Henry and Stephen Crane, anticipating in particular the impressionistic narratives of the latter. After 1897 he was in Washington, D.C., as correspondent for the Hearst newspapers. In 1906 he published the aptly titled *Cynic's Word Book*, later renamed *The Devil's Dictionary*, a collection of ironic and sometimes venomous definitions. In 1913, apparently discontented with American life, Bierce traveled to Mexico and found Pancho Villa; he was last heard from in December of that year and is thought to have died in a battle a month later.

BIGELOW, JACOB (1786–1879), botanist and physician. Born in Sudbury, Massachusetts, on February 27, 1786, Bigelow graduated from Harvard in 1806 and four years later received his M.D. from the University of Pennsylvania. From his interest in botany and his work on drug-producing plants came his *Florula Bostoniensis* in 1814; in its enlarged form of 1824 it remained the standard reference work on New England flora for a quarter of a century. His *American Medical Botany* appeared from 1817 to 1820, and in the latter year he was instrumental in the preparation of the first American Pharmacopoeia. In 1815 he became a professor in the Harvard Medical School; the following year he was appointed to the chair of application of science to the useful arts. From 1847 to 1863 he was president of the American Academy of Arts and Sciences. He died in Boston on January 10, 1879.

BIGLOW, HOSEA see **LOWELL, JAMES RUSSELL**

BILLINGS, JOSH see **SHAW, HENRY WHEELER**

BILLY THE KID see **BONNEY, WILLIAM**

BINGHAM, GEORGE CALEB (1811–1879), painter. Born on March 20, 1811, in Augusta County, Virginia, Bingham lived in Missouri along the Lewis and Clark trail after 1819. He read law and theology, but copied engravings and learned to make his own colors, being encouraged by portraitist Chester Harding. In 1843 he opened an art studio in Missouri. Except for a brief period of training at the Pennsylvania Academy of Fine Arts in 1837, he was self-taught. To support himself he did portrait work, his style varying considerably according to his interest in the sitter. The finest homes in Missouri proudly displayed his portraits. But his major paintings depicted river scenes, pioneer life, and political events in the Missouri valley. "Jolly Flatboatmen," "Raftsmen Playing Cards," "Canvassing for a Vote," "Emigration of Daniel Boone," and "Verdict of the People," completed between 1840 and 1860, were among the most notable examples of his work. During 1856–1858, he visited Düsseldorf, where his studies of old masters led him to change his style; while he continued to be a popular portraitist, his other work lost much of its interest. He became involved in politics, having served in the Missouri legislature in 1848, and being elected state treasurer in 1862, and adjutant general in 1875. He taught art at the University of Missouri for two years before his death in Kansas City on July 7, 1879. His genre paintings slowly came to be recognized as among the best to be produced on the frontier.

BIRKHOFF, GEORGE DAVID (1884–1944), mathematician. Born in Overisel, Michigan, on March 21, 1884, Birkhoff did his undergraduate work at the University of Chicago and at Harvard, graduating from the latter in 1905, and received his Ph.D. from Chicago in 1907. He spent most of his teaching career at Harvard, joining its faculty in 1912 and remaining until his death. His mathematical research was mainly in the fields of analysis and analysis applied to dynamics. His dissertation and much of his later work dealt with the solution of ordinary differential equations and with the associated expansions of arbitrary functions. He made basic contributions to the theory of systems of both differential and difference equations. One of his most striking achievements was the proof, in 1913, of a geometric theorem having applications to dynamics that had earlier been merely conjectured by the great French mathematician Henri Poincaré. Perhaps his most important contribution, however, was the so-called ergodic theorem. This theorem transformed the ergodic hypothesis of the kinetic theory of gases, to which vexing exceptions were known, into a rigorous principle; in the process the exceptions were all made intelligible. He developed his own theory of gravitation, subsequent to Einstein; and he also spent several years in the construction of a mathematical theory of aesthetics, which he applied to art, music, and poetry. He was dean of the Harvard faculty of arts and sciences from 1935 to 1939 and was extraordinarily stimulating as a lecturer and as a director of research. Many of the leading U.S. mathematicians at mid-20th century had either written dissertations under him or studied with him in postgraduate research. He was president of the American Mathematical Society, 1924–1926, and of the American Association for the Advancement of Science, 1936–1937. He died in Cambridge, Massachusetts, on November 12, 1944.

BLACK HAWK (1767–1838), Indian chief. Born in 1767 in the Sauk village at Rock River, Illinois, Ma-ka-tai-me-she-kai-kiak, or Black Sparrow Hawk, resented the Americans as dispossessors of the Spanish, with whom his people had traded since 1769. His hatred grew when members of the Sauk and Fox tribes were persuaded by American Army officers to sign the Treaty of 1804, ceding all their lands east of the Mississippi River to the United States. In the War of 1812 he aided the British, under the command of Shawnee chief Tecumseh, and then, with encouragement from the British, attempted to ally other tribes against the Americans to halt westward expansion. His rival Sauk chief, Keokuk, had accepted American rule and under the treaty moved to lands in Iowa. In April 1832, Black Hawk led his tribe to resettle their disputed homeland, hoping to plant crops and avoid the settlers. Alarmed at the "trespass," the governor of Illinois, John Reynolds, summoned federal troops, which arrived at Rock River under the command of Gen. Henry Atkinson. Two Indian envoys were dispatched to confer with Atkinson, and were shot by a body of Illinois volunteers; thus began the so-called Black Hawk War. Retreating northward through the Rock River Valley, the Indians were slaughtered in the Batlle of Bad Axe River, in Wisconsin, on August 2, 1832. Aid that had been promised from other tribes never materialized. Black Hawk was captured and imprisoned in the East. Taken to meet Pesident Jackson in 1833, he dictated an autobiography that is considered to be a classic statement of Indian resentment against white interlopers. In 1834 he was given over to the custody of Keokuk, in whose village near the Des Moines River he died, on October 3, 1838.

BLACK, HUGO LA FAYETTE (1886–   ), public official and jurist. Born in Harlan, Alabama, on February 27, 1886, Black graduated from the University of Alabama in 1906 and was admitted to the bar in the same year. Moving to Birmingham, he practiced law and entered local politics. During World War I he served as an artillery officer. In 1926 and 1932 he was elected as a Democrat to the Senate. In 1937 President Roosevelt appointed him to the Supreme Court; after considerable debate, his appointment was confirmed. On the bench his strong liberal stance, particularly in matters concerning the rights guaranteed by the First Amendment, effectively silenced critics who had pointed to his earlier connection with the Ku Klux Klan. An advocate of an activist Court, Black rendered a number of notable opinions, often, as in his holding the Smith Act unconstitutional in 1951, in the form of minority dissents.

BLAINE, JAMES GILLESPIE (1830–1893), public official and political leader. Born in West Brownsville, Pennsylvania, on January 31, 1830, Blaine graduated from Washington (now Washington and Jefferson) College in 1847 and for the next six years taught school. In 1854 he moved to Augusta, Maine, and edited the *Kennebec Journal*, making it over into a Republican newspaper and helping to establish the new party in that state. From 1858 to 1862 he was in the state legislature and in the latter year was elected to Congress, where he served until 1876. He was elected speaker of the House in 1868 and was a powerful leader of the Republican ascendancy. In 1876 the shadow of the corruption of Grant's administration lost Blaine the nomination for President; immediately afterwards, however, he was appointed to fill a Senate vacancy. Failing again to attain the nomination in 1880, he became secretary of state in Garfield's cabinet. In this post he took the first diplomatic steps toward the securing of American sovereignty over the later Panama Canal. He also tried to redefine the Monroe Doctrine to make it somewhat less unilateral; but his efforts to organize an inter-American confer-

ence on this and other subjects were halted by his resignation following Garfield's assassination. Blaine finally gained the Republican nomination for President in 1884, only to lose by a narrow margin to Cleveland. Following Harrison's election in 1888, however, Blaine returned to Washington, again as secretary of state. He continued to be concerned with Latin-American relations and anticipated in some ways the more famous policies of Theodore Roosevelt. He was chairman of the first Pan-American Conference, finally held in 1889. He resigned from the Cabinet in June 1892 and died in Washington, D.C., on January 27, 1893.

BLOCK, HERBERT LAWRENCE (1909–   ), "Herblock," editorial cartoonist. Born on October 13, 1909, in Chicago, Block early displayed sufficient talent at drawing to win a scholarship to the Chicago Art Institute at the age of 12. In 1929, after two years at Lake Forest College, he joined the Chicago *Daily News* and, under the pen name of "Herblock," began drawing cartoons for the editorial page. Four years later he moved to Cleveland to work for the Newspaper Enterprise Association and in 1942 won a Pulitzer Prize for his work in the previous year. From 1943 to 1946 he served in the Army's Information and Education Division and in the latter year joined the *Washington* (D.C.) *Post*. From there his cartoons were syndicated to some 200 newspapers around the country. One of the few editorial cartoonists to work from a clear, consistent political philosophy, Block won wide praise for his incisive commentaries on governmental bureaucracy, pork-barrel politicking, and illiberal demagoguery. His scathing attacks on Senator Joseph McCarthy's smear campaign against supposed subversives were particularly notable and were made all the more remarkable for the comparative national silence in which they appeared. In 1952 a collection of his cartoons was published as *The Herblock Book*. His work was widely exhibited, appearing in the Corcoran and Washington National galleries in Washington, D.C., and the Associated American

Artists Gallery in New York. In 1954 he won a second Pulitzer Prize. Other collections of his cartoons included *Herblock's Here and Now*, 1955, *Herblock's Special for Today*, 1958, *Straight Herblock*, 1964, and *The Herblock Gallery*, 1968.

BOAS, FRANZ (1858–1942), anthropologist. Born in Germany on July 9, 1858, Boas was educated at Heidelberg, Bonn, and Kiel. In 1883–1884 he was a member of a German expedition to the Arctic; the studies on Eskimo life made on this journey settled his interests for life. In 1886 he made his first trip to the Pacific Northwest to begin work on his life-long specialty, the study of the Kwakiutl and other primitive Indian tribes of the region. In 1888 he joined the faculty of Clark University and in 1896 that of Columbia University. There he remained for the rest of his life, creating one of the leading anthropology departments in the nation. From 1901 to 1905 he was curator of anthropology at the American Museum of Natural History. In contrast to the 19th-century predilection for anthropological theorizing, Boas carefully accumulated vast amounts of data in the field; in this way he was able to make valuable and original contributions to linguistics, anthropometry, and cultural anthropology. Probably his greatest achievement was in destroying the quasi-scientific justifications for racism, which were subscribed to by a large portion of the world's intelligentsia. Theories of innate racial differences were exposed as entirely specious by his carefully compiled and documented observations. Among his major written works were *The Mind of Primitive Man*, 1911, *Anthropology and Modern Life*, 1928, and *Race, Language and Culture*, 1940. He died in New York City on December 21, 1942.

BOGART, HUMPHREY DeFOREST (1899–1957), actor. Born in New York on December 25, 1899, Bogart was the son of socially prominent parents. He attended Phillips Academy in Andover, Massachusetts, for a time and in 1917 joined the Navy. After the war he returned to New York, where a job in the office of a theatrical producer led eventually to his appearance on the stage in 1922. For years he played mainly in drawing room comedies, though during the early 1930s he made a few Westerns for Fox Studios. In 1934, however, he won the role of the sinister Duke Mantee in Robert Sherwood's *The Petrified Forest*; the play and Bogart were successful and he was starred in the movie version made two years later. From that time on he was a film star, appearing more often than not in "tough guy" roles as in *San Quentin*, 1937, *King of the Underworld*, 1939, *High Sierra*, 1941, *The Maltese Falcon*, 1942 (in which he played Dashiell Hammett's Sam Spade), *Casablanca*, 1942, *To Have and Have Not*, 1944, *The Big Sleep*, 1946, *Key Largo*, 1948, and *The Treasure of Sierra Madre*, 1948. In many of his later films Bogart was able to break the bonds of type-casting and play more sympathetic roles, as in *The African Queen*, 1951, for which he won an Academy Award. In 1954 he played the psychopathic Captain Queeg in *The Caine Mutiny*; his final film, *The Harder They Fall*, was released in 1956. He died on January 14, 1957. During his later years and even after his death the audience for his films of the 1940s was undiminished; they seemed to be taken up with renewed interest by succeeding generations of film-goers, almost to the point of making Bogart—or his image—into a minor folk figure.

BOK, EDWARD WILLIAM (1863–1930), editor and author. Born on October 9, 1863, in den Helder, Netherlands, of a distinguished Dutch family, Bok was brought to New York in 1870. He entered school without knowing a word of English but learned rapidly. Working at various jobs to assist his family, he saved lunch money to purchase an encyclopedia of biography and learned to his satisfaction that many notable men had risen from modest beginnings. In 1882 he began working for the Henry Holt publishing company and two years later joined Charles Scribner's Sons. In the meantime, he edited the *Philomathean*

Review for Plymouth Church in Brooklyn, of which Henry Ward Beecher was president. Writers and politicians whom he befriended through his hobby of collecting autographs contributed articles to the *Review*, which became the *Brooklyn Magazine* in 1884. With a weekly column by Beecher, the youthful editor began a newspaper syndicate. He put together and syndicated a women's page, the famous "Bok page," as well as a column of letters and notes about authors and books, "Bok's Literary Leaves." In 1887 he became advertising manager of *Scribner's Magazine*. With his career well under way, he carefully considered an invitation by Cyrus H. K. Curtis to become editor of the *Ladies' Home Journal*. Despite the advice of many of his friends, he accepted the position. His subsequent great success was born of industry, intelligence, and creativity. Uncertain of the interests of his female readers, he solicited their ideas for new features, and inaugurated personal advice columns, features on child care, health, and religion, and stories and essays by writers such as Mark Twain, Bret Harte, and Rudyard Kipling. He dealt with "untouchable" subjects such as venereal disease, crusaded for wildlife conservation, improvement in Pullman car facilities, and civic reform, and presented views on woman suffrage. Color reproductions of art masterpieces frequently appeared. The magazine's circulation reached two million before he retired in 1919. Thereafter he wrote many books, including his famous autobiography *The Americanization of Edward Bok*, 1920, which won a Pulitzer Prize. He provided funds for important awards in the fields of public service and citizenship, world peace, and education, and endowed several educational institutions. He died in Florida on January 9, 1930, and was buried at the base of the famous "Singing Tower" carillon that he had built in Lake Wales, Florida, the year before.

BONNEY, WILLIAM H. (1859–1881), "Billy the Kid," outlaw. Born on November 23, 1859, in New York, Bonney moved with his family to Coffeyville, Kansas, in 1862. After the death of his father he accompanied his mother to Colorado and then New Mexico, settling in Silver City in 1868. He had little schooling and by the age of 12 commonly passed the time gambling in saloons; he is said to have killed his first man at this time. In 1876 he and a companion robbed and killed three Indians in Arizona, and for a year he ranged through the Southwest and into Mexico performing similar exploits. In 1878 he became leader of one faction in a cattle war and added several more names to his toll of slayings, among them that of Sheriff Jim Brady. In August a truce was secured by the newly appointed governor, Gen. Lew Wallace (who two years later would publish *Ben-Hur*); Wallace was unsuccessful, however, in persuading Billy to lay down his gun. Instead he gathered a band of followers and set out on a spectacular career of killing and cattle rustling. In December 1880 Sheriff Pat Garrett fulfilled his campaign promise by capturing Billy. Convicted and sentenced to hang for the murder of Brady, the Kid escaped from heavy guard, killing two deputies in the process, and remained at large for nearly seven weeks. Finally Garrett discovered him in Fort Sumner, New Mexico, on July 15, 1881, and fatally shot the West's most famous desperado, the smiling, cold-blooded killer of 21 men.

BOONE, DANIEL (1734–1820), hunter and pioneer. Born on November 2, 1734, near what is now Reading, Pennsylvania, Boone probably had no formal education but did learn to read and write. By the age of 12 he was an expert hunter and trapper. He and his family moved in 1750 to North Carolina, where he worked as a blacksmith for his father. In 1755 he accompanied General Braddock's forces, which included George Washington, on an unsuccessful mission to capture Fort Duquesne and escaped from the bloody ambush that ended the expedition. He first visited the Kentucky wilderness briefly in 1767 and in 1769 returned with his brother and several others for two years of hunting and trapping, during which he explored the territory thoroughly. He was twice captured by Indians but, determined to settle, he brought a party of settlers and later his family to the land in 1775. He explored the Wilderness Trail over Cumberland Gap through the Allegheny Mountains; it led to three settlements, one called Boonesborough. In 1776 Kentucky became a county of Virginia and Boone was named captain of the militia. He spent most of his time fighting Indians, trapping, and hunting game for the settlements. He was kidnapped by the Shawnees and adopted by the chief in 1778, but escaped in time to warn Boonesborough of an impending attack and to aid in its defense. In 1781 and 1787 he served in the Virginia legislature; in 1782 he was sheriff and deputy surveyor of Fayette County, Virginia. His extensive land claims in Kentucky were never validated and in 1799, following his son Daniel Morgan Boone, he emigrated to Missouri, then a Spanish possession. He remained in Missouri until his death in St. Charles County on September 26, 1820. His place in American frontier history ranks high, for he was greatly influential in extending the new nation beyond the Alleghenies. In American frontier legend he has no real rival; the publication by John Filson of *The Discovery, Settlement, and Present State of Kentucke,* 1784, which claimed to be Boone's work and which contained an "Autobiography," marked the beginning of a continuing celebration of the great frontiersman.

BOOTH, EDWIN THOMAS (1833–1893), actor. Born on November 13, 1833, near Belair, Maryland, the son of actor Junius Brutus Booth, Edwin toured with his father during childhood, debuted in *Richard III* in Boston in 1849, and played minor roles supporting his father, in 1851 standing in for him in the character of Richard III. After the elder Booth's death in 1852, Edwin toured California, Australia, and Hawaii, finally winning public acclaim in Sacramento in 1856. His style was patterned after his father's, but displayed an individual flair for transmitting pathos and suspense. Triumphant appearances in major U.S. cities eventually established him as the foremost American actor of his day. After 1863 he co-managed the Winter Garden Theater in New York, where he staged Shakespearian tragedies including *Hamlet, King Lear, Macbeth,* and *Othello.* The production of *Julius Caesar* starring him and his two brothers, Junius and John Wilkes, as well as his 100-night appearance as Hamlet, were milestones in American theater. After the assassination of President Lincoln by his brother, he retired from the stage until January 1866, when he returned to the Winter Garden as Hamlet. In 1867 the theater burned to the ground. He had built Booth's Theatre by February 1869 and there continued his brilliant career. Owing to poor business advice, the theater went bankrupt in 1874. He performed for nearly 20 years thereafter in America, the British Isles, and Europe. His final performance was as Hamlet in 1891 at the Brooklyn Academy of Music. He died in New York on June 7, 1893.

BOOTH, JOHN WILKES (1838–1865), actor and assassin. Born in 1838 near Bel Air, Maryland, Booth was the son of Junius Brutus Booth and the brother of Edwin Booth, both noted actors of their day. Educated sporadically in private academies, he made his stage debut at age 17 in Baltimore. He developed into a Shakespearian actor, and was given finer reviews than his brother by some critics. From the late 1850s his sympathies in the growing sectional conflict were strongly Southern. In 1859 he was a member of a Virginia militia company that, under the general command of Col. Robert E. Lee, seized John Brown at Harpers Ferry and during the Civil War he planned the kidnapping of President Lincoln. He and several conspirators were disappointed in their scheme when Lincoln failed to pass the crucial spot on March 20, 1865. After the fall of Richmond and the surrender at Appomattox, Booth decided on assassination, enlisting one accomplice to murder Vice President Johnson and another to kill Secretary of State Seward. On the evening of April 14, 1865, Booth ascended the stairway to the President's box at Ford's Theatre and shot a bullet through Lincoln's head. He leaped to the stage, crying *"Sic semper tyrannis! The South is avenged!"* and escaped through the rear of the theater. His accomplices were unsuccessful in their assassination attempts, although Seward was badly beaten. Booth was not located until April 26th, when he was found hiding in a barn near Bowling Green, Virginia, and was either killed by his captors or died by his own hand; the facts have never been ascertained. Several of his accomplices were hanged on July 7th. A legend arose that he had escaped death and was wandering in Mexico, Texas, and Oklahoma. A man named John St. Helene, who committed suicide in Oklahoma in 1903, was thought to be Booth. St. Helene's body was mummified and exhibited in several states. As late as 1924 historians were still writing articles to disprove the so-called "myth of John Wilkes Booth."

BORAH, WILLIAM EDGAR (1865–1940), public official and political leader. Born near Fairfield, Illinois, on June 29, 1865, Borah completed less than a year of formal study at the University of Kansas. Reading law privately, he was admitted to the bar in Kansas in 1889 and three years later moved to Boise, Idaho. He quickly involved himself in politics while becoming a prominent criminal and corporation lawyer. In 1906 he was elected as a Republican to the Senate, where he was to remain for the rest of his life. While Borah was nominally a Progressive Republican, initiating or supporting a great number of reform measures, he was best characterized as a political maverick. He supported Theodore Roosevelt's industrial policies and led the campaigns for the 16th and 17th Amendments; yet he often opposed conservation proposals, was cold to most of Wilson's domestic reform program, and was, before and during World War I, something of a jingoist. From his bitter opposition to the League of Nations through the remainder of his career he was a strong iso-

lationist; yet he was largely responsible for the Washington Disarmament Conference of 1921 and for the multilateral Kellogg-Briand Pact of 1928, and he consistently advocated the recognition of Soviet Russia. As chairman of the Senate Foreign Relations Committee from 1924 to 1933 he fought foreign entanglements of all kinds while promoting voluntary cooperation and anticipating much of the later Good Neighbor policy. He supported most of the New Deal, though he led Senate opposition to the National Recovery Administration and to Roosevelt's Court-packing plan. He favored the Neutrality Act of 1935 and remained a leading isolationist until his death in Washington on January 19, 1940.

BOUCICAULT, DIONYSIUS LARDNER (c.1820–1890), playwright and actor. Born in Dublin, Ireland, on December 26, 1820 or 1822, Boucicault entered the University of London around 1836, but in 1837 began to act in country playhouses under the name of Lee Moreton. In 1840, living again in London, he offered his first play to Covent Garden. It was turned down, but a second play, *London Assurance,* was produced in 1841 and was a great success. Subsequently he wrote *Old Heads and Young Hearts,* 1844, and adapted *Pauline,* in 1851, and *The Corsican Brothers,* in 1852, from Dumas, and *Louis XI* from Delavigne. In 1853 he emigrated to New York City where his reputation was already established. Of numerous plays that he wrote for the American stage the most notable were *The Young Actress,* 1853, a light musical; *The Poor of New York,* 1857, a surface portrait of the panic of 1837; *Jessie Brown, or the Relief of Lucknow,* 1858, in which he acted; *The Octoroon,* 1859, a milestone in social drama with antislavery implications; *The Collegians,* 1860, the first of several plays, written for Laura Keene's theater, which included a number of Irish comedies, among them *The Colleen Bawn,* 1860, *Arrah-na-Pogue,* 1864, *The O'Dowd,* 1873, and *The Shaughraun,* 1874. In 1858 he became part owner of a theater in Washington, D.C., and the next year he managed the Winter Garden Theater in New York City. From 1862 to 1872 he lived in England, and revised the script of *Rip Van Winkle* in 1865 for Joseph Jefferson. After 1872 he lived in New York City and at the time of his death on September 18, 1890, was teaching drama. Of tremendous influence on the 19th-century American theater, he contributed over 130 plays or adaptations during his career and considerably deepened the treatment of the Irishman as a character. He is also credited with having originated the "long run" by establishing his plays in New York and subsequently taking them on tour with a different cast.

BOURNE, RANDOLPH SILLIMAN (1886–1918), critic and essayist. Born in Bloomfield, New Jersey, on May 30, 1886, Bourne early displayed the keen intelligence that was coupled with a serious physical deformity. Financial difficulties delayed his college education until 1909, when he entered Columbia University. In an intellectual atmosphere dominated by Charles A. Beard, John Dewey, and Franz Boas, he rapidly developed his critical, often iconoclastic, outlook. In 1913, the year of his graduation, a series of articles he had written for the *Atlantic Monthly* was collected and published as *Youth and Life*, an expression of optimism in a coming social and cultural renaissance led by the youth of America. During a year of travel in Europe he was both heartened by signs of a similar spirit he detected in some groups and dismayed by the growing militarism of others. Upon his return he became a regular contributor to the newly established *New Republic*; for it he wrote wide-ranging critical articles on literature, culture, and education. The approach of war, and the failure of Progressive liberalism that it betokened, drove him into a more radical position. His pacifism estranged him from the *New Republic* and he began to contribute to the more radical *Masses* and *Seven Arts*. The suppression of dissident journals by war fever cut off Bourne's outlets. While at work on a novel and a major treatise on the State, he died on December 22, 1918.

BOWDITCH, NATHANIEL (1773–1838), mathematician and astronomer. Born on March 26, 1773, in Salem, Massachusetts, Bowditch received no formal education beyond the age of ten. While at work, however, first in his father's cooperage and later in a ship chandlery, he continued to read and study on his own. He taught himself algebra, geometry, French, and, in order to read Newton's *Principia*, Latin. At fifteen he compiled an almanac. Between 1795 and 1803 he made several sea voyages, the last as master, and continued his studies. In Moore's *Practical Navigator*, then the standard work in the field, he discovered a great number of errors; in 1799 he published the first American edition of the book, incorporating his corrections. Further work and revision led to the publication under his own name of the *New American Practical Navigator*, which, through edition after edition since 1802, has been the "seaman's bible" down to the present. For the rest of his life Bowditch was associated with insurance companies in Salem and Boston; he also continued his scientific interests and published numerous papers, particularly on comets and meteors. For several years he was engaged in translating the first four volumes of Laplace's *Mécanique céleste*; published 1829–1839, this massive work, which included extensive commentary and updating by Bowditch, was a major landmark in the development of American science. Though he declined several professorships, Bowditch was from 1829 until his death president of the American Academy of Arts and Sciences. He died in Boston on March 16, 1838.

BOWDOIN, JAMES (1726–1790), merchant and Revolutionary political leader. Born on August 7, 1726, of a wealthy Boston family, Bowdoin graduated from Harvard in 1745 and entered business. In 1753 he was elected to the Massachusetts General Court and in 1757 to the ruling Council. Here, working closely with John Hancock, James Otis, and Samuel Adams, he spoke and organized for American independence. In 1775–1776 he was a member of the executive council of Massachusetts;

ill health forced his resignation and temporary retirement from public life. Like Franklin, he had deep scientific and literary interests in addition to his public ones; in 1780 he was a founder and thereafter the first president of the American Academy of Arts and Sciences. In the same year he served as president of his state's constitutional convention and from 1785 to 1787 was its governor. During his tenure in this office, he worked to stabilize the state's government and finances and, seeing the great difficulties of conflicting sovereignties under the Confederation, he urged strongly the consideration of a more integrated and permanent union. Bowdoin took prompt and strong action in putting down Shays's Rebellion of disgruntled farmers and debtors in 1787. Shortly thereafter he retired from the governorship; in the following year he was a member of the convention called to ratify the federal Constitution in Massachusetts. He died on November 6, 1790. Four years later the General Court honored his memory by the establishment of Bowdoin College in Brunswick, now part of Maine.

BOWIE, JAMES (1796–1836), Texas revolutionary leader. Born in Logan County, Kentucky, in 1796, Bowie moved with his family to Missouri in 1800 and to Louisiana in 1802. From 1814 he engaged in various enterprises — timbering, slave trading, and sugar cane raising — alone and with his brothers, becoming something of a figure in New Orleans society. He went to Texas in 1828, possibly in consequence of having killed a man in a duel. Settling in San Antonio (then called Bexar), he adopted Mexican citizenship in 1830 and the following year married the daughter of the vice governor, acquiring in the meantime extensive holdings in land. Despite these attachments to the Mexican regime, he sided with the American colonists as agitation for Texan independence developed. In 1835 he was a member of the committee of safety and became a colonel in the revolutionary army. Early in 1836 he joined the force under Col. William Travis at the Alamo. He fell ill during the siege and was discovered dead on his cot when Santa Anna's troops took the stronghold on March 6, 1836. He is generally credited with the invention of the Bowie knife — a stout hunting knife that became widely popular — though it is sometimes attributed to his brother Rezin.

BOWLES, SAMUEL (1797–1851), journalist and editor. Born in Hartford, Connecticut, on June 8, 1797, Bowles was a printer's apprentice at 16 and advanced to foreman of the *New Haven Register*. In 1819 he began publishing the weekly *Hartford Times* in partnership with John Francis, but was unsuccessful and in 1824 moved to Springfield, Massachusetts, to begin the weekly *Springfield Republican*. In 1844, despite the admonitions of business associates, he started a daily evening edition, which his son promised to develop. Made into a morning paper in 1845, the new *Republican* had a system of local correspondents that provided complete coverage of the upper Connecticut Valley and gave every indication of surviving as a leading provincial journal. Bowles died in Springfield on September 8, 1851. His son, **SAMUEL BOWLES II** (1826–1878), was born in Springfield on February 9, 1826. He began working in the *Republican* offices at 17 and through hard work and competitiveness made the daily edition the leading paper in western Massachusetts by 1848. Determined to remain politically independent, he editorially supported the Wilmot Proviso in 1846, denounced the Kansas-Nebraska bill of 1854, supported the Civil War and Reconstruction policies of Lincoln while avoiding the radical views of other editors, but favored the impeachment of President Johnson, and joined the Liberal Republican movement in 1872. His commentaries were authoritative and won for the *Republican* a national audience, exceeding by far its initial promise as a small-town paper, and a reputation for outstanding independent journalism. He traveled for his health after 1862 and published his correspondence from the West in *Across the Continent* and *The Switzerland of America*, both in 1865, and *Our New West*, 1869. He died in Springfield on January 16,

1878. His son, SAMUEL BOWLES (1851–1915), maintained the paper's high standards, developed a school for journalists in its offices, and in 1878 founded the *Sunday Republican*. He died on March 14, 1915.

BRACE, CHARLES LORING (1826–1890), reformer. Born in Litchfield, Connecticut, on June 19, 1826, Brace graduated from Yale in 1846, taught school, and returned to Yale Divinity School a year later. After an extended visit to Europe he moved to New York City where, in 1853, he helped found the Children's Aid Society. He remained for the rest of his life executive secretary of the organization. Concerned mainly with the growing immigrant population of the city, the Society, under Brace's direction, established schools, homes, sanitariums, and camps. The main emphasis of his work was on the realization of the greatest possible degree of self-help. In 1872 he wrote *The Dangerous Classes of New York, and Twenty Years' Work Among Them*, and ten years later *Gesta Christi: a History of Humane Progress Under Christianity*, both of which were major contributions to the literature of philanthropy. He died in Switzerland on August 11, 1890.

BRACKENRIDGE, HUGH HENRY (1748–1816), author and jurist. Born in Scotland, Brackenridge and his family came to America in 1753 and settled in Pennsylvania. Gaining his early education by his own efforts, he entered Princeton in 1768. James Madison and Philip Freneau were classmates, and he collaborated with the latter on *The Rising Glory of America*, their 1771 commencement poem. He studied divinity after graduation and during the Revolution served as a chaplain and wrote and preached in support of independence. He turned to law and in 1781 moved to Pittsburgh where, a few years later, he helped to found the town's first newspaper. He served in the state legislature in 1786–1787 and was a strong supporter of the new Constitution in the period leading up to ratification. In 1799 he was appointed to the state's supreme

court. Between 1792 and 1815 he published his long, rambling novel, *Modern Chivalry*, a satire on many of the people and institutions of the time. He died on June 25, 1816.

BRADFORD, WILLIAM (1590–1657), governor of Plymouth colony. Born in Yorkshire, England, Bradford began at the age of 12 to read the Bible and soon joined a Separatist congregation. He migrated with the Puritans to Holland in 1609 and for 11 years lived and worked quietly in Leyden. In 1620 he sailed on the *Mayflower* and in April 1621, with the settlement nearly decimated by the first harsh winter, became governor of Plymouth. Evidently a man of remarkable tact, honesty, and political ability, Bradford was elected governor in 30 of the succeeding 35 years. It seems to have been largely through his efforts that the colony gained a firm footing despite the extreme hardships of the first years; his handling of unruly elements within and of the Indians surrounding Plymouth averted a number of potential disasters. Though not formally educated, Bradford possessed considerable literary ability; his *History of Plymouth Plantation, 1620–1647*, is a vivid account of the early settlement and the major source of information about it. The work was not published until 200 years after his death in Plymouth on May 9, 1657 (O.S.).

BRADLEY, JOSEPH P. (1813–1892), jurist. Born in Berne, New York, on March 14, 1813, Bradley's intellectual bent was frustrated by poverty until 1833 when he entered Rutgers University. He graduated in 1836 and three years later was admitted to the bar. An astute student of the law, he was counsel for several railroad companies. In 1870 President Grant appointed him to the Supreme Court, where he immediately became involved in the legal problems arising from Reconstruction. In 1877 he was a member of the electoral commission appointed to decide the Hayes-Tilden election; Bradley's was the deciding vote that gave Hayes the presidency. He was dedicated to the maintaining of state powers in the federal system; accordingly, he ruled in 1883 in the Civil Rights Cases that in the internal social relations of the states the 14th Amendment had no power. He was also influential in the molding of the modern view of the relationship of federal and state authority over interstate commerce. Justice Bradley died in Washington, D.C., on January 22, 1892.

BRADLEY, OMAR NELSON (1893–), soldier. Born on February 12, 1893, in Clark, Missouri, Bradley graduated from West Point in 1915 and was commissioned a second lieutenant of artillery. After serving at various Army posts in the West and Midwest he became professor of military science and tactics at South Dakota State College in 1919. A year later he returned to West Point as instructor of mathematics. In 1925 he graduated from the Army Infantry School, in 1929 from the Command and General Staff School, and in 1934 from the War College. From 1934 to 1938 he was again an instructor at West Point, and in the latter year was transferred to duties with the General Staff in Washington, D.C. In 1941 he was promoted to brigadier general. His first combat service came in 1943, when he commanded the U.S. 2nd Corps in North Africa under Gen. Dwight D. Eisenhower; later in the year he took part in the invasion of Sicily, and then moved to England to take command of the U.S. 1st Army and begin planning for the invasion of Europe. He retained this post until August 1944, two months after D-Day, when he assumed command of the 12th Army Group, a force of 1.3 million combat troops and the largest ever to serve under a single American field commander. In 1945 he became a full general. From that year until 1947 he was administrator of veterans' affairs, and in 1948 he succeeded Eisenhower as chief of staff of the Army. After the unification of the armed services he became in 1949 the first chairman of the joint chiefs of staff, a post he held for four years; during that time, in 1950, he was promoted to general of the army. After leaving active service in the Army he followed various business interests, becoming in 1958 chairman of the board of the Bulova Watch Company. In 1951 he published *A Soldier's Story*, a volume of reminiscences.

BRADSTREET, ANNE (c.1612–1672), poet. Born to a family of comfortable means in Northampton, England, Anne came to the New World with her parents and her husband in 1630; they were members of John Winthrop's party, the first settlers in Massachusetts Bay. At first dismayed by the rude life of the colony, she soon reconciled herself to it and, in the midst of her husband's public duties and her private ones as mother of eight, she found time to write poetry. Her early work, largely imitative and influenced by Du Bartas, is conventional, dull, and easily forgotten. It was first published in London in 1650 as *The Tenth Muse Lately Sprung Up in America*. Her later work, unpublished until after her death, is her chief claim to attention; less derivative, it is often, as in "Contemplations," graceful and pleasant. Much of it concerns her deeply personal reflections, and the warmth and frank humanity that pervade them provide a welcome contrast to the Puritan stereotype. She died on September 16, 1672.

BRADY, MATHEW B. (c.1823–1896), photographer. Brady was born in Warren County, New York; apart from that little is known of his background except for his Irish descent and that he received little schooling. Around 1840 he was introduced to Samuel F. B. Morse, who was conducting experiments with daguerreotypes. Soon doing plates of his own, Brady was sufficiently skilled by 1844 to establish a commercial studio. He was rapidly successful, made thousands of portraits, and won awards from the American Institute between 1844 and 1849 that had never been conferred on daguerreotypists before. He experimented with tinting and producing his plates on ivory. The latter were in great demand, and his plan to make portraits of every distinguished American seemed possible to achieve. In 1855 he learned the new wet-plate process of photography from an English expert. Switching to this new medium, he amassed a fortune, which he used to train a team of assistants to photograph the Civil War. They fearlessly tromped through battle-grounds, bivouacs, and officers' quarters, recording every aspect of the conflict. Several collections of the photographs were circulated, one in a book, *Brady's National Photographic Collection of War Views and Portraits of Representative Men*, 1870, another set of 2,000 being sold to the government, another sent to a photographic supply house to repay debts, and others to private collectors. Combined, they form the basis for all pictorial records of the war. In his later years he became ill and impoverished. He died in New York on January 15, 1896.

BRAGG, BRAXTON (1817–1876), Confederate general. Born in Warrenton, North Carolina, on March 22, 1817, Bragg was appointed to West Point and graduated in 1837. He took part in the Seminole Wars of 1837 and 1841 and served with distinction under Zachary Taylor in the Mexican War. In 1856 he retired from the Army to a plantation in Louisiana. Five years later he was called to service in the Confederate States Army. In 1862, after a qualified success at Shiloh, Bragg was given command of the Army of Tennessee. Hoping to secure Kentucky to the Confederacy, he moved north; he retired from an indecisive engagement with Buell in October and from another with Rosecrans in December. Despite severe criticism Bragg retained command. In the following year he won a notable victory at Chickamauga but soon thereafter was routed by Grant at Chattanooga. Bragg surrendered his command and became military advisor to Jefferson Davis. After the war he turned to civil engineering and for four years was commissioner of public works in Alabama. He died in Galveston, Texas, on September 27, 1876.

BRANDEIS, LOUIS DEMBITZ (1856–1941), lawyer and jurist. Born in Louisville, Kentucky, on November 13, 1856, Brandeis graduated from Harvard Law School at the head of the class of 1877. After practising briefly in St. Louis he returned to Boston where he remained until 1916. As a result of his advocacy of public causes, typically without compensation, he became known as the "people's attorney." His involvement in the investigation of the Equitable Life Assurance Society in 1906 led him to devise a low-cost savings bank insurance plan for workingmen. He investigated the railroad industry, revealing wasteful management practices and, from 1907 to 1914, he carried on a number of investigations on behalf of state-enacted labor legislation, for which he employed what became known as the "Brandeis brief," devoted to detailed analysis of the social and economic contexts of such legislation. In 1916 he was appointed to the Supreme Court by President Wilson, the first Jew to be so honored. He was deeply concerned with maintaining a workable federal system and encouraged experimentation in social and economic fields by the states. At the same time a strong civil libertarian, Brandeis was often aligned in dissent with Justice Holmes. He retired from the bench in 1939 and died in Washington, D.C., on October 5, 1941.

BRANT, JOSEPH (1742–1807), Indian chief. Born in 1742 on the banks of the Ohio River, Brant was the son of a Mohawk chief and was known to the Indians as Thayendanegea. He was educated at Moor's Indian Charity School (which later developed into Dartmouth College) in Lebanon, Connecticut. In 1763, soon after leaving school, he served in the French and Indian War as one of the Iroquois contingent aiding the British against Pontiac. In 1774 he became secretary to the superintendent of Indian affairs and when the Revolution broke out remained loyal to the British. After a visit to England, during which he was presented at court, he assumed leadership of the Indians of the Mohawk Valley region, directing devastating raids on settlements on the New York and Pennsylvania frontier. He was particularly prominent at the Battle of

Oriskany in 1777 and at the Cherry Valley Massacre of the following year. Though Brant constantly frustrated attempts by other Indian leaders, notably Red Jacket, to secure an early peace with the Americans, at the war's end he took the lead in pacifying the Indian frontier. He devoted himself thereafter to missionary work, translating the Prayer Book and St. Mark's Gospel into the Mohawk tongue, and attempting to secure the welfare and safety of his people. On a second visit to England in 1786 he obtained funds to purchase settlement lands in Canada and to erect an Episcopal church for the Mohawks. He died on November 24, 1807.

BRATTLE, THOMAS (1658–1713), merchant and philanthropist. Born in Boston on June 20, 1658, into one of New England's wealthiest families, Brattle graduated from Harvard in 1676 and, after extended travel and study in Europe, returned to Boston to enter business in 1689. In 1693 he became treasurer of Harvard College, a post he held until his death, and through substantial personal gifts and wise management greatly increased the institution's resources. In 1698 he organized the Brattle Street Church on a highly liberal basis, dispensing with a number of conventional practices; his deviations from Puritan orthodoxy led to a sustained feud with the powerful Mather family. In line with his liberal outlook he condemned the witchcraft proceedings in Salem as "ignorance and folly." He was an avid amateur mathematician and astronomer and made several valuable observations, one of which aided Isaac Newton in his work. He died on May 18, 1713.

BREASTED, JAMES HENRY (1865–1935), Egyptologist and historian. Born on August 27, 1865, in Rockford, Illinois, Breasted entered NorthWestern (now North Central) College in Naperville, Illinois, at 15, but did not receive his B.A. degree until 1890. An interest in botany and chemistry led him to take apprenticeships in local pharmacies; during 1882–1886 he attended the Chicago College of Pharmacy, graduating in the latter year and beginning his practice. Insufficiently stimulated by this work, however, he began studies in the Congregational Institute (now Chicago Theological Seminary) in 1888, there learning Hebrew and beginning to translate and interpret the scriptures. He transferred to Yale, studying in 1890–1891 under William Rainey Harper, who suggested that he fit himself for a chair in Egyptology at the new University of Chicago, of which Harper had been made president. He received his M.A. degree from Yale in 1892, one year after beginning studies in Egyptology at the University of Berlin, where he took his doctorate in 1894. Returning to the United States, he became an assistant in Egyptology (the first such position in the country) and assistant director of the Haskell Oriental Museum at the University of Chicago. In 1896 he became an instructor in Egyptology and Semitic languages and in 1905 professor of Egyptology and Oriental history. At the beginning of his career with the university he lectured nationally for four years, under the auspices of the University Extension, on the development of ancient Egypt; his subject matter was largely unknown since most histories began with Greek civilization. In the early 1900s he worked primarily in Europe, first for the Prussian Royal Academy of Science to develop with other scholars a dictionary of ancient language from Egyptian texts, then for the academies of Berlin, Munich, Leipzig, and Göttingen to transcribe and sort systematically Egyptian hieroglyphics from European museums for the *Berlin Egyptian Dictionary*. In the course of this work, he collected 10,000 historical documents from which he produced *A History of Egypt*, 1905, and *Ancient Records of Egypt*, in five volumes, published in 1906–1907. As director of the University of Chicago expedition to Egypt and Sudan in 1905–1907, he recorded many inscriptions from formerly inaccessible or deteriorating monuments. In 1907 he was appointed a corresponding member of the Prussian Royal Academy of Sciences. During 1908–1919 he lived and taught in Chicago, offering a course on the ancient Near East. He produced with James Harvey Robinson the high school textbooks *Outlines of European History*, 1914, and *Ancient Times: a History of the Early World*, 1916, the latter reaching audiences beyond the school and tracing the arts and sciences to pre-Greek origins. He published *Development of Religion and Thought in Ancient Egypt* in 1912, based on his Morse lectures of that year given at the Union Theological Seminary, explaining for the first time the progress of ancient Egyptian thought from material to more significant moral and spiritual values. In 1919 he delivered the William Ellery Hale lectures on evolution at the National Academy of Sciences, published from October 1919 to March 1920 in the *Scientific Monthly* as "The Origins of Civilization"; in these he demonstrated the application of scientific reasoning and methods to archeological study, hoping to establish an interrelationship between science and the humanities. Shortly thereafter he became the first archeologist to be elected to the National Academy of Sciences. In 1919 his devotion to uncovering man's earliest history showed fruit in his founding of the Oriental Institute at the University of Chicago, with a grant from John D. Rockefeller, Jr. In its first 40 years the Institute sent 20 expeditions to the Near East and published over 125 scholarly papers. Breasted was relieved of teaching responsibilities in 1925 to assume full control of the Institute and its research projects. His later writings included *Oriental Forerunners of Byzantine Painting*, 1924, *The Conquest of Civilization*, 1926, the *Edwin Smith Surgical Papyrus*, 2 volumes, 1930, and *The Dawn of Conscience*, 1933. He died in New York City on December 2, 1935.

BRECKINRIDGE, JOHN CABELL (1821–1875), public official and soldier. Born on January 21, 1821, near Lexington, Kentucky, Breckinridge graduated from Centre College in Danville in 1839 and after further study at the College of New Jersey (now Princeton) took up law. After a year of study in 1840–1841 at Transylvania University in Lexington he was admitted to the bar; he entered practice in Frankfort, moved to Burlington, Iowa, for two years, and then returned to Kentucky. In 1847 he was commissioned major of a Kentucky volunteer regiment and served briefly in the Mexican War. In 1849 he was elected to the state legislature as a Democrat and two years later won a seat in Congress from a normally Whig district. In 1855, despite having established a national reputation and leadership of Kentucky Democrats, he returned to his law practice. The next year, however, he was nominated for Vice President as James Buchanan's running mate and subsequently elected. His popularity in his home state was such that in 1859 he was elected to the Senate for the term to begin two years later. In 1860, when Southern Democrats withdrew from the national convention in protest against the nomination of Stephen A. Douglas, a splinter convention was held in Baltimore and Breckinridge nominated for President. Though reluctant at first, he soon began to campaign vigorously on a moderate Unionist platform. After the election of Lincoln he continued to preside over the Senate and to work for a compromise solution to the sectional problem until March 1861. He did not actually take his Senate seat until July, when he attempted to maintain the neutrality of Kentucky while voting against Lincoln's war measures. In September military rule was established in Kentucky; he fled to the Confederacy and in December was expelled from the Senate. Commissioned a brigadier general in the Confederate army, he commanded the reserves at Shiloh and in 1862 was promoted to major general. He saw action at Vicksburg, Murfreesboro, Chickamauga, and elsewhere and was a competent division commander. In 1864 he served with Lee in Virginia and was Jubal Early's second-in-command in the Shenandoah campaign. In February 1865 he was appointed Confederate secretary of war by Jefferson Davis. After Lee's surrender in April he fled south with other high-ranking Confederate officials; he escaped to Cuba and then to England, where he remained until 1868. In that year he was permitted to return to Lexington; he resumed his law practice and was active in railroad development in the state. He died in Lexington on May 17, 1875.

BREWER, DAVID JOSIAH (1837–1910), jurist. Born of missionary parents in Smyrna, which is now Izmir, Turkey, on June 20, 1837, Brewer settled with his parents in Connecticut the following year. He attended Wesleyan University and then Yale, graduating in 1856; two years later he was admitted to the bar and traveled West to practise in Leavenworth, Kansas. From 1861 to 1870 he rose through the local judicial ranks and in the latter year was elected to the state's supreme court. In 1884 he was made a federal circuit judge and five years later President Harrison appointed him to the Supreme Court, where he served until his death. Conservatively inclined, Brewer generally expressed in his opinions a strict view of the constitutional limitations on federal power, although he supported such extensions of it as the building of the Panama Canal and the use of labor injunctions. From 1895 to 1898 he helped to arbitrate the boundary dispute between British Guiana and Venezuela; in accordance also with his views on imperialism and international peace, he advocated independence for the Philippines after the Spanish-American War. He died on March 28, 1910.

BRICE, FANNIE (1891–1951), entertainer. Born in New York City on October 29, 1891, Fannie Borach, daughter of a bar keeper on the city's Lower East Side, took "Brice" as a stage name. She appeared first at 13 in a talent contest at Keeney's Theatre in Brooklyn, singing "When You Know You're Not Forgotten by the Girl You Can't Forget," and won first prize. After that she left school to undertake a theatrical career. She was a pianist, singer, and an assistant to the projectionist in a movie theater; at 16 she got a place in the chorus line of the George M. Cohan–Sam Harris production, *Talk of New York*, but was dismissed as soon as it became obvious that she could not dance. In one of the many burlesque houses where she sang, Florenz Ziegfeld discovered and hired her for his Ziegfeld Follies at $75 a week. She became famous as a burlesque comedienne, but she first made her mark introducing a French torch song, "My Man," which became her trademark. She was a Follies perennial after 1910, and her comic routines and parodies were highly popular. She appeared with such major Broadway performers as W. C. Fields, Eddie Cantor, and Will Rogers in the Follies and other shows such as *Music Box Review of 1924* and Billy Rose's *Crazy Quilt*. A role she had played for friends became another Follies favorite—Baby Snooks—and was featured on radio from 1936 until her death. She appeared in one play, Belasco's *Fannie*, in 1925, in the silent film *My Man*, and the movies *Everybody Sing, Be Yourself,* and *The Great Ziegfeld*, in which she played herself. She died on May 29, 1951, in Hollywood. Her life was the subject of *Funny Girl*, a 1964 Broadway musical made into a movie in 1968.

BRIDGER, JAMES (1804–1881), trapper and scout. Born in Richmond, Virginia, on March 17, 1804, Bridger moved with his parents to the vicinity of St. Louis about 1812. Both of his parents died during his youth and he was apprenticed to a blacksmith until 1822 when, in response to a newspaper advertisement, he joined a fur-trapping expedition to the headwaters of the Missouri River. For the next twenty years he remained in the West as a trapper, gaining an incomparable knowledge of the country and becoming the most famous of the "mountain men." In 1824 he became the first white man to see the Great Salt Lake. With the fur trade on the decline, he established Fort Bridger on the Oregon Trail in Wyoming in 1843, and during the following ten years served as scout and guide for a number of exploratory expeditions. About 1849 he discovered the famous Bridger's Pass in southwestern Wyoming. In 1853 he was driven from the region by the recently arrived

Mormons and he retired for a time to a farm near Kansas City. Four years later he returned to the West as an Army guide in the campaign against the Mormons. He remained there, fabled as the "Old Man of the Mountains," until 1868, when he once again retired to his farm. He died on July 17, 1881.

BRIDGMAN, PERCY WILLIAMS (1882–1961), physicist. Born in Cambridge, Massachusetts, on April 21, 1882, Bridgman graduated from Harvard in 1904 and four years later took his Ph.D. in physics. He immediately joined the faculty of Harvard's physics department, where he remained until his retirement in 1954. In 1926 he was named Hollis professor of mathematics and natural philosophy. His field of research through all his active years was the effect of extremely high pressures on materials. Designing equipment capable of producing higher and higher pressures, he tested scores of substances for compressibility, thermal and electrical conductivity, tensile strength, and viscosity. He was eventually able to generate pressures of up to one and a half million pounds per square inch. This work brought him the Nobel Prize for Physics in 1946. In 1939 he startled both academic circles and the general public with the announcement that thenceforward his laboratory and his hopitality would be closed to visitors representing nations under totalitarian governments. In 1949 he was elected a foreign member of the Royal Society of London and in 1950 became Higgins university professor at Harvard. In addition to his extensive laboratory work, he devoted considerable time to philosophical reflection and expressed his views in a number of books, including The Nature of Physical Theory, 1936, The Intelligent Individual and Society, 1938, The Logic of Modern Physics, 1946, and Reflections of a Physicist, 1950. Suffering from terminal cancer, Bridgman took his own life on August 20, 1961, in Randolph, New Hampshire.

BRISBANE, ALBERT (1809–1890), reformer. Born in Batavia, New York, on August 22, 1809, Brisbane received little systematic education;

he studied with a number of tutors and spent several restless years in Europe in search of a guide for his reformist inclinations. In the works of Charles Fourier he discovered a program for the renovation of society that he could fully adopt. In 1834 he returned to the United States and, after a period of ill health, began to interpret Fourierism, which he renamed associationism, to America. He was encouraged on numerous visits by the apparent early success of the Brook Farm community. His book, Social Destiny of Man, attracted the attention of Horace Greeley, who put the columns of the New York Tribune at his disposal. Having expected that a long period of education and preparation would be required for the establishment of Fourierist societies in the United States, Brisbane was overwhelmed when Greeley's publicity prompted the founding of some 30 communities in a very short time. Nearly all were ill-conceived and failed quickly; Brisbane's own North American Phalanx, founded in 1843 and supported by many of the leading reformers of the time, lasted only 12 years. With the fading of public interest, he gradually abandoned Fourierism and turned to personal affairs. He died in Richmond, Virginia, on May 1, 1890.

BRISBANE, ARTHUR (1864–1936), newspaper editor and writer. Born on December 12, 1864, in Buffalo, New York, Brisbane was the son of social reformer Albert Brisbane. He was educated in public schools in New Jersey and New York, and later in Europe. At 19 he became a reporter for Charles A. Dana's New York Sun and later was its London correspondent and night editor. In 1887 he became managing editor of the newly established Evening Sun and was so successful with it that in 1890 Joseph Pulitzer hired him away to fill a variety of editorial and advisory positions with the New York World. In 1896 he became editor of the Sunday World; his predecessor, who had already established a reputation for sensationalism, had gone over to William Randolph Hearst's New York Journal, and a stiff competition for readership was soon underway. Brisbane indulged in such excesses that Pulitzer became alarmed; he ordered his editor to restore the paper to its previous high standards and to cease featuring his own opinions in print. Instead, Brisbane resigned and in 1897 joined the *Journal*. The battle for circulation continued and within seven weeks Brisbane had increased the *Journal's* circulation from 40,000 to 325,000. Relying on the spectacular techniques of "yellow journalism," he won readers by a combination of sensationalism and jingoism. The *World* followed suit; reporting in both papers ran to sheer fiction, and each contributed in major fashion to the growth of the public furor that led to the outbreak of the Spanish-American War in 1898. Brisbane himself was capable of reversing editorial policy on a moment's notice in order to increase circulation. At various times he directed other of Hearst's newspapers and during 1917–1919 owned a number himself. In 1917 he began a daily editorial column, "Today," that was eventually distributed to over a thousand daily and weekly papers and often featured on their front pages. Brisbane invested heavily in real estate in New Jersey and New York City, owned several hotels, and built the Ritz Tower and, with Hearst, the Ziegfeld Theatre, all of which contributed to a fortune estimated at $8 million at his death. A man of enormous energy, he worked ceaselessly until his death on December 25, 1936.

BROOKS, PHILLIPS (1835–1893), clergyman. Born on December 13, 1835, in Boston, Brooks graduated from Harvard in 1855, taught briefly in the Boston Latin School, and attended the Episcopal seminary at Alexandria, Virginia, where he was ordained in 1859. From then until 1869 he occupied the pulpits of two Philadelphia churches. He gained a national reputation in 1865, delivering a compelling sermon at Independence Hall over the body of President Lincoln and speaking at the Harvard commemoration of the Civil War dead. In 1868 his famous Christmas carol "O Little Town of Bethlehem" was first sung. From 1869 to 1891 he was rector of Trinity Church in Boston. He preached to large congregations who appreciated his intelligent, soft-spoken style. His refusal to employ harsh images and thundering oratory, even in response to charges of heresy by contemporary conservatives, won him stature in the eyes of parishioners. A monument to him by the sculptor Saint-Gaudens was later erected outside of Trinity. His teachings, that man, not the Church, was the focus of God's attention, and that the Church was established that men might live better lives, profoundly influenced his community. In contrast to the austerity of the Puritan heritage still strong in New England, he preached a Christianity of joy and liberality. He was consecrated bishop of Massachusetts in 1891 and died 15 months later, on January 23, 1893.

BROOKS, VAN WYCK (1886–1963), critic and essayist. Born in Plainfield, New Jersey, on February 16, 1886, Brooks completed his studies at Harvard in 1907 and began a long career as a distinguished scholar and author. With the exception of a brief period of teaching English at Stanford University during 1911–1913, he devoted his life to writing. His chief interest was in interpreting the cultural, particularly the literary, development of America. His early negative view of the effects of the Puritan heritage, expressed in *The Wine of the Puritans*, 1909, *America's Coming-of-Age*, 1915, and *The Ordeal of Mark Twain*, 1920, was exchanged for a more balanced, even appreciative, treatment in the later *The Flowering of New England*, 1936, *New England: Indian Summer*, 1940, and *The Confident Years*, 1952. These last volumes were part of a history of American literary life entitled *Makers and Finders*. He wrote a number of biographical studies, was an active editor, and translated works by several modern French authors. He died on May 2, 1963.

BROUN, MATTHEW HEYWOOD CAMPBELL (1888–1939), journalist. Born in Brooklyn, New York, on December 7, 1888, Broun left Harvard without a degree in 1910 and continued newspaper work begun in 1908 with the *New York Morning Telegraph*. Moving to the *New York Tribune* in 1912, he developed his unique style as a sports and feature writer and in 1915 became the newspaper's drama critic. He was a correspondent in Europe during America's participation in World War I and his dispatches from France, followed after the war by his literary column in the *Tribune*, won him a rapidly growing readership. In 1921 he began his "It Seems to Me" column in the *New York World*. Eventually syndicated, the column had a huge following; in it, Broun mixed his personal and humorous observations with a strong awareness of social injustice that, on occasions such as the Sacco and Vanzetti case, could be roused to a near fury. In 1930 he ran unsuccessfully for Congress as a Socialist and throughout the Depression he exerted himself on behalf of the unemployed. He was an organizer and first president of the American Newspaper Guild in 1933. *The Nation* and *The New Republic* printed occasional articles of his and for a short time he published his own weekly newspaper, *Broun's Nutmeg*. He died in New York City on December 18, 1939.

BROWDER, EARL RUSSELL (1891–   ), political leader. Born on May 20, 1891, in Wichita, Kansas, Browder left school after the third grade in order to help support his family. Under his father's influence he became a Socialist and later, in Kansas City, he met William Z. Foster, with whom he was associated for many years. He helped edit the *Toiler*, a syndicalist journal, and worked at various jobs until 1919, when he was imprisoned for a year for agitating against military conscription during World War I. In 1921 he moved to New York City and joined the recently organized American Communist Party; he was also managing editor of the *Labor Herald* and a close associate of Foster in the Trade Union Educational League. The two remained prominently among the leadership as the Communist Party emerged from underground and passed through numerous reorganizations.

Browder made several trips to Moscow to attend international conferences and in 1927–1928 was director of the Pan-Pacific Trade Union Secretariat in China. In 1930 he became secretary general of the Communist Party, a post he held for 15 years during the party's period of greatest growth and influence in the United States. In 1936 and 1940 he was the party's nominee for President; in both campaigns he urged strong action against the fascist governments of Spain, Italy, Germany, and Japan, and greater cooperation between the United States and the Soviet Union. His 1940 campaign was conducted while free on bail, and shortly afterwards he served a prison term for irregular use of his passport. In 1944 he announced a new policy of reconciliation between socialism and capitalism and the transformation of the party into the Communist Political Association. Also in that year he became editor of the *Daily Worker*. The following year he was ousted from the post of secretary general and in 1946 was expelled from the party for his coexistence policy. At the 1949 treason trials in Budapest and Prague he and his "Browderist" heresy were formally denounced. Through the years he published numerous books, among them *Communism in the United States*, 1935, *The People's Front*, 1938, *Our Path in War and Peace*, 1944, *War or Peace with Russia*, 1947, and *Marx and America*, 1958.

BROWN, CHARLES BROCKDEN (1771–1810), author. Born of Quaker parents in Philadelphia on January 17, 1771, Brown began to write and dream of a literary career while yet in school. Set to study law by his parents, he held out against his inclinations until 1793; in that year he gave himself entirely to writing. After a treatise on women's rights, in dialogue form, he wrote, in the space of two years, the four novels that constitute his best work: *Wieland*, 1798, *Ormond* and *Edgar Huntly*, both 1799, and *Arthur Mervyn*, 1799–1800. Written under the influence of William Godwin, the four books are Gothic tales of supernaturalism, horror, and psychological aberration transplanted to the American scene. Brown produced a few lesser works during the next year, but his dwindling resources, both literary and financial, forced him to seek a more secure livelihood. He entered business as a merchant and, except for some magazine editing and distinctly minor writing, never returned to the literary life; his best work had won the admiration of Shelley, however, and he had succeeded in becoming for a time America's first professional author. He died on February 21, 1810.

BROWN, JOHN (1800–1859), Abolitionist. Born in Torrington, Connecticut, on May 9, 1800, Brown was for most of his life a restless drifter and business failure. By turns a drover, tanner, farmer, and wool dealer, he succeeded only in amassing a burden of debt and a family of 20. Though he had been of Abolitionist leanings all his life, his first active involvement in the cause came in 1849, when he settled his family in a Negro community that had been established at North Elba, New York, by Gerrit Smith. Two years later he moved to Ohio and became an agent for the underground railroad. Then in 1855 he followed five of his sons to Kansas to join in the battle for control of the territorial government. He quickly became a leader of the free-soil fighters; his fame became national with the Pottawatomie Massacre of 1856 in which Brown, convinced of a divine call to action, and seven others murdered five suspected pro-slavery settlers. During the next three years he continued his crusade while seeking financial support for a plan to establish a guerrilla base in the mountains of Maryland and Virginia, from which escaped slaves and their allies could attack slave-holding regions. Elected "commander" of this "free state," he secured backing from a number of prominent Boston Abolitionists and in 1859 organized a headquarters near Harpers Ferry, Virginia. On October 16 his band entered Harpers Ferry and occupied the federal arsenal; instead of withdrawing to the mountains they remained, and the following night the arsenal was retaken by a company of

United States Marines under the command of Col. Robert E. Lee. Brown was tried and convicted of murder, promoting slave insurrection, and treason against Virginia. Refusing to plead insanity, for which there was considerable evidence, he maintained a solemn and dignified demeanor throughout the trial. His execution on December 2, 1859, made him a martyr in the view of many in the North, and a villain in the South. "John Brown's Body" became probably the most popular Union song during the Civil War.

BROWNE, CHARLES FARRAR (1834–1867), "Artemus Ward," humorist. Born on April 26, 1834, in Waterford, Maine, Browne was a typesetter and a rewrite man on country newspapers before traveling to Boston, where his first literary piece, "The Surrender of Cornwallis," was published in *The Carpet Bag* in 1852. He traveled west, settling in Cleveland. On the staff of the *Cleveland Plain Dealer*, in 1858, he developed the character of "Artemus Ward" or "A. Ward," a traveling showman whose wax museum was supposedly approaching the city. With these articles and a series of letters, whose satirical insights into a wide range of subjects were tempered with comic misspellings and verbal puns, he gained a wide reputation. Joining the staff of *Vanity Fair* in New York in 1860, he produced the sketches and burlesque romances that were compiled in *Artemus Ward: His Book*, 1862. In New London, Connecticut, in 1861, he delivered his first "moral" lecture, "Babes in the Wood." It concerned neither babes nor the wood and employed the same droll humor as his writings; he then set out on a tour, delivering the lecture to appreciative audiences in many cities. A trip to Washington inspired "Artemus Ward in Washington," concerning an imaginary meeting with President Lincoln. Browne's admiration for the President and his pro-Union sympathies became apparent during the Civil War, in such sketches as "High Handed Outrage in Utica" and "The Show is Confiscated." Lincoln greatly admired these works and read the former to his Cabinet in

1862. Delivering lectures in the Pacific states during 1863–1864, Browne encountered the Mormons in Salt Lake City and "Artemus Ward among the Mormons" became his next platform topic. Delighted audiences in England heard him in 1866; during the tour he became ill, and he died in Southampton on March 6, 1867.

BROWNSON, ORESTES AUGUSTUS (1803–1876), clergyman, reformer, and author. Born in Stockbridge, Vermont, on September 16, 1803, Brownson received no formal education during his youth but was a voracious reader. He joined the Presbyterian Church in 1822; two years later he became a Universalist, in which church he was ordained in 1826. His ever-growing liberalism soon estranged him from institutional religion, however, and he became an independent preacher. He was involved in the socialist movements of the period and helped to organize the Workingmen's Party. He became a Unitarian minister in 1832, but four years later again broke away to establish his own church in Boston. In 1838 he founded the *Boston Quarterly Review*, later merged with the *Democratic Review*. He was associated with many of the leading figures of the day, particularly the Transcendentalist group centered around Emerson; he shared their enthusiasms but, even more than they, was too intellectually restless to remain long with one idea. Suddenly in 1844 he found an intellectual and religious home in his rather spectacular conversion to Roman Catholicism. In the same year he resumed his earlier publishing career with *Brownson's Quarterly Review*, a highly personal journal of opinion that appeared from 1844 to 1865 and from 1872 to 1875. In 1875 he moved to Detroit, where he died on April 17 of the next year.

BRUCE, BLANCHE KELSO (1841–1898), public official. Born a slave in Farmville, Virginia, on March 1, 1841, Bruce received his early education from his owner's son. At the beginning of the Civil War he left his master and opened a school for Negroes in Hannibal, Missouri.

After two years of study at Oberlin College, he moved to Mississippi in 1868 and became a prosperous planter. He was sergeant-at-arms of the state senate, assessor and sheriff of Bolivar County, and a member of the Board of Levee Commissioners of the Mississippi. In 1874 he was elected to the Senate, where he was a forceful advocate of civil rights for minority groups, Negroes, Chinese, and Indians alike, and also opposed discrimination against former rebels. The ending of the Reconstruction period prevented Bruce's reelection in 1880; he had been the first Negro to serve a full term in the Senate. He remained in Washington and was appointed Register of the Treasury in 1881 by President Garfield. President Benjamin Harrison appointed him Recorder of Deeds for the District of Columbia in 1889, and in 1895 he was returned to the Treasury post by President McKinley. He retained this position until his death on March 17, 1898.

BRYAN, WILLIAM JENNINGS (1860–1925), political leader and public official. Born in Salem, Illinois, on March 19, 1860, Bryan studied at Illinois College until 1881 and at Union College of Law in Chicago until 1883; for four years thereafter he practised law in Jacksonville, Illinois. Moving to Lincoln, Nebraska, he continued in law and began to speak on political issues, and by 1890 was sufficiently prominent and popular to be elected to Congress as a Democrat from a normally Republican district. His reelection in 1892 was his last successful bid for office. Already in his years in Congress he had become known as a free-silver advocate and as generally agrarian in sympathies. After two years of newspaper editing and lecturing he was sent as a delegate to the Democratic Convention of 1896, where his "Cross of Gold" speech took the meeting by storm and won him the nomination. He campaigned on the silver issue and lost; four years later, after the Spanish-American War, he added anti-expansionism to his campaign and lost by a wider margin. By this time Bryan had become identified, more by association than intent, with the political restlessness among

Western and Southern farmers that had given rise to the Populist Party; he was also to become a spokesman for the closely related fundamentalist reaction against religious modernism. In 1901 he established a popular political weekly, *The Commoner;* through his writings in this newspaper he remained a potent force in the Democratic Party. Although the conservative wing of the party captured the nomination in 1904, Bryan controlled the platform. In 1908 he was again nominated and again defeated. In 1912, demonstrating his power and his complete mastery of political management, he secured the nomination for Woodrow Wilson and subsequently the post of secretary of state for himself. Though not qualified by training for the position, Bryan served creditably; his major accomplishment was a series of bilateral treaties providing for the arbitration of disputes during enforced "cooling-off" periods. His commitment to peace led him to resign in 1915 when, after the sinking of the *Lusitania,* Wilson protested to Germany in terms that Bryan considered unduly strong and insufficiently expressive of a neutralist policy. He continued to support total neutrality until war actually came; thereafter he counseled loyalty to the President's policies. His remaining years he devoted to his newspaper and to lecturing; he attended every Democratic Convention, though he had lost most of his former influence. In 1921 he moved to Miami, Florida, where, three years later, he drafted for the state legislature a resolution banning the teaching of evolution in public schools. In July 1925 he was invited to handle the prosecution of the Scopes trial in Dayton, Tennessee; at the climax of this test of Tennessee's anti-evolution law, the chief defense attorney, Clarence Darrow, placed the theologically and scientifically naive Bryan on the stand to explain his fundamentalist views on creation. Bryan died in Dayton shortly after the trial, on July 26, 1925.

BRYANT, WILLIAM CULLEN (1794–1878), poet and journalist. Born of Puritan stock in Cummington, Massachusetts, on November 3, 1794, Bryant received a limited formal educa-

tion. When his father's financial condition prevented him from continuing his studies at Williams College, Bryant turned to the law. He remained an avid reader, however, and was particularly fond of the Romantic poets. Already, in 1808, he had written a piece, later regretted, in which he castigated President Jefferson. In 1811 he wrote the first draft of what was to be his best-known poem, "Thanatopsis." Admitted to the bar in 1815, Bryant practised law rather unhappily for the next ten years. In 1817 "Thanatopsis" was published in the *North American Review* and secured immediate recognition for the young poet. He published a small volume of verse in 1821, and within four years was firmly established as America's finest poet. In 1825 he went to New York to work for the *New York Review;* he moved to the *Evening Post* in 1827 and two years later became an editor and part owner, a position he held for the rest of his long life. His production of verse dropped sharply, and his volume of collected poems published in 1832 contained fewer than a hundred pieces. He gained prominence as an editor, however; under Bryant's guidance the *Post* became one of the leading Democratic journals in the nation. His liberalism led him to break with the Democrats in 1848 to support the Free-Soilers; he made the breach permanent in 1856 by supporting the new Republican Party. While devoting most of his time to the *Post* he added slowly to his stock of poems during his later years, though never matching the productivity of the 1820's, and he translated Homer and a number of Spanish poets. In April 1878 he struck his head in a fall and lapsed into a coma; he died on June 12th in New York City.

BUCHANAN, JAMES (1791–1868), public official, diplomat, and 15th U.S. President. Born near Mercersburg, Pennsylvania, on April 23, 1791, Buchanan was educated at Dickinson College and, following his graduation in 1809, studied law until his admission to the bar in 1812. He was a highly successful lawyer, and he moved easily into politics. He served in the Pennsylvania legislature from 1814 to 1816 as a moderate Federalist; in 1820 he was elected to Congress and, as the Federalist Party disintegrated, associated himself with the Democrats. In 1832 he began a short term as minister to Russia and upon his return was elected to represent Pennsylvania in the Senate, where he served from 1834 to 1845. He was a loyal Democrat and, slowly defining a conciliatory position on the slavery issue—opposing it in principle while committed to defending it under the Constitution and denouncing the Abolitionists—he was mentioned for the presidency in 1844. When Polk was nominated, however, Buchanan supported him and was given the post of secretary of state. He held this sensitive position during the annexation of Texas, the Mexican War, and the Oregon negotiations. After a short retirement from politics, he was appointed minister to Great Britain in 1853. In 1854 he joined in the writing of the Ostend Manifesto, which further enhanced his popularity in the South; his absence from the country also prevented his having to take a position in the Kansas-Nebraska debates. Upon his return to America in 1856 he was nominated for President by the Democrats and duly elected. He constructed a cabinet with balanced North-South representation and continued with little success to try to pacify the South by preventing antislavery agitation and upholding the Fugitive Slave Law. The growing tension was capped by the election of Lincoln in 1860. Buchanan denounced the secession of South Carolina but was essentially helpless; he managed only to forestall hostilities at Ft. Sumter until Lincoln took office. During the war he supported the Union. He died on June 1, 1868.

BUCK, PEARL (1892–   ), author. Born on June 26, 1892, in Hillsboro, West Virginia, Pearl Sydenstricker was raised in Chenchiang, China, by her Presbyterian missionary parents. Initially educated by her mother and a Chinese tutor, Chinese was her first spoken language. At 15 she attended boarding school in Shanghai. Two years later she entered Randolph Macon College in Vir-

ginia, graduating in 1914 and remaining one semester as an instructor in psychology. In 1917 she married missionary John L. Buck; though later divorced and remarried, she retained the name in her writing. She returned to China and taught English literature in three Chinese universities, then resumed studying in the United States at Cornell University, earning her M.A. degree in 1926. She first submitted articles on Chinese life to American magazines in 1922. Her first published novel, *East Wind, West Wind*, 1930, was written aboard a ship headed for America. *The Good Earth*, 1931, won a Pulitzer Prize, and established her as an interpreter of the East to the West. The story of a Chinese peasant and his wife, a slave, who struggle for property and position, the book was made into a stage play and an Academy Award winning film. With *Sons*, 1932, and *A House Divided*, 1935, it formed a trilogy, *The House of Earth*. She won the Nobel Prize for Literature in 1938. Subsequently, she wrote biographies of her parents, *The Exile* and *Fighting Angel*, both 1936, *The Patriot*, 1939, *Dragon Seed*, 1942, *Imperial Woman*, 1956, and an autobiography, *My Several Worlds*, 1954.

BUFFALO BILL see **CODY, WILLIAM FREDERICK**

BULFINCH, CHARLES (1763–1844), architect. Born on August 8, 1763, in Boston, Bulfinch graduated from Harvard in 1781 and from 1785 to 1787 traveled in England and Europe, studying the many architectural works suggested to him by Thomas Jefferson. Soon after his return to Boston he submitted a design for the Massachusetts State House, which was finally completed in 1798. He followed it with plans for various other buildings and monuments, including the Hollis Street Church, the Beacon monument, the Connecticut State House in Hartford, and the Boston Theatre. During the 1790s he devoted much time to domestic architecture, introducing the finely detailed Adam style (after Robert Adam, an English neoclassical architect) in the Barrell, Derby, and Otis houses and others. He took an active part in civic affairs, serving on Boston's board of selectmen from 1791 to 1795 and again from 1799 to 1817, and acting, during the last few years, as superintendent of police. He was instrumental in securing street lighting in the city and in opening the common schools to girls. Much of his professional activity was also directed to civic improvement; he planned Boston Common and laid out parks on Boston Neck, in South Boston, and at Mill Pond, and designed India Wharf and a large number of public buildings. Others of his works during the period included the Massachusetts General Hospital, the Cathedral of the Holy Cross, and New South Church. In 1817 Bulfinch was invited by President Monroe to succeed Benjamin Latrobe as architect of the national Capitol. He followed Latrobe's plans in completing the wings, but added his own details to the west front and redesigned the dome and rotunda. Before the building was completed in 1830 he also found time to draw plans for the Washington Unitarian Church, the Maine state capitol, and many other works. He retired to Boston and died there on April 4, 1844.

BUNCHE, RALPH JOHNSON (1904–), statesman. Born in Detroit on August 7, 1904, the son of a barber, Bunche graduated from the University of California at Los Angeles in 1927, and received his master's degree in government from Harvard in 1928 and his doctorate in 1934. After 1928 he was an instructor in political science at Howard University; he was chairman of the department from 1929 to 1950 and became a full professor the next year. In addition, he did postdoctoral work at Northwestern, the London School of Economics, and the University of Capetown, in Johannesburg, South Africa. Before World War II he did field work with Gunnar Myrdal for *An American Dilemma* (published in 1945). In 1941 he joined the U.S. Office of Strategic Services and conducted research in French West Africa. By 1946 he was associate chief of the State Department's section on dependent areas, but resigned to become director of the United Nations division of trusteeship. In 1948 he was deputy to UN mediator Bernadotte of Sweden in the Palestinian War. After Bernadotte's assassination he concluded the truce and armistice agreements. Primarily for his work as a UN mediator he won the Nobel Peace Prize in 1950. After 1958 he was UN undersecretary of special political affairs, acting in 1960 as UN special representative in the Congo and in 1963 as head of the UN mission to Yemen. He also carried out difficult assignments in such trouble spots as Suez, Katanga, Kashmir, and Cyprus. In 1965 with Dr. Martin Luther King, Jr., he led a 50-mile march from Selma to Montgomery, Alabama, on a campaign to gain voting rights for Negroes. He received the Spingarn medal in 1949 and numerous other awards and honorary degrees.

BUNTLINE, NED see JUDSON, E. Z. C.

BURBANK, LUTHER (1849–1926), plant breeder. Born on March 7, 1849, in Lancaster, Massachusetts, Burbank was educated in district schools and for four years at the Lancaster Academy. In 1868 he read Darwin's *Variation of Animals and Plants Under Domestication*, a book that he later credited with having determined him upon his career. In 1870 he acquired a small tract of land near Lunenberg, Massachusetts, and began experimenting in growing improved varieties of vegetables. During the five years he spent there he developed the still widely planted Burbank potato. In 1875 he moved to Santa Rosa, California, and there established the nursery that occupied him for the rest of his life. With painstaking care and enormous energy he raised hundreds of thousands of plants representing thousands of different species and varieties, continually grafting new stocks to old in order to combine the superior characteristics of several varieties in one plant. In addition to his 90 varieties of vegetables, he developed 113 new varieties of plums and prunes, and many notable kinds of berries, apples, peaches, quinces, and nectarines. He also devoted much time to ornamental plants — callas, lilies, roses, poppies, and others — and his most famous development in this field was the Shasta daisy. Burbank's goal was always the production of improved varieties of cultivated plants, rather than scientific experimentation for its own sake, and it was his special genius to be able to recognize in one of a thousand seedling plants the potentially larger and better crop. He published numerous catalogues of his developments and wrote *Luther Burbank, His Methods and Discoveries*, 12 vol., 1914–1915, and *How Plants Are Trained to Work for Man*, 8 vol., 1921. He died in Santa Rosa on April 11, 1926; his autobiography, *Harvest of the Years*, was published the following year.

BURNHAM, DANIEL HUDSON (1846–1912), architect and city planner. Born in Henderson, New York, on September 4, 1846, Burnham moved with his family to Chicago in 1855. Failing to gain admission to college, he entered first business and then architecture. The latter was to his liking and in 1873, after working for a Chicago architectural firm, he formed a partnership with John W. Root that was to be highly influential in the development of American commercial building. Their ten-story Montauk Building was the first to be called a skyscraper, and their Flatiron Building in New York was, in 1902, the world's tallest. The firm's greatest opportunity came with the selection of Chicago for the World's Columbian Exposition. With Frederick Law Olmsted supervising the landscaping, they began the massive task of planning and designing the grounds for the fair. Root's death in 1891 left Burnham in sole command. His remarkable ability to create a workable team from many independent designers, combined with his wide vision as a planner, made the Exposition an architectural success. In 1901 he was made chairman of a commission charged with constructing a plan for the development of Washington, D.C. The resulting "Burnham Report" marked the beginning of real city-planning in America. He followed with plans for Cleveland, San Fran-

cisco, and Manila. In 1909 he unveiled his Plan for Chicago, a long-range proposal for city-wide control of industrial, recreational, residential, and transportation resources. In 1910 he was appointed chairman of the National Commission of Fine Arts by President Taft. He died in Heidelberg, Germany, on June 1, 1912.

BURR, AARON (1756–1836), lawyer, public official, and adventurer. Born in Newark, New Jersey, on February 6, 1756, Burr came of a family distinguished on both sides and was a grandson of Jonathan Edwards. His parents died during his infancy and he grew up in the home of an uncle. He graduated from the College of New Jersey (now Princeton) in 1772, of which his father and grandfather had both been president, and in 1774, having briefly attempted and quickly rejected theology, took up the study of law. The next year he enlisted in the Revolutionary Army; he served under Benedict Arnold in the Quebec expedition, was for a short time an aide to Washington (the two parted on less than cordial terms), and fought with some distinction in the New York campaign in 1777–1778. Resigning in 1779, Burr resumed his legal studies and in 1782 commenced to practise. Moving to New York City in 1783, he soon found himself in what was to be a twenty-years' rivalry with Alexander Hamilton. With the aid of the Clinton and Livingston factions of New York Republicans he was elected to the state assembly in 1784, was appointed state attorney general in 1789, and elected to the U.S. Senate in 1790. Defeated for reelection in 1796, he was returned to the assembly. In 1800 he was nominated for Vice President; in the electoral college Burr and Thomas Jefferson were tied and the decision as to which was to be President went to the House of Representatives. After 35 ballots Hamilton's adamant opposition to Burr swung Federalist votes reluctantly to Jefferson and Burr became Vice President. By 1804, though he was nominated for governor of New York by his own followers, he had alienated the Clinton and Livingston groups and was replaced on the national ticket by George Clinton. Hamilton again brought about his defeat in the governor's race and in July Burr, having been apprised of several insults added to the injury, demanded satisfaction. A duel took place at Weehawken, New Jersey, in which Hamilton was fatally wounded. Burr, indicted in both New Jersey and New York, fled to Philadelphia and thence southward. For the next three years he occupied himself with a vague and never fully explained plan to establish an independent nation in the West, comprised of Mexico and several present western states. His co-conspirator was Gen. James Wilkinson, a traitor secretly in the pay of Spain, who was to secure from that nation the assistance that would be required to make the western secession possible. Burr was indiscreet in his associations, and rumors of many sorts —war with Spain, western revolution, invasion of Mexico—soon swept the country, spoiling all chance of secrecy. Wilkinson turned informer and Burr, betrayed while leading a troop of supposed colonists down the Mississippi, fled and was arrested in Alabama early in 1807. Tried for treason in the circuit court presided over by John Marshall, he was acquitted for lack of evidence of overt treasonable acts. Later in the year he went to Europe and spent much time in Paris trying unsuccessfully to interest the French government in various schemes of western adventurism, most of which involved war among some number of nations. His request for a passport back to America was met with considerable delay but he returned finally to New York in 1812. He resumed his law practice and remained out of public notice until his death on September 14, 1836.

BURROUGHS, EDGAR RICE (1875–1950), author. Born in Chicago on September 1, 1875, Burroughs was educated in private schools, and after leaving a military academy in Michigan he enlisted in the Army and served with the cavalry until it was discovered that he was underage. Until 1911 he drifted from job to job, working at various times as a cowboy, a miner, and railroad detective, and engaging in

a number of unsuccessful business ventures. Finally, having failed at everything else, he decided to try to capitalize on his habitual daydreams of high adventure; the result was a short story, "Under the Moon of Mars," published in 1912 in a pulp science fiction magazine under the pseudonym "Normal Bean." He continued to sell stories and in 1914 published his first novel, *Tarzan of the Apes*, about the son of an English nobleman who, lost in the jungle in infancy, was raised by apes and grew to be king of the savage domain. The book enjoyed sufficient success to warrant a sequel, *The Return of Tarzan*, 1915, and then, over a period of 35 years, more than 25 subsequent titles in the series. He also wrote a number of science fiction novels—a long series on Mars, beginning with *A Princess of Mars*, 1917, and books about Venus, a mythical land at the Earth's core, and a great many more. He was an amazingly prolific writer, regularly producing two and sometimes three novels a year. The Tarzan books sold more than 35 million copies and were translated into 56 languages; the figure of the Lord of the Jungle inspired movies, radio and television programs, comic strips, and became almost an industry in itself. With the returns from his early books he invested in real estate in California and settled on a ranch near the town of Tarzana. He interrupted his career during World War II to serve as a war correspondent in the Pacific. He died in Los Angeles on March 19, 1950, leaving 15 unpublished manuscripts.

BURROUGHS, JOHN (1837–1921), naturalist and author. Born on April 3, 1837, near Roxbury, New York, Burroughs early grew to know and love his area of the Catskills. He attended school intermittently and taught from the age of 17. His first essays, including "Expression," 1860, and a series published in the *New York Leader*, "From the Back Country," reflected the ideas and literary style of Emerson. From 1863 to 1873 he worked for the Treasury Department and in Washington in 1863 formed a fruitful friendship with Walt Whitman. He wrote *Notes on Walt Whitman as a*

Poet and Person, 1867, to which Whitman made substantial contributions. A series of nature essays published in the *Atlantic* beginning in 1865 ("With the Birds," "In the Hemlocks," and others) became the kernel of his first nature book, published in 1871 and named by Whitman *Wake-Robin*. The second, *Winter Sunshine*, based on observations in England, was published in 1875 and launched his career, which saw the publication of an average of one book every two years for the rest of his life. After 1873 he lived on a farm in Esopus, New York. His reputation as a naturalist developed into that of a sage and prophet, and his isolated cabin, "Slabsides," attracted many visitors. He spent time traveling in the United States and abroad and in the company of other nature enthusiasts, including John Muir and Theodore Roosevelt. His books, recording deep reflections on the conflict between intuitive philosophy and scientific reasoning, included *Locusts and Wild Honey,* 1879, containing keen observation and common-sense deductions, *Whitman, A Study,* 1896, subordinating scientific achievement to the magnitude of vision achieved by Whitman, *The Light of Day*, 1900, celebrating Darwinian theory, *The Summit of the Years*, 1913, calling on "the great thinkers and prophets, poets and mystics" rather than men of science to explain life, and *Under the Apple Trees*, 1916, viewing World War I as a conflict between morality, in the Allies, and science, in the Germans. His greatest contribution, however, was in developing the nature essay into a finely wrought literary form. He died on March 29, 1921.

BUSHNELL, HORACE (1802–1876), clergyman. Born on April 14, 1802, in Litchfield, Connecticut, Bushnell graduated from Yale in 1827, was literary editor of the *New York Journal of Commerce* until 1829, and then studied law for two years while tutoring at Yale. While waiting for admission to the bar, he decided to enter the Yale Divinity School and in 1833 was ordained in the North (Congregationalist) Church in Hartford, Connecti-cut. He held the pastorate until 1859, when he resigned because of ill health. He advocated religious instruction for the young, lessened the emphasis on adult conversions, and rejected the doctrine of original sin, particularly abjuring its consequences for the theory of the human personality. Seeing a continuity between the sacred and profane and natural and supernatural, he held that God is present in all His creations and that language is inadequate to express His nature, a belief set forth in his book *God in Christ,* 1849, which led to charges of heresy in 1850. The charges were dropped, but criticism by conservatives continued and in 1852 the North Church withdrew from the local consociation to avoid a heresy trial. Called the "father of American religious liberalism," he wrote *Christian Nurture,* 1847, *Christ in Theology,* 1851, *Popular Government by Divine Right,* 1864, *Work and Play,* 1864, *The Vicarious Sacrifice*, 1866, *Moral Uses of Dark Things,* 1868, and *Forgiveness and Law,* 1874. He died in Hartford on February 17, 1876.

BUTLER, BENJAMIN FRANKLIN (1818–1893), lawyer, soldier, and political leader. Born in Deerfield, New Hampshire, on November 5, 1818, Butler graduated from Waterville (now Colby) College in 1838 and two years later was admitted to the bar. He built up a large practice in Lowell, Massachusetts, and entered politics, serving in the state assembly in 1853 and the state senate in 1859. A Democrat, he was a strong supporter of labor and a defender of immigrants. He was a delegate to the 1860 Democratic Convention and was one of the group that bolted to nominate John Breckinridge. When the Civil War began, Butler, as a brigadier general of the Massachusetts militia, strongly supported the Union. In 1861 he occupied Baltimore; in the same year he was promoted to major general and given command of Fort Monroe in Virginia. While in this post he declared escaped slaves to be contraband of war, an interpretation—and a label—which persisted through the war. In 1862 he became military commander of New Orleans; while he improved the city's sanitation and kept order, he aroused the hatred of the citizenry. He strained relations with foreign consuls, executed a citizen for lowering the Union flag, and, in his infamous Order No. 28, warned that any disrespect or contempt shown his men by a female would be taken as evidence of moral disrepute and treated accordingly. He was recalled from this post in December 1862. The remainder of Butler's military career was checkered, and he was relieved of command in January 1865. From 1867 to 1875 and from 1877 to 1879 he was in Congress, as a Radical Republican and then as a Greenbacker. He managed the impeachment trial of President Johnson and became a strong supporter of Grant. He was the Democratic governor of Massachusetts in 1882, and in 1884 was the presidential nominee of the People's Party. He died on January 11, 1893.

BUTLER, NICHOLAS MURRAY (1862–1947), educator. Born on April 2, 1862, in Elizabeth, New Jersey, Butler specialized in philosophy at Columbia University, graduating in 1882 and receiving his doctorate two years later. He studied further at the universities of Berlin and Paris, in Germany meeting Elihu Root, a major influence in his later political life. He returned to Columbia in 1885, becoming an assistant in philosophy. He delved deeply into the theory of education, its application in teaching, and the organization of schools. To implement his methods of training teachers he helped organize the school that became Columbia Teachers College. His teaching methods and curriculum innovations were used in a model school. In 1890 he became professor of philosophy and education, a post he held for 11 years. He made significant reports on state and local teaching systems and edited a number of educational journals, including *Educational Review*, which he founded. In 1901 he became president of Columbia. Thereafter the school witnessed phenomenal growth, expanding its teaching staff, its student body, and its learning facilities. Butler envisioned

the university as a financial holding company and an important business enterprise as well as an institution of learning. His major work outside the university was on behalf of peace. In 1907, 1909, and 1910–1912, he directed conferences on international arbitration, and over the signature "Cosmos" he contributed a series of articles to the *New York Times*, entitled *The Basis of Durable Peace*, that won international recognition. He was a major force in organizing the Carnegie Endowment for International Peace and succeeded Root as its president from 1925 to 1945. In behalf of the Kellogg-Briand Pact outlawing war as a tool of national policy, he traveled to Rome in 1930 to secure approval from Pope Pius XI. With Jane Addams he shared the Nobel Prize for Peace in 1931. He retired from Columbia in 1945 and died in New York City on December 4, 1947.

BYRD, RICHARD EVELYN (1888–1957), naval officer, aviator, and explorer. Born in Winchester, Virginia, on October 25, 1888, Byrd was a direct descendant of William Byrd of early colonial Virginia. After attendance at the Virginia Military Institute and the University of Virginia he entered the U.S. Naval Academy, from which he graduated in 1912. His active service, which included taking part in the 1914 Vera Cruz mission, lasted but three years; forced to retire because of old leg injuries, Byrd nonetheless returned quickly to duty as an aviator. During World War I he commanded a Navy patrol squadron based in Canada and was active afterwards in promoting the development of naval aviation; he was largely responsible for the creation of the Navy bureau of aeronautics and for much necessary legislation, and he contributed several important inventions to aid in aerial navigation. During the early 1920s he helped to plan both transatlantic flights and a dirigible flight over the North Pole. In 1924 he commanded a small flying group attached to a naval Arctic expedition; the next year he returned with his own expedition and on May 9, 1926, made the first flight over the North Pole, a feat that won him the Congressional Medal of Honor, the Distinguished Service Medal, and promotion to commander (retired). In June of the following year he and three companions piloted a multi-engined aircraft across the Atlantic (he had earlier given special training to Charles Lindbergh and, but for equipment difficulties, would probably have beaten him in the race for first crossing). With the status of popular hero combined with considerable skill in public relations, Byrd had little difficulty in securing private sponsors for an Antarctic expedition in 1928–1929; vast new land areas were discovered on this trip and on November 29, 1929, he took off from his base, Little America, and made the first flight over the South Pole. Soon afterward he was promoted to rear admiral (retired). From 1933 to 1935 he was in command of a second Antarctic expedition, during which much more unknown territory was mapped; for five months in 1934 he was alone in a weather observation shack far south of the main base and, nearly dying of carbon monoxide poisoning, he suffered from impaired health thereafter. In 1939, under the aegis of the newly established U.S. Antarctic Service, he led another survey expedition. During World War II he was on the staff of the naval chief of operations. In 1946 he returned to Antarctica in command of a large expedition called Operation Highjump and made a second flight over the pole. In 1955 he was placed in charge of Operation Deepfreeze I, a major scientific and exploratory mission sent to the Antarctic under Navy auspices as part of the International Geophysical Year program. Byrd accompanied the task force to Antarctica, made a last flight over the pole, and returned to the United States. Failing health prevented his rejoining the expedition and he died in Boston on March 11, 1957.

BYRD, WILLIAM (1674–1744), planter and colonial official. Born on March 28, 1674, on his father's Virginia plantation, Byrd was sent to England to be educated. Admitted to the bar in 1695, he returned to Virginia and, thanks to his wealth, education, and social connections,

quickly assumed a position of prominence in the colony. From 1697 to 1705 he was again in England as the colony's agent; during this time also he was made a member of the Royal Society. After his return to his huge plantation he became the colony's receiver-general and colonel of militia, posts his father had held. In 1709 he entered the Council, for which he was the spokesman in a struggle for power against Governor Spotswood. He built a mansion at Westover and there assembled the largest library in the colony. In 1728 he was one of the commissioners appointed to survey the Virginia-North Carolina border; he described the expedition in his witty and satirical *History of the Dividing Line*. In 1737 the future city of Richmond was laid out on his land. Byrd died at Westover on August 26, 1744.

CABELL, JAMES BRANCH (1879–1958), author. Born on April 14, 1879, in Richmond, Virginia, Cabell began his writing career as a newspaper columnist in Richmond after graduating in 1898 from the College of William and Mary. Then he wrote a series of novels and stories about the "First Families of Virginia," among which his own family ranked. *The Cords of Vanity,* 1909, *The Rivet in Grandfather's Neck,* 1915, and *The Cream of the Jest,* 1917, satirized Southern idealism and ancestor worship and, with *Jurgen,* 1919, his best known book, formed part of the 18-volume *Biography of Manuel,* a series of romances set in medieval times in the imaginary province of Poictesme. Suppressed because of obscenity, *Jurgen* won Cabell a wide reputation and, after its official publication, high critical acclaim through the 1920s. Other books of the Poictesme series included *Figures of Earth,* 1921, *The High Place,* 1923, *Something About Eve,* 1927, and *The Way of Ecben,* 1929. He wrote volumes of criticism, among them *Preface to the Past,* 1936, which defended allegory as a literary form, since realism can—perhaps must—distort the spirit of life. Under the name Branch Cabell he published *These Restless Heads*, an autobiographical work, in 1932, several novels, essays, and stories on Virginia, many of which were published in the *American Mercury* by H. L. Mencken, and a trilogy, *Smirt*, 1934, *Smith*, 1935 and *Smire*, 1937. His great popularity during the 1920s faded rapidly and in his later years he was little read or regarded. He died in Richmond on May 5, 1958.

CABLE, GEORGE WASHINGTON (1844–1925), author and social reformer. Born in New Orleans on October 12, 1844, son of a slave-holding Virginian father and a Puritan New England mother, Cable became head of the household when his father died in 1859. In 1863, Union forces entered New Orleans and Cable joined the Confederate army. Serving from 1863 until 1865, he studied mathematics, Latin, and the Bible, presumably during lulls in the fighting. Released from service, he began working as an entertainment columnist for a New Orleans newspaper, but this conflicted with his self-imposed austere style of living. He began a respectable career in a cotton factory, married, fathered seven children, and might have remained comfortable for life in this position, but for the dictates of his Puritan heritage. He was critical of his education; it was too weak; so he studied French and history, and ventured into the archives of New Orleans, uncovering documents which told of the first French and Spanish settlers of the city. He translated these records into fascinating stories, essays, and books, incidentally contributing to the "local color" movement in American literature, but, more significantly, tracing the roots of the temperament of New Orleans, which was, in fact, a unique combination of races, languages, traditions, and moods. In their realism the stories contrasted French aristocracy with mulatto society; as his writing progressed, he became more sophisticated about the essence and gravity of his work. When in 1885 he relocated to Northampton, Massachusetts, his move might have been construed as an escape from a hostile New Orleans citizenry, which previously had either hushed up or comfortably ignored the inequities which pervaded their society, taboos which he exposed

in such works as *The Grandissimas*, 1880, and *The Silent South*, 1885. In fact, however, his relocation placed him closer to other literary figures and social reformers. His writing, travels, and work with various philanthropic societies finally exhausted him. He wrote romantic stories until he was past 70, and died in St. Petersburg, Florida, on January 31, 1925.

CABRINI, FRANCES XAVIER (1850–1917), Roman Catholic saint. Born in Italy on July 15, 1850, Frances Cabrini was determined from her childhood to make religious work her life's vocation. Delicate health prevented her from entering missionary work, but her remarkable efforts in an orphanage, which earned her the name Mother Cabrini, led her bishop to encourage her to take religious vows in 1877; in 1880 she founded the Missionary Sisters of the Sacred Heart. Despite her intention to spread the order's orphanage and missionary work to China, she was directed by Pope Leo XIII to utilize her abilities among the Italian poor in the United States. She arrived in New York in 1889 and from then until her death traveled throughout the Americas and in Europe founding convents, schools, orphanages, and hospitals. She became a naturalized American citizen in 1909. After her death on December 22, 1917, proceedings were instituted that led to her canonization, announced by Pope Pius XII on July 7, 1946. She was the first American citizen to be so honored.

CAGE, JOHN MILTON, JR. (1912–   ), composer. Born on September 5, 1912, in Los Angeles, Cage attended Pomona College from 1928 to 1930 and studied music under a number of masters, including Arnold Schoenberg. He taught at various times at the Cornish School in Seattle, Mills College in California, the School of Design in Chicago, Black Mountain College in North Carolina, and the New School for Social Research in New York City. He premiered in 1943 in New York City in a concert of his own percussion works. The stage was arrayed with such "noninstruments" as buzzers, pottery, and scrap metal, chosen for their quality in making different, not to say startling sounds. The qualities of Cage's music — and controversy over whether his works indeed were music or something else was abundant — were notably silence, sound, and rhythm. No harmony was used. To make a percussion instrument out of such a traditional concert instrument as the piano, he placed nuts, bolts, screws, dolls' arms, and other objects between the strings. For the "prepared piano" he won two awards for expanding the horizons of music. He won note as the musical director for Merce Cunningham's ballet ensemble, and his intricate manuscripts written for concert soloists or conductors were shown in museums as examples of superb calligraphy. Since much of his writing was intended as inspiration for the performer, rather than as finished compositions to be performed as written, his notes offered choices of the number of instruments or noninstruments that might be used, of their kind, and of the various sections of the work that might or might not be included in the concert. His many compositions include *Imaginary Landscape No. 4*, 1951, for 12 radios tuned randomly, 24 performers, and conductor; *Water Music*, 1952, for pianist, radio, whistles, water containers, and deck of cards; *4'33"*, 1954, for any instrument or combination of instruments — which are used only as stage props, the work itself consisting only of silence; *Winter Music*, 1957, for 1 to 20 pianists; *Fontana Mix*, 1958, for magnetic tape; and *Music for Amplified Toy Pianos*, 1960. A performance at New York City's Town Hall in 1958 was recorded as *The Twenty-Five-Year Retrospective Concert of the Music of John Cage*.

CAHAN, ABRAHAM (1860–1951), journalist and author. Born on July 7, 1860, in Vilna, Lithuania, Cahan studied at the Teachers Institute in his native city and taught in a government school. His revolutionary activities over many years made it necessary for him to flee Russia in 1881. He arrived penniless in New York City and, with other Jewish immigrants, found a job in a cigar factory. In a few months he learned English and met Morris Hillquit, a leading figure in the Socialist movement. Together they founded the *New York Arbeiter Zeitung*, a Yiddish newspaper devoted to Socialism, introducing Jewish immigrants to their new surroundings, and improving their living and working conditions. He also edited the papers *Neie Zeit* and *Zukunft* and in 1897 became associated with the *Jewish Daily Forward*, a small paper supported by contributions from Jewish laborers. He later turned to journalism on English-language papers — the *Sun*, the *Evening Post*, and the *Commercial Advertiser* — for five years, becoming well-known for his stories of Jewish life. With compassion and literary skill he related the trials of masses of immigrants as he had witnessed them in factories and ghettoes. In 1896 his first novel, *Yekl, A Tale of the New York Ghetto*, contributed more to the understanding of his people and their condition than any book that had yet been published. Friends convinced him to rejoin the *Forward* in 1902. As editor he changed the entire format of the paper; articles on manners and American customs, theater and the arts, politics, and economics, written for people whose only education had been the Bible, won for it an eventual circulation of 200,000. He became a powerful labor spokesman, advocating the formation of unions and elimination of sweatshops. His later books included *The Imported Bridegroom and Other Stories*, 1898, and *The Rise of David Levinsky*, 1917, his best-known work. He died in New York City on August 31, 1951.

CALDER, ALEXANDER (1898–), sculptor. Born on July 22, 1898, in Lawnton, Pennsylvania, Calder came of a family of artists, but he wished to be an engineer and attended the Stevens Institute of Technology in Hoboken, New Jersey, graduating in 1919. Thereafter he worked as an engineer, a seaman, and a lumberjack before deciding to attend the Art Students' League in New York City in 1923. To support his education he worked as an illustrator for the *Police Gazette*. On assignment to cover the Ringling Brothers and Barnum and Bailey Circus in 1925, he was fascinated by the sight of performers in motion while maintaining perfect balance. His drawings led to small wire sculptures of animals and acrobats, in which the surrounding and interior space became important to the design. In 1926 in Paris he first showed *Le Cirque Calder* whose originality excited such artists as Miró and Cocteau. He added to the miniature circus over many years and filmed it in motion in 1951 in *The Works of Calder*, for which John Cage composed the score. In 1931 he showed the sculptures of wood and metal that Jean Arp called "stabiles." Influenced by Mondrian, the sculptures were nonrepresentational, brightly colored and abstract in form, and suggested motion although they stood in place. In 1932 his first "mobile" (named by Marcel Duchamp) appeared; sections of wire were connected to achieve a delicate balance and from each wire was suspended a sphere or globe. The forms were constantly in motion, initially propelled by motors, but later constructed to move spontaneously at the touch of a fingertip or the slightest breeze. The essential qualities were balance and harmony in every possible configuration that the moving elements would form. Some famous mobiles were used as sets during Martha Graham's dance recitals in the 1930s; and Calder also made a water mobile for the 1939–1940 New York World's Fair, a 45-foot mobile for the Kennedy International Airport in New York, and the 30-foot motorized *Four Elements* at Stockholm. A stabile in Spoleto, Italy, titled "Teodelapio," is 50 feet high and accommodates passing trucks under its huge spindle legs. He also excelled in vigorous opaque watercolors, nonrepresentational and vibrantly hued, and in book illustrations, jewelry, tapestries, and wood and bronze figures.

CALHOUN, JOHN CALDWELL (1782–1850), public official and political theorist. Born in Abbeville district, South Carolina, on March 18, 1782, Calhoun's formal education was some-

what delayed, but at length he graduated from Yale in 1804. Admitted to the bar in 1807, he built up a considerable practice and quickly entered politics; in 1808 and 1809 he was in the state legislature and in 1810 was elected to Congress. Here he immediately joined with Henry Clay in promoting war against England. After the war he continued to support a strong military posture while putting forward a program of internal improvements, a national bank, and a moderate protective tariff. In 1817 he became Monroe's secretary of war. During these years Calhoun was known as a Democrat and a nationalist, largely above sectional dispute. In 1824 he was elected Vice President under Adams and was continued in the post in 1828 under Jackson. He was slowly moving away from protectionism just as he began to be criticized for his earlier pro-tariff stand; in 1827 he cast the deciding vote to defeat the Woolens Bill in the Senate and, after the adoption of the "tariff of abominations" later that year, he openly aided the opposition movement in South Carolina. His *Exposition and Protest* outlined the doctrine of nullification. The tariff of 1832 finally brought on the crisis; a South Carolina convention nullified the tariffs of 1828 and 1832, and Calhoun resigned the vice presidency to enter the Senate and debate the issue with Webster. The threat of military action in Jackson's Force Bill was allayed by Clay's tariff compromise, and Calhoun persuaded South Carolina to accept the new bill. Remaining in the Senate, he once again attempted to support national programs and to reduce sectional strife, but the rise of the Abolitionist movement soon rendered this impossible. He resolutely defended the South's right to its institutions and aggressively opposed efforts to eliminate, modify, or restrict slavery either in the South or in the territories. In 1844–1845 he served briefly as secretary of state and then returned to the Senate, where in 1846 he led the opposition to the Wilmot Proviso, considering it an unwarranted provocation of the South. During these years Calhoun refined his theory of government in two closely reasoned books, *A Disquistion on*

Government and A Discourse on the Constitution and Government of the United States, which detailed his ideas — all based on the absolute sovereignty of the states — of balanced sectional power, concurrent rather than absolute majority rule, and the need for a dual executive. The debate on the Compromise of 1850 was his last; too ill to speak, he sat mute while his final speech in opposition to the compromise was read. He died a short time later, on March 31, 1850.

CAMP, WALTER CHAUNCEY (1859 – 1925), football and athletics promoter. Born on April 17, 1859, in New Britain, Connecticut, Camp graduated from Yale in 1880 and for two years studied at the Yale Medical School. During his six student years he participated in all manner of outdoor sports, but was particularly interested in football. In 1882 he took a job with the Manhattan Watch Company in New York and the next year joined the New York office of the New Haven Clock Company. In 1888 he moved to New Haven, Connecticut, and soon became Yale's athletic director and football coach. The following year he began the practice of selecting an annual All-American football team from among outstanding college players across the nation. From his student days he had devoted considerable attention to the need for formalizing the game and, a long-time member of the Intercollegiate Football Rules Committee, he is given major credit for transforming the sport from a close copy of English rugby into modern American football. Among his contributions were the set scrimmage, the 11-man team, the quarterback position, the gridiron field, signal calling, and the fourth-down rule. Equally important were his development of strategy and his emphasis on clean, sportsmanlike play. Camp wrote numerous books on football, among them Football: How to Coach a Team, 1886, American Football, 1891, and Walter Camp's Book of College Sports, 1893. In 1917 he began organizing classes in physical fitness for New Haven citizens and was soon called to Washington,

D.C., to arrange a similar program for senior government officials. Appointed chairman of a commission charged with maintaining physical fitness among naval personnel, Camp developed his famous "Daily Dozen" exercise routine. He died on March 14, 1925, in New York City.

CANNON, WALTER BRADFORD (1871 – 1945), physiologist. Born on October 19, 1871, in Prairie du Chien, Wisconsin, Cannon earned his B.A. degree in 1896, his M.A. in 1897, and his medical degree in 1900 from Harvard. Remaining there, he taught zoology from 1899 to 1900, physiology until 1906, and was George Higginson professor of physiology until his retirement in 1942. He lectured widely and was an exchange professor to France in 1929 and 1930. A pioneer in X-ray observation of the movements of the stomach and intestines, he published the results of his studies in 1911 in The Mechanical Factors of Digestion. During 1912 he conducted experiments in hunger perception, leading to his theory that peripheral changes such as dryness of throat or stomach contractions account for the sensation of hunger. He served in the medical corps of the U.S. Army in 1918 and during World War I did research into hemorrhagic and traumatic shock, described in Traumatic Shock, 1923. A long series of experiments in emotion perception led to his theory that major emotions are set off by excitation of the sympathetic nervous system. He also showed that the administering of epinephrine duplicates the effects of a stimulated sympathetic nervous system, heightening blood pressure, heart rate, and blood flow to the muscles, concentrating blood sugar, and retarding digestion. In 1929 he published Bodily Changes in Pain, Hunger, Fear and Rage. In 1932 he developed the concept of homeostasis, or the constancy of the internal environment of an organism, in The Wisdom of the Body. He elucidated the action of chemical mediation of nerve impulses in Autonomic Neuroeffector Systems, 1937, with A. Rosenblueth, and in The Supersensitivity of

Denervated Structures, 1949. He also wrote numerous papers and articles on these processes, on medical education, and in defense of medical research. His autobiography, *The Way of an Investigator*, was published in 1945; he died on October 1st of that year.

CAPLIN, ALFRED GERALD (1909–), "Al Capp," cartoonist. Born on September 28, 1909, in New Haven, Connecticut, Al Capp grew up there and in nearby Bridgeport. After graduating from high school he studied art at a succession of schools, including the Academy of Fine Arts, the Designer's Art School, the Philadelphia Museum of Fine Arts, Boston University, and Harvard. In 1932 he took a job as a cartoonist with the Associated Press; his tenure was brief and the next year he was ghost-drawing for other cartoonists. He met Ham Fisher, creator of *Joe Palooka*, and was soon working for him. He introduced some hillbilly characters into the strip and by 1934 had worked out the basic theme for his own comic strip, *Li'l Abner*, which began appearing in a few newspapers that year. Set in the fictitious hamlet of Dogpatch, Kentucky, the series depicted the misadventures of Abner Yokum, a hulking, wholesome, and none-too-bright son of the hills, his family, and assorted odd characters. Deftly drawn caricatures of well-known public figures often appeared in the strip, allowing Capp to inject social and political satire into the cultural isolation of Dogpatch. *Li'l Abner* became a huge success, syndicated within a few years to hundreds of papers and reaching an audience of tens of millions daily. It was one of the few examples of popular art to be studied seriously in academic circles, and it gave rise to at least one minor American institution, "Sadie Hawkins Day," on which unwary males may be captured and married by predatory females. In 1940 he wrote the script for a movie based on the series; in 1956 the Dogpatch characters appeared in a Broadway musical that, in turn, was made into another movie in 1959. He was also the creator and author of a second successful cartoon strip, *Abbie an' Slats*, published under the pseudonym Raeburn Van Buren. He became a popular personality on radio and television and was widely in demand as a public speaker.

CAPONE, ALPHONSE (1899–1947), gangster. Born on January 17, 1899, in Naples, Italy, Al Capone emigrated with his family to the United States, settling in Brooklyn. There he attended school through the fourth grade and later became a member of the notorious Five Points gang, in which he was associated with Johnny Torrio. At some point in his youth he was slashed across the face with a razor and was afterwards known as "Scarface Al." Soon after the beginning of national Prohibition, Torrio, who had moved to Chicago, engaged Capone to come to that city as his lieutenant in an attempt to corner the local market in bootleg whiskey; Capone, fronting as a used-furniture dealer, organized a gang of "rods" —gunmen—and began a campaign of terrorism to drive out competition. The spectacular series of gang wars that followed was highlighted by the murder of rival leader Dion O'Banion in his flower shop in 1924 and the 1926 daylight machine-gun raid by the remaining O'Banions on Capone's headquarters in the Chicago suburb of Cicero. In 1925 Torrio was shot up and prudently decided to retire, leaving Capone in control of the organization. He soon dominated not only the bootlegging but also gambling, prostitution, and dance halls in Chicago. A network of agents smuggled in a constant supply of whiskey from Canada and various Caribbean islands, reaping him a huge fortune. Bribery on a vast scale bought him immunity from police and civic officials; he did not intrude publicly into politics, however, until 1927, when he announced his support for mayoral candidate "Big Bill" Thompson. In a campaign that was dubbed the "pineapple primary" for the use of a novel electioneering device, the hand grenade, Thompson won, further securing Capone's demesne. In 1929 gang warfare reached its peak of brutality and finesse with the St. Valentine's Day Massacre of seven members of Bugs Moran's gang. Finally, in 1931, extensive efforts by agents of the U.S. Treasury Department resulted in an indictment against Capone for income-tax evasion. He was convicted, heavily fined, and sentenced to 11 years in prison. By the time of his release from Alcatraz in 1939 he was a helpless paretic; he retired to his Miami Beach estate and died there on January 25, 1947.

CAPP, AL see **CAPLIN, ALFRED GERALD**

CARDOZO, BENJAMIN NATHAN (1870–1938), jurist. Born in New York City on May 24, 1870, Cardozo received instruction from Horatio Alger before attending Columbia College, where he earned his B.A. degree in 1889 and his M.A. the following year. He studied at Columbia law school and won admission to the bar in 1891 without taking his law degree. Acting as a barrister, or counsel for other attorneys, he earned respect and admiration from his peers while remaining unknown to the public. His extensive practice before the Court of Appeals led to *Jurisdiction of the Court of Appeals of the State of New York,* 1903. In 1913 he was elected a justice of the New York supreme court on a ticket in opposition to a Tammany Hall candidate. Six weeks later the Court of Appeals selected him as temporary associate justice; the appointment was made permanent in 1917, and nine years later he became chief judge of that court. Learned and skilled in the complexities of law, he also brought a flair to common law litigation as shown in *MacPherson* v. *Buick Motor Company,* 1916, in which he established the consumer's right of redress against a manufacturer whose defective product caused him injury. His attitudes on the relation of law to life were clearly expressed in the now classic *Nature of the Judicial Process,* 1921, and in *The Growth of the Law,* 1924, *The Paradoxes of Legal Science,* 1928, and *Law and Literature,* 1931. In 1932 he was named to the U.S. Supreme Court by President Hoover, acting over opposition on the grounds that there were already two New

Yorkers and one Jew on the Court. He handled an unusually large number of cases in six years on the bench, establishing with Justices Holmes and Brandeis the foundation for a later broad interpretation of federal powers. Cognizant of changing social needs, his decisions exhibited an evolutionary application of legal principle and frequently incorporated years of confused precedents, thereby eliminating the need for further reference to them. In *Ultramares Corporation* v. *Touche,* 1931, he further clarified the accountability to third parties for negligent misrepresentation. In *Great Northern Railroad Company* v. *Sunburst Oil and Refining Company,* 1932, he affirmed a court's right to use a previous authority and yet to declare that authority invalid in future cases. His opinion in the Social Security cases of 1937 showed the Constitution an efficient instrument in meeting critical and broad social needs, and in *Palko* v. *Connecticut,* 1937, illuminated the role of the Court in executing the due process clause of the Fourteenth Amendment. His dissent in *Stewart Dry Goods Company* v. *Lewis,* 1935, was a revealing exposition of problems of taxation, and in *Ashton* v. *Cameron County District,* 1936, he argued persuasively that the division of jurisdiction among the federal and state governments did not weaken the structure of either. Throughout his career, he devoted his energies not to agitated disputes on the Court but to the continuing principles of the Constitution. He died in Port Chester, New York, on July 9, 1938.

CAREY, MATHEW (1760–1839), publisher and publicist. Born in Dublin on January 28, 1760, Carey was partially crippled from infancy and received little formal education, though he was markedly studious on his own initiative. He was apprenticed to a printer and began to write occasional articles. In 1779 he published a pamphlet protesting the treatment of Irish Catholics; trouble with the authorities ensued, and he went to Paris, where he met and worked for Benjamin Franklin. He returned to Dublin a year later, but his anti-

English publications again forced him to flee and in 1784 he sailed for America. Arriving in Philadelphia with letters of introduction from Franklin, and receiving an unsolicited loan from Lafayette, whom he had also met in Paris, he became a publisher and produced a series of journals, of which the *American Museum* was most notable. These proved unprofitable, however, and he turned to the book trade, reprinting European books and publishing works by American authors (among which was Mason Weems's *Life of George Washington*). He was active in civic affairs; his most important contribution was the writing of a number of tracts for the Philadelphia Society for the Promotion of National Industry, of which he was a charter member. In these tracts he revived and popularized Hamilton's earlier arguments for the encouragement of domestic manufactures through protective tariffs, becoming a leading advocate of the nationalist school of economics. In other works he advocated internal improvements and universal education; his *Olive Branch*, 1814, was an attempt to heal the widening rift between the Federalists and the Republicans in the War of 1812. In 1829 he published a volume of *Autobiographical Sketches*. He died in Philadelphia on September 16, 1839. His son, HENRY CHARLES CAREY (1793–1879), born in Philadelphia on December 15, 1793, was educated informally and from an early age was trained in his father's economic thought. He became a partner in the publishing house in 1817 and later was its president. The firm came to be a leader in its field in America, publishing works by such authors as Washington Irving, Sir Walter Scott, and Thomas Carlyle. In 1835 Henry left the business to devote himself to the study of economics; in that year he published his *Essay on the Rate of Wages*. It was followed by the 3-volume *Principles of Political Economy*, 1837–1840. In these and subsequent works he outlined an optimistic view of economics in opposition to the dominant tenor of classical English thought, particularly that of Ricardo and Malthus. He saw the workings of

natural laws as conducive to economic and social progress and the mechanics of a generally laissez faire economy as productive of wealth thoughout society. Like his father he was an ardent nationalist and an advocate of protectionism. With the publication of later works — *The Past, the Present, and the Future*, 1848, *Harmony of Interests: Manufacturing and Commercial*, 1851, the 3-volume *Principles of Social Science*, 1858–1860, and *The Unity of Law*, 1872 — he won an international reputation that equalled or exceeded his recognition at home. For several years after 1849 he contributed regularly to Horace Greeley's *New York Tribune*. His home was a center of intellectual life in Philadelphia; he died there on October 13, 1879.

CARNEGIE, ANDREW (1835–1919), industrialist and philanthropist. Born in Dunfermline, Scotland, on November 25, 1835, Carnegie grew up in poverty and received little more than a primary education. In 1848 he emigrated to America with his family, settling in Allegheny, Pennsylvania, where he started work in a cotton factory. A year later he became a messenger boy in a Pittsburgh telegraph office and his diligence — he became one of the first persons able to read telegraph messages by ear — led to his promotion to operator and finally to his employment by the Pennsylvania Railroad. In his 12 years with this company he introduced the first Pullman sleeping cars and rose to become superintendent of the Pittsburgh division. Convinced by his experience with the railroad and in the Civil War of the coming importance of steel, Carnegie resigned to form his own company, the Keystone Bridge Company, in 1865; for several years he had a number of diverse business interests, but from 1873 onwards he concentrated on the steel industry. Gifted with remarkable organizational abilities and great business acumen, he built his steel company into a giant and, weathering the depression of 1892 better than the rest, eventually dominated the industry. In 1889 he published an article entitled "Wealth" — commonly called "The Gospel of Wealth"—in which he outlined his views on the duty of the rich to oversee the distribution of their surplus wealth for the betterment of civilization. It was a novel idea at the time and the article was widely reprinted and discussed. He adhered to his own advice and actively supported a number of philanthropies, among them the building of public libraries, endowing the Carnegie Institute of Technology and the Carnegie Institution, substantially supporting a great many colleges, establishing Hero Funds in America and Great Britain, and financing the construction of the Temple of Peace at The Hague. Carnegie sold his business to J. P. Morgan's United States Steel Corporation in 1901, for $225 million, and thenceforth devoted himself entirely to philanthropy and the promotion of peace. He died on August 11, 1919.

CARROLL, JOHN (1735–1815), Roman Catholic prelate. Born in Upper Marlborough, Maryland, on January 8, 1735, Carroll was, according to the need and custom of the time, sent abroad for his education. He studied in France and then taught in Catholic academies in Liège and Bruges; in 1769 he was ordained and in 1771 he took his vows in the Society of Jesus. The suppression of the Jesuit order forced him to England and in 1774 he returned to Maryland. In 1776, at the request of the Continental Congress, he accompanied Benjamin Franklin and others on a mission to secure Canadian neutrality toward the Revolution. After the war he was active in organizing the American clergy and keeping it free from foreign domination; in 1784 Pope Pius VI named him superior of the American mission. In 1789 Carroll became the first bishop of the Roman Catholic Church in the United States. In the same year he established a Catholic college—now Georgetown University—and in 1791 a seminary in Baltimore. He actively promoted missions to the Indians and welcomed a number of religious orders to the United States. In 1806 he laid the cornerstone for the Baltimore cathedral and two years later, with the organi-

zation of the church firmly established, he became archbishop. He died on December 3, 1815.

CARSON, CHRISTOPHER (1809–1868), trapper, guide, Indian agent, and soldier. Born on December 24, 1809, in Madison County, Kentucky, "Kit" Carson spent his early childhood in Boone's Lick, Missouri. His father was killed by falling timber when he was nine and he received no schooling. In 1825 his mother apprenticed him to a saddlemaker, but he ran away to join the Santa Fe expedition, in which he learned to trap furs and fight Indians, and settled in the region of Taos, New Mexico. He married an Indian girl and had a daughter named Adaline. On a steamboat from St. Louis, he met John Frémont, who subsequently engaged him as a guide on three expeditions. He fought in several battles for the conquest of California, then returned to New Mexico and worked as a guide. In another battle fought to recover Los Angeles, he performed with daring and later, visiting Washington, discovered that he was a national hero. He returned to private life, farming in Taos, driving sheep to Sacramento, and serving as U.S. Indian agent to the Ute tribe. He was extremely effective in this position, even though he was illiterate; he dictated government reports to other people. One of these scribes, an Army surgeon, took down his autobiography but embellished it so much that Carson had to admit it was more fictional than real. He resigned as an Indian agent when the Civil War began, was given the rank of colonel, and successfully battled the Apache, Navajo, Kiowa, and Comanche tribes, which had terrorized settlers for years. But his final battle in Texas in 1864 was a defeat; 5,000 Indians met his poorly armed group of 400 soldiers and retreat was inevitable. Nevertheless, he was brevetted brigadier general of volunteers by President Polk. In 1866 he was named commander of Fort Garland but had to resign the next year due to ill health. He attended a conference in Washington with the Utes although he continued to feel weak, and traveled in the East, hoping to find medical relief. On May 23, 1868, he died at Fort Lyon, Colorado, of a tracheal tumor that had been growing ever since his horse fell on him in a hunt several years earlier. A temperate, modest man, he was given an important place in American frontier legend.

CARSON, RACHEL (1907–1964), biologist and author. Born in Springdale, Pennsylvania, on May 27, 1907, Miss Carson early developed a deep interest in the natural world. She entered Pennsylvania College for Women with the intention of becoming a writer, but soon changed her major field of study from English to biology. Graduating in 1929, she went to Johns Hopkins University for graduate work and in 1931 joined the faculty of the University of Maryland, where she taught for five years. From 1929 to 1936 she also taught in the Johns Hopkins Summer School and pursued postgraduate studies at the Marine Biological Laboratory in Woods Hole, Massachusetts. In 1936 she took a position as aquatic biologist with the U.S. Bureau of Fisheries (later the Fish and Wildlife Service), where she remained until 1952. An article in the *Atlantic Monthly* in 1937 served as the basis for her first book, *Under the Sea Wind*, published in 1941; it was widely praised, as were all her books, for its remarkable combination of scientific accuracy and thoroughness with an elegant and lyrical prose style. *The Sea Around Us*, 1951, became a national best seller and was eventually translated into 30 languages. In 1951 a Guggenheim Fellowship enabled her to begin work on her third book, *The Edge of the Sea*, published in 1955. Her final book, *Silent Spring*, 1962, was also a best seller, but unlike its predecessors it raised a national controversy. In it Miss Carson examined the widespread and still rapidly growing use of chemical insecticides and herbicides for the control of biological "pests" and charged that indiscriminate use of such substances held great danger of permanently upsetting the natural ecological balance in the world. The book aroused public opinion and consequent governmental inquiry into the problem; before any substantive results were achieved, however, she died at her Silver Spring, Maryland, home on April 14, 1964.

CARTWRIGHT, PETER (1785–1872), clergyman. Born on September 1, 1785, in Amherst County, Virginia, Cartwright grew up there and, after 1790, in Logan County, Kentucky, in a frontier atmosphere. Religious instruction from his mother was the bulk of his schooling. At 16 he was converted at a Methodist revival meeting, and, entering the church, began proselytizing among young men in the area, earning an exhorter's license in 1802. The next year he became a traveling preacher, riding a new circuit in parts of Kentucky, Tennessee, Indiana, and Ohio. His physical prowess, courage, and rugged humor gained a ready audience for his message among frontiersmen. Methodism was for him a battle against the devil and rival sects; he denounced Calvinists, Baptists, Presbyterians, and Shakers. His sermons on sin—drinking, gambling, and wearing ruffles, but mainly rejecting Methodism—and of redemption—accepting his church—were delivered in such a vehement manner that many listeners experienced spasms, or "the jerks," before they declared themselves converted. He was ordained a deacon in 1806 by Bishop Francis Asbury and an elder in 1808 by William McKendree. He rode his circuit until 1824 when his hatred of slavery led him to free territory in Sangamon County, Illinois. His antislavery views won him election twice to the Illinois legislature. In 1846 he lost to Abraham Lincoln in a congressional election. He wrote a colorful *Autobiography*, 1856, and *Fifty Years as a Presiding Elder*, 1871, containing his famous letter to the devil. In later years he found it hard to adjust to a more intellectual Methodism and mourned the passage of old-time mass revivals and prayer meetings. Having preached thousands of times and become a major figure in the religious development of the West, he died on September 25, 1872, near Pleasant Plains, Illinois.

CARVER, GEORGE WASHINGTON (c. 1864–1943), agronomist. Born of slave parents on a farm near Diamond Grove, Missouri, about 1864, Carver was left fatherless in his infancy and was stolen and carried into Arkansas with his mother, who was never heard of again. Purchased from his captors for a $300 race horse, he was returned to his former home in Missouri. He worked his way through high school in Minneapolis and later through college, taking his bachelor's degree in 1894 and his master's degree in 1896 from the Iowa State College of Agriculture and Mechanic Arts. In the latter year he accepted an appointment by Booker T. Washington to the faculty of Tuskegee Institute in Albama. There he conducted experiments in soil management and crop production and directed an experimental farm to educate Alabama planters. He urged them to raise peanuts and sweet potatoes, products that would replenish soil minerals, instead of continually planting cotton, which consumed soil minerals and left the land depleted and worthless. In his laboratory he produced hundreds of by-products of the peanut, including milk and coffee substitutes, cheese, flour, ink, dyes, soap, bleach, wood stains, metal polish, shaving cream, linoleum, synthetic rubber, insulating board, and plastics, and of the sweet potato, including flour, vinegar, molasses, and other products. In 1914, at a time when the boll weevil had almost ruined the cotton business, he revealed his experiments and the South turned to peanuts, sweet potatoes, and their derivatives for income. Land that had been exhausted by cotton was renewed, and the South became a major supplier of important new agricultural products. He was awarded the Spingarn medal in 1923 and the Roosevelt medal in 1939. He continued to develop new materials from soil and from soybeans and was the first scientist to make synthetic marble from wood shavings. In 1940 he donated his savings to the establishment of the Carver Foundation for continuing research in agriculture. He worked during World War II to maintain the supply of material dyes formerly imported from Europe, and in all produced 500 different shades. He died in Tuskegee, Alabama, on January 5, 1943.

CARVER, JONATHAN (1710–1780), explorer. Born in Weymouth, Massachusetts, on April 13, 1710, Carver was a sergeant in the British army at the siege of Fort William Henry in 1757. In 1759 he was promoted to lieutenant; the next year he was made captain. In 1766 he commenced his explorations under the command of Maj. Robert Rogers. He traveled west through the Great Lakes region, via the Green Bay-Fox-Wisconsin route, to the Mississippi River, and up the river to the region of the Sioux Indians at the Falls of St. Anthony. He remained during the winter of 1766–1767 in the Sioux camp on the Minnesota River and on his return to Mackinac met at the mouth of the Wisconsin River Capt. James Tute, in charge of a party sent by Rogers to investigate a route to the Pacific Ocean. He joined the party as a draftsman and third in command, ascended the Mississippi, and reached the shores of Lake Superior by the Chippewa and St. Croix rivers, proceeding to the Grand Portage. They returned to Mackinac by the north shore of Lake Superior in 1768. Never properly reimbursed for the journey, he attempted to publish his travel journal, without success, and left for England in 1769 to have it published there (taking a second wife in England in 1774 although his first wife was still alive). But the project met with many delays and he did not benefit when it was finally printed in London two years before his death. Called *Travels Through the Interior Parts of North America in the Years 1766, 1767, 1768,* it became popular at once, the most widely read and enjoyed account of early American travel and adventure. Although the second part on Indian manners and customs was traceable to French authors and brought charges of plagiarism, this did not detract from the book as a whole. His name was later discovered on a *New Universal Geography* published in 1779 and a discourse on raising tobacco. He died in London on January 31,

1780. A second edition of his journal, published posthumously in 1781, mentioned an Indian grant to lands in Wisconsin and Minnesota, which he never claimed.

CASS, LEWIS (1782–1866), soldier, public official, and diplomat. Born in Exeter, New Hampshire, on October 9, 1782, Cass was schooled at Phillips Exeter Academy; upon graduation, in 1799, he joined his father in Marietta, Ohio. There he studied law and was admitted to the bar in 1802. In 1806 he became the youngest member of the Ohio legislature: he was 24. During the war of 1812 he served with distinction under Generals Hull and Harrison; he rose to brigadier general, and his valuable service won him the governorship of Michigan in 1813. For the next 18 years he effectively oversaw the organization and development of the region. He was particularly successful in his relations with the Indians of the territory. In 1831 Cass was appointed secretary of war by President Jackson; he remained in the Cabinet for five years, during which time Indian wars largely occupied him. In 1836 he was sent to France as minister. He remained in the post until his resignation in 1842, occasioned by a dispute with England and with Webster over the rights of search and seizure on the high seas claimed by England in the Quintuple Treaty. Cass represented Michigan in the Senate from 1845 to 1848 and supported the annexation of Texas and the entire Oregon claim. In 1848 he won the Democratic nomination for President, but the breaking away of the Free-Soilers cost his election. He returned to the Senate from 1849 to 1857 and was a strong opponent of the Wilmot Proviso and a supporter of the Compromise of 1850. From 1857 to 1860 he was Buchanan's secretary of state and in this post secured from Britain a relinquishment of its search claims. He resigned in protest against Buchanan's weak reaction to South Carolina's secession. During his retirement Cass published a number of studies based on his experiences with the Indians and in France. He died in Detroit on June 17, 1866.

CASSATT, MARY (1844–1926), painter. Born on May 22, 1844, in Allegheny City, Pennsylvania, Mary Cassatt lived in Paris for five years as a young girl and later, as an artist, chose to live and work in that city. She was tutored privately in art in Philadelphia and attended the Pennsylvania Academy of Fine Arts in 1861–1865. But she preferred learning on her own and traveled to Europe to study the old masters. Her first major showing was one of five annual exhibitions in the Paris Salon in 1872. Two years later she made her residence in Paris permanent and established her studio. She shared with the Impressionists an interest in experiment and in using bright colors inspired by the out-of-doors. Edgar Degas became her friend; his style and that of Courbet inspired her own. Degas was known to admire her drawing especially and to marvel that she could be capable and a woman as well. At his request, she exhibited with the Impressionists in 1879 and joined them in later shows of 1880, 1881, and 1886. Although she was known to be an American artist, she was generally identified with the French group. Her scenes of mothers and children were celebrated examples of her warm, individual style, which featured the combination of delicate colors and strong line. The quality of the etchings she produced was compared to Whistler's. Equally fine were her color prints and pastels. She had a one-man exhibition in the Gallery of Durand-Ruel in Paris in 1891 and another larger one in 1893. Her eyesight began to fail about 1900; she ceased work by 1914 and died in her country home north of Paris on June 14, 1926.

CATHER, WILLA SIBERT (1873–1947), author. Born on December 7, 1873, in Winchester, Virginia, Miss Cather moved with her family to the frontier village of Red Cloud, Nebraska, when she was nine. In 1895 she graduated from the University of Nebraska; she was a journalist for a few years in Pittsburgh and in 1901 became a schoolteacher. In 1903 she published a book of verse, *April Twilights*, and in 1905 a collection of short stories entitled *The Troll Garden*. The latter won her a position as managing editor of *McClure's Magazine*, where she remained until retiring in 1912 to devote herself entirely to writing. Her first novel, *Alexander's Bridge*, 1912, was an unhappily contrived work, but, largely under the influence of regionalist writer Sarah Orne Jewett, she soon found her true literary inspiration in the frontier life of her childhood. *O Pioneers!*, 1913, and *My Antonia*, 1918, set the themes that were to infuse her best work, the heroic spirit of the pioneer and his conquest of hardships. *One of Ours*, 1922, won a Pulitzer Prize, and, with *A Lost Lady*, 1923, mourned the passing of the frontier and the virtues associated with it. Miss Cather's disillusionment deepened with the years and was reflected in *The Professor's House*, 1925, and in the essays collected in *Not Under Forty*, 1936. In *Death Comes for the Archbishop*, 1927, and *Shadows on the Rock*, 1931, she turned to an earlier era, that of the French missionaries in America, to recapture a heroism lost to the modern world. In 1940 she published her last novel, *Sapphira and the Slave Girl*. She died in New York City on April 24, 1947.

CATLIN, GEORGE (1796–1872), artist and author. Born on July 26, 1796, in Wilkes Barre, Pennsylvania, Catlin studied law in 1817–1818 in Litchfield, Connecticut, and practised in Pennsylvania for a short period of time. He relinquished this career in 1823 to begin another in portraiture. In this he was successful, but he developed a greater interest in the Indian tribes that had in the past battled near his birthplace. When, in 1824, he saw in Philadelphia a convention of Indians just arrived from the West, his fascination grew, and after much deliberation, and with encouragement from his adventurous wife, he embarked on a journey into the Western wilderness. Catlin met many different tribes of the Plains; he found it necessary to gain their complete trust before he could start sketching them, since most Indians felt they would surely die if their likenesses were captured on canvas. He pro-

duced hundreds of sketches, engravings, and paintings, as well as notes on the lives of the Indians. His most famous book, *Letters and Notes on the Manners, Customs and Condition of the North American Indians*, 1841, preceded many other written studies, all profusely illustrated with his sketches. While his art is not considered great, it was spontaneous and knowledgeable, perhaps the most reliable record of Indian life prepared by any scholar. It awakened inhabitants of the eastern United States to the existence and conditions of Indian tribes within their own country. He died in New Jersey on December 23, 1872. The controversy that ensued over the disposition of his collection was curious. His work was offered for purchase to Congress. But a Southern faction, fearing that the work might arouse compassion for the Indians and hamper the expansion of slavery into the West, prodded Congress into refusal. Subsequently, much of the collection was donated to the Smithsonian Institution's National Museum.

CHAFEE, ZECHARIAH (1885–1957), lawyer and legal scholar. Born in Providence, Rhode Island, on December 7, 1885, Chafee was graduated from Brown University in 1907 and then, after a short time in his father's business, entered Harvard Law School in 1910. In 1916 he joined the Harvard law faculty, becoming a professor after 1919. The restrictions on freedom of speech that were imposed during World War I roused his concern, and with his study *Freedom of Speech*, in 1920, he quickly became recognized as a leading thinker on the subject of civil liberties. In 1941 an expanded version of the book was published as *Free Speech in the United States*. From 1929 to 1931 Chafee was a consultant to the National Commission on Law Observance and Enforcement. He was a member of the Freedom of the Press Commission from 1943 to 1947 and, from 1947 onward, of the United Nations Subcommission on Freedom of Information and the Press. In 1948 he was a United States delegate to the U.N. conference in Geneva. Among his other written works are *The Inquiring Mind*,

1928, his notable introduction to the *Records of the Suffolk County Court, 1671–1680*, 1933, *Government and Mass Communications*, 2 vol., 1947, and *Blessings of Liberty*, 1956. He died in Boston on February 8, 1957.

CHANNING, WILLIAM ELLERY (1780–1842), clergyman and author. Born April 7, 1780, in Newport, Rhode Island, Channing followed his graduation from Harvard in 1798 with a year and a half as a private tutor in Virginia. During his tenure in the household of David Randolph he decided upon the ministry as his vocation; he also acquired a number of ascetic habits that had an adverse effect on his health. Returning to New England, he studied theology in Newport and at Harvard and in 1803 became pastor of the Federal Street Church in Boston, a position he held for the rest of his life. Though he thoroughly accepted the doctrines and mysteries of Christianity, his rational and moral outlook led him slowly away from Congregational orthodoxy, and particularly from its Calvinist heritage. Against his will he was caught up in the Unitarian controversy; he long resisted being labeled, but when, in 1819, he finally accepted the Unitarian name, he quickly became a leader of the movement. In 1820 he wrote a major document of the time, "The Moral Argument Against Calvinism." His many published essays and reviews won him wide recognition as a scholar. Channing had a deep influence on the men—Emerson, Longfellow, Holmes, and others—who led the great mid-century intellectual movement in New England. He was sympathetic to reform but, in accord with his generally unsocial nature, he was never active in reform organizations. He died in Bennington, Vermont, on October 2, 1842.

CHANUTE, OCTAVE (1832–1910), engineer and aviation pioneer. Born in Paris on February 18, 1832, Chanute emigrated with his parents to the United States in 1838, settling in New York. After 1853 he gained prominence as a civil engineer and a constructor of railroads and railroad bridges. In 1867–1868 he supervised the construction of the first bridge across the Missouri River at Kansas City; he was later a consulting engineer in private practice. In 1886, inspired by the earlier experiments of Otto Lilienthal and others in Europe, Chanute began a rigorous study of aerodynamics; he established a camp on the dunes of Lake Michigan and, though he was already past 60, made some 2,000 glider flights. Always methodical and scrupulous as to detailed records, he developed a number of improved glider designs. The Wright brothers openly acknowledged their debt to Chanute's data and designs, and he made several visits to their Kitty Hawk camp prior to their successful flight of 1903. In 1894 he wrote *Progress in Flying Machines*. He died in Chicago on November 23, 1910.

CHAPLIN, CHARLES SPENCER (1889–   ), motion picture actor. Born in London on April 16, 1889, the son of music-hall performers, Chaplin began his career at the age of seven as a member of a dance troupe. He was soon left on his own and grew up in poverty, shunted from one drab institution to another and sometimes living in the street. At 17 he joined the Fred Karno Company; playing in New York in 1912, he was discovered by Mack Sennett of Keystone Comedies and the next year was signed by the studio for $150 a week. By the time of his second movie, *Kid Auto Races at Venice*, 1914, he had hit upon the costume—baggy trousers borrowed from Fatty Arbuckle, outsized shoes, tight frock coat, derby hat, cane, and false mustache—in which, called variously Charlie the Tramp and the "little fellow," he rose to stardom and wealth. A new contract with Essanay studios in 1915 brought him $1,250 a week; Mutual gave him $10,000 a week and a $150,000 bonus in 1916; and in 1917 First National Exhibitors' Circuit paid him a flat million dollars for eight films. *The Tramp* in 1915 was his first experiment in mixing pathos with comedy in the figure of the little fellow; as the character developed through *Easy Street*, 1917, *Shoulder Arms*, 1918, *The Kid*, 1921, *The Pilgrim*, 1923, *The Gold Rush*, 1925, and *City*

Lights, 1931, he seemed to mellow, losing his early pugnacity and becoming more a representative of the harassed and bewildered victims of circumstance everywhere. These movies enjoyed phenomenal public success throughout the world, and Chaplin was hailed as a comic genius. In 1918 he began to produce his own films and a year later, with D. W. Griffith, Mary Pickford, and Douglas Fairbanks, he formed United Artists to bolster his and their independence. With *Modern Times* in 1936 he began to explore more deeply the potential for social comment that had been growing in his films; in *The Great Dictator*, 1940, his first talking film, he appeared both as the tramp and as a parody of Adolf Hitler. The little fellow did not survive the coming of the talkies, and by the 1940s Chaplin found himself more and more under attack by sundry groups for his presumed personal and political beliefs and for his never having become an American citizen. His personal life—including four marriages, the last to the daughter of Eugene O'Neill, and a paternity suit in 1944—was exploited in newspaper headlines; *Monsieur Verdoux*, a 1947 version of the Bluebeard story, added fuel to the fire, and in 1952 he went into a self-imposed exile in Switzerland. The tramp reappeared for the last time in 1953 in the autobiographical *Limelight*. In 1957 Chaplin produced *A King in New York*, a satire on various aspects of American life, and in 1966 produced and directed *A Countess from Hong Kong*.

CHAPMAN, JOHN (1774–1845), "Johnny Appleseed." Born on September 26, 1774, in Leominster, Massachusetts, Chapman left no record of his early life and virtually nothing is known of him before his appearance in Pennsylvania around 1800. From the apple orchards and cider presses of that state he brought seeds into Ohio and, according to the legend, planted a trail of seedling orchards along the line of the coming migration of settlers into the western territory. During the years he spent in Ohio a great number of stories grew up about him, only a few of them at all verifiable, which were passed on as an oral tradition for decades. He was eccentric in dress, his taste running to a tin plate for a hat, and seems to have supplemented his nursery business by serving also as a religious mystic and Swedenborgian missionary. Many of the anecdotes concerning him involve acts of extraordinary kindness and generosity to men and animals in addition to the more common legendary attributes of great courage and endurance. During the War of 1812 he seems to have set out alone to warn backwoods settlements of the fall of Detroit and the imminence of Indian attacks. By 1828 Chapman had carried his apple orchards as far as Indiana, and he remained there until his death near Fort Wayne in March 1845.

CHASE, SALMON PORTLAND (1808–1873), public official and jurist. Born on January 13, 1808, in Cornish, New Hampshire, Chase attended Cincinnati College, an Episcopal school run by his uncle, a bishop, and Dartmouth, graduating in 1826. He was headmaster of a boys' school in Washington, D.C., having as pupils the sons of most of John Adams' Cabinet members, and with Attorney General William Wirt read law, being admitted to the bar in 1829. Choosing Cincinnati to live and practise in in 1830, he became deeply involved in antislavery activities, writing and lecturing on reforms needed in the law. He also edited the three-volume *Statutes of Ohio*, 1833–1835, a work of great help to his profession. He subsequently gained prominence as a defense attorney in cases involving runaway slaves and was dubbed "attorney general for runaway Negroes." At first a Whig, he was active in the Liberty Party in 1841 and helped organize the Free Soil Party in 1848, elevating the issue of slavery over all other political concerns. Recognizing the need for major party support, he enlisted the Democrats with the Free Soilers in the Ohio legislature to win a Senate seat in 1849. There he vigorously opposed the extension of slavery into the territories and unsuccessfully tried to block the Compromise of 1850. Rejecting the Kansas-Nebraska Bill, he wrote the 1854 "Appeal of the Independent Democrats," calling for bans on slavery to be written into federal law; failing in this he proposed an amendment to the bill that would have allowed residents of a territory to decide whether or not to adopt slavery, but the amendment was also rejected. He joined in the formation of the Republican Party in that year and was elected the first Republican governor of Ohio in 1855, being reelected in 1859. He failed to win the Republican presidential nominations in 1856 and 1860, although he was one of the two strongest Republicans in the nation, the other being William H. Seward. Elected again to the Senate in 1860, he gave up his seat to accept President Lincoln's appointment as secretary of the treasury in 1861. He faced the monumental task of administering the country's finances during the Civil War, developing the national banking system in 1862 and reluctantly issuing "greenbacks" as legal tender to help pay for the war. His opinions on the conduct of the war and reform measures were more aggressive than Lincoln's and led to the formation of an anti-Lincoln faction in the Cabinet. His name was mentioned for the presidency in 1864. He several times presented his resignation to Lincoln; it was finally and abruptly accepted in June 1864. Although put off by Chase's aspirations to the presidency, Lincoln appointed him chief justice of the Supreme Court in October 1864. He became an advisor to President Johnson after Lincoln was assassinated and, though he presided over impeachment proceedings against him, refused to be made a tool of Radical Republicans. In 1868 and again in 1872 his name was prominently mentioned for the presidential nomination. He did not support his party's candidate, Grant, and was at odds with Congress on problems of Reconstruction. In *Ex parte Milligan*, 1866, he ruled that military trials of civilians were illegal unless civil courts were not operative or a region was under martial law. In *Mississippi* v. *Johnson* and *Georgia* v. *Stanton* he avoided political problems by approving the power of the President or Cabinet

members to enforce the Reconstruction Acts. In *Texas* v. *White*, *Cummings* v. *Missouri*, and *Ex parte Garland*, all in 1867, the sanctity of the Union was upheld, secession was declared invalid, and devices for preventing former Confederates from holding office were repudiated. In *Hepburn* v. *Griswold*, 1870, he held unconstitutional the Legal Tender Acts of 1862 that he had administered while secretary of the treasury. When the Hepburn decision was reversed in 1871 he maintained a dissenting position. He died in New York on May 7, 1873.

CHAUNCY, CHARLES (1705–1787), clergyman. Born in Boston on January 1, 1705, Chauncy graduated from Harvard in 1721. In 1727 he began his 60 years of service with the First Church of Boston. A man of keen intellect, he soon gained a prominence and influence that were rivaled only by those of Jonathan Edwards. He was the recognized leader of theological liberalism in New England and as such came into constant conflict with the conservative Edwards. In a battle of pamphlets they debated the Great Awakening, Chauncy criticizing the emotionalism of the wave of revival in his *Seasonable Thoughts on the State of Religion in New England* and other tracts. During the 1760's he devoted his energies to combatting the threatened introduction of episcopacy into New England. Late in his life he openly avowed Universalism and again engaged in debate with Edwards, issuing in 1782 *Salvation for All Men Illustrated and Vindicated as a Scripture Doctrine* and, two years later, *The Mystery Hid from Ages . . . or the Salvation of All Men*. He died in Boston on February 10, 1787.

CHILD, LYDIA MARIE (1802–1880), author and social reformer. Born on February 11, 1802, in Medford, Massachusetts, into an abolitionist family, Lydia M. Francis attended public schools, spent one year in a seminary, and was primarily influenced in her education by her brother, a Unitarian clergyman and later a professor in the Harvard Divinity

School. Her social position could have sheltered her from social ills, but her keen observation of people and conditions led her into humanitarian work. Her first literary ventures, *Hobomok*, 1824, describing early Salem and Plymouth life, and *The Rebels*, 1825, describing pre-revolutionary Boston, were received not for their creativity, but for their interest as re-creations of real life. She subtly wove into her books the idea of social reform. In 1826 she founded America's first monthly magazine for children, the *Juvenile Miscellany*. But this venture, as well as the sale of her books, terminated when, in 1833, she and her recently wedded husband published the *Appeal for That Class of Americans Called Africans*, which was considered an outrageous Abolitionist document in harboring the proposal to educate Negroes. The *Appeal* also won support; it converted some slavery advocates to Abolitionism, and induced a new awareness among groups that previously had ignored the issue. From 1840 to 1844, she and her husband edited the *National Anti-Slavery Standard*, a weekly newspaper. In 1852 they settled permanently on a farm in Weyland, Massachusetts, contributing liberally, from a small income, to the Abolitionist movement. During this time Mrs. Child wrote books on religion, history, and feminism. She spoke firmly against capital punishment. Having persevered for many years in challenging her contemporaries with difficult questions on social injustice, she died in Weyland on October 20, 1880.

CHOATE, JOSEPH HODGES (1832–1917), lawyer, public official, and statesman. Born on January 24, 1832, in Salem, Massachusetts, Choate was a cousin of attorney Rufus Choate. Graduating from Harvard in 1852, he went to law school and was admitted to the bar in Massachusetts in 1855 and in New York in 1856. His lifetime association with the New York law firm of Butler, Evarts and Southmayd began in 1856 and three years later he became a partner. He did important legal work on the wills of Cornelius Vanderbilt and Samuel J.

Tilden, the Standard Oil antitrust case, the Chinese exclusion acts, admiralty actions such as the *Republic* steamship case, railroad suits, and arguments before the Supreme Court, including proceedings in 1895 in which he established the unconstitutionality of the 1894 income tax law. A Republican in politics, he delivered major speeches for party candidates. His efforts against the Tweed Ring in 1871, in forming the Committee of Seventy to investigate graft in the city's finances, led to the disclosure and ruin of the ring. He was a famous after-dinner speaker, his only rival being Chauncy Depew. At the age of 67 he was appointed U.S. ambassador to Great Britain, a post in which he served for six years, settling the Alaskan boundary dispute and securing the abrogation of the Clayton-Bulwer treaty. He was head of the American delegation to the Second Hague Conference of 1907. He presided over the New York State Charities Aid Association, the New York Association for the Blind, and the American Society for the Judicial Settlement of International Disputes, among other cultural and humanitarian organizations. He died in New York City on May 14, 1917.

CHOATE, RUFUS (1799–1859), lawyer and public official. Born on October 1, 1799, in Essex, Massachusetts, Choate was educated at Dartmouth and graduated at the head of his class of 1819. He studied law and was admitted to the bar in 1822. For the rest of his life his primary interest was the practice of law, particularly trial law, and he became the leading trial advocate of his time. He only reluctantly engaged actively in politics; he served in the state legislature briefly and in 1830 was elected to Congress. He resigned from his second term in Congress in order to return to his practice, though he continued to work for the Whig cause in Massachusetts. In 1841 Choate assumed Webster's vacated seat in the Senate and completed the term. He declined opportunities to sit on both the state and federal supreme courts. In his politics he was a staunch and loyal Whig, and his great oratorical ability did much for the party during his brief services.

His final public position was as state attorney general in 1853–1854. Choate was conceded to be the leader of the Massachusetts bar after Webster's death; in criminal law he seems to have had no equal. In what is probably his most famous case, he successfully defended an accused murderer with a plea of somnambulism. He died while on his way to Europe, in Halifax, Nova Scotia, on July 13, 1859.

CLARK, GEORGE ROGERS (1752–1818), soldier. Born near Charlottesville, in Albermarle County, Virginia, on November 19, 1752, Clark received little formal education, but learned surveying from his grandfather and by the time of the Revolution was well known as an explorer in the western frontier region of Virginia, which is now Kentucky. His first military service came during Lord Dunmore's War against the Indians in 1774; when the war with England broke out in 1776 he persuaded the Virginia legislature to provide for the protection of the western region and was made commander of the frontier militia. With the further approval of the legislature he recruited a small force of fewer than 200 men and set out in May 1778 to subdue the Indian allies of the British and to clear the Illinois territory of enemy forces. On July 4 he surprised and captured Fort Kaskaskia; by August he had captured the outposts of Cahokia and Vincennes as well, and won the allegiance of the French settlers in the area. A force from the British stronghold at Detroit recaptured Vincennes in October but failed to maintain the initiative; after a daring and terrible mid-winter forced march, he and his men retook the settlement in February 1779. The failure of Virginia to send reinforcements or supplies made his planned march on Detroit an impossibility, and for the rest of 1779 he remained at Fort Nelson near what is now Louisville. From 1780 to 1782 he conducted several successful campaigns against the Shawnee and defended St. Louis against a British expedition. The Detroit campaign never materialized for lack of support, but Clark had conquered and held the Northwest and this was reflected, though not

explicitly stated, in the terms of the peace treaty in 1783. He and his men had received no pay for their services and he himself had advanced considerable sums of money to the cause; though a large tract of land was granted by Virginia to the "Illinois Regiment," Clark never received his due and found himself considerably in debt. He remained in the West as Indian commissioner and led his last military expedition against the Wabash tribes in 1786. In that same year he was successfully intrigued against by James Wilkinson, secretly a Spanish agent, and was discredited and relieved of his post. During the next several years he became involved in a number of abortive Western schemes initiated by the Spanish and French governments; he accepted commissions freely, apparently reserving his ultimate loyalty to the idea of Western expansion. He took refuge in St. Louis for a time in 1798 rather than surrender his French general's commission. In 1799 he returned to Louisville and there he lived, with the exception of a few years on the Indiana side of the Ohio, until his death on February 13, 1818.

CLARK, JOHN BATES (1847–1938), economist. Born in Providence, Rhode Island, on January 26, 1847, Clark was interrupted for a time in his studies but finally graduated from Amherst College in 1872. He did postgraduate work in economics at Heidelberg and Zürich, where he was strongly influenced by German historical thought. He began to teach economics and history at Carleton College in 1877; four years later he moved to Smith College, and in 1892 returned to Amherst. In 1885 he helped organize the American Economic Association and in the same year published *The Philosophy of Wealth*. It showed German influence in its insistence on the study of actual economic behavior and its strong Christian Socialist tendencies. In 1895 he joined the faculty at Columbia University, where he remained until his retirement in 1923. His major work, *The Distribution of Wealth*, was published in 1899; it is a detailed logical analysis of economics that has had a deep and lasting effect on American economic thought. It was followed by *Essentials of Economic Theory* in 1907 and *The Control of Trusts* in 1912. Clark was an active advocate of peace and from 1910 to 1923 worked with the Carnegie Endowment for International Peace, for which he instituted a comprehensive economic analysis of World War I. He died in New York City on March 21, 1938.

CLARK, WILLIAM (1770 – 1838), soldier, explorer, and public official. Born in Caroline County, Virginia, on August 1, 1770, William was the younger brother of Gen. George Rogers Clark, the conqueror of the West during the Revolution. In 1785 he moved west with his family and settled near Louisville; four years later he followed his brother into military service and participated in several militia campaigns against hostile Indian tribes. In 1792 he was commissioned a lieutenant of the regular Army and served for four years under Gen. "Mad Anthony" Wayne, taking part in 1794 in the battle of Fallen Timbers. Meriwether Lewis, his future partner in exploration, was for a time under his command. He resigned from the Army in 1796 and spent several years in travel and in ordering his estate in Louisville. In 1803 he was invited by Lewis to share command of the government-sponsored expedition to the far West then being organized at the behest of President Jefferson. He quickly accepted and devoted the next three years to this project. (For details of the expedition, see Lewis, Meriwether.) In 1807 Clark was appointed brigadier general of militia and superintendent of Indian affairs for the Louisiana Territory, establishing headquarters in St. Louis. In 1813 he became governor of the Missouri Territory; he led several volunteer military campaigns during the War of 1812 and established the first U.S. outpost in what is now Wisconsin. For several years after the war he was primarily concerned with establishing treaties with various Indian tribes and in 1825 he joined Michigan's territorial governor, Lewis Cass, in calling for and con-

ducting the negotiations at Prairie du Chien that attempted to settle permanently all Indian territorial disputes. He took an important part in the suppression of the uprisings of the Winnebago in 1827 and the Sauk, under the leadership of Black Hawk, in 1832. He died on September 1, 1838.

CLAY, CASSIUS see **ALI, MUHAMMAD**

CLAY, HENRY (1777 – 1852), lawyer and public official. Born on April 12, 1777, in Hanover County, Virginia, Clay received little formal education, but his stepfather's influence and his own industry enabled and assisted his study of law. In 1797 he was admitted to the bar and quickly moved to Lexington, Kentucky, to practise. His reputation grew rapidly and in 1803 he was elected to the state legislature. In 1806 and again in 1809 the legislature sent him to complete unexpired terms in the Senate, and in 1810 he was elected to the House of Representatives, of which he became speaker almost immediately. He led the "war hawks" in pressing for war with England in 1812 and served effectively on the peace commission in 1814. He returned to the House in 1815 and was again chosen speaker. He began developing his earlier advocacy of a protective tariff into his famous "American System" of protected domestic manufactures and internal improvements. The debate over the Missouri Compromise brought Clay to the role of mediator that he played thenceforth; distinctly nationalistic in outlook, he placed primary stress on the preservation of the Union. In 1821 he retired to Kentucky briefly, but two years later he returned to Congress where he remained, again as speaker, until becoming J. Q. Adams' secretary of state amid charges of corrupt bargaining that, though unsubstantiated, clung to him for the rest of his career. Clay had made an unsuccessful bid for the presidency in 1824; after again retiring to Kentucky in 1829, he was returned to the Senate in 1831 in preparation for the next year's election. He was again defeated, but he remained in the Senate as the leader of the opposition to Jackson and his heir, Van Buren. In 1833 he succeeded in effecting a compromise in the nullification controversy. He was bitterly disappointed when the 1840 Whig nomination that he fully and justifiably expected went instead to the obscure Gen. William Henry Harrison; he remained loyal, however, until Tyler's opposition to rechartering the United States Bank, an integral part of Clay's American System and of his earlier fight with Jackson, caused him to resign his Senate seat in 1842. Two years later he was again nominated for President, but his unfortunate maneuvering on the Texas issue lost him the election to the expansionist Polk. He opposed the coming war with Mexico until the nation was actually committed, whereupon he supported its vigorous prosecution. He was again sent to the Senate in 1849 and there proposed his famous "Omnibus Bill," leading to the Compromise of 1850. Clay remained in office until his death on June 29, 1852.

CLEMENS, SAMUEL LANGHORNE (1835–1910), "Mark Twain," humorist and author. Born in Florida, Missouri, on November 30, 1835, Clemens grew up in Hannibal, a village on the Mississippi River that was the scene of many of his later writings. His education was quite limited and at the age of 12 he was apprenticed to a printer; from 1851 to 1853 he worked on his brother's local newspaper and in the latter year set out as an itinerant printer. He had begun already to write occasional short pieces, mostly imitative, in the current style of journalistic humor, but his best work of this time was a letter to a girl friend on the subject of insects. In 1856 he apprenticed himself to a riverboat pilot and remained happily on the Mississippi until the Civil War put an end to river traffic. Partly to avoid service, in 1861 he and his brother set out for Nevada; after failures in prospecting and mining had left him in financial distress he took a job with the *Virginia City Territorial Enterprise* as a feature writer. It was while working for the *Enterprise* that he adopted "Mark Twain"

as his nom-de-plume. In 1864 he moved to San Francisco and continued in journalism. The following year he published his first notable piece, "The Celebrated Jumping Frog of Calaveras County." Reprinted widely, the tale secured him a modest fame. In the next several years he published letters produced during several trips, culminating in *Innocents Abroad*, 1869, a great popular success. In 1870 he settled in Hartford, Connecticut. Then began his most productive period; from that year to 1894 he wrote and published his best-known works: *The Gilded Age* (with C.D. Warner), 1873, *The Adventures of Tom Sawyer*, 1876, *A Tramp Abroad*, 1880, *Life on the Mississippi*, 1883, *The Adventures of Huckleberry Finn*, 1884, *A Connecticut Yankee in King Arthur's Court*, 1889, and *Pudd'nhead Wilson*, 1894. A number of ill-considered investments brought Clemens into bankruptcy in the early '90s, and there followed a world lecture tour and a number of lesser works as he strove to repay his debts. Several deaths in his family, including his wife's, accelerated his late tendency toward a pessimistic and sometimes bitter outlook on humanity; this attitude dominates such late writings as "The Man That Corrupted Hadleyburg" and *The Mysterious Stranger*. In his last years he began an autobiography and wrote numerous articles, many expressing his outrage at man's seemingly innate cruelty. Clemens died on April 21, 1910, in Hartford.

CLEVELAND, STEPHEN GROVER (1837–1908), public official and twice U.S. President. Born in Caldwell, New Jersey, on March 18, 1837, Cleveland was prevented from attending college by the need to support his widowed mother. After four years of study in a law office in Buffalo, he was admitted to the bar in 1859. He immediately joined the Democratic Party. Hiring a substitute for his Civil War service, he entered politics and held a number of local posts, including, in 1870, that of county sheriff. In 1881 he was chosen as Democratic nominee for mayor of Buffalo; pledged to reform, he was elected and surprised a great many people by actually undertaking to reform the city's government. His record in Buffalo, combined with his lack of identification with political bosses, won him the nomination and subsequently the election as governor of New York in 1882. He continued his honest and efficient approach to government and gained a valuable political asset in the open enmity of Tammany Hall. The same qualifications that had made him governor brought him the nomination for President in 1884; in a vicious campaign he defeated the corruption-stained Blaine. In his quiet first term the first Democratic President since the Civil War devoted himself to promoting honest government by means of civil service reform and halting the notorious flow of dubious pension legislation. His advocacy of tariff reduction weakened his position, however, and he failed of reelection in 1888, although he gained a plurality of the popular vote. Cleveland retired to private law practice. In 1892 he was nominated again and elected to a second and stormy term. The Panic of 1893 broke soon after his inauguration, and he alienated the pro-silver West by forcing the repeal of the Sherman Silver Purchase Act. The heavy drains on the Treasury forced him to purchase gold from J. P. Morgan and his associates. In response to the Pullman strike of 1894 he sent federal troops into Illinois over Governor Altgeld's protests. Losing control even of his own party, he was thwarted by Congress in his attempts to lower the tariff. The foreign policy of his second administration was marked by his repudiation of the overthrow of the Hawaiian monarchy by a group of American residents who had had the support of the previous administration, and his forceful dealing with Great Britain in its border dispute with Venezuela. By 1896 he had lost all influence in his party and in the Democratic Convention of that year the opposition to his fiscal policies culminated in the nomination of Bryan. Cleveland retired to live quietly in Princeton, New Jersey, and, his prestige returning with the passage of time, he engaged in private pursuits, including the

successful reorganization of the discredited Equitable Life Assurance Company in 1905. He died on June 24, 1908.

CLINTON, DE WITT (1769–1828), public official. Born in Little Britain, New York, on March 2, 1769, DeWitt was a nephew of George Clinton. He graduated from Columbia College in 1786 and for three years studied law. In 1790 he began his practice and also became secretary to his uncle, then governor of the state. In 1797 he was elected to the state assembly and from 1798 to 1802 served in the state senate; though strongly criticized for his actions as a member of the Council of Appointments—he was charged with introducing the spoils system in New York—he was elected to the U.S. Senate in 1802. Serving only a few months, he resigned in 1803 to become mayor of New York City, an office he held, except for two years, until 1815; during the same period he was a member of the state senate from 1806 to 1811 and lieutenant governor from 1811 to 1813. He advocated and secured many liberal measures during these years, including the opening of New York City's first public school and the removal of political restrictions on Roman Catholics. In 1812 Northern Republicans, resentful of the "Virginia dynasty," nominated him to oppose Madison for the presidency; his campaign was unsuccessful, and his ability to attract Federalist support alienated many in his own party. From 1811 onward Clinton concerned himself primarily with the proposal to construct a canal from Lake Erie to the Hudson River; he was a member of successive commissions appointed to investigate the project and devoted much effort to enlisting public and legislative support. In 1817 he was elected governor and work began on the canal shortly afterward. The growing opposition of the pro-Virginia Tammany Republicans, led by Martin Van Buren, forced him to retire in 1823 after a second term; his removal from the canal commission the next year, however, roused a storm of protest, and he was easily returned to office. He was thus governor when "Clinton's ditch" — the Erie Canal — was opened in October 1825, and remained so until his death on February 11, 1828.

CLINTON, GEORGE (1739–1812), soldier and public official. Born on July 26, 1739, in Little Britain, New York, Clinton went to sea briefly when he was 18, served in the French and Indian War, and about 1762 took up the practice of law. In 1768 he was elected to the New York Provincial Assembly where he served until 1775, when he was elected to the Continental Congress. In the same year he was appointed brigadier general of the state militia and sent to defend New York and the Hudson River. Though he was militarily inept and offered to resign his commission, he was retained, given a second commission by Congress, and in 1777 elected both governor and lieutenant governor of New York. He declined the latter office but remained governor for 18 years. He had a profound distrust of centralized government and strongly opposed New York's ratification of the Constitution in 1788. He was a follower of Jefferson and was instrumental in promoting Aaron Burr's rise to prominence. He retired from the governorship in 1795 but returned for another term in 1800. In 1804 he was elected Vice President and, after an unsuccessful bid for the presidential nomination in 1808, was reelected to the office for a second term. In 1811, in his position as president of the Senate, he cast the deciding vote against the rechartering of the Bank of the United States. He died on April 20, 1812.

COBB, TYRUS RAYMOND (1886–1961), baseball player. Born in Banks County, Georgia, on December 18, 1886, Ty Cobb was the son of a noted Georgia educator and political figure. He began playing baseball seriously at the age of nine and by 1905 was appearing regularly with the Augusta team of the South Atlantic League. He had already been given the nickname "the Georgia Peach" by sportswriter Grantland Rice when, in that year, he was signed by the Detroit Tigers. During his 22

seasons as an outfielder with the Tigers he established himself as baseball's most aggressive and probably greatest player, certainly its greatest hitter. Other players, umpires, even teammates, were fair game when he lost his temper, and even when he didn't he was a force to be reckoned with. A master of the hook and fall-away slides, he was nearly as well known for spiking basemen as for stealing bases. From 1921 to 1926 he managed the Tigers in addition to playing regularly in the outfield; but after two years with the Philadelphia Athletics under Connie Mack he retired in 1928. By that time he had amassed 58 offensive records — a record in itself — and 12 of them still stand, including highest lifetime batting average (.367), batting championships won (12), games played (3,033), seasons batting .300 or better (23), and, perhaps above all, total bases stolen (829). When the first ballot was taken for the Baseball Hall of Fame in 1936 Cobb led all other nominees. After his retirement he returned to Atlanta, Georgia, where he lived quietly and prosperously on the proceeds from prudent investments until his death on July 17, 1961.

CODY, WILLIAM FREDERICK (1846–1917), "Buffalo Bill," frontiersman and showman. Born in Scott County, Iowa, on February 26, 1846, Cody had little education and went to work at the age of 12. By the outbreak of the Civil War he had been by turns a horse wrangler, a mounted messenger for a freight company, an unsuccessful prospector, and a Pony Express rider. The family had moved to Kansas some years before the war came; Cody rode with the Jayhawkers for a time before enlisting in 1863 as a scout with the 9th Kansas cavalry regiment. Later he was a scout with the regular Union Army in operations in Tennessee and Missouri. Soon after the war he took a job as a hunter for a company that had contracted to supply food for the construction crews of the Kansas Pacific Railroad and during 1867–1868 he killed, by his own count, 4,280 buffaloes. For the next four years he was again an army scout in various Indian campaigns; during this time, in 1869, he met E. Z. C. Judson —"Ned Buntline"—who, seeing in him the makings of a popular hero, dubbed him "Buffalo Bill" and proceeded to feature him in a series of highly fictionalized and sensational dime novels. In 1872 Judson wrote a play, *Scouts of the Plains* (later *Scouts of the Prairies*), which successfully toured Eastern cities starring Cody, under his new name, and "Texas Jack" Omohundro, later replaced by "Wild Bill" Hickok. In 1876 Cody returned briefly to scouting and in July of that year killed and scalped Yellow Hand, a Cheyenne leader, in a famous duel. He soon returned to the stage and until 1883 divided his time between show business and his Nebraska ranch. In 1883 he organized his own highly successful "Wild West" show and played to audiences in the East, in Great Britain, and in Europe; the show featured Cody, the famed lady marksman Annie Oakley, and, briefly, Sitting Bull. He later acquired an extensive ranch in Montana where he lived between tours of the "Wild West" troupe. On January 10, 1917, he died suddenly in Denver; after lying in state, his body was buried in a solid rock tomb at the top of nearby Lookout Mountain.

COHAN, GEORGE MICHAEL (1878–1942), composer, playwright, and actor. Born on July 3, 1878, in Providence, Rhode Island, Cohan was called the "Yankee Doodle Dandy" by his father; from then on, his birthdate was advertised as July 4th. He played juvenile roles in productions with his family, a touring vaudeville troop; in his teens he wrote plays and composed songs, and later formed his own group, "The Four Cohans," starring himself, his wife, and his parents. He moved on to legitimate theater, where he wrote his own plays, invariably casting himself in the leading roles, which were often patriotic. His plays' titles identified their themes: *The Wise Guy*, *The Governor's Son*, 1901, *The Man Who Owns Broadway*, 1908, *The Yankee Prince*, 1909, *Get-Rich-Quick Wallingford*, 1910, *The Song and Dance Man*, 1923, and *American Born*, 1925, among many others. He excelled

neither in singing, dancing, nor acting, but he captivated audiences with his stage personality, which was at once unique and endearing. When his cheerful, hand-slapping spectators would become quiet, he roused them once again, characteristically with a patriotic gesture. He would often bring the house down by waving a flag and dancing with it across the stage. One of his songs, "Over There," composed in honor of the American Expeditionary Forces in World War I, won him a special medal from Congress in 1940. Other Cohan songs such as "You're A Grand Old Flag," "Mary's a Grand Old Name," "Give My Regards to Broadway," "I'm A Yankee Doodle Dandy," "Goodbye Flo," "Harrigan," and "Hot Tamale Alley" have entered the American tradition. In a break from performing his own roles, he acted the part of the father in Eugene O'Neill's *Ah, Wilderness!* in 1933. His biography, *Twenty Years on Broadway and the Years it Took to Get There*, was published in 1925, and an academy award winning movie was made based on his life. When he died on November 5, 1942, in New York City, he had achieved the stature of a public hero.

COLE, THOMAS (1801–1848), poet and painter. Born on February 1, 1801, in Bolton-le-Moors, Lancashire, England, Cole traveled with his family to the United States, settling first in Pennsylvania in 1819, then in Steubenville, Ohio, in 1820. There he worked as a wood-block engraver in his father's wallpaper factory for two years. He met a wandering artist who taught him to paint and, desirous of reproducing the vivid colors of the American autumn and the beauty of its spring, he resolved to devote himself henceforth to painting. He set out on foot at the age of 21, wandering through Ohio and Pennsylvania painting portraits, and hoping to make his fortune. In 1823 he settled briefly in Philadelphia, attended the Pennsylvania Academy of Fine Arts, and resumed writing in his spare time, contributing poetry and stories to various magazines. Business called his family to New

York and he joined them there; he continued to paint and exhibited a few landscapes in a shop window, attracting the attention of John Trumbull, Asher Durand, and William Cullen Bryant. Moving to Catskill, Cole began painting the scenes of the Hudson River valley; his work grew in popularity and, joined by Durand and others, he became the acknowledged leader of the Hudson River School, the first native American movement in painting. From 1829 to 1832 he traveled and painted in Europe. On his return he spent four years in New York, during which time he created on commission his great allegorical "Course of Empire," a series of five canvases – "Primeval Nature," "Pastoral Life," "Wealth and Glory," "War," and "Desolation." In 1839 he produced in a similar vein "The Voyage of Life," depicting in four canvases "Childhood," "Youth," "Manhood," and "Old Age." His symbolic work became more religious as he grew older. While working on "The Pilgrim of the Cross," one of a projected series of paintings entitled "The Cross and the World," he became ill and died in Catskill on February 11, 1848.

COLT, SAMUEL (1814 – 1862), inventor and manufacturer. Born in Hartford, Connecticut, on July 19, 1814, Colt worked as a youth in his father's textile factory in Ware, Massachusetts, and attended school until he went to sea in 1830. While on a voyage to India he conceived the idea for a repeating firearm that would utilize an automatically revolving set of chambers, each of which would be brought successively into alignment with a single barrel. He made a wooden model for a pistol and soon after his return to America had two working models, one of which exploded. In order to finance improved prototypes he toured for a time as "Dr. Coult," demonstrating laughing gas and taking up collections. Finally, with good working models, he secured English and French patents in 1835 and a U.S. patent in 1836. In March of that year he founded the Patent Arms Manufacturing Co., in Paterson, New Jersey, to manufacture

his guns by the most efficient methods available: mass production of completely interchangeable parts, assembly line procedure, and inspection of the final product by trained personnel. Though popular with individuals, including Andrew Jackson, the Colt gun failed to interest the Army and the company went out of business in 1842. For the next several years Colt worked on perfecting an underwater mine system for harbor defense; from this he turned to telegraphy and experimented with submarine cable. The outbreak of the Mexican War finally generated a demand for his revolver; many Westerners, particularly Texans, would use no other, and the Army, impressed at last, ordered 1,000 Colts. He hurriedly subcontracted much of the production to Eli Whitney's factory until he began manufacturing in his own factory in Hartford in 1848. Success and fortune secured, he continued to direct the manufacture of his famous .44 until his death in Hartford on January 10, 1862. The revolver, the 19th century's major development in weaponry, went on to play a crucial role in the settlement of the West as well as in warfare.

COLUMBUS, CHRISTOPHER (1451 – 1506), explorer. Born in Genoa, quite possibly of a Spanish-Jewish family, Columbus (Cristóbal Colón) took to sea early in life. In 1476 he was shipwrecked off the coast of Portugal; he made his way to Lisbon, then the center of exploration and discovery. During the next several years he made a number of voyages, to Iceland, the Madeiras, and elsewhere, and was slowly formulating his ideas on sailing to Cathay. He was primarily influenced, not by astronomical considerations, but by the books of Esdras in the Apocrypha. His calculations placed India just where the Americas lie. He proposed an exploration, first to the king of Portugal, who rejected it, to a Spanish nobleman, who could not afford it, and finally to King Ferdinand and Queen Isabella of Spain. From 1486 to 1492 his plan was under consideration; finally, in the latter year, and despite Columbus' extravagant demands for reward, permission and money were granted. On August 3rd the three-ship fleet—the *Niña*, the *Pinta*, and the *Santa Maria*—sailed; after a good deal of indecision and several threats of mutiny, land was sighted on October 12th. Disembarking on the island he named San Salvador, he tarried only briefly and spent the next several weeks looking for gold and the mainland of China. After finding only more islands and leaving a small colony, he set out for Spain in January. He landed in Portugal, was received with great honor in Spain, and was granted huge privileges; he demanded the reward offered to the first to sight land, to the dismay of the sailor who had actually done so. Later that year he returned to the Caribbean as governor; he found more islands and decided that Cuba was the mainland. His administration of the region was tyrannical. He dispatched a shipload of captive Indians to Spain and in 1496 returned himself. Two years later he set out on his third voyage. Again he missed the mainland; his governorship meanwhile resulted in growing hostility among the natives and rebellion among his men, and in 1500 he was replaced as governor. He resisted the change, however, and was returned to Spain forcibly. Ferdinand and Isabella were thoroughly disenchanted with Columbus' administrative abilities by this time, but still indebted to him as an admiral. After toying with the idea of liberating Jerusalem, he decided to return to the New World. In 1502 he made his final voyage; he at last discovered the mainland of Central America, though he apparently did not recognize it as such. He reported that he was quite near to Cathay and that he was being guided by dreams and voices from on high. Beset by difficulties, his fleet disintegrated and he became seriously ill; in 1504 he returned to Spain and died on May 20, 1506, having been, despite his many shortcomings, unquestionably a man of great vision and courage.

COMMONS, JOHN ROGERS (1862–1945), economist. Born on October 13, 1862, in Hollandsburg, Ohio, Commons graduated from Oberlin College in 1888 and for two years pursued further studies at Johns Hopkins University. In 1890 he became an instructor of political economy at Wesleyan University; two years later he returned to Oberlin as professor of sociology. After holding similar positions at Indiana University and Syracuse University, he joined the economics faculty of the University of Wisconsin in 1904. There he devoted himself to the study of American labor and, later, of the role of collective action generally in the development of the American economy. In collaboration with a group of his students he published the 10-volume *Documentary History of American Industrial Society*, 1910–1911, and the 4-volume *History of Labor in the United States*, 1918–1935. He was one of a number of professors at the University of Wisconsin enlisted by Gov. Robert M. La Follette to draft reform legislation for the state; Commons himself was particularly interested in establishing a system of unemployment insurance. From 1913 to 1915 he was a member of the Federal Commission on Industrial Relations, in 1917 he was president of the American Economic Association, and from 1920 to 1928 he was associate director of the National Bureau of Economic Research. His later studies led to the publication of *The Legal Foundations of Capitalism*, 1924, and *Institutional Economics*, 1934, among many other works. He retired as professor emeritus in 1932 and thereafter lived in Fort Lauderdale, Florida, and Raleigh, North Carolina. In 1935 he published *Myself*, an autobiography. He died in Raleigh on May 11, 1945.

COMPTON, ARTHUR HOLLY (1892–1962), physicist and educator. Born on September 10, 1892, in Wooster, Ohio, Compton came of a family that was to be renowned for its educators. He graduated from the College of Wooster, where his father was professor and dean, in 1913 and went on to graduate studies at Princeton, taking his Ph.D. in 1916. After a year teaching physics at the University of Minnesota and a time spent in private industry, he went to Cambridge University for further study. In 1920 he became head of the physics department at Washington University in St. Louis; in 1923 he moved to the University of Chicago and remained there until the end of World War II. In 1923 he published the results of his studies of the scattering of X rays by matter; he observed an increase of wavelength in some of the reflected rays—the Compton effect—and provided an explanation that became a key contribution to the development of the quantum theory of energy. For this work Compton was named a co-winner of the 1927 Nobel Prize for Physics. He later turned to the study of cosmic rays and in the early 1930s supervised a world-wide cosmic ray survey. In 1940 he became chairman of the physics department and dean of the physical sciences division at the University of Chicago. In 1941 he was named chairman of a committee of the National Academy of Sciences formed to study the military applications of atomic energy; the next year he became director of the Metallurgical Laboratory of the Manhattan Project, his goal being the synthesis of sufficient plutonium for one or more atomic bombs. From 1945 to 1953 Compton was chancellor of Washington University and from 1953 to 1961 distinguished service professor of natural philosophy. A man of broadly humanitarian and deeply religious convictions, he published, in addition to his technical works, *The Freedom of Man*, 1935, *The Religion of a Scientist*, 1938, *The Human Meaning of Science*, 1940, and *Atomic Quest*, 1956, the story of the Manhattan Project. Compton served in many high governmental advisory positions and continued to lecture regularly until his death on March 15, 1962, in Berkeley, California.

COMSTOCK, ANTHONY (1844–1915), reformer. Born on March 7, 1844, in New Canaan, Connecticut, Comstock lost his mother at the age of 10, whereupon he elevated her image to an ideal in whose honor he fought during his later career. He attended Wyckoff's Academy and a public high school in Connecticut, then enlisted in the Union Army to replace his younger brother who had been killed in the Battle of Gettysburg. After his discharge he was employed as a shopclerk and a salesman in various towns in Connecticut, Tennessee, and New York. In 1872 he became involved with the Young Men's Christian Association in a crusade against pornographic literature. Such reforms became his life's work, and he lobbied vigorously and effectively in Washington for laws to prevent obscene literature from being sent through the mails. He became a special inspector for the New York City post office and helped to organize the New York Society for the Suppression of Vice, under whose auspices he worked indefatigably to prosecute "criminal offenders," a term that encompassed, in his view, writers and poets, painters working from nude models, quack doctors, abortionists, and fraudulent advertisers. His moral judgments were narrow and often arbitrary; he was denounced for censuring valuable works of art, but praised for prosecuting actual frauds. Among his pamphlets and books for young people were *Frauds Exposed*, 1880, *Traps for the Young*, 1883, *Gambling Outrages*, 1887, and *Morals Versus Art*, 1888. He was responsible for the trial of women's rights crusader Victoria Claflin Woodhull, for the "crime" of exposing a love affair between clergyman Henry Ward Beecher and a parishoner's wife. He instituted legal proceedings against George Bernard Shaw's play, *Mrs. Warren's Profession*, in 1905; Shaw had by this time already coined the term "comstockery" as a disparaging and sarcastic label for puritanical crusading. One of the many commissions on which he served was President Wilson's International Purity Congress. He died in New York City on September 21, 1915.

CONANT, JAMES BRYANT (1893–   ), scientist, diplomat, and educator. Born in Dorchester, Massachusetts, on March 26, 1893, Conant was educated at Harvard, graduating in 1913 and receiving his Ph.D. three years later. After duty with the chemical warfare service in World War I, he joined the faculty at Harvard as an instructor in chemistry, his work in the field of organic chemistry winning him wide recognition as a brilliant investigator. In 1933 he became president of Harvard, a post he retained until his retirement 20 years later. As chairman of the National Defense Research Committee during World War II, he was instrumental in organizing scientific research and development programs in the United States, particularly those leading to the production of the atomic bomb. After the war he was a member of both the Atomic Energy Commission and the National Science Foundation. In 1953 he was appointed United States high commissioner for Western Germany and in 1955 became ambassador to the Federal Republic. Upon his return to America in 1957 he undertook for the Carnegie Foundation an influential study of American high schools. His written work ranges from *Chemistry of Organic Compounds*, 1933, to *On Understanding Science*, 1947, and from *Education and Liberty*, 1953, to his Carnegie report, *The American High School Today*, 1959.

CONKLING, ROSCOE (1829–1888), lawyer and public official. Born on October 30, 1829, in Albany, New York, the son of a New York congressman and federal judge, Conkling attended the Mount Washington Collegiate Institute in New York City from 1842 and studied law in Utica after 1846. He was admitted to the New York bar in 1850. He made campaign speeches for Zachary Taylor and Millard Fillmore in 1848 and gained recognition for his oratorical and legal skills. In 1850 he became Albany's district attorney. Initially a Whig, he helped form the Republican party and in supporting John C. Frémont, its presidential candidate, won New York State for the party in 1856. In 1858 he was elected mayor of Utica and from 1859 to 1867, except for the years 1863–1865, was in Congress. Advocating a vigorous prosecution of the Civil War and repressive measures against the South during Reconstruction, he played a prominent role in bringing impeachment proceedings against President Johnson. He was

elected to the Senate in 1867, 1873, and 1879. As undisputed party leader in his state, he influenced President Grant's Southern policies and was himself a presidential hopeful in 1876, but lost the nomination to Rutherford B. Hayes, whose bitter enemy he was thereafter. In 1880 he led the move to nominate Grant for a third term, but was only successful in splitting the convention. He fought Garfield's nomination even after Chester A. Arthur, one of his chief assistants in the party organization in New York, was selected for the vice presidency. Continually resisting federal control of jobs in the New York Custom House, he finally resigned his Senate seat in 1881 when Garfield sent federal appointees to fill the posts. Offered a Supreme Court justiceship in 1882 by President Arthur, he declined, but sought reelection to the Senate in 1885 to vindicate himself. Finding himself no longer in a controlling position in the Albany legislature, he returned to a successful legal practice and died in New York on April 18, 1888.

CONWELL, RUSSELL HERMAN (1843–1925), lawyer, lecturer, and clergyman. Born in South Worthington, Massachusetts, on February 15, 1843, Conwell grew up on a farm that served as a station on the Underground Railway. His education at Yale was interrupted by the Civil War; he raised a company and was eventually promoted lieutenant colonel. After his admission to the bar in 1865 he moved to Minneapolis to practise; while there he founded the *Minneapolis Daily Chronicle*. Moving to Boston a few years later, he continued to practise law and founded the *Somerville* (Mass.) *Journal*. He became interested in a run-down Baptist church in Lexington and, having successfully revived it, became its minister in 1879. Three years later he was called to perform the same service for the Grace Baptist Church in Philadelphia. He succeeded spectacularly; the huge Baptist Temple opened in 1891, he saw three hospitals established, and a night school he had begun in 1884 became Temple University. With his lecture "Acres of

Diamonds," first delivered in 1861 but often modified afterwards, Conwell achieved widespread fame and became one of the most noted Chautauqua speakers. Little more than a summary of the philosophy of industry and the idea that opportunity is everywhere, the simple speech was delivered more than 6,000 times and eventually earned its author over $8 million. He died on December 6, 1925.

COOKE, JAY (1821–1905), financier. Born near the present site of Sandusky, Ohio, on August 10, 1821, Cooke became a clerk in a local store at the age of 14 and later held a similar job in St. Louis. In 1837 he went to Philadelphia and after two years working for a canal boat company entered the banking house of E. W. Clark and Company. By 1842 he was a partner in the firm. He left Clark in 1858 and three years later established his own banking house, Jay Cooke and Company, which almost immediately floated a $3 million war loan for the state of Pennsylvania. The next year Salmon P. Chase, a friend of Cooke's brother Henry, became secretary of the treasury; the national government was having great difficulty in selling bonds with which to finance the Civil War, and in October 1862 Chase appointed Cooke special agent to sell the securities. Cooke set up a nationwide network of subagent salesmen and by January 1864 had exceeded the $500 million authorized by Congress. Meanwhile he had established national banks in Philadelphia and Washington, D.C. In 1865 Secretary of the Treasury Fessenden again prevailed upon Cooke to aid in the sale of a new bond issue; within six months his reorganized distribution system disposed of some $600 million worth. After the war he extended his banking interests, opening branches in New York and London, and in 1870 plunged most of his available capital into financing the construction of the Northern Pacific, a transcontinental railroad planned to run from Duluth to Tacoma. The speculative bubble in railroad stocks soon burst, however, and in 1873 Jay Cooke and Company failed, precipitating the general financial panic of that year. By 1880 he had repaid his creditors and, through investments in western mining and other ventures, soon recouped his fortune. He died on February 18, 1905, in Ogontz, Pennsylvania.

COOLIDGE, JOHN CALVIN (1872–1933), public official and 30th U.S. President. Born on July 4, 1872, in Plymouth, Vermont, Coolidge graduated from Amherst College in 1895 and two years later began the practice of law. He quietly entered politics and rose steadily from post to post, accumulating a solid reputation for honesty, party loyalty, and completely unspectacular ability. After three terms as lieutenant governor of Massachusetts he was duly elected governor in 1918. His administration would doubtless have passed unnoticed but for the Boston police strike of the following year. In the face of rioting and looting while the police force demanded union recognition, Coolidge delayed action until local authority was clearly paralyzed; he then mobilized the state militia to restore order, and in a message to Samuel Gompers denying reinstatement of the striking police, one sentence—"There is no right to strike against the public safety by anybody, anywhere, any time"—brought him immediate national fame. He was reelected governor later that year and in 1920, after losing the presidential nomination to Harding, easily captured the nomination for Vice President. In his new office he carried on as before, quietly and unremarkably. Harding's death in 1923 made him President; for the remainder of the term and after his reelection in 1924, Coolidge maintained his popularity with his honest, simple, and frugal manner. A strong supporter of business, he encouraged the stock market boom of the 1920s, greatly reduced governmental action against trusts, and promptly vetoed bills of a liberal cast. His foreign policy was not so much one of isolationism as of aloofness. With characteristic resolution and brevity, he declined renomination with the statement: "I do not choose to run for President in 1928." He retired to private business and published occasional articles on public issues. He died on January 5, 1933.

COOPER, GARY (1901–1961), actor. Born on May 7, 1901, in Helena, Montana, Cooper was named Frank James but adopted "Gary" at the start of his movie career. The son of a Montana supreme court justice, he went to high school in Bozeman and attended Wesleyan College and Grinnell College in Iowa until 1924, leaving without a degree. He was a hand on the family ranch during World War I, tending 450 head of cattle, later commenting that the work had been far from romantic. He moved to Los Angeles after college and worked as a salesman for an advertising firm and a photography studio. In 1925 he was hired by Western Studios as a rider at $10 a day. Inspired by Tom Mix, he turned to acting. After playing bit roles in several films he received his first major part opposite Vilma Banky in *The Winning of Barbara Worth* in 1926. After this, successive hits included *It*, with Clara Bow, *The Lives of a Bengal Lancer*, *Wings*, *Mr. Deeds Goes to Town*, *The Virginian*, *The Westerner*, *For Whom the Bell Tolls*, *Saratoga Trunk*, *Desire*, *Friendly Persuasion*, *Along Came Jones*, and *A Farewell to Arms*. So compelling were his heroic roles—in *The Plainsman*, *Cloak and Dagger*, *Task Force*, *Pride of the Yankees*, *The Story of Dr. Wassell*, and *Sergeant York*, among other films—that he came to personify the "all-American male" in the hearts of millions. Lanky, ungrammatical, and seemingly quite ordinary, he personified in his most popular roles the simple, average man who triumphs through courage and goodness of heart. In the homely, laconic western dialect that he made famous, his most celebrated lines were "Yup" and "They went that-a-way." In 1941 he won an Academy Award for *Sergeant York* and in 1953 for *High Noon*. In 1961 actor James Stewart accepted a special Academy Award for him with a brief, emotional tribute. He died that year in Hollywood, on May 13th.

COOPER, JAMES FENIMORE (1789–1851), author. Born in Burlington, New Jersey, on September 15, 1789, Fenimore Cooper grew up in Cooperstown, New York, a settlement founded by his well-to-do father. Without completing his education at Yale, he went to sea in 1806; he served in the Navy from 1808 to 1811, and in the latter year returned to the life of a country aristocrat. Not until he was 30 did he begin to write; then in quick succession he produced *Precaution* in 1820, *The Spy* in 1821, *The Pioneers*, the first of what were to be the Leatherstocking Tales, in 1823, and *The Pilot*, also in 1823. Buoyed by success and already the leading novelist in America, Cooper took his family abroad in 1826 for several years. While traveling in Europe he wrote *The Last of the Mohicans*, 1826, and *The Prairie*, 1827, both in the Leatherstocking series, in addition to a number of lesser romances, political tracts, and travel letters. In 1833 he returned to the United States and continued to produce books at a prodigious rate. In 1838 two novels, *Homeward Bound* and *Home as Found*, and a work of social and political criticism, *The American Democrat*, summed up Cooper's growing dissatisfaction with America; theoretically a democrat but practically an aristocrat, his attempt to synthesize the two views pleased no one, and he found himself constantly at odds with nearly everyone. He instituted a number of libel suits against his less courteous critics and won most of them. In 1838 he also wrote a history of the U.S. Navy and in 1840 and 1841 he published the last two of the Leatherstocking Tales, *The Pathfinder* and *The Deerslayer*. His later works were of lesser note; in all, he wrote 50 major books in his 32-year literary career. At his death, on September 14, 1851, he was probably America's foremost, if not most beloved, man of letters; his fame, however, was quickly overshadowed by that of such men as Emerson and Hawthorne.

COOPER, PETER (1791–1883), manufacturer, inventor, and philanthropist. Born on February 12, 1791, in New York City, Cooper received little formal education and was at 17 apprenticed to a coach maker. He worked in various fields of industry until in 1828 he founded the Canton Iron Works in Baltimore; there, two years later, he built the first American steam locomotive, "Tom Thumb." His business holdings grew rapidly. In 1854 one of his factories produced the first iron structural beams for fire-retardant buildings; two years later he introduced the Bessemer process into American steelmaking. He was a principal supporter of Cyrus Field and was instrumental in the success of the New York, Newfoundland, and London Telegraph Company, of which he was president for 20 years. In 1859 he founded the Cooper Union in New York City; devoted to free public education, particularly for adults, in technical and scientific fields and in art, the Union included among its facilities the city's first free public reading room. In 1876 he was the presidential nominee of the Greenback Party. Cooper died on April 4, 1883, in New York City.

COPLAND, AARON (1900–   ), composer and author. Born on November 14, 1900, in Brooklyn, New York, Copland studied musical composition and orchestration, counterpoint and harmony with Rubin Goldmark in New York until 1921; he then moved to Paris and worked with Nadia Boulanger until 1924. While in France, he observed that the native music reflected the character of French life. No like relation existed between America and its music, and he determined on his return to America to compose music that Americans would appreciate and that would reflect their environment, culture, history, and legends. Some early work, developing his technique and musicianship and identifying him as a singular composer, included *The Cat and Mouse*, 1919, *Symphony for Organ and Orchestra*, 1924, and *Music for Theater*, 1925. Prepared to transcribe his ideas into "native" music, he began work that he hoped would relate to and, consequently, please the American audience. He succeeded. His *Lincoln Portrait* for orchestra and speaker, 1942, and three ballets, *Appalachian Spring*, 1944, *Billy the Kid*, 1938, and *Rodeo*, 1942, used familiar American melodies, drawn from popular recordings, folk songs, and cowboy tunes. As a

result, he was hailed by modern audiences, which had become accustomed to listening to music with little thought for simple enjoyment. An adventurous composer, he produced other works with jazz rhythms, concurrent themes, wide expanses of tone, and unorthodox instrumental combinations. In 1939, he was asked to compose music for the play *Quiet City*. He consented to write the score, and, subsequently, several others for motion pictures, including *Of Mice and Men*, 1939, *Our Town*, 1940, *The Red Pony*, 1948, and *The Heiress*, 1949. He also wrote several books: *What To Listen For in Music*, 1939, *Our New Music*, 1941, *Music and Imagination*, 1952, and *Copland on Music*, 1960.

COPLEY, JOHN SINGLETON (1738–1815), painter. Born on July 3, 1738, into a loyalist family in Boston, Copley learned to paint and engrave from his stepbrother, Peter Pelham. Pelham died in 1751, leaving his business to Copley, who mastered the trade and produced mezzotints, at least one of which still survives. His ambition to be a professional painter was realized at the age of 18. Conforming to the fashion of colonial portraiture, he soon achieved a reputation and acquired great wealth for the period in which he lived. Paintings such as "Paul Revere," "Samuel Adams," and "John Hancock" spread his fame through New England. Commissions from Boston, New York, and Philadelphia encouraged him to go farther afield, and in 1766 he sent "The Boy With a Squirrel" to London for exhibition. It earned for him fellowship in the Society of Artists of Great Britain, as well as an enduring friendship with the prominent artist Benjamin West, who urged Copley to paint in England. During the 1770s, Copley's commissions declined, perhaps because of his affiliations with the Tory party, and he therefore embarked for Europe, vacationing for a year in Italy and in 1775 settling permanently in London. There events of historical and biblical significance dominated his work. English art of the time featured idealism, but Copley retained his direct approach, recreating scenes such as "The Death of Chatham," "The Siege of Gibraltar," "The Arrest of Five Members of the Commons by Charles the First," and "Abraham Offering Up Isaac" with a passion that sometimes shocked refined English patrons of art. But Copley's reputation had been established, and in 1783 he received a full membership in the Royal Academy. He was visited in London by John Adams and John Quincy Adams, who commissioned portraits. Portraiture failed to bring the degree of financial success he had hoped for, however, while his historical paintings, such as "The Siege of Gibraltar" and "The Victory of Lord Duncan," on which he hoped to found his artistic reputation, went relatively unrecognized. Though he was acknowledged during his lifetime as the first great American painter, he continued to labor in frustration until his death in London on September 9, 1815.

CORNELL, EZRA (1807–1874), businessman and philanthropist. Born on January 11, 1807, in Westchester Landing, New York, Cornell grew up and attended school there and in De Ruyter, New York. During his youth he worked at various jobs and exhibited both business ability and a flair for things mechanical. In 1828 he settled in Ithaca, New York, and soon became manager of a flour mill and a plaster mill. Under his direction a larger and mechanically more complex flour mill was built. In 1842 he became associated with Samuel F.B. Morse; developing a method of stringing an insulated telegraph wire along a series of poles, he supervised the construction of the first such line from Washington, D.C., to Baltimore in 1844. During the next 11 years he continued to build telegraph lines connecting many major cities in the East and the Midwest and in 1855, when the number of competing telegraph companies had increased to a threatening degree, he was a leader in unifying the major lines in the Western Union Telegraph Company. For some 15 years he was the principal stockholder of the company and he served as one of its directors until his death. The wealth he accumulated from his holdings he applied to other interests.

He established a model farm near Ithaca and in 1863 built a free public library for the city. The passage of the Morrill Act in 1862 inspired him to found an agricultural college; he developed and broadened plans proposed to him by Andrew D. White and in 1865 formally established Cornell University. Three years later the school opened with White as its first president. In addition to outright gifts totaling about $900,000, the school reaped more than $3 million from Cornell's transactions in public lands on its behalf. From 1861 to 1867 he served in the state legislature. He died in Ithaca on December 9, 1874.

COTTON, JOHN (1585–1652), clergyman. Born in Derby, England, on December 4, 1585, Cotton was educated at Cambridge, where he came under the influence of Puritanism. From 1612 to 1633 he was a parish vicar in Boston, Lincolnshire, where his growing adherence to Puritan heterodoxy finally resulted in charges being brought against him. He fled to London and then, a few months later, to Massachusetts. In October 1633, shortly after his arrival, he was chosen as "teacher" of the First Church of Boston, in which position he remained for the rest of his life. Armed with great learning, he quickly became a leading, even dominating, figure in the colony. He staunchly defended established Puritan institutions against both Anne Hutchinson and Roger Williams. His writings were thorough expositions of Congregational theology and polity; The Way of the Churches of Christ in New England, 1645, and The Way of the Congregational Churches Cleared, 1648, are most notable. He also wrote a children's catechism that was long the New England standard, Milk for Babes, Drawn out of the Breasts of Both Testaments, Chiefly for the Spirituall Nourishment of Boston Babes in either England, but may be of like Use for any Children, which appeared in 1646. Cotton died on December 23, 1652.

COXEY, JACOB SECHIER (1854–1951), businessman and public figure. Born on April 16,

1854, in Selinsgrove, Pennsylvania, Coxey attended public schools in Danville, Pennsylvania, and started work in that city as a stationary engineer in a rolling mill, then entered the scrap iron business. From 1881 to 1929 he was a leader in silica sandstone quarrying. In the financial panic of 1893, he was forced to fire about 40 men from his quarries; in protest he organized 100 men to march from Massillon, Ohio, to Washington, to petition Congress for money to create jobs. On March 25, 1894, "Coxey's Army" set out for the capital and arrived 500 strong on May 1st. They were arrested for trespass (he served 20 days) and received much adverse publicity. But Coxey managed to appear before a House subcommittee, presenting his plan for the federal government to purchase $500,000,000 in municipal bonds to be liquidated at 4 percent annually; the money would enable communities to undertake building and improvement projects to provide work to the unemployed. The proposal was pigeonholed. Nicknamed "General Coxey," he was thereafter identified with the army. On the 50th anniversary of its march he continued a speech from the Capitol steps that had been interrupted by the police in 1894. His only public office, as mayor of Massillon from 1931 to 1934, allowed him to enact his measures on a city-wide scale. He had promised to issue $200,000 in bonds ranging from 25 cents to $10, bearing interest of one-tenth of one percent, to finance public works projects on which the majority of the city's unemployed would have work. But he failed to raise the money and in 1934 lost in the primary. He unsuccessfully sought congressional seats in 1894 as a Populist, in 1916 as an independent, and in 1942 as a Democrat. Nominated for the presidency on the Farm-Labor ticket in 1936, he withdrew to place his support behind Union Party candidate William Lemke. In 1914 he wrote Coxey's Own Story. Never quite understood by the public or the government, he died in Massillon on May 18, 1951.

CRAM, RALPH ADAMS (1863–1942), architect. Born in Hampton Falls, New Hampshire, on December 16, 1863, Cram moved to Boston in 1889 and, with no formal training in the field, opened an architectural office with C.F. Wentworth. Later he formed the firm of Cram, Goodhue, and Ferguson (Cram and Ferguson after the death of Bertram Goodhue in 1924). A thoroughgoing exponent of the Gothic revival, Cram used that style in designing St. Thomas Church, New York City, Emmanuel Church, Cleveland, First Baptist Church, Pittsburgh, and many other such buildings. The firm drew plans for buildings at West Point and at a number of colleges and universities, including Princeton, Rice Institute, and Williams College. Commissioned to redesign the uncompleted Cathedral of St. John the Divine in New York City, Cram and Ferguson changed the originally Romanesque edifice into a Gothic one. On a few occasions Cram worked in the classic or colonial styles, but his predominant medievalism informed the bulk of his work and pervaded his writings and lectures; in these he called for a return to the values of the Middle Ages—the closeness to the land, the feudal stratification of society, and the autocratic government. He was professor of architecture at the Massachusetts Institute of Technology from 1914 to 1921 and from 1915 to 1922 was chairman of the Boston city planning board. Among his many books were Church Building, 1901, The Gothic Quest, 1907, The Ministry of Art, 1914, The Substance of Gothic, 1916, The Nemesis of Mediocrity, 1918, The Great Thousand Years, 1918, My Life in Architecture, 1936, and The End of Democracy, 1937. He died in Boston on September 22, 1942.

CRANE, HAROLD HART (1899–1932), poet. Born on July 21, 1899, in Garrettsville, Ohio, Hart Crane had an unhappy childhood during which he witnessed the dissolution of his family. His education ended with high school and thereafter he worked as a salesman, a warehouse manager, and advertising copywriter. He moved to New York City and in 1926 published his first volume of verse, White Buildings, displaying in it considerable technical mastery and a strong tendency toward a mystical perception of experience. Inspired largely by the democratic faith of Walt Whitman, he broke with the fashionable despair of many of his contemporaries and with an almost religious fervor sought a spiritual affirmation of American life and his experience within it. His quest resulted in *The Bridge,* 1930, in which, in rhapsodic fashion, he explored the mystical essence of the American destiny; the many related poems that comprised the book shared the common unifying image of the Brooklyn Bridge as a symbol of the creative power of man. Though the work won considerable critical appreciation, the overall reaction to it was mixed and served to confirm Crane in his growing insecurity. He spent a great deal of time in travel and on April 27, 1932, while sailing back to the United States from Mexico, he jumped or fell overboard and drowned.

CRANE, STEPHEN (1871–1900), author. Born on November 1, 1871, in Newark, New Jersey, Crane produced in his short life a remarkable body of work, including one undisputed classic of American literature. The son of a Methodist minister, his rather indifferent education ended with a year at Syracuse University apparently devoted largely to baseball. In 1891 he went to New York and pursued a bohemian existence, spending a great portion of his time exploring the Bowery slums, from which experience came *Maggie: A Girl of the Streets* in 1893. Published at his own expense, the book was unsuccessful. He was befriended by Hamlin Garland and William Dean Howells, with whose encouragement he produced *The Red Badge of Courage* in 1895. The vivid realism and psychological perceptiveness of the book were all the more remarkable for Crane's lack of personal experience of war. In the same year his first volume of poetry, *The Black Riders*, was published; its symbolism, stark imagery, and free form made it an important step from Victorian convention to modern poetry. Crane's main work in the following years was in short stories, the best of which displayed a complete mastery of the

form. He moved to England in 1897 and became well acquainted with Henry James, H. G. Wells, and Joseph Conrad. The poverty of his early years in New York, his impulsive stints as war correspondent in Greece and Cuba, and the heedless unconventionality of his life—which was often popularly exaggerated to scandalous proportions—slowly weakened him. He died of tuberculosis on June 5, 1900, in Germany.

CRAZY HORSE (c. 1849–1877), Indian chief. Born about 1849 into the Oglala Sioux tribe, Tashunca-uitco, or Crazy Horse, fought in Red Cloud's War in the Fetterman massacre on December 21, 1866, and the Wagon-Box fight of August 2, 1867, but did not settle on the Sioux reservations established in 1868. He moved north with a band of 1,200 Oglalas and Cheyennes (he married a Cheyenne woman and gained an alliance with the tribe), and joined the nation of Sitting Bull. Noted for his military brilliance, he was the principal military leader in the Sioux War of 1876 and 1877, which broke out as a protest against the order by the U.S. War Department that the Sioux remain on reservations after January 1, 1876. The most famous battle of the war was fought at the Little Bighorn River in Montana on June 25, 1876. Crazy Horse and his Cheyenne warriors surrounded Gen. George A. Custer and his command, assailing them from the north and west, while Gall, chief of the Hunkpapa Sioux, attacked from the south and west. Custer was killed and his entire command destroyed. After the battle the Indians dispersed into bands that went separate ways. Crazy Horse led about 800 warriors back to Sioux territory, hoping to gather supplies, but was relentlessly pursued by forces under Col. Nelson A. Miles. He surrendered on May 6, 1877, with about 1,000 men, women, and children, near Camp Robinson, Nebraska. Promised a limited amount of freedom, he was arrested in September on suspicion of agitating for war among the Oglalas. He was said to have resisted his captors, and was killed on September 5, 1877.

CREVECOEUR, MICHEL GUILLAUME JEAN DE (1735–1813), farmer and essayist. Born on January 31, 1735, in Caen, France, Crèvecoeur emigrated to Canada and served as a map maker during the last part of the French and Indian War. He remained when the war ended and explored extensively in the Great Lakes and Ohio region. In 1765 he became a citizen in New York and settled on a farm. The Revolution put him in a difficult position, for both he and his wife had Loyalist connections, and in 1780 he fled to Europe, leaving his wife and two of his children. In London two years later he published a collection of essays, most of them presumably written while working his New York farm, entitled *Letters From an American Farmer* and signed "J. Hector St. John." The essays were vivid, detailed, and optimistic discussions of American life, particularly in the frontier farming regions, and are a primary source of information about the period. The book was immediately popular, and Crèvecoeur was appointed French consul to three of the new American states. Returning to New York in 1783, he found his house burned, his wife dead, and his children missing, all the result of an Indian raid. He regained his children and became a popular figure in the new states; he knew both Franklin and Jefferson and corresponded with Washington. In 1787 his *Letters* were enlarged and republished. Three years later he left the United States to return to France, where he died on November 12, 1813.

CRITTENDEN, JOHN JORDAN (1787–1863), lawyer and public official. Born near Versailles, Kentucky, on September 10, 1787, Crittenden graduated from William and Mary College in 1807 and began to practise law. In 1809 he was appointed territorial attorney general for Illinois. Returning to Kentucky he saw military service in the War of 1812 and was at the same time elected to the state legislature. In 1817 he was sent to fulfill an unexpired term in the Senate. From the end of his term in 1819 until 1835 he confined his political activities to Kentucky, serving in the legislature,

as district attorney, and as secretary of state. In 1835 he was returned to the Senate, and in 1840 President Harrison named him to his Cabinet as attorney general, in which post he remained until joining the mass Cabinet resignation following Tyler's accession. He was elected again to the Senate in 1842; he now began to be a prominent national leader with his opposition to the annexation of Texas, to strong action in the Oregon dispute, and to the Mexican War. In 1848 he became governor of Kentucky; the following year President Fillmore named him once more attorney general. In 1854 he was once again elected to the Senate where, much disturbed by the slavery issue and the possibility of disunion that it entailed, he opposed the Kansas-Nebraska Act; when the Whig Party disintegrated he joined first the American, or Know-Nothing, Party and then the Constitutional Union Party. Into the crisis occasioned by Lincoln's election he introduced his "Crittenden Resolutions" in December 1860, designed as a compromise to avert secession. When this tactic was defeated by the Congressional radicals he returned to Kentucky and attempted to prevent that state from joining the Confederacy. After serving in 1861 as chairman of a convention of border states that requested the seceded states to reconsider their position, he returned to Congress where he opposed the more radical war measures until his death on July 26, 1863, in Frankfort, Kentucky.

CROCKETT, DAVID (1786–1836), frontiersman. Born in eastern Tennessee on August 17, 1786, Davy Crockett grew up on the frontier with virtually no education. He served as a scout under Andrew Jackson in the Creek War of 1813–1815, and afterwards moved farther west into Tennessee. He was for several years a local magistrate and in 1821 and 1823 he was elected to the state legislature. He was elected to Congress in 1827 and served two terms; defeated in 1831, he returned for a final term in 1833. In 1834 he made a tour of Northern cities in an effort to rouse support for the Whig Party with which he had allied himself; the party's hope was to fashion from Crockett's colorful history as a bear-hunter and largely illiterate frontiersman an answer to the Democrats' Jackson. The determined opposition of the Jackson forces defeated his bid for reelection in 1835. He then left Tennessee to join the war for independence in Texas; he arrived at the Alamo in February 1836 and died in the massacre there on March 6th. The growth of Davy Crockett into a legendary figure began before his death and continued after it with the publication from 1835 to 1856 of a series of Crockett almanacs, containing numerous accounts of mythical adventures in which he, Mike Fink, and other frontier heroes had supposedly been engaged.

CROGHAN, GEORGE (1720?–1782), trader, land speculator, and Indian agent. Born near Dublin around 1720, Croghan immigrated to America in 1741, landing at Philadelphia. He immediately took up trading with the Indians on the Pennsylvania frontier, learning their languages and building a trade empire sufficiently large to induce the French to take strong action. By 1754, with the outbreak of the French and Indian War, his business was ruined; he and a few loyal Indians then joined Washington's and Braddock's disastrous Ohio expeditions. His ability in negotiating with the Indiands led to his appointment in 1756 as deputy superintendent of northern Indian affairs. Through the remainder of the war and afterwards he strove to eliminate the French influence and hostility to the English that were widespread among the Indians beyond the Appalachian frontier. His greatest achievement was the negotiations and treaty that ended Pontiac's War in August 1765. In 1768 he represented the British government at the Fort Stanwix treaty negotiations. His early trading and land speculations had suffered badly from protracted Indian troubles; despite his associations with Washington, Franklin, and others, his later schemes fared no better. In 1778 he finally cleared himself of charges of Tory sympathies arising from some of his speculative ventures, but he died in poverty on August 31, 1782.

CROLY, HERBERT DAVID (1869–1930), journalist and political philosopher. Born on January 23, 1869, in New York City, Croly completed his studies at Harvard in 1899 after many interruptions. From 1900 to 1906 he edited the *Architectural Record*; he maintained a staff connection with the journal until 1913. In 1909 he published *The Promise of American Life*. Embodying the thesis that democratic institutions are dynamic and need to be flexible and innovative in a changing world, the book had a deep influence on both the "New Nationalism" of Roosevelt and the "New Freedom" of Wilson. Five years later he published a sequel, *Progressive Democracy*. In that same year, 1914, he founded *The New Republic*, "A Journal of Opinion," of which he remained editor until his death. Gathering a brilliant staff for the new journal, Croly directed the rapid growth of what was often, though incorrectly, thought to be the official organ of the Wilson administration. Though he and his staff supported American participation in World War I, he broke with the government over the Versailles Treaty; his bitter denunciation of the vindictive peace terms cost him half his readership. In his later years, with the post-war Republican political ascendancy, he slowly lost interest in public affairs. He died on May 17, 1930.

CROSBY, BING (1904–   ), singer and actor. Born on May 2, 1904, in Tacoma, Washington, Crosby was christened Harry Lillis. He grew up in Spokane and while attending Gonzaga University there during 1921–1924 he joined a local band as drummer and vocalist. In 1925 he formed an act called "Two Boys and a Piano" with Al Rinker, and together they played vaudeville circuits and Los Angeles theaters until 1927, when they were hired to sing with Paul Whiteman's orchestra. Joined by Harry Barris, they became the "Rhythm Boys" and were highly successful. The group toured the country and made a number of recordings until disbanding in 1930. In 1932 Crosby began broadcasting regularly on radio and in the same year appeared in his first movie, *The Big Broadcast of 1932*. During the 1930s and 1940s he made a series of recordings — "Pennies from Heaven," "Sweet Leilani," "When the Blue of the Night Meets the Gold of the Day" (his themesong), "White Christmas," and others — that made him the most popular of the crooners; dubbed "the old Groaner," he remained one of the leading American male vocalists for a decade more. He continued his movie career and in addition to the famous series of six *Road* comedies with Bob Hope between 1940 and 1952, he appeared in *Holiday Inn*, 1942, *Going My Way*, 1944, *The Bells of St. Mary's*, 1945, *Blue Skies*, 1946, *A Connecticut Yankee*, 1949, *White Christmas*, 1954, and many others. For his portrayal of Father O'Malley in *Going My Way* he won an Academy Award. In addition to his entertainment career, Crosby engaged in various business pursuits and from real estate and other sources amassed a large fortune. He continued to appear in movies, on radio, and, rarely, on television, but with diminishing frequency; he devoted much of his time to business and to golf, sponsoring an annual benefit tournament in Pebble Beach, California.

CROW, JIM see **RICE, THOMAS DARTMOUTH**

CUMMINGS, EDWARD ESTLIN (1894–1962), poet and artist. Born on October 14, 1894, in Cambridge, Massachusetts, e. e. cummings, as he styled himself, graduated from Harvard in 1915 and took a master's degree the following year. During World War I he served as an ambulance driver in France, where a misunderstanding with French authorities resulted in his spending six months in a detention camp. The incident was recounted in his first book, *The Enormous Room*, 1922. In 1923 he published his first book of verse, *Tulips and Chimneys*; it was quickly followed by *XLI Poems*, 1925, *&*, 1926, and *Is 5*, 1926. The poems, characterized by humorously unorthodox typography and a highly experimental approach to style and diction, were, in the main, celebrations of the possibilities of love, life, and joy in the truly alive individual. At the same time Cummings was capable of biting satire in describing the "unman," the soulless creature sunk in the platitudes and conformity of the masses. He exhibited his drawings and paintings and roused the same controversy that attended his poetry. His first play, *Him*, was produced in 1927; among his other works for the stage were *Tom*, 1935, a satirical ballet based on *Uncle Tom's Cabin*, and *Santa Claus: A Morality*, 1946. His later verse was published in, among others, *ViVa*, 1931, *No Thanks*, 1935, *One Times One*, 1944, and *95 Poems*, 1958. His Charles Eliot Norton lectures at Harvard in 1952–1953 were collected and published in 1953 as *i: six nonlectures*. He died at his farm near North Conway, New Hampshire, on September 3, 1962.

CURRIER, NATHANIEL (1813–1888), lithographer. Born on March 27, 1813, in Roxbury, Massachusetts, Currier became an apprentice to John Pendleton in a pioneer lithographing venture and accompanied him to Philadelphia in 1829 and New York in 1833. Completing his indenture, he set up a lithography house of his own with artist J. H. Buford, and issued "The Ruins of the Merchants' Exchange," 1835, the first of a series of prints that was to continue for seventy years. In 1852 he took **JAMES MERRITT IVES** (1824–1895) into the business as a bookkeeper. Born in New York on March 5, 1824, Ives had improved on his formal education with extensive studies in libraries and art galleries. His abilities as an artist were soon put to use by the firm. He became director of print production, overseeing the staff of artists employed by Currier, and contributing many drawings of his own. He prospered by knowing the taste of the time, selecting such subjects as sports, transportation, political events, scenery, development of the Western frontier, fires and disasters, the California gold rush, flowers and fruit, and portraits of notable Americans. Many of the prints were hand-painted by women who worked in a continuous production line; under his direction technical perfection was mandatory. In 1857 he became a partner and the firm was known as Currier and Ives. Their prints, all signed "Currier and Ives," were sold both retail and wholesale and some by mail order. They were highly popular in America, where as wall decorations they suited the American taste for comfortable living, and were distributed abroad through branch offices in European cities. Currier retired in 1880 and his son Edward West continued the business with Ives. Currier died in New York on November 20, 1888, and Ives on January 3, 1895. Between 1840 and 1890 over 7,000 different prints were issued. More important as manifestations of culture than as art, they became an American institution and are still popular today.

CURTIS, CYRUS HERMAN KOTZSCHMAR (1850–1933), publisher. Born on June 18, 1850, in Portland, Maine, Curtis attended high school until his sophomore year. At 13 he had started a two cent weekly called *Young America*, the first of his many publishing ventures. Its headquarters were destroyed in the Portland fire of 1866 and he moved to Boston; six years later he founded the *People's Ledger*. He moved to Philadelphia in 1876, sold the *Ledger*, and three years later began a magazine called *The Tribune and Farmer*, for which his wife edited a woman's feature page. This became the most popular item in the book, and Curtis built on the idea, starting *The Ladies' Journal*, later *The Ladies' Home Journal*, in 1883. He offered various subscription "specials" to readers, including cash prizes to those who submitted the most names for new subscribers. By 1900 circulation was nearly one million. Editors such as Edward Bok made the *Journal* an innovative, pertinent magazine; Curtis gave free reign to his staff, which he chose with great care on the basis of their creativity and intelligence. He was one of the first publishers to rely heavily for revenue on the sale of advertising space. In 1890 he formed the Curtis Publishing Company. To its

holdings he added *The Saturday Evening Post* in 1897, *The Country Gentleman* in 1911, and newspapers including the *Philadelphia Public Ledger*, the *Philadelphia Evening Telegraph*, the *Philadelphia Press* and the *North American*, the *New York Evening Post*, and the *Philadelphia Inquirer*. He died in Wyncote, Pennsylvania, on June 7, 1933.

CURTIS, GEORGE TICKNOR (1812–1894), lawyer and historian. Born in Watertown, Massachusetts, on November 28, 1812, Curtis graduated from Harvard in 1832, taught for a time, and then went to Harvard law school. He was admitted to the bar in 1836 and began to practise, first in Worcester and then in Boston. He quickly established a reputation as an able lawyer and was, during his career, patent attorney for such famous inventors as Charles Goodyear, Samuel F. B. Morse, and Cyrus McCormick. A Whig and, after the demise of that party, a Democrat, he served in the Massachusetts house of representatives from 1840 to 1843 and later was U.S. commissioner in Massachusetts. In the latter capacity it was his duty in 1852 to send Thomas Sims back to slavery in compliance with the Fugitive Slave Law, an action that offended his antislavery sentiments. He was thus happier in his defense of Dred Scott in the celebrated case that reached the Supreme Court in 1857, and the loss of which by Scott and Curtis helped to precipitate the Civil War. He also appeared before the Supreme Court in the legal tender and greenback cases after the conflict. During the war he moved to New York, where, though a strong unionist, he was critical of the administration; a supporter of General McClellan, he later wrote two vindications of him and his career (1886 and 1887). After about 1870 he spent less time at the law and more in the production of a series of important works in the field of U.S. constitutional history. The best known of these, written from the Federalist-Whig point of view, went through many editions and revisions, the last published in 1896 under the title *The Constitutional History of the United States From Their Declaration of Independence to Their*

Civil War. His legal treatises included a digest of English and American admiralty cases, 1839, *Treatise on the Rights and Duties of Merchant Seamen,* 1841, *Treatise on the Law of Copyright,* 1847, and a two-volume commentary on the courts of the United States, 1854–1858. He also wrote biographies of Daniel Webster (two volumes, 1870) and James Buchanan (two volumes, 1883). He died in New York City on March 28, 1894.

CURTIS, GEORGE WILLIAM (1824–1892), author, orator, and editor. Born in Providence, Rhode Island, on February 24, 1824, Curtis was schooled in Massachusetts and at 15 moved to New York City with his family. He spent two years with the Brook Farm community and was then and afterward strongly influenced by Emerson. From 1846 to 1850 he traveled in Europe and the Near East, sending letters back to New York newspapers that were, after his return, published in book form. In New York again, he held editorial positions with *Putnam's Monthly Magazine, Harper's Weekly,* and *Harper's Magazine;* his essays, also later collected, were very much in the tradition of Irving—graceful, fanciful, and sentimental. In 1856 he delivered a speech on public issues at Wesleyan University in Connecticut. Titled "The Duty of the American Scholar to Politics and the Times" the speech marked the beginning of Curtis' involvement in public affairs. In lectures and, from 1863, as political editor of *Harper's Weekly,* he became a vastly influential publicist; he was a leading Republican from that party's founding, though he refused political office or preferment. He early supported woman suffrage and was a leading advocate of civil service. He was chairman of the National Civil Service Reform Association from its founding to his death, and was appointed chairman of a government commission on civil service in 1871 by President Grant. In 1884, because of nominee Blaine's doubtful political morality, Curtis left the Republican Party to become an Independent. In 1890 he became chancellor of the University of New York, a post he held until his death on August 31, 1892.

CUSHING, HARVEY WILLIAMS (1869–1939), surgeon. Born in Cleveland on April 8, 1869, Cushing was the fourth of his family to enter medicine. He graduated from Yale in 1891 and four years later received his M.D. from Harvard Medical School. In 1896 he joined the staff of the Johns Hopkins Hospital In Baltimore and during the next four years focused on problems of neurosurgery. During 1900 and 1901 he undertook advanced study with leading surgeons and physiologists in England, Switzerland, and Italy, and then returned to Baltimore to open a general surgical practice and to serve in various positions with the department of surgery in the medical school of Johns Hopkins University. He began a thoroughgoing study of brain tumors and, though surgical progress in this field was exceedingly slow, in 1910 successfully removed one from Gen. Leonard Wood. He also devoted much attention to the pituitary gland and in 1912 published a landmark monograph on the function and disorders of the organ. In that year he accepted a position as surgeon-in-chief of the new Peter Bent Brigham Hospital in Boston, becoming also professor of surgery at Harvard. During World War I he directed a base hospital in France and in 1918 published a classic study of wartime brain injuries. In 1925 he published *The Life of Sir William Osler,* a Pulitzer Prize winning biography of his great former mentor at Johns Hopkins. He continued to produce scientific papers of great value, most of them concerning neurosurgical techniques and including exhaustive studies and classifications of tumors. In 1932 he retired from Harvard but accepted appointment as Sterling professor of neurology at Yale, a post he held from 1933 to 1937. From 1937 until his death he was director of studies in the history of medicine at Yale, and to further this field of research he bequeathed his own extensive library to the school. He died in New Haven, Connecticut, on October 7, 1939.

CUSHING, WILLIAM (1732–1810), jurist. Born on March 1, 1732, in Scituate, Massachusetts, Cushing graduated from Harvard in

1751. After teaching for a year, he took up the study of law and was admitted to the bar in 1755. From 1760 to 1772 he was a county official in the district of Maine, still at the time part of Massachusetts; in the latter year he returned to succeed his father as judge of the superior court of Massachusetts. In this post he obeyed the state legislature's order to decline the salary offered by the British government. In 1775 he was appointed to the revolutionary council of state, which after reorganizing kept him as a member of the new supreme judicial court. Two years later, after John Adams resigned as chief justice—a post he had never actually filled—Cushing accepted the position. His most notable act during his twelve years on this bench was his ruling in 1783 that the Massachusetts Bill of Rights implicitly abolished slavery in the state. In 1779 he was a member of the first Massachusetts constitutional convention and in 1788 was vice president of the state's committee to ratify the federal Constitution. When the U.S. Supreme Court was organized he was the first associate justice to be appointed to it. He declined the chief justiceship in 1796 because of ill health, but continued in his duties as associate justice until his death on September 13, 1810.

CUSHMAN, CHARLOTTE SAUNDERS (1816–1876), actress. Born on July 23, 1816, in Boston, Miss Cushman was encouraged by her musically gifted mother to train for the opera and she joined a Boston company, appearing at the age of 19 as Countess Almaviva in *The Marriage of Figaro*. She was engaged to perform in New Orleans, where, allegedly, her instructor attempted to force her natural contralto voice into the soprano range, and her voice failed. She soon met a visiting English actor in New Orleans who offered to give her instruction. Under his guidance, she appeared as Lady Macbeth in a striking performance. She moved to New York and secured engagements with several small theaters. In 1837, she appeared as Nancy Sykes in *Oliver Twist*, as Meg Merrilies in *Guy Mannering*, and as Romeo, in a predictably controversial performance. She was stage manager for the Walnut Street Theater in Philadelphia from 1842 to 1844. Here she met William Macready, a formidable English actor, who took her as a pupil and encouraged her to perform in London; on his advice, she set sail in 1845. There she played Queen Katherine in Shakespeare's *Henry VIII*, Lady Macbeth, Romeo, opposite her sister Susan as Juliet, and other popular roles. From 1849 through 1852 she toured America. She was criticized for taking male roles, not only her favorite, Romeo, but also Hamlet and Cardinal Wolsey in *Henry VIII*; the latter, critics complained, even she could not properly perform. In 1852 she retired, in a fashion, from the stage. She lived in England and continued to make occasional appearances. In 1857 she returned to America, giving a series of farewell performances until 1858. Then she went to Rome. Two years later, back in America, she gave a farewell to New Haven audiences. She returned to Rome and remained there until 1870. Criticized for her farewells and reappearances, she was defended on the grounds of frequent depressions resulting from her continual enactment of tragic characters. The gradual weakening of her body, owing to the cancer from which she had long suffered, was unknown to the public. She died at her home in Boston on February 17, 1876.

CUSTER, GEORGE ARMSTRONG (1839–1876), soldier. Born in New Rumley, Ohio, on December 5, 1839, Custer was appointed to West Point in 1857 and graduated last in his class four years later. Assigned to Civil War service with the cavalry, he quickly acquired a reputation for daring and brilliant leadership. He received numerous field promotions and by the end of the war had been brevetted major general, though his permanent rank was only captain. His greatest achievement during the war was his relentless harrying of Lee's army in its retreat from Richmond, which in no small way helped bring about the surrender at Appomattox; for this Custer won national renown and the high praise of his commander, General Sheridan. In July 1866 he was promoted lieutenant colonel of the regular 7th Cavalry, and was acting commander of the regiment until his death. In the campaign against the Cheyenne in Kansas he directed the telling victory at the Washita River that ended Indian resistance in the Middle Plains region. In 1870 the regiment was disbanded; Custer remained in the West and resumed his position when the 7th was reactivated in 1873. The following year he led an expedition of 1,200 troops and scientists into the Black Hills of South Dakota. The discovery of gold in the area, with the subsequent influx of prospectors, was a major contributing factor to the later Indian wars. In 1876 his regiment was part of a concentrated offensive against the Sioux led by Sitting Bull and Crazy Horse, then encamped on the Little Bighorn River in Montana. Colonel Custer, in command of a separate column, ignored General Terry's plan for encirclement and coordinated attack and, on June 25th, blindly launched his greatly outnumbered troops into the Indian camp. All, including Custer, were killed.

DALLAS, ALEXANDER JAMES (1759–1817), lawyer and public official. Born on June 21, 1759, of Scottish immigrant parents in Jamaica, Dallas was educated in Scotland and England and, after his return to Jamaica in 1780, entered the law. On the recommendation of actor Lewis Hallam he emigrated to the United States in 1783. After fulfilling the required two years' residence he was admitted to the Pennsylvania bar in 1785; he devoted time also to various other pursuits, attempting with Hallam to introduce the drama into Philadelphia, contributing essays on political and literary topics to newspapers, and editing for a time the *Columbian Magazine*. From 1791 to 1801 he served as secretary of the Commonwealth of Pennsylvania and became a leading organizer of the Democratic-Republican Party. In 1801 President Jefferson appointed him U.S. attorney for the eastern district of Pennsylvania, a post he held for 13 years. In 1814 he was

named secretary of the treasury by President Madison. The war with England had brought the Treasury to the brink of bankruptcy, and Dallas immediately set about reestablishing the nation's solvency. His strong message to Congress recommending a greatly increased revenue went far to restore confidence and was approved. For several months during 1815 he served also as acting secretary of war. His plan for a second Bank of the United States was rendered impotent by the Republican opposition in Congress and on his advice was vetoed by the President, but most of his recommendations were incorporated in Calhoun's Bank Bill in 1816 and passed into law. The Tariff Act of the same year was also a result of his analysis of the nation's financial requirements and formed the basis of the system of protection that prevailed for 30 years. He retired from the Treasury in October 1816 to return to his law practice, but died soon afterwards, on January 16, 1817.

DALLAS, GEORGE MIFFLIN (1792–1864), lawyer, public official, and diplomat. Born in Philadelphia on July 10, 1792, the son of Alexander James Dallas, the younger Dallas graduated from Princeton in 1810. After admission to the bar in 1813 he served as secretary to Albert Gallatin on the latter's diplomatic mission to Russia. Returning in 1814, he joined first the treasury department, then headed by his father, and later, in Philadelphia, the legal staff of the Second Bank of the United States. A staunch Democrat, he rose rapidly through numerous political offices and in 1831 was appointed to fill an unexpired term in the Senate. In 1833 he became Pennsylvania's attorney general for two years. From 1837 to 1839 he was minister to Russia; after his return to Philadelphia he devoted himself to his law practice, though maintaining a deep interest in politics and continuing a long-standing rivalry with James Buchanan. In 1844 he was nominated for Vice President and, with Polk at the head of the ticket, elected. At the end of his term, during which he was primarily concerned with the tariff problem, he again returned to private life. In 1856, on President Pierce's request, he succeeded Buchanan as minister to Great Britain; his major accomplishment, a treaty resolving a number of disputes arising from the earlier Clayton – Bulwer Treaty, was nullified by the Senate. He succeeded, however, in obtaining a renunciation of England's claimed right to search on the high seas. He returned to America in 1861 and died on December 31, 1864. The city of Dallas, Texas, was named for him during his vice presidency.

DANA, CHARLES ANDERSON (1819 – 1897), journalist and editor. Born on August 8, 1819, in Hinsdale, New Hampshire, Dana was largely self-taught when he entered Harvard in 1839. His studies were discontinued because of his failing eyesight and financial problems, and during 1841 – 1846 he was a general instructor and managing trustee at Brook Farm. He contributed essays to the community's paper, the *Harbinger,* and to the *Dial* during this period. After fire terminated the experimental colony, he moved to Boston and became assistant editor of the *Daily Chronotype.* He took advantage of a previous meeting with Horace Greeley to gain employment on the *New York Tribune* and was made city editor in 1847. In his 15-year association with the paper he became nearly as influential as Greeley himself. In 1848 – 1849 he witnessed revolutions in Paris and Berlin, becoming disenchanted with his former political ideas. Returning to the *Tribune* in 1849 as managing editor, he was notably more concise in his writing, reflecting a liberal bent, but with a tinge of cynicism. Although he lent valuable support to antislavery forces, he was generally impatient with individual Abolitionists and, as was to be his policy in the future, hostile to labor movements, opposing strikes and advising cooperation with management to correct unfair working conditions. During the Civil War, his attitude toward military and civil policies was notably more aggressive than Greeley's, leading to his resignation in 1862. He was hired by Secretary of War Stanton to observe and report on military operations at the front. Highly impressed with Grant's and Sherman's abilities, he wrote glowing reports that reassured President Lincoln. During 1864 – 1865 he was an assistant secretary of war and recorded impressions of Cabinet members and of Lincoln, which he published in *Recollections of the Civil War,* which did not appear until 1898. Having resigned from government service in 1865, he was editor of a short-lived Chicago paper in 1866 and in 1868 was able to purchase the *New York Sun.* There he became the "newspaper man's newspaper man." Although his political coverage was inconsistent and sometimes reactionary, he made the paper famous, if not notorious, for its news, which featured the human interest story and aggressive reporting. He died at Glen Cove, New York, on October 17, 1897.

DANA, RICHARD HENRY (1815 – 1882), lawyer and author. Born in Cambridge, Massachusetts, on August 1, 1815, the son of a noted poet and essayist of the same name, Dana entered Harvard in 1831. Two years later weakened eyesight forced him to suspend his studies, and he shipped as a common sailor aboard the brig *Pilgrim* from Boston to California, in the belief that the experience would benefit his eyes. Upon his return to Boston in 1836 he reentered Harvard and graduated in 1837. He taught briefly and then, turning to law, was admitted to the bar in 1840. In that same year he published his account of his voyage, *Two Years Before the Mast.* A vivid, detailed description from the viewpoint of an ordinary seaman, the book achieved great popularity and marked the beginning of a new and vital tradition blending the techniques of literature and journalism. In the book, besides telling a wonderful and exciting story, Dana expressed his desire to better the lot of the sailor, a concern he carried also into his law practice. The following year he published *The Seaman's Friend,* a work on practical seamanship and maritime law. He was an early supporter of the Free-Soil Party and later of the

Republican Party. He gave free legal aid to victims of the Fugitive Slave Law and later, during his tenure as U.S. district attorney for Massachusetts from 1861 to 1866, persuaded the Supreme Court to validate the Federal blockade of Southern ports. He ran unsuccessfully for Congress in 1868 and in 1876 his nomination by President Grant as minister to England failed of confirmation by the Senate, partly as a result of the efforts of Simon Cameron, who referred to him as "One of those damned literary fellers." In 1878 he traveled to Rome to continue his study of international law; he died there on January 6, 1882.

DARROW, CLARENCE SEWARD (1857–1938), lawyer. Born on April 18, 1857, near Kinsman, Ohio, Clarence Darrow studied for a year at Allegheny College and for an equally short time at the University of Michigan's law school before being admitted to the bar in 1878. After several years of small-town practice in Ohio he moved to Chicago in 1887, where he became associated with John Peter Altgeld. He was active in the Democratic Party and was appointed city corporation counsel; later he became general counsel for the Chicago and North Western Railway, a position he resigned in 1895 to defend Eugene V. Debs and his associates in the injunction case arising from the Pullman strike. Darrow gained a national reputation as a labor lawyer and subsequently, among other cases, represented the miners in the arbitration of the anthracite strike of 1903 and in 1907 defended William "Big Bill" Haywood and other Western labor leaders on a murder charge. His reputation as a defense attorney, already established in a number of his labor cases, soared in 1924 with his efforts for the defense in the Leopold-Loeb kidnapping and murder trial, in which he introduced novel forms of evidence based on psychiatric examinations. In 1925 he opposed William Jennings Bryan in the Scopes "Monkey Trial," and the following year conducted the defense in the Sweet case in Detroit, involving racial-segregationist violence. His cases were almost invariably,

and usually intentionally, headline material as he tried to use them to educate and persuade the public to his liberal and civil-libertarian views. His rationalism and ingrained skepticism were also expressed in a number of books, among them *An Eye for an Eye*, 1905, *Crime, Its Cause and Treatment*, 1925, and *The Story of My Life*, 1932. A staunch advocate of Progressive reform, particularly the abolition of capital punishment, Darrow was a popular lecturer and debater in addition to his courtroom activities. He died in Chicago on March 13, 1938.

DAVIS, DAVID (1815–1886), jurist and public official. Born in Cecil County, Maryland, on March 9, 1815, Davis was educated at Kenyon College and, after graduating from Yale Law School in 1835, was admitted to the bar. He moved to Illinois and in 1844 was elected as a Whig to the state legislature. He was a leading member of the state constitutional convention in 1847 and the following year began his 14 years as a circuit judge in Illinois. During this time he formed a close friendship with Abraham Lincoln; at the Republican Convention of 1860 Davis was the leader of the Lincoln forces and after the successful campaign accompanied the new President to Washington. In 1862 Lincoln appointed him to the Supreme Court. His political leanings had always been rather vague and subject to change; during his tenure on the bench he began to stray from the increasingly radical Republican Party. In 1872 he was nominated for President by the Labor Reform Convention but, failing to capture the Liberal Republican nomination, which went instead to Horace Greeley, he withdrew from the race. In 1876, while the outcome of the Hayes-Tilden election awaited decision by the Electoral Commission, it was widely assumed that Davis would sit on the commission and, as the supposedly neutral member of the otherwise evenly split panel, cast the deciding vote. Despite the fact that his inclination appeared then to be Democratic, the Democrats in the Illinois legislature suddenly elected him to the Senate, disqualifying him for the Commission and clearing a way for another Republican member to decide the presidency. He remained in the Senate until 1883, the last two years as president pro tem. He died on June 26, 1886.

DAVIS, JEFFERSON (1808–1889), public official, president of the Confederate States of America. Born in southwestern Kentucky on June 3, 1808, Davis moved to Mississippi during his childhood; he was educated at Transylvania University and at 16 was appointed to West Point. After his graduation in 1828 he served in the Army for seven years, mainly in Wisconsin. In 1835 he settled on a plantation in Mississippi; his wife, the daughter of Zachary Taylor, died three months after their marriage, and Davis remained for seven years in the semi-isolation of his plantation. In 1845 he was elected to Congress. The following year he resigned to command a volunteer company in the Mexican War, and his brilliant action at Buena Vista prevented the defeat of General Taylor. Nationally famous for this exploit, he was sent to the Senate in 1847; he resigned four years later to run unsuccessfully for governor of Mississippi. In 1853 President Pierce appointed him secretary of war, in which post he notably improved the nation's military capabilities and brought about the Gadsden Purchase. At the end of his four-year term he reentered the Senate. Though he was a determined and eloquent defender of the South, he discouraged secessionist activity; with his moderate views he enjoyed considerably popularity even in the North and only after secession became a fact in late 1860 did he reluctantly acquiesce. He formally withdrew from the Senate in January 1861 and was immediately commissioned major general of Mississippi's militia. The Confederate convention meeting in Montgomery, Alabama, two weeks later named him provisional president of the Confederacy, and he retained the position in the regular election in October. As president of a new and economically disadvantaged nation, and faced with the immediate prospect of war, Davis performed eminently well. While his military judgment was on occasion at fault, he wisely gave General Lee wide scope in conducting the war. He was constantly hampered by the opposition of extreme states' rights advocates. When, as an inevitable consequence of Northern economic and manpower superiority, defeat was imminent, he left Richmond, the Southern capital, and fled southwards. On May 10, 1865, he was captured by federal troops in Georgia. For two years he was held prisoner in Fort Monroe, Virginia —at first, until Northern public opinion objected, in shackles. He was released on bail in 1867 but, because of legal difficulties, never brought to trial for treason. In his remaining years he lived on the Mississippi plantation of a friend and traveled occasionally in Europe. In 1881 he published the two-volume *The Rise and Fall of the Confederate Government*. He steadfastly refused to request official amnesty and never regained his citizenship. He died in New Orleans on December 6, 1889.

DAVIS, RICHARD HARDING (1864–1916), journalist and author. Born on April 18, 1864, in Philadelphia, Davis was educated at Lehigh and Johns Hopkins universities and in 1886 joined the *Philadelphia Record* as a reporter. He later moved to the *Philadelphia Press* and in 1889 to the *New York Sun*. He had already attracted considerable attention with his colorful and often sensational reporting, and in 1890 he became managing editor of *Harper's Weekly*. During the next several years he undertook extensive travels and his reports to *Harper's* were later collected in a number of volumes: *The West from a Car Window*, 1892, *The Rulers of the Mediterranean*, 1894, *Our English Cousins*, 1894, *About Paris*, 1895, and *Three Gringos in Venezuela and Central America*, 1896. As the best known and most influential reporter in America, he covered every major war in the world from the 1897 Greco-Turkish conflict to World War I, often corresponding with papers in London as well as New York, and his dispatches later filled seven volumes. He also published a great deal of fiction: collections of short stories, such as *Gallegher and Other Stories*, 1891, *Van Bibber and Others*, 1892, *The Lion and the Unicorn*, 1899, *Ranson's Folly*, 1902, *The Scarlet Car*, 1907, and *The Man Who Could Not Lose*, 1911; and novels, including *Soldiers of Fortune*, 1897, *The King's Jackal*, 1898, *Captain Macklin*, 1902, *The Bar Sinister*, 1903, and *The White Mice*, 1909. He wrote 25 plays, some of which were quite successful on Broadway and elsewhere, particularly *Ranson's Folly*, 1904, *The Dictator*, 1904, and *Miss Civilization*, 1906. He died on April 11, 1916, at his home near Mount Kisco, New York.

DAY, BENJAMIN HENRY (1810–1899), printer and journalist. Born on April 10, 1810, in West Springfield, Massachusetts, Day was educated in public schools and in 1824 became a printer's apprentice on the *Springfield Republican*. He opened his own printing business in 1831, which was closed soon after by a financial panic. In 1833 he began printing the *Daily Sun* in New York City. A four-page, three-column daily, it sold for a penny and catered to the average working man, while the majority of papers in the city featured, at six cents, European news and political and financial coverage. The *Sun* covered the proceedings in police court and provided neighborhood news, and reprinted advertisements from other newspapers to make a show of prosperity. It also introduced the institution of the newsboy. Within three months, through shrewd psychology and an innovative policy of street-vending, Day was selling 4,000 copies daily; in two years circulation exceeded that of any paper in the world. The famous "Moon Hoax," written by the *Sun*'s chief reporter, was a factor in boosting circulation. The story told in detail of orange orangutan-like creatures hopping about on the moon, supposedly seen by a British astronomer who was unlikely ever to read the *Sun*. Day took a chance in printing the story, but as it turned out the public was delighted at having been fooled in such an amusing way. In 1838 he

sold the paper to a brother-in-law, a move he later regretted. He founded another penny paper, the *True Sun*, in 1840, and in 1842, *Brother Jonathan*, a magazine that reprinted old British novels. In 1862 he retired from business and died in New York City on December 21, 1889.

DAY, CLARENCE SHEPHARD (1874–1935), writer. Born in New York City on November 18, 1874, the son of a successful Wall Street stock broker and the grandson of editor Benjamin Day, Clarence attended St. Paul's school in Concord, New Hampshire, and graduated from Yale in 1896. Shortly thereafter he became a partner in his father's firm of Clarence S. Day and Company. In 1898 he enlisted in the Navy but saw little action in the Spanish-American War and was mustered out in September. Returning to business, he gradually succumbed to a crippling form of arthritis and retired in 1903. He remained in New York City, and after getting accustomed to the demands of his illness began contributing prose and drawings to magazines. A collection of this material with additional work was published as *This Simian World*, 1920, which had a measure of success. Its witty, pleasant style set the tone of his later works, most notably the autobiographical *God and My Father*, 1932, *Life With Father*, 1935, *Life With Mother*, 1937, and *Father and I*, 1940, the latter two published after his death. *Life With Father*, which was dramatized in 1939 by Howard Lindsay and Russel Crouse, had the longest continuous run of any American play, playing for a decade in New York and on tour. His drawings were humorously distinct caricatures compiled in *Thoughts Without Words*, 1928, and *Scenes from the Mesozoic, and Other Drawings*, 1935. He died in New York City on December 28, 1935.

DAY, DOROTHY (1897–), journalist and social worker. Born in New York City on November 8, 1897, Miss Day grew up there, in California, and in Chicago. In 1914, aided by a scholarship, she entered the University of Illi-

913

nois, where she remained for two years. While a student she read widely among socialist authors and soon joined the Socialist Party. In 1916 she returned to New York and joined the staff of the *Call*, a socialist newspaper; she also became a member of the Industrial Workers of the World. In 1917 she moved from the *Call* to *The Masses*, where she remained until the magazine was suppressed a few months later by the government. After a brief period on the successor journal, the *Liberator*, she spent over a year in 1918–1919 working as a nurse in Brooklyn. For several years thereafter she continued in journalism in Chicago and New Orleans. In 1927, following years of doubt and indecision, she joined the Roman Catholic Church, an act that for some time isolated her from her earlier radical associates. Then in 1932 she met Peter Maurin, a French-born Catholic who had developed a program of social reconstruction — "the green revolution" — based on communal farming and the establishment of houses of hospitality for the urban poor. The program aimed to unite workers and intellectuals in joint activities ranging from farming to educational discussions. In 1933 Miss Day and Maurin founded the *Catholic Worker*, a monthly newspaper, to carry the idea to a wider audience. Within three years the paper's circulation had grown to 150,000, and the original St. Joseph's House of Hospitality in New York was imitated in a number of cities. The *Catholic Worker* took boldly radical positions on many issues and during World War II was a center for pacifism and for Catholic conscientious objectors. In later years both Miss Day and the newspaper agitated against nuclear weaponry and preparations for nuclear war; for several years she was jailed regularly for refusing to comply with New York's compulsory civil defense drills. The number of settlement houses directly connected with the *Catholic Worker* dwindled in later years, but there remained a significant number taking their inspiration from it. Miss Day, like her co-workers, lived in the New York house in voluntary poverty; in addition to the establishment in the city, the organization maintained a farm on Staten Island. In 1952 she published an autobiography, *The Long Loneliness*.

DEBS, EUGENE VICTOR (1855–1926), labor organizer and political reformer. Born in Terre Haute, Indiana, on November 5, 1855, of immigrant parents, Eugene V. Debs left school at 15 to work in the shops of the Indianapolis Railway. In 1875 he became secretary of the newly founded lodge of the Brotherhood of Locomotive Firemen in Terre Haute. In 1879 he was elected city clerk, and the following year became national secretary of the union and editor of its magazine. He was elected to the Indiana legislature in 1885. In 1893 he helped found the American Railway Union and as its president led the successful strike against the Great Northern Railroad the next year. In response to a request from the Pullman strikers later the same year Debs and the A.R.U. agreed to boycott Pullman cars. Debs was cited for conspiracy to obstruct the mails in an injunction issued against the strikers, and again for contempt when he failed to obey the injunction. He was sentenced to six months in jail on the latter charge; during his imprisonment his wide reading led him to adopt socialism as his cause. He supported the Populist movement in 1896 and the following year began to organize what was to become the Socialist Party of America. Debs was the party's presidential nominee four successive times, from 1900 to 1912, polling in the latter year nearly a million votes. In 1905 he helped found the Industrial Workers of the World, though he later disavowed the organization because of its tendency to violence. He supported himself during these years with articles, editorial positions, and lecture tours. In 1918 he publicly denounced the wave of sedition prosecutions that was taking place under the 1917 Espionage Act; for this he was himself charged with sedition and sentenced to ten years' imprisonment. In 1920, while in jail, he was again the Socialist candidate for President and received a larger vote than ever before. He was released on President Harding's order in 1921 and continued to work for the socialist cause until his death on October 20, 1926, in Elmhurst, Illinois.

DECATUR, STEPHEN (1779–1820), naval officer. Born on January 5, 1779, in Sinnepuxent, Maryland, Decatur grew up in Philadelphia and, after a year of study at the University of Pennsylvania, entered a shipping firm in that city. In April 1798 he was commissioned a midshipman in the Navy for service in the naval war with France. He rose quickly and was a lieutenant when, in 1803, he was sent to join the American naval forces in the Mediterranean. In February 1804 he led a daring raid into the harbor of Tripoli to recapture and burn a pirated American frigate. He escaped with but one of his crew injured and was promoted captain. Through 1804 and 1805 he took part in the hostilities off Tripoli; in the latter year he negotiated personally with the Bey of Tunis and returned to the United States with the Tunisian ambassador. For several years he held various commands in home waters. Soon after the outbreak of the War of 1812 Decatur sailed in command of the *United States*; in October 1812 he captured H.M.S. *Macedonian* in one of the war's great naval victories. The following year he was appointed commodore of a squadron defending New York harbor. In January 1815 he ran the British blockade of the harbor in the *President*; pursued, he disabled H.M.S. *Endymion* before being forced to surrender to overwhelming numbers. Later in the year he sailed for the Mediterranean in command of a nine-ship squadron; he successfully ended the corsair raids by Algiers, Tunis, and Tripoli, and secured reparations for damages to American shipping. At a dinner given in his honor shortly after his triumphal return to America, he proposed his famous toast: "Our country! In her intercourse with foreign nations may she always be in the right; but our country, right or wrong." From November 1815 until he died, he served on the Board of Navy Commissioners. His death on March 22, 1820, was the result of a duel with another officer.

DE FOREST, LEE (1873–1961), electrical engineer and inventor. Born on August 26, 1873, in Council Bluffs, Iowa, De Forest grew up there and in Talladega, Alabama, where his father was president of the College for the Colored. He attended school in Mount Hermon, Massachusetts, and then entered Yale's Sheffield Scientific School. He graduated in 1896, took his Ph.D. in 1899, and went to Chicago to work for the Western Electric Company while carrying on research in his spare time. His first of more than 300 patents was granted for an electrolytic detector that made possible the use of headphones with wireless receivers. In 1906 he invented the three-element or triode electron tube, which he called an audion. The device was quickly recognized as perhaps the single most important development in the field of electronics up to that time; its vast potential as a generator, detector, and amplifier of radio signals lay at the basis of the rapid growth of the electronics and communications industries. De Forest patented the audion in 1907, though in the next few years he was involved in several patent litigations. He made a number of musical broadcasts, including one of Enrico Caruso in 1910, but little public note was taken of them. He founded the De Forest Wireless Telegraph Company, the Radio Telephone Company, and the De Forest Radio Company at various times but had little lasting success in these enterprises. By the end of World War I he had sold the rights to the audion and turned to other things. In 1919 he developed a sound system for motion pictures and four years later founded the De Forest Phonofilm Company to produce it. In later years he made important contributions to the electric phonograph, long distance telephony, television, radar, and diathermy. He was an advocate of the educational potential of radio and television and

915

decried the commercialization of those media. Essentially a solitary inventor who preferred independent research to business, De Forest made and lost four fortunes in his life. His autobiography, *Father of Radio*, was published in 1950. He died in Hollywood on June 30, 1961.

DE KOONING, WILLEM (1904 –), painter. Born on April 24, 1904, in Rotterdam, Holland, De Kooning left school at the age of 12 to be apprenticed to a commercial artist. He arrived in America in 1926 as a stowaway on a cattle boat. Supporting himself as a commercial artist, he did not exhibit his own work until 1948. Tremendously influenced by surrealism, by German expressionism, and by Ashile Gorky, a leader in the American movement in abstract art, he became a dominant figure in the abstract expressionist style after World War II. His work was a furious blend of brushwork and color. The most famous of his paintings, based on the theme of "Woman," were first shown in New York City in 1953. From the pattern of lines and color in each work emerged the portrait of a woman so grossly distorted as to become almost comical. He claimed to find no peace in art and transmitted none on the canvas. His paintings appeared to be reactions to objects or people rather than representations of them. But in using a kind of representation and design in his art he was said to be unique among abstract expressionist painters.

DELANY, MARTIN ROBINSON (1812 – 1885), physician, social reformer, soldier, and public official. Born on May 6, 1812, in Charlestown, Virginia (now West Virginia), the grandson of slaves and the son of free Negroes, Delany attended school in Pittsburgh and New York City. In 1843 he began issuing one of the first Negro weeklies, the *Mystery*, a nationalist paper, which he continued in Pittsburgh for four years. Frederick Douglass joined him briefly in partnership in 1846, but he gave up the *Mystery* and from 1847 to 1849 coedited Douglass' *North Star*. In 1849 he entered the medical department of Harvard College, having been refused admission to three other medical schools because of his race, and graduated in 1852. He set up practice in Pittsburgh as a surgeon and specialist in women's and children's diseases. In 1852 he wrote *The Condition, Elevation, Emigration and Destiny of the Colored People of the United States,* the first classic statement of American black nationalism. When the book was censured by white and black Abolitionists, however, for aiding separatists who saw in colonization a way to avoid racial equality, he attempted to withdraw it from sale. In 1854 he spoke at the first convention of the National Emigration Society, which he helped to form. He proposed resettlement in the Caribbean, South or Central America, or eastern Africa. In 1858 the third session of the Society commissioned him to head an expedition to the Niger Valley. He remained in Africa during 1859, conducting scientific research, and signing a treaty with the chiefs of Arbeokuta for land and the expansion of cotton production, with a view toward imminent colonization. From Africa he went on to a meeting of the International Statistical Congress in London and received wide publicity when his brief comments caused a walkout of almost the entire American delegation, leaving only one representative from Boston. He remained in London, delivered a paper before the Royal Geographical Society, and lectured in Europe for nearly seven months on Africa. In 1861 he returned to Canada, the site of the third emigration meeting, to an organized community of fugitive slaves and black expatriates. During the first weeks of the Civil War, he lectured in the United States and then, his attitudes changing with the course of events, he secured permission to recruit free Negroes for an all-black unit of the Union Army. Early in 1865 he conferred with President Lincoln, and shortly thereafter was commissioned major of infantry with the 104th Colored Troops. He worked for three years after the war with the Freedmen's Bureau to gain Negro voting rights. He was a customshouse inspector in Charlestown, South Carolina, and in 1874 ran for lieutenant governor of the state on a Radical Independent Republican ticket, conducting an able campaign and losing only by a narrow margin. In 1876 he switched his support from the radical black Reconstructionist to the moderate white Democratic Party candidate, and after the election secured a position as trial justice, or justice of the peace. In this post he supported an ill-fated movement for the emigration of 206 blacks from Charlestown to Liberia. He published in 1879 *Principia of Ethnology: The Origins of Race and Color,* advocating racial "purity." He briefly resumed his medical practice, moved to Boston, and in January 1885 died in Xenia, Ohio.

DE LEON, DANIEL (1852–1914), political reformer. Born on the Caribbean island of Curaçao on December 14, 1852, De Leon studied in Europe before coming to the United States about 1874. While teaching school he sought further education at Columbia University; in 1878 he received his law degree and went to practise for a time in Texas. He soon returned to New York and in 1883 began teaching at Columbia. His developing interest in social and political issues led him to support the programs of both Henry George and Edward Bellamy; in 1888 he joined the Knights of Labor and two years later the Socialist Labor Party. He became the party's national lecturer and editor of its newspaper and was several times a candidate for public office under its banner. A strictly doctrinaire Marxist, he left the fumbling Knights of Labor in 1895 to found the Socialist Trade and Labor Alliance as a wing of the Socialist Labor Party. A moderate pro-union faction within the S.L.P. withdrew four years later to establish the Socialist Party of America. In 1905 De Leon helped organize the Industrial Workers of the World, with which the S.T.L.A. was merged. Three years later he was ousted from the I.W.W.

when it came under the leadership of antipolitical advocates of direct action tactics. He formed a smaller organization of his followers shortly thereafter that became known as the Workers' International Industrial Union. He continued to advocate his view of socialism and the proper path to it, though with diminishing influence, until his death on May 11, 1914.

DEMILLE, AGNES (1905–   ), choreographer. Born in New York City in 1905, the daughter of a noted American playwright, the niece of Cecil B. deMille, and the granddaughter of Henry George, Miss deMille followed her family's theatrical tradition, studying ballet and choreography under several famous teachers. After years of frustrating penury as a touring dancer and actress in America, England, and the Continent, she got her first real chance when she was asked to join the new Ballet Theatre, for which, among other ballets, she choreographed the famous *Rodeo,* 1942. But it was her dances for *Oklahoma!* the next year that not only made her a leading U.S. theatrical artist, but also introduced dance to a wide American public that might never have known much about it without her. *Oklahoma!* was followed by a long series of successful musicals, among them *Bloomer Girl,* 1944, *Carousel,* 1945, *Brigadoon,* 1947, *Gentlemen Prefer Blondes,* 1949, and *Paint Your Wagon,* 1951. All of these became spectacular movies, as well, and for these, too, she created innovative and memorable dance episodes. Perhaps her best known ballet is *Fall River Legend,* 1948, based on the story of Lizzie Borden. She headed her own company, the Agnes deMille Dance Theatre, which toured 126 cities in 1953–1954. The recipient of many prizes and awards, she was during the 1940s and 1950s the leading choreographer on Broadway and perhaps in America. She wrote several books, among them *Dance to the Piper,* 1952, *And Promenade Home,* 1958, *To a Young Dancer,* 1962, and *The Book of the Dance,* 1963. She married Walter F. Prude in

1943 but continued to use her maiden name in her professional life.

DEMILLE, CECIL BLOUNT (1881 – 1959), motion-picture producer. Born on August 12, 1881, in Ashfield, Massachusetts, deMille (thus he spelled his name) was the son of a noted playwright, Henry Churchill DeMille. After attending Pennsylvania Military College and the American Academy of Dramatic Arts he went on the stage at the age of 19 and later collaborated with his brother, William Churchill deMille, and with David Belasco in writing several plays. In 1913 he joined Jesse Lasky and Samuel Goldwyn in forming the Jesse L. Lasky Feature Play Company (later Famous Players-Lasky) to produce motion pictures. His first film, *The Squaw Man*, was made that year and contributed to the establishment of film as a serious narrative and dramatic medium. He made several innovations in his early works; perhaps the most consequential was the practice of publicizing the leading players. With *The Ten Commandments*, 1923, he began a series of historical and biblical movies produced on a lavish scale and in a spectacular style that was to become his trademark. In 1924 he formed the DeMille Pictures Corporation; in 1928 he joined Metro-Goldwyn-Mayer, and in 1932 moved to Paramount. In a side venture he organized about 1919 Mercury Aviation Company, a pioneering commercial air service. *The King of Kings*, 1927, *The Sign of the Cross*, 1932, *Cleopatra*, 1934, and *The Crusades*, 1935, all played before huge audiences and laid the basis for his large personal fortune. He turned to American themes for *The Plainsman*, 1936, *The Buccaneer*, 1937, *Union Pacific*, 1938, and *Reap the Wild Wind*, 1941; from 1936 to 1945 he also produced the Lux Radio Theatre of the Air. *The Greatest Show on Earth* won the Academy Award for best picture of 1952; in 1956 he brought the cycle of deMille spectaculars to a close with a new and highly successful version of *The Ten Commandments*. In all he produced more than 70 films and was at work on a documentary study of Robert Baden-Powell and the Boy Scout movement when he died in Hollywood on January 21, 1959.

DEMPSEY, JACK (1895 –), boxer. Born in Manassa, Colorado, on June 24, 1895, Dempsey was christened William Harrison. His education ended in the eighth grade and later, while working at various jobs, he trained himself rigorously to become a boxer. He fought for the first time in 1914, as "Kid Blackie," and the next year adopted the name Jack from a boxer of the 1890s. Though he won nearly all of his early fights it was not until 1917, when he met promoter and manager Jack Kearns, that he began his climb to the heavyweight championship. A rather small man for his weight class, he defeated a number of larger fighters, becoming known as "Jack the Giant Killer"; in tribute to his ferocity in the ring and his habit of winning by knockouts he was also dubbed the "Manassa Mauler." On July 4, 1919, he met Jess Willard in Toledo and in the fourth round won the championship. He retained the crown for seven years, attracting an unprecedented popular following. In 1923 he defended his title in a savage fight with Luis Firpo. On September 23, 1926, in Philadelphia, he lost by a decision to Gene Tunney before a crowd of 100,000. A year later, after a program of conditioning and a victory over Jack Sharkey, he met Tunney again in Chicago. Drawing a record gate of over two and a half million dollars, the fight was to be a subject of controversy for years. In the seventh round Dempsey floored his opponent but, dazed himself, lingered in mid-ring; the referee delayed the count until Dempsey retired to a neutral corner and Tunney was able to regain his feet at the count of nine and go on to win in a ten-round decision. Retiring for a time to refereeing, Dempsey attempted a comeback in 1931 but the next year retired permanently from the ring. During his career he had lost only 5 of 69 bouts and 5 times drawn million-dollar gates. He continued to referee until 1940. During World War II he served as director of physical fitness for the Coast Guard and in 1945 was a morale officer for troops in the Pacific. He later became a successful New York restaurateur with extensive business interests.

DEWEY, GEORGE (1837–1917), naval officer. Born on December 26, 1837, in Montpelier, Vermont, Dewey attended Norwich University in Vermont and graduated from the U.S. Naval Academy at Annapolis in 1858. He became a lieutenant in 1861 and during the Civil War served under Admiral Farragut and later with the Atlantic blockade. He rose to commander in 1872, captain in 1884, and commodore in 1896. As chief of the Bureau of Equipment, 1889, and president of the Board of Inspection and Survey, 1895, he became familiar with the modern battleships of the Navy. Assigned to sea duty at his own request in 1897, he received word of the Spanish-American War while in Hong Kong. With orders to capture or destroy Spanish vessels in Philippine waters, he entered Manila Bay with his command, the Asiatic squadron, consisting of four cruisers and two gunboats, on May 1, 1898. He opened fire and sank or destroyed all ten ships of the Spanish fleet, incurring no damage to American vessels and only eight injuries to American seamen. Thus demonstrating the power of the Navy and the superiority of her new ships, the victory earned for the United States the position of major Pacific power. He was promoted rear admiral on May 10, 1898, and formally commended by Congress. In August his fleet assisted in the occupation of Manila and in September 1899 he returned to the United States, where he was given a hero's welcome. In 1899 he was made admiral of the Navy, a rank created especially for him and the highest ever held by an American naval officer. Thereafter he served as president of the General Board of the Navy. He published an *Autobiography* in 1913 and died in Washington, D.C., on January 16, 1917.

DEWEY, JOHN (1859–1952), philosopher, psychologist, and educator. Born on October 20, 1859, in Burlington, Vermont, Dewey graduated from the University of Vermont in 1879

and after two years of teaching school continued his studies, receiving his Ph.D. from Johns Hopkins University in 1884. During the next ten years he taught philosophy at the universities of Minnesota and Michigan, and in 1894 he moved to the University of Chicago. There, two years later, he established the Laboratory School as a testing ground for his educational theories. He remained director of the school until 1904 when he joined the faculty of Columbia University. His educational thought was widely influential and the source of the wave of school reform proceeding under the general name of progressive education. Based on his development of William James's pragmatism into a scientifically oriented "instrumentalism," Dewey's educational views pictured the process of education as the accumulation and assimilation of experience, as an acculturation process whereby the child, through experience and activity, develops into a balanced personality of wide awareness. Such a view, expressed in terms of growth, development, and process, was directly opposed to the more traditional educational methodology of lecture, memorization, and mechanical drill. Dewey was an advisor to several countries on the development of national educational systems and remained throughout his life the leading educational thinker in America. He retired from the Columbia faculty in 1930, but continued to add to his huge bibliography until his death on June 1, 1952. Among his works are *The School and Society*, 1899, *The Child and the Curriculum*, 1902, *How We Think*, 1910, *Democracy and Education*, 1916, *Human Nature and Conduct*, 1922, *Experience and Nature*, 1925, *The Quest for Certainty*, 1929, *Art as Experience*, 1934, *Experience and Education*, 1938, *Freedom and Culture*, 1939, and *Problems of Men*, 1946. He is generally considered one of the two or three greatest philosophers America has produced.

DEWEY, THOMAS EDMUND (1902–   ), lawyer and public official. Born on March 24, 1902, in Owosso, Michigan, Dewey graduated from the University of Michigan in 1923 and earned his law degree from Columbia in 1925. Admitted to the bar the following year, he practised law in New York until 1931. Then he became New York City's assistant district attorney. As a special investigator of organized crime in 1935–1937 he earned the nickname "racket-buster," having secured 72 convictions in 73 prosecutions. On an anti-Tammany Hall ticket in 1937 he was elected district attorney. The next year he ran unsuccessfully for governor on the Republican ticket, but he was victorious in the elections of 1942, 1946, and 1950. As governor he was capable, efficient, and politically moderate. In 1940 he received strong support for the Republican presidential nomination, but lost to Wendell Willkie. That year his first book, *The Case Against the New Deal,* was published. He won the Republican presidential nomination in 1944 and 1948, in the first election losing on a moderate platform to Roosevelt's liberal policies and position as a wartime incumbent, and in 1948 suffering defeat, widely thought to be an upset, by President Truman. He traveled in the Far East during the late 1940s and published *Journey to the Far Pacific* in 1952. That year he rallied strong support for Dwight D. Eisenhower, securing the large New York delegation on behalf of Eisenhower's nomination. His campaigning contributed greatly to Eisenhower's victory. In 1955, when his third term as New York governor ended, he retired from public office and resumed his law practice.

DICKINSON, EMILY ELIZABETH (1830–1886), poet. Born on December 10, 1830, in Amherst, Massachusetts, Emily Dickinson was the daughter of a prominent lawyer who was later a congressman and treasurer of Amherst College. She attended Amherst Academy and spent a year at the Mount Holyoke Female Seminary, but her dislike of being away from home led her to return permanently to her father's house in 1848. Her residence there was interrupted only by brief trips to Washing-

ton and Philadelphia in 1855 and to Boston and Concord in 1864 and 1865. During her youth she was quite lively and outgoing, but she became progressively more reclusive as the years passed. Though she never married she apparently experienced deep, if ambiguous, emotional involvements on two occasions, the latter during the 1850s with the Rev. Charles Wentworth, who may have been the inspiration for the otherwise imaginary lover alluded to in some of her poems. She seems to have written occasional verse from her school days and she continued to write until her death, but the major portion of her work, and the best of it, was produced during the years 1858–1866. Typically short, condensed pieces, her poems combined spare lyricism and metaphysical speculation with highly unorthodox diction and meter; the provinciality of her outer life belied both the scope of her thought and the subtlety of her style. She showed her work to but a few persons outside her family circle. In 1862 she sent a few verses to critic and essayist Thomas Wentworth Higginson, who was at once charmed and baffled by them; in a remarkable correspondence that continued for more than 20 years he gently counseled against publication. During her life none of her poems were published with her consent, though several did appear, one anonymously in 1878 through the agency of Helen Hunt Jackson, a schoolmate and lifelong friend and the shy poet's leading literary champion. Her father died in 1874 and the next year her mother became an invalid. She kept more and more to herself until at length she rarely ventured from the house, but she maintained correspondences with a few intimates until her death on May 15, 1886. Her sister Lavinia subsequently discovered hundreds of poems neatly tucked away; she prevailed upon a still-dubious Higginson to help prepare a slender volume, *Poems by Emily Dickinson,* 1890. The book met with generally unfavorable critical response, but it was sufficiently well received by the public to warrant the publication of *Poems: Second Series,* 1891, and *Poems: Third Series,* 1896. By 1945 nearly all of Emily Dickinson's poetry had been published and her position as one of America's foremost poets was secure.

DICKINSON, JOHN (1732–1808), public official and political publicist. Born in Talbot County, Maryland, on November 8, 1732, Dickinson moved with his family to Delaware and was educated by private tutors until he took up the study of law in Philadelphia and London. In 1757 he returned from London to begin his practice in Philadelphia and, quickly attaining an eminent position at the bar, entered politics, holding a number of public offices in both Pennsylvania and Delaware. In the tense debate that preceded the Revolution he took a conservative, though pro-colonial, position; while he denounced British policies as unjust, he held out hope to the last for conciliation. As a result of a pamphlet he wrote on the Stamp and Sugar Acts he was appointed by the Pennsylvania legislature to the Stamp Act Congress in 1765 and there drafted the resolution of grievances. In 1767–1768 he published a series of *Letters From a Farmer in Pennsylvania* on the proposed non-importation and non-exportation agreements, for which he won wide popularity. He drafted a number of petitions to the king for the Philadelphia legislature and the First and Second Continental Congresses. Though still opposed to precipitate violence and to separation, he was largely responsible for the "Declaration. . . Setting Forth the Causes and Necessity of Their Taking Up Arms" in 1775. The following year, having aided in the drafting of the Articles of Confederation, he voted against the Declaration of Independence. During the war, however, he served in the militia. He represented Delaware in Congress in 1779; in 1781 he was elected president of the Supreme Executive Council of Delaware and, the next year, of Pennsylvania. He was a member of the Constitutional Convention and thereafter supported ratification. His writings through the whole period earned him the title "penman of the Revolution." He died on February 14, 1808.

DILLINGER, JOHN (1902–1934), outlaw. Born in Indianapolis on June 28, 1902, Dillinger attended school until he was 17 and then took a job in a machine shop. In 1920 he moved to Mooresville, Indiana, where he lived for four years, interrupted only by five months in the Navy, from which he deserted. In September 1924 he and a partner attempted to rob a grocery store in Mooresville; Dillinger was apprehended and sent to a reformatory. After twice failing to escape he was declared incorrigible and transferred to a state prison, but in 1933 he was paroled by the governor. Within less than a month he pulled another robbery, this time in Illinois, and then hit the Daleville, Indiana, bank for $3,000. By this time he was leading a gang that successfully raided two more banks before he was again caught in Dayton, Ohio. With the aid of members of his gang he soon escaped; after two raids on police stations to acquire weapons they struck the Greencastle, Indiana, bank on October 21st and got away with $75,000; Dillinger was named Public Enemy Number One by the FBI. Three more bank jobs followed in Wisconsin, Illinois, and Indiana, and in January 1934 he and six companions were arrested in Tucson, Arizona. After a month in jail in Crown Point, Indiana, he escaped with the aid of a mock pistol he had fashioned from wood. In March he was wounded by police in St. Paul, Minnesota, but remained at large. During April he ranged from Mooresville to Minneapolis. He and his gang retired to a resort in Little Bohemia, Wisconsin; police, informed of his whereabouts, attempted to trap him there, but he successfully fought free. By May a total of $50,000 was being offered for his capture; tempted by a share of the reward, a girl friend, the mysterious "Lady in Red," betrayed him and on July 22nd, as he left the Biograph Theater in Chicago, he was shot and killed by FBI agents.

DIMAGGIO, JOSEPH PAUL, JR. (1914–   ), baseball player. Born on November 25, 1914, in Martinez, California, "Jolting Joe" DiMaggio was the son of immigrant Sicilian parents. He played baseball with a local boys' league in his youth and in 1932 joined an older brother on the San Francisco Seals of the Pacific Coast League. During the 1933 season he hit safely in 61 consecutive games, a league record, and batted .340 overall. The next year, despite a knee injury, he was purchased by the New York Yankees; after a final year of experience and exposure with the Seals he joined the Yankees in 1936 and proceeded to bat .323, to amass an excellent fielding record, and to be chosen for the All-Star team. During his 16 years with the Yankees he was consistently its outstanding player; he was on the All-Star team every year and, except for 1946, batted over .300 each season, reaching a peak of .381 in 1939 and compiling a career average of .325; he was three times chosen the American League's Most Valuable Player. His greatest achievement at the plate came in 1941, when he batted safely in 56 consecutive games, a major league record that may never be broken. His fielding was equally remarkable and was all the more impressive for the easy grace of the execution. He was plagued by injuries throughout his career and often played in spite of them; a modest man who declined to play to the stands and whose style of baseball was one of quiet excellence, he was called "the greatest team player of all time" by Connie Mack. In 1949 his salary was raised to an unprecedented $100,000. In 1951 the "Yankee Clipper" retired, citing an accumulation of injuries and a consequent decline in his ability to live up to the expectations of his teammates and his millions of ardent admirers. In 1954, accompanied by vast publicity, he married movie star Marilyn Monroe, but the marriage was dissolved a year later. In 1955 he was elected to the Baseball Hall of Fame. Afterwards he devoted himself to business pursuits and in 1967 became executive vice president of the Oakland Athletics baseball team.

DISNEY, WALTER ELIAS (1901–1966), cartoonist and motion picture producer. Born in Chicago on December 5, 1901, Walt grew up in Marceline and Kansas City, Missouri. After service in World War I—he was too young for the Army or Navy so he drove a Red Cross ambulance—he began working as a commercial artist and cartoonist in Kansas City. He experimented with animated cartoons and from 1923 to 1926 produced a series of films combining live and animated action called *Alice in Cartoonland*. This and the subsequent *Oswald the Rabbit* series failed to achieve much success. Disney persevered, however, trying a new character named Mickey (originally Mortimer) Mouse; the first two films were ignored, but the third, "Steamboat Willie," the first to employ a sound track, was an immediate and smashing success. More Mickey Mouse shorts followed, gaining a worldwide audience, and Disney soon inaugurated a new series, *Silly Symphonies*, and introduced new characters like Donald Duck and Pluto. In 1938 he released *Snow White and the Seven Dwarfs*, the first feature length cartoon movie, which quickly became a classic. There followed a succession of such films, including *Fantasia*, 1940, which combined animation with a sound track by Leopold Stokowski and the Philadelphia Symphony Orchestra, *Pinocchio*, 1940, *Dumbo*, 1941, *Bambi*, 1942, *Cinderella*, 1950, *Alice in Wonderland*, 1951, *Peter Pan*, 1953, and *Sleeping Beauty*, 1959, all of which have remained favorites through periodic revivals. In 1953 Disney began a series of "True Adventure" nature films with *The Living Desert*; this and the succeeding *Vanishing Prairie*, 1954, *The African Lion*, 1955, and *Secrets of Life*, 1956 won for him the title of Officier d'Académie, France's highest artistic decoration. As dozens of other movies—live-action adventure, comedy, and fantasy—flowed from the Disney studios he began branching out into other areas of entertainment with several television shows—*Disneyland*, *The Mickey Mouse Club*, *Zorro*, and *The Wonderful World of Walt Disney* among them—and the Disneyland amusement park in California, which achieved such popularity and world renown that Soviet Premier Khrushchev was bitterly disappointed when security considerations prevented him from visiting it during his 1959 tour of the United States. Disney was the recipient of hundreds of honors and awards from around the world, including a record 29 Academy Awards. He was busily directing construction of a second Disneyland in Florida when he died in Los Angeles on December 15, 1966.

DIX, DOROTHEA LYNDE (1802–1887), teacher, social reformer, and humanitarian. Born on April 4, 1802, in Hampden, Maine, Dorothea Lynde left her unhappy home at the age of 12 to live and study in Boston with her Calvinist grandmother. By the age of 14 she was teaching in a school for young girls, employing a curriculum of her own devising that stressed the natural sciences and the responsibilities of ethical living. During the middle 1830s, bouts with tuberculosis forced her to abandon teaching and leave Boston. She lived for a time in England and wrote several books for children. After two years she returned to Boston, still a semi-invalid, and found to her amazement that she had inherited a large sum sufficient to support her comfortably for life. But her Calvinist beliefs enjoined her from inactivity. Thus in 1841, when a young clergyman approached her to begin a Sunday school class in the East Cambridge House of Correction, she accepted the offer. In the prison she first observed the treatment of insane and disturbed persons, who were thrown in with criminals, irrespective of age or sex. They were left unclothed, in darkness, without heat or sanitary facilities; some were chained to the walls and flogged. Profoundly shocked, she traveled for nearly two years throughout the state, observed the same conditions everywhere, and in 1843 submitted to the Massachusetts legislature a detailed report of her thoroughly documented findings. Her dignity, feverish compassion, and determination, as well as the issue itself, moved the legislators, and despite public apathy, disbelief, and occasional active opposition, a bill was passed for enlargement of the Worcester insane asylum. In the next 40 years, she inspired legislators of 15 different states and in Canada to establish state hospitals for the mentally ill. Her unflagging efforts prompted the building of 32 institutions in the United States, several in Europe, and two in Japan, and fostered the reorganization, enlargement, and restaffing, with well trained, intelligent personnel, of already existing hospitals. She served in the Civil War as superintendent of women nurses. After the war, she returned to her hospitals, touring, advising, and supporting them. When she died on July 17, 1887, it was in a hospital in Trenton, New Jersey, that she had founded.

DOLE, SANFORD BALLARD (1844–1926), public official and first president of the Republic of Hawaii. Born on April 23, 1844, in Honolulu, the son of American missionaries, Dole was educated in missionary schools, and from 1866 to 1868 attended the Williams College law school in Massachusetts. He was admitted to the Massachusetts bar and returned to Honolulu, where he practised law for 20 years. Sympathetic with the principles of democracy, he nevertheless recognized the suitability of a monarchy for the Hawaiian people; but he was critical of the conduct of the monarchy, and by 1880 had helped to bring about the ousting of its irresponsible ministry. He served in the legislature in 1884 and 1886 and supported a revolution in 1887 that secured a more liberal constitution. From 1887 to 1893 he was associate justice of the supreme court of the islands. In the latter year another revolution broke out. Though not one of the original organizers, he soon became a leader of the movement and when the monarchy was overthrown he became head of the new Provisional Government. Answering a letter from Grover Cleveland, in which the President expressed opposition to annexation and asked that the overthrown regime be restored, Dole emphasized his belief that the two governments would eventually unite but was firm in criticizing Cleveland for interfering in his country's policies. In 1894 the Republic of Hawaii was organized with Dole as president. Relations with the United States remained distant until President McKinley took office. In January of 1898 Dole went to Washington and by summer of that year annexation was completed. When the Territory of Hawaii was organized in 1900, Dole was appointed its first governor. He resigned in 1903 to become U.S. district judge for Hawaii and remained in that post until 1915. He died in Honolulu on June 9, 1926.

DONNELLY, IGNATIUS (1831–1901), reformer, public official, and author. Born in Philadelphia on November 3, 1831, Donnelly early took up the study of law and was admitted to the bar in 1852 but, finding practice dull, he set out for Minnesota in 1856. On the banks of the Mississippi he founded Nininger City in the hope of developing a great Western metropolis. He encouraged settlers and saw to it that the town was well supplied with cultural resources. The panic of 1857 destroyed the dream, but Donnelly remained in Nininger City when everyone else left. He entered politics, joined the Republican Party, and was quickly elected lieutenant governor of Minnesota. From 1863 to 1869 he was in Congress. He became estranged from the Republicans and employed his talents as an orator for a succession of small, protest-based parties in the period of growing Western discontent. From 1874 to 1879 he was in the state senate while editing the *Anti-Monopolist*. Turning for a time to literary pursuits, he wrote in 1882 *Atlantis: The Antediluvian World*, a study in support of the theory of the lost continent; the next year appeared *Ragnarok: The Age of Fire and Gravel*, hypothesizing that ages ago the earth had come into contact with a comet. In 1888 appeared his most famous work, *The Great Cryptogram*, in which, with vast ingenuity, he sought to demonstrate that the works attributed to Shakespeare had actually been written by Francis Bacon. *Caesar's Column*, a utopian novel, appeared in 1891. Donnelly had continued all the while his interest in reform politics and took a leading role in the founding of the National People's (Populist)

Party, writing most of its Omaha platform in 1892. Known by this time as the "Great Apostle of Protest," Donnelly served again for a time in the state legislature and ran for Vice President on the Populist ticket in 1900. He died on January 1, 1901.

MR. DOOLEY see **DUNNE, FINLEY PETER**

DORR, THOMAS WILSON (1805–1854), political reformer. Born in Providence, Rhode Island, on November 5, 1805, Dorr was educated at Philips Exeter Academy and Harvard, graduating from the latter in 1823. Four years later he was admitted to the bar and began practice in Providence. In 1834 he was elected to the state assembly. Rhode Island was at the time still governed under the colonial charter of 1663; power was in the hands of a proprietary class and suffrage was limited to freeholders and their oldest sons. The privilege of instituting civil suits was similarly restricted. After a long period of occasional attempts at reform, public resentment came to a head in 1841. In that year a "People's Party" was organized and a convention called, all without authority from the legislature; a constitution was adopted and, in a referendum held on the principle of universal manhood suffrage, overwhelmingly ratified. The legislature, in retreat, called a similar convention in 1842 and proposed a constitution embodying most, but not all, of the reforms demanded by the People's Party. This constitution was defeated in a referendum. In April 1842 Dorr was elected governor in an election held under the People's constitution; Rhode Island thereupon had two governments. The incumbent regime declared martial law; appeals to President Polk by both sides brought lukewarm support of the proprietors. Dorr then decided on actual rebellion; with a small band of followers he attempted to seize the arsenal in Providence. The revolt was a failure and Dorr escaped to Connecticut. He soon returned, gave himself up, and in 1844 was convicted of high treason, for which he received a sentence of life imprisonment at hard labor. His sentence was voided by act of the assembly the following year and in 1851 his civil rights were likewise restored. He died on December 27, 1854.

DOS PASSOS, JOHN RODRIGO (1896–), author. Born on January 14, 1896, in Chicago, Dos Passos graduated from Harvard in 1916 and traveled in Spain intending to study architecture. When the United States entered World War I, he enlisted in the volunteer ambulance corps in the French army, served for a time with the Italian Red Cross, and then became a private in the U.S. Army medical corps. His war experiences led to the publication of his first two books, *One Man's Initiation*, 1917, about an ambulance driver, and *Three Soldiers*, 1921, a bitter portrayal of war's effects on the book's three major characters. In *Manhattan Transfer*, 1925, he developed a literary style that was revolutionary in its combination of naturalism and stream-of-consciousness techniques. A portrayal in hundreds of brief episodes of the expansive, many-faceted life of New York City, the book reflected his outlook on life, which found fuller expression in his major work, the trilogy *U.S.A.*, comprising *The 42nd Parallel*, 1930, *1919*, 1932, and *The Big Money*, 1936. Focusing on deterioration, absurdity, and helplessness in the three decades at the beginning of the 20th century, the trilogy traced the lives of various characters against a fragmented, panoramic background of newspaper headlines, stories, advertisements, and songs of the era. Biographies of notable Americans formed ironic backgrounds for the lives of lesser figures, and "The Camera Eye" revealed the author's opinions of the action in stream-of-consciousness narrative. With the years his work and thought grew gradually more conservative. A second trilogy, *District of Columbia*, 1939–1949, and poetry, essays, plays, and novels dealing especially with politics formed the bulk of the rest of his writing.

DOUGLAS, STEPHEN ARNOLD (1813–1861), public official and political leader. Born in Brandon, Vermont, on April 23, 1813, Stephen A.

Douglas attended school, was for a time apprenticed to a cabinetmaker, and having begun the study of law, drifted west. He finally settled in Jacksonville, Illinois, and was admitted to the bar there in 1834. He became engaged in politics and rose rapidly to influence within the state Democratic organization. He was successively a legislator, land registrar, secretary of state, and justice of the state supreme court. In 1843 he was elected to Congress. He achieved prominence quickly and was an ardent advocate of westward expansion, supporting the annexation of Texas, the Mexican War, the full Oregon claim, and aid for the construction of transcontinental railroads. In 1847 the Illinois legislature elected him to the Senate where he was given the chairmanship of the Committee on Territories. In this position he helped draft the bills organizing territorial governments in Utah and New Mexico that contained provisions for what was to become his "popular sovereignty" doctrine. He was instrumental in securing the adoption of the Compromise of 1850; four years later, however, he introduced his Kansas-Nebraska Act, reopening the slavery issue by replacing the Missouri Compromise with "popular sovereignty" and bringing a great deal of condemnation upon himself. In 1856 Douglas was a serious candidate for the Democratic presidential nomination; he accepted defeat gracefully, however, and warmly supported Buchanan. The next year he broke with the administration over recognition of the fraudulent Lecompton constitution in Kansas. In denouncing it he lost all favor in the South without gaining equally in the North. In 1858, seeking reelection to the Senate, he engaged in the famous series of debates with Abraham Lincoln; though popular support for him dropped sharply, the gerrymandered legislature reelected him. Two years later he was nominated for the presidency by the Northern wing of the split Democratic Party, the full convention having been split by the adoption of his "popular sovereignty" doctrine and the consequent withdrawal of several Southern states. His campaign against

Lincoln was, he himself admitted, hopeless. After the election he fully and openly supported the new President for the short time that remained before his death on June 3, 1861.

DOUGLAS, WILLIAM ORVILLE (1898–), jurist. Born in Maine, Minnesota, on October 16, 1898, Douglas was educated at Whitman College, in Walla Walla, Washington, from which he received his B.A. in 1920, and at Columbia law school, where he gained his LL.B. in 1925. He was a member of the faculty of the Columbia law school from 1925 to 1928, and of that of the Yale law school from 1928 to 1936. He collaborated with the Department of Commerce on studies of bankruptcy from 1929 to 1932 and was named to the Securities and Exchange Commission in 1936. He was chairman of the commission from 1937 to 1939, the year that President Roosevelt appointed him to the Supreme Court. Though relatively young, he had been an exceptional law professor and member of the SEC, and his nomination to fill the seat previously occupied by Justice Brandeis was widely hailed. He soon established himself as a vigorous though controversial member of the Court, writing many of its opinions in cases involving complicated financial questions and making numerous pronouncements in behalf of civil liberties. For example, a majority decision of May 16, 1949, declared that free speech must be guaranteed even to a speaker who "stirs the public to anger, invites disputes, brings about . . . unrest or creates a disturbance." In the course of the opinion he went on to suggest that free speech, in certain circumstances, might serve its fundamental purposes by creating just such conditions. He wrote several notable dissents against the Court's opinion in antitrust cases, arguing that the Court, and indeed all of American law, tended rather to support monopoly than to oppose it. In general, he was found on the liberal side of the Court. Apart from his work, he was an avid outdoorsman, and he wrote a long series of books recounting his experiences in various wilderness and near-wilderness areas of the world, among them *Of Men and Mountains,* 1950, *Beyond the High Himalayas,* 1952, *North from Malaya,* 1953, *West of the Indus,* 1958, *My Wilderness: East to Katahdin,* 1960, *My Wilderness: the Pacific West,* 1961, *Muir of the Mountains,* an account of the great naturalist John Muir, 1961, and *A Wilderness Bill of Rights,* 1965. He was a strong supporter of all conservation measures and spent his vacations every year in some far-off place, often mounted on a donkey. He was married four times, and his last two wives were considerably younger than he, giving his many critics the opportunity to question his prudence; addititional opportunities came in 1969, when his involvement with a foundation that was in turn involved with gambling in Nevada was aired. He resigned from the foundation but did not seem to be fazed by the outcry, which included the threat of impeachment proceedings; a controversial figure all his life, he continued to be an unpredictable and courageous champion of the have-nots in a society dominated by the haves. Other publications by Justice Douglas were *An Almanac of Liberty,* 1954, *We The Judges,* 1955, *America Challenged,* 1960, *A Living Bill of Rights,* 1961, *Mr. Lincoln and the Negroes,* 1963, *The Bible and the Schools,* 1966, and *Points of Rebellion,* 1969.

DOUGLASS, FREDERICK (1817–1895), social reformer, orator, journalist, and public official. Born into slavery in Tuckahoe, Maryland, Frederick Augustus Washington Bailey was sent to Baltimore as a household servant at the age of nine and there learned to read. In 1833 he was returned to his plantation home as a field hand. An attempted escape in 1836 failed and not long thereafter he was apprenticed to a ship caulker in Baltimore. In 1838, disguised as a sailor, he escaped to New York; he soon moved to New Bedford, Massachusetts, and adopted the name by which he has since been known. In 1841 he delivered an extemporaneous speech before a meeting of the Massachusetts Anti-Slavery Society and was immediately hired as an agent of the society. For the next four years he traveled and spoke throughout the North. Disturbed by rumors, based largely on his considerable oratorical ability, that he had not actually been a slave, he published in 1845 his *Narrative of the Life of Frederick Douglass, an American Slave*. Then, to avoid capture, he traveled to Great Britain where he continued his antislavery efforts for two years. Upon his return his freedom was purchased by public subscription and he founded the *North Star* which, later (beginning in 1851) under the name *Frederick Douglass's Paper*, he continued for 17 years. Though at first he followed William Lloyd Garrison, he soon adopted a more conservative approach to Abolition; he fled to Canada briefly in 1859 when he was falsely accused of supporting John Brown's raid. He was active in organizing Negro troops for service in the Civil War. After the war he was assistant secretary to the Santo Domingo Commission, from 1877 to 1881 he was marshal of the District of Columbia, from 1881 to 1886 District recorder of deeds, and from 1889 to 1891 minister to Haiti. He died on February 20, 1895.

DOWNING, ANDREW JACKSON (1815 – 1852), horticulturist, architect, and landscape artist. Born in Newburgh, New York, on October 30, 1815, Downing was inspired as a child by the garden and conservatory that his father had nurtured for many years. Completing formal schooling at the Montgomery Academy at the age of 16, he joined an elder brother in operating the nursery after his father died in 1822. The many fine country estates near the Downing home provided excellent exposure to rural architecture and landscape. Personable and outgoing, he became friendly with many residents of these homes, discussing the botany of the area, the construction of their houses, and the maintenance of their gardens. He wrote essays on these subjects for Boston journals. His work lacked depth and precision, however, and he returned to the nurseries to gather information.

A Treatise on the Theory and Practice of Landscape Gardening, 1841, established him as an authority on rural art and ran through numerous editions. *Cottage Residences,* 1842, applied the principles of design and function stated in *Landscape Gardening* to low-cost housing. The *Fruits and Trees of America,* 1845, written with his brother Charles, was the most complete work of its kind. In 1846 he began to edit a new periodical, the *Horticulturist,* which included a section of correspondence between Downing and his readers. Subsequently, in partnership with Calvert Vaux, he designed and built estates in the Hudson River area: light, wooden houses with overhanging rooftops, assymetrically designed cottages with breezy, skeletal porches, as well as Gothic styled houses. Recognized as the foremost practitioner of the day, he was invited to design the landscaping around the Capitol, the White House, and the Smithsonian Institution, in Washington, D.C., but his plans had to be executed by successors, for a fire aboard a steamship led to his drowning on July 28, 1852.

DREISER, THEODORE (1871 – 1945), author. Born in Terre Haute, Indiana, on August 27, 1871, Dreiser grew up in a family beset by poverty and not a little religious fanaticism. After a year at the University of Indiana he became a newspaper reporter and occasional free-lance writer, working in a number of cities and settling finally in New York. Under the influence of such writers as Balzac, Dickens, T. H. Huxley, and Herbert Spencer, he began to shape his naturalistic view of man as a creature battered by blind forces and his own passions in an amoral, uncaring universe. Translating this attitude into fiction in 1900 with his first novel, *Sister Carrie,* he ran headlong into the first instance of what was to be an entire career of censorship, condemnation, and controversy. The book was virtually suppressed by its publisher and Dreiser suffered a nervous breakdown, apparently as a consequence. He found employment as editor of a chain of cheaply romantic pulp magazines and by

1911 managed to write his second and more successful novel, *Jennie Gerhardt*. He now devoted himself entirely to writing; quickly he produced *The Financier*, 1912, and *The Titan*, 1914, the first two of a trilogy of novels dealing with the world of business and finance, and *The "Genius"*, 1915. The last of these was violently denounced and suppressed; for a number of years thereafter he wrote mainly in minor forms—travel books, sketches, essays, short stories. He finally achieved recognition and success with *An American Tragedy* in 1925. After this date, Dreiser's output fell off sharply; he ventured into social commentary and, in a highly confused manner, into political analysis. The last volume of his trilogy, *The Stoic*, was not published until after his death on December 28, 1945.

DREW, CHARLES RICHARD (1904–1950), physician. Born in Washington, D.C., on June 3, 1904, Drew graduated from Amherst College, where he had an outstanding athletic as well as academic record. He took his medical degree at McGill University in 1933, and taught pathology at Howard University, subsequently enrolling at Columbia to earn his D.Sc. degree. There he conducted research in the properties and preservation of blood plasma. His dissertation, written in 1940, outlined an efficient way to store large quantities of blood plasma in "blood banks." As the authority in the field, he organized and directed the blood plasma programs in the United States and Great Britain during World War II and supervised the American Red Cross blood donor project. Ironically, the Red Cross would not accept his blood because he was a Negro. With his continued protests and the criticism of others, the Red Cross changed its rule and accepted Negro blood, but kept it in separate banks for black men only. In 1943 he was awarded the Spingarn medal for his contributions to science. In 1945 he became professor of surgery at Howard University and chief surgeon at Freedmen's Hospital in Washington, D.C., later becoming chief of staff. Rather than establish a private practice, he spent his time in recruiting young Negroes for medical practice. On April 1, 1950, he was injured in an automobile accident near Burlington, North Carolina. In dire need of a transfusion, he was turned away from a nearby hospital because of his race, and died on the way to a black hospital.

DUANE, WILLIAM (1760–1835), journalist and publicist. Born near Lake Champlain, New York, on May 17, 1760, Duane was taken to Ireland by his widowed mother in 1765. He took up the trade of printer and in 1787 traveled to Calcutta and established the *Indian World*. Sometime later he was deported for his independent and libertarian views and, after a short and unsatisfactory stay in London, he came to Philadelphia. He secured an editorial position with the *Aurora* and from 1798, in sole charge of the paper, made it the leading Jeffersonian journal in America. His views led him to agitate against the Alien and Sedition Laws; early in 1799 he was arrested under the Sedition Act but promptly acquitted. When, in the same year, he denounced the brutality of the irregular army assembled by Federalists who were hoping for war with France, he was mobbed. A short time later he was again charged with sedition; after several postponements of the trial, the charges were ordered dropped by newly elected President Jefferson. Duane's constant opposition to war with France and to the Alien and Sedition Laws was instrumental in securing the election of Jefferson in 1800, and consequently the repeal of the acts. He continued to edit the *Aurora* until 1822 and remained a close friend and valuable supporter of Jefferson. After a visit to South America in 1822–1823, he was appointed prothonotary of the Pennsylvania supreme court, a position he retained until his death on November 24, 1835.

DU BOIS, WILLIAM EDWARD BURGHARDT (1868–1963), scholar, author, editor, and reform leader. Born in Great Barrington, Massachusetts, on February 23, 1868, Du Bois was of French and Dutch in addition to Negro ancestry. He was educated at Fisk and Harvard universities and soon after obtaining his Ph.D. at Harvard in 1895, he joined the faculty of Atlanta University, where he taught economics and history from 1897 to 1910. With his *Souls of Black Folk* in 1903 he announced the intellectual revolt against the accommodationist principles of Booker T. Washington that crystallized two years later in the founding, under Du Bois' leadership, of the Niagara Movement. When this group was merged with the newly founded National Association for the Advancement of Colored People in 1909, he became editor of the association's journal, *Crisis*. In a series of Pan-African Conferences held in 1900, 1919, 1921, 1923, and 1927, he led the call for independence for African colonies. In 1932 he returned to Atlanta University as head of the sociology department; 12 years later he rejoined the N.A.A.C.P. as director of research. He was co-chairman of the 1945 Pan-African Conference; two years later he published *The World and Africa*. During the 1940s Du Bois began to move from his non-ideological radicalism towards a Marxist and pro-Soviet viewpoint; this change culminated in his joining the Communist Party in 1961. The following year he emigrated to Africa; living in Accra, Ghana, where he became a citizen, he was editor of the proposed *Encyclopedia Africana*. He died on August 27, 1963.

DUDLEY, THOMAS (1576–1653), colonial official. Born in Northampton, England, Dudley was, though orphaned early, of a family of means. After commanding a company in an expedition against France in 1597 he became steward to the Earl of Lincoln. At some point he became interested in Puritanism; he was for a time a member of John Cotton's congregation, and he took some part in the formation of the Massachusetts Bay Company. In 1630, along with Governor Winthrop, he sailed for America as deputy governor of the colony. For the rest of his life he was almost constantly in public office, four times as governor, thirteen times as deputy governor,

besides serving on numerous public committees. He helped found Newton (now Cambridge) and later lived in Roxbury. He was active in promoting the establishment of a college in Cambridge, was one of Harvard's first overseers, and as governor in 1650 signed the college's charter. In 1643 he was a delegate to the New England Confederation. A harsh and uncompromising Puritan, Dudley was a leading force in the suppression of heresy and dissent in the colony, once even bringing charges against John Cotton. He died on July 31, 1653.

DUKE, JAMES BUCHANAN (1856–1925), industrialist and philanthropist. Born on December 23, 1856, near Durham, North Carolina, "Buck" Duke was raised in poverty during the Civil War. Having served in the Confederate army, his father, Washington B. Duke, arrived home in 1865 and found his farm plundered. The armies had overlooked some leaf tobacco growing on the land, however, and knowing that a ready market existed in southern North Carolina, Duke made a quick profit. He purchased more tobacco and acquired a large log house in which to process it. The family's subsequent prosperity allowed Buck to attend an academy in Durham, a boarding school, and Eastman Business College in Poughkeepsie, New York. He became an overseer in the tobacco plant and a partner in W. Duke and Sons at 18. Besides catering to the vast market for pipe tobacco, cigars, plug, and snuff, it entered the cigarette business and revolutionized the tobacco industry. All cigarettes had previously been hand-rolled, which satisfied the small demand that existed for them. Duke perfected a machine to roll cigarettes faster than the human hand could do it, initiated an international advertising campaign, and reduced the price of his cigarettes, when a government tax was lowered, before other manufacturers did. He established a branch plant in New York in 1884, capturing the northern and western markets. In 1890 the "tobacco war" among five leading cigarette manufacturers led to the formation of the American

Tobacco Company with Duke as president. The company pursued an aggressive policy and its acquisitions and subsidiaries grew to include the Continental Tobacco Company, the American Snuff Company, the American Cigar Company, the American Stogie Company, and United Cigar Stores Company, formed to provide a major retail outlet. His invasion of the British market led to the formation of the British-American Company. In 1911 the American Tobacco Company was dissolved by the U.S. Supreme Court, Duke being responsible for arranging the dissolution. A principal in founding the Southern Power Company, he created a trust fund for his holdings and heavily endowed Trinity College, in Durham, which changed its name to Duke University, and hospitals, churches, and children's homes in North and South Carolina. He died on October 10, 1925, having helped to revolutionize the life style of Americans.

DULANY, DANIEL (1722–1797), lawyer. Born in Annapolis, Maryland, on June 28, 1722, Dulany was educated in England at Eton and Cambridge. Returning to America, he was admitted to the Maryland bar in 1747. From 1751 to 1754 and again in 1756 he was a member of the legislative assembly and, for his support of the proprietary government, was appointed to the ruling Council the next year. He remained on the Council until the Revolution ended Maryland's colonial status. He was considered one of the best lawyers in America. Though basically a supporter of the established regime, he vigorously protested what he considered unjust acts of government; it was as a man wishing to be thought of as a loyal British subject rather than as a colonial that he wrote his pamphlet, *Considerations on the Propriety of Imposing Taxes in the British Colonies, for the Purpose of raising a Revenue, by Act of Parliament*, against the Stamp Act of 1765. The popularity he gained with this and other writings was largely lost, however, by his support of other governmental actions. He strongly and consistently opposed the growing radicalism in the colonies,

and during the Revolution he remained a Loyalist. In 1781 his property was confiscated; he moved to Baltimore and lived there until his death on March 17, 1797.

DULLES, JOHN FOSTER (1888–1959), lawyer, public official, and diplomat. Born in Washington, D.C., on February 25, 1888, Dulles graduated from Princeton in 1908, studied at the Sorbonne, and received his law degree from George Washington University in 1911. He immediately joined the international law firm of Sullivan and Cromwell, with which he was associated during his entire legal career, becoming head of the firm in 1927. In 1917 he served as a special agent for the State Department in Central America; during World War I he was an officer in the Army Intelligence Service, and in 1918–1919 he was counsel to the American Peace Commission at Versailles. Between the wars he helped oversee the payment of war reparations. Dulles figured prominently in the formation of the United Nations; he helped prepare the charter at Dumbarton Oaks, was a member of the U.S. delegation at the San Francisco conference in 1945, and from 1946 to 1949 was the U.S. representative to the General Assembly. He was an advisor to the secretary of state at the Council of Foreign Ministers meetings from 1945 to 1949. In 1949 he served for a brief period in the Senate and the following year became a consultant for the State Department, in which post he negotiated the treaty of peace with Japan. In 1952 President-elect Eisenhower appointed him secretary of state. In his six years in this position he was the major force in developing U.S. Cold War policy; repudiating Truman's "containment" of Communist expansion, he advocated active opposition and the liberation of "captive" nations. Despite a wealth of knowledge in foreign affairs and vast exertions in behalf of his views, Dulles was often and widely criticized as inflexible and of narrow outlook. He directed the interposition of American naval force between Communist China and the offshore islands of Quemoy and Matsu, he was the architect of the Eisenhower Doctrine in 1957, and he devised and advocated the twin strategies of "massive retaliation" and "brinksmanship." Ill health forced him to resign from the Cabinet in April 1959, and he died in Washington on May 24th of the same year.

DUNBAR, PAUL LAURENCE (1872–1906), poet. Born on June 27, 1872, in Dayton, Ohio, the son of former slaves, Dunbar attended public schools in Dayton, where he was extremely popular with other students, a member of the literary society, editor of the student publication, and composer of the class song at their graduation in 1891. His early ambitions to become a lawyer or a minister, never materialized for one reason or another; to earn his livelihood he operated an elevator. Writing poetry consumed his spare hours; he was published in newspapers and around Christmas in 1893 appeared a collection, *Oak and Ivory*, that was privately printed. He worked in 1894 for Frederick Douglass at the Haitian Exhibition in the Chicago World's Fair. Returning to Dayton he released a second collection of poems, *Majors and Minors,* 1895, which was warmly reviewed by William Dean Howells in *Harper's Weekly,* and subsequently in great demand. *Lyrics of Lowly Life,* 1896, sympathetically introduced by Howells, made him fashionable as a poet and brought him many engagements as a reader, one of which took him to England in 1897. Written in dialect, his verse transmitted the nostalgia for old plantation days and the apprehensive but aggressive and restless feelings about emancipation. A succession of literary novels, including *The Uncalled,* 1896, *The Love of Landry,* 1900, *The Fanatics,* 1901, and *The Sport of the Gods,* 1902, were, to his regret, not as popular as his poems and short stories in dialect. From his return to the United States in 1897 until late 1898 he was an assistant at the Library of Congress. His perseverance and achievement were celebrated among his people, and many schools and societies were named for him. He also wrote the Tuskegee Institute school song. He died in

Dayton on February 9, 1906. His *Complete Poems* was published posthumously in 1913.

DUNCAN, ISADORA (1878–1927), dancer. Born on May 27, 1878, in San Francisco, the daughter of a poet and a musician, Isadora Duncan was the youngest of four children, all theatrically inclined. Soon after she was born her mother and father were divorced, and the family lived in abject poverty. She taught dancing to the children in her neighborhood and with her sister developed a spontaneous style in which, by means of movements and gestures, they attempted to symbolize music, poetry, and the elements of nature. They won attention in San Francisco and traveled on a spare budget to Chicago and New York City, where she formed an alliance with theatrical manager Augustin Daly. She, her mother, a sister, and a brother embarked on a cattle boat to London. While dancing in a public park, she was discovered by a woman who introduced her through a series of private performances to the cultured elite of London. Similar introductions brought her fame in Paris in 1902. She was hailed in Germany, and after traveling briefly in Greece – she had been profoundly influenced by the Greek sculpture she had seen in the British museum – she returned to Berlin to begin a dancing school for children. Disapproving of what she considered the restrictive bonds of matrimony, she bore two children out of wedlock – a daughter born in 1905 and a son in 1908. At the height of her career in 1913, they and their nurse were drowned in an automobile accident. She attempted to forget the tragedy through work, but World War I intervened and she was forced to move the school, first to America, then South America, Athens, and Paris. Finally the school disbanded. The Russian government in 1921 offered her another school in Moscow. There she met and married Sergei Esenin, a dashing, wild poet of the Revolution. On a tour through America in the midst of the postwar "Red" scare, they were everywhere attacked as Bolshevist spies. She made a bitter farewell to America. Impoverished, they made their way back to Russia and had to sell her furniture; but Esenin went berserk, deserted her, and committed suicide in 1925. The school she had created in Russia continued under other management, and although she never performed again, her teaching and dancing freed ballet from its conservative restrictions and presaged the development of modern expressive dance. Her interpretations of music by Gluck, Brahms, Wagner, and Beethoven were not recorded, but her unrestrained performances in bare feet and loose Grecian garb helped to free women's dress and manners in the 20th century. Her last years were spent in France; she died on September 14, 1927, in Nice, strangled when the long scarf she was wearing caught in the wheels of a car in which she was riding.

DUNNE, FINLEY PETER (1867–1936), "Mr. Dooley," humorist and journalist. Born in Chicago on July 10, 1867, of Irish immigrant parents, Dunne entered journalism after graduating from high school. He worked for a number of local newspapers as a reporter and a feature and editorial writer. In 1892 he wrote his first dialect sketch; the following year he introduced the worldly philosopher Martin Dooley. In a rich Irish brogue Mr. Dooley surveyed the social and political scene about him and, with a singular ability to penetrate sham and a determination to champion the disadvantaged, became a Chicago favorite. In 1898 Mr. Dooley's observations on the victory of "his cousin George" Dewey at Manila made him nationally famous. In that year the first of a long and popular series of collections of past columns was published as *Mr. Dooley in Peace and War*. In 1900 Dunne moved to New York and there contributed articles and Dooley columns to a number of newspapers and magazines. He was associated with the leading "muckrakers" of the period and did much to relieve their lack of humor. To his dismay, the articles published under his own name never achieved the popularity of those under Mr. Dooley's. He gave up Dooley in 1915 and the last volume of the series, *Mr.*

Dooley on Making a Will and Other Necessary Evils, appeared in 1919. Dunne continued to write occasionally until his death on April 24, 1936.

DU PONT DE NEMOURS, ELEUTHÈRE IRÉNÉE (1771–1834), industrialist. Born on June 24, 1771, in Paris, the son of French economist and statesman Pierre Samuel Du Pont de Nemours and grandson of Turgot, Eleuthère learned chemistry under Lavoisier in the royal French powder factory until the French Revolution closed it down. He then managed his father's printing house, which was also closed in 1797 by the Jacobins for upholding the loyalist cause. The family came to America in 1799, intending to found a land expedition company in Virginia. But the son had developed an idea for a powder plant after learning of the poor quality and high cost of American artillery explosives. He returned to France to purchase machinery and with funds from his father's company opened a powder mill on an abandoned farm near Wilmington, Delaware, in 1802. He invented a blasting powder far superior to any then available, which he sold to the government, American fur companies, and South American countries. He amassed a fortune during the War of 1812. Selective in his dealings, he refused large orders from the South Carolina Nullifiers in 1833 rather than lose business from the federal government. He operated the factory on a semi-feudal basis, with workers housed on his property. He died of cholera in Philadelphia on October 31, 1834. His descendants, Pierre Samuel, Irénée, and Lammot, developed E. I. Du Pont de Nemours and Company into one of the world's foremost chemical companies.

DURAND, ASHER BROWN (1796–1886), engraver and painter. Born on August 21, 1796, in Jefferson Village, near Newark, New Jersey, the son of an artisan and mechanic, Durand was educated locally and spent time during vacations making small engravings with tools he developed himself. His father apprenticed him to a steel engraver, Peter Maverick, in 1812, and he became his partner after five years. Their most significant commission was an engraving of John Trumbull's "The Signing of the Declaration of Independence"; this was Durand's first major work and won such high praise from Trumbull that the partnership was dissolved and he embarked on an independent career in his own studio, engraving portraits, gift-books, and banknotes. He turned to painting in the 1830s. Living in New York, he was a member of a circle that included Cooper, Bryant, Morse, and other luminaries, many of whom he joined in founding the National Academy of Design in 1826. From 1840 to 1841 he toured Europe, then began to paint landscapes and is credited, with Thomas Cole, with having founded the American, or Hudson River, school of landscape painting. The school's typical composition showed a group of trees in the foreground, with meadows and valleys stretching back into the distance, all rendered with great attention both to detail and to atmosphere. This style was the first native American movement in art and dominated the American art scene through the 1870s. Durand became the first landscape painter to preside over the National Academy of Design, from 1845 to 1861. He died in Jefferson Village on September 17, 1886.

DWIGHT, TIMOTHY (1752–1817), clergyman and educator. Born in Northampton, Massachusetts, on May 14, 1752, Dwight was the most prominent member of a remarkable family. At an early age he displayed great intellectual ability; he graduated from Yale in 1769, having devoted so much time and effort to his studies that his health was damaged, and, after teaching school for two years, returned to Yale as a tutor. In 1777 he resigned to become a chaplain in the Revolutionary army. In 1779 he returned to Northampton, where he established a coeducational school, preached in several churches, and was prominent in local politics. He accepted the pastorate of the Congregational Church in Greenfield Hill in 1783 and remained for twelve

years, founding another coeducational school that achieved considerable success and fame. In 1785 he published an epic poem, "The Conquest of Canaan," written several years earlier as a result of his association with the Connecticut Wits. His other writings, almost all published posthumously, reflect his strongly Calvinist and Federalist outlook. In 1795 he was elected president of Yale; he devoted the remainder of his life to the improvement of the college. He maintained a strenuous teaching schedule and preached in the college chapel in addition to his administrative duties. Under Dwight's guidance Yale became the standard for colleges springing up in other parts of the country. He died on January 11, 1817. His *Travels in New England and New York*, 4 vol., published in 1821–1822, a vivid and intelligent account of the area, remains his most important work.

DYLAN, BOB (1941–   ), songwriter and singer. Born on May 24, 1941, in Duluth, Minnesota, Dylan was named Robert Zimmerman and adopted his later surname from Welsh poet Dylan Thomas. He grew up in Duluth and in Hibbing and at the age of ten began teaching himself to play the guitar and other instruments. He led a rather turbulent youth, running away from home a number of times, and finally, in 1960, after a brief attendance at the University of Minnesota, he set out on his own. He rode freight trains and hitchhiked around the country, "making my own depression," worked at odd jobs from time to time, and wrote songs inspired by country and western music, the blues, and folk music, particularly that of Woody Guthrie. In 1961 he visited Guthrie, then hospitalized with a fatal illness, and then moved to New York City, where he began to sing occasionally in coffeehouses in Greenwich Village. Within a short time he had attracted considerable attention for both his songs and his highly personal singing style, and in the same year his first record album was released. Melodically simple, his songs were nonetheless often powerful statements of protest, though couched in language that ranged from the sardonically humorous to the obscurely allegorical; many were popularized by other performers and some—"Blowin' in the Wind," for example, and particularly "The Times, They Are A-Changin'"—became anthems of the civil rights and student protest movements of the 1960s. His recordings were without exception best sellers and had a profound influence on popular music, most notably in his blending of traditional forms with the rhythmic and instrumental styles of rock and roll into "folk-rock." The lyric of another of his early songs, "A Hard Rain's A-Gonna Fall," marked a trend, later more pronounced, toward a poetic narrative of freely associated images that led some critics to consider Dylan among the leading serious poets of the day. He himself disclaimed such consideration; similarly he disavowed the protest and reform movements that took up his songs, preferring to retain his privacy intact.

EADS, JAMES BUCHANAN (1820–1887), engineer and inventor. Born on May 23, 1820, in Lawrenceburg, Indiana, Eads moved during his childhood to Cincinnati, Louisville, and St. Louis. He attended school until the age of 13, then began working as a Mississippi steamboat purser to help support his family. He devised a means of retrieving sunken steamers and their cargoes with a diving bell of his own invention. He resigned as a purser in 1842 and became a partner in a lucrative steamboat salvaging firm. He left the business three years later to open a glassworks in St. Louis; by 1848 he was heavily in debt, but he returned to the salvage business and within nine years had paid his creditors and made himself a fortune. In 1861, at President Lincoln's request, he submitted plans to the government for fortifying the western rivers. When the war began, he proposed to build a fleet of seven steam driven, armored artillery ships in two months; the first was ready in 45 days and the others quickly followed. The ships incorporated his own inventions for mounted artillery. His major achievement was the Eads Bridge

across the Mississippi at St. Louis. His design solved problems of span and clearance that had been judged insuperable by a team of 27 leading engineers. Work on the bridge began in 1867 and was completed in 1874. He again went against the concensus of less imaginative engineers in proposing to Congress in 1874 to clear the mouth of the Mississippi. Work began the following year in the South Pass and by 1879 his ingenious system of jetties, built to control the direction and speed of flow, had forced the river to clear its own channel by carrying sediment out into the Gulf. During his last years he lobbied Congress unsuccessfully on behalf of a proposed alternative route to the Panama Canal. He died in Nassau on March 8, 1887.

EAKINS, THOMAS (1844–1916), artist. Born on July 25, 1844, in Philadelphia, Eakins was educated at the Pennsylvania Academy of Fine Arts and from 1866 to 1869 at the École des Beaux Arts in Paris, and traveled briefly in Spain, where he was enthralled by the work of Spanish realists, such as Velasquez and Goya. Returning to Philadelphia, he studied anatomy at Jefferson Medical College and in 1873 became a lecturer at the Pennsylvania Academy. He emphasized courses on anatomy and geometrical perspective, believing that technique was as important to a painter as to a draftsman or an engineer. His own work was carefully laid out with enormous attention to detail, creating a feeling of stark realism. His portraits and figure studies were true to sitters, who sometimes took offense because of the acuteness of the portrayal. He also used photographs and experimented in a rudimentary motion picture technique to study the movement of the human body. In 1886 he was dismissed from the Academy for introducing a nude model into a coeducational class. Two of his most famous studies were of scenes in clinics, "The Gross Clinic," 1875, and "The Agnew Clinic," 1889. He also completed sports scenes, notably "Max Schmitt in a Single Scull," 1871, and "Between the Rounds," 1899, and, in sculpture, the "Prophets" for the Witherspoon Building in Philadelphia, and figures for the Trenton Battle monument and for the Soldiers' and Sailors' monument in Brooklyn. He died in Philadelphia on June 25, 1916, and eventually came to be recognized as one of the greatest of American artists.

EARHART, AMELIA (1898–1937), aviator. Born on July 24, 1898, in Atchison, Kansas, Amelia Earhart was an Army nurse in Canada during World War I and a social worker at Denison House in Boston before starting her career in aviation. She learned to fly despite her family's feverish protests and in 1928 (as a passenger) became the first woman to fly the Atlantic; in 1932 she made her own solo crossing, setting a record in the process. She became aviation editor for *Cosmopolitan* in 1928 and published two books, *20 Hours, 40 Minutes,* 1928, and *The Fun of It,* 1932. Married in 1931 to publisher George Palmer Putnam, she retained her maiden name and her complete freedom. In 1930–1931 she was vice president of Luddington Airlines, Inc., an early passenger service in the East. In various airplanes and Autogiros she set a number of altitude and speed records and in 1935 made the first solo flight from Hawaii to the U.S. mainland. In 1937 she attempted a round-the-world flight with a companion in a twin-engined Lockheed Electra. On July 2, flying from New Guinea, trouble developed aboard her plane; radio contact was broken and never resumed. No trace of the plane was ever discovered.

EASTMAN, GEORGE (1854–1932), inventor and manufacturer. Born on July 12, 1854, in Waterville, New York, Eastman moved with his family to Rochester, where he attended school and became interested in photography. In 1880, while working for a bank and an insurance company, he perfected a process for manufacturing photographic dry plates and with a partner established a small factory in Rochester. He developed a paper-backed film in 1884, introduced roll film in 1885, and in 1888 began marketing an inexpensive pre-loaded camera, the Kodak. In 1889 the first flexible, transparent film appeared and in 1891, day-loading film. He expanded the Rochester factory and organized the Eastman Kodak Company in 1892. He dominated the manufacture of photographic equipment, which was constantly improved, and contributed vastly to the development of photography as a popular hobby. By buying out rivals, acquiring patent rights, and holding off foreign competition, Eastman Kodak had a virtual monopoly on photographic equipment in the American market by 1927. A major philanthropist, he donated the bulk of his fortune to various academic and medical institutions, the major recipients being the University of Rochester, which established the Eastman School of Music, and the Massachusetts Institute of Technology; his benefactions eventually amounted to more than $75 million. He also instituted one of America's first profit-sharing plans for employees of Kodak. He died by suicide on March 14, 1932.

EDDY, MARY MORSE BAKER (1821–1910), founder of Christian Science. Born in Bow, New Hampshire, on July 16, 1821, Mary Baker received little formal education but read at home with the aid of her brother. She was from childhood in poor health, subject to seizures and nervous collapse. She married George Glover in 1843 and was widowed the following year. She lived then in retirement with her family until 1853, when she married Daniel Patterson, a dentist and homeopathist. Her long and seemingly hopeless illness roused her interest in spiritual healing, and in 1862 she sought help from the notable practitioner, Phineas Parkhurst Quimby. She was, she attested, cured immediately; she became a disciple devoted to spreading Quimby's methods and fame. He died in 1866 and the same year, having suffered a relapse, Mrs. Patterson obtained a divorce from her husband, resumed the name Glover, and again retired from the world. In 1870 she began her own career of healing and teaching; gradually she abandoned her dependence on Quimby's influence and evolved her own system, and in 1875 published the first of many versions of *Science and Health*, espousing the doctrine that Mind is the sole reality and that the infirmities of the body, like the body itself, are illusory and susceptible to cure by purely mental effort as exemplified in her reading of Christ's words in the New Testament. She gathered a group of followers, one of whom, Asa Eddy, she married in 1877. The "Church of Christ, Scientist" was chartered in 1879; in 1881 the Massachusetts Metaphysical College was founded in Boston and continued under her leadership for 8 years. In 1883 Mrs. Eddy began to publish the *Christian Science Journal*, which enabled her to extend her influence beyond the immediate New England area. In 1895 The Mother Church was founded in Boston; the membership rolls grew, and she created an effective and largely autocratic organization to oversee the affairs of the church. The *Journal* was succeeded by the *Christian Science Sentinel* in 1898 and by the *Christian Science Monitor* in 1908. In 1889 she retired from Boston to Concord, New Hampshire, and later to Chestnut Hill. She maintained control of the church despite disintegrating health—for which she eventually consulted physicians—until her death on December 3, 1910.

EDISON, THOMAS ALVA (1847–1931), inventor. Born in Milan, Ohio, on February 11, 1847, Edison grew up in that town and in Port Huron, Michigan, where, for three months, he received his only formal education. For a time he worked as a railroad newsboy and in 1863 became a telegraph operator. He had since childhood experimented constantly with whatever materials lay at hand, and telegraphy turned his mind to electricity. In 1869 he was granted his first patent for an electrical vote recorder. In that year he moved to New York and became general manager of a stockticker company; he also entered into partnership with Pope, Edison & Co., an electrical engineering consultation firm that was bought out for its patents the next year. With his share of the money Edison opened a manufacturing firm—in reality a research and development company—and in the next few years produced, among other things, quadruplex telegraphy and the carbon transmitter that made practical for wide use the Bell telephone. In 1876 he opened a large new laboratory in Menlo Park, New Jersey; the first major product of the new facility was the phonograph, demonstrated in 1877. Unlike most other of his inventions, which were typically developments of earlier work by other men, the phonograph was Edison's in both concept and execution. In 1879, after an exhaustive period of trial-and-error experimentation, he demonstrated a practical incandescent bulb for illumination. More important than the bulb itself, however, was his subsequent development of a system of wide and efficient power distribution from central generating stations; in the course of this work, a gigantic engineering undertaking, came improvements in motors and dynamos, a practical electric railway, and many other valuable innovations. During his work on the incandescent bulb, Edison had made his only purely scientific discovery, the "Edison effect" of a one-way current between separated electrodes in an evacuated bulb; he paid little attention to the phenomenon, considering it to be of no commercial value, and it was thus left to others to develop the electron tube. In 1887 he moved his laboratory to West Orange, New Jersey. Here four years later Edison patented his "kinetoscope" that, incorporating improvements of his own and others, developed eventually into the motion picture apparatus commonly used today. He returned to his phonograph to improve it, introducing a wax cylinder and later a disc for the recording surface; he devoted time to developing an improved storage battery, a magnetic method for separating iron ore, the manufacture of cement, and many other projects. During World War I he served as a consultant to the Navy on various problems, particularly chemical production and weapons development. In all his work Edison was dedicated to the practical and useful; commercially unprofitable ventures did not interest him, but a potentially beneficial product would elicit from him boundless energy and patience (hence his definition of genius as "one percent inspiration and ninety-nine percent perspiration"). During his life he was granted well over 1,000 patents; he came to symbolize for many the archetypal inventor and the practical American genius of technology. He died in West Orange on October 18, 1931.

EDWARDS, JONATHAN (1703–1758), clergyman and theologian. Born on October 5, 1703, in East Windsor, Connecticut, Edwards was schooled at home and had already displayed great intellectual ability when, not quite 13, he entered Yale. He graduated in 1720 and for two years studied divinity. He served briefly as pastor of a church in New York and then, in 1724, returned to Yale as a tutor. In 1726 he resigned to become the colleague of Solomon Stoddard, his grandfather, in the pulpit of the highly influential church of Northampton, Massachusetts; three years later, upon Stoddard's death, he took sole charge. Edwards' preaching was more than effective; his theology, profoundly influenced by Newtonian science and Lockean psychology, evolved into a masterly system of logical analysis that, though stated in terms of contemporary philosophy, contained a great deal of essentially revanchist Calvinism. His developed system was, however, the product of a profound and original philosophical intellect. In 1734–1735 a small wave of revival followed his sermons on "Justification by Faith Alone"; a much larger wave occurred in 1740–1742 when George Whitefield's evangelistic tour precipitated the "Great Awakening." Though critical of its emotional excesses, Edwards largely approved of the revival and defended it in a number of pamphlets. During this time he delivered his best-known sermon, "Sinners in the Hands of an Angry God," a classically Calvinist exposition of man's natural baseness and God's absolute sovereignty, which described, in vivid detail, the prospects of eternal damnation for the non-elect. His growing insistence on professions, not only of faith, but of regenerative experience, by prospective church members—a requirement that had been allowed to lapse under the "Half-way Covenant" —brought him into conflict with his own congregation in the late 1740s. In 1750 he was dismissed from the Northampton church and the following year answered a call to the frontier and missionary church in Stockbridge, Massachusetts. In his years there he wrote a series of books and pamphlets, including his *Freedom of the Will*, 1754, refuting the Arminianism that, by way of the Episcopal Church, was slowly spreading through New England. In 1757 he was chosen president of the College of New Jersey (now Princeton); he assumed the office in January 1758 but died shortly thereafter, on March 22.

EGGLESTON, EDWARD (1837–1902), clergyman, author, and historian. Born on December 10, 1837, in Vevay, Indiana, Eggleston grew up and was educated there and in other small Indiana communities, all part of what was then virtually the frontier. He became a Bible agent in 1855 and in 1856 a Methodist circuit rider, but poor health forced him to seek a less strenuous profession. In 1858 he went to Minnesota in hopes of restoring his health and during the next several years filled a number of pastorates there. He moved to Evanston, Illinois, in 1866, becoming editor of the *Little Corporal*, a Chicago juvenile paper; early in 1867 he began editing the *National Sunday School Teacher* and in the next three years published several children's books. In 1870 he went to New York to edit the *Independent* until transferring for a year to *Hearth and Home* in 1871. In that year his first novel, *The Hoosier Schoolmaster*, was serialized in *Hearth and Home*; based on his Indiana boyhood, the book was, despite its sentimentalism, a major contribution to the growth of literary realism. Full of local color, it utilized an authentic vernacular style and presented a picture of a rapidly disappearing backwoods way of life. Other novels followed, including *The End of the World*, 1872, *The Mystery of Metropolisville*, 1873, *The Circuit Rider*, 1874, *Roxy*, 1878, *The Graysons*, 1888, and *The Faith Doctor*, 1891. From 1874 to 1879 he was pastor of the Church of Christian Endeavor in Brooklyn; soon afterward he moved to Joshua's Rock, on Lake George, New York, where he lived for the rest of his life. During the 1890s he became interested in history, and he published a number of articles, biographies, and school texts. He planned a *History of Life in the United States* based on cultural developments, but completed only two volumes, *The Beginners of a Nation*, 1896, and *The Transit of Civilization*, 1900. In the latter year he was elected president of the American Historical Association. He died on September 4, 1902.

EINSTEIN, ALBERT (1879–1955), physicist. Born in Ulm, Germany, on March 14, 1879, Einstein moved with his family to Munich as a child and received his first schooling there. Formal education failed to excite him, but on his own he developed a deep interest in mathematics. This continued while he completed his schooling in Switzerland and entered the Federal Polytechnic School to be trained as a physics and mathematics teacher. He graduated in 1900 and, taking Swiss citizenship, was employed in the patent office in Berne. During the next few years he developed his first major contributions to physics, among them the special theory of relativity, the mass-energy equivalence formula ($E = mc^2$), the foundation of the photon theory of light (an important step toward the quantum theory), and the theory of Brownian motion (the existence of which phenomenon, remarkably, he deduced from theoretical considerations, unaware that it had been observed and studied for decades). The papers announcing these discoveries were all published in 1905; in that year he was awarded a Ph.D. by the University of Zürich, and four years later he became a pro-

fessor there. A number of teaching positions followed, at the German University in Prague, at the Swiss Federal Polytechnic School, and finally, in 1913, at the University of Berlin, where he also became director of the Kaiser Wilhelm Institute. In 1916 he published the result of his continuing work in the geometrization of physics and the integration of gravitational, accelerational, and magnetic phenomena, the general theory of relativity. His paper on this theory constituted a revolution in physics comparable only to that of the advent of Newtonian mechanics; from then on, while making a number of contributions to statistical and quantum mechanics, he devoted himself primarily to the development of a "unified field theory," uniting magnetic, electromagnetic, and gravitational phenomena into a single set of equations. He was awarded the 1921 Nobel Prize for physics, largely for his 1905 paper on photons and photoelectricity. In 1932 he made a short visit to the United States; upon his return he resigned his various positions and the following year left Germany, by then under its new Nazi regime, to take up permanent residence in America. For the rest of his career, he was associated with Princeton University and its Institute for Advanced Study. In 1939, at the suggestion of several scientists who, like himself, had become concerned over Germany's apparent efforts to develop a nuclear fission device, he wrote his famous letter to President Roosevelt that led directly to the Manhattan Project and the atomic bomb. Einstein became an American citizen in 1940. He continued to work in physics as well as for a number of social causes, particularly that of peace, until his death on April 18, 1955.

EISENHOWER, DWIGHT DAVID (1890–1969), soldier and 34th U.S. President. Born on October 14, 1890, in Denison, Texas, Eisenhower moved with his family in the following year to Abilene, Kansas, where he grew up in relative poverty. In 1911 he was appointed to West Point; after his graduation four years later he served at a succession of army installations around the world, rising slowly but steadily in rank and responsibility. Soon after the attack on Pearl Harbor in December 1941 he was called to the War Plans Division of the Army's staff headquarters in Washington, D.C. In June 1942 he became commander of the United States forces in Europe; he planned and directed the invasions of North Africa, Sicily, and Italy. In January 1944 he was appointed supreme commander of all Allied forces in Europe, and he remained in this post through the D-Day invasion of June 6, 1944, to the final armistice nearly a year later. In December 1944 he was promoted to the five-star rank of general of the army. After briefly commanding the American occupation forces in Germany, he returned to the United States in November 1945 as Army chief of staff. In 1948 he retired to become president of Columbia University; he published in the same year *Crusade in Europe*, his best-selling war memoir. In 1950 President Truman returned him to duty as commander of the newly organized NATO forces in Europe. Long mentioned by both parties as a potential candidate, Eisenhower finally consented to be considered for the 1952 Republican presidential nomination; he won the nomination and the election, the latter by an overwhelming margin. Intent on remaining above partisanship, and a firm believer in the tradition of separation of powers, he brought to the office a concept of government that he termed, enigmatically, "dynamic conservatism." The problems of postwar America—peace, disarmament, the Cold War, the economy, civil rights—he left largely to the direction of designated subordinates or to Congress. Not until late in his second term (he was reelected in 1956 by an even greater plurality) did he take consistently positive action in behalf of his own policies; then, in 1959, he embarked on a period of unprecedented personal diplomacy that for a time raised worldwide hopes for lasting peace. He retired from office in 1961 to private life; his generally deteriorating health

limited his activities and, after a lengthy hospitalization, he died on March 28, 1969.

ELIOT, CHARLES WILLIAM (1834–1926), educator and editor. Born in Boston on March 20, 1834, Eliot was educated at the Boston Latin School and at Harvard. Following his graduation from the latter in 1853 he taught mathematics and chemistry at the college for ten years. After a tour of Europe he became professor of analytical chemistry at the Massachusetts Institute of Technology in 1865. Two years later he made a second visit to Europe, this time devoting close attention to educational practices there; in 1869 he published the results of his study as "The New Education: Its Organization" in the *Atlantic Monthly*. As one result he was chosen president of Harvard in the same year and began his forty-year career of educational reform and innovation. Under his leadership the university was completely reorganized; the college became the undergraduate nucleus, the professional schools were premised on the college's ability to provide liberal education in both the sciences and the humanities, the graduate school was established (1890), and standards of admission and instruction were raised greatly. He gradually introduced an elective system into the undergraduate college, eliminating the traditional completely prescribed course of study; the professional schools of law and medicine were vastly improved by the raising of standards and the complete revision of methods of instruction. By the end of his tenure in 1909 Eliot had created the modern Harvard University and made it an institution of world renown. His policies spread, affecting not only other colleges and universities, but also the nation's secondary schools, inducing them to raise their own standards. He edited the famous "five-foot shelf of books," the *Harvard Classics*, which appeared in 1909–1910. In 1909 he retired to private life, though he maintained an active interest in educational and public affairs. He died on August 22, 1926, in Northeast Harbor, Maine.

939

ELIOT, JOHN (1604–1690), clergyman, "the Apostle to the Indians." Born in 1604 in Widford, Hertfordshire, England, Eliot came from a prosperous family. He graduated from Cambridge in 1622 and for a time was a teacher. In 1631 a group of Puritan friends persuaded him to emigrate to America with them as their pastor; he settled first in Boston and the next year, having declined an offer to remain as John Wilson's colleague, in Roxbury. He interested himself in the Indians of Massachusetts and in 1646 began preaching to them regularly. By the following year he was preaching in their native Algonkian tongue. His missionary work was supported by the Massachusetts General Court and, from 1649, by the Company for Propagating the Gospel in New England and Parts Adjacent in North America, established in England. In 1653 he published *A Primer or Catechism, in the Massachusetts Indian Language* and his translation of the Bible, 1661–1663, was the first in any language to be printed in America. By 1674 he had settled converted Indians in 14 villages; King Philip's War of the next year scattered them and, because of the treatment that even the Christianized Indians received from the colonists, set back his work irretrievably. Eliot continued his mission, though now handicapped by distrust among the formerly friendly groups, until his death on May 21, 1690.

ELLINGTON, DUKE (1899–   ), composer and band leader. Born on April 29, 1899, in Washington, D. C., Edward Kennedy Ellington was known from childhood as "Duke." He exhibited considerable artistic talent during his youth and was offered a scholarship to the Pratt Institute to study art, but, preferring to devote himself to music, he declined it. A largely self-taught pianist, he was much influenced by jazz and ragtime performers. While working as a sign-painter he began to play professionally and in 1918 founded his own band. In 1923 he moved to New York City and, playing at the Kentucky Club, began gathering the musicians who formed the core of his orchestra—Bubber Miley, Sam Nanton, Harry Carney, and Sonny Greer, among others—and made his first recordings. With no formal training in composition, he nonetheless employed daring and innovative musical devices in his works; blending lush melodies with unorthodox and often dissonant harmonies and rhythmic structures based on "jungle" effects, he wrote and arranged songs tailored to his own band and soloists. Radio broadcasts during an engagement at the fashionable Cotton Club from 1927 to 1932 brought him and his group national recognition, and his recordings—particularly "Saddest Tale," "Echoes of Harlem," "Black and Tan Fantasy," and "Mood Indigo"—spread their fame to Europe. Appearances on Broadway and in movies and tours of Europe and the United States further established the orchestra's reputation. Joined by Barney Bigard, Johnny Hodges, and Cootie Williams, the group continued to produce recordings that became jazz classics—"Ko Ko," "Blue Serge," "Bojangles," "Harlem Air Shaft"—and Ellington began to compose longer and more elaborate works. In 1943 *Black, Brown, and Beige* premiered at Carnegie Hall, in 1947 he wrote *Liberian Suite* for that country's centennial, and in 1950 he was commissioned by Arturo Toscanini to write *Harlem* for the NBC Symphony Orchestra. Others among his most famous songs were "Sophisticated Lady," "In My Solitude," and "Don't Get Around Much Anymore." He composed scores and incidental music for a number of movies and stage productions, including *Anatomy of a Murder, Paris Blues, Beggar's Holiday*, and Shakespeare's *Timon of Athens*. In 1965 his first sacred concert, including a musical sermon, "In the Beginning, God," was performed in New York; in the next year it was heard in Europe while a second such work was premiered at the Cathedral of St. John the Divine in New York. The Ellington orchestra continued to tour America and Europe frequently, at times under State Depart-ent auspices. He was recognized as having broken out of the ranks of jazz musicians to become one of the leading American composers of the century; among his many honors and awards were the Spingarn Medal of the National Association for the Advancement of Colored People and, in 1969, the Presidential Medal of Honor.

ELLISON, RALPH WALDO (1914–   ), author. Born in Oklahoma City on March 1, 1914, Ellison played the trumpet from age eight and took classical music courses in school. He continued in classical composition under composer William Dawson at the Tuskegee Institute, which he attended from 1933 to 1936. In his junior year he visited New York City and studied sculpture briefly. He also met Richard Wright, who inspired him to turn to writing. In 1937 he returned to New York City and began contributing essays, short stories, and reviews to various publications, including *New Masses,* the *Negro Quarterly, Cross Roads,* and *Tomorrow.* Although initially attracted to political radicalism, he later focussed primarily on his role as an artist. Two of his best short stories, "King of the Bingo Game" and "Flying Home," both published in 1944, concerned the black man's place in white society and his relationship to his own complex heritage. In Ellison's most significant work, *The Invisible Man,* 1953, the theme of racial identity was again predominant. The winner of the 1953 National Book Award and named by a Book Week poll in 1965 as the "most distinguished single work" published in the previous 20 years, it earned him a place among major contemporary writers, beyond the sphere of "race" writers. *Shadow and Act,* 1964, a collection of interviews and essays written after 1953, elucidated the shape of his life and expressed his abiding confidence that strong cultural qualities would release his race from the bondage of stereotypes. He lived for two years in Rome and after 1955 taught at Bard College, lectured at the State University of New York at Stony Brook, Long Island, and was a writer-in-residence at Rutgers and a visiting fellow at Yale.

ELLSWORTH, OLIVER (1745–1807), lawyer, jurist, and public official. Born in Windsor, Connecticut, on April 29, 1745, Ellsworth was educated at Yale and Princeton, graduating from the latter in 1766. He studied theology briefly, but soon turned to law and was admitted to the bar in 1771. Moving to Hartford in 1775, his rise in prominence was rapid and he quickly became a political figure; in 1777 he was appointed state's attorney for Hartford County and elected to the Continental Congress, in 1780 he became a member of the Governor's Council of Connecticut, and in 1785 he was named to the state superior court. Little is known of his activities during his six years in the Continental Congress; his national importance dates from the Constitutional Convention in 1787. There he had a major share in developing the "Connecticut Compromise" that constructed the bicameral national legislature with representation balanced between states and populations. His "Letters to a Landholder," published in the *Connecticut Courant* and the *American Mercury,* were of great influence in his state's decision on ratification. In 1789 he was elected one of Connecticut's first two senators; in his seven years in the Senate he became a major force in the new government. He reported the first set of Senate rules, the first 12 amendments to the Constitution, and a bill on organizing the government of the region south of the Ohio; he drafted bills for the admission of North Carolina and for the regulation of the consular service. Most important, he was chiefly responsible for the Federal Judiciary Act of 1789, still the basis of the nation's judicial structure. In 1796 he was appointed chief justice of the Supreme Court. Three years later he was sent by President Adams to assist in the negotiation of a new treaty with France; the resulting treaty of 1800, while unsatisfactory, succeeded in averting war. In that year, his health badly impaired, Ellsworth resigned from the Supreme Court. Upon his return to the United States he retired to private life and died on November 26, 1807.

ELY, RICHARD THEODORE (1854–1943), economist. Born on April 13, 1854, in Ripley, New York, Ely graduated from Columbia in 1876 and for four years continued his studies in several European universities, taking his Ph.D. from Heidelberg in 1879. After returning to the United States in 1880 he engaged in journalism until he was invited to become the first professor of political economy at Johns Hopkins University in 1881. Ely took the lead among younger economists in challenging the naturalistic viewpoints of classical writers and their similarly gloomy descendants, the Social Darwinists. He maintained that the economy was susceptible to control and guidance and that purposeful intervention was necessary to achieve economic justice; he was a particularly vocal supporter of the organization of labor and he advocated the public ownership of natural resources and public utilities. For such views he was regularly denounced as a subversive. During his 11 years at Hopkins he published several books, among them *French and German Socialism in Modern Times,* 1883, and *Introduction to Political Economy,* 1889. In 1885 he helped found the American Economic Association, of which he served as secretary from that year until 1892 and as president from 1892 to 1901. In 1892 he became head of the economics department at the University of Wisconsin, a position he held for 33 years. His advocacy of progressive economics was widely influential and among his books of the period were *Monopolies and Trusts,* 1900, *Studies in the Evolution of Industrial Society,* 1903, and *Foundations of National Prosperity,* 1917. He founded and was director and president of the Institute for Research in Land Economics and Public Utilities (later the Institute for Economic Research, Inc.) and in 1925 moved with it to Northwestern University, where he remained until 1933. Among his later writings were *Elements of Land Economics* (with E. W. Morehouse),

1926, *Hard Times—The Way In and the Way Out,* 1931, and the autobiographical *Ground Under Our Feet,* 1938. The 1937 6th edition of his *Outlines of Economics* (with R. H. Hess) was for many years the principal textbook in the field. Ely died at his home in Old Lyme, Connecticut, on October 4, 1943.

EMERSON, RALPH WALDO (1803–1882), essayist and poet. Born in Boston on May 25, 1803, Emerson came of a long line of New England clergymen. Accordingly, after his graduation from Harvard in 1821, and a few unsatisfactory years spent teaching school to support himself and his widowed mother, he began to study for the ministry. He was licensed to preach in 1826 and three years later assumed the pastorate of the Second Church of Boston. His short time in the pulpit was an unhappy one; his religious doubts and a dislike of being merely the agent of received doctrines and rituals finally culminated in his resignation in 1832. Shortly thereafter he sailed for Europe where he met Coleridge, Wordsworth, and Carlyle, all of whom, particularly the last, had a profound influence on him. His reading of the English, and through them the German, idealists gave direction to his yet unformed philosophy. Upon his return to America he determined upon a literary career; in 1834 he moved to Concord, Massachusetts, his home for the rest of his life. He resumed his preaching, though not connected with any church, and began what was to be a life of lecturing. In 1836 Emerson published *Nature,* a small volume that contained the seeds of his later work and was the first coherent expression of the intellectual ferment then simmering throughout New England. The same year saw the first gathering in Concord of what became the Transcendentalist Club—Emerson, Orestes Brownson, Theodore Parker, Margaret Fuller, Bronson Alcott, and others. In 1837 he was invited to deliver the Phi Beta Kappa address at Harvard; his address, "The American Scholar," was heard as a clarion call for intellectual independence, from Europe, from the past, from all obstacles to originality. The following year his address to the Harvard divinity school roused a storm of denunciation from the pulpit, but it established firmly the breadth and vitality of the new Transcendental spirit of which Emerson was the central figure. His major work appeared in the next few years, transcribed and expanded from his journals to his lectures to *Essays, First Series*, 1841, *Essays, Second Series*, 1844, *Representative Men*, 1849, and *The Conduct of Life*, 1860. Together with *Poems*, 1846, and *May-Day and Other Pieces*, 1867, these constitute the expression of his unique, personal relation to the living, organic universe he felt about him. From 1840 to 1844 the Transcendentalist group published *The Dial*, a journal of literature, philosophy, and social commentary, with Emerson a regular contributor and, for the last two years, editor. In 1847, on a second visit to England, he found himself famous there; he lectured widely, renewed his earlier acquaintances, and made new ones among the leading literary figures. *English Traits*, published in 1856, contained his observations and reflections on this trip. Unlike his Transcendentalist friends, he resisted involvement in the reform movements of the time; only on the slavery issue did he assume a consistent and public stand, supporting the antislavery faction in Kansas and championing John Brown. His lecture tours grew both in extent and popularity and, somewhat ironically, he became an institution. After 1860 he added little that was new to his stock of lectures and essays. In 1867, he again delivered the Phi Beta Kappa address at Harvard, ending the 30-years' exile that had followed his Divinity School Address. A brief tour of California in 1871 and a last trip to Europe and the Near East in 1872–1873 were the only interruptions of his last quiet years in Concord; he declined slowly into a benign senility and died on April 27, 1882.

ERICSSON, JOHN (1803–1889), engineer and inventor. Born in Långbanshyttan, Sweden, on July 31, 1803, Ericsson displayed from an early age a fascination with machinery. At 13 he joined an engineering corps engaged in canal construction and received from his older companions instruction in mathematics, science, and drafting. He later served as a topographer with the Swedish army until 1826, when he went to London. For 13 years he remained there, working as an independent engineer and laying the groundwork for his later achievements. He was particularly interested in developing mechanical sources of motive power; while he made many improvements in steam engine design and construction, he sought to find a more direct and efficient means of utilizing heat energy and through his life constructed various sorts of "caloric" engines, none of which, however, successfully competed with steam. In 1829 he constructed a locomotive for the competition that was won by Stephenson's "Rocket." Later he turned to ship design and propulsion and, striking on the idea of placing the engines below the water line, began using a screw propeller instead of the paddlewheel. In 1837 his ship *Francis B. Ogden* was successfully tested, and he followed it with the *Novelty*, the first propeller-driven commercial vessel. Commissioned by Capt. Robert Stockton of the U.S. Navy to build another such ship, he went to New York in 1839. His new propulsion system was quickly adopted for a number of commercial steamers, and in 1844 the U.S.S. *Princeton* became the first warship to be so powered. In 1848 Ericsson became a naturalized U.S. citizen. In 1861 his proposal for a new type of warship was approved by a government board and in an almost incredibly short time the *Monitor* was built and launched early in 1862. On March 9th it met and defeated the Confederate ironclad vessel *Merrimack* in a much celebrated battle. The *Monitor* opened the age of modern warships; powered solely by steam and propeller, constructed entirely of iron and heavily armored, and armed with heavy mounted turreted guns, it constituted a revolution in naval warfare. Ericsson was widely hailed for his achievement. In 1878 he launched the *Destroyer*, a ship capable of firing submarine torpedoes from its bow. While continuing to work on versions of his "caloric" engine, he also investigated other possible sources of power, particularly solar energy. The great number, variety, and importance of his inventions marked him as one of the most creative and far-sighted engineers of his century. He died in New York City on March 8, 1889, and the following year, at the request of the Swedish government, his body was returned to his native land.

ERSKINE, JOHN (1879–1951), educator, author, and musician. Born in New York on October 5, 1879, Erskine was drawn to music as a child and studied piano for many years, for a time under composer Edward MacDowell. He graduated from Columbia in 1900, took his Ph.D. in 1903, and for six years thereafter was an instructor and associate professor of English at Amherst College. In 1909 he joined the Columbia faculty. During his 28 years there he became a highly popular and influential teacher, numbering among his students Mark Van Doren, Mortimer Adler, Clifton Fadiman, and Rexford Guy Tugwell. The central thesis of his teaching, that liberal education rested upon the reading and assimilation of the major works of learning and literature of the past, was the primary inspiration for the later "great books" programs instituted at many colleges and universities (notably by Hutchins and Adler at the University of Chicago and at St. John's College in Annapolis). Throughout his career he maintained his musical interests; he performed often with private ensembles and occasionally on the concert stage, and was deeply involved with the Juilliard School of Music as trustee from 1927 and as president from 1928 to 1937. He published numerous scholarly works and volumes of poetry, co-edited the *Cambridge History of American Literature*, 1917–1919, and in 1925 created something of a sensation with his thoroughly unacademic novel, *The Private Life of Helen of Troy*, a humorous version of the legend set in the contemporary "Jazz Age" scene. The book was highly successful and was translated into 16 languages. In later books he similarly

treated the figures of Sir Galahad, Adam and Eve, Francois Villón, and others. In 1937 he retired as professor emeritus and devoted himself to writing. His other published works included *The Moral Obligation to Be Intelligent*, 1915, *Democracy and Ideals*, 1920, *The Delight of Great Books*, 1928, *The Start of the Road*, 1938, *Give Me Liberty*, 1940 (the last two on Walt Whitman and Patrick Henry), and *What Is Music?*, 1944. *The Memory of Certain Persons*, 1947, *My Life as a Teacher*, 1948, *My Life in Music*, 1950, and *My Life as a Writer*, 1951, were personal reminiscences. Erskine died in New York on June 2, 1951.

EVANS, GEORGE HENRY (1805–1856), journalist and reformer. Born on March 25, 1805, in Bromyard, Hertfordshire, England, Evans emigrated to the United States with his family in 1820. Apprenticed to a printer in Ithaca, New York, he soon edited his own paper, *The Man*; in 1829, in New York City, he produced the *Working Man's Advocate*, a paper that appeared sporadically until 1845 and that was dedicated, as the name suggested, to the support of the early attempts at labor organization. Evans favored a political approach to the labor problem; his program embraced the natural-rights philosophy of Jefferson and Paine and in many ways anticipated that of the later Henry George. He advocated land reform and a system of free homesteading as a means of drawing off excess labor from the East and maintaining high wage scales, and to this end he organized the National Reform Association to agitate for political action. At intervals from 1837 to 1853 he edited also the *Daily Sentinel* and *Young America*. In 1840 he published his *History of the Origin and Progress of the Working Men's Party*, combining an exposition of his plan of reform, opposition to imported reform movements such as Fourierism, and an analysis of the past failures of labor and agrarian organizations. He died on February 2, 1856.

EVANS, OLIVER (1755–1819), inventor. Born in 1755 near Newport, Delaware, Evans went to school until he was 14, then became indentured to a wagon builder, and continued to study, particularly mechanics and mathematics, on his own time. Throughout his career he suffered from lack of financial support for his inventions and from the failure of the public to understand them. While employed in making card teeth for carding wool, he perfected in 1777 a machine that produced 1,500 cards a minute. In 1780 he joined his brothers in a flour-milling venture and five years later his flour mill with automatic machinery to accomplish every task necessary to change wheat into flour was ready for use. The mill was water powered, used a conveyor system to move the product at various stages of completion through the factory, and required only one operator. Millers refused to adopt the new machinery, fearful of being displaced themselves and reluctant to dismiss their workers. From about 1786 he devoted himself largely to experimenting with steam power. He had arrived at the idea of inventing a steam carriage about 13 years previously, but lack of funds prevented continued work on the project. He now turned to the development of a high-pressure steam engine and again proved his detractors wrong by making it practical. By 1802 he had converted the flour mill to steam power and the next year he started a business to manufacture steam engines, which in 1807 became the Mars Iron Works. In one of his most remarkable achievements, he developed in 1804 a steam powered dredging scow, which he steered through the streets and maneuvered into the water under its own power, thus anticipating both the steamboat and the automobile. In 1817 he planned and built the engines and boilers for the Fairmount Waterworks in Philadelphia. He died in New York City on April 21, 1819.

EVERETT, EDWARD (1794–1865), clergyman, public official, diplomat, and orator. Born in Dorchester, Massachusetts, on April 11, 1794, Everett graduated at the top of his Harvard class of 1811 and turned to the study of divinity. In 1814 he became pastor of the Brattle Street Church in Boston. A year later, having been appointed professor of Greek literature at Harvard, he began four years of study and travel in Europe by way of preparation for the post; he was awarded a Ph.D. from Göttingen in 1817. In 1819 he entered upon his professorial duties and the following year assumed the editorship of the *North American Review*. In 1824 he was elected to Congress and served there for ten years; though already widely noted for his oratory, his politics were vague. From 1835 to 1839 he was governor of Massachusetts, and from 1841 to 1845 minister to England. Following his election as president of Harvard in 1846, a position he held for three years, he withdrew from politics for a time. He served as secretary of state during the last four months of Fillmore's administration and immediately thereafter entered the Senate. Adverse reaction to his strongly Unionist but otherwise conciliatory and compromising stands, particularly on the Kansas-Nebraska Act, caused him to resign in 1854. He then devoted himself to lecturing and was eminently successful. In 1860 he reluctantly accepted the vice-presidential nomination of the Constitutional Union Party and, as he expected, lost badly. The outbreak of war ended his desire for compromise; throughout the war he traveled and spoke in support of the Northern cause. On November 19, 1863, he delivered the two-hour-long principal address at Gettysburg; it was the best speech of a great orator, though it is now overshadowed by the short address that followed it. He achieved vast popularity in these last years; and partially as a result of his exertions, he died in Boston on January 15, 1865.

FAIRBANKS, DOUGLAS ELTON (1883–1939), actor. Born on May 23, 1883, in Denver, Colorado, Fairbanks grew up in his native city and attended the Jarvis Military Academy, East Denver High School, and the Colorado School of Mines. Originally named Douglas Ulman, he and his mother adopted the name Fairbanks (from her first husband) upon her divorce from his father in 1900. His dramatic training came at a neighborhood school, where he met actor Frederick Warde who gave him early encouragement. He and his mother moved to the East in 1900, where he joined one of Warde's repertory theater groups. With them he made his professional debut in Richmond, Virginia, on September 10, 1900, in *The Duke's Jester*. His first major role was the juvenile lead in *A Gentleman From Mississippi*, which played in New York during 1909–1911. In 1915 the lure of Hollywood salaries brought him to the movies. Unlike many former stage actors who could not meet the close demands of the cameras, Fairbanks was photogenic and graceful (he was always in prime physical condition), and delighted in acting before the camera; indeed, his broad, athletic stage manner was perfectly suited to the new medium. With other stars of the silent film—Chaplin, Mary Pickford, and William S. Hart—he was admired and even worshipped by a large part of the movie-going public. He portrayed a succession of quietly heroic young American characters in such early movies as *The Americano*, 1916, *He Comes Up Smiling*, 1918, *Knickerbocker Buckaroo*, 1919, and *The Mollycoddle*, 1925. He wrote several books, *Laugh and Live*, 1917, and *Assuming Responsibilities* and *Making Life Worth While*, both in 1918, in which his real-life philosophies seemed as gallant as his characterizations. As the real-life hero, he married "America's Sweetheart," Mary Pickford, in 1920. They founded, in 1919 with Chaplin and D. W. Griffith, the United Artists Corporation. During the 1920s he made the films for which he is best remembered. In such costume spectaculars as *The Mark of Zorro*, 1920, *The Three Musketeers*, 1921, *Robin Hood*, 1922, *The Thief of Bagdad*, 1924, *Don Q, Son of Zorro*, 1925, *The Black Pirate*, 1926, and *The Gaucho*, 1927, he played the handsome, swashbuckling hero who was never far from a sword, a brilliant smile, and any number of admiring ladies.

When talkies were introduced his popularity gradually declined. In 1935 he and Mary Pickford were divorced and thereafter he spent much of his time in Europe. In 1939 he organized the Fairbanks-International producing company whose first picture, *The Californian*, starred his son. Fairbanks died on December 12, 1939, in Santa Monica, California. DOUGLAS ELTON FAIRBANKS, JR. (1909–), born on December 9, 1909, in New York City, was raised by his mother, Anna Beth Sully, and attended the Harvard military school in Los Angeles, the polytechnic school in Pasadena, and had private tutoring in London and Paris. At 13 his movie debut was made in *Stephen Steps Out*, but he was not recognized as a fine actor, apart from his father's reputation, until 1927, when he appeared in the play *Young Woodley*, in Los Angeles. During the 1930s he became a star in his own right, though in many of his films he continued the line of exhuberant heroes begun by his father; his successful movies included *Dawn Patrol*, 1930, *Morning Glory*, 1933, *Catherine the Great*, 1934, *The Prisoner of Zenda*, 1937, and *Gunga Din*, 1939. During World War II he served in the Navy with distinction, winning an honorary knighthood from the British government. After the war, he became a successful television producer in England and had extensive business interests there and in the United States.

FARMER, FANNIE MERRITT (1857–1915), culinary artist. Born in Boston on March 23, 1857, Miss Farmer attended the Medford high school and there suffered a paralytic stroke that forced her to end her formal education. She recovered sufficiently to help in household duties and developed such an aptitude and fondness for cooking that her parents enrolled her in the Boston Cooking School. She graduated in 1889 and was asked to remain as assistant director; in 1891 she became head of the school. Reticent of publicity, she nevertheless became famous and sought after as a lecturer at schools and social gatherings. She left in 1902 to open Miss Farmer's School of Cookery to train housewives. For a year at Harvard she conducted a course in invalid cooking, and with her sister wrote a regular column for ten years for the *Woman's Home Companion*. Her lasting contribution was two-fold: the introduction of level measurements and the *Boston Cooking School Cookbook*, published in 1896 and still a best seller in a revised and modernized version, *The Fannie Farmer Cookbook*, 1959. Recipes for such classic dishes as Dutch apple cake, Boston baked beans, brown bread, roast duck stuffed with orange slices, Indian pudding, and fish chowder, were accompanied by sections on formal entertaining, proper management of the home and service staff, use of kitchen equipment, and etiquette. Revised editions traced the history of changing food habits. Her largely intuitive knowledge of diet planning presaged the modern science of nutrition. She stressed in her cookbook the "knowledge of the principles of diet [as an] essential part of one's education. Mankind will eat to live, will be able to do better mental and physical work, and disease will be less frequent." Her recipes were all personally tested, and, thanks to accurate measurements, easy to reproduce. She died in Boston on January 15, 1915.

FARMER, JAMES LEONARD (1920–   ), reformer. Born in Marshall, Texas, on January 12, 1920, Farmer was the son of a classical scholar and teacher at Wiley College who had been the first black Texan to receive a Ph.D. He graduated from Wiley in 1938 and turned to medicine only to discover he couldn't stand the sight of blood. He then enrolled at Howard University, studied divinity, and graduated in 1941; but he refused ordination in the Methodist Church because it practised racial segregation. From 1941 to 1945 he was race relations secretary of the pacifist Fellowship of Reconciliation. In 1942 he led a group of University of Chicago students in founding the Congress of Racial Equality, becoming national chairman of the organization. Dedicated to ending racial segregation and discrimination by means of the Gandhian direct-action techniques of passive resistance and the sit-in, CORE grew over the years into a national organization with more than 70 chapters. A Chicago restaurant was the target of the first successful desegregation campaign in 1943, and in 1947 CORE sponsored a Journey of Reconciliation to test the segregation of interstate buses in the upper South. During the 1950s Farmer and CORE worked steadily though largely unnoticed; but widespread publicity came in 1960 when college students in Greensboro, North Carolina, staged a sit-in at a local lunch counter and touched off the civil rights movement of the 1960s. In 1961 CORE mounted the Freedom Rides, the first of which, led by Farmer, met violence and mass arrest in Mississippi. In 1963 he was unable to participate as planned in the March on Washington because he had been jailed for leading a demonstration in Plaquemine, Louisiana, from which he barely escaped with his life. From 1961 to 1966 he was national director of CORE; he was associated with many other civil rights and reform groups and was a director of the League for Industrial Democracy and of the American Civil Liberties Union. In 1965 he became president of the Center for Community Action Education and in 1968 ran unsuccessfully for a New York City congressional seat on the Republican ticket. He was appointed in 1969 to the post of assistant secretary for administration of the Department of Health, Education, and Welfare.

FARRAGUT, DAVID GLASGOW (1801–1870), naval officer. Born near Knoxville, Tennessee, on July 5, 1801, Farragut moved with his family to New Orleans in 1807. At the age of nine he was adopted by Captain David Porter and appointed midshipman in the Navy; apparently in honor of his foster father he changed his first name from James to David about 1814.

From 1811 through the end of the War of 1812 he served under Porter on the *Essex* and, at the age of 12, was briefly in command of a captured prize ship. For the next several years he served on various ships, principally in the Mediterranean, and for a time studied under the American consul to Tunis. He devoted considerable energy to remedying his neglected education and became fluent in several languages. In 1823 he was again with Porter in a campaign to suppress piracy in the West Indies. Farragut was promoted to lieutenant in 1825, to commander in 1841, and to captain in 1855; such progress was slow, however, for his routine duties at sea and ashore during this period, including the Mexican War, failed to engage his distinctive qualities. For several months after the outbreak of the Civil War in 1861 he was given no significant duties, but in December, largely on the recommendation of his foster brother, Commander David Dixon Porter, he was chosen to command the West Gulf Blockading Squadron and ordered to capture New Orleans and gain control of the Mississippi. The New Orleans campaign began in April 1862. Following his instructions, Farragut first attempted to reduce the defending Ft. Jackson by mortar fire; this soon appearing to be fruitless, he decided to run past the fort in the dark. Despite heavy fire Ft. Jackson and Ft. St. Philip beyond were passed, the small Confederate flotilla defeated, and New Orleans captured on April 24th. Within days the two forts likewise surrendered. In July Farragut was promoted to rear admiral. For the next two years he was engaged in the blockade of the Gulf and in controlling traffic on the lower Mississippi and its tributaries, in so doing contributing materially to the capture of Vicksburg and the opening of the entire river to Union control. In 1864 he was given an objective he had long sought, the capture of Mobile Bay. The entrance to the bay was heavily mined except for a narrow channel under the guns of Ft. Morgan. On August 5th Farragut began his approach; the ironclads *Tecumseh* and *Brooklyn* led the fleet into the

channel and as they came abreast of Ft. Morgan the *Tecumseh* struck a mine (or torpedo, as they were then called) and was destroyed. The fleet was thrown into confusion and hesitated; Farragut, on the steam-powered *Hartford*, quickly swung out and headed into the mine field crying "Damn the torpedoes!" Though several mines were contacted, none exploded, and soon the entire fleet was within the bay; the Confederate ironclad *Tennessee* was beaten along with the rest of the defending flotilla and by the end of August all the harbor defenses, including Ft. Morgan, had surrendered. In December Farragut was appointed to the newly created rank of vice admiral. His active service was virtually at an end, for his health was seriously declining. In 1866 the rank of admiral was created especially for him. He died while visiting the naval yard at Portsmouth, New Hampshire, on August 14, 1870.

FARRELL, JAMES THOMAS (1904–   ), author. Born in Chicago on February 27, 1904, Farrell studied for three years, until 1929, at the University of Chicago and then held a succession of small jobs before attaining recognition as a writer. In 1932 he published *Young Lonigan*, the first volume of a trilogy that, with *The Young Manhood of Studs Lonigan*, 1934, and *Judgment Day*, 1935, remains his best-known work. Concerned with the growth of a young man in a decaying Irish neighborhood on Chicago's South Side, the trilogy shows the pervasive influence of both Dreiser and Joyce in its naturalistic outlook and in its use of a stream-of-consciousness narrative technique. A minor character in the Lonigan series, Danny O'Neill, became the central figure of five subsequent novels, *A World I Never Made*, 1936, *No Star Is Lost*, 1938, *Father and Son*, 1940, *My Days of Anger*, 1943, and *The Face of Time*, 1953. Farrell's fiction includes another trilogy, a number of single novels, and several volumes of short stories. He also wrote a number of critical works, including *A Note on Literary Criticism*, 1936, *The League of Fright-*

ened Philistines, 1945, and *Literature and Morality,* 1947.

FAULKNER, WILLIAM CUTHBERT (1897 – 1962), author. Born in New Albany, Mississippi, on September 25, 1897, Falkner (for change of name, see below) moved as a child to Oxford, Mississippi. His education ended after two years of high school; there followed a number of small jobs and a brief period with the British Royal Air Force in World War I during which, however, he saw no combat, the war ending before his training was completed. He returned to Oxford and in 1919 published his first poem, in the *New Republic.* He studied at the University of Mississippi for a year and shortly thereafter left for New York. A year later he was back in Oxford; in 1924 he published *The Marble Faun,* a volume of poetry, on the title page of which, for reasons unknown, he added to his name the "u" that remained for the rest of his life. After brief stays in New Orleans, Europe, and Pascagoula, Mississippi, he settled again in Oxford, this time permanently. His first novel, *Soldier's Pay,* appeared in 1926, and his second, *Mosquitoes,* in 1927. Then, under the combined influences of Sherwood Anderson and Balzac, he began to create his special world of Jefferson (Oxford), and of Yoknapatawpha County. His saga of social change, of the decay of the ante-bellum aristocracy and the rise of the crass and unscrupulous Snopes clan, written in a difficult style and often creating characters of mythic proportions, occupies a long series of books and constitutes Faulkner's major achievement: the first book, *Sartoris,* 1929, was followed by *The Sound and the Fury,* 1929, *As I Lay Dying,* 1930, *Sanctuary,* 1931, *Light in August,* 1932, *Absalom, Absalom!,* 1936, *The Unvanquished,* 1938, *The Hamlet,* 1940, *Go Down, Moses,* 1942, *Intruder in the Dust,* 1948, *The Town,* 1957, *The Mansion,* 1959, and *The Reivers,* 1962. He published a number of other novels, short story collections, and a play, *Requiem for a Nun,* 1951. He won recognition only slowly in America; his reputation abroad, however, was sufficient to win him the 1949 Nobel Prize for literature; belatedly, in 1955, he was also awarded the Pulitzer Prize. In his last years he broke his self-imposed seclusion to make a number of speaking tours in the United States and abroad, and in 1957 and 1958 he was writer-in-residence at the University of Virginia. Faulkner died at home on July 6, 1962.

FERMI, ENRICO (1901 – 1954), physicist. Born in Rome on September 29, 1901, Fermi studied at the University of Pisa and received his doctorate in 1922. After a period of further study in Germany he became a lecturer in physics at the University of Florence; in 1927 he joined the faculty of the University of Rome and remained there for 11 years. Until 1934 his work was concentrated in the theoretical aspects of atomic physics; he developed a mathematics with which to clarify and apply the Pauli exclusion principle and evolved a theory of beta decay. In 1934 news of the discovery of artificial radioactivity led him to turn to experimental work. He methodically proceeded through the periodic table of elements, bombarding each with slow neutrons and noting the results; the reaction of uranium, the final natural element, was puzzling and, because of the then-prevalent belief that nuclear fission was well-nigh impossible, he failed to realize that he had achieved it. In the late 1930s he began planning to leave Italy, for life was becoming unpleasant under the Fascist government, especially for his Jewish wife. In 1938 he was awarded the Nobel Prize for Physics for his work with neutrons; after accepting the award in Stockholm he proceeded on to the United States and joined the faculty of Columbia University. Early in 1939 two German scientists repeated Fermi's experiment with uranium and found that fission had indeed taken place. Fermi, together with several other emigré scientists, sought to interest the U.S. government in the potentials of atomic energy and warned of the danger of its development in Germany; in August they drew up a letter that, signed by Albert Einstein, was sent to President Roosevelt. A small grant to finance work on achieving a sustained nuclear reaction was followed in 1942 by the transfer of Fermi and his team to the Manhattan District project at the University of Chicago. There on December 2 a controlled chain reaction was achieved. Soon thereafter Fermi moved to the new secret installation at Los Alamos, New Mexico, where on July 16, 1945, the first atomic bomb was successfully tested. In 1946 he was awarded the Congressional Medal of Merit for his work; he then returned to the University of Chicago as professor in the Institute for Nuclear Research (later renamed the Enrico Fermi Institute for Nuclear Studies). His work there was concerned mainly with the nature and behavior of mesons. In 1954 he was the first recipient of a $25,000 prize from the Atomic Energy Commission, subsequently known as the Fermi Prize. Shortly after accepting the award he died, on November 28, 1954.

FIELD, CYRUS WEST (1819–1892), businessman and financier. Born in Stockbridge, Massachusetts, on November 30, 1819, the younger brother of David Dudley and Stephen J., Cyrus W. Field chose not to attend college but instead, at 15, took a job in a store in New York City. In 1841, after losing heavily in the bankruptcy of a wholesale paper company of which he was a junior partner, he began his own firm, Cyrus W. Field and Company. Within ten years he had paid his debts and was able to retire from business. In 1854 he became interested in the possibility of a transatlantic telegraph cable. He organized the New York, Newfoundland, and London Telegraph Company and later a similar company in England. With guarantees of business from the U.S. and British governments, the company made its first attempt to lay a cable between Newfoundland and Ireland in 1857; this and two following attempts failed, but the fourth, in 1858, was briefly successful. Queen Victoria sent a message to President Buchanan over

the cable and there was jubilation on both sides of the Atlantic. In the three weeks before this first cable failed the value of such a means of rapid communication was amply demonstrated. In debt again, and delayed by the Civil War, Field continued to promote the idea. More failures in 1865 were followed by complete success the next year. Field traveled widely in subsequent years and advocated the laying of submarine cables throughout the world. In 1877 he bought control of the New York Elevated Railway Company and, as its president from 1877 to 1880, was instrumental in bringing a rapid transit system to the city. He was later associated with Jay Gould in the Wabash Railroad. His affairs suffered sharply in later years and his fortune disappeared. He died on July 12, 1892.

FIELD, DAVID DUDLEY (1805–1894), lawyer and legal reformer. Born in Haddam, Connecticut, on February 13, 1805, the elder brother of Stephen J. and Cyrus W., Field left Williams College in 1825 to take up the study of law. Admitted to the bar in 1828, he began practice in New York City and was soon a recognized authority on common-law and equity pleading. In 1837 he began agitating for reform of the New York legal system, calling for complete codification of the state's laws. By means of letters and articles he successfully induced the state constitutional convention of 1846 to report in favor of such a reform, and the following year the legislature appointed a commission, with Field the leading member, to carry it out. The result was the Civil Code of Procedure, enacted in New York in 1848 and adopted or imitated by many states and foreign nations, including England and Ireland; and a similar code for criminal procedure, adopted in New York several years later. Codes of substantive political, civil, and penal law were created by a subsequent commission under Field's chairmanship between 1860 and 1865, but of these only the penal code was adopted in New York; like the earlier ones, however, these were widely adopted or copied elsewhere. Encouraged by this success, Field devoted much time from 1866 onwards to the elaboration of a code of international law; his *Draft Outline of an International Code* was published in 1872 and in an expanded version in 1876. Originally a Democrat, Field supported the Republican Party from its founding; he seems to have played a part in Lincoln's nomination in 1860, and he served briefly in Congress in 1876. In his legal practice he achieved considerable prominence, arguing several major cases before the Supreme Court, representing Tilden before the Electoral Commission in the dispute following the presidential election of 1876, and, not without controversy, representing Jay Gould and James Fisk in the Erie Railroad litigations. He died on April 13, 1894.

FIELD, MARSHALL (1834–1906), merchant and business leader. Born on August 18, 1834, near Conway, Massachusetts, Field attended school until the age of 16, then worked as a shop clerk in Pittsfield. He moved to Chicago in 1856, where he worked as a traveling salesman and clerk for a wholesale house. His pleasant manner helped to make him a success as a salesman. He became general manager of the business in 1861 and a partner the next year. In 1865 he joined another of the partners and Potter Palmer, an established State Street merchant, in forming Field, Palmer, and Leiter. Palmer left in 1867 and the firm became Field, Leiter and Company. The company survived the great Chicago fire of 1871, the panic of 1873, and another fire in 1877, because of outstanding management and a policy of benefitting the customer in many new ways. Among his important merchandising innovations, Field plainly displayed prices of all merchandise, extended credit, and allowed the return of goods within a reasonable time after purchase. He also was the first to install a restaurant in a department store. In 1881 Leiter sold out his interest and Field and his two brothers were the sole owners, the

business becoming known as Marshall Field and Company. It began manufacturing items and selling them under the company name. Field surpassed his competitors in his ability to anticipate or create consumer demand and to stock for it in advance. By 1895 the store was grossing $40 million a year. He became a noted philanthropist; benefactors of his large fortune included the University of Chicago, the World's Columbian Exposition in Chicago in 1893 (for which he built the Columbian Museum, later known as the Field Museum of Natural History and relocated to a new edifice built with a bequest in his will), and his home town of Conway, where he established a public library. He died on January 16, 1906. His descendants were eminent Chicago business leaders: Marshall Field III established the *Chicago Sun*, which later became the *Sun-Times*; Marshall Field IV became chairman of the board of Field Enterprises, Inc., and published the *Chicago Daily News* and the *Sun-Times*.

FIELD, STEPHEN JOHNSON (1816–1899), jurist. Born in Haddam, Connecticut, on November 4, 1816, Stephen J. Field, the brother of David Dudley and Cyrus W., spent two years as a youth in the Near East, returning In 1833 to enter Williams College. After graduating first in his class four years later he began the study of law; from his admission to the bar in 1841 until 1848 he was in partnership with his brother David. In 1849 he journeyed to California; settling in Marysville, he engaged in land speculation and legal practice in that rough and bustling mining region. In 1850 he was elected to the legislature, where he took the lead in establishing California's civil and criminal codes, which contained very liberal provisions for the protection of debtors and gave legal standing to local miners' customs. In 1857 he was appointed to the state supreme court; there he provided learned leadership in bringing order to a welter of conflicting land and mineral claims. In 1863 he was appointed by President Lincoln to a newly created tenth seat on the Supreme Court. During his tenure Justice Field was most noted for his dissents, many of which were based on a broad view of the 14th Amendment. He opposed the Legal Tender Acts, federal regulation of utilities, the Interstate Commerce Commission, and the income tax. He was mentioned for the Democratic presidential nomination in 1880 and 1884 but was barred by the opposition of California Democrats with whom some of his decisions on the circuit, notably against discriminatory practices toward the Chinese, were highly unpopular. After the longest tenure on the Supreme Court before the 20th century, he retired from the bench in 1897 and died on April 9, 1899.

FIELDS, W. C. (1880–1946), entertainer. Born in Philadelphia on January 29, 1880, William Claude Dukenfield led a turbulent childhood and at 11 ran away from home. He knocked about aimlessly for a time and then, inspired by an act in a traveling show, he began to teach himself juggling. By the time he was 14 he had begun a professional career; from the Atlantic City boardwalk to touring vaudeville, he rose by dint of extraordinary ability and determination to star billing as "W. C. Fields, the Tramp Juggler." In 1901, on a European tour, he played a command performance before Edward VII of England. In 1915 he was engaged for the *Ziegfeld Follies*, with which he remained for six years and in which he shared the stage with Fanny Brice, Will Rogers, and others. His juggling act had long featured a line of comic patter, and in 1924 he appeared on Broadway in his first speaking role, that of the preposterously fraudulent Eustace McGargle in *Poppy*. The show was a success and the next year was made into a film by D. W. Griffith. Several more films, including *So's Your Old Man*, 1926, and *Running Wild*, 1927, and a few seasons in New York followed before he moved to Hollywood permanently in 1931. For Mack Sennett he starred in a number of two-reelers, notably *The Chemist, The Barbershop*, and *The Fatal*

Glass of Beer, and he appeared in numerous Paramount releases, including *Million-Dollar Legs*, 1932, *International House*, 1932, *Tillie and Gus*, 1934, *The Old-Fashioned Way*, 1934, *Mrs. Wiggs of the Cabbage Patch*, 1934, *Mississippi*, 1935, and *The Man on the Flying Trapeze*, 1935. By that time he was one of Hollywood's leading stars and had firmly established the role that remained essentially unchanged from *Poppy* onward—a role composed by turns of bombast, whimsy, chicanery, and an utter disregard for conventions, particularly those concerning children and dogs. He never failed to delight audiences with his rasping drawl, his bulbous nose, and his slightly befuddled sleight-of-hand. His last four major films, made for Universal, have remained perennially popular classics: *You Can't Cheat an Honest Man*, 1939, *My Little Chickadee*, with Mae West, 1940, *The Bank Dick*, for which he wrote the screenplay under the name Mahatma Kane Jeeves, 1941, and *Never Give a Sucker an Even Break*, 1941. He died in Pasadena on December 25 (a day he pretended to detest), 1946. His lifelong distaste for his natal city outlived him in his self-composed epitaph: "On the whole I'd rather be in Philadelphia."

FILENE, EDWARD ALBERT (1860–1937), business leader and reformer. Born on September 3, 1860, in Salem, Massachusetts, Filene was educated in public schools in Lynn, Massachusetts, and briefly attended a German military academy. About the time he planned to enter Harvard, his father opened a store in Boston but had to abandon its management because of poor health. Edward gave up his college plans to assume control of the store with his younger brother. Ambitious and competent, he conducted an energetic enterprise and in the rapid expansion of the department store, which in 1891 became William Filene's Sons Company, had brought several partners into the business by 1911. His innovative ideas included the "Automatic Bargain Basement," which was designed to promote the sale of slow-moving items by featuring low prices that decreased steadily while goods remained in stock. Litigation with his conservative partners stemming from his plans to turn the management of the store over to an employees' cooperative, resulted in his loss of control in 1928, though he remained nominally president. He was active in civic reform. With Lincoln Steffens in 1909 he fostered improvements in municipal, educational, public health, and harbor facilities. He consolidated business groups in Boston's first Chamber of Commerce and provided the impetus for similar state, national, and international associations. He promoted the American credit union movement and in 1919 established the Cooperative League (later the Twentieth Century Fund) to do research on the national economy. He was a strong advocate of consumer cooperatives and foresaw a revised economy of affluence based on high wages and mass distribution. He wrote several books, including *More Profits from Merchandising*, 1925, *Successful Living in This Machine Age*, 1931, and *Next Steps Forward in Retailing*, 1937. He died in Paris on September 26, 1937.

FILLMORE, MILLARD (1800–1874), statesman, 13th U.S. President. Born on January 7, 1800, in Cayuga County, New York, Fillmore received virtually no formal education until he was 18. Six months of schooling were then followed by study in a law office. Supporting himself by teaching school, he was admitted to the bar in 1823. With the aid of Thurlow Weed, Fillmore entered politics in 1828, serving three terms in the state assembly, and in 1833 he was elected to Congress. Sitting out one term, he was elected again in 1836 and remained in Congress until 1843. He had followed Weed out of the Anti-Masonic Party and into the Whig coalition in 1834, and in Congress he was generally counted in the Clay faction. In 1844 he lost both the Whig nomination for Vice President and the governor's contest in New York. In 1848 Clay's support won him the vice presidential nomination, and he was elected with Zachary Taylor. Taylor's death on July 9, 1850, elevated Fillmore to the presidency. He broke his long association with Weed by reversing Taylor's policy of opposition to Clay's "Omnibus Bill"; with the preservation of the Union uppermost in his mind, he approved the Compromise of 1850, including the infamous Fugitive Slave Law. He failed to be renominated by the fractured Whig Party in 1852. In March 1852 he had sent a Navy fleet commanded by Commodore Matthew Perry to Japan with a request for a treaty; Perry left one year later and the treaty was signed in 1854, opening Japan to Western trade. Fillmore accepted the presidential nomination of the strongly nativist American or "Know-Nothing" Party in 1856. Basing his campaign on the need for national unity, he was soundly defeated and retired from public life. He died on March 8, 1874.

FINNEY, CHARLES GRANDISON (1792–1875), clergyman and educator. Born in Warren, Connecticut, on August 29, 1792, Finney grew up on the New York frontier. In 1818, after several years of teaching school and private study, he set about preparing for the bar. In 1821 he underwent a rather violent conversion to Christianity and immediately gave up law to devote himself to evangelism. His legal training remained with him, however, and shaped the style and delivery of his sermons. After a year of theological study he was ordained in the Presbyterian Church in 1824 and immediately began his revival campaign. From the small villages of New York throughout the New England and Middle Atlantic states he preached forcefully, directly, and with great effect; his revivals were wildly emotional scenes, and were much disparaged by regular ecclesiastics. In 1832 he came to New York City as minister of the Second Free Presbyterian Church. He chafed at denominational restrictions, however, and two years later the Broadway Tabernacle was built for him. In 1835 he became professor of theology at the newly founded Oberlin College in Ohio and for two years maintained both this position and his pastorate in New York. In 1837 he resigned from the New York church and became minister of the First Congregational Church in Oberlin. From 1851 to 1866 he was president of Oberlin College; his pastorate continued until 1872, and he taught theology until shortly before his death on August 16, 1875.

FISH, HAMILTON (1808–1893), lawyer and public official. Born in New York City on August 3, 1808, Fish graduated from Columbia College in 1827 and three years later was admitted to the bar. In 1842 he was elected as a Whig to Congress, where he served a single term. In 1847 he was elected lieutenant governor of New York and in the next year became governor. In 1851, with the support of Charles Sumner, he was elected to the Senate; he served as a loyal Whig until near the end of his term, when the party dissolved and he became a Republican. During the war he aided in alleviating the conditions under which Union prisoners of war were held in the South and in arranging for prisoner exchanges. After several years devoted to private interests he reluctantly accepted President Grant's offer of the secretaryship of state in 1869. Contrary to his original intention, he held the post through the next eight years; his services constituted the highest achievements of Grant's administrations, which were otherwise characterized by mediocrity and corruption. Fish held Congressional expansionists in check and successfully managed the arbitration of the "Alabama claims" with England. He managed to deter Grant from annexing the Dominican Republic and, during the Cuban revolution, resisted great pressure from both Congress and Spain in refusing to allow the United States to adopt a partisan position towards the conflict; to this end he even refused to release a presidential proclamation that he deemed ill-advised, later persuading Grant of the wisdom of his action. He was largely responsible for preventing Grant himself from being involved in the corrupt schemes of his associates and finally secured the dismissal of some of the more notorious of them. Fish returned to private life in 1877 and died on September 6, 1893.

FISKE, JOHN (1842–1901), author and lecturer. Born in Hartford, Connecticut, on March 30, 1842, Edmund Fisk Green legally adopted the name John Fisk when he was 13 and added the final "e" five years later. He was a gifted child, read widely, and by the time he entered Harvard had already formed a number of heterodox opinions, particularly on the subject of evolution. He graduated in 1863 and the following year was admitted to the bar. His interest in philosophy and history prevailed over his legal practice, however; in 1869 and again in 1871 he was invited to deliver a series of lectures at Harvard and from 1872 to 1879 he was the college's assistant librarian. During a year's leave from this post in 1874 he visited England and wrote his two-volume *The Outlines of Cosmic Philosophy*, in which he attempted to reconcile the new scientific outlook of evolution with religious tradition. His public lectures in Boston and other places won him wide popularity, and he continued to publish books at an astonishing pace. After about 1855 his written work dealt primarily with American history, particularly the colonial and revolutionary periods. As with his philosophical works, these did not reflect original scholarship; rather they were lucid syntheses of numerous sources and were likewise widely popular. In 1884 Fiske became professor of American history at Washington University in St. Louis, though he continued to live in Massachusetts until his death on July 4, 1901. His primary contribution to American thought was his signal success in popularizing the evolutionary thesis against the adamant opposition of the church.

FITCH, JOHN (1743–1798), metalworker and boatbuilder. Born in Hartford County, Connecticut, on January 21, 1743, Fitch received a few years of schooling as a child and, after a time working on the family farm and brief employment as a sailor, apprenticed himself to a clock maker. From this man and from another craftsman he learned brass working, and he soon opened a brass foundry of his own in East Windsor. In this venture and in a brass and silversmith business he later operated in Trenton, New Jersey, he was unsuccessful, largely because of the disregard for economic prudence and efficiency that was also to contribute to later failures. He served for a short time in the Revolution and then managed a gun factory. From 1780 to 1785 he was engaged in surveying and real estate speculation in Kentucky and the Northwest Territory. Settling in Bucks County, Pennsylvania, in the latter year, he turned his energies to inventing a steam-powered boat. He failed to win financial aid from the Continental Congress and from state legislatures but from several of the latter he secured 14-year monopolies for steamboat operations on inland waters. With these privileges and his working models Fitch persuaded a group of Philadelphians to finance construction of a 45 foot boat. He successfully demonstrated this first full-scale craft on the Delaware River on August 22, 1787, with members of the Constitutional Convention looking on. The next year he built a 60 foot paddlewheeler and in 1790 his third and still larger boat was launched and for a time maintained a regular schedule of trips between Philadelphia and Trenton. In 1791, an earlier dispute over priority having been resolved, he was granted patents by the United States and France. His fourth boat was wrecked in a storm that year and Fitch's financial backers deserted him. He vainly sought aid in France, returned to America in poor health, and after more unsuccessful attempts to find support for his boatbuilding, he moved to Bardstown, Kentucky, where he died on July 2, 1798.

FITZGERALD, FRANCIS SCOTT KEY (1896–1940), author. Born in St. Paul, Minnesota, on September 24, 1896, Scott Fitzgerald was educated in elite private schools and thus, despite a middle-class background, was early exposed to the life and habits of the wealthy with whom he was to concern himself in his writing. He studied at Princeton but left before graduating; in 1917 he joined the Army and during his service began his first novel which, after extensive revision, was published in 1920 as *This Side of Paradise*. The book was successful and Fitzgerald became temporarily wealthy himself. With his collections of short stories, *Flappers and Philosophers*, 1920, and *Tales of the Jazz Age*, 1922, he became the recognized spokesman for the youthful rebellion of the 1920s. In 1922 he published his second novel, *The Beautiful and the Damned*; from 1924 to 1930 he lived in Europe and produced *The Great Gatsby*, 1925, and another collection, *All the Sad Young Men*, 1926. His life during this time, exemplifying in many ways the frenzy and aimlessness he wrote of, began to deteriorate; his wife became mentally ill, he became progressively dependent on alcohol, and his next novel, *Tender Is the Night*, was not finished until 1934. The book was a financial failure, and he recorded his subsequent despondency and emotional emptiness in a series of essays entitled "The Crack-Up," published in 1936. The following year he moved to Hollywood to become a screenwriter; in 1940 he rediscovered the talent he had thought lost and began work on a new novel, *The Last Tycoon*. Before it was completed he suffered a fatal heart attack, on December 21, 1940.

FLEXNER, ABRAHAM (1866–1959), educator. Born in Louisville, Kentucky, on November 13, 1866, Flexner graduated from Johns Hopkins University in 1886 and for the next 19 years taught school. In 1906 and 1907 he pursued graduate studies at Harvard and the University of Berlin, and in 1908 he joined the staff of the Carnegie Foundation for the Advancement of Teaching. He was commissioned to study the state of medical education in America and, taking the excellent medical school at Johns Hopkins as a model, did so critically and in detail. His report, *Medical Education in the United States and Canada*, published in 1910, occasioned a revolution in the field; a large number of institutions were forced to close because of the report's criticism and the publicity that followed, while those that remained raised standards of admission and instruction and were immeasurably strengthened. Modern medical education dates from the appearance of this report. From 1913 to 1925 Flexner was secretary of the General Education Board, and from 1925 to 1928 director of the Board's division of studies and medical education. In 1930 he published *Universities—American, English, German*, a similar study of the whole spectrum of higher education. In the same year he organized the Institute for Advanced Study at Princeton and served as its director until 1939, when he retired to private life. He died on September 21, 1959.

FLINT, TIMOTHY (1780–1840), clergyman and author. Born on July 23, 1780, near North Reading, Massachusetts, Flint graduated from Harvard in 1800 and, after a brief period of teaching, entered the ministry. From 1802 to 1814 he was pastor of the Congregational Church in Lunenburg, Massachusetts. In the next year he began a missionary journey into the Ohio Valley. For a while he tried farming in Missouri and, traveling south to Louisiana, was principal of a seminary in Alexandria. Ill health forced him to return north to Cincinnati. In 1826 he published *Recollections of the Last Ten Years in the Valley of the Mississippi*, an account of the social and economic aspects of the early Western frontier that remains of great value. From 1827 to 1830 he edited the *Western Monthly Review*; in 1828 he published *A Condensed Geography and History of the Western States*, a revised edition of which appeared in 1832. In 1833 he edited briefly the New York *Knickerbocker Magazine*; in the same year he published *The*

Biographical Memoir of Daniel Boone, the First Settler of Kentucky, a book that did much to foster and, through 14 editions, sustain the legend of the trail-blazing pioneer. Flint wrote numerous other works, including four romantic novels. He died on August 16, 1840.

FORD, HENRY (1863–1947), industrialist. Born on July 30, 1863, near Dearborn, Michigan, Ford's formal education ended at 15; he moved to Detroit and held a number of jobs in which he was involved with machinery. In 1892 he built his first gasoline-powered "buggy." Eleven years later, with the success of his racing car "999," he founded the Ford Motor Company to produce standardized, low priced automobiles for a popular market. In 1908 he introduced the Model T, a masterpiece of simplicity and economy. In 1913 he began the use of conveyor assembly line production methods, resulting in a great increase in output and a consequent reduction in cost. Largely because of this method of mass production he was able to manufacture more than 15 million Model T's between 1908 and 1927. He had taken a highly innovative approach in arriving at his low-cost popular automobile, but he was strangely resistant to subsequent change; by the time he introduced the improved Model A in 1927 he had lost his earlier leadership in the market. But in labor relations Ford was similarly in the lead when, in 1914, he announced a new minimum daily wage that was considerably higher than prevailing industry standards, and an employee profit-sharing plan. Again, however, there was a strong conservative element in his resistance to unionization—Ford was the last automobile manufacturer to accept collective bargaining—and in his paternal attitude toward his workers. In 1915, he chartered the Ford Peace Ship and sailed to Europe with a group of pacifists and other reformers in an attempt to bring an end to World War I. In 1918 he ran unsuccessfully for the Senate. The following year he retired as president of the company, turning over control to his son, Edsel B. Ford.

The Ford Foundation, which became one of the leading philanthropic institutions in the country, was founded by father and son in 1936, though it remained relatively insignificant until 1951, when its assets were greatly enlarged. Upon his son's death in 1943 Ford resumed the presidency of the company and held it until his own death on April 7, 1947.

FORD, PAUL LEICESTER (1865–1902), historian. Born in Brooklyn, New York, on March 23, 1865, Ford was of a wealthy and prominent family. He was educated privately and early displayed a marked interest in books. At the age of eleven he prepared and, on a small press, printed a genealogy compiled by his great-grandfather, Noah Webster. With his father's extensive library as a base, he issued during the next several years a number of bibliographical guides, listing the writings of Webster, 1882, Charles Chauncy, 1884, Alexander Hamilton, 1886, and Benjamin Franklin, 1889. He reprinted much valuable but long lost historical material in his *Pamphlets on the Constitution of the United States*, 1888, and in 1890 and 1891 issued, with his brother Worthington Chauncy Ford, the 15-volume *Winnowings in American History*. From 1890 to 1893 he served as editor of the *Library Journal*. In 1892–1899 he edited and published his exhaustively researched *Writings of Thomas Jefferson* in 10 volumes and in 1895 was chosen by the Historical Society of Pennsylvania to edit the works of John Dickinson. In the following year he published *The True George Washington*, a highly popular biography that went far to correct the prevalent narrow view of Washington inspired by earlier moralizing writers. Ford ventured into fiction with *The Honorable Peter Stirling*, 1894, and though his efforts in this direction were more notable for historical richness than literary elegance, he achieved some success with *Janice Meredith*, 1899, which was later dramatized. His scholarly work included a history of the *New England Primer* in 1897 and a biography of Franklin in 1899. A crip-ple from childhood, he was shot and killed on May 8, 1902, by his disinherited and despondent brother Malcolm, who subsequently took his own life.

FORREST, EDWIN (1806–1872), actor. Born on March 9, 1806, in Philadelphia, Forrest left school when he was 13 to help support his family. He began his career as an actor in 1820 as Young Norval in Home's *Douglas* at Philadelphia's Walnut Street Theatre. He then joined a frontier troupe, an itinerant company in the Midwest, a circus, and a New Orleans theater. In 1825 he became a supporting actor under Edmund Kean, who oversaw his development as a Shakespearian actor. He triumphed at the fashionable Park Theatre in 1826 as Othello and was permanently engaged by the less fashionable Bowery Theatre, where audiences responded wildly to the passion of his acting. He returned to the Park in 1829 and offered a series of prizes for plays by native Americans; his power and fortune grew rapidly and by 1834 had won all New York audiences. As one of America's foremost actors, he was hailed in London in the 1830s. Returning to England in 1845, at a time when many English actors, including the formidable William Macready, were unemployed, he received humiliating jeers from the audience as he performed Macbeth. He presumed that Macready had instigated the insult, and subsequently sat in an Edinburgh theater where Macready was performing Hamlet and hissed loudly. The feud thus begun reached its peak in 1849: Macready was acting at New York City's Astor Place Opera House, and crowds of Forrest's nativist and unruly fans attacked the theater. Troops were called to quell the mob; the riot resulted in 22 deaths, numerous injuries, and the complete wrecking of the theater. Although Forrest was elsewhere at the time, it was said that he had encouraged the affair. Stormy and embittered, he aggravated feelings against him in 1851 when he brought suit against his wife for divorce and displayed a brutal temper and coarse language during the sensational trial. But his notoriety packed theaters and people came to hear him give speeches vindicating himself between the acts. Although he continued to pack houses through the 1860s, he was considered as much a curiosity as a great actor. An injury to his back in 1865 eventually put an end to his career. He retired to a large home in Philadelphia, which, after his death on December 12, 1872, became a home for aged actors.

FORTEN, JAMES (1766 – 1842), businessman and social reformer. Born in Philadelphia, on September 2, 1766, of free Negro parents, Forten was largely self-educated, but attended a school run by Quaker Abolitionist Anthony Benezet. At 14 he enlisted in the Revolutionary navy as a powder boy and when his ship was captured escaped being sold into slavery through intercession of the son of the British commander. He spent one year in England and became involved with the Abolitionists. Returning to Philadelphia in 1786 he was apprenticed to a sailmaker, became a foreman at 20, and twelve years later purchased the business. His zeal for Abolitionism grew, especially after 1800, when a petition that he signed to modify the Fugitive Slave Act of 1793 was flatly rejected by Congress. In 1813, when laws were proposed to have free Negro residents of the city register and to ban any further blacks from entering, he led the opposition in five letters published in pamphlet form, "A Series of Letters by a Man of Color." In these he anticipated the fundamental tenet of such Abolitionists as William Lloyd Garrison and Theodore Weld—that Negroes are biologically equal to white men. In 1814 he recruited a force of 2,500 Negroes to secure Philadelphia from the threat of a British attack. Approached in 1816 by the American Colonization Society to support colonization in Liberia, he rejected their plans and their implicit offer to make him ruler of the colony, and began a campaign to convince Negroes and white and black Abolitionists that the Colonization Society was attempting to avoid

the issue of political emancipation and equality in its plan to send Negroes to Africa. He advocated temperance, voting rights, and promoted high standards of living for Negroes. By 1832 he had accumulated a fortune in excess of $100,000 from his sailmaking business, which employed 40 white and black men. Second only to the Tappan brothers in making financial contributions to Abolitionism, he actively supported William Lloyd Garrison and his antislavery journal, the *Liberator*. The American Anti-Slavery Society frequently met in his home. He died in Philadelphia on March 4, 1842, and his eight children continued to fight for his reforms.

FOSTER, STEPHEN COLLINS (1826 – 1864), composer. Born on July 4, 1826, in Lawrenceville, Pennsylvania, Foster had from childhood an inclination toward music and began writing songs at an early age. His formal education included little musical instruction and ended with a month at Jefferson College in 1841. In 1846, although he had published a few pieces, he was sent to work as a bookkeeper for his brother in Cincinnati, where he remained for four years. During this time he wrote a number of songs that gained considerable popularity; "O Susannah," "Away Down South," "Uncle Ned," and others were published in *Songs of the Sable Harmonists* in 1848. The following year he published *Foster's Ethiopian Melodies*, including "Nelly Was a Lady," which was popularized by Christy's Minstrels. Returning to his home, he continued to write songs in his adopted minstrel mode; he concluded a mutually beneficial agreement with E. P. Christy for performance rights, and from then until about 1862 wrote his best songs: "Old Folks at Home" ("Swanee River"), "My Old Kentucky Home," "Massa's in de Cold, Cold Ground," "Old Dog Tray," "Jeanie With the Light Brown Hair," "Old Black Joe," "Beautiful Dreamer." In 1860 Foster moved to New York City. His last years were ones of decline and dissolution; with few exceptions his songs became repetitious and of little value, and he went deeper and deeper in debt. He died on January 13, 1864.

FRANKFURTER, FELIX (1882–1965), jurist. Born in Vienna on November 15, 1882, Frankfurter emigrated with his family to the United States in 1894. He graduated from the City College of New York in 1902 and four years later took his law degree with highest honors at Harvard Law School. Finding private practice unsatisfactory, he became assistant to Henry Stimson, then U.S. attorney for the Southern District of New York. He continued this association when, in 1911, Stimson became secretary of war. In 1914 he joined the law faculty at Harvard, where he was professor of administrative law until 1939. During World War I he was legal advisor to the secretary of war, secretary and counsel to the President's Mediation Commission, and, in 1918, chairman of the War Labor Policies Board. After serving as an advisor at the Versailles treaty conference he returned to Harvard. He participated in the founding, in 1920, of the American Civil Liberties Union; in 1927 he became nationally prominent as a liberal with his critique of the Sacco-Vanzetti trial published in the *Atlantic Monthly*. Among his writings of this period were *The Commerce Clause Under Marshall, Taney, and Waite*, 1937, and *Mr. Justice Holmes and the Supreme Court*, 1938. He had been a close advisor to Franklin D. Roosevelt when the latter was governor of New York; when Roosevelt was elected President, in 1932, Frankfurter declined the office of solicitor general, but in 1939 he accepted an appointment to the Supreme Court. During his tenure on the Court he became, despite his earlier reputation as a liberal, a strong opponent of the latitudinarian interpretations of First Amendment rights favored by some of his colleagues. He held that individual freedom in a highly complex society required constant redefinition and limitation in the light of experience; he further believed that in cases other than clear-cut violations of established law and precedent, the judicial power must defer to popular prerogative and legislative initiative, and he was notably reluctant to employ the judicial veto to invalidate legislative acts. Forced by ill health to retire from the bench in 1962, Justice Frankfurter died on February 22, 1965.

FRANKLIN, BENJAMIN (1706–1790), printer, author, philanthropist, inventor, scientist, diplomat, and statesman. Born in Boston on January 17, 1706, Franklin received a scanty formal education and at the age of 12 was apprenticed to his older brother James to learn the printer's trade. He began also a program of self-instruction and discipline that was to become a lifelong quest for knowledge and virtue, always and characteristically with a primary emphasis on the useful and practical. He left Boston for Philadelphia in 1723, and, in 1724, under the uncertain auspices of Governor Keith, made his first trip to England. He returned to Philadelphia in 1726, became owner of the *Pennsylvania Gazette* in 1730, took as his common-law wife Deborah Read in the same year, and from then until 1748 concentrated on developing his business interests. Circa 1737 he began to publish his immensely popular *Poor Richard's Almanac*. His zealous pursuit of improvement led him at the same time to become a prominent citizen and philanthropist; a series of civic projects and public offices marked the beginning of what was to be a second career of public service. Franklin retired from active business in 1748 to devote himself to his philosophical studies. His most remarkable scientific work, on the nature of electricity, and his achievement thereby of a worldwide reputation came during the next six years. His public career continued and broadened meanwhile and finally, in 1754, when he represented Pennsylvania at the Albany Congress, became his major occupation. He was sent to England in 1757 to represent the Pennsylvania Assembly before the British government in the dispute over the taxation of proprietary estates.

He left England reluctantly in 1762, to return in 1764, again representing the Assembly. The matters that had brought him to England were soon eclipsed by the Stamp Act controversy; with the repeal of the Act, Franklin's reputation at home and abroad grew rapidly. Three other colonies appointed him their agent in London, and he continued to attempt a mediation of the widening rift between England and the colonies until 1775. Convinced at last that conciliation was impossible, he returned to Philadelphia and was immediately appointed to the Second Continental Congress. In October 1776 Congress sent him to France as one of three representatives of the revolutionary government; his fame and popularity, as scientist, diplomat, and creator of Poor Richard, quickly established him as the main, and eventually the sole, negotiator with the French government. In June 1781, he, John Jay, and John Adams were appointed to negotiate peace with Great Britain; the Treaty of Paris was signed in September 1783, but Congress maintained Franklin in France until May 1785. Returning home, he served as president of the executive council of Pennsylvania from 1785 to 1788 and as a member of the Constitutional Convention in 1787. While none of his proposals was adopted by the Convention, his skill as mediator was responsible in large measure for the successful compromises at the meeting. He had begun his most famous written work, the *Autobiography*, in 1771, and he continued writing it intermittently until 1789. When he died, on April 17, 1790, Franklin ended a long career of uninterrupted success and unparalleled diversity; he had been by far the most widely known and respected American of his time, and a leading figure in the cosmopolitan Enlightenment world.

FRAZIER, EDWARD FRANKLIN (1894–1962), sociologist. Born in Baltimore on September 24, 1894, Frazier graduated from Howard University in Washington, D.C., in 1916. For the next three years he taught mathematics at Tuskegee Institute, English and history at St. Paul's Normal and Industrial School in Lawrenceville, Virginia, and French in a Baltimore high school. During 1919–1920 he earned his master's degree in sociology at Clark University, and in 1921 conducted research on the longshoremen of New York City as a fellow of the New York School of Social Work. During 1921–1922 he did research on Danish students under the auspices of the American-Scandinavian Foundation in Denmark. Returning to the United States, he was a sociology teacher at Morehouse College in Atlanta and director of the Atlanta School of Social Work. He published in 1927 "The Pathology of Race Prejudice," whose treatment of the relation between mental disease and race prejudice precipitated a threat on his life and his flight from the city. From 1929 to 1934 he was professor of sociology at Fisk University. He took his doctorate at the University of Chicago in 1931. His dissertation, published as *The Negro Family in Chicago*, and another book, *The Free Negro Family*, appeared in 1932. From 1934 to 1959 he was chairman of the department of sociology at Howard University. His overall concern was the progress, organization, and function of the Negro family; his work in this area is recognized as more far-reaching than any done before him. His most important books were *The Negro Family in the United States*, 1939, and *Black Bourgeoisie*, 1957. He studied racial interaction in Africa, the Caribbean, and, in 1940 and 1941, as a Guggenheim Fellow, in Brazil and the West Indies. In 1935 he was appointed to conduct a survey for Mayor LaGuardia's Commission on Conditions in Harlem. He was president of the International Society for the Scientific Study of Race Relations, a founder of the American Association for the Advancement of Science, and chairman of the UNESCO committee of experts on race. He died in Washington on May 17, 1962.

FRÉMONT, JOHN CHARLES (1813–1890), soldier, explorer, and political leader. Born in Savannah, Georgia, on January 21, 1813, Frémont grew up in Charleston, South Carolina, and was educated at the College of Charleston from 1829 to 1831. He secured a patron in Joel Poinsett, a prominent South Carolina politician, and through his efforts was appointed teacher of mathematics aboard the warship *Natchez* on an extended South American cruise. In 1838 Poinsett arranged Frémont's appointment to the Army's Topographical Corps; he was a member of Nicollet's expedition to explore the plateau region between the Missouri and upper Mississippi rivers and in 1841 led his own exploratory party along the Des Moines River. Upon his return he married Jessie Benton, daughter of Senator Thomas Hart Benton, acquiring in the latter another and greatly influential ally. In 1842, with Benton's support, he was sent to explore the Wind River Mountain region in order to aid emigration to Oregon; his report, prepared with his wife's help, was widely reprinted. In the next year he set out on a much more extensive expedition. Guided, as he had been the year before, by Kit Carson, he crossed Wyoming and Idaho, followed the Columbia River to Fort Vancouver, and turned southeast through Oregon to Nevada; then, in a move bordering on foolhardiness, he made a winter crossing of the Sierra Nevadas into the Sacramento Valley. He traveled south to Los Angeles, explored parts of Arizona and Utah, and finally returned east in 1844. The journey and the report of it that was subsequently published were sensations. With the Mexican War imminent he was sent on a third expedition to California in 1845 with secret orders instructing him, should he find war in progress on his arrival, to convert his party to a military force. Ordered by Mexican authorities to leave shortly after his arrival in December 1845, he refused and briefly raised the American flag. After a northward feint, he supported the Bear Flag revolt and with his largely volunteer army had secured the territory by early 1847. There ensued a conflict of authority over California; after two months as governor, Frémont was arrested by General Kearney for mutiny, disobedience, and con-

duct prejudicial to military order. He was found guilty by a court-martial in 1848 and, although President Polk suspended his sentence, he resigned from the Army. During the next several years he devoted himself to developing his huge estates in California; the discovery of gold made him rich, and he served a brief period as one of California's first senators. In 1856 his wide popularity and his antislavery opinions won him the presidential nomination of the new Republican Party. After his defeat he returned to California. During the Civil War he resumed his army commission; he commanded the western department from St. Louis until political enemies and his own recklessness combined to cause his removal. In his subsequent command in Virginia he was ineffectual against Stonewall Jackson and in 1862 he again resigned. He was dissuaded from seeking the 1864 nomination and thereafter retired to private life. Except for a period as territorial governor of Arizona from 1878 to 1883, he concerned himself with his California properties and with various railroad interests until his death on July 13, 1890.

FRENCH, DANIEL CHESTER (1850–1931), sculptor. Born on April 20, 1850, in Exeter, New Hampshire, French was the son of a prominent attorney. He was first educated in art by Louisa May Alcott, who taught him to build sculptural armatures, and William Morris Hunt, who showed him the significance of color values. At the Massachusetts Institute of Technology, where he studied one year, he developed skill in drawing; later studies included lectures in anatomy in Boston from William Rimmer, one month in J. Q. A. Ward's New York studio, and two years under Thomas Ball in Italy. From 1876 to 1878 he had a studio in Washington, from 1878 to 1887 in Boston and Concord, Massachusetts, and after 1888 he worked in New York. His first commission, in 1873, was "The Minute Man," commemorating the 100th anniversary of the Battle of Concord. The monument was unveiled on April 19, 1875, by Ralph Waldo Emerson and placed on the Old North Bridge in Concord. (During World War II, the "Minute Man" was engraved on the face of defense bonds, postage stamps, and posters.) A constant flow of commissions followed; it was his good fortune to receive wide acceptance for all his work. Most famous among his sculptures were the busts of Emerson and Bronson Alcott, the seated bronze "John Harvard," outside University Hall in Cambridge, 1884, "General Lewis Cass" for the state of Michigan, placed in statuary hall in the National Capitol, 1888, "Dr. Gallaudet and His First Deaf-Mute Pupil," for the founding of the Columbia Institute for the Deaf in Kendall Green, Washington, the 75-foot "Statue of the Republic," which dominated the architecture at the Chicago World's Fair of 1893, "Death and the Sculptor," a tribute to Martin Millmore, in the Forest Hills Cemetary in Boston, 1893, the memorial group to John Boyle O'Reilly in the Boston Fenway, 1896, the equestrian statues "Gen. U.S. Grant" in Fairmount Park, Philadelphia, 1898, and "Washington," in Paris, 1900, the Boston Public Library low relief bronze doors, 1902, the "Four Continents" group, including "Europe," "Asia," "Africa," and "America," for the New York Custom House, 1907, the "Standing Lincoln," in Lincoln, Nebraska, 1912, "Alma Mater" for the Columbia College, 1915, the fountain at DuPont Circle in Washington, and the seated marble statue of Abraham Lincoln at the Lincoln Memorial in Washington, which was dedicated in 1922. The last, probably his greatest work, offered to thousands of visitors every year suggestions of character that each could interpret in his own way. He died in Stockbridge, Massachusetts, on October 7, 1931.

FRENEAU, PHILIP MORIN (1752–1832), poet and editor. Born in New York City on January 2, 1752, Freneau graduated from the College of New Jersey (now Princeton) in 1771. The commencement poem, "The Rising Glory of America," was a joint effort by him and Hugh Henry Brackenridge and was published the following year. For a few years he taught school and maintained his interest in poetry; at the outbreak of the Revolution he began issuing satirical pamphlets aimed at the British and the Loyalists. From 1775 to 1778 he was secretary to a wealthy planter in the West Indies, and during this time he wrote some of his best poetry, notably "The Beauties of Santa Cruz," "The Jamaica Funeral," and, particularly, "The House of Night," which in many ways foreshadowed the coming Romantic period of English literature. Returning to New Jersey, he served in the militia and later as a privateer; in 1780 his ship was captured and he was imprisoned under brutal conditions that he described the following year in *The British Prison-Ship*. For the next three years he was employed by the Philadelphia Post-Office and contributed to that city's *Freeman's Journal*. From 1784 to 1790 he was a sea captain in and around the West Indies. In 1790 he became editor of the New York *Daily Advertiser*; the following year Secretary of State Jefferson secured him a translator's post in the State Department and he began publishing the intensely republican *National Gazette*. The *Gazette* ceased publication in 1793 and Freneau ended his government employment a short time later. For a time he edited the *Jersey Chronical* and then the *New York Time-Piece*; the remainder of his life was divided between the sea and his New Jersey farm, where he died on December 18, 1832. His poetic endeavors had continued throughout his varied life; such poems as "The Wild Honeysuckle," "The Indian Burying Ground," and "Stanzas Written on the Hills of Neversink" marked him as America's leading poet in the period before Bryant and an important precursor of the native strain of nature poetry.

FRICK, HENRY CLAY (1849–1919), industrialist. Born on December 19, 1849, in West Overton, Pennsylvania, Frick received little more than a rudimentary education and from his early youth clerked in stores and worked at various other jobs. In 1871 he organized Frick and Company to construct and operate a number of coke ovens to supply the Pittsburgh steel mills; surviving the panic of 1873, the firm expanded rapidly and by the age of 30 he was a millionaire. In 1882 he became associated with Andrew Carnegie, who bought a portion of Frick and Company, and seven years later he was invited to become chairman of Carnegie's steel company. He instituted a major reorganization program and greatly improved the firm's financial standing; he also overcame Carnegie's reluctance and acquired large holdings in the iron ore region around Lake Superior, a venture that soon proved highly profitable. In 1892 he faced the Homestead steel strike with a degree of adamance remarkable even in that age of extreme measures in relations between labor and capital. He hired a force of 300 Pinkerton guards who attempted unsuccessfully to regain control of the company property occupied by strikers; when they failed, the state national guard was called in. Several pitched battles were required to subdue the strikers and many were killed; Frick himself was shot and stabbed by an anarchist, but he recovered and soon saw the strike broken. He resigned from the steel company in 1900 and the following year played a central role in the negotiations that led to the organization of the United States Steel Corporation under J. P. Morgan. In his later years he continued various business interests while devoting much time to his art collection; he also took up philanthropy, endowing many hospitals and educational institutions and giving a large park and endowment to the city of Pittsburgh. He died in New York City on December 2, 1919. His house, with his art collection, became by bequest a museum and, though small, it remains one of the finest in the city.

FROST, ROBERT LEE (1874–1963), poet. Born on March 26, 1874, in San Francisco, Frost moved with his family to New England at the age of 11. Entering Dartmouth in 1892, he remained for less than a term; for the next several years he lived at home, working at various jobs and writing poetry. His first published poem appeared in 1894. In 1897 he entered Harvard, but ill health forced him to withdraw before completing his studies. For a time he farmed in New England and from 1906 to 1912 he taught school, all the while adding to his stock of as yet unrecognized verse. In 1912 he moved his family to England and the next year his first volume of poems, *A Boy's Will*, was accepted for publication there. *North of Boston* followed in 1914. Early in 1915 he returned to New England to find himself no longer an unknown poet. He held a succession of professorships, fellowships, and residencies at Amherst, the University of Michigan, and Dartmouth; his association with Amherst lasted until his death. From his farm in New Hampshire he issued nine more volumes of new poems, including *West-running Brook*, 1928, *A Further Range*, 1936, *A Witness Tree*, 1942, and *In the Clearing*, 1962. He received four Pulitzer Prizes for poetry, in 1924, 1931, 1937, and 1943. His poetry was throughout marked by the use of everyday language and homely images drawn from his rural New England surroundings; it was his unique ability, however, to build from these elements poems that held hints of transcendant symbolic and metaphysical significance. He was among the most honored of poets during his lifetime; he was awarded over 40 honorary degrees and made a number of good-will trips for the State Department. Late in life he made an impressive appearance at the inauguration of President John Kennedy in 1961, reciting his poem "The Gift Outright." He died in Boston on January 29, 1963.

FULBRIGHT, JAMES WILLIAM (1905–), educator and public official. Born on April 9, 1905, in Sumner, Missouri, Fulbright grew up in Fayetteville, Arkansas, and was educated there. Graduating from the University of Arkansas in 1925, he studied at Oxford on a

Rhodes scholarship until 1928 and then at George Washington University, earning his law degree in 1934. During 1934–1935 he was a special attorney in the Antitrust Division of the Justice Department. In 1935 he joined the law faculty of George Washington University and in 1936 that of the University of Arkansas; from 1939 to 1941 he was president of the latter institution. In 1942 he was elected as a Democrat to Congress and two years later to the Senate. Subsequently reelected in 1950, 1956, 1962, and 1968, Fulbright became a leading figure among Senate liberals and something of an anomaly among his Southern Democratic colleagues. In 1946 he sponsored the Fulbright Act which allotted funds from the sale of surplus war material to finance an educational exchange program between the United States and foreign countries. Under the plan thousands of Fulbright Scholarships have been awarded, with great gains to education and international understanding. In 1959 he became chairman of the powerful Senate Foreign Relations Committee. During the administration of President Lyndon Johnson he gained great prominence with his outspoken and incisive criticism of the conduct of the war in Viet Nam and was an acknowledged leader of dissent within the nation's established political framework.

FULLER, MELVILLE WESTON (1833–1910), lawyer and U.S. chief justice. Born on February 11, 1833, in Augusta, Maine, Fuller graduated from Bowdoin College in 1853 and, after studying law at Harvard, was admitted to the bar in 1855. The following year he moved to Chicago where, over the next 30 years, he built a solid reputation for ability and integrity. He was a member of the Illinois constitutional convention in 1862 and in the same year was elected to the state legislature. Upon the election of Grover Cleveland as President in 1884, Fuller was offered a diplomatic position and the post of solicitor general but declined both. In 1888, however, Cleveland appointed him chief justice of the Supreme Court, a position he accepted and retained until his death. His years on the bench were unspectacular but, as an extremely able administrator, he was acknowledged to be a highly effective chief justice. He took moderate positions on most issues, combining a dedication to the traditional view of the rights of persons and property, a strict-constructionist interpretation of the Constitution, and a broadly humanitarian outlook. He was a member of the arbitration commission in the Venezuela-Great Britain boundary dispute in 1897–1899 and from 1900 to 1910 a member of the Permanent Court of Arbitration at the Hague. He died on July 4, 1910.

FULLER, RICHARD BUCKMINSTER, JR. (1895–   ), inventor and engineer. Born on July 12, 1895, in Milton, Massachusetts, of a prominent Boston family, Fuller was educated at the Milton Academy during 1904–1913 and at Harvard until 1915, when he was dismissed for irregular class attendance. He served apprenticeships with an importer of cotton-mill machinery and at Armour and Company, and was an ensign in the Navy during World War I, gaining valuable supplemental technical training. Upon his discharge he returned to Armour, was a sales manager for a trucking concern for a brief time in 1922, and spent the next five years working for his father-in-law, an architect, in the construction industry. In 1927 he moved to Chicago and began to evolve his unorthodox "comprehensive design" theory, a blend of mathematics, engineering, and philosophy, which materialized in the "Dymaxion" (derived from "dynamic" and "maximum") inventions. His first luxury house, built in 1927, was spacious, comfortable, and portable, supported by one central column, and cost the same as a 1927 Ford sedan; the Dymaxion car would travel 120 miles per hour, cross fields like a jeep, park or turn in its own length, and get 30 to 40 miles per gallon of gasoline. The Dymaxion Corporation, which existed between 1932 and 1935 and in 1941, but eventually dissolved owing to lack of commercial support, also marketed the Dymaxion steel igloo in 1940 and the Dymaxion world map, the first map to receive a U.S. patent, showing the continents "without any visible distortion." The Dymaxion Dwelling Machines Company was established in 1944, producing the Wichita house in 1946, a circular aluminum seven-room luxury home built with airplane construction methods for $6,400. The company was reorganized in 1954 as Geodesics, Inc., and Synergetics, Inc., whose main product was the geodesic dome. Built to provide maximum strength with minimum material, the domes were developed according to his mathematical principle of "energetic synergetic geometry," devised in 1917, which takes into account the paths of force in atoms, molecules, and crystals. The domes were shaped in numerous adjoining tetrahedrons, with supporting struts of high tensile strength alloys—a design that effectively dispersed any force on the dome's surface. Domes for the arctic Distant Early Warning lines were easily flown to location, installed in hours, and stood in 125 miles-per-hour winds; other domes were used by the Air Force to house rotating radar antennas and by the Marine Corps as front line shelters. He designed the Union Tank Car Company dome in Baton Rouge, Louisiana. As the world's largest clearance span building with no interior pillars, it had a diameter of 384 feet and stood as high as a ten-story building. A gold-tinted dome housed the American National Exhibition in Moscow in 1959 and drew such crowds that the State Department erected other exhibition domes in Burma, India, Thailand, Afghanistan, and Japan. Other domes enclosing controlled climates were projected for use in Antarctica, on the ocean floor, and on the moon. Although his early success was uncertain, the acceptance given the geodesic dome secured his later career. Associated at various times with the architectural departments of Yale, Cornell, Princeton, and the Massachusetts Institute of Technology, he lectured on comprehensive design and earned a lifetime professorship in 1959 at Southern Illinois University. He was technical editor of *Fortune* magazine in 1938–1940 and wrote the "Notes on the Future" column in *Saturday Review* after 1964. In 1938 he published *Nine Chains to the Moon* and in 1963 *No More Second Hand God.*

FULLER, SARAH MARGARET, Marchioness Ossoli (1810–1850), author, critic, and reformer. Born in Cambridgeport, Massachusetts, on May 23, 1810, Margaret Fuller was an extremely precocious child. Under the severe tutelage of her father she more than compensated for the inaccessibility of formal education to women of the time, but while she acquired wide learning at a very early age, the strain permanently impaired her health. She taught school for a number of years—for two years at Bronson Alcott's Temple School—and wrote occasional critical essays for the *Western Messenger.* In 1839 she began a series of "conversations" in Boston intended to further the education of women; a brilliant conversationalist, she enjoyed great success and the series was repeated yearly until 1844. In 1840, as a result of her close association with Emerson and the Concord circle, she became editor of the Transcendentalist magazine, the *Dial,* to which she contributed a considerable number of essays, reviews, and poems. In 1844 Horace Greeley invited her to become the literary critic for the *New York Tribune;* during the next two years she established herself as the leading American critic of the time. In 1845 she published her radically feminist work, *Woman in the Nineteenth Century.* The following year a collection of her essays was published as *Papers on Literature and Art.* Shortly thereafter she sailed for Europe where, her reputation having preceded her, she met and mingled with the leading literary figures. In Rome in 1847 she married the Marchese Ossoli, an impoverished Italian nobleman and ardent republican. They both became deeply involved in the Italian revolution led by Mazzini that year; when the revolutionary republic was crushed by France, she fled to Florence and wrote a history of the episode. In 1850 she, her husband, and their child sailed for America; the ship was wrecked off Fire Island and all aboard perished, on July 19, 1850. Her memoirs, edited by Emerson and W. H. Channing, were published the following year.

FULTON, ROBERT (1765–1815), engineer and inventor. Born in Little Britain, Pennsylvania, on November 14, 1765, Fulton grew up and received his schooling in nearby Lancaster. He early exhibited an interest in and a remarkable aptitude for things mechanical; he became an expert gunsmith and as early as 1779 had designed a small paddlewheel boat. In 1782 he moved to Philadelphia and, first as a jeweler's apprentice and later as a painter and miniaturist, he was financially successful. In 1786 he went to England to study under the artist Benjamin West; within a few years his interest in painting gave way to his growing interest in engineering. Particularly fascinated by the promise of canal systems for inland transportation, he devised a method for raising and lowering canal boats to integrate them into a surface railroad system. He also secured patents for machines to saw marble, spin flax, and twist hemp rope. In 1796 he published *A Treatise on the Improvement of Canal Navigation*. He submitted a number of proposals for various engineering projects, complete with detailed plans and cost estimates, to the British government. From 1797 he devoted several years to developing a practical submarine; in France in 1800 his *Nautilus* was successfully demonstrated and its naval potential made clear five years later when, equipped with torpedoes also of Fulton's invention, it sank a heavy brig. He was unable to secure research funds from either France or Great Britain, however, and dropped the project in favor of the steamboat. In partnership with Robert Livingston, then American minister to France, he planned a steamboat for use on the Hudson River. Construction of the *Clermont* was begun soon after his return to the United States in 1806, and on August 17th of the following year the boat steamed up the river from New York City to Albany, completing the round trip in 62 hours. For the remainder of his life, Fulton oversaw the construction of steamboats and the organization of regular freight and passenger lines. His *New Orleans* was in 1811 the first steamboat on the Mississippi. During the War of 1812 he obtained Congressional authority to construct a huge mobile floating fort for the defense of New York harbor; "Fulton the First" or the "Demologus" was launched shortly before the end of the war. He died two months later, on February 24, 1815.

FURMAN, RICHARD (1755–1825), clergyman and educator. Born in Esopus, New York, on October 9, 1755, Furman grew up near Charleston, South Carolina, and received little if any formal education. In 1870 he underwent a religious conversion and joined the Baptist Church; four years later, already an established and popular preacher, he was ordained. He was forced into hiding during the Revolution because of his strong colonial sympathies. After the war he quickly became the leading figure among South Carolina Baptists and in 1787 became pastor of the church in Charleston. Three years later he was a member of the South Carolina constitutional convention. He was long an advocate of the need for a Baptist college in the South. Though he began active preparations for such a school in 1787, it was not until more than a year after his death that it was finally opened; soon afterwards it became Furman University. He was elected first president of the Baptist Triennial Convention organized in Philadelphia in 1814; at the second meeting three years later he was reelected. He met strong opposition to his desire to construct a centralized authority for the Baptist Church and his efforts to this end were long delayed. When, however, the Baptist State Convention in South Carolina was finally formed in 1821 he became its first president. Until his death on August 25, 1825, Furman exercised great influence in both religious and secular matters throughout the South.

GALBRAITH, JOHN KENNETH (1908 –   ), economist and public official. Born in Iona Station, Ontario, on October 15, 1908, Galbraith graduated from the University of Toronto in 1931 and then went to the University of California, where he took his Ph.D. in 1934. From that year until 1939 he was an instructor and tutor at Harvard and from 1939 to 1941 an assistant professor of economics at Princeton. In 1941 he joined the Office of Price Administration as director of price controls and the next year became deputy administrator of the office; the unpopularity inherent in the position led him to resign in 1943. For the next five years he was a member of the editorial board of *Fortune* magazine and in 1945 directed the U.S. Strategic Bombing Survey in Germany and Japan. In addition to serving as director of the State Department's Office of Economic Security Policy in 1946, he held numerous other advisory posts in the government. In 1948 he returned to Harvard as lecturer and the following year became professor of economics. In 1952 Galbraith published *American Capitalism*, in which he analyzed the effects of the creation of huge concentrations of capital and maintained that the principal result was the spontaneous development of opposing groups—labor unions, associations of competing companies, consumer organizations—to wield a "countervailing power" and maintain an economic equilibrium. In *The Great Crash: 1929*, 1955, he recounted with characteristic wit the last days of the boom of the 1920s. *The Affluent Society*, 1958, in which he decried the American economy's overemphasis on private consumer goods, the demand for many of which was artificially created by advertising, and called for greater allocations of wealth to the public good, reached a remarkably wide audience for a work of its kind. In 1961 Galbraith was

appointed ambassador to India by President Kennedy and he served until 1963. In 1967 he was elected chairman of the Americans for Democratic Action. In the same year he published *The New Industrial State*, in which he traced the historical shift of economic power from landowners to capitalists to the "technostructure," a managerial and technical elite that he saw as common to all industrial nations East and West.

GALLATIN, ABRAHAM ALFONSE ALBERT   (1761 – 1849), public official and diplomat. Born on January 29, 1761, in Geneva, Switzerland, Albert Gallatin grew up with all the advantages of wealth and social position in that city of culture. Resisting the claim of tradition, however, he sailed for America, arriving in Massachusetts in 1780. After a brief and unsuccessful attempt to enter business and a short time teaching French at Harvard, he acquired a tract of land in western Pennsylvania and removed there in 1784. A cultured and educated man whose sympathies were nonetheless republican, he naturally became a political figure in the backwoods region; by 1790 he had been elected to the state legislature, where he continued for two more terms. He rapidly gained a reputation for integrity and great ability, particularly in the field of government finance. His election to the Senate in 1793 was disallowed because of the length-of-citizenship requirement, but in 1795 he was elected to the House of Representatives where he remained for six years. In this time he became leader of the House Republicans and maintained a constant pressure on the Federalist administration, especially on Secretary of the Treasury Alexander Hamilton, from whom he demanded fiscal accountability to the House. He brought about the creation of the Committee on Finance (now Ways and Means) and upheld the power of the House to "veto" treaties by withholding appropriations. With the election of Jefferson to the presidency, Gallatin became secretary of the treasury; during his 13 years in this post he sought constantly to reduce the public debt and made great progress to this end, only to be stymied by increasing troubles with England that resulted in the embargo and finally in the War of 1812. In 1813 he was sent to arrange a Russian mediation of the dispute; England refused this move but offered in the next year to negotiate directly. Gallatin resigned his Cabinet post to lead the peace commission in the treaty talks. The successful and satisfactory conclusion of the Treaty of Ghent was largely his work. For the next seven years he remained in France as American minister, declining an offer to resume his position in the Treasury. Soon after his return in 1823 he accepted the vice-presidential nomination of the Republicans but was induced to withdraw by Martin Van Buren. Gallatin retired to his Pennsylvania home; in 1826 President Adams appointed him minister to England. After his return the following year he concerned himself with private interests; settling in New York City, he became president of the National (later Gallatin) Bank and developed an interest in ethnology. In 1836 he published a treatise on the American Indian tribes and in 1842 founded the American Ethnological Society. He died on August 12, 1849.

GALLUP, GEORGE HORACE (1901–   ), public opinion analyst and statistician. Born on November 18, 1901, in Jefferson, Iowa, Gallup earned his B.A. in 1923, his M.A. in 1925, and his Ph.D. in 1928, from the State University of Iowa. He was head of the department of journalism at Drake University from 1929 to 1931, professor of advertising and journalism at Northwestern University during 1931–1932, and then became director of research for the Young and Rubicam agency in New York in 1932. He was made a vice president of the agency in 1937 and held his position there until 1947. He founded the American Institute of Public Opinion in 1935, and originated there the "Gallup polls," statistical surveys of public reactions to nearly every conceivable

issue, but mainly in the fields of news events and radio and television programming. The polls were published regularly in hundreds of newspapers and attracted great attention, particularly during presidential elections. (In the 1948 campaign, Gallup polls indicated a victory for Dewey.) Among other things, the polls seemed to show that the quality of the mass media was held low by business and financial pressures, and, in addition, that educated and uneducated Americans alike seemed to be satisfied with the situation. Gallup himself discussed the need for change and for a new philosophy of education that would stress discovery and self-learning. With a properly educated audience, he felt, the selection of material for mass consumption would ultimately be made by others than profiteers. He authored, among others, *Public Opinion in a Democracy*, 1939, *The Pulse of Democracy*, 1940, and *A Guide to Public Opinion Polls*, 1944.

GARFIELD, JAMES ABRAM (1831–1881), public official and 20th U.S. President. Born near Orange, Ohio, on November 19, 1831, Garfield grew up in poverty but, through his own efforts and those of his widowed mother, secured a good education, graduating from Williams College in 1856. For a time he taught school and, possessed of considerable oratorical skill, became a popular lay preacher. He became interested in politics, supported the Republican Party, and in 1859 was elected to the state senate. Soon after the outbreak of the Civil War he helped recruit a volunteer regiment and shortly thereafter became its colonel; he saw service at Shiloh, was chief of staff for Rosecrans' Army of the Cumberland, and performed with sufficient credit, particularly at Chickamauga, to attain the rank of major general of volunteers. In 1863 he resigned from the Army to enter Congress as representative from Ohio; for the next 17 years he was regularly reelected and was in danger only once, in 1874, for his minor involvement in the Crédit Mobilier scandal.

Garfield was a dutifully partisan Republican, serving as one of the "visiting statesmen" to Louisiana to oversee the election of 1876 and as a member of the electoral commission that awarded the presidency to Hayes. His principal legislative interest was in economic policy and he maintained a sound money position against agitation In western districts—his own included—for inflationary greenback issues. In 1880 Garfield was elected to the Senate for the term beginning in March 1881, but he never occupied the seat. At the 1880 Republican convention he headed the faction favoring John Sherman for the nomination; after his successful fight against the unit rule proposed by the pro-Grant "Stalwarts" the convention was for 34 ballots in a three-way deadlock between Sherman, Grant, and James Blaine. On the 35th ballot there was a break and on the 36th Garfield was nominated. In November he and running mate Chester A. Arthur were elected with a minuscule popular majority. The first months of his administration were taken up by controversy over appointments and consolidating party leadership; he was adamant in his assertion of presidential appointive power and at length was victorious over the Stalwart leader, Sen. Roscoe Conkling of New York. On July 2, 1881, while waiting in a Washington railway station, Garfield was shot by Charles Guiteau, a disappointed office-seeker who, probably insane, shouted that he was a Stalwart and wished to see Arthur become President. For 11 weeks Garfield lingered, incapacitated for his office; the constitutional issue of the conditions of presidential succession was debated publicly and in the Cabinet (Congress was in recess) but remained unresolved when he died in Elberon, New Jersey, on September 19, 1881.

GARLAND, HAMLIN (1860–1940), author. Born in West Salem, Wisconsin, on September 14, 1860, the son of a restless Western farmer, Garland grew up in poverty and frustration in Wisconsin and later in Iowa and the Dakota Territory. Largely self-educated, he moved to Boston in 1884 to seek a literary career. He was encouraged by William Dean Howells; in 1890 he began to write short stories and sketches, some of which were collected in 1891 as *Main-Travelled Roads*. The starkness of this and subsequent books, portraying in vivid detail the ugliness and despair of Western farm life, failed to find a public. In 1893 he moved to Chicago and there published in the following year a set of critical essays entitled *Crumbling Idols*, in which he advocated an unoriginal though, for the time, relatively advanced theory of literary realism, or "veritism." There followed a series of novels, none remarkable, about the far West. In 1917, in something of a critical reversal, he published the autobiographical and somewhat nostalgic *A Son of the Middle Border*; the book was widely popular and was followed by a series of Middle Border sequels, including the Pulitzer Prize-winning *A Daughter of the Middle Border* in 1921. In 1929 he moved to Los Angeles where he lived until 'his death on March 4, 1940.

GARRISON, WILLIAM LLOYD (1805–1879), journalist and reformer. Born on December 12, 1805, in Newburyport, Massachusetts, Garrison received little education and was sent to work at an early age. In 1818 he was apprenticed to a printer; in the office of the *Newburyport Herald* he became an expert compositor while contributing anonymously to its columns. In 1826 he became editor of the local *Free Press*, in which were published Whittier's earliest poems. Later, in 1828, he edited briefly the temperance journal *National Philanthropist* in Boston; later that year he established the short-lived *Journal of the Times* in Bennington, Vermont. In the next year he joined Benjamin Lundy in publishing the Baltimore monthly *Genius of Universal Emancipation*; a libel suit arising from a statement in this paper landed Garrison in jail for seven weeks in 1830 until Arthur Tappan paid his fine. Determined by now to fight both slavery and the temporizing American Colonization

Society, he issued in Boston the first number of the *Liberator* on January 1, 1831. With the famous promise "I am in earnest—I will not equivocate—I will not excuse—I will not retreat a single inch—*and I will be heard*," he began his battle for complete and immediate emancipation. As much a pacifist as an Abolitionist, he relied solely on moral pressure and the mobilization of public opinion to attain this goal. Despite persistent financial difficulties he continued to publish the *Liberator* for 35 years. Garrison was also under the constant threat of physical harm and legal action by pro-slavery elements; the state of Georgia, for example, offered a $5,000 reward for his arrest and conviction. He was active in the organization of the New England Anti-Slavery Society in 1831 and of the American Anti-Slavery Society in 1833. In 1835 at a Boston Abolitionist meeting at which the English Abolitionist George Thompson was scheduled to speak, but which he had been warned to avoid, Garrison was attacked by a mob. His single-minded dedication led him occasionally to treat harshly even potential allies in his cause; he alienated most of the Northern clergy and in 1839–1840, largely as a result of his advocacy of women's participation in the antislavery movement and of women's rights generally, the Abolitionist movement split into two factions. The exclusion of women caused him to boycott the 1840 World's Anti-Slavery Convention in London; in the next year he was elected president of the American Anti-Slavery Society and held the post for 22 years. By this time favoring peaceful disunion, he made lecture tours around the country and in England. While his increasing distaste for the Constitution, with its pro-slavery clauses, led him to burn it publicly in 1854, his overriding pacifism aligned him against John Brown and others who advocated violent action. Though at first opposed to the idea of forcible reunion, he soon came to support Lincoln, who openly acknowledged his services. The preliminary Emancipation Proclamation in 1862 reunited the two Abolitionist factions and in January 1865, with the end of the war in sight, Garrison moved the dissolution of the Anti-Slavery Society; similarly, with the ratification of the 13th Amendment, he brought the career of the *Liberator* to a close. During his last years he made two more trips to England and continued to press for prohibition, woman suffrage, and other reforms. He died on May 24, 1879.

GARVEY, MARCUS (1887–1940), social reformer. Born on August 17, 1887, in St. Ann's Bay, Jamaica, Garvey was largely self-educated and began working as a printer's apprentice at age 14. He moved to Kingston three years later and became foreman of a large printing company. Blacklisted after leading the employees in a strike for higher wages, he worked briefly for the Government Printing Office, founded two nationalistic publications and a political club, and sought more lucrative employment in South America. He observed the poor working conditions in many countries and, continuing on to London in 1912, met and assisted an Afro-Egyptian scholar, learning much of Negro history and culture. He returned to Jamaica in 1914 and founded the Universal Negro Improvement and Conservation Association and African Communities League. In 1916 he came to New York City, establishing the headquarters of UNIA there and founding branches during 1919–1920 in nearly every urban area of the country where there was a substantial Negro population. He also founded the *Negro World,* the weekly UNIA newspaper, which continued from 1919 to 1933. In 1920 he held the first UNIA international convention at Liberty Hall in Harlem; an estimated 25,000 delegates from 25 nations attended. There he delivered remarkable addresses on Negro rights, urging that black men accept a black Deity, exalting African beauty, expounding on the lives and notable achievements of Negroes through history, and projecting plans for Negroes to resettle in Liberia, West Africa, in a "back to Africa" movement.

He began several enterprises, including the Black Star Steamship Line and the Negro Factories Corporation, financed by the sale of stock to UNIA members. Much of his traveling became promotional; he declared that black-owned, black-operated ventures would rebuild the confidence of Negroes in their own people and prepare them for economic independence. Throughout this time he was harassed by both white and black members of middle-class society. In 1924, the Liberian government, fearing that his motives were revolutionary, rejected his plans for resettlement. In 1925 he was convicted of mail fraud in connection with sales of stock in the Black Star Line, which had gone bankrupt. He was sentenced to five years imprisonment, but his sentence was commuted by President Coolidge, and in 1927 he was released and immediately deported to Jamaica. He continued, nevertheless, making fiery speeches, organizing conventions, writing, and briefly participating in Jamaican politics. But his influence and prestige waned considerably. He moved to London in 1935 and died there, obscure and impoverished and nearly forgotten, on June 10, 1940.

GARY, ELBERT HENRY (1846–1927), financier and industrialist. Born near Wheaton, Illinois, on October 8, 1846, Gary studied for a time at the Illinois Institute, a Methodist college in Wheaton, read law in the office of an uncle, and in 1867 graduated from Union College of Law in Chicago. Taking particular interest in corporation law, he soon built up a lucrative practice and served as director of several companies. In 1882 and again in 1886 he was elected judge of DuPage County; though this was his only service on the bench he was ever afterward popularly known as Judge Gary. He took the leading role in the organization of the Federal Steel Company in 1898 and in consequence of his efforts became its president. When J. P. Morgan, who had been Federal's principal backer, set out to create the United States Steel Corporation in 1901 he selected Gary to supervise the actual organization of what was then the largest industrial corporation in the world. Gary became chairman of the executive committee and in 1903 chairman of the board of directors, a position he retained until his death. His standards of business ethics and his attitude toward labor were in some respects remarkably advanced for the time. He saw to it that working conditions at U. S. Steel were conducive to health and safety, introduced a profit-sharing plan for employees, and maintained a high wage scale. In response to the pressure of public opinion, he abolished the 12-hour day and the 7-day week in U.S. Steel's mills. He was, however, an implacable foe of the closed union shop, and his refusal to negotiate on this issue brought on the steel strike of 1919. Judge Gary died on August 15, 1927, in New York City. The city of Gary, Indiana, begun as a company town in 1906, was named for him.

GATES, HORATIO (c.1727–1806), soldier. Born in Maldon, Essex, England, Gates entered the army at an early age; he served in Nova Scotia in 1749–1750 and later in the middle and northern colonies during the French and Indian War. In 1762 he returned to England where, not finding a suitable opportunity in the peacetime army, he remained until 1772. In that year, encouraged by his friend George Washington, he returned to America, settling in Virginia. In 1775 he was commissioned brigadier general by Congress and made adjutant general of the Continental Army. Promoted major general the next year, he commanded the troops retreating from Canada and the following year replaced Schuyler in command of the northern department; there, against the invading British army under Burgoyne, he won the battle of Saratoga. He was appointed by Congress to the Board of War shortly thereafter. During the next several months there developed the "Conway cabal," an intrigue among a number of officers and members of Congress to have Gates replace Washington as commander-in-chief. Gates's implication in the plot is not precisely determined; he was at least, however, not unaware of it. From 1778 to 1780 he resumed command, first in the North and then in the East; there was little combat and his problems were largely those of supply. After a brief retirement to Virginia he was placed in command in the South in 1780. His disastrous defeat at Camden, South Carolina, led Congress to call for an investigation; delays allowed for reconsideration, and no investigation was held, but, except for a brief period under Washington's command in 1782, Gates's military service was over. He retired to his Virginia plantation. In 1790 he freed his slaves and moved to a farm on Manhattan Island, where he died on April 10, 1806.

GEISEL, THEODOR SEUSS (1904–), "Dr. Seuss," author and artist. Born on March 2, 1904, in Springfield, Massachusetts, Geisel graduated from Dartmouth in 1925 and after a few months as a columnist for a home-town newspaper went to Oxford for a year of graduate study in English. Following a period as a successful free-lance cartoonist and illustrator he joined the advertising agency of McCann-Erickson, where he created the popular "Quick, Henry, the Flit!" series. In 1937 he published his first children's book, *And to Think That I Saw It on Mulberry Street*; both written and illustrated by Geisel, the book won critical acclaim and enough popular success to warrant more than 20 printings. The next year he published *The 500 Hats of Bartholomew Cubbins* and in 1940 *Horton Hatches the Egg*, both likewise successful. From 1940 to 1942 he was a political cartoonist for the New York newspaper *PM* and from 1943 to 1946 was engaged in making documentary and indoctrination films for the Army Signal Corps. One of his films, under the title *Hitler Lives*, won an Academy Award in 1946. *Design for Death*, a feature-length documentary on Japanese history, was written by Geisel and his wife and also won an Academy Award in 1947. A cartoon starring his character Gerald McBoing-Boing won another Oscar in 1951. Returning to the field of children's books, he produced *McElligot's Pool*, 1947, *Thidwick the Big-Hearted Moose*, 1948, *Bartholomew and the Oobleck*, 1949, *If I Ran the Zoo*, 1950, *Scrambled Eggs Super!*, 1953, *Horton Hears a Who*, 1954, *On Beyond Zebra*, 1955, *If I Ran the Circus*, 1956, *How the Grinch Stole Christmas*, 1957, *Yertle the Turtle and Other Stories*, 1958, and many others. With *The Cat in the Hat* in 1957, he began a series of primary reading books that, published by Beginner Books, of which he was president, were widely praised by educators. In 1966 *The Grinch* was made into an animated cartoon and has since become an annual holiday presentation on television. In all, Geisel's books, with their zany creatures and their verse and prose that are often nonsense but always delightful, have sold nearly 10 million copies since 1937.

GEORGE, HENRY (1839–1897), journalist, economist, and reformer. Born in Philadelphia on September 2, 1839, George left school at 13 and, after two years as a clerk, went to sea in 1855 on a merchant ship. He returned the next year and entered a printing office. In 1857 he worked his way to California aboard a lighthouse tender, but was unsuccessful in an attempt to share in the gold mining boom. During the next several years he struggled with poverty, often unable to find work but conscientiously applying himself to self-improvement by reading widely. He wrote anonymous articles for various newspapers during his intermittent periods of employment as typesetter and, later, as editor. He became involved also in Democratic politics, though with little success. His intimate knowledge of poverty and a visit to New York during which he observed the paradox of progress and poverty developing hand-in-hand set him to seeking an explanation of the anomalies of capitalistic economics. In 1871 he published *Our Land and Land Policy*, a pamphlet which anticipated his great and fully articulated work to come. In 1876 he was appointed by the governor state inspector of gas meters; with this security he began work on *Progress and Poverty*. Published in 1879, the book analyzed wealth in terms of land and its value; asserting that to work the land is a natural right and that rent demanded by landlords is a violation of economic law and an obstacle to general prosperity, George proposed a government tax upon, and equal to, the rent price of land. Replacing all other forms of taxation, this "single tax" would allow economic laws to operate freely, effect a better distribution of wealth, and raise a surplus revenue to be applied to public works. In 1880 he moved to New York City; on the wave of the popularity that he and his book subsequently enjoyed, he made a number of lecture tours in the United States, Australia, Ireland, and England. He was defeated for mayor of New York in 1886 by the Democratic candidate, though he ran well ahead of Republican Theodore Roosevelt. Ill health and the exertions of a second campaign for mayor in 1897 led to his death on October 29th of that year.

GERONIMO (1829?–1909), Indian leader and warrior. By his own account, Geronimo was born in June 1829 in Arizona and was given the name Goyathlay. He grew up in a period of bloody raiding led by various Chiricahua chiefs, notably Cochise, and, after 1858, when his family was killed, came to be a skillful and courageous leader in raids of revenge against the Mexicans, by whom he was dubbed Geronimo. Other raids in Arizona and New Mexico led to his confinement on a reservation in southern Arizona; but when, in 1876, the Chiricahua were moved to another reservation already occupied by Western Apache, serious trouble ensued. Geronimo and his band escaped to Mexico and during the next ten years alternated raids against American settlers with periodic confinements. In 1886 he agreed to surrender to the Army under Gen. George Crook and to be taken to a Florida reservation. Two days later he again escaped. Crook was replaced by Gen. Nelson A. Miles who, with more than 5,000 troops, required 18 months to recapture him. Placed under military confinement by order of President Cleveland, Geronimo and his followers were sent to Florida, Alabama, and finally Fort Sill, Oklahoma, where they remained. Geronimo eventually adopted Christianity; he was featured at the 1904 World's Fair in St. Louis and in Roosevelt's inaugural procession in 1905. He died at Fort Sill on February 17, 1909.

GERRY, ELBRIDGE (1744–1814), public official. Born on July 17, 1744, in Marblehead, Massachusetts, Gerry graduated from Harvard in 1762 and for ten years thereafter aided in his father's mercantile business. From 1772 to 1774 he was a member of the Massachusetts General Court and served on the Committee of Correspondence; during 1774–1775 he was in the provincial congress and a member of the Committee of Safety. Early in 1776 he entered the Continental Congress as a supporter of separation from Great Britain; he was fully in sympathy with the Declaration of Independence, though illness delayed his signing it until September. He remained in Congress until 1781 and after a time devoted to his business interests he returned in 1783 and served two more years. In the many councils in which he served Gerry constantly impaired his potentially great effectiveness by an inability to maintain settled opinions in practical matters and by a single-minded devotion to a purely theoretical notion of true republicanism. His party affiliations were never clear and always subject to change. In 1787 he was a delegate to the Constitutional Convention, to which he contributed little; his initial opposition to the finished instrument changed later to support, and from 1789 to 1793 he was in Congress as an anti-Federalist who favored Hamilton's fiscal policies. In 1797 he was appointed by President Adams to join John Marshall and Charles Pinckney in a mission to France to negotiate several outstanding disputes. As the "X.Y.Z. Affair" came to light Marshall and Pinckney left in disgust, but Gerry, believing that he could secure concessions from Talleyrand, stayed on for a time and won nothing but criticism at home. Annually from 1800 to 1803 he was the unsuccessful Republican candidate for governor of Massachusetts; in 1810 he ran again and was elected. During his second term a law was enacted redrawing the boundaries of the state's senatorial districts in such a manner as to isolate Federalist strongholds and insure Republican domination of subsequent elections. One of the new districts was thought to resemble a salamander and the derisive term "gerrymander" was quickly coined to describe this form of political maneuver. In 1812 Gerry was nominated for Vice President and with James Madison was elected; he served until his death in Washington, D.C., on November 23, 1814.

GERSHWIN, GEORGE (1898-1937), composer. Born on September 26, 1898, in Brooklyn, New York, of Russian immigrant parents, Gershwin attended public schools on New York City's East Side, but left high school in 1913 to pursue a musical career. Called George from his boyhood, his actual name was Jacob Gershvin; he assumed the professional name of Gershwin. He began working as staff pianist at the Remick publishing company, composing popular songs. In 1918 he moved to Harms publishers, the head of which, Max Dreyfus, promoted his burgeoning career. In 1919 he wrote his first and greatest commercial hit, "Swanee," popularized by Al Jolson. His numerous subsequent productions for the Broadway musical comedy stage included Of Thee I Sing, 1931 (whose lyrics were written by his older brother, Ira), the first musical comedy to win a Pulitzer Prize. Countless song hits emerged from his and his brother's combined efforts, among them "Oh, Lady, Be Good" and "The Man I Love," both 1924, "Fidgety Feet," 1926, "'S Wonderful," 1927, "But Not for

Me," "Strike Up the Band," and "I Got Rhythm," all 1930, and "Nice Work If You Can Get It," 1937. He attempted the larger field of serious music with an epoch-making symphonic jazz score, Rhapsody in Blue, commissioned by Paul Whiteman; the latter introduced it in 1924, as orchestrated by Ferde Grofé. This synthesis of popular American rhythms and themes and traditional classical form (the piano concerto) expanded the artistic horizons of jazz, bringing a new sophistication to the medium, and won Gershwin prosperity and renown previously unequalled by an American composer. His other serious compositions included the Concerto in F, 1925, the symphonic poem An American in Paris, 1928, and the Second Rhapsody, 1932. His folk opera, Porgy and Bess, 1935, with a libretto by Du Bose Heyward and lyrics by Heyward and Ira Gershwin, came to be considered his finest work. Its memorable songs included "It Ain't Necessarily So" and "Summertime." He died in Hollywood on July 11, 1937, at the age of 38; his music became ever more a part of American tradition with the years.

GIBBONS, JAMES CARDINAL (1834–1921), Roman Catholic prelate. Born in Baltimore on July 23, 1834, of Irish immigrant parents, Gibbons grew up in Ireland where his parents had returned in 1837. In 1852 he returned to the United States, settling in New Orleans with his mother. Deciding upon the priesthood as his vocation, he studied at St. Charles College near Baltimore, graduating in 1858, and then at St. Mary's Seminary. He was ordained in 1861. During the Civil War he was pastor of a small parish and chaplain at Fort McHenry; in 1865 he became secretary to the Archbishop of Baltimore. His warm personality and remarkable abilities elevated him rapidly in the hierarchy; consecrated bishop in 1868, he became bishop of Richmond four years later and in 1877 was made archbishop of Baltimore. In the same year he published The Faith of Our Fathers, a clear and eloquent exposition of Catholic doctrine that is still widely popular. Firmly devoted to his native country and to the support of its institutions, he held the U.S. Constitution to be man's greatest achievement in government. Supported by Pope Leo XIII in the belief that the future of the Catholic Church lay in the promotion of democratic institutions, he organized the Third Plenary Council of the American hierarchy, which declared its support of American civil institutions. In 1886 he was appointed the second American cardinal. He was the first chancellor of the Catholic University, which opened in 1889 in Washington, D.C. His patriotism and tolerance made him greatly popular beyond the confines of the Church; the vast numbers of his admirers included several Presidents. He died on March 24, 1921.

GIBBS, JOSIAH WILLARD (1839–1903), mathematical physicist. Born on February 11, 1839, in New Haven, Connecticut, Gibbs graduated from Yale in 1858 and, continuing his studies, took his Ph.D. there in 1863. For three years he was a tutor at the college. From 1866 to 1869 he was in Europe, studying at Paris, Berlin, and Heidelberg; two years after his return to New Haven he was appointed professor of mathematical physics at Yale, a position he held for the rest of his life. The first period of his productive life was devoted to work in thermodynamics. In 1876 and 1878 appeared his two great papers "On the Equilibrium of Heterogeneous Substances," which greatly extended the field of thermodynamics and laid the theoretical groundwork for the science of physical chemistry. Recognition of the importance of his work was, however, long delayed. In the following years he gave his attention to the calculus of quaternions and to vector analysis; his work on the latter was never published, though it was incorporated into a textbook that appeared in 1901. Gibbs published a number of papers on the theory of optics during the 1880s. In 1902 came his last great work, *Elementary Principles in Statistical Mechanics*. He died not long afterwards, on April 28, 1903. Only very slowly in ensuing decades did he come to be recognized as having been up to his time America's greatest theoretical scientist.

GIBSON, CHARLES DANA (1867–1944), illustrator. Born on September 14, 1867, in Roxbury, Massachusetts, Gibson attended schools in Flushing, New York, and the Art Students League in 1884–1885. His black and white illustrations of gay, well-bred people began appearing in *Life*, a humorous weekly, and major publications such as *Scribner's*, *Century*, and *Harper's Magazine*. In much of his work he sought to depict and to glorify the American woman, and he particularly delighted in picturing her in some out-of-doors occupation. His creation of the "Gibson girl" made him famous and much sought after as an illustrator. *Collier's Weekly* paid him $50,000, the highest commission ever paid an illustrator up to that time, for 52 pen and ink sketches. The "Gibson girl" enjoyed an enormous vogue and set a fashion in women's clothing and hairstyles—soft, wide pompadours, high collared starched white shirts and dark ascot ties, and dark-colored skirts with hemlines that just skimmed the floor. "Gibson girls" wore sailor hats and carried parasols in the summer. The fashion persisted through the 1890s to about 1914. Collections of Gibson's drawings appeared as *Sketches in London*, 1894, *Pictures of People*, 1896, *Sketches in Egypt*, 1899, and *The Social Ladder*, 1902. One series, *The Education of Mr. Pipp*, 1899, inspired a play of the same name. He illustrated several books, notably *The Prisoner of Zenda*. He died in New York City on December 23, 1944.

GILBERT, CASS (1859–1934), architect. Born on November 24, 1859, in Zanesville, Ohio, Gilbert studied architecture from 1878 to 1879 at the Massachusetts Institute of Technology and, after a time traveling in Europe, entered the architectural firm of McKim, Mead and

White in 1880. Three years later he began private practice in St. Paul, Minnesota. Business came slowly, but in 1896 he was commissioned to design the Minnesota state capitol and this success enabled him to move his office to New York. He submitted the winning design in a competition for the U.S. Custom House there and followed it with plans for the Union Club. For the 1904 Louisiana Purchase Exposition in St. Louis he designed the Art Building (now the city's art museum) and later built the public library there. In 1913 he achieved a national reputation with his Woolworth Building in New York, considered one of the finest early skyscrapers. Through service from 1910 to 1918 on the National Commission of Fine Arts he secured much work in the national capital, including the U.S. Treasury annex, 1919, the Chamber of Commerce, 1924, and the Supreme Court Building, completed in 1935. Among Gilbert's other major works were libraries in New Haven, Connecticut, and Detroit, the West Virginia state capitol, the New York Life Insurance Building, and the federal court building in New York. His design for the George Washington Bridge was later greatly modified; he also drew plans for the state universities of Minnesota and Texas. His practice was diverse and the body of his work was remarkably large for one man; thoroughly traditional in taste and having a strong dislike for modern functional design, he was much in demand and often honored for his work. He died on May 17, 1934, in Brockenhurst, England.

GILLETTE, KING CAMP (1855–1932), inventor and manufacturer. Born in Fond du Lac, Wisconsin, on January 5, 1855, Gillette was educated in Chicago and after working for a time in a hardware store became a traveling salesman for a succession of companies. He had a strong urge to invent something and in 1891 was advised by his employer, William Painter (inventor of the bottle cap), to concentrate on developing a disposable product for which demand would be constant. Four years later,

faced with a dull straight razor, he suddenly conceived of a razor using a thin, double-edged, and above all disposable steel blade. He soon had a crude model, but it required six years of experimentation and the technical aid of William Nickerson to develop a practical blade and razor. In 1901 the Gillette Safety Razor Company was established. Two years later the product was on the market and the sales for 1903 totaled 51 razors and 168 blades. The easy new method of shaving caught on quickly thereafter, however, and as sales soared into the millions annually beards became steadily less fashionable. Gillette remained president of the company until 1931 and was a director until his death. In his later years he became interested in social and economic reform. In a number of books, including *World Corporation,* 1910, and *The People's Corporation,* 1924, he advocated a reorganization of the economy into a single gigantic trust, an idea similar in many respects to Edward Bellamy's scheme, a planned utilization of the most advanced technology, the organization of labor into efficient production groups, and the communalization of many domestic functions within huge residential units. A World Corporation was established briefly in 1910 and Gillette sought unsuccessfully to persuade Theodore Roosevelt to take charge of it. He died in Los Angeles on July 9, 1932.

GILMAN, DANIEL COIT (1831–1908), educator. Born in Norwich, Connecticut, on July 6, 1831, Gilman graduated from Yale in 1852, studied briefly at Harvard, and in 1853 was appointed an attaché to the American embassy in St. Petersburg. Before his return to the United States in 1855 he spent some time studying in Berlin. Returning to New Haven, he began an association with Yale that was to last 17 years. After drawing up a plan of organization for the Yale Scientific School (later the Sheffield Scientific School), he became professor of physical and political geography as well as assistant librarian and secretary to the governing board. He declined offers of university presidencies in 1867 and 1870 but in 1872 accepted a call from the University of California. His three years there were less than successful, largely because of legislative interference in academic matters. In 1875 he was asked to become first president of the new Johns Hopkins University in Baltimore; he accepted gladly and set about gathering a faculty. In this task he traveled over the country and to Europe seeking men who, more than able lecturers, were also researchers, the seekers of truth that Gilman believed the true university must have. At Johns Hopkins, free from public pressure, legislative meddling, and theological restriction, emphasis was put on original research and the training of graduate students. In 1889 the Johns Hopkins Hospital, with Gilman as director, was opened; four years later the medical school was begun with admission requirements that, while seeming impossibly high at the time — a college degree was requisite — soon became standard throughout the nation. In his quarter-century at Hopkins, Gilman brought to reality his conception of a great university, and his ideas had tremendous impact on other educators and institutions. In 1901 he retired and for the next three years was first president of the Carnegie Institution of Washington. He served also at various times on the General Education Board, as president of the National Civil Service Reform League, and with many other educational and humanitarian organizations. He died in his native city of Norwich on October 13, 1908.

GILMORE, PATRICK SARSFIELD (1829 – 1892), bandmaster and composer. Born near Dublin, Ireland, on December 25, 1829, Gilmore as a child was fascinated by his town's regimental band, whose conductor admitted him into classes on harmony and counterpoint, taught him to play the cornet, and let him tour with the band in Canada in 1846. Several years later he traveled to Salem, Massachusetts, formed his own military band, and went on to Boston to found Gilmore's Band. He was made bandmaster of the 24th Massachusetts Regiment during the Civil War and headed all the Army bands in the Department of Louisiana. His first "monster" concert was organized in New Orleans in 1864. It included 5,000 adults' and children's voices, 500 musicians, trumpeters, drummers, and artillery fire. His National Peace Jubilee in Boston in 1869 featured a chorus of 10,000, a 1,000-piece orchestra, and Gilmore's characteristic rhythm section; it was followed in 1872 by the World Peace Jubilee, also held in Boston, which included a chorus of 20,000, 2,000 instrumentalists, church bells, cannons fired by electricity, and the Boston Fire Department banging out the tune of the "Anvil Chorus" on anvils. Gilmore felt that 100 good musicians would produce twice the amount of good music as 50 good musicians. He and his bands played before enthusiastic audiences throughout the United States, Canada, and Europe. He wrote many of the military band numbers that were played by his and other groups of the time, and composed dance music, popular songs, and, in 1863, the words and music for "When Johnny Comes Marching Home Again," identified with both the Civil and Spanish-American wars. On September 24, 1892, during the St. Louis Exposition, he died suddenly while conducting his band.

GINSBERG, ALLEN (1926–   ), poet. Born on June 3, 1926, in Newark, New Jersey, Ginsberg graduated from Columbia in 1948. He lived in New York until 1953, becoming a close friend of avante-garde writers, including Jack Kerouac and Gregory Corso, and held a variety of jobs until becoming a market research consultant in 1951. Leaving for San Francisco two years later, he stopped in Cuba, explored Yucatán and Guatamala, and lived in San Jose for several months with Neal Cassady, the prototype of Dean Moriarty in Kerouac's On the Road. He worked briefly in market research in San Francisco, but soon turned to writing poetry and living in the bohemian style of the "beat generation." He attended graduate school in 1955 at the University of California at Berkeley. That year he gave the first reading of his long, rambling poem, "Howl," and became immediately famous and revered in the underground, from North Beach in San Francisco to Greenwich Village in New York City. He gave frequent readings thereafter in art galleries, coffee houses, and universities throughout the country, and in the early 1960s at the Lima Museum, the University of Concepción in Chile, Benares Hindu University, Calcutta University, and Oxford. He began to document the various historical, scientific, and religious views among countries on the use of marijuana. His files, which became the most comprehensive on the subject, were the basis of research for students, lawyers, reporters, and others, and for his own articles in underground newspapers and popular magazines. In 1965 he appeared at a gathering of peace marchers in Berkeley, and introduced "flower power"—a strategy of friendly confrontation, passing flowers to armed policemen, spectators, and the press. He was a Guggenheim Fellow in poetry in 1965–1966 and gave readings in Havana, Prague, Moscow, Warsaw, and London. He published *Howl and Other Poems,* 1955, *Empty Mirror,* 1960, *Kaddish and Other Poems,* 1960, *Reality Sandwiches,* 1963, and *Ankor-Wat,* 1967, several editions being published in other languages. He appeared in movies including *Wholly Communion,* 1965, and *Chappaqua,* 1966. He spoke on U.S. military and industrial power on a tour of U.S. colleges in 1968 and was an organizer of the ill-fated Festival of Life in Chicago during the 1968 Democratic National Convention.

GLADDEN, WASHINGTON (1836–1918), clergyman. Born in February 11, 1836, in Pottsgrove, Pennsylvania, Gladden grew up on the farm of an uncle near Owego, New York. He worked for a local newspaper for a time and in 1856 entered Williams College, graduating three years later. He was licensed to preach

soon afterwards and ordained in the Congregational Church in 1860. He served several churches in New England during the next several years and from 1871 to 1875 was religious editor for the *New York Independent.* In 1868 he published *Plain Thoughts on the Art of Living,* the first of his 40 books. He was called to the First Congregational Church of Columbus, Ohio, in 1882; there he remained for the rest of his life. An early advocate of what came to be called the "social gospel," Gladden preached a Christianized social order in which enlightenment and religious conscience would eliminate social and economic evils. He opposed socialism, favoring rather the amelioration of the unpleasant aspects of the established capitalistic system; he was among the very first clergymen to approve of the labor union movement in his *Working People and Their Employers,* 1876. He was a widely popular lecturer; he served on the Columbus city council from 1900 to 1902 and was active in the promotion of civic organizations. From 1904 to 1907 he was moderator of the National Council of Congregational Churches and openly condemned the foreign mission board's solicitation of "tainted" money from John D. Rockefeller. Among his books were *Applied Christianity,* 1887, *Who Wrote the Bible?,* 1891, *Social Salvation,* 1901, and *The New Idolatry,* 1905. He died on July 2, 1918.

GLASGOW, ELLEN ANDERSON GHOLSON (1873–1945), author. Born in Richmond, Virginia, on April 22, 1873, Miss Glasgow was educated privately. In 1897 she published her first novel, *The Descendant*; with *The Voice of the People,* 1900, she began a series of novels depicting the social and political history of Virginia since 1850 that continued in *The Battle-Ground,* 1902, *The Deliverance,* 1904, *The Wheel of Life,* 1906, and others. In *Virginia,* 1913, and *Life and Gabriella,* 1916, she explored the effects of a lingering but long outmoded Southern code of chivalry. *Barren Ground,* 1925, had a deeply tragic theme set in rural Virginia, as did the later *Vein of Iron*, 1935. With an increasingly ironic approach and a brilliant and satiric treatment she examined the decay of Southern aristocracy and the traumatic encroachment of modern industrial civilization in three novels of manners, *The Romantic Comedians*, 1926, *They Stooped to Folly*, 1929, and *The Sheltered Life*, 1932. Her last novel, *In This Our Life*, 1941, had a similar theme and was awarded a Pulitzer Prize. In 1943 Miss Glasgow published a collection of critical essays entitled *A Certain Measure*. She died in Richmond on November 21, 1945; her memoirs were published in 1954 as *The Woman Within*.

GODDARD, ROBERT HUTCHINGS (1882–1945), physicist and rocketry pioneer. Born in Worcester, Massachusetts, on October 5, 1882, Goddard was from an early age fascinated by rockets and what he envisioned as their potential for flight into space. He graduated from Worcester Polytechnic Institute in 1908 and three years later took his Ph.D. at Clark University. He was an instructor in physics at Princeton in 1912–1913 and in 1914 joined the Clark faculty where, after 1919 as a full professor, he remained until 1943. His work with rockets began, possibly as early as 1908, with static tests and experiments with various fuels, and in 1914 he devised a two-step rocket, the first to employ the staging concept. On the basis of a monograph outlining his researches and ideas for further work, Goddard received in 1916 a grant from the Smithsonian Institution, which in 1919 published the report, the now classic "A Method of Reaching Extreme Altitudes." In this paper he predicted the development of rockets capable of breaking free of earth's gravity and traveling to the moon and beyond. Goddard's ideas found little public favor, however, and he was often derided as "moon mad"; the weight of popular opinion was against even his clear demonstration that rockets would operate in a vacuum. During the early 1920s he worked on the use of liquid fuels, settling finally on a combination of gasoline and liquid oxygen; the first liquid-fueled rocket was fired in March 1926. In 1929, with the aid of Charles Lindbergh, he secured a grant from the Guggenheim Foundation and established a large testing range near Roswell, New Mexico. In that year he fired the first rocket to contain an instrument package, consisting of a barometer, a thermometer, and a camera. He began to experiment with gyroscopic guidance systems while improving his fueling apparatus. Goddard's work anticipated much of the progress in rocketry made over the next three decades; he was granted over 200 patents in the field, some of which, though ignored in America, were employed by German scientists in the development of the V-2 rocket in World War II. During the war Goddard moved to Annapolis, Maryland, and worked on developing rocket motors and jet-assisted take-off (Jato) units for naval aircraft. He died on August 10, 1945. In 1960 the U.S. government paid $1 million to the Guggenheim Foundation for infringements upon many of Goddard's patents and in 1962 the National Aeronautics and Space Administration's research facility at Greenbelt, Maryland, was named the Goddard Space Flight Center. On July 17, 1969, while the Apollo XI astronauts orbited the moon in preparation for their historic landing, the *New York Times* printed a formal retraction of a 1920 editorial comment ridiculing Goddard's claim that rockets could fly through a vacuum to the moon.

GODEY, LOUIS ANTOINE (1804–1878), publisher. Born in New York City on June 6, 1804, of French immigrant parents, Godey received little schooling and early began working in printing shops. During the 1820s he moved to Philadelphia and secured a position with the *Daily Chronicle*. In 1830, with a partner, he founded the *Lady's Book*, a periodical modeled on a popular English prototype and dependent on material reprinted from foreign sources. In 1837, however, he bought the *Ladies' Magazine* of Boston and induced its editor, Sarah Josepha Hale, to take charge of the *Lady's Book*. The publication soon came to be known as *Godey's Lady's Book* and became the most popular periodical of its kind, circulation reaching 150,000 by 1858. In addition to the fashion plates and pages of music that were standard fare, the magazine published original stories, essays, and commentaries by native authors, many of them women, and often paid high prices to attract such writers as Hawthorne, Poe, Longfellow, Emerson, and Holmes. Perfectly reflecting the intellectual, moral, and fashion tastes of the day, *Godey's* was considered by many to be the final word on such matters. Godey undertook other publishing ventures as well, founding the *Philadelphia Saturday News and Literary Gazette* in 1836 and holding a part interest in a publishing house that issued, among others, the periodical *Lady's Musical Library* in 1842. The *Lady's Book* remained his principal interest, however, and he retained control of it until 1877. In that year he retired and he died in his Philadelphia home on November 29, 1878.

GODKIN, EDWIN LAWRENCE (1831 – 1902), journalist. Born in Moyne, County Wicklow, Ireland, on October 2, 1831, Godkin graduated from Queen's University, Belfast, in 1851 and went to London to study law. He held a number of journalistic positions and was correspondent for the *London Daily News* during the Crimean War. Returning to Ireland, he was for a time on the staff of the *Belfast Northern Whig*. In 1856 he traveled to the United States; he studied law and was admitted to the New York bar in 1858, but he apparently practised but little. He continued to write for the *London Daily News*; in 1865, declining a partnership in the *New York Times*, he founded the *Nation*. This weekly journal quickly became the most informed and intelligent review in the country; in 1881 the *Nation* became the weekly edition of the *New York Evening Post* — an association that lasted until 1918 — as Godkin became the

Post's associate editor and, two years later, upon the resignation of Carl Schurz, chief editor. In his sixteen years at the head of the paper he made it into one of vast influence; though he was of generally Republican sympathies, he maintained complete independence, contributing greatly to the Mugwump revolt in 1884. In the *Post*, as he had in the *Nation*, Godkin stood firmly for honest, efficient, and sound government; he had a liberal outlook and denounced imperialism and jingoism. He conducted a long and fearless campaign against the corruption of New York's Tammany Hall. He retired from the *Post* in 1899 and died in England on May 21, 1902.

GOETHALS, GEORGE WASHINGTON (1858 – 1928), engineer. Born on June 29, 1858, in Brooklyn, New York, Goethals attended public schools and the College of the City of New York. He had aspired originally toward a medical career, but he transferred to West Point and graduated in 1880. As an officer in the Army Engineer Corps, he was employed on several civil works projects, including improvements on the Ohio and Cumberland rivers and completion of work on the Muscle Shoals Canal on the Tennessee River. From 1885 to 1889 and again from 1898 to 1900 he taught engineering at West Point. In 1907 he was commissioned by President Roosevelt to head construction of the Panama Canal. In addition to the monumental engineering problems involved, he was charged with supervising 30,000 civilian employees of varying nationalities and supplying their food, shelter, medicine, and recreation. Vested with virtually dictatorial powers, he managed to construct an efficient organization while fostering an esprit de corps among the workers. In 1913 the canal was completed and in 1914 it was opened to the world. Goethals was appointed by President Wilson the first governor of the Canal Zone; he was promoted to major general and voted the thanks of Congress in 1915. He retired from the Army in 1916 and resigned as governor in 1917. He continued to serve in government and civil engineering projects until he was recalled to active duty late in 1917 as acting quartermaster general. He was later also made chief of the divisions of Storage, Purchase, and Traffic for the General Staff and a member of the War Industries Board. Retiring again from active duty in 1919, he headed his own engineering firm and was a consultant to many municipalities, and particularly to the Port of New York Authority. He died in New York City on January 21, 1928.

GOLDMAN, EMMA (1869–1940), anarchist. Born on June 27, 1869, in Kovno, Lithuania, Miss Goldman grew up there, in Königsberg, and in St. Petersburg. Her formal education was limited but she read much on her own and in St. Petersburg associated with a student circle. In 1885 she emigrated to the United States and settled in Rochester, New York. There, and later in New Haven, Connecticut, she worked in clothing factories and came into contact with socialist and anarchist groups among fellow workers. In 1889 she moved to New York City, determined to join the anarchist cause; she formed a close association with Alexander Berkman who, in 1892, was imprisoned for an assassination attempt on Henry C. Frick during the Homestead steel strike. The following year she herself was sent to jail for inciting a riot by a fiery speech to a group of unemployed workers. Upon her release she embarked on lecture tours of Europe in 1895, of the United States, and again of Europe in 1899. The assassin of President McKinley claimed to have been inspired by her, though there was no direct connection between them. In 1906 Berkman was freed and they resumed their joint activities. In that year she founded *Mother Earth*, a periodical that she edited until its suppression in 1917. In 1910 she published *Anarchism and Other Essays*. She spoke often and widely, not only on anarchism and social problems, but also on current European drama, which she was instrumental in introducing to American audiences. When World War I broke out in Europe she opposed American involvement, and when this nevertheless came about she agitated against military conscription. In July 1917 she was sentenced to two years in prison for these activities. By the time of her release in 1919 the nation was in the throes of an hysterical reaction to a largely imaginary subversive network of communist elements; Miss Goldman was declared an alien and, along with Berkman and over 200 others, was deported to Russia. Her stay there was brief and two years after leaving she recounted her experiences in *My Disillusionment in Russia*, 1923. She remained active, living at various times in Sweden, Germany, England, France, and elsewhere, continuing to lecture, and writing her autobiography, *Living My Life*, 1931. She joined the anti-fascist cause in Spain and while working in its behalf died in Toronto, Canada, on May 14, 1940.

GOLDWATER, BARRY MORRIS (1909–   ), public official. Born on January 1, 1909, in Phoenix, Arizona, Goldwater was educated at Staunton Military Academy and for a year at the University of Arizona. In 1929 he joined the family department store, Goldwater's, Inc., becoming president in 1937. During World War II he was a pilot with the Army Air Corps's Transport Command and afterwards, a lieutenant colonel, he helped organize the Arizona Air National Guard, serving as its chief of staff from 1946 to 1952. In the Air Force Reserve he rose to major general. In 1949 Goldwater was elected to the Phoenix city council; three years later he was elected by a narrow margin to the Senate. He relinquished the presidency of Goldwater's, becoming chairman of the board in 1953 and subsequently devoting himself entirely to politics. As a staunch and articulate conservative, he soon was the acknowledged leader of the conservative wing of the Republican Party. He was reelected in 1958 and two years later published his widely read *The Conscience of* a *Conservative*. In 1964 he won the Republican presidential nomination; despite an active and spirited campaign, he was overwhelmingly defeated, largely because of fears that, as President, he would attempt to dismantle established welfare programs and pursue a foreign policy leading to war. He remained active in Arizona politics following his defeat, however, and in 1968 was again elected to the Senate.

GOLDWYN, SAMUEL (1882–   ), motion picture producer. Born in Warsaw, Poland, on August 27, 1882, into a poor family, Samuel Goldfish (as his original Polish name was translated) was orphaned at an early age. He ran away to London at 11 and two years later came to the United States. He worked in a glove factory in Gloversville, New York, and rose to salesman and, at 18, partner in the firm. At 30 he owned his own successful glove agency. In 1913 he joined his brother-in-law, vaudeville producer Jesse L. Lasky, and playwright Cecil B. DeMille in founding the pioneer Jesse Lasky Feature Play Company. With DeMille as their novice director, they made the first full-length American film, *The Squaw Man*, which was a great success. They merged with the sole competition, Adolph Zukor's Famous Players, with Goldwyn becoming director and chairman of the board. The same year, 1917, he formed the Goldwyn Pictures Corporation with Broadway producers Edgar and Archibald Selwyn, and in 1918 left the Lasky venture. He changed his name legally to Goldwyn (Judge Learned Hand commenting, "A self-made man may prefer a self-made name") in 1919. That year he founded Eminent Authors Pictures, Inc., with a view to attracting prominent writers to the industry. Although he soon left this enterprise as well, he began the Hollywood tradition of fierce competition for "name" writers. In 1925 he merged Goldwyn Pictures with another company to form Metro-Goldwyn-Mayer. Within the year he sold out and organized Samuel Goldwyn, Inc. Ltd., which he controlled.

From 1926 to 1941 his pictures were distributed by United Artists; after that by RKO. His career was marked by independence and a demand for excellence in artistry and production. He hired, among writers, Ben Hecht and Charles MacArthur, and introduced some of the greatest stars in the industry, including Rudolph Valentino, Pola Negri, Vilma Banky, Will Rogers, and Ronald Colman. The films he produced included *All Quiet on the Western Front*, 1930, *Arrowsmith*, 1931, *Stella Dallas*, 1937, *Wuthering Heights*, 1939, *The Little Foxes*, 1941, *Pride of the Yankees*, 1942, *The North Star*, 1943, *The Best Years of Our Lives*, 1946, and *Porgy and Bess*, 1959.

GOMPERS, SAMUEL (1850–1924), labor leader. Born in London on January 27, 1850, Gompers grew up in a tenement district and ended his formal education at ten. He became, like his father, a cigar maker. In 1863 the family emigrated to the United States, settling on New York's Lower East Side; the next year Gompers joined the Cigarmakers' Union and in 1872 became a naturalized citizen. Under the influence of the socialism then popular among immigrant labor groups as well as the writings of Karl Marx, he developed both a philosophy and a practical plan of labor organization. In 1877 he reorganized the Cigarmakers' Union, introducing high dues and strike and pension funds, and establishing the supremacy of the international over local organizations. He restricted union activities to purely economic ones, seeking higher wages, benefits, and security by the economic leverage of strikes and boycotts, and avoiding political action or affiliations. His success was copied by a number of other unions; in 1881 he helped found the Federation of Organized Trades and Labor Unions of the United States of America and Canada. In 1886 this was reorganized as the American Federation of Labor with Gompers as president, a position that, with the exception of one year, 1895, he held until his death. Under his guidance the A.F. of L. grew slowly but steadily into the largest labor organization in the country. He firmly resisted political alignments or the formation of a labor party; he was equally successful in avoiding all connection with radicalism. Ironically, however, it was the A.F. of L.'s insistence on trade and craft unionism, with no provision for the unskilled laborer, that provided the main impetus to the formation of the radical Industrial Workers of the World in 1905. Viewing the labor union as simply the labor counterpart of the corporation, neither inferior nor superior to it, Gompers early advocated and in the A.F. of L. firmly established the system of negotiation and written contracts that still prevails in labor-management relations. During World War I he served on the Council of National Defense formed by President Wilson and instituted the War Committee on Labor. He attended the Versailles treaty conference to advise on international labor legislation. He continued his activities for the A.F. of L. until his death on December 13, 1924.

GOODRICH, SAMUEL GRISWOLD (1793–1860), "Peter Parley," author and publisher. Born on August 19, 1793, in Ridgefield, Connecticut, Goodrich received only an elementary education before going to work as a clerk in Danbury and later in Hartford. He served in the state militia in the War of 1812 and, after a brief and unsuccessful manufacturing venture, opened a publishing house in 1816. He issued textbooks and juveniles, writing some of them himself, and continued in this line after moving to Boston in 1826. Two years later he published the first issue of the *Token*, an annual giftbook that, during its 15 years of existence, printed early works of Hawthorne, Longfellow, and Lydia Child. In 1827 he published *The Tales of Peter Parley about America*, the first of what became over the years a series of more than a hundred books (not counting the many imitations) bearing the "Peter Parley" name. Treating such subjects as history, geography, science, biography, and morals, the books were easily digestible in-

struction for children and were greatly popular; in 1856 he claimed cumulative sales of some 7 million. Though he wrote a few himself, most were produced under his supervision by others, including on one occasion by Nathaniel Hawthorne. From 1832 to 1834 he edited *Parley's Magazine* and in 1841 established *Merry's Museum*, another children's periodical with which he was connected until 1854. Goodrich also took some interest in public affairs, winning election to the Massachusetts house of representatives in 1836 and to the state senate the following year. From 1851 to 1853 he was U.S. consul in Paris. After his return in 1855 he lived in New York City until his death on May 9, 1860.

GOODYEAR, CHARLES (1800–1860), inventor. Born on December 29, 1800, in New Haven, Connecticut, Goodyear was educated in public school and then obtained a position with a hardware firm in Philadelphia. In 1821 he returned to Connecticut and became a business partner of his father, a hardware manufacturer and inventor of farm implements. Four years later he opened his own store in Philadelphia as a retail outlet for his father's products; but by 1830 both father and son were bankrupt. It was in this year that the India rubber industry came into being; though it enjoyed considerable growth for a short time it soon began to suffer because of the poor quality of goods made with raw rubber—the substance was sticky and could not withstand heat and cold. Goodyear determined to find a method of treatment that would make rubber a practical material for manufactured items. For ten years he worked on the problem, going deeper and deeper into debt and on at least one occasion pursuing his experiments in debtors' prison. In 1836 he had some slight success with a process of treatment with nitric acid, but rubber so treated still melted in the summer. About 1838 he met Nathaniel Hayward, a fellow experimenter who had discovered that sulfur could eliminate the stickiness of rubber; Goodyear acquired Hayward's patent and continued to work with the new process. One day in 1839 he accidentally dropped some rubber mixed with sulfur on a hot stove; the rubber did not melt and seemed greatly improved; by 1844 he had perfected and patented this "vulcanization" process. Soon a number of companies were licensed to use the process and Goodyear exhibited rubber goods at expositions in London and Paris in the 1850s; he failed to secure patents there, however, because of legal technicalities and at home his patent was widely infringed upon. He finally won his rights in 1852 but his lawyer, Daniel Webster, received more in fees than Goodyear ever reaped from his discovery. He died in New York City on July 1, 1860, leaving his family some $200,000 in debt.

GORGAS, WILLIAM CRAWFORD (1854–1920), surgeon. Born on October 3, 1854, in Mobile, Alabama, Gorgas experienced an irregular education, but graduated from the University of the South in Sewanee, Tennessee, in 1875. He wanted to follow a military career, but could not gain admission to West Point; instead, he entered Bellevue Medical College in New York City, graduated in 1879, served an internship at Bellevue Hospital, and was appointed in 1880 a surgeon in the Army Medical Corps. He survived an outbreak of yellow fever while serving in Texas and, thereafter immunized, he was often stationed at posts particularly subject to the disease. He became head of sanitation at Havana in 1898 after its occupation by U.S. forces. He succeeded in greatly improving sanitary conditions in the city, but not until Walter Reed demonstrated that yellow fever was transmitted by a species of mosquito was he able to make headway in eliminating the disease. He immediately began to scour Havana for the mosquito's breeding places and destroy them. The city was quickly rid of mosquitos and the disease disappeared. For this work he won international fame and in 1903 was made a colonel by a special act of Congress. In March 1904 he

became chief sanitary officer of the Panama Canal project. Initiating measures against yellow fever, he was opposed by the Canal Commission, who thought the plans were extravagant. When an outbreak occurred in November 1904 funds were allotted and efforts against the mosquito proceeded. By 1905 yellow fever had been eliminated from the Canal Zone, and sanitary conditions had been vastly improved. In 1914 he was promoted to brigadier general and made surgeon general of the U.S. Army. In addition to instituting exemplary sanitary plans in Panama, he was requested to investigate the control of pneumonia among miners in South Africa and fought yellow fever in South and Central America and West Africa for the International Health Board. During World War I he supervised the Army medical service, retiring in 1918 with the rank of major general. He died in London on July 3, 1920.

GOULD, JAY (1836–1892), financier. Born on May 27, 1836, in Roxbury, New York, Gould was christened Jason but known throughout his life as Jay. He grew up in relative poverty and received little formal education; nonetheless he was possessed of a quick mind and native shrewdness and, untroubled by scruples, he soon began finding opportunities for money-making. His income from three years as a surveyor and from the publication of his *History of Delaware County* in 1856 enabled him to open a tannery in Pennsylvania the next year. By 1860 he had begun speculating in railroad securities; after taking profits from the Rutland and Washington and the Rensselaer and Saratoga and serving as manager of the latter, he became a director of the Erie Railroad in 1867 and with codirectors James Fisk and Daniel Drew engineered a fraudulent sale of stock by means of which they held off Cornelius Vanderbilt's attempted takeover and reaped huge personal gains. By admitting William M. Tweed to their councils and judiciously spreading bribes among state legislators, Gould and Fisk continued to profit.

In 1869 the two attempted to corner the market in gold and to induce President Grant to go along with the scheme; Grant seemed to acquiesce until he finally understood what was afoot, whereupon he ordered a massive sale of government gold that broke the corner at the expense of a disastrous fall in the price of gold on "Black Friday," September 24, 1869. Grant's reputation suffered from his seeming early complicity in the plot. In 1872 Gould was deposed from control of the Erie, whereupon he turned to western railroads. Beginning with the Union Pacific and the Kansas Pacific, stock in which he later sold at a huge profit, he began assembling an empire that included the Missouri Pacific, the Texas and Pacific, and others, and accounted for half the track mileage in the Southwest. He also branched into other fields; from 1879 to 1883 he owned the *New York World*, by 1886 he was in virtual control of the New York elevated railways, and he was a director of the Western Union Telegraph Company. He died on December 2, 1892.

GRADY, HENRY WOODFIN (1850–1889), journalist and orator. Born in Athens, Georgia, on May 24, 1850, Grady graduated from the University of Georgia in 1868 and during the next year studied law at the University of Virginia. During his years as a student he had contributed occasionally to the *Atlanta Constitution*; determining upon a journalistic career, he wrote for and edited a number of Georgia newspapers during the next several years. In 1876–1877 he was the Georgia representative for the *New York Herald*. In 1880 he bought a one-fourth interest in the *Atlanta Constitution* and from then until his death was editor of the paper. He attracted wide attention with his cogent analysis of the South's situation in the post-Civil War era and his realistic program for revitalization, including industrialization, crop diversification, and, not the least, a reasonable accommodation on the race issue. In December 1886 he addressed the New England Club of New York City,

summing up his viewpoint in "The New South." The speech was greatly popular and effective and soon became a standard oratorical piece, and he subsequently delivered a number of addresses on this and related subjects. He died on December 23, 1889, soon after returning from a speaking engagement in Boston.

GRAHAM, MARTHA (1895–   ), dancer. Born in 1895 in Pittsburgh, Pennsylvania, Martha Graham lived in Santa Barbara, California, after she was eight, and after completing her formal education in California schools devoted herself to dancing. She studied with Ruth St. Denis and Ted Shawn in Los Angeles at their tremendously influential Denishawn school and toured in the United States with their company. Her first professional appearance was in 1920 with Shawn; later that year she first performed as a lead dancer, in *Xochitl*, a modern ballet derived from Aztec legend. In 1923 she joined the Greenwich Village Follies, remaining for two seasons as a solo dancer. She subsequently remained apart from any company and further developed her own personal dancing style, which concentrated heavily on improvisation, highly individual choreography, and on new ways of developing a libretto. She taught at the Eastman School of the Theatre in Rochester and experimented with group arrangements. In 1926 she premiered as a solo dancer in New York City, introducing works of her own creation, and began to acquire an audience of select and enthusiastic admirers. Interpretations of Bloch's *Baal Shem* and of Debussy's *Nuages et Fêtes*, and her own *Désir, Tanagar*, and *Revolt*, were several works in her early repertoire. In the 1930s she introduced *Primitive Canticles, Incantation*, and *Dolorosa*, dances that reflected her fascination with Mexican Indians and their religious rituals. She studied in Mexico in 1932 as the first dancer to receive a Guggenheim Fellowship. Later she introduced *Letter to the World*, inspired by the life and poetry of Emily Dickinson, *Deaths and Entrances*, inspired by Emily Brontë, and numerous works based on Greek legend, *Cave of the Heart (Medea), Errand into the Maze (Minotaur), Night Journey (Jocasta),* and *Clytemnestra.* Her sets were frequently designed by modern abstract artists, such as Calder and Noguchi, her costumes were of unconventional materials and designs that heightened the abstract mood of her performance, and her scores were commissioned from such composers as Aaron Copland, Norman Dello Joio, and William Schuman. Her dancing was completely apart from the traditional steps and movements of ballet, fostering personal creativity, also the focus of the training methods she developed. Universally renowned as the foremost exponent of her art, she performed in major cities of the United States, and toured Europe in 1954 and the Far East in 1955–1956 as part of the international cultural exchange.

GRAHAM, WILLIAM FRANKLIN (1918–), evangelist. Born on November 7, 1918, on a farm near Charlotte, North Carolina, of Scotch and Irish Presbyterian parents, Billy Graham was converted at a revival meeting at 16, and his ambitions turned from baseball to preaching. He studied for six months at Bob Jones University, a fundamentalist Baptist college, and in 1937 resumed studying at the Florida Bible Institute (now Trinity College) in St. Petersburg. He had led one gospel meeting and secured 12 conversions before being ordained a Southern Baptist minister in 1939. He earned his B.A. degree in 1943 at Wheaton College in Illinois and briefly was minister of the First Baptist Church in Western Springs, Illinois, before commencing his nationwide evangelistic campaign. He held an eight-week series of tent meetings in Los Angeles in 1949, preaching to 350,000 people, among whom he won 6,000 conversions. In Boston, South Carolina, and Portland, Oregon, during the first six months of 1950, he won over 22,000 "declarations for Christ." In 1957 he held a 16-week campaign at Madison Square Garden in New

York City, part of which was televised, and won 56,426 conversions from the 1,941,200 people who attended, and another 30,523 conversions among his television viewers. In 1958 he was similarly successful in San Francisco at the Cow Palace. His first trip outside the United States was to England and the Continent in 1954–1955; subsequently he toured the Far East (1956), Australia and New Zealand (1959), and Africa and the Holy Land (1960). Compared with John Wesley in winning conversions and with Billy Sunday in his vigorous, magnetic preaching, he used modern communications to reach even wider audiences than they. His Oregon revival was made into a 45-minute film, and a Sunday radio program, *Hour of Decision*, was broadcast nationally, on Canadian networks, and world wide by short wave. Using modern, efficient business methods to handle arrangements for his appearances and to communicate with his followers, he established the Billy Graham Evangelistic Association, Inc. In 1949 he became the first vice president of Youth for Christ International, and from 1949 to 1951 he was president of the Minneapolis Fundamentalist institution, Northwestern Schools. He produced religious films, wrote a daily newspaper column, and published books including *Revival in Our Times*, 1950, *Peace With God*, 1953, *The Secret of Happiness*, 1955, *My Answer*, 1960, and *World Aflame*, 1965.

GRANT, ULYSSES SIMPSON (1822–1885), soldier and 18th U.S. President. Born in Point Pleasant, Ohio, on April 27, 1822, Grant spent his early years working on his father's farm. In 1839 he was appointed to West Point; though he had been christened Hiram Ulysses, an error on the part of his congressman resulted in his being recorded as Ulysses Simpson, and he accepted the change. He graduated in 1843 with a record unremarkable in any field but horsemanship. After service in Missouri and Louisiana he was sent to join General Zachary Taylor in the Mexican War and several times distinguished himself for bravery.

From the end of the war until 1854 he was stationed in California and the Oregon Territory; in that year he resigned his captain's commission and moved to St. Louis. After six unsuccessful years farming and dealing in land he moved to Galena, Illinois, and clerked in the family leather shop. At the outbreak of the Civil War he helped organize the company raised in Galena and worked in the office of the state adjutant general. In June 1861 he was appointed colonel in command of an Illinois volunteer regiment; two months later he was promoted brigadier general. He immediately embarked on a campaign to secure control of the Mississippi. Early in 1862 he captured Forts Henry and Donelson on the Tennessee River; his popularity soared, only to decline in April after the poorly executed and costly battle at Shiloh. From then until July 4th of the next year he concentrated on taking the stronghold of Vicksburg. In this campaign he demonstrated his remarkable and still growing sense of strategy; the victory, and the one following at Chattanooga, made him lieutenant general in command of the Union Army. Developing an overall strategy for the war—a novelty in itself—he determined to engage and wear down the enemy at every opportunity and at any cost. There followed the enormously costly but effective campaigns of the Wilderness, Cold Harbor, Spotsylvania, and Petersburg. The vast number of casualties incurred in these battles aroused the Northern public, but by April 1865 it was clear that Grant's strategy had worked. He accepted Lee's surrender at Appomattox Courthouse on April 9th. He began immediately to be courted as a potential presidential candidate. In 1866 he was appointed general by President Johnson after Congress had revived the rank; but his interim service as secretary of war during the Tenure of Office controversy estranged him from Johnson, and the Republican Party, dominated by the radicals, nominated him for President in 1868. As President he showed poor judgment in selecting aides; of the Cabinet only Hamil-

ton Fish was well chosen as secretary of state, and the conduct of foreign affairs was the high point of Grant's eight years in office. Aside from this and his creditable fiscal policy, his administration was characterized by little else than corruption. Though uninvolved himself, many of his close associates successfully worked major frauds on the government. Upon leaving office he made a world tour; he then returned to Galena, where he lived until he moved to New York City in 1881. After a banking house in which he had invested heavily went bankrupt—again because of the corruption of two of its officers—he was left in poverty. Encouraged by the publication of his article on Shiloh in the *Century Magazine* in 1884, he set to work on his memoirs. These, finished only four days before his death on July 23, 1885, were published by Mark Twain in 1885–1886, and recouped the Grant family fortunes.

GRAY, ASA (1810–1888), botanist. Born on November 18, 1810, in Sauquoit, New York, Gray was educated at the Fairfield Academy in Herkimer County. By the time he graduated from the Fairfield Medical School in 1831 his interest had turned to botany and he never practised medicine. For the next eleven years he was an itinerant, lecturing at various schools and making numerous field trips to study the flora of New York, New Jersey, and other areas. He became associated with John Torrey, also a botanist, and under his tutelage continued his rapid development to scientific maturity. Gray's first publication, *North American Gramineae and Cyperaceae,* 1834–1835, was widely praised and was followed a year later by his first textbook, *Elements of Botany*. With Torrey he published the two-volume *Flora of North America* between 1838 and 1843, and in 1842 appeared his *Botanical Text-Book* (after 1879 called *Structural Botany*), long a standard work. By this time Gray was acknowledged to be the foremost botanist in America, and in 1842 he became Fisher professor of natural history at Harvard, a chair he held until his death. At Harvard he assembled a large botanical library, developed an extensive herbarium, and continued to publish a steady stream of articles, monographs, reviews, and books that placed him among the world's leading naturalists. In 1848 he issued his *Manual of the Botany of the Northern United States*, which has remained the primary work in this field ever since. A pioneer in plant geography, he published in 1859 a study of the botany of Japan and its relation to that of North America, a work that was hailed by scientists around the world as a truly great piece of scientific research. Gray had long been in correspondence with Charles Darwin when the latter sent him an advance copy of *Origin of the Species*; from that time forward he was the chief American defender, and most perceptive critic, of Darwin's thesis; he succeeded in perplexing a number of opponents by subscribing to both the theory of evolution and the Christian religion. He published many popular texts on botany—*How Plants Grow*, 1858, *Field, Forest, and Garden Botany*, 1869, and *How Plants Behave*, 1872, among them—and in 1878 issued his last great work, the *Synoptical Flora of North America*. Gray was for 10 years president of the American Academy of Arts and Sciences, for 14 years a regent of the Smithsonian Institution, and the recipient of a great many honors from universities and societies throughout the world. He died at home in Cambridge on January 30, 1888.

GREELEY, HORACE (1811–1872), editor, reformer, and political leader. Born near Amherst, New Hampshire, on February 3, 1811, Greeley ended his irregular formal education in 1826 when he became an apprentice printer. Five years later, at the age of 20, he made his way to New York and worked for a time as a journeyman printer. Founding with a partner a small printing office of his own, he began to issue in 1834 the *New Yorker*, a magazine of good quality but with persistent financial difficulties. He contributed to other papers during these years, notably the *Daily Whig*, and in 1838 he was offered the editorship of the *Jeffersonian*, a Whig campaign sheet. In 1840 he edited the similar *Log Cabin*; the following year he established the *New York Tribune*, a daily Whig newspaper, which exhibited the highest quality of journalism, growing rapidly along with Greeley's influence. A zealous reformer, he was also something of a faddist, and his enthusiasms found expression in his paper; notable among them was his support of Albert Brisbane and the Fourierist doctrine. He opposed slavery and supported free homesteading as a cure for the industrial ills of the East. The *Tribune* attracted some of the foremost journalists of the day, including Charles A. Dana and Margaret Fuller; by the outbreak of the Civil War it was the leading newspaper in the country outside the South, where it and Greeley were proscribed. In his editorials he opposed the Mexican War and the Kansas-Nebraska Act; he favored the Free-Soil movement and in 1854 finally broke with the Whigs to join the newly founded Republican Party. In 1860, however, he supported Lincoln only reluctantly and in 1864 did so only at the last minute; his various stands during the Civil War epitomized his sometimes poor judgment and his tendency to vacillate on issues that were not morally clear-cut. After the war he advocated total amnesty for former rebels, hoping to heal the wounds of sectional strife; he was among the group that in May 1867 signed a bail bond for Jefferson Davis. On the other hand he generally supported the radical program of reconstruction, particularly the 14th and 15th Amendments. As the *Tribune* grew and control passed to others, Greeley found himself with less and less power; his long-standing political ambitions had also been thwarted, largely through the efforts of his earlier Whig ally, Thurlow Weed. In 1872 he made a final bid for office; joining the Liberal Republican group that was dissatisfied with Grant, he became its presidential nominee and later that also of the Democratic Party. The choice was a poor one, for

Greeley was too easily lampooned to be taken seriously. He was defeated overwhelmingly and, utterly exhausted, died shortly thereafter on November 29, 1872.

GREENE, NATHANAEL (1742 – 1786), soldier. Born on August 7, 1742, in Potowomut, Warwick Township, Rhode Island, Greene spent the years before the outbreak of the Revolution helping to manage his father's iron foundry and served for a short time in the colonial legislature. Though raised a Quaker, he was expelled from the Society for his unseemly interest in military matters. In 1774 he helped organize a company of militia that was kept from going to the scene of conflict in April of the following year in Massachusetts by Rhode Island's Loyalist governor. The legislature, however, authorized the raising of three regiments and appointed Greene brigadier in command. Soon given a similar commission in the Continental Army, he served through the siege of Boston and after briefly commanding the army of occupation there early in 1776, he set out to aid in the defense of New York City. He was promoted major general in August; after his loss of Fort Washington in November he joined Washington in New Jersey and during the next year rendered valuable service at Trenton, Brandywine, and Germantown. In March 1778 he assumed, in addition to his field command, the office of quartermaster general and, in the light of congressional and state recalcitrance in matters of finance and supply, discharged his duties more than creditably until relinquishing the office in August 1780. The next month, with Washington temporarily absent, Greene was in command of the entire army, and it was during this period that Benedict Arnold's plottings came to light. In October Greene was sent to replace Horatio Gates as commander of the Southern department; he arranged an efficient and dependable supply system and soon had the army, demoralized earlier at Camden, again in fighting trim. From the first he faced Cornwallis; shrewdly divid-

ing his army, he sent a force under Daniel Morgan to the victory at Cowpens in January 1781 and then, regrouped, allowed the enemy a Pyrrhic victory at Guilford Court House in March. Greene continued to hound the British, giving them another expensive win at Hobkirk's Hill in April. By this time the movements and battles forced by Greene had exhausted the British and induced Cornwallis to give up his plans for Southern conquest and to retire with the bulk of his army northward to Yorktown. In September, after a prolonged rest, Greene's forces won a major victory at Eutaw Springs and by December they had laid siege to the last British stronghold in the South, Charleston. After the war Greene experienced financial difficulties resulting from the mismanagement of funds and supplies by subordinate officers and government contractors and from the reluctance of the government to reimburse his heavy personal expenses in supporting his army. He retired to an estate near Savannah, Georgia, and died there on June 19, 1786.

GREENHOW, ROSE O'NEAL (? –1864), Confederate spy. Born in Washington, D.C., and reared in the elegance of prewar Southern society, Rose O'Neal was the widow of prominent physician and historian Robert Greenhow and was living in Washington when the Civil War began. A staunch Southerner, she was appalled at the desolation and destruction caused in the South by the war and blamed it all on Northern influence. She remained in Washington during the first year of the war, and was suspected then of spying, but her methods were unknown. Even when she was tried for treason, on March 25, 1862, the evidence supporting the charge was vague. She remained self-confident and polite throughout the trial; this frustrated the judges, who could not severely chastise her. An exile was imposed — she was to remain in the South, at least stay away from Washington. As a matter of fact, Mrs. Greenhow had amassed large amounts of information on Northern battle strategy, which she then passed to Southern generals. Several Confederate victories were apparently due to her counsel. Following her trial, she escaped to England, where, in two years' time, she stockpiled a huge amount of gold for the Confederacy. Her plan was to smuggle it through the Union naval blockade off the North Carolina coast; but before reaching her destination, she was shipwrecked and drowned.

GREENOUGH, HORATIO (1805 – 1852), sculptor. Born on September 6, 1805, in Boston, the son of a prosperous merchant, Greenough was reared in cultured surroundings. At the age of 12, inspired by a sculpture in his father's garden, he began his artistic endeavors by fashioning a figure out of chalk. He subsequently completed several more miniature figures from chalk and plaster. Throughout his school career he studied drawing and painting, clay modeling, and stonecutting, with local teachers. He graduated from Harvard in 1825, then left for Italy, becoming the first American to study sculpture there. He worked diligently, but contracted malaria in 1827 and had to return to Boston. Regaining his strength, he modeled John Quincy Adams from life and did several portraits, including one of Chief Justice Marshall. In 1828 he returned to Italy and established his studio in Florence, fulfilling commissions for portraits, busts, and sculptured groups. Requested by James Fenimore Cooper to model a group based on a painting by Raphael, he completed "Chanting Cherubs," which prompted much criticism when seen in America, for the display of nude infants horrified many. But Greenough successfully defended his work and a similar piece, "The Child and the Angel," was subsequently received without protest. In 1833, largely through Cooper's influence, he was commissioned by the U.S. government to create a statue of George Washington to be placed in the Capitol rotunda. All of his patriotism and republican feeling converged in this statue, on

which he worked for eight years, and which evolved into a colossal, half-draped marble figure, more reminiscent of a Roman senator than of an American President. The work was moved to America, but when placed in the Capitol building it shook the floor, and was immediately removed to the grounds outside, to the regret of almost no one but Greenough at the time. It was later moved to its permanent place in the Smithsonian Institution. In 1851 he completed a group called "The Rescue," which depicted a pioneer family under attack by Indians, and which was placed on the portico of the Capitol building. In the same year he was forced to abandon his studio in Florence because of political instability there. He reestablished himself in Newport, Rhode Island. His *Aesthetics in Washington*, 1851, and *Travels, Observations and Experiences of a Yankee Stonecutter*, 1852, in which he propounded a theory of functionalism, have come to be considered, more than his sculpture, his major contributions to the development of American art. In addition, he optimistically defended American art against European critics and helped raise the opinion of art in the minds of many skeptical Americans. He died in Somerville, Massachusetts, on December 18, 1852.

GREGG, WILLIAM (1800 – 1867), industrialist. Born on February 2, 1800, near Carmichaels, in what is now West Virginia, Gregg apparently received no schooling. He was apprenticed to a watchmaker uncle with whom he also operated a small cotton factory during the War of 1812. By 1824 he had completed his training and begun his own watchmaking business in Columbia, South Carolina. Within ten years ill health forced his retirement, but he had amassed a modest fortune and was free to follow his growing interest in manufacturing. He acquired an interest in a small cotton factory and quickly reorganized it into a profitable enterprise. In 1838 he moved to Charleston, then in many respects the capital city of the South, and began to develop his ideas on the need for industrialization in the one-crop "Cotton Kingdom." In 1844, as a result of a tour of the textile manufacturing areas in New England and the Middle States, he published a series of articles on this subject in the *Charleston Courier*; they appeared as a pamphlet, *Essays on Domestic Industry*, in the following year. The effect was immediate. A factory was begun in Charleston and in 1846, after obtaining with great difficulty a charter of incorporation from the reluctant South Carolina legislature, Gregg began erecting a factory and accompanying town near Aiken. Opened two years later, the enterprise was highly successful; landless whites, having no place in the dominant cotton culture, eagerly took up factory work and Graniteville quickly reached a population of 900. With this example, similar factories were built through the South; Graniteville's success was such that in 1858 Gregg could, in South Carolina, openly advocate a protective tariff. In 1856 and 1857 he served in the state assembly, but apart from this interruption he devoted himself to his town. He supported the secession movement in 1860 and during the Civil War was able to maintain the factory's production. In 1867 a flood seriously damaged the factory, and the exhaustion and exposure that he suffered in his efforts to save or repair as much of the plant as possible led to his death on September 13th of that year.

GREW, JOSEPH CLARK (1880–1965), diplomat. Born in Boston on May 27, 1880, Grew came of a patrician banking family. He was educated at Groton and Harvard, taking his degree in 1902. He then embarked on a world tour, spending most of his time in the Far East. An incident involving a tiger described in his published account of his travels, *Sport and Travel in the Far East*, attracted the attention of President Theodore Roosevelt; in 1904 Grew obtained a clerk's position at the American consulate in Cairo and soon afterwards became deputy consul general. During the next several years he served in a number of consulates in Mexico, and in St. Petersburg, Berlin, and Vienna. In 1918 he returned to Washington as chief of the State Department's Division of Western European Affairs and the following year was in attendance at the Versailles treaty conference. After a series of diplomatic assignments of increasing responsibility he became in 1924 undersecretary of state and oversaw the transition of the foreign service from political patronage to a professional career basis. In 1927 he was named ambassador to Turkey; four years later President Hoover appointed him ambassador to Japan. During his ten years there he struggled constantly to stem the growing conflict between Japanese and American claims in the Far East; he was one of few Americans to gain the real respect of the Japanese government, though it was in the end of no avail. Early in 1941 he warned the American government of the possibility of a Japanese attack on Pearl Harbor; when war came late in that year he returned to the State Department. For eight months in 1944–1945 he was again undersecretary of state, but in the latter year he retired to private life. He published his two-volume autobiographical *Turbulent Era: A Diplomatic Record of Forty Years* in 1952. He died on May 25, 1965.

GRIFFITH, DAVID LEWELYN WARK (1875–1948), motion picture actor, director, and producer. Born in Oldham County, Kentucky, on January 22, 1875, D. W. Griffith was the son of an aristocratic but, since the Civil War, ruined Southern family. At 16 he took a job in a newspaper office; in 1897 he won a small part in a production by the Mefert stock company, and for several years toured with this and other theater groups, working at odd jobs all the while. In 1907 a play he had written was staged unsuccessfully; a scenario for a movie version of the opera *Tosca* was rejected but gained him a job as a movie actor. After a brief time at Thomas A. Edison's studio he moved to the Biograph company; he advanced quickly and directed his first film in 1908. During the next 23 years he directed or produced nearly 500 films and was the single most important figure in establishing the basic techniques of cinematic art. On the technical side, his innovations and improvements, all soon part of the cinematographer's essential repertoire, include the close-up, the fade-in and fade-out, high- and low-angle shots, the pan, the flashback, soft focus, the moving camera, and others. At the same time he gave serious attention to content and opened the film to history, philosophy, and social comment. *The Birth of a Nation,* his first great film, opened in 1915 and was a sensation, both for its obvious artistic merit and for its controversial racial aspects. It was followed by the epic *Intolerance* in 1916, *Broken Blossoms* in 1919, *Way Down East* in 1920, *Orphans of the Storm* in 1922, *America* in 1924, and *Abraham Lincoln* in 1931. Griffith also had a keen perception of potential talent and the list of stars he introduced to motion picture audiences included Mary Pickford — "America's Sweetheart" — Dorothy and Lillian Gish, Lionel Barrymore, Joseph Schildkraut, Harry Carey, Mack Sennett, and Donald Crisp. In 1919 he had formed the United Artists Corporation with Mary Pickford, Douglas Fairbanks, and Charlie Chaplin. He made no more films after 1931; he retired to private life and sold his interest in UA in 1933. He died on July 23, 1948.

GRIMKÉ, SARAH MOORE (1792–1873) and AN-
GELINA EMILY, (1805–1879), social reformers. Born in Charleston, South Carolina, Sarah on November 26, 1792, and Angelina on February 20, 1805, the Grimké sisters came of a wealthy and aristocratic family. They early developed an antipathy toward both slavery and the limitations on the rights of women. Sarah made a number of visits to Philadelphia where she became acquainted with the Society of Friends; at length, in 1821, she became a member and left her Southern home permanently. Angelina followed and also became a Quaker in 1829. In 1835 Angelina wrote a letter of approval to William Lloyd Garrison that was subsequently published in the *Liberator;*

from this time on, the sisters were deeply involved in the Abolitionist movement, Angelina always taking the lead. In 1836 she wrote a pamphlet, "An Appeal to the Christian Women of the South," in which she urged those addressed to use their moral force against slavery. The institution, she argued, was harmful not only to the Negro but to women generally. Sarah followed with "An Epistle to the Clergy of the Southern States." Under the auspices of the American Anti-Slavery Society, they began to address small groups of women in private homes; this practice grew naturally into appearances before large mixed audiences. The General Association of Congregational Ministers of Massachusetts issued a pastoral letter strongly denouncing women preachers and reformers, and the sisters found it necessary to crusade equally for women's rights. There followed Angelina's *Appeal to the Women of the Nominally Free States,* 1837, and Sarah's *Letters on the Equality of the Sexes and the Condition of Woman,* 1838. In 1838 Angelina married the Abolitionist Theodore Dwight Weld, and both sisters soon afterwards retired from public activity. They assisted in Weld's school in New Jersey for a time; later all three moved to Hyde Park, Massachusetts. There the sisters died, Sarah on December 23, 1873, and Angelina on October 26, 1879.

GRONLUND, LAURENCE (1846–1899), political reformer. Born in Denmark on July 13, 1846, Gronlund received his M.A. degree from the University of Copenhagen in 1865 and began to study law. Two years later he emigrated to the United States and became a teacher of German in Milwaukee. He continued to study law and was admitted to the Chicago bar in 1869. He apparently did not find legal practice agreeable and as he became increasingly interested in socialism, a development that he obscurely attributed to his reading of Pascal's *Pensées,* he gradually gave it up entirely. In 1878 he published *The Coming Revolution: Its Principles;* this was followed in 1884 by his major work, *The Cooperative Common-*

wealth. In this book he presented, in a form somewhat modified to fit particular American circumstances, essentially a Marxist prescription for socialist revolution against a rigid and moribund capitalist system. During his remaining years he traveled widely lecturing on socialism. He consistently opposed half-way measures such as the Single Tax movement, though he supported Henry George's campaign for mayor of New York in 1886. In 1888 he became a member of the executive committee of the Socialist Labor Party. His views slowly mellowed as events such as the passage of the Interstate Commerce Act and the Sherman Antitrust Act indicated that American capitalism had a reserve of adaptability and might after all be viable. He gradually abandoned revolution in favor of government leadership in the evolution of a socialist state, an idea he developed in *New Economy; A Peaceable Solution of the Social Problem*, 1898. Shortly after joining the staff of the *New York Journal*, he died on October 15, 1899.

GROPIUS, WALTER ADOLF (1883–1969), architect. Born in Berlin on May 18, 1883, Gropius attended the technical institutes in Munich in 1903 and in Berlin from 1905 to 1907. He was head assistant to Professor Peter Behrens in Berlin until 1910, when he founded his own architectural firm. His prewar designs included factories and residences, as well as furniture, interior designs, and a benzene-powered locomotive, and were notable for their functional, sparse lines and innovative use of materials. His Fagus factory at Alfeld, built in 1911, employed a steel skeleton as the entire support of the structure; the only walls were "curtain walls" of glass. At the Werkbund Exhibition at Cologne in 1914 he created a stir with his model factory and its adjacent headquarters building, introducing a transparent staircase, glass-enclosed office units, and a roof garden. In 1918 he combined two German art schools at Weimar under the name Staatliches Bauhaus. As director of the revolutionary center, he embraced art, science, technology, and humanism as partners. Students working with extremely talented painters, typographers, weavers, furniture designers, and other practitioners in the applied arts learned skills in production as well as design. In 1925 the Bauhaus, which developed a reputation for teaching "architectural socialism," was moved to Dessau, where it was housed in his Bauhaus building, 1925–1926. He maintained a private practice in Berlin from 1928 to 1934. In 1933 the school was closed by the Nazi regime. Gropius remained in self-imposed exile in England from 1934 to 1937, working during the time with London architect Maxwell Fry, with whom he designed the Village College residence in Cambridgeshire, 1936–1937. In the latter year he was called to Harvard as professor of architecture, and remained in the United States thereafter. He continued Bauhaus methods at Harvard, where he was made chairman of the Department of Architecture in 1938, and at the New Bauhaus in Chicago, later called the Institute of Design, founded with Moholy-Nagy in 1937. He collaborated with Marcel Breuer on many projects, including a 250-unit defense housing project called Aluminum City in New Kensington, Pennsylvania, in 1941. In 1946 he established the Architects' Collaborative, and with his colleagues completed the Container Corporation of America plant in Greensboro, North Carolina, the American Embassy in Athens, 1957, and his famous Harvard graduate center in 1949–1950, comprising seven dormitory buildings and a community center, with buff-colored brick facing, framed in concrete, and adjoined by enclosed walkways. Among his many books were *The New Architecture and the Bauhaus*, 1935, *The Bauhaus, 1919–1928*, 1938, *Rebuilding Our Communities*, 1946, and *Scope of Architecture*, 1955. He died in Boston on July 5, 1969.

GUGGENHEIM, MEYER (1828–1905), industrialist. Born on February 1, 1828, in Lengnau, Switzerland, Guggenheim emigrated to the United States at the age of 19, settled in Philadelphia, and for many years engaged in various mercantile pursuits, including peddling. In 1872 he founded with a partner the firm of Guggenheim and Pulaski, importers of Swiss embroidery. In 1881 the business was reorganized as M. Guggenheim's Sons with his four oldest sons as partners. A venture in copper-mine stock in 1887 led to the abandonment of the lace business and the formation of the Philadelphia Smelting and Refining Company a year later. A second smelter was established in Mexico in 1891 and a third, also in Mexico, in 1894; as the company's installations multiplied, Guggenheim was able to rely heavily on his seven sons, principally the oldest, DANIEL (born in Philadelphia on July 9, 1856), to manage operations in the field. In 1899, the American Smelting and Refining Company was formed to consolidate the leading operators; Guggenheim, however, refused to join and instead decided to compete with the trust for business. He outbid it at the mine, formed alliances with and rendered financial aid to mine owners, and established the Guggenheim Exploration Company to seek new ore deposits throughout the world. Within two years he had demonstrated the superiority of his methods and in 1901 merged with American Smelting, taking control of the entire combine. Daniel became chairman of the executive committee and four of the sons were on the board of directors. Meyer Guggenheim died in Palm Beach, Florida, on March 15, 1905. His policies were continued by Daniel, who extended the company's holdings and processing operations into copper and nitrate fields in Chile, tin in Bolivia, gold in Alaska, and diamonds and rubber plantations in the Belgian Congo. His administration of the company was marked by his insistence upon employing the most modern and efficient techniques available and by his enlightened, though paternalistic, views on labor. He continued as chairman or president until 1919. He founded the philanthropic Daniel and Florence Guggenheim Foundation and in 1926 the Daniel Guggenheim Fund for the Promotion of Aeronautics. He died at his Long Island home on September 28, 1930. Another Guggenheim son, SIMON (born in Philadelphia on December 30, 1867), played a prominent role in the growth of the family holdings. He was a U.S. senator from Colorado from 1907 to 1913 and from 1919 until his death was president of the American Smelting and Refining Company. In 1925 he established the John Simon Guggenheim Memorial Foundation, named for his son, to provide financial support to scholars and artists pursuing advanced study abroad. He died in New York City on November 2, 1941.

GUTHRIE, WOODROW WILSON   (1912–1967), folksinger and composer. Born on July 14, 1912, in Okemah, Oklahoma, Woody Guthrie was one of five children reared in an atmosphere of guitar playing, ballad singing, prize fighting, Indian square dancing, and Negro blues. His formal schooling ended in the tenth grade. Subsequently the family suffered a series of tragedies: his father went bankrupt, their house burned down, his sister died, and his mother developed Huntington's chorea, a fatal and hereditary degenerative disease. Thus, at the age of 15, Guthrie got the urge to travel. He left for Houston, played the harmonica there in barbershops and poolhalls, then went back to Okemah and learned to play the guitar. The Depression and dust storms hit the Southwest soon after, and he left for California by freight train, singing in saloons for his dinner, observing people and situations wherever he stopped off. He allied himself firmly with the union movement, having witnessed mistreatment of migrant workers throughout the land. He began writing songs, such as "So Long (It's Been Good To Know Yuh)," "Hard Traveling," "Blowing Down This Old Dusty Road," "Union Maid," and "Tom Joad" (from a character in Steinbeck's Grapes of Wrath), expressing both his understanding of and his impatience with social ills. Growing short of money on the West Coast, he traveled to New York, sang first in hobo camps, then in waterfront taverns, to the workingmen in Madison

Square Garden, and, eventually, to the upper classes in Town Hall. He joined folksingers Pete Seeger, Lee Hays, and Millard Lampell in the Almanac Singers, entertaining primarily union groups and audiences of farm and factory workers. He joined the merchant marine in 1943, survived three invasions, and sailed on two ships that were torpedoed. In 1944 he rejoined the Almanac Singers briefly and wrote *American Folksongs*, a collection of 30 songs and sketches. He wrote over 1,000 songs that spoke as fervently of the goodness of the American people and the beauty of the American land as of the imperfections of the American system. One of his last, and probably his most famous productions, "This Land Is Your Land," was taken up as an anthem by many civil-rights and other reform movements of the 1950s and 1960s. Guthrie's final 13 years of life were spent in a losing battle against Huntington's chorea and he died, already almost a legend, on October 4, 1967, in New York.

HADLEY, ARTHUR TWINING (1856–1930), economist and educator. Born in New Haven, Connecticut, on April 23, 1856, Hadley was an exceptional student and graduated first in his Yale class of 1876. He remained at Yale for a year of additional study and then spent two years at the University of Berlin. Upon his return in 1879 he became a tutor at Yale and four years later an instructor in political science. In 1885 he published his first book, *Railroad Transportation, Its History and Its Laws;* in it he demonstrated the fallacy of the Ricardian theory of free competition as applied to industries having relatively large permanent investments, and he pinpointed precisely this high proportion of fixed to variable costs as a source of instability and tendency toward combination. He was soon called to testify before a Senate committee then drafting the Interstate Commerce Act and shortly thereafter was appointed commissioner of labor statistics for Connecticut. He continued his teaching at Yale while contributing articles on economics and railroads to various publications. In 1876 he published *Economics: An Account of the Relations between Private Property and Public Welfare*, his most influential work, in which he argued that expanding governmental powers would not answer the challenge of concentrated private economic power, and that only a morally enlightened public could solve the problem. Three years later Hadley was elected president of Yale. During his long tenure in this office he relinquished his teaching, but traveled and spoke widely while overseeing an unprecedented growth of the university. He retired in 1921; he was a director of a number of railroad companies and was mentioned as a possible political figure. In 1925 he published his last major work, *The Conflict between Liberty and Equality*. While on a world tour he died in Kobe, Japan, on March 6, 1930.

HALE, EDWARD EVERETT (1822–1909), clergyman and author. Born in Boston on April 3, 1822, Hale was educated at the Boston Latin School and Harvard, graduating from the latter in 1839. For two years he taught school and studied for the ministry; he began to preach in 1842 and four years later was ordained minister of the Church of the Unity in Worcester, Massachusetts. In 1856 he became pastor of the South Congregational (Unitarian) Church in Boston. He was a prolific writer, producing some 150 books and pamphlets during his lifetime; he readily lent his pen to a wide spectrum of popular causes and reforms. In 1863 he published his most famous tale, "The Man Without a Country." This and other stories were collected in *If, Yes, and Perhaps* in 1868. There followed a steady stream of collections and novels, including *Four Possibilities and Six Exaggerations, with Some Bits of Fact*, 1868, *The Ingham Papers*, 1869, *Ten Times One Is Ten*, 1871, and *In His Name*, 1873. In his writings as in his preaching he was a powerful advocate of the renovation of society through the influence of a liberal Christianity; he was thus an early apostle of the "social gospel" movement that developed in the last decades of the 19th century. From 1870 to 1875 he edited the Unitarian journal *Old and New*. Notable among his later works are *A New England Boyhood*, 1893, *James Russell Lowell and his Friends*, 1899, and *Memories of a Hundred Years*, 1902. In 1903 he was elected chaplain of the United States Senate; he held this position until his death on June 10, 1909.

HALE, NATHAN (1755–1776), Revolutionary soldier. Born on June 6, 1755, in Coventry, Connecticut, Hale graduated from Yale in 1773. He taught school from then until July 1775, when, war having broken out, he was commissioned a lieutenant in the Connecticut militia. He soon joined the Continental Army, served at the siege of Boston, and on January 1, 1776, was promoted captain. In March of that year the Army removed to New York. According to legend, in May 1776 Hale led a small band of men in seizing a provision sloop from under the guns of a British man-of-war. In September he volunteered to undertake a reconnaissance mission behind enemy lines; disguised as a Dutch schoolmaster, he gathered the required intelligence and was returning to his regiment when he was captured on September 21st. Brought before General Howe, he was ordered hanged the next day. On the gallows he made a brief speech, ending, again according to tradition, with the words, "I only regret that I have but one life to give for my country." Since that time he has been revered as a martyr to American independence and as a model for American youth.

HALE, SARAH JOSEPHA BUELL (1788–1879), editor and author. Born on October 24, 1788, in Newport, New Hampshire, Sarah Hale was educated by her mother and an older brother and by her husband, David Hale, a lawyer, whom she married in 1813. She submitted some articles to newspapers but was basically a housewife, raising five children, until her husband died in 1822. In financial straits, she then embarked on a literary career. Her poems, written over the signature "Cornelia," were printed in local journals and gathered in *The Genius of Oblivion*, 1823. A novel, *Northwood, a Tale of New England*, 1827, brought her an offer to go to Boston as editor of a new publication, the *Ladies' Magazine*, which she did, with her children, in 1828. As editor she composed the bulk of each issue herself — literary criticism, sketches of American life, essays, and poetry — supported patriotic and humanitarian organizations, and staunchly advocated education for women and opportunities for women to teach; however, she always remained apart from formal feminist movements. She also published during this period *Poems for Our Children*, 1830, containing "Mary Had a Little Lamb." In 1837 Louis A. Godey purchased the *Ladies' Magazine* and established Mrs. Hale as literary editor of the new *Godey's Lady's Book*. After 1841 she worked in Philadelphia, and with Godey made the *Lady's Book* into the most influential and widely circulated ladies' magazine published in the country up to that time. She continued to call for female education in the liberal arts and in medicine, and for women teachers (her articles aided the founding of Vassar College), and wrote of women as America's cultural and moral cornerstone, always advocating that their influence be wielded in the home and in schools and not through political power. Of her other activities, notably in child welfare, and publications, including cookbooks, poetry, and prose, her major achievement was the *Woman's Record, or Sketches of Distinguished Women*, 1853, 1869, 1876; in the course of this ambitious project she completed some 36 volumes of profiles of women, tracing their influence through history on social organization and literature. She retired two years before her death in Philadelphia on April 30, 1879.

HALL, GRANVILLE STANLEY (1844–1924), psychologist. Born on February 1, 1844, in Ashfield, Massachusetts, Hall graduated from

Williams College in Williamstown, Massachusetts, in 1867, and studied for a year at the Union Theological Seminary before going to Germany, where he remained until 1872, to study experimental psychology. Returning to the United States, he was professor of psychology at Antioch College for four years, and in 1876–1877 taught English at Harvard, where he completed his doctoral studies in 1878 under William James. He continued his studies in Germany before becoming a lecturer in the new field of educational psychology at Harvard in 1880–1881. For seven years thereafter he was a lecturer and professor of psychology and pedagogics at Johns Hopkins University, where he established in 1883 one of the first psychological laboratories in the country. In studies there he applied the ideas of Darwin, Wilhelm Wundt, and Sigmund Freud, among others, to strengthen and enlarge the base of psychology. His many outstanding students and followers included John Dewey. In 1891 his efforts bore fruit in the founding of the American Psychological Association, of which he was first president. At various periods he edited journals that he also established, among them the *American Journal of Psychology*, founded in 1887, the *Pedagogical Seminary*, 1891, the *Journal of Religious Psychology and Education*, 1902, and the *Journal of Applied Psychology*, 1915. His 489 published works touched on every significant branch of psychology. *The Contents of Children's Minds on Entering School*, 1883, launched the new field of child psychology. Other major works were *Youth*, 1906, *Educational Problems*, 1911, *Founders of Modern Psychology*, 1912, and *Senescence, the Last Half of Life*, 1922. Recognized as the most prominent authority on educational standards in the country, he was chosen, in 1888, as the first president of Clark College, Worcester, Massachusetts. There he founded the first institute of child psychology in the country and established a highly praised curriculum in graduate studies in the fields of education and psychology. He resigned in 1920. In 1923 appeared his autobiography, *Life and Confessions of a Psychologist*. He died the next year, on April 24th, in Worcester.

HALL, JAMES (1793–1868), lawyer, jurist, and author. Born in Philadelphia on August 19, 1793, of a literary family, Hall was educated largely at home. He began to study law but broke off to serve in the War of 1812; he saw considerable action and performed commendably, but in 1817, after some difficulty with his commander, he was court martialed and convicted. Though he was restored to rank by presidential order he resigned the following year, after his admission to the bar. In 1820 he traveled west to Illinois. Settling in Shawneetown, he quickly attained local prominence and was elected circuit prosecuting attorney; four years later he became circuit judge. In 1828 he compiled the *Western Souvenir* and published *Letters from the West*. From 1829 to 1832 he edited the *Illinois Intelligencer* and in 1830 began editing the *Illinois Monthly Magazine*; the latter became, upon Hall's removal to Cincinnati in 1832, the *Western Monthly Magazine*, which continued for four more years. Also in 1832 he published *Legends of the West*; among his valuable factual works about the region are *Sketches of History, Life, and Manners in the West, 1834–1835*, *Statistics of the West at the Close of the Year 1836*, and *The Romance of Western History*, 1857. In addition he produced a considerable amount of fiction, including *Harpe's Head*, 1833, and *Tales of the Border*, 1835. In all his writings he drew an accurate and vivid picture of the early Western frontier and much of his work is invaluable in this respect; at the same time he did much, through his editorial activities, to hasten the civilization of that same frontier. He died in Cincinnati on July 5, 1868.

HALSEY, WILLIAM FREDERICK (1882–1959), naval officer. Born on October 30, 1882, in Elizabeth, New Jersey, Halsey was the son of a Navy captain. He graduated from the Naval Academy in 1904 and after service on the *Missouri* and the *Don Juan de Austria* was commissioned ensign in 1906. After various other assignments he was placed in command of the First Group, Torpedo Flotilla, in the Atlantic in 1913. From 1915 to 1917 he was an executive officer on the staff of the Naval Academy, and during World War I he commanded a number of destroyers assigned to patrol and escort duty and based in Ireland, for which service he won the Navy Cross. From 1918 to 1921 he held several Destroyer Division commands and then spent a year with the Office of Naval Intelligence. After nearly two years in naval attaché duty in Germany, Denmark, Norway, and Sweden, he returned to the line and held a succession of commands, including that of the Naval Academy's station ship. From 1932 to 1934 he studied at the Navy and Army War colleges and then took flight training at Pensacola, Florida, qualifying as an aviator in 1935 at the age of 52. The next five years were spent with the carriers *Yorktown* and *Saratoga* and for a time as commander of the Pensacola station. In 1938 Halsey was promoted to rear admiral and in 1940 to vice admiral. When the Japanese attacked Pearl Harbor on December 7, 1941, he was commanding a force of ships returning from Wake Island, and his was left virtually the only operational battle force in the Pacific. In February 1942 he led the first American offensive in the area, a strike at the Gilbert and Marshall islands. After several other minor battles he was placed in command of the South Pacific force and South Pacific area in October; by now an admiral, in that month he defeated the Japanese in the Battle of Santa Cruz and in November beat them again at Guadalcanal. In June 1944 he became commander of the Third Fleet and engaged in operations throughout the western Pacific islands. Living up to his motto "Hit hard, hit fast, hit often," he was noted for his daring and imaginative tactics and made brilliant use of air power in delivering crushing blows to Japanese forces. "Bull" Halsey, as he was dubbed, helped turn the Battle of Leyte Gulf into the most overwhelming victory in naval history and then,

during 1945, brought the war to the Japanese homeland with naval and air strikes at Tokyo and other cities. On September 2 the surrender terms were signed aboard his flagship, the *Missouri*. In December 1945 he was promoted to the five-star rank of fleet admiral. After his retirement in 1947 he served on the boards of several major corporations until his death on August 16, 1959.

HAMILTON, ALEXANDER (1755 – 1804), political leader and public official. Born on Nevis, one of the Leeward Islands of the Caribbean, on January 11, 1755, Hamilton had a family life and an early education that were both irregular. Deserted by his father, his mother died when he was 13 and he spent the next four years working in a general store. His obviously remarkable abilities induced his relatives and friends to further his education; in 1772 he was sent to school in New Jersey and the following year he entered King's College (now Columbia University) in New York City. He interrupted his studies to join in the public debate on revolution; three pamphlets written by him in 1774 – 1775 in defense of the patriot cause were highly effective; at least one, written before he was 20, was widely assumed to be the work of John Jay and John Adams. When war broke out he organized a company and served with distinction in New York and New Jersey. In 1777 Washington appointed him aide-de-camp and personal secretary; four years later, hopeful of military glory, he impetuously resigned and performed creditably in command of a battalion at Yorktown. In 1781 he moved to Albany, New York, to study law and the next year was admitted to the bar; he had published a number of newspaper essays advocating the formation of a strong federal government and as a member of Congress in 1782 – 1783 he worked for this same cause. In the latter year he moved to New York City, where in the courts as well as in the press he effectively defended Loyalists against discrimination. In 1786 he was a delegate to the Annapolis Convention and introduced there a resolution to hold what came to be the Constitutional Convention in the following year. To that meeting he was also a delegate, though he contributed little to the final document. On his return to New York, however, he began a campaign to secure New York's ratification of the Constitution; after publishing a series of ineffectual letters to this end, he joined with James Madison and John Jay in writing the 85 *Federalist* papers that succeeded in winning over a majority in New York. Hamilton was author of at least two-thirds of the essays in *The Federalist*; at the New York ratifying convention in 1788 he led and won the fight for approval. In 1789, as the new government was organized, President Washington appointed him secretary of the treasury. He immediately set about stabilizing the nation's finances; by insisting upon full payment of the national debt, the assumption of state war debts, and a system of taxation to pay for it all, he intended firmly to establish the nation's credit while increasing the power of the central over the state governments. In his reports to Congress he also proposed the creation of the Bank of the United States and suggested a system of protective tariffs to encourage the growth of domestic industry. The Whiskey Rebellion of 1794, brought on by his excise tax on distilled liquor, provided him with an opportunity to strengthen further the supremacy of the federal government and to satisfy his taste for military action, and he took a leading part in the militia force sent by Washington to suppress the outburst. As factionalism developed within the government, giving rise to the Federalist and Republican Parties, Hamilton emerged as the leader of the former; his main opponent was Secretary of State Thomas Jefferson, and between the two men friction increased to feud proportions. Hamilton thought of himself more or less as Washington's prime minister and constantly interfered in other departments, particularly Jefferson's. The dispute reached its highest pitch during the war between England and France that began in

1793. Jefferson had long advocated close ties with France, Hamilton with England; the latter persuaded Washington to issue a proclamation of neutrality that was generally interpreted as pro-English and seriously usurped Jefferson's position by arranging for John Jay to be sent to England to negotiate a treaty. Jay's Treaty of 1795 was unpopular, but Hamilton managed to secure its ratification. In that year he left the Cabinet but retained considerable influence in the government. He wrote most of Washington's "Farewell Address" of the next year and in 1798 he secured, through Washington's influence, an appointment as inspector general of the Army. With the rank of major general, he organized the Army to resist a possible French invasion. Nothing came of the episode; war was averted by diplomacy and in 1800 he resigned his major general's commission. In that year, in an attempt to prevent the reelection of his rival for Federalist leadership, President Adams, he wrote an intemperate attack on Adams; a copy of the privately circulated letter was obtained by Aaron Burr and published. Adams was defeated, but in the tied election that resulted Hamilton broke with most Federalists by supporting Jefferson against Burr. In 1804, when Burr was a candidate for governor of New York, Hamilton again opposed him; after his defeat Burr demanded a duel of honor because of some derogatory remarks attributed to his enemy. Hamilton reluctantly agreed and was seriously wounded; he died the next day, July 12, 1804.

HAMMERSTEIN, OSCAR II (1895–1960), lyricist. Born on July 12, 1895, in New York City, the grandson of the composer and opera impressario of the same name, Hammerstein attended the Hamilton Institute in New York City from 1904 to 1912 and graduated from Columbia in 1916. He practised law for a year and then turned to a career as a lyricist for musical productions. As his reputation grew, he worked with top composers, producing the musical, *Rose Marie,* 1924, and songs including "Indian Love Call" and "Rose Marie" with Rudolf Friml; *Show Boat,* 1927, and "All the Things You Are," "I've Told Ev'ry Little Star," "Ol' Man River," and "Who?" with Jerome Kern; *Desert Song,* 1926, and *New Moon,* 1928, and "Lover, Come Back to Me," "Stout Hearted Men," "When I Grow Too Old to Dream," and "Blue Heaven" with Sigmund Romberg; "Bambalina" and "Wildflower" with Vincent Youmans; and *Oklahoma!,* 1943, *Carousel,* 1945, *South Pacific,* 1949, *The King and I,* 1951, and *The Sound of Music,* 1959, and "Bali Ha'i," "Climb Every Mountain," "Hello, Young Lovers," "It Might As Well Be Spring," "My Favorite Things," "Oh, What a Beautiful Mornin'," "Some Enchanted Evening," "You'll Never Walk Alone," and "Younger Than Springtime," all with Richard Rodgers, with whom he worked exclusively after 1943. His lyrics were typically nostalgic, conveying sentiments that were both recognizable and sincere. His musicals with Rodgers were notable for their themes, which often involved social criticism, and for their unprecedented success; some ran for years on Broadway and *Oklahoma!* went through more than 2,200 performances. Hammerstein died in Doyleston, Pennsylvania, on August 23, 1960.

HAMMETT, SAMUEL DASHIELL (1894–1961), author. Born on May 27, 1894, in St. Mary's County, Maryland, Hammett left school at 13 and for years worked at a succession of jobs, including newsboy, freight clerk, and railroad laborer. For eight years he was a detective for the Pinkerton agency. During World War I he served in the Motor Ambulance Corps and soon after his discharge began writing detective stories, a great number of which he published in *Black Mask* magazine under the name Dashiell Hammett. In 1929 appeared his first two novels, *Red Harvest* and *The Dain Curse,* both drawing heavily on his Pinkerton experiences. The next year he published *The Maltese Falcon,* probably his finest work, in which, through his protagonist, Sam Spade,

he brought a new style of hard-bitten realism to the realm of detective fiction. His characterization and dialogue were esteemed highly by many critics and compared to those of Hemingway by some. After *The Glass Key,* 1931, and *The Thin Man,* 1934, he wrote no more novels. The latter book introduced a new hero, Nick Charles, who combined the toughness of Sam Spade with an air of wit and urbanity and who became the subject of a number of movies and of a radio series written by Hammett. In 1942 *The Maltese Falcon* was made into a perennially popular movie starring Humphrey Bogart. During World War II Hammett, then 48, enlisted and served for two years in the Aleutian Islands. Long a supporter of left-wing political causes, he encountered considerable harassment in the early 1950s; his refusal in 1951 to divulge the names of members of an allegedly subversive organization brought him a contempt citation and six months in prison, and in 1953 his books were for a time removed from American libraries overseas. He died in New York City on January 10, 1961.

HANCOCK, JOHN (1737–1793), merchant and public official. Born in Braintree (now Quincy), Massachusetts, on January 12, 1737, Hancock moved as a child to Boston and was raised by a wealthy uncle. He graduated from Harvard in 1754, entered his uncle's mercantile business, and ten years later inherited it along with a large estate. His identification with the patriot cause dated from the Stamp Act, which, as a leading merchant, he both protested and evaded by smuggling. In 1769, soon after the impounding of one of his ships, he was elected to the General Court, remaining a member until 1774. In 1770 he was made chairman of the town committee formed as a result of the "Boston Massacre." He was elected president of the first and second provincial congresses in 1774–1775 and in the latter year was forced to flee to Lexington and then on to Philadelphia as one (with Samuel Adams) of the men specifically excepted from the pardon offered by General Gage. From 1775 to 1780 Hancock was a delegate to the Continental Congress, serving as president for his first two years, and in 1776 he was the first to sign the Declaration of Independence. Though wealthy and popular, he was a man of limited ability and was sorely disappointed when denied command of the Continental Army, a position he had eagerly sought. In 1780 he served in the convention to frame the Massachusetts constitution and under it was elected governor; he served until 1785 and was then elected to Congress. In 1787 he returned to the governorship and the next year presided over the Massachusetts constitutional ratifying convention. Regularly reelected as governor, Hancock was in his ninth term when he died in Quincy on October 8, 1793.

HAND, LEARNED (1872–1961), jurist. Born on January 27, 1872, in Albany, New York, Hand was the son and grandson of noted New York judges. He graduated from Harvard in 1893 and received his law degree three years later. He practised law in Albany and New York until his appointment as U.S. district judge in New York in 1909. He held the post until 1924, when he was appointed to the Federal Court of Appeals for the Second Circuit. In 1939 he became chief judge. He retired from this position in 1951, but continued to sit on special cases. During his long service in the federal judiciary he rendered verdicts in nearly every field of law; most notable were those in an antitrust suit against the Aluminum Company of America in 1945, later upheld by the Supreme Court, and in the prosecution of 11 Communist Party members under the Smith Act in 1950, later reversed. Although never serving on the U.S. Supreme Court, he was sometimes referred to, because of the reverence owed his opinions, as the "tenth man" on that court. In 1958 Hand delivered the Holmes addresses at Harvard in which he cautioned judges against the temptation to go beyond their constitutionally lim-

ited function and legislate from the bench. He did not support, however, a congressional attempt to place severe limits on judicial discretion. The lectures were published as *The Bill of Rights* in 1958. On April 10, 1959, he was honored by the national bench and bar for his 50 years of service. He died on August 18, 1961.

HANDY, WILLIAM CHRISTOPHER (1873–1958), musician and composer. Born in Florence, Alabama, on November 16, 1873, Handy was the son of former slaves. His deeply religious family intended him for the ministry and strongly disapproved of his interest in secular music; he left home after finishing his schooling to continue the study of music and his chosen instrument, the cornet. He walked to Birmingham, taught school for a time, and worked in a steel mill. In 1893, in the midst of that year's business depression, he organized a quartet to perform at the World's Columbian Exposition in Chicago; for several years thereafter he drifted and worked at numerous jobs, only some of them connected with music. Finally he settled in Memphis, Tennessee, and began to work seriously on developing the musical form that came to be called "blues." Assimilating the music he had grown up with—spirituals, work songs, rambling folk ballads, and particularly the infant school of "jass"—he produced, in written form, a type of song that combined elements of all—basically ragtime, modified by a strongly nostalgic or melancholy feeling. For a candidate in the Memphis mayoralty election of 1909 he wrote a campaign song, "Mr. Crump"; in 1911, somewhat altered, it was published as "Memphis Blues." There followed in the next few years a flood of songs in the new mode: the immortal "St. Louis Blues" in 1914, "Beale Street Blues," "Yellow Dog Blues," and some 60 others published in his several anthologies of Negro music. In 1941 his autobiography appeared under the title that had long been acknowledged to be his, *Father of the Blues*. Though blind and in poor health in his late years he continued to direct his own music publishing company until his death in New York City on March 28, 1958.

HANNA, MARCUS ALONZO (1837–1904), industrialist and political leader. Born in New Lisbon (now Lisbon), Ohio, on September 24, 1837, Mark Hanna moved with his family to Cleveland in 1852 and attended Western Reserve College for only a few months before joining his father's wholesale grocery business. In 1864 he served briefly in the Union Army and three years later became a partner in his father-in-law's coal and iron business. During the next several years he devoted himself to this and other business interests, always with great success; he helped organize the Union National Bank and bought the *Cleveland Herald*, the city's opera house, and a good deal of the street railway system. In 1885 the coal and iron company was reorganized as M. A. Hanna & Company. As his business connections widened and his fortune increased, Hanna became interested in politics; he saw that the continued growth of industry necessitated a recognized interdependence between business and government, and he became convinced that the latter could safely be entrusted only to the Republican Party. Accordingly in 1880 he contributed heavily to Garfield's presidential campaign and actively organized the businessmen of Cleveland in his support; in 1888 he promoted Ohio Senator John Sherman, though unsuccessfully. He then took another Ohio politician, Congressman William McKinley, under his wing. McKinley was defeated for reelection to the House in 1890, largely because of his sponsorship of the tariff bill of that year, but in 1891 won the governorship of Ohio; two years later Hanna directed his reelection to this office and, retiring from business, began planning for the presidential election of 1896. With a large staff paid for out of his own pocket he set about convincing party leaders of McKinley's suitability; he succeeded so well that the governor was

nominated on the first ballot. Named chairman of the Republican National Committee, Hanna raised a campaign fund of unprecedented size by adding to the normal solicitation of contributions a regular system of assessments on large businesses. The campaign was a great success; declining the office of postmaster general, Hanna accepted an appointment to John Sherman's vacated seat in the Senate in 1897; he was reelected the following year and quickly became a leader in the Republican inner circle as well as the President's closest advisor. He directed the campaign of 1900 and was again eminently successful in raising large sums of money from the business community. He remained a major power in the Republican Party until his death on February 15, 1904, in Washington, D.C.

HARDING, WARREN GAMALIEL (1865–1923), public official and 29th U.S. President. Born on November 2, 1865, in Morrow County, Ohio, Harding followed his schooling with three years of study at a nearby academy. In 1882 he moved with his family to Marion, Ohio, and there, after a short and unsatisfactory period studying law, he gained a position with the *Marion Democratic Mirror*. In 1884 he and a partner bought the *Marion Star* and for the next several years he devoted himself to making it a success; as Marion's population grew the newspaper prospered and his interests and influence gradually expanded. He became involved in local Republican politics and with his impressive oratorical abilities soon gained a measure of prominence. In 1898 he was elected to the state senate; after a second term he was elected lieutenant governor in 1902, but two years later he declined renomination and returned to his newspaper business. In 1910 he ran for governor and was defeated badly. Though he thought his political career ended, his reputation as a public speaker led to his being chosen to present William H. Taft's name to the Republican convention of 1912; two years later he was elected to the Senate by a huge majority and in 1916 gave the Republican convention's keynote address. His Senate career, like his earlier political life, was completely undistinguished by any quality other than party regularity. This very quality, however, combined with his geniality and lack of pretension, enabled him to emerge as a dark-horse compromise candidate from the 1920 Republican convention despite the fact that a campaign begun the previous year by his old Ohio political ally, Harry Daugherty, had revealed an almost total absence of popular support. Conducting a colorless, inactive, and confusing campaign—he was endorsed by various Republican factions as both an opponent and a supporter of the League of Nations—he won the election by a large margin, primarily because of national ennui and his own call for a "return of normalcy." His administration proceeded much as had Grant's after the Civil War: he made a large number of ill-advised appointments and was unknowingly surrounded by corruption. Leadership was left to the ruling party clique in the Senate and the high point of his term, the Washington Naval Conference of 1921–1922 and the subsequent arms-limitation treaty, came through the initiative of others. By 1923 Washington was rife with rumors of widespread corruption in various government departments and a Senate investigation into the Teapot Dome oil lease transfers was begun. In June Harding set out on a transcontinental tour; while in Alaska he received a long cipher message from Washington, apparently informing him of the extent of the corruption that was about to be exposed. Deeply shaken, he traveled south toward San Francisco and was soon reported to be suffering from ptomaine poisoning and other complications; he died in that city on August 2, 1923, under circumstances that are still not completely clear.

HARLAN, JOHN MARSHALL (1833–1911), public official and jurist. Born in Boyle County, Kentucky, on June 1, 1833, Harlan was educated at Centre College in Danville. After his graduation in 1850 he entered Transylvania University to study law and was admitted to the bar three years later. Taking up practice in Frankfort, he was elected county judge in 1858; on completing his term the next year he ran unsuccessfully for Congress and in 1860, not yet reconciled to the policies of the Republicans, he was a presidential elector for the Constitutional Union Party. During the Civil War he commanded an infantry regiment until resigning his commission in 1863; in the same year he was elected state attorney general. In 1864 he opposed Lincoln's bid for reelection and supported General George B. McClellan. The next year he won a second term as attorney general, upon the completion of which, in 1867, he retired to private practice. He moved slowly from the conservative to the radical wing of the Republican Party and was its unsuccessful candidate for governor of Kentucky in 1871 and 1875. As head of the Kentucky delegation to the Republican convention in 1876 he was instrumental in securing the nomination of Rutherford B. Hayes; in gratitude Harlan was offered a diplomatic post but declined it. In 1877 Hayes appointed him to a commission sent to resolve the conflict between two rival state governments in Louisiana and later in the year he was named to the Supreme Court. During his nearly 34 years on the bench he was a powerful advocate of a balanced view of national sovereignty and states' rights. He was never the least inclined to muffle a dissent; most of his notable opinions were such and verged occasionally on bitterness as he seemed to flourish in the heat of controversy. In the Civil Rights Cases he dissented from the Court majority in upholding a broad interpretation of the 13th and 14th Amendments. He was also in the minority in holding, in the Insular Cases, that the Constitution "follows the flag"; in upholding in 1895 the right of the federal government to tax personal income; and in declaring, in *Plessy* v. *Ferguson* in 1896, that segregated schools did not constitute equal treatment under law and that the Constitution is "color-blind." He vigorously opposed judicial legislation, particularly when the Court read the word "unreasonable" into the Sherman Antitrust Act's prohibition of practices resulting in "restraint of trade." In 1892 he was called upon by President Benjamin Harrison to aid in the arbitration of the Bering Sea seal hunting dispute with Great Britain. He continued his Court duties until his death on October 14, 1911, in Washington, D.C.

HARPER, WILLIAM RAINEY (1856–1906), scholar and educator. Born on July 26, 1856, in New Concord, Ohio, Harper graduated from Muskingum College at the age of 14. After a few years spent working in his father's dry-goods store and studying languages on his own he began graduate work at Yale and was awarded a Ph.D. in 1875, shortly before his 19th birthday. In succeeding years he taught at several small colleges and in 1879 was called to the Baptist Union Theological Seminary in Chicago, where he had his first opportunity to teach in his field of primary interest, the Hebrew language. In Chicago he founded *The Hebrew Student* and *Hebraica* and developed a correspondence course in Hebrew. He published a number of textbooks and study aids and established the American Institute of Hebrew. In 1886 he became professor of Semitic languages at Yale; during his tenure there he achieved national recognition as an educator. Particularly effective as a teacher and organizer, he was selected as the first president of the University of Chicago when it opened in 1891. Determined from the outset to create a major educational and research institution, Harper insisted upon complete academic freedom for the brilliant faculty he soon gathered. While he was seldom really innovative in his plans, his ability to form and execute a comprehensive program of development for the university rendered his services invaluable. While carrying on his extensive duties as president he continued to teach full

time and was head of the department of Semitic languages. Among his writings, his most important works appeared near the end of his life: *A Critical and Exegetical Commentary on Amos and Hosea* and *The Trend in Higher Education,* both 1905. He died on January 10, 1906.

HARRIMAN, EDWARD HENRY (1848–1909, financier and railroad executive. Born February 25, 1848, in Hempstead, New York, Harriman left school at 14 to become a broker's clerk in Wall Street. By 1870 he was in a position to buy a seat on the Stock Exchange. He first became interested in railroads in 1881 when he acquired the Lake Ontario Southern, reorganized it, and reaped a large profit from its sale. Two years later he became a director of the Illinois Central and in 1887 vice-president. In 1897 he allied himself with the banking firm of Kuhn, Loeb, & Company, which was reorganizing the bankrupt Union Pacific Railroad; the next year he became chairman of the line and the dominant figure in its administration. Displaying a broad, detailed knowledge of railroading as well as great financial acumen, he directed the revitalization of the company with such skill and energy that within three years it was showing a profit and expanding its facilities. Early in 1901 he acquired control of the Southern Pacific and of its subsidiary, the Central Pacific, setting up a highly efficient central administration for the entire system. Later in the year, seeking control of the Chicago, Burlington, & Quincy Railroad in order to have clear access to Chicago, he entered upon a titanic struggle with James J. Hill of the Northern Pacific. The contest triggered a serious panic on Wall Street in May. A settlement was reached in the forming of the Northern Securities Company to hold the contested property in trust, but in 1904 the company was ordered dissolved by the Supreme Court and Harriman was left in a minority position, which, however, he was able to convert into a huge cash profit. President of the Union Pacific from 1903, he began buying stock in other lines, extending his influence eventually over some 60,000 miles of track. Prompted by President Roosevelt, the Interstate Commerce Commission launched an investigation into the Harriman holdings in 1906; revelations of his ruthless business methods, combined with his staunch refusal to excuse them, roused a storm of public opprobrium. He died on September 9, 1909.

HARRIMAN, WILLIAM AVERELL (1891–), businessman, public official, and diplomat. Born in New York City on November 15, 1891, Harriman was the son of Edward H. Harriman of the Union Pacific Railroad. He graduated from Yale in 1913 and two years later became a vice president of the Union Pacific and a director of the Illinois Central Railroad. In 1917 he became chairman of the board of the Merchant Shipbuilding Corporation, a post he held for eight years. He held high positions in many other firms and from 1932 to 1946 returned to the Union Pacific as chairman of the board. At the request of President Franklin Roosevelt he entered government service in 1934 as a divisional administrator for the National Recovery Administration. He remained with the NRA for a year; in 1941, after three months in the Office of Production Management, he was sent to Great Britain and then to the Soviet Union as special representative of the President. During 1942 he continued to represent the United States on a number of joint boards in London and in 1943 was appointed ambassador to the U.S.S.R. Three years later he became ambassador to Great Britain, a position he had held only six months when he was named secretary of commerce by President Truman. From 1948 to 1951 he represented the United States in various capacities in Europe and for two years thereafter was director of the Mutual Security Agency. In 1954 he was elected governor of New York; he ran again in 1958 but was defeated. In 1961 President Kennedy appointed Harriman assistant secretary of state for Far

Eastern affairs, and two years later he became undersecretary of state for political affairs. In 1965 he was named ambassador-at-large by President Johnson and undertook a number of roving assignments, notably, from 1968 to 1969, as chief American negotiator at the Vietnam peace talks in Paris.

HARRIS, JOEL CHANDLER (1848–1908), journalist and author. Born on December 9, 1848, in Eatonton, Georgia, Harris ended his schooling in 1862 when he became an apprentice on a local plantation newspaper, *The Countryman*. Here and on a succession of other Southern newspapers he gradually established a reputation as a humorist. In 1876 he joined the *Atlanta Constitution*, with which he was associated for the next 24 years. With painstaking care he developed a written transcription of the plantation Negro speech with which he was intimately familiar and in 1879 published "The Tar-Baby Story," the first of the Uncle Remus series. The fidelity of the dialect and the warmth and humor of this and subsequent tales made them immediately and widely popular; a collection entitled *Uncle Remus: His Songs and Sayings* was published in 1880 and followed by a number of sequels, including *Nights with Uncle Remus*, 1883, *Daddy Jake, the Runaway*, 1889, *Uncle Remus and His Friends*, 1892, *The Tar Baby*, 1904, and *Uncle Remus and Brer Rabbit*, 1906. As the foremost of the local colorists of the 1870s and '80s, Harris wrote in addition to the animal fables of Uncle Remus a number of books reflecting the Georgia scene; most notable of these are *Mingo, and Other Sketches in Black and White*, 1884, and *Free Joe and Other Georgia Sketches*, 1887. In 1907 he established *Uncle Remus's Magazine* and continued to edit it until his death in Atlanta on July 3, 1908.

HARRIS, WILLIAM TORREY (1835–1909), philosopher and educator. Born in North Killingley, Connecticut, on September 10, 1835, Harris was educated at a number of schools and academies and after a little more than two years of study at Yale began to teach school himself in St. Louis in 1857. He was notably successful as a teacher and rose rapidly in the city's public school system, becoming its superintendent in 1868. At the same time, under the influence of Bronson Alcott and Theodore Parker, he began reading deeply in the German idealistic philosophers, particularly Hegel. In 1867 he founded the *Journal of Speculative Philosophy*, which, continuing until 1893, contained original translations of Hegel, Schelling, and Fichte; it also published the early writings of the American philosophers Peirce, Royce, James, and Dewey. As an educator Harris was highly effective; though seldom innovative himself he was receptive to ideas and was a leader in developing a broad curriculum for the schools. His annual reports served widely as models of their kind. In 1880 he resigned his position and moved to Concord, Massachusetts, to help Alcott establish the Concord School of Philosophy. The school endured for several years but had little effect on the course of American philosophy; the vitality of Transcendentalism was long gone, and idealism in all its forms was in general retreat from naturalism. In 1889 he was appointed U.S. commissioner of education, a position he held until 1906. During these years he published the most important of his nearly 500 titled works: *Introduction to the Study of Philosophy*, 1889, *The Spiritual Sense of Dante's Divina Commedia*, 1889, *Hegel's Logic*, 1890, and *The Psychologic Foundations of Education*, 1898. He also held a number of editorial positions, including that of editor-in-chief of the first *Webster's New International Dictionary*, 1909. He died on November 5, 1909, in Providence, Rhode Island.

HARRISON, BENJAMIN (1833–1901), lawyer, public official, and 23rd U.S. President. Born in North Bend, Ohio, on August 20, 1833, of a long line of political figures, including his grandfather, President William Henry Harrison, Benjamin was educated at the nearby Farmers' College and Miami University, graduating from the latter in 1852. He was admitted to the bar two years later and moved to Indianapolis to begin practice. As he advanced in his profession he developed an interest in politics, becoming an ardent Republican and holding some minor party and public offices. At the outbreak of the Civil War he raised an infantry regiment and as its colonel commanded it for three years, first in relatively quiet duties in Kentucky and Tennessee, and from 1864 as part of Sherman's forces at Atlanta. In March 1865 Harrison was brevetted brigadier general. Returning to Indiana after the war, he continued to gain in prominence in both his legal practice and state politics. He supported the Radical Republican program, opposing both the Liberal Republican and the Greenback parties. He failed to win the nomination for governor in 1872; four years later he was nominated but lost the election. The campaign of that year, however, brought him national attention. In 1880 he was chairman of the Indiana delegation to the Republican national convention and was instrumental in securing Garfield's nomination; shortly thereafter he declined the offer of a Cabinet post, accepting instead election to the Senate. There he was a strong supporter of civil service reform, the Interstate Commerce Act, and the tariff, and took great interest in Indian and territorial affairs. He failed to be reelected in 1887 but the next year was Indiana's favorite son candidate at the Republican convention; he was nominated and, though he lost the popular vote to Cleveland, won the presidency in the electoral college. Most of the notable achievements of his administration were in the field of foreign affairs, where an active policy resulting in a number of international conferences and treaties overseen by Harrison and his capable secretary of state, James G. Blaine, marked something of a departure in American relations with the rest of the world. On the domestic side, Harrison's four years were less successful; while the Sherman Anti-Trust Act was passed in 1890, the same year saw the passage of the highly unpopular McKinley Tariff and the politically motivated Sherman Silver Purchase Act. The Veterans Bureau, released from Cleveland's strict scrutiny, embarked on a program of extravagance that acquired sufficient notoriety to force the resignation of the pension commissioner. Largely because of the tariff, Congress came under Democratic control after 1890; growing popular discontent, primarily over financial and labor issues, led to Harrison's defeat in his bid for reelection in 1892. He returned to Indianapolis and resumed his legal practice. He published a number of articles and speeches in various periodicals, many of which were collected in *This Country of Ours*, 1897, and *Views of an Ex-President*, 1901. His legal reputation was such that he was chosen by Venezuela as its chief counsel in the arbitration of its boundary dispute with Great Britain in 1898–1899. Harrison died in Indianapolis on March 13, 1901.

HARRISON, WILLIAM HENRY (1773–1841), soldier, public official, and 9th U.S. President. Born at "Berkeley," his father's Charles City County, Virginia, plantation, on February 9, 1773, Harrison was the son of a wealthy and politically prominent father. He studied for three years at Hampden-Sidney College and then, in 1790, moved to Philadelphia where he attended the College of Physicians and Surgeons and worked under Dr. Benjamin Rush. In 1791 he joined the Army and was sent to the Northwest Territory; there, as aide-de-camp to Gen. Anthony Wayne, he participated in the campaign against the Indians and the final battle of Fallen Timbers in 1794. In 1798 he resigned his captaincy and was appointed secretary of the Northwest Territory; the following year he was sent by the Territory to Congress. In 1800 he was appointed governor of Indiana Territory, a position he retained until 1812. He negotiated a number of land-cession treaties with the Indians and when growing dissatisfaction among the tribes cul-

minated in the hostile confederacy under Tecumseh and his brother "The Prophet," Harrison led a successful military campaign against the Indian encampment at the Tippecanoe River in November 1811. Though the battle was actually inconclusive, Harrison won an immediate military reputation. His plans for a further Indian campaign were interrupted by the war with Great Britain the next year, and he became major general of the Kentucky militia and later brigadier general in command of the regular Army in the Northwest. Under his leadership the decisive victory at the Thames River was won in October 1813, permanently securing the territory against the British. He resigned from the Army in 1814 and in the same year oversaw the negotiations for a final peace treaty with the Indians. Settling at North Bend, Ohio, he served in Congress from 1816 to 1819, in the Ohio legislature from 1819 to 1821, and in the Senate from 1825 to 1828. For a little more than eight months in 1829 he was minister to Colombia and in that time provoked considerable controversy by his connection with Colombian revolutionaries. For the next several years he remained largely out of the public notice; then in 1835 he was chosen by dissident Whigs to head a presidential ballot against Martin Van Buren in the next year's election. Though he lost, plans were immediately laid for 1840; in that year he won the regular Whig nomination and after a remarkable campaign—employing campaign songs, the "log cabin and hard cider" symbols, and the slogan "Tippecanoe and Tyler too!"—was overwhelmingly elected. Left in a state of exhaustion by the campaign and the hordes of office-seekers who immediately appeared, he contracted pneumonia and died on April 4, 1841, one month after his inauguration.

HARTE, FRANCIS BRETT (1836–1902), author. Born in Albany, New York, on August 25, 1836, Frank, as he was familiarly known, spent an unsettled childhood, moving often until alighting in New York following his father's death in 1845. At 13 he ended his irregular education and went to work. In 1853 his mother traveled to California and the next year he joined her there. For the next several years his situation was precarious; he taught for a while, was briefly employed by Wells Fargo, and made a short visit to a mining district. For two years he worked on the *Northern Californian* in Union (now Arcata) until his editorial denunciation of the massacre of some 60 peaceful Indians forced him to leave town in 1860. During these years he wrote constantly, both poetry and prose sketches; some were published but few showed any promise. Moving to San Francisco, he took a job on the *Golden Era* and published a number of pieces in this newspaper during the next several years. In 1861 he secured an appointment in the surveyor general's office and two years later a clerkship in the U.S. Branch Mint. In 1864 he began to contribute to the newly established *Californian* and occasionally served as its editor. Four years later he became the first editor of the *Overland Monthly* and, assigned to produce some sketches of local life, soon published "The Luck of Roaring Camp" and six months later "The Outcasts of Poker Flat." Under his pen name, Bret Harte, the stories were a sensation in the East; after the further success of his poem "Plain Language from Truthful James" (commonly known as "The Heathen Chinee") and his collection *The Luck of Roaring Camp and Other Sketches*, 1870, he left California for Boston in 1871. He was accepted in the highest literary circles and offered an extremely lucrative contract by the *Atlantic Monthly*, which, however, he fulfilled only with difficulty and which was not renewed. Within a short time his success and prosperity had largely ended. Through his use of scenes and dialect from the exotic California mining regions, his colorful characters and attention to detail, he had produced novelties that were technically skillful but superficial. As his limited stock of experience became exhausted, his work became repetitious and the benefits of

novelty were lost. After *Tales of the Argonauts* in 1875 little was left; in financial difficulty, he finally accepted a consulship in Germany in 1878 and in Glasgow, Scotland, two years later. His popularity in England had not waned and at the end of his term of office in 1885 he moved to London where he remained for the rest of his life. There he continued to write, reworking his worn and formulaic material and retaining at least his English reputation until his death on May 5, 1902.

HAWTHORNE, NATHANIEL (1804–1864), author. Born in Salem, Massachusetts, on July 4, 1804, Hawthorne (Hathorne, as it was spelled until he changed it while in college) was of a long Puritan line that included one of the judges in the Salem witchcraft trials. When he was four years old his father died and his mother became a virtual recluse; he thus early gained the habits of solitude and self-sufficiency that he retained throughout life. In 1825 he graduated from Bowdoin College, where he was a classmate of Longfellow and a close friend to Franklin Pierce. He returned to Salem and devoted himself to writing; a good deal of his work he burned, but numerous sketches and stories appeared in various periodicals. Dismissing the forgettable *Fanshawe*, published anonymously in 1828 and later regretted by its author, his first volume was a collection of stories under the title *Twice-Told Tales*, published in 1837. Hawthorne's finances were perennially precarious; in 1839–1840 he held a political patronage job in the Boston customhouse and when the Whig victory of 1840 deprived him of this security he joined the Brook Farm association for a brief time. In 1842 he moved with his new wife to Concord and became a somewhat reserved member of the famous circle of notables there. In the same year appeared the second series of *Twice-Told Tales*; four years later the results of his happy years in Concord were contained in another collection, *Mosses from an Old Manse*. In that year, 1846, having returned to Salem, he received another customhouse position and remained in it for three years. Shortly afterward, in 1850, he published *The Scarlet Letter*. He moved to Lenox, Massachusetts, became a close friend of Herman Melville, and in the next two years produced *The House of the Seven Gables* and *The Blithedale Romance*. In 1852 he returned to Concord; the following year, as a result of having written a campaign biography for President Pierce, he was appointed to the consulate in Liverpool. Four years in this post were followed by two in Italy and another in England; early in 1860 appeared *The Marble Faun*, and later in the year Hawthorne returned again and finally to Concord. His last major work, *Our Old Home*, based on his experiences in England, was published in 1863; on May 19th of the next year he died after a long and undetermined illness. He left a legacy of writings that are among the best of American literature. His dark and brooding preoccupation with evil was during his lifetime always in sharp contrast with the prevailing optimism of the Concord circle as he himself was always something apart; in coming to terms with his Puritan heritage while surrounded by the Transcendentalists' rebellion, he achieved a breadth of view and a depth of analysis that far surpassed theirs. In expressing all this in clear and precise prose and, most importantly, in dealing with it in richly symbolic terms, he created works of art at once American and universal. His masterwork, *The Scarlet Letter*, must stand as one of the very few great American novels.

HAY, JOHN MILTON (1838–1905), author and diplomat. Born in Salem, Indiana, on October 8, 1838, Hay graduated from Brown University in 1858 and, after studying law in Springfield, Illinois, in an office next door to that of Abraham Lincoln, was admitted to the bar in 1861. Immediately afterwards he accompanied the President-elect to Washington as assistant private secretary. In March 1865 he was appointed secretary to the legation in Paris; he remained there until 1867 and from 1867 to 1870 was attached to the legations in Vienna and Madrid successively. In 1870 he returned to the United States and for the next five years was an editorial writer for the *New York Tribune*. He published a notable volume of poetry in 1871, *Pike County Ballads and Other Pieces*; later in the same year appeared *Castilian Days*, a record of travel and impression in Spain. In 1875 he moved to Cleveland and remained there until his appointment as assistant secretary of state in 1879; he remained in Washington after resigning his office in 1881, continuing to write while closely associated with Henry Adams and Clarence King and becoming a fixture of the city's social scene. In 1883 he published anonymously a novel, *The Bread-Winners*; in 1890, with his co-author John G. Nicolay, he published the ten-volume *Abraham Lincoln: A History*, earlier serialized in the *Century* and long the standard Lincoln biography. In 1897 President McKinley continued the tradition of choosing literary figures as ambassadors to Great Britain by appointing Hay. After successfully maintaining England's good will during the Spanish-American War, he was named secretary of state the following year. His first task in this post was to oversee the peace negotiations with Spain, and in this he fully supported the decision to retain the Philippines; he was a determined though not aggressive protector of American interests throughout the world, his most notable contribution to foreign affairs being the Open-Door Policy promulgated in 1899–1900. In two notes circulated among the European powers with interests in China he proposed a cooperative effort to guarantee Chinese territorial and administrative integrity. The actual policy was not Hay's, but the timing and skill of its publication were completely so and were primarily responsible for the general acceptance of the Open Door. In 1901 he negotiated the Hay-Pauncefote treaty with Great Britain, abrogating the 1850 Clayton-Bulwer treaty and opening the way for the Panama Canal maneuvers that followed; by 1903 and the Colombian revolution, President Roosevelt had taken over direction of a great deal of American foreign policy and Hay's individual role is unclear. In that year, however, he won a diplomatic victory in the settlement of the Alaskan boundary. He was increasingly beset by ill health and died on July 1, 1905, in Newburg, New Hampshire.

HAYDEN, FERDINAND VANDEVEER (1829–1887), geologist and explorer. Born on September 7, 1829, in Westfield, Massachusetts, Hayden graduated from Oberlin College in 1850 and three years later was awarded an M.D. from Albany Medical College. Under the influence of James Hall, the paleontologist, he deferred medical practice, however, and made a collecting trip to the South Dakota Badlands in 1853; his enthusiasm for geology and exploration dates from this trip, and during the next six years he made numerous expeditions into the West and Northwest, often under Army auspices. He joined the Army as a surgeon when the Civil War broke out and by June 1865 had been brevetted lieutenant colonel. In 1865 he was appointed professor of geology at the University of Pennsylvania, retaining this position until 1872 while beginning in 1867 a 12-year series of explorations and scientific investigations of the Western territories, primarily in the middle- and upper-mountain regions. His work was celebrated throughout the world and played an important part in laying the foundations for the U.S. Geological Survey, organized in 1879, and in securing the creation of Yellowstone National Park, established in the same year. He remained as a geologist with the Survey until his retirement in 1886. He died in Philadelphia on December 22nd of the following year.

HAYES, HELEN (1900–), actress. Born on October 10, 1900, in Washington, D.C., Helen Hayes Brown made her professional debut with a Washington company, the Columbia Players, in 1905, as Prince Charles in The

Royal Family. She went to New York in 1909 and performed in *Old Dutch* and other plays, returning to Washington after two years to resume acting with the Columbia Players and to study at the Sacred Heart Convent, where she graduated in 1917. That year she appeared again on Broadway in *Pollyanna,* beginning a long and distinguished career paralleled only by that of Ethel Barrymore. She was hailed for her performances in *Penrod,* in *Dear Brutus,* 1918, as Cleopatra in Shaw's *Caesar and Cleopatra,* 1925, as Maggie Wylie in Barrie's *What Every Woman Knows,* 1926, in *Coquette,* 1927, in *Mr. Gilhooley* and *Petticoat Influence,* 1930, in Maxwell Anderson's *Mary of Scotland,* written for her, 1933–1934, in Laurence Housman's *Victoria Regina,* generally regarded as her most brilliant role, 1935–1939, in *Ladies and Gentlemen,* 1937, as Viola in Shakespeare's *Twelfth Night,* 1940, in Maxwell Anderson's *Candle in the Wind,* 1941–1942, as Harriet Beecher Stowe in *Harriet,* 1944, in J. M. Barrie's *Alice-Sit-by-the-Fire,* 1946, as Addie in Anita Loos's *Happy Birthday,* 1946–1947, as Amanda Wingfield in Tennessee Williams' *The Glass Menagerie* in London in 1948, again on Broadway in Joshua Logan's *The Wisteria Trees,* 1950, and as Mrs. Howard V. LaRue 2nd in Mary Chase's *Mrs. McThing* in 1952, and in Paris as Mrs. Antrobus in a revival of Thornton Wilder's *The Skin of Our Teeth* in 1955. Her movie career included warmly received roles in *The Sin of Madelon Claudet,* 1931, for which she won an Academy Award, *Arrowsmith* and *A Farewell to Arms* in 1932, *The White Sister, Another Language,* and *Night Flight,* 1933, *What Every Woman Knows,* 1934, *Vanessa—Her Love Story,* 1935, *My Son John,* 1952, and *Anastasia,* 1956. In radio she starred in 1935 in the *New Penny* programs, in 1936 in the *Bambi* series, in 1940 and 1941 in the *Helen Hayes Theatre,* in 1945 in *This Is Helen Hayes,* in 1948–1949 in *Electric Theatre,* and in 1956 in *Weekday.* She acted in television productions of *Dear*

Brutus and other plays. In 1955 New York's Fulton Theatre was renamed in her honor the Helen Hayes Theatre.

HAYES, RUTHERFORD BIRCHARD (1822–1893), lawyer, soldier, public official, and 19th U.S. President. Born in Delaware, Ohio, on October 4, 1822, Hayes graduated from Kenyon College in 1842. He studied law privately and then at Harvard Law School and took his degree in 1845. For the next few years he practised in Lower Sandusky, Ohio, but was not notably successful until his removal to Cincinnati in 1849. There he became socially prominent and involved himself in politics, first with the Whigs and later with the Republican Party. In 1861 he was commissioned a major in an Ohio volunteer regiment; he served capably in a number of capacities and by the time of his resignation in June 1865 was a brigadier general and brevet major general of volunteers. In 1864 he had been nominated and, with no campaigning on his part, elected to Congress. He generally supported the Republican leadership in Congress, though he shied away from the extreme radicals. He was reelected in 1866, but resigned the following year to run for governor of Ohio. He was successful in this campaign and again in 1869; after four years of competent and mildly reformist administration he stood by precedent and declined renomination. Heavy Democratic gains and presidential ambition induced him to stand again, however, in 1875, and he was duly elected after a campaign that attracted national attention. The next year he defeated James G. Blaine for the Republican presidential nomination and managed to unify his party for the election. In that famous election the Democrat Samuel J. Tilden appeared at first to have won; Republicans, however, challenged the returns from four states—South Carolina, Louisiana, Florida, and Oregon—and two sets of electoral votes were submitted to Congress from each. The solution was the creation of a 15-member Electoral Commission, five from each house of Congress and five from the Supreme Court, to decide the dispute. The Republicans had an 8 to 7 majority on the commission and the contested electoral votes were awarded to Hayes by precisely this margin. Meanwhile a bargain had been struck whereby the Southern Democrats agreed to accept the verdict in return for the withdrawal of all remaining federal troops from South Carolina and Louisiana. After a private ceremony on March 3rd, Hayes was publicly inaugurated on March 5, 1877, and the troop withdrawal was completed by May, ending Reconstruction and returning the South to white rule. The new President soon alienated much of his own party by insisting on merit-based appointments and thoroughgoing reforms in a number of government departments. In one such dispute he secured, against the opposition of Senator Roscoe Conkling, the dismissal of Chester A. Arthur as port collector in New York. He conducted a sound fiscal policy in which specie payments were resumed and the coinage of silver begun only over his veto. Despite his sympathy for labor he took a firm stand in the railroad strike of 1877; he vetoed a Chinese exclusion bill because it violated a treaty; and during 1879 he defeated a sustained attempt by Congress to usurp presidential power by attaching to appropriations bills riders nullifying federal election laws. Hayes adhered to an earlier pledge to not seek reelection in 1880; he returned to Ohio and busied himself in various humanitarian and reform causes. He was active in promoting education, was from 1883 president of the National Prison Association, and, as he became increasingly disturbed at the concentration of wealth and power in a few hands, evinced some agreement with socialist ideas. He died on January 17, 1893, at Fremont, Ohio.

HAYWOOD, WILLIAM DUDLEY (1869–1928), labor leader. Born in Salt Lake City on February 4, 1869, Haywood got his first taste of mining at the age of 9. Several odd jobs followed in the next few years, along with a little rudimentary schooling, and at 15 he was again a miner in Nevada. For a time he tried his hand at being a cowboy and a homesteader, but soon returned once again to the mines. In 1896 he became a charter member of the Silver City, Idaho, local of the Western Federation of Miners; three years later he was a member of the national executive board and in 1900 was named secretary-treasurer of the W.F.M.'s Denver headquarters. Closely attuned to the mood of the rank and file membership and a highly aggressive advocate of industrial unionism, "Big Bill" Haywood soon became the W.F.M.'s principal leader and spokesman, a position he retained through the violent 1900–1905 period when the western mining regions were torn by industrial war. He presided over the founding of the Industrial Workers of the World in Chicago in June 1905. Later that year Frank Steunenberg, the anti-union former governor of Idaho, was murdered, and a W.F.M. member arrested for the crime implicated Haywood and others, who were promptly jailed. Labor rallies around the country raised money to engage Clarence Darrow for the defense, and with William E. Borah leading the prosecution, the trial received wide publicity. In 1907 the acquittal that followed the disclosure of perjury on the part of the accuser made Big Bill something of a popular hero. In that year the W.F.M. withdrew from the I.W.W., objecting to its predilection for violent direct-action tactics, and in 1908 Haywood was dismissed from its leadership. At the head of the I.W.W., however, he continued to organize, write, and speak in behalf of the ideals of "one big union" encompassing all workers and the destruction of the class of idle capitalists. From 1901 to 1912 he was a member of the Socialist Party as well, though he was finally dismissed from its inner councils because of his advocacy of violence. In 1917 he was one of the large number of I.W.W. leaders and members arrested for sedition—they denounced the World War as a capitalist attack on the worldwide working class—and the next year was convicted and sentenced to 20 years in prison. While temporarily free on bond in 1921 he escaped to the Soviet Union, where he remained until his death on May 18, 1928.

HEARN, LAFCADIO (1850–1904), author, translator, and critic. Born on June 27, 1850, on Santa Maura in the Greek Ionian Islands, Hearn was of English and Greek parentage and was given the name Patricio Lafcadio Tessima Carlos. From the age of six he was reared by a great-aunt in Dublin who sent him to schools in England and France. In 1869 he went to the United States; after a time in New York City he moved to Cincinnati and barely supported himself with menial jobs until he met Henry Watkin, a printer who took him under his wing and taught him typesetting and proofreading. Hearn soon found a place on a newspaper; during the next several years he reported for a succession of Cincinnati journals, wrote feature articles that won considerable attention, and did translations from French literature. In 1877 he went to New Orleans, where for four years he led a marginal existence. Finally, in 1881, he joined the *Times-Democrat* and conducted a column of translations from French and Spanish that led to the publication of his first book, *One of Cleopatra's Nights*, 1882. It was followed by *Stray Leaves from Strange Literatures*, 1884, *Gombo Zhèbes*, 1885, *Some Chinese Ghosts*, 1887, and his first novel, *Chita*, 1889. At the same time he contributed to *Century Magazine*, *Harper's Weekly*, and *Harper's Bazaar* articles on folklore, legend, and, after leaving New Orleans in 1887, on the West Indies. In 1890 he was commissioned by *Harper's New Monthly* to send articles back from Japan, but soon after arriving in that country he broke with the magazine. He obtained a teaching position in Matsue and the next year married a Japanese woman of a noble samurai line. In 1893 he began teaching at the government college in Kumamoto. He published *Glimpses of Unfamiliar Japan* in 1894, the first of a series of brilliant books that gave Western readers their first studied, sympathetic view of Japanese culture. In 1895 he became a Japanese citizen and the following year transferred to the Imperial University of Tokyo. In rapid succession he published *Gleanings in Buddha-Fields*, 1897, *Exotics and Retrospectives*, 1898, *In Ghostly Japan*, 1899, *Shadowings*, 1900, and *A Japanese Miscellany*, 1901. In 1903 he was invited to lecture at Cornell University; the invitation was later withdrawn, but Hearn published his prepared lectures as *Japan: an Attempt at an Interpretation*, 1904, and this became his best-known work. He died on September 26, 1904, in Okubo.

HEARST, WILLIAM RANDOLPH (1863–1951), publisher. Born in San Francisco on April 29, 1863, Hearst was the son of a powerful and wealthy California figure. He studied at Harvard, leaving in 1885 without a degree. He became interested in journalism and in 1887 persuaded his father, who had acquired the *San Francisco Examiner* for a bad debt, to let him take over the newspaper. He was successful in making the *Examiner* a paying venture and in 1895 invaded the domain of Joseph Pulitzer by buying the floundering *New York Morning Journal*. Lowering the price to a penny, he introduced a number of circulation-building features — colored comic strips, a color magazine section, sensational crime reporting, society gossip, and a jingoist approach to foreign affairs — and soon attained record sales. Under his editorial control the *Journal*, and its evening counterpart introduced the next year, carried a strong anti-British bias and was generally Populist in outlook. Hearst supported Bryan in 1896 and the following year published a spectacular series of articles and editorials that did much to rouse public clamor for war with Spain. As he began to assemble his publishing empire by acquiring or establishing newspapers across the country, his growing political ambition was rewarded

by his election to Congress from New York in 1902; during this and his subsequent term he generally supported the liberal and progressive programs but aroused little attention. In 1904 he was considered for the Democratic presidential nomination; the following year he narrowly missed election as mayor of New York, and in 1906 lost the governor's race. In his last political campaign in 1909 he was again defeated for mayor. He continued. to add to his publishing holdings by purchasing several magazines, including *Cosmopolitan* and *Harper's Bazaar*. He also became interested in the young movie industry and in 1913 one of his companies produced *The Perils of Pauline*. His isolationism and dislike of England led him to oppose America's entry into World War I; when peace came he campaigned vociferously against the League of Nations while demanding full repayment of war loans from allied nations. In 1922 he tried again for political office by seeking the Democratic nomination for senator. He failed when the nominee for governor, Alfred E. Smith, refused to run on the same ticket with Hearst; in an earlier series of articles and cartoons in the Hearst papers, Smith had been linked with the milk trust. In that year Hearst's holdings consisted of 20 major newspapers, 2 news services, a feature syndicate, and 5 leading magazines. In 1927 he moved permanently to his 240,000 acre ranch at San Simeon, California. Long an avid, though untutored, collector, he amassed a huge miscellany of art treasures and curios that filled several warehouses and included Etruscan tombs, Egyptian mummies, a Spanish monastery disassembled and shipped to the United States at enormous cost, and large collections of paintings, furniture, silver, and armor. At the peak of his fortunes, in 1935, he owned another 8 newspapers, 13 magazines, 8 radio stations, 2 movie companies, a castle in Wales, and extensive real estate in New York City, California, and Mexico. But within two years the Depression had made such inroads on his empire that it was necessary to reorganize his holdings, pruning away unprofitable properties. In 1937 most of his art collection had to be disposed of, much of it being sold in department stores during the next several years. By 1940 the Hearst enterprises were stabilized, but he had lost all but nominal control. World War II brought prosperity back, but he was largely out of public notice; his last years were spent in virtual seclusion and he died on August 14, 1951, at Beverly Hills, California.

HEFNER, HUGH MARSTON (1926–), editor and publisher. Born in Chicago on April 9, 1926, of strict Methodist parents, Hefner grew up forbidden to smoke, drink, or attend movies on Sundays. Although encouraged to discuss literature and political and social issues, he was chastized for broaching the subject of sex. After two years of service in the Army he enrolled at the Universtiy of Illinois and graduated in three years, in 1949. He did one semester of post-graduate work in psychology at Northwestern University, and worked as a personnel manager, a department store advertising copywriter and a subscriptions writer for *Esquire* magazine until 1952, when he resigned with plans for a new magazine in his head. With about $10,000 capital he put together the first issue of *Playboy* magazine, which appeared on the newsstands in December 1953. Its most celebrated feature was a nude calendar photograph of Marilyn Monroe. Regular features on dining, drinking, fashions, and personal problem-solving, in addition to the monthly "playmate," put forth the image of the modern "playboy," which he sought to personify in his 48-room mansion equipped with personal luxuries. He used a pipe, frequently without tobacco, as a prop. The literary quality of the magazine — fiction and nonfiction articles and interviews with notable figures in the arts, politics, and sports — was consistently high. He purchased in 1965 what had been the Palmolive building, long a Chicago landmark, and not without attendant controversy renamed it the Playboy Building. It houses the editorial employ-ees of the magazine and those of its subsidiary Playboy Clubs International, Inc., Playboy Products, and the Playboy Press. In 1968 the magazine was 12th in the nation with a circulation of over 5 million.

HEINLEIN, ROBERT ANSON (1907–), author. Born in Butler, Missouri, on July 7, 1907, Heinlein grew up there and in Kansas City. He won appointment to the U.S. Naval Academy and following graduation in 1929 served as a line officer until receiving a discharge for a physical disability in 1934. He entered the University of California at Los Angeles to pursue graduate studies in mathematics and physics but ill health forced him to withdraw after a short time. For four years he held various jobs and in 1939 he published his first magazine story, launching a writing career that, except for service as a mechanical engineer at the Naval Air Material Center in Philadelphia during World War II, was thereafter uninterrupted. His first book, *Rocket Ship Galileo*, 1947, was the basis of his scenario for the 1950 movie *Destination Moon*. While producing a steady stream of stories for numerous magazines, he published several more books — *Beyond this Horizon*, 1948, *Red Planet*, 1949, *Sixth Column*, 1949, *The Man Who Sold the Moon*, 1950, *Waldo; and Magic, Inc.*, 1950 (from which came the term "waldo," referring to the pantograph gauntlets used to handle radioactive materials), *The Green Hills of Earth*, 1951, *The Puppet Masters*, 1951, *Revolt in 2100*, 1953, *Starman Jones*, 1953, *Tunnel in the Sky*, 1955, *The Door Into Summer*, 1956, and others. He became firmly established as the foremost of American science fiction writers. His writings relied heavily on his own rich background in science and engineering and proceeded carefully from the known to the speculatively reasonable. Utilizing as well a vivid narrative style, a wide range of characters, and a coherent and generally optimistic view of man in the universe, Heinlein went far in his work to raise the general level of science fiction above that of the "bug-eyed monster" school. Others among his major books were *The Menace from Earth*, 1959, *Starship Troopers*, 1959, *Stranger in a Strange Land*, 1961, *Farnham's Freehold*, 1964, and *The Moon is a Harsh Mistress*, 1966.

HELPER, HINTON ROWAN (1829–1909), author and publicist. Born in Rowan (now Davie) County, North Carolina, on December 27, 1829, Helper graduated from a local academy and clerked in a store until, in 1850, he traveled to New York and by sea to California. In 1853 he returned to North Carolina and wrote *The Land of Gold*, published in 1855. Two years later he published *The Impending Crisis of the South: How to Meet It*, in which he attacked slavery as the cause of the South's economic weakness. Marshaling statistics to support his thesis, he demonstrated that the free labor of slaves was responsible for the depressed condition of non-slaveholding whites and of the South generally; he waxed violent in his denunciation of slavery and soon found it expedient to leave the South for New York. The book was a sensation: the Southern reaction was so extreme that it could hardly be read, even for the purpose of refutation; it was banned by several state legislatures and, as was not even the case with *Uncle Tom's Cabin*, a number of men were lynched for possessing it. In the North its already wide circulation was increased as a result of the 1860 Republican campaign. Largely overlooked at the time was the fact that Helper's attack on the institution of slavery included no sympathy for the slaves themselves. After serving as consul in Buenos Aires from 1861 to 1866 he clarified this point in three more book, *Nojoque*, 1867, *Negroes in Negroland*, 1868, and *Noonday Exigencies*, 1871, in which he expounded an explicitly racist viewpoint and advocated the deportation of all Negroes. He maintained a deep interest in South America, particularly in its commerical and transportation development; a plan for a railroad from Hudson Bay to the Strait of Magellan grew into an obsession, and he spent his last years in fruitless lobbying, letter-writing, and publishing to achieve this dream. He committed suicide in Washington, D.C., on March 9, 1909.

HEMINGWAY, ERNEST MILLER (1899–1961), author. Born on July 21, 1899, in Oak Park, Illinois, Hemingway did not attend college but instead went to work as a reporter for the *Kansas City Star*. He served with a volunteer ambulance unit in Italy in World War I until he was seriously wounded and forced to remain in Milan. Recovering from his wounds, he became a European correspondent for the *Toronto Star*. He settled in France, where he mingled with a group of expatriate artists and writers and was especially influenced by Gertrude Stein and Ezra Pound. His early short stories, compiled in *Three Stories and Ten Poems*, 1923, and *in our time*, 1924, shared with his novels, *The Torrents of Spring*, 1926, and *The Sun Also Rises*, 1926, the theme of shattered individuals seeking refuge from the demands of a world they had never made. *A Farewell to Arms*, 1929, portrayed an English nurse and an American ambulance lieutenant whose intense relationship was in stark contrast to the background of war. *Death in the Afternoon*, 1932, concerning one of his obsessions, bullfighting, and *The Green Hills of Africa*, 1935, concerned with another, big game hunting, focused on the corruption of individual goodness by mass culture. He acknowledged the possibility of men triumphing over social problems in *To Have and Have Not*, 1937, and attempted to show that the bondage of one people leads to the bondage of all in his novel of the Spanish Civil War, *For Whom the Bell Tolls*, 1940. A foreign correspondent during World War II, he was involved in most of the major European campaigns and was present at many battles, and he was one of the first Americans to return to Paris after it was retaken by Allied forces in 1944. His sardonic, not to say bitter, view of war and especially of World War II was reflected in *Across the River and Into the Trees*, 1950. This novel was not a success, and his critics exulted that he had lost whatever greatness he had had. But *The Old Man and the Sea*, a short novel about an aged Cuban fisherman's lonely expedition in search of a great fish, appeared in 1952 and is probably his most lasting work. The book won a Pulitzer Prize and was instrumental in gaining Hemingway the Nobel Prize for Literature in 1954. His generally terse, journalistic style had great emotional impact and influenced a generation of American writers. He died at his home in Ketchum, Idaho, by suicide, on July 2, 1961. Sketches of his life in Paris in the early 1920s appeared posthumously as *A Moveable Feast*, 1964.

HENRY, JOSEPH (1797–1878), physicist. Born on December 17, 1797, in Albany, New York, Henry displayed little interest in his schooling and after a brief apprenticeship to a watchmaker became involved with an amateur theatrical group. By age 16, however, he had become fascinated by natural science and entered Albany Academy, supporting himself by teaching in country schools and later in the Academy itself. His intention was to study medicine after graduation, but this was altered by his appointment in 1825 to a state surveying party. His interest switched to engineering, and the following year he became professor of mathematics and natural philosophy at Albany Academy. Here, in his spare time, he embarked on a series of investigations into electrical phenomena, particularly those related to magnetism. His first major achievement was his powerful electromagnet, for which he developed insulated wire in order to wind a close coil of several layers, a type still generally employed. He discovered and formulated the basic principles governing the behavior of various sorts of coils and by 1829 had constructed primitive versions of the telegraph and the electric motor. In 1832 he was appointed professor of natural philosophy at the College of New Jersey (now Princeton) and there continued his research. In 1832 he read Michael Faraday's published announcement of the discovery of the self-induction of current in a coil; he promptly resumed his own earlier investigations of this phenomenon and, though he never attempted to claim credit, clearly established that he had independently observed it, possibly as early as 1830. In recognition of his work his name was given to the unit of electrical induction by international agreement in 1893. Continuing this line of research, Henry discovered the induction of a current in one coil by that in another, showed how the induced current could be varied by different coil arrangements, and thus laid the groundwork for the development of the transformer. He found that an induced current could also be generated by an electrical discharge, or spark; in one such experiment in which a current was set up in a coil by a miles-distant lightning flash, he appears to have been the first to record the action of electromagnetic waves, though he himself was unaware of their existence. Subsequently, in 1842, he correctly concluded that such discharges are oscillatory in nature. He collaborated with his brother Stephen in work on solar radiation and determined that sunspots are cool relative to the surrounding areas of the sun's surface. In 1846 he was chosen first secretary and director of the newly established Smithsonian Institution. In this position he prevented the institution from becoming merely a curator of knowledge by developing a program of active support for basic scientific research; he organized a corps of volunteer weather observers whose work led eventually to the creation of the U.S. Weather Bureau; and he began a program of publication and distribution of scientific papers. From 1852 he was a member of the federal Lighthouse Board and was its chairman after 1871; he participated in the organization of the American Association for the Advancement of Science and the National Academy of Sciences, serving as president of the latter from 1868. He died in Washington, D.C., on May 13, 1878.

HENRY, PATRICK (1736–1799), orator, political leader, and public official. Born in Hanover County, Virginia, on May 29, 1736, Henry showed little promise for the future in his early years; after an indifferent education he proceeded to fail as a farmer and twice as a storekeeper and by 1759 was deeply in debt. He turned at last to law, was admitted to the bar in 1760, and within a short time had achieved great success and a wide reputation. In a case in 1763 known as the Parson's Cause, in which a minister of the established church challenged the authority of the colonial legislature to pay clerical salaries in money when tobacco, the usual medium, was scarce, Henry appeared for the defense and won a virtual victory over a Crown veto by invoking the doctrine of natural rights. In 1765 he entered the House of Burgesses and quickly became a leader of the growing opposition to the low-country aristocrats. With the announcement of the Stamp Act of that year he introduced a number of radical resolutions against it and with his first great speech, concluding in the famous observation "Caesar had his Brutus, Charles the First his Cromwell, and George the Third—may profit by their example," he succeeded in carrying several of them. Through the next several years he was the recognized leader of the radical faction in Virginia and increasingly prominent throughout the colonies. He was a member of his state's first committee of correspondence and a delegate to the first and second Continental Congresses. In 1775, at the Virginia convention that met in place of the legislature dissolved by the governor, he introduced a number of revolutionary resolutions, including one for the arming and training of the militia, and carried the convention with the speech containing the words "I know not what course others may take, but as for me, give me liberty or give me death." He became commander of the Virginia militia, but resigned in 1776 because of the opposition of political enemies. In that year he helped draft the state's constitution and under it was elected governor. He was reelected in the two succeeding years; an effective wartime governor, he authorized George Rogers Clark's 1778 military expedition into the Illinois country. After a brief retirement he was in the legislature from 1780 to 1784, during which time, after the peace treaty in 1783, he surprised his followers, and alienated some, by advocating equitable treatment for former Loyalists. From 1784 to 1786 he was again governor, and from 1787 to 1790 again in the legislature. He opposed the Constitutional Convention in 1787 and refused to be a delegate to it; when the Constitution was being considered in Virginia, he led the opposition to ratification. He acquiesced in its adoption but immediately began a campaign that resulted in the adoption of the ten Bill of Rights amendments. In 1788 he retired to his legal practice and private life; through succeeding years he became gradually estranged from the Republican leaders Jefferson and Madison as he reconciled himself to the new federal government. He declined several high government offices but finally, in 1799, he was prevailed upon by George Washington to seek another term in the state legislature in order to oppose the Virginia and Kentucky resolutions. He was elected, but before taking his seat he died on June 6th at his Virginia estate.

HERBLOCK see **BLOCK, HERBERT**

HERSEY, JOHN RICHARD (1914–   ), author. Born on June 17, 1914, in Tiensin, China, of American missionary parents, Hersey was fluent in Chinese before he learned English. He attended the Chinese and American grade schools in Tiensin. At 10, moving to the United States, he entered the Hotchkiss school. He graduated from Yale in 1936 and took a year of post-graduate work at Clare College in Cambridge, England. In the summer of 1937 he became personal secretary to Sinclair Lewis. That autumn he was employed as a writer by *Time* magazine, fulfilling a long-time career aspiration. Later he became an editor of *Time* and a senior editor of *Life* magazine and was a prominent correspondent for major periodicals, including the *New Yorker*. His first overseas assignment for *Time* in 1939 was to cover the Far Eastern situation. In the Orient he interviewed such prominent figures as Chiang Kai-shek. He compiled *Men on Bataan*, 1942, from information gathered in the Far East, from statements of friends of Gen. Douglas MacArthur and families of soldiers, and with the aid of *Time's* vast library of news dispatches and clippings. The book was the first of a series of extremely popular war documentaries highlighting the human aspects of major news stories: they included *Into the Valley*, 1943, based on his experiences with a Marine company on Guadalcanal, *A Bell for Adano*, 1944, awarded a Pulitzer Prize and made into a motion picture, a radio drama, and a Broadway play, *Hiroshima*, 1946, a powerful account of the bombing and aftermath of nuclear holocaust, and *The Wall*, 1950, describing the ill-fated rebellion of Warsaw's ghetto against the Nazis. He also wrote, among others, *The Marmot Drive*, 1953, *A Single Pebble*, 1956, *The War Lover*, 1959, *The Child Buyer*, 1960, *White Lotus*, 1965, and *Under the Eye of the Storm*, 1967.

HIGGINSON, THOMAS WENTWORTH STORROW (1823–1911), reformer, soldier, and author. Born on December 22, 1823, in Cambridge, Massachusetts, Higginson graduated from Harvard in 1841 and after two years of teaching returned to the college to pursue a rather aimless course of study. Finally in 1846 he enrolled in the divinity school and graduated the following year. He became the pastor of the First Religious Society of Newburyport, Massachusetts, and immediately launched into a number of reform activities. He founded an evening school for workers, wrote frequent editorials for newspapers, ran for Congress on the Free-Soil ticket in 1848, and so often infused his sermons with radical declarations on women's rights, Abolitionism, and other causes that after two years he was at odds even with his liberal Unitarian congregation and was relieved of his duties. He had for some years been advocating extreme antislavery action, and in 1851 he joined the Boston Vigilance Committee organized to oppose execution of the Fugitive Slave Law. In 1852 he became pastor of the Free Church in Worcester, a position he retained until 1861. In 1854, when Anthony Burns, an escaped slave, was being held in Boston pending forcible return to the South, Higginson purchases axes and led in breaking down the courthouse door and liberating Burns. He aided in sending antislavery settlers and supplies to Kansas and in 1856 made a visit to the state and met John Brown. A series of letters to the *New York Tribune* on the trip were collected in *A Ride Through Kansas*, 1856. In 1861 he helped raise a company of Massachusetts troops; the next year he resigned as its captain to accept a commission as colonel of the 1st South Carolina Volunteers, the first Negro regiment in the Union Army. He continued to serve until 1864 and recorded his experiences in *Army Life in a Black Regiment*, 1870. From the end of the war until 1878 he lived in Newport, Rhode Island; there he became a regular contributor to the leading magazines—*Scribner's*, *Harper's*, *Atlantic Monthly*, *North American Review*—and wrote his only novel, *Malbone*, 1869. In 1875 he published his popular *Young Folks' History of the United States* and ten years later a *Larger History of the United States*. From 1878 until his death he lived again in Cambridge. He continued to produce a steady stream of magazine articles on a wide range of subjects, many of which were collected into books, and he wrote a number of biographies, notably of Longfellow, Whittier, and Margaret Fuller. He was, in a remarkable correspondence that spanned more than 20 years, one of the very few people to whom

Emily Dickinson revealed herself as a poet, and though he was often baffled by her unorthodox manner and had serious doubts about publishing her work, after Emily's death he joined her sister in editing *Poems by Emily Dickinson*, 1890, and *Poems: Second Series*, 1891. He died in Cambridge on May 9, 1911.

HILL, JAMES JEROME (1838–1916), financier and railroad magnate. Born near Guelph, Ontario, Canada, on September 16, 1838, Hill ended his formal education at 14 and thereafter clerked in a store until setting out, four years later, to seek his fortune in the Orient. He could find no suitable opportunity to this end and in 1856 settled instead in St. Paul, Minnesota. He obtained a position with a trading company that operated a number of steamboats and gradually took on more and more responsibility in it; by 1865 he was venturing into business on his own. His interests grew to include railroad transportation and in 1878, with three Canadian partners, he bought the bankrupt St. Paul & Pacific Railroad. With Hill as general manager the company was reorganized the next year. as the St. Paul, Minneapolis, & Manitoba Railway and a vigorous expansion program was undertaken. In 1882 he became president; eight years later the Great Northern Railway Company was organized to absorb the S.P.M. & M. and a number of smaller lines into one system. The railroad was extended to Seattle in 1893; Hill's foresighted and closely personal supervision of the company's activities made it highly profitable and the most successful of the transcontinental systems. With his associates he acquired a large interest in the Northern Pacific Railroad, and the two companies obtained joint control of the Chicago, Burlington, and Quincy in 1901. In that same year he organized the Northern Securities Company, a holding company for his vast interests; in 1904 the Supreme Court declared the arrangement in violation of the Sherman Anti-Trust Act and the company was dissolved. He had extensive holdings in banks and played an important role in the development of the Mesabi iron ore range. He retired as president of the Great Northern in 1907, serving as chairman of the board from then until 1912. He died on May 29, 1916, in St. Paul.

HILL, JOE (1872?–1915), labor organizer and songwriter. Born in Sweden about 1872, Joe Hill was originally named Joel Emmanuel Haaglund or Hagglund, though some sources give it as Joseph Hillstrom. He worked as a seaman and came to the United States about 1901. Virtually nothing is known of him—he was reticent about biographical details—until 1910, by which time he had joined the Industrial Workers of the World, a radical syndicalist labor organization founded five years earlier. He took part in organizing and strike activities among dock workers in San Pedro, California, and in a short-lived communalist revolution in Tijuana, and late in 1913 appeared in Utah. During these years of hobo life he was one of the I.W.W.'s staunchest supporters and became well known to its growing membership through the pages of the *Industrial Worker* and *Solidarity*, which printed his essays, letters, and songs. It was the songs that won the greatest attention; the most famous, "The Preacher and the Slave," contained the phrase "pie in the sky" that became a part of the American lexicon. Others of his best songs were "Casey Jones—the Union Scab," "Coffee An'," "There is Power in a Union," "Nearer My Job to Thee," and "The Rebel Girl." Hill's works were the mainstay of a movement that had a remarkable penchant for singing. In January 1914 he was arrested in Salt Lake City on a murder charge; tried in June, he was quickly convicted on circumstantial evidence that left, for many, considerable doubt of his guilt. Hill and the I.W.W. claimed that the charge had been trumped up simply to eliminate him. He remained in prison for 22 months while various appeals were entered and denied. By October 1915 the Swedish ambassador, Samuel Gompers, and President Wilson had tried unsuccessfully to intercede and secure a new trial. Utah officials remained adamant and on November 19th Hill was executed by a firing squad. The night before his death he had wired to I.W.W. head William "Big Bill" Haywood: "Don't waste any time in mourning. Organize." The message, and the massive funeral observances in Salt Lake City and Chicago, confirmed his martyrdom, and his reputation grew in time to legendary proportions.

HILLMAN, SIDNEY (1887–1946), labor leader. Born on March 23, 1887, in Zagare, Lithuania, Hillman studied to be a rabbi but his participation in the abortive revolution of 1905 led to his imprisonment for several months. After his release he went to England and in August 1907 came to the United States. In Chicago he found a job with Sears, Roebuck & Company; in 1909 he became an apprentice cutter at Hart, Schaffner, & Marx and was soon deeply involved in union activities. He led the strike against the company in 1910–1911 and was the labor spokesman when negotiations were finally begun. The resulting contract, largely his work, soon came to be considered a model labor-management agreement; it clearly defined the interests of the contracting parties and established a permanent mechanism for discussion and arbitration of disputes. In 1914 Hillman went to New York City to become chief clerk for the Cloakmakers Joint Board and later in the year became the first president of the Amalgamated Clothing Workers of America, a position he held for the rest of his life. Through his strenuous efforts the 40-hour week became nearly universal in the men's clothing industry by the end of World War I; by 1940 the union numbered 350,000 members and had 96 percent of the industry under contract. He secured contracts providing for uniform wage scales across the nation, thus ending the threat of the "runaway shop," the moving of a factory to an area where low wages prevailed. Services to union members included two banks, unemployment insurance, and a housing development, while, consonant with Hillman's insistence on cooperation as the cornerstone of industrial relations, union funds were occasionally loaned to companies in temporarily straitened circumstances and the union's research staff offered suggestions on improving the manufacturing process. In 1935–1938 Hillman joined John L. Lewis and others in forming the Congress of Industrial Organizations. President Roosevelt appointed him to the National Defense Advisory Commission; in 1941 he became associate director-general of the Office of Production Management and the next year was named director of the labor division of the War Production Board. In 1943 Hillman left government service to become chairman of the C.I.O. Political Action Committee, playing a major role in Roosevelt's reelection campaign of 1944. He was also a vice chairman of the World Federation of Trade Unions from its organization in 1945. He died at his Long Island home on July 10, 1946.

HILLQUIT, MORRIS (1869–1933), lawyer, reformer, and author. Born in Riga, Russia, on August 1, 1869, Hillquit (or Hillkowitz, as it was originally) emigrated to the United States in 1886; for a brief time he attended high school in his adopted city of New York, but soon was forced to go to work. Like many other young immigrants he joined the Socialist Labor Party; he also became involved in labor union organization and in 1888 helped found the United Hebrew Trades. He worked for the *Arbeiter Zeitung*, the first Yiddish newspaper in America, and in 1891 entered the law school of the University of the City of New York, graduating two years later. Devoting himself from this time on to the socialist cause, he soon became a prominent leader and unofficial spokesman for the Socialist Labor Party and later for the coalition Social Democratic Party of Eugene V. Debs. He spoke before a great number of audiences and engaged in a number of debates, including one with Samuel Gompers before a congressional committee in 1909. The party's policy on peace, announced soon after the outbreak of World War I, was largely Hillquit's work, as was its later condemnation of American participation in what was deemed the immoral yet inevitable outcome of capitalist imperialism. The Espionage Act of 1917 greatly increased demands for his legal services as numbers of Socialists and others were prosecuted for generally dubious reasons. He had already been three times a candidate for Congress when in the same year he ran unsuccessfully for mayor of New York; despite the prevalent antisocialist mood that often approached hysteria, he won a remarkably large portion of the vote. Tuberculosis interfered with his activities after 1917, but he managed to be twice more a candidate for Congress and in 1932 again for mayor. He continued to work, speak, and write on behalf of Socialism until his death on October 7, 1933. Among his published works are *History of Socialism in the United States*, 1903, *Socialism in Theory and Practice*, 1909, and *Socialism Summed Up*, 1912.

HOCKING, WILLIAM ERNEST (1873–1966), philosopher and educator. Born in Cleveland on August 10, 1873, Hocking grew up there, in Maryland, Michigan, and in Joliet, Illinois. After graduating from high school he became a surveyor. He attended Iowa State College for two years and in 1895, upon reading William James's *Principles of Psychology*, determined to attend Harvard. After four years of schoolteaching in Davenport he did so and pursued studies in psychology and philosophy under James, Josiah Royce, George Santayana, and George Palmer. Graduating in 1901, he remained to take his M.A. the next year and, after a year of study in several German universities, returned to Harvard for his Ph.D. in 1904. From that year to 1906 he was an instructor at both Harvard and at Andover Theological Seminary. From 1906 to 1908 he taught at the University of California and then joined the faculty at Yale. In 1912 he published his first major work, *The Meaning of*

God in Human Experience, outlining a philosophical view that reflected the influence of both Royce and James in modifying the absolute idealism of the one with the pragmatism of the other. In 1914 he became professor of philosophy at Harvard, where he remained, after 1920 as Alford Professor and after 1937 as chairman of the philosophy department, until his retirement as professor emeritus in 1943. In 1917, at the request of the British government, he undertook a study of the psychology of morale; the results of his investigations among British and French combat troops were published as *Morale and Its Enemies*, 1918. During 1931-1932 he headed the Laymen's Foreign Missions Inquiry Commission in the Far East and was coauthor and editor of its report, *Re-Thinking Missions*, 1932. In his writings Hocking continually expressed his belief that a philosophy, even though idealistic, ought to have real implications for the common man, and he applied his own system to concrete problems in such works as *Human Nature and Its Remaking*, 1918, *Man and the State*, 1926, *The Spirit of World Politics*, 1932, *Lasting Elements of Individualism*, 1937, *Freedom of the Press*, 1947, *The Coming World Civilization*, 1956, *The Meaning of Immortality in Human Experience*, 1957, and *Strength of Men and Nations*, 1958. Hocking died in the stone house he had built himself in Madison, New Hampshire, on June 12, 1966.

HOLIDAY, BILLIE (1915–1959), singer. Born on April 7, 1915, in Baltimore, Miss Holiday was the daughter of a professional guitarist who for a time played with the great Fletcher Henderson band. Christened Eleanora, she later adopted the name Billie from a favorite movie actress, Billie Dove. She grew up in poverty in a ghetto area of Baltimore; as a child, in return for running errands for a local brothel keeper, she was allowed to linger and listen to recordings by blues singer Bessie Smith and trumpeter Louis Armstrong. In 1928 she moved with her mother to New York City and after three years of subsisting by various marginal means she found a job singing in a Harlem nightclub. She had no musical training whatsoever and got the job only by chance; but with an almost instinctive sense of musical structure and with a wealth of experience gathered at the root level of jazz and blues she developed a singing style that was deeply moving, individual, and inimitable. In 1933 she made her first recordings with Benny Goodman and others; two years later a series of recordings with Teddy Wilson and members of Count Basie's band brought her wide recognition and launched her career as the leading jazz singer of her time. She toured with Basie and with Artie Shaw in 1937 and 1938 and in the latter year opened at the plush Cafe Society in New York. From about 1940 she performed exclusively in cabarets and in concert. Her recordings between 1936 and 1942 marked her peak years; during that period she was professionally and personally associated with saxophonist Lester Young, who gave her the nickname "Lady Day" (it was she, in turn, who dubbed him "Pres"). In 1947 she was arrested for a narcotics violation and spent a year in a rehabilitation center; no longer able to obtain a cabaret license, she nonetheless packed Carnegie Hall ten days after her release. She continued to perform in concert and made several tours during her later years. The constant struggle with heroin addiction more and more affected her voice, though not her style. She died in New York on July 17, 1959.

HOLLEY, ALEXANDER LYMAN (1832–1882), author and engineer. Born in Lakeville, Connecticut, on July 20, 1832, Holley graduated from Brown University in 1853. While in college he received his first patent for a steam engine cut-off. Between 1853 and 1855 he worked for companies engaged in the manufacture of railroad locomotives and then, from 1855 to 1857, published *Holley's Railroad Advocate*. In the latter year he and an asso-

ciate traveled to Europe under the auspices of several railroad companies to inspect European railroads and study their practices, publishing a comprehensive report upon their return the next year. In 1858 he began an association with the *New York Times* that lasted for nearly 20 years; he was technical editor for the *American Railway Review* and in 1860 published *American and European Railway Practice*. He engaged in a number of engineering projects until 1862 when, while on business in England, he became acquainted with the new Bessemer process for steelmaking. The following year he obtained patent rights for using the process in America and within two years had a steel plant in operation in Troy, New York. By 1867 the experimental stage was completed and the first steel rails were produced. For the rest of his life Holley designed and built steel plants all over the country and patented a number of improvements on the Bessemer process. He was foremost in his field and largely responsible for laying the foundations of the steel industry in the United States. He died on January 29, 1882, in Brooklyn, New York.

HOLMES, OLIVER WENDELL (1809–1894), physician, educator, and author. Born in Cambridge, Massachusetts, on August 29, 1809, Holmes graduated from Harvard in 1829. Though tempted by a life of letters, he chose to undertake a more secure profession and entered the Harvard Law School; the following year, finding law a dull study, he transferred to a private medical school. In that same year, 1830, he achieved his first recognition as an author when his poem "Old Ironsides" appeared in the *Boston Daily Advertiser*; a year later he published an article in the *New England Magazine* entitled "The Autocrat of the Breakfast-Table," which was followed by another of the same name in 1832. In 1833 he sailed to France for two more years of medical study; upon his return he completed his studies at Harvard Medical School and in 1836 was granted an M.D. In the same year he published his volume of *Poems*. During the next several years his literary activities were greatly diminished as he devoted himself to practice, to research—for which he was recognized with three Boyleston prizes though little of his work was particularly original—and teaching, first at the Tremont Medical School, which he helped to found, at Dartmouth, and finally, from 1847, at Harvard. Along with his popularity at Harvard there developed a demand for Holmes as a public lecturer; by 1857 his reputation was such that when James Russell Lowell was asked to be the first editor of the *Atlantic Monthly*—the name was Holmes's—he accepted only on condition that the doctor be secured as a contributor. In the first issue that year appeared the first of a series of articles under the revived title of 25 years earlier, "The Autocrat of the Breakfast-Table." Beginning "I was just going to say when I was interrupted," the piece and the ones that followed were widely read and appreciated; the series was collected in book form and published the next year. There followed three similar series of witty, conversational pieces, all later published as separate volumes, *The Professor at the Breakfast-Table*, 1860, *The Poet at the Breakfast-Table*, 1872, and *Over the Teacups*, 1891. In addition to these and his poems, Holmes wrote three novels, all following the same pattern of publication and based on his preference for a psychological rather than religious interpretation of morality and behavior, of which only *Elsie Venner*, 1861, is memorable. He retired from the medical faculty at Harvard in 1882; four years later he visited Europe for a second time and was received with great honor. He continued to write, publishing several volumes of verse, some collections culled from his earlier work, and biographies of John Lothrop Motley and Ralph Waldo Emerson, among others. He died in Boston on October 7, 1894, having outlived the rest of the generation of great New England literary figures who had been his contemporaries and companions.

HOLMES, OLIVER WENDELL (1841–1935), jurist. Born on March 8, 1841, in Boston, Holmes was the son of the famed author and physician of the same name. His formal education occurred in private schools and at Harvard; his informal education, which was perhaps more important, was at the hands of the leading intellectuals of Boston who formed his father's circle: Lowell, Longfellow, Whittier, Emerson, Agassiz, and others. Shortly before his graduation from Harvard in 1861 he enlisted in the army and soon after receiving his degree he went to war as a second lieutenant. In three years of service he was wounded three times, returning each time to his regiment. At the expiration of his enlistment in 1864 he returned to Boston and entered Harvard Law School; he took his degree in 1866 and was admitted to the bar the following year. He worked for and with a number of prominent attorneys, becoming a partner in the firm of Shattuck, Holmes, and Monroe. From 1870 to 1873 he was editor of the *American Law Review* and in the latter year produced the 12th edition of Kent's *Commentaries on American Law*. Approaching the law with deep philosophical insight and a thoroughgoing skepticism, Holmes sought constantly to probe to the roots of the body of law, to discover both its rational essence and its mode of development in an ever-changing context. The opportunity to systematize his thoughts and earlier writings on this subject came with an invitation to deliver a series of lectures at Boston's Lowell Institute; these were published as *The Common Law*, 1881, a book of tremendous impact on American judicial thought and practice. Almost immediately he was offered the Weld professorship by Harvard; he accepted, but resigned a year later to join the Massachusetts supreme judicial court. In his twenty years on this bench, the last three as chief justice, he delivered nearly 1,300 opinions and became widely known and influential for his detached, rational analyses, his ability to penetrate to the heart of an issue, and his open, even cavalier, disregard for precedent. In 1902 President Theodore Roosevelt appointed Holmes to the Supreme Court. In his 29 years of service on the national bench he achieved an eminence equaled only by that of John Marshall; though he delivered numerous important decisions and dissents, notable among which were *Northern Securities Co.* v. *U.S., Lochner* v. *New York, Adair* v. *U.S., Schenck* v. *U.S., Sanitary District* v. *U.S.,* and many others, his primary contribution to the Court and to judicial process generally was philosophical. A strong advocate of judicial restraint, he constantly opposed the use of judicial power either to force change by judicial legislation or to oppose it through blind adherence to precedent. His influence was profound and lasting. On January 12, 1932, at the age of 90, he resigned from the Court. He died on March 6, 1935, leaving the major portion of his estate to the United States; it was finally used to finance a history of the Supreme Court.

HOMER, WINSLOW (1836–1910), painter. Born on February 24, 1836, in Boston, Homer was apprenticed to a lithographer in 1855. Two years later he opened his own studio and began a career of illustrating for *Ballou's Pictorial* and *Harper's Weekly. Harper's* sent him to Washington to sketch Lincoln's inauguration. Later he drew camp scenes, episodes from Army life, and battle scenes from Virginia, the emotion and intensity of this Civil War experience affecting much of his later work. After returning to his studio he continued to paint war subjects producing, among others, "Sharpshooter on Picket Duty" and "Prisoners from the Front," and exhibited at the National Academy of Design and elsewhere. After a trip to France he turned to landscape painting. He continued to contribute to *Harper's* and other periodicals and traveled extensively in search of subject material for his paintings. He produced "Snap the Whip" in 1872 and showed it at the Centennial Exposi-

tion in Philadelphia four years later. A trip to England in 1881–1882 reawakened his boyhood love of the sea. He turned away from city life to settle at Prouts Neck, near Scarboro, Maine, in 1883. His works in watercolor and oil portraying the drama of the sea made him famous as both critical and popular acceptance came to him during the 1880s. Outstanding among them were "The Fog Warning," "Banks Fisherman," "Eight Bells," "Gulf Stream," "Rum Cay," "Mending the Nets," and "Searchlight, Harbor Entrance, Santiago de Cuba." Although his style was realistic, it was never merely pictorial, instead conveying the dignity and vitality of its subject matter. He died at Prouts Neck on September 29, 1910.

HOOVER, HERBERT CLARK (1874–1964), engineer, relief administrator, public official, and 31st U.S. President. Born on August 10, 1874, in West Branch, Iowa, of Quaker parents who died during his childhood, Hoover grew up in the home of an uncle in Oregon. His early education was irregular, but chance and a determination to better himself brought him to the newly opened Stanford University in 1891. He worked his way through Stanford, studying mining engineering, and graduated in 1895; his first job out of college was pushing a mine cart for two dollars a day. His rise in his profession was rapid, however; in 1897 he joined Bewick, Moreing & Company, an international mining concern, and was sent to oversee operations in Australia and later in China, where he witnessed the Boxer Rebellion. In 1908 he organized his own firm, was highly successful, and by 1914 was worth some $4 million. In that year, in London, the U.S. ambassador called on him to organize the evacuation of the more than 100,000 Americans trapped in the outbreak of war in Europe; later in the same year he became chairman of a volunteer agency devoted to obtaining money and food for the relief of devastated Belgium, and in the course of three years he directed the expenditure of $1 billion to this end. With the American entry into World War I in 1917 Hoover was appointed by President Wilson as U.S. food administrator, and his effective supervision of voluntary rationing and conservation of food throughout the nation added the verb "hooverize" to the American vocabulary. As the war drew to a close he was given responsibility for general relief in Europe; 23 million tons of food were distributed to more than 30 nations, and when the signing of the peace treaty ended his official duties he organized a volunteer agency to continue the work. He returned to the United States in 1919 and in 1921 President Harding named him secretary of commerce, a position he retained, under President Coolidge, until 1928. As secretary, Hoover worked constantly through numerous committees to establish regular methods of voluntary cooperation among the nation's many economic interest groups. His insistence on voluntary action as opposed to government regulation was characteristic, and in 1922 he explained his view of American society in *American Individualism*. In 1927 he again showed his skill in directing relief operations during the disastrous Mississippi flood of that year. With the retirement of Coolidge from politics in 1928, Hoover became a prominent presidential possibility; at the Republican convention he was nominated on the second ballot and in the ensuing election easily defeated Al Smith. The prospect of a mildly successful administration led by a moderate Republican deeply interested in governmental efficiency and economy was ruined within a few months after the inauguration when the nation's financial structure, weakened by unsecured credit, crumbled suddenly in October 1929; warning signs had been disregarded by previous administrations and Hoover had had no time to stem the speculative boom on Wall Street. Democratic gains in the congressional elections of 1930 severely limited his scope of remedial action; despite a tax cut, a moratorium on German war reparations payments, and the creation of the Reconstruction Finance Corporation — later

a mainstay of the "New Deal" — the Republican Party and the President in particular bore the onus of the Depression, and against his dire warnings, Hoover was rejected in favor of Franklin D. Roosevelt in the 1932 election. He retired to private life until the end of World War II, which brought him back to public service to organize European relief operations. In 1947 he was named chairman of a commission — popularly known as the Hoover commission, a term since used to designate any such body — created by Congress to examine and make recommendations on the organization of the executive branch of government. The suggestions of this and a second commission appointed in 1953 were largely adopted. Among his published works were *Addresses Upon the American Road*, 1938–1955, his *Memoirs*, 1951–1952, *The Ordeal of Woodrow Wilson*, 1958, and *An American Epic*, 1959–1964, a record of relief work since World War I. He died in New York City on October 20, 1964.

HOOVER, JOHN EDGAR (1895–   ), lawyer, public official, and criminologist. Born in Washington, D.C., on January 1, 1895, Hoover was intended by his parents for the ministry but following his graduation from high school, he became a messenger in the Library of Congress while studying law at night at George Washington University. He took his degree in 1916, added a master of laws the next year, and found employment as a file reviewer for the Department of Justice. In 1919 he became special assistant to Attorney General A. Mitchell Palmer and was assigned to oversee the large number of deportation cases then arising from the Red Scare hysteria of the postwar years. Two years later he became assistant director of the department's Bureau of Investigation; the bureau shared in the scandal and disrepute of the Harding era and when, in 1924, Hoover became director, he immediately set about reorganizing it on a fully professional basis. As the scope of the bureau's jurisdiction was increased, its standards were correspondingly raised; by 1935, when the name was changed to the Federal Bureau of Investigation, he had instituted a vast fingerprint file, a crime laboratory, and a training academy. During the 1930s he mounted a publicity campaign to offset the glamorous image that often attended crime and criminals and, for a time at least, "G-men" were included among the heroes of American children. He wrote *Persons in Hiding*, 1938, and, as part of his remarkably tenacious campaign against Communism in later years, *Masters of Deceit*, 1958. He was the recipient of numerous honors and awards and active in many organizations, among them the Boys' Clubs and the Boy and Girl Scouts.

HOPKINS, HARRY LLOYD (1890–1946), social worker and public official. Born in Sioux City, Iowa, on August 17, 1890, Hopkins graduated from Grinnell College in 1912 and immediately entered the social-work field, becoming director of a boys' camp in New York. During the next several years he was connected at various times with the Association for Improving the Condition of the Poor, the New York City Board of Civil Welfare, the American Red Cross, and the New York Tuberculosis and Health Association. In 1931 New York Governor Franklin D. Roosevelt called on him to head the state's Temporary Emergency Relief Administration. Two years later with Roosevelt in the White House, Hopkins became administrator of the new Federal Emergency Relief Administration. In a little more than five years some eight to ten billion dollars passed through his hands and he was dubbed "the world's greatest spender." He was active in organizing the Works Progress Administration and was one of its staunchest defenders. In 1938 he became secretary of commerce. A close and trusted adviser and confidant whom Roosevelt found increasingly valuable, he directed the Roosevelt forces at the 1940 Democratic convention; ill health, however, forced him to resign from the Cabinet later that year. In 1941 he began

a long series of services in foreign affairs when he went to England as Roosevelt's personal representative to discuss American assistance for Britain's war effort. After discussions with the British government and King George VI, and later with Stalin in Moscow, he returned to the United States to direct the operation of the Lend-Lease program and to serve on a number of advisory and directory boards, becoming thereby a member of the so-called "Little War Cabinet." He attended every major Allied conference during the war except for the last one at Potsdam, which, however, he had arranged for during another trip to Moscow in early 1945. Ill health had long plagued him and he died on January 29, 1946.

HOPKINS, MARK (1802–1887), educator. Born in Stockbridge, Massachusetts, on February 4, 1802, Hopkins graduated from Williams College in 1824. He turned to medicine but his study for this profession was interrupted by two years as a tutor at Williams; he was granted his M.D. in 1829 and moved to New York City, but practised only a short time. In 1830 he returned to Williams as professor of moral philosophy and rhetoric; from that year until his death he was in charge of instruction for the senior class. In 1836, though he had no training in theology, he was ordained in the Congregational Church and became in the same year president of the college, a post he held until 1872. He was neither a scholar nor a creative thinker, but as a teacher he was greatly effective; his teachings, both in the classroom and in the pulpit, embodied the secularized Puritanism that marked much of the theology of the 19th century. Often called the "gospel of wealth," it stressed individualism, the pursuit of wealth and progress, and the idea that possession is a form of stewardship; property as a mark of personal worth is to be held and administered as a trust for the benefit of society. Hopkins delivered a number of lecture courses at the Lowell Institute in Boston and these were published in books that enjoyed great popularity. At a dinner meeting of Williams alumni in New York City in 1871, President James Garfield, class of 1856, declared, "Give me a log hut, with only a simple bench, Mark Hopkins on one end and I on the other, and you may have all the buildings, apparatus, and libraries without him." Hopkins continued to teach and deeply influence the students in his charge until his death on June 17, 1887.

HOPKINS, SAMUEL (1721–1803), clergyman. Born on September 17, 1721, in Waterbury, Connecticut, Hopkins graduated from Yale in 1741 and the following year was licensed to preach by the Congregational Church. After studying theology privately under Jonathan Edwards he was ordained minister of the Congregational Church in Great Barrington, Massachusetts, in 1743. His association with Edwards resumed in 1751 when the latter took charge of the church in nearby Stockbridge and continued until 1758, when Edwards became president of the College of New Jersey. Not merely a disciple, Hopkins modified the theology of Edwards and presented it in a form that, while as logically rigorous as the work of his master, was more palatable and more suited to the age. "Hopkinsianism" was long a major school of Congregational theology. The titles of some of his published works indicate the trend of his thought: *Sin, thro' Divine Interposition, an Advantage to the Universe*, 1759, *An Enquiry Concerning the Promises of the Gospel. Whether Any of Them Are Made to the Exercises and Doings of Persons in an Unregenerate State*, 1765 (answered, of course, in the negative), and *The True State and Character of the Unregenerate, Stripped of All Misrepresentation and Disguise*, 1769. In this last year, having alienated a number of his parishioners with his stern, unemotional, and demanding sermons, he was dismissed from his church. The following year he assumed the pastorate of the First Church in Newport, Rhode Island, where, with the exception of the years 1776–1780, when the

town was under British occupation, he remained for the rest of his life. During the early 1770s he began to speak out against slavery, becoming one of the first Congregationalists to do so, and worked to establish missions to Africa. In 1776 he published *A Dialogue Concerning the Slavery of the Africans; Shewing It To Be the Duty and Interest of the American States to Emancipate all Their African Slaves*. His theological summa appeared in 1793 as *A System of Doctrines Contained in Divine Revelation*. Hopkins died on December 20, 1803.

HOPKINSON, FRANCIS (1737–1791), lawyer, author, musician, and public official. Born in Philadelphia on September 21, 1737, Hopkinson studied at the College of Philadelphia and was granted that institution's first degree in 1757. He was awarded an M.A. three years later and in 1761 began the practice of law. A man of wide interests and talents, he published a number of poems in various periodicals, was an accomplished harpsichordist, and composed several songs and hymns. His professional life was unsettled; he gave up law for a time, holding some minor government posts and operating a drygoods store. In 1773 he moved to Bordentown, New Jersey, and resumed his law practice; he was successful and by 1776 had achieved sufficient prominence to be elected to the Continental Congress. He was a signer of the Declaration of Independence. His career as a political satirist and pamphleteer had begun two years earlier with *A Pretty Story*; during the Revolution, while serving in a number of government positions, he kept up a steady barrage of anti-British writings: *A Letter to Lord Howe, A Letter Written by a Foreigner*, and *An Answer to General Burgoyne's Proclamation* in 1777, *A Letter to Joseph Galloway* and his famous poem "The Battle of the Kegs" in 1778, and many others. In 1777 he helped design the first national flag authorized by Congress. He was judge of admiralty for Pennsylvania from 1779 to 1789 and from the latter year until his death federal district judge for eastern Pennsylvania. He strongly supported the adoption of the Constitution and wrote several articles favoring it. In his later years he maintained his wide interests and wrote prolifically; in 1788 he published *Seven Songs for the Harpsichord or Forte-Piano*. He died on May 9, 1791.

HOPPER, EDWARD (1882–1967), painter. Born on July 22, 1882, in Nyack, New York, Hopper moved to New York City in 1899 to study commercial illustration and entered the New York School of Art in 1900, studying under Robert Henri. Except for brief periods in Europe and summers in New England, he lived and worked in New York City for the rest of his life. Throughout his career, despite changes in art fashions, he continued to paint starkly realistic, and somber though brightly colored scenes of contemporary life. His subjects included city streets, New England cottages, finely detailed Victorian houses, roadside lunch counters, theater interiors, and barren apartments, all depicted with a pervading calm, devoid of urban hubbub. His most famous paintings were "Early Sunday Morning" and "Nighthawks." He exhibited at the Armory Show in 1913 and had major retrospective shows at the Museum of Modern Art and the Whitney Museum in New York City. He produced but a few paintings each year, and was known as the painter of loneliness. He died on May 15, 1967.

HOUDINI, HARRY (1874–1926), magician. Born on April 6, 1874, in Appleton, Wisconsin, the son of Hungarian immigrants, Houdini was named Ehrich Weiss but later legally changed his name. He began the study of magic at an early age, reading books on the subject and attending performances in circuses and side shows. In 1882 he was a trapeze artist in New York, where he had moved to earn money for his family. When the family joined him he developed a magic act with his brother, called "Hardeen," as his assistant; in 1894 he married, and his wife became his assistant, performing under the name Beatrice Houdini. They made appearances in circuses and in 1895 at Tony Pastor's theater, and then in a chain of vaudeville houses, but remained relatively unknown, despite Houdini's remarkable skill. Though he was highly skilled in many forms of magic, his forte was escape acts, in which he extricated himself from ropes, shackles, and various locked containers. Determined to make his mark, he went abroad in 1900 and executed an escape from Scotland Yard, gaining wide publicity and becoming a main attraction at the Alhambra Theatre in London. He successfully toured the Continent for four years. Returning to the United States, he received international news coverage for his escapes, which completely baffled audiences. In one feat, he was shackled with irons and locked into a roped, weighted box that was dropped from a boat into water; he returned to the boat, having broken loose under water. In another act, he was suspended upside down 75 feet in the air and in this position freed himself from a strait jacket. If success depended on muscular power or adroitness, he would escape in front of spectators; but frequently his acts depended on his extensive knowledge of lock mechanisms, and his more complicated feats were done in enclosures. He occasionally used an unseen tool or assistant; but he stressed that supernatural forces did not aid him. He undertook a study of Robert-Houdin, the French magician from whom he had adopted his name. In the course of gathering information, he discovered that Houdin's dexterity had been exaggerated and wrote, instead of the planned tribute, *The Unmasking of Robert-Houdin*, 1908. He also published *Miracle Mongers and Their Methods*, 1920, and *A Magician Among the Spirits*, 1924, to discredit mind readers and mediums; he had discovered their tricks in the course of several attempts to contact his dead mother. Nevertheless, he planned with his wife an experiment in supernaturalism—whoever died first would attempt to contact the other through a medium. He died in Detroit on October 31, 1926, when a stomach injury led to peritonitis; his wife revealed the failure of the experiment before her death in 1943. Houdini also edited and was the major contributor to *Conjurers' Monthly* during 1906–1908. He established the London Magicians' Club and the Society of American Magicians. His books and papers on spiritualism and magic were bequeathed to the Library of Congress.

HOUSTON, SAMUEL (1793–1863), soldier and public official. Born on March 2, 1793, near Lexington, Virginia, Houston grew up there and, after his father's death, on the Tennessee frontier. He received little schooling and at the age of 15, rather than take a clerkship in a local store, he moved into the woods and for three years lived among the Cherokee Indians. He served in the War of 1812 under Andrew Jackson and took part in the battle of Horseshoe Bend against the Creeks. Remaining in the Army after the war, he became an Indian agent and helped oversee the removal of the Cherokee from Tennessee to Arkansas. The next year he resigned and took up the study of law; he was soon led into politics and in 1823 was elected to Congress, remaining there for two terms. Returning to Tennessee in 1827 he was elected governor; soon after his reelection in 1829, however, his wife of three months deserted him and he resigned and returned to the Cherokee. Houston was formally adopted by the Cherokee nation and for a few years operated a trading post in their territory. He made several trips to Washington, D. C., to plead for equitable treatment of the Indians and in 1832 was sent by President Jackson to negotiate with several tribes in Texas. He was caught up in the growing agitation for Texan independence and in 1833 attended the convention that drew up a petition to the Mexican government requesting statehood and wrote a constitution. By 1835 he had settled permanently in Texas and was appointed commander of the small army then being organized. In April 1836 he engaged the Mexi-

can army under Santa Anna and, though outnumbered by more than two to one, dealt it a smashing defeat at San Jacinto. In September Houston was elected president of the Republic of Texas. From 1838 to 1840 he was in the legislature and from 1841 to 1844 was again president. The next year, with the admission of Texas to the Union, he was sent to the Senate where he remained for nearly 14 years. He spoke and voted always as a Union Democrat rather than as a Southerner and strongly opposed the Kansas-Nebraska Bill of 1854. In 1859, having become unpopular with the legislature, he left the Senate but was elected governor. He vigorously opposed but finally acquiesced in secession; refusing to swear allegiance to the Confederacy, however, he was deposed in March 1861. He retired to Huntsville, Texas, and died on July 26, 1863.

HOWE, ELIAS (1819–1867), inventor. Born on July 9, 1819, in Spencer, Massachusetts, Howe was raised on a farm and received only brief formal schooling. Interested in machinery and tools, he worked in his father's gristmill and sawmill and later was an apprentice in several machine tool shops between 1835 and 1837. Traveling then to Boston, he went to work for a watchmaker and one day overheard a conversation in which the idea of a sewing machine was discussed. He at once began to try to construct such a device and by 1845 had created one that featured an eyed needle and a threading device, which together worked to fasten stitches at regular intervals in fabric. He secured patent rights in 1846 but could not sell the machine. He sold one machine and British patent rights to an English corset-maker, and went there to develop it further, returning to Boston in 1849. He discovered that other inventors, notably Isaac M. Singer, had created sewing machines based on his invention and were blatantly violating his patent. Litigation through 1854 finally secured his claim and awarded him royalties on all sewing machines sold in the United States until the expiration of his patent in 1867. Having created a manufacturing revolution with a machine that made possible the mass production of clothing, he died in Brooklyn, New York, on October 3, 1867.

HOWE, JULIA WARD (1819–1910), author and reformer. Born in New York City on May 27, 1819, Miss Ward came of a wealthy and cultivated family. In 1843 she married Samuel Gridley Howe, the educator and reformer. Always of a literary mind, she published her first volume of poetry, *Passion Flowers*, in 1854; this and subsequent works had little success. For a while she and her husband published *The Commonwealth*, an Abolitionist newspaper. In February 1862 the *Atlantic Monthly* published her poem "Battle Hymn of the Republic," to be set to an old folk tune also used for "John Brown's Body." The song was adopted as the semiofficial war song of the Northern Army and Mrs. Howe became immediately famous. After the war she involved herself in the woman suffrage movement and was the first president of the New England Woman Suffrage Association. She also took up the cause of peace and in 1870 published an "Appeal to Womanhood Throughout the World," a call for an international conference of women on the subject of peace. In 1871 she became first president of the American Branch of the Woman's International Peace Association. She continued to write throughout her life, her publications including travel books, poetry, collections of essays, and biographies, notably that of Margaret Fuller. She died on October 17, 1910, in Newport, Rhode Island.

HOWE, SAMUEL GRIDLEY (1801–1876), educator and reformer. Born in Boston on November 10, 1801, Howe graduated from Brown University in 1821 and then entered Harvard Medical School, taking his M.D. in 1824. Soon thereafter he sailed to Greece to aid in that country's revolution; for six years he fought, was a surgeon for the fleet, and helped in the recon-

struction that followed. In 1831, having returned to Boston, he accepted an offer to direct a newly founded school for the blind. During an inspection tour of such schools in Europe he was imprisoned for aiding the revolt in Poland; he returned the following year and in August opened a new school in his father's house. He was eminently successful in educating blind children to lead happy and useful lives; his triumph was in the case of Laura Bridgman, a blind deaf-mute child who entered the school (by then the Perkins School) in 1837. His success in communicating with Miss Bridgman roused the enthusiasm of Charles Dickens during his visit to America in 1842. In 1843 Howe married Julia Ward, later to write "The Battle Hymn of the Republic." He worked for a great number of causes: he supported Horace Mann in the crusade for common and normal schools; pioneered in the education of mentally retarded children; worked for prison reform; and aided Dorothea Dix in improving the care accorded the mentally ill. With his wife he published for a time *The Commonwealth*, an Abolitionist newspaper; in 1846 he ran unsuccessfully for Congress as a Conscience Whig. He was chairman of the Massachusetts Board of State Charities from 1865 to 1874. He died on January 19, 1876.

HOWELLS, WILLIAM DEAN (1837–1920), author and critic. Born in Martin's Ferry, Ohio, on March 1, 1837, Howells was the son of an itinerant printer and was taken into the trade himself at the age of nine. He spent his early years in a succession of small Ohio towns and received scant formal education. His determination to become a writer, however, led him to study long hours on his own; after four years as editorial writer for the *Ohio State Journal* in Columbus, he published in 1860 his first book of verse—*Poems of Two Friends*, with John J. Piatt—and his first book of prose, a campaign biography of Lincoln. The latter was the more important; it allowed him to visit New England and meet James Russell Lowell and the Boston circle and it won him the consulate in Venice, a position he held from 1861 to 1865. Upon his return to the United States he was briefly on the staff of the *Nation* and then in 1866 commenced his long association with the *Atlantic Monthly*, beginning as assistant editor. In the same year he published his observations of four years as *Venetian Life*. He quickly made himself a part of the social and intellectual life of Cambridge and Boston and in 1871 became editor-in-chief of the *Atlantic*; for the next ten years he made the magazine into one of national importance and influence and a champion of young and unorthodox writers. In particular he encouraged two men who were perhaps polar opposites in literature, Henry James and Mark Twain, and in doing so demonstrated a truly remarkable breadth of appreciation. At the same time he was developing his own literary career with a number of travel and international novels, including *Their Wedding Journey*, 1872, *A Foregone Conclusion*, 1875, and *The Lady of the Aroostook*, 1879. In 1881 he severed his connection with the *Atlantic* and for several years his novels were serialized in the *Century Magazine*. These years saw the growth of Howells' consciousness of the need for a realistic portrayal of and even involvement in the society surrounding the author; his realism, though later often dismissed as meek and compromising, showed a steady development of awareness and understanding while it was always restrained from belonging in the naturalistic school by a certain moral optimism. *The Undiscovered Country*, 1880, was followed by *Dr. Breen's Practice*, 1881, *A Modern Instance*, 1882, one of his very best, and *The Rise of Silas Lapham*, 1885, probably his best-known. He became associated with *Harper's Magazine* and from 1886 to 1892 wrote a long series of critical articles for the "Editor's Study," many of which were collected as *Criticism and Fiction*, 1891. He again demonstrated his catholic yet discriminating taste in approving such diverse writers as Emily Dickinson, Hamlin Garland,

Stephen Crane, Frank Norris, and Thorstein Veblen. His removal to New York in 1888 marked something of a turning point in his outlook; a starker vision of life entered his work and he began to express a view of social complicity very like that of Tolstoi. In *Annie Kilburn*, 1889, he took up the cause of labor; there followed *A Hazard of New Fortunes*, 1890, *The Quality of Mercy*, 1892, and *The World of Chance*, 1893. Finally, in 1894, he published *A Traveler from Altruria*, an explicitly utopian novel that pictured a genial socialist commonwealth more clearly delineated in *Through the Eye of the Needle*, 1907. His last major novel, *The Landlord at Lion's Head*, appeared in 1897. From 1900 until his death Howells conducted the "Easy Chair" column in *Harper's* and continued to add to his voluminous bibliography of travel sketches, biography, drama, and reminiscence. As the acknowledged "dean of American letters" he was awarded numerous honorary degrees; his long and productive life ended on May 10, 1920.

HUBBARD, FRANK McKINNEY (1868–1930), humorist. Born on September 1, 1868, in Bellefontaine, Ohio, Hubbard was the grandson of Capt. John B. Miller who acted in a wagon-theater that traveled through the Midwest, and the son of the publisher of the *Bellefontaine Examiner*. Known throughout his life as "Kin," he regularly attended circuses and theaters and produced his own popular blackface minstrel shows. He taught himself to sketch, went to local schools, and learned the printer's trade from his father. In 1891 he became a police reporter and artist on the *Indianapolis News*, and about 1894 returned to Bellefontaine to work in the post office for his father, who had become postmaster. He was subsequently employed on the *Cincinnati Commercial Tribune* and the *Mansfield* (Ohio) *News*. In 1901 he rejoined the *Indianapolis News* and remained there the rest of his life. In 1904, while riding on a political-campaign train, he made sketches of several Hoosier characters, and printed them in the *News* with succinct captions like "Ther's some folks standin' behind th' President that ought t' git around where he kin watch 'em." The feature appealed to the editor who encouraged him to do a series, and thus, Abe Martin, a farmer from Brown Country, Indiana, was born. Since the caricatures were merely signed "Hub.," it was Abe Martin, the character, who became identified with the "home-cured philosophy" that accompanied them — "Very often the quiet feller has said all he knows," or "If capital an' labor ever do git t' gether it's good night fer th' rest of us," or "Ther ought t' be some way t' eat celery so it wouldn' sound like you wuz steppin' on a basket." Soon syndicated (as were his weekly essays "Short Furrows"), the sketches and sayings were collected and published at least once a year from 1906 to 1929. Hubbard made an international tour as Abe Martin in 1924 but usually declined radio and stage appearances, preferring to remain at home ("of all th' home remedies a good wife is th' best") and cultivate his garden. He died on December 26, 1930, in Indianapolis.

HUBBLE, EDWIN POWELL (1889–1953), astronomer. Born in Marshfield, Missouri, on November 20, 1889, Hubble graduated from the University of Chicago in 1910 and subsequently studied at Oxford on a Rhodes Scholarship. Taking a B.A. in jurisprudence, he returned to the United States and for a year practised law in Kentucky, but his interest in science drew him back to the University of Chicago where he received his Ph.D. in 1917, having begun his astronomical researches at the university's Yerkes Observatory. During World War I he served in France as chief ballistician for Army Ordnance. In 1919 he joined the staff of Mount Wilson Observatory in California, with which he was connected for the rest of his life. His primary interest was in the study of nebulae, huge agglomerations of stars about which little was then known. With his discovery in 1923 of a Cepheid variable star — one whose period of variation in brightness is directly related to its actual luminosity and whose distance can therefore be accurately determined — in the Andromeda nebula, he succeeded in demonstrating that that nebula and others like it were independent galaxies and lay at vast distances from our own. He undertook a sky survey of the density and distribution of these extragalactic nebulae; on the basis of this survey he developed a classification scheme for the various forms of nebulae based on a suggested evolutionary pattern. In 1929 he announced the results of his investigations concerning the spectral red-shifts displayed by these nebulae, a phenomenon interpreted as an instance of the Doppler effect whereby the frequency of wave radiation — in this case light — is changed by the speed of approach or recession of the radiating object relative to the observer. A shift towards the red end of the spectrum had been observed in the light from distant galaxies and this was taken to indicate that they were all receding away from ours. Hubble's research demonstrated a simple relation between a galaxy's distance and its speed of recession, and further assigned a numerical value to the still-accepted "Hubble's constant." This discovery had a profound effect on cosmology and stimulated the formulation of numerous cosmological models. His work strained the capabilities of the 100-inch Mount Wilson telescope to their limit and provided a strong impetus for the building of the great 200-inch instrument at Mount Palomar, opened in 1948. Hubble continued his investigations into the nature of extragalactic nebulae until his death on September 28, 1953, in San Marino, California.

HUGHES, CHARLES EVANS (1862–1948), jurist and public official. Born on April 11, 1862, in Glens Falls, New York, Hughes was educated at Madison (now Colgate) and Brown Universities, graduating from the latter in 1881. After a period of teaching and private law study he entered the law school at Columbia

University and was granted a degree in 1884; he began practice and for three years was a tutor at Columbia. He taught in the law school at Cornell University from 1891 to 1893 and then returned to his practice in New York City. His public career began in 1905 when he served as counsel to a legislative committee investigating the gas and electric lighting industries; as a result of this work he was considered for mayor of New York, but he declined in order to aid in a similar investigation of the practices of insurance companies. In 1906, however, he was nominated for governor and defeated William Randolph Hearst. His two terms, 1906–1910, were marked by extensive reforms of the state's government. In 1910 he was appointed to the Supreme Court by President Taft. He had been prominently mentioned for the presidency since 1908 but had consistently refused to be considered; finally, in 1916, he accepted a Republican draft and resigned from the Court to campaign. After being narrowly defeated by the incumbent Woodrow Wilson he returned to his law practice, serving also as chairman of New York City's draft appeals board and in an investigation of the aircraft industry. With the election of Warren G. Harding as President in 1920, Hughes became secretary of state. He was unsuccessful in his advocacy of American membership in the League of Nations and was forced therefore to negotiate a separate peace treaty with Germany. He was the chief organizer of the Washington naval conference in 1921–1922 that produced an arms-limitation treaty and he succeeded in maintaining both the Open Door policy in China and American interests in the Pacific. At the Pan-American Conference in Santiago in 1923 he negotiated a 15-nation treaty arranging for the arbitration of disputes by commission. After leaving the Cabinet in 1925 he aided in the reorganization of the state government in New York, represented the U.S. at two further Pan-American conferences, was a member of the International Permanent Court of Arbitration,

and in 1929 served as a judge on the Permanent Court of International Justice at The Hague. In 1930 President Hoover appointed him chief justice of the Supreme Court. He took generally a liberal stand, particularly on civil-rights cases, and preferred a loose-constructionist interpretation of the Constitution. As the Supreme Court began to invalidate the early New Deal legislation in the 1930s, Hughes occupied a middle ground, often dissenting from the Court's conservatism but joining in its opposition to the National Industrial Recovery Act in 1935. When President Roosevelt proposed his "court-packing" plan in 1937, Hughes denounced it and was instrumental in its defeat; he later denied that the approval by the Court of several major New Deal acts at the same time or a little later was an accommodation to the President. He retired from the Court in 1941 and died on August 27, 1948, on Cape Cod.

HUGHES, HOWARD ROBARD (1905–   ), industrialist, aviator, and motion picture producer. Born in Houston on December 24, 1905, Hughes was the son of an oil-well drilling equipment developer, the owner of Hughes Tool Company in Houston. He was educated at the Rice Institute in Houston and the California Institute of Technology. While he was still in his teens his father died, and he assumed control of the tool business shortly thereafter. With an estimated income at age 20 of $2 million he went to Hollywood to produce motion pictures. Among his box-office hits were *Two Arabian Nights*, winner of the Academy Award in 1928, *Hell's Angels*, starring the yet-unknown starlet, Jean Harlow (Academy Award in 1930), *Scarface*, which introduced Paul Muni and began a trend in gangster movies, *The Front Page, The Sky Devils, The Racket*, and, after purchasing RKO films in 1939 (an unsuccessful venture), *The Outlaw*, 1941. He organized and became president of an experimental aircraft enterprise, Hughes Aircraft Company. In a plane of his own design in September 1935, he set the world's air speed record, 352 miles per hour. In January 1937 he broke his own transcontinental flying record made a year earlier with a new time of 7 hours, 28 minutes, 25 seconds. In July 1938, in a twin-engine Lockheed, he set an around-the-world flight record of 3 days, 19 hours, 8 minutes, 10 seconds. He designed, built, and flew a 220-ton plywood flying boat—then the world's largest plane —on November 2, 1947. In 1939 he had, through Hughes Tool, begun buying stock in the company that later became Trans World Airlines, and by 1959 he held three-fourths of the common; his control of the company met with considerable opposition and litigation, however, and in 1966 he sold out in one of the largest stock transactions in history, amounting to over a half billion dollars. Hughes Tool was also the major stockholder in Northeast Airlines from 1962 to 1964. In the late 1960s he purchased huge tracts of land in and near Las Vegas, becoming virtual owner of the famous Las Vegas "strip." He took residence in the top floors of one of his hotels and continued to live, as he had for years, in total seclusion.

HUGHES, JAMES MERCER LANGSTON (1902–1967), author. Born in Joplin, Missouri, on February 1, 1902, Langston Hughes—he habitually ignored the first two of his names —moved often as a child until his family settled in Cleveland when he was 14. In 1921, shortly after he graduated from high school, his first poem, and one that remains perhaps his best-loved, "The Negro Speaks of Rivers," was published in the *Crisis*. After an extended visit to Mexico he entered Columbia University in 1921 but left the following year. For several years he drifted, working his way to Africa on a freighter and living for a time in Paris and Rome. While working as a busboy in a Washington, D.C., hotel in 1925, he showed some of his work to Vachel Lindsay who immediately arranged for its publication. Hughes was awarded the Opportunity Prize for Poetry that year and was granted a scholarship to Lincoln

University. His first volume of poetry, *The Weary Blues*, appeared in 1926 and was followed the next year by *Fine Clothes to the Jew*. In 1926 he received the Witter Bynner Undergraduate Poetry Award; he graduated from Lincoln in 1929 and the next year published his first prose work, *Not Without Laughter*. Poetry continued to be his primary interest and he came to be called "the poet laureate of Harlem" through his collections including *The Dream Keeper*, 1932, *Scottsboro Limited*, 1932, *Shakespeare in Harlem*, 1942, and *Fields of Wonder*, 1947. He employed other literary forms, however, producing dramas, including *Mulatto* and *Simply Heavenly*; song-plays like *Black Nativity* and *Jerico Jim Crow*; a collection of stories under the title *The Ways of White Folks*, 1934; and newspaper columns in the *New York Post* and the *Chicago Defender*. In these columns he chronicled the adventures and philosophy of his fictional character Jesse B. Semple, usually known as Simple, and many of them were collected in book form as *Simple Speaks His Mind*, 1950, *Simple Stakes A Claim*, 1957, and others. In later years Hughes edited a number of anthologies of Negro authors and wrote several books and articles on outstanding Negro figures. He died in New York City on May 22, 1967.

HUGHES, JOHN (1797–1864), clergyman. Born on June 24, 1797, in Annaloghan, County Tyrone, Ireland, Hughes emigrated to the United States in 1817. In 1820 he began religious training at Mount St. Mary's College in Emmitsburg, Maryland, and in 1826 was ordained a priest. He became prominent as a "fighting Irish priest," while at the head of two Philadelphia parishes, during which time he debated with Protestant clergymen over nativism, and settled the issue of trusteeism. In 1838 he was made bishop co-adjutor of New York and was immediately identified as a champion of the interests of the growing Eastern population of Irish and German Catholic immigrants. Succeeding to bishop of the see in 1842, he saw an end to the lay trustee system in New York, securing state legislation to remove the control of church property from secular administrators and giving title to the bishop (later the archbishop), or his designates, on behalf of the Church. His proposal to establish properly equipped and well staffed parochial schools for all Catholics led to a fierce battle in which the Protestant dominated public schools were finally secularized in 1841, and his people were pledged to the development of a parochial school system. Threats and abuse from the Nativist and Know-Nothing Parties, reaching heights in 1844 and 1854, prompted his own threat to use force if necessary to defend Catholic institutions. In 1850, when New York was elevated to an archbishopric, he became its first archbishop, and thereafter made frequent trips to Europe and the Vatican, becoming the foremost spokesman for American Catholics. In 1854 he battled the radical Irish press set up in New York by political exiles and denounced a movement calling for Irish immigrants to settle away from the urban centers of the East. During the Civil War he was an active pro-Unionist and, as a special representative of President Lincoln, promoted the Union cause in Europe. His personal appeal was a major factor in bringing the draft rioting of 1863 to an end. In his 25-year reign as bishop and archbishop, he built more than 100 new churches and established many Roman Catholic societies. He helped to found St. Joseph's Provincial Seminary in Troy, New York, and the North American College in Rome. In 1858 he began construction of St. Patrick's Cathedral. His influence extended far beyond religion into the social, political, and educational spheres. He died in New York on January 3, 1864.

HULL, CORDELL (1871–1955), lawyer and public official. Born on October 2, 1871, in Overton County, Tennessee, Hull was educated in a one-room school and at Montvale College in Celina, Tennessee. An ardent Democrat before he was 20, he entered National Normal University at Lebanon, Connecticut, in 1889, transferred to Cumberland University Law School the following year, and graduated and was admitted to the bar in 1891. A brief law practice in Celina preceded his election to the state legislature in 1893; in 1897 he left to recruit a volunteer company for the Spanish-American war. They went to Cuba as part of the 4th Tennessee Regiment but saw little action. In 1903 he was elected a Tennessee circuit court judge and from 1907 to 1931, except for 1921, served in Congress, where his concerns focused on tax and tariff problems. He authored the first federal income tax bill in 1913 and the later revised act, and the Federal and State Inheritance Tax Law in 1916. An advocate of President Wilson's economic program and of the League of Nations, he was determined by 1919 that low tariffs and the removal of other trade barriers would promote if not secure world peace. In 1931 he was elected to the Senate and in 1933 became secretary of state under Franklin D. Roosevelt. He was successful in a number of Pan-American conferences—at Montevideo in 1933, at Buenos Aires in 1936, at Lima in 1938, and at Havana in 1940—in formulating a "good neighbor" policy and establishing a united front against aggression in case of war with Europe. In 1934 he won passage of the Trade Agreements Act, designed to stimulate trade with Latin America by giving the President the power to adjust tariffs within limits. He blamed the disintegration of world peace in the 1930s on U.S. rejection of the League of Nations. As neutrality became impossible in 1940, he supported President Roosevelt in drawing the United States closer to the Allies. Despite his steadily weakening health he led a U.S. delegation to a foreign ministers' conference in Moscow in 1943. He also played a major role in the Dumbarton Oaks conferences in Washington that laid the groundwork for the San Francisco conference in 1945, where the United Nations was founded. He was called by President Roosevelt the "father of the

United Nations," and for his contribution won the Nobel Prize for Peace in 1945. He resigned from the Cabinet after the 1944 presidential election, owing to his health, and died on July 23, 1955, at Bethesda, Maryland.

HUMPHREY, HUBERT HORATIO (1911–), public official. Born in Wallace, South Dakota, on May 27, 1911, Humphrey attended the public schools of Doland, South Dakota, where his family had moved. He studied at the Denver College of Pharmacy in 1932– 1933 and, after working as a pharmacist for several years, received his B.A. from the University of Minnesota in 1939 and his M.A. from the University of Louisiana in 1940; while at Louisiana he also taught political science there, and after receiving his degree went back for a year of teaching at Minnesota. From 1942 to 1945 he served in several federal posts in Minnesota, was an instructor with the Army Air Forces, worked as a radio news commentator, and acted as the state campaign director for Franklin Roosevelt during the 1944 campaign. During this period he helped to merge the Democratic and Farmer-Labor parties in the state and on a combined ticket he was elected mayor of Minneapolis in 1945. He was elected to the U.S. Senate in 1948 and reelected in 1954 and 1960; in 1956 he served as U.S. delegate to the UN General Assembly. In 1960 he made a bid for the Democratic presidential nomination, but after the West Virginia primary campaign he was out of the running and John F. Kennedy was chosen as the party's candidate. Known as a liberal, he was elected by his fellow senators as assistant majority leader in 1961 and chosen to manage the 1964 civil rights bill. With strong bipartisan support, and despite a three-month filibuster by the opponents of the bill, he was able to marshall enough votes for passage. At the 1964 Democratic convention President Johnson announced that he had chosen Humphrey for his running mate, and he campaigned ably for the national ticket and shared Johnson's landslide victory that

year. As Vice President he was given important posts by Johnson—membership on the National Security Council, chairman of the National Advisory Council of the Peace Corps, coordinator of the antipoverty program, and chairman of the Civil Rights Council, among others—but it appeared that he was not always taken into the President's confidence on all matters, and he found himself in the position of defending policies, particularly with regard to the Vietnam War, that he either did not fully understand or did not fully approve. He nevertheless made many trips abroad in behalf of the President's policies, acting as a sort of roving ambassador of the United States. He announced his intention to seek the Democratic nomination in 1968 shortly after Johnson withdrew in March of that year, and emerged as the front-running candidate after the murder of Robert F. Kennedy in June. He was nominated by his party at a chaotic convention in Chicago in August but, after a somewhat confused and confusing campaign, lost by a narrow margin to Richard M. Nixon in November. After the election he accepted a position as a professor at the University of Minnesota and also devoted himself to various business interests.

HUNTINGTON, COLLIS POTTER (1821–1900), railroad executive. Born on October 22, 1821, in Harwinton, Connecticut, Huntington left school and went to work at 14. From 1836 to 1842 he was an itinerant peddler and in the latter year opened a store in Oneonta, New York. After seven successful years he joined the rush to California in 1849, taking a load of merchandise to Sacramento. There he established a new store; he later took in a partner and Huntington & Hopkins became a prosperous mercantile company. In 1860, with Leland Stanford and others, he financed a survey for a possible railroad route eastward across the Sierra Nevada Mountains; he went to Washington, D.C., to assist in securing government grants to underwrite construction costs and remained in the East as agent for the company. The line, the Central Pacific Railroad of California, was completed and joined to the Union Pacific at Promontory Point, Utah, in 1869. Work was begun on a new route leading south through California, and in 1884 this and the Central Pacific were merged into the Southern Pacific Company, with Stanford president and Huntington vice president and chief executive. He spent most of his time in the East, improving the company's financial status and carrying on lobbying activities in Washington. On his own he invested in several other railroads, particularly the Chesapeake & Ohio, which he improved and extended, founding the town of Newport News, Virginia, as its eastern terminus. He also had interests in a number of steamship companies. In 1890 he succeeded Stanford as president of the Southern Pacific system, which by then encompassed over 9,600 miles of track. He died near Raquette Lake, New York, on August 13, 1900.

HUNTINGTON, ELLSWORTH (1876–1947), geographer. Born in Galesburg, Illinois, on September 16, 1876, Huntington received his B.A. degree from Beloit College in 1897, his M.A. from Harvard in 1902, and his Ph.D. from Yale in 1909. He taught geography from 1897 to 1901 at Euphrates College in Harput, Turkey, and in 1907 at Yale, and was assistant professor of geography at Yale from 1910 until he was promoted to research associate in 1917, with the rank of professor. His researches dealt primarily with climatic effects on land structure, population, and family and social organization. In 1901 he explored the canyons of the Euphrates River, winning the Gill Memorial of the Royal Geographical Society. During 1903–1904 he participated in the Pumpelly expedition to Russian Turkestan, remaining there and in Persia until 1905, and from that year to 1906 he was with the Barrett expedition in India, China, and Siberia. He published *Explorations in Turkestan*, 1905, and *The Pulse of Asia*, 1907. In 1909 he led an eight-month Yale expedition to Palestine, the Syrian desert, and Asia Minor, and was special correspondent on the mission for *Harper's*. *Palestine and Its Transformation* appeared in 1911. During 1910–1913 he conducted investigations of climate in Mexico, Central America, and the United States as research associate of the Carnegie Institution of Washington. He published in 1914 *The Climatic Factor*, in 1915 *Civilization and Climate*, and in 1922, with S. S. Visher, *Climatic Changes*. During 1918–1919 he was a captain in military intelligence. His *World Power and Evolution* appeared in the latter year. Other publications included *Earth and Sun*, 1923, *The Character of Races*, 1924, *The Pulse of Progress*, 1926, and *Tomorrow's Children—The Goal of Eugenics*, 1935. *Mainsprings of Civilization*, 1945, was the fruition of all his research. Recipient of numerous awards, he retired from the active Yale faculty as professor emeritus in 1945 and died in New Haven, Connecticut, on October 17, 1947.

HUTCHINS, ROBERT MAYNARD (1899–   ), educator. Born in Brooklyn, New York, on January 17, 1899, Hutchins was the son of a Presbyterian minister who became president of Berea College in Kentucky. After two years of study at Oberlin College, he served in the ambulance service of both the U.S. and the Italian armies, then entered Yale, from which he graduated in 1921. He received his LL.B. from the Yale law school in 1925 and immediately began to teach there; he was named dean in 1927. In 1929, at the age of 30, he was elected president of the University of Chicago, where he remained until 1951, for the last six years as chancellor. At Chicago he was an effective but highly controversial administrator. Among his many important innovations, some of which brought savage attacks on him, were the abolition of big time football, the introduction of a Great Books program, the reorganization of the graduate school, and the institution of the so-called Chicago Plan—a four-year liberal arts program starting after the sophomore year in high school. Early educational specialization was discouraged, and students were required to take courses in the mathematical, physical, biological, and social sciences, and in the humanities. At the same time he wrote a number of books that argued eloquently for his ideas, among them *No Friendly Voice*, 1936, and *The Higher Learning in America*, 1936. He left Chicago in 1951 to become associate director of the Ford Foundation and president of its Fund for the Republic, which soon split off from the parent organization; the Fund then founded the Center for the Study of Democratic Institutions, first in Pasadena and then in Santa Barbara, California, which he continued to head. The Center, by means of a widely read magazine, occasional papers and other publications, and influential convocations of scholars and politicians, was principally "directed at discovering," as he said, "whether and how a free and just society may be maintained under the strikingly new . . . conditions of the second half of the 20th century." His later books, in which, among other things, he defended nonconformity and protest, included *The Conflict in Education*, 1953, *University of Utopia*, 1953, *Some Observations on American Education*, 1956, *Education for Freedom*, 1963, and *Education: The Learning Society*, 1968. Chairman of the board of editors of *Encyclopaedia Britannica* from 1943, he was editor-in-chief of *Great Books of the Western World*, 1952, and coeditor of an annual, *The Great Ideas Today*, from 1963.

HUTCHINSON, ANNE (1591–1643), religious leader. Born in Lincolnshire, England, in 1591, Anne Marbury was the daughter of a clergyman and grew up in an atmosphere of learning. In 1612 she married William Hutchinson. She became a follower of John Cotton and in 1634, a year after he had gone to Massachusetts, she sailed for Boston with her husband and family. Her kindliness and intellect soon won her a position of influence in the community and when she organized regular religious meetings in her home she attracted large numbers of people, including many ministers. At first concerned only with discussion of recent sermons, she gradually began using the meetings to expound her own theological views; in opposition to the orthodox "covenant of works" she set forth a "covenant of grace," holding that faith alone was necessary or sufficient for salvation. Her teachings were viewed by conservatives as a veiled attack on the theocratic polity of the Puritan settlements and factions quickly formed in what came to be known as the Antinomian Controversy. Principal among her supporters were her brother-in-law, the Rev. John Wheelwright, John Cotton, and the governor, Sir Henry Vane; ranged against them were Deputy Governor John Winthrop and the Rev. John Wilson. In 1637 Winthrop won the governorship from Vane, who returned to England, and a synod of churches was called at which Mrs. Hutchinson and the Antinomians were denounced. Cotton recanted and Wheelwright was banished. After being convicted by the General Court of "traducing the ministers," Mrs. Hutchinson was also banished, and a short time later was formally excommunicated. Early in 1638 she removed with her family and others to the island of Aquidneck in what is now Rhode Island. Following the death of her husband in 1642 she resettled on Long Island Sound, where in August 1643 she was killed by Indians in what was considered an act of divine judgment.

INGERSOLL, ROBERT GREEN (1833–1899), lawyer, orator, and public official. Born in Dresden, New York, on August 11, 1833, Ingersoll was the son of a stern, itinerant Congregational minister. He received little formal education as the family moved to Ohio, to Wisconsin, and finally to Illinois; his efforts at self-education, however, enabled him to be admitted to the Illinois bar in 1854. Three years later he took up residence in Peoria and soon became locally prominent. During the Civil War he commanded a volunteer cavalry regiment; in late 1862 he was captured by Confederate forces and by June 1863 had been paroled and discharged from the Army. He had been in 1860 an unsuccessful Democratic candidate for Congress; in 1867, having converted to Republicanism, he was elected attorney general of Illinois for two years, and this was to be his only public office in over 30 years of political activity. As the spread of Darwinism provoked wide and violent controversy, Ingersoll took to the lecture platform as a powerful advocate of scientific and humanistic rationalism and propounded a view called by T. H. Huxley "agnosticism." In a time when Darwinians were generally shunned, Ingersoll was widely in demand as a speaker, his personality and integrity clearly giving the lie to the charges commonly lodged against men of his persuasion. Among his famous addresses were "The Gods," "Some Mistakes of Moses," "Why I Am an Agnostic," and "Superstition." He was an active campaigner for the Republican Party as well; at the 1876 convention he presented the name of James G. Blaine for the nomination, dubbing him "the plumed knight." He moved to Washington, D.C., in 1879 and continued both his lecturing and his law practice. He was chief counsel for the defense in the trials resulting from the Star Route Scandal of 1882. Three years later he moved to New York City and continued to work as lawyer, lecturer, and political orator until his death on July 21, 1899.

INNESS, GEORGE (1825–1894), painter. Born on May 1, 1825, on a farm near Newburgh, New York, Inness was frail as a child but possessed a strong temperament and was both obstinate and ambitious. In school at Newark, New Jersey, he frequently missed classes because of poor health; but he was generally indifferent to lessons even when attending. With the consent of his father, he left school to study art with a local teacher who soon taught him as much as he knew. He went on to New York City in the 1840s and worked for a map

engravers' firm for a year. He painted country landscapes and studied briefly, then set up a studio in 1845. His art was immensely serious to him, so that painting a cloud was a test of perfection. The result was a period of strained, technical painting. Within a few years after 1847 he married twice, made several brief trips to Europe, and came under the influence of the Barbizon school, which emphasized spontaneity and suggestion in landscape painting, with the result that his work became more individual and less reminiscent of the Hudson River School. He moved to Boston in 1859, and lived in Medfield, Massachusetts, in the 1860s; there he concentrated on tonal variations, intensities of light, and contrasts between the earth, air, and sky. During the 1870s his initial preoccupation with structure and technique gave way to mystical, extremely personal visions of landscapes that were characterized by glistening colors and vagueness of form. His conversion to Swedenborgianism about that time may have prompted the change; whatever its springs, his final period saw the creation of many of his finest and most compelling works, including "Evening at Medfield" and "Autumn Oaks." He argued hotly over social issues, espousing the single tax and Abolitionism. During his last years he had several generous patrons, and though he was the most prosperous landscape painter of his time he remained, as always, indifferent to money. Traveling in Scotland in 1894, he died at Bridge of Allan on August 3rd.

IRVING, WASHINGTON (1783–1859), author. Born in New York City on April 3, 1783, Irving was indulged as a child, and though he grew up in an atmosphere of learning and refinement he cared little for school and not at all for college. In 1798, however, he undertook to fit himself for the law. His period of desultory study stretched over six years, during which he found entertainment in travel, in the gay life of cosmopolitan New York, and in writing a series of lightly satirical "Letters of Jonathan Oldstyle, Gent." for his brother's

Morning Chronicle. During 1804–1806 he toured Europe for his health and then returned to New York and was admitted to the bar. He found writing more to his liking, however, and in 1807–1808, with several associates including James Kirke Paulding, he published a series of papers entitled *Salmagundi: or, the Whim-Whams and Opinions of Launcelot Langstaff, Esq. and Others*. These, like his earlier letters, were largely genteel satires on fashionable society. In 1809 he published *Diedrich Knickerbocker's History of New York,* which had grown from a parody of a pretentious guidebook into a richly comic history of Dutch New York. During the next six years he wrote little; he published an American edition of Thomas Campbell's poetry and edited the *Analectic Magazine* in 1813–1814, but lobbying efforts on behalf of his brothers' importing firm and a position on the governor's military staff during the War of 1812 occupied most of his time. In 1815 he sailed for England, again on behalf of the family business, but meetings with Sir Walter Scott and other literary figures turned him back to the pen. A number of occasional essays, tales, and travel pieces were collected in 1819–1820 as *The Sketch Book of Geoffrey Crayon, Gent.,* published in London and an immediate success there and in America. Among the contents were "Rip Van Winkle," "The Legend of Sleepy Hollow," and "The Spectre Bridegroom," which have been called the first modern short stories. The voluminous travel notes that Irving had accumulated enabled him to issue a sequel, *Bracebridge Hall,* 1822, that, while not of the quality of *The Sketch Book,* was equally popular and firmly established him as America's leading man of letters. He remained in Europe, traveling on the Continent and gathering notes; *Tales of a Traveller,* 1824, the result of a visit to Germany, was a weak effort and was poorly received. Early in 1826, at the invitation of Alexander H. Everett of the American legation in Madrid, he journeyed to Spain to produce a translation of a recent scholarly biography of

Columbus. He quickly decided to write an original work instead and in 1828 appeared *History of the Life and Voyages of Christopher Columbus,* which was followed three years later by *The Companions of Columbus.* His sojourn in Spain awakened a deep interest in Spanish history and folklore and resulted in *A Chronicle of the Conquest of Granada,* 1829, and, in *Sketch Book* style, *The Alhambra,* 1832. In the latter year he returned at last to the United States, where he was received as a hero, and settled at "Sunnyside" on the Hudson near Tarrytown. A western trip inspired him to write *A Tour on the Prairies,* 1835, *Astoria,* 1836, and *The Adventures of Captain Bonneville, U.S.A.,* 1837. From 1842 to 1846 he served as minister to Spain, afterwards returning to "Sunnyside" permanently. Like his books on the West, his later works were not memorable; they were principally biographical and included *Oliver Goldsmith,* 1849, *Mahomet and his Successors,* 1849–1850, and a five-volume *George Washington,* 1855–1859. He died at home on November 28, 1859.

IVES, CHARLES EDWARD (1874–1954), composer. Born in Danbury, Connecticut, on October 20, 1874, Ives was the son of a military bandmaster who encouraged an early interest in music and gave him his first instruction. He later studied music at Yale, but composition was to be an avocation; upon graduation from Yale in 1898 he entered the insurance business, in which he remained until 1930. Illness forced him to give up composition relatively early; by far the greatest portion of his major work was done in the eighteen years after leaving Yale. His music was largely ignored until the end of his life. He received the Pulitzer Prize in 1947 for his Third Symphony, composed 36 years earlier. The Second Symphony was first performed in 1952, the Fourth in 1965. Exceedingly complex, his work combines polytonal and polyrhythmic structures with vernacular elements, such as popular melodies, march music, and hymns, drawn primarily from his native New England. Concerned with the evocation of whole scenes of life, the music is often dissonant and occasionally seems disjointed or amorphous. As the titles of some of his works imply—"Concord, Mass.," "Central Park in the Dark," "Three Places in New England," and "Thanksgiving," for example—his music was by intent distinctly and distinctively American. Ives died in New York City on May 19, 1954.

IVES, JAMES MERRITT see **CURRIER, NATHANIEL**

JACKSON, ANDREW (1767–1845), lawyer, soldier, public official, and 7th U.S. President. Born on March 15, 1767, in the Waxhaw settlement on the Carolina frontier—probably in what is now South Carolina—Jackson received little formal schooling. The backcountry warfare during the Revolution left him without a family at 14; in 1784 he began the study of law in Salisbury, North Carolina, was admitted to the bar in 1787, and the next year traveled west to the trans-Appalachian region that was to become Tennessee. He soon gained appointment as prosecuting attorney for the district and with the collection of debts as his principal duty in that unsettled area he became allied with the comparatively wealthy class. He engaged in land speculation, trade, and planting, and in 1795 established his home at the "Hermitage" near Nashville. The following year he helped draft the constitution of the new state of Tennessee and was immediately elected to its one seat in the House of Representatives. He served for three months, during which he was prominent only for disapproving of Washington's Farewell Address as being pro-British. In 1797 he was elected to the Senate but was forced by financial reverses at home to resign a year later; he was soon appointed to the state superior court and he served there until 1804 when he resigned for similar reasons. In 1802 he had been elected major general of the state militia and from 1804 to 1812 this was his only connec-

tion with public life; in the latter year it ceased to be a largely honorary position with the outbreak of war with England. The next year he set out in command of the militia to subdue the Creek Indians, allies of the British who had perpetrated a massacre at Fort Mims in Mississippi, and at the Battle of Tohopeka, or Horseshoe Bend, in March 1814, he succeeded completely, wresting from the tribe a vast region in what is now Georgia and Alabama. He proceeded to Pensacola, Florida, capturing it in November, and then hurried to New Orleans where he repulsed the attempted British invasion on January 8, 1815. News of his victory reached Washington shortly ahead of news that the peace had been restored two weeks earlier by the Treaty of Ghent. Jackson—"Old Hickory" —was a national figure and already was considered by many a potential President. He retained his major general's commission in the regular Army that had come after the victory over the Creeks and was made commander of the Southern district. In 1818 he was sent to subdue the Seminole Indians and in doing so invaded Spanish Florida; in capturing Spanish territory and in executing two British subjects for stirring up Indian trouble, he raised a diplomatic and political storm in which J. Q. Adams was his staunchest supporter. By virtue of his frontier origin, his expansionism, his exploits against the Indians and the British, and his obvious independence, Jackson was by now the hero of the West and South and, by association at least, the representative of the growing democratic spirit in those sections. Though for a time he disavowed presidential aspirations, friends and supporters began preparing for 1824; after a brief period as territorial governor of Florida in 1821 he retired to the "Hermitage" until his election to the Senate in 1823. At the end of the balloting in the next year's election he led the other three candidates for President; the contest went to the House, which chose J. Q. Adams, and when Henry Clay became secretary of state the Jackson group raised the cry of "corrupt bargain." Organizing and campaigning began immediately for 1828, however, and that year Jackson defeated Adams decisively. Almost from the beginning his administration was beset by controversy; objections to the much-exaggerated awarding of public offices as spoils were followed closely by the social ostracism of the wife of the secretary of war by other Cabinet wives, an affair which began the split between Jackson and Vice President Calhoun. In 1830 the protective tariff became a crucial issue and both men adopted clear and completely opposed positions; in 1832 South Carolina, with Calhoun's support, nullified the tariff. Jackson immediately and vehemently denounced the move and in March 1833 secured from Congress both the authority to use federal troops to insure the state's compliance with federal law and a reduction of the objectionable rates. South Carolina then withdrew its earlier proclamation but saved face by nullifying the Force Bill; the states' rights issue was thus postponed. Meanwhile Jackson had been re-elected over Henry Clay—and Calhoun replaced by Martin Van Buren—in a campaign based primarily on the issue of the Bank of the United States. The President had vetoed a rechartering bill earlier in the year and thereby reinforced his popularity; he was vindicated in the election and thereafter continued his war against the bank by withdrawing from it all deposits of federal money. By the time the bank's charter expired in 1836 the government's money had been distributed among several state banks; this action, combined with the policy begun the same year of demanding only gold or silver in payment for public land, led directly to a financial panic in 1837, after Jackson had been succeeded by Van Buren. When Jackson left office in March 1837, the general but disorganized movement, largely of Westerners and Southerners, that had originally elected him had been transformed into the Democratic Party; despite the fact that he had often had little sympathy for the movement, had in fact often allied himself with opposing interests, his name became firmly attached to it. He was in many ways more the accepted symbol than the living representative of "Jacksonian Democracy." He retired to the "Hermitage" and remained there in declining health until his death on June 8, 1845.

JACKSON, THOMAS JONATHAN (1824–1863), soldier. Born on January 21, 1824, in Clarksburg, Virginia (now West Virginia), Jackson was orphaned early in life and was cared for by relatives. Despite his very limited schooling he received an appointment to West Point in 1842 and graduated with a creditable academic record four years later. Commissioned a second lieutenant of artillery, he was immediately sent to join the Army in Mexico; he distinguished himself in several battles and had been brevetted a major by the time he returned to the United States in 1848. For three years he served at various posts, but in 1851 he accepted an appointment as professor of artillery tactics and natural philosophy at the Virginia Military Institute and resigned his commission. For the next ten years he lived quietly in Lexington, Virginia; he was neither popular nor particularly successful as a teacher, and he took no part in public affairs. With the outbreak of the Civil War in 1861, however, he was ordered to bring his cadet corps to Richmond; he was commissioned colonel and sent to fortify Harpers Ferry. In July, now a brigadier general, he was ordered to the field at Bull Run (Manassas), and there his stout resistance to the Northern advance earned him the nickname "Stonewall." In October Jackson was promoted to major general and a month later assumed command of the forces in the Shenandoah Valley; there, early in 1862, he began the famous Valley Campaign in which, by rapid movements of his forces, he tied up much greater numbers of Northern troops, prevented reinforcements being sent to McClellan's campaign against Richmond, and threatened Washington. In June he won successive victories at Cross Keys and Port Republic and the Northern invasion was checked. By this time Jackson was working closely with Lee and the two formed an apparently invincible team. In August Stonewall Jackson and his famed "foot-cavalry" executed an encircling movement and at the second battle of Bull Run again drove the Northern forces back to the Potomac. In October he was made lieutenant general and placed in command of one of Lee's two corps. In early May 1863 Jackson performed his last great service. Outnumbered by more than 2 to 1, Lee's forces were threatened at Chancellorsville; Jackson was sent in another encircling movement and took the enemy completely by surprise, rolling up Hooker's flank and forcing him to retreat. In the confusion of this twilight attack, however, Jackson was shot by his own men; he died eight days later on May 10, 1863.

JAMES, HENRY (1843–1916), author. Born in New York City on April 15, 1843, James was named for his father, a widely-known author, religious thinker, and conversationalist, and was the younger brother of William James, the philosopher and psychologist. His early life and education were unsettled; his father determined that the children should be given as wide a view of the world as possible and moved the family back and forth across the Atlantic while engaging a succession of tutors to provide formal education. In 1860 the family settled, more or less, in Newport, Rhode Island; two years later Henry began a brief period of study in the Harvard Law School, but literature soon claimed him and his first story was published anonymously in 1864. While writing criticism regularly for the *Nation* from 1865 to 1869, he was greatly encouraged to continue his work in fiction by William Dean Howells, who published his stories in the *Atlantic Monthly*. Until 1875 he oscillated between America and Europe, accumulating the experiences that found expression in his early international stories and novels and publishing in 1871 the first of these,

"A Passionate Pilgrim." In 1875 he finally chose Europe as his permanent home; at first he lived in Paris, where he was close to Turgenev and was a member of Flaubert's circle, but the following year he moved to London. During the next several years he concentrated in his writing on the contrast and conflict of America and Europe, the one young, rude, brash, naive, the other old, civilized, corrupt yet wise. The first novel of the period was *Roderick Hudson*, 1875; there followed, among others, *The American*, 1877, *The Europeans*, 1878, *Daisy Miller*, 1879, and perhaps the masterwork of the genre, *The Portrait of a Lady*, 1881. In 1881 he also published one of his very few novels with an exclusively American scene and cast of characters, *Washington Square*. The next two decades were an extended transitional period for James, during which international conflict ceased to be central in his work and he concentrated, with vast sensitivity and perception, on people as they developed morally and intellectually and as they formed relationships of various sorts with others. This period saw the publication of *The Siege of London*, 1883, *The Author of Beltraffio*, 1885, *The Bostonians*, 1886, *The Princess Casamassima*, 1886, *The Aspern Papers*, 1887, *The Real Thing and Other Tales*, 1893, *The Spoils of Poynton*, 1897, *What Maisie Knew*, 1897, "The Turn of the Screw," 1898, *The Awkward Age*, 1899, and *The Sacred Fount*, 1901, among many others. During the early 1890s he tried unsuccessfully to apply his writing to the theater, and despite his disappointment with failure, his subsequent work showed increasingly a concern for the dramatic, while the number of characters diminished in order to portray more vividly and analyze more deeply the tensions and forces of relationships. In addition to his fiction, James maintained all the while a steady flow of criticism, essays, and travel books, notable among which were *French Poets and Novelists*, 1878, *Hawthorne*, 1879, *A Little Tour in France*, 1885, *Partial Portraits*, which included his essay "The Art of Fiction," 1888, and

Essays in London, 1893. With the turn of the century he began his final period of fiction, represented by three large novels in which, through diverse characters and situations, he delved into the relation of the individual to society and developed an ethical framework upon which, in his view, depended both the rational growth of the individual and the maintenance of civilized society. The first of these books to be written was *The Ambassadors*, published in 1903; it was preceded in publication by *The Wings of the Dove*, 1902, and followed by *The Golden Bowl*, 1904, his last completed novel. In his remaining years he continued to write in his favorite non-fiction modes, publishing *English Hours*, 1905, and *Italian Hours*, 1909, along with several other books of criticism and essays; he returned briefly to the drama and late in life produced several autobiographical works. A trip to the United States in 1904–1905, during which for the first time he traveled the length and breadth of the country, resulted in his penetrating analysis of *The American Scene*, 1907. In 1915, prompted by his sympathy for England and its allies in the Great War and much dismayed by America's determined isolationism, he became an English citizen after 40 years' residence there. He died soon afterwards, on February 28, 1916.

JAMES, JESSE WOODSON (1847–1882), outlaw. Born near Centerville (now Kearney), Missouri, on September 5, 1847, Jesse grew up a farm boy and had little schooling. His father died when he was 4 and his mother twice remarried. The family, like many of the region's people, was openly sympathetic to the South, and during the Civil War their home was raided twice by Northern militiamen. At 15 Jesse joined the pro-Southern guerillas of Quantrill's Raiders. At the end of the war he surrendered with the others but was shot and in 1866 became a fugitive. He formed a gang with his brother Frank, the Younger brothers, and a few others, and embarked on a career of robbery that lasted 15 years. In July 1873

they opened up new possibilities by robbing a Rock Island train in Iowa. The most famous of their exploits, and possibly the least successful, was an attempt on a bank in Northfield, Minnesota, in September 1876; all of the band except Jesse and Frank were killed or captured. The brothers ceased their activities until 1879 when they resumed with a new gang. Until 1880 they enjoyed the sympathy and protection of a great number of people in and around their native region; in that year public sentiment shifted against them and concerted efforts began for their capture. Jesse had been living quietly in St. Joseph, Missouri, under the name Thomas Howard when, prompted by a large reward offered by the state's governor, Robert Ford, a member of his outlaw band, shot him in the back of the head on April 3, 1882. The legend of Jesse James, already begun during his lifetime, grew steadily after his death until he became one of America's genuine folk heroes, celebrated in ballad and story. Later that year Frank surrendered, was twice tried and acquitted, and retired to obscurity on his Missouri farm until his death in 1915.

JAMES, WILLIAM (1842–1910), psychologist and philosopher. Born in New York City on January 11, 1842, William was the son of Henry James, a noted religious thinker and brilliant conversationalist, and the elder brother of Henry James, the novelist. His early life and education were irregular for, prompted by the father's determination that the children develop as broadly cosmopolitan an outlook as possible, the family was almost constantly on the move between New York, New England, and various places in Europe, using private tutors and private schools as occasion allowed. By 1860 James had accumulated a basic liberal education and, choosing among his interests, began to study art under William Hunt; within a year he changed his mind and in 1861 entered the Lawrence Scientific School at Harvard. Three years later he enrolled in the Harvard Medical School. He interrupted his studies in 1865 to accompany Louis Agassiz on an exploring and collecting expedition to the Amazon; he returned in poor health and after a brief resumption of his studies sailed for Europe. He studied and sought in vain to restore his health for 18 months; he returned to Harvard late in 1868 and took his medical degree the following year. The next three years, during which he was virtually an invalid, were a crucial period; he continued to read widely and in the writings of Charles Renouvier, a French psychologist, he apparently found the intellectual strength to overcome his chronic morbidity and depression and to adopt free will as an active, operative principle. In 1872 he was appointed instructor in physiology at Harvard; by 1880 he had shifted to psychology, created the country's first experimental laboratory for psychological research, and been transferred to the department of philosophy. On an extended European visit in 1882–1883 James formed numerous close associations with leading psychologists and philosophers and began an active interest in parapsychological phenomena. During the 1880s his teaching at Harvard came more and more to be concerned with ethical and religious problems, and his interest in pure psychology ended with the publication of his monumental work of 12 years, *The Principles of Psychology*, in 1890. Both definitive and seminal, the work gained wide acceptance not only in scientific circles but, with its clear and vivid prose, also among the general public. In his subsequent teaching, lecturing, and writing, James went beyond his radically empiricist psychology, using it as a tool to explore philosophical questions. Nearly all of his books were collections of earlier articles or of lectures; thus, for example, *The Will to Believe and Other Essays in Popular Philosophy*, published in 1897, was actually begun in 1879. Similarly, his Gifford lectures at the University of Edinburgh in 1901 and 1902 were published as *The Varieties of Religious Experience*, 1902. In this book James achieved a reconciliation

of sorts between science and religion by investigating the claims of the latter from a standpoint of thoroughgoing empiricism and concluding that the weight of evidence lay in favor of the existence of dimensions of consciousness beyond the realm of everyday experience. The work remains a classic in its field. His Lowell lectures in Boston in 1906 were collected and published the next year as *Pragmatism: A New Name for Some Old Ways of Thinking*; the term he had borrowed from C. S. Peirce was thereafter firmly attached to his own philosophy. James's later works, many of which were directed to the controversy raised by *Pragmatism*, included *A Pluralistic Universe* and *The Meaning of Truth*, both 1909, and, posthumously, *Some Problems of Philosophy*, 1911, and *Essays in Radical Empiricism*, 1912. His teaching career at Harvard ended in 1907; he was increasingly beset by ill health, and shortly after returning from a trip to Europe to seek relief, he died in Chocorua, New Hampshire, on August 26, 1910.

JARVES, JAMES JACKSON (1818–1888), art critic and collector. Born in Boston on August 20, 1818, Jarves received his formal schooling in Boston at Chauncey Hall, but acquired the better part of his education by reading and by collecting and observing natural objects. His plans to attend Harvard were ended when impairment of his vision forced him to abandon his studies. He began traveling, first to California, then to Mexico and Central America, noting for future books the things he saw. He settled in Honolulu in 1838, and founded there the first newspaper in the Hawaiian (then the Sandwich) Islands, the *Polynesian*. Appointed in 1848 as special commissioner for the Hawaiian monarchy to make commercial treaties with the United States, France, and Great Britain, he traveled to Europe, and found the atmosphere there so pleasant, especially in Italy, that he established a permanent residence in Florence. He began to purchase paintings by the early Italian masters, and eventually developed a collection that in quantity and quality surpassed any in the United States. But it was not received warmly when shown in the United States in 1860. There were no offers for purchase, and although Jarves probably could have sold items individually, he was reluctant to do so, since he recognized the value of the collection as a whole for the study of early Christian art. Finally, in 1871, the paintings were sold at auction to the Yale Art School, the only bidder; the collection is today considered priceless. In 1881 he donated his Venetian glass to the Metropolitan Museum of Art in New York City, and in 1887 he sold his collection of rare Venetian laces and costumes and Renaissance fabrics. Although his personal fortune was spent on his collections, he accomplished his main purpose, to bring European art to America, though the value of his efforts was not recognized for a generation. Among his writings were *Scenes and Scenery in the Sandwich Islands*, 1843, *Scenes and Scenery in California*, 1844, *Parisian Sights*, 1852, *Italian Sights*, 1856, *Art Hints*, 1855, *Art Studies*, 1861, and *The Art Idea*, 1864. He died in Switzerland on June 28, 1888, and was buried in the English cemetary in Rome.

JAY, JOHN (1745–1829), public official, jurist, and diplomat. Born in New York City on December 12, 1745, Jay came of a wealthy, aristocratic family. After graduation from King's College (now Columbia University) in 1764, he began the study of law; he was awarded an M.A. by King's in 1767 and the next year admitted to the bar. For six years he practised law and prospered; then, in 1774, he was elected to the first Continental Congress. There, a staunch conservative and opposed to independence for the colonies, he drafted the *Address to the People of Great Britain*. In May 1776, still a delegate to Congress, he began serving also in the New York provincial congress and thus was absent from the signing of the Declaration of Independence; nonetheless, and despite his earlier opposition to the step, he supported it after the fact and drafted the resolutions whereby New York ratified independence. In 1777 he wrote the state's first constitution and shortly thereafter was elected its first chief justice, a position he held until December 1778. He returned then to Congress and was elected its president. In September 1779 he was appointed by Congress minister plenipotentiary to Spain and sent to Madrid to secure Spanish recognition and aid; the former request was refused flatly and the latter met with minimal response even after Congress, against Jay's own judgment, offered to retract all claims to navigation on the Mississippi River. In 1782 Jay joined the peace commission in Paris, where his insistence on a point of protocol resulted in the delay of peace negotiations for a year; meanwhile, he convinced John Adams and Benjamin Franklin that they should violate their instructions from Congress by entering into a preliminary agreement with Great Britain without informing France. Soon after the complicated maneuverings among the American states, Great Britain, France, and Spain were completed and the Treaty of Paris signed in 1783, Jay returned to New York, intending to resume his law practice. Instead, Congress had appointed him secretary for foreign affairs, and for six years he struggled against the narrow confines of this office and of national power generally. He strongly supported the Constitution and in New York contributed five essays to the *Federalist* as part of the campaign for ratification. When the new government was organized he was appointed the first chief justice of the Supreme Court, turning over his duties in foreign affairs to Secretary of State Thomas Jefferson. In his five years on the bench he was primarily responsible for organizing the Court and establishing its procedures. His most significant decision was in *Chisholm* v. *Georgia*, in which he ruled that a citizen of one state could sue another state in federal court; this opinion was almost immediately nullified by the passage of the 11th Amendment. In 1794, largely at Alexander Hamilton's behest, he was sent to England to arrange a treaty of commerce and seek redress for a number of American grievances; the resulting Jay's Treaty was roundly denounced at home and became a bitter partisan issue, for while it provided for British evacuation of the Northwest—an unfulfilled provision of the Treaty of Paris—and set up mixed claims commissions, it made no mention of England's violations of maritime law, particularly the impressment of American sailors. By averting possible war with England in this way, moreover, the treaty brought on a crisis in relations with France. The Federalists managed to effect ratification in the Senate by the barest possible margin. Returning to the United States in 1795, Jay found himself the elected governor of New York; he resigned from the Supreme Court and served in his new position for two terms. Upon leaving office in 1801 he retired to his farm near Bedford, New York, and lived there until his death on May 17, 1829.

JEFFERS, JOHN ROBINSON (1887–1962), poet and dramatist. Born in Pittsburgh on January 10, 1887, Jeffers was educated by his father, a classical scholar, and in a number of private schools. He studied for a year at the University of Western Pennsylvania (now Pittsburgh) and then, his family having moved to California, at Occidental College, graduating in 1905. Unsure of his vocation, he pursued graduate studies at the University of Southern California, at Zürich, and at the University of Washington as his interests shifted from English to medicine to forestry. A bequest from a distant relative in 1912 gave him financial security and he was able to devote himself to writing; after the outbreak of World War I disrupted plans to live in Europe, he and his wife settled amid the magnificent scenery of the California coast near Carmel. There he built with his own hands "Tor House," a house and tower of native granite, and there he lived for the rest of his life. His first important volume of verse, *Roan Stallion, Tamar, and Other Poems*, 1924, published, as were all his works, under his preferred name Robinson Jeffers, established his reputation as an original and deeply disturbing poet. In this and subsequent books, *The Women at Point Sur*, 1927, *Cawdor*, 1928, *Thurso's Landing*, 1932, *Give Your Heart to the Hawks*, 1933, *Solstice*, 1935, *Be Angry at the Sun*, 1941, and others, he developed a view of humanity that was profoundly pessimistic; accepting much of 20th-century science at face value, he constructed a cosmic scheme in which the smallness, transience, and meanness of humanity contrasted unfavorably with the brooding sea and mountains that surrounded him, and even those passed into insignificance before the eternal night and a strangely dark and impersonal pantheism. In 1946 his adaptation of Euripides' *Medea* was successfully produced in New York; other plays, *The Cretan Woman* and *The Tower Beyond Tragedy*, were also staged with some success. Later volumes included *The Double Axe*, 1948, *Hungerfield*, 1954, and *The Beginning and the End*, 1963. He remained at "Tor House," something of a recluse and traveling infrequently, until his death on January 20, 1962.

JEFFERSON, JOSEPH (1829–1905), actor. Born on February 20, 1829, in Philadelphia, the son and grandson of actors, Jefferson made his debut at age three in Kotzebue's *Pizarro*, and the following year supported Thomas Dartmouth Rice as a miniature "Jim Crow." His education came from travel and experience with troupes throughout the country. After his father's death he acted and managed theaters in the South. Arriving in New York in 1849, already a seasoned performer at the age of 20, he organized his own troupe, but enjoyed only a minor success. He toured Europe in 1856. With Laura Keene's celebrated company in New York after 1856, he achieved success in roles including Dr. Pangloss in *The Heir at Law*, Asa Trenchard in *Our American Cousin*, and Bob Acres in *The Rivals*. The years 1861–1864 were spent touring Australia. In 1859 he had adapted Washington Irving's "Rip Van Winkle" for the stage, with himself in the title role, but he did not achieve success in it until Irish playwright and actor Dion Boucicault revised the script. Jefferson's appearance in the new version in 1865 at the Adelphi Theater in London was a triumph. He became identified with the role, and it was conceded that no other actor could approach him in it. From then until the end of his 72-year career, "Rip" was the mainstay of his repertoire as the play was of the American theater. Succeeding Edwin Booth as president of the Players' Club in 1893, he delivered vivid lectures on acting, and wrote a perceptive *Autobiography*, 1889. He died in Palm Beach, Florida, on April 23, 1905.

JEFFERSON, THOMAS (1743–1826), public official, political leader, philosopher, and 3rd U.S. President. Born on April 13, 1743, on his father's plantation "Shadwell" in Goochland (now Albemarle) County on the western fringe of settlement in Virginia, Jefferson graduated from the College of William and Mary in 1762 and, after an unusually diligent and comprehensive study of law, was admitted to the bar five years later. He entered politics as a matter of course, advancing from county positions to the House of Burgesses in 1769. He served in that body until its dissolution in 1775; he early identified himself with the more radical faction, was a member of the committee of correspondence, and in 1774 wrote the officially rejected but nonetheless widely circulated and highly influential *Summary View of the Rights of British America*. In 1775 he was sent as a delegate to the Continental Congress. He was not an orator and confined his work to committees; his ability and literary gifts were acknowledged in his selection as a member of the committee charged to draft the Declaration of Independence and in the deference shown by the other committee members to his powers of composition; his draft, with a few changes, some of them significant, became the adopted text. In October of that year he returned to the Virginia legislature, by now the House of Delegates, and set about reorganizing the government and laws of the state on republican principles under its new constitution. Within ten years his proposals for the abolition of the slave trade and of the laws of entail and primogeniture, and for the adoption of complete freedom of religion, were adopted. In 1779 he was elected governor, but this first and a subsequent term were not notably successful; he had to bear responsibility for the events of the British invasion in 1781 and barely escaped capture himself. He retired to his home, Monticello, near Charlottesville, later that year. In 1783 he was returned to Congress and there, again in committee work, he made important contributions: he advocated a decimal monetary system and submitted a series of reports on the organization of government in the western territory, the proposals contained in which were almost without exception included in the later Northwest Ordinance of 1787. In 1784 he was sent to France to aid in the negotiation of commercial treaties and the following year succeeded Benjamin Franklin as minister to France. The publication in France in 1785 of his *Notes on the State of Virginia* greatly enhanced his already high reputation and extended it into the fields of science and general scholarship. During his years in Europe he traveled widely, gathering impressions and knowledge that were later useful in the United States. He kept closely in touch with developments at home and generally favored the adoption of the Constitution, though he was critical of its failure to include a Bill of Rights. He returned to Monticello late in 1789 and in March 1790 became the first secretary of state. The next three years were a period of difficulty and disappointment for him: strongly opposed to factionalism, he came reluctantly but necessarily to the leadership of a faction; convinced of the danger of monarchism in the opposing faction, he fought constantly and with but little success against the influence and interference of its leader, Alexander Hamilton. The philosophies of the two men, and of the parties of which they were the acknowledged if unofficial leaders, were best expressed in 1791 in their written opinions on the constitutionality of a national bank, in which they exemplified the strict- and loose-constructionist approaches to the Constitution. Jefferson resigned from the Cabinet at the end of 1793 but remained the leader of the Democratic-Republican Party; his retirement to Monticello ended with the presidential election of 1796 in which he ran second to John Adams, a Federalist, and thus became Vice President. He played little part in the opposition administration but when the Federalists forced the passage of the Alien and Sedition Laws in 1798, he drafted the Kentucky Resolutions of 1798—the similar Virginia Resolutions were the work of his close colleague James Madison—in which he developed the states' rights theory that the sovereignty delegated by the states to the federal government can be retracted when the latter oversteps its authority; that is, an act of the federal government may be nullified by a state on grounds of unconstitutionality. In the election of 1800 the Republican candidates for President, Jefferson and Aaron Burr, defeated the Federalists but were themselves tied in the electoral college; in the House of Representatives Jefferson was chosen and he was the first President to be inaugurated in Washington, D.C. There soon followed a controversy over federal appointments as, though his actions were greatly exaggerated by the Federalists, Jefferson first introduced something like a spoils system. His first administration was signalized, however, by the Louisiana Purchase, an action that, in the irony of practical affairs, violated Jefferson's political principles in having no constitutional authority behind it. Nonetheless, he demonstrated his freedom from doctrinaire policy by seizing the opportunity to capitalize on France's financial difficulties and to acquire a vast new territory for American expansion. Soon after his reelection in 1804 he was faced with the almost impos-

sible problem of maintaining neutrality in the war between England and France; determined to avoid war he resorted finally to the Embargo Act of 1807, which, though based on firm constitutional grounds, was again a great extension of federal power and was widely criticized. In 1809 he retired permanently to Monticello and remained there for the rest of his life. He continued active in his many fields of interest, however, particularly in the establishment of state-supported education in Virginia; after long and arduous efforts he secured the chartering of the University of Virginia in 1819. The organization, the design and architecture, and the curriculum were all his, and he supervised them closely. An accomplished architect, he designed the state capitol in addition to the buildings of the university and his own and other homes, and was instrumental in bringing about the classical revival in America. He continued his scholarly pursuits and was from 1797 to 1815 president of the American Philosophical Society. In 1813 he and John Adams, who was also in retirement, became reconciled and began a voluminous correspondence between Monticello and Quincy, Massachusetts; the experience and perspective that the two elder statesmen brought to bear on the problems and future of their country were unmatched, and the result was one of the most remarkable and extensive exchanges of views ever recorded. On July 4, 1826, the 50th anniversary of the Declaration of Independence, both men died. At his own direction, Jefferson's tombstone recorded the three achievements that he himself valued most highly: ". . . author of the Declaration of American Independence, of the statute of Virginia for religious freedom, and father of the University of Virginia."

JENNEY, WILLIAM LE BARON (1832–1907), engineer and architect. Born on September 25, 1832, in Fairhaven, Massachusetts, Jenney attended the Phillips Academy in Andover, Massachusetts, Harvard's Lawrence Scientific School, and the École Centrale des Arts et

Manufactures in Paris, graduating in 1856. Settling in New Orleans, he became an engineer with the Tehuantepec Railroad Company. But he returned to Paris to further his studies in architecture, remaining from 1859 to 1861. Returning to the United States, he enlisted in the Union Army and served capably as an engineer with Grant and Sherman, having earned the rank of major by 1866, when he resigned. He worked in Pennsylvania as an engineer until 1868. Then he established an architectural and engineering firm in Chicago that, with the addition of two partners, became Jenney, Mundie, and Jensen. In his early building, mainly of office structures, he strove to get maximum light and to make hallways and entrances as spacious and attractive as possible. His concepts were developed in *Principles and Practice of Architecture*, which he published in 1869. With the Home Insurance Company building, his major contribution, built in 1884–1885, he inaugurated "skeletal" construction, an internal framework of iron and steel beams that supported the walls and roof of the building and determined its outer form. It was the first structure of its kind to use steel as a building material, and also introduced the best plumbing system yet developed in an office building of its size. He went on to design the Leiter building in 1889–1890, the Fair store in 1890–1891, and other structures in Chicago, further developing the steel skeletal construction. He was later honored by the Bessemer Steamship Company of New York for his service to the steel industry by having one of their ships named after him. In 1905 he retired and moved to Los Angeles, where he died on June 15, 1907.

JEWETT, SARAH ORNE (1849–1909), author. Born on September 3, 1849, in the village of South Berwick, Maine, Miss Jewett was often taken by her father, a physician, on visits to the fishermen and farmers of the area, developing thereby an appreciation of their way of life and of the sights and sounds of her surround-ings. These experiences, and reading in her family's ample library, formed the bulk of her education; although she also attended the Berwick Academy, she considered this insignificant compared to the learning she gained on her own. During her childhood she began to write of the perishing farms and neglected, shipless harbors around her. She published her first story, "The Shipwrecked Buttons," in a children's magazine in 1869. Numerous later sketches of a New England town, "Deephaven," that resembled South Berwick, were published by the *Atlantic Monthly* and were collected in *Deephaven*, 1877, her first major book. There followed *A Country Doctor*, 1884, *A Marsh Island*, 1885, *A White Heron*, 1886, *A Native of Winby*, 1893, and other novels and collections of stories, children's books, and vignettes published in *Century* and *Harper's*, as well as in the *Atlantic*. Her best novel, *The Country of the Pointed Firs*, 1896, portrayed, like *Deephaven*, the isolation, unique humor, and loneliness of a declining seaport town. The portrayal of this provincial and rapidly disappearing society made her an important local color novelist, and in this she was a profound influence on Willa Cather. The best of her writing resembled 19th-century French fiction, especially that of Flaubert, whom she greatly admired, in its naturalism, precision, and compactness. She frequently visited Boston and other large cities, but lived and wrote in the same house in which she was born. Her writing career ended after a disabling accident in 1902. She died in South Berwick on June 24, 1909. Her collected poems were published posthumously as *Verses*, 1916.

JOHNSON, ANDREW (1808–1875), public official and 17th U.S. President. Born in Raleigh, North Carolina, on December 29, 1808, Johnson received no formal education as a child and was early apprenticed to a tailor. In 1826 he moved with his mother and stepfather to Tennessee and settled at length in Greeneville, opening his own tailor shop. He had by this time taught himself to read; his wife, whom he married the following year, helped him to further his education. Becoming interested in politics, he identified himself with the cause of workingmen and was elected three times alderman and once mayor of Greeneville; he was elected to the state legislature in 1835 and 1839, to the state senate in 1841, and to Congress in 1843, where he remained for ten years. In 1853, gerrymandered out of his district by Tennessee's Whig legislature, he ran successfully for governor and was re-elected in 1855. During all these years he supported a number of democratic reforms, governmental economy, education, and, breaking here with his party, a homestead program for Western lands. In 1857 he was elected to the Senate where he voted and spoke as an orthodox Southern Democrat until his sectional interests were overridden by his devotion to the Union; he opposed secession and campaigned against it in his own state, and when Tennessee finally broke away in June 1861 he alone among Southern senators remained in his seat and refused to join the Confederacy. This action was hailed throughout the North and made Johnson a major political figure. In 1862 Lincoln appointed him military governor of Tennessee, and in the face of strong opposition he managed to restore civil government to the state before the Civil War ended. In 1864 he was the obvious choice for the vice-presidential nomination of Lincoln's coalition National Union Party; he was duly elected and on April 15, 1865, succeeded the assassinated Lincoln as President. The task before him was that of reconstructing the defeated Southern states, and in this he wished to follow the policy of moderation that had been outlined by Lincoln and that he himself had applied in Tennessee. The Radical Republicans in Congress, released from the restraint of Lincoln's power and prestige, began formulating their own program. During 1865 Johnson oversaw the reestablishment of civil government in the South; secession was formally retracted, slavery abolished, and the 13th

Amendment ratified in all but one of the former Confederate states. The issue of suffrage he left to state determination. In December Congress met and, under Radical leadership, began dismantling the President's program and substituting its own; the Radical strength in both houses, enough to override any presidential veto, had, by late 1866 and in spite of Johnson's plea for moderation during that year's congressional elections, completely eclipsed executive authority. Radical Reconstruction began early in 1867; Johnson was faithful in administering laws that he was powerless to keep from the books, though he employed the narrowest possible interpretation of them in doing so. On March 2, 1867, the date of the first Reconstruction Act, Congress also passed the Tenure of Office Act, forbidding the President to dismiss any office holder appointed with the Senate's advice and consent before obtaining the same legislative concurrence. Convinced of the act's unconstitutionality, and seeking to test it in the courts, Johnson asked for the resignation of Secretary of War Edwin M. Stanton, long a secret collaborator with congressional Radicals; Stanton refused and Johnson suspended him, appointing Gen. U. S. Grant to serve in his place. In January 1868, Congress restored Stanton, and in February Johnson dismissed him; on February 25th the President was formally impeached for high crimes and misdemeanors. The trial began on March 5th, and though the eleven articles of impeachment dealt almost exclusively with the Tenure of Office Act, masses of irrelevant and even fraudulent charges and testimony turned the trial into a mockery—some even wished to implicate Johnson in the murder of Lincoln. Finally, on May 16th and 26th, votes were taken on three of the articles, and seven Republicans joined the pro-Johnson men in acquitting the President by a single vote. The other charges were then dropped. Embittered, Johnson left office in March 1869 and returned to Tennessee. After several unsuccessful attempts, he achieved a vindication of sorts with his election to the Senate in 1875; but less than five months after taking his seat he died, on July 31, 1875.

JOHNSON, HIRAM WARREN (1866–1945), public official. Born in Sacramento, California, on September 2, 1866, Johnson attended the University of California through the junior year, until he was 20. In 1888 he was admitted to the California bar and began to practise law with his father, Grove Johnson, and his brother. He began a record of opposition to the political machine over which his father presided by waging a vigorous campaign for a reform mayor. In 1902 he and his brother moved their practice to San Francisco, but he soon dissolved the partnership and became a prominent trial attorney. In 1906 he joined the prosecution in bribery cases connecting major city officials in the Union Labor Party with the city's public utility corporations. In 1910, on a reform program, he was elected governor of California and won reelection in 1914. His administration was one of the most progressive in the nation and was successful in ending the domination of the state government by the Southern Pacific Railroad, for which his father was an attorney. In 1912 he ran for the vice presidency on the ticket of the National Progressive Party, which with presidential candidate Theodore Roosevelt he had helped to organize, calling for a change in party machinery and for aggressive social legislation. Elected to the Senate in 1917, he earned a reputation for implacable isolationism. He opposed U.S. entry into World War I, the League of Nations, the World Court, and such preparedness measures as conscription and Lend-Lease. He supported the neutrality acts of the 1930s and later advocated a federal ban on loans to governments in default of their war debts. He also resisted the formation of the United Nations. Elected to a fifth Senate term in 1940, he died in Bethesda, Maryland, on August 6, 1945.

JOHNSON, JAMES WELDON (1871–1938), author, diplomat, reformer, and anthologist. Born in Jacksonville, Florida, on June 17, 1871, Johnson attended Atlanta University for both his secondary and college education, there being no high school for Negroes in Jacksonville. He took his B.A. in 1894 and returned to his home city; he became principal of a Negro school there and organized a program of secondary education. At the same time he studied law and was admitted to the bar in 1897. With his brother John Rosamond Johnson, a talented composer, he began to write songs and soon produced "Lift Every Voice and Sing," often called the Negro national anthem. In 1901 the brothers moved to New York City and for several years were successful songwriters for Broadway. Johnson continued his studies during this time and in 1904 was awarded an M.A. from Atlanta University. He later studied also at Columbia University. As a result of his efforts for the Republican campaign in 1904, he was appointed by President Theodore Roosevelt consul to Puerto Cabello, Venezuela, in 1906; in 1909 he assumed the consulate in Corinto, Nicaragua, and served there through that country's revolution until 1914. In 1912 he published anonymously a novel, *Autobiography of an Ex-Colored Man*; with the end of his diplomatic career he became editor of the *New York Age* and during his ten-year association with this newspaper continued his literary career with *Fifty Years and Other Poems*, 1917. In 1916 he joined the National Association for the Advancement of Colored People as a field secretary and was highly effective in organizing new branches of the association throughout the country; from 1920 until his resignation in 1930 he was its executive secretary. He was one of the leading spokesmen and interpreters of the cultural movement of the 1920s known as the "Harlem Renaissance." In 1922 he published his *Book of American Negro Poetry*, and in 1925 and 1926 two collections with the same title, *Book of American Negro Spirituals*; his prefatory and critical essays in these volumes were intelligent and influential appraisals of Negro contributions to American culture. In 1927 he published *God's Trombones*, a book of seven

Negro folk sermons in verse. Johnson's later works include *Black Manhattan*, 1930, an informal history; *Saint Peter Relates an Incident of the Resurrection Day*, 1930, a verse satire on racial prejudice; and *Along This Way*, 1933, his distinguished and valuable autobiography. From 1932 until his death he was professor of creative literature at Fisk University and from 1934 was a regular visiting professor at New York University. He died in an automobile accident on June 26, 1938.

JOHNSON, JOHN ARTHUR (1878–1946), boxer. Born in Galveston, Texas, on March 31, 1878, Jack Johnson learned to box at the Galveston Athletic Club. In 1901 he was jailed briefly for fighting Joe Choynski and in his cell learned from the latter much of the skill that would later make him the craftiest boxer of his time. From 1902 to 1908 he fought all over the country, losing only three bouts in that time. After two years of trying he finally broke the color-line in boxing by persuading heavyweight champion Tommy Burns to accept his challenge. On Christmas Day, 1908, in Sydney, Australia, Johnson knocked out Burns, becoming the first Negro to win the title. The public outcry that followed became a call for a "white hope" to retrieve the title; James J. Jeffries, who had earlier quit boxing with an undefeated record, was coaxed out of retirement to meet Johnson. On July 4, 1910, in Reno, Nevada, the "Galveston Giant" ended all dispute with a decisive victory. His record purse of $120,000 was the beginning of the small fortune that he amassed in the next few years and that he almost as quickly lost in ostentatiously lavish living. The already shaken white boxing public was further alienated by his marriage to a white woman. In 1912 he was convicted of violating the Mann Act and, while free on bond, he fled to Canada and then to Europe. There he continued to fight and to live in kingly fashion. In 1915 he traveled to Havana, Cuba, to meet Jess Willard; in the 26th round of their title bout he lost the heavyweight crown (he later claimed to have thrown the fight). His wealth dissipated, he returned to the United States in 1920, surrendered himself, and served out his one-year sentence. After his release he had a few more fights and made numerous personal appearances at carnivals and in vaudeville theaters. He died in Raleigh, North Carolina, on June 10, 1946, following an automobile accident.

JOHNSON, LYNDON BAINES (1908–   ), public official and 36th U.S. President. Born on a farm near Stonewall, Texas, on August 27, 1908, Johnson grew up there and in Johnson City (named for his grandfather). For three years after graduating from high school he worked at odd jobs at home and for a time in California; in 1927 he entered Southwest Texas State Teachers College and graduated in 1930. He taught high school in Houston for a year and then accepted an invitation to accompany a Texas congressman to Washington. In 1935 he was appointed Texas director of the National Youth Administration, a New Deal agency, and two years later, running as a New Dealer, he was elected to Congress. For 11 years he faithfully represented his district, remaining relatively obscure but gaining valuable experience and guidance from his fellow Texan, Sam Rayburn. Early in World War II he served for a few months with the Navy in the Pacific but returned to Washington when President Roosevelt recalled all legislators from the armed forces. In 1948, after a Democratic primary runoff election in which he won by 87 out of nearly a million votes, Johnson was elected to the Senate. His progress in that body was rapid; he became Democratic whip in 1951 and the party's Senate leader in 1953. Then and as majority leader after 1955 he demonstrated a mastery of the legislative process and of the problems of party discipline; though his policies of constructive cooperation with and only muted criticism of the Eisenhower administration were debated within the party, the technical brilliance of his leadership was universally conceded. He was primarily responsible for securing passage of the civil rights bills of 1957 and 1960 and supported extensions of welfare programs. In

1960 he mounted a strong campaign to win the Democratic presidential nomination; when John F. Kennedy was instead chosen, the nation was astonished by the choice of Johnson as Kennedy's running mate. He accepted and was later credited with attracting enough Southern and Western support to enable the ticket to win a slim victory over Republican Richard Nixon. For the next two and a half years Johnson, though seeming at times out of place in the Kennedy group, dutifully filled the frustrating office of Vice President. Then, on November 22, 1963, Kennedy was assassinated in Dallas and Johnson was promptly sworn in as President. He quickly took the initiative and secured from Congress passage of civil rights and other legislation earlier proposed by Kennedy. In August 1964, on the basis of a report, later shown to be highly dubious, of an attack by North Vietnamese forces on Navy ships in the Gulf of Tonkin, he ordered retaliatory air and sea action against that country and obtained from Congress the "Gulf of Tonkin resolution" permitting him discretionary powers to respond with force to further provocations. Soon after his reelection in 1964, when he defeated Sen. Barry Goldwater by the largest popular margin in history, international affairs began to dominate the administration's attention and to divert both time and money from Johnson's campaign proposals to create the "Great Society" at home. In April 1965 several thousand troops were dispatched to the Dominican Republic to meet the much exaggerated danger of a Communist takeover in that country. Soon thereafter, with the Tonkin resolution as authority, the President ordered the beginning of a rapid buildup of U.S. forces in South Vietnam to prevent the defeat of the pro-Western regime by Northern Communists. Intensive bombing of the North was continued while the troop level in the South grew to more than half a million. Hopes for a quick victory dimmed as the war dragged on through 1966 and 1967, and at home opposition to the administration's policy grew apace.

Johnson's popularity ebbed seriously and in March 1968, in the New Hampshire Democratic presidential primary, he outpolled challenging Sen. Eugene McCarthy by a margin so slim as to constitute a defeat for an incumbent. On March 31st he addressed the nation, announcing a reduction of the highly controversial bombing of North Vietnam and, in a move that stunned the nation, declared that he would neither seek nor accept renomination, but utilize the remainder of his term in a non-partisan search for peace. He did not, however, remain aloof from politics; his influence brought the Democratic nomination to his Vice President, Hubert Humphrey, at the tragically strife-ridden convention in Chicago in August. In January 1969 he retired to Johnson City, Texas, to work on his memoirs and to aid in assembling the documents of his administration for the Johnson library at the University of Texas.

JOHNSON, REVERDY (1796 – 1876), lawyer, public official, and diplomat. Born on May 21, 1796, in Annapolis, Maryland, Johnson graduated from St. John's College in 1811 and five years later was admitted to the bar. Commencing his practice in Upper Marlboro in 1816, he served that year and the next as deputy attorney general of Maryland; in 1817 he moved to Baltimore and in 1821 was elected as a Whig to the state senate. He was reelected in 1826 but resigned two years later to devote more time to his law practice. As a lawyer, Johnson became nationally prominent; he was a leading expert on constitutional law and appeared in a number of important cases before the Supreme Court, including *Brown* v. *Maryland* in 1827, the Wheeling Bridge cases in 1852 and 1856, *Seymour* v. *McCormick* in 1854, and, for the defense, *Dred Scott* v. *Sanford* in 1857. In 1854 he was elected to the Senate and was a generally regular Whig; he served until 1849 when President Zachary Taylor appointed him attorney general. He joined the mass resignation of the Cabinet following Taylor's death in 1850. He soon allied himself with the Democratic Party and in 1860 and 1861 was again in the Maryland legislature, where he led the fight to keep Maryland in the Union. In 1862 he was sent by President Lincoln to investigate the complaints against the military governor of New Orleans and in 1863, upon his return, he again entered the Senate. During his five years in that body he exhibited so conciliatory and mediatory an approach to vital issues that he was known as "the trimmer." He was privately moderate and publicly radical on Reconstruction; he opposed Negro suffrage but voted for the 14th Amendment; he sought a quick end to military occupation of the South but later voted for the bill that organized military government by district there. He voted for acquittal in the impeachment trial of Andrew Johnson. In 1868 he resigned from the Senate to succeed Charles Francis Adams as minister to Great Britain and in his year of service in this position performed creditably. In 1869 he returned to his Maryland practice; he pleaded for the defense in a number of loyalty cases and won an acquittal in *U.S.* v. *Cruikshank*, a landmark case that established a narrow construction of the 1870 Enforcement Act. He died on February 10, 1876.

JOHNSON, RICHARD MENTOR (1780–1850), lawyer, soldier, and public official. Born in Beargrass, an early settlement on the site of present-day Louisville, Kentucky, in 1780, Johnson received little education, but he studied law under professors at Transylvania University and was admitted to the bar in 1802. In 1804 he was elected to the state legislature and served there until he entered Congress in 1807, to which he was reelected as a Democrat five successive times. With the outbreak of the War of 1812 he became colonel of a Kentucky regiment of mounted riflemen; serving under General William Henry Harrison, he performed gallantly at the Battle of the Thames in 1813, sustaining serious wounds and reputedly killing Tecumseh. He returned to his seat in Congress as soon as he re-

covered and in 1818 was honored by a congressional resolution and ceremonial sword. The following year he retired from Congress, was elected to the Kentucky legislature and subsequently by that body to the Senate, where he served for ten years. He was a leading advocate of the abolition of imprisonment for debt, and he kept up a campaign to this end until the Senate approved his bill in 1832. He later added to his national reputation by his authorship in 1829 of a committee report on religious freedom occasioned by a heated public controversy over the propriety of operating post offices on Sunday. He was defeated for reelection in 1829 but was elected instead to the House of Representatives. He was a thoroughly regular Democrat and an even more regular Jacksonian; he was a close and trusted assistant to the President and in 1836 was hand-picked by the latter to be Van Buren's Vice President. The selection was ratified by the party but in the election, none of the four candidates for Vice President received a majority of the electoral vote. In the only such occasion in U.S. history, Johnson was chosen for the post by the Senate. His four year term was uneventful, but he became estranged from party leaders and his candidacy for renomination in 1840 was repudiated when the party refused to nominate anyone for Vice President. He returned to Kentucky, served again for a brief time in the legislature, and died on November 19, 1850.

JOHNSON, WALTER PERRY (1887–1946), baseball player. Born on November 6, 1887, in Humboldt, Kansas, Johnson drifted to the West Coast when he was 18 and was soon offered a contract to play baseball with a team in Tacoma, Washington. For some reason he did not accept, but in 1907 he signed with the Washington Senators, of the American League. During the next 21 years, a record-length service with a single major league team, he pitched 802 games, won 414, and amassed over 40 other records; he recorded 113 shutouts (in 1908 pitching 3 in 4 days) and 3,497 strikeouts, and pitched a total of 5,923 innings. At one point he pitched 56 consecutive scoreless innings; in 1913 he won 36 games while losing only 7. His 414 victories—the second highest total ever achieved by a pitcher and the highest of any pitcher in this century—were the more remarkable for having been gained for a perennial second division team. His fastball was the principal weapon in his arsenal and it was considered to be the fastest of all time, earning him the nickname "Big Train." In 1924 he was voted the American League's most valuable player. After his retirement from playing in 1927 he managed the Senators from 1929 to 1932 and the Cleveland Indians from 1933 to 1935. In 1936 he was one of the first five men chosen for membership in the Baseball Hall of Fame in Cooperstown, New York. Johnson served for a time as president of the Association of Professional Baseball Players and appeared on radio as a sports broadcaster. He later became prominent in Republican politics in Maryland and in 1940 ran unsuccessfully for Congress. He died in Washington, D.C., on December 10, 1946.

JOHNSTON, JOSEPH EGGLESTON (1807–1891), soldier. Born near Farmville, Virginia, on February 3, 1807, Johnston entered West Point in the same class as Robert E. Lee and graduated in 1829. For eight years he served as an artillery officer, seeing action in the Seminole War, and then resigned in 1837 to become a civil engineer. A year later Indian troubles in Florida brought him back into the Army as a lieutenant in the topographical engineers. He performed with distinction during the Mexican War and was brevetted colonel; by 1860 he had attained the rank of brigadier general and was quartermaster general of the Army. He resigned his commission when Virginia seceded from the Union and offered his services to his native state. He was named brigadier general of the Confederate forces and placed in command of the Army of the Shenandoah. In July 1861 he evaded the federal force that was intended to tie him down at Harpers Ferry and joined Beauregard at the first battle of Bull Run (Manassas); he was the ranking officer at this first major Confederate victory and was subsequently promoted to general. The next spring he was charged with opposing McClellan's drive on Richmond from the Yorktown peninsula. Johnston withdrew toward Richmond as McClellan consolidated his position, fighting a rearguard action at Williamsburg and then making a poorly coordinated attack at Seven Pines (Fair Oaks) during which he was badly wounded. Upon his recovery in November 1862 he was sent west to direct the Tennessee and Mississippi forces. In May 1863 he took personal command as Grant threatened Vicksburg; his evacuation order was countermanded by Jefferson Davis and Johnston, cut off from the city, could only watch as Vicksburg surrendered in July. In December he took command of the Army of Tennessee; too weak to move northward, the army entrenched itself near Dalton, Georgia, awaiting attack by Sherman's forces from the north. Sherman preferred to maneuver and Johnston found himself, outnumbered and outflanked, forced to retreat slowly towards Atlanta. Only one battle stood out from the constant skirmishing and in that, at Kenesaw Mountain, Johnston was briefly victorious. In July 1864, with his back to Atlanta, he was relieved of his command. In February 1865 Lee restored him with orders to oppose Sherman's march northward through the Carolinas. After two months of maneuvers and minor engagements he was forced to surrender to Sherman on April 26 at Durham Station, North Carolina. In the years following he engaged in the insurance business in Savannah and in 1878 was elected to a term in Congress. He remained in Washington, D.C., thereafter and in 1885 was appointed railroad commissioner by President Cleveland. He died on March 21, 1891.

JOLSON, AL (1886–1950), entertainer. Born on May 26, 1886, in Srednick, Russia, Asa Yoelson was the son of a Jewish cantor. He arrived in the United States at seven and grew up in Washington, D.C., where he made his stage debut. He was in *The Children of the Ghetto* in New York's Herald Square Theater in 1899, and traveled in vaudeville and circuses, performing for a time with Jolson, Palmer, and Jolson, composed of himself, a friend, and his brother. In Brooklyn about 1909 he first sang in black-face, thereafter a trademark. In that year he signed with Lew Dockstader's minstrel company and, moving rapidly to phenomenal success as a singer and entertainer, he appeared in the musical comedies *La Belle Paree*, 1911, and *Honeymoon Express*, 1913. Some of his greatest performing triumphs were scored with songs introduced in Lee Shubert's New York Winter Garden shows, among them *Sinbad*, 1918, *Bombo*, 1921, *Big Boy*, 1925, and *Artists and Models*, 1926. By 1921 he was considered the country's top entertainer and was one of few stars to have a theater named in his honor. His motion picture debut was in *The Jazz Singer*, 1927, the first major talking picture. He also appeared in *The Singing Fool*, 1928, *Say It With Songs*, 1929, and other movies, and sang the sound tracks for two screen accounts of his life, *The Jolson Story*, 1946, and *Jolson Sings Again*, 1949. In these were featured his famous standards, including "You Made Me Love You," "Waiting for the Robert E. Lee," "I Want a Girl Just Like the Girl That Married Dear Old Dad," "Liza," "April Showers," "Rock-a-Bye Your Baby With a Dixie Melody," "Swanee," and "My Mammy." He collaborated on writing many of his hits, including "Back in Your Own Back Yard," "California Here I Come," "Keep Smiling at Trouble," "Me and My Shadow," "Sonny Boy," "There's a Rainbow 'Round My Shoulder," "Yoo Hoo," and "You Ain't Heard Nothin' Yet," the last inspired by his favorite remark to his audiences. He sang on every war front during World War II, and had just returned to San Francisco after visiting the troops in Korea when he died, on October 23, 1950.

JONES, JOHN PAUL (1747–1792), sailor and naval officer. Born in Kirkcudbrightshire in southwestern Scotland on July 6, 1747, John Paul (for change of name, see below) received little schooling and at the age of 12 was apprenticed to a merchant shipper. He sailed as a cabin boy to Fredericksburg, Virginia, and there visited his elder brother, a tailor. In 1766 his apprenticeship ended when his master's business failed and for two years he engaged in the slave trade. By 1769 he had his own command, the merchant ship *John*; the following year he flogged the ship's carpenter, who then shipped on another vessel and soon died, and in Scotland in November Paul was arrested for murder. He was eventually cleared, but in 1773, again commanding a ship in the West Indian trade, he killed the leader of a mutiny and was advised to flee. He returned to Fredericksburg and added "Jones" at the end of his name. With the outbreak of hostilities between Great Britain and the American colonies he traveled to Philadelphia and in December 1775 was commissioned senior lieutenant of the Continental Navy. Assigned to the *Alfred*, he raised the first Grand Union flag and sailed with the small fleet under Esek Hopkins to the Bahamas; his knowledge of the islands aided greatly in the capture of a large quantity of ordnance there and he soon was given command of the sloop *Providence*. He was commissioned captain in August 1776 and in a six-week cruise captured eight vessels and destroyed eight more. In October he took over the *Alfred* and returned from another highly successful cruise in December. He found himself barred from promotion, largely because of intra-service politics and jealousy; he was promised command of a frigate, however, in recognition of his services. In November 1777 he sailed the *Ranger* to France to receive the frigate *Indien* from its French builders, only to have politics interfere again when the *Indien* was sold to France instead. From February to May 1778 he sailed the *Ranger* around the British Isles, made two partially successful shore raids, and captured a British naval sloop. He saw no further action until August 1779, when he set sail in command of a refitted merchant ship that he renamed *Bonhomme Richard* in honor of Benjamin Franklin, creator of *Poor Richard*. Again he sailed around the British Isles and in September came upon the Baltic trading fleet and its naval escorts, *Countess of Scarborough* and *Serapis*. Jones engaged the latter, though heavily outgunned and outmanned, and in three and a half hours of one of the fiercest and bloodiest naval battles on record simply wore down the enemy with his blank refusal to give up; at length the *Serapis* surrendered and Jones transferred his crew to the British ship, the *Bonhomme Richard* sinking two days later. From October 1779 to April 1780 he cruised aboard the *Alliance*; in the latter month he returned to Paris and was lionized. Louis XVI presented him with a sword and made him, with the permission of Congress, a chevalier of France. In December, capitalizing on his great fame, he borrowed the French ship *Ariel* and returned to America. In 1781, by way of thanks, Congress appointed him to command the huge *America*; delays in construction were followed by the decision to give the ship to France instead, and Jones's services to the Revolution were over. In 1783 he was sent to France to negotiate payment on captured prize ships held by France, and in 1788 he performed a similar service in Denmark. On his last visit to America in 1787 Congress honored him with the only gold medal given to a Continental naval officer. In 1788 he accepted a commission from Empress Catherine as rear admiral of the Russian Navy; his services were valuable in the war with Turkey, but he was intrigued against and finally dismissed in 1789. He retired to Paris and remained there in declining health until his death on July 18, 1792. His unmarked grave lay undiscovered for over a century, but in 1905 his supposed remains were returned to America by an escort of U.S. naval vessels and installed in a crypt in the chapel of the Naval Academy in Annapolis, Maryland.

JONES, LEROI (1934–), poet and playwright. Born on October 7, 1934, in Newark, New Jersey, the son of a postman, Jones attended Rutgers and graduated from Howard University in Washington, D.C. in 1954, doing further study in German literature at Columbia and in philosophy at the New School for Social Research. He served in the Air Force, visiting Puerto Rico, Europe, Africa, and the Middle East, and taught at the New School for Social Research. His first book was published in 1961: *Preface to a Twenty-Volume Suicide Note*, a collection of poems written after 1957 in a highly personal, erudite manner that among other things seemed to identify a Negro movement in the arts. He showed contempt for white society and expressed the revolutionary conception of the black artist as one who was called upon to expose a corrupt society and destroy it. His play *The Dutchman*, 1964, won the Obie Award as the best American play produced off-Broadway in the 1963–1964 season. It was released in a film version in 1967. Notable among his other plays were *The Toilet* and *The Slave*, which won second prize in drama at the 1966 first World Festival of Negro Arts in Dakar, Senegal, West Africa. Both plays were produced off-Broadway in 1964. His autobiographical novel, *The System of Dante's Hell*, appeared in 1965, a collection of *Tales* in 1967, and the nonfiction works *Blues People: Negro Music in White America*, in 1963, and *Home: Social Essays* in 1966. His works were published in *Poetry*, the *Nation*, the *Evergreen Review*, *Saturday Review*, and *Esquire*, and he wrote articles on jazz for *Downbeat*, *Metronome*, and the *Jazz Review*.

JONES, ROBERT TYRE, JR., (1902–), golfer. Born in Atlanta, Georgia, on March 17, 1902, Bobby Jones began to play golf during his childhood. He won a junior tournament when he was only 9, and at 14 he advanced as far as the third round of the 1916 U.S. National Amateur tournament. While pursuing his education—he graduated from the Georgia

School of Technology in 1922, took a second degree in English literature from Harvard in 1924, and studied law at Emory University in 1926–1927—he became one of the most idolized of sports heroes of the 1920s, in so doing also firmly establishing the popularity of golf in America. At the U.S. Open in 1923 he won his first major tournament; he subsequently won the Open in 1926 and 1929, the U.S. Amateur in 1924, 1925, 1927, and 1928, and the British Open in 1926 and 1927. In 1930 he capped his career with the unprecedented and probably never to be equaled feat of winning the "Grand Slam," the Open and Amateur tournaments in both the United States and Great Britain. He won in all a record total of 13 major championships. In 1922, 1924, 1926. 1928, and 1930 he was a member of the U.S. Walker Cup team. Following the 1930 season he made a series of golf instructional films, thus relinquishing his amateur standing, and with no further heights to reach he retired from the game. Having been admitted to the Georgia bar in 1928, he opened a law practice in Atlanta and in Augusta helped establish the Augusta National Golf Club. In 1934 he founded there the annual Masters Tournament, which became one of the most prestigious in the country. Confined to a wheelchair after suffering a spinal injury in 1948, he continued to pursue various business interests from his Atlanta home. In 1958 he became the first American since Benjamin Franklin to be honored with the freedom of the burgh of St. Andrews, Scotland, site of the world's most famous golf course.

JORDAN, DAVID STARR (1851–1931), naturalist, educator, and philosopher. Born near Gainesville, New York, on January 19, 1851, Jordan received his early schooling in local institutions while developing at an early age a deep interest in botany. In 1869 he entered Cornell University; his knowledge in his chosen field was already so extensive that in his junior year he was appointed to an instructorship. He

graduated with an M.S. in 1872 and in the next two years taught at small colleges in Illinois and Wisconsin; in 1874 he began a year of teaching high school in Indianapolis during which he also earned an M.D. from the Indiana Medical College. The next year he joined the faculty of Northwestern Christian University (now Butler University), where he remained for four years. In 1876 he published the first of many editions of his influential *Manual of the Vertebrates of the Northern United States*. He became head of the department of natural sciences at Indiana University in 1879 and six years later was its president; to his well-established reputation as a biologist was now added an increasing respect for his administrative talents, and the result was a call to become first president of Stanford University in 1891. He held this post until 1913, becoming in that year chancellor of the university and in 1916 chancellor emeritus. Despite the burdens of organizing and stabilizing the new and sometimes shaky institution, Jordan maintained his intellectual pursuits that were now leading him into more philosophical questions. While he remained one of the nation's leading biologists—he made numerous reports to the government on fish and fisheries and was the acknowledged master of the field—he began also to speak out against war. War violated, in his view, the process of natural selection by killing off precisely the strongest and most capable members of the human species; it was, that is, dysgenic. He became a champion of international arbitration, progressive reform, and world federalism. He wrote constantly to promote these causes; among his books were *The Care and Culture of Men*, 1896, *Imperial Democracy*, 1899, *The Human Harvest*, 1907, *War and Waste*, 1914, and *Democracy and World Relations*, 1918. He opposed American entry into World War I, though he supported the "democratic crusade" afterwards; in his concern with human heredity and his advocacy of eugenic practices he joined also in the period's wave of theorizing on Nordic racial superiority. In 1922 he published his autobiographical *The Days of a Man*, and in 1924 his *Plan of Education to Develop International Justice and Friendship* won a $25,000 prize. He died on September 19, 1931.

JOSEPH (c.1840–1904), Indian chief. Born around 1840, probably in Oregon's Wallowa Valley long inhabited by the Nez Percé, Joseph was given the Indian name Hinmaton-yalatkit, meaning "thunder coming up over the land from the water." His father, also known as Joseph, was leader of one of the major Nez Percé bands, one which in 1863, the year gold was discovered on their lands, refused to participate in a renegotiation of the land-cession treaty of 1855. Other bands did take part, however, and white authorities held the new treaty binding on all Nez Percé. Upon the death of his father in 1873, Joseph succeeded him as leader of the resisting Nez Percé and, as Chief Joseph, he continued his father's policies of passive noncompliance. After years of delay, the government finally took action in 1877; through Gen. O. O. Howard an ultimatum was issued, ordering Joseph and his people to leave the contested lands or be removed forcibly. His decision to leave was not easy: "I would give up everything rather than have the blood of my people on my hands. . . . I love that land more than all the world. A man who would not love his father's grave is worse than a wild animal." In his absence, however, Nez Percé braves killed several whites; on hearing of this Howard dispatched troops to capture the tribe. In the ensuing battle of White Bird Canyon the soldiers were nearly annihilated by the Nez Percé, led by chiefs other than Joseph. During this and 18 subsequent conflicts, he guided his warriors' decisions, counselled his people, and cared for the women, children, aged, and wounded. The Army assumed that he was the battle leader, however, and his reputation grew to legendary proportions. After two days' fighting near Kamiah, Idaho, Howard and 600 soldiers finally weakened the tribe. Joseph,

rather than surrender, executed a masterly retreat. Heading for the Canadian border and the huge nation of Sitting Bull, he led 750 people through four states, twice over the Rockies, across what is now Yellowstone Park, and over the Missouri River, a distance of more than 1,500 miles. They outfought pursuing troops and were in Montana near the Bear Paw Mountains, within 30 miles of the Canadian border, when fresh troops surrounded them, on October 5, 1877. He surrendered with dignity, renouncing armed resistance forever, and devoted himself thereafter to the tribe's welfare. He and his band were sent to Indian Territory (Oklahoma) until 1885, when they were moved to the Colville Reservation in Washington; there he died on September 21, 1904.

JUDSON, EDWARD ZANE CARROLL (1823–1886), "Ned Buntline," author and adventurer. Born in Stamford, New York, on March 20, 1823, Judson ran away to sea as a youngster; after a time as a cabin boy he became an apprentice in the Navy and by 1838 had earned a midshipman's commission. He left the Navy in 1842 and served, he later claimed, in the Seminole War. In 1844 he was in Cincinnati and founded two successive and equally short-lived newspapers; he had already begun to write stories in the action-and-violence manner, some of which were published in the *Knickerbocker Magazine*, and the pseudonym he used for these efforts was given also to the first of his Cincinnati ventures, *Ned Buntline's Magazine*. In Kentucky in 1845 he successfully tracked down and captured two fugitive murderers and then established the sensational *Ned Buntline's Own* in Nashville, Tennessee. The following year he shot and killed the husband of his alleged mistress and was arrested; he escaped being lynched and left for New York. He reestablished *Ned Buntline's Own* there and made it a jingoist, nativist, unruly, and highly popular sheet. There developed a heated public controversy in 1849 over the respective merits of Edwin Forrest, a popular

American actor, and William Charles Macready, an English counterpart; the culmination was the May riot at the Astor Place Opera House, led by Judson, in which over a score were killed and the theater nearly destroyed. He was fined and jailed for a year. Three years later, in St. Louis, he was involved in another riot, this one precipitated by an election. He was a leading organizer of the American Party and was said to be the source of its alternate and better known name, Know-Nothing. He had been continuing his literary career all the while, publishing his stories in cheap pamphlet form and thus becoming one of the chief creators of the "dime novel" genre. In 1856 he removed to a farm in New York; he joined the Union Army during the Civil War and was dishonorably discharged in 1864. On a trip to Nebraska in 1869 he met William F. Cody, whom he immediately dubbed "Buffalo Bill" and cast as the hero of a long series of his dime novels. In 1872 he wrote and produced a play, *The Scouts of the Plains* —later *Scouts of the Prairies*—which starred Cody and J. B. Omohundro ("Texas Jack," also a dime novel hero) and was highly successful in Chicago, St. Louis, and New York. Cody soon found another and more generous manager, and Judson retired to his birthplace, where he died on July 16, 1886.

KAUFMAN, GEORGE S. (1889–1961), playwright and director. Born in Pittsburgh on November 16, 1889, Kaufman attended city schools in Pittsburgh and Paterson, New Jersey, studied law for three months, and became a salesman. He contributed humorous quips and verse regularly to Franklin P. Adams' satirical column in the *New York Mail* and in 1912, through F.P.A.'s influence, got his own humor column in the *Washington Times*. In 1914 he took over Adams' column in the *Evening Mail* and the next year became a writer in the drama department of the *New York Herald Tribune*, working under Heywood Broun. He became drama editor of the *New York Times* in 1917 and remained with the paper until

1930. His first successful play was based on Dulcinea, a character created by F.P.A. *Dulcy*, written with Marc Connelly, was the hit of the 1921–1922 Broadway season. He wrote seven other plays with Connelly, the most famous of which were *Merton of the Movies* and *To the Ladies*, both 1922, and *Beggar on Horseback*, 1924. In that year he wrote *The Butter and Egg Man*, with no collaboration, and in 1925 he completed the book for a Marx brothers' musical, *The Coconuts*. With Edna Ferber he wrote *The Royal Family*, 1927, *Dinner at Eight*, 1932, *Stage Door*, 1936, and *The Land Is Bright*, 1941. He shared Pulitzer Prizes in drama for *Of Thee I Sing*, 1931, written with Morrie Ryskind and Ira Gershwin, with a score by George Gershwin, and for *You Can't Take It With You*, 1936, written with Moss Hart. He also collaborated with Hart on *Once in a Lifetime*, 1930, *The Man Who Came to Dinner*, 1939, and *I'd Rather Be Right*, 1938, which starred George M. Cohan as Franklin D. Roosevelt. He wrote *The Solid Gold Cadillac* with Howard Teichmann in 1953, and *Silk Stockings* with Abe Burrows in 1955, and through the years directed Broadway productions of the plays *June Moon, Let 'Em Eat Cake, Bring on the Girls, Of Mice and Men, My Sister Eileen, Guys and Dolls, Romanoff and Juliet,* and *The American Way*. He wrote or directed at least one hit on Broadway every year from 1921 to 1941; during those 20 years he was often referred to as the funniest man in America. He died in New York City on June 2, 1961.

KELLER, HELEN ADAMS (1880–1968), author and lecturer. Born on June 27, 1880, near Tuscumbia, Alabama, Helen Keller was afflicted at the age of 19 months with a severe disease that left her blind, deaf, and mute. She was examined by Alexander Graham Bell at about the age of 6; as a result he sent to her a 20-year-old teacher, Anne Mansfield Sullivan, from the Perkins Institution, which Bell's son-in-law directed. Miss Sullivan (later Mrs. John A. Macy), a remarkable teacher, remained with Helen from March 2, 1887, until her death in 1936. Within months Helen had learned to feel objects and associate them with words spelled out by finger signals on her palm, to read sentences by feeling raised words on cardboard, and to make her own sentences by arranging words in a frame. During 1888–1890 she spent winters in Boston at the Perkins Institution learning Braille. Then she began a slow process of learning to speak—feeling the position of the tongue and lips, making sounds, and imitating the motions—at the Horace Mann School for the Deaf. She also learned to lip-read by placing her fingers on the tongue and throat of the speaker. At 14 she enrolled in the Wright-Humason School for the Deaf in New York, and at 16 entered Cambridge School for Young Ladies in Massachusetts. She won admission to Radcliffe, entering in 1900, and graduated cum laude in 1904. Having developed skills never approached by any person so handicapped, she began to write of blindness, a subject then taboo in women's magazines because of its relation to venereal disease. The pioneering editor Edward Bok accepted her articles for the *Ladies' Home Journal*, and other major magazines—*Century*, *McClure's*, and the *Atlantic Monthly*—followed suit. She wrote of her life in several books, including *The Story of My Life*, 1902, *Optimism*, 1903, *The World I Live In*, 1908, *Song of the Stone Wall*, 1910, *Out of the Dark*, 1913, *My Religion*, 1927, *Midstream*, 1929, *Peace at Eventide*, 1932, *Helen Keller's Journal*, 1938, and *Let Us Have Faith*, 1940. In 1913 she began lecturing, primarily on behalf of the American Foundation for the Blind, for which she established $2 million endowment fund. Her efforts to improve treatment of the deaf and blind were influential in removing the handicapped from asylums. She also prompted the organization of commissions for the blind in 30 states by 1937. She died in Westport, Connecticut, on June 1, 1968, universally acknowledged as one of the great women of the world.

KELLY, WILLIAM (1811–1888), manufacturer and inventor. Born in Pittsburgh on August 21, 1811, Kelly received his education from public schools and until 1846 engaged in the dry goods business in Philadelphia. Moving to Eddyville, Kentucky, he operated the Suwanee Iron Works & Union Forge, manufacturing sugar kettles. As charcoal became scarce he began casting about for an alternate method of heating pig iron; observation and experiment led to the development of a process whereby a blast of air was shot through the molten pig iron, causing combustion of the carbon dissolved in it and greatly increasing the total heat. The unwanted impurities were thus got rid of and a low grade of steel obtained. Kelly built several furnaces to employ this "pneumatic process" but kept his discovery secret. When Henry Bessemer in England announced his independent discovery of the same process and applied for a U.S. patent Kelly revealed his work and with his patent in 1857 established his priority. In 1862 he built a converter for the Cambria Iron Works in Johnstown, Pennsylvania; before it was completed, however, Kelly-process steel had been poured at the Wyandotte Iron Works in Michigan in 1864. Kelly's patent came under the control of the Kelly Pneumatic Process Company, with which he had nothing to do and which later merged with the company of Alexander L. Holley, Bessemer's sole American licensee. The Bessemer name came into exclusive use for the air-blown steel process and Kelly remained in relative obscurity, receiving for his discovery less than a twentieth of the royalties paid to his more fortunate counterpart. After 1861 he operated an axe manufactory in Louisville, Kentucky, and died there on February 11, 1888.

KENNEDY, JOHN FITZGERALD (1917–1963), author, public official, and 35th U.S. President. Born on May 29, 1917, in the Boston suburb of Brookline, Kennedy was the son of a prominent businessman and political figure. Educated in private schools, he entered Princeton at 18 but, after a short illness, transferred to Harvard; he graduated in 1940 and his senior thesis, a study of England's reaction to the rise of European fascism, was published the same year as *Why England Slept* and became a best-seller at the time. After brief graduate study In business at Stanford University he enlisted in the Navy in 1941; during World War II he served as commander of a PT-boat in the Pacific and in 1943 his craft was sunk in an episode later much publicized. In 1945 he received his discharge from the Navy and the next year entered politics. With the unusually vigorous campaigning that came to be characteristic he won election to Congress from a Boston district, and his support of the New Deal legacy in domestic affairs and his close attention to the needs of his constituents gained him reelection in 1948 and 1950. In 1952 he widened his scope and demonstrated his effectiveness as a campaigner by defeating the incumbent Henry Cabot Lodge for U.S. senator from Massachusetts. While convalescing from two major spinal operations in 1954 he wrote *Profiles in Courage*, published in 1956 and awarded a Pulitzer Prize. Kennedy gradually became more interested in international affairs and less a merely local politician during his Senate years, and by 1956 was able to wage a vigorous battle for the Democratic vice presidential nomination. He lost, but he began almost immediately to lay the groundwork for a presidential campaign in 1960; he traveled and spoke widely, wrote numerous articles, was reelected to the Senate in 1958 by a record margin, and by 1960 was far and away the leading candidate. The Democrats nominated him on the first ballot and in November he won the election with the smallest of pluralities in the popular vote. He was inaugurated the youngest man and first Catholic ever elected to the presidency and in his address laid down the famous challenge: "Ask not what your country can do for you—ask what you can do for your country." The image of youth and vigor constantly projected and cultivated by Kennedy and his family

made him immensely popular at home and abroad; however, his legislative program, the "New Frontier," emphasizing domestic social programs and increased foreign aid, met with mixed reactions in Congress and was only in part effected. In April 1961, with the ill-fated invasion of Cuba at the Bay of Pigs by Cuban refugees supported, trained, and equipped by the State Department and the Central Intelligence Agency, the prestige of the United States and of the President was dealt a severe blow. Kennedy was forced to deal with a series of challenges in foreign affairs, including the building of the Berlin Wall, the Cuban missile crisis in October 1962, the world's closest approach yet to nuclear war, and increasing conflicts in Laos and Vietnam. At home the scene was dominated by the civil rights movement; the President sent federal troops to open the University of Mississippi to a Negro student and maintained a liberal position favoring integration and the efforts of such leaders as Rev. Martin Luther King, Jr. A significant step toward eventual disarmament was taken in September 1963 with the signing by the United States and the Soviet Union of a treaty banning all but underground tests of nuclear devices. On a visit to Dallas on November 22, 1963, the President was shot by a sniper while riding in a motorcade through the city, dying almost immediately. The alleged killer was himself shot two days later, but despite the researches of a presidential commission, the facts surrounding the assassination remained somewhat in question.

KENNEDY, ROBERT FRANCIS (1925–1968), public official. Born in Brookline, Massachusetts, on November 20, 1925, Robert F. Kennedy was the son of Joseph P. Kennedy and the younger brother of President John F. Kennedy. He graduated from Harvard in 1948 and from the law school of the University of Virginia in 1951, and almost immediately entered public service as an attorney for the criminal division of the Department of Justice. He resigned his post to manage his brother's

1952 senatorial campaign but returned to Washington shortly thereafter, serving on the staffs of several Senate committees and, from 1957 to 1960, as chief counsel of the Select Committee on Improper Activities in the Labor or Management Field. During these years he devoted much of his energy to the government attack on Teamster Union president James Hoffa, who was finally jailed on the basis of information unearthed by Kennedy. In 1960 he managed his brother's campaign for the Democratic nomination and then for the presidency. He was appointed attorney general after the Kennedy electoral victory, one of the youngest men ever to hold the post, and served with distinction as the administration's chief strategist in civil rights activities and in litigation concerning trusts and rackets. After his brother's death in November 1963, he stayed on as attorney general under President Johnson, but he resigned the post in 1964 to run for the Senate from New York and was elected in November of that year. He soon emerged as a national leader and as a spokesman for the liberal wing of his party, and in March 1968 he announced his candidacy for the Democratic presidential nomination. When Johnson withdrew later in the month he seemed to have a good chance, but his fortunes in various state primaries were mixed—he won in Indiana and Nebraska but lost in Oregon, the first time a member of the Kennedy family had ever lost a public election. It appeared that the California primary, early in June, might be decisive, and he won it; but while celebrating his victory on June 5th, he was shot and fatally wounded by Sirhan Sirhan, a Jordanian-born resident of Southern California. Senator Kennedy died on the morning of June 6, 1968, in Los Angeles. His younger brother, **EDWARD MOORE KENNEDY** (1932–), born in Brookline on February 22, 1932, graduated from Harvard in 1954 and from the University of Virginia law school in 1959. He managed his brother John's second senatorial campaign in 1958 and with Robert helped to win the presidency for him

in 1960. In 1962 he was elected to fill the last two years of John's unexpired Senate term and was elected to a full term in 1964. After Robert's death in June 1968, he was spoken of as a candidate for the Democratic presidential nomination that year, but he firmly refused to allow his name to be put forward for the office. After Nixon's victory, however, he emerged as probably the leading Democratic contender for 1972; but an automobile accident involving the drowning of a young woman on Martha's Vineyard Island, in the later summer of 1969, the details of which remained puzzling, seemed to redound to his discredit, and he was thereafter apparently out of contention.

KENT, JAMES (1763–1847), lawyer and jurist. Born in Fredericksburg, New York, on July 31, 1763, Kent was schooled privately and then entered Yale, graduating in 1781. He took up the study of law, was admitted to the bar in 1785, and began practice in Poughkeepsie. In 1793 he moved to New York City and, through the influence of his Federalist friends John Jay and Alexander Hamilton, was appointed professor of law at Columbia College; his lecture courses were not particularly successful and in 1798 he resigned. He had by this time held two public offices, both at the pleasure of Governor Jay: master in chancery and recorder of the City of New York. In 1798 he was appointed to the state supreme court where he remained until 1814, after 1804 as chief justice, and in 1814 he became chancellor of the New York court of chancery, remaining there until his compulsory retirement (at age 60) nine years later. His decisions while on the bench were recorded by his friend William Johnson in a long series of *Reports for New York*, and these were widely circulated and influential in other states. In 1824 and 1825 he resumed his professorship at Columbia, again with little success; in the latter year, however, he set about revising and expanding his lectures for publication. The result was *Commentaries on American Law* in four volumes, 1826–1830. Relying, as he had on the bench, on English common law whenever possible and otherwise on Roman law, Chancellor Kent produced the first major systematic work on Anglo-American law; his discussion of international law was widely admired and his treatment of constitutional law was for long the standard Federalist interpretation. The *Commentaries* appeared in five subsequent editions during his life and under his editorship, and numerous translations were made of various portions of the work. Kent died in New York City on December 12, 1847.

KETTERING, CHARLES FRANKLIN (1876–1958), engineer and inventor. Born on August 29, 1876, near Loudonville, Ohio, Kettering received mechanical and electrical engineering degrees from Ohio State University in 1904. Employed by the National Cash Register Company of Dayton, he devised on assignment an electric motor for cash registers. After becoming head of the inventions department, he left in 1909 and, with the company's former works manager, Edward A. Deeds, formed the Dayton Engineering Laboratories Company (later called Delco) to develop improved automobile electrical equipment. In the first two years of his work he developed and produced an improved ignition and lighting system and the first self-starter for automobiles; both were installed in Cadillacs and made him famous as an inventor. In 1914 he established the Dayton Metal Products Company and the Dayton-Wright Airplane Company. Two years later Delco was purchased by the United Motors Corporation, which in 1919 became the General Motors Corporation. In 1925 Delco's independent research facilities were moved to Detroit and merged with GM's laboratories to form the General Motors Research Corporation, of which he became president and general manager. In this position he led advanced investigations into maximum engine performance and the nature of friction and combustion, in addition to contributing vastly to the development of such products and improvements as leaded (ethyl) gasoline and high octane fuels, fast-drying lacquer, chromium plating, crankcase ventilators, balancing machines, engine-oil coolers, two-way shock absorbers, variable speed transmissions, the high-speed diesel engine for trains, and the high-compression automobile engine. He established at Antioch College the Charles Franklin Kettering Foundation for the Study of Chlorophyll and Photosynthesis, co-founded the Sloan-Kettering Institute for Cancer Research, and sponsored the Fever Therapy Research Project at Miami Valley Hospital in Dayton, which developed the hypertherm, or artificial fever machine, for use in disease treatment. In June 1947 he resigned from General Motors. He died in Dayton on November 25, 1958.

KEY, FRANCIS SCOTT (1779–1843), lawyer. Born in Frederick (now Carroll) County, Maryland, on August 1, 1779, Key graduated from St. John's College in 1796 and began the study of law. He commenced practice in 1801 and the next year moved to Georgetown, near Washington, D.C., becoming there a moderately successful attorney. In September 1814 he was sent to secure the release of a Maryland physician, Dr. William Beanes, who had been taken prisoner by British troops retiring from the burning of Washington and was being held aboard a British ship. Key was successful in his mission; his return to the District was delayed, however, by the British attack on Baltimore during the night of September 13–14. His ship lay off the besieged Fort McHenry through the bombardment; when morning revealed the U.S. flag still flying over the fort, Key exultantly dashed off some descriptive verses that were circulated as a broadside in Baltimore the next day under the title "Defense of Fort M'Henry." Within a few days the poem was published in a newspaper and was already linked to the tune of a popular English drinking song, "To Anacreon in Heaven"; soon the new song was being sung throughout the nation. Key's few other verse works were of little note; he remained in Georgetown and Washington for the rest of his life and from 1833 to 1841 was U.S. attorney for the District. He died on January 11, 1843. The song, known from about 1815 as "The Star-Spangled Banner," grew in popularity and became something of an unofficial national anthem; this status was bolstered when it was adopted by the Navy in 1889 and by the Army in 1903. Finally the objections to the song—among them its virulently anti-British language and its musical difficulty—were overridden and it was officially adopted by Congress in 1931.

KING, CLARENCE (1842–1901), geologist. Born on January 6, 1842, in Newport, Rhode Island, King graduated from Yale's Sheffield Scientific School in 1862. The following year he and a companion set out to cross the continent on horseback; upon reaching California he joined the state geological survey and for nearly three years performed much exploratory work, particularly in the desert and mountain regions of the south. In 1866 he returned east and secured congressional approval for his plan for a government-sponsored survey along the 40th parallel from eastern Colorado to California. With King in charge, the survey was a masterful work of scientific exploration; the field and laboratory work occupied some ten years and King's contribution to the seven-volume *Report* was *Systematic Geology*, 1878, which combined scientific and literary excellence. On his urging, Congress unified the many government surveys into the single U.S. Geological Survey in 1879, and he served as its director for two years, assembling the staff and organizing its activities with great administrative skill. After 1881 he devoted his time primarily to geological research, serving also as a consulting mining engineer on many occasions. A series of articles in the *Atlantic Monthly* were collected and published in 1872 as *Mountaineering in the Sierra Nevada*, his only other major written work. In poor health during his last years, King died on December 24, 1901, in Phoenix, Arizona.

KING, MARTIN LUTHER, JR. (1929–1968), clergyman and reformer. Born on January 15, 1929, in Atlanta, King was christened Michael Luther by his father who later changed both their names in honor of the great Protestant reformer. He entered Morehouse College at 15; in 1947 he was ordained to the ministry in his father's Ebenezer Baptist Church in Atlanta, and the next year took his B.A. from Morehouse. He pursued his studies at Crozer Theological Seminary in Chester, Pennsylvania, where he was awarded a B.D. in 1951, and at Boston University, where he took his Ph.D. four years later. He was installed as pastor of the Dexter Avenue Baptist Church in Montgomery, Alabama, and was still new and relatively unknown in the city's Negro community when, in December 1955, Mrs. Rosa Parks was arrested for refusing to give up her bus seat to a white man and the Montgomery bus boycott began. King was placed in charge of the boycott and after more than a year of pressure and agitation on both sides the Supreme Court ruled in favor of the strikers. Early in 1957 the Southern Christian Leadership Council was formed with King as its president; through this organization he was able to broaden his civil rights activities to include the entire South. He developed a Gandhian strategy of nonviolent but active and massive confrontation with injustice and the unresponsive institutions of white society; his insistence on nonviolence, later rejected by more militant black activists, was in this early period often overlooked in the widespread criticism of his policy of confrontation. In 1959 he moved to Atlanta, becoming co-pastor of his father's church. During the early 1960s he continued to build up the movement and became the major figure in the struggle for civil rights through his leadership at Selma and Birmingham, Alabama, at Albany, Georgia, and at the massive March on Washington assembly in 1963, where he delivered his famed sermon-speech, "I Have a Dream." In December 1964 King was awarded the Nobel Prize for Peace. By 1966 he had begun to bring his campaign to Northern cities where de facto segregation was subtle and all-pervading. He was in great demand as a speaker, and he found time to publish several books about his work: *Stride Toward Freedom*, 1958, *Why We Can't Wait*, 1964, *Where Do We Go From Here: Chaos or Community?*, 1967, and others. During this last period he also turned against the war in Vietnam, declaring that it was an immoral adventure that was draining away resources .needed to eliminate poverty and hunger in America. Throughout his 12 years of active involvement in the civil rights movement he had met with strong and often violent opposition; he had been jailed, stoned, and beaten, his house had been bombed, and many threats had been made against his life. In the spring of 1968 he was in Memphis, Tennessee, to help the struggle of city workers, largely black, to improve the conditions of their employment; on April 4th he was shot to death by a sniper.

KING, RUFUS (1755–1827), public official and diplomat. Born in Scarboro, Massachusetts (now Maine), on March 24, 1755, King graduated from Harvard in 1777 and three years later was admitted to the bar. He served in the Massachusetts legislature from 1783 to 1785 and was elected by that body a delegate to the Continental Congress from 1784 on, serving until 1787. He was a member of the Constitutional Convention of 1787, and there reversed his earlier opinion by favoring a strong central government; he was later instrumental in securing ratification by Massachusetts. In 1788 he moved to New York City and the next year was elected to the state legislature, which in turn elected him one of New York's first U.S. senators. In the Senate he was a leading Federalist and strongly supported all of Alexander Hamilton's programs; soon after his reelection in 1795 he resigned to accept President Washington's offer of the ministry in London. He performed creditably during his tenure, 1796–1803, and on his return to America began a period of semi-retirement on his Long Island estate while the Republican Party was in its ascendancy. He was the unsuccessful Federalist candidate for Vice Presi-

dent in 1804 and 1808, but in 1813 was elected again to the Senate. In 1816 he was a candidate for President and was again defeated. During his last term in the Senate, from 1819, he became a strong opponent of slavery, denouncing the Missouri Compromise of 1820 for merely delaying an inevitable showdown between North and South. He declined reelection in 1825 and was appointed minister to Great Britain by President J. Q. Adams. He began his second term of service in this office in June 1825 but was forced to resign a year later because of ill health. He returned to Long Island and died on April 29, 1827.

KROEBER, ALFRED LOUIS (1876–1960), anthropologist. Born in Hoboken, New Jersey, on June 11, 1876, Kroeber took his B.A. degree in 1896, his M.A. in 1897, and his Ph.D. under Franz Boas at Columbia in 1901. That year he established a department of anthropology at the University of California at Berkeley and was attached to it, as a professor of anthropology after 1919, until 1946. His major anthropological expeditions were to New Mexico in 1915–1920, to Mexico in 1924 and 1930, and to Peru in 1925, 1926, and 1942. His research focused on the Indians of California, but also encompassed the Zuñi and plains tribes; he extended the domain of archeology—especially that of California, Mexico, and Peru—to include linguistics, folk culture, family structure, and social organization. He analyzed such cultural manifestations as art, fashion, and language for their repetitive features among civilizations. His textbook, *Anthropology*, 1923, revised in 1948, was regarded as the most authoritative in the field. Among numerous other publications were *Handbook of the Indians of California*, 1925, *Three Centuries of Women's Dress Fashions*, with Jane Richardson, 1940, *Peruvian Archeology in 1942*, 1944, *Configurations of Culture Growth*, 1944, *A Mohave Historical Epic*, 1951, *Style and Civilizations*, 1957, *Sparkman Grammar of Luiseño*, with G. Grace, 1960, and *A Roster of Civilizations and Culture*, 1962. He was a founder of the American

Anthropological Association and its president in 1917, a member of numerous other scientific organizations, and winner of many honorary degrees and awards, including the Huxley and Viking medals. He died in Paris on October 5, 1960.

KRUTCH, JOSEPH WOOD (1893–1970), author and naturalist. Born in Knoxville, Tennessee, on November 25, 1893, Krutch grew up there and received a B.S. from the University of Tennessee in 1915. He went to New York to study English at Columbia University, where he received his M.A. in 1916 and his Ph.D. in 1923. An instructor of English at Columbia in 1917–1918, he taught the subject at Brooklyn Polytechnic Institute from 1920 to 1923, at Vassar College in 1924–1925, at Columbia's School of Journalism from 1925 to 1931, and at the New School for Social Research from 1932 to 1935. He returned to Columbia's regular faculty of English in 1937, remaining until 1952, the last nine years as Brander Matthews Professor of Dramatic Literature. His doctoral dissertation, published as *Comedy and Conscience After the Restoration* in 1924, had initiated his lifelong interest in the theater, and he was drama critic of the *Nation* for nearly three decades, from 1924 to 1952, and served in 1940–1941 as president of the New York Drama Critics Circle. During these years he also wrote a series of scholarly books. A study of Poe appeared in 1926; *Five Masters*, treating the lives and works of Boccaccio, Cervantes, Richardson, Stendhal, and Proust, in 1930; and his biography of Samuel Johnson was published in 1944. He resigned his Columbia post in 1952. His achievements as a drama and literary critic, as an inspiring teacher, and as a raconteur already constituted a full career. Yet, he set out upon another, in the course of which he gained his greatest fame. In the later 1940s he had begun to travel to the Southwest, partly for his health, and he developed a passion for the desert and the mountains. A superb biography of Thoreau had appeared in 1948, and now, partly in emula-

tion of Thoreau, he retired to Tucson to live in an adobe house in the desert. Books flowed from his desert study. *The Twelve Seasons,* a dozen essays, each on a month, had appeared in 1949; 1952 saw the publication of *The Desert Year,* a lyrical study of his new environs; and *The Best of Two Worlds,* 1953, *The Voice of the Desert,* 1955, *The Great Chain of Life,* 1957, *Grand Canyon: To-day and All Its Yesterdays,* 1958, *The Gardener's World,* 1959, *The Forgotten Peninsula* (about Baja), 1961, *The World of Animals,* 1961, *Herbal,* 1965, and *The Best Nature Writings of Joseph Wood Krutch,* 1970, all expressed his deep concern with and affection for the natural world; and he wrote and narrated three television specials, on the Sonora Desert in 1963, on the Grand Canyon in 1965, and on the Baja Peninsula in 1968. He also continued to contribute articles and essays to many publications, to edit collections of these and of the works of others, and to write occasional drama criticism. He produced in 1954 *The Measure of Man,* a study of humanity that won a National Book Award and that was in some degree an updating of an early, famous book, *The Modern Temper,* whose pessimism had shocked readers when it first came out in 1929; *Human Nature and the Human Condition,* 1959, and an autobiography, *More Lives Than One,* 1962, which drew together all the strains of his thought and experience in an eloquent plea for a sane relationship between man and nature. He died in Tucson, one of the major prophets of the ecological revolution, on May 22, 1970.

LA FARGE, JOHN (1835–1910), artist and author. Born in New York City on March 31, 1835, of French parentage, La Farge was reared in a home decorated with fine paintings and dedicated to learning and refinement. When he was six he asked his grandfather, a miniaturist, to teach him to paint. This interest persisted throughout his formal schooling. When he graduated from Mount St. Mary's College, Maryland, in 1853, he studied law briefly and without enthusiasm, then went to Paris in 1856 to become involved in the cultural scene. For a short time he joined classes taught by the painter Couture, but he gained his training primarily in galleries and museums; he continued to travel through Europe, studying the old masters and developing more and more of an inclination to paint. He returned to America in 1858, briefly resumed reading law, and then studied painting again with William Morris Hunt in Rhode Island. He concentrated on the relationships of light and color, executing a work, "Paradise Valley," in 1866–1868 that anticipated French impressionism. He painted flowers and landscapes, contrasting the delicacy of flowers to solid objects. Invited by architect H. H. Richardson to decorate the interior of Trinity Church in Boston in 1876, he produced a series of murals that were beautifully unified by color and design. Many commissions followed, including his foremost work of this nature, "The Ascension," in the Church of the Ascension in New York City, for Stanford White. He became preoccupied with medieval stained glass and invented an opalescent glass that he used in windows of his own design. His work began a revival of the nearly lost craft and secured his own worldwide fame. His travels with Henry Adams through the South Seas and to Japan were recorded in a series of watercolors and two books, *An Artist's Letters from Japan*, 1897, and *Reminiscences of the South Seas*, 1912. His other books examined artists and art movements with depth and precision and included *Considerations on Painting*, 1895, *Great Masters*, 1903, and *The Higher Life in Art*, 1908. He died in Providence, Rhode Island, on November 14, 1910.

LA FOLLETTE, ROBERT MARION (1855–1925), public official. Born in Dane County, Wisconsin, on June 14, 1855, La Follette worked his way through the University of Wisconsin, graduated in 1879, and the following year was admitted to the bar. At the same time he began his practice he also entered politics and was elected district attorney; characteristically, he had campaigned by himself, ignoring the Republican Party organization. He was reelected in 1882 and then from 1885 to 1891 served three terms in Congress. He was, in outlook and voting record, a reasonably regular Republican at this time, in his last term helping to draft the McKinley tariff legislation. He lost his seat in the popular reaction against the tariff in 1890 and returned to his law practice in Madison; the next year, however, he opened a campaign against the established party leadership in Wisconsin with charges of corruption and bribery and for ten years, while evolving a legislative reform program, he maintained his war against the bosses. In 1900 he won the governorship; in 1902 he was reelected and given a friendly legislature that proceeded to institute his program of direct nominating primary elections, state civil service, and state regulation and equitable taxation of the railroads. In 1906 he resigned from his third term to enter the Senate, to which he was also twice returned. In the Senate his independence and progressive views estranged him from party leaders; his name was placed in nomination for the presidency at the 1908 Republican convention but the dominant conservatives easily secured Taft's victory. To broaden the movement for reform he founded *La Follette's Weekly Magazine* in 1909 and two years later organized the National Progressive Republican League; as the League's revolt against Taft gained in credibility Theodore Roosevelt became interested and, when La Follette's health failed in 1912, he incorporated it into his own Bull Moose campaign. La Follette rejected Roosevelt's pragmatic politics and after 1912 cooperated with the reform program of Democrat Woodrow Wilson, breaking with him, however, over American policy in World War I and the League of Nations. He lost some of his support when a false newspaper report in 1917 seemed to show him as imperfectly patriotic, but the national reaction that followed the war restored him completely to public favor. In 1924 a coalition of liberal and reformist groups under the Progressive name nominated him for President; and he and his running mate, Sen. Burton K. Wheeler, polled nearly 5 million votes, one-sixth of the total. He died in Washington, D.C., on June 18th of the next year.

LA GUARDIA, FIORELLO HENRY (1882–1947), public official. Born in New York City on December 11, 1882, La Guardia attended high school in Prescott, Arizona, and was for a time employed as a reporter for the *St. Louis Dispatch*. At 16 he went to Budapest and worked at the U.S. consulate. After working at the consulates at Trieste and Fiume he returned to the United States, and became an interpreter at Ellis Island. He graduated from New York University law school in 1910 and was admitted to the bar. Having established a legal aid bureau to represent poor people in court for no fee, he became well known to immigrants of the 14th congressional district, who elected him to Congress on the Republican ticket in 1916. He allied himself with progressive forces and voted to liberalize House rules. When the United States entered World War I he resigned to join an Air Service bombing squadron to the Italian front. He returned to Congress in 1918 and was reelected in 1922. Called a "chronic dissenter," he fought for child labor laws and woman suffrage, vigorously opposed Prohibition and pork-barrel legislation, and prompted resignations by Federal judges whom he exposed for graft. He was co-sponsor of the 1932 Norris-La Guardia Act that restricted the use of injunctions and helped establish labor's right to strike, picket, and conduct boycotts. In 1933, on a reform-fusion ticket, he unseated Tammany Hall in New York City's mayoral election. Twice reelected, in his 12 years he began slum clearance and low-cost housing projects, improved the operations of the police and fire departments, battled gangsters, slot machines, and official corruption, and built recreational facilities, health clinics, roads

and bridges, and La Guardia Airport. In 1941 he was named director of the Office of Civilian Defense and he became director general of the United Nations Relief and Rehabilitation Agency in March 1946, but resigned in December. He died in New York City on September 20, 1947, the city's most controversial and beloved mayor.

LAMAR, LUCIUS QUINTUS CINCINNATUS (1825–1893), public official and jurist. Born in Putnam County, Georgia, on September 17, 1825, Lamar graduated from Emory College in 1845 and two years later was admitted to the bar. In 1849 he moved to Oxford, Mississippi, and served as adjunct professor of mathematics at the University of Mississippi there while practising law. He went back to Georgia in 1852, served a year in the state legislature, and in 1855 returned permanently to Mississippi. In 1857 he was elected to Congress; reelected in 1859, he served until the eve of the Civil War and then, in December 1860, resigned, returned to Mississippi, and drafted the state's ordinance of secession. He served in the Confederate Army for over a year until ill health forced his resignation, whereupon in November 1862 he was appointed special commissioner to Russia by President Davis. After several months in Paris vainly waiting for legislative confirmation of his mission he returned to the Confederacy early in 1864. He continued to work in support of the South and the Davis administration until the war ended, when he resumed his law practice and taught metaphysics and law at the University of Mississippi. In 1872, as the grip of Reconstruction began to relax, Lamar was elected Mississippi's first postwar Democrat in Congress. He quickly became a leading Southern figure and highly prominent nationally as he fought the vestiges of radical Reconstruction and spoke and, more importantly, acted for reconciliation. He supported the ultimate resolution of the presidential election of 1876 and was that year elected to the Senate where he became the leading spokesman for the "new South." In 1885 President Cleveland offered him the post of secretary of the interior; primarily to further the reunion of North and South, he accepted and served well for over two years. Then, in 1887, the President appointed him to the Supreme Court. In his short tenure on the bench he delivered few opinions, but the learning, intelligence, and judgment he brought to the Court were later attested to by his colleagues. Lamar died in Macon, Georgia, on January 23, 1893.

LAND, EDWIN HERBERT (1909–), inventor and businessman. Born in Bridgeport, Connecticut, on May 7, 1909, Land attended Harvard University; while still a student he made his initial discoveries in the field of polarized light. After developing a plastic film, called Polaroid, that was capable of polarizing light passed through it, he left school in 1932 and, with a former Harvard physics instructor, opened the Land-Wheelwright Laboratories in Boston. In 1935 they began manufacturing polarizing filters for cameras and the next year introduced sunglasses employing Polaroid lenses. In 1937 Land organized the Polaroid Corporation and served thereafter as its president, chairman of the board, and director of research. In 1941 he developed a technique for producing three-dimensional photographs by means of differently polarized double exposures. During World War II he performed research for the Army, developing many optical devices for night reconnaissance, range finding, and weapon sighting, and was a consultant on guided missiles. In 1947 he announced his invention of a one-step photographic process whereby a finished picture was produced inside the camera within a minute after the exposure. The Polaroid Land camera was a huge commercial success —sales passed the million mark by 1956—and it was later refined to deliver color prints. The same process was applied to a dosimeter, a device used to monitor the radiation exposure of persons working with radioactive materials. In 1948 he developed a color-translation technique that made possible full-color still and motion pictures of living cells. He was the recipient of numerous honors from scientific organizations; he served on the Harvard Board of Overseers and was president of the American Academy of Arts and Sciences; and by 1970, in the course of less than a generation, he had amassed one of the great American fortunes.

LANGLEY, SAMUEL PIERPONT (1834–1906), astronomer and aviation pioneer. Born on August 22, 1834, in Roxbury, Massachusetts, Langley early developed a deep interest in astronomy and as a boy built his own telescopes. His formal education ended with graduation from high school in 1851 and for the next 14 years he was occupied mainly in civil engineering and architecture in the Midwest. In 1865 he was granted an assistantship in the Harvard Observatory; after a year there and another as assistant professor of mathematics and director of the observatory at the Naval Academy, he joined the faculty of Western University in Pennsylvania in 1867, taking charge also of the Allegheny Observatory. During his 20 years in these two posts Langley pursued a line of research into solar phenomena that, in addition to being a highly valuable pioneering study in itself, contributed significantly to the reorientation of astronomy from a geometrical to a physical basis. In 1878 he invented the bolometer, a device with which he was able to measure the sun's energy output at chosen points along its radiation spectrum; for the first time solar radiation in the infrared region was investigated, and in 1881 he set up his equipment on Mount Whitney in order to determine the constant of solar radiation and the transmission characteristics of the atmosphere. In 1887 Langley was appointed assistant secretary and later in the year secretary of the Smithsonian Institution. Under his administration the National Zoological Park and the Astrophysical Observatory were founded. At the latter he continued his researches, constructing a map of the solar spectrum including the Fraunhofer absorption lines in the infrared region, and making the first energy measurement of the solar corona.

At the same time he was investigating the problem of heavier-than-air flight; in 1893 he offered the first fully reasonable explanation for the flying ability of birds and began experimenting with various wing shapes for a powered aircraft. By 1896 he had successfully flown a steam-powered pilotless plane for a distance of 4200 feet. With a grant from the War Department he began constructing a larger machine, powered by a gasoline engine, and capable of carrying and being controlled by a man. It seems likely that with continued work Langley would have achieved powered, controlled, heavier-than-air flight by a man before the Wright brothers, but unfortunate accidents exhausted his funds before he could complete his work. He died on February 27, 1906.

LANGMUIR, IRVING (1881–1957), chemist. Born on January 31, 1881, in Brooklyn, New York, Langmuir early developed a strong interest in scientific subjects and during his school years carried on independent studies in a home laboratory. In 1903 he graduated from the Columbia School of Mines and three years later took his Ph.D. from the University of Göttingen. From 1906 to 1909 he taught chemistry at the Stevens Institute of Technology in Hoboken, New Jersey, and in the latter year joined the research staff of the General Electric Company's laboratory in Schenectady, New York, where he remained for over 40 years. His first major accomplishment came in 1912, when he discovered that filling incandescent light bulbs with inert gases greatly increased the working life of the tungsten filaments. Later work led to the development of atomic hydrogen welding in 1927, the mercury condensation vacuum pump in 1930, and subsequent progress in high-vacuum electron tubes. In 1932 his investigations into the nature of molecular films and the chemistry of surfaces, which opened an entirely new field of study, were recognized with a Nobel Prize for Chemistry. Also in that year he became associate director of the laboratory. During World War II he did research for the Army,

developing a smoke generator for use as camouflage and working on the problem of ice formation on aircraft wings. The latter line of research led to his development in 1946 of a method of artificially producing rain by seeding clouds with dry ice and silver iodide. In 1950 Langmuir retired from General Electric, continuing, however, to serve as a consultant to the company and to the Army's Project Cirrus, begun in 1947 to develop his cloud-seeding technique. He died on August 16, 1957, in Falmouth, Massachusetts.

LANIER, SIDNEY (1842–1881), poet and musician. Born in Macon, Georgia, on February 3, 1842, Lanier early developed deep interests in music and literature but did not allow them full expression for many years. He graduated from Oglethorpe University, near Milledgeville, Georgia, in 1860 and after a brief period as a tutor joined a volunteer regiment to fight for Southern independence. After more than three years of service he was captured in November 1864 and imprisoned in Point Lookout, Maryland; while in prison he contracted tuberculosis. He was released early in 1865 and returned to Macon where he worked in his father's law office while writing his first book, a novel entitled Tiger-Lilies, 1867. With his health slowly slipping away, he decided to devote himself to his two chosen arts: in 1873 he moved to Baltimore and became first flutist with the Peabody orchestra; giving more time to poetry, he published in 1875 two of his finest pieces, "Corn" and "The Symphony," and gained immediate national attention. His "Centennial Meditation" for the 1876 exposition in Philadelphia was less well received, but it led him to begin a series of studies of versification that resulted in The Science of English Verse, 1880. This book and The English Novel, 1883, also reflected the research done for his lectures at Johns Hopkins University, begun in 1879. In these years he wrote also a number of lesser books—"pot-boilers"—for quick return; but his poetry, at its best as in "The Marshes of Glynn," remains his primary contribution to American literature.

His attempts to regain his health failed and he died on September 7, 1881.

LARDNER, RINGGOLD WILMER (1885–1933), journalist and author. Born on March 6, 1885, in Niles, Michigan, Ring Lardner attended public high school and the Armour Institute of Technology for one term. In 1905 he turned to a career in journalism, worked for two years as a sportswriter on the *South Bend* (Indiana) *Times*, then for various papers in Chicago, Boston, and St. Louis, and returned to the *Chicago Tribune* from 1913 to 1919 to write a feature column, "In the Wake of the News." In 1919 he was employed by the Bell Syndicate, which distributed his work widely and increased his popularity. From journalism he graduated to fiction writing. He submitted a series of "Jack Keefe" letters to the *Saturday Evening Post*, compiled in *You Know Me, Al*, 1916, a title that became a catch phrase for admissions of personal stupidity. Keefe was a fictitious baseball player with a mind as small as his ego was large. Lardner's disdain for the heroic stature accorded sports figures by the public was well expressed by these letters and by books that followed—*Treat 'Em Rough*, 1918, *The Real Dope*, 1919—in which Keefe was the major character. With a complete mastery of the American vernacular and a new sardonic twist to his humor, Lardner wrote *How to Write Short Stories (With Samples)*, 1924; *Round Up*, 1929, contained "Hair Cut," his supremely ironic portrayal of the life of a small Midwestern town. His deft and often wildly funny stories simulated reportage of living characters, generally either stupid or despicable, and showed him to be a master of the form. He also wrote for the theater, collaborating with George M. Cohan on *Elmer the Great*, 1928, and with George S. Kaufman on *June Moon*, 1929. He died in East Hampton, Long Island, on September 25, 1933.

LATROBE, BENJAMIN HENRY (1764–1820), architect and engineer. Born in Fulneck, near Leeds, England, on May 1, 1764, Latrobe was educated in England and Germany and in 1786 began to study engineering and architecture. In 1796 he sailed to America, landing in Virginia; the next year he designed and supervised the construction of a penitentiary in Richmond and completed, with modifications, Jefferson's state capitol building. In December 1798 he moved to Philadelphia in order to oversee the execution of his design for the Bank of Pennsylvania, the beginning of Greek Revival architecture in the United States. By 1801 he had constructed a water supply system for the city; he received numerous private commissions as well and built several distinguished residences that were long Philadelphia landmarks. In 1803 he was appointed by President Jefferson to the newly created post of surveyor of public buildings; moving to Washington, he immediately set about the completion of the south wing (Hall of Representatives) of the Capitol. During his government service, which lasted until 1817, he designed, built, or remodeled a great number of public structures. His private practice flourished at the same time; he built many private homes, performed engineering tasks for canal companies, and donated designs for buildings to several educational institutions. From 1805 to 1818 he was engaged in the design and construction of the Baltimore Cathedral, for which work, like that for schools and colleges, he accepted no pay. In 1813 he retired briefly from government service and moved to Pittsburgh, where he was involved with Robert Fulton in a scheme that ultimately bankrupted him. The burning of Washington by the British in 1814 necessitated his return there to rebuild the Capitol. He later designed the second Bank of the United States—completed after his death—and in 1820 journeyed to New Orleans to complete work on a water supply system begun by his son. Like his son, he succumbed soon after his arrival to yellow fever and died on September 3, 1820. Latrobe is credited, above and beyond his specific works, with having professionalized both architecture and engineering in the United States and with establishing high standards of integrity in both design and performance that were carried on by his many able students.

LAWRENCE, ERNEST ORLANDO (1901–1958), physicist. Born in Canton, South Dakota, on August 8, 1901, Lawrence was educated at St. Olaf's College and the University of South Dakota, graduating from the latter in 1922. After further study at the University of Minnesota and the University of Chicago he went to Yale in 1925 as a National Research fellow in physics. Taking his Ph.D. in 1925, he remained at Yale until moving to the University of California in 1928 as an associate professor of physics. He became a full professor two years later. In the same year he demonstrated his first model cyclotron, a device in which, by means of an alternating electrical field within a permanent magnetic field, atomic particles can be accelerated to extremely high speeds and energies. In 1933 the first large-scale cyclotron was completed, employing an 80-ton magnet. With this machine and larger ones built under his direction in 1938 and 1942 he was able to convert stable forms of many elements into radioactive isotopes, some of which were subsequently employed as tracers in biological and medical research and in the treatment of cancer. In 1936 he became director of the University of California's Radiation Laboratory and three years later was awarded the Nobel Prize for Physics. During World War II he was associated with Arthur H. Compton and Harold C. Urey in the production of plutonium for the first atomic bombs, and in 1957 he was named recipient of the Fermi Prize by the Atomic Energy Commission. He died in Palo Alto, California, on August 27, 1958.

LAZARUS, EMMA (1849–1887), poet and essayist. Born in New York City on July 22, 1849, Emma Lazarus came of a wealthy family and was educated privately. She early displayed an inclination and talent for poetry and her first book, *Poems and Translations*, 1867, was praised by Ralph Waldo Emerson, to whom her next, *Admetus and Other Poems*,

1871, was dedicated. These and subsequent volumes—the prose *Alide: an Episode of Goethe's Life*, 1874, a verse tragedy, *The Spagnoletto*, 1876, and a fine translation, *Poems and Ballads of Heinrich Heine*, 1881 —were pleasant, international in flavor, sometimes excellent, but often lacking in real distinction. About 1881, however, with the wave of immigration from European and Russian ghettoes, she took up the defense of Jews and Judaism. She published numerous essays in behalf of this persecuted minority and in 1882 produced *Songs of a Semite*, which included such powerful pieces as "The Dance to Death," "The Banner of the Jew," and "The Crowing of the Red Cock." Her sonnet on the Statue of Liberty, "The New Colossus," was chosen to be inscribed on the base of the monument; it remains a most moving and eloquent expression of an American ideal since lost. Her last book, a series of prose poems under the title *By the Waters of Babylon*, appeared in 1887; she died on November 19th of that year.

LEADBELLY see LEDBETTER, HUDDIE

LEDBETTER, HUDDIE(1888–1951), folksinger and composer. Born about 1888 near Shreveport, Louisiana, "Leadbelly," as he came to be known, was raised by his Negro-Cherokee parents on a farm near the state's western border. From childhood his main interest was in music; he was given a small accordion, then a guitar, and he finally acquired the 12-string guitar that he made famous. Until 1934, when he was 45, his life centered around music, liquor, and women, and he often was in trouble with the law, being sent to prison on numerous occasions. But he never stayed long in jail, for he always managed to gain the attention of some prison or government official, for whom he sang, and who rewarded him by reducing his sentence or giving him an outright pardon. In 1934 he met Alan and John Lomax, who, recognizing his great talent, befriended him thereafter. The three men toured the country for some 15 years, with Leadbelly helping them to gather songs from prisons and in small towns in the South, the Lomaxes sponsoring him in the professional folksinging world. Finally reaching New York, he gave concerts in Town Hall, appeared on national radio and television programs, and won world wide fame. He toured college campuses, performed in Hollywood, and gave a notable concert in Paris. He was a true artist of the folk tradition; he could transform a simple tune into a strange and beautiful composition, but he also composed original songs, among them his well known theme song, "Good Night, Irene." He entranced his audiences by his presence and delivery; frequently he introduced a song by telling a little story in order to get the audience, as he said, into his mood. His style was individual and spontaneous and seemed to have sprung from a world other than the impersonal, fast-paced one that heard and applauded him. He died on December 6, 1951; later that month the many singers whom he had inspired marked his death by a memorial concert in New York.

LEE, IVY LEDBETTER (1877–1934), public relations consultant. Born on July 16, 1877, in Cedartown, Georgia, the son of a Methodist minister, Lee graduated from Princeton in 1898. After graduation he went to New York where he worked as a reporter for four New York papers, the *Journal, Sun, Times,* and *World,* while studying political science at Columbia University in the evenings. In 1903 he managed a mayoral campaign for a citizens' committee and the following year was hired as a press agent for the Democratic National Committee. He admired businessmen and was fascinated by the operations of industry; he formed friendships easily and was thus able to learn the workings of many major corporations. In 1906–1907 he acquired two accounts, the Pennsylvania Railroad, and a group of mine owners in Pennsylvania who had been struck by their employees and were being severely criticized by the press. His philosophy was tested when a train crash threatened the reputation of the Pennsylvania Railroad. In contrast to the traditional practice of distorting or suppressing information, he provided transportation for newsmen to the accident and answered their questions honestly. To his shocked client he pointed out that a company would always receive bad publicity if the situation warranted it; but that a frank admission of the facts would promote respect for the company's integrity and possibly arouse public sympathy. In 1910 he went to Europe to organize offices for a London banking firm, and during 1911 and 1912 lectured at the London School of Economics. In 1912 he returned to New York and met John D. Rockefeller, Jr. Two years later, following the Ludlow Massacre, in which striking workers at the Rockefeller-owned Colorado Fuel and Iron works at Ludlow had been fired at by troops using machine guns, and a number of women and children had been killed, Lee persuaded Rockefeller to travel to Colorado and talk to the miners personally, and this simple but characteristically human idea soon healed the rift between the wealthy Rockefellers and the outraged public. The Rockefeller family retained his services and soon John D. Rockefeller, Sr., was attracting unusually favorable publicity by handing out dimes to children. He represented numerous and varied organizations, including the Portland Cement Company, Harvard, the Red Cross, Bethlehem Steel, the Republic of Poland, and the Episcopal diocese of New York. He expressed his opinions of his employers' enterprises honestly, urging improvements so that there would be no need to withhold information from the public; he became known as the "physician to corporate bodies." He died in New York City on November 9, 1934, haveing almost single-handedly made of public relations a respectable profession.

LEE, RICHARD HENRY (1732–1794), public official. Born on January 20, 1732, at the family estate, "Stratford," in Westmoreland County, Virginia, Lee was of a wealthy and distinguished family. His education began with private tutoring and was completed in England; he returned to Virginia about 1752. In 1757, following a family tradition of public service, he became a justice of the peace, and the next year entered the House of Burgesses, beginning 17 years of continual service in that body. He quickly established himself as an advocate of liberal policies and, as the friction between Great Britain and the colonies increased during the period of the Stamp and the Townshend Acts, he was firmly on the American side. In 1766 he organized a local non-importation association, the first such group in the colonies; he drafted a number of petitions and protests for the House and became closely associated with Patrick Henry and Thomas Jefferson. In 1773 he proposed the system of intercolonial correspondence committees to coordinate the efforts of the several colonies, and the following year he was chosen one of Virginia's delegates to the first Continental Congress. He remained in Congress for five years. In June 1776 he introduced a resolution that led directly to the Declaration of Independence on July 4th; another of his resolutions called for a confederation among the colonies and, in order to achieve this end, he later worked to induce Virginia to relinquish its western land claims. He retired from Congress in 1779 because of ill health but the next year was elected to the Virginia legislature, remaining there until being returned in 1784 to Congress, where he served three years, the first as president. He refused to be a delegate to the Constitutional Convention in 1787 because of his membership in Congress, and he opposed ratification of the resulting Constitution because of its strong central government and its lack of a bill of rights. After losing the battle over ratification in Virginia, Lee was chosen one of that state's first senators in the new government. In the Senate he proposed a number of resolutions to correct the oversights in the Constitution and several of these were adopted as part of the Bill of Rights, the first ten amendments. He continued in the Senate until ill health

again forced his resignation in 1792; he retired to his Virginia estate and died on June 19, 1794.

LEE, ROBERT EDWARD (1807–1870), soldier. Born at "Stratford," the family estate in Westmoreland County, Virginia, on January 19, 1807, Lee was the son of a famed Revolutionary cavalry officer and a member of a family long distinguished in public and military service. He grew up and was schooled in Alexandria and in 1825, seeking a means to continue his education cheaply, he won appointment to West Point. He graduated second in his class four years later and for nearly twenty years was engaged in various projects with the corps of engineers, acquiring a reputation as a highly competent engineer in his work on Mississippi flood control and Atlantic coastal defenses. In 1846 he was ordered to Texas and the next year joined the command of Gen. Winfield Scott in Mexico; he distinguished himself on several occasions and when the Mexican War ended in 1848, Lee held the rank of brevet colonel. For four years he was again with the corps of engineers and then in 1852 was appointed superintendent at West Point. Three years later he was sent to command a frontier cavalry regiment but found himself confined largely to court-martial duties and this, combined with his father-in-law's death and his wife's chronic illness, led him to consider resigning from the Army. He was on leave at his Arlington home when, in October 1859, he was ordered to Harpers Ferry to dislodge John Brown and his raiders from the federal arsenal there. As sectional strife became secession Lee maintained a devotion to the Union, but as his own state of Virginia began to talk of breaking away he wavered; he declined the command of all federal forces because he could not fight his own people and, hoping to stay out of the hostilities, resigned his commission in April 1861 and retired to his home. Within three days, however, he had been appointed commander of Virginia's forces and had accepted.

For several months he was concerned solely with preparing defenses for the anticipated invasion of Virginia and did not assume field command until the campaign in which West Virginia was lost to the Union. His prestige shaken by this failure, he was nonetheless retained by President Jefferson Davis and sent to fortify the southern Atlantic coastal region. In March 1862 he became military advisor to Davis and, despite his lack of direct authority, managed to work through and around Davis and the Confederate commander, Gen. J. E. Johnston, to send Gen. "Stonewall" Jackson on his spectacular Valley campaign. When Johnston was incapacitated, Lee assumed command of the new Army of Northern Virginia on June 1, 1862. Already a masterly strategist, he soon gained, under the pressure of dealing with often incompetent or recalcitrant subordinates, considerable tactical skill as well. In the Seven Days' Battle (June 26th–July 2nd) he forced McClellan to retreat from his position threatening Richmond and then, in a brilliantly conceived and executed maneuver, and relying on Jackson as his most able lieutenant, he defeated Pope at the second battle of Manassas (Bull Run). An attempt to carry the war to the North by invading Maryland was stymied by the interception of Lee's general orders by federals and his subsequent near-defeat by McClellan at Sharpsburg (Antietam). Two months later, in November 1862, he dealt heavy casualties in repulsing Burnside's attack at Fredericksburg. After a long hard winter, action resumed in May when Hooker attempted to move south to Richmond; another daring plan gave Lee a major victory at Chancellorsville, but cost him the invaluable Jackson. He struck north again, this time into Pennsylvania, in the summer of 1863; the lack of cooperation from various subordinates culminated in the disastrous defeat at Gettysburg in July. There was little significant action then until May 1864, when Grant headed for Richmond with a force outnumbering Lee's nearly two to one. The chronic shortages of men and material that

Lee had so far overcome now became decisive; limited to a strictly defensive role, Lee slowly retreated through Spotsylvania and Cold Harbor, sending Grant's casualty list up to 50,000 in a month. Finally and hopelessly entrenched at Petersburg, Lee could only watch as Grant developed his siege lines during the winter of 1864–1865. With retreat impossible, Lee at last ended the bloodshed by surrendering at Appomattox Courthouse on April 9, 1865. He was released on parole; in September he accepted appointment as president of Washington College in Lexington, Virginia, and he held this post until his death. He counseled acceptance of the defeat and hard work to restore the Union; his own application for amnesty and pardon was unanswered. He died on October 12, 1870, and subsequently the college changed its name to Washington and Lee.

LEHMAN, HERBERT HENRY (1878–1963), banker, public official, and philanthropist. Born in New York City on March 28, 1878, Lehman was of a wealthy banking family. He attended private schools and graduated from Williams College in 1899; after working for a textile concern, of which he became a vice president, he joined the family investment house of Lehman Brothers in 1908. In 1914 he was a co-founder of what became the American Joint Distribution Committee, an international Jewish relief fund. Too old for combat duty in World War I, he served for a time in the office of Assistant Secretary of the Navy Franklin D. Roosevelt and then received a captain's commission in the Army; he was concerned with procurement and expediting war material and for his services was promoted colonel and awarded in 1919 the Distinguished Service Medal. During the 1920s he became interested in politics; he was a close friend of Al Smith and managed his gubernatorial campaign in 1926. In 1928 he was nominated by the Democratic Party as Roosevelt's lieutenant governor and both were elected; reelected in 1930, he became the successful candidate for governor in 1932 when Roosevelt left New York for the presidency. In his ten years as governor, Lehman oversaw a period of government in New York marked by unquestioned integrity and dedication to liberal principles. His legislative program was dubbed the "Little New Deal" in recognition of both its similarity to Roosevelt's national program and his own close personal association with the President. In 1935, in a move that demonstrated his remarkable sincerity in promoting honest government, he appointed Republican Thomas E. Dewey as special prosecutor assigned to clean up the corruption in the Democratic borough of Manhattan; three years later he was reelected over Dewey, whose political career dated from his 1935 investigations. Upon leaving the State House in 1942 Lehman was appointed by Roosevelt director of the Office of Foreign Relief and Rehabilitation and remained in charge when the agency merged into the United Nations Relief and Rehabilitation Agency the next year; he served in this capacity without salary until 1946. In that year he ran unsuccessfully for the Senate; three years later he was elected to fill an unexpired term in that body and retained his seat in the 1950 election. He quickly became the chief liberal spokesman in the Senate and was one of few who dared to oppose openly Sen. Joseph McCarthy's infamous campaign; Lehman came during these years to be called "the conscience of the Senate." In 1956 he retired from national public life but retained his interest in state politics. He continued his life-long program of philanthropy; the number and size of his gifts he never revealed, but he was conceded to be, if anything, even more liberal in this respect than in politics. He died in New York City on December 5, 1963, the day before he was to receive the Presidential Medal for Freedom from Lyndon B. Johnson.

L'ENFANT, PIERRE CHARLES (1754–1825), engineer and architect. Born in Paris on August 2, 1754, L'Enfant studied for a time under his father, a painter, but in 1776 enthusiastically joined the American Revolutionary army. He was commissioned lieutenant of engineers and two years later promoted captain; after much disappointingly dull service in the North he transferred to the Southern theater of war, was wounded at Savannah, and captured in Charleston in May 1780. Finally released in 1782, he was soon honored by Congress with a promotion to major. In 1783 his designs for the medal and diploma of the Society of the Cincinnati, a fraternal organization of Revolutionary officers of which he was a member, were accepted and he was sent to Paris to have them executed and to organize the French branch of the Society. Returning the next year, he settled in New York City and began his architectural career; in 1787 he planned and oversaw the conversion of the old city hall into the temporary seat of the new federal government. Four years later he was engaged by President Washington to survey the site chosen for the new capital city and to create an overall plan for it. L'Enfant threw himself into the task with vast energy and, assuming an imperious and proprietary attitude toward the entire federal project, soon antagonized nearly everyone with whom he was associated. His basic plan of radial boulevards, formal parks, and an imposing, monumental atmosphere not unlike that of Versailles, was widely approved; he ordered work begun on a large scale even before the plans were complete, however, and sought constantly to override the authority of the District commissioners and even of the President. His immediate undertakings far exceeded his budget; at one point he discovered that the home of a prominent citizen lay in the path of a projected street and, with no authority whatever, had it torn down. Finally he was dismissed in February 1792. He continued to practise privately and was associated with Alexander Hamilton and Robert Morris in planning an industrial city in New Jersey, but he soon was at odds with the directors of the enterprise and was relieved of his position. Morris engaged him to design and build a house in Philadelphia; the grandiose plans that L'Enfant carried over Morris' objections were never fulfilled, but the expense contributed to the latter's bankruptcy in 1798. He obtained a number of small commissions from the government in later years, but his claim of $95,000 for his services in the planning of Washington was rejected and Congress awarded him $3,800 instead. In 1812 he declined a professorship of engineering at West Point. His last years were spent at the estate of a friend in Maryland where he died penniless on June 14, 1825. In 1909 his remains were moved to the Arlington National Cemetery.

LEVINE, JACK (1915–), painter. Born on January 3, 1915, in Boston, the son of a shoemaker who immigrated from Lithuania, Levine received his first art training at the Jewish Welfare Center. Later, while studying at the Boston Museum of Fine Arts, devoting his attention to the drawing techniques of the old Italian masters, he won the patronage of Dr. Denman Ross, a lecturer in design theory at Harvard, who was his teacher from 1929 to 1931. In 1935 he began working for the WPA Artists' Project in a studio in a poor section of Boston, and began painting scenes that expressed his sensitivity to social and political ills; these eventually made him famous and ranked him with protest painters like Ben Shahn. His style was expressionistic and combined tense brushwork, hot colors, and dramatic exaggerations, recalling the painters Roualt, Soutine, and Kokoschka. In this period, he completed "Brain Trust," "The Feast of Pure Reason," "The Street," "String Quartet," and other works. In 1945, having spent three years in the Army, he received a Guggenheim fellowship, and in 1946 an American Academy of Arts and Letters grant and, continuing in the genre of satirical commentary, produced "Welcome Home," "Apteka," "The Tombstone Cutter," "Every Inch a Ruler," "The Royal Family," "Pawnshop," "Gangster Funeral," and "The Trial." He was featured in many important exhibitions and won several awards. In 1955 he was given a retrospective show at the Whitney Museum in New York City. His work was collected by major museums throughout the country.

LEWIS, JOHN LLEWELLYN (1880–1969), labor leader. Born near Lucas, Iowa, on February 12, 1880, of Welsh immigrant parents, Lewis grew up in a coal-mining district surrounded by the turmoil of early labor organization; his father was blacklisted for several years for union activities. John left school after the seventh grade and at 15 entered the mines; possessed of a strong drive for self-improvement, he read widely and deeply, and was in later years recognized as something of an expert on English literature, American history, and the Bible. He wandered about the West for a few years in his early twenties, then returned to the mines and joined the United Mine Workers of America. In Lucas and later in Panama, Illinois, he advanced to president of the local, to Illinois lobbyist for the union, and in 1911 to general field agent of the American Federation of Labor. Finally, in 1920, he was elected president of the U.M.W., a position he held for 40 years. While his rapid consolidation of power gave him extensive control over a major American union, his period of great national prominence and influence did not begin until 1935; in that year he joined with several other labor leaders to form the Committee on Industrial Organization, a group within the A.F. of L. but intended to promote industrial unionism as an alternative and a necessary complement to the A. F. of L.'s steadfast devotion to trade and craft unionism. The A.F. of L., however, refused to countenance any challenge to its own sovereignty and, after an order to disband had been ignored, expelled ten unions, including the U.M.W. The Committee then reorganized itself as the independent Congress of Industrial Organizations and elected Lewis its first president. In the next few years he presided over the often violent struggle to introduce unionism into previously unorganized industries, particularly steel and automobiles; these were the years of the Little Steel strike, the Chicago Massacre, and the great sitdown strike against General Motors. In 1940 he reversed his earlier support of Franklin D. Roosevelt and attempted to rally labor against the President's third-term bid; taking Roosevelt's success as a repudiation, he resigned as president of the C.I.O. In 1942 he withdrew the U.M.W. from the C.I.O.; in 1946 he led the union back to the A.F. of L., only to withdraw from it two years later. A series of miners' strikes during World War II won wage increases but alienated large segments of the public and is held to have been responsible in part for the passage of the Smith-Connally and Taft-Hartley acts, both of which placed new restrictions on labor unions. In 1946 Lewis called for a strike of bituminous coal miners; President Truman countered by ordering a government seizure of the mines, and the strike ended immediately with some concessions to the miners that were soon extended to anthracite workers as well. Within a few months, however, Lewis called for another strike and ignored a federal court injunction to the contrary; early in 1947 he was found guilty of contempt of court and both he and the union were fined heavily. In 1948 he was convicted of contempt and fined again for ignoring another injunction against a strike called over a pension dispute. In 1952, with the extra impetus provided by an Illinois mine disaster of the previous year, in which 119 men were killed, he succeeded in persuading Congress to set federal safety standards for mines. He remained president of the U.M.W. until his retirement in 1960, after which time, as president emeritus, he served as chairman of the board of trustees of the union's welfare and retirement fund until his death on June 11, 1969.

LEWIS, MERIWETHER (1774–1809), soldier, explorer, and public official. Born in Albemarle County, Virginia, on August 18, 1774, Lewis grew up there, among the Virginia aristocracy, and in Georgia, where his family moved when he was ten. He returned alone to Virginia three years later to be educated by private tutors and was still there when, a member of the local militia, he was sent to take part in the suppression of the Whiskey Rebellion in 1794. A year later he enlisted in the regular Army and served several years, including a brief period under his future companion in exploration, William Clark. In 1801 President Jefferson offered him the position of private secretary and he immediately accepted; for two years thereafter he lived in the executive mansion in Washington, D.C., while Jefferson laid plans for an exploring journey across the continent and trained Lewis to lead it. He was sent to Philadelphia to learn map-making and other needed scientific skills. Finally, in 1803, with a $2500 appropriation from Congress and detailed instructions from Jefferson, Lewis set out for Illinois to recruit and train an exploring party. At his request, a share of the command had been offered to William Clark, and the names of the two men were thenceforth linked. Training and equipping some 40 men occupied the winter and early spring of 1803–1804; in May 1804 they set out "under a jentle brease up the Missourie" in their three well-stocked boats and by November had reached the villages of the Mandan Sioux, where they built Fort Mandan and wintered near what is now Bismarck, North Dakota. The next April, 16 men were sent back to St. Louis to report on the expedition's progress, and the rest continued up the Missouri to the three forks, which they named the Jefferson, the Madison, and the Gallatin rivers. They were accompanied now by a French-Canadian interpreter and his Indian wife, Sacagawea, who is often incorrectly credited with guiding the expedition. Procuring horses from the Shoshone, they crossed the continental divide and then made their way by canoe down the Clearwater, Snake, and Columbia rivers, arriving at the Pacific coast in November 1805. The following March they began the return journey; just beyond the Great Falls of the

Missouri the party split, Lewis exploring northward along the Marias River, and Clark striking south to the Yellowstone. They rejoined at the Missouri-Yellowstone junction and continued eastward. Their arrival in St. Louis in September 1806 was cause for national celebration, not the least because in their overlong absence they had been given up. The maps and specimens they brought back were invaluable scientific acquisitions, and among the remarkable accomplishments of the entire project was the fact that in more than two years of exploring unknown territory and dealing with sometimes hostile Indians, only one man had died. In November Lewis was appointed governor of the Louisiana Territory and for nearly two years he executed his office with great skill. In 1809, finding that some of his drafts on the government had not been honored, he set out for Washington to clear up the matter; he was near Nashville when, under mysterious circumstances, he died on October 11, 1809.

LEWIS, SINCLAIR (1885–1951), author. Born on February 7, 1885, in Sauk Centre, Minnesota, Lewis entered Yale in 1903. In his senior year he left college to join Helicon Hall, Upton Sinclair's socialist community in New Jersey, but he returned to graduate in 1908. For several years he was a reporter and editorial writer for various newspapers and magazines, and he worked for a number of publishing companies. His first novel, a juvenile book, was published in 1912; a series of minor novels followed, and from about 1915 his short stories were appearing regularly in popular magazines. In 1920 his first major work, *Main Street*, was published; a satirical, iconoclastic, and markedly sociological treatment of the American myth of the Small Town, the book won Lewis immediate fame and recognition as a serious author, and began a controversy that his work was to continue to feed throughout his life. Two years later he published *Babbitt*, a study of the typically complacent, conservative, conformist

American businessman that added a highly pejorative term to the vocabulary of popular sociology. *Arrowsmith*, about the frustrations of a man of science, appeared in 1925 and the next year was awarded a Pulitzer Prize, which Lewis declined. *Elmer Gantry*, 1927, was concerned with a religious evangelist and charlatan; *Dodsworth*, 1929, portrayed a retired industrialist touring in Europe. In 1930 Lewis became the first American to win the Nobel Prize for Literature. He was the most popular and most effective of the debunking writers between the World Wars; unlike the expatriates, however, he remained in the United States and founded his incisive criticisms and satirical characterizations on an underlying optimism and a profound sense of humor. Most notable among his later works were *It Can't Happen Here*, 1935, a description of a future Fascist takeover in the United States, *Cass Timberlane*, 1945, and *Kingsblood Royal*, 1947. In all he produced 22 novels, along with three plays, *Jayhawker* and *Dodsworth*, 1934, and *It Can't Happen Here*, 1936. He died in Rome on January 10, 1951, and his remains were returned to Sauk Centre.

LIBBY, WILLARD FRANK (1908–), chemist. Born in Grand Valley, Colorado, on December 17, 1908, Libby moved with his family to California about 1913. He graduated from the University of California at Berkeley in 1931 and remained to take his Ph.D. in 1933. Appointed an instructor in that year, he did research on, among other topics, radioactive materials, the gaseous state, and the behavior of neutrons. This work led in 1941 to his involvement with the Columbia University division of the Manhattan Project, to which his principal contribution was the development of a gaseous diffusion method for separating the various isotopes of uranium. With the successful completion of the atomic bomb program he moved in 1945 to the University of Chicago, becoming professor of chemistry and a member of the Institute for Nuclear Studies. On the basis of reports by other investigators that cosmic ray bombardment of the earth's upper atmosphere produced free neutrons and that neutrons could react with nitrogen to produce radioactive carbon 14, Libby hypothesized that such a transmutation process did in fact take place, that it had been going on long enough to establish an equilibrium in the amount of carbon 14 present in the biosphere, and that minute quantities were therefore present in all living things. Careful experiments confirmed this idea. He then went on to show that since the proportion of carbon 14 in organic matter was kept constant by life processes but at death began to diminish at a known rate (the half-life of the isotope), sensitive measurements of the amount of carbon 14 in formerly living material — wood, charcoal, or bone, for example — could be used to ascertain with considerable precision the age of a specimen. Announced in 1949, the radiocarbon dating technique provided a powerful and even revolutionary tool to archaeologists. From 1955 to 1959 Libby was a member of the Atomic Energy Commission and in the latter year became professor of chemistry and director of the Institute of Geophysics and Planetary Physics at the University of California at Los Angeles. In 1960 he was awarded the Nobel Prize for Chemistry for his radiocarbon work.

LIEBER, FRANCIS (1800 – 1872), political scientist. Born in Berlin on March 18, 1800, Lieber studied at the universities of Jena, Halle, and Dresden, and was awarded a Ph.D. from the first of these in 1820. In 1822 he joined the large number of liberal young Germans who enlisted in the Greek revolt against Turkish rule; he found the experience disillusioning and soon went to Rome where he met and was profoundly influenced by the German diplomat-historian B. G. Niebuhr. In 1823 he returned to Berlin and continued studying mathematics until he was imprisoned in 1824 for his liberal views. In 1826 he went to England, was employed for a time as a tutor, and the next year emigrated to the United States. He soon embarked upon his first major scholarly enterprise, founding and editing the *Encyclopedia Americana,* which appeared in 13 volumes from 1829 to 1833. In 1835 he accepted a professorship of history and political economy at South Carolina College (now the University of South Carolina) where he remained for 21 years. During this time he established a reputation as the nation's leading political theorist and the first to construct a rigorous and systematic philosophy of political science. His major writings, *Manual of Political Ethics,* 1838 – 1839, *Legal and Political Hermeneutics,* 1839, and *On Civil Liberty and Self-Government,* 1853, were widely read and highly praised. Lieber was a strong advocate of nationalism, though he opposed the centralization of political power. Among his many shrewd insights into the political functioning of a modern state was his crediting of the vast complex of voluntary and non-political associations in society with the maintenance of civil liberty. In 1857 he was invited to the chair of history and political science at Columbia College (then becoming a university) and he retained this post until transferring to the law school in 1865, where he remained for the rest of his life. During the Civil War he devised for the War Department his *Instructions for the Government of the Armies of the United States in the Field;* this work, the first such code of military law and procedure in the world, was adopted as *General Orders No. 100* in 1863. It was later adopted by the armed forces of several nations and became international law at the Hague conventions in 1899 and 1907. Lieber died in New York City on October 2, 1872.

LINCOLN, ABRAHAM (1809 – 1865), lawyer, public official, and 16th U.S. President. Born in a log cabin near Hodgenville, Kentucky, on February 12, 1809, Lincoln grew up in the poverty of a frontier farming family. At the age of seven he moved with his family to Indiana and two years later his mother died; the father remarried in 1819 and of his stepmother Lincoln long retained fond memories. He received little formal education, and that sporadically, but he early evinced a desire for learning, and his endeavors to this end — reading by firelight, walking miles to borrow books — have become legendary. He seems not to have been particularly happy with life on his father's farm; he did odd jobs on his own when possible, and in 1828 he made a brief trip to New Orleans. Two years later the family removed to Illinois; Lincoln was now of age and ready to strike out on his own, and after a second trip to New Orleans he settled at New Salem, Illinois, in 1831. For five years he worked at various jobs and served as captain of militia in the Black Hawk War of 1832; in his spare time he studied law and a year after his admission to the bar in 1836 he moved to the state capital of Springfield to further his practice. His first political involvement had been as a member of the state legislature for four terms from 1834 to 1841; though deeply democratic in spirit, his views on national policy, especially in economics, led him into the Whig Party. His later career was foreshadowed only by his reaction to the Alton riot of 1837 and the legislature's subsequent resolutions against antislavery agitation; in his protest against the latter he disapproved of both slavery and Abolitionists. His law practice in Springfield and on the circuit was successful, and in addition to his criminal and civil cases he was an effective lobbyist and counsel for the Illinois Central Railroad. In his most notable case he saved the first bridge across the Mississippi from being torn down by shipping interests. During these years he made only a brief return to politics with one term as Illinois' only Whig in Congress in 1847–1849; there he was a party regular, opposing the Mexican War and stumping for Zachary Taylor in 1848. His party efforts went unrewarded and his political career seemed at an end; but the Kansas-Nebraska Bill of his Illinois rival Stephen A. Douglas brought him back to the public eye and launched the great phase of his life. Speaking widely against the measure, he regained and surpassed his earlier prominence in Illinois politics, though he was unsuccessful in a bid for the Senate in 1855. The next year, however, he joined the migration of disorganized Whigs to the Republican Party and soon was its recognized leader in the state. In 1858 he challenged Douglas directly in the campaign for the latter's Senate seat and in a series of famous debates hammered away at the incumbent's avoidance of the moral aspect of the slavery issue and his paradoxical advocacy of his "popular sovereignty" doctrine, on the one hand, and of certain implications of the Dred Scott case, on the other. The tactic was successful; though he lost the election, he gained a national reputation that continued to grow, reaching sufficient proportions to win him the presidential nomination at the Republican convention two years later. While taking no active part, he maintained close control over the campaign from Springfield; the vote split on sectional lines and, though he failed of a majority in the popular vote, Lincoln was elected to the presidency by the Electoral College. From 1854, through the Douglas debates, in the campaign of 1860, and at his inauguration in March 1861, he maintained a moderate position on slavery; he was willing to allow it to remain, with full federal sanction, in the South, but he was adamantly opposed to its extension into the territories. Little faith was placed in Northern moderation among the councils of the slave states, however, and upon taking office Lincoln was already faced with a hostile Confederacy of seven former, now seceded states. Further, Fort Sumter, in Charleston harbor, was being threatened by South Carolina forces. After considerable hesitation, the President tried a characteristically conciliatory approach: apprising the governor of South Carolina of his intentions, he dispatched a relief expedition to bring needed supplies to the fort, but no arms or reinforcements, thus demonstrating both a dedication to peace and a determination to maintain the federal presence despite secession. The plan did not conciliate; on April 12, 1861, Charleston harbor batteries fired on Sumter and opened four years of bloody conflict. With Congress in recess, Lincoln quickly assumed broad executive powers, proclaiming a blockade of Southern ports, issuing calls to the states for troops, suspending habeas corpus, and initiating unappropriated expenditures. His acts were ratified and his assumed powers confirmed when Congress assembled in July, but by then he was faced with the tangled problems of military organization and strategy. Lacking either a fully competent commander or military knowledge, he suffered through the disastrous Union defeat at First Bull Run and several subsequent setbacks. The search for a viable system of command and for a man equal to the task was long and frustrating; not until he brought Gen. Ulysses S. Grant from the western theater in 1864 did the Union Army begin to function efficiently and with an integrated overall strategy. Meanwhile, domestic political problems diverted much of the President's energy from the prosecution of the war. In forming his Cabinet he had created a somewhat unstable coalition of conservative and radical advisors, and this was a source of constant and increasing friction; and as the war dragged on, Northern popular sentiment began to shift against him, particularly since war requisitions, conscription, and high casualty rates were placing a heavy burden on the public. In contrast to popular feeling, Congress was coming more into the hands of Radicals, and Lincoln, always an astute politician, found it expedient to accommodate them to a degree, and this, in addition to the humanitarian impulse, was a significant force behind the preliminary and final Emancipation Proclamations of September 1862 and January 1863, respectively. Though the Proclamation was largely symbolic — it applied only to areas not under federal control — and, he believed, probably unconstitutional, it cast a new light on the war to preserve the Union, won additional and needed liberal support abroad, and

forestalled the Radical schism. The establish ment of a new rationale for the war was fur thered in November 1863 when he spoke a the dedication of a national cemetery on the site of the Battle of Gettysburg, fought the preceding July; the emphasis was now placed on the preservation of popular government rather than simply the Union. Lincoln's Gettysburg Address remains, in its brevity and utter simplicity, the most eloquent expression, not merely of the administration's war aims, but also of a large part of the American faith. As the election of 1864 approached, Lincoln's prospects for reelection appeared dim; military failures had given rise to a widespread desire for peace, and the nomination by the Democrats of former Union commander Gen. George B. McClellan on a peace platform seemed ominous. In the few months before the election, however, Northern military fortunes rose as Sheridan routed the Confederate forces in the Shenandoah Valley and Sherman captured Atlanta. Lincoln was easily reelected; by the inauguration in March 1865, victory was in sight, and the President was already calling for patience and moderation in the reorganizing of the South. While he pushed the 13th Amendment through Congress and submitted it to the states, he was slowly developing a reconstruction policy; but he had vetoed the Radical-sponsored Wade-Davis plan the summer before and was now faced with increasing hostility in Congress. The reconstructed governments of Louisiana, Arkansas, Tennessee, and Virginia failed to receive congressional recognition; it seems certain that, had he lived out his term, he would have met the same rancorous opposition from the Radicals that wrecked his successor's administration. On April 11, 1865, two days after Lee's surrender at Appomattox, Lincoln made his final public address and, without proposing a specific plan for reconstruction, again called for the swift readmission of the Southern states, a general policy of leniency and forgiveness, and a rededication to harmonious union. Three days later, on the evening of

April 14, he was shot by a crazed actor, John Wilkes Booth, while attending a performance at Ford's Theater. He died the next morning and was buried amid deep national mourning in Springfield. In the years and decades that followed the figure of Abraham Lincoln gathered about itself the trappings of a towering legend, until he became in every sense a mythic hero. His rise from poor frontier farmer to great national leader, his ingrained democracy and humanity, and perhaps most of all his image as one more saddened than angered by treachery and treason, touched a deep chord in the American imagination as it had never before, nor has it since, been touched.

LINDBERGH, CHARLES AUGUSTUS (1902–), aviator. Born in Detroit on February 4, 1902, Lindbergh entered the University of Wisconsin in 1920, but left college to enroll in the flying school in Lincoln, Nebraska, run by the Nebraska Aircraft Corporation. In 1923 he bought a World War I surplus Curtiss "Jenny" and made his first solo flight, subsequently making barnstorming trips through the southern and midwestern states. He entered the Army flying school at Brooks Field, Texas, in 1924, completed his training in about a year, and was commissioned a captain in the U.S. Air Service. In 1926 he became an airmail pilot on the St. Louis-Chicago route. Drawn by a $25,000 prize offered by Raymond B. Orteig for the first nonstop flight from New York to Paris, in 1927, with several St. Louis businessmen as his backers, he purchased a Ryan monoplane with a single radial air-cooled engine, which he christened *The Spirit of St. Louis*. On May 10th he flew from the factory in San Diego to Curtiss Field on Long Island, making one stop in St. Louis and setting a transcontinental record of 21 hours and 20 minutes. After being delayed by bad weather, he embarked on May 20th from Long Island's Roosevelt Field, crossed the Atlantic, and 33 1/2 hours later arrived at Le Bourget airport near Paris. He was met by a tumultuous crowd, who were only with diffi-

culty restrained from wrecking the *Spirit* for souvenirs, given a reception by the French government, and returned to America to be greeted with New York's greatest ticker-tape parade. He was received as the greatest hero of the adulatory decade of the 1920s and was voted the Medal of Honor by special act of Congress. In December he arrived at Mexico City from Washington after a 27-hour 10-minute flight and at a reception held in his honor he met Anne Spencer Morrow, daughter of U.S. ambassador Dwight Morrow. They were married in 1929; in 1932 their two-year-old son was kidnapped and murdered and the attendant publicity made it the most sensational crime of the 1930s. A carpenter, Bruno Richard Hauptman, was convicted of the crime and executed in 1936. Until 1939 they lived in Europe, during which time he was able to survey German air power and make significant reports to the U.S. government. In the United States during 1940–1941 he was a leading member of the America First Committee and made speeches across the nation urging that America remain out of the war. For these activities he was criticized by President Roosevelt, and in April 1941 he resigned his commission from the Air Corps. When the United States entered the war he found it difficult to obtain security clearance for defense work; finally he was employed in a civilian capacity as consultant to the Ford Motor Company and the United Aircraft Company, for which he accompanied 50 combat missions in the Pacific. After the war he went to Germany with a naval commission to survey the progress of German jet aircraft, rocket, and guided missile development. He then settled in Darien, Connecticut. He was named brigadier general in the Air Force Reserve by President Eisenhower in 1954 and was a consultant to the Department of Defense and to Pan American World Airways. For his story of the flight to Paris, *The Spirit of St. Louis*, 1953, he won a Pulitzer Prize. He also wrote the autobiographical *We*, in 1927 and *Of Flight and Life*, 1948.

LINDSAY, NICHOLAS VACHEL (1879–1931), poet. Born on November 10, 1879, in Springfield, Illinois, Vachel Lindsay studied for three years at Hiram College and in 1900 moved to Chicago. He attended night classes at the Art Institute from then until 1903 and later, in 1904–1905, continued his art studies at the New York School of Art. Devoutly religious, he also lectured on behalf of the Y.M.C.A. and the Anti-Saloon League. In 1906 he set out on foot to wander through the South, trading poems for food and lodging. He spent a few years in Illinois, again lecturing, and in 1912 walked west to New Mexico. During these years he was writing and polishing his early poems and in 1913 *Poetry* magazine published his "General William Booth Enters Into Heaven," an elegy on the founder of the Salvation Army. Highly original in all respects, the work was particularly remarkable for its rhythmic qualities. During the next several years he published a number of volumes of verse containing his best pieces—"The Congo," "Bryan, Bryan, Bryan, Bryan," "Abraham Lincoln Walks at Midnight," "The Santa Fe Trail," "The Eagle that is Forgotten." In addition to the compelling rhythms of the poems, he worked with a seemingly intuitive understanding of the appeal of popular and cult heroes and made them the subjects of many of his finest compositions. As his poetry grew rapidly in popularity he toured the country giving recitals. His chanting of his works attracted large audiences, and his success was crowned in 1920 when he became the first American poet to be invited to recite at Oxford. His later writings were, however, almost uniformly without interest. He died in Springfield on December 5, 1931.

LINDSEY, BENJAMIN BARR (1869–1943), jurist. Born on November 25, 1869, in Jackson, Tennessee, Lindsey moved to Denver at the age of 16 and was admitted to the Colorado bar in 1894. He secured legislation to establish the first juvenile court in the United States in 1899 and as its presiding judge from 1900 to 1927 made it the model for others that were subsequently established throughout the country. Based on his philosophy that juvenile delinquency was not an isolated problem, but one that related to many other social factors, he introduced reforms that protected juvenile offenders and made them wards of the court. He felt that juveniles should be treated rather than punished. He moved to California in 1928 and, as judge of the Superior Court from 1934, he became known as a political reformer, contending vigorously against the outmoded political system that made individualized legal treatment impossible. In Los Angeles in 1939 he helped establish and presided over a new "conciliation court," which dealt specifically with divorce cases that might be susceptible to reconciliation. He proposed a family court that would deal simultaneously with cases involving both divorce and delinquency. He also advocated "companionate marriage," in which couples would practise birth control and, if childless and if their marriage proved unsound, could separate at any time by mutual consent without legal proceedings. He was throughout his career a leading and highly controversial reformer. Among his written works were *Problems of the Children*, 1903, *Children in Bondage* (with George Creel), 1914, and *Childhood, Crime, and the Movies*, 1926. He died in Los Angeles on March 26, 1943.

LIPPMANN, WALTER (1889–   ), journalist and author. Born in New York City on September 23, 1889, Lippmann graduated from Harvard in 1910. He joined Lincoln Steffens briefly on *Everybody's Magazine*, and in 1913 his first book appeared, *A Preface to Politics*, containing penetrating criticism of popular prejudices. In 1914 he was a founder of the *New Republic*, a liberal weekly, and became its associate editor. In numerous contributions his praise of the Progressive Party principles of 1912 influenced President Wilson, who conferred personally with Lippmann and selected him to assist in formulating the Fourteen Points and in developing the concept of the

League of Nations. In 1917 he was an aide to Secretary of War Newton D. Baker and during World War I was a captain in U.S. Military Intelligence. He attended the peace conference at Versailles and returned to the United States in 1919, rejoining the *New Republic*. In 1921 he became editor of the *New York World*. Two thousand or more of his editorials were printed in that paper before he left it in 1931 and began to produce "Today and Tomorrow," for the *New York Herald Tribune*. Syndicated internationally in at least 200 newspapers, the column won Pulitzer Prizes in 1958 and 1962, earned him a wide following and established him as the foremost analyst of social, political, and ethical problems in the United States. An acute and highly individual analyst of the contemporary scene, he sought a "liberal democracy" and warned against the forces in modern society that led away from that goal. He contributed articles to more than 50 magazines, wrote a large number of books on famous men and events, and ten books of political philosophy, the most significant of which were *Public Opinion*, 1922, *A Preface to Morals*, 1929, *The Good Society*, 1937, and *Essays in the Public Philosophy*, 1955. HIs contributions to political thought were compiled in *The Essential Lippmann*, 1963.

LIVINGSTON, EDWARD (1764–1836), lawyer, public official, and diplomat. Born in Columbia County, New York, on May 28, 1764, the younger brother of Robert R., Livingston graduated from the College of New Jersey (now Princeton) in 1781. An additional year of study under private tutors was followed by his entering a law office where, with Alexander Hamilton, Aaron Burr, and James Kent, he studied until his admission to the bar in 1785. He began practice in New York City and attained considerable prominence. In 1794 he was elected as a Republican to Congress; there he led the continuing opposition to Jay's Treaty through the withholding of appropriations. He was continued in office until 1801 and in that year, when the House was called upon to decide the presidency, supported Jefferson over Burr. In that year also he was appointed U. S. attorney for New York and elected mayor of the city; two years later, recovering from yellow fever, he discovered that a confidential clerk had absconded with a large amount of government money and, taking responsibility upon himself, he resigned both his offices, relinquished his property, and shortly thereafter left New York for New Orleans. The sale of his property and the large law practice he soon established in his new home enabled him to repay his government and private debts with interest by 1826. During the War of 1812 Livingston was active in organizing the defense of Louisiana against the British and served as an unofficial advisor to Gen. Andrew Jackson in New Orleans. In 1820 he was elected to the state legislature and the next year appointed by that body to prepare a code of criminal and penal law; completed in 1824, the code was accidentally burned but was finally presented the next year. Though not adopted in Louisiana, the code was widely praised and gained serious attention and influence throughout the world. In 1822 he was elected to Congress, where he remained until 1829, when he entered the Senate. To that body he submitted his proposed *System of Penal Law for the United States of America*, but no action was taken. In 1831 President Jackson appointed him secretary of state, and as one of the President's closest advisors he drafted the 1832 proclamation on nullification and several other state papers. In 1833 he became minister to France, where he attempted to secure reparations for maritime spoliation suffered under the Berlin and Milan decrees of the Napoleonic period; after two years of diplomatic muddle, he resigned and returned to his recently inherited New York estate where he died on May 23, 1836.

LIVINGSTON, ROBERT R. (1746–1813), lawyer, public official, and diplomat. Born on November 27, 1746, in New York City, Livingston was the elder brother of Edward and a member of a long-prominent New York family. He graduated from King's College (now Columbia University) in 1765 and in 1770 was admitted to the bar. He was appointed city recorder in 1773, but two years later his colonial sympathies led to his dismissal from that post and his election to the Continental Congress. In this and his subsequent periods of service in Congress, he was especially noted for his wide-ranging activity and influence in committee, though his membership on the committee charged with drafting the Declaration of Independence bore little result and he was absent from the signing. Having returned to New York in 1776, he aided in the drafting of the state's first constitution and under it became the first chancellor of New York in 1777. From 1779 to 1781 he was again in Congress and was again one of its busiest members; in the latter year he was appointed secretary of the newly created department of foreign affairs and in this position supervised the instructing of the peace negotiators in Paris and made considerable progress in securing proper recognition of American representatives in world capitals. In June 1783 he returned to New York and in addition to another term in Congress in 1784–1785, was active in state affairs. In 1788 he was a leading advocate for ratifying the Constitution and the following year administered the oath of office to George Washington in New York City. Receiving what he considered insufficient recognition for his efforts on behalf of the Constitution, he became an anti-Federalist, opposing Jay's Treaty and, in a gubernatorial election, Jay himself. Soon after the Republican victory of 1800, however, came appointment as minister to France; he resigned his chancellorship and sailed for France in October 1801. There, after some preliminary diplomacy concerning the purchase of New Orleans, he was joined by James Monroe in April 1803, and the two proceeded, without authority, to purchase the entire Louisiana Territory from France. While in France he met Robert Fulton and provided him technical and financial assistance in developing a steamboat that

was successfully tested on the Seine in 1803. Livingston had long been interested in the possibilities of steam navigation and had secured from New York a monopoly on operations of this kind on the state's rivers in 1798; he now renewed the monopoly with Fulton and, resigning his office, returned to New York in 1804 to continue experimentation. The first successful boat in 1807 was named for Livingston's estate, "Clermont." Livingston continued his interests in steam navigation, scientific farming, and other intellectual pursuits, and remained out of public life; he died at "Clermont" on February 26, 1813.

LLOYD, HENRY DEMAREST (1847–1903), journalist, author, and social reformer. Born in New York City on May 1, 1847, Lloyd was educated at Columbia College and Law School, was admitted to the bar, and engaged for a time in reform activities in New York, including the campaign against Tammany Hall. In 1872 he joined the staff of the *Chicago Tribune* as financial and literary editor and editorial writer; during his 13 years on the paper his continuing interest in reform led him to conduct numerous investigations into abuses of public interest, particularly those perpetrated by corporations and trusts, and to publish his findings in articles that, by their thorough documentation and crusading tone, became sensations. Such articles as "The Story of a Great Monopoly," published in the *Atlantic Monthly* in 1881, made Lloyd the first of the "muckrakers." In 1885 he left the *Tribune* and devoted himself to the cause of progressive reform. He wrote a number of books on problems of labor and monopoly, his most famous being his study of the Standard Oil Company, *Wealth Against Commonwealth*, 1894. In the same year he defended Eugene V. Debs in the legal battles growing out of the Pullman strike and accepted the nomination of the National People's Party for Congress. During his last years he traveled extensively, particularly in England and New Zealand where he studied new methods of dealing with the problems of labor; his observations and his advocacy of similar reforms in the United States were contained in several books, among them *Labour Copartnership*, 1898, and *A Country Without Strikes*, 1900. He was one of the principal spokesmen for the anthracite miners in the negotiations that followed the great strike of 1902. He died while engaged in a campaign for public ownership of street railways in Chicago, on September 28, 1903.

LOCKE, DAVID ROSS (1833 – 1888), "Petroleum V. Nasby," journalist. Born in Vestal, New York, on September 20, 1833, Locke began at the age of ten a seven years' apprenticeship on the *Democrat*, a political journal in nearby Cortland. For two years thereafter he was an itinerant printer throughout the country, and in 1852 settled in Plymouth, Ohio, long enough to help found the *Plymouth Advertiser*. He soon resumed wandering from town to town in Ohio and was editor of the *Findlay Jeffersonian* when, in March 1861, he published the first of his letters over the signature of Petroleum Vesuvius Nasby. The character Nasby—later depicted by cartoonist Thomas Nast—was the embodiment of everything Locke detested: dissolute, intemperate, illiterate, dishonest, cowardly, hypocritical. Through the ironic manipulation of this "late pastor uv the Church uv the New Dispensation, Chaplain to his excellency the President, and p.m. at Confederate x roads, kentucky," Locke maintained a running attack on slavery, Copperheads, and the Democratic Party. Nasby wrote, as the humorous fashion of the day required, with unorthodox spelling and tortured grammar, and his logical processes were absurd. The Nasby letters were a great success, enjoyed even by President Lincoln, who was known to read them to his Cabinet on occasion. A collection in book form, *The Nasby Papers*, appeared in 1864 and the next year Locke became editor of the *Toledo Blade*, soon acquiring a controlling interest in it. He refused offers of government employment from both Lincoln and Grant; in 1871

he went to New York to join the *Evening Mail*, but before long had returned to Ohio. He became a highly popular lecturer on the lyceum circuit; the Nasby letters continued to appear in collections, and others of Locke's publications included *The Morals of Abou Ben Adhem*, 1875, and *The Demagogue*, 1881. The final Nasby letter was published in December 1887 and Locke died two months later, on February 15, 1888.

LODGE, HENRY CABOT (1850 – 1924), author and public official. Born in Boston on May 12, 1850, Lodge graduated from Harvard in 1871 and entered the Law School, taking his law degree in 1875. Meanwhile he had been assisting Henry Adams in editing the *North American Review* from 1873 to 1876, and in the latter year was awarded his Ph.D. and admitted to the bar. From 1876 to 1879 he lectured on American history at Harvard; in 1880 – 1881 he was a member of the Massachusetts legislature and after suffering defeat in the Mugwump revolt in 1884 was elected as a Republican to Congress in 1886. In his three terms in the House he increased his reputation for party regularity while championing the protection of voting rights and civil service reform. He had continued his scholarly career during these years as well, publishing several distinguished biographies — *Alexander Hamilton*, 1882, *Daniel Webster*, 1883, and *George Washington*, 1889 — and a number of historical studies, and editing a nine volume *Works of Alexander Hamilton*, 1885 – 1886, and *The Federalist*, 1891. In 1893 he was elected to the Senate and he remained in that body for the rest of his life. He rose steadily in prominence both within his party and nationally; he was a member of the Alaskan Boundary Commission in 1903 and of the U.S. Immigration Commission from 1907 to 1910. Staunchly Republican and conservative, he was a leading opponent of the Populist free-silver campaign and an equally strong supporter of the imperialist policies that stemmed from the Spanish-American War. With little sympathy for progressive reform legislation, and far from an idealist in practical affairs, he became soon after the election of 1912 the principal critic of the Wilson administration. He called for American entry into World War I after the sinking of the *Lusitania*, supported vigorous action when war did finally come, and advocated harsh peace terms. He had long arrogated to himself leadership in the field of foreign affairs when, in 1918, he became both Republican floor leader in the Senate and chairman of the foreign relations committee. Utilizing the powers of both positions he organized the Senate opposition to the League of Nations. When the Versailles peace treaty, which included, against his wishes, the League Covenant, was submitted for ratification he reported it out of committee with a number of amending reservations; these, intended to retain what he considered an essential degree of national sovereignty, were unacceptable to the President. The amendments were approved by the Senate, whereupon Wilson directed Democratic senators to vote against the treaty, which was duly defeated. Lodge's prestige rose greatly as a result of this victory. In 1921 he was one of the four American delegates to the Washington conference on arms limitation and later led the opposition to Harding's proposal to join the World Court. Lodge died on November 9, 1924.

LOEB, JACQUES (1859–1924), biologist. Born on April 7, 1859, in Mayen, Germany, Loeb was educated at the universities of Berlin, Munich, and Strasbourg, taking his M.D. from the last in 1884. He began his research work at the University of Würzburg in 1886 and two years later moved to Strasbourg; from 1889 to 1891 he was at the biological station in Naples. During these years he was primarily concerned with investigating the so-called instinctual behavior of animals and plants, and was able to demonstrate that many such responses were actually explicable in relatively simple chemical terms and were evoked auto-

matically by specific stimuli. His observations led him to formulate his famous theory of tropisms, which, like the hypothetical instincts, were inherited, but which, unlike them, were demonstrably mechanically determined by the subject's physiology. In 1891 he traveled to the United States and joined the faculty of Bryn Mawr College; the next year he moved to the University of Chicago and in 1902 went to the University of California at Berkeley. His work with tropisms led him to investigate, from a mechanist viewpoint, sexual attraction and reproduction in lower animals. By introducing controlled variations in the chemical and physical environment he was able to induce parthenogenetic reproduction in the eggs of sea urchins and frogs. He also demonstrated that the phenomenon of regeneration, the replacement of lost tissues or members, was also chemically determined and therefore subject both to error and to the control of the experimenter. All of Loeb's researches were dominated by his desire to substitute rigorous scientific for superstitious and mystical explanations of the life process. In 1910 he joined the Rockefeller Institute for Medical Research; there he continued his experimental work and in his last years made valuable contributions to the chemistry of colloids. He died while vacationing in Bermuda on February 11, 1924.

LOEB, JAMES MORRIS (1867–1933), banker and philanthropist. Born in New York City on August 6, 1867, Loeb graduated in 1888 from Harvard, where he studied under and formed a close friendship with Charles Eliot Norton. In deference to his father's wishes, he joined Kuhn, Loeb & Company, bankers, and remained there until his father died in 1905. During that period he contributed substantially to education and civil and political reform. He made numerous gifts to Harvard, in 1902 establishing the Charles Eliot Norton traveling fellowship to enable Radcliffe and Harvard students to attend the American School of Classical Studies in Athens. In 1905, as a memorial to his mother, he endowed the American Institute of Musical Art in New York City, which later was combined with the Juilliard Musical Foundation. After that year he resided in Europe, first in Munich and after 1913 in Murnau, Bavaria, and devoted himself to collecting, playing the cello and piano, and to various literary endeavors. He translated many important works on Greek drama and poetry by French scholars, among them Paul Delcharme's *Euripides and the Spirit of His Dreams* in 1906, and Maurice Croiset's *Aristophanes and the Political Parties at Athens* in 1909. In 1910 he founded the Loeb Classical Library, eventually comprising 360 volumes of Greek and Latin literature, with complete edited original texts opposite their English translations. The translating and editing was done by outstanding American and British scholars. He was active in societies to further studies of ancient Greece and Rome, in the Archeological Institute of America, and humanistic organizations in Germany. He died in Murnau on May 28, 1933. In his will large endowments were made to Harvard's department of classics, to the American School of Classical Studies in Athens, Columbia, the Murnau town council, and the German Institute for Psychiatric Research, which he also founded and maintained. His collections of ancient pottery, bronzes, vases, gold ornaments, and engraved gems were left to the Museum Antiker Kleinkunst in Munich.

LONDON, JOHN GRIFFITH (1876–1916), author. Born on January 12, 1876, in San Francisco, Jack London grew up in poverty and at 14 left school to lead a wandering and adventurous life. Though employed briefly by the fish patrol in San Francisco Bay, he spent more time on the other side of the law as an oyster pirate. His passionate interest in the sea led to little more than waterfront loafing until 1893, when he shipped as a common sailor aboard a sealing vessel that ventured as far as Japan. Upon his return he drifted from job to job and finally in 1894 traveled east in the rearguard of Kelly's Army (similar to the more famous Coxey's Army). He wandered in the East, was jailed for a month for vagrancy in New York, and then, determined to make something of himself, returned to California and to school. He completed high school in a year and entered the University of California in 1896. His experiences as a hobo and an occasional worker, and his wide reading, particularly of Herbert Spencer, had made him by this time a Marxian socialist. He left college after a few months, and failing to find a market for his writing, in mid-1897 joined the Klondike gold rush; ill health forced him to return the next year and he turned again to writing. His stories finally began to be accepted by various periodicals and many of them were collected for his first book, *The Son of the Wolf*, 1900. In these, as in most of his writings, he relied heavily on his personal experiences: from the far North came *The Call of the Wild*, 1903, and *White Fang*, 1906; his earlier sea voyage resulted in *The Sea Wolf*, 1904; and a period in 1903 spent in the slums of London furnished him with the material for *The People of the Abyss*, 1903. In 1904 he spent six months as a correspondent in the Russo-Japanese War and the following year he settled permanently in Glen Ellen, California. In 1907 he sailed to the South Pacific in his ketch and four years later recounted his experiences in *The Cruise of the Snark*. In much of his writing London displayed a fascination with strength, violence, and the primitive; his popularity rested on the action and adventure contained in his tales and owed little to the constant tension between his Nietzschean predilections and socialistic convictions, a conflict he made explicit in *The Iron Heel*, 1907. His later writings include *Martin Eden*, 1909, *Burning Daylight*, 1910, and *The Valley of the Moon*, 1913; three autobiographical books, *Tales of the Fish Patrol*, 1905, *The Road*, 1907, and *John Barleycorn*, 1913; and numerous essays and stories. London died at his Glen Ellen ranch on November 22, 1916.

LONG, HUEY PIERCE (1893–1935), public official. Born near Winnfield, Louisiana, on August 30, 1893, Long graduated from high school and in brief periods of study at the law schools of the University of Oklahoma and Tulane University acquired enough legal knowledge to be admitted to the bar in 1915. Three years later he was elected to the Louisiana Railroad Commission and in his ten years in this post (the board's name was changed to the Public Service Commission in 1912) he made valuable contributions to the equitable regulation of public utilities, and this performance gave substance to his claim to represent the poor, dispossessed, rural folk of the state. Long's campaign style, flamboyant, democratic, and unconventional, was perfectly attuned to the mounting grievances and long-suppressed agrarian populism of the majority outside the cities, and after an initial defeat in 1924, he captured the governorship and great political power in 1928. Though he managed to institute most of his promised public works program—a vast and useful one including roads, bridges, and a major expansion of Louisiana State University—he was hampered by the opposition of the New Orleans-based Democratic Party machine; he forced the Old Regulars into his camp in 1930 by being elected to the Senate while retaining the governor's seat. The latter post he kept until he could hand it over to a trusted lieutenant and in January 1932 he formally entered the Senate. "Kingfish," as he was widely known, appeared to most of the nation to be merely a backwoods buffoon; while retaining his nearly complete control of state affairs, however, he embarked in 1933 on a campaign to gain national power. Reversing his earlier support of the New Deal, he formulated his own "Share the Wealth" program, which while economically unsound, appealed strongly to great numbers of people. He explained the program in his book *Every Man a King*, 1933. In 1934 a challenge to his control in Louisiana called him home, and by means of a number of new laws that he forced through the legislature he abolished local government in the state and became a virtual dictator. In 1935, with the Rev. Charles Coughlin and the Rev. Gerald L. K. Smith, both popular agitators, anti-Semites, and radical reformers, he founded the National Union for Social Justice. In August of that year he announced his intention to run for President, a move that was seen as a real threat to Roosevelt. A month later he was shot while at the state capitol in Baton Rouge and died two days later, on September 10, 1935.

LONGFELLOW, HENRY WADSWORTH (1807–1882), poet. Born in Portland, Maine (then a part of Massachusetts), on February 27, 1807, Longfellow was educated in private schools and at Bowdoin College, from which he graduated in 1825, having been a classmate of Nathaniel Hawthorne. Determined from an early age upon a literary career, he resisted pressure to go into law and accepted an offer to return to Bowdoin as professor of modern languages provided he first pursue further study in Europe; in 1835, after six years at Bowdoin, he received a similar offer from Harvard, and following an additional year in Europe, he became head of the modern language program there, a demanding position that he held for 18 years. He had had poems published in periodicals from time to time since his youth—"The Village Blacksmith" appeared in 1840—and at Bowdoin he had become a noted translator and critic of European literature; his trips to Europe exposed him to German romanticism, a major influence on his writing, and soon after taking up residence in Cambridge he published his first book of verse, *Voices of the Night*, 1839. Despite his burdensome duties at Harvard, he continued to publish his poetry regularly and it enjoyed an increasing popularity; *Ballads and Other Poems*, 1841, was followed by *Poems on Slavery*, 1842, *Poems*, 1845, *The Belfry of Bruges and Other Poems*, 1846, the widely celebrated *Evangeline*, 1847, *The Seaside and the Fireside*, 1850, and *The Golden*

Legend, 1851. In 1854 he gave up teaching and soon produced *The Song of Hiawatha*, 1855, *The Courtship of Miles Standish, and Other Poems*, 1858, and *Tales of a Wayside Inn* (which began with "Paul Revere's Ride"), 1863. The death of his second wife in 1861 had a profound and lasting effect on Longfellow; for solace he turned to Dante's *Divine Comedy* and his distinguished translation finally appeared in 1865–1867. By this time he was America's best known and best loved poet, and his fame was worldwide; he received honorary degrees from Oxford and Cambridge in 1868 and his home, long a center of Boston intellectual life in its greatest period, now attracted the outstanding men of the world. Sweetness, gentleness, romantic vision shaded by melancholy, were the characteristic features of both his poetry and himself; universally venerated in old age, he continued to live quietly in Cambridge and to write: among others, *The Divine Tragedy*, 1871, *Christus, a Mystery*, which he intended as his masterwork, 1872, *The Hanging of the Crane*, 1874, *Ultima Thule*, 1880, and, published posthumously, *Michael Angelo*, 1883. Longfellow died on March 24, 1882, and two years later was honored by the placing of a memorial bust in Poet's Corner of Westminster Abbey.

LOUIS, JOE (1914–   ), boxer. Born on May 13, 1914, in a sharecropper's shack in Lexington, Alabama, Joseph Louis Barrow grew up in Detroit. He sold newspapers, shined shoes, and drove an ice wagon until he became a sparring partner in a local gym at the age of 16. In his first fight he was floored six times in three rounds. Rapidly improving his style, he won 50 of 59 amateur bouts, 43 by knockouts, and was a Golden Gloves champion. He turned professional in Chicago's Comiskey Park on July 4, 1934, knocking out Jack Cracken in the first round. In his first year of professional boxing, he won 10 out of 12 fights with knockouts, establishing a reputation in the Midwest for his paralyzing punches. He went East to fight former champion Primo Carnera, scored a six-round knockout, and was called thereafter the "Brown Bomber." On June 22, 1937, he knocked out James Braddock for the heavyweight championship of the world. He was the youngest fighter ever to hold the crown. He defended it 25 times, more than the eight preceding champions combined, scored knockouts against 21 of the challengers, and won four bouts by decisions. In 71 professional fights he knocked out six world champions—Carnera, Jack Sharkey, Braddock, Max Baer, Max Schmeling, and Jersey Joe Walcott. In the Army during World War II he fought exhibition matches for the troops and won two title fights, donating his share of the purse to Army and Navy relief. He retired undefeated in 1949, one of the most beloved, sportsmanly figures in boxing. He grossed an estimated $4,225,000 and drew three million-dollar gates, but because of huge tax liabilities was never a millionaire. He made unsuccessful comeback attempts against Ezzard Charles and Rocky Marciano to try to pay the government. Thereafter he was an executive of the International Boxing Club. He never lost his large popular following and in 1954 was elected to boxing's Hall of Fame.

LOVEJOY, ELIJAH PARISH (1802–1837), Abolitionist editor. Born on November 9, 1802, in Albion, Maine, Lovejoy graduated from Waterville (now Colby) College in 1826. He taught school in Maine and from 1827 in St. Louis. He studied for the ministry at Princeton, was licensed in 1833, and returned to St. Louis to edit the Presbyterian newspaper, the *St. Louis Observer*. He used the weekly as a vehicle for social protest, supporting in editorials the temperance and gradual emancipation movements. He incurred the wrath of the St. Louis citizenry but refused to alter the paper's content, and in 1836 moved to Alton, Illinois, where he anticipated support from the New England immigrant population. He was not welcomed, however. His press was shipped from St. Louis on a Sunday while he was observing the Sabbath and was pushed into the river. He was assured of funds for a new press by the townsfolk, who politely voiced their hope that he would temper his treatment of the slavery issue; but to their dismay, the *Alton Observer* covered activities of many antislavery groups as Lovejoy himself embraced Abolitionism. Time and time again the paper's press was smashed, but each time the Ohio Anti-Slavery Society sent him a new one. On November 7, 1837, soon after another new press had been delivered, a group of Abolitionists determined to defend it stood guard as an armed band of citizens approached the warehouse where the press was being stored. Lovejoy dashed into the street as he saw one of the citizens attempt to set fire to the warehouse and was shot. News of his death stunned the nation. He became a martyr to Abolitionists who used the circumstances of his death to illustrate the incongruity of the existence of slavery in a democracy.

LOWELL, AMY (1874–1925), poet and critic. Born on February 9, 1874, in Brookline, Massachusetts, Amy Lowell came of a long-prominent Massachusetts family. She was educated in private schools and by her mother and until she was 28 did little but alternately live at home and travel abroad, the latter an activity always taxing on her nervous constitution. About 1902 she decided to devote her energies to poetry, though it was eight years before her first piece was published and two more before her first volume, *A Dome of Many-Colored Glass,* appeared. On a visit to England in 1913 she met Ezra Pound and discovered his circle, the Imagists, and the following year her second book, *Sword Blades and Poppy Seed,* included her first experimental work with free verse and "polyphonic prose." She edited the three numbers of *Some Imagist Poets,* 1915–1917, and subsequent volumes of her own work include *Men, Women, and Ghosts,* 1916, *Can Grande's Castle,* 1918, *Pictures of the Floating World,*

1919, *Fir-Flower Tablets,* a collection of translations from the Chinese (with Florence Ayscough), 1921, and, posthumously, *What's o'Clock,* 1925, *East Wind,* 1926, and *Ballads for Sale,* 1927. Her critical work included a study of *Six French Poets,* 1915, *Tendencies in Modern American Poetry,* 1917, and a biography of *John Keats,* 1925, undertaken after delivering at Yale an address commemorating the centennial of his death in 1921. Miss Lowell became the leading exponent of the modernist movement in poetry in America and succeeded Ezra Pound as the guiding spirit of Imagism. She was a brilliant and popular conversationalist and lecturer; highly unconventional in her life as in her poetry — she was a habitual cigar smoker — her fame edged occasionally into notoriety. In 1922 she published *A Critical Fable,* a playful verse treatment of several contemporary poets patterned on the *Fable for Critics* of her collateral ancestor, James Russell Lowell. She died suddenly on May 12, 1925, in Brookline.

LOWELL, JAMES RUSSELL (1819–1891), author, educator, and diplomat. Born in Cambridge, Massachusetts, on February 22, 1819, Lowell graduated from Harvard in 1838 and two years later took his Ll.B. from the Law School. In 1841 his first volume of poetry appeared, entitled *A Year's Life;* in 1843 he began another facet of his career by editing the short-lived *Pioneer* and publishing in it works by Poe, Hawthorne, and Whittier; and in 1845 he published his first critical work, *Conversations on Some of the Old Poets.* Under the influence of his wife, a reformer and poet in her own right, he took up the cause of abolition and contributed a great number of articles on the subject to various periodicals; in 1846 he began to publish a series of "letters" in dialect in which Hosea Biglow, a shrewd Yankee character, commented satirically upon the Mexican War and the prospect of the extension of slavery. The collected *Biglow Papers* appeared in 1848, along with the *Fable for Critics,* a broadly humorous survey of the contemporary literary scene, and *The Vision of Sir Launfal*. After a period of writing and traveling he succeeded Longfellow in 1855 as professor of modern languages at Harvard, a position he held for some 20 years. In 1857 he began a four-year period as editor of the *Atlantic Monthly*, during which the magazine became the center of the New England renaissance. During the Civil War the second series of *Biglow Papers* was published in the *Atlantic* and appeared in book form in 1867. From 1864 to 1872 Lowell assisted Charles Eliot Norton in editing the *North American Review* and published in its pages a number of critical and biographical articles. He produced numerous books of essays, including *Fireside Travels*, 1864, *Among My Books*, 1870, *My Study Windows*, 1871, and of poetry, such as *Under the Willows*, 1869, and *Three Memorial Poems*, 1877. In 1876 Lowell contributed his services to the presidential campaign of Rutherford B. Hayes, and the following year was rewarded by being appointed minister to Spain. His diplomacy in Madrid was entirely satisfactory and after three years he was appointed minister to Great Britain, a post he conducted with grace and skill for five years, 1880–1885. In the six remaining years of his life he lived in Cambridge, though making several more visits to England, and continued to produce poetry, criticism, and political essays as America's acknowledged leading man of letters. He died on August 12, 1891.

LOWELL, PERCIVAL (1855–1916), astronomer. Born in Boston on March 13, 1855, Lowell was a member of a distinguished family and the elder brother of Amy Lowell, the poet. He graduated from Harvard in 1876, traveled for a year, and then devoted himself to diverse business interests until 1883; for the next decade he traveled in the Orient and published his experiences and reflections in a series of books: *Chöson*, 1885, *The Soul of the Far East*, 1888, *Noto*, 1891, and *Occult Japan*, 1895. He had maintained all the while an interest in astronomy, and at the end of his

travels he decided to devote himself to it. After careful consideration he selected a mesa near Flagstaff, Arizona, as the site for his observatory, and in 1894 observation was begun on a regular basis. His primary interest was the planet Mars; having confirmed Schiaparelli's earlier reports of fine markings, or "canals," on the surface, Lowell elaborated a theory of intelligent life fighting the slow disappearance of water from the planet. His and the staff's observations of Mars and other planets were among the most advanced being carried on at the time. He described his work and his theory in several books, including *Mars*, 1895, *Mars and Its Canals*, 1906, and *Mars as the Abode of Life*, 1908. Mathematical investigations of anomalies in the orbit of Uranus led him in 1905 to postulate the existence of an undiscovered planet beyond Neptune; a systematic search was begun that culminated in the discovery of Pluto in 1930, 14 years after Lowell's death on November 12, 1916. The Lowell Observatory continued to grow and carry on significant astronomical research with a permanent endowment fund.

LOWELL, ROBERT TRAILL SPENCE, JR. (1917–   ), poet. Born in Boston on March 1, 1917, Robert Lowell was the most eminent living representative of a family long prominent in the political, commercial, and intellectual life of New England and indeed of the United States. He graduated summa cum laude from Kenyon College, Ohio, in 1940, after having been a student at Harvard during 1935–1937. He was an editorial assistant at the New York publishing house of Sheed and Ward in 1941–1942 and was a conscientious objector during World War II. His first book of poems, *Land of Unlikeness*, appeared in 1944, by which time he had already determined on a literary career. *Lord Weary's Castle* was published in 1946 and received a Pulitzer Prize the next year. He received a Guggenheim Fellowship in 1947–1948 and during the same time also served as a consultant in poetry to the Library of Congress. Later books were *The Mills of* the Kavanaughs, 1951, Life Studies, 1959, for which he received a National Book Award, Phaedra and Imitations, 1961, for the second of which he received a Bollingen prize for translations, For the Union Dead, 1964, Near the Ocean: Poems, 1967, and Notebook of a Year, 1969. He has also published distinguished translations of Aeschylus, Baudelaire, and others, as well as essays and reviews in many periodicals.

LUCE, HENRY ROBINSON (1898–1967), editor and publisher. Born on April 3, 1898, in Tengchow, China, the son of a Presbyterian missionary, Luce came to the United States at 15 to study at the Hotchkiss School in Connecticut. There he met Britton Hadden. Together they attended Yale from 1916 to 1920, and served in World War I in 1918. Luce went to Oxford for a year after graduation and following a stint as a reporter on the Chicago Daily News he joined Hadden on the Baltimore News. They resigned in 1922 and by rewriting articles from such papers as the New York Times, put together the first issue of Time, a weekly news magazine they had been planning since college, and published it on March 3, 1923. Successful at once, it doubled its initial circulation of 12,000 within a year. Hadden established its nimble style with word inventions (like "GOPolitics," "cinemaddict," "socialite," and "tycoon"), inverted sentences, and an innovative format, and these were carried on after his death in 1929 by Luce, who projected his broad personal philosophy into its editorial stance. Credited with developing group journalism and creating the modern news magazine, he treated news coverage as a continuing story. A staunch Republican, he defended big business and free enterprise and advocated aggressive opposition to world Communism. In 1930 he began Fortune, a monthly business magazine, in 1936 Life, a weekly pictorial journal, and in 1954 Sports Illustrated. He purchased Architectural Forum in 1932, drew from it House and Home in 1952 (purchased by McGraw-Hill in

1964), and consolidated it under Fortune in 1964. Having started with $86,000, the Time Inc. enterprises had an income in 1966 of $503 million. In 1967 Time had a weekly circulation of 3.5 million and Time and Life together had 2 million subscribers to 4 foreign editions. He retired as editor-in-chief in 1964 and became editorial chairman of the publications. He also produced television programs, operated five radio and six television stations, and sponsored the March of Time radio broadcasts and movie shorts from 1928 to 1943. He died in Phoenix, Arizona, on February 28, 1967. His wife, **CLARE BOOTHE LUCE** (1903–   ), was born in New York City on April 10, 1903, and educated in private schools. Employed by Condé Nast publications from 1930, she was associate editor of Vogue during that year and edited Vanity Fair in 1930–1934. After her marriage to Luce in 1935 she wrote several plays, including The Women, 1936, Kiss the Boys Goodbye, 1938, and Margin for Error, 1939. She also wrote books including Stuffed Shirts, 1931, and Europe in the Spring, 1940. During 1943–1947 she was congresswoman from Connecticut, serving in the 78th and 79th congresses, and was U.S. ambassador to Italy from 1953 until her retirement in 1956. In 1959 President Eisenhower appointed her ambassador to Brazil, but she resigned a month later.

McADOO, WILLIAM GIBBS (1863–1941), railroad executive and public official. Born near Marietta, Georgia, on October 31, 1863, McAdoo attended the University of Tennessee for a brief period and then, in 1882, became a deputy clerk in the U.S. circuit court at Chattanooga, where he read law in his spare time. He was admitted to the bar in 1885, but his practice disappointed him and he lost what money he gained in an attempt to reorganize the street railway system in Knoxville. He went to New York, where during the next few years he organized and headed two companies, later consolidated as the Hudson and Manhattan Railway Company, that dug tunnels under the Hudson River and ran trains to New Jersey. He met Woodrow Wilson around 1910 and was an early supporter of the campaign to make him President. Wilson appointed him secretary of the treasury and he was one of the leading figures in the administration, serving as chairman of the Federal Reserve Board and as director-general of the U.S. railroads from 1917 to 1919, when they were being run by the government. He also successfully directed four Liberty Bond drives during the war. In 1914, his wife having died two years earlier, he married Wilson's daughter Eleanor in a White House ceremony. He left the Cabinet in 1919 and resumed his law practice. After 1920 he was the acknowledged leader of one branch of the Democratic Party, and he came close to gaining the nomination at the San Francisco convention of that year. In 1924 he came even closer; the convention was deadlocked and only on the 103rd ballot was John W. Davis nominated as a compromise candidate. Living in California, McAdoo was active in local politics and was elected to the U.S. Senate in 1932. He resigned in 1938 and died in California on February 1, 1941. An autobiography, *Crowded Years*, appeared in 1931.

MacARTHUR, DOUGLAS (1880–1964), soldier. Born on an army post near Little Rock, Arkansas, on January 26, 1880, MacArthur was the son of a distinguished career soldier who had won the medal of honor at Missionary Ridge. He gained appointment to West Point and graduated first in his class of 1903; choosing to join the corps of engineers, he was sent to survey and study the Philippines, where his father had been military governor a few years earlier, and other Far Eastern nations. He participated in the expedition to Veracruz in 1914. With American entry into World War I, he helped organize the "Rainbow" Division and, with the temporary rank of brigadier general, was its commander. He soon displayed the independence and preference for his own judgments that marked

his entire career; he won the Distinguished Service Cross and Medal, and at the end of the war was placed in command of the U.S. occupation zone. From 1919 to 1922 he was superintendent of West Point, from 1928 to 1930 department commander in the Philippines, and from 1930 to 1935, a longer period than any of his predecessors, Army chief of staff. In this last post he was called upon by President Hoover in the summer of 1932 to rout the Bonus Army from Washington in an action that came to be known sardonically as the Battle of Anacostia Flats. In 1935 he was sent to organize the defense forces of the Philippines in anticipation of the islands' independence; he was appointed field marshall of the Philippines and in 1937, rather than be transferred to other duties before his task was complete, he resigned from the Army. He was still in the islands when, in response to increasing tension in the Far East, the Philippine army was merged with the U.S. forces still there in July 1941; MacArthur was placed in command of the combined forces with the rank of lieutenant general. On the same day that Pearl Harbor was raided—December 7, 1941—Japanese forces invaded the Philippines; overwhelmed, MacArthur and his men retreated onto Bataan peninsula and finally to the island of Corregidor. In February 1942, two months before the garrison surrendered, he was ordered to leave the Philippines for Australia. Appointed overall commander of the Southwest Pacific area, he began his counteroffensive in the fall of that year and oversaw the "island-hopping" strategy that led the Allied forces slowly toward Japan. In October 1944 he fulfilled his famous promise of more than two years earlier by returning to the Philippines; two months later he was promoted to the rank of general of the army. The Philippines were finally secured in July 1945 and on September 2nd of that year, MacArthur received the surrender of Japan aboard the U.S.S. *Missouri*. Appointed commander of the Allied occupation of Japan, he spent the next six years reorganizing the government and the economy of the former enemy; the remnants of feudalism were destroyed and a democratic regime instituted, while the emperor was relegated to the position of benign figurehead. When, in June 1950, North Korea launched the invasion that began the Korean War, MacArthur was ordered to provide assistance to the poorly prepared army of South Korea. Following UN resolutions that established concerted military assistance and unified command, he was made supreme commander of the UN forces in Korea; the suddenness of the initial attack, the weakness of the South Korean army, and the delay in dispatching American forces allowed the North Koreans to overrun almost the entire peninsula and to bottle up the UN forces in a small area around Pusan. Carrying his plan over the objections of the joint chiefs of staff and others, MacArthur launched the daring counterinvasion at Inch'on in September 1950 and a few days later recaptured Seoul, the South Korean capital. The forces at Pusan broke out and swept northward. By October they had reached the 38th parallel, the border between North and South Korea; following President Truman's instructions, which were only later ratified by the UN, MacArthur ordered the invasion of the North and by late November some units of the UN forces had reached the Yalu River, the border of China. Faced with conflicting intelligence reports concerning the massing of Chinese forces just north of the Yalu and the substantial numbers of Chinese already in Korea, MacArthur chose to discount the likelihood of Chinese intervention and to press on to the river. In late November, as the last advance was begun, the Chinese poured vast numbers of troops across the Yalu, driving the UN forces back to and across the 38th parallel. The commander, convinced that the entry of China meant a "new war" and that the fighting should be carried by air directly to the new enemy, publicly disagreed with settled American policy on war aims; ordered to refrain from public disputation by Truman, he persisted in calling for action against China and on April 11,

1951, was relieved of his command by the President. His return to the United States was that of a hero; immense crowds greeted him in city after city, and this, combined with his stirring address to a joint session of Congress, seemed to make him a potential political figure. He retired to private life, however, retaining his rank and active status and becoming in 1959 the senior officer of the army. He died in Washington, D.C., on April 5, 1964.

McCARTHY, JOSEPH RAYMOND (1908–1957), public official. Born in Grand Chute, Wisconsin, on November 14, 1908, McCarthy left school at 14, worked for a time, and then returned to complete high school in a single year. In 1930 he entered Marquette University in Milwaukee to study engineering but soon switched to law; he graduated and was admitted to the bar in 1935. He quickly became interested in politics and was at this time a Democrat, but in his first successful bid for office, in which he was elected a state circuit judge in 1939, he ran as a Republican and was thenceforth identified with that party. In 1942, retaining his office, he was commissioned a lieutenant in the Marine Corps and served in the Pacific and at home. In 1944, a year before his discharge, he campaigned unsuccessfully for the Senate; two years later he sought the Senate seat then held by Robert LaFollette, Jr., and won a surprising victory, despite widespread rumors that he was being supported by Wisconsin Communists. McCarthy's career in the Senate was quiet and undistinguished until 1950 when, in a speech to a Republican women's club in Wheeling, West Virginia, he created a furor by claiming to have a list of some large number (the precise figure was never determined) of "known Communists" currently employed by the State Department. The sensation caused by this and subsequent speeches led to his being called to testify before a subcommittee of the Senate Committee on Foreign Relations; unable to produce proof or even real evidence of Communist affiliation on the part of any government employee, he was excoriated for having perpetrated "a fraud and a hoax" by the chairman, Millard Tydings, a Democratic Senator from Maryland. In the fall elections McCarthy and several aides carried on a secret smear campaign that succeeded in defeating Tydings. Despite repudiation in the Senate, however, he won an increasing amount of popular support by capitalizing on the post-war fears and frustrations of the nation; his position was secure enough by 1951 to enable him to attack Gen. George C. Marshall, formerly chief of staff and secretary of state. In 1952 he was reelected, though he ran behind the Republican ticket in Wisconsin, and in the reorganization of Congress he acquired the chairmanship of the Permanent Subcommittee on Investigations. For the next two years he was constantly in the public eye, investigating the State Department, the Voice of America, and innumerable individuals; though he failed to present an actionable case against anyone, a number of persons lost their jobs or were brought into public disrepute through his efforts. He charged that America had seen "twenty years of treason" under the administrations of Roosevelt and Truman, and he finally broke with leaders of his own party to include Eisenhower in his list of traitors. The climax of his anti-Communist crusade came in 1954, when his committee investigations of a number of army officers were televised nationwide. The detailed exposure of his interrogative tactics dismayed many supporters; in August a Senate committee was appointed to investigate his activities and make recommendations and on December 2, having lost his chairmanship in the fall elections, he was formally condemned on two counts: his refusal to explain a financial transaction of several years before, and his abuse of fellow senators. His popularity and power dropped sharply and were never regained; he died suddenly on May 2, 1957.

McCLELLAN, GEORGE BRINTON (1826–1885), soldier. Born in Philadelphia on December 3, 1826, McClellan won appointment to West Point at 15, and graduated second in his class

of 1846. He was assigned to Gen. Winfield Scott's command in the Mexican War and, distinguishing himself in several actions, was twice brevetted, emerging from the war a captain. From 1848 to 1851 he was an instructor in military engineering at West Point, and from 1851 he engaged in a number of Army projects, including river and harbor work, railroad surveys, a secret mission to Santo Domingo in 1854 to evaluate its potential naval value, and an observation mission to Europe and the Crimea in 1855. In that year he submitted a new design for cavalry saddles that was adopted and retained for many years as the "McClellan saddle." In 1857 he resigned his commission to become chief engineer for the Illinois Central Railroad. At the outbreak of the Civil War he was commissioned major general of the Ohio volunteers and a month later, upon being commissioned in the regular Army, assumed command of the Department of the Ohio. By July 1861 he had secured the territory that later became West Virginia from Confederate occupation; in that month he went to Washington to take command of the Department of the Potomac, in great confusion and disrepute since the defeat at Bull Run, and by November, when he succeeded General Scott as general-in-chief of the Union armies, he had effectively organized, equipped, and trained the Army, restored its morale, and made it into a capable and eager fighting force. He hesitated, however, to undertake offensive operations, and his hesitation lasted so long that Lincoln, losing patience, finally issued his General War Order No. 1 in January 1862, ordering a general Union advance. McClellan delayed while obtaining permission to substitute his own plan to approach Richmond along the Yorktown peninsula; in March the campaign was begun with McClellan in command of the new Army of the Potomac, relinquishing his position as commander-in-chief. He was overly cautious, consistently overestimating his opponent's strength, and as the campaign dragged on no decisive victories were won by either side; after the Seven Days' Battle in

July, in which he repulsed Lee's all-out attack but failed to press his advantage, he and his army were withdrawn from Virginia. Returning to Washington, he again exercised his great organizational talents in preparing for the defense of the capital. As Lee invaded Maryland, McClellan moved to meet him, but even with the advantage of having come into possession of a copy of the Confederate general's orders, he moved too slowly; instead of the overwhelming victory that was within reach, there came only the check at Antietam, and again McClellan failed to pursue the retreating Lee. In November 1862 he was finally removed from command. In 1864 the Democratic Party nominated him for President on a peace platform; he had been and still was an advocate of vigorous prosecution of the war, but he nonetheless accepted the nomination and tried with little success to reconcile his views with the platform. The Democrats were soundly defeated in the election and McClellan resigned his commission and sailed to Europe for a three year visit. Upon his return he declined two college presidencies, served as chief engineer for New York City's Department of Docks, and was from 1878 to 1881 governor of New Jersey. He died on October 29, 1885.

McCLURE, SAMUEL SIDNEY (1857–1949), editor. Born on February 17, 1857, in County Antrim, Ireland, McClure was brought to America at age nine. He worked his way through Knox College, earning his B.A. degree in 1882 and his M.A. degree in 1887. He was editor and manager of The Wheelman, a small publication for bicyclists, in 1882, and an employee of New York's De Vinne Press during 1883–1884. In 1884 he founded McClure's Syndicate, the first newspaper syndicate in the country. At first he offered reprints of previously published stories to newspapers across the country for simultaneous publication; as the syndicate became more prosperous he purchased novels from such writers as Kipling, Hardy, and Stevenson, for simultaneous serialization. He founded McClure's Magazine in 1893. Initially he planned to present contemporary American and English literature and news of scientific discoveries and world events. Having hired Ida Tarbell in the late 1890s, he assigned her to write a story of the Standard Oil Company, anticipating an account of the trust's services to the public, but was shocked to receive her carefully documented exposé of the bribery, coercion, and violence used by the company to gain power. He nevertheless published the story and thus launched the age of the "muckrakers." Hiring other noted journalists—including Ray Stannard Baker, William Allen White, and Lincoln Steffens—he financed their research into nearly every aspect of American life. Subsequent articles created public enthusiasm for reform and unprecedented legislative action. Advertisers, rather surprisingly, were anxious to be represented in it, since this was considered as a mark of integrity. McClure's became far more potent in shaping public opinion than the daily newspapers. In 1906 he disclosed plans for a model community to enact his theories on social organization; this led to discontent among the staff, and Miss Tarbell, Steffens, and Baker resigned to found another muckraking journal, the American Magazine. McClure's was sold and he relinquished his business ties. He began a scholarly retirement, writing My Autobiography, 1914, Obstacles to Peace, 1917, The Science of Political and Historical Self-Organization, and the Influence of Human Organization on History, 1934, The Achievements of Liberty, 1935, and What Freedom Means to Man, 1938. He died on March 21, 1949.

McCORMICK, CYRUS HALL (1809–1884), inventor and manufacturer. Born on February 15, 1809, in Rockbridge County, Virginia, McCormick received little formal education but was strongly influenced by his father, an inventor of agricultural implements who had long sought to perfect a mechanical reaper. In 1831 the son succeeded where the father had not; the principles and basic construction of this first reaper have remained virtually unchanged down to the present. Not until 1834, faced with the threat of competing inventors, did McCormick obtain a patent, and he kept his reaper from the market for several years more as he continued to make improvements in the mechanism. In 1844 he attempted to gain a national market by licensing manufacturers in a number of cities, but quality suffered and in 1847 he concentrated in one plant in Chicago. For the rest of his life, McCormick demonstrated his reaper at home and abroad, continually improved it, and fought countless patent suits to maintain his pioneering and preeminent position in his field. In later years he became interested in the Presbyterian Church and made generous contributions to what became, after his death, McCormick Theological Seminary. He was also active in the Democratic Party in Illinois, and had diverse business interests throughout the country. He died in Chicago on May 13, 1884.

McCORMICK, ROBERT RUTHERFORD (1880–1955), editor and publisher. Born in Chicago on July 30, 1880, McCormick was the grandson of Joseph Medill and the son of U.S. diplomat Robert Sanderson McCormick. He graduated from Yale in 1903 and entered Northwestern University law school, winning admission to the bar in 1908. He was the Republican alderman from Chicago's 21st ward from 1904 to 1906 and from 1905 to 1910 was president of the board of trustees of the city's Sanitary District. With the death of Robert W. Patterson in 1910 he became editor and publisher of the Chicago Tribune, with his cousin Joseph Medill Patterson. In 1911 he became president of the Tribune company. He was a war correspondent on the eastern front in 1915 and in 1917 and 1918 was an artillery officer in France. In 1925 he became sole editor and publisher of the Tribune, while Patterson founded the New York Daily News. A staunch and unwavering Republican, he espoused the causes of freedom of the press,

big business, and nationalism; denounced labor unions, Jane Addams and the Chicago school board, the Russian Bolsheviks, the New Deal, and the Fair Deal; and adhered to isolationist doctrines throughout his career, opposing U.S. entry in both world wars, although supporting the war efforts after entry. He gave frequent public and radio addresses to bolster his provocative newspaper campaigns. When he first joined the Tribune, the daily circulation was 200,000; at his death it had grown to 892,058. The Sunday circulation was 1,392,384, and the paper was the world leader in advertising revenue. He enlarged its empire to include paper mills in Quebec and Ontario, Canadian forest lands, hydroelectric installations, shipping companies, radio and television stations, and publishing houses. He died in Wheaton, Illinois, on April 1, 1955.

McDOUGALL, WILLIAM (1871–1938), psychologist. Born on June 22, 1871, in Chadderton, Lancashire, England, McDougall attended the Real-Gymnasium in Weimar for a year, Owen's College in Manchester from the age of 17, and St. John's College, Cambridge, from 1890, receiving his B.A. degree in 1894. He completed his medical studies at St. Thomas Hospital in London in 1897, taking his M.A. degree in the same year. In 1898 he became a fellow of St. John's, subsequently shifting his concern from medicine to psychological research. He left his internship to participate in a Cambridge anthropological expedition to the Torres Straits, his function being to ascertain the sensory capacity of the natives by means of modern psychological methods. During this expedition, he also aided Dr. Charles Hose in his study of headhunters in Borneo; together they produced The Pagan Tribes of Borneo, 2 vols., 1912. On his return to Cambridge he heard lectures by Henry Sidgwick and James Ward, and in Göttingen in 1900 studied under G. E. Muller the techniques of experimental psychology. Of prime influence on him were the theories of William

James, which underscored his own interest in the broad theoretical and humanistic implications of psychology rather than the precise methodology favored by the Germans. He returned to England late in 1900 as a reader at University College, London, and assistant to James Sully in the school's new experimental laboratory. For four years he conducted research in the psychophysics of vision, publishing the results of a series of experiments designed to confirm Thomas Young's three-color hypothesis of vision. Other research in mental concentration (which he identified with conscious perception), and its relation to neurological processes, led to his theory that the foundation of intellectual operations is a major system of neural circuits. He argued for the merit of his position over the traditional philosophical view in *Physiological Psychology,* 1905, and *Psychology, the Study of Behavior,* 1912. In 1904 he became a reader in mental philosophy at Oxford, where he propounded Sir Francis Galton's methods for statistical measurement of personality traits. In 1920 he came to the United States as professor of psychology at Harvard. In a series of lectures published in 1921 under the title *Is America Safe for Democracy?*, he declared the supremacy of the Nordic "race" on the basis of Army mental tests and noted class differences according to mental ability. This view was decried by the press and by many of his peers; their hostility never entirely subsided and overshadowed his significant contributions to scientific psychology. While at Harvard, he also published *Outline of Psychology,* 1923, exploring the role of purpose in action, and *Outline of Abnormal Psychology,* 1926, developing the "hormic" psychology, in which desire for survival is the primary motivation. In 1927 he moved to Duke University as professor of psychology, furthering his research on acquired behavior characteristics, and publishing among other works *The Riddle of Life,* 1938, on his theory of interaction between the body and the soul. He died

in Durham, North Carolina, on November 28, 1938.

MacDOWELL, EDWARD ALEXANDER (1861–1908), pianist and composer. Born on December 18, 1861, in New York City, MacDowell was an ambitious, precocious child. He began his music studies at an early age and after studying for several years with Teresa Carreño in New York, he went to Paris in 1876 to enroll in the Conservatoire. His training there was rigorous and significant for the discipline it instilled in him. He was not comfortable with French music, however, and went to Germany in 1878, where he studied at the Frankfurt Conservatory. There he found his métier, and three years later he was made an instructor at the Darmstadt Conservatory and began to compose with fervor. Encouraged by fellow musicians and composers, he took his A-minor concerto to Franz Liszt, who was extremely impressed. Liszt arranged to have his *First Modern Suite* performed in Zürich in 1882. The reception of this composition stimulated him to spend the next several years composing songs, piano sonatas, and symphonic poems, many inspired by the German landscape, others by legend and literature, among them *Hamlet and Ophelia,* 1885, and *Lancelot and Elaine,* 1888. In 1884 he returned to the United States where he married. He took his bride back to Germany where they lived in Wiesbaden until 1888, when they returned to Boston. Even though he had not lived in his native country for many years, he drew on America's historic themes and environment for some of his finest works, including *Indian Suite,* 1892, *Woodland Sketches,* 1896, *Sea Pieces,* 1898, and *New England Idylls,* 1902. He accepted an invitation from Columbia University to head a new department of music in 1896. He formed an orchestra and chorus and attempted to integrate the musical arts with the academic curriculum, but was faced with strong opposition from conservative academicians, and with the argument that talented pupils did not study in American universities but went to European conservatories for musical training. He resigned in bitterness in 1904 and retreated to his Peterborough, New Hampshire, farm. He continued to compose but made only rare public appearances before he died in New York City on January 23, 1908. After his death, his wife organized the MacDowell Colony at their New Hampshire farm for American composers and writers to use as a summer residence. His works are considered to have been unsurpassed by any previous American composer, and are still performed in Europe and America.

McGILLICUDDY, CORNELIUS (1862–1956), "Connie Mack," baseball player and manager. Born on December 23, 1862, in East Brookfield, Massachusetts, McGillicuddy began his baseball career while working in a shoe factory. The limited space on scoreboards then used led him to shorten his name to Connie Mack, and he was thus universally known for the rest of his life. The East Brookfield team won the central Massachusetts championship in 1883 and Mack, a catcher, was signed by the professional team in Meriden, Connecticut. Through the next several years he played for teams in Washington, Buffalo, Pittsburgh, and Milwaukee. His career as a manager began in Pittsburgh in 1894, and he continued to double as a catcher until 1901, when, under the auspices of the newly formed American League, he became manager and part owner of the Philadelphia Athletics. Mack's managing technique, based on infinite patience and a respectful treatment of his players, was unique in a day when physical punishment for mistakes on or off the playing field was not uncommon. The Athletics won their first league pennant in 1902; they won again in 1905 and that year played and lost to John J. McGraw's Giants in the first official World Series. League champions in 1910, 1911, 1913, 1914, 1929, 1930, and 1931, the Athletics were also world champions in all but 1914 and 1931. In 1914 and

again in 1933 Mack startled the baseball world by disassembling star player combinations and undertaking slow rebuilding programs for the Athletics; he became known as a discoverer and mentor of young players on their way up and numbered among his great proteges Chief Bender, Rube Waddell, Lefty Grove, and Jimmy Foxx. When, during the "centennial" of baseball in 1939, the first 13 men were installed in the new Baseball Hall of Fame in Cooperstown, New York, Mack was the only living member. His bust in the Hall of Fame was inscribed with the title that was his by acclamation, "Mr. Baseball." From 1940 he had a controlling interest in the Athletics; he retired from active management in 1951 and finally sold the club early in 1955. He died in Philadelphia on February 8, 1956, at the age of 93.

McGUFFEY, WILLIAM HOLMES (1800–1873), educator. Born near Claysville, Pennsylvania, on September 23, 1800, McGuffey moved with his parents to the Western Reserve region of Ohio two years later. He received little formal schooling but, possessed of a prodigious memory, worked diligently to educate himself; he began to teach in rural schools in Ohio and Kentucky at the age of 13 and supplemented his independent studies with occasional periods under private tutors and later at Greersburg Academy. Finally, he entered Washington College and graduated in 1826. The previous year he had been appointed instructor in ancient languages at Miami University in Oxford, Ohio; the awarding of his A.B. degree was followed by a promotion to professor at the University. In 1829 he was ordained in the Presbyterian Church; though he never had a congregation of his own, he was a frequent and popular guest preacher. He became head of the department of mental philosophy and philology at Miami in 1832; in addition to his own teaching duties he took a great interest in improving the standards of teaching in elementary schools. In 1836 he accepted the presidency of Cincinnati College. In the same year appeared the first and second *Eclectic Readers*, which McGuffey had prepared at the request of a Cincinnati publishing house; the third and fourth *Readers* were issued in the next year. During his years in Cincinnati he was instrumental in founding the common school system in Ohio. In 1839 he became president of Ohio University in Athens, but the institution closed four years later. In 1845 he was appointed professor of mental and moral philosophy at the University of Virginia, a post he held until his death on May 4, 1873. The *Reader* series was extended to a fifth in 1844 and a sixth in 1857 and was supplemented by a spelling book prepared by McGuffey's brother, Alexander Hamilton McGuffey, in 1846. The *Readers*, anthologies of selections from English and American literature, represented a great improvement over the textbooks generally available to small schools; they were immediately and vastly popular, running through many editions as they were employed as standard texts for nearly a century in the Middle West. The eventual sales reached an estimated 122,-000,000. In addition to the high intellectual level of much of the material, the *Readers* were characterized by an all-pervading emphasis on morality, though it was often the degenerated Puritan morality in which virtue and vice are immediately and materialistically rewarded and punished. *McGuffey's Eclectic Readers* exerted a profound influence on generations of Americans, and they have been credited with playing a vital role in the development of American nationalism.

MACK, CONNIE see McGILLICUDDY, CORNELIUS

McKAY, CLAUDE (1889–1948), poet. Born on September 15, 1889, near Clarendon Hills, Jamaica, McKay lived with his parents until he was six. Then an older brother, a schoolteacher and a lay preacher in the Anglican Church, became his guardian. His brother exposed him to such writers as Huxley and Gibbons and introduced him to an English squire, an authority on Jamaican dialect and folklore, who taught him to write poetry and to incorporate dialect into it. McKay wrote two books of verse in dialect, *Songs of Jamaica* and *Constab Ballads*, in 1912, and emigrated to America that year. He entered the Tuskegee Institute but transferred to Kansas State University, where he majored in agriculture. After two years of study he left and attempted to work as a freelance writer. He was offered menial jobs instead. His poems, contributed to the *Liberator*, became intense and angry as he grew more aware of the inferior status allotted him in his new homeland. In 1919, a year marked by race riots throughout the country, he wrote "If We Must Die." This poem, and two volumes of verse, *Spring in New Hampshire*, 1920, and *Harlem Shadows*, 1922, marked the beginning of the Negro civil rights movement of the 1920s, and of a development in the arts known variously as the "New Negro Movement" and the "Harlem Renaissance." One of the movement's most militant spokesmen, he encouraged his people to fight for their honor and freedom. From 1922 to 1934 he lived abroad in Russia and Europe. His subsequent writings emphasized the distinction between the black and white races; he sought to discover and encourage the wellsprings of a black culture and in doing so moved away from the integrationists toward a mild form of black nationalism. He became a U.S. citizen in 1940, a convert to Catholicism in 1944, and worked with youth in Chicago ghettos with Bishop Bernard J. Sheil. Others among his works were three novels, *Home to Harlem*, 1938, *Banjo*, 1929, and *Banana Bottom*, 1933, a short-story collection, *Gingertown*, 1932, and the autobiographical *A Long Way from Home*, 1937. He died in Chicago on May 22, 1948.

McKAY, DONALD (1810–1880), ship builder. Born in Nova Scotia on September 4, 1810, McKay moved to New York City in 1827 and became an apprentice ship carpenter.

For several years after the completion of his indenture he was a journeyman shipwright, and he established a firm reputation with a number of fine vessels. In 1845 he opened his own shipyard in East Boston; for five years he concentrated on building packet ships, but in 1850 launched his first clipper, the *Stag Hound*. The clipper, a product of long experimentation in fast sailing ships and the triumph of art in marine architecture, was brought to its highest development by McKay during the next five years. The demand for rapid transportation to California provided the occasion for his *Flying Cloud* of 1851, which set a record for the New York-to-San Francisco run around Cape Horn of 89 days. Ignoring widespread scepticism, he built the huge *Sovereign of the Seas*, registered at 2,421 tons, in 1852 and won worldwide fame when it proved practical. The next year he began work on the largest clipper ever attempted, the *Great Republic*, of 4,555 tons; though it burned before launching, it was rebuilt and became the pride of the American fleet. His *James Baines* set standing records for the Boston-to-Liverpool and around-the-world passages, and the *Lightning* once covered 436 nautical miles in 24 hours, also a standing record for sail. By 1855 the era of the extreme clipper was at an end and the economic depression forced him to close his yard two years later. A trip to England convinced him of the superiority of ironclad, steam-powered vessels for naval use, but he was unable to convince the U.S. government to order them. In 1863 he reopened his yard to build iron ships and produced several vessels for the Navy, among them the monitor *Nausett*. He was financially unsuccessful, however, and in 1869, shortly after launching his last sailing ship, the *Glory of the Seas* (which lasted until 1923), he sold the yard. He died at his farm near Hamilton, Massachusetts, on September 20, 1880.

MacKAYE, JAMES MORRISON STEELE (1842 – 1894), actor, inventor, theater manager, and playwright. Born on June 6, 1842, in Buffalo, New York, Steele MacKaye was indulged as a youth by wealthy parents, educated in Paris at the École des Beaux Arts with an unlimited allowance, and permitted to tinker with painting, acting, or anything that struck his fancy. He joined the 7th regiment in the Civil War and in the regimental theater made his stage debut as Hamlet. After the war he painted, purchased and managed an art gallery, invented "photosculpture" and tried to market it through a company he formed. In 1869 his father denied him further financial support. He sailed to France to study acting with Delsarte, whose method involved the study of gymnastics to achieve coordination of body and voice; he became an avid devotee and returned to the United States to introduce the system, lecturing at Harvard and elsewhere. In New York he acted in 1872 in *Monaldi* in a theater of his own reconstruction. In 1873 he appeared in London as Hamlet, becoming the first American to play the role in England. He returned to the United States and opened a "school of expression" for student actors. Two of his plays were produced with enough success to finance his rebuilding of the renamed Madison Square Theater. There he introduced such innovations as artificial ventilation, overhead and indirect lighting, and the elevator stage. In 1880, *Hazel Kirke*, the play for which he is best known, opened at his theater and played for more than a year, a phenomenal success for the time. The profits from these productions could have reaped him a fortune, but his inexperience with money matters left him often short of funds. He lost the controlling interest in his theater, but built another, the Lyceum, where he established the first professional acting school in America, now the American Academy of Dramatic Art. An accomplished teacher, he also wrote nearly 30 plays, and lectured on the social aspects of the theater and the educational value of dramatic study. For the World's Columbian Exposition in Chicago in 1893 he proposed a fantastic auditorium, the massive "Spectatorium," seating 12,000 and containing 25 moving stages on which *The World Finder*, his epic drama of Columbus' discovery of America, would be enacted. For the production Anton Dvorak composed his *New World Symphony*. Completion of the project was prevented by dwindling funds, and only a working model resulted. En route to California, MacKaye died in Timpas, Colorado, on February 25, 1894.

McKIM, CHARLES FOLLEN (1847–1909), architect. Born on August 24, 1847, in Isabella Furnace, Chester County, Pennsylvania, McKim, the son of a noted Abolitionist, was educated at Theodore Weld's school, in public school in Philadelphia, and for a year in 1866–1867 at Harvard's Lawrence Scientific School. From 1867 to 1870 he studied architecture at the École des Beaux Arts in Paris, and in the latter year he returned to America and entered the office of Henry H. Richardson, then busy with the construction of Trinity Church in Boston. In 1878 he formed a partnership with two other young architects and the following year the company became McKim, Mead, and White, for many decades the leading American architectural firm. For several years the company subsisted on private commissions for city residences and summer homes as McKim developed his ideas on the necessity of basing sound design on classical precedents, a view strongly opposed to that of his early mentor, Richardson. His first monumental work, the Boston Public Library, was begun in 1887; engaging the services of John Singer Sargent and Augustus Saint-Gaudens, among others, McKim produced a model of functional planning within a thoroughly classical context. With this and his later designs, he became the leading exponent of the neoclassical revival in American architecture. In 1893 the Chicago Columbian Exposition featured McKim's Agricultural Building and the New York State Building, and in 1899 he designed the University Club in New York City. In 1901 he joined Daniel Burnham, Saint-Gaudens,

and Frederick Law Olmsted under commission to study and make recommendations for the development of Washington, D.C. He was primarily responsible for the central region about the Capitol and made the preliminary sketches for the Lincoln Memorial, which were elaborated later by one of his associates. During 1902–1903 he supervised the faithful restoration of the White House; in subsequent years his outstanding works included the Morningside Heights campus of Columbia University, the Pierpont Morgan Library, and the Pennsylvania Station, all in New York City. Throughout his life he was deeply interested in improving the training available to young artists; his own office was an excellent school for those whose field was architecture, and from 1894 onward he supported and supervised his major contribution to the future of American art, the American Academy in Rome. McKim retired in 1908 and died a year later, on September 14, 1909.

McKINLEY, WILLIAM (1843–1901), public official and 25th U.S. President. Born in Niles, Ohio, on January 29, 1843, McKinley studied for a year at Allegheny College before illness and his family's limited means curtailed his formal education. For a time he taught school and in 1861 he enlisted in the Union Army. He served with distinction, became an aide to Col. Rutherford B. Hayes, and at the time of his discharge in 1865 held the brevet rank of major. He took up the study of law and began practice in 1867 in Canton, Ohio. He was soon involved in politics and in 1876 was elected as a Republican to Congress where, except for one term, he remained until 1891. An ardent advocate of the protective tariff, he employed his position as chairman of the Ways and Means Committee during his final term to secure passage of what soon became known as the McKinley Tariff; popular reaction against this measure led to a sweeping victory for the Democratic Party in the 1890 election and McKinley was one of many Republican victims. His reputation was nonetheless secure in Ohio and was growing steadily on the national scene. With the aid of Mark Hanna, a Cleveland businessman who was rich, Republican, and an incomparable political manager, he was elected governor of Ohio in 1891 and again in 1893. In 1896 he was chosen by the Republicans to oppose William Jennings Bryan in a presidential campaign fought mainly over the issue of free silver. He remained relatively passive while Hanna organized the nation's business interests; representing the conservative, pro-tariff, antisilver position, McKinley was elected by a substantial margin. The record-high Dingley Tariff passed by Congress early in 1897 marked the beginning of what might have been a quiet Republican administration; the following year, however, the current revolt against the Spanish colonial government in Cuba began to capture public attention, and a series of incidents culminating in the mysterious sinking of the U.S.S. *Maine* in Havana Harbor on February 15th, along with a great deal of sensational, if not always accurate, journalism, created a wave of war sentiment with which McKinley was unprepared to deal. He attempted to soothe a rankled public and Congress with diplomacy, but finally gave Congress its head; war was effectively declared on April 20th when a joint resolution called for U. S. intervention to secure Cuban independence. This limited aim was quickly forgotten as the first victory of the war came with the destruction of the Spanish fleet at Manila on May 1st, and the subsequent capture of the Philippine Islands by the Pacific fleet commanded by Commodore George Dewey. Santiago, Cuba, was taken in June, and in August all hostilities ceased. With the signing and ratification of the peace treaty (December 1898, February 1899), the United States was suddenly in possession of an empire, and McKinley faced unforeseen problems. As the details of colonial administration were slowly being worked out, imperialism was becoming a partisan issue. In the election of 1900 the Democrats, while retaining their free-silver plank and Bryan, gave it priority; McKinley was reelected despite a not inconsiderable amount of anti-imperialist disaffection within his own party. Garret Hobart, his first-term Vice President, had died in 1899, and into the vacancy came Theodore Roosevelt, nominated largely at the behest of New York Republicans who hoped thereby to deactivate a rising political figure with disturbingly reformist ideas. Soon after beginning his second term, McKinley found confirmation for his colonial policies when the Supreme Court decided in the Insular Cases that the Constitution did not necessarily follow the flag: Guam, Puerto Rico, and the Philippines were not within the area of free trade. There is reason to suspect that before his death the President was moving away from his firm belief in protection toward a position favoring freer, if not free, trade. Before he was able to elaborate his new views to the nation, however, he was shot by Leon Czolgosz, an anarchist, while visiting the Pan-American Exposition in Buffalo, New York. He died eight days later, on September 14, 1901.

MacLEISH, ARCHIBALD (1892–   ), public official and poet. Born in Glencoe, Illinois, on May 7, 1892, a member of a wealthy Midwestern mercantile family, MacLeish was educated at private schools, at Yale, from which he graduated in 1915, and at the Harvard law school, from which he received his LL.B. in 1919. After Army service overseas in 1917–1918, he practised law for three years, from 1920 to 1923, but then turned to poetry full time. During the 1920s an expatriate, living in Paris and other European cities and moving in a literary circle that included Hemingway, Fitzgerald, Gertrude Stein, and others, he published several books of poetry, among them *The Happy Marriage*, 1924, *Streets in the Moon*, 1926, and *The Hamlet of A. MacLeish*, 1928, that showed the influence, then extremely fashionable, of Pound and Eliot. But in 1928 he returned to the United States, became a writer for *Fortune* (from 1930), and published another book, *New Found Land*, 1930, whose simple lyric eloquence and deep patriotism sounded a note that came to be typical of him thereafter. In the 1930s he became deeply concerned about the threats to American society and to world democracy, particularly the menace of Fascism. *Conquistador*, 1932, dealing with the Spanish conquest of Mexico, was the first of his "public" poems and won him the first of three Pulitzer Prizes. Other works from the decade, during which he continued to protest against what he considered America's blindness to its peril, were *Frescoes for Mr. Rockefeller's City*, 1933, *Fall of the City*, 1937, *Public Speech*, 1936, *Air Raid*, 1938, *America Was Promises*, 1939 — the use of the past tense in the last title being intended to shock readers into an awareness of their condition — and *The Irresponsibles*, 1940. In 1939 he was named librarian of the Library of Congress, serving in this capacity until 1944; he also performed other public duties during the war years, and was assistant secretary of state from 1944 to 1945. He aided in the foundation of UNESCO and, in the years after World War II, continued to speak out in defense of American democracy. Among his most notable works of these years were *Actfive and Other Poems*, 1948, and *Collected Poems 1917-1952*, 1952, which won both a Pulitzer Prize and a National Book Award. *J.B.*, 1958, a biblical allegory in verse, not only won a Pulitzer Prize for drama but also enjoyed a triumphant production on Broadway. He was named Boylston Professor of Rhetoric at Harvard in 1949, where he taught until his retirement.

McPHERSON, AIMEE SEMPLE (1890–1944), evangelist. Born on October 9, 1890, in Ontario, Canada, Sister Aimee, as she was called by her followers, was married first to a Pentecostel evangelist, Robert Semple, with whom she did missionary work in China. After his death she returned to the United States, and later married Harold McPherson. Her marriage ended when she decided to devote her life to preaching and healing. She traveled through America, England, Canada, Australia, and other countries, finally settling in 1918 in Los Angeles, penniless, but with a large following. She founded a religious movement that she called the International Church of the Foursquare Gospel, a name derived from her vision of heaven with four walls. Based on tenets of hope and salvation for the needy, it especially appealed to migrant Southerners and Midwesterners, frustrated by the complexities of urban Los Angeles. They provided the funds to build the huge Angelus Temple, where her sermons were heard and broadcast simultaneously over the radio station she had also purchased. Sunday services at the temple were attended by thousands of worshippers, who sat spellbound throughout the extravaganzas that included patriotic and quasi-religious music played by a 50-piece band, the breathtaking entrance of Sister Aimee, singing and prayers, all concluded by a dramatic sermon. Theologically fundamentalist, she based much of the appeal of her movement on faith-healing, adult baptism by immersion, and a pervading aura of optimism and spectacle. She compiled a book of sermons, *This Is That*, 1923, and wrote *In the Service of the King*, 1927, and *Give Me My Own God*, 1936. She frequently made newspaper headlines and was accused of a number of improprieties, but none was proved and none detracted from her following. She died on September 27, 1944, from an overdose of sleeping powders. Her son continued the movement, which claimed nearly 90,000 adherents in the late 1960s.

MADISON, JAMES (1751–1836), political philosopher, public official, and 4th U.S. President. Born in Port Conway, King George County, Virginia, on March 16, 1751, Madison was of a moderately wealthy family of Virginia planters. He was educated at the College of New Jersey (now Princeton) and continued his studies for a year beyond his graduation in 1771, possibly with a thought of entering the ministry. He returned home in 1772 and two years later began his long political career by being chosen a member of his county's committee on public safety. In 1776 he was elected to the Virginia constitutional convention and became *ex officio* a member of the first state legislature the following year. His prominence in the convention, where he fought for the establishment of complete freedom of religion, secured him a place on the governor's council early in 1778 and he remained in that body until his election to Congress nearly two years later. During his single term, 1779–1783, he became an outspoken advocate of revision of the Confederation in order to strengthen the central government. During 1784–1786 he was a member of the Virginia House of Delegates where again he spoke for the establishment of complete religious freedom, introducing and securing passage of Jefferson's famous bill to that end. Beginning in 1785 he proposed a series of interstate conferences that led to the Annapolis Convention of 1786 and culminated in the Constitutional Convention the next year. At the Convention he was a dominant figure; a number of proposals for an effective central government, outlined by him in a letter to Washington in April 1787, became the basis of the "Virginia Plan" introduced into the Convention by Edmund Randolph. Madison managed the Convention with great skill, was responsible for many of the crucial compromises, and all the while diligently kept the only nearly complete record of the proceedings and deliberations. During the campaign for ratification he joined with Alexander Hamilton and John Jay in writing the *Federalist* papers; 29 of the 85 essays appeared over his pseudonym, "Publius." He also led the proratification forces in the Virginia convention. Elected a representative to the first Congress, he took the lead in organizing the new government and in adding to the Constitution the Bill of Rights amendments. Though strongly identified up to this time with the nationalist view, Madison slowly shifted his position during his years in Congress; he opposed Hamil-

ton's financial policies vigorously and as party alignments developed he emerged as the congressional leader of the Jeffersonian Republicans. He shared Jefferson's preference for close relations with France rather than with England, and he denounced Washington's seemingly pro-British Neutrality Proclamation of 1793 along with Jay's Treaty in 1795. He remained in Congress until 1797; from his home, "Montpellier," in Virginia he kept close watch on public affairs and in 1798, when Federalist hysteria produced the Alien and Sedition Acts, he and Jefferson wrote, respectively, the Virginia and Kentucky Resolutions, protesting the unconstitutionality of the measures and raising—although this interpretation was later denied by Madison —the specter of nullification. When Jefferson was elected to the presidency in 1800, Madison was the immediate choice for secretary of state; during the next eight years the two men worked in perfect harmony through the succession of crises occasioned by the war between Britain and France and the constant harassment of American neutral shipping that was, for America, its central feature. In 1808 he was the clear successor to the presidency; he won a strong victory over his Federalist opponent and continued the policies of Jefferson unaltered. The difficulties with Britain and France continued and worsened, particularly with the former; Madison was apparently deceived by Napoleon into issuing a nonintercourse proclamation against Great Britain in November 1810, making war with that country virtually inevitable. In June 1812 war was formally declared, beginning a painful and dangerous period for the nation, which was totally unprepared and part of which, New England, was totally unsympathetic. Military disasters fostered the growth of popular discontent; New England seriously considered secession, great areas of the Northwest were lost to British forces from Canada, and Washington, D.C., was burned. Nevertheless, Madison managed to win reelection in 1812. The war was ended by the Treaty of Ghent in

December 1814 with the United States having failed to gain a single one of its war aims, and having had to bargain from weakness simply to regain its territory. But the mere fact that the war was over, coupled with a few spectacular though belated victories—notably by Gen. Andrew Jackson at New Orleans—restored to the President much popular favor. The remainder of his administration was marked most prominently by his brief backing away from Jeffersonian principles in approving both the charter of the second Bank of the United States and a system of protective tariffs. Madison retired to "Montpellier" in 1817; his public service after that time was limited to participation in the Virginia constitutional convention of 1829 and, upon the death of Jefferson in 1826, acting as rector of the University of Virginia until his own death on June 28, 1836.

MAHAN, ALFRED THAYER (1840–1914), naval officer and historian. Born on September 27, 1840, in West Point, New York, Mahan was the son of a professor of military engineering at the U.S. Military Academy. After two years at Columbia College he entered the U.S. Naval Academy, from which he graduated in 1859 at the age of 18. During his nearly 40 years of active duty in the Navy he served in numerous capacities at sea and ashore. He progressed steadily in rank and responsibility; in 1885 he was promoted to captain and the following year, in recognition of his abilities and his reputation for scholarship, he received a call to lecture on naval history and strategy at the Naval War College in Newport, Rhode Island. He soon became the institution's president and held the post until 1889. The next year his lectures were published under the title *The Influence of Sea Power Upon History, 1660–1783*; a thoroughgoing analysis of sea power in its broadest manifestations, the book broke new ground in the examination of international affairs and won immediate recognition abroad. In 1892 Mahan's second major work appeared, entitled *The Influence of Sea Power Upon the French Revolution and Empire, 1793–1812*, and, like the first, became a classic. Assiduously studied in translation, the two books greatly influenced the worldwide buildup of naval forces in the period prior to World War I. In 1892–1893 he was again president of the War College, and in 1893, on a cruise in European waters, he was publicly honored by the government of Great Britain and awarded honorary degrees by both Oxford and Cambridge. He retired from the Navy in 1896 but was recalled to service on the naval strategy board during the Spanish-American War. He was a member of the American delegation to the peace conference at The Hague in 1899, and in 1902 was elected president of the American Historical Association. Notable among Mahan's many other works were *The Life of Nelson*, 1897, *The Interest of America in Sea Power, Present and Future*, 1897, and *The Major Operations of the Navies in the War of American Independence*, 1913. He died on December 1, 1914.

MAILER, NORMAN (1923–   ), author. Born on January 31, 1923, in Long Branch, New Jersey, Mailer grew up in Brooklyn and graduated from Harvard in 1943 with a degree in engineering. He had begun to write short stories in college and won *Story* magazine's college competition in 1941 with "The Greatest Thing in the World." Drafted into the Army in 1943, he was an infantryman in the Philippines during World War II and afterwards served in Japan. He returned to New York City in 1946 and spent 15 months producing an open, searing novel of the war, *The Naked and the Dead*, 1948, which brought him immediate fame and critical praise and was compared in its expression of bitterness toward war to Hemingway's *A Farewell to Arms*. In the late 1940s he went through a period of political search that left him hostile to both Communism, as reflected in his book *Barbary Shore*, 1951, and to the authoritarianism he saw in the United States. After a brief time as a script writer in Hollywood, he completed *The Deer Park*, 1955, a picture of a Hollywood psychopathic personality, which he adapted for an off-Broadway stage production in 1967. He settled in New York City's Greenwich Village in late 1951 and aided in organizing the *Village Voice*, becoming a frequent contributor. His pithy essays also appeared in *Partisan Review*, *Commentary*, *Esquire*, and *Dissent*, the last of which introduced his definitive treatise on "hipsterism," "The White Negro," in 1957. Numerous works followed: *Advertisements for Myself*, 1959, autobiographical-confessional essays, *The Presidential Papers*, 1963, magazine essays on President Kennedy, *Deaths for the Ladies, and Other Disasters*, 1962, a book of verse, *Cannibals and Christians*, 1966, a miscellaneous collection of writings, and two allegorical novels, *An American Dream*, 1965, and *Why Are We in Vietnam?*, 1967. He won the National Book Award and shared a Pulitzer Prize in nonfiction for *The Armies of the Night*, 1967, a report on the 1967 march on the Pentagon by antiwar demonstrators in which he participated prominently. The next year he wrote *Miami and the Siege of Chicago*, on the presidential nominating conventions of 1968. He ran unsuccessfully for mayor of New York City in June 1968 on a secessionist platform calling for the city to become the 51st state. A restless, unruly personality, he was recognized as a driving force in modern American literature.

MALCOLM X (1925–1965), political and religious leader. Malcolm Little was born on May 19, 1925, in Omaha, Nebraska. His father, a Baptist preacher and follower of Marcus Garvey, soon moved the family to Lansing, Michigan; his death under unclear circumstances in 1931 led to Malcolm's separation from his family, first to a foster home, and finally, in 1938, to a reform home in Mason, Michigan. He completed the 8th grade there, and from 1941 to 1946 he lived in Boston and Harlem. Known as "Detroit Red," he was involved in a number of petty criminal activities. In 1946 he was convicted on several counts of robbery and sentenced to 7 years in prison. While in prison he became acquainted with the teachings of Elijah Muhammad, leader of the "Nation of Islam" or the Black Muslims. Adopting this faith, he set about educating himself and, upon his release in 1952, changed his name to Malcolm X and devoted himself to religious work. A remarkable orator and an assiduous follower of Elijah Muhammad, Malcolm rose quickly in the organization, becoming the sect's first "national minister" in 1963. The Black Muslims enjoyed great gains in membership and publicity as a result of the increasing national attention given Negro rights, status, and culture; however, the Muslim insistence on black separatism and avoidance of active participation in the civil-rights struggle gradually alienated Malcolm. Finally, in March 1964, he broke publicly with Elijah Muhammad, forming his own Muslim group. This was succeeded, following visits to Mecca and several new African states, by the Organization of Afro-American Unity. Malcolm's speeches, often brilliantly eloquent, were militant, even strident, calls for conscious black identity and pride. In his last months, as a result of his African experiences, he began to approach in his thinking a socialist alternative to American capitalism. On February 21, 1965, Malcolm X was fatally shot while preparing to speak in a Harlem auditorium. In the wake of his death, his often radical disagreements with other black leaders were largely forgotten, and he quickly assumed the charismatic stature of a cultural hero for a new and activist generation of black Americans.

MANN, HORACE (1796–1859), educator. Born on May 4, 1796, in Franklin, Massachusetts, Mann suffered an unhappy childhood marked by poverty and hard work. His education was sporadic and of inferior quality until, in 1816, he studied with an itinerant teacher who in six months prepared him for college. He entered the sophomore class at Brown University and graduated in 1819. After a brief time in a law office he became a tutor at Brown; in 1821 he entered the law school in Litchfield, Connecticut, and two years later was admitted to the bar. For ten years he practised in Dedham, Massachusetts, and in 1833 moved to Boston. In 1827 he was elected to the state house of representatives and served there for six years; in 1835 he was elected to the senate, where he remained two years, the last as president. In 1837 a bill was enacted creating a state board of education to supervise the common school system. He relinquished his law practice and a promising political future to accept the post of secretary to the board, a position of little power but of potentially great influence. The school system of Massachusetts, which dated back to the early colonial period, had deteriorated seriously in the preceding 40 or 50 years, largely because of decentralized control and dwindling financial support. Wielding little more than moral suasion, Mann worked a virtual revolution during his 12 years as secretary. He organized county educational conferences, promoted the establishment of the first normal schools, founded the *Common School Journal* in 1838, secured enlarged appropriations for salaries and facilities and a minimum school-year law, and issued 12 annual reports in which he argued powerfully for free, public-supported common education, nonsectarian, professionally conducted, and dedicated to training citizens for a democracy. The annual reports and the reforms they outlined traveled beyond Massachusetts and profoundly affected educational practices throughout the nation. In 1848 Mann resigned the secretaryship to succeed to John Quincy Adams' seat in Congress. In 1852 he ran unsuccessfully for governor as a Free-Soiler. The next year he accepted the presidency of Antioch College in Yellow Springs, Ohio, where he remained until his death on August 2, 1859.

MARIN, JOHN CHERI (1872–1953), painter. Born on December 23, 1872, in Rutherford, New Jersey, Marin studied architecture at the Stevens Institute of Technology and later turned to art at the Pennsylvania Academy of Fine Arts and the Art Students League in New York. In Europe during 1905–1911, he was deeply influenced by the individuality of Whistler's watercolors and etchings. His own expressionist style was technically experimental, using short, blunt brush strokes and bold contrasts that imparted a vigorous, dynamic quality. Famous by 1920 for his watercolors (including "Sunset, Casco Bay" and "Lower Manhattan from the River") he also later achieved great success in oils. His paintings of the Maine seacoast, completed in the later part of his career, reflected the influence of Cubism. He was among the American modern artists to be introduced and promoted by Alfred Stieglitz in the "291" gallery, and in 1936 was the subject of a retrospective showing in the Museum of Modern Art in New York City. He received the Fine Arts Medal of the American Institute of Architects in 1948. By the time of his death in Addison, Maine, on October 1, 1953, he was represented in major museums and private collections throughout the United States.

MARSHALL, GEORGE CATLETT (1880–1959), soldier and public official. Born in Uniontown, Pennsylvania, on December 31, 1880, Marshall graduated from Virginia Military Institute in 1901 and a year later received a commission as second lieutenant in the Army. After service in the Philippines he attended the School of the Line and the Command and General Staff School in 1907 and 1908. During World War I he served in high planning and administrative posts for the American Expeditionary Force in Europe; already his great abilities as a staff officer were recognized and his request for a combat command was refused. From 1919 to 1924 he was an aide to Gen. John J. Pershing, and after three years in China he became assistant commander of instruction at the Army's infantry school at Fort Benning, Georgia. In 1933 he seemed for a time to have been consigned to obscurity when he was assigned as senior instructor for the Illinois National Guard, but in 1939 he was chosen over the heads of several senior officers to become Army chief of staff. He served in this position until 1945, carrying the major responsibility for organizing, training, supplying, and deploying American troops in World War II. He was also a principal advisor to the President on strategy and attended the major Allied planning conferences from Casablanca to Potsdam. Soon after resigning as chief of staff in November 1945 Marshall was sent by President Truman to attempt — unsuccessfully—a mediation of the civil war in China. In 1947 he was appointed secretary of state; in June of that year, in a speech at Harvard, he proposed a massive program of aid to the devastated nations of Europe that was undertaken the following year and known universally as the Marshall Plan. In January 1949 he resigned from the Cabinet, but returned in September 1950 as secretary of defense, a post he held for a year during the early phase of the Korean War. He retired permanently from public service in 1951. In 1953 he was awarded the Nobel Prize for Peace, primarily for his Marshall Plan for European recovery. He died on October 16, 1959.

MARSHALL, JOHN (1755–1835), lawyer, public official, and jurist. Born on September 24, 1755, near Germantown (now Midland), Virginia, of moderately successful and, particularly for a frontier region, well educated parents, Marshall grew to manhood with little formal schooling and little exposure to the world beyond Fauquier County. In 1775 he joined a regiment of Virginia minutemen and the next year enlisted in the Continental Army; he served through Brandywine, Germantown, Monmouth, and Valley Forge and in 1779 returned home. After a brief period studying law, he began practice and from 1780 onward he was increasingly involved in state politics. Several terms in the legislature and on the executive council were followed by election to the constitutional ratifying con-

vention in 1788 where he supported ratification. This support, along with his rising prominence at the bar, led Washington to offer him the post of U.S. attorney for Virginia; Marshall declined, remaining in Richmond to become the leader of the Federalist Party there. In 1797–1798 he was one of the commissioners to France who became embroiled in the "X.Y.Z. Affair." In 1799 he finally accepted federal service by successfully running for Congress; the next year he declined the post of secretary of war offered by President Adams but was persuaded to become secretary of state. Before the administration's term had expired, Adams nominated him for chief justice of the Supreme Court; Marshall accepted and the nomination was confirmed by the Senate, but the post remained virtually empty until the State Department could be turned over to a successor in March 1801. In that month Marshall began his 34 years as the nation's highest magistrate, taking as his primary task the elaboration of a set of principles and policies aimed at creating a strong and effective national government. He immediately ended the Court's practice of producing separate opinions from each judge on each case and substituted a single majority opinion that during his tenure was usually written by himself. His first major policy-making opinion, and his most famous, came in 1803 in the case of Marbury v. Madison. Marbury, one of President Adams' "midnight appointments" to a federal judgeship, was suing for delivery of his commission by a reluctant Republican administrator; Marshall held that Marbury's claim was valid but that Section 13 of the 1789 Judicial Act, under which the suit was brought, conflicted with the constitutional limitations on the Supreme Court's area of original jurisdiction and was therefore invalid. Though judicial review was not unknown at the time, and though many had assumed it would be practised under the new government, this was the first instance of its use and the chief justice established it firmly in his decision. In subsequent cases—for example, U.S. v. Peters, 1809, Cohens v. Virginia,

1821, and *Gibbons* v. *Ogden*, 1824—he established the unity of the federal court system and its authority over state actions where federal law was concerned. In *McCulloch* v. *Maryland*, 1819, he upheld Congress' power to create the Bank of the United States on essentially the same grounds that Alexander Hamilton had argued in 1790, that of powers implied though not enumerated in the Constitution. In these and many other decisions, Marshall exerted a profound influence on the legal and judicial history of the United States and in this field he remains the preeminent figure; more effectively perhaps than any other man he oversaw the transition from confederation to nation. He died in Philadelphia on July 6, 1835.

MARSHALL, THURGOOD (1908–), jurist. Born in Baltimore on July 2, 1908, Marshall was the great-grandson of a slave "of independent spirit," and the son of a steward in a country club. He worked as a grocery clerk, waiter, and baker to earn his tuition at Lincoln University in Pennsylvania, graduating cum laude in 1930, and took his law degree magna cum laude from Howard University in Washington, D.C., in 1933, being admitted to the bar that year. Beginning private practice in Baltimore, he concentrated on the field of civil rights, and argued a number of cases for the local branch of the National Association for the Advancement of Colored People. In 1938 he was named special counsel for the NAACP and two years later became head of its legal services division. Serving with the organization for 23 years, he presented 32 cases and won 29. He established major constitutional precedents in *Smith* v. *Allwright,* securing Negro voting rights in Texas primary elections; *Morgan* v. *Virginia,* declaring unconstitutional segregated seating on interstate buses; *Sweatt* v. *Painter,* winning admission of a qualified Negro pupil to the University of Texas law school; and *Shelley* v. *Kraemer,* declaring state implementation of segregated housing agreements to be a violation of the Fourteenth Amendment. He won a reversal of the *Plessy* v. *Ferguson* "separate but equal" accommodations ruling in the historic *Brown* v. *Board of Education* case in 1954, in which the Court held unanimously that racial segregation in public schools was a denial to Negro pupils of their rights under the Fourteenth Amendment. In 1961 he was nominated to the U.S. Court of Appeals by President Kennedy. Renominated in 1962 he was approved over the bitter protests of Southern senators in a floor vote. In 1965 President Johnson appointed him U.S. solicitor general, the first Negro to hold this position, and in 1967 he became the first Negro member of the Supreme Court.

MARX, GROUCHO (1895–), humorist. Born in New York City, on October 2, 1895, Julius Henry Marx made his stage debut in 1906 as a soprano in *The Messenger Boys.* Two years later he went on tour with the LeRoy Trio, who mimicked female singers, but his voice changed and he returned to New York. He next performed around 1911 in a group called the Three Nightingales, organized by his mother, the daughter of a German ventriloquist and a yodelling harpist and the sister of Al Sheean of the team of Gallagher and Sheean. The group was reorganized first as the Four Nightingales and then as the Six Mascots before finally becoming the Four Marx Brothers—Adolph, who took the name Arthur ("Harpo"), Milton ("Gummo"), and Leonard ("Chico"). After World War I Milton went into the raincoat business and was replaced by the youngest brother, Herbert ("Zeppo"). Their nicknames were created by monologist Art Fischer, and over their vaudeville years evolved the stage personalities: Groucho, the crack-shot wit; Harpo, the idiot, a mute harpist; Chico, a pianist, soliloquist, and Harpo's interpreter, who spoke in incorrigibly broken English; and Zeppo, the "straight man" of the group. One of their most memorable early vaudeville shows was *On the Mezzanine.* In 1924 they conquered the musical stage with

I'll Say She Is, followed with *Coconuts,* 1926, and *Animal Crackers,* 1928, the last two of which were made into movies in 1929. Their one silent film was *Humor Risk,* 1919, a travesty on *Humoresque.* Their talking films included *Monkey Business,* 1931, *Horsefeathers,* 1932, and *Duck Soup,* 1933. Zeppo left the group after the last film to open a theatrical agency, and the remaining trio was then seen in *A Night at the Opera,* 1935, *A Day at the Races,* 1936, *Room Service,* 1938, *A Day at the Circus,* 1938, *Go West,* 1940, *The Big Store,* 1941, *A Night in Casablanca,* 1946 (for which Harpo refused a large sum of money to speak one word), and *Love Happy,* 1948, their last film together. Groucho, usually acknowledged as the group's mainstay, wrote many of their zany routines (other screenplays and stage scripts were provided by such notables as George S. Kaufman, S. J. Perelman, and Ben Hecht), and also contributed to the screenplay for *The King and the Chorus Girl,* 1937, and the play *Time for Elizabeth,* 1948. He appeared in *Copacabana,* 1947, *It's Only Money,* 1951, and *A Girl in Every Port,* 1951, moderated the quiz show *You Bet Your Life* on radio and television, and wrote *Beds,* 1930, *Many Happy Returns,* 1940 (about income tax problems), and the autobiographical *Groucho and Me,* 1959. Fascinated by words, his devastating and atrocious puns made mincemeat of logic or of notable personalities or of guests on *You Bet Your Life.* As much a part of his humor as verbal twists were his Rabelaisian leer, wagging eyebrows, bent-over gait, frock coat, mustache, and cigar. He was the last Marx brother to remain prominent in show business.

MASON, GEORGE (1725–1792), planter and public official. Born in 1725 in Fairfax County, Virginia, Mason received little formal education but through his own efforts and those of his guardian uncle he read much and accumulated a wide knowledge of law. Throughout his life he considered himself a private citizen and his periods of public service were undertaken with reluctance and sometimes, from his low esteem for the common run of politicians, with outright distaste. Nonetheless as a large landowner he naturally became involved in public affairs, first locally and by 1759 in the Virginia House of Burgesses. After a single term in this body he withdrew to private life, but during the mounting conflict between the colonies and Great Britain in the 1760s and 1770s he wrote numerous tracts defending the colonial position. In 1775 he was a member of the July Convention and the next year of the state's committee of safety; in May of 1776 he drafted Virginia's first constitution, including a Declaration of Rights that, with its doctrine of inalienable rights, was drawn upon by Jefferson in the Declaration of Independence. The constitution itself served as a model for those of several other states. A member of the Virginia House of Delegates from 1776 to 1788, Mason was active in supervising the organization of the new state government and was instrumental in arranging George Rogers Clark's western expedition. In 1787 he was a delegate to the Constitutional Convention in Philadelphia and was one of its most active members. As a lifelong opponent of slavery, he objected to the compromise that allowed continuation of the slave trade until 1808. Though he had favored replacing the Articles of Confederation with a stronger instrument, he decided at length that the proposed Constitution went too far in the direction of centralization and he left the Convention early, returning to Virginia to oppose ratification. His objections, clearly and forcefully maintained, were in large part responsible for the adoption of ten amendments—the Bill of Rights—to the Constitution, which again were influenced greatly by his earlier Declaration of Rights. Mason declined public office thereafter, retired to his plantation, and died on October 7, 1792.

MASTERS, EDGAR LEE (1869–1950), poet and novelist. Born on August 23, 1869, in Garnett, Kansas, Masters moved during his childhood to Lewistown, Illinois. He attended Knox College for a year, was admitted to the bar in 1891, and moved to Chicago. His law practice was slow to develop and he found ample time to write; he published a volume of poetry in 1898 and several other books afterwards, none of which was successful or significant. During 1914, however under the pseudonym Webster Ford, he published a number of poems in *Reedy's Mirror*, a St. Louis literary paper; the series, consisting of free-verse monologues the speakers in which were an assortment of persons who spoke from the graveyard where they lay buried in Spoon River, a fictitious Illinois town, attracted encouraging attention and was published in book form as *Spoon River Anthology* in 1915. The book was a sensation on the American literary scene. By 1940 it had gone through 70 editions and had been translated into several foreign languages; the success ruined Masters' legal practice, however, and, moving to New York, he devoted himself to writing thereafter. Though he was immensely prolific, none of his later works attained either the quality or the attention of the *Anthology*. *Domesday Book*, 1920, was accounted by many critics and by Masters himself the best of his later verse, and his biography *Vachel Lindsay, A Poet in America*, 1935, was awarded the Mark Twain Medal. His biography of Abraham Lincoln in 1931 took a harshly debunking approach to an American mythic hero and aroused a storm of controversy. In 1936 he published *Across Spoon River*, his autobiography. He died in Philadelphia on March 5, 1950.

MATHER, COTTON (1663–1728), clergyman. Born in Boston on February 12, 1663, Cotton Mather was the eldest son of Increase and grandson of Richard and of John Cotton, for whom he was named. He graduated from Harvard in 1678 and, sharing his father's interest in science, studied medicine for a time. He turned to the ministry, however, and in 1685 joined his father in the pulpit of Boston's Second Church where he remained for the rest of his life. He worked always closely with his father and during the latter's absence in England where he sought the restoration of the colonial charter revoked by James II, Cotton led the revolt against the Stuart-appointed royal governor, Sir Edmund Andros. His scientific curiosity, combined with his marked proclivity for mysticism, led him into the study of spiritualism and possession; his *Memorable Providences, Relating to Witchcrafts and Possessions*, 1689, made a public issue of the subject and contributed to the hysteria that resulted in the witchcraft trials of 1692. Mather did not participate in the trials, and disapproved of the excesses and lapses of reason displayed by the judges. *Wonders of the Invisible World*, 1693, was a narrative of some of the trials. After this time his political influence, which through his association with his father in the charter dispute had been considerable, began to wane as the new charter of 1691 proved less than unanimously popular and as colonial politics became increasingly secular. His devotion to the church was undiminished, however, and through his tireless efforts in the cause of orthodox Congregationalism and his vast body of written work — some 450 separate titles — his fame continued to grow. His most famous work, *Magnalia Christi Americana*, was published in 1702 and remained the most complete history of New England for many years. His struggle against heterodoxy was unavailing. Dissenting churches, such as the Brattle Street Church founded in 1698, flourished and Harvard became less and less strictly Congregational in policy; in 1703 he resigned his fellowship in the college after 13 years and promoted the founding of Yale as a new bastion of the faith. He took great interest in the proper training of children, organized a school for the education of Negroes, and concerned himself with ministering personally to his parishioners. In 1713 he was elected to the Royal Society; in 1721 he joined his father in the often unpopular campaign to promote inoculation against smallpox. At the time of his death on February 13, 1728, Cotton Mather was probably the best known of Americans; he remains the most famous of the American Puritans.

MATHER, INCREASE (1639–1723), clergyman and statesman. Born in Dorchester, Massachusetts, on June 21, 1639, Increase was the son of the renowned preacher, Richard Mather. He graduated from Harvard in 1656 and the next year sailed to England; in 1658 he took his M.A. degree from Trinity College, Dublin, and remained in the British Isles serving in various churches until the restoration of the Stuarts made Puritanism again uncomfortable in England. Returning to Massachusetts in 1661, he joined his father at the church in Dorchester and remained there until he became teacher of Boston's Second Church in 1664. His strong personality, forceful preaching, and broad scholarship won him increasing prominence; in 1674 he was appointed licenser of the press, in 1675 a fellow of Harvard, and ten years later president of the college. He was a prolific writer and though most of his works were theological in nature, he wrote also on history, science, and politics. Prominent among his books were *The Life and Death of that Reverend Man of God, Mr. Richard Mather*, 1670, *A Brief History of the Warr with the Indians*, 1676, *A Relation of the Troubles Which Have Hapned in New-England by Reason of the Indians There*, 1677, and *Essay for the Recording of Illustrious Providences*, 1684. Although always first and foremost devoted to his ministry, he was drawn into political affairs by the dispute over the Massachusetts charter during the 1680s. He led the protest against revocation of the charter and in 1688 sailed to England in an attempt to have it restored. Negotiations with powerful politicians of the Stuart court and with James II himself came to naught; but in 1690 he was appointed an official agent of the colony and managed to win some concessions from William III in the new charter of 1691. He returned to Boston the next year with the new royal governor whom the King had allowed him to nominate. Mather was identified strongly with both the governor and the charter and when they proved unpopular with a large segment of the colony, he found himself embroiled in a political controversy that eventually, in 1701, cost him the presidency of Harvard. During the period of the witchcraft trials in 1692 he expressed private disapproval of the proceedings but publicly held his peace until October when he wrote *Cases of Conscience Concerning Evil Spirits*, a book that was circulated widely and played a vital role in ending the period of hysteria. After leaving Harvard he largely forsook politics but remained a leader of New England Congregationalism. He died on August 23, 1723. His eldest son, Cotton Mather, became the most famous of Puritan clergymen.

MATHER, RICHARD (1596–1669), clergyman. Born in 1596 in Lowton, Lancashire, England, Mather taught grammar school for several years before spending a few months in 1618 studying at Brasenose College, Oxford. In November of that year he was called to the pulpit at Toxteth Park Chapel (now part of Liverpool). During the course of his ministry there he displayed an increasing tendency toward Puritanism, with the result that in 1633 and again in 1634 he was suspended by ecclesiastical authorities. In 1635 he decided upon emigration to America; he set sail with his family in May and on August 17th landed in Boston. Immediately offered several pulpits, he chose that of Dorchester, where he remained as teacher for the rest of his life. He quickly became a leader of New England Congregationalism and a central figure in the elaboration of both doctrine and polity. One of his earliest written works, done in collaboration with two other ministers, was *The Whole Booke of Psalms*, 1640, better known as *The Bay Psalm Book*. Other major works by Mather were *Church-Government and Church-Covenant Discussed*, 1643, and particularly *A Platform of Church Discipline*,

1649, which under the common title of the "Cambridge Platform" served for many years as the basic document of New England Congregationalism. He was a chief proponent of the "Half-Way Covenant," which broadened church membership and helped maintain ecclesiastical power in the colony. Of his six children, four became ministers; the youngest, Increase Mather, became one of the most prominent and influential of all New England clergymen. Richard Mather died on April 22, 1669.

MAULDIN, WILLIAM HENRY (1921–), editorial cartoonist. Born on October 29, 1921, in Mountain Park, New Mexico, Mauldin studied cartooning at the Chicago Academy of Fine Arts in 1939 and began to train with the 45th Infantry Division of the U.S. Army in 1940. He became a staff cartoonist for the *45th Division News* and, going overseas in 1943, joined the Mediterranean staff of *Stars and Stripes*, covering campaigns in Italy, France, and Germany. He developed the cartoon soldiers named Willie and Joe, whose progressively deteriorating appearance and disenchanted attitudes reflected those of many American soldiers overseas. The cartoons were featured in 100 newspapers in the United States, collected in several volumes, including *Up Front*, 1945, and made Mauldin famous. He won a Pulitzer Prize in 1945 for a cartoon captioned "Fresh American troops, flushed with victory," which showed grimy soldiers plodding through a storm in the mud. His postwar depictions of Willie and Joe trying to adjust to civilian life (collected in *Back Home*, 1947) and his new series of cartoons mocking racists, overzealous patriots, and stereotyped liberals were distributed, at one point to some 180 newspapers, by the United Features Syndicate. During 1950–1951 he worked in Hollywood as a technical consultant and an actor in the war film *Teresa* and as the star of *The Red Badge of Courage*, both released in 1951. Also released that year was *Up Front*, a movie based on the Willie

and Joe cartoons. *Bill Mauldin in Korea*, 1952, was published after he visited that war zone. In 1956 he ran unsuccessfully for Democratic congressman from New York. Two years later he became editorial cartoonist for the *St. Louis Post Dispatch*, his work from there being syndicated eventually to 141 newspapers. Finding his postwar métier in satirical social and political commentary, he became the first formidable rival to Herblock of the *Washington Post*. In 1958 he won a second Pulitzer Prize for his impression of Boris Pasternak's fate: "I won the Nobel Prize for Literature. What was your crime?" In 1962 he joined the *Chicago Sun Times*, which distributed his editorial cartoons to more than 200 newspapers. He wrote and illustrated numerous articles for popular magazines and published other collections, including *Sort of a Saga*, 1949, and *What's Got Your Back Up*, 1961.

MAURY, MATTHEW FONTAINE (1806–1873), naval officer and oceanographer. Born in Spotsylvania County, Virginia, on January 14, 1806, Maury grew up there and, from the age of five, on a farm near Franklin, Tennessee. In 1825 he entered the Navy as a midshipman and in the following nine years made three lengthy cruises, the second of which was a circumnavigation of the globe on the *Vincennes*. Under various pseudonyms, he published a number of articles criticizing the administration of the Navy and suggesting reforms. An accident in 1839 rendered him permanently lame and unfit for sea duty, but three years later he was appointed superintendent of the Navy's Depot of Charts and Instruments and Naval Observatory (after 1854 the U.S. Naval Observatory and Hydrographic Office). He launched an intensive program of research into winds and currents and in 1847 published his *Wind and Current Chart of the North Atlantic*; this manual, with later supplements, proved highly valuable in reducing sailing times. It produced worldwide interest in his work, which culminated in

1853 in an international conference in Brussels. He represented the United States at the meeting and secured the adoption of a plan for international cooperation in the gathering and collating of oceanographic data. With new sources of information available he revised his earlier work and compiled charts for other ocean areas. In 1855 he published *The Physical Geography of the Sea*, considered the first work of modern oceanography. In that year a naval board convened to review the officer list placed him on leave of absence, possibly because of jealousy of his growing reputation; in 1858 President Buchanan restored him to active service with the rank of commander, retroactive to 1855. In 1861, shortly after the secession of Virginia, he resigned from the U.S. Navy and was promptly commissioned a commander in the Confederate Navy. Placed in charge of coast, harbor, and river defenses, he conducted experiments with an electric torpedo, continuing the work in England, where he was sent in 1862 as special agent of the Confederacy. His reputation gained him considerable influence there, and he secured a number of warships for the South. While returning to America in 1865 he learned of the fall of the Confederacy and went instead to Mexico. He was appointed imperial commissioner of Immigration by Emperor Maximilian and attempted unsuccessfully to establish a colony of Virginians in that country. From 1866 to 1868 he was again in England, but in the latter year he returned to the United States to become professor of meteorology at the Virginia Military Institute. He died in Lexington, Virginia, on February 1, 1873.

MAYO, WILLIAM JAMES (1861–1939) and CHARLES HORACE (1865–1939), physicians. Born in Minnesota, William in Le Sueur on June 29, 1861, and Charles in Rochester on July 19, 1865, the Mayo brothers were sons of William Worrall Mayo (1819–1911), who had emigrated from England in 1845, studied medicine in Indiana and at the University of Mis-

souri, and settled in Minnesota in 1855 to become the region's most prominent physician. Both sons aided their father in his medical practice from early youth and in due time studied medicine formally; William took his medical degree from the University of Michigan in 1883 and Charles graduated from the Chicago Medical College (now part of Northwestern University) in 1888. In the aftermath of a disastrous tornado that struck Rochester in 1883, the Sisters of St. Francis began erecting a permanent hospital in the town; it opened in 1889 with the Mayos as its sole staff. St. Mary's Hospital had the only adequate surgical facilities accessible to much of Minnesota and Iowa and all of the Dakotas, and consequently the three doctors enjoyed a huge practice. The brothers traveled regularly to other medical centers to keep abreast of progress in medical and surgical techniques; as their proficiency increased, so did their practice and reputation. Gradually other doctors were attracted to Rochester for advanced study in surgery, and as the staff of St. Mary's thus multiplied a form of group practice was evolved, the first such system to be applied in private practice. The cooperative clinic was broadened to include specialists in various medical fields and was able to attract highly skilled practitioners. The Mayos, who until 1905 had performed all the surgery at St. Mary's, were able to specialize as well, William in surgery of the stomach and Charles in surgery of the thyroid and the nervous system. In 1907 William became a member of the board of regents of the University of Minnesota, a position he held until his death, and from 1915 to 1936 Charles held positions on the university's surgical faculty. In 1915 they established the Mayo Foundation for Medical Education and Research with an endowment of $1.5 million (later much increased), and two years later the foundation was transferred to the University of Minnesota as part of its graduate school. In 1919 the bulk of the rest of their holdings was vested in the Mayo Properties Association, a perpetual charitable and educational organization. With the clinic reorganized from a partnership into a voluntary association, the brothers retired from medical practice, William in 1928 and Charles in 1930. Both died in 1939, Charles in Chicago on May 26 and William in Rochester on July 28.

MEAD, MARGARET (1901 –   ), anthropologist. Born on December 16, 1901, in Philadelphia, Margaret Mead was the daughter of an economics professor and a sociologist. The teaching of Franz Boas and Ruth Benedict at Columbia, where she received her B.A. in 1923 and her M.A. in psychology in 1924, led her to choose anthropology as her field. She took her doctorate in 1929. In 1925–1926 she made the first of many field trips to the South Seas, to the island of Tau in the Samoas, where she observed the development of native children through adolescence (*Coming of Age in Samoa*, 1928). On the second trip, during 1928–1929, she investigated the development of social behavior in children of the Manus tribe in the Admiralty Islands in the western Pacific (*Growing Up in New Guinea*, 1930). Her expedition of 1931–1933 was also to the New Guinea area, where she studied three primitive tribes, the Arapesh, Mundugumor, and Tchambuli (*Sex and Temperament*, 1935). The three books appeared together as *From the South Seas* in 1939. In a format frequently used in subsequent volumes — contrasting the values of two or more cultures — she prompted significant questioning of rigid social standards. Like Ruth Benedict, she stressed the impermanence of human values and their dependence on time and environment. She was one of few ₋nthropologists to reach popular as well as scientific audiences. In 1932 she published the results of her study of an anonymous American Indian tribe ("the Antlers") in *The Changing Culture of an Indian Tribe*. In 1935 she edited 13 papers of Columbia graduate students, publishing them as *Cooperation and Competition Among Primitive Peoples* in 1937, to refute the notion of society as a Darwinian jungle. During 1936–1939 she

did field work in Bali and New Guinea, producing *Balinese Character: A Photographic Analysis* (with Gregory Bateson), 1941, and *Growth and Culture; a Photographic Study of Balinese Childhood* (with Frances MacGregor), 1951. With her knowledge of primitive cultures she explored American cultural standards in *And Keep Your Powder Dry*, 1942. During World War II she wrote pamphlets for the Office of War Information to aid communication between British and American troops. One of her most important books appeared in 1949, *Male and Female: A Study of the Sexes in a Changing World*. It examined traditional male-female relationships using observations in the Pacific and East Indies for reference in discussing such topics as the mother's influence in perpetuating male and female roles and concepts of marriage. She also published *Soviet Attitudes Toward Authority*, 1951, *Childhood in Contemporary Cultures* (with Martha Wolfenstein), 1955, *New Lives for Old*, 1956, *An Anthropologist at Work* (about Ruth Benedict), 1958, *Continuities in Cultural Evolution*, 1964, and numerous anthropological papers. She became assistant curator of ethnology in 1926, associate curator in 1942, and curator in 1964 of the American Museum of Natural History. She served on national public and mental health councils and was a frequent visiting lecturer at American universities.

MEADE, GEORGE GORDON (1815 – 1872), soldier. Born of American parents in Cadiz, Spain, on December 31, 1815, Meade graduated from West Point in 1835, was commissioned in the artillery, and was immediately ordered to Florida for service in the Seminole War. In 1836 he resigned from the Army and for six years engaged in engineering work for the Alabama, Florida & Georgia Railroad and in surveying the Texas and Maine boundaries. In 1842 he reentered the Army as a second lieutenant in the Topographical Engineers. He remained with the Maine survey for a year and then was transferred to Philadelphia to work on lighthouse construction. After service in the Mexican War he again engaged in engineering and survey duties in Philadelphia, Florida, and the Great Lakes region. In 1861 he was appointed brigadier general of volunteers in Pennsylvania. He took part in McClellan's Peninsula campaign in 1862 and later in the year was seriously wounded at Glendale; he recovered sufficiently to command his brigade at Second Bull Run in August and a month later, at Antietam, he temporarily took command of the I Corps when Gen. Joseph Hooker was wounded and taken from the field. In November he was promoted to major general of volunteers and in December, following the Union defeat at Fredericksburg, he was given command of the V Corps. On June 28, 1863, a month after the battle of Chancellorsville, President Lincoln named Meade to succeed Hooker as commander of the Army of the Potomac. He reluctantly accepted; just three days later contact was made with Lee's army at Gettysburg and Meade displayed great tactical skill in repulsing the Confederate forces, though, like many of his predecessors, he failed to press his advantage. He was made brigadier general in the regular Army and in January 1864 was voted the thanks of Congress. He retained command of the Army of the Potomac, but when Grant was placed in command of all Union forces and joined the Army in the field, Meade's independence was greatly reduced. He gave complete loyalty to Grant, however, and in August 1864 was promoted to major general. After the war he commanded the Military Division of the Atlantic and later the Department of the East. From 1868 to 1869 he was commander of Georgia, Alabama, and Florida in the Department of the South, and then returned to his earlier post with the Military Division of the Atlantic. He died in Philadelphia on November 6, 1872.

MEDILL, JOSEPH (1823–1899), journalist. Born on April 6, 1823, in New Brunswick, Canada, of a family of Irish shipbuilders, Medill studied law in Massillon, Ohio, and was admitted to the bar in 1846. He opened a practice but soon turned to journalism and joined three younger brothers in purchasing the Coshocton (Ohio) Whig, which he renamed the Republican. Moving to Cleveland in 1851, he founded the Daily Forest City, combined it with a Free-Soil journal, and renamed it the Cleveland Leader. Formerly active in Whig politics, he could foresee the demise of the party after the election of 1852. He began organizing a new antislavery party, which he suggested be named "Republican"; the party was founded in 1854. In 1855 he bought a share in the Chicago Tribune and with its resources and his own influence united disgruntled factions under the Republican banner. He firmly advocated Lincoln's nomination for President in 1860 and supported Republican Civil War policies, promoting even harsher moves against the South than were being taken with regard to property confiscation and emancipation. He conducted effective editorial campaigns for the adoption of laws to provide soldiers in battle with the opportunity to vote in elections, and for the eradication of political corruption in the city. He was elected to the Illinois Constitutional Convention in 1869 and was elected mayor of Chicago one month after the great fire of 1871. He oversaw the reorganization of the government and the rebuilding of the city, and projected the building of the Chicago Public Library. In 1874 he resigned as mayor and purchased a controlling interest in the Tribune. As its editor-in-chief he guided the paper's conservative, pro-business, and sometimes, as during the events leading to the Spanish-American War, jingoistic editorial position until his death in San Antonio, Texas, on March 16, 1889. His son-in-law, Robert W. Patterson, became editor-in-chief of the Tribune; in 1900 a grandson, Joseph McCormick, became manager of the paper, and in 1914 another grandson, Robert R. McCormick, gained control. Still another grandson, Joseph M. Patterson, became publisher of the New York Daily News; and

Eleanor M. Patterson, a granddaughter, founded and edited the *Washington Times Herald* to compete with the Hearst papers. The family established the Medill School of Journalism at Northwestern University in Evanston, Illinois, and dedicated it to the memory of Joseph Medill.

MEIKLEJOHN, ALEXANDER (1872–1964), educator. Born on February 3, 1872, in Rochdale, England, Meiklejohn was brought to America in 1880. He graduated from Brown in 1893, received an M.A. from that university in 1895, and a Ph.D. from Cornell in 1897. He taught philosophy at Brown from 1897 to 1912, the last six years as professor of logic and metaphysics, and he was dean from 1901 to 1912. He was named president of Amherst College in the latter year, a post that he retained until 1924. In 1926 he became a professor of philosophy at, and director of, the Experimental College at the University of Wisconsin. There, until his retirement in 1938 as professor emeritus, he oversaw many educational innovations, and gave strong support to the great books programs installed during those years at the University of Chicago and at St. John's College. In the course of his work at Wisconsin he found time to serve as the chairman of the School for Social Studies at San Francisco, 1933–1936, and after his retirement he continued to be active in education, serving as a visiting professor at Dartmouth in 1938, and at St. John's in 1940, among other positions. He was the author of a number of books, among them *The Liberal College*, 1920, *The Experimental College*, 1932, *What Does American Mean*, 1935, *Education Between Two Worlds*, 1942, probably his best known book, and *Free Speech and Its Relationship to Government*, 1948. He received the Presidential Medal of Freedom in 1963, and died in California on September 16, 1964, at the age of 92.

MELLON, ANDREW WILLIAM (1855–1937), financier and public official. Born in Pittsburgh on March 24, 1855, Mellon was educated in the city's public schools and at Western University of Pennsylvania (now the University of Pittsburgh), which he left, however, shortly before the graduation of his class of 1872. He opened a successful lumber firm and two years later, having demonstrated considerable business ability, entered the family banking firm. Within ten years ownership of the business was in his hands. Thoroughly grounded in sound business practices, possessed of great acumen in finance, and particularly able to judge accurately the potential in a prospective venture, he quickly expanded his interests; he backed the founding and growth of a number of companies that became industrial giants, among them the Aluminum Company of America, the Gulf Oil Corporation, Union Steel Company (later merged with U.S. Steel), and many others. In 1902 the banking house at the center of his financial empire became the Mellon National Bank. While becoming one of the major figures in American capitalism and one of its richest men, Mellon nevertheless remained largely unknown to the country. Not until 1921 did he achieve national prominence; in that year he was chosen by President Harding to serve as secretary of the treasury. For the next 11 years he presided over the greatest business boom and the beginning of the worst depression in American history. A staunch conservative, he urged constantly upon Congress schedules of taxation that rested as lightly as possible upon the wealthy and upon business; his program embodied the view that the nation's greatest interest was business, that to aid business government should allow it to retain a maximum of profit for reinvestment and expansion, and that wealth retained or created at the top would filter down to the lower classes. Despite considerable congressional opposition from progressives of both parties, this program was widely popular, though somewhat less so after 1929. In handling the repayment of war loans by European allies, he followed currently popular opinion and resisted a realistic view of European finance; the result was a system whereby huge amounts of capital were loaned to Germany, used by that country to cover reparations payments to other nations, and then returned to the United States as loan repayment. Mellon's popularity—he was commonly considered the greatest secretary of the treasury since Hamilton—declined after the stock market crash in October 1929. In 1932 President Hoover replaced him and he became ambassador to Great Britain, a position he held for just over a year. He returned to his private business interests in 1933. In 1937 he donated his large art collection— valued at $35 million—to the federal government, along with sufficient funds to construct and endow the National Gallery of Art. While work was in progress on this great project, he died on August 26, 1937.

MELVILLE, HERMAN (1819–1891), author. Born on August 1, 1819, in New York City, Melville was of a family long distinguished on both sides but which suffered successive financial reverses until left virtually destitute by his father's death in 1832. At 15 he ended his formal schooling and at 19, after holding a series of small jobs, he signed as a cabin boy aboard a New York-to-Liverpool packet. The experiences of the four-month round trip journey were the core of his largely autobiographical work, *Redburn*, 1849. In January 1841 he set sail again aboard a whaler bound for the South Seas; for the next four years he wandered and accumulated the material for most of his writings. His four weeks in benevolent captivity among the Taipi tribe on Nuku Hiva, one of the Marquesas Islands, became *Typee*, his first book; his life on Tahiti and the nearby island of Eimeo, whither he escaped from the Taipis, was described in *Omoo*; and his service as a seaman aboard a Navy frigate furnished him with the basis for *White-Jacket*, 1850. In October 1844 he returned to his mother's home near Troy, New York, and began to write of his experiences. *Typee* appeared in 1846 and was followed a year later

by *Omoo*; the two books, full of high adventure and romantic visions of South Seas life, secured him considerable fame, though his harsh depiction of hypocrisy and venality among Christian missionaries to the islands roused a storm of controversy. In 1847 he moved to New York City and produced *Mardi*, 1849, another sea story that was, however, more allegorical and less successful than its predecessors, and followed with *Redburn* and *White-Jacket*. In 1850 he purchased a farm near Pittsfield, Massachusetts, and began work on his greatest book, *Moby-Dick*, completed and published the next year. At Pittsfield he formed a close friendship with his near neighbor, Nathaniel Hawthorne, to whose influence much of the power and insight of *Moby-Dick* are probably due. The book, though a critical and popular failure at the time, has come to be recognized as one, perhaps the best, of the very few truly great American novels. The visions of evil in the white whale and in the growing and corrupting monomania of Ahab, the pervading mystical atmosphere, and the richly and subtly symbolic narrative show Melville at the height of his powers. In 1852 appeared *Pierre*, a psychological study that anticipated much later literature. After this time his work suffered a decline. A few short stories, published in magazines and collected in 1856 as *The Piazza Tales*, remain noteworthy, particularly "The Encantadas," "Bartleby," and "Benito Cereno"; with the exception of *The Confidence-Man*, 1857, a dense allegory of American materialism, he wrote little prose thereafter, and his poetry, except for a few of his *Battle-Pieces*, 1866, was undistinguished. He journeyed to the Holy Land and to Europe in 1856–1857 and briefly visited Hawthorne, then U.S. consul in Liverpool; in 1863 he left the farm to return to New York City. In 1866 he obtained a long sought government sinecure as a customs inspector, a post he held until 1885. In these last years he lived in utter obscurity. He regained his former literary powers in his last complete work, *Billy Budd*,

Foretopman, completed in 1891 but not published until 1924. He died on September 28, 1891. His work remained largely unknown until the 1920s, when a revival of interest in American literature brought about a critical and public rediscovery of him and of many similarly forgotten authors.

MENCKEN, HENRY LOUIS (1880 – 1956), journalist and critic. Born in Baltimore on September 12, 1880, Mencken graduated from the Baltimore Polytechnic Institute, a high school, and in 1899 joined the staff of the *Baltimore Morning Herald* as a police reporter. Four years later he was city editor and in 1906 switched to the *Baltimore Sun*, with which he was associated at intervals throughout his career. In 1908 he was hired to review books for *The Smart Set*, a witty, urbane periodical that also featured the drama reviews and criticism of George Jean Nathan; in 1914 the two assumed co-editorship of the magazine. In 1923 they departed from *Smart Set* to found the *American Mercury*, and for ten years Mencken continued to dominate American criticism in its pages. A vigorous and colorful writer, he consistently and gleefully attacked every sacred cow within reach; in his omnivorous iconoclasm he was particularly caustic toward sham, prudery, Prohibition, the middle class (or "booboisie"), and, later, the New Deal. While belittling the excesses and deficiencies of currently popular sentimental literature, he promoted such younger writers as Theodore Dreiser, Sherwood Anderson, and Sinclair Lewis. The Scopes "monkey trial" in 1925, which he reported from the scene, provided a golden opportunity for Mencken to exercise his acerbic wit. Many of his reviews and essays were collected in the six series of *Prejudices*, 1919 – 1927. His most lasting work came in a surprisingly uncharacteristic form: *The American Language*, 1919, a solid, thorough, and scholarly treatment of the subject that, together with two supplements issued in 1945 and 1948, constituted an effort of primary value and established him as the leading authority on American English. The radical change in the temper of the country brought on by the Depression lessened the popular appeal of a perennial cynic; he continued to report on the American scene after 1933, but with diminished influence. He published numerous books of essays and criticism and three autobiographical works, *Happy Days*, 1940, *Newspaper Days*, 1941, and *Heathen Days*, 1943. In 1948 he suffered a stroke from which he never fully recovered; he died on January 29, 1956.

MENNINGER, KARL AUGUSTUS (1893 –   ), psychiatrist. Born on July 22, 1893, in Topeka, Kansas, the son of psychiatrist Charles Frederick Menninger, Karl graduated from the University of Wisconsin in 1914 and received his medical degree from Harvard in 1917. He interned in the Kansas City General Hospital during 1918 – 1919 and was an assistant physician in the Boston Psychopathic Hospital in 1920. That year he founded the Menninger Clinic for psychiatric research in Topeka with his father. He and his brother, also a psychiatrist, established the Menninger Foundation in 1941, to provide clinics for research, professional education, and diagnosis and treatment, and programs on the relation of psychiatry to law, religion, industry, and education. He made the community in Topeka aware of the aims of the clinic through various public appearances, working on the principle that knowledge of psychiatry's basic concepts would overcome prejudice. Kansas revamped its entire mental health program under his guidance and became a model for the nation. After World War II he helped establish the Winter Veteran's Administration Hospital, and remained there as manager until 1948. During 1946 – 1962 he was clinical professor of psychiatry at the University of Kansas. State and national organizations enlisted his services as mental health advisor, among them the Illinois State Department of Welfare, the Office of Vocational Rehabilitation of the Department of Health, Education and Welfare, and the prison bureau of the Department of Justice. He edited the *Bulletin* of the Menninger Foundation and wrote *The Human Mind*, 1930, *Man Against Himself*, 1938, *Manual for Psychiatric Case Study*, 1952, and *Theory of Psychoanalytic Technique*, 1958.

MERGENTHALER, OTTMAR (1854–1899), engineer and inventor. Born on May 11, 1854, in Hachtel, Germany, Mergenthaler wanted to be an engineer when he finished school and at 14 he became an apprentice to a watchmaker and developed, in the course of his four-year indenture, a keen ability in precision instrument making and a refined sense of the interrelationship of parts in a machine. Emigrating to the United States in 1872 (he was naturalized in 1878), he joined the business of August Hahl, his former master's son, a scientific equipment manufacturer, in Washington, D.C., and after 1876 in Baltimore. They were commissioned to construct a patent model of a typewriting device, which used rudimentary papier-mâché molds for type-casting. Although the device proved unworkable, its intent—to eliminate the laborious task of hand type composition—stimulated Mergenthaler to seek an efficient mechanical typesetter. In developing the final model, he passed through various stages—attempting to avoid type completely by directly making an inked transfer for lithographic reproduction, and also using the basics of stereotyping to successively punch letters into papier-mâché molds for casting in metal. Finally he employed sturdy individual copper molds, or matrices, for each character; by quickly stamping the matrices, depressed with the impressions of characters, onto a molten but fast-cooling alloy, he rapidly produced column-widths of type. The machine was named the Linotype when Whitelaw Reid of the *New York Tribune* (the first enterprise to use the machine commercially) examined a line-long "slug" and cried, "It's a line of type!" The first patent was obtained by Mergenthaler in 1884. He had begun his own

business the year before, and did secure patents on other successful inventions, but the Linotype remained his major concern. He constantly made and patented improvements on the original and was widely honored for his invention. At the time of his death in Baltimore, on October 28, 1899, three Mergenthaler Linotype manufactories in New York, England, and Germany, were in full operation, and over 3,000 Linotypes were being used. More than any other invention of its time, the Linotype brought about a dramatic surge in publishing and a rapid rise in the level of world literacy.

MICHELSON, ALBERT ABRAHAM (1852–1931), physicist. Born on December 19, 1852, in Strelno, Prussia, Michelson came to the United States with his parents in 1854, and grew up in Virginia City, Nevada, and San Francisco. He won appointment to the Naval Academy, graduated in 1873, and after two years of regular duty returned there as an instructor in chemistry and physics. After four years of teaching he returned to his own studies in Germany and France, resigning from the Navy in 1881. In 1883 he became professor of physics at the Case School of Applied Science in Cleveland and in 1889 moved to Clark University in Worcester, Massachusetts; finally, in 1892, he was appointed head of the physics department of the newly organized University of Chicago and there remained until his retirement. Throughout his life his main interest was the study of light. His first published paper in 1878 concerned the measurement of the speed of light; this problem and that of optical interference were the subjects of the bulk of his researches and writings. His major work was in the latter field and began in 1881 with his invention of the interferometer, a device for studying the nature and behavior of light on the nearly infinitesimal scale of the single wavelength. At the time it was generally believed that electromagnetic phenomena —light, for example—occurred in and were transmitted by a universal substrate or medium called the ether. The ether was presumed to be uniform, and it was therefore predicted that the earth, moving at high speed in a constantly changing direction along its curved orbit, ought to show a changing velocity with respect to it. This change would appear as a slight difference in the speed of light rays traveling in different directions. After some preliminary experiments in 1881 Michelson collaborated with Edward Morley to conduct the famous Michelson-Morley experiment in 1887 that demonstrated the absence of the "ether wind." This result, confirmed many times, was a major foundation for Einstein's analysis of motion and reference systems in his theory of relativity. In later work Michelson continued to refine the determination of the speed of light, redefined the meter in terms of a new standard, the wavelength of cadmium light, and in 1920 used his stellar interferometer to make the first reliable measurement of the diameter of a star. During World War I he was called to service in the naval reserve and contributed much valuable work, particularly the development of a range-finder. He was the recipient of a large number of honors and awards and a member of the world's leading scientific societies. In 1925 he became the first distinguished service professor at the University of Chicago; he retired in 1931 and died shortly thereafter, on May 9, 1931, in Pasadena, California.

MIES VAN DER ROHE, LUDWIG (1886–1969), architect. Born on March 27, 1886, in Aachen, Germany, Ludwig Mies (he added van der Rohe later in life) learned the fundamentals of architecture from his father, a mason and stonecutter. He attended a trade school at Aachen and became a draftsman's apprentice. From 1905 to 1907 he worked with furniture designer Bruno Paul in Berlin, and from 1908 to 1911 he studied under Peter Behrens, who also influenced architects Le Corbusier and Walter Gropius. He opened an office in Berlin in 1913, and served in the German army as a bridge and road constructor during World War I. In 1919 and 1921 he planned the first steel and glass skyscrapers, which became his trademark. He introduced "ribbon windows," rows of glass evenly divided by concrete slabs, in an office building in 1922. His concrete house, developed in 1924, anticipated the California ranch house. International recognition came from his German Pavilion at the Barcelona World Exhibit in 1929, and from his contemporary Tugendhat House in Brno, Czechoslovakia, completed in 1930. Between 1926 and 1932 he led a group of German architects whose purpose was to adapt art to the technological age. In 1930 he became head of the Bauhaus School of Design at Dessau, which was closed in 1933 by the Nazis for being "un-German." He came to the United States in 1938 to direct the school of architecture at the Illinois Institute of Technology, a post he held until 1958. He became an American citizen in 1944. During the rapid increase in building after World War II, his designs materialized in cities across America. Based on his concepts of order, logic, and clarity, they used minimal ornamentation to achieve striking effects. Among the most famous were the Seagram Building in New York City, a dark glass tower in a spacious concrete plaza; Crown Hall at the Illinois Institute of Technology, a "glass house" with mobile space dividers, one of 20 buildings he planned for the campus; the Chicago Federal Center, a symmetrical group of high- and low-rise structures; and twin glass apartment towers in Chicago overlooking Lake Michigan. His chairs became as famous as his buildings, among them the MR of cane and tubular steel; the steel-framed, leather-upholstered Tugendhat, whose design forms a square S; the Brno, which forms a curved S; and the Barcelona, whose legs form an X. A master of 20th-century architecture, he died in Chicago on August 18, 1969.

MILLAY, EDNA ST. VINCENT (1892–1950), poet. Born on February 22, 1892, in Rockland, Maine, Miss Millay was raised with two younger sisters by their widowed mother, who recognized and encouraged her talent in writing poetry. At 19 she entered "Renascence," a poem of about 200 lines, in an anthology contest, and although she did not win a prize, she attracted critical recognition and a patron who sent her to Vassar. She enrolled at 21 and graduated in 1917, in that year publishing *Renascence and Other Poems* and moving to Greenwich Village in New York City. There she submitted verse and short stories under the pseudonym "Nancy Boyd" to magazines, and to augment her modest income wrote skits for the Provincetown Players and joined them briefly as an actress. In 1920 she published *A Few Figs From Thistles,* her second book of verse, and in 1921 *Second April.* In the latter year she also published three plays, *Aria Da Capo, Two Slatterns and a King,* and *The Lamp and the Bell.* She won a Pulitzer Prize in 1923 for *The Harp-Weaver and Other Poems.* She also married in 1923 and lived thereafter in a large, isolated home in the Berkshire foothills near Austerlitz, New York. In 1925, the Metropolitan Opera Company commissioned her to write an opera with Deems Taylor; the resulting work, *The King's Henchman,* first produced in 1927, became the most popular American opera up to its time and, printed in book form, sold out four printings in 20 days. Her youthful appearance, the independent, almost petulant tone of her poetry, and her political and social ideals made her a symbol of the youth of her time. In 1927 she donated the proceeds from "Justice Denied in Massachusetts" to the defense of Sacco and Vanzetti and personally appealed to Governor Fuller for their lives. The night of their execution she was arrested in the death watch outside the Boston Court House. Three later books, *There Are No Islands Any More,* 1940, *Make Bright the Arrows,* 1940, and *The Murder of Lidice,* 1942, expressed her concern with contemporary politics. She also published *The Buck in the Snow and Other Poems,* 1928, *Fatal Interview,* 1931, *Wine From These Grapes,* 1934, *Conversation at Midnight,* 1937, and *Huntsman, What Quarry?,* 1939. She died in Austerlitz on October 19, 1950.

MILLER, ARTHUR (1915–   ), author and playwright. Born on October 17, 1915, in New York City, Miller was raised in modest circumstances, attending local public schools. When the Depression struck he had to find a job to sustain himself and earn tuition for college. Combining studies with full-time jobs, he completed a four-year course at the University of Michigan in six years and graduated in 1938. He began writing in college and won a measure of fame when his first novel *Focus,* about anti-Semitism, was published in 1945. He had written an earlier play, *The Man Who Had All the Luck,* 1944, and a book about life in the Army, *Situation Normal,* also 1944. His first successful play was *All My Sons,* 1947, which explored the guilt of a manufacturer of inferior war supplies and the effect of his crime on his family; it won the New York Drama Critics' Circle Award. *Death of a Salesman,* 1949, won a Pulitzer Prize. It pictured a salesman's struggle to maintain his life on illusion. In *The Crucible,* 1953, Miller's account of the Salem witch trials closely paralleled political events of the time in 20th-century America. His other plays typically placed characters in rigid social structures, the drama being produced by the character's attempt to overcome the system and achieve self-determination. He became known as an intellectual, and his marriage to movie actress Marilyn Monroe in 1956 was regarded as bridging a culture gap. Other plays included *A View From the Bridge,* 1955, *After the Fall,* 1963, *Incident at Vichy,* 1964, and *The Price,* 1968. Adapted to the screen were *Death of a Salesman* in 1951, *The Crucible* in 1958, and *A View From the Bridge* in 1962. In 1961 he wrote the screenplay for *The Misfits* for Miss Monroe, her last movie. His other published works included a collection of stories, *I Don't Need You Any More,* 1967, and stories and essays for *Harper's, Life, Esquire, Holiday, The Nation,* and other magazines.

MILLER, SAMUEL FREEMAN (1816–1890), jurist. Born on April 5, 1816, in Richmond, Kentucky, Miller studied medicine at Transylvania

University and received his M.D. degree in 1838. While carrying on his practice in Barbourville, he read law and in 1847 was admitted to the bar. The Kentucky constitutional convention of 1849 reaffirmed the legality of slavery in the state and Miller, mildly Abolitionist in sentiment, decided to leave; in 1850 he settled in Keokuk, Iowa, and opened a law office. He became prominent at the bar and increasingly involved in organizing and supporting the Republican Party. In 1862 his name was put forward by the Iowa delegation in Congress for appointment to the Supreme Court; Lincoln accepted the proposal and Miller was confirmed by the Senate on July 16. Though he had had little formal preparation for the post, he was throughout his 28 years on the bench particularly sensitive to the main issues of justice that often tended to be obscured by the technicalities of particular cases. He was, moreover, acutely aware of larger constitutional implications in the cases he heard. He dissented when, in 1869, the Court ruled against the applicability of wartime paper currency to previously incurred debts, and was with the majority when the Court reversed itself on this point in the Legal Tender Cases two years later. His most important contribution came in 1873, when he wrote the majority opinion in the Slaughterhouse Cases, the first in which the Court was called upon to construe the 14th Amendment; pointing out the violence any other view would do to the federal system, he held that the "privileges and immunities" clause applied to federal rather than to state citizenship and that the Supreme Court was charged with supervising only the former. Despite the nationalizing intentions of the authors of the amendment, he effectively precluded the possibility of the Court's interposing itself between a state and its citizens; while this decision preserved the federal system, it had as an unfortunate by-product a virtual validation of discriminatory state legislation in the area of purely intra-state jurisdiction. He remained a powerful and steadfastly conscientious figure on the Court throughout his career; he contin-

ued to serve until his death on October 13, 1890.

MILLIKAN, ROBERT ANDREWS (1868–1953), physicist. Born on March 22, 1868, in Morrison, Illinois, Millikan grew up there and in Maquoketa, Iowa. He graduated from Oberlin College in 1891; after taking his Ph.D. at Columbia University in 1895 he spent two years in further study at Berlin and Göttingen. Upon his return to the United States in 1896 he was appointed to an instructorship at the University of Chicago; he remained at that institution until 1921, becoming a full professor of physics in 1910. His earliest major researches concerned the electron and particularly the determination of its electrical charge. By improving upon the techniques of his predecessors he was able to arrive at an accurate determination of the charge and then, by isolating the electron, to show that the charge was a discrete constant rather than a statistical average. In 1913 this work brought him the Comstock Prize of the National Academy of Sciences. Turning to an examination of the photoelectic effect, he was able to obtain experimental confirmation of Einstein's photoelectric equation and to derive a most accurate evaluation of Planck's constant. During World War I he served as chief of the science and research division of the Army Signal Corps with a lieutenant colonel's commission; afterwards, from 1922 to 1932, he represented the United States on the League of Nations committee for intellectual cooperation. In 1921 he left the University of Chicago to become director of the Norman Bridge Laboratory of the California Institute of Technology in Pasadena, and became also chairman of the Institute's executive council. In 1923 he was awarded the Nobel Prize for Physics for his work on electrons and photoelectricity. During the 1920s he devoted much of his time to an attempt to discover the cause of a long-noted and puzzling phenomenon, the apparently spontaneous discharge of a charged electroscope over time. Examining the rates of discharge in various circumstances, from balloons ten miles in the air to the bottoms of mountain lakes, he finally evolved the theory, later fully confirmed, that the cause lay in radiation coming to the earth from outer space. These "cosmic rays," as he called them, he thought to be the "birth cries" of new atoms. During World War II he worked on developing jet and rocket propulsion systems for practical military use. Among his many publicatons, in addition to his technical papers and textbooks, were *Evolution in Science and Religion,* 1927, *Science and the New Civilization,* 1930, and an *Autobiography,* 1950. He died at home in San Marino, California, on December 19, 1953.

MILLS, ROBERT (1781–1855), architect and engineer. Born on August 12, 1781, in Charleston, South Carolina, Mills was educated at the College of Charleston and then, determining to prepare himself for a career in architecture, moved to Washington, D.C., in 1800 to study under the Irish-born architect James Hoban. Three years later he took up residence at Monticello as he continued his training under the guidance of Thomas Jefferson; at the latter's suggestion he entered the office of Benjamin Latrobe and remained there until 1808, absorbing the principles of Greek design and gradually taking on work of his own. Thus thoroughly prepared, he entered upon an independent career as an architect, the first native American to follow this profession. From 1808 to 1817 he practised in Philadelphia; his work included residences, churches, the State House in Harrisburg, and the rebuilding of Independence Hall. In 1814 the city of Baltimore held a competition for designs for a proposed monument to George Washington and his design was adopted; begun in 1815, the structure was completed 14 years later. In 1817 he moved to Baltimore, but in 1820 he returned to Charleston where he remained for ten years, carrying on his private practice while serving as chief engineer for the state Board of Public Works. In this capacity he oversaw an ambitious program of internal improvements, including many roads and canals, while designing a number of public buildings, particularly notable among which was his State Hospital for the Insane, remarkable for being precisely that rather than, as was the nearly universal practice, a prison. In 1830 he moved to Washington and his work on federal buildings led to his appointment six years later as architect of public buildings. His major works there were the Treasury, 1836–1842, and the Patent Office, 1839. In 1836 a competition was held to select a design for a Washington monument in the capital and he was again successful. Work was begun in 1848, but lack of funds postponed completion until 1884. In 1851 he retired from his public post and thereafter did little work; he died in Washington on March 3, 1855.

MITCHELL, WILLIAM (1879–1936), aviator. Born of American parents in Nice, France, on December 29, 1879, Billy Mitchell, as he was called throughout his life, grew up in Milwaukee. He was educated at Racine College and at Columbian University (now George Washington University); he left the latter school in 1898 before graduating to enlist in the Spanish-American War. He served in Cuba and the Philippines and in 1901 was commissioned in the regular Army and attached to the Signal Corps. After a number of assignments around the world he attended the Army Staff College and in 1912 became the youngest member of the General Staff. In 1915 he was assigned to the aviation section of the Signal Corps; he learned to fly the following year and began his twenty-years' advocacy of military air power. He was already in Europe as an observer when the United States entered World War I, and as the war progressed he advanced rapidly in rank and responsibility as he proved a highly effective air commander. In September 1918 he successfully attempted a mass bombing attack with nearly 1500 planes, and in October he led a large bombing force in a behind-the-lines air strike; in that month he was promoted brigadier general. His plans for strategic bombing of the

German homeland and for massive parachute invasions were cut short by the Armistice and he returned home as assistant chief of the Air Service. He outspokenly advocated a separate air force and continued research and development to secure better machines and techniques. He claimed that the airplane had rendered the battleship obsolete and, over the vociferous protests of the Navy Department, proved his point by sinking from the air several captured and overage battleships in 1921 and 1923. He was persistently critical of the low state of preparedness of the tiny Air Service and of the poor quality of its equipment; but his harrying of the upper military echelons won him only a transfer to an obscure post in Texas and the rank of colonel. When, in September 1925, the Navy's dirigible *Shenandoah* was lost in a storm, he made a formal statement to the press charging "incompetency, criminal negligence, and almost treasonable administration of the national defense by the War and Navy Departments." He was, as he expected, immediately court-martialed and, after making the trial a platform for his views, convicted of insubordination and sentenced to five years' suspension from rank and pay. On February 1, 1926, he resigned from the Army. He continued to advocate air power and warned against the danger of developments in this field by other nations, particularly Japan. He hypothesized a possible attack by Japanese aircraft launched from great ships and directed at the Hawaiian Islands. He died in New York City on February 19, 1936. Subsequent events proved the validity and the striking accuracy of many of his ideas, and in 1946 Congress authorized a special medal in his honor that was presented to his son two years later by Gen. Carl Spaatz, chief of staff of the newly established independent Air Force.

MONROE, JAMES (1758–1831), public official, diplomat, and 5th U.S. President. Born in Westmoreland County, Virginia, on April 28, 1758, Monroe studied for two years at the College of William and Mary, cutting his education short to take part in the Revolution. He saw action in several important battles and rose to the rank of major; but in 1780 he left the Army and took up the study of law under the tutelage of Thomas Jefferson, then governor of Virginia. In 1782 he was elected to the Virginia legislature and from 1783 to 1786 served in Congress. In 1787 he was in the Virginia House of Delegates and the following year was a member of the state's constitutional ratifying convention, where he was among the opposition. Beaten by James Madison for election to Congress that year, he succeeded in winning a Senate seat in 1790 and, as became a long-time friend of Jefferson, aligned himself firmly with the Republicans. Despite political differences, Washington appointed him minister to France in 1794; in his two years in that position his service was less than satisfactory, particularly his unwillingness to attempt to justify to the French government the apparently pro-British Jay's Treaty. Monroe returned to America in 1797 and from 1799 to 1802 was governor of Virginia. In 1803 he was sent by President Jefferson to aid Robert Livingston in the negotiations that resulted in the purchase of Louisiana. Shortly before the treaty was concluded he was appointed minister to Great Britain; he undertook the duties of this post in July and, with the exception of a few months spent in Madrid in 1804–1805 unsuccessfully trying to purchase the Floridas from Spain, he remained in London until December 1807. While there he negotiated a treaty that was originally intended to rectify the omissions and unfortunate provisions of Jay's Treaty; the result was, if anything, worse, and Jefferson refused to accept it. In 1810 he was again in the Virginia legislature and served as governor during 1811; in November of that year President Madison appointed him secretary of state and in September 1814 he took on for six months the additional duties of secretary of war. In March 1817 he was inaugurated as President, having followed the regular pattern of succession. Reelected in 1820 by all but one vote of the electoral college, he presided over eight years of calm prosperity that have come to be known as "the era of good feeling." The principal events of the period were the acquisition of the Floridas in 1819–1821, the Missouri Compromise of 1820, which he signed despite doubts about its constitutionality, and the formal announcement of U.S. foreign policy with regard to relations between the hemispheres. In this message, delivered in December 1823, Monroe concisely summed up policies that had actually been unstated though followed for some time; their formulation owed as much to Secretary of State John Quincy Adams as to Monroe, but the decision to publish was the President's. Referred to at the time as "the principles of President Monroe," the policy statement came eventually to be called the Monroe Doctrine and to be accepted as an axiom of American foreign policy. In 1825 he retired to his Virginia home; his public service after that time was limited to acting as regent of the University of Virginia from 1826 and presiding over the state constitutional convention in 1829. He died in New York City on July 4, 1831.

MONROE, MARILYN (1926–1962), actress. Born in Los Angeles on June 1, 1926, Norma Jean Mortenson later took her mother's name, Baker. With her mother frequently confined in an asylum, she was reared by 12 successive sets of foster parents and for a time lived in an orphanage. In 1942 she married a fellow worker in an aircraft factory. She was divorced soon after World War II, became a popular model, and in 1946 signed a short-term contract with Twentieth Century-Fox, taking as her screen name Marilyn Monroe. After a few brief appearances in movies from Fox and Columbia studios she found herself jobless; supporting herself by modeling for photographers, she posed for a nude calendar picture that later became a national sensation. In 1950 she played a small uncredited role in The Asphalt Jungle that reaped a

mountain of fan mail; another appearance in All About Eve, 1950, won her another contract from Fox and an intense publicity campaign soon made her name a household word. In a succession of movies, including Let's Make It Legal, 1951, Don't Bother to Knock, 1952, and Monkey Business, 1952, she advanced to star billing on the strength of her studio-fostered image as "Love Goddess." In 1953 she starred in Gentlemen Prefer Blondes and How to Marry a Millionaire; her fame grew steadily and became international, and she was the object of unprecedented popular adulation. In 1954 she married baseball hero Joe DiMaggio and her publicity reached new heights. With the end of their marriage less than a year later she began to grow discontented with the insubstantiality of her career; she studied for a time with Lee Strasberg at the Actors Studio in New York, and in There's No Business Like Show Business, 1954, The Seven-Year Itch, 1955, and Bus Stop, 1956, she began to emerge as a talented comedienne. In 1956 she married playwright Arthur Miller and retired for a time from Hollywood, though she co-starred with Sir Laurence Olivier in The Prince and the Show Girl, 1957. In 1959 she won critical acclaim for Some Like It Hot. In 1960 she appeared in Let's Make Love and in 1961, in her last role, in The Misfits, written by Miller, whom she had divorced the year before (the movie also featured Clark Gable's final performance). Her 23 movies since 1950 grossed among them more than $200 million and her fame surpassed that of any other entertainer. After several months as a virtual recluse, Miss Monroe died in her Hollywood home on August 5, 1962, having taken a massive overdose of sleeping pills.

MOODY, DWIGHT LYMAN (1837–1899), evangelist. Born on February 5, 1837, in East Northfield, Massachusetts, Moody attended school until he was 13, moved to Boston at age 17, and worked in his uncle's shoe store. Although baptized by a Unitarian minister, he attended a Congregational Church in Boston and received full membership in 1856. He moved to Chicago in that year and worked as a shoe salesman. His interest in religion grew and he formed a church school for slum children in 1858. Two years later, he decided on evangelism as his life's work, intending to devote himself to the underprivileged. He became president of the Chicago branch of the Young Men's Christian Association in 1866, after organizing and leading volunteers from the association to the aid of soldiers on the battle fronts of the Civil War. During 1873–1875 he conducted tours through Scotland, Ireland, and England, in association with Ira D. Sankey, organist and composer; the tour was highly successful and upon returning to the United States Moody found himself in great demand. He established his headquarters in Northfield and soon set out on the first of a series of evangelistic tours that eventually encompassed the whole country. His great success was due mainly to his manner in preaching; he spoke directly to the common man with a sincere, friendly approach that inspired religious renewal in thousands. Never ordained himself, he was careful to seek cooperation from established religious leaders; his background attracted support from businessmen and his business-like administrative methods presaged those of the 20th-century evangelists. The substance of his preaching was a simple, conservative, personal Christianity sharply in contrast with the Social Gospel movement of the same period. His visits to universities inspired the formation of Y.M.C.A. branches on campuses, and Student Volunteer Associations to send missionaries abroad. Contributions maintained these ventures and supported his Northfield Seminary for girls, founded in 1879, Mount Hermon School for boys, founded in 1881, and the Chicago (later Moody) Bible Institute in 1889, for men and women who desired training as lay church workers or missionaries, but who could not afford college. He died in Northfield on December 22, 1899.

MOODY, WILLIAM VAUGHN (1869–1910), poet and playwright. Born in Spencer, Indiana, on July 8, 1869, Moody entered Harvard in 1889, completed four years of work in three, and spent his final year touring Europe and tutoring. He graduated in 1893 and stayed on for two years, the first to obtain his A.M. degree and the second as an instructor in English literature. In 1895 he joined the faculty of the University of Chigago where, except for the year 1899–1900, he remained until 1907. Long interested in literature as a vocation as well as a field of study, Moody had contributed substantially to and helped edit the *Harvard Monthly* in his undergraduate days; throughout his teaching career he continued to write and when he resigned his professorship it was to devote full time to this activity. His first major published work appeared in 1900; it was a verse drama, *The Masque of Judgment*, and the first of a projected trilogy depicting the innate rebelliousness of man, his alienation from God, and a final reconciliation achieved through the mediation of woman. The trilogy was continued in *The Fire-Bringer*, 1904, and *The Death of Eve*, not yet completed when he died. In 1901 appeared *Poems*, which included his "Ode in Time of Hesitation," first published in the *Atlantic Monthly* the previous year, in which he expressed his reaction to the problems of contemporary civilization, particularly that presented by American imperialism in the Philippines. His best work was a prose drama, *The Great Divide* (originally *The Sabine Woman*), 1906, in which he portrayed opposing strains in the American character, the inhibited Puritan heritage and the open, wide-ranging Western outlook. This alone among his plays enjoyed success on the stage and was the leading contribution to American drama in the first decade of the 20th century. Moody's career was cut short by a brain tumor; he died on October 17, 1910.

MOORE, MARIANNE CRAIG (1887–   ), poet. Born on November 15, 1887, in St. Louis, Missouri, Marianne Moore graduated from Bryn Mawr in 1909, attended Carlisle Commercial College in Pennsylvania, and subsequently gave vocational training to Indian students in a school at Carlisle. She was later an assistant librarian in the New York Public Library and acting editor of the *Dial* from 1925 to 1929. She lived most of her life in New York City. Her verse and literary criticism appeared in many journals and periodicals in England and the United States. *Poems,* 1921, published by friends in London, was followed by American publication of *Observations,* 1924, *Selected Poems,* 1935, *The Pangolin and Other Verse,* 1936, *What Are Years,* 1941, *Nevertheless,* 1944, and her Pulitzer Prize winning *Collected Poems,* 1951. From the start of her writing career she used highly personal metrical forms, consistent in themselves but inimitable. The content of her poetry, as well as its intense, sometimes ironic treatment, was a clue to her personality. Among her other writings were a translation of *The Fables of La Fontaine,* 1954, and *Predilections,* 1955, a collection of essays on her favorite authors. Other books included *Like a Bulwark,* 1956, *O To Be a Dragon,* 1959, *The Arctic Ox,* 1964, and *Tell Me, Tell Me,* 1966. She won many honors, among them the Dial Award, the Bollingen Prize, the National Book Award, and the Gold Medal of the National Institute of Arts and Letters.

MORE, PAUL ELMER (1864–1937), philosopher and critic. Born on December 12, 1864, in St. Louis, More attended Washington University, receiving his B.A. in 1887 and his M.A. in 1892. He took a second M.A. at Harvard in 1893, where he met Irving Babbitt, and taught Sanskrit there during 1894–1895 and Sanskrit and classical literature at Bryn Mawr from 1895 to 1897. He began a career in literary criticism in 1901 as literary editor of the *Independent,* moving to the *New York Evening Post* from 1903 to 1909 and remaining editor of the *Nation* for the next five years. In this he was responsible for developing an out-

standing corps of reviewers and for raising the quality of literary comment to unparalleled standards. In 1914 he returned to studies and lecturing at Princeton, and retired in 1934. The 11-volume *Shelburne Essays,* 1904–1921, reflected the scope of his literary interests based on his thorough training in the classics. His other books of criticism included *Life of Benjamin Franklin,* 1900, *Nietzsche,* 1912, *Platonism,* 1917, *The Religion of Plato,* 1921, *Hellenistic Philosophies,* 1923, and *New Shelburne Essays,* 1928–1936. His judgments followed the standards of reserve and rationalism of the classics. He shunned the idealistic concepts of humanitarianism and equality, attacked liberal politics, and mistrusted the romantic movement in all its manifestations. During the 1920s he joined Babbitt in the New Humanist movement, an attempt to revive the classical virtues and values. He was often rebuked for his patricianism, especially during the Depression, but was nonetheless held in high esteem for the enduring worth of his work. He died at Princeton on March 9, 1937.

MORGAN, JOHN PIERPONT (1837–1913), financier. Born on April 17, 1837, in Hartford, Connecticut, J. P. Morgan graduated from English High School in Boston in 1854 and studied for two years at the University of Göttingen. His banking career began in 1857 when he joined the New York firm of Duncan, Sherman and Company, American agents of George Peabody and Company, of which his father, Junius Spencer Morgan, was a partner. In 1860 he became special agent in the United States for George Peabody and Company (later J. S. Morgan and Company). From 1864 to 1871 he was a member of Dabney, Morgan and Company, and in 1871 he joined in forming Drexel, Morgan and Company, which, through his ability and leadership and Drexel's death, became J. P. Morgan and Company in 1895. The most prosperous private banking house in the country, it was able to replenish the federal reserve with $62 million in gold in

1895. Having obtained control of the Albany and Susquehanna Railroad in 1869, Morgan concentrated on railroad development and by 1890 owned a controlling interest in many of the country's major railroads. More important than his ownership, however, was his great ability as an organizer; in contrast with the financial raiders of the day—Fiske, Gould, and the like—Morgan's was a rationalizing and stabilizing influence. As more and more economic power came into his hands, he was quick to eliminate inefficiency, costly competition, and instability. And, as his reputation grew, he was much sought-after to perform such services. In 1901 he purchased the interests of Andrew Carnegie, merging them with his own and others to form the world's largest corporation, the United States Steel Corporation. He was also active in the formation of the General Electric and International Harvester corporations, as well as the unsuccessful International Mercantile Marine and the short-lived Northern Securities Company. In 1907 he headed a group of bankers who preserved the solvency of major U.S. banks and corporations to halt an impending financial panic. By this time he was the preeminent figure in American finance, the symbol of concentrated economic power. In 1912 Congress formed the Pujo Committee, largely to investigate the extent of his holdings, and found, among other things, that 11 House of Morgan partners held 72 directorships in 47 major corporations. This industrial domination was widely criticized, although Morgan himself was little affected, feeling as he did morally bound to protect the interests of stockholders in his organizations. He made large contributions to trade schools, hospitals, libraries, churches, and museums, though his philanthropies, unlike those of Rockefeller, were unsystematic. He acquired an enormous personal art collection, much of which, after his death, was given to the Metropolitan Museum of Art. His great book collection, housed in a magnificent marble building, became a public library in 1924. An avid yachtsman, he built the *Columbia,* which won prizes in several international competitions. He died on March 31, 1913, in Rome, leaving a vast estate that has been greatly increased by successive generations of Morgans.

MORGAN, LEWIS HENRY (1818–1881), ethnologist and anthropologist. Born on November 21, 1818, near Aurora, New York, Morgan graduated from Union College, Schenectady, in 1840. He went to Rochester about 1844 and there practised law for many years. In the 1840s he began to make intensive studies of the social organization and material culture of the Iroquois Indians, which led to the publication in 1851 of his first book, *The League of the Ho-dé-no-sau-nee, or Iroquois.* He thereupon undertook field trips to the West and Southwest and to the Hudson's Bay area and began work on his monumental study, *Systems of Consanguinity and Affinity of the Human Family,* 1871, in which he founded the scientific study of kinship. *Ancient Society; or Researches in the Line of Human Progress From Savagery Through Barbarism to Civilization* appeared in 1877, with a revised edition the next year. The work was taken up by the Marxists and became the subject of Engels' *The Origin of the Family, Private Property, and the State.* Its theory of the evolution of the family, from promiscuity to monogamy, has long been considered obsolete, but many of its theses remain valid, notably the distinction between primitive and civil society, and the notion of the importance of technology in cultural evolution. Among his other books were *The American Beaver and His Works,* 1868, a delightful account of this remarkable animal, and *Houses and House-Life of the American Aborigines,* 1881. He was a member of the National Academy of Sciences and was president of the American Association for the Advancement of Science in 1880. Active in state politics, he served as assemblyman from 1861 to 1868 and as a state senator in 1868–1869.

He died in Rochester on December 17, 1881. He is often called the "father of American anthropology."

MORGAN, THOMAS HUNT (1866–1945), biologist. Born on September 25, 1866, in Lexington, Kentucky, Morgan attended the State College of Kentucky, graduating in 1886 and taking his M.S. in 1888. In 1890 he received his doctorate from Johns Hopkins University and the next year joined the faculty of Bryn Mawr College. In 1904 he moved to Columbia University as professor of experimental zoology. His early work was principally concerned with embryology, but about 1909 he turned his attention to the study of the mechanism of heredity. Doubtful himself, Morgan set out to seek evidence of the existence of physical units of heredity, the genes whose existence was then only postulated. Working closely with a number of students, including Hermann Muller, he undertook a series of experiments in breeding varieties of *Drosophila,* the common fruit or vinegar fly. In *Mechanism of Mendelian Heredity*, 1915, they described their findings: genes did indeed exist as discrete entities and were found at specific locations along the chromosomes of cell nuclei. In this work and the subsequent *Theory of the Gene*, 1926, Morgan and his associates laid the foundation of the science of genetics. In 1928 he became director of the newly established Kerckhoff Laboratories of Biological Sciences at the California Institute of Technology in Pasadena, where he remained for the rest of his life. From 1927 to 1931 he served as president of the National Academy of Sciences and in 1929–1930 was president of the American Association for the Advancement of Science. In 1933 he was awarded the Nobel Prize for Medicine for his pioneer work in genetics; he was the first native American and the first non-physician to receive the award. In his later work he returned to embryology; his publications included *Experimental Embryology*, 1927, *The Scientific Basis of Evolution*, 1932, and *Embryology and Genetics*, 1933. He died in Pasadena on December 4, 1945.

MORRILL, JUSTIN SMITH (1810–1898), public official. Born in Strafford, Vermont, on April 14, 1810, Morrill attended the common schools and two local academies but left school when he was 15 to go to work in a general store. He became a partner in 1831 when he turned 21, and amassed a sufficient fortune to be able to retire at 38, when he went to live on a country estate near Strafford, there engaging in horticulture and agriculture. His long congressional career—nearly 44 years of service in the House and Senate —began in 1854 when he was elected as a Whig to the Thirty-fourth Congress, taking his seat in March 1854. He served in the House until 1867, as chairman of the Ways and Means Committee after 1865, whereupon he entered the Senate, to remain until his death. He was elected for the first time in 1866 and reelected in 1872, 1878, 1884, 1890, and 1896, as a Republican. A financial conservative, he sponsored the tariff act of 1861 that inaugurated the era of protectionism, and thereafter was a potent foe of free traders. Also a champion of "sound" money, he opposed all of the schemes to adopt paper currency during and after the Civil War and disapproved of silver as a monetary standard. For special needs, and to supplement tariff revenues, he favored internal revenue taxes. In his long career he made many contributions to the appearance of the national capital, being influential in the landscaping of the Capitol grounds, the building of the Washington Monument and the Library of Congress, and other projects. But his most enduring achievement is doubtless the Morrill Act of 1862, which provided grants of land to state colleges in which the leading object was to be the teaching of subjects "related to agriculture and the mechanic arts," without, however, excluding the general sciences and classical studies. He first proposed such a measure in 1857, but President Buchanan vetoed it; President Lincoln signed it into law five years later, and from it flows our present system of state universities. The Morrill Act was supplemented in 1890 by a second Morrill Act, which provided monetary grants to the colleges and universities, thus establishing the principle of federal aid to education. Morrill died in Washington on December 28, 1898.

MORRIS, GOUVERNEUR (1752–1816), public official and diplomat. Born in the family manor house in Morrisania, New York, on January 31, 1752, Morris graduated from King's College (now Columbia University) in 1768 and was admitted to the bar three years later. A political conservative, he at first opposed the separation of the colonies from Great Britain, but soon adopted a middle position between the democratic radicals and the Loyalists; he acted as something of a mediator in the New York provincial congress that succeeded the colonial legislature and in the constitutional convention of 1776, where he was successful in securing a provision for religious freedom, though not for the abolition of slavery. From 1777 to 1779 he was in the Continental Congress where, in 1778, in response to Lord North's conciliation offer, he drafted the report that declared independence to be a prerequisite of peace. Shortly after his defeat for reelection to Congress in 1779 he moved to Philadelphia. A series of articles on finance that appeared in the *Pennsylvania Packet* in 1780 led to his appointment as assistant to the superintendent of finance, Robert Morris (no relation). During his tenure in this office, 1781–1785, he submitted a proposal that, modified by Jefferson, became the basis for the national currency. Elected to the Constitutional Convention in 1787, he seems to have spoken more often than anybody; he was an advocate of a strong central government including such features as a president with life tenure and senators appointed by him also for life. Shortly after the Convention adjourned he

returned to New York; his pronounced anti-democratic sympathies barred him from public office, and in 1789 he sailed to Europe, where he remained for nearly a decade. In Paris he watched and recorded in his diary the progress of the French Revolution; he was appointed minister to France in 1792 but his often and publicly stated antipathy to the later radical developments of the Revolution led to a request for his recall in 1794. Business interests and travel delayed his return to the United States until 1798. He served briefly in the Senate from 1800 to 1803, his last public office. In private life he continued to align himself with the extreme Federalists and even supported the idea of Northern secession during the War of 1812. He died on November 6, 1816.

MORRIS, ROBERT (1734–1806), merchant, financier, and public official. Born on January 31, 1734, in Liverpool, England, Morris came to America in 1747, joining his father in Maryland. With little schooling he entered a large mercantile house in Philadelphia, and such were his talents in business that at the age of 20 he became a member of the firm. His sympathies lay with the colonies at the outbreak of the Revolution, though he took a conservative position and was slow to accept the idea of separation from Great Britain; he served as vice president of the Pennsylvania Committee of Safety in 1775–1776 and as a delegate to the Continental Congress from 1775 to 1778. He opposed the Declaration of Independence and after its adoption delayed signing it for some weeks. In Congress he served on several committees, particularly those concerned with finance and trade. Upon leaving Congress he was immediately elected to the Pennsylvania Assembly, where he remained until 1779. In that year charges were brought against him for having taken personal advantage of his central role in congressional finance; but though he had never failed to direct public business to his own firm when possible and to collect a regular profit, several investigations cleared him of profiteering. In 1780–1781 he was again in the Assembly and in the latter year accepted the urgent call of Congress to assume the sole responsibility of supervising the public finances under a new unified system. One of his first acts was to establish the Bank of North America in Philadelphia. Only Morris' great organizational ability and his own personal credit prevented utter bankruptcy; he was able to secure the money needed to transport Washington's army from New York to Yorktown in order to force the surrender of Cornwallis in 1781, and yet the future of the nation appeared so doubtful to one even of his great resourcefulness that in 1783 he was only with difficulty persuaded to retain his post. In 1784 he resigned and from 1785 to 1787 was in the Pennsylvania Assembly; he was a delegate to the Annapolis Convention in 1786 and to the Constitutional Convention the next year. He was elected one of Pennsylvania's first senators, serving from 1789 to 1795 as a Federalist and supporter of Alexander Hamilton's financial policies. He had liquidated his mercantile interests and invested heavily in western lands; when this speculative venture failed to yield returns, he found himself bankrupt and from 1798 to 1801 was held in debtor's prison. His last years were spent in declining health in Philadelphia, where he died on May 7, 1806.

MORROW, DWIGHT WHITNEY (1873–1931), lawyer, financier, and diplomat. Born on January 11, 1873, in Huntington, West Virginia, Morrow was educated at Amherst College, where he was a classmate of Calvin Coolidge, graduating in 1895. The next year he entered the law school of Columbia University and upon graduating in 1899 joined the law firm of Reed, Simpson, Thacher and Barnum. He became a partner in 1905 and attained a reputation in the field of corporation law. In 1911 he drafted a workmen's compensation law for New Jersey and in 1917 was chairman of a commission called to investigate the

state's prison system. In 1914 he became a partner in the banking house of J. P. Morgan and Company, where, in addition to his regular business activities, which included the organization of the Kennecott Copper Corporation, he was involved in arranging for financial and material aid to the Allied powers In Europe. Soon after the United States entered the World War he became an adviser to the Allied Maritime Transport Council; he was also an adviser on transportation problems to Gen. John J. Pershing, commander of the American forces in Europe, and for this work was awarded the Distinguished Service Medal. After the war he served as a consultant to the government of Cuba and succeeded in restoring that country's finances. In 1925 he was chairman of the President's Aircraft Board, which helped formulate national policy on civil and military aviation. He was appointed ambassador to Mexico by President Coolidge in 1927 and during his three years in the post reestablished cordial relations between that nation and the United States, settled or arranged for future settlement of the outstanding grievances between them, and helped restore harmony between the Mexican government and the Catholic Church. In 1930 President Hoover named him a delegate to the London Naval Conference. Later in the same year he was elected to the Senate from New Jersey; he died at his home in Englewood a short time later, however, on October 5, 1931. His daughter Anne married aviator Charles Lindbergh in 1929.

MORSE, SAMUEL FINLEY BREESE (1791–1872), artist and inventor. Born on April 27, 1791, in Charlestown, Massachusetts, Morse was the oldest son of the noted clergyman and geographer, Jedidiah Morse. He graduated in 1810 from Yale, where he had developed a strong interest and considerable facility in painting; overcoming his parents' objections, he sailed to England in 1811 to study art under Washington Allston and Benjamin West. On his return in 1815 he opened a studio in Boston;

but his high ambitions were shattered by the discovery that the American public had little taste for any save portrait art, and little money for that. His earnings were meager and irregular and did not improve significantly when he moved to New York City in 1823. His social and intellectual life was altogether satisfactory, however, and his devotion to art led him to be the principal founder of the National Academy of Design in 1826 and to serve as its first president from that year until 1845. In 1829 he left New York for a three-year period of study and travel in Europe; on the return voyage in 1832 a chance conversation on recent discoveries in electromagnetism sparked in him the idea for an electrical device for the transmission of information. He drafted preliminary sketches of a telegraph while still on board but for several years made little progress on the idea. For a few years he was caught up in the wave of nativist agitation and in 1836 ran unsuccessfully for mayor of New York on the Native-American ticket. He continued to paint and taught art at the University of the City of New York (now New York University). In 1837 he was introduced to the work of Joseph Henry, who had published a detailed proposal for a telegraph six years earlier; the two corresponded on the idea and by 1838 Morse had both a working model and a usable code for translating letters and numbers into dots and dashes. His major innovation in developing practical telegraphy was a relay device that, placed at intervals along the wire, enabled messages to be sent over great distances. Public interest was difficult to arouse, but finally in 1843 Congress appropriated $30,000 to construct a telegraph line from Washington to Baltimore. On May 24, 1844, Morse tapped out the first message—"What hath God wrought!"—from the Supreme Court chamber in the Capitol. For the next several years he was caught up in a storm of litigation over patent rights and with a few unfortunately chosen partners. His patent claim was finally validated by the Supreme Court in 1854; in 1857–1858 he was

associated with Cyrus Field in laying a transatlantic telegraph cable; and in 1858 he was honored by a number of European nations. In 1861 he was again president of the National Academy of Design; in the same year he helped found Vassar College and was throughout his later years a prominent philanthropist. He died in New York on April 2, 1872.

MORTON, WILLIAM THOMAS GREEN (1819–1869), dentist and pioneer anaesthetist. Born on August 9, 1819, in Charlton, Massachusetts, Morton attended New England common schools until he was 17, then studied dentistry in 1840 at the Baltimore College of Dental Surgery. He practised in Farmington, Connecticut, for two years, and moved to Boston, hoping to further his education at Harvard, but was deterred by financial problems. For a time he practised in partnership with Horace Wells, who experimented in using nitrous oxide gas as an anaesthetic. Later, learning through Prof. Charles T. Jackson that inhalation of "sulphuric ether" created total loss of consciousness, Morton experimented with the chemical for use in oral surgery. By inhaling it himself and administering it to various animals, he determined that the patient always returned to normal consciousness. On September 30, 1846, he used ether on a patient and quickly completed a painless tooth extraction. On October 16th he administered ether to a patient at the Massachusetts General Hospital in preparation for removal of a neck tumor. Several more publicized anaesthetizations followed. Controversy over his lay status and his refusal to disclose the components of the anaesthetic was overcome, and he received a patent, calling the drug "letheon," and prepared to license its use by hospitals and doctors. He sought additional financial rewards from Congress and various petitions to that end were introduced and debated until the Civil War. Wells, Jackson, and Crawford W. Long, who, it was discovered, had used ether during an operation in 1842, challenged Morton's claims to sole credit for the discovery. Litigation and controversy dragged on until, totally impoverished, Morton died of apoplexy in New York City on July 15, 1868. Despite the justifiable claims of others, it was he who brought ether into common use.

MOTLEY, JOHN LOTHROP (1814–1877), diplomat and historian. Born in the Dorchester district of Boston on April 15, 1814, Motley spent two years at the experimental Round Hill school run by George Bancroft and J. G. Cogswell and then went to Harvard, from which he graduated in 1831. He studied rather desultorily for two years in Germany, ostensibly reading law but in reality living the easy life of a wealthy Bostonian abroad and making the acquaintance of young German scholars and nobles, among them Bismarck, and then spent two years traveling in Britain and the Continent, once more extending his acquaintance. He returned to Boston in 1835, determined to devote his life to literature. He married and took up residence in a house built for him by his father on his Boston estate. His first productions were two undistinguished novels; their lack of success seems to have turned his ambitions to a diplomatic career, and he spent a few months in 1841 as secretary to the U.S. legation in St. Petersburg. But he did not like the climate and found living expensive, and he returned to Boston. Around 1847 he decided upon the subject matter of his life's work—the history of the Netherlands in the 16th and 17th centuries. He threw himself into his researches, discussed his discoveries endlessly with his wide circle of distinguished friends—among them Holmes, Prescott, Longfellow, Emerson, Hawthorne, Lowell, Agassiz, Dana, and Sumner—and finally, in 1856, brought out the work by which he is best known, *The Rise of the Dutch Republic*. No longer considered to be historically valid, and even at the time sharply criticized by Dutch historians, the book was nevertheless tremendously popular and influential. Written in a brilliant style, it emphasized the drama of the exciting events of which it told, and was embued throughout with its author's strong feeling for liberty and democracy and his prejudice against Spanish Catholic absolutism. Indeed, Motley once said that his prime motive in writing it had been to point out the analogues between the Dutch struggle for independence from Spain and America's struggle with England. He served as minister to Austria from 1861 to 1867 and as minister to England in 1869–1870—in neither post did he perform with memorable distinction—and at the same time continued his researches. *The History of the United Netherlands, 1584–1609* appeared in four volumes from 1860 to 1867, and *The Life and Death of John of Barneveld* in two volumes in 1874, but neither of these works had the fire or popularity of his earlier book. He planned to carry his history down to 1648, but he died in England on May 29, 1877, before he could complete it.

MOTT, LUCRETIA COFFIN (1793–1880), social reformer. Born on January 3, 1793, in Nantucket, Massachusetts, Lucretia Coffin attended public school for two years in Boston in accordance with her father's wish that she become familiar with democratic principles. Later she was enrolled in a boarding school of the Society of Friends and studied and taught there until she moved back to her father's home, by now in Philadelphia. In 1811 she married James Mott, a fellow teacher from the school. About 1818 she began to speak at religious meetings with such fervor that she was accepted as a minister of the Friends. She joined the less conservative Hicksite branch of the Society when a rift occurred in the 1820s and traveled across the country lecturing on religion and social reform. She and her husband opened their home to runaway slaves after the Fugitive Slave Law was adopted. But she met opposition within the Society when she spoke of Abolition, and attempts were made to strip her of her ministry and membership. Rebuffed because she was a woman at the world antislavery convention in London in

1840, she still managed to make her views known. With Elizabeth Cady Stanton, she helped found the women's rights movement at the Seneca Falls convention of 1848. A fluent, moving speaker, she retained her poise and femininity before the most hostile audiences. Her last address was given to the Friends' annual meeting in 1880. She died that year, on November 11th, in her home outside of Philadelphia.

MOZEE, PHOEBE ANNE OAKLEY (1860–1926), markswoman. Born on August 13, 1860, on a farm in Darke County, Ohio, Annie Oakley, as she came to be known, early developed an amazing proficiency with firearms. As a child she hunted game with such success that, by selling it in Cincinnati, she was able to pay off the mortgage on the family farm. When she was about 15 she won a shooting match in Cincinnati with Frank E. Butler, a vaudeville marksman; some years later they were married, and until 1885 they played vaudeville circuits and circuses as a team. In that year they joined "Buffalo Bill" Cody's Wild West Show and "Little Missy," billed as "Miss Annie Oakley, the Peerless Lady Wing-Shot," was one of its star attractions for 17 years. She never failed to delight her audiences, and her feats of marksmanship were truly incredible. At 30 paces she could split a playing card held edge-on; she hit dimes tossed into the air; she shot cigarettes from her husband's lips; and, a playing card being thrown in the air, she riddled it before it touched the ground (thus giving rise to the custom of referring to punched complimentary tickets as "Annie Oakleys"). She was equally successful touring Europe and in Berlin performed her cigarette trick with, at his insistence, Crown Prince Wilhelm (later Kaiser Wilhelm II) holding the cigarette. A train wreck in 1901 left her partially paralyzed for a time, but she recovered and returned to the stage to amaze audiences for many more years. She died on November 3, 1926, in Greenville, Ohio.

MUHAMMAD, ELIJAH (1897–   ), religious leader. Elijah Muhammad was born Elijah Poole on a tenant farm near Sandersville, Georgia, on October 10, 1897. The son of former slaves (his father became a Baptist minister and sharecropper), he was schooled through the fifth grade and left home at 16. He lived for a time in Atlanta, married in 1919, and moved with his family to Detroit in 1923. He held a variety of jobs, encountering racial discrimination and later the effects of the Depression, living from 1929 to 1931 on relief. For a brief period he was a Baptist preacher. In 1931 he met and became an assistant to Wali Farad, who founded the Nation of Islam, a Moslem sect. Farad's doctrines included a denunciation of Christianity as a deceptive tool of white men to keep blacks in a state of servility. In what came to be an Islam tradition, Elijah was relieved of his "slave" name and given an Islamic surname, Karriem; later he was rechristened Muhammad to indicate his position of leadership in the movement. In 1934, under Farad's direction, he established Muhammad's Temple of Islam No. 2 in Chicago; Farad had established the original mosque in Detroit in 1931. Shortly thereafter, in a way that baffled police and FBI investigators, Farad disappeared, and Elijah was named the Messenger of Allah and head of the burgeoning organization. In *The Supreme Wisdom: Solution to the So-Called Negroes' Problem*, which came to be a sacred text of the movement, Elijah perpetuated the myth of Farad as a deity, the incarnation of Allah, and spread the conviction that blacks would one day rule the world. His nationalist philosophies, which paralleled those of Marcus Garvey in the 1920s, helped create the intricately structured, prosperous "Black Muslim" movement. He advocated strict morals and economic prudence, thus aiding the welfare of tens of thousands of blacks. He organized temple-sponsored business enterprises in Chicago and Detroit, as well as parochial schools. In 1934 he was arrested and paroled on charges of contributing to the delinquency of a minor, after refusing to withdraw his son from a Moslem school and enter him in a public school in Detroit. He lived in Washington, D.C., from 1935 to 1941 and spent the next six years in prison for violating selective service laws by speaking at an induction center on the similarity of prejudice against Japanese and Negroes. Even while he directed the movement from jail, the size of his following increased. On his release, he moved to Chicago, supervised the business of Temple No. 2, and formulated and administered his national policies through his own fiery preaching and through the work of his ministers, most notably his principal disciple, Malcolm X. By 1962 there were at least 49 Temples of Islam in areas of large Negro population in the United States and an estimated quarter of a million Black Muslims. He was allowed to make the traditional Moslem pilgrimage to Mecca on a tour of Moslem countries in Africa and the Middle East during 1959–1960. He made numerous radio broadcasts, wrote special publications, and contributed articles to newspapers and to journals of the movement.

MÜHLENBERG, HENRY MELCHIOR (1711–1787), clergyman. Born in Einbeck, Hanover, Germany, on September 6, 1711, Mühlenberg studied theology at the University of Göttingen and in 1738–1739 was a teacher in the Waisenhaus, an orphan school in Halle. In 1739 he was ordained a Lutheran minister in Leipzig, and in 1741 he accepted a call from the United Congregations, the Lutheran churches in Philadelphia, New Providence (now Trappe), and New Hanover, Pennsylvania. His position, though technically limited to the three congregations, made him virtual leader of all American Lutherans. Soon after his arrival in 1742 he managed to head off an incipient schism in the church. He traveled throughout the colonies, particularly in New Jersey, Maryland, and New York, and in 1748 organized the first Lutheran synod in America,

the Evangelical Lutheran Ministerium of Pennsylvania. His home, when not on one of his many journeys to other Lutheran settlements, remained in New Providence until 1761. From that year until 1776 he lived in Philadelphia, but with the outbreak of the Revolution he returned to New Providence where he stayed for the rest of his life. After 1779 his activities were restricted, and his last appearance before the synod was in 1781. In 1784 he was awarded the degree of Doctor of Divinity by the University of Pennsylvania. Three years later, on October 7, 1787, he died at home.

MUIR, JOHN (1838–1914), naturalist and author. Born on April 21, 1838, in Dunbar, Scotland, Muir emigrated with his family to a homestead near Portage, Wisconsin, in 1849. His early education was obtained largely by his own efforts, but from 1859 to 1863 he studied at the University of Wisconsin, taking no degree, however, because of his refusal to follow a curriculum of required courses. He made extensive exploratory journeys on foot through the Midwest and into Canada. He had a remarkable aptitude for mechanical invention that he pursued until an accident in 1867 damaged an eye and he turned to the study of nature. In that year he walked to the Gulf of Mexico, keeping a detailed journal of the trip that was published in 1916 as *A Thousand-Mile Walk to the Gulf*. In 1868 he went to California and for several years devoted himself to nature study, giving particular attention to trees, forests, and glaciers, and ranging into Utah, Nevada, the Northwest, and Alaska. The center of his interest, however, was the Yosemite Valley. From 1880 to 1891 he engaged in horticulture with sufficient success to enable him to retire in the latter year and devote the rest of his life to his studies. In 1890 a decade of effort, recorded primarily in several brilliant articles in *Scribner's Monthly* and *Century* magazines, culminated in the passage of the Yosemite National

Park bill by Congress; to this was added the next year a bill empowering the President to create forest preserves from the public domain. Muir was appointed an advisor to the Forest Commission in 1896 and, when the forest preserves established as a result of the Commission's report were threatened by commercial interests, he wrote articles for *Harper's Weekly* and the *Atlantic Monthly* that succeeded in rousing public concern and saving the preserves. He later influenced President Theodore Roosevelt to increase greatly the amount of protected public land. Among Muir's other books were *The Mountains of California*, 1894, *Our National Parks*, 1901, and *The Yosemite*, 1912. He died in Los Angeles on December 24, 1914.

MULLER, HERMANN JOSEPH (1890–1967), biologist. Born on December 21, 1890, in New York City, Muller studied at Columbia University; he graduated in 1910, took his M.A. in 1911, and, after a time at the Medical School of Cornell University, returned to Columbia for his doctorate in 1916. He worked closely during this time with Thomas Hunt Morgan in the experiments that revealed the existence of genes as carriers of heredity and was a co-author of *The Mechanism of Mendelian Heredity*, 1915. From 1915 to 1918 he was an instructor in biology at Rice Institute in Houston; after two years on the Columbia faculty he went to the University of Texas in 1920. Muller continued his research into heredity and was able to explain the various modes of arrangement and combination of genes and to clarify the manner of occurrence of mutations. During the 1920s he began to use X-ray bombardment on *Drosophila* fruit flies and in 1927 successfully produced artificial mutations. From 1933 to 1937 he was senior geneticist at the Institute of Genetics in Moscow; but he became much disillusioned with Marxism, and particularly with the Soviet policy of forcing scientific fact to fit the spurious Lysenko theory of heredity. He lectured at the University of Edinburgh from 1937 to 1940,

from 1940 to 1945 was at Amherst College, and from 1945 until his death was associated with the University of Indiana. In 1946 he was awarded the Nobel Prize for Medicine for his pioneering work on mutations. In his later years he was a controversial figure among scientists; he proposed the establishment of a sperm bank to preserve for the race the genetic characteristics of outstanding men, and issued solemn and eloquent warnings against the use of nuclear weapons because of their potential for creating harmful mutations in human genes. In 1953 he became distinguished service professor of zoology at Indiana (emeritus from 1964). He died in Indianapolis on April 5, 1967.

MUMFORD, LEWIS (1895–   ), author and social critic. Born in Flushing, New York, on October 19, 1895, Mumford was educated in the public schools of New York City and attended Columbia and New York universities, the College of the City of New York, and the New School for Social Research. He did not graduate from any of them, although he later received several honorary degrees, including an LL.D. from the University of Edinburgh in 1965 and a D. Arch. from the University of Rome in 1967. He determined on a literary career early in his life and supported himself and his family by writing a long series of articles and books. Apart from his periodical articles, some of them of profound influence on his contemporaries, his books included *The Story of Utopias*, 1922, *Sticks and Stones*, 1924, *The Golden Day*, 1926, *Herman Melville*, 1929, *The Brown Decades*, 1931, *Technics and Civilization*, 1934, *The Culture of Cities*, 1938, *The Condition of Man*, 1944, *The Conduct of Life*, 1951, *Art and Technics*, 1952, *The Human Prospect*, 1955, *The Transformation of Man*, 1956, *The City in History*, 1961, for which he won a National Book Award, *The Highway and the City*, 1963, *The Myth of the Machine*, 1967, and *The Urban Prospect*, 1968. These books ranged over a wide variety of subjects, from architecture, of which he was accepted as perhaps the leading American critic of the 20th century, to literature and literary history, and to speculations on human progress. He was professor of humanities at Stanford from 1942 to 1944, professor of city and regional planning at Pennsylvania from 1951 to 1959, research professor in that institution from 1959 to 1961, and visiting professor at the Massachusetts Institute of Technology from 1957 to 1960. The recipient of many medals and awards, he was president of the American Academy of Arts and Letters from 1962 to 1965.

MURRAY, PHILIP (1886–1952), labor leader. Born on May 25, 1886, in Blantyre, Lanarkshire, Scotland, Murray received only elementary schooling before entering the coal mines at the age of 10. In 1902 he emigrated with his father to the United States, settling in Pittsburgh and finding employment again as a coal miner. He joined the United Mine Workers of America and soon was elected president of his local. By the age of 26 he was on the international executive board of the U.M.W. and at 34 was vice president, a post he held for 22 years. When his superior, John L. Lewis, helped form the Committee for Industrial Organization to promote the growth of mass industrial unions, Murray was charged with the immensely important and difficult task of organizing the steel industry. As head of the Steel Workers Organizing Committee from 1936 he successfully directed the campaigns against "Big Steel" and "Little Steel" and became president of the United Steel Workers of America. In 1938 he was elected vice president of the independent Congress of Industrial Organizations and two years later president, a position he held along with his U.S.W.A. post until his death. During both World War II and the Korean War he committed his leadership to full support of the nation's wartime economic policies, but in peacetime he fought hard and successfully for an increased standard of living, for pensions and other benefits, and for fair treatment for the workers to whom he was responsible. He led the campaign to expel from the C.I.O. all Communists and Communist-dominated unions. He died suddenly in San Francisco on November 9, 1952.

MURROW, EDWARD ROSCOE (1908–1965), newscaster. Born on April 25, 1908, in Greensboro, North Carolina, Murrow moved to Blanchard, Washington, when he was four years old. He was a compassman and topographer for timber cruisers in Washington for two years before entering college. In his sophomore year he changed his first name from Egbert to Edward. He attended Stanford University and the University of Washington and graduated from Washington State College in 1930, after which he traveled for two years to American and European colleges arranging for debates and travel as president of the National Student Federation. From 1932 to 1935 he was assistant director of the Institute of International Education. In 1935 he began working for CBS as director of talks and education. Summoned to London in 1937, he became director of the CBS European bureau, hiring William L. Shirer to aid him in reporting prewar events on the Continent. During World War II he hired and trained a corps of war correspondents, which included Eric Sevareid, Charles Collingwood, Howard K. Smith, and Richard Hottelet. His own broadcasts, beginning "This. . . . is London," and then from North Africa and the Continent, familiarized millions of Americans with his terse, authoritative, and highly descriptive style. In 1941 selections from his London broadcasts were published as *So This Is London*. In 1946, returning to the United States, he became CBS vice president and director of public affairs. He resigned in 1947 to return to radio news broadcasting, and from 1950 to 1951 narrated and produced the *Hear It Now* series, presenting weekly news summaries through phonograph records made at the scene of events. The series provided the format for the 1951–1958 television broadcasts, *See It Now*, which he narrated and co-produced. From 1958 to 1960 he moderated and produced *Small World*, remote telecast discussions between world figures at various points on the globe. The informal *Person to Person*, which he began in 1953, became his most popular program. In 1961 he was appointed by President Kennedy to head the U.S. Information Agency, remaining in the post through 1964. His other activities included lecturing on international relations and contributing articles to educational journals and magazines. He died of cancer on April 27, 1965.

NABOKOV, VLADIMIR VLADIMIROVICH (1899–), author. Born in St. Petersburg (Leningrad), Russia, on April 23, 1899, into a family of old Russian nobility, Nabokov attended Prince Tenishev Gymnasium in St. Petersburg. He left Russia with his family in 1919 and entered Cambridge University, earning his B.A. from Trinity College in 1922. For the next 18 years, he lived in Germany and France. His poetry, plays, short stories, and novels of the period, written in Russian and translated into many languages, established him as the major post-1917 émigré writer. Among his early novels, later translated into English, were *The Defense*, 1930 (English, 1964), *Kamera Obskura*, 1932 (published in the United States in an altered version as *Laughter in the Dark*, 1938), *Despair*, 1934 (1966), *Invitation to a Beheading*, 1935 (1959), and *The Gift*, 1937 (1963), the latter introducing parody as a major device in his work. In 1940 he came to the United States and taught for one year at Stanford University. From 1941 to 1948 he was a lecturer and professor of literature at Wellesley College, from 1948 to 1959 professor of Russian literature at Cornell University, and in 1952 a visiting lecturer at Harvard. After 1959 he devoted himself to writing. His works written in English included two novels, *The Real Life of Sebastian Knight*, 1941, and *Bend Sin-*

ister, 1947, *Nikolai Gogol*, 1944, an important critical work, *Nine Stories*, 1947, *Conclusive Evidence: A Memoir*, 1950, an account of his life in pre-revolutionary Russia, *Pnin*, 1957, a short satirical work, *Nabokov's Dozen*, a collection of 13 stories, *Poems*, 1959, and *Speak, Memory!*, 1967, an autobiographical work. With the controversial, best-selling *Lolita*, 1955, he gained a popular audience and some notoriety. Its subject matter, the love of a middle-aged European man for a 12-year-old American girl, was tempered for a popular 1962 motion picture version. His major English work was considered to be *Pale Fire*, 1962, which displayed the heights of his verbal skill and intricate structural effects. He published English translations of the works of Pushkin and Lermontov and also contributed essays and short stories to such magazines as the *New Yorker*, *Atlantic Monthly*, *Harper's*, and *Esquire*. Also a noted lepidopterist, he was a research fellow in entomology from 1942 to 1948 at Harvard's Museum of Comparative Zoology and published in its journal the authoritative "Nearctic Members of the Genus *Lycaeides* Hübner," 1949.

NASBY, PETROLEUM V. see LOCKE, DAVID ROSS

NASH, OGDEN (1902–), author. Born on August 19, 1902, in Rye, New York, of predominantly Southern forebears (among whom the brother of his great-grandfather gave his name to Nashville, Tennessee), Nash grew up in various cities along the East coast, from Georgia to New England. He attended Harvard during 1920–1921, and taught at St. George's School in Newport, Rhode Island, where he had formerly been a student, but left after one year because of harassment by the fourteen-year-olds. During the late 1920s he worked in New York City as a bond salesman, an advertising copywriter, and a manuscript reader, and began contributing his verse—a unique and eccentric meeting of words and rhyme—to numerous magazines, including the *New Yorker*, whose editorial staff he joined. Numerous books were published containing his reflections on little boys, women's hats, salads, parsley, diets, bankers, debt, animals, literature, and other such phenomena. They included *Hard Lines*, 1931, *Bad Parents' Garden of Verse*, 1936, *The Face Is Familiar*, 1941, *Musical Zoo*, 1947, *Versus*, 1949, *Parents Keep Out*, 1951, and *You Can't Get There From Here*, 1957. He wrote librettos in 1943 for the Broadway musical *One Touch of Venus* (with S. J. Perelman) and in 1958 for the television special *Art Carney Meets Peter and the Wolf*. He appeared on radio and television and gave lectures and poetry readings throughout the country.

NAST, THOMAS (1840–1902), political cartoonist. Born in Germany on September 27, 1840, Nast came to the United States with his mother in 1846. An early love of drawing led him to study art at the National Academy of Design in his adopted home, New York City. At 15 he was hired as a draftsman for *Frank Leslie's Illustrated Newspaper*; in 1859 his work first appeared in *Harper's Weekly*. He joined the newly established *New York Illustrated News* the same year, covering John Brown's funeral and, in England, the first International heavyweight boxing title match between the English and American champions. He extended his English trip to go to Italy to cover Garibaldi's revolt. In 1862 he became a regular staff artist for *Harper's*, a position he held until 1886. His work during the Civil War brought him the great influence he was to retain for the remainder of his career; his effective support of a vigorous prosecution of the war was acknowledged even by President Lincoln. His most famous work was done in his campaign against Tammany Hall's "Tweed Ring" in 1869–1872; his efforts were triumphantly climaxed when one of his caricatures led to Tweed's arrest in Spain. The donkey and elephant symbols of the Democratic and Republican parties were both invented by Nast

and were firmly established by 1874. Beset by financial difficulties, he did little work of note after leaving *Harper's*. In 1902 he was appointed consul general at Guayaquil, Ecuador, by President Theodore Roosevelt. He died there on December 7th of the same year.

NATHAN, GEORGE JEAN (1882–1958), editor and drama critic. Born in Fort Wayne, Indiana, on February 14, 1882, Nathan grew up in Cleveland where his family moved when he was four. He graduated from Cornell University in 1904 and, after a year of additional study at the University of Bologne, became a reporter for the *New York Herald*. In 1906 he became associate editor and drama critic for *Outing* and *Bohemian* and began his half-century as the nation's most influential observer of the theater. From 1914 to 1923 he was, with H. L. Mencken, coeditor of *Smart Set*, and in 1924 the two—the "critical Katzenjammer Kids"—founded the *American Mercury*. By 1925 Nathan was estimated to be the most widely read and the highest paid drama critic in the world. He severed his connection with the *Mercury* about 1930 and two years later joined Theodore Dreiser, Eugene O'Neill, Sherwood Anderson, and others in founding the *American Spectator*, which, like *Smart Set* and *Mercury* before it, was a magazine of literature and the arts, much given to a satirical view of American life and culture. Such was Nathan's influence that in 1932 he was threatened with investigation by a Congressional subcommittee on the ludicrous grounds that criticism such as his had destroyed native theater; in a more realistic view, he was acknowledged by the end of his career to have done more than any other person to elevate the standards of the stage and of audiences in America. During his career he was associated with over 30 periodicals, and he published an annual *Theatre Book of the Year* from 1943 to 1951. He was first-string critic for the *New York Journal-American* when illness forced his retirement in 1956. He died in New York on April 8, 1958.

NATION, CARRY AMELIA MOORE (1846–1911), social reformer. Born on November 25, 1846, in Garrard County, Kentucky, Carry Moore attended school sporadically as her family moved back and forth between Kentucky, Missouri, and Texas. She secured a teaching certificate from the Missouri State Normal School and taught school for a brief period. Her mother was insane, suffering from delusions of being Queen Victoria. Her father, a prosperous land owner before the Civil War, was ruined by it and moved to Belton, Missouri, where Carry met her first husband, an alcoholic who resisted her efforts at reform and died, leaving her with a hatred for liquor and bars. Her second husband, David Nation, a lawyer and minister, divorced her for desertion in 1901. She had become by that time deeply involved with her own version of the temperance movement, proclaiming that any property connected with liquor as well as liquor itself was doomed to destruction. She began in the 1890s a series of hatchet-swinging "missions" through bars in small towns in Kansas and later moved on to large cities across the country. Alone or with a few hymn-singing supporters, she invaded "joints," castigated the "rummies" present, and concluded with a highly destructive "hatchetation" of the property. Frequently arrested for disturbing the peace, she paid her fines by selling souvenir hatchets. She published newsletters called *The Smasher's Mail, The Hatchet,* and *The Home Defender,* and an autobiography in 1904. She was for a time much in demand as a lecturer and she appeared in her customary deaconess's uniform, holding a hatchet. Poor health finally forced her to retire to the Ozark Mountains. She died after a period of hospitalization in Leavenworth, Kansas, on June 9, 1911. Despite her spectacular campaign, it was largely the result of the efforts of more legitimate reform groups, who had been reluctant to support her, when national prohibition went into effect less than ten years later.

NEWCOMB, SIMON (1835–1909), astronomer. Born on March 12, 1835, in Wallace, Nova Scotia, Newcomb, the son of an itinerant school teacher, himself received little or no formal schooling. He early developed an avidity for study, however, and was particularly fascinated by mathematics. After about two years as an apprentice to a quack herbalist, he traveled at the age of 18 to Maryland, and for several years taught in country schools while spending his spare time in Washington, D.C., studying under the occasional guidance of Joseph Henry. On the latter's recommendation he was taken into the office of the *American Ephemeris and Nautical Almanac* in Cambridge, Massachusetts, in 1857. While working as a computer for the *Ephemeris* he enrolled in Harvard's Lawrence Scientific School and graduated in 1858. In 1861 he was named professor of mathematics by the Navy and assigned to the Naval Observatory. His work there was an extension of that done for the *Ephemeris;* he set about finding and correcting errors in published values for the positions and motions of various celestial objects, including a large number of reference stars, the moon, several planets, and the sun. His work on the orbits of Neptune and Uranus and on the solar parallax was particularly valuable and widely hailed. In 1877 he became superintendent of the *Ephemeris* office and commenced the monumental task of thoroughly revising the motion theories and position tables for all the major celestial reference objects. Assisted by George W. Hill, he carried on the vastly complex computations required to construct new tables of values that came into standard use throughout the world, and some of which remain so yet. In 1879 he inaugurated a series of *Astronomical Papers Prepared for the Use of the American Ephemeris and Nautical Almanac* to publish the results of these researches. He also found time to lecture at various colleges and in 1884 was appointed professor of mathematics and astronomy at Johns Hopkins University. In 1896 he attended an international conference in Paris, held primarily at his instigation, at which it was decided to eliminate the reigning confusion by adopting for worldwide use a common system of astronomical constants; the system adopted was largely his, and a similar conference in 1950 reaffirmed that decision. In 1897 he reached the compulsory retirement age for Navy captains; he continued his work thereafter under grants from the Carnegie Institution of Washington. In 1899 he helped found and for the next six years was the first president of the American Astronomical Society; he was a member of all the leading scientific societies in the world, and to his many honors was added in 1906 promotion to the rank of rear admiral (retired). He died in Washington on July 11, 1909.

NIEBUHR, REINHOLD (1892–), theologian. Born on June 21, 1892, in Wright City, Missouri, the son of a clergyman, Niebuhr attended Elmhurst College, Eden Theological Seminary, and Yale Divinity School, where he earned his B.D. in 1914 and his M.A. in 1915. Ordained to the ministry of the Evangelical Synod of North America in 1915, he was pastor at Detroit's Bethel Evangelical Church until 1928, when he joined the staff of the Union Theological Seminary in New York City as associate professor of the philosophy of religion. He became professor of applied Christianity in 1930, retiring as professor emeritus in 1960. Initially a religious liberal and social idealist, he came into increasing contact with the realities of mundane life, notably during his pastorate in Detroit, and gave deep consideration to the nature of international conflicts, resulting in a stern and realistic shift in his theological outlook. His book, *Moral Man and Immoral Society*, 1932, marked the beginning of the Neo-orthodox movement in the United States. It attacked the form of Christi-

anity whose focus on a "gospel of love" rendered it inadequate to deal with such real and active problems as political coercion. He aimed for and achieved a reinterpretation of the teachings of Christianity that took into account the social and political problems of modern times. In defiance of optimism, idealism, and the like, he argued that the true character of nations and people made essential the doctrines of sin and repentance. His concept of "human nature and destiny" was based on Augustinian theology, and emphasized that at the root of men's highest achievements was the taint of ambition and self-love. Though he had earlier embraced radical socialism, after World War II he turned against totalitarian communism, as well as doctrinaire socialism, though without losing his deep social concern. His developed theological position— which placed the Augustinian-Reformation view of man in an existentially interpreted environment—was stated more completely in his Gifford lectures, published as *The Nature and Destiny of Man*, 2 vol., 1941–1943. He paid greater attention to history and man's fundamental historicity in his later writings, including *Faith and History*, 1949, *The Irony of American History*, 1952, *The Self and the Dramas of History*, 1955, and *The Structure of Nations and Empires*, 1959.

NIMITZ, CHESTER WILLIAM (1885–1966), naval officer. Born on February 24, 1885, in Fredericksburg, Texas, Nimitz entered the Naval Academy at the age of 15 and graduated in 1905. After serving the required two years of sea duty, he became a lieutenant and received command of the destroyer *Stephen Decatur*. He went to Germany in 1913 to study advancements in diesel engines in that country and in Belgium; returning to the United States he was able to supervise the construction of the first diesel engine for the Navy. During World War I he was chief of staff to the commander of the submarine division of the Atlantic Fleet. From 1926 to 1929 he was at the University of California, and organized the first training division for officers in the naval reserve. Before World War II he furthered his education at advanced naval schools and had earned the rank of rear admiral by 1938. The next year he was made chief of the Bureau of Navigation and immediately after the Japanese attack on Pearl Harbor on December 7, 1941, he was named commander in chief of the Pacific Fleet. With both sea and land forces under his command, he directed a series of battles—of Midway, 1942, of the Solomon Islands, 1942–1943, of the Gilbert Islands, 1943, the Marshalls, Marianas, Palaus, and Philippines, 1944, and Iwo Jima and Okinawa, 1945—which, combined with the operations under Gen. Douglas MacArthur, won victory over Japan for the United States. In 1944 he was promoted to the newly created rank of fleet admiral. On September 2, 1945, the peace treaty was signed aboard his flagship, the U.S.S. *Missouri*. During 1945–1947 he was chief of naval operations and afterwards served as special assistant to the secretary of the Navy. He coedited with E. B. Potter *Sea Power, a Naval History*, 1960. He died near San Francisco on February 20, 1966.

NIXON, RICHARD MILHOUS (1913–), public official and 37th U.S. President. Born in Yorba Linda, California, on January 9, 1913, Nixon was the child of Quaker parents. He graduated in 1934 from Whittier College in California, and then went to Duke University law school, where he received his LL.B. in 1937. After five years of legal practice in Whittier he joined the Navy, being discharged in 1946 as a lieutenant commander. In the fall of 1946 he challenged the veteran Democratic representative of California's 12th congressional district, H. Jerry Voorhis, and after a series of joint platform debates defeated him in the November election. He was unopposed for reelection in 1948. While in the House of Representatives he helped write the Taft-Hartley Labor Relations Act and played a large part in preparing the congressional investigation of Alger Hiss, who was later convicted of perjury in connection with Communist espionage activity. On the strength of the reputation gained in this affair, and after a campaign marked by innuendoes about the loyalty of his opponent, Mrs. Helen Gahagan Douglas, he defeated her in the senatorial race in California in 1950. He was nominated by the Republicans at their convention in 1952 as General Eisenhower's running mate. The campaign opened with charges that he had benefited illegally from a fund raised by his supporters, and he was asked, though not by Eisenhower, to withdraw. Instead he made a dramatic and successful defense in a nationwide television broadcast and was elected with Eisenhower by a decisive margin. As Vice President he was a leading spokesman of the administration, particularly during the periods when Eisenhower was incapacitated by illness. He presided over meetings of the Cabinet and the National Security Council in the President's absence and represented the government in several trips throughout the world, on most of which he was well received although he encountered mob violence and an assassination threat in Venezuela in 1958. In 1959, at the opening of the first American exposition in Moscow, he met Premier Khrushchev of the Soviet Union in the course of touring the exhibition and engaged him in a famous "kitchen debate," from which Nixon was felt by American observers to have emerged victorious. With Eisenhower's blessing he was nominated by the Republicans as their candidate in 1960, but though he campaigned vigorously he was defeated by an extremely narrow margin by John F. Kennedy. The turning point in the campaign was probably a series of television debates, which it was thought that Nixon lost. He returned to California and prepared to run for governor against incumbent Democrat Edmund G. Brown. After another difficult campaign, in 1962, he lost again, whereupon, in an emotional speech to newspapermen, he announced his intention to retire from politics. In *Six Crises*, published that year, he told the story of the turning points of his career. He went to New York in 1963, established a lucrative law practice, and remained out of contention for many months, but in 1966 he actively campaigned for Republican congressional candidates, and it became obvious that he did not mean his retirement to be permanent. As 1968 approached, he was more and more clearly the leading Republican candidate for the nomination, and he was chosen in Miami Beach on the first ballot. Declaring that his primary intention was to unify the country, he conducted a relatively muted campaign, particularly after the Democrats had shown the rifts within their party at Chicago in August, and won in November over Hubert Humphrey. He was inaugurated on January 20, 1969. His daughter Julie married David Eisenhower, the grandson of the ex-President, in 1969.

NOCK, ALBERT JAY (1870–1945), author and editor. Born in Brooklyn, New York, on October 13, 1870, Nock grew up there and, from the age of nine, in Alpena, Michigan, where his father was a clergyman. He went to boarding school when he was 14 and later attended St. Stephen's College, Annadale, New York. When he was a young man he played semi-professional baseball, then taught classics at various schools, and was eventually ordained an Episcopalian minister. In 1910, dissatisfied with his life up to that point, he moved to New York in search of a literary career. He started with the *American Mercury* and during the next ten years wrote astute and entertaining articles for most of the leading magazines of the day. From 1920 to 1924 he was editor of *The Freeman*, which during its brief life was a vehicle for his personal philosophy. From 1925 to 1940 he lived much of the time abroad, chiefly in Belgium. When World War II came he returned to the United States, spending his declining years in the hills of Connecticut and Vermont. Most of his books were written in the last 20 years of his life,

notably *Jefferson*, 1926, *On Doing the Right Thing, and Other Essays*, 1928, *The Theory of Education in the United States*, 1932, *Our Enemy, the State*, 1935, and *Henry George; an Essay*, 1939. None of these books was especially popular, but in them he developed his political and social theories, which were antidemocratic in the extreme and verged on a kind of gentlemanly anarchism. His ideas bore their richest fruit in his informal autobiography, *Memoirs of a Superfluous Man*, 1943, in which he expressed his dislike of practically everything that was happening not only in the United States but also in Russia and the rest of the world. Written in an engagingly personal style, it was a best seller for several months and has become a minor classic. Several books, including a collection of his letters, were published after his death, which occurred in New Canaan, Connecticut, on August 19, 1945.

NOGUCHI, HIDEYO (1876–1928), bacteriologist. Born in Inawashiro, Fukushima, Japan, on November 24, 1876, Noguchi graduated from Tokyo Medical College in 1897 and during the next year was a special assistant at Tokyo General Hospital and a lecturer in general pathology and oral surgery at Tokyo Dental College. He served at the Government Institute for Infectious Diseases in 1898–1899 and was sent to New Chwang, China, as physician in charge of the Central Hospital and bacteriological laboratory during an outbreak of bubonic plague. Returning to Tokyo at the start of the Boxer movement, he completed several texts on bacteriology, pathology, and dentistry. He came to the University of Pennsylvania in 1899 to work in Simon Flexner's pathology laboratory. There he assisted in Dr. S. Weir Mitchell's research on snake venoms, showing himself to be a dedicated, industrious, and adroit experimenter. He published in 1904 *The Action of Snake Venom upon Cold-blooded Animals*, which secured his reputation. In 1904 he began an association with the Rockefeller Institute for Medical Research in New York City, under whose auspices he worked for the rest of his career. Immediately he turned to clarification of Wassermann's principles and method for diagnosing syphilis, and, using a subtle variation of Theobald Smith's method of obtaining pure cultures of spiral organisms, he isolated the spirochetes of syphilis (*Treponema pallidum*) and grew them free of contaminating bacteria, making possible the preparation of extract luetin. He introduced the luetin reaction, or skin test for syphilis. In 1913, with J. W. Moore, he observed the presence of *Treponema pallidum* in the brain of patients dead of paresis. He also demonstrated the presence of the organism in the central nervous system of patients dying of general paresis and of tabes dorsalis, thus establishing syphilis as the cause of both disorders. The first to produce cultures of numerous pathogenic spiral organisms and saprophytic forms, he grew the globoid bodies of poliomyelitis, but erroneously identified them as causative agents. (Viruses were later shown to cause poliomyelitis.) He was successful in demonstrating that the clinically diverse processes of Oroya fever (Carrión's disease) and Verruga peruana were produced by the same agent, *Bartonella bacilliformis*. He made several trips to South America to conduct these and other investigations into yellow fever. Relinquishing the results of his own earlier work on the disease, in 1927 he joined other bacteriologists in British West Africa, after it was learned that the etiological agent in yellow fever was a virus. In the course of his work he contracted yellow fever and died, in Accra, on May 21, 1928.

NOGUCHI, ISAMU (1904–   ), sculptor. Born in Los Angeles on November 7, 1904, Noguchi was the son of a Japanese poet and art historian and of an American writer. He resided in Japan from the age of 2 until returning to the United States at 13 to attend high school in Indiana. Thus he was able to view and receive early influence from Japanese primitive carving and earthenware. After graduation he studied sculpture with Gutzon Borglum, creator of Mount Rushmore, who discouraged him from furthering his training. He entered Columbia University as a pre-medical student, completing the two-year course. He returned to his art and in 1926 won a Guggenheim Award to go to Paris and study sculpture under Constantin Brancusi. In 1927 and 1928 he studied in Europe, also as a Guggenheim Fellow, but several unsuccessful showings prompted him to do a series of realistic heads in bronze, which he exhibited with great success in New York in 1930–1931. He was able to travel around the world from his sales, furthering his studies of primitive art in the Orient, and working in London in 1933 and in Mexico in 1936, where he completed a relief sculpture of colored cement 65 feet long. Returning to the United States, he submitted the award-winning design for a plaque to decorate the entrance of the Associated Press building in New York City's Rockefeller Center. Cast in stainless steel at his behest, the sweeping, rhythmical design was enthusiastically received at its unveiling in 1941. Thereafter he completed many works, including the "Kuros," 1945, and was exhibited in museums in New York and Japan and in numerous galleries. In 1958 he designed a garden for the UNESCO building in Paris. His art naturally extended into practical environment, using the shapes and materials (stone, terracotta, plastic) of plant, animal, and geographic formations. His chair, lamp, and table designs, playground equipment, fountain at the 1939 New York World's Fair, backdrops for Martha Graham's dance recitals, and bridge at Hiroshima contributed immensely to the extension of the modern abstract art movement.

NORRIS, BENJAMIN FRANKLIN (1870–1902), author. Born in Chicago on March 5, 1870, Frank Norris, as he was always known, moved with his family to San Francisco in 1884. In 1887, having demonstrated considerable artistic ability, he was enrolled in the Atélier Julien in Paris; two years later, having decided that literature was his true vocation, he withdrew, returned to America, and entered the University of California in 1890. He remained there four years and, though he failed to graduate, continued his studies for another year at Harvard. During 1895–1896 he was in South Africa as a correspondent for the *San Francisco Chronicle*; he returned in the latter year and joined the *San Francisco Wave*, a literary journal. In 1898 he moved to New York, joined the staff of *McClure's Magazine*, and went to Cuba as a war correspondent. In that year also he published his first book, *Moran of the Lady Letty*, a sea adventure and love story earlier serialized in the *Wave*. In 1899 he returned to New York and published *Blix*, a partially autobiographical novel, and *McTeague*, a story of greed and violence and the first of his characteristic novels in the naturalistic vein inspired by Zola. With this book and those that followed, he joined Theodore Dreiser in the front rank of American literature. In 1901 appeared *The Octopus*, the first book of a projected trilogy entitled *The Epic of the Wheat*. The first volume concerned California wheat growers and their struggle against the railroad trust; the second volume, *The Pit*, 1903, was a tale of the Chicago Board of Trade, where the wheat passed from speculator to speculator; the final volume, *The Wolf*, unwritten at his death, was to have shown the wheat, as bread, feeding a famine-stricken village in the Old World. Another novel, *Vandover and the Brute*, was published in 1914, long after his death. In 1902 he returned to California; on October 25th of that year he died.

NORRIS, GEORGE WILLIAM (1861–1944), public official. Born in Sandusky County, Ohio, on July 11, 1861, Norris early in life became his family's main support. Unable to attend school regularly, he gained his early education largely on his own. He obtained a law degree from Northern Indiana Normal School (now Valparaiso University) in 1882 and moved to Beaver City, Nebraska, in 1885. He soon entered local politics, serving as county prosecuting attorney for three terms and, from 1895 to 1902, as district judge. In 1902 he successfully campaigned for Congress as a Republican and continued to represent his district until 1912, during which time he led the House progressives in their struggle to strip the speaker of his autocratic prerogatives. In 1912 he began his 30-year career in the Senate. Staunchly independent, he opposed American entry into World War I and participation in the League of Nations and denounced the Treaty of Versailles. He fought for a number of political reforms and sponsored the Norris-La Guardia Anti-Injunction Act in 1932 and the 20th Amendment to the Constitution in 1933. His major efforts were directed to securing public ownership and operation of hydroelectric resources; though he was twice stymied by presidential veto, his work finally resulted in the creation of the Tennessee Valley Authority. The first dam completed in the program was named in his honor. Nominally a Republican, he was far from a strict partisan; he supported Theodore Roosevelt's Bull Moose candidacy in 1912, Progressive Robert La Follette in 1924, and Democrat Franklin Roosevelt in his four campaigns. He ran as an Independent Republican in 1936. Defeated for reelection in 1942, he retired from public life and died on September 2, 1944, in McCook, Nebraska.

NORTON, CHARLES ELIOT (1827–1908), author, editor, and educator. Born in Cambridge, Massachusetts, on November 16, 1827, Norton graduated from Harvard in 1846 and entered business. After three years with a mercantile house he spent two years traveling and studying in Europe and the Orient. From 1851 to 1855 he managed his own importing firm and then spent another two years in Europe. For several years he wrote articles and reviews for the *Atlantic Monthly*, edited by James Russell Lowell, and in 1864 he became coeditor with Lowell of the *North American Review*. A year later he was one of the founders of the *Nation*. He was a central figure in the Boston-Cambridge-Concord intellectual circle and was a close friend of many European personalities, particularly Thomas Carlyle and John Ruskin; much of his contribution to literature consisted of volumes of letters by the great men who were his friends. In 1873 he began to lecture at Harvard on the history of art, a new course introduced by his cousin Charles W. Eliot, the innovative president of the college. Norton gave the course until 1897 and his skill, scholarship, and lasting influence were attested by hundreds of students. In 1891–1892 he published his prose translation of Dante's *Divine Comedy*; notable among works he edited were *The Poems of John Donne*, 1895, *The Poems of Mrs. Anne Bradstreet*, 1897, and *The Love Poems of John Donne*, 1905. He died on October 21, 1908, in Cambridge.

NOYES, JOHN HUMPHREY (1811–1886), social reformer. Born on September 3, 1811, in Brattleboro, Vermont, Noyes graduated from Dartmouth College in 1830 and then studied law. During a tour by the great revivalist, Charles Finney, he was converted and shortly thereafter entered Andover Theological Seminary, later transferring to Yale. He proclaimed to his teachers that total release from sin could be attained by any individual by will and self-determination. In 1834 he announced that he had attained to perfection and his license to preach was promptly revoked. He traveled about the country, becoming convinced of the evils existing in the secular world. Under his leadership a Bible group that he had formed became a community in 1836; based on perfectionism, it was an association of "Bible communists" who hoped to revive the communal living of early Christianity. In 1837 Noyes proclaimed the doctrine of free love. Noyes and several of his followers were arrested for adultery, but escaped and fled to central New York to found the similar but larger and more elaborately structured Oneida

community. Also devoted to perfection, the community practised "complex marriage," in which each woman in the group was considered each man's wife, and each man, each woman's husband. Male continence was stressed, mutual consent to sexual activities made mandatory, and child-bearing was founded on a program of eugenics. Noyes's control over the group continued undisputed for 30 years and the community was the most successful of the many utopian experiments of the period. But by 1879 tension within and around the community prompted him to end Oneida's bizarre sexual teachings and to move to Canada, where he was safe from legal proceedings. He died in Niagara Falls, Ontario, on April 13, 1886.

OAKLEY, ANNIE see **MOZEE, PHOEBE ANNE OAKLEY**

OCHS, ADOLPH SIMON (1858–1935), newspaper publisher. Born in Cincinnati on March 12, 1858, of German immigrant parents, Ochs moved with them to Knoxville, Tennessee, in 1865. He received fairly regular schooling until he was 11, when he became an office boy for the *Knoxville Chronicle*. With but a few interruptions he remained in the newspaper business for the rest of his life. At 14 he was a printer's devil; he moved to Chattanooga and worked on the *Dispatch* until it failed, whereupon at the age of 20 he borrowed some money and bought control of the faltering *Chattanooga Times*. Within a short time he had brought the paper to a position of financial and journalistic soundness from which it progressed to become one of the leading Southern journals. In 1891 he helped found the Southern Associated Press and was its chairman for its first three years. In 1896 he gained control of the *New York Times*; though once powerful, the *Times* had been declining for several years and was considered moribund by many in the business. Explaining his philosophy of journalism in the simple masthead slogan he introduced—"All the News That's Fit to Print"—Ochs set about rebuilding the *Times* in competition with the much more popular exponents of "yellow journalism." Eschewing sensationalism, he insisted upon an accurate, complete coverage of the news directed to the intelligent reader. In 1898 he reduced the cost of the *Times* to one cent, a price then considered the emblem of the yellow sheets, and within a year circulation tripled. While setting high and influential standards for integrity—he refused to follow the then-common practice of allowing major advertising clients to dictate editorial policy—the *Times* achieved financial security and grew into one of the world's leading newspapers. He introduced many new features, including rotogravure illustration and the book review supplement. Retaining ownership of the *Chattanooga Times,* he also published the *Philadelphia Public Ledger* (merged with the *Philadelphia Times*) from 1901 to 1912. From 1900 to his death he was a director of the Associated Press, and in 1913 he began to publish the *New York Times Index,* the only such service in the United States. He was the principal financial backer for the compilation and publication of the *Dictionary of American Biography*, advancing a half-million dollars for the project. He died in Chattanooga on April 8, 1935.

ODETS, CLIFFORD (1906–1963), playwright. Born on July 18, 1906, in Philadelphia, the son of a printer, Odets was raised in the Bronx. He left high school to become a poet, then turned to acting on radio and in repertory theater. He was associated with the Theatre Guild and in 1931 helped to found the Group Theater with Lee Strasberg and others. In 1935 he attempted writing plays himself and was an immediate success with *Waiting for Lefty* and *Awake and Sing*, both performed by the Group in 1935. The two plays immediately established him as the leading proletarian playwright in America and, in the turmoil of the Depression, enjoyed a great vogue. He began writing movie scripts with *The General Died at Dawn* in 1936. His great success,

Golden Boy, appeared on the stage in 1937. He directed the film *None But the Lonely Heart*, selected best movie by the National Board of Review in 1949. His play, *The Big Knife*, was also produced in 1949, followed by *The Country Girl*, 1950, and his last play, *The Flowering Peach*, 1954. In 1960 he again took up film directing with *The Story on Page One*. At his death in Los Angeles on August 15, 1963, he was completing the script for a television series and three plays, and had finished a musical version of *Golden Boy* (produced in 1964). His work never achieved its potential, and the Hollywood influence that appeared only subtly in his first plays marred his final endeavors.

O. HENRY see **PORTER, WILLIAM SIDNEY**

OLMSTED, FREDERICK LAW (1822–1903), landscape architect. Born on April 27, 1822, in Hartford, Connecticut, Olmsted was prevented by weak eyesight from entering Yale in 1837, as he had planned. Instead he studied engineering for a time, worked for two years in a New York mercantile house, attended lectures at Yale for a year, and sailed to the Orient aboard a trading vessel. In 1844 he embarked on a farming career; he studied scientific methods of agriculture, served virtual apprenticeships on prize farms, and in 1847 began his own operations, which included a small nursery business. In 1852, on commission from the *New York Times,* he traveled down the Atlantic coast into the South and later wrote a clear, unbiased report of his findings, *A Journey in the Seaboard Slave States,* 1856. Subsequent trips resulted in *A Journey Through Texas,* 1857, and *A Journey in the Back Country,* 1860, and in 1861 the three books were condensed into one, *Journeys and Explorations in the Cotton Kingdom,* which was particularly influential in England during the Civil War. In 1857 he was appointed superintendent of New York's Central Park, then in process of construction. A competition was held to select a new plan for the park, and he collaborated with Calvert Vaux in developing the successful design. In 1858 he became chief architect of the park and from then until 1861 worked assiduously to create a park that would be both a work of art and a functional part of the city. From 1861 to 1863 he was secretary of the U.S. Sanitary Commission, the forerunner of the Red Cross. From 1863 to 1865 he was in California, where he secured the establishment of the magnificent Yosemite Valley as a state park and served as its first commission president. In 1865 he returned to New York to continue work on Central Park. Thereafter, for several decades, he created parks and landscaped settings all over the country: Brooklyn's Prospect Park, Philadelphia's Fairmount Park, Riverside and Morningside parks in New York, the grounds of Stanford University, those of the Capitol in Washington, D.C., Mount Royal Park in Montreal, the park system of Boston, and many others. He was the outstanding landscape architect of his time and his works stand yet unchallenged. In 1892–1893 he helped to design and supervised the execution of the grounds for the World's Columbian Exposition in Chicago, and during the last year of his career he devoted much time to the landscaping of "Biltmore," the famed Vanderbilt estate in Asheville, North Carolina. He retired in 1895 and lived quietly until his death on August 28, 1903.

O'NEILL, EUGENE GLADSTONE (1888–1953), playwright. Born on October 16, 1888, in a Broadway hotel in New York City, O'Neill was the son of James O'Neill, an itinerant actor, and grew up on the road. His family life was highly unstable; he was educated at boarding schools and during 1906–1907 attended Princeton. The next six years of sea and waterfront life and alcoholism climaxed in a suicide attempt. He worked briefly in 1912 for the New London (Connecticut) Telegraph. While confined to a tuberculosis sanitarium he began to experiment with drama and during 1914–1915 he studied at George

P. Baker's 47 Workshop at Harvard. In 1916 the Provincetown (Massachusetts) Players produced his Bound East for Cardiff, a one-act play that was also staged later in the year by the Playwrights Theater in New York City. Several more short works followed and in 1920 his first full-length drama, Beyond the Horizon, opened on Broadway and won the first of his four Pulitzer Prizes. During the next 23 years he completed more than a score of plays and rose to the forefront of the American theater. His major works included The Emperor Jones, 1920, Anna Christie, 1922 (Pulitzer Prize), Desire Under the Elms, 1925, The Great God Brown, 1926, Strange Interlude, 1928 (Pulitzer Prize), Mourning Becomes Electra, 1931, Ah, Wilderness!, 1933 (his only comedy), The Iceman Cometh, written in 1939 but produced and published in 1946, and the semi-autobiographical Long Day's Journey into Night, written by 1941 but not produced until 1956 (Pulitzer Prize). In treating the drama as literature and in utilizing characters—drug addicts, prostitutes, derelicts of all sorts—previously confined to the novel, O'Neill set a new high standard for American drama and became, both at home and abroad, the best known and most widely admired American dramatist. In 1936 he became the first American playwright to be awarded the Nobel Prize for Literature. After 1943 a crippling disease ended his writing. His last ten years were spent in frustration; he died in Boston on November 27, 1953.

OPPENHEIMER, J. ROBERT (1904–1967), physicist. Born in New York City on April 22, 1904, Oppenheimer was educated at the Ethical Culture School and at Harvard, from which he graduated after three years in 1925. He continued his studies at Cambridge University and from there, at the invitation of Max Born, went to Göttingen, where he received his doctorate in 1927. After two more years at Leiden and Zürich, he returned to the United States and joined the faculties of the California Institute of Technology and the University of California. He was a remarkable teacher and inspired great devotion in his students; in his particular field, while he made numerous theoretical contributions, he was especially noted for his broad grasp of the entire range of quantum and nuclear physics. In 1941 he became associated informally with the project to develop the atomic bomb, code-named the Manhattan Engineering District; by the next year he was in a position of great authority, helping to select and then taking charge of the huge staff—which included Enrico Fermi and Niels Bohr—of the government laboratory at Los Alamos, New Mexico. His leadership and administrative ability contributed so much to the success of the project that afterwards he was publicly hailed, more so than any of the purely scientific staff, as the father of the atomic bomb. In 1946 he was awarded the Presidential Citation and Medal of Merit. He served as a top government advisor on atomic policy; from 1946 to 1952 he was chairman of the General Advisory Committee of the Atomic Energy Commission and was the principal author of the Acheson-Lilienthal Report and the subsequent Baruch Plan for United Nations control of atomic energy. In 1947 he became director of the Institute for Advanced Study in Princeton, New Jersey. In 1954 charges were lodged against him accusing him of disloyalty, Communist sympathies, and possible treason. His security clearance was removed by President Eisenhower, cutting him off from government research. An investigative board cleared him of the serious charges but held him to have been imprudent in his associations and upheld the revocation of his security clearance. The decision, not unanimous, was protested by scores of his fellow scientists, who saw the action as a manifestation of repression inspired by the McCarthy hysteria. The official proscription of Oppenheimer eased in later years and seemed to come to a symbolic end in 1963 when he was awarded the AEC's highest honor, the Fermi Prize, by President Johnson. He retired from the Institute in 1966 and died in Prince-

ton on February 18, 1967. A man of wide cultural interests, he concerned himself with the role of science and the scientist in the world; he writings included *Science and the Common Understanding,* 1954, *The Open Mind,* 1955, and *Some Reflections on Science and Culture,* 1960.

OTIS, ELISHA GRAVES (1811–1861), inventor and manufacturer. Born on August 3, 1811, in Halifax, Vermont, Otis was educated in public schools and worked variously in the construction and trucking businesses, and in a grist mill, a carriage shop, machine shop, saw mill, and bedstead manufactory. In the latter enterprise he became in 1852 supervisor of construction of a new plant in Yonkers, New York; there, for working convenience, he developed a mechanical elevator with an innovative safety device to prevent it from falling even if the lifting chain broke. In 1853 he planned to leave the firm and join the California gold rush, but two New York firms whose representatives had seen the safety elevator requested copies of it. He purchased space in the Yonkers plant and began manufacturing elevators. Demand for the device was small, however, until he publicly demonstrated its safety at the New York Crystal Palace Exhibition of 1854, standing in an elevator and ordering the rope cut. With the safety device proven, orders from industry for freight elevators gradually increased. In 1857 he installed the first passenger elevator in the Haughwout store in New York City. It was immediately popular and caused a revolution in the construction industry and in architecture. Providing a safe, efficient means of vertical transportation, it helped make possible the skyscraper, which soon followed. He died in Yonkers on April 8, 1861, leaving the business to his sons who oversaw its becoming a million-dollar firm by 1889.

OTIS, JAMES (1725–1783), lawyer, public official, and publicist. Born on February 5, 1725, in West Barnstable, Massachusetts, Otis graduated from Harvard in 1743, was admitted to the bar in 1748, and then settled in Boston. In the next ten years he established himself as a leader of the bar and served for a time as king's advocate general of the vice-admiralty court. In 1760 the long-disregarded provisions of the 1733 Stamp Act were revived by the British government and royal officials in Massachusetts sought to renew their writs of assistance. When the case came to court in February 1761 Otis was the chief spokesman for the opposition; he raised the doctrine of natural law underlying the rights of citizens and declared that even if affirmed by Parliament, such writs would be void. He lost the case but was elected almost immediately to the Massachusetts General Court where, with his father, who was speaker of the house, he led the opposition to the royal governor. In September 1762 he published the first of his many political pamphlets, *A Vindication of the Conduct of the House of Representatives of the Province of Massachusetts Bay*. He continued in the General Court and until 1769 was the major political leader in the province, as his writings were the basic and most prominent documents in the early part of the revolutionary struggle. In 1764 he wrote *The Rights of the British Colonies Asserted and Proved* and in 1765 instigated, organized, and served in the inter-colonial Stamp Act Congress. In that year also he wrote several powerful pamphlets, notably *Considerations on behalf of the Colonists, in a Letter to a Noble Lord* and *A Vindication of the British Colonies Against the Aspersions of the Halifax Gentleman*. Though a stout defender of the rights of the colonists, Otis opposed throughout his career the use of violence, and considered separation from Great Britain unthinkable. He was instrumental in organizing the non-importation movement that followed the Townshend Acts in 1767, but exerted himself equally in preventing active opposition to British occupation of Boston. Despite such scruples, he was branded by royal officials as an incendiary and threatened with trial for treason. On September 5, 1769, in a scuffle with a crown officer, Otis was struck a severe blow to the head; he had for some time been exhibiting signs of instability and from this time on he was clearly unbalanced. Though reelected to the General Court during a lucid period in 1771, his public career was, to all intents and purposes, over. He was struck and killed by lightning on May 23, 1783.

OWENS, JESSE (1913 –), athlete. Born on September 12, 1913, in Danville, Alabama, James Cleveland Owens set his first track record while attending Fairview Junior High School in Cleveland, running the 100-yard dash in 10 seconds flat. In 1932, while attending East Technical High School in Cleveland, he won national attention by running 10.3 in the 100-meter dash and, the next year, as a triple winner in the National Interscholastic Championships held at the University of Chicago. In 1934 he enrolled in Ohio State University, where his career in track and field was little short of phenomenal. In one day — May 25, 1935 — at the Big Ten (Western Conference) track and field championships, he broke world records in the 220-yard dash (20.3 seconds), the 220-yard low hurdles (22.6 seconds), and the running broad jump (26'8 1/4" — a record that was not broken for 25 years), and tied a fourth world record for the 100-yard dash (9.4 seconds). He went on to win four gold medals in the 1936 Olympic games at Berlin, tying the Olympic record in the 100-meter sprint (10.3 seconds), setting the Olympic and world records in the 200-meter sprints (20.7 seconds), setting the Olympic and world records for the running broad jump (26'5 5/16" — his jump in 1935 had not yet been officially accepted), and running anchor on the world record-breaking U.S. 400-meter relay team (39.8 seconds). Rather than present Owens, a Negro, with the victory medals, Adolph Hitler left the stadium, his Aryan "master race" seriously embarrassed. The attendant publicity brought even wider fame to Owens, who nevertheless chose to leave sports after the Olympics. He graduated from Ohio State in 1937 and ventured into show business, public relations, a dry cleaning establishment, and the stockmarket, eventually becoming secretary of the Illinois Athletic Commission, a post he left in 1955 to embark on a goodwill tour of India for the U.S. State Department. Thereafter he established the "junior sized Olympic games" and a sports clinic for boys with major athletes as instructors under the aegis of the Illinois Youth Commission.

PAGE, WALTER HINES (1855 – 1918), author, editor, and diplomat. Born on August 15, 1855, in Cary, North Carolina, Page was educated at Trinity College (now Duke University), Randolph-Macon College, and Johns Hopkins University, though he failed to obtain a degree. After a few months teaching school he found a position as reporter for the *St. Joseph* (Mo.) *Gazette* in 1880 and in a short time was its editor. In the summer of 1881 he toured the South, recording his observations and recommendations in a series of articles that he successfully offered for syndicated newspaper publication. Later that year he was commissioned by the *New York World* to make a similar tour of the West. By 1882 he was literary editor and regular literary critic of the *World.* From 1883 to 1885 he was in Raleigh, North Carolina, editing his own *State Chronicle*, a newspaper that distinguished itself by its outspoken and unconventional editorial opinions. In it Page advocated strongly a "New South" program of primary education for both races, scientific agriculture, industrialization, and, above all, a long overdue deemphasis of the Civil War. In 1887, back in New York, he joined the staff of *Forum*, a monthly review in financial straits; within four years he had assumed control and by the time he resigned as editor in 1895, *Forum* was one of the country's leading periodicals. In 1895 he accepted an offer to become literary advisor and associate editor of the *Atlantic Monthly* and three years later became editor. In 1900,

by now a partner in the publishing house of Doubleday, Page, & Co., he founded *World's Work*, a magazine of politics and public affairs of which he was editor until 1913. He wrote two books embodying his views on the revitalization of the South, *The Rebuilding of Old Commonwealths*, 1902, and *The Southerner*, 1909, a semi-autobiographical novel published under the pseudonym Nicholas Worth. He was active in many public and philanthropic activities, including the Southern Education Board, the program to eradicate the hookworm, and President Roosevelt's Country Life Commission. A lifelong Democrat, he was an early supporter of Woodrow Wilson for the presidency in 1912; after the election he was rewarded with an appointment as ambassador to Great Britain. For the first year, Page and Wilson were in complete harmony as the ambassador strove to eliminate frictions in Anglo-American relations; after the outbreak of World War I in 1914, however, the two drifted apart as Page ardently supported the Allied cause while Wilson insisted upon American neutrality. Never in open opposition, Page nonetheless kept up a barrage of pro-Allied notes and memoranda to the President and, after the sinking of the *Lusitania*, called in them for a declaration of war on Germany. When Wilson at length did request a declaration of war from Congress, he did so in terms and with arguments directly from Page's communiqués covering nearly three years. In declining health, Page was finally forced to resign his post in August 1918; he returned to his North Carolina home and died on December 21st of that year.

PAIGE, LEROY ROBERT (1906–), baseball player. Born, according to his mother, in 1906 in Mobile, Alabama, "Satchel" Paige started pitching professional baseball in the Negro Southern Association in the mid-1920s with teams like the Birmingham Black Barons, the Nashville Elite Giants, the New Orleans Black Pelicans, and the Black Lookouts of Chattanooga, who gave him his nickname because of his "satchel-sized" feet. He played winter ball during the 1930s in South and Central America and the Caribbean, and summer ball in the Northwest, at one time or another with teams in Mexico, Puerto Rico, Venezuela, Cuba, the Dominican Republic, Denver, Colorado, and Bismarck, South Dakota. He built an extraordinary record and in his heyday charged $500 to $2,000 to pitch a game, frequently traveling some 30,000 miles in a season. In 1933 he pitched 31 games and lost 4. In 1934 he started 29 games in 29 days with the Bismarck team, which reportedly won 104 of 105 games. In the Negro National League he pitched for the Crawford Giants of Pittsburgh, the Homestead Grays of Baltimore, and the Kansas City Monarchs—clinching the Monarchs' victory in the Negro World Series in 1942 and pitching 64 scoreless innings in 1946 in another winning pennant drive. He encountered top major league players—including Rogers Hornsby (whom he struck out 5 times in one game), Jimmy Foxx, and Charley Gehringer—in exhibition games. In 1934 he broke Dizzy Dean's 30-game winning streak on the St. Louis Cardinals in a Hollywood All-Stars game by striking out 17 men and allowing no runs, while Dean struck out 15 and let one run in. Though past his prime, he finally broke the color bar in 1948 and was signed by Bill Veeck of the Cleveland Indians. The team won the American League pennant and the World Series. His drawing power undiminished, he attracted 200,000 fans in three games. In 1950 he moved to the St. Louis Browns and was their most valuable relief pitcher in 1951, 1952, and 1953. He continued to play in exhibition games and on the Harlem Globetrotters' barnstorming circuit. Called by Joe DiMaggio in 1937 "the best pitcher I ever faced," he was one of the all-time great American baseball players.

PAINE, THOMAS (1737–1809), author, publicist, and humanitarian. Born in Thetford, Norfolk, England, on January 29, 1737, Paine received little formal education and spent the first 37 years of his life in poverty, wandering from job to job with few prospects for the future. A fortuitous meeting with Benjamin Franklin in London encouraged him to seek his fortune in America and in November 1774 he arrived in Philadelphia. He worked for a time for the *Pennsylvania Magazine*. In January 1776 he published the pamphlet *Common Sense*; in powerful and stirring language he called for independence from England and marshalled a number of supporting arguments for his thesis. The pamphlet was a huge success and sales of it have been estimated as high as half a million. Paine soon enlisted in the army, became an aide to Gen. Nathanael Greene, and began a series of pamphlets entitled *The Crisis*; the first of these appeared in December 1776 and began with the memorable line "These are the times that try men's souls." In April 1777 he was appointed secretary of the congressional committee on foreign affairs, a post he held until forced to resign two years later for his indiscreet publication of certain secret papers. In November 1779 he became clerk of the Pennsylvania Assembly, in 1781 he accompanied John Laurens to France to seek money and supplies for Washington's army, and he continued writing effectively in support of the Revolution and of the government's policies; as a result he was given a Loyalist's confiscated farm by New York and a sum of money by Pennsylvania at the war's end. Until 1787 he lived rather quietly, working on a pierless iron bridge he had invented and was trying to perfect. In that year he went to England to market his bridge, but again was caught up in politics; in answer to Burke's highly critical review of the French Revolution he issued in 1791 the first part of his *Rights of Man*, to which a second part was added the next year. The American publication of the work was arranged for by Jefferson as a means of combatting the "Federalist heresy." The book, an extended and detailed piece of republican and constitutional propaganda, sold so well in England that the government indicted Paine for treason; he escaped to Paris and, having already been made an honorary French citizen along with Washington, Madison, and Hamilton, was elected to the Assembly in September 1792. When the Revolutionary moderates fell from favor, Paine, who had advocated exile rather than execution for the King, was imprisoned for a year, 1793–1794, by Robespierre. In 1794 and 1796 appeared the first and second parts of *The Age of Reason*, a long work of deistic and humanistic apologetics that won its author the unwarranted reputation of an atheist. This latter imputation weighed more heavily with many people than did Paine's undeniable and invaluable services to the American Revolution; when he returned to New York in 1802 he was not welcomed, and he lived in disrepute until his death on June 8, 1809. In 1819 his remains were taken to England by William Cobbett and eventually lost.

PARKER, CHARLIE (1920–1955), jazz musician. Born in Kansas City, Kansas, on August 29, 1920, Parker was a professional on the alto saxophone at age 17. He played with the best bands in Kansas City before moving to Harlem in 1939. There, in the early 1940s, he joined the bands of Noble Sissle, Earl "Fatha" Hines, Cootie Williams, and Andy Kirk, as well as the first Billy Eckstine group. He joined the jam sessions at Minton's Play House, where trumpeter John "Dizzy" Gillespie, drummer Kenny Clarke, and pianist Thelonius Monk were the other participants in the founding of bop, a progressive jazz movement that emphasized listening over dancing. Known as Yardbird or simply Bird, Parker made records in 1944 with Lloyd "Tiny" Grimes and in 1945 with Gillespie—notably "Hot House" and "Salt Peanuts"—that made him the leading exponent of bop and the idol of young musicians. His extemporaneous style was endlessly creative, an amazing synthesis of rhythm, tone, melody, harmony, and form. Bebop (named for a rhythmic device) featured the soloist, who improvised on chords rather than themes, effecting continually new melo-

dies and rhythms. Parker formed a quintet in 1947 with Max Roach, Miles Davis, and others; their recordings were especially acclaimed and reissued many times after his death. While his last years were marked by physical decline (he succumbed to narcotics and alcohol), his music was constantly played and his style influenced a generation of jazz musicians. In 1955 he made his last appearance at Birdland, a Broadway jazz hall named in his honor. He died on March 12, 1955, in New York.

PARKER, FRANCIS WAYLAND (1837–1902), educator. Born on October 9, 1837, in Bedford, New Hampshire, Parker was orphaned in his early childhood and raised by a farmer who permitted him to go to school only eight weeks each winter. When he was 13 he enrolled in a school in Mount Vernon, New Hampshire, and separated from his guardian. He excelled in his studies, and at 16 began to teach. When he was 21 he was invited to become principal of a school in Carrolton, Illinois. He filled this post until the Civil War, in which he served for nearly four years, and afterwards he returned to teaching in Dayton, Ohio. Fascinated with the ideas for liberal teaching propounded by Dr. E. A. Sheldon in *Object Lessons*, he attempted to enact them in his own classes, with encouraging results. He sailed to Germany in 1872 to observe the teaching methods and liberal school environment pioneered by Froebel, Pestalozzi, and others, and, much impressed, returned to the United States in 1875 to become superintendent of schools in Quincy, Massachusetts. There and, from 1880 to 1883 in Boston, he inaugurated his program of "progressive education." His liberal system stressed the development of both teacher and student as individuals on different levels. It encouraged activity and self-expression for students and allowed teachers to practise instruction as an art. Called to Chicago as principal of the Cook County Normal School in 1883, he revamped the entire curriculum and instituted his own pedagogic creed. In 1899 he received a large endowment to found the Chicago Institute, incorporated in 1901 into the University of Chicago as the School of Education with Parker as its first director. The move to introduce education as a discipline into the university curriculum was an innovation that Parker and the university welcomed. During his brief tenure he was associated with John Dewey. Among his writings, his *Talks on Pedogogics*, 1894, and *Talks on Teaching*, 1896, expressed views that generally were warmly received by communities that had grown tired of the stern, repressive methods of traditional school teachers. He died in Chicago on March 2, 1902.

PARKER, THEODORE (1810–1860), clergyman. Born in Lexington, Massachusetts, on August 24, 1810, Parker received little schooling but was an intellectually and spiritually precocious child. Admitted to Harvard in 1830, he was barred by poverty from attending; in 1834, however, he entered the Harvard Divinity School and graduated two years later. By this time he was conversant in 20 languages. In June 1837 he began his ministry at the Unitarian Church in West Roxbury. He was closely associated with the progressive spirits of the time and place—the Channings, Wendell Phillips, Emerson, Alcott, and others—and became himself a leader, never a disciple, in liberal thought. A growing tendency toward a rational approach to religion and a scientifically critical appraisal of the Bible became slowly apparent in Parker's sermons; in May 1841 he delivered one entitled "The Transient and Permanent in Christianity" that provoked nearly as hostile and violent a reaction as had Emerson's Divinity School Address three years earlier. A series of lectures published as *A Discourse of Matters Pertaining to Religion*, 1842, followed the next year by his translation of one of the pioneer works of German "higher criticism," De Wette's *Beiträge zuer Einleitung in das Alte Testament*, widened the schism between Parker and the regular clergy. He returned from a year in Europe in September 1844 and the following January resigned from the West Roxbury pulpit to take charge of the newly organized Twenty-Eighth Congregational Society of Boston. He became a leader in reform movements of all sorts, those for education, prison reform, temperance, and most particularly for the abolition of slavery. He was prominent in the resistance to the Fugitive Slave Law and a strong supporter of John Brown's guerilla war plans, not because they might succeed but because they would precipitate the civil war that Parker saw as inevitable. He lectured widely, carried on voluminous correspondence with public leaders, and is thought to be the source of the phrase "government of the people, by the people, for the people" utilized by Lincoln. His health began to fail in 1857; two years later he withdrew completely from public affairs and, seeking a restoration of his health in European travel, died in Florence, Italy, on May 10, 1860.

PARKMAN, FRANCIS (1823–1893), historian. Born in Boston on September 16, 1823, Parkman was of an old Puritan family and heir to a mercantile fortune. He graduated from Harvard in 1844, entered the law school, and took his degree in 1846. Primarily interested in the rigor of legal training, he did not seek admission to the bar but instead traveled west to Independence, Missouri, the jumping-off point for Western emigrants. He set out on the Oregon Trail; in the months that followed he lived with the Sioux, worked and talked with frontiersmen of all sorts, and absorbed the sights and sounds and feel of unsettled, almost unexplored, territory. In October 1846 he returned to Boston; his health, always marginal, had worsened during the trip and was to decline throughout his life. He described his journey in a series of articles in the *Knickerbocker* that appeared in book form in 1849 as *The California and Oregon Trail* (now known simply as *The Oregon Trail*, the serial title). He then undertook his long contemplated massive work of history, *France and England in North America*; from 1848 to 1851, hampered by a nervous disability and eyesight that rendered reading impossible, he worked on the first volume, *History of the Conspiracy of Pontiac*. For several years thereafter he was unable to continue and contrived to pass the time by writing a novel, *Vassal Morton*, 1856, and by developing an interest in horticulture that led eventually to his *Book of Roses*, 1866, and a professorship at Harvard in 1871. Meanwhile his faculties had revived sufficiently for him to continue work on his magnum opus. He employed copyists to research European archives, and his extensive and critical use of documentation was one of his major contributions to historiography. Subsequent volumes of his history were *Pioneers of France in the New World*, 1865, *The Jesuits in North America*, 1867, *The Discovery of the Great West* (later *LaSalle and the Discovery of the Great West*) 1869, *The Old Regime in Canada*, 1874, *Count Frontenac and New France under Louis XIV*, 1877, *Montcalm and Wolfe*, 1884, and *A Half-Century of Conflict*, 1892. Long before the series was complete, Parkman was established as America's foremost historian. He died on November 8, 1893.

PARRINGTON, VERNON LOUIS (1871–1929), educator and literary historian. Born in Aurora, Illinois, on August 3, 1871, the son of a public school principal, Parrington grew up in the Midwest (for which he retained a bias throughout his life), attended the College of Emporia (Kansas) for several years, and graduated from Harvard in 1893. Returning from Cambridge, where he had been uncomfortable, he began to teach at the College of Emporia, moved to the University of Oklahoma four years later, where he taught until 1908, and then went to the University of Washington, where he was successively assistant professor and professor of English until his death. At Washington he was an effective teacher, much beloved by his students, and he de-

veloped a notable series of courses in American literature; but his failure to publish was an obstacle to administrative and public recognition. However, the publication in 1927 of the first two volumes of *Main Currents in American Thought: An Interpretation of American Literature from the Beginning to 1920* changed all that. This work, besides winning a Pulitzer Prize, was immediately recognized as a classic in its field, and its author was lionized both in the United States and in England. Happy in his new fame, he continued work on the third volume, *The Beginnings of Critical Realism in America*, which he did not have time to finish before his sudden death in England on June 16, 1929, and which appeared in the form in which he left it in 1930. Among his other books were *The Connecticut Wits*, 1926, and *Sinclair Lewis, Our Own Diogenes*, 1927, but it is on *Main Currents* that his reputation continues to rest. Influenced by Morris, Ruskin, Taine, and the political program of the Populists, the work was not so much a history of American literature as an interpretation of the development of American thought in terms of the idea of democratic idealism, which he saw as the characteristic American idea.

PATTON, GEORGE SMITH, JR. (1885–1945), soldier. Born on November 11, 1885 in San Gabriel, California, Patton studied for a year at the Virginia Military Institute and in 1904 won appointment to West Point, from which he graduated in 1909. Commissioned second lieutenant and assigned to the cavalry, he served at a number of Army posts, quickly gaining a reputation for ability and driving energy. After taking part in Gen. John J. Pershing's expedition into Mexico in 1916 he was assigned to Pershing's staff at the head of the American Expeditionary Force sent to France in 1917. He received training in the use of tanks, then a new weapon, and commanded a tank brigade at St. Mihiel and Meuse-Argonne. After the war he returned to the United States and during the next 20 years fulfilled assignments in Massachusetts, Texas, Hawaii, and, principally, at Fort Myer, Virginia, where in 1938 he assumed command of the 3rd Cavalry. In 1940, with war seeming imminent, he was assigned to the 2nd Armored Division at Fort Benning, Georgia, and the following year became divisional commander. There and later in California he molded the 2nd, and then the larger 1st Armored Corps, into a highly efficient force. By this time a major general, he was sent with his command to take part in the North Africa campaign in November 1942; he occupied Morocco and early in 1943 took charge of the 2nd Corps in Tunisia. In July he commanded the 7th Army in the invasion and rapid capture of Sicily. It was during this campaign that, in an incident later much publicized, he slapped two hospitalized soldiers whom he suspected of malingering; he was sharply reprimanded by General Eisenhower and was widely criticized in the press. In the invasion of France that began on June 6, 1944, Lieutenant General Patton commanded the 3rd Army, which, in a series of rapid and boldly unconventional armored sweeps, advanced to the Rhine by March 1945 and then sped across Germany, cutting the country in half. Throughout this final campaign of the war, "Old Blood and Guts," as he was known, displayed at their height his characteristic qualities of courage, daring, and ruthlessness, wearing all the while his matched ivory-handled revolvers. He died in an automobile accident in Germany on December 21, 1945.

PAULING, LINUS CARL (1901–   ), chemist. Born in Portland, Oregon, on February 28, 1901, Pauling attended Oregon State College and after graduating in 1922 went to the California Institute of Technology where he took his Ph.D. in 1925. His primary interest was in the field of physical chemistry, and during 1926–1927, aided by a Guggenheim Fellowship, he studied atomic and quantum physics with leading European scientists in Munich, Zürich, and Copenhagen. In 1927 he returned to Caltech as assistant professor of chemistry, becoming a full professor four years later. His early investigations into the structure of crystals led him to consider the nature of chemical bonds and the structure of molecules, a line of research that was to prove the most fruitful in modern chemistry. Applying quantum mechanics to the problem, he developed his resonance theory of chemical valence by means of which he was able to construct a model for the benzene molecule, which had been inexplicable in conventional chemical terms. He published the results of these early researches in *The Nature of the Chemical Bond and the Structure of Molecules and Crystals*, 1939. In 1937 he became chairman of the division of chemistry and chemical engineering and director of the Gates and Crellin laboratories at Caltech. He began to turn his attention to more complex chemical structures, particularly the amino acids and peptide chains that constitute proteins. His researches were interrupted during World War II when he served on a number of government scientific boards, for which he was awarded the Presidential Medal of Merit in 1948. His work on protein structure was announced in a series of papers that won him the Nobel Prize for Chemistry in 1954. During his investigations of organic proteins he discovered a structural fault in blood hemoglobin that was responsible for hereditary sickle-cell anemia; and as he continued to look into hereditary defects and diseases that might be traceable to structural errors on the molecular level, he became increasingly concerned over the threat to humanity posed by radioactive fallout from the testing of nuclear weapons. He spoke and wrote in favor of a cessation of such testing, publishing *No More War!* in 1958. The same year he presented to the United Nations a petition signed by more than 11,000 scientists calling for a halt to nuclear testing. On October 10, 1963, the starting date for the U.S.-Soviet partial test ban treaty, Pauling was awarded the 1962 Nobel Prize for Peace, becoming the first person to win two Nobel prizes alone. (Marie Curie also won two, but one was for joint work with two other physicists.) In 1964 he resigned his professorship at Caltech, having given up his administrative posts six years earlier; from 1963 until 1969 he was associated with the Center for the Study of Democratic Institutions, and from 1967 was a member of the faculty of the University of California.

PEALE, CHARLES WILLSON (1741–1827), painter and naturalist. Born on April 15, 1741, in Queen Annes County, Maryland, Peale was apprenticed to a saddler at 13. He opened his own saddlery in 1762 but the business was closed down by Loyalist creditors when he joined the Sons of Freedom. He developed an interest in portraiture, seeking instruction from John Hesselius and advice from John Singleton Copley, and received funds from several men for study with Benjamin West in London from 1767. He returned to live in Annapolis, Maryland, in 1769, and his work was warmly received. In 1776 he moved to Philadelphia and painted government officials and important visitors to the country, becoming one of the foremost portraitists in America. He helped to recruit soldiers for the Continental Army and was made captain after serving in the battles at Trenton and Princeton in 1777. He was elected to the Pennsylvania General Assembly in 1779 but returned to painting after 1780. Most famous for his portraits of Washington, he completed nearly 60 based on seven actually from life; that of 1772 was the first painting of Washington ever done. Conservative rather than romanticized visions, they probably are accurate portrayals of the first President. He founded a museum (later the Philadelphia Museum and later still Peale's Museum) and supplied it with paintings and collections of natural objects, including the bones of a mastodon unearthed in 1801 in the course of the first American scientific expedition. He helped establish the Pennsylvania Academy of Fine Arts in 1805. He also wrote several books, including An Essay

on Building Wooden Bridges, 1797, Introduction to a Course of Lectures on Natural History, 1800, and An Epistle to a Friend on the Means of Preserving Health, 1803. He was accomplished also in the fields of taxidermy, shoemaking, carpentry, dentistry, and optometry. He taught all of his children to paint, and several—notably Raphaelle, Rembrandt, and Titian Ramsay—became noted artists and naturalists. He died in Philadelphia on February 22, 1827.

PEARY, ROBERT EDWIN (1856–1920), explorer. Born in Cresson, Pennsylvania, on May 6, 1856, Peary graduated from Bowdoin College in 1877 and two years later joined the U.S. Coast and Geodetic Survey. In 1881 he was commissioned a lieutenant in the Navy's civil engineering corps. From 1884 to 1888 his official duties were concerned with the surveying of a proposed canal route through Nicaragua, but during a six-month leave in 1886 he began his real career with an exploratory journey to the interior ice of Greenland. In 1891, with an 18-month leave, he returned to Greenland, wintered there, and the following spring sledged northward far enough to gain substantial evidence of the insularity of Greenland. The daring and difficult journey, during which valuable scientific observations were made, won Peary a considerable recognition which eased the problem of financing his explorations. He made more trips to Greenland in 1893–1894, 1896, and 1897, and transported two huge meteorites from the ice fields to the United States. In 1898 he published a record of his Arctic experiences in Northward over the "Great Ice" and announced his intention of reaching the North Pole. Securing a five-year leave from the Navy, he surveyed northern routes and passages from 1898 to 1902, failing, however, to reach the Pole. In 1905–1906, with the ice-breaking ship Roosevelt, built to his specifications and underwritten by the Peary Arctic Club, he sailed and sledged to within 175 miles of the Pole. After publishing Nearest the

Pole in 1907 he set out in 1908 on his final Arctic journey; accompanied only by his personal aide and four Eskimos, he reached the North Pole on April 6, 1909. On his return to the United States he learned that Dr. Frederick Cook, who had been with him in 1891, had claimed to have reached the Pole a year earlier, and a long and unpleasant controversy ensued. Nonetheless, after publishing *The North Pole* in 1910, Peary was voted the thanks of Congress and given the naval rank of rear admiral (retired) in 1911. In his later years he was much interested in aviation and during World War I organized the National Aerial Coast Patrol Commission and served as chairman of the National Committee on Coast Defense by Air. He died in Washington on February 20, 1920.

PEGLER, JAMES WESTBROOK (1894–1969), journalist. Born in Minneapolis on August 2, 1894, the son of a Hearst reporter, Pegler began working for the United Press in Chicago in 1910. He spent two years in high school and resumed work with UP, going to London as a foreign correspondent in 1916. During World War I he served in the Navy. Returning to the United States, he turned to the lucrative field of sportswriting. On the advice of a colleague, he changed his byline from J. W. Pegler to Westbrook Pegler. He was so successful with his brawny, rough reporting style and his choice of amusing or unexpected events to enliven the column, that he was hired in 1925 to write a nationally syndicated sports feature for the *Chicago Tribune*. On days when there was little news in sports, he turned to the world of international events, the subject of much of his later controversial reportage. He was hired by the *New York World-Telegram* in 1933 to write a nationally syndicated column of general commentary, called "Fair Enough." In it he vented what he called the opinions of the "average man." He attacked the Supreme Court, the Newspaper Guild, wealthy people, the income tax, other journalists including Heywood Broun and Walter Winchell, Upton Sinclair, and national figures from Elsa Maxwell to Franklin D. Roosevelt. He moved to the Hearst-owned King Features Syndicate in 1944, changing his column's name to "As Pegler Sees It." In 1954 Quentin Reynolds became the first to challenge his abuse in a libel suit and was awarded the highest amount in punitive damages ever paid by an American court. In 1962, after being edited frequently over his protests, he broke with the Hearst enterprises, and for two years wrote for *American Opinion*, the organ of the John Birch Society. He died in Tucson, Arizona, on June 24, 1969.

PEIRCE, CHARLES SANDERS (1839–1914), mathematician and philosopher. Born in Cambridge, Massachusetts, on September 10, 1839, Peirce was the son of Benjamin Peirce, the foremost American mathematician of his time. Educated largely by his father, Charles entered Harvard in 1855 and graduated after four years with a less than mediocre record. His interests were broad, ranging from physics through logic to philosophy, and for most of his life he pursued them concurrently. In 1861 he joined the U.S. Coast Survey and during his 30 years' association with it performed gravity research, helped compile a nautical almanac, and represented it at international conferences. He was awarded an M.A. by Harvard in 1862 and an Sc.B., the first such degree, the next year. He lectured at Harvard on the philosophy of science in 1864–1865, later lectured on logic, and carried on research at the Harvard Observatory. In 1867 he read a paper to the American Academy of Arts and Sciences in which he discussed the symbolic logic of George Boole, until then virtually unknown in America, and from then until the end of his life he was probably the world's leading logician. Little of his work was published, and an appreciation of his originality and brilliance in this field was long delayed. From 1879 to 1884 Peirce lectured on logic at Johns Hopkins University. As his work in logic had grown out of his concern with the foundations of science and mathematics, so he was led at the same time into a study yet more basic, an inquiry into ontology and epistemology. Departing from the realism of the medieval philosopher Duns Scotus, he gradually developed his own philosophical system, which he called pragmatism. He first clearly explicated this idea in 1878 in an article in *Popular Science Monthly*; he continued to develop his philosophy in considerable detail throughout his life, but again his work was considered too recondite by publishers and little of it came to public notice. In 1887 he retired to a remote home near Milford, Pennsylvania, and spent the rest of his life there in research and writing. Apart from the few articles he managed to have published in periodicals he had little income and was at times forced to accept financial aid from William James—in whose honor he adopted the middle name "Santiago" or Saint James—and others. His "pragmatism" became, in the hands of James and John Dewey, the distinctive American philosophy, though Peirce rejected much of James' interpretation and modification and eventually applied the term "pragmaticism" to his own work in order to preserve its identity. He died on April 19, 1914; his reputation grew apace as his many papers and assorted manuscripts were found, assembled, and published.

PENN, WILLIAM (1644–1718), religious reformer and founder of Pennsylvania. Born in London on October 14, 1644, the son of Admiral Sir William Penn, the younger Penn studied for a year at Oxford, was dismissed for Puritan leanings in religion, continued his education during an extended European tour, and finally spent a year in law study at Lincoln's Inn in 1665. The next year he went to Ireland to oversee his father's estates and soon came under the influence of Thomas Loe, a powerful Quaker preacher. In 1667 he was briefly imprisoned for attending a Quaker meeting and in 1669, back in London, he was incarcerated in the Tower for writing heterodox theological

texts. While there he composed *No Cross, No Crown*, an influential exposition of Quaker-Puritan morality. In 1670 he was again arrested for street preaching; he pleaded his own case, persuaded the jury and, contrary to the judge's direction, was acquitted, whereupon the jury was arrested. The eventual vindication of the jurymen in this "Bushell's case" was a landmark in English law. In that same year he wrote his lucid and thorough work on religious toleration, *The Great Case of Liberty of Conscience*. Upon the death of his father, also in 1670, Penn inherited a moderate fortune and a large claim upon the King for loans the admiral had made for the Crown. For several years he concerned himself with writing religious tracts and with missionary travels through Europe. He became a trustee of the West New Jersey province and played a considerable role in establishing in 1677 the "Concessions and Agreements" for its government; this document was a remarkable outline of libertarian and democratic principles and was unique in its provisions for the fair treatment of Indians. In 1681, in order to create a commonwealth of toleration for Quakers and other dissenters, he pressed his claim against the King and was granted the huge tract of land in America that he named, at the King's urging, Pennsylvania in his father's honor. The following year he secured the "lower counties" (now Delaware) from the Duke of York. The Frame of Government that he drew up for Pennsylvania was not so radical a departure as the Concessions for New Jersey had been, but it contained an innovation that made it a workable and self-adjusting constitution—an explicit amendment clause. He laid out the city of Philadelphia on a modern grid plan and took care to establish and preserve friendly and honorable relations with the Indians. From late 1682 until mid-1684 Penn was in America, inspecting his province and visiting other colonies; but a boundary dispute called him back to England, where, in the court of James II—formerly the Duke of York—he enjoyed considerable influence and prestige. Soon after the accession of William and Mary, however, he fell under suspicion and during 1693–1694 Pennsylvania was removed from his proprietorship. During these years of virtual retirement he wrote several important works, including *An Essay Towards the Present and Future Peace of Europe*, 1693, in which he proposed a system of arbitration among disputing nations, and, for the Board of Trade in London, a plan of union for the American colonies. At last, his troubles at home somewhat cleared and new ones developing in Pennsylvania, he returned there in December 1699; he successfully solved many of the province's problems but new difficulties with his affairs in England prevented his remaining in America and he left late in 1701. His last years were difficult; his deputy governors for Pennsylvania were ill-chosen, his oldest son was a disappointing prodigal, and he spent several months in debtors' prison for the malfeasance of his steward. He was at the point of selling Pennsylvania to the Crown when a stroke rendered him virtually helpless; he died on July 30, 1718.

PERKINS, FRANCES (1882–1965), public official. Born in Boston on April 10, 1882, Miss Perkins graduated from Mount Holyoke College in 1902 and for some years taught school and served as a social worker for the Episcopal Church. She worked for a time with Jane Addams at Hull House in Chicago and then resumed her studies at the Wharton School of Finance and Commerce, the University of Pennsylvania, and Columbia University, where she took an M.A. in social economics in 1910. From that year until 1912 she was executive secretary of the Consumers League of New York, directing studies of working conditions and hours and female and child labor. She led the lobbying efforts that resulted in state legislation on factory safety standards in 1911 and on hours and wages in 1913. She was appointed in 1919 to head the State Industrial Commission by Governor Al Smith and was retained in that position by his

successor, Franklin D. Roosevelt, who in 1929 appointed her state industrial commissioner. She was, both before and after the onset of the Great Depression in 1929, a strong advocate of unemployment insurance and close government supervision of fiscal policy. When Roosevelt assumed the presidency in 1933 he named Miss Perkins secretary of labor, making her the first woman to serve in a Cabinet position. For twelve years she oversaw an unprecedented program of government interest in labor, during a period when labor itself was experiencing great new problems. She was directly responsible for supervising New Deal labor legislation, particularly the Fair Labor Standards Act. During her tenure the Department's activities were greatly extended, and much of the controversy surrounding the New Deal devolved upon her. She left the Cabinet in June 1945; from 1946 to 1953 she was a civil service commissioner in Washington, D.C., and in subsequent years was a much sought after lecturer on labor and industrial problems. *The Roosevelt I Knew*, a record of her association with the late President, was published in 1946. She died in New York on May 14, 1965.

PERRY, MATTHEW CALBRAITH (1794–1858), naval officer. Born on April 10, 1794, in South Kingston, Rhode Island, Mathew was the younger brother of Oliver Hazard Perry. He joined the Navy as a midshipman in 1809 and saw his first service aboard the *Revenge*, commanded by his brother. His varied duties took him to the Mediterranean and Africa, to the West Indies to suppress piracy, and to Russia, where the Czar offered him a post in his naval service. From 1833 to 1837 he was second officer of the New York naval yard. Perry took a deep interest in naval education; he successfully advocated an apprentice system for the training of seamen, helped establish the course of instruction at the Naval Academy, and was an active supporter and officer of the Naval Lyceum. He was likewise a strong proponent of naval modernization and in 1837, taking command of the country's first steam warship, the *Fulton II*, he organized the first corps of naval engineers. From 1841 to 1843 he was chief of the New York yard and in the latter year assumed command of the African Squadron sent, pursuant to provisions in the Webster-Ashburton Treaty, to suppress the slave trade. During the Mexican War he commanded the expedition that captured Frontera, Tabasco, and Laguna in 1846 and the following year was in charge of naval support for the siege and capture of Veracruz. In November 1852 he sailed in command of a squadron, on his recommendation much strengthened, to attempt to secure a treaty with Japan, whose rulers were then pursuing a policy of total isolation from the West. Determined "to demand as a right, and not to solicit as a favor, those acts of courtesy which are due from one civilized country to another," he arrived in the harbor near Yedo, the capital, in July, 1853, and demanded an interview with the highest possible official in order to deliver President Fillmore's letter, threatening to use force ashore if necessary. The Japanese government acceded and Perry soon left, promising to return in a year to receive a reply. He returned in February 1854, distributed boat-loads of gifts, and accepted a treaty providing for hospitable treatment of shipwrecked sailors and for fueling and supply privileges at two Japanese ports. Perry returned to the United States in 1855; the next year the report of his mission was published as *Narrative of the Expedition of an American Squadron to the China Seas and Japan*. He died in New York City on March 4, 1858.

PERRY, OLIVER HAZARD (1785–1819), naval officer. Born in South Kingston, Rhode Island, on August 23, 1785, Perry, the older brother of Mathew C., entered the Navy as a midshipman in 1799. He served in the West Indies and the Mediterranean and from 1807 to 1809 was engaged in building and commanding coastal gunboats to enforce the Embargo. In February 1813 he was ordered to Erie,

Pennsylvania, to direct the construction of a naval fleet—consisting of ten small ships —for service on the Great Lakes. The building occupied most of the summer; in May Perry participated in the capture of Fort George on Lake Ontario and in August the fleet at Erie was ready for action. He moved his base of operations to Put-in-Bay, north of Sandusky, and awaited the appearance of the British fleet under Capt. Robert Barclay. Early on September 10th Perry sighted the enemy; the battle was joined shortly before noon, the main burden being borne by Perry's flagship, the *Lawrence*, which, despite the overall American superiority in firepower, was virtually destroyed. Perry transferred to the *Niagara*, continued the fight, and soon forced the British to surrender. Lake Erie was securely under American control and Perry sent to Gen. William Henry Harrison his famous message: "We have met the enemy and they are ours." Shortly thereafter he joined Harrison in the battle of the Thames and in October returned to the East. In January 1814 he was voted the thanks of Congress and was everywhere received as a great hero. After the war he saw further service in the Mediterranean and in 1819 was given command of a fleet sent on a South American mission. He contracted yellow fever and died on the Orinoco River on August 23, 1819.

PERSHING, JOHN JOSEPH (1860–1948), soldier. Born on September 13, 1860, in Laclede, Missouri, Pershing worked on his father's farm and taught school during his youth. He graduated from the Kirksville (Missouri) Normal School in 1880 and, though not planning an Army career, entered West Point, from which he graduated as senior cadet captain in 1886. Assigned to the 6th Cavalry, he participated in several Indian campaigns, including that against Geronimo and the Battle of Wounded Knee against the Sioux. He was a military instructor at the University of Nebraska for a time and there took a law degree in 1893. After further service in the West he was sent to West Point as an instructor in tactics. In 1898, a captain, he served in Cuba and shortly thereafter, having organized the Insular Bureau to administer Puerto Rico and the Philippines, was sent to the latter as adjutant general of the Mindanao province. He led his troops successfully against the Moro insurgents there in 1903, for which he was congratulated by President Theodore Roosevelt. In 1906, having fulfilled assignments with the General Staff in Washington and as military attaché in Tokyo, he was promoted from captain to brigadier general—over the heads of 862 senior officers—by an enthusiastic Roosevelt. After further service in the Philippines—where he put down another Moro rebellion in 1913—as an observer in the Balkans, and as commander of the 8th Brigade in San Francisco, he was sent to patrol the troubled Mexican border in 1915. The following March, after Pancho Villa's bloody raid on Columbus, New Mexico, Pershing led a large force into Mexico in pursuit of the bandit; but a year later the search ended without success. In 1917, now a major general, he was named to command the American Expeditionary Force to be sent to Europe; he arrived there ahead of his troops and set about planning for their deployment. Determined, with the support of the U.S. government, to preserve the identity and integrity of the AEF, Pershing was constantly at loggerheads with the Allied command and, except for a time of crisis early in 1918, adamantly refused to split his forces into replacement units for the French and British armies. Finally in September 1918, Allied commander-in-chief Marshal Foch gave Pershing and the independent AEF a combat assignment, the assault on the St. Mihiel salient. Success there was followed by the Meuse-Argonne offensive that led to the Armistice. Pershing returned to the United States in September 1919, was greeted as a hero, and by special act of Congress was made general of the armies, a rank never held before (though it had been created by Congress in 1799 for George Washington) or since. From July 1921 to September 1924 he was Army

chief of staff; after his retirement he remained, according to the terms of his rank, on active duty as the senior officer of the Army. He maintained an office in the War Department that was later transferred to the Pentagon. In 1931 he published his widely read memoirs, *My Experiences in the World War.* From 1941 he made his permanent residence in a special wing of the Army's Walter Reed Hospital in Washington, D.C., where he died on July 15, 1948.

PHILIP (c. 1639–1676), Indian chief. Born about 1639, in the region of the Wampanoags (part of what is now Massachusetts and Rhode Island), Metacomet, who was called Philip by the English, was the son of Massasoit, chief of the Wampanoag Indians. When his older brother, Wamsutta, or Alexander, died in 1662, Philip succeeded him as chief and promised to honor the peace treaty and generous land grants that their father had made with the Mayflower pilgrims. But conflict over interpretation of the land treaties created tension. The Indians were willing to let the settlers use the land, but had not conceived of being barred from it for hunting and fishing, while the English had definite concepts of "boundary" and "trespass." Despite Philip's promise, he was suspected as early as 1671 of planning revolt, and in that year was fined and partially disarmed. In 1675 an Indian informer called John Sassamon revealed Philip's plans for revolt and was murdered, purportedly by three Indians whom the colonists identified as the culprits and executed. Furious at this violation of their judiciary, the Indians began war before strategy was even decided upon. Philip's role as a war chief was not clear, but he is not now regarded as the leader that the colonists thought him to be; indeed, he may have tried unsuccessfully to restrain the younger braves from going on the warpath. Called "King Philip's War," the fighting began around Narragansett, raged through Plymouth and Massachusetts, and extended as far west as the Connecticut River. The Wampanoags were aided by the Nipmuck, Sakonnet, and Pocasset tribes, and were completely victorious until the opposition began ruining their corn crops, capturing their women and children, and offering amnesty to those who would disavow Philip's rule. Twelve towns were completely destroyed and thousands of settlers killed. In the final battle, on August 12, 1676, at Kingston, Rhode Island, the Indians were overwhelmed by colonists aided by Mohegans. Philip sought refuge in a swamp near Mt. Hope, in what is now Bristol, Rhode Island, but was found the day of the battle, and killed by an Indian aiding the English.

PHILLIPS, WENDELL (1811–1884), social reformer. Born on November 29, 1811, in Boston, of a wealthy and influential family, Phillips was educated in the Boston Latin School, at Harvard College, from which he graduated in 1831, and at the Harvard law school. Admitted to the bar in 1834, he practised briefly in Boston, but gave up his career to embrace the cause of Abolitionism. In 1837, after the murder of Elijah P. Lovejoy in the Alton, Illinois, riot, he responded passionately at a public gathering and delivered a spontaneous address that drew cheers. After that he traveled across the nation, using his oratorical skills to gain support for Abolitionism, prohibition, woman suffrage, penal reform, concessions to the Indians, regulation of corporations, and the union movement. He was a forceful and uncompromising speaker and on several occasions was nearly mobbed. He allied himself with William Lloyd Garrison on the slavery issue and contributed frequently to his newspaper, the *Liberator*. They agreed that the Constitution compromised weakly on the issue of slavery, that the North should separate from the South, and that Abolitionism should continue to have no political party affiliations, though Phillips did not follow Garrison in insisting upon nonviolence. It was over the issue of disbanding the American Anti-Slavery Society that the two broke apart in 1865; Phillips succeeded Garrison as president of the society

until it was finally dissolved in 1870. That year he was nominated by both the Labor Reform and Prohibition Parties for the governorship of Massachussetts. Unsuccessful in his campaign, he resumed traveling and speaking tours. He became a champion of labor, being far advanced of his time in this regard. Vigorously railing at academic conservatives at the age of 70, he espoused youth and progress. He always retained the prestige of his New England heritage, was impervious to criticism, and spoke to hostile and friendly audiences alike. He died in Boston on February 2, 1884.

PHYFE, DUNCAN (c. 1768–1854), cabinet maker. Born about 1768 near Inverness, Scotland, of a family named Fife, Duncan came to America in 1784 and settled with his family in Albany, New York. At first he was apprenticed to an Albany cabinet maker. In 1792 he moved to New York City and opened a joiner's shop, which came eventually to employ at least 100 workmen—carvers and cabinet makers—and made furniture for the wealthy families of the city. The finest American furniture maker of his day, Duncan Phyfe (he changed the spelling of his name around 1793) was unsurpassed in using mahogany, in heightening its texture and color, and in achieving perfect proportion, line, and detail. Precision in wood carving, design, and final construction made his pieces—notably couches, chairs, and tables—as sturdy as they were beautiful. His earlier designs were drawn from the Adam, Hepplewhite, and Sheraton traditions in English furniture. His decorations typically were period ornaments such as harps, lyres, bow knots, and acanthus leaves. After 1825 his designs reflected the popular taste for heavier furniture, the so-called American Empire style. His "butcher's furniture," as he himself called it, of the period 1830-1847, although characteristically well made, was a bow to popular taste and inferior to his earlier work. In 1837 his sons joined the firm, which became Duncan Phyfe and Sons. Ten years later he sold the business and retired. He died in New York City on August 16, 1854.

PICKERING, TIMOTHY (1745–1829), soldier, public official, and political leader. Born in Salem, Massachusetts, on July 17, 1745, Pickering graduated from Harvard in 1763, returned to Salem, and was there admitted to the bar five years later. He held numerous town and county offices and from 1766 was a member of the militia. In 1775 he published a drill and discipline manual that was widely adopted by state militias and by the Continental Army. In the same year he became colonel of his regiment, and his valuable services in the early phase of the Revolution led to his appointment by Washington to the post of adjutant general in 1777. He became a member of the board of war and from 1780 to 1785 was quartermaster general. In 1786 he moved to Pennsylvania and in 1787 to Luzerne County, bringing with him a commission from the state government to organize the county and settle disputes with Connecticut settlers in the region. His three years there were difficult but fruitful; he helped found the town of Wilkes-Barre and was elected to both the Constitutional ratifying convention and the Pennsylvania constitutional convention in 1788 and 1789. In 1790 he applied to President Washington for the office of postmaster general; he received instead a mission to the Seneca Indians. He was offered his desired Cabinet post in 1791 and held it for four years while continuing as Indian commissioner. In 1795 he became secretary of war and later that year, following the dismissal of Edmund Randolph, he took what was intended to be temporary charge of the State Department as well. He resigned his war portfolio in 1796 but was retained as secretary of state by President Adams; a Hamiltonian Federalist, Pickering came at length into conflict with Adams and was himself dismissed in 1800. Moving back to Massachusetts, he remained an influential Federalist leader and was in the Senate from 1803 to 1811. There and in the House of Representatives, from 1813 to 1817, he strongly opposed the policies of Jefferson and Madison, most particularly the Embargo and the War of 1812. He seriously considered secession on the part of New England and conducted private discussions and even agitated to that end. After 1817 he devoted himself to farming, in which he was a noted experimenter and advocate of scientific practice and education. He died in Salem on January 29, 1829.

PICKFORD, MARY (1893–   ), actress. Born on April 8, 1893, in Toronto, Gladys Mary Smith began acting at five. She went on tour at eight and four years later received a part in a play in which her mother was also appearing. At 13 she was brought to New York by producer David Belasco. She adopted the name Mary Pickford and starred in *The Warrens of Virginia*, for which she created the role of Betty Warren. She began working in the movies at 15 as an extra for D. W. Griffith, but returned to Belasco and played the ingénue lead of Juliet in *A Good Little Devil*. She had a screen hit with *Hearts Adrift* and in 1913 turned entirely to movie acting. Within two years her salary rose from $40 a week to $10,000 plus a share of the profits. She organized the Mary Pickford Corporation in 1916 to produce her films, among them *Daddy Long Legs*. Then, in 1919, she joined Charlie Chaplin, D. W. Griffith, and Douglas Fairbanks in establishing the United Artists Corporation. Her innocent gestures and facial expressions in ingénue roles won for her the title "America's Sweetheart." The public responded with enthusiasm to her marriage of 1920 to Douglas Fairbanks; during their 16 years of marriage they were Hollywood's leading couple. Her other famous films included *Tess of the Storm Country, Stella Maris, Pollyanna, Rebecca of Sunny Brook Farm, Poor Little Rich Girl, Little Lord Fauntleroy*, and *Coquette*, for which she won an Academy Award. She retired from the screen in 1932; she returned to the stage briefly in *Coquette*, 1935, and thereafter devoted herself to business and to various public service and charity activities. She published an autobiography, *Sunshine and Shadow*, in 1955.

PIERCE, FRANKLIN (1804–1869), public official and 14th U.S. President. Born on November 23, 1804, in Hillsboro, New Hampshire, Pierce was the son of a prominent Democratic politician in the state. He graduated from Bowdoin College in 1824, was admitted to the bar in 1827, and two years later was elected to the state legislature as his father began a second term as governor. He remained in this post for four years, the last two as speaker, and in 1833 was elected to Congress. In two terms in the House and from 1837 to 1842 in the Senate he was a quietly regular Democrat. From 1842 he served as federal district attorney for New Hampshire and practised law in Concord; he declined appointments to the Senate and as attorney general, but remained active in local Democratic politics. He served in the Mexican War as colonel and then brigadier general of volunteers under Gen. Winfield Scott. As the Democratic convention of 1852 approached, friends of Pierce prepared to nominate him for the presidency in the event of an expected deadlock among the leading candidates, Lewis Cass, James Buchanan, and Stephen Douglas. All went as anticipated and Pierce, unknown and unqualified, was elected President by a large margin over the Whig candidate, his former commanding officer. A nationalist before all, the new President tried to promote sectional unity in the composition of his Cabinet; taking his election as an expression of popular approval of the Compromise of 1850, he made every attempt to end the slavery controversy, but was altogether unsuccessful. In other respects, his domestic policy was marked by encouragement of transcontinental railroads; for one possible southern route a tract of land, the Gadsden Purchase, was acquired from Mexico in 1853, completing the outline of the United States that would remain unchanged for over 100 years. In 1854 he approved the Kansas-Nebraska Act that, while establishing two new territories and encouraging railroads and settlement, abolished the Missouri Compromise; with his power to appoint territorial officials, Pierce stood responsible for the preservation of peace in an area that in a very short time was the scene of a miniature civil war. Later in the same year a communication arrived at the Department of State from Pierre Soulé, U.S. ambassador to Spain whom Pierce had directed to meet with the ambassadors to Great Britain and France, James Buchanan and John Mason, to discuss the possible acquisition of Cuba; intended to be secret, the message leaked to the public and the Ostend Manifesto, as it came to be known, caused widespread concern, for it advocated forcible seizure of the island should Spain continue to refuse to sell it. The publicity effectively ended all such plans. In 1856 the administration extended recognition to the dictatorship established in Nicaragua by William Walker, an American adventurer who had led an armed party into that country, captured it, and who sought to introduce slavery there, with an eye to annexation by the United States. In the Democratic convention of 1856 Pierce was repudiated by being ignored; his ineptness rendered a second term out of the question. He retired to Concord and died there in obscurity on October 8, 1869.

PIKE, ZEBULON MONTGOMERY (1779–1813), soldier and explorer. Born on January 5, 1779, in Lamberton, New Jersey, the son of an Army officer, Pike attended school until entering his father's unit as a cadet at the age of 15. In five years he reached the rank of lieutenant. He was sent by Gen. James Wilkinson in 1805 to lead a party of 20 men to the source of the Mississippi River and to assert American claim to the area. He returned in eight months, mistakenly reporting Leech Lake as the source of the Mississippi, but he had informed Indians in the area that they must accede to American rule and warned British officers and citizens that they were violating American territorial rights by remaining in the area. In July 1806 he was ordered to travel southwest to the Arkansas River and gain information about the Spanish territories. Passing through Colorado, he attempted to scale the peak now named after him, but failed. On entering Spanish territory, he was taken without resistance to Santa Fe by New Mexican troops. Tried by authorities in Chihuahua, he was released in July 1807, but deprived of his notes and maps. His *Account of the Expeditions to the Sources of the Mississippi and through the Western Parts of Louisiana*, 1810, contained accounts of Santa Fe and Mexico that encouraged the American expansionist movement. Upon his return from Mexico, he was interrogated concerning his possible connection with the conspiracy of Aaron Burr and General Wilkinson to build an empire in the Southwest. He was cleared of all charges by the secretary of war. A brigadier general in the War of 1812, he was killed on April 27, 1813 while leading a victorious attack on York (now Toronto), Canada.

PINCHOT, GIFFORD (1865–1946), forester and public official. Born on August 11, 1865, in Simsbury, Connecticut, Pinchot graduated from Yale in 1889 and for a time studied in Europe, primarily at the École Nationale Forestière in France. In 1892, at the Vanderbilt Forest in Biltmore, North Carolina, he undertook the first systematic forestry work done in the United States. Four years later he became a member of the National Forest Commission created to draw up a plan for government forest reserves. In 1897 he became an adviser to the secretary of the interior on these reserves and the next year was named chief of the Division of Forestry (later the Bureau of Forestry and later still the Forest Service), a post he held until 1910. Under his guidance the service was greatly extended and a heightened awareness of conservation problems was brought home to the American public. In 1902 he toured and made recommendations on the management of the forests in the Philippines. The following year he became professor of forestry at the Yale School of Forestry, which he had founded, and held the position until retiring as professor emeritus in 1936. He served on a large number of governmental bodies, including the Committee on Public Lands in 1903, the Inland Waterways Commission in 1907, and as chairman of the President's Commission on Country Life in 1908. Also in 1908 he became chairman of the National Conservation Commission and from 1910 to 1925 was president of the National Conservation Association. He actively supported Theodore Roosevelt in the formation of the Bull Moose Party in 1912 and two years later ran unsuccessfully for the Senate in Pennsylvania on that ticket. From 1920 to 1922 he was commissioner of forestry in Pennsylvania and in the latter year, successfully bucking the regular Republican organization, was elected governor. His administration was marked by governmental and financial reform; he served another term from 1931 to 1935. He died in New York City on October 4, 1946. Among his many written works were *A Primer of Forestry*, 1899, *The Fight for Conservation*, 1909, *The Training of a Forester*, 1917, and his autobiography, *Breaking New Ground*, 1947.

PINKERTON, ALLAN (1819–1844), detective. Born on August 25, 1819, in Glasgow, Scotland, the son of a police sergeant, Pinkerton emigrated to America in 1842 and, after a year in Chicago, opened a cooper's shop in Dundee, Illinois. Working on a desolate island one day, he discovered a gang of counterfeiters and later led in capturing them. Similar successful exploits followed and in 1846 he was elected deputy sheriff of Kane County. An Abolitionist, he converted his shop into a way station for the Underground Railroad. He moved to Chicago when appointed deputy sheriff of Cook County, and joined the police force in 1850 as its first and only detective. During a series of railway and express robberies, in 1850, he opened his own firm, the Pinkerton National Detective Agency, a pioneer venture in America. The agency solved many of the railroad crimes and in 1861 disclosed a plot to assassinate Abraham Lincoln while the President-elect was passing through Baltimore on the way to his inauguration. Plans for Lincoln's journey were changed and the plot foiled. At Gen. George B. McClellan's request, Pinkerton organized the secret service in the area of his command and followed him to Washington to head a department of counter-espionage, working in disguise under the name of Maj. E. J. Allen. He resigned in 1862 and after the Civil War resumed control of his own detective agency, though after 1869 he relinquished field work to his subordinates. The agency became particularly prominent for anti-labor union work, and the most famous "Pinkerton," James McParlan, was primarily responsible for crushing the terroristic Molly Maguires in the Pennsylvania coal fields. Pinkerton's files became invaluable to law enforcement bodies and he published a number of popular accounts of his work, including *The Molly Maguires and the Detectives*, 1877, *Strikers, Communists, Tramps and Detectives*, 1878, *The Spy of the Rebellion*, 1883, and *Thirty Years a Detective*, 1884. He died in Chicago on July 1, 1884.

PLATT, THOMAS COLLIER (1833–1910), businessman, public official, and political leader. Born on July 15, 1833, in Owego, New York, Platt studied for a time at Yale and then became a druggist in his home town. He was elected county clerk as a Republican in 1859 and soon became chairman of the Tioga County Republican Committee, meanwhile extending his business interests into banking. From 1870 he was a close friend and political ally of Roscoe Conkling and with him became a leader of the Republican "Stalwart" faction. He served in Congress from 1873 to 1877 and, as in all his public positions, was altogether unimpressive. In 1879 he became secretary and in the following year president of the United States Express Company, holding the latter post until his death. In March 1881 he joined Conkling in the Senate; in a dispute with President Garfield over New York patronage—Garfield insisted on awarding the choice job of collector of the port of New York to a "Half-Breed"—they both resigned in May of the same year. An appeal to the state legislature for vindication was denied and Conkling retired from politics, leaving Platt, the very type of a political boss, in control of the Republican machine. While his power within the state was enormous, his national influence declined. In 1896 he was again elected to the Senate and served there as an unobtrusive regular party man. He reluctantly supported Theodore Roosevelt for governor of New York in 1898, but soon became exasperated by his reformist notions and in 1900, in an attempt to remove Roosevelt from influence in the state, promoted his nomination for Vice President. But the death of McKinley elevated Roosevelt to the White House, and by 1903, when he was reelected to the Senate, Platt's power in New York was rapidly disintegrating. He left the Senate in 1909 and died in New York City on March 6, 1910.

POE, EDGAR ALLAN (1809–1849), author and critic. Born in Boston on January 19, 1809, Poe was the son of actors and before he was three was left an orphan. He was taken into the home of John Allan of Richmond, Virginia; with the Allan family he lived in England and Scotland from 1815 to 1820 and was schooled there and afterwards in Richmond. During 1826 he attended the University of Virginia, but his foster father's meager financial support and his own gambling losses brought about the end of his formal education. Relations with Allan deteriorated seriously and in 1827 Poe went to Boston, where he published a slim volume, *Tamerlane and Other Poems*, which failed to attract attention and left him in extremely straitened circumstances. Later in the same year he enlisted in the Army under the name Edgar. A. Perry. In 1829, on the death of his foster mother, he and Allan were temporarily reconciled. With Allan's aid he sought appointment to West Point. While awaiting his acceptance he published *Al Aaraaf, Tamerlane, and Minor Poems*, 1829. In 1830 he entered West Point, but after a few months another break with Allan prompted him to neglect his duties and early in 1831 he was dismissed. Traveling to New York City, he issued *Poems*, 1831, containing early versions of "Israfel" and "The Doomed City." For the next four years he was in Baltimore and began writing short stories; "Metzengerstein" appeared in 1832 and the next year "Manuscript Found in a Bottle" won a competition sponsored by the *Baltimore Saturday Visiter*. In 1835 he returned to Richmond as editor of the *Southern Literary Messenger*, which grew, under his guidance and because of the stories, poems, and criticism he contributed, into an influential periodical. He married his 13-year-old cousin in 1835; by late 1836 he had begun to drink heavily, was dismissed from the *Messenger*, and in 1837 went to New York. In 1838 he published *The Narrative of Arthur Gordon Pym* and engaged in free-lance journalism until becoming in 1839 editor of *Burton's Gentleman's Magazine*, in which he published "The Fall of the House of Usher" and other pieces. In the same year appeared *Tales of the Grotesque and Arabesque*. He resigned his position in 1840 but in 1841 became editor of the successor *Graham's Lady's and Gentleman's Magazine* in which appeared "The Murders in the Rue Morgue," credited with being the first detective story, and "The Masque of the Red Death." In 1842 drink and ill health lost him his job. In 1843 "The Gold Bug" was published in the *Philadelphia Dollar Newspaper*, winning a $100 prize and wide recognition for its author. "The Tell-Tale Heart" appeared in the same year. His reputation grew rapidly after his return to New York in 1844 and the publication of his most famous poem, "The Raven." Holding posi-

tions with the *New York Evening Mirror*, 1844–1845, the *Broadway Journal*, 1845–1846, and *Godey's Lady's Book*, 1846, he established himself as a leading, if often contentious, literary critic of the day while publishing *The Raven and Other Poems* and *Tales*, both 1845. During these years he produced "The Pit and the Pendulum," "The Premature Burial," "The Cask of Amontillado," and other stories that combined his power of cold analysis with his frenzied imaginations of horror and mystery. From 1847 he fell deeper into poverty and became more erratic than ever. He sought solace with a succession of women and occasionally fell victim to alcohol; to the same period, however, belong some of his best verse—"The Bells," "Ulalume," "Annabel Lee," "El Dorado," and others. After a relatively quiet summer in Richmond he traveled to Baltimore, where a final spree led to his death on October 7, 1849. His personal life had been almost continuously miserable, but his very misery found an answering chord in the great French poet Baudelaire, who studied him and translated many of his works in the 1850s, so that Poe became the first American author to be widely read and admired in France.

POLK, JAMES KNOX (1795–1849) public official and 11th U.S. President. Born on November 2, 1795, in Mecklenberg County, North Carolina, the son of a wealthy farmer, Polk suffered at an early age from frail health which left him incapable of farm chores. He labored therefore in preparatory schools, and at the age of 20 he entered the University of North Carolina, where he did particularly well in mathematics and the classics. He graduated in 1818 as salutatorian of his class. He entered the bar in 1820 and established a thriving practice. Socializing with influential members of the Democratic Party, he gained a following which aided his advance in state politics, where, once established, he displayed an ardent loyalty to Democratic principles and the industry and efficiency of an exceptional executive. Andrew Jackson, already a prominent figure in the party, was especially impressed by Polk's ability to communicate with both politicians and the populace. With Jackson's support, he entered the House of Representatives in 1825, where he remained for 14 years, and in 1835 was elected speaker. Deferring to the wishes of his party in 1839, he accepted the nomination for governor of Tennessee and was elected. But his interest was in national politics, and after two unsuccessful tries for a second term as governor, he returned to Washington. He allied himself once again with Jackson on two burning issues of the day: the annexation of Texas, and the acquisition of the Oregon territory from Great Britain, which occupied it jointly with the United States according to previous treaty. It became clear that Polk was the most able and articulate advocate of expansionism in the party. Jackson therefore endorsed him for the presidential nomination over Martin Van Buren. The country applauded him for his aggressive stance, and he was nominated as his party's first dark horse candidate in 1844. At the age of 49, he was the youngest man yet to be elected President. Though the Democrats had campaigned on Polk's expansionism and on the slogan "54°40' or fight," he approached the Oregon question open to compromise, and by dint of hard-nosed diplomacy secured agreement to a division along the 49th parallel in 1846. By that time, however, relations with Mexico had deteriorated completely; an attempt to settle outstanding claims and to buy California had been rebuffed by the Mexican government late in 1845 and Polk had immediately ordered U.S. troops under Gen. Zachary Taylor into the disputed border area between the Rio Grande and the Nueces. The President was already considering war when news was received in Washington that Mexican forces had crossed the Rio Grande and skirmished with American troops. War was declared on May 13, 1846. Though a military success, the two-year war was was heavily criticized at home, particularly by Abolitionists, who saw

it as a not-so-subtle way of extending the domain of slavery. With the signing of the Treaty of Guadalupe Hidalgo on February 2, 1848, the United States came into possession of California, and nearly all the territory of the Southwest. Despite having thus fulfilled the major promises of his campaign — and having covered others with the Walker Tariff and the independent treasury bill in 1846 — Polk lost popular support steadily during his administration, largely through his equivocation on the slavery dispute. A highly efficient and competent President, and one who was remarkably facile in handling Congress, Polk was nonetheless exhausted by his labors. He retired from the White House to Nashville and died three months later, on June 15, 1849.

POLLACK, JACKSON (1912 – 1956), artist. Born on January 28, 1912, in Cody, Wyoming, of Scotch-Irish ancestry, Pollack grew up with the western landscape, but became fascinated with the movement and activity of big cities. After completing his secondary schooling, he went to New York City, where he enrolled in the Art Students League under the tutelage of Thomas Hart Benton, a leading proponent of regionalism, who introduced him to the work of the Italian masters. Pollack reacted against the realism then current in American painting, turning instead to his own form of artistic expression. He unrolled yards of canvas onto the floor, splashing and weaving lines and splotches of many colors, textures, rhythms, and hues, claiming that his work was personal, controlled by his moods and not by objects. From these vast canvases portions were cut and shown as individual paintings. These compositions were the start of abstract expressionism, a movement that radically altered the path of American art. He held his first one-man show in 1943; several more followed as Pollack was recognized as being in the forefront of the new movement. Abandoning the use of brushwork completely by 1950, he poured paintings out of paint cans, walked about in them, and said that they had a life of their own. Pollack died in Easthampton, Long Island, New York, on August 11, 1956.

PONTIAC (1720?–1769), Indian chief. Born, probably around 1720, near the Maumee River in northern Ohio, Pontiac was the son of an Ottowa father and an Ojibwa mother. By 1755 he was chief of the Ottowa. After the victory of the English in the French and Indian War, he and the loosely knit confederation of tribes that he headed grew resentful of the British who, unlike the French before them, did not welcome Indians into their forts and planted and settled on Indian lands. In 1762 he enlisted in the confederacy nearly all the tribes of the trans-Appalachian region in a plot that came to be known as Pontiac's Conspiracy. British forts along the frontier were to be attacked simultaneously and frontier settlements then destroyed. In May 1763 Pontiac himself led a surprise attack on the garrison of Detroit under the command of Maj. Henry Gladwin. The siege lasted for a year, and when the British finally gained control of the region, it was discovered that nearly every Western fort had been ransacked and that settlements from Niagara to Virginia had been burned. After a preliminary truce arranged by George Croghan in 1765, he attended peace talks with Sir William Johnson in 1766 and signed a treaty, by which he thereafter abided. The figure of Pontiac as a symbol of Indian resistance appealed to popular imagination, and he became almost a legend in his own lifetime. There are various accounts of his death in 1769, but he was probably killed in Illinois by another Indian who had been bribed by an English trader.

PORTER, COLE (1893–1964), lyricist and composer. Born on a farm in Peru, Indiana, on June 9, 1893, Porter could play the violin well at 6 and the piano well at 8. His first song was published when he was 10, "The Bobolink Waltz." Despite these manifest talents, he went to Worcester Academy and Yale (where he wrote "Bingo Eli Yale" and the "Yale Bull-

dog Song") to study law at the encouragement of his grandfather. He entered Harvard Law School in 1914, but transferred to the school of music at the dean's suggestion, and wrote with a classmate, T. Lawrason Riggs, the musical *See America First*, which was unsuccessful on Broadway in 1916. That year he joined the French Foreign Legion and during World War I earned the Croix de Guerre for comradeship; he entertained troops with a portable piano that was devised for him. In 1918 he contributed to the score of the review *Hitchy Koo* and in 1924 to the Greenwich Village Follies. In 1928 five of his songs were used in a musical play, *Paris*, one of the songs being the amusing "Let's Do It," which enjoyed a warm reception and launched his career. The first of his successful Broadway musicals, *Fifty Million Frenchmen*, containing "You Do Something to Me," and *Wake Up and Dream*, with "What Is This Thing Called Love," appeared in 1929, followed by *The New Yorkers*, containing "Love for Sale," in 1930, *The Gay Divorcée*, with "Night and Day," 1932, *Anything Goes*, with "I Get a Kick Out of You," "You're the Top," "All Through the Night," and the title song, 1934, *Jubilee*, with "Begin the Beguine," "Just One of Those Things," and "Why Shouldn't I," 1935, and *Red, Hot and Blue*, with "It's Delovely" and "Down in the Depths on the 90th Floor," 1936. In 1937 he was injured in a fall from a horse and was confined to a wheelchair for the rest of his life. He continued writing, however, and in 1938 appeared *Leave It To Me*, containing "My Heart Belongs to Daddy," in 1939 *Dubarry Was a Lady*, containing "Friendship," and in 1948 his greatest artistic and commercial success, *Kiss Me Kate*, derived from Shakespeare's *The Taming of the Shrew*, containing songs that combined his own and Shakespearian idioms, "I've Come to Wive It Wealthily in Padua," "I Am Ashamed that Women Are So Simple," "I Hate Men," and "Were Thine That Special Face." In 1953 appeared *Can-Can* and in 1955 *Silk Stockings*. For the films *Born to Dance*, in 1936, he wrote "I've Got You Under My Skin" and "Easy to Love"; for *Rosalie,* 1937, "In the Still of the Night" and "Rosalie"; for *Broadway Melody,* 1940, "I Concentrate on You"; and for *Something to Shout About,* 1943 "You'd Be So Nice to Come Home To." In the genre of urbane, witty lyrics and sinuous music that came to be known as "the Cole Porter song," other memorable hits included "All of You," "Blow, Gabriel, Blow," "Don't Fence Me In," "From Now On," "From This Moment On," "I Love Paris," "Miss Otis Regrets," "True Love," "Why Can't You Behave," and "Wunderbar." He died in Santa Monica, California, on October 15, 1964.

PORTER, DAVID DIXON (1813–1891), naval officer. Born on June 8, 1813, in Chester, Pennsylvania, Porter received little formal education and at the age of ten made his first sea cruise, a pirate-hunting expedition commanded by his father, Capt. David Porter. When the latter became commander in chief of the Mexican navy in 1826, the younger Porter joined also, serving as a midshipman for three years. In 1829, after being released by Spanish authorities from imprisonment that followed the capture of his ship, he enlisted In the U.S. Navy, and for many years served with the Coastal Survey, the Naval Observatory, and on various routine cruises. In 1841 he was promoted to lieutenant. During the Mexican War he participated in the naval bombardment of Veracruz and Tabasco and for a time commanded the steamer *Spitfire.* After the war he returned to his earlier duties but, dissatisfied with his failure to advance, soon left to enter the merchant service. He rejoined the Navy in 1855, made two voyages to the Mediterranean to obtain camels for the Army's use in the Southwest, and from 1857 to 1860 was assigned to the Portsmouth Navy Yard. He was on the verge of resigning again when he was ordered to command the *Powhatan* on a relief mission to Fort Pickens, Florida, in April 1861. Promoted commander, he performed blockade duty along the Gulf Coast and made a short cruise in the West Indies. From November 1861 until April 1862 he helped plan a naval offensive against New Orleans; he recommended his foster brother, Commander David G. Farragut, for chief command, and was himself placed in charge of the mortar flotilla. The bombardment inflicted by Porter's command on Fort Jackson on April 24 opened the mouth of the Mississippi; later the same service was performed at Vicksburg. In October Porter was made acting rear admiral in command of the Mississippi Squadron and during 1863 he provided the necessary naval support for Union victories at Arkansas Post, Grand Gulf, and most importantly at Vicksburg; for his actions in the last campaign he was given the official thanks of Congress. After further campaigns on the western rivers he was called in 1864 to command the North Atlantic Blockading Squadron. In two expeditions he reduced Fort Fisher, defensive stronghold of Wilmington, North Carolina, and was again formally thanked by Congress. From 1865 to 1869 he was superintendent of the U.S. Naval Academy and there introduced many excellent improvements in organization and training. In 1866 he was promoted vice admiral. During 1869–1870, as advisor to Secretary of the Navy Adolph Borie, Porter was in virtually complete command of the Navy. In 1870, upon the death of Farragut, he became admiral. Nominally the senior officer of the service, he nonetheless found himself powerless and frustrated in these last years; his duties were limited to membership on the Board of Inspection. He died in Washington on February 13, 1891.

PORTER, WILLIAM SIDNEY (1862–1910), "O. Henry," journalist and author. Born on September 11, 1862, in Greensboro, North Carolina, Porter left his poverty-stricken home after a brief formal education and settled in Texas, trying various odd jobs including publishing a humorous weekly and writing a column for a Houston newspaper. In 1896 he was charged with embezzling funds from an Austin bank where he had worked from 1891 to 1894. He fled to Honduras rather than be tried and returned only upon reports of his wife's serious illness. She died in Austin, and he was thereafter convicted and imprisoned for three years. He began to write short stories in prison, publishing them under the pseudonym "O. Henry." Released for good behavior, he went to New York City in 1902 to devote himself to writing. Fascinated with the details of life in "Bagdad on the Subway," he concerned himself with the intricacies of the lives of anonymous people of the city. With the bustle of the urban environment as a backdrop he wrote episodic stories that featured irony, fate, sentiment, and coincidence. He never left the genre of the short story. His most famous works, like "The Gift of the Magi" and "The Furnished Room" (both collected in *The Four Million*, 1906) typically pictured the rather dull lives of ordinary people and then often surprised the reader with trick endings. He wrote prolifically, delivering a story every week to the *New York World*, as well as to other periodicals. Collections of his stories appeared in books regularly from 1904, and included *Cabbages and Kings*, 1904, *Heart of the West*, 1907, *The Trimmed Lamp*, 1907, *The Gentle Grafter*, 1908, *The Voice of the City*, 1908, *Roads of Destiny*, 1909, *Whirligigs*, 1910, and several posthumous volumes, among them *Sixes and Sevens*, 1911, *Rolling Stones*, 1913 and *Waifs and Strays*, 1917. He died in New York on June 5, 1910.

POST, EMILY PRICE (1873–1960), author. Born in Baltimore on October 30, 1873, the daughter of an architect, Emily Price Post was educated in private schools in New York City, among them Miss Graham's Finishing School for Young Ladies. A popular debutante, she was feted by Ward McAllister, author of the term "the 400." At the turn of the century financial circumstances compelled her to begin to write newspaper articles on architecture and interior decoration, and light novels, in one of which she unfavorably compared American social customs with the European. At the request of her publisher, she brought out *Etiquette—The Blue Book of Social Usage*, in 1922. Immediately popular, her charming presentation differed from other guides to manners in being directed to popular audiences rather than merely to the upper classes. It laid down fundamental rules that remained unchanged through the book's many printings ("corn on the cob, eating of," "fish, removing bones from," "nuts, at dinner or lunch"). Proper behavior, she believed, was a form of consideration of other people. Sections of the first edition reflected her own upbringing (Chaperons and Other Conventions) and were later modified to reflect modern customs (The Vanishing Chaperon and Other New Conventions). She added to later editions guides to television, telephone, airplane, and business etiquette. After 1931 she was a radio speaker and contributed a column on good taste to the Bell Syndicate; it appeared daily in some 200 newspapers after 1932. Her other books included *The Personality of a House*, 1930, *Children are People*, 1940, and *Motor Manners*, 1950. At her death in New York City on September 25, 1960, *Etiquette* was in its 10th edition.

POUND, EZRA LOOMIS (1885–   ), poet and literary critic. Born on October 30, 1885, in Hailey, Idaho, Pound was educated in romance philology at the University of Pennsylvania and at Hamilton College, from which he graduated in 1905. He taught briefly at Wabash College but was dismissed despite his academic brilliance because he would not bow to academic regulations. He went abroad to live in 1908, settling first in Italy, where he published his first book, *A Lume Spento*, then in London from 1908 to 1920, in Paris from 1920 to 1924, and in Italy from 1925 to 1945. In 1909 he published *Personae* and *Exultations*; more volumes followed, including *Ripostes*, 1912, and *Hugh Selwyn Mauberly*, 1920. His verse quickly attracted attention. It was personal both in content and treatment and highly unorthodox in style. His knowledge of medieval literature, Provençal singers, and troubador ballads pervaded much of his work, which often dwelt on obscure lore. He defined a poet's duty as interpreting his knowledge for his contemporaries, and he gave invaluable support and help to then unknown writers such as Robert Frost and T. S. Eliot. He fought for publication of Joyce's controversial *Portrait of the Artist As A Young Man* and *Ulysses*, and Wyndham Lewis' *Tarr*, and he carved *The Wasteland* out of Eliot's massive manuscript. He produced many notable works of translation, among them *Cathay*, 1915 and the *Noh* plays of Japan in 1916. His lifetime project, *The Cantos*, a huge, rambling work dealing with ancient history, the Renaissance, American history, and current events, was begun in 1917 and by 1959 had attained a total of 109 cantos. Its concept of individual morality rests on Confucian thought, of social mores on Pound's interpretation of Jeffersonian economics. Often highly esoteric, the work even utilized Chinese ideographs, and despite its difficulty had a profound and liberating influence on modern poetry. Pound's own theory of poetry, imagism and later vorticism, attempted to place verse in relationship to the other arts. In 1945 he was arrested and charged with treason for his pro-Fascist propaganda broadcasts from Italy during World War II. Judged mentally unfit to stand trial, he was confined to St. Elizabeth's Hospital in Washington, D.C., in 1946. Upon his release in 1958 he returned to Italy. In his later years he traveled extensively and was said to be revising *The Cantos*.

POUND, ROSCOE (1870–1964), educator and legal historian. Born in Lincoln, Nebraska, on October 27, 1870, Pound studied at the University of Nebraska, from which he received a degree in botany in 1888. Continuing his studies in botany, he received an M.A. from Nebraska in 1889, then went to Harvard to study law. But he stayed only one year, returned to Nebraska, passed the bar examination without a law degree, and practised until 1907. During the same time he continued his work in botany at the University of Nebraska, earned a Ph.D. in 1897, and directed the botanical study of the state from 1892 to 1903; he was the discoverer of the rare lichen *Roscopoundia*. He also taught at the university from 1899 to 1903, was dean of the law department from 1903 to 1907, and was a legal advisor to the state from 1904 to 1907, holding the post of commissioner of uniform state laws. The bifurcation of his career came to an end, for all practical purposes, in 1907, when he joined the law faculty at Northwestern; he went to the University of Chicago in 1909–1910, and then joined the Harvard law faculty; he was dean of the Harvard law school from 1916 to 1936. Resigning the deanship in the latter year, he was given a "roving professorship" and taught a variety of subjects until his retirement in 1947. After his retirement, at the age of 77, he continued to be active in many legal, editorial, and educational positions. Among other activities, he spent several years in Formosa reorganizing the Nationalist Chinese government's judicial system. During his long career he studied, taught, and wrote on many different fields of law. Among his many books were *Readings on the History and System of the Common Law*, 1904, *Readings on Roman Law*, 1906, *Outlines of Lectures on Jurisprudence*, 1914, *The Spirit of the Common Law* (perhaps his best-known book), 1921, *Law and Morals*, 1924, and *Criminal Justice in America*, 1930. During his later years he shared with Learned Hand the reputation of being America's leading jurist not on the U.S. Supreme Court. He died in Cambridge, Massachusetts, on July 1, 1964.

POWDERLY, TERENCE VINCENT (1849–1924), labor leader and public official. Born in Carbondale, Pennsylvania, on January 22, 1849, of Irish immigrant parents, Powderly went to work on the railroad at 13. Four years later he was apprenticed to a machinist and from

1869 to 1877 he followed that trade. His involvement in labor organization began in 1871, when he joined the Machinists' and Blacksmiths' Union; later he joined the Industrial Brotherhood and worked as an organizer in Pennsylvania. In 1874 he joined the Knights of Labor, at that time still a secret organization. He rose quickly in the Knights, serving on the committee on constitution at the first General Assembly in 1878, and in 1879 became Grand Master Workman, a position he held until 1893 (the last ten years as General Master Workman). His leadership of the Knights thus spanned the period of the organization's public (after about 1880) and major influence. Powderly was at the same time active politically; from 1878 to 1884 he was the Greenback-Labor mayor of Scranton, Pennsylvania, and he stumped often and in many states for candidates sympathetic to labor. He resisted always, however, efforts of others to form a labor party. More idealistic and optimistic than many other labor leaders, Powderly sought through the Knights to create a union for all workers, skilled and unskilled, to discard the use of the strike and other coercive measures, and to found labor-management relations on the basis of cooperation and arbitration. The Knights of Labor was at the time the largest and most powerful union organization ever established, its membership reaching nearly a million in 1886. In that year, however, Samuel Gompers led his cigar-makers union out of the Knights to establish the American Federation of Labor, and the Knights declined steadily thereafter, to a large degree because of the conflict with the A.F. of L. over the issue of craft unionism. Powderly was admitted to the Pennsylvania bar in 1894; in 1897 he was appointed by President McKinley, for whom he had campaigned, commissioner general of immigration. Removed from the post by President Roosevelt in 1902, he became four years later a special representative of the Department of Commerce and Labor to study the causes of European immigration. From 1907 to 1921 he headed the Division of Information of the Bureau of Immigration. He wrote many articles and pamphlets on the problems of labor and immigration, of which the most notable was *Thirty Years of Labor*, 1889. He died in Washington, D.C., on June 24, 1924.

POWELL, JOHN WESLEY (1834–1902), geologist and ethnologist. Born in Mount Morris, New York, on March 24, 1834, Powell made with his family successive moves to Ohio, Wisconsin, and finally to Wheaton, Illinois. He received his formal education from Wheaton College, Illinois College, and Oberlin College in Ohio, but took no degree. Though he had intended to follow his father into the ministry, an interest in natural science deepened and soon displaced the earlier ambition; he made long observing and collecting trips throughout the eastern Great Plains and became secretary of the Illinois Society of Natural History. He enlisted in the Army at the beginning of the Civil War, served with distinction, and emerged in 1865 as a major of artillery and with his right arm amputated at the elbow. He was quickly appointed professor of geology at Illinois Wesleyan College and in a short time became lecturer and museum curator at Illinois Normal University as well. In 1867 he made the first of his many exploratory journeys into the Rocky Mountain region; the earlier trips were intended as field work and training for students, but in 1869 he led a fully professional expedition, financed by the Smithsonian Institution and by Congress, down the Colorado River and through the Grand Canyon by boat. He continued to make government-sponsored explorations and in 1875 was placed in charge of the United States Geographical and Geological Survey of the Rocky Mountain Region. In addition to his work in geology, Powell had made on his many trips close scientific observations of the western Indians and was the first to establish a definitive scheme of classification of Indian languages. In 1879 he became the first director of the Bureau of American Ethnology; in the same year his survey group was merged into the newly unified U.S. Geological and Geographical Survey, of which he became director two years later. For both the Bureau and the Survey he was an able and farsighted administrator, and in both agencies he inaugurated a program of regular publication of proceedings and activities that greatly enhanced the scope and significance of the scientific work being done and did much to interest the public in the human and natural history of the continent. He resigned from the Survey post in 1894 but continued to direct the work of the Bureau until his death on September 23, 1902, in Haven, Maine.

PRESCOTT, WILLIAM HICKLING (1796–1859), historian. Born in Salem, Massachusetts, on May 4, 1796, Prescott was of a wealthy New England family; his grandfather had commanded the colonial troops at the Battle of Bunker Hill and his father was a well known lawyer. After entering Harvard College in 1811, he suffered an accident that affected his entire later life. While dining in commons, another student threw a crust of bread across the table; it struck and blinded him in one eye. In spite of this he completed his studies, graduating with honors in 1814; but though he hoped to enter his father's law office, his doctors warned that the sight would dim in his other eye—it was already affected—and he instead chose a literary career. He worked in a darkened study while assistants read to him; he took notes with a machine known as a noctograph, which guided his hand; an assistant then read the notes back, and he committed them to memory. His first book, the *History of the Reign of Ferdinand and Isabella, the Catholic*, three volumes, 1837, established his reputation as an historian. Profoundly interested in Spanish history, he followed this with the *History of the Conquest of Mexico*, three volumes, 1843, which was translated into many languages and became one of the most widely read histories in the English-speaking world. His *History of the*

Conquest of Peru, 1847, was almost as popular. He then embarked on a *History of the Reign of Philip the Second, King of Spain*; two volumes were published in 1855, another in 1858, but the work was incomplete at his death, on January 28, 1859. Possessing a vivid historical imagination, Prescott dramatized the lives and achievements of the early Spanish explorers of America sometimes to excess; he was occasionally verbose and inattentive to details. But despite minor changes that have been made by later anthropological research, his accounts have generally stood the test of time, and they remain, of course, wonderfully readable.

PRESLEY, ELVIS ARON (1935–), entertainer. Born on January 8, 1935, in Tupelo, Mississippi, Presley first sang in a church choir and at revival meetings, and on his 12th birthday began teaching himself to play the guitar (he never learned to read music). In 1953, having moved to Memphis, he graduated from high school and began driving a truck, while attending school at night to become an electrician. As a surprise for his mother, he cut a personal record that year at the Sun Record Company that was accidentally heard by the company's president. Signed to a recording contract, he made his first commercial record in 1954—"That's All Right, Mama" and "Blue Moon of Kentucky"—and achieved considerable local success. That year he toured the South as The Hillbilly Cat, performed on the *Louisiana Hayride* over a Shreveport radio station, and in 1955, after singing at a disc jockeys' convention in Nashville, made a lucrative agreement with RCA Victor, which released five of his records simultaneously, bringing him national fame. His first national television appearance was in 1955 on the Jackie Gleason *Stage Show*. In 1956 he began a seven-year movie contract, making *Love Me Tender*, followed in 1957 with *Loving You, Jailhouse Rock*, and *King Creole*, the last of which was released in 1958, while he was serving in Germany with the U.S. Army. He had by that time become a veritable industry, with innumerable products bearing his name, picture, or the titles of his songs, bringing billions of dollars in international sales. His music combined country and western and rhythm and blues strains into a more emotional, if sometimes less lyrical, style that came to be known as "rockabilly" and then "rock and roll." As rock and roll grew to the proportions of national mania among teenagers, Presley remained for years the dominant figure, creating instantaneous fads, calling up scores of imitators, and eliciting the same responses from audiences (and from disapproving elders) that, a decade or two before, had greeted Bing Crosby or Frank Sinatra. Though the obvious target for attacks on or analyses of the rock phenomenon, he remained apparently unaffected by the controversy; he performed as he pleased and in later years won a new audience with a series of recordings of favorite hymns, winning a Grammy Award in 1967 for the best sacred recording. His most popular records included "Blue Suede Shoes," "Hound Dog," "Don't Be Cruel," "All Shook Up," "Love Me Tender," "A Fool Such As I," "I Want You, I Need You, I Love You," and "Heartbreak Hotel."

PULITZER, JOSEPH (1847 – 1911), editor and publisher. Born on April 10, 1847, in Mako, Hungary, Pulitzer was tutored in Budapest and emigrated to Boston in 1864. He served in the Union Army until 1865, then held various jobs until becoming a reporter for the *St. Louis Westliche Post* in 1868. He became active in politics and was a leading figure in the Liberal Republican movement. In order to support his legal studies, he earned money by purchasing a defunct St. Louis newspaper and selling its Associated Press subscription to the *St. Louis Daily Globe*. Admitted to the District of Columbia bar in 1876, he nevertheless chose a career in journalism, purchasing the *St. Louis Dispatch* in 1878, combining it with the *Post*, and becoming sole owner by 1880. His editorial targets were soft money, high tar-

iffs, and corrupt politicians. The paper was immediately successful, but a scandal involving its chief editorial writer turned the public against Pulitzer; profits declined and he sought other involvements. In 1883 he purchased the *New York World* from Jay Gould and developed it into a respected paper, espousing the rights of the working class. For a few months during 1885 – 1886 he served in Congress. In 1887 he founded the *Evening World*. Failing eyesight forced him to abandon management in 1887 and in 1890 he gave up the editorship; he continued to exercise close watch on the paper's policies, however, and when a fierce competition began with William Randolph Hearst's *New York Journal*, involving outrageous sensationalism that prompted the phrase "yellow journalism," Pulitzer resumed control and went back to the original conservative and responsible format. At his death, the *World* was noted for concise, intelligent, accurate reporting, political independence, and fearlessness in exposing corruption in civic and national government. In 1903 he announced that his will would provide for the endowment of the Columbia School of Journalism, opened in 1912, and the establishment of Pulitzer Prizes for journalism, letters, music, and other specialized categories. He died in Charleston, South Carolina, on October 29, 1911.

PULLMAN, GEORGE MORTIMER (1831 – 1897), inventor and industrialist. Born on March 3, 1831, in Brocton, New York, Pullman left school at 14 to become a store clerk. In 1848 he was apprenticed to his brother, a cabinet maker, and in the course of seven years undertook independent contracting work, which he found more lucrative in Chicago, and moved there in 1855. Working on streets and buildings he accumulated enough capital to realize his earlier ideas for railroad cars with sleeping facilities. In 1858 he contracted with the Chicago and Alton Railroad to remodel two day-coaches into sleeping cars, using his principle of hinging an upper berth to the sides of the car, and in 1859 he built a third car. Although passengers were delighted with the new accommodations, the railways were reluctant to adopt them. He moved to Colorado in 1859 and ran a store for four years, in the meantime developing his plans for the Pullman car. About 1864 he returned to Chicago and applied for a patent on the folding upper berth and in 1865 on the lower berth, both inventions remaining unchanged in principle in contemporary cars. In 1865 the first Pullman car—"The Pioneer"—was introduced. Again public response was enthusiastic and this time several railroad companies ordered cars, despite their expense and their large size, which necessitated adjustments in bridges and station platforms. In 1867 the first combined sleeping and restaurant car was completed, followed by the first dining car in 1868, the first chair car in 1875, and the first vestibule car in 1887. In 1867 he organized and became president of the Pullman Palace Car Company, which grew to be the greatest car manufacturer in the world. He opened the first manufacturing plant in Palmyra, New York, then moved it to Detroit, and added plants in St. Louis, Elmira, New York, Wilmington, Delaware, San Francisco, and Pullman, Illinois, the latter being a controversial town south of Chicago built entirely by the company for the accommodation of employees. He was forced to relinquish its control by the state, after Eugene V. Debs's American Railway Union strike in 1894 against the Pullman Company. Outside of his own business, he owned the Eagle Wire Works in New York and was president of the Metropolitan Elevated Railroad in New York. At his death in Chicago on October 19, 1897, he left $1,200,000 for the founding of a free manual training school in Pullman.

PUPIN, MICHAEL IDVORSKY (1858–1935), physicist. Born on October 4, 1858, in Idvor, Hungary (now Yugoslavia), Pupin was the son of poor and illiterate parents who nonetheless encouraged him to seek an education. Having received his elementary schooling in his native town, in nearby Pancevo, and in Prague, he emigrated to the United States, landing in New York in March 1874. For the next several years he worked at various jobs while devoting his spare time to mastering English and qualifying himself for college. In 1879 he entered Columbia University, where he distinguished himself in mathematics; after graduation in 1883 he continued his studies at Cambridge University and, as the first John Tyndall Fellow, at the University of Berlin, where he studied under Helmholtz. He took his Ph.D. in 1889 and the following year was appointed instructor in mathematical physics at Columbia. In 1892 he became adjunct professor of mechanics and in 1901 professor of electromechanics. Among his major achievements were his invention of an electrical resonator device for determining the harmonic structure of an alternating electrical current, and his thorough analysis of the wave pattern in a vibrating string. The latter work, applied by analogy to electrical wave behavior, led to his development of a system of spaced inductance coils that greatly increased the efficiency of long-distance telephony and that was quickly put into operation in America and Europe. Soon after Roentgen announced his discovery of X rays in 1895, Pupin began experimenting with the new form of radiation and the next year, having constructed a machine with which he produced the first X-ray photograph in America, developed a method of greatly reducing the exposure time required for such a picture by means of fluorescence; he also discovered the phenomenon of secondary X-radiation. Pupin's autobiography, *From Immigrant to Inventor*, 1923, won a Pulitzer Prize, and his inventions made him a wealthy man. He retired from Columbia in 1931 and died in New York on March 12, 1935.

PYLE, ERNEST TAYLOR (1900–1945), journalist. Born on August 3, 1900, near Dana, Indiana, Ernie Pyle studied journalism at Indiana University and in 1923 accepted a position with a local newspaper shortly before graduation. He served in many editorial capacities in Washington and New York, finally securing a traveling assignment for the Scripps-Howard newspaper chain. His daily experiences were recorded in a column that was enthusiastically received and subsequently published in nearly 200 newspapers. His sensitive reports of the bombings of London in 1940 prompted his World War II writing assignments, which led him on campaigns with American troops into North Africa, Sicily, Italy, and France. His columns became immensely popular, in large part because of his comradeship with and understanding of the ordinary soldier in war. In 1944 he won the Pulitzer Prize, among other awards, for the stories he sent back home. Collections of his pieces were published as *Ernie Pyle in England*, 1941, *Here Is Your War*, 1943, and *Brave Men*, 1944. During the Pacific campaign on the islands of Iwo Jima and Okinawa, he visited a neighboring island, Ie Shima. There on April 18, 1945, he was felled by enemy machine-gun fire. He became a national hero, his last articles being published posthumously in *Last Chapter*, 1946.

PYLE, HOWARD (1853–1911), artist and author. Born on March 5, 1853, in Wilmington, Delaware, Pyle decided not to attend college but to study art with a private teacher in Philadelphia. Some years passed before he seriously undertook art as a profession, but in 1876 he moved to New York City, pursued further study at the Art Students League, and by 1878 had begun contributing illustrations regularly to various magazines, particularly *Harper's Weekly* and its related publications. In 1880 he returned to Wilmington and was soon established as one of the country's leading illustrators. In 1883 he published *The Merry Adventures of Robin Hood*, written and illustrated by himself; it was the first of a long series of highly popular children's books, most of them dealing with medieval England

or with pirates. Among them were *Pepper and Salt*, 1886, *Otto of the Silver Hand*, 1888, *Men of Iron*, 1892, *The Story of Jack Ballister's Fortunes*, 1894, and *The Ruby of Kishmoor*, 1908. At the same time he provided illustrations for works by Woodrow Wilson, Henry Cabot Lodge, Oliver Wendell Holmes, and James Branch Cabell; his renderings of American historical subjects were particularly noteworthy. He taught classes in illustration at the Drexel Institute in Philadelphia from 1894 until 1900, when he established a free art school in Wilmington; among his many students were Maxfield Parrish and N. C. Wyeth. Late in his life he turned to mural decoration and executed works for the Minnesota state capitol and other public buildings. In 1910 he traveled to Italy to study the old masters. He died in Florence on November 9, 1911.

QUINCY, JOSIAH (1772–1864), public official, reformer, and college president. Born on February 4, 1772, in Quincy, Massachusetts, the son of lawyer Josiah Quincy, known for his defense (with John Adams) of the British soldiers accused of murder in the so-called Boston massacre of 1770, young Quincy graduated from Harvard in 1790 and began his career in politics as a Federalist congressman from Massachusetts in 1805. As minority leader, 1805–1813, he stressed free trade and open communication among nations. He shocked the country early in 1811 by declaring it his opinion that the accession of new territory, if not unanimously agreed upon by the 13 original states, would invalidate and in effect dissolve the American union. His violent opposition to the country's involvement in the War of 1812, although manifesting party loyalty, was unpopular with his constituents, and he resigned from Congress in 1813. He returned home to devote himself to the affairs of Boston, serving also during the following decade in the state senate and house. He was elected mayor of Boston in 1823 and reelected five times. He was a great reforming mayor and instituted many changes in municipal government; on the strength of his name, his son Josiah and his great-grandson Josiah were both elected mayor of the city. Defeated by his enemies in 1828, he was named president of Harvard, in which post he served from 1829 to 1845. There, faced by a potent conservative element, he upheld the liberal traditions of the university, bringing the law school up to a professional level, building a conservatory, and hiring outstanding members of the faculty, including Longfellow and Benjamin Peirce. But he fell foul of student protests and riots, and was burned in effigy in 1841. His works were voluminous; *The History of Harvard University*, 2 vols., 1840, is perhaps the best known. Quincy spent the last 20 years of his long life in retirement, although after 1850 he wrote numerous political pamphlets in which he expressed his deep dislike, shared by other New England conservatives, of the West, of industrialism, and of democracy. But in his last public address, delivered at the age of 91, he strongly supported Lincoln and the Union that he had once attacked. Although he had been drummed out of the party in 1820, he called himself a Federalist until the day of his death, in Boston, on July 1, 1864.

QUINE, WILLARD VAN ORMAN (1908–), philosopher. Born in Akron, Ohio, on June 25, 1908, Quine graduated summa cum laude from Oberlin College in 1930 and received his M.A. and Ph.D. degrees from Harvard in 1931 and 1932. After study abroad he joined the philosophy department of Harvard, where he remained, after 1955 as Edgar Pierce Professor of Philosophy, for the rest of his academic career, and of which he was chairman in 1952–1953. He was a visiting professor at the University of São Paulo, at Oxford, at the University of Tokyo, and at the University of Adelaide, and was a fellow of Balliol College, Oxford, in 1953–1954. He served in the U.S. Navy in World War II. He was a fellow of the Institute for Advanced Study, at Princeton, in 1956–1957, and in 1958–1959 a fellow of the Center for Advanced Study in the Behav-

ioral Sciences, Palo Alto. A contributor to many of the learned journals in his field, he was also the author of a number of books, some of them quasi-popular in nature, among them *A System of Logistic*, 1934, *Mathematical Logic*, 1940, *Elementary Logic*, 1941, *Methods of Logic*, 1950, *From a Logical Point of View*, 1953, *Word and Object*, 1960, *Set Theory and Its Logic*, 1963, *The Ways of Paradox*, 1966, and *Selected Logic Papers*, 1966. He was also the coauthor of studies of A.N. Whitehead and Rudolph Carnap.

RABI, ISIDOR ISAAC (1898–), physicist. Born in Rymanow, Austria, on July 29, 1898, Rabi was brought to the United States in infancy. He received his B. Chem. from Cornell in 1919 and a Ph.D. from Columbia in 1927, whereupon he spent two years abroad, doing postgraduate work in Munich, Copenhagen, Hamburg, Leipzig, and Zürich. Until that time almost all of his work had been done in chemistry—he never formally studied physics, he once said, because that was the subject that most interested him, and he did not have to study it—although he had taught physics at the College of the City of New York from 1924 to 1927. In 1929, upon returning to the United States, he joined the Columbia physics department, where he remained until 1964, when he became a university professor, without departmental responsibilities and able to teach whatever he pleased. His major contribution to physics occurred in 1937, when he invented the atomic and molecular beam magnetic resonance method for observing spectra in the radio-frequency range. The development, subsequently by many other workers, of several different kinds of spectroscopic methods over a wide range of frequencies, depended greatly on his pioneering studies, for which he received the Nobel Prize for Physics in 1944. After 1940 he became deeply involved in the administration of research, serving from 1940 to 1945 as associate director of the Radiation Laboratory of the Massachusetts Institute of Technology, and after 1945 on many government commissions, including the general advisory committee of the Atomic Energy Commission. He was a delegate to UNESCO in 1950 and vice president of the 1955 Geneva conference on the peaceful uses of atomic energy. From 1962 he was a member of the general advisory committee of the U.S. Arms Control and Disarmament Agency. He was a visiting professor at many universities and institutions, received numerous honors and awards, and was involved in one way or another with almost all of the advances in his field of atomic and nuclear physics in his time. He published an autobiography, *My Life and Times as a Physicist*, in 1960.

RANDOLPH, ASA PHILIP (1889–   ), labor leader. Born on April 15, 1889, in Crescent City, Florida, the son of a Negro minister, Randolph attended grade school and the Cookman Institute in Jacksonville before traveling to New York City to gain a college education. He had worked as an attendant in his family's tailor shop, an errand boy for a white grocer, and a section hand on a railroad. In New York he held various small jobs while studying political science, economics, and philosophy at the City College of New York. While working as a waiter on a ship of the Fall River Line, he organized a protest against the filthy living quarters of the crew and was fired and blackballed by other shipping lines. He attempted to unionize shipyard workers in Virginia during the early years of World War I, but Negroes were physically beaten for participating in any movements toward unionization. He founded a magazine, the *Messenger*, to inform Negroes of their importance to war production and to encourage them to take advantage of it by demanding higher wages. After the war he addressed Negroes working in laundries, motion picture theaters, and the garment industry, expressing his belief that unionization alone would create pride among the members of his race and bring about their equal treatment and recognition in industry.

In 1925 he began his campaign to organize sleeping car porters. Having discovered that dues collected from Negroes for a purported "Benefit Association" were actually paid to spies to identify union "agitators," he waged a daring fight with the Pullman Company, via the *Messenger*, the press, and public lectures and debates. He appeared before the Interstate Commerce Commission, the Federal Mediation Board, and several courts. Against all odds, and the fear of the porters that supporting the movement would mean losing their jobs, he won legislative recognition for the Brotherhood of Sleeping Car Porters. In 1934 he secured an amendment to the Railroad Labor Act to include Negroes under its provisions. By 1937 the Brotherhood was strong enough to win long-overdue wage increases and other concessions from the Pullman Company. In 1941 he threatened President Roosevelt with a march on Washington of 50,000 Negroes to protest unfair employment practices in war industries and the government. Along with persistent lobbying, his demands on the President won establishment of the Fair Employment Practices Commission. In 1942 he was awarded the Spingarn Medal by the National Association for the Advancement of Colored People. He conferred in 1948 with President Truman and stimulated the executive order to desegregate the military. In 1955 Randolph was named a vice president of the newly merged AFL-CIO. In 1960 he established a branch of the AFL-CIO, the Negro American Labor Council, to clarify Negro grievances for the larger organization. In 1963 he directed the 200,000-strong March on Washington for Jobs and Freedom, the largest such protest expression in the history of the United States.

RANDOLPH, EDMUND JENNINGS or **JENINGS** (1753–1813), public official. Born near Williamsburg, Virginia, on August 10, 1753, Randolph was of a prominent colonial family. He was educated at William and Mary College and then took up the study of law under his father.

At the outbreak of the Revolution in 1775 his family returned to England as fugitive Loyalists while he became an aide-de-camp to General Washington. The next year he returned to Virginia to oversee the estate of a deceased uncle and was promptly elected to the state constitutional convention; he was also elected mayor of Williamsburg and became attorney general under the new state government. He was sent to the Continental Congress in 1779 and elected governor of Virginia in 1786, in which year also he led the Virginia delegation to the Annapolis Convention. He was sent the next year to the Constitutional Convention, where he proposed the "Virginia Plan" for the government of the states. He also served on the committee on detail, charged with writing the final draft of the Constitution. Considering the frame of government outlined in the final document to be insufficiently republican, he refused to sign his name to it; by the time of the Virginia ratifying convention in 1788, however, he had reconciled himself to it and joined James Madison in urging its adoption. When the new government was organized, he was the first attorney general; caught in the growing feud between Jefferson and Hamilton, he remained strictly neutral, and when at length Jefferson resigned in December 1793 Randolph succeeded him as secretary of state. Maintaining a middle course between then-warring France and Great Britain, and thereby between the Republicans and the Federalists, he was rewarded with harsh criticism from both parties. He drafted the instructions for John Jay's mission to London; the resulting Jay's Treaty demonstrated that his instructions had been ignored, and he was faced with the difficult task of mollifying France and the Federalists. In neither case was he entirely successful. Before he left the Cabinet, negotiations were begun with Spain that culminated in the Treaty of San Lorenzo, or Pinckney's Treaty, guaranteeing free use of the Mississippi to the United States. Charges of impropriety stemming from an intercepted message to the French government from its minister to America—in which it was hinted that Randolph might be susceptible to bribery—led him to resign in August 1795. He returned to Virginia and became a leader of the bar in that state; his most notable case was the defense of Aaron Burr in the treason trial of 1807. He died at home, Carter Hall, near Millwood, on September 12, 1813.

RANDOLPH, JOHN (1773 – 1833), public official. Born on June 2, 1773, at the "Cawsons" plantation in Prince George County, Virginia, Randolph was of a highly prominent family and counted Pocahontas among his ancestors. He studied for brief periods at Princeton, Columbia, and William and Mary, and for a time was under the tutelage of his relative Edmund Randolph, then attorney general of the United States. Until 1799 he was a rather carefree young aristocrat; in that year, however, he was persuaded to run for Congress and was elected. His rise to leadership was amazingly rapid, and at the opening of the Seventh Congress in 1801 he was made chairman of the Committee on Ways and Means and was thus leader of the House Republicans. A brilliant orator, with a sharp and acerbic wit that often became biting sarcasm, Randolph was at the same time a master of parliamentary procedure. His Republicanism was never strictly regular and, though he supported the Louisiana Purchase, he eventually broke with the administration over constitutional issues, on which he was a pure strict-constructionist. From his unsuccessful management of the impeachment trial of Supreme Court Justice Samuel Chase in 1804 and his opposition to Jefferson's attempts to obtain Florida, until the end of his long career, he was a political maverick, standing firmly and disinterestedly on principle. About 1810, in order to distinguish himself from a distant and despised relation, he began to add "of Roanoke" to his name. An aristocrat and a strong defender of states' rights, he opposed all nationalizing legislation in Congress; his opposition to the War of 1812 lost him reelection in 1813, but he was back two years later denouncing the tariff and the Bank of the United States. He declined reelection in 1817 because of ill health, but returned to the House in 1819 and remained for three more terms. From 1825 to 1827 he filled an unexpired term in the Senate and, defeated for reelection to that body by John Tyler, he returned to the House for a final term from 1827 to 1829. During the 1820s Randolph, who had always tended to be erratic, became at times unstable almost to the point of insanity; his rhetoric remained brilliant, but his subject matter often drifted to the irrelevant. In 1826, as a result of his comments on the election of 1824, he fought a duel with Henry Clay in which neither man was wounded. In 1829 he served prominently in the Virginia constitutional convention and the next year was appointed special minister to Russia by President Jackson. His health broke shortly after his arrival in St. Petersburg and he returned to Virginia in April 1831. He continued to decline mentally and physically until his death on May 24, 1833.

RANSOM, JOHN CROWE (1888–   ), poet and critic. Born on April 30, 1888, in Pulaski, Tennessee, Ransom graduated from Vanderbilt University in 1909 and was a Rhodes Scholar at Oxford from then until 1913. He taught English at Vanderbilt from 1914 to 1937, holding a professorship from 1927 to 1937. At Kenyon College he was professor of poetry from 1937 and editor of the *Kenyon Review* from 1939 to 1958, when he retired. His typically sardonic criticism appeared in many periodicals and reviews and was collected in, among others, *The World's Body*, 1938, and *The New Criticism*, 1941. *Poems About God*, his first book of verse, appeared in 1919, and was followed by *Chills and Fever*, 1924, *Two Gentlemen in Bonds*, 1926, and *Selected Poems*, 1945. A revised and enlarged edition of the last appeared in 1963. His total output was relatively small, but he was an important figure on the Southern literary scene in the period between wars, not least because of a succession of distinguished students at Vanderbilt and Kenyon. He joined a number of other Southern "agrarians" in publishing *I'll Take My Stand*, 1930, a collection of essays advocating a return to what can be described as a Jeffersonian way of life.

RAUSCHENBUSCH, WALTER (1861–1918), clergyman. Born on October 4, 1861, in Rochester, New York, Rauschenbusch was the son of an immigrant German minister. After schooling in Rochester he was sent to study in Germany, and in 1884, a year after his return, he was granted a degree from the University of Rochester. Two years later he graduated from the Rochester Theological Seminary, was ordained, and assumed the pulpit of the Second German Baptist Church in New York City. The living conditions of the lower working class people to whom he ministered made a deep impression on him, as did the writings of Tolstoy, Marx, Bellamy, and Henry George, with whom he was acquainted. With two colleagues he founded the Society of Jesus—later renamed the Brotherhood of the Kingdom—and began in 1889 to publish *For the Right*, a Christian Socialist periodical that continued for a little more than a year. During 1891–1892 he was again in Europe studying, this time with an emphasis on economics and social problems, and he returned to New York in time to witness, and be reinforced in his developing socialist beliefs by, the hardships of the economic depression of 1893. In 1897 he left the pulpit to become professor of New Testament exegesis at the Rochester Theological Seminary; in 1902 he became professor of church history, a position he retained until his death. His first book, *Christianity and the Social Crisis*, was published in 1907 and made him almost immediately a prominent national figure, the acknowledged leader of the "social gospel" movement that, though never organized, sought in various ways the amelioration of social problems through the workings of individual and social conscience and the establishment of a social order that

Rauschenbusch called "the Kingdom of God." Subsequent books maintained and further developed this position: *Prayers for the Social Awakening*, 1910, *Christianizing the Social Order*, 1912, *The Social Principles of Jesus*, 1916, and *A Theology for the Social Gospel*, 1917. The outbreak of World War I was a profound shock to Rauschenbusch; before it ended he died, on July 25, 1918.

RAYBURN, SAMUEL TALIAFERRO (1882–1961), public official. Born on January 6, 1882, in Roane County, Texas, of Scotch-Irish parents, Rayburn grew up on a farm in northern Texas. He attended a one-room schoolhouse in Flag Springs, traveling to Commerce to attend East Texas State College at 18. Having decided to enter politics, and with the stated ambition of one day becoming speaker of the House, he studied law and after receiving his degree practised in Bonham, Texas. He was elected to the state house of representatives in 1907 and became speaker in 1911. The following year he was elected to Congress and was re-elected 24 times, for a total service of 48 years and 8 months, a record. During 1931–1937 he helped mold much controversial New Deal legislation, including the Securities Act of 1933, the Securities Exchange Act of 1934, and the Public Utility Holding Company Act. His homely personality and remarkable aptitude advanced him in the House; elected Democratic leader in 1937, he became speaker of the House three years later and retained the post until 1957, also a record tenure. Firmly devoted to his party and his country, he held himself to be a Democrat "without prefix, without suffix, and without apology." In the belief that he was no orator, he made few political speeches, but he won members of both parties to his policies through personal contacts. He was considered one of the most powerful speakers in the history of the country, and was a master of legislative process. His patriotism and honesty made him a trusted adviser beyond the bounds of party; the numbers of his confidants included Presidents Roosevelt, Truman, Eisenhower, and Kennedy. He died in Bonham on November 16, 1961.

REED, JOHN (1887–1920), journalist and revolutionary. Born in Portland, Oregon, on October 22, 1887, Reed belonged to a wealthy family of social standing, and after completing his secondary education in Portland he entered Harvard. There he had a splendidly successful career, graduating in 1910. The next year he joined the staff of the *American Magazine* and proceeded to write and publish poems that were highly regarded at the time. He met Lincoln Steffens and Ida Tarbell in the course of his journalistic work and was aroused by them to an interest in social problems; but he quickly went beyond them and, in 1913, joined the staff of *The Masses*. The first of many arrests occurred in 1914, for attempting to speak in behalf of some Paterson, New Jersey, strikers. In the same year he was sent by the *Metropolitan Magazine* to Mexico to report on Pancho Villa's revolution; four months spent with Villa's army resulted in a series of brilliant articles that brought him a national reputation as a left-wing correspondent. The articles were reprinted as *Insurgent Mexico*, 1914. When war broke out in Europe, *Metropolitan* sent him to Germany, and articles recounting his experiences with the German, Serbian, Bulgarian, Rumanian, and Russian armies were collected in *The War in Eastern Europe*, 1916. He returned to the United States for an operation, married, and left again in August 1917, to arrive in Russia in time to observe the October Revolution. An enthusiastic supporter of the Bolsheviks, he became a close friend of Lenin's, wrote much of the Bolshevist propaganda dropped over the German lines, and wired articles and reports to the *The Masses* that led to an indictment of the magazine for sedition. He returned to America to help in the magazine's defense, was arrested several times for "incendiary" speeches, and published, in 1919, the book by which he is best known—*Ten Days That Shook the World*, an account of events in Russia in 1917. A member of the left wing of the Socialist Party, he was expelled from it for his radical views in August 1919, whereupon he helped to found the Communist Labor Party (as distinguished from the Communist Party, which in fact was bitterly opposed to his faction). The Red Scare of 1919 was by now in full swing, and he was indicted for sedition. By means of a forged passport, he made his way to Finland, was there imprisoned, but managed to reach Russia, where he was making speeches at the same time that a nation-wide search for him was going on in America. Excitable, with enormous energy and the possessor of an eloquent style, he seemed to be at the height of his career when he was stricken by typhus and died, in Moscow, on October 17, 1920. His body was buried within the Kremlin.

REED, THOMAS BRACKETT (1839–1902), public official. Born in Portland, Maine, on October 18, 1839, Reed graduated from Bowdoin College in 1860 and took up the study of law. In 1861 he went to California and was there admitted to the bar two years later; he returned to Portland and was admitted to the Maine bar in 1865. He quickly entered politics. He was elected as a Republican to the state house of representatives in 1867 and 1868 and to the senate in 1869; from 1870 to 1873 he was state attorney general and in 1876 he was elected to Congress, where he served until 1899. While not an orator in the grand tradition, Reed was an extremely effective debater, a skilled parliamentarian, and the possessor of a mordant wit. In 1882 he was appointed to the committee on rules and was soon the acknowledged leader of the House Republicans. He began his long campaign for the reform of the House procedural rules as a member of the minority, and not until the Republican victory of 1888 was he able to count on success. The next year he was chosen speaker and, with William McKinley and Joseph Cannon, devised a new set of rules for the more expeditious handling of

business: the most significant changes were the redefinition of quorum in terms of members present rather than members voting, and the grant to the speaker of discretionary powers in refusing to hear dilatory motions. He introduced the changes suddenly, assuming and wielding powers of his position in so vigorous a manner as to earn the title "Czar" Reed from opponents. After a little more than two weeks the Reed Rules were formally adopted on February 14, 1890. There followed a flood of Republican legislation, including the McKinley Tariff that brought the Democrats back into power in that year's election. After a brief period under the old regime, the Reed Rules were again adopted with his resumption of the speakership in 1895, a post he held until his resignation in 1899. His leaving Congress was the culmination of a break with the administration that centered on his bitter opposition to its imperialist policies in Cuba and Hawaii. He moved to New York City and enjoyed a lucrative law practice until his death on December 7, 1902.

REED, WALTER (1851–1902), physican. Born on September 13, 1851, in Gloucester County, Virginia, Reed was educated at the University of Virginia, where he was granted an M.D. after two years, and at Bellevue Hospital Medical College in New York City, where he received a second M.D. a year later. After working for several years for the boards of health of New York and Brooklyn, he gained a commission in the Army Medical Corps in 1875. For more than 20 years he served inconspicuously as a surgeon in New York, Arizona, and Baltimore, as professor of bacteriology and clinical microscopy at the Army Medical School, and as curator of the Army Medical Museum. In 1898 he headed a committee directed to investigate the outbreak of typhoid fever in Army camps; their report contributed significantly to the understanding of the modes of infection and thus the means of control of the disease. The following year he and an associate published the results of their investigation of yellow fever; they had demonstrated the falsity of the belief, then widely accepted, that the disease agent was a specific bacillus. In 1900, when yellow fever broke out among U.S. troops in Cuba, he was sent to head an investigative committee to do research into the cause and means of transmission of the disease. The idea that a particular species of mosquito served as the exclusive carrier of yellow fever had been proposed some time previously; Reed's observation led him to consider this possibility. In a long series of carefully controlled experiments he demonstrated that yellow fever was spread only by the *Aëdes aegypti* mosquito (then known as *Stegomyia fasciata*), and by it only under certain conditions. The researches were complete by February 1901; several co-workers had died of yellow fever during the course of the investigations, but the disease could now be completely controlled. A program to wipe out the mosquito vector was instituted by Army sanitary engineers under Maj. William C. Gorgas and had spectacular results: in 1900 there had been 1400 reported cases of yellow fever in Havana alone, but by 1902 there were none in all of Cuba. Dr. Reed returned to Washington, D.C., in 1901 and resumed his teaching position. He died suddenly of appendicitis on November 23, 1902.

REID, WHITELAW (1837–1912), journalist and diplomat. Born near Xenia, Ohio, an October 27, 1837, Reid graduated from Miami University of Ohio in 1856 and immediately began his lifelong efforts in behalf of the Republican Party, speaking throughout the state for Frémont, the party's presidential candidate that year. After the election, which Frémont lost, he entered journalism, beginning to write occasional articles and then becoming a correspondent in Columbus for several papers, including the *Cincinnati Gazette*, of which he was made city editor in 1861. He was a war correspondent for the *Gazette* in 1861–1862, and its Washington correspondent from 1862 to 1868. Horace Greeley, head of the *New York Tribune*, had observed his career with favor, and in the latter year prevailed upon him to join the *Tribune* as second in command in editorial matters. In 1869 Reid became managing editor. A loyal friend and supporter of Greeley, he tried to persuade him not to enter the presidential race in 1872; but when Greeley insisted, and was nominated by the Liberal Republicans, Reid, who took over the paper temporarily, supported him ably. After his defeat Greeley returned to head the *Tribune* again, but he soon died, and after a short but bitter struggle for control Reid emerged victorious. At the age of 35 he was thus the head of the most powerful American newspaper. He maintained its reporting at a consistently high level, which was all the more remarkable in an era when his great competitors, Dana, Pulitzer, and Hearst, were in varying degrees depending on sensationalism. He spent liberally to gather a glittering staff, and once proclaimed: "In making a newspaper, the heaviest item of expense used to be the white paper. Now it is the news. By and by, let us hope, it will be the brains." After 1882 he directed the paper's fortunes in a more leisurely fashion than before. He was a strong supporter of Harrison in 1888 and was rewarded with the ministry to France; he spent three happy years in Paris, entertaining lavishly, making many important new friends, and doing his country's business quietly and well. He was the Republican vice-presidential nominee in 1892, and his and Harrison's defeat by Cleveland embittered him, though he had supported Cleveland's reform administration in New York State previously. He was an early supporter of McKinley, who rewarded him by special diplomatic assignments — for example, special ambassador to England at Queen Victoria's jubilee — and transferred his loyalty to Roosevelt after some initial suspicion. He was named ambassador to Great Britain in 1905, and before sailing for London, in May of that year, relinquished editorial though not financial control of the *Tribune*. He died in London after a brief illness on

December 15, 1912; during his last years he enjoyed the esteem of most of his compatriots, and he is still regarded as one of the most distinguished journalists of his time.

REMINGTON, FREDERIC (1861–1909), illustrator and sculptor. Born on October 4, 1861, in Canton, New York, Remington was educated at the School of Fine Arts at Yale (where he was on the football team with Walter Camp) and the Art Students League in New York City. He traveled West, became a cowboy, and worked on a mule and sheep ranch. He sketched constantly and resolved to become an illustrator. All the time and money he could muster were used for traveling and illustrating: he visited Germany, Russia, North Africa, and Cuba—where he was an artist and correspondent during the Spanish-American War—and he spanned the North American continent. He chose for subjects men living close to nature—cowboys, Indians, soldiers, and frontiersmen. He painted bucking broncoes and modeled them in bronze relief sculpture; his human beings were alive with motion and all his works were remarkable for capturing the action and mood of a moment. Dedicated to accuracy in the smallest detail, he kept a reference collection of cowboy, Indian, and Army garb in his studio. Notable examples of his sculpture were "The Bronco Buster" and "The Wounded Bunkie." His books were illustrated profusely, written in a concise, journalistic style, and dealt with the subject matter of his art. They included *Pony Tracks*, 1895, *Men with the Bark On*, 1900, and *The Way of an Indian*, 1906. He died in his home in Ridgefield, Connecticut, on December 26, 1909.

UNCLE REMUS see HARRIS, JOEL CHANDLER

REUTHER, WALTER PHILIP (1907–1970), labor leader. Born in Wheeling, West Virginia, on September 1, 1907, Reuther studied for three years at Wayne University but left without a degree. He began as an apprentice tool and die maker in Wheeling when he was 17 and then, moving to Detroit, worked for the Briggs Manufacturing Company, for General Motors, and for Ford, from 1927 to 1932, for the last two years as a foreman at Ford. From 1932 to 1935 he toured through Europe on a bicycle, observing automobile plants and tool and machine shops, and returned to the United States determined to aid in the organization of automobile workers. In 1935 he founded and served as the president of Local 174 of the United Automobile Workers; he was associated with the UAW for the rest of his career, serving as president of the international union after 1946. He was president of the Congress of Industrial Organizations from 1952 to 1955, when he became president of the CIO division of the newly merged American Federation of Labor—Congress of Industrial Organizations. He made a notable contribution to the war effort in World War II by proposing a plan to produce aircraft by mass production methods in automobile plants, and he served on various government manpower and production boards during the conflict. He led the 113-day UAW strike against General Motors from November 1945 to March 1946, which ended with his union winning important wage increases and improvements in working conditions. A general or labor member of many government and philanthropic boards after the war, he was also active in civic work in Detroit. Author of numerous articles and speeches, he published *Selected Papers of Walter Reuther*, 1961, and *Education and the Public Good* (with Edith Green), 1963. He died in an airplane crash in northern Michigan on May 10, 1970.

REVERE, PAUL (1735–1818), silversmith and patriot. Born on January 1, 1735, in Boston, the son of a silversmith, Revere attended local schools and pursued his father's trade. In 1756 he joined a military expedition against Crown Point, a French fort where major fighting occurred during the French and Indian War. In six months he returned to Boston. By

1765 his silver shop was also a purveyor of copper engravings of portraits, music sheets, surgical instruments, crude political cartoons bolstering the patriot cause, carved picture frames, many for John Singleton Copley's portraits, and dental plates. Active in local politics, especially in recruiting volunteer political workers, he was appointed one of three advisors in the tea crisis and was a leader of the Boston Tea Party. He was the principal express rider for the Boston Committee of Safety and, when formally appointed a messenger for the Massachusetts provincial assembly, he was already a celebrated figure in the colonies. His ride to Lexington on April 18, 1775, warning the fugitive Hancock and Adams and the entire Middlesex countryside of approaching British troops, was immortalized in Longfellow's poem, "Paul Revere's Ride." He engraved the first Continental money and the official seal of the colonies; his military services were of minor value and after the Revolution he returned to his many crafts. His silverware was the finest in the nation and is highly prized today. He was also involved in the manufacture of gunpowder, copper bells and cannons, copper plating, and bolts and parts for frigates, including the Constitution — "Old Ironsides." He worked with Robert Fulton in developing copper boilers for steamboats. He daily wore uniforms of the Revolution until his death in Boston on May 10, 1818.

RICE, THOMAS DARTMOUTH (1808–1860), actor. Born on May 20, 1808, in New York City, Rice was reared in poverty. He learned the wood carver's trade, but became fascinated by the theater, working for a time at the Park Theater in New York and going on to Louisville to Smith's Southern Theater, where he was employed as a carpenter, lamplighter, and handyman. Through his persistence, he convinced the theater manager that he could perform "bit" parts, demonstrated his talent, and was allowed to create and put on solo skits between scenes. One of these, a song

and dance act called "Jim Crow," was first played to a receptive audience in 1828. The routine was based on Rice's observations of a Negro stable boy, jumping about and whistling as he washed down the horses. His impersonation of the boy's manner, dress, and shuffling dance established a stereotype that helped launch and maintain the highly popular minstrel shows of the 19th century. His subsequent blackface characters included jovial or shiftless plantation workers and Negro dandies. The tune of "Jim Crow" became a hit in America and England and hundreds of stanzas were added to its original chorus to suit various locales and occasions. Rice brought "Jim Crow" to New York in 1832, played in other major cities, and during 1836–1837 made a highly successful appearance in London. He wrote plays, among them Long Island Juba, 1833, Jumbo Jim, Ginger Blue, and Jim Crow in London, 1837, and Negro opera burlesques, one on "Othello." Joining in but few of his company's productions, he preferred to perform alone. He earned a fortune as a box office star, but his lavish style of life and erratic personal behavior led him to poverty. He died in New York City on September 19, 1860.

RICHARDS, THEODORE WILLIAM (1868–1928), chemist. Born on January 31, 1868, in Germantown, Pennsylvania, Richards graduated from Haverford College in 1885 and then enrolled at Harvard, where he took a second bachelor's degree in 1886 and his doctorate in 1888. After another year of study in Europe he returned to Harvard as an assistant, became an instructor in 1891, and by 1912 had risen to the Erving chair in chemistry. As a graduate student he had become interested in the precise determination of the atomic weights of chemical elements and this line of work occupied the major portion of his career. In making his investigations he insisted upon the utmost possible accuracy; he was particularly ingenious at discovering hidden sources of error in the purification of samples, the conducting of reactions, and in the measurements required throughout the process, and he devised a number of experimental tools and procedures to guard against them. Among his innovations were the use of quartz weighing apparatus, the "bottling process" to prevent contamination of samples by moisture, and the nephelometer to measure the concentration of particulate substances in suspension. The results of his work were a great refinement in the atomic weight values for a large number of elements (his measurements of lead helped confirm the existence of isotopes) and, perhaps more importantly, a great contribution to the development of chemistry into a precisely quantitative science. In 1914 Richards was awarded the Nobel Prize for Chemistry. In later researches he concentrated on studying the physical properties of solids, with special attention to thermochemistry and thermodynamics, atomic volumes, and compressibilities, and to each of these subjects he made notable contributions. In 1925 the Richards chair of chemistry was endowed at Harvard in his honor. He continued to occupy the Erving chair until his death in Cambridge on April 2, 1928.

RICHARDSON, HENRY HOBSON (1838–1886), architect. Born on September 28, 1838, in St. James Parish, Louisiana, the son of a cotton industry executive, Richardson attended public and private schools in New Orleans and excelled in mathematics. He attended the University of Louisiana and graduated from Harvard in 1859. He had intended to become a civil engineer, but his interest had turned to architecture in college, and his family sent him to Paris to study at the École des Beaux Arts. He worked in several architectural offices during the day and attended classes in the evening. When he settled in New York in 1866, he had achieved a reputation with his already individual style. He won two competitions in 1866, for the First Unitarian Church in Springfield, Massachusetts, and the Episcopal Church in West Medford. Two more awards,

for the Brattle Street Church in 1870 and the Trinity Church in 1877, both in Boston, established his nationwide fame. The latter design was a combination of French and Spanish Romanesque that came to be called "Richardsonian." In 1878, owing to the frequency of his work in Boston, he moved his office there. In 1882 he toured Europe and studied the Romanesque style of northern Spain, which he had incorporated in his own designs. He tempered his own sense of daring with a functional approach in his most successful buildings and his work was marked by engineering as well as architectural innovations. This was seen, for example, in the Pittsburgh Jail and Court House, 1880, the Marshall Field building in Chicago, 1887, and in the Boston and Albany Railroad stations at Auburndale and Wellesley, Massachusetts. His shingled country houses, among them the Stoughton house in Cambridge, relied on simple mass for their effect. Characteristic of his style was the use of graceful, expansive arches, interior ornamentation, and materials with inherent beauty, such as quarry-faced stone, which he had laid according to the texture and shape of each piece. Other architects, such as Charles McKim, John Wellborn Root, and especially Louis Sullivan, were inspired by the originality and spontaneity of his work; through them his influence extended into the 20th century. Richardson was a popular man who knew and worked well with his peers. He assisted the sculptor Saint-Gaudens, and used many of his designs for interior figures in the Trinity Church, as well as the stained-glass work of John LaFarge. He designed homes for John Hay and Henry Adams in Washington. Other major works included Sever Hall, 1878, and Austin Hall, 1881, at Harvard; the Ames and Pray wholesale house buildings in Boston, 1882 and 1886; the summer cottage of Rev. P. Browne in Marion, Massachusetts, 1881; and stone houses for J. J. Glessner and Franklin MacVeagh in Chicago, 1885. Having worked vigorously for many years despite weakening health, he died in Boston on April 27, 1886.

RICKENBACKER, EDWARD VERNON (1890–), aviator and businessman. Born on October 8, 1890, in Columbus, Ohio, Rickenbacker adopted his middle name and dropped the Germanic spelling of his surname, Rickenbacher, during World War I. With little formal schooling and a succession of jobs behind him, he began working for a railroad car manufacturing firm in 1905 and there discovered a deep interest in internal combustion engines and engine-powered vehicles. He began driving racing cars at 16. By the time the United States entered World War I, he was internationally famous as a daredevil speed driver with a world speed record of 134 miles per hour to his credit, and was rated 3rd among American drivers. In 1917 he enlisted in the Army and went to France as a member of Gen. John J. Pershing's motor car staff. With help from Col. William Mitchell he took pilot's training and was assigned to the 94th Aero Pursuit Squadron, which adopted the famous hat-in-the-ring insignia and was the first American flying unit to participate actively on the Western front, fighting the "flying circus" commanded by the German ace, Baron von Richthofen; by the end of the war the 94th had downed 69 enemy craft, of which Captain Rickenbacker accounted for 26. He earned nearly every decoration possible, including the Medal of Honor. His account, *Fighting the Flying Circus*, appeared in 1919. Returning to the United States, he organized the Rickenbacker Motor Company; the company dissolved in 1926, and the next year he bought a controlling interest in the Indianapolis Speedway, which he retained until 1945. He began working for the Cadillac Motor Car Company, and then for a number of airlines, including General Aviation Manufacturing Company, American Airways, and North American Aviation, Inc. In 1935 he became general manager and vice president of Eastern Airlines, and three years later became president and director of the line. The technical knowledge he gained throughout his career prompted his appointment as special representative of the secretary of war to inspect Pacific air bases in 1942. On his second mission over the Pacific, his B-17 was forced down and he and seven men (one of whom died) were set adrift on rubber rafts with only fish and rainwater to sustain them. After 23 days he was rescued and with a two-week rest, resumed his tour of battle fronts. In 1943 he published *Seven Came Through*. A film biography, *Captain Eddie*, was released in 1946. After the war he returned to Eastern Airlines until his retirement in 1963.

RIIS, JACOB AUGUST (1849–1914), journalist and social reformer. Born in Ribe, Denmark, on May 3, 1849, Riis was educated by his father and by a private tutor. He came to the United States in 1870 and after wandering from job to job for several years he was able to secure a position as a reporter with the *New York Tribune* in 1877. Eleven years later he joined the *Evening Sun* as a police reporter. He followed detectives into tenement areas and photographed children in rags, garbage-filled alleyways, and infested halls of apartment houses. His stories concentrated on the utter horror of slum conditions and exposed the institutions that perpetuated them. He made many foes among politicians and landlords but crusaded with great success among the people. Among his most influential supporters was Theodore Roosevelt, who responded to his work with enthusiasm. In 1890 he published *How the Other Half Lives*, a book that promptly shocked the nation's conscience and led to the first organized efforts to wipe out the worst aspects of tenement life. He carried on his crusade in several subsequent books—*The Children of the Poor*, 1892, and *Children of the Tenements*, 1903, among them—and in a steady stream of articles and lectures. His work anticipated and in part stimulated the "muckraking" period of American journalism. In 1901 he published an autobiography, *The Making of an American*. He died at Barre, Massachusetts, on May 26, 1914.

RILEY, JAMES WHITCOMB (1849–1916), poet. Born on October 7, 1849, in Greenfield, Indiana, Riley left school at 16 and worked at various careers from house painting to assisting in patent medicine shows, during this time becoming familiar with the habits, speech, and outlook of rural Indiana folk. As editor of the Greenfield local newspaper, he began writing poetry, and after joining the *Indianapolis Journal* in 1877 he achieved great popularity with a series of whimsical, friendly verses, written in a Hoosier dialect, and purportedly composed by "Benj. F. Johnson, of Boone." The series, which included "When the Frost is on the Punkin," was collected in *The Old Swimmin' Hole and 'Leven More Poems*, 1883. Although they were often obtrusively sentimental, the poems constituted a significant contribution to American letters in depicting rustic life and characters. Others among his numerous collections included *Afterwhiles*, 1887, *Pipes o' Pan at Zekesbury*, 1888, *Rhymes of Childhood*, 1890, *Poems Here at Home*, 1893, and *Home Folks*, 1900. In 1885 he retired from the *Journal*. Throughout his career he was sought after to read his verse and often shared the podium with humorist Edgar Wilson "Bill" Nye. He died in Indianapolis on July 22, 1916.

RIPLEY, GEORGE (1802–1880), editor and reformer. Born in Greenfield, Massachusetts, on October 3, 1802, Ripley graduated from Harvard in 1823, entered its divinity school, and was ordained a Unitarian minister of the Purchase Street Church in Boston in 1826. During 1830–1840 he wrote ten articles for the *Christian Examiner,* in which he displayed an attitude even more liberal than the broad Unitarian doctrine. Criticism led him to resign his ministry in 1841. In 1838, with F. H. Hedge, he began to edit *Specimens of Foreign Standard Literature* (eventually 14 volumes), which contained the translations of such philosophers as Schleiermacher that provided the New England Transcendentalists—among them Emerson, Amos Bronson Alcott, Orestes A. Brownson, Theodore Parker, and Margaret Fuller—with their basic doctrine, a belief that intuition rather than experience or logic reveals the most profound truths. He was a founder, editor, and contributor to the organ of the movement, the *Dial*, published between 1840 and 1844. In 1841 he helped organize the Brook Farm colony, which attempted to put their social ideals into practical use. One of several 19th-century communal experiments, Brook Farm achieved lasting fame because of its modern educational and disciplinary methods, and because almost all of the Transcendentalists taught or lived there at some point or contributed to its journal. He was editor of its weekly *Harbinger* magazine (the successor to the *Dial*) between 1845 and 1849, and president of the community throughout its existence. When its finances were finally exhausted in 1847, he moved to Flatbush, Long Island, and continued publishing the *Harbinger*. From 1849 until his death he was literary critic of the *New York Tribune,* and during that time recognized and commented upon the most significant books published in America, among them Darwin's *Origin of Species* and Hawthorne's *Scarlet Letter.* He was a founder of *Harper's New Monthly Magazine* in 1850 and editor of its literary department until 1854. Between 1858 and 1863 he produced with Charles A. Dana the 16-volume *New American Cyclopaedia.* From 1872 to 1880 he was president of the Tribune Association. He died in New York City on July 4, 1880.

ROBESON, PAUL BUSTILL (1898–   ), singer and actor. Born on April 9, 1898, in Princeton, New Jersey, of African and Indian descent, Robeson attended Rutgers University in New Brunswick, New Jersey, where he was named by Walter Camp to the All-American football team as an end in 1917 and 1918, and became a Phi Beta Kappa student in his junior year. He graduated in 1919 and entered the Columbia University law school, taking his law degree in 1923. He had been seen the year before in an amateur Y.M.C.A. stage production by Eugene O'Neill, who in 1922 offered him a part in The Emperor Jones. He refused this role but accepted another, in Taboo; his performances in 1923 in The Emperor Jones and in All God's Chillun Got Wings established him as an actor. With apparently more opportunity open to him in the theater than in the law, where he had experienced racial discrimination, he remained in acting. He became prominent as a singer as well, although he had never taken a voice lesson in his life. In 1926 he gave successful concerts of spirituals and gospel songs at the Greenwich Village Theatre and in New York City's Town Hall. He subsequently appeared in concert in Boston, Philadelphia, and Baltimore, and played as well in Black Boy, Porgy, and Stevedore. In 1930 he went to England to appear in Show Boat, Othello, and The Hairy Ape, and returned to Broadway an international star in 1934. For the next five years he traveled internationally, making the first of many visits to the Soviet Union, and appearing on the battlefield in the Spanish Civil War, singing Negro spirituals to the Loyalist soldiers. He claimed that his social and political views were subserved by his performing. In 1943–1944 he performed on Broadway in Othello, establishing the longest Shakespearian run in the American theater. In 1950 he was denied a passport by the U.S. State Department for refusing to sign an affidavit stating whether he was or ever had been a member of the Communist Party. In 1958 the government's action was disallowed by the Supreme Court. He appeared in concert in San Francisco and at Carnegie Hall and in 1959 again played Othello at Stratford-on-Avon. He lived in England and made concert tours of Europe and Russia until returning to the United States in 1963. After 1933 he appeared in the movies Emperor Jones, Showboat, Sanders of the River, King Solomon's Mines, Dark Sands, Jericho, and Song of Freedom.

ROBINSON, EDWIN ARLINGTON   (1869–1935), poet. Born on December 22, 1869, in Head Tide, Maine, Robinson was a collateral descendant of Anne Bradstreet. He grew up in Gardiner, Maine, and from 1891 to 1893 studied at Harvard. He spent six years in Boston and in Gardiner, working at various jobs and attempting to find an audience for his early poetry. At his own expense he published The Torrent and the Night Before, 1896, and the next year appeared The Children of the Night, both of which were unsuccessful. In 1899 he moved to New York and continued to lead a precarious existence until President Theodore Roosevelt, who had favorably reviewed The Children of the Night, offered him a customs-house job in 1905. In 1910 he issued The Town Down the River and in 1916 The Man Against the Sky. Much of his early verse was in the form of dramatic lyric and concerned the residents of "Tilbury Town," a provincial New England village modeled on his native Gardiner. With finely wrought structure and abundant evidence of wide learning, his poetry often seemed dark and pessimistic. His Collected Poems, 1921, won a Pulitzer Prize. With Merlin, 1917, he entered the realm of Arthurian legend from which he also drew Lancelot, 1920, and Tristram, 1927, the last a popular success and Pulitzer Prize winner. Other later volumes, which were primarily blank-verse narratives of considerable skill, included Roman Bartholow, 1923, The Man Who Died Twice, 1924 (Pulitzer Prize), Dionysus in Doubt, 1925, Cavender's House, 1929, Matthias at the Door, 1931, Amaranth, 1934, and King Jasper, 1935. He died in New York City on April 6, 1935.

ROCKEFELLER, JOHN DAVISON (1839–1937), industrialist and philanthropist. Born on July 8, 1839, in Richford, New York, Rockefeller moved with his family to Moravia, Owego, and in 1853 to Cleveland, Ohio, where he completed his formal education with high school. In 1855 he entered the office of a mercantile firm of that city and by 1859 felt competent to strike out independently in business as a partner in Clark & Rockefeller, a commodity trading operation that, with the Civil War economic boom, did quite well. In 1863, with the four-year-old petroleum industry already a thriving enterprise, he organized a new company with four partners to build an oil refinery in Cleveland; two years later he left the commission merchant business, bought out three of his oil partners, and devoted himself to Rockefeller & Andrews, within months Cleveland's largest refinery. Bringing his brother William into the business, John D. built a second refinery that in 1867 was merged with the first in Rockefeller, Andrews, Flagler, & Company; within three years the company had grown and had expanded vertically—including by then timber tracts, cooperage plants, sulfuric acid manufactories, warehouses, and tanker cars and wagon fleets—to such an extent that it required reorganization. A joint stock company, the Standard Oil Company of Ohio, with Rockefeller as president, was incorporated on January 10, 1870. The fierce competition among oil companies at that time manifested itself largely in the jockeying of transportation agreements and the playing off of one railroad against another in order to obtain preferential shipping rates and rebates. Standard, efficiently organized, managed with great foresight, and wielding tremendous economic leverage, secured highly favorable contracts from its shippers and was in a position to consolidate the greater part of the industry under a single unified command. Able to survive temporary depressions as smaller or less efficient companies could not, Standard, under Rockefeller's guidance, set about buying up other companies, driving many others out of business by sheer economic weight, and extending its vertical structure to include pipeline systems and direct marketing facilities. By 1878 Rockefeller dominated the entire industry. In 1882, in a move to circumvent state corporation laws, the various Standard subsidiary companies were entrusted to a nine-man directorate that was itself incorporated; the result was the Standard Oil Trust, the first of many such industrial combinations that allowed a long-developing public antipathy to monopolies to crystallize finally in the Sherman Antitrust Act of 1890. The Trust was ordered dissolved by the Ohio Supreme Court in 1892, and seven years later a new combination was effected under the head of the Standard Oil Company of New Jersey. By this time, though the public was unaware of it, Rockefeller had retired from active business and was devoting himself full time to philanthropy. To this he brought the same organizational skills that had built an industrial empire; at first he gave to specific institutions, such as the University of Chicago, founded in 1891 and ultimately the recipient of $35 million of Rockefeller money, but soon he turned to the idea of endowed philanthropic foundations. Of these he established four: the Rockefeller Institute for Medical Research in 1901, the General Education Board in 1902, the Rockefeller Foundation in 1913, and the Laura Spelman Rockefeller Memorial Foundation, named for his late wife, in 1918. His total benefactions during his lifetime totalled about $530 million. In his later years he kept much to himself, though he was not so averse to publicity as he had been during his business days. He died in Ormond Beach, Florida, on May 23, 1937.

ROCKNE, KNUTE KENNETH (1888–1931), football coach. Born on March 4, 1888, in Voss, Norway, Rockne emigrated with his family to the United States in 1893. He grew up and attended school in Chicago and, after several years working at various jobs, entered the University of Notre Dame in 1910. He starred on the Notre Dame football team and his brilliant use of the forward pass against Army in 1913 is generally held to mark a turning point in the evolution of the game. Upon graduation in 1914 he became an instructor in chemistry and assistant football coach at Notre Dame and four years later was made head coach. During the next 13 years he fielded teams that amassed an overall record of 105 wins, 12 losses, and 5 ties. Rockne developed an approach to football that featured speed, agility, and deception, rather than sheer brute force, and perfected the "Notre Dame shift" maneuver. He instituted the practice of substituting entire teams — his "shock troops" — during a game and was widely renowned for the fervor of his exhortations to his players. His backfield of 1924 was immortalized by sportswriter Grantland Rice as the "Four Horsemen." The success of his teams, combined with Rockne's own colorful and ebullient personality, attracted a huge national following. His career was cut short when an airplane in which he was traveling crashed in Kansas on March 31, 1931.

RODGERS, RICHARD (1902–), composer. Born on June 28, 1902, in Hammels Station, Long Island, New York, Rodgers learned to play the piano at 4 and wrote his first song, "My Auto Show Girl," at 14. He entered Columbia College and in his freshman year wrote the annual varsity show, *Fly With Me*, meeting Lorenz Hart, a recent Columbia graduate, shortly thereafter. They agreed to collaborate on songs with Rodgers as composer and Hart as lyricist. Their first song was "Any Old Place With You" for Lew Fields's production of *A Lonely Romeo*, 1919. Rodgers left Columbia in 1921 and studied under Walter Damrosch for two years at the Institute of Musical Art. In 1920 he had contributed to Sigmund Romberg's score for *The Poor Little Ritz Girl*. After a number of amateur productions, he and Hart created the Theatre Guild's *Garrick Gaieties* of 1925, for which they wrote "Manhattan" and "Sentimental Me." Their success was repeated in *Dearest Enemy*, containing "Here in My Arms," and *The Second Garrick Gaieties*, containing "Mountain Greenery," in 1925, *The Girl Friend* and *Peggy* *Ann*, 1926, *Connecticut Yankee*, containing "Thou Swell" and "My Heart Stood Still" and *She's My Baby*, 1927, *Present Arms*, 1928, *Spring Is Here*, containing the title song and "With a Song in My Heart," and *Heads Up*, 1929, *Simple Simon*, containing "Ten Cents a Dance," 1930, *America's Sweetheart*, 1931, *Jumbo*, 1935, *On Your Toes*, 1936, *I'd Rather Be Right*, containing "Have You Met Miss Jones," and *Babes in Arms*, containing "Where or When," "The Lady Is a Tramp," "My Funny Valentine," and "Johnny One Note," 1937, *I Married an Angel* and *The Boys from Syracuse*, containing "This Can't Be Love" and "Falling in Love with Love," 1938, *Too Many Girls*, containing "I Didn't Know What Time It Was," 1939, and *Pal Joey*, containing "Bewitched, Bothered, and Bewildered," 1940. In 1943 Rodgers began working with lyricist Oscar Hammerstein II. Together they produced *Oklahoma!*, 1943, containing the title song, "Oh What a Beautiful Mornin'," "People Will Say We're in Love," "Kansas City," and "The Surrey with the Fringe on Top"; *Carousel*, 1945, containing "If I Loved You," "You'll Never Walk Alone," and "June Is Bustin' Out All Over"; *South Pacific*, 1949, containing "Bali Ha'i," "Happy Talk," "There Is Nothin' Like a Dame," "Some Enchanted Evening," "I'm in Love with a Wonderful Guy," "I'm Gonna Wash That Man Right Outa My Hair," and "Younger Than Springtime"; *The King and I*, 1951, containing "Getting to Know You," and "Hello Young Lovers"; *Flower Drum Song*, 1958, containing "A Hundred Million Miracles," "I Enjoy Being a Girl," and "Love, Look Away"; and *The Sound of Music*, 1959, containing, besides the title song, "Climb Every Mountain," "Do Re Mi," and "My Favorite Things." They also wrote the motion picture score for *State Fair*, in 1945, containing "It Might As Well Be Spring." Rodgers wrote both words and music for the musical *No Strings* in 1962. Among numerous honors and awards received by him were a special Pulitzer award in 1944 for

Oklahoma! and the Navy's Distinguished Public Service Award for the motion picture score for *Victory at Sea*, 1952, later also a popular television series.

ROEBLING, JOHN AUGUSTUS (1806–1869), engineer. Born on June 12, 1806, in Mulhhausen, Prussia, Roebling studied engineering and philosophy (under Hegel) at the Royal Polytechnic Institute in Berlin and graduated in 1826. He emigrated to America in 1831 and purchased a large farm in Pennsylvania, but in 1838 he obtained an official position as an engineer on state canal projects. He invented twisted wire cable to replace hemp ropes in hoisting canal boats onto barges and in 1841 established a factory in Saxonburg, Pennsylvania, to produce it. In 1845 he constructed a wooden aqueduct over the Allegheny River; the next year he built a suspension bridge over the Monongahela at Pittsburgh. Thereafter he concentrated on designing suspension bridges, using wire rope from his new factory in Trenton, New Jersey, instead of chain cable. His great Niagara Falls double roadway bridge, completed in 1855, demonstrated the reliability of his methods, which subsequently were adopted by bridge builders throughout the world. In 1867 he completed a larger span over the Ohio River at Cincinnati that firmly established his reputation. His most famous design was for the Brooklyn Bridge. Its vast length, connecting Brooklyn and Manhattan over the East River, and its long open span, which removed all obstacles to navigation, were both revolutionary and, to some, unbelievable. His plans, which were originally submitted to city officials in 1857, were finally approved in 1869 and work was begun immediately. At the site, he sustained a relatively minor injury, but contracted tetanus, and died on July 22, 1869. His son, WASHINGTON AUGUSTUS ROEBLING (1837–1926), was born in Saxonburg, Pennsylvania, on May 26, 1837, and graduated from Rensselaer Polytechnic Institute in 1857. After a year in the wire-rope factory in Saxonburg, he joined his father in the construction of bridges. He served in the Army for four years during the Civil War, attaining the rank of brevet colonel. He again assisted his father on the Ohio River bridge at Cincinnati and then spent a year studying new engineering techniques in Europe. He was a principal assistant on the Brooklyn Bridge project from its beginning in 1869 and on the death of the elder Roebling shortly thereafter he succeeded him as chief engineer. He insisted upon overseeing every detail of the work and by 1872 had ruined his health. From his home in Brooklyn to which he was confined he continued to direct the project until the opening of the bridge in 1883. After four years in Troy, New York, he retired permanently to Trenton, New Jersey, in 1888 and lived quietly until his death on July 21, 1926.

ROGERS, WILLIAM PENN ADAIR (1879–1935), humorist and entertainer. Born on November 4, 1879, near Oologah in the Indian Territory that later became Oklahoma, Will Rogers grew up in cattle country and became highly adept with the lasso. Sent to a succession of boarding schools, he found formal education confining and finally gave it over entirely in 1898. After a time as a cowboy in Texas he took to travel and in 1902, in South Africa, joined Texas Jack's touring Wild West Circus as a rope artist. Two years later he returned to America and continued to perform in various Wild West and vaudeville shows, gradually introducing into his act humorous patter that, spoken with a distinct Southwestern drawl and delivered in an offhand and rather diffident manner, proved a delight to his audiences. Rogers rose quickly to stardom on Broadway, appearing in a number of musical revues and, after 1915, regularly in the Ziegfeld Follies. His wry humor—homely and good-natured but with a potential for sharp satire underneath—became even more popular as he turned to political topics. In 1922 he began writing a weekly column for the *New York Times* that was soon syndicated nationally; in 1926, while touring Europe as President Coolidge's unofficial goodwill ambassador, he began submitting daily reports to his readers and reached an audience estimated at 40 million. He wrote a number of books as well, including *The Cowboy Philosopher on Prohibition,* 1919, *The Illiterate Digest,* 1924, *There's Not a Bathing-Suit in Russia,* 1927, and *Ether and Me,* 1929. As early as 1918 Rogers appeared in motion pictures, but it was after about 1929 that he achieved real success in that medium; among his most popular films were *A Connecticut Yankee,* 1931, *State Fair,* 1933, and *David Harum,* 1934, Rogers died with pilot Wiley Post in an airplane crash near Point Barrow, Alaska, on August 15, 1935.

ROOSEVELT, ANNA ELEANOR (1884–1962), author, diplomat, and humanitarian. Born in New York City on October 11, 1884, Miss Roosevelt was of a prominent, well established family and the niece of Theodore Roosevelt. Her parents died during her childhood and she grew up in the home of her grandmother, who sent her to be schooled in England. In 1905 she married her distant cousin, Franklin D. Roosevelt, and was given away by her uncle, then President. She provided constant support and aid to her husband, particularly after his attack of polio in 1921 and during his long convalescence. She cultivated an interest in politics and public affairs that she maintained, though somewhat subdued, after Roosevelt was elected governor of New York in 1928. With his elevation to the presidency in 1932 she began her 12 years as First Lady, during which she shattered many precedents, set many more, and made her position into one of great, if unofficial, influence. Her newspaper column "My Day," which she wrote for many years, changed in emphasis from women's affairs to public affairs about 1939; in that year she used it to announce her resignation from the Daughters of the American Revolution in consequence of that organization's refusal to allow Negro singer Marian Anderson the use of its Constitution Hall for a concert. She actively promoted liberal causes, worked effectively for civilian defense early in World War II, and succeeded in becoming nearly as controversial a figure as her husband. Soon after the latter's death in 1945 she was named a delegate to the United Nations by President Truman. As chairman of the UN Commission on Human Rights she took a central role in drafting and securing the adoption of the Universal Declaration of Human Rights in 1948. She resigned her post in 1952 and for the next ten years traveled constantly, promoting her chosen causes, particularly the work of the UN. She was welcomed by heads of state around the world and was widely acknowledged to be the world's most admired woman. She remained active in Democratic politics, speaking at party conventions and campaigning in its behalf. She wrote prolifically, both books and articles; among the former were *This Is My Story,* 1937, *The Moral Basis of Democracy,* 1940, and *On My Own,* 1958. In 1961 she was reappointed to the U.S. delegation to the United Nations by President Kennedy. She died in New York on November 7, 1962.

ROOSEVELT, FRANKLIN DELANO (1882–1945), public official and 32nd U.S. President. Born on January 30, 1882, in Hyde Park, New York, Roosevelt was of a wealthy and patrician family. He was educated at Groton and Harvard, graduating from the latter in 1904. He studied for a time at the Columbia University School of Law, was admitted to the bar, and entered the office of a distinguished New York law firm. In 1904 he married Eleanor Roosevelt, niece of Theodore Roosevelt and his own distant cousin. His political career began in 1910 with his unexpected victory as a Democrat in a campaign for the state senate; during his tenure in that body he became identified with the interests of upstate farmers and with progressive legislation and reform generally. During the 1912 campaign he was easily reelected but his term was cut short, when, in payment for his strong support, President Wilson appointed him assistant secretary of the Navy in 1913. He held this post until 1920 when he was nominated for Vice President at the Democratic convention; defeated in the Republican sweep that year, he entered private business until, in 1921, he was stricken with polio. He maintained his political interests and connections during his long and difficult convalescence and, though by that time he had not regained full use of his legs, he accepted the nomination for governor in 1928. He outpolled Al Smith, the outgoing governor and Democratic candidate for President, and embarked on a progressive administrative program that won him easy reelection in 1930. He reacted swiftly and vigorously to the Depression and in 1931 secured the establishment of the nation's first state relief agency. He was the leading contender for the presidential nomination in 1932 and, with the skillful management of his close associate James A. Farley, won it on the third ballot. In the November election, which turned solely on the Depression issue, he won easily over Herbert Hoover and carried Democratic majorities into both houses of Congress. Between election and inauguration Roosevelt and his advisors — the "brain trust" — planned in detail what had until then been a relatively vague intent to relieve and reform the economy; on March 4th began the famous "hundred days" during which was enacted a sweeping, though unintegrated, program of legislation known as the New Deal. Government assumed new functions and powers and the nation was confronted by a proliferation of initialled agencies. The already existing Reconstruction Finance Corporation (RFC) was strengthened, banking was reformed and underwritten by the Federal Deposit Insurance Corporation (FDIC), and the Federal Emergency Relief Agency (FERA) began the work of alleviating human suffering among the 13 million unemployed. Other primary agencies included the Tennessee Valley Authority (TVA), the Civilian Conservation Corps (CCC), the

Farm Credit Administration (FCA), and the Home Owners' Loan Corporation (HOLC). Most important of all were the Agricultural Adjustment Administration (AAA), and the twin agencies of the National Recovery Administration (NRA) and the Public Works Administration (PWA). A second major legislative program, with its emphasis on reform, occupied 1934–1935 and is often referred to as the second New Deal. Major new agencies included the Federal Housing Administration (FHA), the Securities and Exchange Commission (SEC), the Works Progress Administration (WPA), the Social Security Administration (SSA), and the National Labor Relations Board (NLRB) established under the Wagner Act. Roosevelt won reelection by a landslide, carrying all but two states in 1936. (The election ended Maine's reputation as national political bellwether and occasioned Farley's famous variation on an old saw: "As Maine goes, so goes Vermont." His second administration was beset by serious difficulties. The Supreme Court had invalidated NRA in 1935 and AAA in 1936 and seemed likely to cripple the New Deal still further; Roosevelt thus proposed a plan to reform the Court by, among other things, adding up to six more members. This "court-packing" plan roused great opposition among already alienated conservatives and others, and only the Court's late approval of Social Security and the Wagner Act in 1937 averted a head-on collision between the President and the Congress as Roosevelt allowed the plan to die. The Wagner Act, "labor's Magna Carta," was also a source of trouble, for the guarantees of section 7a prompted a wave of union activity that often came to violence for which many charged Roosevelt with responsibility. The continued popularity of the New Deal among farmers and workers was never, however, threatened. The New Deal encouraged recovery, but to a degree impossible to determine; a cutback on government spending in 1937 caused a sharp recession, and its resumption ended it in 1938, but within a year foreign policy was engaging more attention than domestic problems and complete economic recovery became ultimately a function of war mobilization. Japanese aggression in China and the rise of Hitler in Germany brought about a slow deterioration of U.S. relations with both countries, but until 1939 Roosevelt held to a firmly neutral policy. In that year, however, following the invasion of Poland, he called for a "cash-and-carry" plan to modify the ban on arms sales to belligerents contained in the Neutrality Acts of 1935 and 1937, of which he had at the time approved. In 1940, by executive authority, he traded 50 overage naval destroyers to Britain for military bases in British possessions and finally, in 1941, the Lend-Lease Bill was enacted at his request. Roosevelt accepted the nomination for and election to an unprecedented third term in 1940, though by a much diminished margin. During 1941 the international situation worsened steadily as Germany overran nearly .all of Europe and Japan approached the establishment of absolute hegemony in the Pacific. Opposition to Roosevelt passed from the hands of economic conservatives to isolationists as he persisted in his aim of rendering to the Allies "all aid short of war." In August he met with British Prime Minister Winston Churchill, and the two issued jointly the Atlantic Charter, proclaiming what were in effect war aims. Finally, on December 7th, Japanese forces attacked Pearl Harbor in Hawaii; the President obtained a declaration of war from Congress the next day and similar declarations against Germany and Italy a few days later. Economic mobilization was the first imperative, and authority for it was given to the War Production Board (WPB) and the Office of War Mobilization (OWM). Roosevelt concerned himself primarily with securing close cooperation among the Allies, and the course of the war was marked by a series of meetings with heads of state — primarily Churchill and Joseph Stalin — to plan overall war strategy (as at Casablanca in 1943) and the structure of the postwar world (at Teheran, 1943, and Yalta, 1945). He was most anxious to establish good working relations with the Soviet Union, both during the war and afterwards, but was disappointed in this aim, especially when, soon after Yalta, it appeared that the U.S. and the U.S.S.R. placed differing interpretations on the agreements reached there. By this time he was in poor health; this had been an issue in the election of 1944 when he nonetheless won a fourth term, and it was now a serious problem. He retired to Warm Springs, Georgia, to rest for the forthcoming meeting in San Francisco to draft the United Nations charter; two weeks before the meeting he died, on April 12, 1945.

ROOSEVELT, THEODORE (1858 – 1919), public official and 26th U.S. President. Born in New York City on October 27, 1858, Roosevelt was of a well-to-do family long established in New York. In his youth he set about overcoming his physical weakness and developed a taste for the vigorous, rugged life that was to become a trademark. He graduated from Harvard in 1880 and entered the Columbia University Law School but soon withdrew to run successfully for the state assembly in 1881. During his three terms in that body he was nominally a Republican, but he acted and voted as an outspoken independent. During these years also he undertook the writing of history as a serious and continuing avocation, beginning with *The Naval War of 1812*, 1882. With the defeat of the progressive anti-Blaine faction at the Republican convention of 1884, and the death of his wife in the same year, Roosevelt retired to a ranch in the Dakota territory where he remained until called back to New York for the mayoral election of 1886, in which he ran third to the Democratic candidate and Single-Taxer Henry George. He again retired from politics and devoted himself largely to writing, publishing in 1889 the first two volumes of his *Winning of the West* (the third and fourth volumes followed in 1894 and 1896). In that year he was appointed civil service commissioner by President Harrison and served in that position until 1895, when he became president of New York's Board of Police Commissioners. He maintained his reputation as a reformer and this, together with his strong support of McKinley in the 1896 election, won him appointment as assistant secretary of the Navy. In this post he advocated a strong military stance for the United States and acted to achieve his aim, sometimes undercutting or assuming the authority of his superior. In May 1898 he resigned to join Leonard Wood in organizing the 1st U.S. Volunteer Cavalry for service in Cuba; as commander of the "Rough Riders" he cut a spectacular figure, and the much-publicized charge up Kettle Hill (not San Juan Hill, as is often stated) made him a national hero. Immediately upon his return home he was nominated for and elected governor of New York. In his two years in Albany his reform views and insistence on competence in officeholders so exasperated the Republican machine leaders that, in order to remove him from New York politics, they pushed for his nomination for Vice President in 1900. He accepted the bid but soon after the election found himself bored with the empty job and considered returning to law or joining a university faculty. Six months after his inauguration, on September 14, 1901, McKinley died of an assassin's bullet and Roosevelt became President. While pledging a continuation of his predecessor's policies, he in fact pursued a course more in line with Western populist ideas than with the business-oriented views of Mark Hanna and his late protégé. Faced with a conservative, hostile Congress, however, the President chose to work through an expansion of the ill-defined power of executive authority. He began by revitalizing the Sherman Anti-Trust Act of 1890 and, through Attorney General Philander C. Knox, hauled more than 30 corporations into court on antitrust charges, the most notable of which were the Northern Securities Company and Standard Oil Company of New Jersey, ordered dissolved by the Supreme Court in 1904 and 1911 respectively. When the anthracite coal strike of 1902 began

to cause massive coal shortages, he forced the recalcitrant operators to negotiate with the miners' union by threatening to use the Army to work the mines. In 1903, on his recommendation, a Cabinet-level Department of Commerce and Labor was created by Congress. In foreign affairs he exercised power even more vigorously. In 1902 and 1903, when first Venezuela and then the Dominican Republic were faced with European occupation because of defaulted debts, he intervened and assumed for the United States responsibility for the payment of debts by Latin American nations; in 1904, with Secretary of State Elihu Root, he announced what came to be known as the Roosevelt corollary to the Monroe Doctrine, stating that the United States would be, in effect, the armed policeman and defender of the Western Hemisphere. In the Dominican Republic the United States took full control of national finance through an appointed comptroller. In 1903 the government of Columbia rejected a treaty allowing construction of a canal through a U.S.-controlled section of the Isthmus of Panama; but Roosevelt saw to it that a revolutionary secession by Panama was encouraged and protected by the presence of Navy warships, and shortly thereafter the Canal Zone was ceded by the new nation. The President maintained a close interest in the construction of the canal and, in visiting the site later, became the first incumbent President to leave United States soil. In 1904 he was reelected easily, and announced that he would construe his first three years in the White House as constituting a first term and would therefore not run again in 1908. During his second term he secured passage of the Pure Food and Drug Act and the Hepburn Act, which greatly strengthened the Interstate Commerce Commission. In 1905 he took the initiative in arranging negotiations to end the Russo-Japanese War, a service for which he was awarded the Nobel Prize for Peace. Throughout his seven years as President, he worked for an expanded government role in the conservation of natural resources, increasing the extent of national preserves nearly five-fold. As 1908 approached he began to regret his promise not to run, but arranged to have William Howard Taft, then secretary of war, nominated as his successor. Soon after leaving office he set out on an extended African safari, followed by a tour of Europe during which he consulted with many heads of state. Returning in 1910, he immediately resumed his political activity; as Taft slowly allied himself with the conservative wing of the Republican Party, Roosevelt's views moved leftward and the breach between the two was mirrored in the party ranks. On a Western speaking tour that year Roosevelt delivered his famed "New Nationalism" address. As the 1912 convention approached he began to gather delegate votes for a showdown with Taft; he won several state primaries, but the President controlled the party machinery and the convention. Rejected by the Republicans, he immediately formed the Progressive Party—soon dubbed the Bull Moose Party after a comment by Roosevelt on his fitness—and, displacing Sen. Robert LaFollette, accepted its nomination. The Republican split caused by the Progressive defection allowed Democrat Woodrow Wilson to win a minority election. Roosevelt took an active dislike to Wilson and his policies, particularly that of neutrality toward the European war, and in 1916, though again losing the Republican nomination, campaigned against him. When the United States entered World War I he unsuccessfully sought a military command and spoke widely in support of the war effort. He continued to publish books and articles, among the former *Progressive Principles*, 1913, *History as Literature*, 1913, and *America and the World War*, 1915. He still had hopes for the Republican nomination in 1920 when, weakened by a lingering illness contracted during a South American journey, he died suddenly on January 6, 1919.

ROOT, ELIHU (1845–1937), lawyer, public official, and diplomat. Born in Clinton, New York, on February 15, 1845, Root graduated from Hamilton College in 1864 and after a year teaching school entered the Law School of New York University. He graduated in 1867, was admitted to the bar, and, soon forming his own law firm, became within a few years one of the nation's leading corporation lawyers. Though not actively involved in politics, he was identifiably a Republican with leanings towards the party's conservative wing. He nonetheless became a close friend and advisor to Theodore Roosevelt while the latter was in New York state politics, and he maintained the association for many years. In 1894 he played a leading role in the state constitutional convention. He became secretary of war in 1899 at President McKinley's invitation and in his four years in that office directed the department's activities more effectively than had any of his predecessors since the Civil War. Charged with the administration of territories acquired in the Spanish-American War, Root quickly arranged for an effective, conservative management of Puerto Rico through the Foraker Act of 1900, granting the island dependency much-needed tariff advantages, and turned to the more difficult problem of Cuba. He chose Gen. Leonard Wood as military governor and in 1901 drafted the Platt Amendment, outlining safeguards for American interests in Cuba to be included in the island's new constitution that took effect with independence the following year. In the Philippines there was open insurrection against American occupation; Root dispatched new troops there and in 1900 sent a governing commission, headed by William Howard Taft, with detailed instructions that amounted to a constitution and a legal and judicial code. The instructions were affirmed by Congress in the Organic Act of 1902. Of the Army itself Root effected a reorganization that greatly improved its efficiency and readiness; the general staff concept was introduced along with rotation of staff and line assignments, the Army War College was established, and the state National Guards were transformed into a national militia. He resigned from the Cabinet in 1903 and returned to law, only to be recalled by President Roosevelt to succeed the late Secretary of State John Hay in 1905. He managed, despite Roosevelt's "gunboat diplomacy," to improve greatly U.S. relations with Latin America during a tour in 1906; U.S.-Japanese affairs were smoothed by the Gentleman's Agreement of 1907 and the Root-Takahira Agreement of 1908; and he negotiated numerous arbitration treaties with European nations. For these accomplishments and for his earlier success in constructing an enlightened colonial policy, he was awarded the Nobel Prize for Peace in 1912. He also made considerable progress in professionalizing the diplomatic corps. Root resigned his post in 1909 and was immediately elected to the Senate where he remained until 1915, a Taft Republican and leading opponent of President Wilson. His long friendship with Roosevelt ended in 1912 when he presided over the Republican convention that ignored the former President and obligingly renominated Taft. Out of the Senate, Root continued to oppose Wilson until the United States entered World War I. In April 1917 he was sent by Wilson to Russia in a futile attempt to bolster the Kerensky government. He supported, with minor reservations, the Versailles Treaty and the attached League of Nations Covenant, breaking with Henry Cabot Lodge on that issue. In 1920 he was appointed to a commission of jurists charged with framing the statute for the Permanent Court of International Justice and in 1929 he helped revise the statute; he was a constant though unsuccessful advocate of U.S. membership in the Court. President Harding appointed him one of the U.S. delegates to the 1921 Washington arms-limitation conference. In his later years he was active in the direction of a number of Andrew Carnegie's philanthropic activities, particularly the Carnegie Endowment for International Peace, of which he was president from 1910 to 1925. He died in New York City on February 7, 1937.

ROSENWALD, JULIUS (1862–1932), merchant and philanthropist. Born on August 12, 1862, in Springfield, Illinois, Rosenwald attended local public schools and began his career in 1879 with Hammerslough Brothers, wholesale clothiers in New York. In 1885 he established and became president of Rosenwald and Weil in Chicago. He began a lifelong association with Sears, Roebuck and Company in 1897 as vice president, becoming president in 1910 and chairman of the board in 1925. His success depended largely upon his ability to choose competent, efficient associates. He believed in the mail order system, actively promoted it, and the business thrived. He was named to several more or less honorary government posts; for instance, to the Counsel of National Defense in 1916, and to the second National Industrial Conference in France, 1919. Enormously wealthy, he became a generous and astute philanthropist. The Julius Rosenwald Fund, established in 1917 and endowed by 1928 with $40 million to be used for "the welfare of mankind," was his largest benefaction. He refused to try to influence the enterprises he assisted; his faith was in men's ability to work out their destinies, and his purpose was to provide equipment and facilities where men could learn. He did not believe in permanent endowments — the Fund was charged with expending all of its assets within 25 years of his death — and insisted on matching local funds and self-help. He made sizeable contributions to 25 Y.M.C.A. buildings in areas of cities with large Negro populations, and the Fund helped build more than 5,000 public schools for Negroes in the South. He contributed to Jewish agricultural colonization in Russia, and to the relief of German children after World War I. As a member of the American Jewish Committee, he fought both anti-Semitism and Zionism. Other principal benefactors of his wealth were the Museum of Science and Industry in Chicago and the University of Chicago. His gifts, exclusive of the Fund, totaled more than $22 million. He died on January 6, 1932.

ROSS, HAROLD WALLACE (1892–1951), editor. Born in Aspen, Colorado, on November 6,

1892, Ross attended high school in Salt Lake City but did not go to college. He first went to work as a reporter for the *Salt Lake City Tribune* in 1906, at the age of 13. In 1910 he moved to California and worked as a reporter for the *Marysville Appeal*. He joined the *Sacramento Union* In 1911 and the *Panama* (Republic) *Star and Herald* in 1912, and worked for the *New Orleans Item*, the *Atlanta Journal*, and the *San Francisco Call* from 1915 to 1917. In the latter year he enlisted in the Railway Engineer Corps of the U.S. Army but did not do much railroading. Instead, he became an editor of *Stars and Stripes*, the Army newspaper, and is said to have realized for the first time his latent ability to recognize good humorous writing. After the war he worked for a time for the Butterick Publishing Company, was editor of the *American Legion Weekly* from 1921 to 1923, and in 1924 was editor of *Judge. The New Yorker* began publication in February 1925, with Ross as editor, Raoul Fleishman as publisher, and, for a time at least, with James Thurber as managing editor. The new magazine quickly caught on and ultimately had great influence on the development of American humorous writing, reporting, and cartooning over the next quarter-century. Ross was an unpredictable but brilliant editor who always knew exactly what he wanted although he was not always able to make this absolutely clear to contributors. Emphasis was on the content of stories and articles, not on authors' names; the magazine carried no table of contents until the later 1960s, but it nevertheless helped to make the reputations of many writers, among them Thurber, Clifton Fadiman, Edmund Wilson, John O'Hara, and Truman Capote. Reporting was on a high level, for Ross demanded documentary proof of every statement. One of the glories of the magazine was its cartoons. *The New Yorker* was the inventor, or reinventor, of the one-line joke, and Ross insisted obsessively that all his cartoonists make their point in the drawing, not in lengthy, complex captions. A number of cartoonists were made famous by the magazine, among them Gluyas Williams, Mary Petty, Charles Addams, and Peter Arno. The magazine printed a weekly review of events in New York, fine poetry, excellent book reviews, and enjoyed from about 1940 on the highest advertising revenues of any periodical in the nation. Ross devoted himself completely to it, and did almost nothing else but worry about it, edit all of the copy, and plan for the future. He died on December 6, 1951; Thurber, probably his greatest discovery, wrote an entertaining biography of him, *The Years with Ross*, in 1959.

ROWLAND, HENRY AUGUSTUS (1848–1901), physicist. Born in Honesdale, Pennsylvania, on November 27, 1848, Rowland broke the long family line of Yale-educated clergymen by taking his degree in civil engineering at Rensselaer Polytechnic Institute in 1870. After teaching for a short time at Wooster University in Ohio he returned to Rensselaer as an instructor in physics in 1872. In 1875 he was invited to become professor of physics at the newly founded Johns Hopkins University and he retained that position for the rest of his life. His earliest researches were in the field of magnetism and electromagnetism. His paper on magnetic lines of force and magnetic permeability was published in England in 1873 by James Clerk Maxwell and two years later, while working in Von Helmholtz's laboratory in Berlin, he demonstrated the similarity in magnetic effect of an electric current and a high-speed electrostatic charge. Later he made new and precise determinations of the mechanical equivalent of heat, of the value of the ohm, and of the ratios of electrical units. His interest turned to spectrometry, and he constructed a machine for making diffraction gratings on a spherical surface at an accuracy of 14,000 to 20,000 lines per inch, a great improvement over previous plane gratings. He made several detailed studies of various spectra and improved determinations of spectral line wavelengths. He became a leading expert on both the theoretical and practical aspects of alternating currents and was consulted on the installation of electrical generators at Niagara Falls. In all his work he combined the mathematical background of pure science with great engineering skill, and his mechanical devices were of a value equal to his theoretical contributions. In 1899 he was elected to the Royal Society and during 1899–1900 he served as first president of the American Physical Society. He died in Baltimore on April 16, 1901.

ROWSON, SUSANNA HASWELL (c.1762–1824), author, actress, and educator. Born about 1762 in Portsmouth, England, Miss Haswell spent much of her childhood in Nantasket, Massachusetts, where her father, a naval lieutenant, was stationed. In 1778 they returned to England. Her education consisted of wide reading in Shakespeare, Spenser, and the Pope and Dryden translations of Homer and Virgil. She published her first novel, *Victoria,* in 1786, and later that year married William Rowson. Several other works, including a book of theatrical criticism, *A Trip to Parnassus,* 1788, appeared before her greatest success, *Charlotte, a Tale of Truth,* 1791. Reprinted in Philadelphia in 1794, this sentimental story of Charlotte Temple was the first "best seller" in America. Later in 1791 appeared her essays on education, *Mentoria, or the Young Lady's Friend,* and in 1792 a semiautobiographical work, *Rebecca, or the Fille de Chambre.* The failure of her husband's business led them to seek theatrical careers. During 1792–1793 they played in Edinburgh and other cities, and in 1793 came to the United States. They appeared in Baltimore, Annapolis, and Philadelphia, where she wrote a comic opera, *Slaves in Algiers,* 1794, and a light musical, *The Volunteers,* 1795. Her preoccupation with American patriotism in these and other works led to a much-publicized interchange in which William Cobbett intimated her betrayal of England in *A Kick for a Bite,* 1795, and she responded in *Trials of the Human Heart,* also 1795, calling him a "kind of loathsome reptile." She retired from the theater in 1797 and from that year until

her death on March 2, 1824, operated a successful boarding school for young ladies in or near Boston. She wrote texts, songs, and poetry for her pupils, edited the *Boston Weekly Magazine* during 1802–1805, wrote for its successor, *The Boston Magazine,* and other publications, and completed several novels, among them *Sarah, the Exemplary Wife,* 1813, and a sequel to Charlotte Temple, concerning a certain Lucy Temple. The book was titled *Charlotte's Daughter, or The Three Orphans,* and it was published posthumously in 1828.

ROYCE, JOSIAH (1855–1916), philosopher. Born on November 20, 1855, in Grass Valley, California, of English immigrant parents who had joined the California Gold Rush, Royce graduated from the University of California in 1875. For a year he studied philosophy at the universities of Leipzig and Göttingen and in 1876 accepted an invitation to be one of the first group of fellows at Johns Hopkins University, where two years later he took his Ph.D. He returned to the University of California for four years as instructor of English. Though literature had been the primary focus of his undergraduate studies, he was drawn more and more to philosophy and in 1881 published *Primer of Logical Analysis for the Use of Composition Students,* neatly bridging the two subjects. The opportunity to follow his chosen field came in 1882 when he was invited to substitute for William James at Harvard during the latter's absence. Royce remained at Harvard for the rest of his life, becoming assistant professor in 1885 and professor in 1892. The bulk of his thought and writings fell into two general areas: logic and mathematics, on which he published a number of important papers; and religion and metaphysics, the subjects of his major books. An idealist, he gradually evolved a philosophical system based on his conception of the Absolute, the single mind and will that encompasses all others; that, as the principle of unity and relation in the universe, is the ground of all consciousness and knowledge; and that, as the ultimate being, is the proper object of worship. In his later thought, he elaborated the parallel and supplementary idea of the "beloved community," consisting of all humanity, the object of ultimate personal loyalty and the source of ethical values. He argued his position with great dialectical skill, drawing often from his deep knowledge of logic and scientific method. William James, long his colleague and friend, once commented that Royce's brand of idealism was the only idealistic philosophy that tempted him to relinquish his own pluralistic pragmatism. His major works were many: *The Religious Aspect of Philosophy*, 1885, *The Spirit of Modern Philosophy*, 1892, *The Conception of God*, 1897, *Studies of Good and Evil*, 1898, *The World and the Individual*, 1900 – 1901 (from his Gifford lectures at the University of Aberdeen, 1899 – 1900), *The Conception of Immortality*, 1903, *Race Questions, Provincialism, and Other American Problems*, 1908, *The Philosophy of Loyalty*, 1908, *The Sources of Religious Insight*, 1912, *The Problem of Christianity*, 1913, and *The Hope of the Great Community*, posthumously 1916. In 1914 he succeeded to the Alford chair of philosophy at Harvard; he died in Cambridge on September 14, 1916.

RUFFIN, EDMUND (1794 – 1865), agriculturalist and author. Born on January 5, 1794, in Prince George County, Virginia, Ruffin entered the College of William and Mary in 1809 but remained only briefly. He served for six months in the Army during the War of 1812 and in 1813 returned home to take charge of his late father's farm. As was true of much of Virginia at the time, the soil on Ruffin's farm had been depleted by inefficient one-crop cultivation and overuse. He set about experimenting with various treatments and methods to revitalize the soil; by 1818 he was able to announce his considerable success in using marl (an earth containing a large proportion of calcium carbonate) on the soil

before fertilizing, crop rotation, and improved patterns of plowing and drainage. A published article detailing his results grew into a widely influential book, *An Essay on Calcareous Manures*, in 1832 and continued to expand through several editions. He was elected as a Whig to the Virginia senate in 1823 and remained in that body for three years. From 1833 to 1842 he published the *Farmer's Register*. In 1842 he became agricultural surveyor for the state of South Carolina; two years later he declined the first presidency of the Virginia State Agricultural Society but accepted the post in 1852. He continued to publish articles and books on the improvement of agriculture and was a much-sought lecturer. In his later years he changed his political affiliations from Whig to Democrat as, with the sectional crisis worsening, he became an outspoken defender of slavery and states' rights and an early advocate of Southern secession; his views were given wide circulation in Southern newspapers, in *DeBow's Review*, and in his many pamphlets. Finally, as a member of the Palmetto Guards of Charleston, he was granted the honor of firing the first shot on Fort Sumter on April 12, 1861. He served sporadically in the Confederate army during the ensuing war; despondent over the South's defeat, he took his own life on June 18, 1865.

RUSH, BENJAMIN (1745/6 – 1813), physician and educator. Born near Philadelphia on December 24, 1745 O.S. (January 4, 1746 N.S.), Rush graduated from the College of New Jersey (now Princeton University) in 1760. He studied for six years in the office of a Philadelphia physician and then spent two years at the University of Edinburgh, taking his M.D. degree in 1768. He returned to Philadelphia the following year and immediately entered upon the practice of medicine. At the same time he became professor of chemistry at the College of Philadelphia. In addition to his scientific pursuits, he maintained a keen interest in politics and reform; he strongly supported the colonial side in the growing dispute with

Great Britain and in 1776 was elected to the Continental Congress in time to become a signer of the Declaration of Independence. In 1777 he was appointed surgeon general of the armies of the Middle Department but his involvement in the abortive Conway Cabal, aimed at the removal of Washington as commander-in-chief, led to his leaving the position a year later. He began to lecture at the University of the State of Pennsylvania in 1780. He enjoyed a large practice and an increasing popularity as a teacher. He established the nation's first free dispensary in 1786, and strongly urged the abolition of slavery and capital punishment, prison reform, the broadening of educational opportunities for women and the poor, the rational and humane treatment of the mentally ill, and, unfortunately, a simplistic view of disease that insisted upon the great value of bleeding and purging under most circumstances. He was a leading member of the Pennsylvania ratifying convention and of the movement that led to the state constitution of 1790. In 1791 he joined the medical faculty of the newly unified University of Pennsylvania. During the yellow fever epidemic in Philadelphia in 1793 he performed devoted service, though of limited value in light of his therapeutic methods, and his *Account of the Bilious Remitting Yellow Fever As It Appeared in the City of Philadelphia in the Year 1793*, 1794, was a graphic and valuable description of the disease that won recognition in Europe. Despite his dogmatic approach to medicine, he made valuable contributions to the science, particularly with his observations of cholera infantum, dengue, and focal infection of the teeth. In 1797 he was appointed treasurer of the United States Mint by President Adams and retained the position until his death. Among his other notable written works were his collected *Essays, Literary, Moral, and Philosophical*, 1798, and *Medical Inquiries and Observations Upon the Diseases of the Mind*, 1812, the first systematic treatment of the subject in

America. He died in Philadelphia on April 19, 1813.

RUSH, RICHARD (1780–1859), lawyer, public official, and diplomat. Born in Philadelphia on August 29, 1780, the son of the physician Benjamin Rush, Richard Rush graduated from the College of New Jersey (now Princeton University) in 1797, studied law, and was admitted to the bar in 1800. His law practice was unspectacular and he gained prominence but slowly. In 1811 he was appointed attorney general of Pennsylvania and, later in the same year, comptroller of the U.S. Treasury (his father was at the time treasurer of the U.S. Mint). He accepted President Madison's invitation to become U.S. attorney general in 1814. With the inauguration of President Monroe in March 1817 he became ad interim secretary of state until John Quincy Adams' return from Europe in September; during this time he negotiated the Rush-Bagot convention providing for mutual American and British disarmament on the Great Lakes. In October of that year he was appointed minister to Great Britain. During his eight years in this position he discharged his duties well, negotiating several agreements of which the most notable was the convention of 1818, which extended the U.S.-Canadian border westward from the Lake of the Woods along the 49th parallel and provided for joint U.S.-British occupation of Oregon. His reports of conversations with the British foreign minister in 1823, relating to British and French policy in Latin America, contributed directly to the enunciation of the Monroe Doctrine in December of that year. In 1825 he returned to America to become secretary of the treasury under President Adams; he was Adams' running mate in the election of 1828 and with him was soundly defeated. For the next eight years he returned to his private practice of law and dabbled briefly in Antimasonic politics. In 1836 he went to England to take part in the litigation surrounding the bequest of James

Smithson of his large estate to the United States; two years later the case was cleared and Rush brought back the money that was used, according to the terms of the will, to establish the Smithsonian Institution. During his last years his only public service was as minister to France from 1847 to 1849. He died in Philadelphia on July 30, 1859.

RUSSELL, CHARLES TAZE (1852–1916), religious leader. Born in Pittsburgh on February 16, 1852, Russell was educated in the city's common schools. Though raised in the Congregational Church, he at length rejected its teachings, particularly the doctrine of eternal punishment, and began to study the Bible closely for verification of his own beliefs. In 1872 he published a booklet, *The Object and Manner of Our Lord's Return*, in which he announced that the second coming of Christ would occur invisibly in the fall of 1874. The ascension to the throne and the end of the Gentile times would come in 1914 and, after a period of world-wide strife marked by class warfare and consequent chaos, the millenial kingdom would begin. Pastor Russell (commonly so called, though he was never ordained in any church) organized the International Bible Students Association in Pittsburgh in 1872 and in 1879 began publishing *The Watch Tower and Herald of Christ's Presence*, later known as *Zion's Watch Tower* and finally simply as *The Watch Tower*. In 1881 he published his most influential book, *Food for Thinking Christians*, in which he outlined a pattern of unworldly devotion and warned against political and social allegiance or involvement on the part of true Christians. The book was reissued in 1886 as the first volume of *Millenial Dawn* and still later as part of his six-volume *Studies in the Scriptures*. In 1884 he founded the Watch Tower Bible and Tract Society to publish his books, pamphlets, and periodicals. The original congregation in Pittsburgh was followed by branches throughout the country, in Canada, England, and in Eu-

rope. His growing influence was unaffected by numerous highly publicized incidents smacking of impropriety. He traveled and preached all over the world; on one such trip he died, in Pampa, Texas, on October 31, 1916. The International Bible Students Association continued to grow and In 1931 was renamed the Jehovah's Witnesses.

RUSSELL, LILLIAN (1861–1922), entertainer. Born on December 4, 1861, in Clinton, Iowa, Helen Louise Leonard adopted the stage name Lillian Russell while appearing at Tony Pastor's Theatre in 1880. From the age of four she lived in Chicago; she attended the Sacred Heart Convent, where she sang in the choir, and the Park Institute, a finishing school. Her early training in voice and violin was supplemented by a year of opera study under Leopold Damrosch. Her first stage role was in the chorus of Rice's *H.M.S. Pinafore* company in 1879. After appearing as a ballad singer at Pastor's Theatre in New York she continued her studies in voice and acting, and then toured California as the lead in *Babes in the Wood*. Returning to New York, she attained stardom as D'Jemma in Edwin Audran's comic opera, *The Great Mogul: or, the Snake Charmer*, in October 1881, and then played in Gilbert and Sullivan's *Patience* and *The Sorcerer*. By 1883 she was the prima donna of the McCaul Opera Company. She made her London debut at the Gaiety Theatre in July 1883 in Solomon's *Virginia and Paul*. Returning to the United States in 1884, she was in the news frequently because of her flamboyant personal life and numerous contract disputes; at one time she sought an injunction to keep any theater manager from having her appear in silk tights. Celebrated for her beauty and her clear, pleasant, soprano voice, not yet so trained as to be beyond popular audiences, she was dubbed "airy, fairy Lillian." Her most difficult roles were in two Offenbach operas, as Fiorella in *The Brigands*, in 1889, and in the title role in *The Grand Duchess* in 1890.

She joined Weber and Fields' burlesque company in 1890 and sang in *Fiddle-dee-dee* and *Whoop-dee-doo*. With *Barbara's Millions* in 1906 she entered straight comedy and was successful thereafter in this genre in *Wildfire* and *Hokey-Pokey*. After 1912 she appeared only rarely on the stage. She wrote articles on beauty for the women's pages of the *Chicago Herald* and the *Chicago Daily Tribune* and in 1913 toured the country delivering a lecture on "How to Live a Hundred Years." During World War I she was active in the Red Cross and Liberty Loan campaigns. She died in Pittsburgh on June 6, 1922, 40 years short of her goal.

RUTH, GEORGE HERMAN (1895–1948), baseball player. Born in Baltimore on February 6, 1895, Ruth grew up amid poverty and an irregular family life. From the age of seven he spent much time in St. Mary's Industrial School and there, encouraged by an interested priest, developed a passionate love of baseball. In 1914 he was signed by the Baltimore Orioles and later in the year sold to the Boston Red Sox. By 1919 he was the best left-handed pitcher in the American League, indeed one of the best ever, but his obvious potential for even more spectacular results with a bat led to his transfer to the outfield. In that year he broke the major league home run record with 29. In 1920 he was sold to the New York Yankees, then a struggling team that rented the Giants' Polo Grounds for home games. The Babe hit 54 home runs that year and 59 the next, and the Yankees won their first pennant. Beyond boosting his own team into prominence, he was credited with helping greatly to save baseball from a fatal loss of popularity that was feared might follow the "Black Sox" scandal of 1919–1920. Yankee Stadium, opened in 1923, was aptly dubbed "The House That Ruth Built." He slumped somewhat during 1924 and 1925, in the latter year drawing a $5,000 fine for "misconduct off the ball field," but soon gave up the high life and rededicated himself to baseball and

his legion of fans. In 1927 the "Sultan of Swat" set the standing record for home runs in a 154-game season with 60. In 1935 he moved to the Boston Braves and ended his playing career in June of that year. In addition to his home run record he held 53 more, including career home runs (714), runs batted in (2,209), bases on balls (2,056), and strikeouts (1,330). He played in 10 World Series and in 1928, when the Yankees swept the Series in 4 games, he scored 9 runs. In 1936 he was one of the first five men elected to the Baseball Hall of Fame in Cooperstown, New York. During the 1938 season he coached the Brooklyn Dodgers, but he never realized his ambition to manage a major league team. In his later years he devoted much time to charity and his last home run, hit in 1942 against Walter Johnson, was in a benefit performance in Yankee Stadium for war service organizations. During World War II American Marines fighting in the Pacific were startled to hear Japanese soldiers shouting "To hell with Babe Ruth!" as a battle cry; the fact was a tribute, however, to both his worldwide fame and his heroic stature in America. He died in New York City on August 16, 1948.

RYDER, ALBERT PINKHAM (1847–1917), painter. Born on March 19, 1847, in the seaport town of New Bedford, Massachusetts, Ryder was haunted all his life by the sea. He attended school locally and painted from an early age, but grew frustrated at his inability to recreate nature on the canvas. The family moved to New York in 1868, and he studied art formally with William E. Marshall and at the National Academy of Design. His paintings brought him a very small income; being totally naive in money matters he left checks about the house and frequently gave what little he had to a beggar. Content to live in his dusty attic studio, he traveled abroad once but returned to New York unaffected by his exposure to Europe; he had no taste for travel and felt that an artist should dedicate himself totally to his work. He often walked in solitude in the park or visited Cape Cod, where he made sketches for his famous lunar landscapes. To achieve fresh, brilliant color he piled layer upon layer of rich, heavy enamel; he completed only some 150 paintings in 70 years. Many were small and all were worked and reworked with patience and care. Outstanding among his works were "The Race Track" (sometimes called "Death on a Pale Horse"), "Toilers of the Sea," and "The Flying Dutchman." His death after a long illness occurred in a friend's home in Long Island, New York, on March 28, 1917. His marine and pastoral paintings and several still lifes were hailed as the work of a genius after his death; because of his unfortunate lack of technical concern, many of his works have deteriorated seriously.

SAARINEN, GOTTLIEB ELIEL (1873–1950), architect. Born on August 20, 1873, in Rantasalmi, Finland, Eliel Saarinen was his country's foremost architect when he emigrated to the United States in 1923. Public buildings such as the Helsinki railroad station, 1905–1914, and urban housing and development projects for Reval, Estonia, and Canberra, Australia, earned his reputation. In 1922 he entered a design in the *Chicago Tribune* competition. It did not win the prize—a Gothic tower was erected instead—but it nevertheless exerted a strong influence on the development of the skyscraper in the United States. He designed the Cranbrook Foundation in Michigan, where he headed the Academy of Art and supervised its departments of architecture and city planning. His Tabernacle Church of Christ in Columbus, Indiana, 1942, and Christ Lutheran Church in Minneapolis, 1950, were especially notable among his works. Together with his son Eero he received awards from the American Institute of Architects in 1948 for a design for the new annex to the Smithsonian Institution in Washington, D.C. His writings included *The City: Its Growth, Its Decay, Its Future*, 1943, and *Search for Form*, 1948. He died at Bloomfield Hills, near Detroit, on July 1, 1950.

EERO SAARINEN (1910–1961), was born on August 20, 1910, in Kirkkonummi, Finland, graduated from Yale in 1934, and worked with his father from that time until the latter's death. Highly innovative in his own right, he designed structures having a sculptural quality that inspired, he said, an endless "search for form." Examples of his stainless steel and glass buildings with curving rooftops and convex walls are the Davis S. Ingalls hockey rink at Yale, 1958, the Trans World Airlines Terminal at Kennedy Airport in New York City, 1962, and the Dulles Airport near Washington, 1962. His winning design for the St. Louis Jefferson National Expansion Memorial competition, a stainless steel arch, was executed in 1968. Often called the most creative architect of his day, he died in Ann Arbor, Michigan, on September 1, 1961.

SAINT-GAUDENS, AUGUSTUS (1848–1907), sculptor. Born in Dublin on March 1, 1848, Saint-Gaudens emigrated with his parents to the United States later in the same year. Settling in New York, he was apprenticed to a cameo cutter at 13 and from 1861 to 1865 spent his evenings studying art at Cooper Union and for another year at the National Academy of Design. In 1867 he went to Paris, and after a few months of travel enrolled in the École des Beaux Arts. Three years later he moved to Rome, where he continued to study and develop his skill in modeling while supporting himself by cameo cutting. His "Hiawatha" was the major work of these years. Except for a brief visit to New York in 1872–1873 he remained in Rome until 1875; by the time of his return he was an established sculptor. He became associated with a number of leading artists and architects, notably H. H. Richardson, Charles F. McKim, Stanford White, and John La Farge; for the last he carved "Adoration of the Cross by Angels," a relief reredos for St. Thomas' Church, New York, in 1877. In the same year he executed a memorial statue of Admiral Farragut, mounted on a pedestal designed by White, and placed in Madison

Square, New York. A flood of major works followed, most notable among which were "The Puritan," 1885, "Amor Caritas," 1887, the hooded figure on the memorial to Mrs. Henry Adams in Washington, 1891, and the "Diana" for Madison Square Garden, 1892. He was an active member of the Society of American Artists from its founding in 1877, taught from 1888 to 1897 at the Art Students League in New York, and was a staunch supporter of McKim's American Academy in Rome. From 1885 he spent much of his time at a home and studio he established near Cornish, New Hampshire. In addition to his large pieces, he produced a great number of smaller busts, portraits, plaques, and medallions, and in 1907 he designed the U.S. $20 gold piece and the head on the $10 gold piece. He died on August 3, 1907.

SALINGER, JEROME DAVID (1919–   ), author. Born in New York City on January 1, 1919, Salinger attended public schools in New York City and a military academy in Pennsylvania, and took classes at New York University and Columbia. He began writing when he was 15 and published his first short story in 1940 in *Story* magazine. From 1942 to 1946 he was in the Army, his experiences inspiring such stories as "For Esmé—With Love and Squalor," 1950. With his first novel, *Catcher in the Rye*, 1951, he won a legion of admirers, young and old, who found their lives reflected in that of the hero, 16-year-old Holden Caulfield. As Salinger described it—in free-associative language, replete with adolescent slang—Holden's flight from the "phonies" to the good, the pure, and the true, was everyone's quest. In 1953 he published *Nine Stories*, which included "For Esmé," "A Perfect Day for Bananafish," "Uncle Wiggly in Connecticut," and others, followed by *Franny and Zooey*, 1961, *Raise High the Roof Beam, Carpenters; and, Seymour; an Introduction*, 1963, (earlier published in the *New Yorker*), the last two on the life and activities of the Glass family. In his work children—as possessors of an inno-

cence lost too soon—were precisely, almost eerily described, with painstaking accuracy, and, particularly in the Glass family, they were possessed of a precocious wisdom usually far beyond the grasp of adults. His stories were published after 1945 in the *New Yorker*, *Harper's*, *Saturday Evening Post*, *Esquire*, and other popular magazines.

SALK, JONAS EDWARD (1914–   ), epidemiologist. Born in New York City on October 28, 1914, Salk earned his B.S. degree in 1934 from the City College of New York, his M.D. degree in 1939 from New York University's medical college, where he stayed on briefly as a fellow in bacteriology, and was an intern for two years at the Mount Sinai Hospital in New York. In 1942, on a fellowship in epidemiology from the University of Michigan, he began studies of the influenza virus with Dr. Thomas Francis, Jr., in order to produce commercial vaccines. He became a research fellow in 1943, research associate in 1944, and a professor of epidemiology in 1946 in the university's School of Public Health. In 1947 he went to the University of Pittsburgh as research professor of bacteriology and director of the Virus Research Laboratory. He continued his research on the influenza virus, but by 1949 was interested in developing a serum against poliomyelitis. He was made a director of a three-year project to investigate the polio virus sponsored by the March of Dimes of the National Foundation for Infantile Paralysis. The project disclosed three strains of virus capable of producing the disease, all of which had to be neutralized by a vaccine if it were to be considered effective. Using this foundation, as well as technical accomplishments of others which made it possible to cultivate polio virus in the kidney tissue of monkeys, and to enhance the potency, he was able to produce an inactivated-virus vaccine. He announced its experimental success in 1953, just one year after a polio epidemic had struck 57,626 people and killed 3,300 in the United States. Mass innoculation of school children was undertaken by the National Foundation in 1954, and by 1955 the Salk vaccine was proven effective. In 1953 he also published the results of experimental innoculations of 20,000 persons with a flu vaccine, which had produced immunity for as long as two years and also went into wide use. A winner of numerous honors and awards, he became Commonwealth professor of preventive medicine at Michigan in 1956, of experimental medicine in 1957, and was a fellow and director of the Salk Institute for Biological Studies after 1963. A major part of his later work was concerned with developing a vaccine against cancer.

SANDBURG, CARL (1878–1967), poet and folklorist. Born on January 6, 1878, in Galesburg, Illinois, the son of a Swedish blacksmith, Sandburg worked from the age of 11, combining schooling with various jobs, then went to Puerto Rico to fight in the Spanish-American War. Upon his return, he worked his way through Lombard College in Galesburg, graduating in 1902. His wanderings continued; he recruited members for the Socialist-Democratic party in Wisconsin, serving as secretary to the Socialist mayor of Milwaukee from 1910 to 1912. He moved to Chicago in 1913. Although he had published his poems as early as 1904, they did not gain much attention until they appeared in *Poetry* magazine, starting in 1914. Including "Fog" and "I Am the People, the Mob," his first book, *Chicago Poems*, 1916, was successful from the outset. His style was compared to Whitman's for freedom and authenticity, but his knowledge of the land was deeper and born of personal experience. He used conspicuous colloquialisms, portraying everyday people and common things, embracing both the delicate and the crude. He turned to journalism, becoming feature editor for the *Chicago Daily News* by 1919, and issued subsequent volumes of poetry, including the Pulitzer Prize winning *Cornhuskers*, 1918, *Smoke and Steel*, 1920, and *Slabs of the Sunburnt West*, 1922. His six-

volume biography of Lincoln, 1926–1939, was begun as a study for young people, but it expanded far beyond that and received another Pulitzer Prize, in 1940. His democratic faith in the wisdom of the people pervaded *The People, Yes*, 1936, and his interest in American lore, especially that of his native Midwest, prompted him to give folksong recitals throughout the country. Important collections of such songs appeared as *The American Songbag*, 1927, and *New American Songbag*, 1950. He wrote several charming children's books, notably *Rootabaga Stories*, 1922, *Rootabaga Pigeons*, 1923, and *Potato Face*, 1930. His later publications included *Remembrance Rock*, 1948, a history of America from Plymouth Rock through the events of World War II, *Complete Poems*, 1950, which won a Pulitzer Prize the next year, and *The Sandburg Range*, 1957, selections from previous works and many interesting photographs. He died at his home at Flat Rock, North Carolina, on July 22, 1967.

SANGER, MARGARET HIGGINS (1883–1966), social reformer. Born on September 14, 1883, in Corning, New York, Margaret Higgins completed her nurse's training at the White Plains Hospital in New York and at the Manhattan Eye and Ear Clinic. In 1900 she married William Sanger, retaining that surname, by which she was well known, after they were divorced and she remarried. In New York City she contributed articles on health to the Socialist Party's *Call*, later collected in *What Every Girl Should Know*, 1916, and *What Every Mother Should Know*, 1917. In her nursing career she ministered primarily to maternity cases from the city's crowded Lower East Side, coming directly into contact with her patients' desperate financial and mental conditions and witnessing many deaths from self-induced abortions. She gave up nursing in 1912 to devote herself to the cause of birth control. Gathering and disseminating information, however, was nearly impossible because of the Comstock Act of 1873, which classified contraceptive data as obscene. Late in 1913 she traveled in Scotland and France to view the situations there. In 1914 she returned to the United States and began publishing the *Woman Rebel*, a magazine addressed to her cause, and was indicted for sending an obscene publication through the mails. Her case was dismissed before coming to trial. Also in 1914 she founded the National Birth Control League. Soon after setting up the nation's first birth control clinic in the Brownsville district of Brooklyn, she was sent to the workhouse in 1917 for 30 days on charges of creating a public nuisance. But her appeal, bolstered by mounting public sympathy, led to a favorable decision from the New York Court of Appeals, granting doctors the right to give advice about birth control to their patients. In 1936 a further modification granted doctors the right to import and prescribe contraceptive devices. She organized numerous conventions in the United States and abroad, beginning with the First National Birth Control Conference in New York in 1921. That year she also established the American Birth Control League, serving as its president until 1928, after which she founded the National Committee on Federal Legislation for Birth Control. In 1939 the League combined with the Education Department of the Birth Control Research Bureau and became the Birth Control Federation of America, renamed in 1942 the Planned Parenthood Federation. As first president of the International Planned Parenthood Federation, organized in 1953, she furthered the cause in Far Eastern countries, notably India and Japan. In 1935 she began the *Journal of Contraception* (later called *Human Fertility*). Her numerous books included *Women, Morality, and Birth Control*, 1922, *Happiness in Marriage*, 1926, *Motherhood in Bondage*, 1928, *My Fight for Birth Control*, 1931, and *Margaret Sanger: an Autobiography*, 1938. She died in Tucson, Arizona, on September 6, 1966.

SANTAYANA, GEORGE (1863–1952), philosopher, poet, novelist, and critic. Born in Madrid on December 16, 1863, Santayana was brought up by his father in Ávila, joining his mother in Boston when he was eight, in 1872. Educated at the Boston Latin School and at Harvard, he graduated from the latter in 1886, after which he studied in Germany, returning to Harvard in 1888 to receive his doctorate. He joined the Harvard philosophy department the next year, remaining a member of its distinguished faculty—which included William James and Josiah Royce—until 1912, when a small inheritance allowed him to retire. He lived in England for several years, then in Paris, and in 1925 finally settled in Rome. His first major philosophical work, *The Sense of Beauty*, had appeared in 1896; in it he attempted to set forth a complete aesthetic theory, which he later developed further in *Reason in Art*, 1905, Vol. IV of *The Life of Reason*. The other parts of this five-volume treatise were published in 1905–1906, dealing, in order, with reason in common sense, society, religion, and science. *The Life of Reason*, subtitled *The Phases of Human Progress*, was "a presumptive biography of the human intellect" that reflected his intense interest in psychology and also his desire to avoid the errors of the German idealists and transcendentalists. In 1923 appeared *Scepticism and Animal Faith*, in which he undertook an extensive recasting of his whole system of thought. Developed in the four volumes of *Realms of Being*, 1927–1940, this took the form of a careful and detailed analysis of the four major modes of being that emerge from the skeptical investigation of consciousness. These four modes are essence, matter, truth, and spirit. Santayana's philosophy was basically personal and idiosyncratic, although he doubtless owed more to his contemporaries than he liked to admit. A graceful and intelligent writer, he produced, besides his philosophical studies, many works of criticism, both philosophical and aesthetic, a novel, poems, and an autobiography. In his criticism, which includes *Three Philosophical Poets*, 1910, *Winds of Doctrine*, 1926, *Character* *and Opinion in the United States*, 1920, and *Some Turns of Thought in Modern Philosophy*, 1933, he expressed his often quite individualistic opinions in a style that helped even the objects of his attacks to forgive him. His novel, *The Last Puritan*, 1936, was by way of being a best seller, and is also a "memoir" of considerable psychological interest. His poetry, written mostly during his years at Harvard, is classical in tone and approach, and runs counter to most of the prevailing schools of the time. His three-volume autobiography, *Persons and Places*, 1944–1953, is one of his most delightful though crusty works. In it he revealed himself as a confirmed opponent of democracy and liberalism; instead he advocated, though he admitted that he did not expect, a return to the "natural" aristocratic societies of the past. As he grew older, he became more and more alienated from the modern world, and during World War II he took refuge in the convent of an order of English nuns in Rome. He died there on September 26, 1952.

SARGENT, JOHN SINGER (1856–1925), painter. Born on January 12, 1856, in Florence, of American parents, Sargent received lessons in the Academy of Fine Arts at Florence and sketched profusely as the family traveled through southern Italy, France, and Germany during his childhood. His formal studies began at the École des Beaux Arts in 1874. In 1876 he visited the United States and acquired American citizenship, which he never relinquished, but he then returned to Paris. Confidently painting his subjects from life in oils, he developed a style marked by understated tones with brilliant highlights. He mingled with other artists but for years could not find patrons. His style was in advance of the academic painting fashionable in Paris and London, but he nevertheless continued to work in his own way; he created a scandal in Paris with his brilliantly conceived portrait of "Madame X." In 1885 he moved to London. His work continued to be poorly received; the unorthodox composition of "The Misses Vickers" was particularly savagely criticized. In 1887 he exhibited a painting of two children in a flower garden, "Carnation, Lily, Lily, Rose," which warmed the public toward his work. He was deluged with portrait commissions; those that he painted mirrored the elegance of the Edwardian age. His renderings were not psychologically profound, but his remarkable brushwork gave directness and spontaneity to his style. Recognized as the leading practitioner of the day, he nonetheless tired of portraiture and switched to decorative work and landscapes. He executed a series of large murals in the Boston Public Library, 1890–1910, and the interior design for the Boston Museum of Fine Arts. He traveled constantly between Europe and America, after 1910 spending summers in Italy and the Alps working freely in watercolors. In 1918 he was commissioned an official war artist by the British government; he produced "Gassed" and "General Officers of the Great War." Reputed to be merely a society painter, he was seriously devoted to his work and received numerous honors for his painting during his life. He died in London on April 15, 1925.

SARNOFF, DAVID (1891–   ), engineer and industrialist. Born in Uzlian, Minsk, Russia, on February 27, 1891, Sarnoff was brought to the United States at the age of nine. He was educated in public schools in Brooklyn, New York, and studied electrical engineering at Pratt Institute. He began his work with wireless communications systems as early as 1906, when he was only 15. He joined the Marconi Radio Company in 1913 as chief radio inspector and assistant chief engineer, and rose through the ranks of this company until it was absorbed in 1919 by the Radio Corporation of America. At that time commercial manager of Marconi, he was taken over in the same capacity in the new organization. He was elected general manager of RCA in 1921, vice president and general manager in 1922, executive vice president in 1929, president in 1930, and chairman of the board in 1947. An imaginative and innovative businessman, General Sarnoff, as he liked to be called—he was a brigadier general (retired) in the regular Army—made at least three important and far-reaching decisions in the course of his career, to each of which he stuck despite tremendous pressures both from within and from outside his company. In the 1920s RCA was the leading manufacturer of radio sets, and he insisted upon the founding of the National Broadcasting Company as a subsidiary, in order to insure that something could be heard over the radios. NBC lost money at first but eventually justified his faith in it. In the 1930s he was one of the first to see that television would replace radio, and he invested large sums in research in the new medium. World War II intervened, and no television sets could be manufactured; but after the war was over his faith was again confirmed. Finally, in the late 1940s, he decided that color television would eventually replace black and white. RCA began to manufacture color sets, and NBC broadcast in color as often as possible. But for several years other manufacturers did not join in, nor did the other networks. RCA was said to have lost nearly half a billion dollars during the period. But Sarnoff triumphed again when color became almost universal. He retired as chairman of the board in 1970.

SCHAFF, PHILIP (1819–1893), theologian and church historian. Born on January 1, 1819, in Chur, Switzerland, Schaff was educated at the universities of Tübingen, Halle, and Berlin, receiving the degree of licentiate of theology from the last in 1841. He remained at Berlin as *privatdozent* and had already attracted considerable attention as a brilliant scholar when he accepted a call from the Theological Seminary of the German Reformed Church, Mercersburg, Pennsylvania, in 1844. At his inauguration as professor of church history and biblical literature he delivered an address on "The Principle of Protestantism," in which he viewed the Protestant movement as an inspired evolution of the Church out of the best strains of Catholicism rather than as a revolutionary (or reactionary) development. His further statements looking toward the eventual possible unification among Christian sects raised charges of heresy of which he was cleared by the Synod the following year. He remained at Mercersburg for 19 years, during which he founded *Der Deutsche Kirchenfreund*, a theological journal, in 1846, published, among other works, *What is Church History? A Vindication of the Idea of Historical Development*, 1846, and began his massive *History of the Christian Church*, 7 volumes, 1858–1892. His 25-volume edition of Lange's *Commentary* began to appear in 1864; the following year he resigned his professorship and moved to New York City. From 1864 to 1870 he was secretary of the New York Sabbath Association and in the latter year joined the faculty of Union Theological Seminary, where he remained until his death. He published his *Bibliotheca Symbolicae Ecclesiae Universalis: The Creeds of Christendom* in 1877 and edited the Schaff-Herzog *Encyclopedia of Religious Knowledge*, 1884. From 1881 to 1885 he headed the American Committee in the international work on revision of the English Bible. He founded and was first president of the American Society of Church History in 1888. He wrote or edited more than 80 published works and became, through both quantity and quality of effort, known worldwide as a great theological scholar. He died in New York on October 20, 1893.

SCHOOLCRAFT, HENRY ROWE (1793–1864), explorer and ethnologist. Born in Albany County, New York, on March 28, 1793, Schoolcraft was educated at Union and Middlebury colleges, where he studied especially geology and mineralogy. After leaving college he went on a collecting trip through the Indian country of Missouri and Arkansas. One of the fruits of this trip was a book, *A View of the Lead Mines* of Missouri, 1819; another was an appointment as topographer on the Lewis Cass expedition to the copper regions around the Upper Mississippi and Lake Superior. There he became increasingly interested in Indian life, and in 1822 he was appointed Indian agent to the tribes of the Lake Superior region. Shortly afterwards he married an Indian girl, or at least a girl of Indian extraction—a member of the Ojibwa tribe, which soon became his special study. He was superintendent of Indian affairs for Michigan from 1836 to 1841, and in this capacity he supervised a treaty, promulgated March 28, 1836, whereby the Ojibwa ceded much of northern Michigan to the United States. In the meantime he had continued to write. *Narrative Journal of Travels through the Northwestern Regions of the United States . . . to the Sources of the Mississippi River* appeared in 1821, after his return from the Cass expedition. A later exploring trip to the same area, in the course of which he discovered Lake Itasca, the source of the Mississippi, was described in *Narrative of an Expedition . . . to Itasca Lake,* 1834. *Algic Researches* appeared in 1839; a study of Indian mentality, it was reissued in 1856 as *The Myth of Hiawatha,* and in this form was the inspiration for Longfellow's poem. His principal contribution to ethnology was *Historical and Statistical Information Respecting the History, Condition, and Prospects of the Indian Tribes of the United States.* Issued in six parts from 1851 to 1857, and illustrated by engravings from paintings by Seth Eastman, the work was almost unusable owing to its disorganization. But it contains much invaluable lore, and an index prepared by the Bureau of American Ethnology and published in 1954 made its information accessible to the modern student. Schoolcraft died in Washington, D.C., on December 10, 1864.

SCHURZ, CARL (1829–1906), journalist, reformer, political leader, and public official. Born in Liblar, near Cologne, Germany, on March 2, 1829, Schurz studied at the University of Bonn. His deep involvement in the revolutionary movement of 1848–1849 forced him to flee to France and then Switzerland, returning to Germany briefly in 1850 to execute a daring rescue of an imprisoned former teacher and revolutionary comrade. After a stay in England he came to the United States in 1852; he lived in Philadelphia until 1855, then moved to Watertown, Wisconsin. His reformist spirit led him into the Abolitionist cause and thence to the Republican Party; he campaigned in both English and German for Frémont in 1856 and for Lincoln in 1858 and again in the national election of 1860. In return he was named minister to Spain, but he remained there only until January 1862; he resigned in April and was commissioned brigadier general. He saw action at second Bull Run, Chancellorsville, and Gettysburg, and was promoted to major general in 1863. Though without military training, Schurz was thoroughly competent and one of the best of the politically appointed generals. Soon after the war's end he was asked by President Johnson to tour and report on conditions in the South; his report, containing strong recommendations for Negro suffrage and civil rights, was shelved by the President and published only at Congressional insistence. After a brief time as Washington correspondent for Greeley's *New York Tribune* Schurz became editor of the newly-founded *Detroit Post* in 1866; the next year he moved to St. Louis and was co-editor of the *St. Louis Westliche Post.* In 1869 he was elected to the Senate from Missouri and served there a single term, during which he was an outspoken critic of Grant's casual administration, official corruption, and the effort to annex Santo Domingo, and sought the establishment of a merit-based system of civil service. Such was his disgust with the regular Republican Party that in 1872 he was the chief organizer of the Liberal Republicans and campaigned vigorously for the party's ticket despite its unfortunate nomination of Horace Greeley for President. In 1876, out of the Senate, Schurz returned to the party ranks and supported Hayes, who subsequently appointed him secretary of the interior. In this post he followed an enlightened policy toward the Indians and continued his efforts at civil service reform. From 1881 to 1883 he was an editor for the *New York Evening Post.* His consistently lofty approach to politics led him to bolt the Republican Party twice more, in 1884 as leader of the Mugwump revolt against Blaine, and in 1900 when he reluctantly supported Bryan against McKinley on the issue of imperialism. From 1892 to 1901 he was president of the National Civil Service Reform League and during about the same period was an editorial writer for *Harper's Weekly*, a connection that Schurz ended himself in refusing to support the agitation for war with Spain. He died in New York City on May 14, 1906.

SCHWAB, CHARLES MICHAEL (1862–1939), industrialist. Born on February 18, 1862, in Williamsburg, Pennsylvania, Schwab grew up in the village of Loretto, Pennsylvania. After finishing high school, he entered the Carnegie-owned Edgar Thomson Steel Works in Braddock, Pennsylvania, as a laborer. His flair for handling people and receptiveness to new industrial methods elevated him rapidly in the business; made general superintendent of the Thomson plant in 1889, he became manager of both the Thomson and Homestead works three years later and in 1897 was appointed president of the Carnegie Steel Company, Ltd. He stimulated and negotiated the sale of the Carnegie properites to a group headed by J. P. Morgan and directed the formation of the United States Steel Corporation, its successor corporation, becoming, at 39, its first president. In the meantime, he had purchased a controlling interest in the small Bethlehem Steel Company and merged it with the defunct U.S. Shipbuilding Company. In 1903 he resigned from U.S. Steel to preside over the new enterprise, which became the Bethlehem Steel Corporation in 1904. Firmly devoted to profit-sharing and incentive wages and to giv-

ing freedom to his executives, he built the company into U.S. Steel's most formidable rival. With lucrative contracts during World War I, he saw production rise to levels that made Bethlehem a prime arsenal for the Allies. At its height, his fortune was estimated at $200 million. Unsound ventures outside the steel industory depleted his resources, however, and he died insolvent on September 18, 1939.

SCOTT, WINFIELD (1786–1866), soldier. Born on June 13, 1786, near Petersburg, Virginia, Scott attended the College of William and Mary briefly in 1805 and took up the study of law. In 1807, following the *Chesapeake-Leopard* affair, he enlisted in a local cavalry troop; he soon returned to law but the next year was commissioned captain of light artillery and remained a military man thereafter. In 1812 he was made lieutenant colonel and saw action on the Niagara frontier, where he was captured by British forces. Soon after his release he participated in the attack on Fort George and in 1813 took command of the captured stronghold. In 1814, promoted to brigadier general, he fought at the battles of Chippewa and Lundy's Lane; he was wounded twice at the latter, but his success there made him a national hero, his evident ability receiving extra emphasis amid the general mediocrity of American commanders. He was brevetted major general, made a department commander, and settled in New York City. He made several trips to Europe to study military tactics and took a deep interest in maintaining a well trained and disciplined American Army. In 1838 he was charged with overseeing the pacification and removal of the Cherokee Indians to reservations beyond the Mississippi River; immediately afterward President Van Buren sent him to the far Northeast where he successfully smoothed the border conflict of the "Aroostook War." In 1841 he succeeded to the command of the entire Army. With the outbreak of the Mexican War he recommended Zachary Taylor for command of the U.S. troops; when the latter appeared to be making little progress, however, he set out himself with a supplementary force, captured Veracruz in March 1847, and six months later, after a series of victories, entered Mexico City. He remained there until April 1848, governing the city with notable justice and humanity; unfounded charges by junior officers led President Polk to call a board of inquiry to investigate his conduct of the war, but soon after his return to the United States the charges were dropped in the national celebration of his great success. Though he was by far the most capable military leader of his time, Scott was ever beset by political opposition, and though highly popular with his men, his insistence upon fine points of military propriety earned him the nickname "Old Fuss and Feathers." In 1852 he received the Whig nomination for President but was soundly beaten by Franklin Pierce. In 1855 he was promoted to lieutenant general, the first man since Washington to hold that rank. He was still commander-in-chief when the Civil War began in 1861; his advice was largely ignored and his proposed "anaconda" strategy of splitting the Confederacy—the plan eventually adopted—was widely ridiculed. In the fall of that year he retired, pleading age and infirmity. He died at West Point on May 29, 1866.

SEABORG, GLENN THEODORE (1912–   ), chemist. Born on April 19, 1912, in Ishpeming, Michigan, Seaborg grew up there and, after 1922, near Los Angeles. He graduated from the University of California at Los Angeles in 1934 and moved to the university's Berkeley campus for graduate work, taking his Ph.D. in 1937. He remained there as a research associate and in 1939 was appointed an instructor. Until 1940 his work was concerned primarily with the production of isotopes of common elements. In that year Edwin M. McMillan produced the first synthetic element, neptunium (atomic number 93), by bombarding uranium with neutrons by means

of a cyclotron; Seaborg joined him and later in the same year they produced plutonium (94). An isotope of plutonium promised a higher energy yield from nuclear fission than uranium and in 1942 Seaborg moved to the metallurgical laboratory of the Manhattan Project at the University of Chicago in order to seek means of producing and isolating usable quantities of plutonium for the atomic bomb. During the course of his work he and his staff discovered that extremely minute quantities of neptunium and plutonium occur in nature as the result of natural radioactive processes in uranium. His group also discovered two new elements, americium (95) and curium (96), in 1944, and confirmed his hypothesis that the transuranium elements form part of a transition series (the actinide series) similar to the lanthanide series of rare earths. In 1946 he returned to Berkeley as professor of chemistry and associate director of the Lawrence Radiation Laboratory. During the next 12 years his team of researchers discovered 6 more elements: berkelium (97) in 1949, californium (98) in 1950, einsteinium (99) in 1952, fermium (100) in 1953, mendelevium (101) in 1955, and nobelium (102) in 1958. In 1951 he was awarded the Nobel Prize in Chemistry jointly with McMillan. In 1954 he became director of the Radiation Laboratory and in 1958 he gave up research to become chancellor of the Berkeley campus. In 1959 he won the Enrico Fermi Award of the Atomic Energy Commission, and in 1961 he left the university to become, at President Kennedy's request, chairman of the A.E.C., the first scientist to hold the position. He represented the United States at international conferences on atomic energy and was a member of numerous scientific and educational organizations and advisory boards.

SEABURY, SAMUEL (1729–1796), clergyman. Born on November 30, 1729, in Groton, Connecticut, Seabury graduated from Yale in 1748, studied medicine at the University of Edinburgh, and was ordained a priest by the bishop of London in 1753. He was sent to New Brunswick, New Jersey, as rector in 1754, was transferred to Jamaica, New York, in 1757, and was installed as rector in Westchester, New York, in 1761. Before the American Revolution, he wrote several pamphlets and circulated them in New England under the pen name "A. W(estchester). Farmer," encouraging Americans to accept British authority and forego ideas of independence. He and his pamphlets became notorious. He was imprisoned for a time in Connecticut and after his release returned to Westchester. He served British forces as a chaplain and as a guide around New York. For the major part of the Revolution he resided far from the battle in New York City. In 1783 the Episcopal clergy of Connecticut met to choose a candidate for bishop; when their first choice declined, they turned to Seabury, who subsequently sailed for England to be consecrated. Legal problems were raised there and he turned instead to Scotland, where he was consecrated bishop of Connecticut and Rhode Island late in 1784. Upon his return to America he settled in St. James' Church in New London. When other bishops from the middle and southern colonies were consecrated in England in 1787 a movement was begun to reunite the English and Scottish factions of the American church. At the General Convention of 1789 the reunification came about and in 1792 the four American bishops met to conduct the first American consecration. Seabury continued as rector of St. James' and as bishop until his death in New London on February 25, 1796.

SEARS, RICHARD WARREN (1863–1914), merchant. Born on December 7, 1863, in Stewartville, Minnesota, Sears began working in Minneapolis for the Minneapolis and St. Louis Railway about 1880, and then was transferred to Redwood Falls, Minnesota. Various other occupations included selling lumber and coal. In 1886 a shipment of watches was left abandoned in the station and Sears got permission to sell them. He promoted them in letters, offering them at bargain rates, and sold the lot

rapidly and at a profit. He renewed his supply of watches, advertised them in St. Paul newspapers, and by 1886 was secure enough to leave railroading and start the R. W. Sears Watch Company, a mail order business, in Minneapolis. Within a year he had issued a catalogue, moved to Chicago, and engaged Alvah C. Roebuck, a watchmaker, to fix watches that were returned for adjustments. He sold out in 1889 and agreed to refrain for three years from selling watches in Chicago, settling in Iowa as a banker. But this career did not suit his entrepreneurial temperament and he returned to Minneapolis, again engaged Roebuck, and started another mail order watch and jewelry outlet. In 1893 they settled again in Chicago and the firm was renamed Sears, Roebuck and Company. Its catalogue, which at first offered 25 watches, progressively expanded to general merchandise at prices that reflected the economy of large-scale purchasing, efficient handling, and mail instead of retail sales. The bulk of their customers (though later including millions in cities) were in remote rural areas, inadequately served by retail outlets. Sears's catalogue advertising, liberally sprinkled with adjectives, was "folksy" enough to be readable as popular fare. The success of his business, however, relied on firm policies—fixed prices, guarantees, and a liberal adjustment plan—standards which, in themselves, fostered quality merchandise and an improvement in the conduct of competitive retailers. In 1897 Julius Rosenwald became vice president of the company. He rose to president in 1910, succeeding Sears, who had retired the year before to his farm north of Chicago. Sears died in Waukesha, Wisconsin, on September 28, 1914.

SEEGER, PETE (1919–), folk singer and composer. Born in New York City on May 3, 1919, into a musical family, Seeger attended Harvard from 1936 to 1938, before he began to travel. By 1940 he had passed through the 48 states, mostly by freight train and hitchhiking, and had acquired along the way a vast repertoire of songs—ballads, blues and country songs, hymns and spirituals, work songs, and dance tunes—and new ways of playing his favorite instrument, the five-string banjo. That year he organized the Almanac Singers, with Millard Lampell, Lee Hays, and Woody Guthrie, and they toured the country in 1941, entertaining primarily in union halls and at farmers' and factory workers' meetings, with industrial ballads and songs that he and Guthrie wrote. He made broadcasts overseas for the Office of War Information during World War II, and after the war briefly rejoined the Almanac Singers. In 1948 he organized the Weavers, a singing group, with Hays, Fred Hellerman, and Ronnie Gilbert, and himself singing and playing banjo. Achieving great popularity, they appeared on national radio and television, in nightclubs, concert halls, and theaters, and made numerous recordings. In 1958 he reluctantly left the group to attend to his individual activities. He played and sang in high schools and colleges, churches, taverns, backyard theaters, and Town Hall and Carnegie Hall, and on hundreds of radio and television programs. He was in the short film *To Hear My Banjo Play* in the 1940s and in a Los Angeles Repertory Theatre revival of the folk play *Dark of the Moon*. In the 1950s he appeared in the National Folk Festival in St. Louis and gave six concerts with commentary on "American Folk Music and Its World Origin" at Columbia. In 1963–1964, he undertook a global singing tour with his family. A virtuoso and authority on the five-string banjo, he published an instructional manual replete with anecdotes, history, and biographical sketches, *How to Play the 5-String Banjo*, 1948, rev. 1954. Among the songs he wrote or collaborated on were "Where Have All the Flowers Gone," "If I had a Hammer," "Kisses Sweeter than Wine," and "Turn, Turn, Turn." An inspiration to countless young artists, he was one of the most beloved figures in the folk music world.

SENNETT, MACK (1884–1960), motion picture producer and director. Born on January 17, 1884, in Richmond, Quebec, Canada, Sennett moved to New York City at age 20 from East Berlin, Connecticut, where he had been an iron worker. Intent upon a stage career, he changed his name from Michael Sinnott. He performed in burlesque and circuses, and secured minor parts in Broadway plays, once in *The Boys of Company B*, in whose cast also was John Barrymore. In 1909 he began working for D. W. Griffith at the Biograph Studios. Late in 1911 he opened his own studio, the Keystone Company, where three years later *Tillie's Punctured Romance*, the first American feature-length comedy was produced. Between 1919 and 1924 the company produced a number of biting satires and parodies of industrialism, but Sennett became most famous for the broad comedy and burlesque known as slapstick. The legend, "A Mack Sennett Comedy," signified incredible chases, the Mack Sennett Bathing Beauties, and custard pies. (The original custard pie was flung spontaneously into the face of Ben Turpin by actress Mabel Normand.) At first he acted in his films, but later he devoted himself to being a director of such stars as Charlie Chaplin, W. C. Fields, Gloria Swanson, Marie Dressler, Harold Lloyd, Wallace Beery, Buster Keaton, Miss Normand, and Turpin. He created the Keystone Kops, whose hilarious antics featured performances by Harry Langdon, Edgar Kennedy, Slim Summerville, and Roscoe ("Fatty") Arbuckle, and which were frequently improvised at the scene of actual events—fires or parades—that would have been too expensive to stage. The studio was responsible for some 1,000 short subjects before its demise in 1933, largely because of the Depression and the advent of talking and double-feature films. He was honored by the Academy of Motion Picture Arts and Sciences in 1937 and drifted gradually into oblivion. He died in Woodland Hills, California, on November 5, 1960.

SEQUOYA (c.1770–1843), Indian leader. Born about 1770 in a Tuskegee village on the Tennessee River, the present site of Loudon County, Tennessee, Sequoya (or Sequoyah) was probably the son of an English trader, Nathaniel Gist, and a part-Cherokee woman. Raised by his mother, he never learned English and understood his English surname to be Guess. He was a silversmith, a hunter, and a fur trader, and served with the Army in the Creek War in 1813–1814. Wounds incurred either in battle or on a hunting trip left him lame in one leg. He began work about 1809 on an alphabet for the Cherokee language, having always been fascinated by the "talking leaves" or papers with the written language of the white man. He first experimented with pictographs, but by 1821 arrived at a syllabary of 86 characters adapted from the English, Greek, and Hebrew alphabets, which he studied in mission school books. His people had thought him foolish or a witch—at one time all of his records were burned—but his successful demonstration of the alphabet with his six-year-old daughter won the approval of the chieftains. In 1822 he visited the Cherokees of Arkansas and sent written communications from them to the tribe in the East. He moved with them to Oklahoma in 1828 and became a teacher in schools that were established, and a political envoy, traveling in 1828 to Washington. In 1824 parts of the Bible were printed in Cherokee and in 1828 appeared the *Cherokee Phoenix,* a weekly newspaper printed in English and Cherokee. In 1841 he was voted an allowance for his contribution and two years later the tribe's legislature voted him a lifetime pension—the first in an Indian tribe. He made trips to other villages to compare their grammar and speech. In 1843 he set out to find a band of Cherokees thought to have crossed the Mississippi at the time of the Revolution. On this journey, probably while in Tamaulipas, Mexico, he died. A national park and a species of giant redwood trees in California were named for him. A statue of him was placed in Statuary Hall in the national Capitol by the state of Oklahoma.

DR. SEUSS see **GEISEL, THEODOR SEUSS**

SEWALL, SAMUEL (1652–1730), merchant, jurist, and diarist. Born on March 28, 1652, in Bishopstoke, England, Sewall traveled with his New England parents to Boston in 1661. He graduated from Harvard in 1671 and five years later married the daughter of wealthy shipowner John Hull, thereby acquiring a sizeable fortune. A member of the General Court, he also held a lifetime position on the governor's advisory council. Although his training was not primarily in the law, he was named a judge of the Superior Court of the colony and in 1718 became its chief justice. Noted throughout the colony for clarity and compassion in his rulings, he stood alone before the people five years after the 1692 Salem witchcraft trials to disclaim his decisions, while the other nine judges who had sat on the bench during the trials remained silent. His essay, *The Selling of Joseph,* 1700, was one of the first American appeals for an end to slavery. His diary, published initially by the Massachusetts Historical Society in 1878–1882, covers the period from 1673 to 1729, with the omission of eight years from 1677 to 1685, and is unique and historically greatly valuable in its depiction of the values and character of a typical New England Puritan. He died in Boston on January 1, 1730.

SEWARD, WILLIAM HENRY (1801–1872), public official. Born in Florida, New York, on May 16, 1801, Seward graduated from Union College in 1820, was admitted to the bar two years later, and began the practice of law in Auburn, New York. He soon became actively interested in politics and began what was to be a lifelong association with Thurlow Weed; he allied himself with the rising Antimason Party and was elected to the state senate in 1830. As the Antimason movement subsided and the opposition to the Jacksonian Democrats coalesced in the Whig Party, Seward followed suit. Defeated for governor on the Whig ticket in 1834, he was elected in 1838 and again in 1840. During his four years in this office he took boldly liberal stands on several issues, advocating the admission of foreign-born and Catholic teachers to the public school system, public expenditures for internal improvements, and, most significantly, resistance to the extradition of fugitive slaves. In 1843 he returned to his law practice but maintained his political interest and connections and in 1849 was elected to the Senate. His national political career began with his opposition to the Compromise of 1850 and his controversial appeal—later retracted in some confusion—to "a higher law than the Constitution." He strongly opposed the Kansas-Nebraska Bill in 1854 and led the remnants of the shattered Whig Party into the new Republican Party. He supported the admission of Kansas as a free state and denounced the Dred Scott decision in 1858, and it was he who, in a speech of that year, referred to the "irrepressible conflict" between the slave and free sections. As the preeminent figure among Republicans, he had justifiable hopes for the presidential nomination in 1856 and 1860, but in both years was passed over for candidates with less previous political identification. Lincoln chose Seward for secretary of state and he took office confident that he would dominate the President and the government; he suggested to Lincoln that a war with one or more European nations would unite the country and, conferring with Southern emissaries, he made unauthorized statements to the effect that Fort Pickens and Fort Sumter would be surrendered. He interfered in the Sumter expedition but to no avail; soon brought to heel by Lincoln, he performed the functions of his office with great skill thereafter. He successfully handled the problem of maintaining European neutrality during the Civil War and secured valuable advantages from the *Trent* and *Alabama* affairs. His diplomatic conduct concerning the French intervention in Mexico was masterful, succeeding at length in obtaining Maximilian's withdrawal. On April 13, 1865, as Lincoln was being assassinated, Seward was attacked by a co-conspirator of John Wilkes

Booth; already in poor health from an injury sustained some days earlier, he nonetheless regained his powers sufficiently to remain in office under President Johnson. In 1867 he negotiated the purchase of Alaska—"Seward's Folly"—from Russia and looked forward to the annexation of Santo Domingo and Hawaii. He fell from political grace by siding with Johnson in the battle over Reconstruction and left office with him in 1869. After a world tour he returned to his Auburn home and died there on October 10, 1872.

SHAHN, BENJAMIN (1898–1969), painter. Born on September 12, 1898, in Kaunas (Kovno), Lithuania, the son of a carpenter, Shahn came to New York at age eight and grew up in a Brooklyn slum. Trained as a lithographer at 15, he worked while taking evening courses at the City College, New York University, and the National Academy of Design. He traveled through France, Italy, North Africa, and Spain in 1925 and 1927–1929. Returning to the United States, he devoted his work to social and political causes, changing his expressionistic painting style to a realism that was highly personal and that often bordered on surrealism. He completed in 1931–1932 a series of 23 small gouache paintings and two large panels on the trial and execution of Sacco and Vanzetti, and executed 15 paintings and a panel on the trial of labor leader Tom Mooney in 1933. Between 1933 and 1943 he worked under the Federal government's Public Works of Art project, completing eight temperas on life during Prohibition, and several epic murals, among them a fresco for a housing project for garment workers in New Jersey, a 13-panel mural in the Bronx Central Annex post office depicting American city and country life, and the story of American welfare under social security in the Social Security building in Washington D.C. These and other murals were influenced by the concepts of the Mexican artist Diego Rivera, whom he assisted for several years. He designed posters in 1943 for the Office of War Information, in

1944 for the Political Action Committee of the Congress of Industrial Organizations, and in his later career for the presidential campaign of Eugene McCarthy. Simultaneously with his mural and poster work he completed paintings of urban life, including "Handball," 1939, and "Girl Jumping Rope," 1943, and others with labor messages or views of social significance, such as "The Red Stairway," 1944, and "Liberation," 1945, "Hunger" and "The World's Greatest Comics," both 1946, and "Death of a Miner," "The Violin Player," and "East Twelfth Street," all in 1947. In 1956 he delivered the Charles Eliot Norton lectures at Harvard, published as *The Shape of Content,* 1957. His works were shown in museums, galleries, and universities throughout the United States and in Europe. He died in New York City on March 14, 1969.

SHAPLEY, HARLOW (1885–), astronomer. Born in Nashville, Missouri, on November 2, 1885, Shapley graduated from the University of Missouri in 1910 and received his M.A. and Ph.D. degrees from Princeton in 1911 and 1913. He joined the staff of the Mount Wilson Observatory in 1914, remaining until 1921, when he became a professor of astronomy at Harvard. He was director of the Harvard observatory from 1921 to 1952, remained as a professor until 1956, and was subsequently an emeritus professor at Harvard and a visiting lecturer at several other institutions. A bold and imaginative researcher and theorist, his first important work concerned eclipsing binary stars. As early as 1913, with H. N. Russell, he devised a method of determining the dimensions of the component stars of these systems from measurements of the light variation during eclipse. He was the first to show that Cepheid variables cannot be eclipsing binaries and was also the first to propose the theory, now accepted, that they are instead single pulsating stars. He then went on to study star clusters, especially globular clusters, and was one of the first to employ variable stars (Cepheids and RR Lyrae stars) as indicators of distance. He was thus able to make a map of

star clusters by distance and on the basis of this made the novel hypothesis, later substantiated, that the globular clusters form a fairly symmetrical swarm around the center of our galaxy and that our sun must therefore be in the outer regions of the galaxy, some tens of thousands of light years from the center. He studied our own Milky Way galaxy in relation to other nearby galaxies, such as that in the constellation of Andromeda, and was able to show that galaxies themselves tend to occur in clusters and that the Milky Way is a member of one such cluster. He wrote a number of books and articles, most of them of a highly technical nature, but also including such more or less popular works as *Star Clusters,* 1930, *Flights from Chaos,* 1930, *Galaxies,* 1943, *Inner Metagalaxy,* 1957, *Of Stars and Men,* 1958, and *The View from a Distant Star,* 1964. He was the recipient of many honors and awards, and was president of the American Academy of Arts and Sciences from 1939 to 1944 and of the American Association for the Advancement of Science in 1947.

SHAW, HENRY WHEELER (1818–1885), "Josh Billings," author and humorist. Born on April 21, 1818, in Lanesboro, Massachusetts, Shaw briefly attended Hamilton College and led an unsettled life, being at various times a farmer, explorer, real estate salesman, riverboat man, and auctioneer for the first 40 or more years of his life. Then he began writing burlesques of news items, featuring misspelled words, distorted syntax, anticlimax, and numerous other humorous devices. He joined the staff of the *New York Weekly* in 1867 and won a national reputation for his work, but he had made his first great hit in 1860, with his "Essa on the Muel," which began: "The muel is haf Hoss and haf Jackass, and then kums tu a full stop, natur diskovering her mistake." His books included *Josh Billings, His Sayings,* 1865, annual *Allminax* published from 1869 to 1880, and *Josh Billings Struggling With Things,* 1881. Unlike other contemporary humorists, his work was not based on current events but was intended to be universal.

He died in Monterey, California, on October 14, 1885.

SHAW, LEMUEL (1781–1861), jurist. Born on January 9, 1781, in Barnstable, Massachusetts, Shaw graduated from Harvard, studied law in Boston, and was admitted to the bar in 1804. A distinguished career followed as a civic official and as a counsel to many important commercial interests. In 1822, with few or no precedents to guide him, he wrote Boston's first city charter, which endured for more than 90 years. By 1830, when he was offered the post of chief justice of the Massachusetts supreme court, he was making upwards of $20,000 a year, an immense sum for the time. He accepted the post and served for 30 years, until his retirement in 1860. His long tenure on the bench coincided with the rise and evolution of important social and economic issues, and he left his mark on the structure and development not only of Massachusetts but also of U.S. law. Two cases were particularly notable. In the first, *Commonwealth* v. *Hunt*, 1842, he ruled in favor of a striking labor union, thus freeing unions generally of the abusive application of the law of conspiracy; in the second, *Roberts* v. *Boston*, though personally opposed to slavery, he ruled that racial segregation in the city's schools did not create constitutional inequalities. This "separate but equal" doctrine was later extended nationwide by the Supreme Court in *Plessy* v. *Ferguson*, 1896; but in Massachusetts it had the contrary effect, for a state desegregation law was soon passed, the only one to be enacted by a state until the 20th century. Shaw sponsored many charitable institutions and was a fellow and overseer of Harvard. He died on March 30, 1861. His only daughter, Elizabeth, was the wife of Herman Melville.

SHAYS, DANIEL (1747?–1825), Revolutionary soldier and rebel. Shays was probably born in Hopkinton, Massachusetts, around 1747, although the town's records do not mention his name. Little is known of his early life, but he responded to the call for volunteers at the outbreak of the Revolution and served with distinction at Bunker Hill, Ticonderoga, Saratoga, and Stony Point, being commissioned captain in the 5th Massachusetts at the beginning of 1777. He was a popular and effective officer and was rewarded, toward the end of the war, with a handsome sword that was presented to him by Lafayette, but later poverty forced him to sell it. He resigned from the army in 1780 and settled in Pelham, where he held several town offices. The end of the war was followed by a period of prosperity, but this soon gave way to a severe country-wide depression. The Massachusetts legislature refused to heed demands for redress of grievances, especially vocal in western Massachusetts, and the situation deteriorated there in the latter part of 1786 to armed rebellion. Shays was but one of several leaders, but his name became associated with the revolt, mainly because of a confrontation in Springfield on September 26th between a group of about 800 armed farmers and about the same number of militia. The question was whether the state supreme court should be allowed to sit, for the farmers feared that it would return indictments against them. An agreement was reached, but it was followed by a period of chaotic relations between the two parties, and actual fighting broke out during the winter. After confused rallyings, a band under Shays was defeated at Petersham, on February 2, 1787. He fled to Vermont and was one of the few who were exempted from a general pardon later in the year. He was condemned to death in absentia, but in February 1788 he petitioned for pardon and was granted it on June 13th. He later moved to New York State, where he lived until his death, in Sparta, on September 29, 1825. In his later years he was given a pension for his service in the Revolution; and he always insisted that he had fought then and in the rebellion that bears his name for exactly the same principles.

SHERIDAN, PHILIP HENRY (1831–1888), soldier. Born on March 6, 1831, Sheridan gave his birthplace variously as Albany, Boston, and Somerset, Ohio. It is certain, at least, that he grew up and received his rather scanty schooling in the last-named town. In 1848 he entered West Point and graduated in 1853, having been suspended for a year for fighting. He served in several Indian campaigns in the West and at the outbreak of the Civil War was a captain and quartermaster officer in Missouri. His much wished-for opportunity for combat came in May 1862 when he was appointed colonel in command of the 2nd Michigan Cavalry. On July 1st he performed brilliantly at Booneville, Mississippi, was commended by General Rosecrans, and was promoted to brigadier general of volunteers. At the head of the 11th Division, Army of the Ohio, he won victories at Perryville and Stones River and was made major general. Taking command of the 20th Corps, Army of the Cumberland, in 1863, he fought at Chickamauga and then ended his service in the western theater with his famous charge up Missionary Ridge that contributed in large fashion to Grant's victory at Chattanooga. When Grant went east to take over the Army of the Potomac, Sheridan followed to command the cavalry. During the Wilderness campaign and the action around Richmond in 1864 his troops destroyed Confederate supplies and lines of communication and constantly harassed the enemy. In August he took command of the Army of the Shenandoah. After weeks of careful planning he set about clearing and securing the Shenandoah Valley; he defeated Jubal Early at Winchester, Fisher's Hill, and Cedar Creek and was made brigadier and then major general of the regular Army. In March 1865 he began maneuvering around the enemy's rear at Petersburg; after victories at Dinwiddie Court House and Five Forks he cut off Lee's line of retreat from Appomattox and the Southern surrender followed promptly. Sheridan was sent after the war to command troops along the Gulf and the Mexican border, where his aid and demonstrations of force helped hasten the fall of Emperor Maximilian. Early in 1867 he was made military governor of Louisiana and Texas, but his harsh administration led to his removal soon thereafter. He returned to the Indian campaigns in the West and in 1869 became lieutenant general in command of the Divison of the Missouri. He was sent to observe the Franco-Prussian War in 1870–1871. In 1883 he became commander-in-chief of the Army, succeeding Sherman, and on June 1, 1888, was promoted by act of Congress to the rank of general. He died shortly thereafter, on August 5, 1888, in Nonquitt, Massachusetts.

SHERMAN, JOHN (1823–1900), public official. Born in Lancaster, Ohio, on May 10, 1823, a younger brother of William Tecumseh Sherman, John Sherman received little formal education but studied law with an uncle and was admitted to the bar in 1844. He achieved prominence as a lawyer quickly and involved himself in Whig politics, though he did not run for office until 1854 when he was elected to Congress primarily on the anti-Nebraska issue. In 1856 he drafted the report of a committee investigation into the situation in Kansas. Moving easily into the Republican Party, he remained in the House until being elevated to the Senate in 1861. In 1867 he became chairman of the finance committee; this subject Sherman considered to be his special competence and, as a generally conservative Republican from a largely agrarian region, he attempted constantly to mediate inflationist and sound-money factions, usually by compromise though occasionally by wavering. He was persuaded to hold out against the cancellation of Civil War greenbacks, whose issue he had supported, until 1875, when he played a central role in the passage of the Specie Resumption Act. Two years later he became Hayes's secretary of the treasury and for two years very skillfully administered a program leading to specie resumption and retirement of greenbacks in 1879. In 1881 he returned to the Senate. His next 16 years in that body were marked most notably by the Anti-Trust and Silver Purchase acts of 1890, both of which bore his name, but which were compromise measures having only his partial approval. In 1880, 1884, and 1888 his name was mentioned as a possibility for the Republican presidential nomination, but he attracted little real support. In 1897 President McKinley appointed him secretary of state in order to create a Senate vacancy for Mark Hanna. Sherman found the duties of this office beyond his capacities; he was, moreover, in profound disagreement with popular expansionist clamor, and when the decision for war with Spain was made he resigned. He died in Washington on October 22, 1900.

SHERMAN, ROGER (1721–1793), public official. Born on April 19, 1721, in Newton, Massachusetts, Sherman grew up in Stoughton, working his father's farm and learning the trade of cordwainer. His formal education was scant but on his own he was an avid student of theology, mathematics, and law. In 1743 he moved to New Milford, Connecticut, and opened a cobbler shop. In 1745 he was appointed county surveyor and began to accumulate what eventually amounted to considerable wealth. He served in a succession of local offices while carrying on a mercantile business and publishing a series of almanacs. In 1754 he was admitted to the bar and during the next several years served on the county court, in the legislature, and in other public offices. In 1761 he moved to New Haven, where he became a benefactor and for several years treasurer of Yale College. His public duties increased continually until he was forced to retire from business in 1772. In 1774 he was elected to the First Continental Congress and, a staunch though conservative supporter of the colonial cause, there signed the Non-Importation Articles of Association; he remained in Congress until 1781 and served again in 1783–1784, becoming a signer of the Declaration of Independence and helping to draft the Articles of Confedera-

tion, which he also signed. He was an indefatigable worker in committee and became an experienced and highly adroit legislator. Through the war he was often a member of the Connecticut Council of Safety and in 1783 helped revise and codify the state laws. In 1787 he was a delegate to the Constitutional Convention and there introduced the famous "Connecticut Compromise" that provided for the dual system of representation in Congress and prevented a deadlock between large and small states. By signing the Constitution he became the only person to have signed the Articles of Association and of Confederation, the Declaration of Independence, and the Constitution. He was held in high regard by his contemporaries, among whom he was known as a man of unimpeachable honesty; he was in the House of Representatives from 1789 to 1791 and in the Senate from 1791 until his death on July 23, 1793, in New Haven.

SHERMAN, WILLIAM TECUMSEH (1820–1891), soldier. Born on February 8, 1820, in Lancaster, Ohio, Sherman was the son of an Ohio supreme court judge and an elder brother of John Sherman. Left fatherless at nine, he grew up in the home of Thomas Ewing, prominent Ohio politician and later first secretary of the interior, who procured for him an appointment to West Point in 1836. Graduating in 1840, he served in Florida and other points in the South until the outbreak of the Mexican War; after holding several staff positions despite his eagerness for line duty, he became adjutant to the commander of the Division of the Pacific and thereby effectively chief administrative officer of California until the state government was organized in 1848. In 1853 he resigned his commission and joined a St. Louis banking firm, managing its San Francisco branch; he was later in New York for a short time and after the failure of the firm in 1857 he practised law briefly in Leavenworth, Kansas. In 1859 he obtained the position of superintendent of a new military college in

Alexandria, Louisiana, a post he held until 1861 when the secessionist movement in the South forced him to move to St. Louis. In May of that year he was appointed colonel of the 13th Infantry; he led a brigade at first Bull Run and soon was made brigadier general of volunteers. Sent to Kentucky, he soon assumed command there, but held it only briefly; he then joined Grant's command and took part in the battles of Shiloh and Corinth. He was promoted to major general of volunteers and sent to fortify Memphis in preparation for the Vicksburg campaign; he played a conspicuous part in the final defeat of Vicksburg in July 1863 and was promoted to brigadier general of the regular Army. When Grant was placed in charge of all Western forces, Sherman succeeded to command of the Army of the Tennessee. He took part in the battle of Chattanooga in November 1863; the following March, when Grant went east to assume command of all Union forces, Sherman again succeeded him, becoming commander of the Division of the Mississippi. In May he assembled his armies—numbering about 100,000 men—and began his invasion of Georgia. He had forced Confederate Gen. Joseph Johnston back to Atlanta by July; he continued to pressure his outnumbered opponent and on September 1, J. B. Hood, who had replaced Johnston, abandoned Atlanta. Sherman was promoted to major general. In November, leaving behind a force to deal with Hood, he cut loose from his supply base and led 60,000 men to Savannah, living off the land and destroying everything of military value in his path. The Georgia campaign, intended to bring the war home to the Southern citizenry, roused bitter controversy but was undeniably effective; looting along the route of march was inevitable but, despite Southern memories of the matter, was in fact held to a minimum. Savannah was reached on December 21st and in January Sherman turned northward through the Carolinas. Johnston was called east to oppose him but could offer little resistance; the Confederate general accepted Sherman's liberal surrender terms on April 17, 1865, eight days after Lee had surrendered to Grant. Sherman returned to St. Louis in command of the Division of the Mississippi and, while restraining the Indians, aided in the construction of the transcontinental railroad. He became lieutenant general in 1866 and in 1869, when Grant was inaugurated President, assumed command of the entire Army. He held this post until November 1883 and a few months later retired from active duty. In 1884 his name was proposed to the Republican convention as a presidential possibility; he ended such speculations by sending a message to clarify his position: "If nominated, I will not accept. If elected, I will not serve." He moved to New York City in 1886 and died there on February 14, 1891.

SHERWOOD, ROBERT EMMET (1896–1955), author and playwright. Born on April 4, 1896, in New Rochelle, New York, Sherwood attended Milton Academy and Harvard, where he showed more interest in the *Lampoon* and in various theatrical productions than in his studies. He left college in 1917 to enlist in the Canadian army and was discharged two years later, having received a dose of poison gas. He returned to New York and became drama editor of *Vanity Fair*. There his coworkers, Dorothy Parker and Robert Benchley, introduced him to the exclusive New York literary circle, with whom he subsequently associated at the Algonquin Round Table, the center of literary society. He was an editor of *Life*, a humor magazine, from 1920 to 1928. His first play was *The Road to Rome*, 1927. It was followed by *The Petrified Forest*, 1935, and a 1936 Pulitzer Prize winner, *Idiot's Delight*, both focusing on selfish heroes who find that their lives only become meaningful when they sacrifice themselves for other people. *Abe Lincoln in Illinois*, 1938, and *There Shall Be No Night*, 1941, also won Pulitzer Prizes. So impressed with his play about Lincoln was Mrs. Eleanor Roosevelt that she introduced him to the President, with whom he became closely allied. He eventually became Roosevelt's chief speech writer, and his sensitivity in interpreting the President's views helped to end the disfavor in which speech writing was generally held. He won a fourth Pulitzer Prize for the biographical *Roosevelt and Hopkins*, 1949, based on his friendship with the two men. Between 1940 and 1945 he served in various government posts, including assistant to the secretary of war and the secretary of the Navy and director of the overseas division of the Office of War Information. He wrote little for the stage after the war, but a screenplay, *The Best Years of Our Lives*, 1946, won an Academy Award. He died in New York on November 14, 1955.

SHUBERT, LEE (1875–1953), and JACOB J. (1880–1963), theater managers and producers. Born in Syracuse, New York, Lee on March 15, 1875, and J. J. on August 15, 1880, the Shuberts as young men entered the theater business. With a third brother, Sam S. (1876–1905), they began by organizing several touring companies in Syracuse for the comedies of Charles A. Hoyt. At the time—the later 1890s—the Theatrical Syndicate, headed by Marc Klaw, A. L. Erlanger, and others, owned and operated most of the New York theaters and many playhouses outside the city. This trust had enormous power and was able—and was charged with desiring—to discriminate against some independent producers, among them David Belasco. In 1900 the Shuberts leased the Herald Square Theatre in New York City and thereupon began to acquire, by lease and purchase, other theaters both inside and outside of New York. For about ten years the war between the Shuberts and the syndicate was waged relentlessly, but in the end—by about 1910—the Shuberts emerged triumphant. At first, the Shuberts rented their theaters to producers discriminated against by the syndicate; but soon they became producers also, putting on their own shows in their own houses, and once again this had the effect of limiting the availability of theaters for the independents. Thus the Shuberts came to be hated as the syndicate had been; they were charged with demanding exorbitant rentals and with insisting on harsh contracts, particularly for neophyte producers. In 1950 the U.S. government filed a civil antitrust suit against the Shubert Theatre Corporation, charging the brothers with monopolistic practices, but the suit was dropped before coming to trial. At that time, the Shubert combine was said to control some 37 theaters (including 17 in New York) and a large part of the theatrical bookings of the nation. These revelations were hardly news to those within the theater, but they led to a series of charges that the Shuberts were stifling American theatrical creativity. Sam S. died in 1905; a New York theater was later named after him by his surviving brothers. Lee died on Christmas Day, 1953, whereupon J. J. Shubert became head of all the family enterprises, which included, besides theaters, a company controlling production rights to a large number of plays, a music publishing company, and one of the leading purveyors of stage costumes. Known as "the man who produced a thousand shows," J. J. included among his credits the staging of vast open air operettas in cities from Miami to Los Angeles, and the introduction to American audiences of such stars as Al Jolson, Eddie Cantor, Ed Wynn, Fanny Brice, the Dolly sisters, Ray Bolger, Bert Lahr, and many more. He died exactly ten years after his brother Lee, on Christmas Day, 1963.

SIKORSKY, IGOR IVANOVITCH (1889–   ), aeronautical engineer. Born in Kiev, Russia, on May 25, 1889, Sikorsky was educated in Kiev, Petrograd, and Paris. Interested in aviation from his youth, his earliest ideas came from drawings of flying machines by Leonardo da Vinci. He went to France and Germany before he was 20 and studied the accomplishments of Blériot and the work being done on Zeppelin's dirigible. In 1909 he designed and built his first aircraft, a helicopter, which was as yet impractical, however. He turned to construction of fixed-wing aircraft and by 1911 was not only an experienced pilot, but had produced five successful airplanes. His S-5 made a world record flight in 1911 with three men on board, 30 miles cross-country at 70 miles per hour. During 1912–1918, as head of engineering of the aviation plant at Russo-Baltic Railroad Car Works, he designed, built, and piloted planes of unsurpassed flying range and size. The most important of these, built in 1913, was the first successful four-engine plane in the world. Leaving Russia during the Revolution, he stayed briefly in London and Paris before emigrating to the United States in 1919 (he was naturalized in 1928). Settling in New York, he taught mathematics at a school for Russian immigrants until, in 1923, he was financially able to found his own aircraft manufacturing firm, the Sikorsky Aero Engineering Corporation, which in 1929 became a subsidiary of the United Aircraft Corporation. The enterprise turned out a variety of aircraft for commercial and military uses. Among these were the S-29, a twin-engine 14-passenger plane with a speed of 115 miles per hour; the huge S-38 amphibian; and the S-40 "American Clipper," the first of a series of four-engine Clipper ships, which pioneered transoceanic commercial routes in the 1930s. In 1939 he resumed work on the helicopter, and in that year built and flew the first workable direct-lift machine in the country. Able to take off and land vertically, to hover in the air, and to move in any direction, the helicopter was quickly recognized as a highly versatile craft with a multitude of applications in civil and military operations. As a cargo, air-bus, and rescue vehicle, it soon became the work-horse of the air. Sikorsky continued to produce and improve helicopters until retiring from United Aircraft in 1957, after which he served on a consulting basis. He was named to the International Aerospace Hall of Fame in 1966 and the next year received the National Medal of Science. He wrote *The Winged S*, 1938, *The Message of the Lord's Prayer*, 1942, and *The Invisible Encounter*, 1947.

SILLIMAN, BENJAMIN (1779–1864), scientist and educator. Born in North Stratford (now Trumbull), Connecticut, on August 8, 1779, Silliman graduated from Yale in 1796. Two years later he returned to New Haven to study law and in 1799 became a tutor at Yale; in 1802, after his admission to the bar, he was appointed Yale's first professor of chemistry and natural history. For two years he pursued his studies with prominent American scientists and in 1804 assumed his teaching duties. In 1805 he sailed to Europe to further his studies and published a popular account of his travels and associations in 1810 as *A Journal of Travels in England, Holland and Scotland*. Beginning in 1808 he also lectured in public on topics in chemistry and geology, becoming eventually a speaker in great demand throughout the nation, and he delivered the first Lowell Lectures in Boston in 1839–1840. He played a leading role in the establishment of the Yale Medical School in 1813 and served it thereafter as professor of chemistry. In 1818 he issued the first number of *The American Journal of Science and the Arts*; remaining under his editorship until passed on to his son, "Silliman's Journal," as it was popularly known, became one of the world's leading scientific periodicals. In addition to American editions of standard English texts in chemistry and geology, he published in 1830 his own *Elements of Chemistry*. In 1847 he secured the establishment of the Department of Philosophy and the Arts that became in time the Yale and finally the Sheffield Scientific School. He was also instrumental in the founding of Yale's Trumbull Gallery. He retired as professor emeritus in 1853 and ten years later was, with his son, an original member of the National Academy of Sciences. He died in New Haven on November 24, 1864. His son, BENJAMIN SILLIMAN, JR., born in New Haven on December 4, 1816, graduated from Yale in 1837 and became immediately his father's assistant. The younger Silliman aided in the founding of the Scientific School and gradually took over editorship of the *Journal*, serving in that capacity until his death. During 1845–1846 he delivered what is believed to be the first course on agricultural chemistry in a series of lectures in New Orleans; in the latter year he was appointed professor of chemistry at Yale. From 1849 to 1854 he lectured at the University of Louisville and then returned to Yale to succeed to his father's twin professorships. In 1855 he published his *Report on the Rock Oil, or Petroleum, from Venango County, Pennsylvania*, in which he described the first analysis of crude oil, the method of fractional distillation into several components, and the superior usefulness of various portions for lubrication, illumination, and the manufacture of parrafin, thus outlining the economic potential of the great industry that was to begin four years later. Others of Silliman's publications included *First Principles of Chemistry*, 1846, and *First Principles of Physics, or Natural Philosophy*, 1858. He retired from the Scientific School in 1869 and from the College in 1870, but continued to lecture at the Medical School until his death in New Haven on January 14, 1885.

SIMMS, WILLIAM GILMORE (1806–1870), author. Born on April 17, 1806, in Charleston, South Carolina, Simms grew up motherless and, after his father left to serve under Jackson in the Creek campaigns and at New Orleans, he was reared by his grandmother. He was a precocious student and, having already fairly mastered four languages, entered the College of Charleston at 10. Two years later he was apprenticed to a druggist and during the next few years contributed poetry to Charleston newspapers, did editorial work, and took up the study of law. Though he was admitted to the bar in 1827 he had by that time decided to devote his energies to literature. He became editor of the Charleston *City Gazette* about 1828, but lost the job when he took a highly unpopular stand against nullification in 1832. Following the death of his wife in the same year, he traveled to New York, where he formed valuable friendships with William Cullen Bryant and other literary figures and wrote his first novel, *Martin Faber*, 1833. It was fol-

lowed by *Guy Rivers*, 1834, and *The Yemassee*, 1835, his best known work. In 1835 he returned to Charleston; the next year he married the daughter of a wealthy plantation owner and until about 1842 he continued to produce romantic novels, including *The Partisan*, 1835, *Mellichampe*, 1836, *Richard Hurdis*, 1838, and *The Kinsmen*, 1841. The larger portion of his fiction dealt with various periods of Southern history and, while his major characters tended to be formulaically aristocratic, in his secondary figures he presented accurate and engaging portraits of a wide range of Southern types—backwoodsmen, Indians, slaves, adventurers, outlaws, gamblers, and the rest. Simms's work as a whole suggested a Southern parallel, remarked at the time, to that of James Fenimore Cooper in the North. His reputation, at least during the early part of his career, was higher in the North, primarily because his social station was such as to retard recognition in conservative Charleston. During the 1840s he wrote a history and a geography of his native state, biographies of several Southern figures, and a good deal of criticism. He returned to the historical novel with *Katherine Walton*, 1851, and followed with *The Sword and the Distaff*, 1853 (revised as *Woodcraft*, 1854), *The Forayers*, 1855, and *Eutaw*, 1856. His collected *Poems* appeared in 1853, the most notable of his 19 volumes of verse. He threw himself vigorously into the growing sectional dispute, becoming a noted lecturer on the South and editing from 1849 to 1856 the pro-slavery *Southern Quarterly Review*. During the Civil War he suffered the loss of his second wife and two of his children and the burning of his home and library. In his remaining years he wrote little of note; a novel, *Joscelyn*, appeared in 1867 and in the same year he edited the *War Poetry of the South*. In all he produced some 82 volumes during his life. He died in Charleston on June 11, 1870.

SIMS, WILLIAM SOWDEN (1858–1936), naval officer. Born on October 15, 1858, in Port Hope, Ontario, of an American father, Sims moved with his family to Pennsylvania in 1872. In 1876, having once been rejected, he gained admission to the Naval Academy and graduated four years later. From 1880 to 1897 he was almost continuously on sea duty; a part of the time he devoted to writing a navigation text that was long used by both the Navy and the merchant marine. From 1897 to 1900 he was naval attaché at the American embassies in Paris and, briefly, St. Petersburg. By the time he resumed sea duty on the China Station in 1900 he had become convinced of the relative inferiority of the U.S. Navy in matters of ship design, tactics, and gunnery, the victories of the Spanish-American War notwithstanding . In the Orient he met Capt. Percy Scott, developer of the new technique of continuous-aim firing; he wrote a series of memoranda to the Navy Department describing and advocating the adoption of this method, but received no satisfactory reply. Finally, in 1901 and again in 1902, he wrote directly to President Roosevelt—an act of technical insubordination—and as a result was brought to Washington as inspector of target practice. Remaining in that post until 1909, and, after 1907 serving additionally as naval aide to the President, he wrought an almost revolutionary improvement in the state of naval gunnery. At his instigation a commission was appointed to investigate and make recommendations on the organization of the Navy Department, but this, like an earlier congressional investigation into faulty battleship design for which he was also indirectly responsible, led to no conclusive reform. In 1910, while captain of the battleship *Minnesota*, he made an unauthorized speech in England pledging the full support of the United States in the event of an attack on the British Empire and was reprimanded by President Taft. From 1913 to 1915 he was commander of the Atlantic Torpedo Flotilla and developed a tactical doctrine for the deployment of the newly introduced naval destroyer. In 1917 he was promoted to rear admiral and appointed president of the Naval War College. When the United States entered World War I in April of that year he was placed in command of the U.S. Naval Forces Operating in European Waters. Working closely with the naval departments of Allied nations, he secured the adoption of the convoy system. In 1918 he was made full admiral and in 1919 returned to the War College. Angered by the award of honors in a manner he considered arbitrary, he refused to accept the Distinguished Service Medal. His report on mismanagement in the conduct of naval affairs during the war led to another congressional investigation, but 1920, like 1908, was an election year and the results were partisan and inconclusive. Despite such disappointments, Sims was acknowledged to be the most influential officer in American naval history. He retired in 1922, but continued to write and speak on topics of public and military interest until his death in Boston on September 28, 1936.

SINCLAIR, UPTON BEALL (1878–1968), author and social reformer. Born on September 20, 1878, in Baltimore, Maryland, of an eminent but financially straitened family, Sinclair earned money by writing from the age of 15. He graduated from the City College of New York in 1897, then did graduate work at Columbia while supporting himself by doing various kinds of hack work. He published several novels, none of which won much attention. His first success came with his sixth novel, *The Jungle*, 1906, an account of immigrant workers in the Chicago stock yards. Commissioned by a Socialist weekly, it was intended to bring laborers under the Socialist Party wing; but, ironically, the wheels of democracy began to turn in response to the book's horrifying revelations of meat packing conditions and subsequent congressional investigations led to the passage of the Meat Inspection Act of 1906, a milestone in consumer protection. "I aimed at the public's heart," he said of the book, "and hit it in the stomach." Sinclair repeatedly tried to demonstrate the falseness of American society and instead to show forth a Socialist alternative, as in *King Coal*, 1917, *The Profits of Religion*, 1918, an interpretation of religion as a capitalist instrument, *Oil!*, 1927, about the political scandals of the 1920s, and *Boston*, 1928, covering events of the Sacco and Vanzetti case. His Lanny Budd series, 11 novels written between 1939 and 1949 but involving the hero in national and international affairs in the period 1913–1949, stressed social reform, but did not propose Socialism as the remedy. The volume covering 1930–1934, *Dragon's Teeth*, won a Pulitzer Prize in 1942. He ran five times unsuccessfully on the Socialist Party ticket between 1906 and 1930 —for Congress, the Senate, and governor of California. He finally broke with the party in 1934 and formed the EPIC league—"End Poverty in California." On this platform he narrowly missed the governorship of California on the Democratic ticket in 1934. He succeeded in uniting unemployed workers with liberals and paved the way for a Democratic victory in 1938. An autobiography, revised and enlarged from an early version of 1932, appeared in 1962. He died in Bound Brook, New Jersey, on November 25, 1968.

SINGER, ISAAC BASHEVIS (1904–   ), author. Born on July 14, 1904, in Radzymin, Poland, Singer was the son and grandson of rabbis; his family intended that he become a rabbi and a theological scholar. At four he moved to Warsaw, where his family lived in a Jewish ghetto and his father had a *Beth Din*, or rabbinical court, where the people came to discuss their religious and worldly lives. He commenced a traditional Jewish education, attending the Tachkemoni Rabbinical Seminary in Warsaw, but in the early 1920s followed the example of his older brother and became a journalist. He wrote first in Hebrew but soon turned to Yiddish. His stories and book reviews appeared in the Yiddish journals *Literarishe Bleter* and *Globus*, the last of which he coedited from 1932 until 1935, when he came to New York City. His articles, book reviews, and stories were published in the original Yiddish in the *Jewish Daily Forward* (regularly after 1943), and in other Yiddish papers throughout the world. He was soon established as the leading Yiddish writer of the time and a story teller in the tradition of Sholom Aleichem. His work, permeated by traditional Jewish folklore, legend, and mysticism, was sympathetic to the foibles and temptations of his fellows and frequently depicted life as he had known it in the disintegrated Jewish towns of eastern Europe. Popular English versions of his novels included *The Family Moskat*, 1950, *The Magician of Lublin*, 1960, *In My Father's Court*, 1966, *The Manor*, 1967, and *The Estate*, 1969. English translations of his stories were collected in *Gimpel the Fool and Other Stories*, 1957, *The Spinoza of Market Street*, 1961, *Short Friday and Other Stories*, 1964, and *The Seance and Other Stories*, 1968. Among his children's books were *Mazel and Schlimazel; or, The Milk of a Lioness*, 1967, and *When Schlemiel Went to Warsaw and Other Stories*, 1968. He also contributed to popular English-language magazines, including the *New Yorker, Playboy, Harper's, Commentary*, and *Encounter*.

SINGER, ISAAC MERRIT (1811–1875), inventor and manufacturer. Born on October 27, 1811, in Rensselaer County, New York, of German immigrant parents, Singer attended public schools in Oswego until he was 12, then ran away from home and became a machine shop apprentice in Rochester. Between 1830 and 1850 he was a roving actor and occasional mechanic. Among his early inventions were a rock-boring device and a carver. In 1851 he had an opportunity to study a sewing machine and in 11 days built a greatly improved model. It embodied a horizontal table on which the material was spread, with the toothed rotating feed mechanism projecting through the table top. A vertical spring presser foot secured the material as the wheel fed and the needle stitched. The model enabled uninterrupted sewing, both straight and curved, and made it possible to stitch any place on the material. But the basic eye-pointed needle and lockstitch were first developed and patented in 1846 by Elias Howe, who won damages in 1856, after three years of involved litigation, in the form of royalties from the four major sewing machine producers, one of whom was Singer. Singer had gone into partnership in 1851 with an attorney, Edward Clark, and they were, by 1860, the world's foremost sewing machine manufacturers. Clark supervised advertising and marketing of the machine, introducing traveling salesmen, installment buying, and trade-in allowances to stimulate domestic buying. Singer continued to make and patent improvements on the machine. In 1863 the Singer Manufacturing Company was incorporated. Singer moved to England to live in a palace (called the Wigwam), which he had built on the English coast. By the time he died, on July 23, 1875, his sewing machine had not only helped women with the chores of family sewing, but had also fostered a major industry.

SITTING BULL (c.1831–1890), Indian chief. Born about 1831 into the Hunkpapa Sioux tribe, on the Grand River in what is now South Dakota, Tatanka Iyotake, or Sitting Bull, son of Jumping Bull, was a warrior by the age of 14, and about 1856 became head of the Strong Heart warror society. He engaged in conflict with the Army after the entire Sioux nation was brought into disrepute by the so-called Minnesota Massacre of 1862, in which the Santee Sioux under Little Crow rebelled against white encroachments and killed more than 350 settlers. In 1866 he became chief of the northern hunting Sioux, with Crazy Horse, leader of the Oglala branch, as his vice chief. In 1868 he accepted peace on the basis of a guaranteed reservation north of the North Platte River, with hunting privileges off the reservation. In 1874 gold was discovered in the area of the Black Hills, and miners invaded the Indian territory. Discontented Sioux, Arapahoe, and Cheyenne assembled at his camp, eventually growing to a force estimated at 2,500 to 4,000, and in 1875 he was made head of the Sioux Confederacy war council. He did not obey the Army's order that the Sioux return to their reservations by the end of January. He was said to have beheld visions of the subsequent battles in a Sun Dance that he performed in June 1876. On the 17th of that month, forces under the command of Gen. George Crook were defeated by Crazy Horse; on the 25th, Gen. George A. Custer was killed and his entire command destroyed in the Battle of Little Bighorn, by warriors led by Crazy Horse and Gall. Sitting Bull "made medicine" during the battle and took no part in the fighting. When the encampment at Little Bighorn broke up, he led his remaining people to Canada in May 1877, but could not convince the Canadian government to assist them. Suffering from famine and disease, he and 187 tribesmen finally surrendered to the Army in July 1881. He was imprisoned at Fort Randle for two years and in 1883 moved to the Standing Rock reservation. For a year he toured with Buffalo Bill's Wild West show and became a legendary figure, but he never acquiesced to white rule or considered himself other than leader of the Sioux. He was rumored to be at the head of the religious agitation that swept Sioux camps around 1889, and was ordered arrested. As Sioux warriors attempted to rescue him, he was shot by Indian police at Grand River on December 15, 1890.

SLATER, SAMUEL (1768–1835), inventor and manufacturer. Born on June 9, 1768, in Belper, Derbyshire, England, the son of a farmer, Slater was apprenticed in a manufactory of cotton machinery from 1783 to 1789. During his indenture, he learned of the need in America for skilled mechanics and efficient textile machinery. He supervised the construction of such machinery in his former master's new plant and sailed for America in 1789 with plans for a cotton mill in his mind. He was necessarily in disguise, for trained mechanics were forbidden to leave England, and machinery could not be exported. He arrived in New

York and was there employed by the New York Manufacturing Company. Having communicated with the Almy and Brown textile manufacturing firm in Providence, Rhode Island, he was welcomed and offered a consultantship which he accepted. Beginning in 1790, he reworked their machinery, from the smallest tools to the most complex carding and spinning devices, and trained American mechanics to execute his intricate designs. The new mill was completed by 1793, under the firm name of Almy, Brown and Slater; it marked the beginning of the textile industry in America. Meanwhile, Slater's wife had developed a fine thread from cotton that was more efficient than linen thread, and Samuel Slater and Company opened a factory to manufacture it. With other relatives, Slater opened a textile plant near Pawtucket. By 1812 he controlled 12 companies — mills or manufactories. An eager teacher and a willing consultant to other industrialists, he was active in the cotton industry until his death in Webster, Massachusetts, on April 21, 1835. In 1955 his Pawtucket plant was opened to the public.

SLOAN, JOHN FRENCH (1871–1951), painter. Born in Lock Haven, Pennsylvania, on August 2, 1871, Sloan began studying art at 16 in the evening classes of the Pennsylvania Academy of Arts, part of the time under the realist Robert Henri. He did sketches for the *Philadelphia Press*, and sometimes drew the Sunday puzzles and cartoons. He illustrated for major magazines, including *Harper's*, *Scribner's*, *Everybody's*, and *Collier's*, and contributed to *The Masses* before the United States entered World War I. In 1904 he went to New York, establishing himself in a Greenwich Village studio that was a hub of New York artists for three decades. His first fame — a kind of notoriety — was achieved in 1908 in an historic showing with Henri and six other realists dubbed the "ash can school" or the "apostles of ugliness." Although they did not share styles or constitute a movement, their common themes were city life — waterfronts,

slums, and other scenes — depicted with uncompromising veracity. Several of them helped organize the Armory Show in 1913. Sloan also painted scenes of Santa Fe, New Mexico, the site of his summer studio, Gloucester, Maine, and Philadelphia. He used watercolors and oils, was an etcher and a book illustrator, and a teacher at the Art Students' League from 1914 to 1930 and 1932 to 1938. His paintings included "The Coffee Line," "Madison Square in a Dust Storm," "Bleecker Street on Saturday Night," "Scrubwomen in the Old Astor Library," "McSorley's Bar," "Sunday, Women Drying Their Hair," "Backyards, Greenwich Village," and "Spring in Washington Square." In 1939 he published the autobiographical critique, *The Gist of Art*. He also helped to organize the Society of Independent Artists and was its president for many years. He died in Hanover, New Hampshire on September 8, 1951.

SMITH, ALFRED EMANUEL (1873–1944), public official. Born in New York City on December 30, 1873, Smith received little education and worked at the Fulton Street fish market until taken into the Tammany Hall fold in 1895. Given a small political job that year, he supplemented his meager formal education with close-hand experience in city politics and in 1903 was elected to the state assembly, where he remained until 1915. He served as speaker during his last two years. In 1915 he became sheriff of New York County and two years later president of the Greater New York board of aldermen. In 1918 he ran for governor and won an upset victory over the Republican candidate. He was defeated for reelection in 1920 though he ran far ahead of the Democratic presidential candidate. He turned to business but in 1922 again entered the governor's race and was elected; reelected in 1924 and 1926, he was the first man to serve four terms as governor of New York. His administrations were characterized by clean, efficient government operations. Al Smith himself was a colorful character with his picturesque, low-key speech and his ever-present derby hat and cigar; his Catholicism and outspoken opposition to Prohibition, however, were political liabilities hampering his further political progress. He was a contender for the presidential nomination at the 1924 Democratic convention that was deadlocked until a compromise candidate was selected on the 103rd ballot. In 1928 Smith won the nomination on the first ballot and, dubbed "The Happy Warrior" by his protégé, Franklin D. Roosevelt, conducted a vigorous campaign; antipathy to his religion and his stand on Prohibition lost him support in rural areas and, combined with the continuing "Republican prosperity," led to his defeat by Herbert Hoover. His later years were unhappy, marked by financial setbacks and a major break with Roosevelt. He died on October 4, 1944.

SMITH, CHARLES HENRY (1826–1903), "Bill Arp," journalist. Born on June 15, 1826, in Lawrenceville, Georgia, Smith attended Franklin College in Athens until 1848, studied law, and was admitted to the Georgia bar in 1849. A staunch Southerner and a keen political observer, he left his practice to enlist in the Confederate army in 1861. During the first year of the Civil War, a series of letters began to appear in the *Southern Confederacy* addressed to "Mr. Abe Linkhorn" from a "Bill Arp." They purportedly expressed the opinions of a foolhardy Northerner and sympathized with Yankee aims, but in fact, by means of a contrived ineptitude, they shrewdly satirized the North. As the letters continued and appeared in other papers, including the *Atlanta Constitution* and the *Louisville Home and Farm,* they gradually dropped the comic devices of dialect and misspelling initially employed and began to rely on acute commentary and direct satire to express their author's opinions on women's rights, Negroes in America, the income tax, agricultural policies, and other issues as they arose. The character evolved at the same time into a benign cracker-barrel philosopher. The letters were popular and eagerly anticipated by many ordinary folk, who found their own views reinforced by Bill Arp's homespun philosophizing. Smith was elected to the Georgia state senate in 1865 and became mayor of Rome in 1868. He continued his law practice until 1877, after which he devoted the rest of his life to writing. His works were compiled in books including *Bill Arp, So Called,* 1866, *Bill Arp's Peace Papers,* 1873, *Bill Arp's Scrap Book,* 1884, *The Farm and Fireside,* 1891, and *Bill Arp: From the Uncivil War to Date,* 1903. He died in Cartersville, Georgia, on August 24, 1903.

SMITH, JEDIDIAH STRONG (1799–1831), explorer and trader. Born on January 6, 1799, in Jericho (now Bainbridge), New York, Smith received a basic elementary education before going to work in the Lake Erie trade. At a date unknown, possibly as early as 1816, he went to St. Louis to join a fur trade expedition into the West; his first journey was made in 1822 as part of the Ashley-Henry Rocky Mountain venture that effectively brought the fur territory outside of the English-dominated Oregon region under American control. He ascended the Missouri again in 1823 and early the next year rediscovered the South Pass, a major gateway to the Northwest in what is now Wyoming (the original discovery, made some years earlier, had not been adequately reported). In 1826 Smith and two partners formed a trading company at Great Salt Lake, Utah. That year he led a party from Great Salt Lake across the Mojave Desert into California; from San Gabriel he then journeyed northward to the American River (just east of Sacramento) and in May 1827 crossed the Sierra Nevadas and the Great Basin back to Great Salt Lake, the first man to follow that route. Later in the year he retraced his path to San Gabriel, surviving an attack by Mojave Indians, and up to the Sacramento Valley; the next spring, contrary to the wishes of the Mexican government, he continued north to Fort Vancouver on the Columbia River in Oregon, opening up the coastal route to that territory. In 1830 he and his partners sold their fur business to a new company organized by Jim Bridger and others. In 1831 he joined the Santa Fe trade and on his way there was killed by Comanche Indians on the Cimarron River on May 27, 1831. His explorations were exceeded in importance only by those of Lewis and Clark; but his geographical discoveries were passed on orally among mountain men while his maps were published in obscure works and remained virtually unknown for years.

SMITH, JOHN (c.1580–1631), explorer and colonizer. Born about 1580 in Willoughby, Lincolnshire, England, Smith attended school until the age of 15, then was apprenticed to a wealthy merchant. He began to travel in Europe at the age of 16 and four years later joined the fighting in Transylvania, where he was taken prisoner and made a slave by the Turks. He escaped, traveled further in Russia and Europe, and returned to England in 1604. In London he learned of the Virginia Company and actively promoted its plan to found a colony in America. He sailed in 1606 and arrived with the first settlers in 1607, helping to found Jamestown. He was appointed to the governing council and began to explore the region. He ventured alone many times into Indian territory to obtain food. On one occasion, according to his own account, he was captured by Indians and was sentenced to death by their chief, Powhatan, and escaped death only by the intervention of Powhatan's daughter, Pocahontas. On his return to Jamestown in 1608, he found the government in the hands of personal enemies and he was sentenced to be hanged for having lost the men of his exploring party. New supplies arrived at the impoverished colony shortly thereafter and he was released and restored to his position on the council. In 1608 he was elected president of the colony and with great resourcefulness brought it through many hardships. He was constantly involved in quarrels over the leadership and, principally because of

a severe injury, he finally returned to England in 1609. In 1614 he returned to America and explored the coast of the region he named New England. He became a strong advocate of colonization of the area and publicized widely its attractions. In 1615, on his way again to New England, he was captured by pirates, with whom he was forced to remain for several months. During this time he wrote *A Description of New England*, including the most accurate map of the region yet produced. It provided a rosy picture of the region and was instrumental in bringing settlers to it. When released, he returned to England and offered his services as a guide to the Pilgrims, but they felt his books and maps would suffice. He remained in England thereafter, actively promoting colonization and persuading settlers to emigrate. In 1624 he published a *Generall Historie of Virginia, New England and the Summer Isles* and in 1630 *The True Travels, Adventures, and Observations of Captaine John Smith in Europe, Asia, Africa and America*. He died in London in June 1631.

SMITH, JOSEPH (1805–1844), religious leader and prophet. Born in Sharon, Vermont, on December 23, 1805. Smith moved with his parents to Palmyra, New York, in 1816. Little is known of his childhood; by his own account he was subject from about 1820 onward to visions in which God or Jesus Christ would grant revelations of true Christianity to him. In one of these he was directed to a hill near Manchester, New York, where he found golden plates on which was inscribed the history of the true church in America as carried by ancient Indian descendants of lost Hebrew tribes. He deciphered the inscriptions, written in "reformed Egyptian," by means of magic stones called Urim and Thummim, and published them as *The Book of Mormon* in 1830. The book reflected the current social, political, and religious ferment of Smith's region and combined this with Indian legend in a work of quasi-biblical style that is remarkable considering Smith's presumably rudimentary education. On April 6, 1830, he organized the Church of Jesus Christ of Latter-Day Saints and began immediately to win converts. The next year he led his congregation to Kirtland, Ohio. Church polity, as outlined in *A Book of Commandments for the Government of the Church of Christ*, 1833, and *Doctrine and Covenants of the Church of the Latter-Day Saints*, 1835, involved church ownership of all property, exercised for the communal good, the vesting of all power in the church, and the ultimate authority of the president— Smith—to whom alone was vouchsafed direct revelation. In 1838 the Mormons journeyed to western Missouri, but friction with other settlers forced them to leave and they established themselves anew at Nauvoo, Illinois. There the church was granted considerable autonomy by the state, even to the point of fielding its own militia. Again there was constant trouble with non-Mormon neighbors, generated particularly by rumors of polygamy (Smith apparently followed this practice pursuant to a revelation in 1831, but it was not publicly proclaimed until 1852 by his successor, Brigham Young), and by the communalism and the impressive size of the colony. By 1844 Nauvoo held about 18,000 Mormons. In June of that year a small dissenting Mormon group published an attack on Smith and he ordered their press destroyed. He and his brother were imprisoned in Carthage, Illinois, and on June 27, 1844, were dragged from the jail by a mob of anti-Mormons and shot. There followed a schism in Mormon ranks and control of the major group passed to Brigham Young.

SOUSA, JOHN PHILIP (1854–1932), bandmaster and composer. Born on November 6, 1854, in Washington, D. C., Sousa early showed a marked aptitude for music. He studied violin and in 1867 took up the trombone. For about five years he played with the United States Marine Band. In 1872 he returned to the violin and played in and conducted a number of theater orchestras during the next few years. In 1876 he played in Offenbach's orchestra at the Philadelphia Centennial Exhibition. In 1880 he was given charge of the U.S. Marine Band, considerably improving its standards until he left in 1892 to form his own group. During this period he began to compose the marches that won him the title of "March King"—"Semper Fidelis" in 1888, "The Washington Post" in 1889, and "The Liberty Bell" in 1893. With his own band he toured the United States and Europe and met outstanding success. In 1897 he wrote "The Stars and Stripes Forever," his most popular piece, and in 1899 "Hands Across the Sea." During the Spanish-American War he was music director for the VI Army Corps and during World War I director of all Navy bands. After the latter war he resumed his tours. In all he composed over 100 marches, celebrated for their rhythm and ingenious orchestration, 10 comic operas, the most successful of which were *El Capitan*, 1896, and *The Bride-Elect*, 1897, and many other songs and miscellaneous compositions. He compiled a potpourri of songs of foreign nations for the U.S. Naval Department, wrote three novels, dissertations on the trumpet and violin, and an autobiography, *Marching Along*, 1928. He died in Reading, Pennsylvania, on March 6, 1932.

SPARKS, JARED (1789–1866), editor, historian, and educator. Born on May 10, 1789, in Willington, Connecticut, Sparks grew up in poverty and with few opportunities for schooling. His efforts at self-education, however, finally won him a scholarship to Phillips Exeter Academy and from there he went to Harvard in 1811. Graduating four years later, he continued his studies in the Harvard Divinity School, took his master's degree in 1819, and in the same year became pastor of the First Independent Church (Unitarian) of Baltimore. His ministry lasted four years; in 1823 he purchased the *North American Review* and edited it for seven years, during which time it became the leading literary journal in America.

About 1827 he began seeking out and collecting materials — original documents, correspondence, and first-hand accounts — for his historical works. After *The Life of John Ledyard*, 1828, appeared *The Diplomatic Correspondence of the American Revolution* in 12 volumes in 1829–1830; the 3-volume *Life of Gouverneur Morris*, 1832; the 12-volume *Writings of George Washington*, 1834–1837; and *The Works of Benjamin Franklin*, 10 volumes, 1836–1840. Sparks also edited and contributed to *The Library of American Biography*. He uncovered and published a great deal of valuable historical material in the course of his researches, which extended to European as well as American archives, and his work as a whole fostered a new interest in American history and historiography. The enduring value of his efforts was severely impaired, however, by his bowdlerization of his materials; he edited, omitted, and rewrote whole passages, often to prevent giving offense to any person or government and sometimes simply to polish the finished product. In 1839 he assumed the McLean Professorship at Harvard, becoming the first professor of secular history in the United States. Ten years later he was chosen president of Harvard. Beset by heavy administrative duties and ill health, he remained in this position only four years, and his administration, with its somewhat reactionary academic policy, was not markedly successful. After his retirement in 1853 he lived quietly in Cambridge until his death there on March 14, 1866.

SPELLMAN, FRANCIS JOSEPH CARDINAL (1889–1967), Roman Catholic prelate. Born in Whitman, Massachusetts, on May 4, 1889, of Irish descent, Spellman chose the priesthood as his vocation shortly before receiving his B.A. degree from Fordham University in New York City in 1911. Completing his doctorate at the North American College in Rome, he was ordained on May 14, 1916, in St. Apollinaris' Church in Rome. In 1918, after two years as an assistant at the All Saints' Parish in Roxbury, Massachusetts, he joined the staff of the Cathedral of the Holy Cross in Boston and supervised literature for the diocese, later editing the weekly *Boston Pilot*. Four years later he was appointed vice-chancellor of the archdiocese of Boston and in 1925 became the first American attaché in the office of the Vatican Secretary of State. There he was responsible for translating Papal broadcasts and encyclicals into English and for issuing foreign language translations to Roman Catholics around the world. His enthusiasm, remarkable administrative capabilities, and intelligence elevated him rapidly in the hierarchy; consecrated titular bishop of Sila on September 8, 1932, he soon afterwards became auxiliary bishop of Boston with the Sacred Heart Chapel in Newton Center, Massachusetts, as his parish, and in 1939 was named archbishop of New York by Pope Pius XII. In the same year he was designated military vicar for the United States, a post that took him throughout the world to wherever American troops were stationed in World War II, the Korean War, and the war in Vietnam. Having achieved in his early years a reputation for social and political conservatism, he remained preoccupied with the welfare of Catholics in the years of new ecumenical and socially-oriented Catholicism, dealing with personal sins rather than directly with major social issues. In 1946 he was created a cardinal of his church. In 1953 he defended Senator Joseph McCarthy's investigations into Communist infiltration of the government and in later years supported the U.S. presence in Vietnam. His rule over the huge New York diocese was the epitome of efficiency and discipline. Successful in doubling his flock between 1939 and 1967, he erected churches, schools, and hospitals, and was outstanding for his generosity to charities and his sympathetic handling of personal problems in the laity. He wrote numerous articles for newspapers and popular magazines, as well as books, including *The Road to Victory*, 1942, *The Risen Soldier*, 1944, *The Foundling*, 1951, and *What America Means to Me* *and other Poems and Prayers,* 1953. One of the most influential prelates in American history, he died in New York on December 2, 1967.

SPOCK, BENJAMIN McLANE (1903–), physician. Born in New Haven, Connecticut, on May 2, 1903, Spock attended Phillips Academy in Andover, Massachusetts, took his B.A. degree from Yale in 1925, attending medical school there, and completed his M.D. degree at Columbia's College of Physicians and Surgeons in 1929. He interned at Presbyterian St. Luke's Hospital in New York City, served residencies in pediatrics at the New York Nursery and Children's Hospital (1931–1932) and in psychiatry at the New York Hospital (1932–1933), and completed six years of training at the New York Psychoanalytic Institute. During 1933–1943 he practised in New York City and taught pediatrics at Cornell University's Medical College. During the next two years he was a psychiatrist in the U.S. Naval Reserve and completed, in this period, *The Common Sense Book of Baby and Child Care,* 1946 (later *Baby and Child Care*), which became so popular—it was one of the all-time best sellers—that "Dr. Spock" became a household word. His attitude toward child rearing was kindly and understanding in contrast to the traditional parents' manuals of stern, inflexible edicts. He reassured parents—"You know more than you think you know"—emphasized the fact that babies' personalities differ and that flexibility is thus required, and provided insights into child psychology. In 1947 he taught psychiatry at the University of Minnesota and was professor of child development at the University of Pittsburgh from 1951 to 1955 and at Western Reserve University from 1955 until he retired in 1967. Articles collected in *Dr. Spock Talks with Mothers,* 1961, and *Problems of Parents,* 1962, first appeared in the *Ladies' Home Journal,* where his column was published regularly during 1954–1963, his articles after that time appearing in *Redbook.* He had long worked on behalf of the National Committee for a Sane Nuclear Policy (SANE), warning of the effects of radioactive pollution, and was co-chairman from 1963 to 1967. In 1963 he became publicly identified with the opposition to the Vietnam war. He was conspicuous at numerous protest rallies and marches in New York, Washington, and other U.S. cities. In 1968 he was indicted with four other prominent members of the peace movement for conspiring to violate selective service laws. He was found guilty, fined, and given a two-year prison sentence; the conviction was reversed, however, by the Court of Appeals in 1969. Out of this controversy he produced *Decent and Indecent,* 1969, which elucidated his concerns beyond child rearing, for the fate of adults and of the country.

SQUIBB, EDWARD ROBINSON (1819–1900), physician and pharmaceutical manufacturer. Born on July 4, 1819, in Wilmington, Delaware, Squibb was reared in the Quaker tradition and tutored privately. He earned his medical degree from Jefferson Medical College in Philadelphia in 1845. For two years he practised and taught anatomy at the college and then became an assistant surgeon in the Navy. While serving at sea he discovered that many of the drugs supplied to him were impure or of poor quality. Objecting strongly and bringing the situation to the attention of the authorities, he gained permission in 1851 to establish a laboratory in the Brooklyn naval hospital to produce chemicals and drugs for the armed forces. There he worked for six years, until the failure of the Army to provide funds forced him to resign. He took a position with the Louisville Chemical Works in Kentucky, but in 1858, in the expectation that the Army would purchase his products, he opened his own laboratory in Brooklyn. Fire demolished the premises soon after he moved in, but another laboratory was built to his specifications in 1859. Massive orders for drugs during the Civil War secured the success of the business, but even during the boom his high standards for his products were never compromised. He continually scored unlicensed medical practitioners, medical advertising, and ineffectual commercial preparations, and was a leading advocate for the revision and improvement of the official U.S. Pharmacopeia. After 1882 he published sporadically *An Ephemeris*, a pharmaceutical journal. He drafted the model for the first pure food and drug laws in New York and New Jersey. When his sons entered the business in 1892 the company became E.R. Squibb & Sons. He retired in 1895 and died in Brooklyn on October 25, 1900. The company grew into one of the country's leading pharmaceutical houses and in the 1950s was purchased by the Mathieson Chemical Company (later the Olin Mathieson Chemical Company).

STAGG, AMOS ALONZO (1862–1965), football coach. Born in West Orange, New Jersey, on August 16, 1862, Stagg attended Yale and while studying for the ministry played both baseball and football. In 1888, the year he pitched the Yale team to a victory over the Boston Braves, he turned down six offers from professional baseball teams. In 1889 he was selected by Walter Camp for the first All-American football team, and the next year, having graduated from Yale, he went to Springfield (Massachusetts) College, where he coached and played on the football team. Two years later he became coach at the University of Chicago; he remained there for 41 years, molding the "Giants of the Midway" into one of the football powerhouses of the early part of the century and developing such innovations as the huddle, the shift, the man-in-motion, the end-around play, and the since-outlawed hidden ball trick. In addition to his coaching success—5 undefeated seasons, 6 conference championships, and an overall record of 268 wins and 141 losses—Stagg was the first college athletic director to hold full faculty status. In 1933, at the age of 70, he refused promotion to the largely honorary position of superintendent of athletics and instead resigned to assume the coaching job at the College of the Pacific in Stockton, California. In 1946 he went to Susquehanna (Pennsylvania) College in an advisory capacity and in 1953 returned to Stockton, where he was an advisor at the city junior college until his retirement in 1960. Known affectionately as the "grand old man of football," Stagg was elected to the Football Hall of Fame in 1951, one of the first men chosen and the only one honored both as a player and a coach. He died in Stockton on March 17, 1965, at the age of 102.

STANFORD, AMASA LELAND (1824–1893), railroad executive and public official. Born on March 9, 1824, in Watervliet, New York, Leland Stanford was educated in local schools, at the Clinton Liberal Institute, and at Cazenovia Seminary. In 1845 he took up the study of law and was admitted to the bar three years later. He moved to Port Washington, Wisconsin, to begin practice and remained there for four years before following the example of his brothers and moving to California. There he engaged in retail trade, became involved in Republican politics, and in 1861 was elected governor. In the same year he joined Collis P. Huntington and others in organizing the Central Pacific Railroad, of which he served as president for the rest of his life. During the next two years he freely employed his official position to aid the company; after leaving office in 1863 he devoted himself to the railroad and, with his political connections, was primarily responsible for its finances and for maintaining good relations with California governmental bodies. The Central Pacific was completed and joined to the Union Pacific in 1869, and the partners began looking toward the extension of the line through southern California and, ultimately, toward the construction of a second transcontinental route. The Southern Pacific Railroad was built and in 1885 was absorbed along with the Central Pacific in a holding company, the Southern Pacific Company, of which Stanford was president until 1890. In 1885, in memory of his son who had died the year before at the age of 15, he founded Leland Stanford, Jr., University near Palo Alto, with a 9,000 acre gift of land and a $21 million endowment. Also in 1885 he was elected to the Senate by the California legislature; though he possessed few qualifications for the post and contributed nothing of value to the work of the body, he was reelected in 1890. He died at his palatial Palo Alto home on June 21, 1893.

STANTON, EDWIN McMASTERS (1814–1869), lawyer and public official. Born in Steubenville, Ohio, on December 19, 1814, Stanton entered Kenyon College in 1831 but was forced by financial difficulties to withdraw before graduating. He turned to law and was admitted to the bar in 1836. He soon won recognition as an industrious and highly capable attorney; he moved to Pittsburgh in 1847 and to Washington, D.C., in 1856, gaining constantly in prominence and coming to national notice in 1851 when he represented Pennsylvania in a suit against the Wheeling & Belmont Bridge Company before the Supreme Court. In 1858 he represented the United States in a series of California cases involving land claims based on fraudulent Mexican titles. In December 1860 President Buchanan reorganized his Cabinet and named Stanton attorney general; he opposed the abandonment of Fort Sumter and was so fearful of the ineffectiveness of Buchanan's responses to secession that he secretly met with Republican leaders in Congress to inform them of Cabinet matters. He left the Cabinet with Lincoln's inauguration in March 1861, but soon afterward, though a Democrat, became legal advisor to Secretary of War Simon Cameron; when Cameron was dismissed, Stanton succeeded him in January 1862. As the civilian head of the Union armed forces through the remainder of the Civil War, he applied his energy and ability with great effect, though his abrasive personality brought him often into conflict with other civil and military leaders and his brusque and summary conduct of his office made him widely unpopular. His origi-

nal antipathy to Lincoln mellowed over three years of association; for President Johnson, by whom he was retained, he had little regard. He again collaborated with congressional leaders against the President's Reconstruction policies and on many occasions usurped his executive authority. Finally, in August 1867, Johnson requested his resignation. Stanton refused, claiming the protection of the Tenure of Office Act that had earlier been passed over Johnson's veto (ironically, Stanton had helped write the veto message). Johnson then suspended him, but in January 1868 the Senate refused to confirm the action and Stanton returned. A month later Johnson dismissed him outright; Stanton barricaded himself in the War Department, posted a guard, and remained until the impeachment charges against Johnson failed in May and he was forced to resign. In 1869 President Grant nominated him to the Supreme Court, but four days after his confirmation by the Senate he died, on December 24, 1869.

STANTON, ELIZABETH CADY (1815–1902), social reformer. Born on November 12, 1815, in Johnstown, New York, the daughter of an eminent lawyer, Elizabeth Cady received a superior education and often sat with her father observing him practise his profession. Many times she heard him explain to tearful women the details of laws that deprived them of their property and even their children. She resolved at an early age to reform those statutes that placed women in a lower status in church, state, and society. In 1840 she married Abolitionist Henry Brewster Stanton, insisting that the word "obey" be dropped from the ceremony. With Lucretia Mott she organized the first women's rights convention in Seneca Falls, New York, in 1848. For it she drew up a Declaration of Sentiments, modeled on the Declaration of Independence, that detailed the inferior status of women and that, in calling for extensive reforms, launched the women's rights movement. The convention was followed by several more; as the movement gained momentum, Mrs. Stanton remained in the forefront. Her suffrage proposals met with the greatest opposition, even among women, and her reputation as a radical was secured when she later suggested that a husband's drunkenness or brutality be made grounds for divorce. From 1851 she worked closely with Susan B. Anthony and together they remained active for 40 years after the first convention, planning campaigns, speaking before legislative bodies, addressing gatherings in conventions, lyceums, and on the streets. By 1860 New York laws had been amended to grant women joint guardianship of their children, the right to sue in court, to receive and keep wages, and to own real and personal property. With Miss Anthony as her business manager, she edited and wrote militant articles for *The Revolution,* 1868–1870, a women's rights newspaper. Almost continuously from the founding in 1869 until 1890 she presided over the National Woman Suffrage Association. She helped to compile the first three volumes of the six-volume *History of Woman Suffrage,* 1881–1922, contributed articles to newspapers and periodicals, and published an autobiography, *Eighty Years and More,* in 1898. She died in New York on October 26, 1902.

STEFFENS, JOSEPH LINCOLN (1866–1936), journalist and reformer. Born in San Francisco on April 6, 1866, Steffens grew up there and in Sacramento. In 1889 he graduated from the University of California and for three years traveled and studied in Europe. Upon his return he became a reporter for the *Evening Post* in New York; there he observed the exposures of corruption in the police department and during the investigations met Theodore Roosevelt, with whom he remained friends for many years. From 1897 to 1901 he was city editor of the *Commericial Advertiser* and in the latter year, after a brief and abortive attempt to write a novel, he became managing editor of *McClure's Magazine.* With colleagues Ida Tarbell and Ray Stannard Baker,

he inaugurated the era of journalistic "muckraking—so called by Roosevelt—by publishing a series of exposés of corruption in business and politics. Beginning with "Tweed Days in St. Louis," written with Claude Wetmore, he contributed articles on corruption in municipal governments across the country that were later collected as *The Shame of the Cities,* 1904. In this book, in his subsequent *Struggle for Self-Government,* 1906, and *Upbuilders,* 1909, and on his many successful lecture tours, he avoided the often empty sensationalism of lesser muckrakers and confronted his audiences with factual case studies in order to clarify the conflict of public and private interests, leaving the solution to enlightened public action. In 1906 he left *McClure's* and, with Miss Tarbell, Baker, and others, took over the *American Magazine;* they quickly made it into the nation's leading journal of reform. He resigned in 1907 and from then on worked as a free-lance journalist. He gradually lost faith in the efficacy of spontaneous popular reform movements and turned more and more toward revolution and charismatic leadership, in the process losing most of his audience. In 1914 he traveled with Carranza, the Mexican revolutionary leader, and in 1917 and 1919 visited Russia. On the latter trip he met Lenin and returned much impressed; he wrote a friend, "I have seen the future, and it works." From 1919 to 1927 he lived in Europe; upon his return he settled in Carmel, California. In 1931 he published his *Autobiography,* which was highly successful, and for several years he was again a popular lecturer. He died on August 9, 1936.

STEICHEN, EDOUARD JEAN (1879–   ), photographer. Born in Luxembourg on March 27, 1879, Steichen favored spelling his first name "Edward" during his career. He emigrated with his parents to Hancock, Michigan, at the age of three, and in 1889 settled in Milwaukee. At 15 he left school to assume a four-year apprenticeship in a lithography house. He bought his first camera at 16 and made profitable hobbies of photography and painting. His early camera work was impressionistic; he was preoccupied with conveying mood and used soft-focus and such techniques as raindrops on his camera lens. *The Lady in the Doorway* was shown in a Philadelphia salon in 1889 and brought him early attention; he also exhibited in a Chicago salon in 1900. On the way to Paris that year, he stopped in New York to show samples of his work to Alfred Stieglitz, who encouraged him to continue. In London he created a stir with several photographs in a show in 1900 and in Paris he became associated with the movement in modern art. There he photographed many notable Europeans, including Rodin, whom he studied for a year before producing *Rodin — Le Penseur*, 1902, which won first prize in a 1904 contest at The Hague. He returned to New York in 1902 and opened a studio at 291 Fifth Avenue, where in 1905 Stieglitz and the "photo-secessionists," among whom was Steichen, opened the "291" gallery. From 1906 until the beginning of World War I he was in France, conducting experiments in plant breeding, painting, and photography. In 1917 he became a lieutenant colonel in the photography section of the air service of the Army Signal Corps and did important work in aerial photography. Returning to New York in 1923 he became head of photography for Condé Nast Publications. His portraits of such people as Garbo, Valentino, Chaplin, and the Barrymores appeared regularly in *Vanity Fair* and his fashion photography glorified *Vogue*. In 1938 he closed his New York studio and spent much time at his farm in West Redding, Connecticut, cultivating hybrid delphiniums. (These were first shown at the Museum of Modern Art in 1936 in an unprecedented display of creative flower breeding.) In 1941 he entered the Navy as lieutenant commander and rose to captain by 1946, having supervised all combat photography during World War II. He produced the film *The Fighting Lady*, 1944, published *The Blue Ghost; A Photographic Log and Personal Narrative of the Aircraft Carrier U.S.S. Lexington in Combat Operation*, 1947, and compiled two pictorial exhibitions, "Road to Victory," 1942, and "Power in the Pacific," 1945, for the Museum of Modern Art. He was appointed director of the museum's photography department in 1947. Of the many outstanding exhibitions he organized, the most acclaimed was "The Family of Man," 1955. He retired in 1962.

STEIN, GERTRUDE (1874–1946), author. Born on February 3, 1874, in Allegheny, Pennsylvania, Miss Stein grew up in Oakland and in San Francisco, California. She attended Radcliffe from 1893 to 1897, where she studied psychology under William James, and Johns Hopkins Medical School from 1897 to 1902, specializing in brain anatomy. In 1903 she moved to Paris, where she lived on an independent income, and returned to the United States only once, on a lecture tour in 1934. She became famous as the center of the American expatriate movement of the 1920s and dubbed its members the "lost generation" (quoted in the epigraph to Hemingway's *The Sun Also Rises*). An early patron of such artists as Picasso, Braque, Matisse, and Gris, she built up a fabulous collection of their art before they became famous. Among numerous others who frequented her home were Ernest Hemingway, Sherwood Anderson, Wyndham Lewis, André Gide, Carl Van Vechten, Ezra Pound, Ford Madox Ford, Paul Robeson, Clive Bell, John Reed, Eliot Paul, and Jo Davidson. Her writing was for the most part unintelligible. Concerned with sound and the rhythm of words rather than their conventional meanings, it was, she claimed, a literary counterpart of Cubism, and was characterized by sentences such as "Rose is a rose is a rose." A second famous phrase, "pigeons in the grass alas," was from her libretto for the opera *Four Saints in Three Acts* (which neither concerned four saints nor was presented in three acts), with music by Virgil Thomson, first produced in America in 1934. Her books included *Three Lives,* 1908, *Before the Flowers of Friendship Faded Friendship Faded,* 1931, *How to Write,* 1931, *The Autobiography of Alice B. Toklas,* 1933, *Picasso,* 1938, and *Brewsie and Willie,* 1946. She died in Paris on July 27, 1946.

STEINBECK, JOHN ERNST (1902–1968), author. Born on February 27, 1902, in Salinas, California, Steinbeck grew up near Monterey and attended Stanford University off and on from 1920 to 1925. He moved to New York and was a newspaper writer and a bricklayer; returning to California in 1926 he lived on an estate in the High Sierra as a caretaker, completing in the course of two winters his first novel, *Cup of Gold,* published in 1929. The following two novels, *The Pastures of Heaven,* 1932, and *To a God Unknown,* 1933, although promising, contributed little to his reputation. *Tortilla Flat,* however, published in 1935, became a best-seller, won a book-of-the-year medal from a California group, was adapted to the stage and sold to Hollywood, and was criticized by the Monterey Chamber of Commerce as a possible deterrent to the tourist traffic. Concerned with the colorful and unique "paisanos" working in Monterey, it was filled with ideas and moral attitudes that later appeared in *Cannery Row,* 1945, *The Wayward Bus,* 1947, and *Sweet Thursday,* 1954. His distinguished collection of stories, *The Long Valley,* 1938, included those published separately in 1937 as *The Red Pony.* Its theme of leadership was foreshadowed by *In Dubious Battle,* 1936, a chilling, vivid portrayal of a California strike in the 1930s. His celebrated allegory of self-determination and need, *Of Mice and Men,* 1937, was initially conceived as a stage drama but was only later adapted for that medium following its reception as a novel, and won the 1937 New York Drama Critics' Circle Award. He was at that time accompanying several migrant workers to California on a journey that he described in *The Grapes of Wrath,* 1939, a novel that provoked almost as wide and shocked reaction as Harriet Beecher Stowe's *Uncle Tom's Cabin.* Appearing at the end of the Depression, the story of the dispossessed "Okie" Joad family became symbolic of the hardships of everyone. The book won a 1940 Pulitzer Prize and was made into a motion picture. During World War II he produced *Bombs Away* and *The Moon is Down,* both in 1942, and was a correspondent for the *New York Herald Tribune,* his dispatches later being collected in *Once There Was A War,* 1958. He wrote movie scripts for *The Red Pony, The Pearl,* published as a novel in 1947, and *Viva Zapata!,* 1952. Although his critical reputation suffered a decline, his later realistic novels, *East of Eden,* 1952, and *The Winter of Our Discontent,* 1961, were significant additions to the corpus of his work, for which he won the 1962 Nobel Prize for Literature. He died in New York City on December 20, 1968.

STEINMETZ, CHARLES PROTEUS (1865–1923), electrical engineer. Born on April 9, 1865, in Breslau, Germany, Steinmetz was christened Karl August Rudolf. In 1883 he entered the University of Breslau and undertook a rigorous course in mathematics, the physical sciences, and electrical engineering. He studied there and at Berlin until his editorship of a Socialist newspaper brought him into conflict with the authorities in 1888 and he was forced to flee. After a year in Switzerland, during part of which he attended the University of Zürich, he came to New York in 1889 and took a job as a draftsman with an electrical engineering firm in Yonkers. When he applied for citizenship he anglicized Karl to Charles and adopted as a middle name Proteus, a nickname from his university days. His great knowledge of electricity and mathematics quickly won him advancement from draftsman, and he began to undertake independent research. His first major accomplishment was the discovery of the law of hysteresis, the residual magnetism in the electromagnets of electrical generators and motors that causes power loss; his quantification of this hitherto little understood phenomenon made possible great progress in generator and motor design. His papers on hysteresis were presented in 1892 and firmly established his reputation; in the same year his firm was merged into the General Electric Company and he soon became a consulting engineer with the new company in Schenectady, New York. In 1893 he announced the results of his theoretical studies of alternating currents, a symbolic method of calculation that eventually brought this highly complex field within reach of the average practising engineer and helped make it commercially feasible. His *Theory and Calculation of Alternating Current Phenomena*, 1897, and subsequent texts, were long standard works. He later turned to the investigation of lightning, a line of research that led to the production of artificial lightning in the laboratory and his development of lightning arresters for the protection of electrical power lines. From 1902 until his death he supplemented his work at General Electric by serving as professor of electrical engineering and later of electrophysics at Union College in Schenectady. In addition to his theoretical contributions to electrical engineering, he also made many practical innovations and held some 200 patents in the field. He died in Schenectady on October 26, 1923.

STEPHENS, ALEXANDER HAMILTON (1812–1883), public official. Born on February 11, 1812, in Wilkes (now Taliaferro) County, Georgia, Stephens graduated from the University of Georgia in 1832 and, after a time teaching school and reading law, was admitted to the bar in 1834. Two years later he was elected to the state legislature; he was a member of the state house of representatives until 1841 and in 1842 was elected to the state senate. As the shifting political alignments in Georgia stabilized, he emerged as a leading Southern Whig and as such was elected to Congress in 1843. At the outset of his career he had opposed the doctrine of nullification but upheld the theoretical right of secession; he continued to hold

to the latter position while counseling all possible forbearance short of surrendering states' rights altogether. He supported the annexation of Texas as a means of increasing Southern representation in Congress and in 1850 not only supported but placed great hope in the compromise measures of Clay's Omnibus Bill; two years later he broke with the Whig Party when it nominated for the presidency Gen. Winfield Scott, who refused to endorse the compromise. Stephens moved into the Democratic Party and retained his seat in Congress. He was instrumental in securing passage of the Kansas-Nebraska Bill in 1854. As the conflict over slavery deepened, he became more and more a defender and even an advocate of the institution, though he still hoped secession could be prevented. He left Congress in 1859 and returned to Georgia; there he continued to preach patience, but when secession was declared early in 1861 he acquiesced. Sent as a Georgia delegate to the Montgomery convention, he was chosen vice president of the Confederacy on February 9, 1861. His official duties were minimal and, a firm believer in the precedence of principle over expediency, he was frequently at odds with President Davis over infringements of personal and states' rights in such matters as conscription, martial law, and suspension of habeas corpus. During the war he constantly urged a program of prisoner exchange, and in February 1865 he headed the Confederate delegation to the unsuccessful armistice conference at Hampton Roads, Virginia. On May 11th, shortly after the Southern surrender, he was arrested at his home by Federal troops and until October was imprisoned in Boston. Returning home, he was elected to the Senate in 1866 but was refused his seat. He wrote a tedious but at the time quite successful *Constitutional View of the Late War Between the States*, 1868–1870, and reprinted and rebutted many of his critics in *The Reviewers Reviewed*, 1872; he also published in 1875 *A Compendium of the History of the United States*. In 1872 he was returned to Congress and remained there for ten years; in 1882 he was elected governor of Georgia but died after only a few months in office on March 4, 1883.

STEVENS, THADDEUS (1792–1868), public official. Born in Danville, Vermont, on April 4, 1792, Stevens graduated from Dartmouth College in 1814 and two years later, having moved to Pennsylvania, was admitted to the bar and began the practice of law in Gettysburg. As he gradually attained success as a lawyer he invested in real estate and the iron business and developed an interest in politics. In 1833 he was elected as an Antimason to the Pennsylvania legislature; he remained in that body until 1842, supporting measures for public education and internal improvements and staunchly opposing all proposals that to him smacked of privilege or class distinction. After a few years in private law practice he returned to politics and was elected as a Whig to Congress in 1848. During his two terms he furthered his reputation for harsh, uncompromising views while opposing the Compromise of 1850 and particularly the Fugitive Slave Law. In 1853 he again retired from office but not from politics; he was soon deeply involved in organizing the new Republican Party and in 1859 returned to Congress as a Republican to begin the major phase of his career. He was a skilled parliamentarian, but more important was his stern, absolute, and sometimes blind devotion to radically democratic principles and his great power in debate. A master of sarcasm and invective, he lavished abuse on Southern Congressmen and moderate Northerners alike, on numerous occasions bringing the House to near violence with his oratory. During the Civil War he urged an impossibly vigorous prosecution of military operations and on this subject was often in conflict with President Lincoln. As chairman of the ways and means committee, however, he rendered invaluable aid to the administration in securing the fiscal legislation—notably the issue of greenbacks—necessary to carry on the war. Viewing secession as utter treason, he advocated confiscation of rebel-owned property, wholesale arrest and execution, and arming of slaves; as the war came to a close he declared the South to be a conquered province to which the Constitution had no application. Against Lincoln's moderate plan for reconstruction he proposed much more rigorous measures, and when President Johnson indicated his intention to continue Lincoln's policies Stevens moved into open and complete opposition. The acknowledged leader of House Republicans, he obtained the exclusion of newly elected Southern Congressmen in 1866 and established the joint Committee on Reconstruction, becoming its dominant member. He secured passage of the Civil Rights and Freedmen's Bureau acts over Johnson's vetoes, directed the preparation and passage of the 14th and 15th Amendments, and used Republican gains in the 1866 election to force through the harsh Reconstruction measures of 1867, establishing military rule to guarantee Negro suffrage in the South. Early in 1868 he introduced a resolution for the impeachment of Johnson, helped draw up the articles of impeachment, and managed the subsequent trial; the charges were flimsy and Johnson was acquitted in May, to the deep disappointment of Stevens. His health had failed by that time and he died in Washington on August 11, 1868. He was buried in Lancaster, Pennsylvania, amid the graves of Negroes, in order, he explained in an epitaph he had composed himself, "that I might illustrate in my death the principles which I advocated through a long life—Equality of Man before his Creator."

STEVENS, WALLACE (1879–1955), poet and businessman. Born in Reading, Pennsylvania, on October 2, 1879, Stevens spent three years at Harvard and was a reporter for the *New York Herald Tribune* before graduating from New York Law School in 1904 and being admitted to the bar. Around that time he began writing poetry and opened a general law practice in New York City. His poems were first published in *Poetry* magazine in 1914 and then appeared in other similar publications. In 1916 he joined the Hartford Accident and Indemnity Company in Connecticut and rose steadily in its ranks, becoming vice president in 1934. In 1923, when he was 44 years old, his first book of poetry was published, *Harmonium*, which was followed by numerous volumes, including *Ideas of Order* and *Owl's Clover*, both 1936, *The Man With the Blue Guitar*, 1937, *Parts of a World*, 1942, and *The Auroras of Autumn*, 1950. He was a subtle, intellectual, but at the same time lively and engaging poet whose writing relied on the rhythm and sound of words as much as on their conventional meanings. The intent of his work, elucidated in his critical work, *The Necessary Angel*, 1951, was to contrast reality with imagination, an aim perhaps best achieved in one of his best-known poems, "The Emperor of Ice Cream." He became a vice president in the Hartford Livestock Insurance Company while, in his other sphere of activity, winning the Bollingen Prize in 1949, and the National Book Award in 1950 and 1954, the latter for his *Collected Poems*, 1954, which also won a 1955 Pulitzer Prize. He died in Hartford on August 2, 1955.

STEVENSON, ADLAI EWING (1900–1965), lawyer, public official, and diplomat. Born on February 5, 1900, in Los Angeles, Stevenson was the son of a newspaper executive and the grandson of Adlai E. Stevenson, Vice President during Grover Cleveland's second administration. Raised after 1906 in Bloomington, Illinois, the family home, he attended Choate Preparatory School in Wallingford, Connecticut, graduated from Princeton in 1922, and entered Harvard Law School. After two years of study, he rejoined his family in Bloomington and became assistant managing editor of the *Pantagraph*, a local newspaper of which his mother was part owner and that had been in the family for several generations. Returning to law school at Northwestern University, he graduated in 1926 and was admitted to the

bar that year. He opened a practice in Chicago. In 1933 he was one of the many lawyers who flocked to Washington to help plan the New Deal. For two years he was an adviser to the Agricultural Adjustment Administration, touring the country to interview farmers and relay their problems back to the administration. In 1935 he returned to Chicago, where his law practice was interrupted by his service in various public posts. Called back to Washington in 1941 as legal assistant to the secretary of the navy, he served in 1943 as head of a mission to Italy planning for military occupation, and in 1946 as a senior adviser to the American delegation to the U.N. General Assembly. He returned to Chicago in 1947 and was nominated for governor on a Democratic reform ticket. He won the 1948 election and, as governor, secured the passage of 78 "clean up" measures. In 1952 he was chosen as the Democratic candidate for President, despite his previous refusal to seek the nomination. But he waged a vigorous campaign that was marked by eloquent speeches whose wit was often memorable. He lost the election to General Eisenhower, but he gained national prominence and the undisputed role of leader of his party. In 1956 he formally declared his candidacy and once again gained the nomination. His second campaign paid heed to voter preferences; but he could not escape his identity as the "intellectual's" candidate, and to some extent this cost him the race. He returned to his law practice, traveled extensively, and in 1960 received strong support for a third nomination, but John F. Kennedy was chosen on the first ballot. In 1961 Kennedy appointed him U.S. ambassador to the United Nations, with Cabinet rank. In this role he was unsurpassed as a speaker and was respected by all the delegates. He died in London while visiting friends on July 14, 1965. Among his writings were *Call to Greatness*, 1954, *What I Think*, 1956, *The New America*, 1957, *Friends and Enemies*, 1959, *Putting First Things First*, 1960, and

Looking Outward: Years of Crisis at the U.N., 1963.

STIEGLITZ, ALFRED (1864–1946), photographer. Born in Hoboken, New Jersey, on January 1, 1864, the son of a wool merchant, Stieglitz moved to New York City with his family at the age of seven. He attended private and public schools and studied engineering at the City College from the age of 17. In 1881 he enrolled at the Berlin Polytechnic Institute in Germany. He soon became interested in photography and began at once to experiment and take pictures then considered impossible—at night, in the snow and rain, and of reflections in windows—earning a reputation as a "revolutionary." His pictures of a trip to Tyrol, Italy, won top honors and international acclaim in London three years before he returned to the United States, in 1890, and commenced pioneer experiments in three-color photography. He produced a collection of prints on the development of New York City, containing the classic "Winter—Fifth Avenue" (showing a horsecar moving up a hill in a blizzard) and "The Terminal—Streetcar Horses" (of the steaming horses being watered at a train depot after the storm). He was the first to photograph skyscrapers, clouds, and views from an airplane. He used no retouching, would not make mechanically duplicated prints, or use eccentric camera angles; all of his effects relied on vision, timing, and perfect focusing. In 1905, with a group of photographers that he dubbed the "photo-secessionists," he opened a gallery at 291 Fifth Avenue in New York City—the famous "291." In its first three years, the gallery showed only photographs. In 1908 he began to show and promote experimental paintings and sculpture of the burgeoning modern art movement. He gave the first American showings of Matisse, Brancusi, Rousseau, Picasso, Cézanne, Toulouse-Lautrec, and other European artists, defended them to the outraged press and public, and introduced African sculpture as an art form.

Then he began exhibiting the work of John Marin, Charles Demuth, Georgia O'Keeffe (his wife), Arthur Dove, Max Weber, and other unknown American artists whose contemporary (and shocking) styles were slow to be accepted by the art public. The "291" closed in 1917 and was followed by the Intimate gallery and in 1929 by An American Place. He edited and published *Camera Work*, 1903–1917. He died in New York City on July 13, 1946.

STIMSON, HENRY LEWIS (1867–1950), public official. Born on September 21, 1867, in New York City, Stimson graduated from Yale in 1888, took his M.A. at Harvard the next year, and after further study at the Harvard Law School was admitted to the New York bar in 1891. In 1893 he joined Elihu Root's law firm and remained with it until appointed U.S. attorney for the southern district of New York by President Theodore Roosevelt in 1906. In his four years in this office he pursued a vigorous program of prosecutions of large companies, particularly for railroad rebate practices, and became a close associate of Roosevelt. The latter persuaded him to run for governor of New York in 1910; the campaign was unsuccessful, but the following year Stimson was appointed secretary of war by President Taft. During World War I he served a short time in France as colonel of artillery and then from 1918 to 1926 enjoyed a lucrative private law practice. In 1926 he was sent to attempt a negotiation of the Tacna-Arica dispute between Chile and Peru and in the next year went to Nicaragua to arrange an armistice in that country's civil war. In 1927, despite his intention to retire from both business and public life, he was named to succeed Gen. Leonard Wood as governor general of the Philippines. After effectively dismissing the question of Philippine independence and implementing a program of economic development, he returned to the United States in 1929 to become President Hoover's secretary of state. For his handling of the major problem of his four year term, the Japanese invasion of Manchuria, he was widely criticized; eschewing strong diplomatic or direct action, he proposed a policy of non-recognition—the Stimson Doctrine—that, though adopted by the League of Nations, had no effect on Japanese aggression. In 1933, before leaving office, he supervised the transition from Hoover's to Franklin D. Roosevelt's administration. In 1940, at the age of 72, he was called back to service as Roosevelt's secretary of war, becoming one of the two Republicans in the President's war cabinet. Stimson oversaw the mobilization, training, and operations of the American armed forces throughout World War II and served as chief presidential advisor on atomic policy. In 1945 he made the final recommendation to President Truman to use the atomic bomb against Japan. On September 21, 1945, he left office and retired to his Long Island estate where he died on October 20, 1950.

STOKOWSKI, LEOPOLD ANTONI STANISLAW BOLESLAWOWICZ (1882–), conductor. Born in London on April 18, 1882, the son of a Polish anthropologist, Stokowski was skilled on the violin, piano, and organ by the age of 16. Under teachers including Sir Edward Elgar he studied composition at Queens College, Oxford, from which he graduated in 1903. In 1905, after furthering his studies at the Paris Conservatoire and in Germany, he arrived in the United States; he was naturalized in 1915. He played the organ for three years for New York's fashionable St. Bartholomew's Church before making his first appearance as a conductor in Paris in 1908 and leading a concert series that year in London. Returning to the United States in 1909, he became, at 27, the principal conductor of the Cincinnati Symphony Orchestra. In that post for three years, he gained national attention with his unorthodox and impassioned interpretations, especially of the music of Bach, Beethoven, Brahms, and Tschaikovsky. Invited in 1912 to become conductor of the Philadelphia Sym-

phony, he brought the group to prominence, and in 1937 became co-conductor with Eugene Ormandy, finally resigning in 1941. During the next four years he conducted radio concerts with the NBC Symphony Orchestra, supplementing the music with lectures. He founded the New York Symphony, becoming its conductor in 1944 and 1945, and in the latter year led the Hollywood Bowl Symphony Orchestra. From 1947 to 1950 he conducted the New York Philharmonic, and in 1955 became permanent conductor of the Houston Symphony. He formed the American Symphony Orchestra in New York in 1962. A driving experimentalist, he was one of the first symphonic conductors to pay heed to jazz and to employ young and female musicians. He introduced young people's concerts, with special rates and programs, in 1933, organized the All-American Youth Orchestra in 1940 (with whom he toured extensively in the United States, Canada, and Latin America), and in 1953 founded the Contemporary Music Society. A great success with commercial recordings, he also appeared in the motion pictures *The Big Broadcast of 1937*, *One Hundred Men and a Girl*, and Walt Disney's innovative *Fantasia*. He was praised and criticized alike for his "popularization" of the concert medium, as well as for his lush interpretations and his willingness to introduce contemporary and controversial music.

STONE, EDWARD DURELL (1902–), architect. Born on March 9, 1902, in Fayetteville, Arkansas, Stone early displayed talent in design and won a prize for a bird cage overlayed with sassafras branches at the age of 14. In 1923, after three years as an art student at the University of Arkansas, he began his architectural career in Boston and, on a scholarship, furthered his studies at Harvard's Architectural School (1925–1926) and at the Massachusetts Institute of Technology (1925–1927). For two more years he studied in Europe. In 1930 he moved to New York to work for the Rockefeller Center Architects and Wallace K.

Harrison and with them contributed to the designs for the Waldorf-Astoria Hotel, Rockefeller Center, and Radio City Music Hall. From 1935 to 1940 he taught advanced design at New York University and in 1936 founded his own architectural firm in New York City. During World War II he headed the Army's planning and design section and in 1946 he became a professor of architecture at Yale, leaving in 1951 to devote himself to building. His plans with Philip L. Goodwin for New York's Museum of Modern Art (1937) typified the functional, clean lines of the "international style." As his work progressed, however, he exhibited a more traditional approach, frequently using central courtyards and gardens to unify the interior and exterior designs. Experimental in his choice of decoration and materials, he achieved complex lighting effects and airy, serene moods with mesh, grillwork, skylights, pools, hanging gardens, and raised roofs. He was noted for the El Panama Hotel, Panama City, 1949, the Bay Roc Hotel, British West Indies, 1952, the Social Security Hospital, Lima, Peru, 1957, the U.S. Embassy, New Delhi, India, 1958, the Hotel Phoenicia, Beirut, Lebanon, 1958, and the American Pavilion at the Brussels World's Fair, 1958. In the United States he completed the Fine Arts Center at the University of Arkansas, 1951, Philadelphia's Commercial Museum, 1955, a pharmaceutical plant for the Stuart Company, Pasadena, California, 1958, and many other public buildings, university centers, and homes.

STONE, HARLAN FISKE (1872 – 1946), jurist. Born on October 11, 1872, in Chesterfield, New Hampshire, Stone enrolled in Massachusetts Agricultural School, intending to become a scientific farmer. But his interest turned to medicine and he transferred to Amherst College, where instead he studied law, graduating in 1894. He earned his law degree at Columbia University in 1898. From 1899 to 1924 he practised in New York City and taught at Columbia. In 1910 he became dean of the Columbia law school. There he attempted to extend to five the number of years required for earning a law degree, and to improve the quality and methods of teaching. Preaching simplification of the law, he attacked complex statutes that hindered social and economic progress. In 1924 he was appointed U.S. attorney general by President Coolidge, in which position he oversaw the reorganization of the Federal Bureau of Investigation. He was named to the Supreme Court in 1925 and became chief justice on July 1, 1941. As a member of the liberal wing of the court, with Justices Holmes and Brandeis, he affirmed the far-reaching reforms instituted by many New Deal acts. In 1934 he wrote the opinion upholding the Crosser-Dill Act or Railway Labor Act providing for collective bargaining with employees. In 1937 he supported the Social Security Act, upholding unemployment insurance, old age pensions, and auxiliary state laws to enforce it. This led to the enactment of the Fair Labor Standards Act of 1938, providing minimum wages and maximum hours for adults engaged in production for interstate commerce and defining appropriate labor for children. In 1936, in U.S. v. Butler, he stood with the minority in support of the Agricultural Adjustment Act of 1933, which had provided farmers with government subsidies. He noted that, unlike the legislative and executive branches of the government, which were reviewed by the judicial branch, the latter had nothing but its own sense of restraint as a review of its own actions; and it was said that Stone would not have voted for the act as a legislator, but that his obligation as a Supreme Court jurist led him to disregard personal philosophies. In 1940, in Minersville v. Gobitis, he was the only member of the court to oppose a state's power to force a member of the Jehovah's Witnesses to salute the flag against his religion. The court reversed its position in 1943 in West Virginia Board of Education v. Barnette, and adopted Stone's earlier dissent. He upheld a traditional position of the Supreme Court in deciding

1253

against the power of a state to control inter-state commerce in 1945 in *Southern Pacific Co. v. Arizona*, invoking the Court's power to invalidate local laws that affected the people of other states. In his last opinion in 1946, in *Girouard* v. *U.S.*, he reversed his 1931 dissent that a congressional act could not be so inter-preted as to bar naturalization of an immi-grant who refused to bear arms for religious reasons. In this case, the majority switched to his original dissent but, in deference to legis-lative prerogative, he changed his opinion on the basis of further clarification by Congress of the act's intent. He died in Washington, D.C., on April 22, 1946, having written over 600 opinions and dissents, notably in the field of constitutional law.

STONE, ISIDOR FEINSTEIN (1907 –   ), journal-ist. Born on December 24, 1907, in Philadel-phia, Stone published his first newspaper, *The Progress*, at the age of 14. From 1924 to 1927 he studied at the University of Pennsyl-vania, at the same time working as a reporter for a series of newspapers in the Philadelphia area. In 1933 he became an editorial writer for the *Philadelphia Record* but soon moved to New York to join the *Post*. From 1938 to 1946 he was with the *Nation* as associate edi-tor and later Washington editor. He had by this time established a reputation as a re-sourceful reporter and a particularly hard-headed and lucid editorial writer. He was connected at various times during the 1940s and early 1950s with several other publica-tions, notably the New York newspaper-mag-azine *PM*. In 1953 he severed his ties with all of them and in Washington began to write and publish his own four-page newsletter, *I.F. Stone's Weekly*. Beginning with a circulation of 5,500 the small paper grew steadily, large-ly by word-of-mouth recommendations, to 45,000 by 1968, by which time, however, it had become a biweekly. Generally thought of as a radical, Stone was nevertheless not to be labelled; his absolute independence led him to alienate his own avid readers by sternly criti-cizing Israel's policies in the Middle East, de-scribing Russian society as "bourgeois," and ascribing the many denunciations of the War-ren Commission's report on President Kenne-dy's assassination to forms of paranoia. He delighted in quoting official government pro-nouncements alongside contradictory quotes from the same sources of a week or a month or a year before, and his trenchant analyses of persons and policies won high praise from journalistic colleagues as well as from his readers. He was a regular contributor to the *New York Review of Books* and published several collections of his essays, editorials, and reviews. Among his many books were *Business as Usual*, 1941, *This is Israel*, 1948, *The Hidden History of the Korean War*, 1952, *The Haunted Fifties*, 1964, and *In a Time of Torment*, 1967.

STORY, JOSEPH (1779 – 1845), jurist and educa-tor. Born on September 18, 1779, in Marble-head, Massachusetts, Story graduated from Harvard in 1798 and read law, for a time in the office of Samuel Sewall, until his admis-sion to the bar and commencement of prac-tice in Salem in 1801. Though a Jeffersonian Republican — a political rarity in his region — he was elected to the Massachusetts legisla-ture for three terms, 1805 – 1807; in 1808 – 1809 he filled the final months of a term in Congress, and in 1810 he returned to the state legislature where he became speaker of the house. In November 1811 President Madison appointed him to the Supreme Court in the hope that his Republicanism would help offset the strongly Federalist views of Chief Justice John Marshall. Instead, he became a Federal-ist ally and during the course of his long ca-reer, which outlasted the chief justice's by ten years, achieved a lasting influence on Ameri-can jurisprudence that was the closest chal-lenge to Marshall's preeminence. His first major contribution, however, issued from his work on his circuit; the War of 1812 pro-duced a flood of admiralty and prize cases and he brought his scholarly mind to bear on them, creating for the first time a unified, coherent body of opinion in this hitherto chaotic area of American law. His first major opinion on the Supreme Court was in the 1816 case of *Martin* v. *Hunter's Lessee*, in which he ruled that the Court had appellate jurisdiction, hence supremacy, over state courts in civil cases arising from constitutional or federal law or treaties. Of his 286 opinions, only 14 were in dissent; in one of these, *Ogden* v. *Saunders*, 1827, he joined Marshall in the first opinion on constitutional law in which the latter was in a minority. After Marshall's death in 1835, Story presided over the Court until the appointment of Roger B. Taney as chief justice; Taney, a Jacksonian, altered considerably the complexion of the Court and Story found himself more and more in dissent, most notably in *City of New York* v. *Miln, Briscoe* v. *Bank of Kentucky*, and *Charles River Bridge* v. *Warren Bridge*, all in 1837, the last of which was considered by Daniel Webster to be his best opinion. In 1829 he became, by explicit direction in the endowment, first Dane Professor of Law at Harvard. In this position, which he held along with his justiceship until his death, he contributed greatly to the improvement of legal education in the United States; his lectures led to the publication of his nine great *Commentaries* on various kinds of law between 1832 and 1845. Among his many other written works was *Constitutional Classbook*, 1834. He drafted several pieces of legislation and found time to act as advisor to numerous business firms and committees. He died on September 10, 1845, in Cambridge, Massachusetts.

STOWE, HARRIET ELIZABETH BEECHER (1811–1896), author and reformer. Born on June 14, 1811, in Litchfield, Connecticut, Harriet Beecher was a member of one of the 19th century's most remarkable families. The daughter of Lyman Beecher, whose Calvinist influence was offset somewhat by the liberality of her sister Catherine and her brothers Henry Ward and Edward, she grew up in an atmosphere of learning and moral earnestness. She studied and then taught at Catherine's school in Hartford and in 1832 accompanied Catherine and their father to Cincinnati, where he became president of Lane Theological Seminary and she taught in the Western Female Institute founded by Catherine. In 1836 she married Calvin Stowe, a professor at Lane. She supplemented their meager income by writing stories and sketches for various periodicals and published a collection, *The Mayflower*, in 1843. In 1850 she moved to Brunswick, Maine, where her husband joined the faculty of Bowdoin College. She began writing a long tale of slavery, based on her observations in Ohio and Kentucky, and published it serially in the *National Era*; in 1852 it appeared in book form as *Uncle Tom's Cabin; or, Life Among the Lowly* and was an immediate sensation. It was taken up eagerly by Abolitionists and, along with its author, vehemently denounced in the South, where reading or possessing the book became an extremely dangerous undertaking. With sales of 300,000 in the first year, the book exerted an influence equalled by few others; it helped solidify both pro- and antislavery sentiment and fanned the flames that were to become the Civil War. Mrs. Stowe was enthusiastically received in England in 1853 and there formed friendships with many leading literary figures. In the same year she published *A Key to Uncle Tom's Cabin*, a compilation of documentary evidence in support of disputed details of her indictment of slavery. In 1856 appeared *Dred: a Tale of the Dismal Swamp*, another antislavery novel. From 1852 to 1863 she lived in Andover, Massachusetts, and from 1863 onwards in Hartford. She traveled widely in the United States and to Europe and continued to produce articles and stories, many of which appeared in the *Atlantic Monthly*, and novels, including *The Minister's Wooing*, 1859, *The Pearl of Orr's Island*, 1862, and *Oldtown Folks*, 1869. An article she published in 1869 in which she alleged that Lord Byron had had an incestuous affair with his sister created an uproar and cost her much of her English popularity, but she remained a leading author and lyceum lecturer in America. After the death of her husband in 1886 she remained at home in Hartford until her own death on July 1, 1896.

STRAVINSKY, IGOR FEDOROVICH (1882–), composer. Born on June 5, 1882 (O.S.), in Oranienbaum, near St. Petersburg (now Leningrad), Russia, the son of the leading bass singer in the Imperial Opera, Stravinsky grew up in a musical environment but was intended for a law career. He began composing on the piano at the age of 9 and continued his studies in harmony while attending law school at the University of St. Petersburg. He graduated in 1905 and, abandoning the law, took up the study of orchestration and composition under the composer Rimski-Korsakov, remaining in a close apprenticeship until the latter's death in 1908. The romantic themes and lush orchestral usage of his mentor pervaded his early compositions, including *Symphony in E-flat*, 1905–1907, the symphonic poem *Fireworks*, 1908, and *The Firebird*, 1910, which was commissioned by impressario Sergei Diaghilev for the Ballet Russe, the major producer of his stage works for the next 20 years. The ballet *Petrouchka*, 1911, marked a change from his early romanticism to completely unconventional meters and syncopation and also introduced bitonality. It prefaced the style of the ballet *The Rite of Spring*, later recognized as the beginning of an epoch in 20th-century music, but whose tumultuous rhythms and wild dissonances provoked violent demonstrations by the outraged audience at the premiere performance in Paris in 1913. By this time he was considered an extremely gifted but most controversial composer. The Russian Revolution, severed him from his home and property while he was visiting Switzerland, and he decided to remain in that country. During these years he wrote the innovative stage works *Reynard*, 1915–1916, and *The Soldier's Tale*, 1918.

After World War I he moved to France, becoming a citizen in 1934. His ballet *Pulcinella*, 1919–1920, marked a conversion from his dissonant mood to the predominant European musical tradition. He began a second career as a pianist and conductor, and composed *Capriccio* for piano and orchestra, 1929, and *Concerto* for two pianos, 1934–1935, for his own performances, and the *Violin Concerto*, 1931, for the violinist Samuel Dushkin. The last of his ballets to be produced by Diaghilev also was written in this period, *Apollo Musagetes*, 1928, as were *The Fairy's Kiss*, 1928, and *Persephone*, 1933–1934, both for Ida Rubenstein's ballet company, and *The Card Party*, 1936, for the American Ballet. The high points of his neoclassical period were the opera-oratorio *Oedipus Rex*, 1926–1927, and *Symphony of Psalms*, 1930. When World War II began he moved to the United States, becoming naturalized in 1945. A consolidation of all of his previous styles and techniques took place in *Symphony in C*, 1938–1940, *Symphony in Three Movements*, 1942–1945, the ballet *Orpheus*, 1947, reflecting his interest in jazz, the *Mass in C*, 1948, and an opera, *The Rake's Progress*, 1951, with libretto by W. H. Auden. To the amazement of listeners he took up the twelve-tone system in numerous works including *In Memoriam Dylan Thomas*, 1954, *Canticum Sacrum*, 1955, the ballet *Agon*, 1953–1957, and the completely atonal *Movements*, 1958–1959, *The Flood*, 1961–1962, and *Requiem Canticles*, 1965–1966. The range of his styles, forms, and techniques, while outrageous to many critics, marked him as one of the most fertile and influential of 20th-century composers.

STRONG, JOSIAH (1847–1916), clergyman. Born on January 19, 1847, in Naperville, Illinois, Strong graduated from Western Reserve College in 1869, then attended Lane Theological Seminary, and was ordained in 1871. Although he held many Congregational pulpits and was successful as a minister, he was dissatisfied with his work and did not discover his true métier until he wrote *Our Country*, 1885, a revision of the manual for the Congregational Missionary Society of Cincinnati. His ideas were revolutionary, proposing religious solutions of social and industrial problems. His second book, *The New Era*, 1893, went further, affirming that it was God's intention that Christians aspire to the kingdom through social work for the common good. His philosophy, called "Christian Socialism," spread far beyond the Missionary Society. The book was translated into many languages, and he became celebrated internationally as a lecturer. He was made secretary of the American Evangelical Alliance, which he hoped to use to unite churches in a concerted response to what he considered their social responsibilities. Resistance from orthodox clergymen was vigorous, however, and he resigned from the Alliance and formed the League for Social Service in 1898, which became in 1902 the American Institute for Social Service. Under the auspices of the Institute, he wrote pamphlets and books, gave lectures, and initiated the "Safety First" movement, which he extended to South American countries. He founded a British Institute for Social Service, and furthered the establishment of the American Federal Council of the Churches of Christ. He died in New York on April 28, 1916.

STUART, GILBERT CHARLES (1755 – 1828), painter. Born on December 3, 1755, near Narragansett, Rhode Island, Stuart was raised and educated in Newport and subsequently tutored by a Scottish painter living in Rhode Island. He traveled to Edinburgh with his master in 1771 and tried to earn his living by painting, but failed and returned to Newport the next year. In 1775 he sailed to England, where he lived in poverty for a year before approaching Benjamin West, who welcomed him to his studio as a pupil. He spent nearly six years with West, progressed rapidly in portraiture, and by 1777 he was exhibiting successfully at the Royal Academy. His painting "Portrait of a Gentleman Skating," 1782, won special favor and led to several commissions. Ranked among the leading portrait artists in England, he was nevertheless naive about money matters and fell into debt. In order to avoid prosecution he traveled to Ireland in 1787; there he painted with equal success but again met with financial disaster. He left for New York City in 1793 and in late 1794 opened a successful studio in Philadelphia. He completed a famous series of female portraits and two paintings of President Washington, a profile in 1795 and a full length portrait from life in 1796. Later that year he executed the famous unfinished "Athenaeum Head" of Washington, a highly romanticized version that has remained the most popular portrait of the man. In 1803, in a new studio in Washington, he completed portraits of Jefferson, Madison, and Monroe, among other distinguished public figures. His paintings were noted for their elegance, perception, and vibrant colors. Living in Boston after 1805, he remained successful but was chronically in debt. He showed symptoms of paralysis after 1825 but continued to paint. Well mannered, happy, and congenial into his 70s, he died in Boston on July 9, 1828.

STUART, JAMES EWELL BROWN (1833 – 1864), soldier. Born in Patrick County, Virginia, on February 6, 1833, Stuart attended Emory and Henry College for two years before entering the U.S. Military Academy in 1850. He graduated in 1854, was commissioned in the cavalry, and for six years was assigned to duty in Texas and Kansas. During a visit to the East in 1859 he served as aide to Col. Robert E. Lee in the expedition that defeated John Brown's raiding party at Harpers Ferry, Virginia. In May 1861 Stuart, by now a captain, resigned his commission and returned to Virginia, where he was commissioned lieutenant colonel of infantry. Two weeks later he was commissioned captain of cavalry in the Confederate army. Jeb Stuart (the nickname derived from his initials) distinguished himself quickly at first Bull Run (Manassas) in July and two months later was promoted to brigadier general. In command of the cavalry of the Army of Northern Virginia, he covered the retreat from the Peninsula in the spring of 1862. In June he was sent to scout McClellan's right just before the Seven Days' Battle; he completely circled the Union force and returned to Richmond with a quantity of captured supplies and prisoners. In July he became a major general and all Confederate cavalry was placed under him. He performed brilliantly at second Bull Run and at Fredericksburg and was highly valued by Lee as an intelligence officer of foremost ability. When "Stonewall" Jackson was wounded at Chancellorsville in May 1862 Stuart was given command of the 2nd Corps. His conduct at Gettysburg was long a subject of controversy: ordered to deploy his cavalry as a screen for the advancing Confederate army and to subordinate all other activity to this end, he nonetheless struck into Pennsylvania on a raid, was delayed, and arrived at Gettysburg too late to provide Lee with vital information on the position and movement of Union troops. In 1864 he again was invaluable in providing information on and a shield from Grant's advance, but by this time the Union cavalry under Sheridan had been greatly improved. Heavily outnumbered, Stuart met Sheridan at Yellow Tavern on May 11th; his force was partially defeated and Stuart himself was mortally wounded. He died the next day, May 12, 1864.

STUDEBAKER, CLEMENT (1831–1901), manufacturer. Born in Pinetown, near Gettysburg, Pennsylvania, on March 12, 1831, Studebaker moved with his family to Ohio, where he attended school and worked in his father's blacksmith shop. He moved to South Bend, Indiana, in 1850 and taught school until 1852, when he and his brother Henry formed the H.&C. Studebaker blacksmith and wagonmaking company. The growing demand for wagons in the Midwest, combined with the brothers' scrupulously maintained high standards of quality, allowed the business to prosper. Another brother, John, replaced Henry in 1858, and soon government contracts occasioned by the Civil War created further expansion. In 1868 Peter, yet another brother, came into the fold and the company was reorganized as the Studebaker Brothers Manufacturing Co., with Clement as president. A fifth and final brother, Jacob, joined them in 1870, in which year a branch was opened in St. Joseph, Missouri, to provide wagons for Western settlers. By this time the company was the world's largest manufacturer of wagons. Clement Studebaker became prominent in the Republican Party and enjoyed personal friendships with Presidents Grant, Harrison, and McKinley; in 1889 he was appointed a delegate to the Pan-American Congress by Harrison. About 1897 he began to experiment with self-propelled vehicles and these became, after his death, the company's major product. During its history the Studebaker company produced over 750,000 wagons before turning to powered automobiles in 1902. Clement Studebaker died on November 27, 1901.

SULLIVAN, HARRY STACK (1892–1949), psychiatrist. Born on February 21, 1892, in Norwich, New York, Sullivan earned his M.D. degree from the Chicago College of Medicine and Surgery in 1917 and studied after 1919 under William A. White at St. Elizabeth's Hospital in Washington, D.C. From 1923 to 1930 he did clinical research at Sheppard and Enoch Pratt Hospital in Towson, Maryland. In 1936 he helped to organize the Washington School of Psychiatry. A leader in the interpersonal school of psychiatry, he conceived of anxiety as a disturbance in interpersonal relations, having its first appearance in the relationship between a mother and child and continual application in the response of an individual to life situations. He rejected the idea of an individual personality and contended that character traits were a result of cultural and personal interactions. By using group treatment methods, he brought some forms of schizophrenia from the realm of incurable disorders to that of common mental diseases, showing them to be caused by anxiety and lack of self-esteem. At the beginning of World War II he was a consultant in the selective service program. After the war he attempted to apply his theories to understanding international tensions. He wrote several books, including *Conceptions of Modern Psychiatry*, 1947, *The Interpersonal Theory of Psychiatry*, 1953, *The Psychiatric Interview*, 1954, *Clinical Studies in Psychiatry*, 1956, and *The Fusion of Psychiatry and Social Science*, 1964. He died in Paris on January 14, 1949.

SULLIVAN, JOHN LAWRENCE (1858–1918), boxer. Born in Boston on October 15, 1858, Sullivan attended school, studied briefly at Boston College, and worked at various jobs until, at 19, he made his first appearance as a fighter. For several years he fought exhibition matches, gathering a reputation for great strength; in 1882, in Mississippi City, Mississippi, he knocked out Paddy Ryan for the world heavyweight championship. For a decade thereafter the "Great John L." reigned supreme in American boxing, attracting a large popular following and accumulating a small fortune that he as quickly lost, however, by living on a spectacular scale. In 1887 he was lionized while visiting England and was eagerly sought out by the Prince of Wales. In 1889 in Richburg, Mississippi, he knocked out Jake Kilrain in the 75th round of the last bare-knuckle bout in professional boxing. Finally, on September 7, 1892, in New Orleans, the "Boston Strong Boy" was defeated by James J. "Gentleman Jim" Corbett. From the ring Sullivan addressed the crowd: "I fought once too often. But I'm glad that it was an American who beat me and that the championship stays in this country. Very truly yours, John L. Sullivan." For a time he toured in plays and in

vaudeville and later opened a bar in New York. In 1905 he reformed and began lecturing on temperance. Sullivan died in near-poverty on February 2, 1918.

SULLIVAN, LOUIS HENRI (1856–1924), architect. Born on September 3, 1856, in Boston, Sullivan was trained in architecture at the Massachusetts Institute of Technology, 1872–1873, the École des Beaux Arts in Paris, 1874–1875, and in the offices of various architectural firms in Chicago, including that of William Le Baron Jenney. He had established a name as a competent draftsman in Chicago when he joined in partnership with Dankmar Adler in 1881. Their firm gained international fame upon completion of the Auditorium building in Chicago in 1890. Its interior design, planned largely by Sullivan, was intricate and wholly magnificent, and the receding, elevated pattern of seat rows produced near-perfect acoustics. Among Sullivan's apprentices at this time was Frank Lloyd Wright, who regarded his ideas on design as gospel. Sullivan completed several buildings based on his own structural theories: the Wainwright in St. Louis, generally thought to be the first true skyscraper, the Transportation Center at the World's Columbian Exposition and the Gage Building in Chicago, and the Prudential Building in Buffalo, New York. When Adler died in 1900 his financial resources diminished, primarily because his advanced ideas often bewildered potential clients. He was able, however, to erect the Carson Pirie Scott department store in Chicago and several banks in small midwestern towns. Through lectures, articles, and books, he expounded the theory that design should relate to use and materials and that architecture should be a response to the milieu—a principle made famous by the phrase "form follows function." This became the groundwork for all modern design. He was called the founder of the "Chicago School" of architecture, one diametrically opposed to useless tradition and devoted to modernism, uniquely represented by the skyscraper. He wrote, among other books, *The Autobiography of an Idea*, 1924. He died in Chicago on April 14, 1924.

SULLY, THOMAS (1783–1872), painter. Born on June 8 or 19, 1783, in Horncastle, England, the youngest son of actor parents, Sully came to the United States as an infant, was raised in South Carolina and moved to Virginia around 1799 to study art with his brother, a miniaturist. In 1801 he began indexing his work. By the end of his career, his portraits numbered 2,000 and his historical subject paintings over 500. In 1806 he moved to New York City. He studied briefly in Boston with Gilbert Stuart in 1807, and after establishing residence in Philadelphia in 1808 he spent a year in London, where he studied with Benjamin West and others. He was unmatched in portraiture after the deaths of Charles Willson Peale and Gilbert Stuart in 1827 and 1828. His works included studies of Lafayette, Jefferson, Madison, and Jackson, and, in 1838, young Queen Victoria of England. The most famous of his historical works, "Washington Crossing the Delaware," was executed about 1818. Commissions and social acceptance were assured him. Although his portraits failed to capture the personality that Stuart's work did, they were warm and exquisite in color. He remained the leading portraitist in Philadelphia until his death on November 5, 1872.

SUMNER, CHARLES (1811–1874), public official. Born in Boston on January 6, 1811, Sumner graduated from Harvard in 1830 and from Harvard Law School in 1834. He found the practice of law rather dull and in 1837 traveled to Europe for a stay of nearly three years, during which time he met prominent men of affairs and of letters and acquired a great deal of knowledge of European politics. He returned to his law practice and began lecturing at Harvard; he involved himself in several reform movements, notably those directed toward world peace, educational improve-

ment, and the abolition of slavery. He was a noted speaker and attracted wide, if sometimes unfavorable, attention with his strong and powerfully stated views. In 1851 he was nominated for the Senate by a Democratic-Free-Soil coalition and, after several months of deadlock in the legislature, elected. In his first major address, in August 1852, he reopened the issue of the Compromise of 1850 by proposing the repeal of the Fugitive Slave Law. His oratory typically was of the nature of tirade; in vituperation he was peerless, and his uncompromising stand on slavery made him the favorite, and most powerful, of Abolitionists. He bitterly opposed the Kansas-Nebraska Bill in 1854 and in May 1856, in a debate on the admission of Kansas, made his most famous address, "The Crime Against Kansas." He scorned the Act as a "swindle" and heaped invective upon its authors, Senators Butler and Douglas, in the most vindictive terms. Two days later, while at his desk in the Senate chamber, he was severely beaten by Preston Brooks, a Congressman from South Carolina and nephew of Senator Butler. For three years Sumner was unable to resume his official duties, but the outraged Massachusetts legislature nonetheless reelected him in 1857. He took a leading role in organizing the Republican Party and was its Senate leader when it came into control in 1860. During the Civil War, as chairman of the foreign relations committee, he rendered service of great value in helping prevent intervention by European powers; to this end he counseled the return of Mason and Slidell in the "Trent" affair and prevailed over more reckless heads. His extremist position on slavery and on rebellion led him to assert the belief that the defeated South would be a conquered province outside the protection of the Constitution; against Lincoln and later Johnson he worked in tandem with Thaddeus Stevens to secure enactment of the radical Reconstruction bills providing for military occupation of the South and making Negro suffrage a precondition for readmission to the Union. Also with Stevens he sought the impeachment and conviction of Johnson. He opposed President Grant's policies almost without exception and was instrumental in defeating the latter's plan to annex Santo Domingo in 1870, apparently in retaliation for which he was removed from the chairmanship of the foreign relations committee. His major accomplishments in his last years were the ratification of the 1871 Treaty of Washington, providing for arbitration of U.S.-British grievances (notably the *Alabama* claims) and a bill in 1872 that directed the removal from battle rolls and regimental flags of the names of all "battles with fellow-citizens." For the latter action he was at first censured by the Massachusetts legislature; in 1874, however, the censure was rescinded, but the day after the reversal was reported to the Senate, he died, on March 11, 1874.

SUMNER, WILLIAM GRAHAM (1840–1910), social scientist and educator. Born on October 30, 1840, in Paterson, New Jersey, Sumner grew up in Hartford, Connecticut, and graduated from Yale in 1863. During the next three years he studied abroad, at Geneva, Göttingen, and Oxford, intent on entering the ministry. From 1866 to 1869 he was a tutor at Yale and in the latter year was ordained an Episcopal minister in New York City. In 1870 he moved to Morristown, New Jersey, and led the church there until, no longer satisfied within the confines of clerical activity, he accepted an invitation to join the Yale faculty as professor of political and social science in 1872. In this position, which he held until his death, he became nationally influential, while devoting great energy to the study of social institutions from a viewpoint much like that of Herbert Spencer. In his economic and social outlook, Sumner was a Social Darwinist, holding that distinctions of wealth and status among men were the direct result of inherently different capacities, that this stratifying tendency worked to the good of society by eliminating weaker and encouraging stronger strains (as natural selection does among animals and plants), and that this tendency should not be interfered with by sentimental, unintelligent attempts to hedge the free play of economic forces and personal abilities. Sumner thus championed laissez faire as the only true principle of government; in lectures and written works with such titles as "The Absurd Attempt to Make the World Over" and *What Social Classes Owe to Each Other*, 1883, he decried any and all movements that pointed to a welfare state to the detriment of "The Forgotten Man" (an 1883 lecture title), the ordinary man of the middle class at whose expense government welfare programs were undertaken. He was throughout his life an opponent of inflationary fiscal policies and of the protective tariff. His interest in human institutions led him to study them at deeper and more basic levels, and in 1906 he published his great work on customs and mores, *Folkways*. He died in Englewood, New Jersey, on April 12, 1910. His notes and drafts for a major work on the entire range of sociology, left unfinished at his death, were edited and published in 1927–1928 as *The Science of Society*.

SUNDAY, WILLIAM ASHLEY (1862–1935), evangelist. Born in Ames, Iowa, on November 18 or 19, 1862, "Billy" Sunday grew up fatherless and in poverty. He completed high school and held a number of small jobs until he joined the Chicago White Sox baseball team in 1883. He played professional baseball for eight years, during which time, in 1887, he was converted to Christianity. In 1891 he began working with the YMCA in Chicago. After serving as assistant to another evangelist, he began traveling and preaching on his own in 1896. In 1903 he was ordained by the Presbyterian Church. Sunday was a flamboyant preacher and much given to sensationalism. He preached a fundamentalist theology, denouncing among other things science and political liberalism. In tune with the prevailing mood of much of rurally oriented America, he quickly gained an enormous following and, from the "free-will offerings" of his audiences, reputedly amassed a fortune. He is credited with having encouraged a number of local reform campaigns; his zealous advocacy of an essentially Puritanic morality was of considerable effect in the popular agitation for Prohibition. He reached the peak of his career in the decade between 1910 and 1920; after that his popularity decreased, though he continued to preach until his death in Chicago on November 6, 1935.

SWIFT, GUSTAVUS FRANKLIN   (1839–1903), butcher and meat packer. Born on June 24, 1839, near Sandwich, Massachusetts, Swift was educated in public schools and at the age of 14 joined his brother in the meat business. After butchering his own heifer and selling it door-to-door at a profit, he opened a butcher shop in 1859. First in Eastham, Massachusetts, and then in Barnstable, he established his trade by innovations such as the display of meat to the customer and packaging that made by-products like sausage look especially attractive. He opened markets in Freetown and Clinton and served customers in surrounding areas with meat wagons that traveled regular routes. Forming a partnership with James Hathaway in 1872, Swift soon moved to Chicago, the new center of the cattle market. He there developed his idea of shipping already butchered, packed, dressed beef to eastern cities in order to avoid the cost of shipping livestock. Anticipating failure, Hathaway sold his share of the business while Swift had a rudimentary refrigerator car developed to prevent the meat from deteriorating while in transit. He hired a railroad that had not shipped livestock previously, since other lines asked exorbitant rates to compensate for the loss they would suffer owing to reduced tonnage. The first shipment arrived in Boston in 1877 and the new method of distribution was quickly accepted. He fought increasing competition from other Chicago firms that began shipping dressed meats by developing innumerable by-products such as margarine, soap, glue, ferti-

lizer, and various pharmaceuticals. In 1885 Swift and Company was incorporated. Branch houses were established in other U.S. cities as well as in Great Britain and the Far East. Swift died in Chicago on March 29, 1903, and his sons continued to manage and control the company, which by that time had increased its capital worth more than eighty-fold.

TAFT, ROBERT ALPHONSO (1889–1953), public official. Born on September 8, 1889, in Cincinnati, the son of William Howard Taft, Robert Taft graduated from Yale in 1910 and from Harvard Law School in 1913. Admitted to the Ohio bar in the same year, he began his practice in Cincinnati and, with several successful business investments and an inheritance, soon became a man of some wealth. In 1920 he was elected as a Republican to the Ohio legislature, where he served for six years, the last as speaker of the house, and from 1930 to 1932 he was in the state senate. In 1938 he entered the U.S. Senate and immediately became an outspoken critic of President Roosevelt's policies, both domestic and foreign. The New Deal he labeled "socialistic" while calling for reduced and balanced government expenditures and an end to the concentration of power in Washington; in foreign affairs he was, until the Japanese attack on Pearl Harbor, a firm isolationist, and he stoutly opposed Roosevelt's internationalist tendencies. In the period of Republican resurgence that followed the party's defeats early in the Depression, Taft came quickly to a position of power and leadership within the party; as his preeminence grew he came eventually to be known as "Mr. Republican." Reelected in 1944 and 1950, he served in the Senate until his death; during this time he held such influence over legislation that he incurred the special wrath of President Truman for his blocking of Fair Deal measures. His principal legislative achievement was the 1947 Taft-Hartley Act, which restricted the activities of organized labor and nullified many of the concessions won in the earlier Wagner Act of the New Deal. He opposed American membership in the NATO alliance, attacked the administration for its "soft" response to Communist challenges, and lent support to Sen. Joseph McCarthy's investigations of Communist infiltration and subversion. Mentioned as a possible presidential candidate as early as 1940, Taft actively sought the nomination in 1948 and 1952; in the latter year he was thought to be the strongest candidate and lost to Gen. Dwight Eisenhower only after a long and bitter struggle that threatened for a time to split the party. He remained a faithful Republican, however, supporting the Eisenhower ticket fully and becoming Senate majority leader in the new Congress and one of the President's closest advisors. A few months later he died, on July 31, 1953.

TAFT, WILLIAM HOWARD (1857–1930), public official, jurist, and 27th U.S. President. Born in Cincinnati, Ohio, on September 15, 1857, Taft graduated from Yale in 1878 and two years later took his law degree at the Cincinnati Law School. Almost from the first he supplemented his law practice with involvement in local Republican politics, and after holding a number of minor public offices was appointed to fill an unexpired term on the superior court of Ohio in 1887. Elected to a full term the next year, he served only until 1890 when he became U.S. solicitor general under President Harrison. In 1892 he became presiding judge for the sixth federal circuit (Tennessee, Kentucky, Ohio, and Michigan). During his eight years on this bench Taft established himself as a thorough and effective legal arbiter but acquired a reputation for conservatism that was not wholly deserved. His judgments against union activities were based, not on antipathy to labor, whose right to organize and strike he never questioned, but on his view of the proper limits of such activities; in the major cases for which he was criticized for antiunion bias, his opinions were rendered against the use of secondary boycotts and the

violence accompanying strikes. His use of the injunction power applied as well to businesses under the antitrust laws. In 1900 President McKinley appointed Taft president of the Philippine Commission; arriving in the islands, he immediately set about organizing a civil government to supplant military rule and became civil governor in 1901. He effectively brought peace to the islands, negotiated a settlement with the Roman Catholic Church for confiscated property, and began a program of economic development and internal improvements. While in the Philippines he twice declined offers from President Roosevelt of a seat on the Supreme Court because he felt his work as governor was incomplete, but in 1904 he accepted an offer to become secretary of war, a post that would allow him to remain in touch with the new government. In Washington he became Roosevelt's most trusted advisor and assistant, acting as troubleshooter to quell a potential rebellion in Cuba, to organize the construction of the Panama Canal, and was chosen by Roosevelt to succeed him to the presidency in 1908. He was nominated and elected easily that year, but found the office trying and disappointing. Despite the influence of Roosevelt he allied himself more and more with the conservative wing of the party; pledged to tariff reduction, he approved of the Payne-Aldritch Tariff, with its negligible concessions to reduction, as the best bill obtainable and further alienated progressives. His administration was effective and efficient at the departmental level, but in a quiet way not calculated to win popular support. His major achievements, arbitration treaties with England and France and a trade agreement with Canada, failed of ratification, the first two by Senate recalcitrance. Though obscured by lack of publicity, the antitrust activities of the federal government under Taft were actually more extensive than had been the case under Roosevelt. The former President returned to America in 1910 and soon the conservative-progressive split in the Republican Party widened as Roosevelt formulated his "New Nationalism." Taft, at the head of the party machinery, was the inevitable if reluctant nominee of the 1912 Republican convention, but Roosevelt's challenge led to charges that he had "stolen" the nomination. The schism created by Roosevelt's Bull Moose (Progressive) Party made a Democratic victory certain; Taft ran a poor third, winning only eight electoral votes. He became Kent Professor of Law at Yale on leaving the White House in 1913. During World War I he served as joint chairman of the National War Labor Board and afterwards was a strong advocate of American entry into the League of Nations. In 1921 President Harding appointed him chief justice of the Supreme Court, a position he found completely suited to his wishes, his temperament, and his abilities. Again, his most effective work for the Court was as an administrator; he successfully eliminated the large backlog of cases on the docket and in 1925 secured passage of the Judges Act, providing for greater discretion by the Court in accepting cases and in considering them in order of national priority. His most important opinions included the majority opinion in *Bailey* v. *Drexel Furniture Co.*—the Child Labor Case—in 1922, holding that Congress had exceeded its authority in using the tax power for social reform to the destruction of state sovereignty; a dissent in *Adkins* v. *Children's Hospital*, 1923, in which revealed his liberal side by arguing that a 1918 women's minimum wage law in the District of Columbia was in the public interest; and the majority opinion in *Myers* v. *U.S.*, 1926, extending and clarifying the President's power to remove executive office holders. Ill health forced him to resign early in 1930; a month later, on March 8, he died in Washington.

TANEY, ROGER BROOKE (1777–1864), public official and jurist. Born in Calvert County, Maryland, on March 17, 1777, Taney was of the landed aristocracy in his region. He graduated from Dickinson College in 1795, was admitted to the bar in 1799, and two years later set-

tled in Frederick, Maryland, to establish his practice. While there he married, in 1806, the sister of Francis Scott Key. He became prominent in the Federalist Party in his state, serving on occasion in the legislature, and in 1812 was the leader of the pro-war faction, the "Coodies." As the split among Federalists failed to heal, the party slowly disintegrated, and soon after moving to Baltimore in 1823 Taney switched his allegiance to Andrew Jackson. A recognized leader of the Maryland bar, he was appointed state attorney general in 1827 and in 1831, by Jackson's appointment, became U.S. attorney general. By this time he had come to view the Bank of the United States as a dangerous institution; though in many ways a useful instrument, it had abused its powers and was now seeking an early renewal of its charter. Taney persuaded Jackson to veto the new charter passed by Congress and drafted much of the veto message; in the midst of the ensuing controversy he further pressed for a withdrawal of federal deposits from the Bank. Jackson agreed and when Secretary of the Treasury Duane refused to do so Taney was appointed in September 1833 to replace him. The appointment came during a congressional recess, and nine months later the Senate, led by Whigs, refused to confirm him, though by this time the redistribution of federal money among selected state banks had already been effected. Taney returned to his law practice. In 1835 his nomination as an associate justice of the Supreme Court was also rejected by the Senate, but changes in that body enabled his appointment as chief justice to stand the following year. Succeeding John Marshall, he immediately began to change the tenor of the Court by reversing the earlier trend toward strong centralization of governmental powers. In his first major opinion, *Charles River Bridge* v. *Warren Bridge*, 1837, he established a narrow construction of corporate charters granted by states, the charter powers and privileges being balanced against the public good. The reversal of Federalist tendencies was not so extreme as many had feared it might be; rather than being a spokesman for the radical states' rights position, Taney held consistently—in *Bank of Augusta* v. *Earle*, 1839, the 1847 License Cases and the 1849 Passenger Cases—that in the absence of federal legislation, states were competent to regulate commerce in any way that was not an invasion or contradiction of federal jurisdiction or law, a much more moderate view. On the other hand, he maintained the supremacy of federal over state courts and produced a masterly analysis of the power relations of federalism in *Ableman* v. *Booth*, 1859. In March 1857 he succumbed to the temptation to settle the question of congressional authority over slavery judicially. In his decision in the case of *Dred Scott* v. *Sandford* he dismissed Scott's plea by holding that a Negro could not be a citizen and therefore could not sue in federal court; he then went on, in what many thought to be an ill-considered *obiter dictum*, to declare that Congress had never had the authority to ban slavery from the territories, thus effectively branding the 1820 Missouri Compromise unconstitutional. The decision roused a bitter controversy, and Republicans and Abolitionists made it a major issue in the 1860 elections. The prestige of the Court dropped sharply, and during the Civil War it and particularly Taney were viewed with suspicion. He exacerbated such feelings by finding several governmental war measures unconstitutional, notably in *Ex Parte Merryman*, 1861, when, sitting as circuit judge, he overruled a military suspension of habeas corpus in Baltimore. He died, publicly unlamented, on October 12, 1864, in Washington.

TAPPAN, ARTHUR (1786–1865) and **LEWIS** (1788–1873), merchants, philanthropists, and reformers. Born in Northampton, Massachusetts, Arthur on May 22, 1786, and Lewis on May 23, 1788, the Tappan brothers moved to Boston upon completing school and entered the dry goods business. About 1807 Arthur established his own firm in Portland, Maine,

moving it later to Montreal. In 1826 he founded a new company in New York City and was joined two years later by Lewis. The firm lasted until 1837; four years later Lewis opened the first commercial credit rating agency in America and Arthur became a partner in 1849. Between the two, In various ventures, a considerable fortune was amassed, and they soon began to devote a major portion of their time to distributing it among several worthy institutions and causes. Arthur founded the *New York Journal of Commerce* in 1827 to serve as a model of moral and reformist journalism; Lewis took over the paper after a year and continued it until 1831 when it was sold. They supported the revivalist Charles Grandison Finney and were primarily responsible for the construction of the Broadway Tabernacle for him. Money was contributed toward the establishment of Kenyon College, Auburn and Lane Theological seminaries, and especially Oberlin College. They helped organize the American Anti-Slavery Society in 1833 with Arthur as its first president; the next year Lewis' house was sacked by a mob for his Abolitionist activities. Both men worked closely with William Lloyd Garrison until his insistence on linking other reforms with Abolitionism caused them to break with him and form the American and Foreign Anti-Slavery Society in 1840, again with Arthur as president. In 1843 Lewis went to England to attend an international conference on the abolition of slavery and made valuable contacts for the American group. In 1846 they helped found the American Missionary Association, in which both held high offices. Both Tappans were originally moderate Abolitionists, hoping to achieve their goal by legal action and reform under the Constitution and within the Union, but after passage of the Fugitive Slave Law in 1850 their position became more radical as they openly defied the law and supported the Underground Railroad. By the late 1850s both found their activities limited by the restraints of age. Arthur retired to New Haven, Connecticut, where he died on July

23, 1865; Lewis published a biography of his brother in 1870 and continued to work with the American Missionary Association until his death on June 21, 1873.

TARBELL, IDA MINERVA (1857–1944), author. Born on November 5, 1857, in Erie County, Pennsylvania, Ida Tarbell graduated from Allegheny College in Meadville, Pennsylvania. Intent on a career in journalism, she became an associate editor of the *Chatauquan* in 1883. She resumed her studies at the Sorbonne and the College de France, 1891–1894. From 1894 to 1906 she was an editor of the leading muckraking journal of the day, *McClure's Magazine*, which through articles and editorials exposed political and industrial corruption and emphasized the need for reforms, thus giving impetus to the Populist and Progressive movements. Her own exhaustively researched articles for *McClure's* on the Rockefeller oil interests were collected in *The History of the Standard Oil Company*, 1904. The articles and the book aroused public opinion and led to federal investigations into the activities of the Standard Oil Company of New Jersey, which was ultimately dissolved in 1911 under the Sherman Antitrust Act. In 1906 she left *McClure's* and with Lincoln Steffens, Ray Stannard Baker, William Allen White, and Finley Peter Dunne, purchased the *American Magazine*, of which she was associate editor until 1915. She wrote biographies of business leaders and politicians, including Judge Gary and Owen D. Young, and in all produced eight books on Lincoln. Other writings included *The Business of Being a Woman*, 1912, *The Ways of Women*, 1915, and an autobiography, *All in a Day's Work*, 1939. She died at her home in Bethel, Connecticut, on January 6, 1944.

TARKINGTON, NEWTON BOOTH (1869–1946), author. Born in Indianapolis on July 29, 1869, Tarkington was educated at Phillips Exeter Academy, Purdue University, and Princeton. He lived in Maine and abroad at various times, but considered himself a Hoosier writer. His first book, *The Gentleman From Indiana*, 1899, was an immediate success, and was followed by *Monsieur Beaucaire*, 1900, which later in its stage adaptation provided Rudolph Valentino with one of his most brilliant roles. Immensely versatile and prolific, producing some 40 popular novels in his career, he was famous for stories of boyhood life—*Penrod*, 1914, its sequels, and *Seventeen*, 1916—for portrayals of midwestern life and character—*The Turmoil*, 1915, *The Magnificent Ambersons*, 1918, which won a Pulitzer Prize, *The Midlander*, 1923, and *The Plutocrat*, 1927—and for his portrayals of female personalities—*Alice Adams*, 1921, which won his second Pulitzer Prize, *Claire Ambler*, 1928, *Mirthful Haven*, 1930, and *Presenting Lily Mars*, 1933—and for numerous plays, many of which were adaptations from his novels. He died in Indianapolis on May 19, 1946.

TAYLOR, EDWARD (c. 1645–1729), poet. Born about 1645 in Leicestershire, England, in or near Coventry, Taylor is thought to have come from a dissenting family. In any event, unwilling to subscribe to the oath of conformity required of schoolteachers, he gave up his profession and emigrated to New England, where he arrived in 1668. Already 23 and a man of some education, he was immediately admitted by President Increase Mather as a sophomore at Harvard, and he graduated from the college in 1671. He then went to Westfield, Massachusetts, as physician and minister, and remained there until his death in 1729. He married twice and became the father of 13 children, most of whom he outlived. His grandson, Ezra Stiles, was president of Yale during the Revolution and was in addition the inheritor of his manuscripts and the greater part of a library of some 200 volumes. The manuscripts included a 400-page "Poetical Works" that, by its author's express desire, was not published by his heirs. But it came into the possession of Yale in 1883 by the gift of a descendant, and Taylor's poems first began to be published in the late 1930s. The occasion was a momentous one, for he was immediately recognized as the best American poet of the 17th century. The important poems fall into two main divisions. "God's Determinations Touching His Elect" is an extended verse sequence setting forth the drama of sin and redemption. "Sacramental Meditations," about 200 shorter poems on various subjects, were written over a period of 44 years, from 1682 to 1725; the author described them as "Preparatory Meditations Before My Approach to the Lord's Supper." The poems are interesting not only in themselves but also for the light they throw on the English poetic tradition; for Taylor was still writing like the metaphysical poets he had read in his youth — Donne, Herbert, and Crashaw, for example — long after the extravagant tropes that marked their work were completely passé, and sharply disapproved of, in England itself. *The Poetical Works of Edward Taylor*, edited by T. H. Johnson, a selection together with a biographical sketch, a critical introduction, and notes, appeared in 1939. *The Poems of Edward Taylor*, edited by Donald E. Stanford, 1960, is a comprehensive edition including the complete text of the "Meditations." *Christographia*, a collection of sermons delivered in 1701–1703, was published in 1962.

TAYLOR, FREDERICK (1856–1915), inventor and efficiency engineer. Born on March 20, 1856, in Germantown, Pennsylvania, Taylor intended to become a lawyer, but suffered an eye defect that disrupted his plans to attend Harvard law school. He worked in several Philadelphia factories, then in a steel mill, and observed and sympathized with his co-workers who frequently dropped of exhaustion trying to meet their employers' demands. For 12 years he remained in the steel company and rose to become its chief engineer. During this time, he attended night school at the Stevens Institute of Technology and graduated in 1883. From his position of authority, he commenced investigations of the real power of the machinery that was being used and related that information to the amount of work that could reasonably be expected of a man in one day. It became obvious that the demands being made were not feasible. With two objectives in mind, to eliminate the hostility between labor and management and at the same time to increase daily output, he began to devise more powerful machinery and to study the amount of time that was involved in performing every operation in the plant. He invented the largest steel hammer in the United States in 1890; and his application of the data obtained from his "time and motion studies" led to reasonable work loads, better relations among employees and overseers, an incentive system of wages, and increased efficiency throughout the plant. "Taylorization" was adopted with great success in shops, offices, and industrial plants throughout the nation. In 1898 he was retained by the Bethlehem Steel Company to apply his theories and revise their entire complex. At that time he met J. Maunsel White; together they studied methods for tempering tool steel and in 1898 developed the Taylor-White process that increased steel cutting capacity by 300 percent. He resigned his post at Bethlehem Steel to devote himself to spreading his ideas. He offered his services to any company that was interested in Taylorization and completed, by 1911, *The Principles of Scientific Management* and a report to Congress on the fairness and reliability of his plan. His other works included *The Adjustment of Wages to Efficiency*, 1896, and *Shop Management*, 1903. He died in Philadelphia on March 21, 1915.

TAYLOR, JOHN (1753–1824), public official and publicist. Born on December 19 (?), 1753, in either Orange or Caroline County, Virginia, Taylor later resided in and is usually identified with the latter place, being commonly known as John Taylor of Caroline. He studied for a time at the College of William and Mary and after reading law began to practise in 1774. During the Revolution he served with the Army in Virginia, Pennsylvania, and New York, attaining the rank of major before resigning in 1779; two years later he was appointed lieutenant colonel of his home militia and served through the final campaigns in Virginia. He was elected to the Virginia House of Delegates regularly except for one year from 1779 to 1785 and served again from 1796 to 1800. On three occasions he filled out unexpired terms in the Senate, 1792–1794, 1803, and 1822–1824. It was through his political writings, however, that he became widely known; like so many Virginians at the time, he was an ardent democrat and staunchly opposed all efforts to establish a strong central government that, in his view, would inevitably usurp the rights and powers of the states and ultimately of the people. He joined Patrick Henry in opposing ratification of the Constitution in Virginia and then, having failed in that aim, attempted to stem the federalist drift of the new government. *A Definition of Parties* and *An Enquiry into the Principles and Tendencies of Certain Public Measures*, both 1794, were directed against the fiscal policies of Alexander Hamilton; in 1798 he introduced into the legislature Madison's Virginia Resolutions against the Alien and Sedition acts and in 1805 published *A Defence of the Measures of the Administration of Thomas Jefferson*. His major writings came later: *An Inquiry into the Principles and Policy of the Government of the United States*, 1814, a rebuttal of John Adams; *Construction Contrued and Constitutions Vindicated*, 1820, an attack on the growing power of the federal courts under John Marshall's leadership; *Tyranny Unmasked*, 1822, denouncing the protective tariff; and *New Views of the Constitution of the United States*, 1823. These works, despite their wordy and infelicitous style, are among the best and most thorough expositions of the agrarian liberal democracy that remains one of the major strains in American political thought. Taylor was, in addition,

an agriculturalist of note and made significant experiments with crop rotation and other methods of improved cultivation. He died on August 21, 1824.

TAYLOR, ZACHARY (1784–1850), soldier and 12th U.S. President. Born on November 24, 1784, in Orange County, Virginia, Taylor grew up near Louisville, Kentucky, where his family moved in 1785. He received little formal education. He first saw military service as a short-term volunteer in 1806; two years later he was commissioned a regular lieutenant and by the end of the War of 1812, during which he served under Gen. William Henry Harrison, he had been brevetted major. The reduction in forces that followed the war returned him to captain and he resigned, but in 1816 President Madison recommissioned him as a major and for the next 21 years he saw garrison duty along the western frontier from Louisiana to Wisconsin, where, in 1832, he took part in the Black Hawk War. In 1837 he was ordered to Florida to help prosecute the war against the Seminole Indians; he won a major victory at the Battle of Lake Okeechobee in December and was brevetted brigadier general. In May 1838 Taylor—now nicknamed "Old Rough and Ready"—became departmental commander in Florida and for two years oversaw the frustrating and inconclusive campaign. Relieved at his own request in 1840, he returned to Louisiana and a year later became departmental commander at Ft. Smith, Arkansas. In 1845 he was ordered to prepare for a possible invasion of newly annexed Texas by Mexican forces. Early in May 1846, before war was declared, he won minor victories at Palo Alto and Resaca de la Palma and was brevetted major general. In September he captured Monterrey and granted the Mexicans an eight-week armistice; this action was repudiated by President Polk and Taylor began to suspect Polk and Secretary of War Marcy of political intrigue aimed at his own growing popularity. His conviction was strengthened when Gen. Winfield Scott commandeered many of his seasoned troops for the Vera Cruz invasion, leaving him with orders to concentrate at Monterrey and to pursue a strictly defensive policy. Instead he advanced to the south and, though outnumbered four to one, defeated Santa Anna's army at Buena Vista in February 1847. Now a national hero, he began to receive serious consideration by the Whigs as a presidential candidate; he was already something of a Whig, though he had never voted in a presidential election, and his status as a slaveholder would attract Southern support for a party suspected of Northern sympathies. At the 1848 Whig convention he was nominated over Clay, Webster, and Scott, and, aided by a Democratic split, was elected President. He took office with virtually no knowledge of the political process; though he adapted himself to the patronage system, he soon came into conflict with other party leaders over the admission of California and New Mexico to the Union. He strongly resented opposition to his own policy of encouraging admission and was himself opposed to the injection of sectionalism into the issue. He was contemptuous of Southern leaders who threatened secession should California enter the Union as a free state, and he referred with disdain to the Compromise measures of 1850 as the "Omnibus Bill." In mid-1850 he was further troubled by a scandal involving three of his Cabinet advisers and decided to reorganize the entire Cabinet; before any of these matters was resolved, however, he became seriously ill following a July 4th celebration and died on July 9, 1850.

TECUMSEH (1768–1813), Indian chief. Born in March 1768 near what is now Oldtown, Ohio, Tecumseh was noted everywhere on the frontier for his courage and integrity. He wished to establish a powerful Indian nation to halt American agricultural settlement in the Ohio Valley. He maintained that the frontier as a whole belonged to all the Indians who, throughout history, had changed the location of their homeland without any concept of ownership of particular regions. He emphasized that the Treaty of Greenville, 1795, had been negotiated with all Indian tribes, assuring them that unceded lands would be theirs. Ohio Gov. William Henry Harrison, who recognized the implications of this treaty, maneuvered individual tribes to sign cession treaties, frequently under conditions of trickery or deceit. Tecumseh traveled among the tribes, trying to unite them and to convince them to refuse white men's gifts, to work in agriculture, and to live on what they earned. He acquired great influence and nearly perfected his confederation with the aid of the British, who supplied guns and ammunition. Despite his exertions, however, Governor Harrison continued to gain lands. In 1811, while he was absent, his brother Teuskwatawa, "the Prophet," was killed by Harrison at Tippecanoe, a battle that scattered his finest warriors and led to the destruction of the provisions he had stockpiled as security. When the War of 1812 broke out, he joined the British forces as a brigadier general. They captured Detroit and he rallied more warriors to fight on the British side. When he learned of their plan to burn Detroit and retreat eastward, he was angry and demanded arms so that he and his warriors could fight for the Western land or die upon it. He remained with the British troops, however, until the Battle of the Thames, in Canada, on October 5, 1813, in which he commanded the right wing of the army. He was killed in the battle.

TELLER, EDWARD (1908–), physicist. Born in Budapest, Hungary, on January 15, 1908, Teller studied at the technological institute in Karlsruhe, Germany, and took his Ph.D. from the University of Leipzig in 1930. From 1931 to 1933 he was a research associate at the University of Göttingen, in 1934 he studied with Niels Bohr in Copenhagen, and in 1935 he fled the Nazi regime and, after a brief time as a lecturer at the University of London, he became a visiting professor at George Washington University. In 1941, the year he became a naturalized citizen, he moved to Columbia University to join Enrico Fermi in research on atomic fission and later in the year became a member of the Manhattan Project group working on development of the atomic bomb. For five years he was concerned with the project, first at Columbia and later at the University of Chicago, the University of California at Berkeley, and the Los Alamos Laboratory in New Mexico. At the same time he began formulating the theoretical foundations for a hydrogen fusion bomb and was a major proponent of its development. In 1945 he returned to the Institute for Nuclear Studies at the University of Chicago and the following year became professor of physics there. In 1949 he was named assistant director of the Los Alamos facility and remained there until 1951, by which time the principal theoretical and practical problems of the H-bomb had been solved. After another year at the University of Chicago Teller joined the staff of the Atomic Energy Commission's new laboratory in Livermore, California, and in 1953 became professor of physics at the University of California. From 1954 he was associate director of the university's Lawrence Radiation Laboratory and during 1958–1960 was director of the Livermore laboratory; in 1960 he became professor at large. He was a strong advocate of the continued testing and improvement of nuclear weapons and was critical of those favoring test moratoriums and bans. In 1954 he was a major figure in the security hearings for J. Robert Oppenheimer and testified that Oppenheimer had, by lack of "moral support," delayed the development of the H-bomb by several years. Teller wrote a number of books on the history and future of nuclear weapons, including *Our Nuclear Future* (with A.L. Latter), 1958, and *The Legacy of Hiroshima*, 1962. In 1962 he was awarded the Atomic Energy Commission's Fermi Prize.

TENNENT, GILBERT (1703–1764), clergyman. Born on February 5, 1703, in County Armagh, Ireland, Tennent was the son of a noted Presbyterian minister who brought him to America in 1718. Well educated by his father, he entered the ministry in 1725; the following year he accepted a pastorate in New Brunswick, New Jersey, and, associated there with the Dutch evangelist T. J. Frelinghuysen, soon developed into a zealous and rousing preacher. Joined by other students of his father's "Log College," he became the central figure of the rapidly growing wave of revivalism that came to be known as the Great Awakening. In 1739 the group was joined by the great English revivalist George Whitefield, and during 1739–1740 Whitefield and Tennent traveled throughout the middle colonies and into New England, fervently preaching the awesome power and wrath of God and the imminent damnation of sinners. The conservative majority of Presbyterian leaders was soon roused to concern and in 1741 the church split into the traditional Old Side and the evangelistic New Side. In 1743 Tennent became pastor of a New Side church organized by Whitefield in Philadelphia; he retained the position for the rest of his life and continued to be a controversial figure, though in later years he appeared to regret his earlier contentiousness and led the movement that resulted in the reunification of the Presbyterian Church in 1758. In 1753 he traveled to England with Samuel Davies and raised money for the construction of Nassau Hall at the newly founded College of New Jersey (now Princeton). He died on July 23, 1764.

TESLA, NIKOLA (1856–1943), electrical engineer and inventor. Born on July 10, 1856, in Smiljan in what is now Yugoslavia, Tesla studied mathematics, physics, and engineering at the polytechnic school in Gratz for four years and then, from 1878 to 1880, was enrolled at the University of Prague, where he concentrated on philosophy. In 1881 he went to Paris to work as an electrical engineer and three years later came to the United States. For a time he was employed by Thomas Edison and later by George Westinghouse, but his preference was for independent research; his Tesla Electric Company, formed in 1887, soon failed, and he spent most of his life working alone. His was a fertile genius for invention; he claimed some 700, beginning with his 1881 construction of a telephone repeater, but he never reaped the material rewards that might have been his. In 1888 he developed his idea of a rotating magnetic field into a practical motor run by an alternating electric current. The induction, synchronous, and split-phase motors were all of Tesla's invention, as were new and improved generators and transformers, together constituting a workable system for the production and distribution of A.C. electric power. From about 1890 he devoted much time to the study of high frequency current, developing several forms of oscillators and the famous Tesla coil. By 1893 he had worked out a method of transmitting intelligence by wireless telegraphy. He became convinced that the power distribution system of the future would be by wireless broadcast from tall, centrally located towers, and he concentrated his energies on developing this method for practical application. He secured backing from J. P. Morgan to erect a tower on Long Island, but the financier's death interrupted the project; later he worked on designing such a system for the Niagara Falls power plant. A visionary as well as a practical engineer, he foresaw the harnessing of solar energy for man's use and around the turn of the century announced that he had been attempting wireless communications with other planets, which he was convinced were inhabited. He died in New York City on January 7, 1943.

THOMAS, GEORGE HENRY (1816–1870), soldier. Born in Southhampton County, Virginia, on July 31, 1816, a member of a wealthy Virginia family, Thomas graduated from West Point in 1840 and served in the artillery during the Seminole Indian War in Florida and in the Mexican War. After 1848 he was an instructor at West Point and in 1855 was promoted major in the 2nd Cavalry. When the Civil War broke out in 1861, he, unlike some of his better known Virginia contemporaries, remained faithful to his Army oath and to the Union. He was made commander of an independent force in eastern Kentucky, and at Mill Springs, on January 19, 1862, he gained the first important Union victory in the west. He served under Gen. Don Carlos Buell and was offered the chief command but refused it; under Gen. W. S. Rosencrans he was engaged at Stone River early in 1863 and was in charge of most of the important maneuvering that led up to the Battle of Chattanooga, later in the year. At the Battle of Chickamauga, on September 19th, he held Rosencrans' left wing against heavy odds, and gained the sobriquet "the Rock of Chickamauga." He succeeded to the command of the Army of the Cumberland shortly before the great victory at Chattanooga in late November. At the time Grant was the chief Union officer in the west; when he departed for Washington as commander in chief, Sherman replaced him in the west, but Thomas remained as second in command in the area. In the autumn of 1864 Gen. J. B. Hood broke away from Atlanta and menaced Sherman's extended lines of communications, and Sherman left to Thomas the task of containing Hood. A delaying action checked Hood on November 30th, and Thomas thereupon attacked him at Nashville on December 15th–16th, inflicting the worst defeat sustained in the open field by any army on either side during the war. Thomas was made a major general in the regular Army and received the thanks of Congress. After the war he commanded military departments in Kentucky and Tennessee; in 1869 he was placed in charge of the division of the Pacific, with headquarters in San Francisco. He died there on March 28, 1870.

THOMAS, ISAIAH (1749–1831), printer and publisher. Born in Boston on January 19, 1749 (O. S.), Thomas had just 6 weeks of schooling and at age 6 began to learn printing from the local printers, so that he was well qualified in the field by the age of 17. With his apprenticeship still in effect, he went to Nova Scotia in 1766 and obtained employment with the *Halifax Gazette*, hoping to continue to London and further his training. His refusal to comply with the Stamp Act, however, led him back to Boston, where he was released from his indenture. Then traveling south in the United States, hoping to reach England through the West Indies, he stopped in Charlestown and worked on the *South Carolina and American General Gazette*. With dim prospects for reaching England, he went back to Boston in 1770 and established with his former master, Zechariah Fowle, the *Massachusetts Spy*. Soon becoming the sole owner of the paper, he took up the patriot cause and became notorious with the royal government, and famous among the people. Driven from Boston by the British occupation in 1775, he sent his printing equipment to Worcester and on the way there helped Paul Revere to warn the countryside on April 18th and was a Minute Man in the battles of Lexington and Concord. He set up offices in Worcester on April 20th and became the official printer for the patriots. In 1778, having spent a brief time in business in Salem, he resumed issuing the *Spy*. Opening offices throughout New England, he issued textbooks (including Nicholas Pike's arithmetic and William Perry's speller and dictionary), Blackstone's *Commentaries*, illustrated editions of children's books (including *Mother Goose's Melody* and *The History of Little Goody Two-shoes*), and almanacs, magazines, religious works, sheet music, and the first native American novel, *The Power of Sympathy*, 1789. He was also the first postmaster of Worcester (1775–1801), compiled a *History of Printing in America*, 2 volumes, 1810, and founded and incorporated the American Antiquarian Society in 1812, becoming its first president. He died in Worcester on April 4, 1831.

THOMAS, NORMAN MATTOON (1884–1968), social reformer and political leader. Born on November 20, 1884, in Marion, Ohio, Thomas was educated at Bucknell University and at Princeton, graduating from the latter at the head of his class of 1905. After devoting some time to travel and to social settlement work he entered Union Theological Seminary. He graduated in 1911, was ordained in the Presbyterian Church, and became pastor of the East Harlem Church in New York City. In his pastorate and in his work with the American Parish, a settlement house, he was deeply impressed with the problems of poverty; abandoning his youthful conservatism, he gradually adopted the "Social Gospel" ideas of Walter Rauschenbusch. The outbreak of World War I strengthened his conviction that the major political parties were incapable of solving the overriding problems of society. By 1918 he had moved from pacifism to socialism. Resigning from his church and joining the Socialist Party in that year, he also became secretary of the Fellowship of Reconciliation and founded *The World Tomorrow*, which he edited until 1921. In 1920 he helped found the American Civil Liberties Union. From 1921 to 1922 he edited *The Nation* and from then until the mid-1930s was co-executive director of the League for Industrial Democracy. He was the Socialist Party candidate for governor of New York in 1924, for mayor of New York City in 1925 and 1929, and, becoming the leader of the party after the death of Eugene V. Debs in 1926, ran for President in every election from 1928 to 1948. He was an indefatigable speaker and writer, and notable among his many books were *Is Conscience a Crime?*, 1927, on conscientious objection to military service, *As I See It*, 1932, *Socialism on the Defensive*, 1938, *We Have a Future*, 1941, *A Socialist's Faith*, 1951, *The Test of Freedom*, 1954, *The Prerequisites for Peace*, 1959, and *Socialism Reexamined*, 1963. He effectively shaped the policies of the Socialist Party for over 40 years, and, while offering the party's program as an alternative to capitalism, was remarkably successful in keeping it free of the taint of Communism in the mind of the American public. Many of his proposals — low-cost housing, the five-day work week, minimum wage laws, and the abolition of child labor among them — ultimately found their way into legislation. A brilliant orator, he was constantly in demand and continued to lecture several times weekly until his death in New York City on December 20, 1968.

THOMSON, VIRGIL GARNETT (1896 –), composer and music critic. Born in Kansas City on November 25, 1896, of Scottish and Irish ancestry, Thomson studied piano and organ from the age of five, and musical theory and voice, also from an early age. He graduated from the Kansas City Polytechnic Institute and Junior College and enlisted in the Army in 1917. He entered Harvard and wrote his first piece, a song based on Amy Lowell's poem *Vernal Equinox*, in 1920. In 1922 he studied under Nadia Boulanger in Paris. He graduated from Harvard in 1923 and studied counterpoint and conducting for one year in New York City at the David Mannes School of Music, returning to Harvard as an instructor. In 1925 he settled in Paris for ten years. There he wrote the dissonant but traditionally formed *Sonata da Chiesa* in 1926, the ultramodern *Symphony on a Hymn Tune* in 1928, and the more simply stated *Symphony Number 2* in 1931, both of the latter works drawing from American folk themes. He based a cantata on Gertrude Stein's *Capitals, Capitals*, shortly after meeting her in 1926, and collaborated with her as librettist on the opera burlesque *Four Saints in Three Acts*, which premiered in 1934, and *The Mother of Us All*, first performed in 1947, the latter an opera-collage of American historical, folk, and contemporary musical themes, depicting the life of Susan B. Anthony. He wrote musical accompaniments to Broadway plays and to films including *The Plow That Broke the Plains*, 1936, *The River*, 1937, *Louisiana Story*, 1948, for which he won a Pulitzer Prize, Chayevsky's *The Goddess*, 1958, and Houseman's *Voyage to Amer-*

ica, 1964. He wrote over 100 orchestral "portraits" of personalities such as Picasso, Aaron Copland, Fiorello LaGuardia, and Dorothy Thompson, and "landscapes" — of Paris, *The Seine at Night*, 1947, and of Missouri, *Wheat Fields at Noon*, 1948. He also wrote liturgical music, including *Missa Pro Defunctis*, which premiered under his direction in 1960, the ballet *Filling Station*, 1937, organ music, piano sonatas, flute and cello concertos, and songs based on American folk themes and French, Spanish, and Latin texts. As music critic for the *New York Herald Tribune* from 1940 to 1954 he wrote articles gathered with other essays in *The Musical Scene*, 1945, *The Art of Judging Music*, 1948, and *Music Right and Left*, 1951. He also wrote *The State of Music*, 1939, which established him as a witty, opinionated commentator, in favor of music as entertainment, and *Virgil Thomson on Virgil Thomson*, 1966.

THOREAU, HENRY DAVID (1817 – 1862), naturalist, philosopher, and author. Born in Concord, Massachusetts, on July 12, 1817, Thoreau was able, despite his family's lack of means, to enter Harvard in 1833; he graduated four years later in the same week that Emerson, also of Concord and Thoreau's principal mentor, delivered his famous "American Scholar" address to the Harvard Phi Beta Kappa Society. After a brief and unpleasant time teaching school in Concord — he resigned when his refusal to employ corporal punishment was objected to — he turned to the family industry of pencil making until 1839 when, with his brother John, he opened a private school. The school lasted two years, during which the two introduced an educational innovation, nature-study field trips. Henry then accepted an invitation to live with Emerson, nominally earning his keep as general handyman while devoting much of his time to reading, writing poetry and essays, talking with the members of the Transcendentalist Club that met with Emerson, and rambling through the woods and fields. His reading from college days onward was concentrated in the English nature and mystical poets, Oriental philosophy, and the contemporary romantic literature of Europe; his writing was encouraged by Emerson, who proposed subjects, edited, and sought publication for it. In 1843 he went as tutor to the home of Emerson's brother William on Staten Island and during his year there confirmed his dislike for urban society by his visits to New York City. He returned to Concord in 1844 and resumed his pencil making. The following year he brought to fruition a project long planned. Moving to the shore of nearby Walden Pond, on land provided by Emerson, he built a house, planted a garden, and settled down to a two-year experiment in living the simple, self-reliant, contemplative life of a free spirit. While recording his experiences, observations, and reflections in his voluminous journals, he also wrote his first book, *A Week on the Concord and Merrimack Rivers*, which, while cast in the form of a record of a boat trip made with his brother in 1839, was largely drawn from his journals of that and subsequent years. His earlier failure to find a publisher for his work was repeated and in 1849 he issued the book, unsuccessfully, at his own expense. He was meanwhile at work on his second book, *Walden, or Life in the Woods*; this, too, depended upon several years of journal entries as well as the two years at Walden. Discouraged and in debt, he withheld it from publication until 1854. In 1849 he published his famous essay "Resistance to Civil Government" (later "On the Duty of Civil Disobedience") in a minor periodical. In it he told of his one-day imprisonment in 1845 for refusing to pay a poll tax levied to support the Mexican War; the essay was to be his most influential work, numbering Mohandas Gandhi and Martin Luther King, Jr., among its close students. After a second period, 1847–1849, under Emerson's roof, he returned to his family home and remained there for the rest of his life, making pencils and surveying for his living and traveling occasionally to the Maine woods, Canada, and Cape Cod, records of which were published posthumously in book form. In all his works, Thoreau urged the claim of the single, free individual, determined to find and confront the world of reality; the civilization built on industrialization and commerce and their inauthentic concerns he viewed as a madness leading men blindly into "lives of quiet desperation." He prescribed no single alternative life; he counseled men only to examine themselves, to know nature, and to act and live truthfully in light of their own discoveries. He was confident, though, that a life lived in harmony with nature and itself would have as its first precept "Simplify, simplify." Through most of his life he had little contact, apart from his slight success at the local lyceum, with the public or its causes; during the 1850s, however, the movement to abolish slavery enlisted his sympathy, and he spoke often in its behalf. In 1859 he sprang to the defense of John Brown after the Harpers Ferry raid and did much to make him into a martyr. Thoreau's last years were spent under the shadow of tuberculosis; he died in Concord on May 6, 1862.

THORNDIKE, EDWARD LEE (1874–1949), psychologist. Born on August 31, 1874, in Williamsburg, Massachusetts, Thorndike earned a B.A. from Connecticut Wesleyan University in 1895 and a second B.A. in 1896 and his M.A. in 1897 from Harvard. His dissertation for a doctoral degree from Columbia in 1898 was in the revolutionary area of animal psychology. He taught for one year in the women's college of Western Reserve University in Cleveland, Ohio, and spent the rest of his career (after 1899) at Columbia's Teachers' College, becoming a full professor in 1904. His theories of experimental psychology and quantitative measurement were of far-reaching influence in the development of learning theory. In the field of education, he wrote many basic textbooks. A pioneer in applying the results of animal experiments to human psychology, he devised such standard testing methods as the maze, puzzle box, and signal or choice reaction. He applied scales of quantitative measurement to skills in reading, composition, language, and handwriting, and to behavior, intelligence, vocational aptitude, human nature, motivation, the effects of heredity on intelligence and character, and the interrelation of abilities. During World War I he devised intelligence tests for the Army. He retired from teaching in 1940 and continued writing, producing alone or in collaboration more than 500 articles and books, best known among which were his *Educational Psychology*, 3 volumes, 1913–1914, *Human Nature and Social Order*, 1940, and *Man and His Works*, 1943. He also compiled the *Thorndike—Century Senior Dictionary* and *The Teacher's Book of 30,000 Words*, the latter with Dr. Irving Lorge. He died on August 9, 1949, in Montrose, New York.

THORPE, JAMES FRANCIS (1888–1953), athlete. Born on May 28, 1888, near Prague, Oklahoma, of Indian descent, Jim Thorpe received some education and, mainly because of his athletic skills, was able to matriculate at Carlisle (Indian) Institute in Pennsylvania in 1908. There he devoted himself primarily to football, which he played extraordinarily well. He was named a halfback on Walter Camp's All-America teams in 1911 and 1912, and he helped make Carlisle a football power in the country. In 1912 he scored 25 touchdowns and 198 points. That same year he went to Stockholm to participate in the Olympics, and achieved the unprecedented and never-to-be-repeated feat of winning gold medals in both the decathlon and pentathlon. He could justifiably claim to be the world's greatest athlete on the strength of the performance. Later, however, he admitted that he had played semiprofessional baseball during the summer of 1911, thereby losing his amateur status, and his gold medals and his trophy were taken from him and his name was expunged from the record books. In the meantime he had begun to play baseball seriously. He was

signed by John McGraw in 1913 for $4,500, but he spent most of his time with the Giants on the bench. He finished his baseball career in 1919 with the Boston Braves, where he played in 60 games and batted .327. He had also played professional football during these years, most of the time for the Canton Bulldogs, which also was a power in the land because of his strength and skill. He was totally contemptuous of training rules and a terror on defense, wearing a "slightly illegal" shoulder pad with an outer covering of sheet metal that destroyed opposing ball carriers. Few records remain of his achievements before 1920, and by that year, when the American Professional Football Association was formed, his career was nearing its end. But he was the most famous football player in the country, and the league named him its first president. Lighthearted, erratic, and unpredictable, he was a bad executive, and he was replaced in 1921. He played for a few years longer, but with lessening distinction, and died in Lomita, California, on March 28, 1953. The towns of Mauch Chunk and East Mauch Chunk, Pennsylvania, were joined and renamed Jim Thorpe in his honor in 1954.

THURBER, JAMES GROVER (1894–1931), author and cartoonist. Born on December 8, 1894, in Columbus, Ohio, Thurber was the son of a tall, slender man who favored derby hats and lost continually in efforts to establish himself in politics, and a hearty woman who once aspired toward an acting career and staunchly refused to wear black when she passed 80 because she insisted it would make her look old. At the age of six, through an accident while playing with his brother, he lost total vision in his left eye. Although he continually bumped into furniture and missed doorways about the house, he made light of his injury and at a later age joked that if ever he wrote his memoirs they would surely be called "Long Time No See." He attended Columbus public schools and matriculated at Ohio State University in 1913, where he was bookish and apparently rather mangy in appearance. There he met Elliot Nugent, a big man on campus, later to become a collaborator with him on plays and other ventures. When World War I began, he left school to enlist but was rejected because of his eye. Depressed but not daunted, he proceeded to France where he obtained a job as a code clerk for the U.S. State Department. Returning to Columbus in 1922, he reported for the *Dispatch*, married, returned to Paris with his wife, and reported for the European edition of the *Chicago Tribune* and for the *Paris Herald*. Unfortunately, his total salary was $12 a week and the Thurbers left Paris in financial straits. They went to New York where he began writing for the *Evening Post*. Intrigued by the *New Yorker*, which had begun publication in 1925, he began submitting stories and after 20 rejection notices was finally published. After that he became a leading contributor to the magazine. He met E. B. White, editor of the chatty "Talk of the Town" section of the magazine, at a social affair and convinced him that he should be made a staff member. When Thurber reported for work he found that he was to be managing editor of the magazine. But he did not like administration and transferred back to work with White on "Talk of the Town." He left the magazine in 1933 to devote full time to writing and completed numerous short stories, plays, and novels, including *My Life and Hard Times*, 1933, *Let Your Mind Alone!*, 1937, *Fables for Our Time*, 1940, *The Beast in Me and Other Animals*, 1948, and *The 13 Clocks*, 1950. His most famous short story, "The Secret Life of Walter Mitty," pictured a humble little man with a vivid imagination, which led him into scenes of passion and adventure. Constantly jolting him back to reality was his bombastic wife, who inevitably reminded him that he hadn't dumped the garbage or bought food for the dog. The character became a prototype and the story a part of American tradition. Its qualities typified Thurber's work, which poked fun at moderns who made tragedies out of their

maladjustments. He treated the devilish aspects of life as if they were commonplace and in his writing and drawing transformed them into so much hysteria. He lived for many years in West Cornwall, Connecticut, and died in New York City on November 2, 1961.

TICKNOR, GEORGE (1791–1871), educator and author. Born in Boston on August 1, 1791, Ticknor graduated from Dartmouth in 1807 and continued to study Latin and Greek privately; he read law for three years and was admitted to the bar in 1813. His interest in classical studies prevailed, however, over the law, and in 1815 he sailed for Europe, remaining for two years at the University of Göttingen, where he devoted himself to learning the German language and studying Greek and German literature. During this time he was invited to fill the new post of Smith professor of French and Spanish at Harvard; accepting in 1817, he spent the next two years in France, Italy, and Spain, acquainting himself with the languages and literatures of those countries. He assumed the professorship at Harvard in 1819 and remained there until 1835. His attempts to liberalize the organization of the university met stubborn resistance and eventually led to his resignation. But his influence on the school was great. He was successful in making modern language studies respectable, and he consolidated all of the language courses into one department. Although criticized by his conservative peers, his lectures attracted large audiences both inside and outside the university. Upon his resignation in 1835 his chair was filled by Henry Wadsworth Longfellow. During 1835–1838 he lived in Europe. For the next ten years he worked on his celebrated *History of Spanish Literature*, published in 1849. Written for popular audiences as well as for scholars, the study was the first to view the whole of Spanish letters and prompted continued research in the area. His other writings included *Remarks on Changes Lately Proposed or Adopted in Harvard University*, 1825, *Lecture on* the Best Methods of Teaching the Living Languages, 1833, and Life of William Hickling Prescott, 1864. Independently wealthy, he was prudent but generous in contributing to charities and various public institutions, including the Massachusetts General Hospital and the Boston Public Library, which he helped found in 1852. He died in Boston on January 26, 1871.

TIFFANY, CHARLES LEWIS (1812–1902), jeweler. Born on February 15, 1812, in Killingly, Connecticut, Tiffany spent two years in an academy in Plainfield, Connecticut, before joining the cotton manufacturing business of his father, Comfort Tiffany. In 1837 he and a friend, John B. Young, began a small fancy goods shop in New York City, which in 1841 became Tiffany, Young and Ellis. Eventually featuring jewelry, glass, and porcelain, the shop was known for superior standards of quality, beauty, and taste, a reputation enhanced when in 1851 they put English silver standards into effect and consequently gained American acceptance of the designation "sterling." In 1848 they began to manufacture their own jewelry in addition to importing it. Their collection of historic gems included those of Hungarian Prince Esterhazy and the crown jewels of the Second French Empire. A Paris branch was opened in 1850 and three years later the firm was reorganized as Tiffany and Company. In 1858 he sold as souvenirs pieces of a surplus section of the newly laid Atlantic cable. During the Civil War he produced such useful items as medals and swords. In 1868 the company was incorporated and branches established in London and Geneva. Tiffany became the most prominent jeweler in the United States and Europe, catering to European nobility, and in 1878 was made a chevalier of the Legion of Honor. He was also a founder of the New York Society of Fine Arts. He died in Yonkers, New York, on February 18, 1902. His son, LOUIS COMFORT TIFFANY (1848–1933) was born on February 18, 1848, in New York City. He completed

high school and studied art with several teachers, among them landscape artist George Inness. In 1875 he began working with stained glass and three years later opened a glass manufactory. His technique of adding color to glass while the glass was being made, rather than applying a stain or burning a pigment into already hardened glass, produced incomparably iridescent and beautifully colored results. He molded the pieces into free-form shapes and kneaded folds and other textural effects into the material while still hot. Among his many famous windows was the huge glass curtain in Mexico City's Palacio de Bellas Artes, 1911. He also designed vases, chandeliers, jewelry, and tiles made of his "favrile" glass and won a great popular reputation for these pieces, which were the height of fashion during 1890–1915 and again in the 1950s. He was vice president and a director of Tiffany and Company jewelers and founded a New York interior decorating firm (later called Tiffany Studios), which served the elite, designed church interiors, and refurbished the reception areas of the White House. In 1919 he established the Louis Comfort Tiffany Foundation for art students at his elegant estate on Long Island. He died in New York City on January 17, 1933.

TILDEN, SAMUEL JONES (1814–1886), lawyer and statesman. Born in New Lebanon, New York, on February 9, 1814, Tilden had a somewhat desultory formal education but learned a good deal about practical politics by serving for several years after 1834 as a writer of political tracts and treatises in support of the policies of his friend Martin Van Buren, President from 1837 to 1841. He attended the law school of the University of the City of New York (later New York University) from 1838 to 1841 and was admitted to the bar in the latter year. Suffering throughout his life from frail health, he nevertheless soon became a power in New York Democratic circles and by the time he was 35 had developed a lucrative law practice and gained a reputation as a corporation and railroad lawyer of great skill. A leader of the Free-Soil or Barnburner element among New York Democrats, he supported the Union cause when the Civil War broke out, but he strongly opposed certain policies of the Lincoln government, in particular disapproving of what he thought was a too great amalgamation of federal power in Washington. He was prominent nationally in the necessary reorganization of the Democratic Party after the war and, in his own state, was a leader in the successful effort to overthrow the notorious Tweed Ring. Nominated for governor in 1874, he ran on a reform ticket, was elected, and enjoyed notable success as a reforming administrator, among other achievements exposing and breaking up the so-called Canal Ring, a conspiracy of politicians and contractors that was defrauding the state in the course of canal repairs. In 1876, with an unbroken series of triumphs behind him, he was the obvious choice of the Democrats for the presidency, and he was nominated at St. Louis in June. But the campaign was exceptionally bitter, memories of the war were still vivid—Republican candidates who reminded voters of it were said to be "waving the bloody shirt"—and although Tilden won a majority of the popular vote, the Republicans disputed the returns from four states, Oregon, Florida, Louisiana, and South Carolina. He agreed to abide by the decision of a supposedly impartial electoral commission composed of five members each from the Senate, the House, and the Supreme Court. The commission included seven Democrats and seven Republicans and one supposed independent who; however, was in sentiment a Republican; the commission finally decided everything by votes of 8 to 7, giving Rutherford B. Hayes all four disputed states and the presidency. Tilden is said to have failed to exert vigorous and direct leadership in the crisis; in any event, after it was over, he remarked: "I can retire to private life with the consciousness that I shall receive from poster-

ity the credit of having been elected to the highest position in the gift of the people, without any of the cares and responsibilities of the office." He thereupon returned to New York, taking up his law practice again and remaining until his death an important figure in his party. He died in New York on August 4, 1886, leaving the bulk of the great fortune he had amassed to be used for establishing a free public library for the city.

TILDEN, WILLIAM TATEM (1893–1953), tennis player. Born on February 10, 1893, in Germantown, Pennsylvania, Big Bill Tilden played tennis from his childhood. In 1920 he won his first national championship; in the same year he became the first American to win the men's singles at Wimbledon. He retained the national amateur championship each year through 1925 and won it again in 1930, while winning again at Wimbledon in 1921 and 1930. From 1920 through 1930 he played on the United States Davis Cup team, leading it to victory in seven consecutive years; in Davis Cup singles play he was unbeaten from 1920 to 1925 and lost only one doubles match. In 1928 he was captain of the team, but a minor rules infraction led to his suspension by the U.S. Lawn Tennis Association shortly before the finals in France; the French were so incensed by the prospect of not having an opportunity to face him that at length the U.S. ambassador interceded and secured Tilden's reinstatement. In absolutely dominating world tennis from 1920 to 1925 he became one of the leading figures in the sports-conscious decade of the 1920s. In 1931 he turned professional and continued to play a powerful game. He was pro singles champion in 1931 and 1935 and with Vincent Richards won the pro doubles title in 1945 at the age of 52. He made numerous short movies on tennis, wrote numerous books and pamphlets on the subject, and for a time published and edited Racquet magazine. In 1950 an Associated Press poll voted him overwhelmingly the greatest tennis player of the first half of the 20th century. He died in Hollywood on June 5, 1953.

TILLICH, PAUL JOHANNES (1886 – 1965), philosopher and theologian. Born in Starzeddel, Brandenburg, on August 20, 1886, the son of a pastor and district superintendent in the Prussian territorial church, Tillich studied at the University of Berlin and other German universities, receiving his Ph.D. from Breslau in 1911 and the licentiate in theology from Halle in 1912. He served in the German army as a chaplain from 1914 to 1918. After the war he taught in the universities of Berlin, Marburg, Dresden, and Leipzig, and in 1929 became professor of philosophy at Frankfurt am Main. But his early writing and teaching were not calculated to endear him to the Nazis, and he was one of the first professors, and the first non-Jewish professor, to be removed from his post by the new regime. He came to the United States in 1933 and was named professor of philosophical theology at the Union Theological Seminary in New York City. He remained there until 1955, when he became a university professor at Harvard; from 1962 until his death he was Nuveen professor of theology at the divinity school of the University of Chicago. His thesis, published in Germany before World War I, was on Schelling, who, along with Jakob Böhme, was an important influence on his thought. During the 1920s, in the heyday of the Weimar Republic, he was associated with the Religious Socialists who sought to combine a spiritual revival with political reforms. He was an outspoken critic of the Nazis from their first appearance. In two books published shortly before he left Germany, *Religious Realization* and *The Religious Situation*, he analyzed with clarity and force the religious and cultural dilemmas of his time. The books that made his worldwide reputation, however, appeared after he arrived in the United States, and indeed after he had become a U.S. citizen in

1940. *The Protestant Era* was published in 1948, and *The Shaking of the Foundations*, a collection of sermons, appeared the same year. *The Courage to Be*, 1952, *Love, Power and Justice*, 1954, and *Biblical Religion and the Search for Ultimate Reality*, 1955, were other theological works, while more sermons were collected in *The New Being*, 1955, and *The Eternal Now*, 1963. Perhaps his major contribution, certainly the one on which he worked longest and hardest, was *Systematic Theology*, 3 volumes, 1951 – 1963. Including within its purview depth psychology, existentialism, and all kinds of artistic expression, it was an attempt to include in one system – primarily religious – all of the culture of man, or at least of Western man. Like his other works, it was infused with a deep and sometimes mystical piety; this made it difficult for some analytical theologians to read and appreciate him, but at the same time won him devoted disciples in many countries. A member of the United Church of Christ, he died in Chicago on October 22, 1965.

TITCHENER, EDWARD BRADFORD (1867 – 1927), psychologist. Born on January 11, 1867, in Chichester, England, Titchener earned his B.A. degree from Oxford in 1890, and took his doctorate under Wilhelm Wundt at the psychological laboratory in Leipzig in 1892. While residing in the United States, he submitted work to Oxford, earning his M.A. degree in 1894 and his D.Sc. degree in 1906. An instructor in psychology after 1893 at Cornell University, he became Sage professor in 1895 and a research professor in the graduate school in 1909. A leader of the "structuralist" school, he emphasized the scientific aspects of his field and recognized as the only problem of psychology the contents of the mind. This introspective approach was opposed to functional or applied psychology, which, in the form of educational psychology and mental testing, was concerned only with manifest acts and functions. He completed 11 English translations of German texts, eight original psychology books, among them the monumental *Experimental Psychology*, 4 volumes, 1901–1905, and more than 200 papers and articles. From 1894 to 1921 he was the American editor of *Mind*, and was from 1895 to 1921 associate editor and from 1921 to 1925 editor of the *American Journal of Psychology*. In 1904 he founded the Society of Experimental Psychology. He died on August 3, 1927.

TOSCANINI, ARTURO (1867–1957), conductor. Born in Parma, Italy, on March 25, 1867, the son of a tailor, Toscanini attended the Parma Conservatory from the age of 9, intending to become a cellist, and graduated at age 18. In 1886 he was engaged as first cellist and assistant chorus master with Claudio Rossini's opera company, which was appearing in Rio de Janeiro. He was called upon to substitute for the conductor, and was so successful in leading *Aida* that he conducted the performances for the rest of the season. For 12 years he conducted in opera houses in Genoa, Bologna, Treviso, and Turin. In 1898 he became the conductor at Teatro La Scala in Milan, remaining there until 1908, when he arrived in New York City to become conductor of the Metropolitan Opera. He also made his first appearance as a symphonic conductor about this time. In 1915 he returned to Milan and conducted several benefit concerts until the end of World War I. He then organized his own orchestra and with it toured the United States during 1920 and 1921. From 1921 to 1929 he was again conductor at La Scala, appearing in 1926 and 1927 as a guest conductor of the New York Philharmonic Orchestra. In 1928 he was appointed conductor of the newly merged New York Philharmonic-Symphony Orchestra. He remained in this position until 1936, making a highly successful European tour in 1930. He also led the music festivals at Bayreuth, 1930–1931, Salzburg, 1934–1937, and Lucerne, 1938–1939, and conducted prominent European orchestras such as the Vienna Philharmonic Orchestra, the BBC Orchestra, and the newly organized Palestine Orchestra. In 1937, at the age of 70, he became conductor of the NBC Symphony, a group created especially for him, with virtuoso players from many nations. They broadcast weekly performances until he retired in 1954, and also made extensive tours in South America (1940) and the United States (1950). Toscanini came to be considered by many the world's greatest conductor. His reverence for music and his driving stamina evoked a similarly deep and vigorous musical response from his orchestra. He chose not to use a studied conducting technique, but intuitive gestures associated with the mood and tempo of each musical phrase. His tremendous feeling for the styles and traditions of the old masters—notably Beethoven and Verdi—gave to his performances great vitality and emotional force. He died in New York City on January 16, 1957.

TRUMAN, HARRY S. (1884–   ), public official and 33rd U.S. President. Born in Lamar, Missouri, on May 8, 1884, Truman grew up on a farm near Independence, Missouri, and managed to finish high school, but there was no money for college. He went to Kansas City and became a bank clerk, but after five years he returned to the farm. World War I gave him his first opportunity. He had joined the National Guard; now he was called up and sailed for France as a 1st lieutenant of artillery. In action he was a capable officer, liked and respected by his men. He was promoted captain, returned to the United States, and in June 1919 married Bess Wallace. Truman set up a clothing store in Kansas City with an Army comrade, but the store failed after the depression of 1921 and he was left with about $20,000 in debts. He refused to declare himself a bankrupt and eventually paid back every penny. In his search for a job, he got in touch with another comrade from his Army days, who introduced him to Thomas J. Pendergast, boss of the Democratic machine in Kansas City, who appointed him overseer of highways and then, after a year, managed to get him elected to the county court of Jackson County. He served in the post from 1922 to 1924, was defeated for reelection, but won a second two-year term in 1926. This time he was elected presiding judge, a post he held until 1934. Although state law did not require that he be a qualified lawyer, he studied law at night from 1923 to 1925. His real opportunity came in 1934, when he was selected by Pendergast as Democratic nominee for the Senate. He won the primary and was elected. His first term was undistinguished, and it was predicted that he could not win reelection in 1940. (In the meantime the Pendergast machine had collapsed: Scores of his cohorts had been convicted for voting frauds, and Pendergast himself was in federal prison for income tax evasion.) But Truman won nevertheless; no one had ever even charged him with being involved in the corruption of his political mentor, and his personal integrity was unquestioned. During his second term in the Senate he began to make his mark. He was appointed chairman of a special Senate "watchdog" committee to investigate national defense projects. The Truman Committee did an excellent and impartial job, uncovering instances of waste and of collusion between corporations and certain Army agents, and saving the government hundreds of millions of dollars. By now a national figure, he was proposed to President Roosevelt as a running mate in the 1944 campaign, to replace Henry Wallace, who was thought to be too liberal for Southern voters. Truman was nominated on the second ballot and was elected when Roosevelt won his fourth term. When Roosevelt died, on April 12, 1945, Truman became President. He had not been taken into the President's confidence during the previous five months, and he knew almost nothing when he assumed office about confidential government policy; but he had little to do during his first few months except to oversee the military victories over Germany and Japan that had

already been planned and prepared. He presented his domestic program to Congress in September of that year. Called the Fair Deal, it proposed far-reaching reforms, but conservatives in both major parties blocked most of the measures, and he finally largely abandoned it. (Much of the legislation was later passed under President Lyndon B. Johnson.) Foreign affairs soon became dominant in his administration. In February 1947 Great Britain informed the U.S. government that it could no longer supply military and economic aid to Greece and Turkey in their fight against a Soviet takeover. The Truman Doctrine was the U.S. answer, in which the President announced that this country would take over the responsibilities. The first monies for Greece and Turkey were approved by Congress in May 1947; in June, after an address by Secretary of State George C. Marshall at Harvard, the so-called Marshall Plan for European Recovery began to go into effect, involving the expenditure during 1948–1951 alone of over $12 billion. Meanwhile an election loomed. Thomas E. Dewey, governor of New York State and the defeated Republican candidate in 1944, was again the Republican standard-bearer, and all polls and most political observers predicted that Truman could not win. But he took his cause to the country, embarking on a "whistle stop" campaign, and despite a states' rights challenge in the South, and the candidacy of Wallace on an ultra-liberal platform, Truman won. The major events of his second term were two: the Korean War and the right-wing challenge of Sen. Joseph R. McCarthy of Wisconsin. The President intervened in Korea without congressional approval, although he later received it, on the grounds that the authority of the United Nations was being directly attacked by the North Korean Communists. The war, which began in June 1950, was indecisive. Gen. Douglas MacArthur, American commander in the area, did not see matters as Truman did, and the conflict between them was only resolved in April 1951, when MacArthur was removed from his command. On the domestic scene, McCarthyism was rampant, and the President was able to make little headway against it, although he apparently would have preferred to. In March 1952 he announced his intention not to run again. He retired to Independence, where in 1957 the Harry S. Truman Library, a part of the national archives, was dedicated. His *Memoirs* were published in two volumes in 1955–1956.

TRUMBULL, JOHN (1756–1843), artist. Born on June 6, 1756, in Lebanon, Connecticut, the son of the state's governor, Trumbull showed talent for drawing at an early age. He graduated from Harvard in 1773, taught school in Lebanon, assisted his father by drawing maps of Connecticut's western land claims, and dabbled in painting until the outbreak of the American Revolution. From 1775 to 1777 he served in the Continental Army, first in a Connecticut regiment and later as an aide to General Washington and then to General Gates, and attained a colonelcy before he was 21. He resigned his commission in 1777, incidentally volunteered his services in the Rhode Island campaign of 1778, but for the following two years studied art in Boston. In 1780 he sailed to London to the studio of Benjamin West. There he was seized and imprisoned, apparently in reprisal for the hanging of Major André in the Benedict Arnold affair, but used his time profitably in the study of art and architecture. Upon release (for which Edmund Burke was largely responsible) he went to Amsterdam and completed a full-length portrait of George Washington that was engraved and distributed throughout Europe, the first authentic likeness of Washington to be seen abroad. After an unproductive time in America, he returned to London and West's studio in 1784. A series of small-scale paintings including "The Battle of Bunker's Hill" and "The Death of General Montgomery at the Attack of Quebec" led to encouragement from Thomas Jefferson to recreate in painting the scenes of the Revolution that he had witnessed. Trumbull returned to America in 1789

to paint portraits, revisit scenes of great battles, and study documents, uniforms, and equipment that related to his subject. His much larger work, "The Declaration of Independence," included 48 portraits, more than two-thirds of them painted from life, the others from portraits or from memory. In 1794 John Jay invited him to serve as his secretary during the negotiation of Jay's Treaty in England; he accepted and remained abroad as a member of the treaty commission until 1804. When his service was completed, he returned to portraiture, but his ten-year absence from painting had had no small effect on the quality of his work. During 1804–1808 he was in New York and for five years thereafter again in London. In 1813 he returned to America and set up a studio in New York. To the consternation of many young American painters, he was given in 1817 a congressional commission to execute four large pictures for the Capitol rotunda. The four pictures, already completed in miniature, took him seven years to transfer to large canvases; titled "The Surrender of Burgoyne," "The Surrender of Cornwallis," "Washington Resigning his Commission," and most notably "The Declaration of Independence," they constitute Trumbull's best known work. From 1817 to 1836 he was president of the American Academy of Fine Arts, and it was his dictatorial manner that prompted a secession of younger artists led by Samuel F. B. Morse and the founding of the rival National Academy of Design in 1826. Long past his prime as a painter and with fewer and fewer commissions, he spent much of his old age in financial insecurity. Finally in 1831, through the agency of Benjamin Silliman, he donated his unsalable paintings to Yale in exchange for an annuity. The university established the Trumbull Gallery, the first art gallery to be affiliated with an educational institution in America. He wrote an *Autobiography* in 1841 and died in New York on November 10, 1843.

TUBMAN, HARRIET (c. 1820–1913), Abolitionist. Born a slave in Dorchester County, Maryland, about 1820, Harriet was first named Araminta, but later adopted her mother's name; the name Tubman came with a marriage forced upon her by her master in 1844. In her childhood and youth she was a field hand, but in 1849 she escaped from the plantation and made her way North with the aid of the loosely organized Underground Railroad. During the next decade she became the most famous and successful of conductors on the Railroad; she made 19 trips into the South to aid escaped slaves and brought more than 300 to safety in the North and, after passage of the Fugitive Slave Law, in Canada. In 1857 she even managed to rescue her aged parents. A woman of great strength, resourcefulness, and intelligence, she stoutly withstood spells of dizziness and unconsciousness stemming from a childhood head injury and maintained an iron discipline among her charges. She always evaded capture despite huge rewards offered for her, and she became known as the "Moses of her people." She met and worked with leading white Abolitionists of the time—Emerson, Seward, Phillips, and others—and was consulted by John Brown before his raid on Harpers Ferry. During the Civil War she attached herself to the Union forces operating in South Carolina as a cook, laundress, and nurse, and rendered valuable service as a guide and occasional spy. Later she settled in Auburn, New York, where she lived until her death on March 10, 1913.

TURNER, FREDERICK JACKSON (1861–1932), historian. Born on November 14, 1861, in Portage, Wisconsin, Turner graduated from the University of Wisconsin in 1884. After a short time working for a newspaper he returned to the University to pursue graduate studies in history; he took his master's degree in 1888 and then studied for a year at Johns Hopkins University, where he formed a close friendship with Woodrow Wilson. In 1889 he joined the faculty at Wisconsin, received his Ph.D. from Hopkins the next year, and was made full professor of American history in 1892. In 1893, during the World's Columbian Exposition in Chicago, he presented a paper to a meeting of the American Historical Association in which he outlined a revolutionary interpretation of American history. Where earlier historians had focused on single issues and institutions—religious liberty, nationalism, slavery, or others—Turner, in "The Significance of the Frontier in American History," suggested not only a new viewpoint but also a complex of political and environmental forces as the key to the development of American civilization. He saw in the frontier the source of the individualism, restless energy, self-reliance, and inventiveness that are characteristically American. The "Turner thesis" sparked considerable controversy and was eagerly adopted by many of his colleagues and students, though often with less flexibility than he himself displayed in his continual revisions and modifications in light of opposing theories. During 1909–1910 he was president of the American Historical Association, and in 1910 he moved to Harvard where he remained for 14 years. In 1920 he published *The Frontier in American History* and in 1932 *The Significance of Sections in American History*, which was awarded a Pulitzer Prize. Following his retirement in 1924 he became a research associate at the Huntington Library in San Marino, California; he died there on March 14, 1932.

TURNER, NAT (1800–1831), slave insurrectionist. Born on October 2, 1800, in Southampton County, Virginia, Nat Turner grew up a slave in a relatively permissive environment; recognized for his exceptional intelligence, he received instruction in reading, writing, and religion from the family of his first master, Benjamin Turner. In the early 1820s, in a period of financial straits, the Turners were forced to sell him to an almost illiterate farmer who gave him much work to do but no constructive outlet for his mental energy. He nourished an increasing religious ardor with trips into the woods, where he believed that he felt the presence of God and that he saw "white spirits and black spirits engaged in battle, and blood flowing in streams." Assuming the role of "preacher" to the slaves, he convinced many of his belief that he was chosen through divine inspiration to lead the Negro from slavery. In 1830 he became a slave of a craftsman, Joseph Travis. Shortly thereafter, in 1831, an eclipse of the sún convinced him the time was near. He secured the support of four other slaves, but the uprising was abandoned. After a new sign, they set August 21, 1831, as the day of deliverance. With seven others he attacked the Travis family in their sleep and murdered them all. With about 75 undisciplined insurgents he killed in two days and two nights 55 white persons on the way to Jerusalem, Virginia. The state militia and armed townsmen put a stop to the raid about three miles from Jerusalem. He escaped while the others were dispersed and either captured or killed. After six weeks he was found, tried, convicted, and sentenced to death. He was hung in Jerusalem on November 11, 1831. Sixteen of his companions were also hung. As a result of his insurrection, nearly every Southern state passed more severe slave codes. The fear of another rebellion remained through the time of the Civil War.

TWAIN, MARK see CLEMENS, SAMUEL LANGHORNE

TWEED, WILLIAM MARCY (1823–1878), public official and political leader. Born in New York City on April 3, 1823, Tweed received only elementary schooling before serving apprenticeships to a chairmaker and later a saddler. At 17 he became a bookkeeper in his father's brush factory. His involvement in politics sprang from his work as a volunteer fireman, a not uncommon stepping-stone at the time; he became foreman of his company in 1850 and the next year was elected alderman. From 1853 to 1855 he served in Congress while retaining his aldermanic seat. He gradually strengthened his position in Tammany Hall, the New York Democratic organization, and began to collect the associates who would form the infamous "Tweed Ring." In 1856 he

was elected to the Board of Supervisors, a group created to stamp out corruption but which, with Tweed's help, became a center for political graft. He became a sachem of Tammany and served as school commissioner, deputy commissioner of public works, and deputy street commissioner, at the same time elevating his friends to positions of influence. In 1860 he opened a law office to serve as a channel for graft payments from various corporate sources, among them the Erie Railroad. In 1867 he was elected to the state senate; the next year he became grand sachem of Tammany, placed his own candidate in the governor's seat, and was virtual dictator of New York politics. A systematic plundering of the city and state treasuries was instituted on a formula that eventually called for 85 percent fraud in all bills charged to New York City and County; the program was aided by the new city charter of 1870 (procured at a cost of about a million dollars) that provided for a board of audit that quickly came under the control of the Ring. The amount of public money eventually diverted into the hands of Tweed and his men is estimated to have been between 45 million and 200 million dollars. *Harper's Weekly* began an editorial campaign against the Ring in 1870, counting among its most potent weapons the cartoons of Thomas Nast, who was offered $500,000 to stop publishing them; the *New York Times* joined in later in the year, and late in 1871 Tweed was arrested and charged with forgery and larceny. Convicted in 1873, he was sentenced to a short term in prison and after his release in 1875 was rearrested on a civil charge. In December he escaped from jail and fled, disguised as a sailor, first to Cuba and then to Spain. There, with the aid of a Nast cartoon, he was recognized, apprehended, and returned to imprisonment in New York, where he died on April 12, 1878.

TYLER, JOHN (1790–1862), public official and 10th U.S. President. Born in Charles City County, Virginia, on March 29, 1790, Tyler was of a family of aristocratic planters. He graduated from the College of William and Mary in 1807 and after studying law under his father, then governor of Virginia, began to practise in 1809. From 1811 to 1816 he served as a Jeffersonian Republican in the state legislature and in the latter year was elected to Congress, where he served until ill health forced his resignation in 1821. He was firm in his belief in a strict construction of the Constitution with an emphasis on states' rights; he opposed the Bank of the United States, Clay's nationalistic program of internal improvements and tariffs, and, though he disliked the institution and hoped to see it disappear, was especially harsh toward congressional attempts to regulate slavery as in the Missouri Compromise of 1820. In 1823 he was returned to the Virginia legislature and from 1825 to 1827 served as governor, resigning when he was elected to the Senate by the anti-Jackson element in the legislature. In 1828, however, he supported Jackson for President, preferring him to John Q. Adams as the lesser of two evils. Tyler opposed the tariff bills of 1828 and 1832 and, while disagreeing with South Carolina's nullification stand, stood also against Jackson by casting the only Senate vote against the Force Bill. It was at his initiative that the compromise tariff of 1833 was negotiated and the crisis ended. He supported the President's vetoes of the Maysville Road bill and the rechartering of the Bank of the United States but, soon after his reelection in 1833, he joined in the Senate censure of Jackson for his removal of federal deposits from the Bank. In 1836 the Virginia legislature instructed him to support Sen. Thomas Hart Benton's resolution to expunge the censure from the record, but rather than do so he resigned his seat. His tenuous connection with the Democrats broken, he became loosely allied with the Whigs; in 1838 he was again in the state legislature and two years later was nominated and elected Vice President on that ticket. President Harrison died a month after the inauguration and Tyler, overcoming efforts to deny him the succession, became the first Vice President to attain to the presidency. Clay, the Whig leader, immediately introduced a number of nationalistic measures for Senate approval; Tyler vetoed two successive bank bills that he considered detrimental to state sovereignty and, at Clay's behest, the entire Cabinet resigned except for Daniel Webster, secretary of state, who remained only long enough to negotiate the Webster-Ashburton Treaty settling the northeastern U.S.-Canadian border controversy. Tyler now had no party. Nonetheless, his administration was not without achievement; the Navy was reorganized and steps were taken toward the establishment of the Naval Observatory, the Seminole War and Dorr's Rebellion were settled, a trade agreement was reached with China, and Texas was annexed. The President had been working for the last through 1844, but Congress had delayed; the Democratic convention of that year endorsed expansion but passed over Tyler and chose Polk for the nomination. Tyler at last called for annexation by joint resolution of Congress, and this came just before he left the White House in March 1845. He retired to his Virginia plantation and remained out of active politics until the eve of the Civil War; he emerged in 1860 as a strong voice for moderation and deliberation in the South. He organized and presided over the unsuccessful Washington Peace conference in 1861, and only when all compromise seemed impossible did he endorse secession. He was elected to the provisional Confederate congress and then to the permanent congress but, before taking his seat in the latter, he died in Richmond, Virginia, on January 18, 1862.

UREY, HAROLD CLAYTON (1893–   ), physical chemist. Born on April 29, 1893, in Walkerton, Indiana, Urey overcame obstacles to gain his high school diploma but thereupon interrupted his education to teach in country schools in Indiana and Montana. Having saved enough to go to college, he matriculated at Montana State University in 1914 and received his B.S. in 1917. He worked for a chemical company in Philadelphia during the war, taught chemistry at Montana State from 1919 to 1921, and then went to the University of California at Berkeley to study physical chemistry. He received his Ph.D. in 1923. He studied for a year under Niels Bohr in Copenhagen and returned to the United States to become an associate in chemistry at Johns Hopkins, but he moved from there to Columbia in 1929. He was a professor of chemistry at Columbia until 1945, when he moved to the University of Chicago; in 1958 he was named professor at large of chemistry at the University of California, La Jolla. In December 1931 he announced that, working with two other investigators, he had discovered the existence of heavy water, in which the molecules consist of an atom of oxygen and two atoms of deuterium, a rare isotope of hydrogen. This discovery is considered one of the most important in the history of modern science, and for it he was awarded the Nobel Prize for Chemistry in 1934. After his discovery, he continued at Columbia to study the problem of isotope separation and developed the gas distillation process that was successfully used in the creation of the first atomic bomb. By 1940 he was one of the first Americans to realize fully that such weapons could be made, and he was the director of an important section of the Manhattan Project which produced the bomb. After Hiroshima, however, he joined with other scientists in urging consideration of the ethical problems involved in its use. Among his other significant contributions were an oxygen thermometer that made possible the measurement of temperatures in the ancient seas and a now widely accepted theory of the origin of the solar system, which he advanced in *The Planets: Their Origin and Development*, 1952. He was the recipient of many awards and honorary degrees and after 1960 served as an advisor to the national space effort.

VALENTINO, RUDOLPH (1895–1926), actor. Born in Italy on May 6, 1895, Rodolfo Alfonzo Raffaelo Pierre Filibert Guglielmi di Valentina d'Antonguolla arrived in the United States in 1913. He was a dishwasher and a gardener and then entered vaudeville as a dancer. He joined a musical comedy company and went to San Francisco and later to Hollywood, where he became a bit player in films in 1918. He was promoted by a scenario writer, June Mathis, and received the role of Julio in *The Four Horsemen of the Apocalypse* in 1921. In this performance his dash and smoldering appeal transfixed countless female movie-goers and he was elevated to stardom. He played in *The Sheik*, 1921, *Blood and Sand*, 1922, *The Young Rajah*, 1922, *Moran of the Lady Letty*, 1922, *Monsieur Beaucaire*, 1924, *A Sainted Devil*, 1924, *Cobra*, 1925, *The Eagle*, 1925, and *The Son of the Sheik*, 1926. The paradigm matinee idol, he attracted a huge following, but at the height of his career he contracted a combination of pneumonia and peritonitis and died on August 23, 1926, in New York City. Skillful press agentry made his lying-in-state—attended by an 11-block-long crowd—and his funeral events of the decade. Ladies in black appeared frequently at his grave site and were reported to be former mistresses and great beauties, but were later exposed as shills selling memorial flowers.

VALLANDIGHAM, CLEMENT LAIRD (1820–1871), public official. Born on July 29, 1820, in New Lisbon, Ohio, Vallandigham studied for a time at Jefferson College, Canonsburg, Pennsylvania, and was admitted to the Ohio bar in 1842. He quickly became involved in politics and from 1845 to 1847 was a Democratic member of the Ohio legislature, the last year serving as speaker of the house. He returned to law in Dayton, edited a newspaper for a time, and served as brigadier general of the state militia. After two previous defeats he was elected to Congress in 1856 and remained there until 1863. He called for an end to sectionalism and denounced extremists on both sides of the growing controversy, but held Northern radicals especially responsible. He was particularly venomous in his indictment of the Republican Party; he supported Douglas for President in 1860, and when Lincoln's election was followed by secession and war he maintained a bitter opposition to the administration's war measures, claiming that Lincoln was destroying constitutional rule. The acknowledged leader of the Peace Democrats, or "Copperheads," he incurred the intense hatred of Republicans and War Democrats alike. He was defeated for reelection to Congress in 1862 and returned to Ohio the next year; in defiance of an order issued by Gen. Ambrose Burnside, commander of the military district of Ohio, he spoke out against the war and was arrested. Convicted of expressing treasonable sentiments, he was imprisoned until Lincoln changed his sentence to banishment to the Confederacy. From there Vallandigham made his way to Canada. Later in 1863 the Ohio Peace Democrats nominated him for governor, but he was defeated. In 1864 he returned to Ohio and was allowed to remain there unmolested; at the Democratic convention of that year he wrote a denunciation of the war as a failure into the platform. After Lincoln's assassination he continued to oppose the Republicans on the issue of Reconstruction, but by 1870 he had concluded that the Civil War and its results had to be accepted and new issues found. Before he could develop his position or his political influence further he died, on June 17, 1871, as a result of an accidentally self-inflicted bullet wound.

VAN BUREN, MARTIN (1782–1862), public official and 8th U.S. President. Born on December 5, 1782, in Kinderhook, New York, Van Buren received no formal education beyond the local schools. He read law for a number of years, however, and in 1803 began to practise in his native town. He was elected as a Republican to the state senate in 1812, campaigning on the antibank issue; he served two four-year terms and from 1816 to 1819 was concurrently state attorney general. At the head of the "Bucktail" faction, Van Buren was in constant rivalry with De Witt Clinton for the leadership of the New York Republicans and developed great skill in political organization and maneuver. After playing a major role in calling and expediting the state constitutional convention of 1821 he was elected to the U.S. Senate, leaving behind in New York a group of associates known as the "Albany regency" to carry on his battle with Clinton. He led the Crawford group in the three-way presidential contest of 1824; later, having supported the tariff and opposed internal improvements measures, he drew close to Andrew Jackson. Reelected to the Senate in 1827, he managed the passage of the Tariff of Abominations the next year to bolster Jackson's popularity and, Clinton having died, then resigned to become governor of New York and solidify his leadership there. Less than three months later he resigned this office to become Jackson's secretary of state. He was the President's most trusted advisor, and by this time his consummate political skill had earned him the title "Little Magician." His conduct of foreign affairs was altogether creditable; the dispute with Great Britain over the West Indian trade was settled, a commitment was secured from France for payment of spoliation claims dating from the Napoleonic wars, and a treaty was signed with Turkey, granting the U.S. most-favored-nation trade privileges and access to the Black Sea. In 1831 he resigned to become minister to Great Britain, but Senate confirmation of his appointment was blocked by Vice President Calhoun. By the time he returned to America he had been nominated for Vice President himself. With his election and his effective support of the President through the nullification crisis and the next four years he became Jackson's clearly designated successor. Van Buren was duly nominated and elected President in 1836. He was faced immediately with the panic of 1837; while continuing Jackson's general fiscal policies, he proposed the establishment of an independent treasury as a depository for federal money that had been in state banks since its withdrawal from the Bank of the United States. This legislation he finally secured in 1840. In the growing sectional controversy Van Buren maintained a middle ground, supporting slavery in the South but opposing its extension into the territories. Popular support of the revolution in Canada created diplomatic difficulties with Great Britain, and subsequent armed clashes along the Maine-Canada border—the "Aroostook War"—further complicated matters. He lost popularity by the Seminole Indian War and particularly by his refusal to annex Texas, a position he took in order to avoid war with Mexico and to prevent the creation of another slave state. Renominated in 1840, he lost the election to the Whig candidate, Gen. William Henry Harrison, in a campaign marked by a great deal of emotionalism and ballyhoo and a total lack of discussion of the issues. He was a leading contender for the Democratic nomination in 1844 but again his stand on Texas lost him needed support. In 1847 the antislavery faction of the New York Democrats—the "Barnburners"—proposed him for President; the next year he was also nominated by the Free-Soil Party, a coalition of Barnburners, "conscience" Whigs, and others. After an unsuccessful campaign he continued to take an active interest, but little part, in politics until his death in Kinderhook on July 24, 1862.

VANDENBERG, ARTHUR HENDRICK (1884–1951), statesman and public official. Born in Grand Rapids, Michigan, on March 22, 1884, Vandenberg entered the University of Michigan law school after graduating from high school, but because of family financial troubles remained only a year. He joined the staff of the *Grand Rapids Herald* and became its editor in 1906; an ardent Republican, he soon acquired considerable influence in the state party organization and in 1928 was appointed to fill an unexpired term in the Senate. He survived the Democratic election sweeps of the 1930s and held his seat until his death. He was a strong though not unreasonable critic of the New Deal, agreeing with much of its purpose but differing on matters of method and efficiency. His major opposition to President Roosevelt was in the field of foreign affairs; he was a member of the Nye Committee investigating the operations of the munitions industry during World War I and was a leading spokesman for isolationism, or, as he called it, "insulationism." He was widely mentioned as a presidential possibility in 1936 and openly sought the Republican nomination in 1940. Having supported the series of Neutrality Acts of the late 1930s, he began to modify his stand after Pearl Harbor. He fully supported the American war effort and in January 1945 announced in a Senate speech the complete reversal of his earlier stand on American participation in political and military alliances. He was a delegate to the San Francisco conference to organize the United Nations, and his support ensured Senate ratification of American membership in the organization. In 1948 he sponsored the Marshall Plan legislation in the Senate and introduced the Vandenberg Resolution by which the Senate approved foreign alliances; the next year he effectively supported the forming of the North Atlantic Treaty Organization. A leading member of the Senate Foreign Relations Committee, and chairman from 1946 to 1948, he was the chief architect of the bipartisan foreign policy of the post-World War II period. He died in Grand Rapids on April 18, 1951.

VANDERBILT, CORNELIUS (1794–1877), industrialist. Born on May 27, 1794, in Staten Island, New York, the son of a humble farmer, Vanderbilt was a willful child and refused to attend school past the age of 11. At 16 he purchased a small sail boat with a loan from his parents and used it to carry passengers between Staten Island and New York. He was authorized during the War of 1812 to transport provisions to regiments around New York City. He soon had a small fleet engaged in river and coastwise trade. In 1818 he sold his boats and began working for a ferry boat owner, in competition with Robert Fulton for the control of mail, freight, and passenger service between Philadelphia and New York. Operating for years illegally, he managed by 1824 to have Fulton's monopoly on the waters voided by the Supreme Court in *Gibbons* v. *Ogden*. Vanderbilt formed his own company in 1829. To the dismay of established firms on the Hudson River, he quickly came to dominate the business by charging lower fares and converting his passenger boats into luxury liners. He was paid royally to move his boats elsewhere and went to Long Island Sound, then to Boston and Providence. By 1846 he was a millionaire. He formed a line to operate from New Orleans and New York through Nicaragua to the Pacific and San Francisco, under the name Accessory Transit Company, to capitalize on the traffic from the Gold Rush of 1849. Two subordinates attempted to wrest control of the company from him and, when that failed, they enlisted the aid of William Walker, an American filibuster who made himself dictator of Nicaragua in 1855. Walker seized the company's Nicaraguan property, claiming charter violations, and turned it over to Vanderbilt's rivals. Vanderbilt then organized a Central American coalition that in 1857 succeeded in driving Walker out. Vanderbilt built a personal yacht in 1853, the "North Star," which he sold five years later for $400,000 to Panama shipping companies whose businesses he had nearly ruined, agreeing at the same time to discontinue, for a monthly indemnity of $40,000, all operations of Accessory Transit. From 1855 to 1861 he operated three vessels between New York and Le Havre, France, sold two in 1861 for a large sum, and donated the third, the "Vanderbilt," to the government as a warship. He immensely enlarged his fortune by buying up old harbor vessels and selling them to the Navy for blockade duty during the Civil War. He began purchasing stock in the New York and Harlem Railroad in 1862; by 1863 he controlled the line and used it to initiate New York street car service. Succes-

sively he acquired the Hudson River Railroad, the New York Central, the Lake Shore and Michigan Southern Railway, and the Canadian Southern Railway, each time improving equipment and service, and frequently fighting competitors at the outset of operations. His attempt in 1868 to buy the Erie Railroad was thwarted by Daniel Drew, Jim Fisk, and Jay Gould, who flooded the market with a fraudulent stock issue. He remained secure during the panic of 1873 and, in ordering construction of Grand Central Terminal in New York, offered jobs to thousands of unemployed. At his death on January 4, 1877, his wealth was estimated at $100 million. His principal benefactions, outside of his family, were to Central University in Nashville, which became Vanderbilt University. Successive generations of Vanderbilts maintained and enlarged his fortune; a grandson, George Washington, established the fabulous "Biltmore" estate in Asheville, North Carolina.

VAN DOREN, CARL CLINTON (1885 – 1950), author. Carl Van Doren was born on a farm near Hope, Illinois (a small town that, like its neighbors Faith and Charity, no longer exists), on September 10, 1885. He graduated from the University of Illinois, his doctor father having moved to Urbana in order to put his five sons through the university, in 1907, whereupon he went to New York to do further study in literature. He received his Ph.D. from Columbia in 1911 and that year joined its English department, where he taught until 1930. He was involved in the revival of interest in American literature that marked Columbia in those years, was managing editor of the *Cambridge History of American Literature* from 1917 to 1921, and was literary editor of the *Nation*, 1919 – 1922, and of *Century Magazine*, 1922 – 1925. He also wrote *The American Novel*, 1921 (revised 1940), *Contemporary American Novelists*, 1922, *American and British Literature Since 1890* (with his brother Mark), 1925, and studies of Thomas Love Peacock, 1911, *James Branch Cabell*,

1925, *Swift*, 1930, and *Sinclair Lewis*, 1933. In the 1930s he turned from literature to American history. A biography of Benjamin Franklin appeared in 1938, for which he received a Pulitzer Prize; still probably the standard biography, it was also a best-seller. Among his other historical works were *Secret History of the American Revolution*, 1941, *Mutiny in January*, 1943, and *The Great Rehearsal*, 1948. The last is an account of the Federal Convention of 1787; its main thesis is that the creation of the American Union, with its consequent giving up of sovereignty by the 13 original states, shows that the nations of the world could create a world government. He was married to Irita Bradford, for many years editor of the *New York Herald Tribune Book Review*. He died in Torrington, Connecticut, on July 18, 1950. His autobiography, *Three Worlds*, appeared in 1936. MARK VAN DOREN (1894–   ) was born near Hope on June 13, 1894. His career paralleled that of his brother for many years; he graduated from the University of Illinois in 1914, received his Ph.D. from Columbia in 1920, joined its English department (where he taught from 1920 to 1959), and was literary editor of the *Nation*, 1924–1928. He also wrote a number of works of literary criticism, among them studies of Thoreau, 1916, Dryden, 1920, Shakespeare, 1939, and Hawthorne, 1949; *The Private Reader*, 1942, and *The Happy Critic*, 1961, were collections of occasional literary pieces. But Mark's literary interests tended to diverge from those of his brother as the years wore on. Perhaps best known as a poet, he produced his first book of poems, *Spring Thunder*, in 1924. It was followed by a long series of others, culminating in *Collected Poems*, 1939, which won a Pulitzer Prize, *Selected Poems*, 1954, *Collected and New Poems 1924–1963*, 1963, and *Narrative Poems*, 1964; the last included his *Winter Diary*, an account in verse of a year spent on a New England farm that had been issued separately in 1935. He became a permanent resident of the farm in 1959. Apart

from poetry he also produced novels (*The Transients*, 1935; *Windless Cabins*, 1940); short stories, collections of which were published in 1962, 1965, and 1968; and plays (*The Last Days of Lincoln*, 1959; *Three Plays*, 1966). *Liberal Education* appeared in 1959. A book of new poems, *That Shining Place*, was published on his 75th birthday in 1969. He married Dorothy Graffe in 1922; she was also an editor of the *Nation* (1919–1936) and the author of a number of books. His autobiography was published in 1958.

VASSA, GUSTAVUS (1745–1801), freedman and author. Born in the village of Benin in what is now Nigeria, Olaudah Equiano, or Gustavus Vassa as he came to be known, was the youngest of seven children, was schooled by his mother, and was taught the ways of farming and warfare. One day in 1765 he and his sister were left alone in the house and kidnappers broke in, taking the children many miles and eventually separating them. Within Africa he was sold several times. Eventually he spent two months with a family that treated him as a son. But he was kidnapped again, and after about seven months was thrown into a slave ship bound for the Barbados. After a terrible passage on the crowded, filthy ship, he was herded to a slave auction and sold to a Virginia planter. A sea captain named Pascal negotiated with the planter for the boy, intending to give him to two ladies in England. The bargain was made, and he commenced a two-year voyage on Pascal's ship; he was treated kindly and befriended by a white boy who became his dearest friend. On this ship he was renamed Gustavus Vassa, after a king of Sweden. He reached the house of the two ladies in England and learned to read the Bible. No sooner had he become accustomed to this arrangement than he was sold three more times and once again was at sea headed for the West Indies. For the sum of $24 he persuaded the mate to teach him navigation. His next master was a Philadelphia Quaker who allowed him to work for wages and thereby purchase his freedom; he did so within three years, in 1767. He went back to England and tried to further his education, but was hampered by lack of funds. Accustomed to the sea by now, he joined an expedition headed for India, but landed on the coast of Greenland instead. He finally reached India, then visited the United States. In 1785, when the British government was attempting to return Africans to their homes, he was appointed to a post with the commissary department supplying necessary items to the returnees. When he reported thievery by his English coworkers, he was dismissed from his post. In 1788 he issued a plea to Queen Charlotte to let his people rise from slavery and regain their dignity. His autobiography, published in 1789, accounts for his fame. The *Interesting Narrative of the Life of Olaudah Equiano or Gustavus Vassa, The African*, described his initiation into slavery, the conditions he observed and was subjected to, the effects of slavery on master and slave. The book went through several editions in England and the United States and is invaluable as a source of historical information. Vassa died in England in 1801.

VEBLEN, THORSTEIN BUNDE (1857–1929), social scientist. Born on July 30, 1857, in Manitowoc County, Wisconsin, Veblen came of Norwegian immigrant stock and was raised in an area of Minnesota where the rural patterns of life and the attitudes of the transplanted Norwegian dwellers contrasted sharply with those of more assimilated Americans. Only because of his father's passion for education did he arrive in 1874 at Carleton College in Northfield, Minnesota. He received his B.A. in 1880 and did graduate work at Johns Hopkins and Yale, taking a Ph.D. in philosophy, but he found, to his dismay, that no teaching post was open to him. He returned home, spent seven tortured years on the farm doing work that he was no longer suited for, reading aimlessly, and following events of the day and railing at mercenary businessmen and religious leaders. In 1891 he finally obtained a special fellowship at

Cornell. That same year he published his first essay, "Some Neglected Points in the Theory of Socialism." Eager to study and teach in what seemed to be his first real place in the academic world, he accepted an offer from the University of Chicago and taught political economy from 1892 to 1906 and privately pursued anthropological and psychological studies. He helped to launch in 1892, and edited until 1905 the *Journal of Political Economy*, in which appeared many of his essays, among them "The Economic Theory of Women's Dress," "The Instinct of Workmanship and the Irksomeness of Labor," and "The Barbarian Status of Women." His views were marked by fantastic polysyllabic terminology and cryptic insinuations. In 1899 his first book, *The Theory of the Leisure Class*, brought him immediate fame. A bristling account of the mercenary business classes, it presaged *The Theory of Business Enterprise*, 1904, which further clarified his views concerning the American economy. He had gained much notoriety by this time, and his impertinence so enraged other faculty members, as well as the board of trustees, that he was forced to resign his post. He held a position at Stanford from 1906 to 1909, but his entanglements with women, who virtually clung to him, plagued his life and career and resulted in his leaving that university as well. From then on he was affiliated with a number of universities, but he encountered many of the same problems, and his manner and writings became more revolutionary. *An Inquiry Into the Nature of Peace*, 1917, attributed the lack of world peace to patriotism and big business; *The Higher Learning in America*, 1918, denounced the control by business of educational institutions; *The Vested Interests and the State of the Industrial Arts*, 1919, accused business of trying to stunt production to maximize profits; *The Engineers and the Price System*, 1921, prophesied eventual business control of the whole country. In all his writing, little trace of the influence of other American authors could be found; he retained throughout his life the attitudes of his hard-bitten, rural heritage. Far from being simplistic, however, his ideas helped to jolt America away from a trend toward business domination to a more rational approach to the control of the economy. He died on August 3, 1929, in his cabin retreat near Palo Alto, California.

VILLARD, HENRY (1835–1900), journalist and financier. Born on April 10, 1835, in Speyer, Bavaria, Ferdinand Heinrich Gustav Hilgard attended the universities of Munich and Würzburg and came to America in 1853. He assumed the name Villard to avoid being called back to the German army by his father, a Bavarian supreme court jurist, whose political philosophy had precipitated his son's emigration. He settled with relatives in Belleville, Illinois, and concentrated on mastering the English language. In 1858 he began a career in journalism with the *New York Staats-Zeitung*, covering the Lincoln-Douglas debates and gaining the confidence of Lincoln. Desirous of exploring the Pike's Peak region of Colorado, he secured a position with the *Cincinnati Daily Commercial* to cover the gold rush in 1859. In 1860 he covered the Republican convention in Chicago. He was selected as a special correspondent in Springfield after Lincoln's election, and sent stories to the *New York Herald*, which distributed them through the New York Associated Press. The *Herald* and the *New York Tribune* printed his dispatches from the battlefronts during the Civil War. In 1864 he organized his own news agency and served as its Washington correspondent through 1865, and as a free lance writer in America and Europe through 1868. He then became secretary of the American Social Science Association in Boston, where he studied the financial structure of banks and railroads. Visiting Germany in 1873, he met bondholders of the Oregon and California Railroad and agreed to go to Oregon in 1874 to oversee their interests. He instituted reforms in the operations of the railway and became its president in 1876. He improved other local trans-portation companies and also in 1876 became president of the Oregon Steamship Company. While representing the interests of the Kansas Pacific Railroad in the 1870s, he saved the line from dissolution with his reforms, and was named receiver of it in 1876. In 1879 he bought the Oregon Steam Navigation Company, formed the Oregon Railway and Navigation Company, and proceeded to build a railway line along the Columbia to Portland; when, in 1881, the approaching Northern Pacific threatened to break his monopoly on Oregon coastal outlets, he bought it out, securing from friends subscriptions amounting to millions of dollars with which to purchase stock. The Northern Pacific then completed its transcontinental line, but by 1883 heavy expenses had put it deeply in debt and Villard was removed from the presidency. After a nervous breakdown and two years in Germany he became a New York agent for a German bank. He was soon involved in railroads again, however, and in 1889 returned to the Northern Pacific as chairman of the board, a post he held until 1893. He gave financial support to Thomas Edison, and in 1890 purchased the Edison Lamp Company and the Edison Machine Works, which he combined into the Edison General Electric Company. He presided over this company until 1893, when it was reorganized as the General Electric Company. He had purchased the controlling interest in the *New York Evening Post* in 1881 and hired Horace White, Carl Schurz, and E. L. Godkin, as its editors, the last of whom brought with him *The Nation*, a distinguished journal of current affairs. He died in Dobbs Ferry, New York, on November 12, 1900. His widow, Helen Frances, the only daughter of Abolitionist William Lloyd Garrison, was active in the formation of the National Association for the Advancement of Colored People in 1909, and organized the Women's Peace Society in 1919. Their son Oswald Garrison Villard became president of the *New York Evening Post* and editor and owner of *The Nation*.

VILLARD, OSWALD GARRISON (1872–1949), journalist. Born on March 13, 1872, in Wiesbaden, Germany, the son of journalist and financier Henry Villard and the grandson of Abolitionist William Lloyd Garrison, Villard graduated from Harvard in 1893 and began a career in journalism with the *Philadelphia Press*. In 1897 he joined the staff of his father's *New York Evening Post* and became its president and owner after the elder Villard's death in 1900. Under his control, the paper became a leading liberal organ with a nationwide circulation. Like his grandfather, Villard was a pacifist, and his feelings permeated the newspaper's editorial position. When his negative stance on U.S. entry into World War I adversely affected circulation, he sold the paper, but retained control of its weekly periodical, *The Nation*, which he molded into a journal of social protest with astute commentary on politics and the arts. His controversial editorials, written at a time when pacifism was highly suspect, led to issues of *The Nation* being detained by U.S. postal authorities, though they were finally released. Despite his feelings that the power to declare war should be placed in the hands of the people, and that war would thereby be eliminated, his editors supported the government's defense program. Unable to sway them, he stepped down to the position of contributing editor in 1933 and two years later sold the magazine. Thereafter he contributed articles and letters to many newspapers and magazines, protesting war and oppression in any form. He was a founder, in 1909, of the National Association for the Advancement of Colored People and was an active member of several antiwar organizations. His book *The Disappearing Daily*, 1944, denounced the shift of emphasis in American journalism from news coverage to entertainment. He also wrote an autobiography, *Fighting Years*, 1939. He died in New York City on October 1, 1949.

VINCENT, JOHN HEYL (1832–1920), clergyman and educator. Born in Tuscaloosa, Alabama, on February 23, 1832, Vincent grew up in Pennsylvania and after holding a number of jobs became a Methodist preacher in 1850. In 1852 he studied for a short time at the Wesleyan Institute in Newark, New Jersey; after several years in that state he moved to Illinois and served a number of churches before assuming the pastorate of Trinity Church in Chicago in 1864. Setting himself the task of making over the institution of the Sunday School into an effective and truly educational program, he founded the Union Sunday School Institute for the Northwest and began publication of a journal to promote organization and uniformity in lessons and standards. In 1866 he became general agent of the Methodist Episcopal Church's Sunday School Union in New York City and during the next twenty years supervised the unified program and edited its publications, including the *Sunday School Journal*. In 1874, in association with Lewis Miller, he organized a national assembly and training institute for Sunday School teachers at Lake Chautauqua, New York. The great success of the idea allowed the program to expand into a regular summer study and training institute, and in 1878 Vincent drew up proposals for the Chautauqua Literary and Scientific Circle, a four-year program of prescribed reading followed by an examination and a diploma. Soon hundreds of "Chautauquas" were organized across the country and noted scholars, lecturers, and literary figures were touring the circuit, supplementing the directed program of adult home study. Vincent continued to direct both Chautauqua and the Sunday School Union until 1888 when he was elected a bishop of his church; from 1888 to 1892 he was bishop of Buffalo, New York, from 1892 to 1900 of Topeka, Kansas, and from 1900 to his retirement in 1904 of Zürich, Switzerland, where he directed Methodist activities for all of Europe. He died on May 9, 1920.

VON BRAUN, WERNHER (1912–), rocket engineer. Born on March 23, 1912, in Wirsitz,

Germany, Von Braun as a youth became fascinated with the possibilities of using rockets to explore outer space and in 1930 joined the Verein für Raumschiffahrt, a group of amateur rocket enthusiasts in Berlin. He studied engineering at technological institutes in Zürich and Berlin, took his degree in 1932, and later in the same year became chief of a rocket research station established by the German army. Two years later he was awarded a Ph.D. by the University of Berlin. In 1936 Hitler became interested in rockets as potential weapons and ordered construction of a large research facility at Peenemünde, where Von Braun and his group continued their work with greatly improved resources. By 1938 a first model of the Vergeltungswaffe Zwei (V-2, "revenge weapon two") had been developed. Over the next six years it was enlarged and improved until it was capable of carrying a warhead of nearly a ton over 190 miles in 5 minutes. V-2 launchings against London and Antwerp began in September 1944 and numbered about 3,600 before the end of the war. By that time Von Braun and a large number of his colleagues had fled from the advancing Russian army and surrendered to U.S. forces. In 1945 he came to the United States and became technical director of the Army missile proving grounds at White Sands, New Mexico. In 1950 he was made director of the missile research facility at Huntsville, Alabama. Under his supervision the Redstone, Jupiter-C, Jupiter, and other rockets were developed. He continued to press for a program of space exploration and wrote numerous papers, articles, and books on the subject, including *Conquest of the Moon* (with Fred Whipple and Willy Ley), 1953, and *Exploration of Mars*, 1956. He became a U.S. citizen in 1955. Lack of government support retarded progress on the development of an earth satellite until the Russian Sputnik I in October 1957 provided the necessary impetus. In January 1958 the Huntsville group orbited Explorer I, the first American satellite. Two years later the group became part of the National Aeronautics and Space Administration; Von Braun remained director of the renamed George C. Marshall Space Flight Center at Huntsville and worked on the development of new launch vehicles, notably the huge Saturn V employed in the Apollo manned moon landing program. Others among his published works were *First Men to the Moon*, 1960, and *Space Frontier*, 1967.

VON NEUMANN, JOHN (1903–1957), mathematician. Born in Budapest on December 28, 1903, and christened Janos, Von Neumann was a scientific prodigy, receiving simultaneously in 1923, before he was 20, a Ph.D. in mathematics from the University of Budapest and a degree in chemical engineering from the Federal Institute of Technology in Zürich. He was a lecturer at the University of Berlin from 1926 to 1929, when he became an assistant professor at the University of Hamburg. He was a visiting lecturer at Princeton the next year, and soon came to the United States to stay. He was named professor of mathematics at the Institute for Advanced Studies when it was founded at Princeton in 1933, and he remained associated with that organization until his death. His scientific interests were extraordinarily wide and he made many contributions to mathematical and physical theory. His best known early work was his invention of the theory of rings of operators—the so-called Von Neumann algebras—begun in the late 1920s; his *Mathematical Foundations of Quantum Mechanics*, published in German in 1926 and in an English translation in 1955; and his elaborate and beautiful theory of numbers as sets, published as early as 1923. His most famous achievement, *The Theory of Games and Economic Behavior*, was written with Oskar Morgenstern and published in 1944. He also did immensely important work in pure mathematics during his first years at Princeton—for example, on operator rings and continuous groups—which showed that the branch of mathematics known as analysis had interesting and hitherto unsuspected connections with geometry and algebra, the other two classical divisions of the subject. He thus was a leading figure in the 20th-century movement toward the unification and integration of all mathematics. In the later 1930s he began to do consultant work for the government and for the Army and Navy. He was instrumental in quickening research on the atomic bomb and from 1945 to 1954 was director of the federal electronic computer project, his efforts speeding development of the hydrogen bomb. He was named to the Atomic Energy Commission in 1954 and in 1956 won its Enrico Fermi Award. He contracted cancer in 1956 but continued to work for the commission from his bed at Walter Reed Hospital in Washington, D.C. He died there on February 8, 1957. His *Theory of Self-reproducing Automata* appeared in 1966, edited from manuscripts by A. W. Burks. This astounding work was an attempt to produce a general cybernetic theory that would generate increasingly sophisticated computers and eventually robots that could reproduce their kind.

WADE, BENJAMIN FRANKLIN (1800–1878), lawyer and political leader. Born in Springfield, Massachusetts, on October 27, 1800, Wade grew up amid the hardships of a farm and could attend school only in the winter months. In 1821 the family moved to Andover, Ohio, where he undertook various jobs, including school teaching. In 1825 he settled down to the study of law in Canfield, Ohio, was admitted to the bar in 1827, and in 1831 became a partner of Joshua R. Giddings. He gained a successful practice in northeastern Ohio and served a term, in 1835–1837, as prosecuting attorney for Ashtabula County until his election to the state senate. His outspoken antislavery stand cost him reelection in 1839, but he was returned to the senate for another term in 1841. He was chosen judge of the Third Judicial District in 1847 and the Whig-controlled legislature elected him to the U.S. Senate in 1851. He was uncompromis-

ingly opposed to the extension of slavery and vigorously fought the passage of the Kansas-Nebraska Bill (1854). Returned to the Senate as a Republican in 1857 and in 1863, he stood with the Radical group in their demands for decisive prosecution of the war, emancipation of the slaves, and severe punishment of the South. He helped set up the Joint Congressional Committee on the Conduct of the War and as its chairman played a prominent and controversial role in investigating all aspects of the Union military effort. In 1864 his cosponsorship with Henry W. Davis of the Wade-Davis Bill, which declared Reconstruction of the Southern state governments a legislative and not an executive concern, brought him into direct conflict with President Lincoln. Beaten by Lincoln's pocket veto, Wade and Davis published a manifesto in the *New York Tribune* denouncing the President's "studied outrage on the legislative authority." They joined in the effort to replace Lincoln as the Republican candidate in 1864, but the project failed and Wade supported the President's reelection. After Lincoln's assassination, Wade backed President Johnson until it was plain that he, following Lincoln, favored a lenient plan of Reconstruction. In 1867 Wade was elected president pro tempore of the Senate, a position that would have elevated him to the Presidency had Johnson been removed in the impeachment trial of 1868. Sure of success, Wade began selecting his Cabinet, and the acquittal of Johnson bitterly disappointed him. A Democratic majority in the Ohio legislature denied him a fourth term in the Senate and the Republican convention of 1868 nominated another man to be Grant's running mate. In 1869 he resumed his Ohio law practice; he became general counsel of the Northern Pacific Railroad and served as a government director of the Union Pacific. In 1871 President Grant appointed him a member of the commission sent to investigate Santo Domingo, and he recommended its annexation. He died in Jefferson, Ohio, on March 2, 1878.

WAITE, MORRISON REMICK (1816–1888), jurist. Born in Lyme, Connecticut, on November 29, 1816, Waite was the son of the chief justice of Connecticut. He graduated from Yale in 1837 and moved to Maumee City, Ohio, the following year to enter a law firm. He was admitted to the bar in 1839 and after failing in a run for Congress in 1845, was elected to the state legislature in 1849. He moved to Toledo in 1850 and developed a substantial practice in railroad and other corporate matters that led him to argue 31 cases before the Ohio supreme court in the next ten years. In 1862 he ran as an independent Republican for Congress and was again defeated. He declined appointment to the state supreme court in 1863. During the Civil War he was the leader of nearly every local meeting or movement that promoted the Union cause. In 1871 President Grant appointed him one of the American counsel in the *Alabama* claims arbitration; he wrote 5 of the 13 chapters of the American *Argument*, and was noted for his "excellent tone and temper" with the British representatives. Returning from Geneva, he was elected as a delegate to the Ohio constitutional convention of 1873 and made its president. While in session he learned of his nomination as chief justice of the United States by President Grant. Although Waite had no judicial experience, had argued no cases before the Court, and had little reputation beyond his service in the *Alabama* arbitration, the appointment was well received by the nation's bar and the Senate unanimously confirmed him the seventh chief justice on January 21, 1874. He immediately assumed a large share of the work of the Court and in his 14 years on the bench gave the opinion of the Court in over 1,000 cases. It was the main task of his Court to interpret the amendments to the Constitution, particularly the 14th, that were adopted after the Civil War. His major contribution was his interpretation of the due process clause of the 14th Amendment: businesses "clothed with a public interest" could be subject to regulation by states. His decisions established or confirmed many of the accepted principles of constitutional law. Although active in civic affairs, he tried to disassociate his office from politics; he refused to allow his name to be considered among the presidential nominees of 1876 and he would not serve on the electoral commission in the Tilden-Hayes controversy. He died in Washington on March 23, 1888.

WAKSMAN, SELMAN ABRAHAM (1888–), biochemist. Born in Priluka, Russia, on July 22, 1888, Waksman emigrated to the United States in 1910 and was naturalized in 1916. He received his B.S. from Rutgers in 1916, his M.S. in 1916, and he gained a Ph.D. from the University of California, Berkeley, in 1918. After a few years of work as a bacteriologist and research biologist at commercial laboratories, he joined the Rutgers faculty. He was a lecturer in soil microbiology, 1918–1924, associate professor of that subject from 1924 to 1930, and professor from 1930 to 1942; he was professor of microbiology from 1942 to 1958, after which he was professor emeritus. He was a microbiologist for the New Jersey agricultural experiment station at New Brunswick from 1924 to 1951 and he organized and headed a division of marine microbiology at Woods Hole Oceanographic Institute, Woods Hole, Massachusetts, from 1930 to 1942. He was considered one of the world's leading authorities on soil microbiology and on antibiotics. His most important studies concerned filamentous bacteria, the actinomycetes, which include many antibiotic-producing organisms. With his co-workers he discovered many new species, including *Streptomyces* in 1944 and *Neomyces* in 1949. Streptomycin was the first specific agent effective in the treatment of tuberculosis, and for its discovery he was awarded the 1952 Nobel Prize for Medicine. Neomycin is widely used in the treatment of infectious diseases of man, domestic animals, and plants. Apart from papers in technical journals and books describing his discoveries—such as the massive *The Actinomycetes*, 3 vols., 1959–1962—he also wrote two popular books, *My Life with the Microbes*, 1954, and *The Conquest of Tuberculosis*, 1964.

WALD, LILLIAN D. (1867–1940), nurse and social worker. Born on March 10, 1867, in Cincinnati, Miss Wald grew up there and in Rochester, New York. She early became interested in nursing and in 1891 graduated from the New York Hospital Training School for Nurses. She later supplemented her training with courses at the Women's Medical College. In her work she observed at first hand the wretched conditions prevailing in New York City's largely immigrant Lower East Side and in 1893, with a companion, she moved to the neighborhood and offered her services as a visiting nurse. Two years later she took larger accommodations and opened the Henry Street Settlement House. As the number of nurses attached to the settlement grew, services were expanded to include nurses' training, educational programs for the community, and youth clubs. In 1902 nursing service was experimentally extended to a local public school; the project was so successful that the Board of Health soon instituted the first city-wide public school nursing program. The organization of nursing programs by insurance companies and of the district nursing service of the Red Cross were both at her suggestion and in 1912 she helped found and became first president of the National Organization for Public Health Nursing. In the same year Congress established the Children's Bureau, also in no small part owing to her suggestion. She was active in other areas of reform, particularly the National Women's Trade Union League and the American Union Against Militarism. In 1933 ill health forced her to leave Henry Street. She settled in Westport, Connecticut, and died there on September 1, 1940.

WALKER, AMASA (1799–1875), economist and legislator. Born in Woodstock, Connecticut, on May 4, 1799, Walker was raised in Brookfield, Massachusetts, attended the district school, and worked on the family farm and at a card manufacturer's in Leicester until he was 15 years old. For the next six years he clerked in a country store, farmed, and taught school in an unsuccessful attempt—mainly because of bad health—to gain admission to Amherst College. At 21 he bought part interest in a store that he sold three years later in order to become a manufacturer's agent. In 1825 he and a partner opened a shoe store in Boston. In 1835 he wrote a series of articles for the *Boston Daily Advertiser and Patriot* calling for the building of a railroad from Boston to Albany. Four years later a St. Louis audience laughed when he told them that sleeping and dining cars would one day arrive at the Mississippi by rail from Boston. In 1840 he retired from business and visited Florida for his health. Influential in the founding of Oberlin College, he lectured there on political economy from 1842 to 1849. An advocate of world peace, he was vice president of the International Peace Congress held in England in 1844 and of the Paris Congress of 1849. He served in the Massachusetts House of Representatives in 1848, the state senate in 1849, and was secretary of state of Massachusetts, 1851–1852. He was examiner in political economy at Harvard from 1853 to 1860. His primary interest was the monetary system, and his study of the financial panic of 1837 led to a series of articles in *Hunt's Merchants Magazine and Commercial Review* that were reprinted as *The Nature and Uses of Money and Mixed Currency* in 1857, the year of another panic. His advice to Boston businessmen to stop specie payments was ignored, only to be proved correct a short time later. He was elected to another term in the Massachusetts House in 1859 and was appointed to fill a vacancy in Congress, 1862–1863. He finally went to Amherst College as a lecturer from 1860 to 1869. His chief work, *The Science of Wealth: A Manual of Political Economy*, appeared in 1866 and was long a popular textbook of economics. He died in Brookfield on October 29, 1875.

WALKER, FRANCIS AMASA (1840–1897), economist. Born in Boston on July 2, 1840, the son of Amasa Walker, Francis entered Amherst College at 15 but his graduation was delayed until 1860 by his poor eyesight. After a year studying law in Worcester, he joined the Union Army as a private and rose to the rank of brigadier general. Long after the war, in 1886, he published a *History of the 2nd Corps in the Army of the Potomac*. From 1865 to 1868 he taught Latin and Greek at Williston Seminary in Easthampton, Massachusetts, and spent the next year as an editorial writer for the *Springfield Republican*. In 1869 he was appointed to direct the Bureau of Statistics, with his primary task the supervision of the census of 1870. Difficulties with an appropriation for the Bureau led President Grant to appoint him U.S. Commissioner of Indian Affairs, in which post he continued and completed his work on the census. He nevertheless found time to perform his official duties, and his *Indian Question*, 1874, was notable for its common sense and honesty. While serving as a professor of economics at the Sheffield Scientific School at Yale, 1873–1881, he was appointed to direct the Tenth Census, the major work on which was done from 1879 to 1881. Many innovations in the census questions were devised by Walker at this time, and he was also allowed greater freedom to employ good census takers, since a new law removed the department from the realm of political patronage. The first of his important economic treatises, *The Wages Question*, 1876, earned him an international reputation and was widely adopted as a textbook in the United States and abroad. Notable among his other works were *Money*, 1878, *Political Economy*, 1883, *Land and Its Rent*, 1883, and *International Bimetallism*, 1896. One of his powerful theoretical insights was his notion of the importance of the entrepreneur, as opposed to the capitalist, in industrial development; and his influence was decisive in discrediting the myth that the total wage bill in the national economy was determined by the capital set aside for labor. He employed the wealth of statistics he had gathered in his years with the census in all of his work, and emphasized the problems of immigration and population growth in his analyses of the economic circumstances of the country. He was named president of the Massachusetts Institute of Technology in 1881 and served in this post until his death, in Boston, on January 5, 1887.

WALKER, JAMES JOHN (1881–1946), public official. Born in New York City on June 19, 1881, Jimmy Walker studied for a year at St. Francis Xavier College, entered the New York Law School, and was admitted to the bar in 1912. During his school days he was active in amateur theatrics and wrote several popular songs, including "Will You Love Me in December As You Do in May?" He early became involved in Democratic politics and in 1909 was a successful Tammany candidate for assemblyman. Under the tutelage of Al Smith and others he was elevated in 1914 to the state senate, where seven years later he became leader of his party. He was noted for his liberal views, and not a little of his remarkable popularity stemmed from his sponsorship of a bill legalizing prize fighting in New York. In 1925 he was elected mayor of New York City. During his tenure in that office he became a world celebrity; equally at ease among workers and socialites, he delighted everyone with his ready wit and expansive, jovial manner. He was particularly fond of Broadway and the entertainment world and often referred to himself as the "night mayor." Under his administration the city's vast subway system was advanced, the hospital system unified, the Department of Sanitation created, and other steps taken toward centralized city planning and management. Soon after his reelection in 1927 by a huge plurality over Fiorello La Guardia, charges of graft and corruption at many levels of city government prompted a full legislative investigation. Walker himself was called on to explain certain financial transactions and was charged with several counts of impropriety. He denounced as a judicial travesty a hearing before Gov. Franklin D. Roosevelt and resigned as mayor on September 1, 1932. He spent several years in Europe and returned to New York to find his popularity undiminished. In 1940 Mayor La Guardia appointed him arbiter of the National Cloak and Suit Industry. He died in New York on November 18, 1946.

WALKER, ROBERT J. (1801 – 1869), lawyer and public official. Born in Northumberland, Pennsylvania, on July 19, 1801, Walker was educated at town schools and by private tutors and graduated first in his class at the University of Pennsylvania in 1819. Admitted to the Pittsburgh bar in 1821, he joined with the Jeffersonian movement and became the acknowledged Democratic leader in the state. In 1826 he moved to Natchez, Mississippi, to join his brother in a lucrative law practice. His speculations in plantations, slaves, and wild lands were huge, involving a debt of hundreds of thousands of dollars. In 1835 he was elected to the first of his two terms in the U.S. Senate. He was an ardent supporter of Democratic policies, particularly the annexation of Texas, and took charge of the 1844 Democratic campaign. President Polk appointed him secretary of the treasury, 1845 – 1849, and his report of 1845 on the state of the finances became a classic of free-trade literature. He was largely responsible for the Tariff Bill of 1846, which prepared British public opinion for acceptance of a compromise on the Oregon boundary. His financing of the Mexican War was carried out with simplicity and success. He initiated the warehousing system for the handling of imports, and he was mainly responsible for the creation of the Department of the Interior in 1849. His administration, often considered the ablest in the history of the treasury, ended when Polk left office. Walker stayed on in Washington, practising before the Supreme Court and managing his extensive business affairs. He visitied England during 1852 – 1853 to sell securities for the Illinois Central Railroad. In 1853 he accepted the mission to China, but he finally rejected the appointment because of a disagreement with President Pierce. He supported Buchanan in the 1856 election and was appointed governor of the Kansas Territory in 1857. An enemy of slavery, he resigned the same year when the President failed to back him in permitting the people to decide the slavery issue themselves. During the Civil War, he served the Treasury Department abroad, selling federal bonds and undermining Confederate credit. He resumed his law practice after the war and played a part in getting the Alaska Purchase Bill through Congress. He died in Washington on November 11, 1869.

WALKER, WILLIAM (1824 – 1860), adventurer and filibuster. Born in Nashville on May 8, 1824, Walker graduated from the University of Nashville in 1838 and five years later took his M.D. degree from the University of Pennsylvania. After two years of study and travel in Europe he returned to the United States, became interested in the law, and was admitted to the bar in New Orleans. While practising law he also dabbled in journalism as an editor and part owner of the *Daily Crescent*. In 1850 he moved to California and in San Francisco and later Marysville he continued in law and journalism for three years. In 1853 he organized a party of American "colonists" and sailed to La Paz in Baja California; upon landing he proclaimed a republic with himself as president and two months later announced the annexation of Sonora. Needed reinforcements and supplies were held up in San Francisco by U.S. authorities, and in May 1854 Walker and his men were forced to flee back to the United States. He was acquitted of charges of violating neutrality laws. In 1855 he led a party to Nicaragua at the invitation of a revolutionary faction there. By the end of the year he was virtual dictator of the country; the new regime was recognized by the United States in May 1856 and two months later Walker became president. His grandiose but rather vague plans for Central American development came to naught, for he entered into a scheme to wrest control of the Accessory Transit Company, which operated several facilities in Nicaragua, from Cornelius Vanderbilt. On the pretext of charter violations he seized the company's property in that country and turned it over to Vanderbilt's rivals. Vanderbilt then sent agents into other Central American nations to aid in a joint effort to oust Walker. To avoid capture, Walker surrendered himself to a U.S. Navy officer on May 1, 1857. Still claiming the presidency, he returned to Nicaragua in November but was soon captured and sent back. In 1860 he made a final attempt to return to Nicaragua by way of Honduras; he was captured by a British naval officer, turned over to Honduran authorities, and executed on September 12, 1860.

WALLACE, HENRY AGARD (1888–1965), agriculturist and public official. Born in Adair County, Iowa, on October 7, 1888, Wallace was the son of Henry C. Wallace, magazine editor and secretary of agriculture under Harding and Coolidge. He graduated from Iowa State College in 1910 and joined his family's magazine, *Wallace's Farmer*, as associate editor. His study of farm prices produced the first hog-ratio charts and forecast the farm-price collapse of 1920. He became the magazine's editor in 1924 and shifted from the Republican to the Democratic Party in 1928. The magazine merged with another in 1929 to become *Wallace's Farmer and Iowa Homestead*; he remained editor until President Roosevelt appointed him secretary of agriculture in 1933. He helped formulate and administer the New Deal policies of soil conservation, store reserves, controlled production, and higher farm prices. Roosevelt chose him as his running mate in 1940 and, as Vice President, Wallace became the goodwill ambassador to Latin America. During World War II he assumed many duties beyond those traditional to the vice presidency. Passed over for renomination in 1944,

he became secretary of commerce in 1945, a position he continued to hold, after Roosevelt's death, under President Truman. His plans to revitalize the department were overshadowed by his criticism of the President's "get tough" policy with Russia and he was forced to resign in 1946. He edited the *New Republic* during 1946–1947. In 1948 he campaigned for President on the Progressive ticket, calling in his platform for close cooperation with Russia, reduction of armaments, and United Nations supervision of foreign aid. He received over a million popular votes but no electoral votes. He later broke with the Progressive Party and returned to private life. His many books included *Agricultural Prices*, 1920, *America Must Choose*, 1934, *The Century of the Common Man*, 1943, *Sixty Million Jobs*, 1945, and *The Look Ahead*, 1960. He died in Danbury, Connecticut, on November 18, 1965.

WANAMAKER, JOHN (1838–1922), merchant. Born in Philadelphia on July 11, 1838, Wanamaker started working at 14 as a delivery boy for a bookstore and at 18 entered the retail men's clothing business. During 1857–1861 he was secretary of the Philadelphia Young Men's Christian Association. He returned to the clothing industry in 1861 with his brother-in-law, Nathan Brown. That year they founded Brown and Wanamaker, which in ten years was the leading men's retail clothier in the country. Wanamaker served a more fashionable clientele at John Wanamaker and Company, which he established in 1869. He opened a clothing and dry goods business in 1875 in the old freight depot of the Pennsylvania Railroad Company, inviting merchants in other lines to lease space from him. They did not, and in 1877 he himself established a number of small specialty shops under the depot's roof—a "new kind of store"—and thus founded one of the first major department stores in the country. In 1896 he purchased A. T. Stewart's in New York, broadened its general stock, created departments, and had a second department store. Innovation and continual reorganization were the root of his success. He was one of the first American businessmen to use advertising and advertising agencies. Paternalistic toward his employees, he created a mutual benefit program and training classes for clerks, which in 1896 evolved into the John Wanamaker Commercial Institute. He chose reliable relatives and associates to manage his stores and consequently was free to become involved in religious and political work. He was an active temperance worker, several times sought public office, and in 1888 led a fund-raising drive for Benjamin Harrison's presidential campaign and then served as postmaster general from 1889 to 1893. He died in Philadelphia on December 12, 1922.

WARD, AARON MONTGOMERY (1843–1913), merchant and business leader. Born on February 17, 1843, in Chatham, New Jersey, Ward attended school until he was 14, then worked for various dry goods firms, in St. Louis, Chicago, and St. Joseph, Michigan. Traveling for a St. Louis wholesale house, he became acquainted with the problems of farmers, who had to pay extremely high prices, relative to the money they earned in crop production, for a small selection of inferior goods. He thought of solving their needs with a store that would purchase goods wholesale in mass quantities and offer them by mail at a very small markup, eliminating the expense of running a retail outlet by eliminating the middleman. In 1872 he opened a mail order dry goods business in Chicago and published a one-page catalog offering 30 items; his brother-in-law joined the business a year later. The business was immediately successful; unquestioned return of goods was allowed and the steadily increasing selection of previously unobtainable goods accounted for the growth of the firm, which was continually expanded and relocated, finally, in 1900, to the Ward Tower at Michigan Boulevard and Madison Street. By 1888 annual sales were

one million dollars. Retiring from the business in 1886—though remaining its president —Ward thereafter fought vigorously for an unobstructed lakefront and the preservation of Grant Park. He died in Highland Park, Illinois, on December 7, 1913. His fortune was distributed to various charities; the principal benefactor was Northwestern University, which established a medical and dental school in his memory.

WARD, ARTEMUS see **BROWNE, CHARLES FARRAR**

WARD, LESTER FRANK (1841–1913), sociologist. Born in Joliet, Illinois, on June 18, 1841, Ward was raised in poverty on the Illinois and Iowa frontier and was largely self-taught. At 17 he joined his brother, Cyrenus O. Ward, in Meyersburg, Pennsylvania, in the manufacture of wagon hubs. In 1862, after four terms at the Susquehanna Collegiate Institute at Towanda, he enlisted in the Union army and as a result of wounds received at Chancellorsville was discharged in November 1864. He went to Washington, D.C., and obtained a position with the Treasury Department in 1865; he continued his studies at Columbian College (now George Washington University); he graduated in 1869 and earned his law degree in 1871. Rather than law, however, he devoted himself to geology, paleontology, and to botany, to which he contributed his notable theory of sympodial development. In 1881 he joined the U.S. Geological Survey, where he was appointed geologist in 1883 and paleontologist in 1892. In 1883 appeared his two-volume *Dynamic Sociology*, a pioneer work in evolutionary sociology that made him the leader in the field. He developed the theory of what he called "telesis," whereby man, through education and development of intellect, could direct the course of social evolution. In 1906 he became professor of sociology at Brown University. In 1903 he was president of the Institut International de Sociologie. His books included *The Psychic Factors of Civilization*, 1893, *Outlines of Sociology*,

1898, *Pure Sociology*, 1903, *Applied Sociology*, 1906, and a "mental autobiography," *Glimpses of the Cosmos*, 6 vols., 1913–1918. He died in Washington on April 18, 1913.

WARD, NATHANIEL (c.1578–1652), clergyman. Born in Haverhill, England, about 1578, of a notable Puritan family, Ward earned his B. A. degree in 1599 and his M.A. degree in 1603 from Emmanuel College, Cambridge, was admitted to the bar and practised until, in Heidelberg in 1618, he met a famous theologian, David Pareus, who inspired him to join the ministry. Returning to England in 1624 he was a preacher in London until dismissed for nonconformity in 1633. The next year he emigrated to Massachusetts Bay and became minister at Agawam (now Ipswich), and endeavored to instill religious orthodoxy in the community. In 1638, having resigned his pulpit, he was engaged by the Massachusetts General Court to assist in compiling a code of law for the state. The resulting "Massachusetts Body of Liberties," enacted in 1641, constituted the first real bill of rights in America. Yet Ward typified the conflict of the time between social and political liberalism and religious orthodoxy. He issued a booklet in 1647 that satirically but powerfully attacked religious toleration. It was called *The Simple Cobler of Agawam . . . Willing to Help 'mend his Native Country, Lamentably Tattered, Both in the Upper-leather and Sole, with All the Honest Stitches He Can Take.* Its putative author, the "cobler," also diverted his readers with offhand remarks on a variety of subjects. He settled in the ministry after 1648 in Shenfield, England and died there in 1652.

WARHOL, ANDY (c. 1930–   ), painter and movie maker. Born about 1930, Warhol was secretive about the date and the place of his birth, which was recorded variously as Cleveland, Philadelphia, Pittsburgh, and McKeesport, Pennsylvania. He was early attracted to comic strip pictures and studied art at the Carnegie Institute of Technology, later working as a window decorator in Pittsburgh. Moving to New York City in his early twenties, he was first an advertising illustrator and won the Art Director's Club Medal in 1957 for a giant shoe ad. About 1959 his paintings of repeated rows of Campbell's soup cans, dollar bills, trading stamps, typewriters, telephones, Marilyn Monroe, and Dick Tracy, heralded the start of a new movement called "pop" art, whose other major exponents included Robert Rauschenburg, Roy Lichtenstein, and Claes Oldenburg. Different from the abstract expressionist trend that dominated the 1950s, "pop" art, especially as Warhol conveyed it, was impersonal, frequently mass-produced, and often executed by studio assistants, and was significant in legitimizing commercial products as subject matter. The acknowledged leader of the movement by 1962, he turned in 1964 to commercial silk screen reproduction of paintings and photographs on canvas. Famous in this series were pictures of Elvis Presley, Jacqueline Kennedy, and an electric chair; an entire exhibition at New York City's Stable Gallery in 1964 contained his silk screened paintings of Brillo soap pad and Heinz tomato catsup labels glued onto wooden boxes. His works were shown in major U.S. cities as well as in Toronto, Paris, Buenos Aires, Stockholm, and Turin. In 1965 he began making experimental movies that were popular with "underground" audiences, whether because or in spite of their often monumental length. They included *Haircut, Empire, Eat, Sleep, The Chelsea Girls, My Hustler,* and *I, a Man,* and raised to a kind of dim stardom Baby Jane Holzer, Gerard Tenanga, Viva, and Ingrid Superstar. He also managed an electronic rock group, the Velvet Underground. Perenially controversial, he reached mythic proportions in the 1960s largely because his motives were almost totally obscure.

WARREN, EARL (1891–   ), public official and jurist. Born in Los Angeles on March 19, 1891, Warren was raised in Bakersfield and graduated from the University of California at

Berkeley in 1912 and from the Law School in 1914. Admitted to the California bar, he practised law in San Francisco and Oakland for three years. He then served in the Army, 1917–1918, as a first lieutenant in the infantry. He became clerk of a California state legislative committee in 1919 and was deputy city attorney for Oakland during 1919–1920, before serving Alameda County as deputy district attorney, 1920–1925, and district attorney, 1925–1939. For the next four years he was attorney general of California. With wide popular support from both parties, he was elected governor of California in 1943 and was twice reelected. As Republican candidate for Vice President in 1948 he suffered the only political defeat of his career. In 1953 President Eisenhower named him chief justice of the Supreme Court. In the following year the school segregation cases, principally *Brown* v. *Board of Education*, brought forth one of the most notable rulings of the Warren court. "In the field of public education," he stated for the unanimous court, "the doctrine of 'separate but equal' has no place. Separate educational facilities are inherently unequal." In other notable opinions Warren spoke for the court: *U.S.* v. *Harriss*, 1954, in sustaining the constitutionality of the Federal Lobbying Act; *Quinn* v. *U.S.*, 1955, and *Watkins* v. *U.S.*, 1957, in protecting the rights of witnesses before congressional investigating committees; *Pennsylvania* v. *Nelson*, 1956, in barring enforcement of state sedition laws that duplicated federal legislation on the same subject; *Trop* v. *Dulles*, 1958, in invalidating a federal statute revoking the citizenship of deserters; *Reynolds* v. *Sims*, 1964, in holding that state legislatures must be apportioned on the basis of population ("one man, one vote"); and *Miranda* v. *Arizona*, 1966, in upholding the rights of suspects held in custody by the police. He also served as chairman of the Presidential Commission to Investigate the Assassination of John F. Kennedy. Perhaps the most controversial judge of his time, Warren resigned from the Court, effective at the end of

the 1968–1969 term, June 1969. He continued to live in Washington, maintaining an office at the Supreme Court and working with retired Supreme Court Justice Tom Clark, director of the Federal Judicial Center, in order to help improve the federal judiciary.

WARREN, JOSEPH (1741–1775), Revolutionary officer and physician. Born in Roxbury, Massachusetts, on June 11, 1741, Warren graduated from Harvard in 1759. He taught at the Roxbury Grammar School for a year before going to Boston to study medicine. He established a good medical practice but his interest in the Whig cause led him to neglect it for politics. With the passage of the Stamp Act in 1765, he became active with prominent Whigs in their political clubs. His frequent writings in the press and his speeches made him a leader of the popular party. He helped prepare the "Suffolk Resolves" that denounced the coercive measures passed by the British Parliament after the Boston Tea Party, called Massachusetts to arms, and recommended eonomic sanctions against Great Britain. Paul Revere carried these resolves to the Continental Congress in Philadelphia where they were endorsed In 1774. Warren was a member of the first three provincial congresses held in Massachusetts, was president of the third, and actively served the committee of Public Safety. He was named major general on June 14, 1775, but before receiving his commission he took part in the battle of Bunker Hill and was killed by enemy fire on June 17, 1775.

WASHINGTON, BOOKER TALIAFERRO (1856–1915), educator and reformer. Born a slave on April 5, 1856, in Franklin County, Virginia, Washington was taken by his mother, with her two other children, to Malden, West Virginia, after emancipation. There poverty necessitated his working from the age of nine in a salt furnace and then a coal mine. He attended a school for Negroes and there identified himself as Booker Washington, only later to learn that his mother had named him Booker Taliaferro; he ultimately combined all three names. Having always been anxious to acquire an education, he went to the Hampton Normal and Agricultural Institute in Virginia in 1872, and there studied for three years, working as a janitor to pay his expenses. Returning to Malden after graduation, he taught children in the daytime and adults in the evenings. During 1878–1879 he attended the Wayland Seminary in Washington, D.C. Then, summoned back to Hampton, he joined the faculty in a trial program of education for American Indians. The founding of Tuskegee Institute, a Negro normal school in Tuskegee, Alabama, in 1881, and the choice of Washington as its first president, began his major career. The school was provided with two converted, unequipped buildings, a small appropriation, and a student body of 40 unschooled blacks from local farms. Thirty-four years later, at his death, Tuskegee had more than 100 well equipped buildings, a student body of over 1,500, a faculty of almost 200, and an endowment of nearly $2 million. He was extremely successful in promoting good will and in gaining funds for the school and won a national reputation as the most prominent Negro in the country. The school became famous for its hard-working, reliable graduates. A staunch believer in industrial training for Negroes rather than a liberal arts education, he was shunned by many black intellectuals, notably W. E. B. Du Bois, who saw in his philosophy the guarantee of continued Negro servility. Among the organizations he established for uplifting and benefitting black men was the National Negro Business League. He wrote numerous books, including the autobiographical *Up From Slavery*, 1901, and *My Larger Education*, 1911. Exhausted from overwork, he died at Tuskegee on November 14, 1915.

WASHINGTON, GEORGE (1732–1799), soldier, public official, and 1st U.S. President. Born on February 22 (N.S.), 1732, in Westmoreland County, Virginia, Washington grew up on the family plantation. Little is known of his childhood and much that was later written about it—notably Mason Weems's cherry-tree story—is apocryphal. In 1743 his father died and he came into the care of his older half-brother Lawrence. His irregular schooling came to an end at 15 and he turned to surveying as a profession; in 1748 he joined a surveying party sent by Lord Fairfax into the Shenandoah Valley and the next year was appointed official surveyor of Culpeper County. In 1751 he accompanied Lawrence, then suffering from tuberculosis, to the Barbados; the deaths of Lawrence and his daughter in 1752 left George in possession of the Mount Vernon estate, one of the best in the colony, at the age of 20. Shortly thereafter he was named adjutant for the southern district of Virginia by Governor Dinwiddie. In 1753 he became adjutant of the Northern Neck and Eastern Shore and volunteered to carry a warning from Dinwiddie to French forces encroaching on the Ohio Valley claims. The journey was perilous and Washington's account of it, emphasizing the French refusal to leave, was published by the governor and widely read. In 1754 he was commissioned lieutenant colonel of a Virginia regiment and sent back to the Ohio territory; near the French Fort Duquesne he built Fort Necessity and on May 28th defeated a small French detachment. Promoted colonel and given reinforcements, he was nonetheless compelled to surrender on liberal terms to a much superior enemy force in July. In October he resigned his commission, largely because of conflicts with British regular officers who, though of inferior rank, assumed authority because they held king's commissions. Early in 1755 Gen. Edward Braddock arrived in Virginia with a fresh army and offered Washington a position as aide-de-camp. An expedition was mounted against Fort Duquesne and Washington, in poor health much of the time, joined the vanguard just one day before the column was ambushed and dispersed by Indians. Braddock was killed and Washington succeeded in turning the rout into an orderly retreat, after which he was made commander of all Virginia forces. For the next three years of the French and Indian War he was primarily concerned with defense of the frontier, for which he was given insufficient support by the colonial government. He accompanied the British force that erected Fort Pitt on the site of the abandoned and razed Fort Duquesne in 1758. Shortly after his election to the House of Burgesses that year he resigned his commission. Early the next year he married Martha Dandridge Custis, a wealthy widow, and settled down to 15 years as a farmer. He remained a burgess and from 1760 to 1774 was a justice of the peace; Mount Vernon and other properties waxed in value as he devoted himself to his favorite occupation. As tension between the colonies and Great Britain grew he sided unequivocally with his native country; he took part in the irregular meetings of the burgesses at the Raleigh Tavern in 1770 and 1774, declared himself in favor of armed resistance to unlawful authority, and in the latter year was elected to the First Continental Congress. The next year he was a delegate to the more radical Second Continental Congress and in June, as part of a compromise between Virginia and Massachusetts, leaders of the southern and northern factions, he was chosen commander-in-chief of the Continental Army. He arrived at Boston shortly after the Battle of Bunker Hill and spent several months training the ill-equipped troops. In March 1776 he seized Dorchester Heights, brought in cannon captured earlier at Fort Ticonderoga by Ethan Allen, and forced General Howe to evacuate the city. He then moved south to New York, where, outmanned and outmaneuvered, he lost Long Island and Manhattan and in a brilliant delaying retreat was forced into New Jersey and across the Delaware. Unable to cross the river themselves, the British forces and their Hessian mercenaries encamped at Trenton, Princeton, and elsewhere. On Christmas night Washington ferried his troops back across the Delaware, overwhelmed the Trenton encampment, slipped away in the night from a superior force, and captured Princeton the next day. The year 1777 was marked by the constant struggle to maintain the Army despite short-term enlistments, desertions, and lack of congressional and state support in money and supplies, by the desperate battle at Brandywine and the subsequent loss of Philadelphia, and by the Conway Cabal, wherein several of Washington's military rivals and their allies in Congress sought to have him replaced by Gen. Horatio Gates. After a final unsuccessful battle at Germantown in October the Army made camp at Valley Forge; the winter of 1777–1778 was perhaps the darkest moment of the Revolution, as the Army starved and dwindled, Congress meddled, and only the personal strength of the commander held the tatters together. In 1778 the alliance with France was sealed and, in anticipation of the arrival of a French fleet, the British abandoned Philadelphia and withdrew toward New York. Washington met Clinton's army at Monmouth and was kept from a major victory only by the incompetence and possible treachery of Charles Lee, commander of the American advance column. Clinton occupied New York, the American forces surrounded the city, and little action occurred in the northern department for the remainder of the war. In August 1781 Washington, reinforced by French troops and a fleet under Admiral De Grasse, marched south to face Cornwallis, who entrenched himself at Yorktown, Virginia. On October 19th, a month after arriving, the allied armies forced Cornwallis to surrender and the Revolutionary War was effectively ended. Washington remained in command of the Army, continued to plead with Congress to pay the soldiers, and put down a scheme concocted by certain officers to displace Congress and make the commander king. Soon after the occupation of New York in November 1783 he bid his officers farewell, resigned his commission to Congress at Annapolis, and on Christmas Eve returned to

Mount Vernon. Much of his money had gone to the war effort and he had accepted no compensation for the work of eight years; in addition, his properties had suffered greatly during the war, and he now devoted his energies to restoring them to prosperity. Washington shared in the rapidly growing concern that the Articles of Confederation were incapable of providing the unity and security necessary for the new nation. In 1785 a meeting was held at his home between representatives of Virginia and Maryland to settle the navigation of the Potomac; the conference led to the larger Annapolis Convention of 1786, which in turn produced the Federal Convention held in Philadelphia in 1787. Sent as a Virginia delegate, he was unanimously chosen to preside over the Convention. He approved of the Constitution and played a prominent role in securing ratification in Virginia. When the state electors met early in 1789 to select the first President they ratified without exception the long-obvious choice of George Washington. On April 30th he was inaugurated at Federal Hall in New York City. As the first President of a new and unsure government, not the least of his responsibilities was to avoid creating potentially harmful precedents. He constructed his Cabinet with an eye to sectional and ideological balance, strove to the utmost to maintain cordial relations with and among all his officers, and conducted himself with republican decorum and restraint. His first term passed without major crisis, but his second witnessed a heated and inevitable clash between Jefferson and Hamilton, the resignation of the former, and the polarization of politics into party camps. While seeking to steer a middle course, he more often than not found himself aligned with the Hamiltonian Federalists, particularly in issuing his proclamation of neutrality upon the outbreak of the Anglo-French war in 1793, in sending troops under Hamilton to suppress the Whiskey Rebellion in western Pennsylvania in 1794, and in signing the Jay Treaty with England in 1795. The treaty provoked a particularly bitter attack from the opposition, and the President resisted an attempt by the House of Representatives to gain a share of the treaty-making power. In 1796 he firmly rejected pleas that he accept a third term (setting a precedent that endured for 144 years and that was later made law) and in September he delivered before Congress his "Farewell Address," which owed much to Hamilton, and in which he advised his country on its future course. In March 1797 he returned once again to Mount Vernon. The apparent imminence of war with France in 1798 led to his appointment as lieutenant general in command of the Provisional Army, but the crisis passed without his having taken the field. He died at home on December 14, 1799, as the result of exposure. He has remained in the century and three-quarters since his death, in the words of Henry Lee's famous eulogy, "first in war, first in peace, and first in the hearts of his countrymen."

WATERHOUSE, BENJAMIN (1754–1846), physician. Born in Newport, Rhode Island, on March 4, 1754, Waterhouse apprenticed himself to a surgeon at 16 and went abroad in 1775 to complete his medical education. He studied in London for three years and in Edinburgh before going to Leyden in 1778 for more training. There he stayed with the American ambassador, John Adams. In 1782 he returned to America and settled in Newport, but the founding of a medical school at Harvard in the following year led to his appointment, as one of the best-educated physicians in America, as professor of the theory and practice of physic. The first part of his *Synopsis of a Course of Lectures, on the Theory and Practice of Medicine* appeared in 1786. A discourse emphasizing experimental investigation was published in 1792 as *The Rise, Progress, and Present State of Medicine*. He publicized the work of Jenner, the English developer of smallpox innoculation, in 1799 and the next year received some of the cowpox vaccine from England. Successfully innoculating his five-year-old son and other members of the household, he became the first American physician to establish Jenner's method as a general practice. But in the anti-innoculation furor of the time, a serious epidemic was blamed on Waterhouse. He demanded that the Boston board of health investigate and their committee concluded that "the cow-pox is a complete security against the small-pox." Vaccination became known in the neighboring states, and President Jefferson had hundreds of persons vaccinated with the cowpox Waterhouse sent him. His articles on vaccination appeared in many newspapers, and in 1810 he abstracted all previous publications to form *Information Respecting the Origin, Progress, and Efficacy of the Kine Pock Innoculation*. He was honored with memberships in various scientific societies in the United States, Great Britain, and France. His most popular book, *Shewing the Evil Tendency of the Use of Tobacco*, had already appeared in German and French translations, and ran through five American editions beginning in 1805. His lectures on natural history, particularly mineralogy and botany, were also published and he was a founder of the Massachusetts Humane Society. His relations with his Harvard colleagues became strained, however, and he was forced to resign in 1812 because of his opposition to the reestablishment of the medical school in Boston. He stayed on at the United States Marine Hospital, with which he had been connected since 1808 when he wrote their first *Rules and Orders*, and President Madison appointed him medical superintendent of all military posts in New England, 1813–1820. Of considerable note was his work in 1817 on the diagnosis and treatment of dysentery. Most of his later writings were not medical; in 1833 he edited and published a book on Oregon in order to deter immigration to the West. He died in his home in Cambridge on October 2, 1846.

WATSON, JAMES DEWEY (1928–), biochemist. Born in Chicago on April 6, 1928, Watson attended Chicago schools and then attended the University of Chicago, which he entered after only two years of high school; during his four years there he earned a Ph.B. and a B.S., both conferred in 1947, when he was still only 19. Interested in bird study, he went to the University of Indiana, where he came under the influence of a brilliant group of researchers in genetics, including Hermann J. Muller. He received his Ph.D. in 1950, and was named a National Research Council fellow, which took him to Copenhagen for further work. After a year there, however, he moved to Cambridge, where he met Francis H.C. Crick, a nonconformist and somewhat controversial geneticist. Having a small fellowship from the National Foundation for Infantile Paralysis, he joined with Crick in a series of genetic experiments carried out in a shabby building called The Hut. Obsessed with the problem of the molecular structure of deoxyribonucleic acid, or DNA, they worked for months on their three-dimensional jigsaw puzzle, making various models of the DNA molecule out of pieces of wire and colored beads and pieces of sheet metal. Finally they were successful in producing a model that met all requirements, and they described it in a now-classic one-page article in *Nature* on April 25, 1953. "We wish to suggest a structure for the salt of deoxyribose nucleic acid (DNA)," they modestly began. "This structure has novel features that are of considerable biological interest." The problem was to build a model that would show how the genetic material in the cell could duplicate itself; and their model, of a helical ladder, one side of which determined the other side, was exactly what was needed. This, indeed, was the core of their discovery, which has been compared, for its importance in the history of science, with Newton's laws of motion, Darwin's theory of evolution, and Einstein's theory of relativity. In the May 30th issue of *Nature* Watson and Crick developed some of the implications of their model, and researchers the world over immediately began to do experiments that soon confirmed it triumphantly; one worker, Arthur Kornberg of Stanford University, received the 1959 Nobel Prize in Medicine for his efforts. Watson and Crick's Nobel Prize, shared with another scientist, was conferred in 1962. Meanwhile, Watson had joined the Harvard faculty, where he was a professor of biology from 1961 on. He was also the recipient of many other awards and prizes, and was famous the world over by the time he was 30. *The Molecular Biology of the Gene,* a highly technical study of the subject, appeared in 1965; in 1968 he published a popular best seller, *The Double Helix,* which, in candid and unsophisticated prose, told the story of his life and of his great discovery, in the process revealing much about the politics of science. Watson's later work was on the molecular structure of viruses and the mechanism of protein biosynthesis, where once again he made a number of notable contributions.

WATSON, JOHN BROADUS (1878–1958), psychologist. Born on January 9, 1878, in Greenville, South Carolina, Watson earned his M.A. degree from Furman University in Greenville in 1900 and his Ph.D. from the University of Chicago in 1903. In 1908 he became professor of psychology at Johns Hopkins University and remained there for 12 years. His principal work was in founding the behaviorist school of psychology, whose principles were first formally stated in his paper of 1913, "Psychology as the Behaviorist Views It." He came into direct and successful opposition to the methods of introspective psychology, which had dominated the field. He based his "psychology of behavior" on extensive experiments at Johns Hopkins, many on animals, using the devices of Edward Lee Thorndike, and concluded that personality and habits were a result of training or conditioning rather than of inborn mental constitution. Contending that human beings could be trained to do or be anything, he denied instinct and heredity and stressed the effects of learning and environment. The only legitimate subject matter for behaviorist psychology was the strictly observable and measurable responses to outside stimuli. His books included *Behavior: an Introduction to Comparative Psychology,* 1914, *Psychology From the Standpoint of a Behaviorist,* 1919, *Behaviorism,* 1925, and *Psychological Care of Infant and Child,* 1928. In 1920 he was forced by the scandal of a divorce to resign. He entered the advertising business, became an agency vice president in 1924, and retired in 1945. He died in New York City on September 25, 1958.

WATSON, THOMAS JOHN (1874–1956), businessman. Born in Campbell, New York, on February 17, 1874, Watson was educated at the Addison (New York) Academy and at the Elmira School of Commerce. He did not receive a B.A., but he later garnered some 32 honorary degrees. He went to work in 1899 for the National Cash Register Company, serving successively as business manager, special representative, and general sales manager; in 1914 he left NCR to become president of his own firm, Computing-Tabulating-Recording Company, which became International Business Machines in 1924. He was president and a director of IBM from then until 1949, when he was elevated to chairman of the board and chief executive officer. He remained in that position until his death. An astute and capable executive, he saw a revolution coming in the computing, tabulating, and recording of information. He was also a canny psychologist and felt that the constant reminder of duty would inspire employees—hence the slogans that became famous, among them "Serve and Sell," "Make Things Happen," "Be Better Than Average," and, of course, "Think." He not only instigated thinking in human beings, but he also pioneered in the invention, development, and manufacture of machines that did something like thinking, and thereby made the initials of his company almost synonymous with the so-called Second Industrial Revolution, which saw the computer and other cybernetic devices take over—and perform quicker and better—many onerous business tasks. He died on June 19, 1956. His son, **THOMAS JOHN WATSON, JR.,** (1914–   ), was born in Dayton, Ohio, on January 8, 1914. At the age of 5 he made his first tour of the IBM plants; at 9 he toured its European installations; at 12 he made his first speech to its salesmen. He graduated from Brown in 1937 and soon after joined the company as a salesman in its Manhattan district. He was astoundingly successful, scoring 231% of his sales quota. His career was interrupted by World War II, in which he served in the Army Air Force, being discharged with the rank of lieutenant colonel. He returned to IBM in 1946 as assistant to the vice president in charge of sales, a position he assumed himself, on the death of the incumbent, in 1947. In 1949 he was named executive vice president and in 1952 president of the company. He was chairman from 1961. No less capable than his father, he oversaw the expansion of IBM into many fields, including publishing; also like his father, he served on many boards and commissions, was involved with many philanthropies, and was generally reputed as one of the most enlightened corporation executives in the nation.

WATTERSON, HENRY (1840–1921), journalist and political leader. Born in Washington, D.C., on February 16, 1840, Watterson, the son of a Tennessee congressman, received little formal education. Poor sight in his right eye, which later became blind, ended musical studies and a possible career as a pianist. In 1858 he left Tennessee for New York, where he was briefly a reporter on the *Times*, before returning to Washington to join the staff of the *Daily States*. Although a Unionist and drawn to Lincoln, his sectional sympathies led him to join the Confederate army in 1861. He was attached to the staffs of Generals Forest, Hood, and Polk; was chief of scouts in the Johnston-Sherman campaign; and edited the *Rebel* in Chattanooga. At war's end the "Marse Henry" of editorials and cartoons was running a newspaper in Montgomery, Alabama. After editorial stints in Cincinnati and Nashville, he became an editor of the *Louisville Daily Journal*, which in 1868 he merged with the competing *Courier* and *Democrat*. Under his editorship, the *Courier-Journal* became one of the nation's best known newspapers. His editorials were carried by telegraph across the country and considered news in their own right. Watterson's complete integrity made the paper a leading influence in the South. He advocated civil rights for Negroes and the restoration of Southern home rule; he joined Carl Schurz and Horace Greeley in the unsuccessful Liberal Republican campaign of 1872; and it was he who built up Samuel J. Tilden, "the ideal statesman," to win the Democratic presidential nomination in 1876. He filled a congressional vacancy in order to serve as Tilden's floor leader in the House, 1876–1877, until Hayes was finally certified as President. He sharply criticized Grover Cleveland, approved of William Jennings Bryan and free silver, crusaded against "the man on horseback" Theodore Roosevelt, and did not support Woodrow Wilson until 1916. *"Marse Henry": An Autobiography* appeared in two volumes in 1919, and in the same year he retired because of his opposition to the League of Nations. He died in Jacksonville, Florida, on December 22, 1921. *The Editorials of Henry Watterson* were collected by Arthur Krock in 1923.

WEAVER, JAMES BAIRD (1833–1912), soldier, lawyer, and political reformer. Born in Dayton, Ohio, on June 12, 1833, Weaver was raised on farms amid the forests of Michigan and on the prairies of Iowa; he attended school in Bloomfield, Iowa, and became a local mail carrier for four years. In 1853 he went to California with a relative but was cured of his "gold fever" in a few months. Returning to Iowa, he worked in a store in Bonaparte but refused a partnership in order to attend the Cincinnati Law School, 1855–1856. After graduation, he began practising law in Bloomfield. He had been a Democrat, but he was attracted to Free-Soil principles and from 1857 to the outbreak of the Civil War was active in local Republican circles. When Lincoln called for troops in 1861 he volunteered. He fought at Fort Donelson, Shiloh, and Corinth, rising from the rank of first lieutenant to colonel. At the end of his enlistment in 1864 he returned to Iowa and was made a brigadier general the following year. He failed, however, to obtain the nomination for lieutenant governor in 1865. Although he was elected district attorney to the Second Iowa Judicial District in 1866, and was appointed the federal assessor of internal revenue for the First District from 1867 to 1873, he continued to lose ground with state Republican leaders, for he was an ardent prohibitionist, denounced the politically powerful railroads and other predatory corporations, and strenuously objected to the party stand on the currency question. He was outmaneuvered in his attempt to get the Republican nomination for Congress in 1874 and for governor in 1875. As a Greenbacker, he won election to Congress in 1878 and was the presidential candidate for that party in 1880. Defeated for Congress in 1882, he was reelected in 1884 and 1886. When the Farmers' Alliance succeeded the Greenbackers as the chief exponent of soft-money views, he led in transforming it into the Populist Party. As their presidential candidate in 1892, he won over a million popular votes and 22 votes in the electoral college. The fusion of the party with the Democrats left him and other Populist leaders without a political future. In his *Call to Action*, 1892, he set forth his political principles as one of the first "progressives." Virtually all of the social and industrial legislation he called for was eventually enacted into law by the major parties. From 1904 to 1906 he was mayor of Colfax, Iowa; he died in Des Moines on February 6, 1912.

WEBSTER, DANIEL (1782–1852), lawyer, orator, and statesman. Born in Salisbury, New Hampshire, on January 18, 1782, Webster received only rudimentary schooling, but his father, through great hardship, sent him to Phillips Exeter Academy and to Dartmouth College, where he graduated in 1801. While at Dartmouth he acquired, because of his swarthy complexion, the nickname "Black Dan." He studied law with a Salisbury firm and, after a time teaching in an academy at Fryeburg, was admitted to the Boston bar in 1805. Family obligations forced his return to New Hampshire and he began practising law in Portsmouth in 1807. He promptly won distinction and developed a successful practice as champion of New England shipping interests during the Anglo-French War. He voiced the Federalist opposition to President Jefferson's policies in *Considerations on the Embargo Laws*, 1808. His speeches opposing the War of 1812—but opposing also the extremists who called for New England secession—earned him a Federalist seat in Congress, 1813–1817. He then restricted himself to his profitable law practice in Boston and to delivering holiday addresses that earned him a reputation as one the great orators of all time. He returned to politics in 1823, representing Massachusetts in the House, and in 1827 was elected to the Senate. As the aggressive spokesman of Massachusetts industry, he clashed with Southern leaders who wanted low tariffs for the sake of their cotton and slave economy. He became a leading political figure, supporting President Jackson against South Carolina's nullification of the tariff and in the election of 1832. But he had many disagreements with the President, particularly on fiscal policies, and with Henry Clay he became a leader of the Whig Party. In 1836 he was the presidential candidate of the New England Whigs, but he won only the vote of the Massachusetts delegation. He returned to his law practice until President Harrison appointed him secretary of state in 1841. Webster, alone of the Whigs, stayed on in the Cabinet after Polk became President that same year. He completed the negotiations of the Webster-Ashburton Treaty, settling the northeast boundary dispute with England, before resigning in 1843. He returned to the Senate, 1845–1850, where he opposed the annexation of Texas and the war with Mexico. His belief that the evil of disunion was worse than the evil of slavery finally led to his support of the Compromise of 1850, which lost him the support of antislavery advocates in his own party; the once-honored hero of New England was denounced as "Black Dan Webster." Passed over for Fillmore for the presidential nomination in 1848, he again became secretary of state in 1850, in which post he championed the government's right to recognize the new Hungarian Republic and other popular governments. In 1852, poor health forced him to return to his home in Marshfield, Massachusetts, where he died on October 24th.

WEBSTER, NOAH (1758–1843), lexicographer. Born in West Hartford, Connecticut, on October 16, 1758, Webster was the son of a farmer and descendant of a Connecticut governor. He entered Yale in 1774 and, after serving briefly in the Revolutionary War, graduated in 1778. He taught school and did clerical work while studying law and was admitted to the bar in 1781. In the following year, while teaching in Goshen, New York, his dissatisfaction with the texts for children led him to write *The American Spelling Book*, 1783, the first part of *A Grammatical Institute of the English Language*. He completed the *Institute* with a grammar, 1784, and a reader, 1785. His principle that "grammar is formed on language, and not language on grammar" anticipated the modern doctrine of usage. A fervent nationalist, he instituted spelling reforms that were largely responsible for the differences between American and British spelling. The difficulty in copyrighting his work in 13 states led to his lobbying for a national copyright law, enacted in 1782, and to his support of the Federalist cause. The *American Magazine*, which he founded in New York in 1788, was short-lived, but after practising law in Hartford he returned to New York in 1793 to

found the *American Minerva*, a pro-Federalist daily newspaper, and the *Herald*, a semi-weekly. He sold both papers in 1803 when the income from his speller allowed him to retire from journalism. Back in New Haven, he brought out the *Compendious Dictionary of the English Language*, 1806, recording non-literary words as well as "Americanisms" in a work that included 5,000 words not included in previous dictionaries. But he considered it only preparatory to the *American Dictionary of the English Language*, on which he labored steadily for 20 years and which was finally published in 1828. The great work was received as a scholarly achievement of the first order in the United States and abroad. In 1833 he published for American readers a revision of the Authorized Version of the English Bible. Besides his many publications and revisions in the field of lexicography, other writings added to his reputation. His *Brief History of Epidemic and Pestilential Diseases*, 1799, was a standard medical work of the day. Webster's political writings included the "Curtius" articles on the Jay Treaty in 1795; the "Aristides" letter to Hamilton, 1800; and *Ten Letters to Dr. Joseph Priestley*, 1800. His *Experiments Respecting Dew*, 1809, a pioneer work in the physical sciences, foreshadowed work of later census and weather bureaus. He was a founder of the Connecticut Academy of Arts and Sciences and served in the Massachusetts legislature in 1815 and in 1819, the same year he helped found Amherst College. He died in New Haven, Connecticut, on May 28, 1843. For generations his speller was used by pioneers to teach their children to read; annual sales passed the 1 million mark by 1850.

WEED, THURLOW (1797–1882), journalist and political leader. Born on November 15, 1797, in Cairo, New York, Weed had little formal education but his newspaper work, which began when he was 12, provided a thorough schooling in political affairs. For many years he was a journalist and printer and traveled throughout the state until settling in a position with the *Rochester Telegraph* in 1822. Two years later he was sent as a lobbyist to the state capital at Albany and there set about effecting a union of political factions opposed to Van Buren's group. Later he stumped through western New York for Adams and was himself elected to the legislature. He bought the *Telegraph* in 1825; a year later, however, he joined the rising tide of antimasonic sentiment and began a new journal, the *Anti-Masonic Enquirer*. He soon became the principal leader of the Antimason Party and saw to it that its candidates were, when possible, drawn from the ranks of the National Republicans. In 1829 he was again elected to the legislature and in 1830 began publishing the *Albany Evening Journal* as a party organ. With William H. Seward he realized that the Antimason Party was too narrowly based to become a national organization; accordingly he began slowly reorienting it along anti-Jacksonian lines and soon merged it into the newly formed Whig Party. He converted his newspaper to the new doctrine and his influence, preeminent in New York, grew to national proportions. He eschewed office himself, preferring to manage affairs from the background; he took a liberal view of the corrupt methods of political maneuver and was a master of all of them, yet is said to have been himself personally incorruptible. After the Whigs split over the Compromise of 1850 he went with Seward, then in the Senate, into the new Republican Party, formed in 1854, and six years later managed Seward's unsuccessful bid for the presidential nomination. In 1861 he was sent by Seward, then secretary of state, as a special agent to England to conciliate public opinion there and in France following the *Trent* affair. By 1863, with the Radicals ascendent, he found himself estranged from his party; he sold the *Evening Journal* and retired from politics. Moving to New York City in the same year, he edited for a time the *Commercial Advertiser* but remained out of public notice and affairs. He died on November 22, 1882.·

WELCH, WILLIAM HENRY (1850–1934), pathologist. Born on April 8, 1850, in Norfolk, Connecticut, the son and grandson of doctors, Welch graduated from Yale in 1870 and earned his M.D. degree in 1875 from Columbia's College of Physicians and Surgeons. He broadened his knowledge of the sciences and was inspired by many of the latest advances, while studying in Germany until 1878 under leading medical scientists. Becoming professor of pathology and anatomy at the Bellevue Hospital Medical College (later New York University) in 1879, he developed the first pathology laboratory in the country. In 1884 he began a long and distinguished career at Johns Hopkins University in Baltimore, as professor in the newly created department of pathology. There he earned a reputation as a stimulating educator, influencing numerous outstanding associates in his laboratory, where he discovered, with G. H. F. Nuttall, the so-called "gas bacillus," *Clostridium welchi*, the cause of gas gangrene. He was extremely influential in the founding of the university hospital in 1889, and the medical school in 1893, of which he was the first dean. He secured prominent staffs in both institutions, which he developed into major teaching, research, and clinical centers. In 1896 he founded the first journal to publish the results of major medical research projects, the *Journal of Experimental Medicine*, which he edited until 1906. From 1916 to 1926 he was director of the new school of hygiene and public health, in the latter year becoming the university's first professor of the history of medicine. In 1930 he retired. One of the most prominent figures in U.S. medicine, he was active in scientific and medical associations and a consultant to research foundations, notably the Rockefeller Institute of Medical Research, which he helped to establish, and the Carnegie Foundation. He received honorary degrees from universities in the United States and abroad and many other awards. He died in Baltimore on April 30, 1934.

WELD, THEODORE DWIGHT (1803 – 1895), social reformer. Born in Hampton, Connecticut, on November 23, 1803, Weld grew up near Utica in western New York. Converted by the Presbyterian revivalist Charles G. Finney, he joined Finney's "holy band" of crusaders, and preached primarily among the young men of New York for two years. About 1825 he entered the Oneida Institute in Whitesboro, New York, to prepare for the ministry, and scores of his followers entered too. During vacations he continued preaching for temperance and traveled around the country as a representative of the Society for Promoting Manual Labor in Literary Institutions, which was sponsored by the philanthropists Arthur and Lewis Tappan, also patrons of Finney. He was brought into the antislavery movement about 1830, primarily through the English reformer Charles Stuart, a friend and patron since childhood. His first converts to Abolitionism were the Tappans. He convinced them to sponsor the Lane Seminary, then being built in Cincinnati, and they secured Lyman Beecher as president in 1832. Weld entered Lane, bringing a large enrollment from the participants in Finney's crusade. In 1834 he organized the famous antislavery debates at the school, in which the students and Beecher's children, including Henry Ward and Harriet, participated. In the meantime the Tappans founded the American Anti-Slavery Society and incurred much ill will and misunderstanding in a campaign for "immediate emancipation." Under fire from the trustees of Lane who now forbade students to discuss antislavery, in 1834 Weld led the majority of the student body to Oberlin College and set out to rouse popular support for the Society. Using Finney's revival methods, he preached emancipation and won to the cause hundreds of advocates and workers, among them Angelina Grimké, whom he mar-

ried in 1838. His voice broken from constant preaching, he resigned soon after his marriage and with his wife opened a number of schools in New Jersey and Massachusetts. He wrote *The Bible Against Slavery*, 1837, and *Slavery As It Is*, 1839, the latter providing inspiration for a part of Charles Dickens' *American Notes* and for Harriet Beecher Stowe's *Uncle Tom's Cabin*. In 1841 – 1843 he was successful in establishing an antislavery bloc among insurgents in the Whig Party, who then were able to defeat the "gag rule" in the House of Representatives, illustrating the value of the lobby to Abolitionism. As the antislavery movement spread to the West, its leaders were nearly without exception Weld's followers or pupils. Called the greatest Abolitionist, he died in Hyde Park, Massachusetts, on February 3, 1895.

WELLES, GEORGE ORSON (1915 –), actor and director. Born in Kenosha, Wisconsin, on May 6, 1915, Orson Welles grew up in an atmosphere of wealth, culture, and sophistication. After graduating in 1930 from the progressive Todd School for Boys in Woodstock, Illinois, he studied briefly at the School of the Art Institute of Chicago and made a sketching trip by pony cart through Ireland. He won his first professional stage role at the age of 16 in Dublin's famous Gate Theatre, as the Duke of Württemberg in *Jew Süss*. Returning to Woodstock in 1933, he coedited with Roger Hill, his former acting coach at Todd, a popular text, *Everybody's Shakespeare*, 1933, and the illustrated acting editions of Shakespeare's *Julius Caesar*, *Twelfth Night*, and the *Merchant of Venice*, all published in 1934. He was engaged by the Katherine Cornell players, with whom he toured in 1933; he played Mercutio in Romeo and Juliet, made his Broadway debut in the same play in 1934 as both the Chorus and Tybalt, and later acted, opposite Miss Cornell, as Marchbanks in Shaw's *Candida* and as Octavius Barrett in *The Barretts of Wimpole Street*. In 1934, again with Hill, he organized and directed the Woodstock summer drama festival, and appeared as Hamlet. In 1934 he took part in a radio adaptation of Archibald MacLeish's *Panic*, and during 1934–1935 narrated the *March of Time* series. In 1936, under the aegis of the Federal Theatre Project, he codirected an extremely successful version of *Macbeth* at the Negro People's Theatre in Harlem. He and Houseman also produced *Dr. Faustus* for the FTP and in 1937 founded the Mercury Theatre, which staged a modern dress *Julius Caesar*, Dekker's *Shoemaker's Holiday*, Büchner's *Danton's Death*, and Shaw's *Heartbreak House*. Welles also became known for his role as Lamont Cranston in the popular radio thriller, *The Shadow*. In 1938 the Mercury company presented a series of radio dramatizations of famous novels. Notorious in this series was their version of H. G. Wells's *War of the Worlds*, which was so realistic that near-panic resulted in many locales. In 1940 he went to Hollywood and embarked on the writing, production, direction, and enactment of the title role in his next triumph, *Citizen Kane*. Released in 1941, the allegory of a power-corrupted idealist (a thinly veiled portrait of William Randolph Hearst) marked an epoch in movie-making in its powerful use of sound and editing technique. His movie adaptation of Booth Tarkington's *The Magnificent Ambersons*, 1942, was less successful. In 1941 he staged a highly praised adaptation of Richard Wright's *Native Son*. During World War II he wrote and delivered weekly *Hello, Americans* radio broadcasts, and wrote a syndicated column for the *New York Post*. In 1946 he adapted and staged a Broadway musical extravaganza, *Around the World*, from Jules Verne's *Around the World in Eighty Days*. For the next ten years he was in Europe and produced and starred in films of *Macbeth*, 1948, *Othello*, 1955, and *The Third Man*, 1950, and acted the lead in London in a 1951 production of *Othello*. Returning to New York in 1956 he starred on stage as King Lear and in 1958 appeared in *The Long Hot Summer*.

He directed and designed Ionesco's *Rhinoceros* in London in 1960, and three years later directed a film adapted from Kafka's *The Trial*. In 1967 he played Cardinal Wolsey in the movie *A Man for All Seasons*.

WELLES, GIDEON (1802–1878), public official and political leader. Born in Glastonbury, Connecticut, on July 1, 1802, Welles attended the Episcopal Academy in Cheshire and the American Academy (now Norwich University) in Northfield, Vermont, for three years before taking up the study of law in Hartford, Connecticut. In 1826, however, he became part owner and editor of the *Hartford Times* and made it the official spokesman for Jacksonian democracy in southern New England. He was also elected to the state legislature in 1826, where he remained for nine years and fathered legislation to end the debtor's prison, to free voting from property and religious requirements, and to establish Connecticut's model general incorporation law. He was elected state comptroller in 1835 and President Jackson appointed him postmaster of Hartford in 1836. Reelected as comptroller in 1842 and 1843, he then served as chief of the Bureau of Provisions and Clothing for the Navy from 1846 until 1849. He ran unsuccessfully for the Senate in 1850, as he had for Congress in 1834. Breaking with the Democrats in 1854 on the slavery issue, he helped in organizing the Republican Party. He became a founder of the *Hartford Evening Press*, one of the first Republican papers in New England. Although defeated as the party candidate for governor in 1856, his party activities led President Lincoln to select him as New England's representative in the first Republican Cabinet in 1861. As secretary of the Navy, Welles was an early supporter of the development of the ironclads that revolutionized naval warfare. He made the blockade of the Confederacy an effective factor in the Union victory. Although he opposed Lincoln's suspension of habeas corpus and the suspension of critical newspapers, Welles nevertheless backed the Emancipation as a war measure and stood behind President Johnson in the impeachment proceedings. He remained in the Cabinet until 1869, serving the longest term of office to that time for a Navy secretary. He gave the Liberal Republicans his support in 1872, but voted for Tilden in 1876. Welles died in Hartford on February 11, 1878. The *Diary of Gideon Welles*, one of the most important documents of the Civil War period, appeared in three volumes in 1911.

WELLS, DAVID AMES (1828–1898), economist. Born in Springfield, Massachusetts, on June 17, 1828, Wells was a descendant of the colonial governor of Connecticut, Thomas Welles. He graduated in 1847 from Williams College, where he assisted in the publication of its *Sketches*. He joined the staff of the *Springfield Republican* in 1848 and invented a device for folding paper that was attached to the power presses of the newspaper. In 1851 he graduated from Lawrence Scientific School at Harvard, where he was a special student of Louis Agassiz. From 1850 until 1866 Wells and George Bliss published *The Annual of Scientific Discovery*. Wells's important improvements in textile manufacture were introduced in 1856. As a special partner in the publishing firm of G. P. Putnam, 1857–1858, he compiled *The Science of Common Things* and *Wells' Principles and Applications of Chemistry*. These books were followed by *Wells' First Principles of Geology*, 1861, and *Wells' Natural Philosophy*, which appeared in 1863 and went through 15 editions. He achieved international prominence in 1864 with the publication of his first work in economics, *Our Burden and Our Strength*. Demonstrating the economic dynamism of the North, the rapid capital accumulation and constantly improved labor-saving devices, the pamphlet reassured Northerners and foreign investers of the government's ability to pay the increasing debts caused by the Civil War. In 1865 Lincoln appointed Wells to chair the National Revenue Commission and its report

the following year made recommendations that were incorporated into law. The post of special commissioner of the Revenue was created for him, and his *Reports*, 1866–1869, thoroughly covering the subject of indirect taxes for the first time, recommended the use of stamps in collecting liquor and tobacco revenues. His visit to Europe in 1867, where he saw the relatively backward ways of foreign manufacture, converted him from protectionism to free trade. His anti-tariff advocacy cost him his job in 1869 when President Grant deliberately abolished the office of special commissioner. Wells immediately became head of the New York State Tax Commission and its report on *Local Taxation*, 1871, was considered the first competent study of the subject. In 1875 he helped reorganize the Erie Railway and in 1876 he was one of the receivers for the Atlanta and Chattanooga Railroad. In 1878 he became a member of the board of arbitration of the Associated Railways, deciding on questions of pooling. Actively interested in politics, he was several times a delegate to Democratic conventions. He was an advisor on tariff matters to Presidents Garfield and Cleveland; he ran unsuccessfully for Congress from Connecticut in 1876 and 1890. Others among his many books included *Robinson Crusoe's Money*, 1876, *Our Merchant Marine*, 1882, and *The Theory and Practice of Taxation*, 1900. He opposed personal income tax and was among the first to appreciate the importance of "technological unemployment." He died in Norwich, Connecticut, on November 5, 1898.

WEST, BENJAMIN (1738–1820), artist. Born on October 10, 1738, near Springfield, Pennsylvania, West began drawing and painting before he started his formal education. Upon graduation in 1756 from the College of Philadelphia he opened a studio as a self-taught portrait painter. The number of commissions he received was encouraging, and he successfully solicited further work in New York. With the help of friends he financed a trip to Italy in

1759, where as the first American to study art in that country he received much attention. The neoclassical movement was just becoming popular, and he was directed to the galleries and towns that exhibited the style. In his extensive studies of Baroque and Renaissance painting, he was especially impressed by Titian and Raphael. Going to London in 1763, he soon became one of the foremost artists there; his interesting background and pleasant manner secured him friends and patrons. His work, "Agrippa with the Ashes of Germanicus," won the esteem of King George III, who subsequently appointed him a charter member of the Royal Academy. His style leaned more and more toward the Italian neoclassical, featuring auburn colors and modulated tones, while other British artists busied themselves with vigorous subjects and robust hues. In 1771 he flustered the Academy with his "Death of Wolfe," which placed contemporary figures in a classical composition. The work won him an appointment as a painter to the king. In this capacity he executed portraits of the royal family and other works that conformed to the king's wishes. But his delicate brushwork and muted colors limited the effect of his canvases, which were typically large and well designed. He became president of the Royal Academy in 1792 and provided help to many American pupils, among them Copley, Stuart, and Trumbull. Around 1801 his position at court became less secure, and he left for France the next year. His sketches for "Death on a Pale Horse," 1817, exhibited in Paris, presaged the French romantic movement. He completed about 400 canvases in his career and dominated painting in England and America for many years. Although he never returned to the United States, he stayed loyal to his Quaker heritage and rejected the knighthood that was offered him. When he died in London on March 11, 1820, his body lay in state in the Royal Academy before burial with great ceremony in St. Paul's Cathedral.

WEST, NATHANAEL (1903–1940), author. Born in New York City on October 17, 1903, Na-than Wallenstein Weinstein attended city schools and graduated from Brown University in 1924. He went to Paris for 15 months, during which time he completed his first novel, *The Dream Life of Balso Snell*, which was published under the pen name of Nathanael West in 1931. It was one of four short novels that he wrote and constructed in a style derived from the Dadaist and Surrealist movements in the arts; all four ridiculed the superficial aspirations of contemporary men. *Miss Lonelyhearts*, 1933, was executed with extraordinary skill, and was considered his masterwork. It concerned a newspaper advice columnist who met and became involved with several of the people behind the letters. As if emphasizing the conclusion of *Miss Lonelyhearts*, his next work, *A Cool Million*, 1934, did not share the stark narrative or striking imagery of his other novels, but used broad, burlesque humor to parody Horatio Alger's theme of fortitude in the face of frustration. His last book, *The Day of the Locust*, 1939, was a portrayal of the hypocritical life and activities of Hollywood, which he observed toward the end of his career, when he worked as a motion-picture scriptwriter. The book pictured a center of luxury and wickedness, whose society's underdogs were incited to destroy the city, in an attempt to satisfy their spiritual hunger. He was killed in an automobile accident near El Centro, California, on December 22, 1940.

WESTINGHOUSE, GEORGE (1846–1914), inventor and manufacturer. Born on October 6, 1846, in Central Bridge, New York, Westinghouse joined the Union Army at the age of 16 and later served in the Navy as well. After his discharge in 1865 he attended Union College in Schenectady briefly and then returned home to a position in his father's agricultural implement factory. At the age of 19 he was granted the first of his 400-odd patents. Many of his early inventions were designed for use on railroads, and his major single development came in this field in 1869—the air brake. The device made it possible for the engineer to brake an entire train all at once, where previously it had been necessary to hand-set the brakes on each car individually; with the new system trains could begin to operate safely at high speeds. Westinghouse organized the Westinghouse Air Brake Company in the same year; subsequent improvements, notably the automatic features introduced in 1872, led to the rapid adoption of the air brake by American railroads. He later turned his attention to developing an integrated automatic signalling system for railroad use and in 1882 began production with another company in Pittsburgh. From about 1885 he became interested in the potential use of alternating current for the wide distribution of electrical power; aided by several brilliant engineers, among them Nikola Tesla, he eventually worked out a practical system of generation, transmission, and conversion of A.C. power and saw it develop over considerable opposition into the method used almost exclusively. The Westinghouse Electric Company was founded in 1886 to produce the dynamos, transformers, and motors for A.C. power systems, and the company's equipment was used for the Niagara Falls power plant and for the rapid transit systems in New York and London. In 1893 Westinghouse contracted to supply the lighting for the World's Columbian Exposition in Chicago. After 1907 he lost his control over most of the companies he had founded, but he continued to invent and improve earlier inventions until illness intervened in 1913. He died in New York City on March 12, 1914.

WHARTON, EDITH NEWBOLD JONES (1862–1937), author. Born in New York City on January 24, 1862, Edith Newbold Jones was of a distinguished New York family. She read voraciously and was educated by private tutors and governesses at home and in Europe. She married Edward Wharton, a wealthy Boston banker, in 1885. Although she began publishing at 16, her first popular work was *The House of Mirth*, 1905, which analyzed the stratified society she knew and its reaction to

industrialism. Her preoccupation with aristocratic values ebbed with her most famous work, a novelette of simple New England people, *Ethan Frome*, 1911, which eloquently expressed the anguish of an individual doomed to live within the barriers of convention. *The Age of Innocence*, 1920, which won her a Pulitzer Prize, was considered her best-wrought novel. A highly moral work, it was infused with ironical observations on social affectation and foolishness. In all, she published over 50 books, including fiction, short stories, travel books, historical novels, and criticism, and published early poetry in magazines. She died on August 11, 1937, at St. Brice-sous-forêt near Paris.

WHEATLEY, PHILLIS (c. 1753–1784), poet. Born in Senegal, Africa, Miss Wheatley was kidnapped and brought to Boston on a slaveship about 1761 and purchased by a tailor, John Wheatley, as a companion for his wife. In less than two years, under Mrs. Wheatley's tutelage, she had mastered the English language; she went on to Greek and Latin and caused a stir among Boston scholars by translating a tale from Ovid. From the age of 13 she wrote exceptionally mature poetry, including "To the University of Cambridge in New England," "To the King's Most Excellent Majesty," and "On the Death of Rev. Dr. Sewall." When the authenticity of her work was challenged, she was defended by many people, including Thomas Jefferson, even though he did not fancy her work. She was escorted by Mr. Wheatley's son to London in 1773 and there her first book, *Poems on Various Subjects, Religious and Moral*, was published. She returned to Boston shortly thereafter because of the sickness of her mistress; both Mr. and Mrs. Wheatley died soon thereafter and Phillis was freed. In 1778 she married an intelligent but irresponsible free Negro who eventually abandoned her. She died in Boston on December 5, 1784. Two books issued posthumously were *Memoir and Poems of Phillis Wheatley*, 1834, and *Letters of Phillis Wheatley, the Negro Slave-Poet of Boston*, 1864. Her work was used by Abolitionists to combat notions of innate intellectual inferiority among Negroes and to promote educational opportunities for her race.

WHISTLER, JAMES ABBOT McNEILL (1834–1903), painter and etcher. Born on July 10, 1834, the son of a railway engineer, Whistler lived in Russia during 1843–1849, while his father directed the building of a line for Czar Nicholas I. From 1851 to 1853 he studied at the Military Academy in West Point, New York, but was obliged to leave, owing to his failure to understand chemistry. During 1854 he was a draftsman and map engraver for the Coast and Geodetic Survey in Washington. He left for Paris in 1855 (never to return to the United States) to become an artist. Of prime influence on him were the styles of Legros and Fantin-Latour, who relied on recollections of a scene, the realist Courbet, and Velazquez. Such early paintings as "At the Piano" and "The Blue Wave" showed the realist influence, but their tonal treatment anticipated his later marked preoccupation with mood. In 1859 he moved to London and commenced a controversial career. His "White Girl," which had formerly been rejected by the Paris Salon and the British Royal Academy, was a huge success at the Salon des Refusés in Paris in 1863. He renamed the work "Symphony in White No. 1," the first in his series of "Symphonies" and "Nocturnes," which grew progressively more delicate and depended strongly on the spatial relationships of colors and forms. His most famous painting in this genre was "Mrs. George Washington Whistler," 1872, which he also described as "Arrangement in Grey and Black No. 1." Subsequent portraits included "Thomas Carlyle," 1873, "Miss Cicely Alexander," 1873, "Yellow Buskin," 1878, and the "Sarasate," 1884. In 1878 Whistler, with much publicity, sued the celebrated English art critic, John Ruskin, for libel after Ruskin, in the course of a criticism of "Nocturne in Black and Gold: the Falling Rocket," 1874, had made remarks about Whistler's character and artistic motives that seemed to him slanderous. At the trial, Whistler declared that a picture of a bridge was not that but instead a blending of colors based on his own personal feeling about the bridge. His sarcasm so upset the judge, however, that although he won the case, the damages were set at one farthing and the expense of the trial left him penniless. His book *The Gentle Art of Making Enemies*, about the suit, was published in 1890. During 1879–1880 he lived in Venice and produced his finest series of etchings. Returning to London, he enjoyed a new popularity and was sought as a portraitist. In his "Ten O'Clock" address of 1885 he summarized his feelings about art as they were manifested in his work. Always a step ahead of conservative academicians, however, he was never fully endorsed by the critics, although by 1886 he was asked to preside over the Royal Academy; he also organized the newly founded International Society of Sculptors, Painters and Gravers during 1897. He settled again in Paris in 1892, but died in London on July 17, 1903.

WHITE, ANDREW DICKSON (1832–1918), educator and diplomat. Born in Homer, New York, on November 7, 1832, White graduated from Yale in 1853 and thereupon went to Europe to study. He stayed three years, spending part of the time as attaché to the U.S. legation in St. Petersburg, 1854–1855. He returned to the United States in 1856, spent a year in graduate study at Yale, and then accepted the post of professor of history and English literature at the University of Michigan. An effective teacher, he also devoted himself to developing his plan for a state university for New York that would, as he wrote a friend, exclude "no sex or color, [battle] mercantile morality and [temper] military passion, . . . [and] afford an asylum for science where truth shall be sought for truth's sake." Inheriting considerable wealth from his father, who died in 1860, he propagandized widely in support of his ideal. But his health broke down, and he took the first of many trips abroad in pursuit of the renewal of his strength in 1862. He returned late the next year to discover that he had been elected a New York State senator. As chairman of the senate committee on education in 1864 he helped to codify the state's school laws and to create a system of normal schools, and in addition used the position to further his aim. He won over the philanthropist Ezra Cornell, who provided large sums of working capital, employed land given New York under the Morrill Act, and founded a university at Ithaca, New York, that bore Cornell's name. The charter, written by White, provided for the common teaching of the sciences, humanities, and technical arts, for equal degrees based on various courses of study, for equal status for modern languages and history and political science with the classics, for the use of eminent scholars as "nonresident professors," and for the treatment of students as men, not boys. Upon Cornell's insistence, he resigned his professorship at Michigan and became president of the new institution, reserving the chair of European history for himself. The university opened in 1868 with a young faculty supplemented by distinguished nonresidents, among them Agassiz and James Russell Lowell. Apart from teaching, he defended the university from attacks on its methods and saw it through a financial crisis when Cornell's benefactions turned out to be less valuable than foreseen. He continued to struggle with these difficulties until 1885, when he resigned the presidency. In the meantime he had spent several years abroad and had served as U.S. minister to Germany, 1879–1881. In 1884 he helped to found the American Historical Association and was elected its first president. After still another recuperative trip to Europe, 1885–1889, he resumed his researches and lectured widely, was minister to Russia, 1892–1894, served as ambassador to Germany, 1897–1902, and headed the U.S. delegation to the Hague Peace Conference in 1899; he considered the last post the summit of his diplomatic career. Among his many books were the remarkable *History of the Warfare of Science with Theology in Christendom,* 1896, *Seven Great Statesmen in the Warfare of Humanity*

with Unreason, 1910, and an autobiography, 1905. He died at Ithaca on November 4, 1918, leaving his valuable library to the university.

WHITE, DAVID (1862–1935), paleobotanist and geologist. Born near Palmyra, New York, on July 1, 1862, White received his B.S. from Cornell in 1886. He went to work for the U.S. Geological Survey almost immediately and was associated with it for the rest of his life, from 1912 to 1922 as chief geologist. He was curator of paleobotany of the U.S. National Museum from 1903 to 1935 and was also an associate of the Carnegie Institution. His most important research was done before 1912; after that, administrative duties occupied most of his time and energy. A keen observer, he was not content with mere descriptions of fossils, but instead interpreted them in terms of their chronology and environment; this was especially so when they had been found in association with beds of coal. More precise in his methods than earlier scientists, he was able to disprove prevailing theories about the Appalachian coal basin and to show that coals could be classified according to the degree of deoxygenation. In 1915 he announced a generalization from this work — the so-called carbon-ratio hypothesis — that allowed the determination of the rank of a coal on the evolutionary scale. The idea soon became economically important when it became clear that it was now possible to predict the occurrence of liquid and gaseous hydrocarbons in association with certain kinds of coal. He was thus one of the founders of the 20th-century petroleum industry. His theory of the carbon ratio was developed in a paper, "Metamorphism of Organic Sediments and Derived Oils," 1935. Among his books were *Fossil Flora of the Lower Coal Measures of Missouri,* 1899, and *Flora of the Hermit Shale, Grand Canyon, Arizona,* 1929. He died in Washington, D.C., on February 7, 1935.

WHITE, EDWARD DOUGLASS (1845–1921), public official and jurist. Born in Lafourche Parish,

Louisiana, on November 3, 1845, White was educated at Catholic schools in New Orleans and Maryland and in 1857 entered Georgetown College in Georgetown, D.C. At 15 he left college to join the Confederate army and was soon captured. Upon his parole he settled in New Orleans, took up the study of law, and was admitted to the bar in 1867. He quickly became involved in politics and was elected to the state senate in 1874 and 1876. From 1879 to 1880 he served on the state supreme court, his tenure being cut short by the reorganization of the court under a new state constitution. For the next ten years he remained out of office, though maintaining his political ties, and aided in the founding of Tulane University. In 1891 he was elected to the Senate and three years later was appointed to the Supreme Court by President Cleveland. Though not a legal scholar, White achieved a high reputation on the Court, principally through his dissents in the Income Tax Cases in 1895 and his opinions, both concurring and dissenting, in the Insular Cases of 1901, arising from the territorial acquisitions of the Spanish-American War, in which he formulated the White Doctrine of incorporated and unincorporated territories. In other major cases of the period he concurred with the majority in *U.S.* v. *E.C. Knight Co.*, 1895, *In re Debs*, 1895, and *Adair* v. *U.S.*, 1908, and dissented in *Northern Securities Co.* v. *U.S.*, 1904, and *Lochner* v. *New York*, 1905. In 1910 he was named by President Taft to succeed the late Chief Justice Melville W. Fuller, becoming the first associate justice to be so promoted. In his remaining years on the bench his major contribution to jurisprudence was a controversial one, his "rule of reason" invoked to interpret the Sherman Anti-Trust Act in *Standard Oil Co. of New Jersey* v. *U.S.* in 1911. In all he wrote nearly a thousand opinions and was a strong conservative and nationalistic voice on the Court. He died in Washington on May 19, 1921.

WHITE, ELWYN BROOKS (1899–), humorist and essayist. Born in Mount Vernon, New York, on July 11, 1899, White attended Cornell University and graduated, after military service in World War I, in 1921. He was a reporter on the *Seattle Times* and a ship's messboy on the Alaska run before he moved to New York. While working for an advertising agency he wrote poems and pieces that he submitted to the *New Yorker* and which earned him a staff position with that magazine. For 11 years he wrote most of its "Talk of the Town" section. His collection of poems, *The Lady Is Cold*, appeared in 1929, as did his book written with James Thurber, *Is Sex Necessary?* His essays, editorials, and parodies on any subject—in prose or verse—led some critics to call him "a writer's writer." His "One Man's Meat" column appeared in *Harper's Magazine* from 1938 to 1943 and in book form under the same title in 1942 (revised and enlarged, 1944). His versatility was shown in *The Wild Flag*, 1946, a serious satire about world government, and "Across the River and Into the Bar," a hilarious parody of Ernest Hemingway. The gentle fantasy of his two children's books, *Stuart Little*, 1945, and *Charlotte's Web*, 1952, proved equally delightful to adults. Among his other books were *Every Day Is Saturday*, 1934, *The Fox of Peapack*, 1938, and *Quo Vadimus?*, 1939. *Here Is New York*, 1949, reprinted his famous *Holiday* magazine essay. *The Second Tree from the Corner* appeared in 1953, and *The Points of My Compass* in 1962. The anthology he edited with his wife, *A Subtreasury of American Humor*, first appeared in 1941.

WHITE, STANFORD (1853–1906), architect. Born in New York City on November 9, 1853, White was the son of a well known scholar and literary critic, Richard Grant White. After a rather desultory education, in the course of which he showed great artistic talent but was discouraged in his ambition to be a painter by John La Farge, a family friend, he joined, at the age of 19, the architectural firm of Gambrill & Richardson. H. H. Richardson was then the most influential architect in America and also a family friend, and he took young

White under his wing, teaching him personally to draw, and involving him in the work on one of his own major achievements, Boston's Trinity Church. In 1878 White went to Europe to study, to live with the Saint-Gaudens family in Paris, and to design the pedestal for the statue of Farragut that the great sculptor was creating for Madison Square in New York. The next year, together with two friends of long standing, White formed the famous firm of McKim, Mead & White, the most important architectural group in American history until the later 20th century. White was known as the Cellini, McKim as the Bramante, and Mead was popularly supposed to bear the burden of being associated with his two flighty friends, but in fact all three were exceptionally talented, although White was probably the most creative and imaginative. White worked in a large number of styles, always with great skill; he maintained throughout his career that any two or more things that were beautiful in themselves could be combined in a harmonious and beautiful whole, and he exemplified this eclecticism, among other places, in his own Long Island home, a made-over farmhouse embellished with gilded Spanish columns, Renaissance fireplaces, Persian rugs, Roman fragments, and Dutch tiles. Until about 1887 the firm specialized in enormous shingled buildings, notably White's Casino at Newport, Rhode Island, 1881. Slowly, over the years, the firm turned from the Romantic style of Richardson to a Classic or Renaissance style that is best known to this day as that of White himself. Among the celebrated examples of his formal planning are the Villard houses, completed in 1885, the Century and Metropolitan clubs, the Herald Building, Madison Square Garden Presbyterian Church (torn down for a commercial replacement in 1919), and Madison Square Garden itself, all in New York, as well as many luxurious homes in New York, Newport, and the Berkshires. Among other buildings in different styles were the Judson Memorial, in Washington Square Park, and his restoration of the Rotunda after a fire and designs for several accompanying buildings at the University of Virginia, where he worked reverently in the spirit of the original designer, Thomas Jefferson. Perhaps his most famous structure is the Washington Arch, at the foot of Fifth Avenue in New York City, which still stands, but his favorite was probably Madison Square Garden, now long since gone, in the tower of which he built an apartment for himself. His dinners in this eyrie were famous, but after one of them, on the night of June 25, 1906, he was set upon by Harry K. Thaw, a wealthy rival for the hand of a chorus girl, and shot to death. Thaw was adjudged insane but later escaped from confinement and married the girl.

WHITE, WALTER FRANCIS (1893–1955), author and civil rights leader. Born on July 1, 1893, in Atlanta, Georgia, the son of parents of mixed ancestry, White was by personal choice a Negro although his features were predominantly Caucasian. He attended Atlanta Preparatory School and graduated from Atlanta University in 1916. In 1918 he went to New York, where he became assistant secretary of the National Association for the Advancement of Colored People. For the next ten years, passing as a white reporter in the South, he investigated some 40 lynchings and eight race riots. He interviewed members of lynch mobs and many state officials. In 1930 he became secretary of the N.A.A.C.P., and began to work for civil rights legislation. His first-hand knowledge of the attitudes and conditions in the South gave impetus to his fight for legislation to bar lynching and segregation. He lobbied effectively to keep a North Carolina segregationist from being seated on the Supreme Court. In 1937 he was awarded the Spingarn Medal by the N.A.A.C.P. He was consulted by Presidents Roosevelt and Truman, and was able to stimulate the formation of a Fair Employment Practices Commission during World War II and to secure a more liberal stance on civil rights in both administrations. In 1939, when singer Marian Anderson was refused the use of Constitution

Hall in Washington by the Daughters of the American Revolution, he staged an open air concert for her at the Lincoln Memorial that attracted 75,000 people. In 1945 and 1948 he served as a consultant to the U.S. delegations to the United Nations and he was a consultant to and a member of many state, national, and international civic and governmental organizations concerned with civil liberties. His books included *Rope and Faggot; a Biography of Judge Lynch*, 1929, *A Rising Wind: a Report of the Negro Soldier in the European Theater of War*, 1945, *A Man Called White*, an autobiography, 1948, and *How Far the Promised Land*, 1955. He died in New York City on March 21, 1955.

WHITE, WILLIAM ALLEN (1868–1944), journalist. Born on February 10, 1868, in Emporia, Kansas, White attended the University of Kansas and held positions on the *El Dorado* (Kansas) *Republican* and the *Kansas City Star* before purchasing the *Emporia Daily and Weekly Gazette* in 1895. Through his editorials in the *Gazette* he became a rural spokesman for liberalism in the Republican Party and in the nation. His paper had a small circulation, but his editorials were reprinted and quoted by papers throughout the nation. He first won recognition in August 1896 for "What's the Matter With Kansas?," an editorial that attacked the Populists and boosted McKinley's campaign for the presidency. He won the Pulitzer Prize for editorial writing in 1923. Collections of his editorials were published in *The Editor and His People*, 1924, and *Forty Years on Main Street*, 1937. He was usually a loyal Republican, but he proved himself an individualist when in 1912 he actively promoted Theodore Roosevelt's Bull Moose Party. Others among his numerous books, some of them novels, were *Strategem and Spoils*, 1901, *A Certain Rich Man*, 1909, and *In the Heart of a Fool*, 1918; his *Autobiography* was published posthumously in 1946 and awarded a Pulitzer Prize. He died in Emporia on January 29, 1944.

WHITEHEAD, ALFRED NORTH (1861–1947), philosopher and mathematician. Born in Ramsgate, Kent, England, on February 15, 1861, Whitehead entered Trinity College, Cambridge, in 1880, remaining as student and fellow until 1910. From 1911 to 1914 he was a lecturer at University College, London, and from 1914 to 1924 chief professor of mathematics and from 1921 to 1924 dean of the Imperial College of Science and Technology of the University of London. He was by then 63 years old, and faced with the necessity of retiring if he remained in England. He therefore accepted a professorship at Harvard, which he held from 1924 until his death, after 1936 as professor emeritus. He enjoyed the freedom that he found in America: "From twenty on I was interested in philosophy, religion, logic, and history," he once said. "Harvard gave me a chance to express myself." He was senior member of Harvard's Society of Fellows in his later years and was one of the intellectual monuments of Cambridge. He published his first important book in 1898, *A Treatise on Universal Algebra*; an attempt to house all mathematics under one roof, it recorded, in its introduction, a debt to a young student, one B. Russell. This was Bertrand Russell, then 26, with whom Whitehead set to work to deduce the whole of mathematics from a few logical principles. The result was *Principia Mathematica*, 3 volumes, 1910–1913, a fundamental study of the structure of mathematical and logical thought that has been called one of the greatest contributions to logic since Aristotle and has been compared with Newton's *Principia* for its mathematical power and innovation. Other books by Whitehead that were written before he left England were *An Introduction to Mathematics*, 1910, *The Organization of Thought*, 1916, *The Principles of Natural Knowledge*, 1919, *The Concept of Nature*, 1920, and *The Principle of Relativity*, 1922. But his most popular and widely read works appeared after he moved to America. *Science and the Modern World* was published in 1925; *Religion in* the Making in 1926; The Aims of Education in 1928; Process and Reality in 1929; and Adventures of Ideas in 1933. These and other books stressed individuality, creative interaction, and a pantheistic approach to religion, and were attempts to modify what he felt to be a contemporary overemphasis on science and deterministic philosophy. The works were often abstruse but included illuminating references to history and everyday life. The wise man showed through the thicket of technicalities and won Whitehead a large number of devoted disciples. One of the major philosophers of the 20th century, he died in Cambridge, Massachusetts, on December 30, 1947.

WHITMAN, WALTER (1819–1892), poet. Born in West Hills, Long Island, on May 31, 1819, Whitman grew up there and, from the age of four, in Brooklyn. He attended school until he was 12 and then became a printer's devil, working on a succession of newspapers on Long Island and around New York City. He taught school occasionally as well until he established himself as a competent, if somewhat itinerant, journalist. He held positions with and contributed to several leading magazines, including Brother Jonathan, American Review, and Democratic Review, and from 1846 to 1848 was editor of the Brooklyn Eagle, finally losing his position because of his Free-Soil inclinations. Of his early published prose and verse nothing was remarkable. He traveled to New Orleans, worked briefly there for the Crescent, and returned to New York; while supporting himself by journalism and later by house-building, he began to experiment with radically new verse forms. Under the influence of Carlyle and Emerson and others his thoughts on man expanded into a triumphant vision of the robust individual and the robust democratic society; to keep pace with the vision, his poetry quickly lost all trace of convention and became a blend of rhythmically rambling discourse, mystical imagery, and epic cataloguery. In 1855 he assembled 12 poems, including those later titled "Song of Myself," "I Sing the Body Electric," and "There was a Child Went Forth," prefaced by a lengthy introduction, and published them at his own expense as Leaves of Grass. The book featured an engraved likeness of himself in loose workman's clothes (he had once been something of a dandy about New York) with a jaunty, self-confident demeanor, and gave the author's name as Walt Whitman. It was a failure with the public and drew mixed critical response; Emerson, however, to whom he sent a copy, wrote back that he found it "the most extraordinary piece of wit and wisdom that America has yet contributed. . . . I greet you at the beginning of a great career." Though Emerson later tempered his praise, Whitman seized upon the second sentence and had it stamped on the cover of the enlarged second edition in 1856. Not until the third edition of 1860 did sales of the book become noticeable; by that time "By Blue Ontario's Shore," "Crossing Brooklyn Ferry," "Song of the Open Road," "Out of the Cradle Endlessly Rocking," and many other new poems had been added and the book was divided into more-or-less topical sections. Late in 1862 he traveled to Virginia to locate his wounded brother on a battlefield and then took up residence in Washington, D.C., where he devoted himself to caring for wounded soldiers. The publication of his war poems in 1865 as Drum Taps, to which "When Lilacs Last in the Dooryard Bloom'd" was appended and all of which was later incorporated into Leaves of Grass, marked the beginning of a mellower, maturer period during which his image was slowly transformed from that of the barbaric young man to that of the Good Gray Poet (the title of an 1866 pamphlet by a devoted disciple). Nonetheless, soon after obtaining a clerkship in the Department of the Interior in 1865 he was discharged for being the author of Leaves of Grass, a book supposedly replete with scandalously explicit sexual references. He found another position in the attorney general's office and remained in Washington until suffering a paralytic stroke in 1873, whereupon he moved to Camden, New Jersey. Larger and reorganized editions of *Leaves of Grass* continued to appear until the definitive "deathbed" version of 1892; he also published two remarkable works in prose, *Democratic Vistas*, 1871, and *Specimen Days*, 1882. His reputation grew more rapidly in Europe than in America during his lifetime, and his poetry was translated into many languages. His fame at home developed at the hands of younger champions, notably John Burroughs, but it did not begin to match his literary significance until after his death in Camden on March 26, 1892.

WHITNEY, ELI (1765–1825), inventor. Born in Westboro, Massachusetts, on December 8, 1765, Whitney showed little fondness for school at first, but was particularly apt in his father's shop at making and repairing violins and had a business during 1781–1783 manufacturing nails and hatpins. He taught school in Pennsylvania to support his education at the Leicester Academy and graduated from Yale in 1792. Traveling to Georgia where he had been engaged as a tutor, he met Mrs. Nathanael Greene and her plantation manager Phineas Miller; through them he learned of the pressing need in the South for a device that could be used to separate short staple upland cotton from its seeds. Within a matter of weeks he designed and built a hand-operated cotton gin, which, by April 1793, he had improved so that one operator could use it to clean 50 pounds of cotton daily. He went into partnership with Miller to patent and manufacture cotton gins, and although they received a patent in 1794, throngs of other inventors had seen the original and duplicated it; the subsequent infringements and litigation left them with practically no return. Whitney's claim was finally validated in 1807. He had anticipated financial problems and in 1798 obtained a government contract to supply 10,000 muskets on the basis of his system of manufacturing interchangeable parts. He purchased a mill site near New Haven, Connecticut, an area now known as Whitneyville, and built nearly all the tools and machinery for the factory, among which was what is believed to be the first successful milling machine. The system of interchangeable parts manufactured and assembled by workers who required little skill was of vast significance in industrial development and eventually brought him liberal compensation. In the meantime, the cotton industry had been revolutionized and firmly fastened to the South. By 1795, U.S. exports were more than 40 times greater than the year before the invention of the cotton gin. Whitney became one of the most celebrated inventors in American history. He died in New Haven on January 8, 1825.

WHITTIER, JOHN GREENLEAF (1807–1892), poet and Abolitionist. Born on December 17, 1807, near Haverhill, Massachusetts, Whittier had little schooling as a child but was an avid reader and early developed a love of poetry. He was throughout life a devout Quaker. In 1826 his sister sent one of his poems, "The Exile's Departure," to William Lloyd Garrison, who printed it in his *Newburyport Free Press*. During 1827–1828 he attended Haverhill Academy and continued to write poetry. From 1829 he engaged in journalism and from 1830 to 1832 was editor of the *New England Weekly Review*. His first book, *Legends of New England*, appeared in 1831 and was followed the next year by *Moll Pitcher*. After 1833 he devoted himself to the cause of Abolitionism; he lectured and lobbied throughout New England and on several occasions barely escaped bodily harm. He favored regular political action—an issue over which he broke with Garrison—and in 1835 sat in the Massachusetts legislature. He was associated with several periodicals at various times, notably as editor of the *Pennsylvania Freeman* in 1838–1840 and for many years as contributing editor of the *National Era*. Much of his poetry was chiefly concerned with the moral crusade against slavery and was collected in *Voices of Freedom*, 1846, which included "Massachusetts to Virginia." Other volumes — *Lays of My Home*, 1843, *Songs of Labor*, 1850, *The Chapel of the Hermits*, 1853, *The Panorama*, 1856, which included "Maud Muller" and "Barefoot Boy," *Home Ballads*, 1860, with "Telling the Bees," and *In War Time*, 1864, containing "Barbara Frietchie" — brought him to the front rank of American poets, one of the "household poets" along with Bryant and Longfellow. Other notable single pieces of the period were "Ichabod," a denunciation of Webster's "Seventh of March Address," and "Laus Deo!" in celebration of the ratification of the 13th Amendment. Living quietly in Amesbury and later Danvers, Massachusetts, after the Civil War, Whittier enjoyed an ever-growing popularity as a poet of homely faith and joy. In 1866 *Snowbound*, his most famous work, appeared; there followed *The Tent on the Beach*, 1867, *Among the Hills*, 1869, *Hazel-Blossoms*, 1875, and *At Sundown*, 1890, among many others. Though his poetry was later to suffer a decline in critical estimation, he was during the last years of his life a celebrated figure; a member of the Saturday Club, his 70th and 80th birthdays were public events. He died in Hampton Falls, Massachusetts, on September 7, 1892.

WIENER, NORBERT (1894–1964), mathematician. Born in Columbia, Missouri, on November 26, 1894, Wiener learned to read and write by the time he was three. He graduated from Tufts College in 1909 and pursued graduate work in mathematics at Harvard and Cornell, taking his Ph.D. from the former in 1913, before he was 19. After two years of further study at Cambridge, Göttingen, and Columbia, he lectured at Harvard and at the University of Maine, worked for a time for the *Encyclopedia Americana* and the Boston *Herald*, and in 1919 joined the faculty of the Massachusetts Institute of Technology, with which he was associated for 41 years. In his mathematical researches he was principally con-

cerned with logic and the foundations of mathematics. During World War II he worked for the government, helping to develop and refine techniques in radar and missile guidance; this work, relying heavily on the use of automatic information processing and control by machine, led him to a deeper study of such computers and their similarities to animal nervous systems. In 1948 he published *Cybernetics*, summarizing the results of his investigations into information control and communication; the book enjoyed wide popular attention despite its technical nature, and the title, a word he coined from the Greek for "steersman," came into common use as designating the whole field of automated machine control of information. Wiener continued to elaborate on the possibilities of cybernetics and also to warn of its dangers, particularly that of man, through intellectual laziness, relinquishing control to the machines of his creation. He made significant contributions to the study of harmonic functions and of random (stochastic) processes. Others among his books were *The Human Use of Human Beings*, 1950, *Non-Linear Problems in Random Theory*, 1958, *God and Golem, Inc.*, 1964, and two autobiographical works, *Ex-Prodigy*, 1953, and *I Am a Mathematician*, 1956. In 1960 he retired from M.I.T. as professor emeritus; he died in Stockholm on March 18, 1964.

WILDER, THORNTON NIVEN (1897–), author and playwright. Born on April 17, 1897, in Madison, Wisconsin, Wilder was raised in China and the United States. He received his B.A. from Yale in 1920 and his M.A. from Princeton in 1925. He was a schoolmaster at the Lawrenceville School in New Jersey, taught at the University of Chicago from 1930 to 1937, and was a professor at Harvard in 1950 and 1951. His first book to win public attention was a novel, *The Bridge of San Luis Rey*, 1927, which was awarded a Pulitzer Prize. The action focused on five characters whose lives were externally quite different but end in the same way. The implication was that lives are essentially similar, regardless of race, class, time, or place; the idea reappeared in most of his prominent works. His historical novels, *The Woman of Andros*, 1930, *Heaven's My Destination*, 1934, and *The Ides of March*, 1948, all stressed repeating or unchanging nature and events through different periods of time. His Pulitzer Prize winning play *Our Town*, 1938, called for no scenery, suggesting that the action might occur anywhere, not only in the small New England town in which it was nominally placed. *The Skin of Our Teeth*, 1942, which won another Pulitzer Prize, contained intentional anachronisms and shifted characters from one time and place to other times and places. In *The Matchmaker*, 1956, stage characters addressed the audience, as though to bring the play's action as close as possible to real life. His plays have a simplicity and universality that has made them widely popular, and they are frequently revived.

WILKES, CHARLES (1798–1877), naval officer and explorer. Born in New York City on April 3, 1798, Wilkes entered the merchant service in 1815 and three years later was commissioned a midshipman in the Navy. For several years he alternated routine sea cruises in the Mediterranean and the Pacific with periods of shore duty and study. In 1826 he was promoted to lieutenant and four years later placed in charge of the Depot of Charts and Instruments in Washington, D.C., which later became the Naval Observatory and Hydrographic Office. In 1838, despite his junior rank, he was appointed to command a naval scientific expedition to the South Seas. Setting out in August with six ships, he was accompanied by a team of scientists in various fields. After stops in South America, islands of the South Pacific, and Australia, the squadron sailed through the Antarctic Ocean and made several successive sightings of land. Wilkes claimed on the basis of these observations to have discovered Antarctica as a continent; though long disputed, his claim was later substantiated and the large

region he had seen named Wilkes Land. The expedition sailed northward, visiting the Fiji and Hawaiian Islands, and made explorations along the North American coast that served to bolster U.S. claims to the Oregon Territory. After circling the globe westward, Wilkes and his party returned to America in 1842. In matters of discipline he was something of a martinet, and soon after his return he was court-martialled for having improperly administered punishment to some of his crew, but in 1843 he was nonetheless promoted to commander. From 1844 to 1861 he was engaged in preparing the report of the expedition; of the 19 volumes, he himself wrote the 5-volume *Narrative of the United States Exploring Expedition*, 1844, and the single volumes on *Meteorology*, 1851, and *Hydrography*, 1861. He was made captain in 1855. In November 1861, in command of the *San Jacinto*, he stopped the British mail ship *Trent* and forcibly removed two Confederate agents, Mason and Slidell; though publicly acclaimed, his action was of necessity officially disavowed. In 1862 he was promoted to commodore and placed in command of a squadron sent to supress Confederate raiding on commerce in the West Indies; the mission was largely a failure and aroused considerable diplomatic friction. In 1864 he was court-martialled for insubordination and conduct unbecoming an officer and suspended from duty. He retired before the expiration of his suspension and in 1866 was given the rank of rear admiral (retired). He died in Washington, D.C., on February 8, 1877.

WILKINS, ROY (1901–   ), social reformer. Born in St. Louis on August 30, 1901, Wilkins attended the University of Minnesota, where he was night editor of the school paper. Before his graduation in 1923 he was also editor of the *St. Paul Appeal*, a Negro weekly. For the next eight years he edited the leading Negro weekly, the *Kansas City Call*. In 1931 he began his long career with the National Association for the Advancement of Colored

People. He served as assistant secretary and in 1934 became editor of its official publication, *Crisis*. In 1949 he became acting secretary of the organization, and in 1950 its administrator of internal affairs. He served as executive secretary from 1955 to 1965, and as executive director from 1965. He wrote for many publications, testified on many occasions before congressional hearings, and served in 1950 as chairman of the National Emergency Civil Rights Mobilization, a union of groups lobbying for civil rights and fair employment legislation. He never wavered in his determination to use all constitutional means at his disposal to help blacks achieve full citizenship within the democratic framework of American society.

WILKINSON, JAMES (1757–1825), soldier and adventurer. Born in 1757 in Calvert County, Maryland, Wilkinson was studying medicine in Philadelphia when the Revolution began. He was commissioned a captain in 1776, served under Arnold in the Montreal expedition that year, and then became adjutant general to Gen. Horatio Gates. In 1777 he was brevetted brigadier general; in 1778 he became secretary to the board of war and was a member of the Conway Cabal against Washington, the exposure of which forced his resignation. He settled in Bucks County, Pennsylvania, was appointed brigadier general of militia, and in 1783 was elected to the legislature. The next year he moved to Kentucky, became a merchant, and gained considerable influence in the region, largely by playing on westerners' fears of being cut off from the commercially vital Mississippi River and the port facilities of New Orleans. While agitating in Kentucky for separate statehood, he established valuable commercial connections in New Orleans and in 1787 swore allegiance to Spain, promising to work for the secession of the western settlements and the extension of Spanish influence. For these services he collected until 1800 an annual $2000 pension from the Spanish authorities; he also secured

several sizeable loans and outright gifts to finance his activities. At the same time, however, he was actively working against the Spanish; his reports to them concerning his efforts in their behalf were greatly exaggerated, and in 1791, his various business ventures having failed to prosper, he returned to the military service of the United States. The next year, now a brigadier general, he was placed under Gen. Anthony Wayne, against whom he intrigued until Wayne's death in 1796, after which he became the ranking officer in the Army. In 1798 he became military commander on the southern frontier; his vague collusion with the Spanish in New Orleans continued until 1803 when he was one of the commissioners appointed to receive the Louisiana Territory. In 1804–1805 he met often with Aaron Burr and with him formed a plan to separate the western territory from the United States, invade Mexico, and establish an independent nation. In 1805 he became governor of a portion of the Louisiana Territory with headquarters in St. Louis. While conducting a highly unpopular rule he sent out several expeditions, notably that of Zebulon Pike, to survey military routes into Spanish territories to the southwest. In 1806 he was transferred to New Orleans; as numerous rumors about his and Burr's plans were confirmed by the admissions of an accomplice, Wilkinson, with characteristic bravado, declared martial law and arrested scores of persons for alleged involvement with Burr. Burr himself approached down the Mississippi with a party of followers, and Wilkinson had him arrested. At the treason trial in Richmond, Virginia, in 1807, Wilkinson testified for the prosecution and barely escaped indictment. Courts of inquiry and congressional investigations in 1807, 1809, and 1811 cleared him of wrongdoing and in 1812 he was restored to his command in New Orleans. In 1813 he was promoted to major general and ordered to the St. Lawrence frontier; the spectacular failure of the Montreal campaign that year ended his military career. He returned to an estate near New Orleans.

In 1821 he went to Mexico City and for several years sought a land grant in Texas. He died in that city on December 28, 1825.

WILLARD, EMMA HART (1787–1870), educator. Born on February 23, 1787, in Berlin, Connecticut, Emma Hart was raised in a well informed, communicative family so that even as a child she became interested in world affairs. She graduated from the Berlin Academy, where she also taught while furthering her studies in private schools. Subsequently she held teaching positions in Westfield, Massachusetts, and Middlebury, Vermont. She exhibited an unusual flair for her profession; but she married in 1809 and resigned her position. Her husband's nephew, a student at Middlebury College, lived with them for a time and acquainted her with the curriculum of his college. It included subjects to which female students had never been exposed, and she studied his textbooks on geometry, philosophy, and so forth. When her husband's business declined she opened her own Female Seminary in Middlebury. Its curriculum was designed to prepare the female graduate for college, an unheard-of idea at the time. In 1818 she wrote a letter to the governor of New York requesting funds for the establishment of schools for girls and outlining an ambitious course of study. She was met with some sympathy, but her proposals were dismissed by the majority of the legislature as being contrary to God's will for women. She moved her school to Waterford, New York, but was unsuccessful in finding financial support. At last, in 1821, a building was provided by the citizens of Troy, New York. Her students were as eager to learn as she was to teach, and the curriculum expanded rapidly. She developed new methods of teaching and published widely used textbooks on geography and history. Stressing the importance of education, she trained many able female teachers. She retired from the Troy Seminary in 1838 to devote all of her time to improving public schools. She organized teachers' con-

ventions, developed three model schools in Connecticut, and lectured in the southern and western United States on the significance of proper teaching, adequate salaries, and good textbooks and schoolhouses. Her attempts to provide equal educational opportunities for women led to many more female schools and eventually to the coeducational school system. She died in Troy on April 15, 1870.

WILLARD, FRANCES ELIZABETH CAROLINE (1839–1898), educator and reformer. Born on September 28, 1839, in Churchville, New York, Frances Willard moved with her family to Ohio and later to Wisconsin. Her parents were teachers and, particularly her father, sternly religious. She entered the Milwaukee Female College at 17 and after a year transferred to North-Western Female College in Evanston, Illinois. Following her graduation in 1859 she became a teacher at a succession of schools in Illinois, Pennsylvania, and New York. During 1868-1870 she traveled in Europe; in 1871 she accepted the presidency of the Evanston College for Ladies, becoming in 1873 dean of women at Northwestern University when the two schools merged. She had by this time already developed temperance sentiments and in 1874 she resigned her position to join the growing national crusade against liquor. She became corresponding secretary of the National Woman's Christian Temperance Union and five years later was named president, a post she held for the rest of her life. In 1883 she organized and was first president of the World Woman's Christian Temperance Union. A powerful speaker and an expert in mobilizing public and legislative support, she toured the country speaking on behalf of temperance and other reforms, notably woman suffrage. She attempted political action as well, helping to organize the Prohibition Party in 1882 and ten years later taking part in the Industrial Conference in St. Louis that grew into the Populist Party. In 1888 she was elected president of the National Council of Women. Among her many writings were

Woman and Temperance, 1883, and *Glimpses of Fifty Years*, 1889. She died in New York City on February 18, 1898.

WILLIAMS, ROGER (c.1603–1683), religious leader and public official. Born in London about 1603, Williams graduated from Pembroke College, Cambridge, in 1627 and was ordained about 1628. A religious nonconformist, he came to America with the founders of the Puritan colony at Massachusetts Bay in 1630, seeking free expression of his ideals. In 1631, when called a serve as pastor of a church in Boston, he refused, insisting upon open repudiation of the Church of England. At Plymouth, where the church was avowedly separatist, he was pastor from 1632 to 1633. He severely criticized the Puritans for enforcing religious principles with the powers of civil government and for expropriating Indian lands. In 1634 the civil rulers of the colony denied him permission to become minister of the Salem church; in defiance of the General Court he took the pulpit anyway. In 1635 he was brought to trial and found guilty of spreading "dangerous opinions." Banished from the colony, he attempted to organize the Salem congregation into a separate colony in Narragansett Bay, but was pursued by Puritan leaders and compelled to leave Massachusetts. In 1636, with a group of followers, he successfully founded the town of Providence and the colony of Rhode Island in the Narragansett area. The colony became known for its democratic institutions, including a town government, the separation of church and state, and religious toleration. In 1639 he called himself a Seeker, identifying with no sect but believing in the basic tenets of Christianity. Although he mistrusted many new religions, he defended the right of all to worship as they pleased. He went to England in 1643 to obtain a patent to govern the four settlements that developed in Rhode Island. He received a charter for the Providence Plantations in 1644, over the claims of the Puritan colonies, which had dispatched delegates to London to negotiate for a Narragansett patent. In England he wrote *The Bloudy Tenent of Persecution*, 1644, a famous defense of religious liberty. He went again to England in 1651 to have the charter confirmed, after William Coddington, a settler of Newport, had attempted to split the colony and establish himself as governor. From 1654 to 1657, when Williams was the first president of Rhode Island, the colony harbored religious groups — Jews and Quakers — who were persecuted by the Puritans. He respected and was respected by the Narragansett Indians, and served as a peacemaker even on behalf of Massachusetts Bay. But his skepticism of existing churches made him give over attempts at conversion. It was beyond his power to maintain peace in 1675; he reluctantly fought in King Philip's War, in which Providence and Warwick were burned. He remained in public office until his death in 1683. Others among his many writings on religion were *Christenings Make Not Christians*, 1645, *The Hireling Ministry None of Christ's*, 1652, and *George Fox Digg'd Out of His Burrows*, 1676, against the Quaker leader.

WILLIAMS, TENNESSEE see WILLIAMS, THOMAS

WILLIAMS, THOMAS LANIER (1911–), playwright. Born in Columbus, Mississippi, on March 26, 1911, Williams came of a family of Tennesseans and himself chose the name by which he is known, "Tennessee." Raised in a Southern Puritan environment, largely by his grandfather, an Episcopalian minister, he and his family moved, when he was about 13, into a St. Louis slum. He worked in a shoe company, a job he detested, and attended the University of Missouri from 1931 to 1933, Washington University in St. Louis, 1936–1937, and the University of Iowa, from which he graduated in 1938. Journeying throughout the country, he lived frugally on the proceeds of meager jobs and spent much time writing, producing several short plays that were performed by community theaters. His great success with his first Broadway play, *The Glass Menagerie*, 1944, which won the New York Drama Critics' Circle Award, was followed by three more Circle Awards—for *A Streetcar Named Desire*, 1947 (also a Pulitzer Prize winner), *Cat on a Hot Tin Roof*, 1955 (which won his second Pulitzer Prize), and *Night of the Iguana*, 1962. His other plays included *Summer and Smoke*, 1948, *Rose Tatoo*, 1950, and *Sweet Bird of Youth*, 1959. Many of his dramas were adapted for motion pictures, the medium for which *Suddenly Last Summer*, 1959, was directly written. His works included, besides 15 full-length plays, numerous one-act plays, a book of poems, many short stories, and a novel. The South, colorful but tense, was the typical setting in which his characters acted out a struggle between virtue and passion, frequently being destroyed by the latter. They were often portrayed as virtual psychopaths, the victims of their emotions in a world indifferent to them.

WILLIAMS, WILLIAM CARLOS (1883–1963), poet and physician. Born on September 17, 1883, in Rutherford, New Jersey, Williams attended small-town schools, traveled in France and Switzerland, attended secondary school in New York City, received his M.D. from the University of Pennsylvania in 1906, and interned in New York City hospitals. His graduate work in pediatrics at the University of Leipzig preceded a brief tour through Italy and Spain. In 1910 he settled once again in Rutherford and opened his medical practice. As his practice enlarged, he was inspired to write poetry. He had already published a small, imitative volume, *Poems*, 1909, but he grew more inventive and his works were solicited by avant-garde journals. At his best, his poetry was totally direct, realistic, and unembellished by traditional poetic formality either in language or structure. He referred to his practice of verse as objectivism, which he viewed as a further development of the imagism of Pound and others. Subsequent volumes included *Sour Grapes*, 1921, *Spring and All*,

1922, *An Early Martyr*, 1935, *Adam and Eve in the City*, 1936, and *The Wedge*, 1944. His most famous poem, *Patterson*, 1946, grew with additions in 1948, 1949, 1951, and 1958, into an epic vision of modern America. He also wrote considerable prose, including a trilogy—*White Mule*, 1937, *In the Money*, 1940, and *The Build-up*, 1952—and *The Farmers' Daughters*, 1961, a collection of stories. His *Pictures from Brueghel, and Other Poems*, 1962, won a posthumous Pulitzer Prize. He died in Rutherford on March 4, 1963.

WILSON, EDMUND (1895–), author and critic. Born in Red Bank, New Jersey, on May 8, 1895, Wilson was educated at the Hill School in Pennsylvania and at Princeton, from which he graduated in 1916. He began as a reporter on the *New York Evening Sun*, but his career was interrupted by two years of service in the U.S. Army Intelligence Corps, in 1917–1919. He was managing editor of *Vanity Fair* in 1920–1921, associate editor of the *New Republic* from 1926 to 1931, and book reviewer for the *New Yorker* from 1944 to 1948. In the interims between these positions, and after 1948, he was a free-lance writer, writing articles and books on subjects that interested him. Two collections of poetry and short plays appeared in the early 1920s; his first truly distinctive book was a novel, *I Thought of Daisy*, 1929. It was followed by, among others, *Axel's Castle*, a collection of critical pieces, 1931, *Travels in Two Democracies*, 1936, *The Triple Thinkers*, 1938, *To the Finland Station*, a study of the career of Lenin up to the Russian Revolution, 1940, *The Wound and the Bow*, more literary criticism, 1941, *The Shock of Recognition*, an influential collection of literary pieces, 1943, *Memoirs of Hecate County*, a rambling fictional account that for a time was banned in the United States, 1946, *Europe Without Baedecker*, 1947, *The Shores of Light*, 1950, *Classics and Commercials*, 1952, *The Scrolls from the Dead Sea*, a best-selling account of then recent discoveries in the Near East, 1955, *Apologies to the Iroquois*, a sympathetic history of the Indian tribes of upper New York State, 1959, and *Patriotic Gore*, a study of the Civil War and particularly of its influence on literature, 1962. He refused or at least failed to pay federal income taxes in the late 1950s and early 1960s and got into trouble with the Internal Revenue Service; an account of the affair appeared in 1963 as *The Cold War and the Income Tax*. He was recognized as one of the most distinguished American critics of the 20th century and in 1963 was awarded the Presidential Medal of Freedom.

WILSON, JAMES (1742–1798), lawyer and political philosopher. Born in Fifeshire, Scotland, on September 14, 1742, Wilson studied at St. Andrews, Glasgow, and Edinburgh universities until his father's death interrupted his education. He tried tutoring and bookkeeping before emigrating to America in 1765. Arriving in Philadelphia with a letter of introduction to an authority at the College (now the University of Pennsylvania), he was made a Latin tutor in February 1766. Three months later he successfully petitioned for an honorary M.A. degree. Aftery studying for a year in John Dickinson's law office, he was admitted to the bar. He practised in Reading and in 1770 settled in Carlisle, where he soon developed a reputation as the best lawyer in Pennsylvania. For six years he also lectured on English literature at the College of Philadelphia. He was nominated, but not elected, to the First Continental Congress in 1774. He then revised his *Considerations on the Nature and Extent of the Legislative Authority of the British Parliament*, 1774, for members of the Congress. The work, which concluded that there was no "power of Parliament over us," anticipated Britain's modern Commonwealth of Nations and exhibited intellectual power equal to that of John Adams and Thomas Jefferson. Wilson was elected to the Second Continental Congress, 1775–1777, and signed the Declaration of Independence. He

became advocate general for France in 1779 and represented that country in cases arising out of its alliance with the American colonies. He wrote the argument for the Bank of America and supported the struggle for currency reform after 1781. He served as Pennsylvania's counsel in the dispute with Connecticut over the Wyoming Valley in 1782. His role at the federal Constitutional Convention was central; it was he who thought to the heart of the problem of establishing a central authority necessary to a union of states while, at the same time, preserving the local rights insisted upon by Americans. In addition to being a leading influence in framing the Constitution, he was also mainly responsible for its ratification by Pennsylvania and, in 1790, for writing that state's constitution. President Washington appointed him associate justice to the first U.S. Supreme Court in 1789. He also became the first professor of law at the College of Philadelphia and lectured in 1790 in an attempt to interpret the national and state constitutions in the manner in which Blackstone had treated English law. His lectures enunciated the arguments Chief Justice Marshall later used to declare an act of Congress unconstitutional; they remain landmarks In the history of American jurisprudence. Wilson participated in all the notable decisions of the Court and himself spoke for the majority in the case of *Chisholm* v. *Georgia*, which led to the 11th Amendment to the Constitution in 1798. His land speculations during the panic years of the 1790s involved him in financial ruin and undermined his health. He died in Edenton, North Carolina, on August 21, 1798.

WILSON, THOMAS WOODROW (1856–1924), educator, public official, and 28th U.S. President. Born on December 28, 1856, in Staunton, Virginia, Wilson, the son of a Presbyterian minister and teacher, grew up in Georgia and the Carolinas. After a year at Davidson College in North Carolina he went to the College of New Jersey (after 1896 Princeton University) and graduated in 1879; he studied law briefly at the University of Virginia, entered upon a short and unsuccessful practice in Atlanta, and in 1883 took up graduate studies at Johns Hopkins University. Three years later he was granted a Ph.D., his thesis being *Congressional Government*, 1885, a brilliant analysis of the power relations between the legislative and executive branches of the national government. From 1885 to 1888 he taught history and political economy at Bryn Mawr College; for two years thereafter he was on the faculty of Connecticut Wesleyan University, and in 1890 he returned to Princeton as professor of jurisprudence and political economy. In 1902 he was elected president of the university. During his eight years in this office he attempted to revolutionize the atmosphere of Princeton and to create what would truly be a community of scholars; his two avenues of approach, the preceptorial system and the quadrangle plan, were designed to encourage the growth of close personal contacts between students and teachers and to establish a collection of small communities much like those of Cambridge and Oxford. These ideas, strongly democratic in tendency, roused heated opposition at Princeton, long a club-dominated and class-conscious campus, but they were later adopted at many major universities. In 1910 Wilson, now with a national following and a reputation as a strong and incorruptible democrat, was offered the Democratic nomination for governor of New Jersey; he accepted and was easily elected. To the dismay of many of the Democratic professionals, he soon demonstrated that he took campaign promises seriously and actively pushed through the legislature a series of reform measures, maintaining his leadership even after Republicans captured control of both houses. In 1912 he was a prominent, though not leading, candidate for the presidential nomination; on the 46th ballot, however, and after his public disavowal of Tammany Hall, he was nominated. The Taft-Roosevelt split in the Republican Party en-

abled him to gain the largest electoral victory in history. On the crest of progressive enthusiasm aroused by his "New Freedom" campaign he again began his administration by carrying through a vigorous program of reform legislation, notably the Underwood Tariff that, in addition to lowering rates substantially, also included an income tax, the Federal Reserve Act, the establishment of the Federal Trade Commission, and the Clayton Anti-Trust Act, which recognized the legality of labor unions and of their use of strikes and boycotts. In foreign affairs he faced more difficult problems. Certain outstanding conflicts were resolved quickly as "dollar diplomacy" was repudiated, the Panama Canal toll exemptions that had angered Great Britain were revoked, and a public position favoring the protection of the independence of smaller nations was clearly elaborated. But it became apparent that high idealism and moral uprightness failed to answer all the demands of international politics. The revolution and civil war in Mexico was the thorniest question. Wilson refused on principle to recognize the Huerta government and adopted a "watchful waiting" policy; in April 1914, after a minor incident with American sailors in Tampico and with the approach of a shipment of German arms, the terminal facilities at Vera Cruz were seized by U.S. armed forces. The imminent war was averted by the mediation of Argentina, Brazil, and Chile (the "ABC powers") and the subsequent resignation of Huerta. In November U.S. forces were withdrawn and the new government recognized; but friction developed again in 1916 when, after a raid into New Mexico by Pancho Villa, Wilson ordered Gen. John J. Pershing to lead an American force into Mexico in pursuit of the bandit. During 1915 American protectorate governments had been established in Haiti and Santo Domingo. By this time, however, world attention centered on the European war, and Wilson was embroiled in the problems of maintaining and defending American neutrality.

The first manifestations of the problem, brought about by Britain's blockade of Germany, were soon overshadowed by Germany's declaration of unrestricted submarine warfare. When loss of American lives and property began, and particularly after the sinking of the *Lusitania* in May 1915, Wilson protested vigorously (so much so as to cause the resignation of William Jennings Bryan, secretary of state and a pacifist). Stronger protests followed until, early in 1916, a halt to such acts was secured; this victory was a major gain to the President's bid for reelection that year, and the slogan "He kept us out of war" helped him in a very close race. In the meanwhile diplomatic maneuvers were being made in an attempt to bring the belligerents to the conference table; to bring public opinion to bear and to forestall a possible resumption of open submarine warfare by Germany, Wilson had already planned a public appeal for a peace conference when, in December 1916, Germany announced its willingness to negotiate. A week later Wilson made his proposal for a conference and in mid-January outlined his ideas on the shape of the settlements to be made in a "peace without victory." But by this time German leaders had decided to resume unlimited submarine operations; relations with Germany were immediately broken and, several more ships having been lost, on April 2nd Wilson requested a declaration of war, receiving it four days later. Throughout the war Wilson's role was primarily that of moral leader; delegating much of the necessary practical work to others, he concerned himself with enlisting support for the war on his own terms—"making the world safe for democracy" in a moral crusade—and with planning the peace. To the latter end his major contribution was the Fourteen Points announced in a speech in January 1918. Among these, which were mostly concerned with adjustment of territorial and colonial claims, were proposals for arms reductions, open diplomacy, trade liberalization, and "a general association of nations." He continued to advocate his peace program through 1918. In October, Germany suddenly accepted it as a basis for peace negotiations; until this time the Allies had paid little attention to it, but now, faced with pressure from Washington and the prospect of shortening the war by several months, they also accepted and the armistice was signed on November 11th. Wilson, now the preeminent figure in the world, committed a political blunder in trying to make the congressional elections of that month into a referendum on his policies. In December he sailed for Europe and was hailed almost as a savior by the people of the countries he visited; at the peace conference, however, he soon met major obstacles to his plans. Earlier secret agreements among the Allies came to light, and the idealism of the Fourteen Points paled before nationalistic fervor. He secured agreement to the League of Nations Covenant but was forced into painful compromises on territorial matters and arms reduction. In July he returned to the United States with the Versailles Treaty and its included League Covenant. Ill and disgusted with compromise, he soon made it clear that he had no intention of making concessions to the "reservationists" in the Senate. Instead he set off on a cross-country speaking tour to arouse public support for the Treaty; but in September he suffered a collapse and was brought back to Washington, where his condition worsened. The Senate, under Henry Cabot Lodge's leadership, approved a number of reservations to be added to the treaty before ratification. More adamant than ever, Wilson refused to consider negotiating the reservations and called on his supporters to defeat ratification rather than accept any part of the Lodge policy. On November 19th and again on March 19, 1920, the Treaty was voted down. Wilson's hope to make the 1920 presidential election a "solemn referendum" on the Treaty failed to materialize; he himself was too ill to take part in the campaign. In

December he was awarded the 1919 Nobel Prize for Peace. After Harding's inauguration he retired to a small house in Washington, D.C., where he remained, largely inactive and out of public life, until his death on February 3, 1924.

WINTHROP, JOHN (1588–1649), lawyer, colonial leader, and first governor of Massachusetts Bay Colony. Born in England at Edwardstone, Suffolk, on January 12, 1588, Winthrop went to Trinity College, Cambridge, in 1603 but left after two years in order to marry. To augment the income from his lands, he studied law, was admitted to the bar at Gray's Inn in 1613, and established a legal practice in London. His success was undermined by the economic confusion of the times and the demands of his social position. A Puritan of deep religious convictions, he was troubled by the future of religion and morals. In 1629 he joined other Puritans in the Cambridge Agreement, a pledge to move to New England if the patent and the government of the Massachusetts colony could be transferred there. He was chosen its first governor and, with royal approval, the group sailed in March 1630 on the *Arabella*, reaching Salem in June. They went to the Shawmut Peninsula and founded the settlement that became Boston. Chosen as governor of the colony 12 times by annual election, Winthrop strongly opposed democratic tendencies by resisting the efforts of the clergy to share control of the colony with the duly constituted officers. He took the lead in preparing the colony for the possibility of coercion by England. After being rebuked by the clergy for his leniency toward dissenters, he forcefully opposed the Antinomian beliefs of Anne Hutchinson and her followers, 1636–1638. In 1643 he headed the United Colonies of New England in their defense against the Indians. He defended the colony from parliamentary interference again in 1645–1646. Winthrop's influence on the history of colonial Massachusetts was enormous. He died in Boston on March 26, 1649. Two volumes of his richly informative *Journal* were published in 1790, and with a third appeared in 1825–1826 as *The History of New England from 1630 to 1649.*

WISE, ISAAC MAYER (1819–1900), rabbi. Born on March 29, 1819, in Steingrub, Bohemia, Isaac Weis attended Hebrew day schools, several rabbinical schools, the Prague Gymnasium, the University of Prague, and the University of Vienna. He became a rabbi at the age of 23, and officiated at Radnitz, Bohemia, where Jews were constantly and brutally harassed by citizens and the government. In 1846 he came to America and was installed as a rabbi at Albany, New York. At this time he changed the spelling of his name. In 1854 he moved to the Bene Yeshurun congregation in Cincinnati, where he served for the rest of his life. Dismayed at the disunity among Jews across the nation, and feeling that the only way to defeat anti-Semitism was to develop a universal pride in Judaism and to adapt its doctrines to American life, he espoused a gradual movement toward liberal or reform Judaism, which, by the time of his death, was a major branch of his religion. He communicated with his people through a newspaper, the *American Israelite*, as well as a German paper, *Die Deborah*, and wrote a prayerbook, *Minhag America*, plus plays, hymns, novels, and several histories of Judaism. A major step towards unity was taken in the founding of the Union of American Hebrew Congregations in 1873; at first only a regional organization, it grew to encompass the entire nation. From the time of his emigration he urged the founding of an American theological seminary to provide native-trained rabbis. This was realized in the founding of the Hebrew Union College in 1875, of which he was president until his death, and from which the first American rabbis were ordained. He also proposed a conference of rabbis, realized in 1889 in the Central Conference of American Rabbis in Detroit. He is accepted as the founder of Reform Judaism in America; a universalist, he was strongly opposed to all manifestations of Jewish nationalism or separatism. He died in Cincinnati on March 26, 1900. His *Reminiscences* were published in 1901.

WISE, STEPHEN SAMUEL (1874–1949), religious leader. Born in Budapest, Hungary, on March 17, 1874, the descendant of seven generations of rabbis, Wise came to New York City with his father in 1875. He attended the City College and Columbia University, earning his B.A. in 1892 and his Ph.D. in Semitic languages in 1901. He studied religion with many private teachers. After serving in the pulpit at Congregation B'nai Jeshurun in New York City from 1893 to 1900, he moved to Temple Beth Israel in Portland, Oregon, where he drafted the state's first child labor laws and organized a conference on charities and correction. An ardent spokesman for Zionism, he was in demand as a lecturer, and in 1898 founded the Zionist Organization of America. In 1906 he declined a call to Temple Emanu-El in New York City, fearing censorship of his sermons by its conservative board of directors. He resigned his pulpit in Portland and returned to New York City in 1907, founding the Free Synagogue, where he was consistently controversial as its rabbi. A staunch non-assimilationist, he declared that being a Jew and being an American were two separate things, of individual import. He spoke for civic reform, attacking Tammany Hall leaders from his pulpit, and contributing to the downfall of Richard "Boss" Croker and Mayor James J. Walker. Perhaps his greatest desire was for the establishment of Palestine as a national home for Jews. In 1915–1916 he joined Supreme Court justices Brandeis and Frankfurter, and other leaders, in the American Jewish Congress, later serving as its president, and, in 1919, as one of its spokesmen at the peace conference in Versailles. He served as president of the World Jewish Congress, founded the Institute of Religion to train young men for the rabbinate, founded and edited the magazine *Opinion*, and authored numerous pamphlets and books including *The Improvement of Moral Qualities*, 1902. He was one of the major spokesmen against Hitlerism in the 1930s. His Sunday services held for many years at Carnegie Hall attracted multitudes of Jews and non-Jews alike. He died in New York City on April 19, 1949.

WISTER, OWEN (1860–1938), author. Born in Philadelphia on July 14, 1860, Wister was the favorite grandson of the great English actress Fanny Kemble. Brought up in an intellectual household, he graduated from Harvard in 1882, intending to devote himself to a musical career; but after two years of unproductive study in Paris he returned to the United States to restore his health and spent the summer of 1885 in Wyoming. There he came in contact with cowboys, and their way of life, along with the beauty of the Western scenery, filled him with fascination. He nevertheless went back to Harvard to study law, was admitted to the bar in 1889, and practised in Philadelphia for two years. But he continued to spend his summers in the West, and in 1891, after the acceptance by *Harper's* of two sketches about the region, he decided on a literary career. Two early books, *Red Men and White*, 1896, and *Lin McLean*, 1898, were moderately successful, and contributed to the legends of the cunning horse thief, the chivalrous rancher, and the vanishing but noble red man. But his most memorable book, and the only one that is still read, was *The Virginian*, a humorous account of the midadventures of a "tenderfoot" in Wyoming that was published in 1902. It did as much as any single work to create the modern image of the cowboy, and it contained one line of dialogue—"When you call me that, *smile!*"—that is probably as famous as anything ever written by an American. Wister also wrote other novels, among them *Philosophy 4*, 1904, and *Lady Baltimore*, 1906; biographies of U.S. Grant and of Theodore Roosevelt, a classmate at Harvard and life-time friend; and political works on Anglo-American relations, but none approached the fame and popularity of *The Virginian*. His journals and letters from 1885 to 1895 were published· in *Owen Wister Out West*, 1958. A decided conservative in politics, he disapproved of almost everything about Franklin D. Roosevelt and the New Deal. He died in North Kingstown, Rhode Island, on July 21, 1938.

WITHERSPOON, JOHN (1723?–1794), clergyman, educator, and public official. Born in Gifford, Scotland, probably on February 5, 1722 or 1723, Witherspoon was educated at the University of Edinburgh, where he took his M.A. in 1739 and a divinity degree in 1743. He was licensed to preach by the Presbyterian Church in the latter year and ordained at Beith in 1745, remaining there until called to Paisley in 1757. A sternly conservative, orthodox churchman, he carried on for more than 20 years a running battle with what he saw as the decadence of the church in his day; in sermons and debates, and in diatribes like *Ecclesiastical Characteristics*, 1753, and *Essay on Justification*, 1756, he displayed a keenly logical mind and a marked talent for satire. In 1768 he was called to America to become president of the College of New Jersey (now Princeton University) in Princeton. For eight years he devoted himself to enlarging and improving the college, making of it much more than a training school for ministers, and at the same time he came to a position of leadership among American Presbyterians. He stood firmly with the colonies in the growing dispute with Great Britain, and by 1776, when war forced the closing of the college, he had already served on a number of provincial committees and conventions. In that year he was elected to the Continental Congress and was the only clergyman to sign the Declaration of Independence; he served in that body, with a brief interruption, until 1782, playing a prominent role in the work of a large number of committees. In 1782 he returned to Princeton to reopen and rebuild the college. He remained active in public affairs, serving twice in the New Jersey legisla-

ture and in the state's constitutional ratifying convention. At his suggestion, and after years of effort, the first General Assembly of the Presbyterian Church was held in 1789 with Witherspoon as moderator. He died near Princeton on November 15, 1794.

WOLCOTT, ROGER (1679–1767), colonial governor and author. Born on January 4, 1679, in Windsor, Connecticut, Wolcott was the third generation of Wolcotts to live in Windsor, his grandfather, Henry (1578–1655), having emigrated from England in 1628 and, in 1635, helped to found the town. He was apprenticed to a clothier and never attended school, but through his own efforts and those of his mother he obtained some education and managed to author the first volume of verse produced in Connecticut (*Poetical Meditations*, 1725). He was a member of his state's general assembly in 1709, a judge the following year, in 1711 commissary of the Connecticut forces in the expedition against Canada, and a member of the state council in 1714. He was again a judge in 1721 and a justice of the superior court in 1732; in 1741 he was chief justice of this court and also deputy governor. In the expedition of 1745 against Louisburg, in Canada, he was second in command to Sir William Pepperrell, with the rank of major general. He was elected governor of Connecticut in 1751 and served in this post until 1754. He died in what is now East Windsor on May 17, 1767. Among his other works are an epic poem about John Winthrop and a journal recording events of the siege of Louisburg. His son **OLIVER** (1726–1797), born in Windsor on November 20, 1726, graduated from Yale in 1747 and studied medicine with his brother Alexander. Lands in the northwestern portion of the state were opened up for settlement in the late 1730s, and Oliver was made sheriff of the newly established Litchfield County in 1751 and practised law in Litchfield, a town famous for the establishment, somewhat later, of the first law school in America. He was a member of the council from 1774 to 1786 and was a delegate to the Continental Congress in 1775 – 1776, 1778, and 1780 – 1784. He was commissioner of Indian affairs for the Northern Department in 1775. He was a signer of the Declaration of Independence and during the Revolution was active in raising militia in Connecticut. In August 1776 he was in command of the Connecticut militia in the defense of New York City, and he served in the campaign against Burgoyne in 1777 and in the defense of Connecticut when the British invaded it in 1779. In 1784, again as a commissioner of Indian affairs, he negotiated the Treaty of Fort Stanwix settling the boundaries of the Six Nations. He was lieutenant governor of Connecticut from 1786 to 1796 and in 1787 was a member of the state convention that ratified the Constitution. He became governor in 1796 upon the death of Samuel Huntington and served until his own death, in Hartford, on December 1, 1797. His son OLIVER (1760 – 1833), born in Litchfield on January 11, 1760, was graduated from Yale in 1778, studied law at Litchfield, and was admitted to the bar in 1781. He was appointed, with Oliver Ellsworth, a comissioner to adjust the claims of Connecticut against the United States in 1784. He served as auditor of the federal treasury, became controller of the treasury in 1791, and in 1795 succeeded Alexander Hamilton as secretary of the treasury. He resigned the post in 1800 after a particularly bitter attack on him in the press. He soon reentered politics as a leader of the Toleration Republicans and in 1817 was elected governor of Conecticut, in which post he served for ten years. In 1818 he presided over the state convention that adopted a new constitution. He died in New York City on June 1, 1833. The lifespans of these three generations of Connecticut Wolcotts, all governors of their state, covered 154 years of eventful history in America.

WOLFE, THOMAS CLAYTON (1900 – 1938), author. Born on October 3, 1900, in Asheville, North Carolina, Wolfe was educated privately and entered the University of North Carolina at 15. He graduated in 1920, determined to be a dramatist. He had written and acted in several one-act plays, and he was encouraged to go to Harvard to study under Prof. George Pierce Baker in his famous · 47 Workshop. There he wrote more plays, expanding his vision from that of his rural background to an urban setting, but none was particularly successful. He received an M.A. in English in 1922 and, to support himself, went to New York to teach sporadically at New York University. In 1925 he went to Europe for a year, and on this trip he met a wealthy stage designer, Mrs. Aline Bernstine, who gave him love and encouragement and supported his growing interest in his personal background, which he thereupon decided to make the subject of an autobiographical novel. In 20 months he produced an enormous manuscript that was rejected by many publishers. But the chief editor at Scribner's, Maxwell Perkins, recognized its virtues, helped him to cut it drastically, and saw it through to publication in 1929 as Look Homeward, Angel. The book, quite literally autobiographical – the Gant family of the novel being in fact the Wolfe family of Asheville – was a great critical success but was considered by Asheville to be a scandalous libel. Wolfe now decided to devote himself to a literary career, gave up his job at N.Y.U., and set to work on another book. But though he could write vast amounts, he had extraordinary difficulty in arranging his productions, and it was six years before Of Time and the River appeared, and only then after extreme measures on the part of Perkins, who in the end felt it necessary to publish the work before Wolfe considered it finished. The Story of a Novel, 1936, was an account by Wolfe of the ordeal he had undergone to produce the book; it contains a generous description of Perkins' help. He embarked on a new manuscript concerning another autobiographical character, George Webber, and his family. But he did not live to see any of this work published; on a trip to the West Coast in 1938 he fell ill and died in Baltimore on September 15th. Edward Aswell, his editor at

Harper's, his new publishers, fashioned three books out of the manuscript Wolfe had left — *The Web and the Rock*, 1939, *You Can't Go Home Again*, 1940, and *The Hills Beyond*, 1941. *Look Homeward, Angel*, a play based on his first novel, was a hit on Broadway in the later 1950s and was adapted into a successful movie. Wolfe also wrote short stories, a collection of which appeared as *From Death to Morning*, 1935, and lyrical passages from his novels were published in 1939 and 1946 as *The Face of a Nation* and *A Stone, A Leaf, A Door*.

WOOD, GRANT (1892–1942), painter. Born on a farm near Anamosa, Iowa, on February 13, 1892, Wood showed an early talent for drawing with charcoal. Left fatherless at 10, he grew up in Cedar Rapids, Iowa, completed high school there, and after graduation attended the Minneapolis School of Design and Handicraft. He moved to Chicago in 1913 where he studied at the Art Institute during the evenings and worked as a craftsman on metal hand-made jewelry at the Kalo silversmith shop. In 1918 and 1919 he was with the Camouflage Division of the U.S. Army. For five years thereafter he taught art in the public schools of Cedar Rapids, spending the summer of 1920 in Europe, and in 1923 attending the Académie Julian in Paris. Returning to Iowa, he met his first major patron, a mortician, and set up a studio and home in his garage. A commission in 1928 for a stained-glass window for the Cedar Rapids Memorial building of the American Legion took him to Munich in search of craftsmen. There he was influenced by the work of 15th-century Flemish primitives, including Albrecht Dürer and Hans Holbein, and by the realists Wilhelm Leibl and Otto Dix. His own painting style had been pseudo-impressionistic, but he now changed to an expressive, fine-lined realism. One of his initial works in this style was "Woman With Plants," 1929, a portrait of his mother. Another, and his most famous work, "American Gothic," 1930, portrayed his sister

and his dentist as rural Iowa farm folk, and launched the American native regionalist style, whose other major exponents were John Steuart Curry and Thomas Hart Benton. The painting was first shown at the American Exhibit in the Art Institute of Chicago, won the Harris bronze medal and prize, and was purchased for the museum by the Friends of American Art. His paintings and lithographs achieved high honors and great popularity, among them "Daughters of the Revolution," "Dinner for Threshers," and "John B. Turner, Pioneer." After 1934 he was a professor of graphic and plastic arts at Iowa State University. Called the "Painter of the Soil," he died on February 12, 1942.

WOOD, LEONARD (1860–1927), soldier. Born on October 9, 1860, in Winchester, New Hampshire, Wood entered Harvard Medical School and took his M.D. in 1884. The following year he became a civilian contract surgeon with the Army. Ordered to Arizona, he became involved in the campaign against Geronimo and for his participation in this action was later, in 1898, awarded the Medal of Honor. He was commissioned in the regular Army in 1886 and in 1895 transferred to Washington, D.C. At the outbreak of the Spanish-American War he organized, with Theodore Roosevelt, the U.S. 1st Volunteer Cavalry — the Rough Riders — and was its colonel in Cuba. For his performance there he was promoted to brigadier and then major general of volunteers; in 1898 he became military governor of Santiago and the next year of the entire island, and for the next three years he directed Cuban affairs and organized a new government with great skill. In 1903 he was made governor of the Moro Province in the Philippines and given the rank of major general in the regular Army. From 1906 to 1908 he was in command of the Philippine Division; returning to the United States, he became chief of staff in 1910. Four years later he was named for the second time commander of the Eastern Department. The beginning of

World War I in Europe prompted him to become an advocate of military preparedness, and he joined Roosevelt in organizing the Plattsburg volunteer officer training camp. Though senior officer of the Army, he was passed over for command of the American Expeditionary Force and was sent instead to supervise training at Camp Funston, Kansas. His work in the preparedness movement had made him a well known and popular figure and, thought by many to be Roosevelt's political heir, he was a leading contender for the 1920 Republican presidential nomination; his supporters were unorganized, however, and the nomination went to Harding. In 1921 he headed a special mission to the Philippines and remained there as governor general. He died following surgery in Boston on August 7, 1927.

WOODHULL, VICTORIA CLAFLIN (1838–1927), social reformer. Born on September 23, 1838, in Homer, Ohio, of a poor and eccentric family, Victoria Claflin traveled with their medicine and fortune-telling show, giving demonstrations in spiritualism with her younger sister, Tennessee, and married Dr. Channing Woodhull before she was 16. (They were divorced in 1864; she was subsequently twice remarried.) The sisters traveled to New York in 1868, where they met Cornelius Vanderbilt, who was interested in spiritualism. He set them up in a stock brokerage firm, Woodhull, Claflin and Company, which was quite successful. With considerable profits, they founded in 1870 *Woodhull and Claflin's Weekly*, a women's rights magazine that espoused a single moral standard for men and women, as well as free love. Much of each issue was written by Stephen Pearl Andrews, leader of the Socialist cult "Pantarchy." Victoria's ardent speeches on women's rights, notably in 1871 before the House Judiciary Committee, won the acceptance of woman suffrage leaders, who had been put off by her moral attitudes. In 1872 she became the first woman to be nominated for the presidency,

with Abolitionist and former slave Frederick Douglass as her running mate. Although she of course anticipated losing the election, she retained her enthusiasm for her movement and made a much-publicized though futile attempt to vote. In the most sensational scandal of the day she printed in the November 2, 1872 issue of the *Weekly* an exposé of an alleged affair between the already-controversial clergyman Henry Ward Beecher and her own former lover's wife. Intended mainly to discredit Beecher's sisters, who opposed her stand on free love, the article led to Beecher's trial and subsequent exoneration and to charges against Victoria and Tennessee for libel. Charges were also brought against them in 1873 by Anthony Comstock for printing and mailing the first English translation of Marx and Engels' *Communist Manifesto* in 1872; once again they were acquitted. In 1877, purportedly with money left in Vanderbilt's will, they moved to England. Victoria continued to lecture, write books and pamphlets, and work for charities; after a marriage to a wealthy English banker, she was eventually received by London society. She wrote with her sister *The Human Body the Temple of God*, 1890, and by herself *Stirpiculture, or the Scientific Propagation of the Human Race*, 1888, and *Humanitarian Money*, 1892. From 1892 to 1910 she published with her daughter, Zulu Maud Woodhull, the *Humanitarian* magazine. Although she returned on occasion to the United States, she resided in England until her death at Norton Park, Bremons, Worcestershire, on June 10, 1927.

WOOLMAN, JOHN (1720–1772), reformer and religious leader. Born on October 19, 1720, at Ancocas, in the present Burlington County, New Jersey, Woolman worked on his father's farm until moving to Mt. Holly, New Jersey, in 1741. Deeply religious from his early youth, he had a Quaker education and read voraciously. At 23 he took up the Quaker ministry and opened a tailor shop to support himself. During 1743–1771 he traveled throughout

America attending meetings of the Society of Friends, and spread the Quaker doctrine from North Carolina to New Hampshire. Through his travels and writings—*Some Considerations on the Keeping of Negroes*, 1754, 1762, *Considerations on Pure Wisdom and Human Policy, on Labour, on Schools, on the Right Use of the Lord's Outward Gifts*, 1758, and *Considerations on the True Harmony of Mankind, and How It Is to Be Maintained*, 1770—he influenced the Philadelphia Yearly Meeting of 1776 to forbid its members to own slaves. He aided Moravian missionaries in Indian camps on the Pennsylvania frontier in securing conversions, in stopping the sale of liquor to the Indians, and in attempting to secure more just land policies. He gave up his tailor shop because it was making more money than he needed and abandoned horseback riding as a vanity, making his later trips on foot. He ate no sugar because it was produced by slaves, and wore clothing of undyed material because fabric dyes were often injurious to workers. While working with the poor in England he contracted smallpox and died in York on October 7, 1772. His famous *Journal*, which he began when he was 35 and continued until his death, was first published in 1774 and often republished.

WOOLWORTH, FRANK WINFIELD (1852–1919), merchant. Born on April 13, 1852, near Rodman, New York, Woolworth attended country schools and spent a brief time in business school at Watertown, New York. He worked on his father's farm, although he craved a mercantile career and attempted to obtain jobs as a store clerk. Inexperienced and awkward, he consented to work for negligible wages in various concerns. By the time he was 21, still on a tiny salary, he convinced his employer that a five cent counter he had seen in another store would work. Goods that were slightly damaged or overstocked were placed on a special counter and priced at five cents. They sold immediately. In 1879 Woolworth began a store of his own in Utica, New

York, which contained a variety of goods, all priced at five cents. The store was unsuccessful, but later in the year he opened another store in Lancaster, Pennsylvania, offering goods up to ten cents, and was successful. Even frugal housewives bought such luxury items as toothpaste and cold cream. Subsequently he opened stores in Buffalo, Erie, and Scranton, and elsewhere; he acquired several partners, four of whom began their own chains of stores. In 1912 the four chains were merged into the F. W. Woolworth Company. As a business manager, he kept a careful watch on his stores, paying them unexpected visits, and attempting to shoplift items to test his managers' keenness. He paid extremely low wages to female employees; when they struck for more pay, he acknowledged their demands as long as business was good but fired them after business declined. By 1900 he had 59 stores; sales surpassed $5 million. He incorporated in 1905. In 1909 he opened his first stores in England and by 1919 had a chain of over 1,000 stores and sales in excess of $107 million. The Woolworth Building in New York City, then (at 792 feet) the tallest in the world, was opened in 1913. He died at Glen Cove, Long Island, on April 8, 1919, leaving a fortune estimated at $65 million.

WORCESTER, JOSEPH EMERSON (1784–1865), lexicographer. Born on August 24, 1784, in Bedford, New Hampshire, Worcester was delayed in his education by his family's limited means but he finally graduated from Yale in 1811. For five years he taught school in Salem, Massachusetts (Nathaniel Hawthorne was one of his students), while preparing his *Geographical Dictionary, or Universal Gazetteer, Ancient and Modern*, published in 1817. After a brief stay in Andover he settled permanently in Cambridge and during the next nine years published several more books on geography and history. In 1828 appeared his edition of *Johnson's English Dictionary, . . . with Walker's Pronouncing Dictionary, Combined*; a year later it was followed by an abridgment of Noah Webster's *American Dictionary*. In 1830 he produced his first original dictionary, the *Comprehensive Pronouncing and Explanatory Dictionary of the English Language*, initiating the "Dictionary War" between Worcester and Webster. Webster charged plagiarism, a claim bolstered by the appearance of an English edition of Worcester's 1830 work with an unauthorized and false acknowledgment to Webster. While working on his next dictionary, Worcester served as editor of *The American Almanac and Repository of Useful Knowledge* from 1831 to 1842. *A Universal and Critical Dictionary of the English Language* appeared in 1846; in its 1855 revision, in addition to the previously introduced "compromise vowel," midway between the *a* of *hat* and of *father*, it featured the innovative use of synonymy and an etymological list of common surnames. Worcester's final and major dictionary was his illustrated *Quarto Dictionary of the English Language*, 1860. In this as in previous works he displayed a more conservative approach to spelling and etymology than did Webster, and his dictionaries were generally preferred for academic and literary use; lacking Webster's zeal and promotional ability, however, he could not seriously compete in the popular market. He died on October 27, 1865; his dictionaries, unlike those of his rival, saw little subsequent publication.

WORK, HENRY CLAY (1832–1884), songwriter. Born in Middletown, Connecticut, on October 1, 1832, Work moved with his family to Quincy, Illinois, where his father used their home as a station on the Underground Railroad. Over 4,000 runaway slaves were helped to escape before his father's imprisonment. The family returned to Connecticut upon his father's release in 1845, and Henry finished his schooling in Hartford, where he became a printer's apprentice. Finding a melodeon above the shop, he practised with it, studied harmony, and wrote songs for his friends. In 1854 he went to Chicago as a printer but continued to write songs. He finally achieved success with the song, "We're Coming, Sister Mary," written for the Christy Minstrels. His publisher encouraged him to compose for the Northern cause and "Kingdom Coming!," 1861, was the result. Its success earned him a contract to write songs and he was able to quit printing. Among the partisan songs he wrote during the Civil War were "Babylon Is Fallen!" 1863, "Wake Nicodemus," 1864, and "Marching Through Georgia," 1865. In 1864 his temperance song, "Come Home, Father," was published, and it was sung every night for years in the play, *Ten Nights in a Barroom*. "Grandfather's Clock," 1876, is said to have sold 800,000 copies. The Chicago Fire of 1871 destroyed the plates of his songs and ruined his publisher. Work moved to Philadelphia and then to Vineland, New Jersey, where he joined his brother and uncle in land speculation that proved unsuccessful. By 1875 his publisher was reestablished and he returned to Chicago, resuming his career with songs that brought him even greater financial success than before. He died while visiting Hartford on June 8, 1884.

WRIGHT, CARROLL DAVIDSON (1840–1909), statistician, public official, and educator. Born in Dunbarton, New Hampshire, on July 25, 1840, Wright was the son of a Universalist minister. He grew up in Washington, New Hampshire, where he went to local schools and worked on his father's farm. After attending academies in the various New Hampshire and Vermont parishes to which his father moved, he began reading law in a Keene, New Hampshire, firm in 1860 and paying his way by teaching in country schools. He moved to Boston to continue his legal studies, but in 1862 enlisted as a private in the New Hampshire Volunteers. Rapidly promoted, he held responsible assignments in Washington, D.C., before joining Sheridan's staff in the Shenandoah campaign and becoming colonel of his own regiment. In 1865 he returned to New Hampshire, was admitted to the bar, and finally established a successful practice in patent cases in Boston. Living in Reading, he was elected in 1871 and 1872 to represent his district in the Massachusetts senate. In 1873 the governor appointed him chief of the Massachusetts Bureau of Statistics for Labor. In 1883 he organized the National Convention of Chiefs and Commissioners of Bureaus of Statistics and was its president for two decades. He stimulated objective research on labor problems and was an advocate of collective bargaining and of the sliding scale in wage adjustment. In 1885 President Arthur appointed him the first commissioner of the Bureau of Labor, a post he retained until resigning in 1905. In 1894 he was chairman of the investigation of the Pullman strike, and in 1902 he was recorder of the commission inquiring into the anthracite miners' strike. He was called in to complete the Eleventh Census. After 1895 he also taught social economics and statistics at Catholic University and Columbian (now George Washington) University and at Clark College (now University) after becoming its president in 1902. He planned and supervised the first volumes of the economic history of the United States financed by the Carnegie Institution. Among his own works were *The Industrial Evolution of the United States,* 1895, and the *Outline of Practical Sociology,* 1899. He was president of the American Statistical Association from 1897 until his death on February 20, 1909, in Worcester, Massachusetts.

WRIGHT, FRANCES (1795–1852), reformer. Born in Dundee, Scotland, on September 6, 1795, Miss Wright was the daughter of a well-to-do Scotch radical who had circulated the work of Thomas Paine in northern Britain. Her parents died and left her a fortune when she was two, and she was raised in London by conservative relatives. As soon as her legal status permitted she returned to Scotland and, at 18, wrote *A Few Days in Athens,* 1822, a novelistic sketch of a disciple of Epicurus that contained the well worked-out materialistic philosophy she followed throughout her life. Her guardians

suggested a European tour to cap her education but she preferred to go to America. She arrived in New York with her sister in 1818 and the following year saw the production and publication of her play *Altorf,* a tragedy of the Swiss struggle for independence. She toured the northern and eastern states and the enthusiasm of her *Views of Society and Manners in America,* published in England in 1821, won her the friendship of Lafayette. She timed her return to New York in 1824 with his triumphal tour of America and joined him in his visits with Jefferson and Madison. Slavery was discussed and they approved of her plan for gradual emancipation through purchase and colonization. She invested a large part of her fortune in a tract of land in western Tennessee that she called Nashoba. Slaves were purchased in 1825, established at Nashoba, and later colonized (1830) in Haiti, but socialist recruits in the Tennessee colony introduced free unions, as opposed to marriage, which led to its failure. She moved to New Harmony, Indiana, to edit the *Gazette* with Robert Dale Owen in 1828. She also lectured – an activity then considered scandalous for a woman – and her *Course of Popular Lectures* (1829 and 1836) attacked religion, church influence in politics, and authoritarian education, and defended equal rights for women and the replacement of legal marriage by a union based on moral obligation. In 1829 she settled in New York where with Owen she published the *Free Enquirer* and led the free-thinking movement there, calling for a reformed, free education run by the state and for the political organization of the working classes. Her sister died in 1831, and she married William D'Arusmont, a Frenchman who had been a co-worker in New Harmony and New York. She continued writing and lecturing on modern causes, including birth control and a more equal distribution of property, as well as women's rights and the gradual emancipation of slaves and colonization of freemen outside the United States. In 1836 she supported Andrew Jackson's attack on the banking system and advocated an independent treasury. In her last years she lived in Cincinnati and continued her efforts at reform until her death on December 13, 1852.

WRIGHT, FRANK LLOYD (1869–1959), architect. Born on June 8, 1869, in Richland Center, Wisconsin, Wright studied civil engineering at the University of Wisconsin from 1884 to 1888, was apprenticed to Louis Sullivan for five years in Chicago, and opened his own business as an architect in 1893 in Oak Park, Illinois. His concepts of architectural design were highly unorthodox, unlike either the popular neoclassical and neo-Gothic styles of the 19th century or the 20th century glass and steel highrise structures. He used the colors, forms, and textures of nature in the "organic architecture" of his buildings. His "Prairie style" was intended to blend with the expansive, horizontal aspect of western landscape and it featured houses of long, low proportions, wide windows, and open terraces. His windows curved around trees and balconies sat in hollows in the wall. Interior space flowed from room to room, unifying the entire structure. He adapted his buildings to their environments as well as to the needs of the people who were to inhabit them. In designing commercial buildings, he used modern materials and innovated mechanical ventilation and steel furnishings. His engineering skill defied his many skeptical critics; his Imperial Hotel in Tokyo, a controversial structure completed in 1922, was the only major building to survive the earthquake of 1923. Among his most famous creations were the Fallingwater house in Bear Run, Pennsylvania, 1936; his own home, Taliesin West in Phoenix, 1938; the Johnson Administration building in Racine, Wisconsin, 1939; the Hanna House in Palo Alto, California, 1937; the First Unitarian Church in Madison, Wisconsin, 1951; and the Guggenheim Museum, a daring spiral structure, in New York City, opened in 1959. In his home he conducted a school for apprentices and he set down his ideas in

several books, including *An Organic Architecture,* 1939, and *An American Architecture,* 1955. He died in Phoenix on April 9, 1959.

WRIGHT, RICHARD (1908–1960), author. Born on a plantation near Natchez, Mississippi, on September 4, 1908, Wright was the grandson of slaves. Despite an underprivileged childhood in Memphis, he became self-educated and his first story was published when he was 16. In 1927 he moved to Chicago but could find only menial work. The Depression forced him on relief and in 1932 he joined the Communist Party. The publication of a second story in 1931 and a poem in 1934 finally enabled him to write full time as a member of the Federal Writers' Project. This resulted in his *Uncle Tom's Children,* four long stories of racial prejudice and brutality in the South, which was published in 1938 and won the *Story* prize for the best book submitted by anyone from the Federal Writers' Project. He was then in New York, where he had moved in 1937 to edit the Communist Party's *Daily Worker,* and also received a Guggenheim Fellowship. The publication in 1940 of his novel *Native Son* brought him recognition as being more than America's leading Negro author; it became a Book of the Month Club selection and he was acclaimed as a major heir to the naturalistic tradition. The novel was dramatized successfully the following year by him and Paul Green, and he later made a film of it in Argentina with himself playing the leading role. In 1941 he took part in producing *12 Million Voices,* a pictorial history of the American Negro. *Black Boy,* the autobiography of his childhood and youth, appeared in 1945. After the war he broke with the Communists and, in protest against the treatment of Negroes in the United States, he became an expatriate in Paris. *The Outsider,* a sensational story of a Negro's life and his fatal involvement with the Communist Party, appeared in 1953 and was hailed as America's first existential novel. His trip to the Gold Coast was recorded in *Black Power,* 1954. He reported the Bandung Conference in *The Color Curtain* in 1956, and an account of his life in *Pagan Spain* appeared in 1957. Lectures that he delivered in Europe from 1950 through 1956 were published as *White Man, Listen!* in 1957. His novel of corruption in the South, *The Long Dream*, appeared in the following year. After his death in Paris on November 28, 1960, were published *Eight Men*, 1961, and *Lawd Today*, 1963, a novel of the life of a Negro postal clerk in Chicago that had been written before *Native Son*.

WRIGHT, WILBUR (1867–1912) and **ORVILLE** (1871–1948), inventors, aviators, and manufacturers. Wilbur, born on April 16, 1867, near Millville, Indiana, and Orville, born on August 19, 1871, in Dayton, Ohio, were sons of a minister who later became a bishop of the United Brethren Church. Both early displayed great mechanical skill and ingenuity; while Orville was still in high school they built a large printing press and began publishing a local newspaper. In 1892 they opened a bicycle sales and repair shop in Dayton and were soon manufacturing their own bicycles. Their reading about the glider experiments of Otto Lilienthal in Germany and Octave Chanute in America kindled an interest in flying. They obtained all the information available on aerodynamics and set about constructing an improved glider. They first concentrated on the problem of control in three dimensions and came up with the method of "warping," or controlling the lift of the wings by twisting them; this method later evolved into the movable aileron. Through much of their experimental work they received advice and encouragement from Chanute. In 1900 they consulted the U.S. Weather Bureau to find a suitable location for extended glider flights and that summer made their first trip to the sand hills near Kitty Hawk, North Carolina. Their glider experiments of that year revealed large errors in published tables of lift-pressures for various wing surfaces and wind

speeds and, back in Dayton in 1901, they devised the first wind tunnel and conducted a long series of experiments to construct their own tables. In 1902 they returned to Kitty Hawk with an improved glider and in the course of nearly a thousand flights perfected their control system. Now ready to attempt powered flight, they built a small but powerful engine and designed a highly efficient airscrew for propulsion. The new airplane was brought to Kitty Hawk in September 1903; bad weather delayed testing for many weeks, but on December 17th Orville climbed aboard and piloted the craft through a 12-second, 120-foot flight. Later in the day Wilbur flew for 59 seconds, covering 852 feet. During the next two years they built two more airplanes, constantly improving their design and increasing the reliability and range of flight. In 1906 they were granted a U.S. patent for a flying machine. In the United States interest in flying was slow to develop, but the Wrights were soon negotiating with the British and French governments for the manufacture of aircraft. In 1908, however, the U.S. War Department awarded them a contract for a machine capable of flying 40 miles per hour for 10 miles carrying a pilot and a passenger. Later that year and into 1909 the brothers were busy demonstrating their airplanes to government officials and the public, Wilbur in Europe and Orville in the United States. In 1909 the Wright Company was incorporated and both Wrights devoted themselves to the manufacture and improvement of their airplane and the training of pilots. Wilbur died of typhoid fever on May 30, 1912, and for two years Orville continued to direct the Wright Company. In 1914 he retired from the business to carry on his private research; during World War I he served as a consultant to the Aviation Service of the Army Signal Corps. He died in Dayton on January 30, 1948. On December 17th of that year the original Kitty Hawk machine of 1903 was installed in the Smithsonian Institution.

WRIGLEY, WILLIAM, JR., (1861–1932), industrialist. Born in Philadelphia on September 30, 1861, the son of a soapmaker, Wrigley began his own business in 1891 in Chicago, selling soap, baking powder, and chewing gum. Through salesmanship, organization, special incentive offers to dealers, and sheer persistence, he developed a vast trade, eventually discontinuing his lines in soap and baking powder and concentrating on the burgeoning market in chewing gum. In 1899 he announced an addition to his many gum flavors—"Spearmint"—which brought $1,345,862 in sales in 1908, directly attributable to the previous year's advertising. In 1911 he purchased the Zeno Company, gum manufacturers, and consolidated it in the William Wrigley, Jr. Company. He established branches in New York City, Brooklyn, Toronto, Berlin, Frankfurt, and London, and before his death had yearly sales of $75 million. Diversifying his interests, he gained a controlling interest in the Chicago Cubs National League Baseball team during 1916–1921, and bought the Los Angeles and Reading, Pennsylvania baseball teams as well. He purchased and redeveloped Santa Catalina Island, making it a major resort, directed banks, including the National Boulevard Bank of Chicago, and held interests in hotels and mines. The Wrigley Building, one of the most famous skyscrapers in Chicago, was completed in 1924. On January 26, 1932, Wrigley died in Phoenix, Arizona. Control of his enterprises passed to his son, Philip Knight Wrigley (1894–), who perpetuated the Wrigley name as the world's foremost manufacturer of chewing gum.

WYETH, ANDREW NELSON (1917–), painter. Born on July 12, 1917, in Chadds Ford, Pennsylvania, Wyeth received his training in drawing and anatomy from his father, noted illustrator N. C. Wyeth. He was adept at drawing from memory, and his early watercolors were brisk and impressionistic in style. His first notable achievements were in illustrating the Brandywine edition of Pyle's *The Merry Adventures of Robin Hood* at age 12 and Rob White's *The Nub* at age 14. In 1936 he had his first one-man showing at the Art Alliance in Philadelphia. The following year he exhibited his watercolors in New York City. The use of egg tempera, an exacting medium, disciplined his style, so much so that it was called photographic. But visitors to areas he painted were frequently disappointed to find that what they saw differed substantially from what he drew. He created from the barns, fields, rooms, and people of his surroundings in Chadds Ford, Brandywine Valley, and Cushing, Maine, paintings that were personal and richly symbolic. His watercolors included "The Coot Hunter," 1941, "Muddy Road by Adam Johnson's," 1943, and "Young Buck," 1945. Among the most notable of his tempera paintings were "Four Poster," 1946, "Wind From the Sea," 1947, "Young America," 1950, "Northern Point," 1950, "Faraway," 1952, "Nicholas," 1955, "Ground Hog Day," 1959, "Albert's Son," 1959, "Distant Thunder," 1961, "Day of the Fair," 1963, "Christina's World," 1963, and "Grape Wine," 1966. The recipient of many honors and awards, he was perhaps the most successful of American painters, his canvases bringing enormous prices. Critical opinion concerning the lasting value of his work was divided but largely favorable.

WYTHE, GEORGE (1726–1806), lawyer, public official, jurist, and educator. Born in Elizabeth City County, Virginia, in 1726, Wythe had little formal education when he began the study of law. He was admitted to the bar in 1746 and for several years practised in Spotsylvania County. During 1754–1755 he served in the House of Burgesses and in 1758 began ten years of membership in that body. By 1760, having devoted much time to study in law and the classics, he was one of the leading lawyers and legal scholars in the colony, and from 1762 to 1767 Thomas Jefferson studied in his office. In 1764 he was charged with drafting the Virginia remonstrances to the House of Commons protesting the Stamp Act; his language was considered too strong and was much attenuated in the final version. In 1775 he was elected to the Continental Congress and remained there through 1776, becoming a signer of the Declaration of Independence. Upon his return to Virginia he was appointed with Edmund Pendleton and Jefferson to revise the laws of the commonwealth in the light of its recently achieved independence. After serving in the House of Delegates he was named a judge of the Chancery Court in 1778; he held this position until his death, and between 1788 and 1801 was the sole judge of the court. Noted for his erudition and disinterested administration of justice, he was one of the first judges to enunciate the doctrine of judicial review, in *Commonwealth* v. *Caton*, 1782. Largely by the efforts of Jefferson, then governor, he was appointed in 1779 to the newly created professorship of law and police at the College of William and Mary, the first such chair in an American college. His judicial duties forced him to resign the chair in 1789, but in his ten years there he exerted a powerful influence on the course of American legal education, supplementing his lectures with moot courts and moot legislatures held by his students, among whom was John Marshall. He served in 1787 in the Consitutional Convention and the next year in the Virginia ratifying convention. After leaving the College, he moved to Richmond to conduct his duties on the bench and there opened a private law school; among his students was Henry Clay, who served also as clerk of his court. He died in Richmond on June 8, 1806, apparently poisoned by a relative who was also his principal heir, but who was acquitted of the crime for lack of evidence.

YANCY, WILLIAM LOWNDES (1814–1863), lawyer and public official. Born on August 10, 1814, in Warren County, Georgia, Yancey attended Williams College in Massachusetts. In 1833 he went to Greenville, South Caro-

lina, and was a pro-Union editor of the *Greenville Mountaineer* during the furor over nullification. He also studied law in Greenville and was admitted to the bar. In 1837 he moved to Alabama and purchased, with his brother, the *Wetumpka Commercial Advertiser* and the *Argus*. He soon rose to prominence in the state and was elected to the Alabama legislature in 1841 and became a state senator in 1843. He won election to the House of Representatives in 1844 and was reelected in 1845. He resigned on September 1, 1846, to devote himself to combatting Abolitionism. In response to the Wilmot Proviso he drew up the Alabama Platform in 1848 calling for positive congressional action on behalf of the rights of slaveholders and calling upon the Democratic Party to endorse pro-slavery presidential and vice-presidential candidates. At the party's national convention in Baltimore in 1848, he attempted unsuccessully to have the statement included in the Democratic platform. Following the Compromise of 1850, he openly advocated secession and organized non-partisan Southern rights associations to take a united stand for Southern interests. He founded the League of United Southerners in 1858 and called for the repeal of laws against the slave trade. In 1860 he delivered the final statement of Southern delegates before their withdrawal from the National Democratic Convention in Charleston. He then organized the Constitutional Democratic Party, which nominated John Breckinridge for President, and toured the country making campaign speeches for him. He personally drafted the ordinance of secession of the Alabama Convention. Declining a cabinet post in Jefferson Davis' administration, he went to England and France in 1861 and 1862 to try to secure recognition of the Confederacy. In 1862–1863 he was a member of the Confederate senate. He died in Montgomery, Alabama, on July 27, 1863.

YOUNG, BRIGHAM (1801–1877), religious leader. Born in Whitingham, Vermont, on June 1, 1801, Young was raised in western New York

State and received only a few months of formal schooling in the towns where his poverty-stricken family drifted. He grew up to be a farmer, carpenter, painter, and glazier, and in 1829 he settled in Mendon, New York. Joseph Smith's *Book of Mormon* was published the following year in nearby Fayette, and Young was baptized into Smith's new church on April 14, 1832. After several successful missionary tours for the church in the fall of 1833, he "gathered" with the Saints in Kirtland, Ohio, and joined in the march of Zion's Camp to Missouri, a fruitless effort to help dispossessed Mormons regain their lands. For his faith and works, he was named one of the Twelve Apostles when Smith organized this quorum in 1835. The failure of the Mormon bank made it necessary for Young, like Smith and other Mormon leaders, to flee to northwestern Missouri in 1838. By the following year, when they were also driven from Missouri, two older apostles had died or left the church and Young became senior member of the quorum. A chief figure in the successful founding of Nauvoo, Illinois, he then went to England, where he preached the gospel for a year and established a mission that was to contribute many British converts to the church in America during the next half century. Returning home in 1841, he lived quietly among the Saints in Nauvoo until the assassination of Smith in June 1844. Young succeeded in his bid to head the church and early in 1846 the pressure of unfriendly neighbors forced him to lead the Saints out of Illinois. They spent the summer at the Missouri River and in 1847 he conducted a pioneer company to the Rocky Mountains, where the site of Salt Lake City was chosen as a gathering place for the Saints. He led the immigration of the whole church to Utah in 1848, and Salt Lake City became the base of a colonizing endeavor in which the Saints preempted all the irrigable land and settled every feasible locality, including areas in what are now the four surrounding states as well as California. As the supreme authority in the cooperative theocracy, he supervised the most minute details of the settlement, and their agricultural community enjoyed phenomenal growth and prosperity. When Congress changed their provisional state of Deseret to the Territory of Utah in 1850, he continued as governor. He was appointed to a second term in 1854, but grinding friction between the Mormons and the federal judiciary over the Mormon practice of polygamy and their economic power finally led President Buchanan to replace Young in 1857. An Army force was sent to establish the primacy of federal rule in Utah, and he resisted the incoming troops until the spring of 1858. His statesmanship avoided a real break with the United States, however. Although he never again held political office, he effectively ruled the people of Utah as president of the Mormon church. Having accepted the doctrine of plural marriage, he took dozens of wives—some merely "sealed" to him—17 of whom survived him, along with 47 children, on his death in Salt Lake City on August 29, 1877.

ZAHARIAS, MILDRED ELLA DIDRIKSON (1914–1956), athlete. Born at Port Arthur, Texas on June 26, 1914, "Babe" Didrikson was an all-American basketball player in 1930, while she was still in high school, and from that year until 1932 won eight events and tied for a ninth in women's national track and field. In the Olympic games of the latter year, at Los Angeles, she won two gold medals, setting a new record of 143' 3 11/16" in the javelin throw and establishing a U.S. outdoor mark of 11.7 seconds in the 80-meter hurdles. Shortly after the games she turned professional and gave athletic exhibitions throughout the country for the next several years. In 1935 she took up golf and, regaining her status as an amateur, soon became the leading woman golfer in the United States. In 1947 she won 17 straight golf titles, including the British Women's Amateur, of which she was the first U.S. winner. She later became a professional golfer and continued to win most of the tournaments in which she participated. But by 1952 it was obvious that she was very ill, and the next year she underwent a cancer operation. She appeared to have recovered when she won the U.S. Open and the All-American Open in 1954. But she was operated on once again for cancer in 1956 and died that year in Galveston, Texas, on September 27th. She married the wrestler George Zaharias in 1938 and published an autobiography, *This Life I've Led*, in 1955. The book revealed her as a delightful and courageous woman as well as one of the greatest woman athletes in history.

ZENGER, JOHN PETER (1697 – 1746), editor. Born in Germany, Zenger emigrated to New York in 1710 and was indentured to the colony's foremost printer, William Bradford, until 1719. He joined Bradford in partnership in 1725 and the next year formed his own business in Maryland, translating religious and polemic articles from the Dutch, and issuing *Arithmetica*, America's first mathematics text. In 1733, during conflict over Gov. William Cosby's dismissal of chief justice Lewis Morris, Zenger was installed as editor of an anti-government paper, the *New-York Weekly Journal*. Its articles aggressively attacked the opinions and actions of the governor; particularly hostile issues were confiscated and burned in 1734. Shortly thereafter Zenger was arrested for seditious libel, but the paper continued on his instructions under his wife's supervision. The defense in August 1735 was handled by a noted Philadelphia lawyer, Andrew Hamilton, who, despite the judge's charge to the contrary, requested the jury to consider the truth as well as the simple fact of the allegedly libelous statements. On doing so the jury acquitted Zenger; while no legal precedent was set by the action, popular sentiment was aroused in favor of both freedom of the press and a wider scope of responsibility for juries. Zenger's name thereafter was linked with the individual's right publicly to discuss and criticize his government. He died on July 28, 1746, and the paper continued under his wife's and his son's management until 1751.

ZIEGFELD, FLORENZ (1869 – 1932), theatrical producer. Born in Chicago on March 21, 1869, Ziegfeld attended Chicago public schools and entered show business in 1892, engaging orchestras and musical atttractions for the World's Fair of 1893. He also managed Eugene Sandow the Strongman at the Fair and later in country-wide appearances. In 1896 he turned to theatrical management, introducing a French starlet, Anna Held, in *A Parlor Match*, and filling newspapers, magazines, and billboard advertisements with enticing pictures and descriptions of her milk baths. She became famous and appeared in his lavish musical comedy productions of *Papa's Wife*, *The Little Duchess*, *The Parisian Model*, and *Mlle. Napoleon*, all of which were a prelude to *The Follies of 1907*, an experiment with a "revue," a new type of musical production in America. The first *Follies* was staged on the roof of the New York Theatre and was followed by editions seen, except for 1926, 1928, and 1929, every year on Broadway until 1931. They featured in the chorus line through the years the most beautiful women ever to walk across an American stage, all personally chosen by Ziegfeld, whose major aim was to glorify the American girl. With a fine sense of the right effect, he also selected the music for the shows, approved the opulent costuming and great stage effects, and directed the production of each number. His taste and standards popularized the revue and brought to the musical stage levels of artistry and production never before achieved. The contemporary ideal of slenderness in women was attributed to the girls in the *Follies*. Contributing to the scores of various productions, some of which cost over $200,000, were such eminent composers as Irving Berlin, Jerome Kern, Rudolf Friml, and Victor Herbert. Featured entertainers wrote their own material; among the stars he developed were Eddie Cantor, Fannie Brice, W. C. Fields, Will Rogers, Ann Pennington, and Ed Wynn. The songs introduced included "Shine On, Harvest Moon," sung by Nora

Bayes in 1908, "By the Light of the Silvery Moon," by Lillian Lorraine in 1909, "Be My Little Baby Bumble Bee," sung by the Dolly Sisters in 1911, "A Pretty Girl Is Like a Melody," composed by Irving Berlin and used as the *Follies* theme song after 1919, "My Blue Heaven," introduced by Eddie Cantor in 1927, and "My Man," by Fannie Brice, also in 1927. Besides the *Follies* he produced *Sally* with Marilyn Miller in 1920, *Show Boat* and *Rio Rita*, which opened the specially designed Ziegfeld Theatre, in 1927, and *Bitter Sweet* in 1929. He died in Hollywood on July 22, 1932.

ZORACH, WILLIAM (1887–1966), sculptor. Born in Eurburg, Lithuania, on February 28, 1887, Zorach was brought to the United States by his parents at the age of four. He was raised in Cleveland, where he studied at the Cleveland School of Art. First a painter, he was strongly influenced by the work of Matisse and the Cubists, with which he came in contact during a year in Paris in 1910–1911. So strong was this influence that he was numbered among the *fauve* or "wild" young painters who dominated the Paris art world at the beginning of the century, and who shocked art lovers elsewhere. He settled In New York City in 1912 and remained there, except for extended sojourns on a farm that he bought in 1923 in Robinhood, Maine, until his death. In 1917 he did his first direct carving—a very old process in which the sculptor hews out the image that he senses in the material without the aid of models, pointing machines, or other mechanical devices. Becoming fascinated by this traditional technique, he became at the same time more traditional, even conservative, in his approach and subject matter. In 1922 he gave up oils for sculpture, although he did watercolors sporadically for the rest of his life. His later and best known work was often monumental, simple in composition and in conception. He exerted an influence on many younger artists through his classes at the Art Students League in New York, where he taught after 1929. He was honored in 1959 by a retrospective exhibition at the Whitney Museum of American Art. Among his public commissions were "Spirit of the Dance," at Radio City Music Hall in New York, 1932; the Mayo Clinic reliefs at Rochester, Minnesota, 1954; and "The Spirit of the Sea" at Bath, Maine, 1962, in which town he died on November 16, 1966.

ZWORYKIN, VLADIMIR KOSMA (1889–   ), engineer and inventor. Born in Mourom, Russia, on July 30, 1889, Zworykin graduated from the St. Petersburg Institute of Technology in 1912 and then went to Paris to do graduate work at the Collège de France. After service in the Russian army in World War I, he emigrated to the United States in 1919, becoming a naturalized citizen in 1924. He worked first as a researcher on the staff of the Westinghouse Electric Corporation in Pittsburgh, and in 1926 received his Ph.D. from the University of Pittsburgh. In 1929 he joined the Radio Corporation of America as head of its electronic research laboratory, first at Camden, New Jersey, then at Princeton. From 1954 he was an honorary vice president of RCA as well as a consultant on various technical problems. Probably his greatest contribution was his invention of the first iconoscope, the camera tube that made possible the development of the all-electronic television system. But he also made many other contributions to the development of this industry and is known as "the father of television." He made contributions to other fields of electronics and scientific instrumentation as well, among others the electron microscope. He was the recipient of a large number of prizes and awards, including the Rumford medal of the American Academy of Arts and Sciences, in 1941, and the National Medal of Science in 1967. From 1954 to 1962 he was director of the medical electronics center of the Rockefeller Institute for Medical Research, in New York. He lived during most of his later life in Princeton.

INDEX

References in the index are listed in strict order of pagination, and abbreviations are used to distinguish several different kinds of citation. Text references are indicated simply by a page number, while references to quotations are preceded by the symbol "q.", to maps by the symbol "m.", to tables by the symbol "t.", and to illustrations by the symbols "il." or "il. fol.", the latter abbreviation identifying references to unnumbered illustration pages. A number in boldface type indicates the page on which a biographical sketch appears.

The lists of popular plays, songs, magazines, books, and movies on pp. 779–792 of Part II were not indexed for two reasons. First, the lists were conceived as historical continua, valuable in showing pattern rather than detail; second, it was thought that page references to such concentrations of material would be of negligible usefulness.

Acknowledgements continued—

Emily Davie for Red Cloud, Sioux Chief—Speech made at a reception held in his honor at Cooper Institute, July 17, 1870, from *Profile of America*, ed. by Emily Davie, N.Y.: Grosset & Dunlap, Inc.

The Dial Press for "My Dungeon Shook," from *The Fire Next Time*, by James Baldwin, Copyright © 1963, 1962 by James Baldwin.

Helen Hartness Flanders for "Ye Parliament of England," as published in *Ballads Migrant in New England*, Farrar, Straus & Young, 1953; Books for Libraries, 1968.

Harcourt Brace Jovanovich, Inc., for "the Cambridge ladies," from his volume, *Poems 1923-1954*, Copyright 1923, 1951 by E. E. Cummings. Also for "next to of course god," from his volume, *Poems 1923-1954*, Copyright 1926 by Horace Liveright; renewed 1954 by E. E. Cummings.

Holt, Rinehart and Winston, Inc., for "Mending Wall," from *The Poetry of Robert Frost*, ed. by Edward Connery Lathem, Copyright 1930, 1939, © 1969 by Holt, Rinehart and Winston, Inc., Copyright © 1958 by Robert Frost, Copyright © 1967 by Lesley Frost Ballantine. Also for "Chicago," from *Chicago Poems*, by Carl Sandburg, Copyright 1916 by Holt, Rinehart and Winston, Inc., Copyright 1944 by Carl Sandburg.

Houghton Mifflin Company for a selection from "Patterns," from *The Complete Poetical Works of Amy Lowell*, Boston: Houghton Mifflin Company.

International Publishers Co., Inc., for "Address of the International Workingmen's Association to Abraham Lincoln," from *Letters to Americans 1848-1895*, by Karl Marx and Frederick Engels, Copyright 1953 by International Publishers Co., Inc.

The Jewish Publication Society of America and American Jewish Committee for Letter by Louis Marshall to President Coolidge, May 22, 1924, from *Louis Marshall, Champion of Liberty: Selected Papers and Addresses*, ed. by Charles Reznikoff, Vol. I.

Life Magazine for "A Dark Night to Remember," by Loudon Wainwright, from *Life Magazine*, November 19, 1965, © 1965 by Time Inc. Also for "Amid Gold Medals, Raised Black Fists," by Jeremy Larner and David Wolf, from *Life Magazine*, November 1, 1968 © 1968 by Time Inc.

Walter Lippmann for "The Portent of the Moon," from *New York Herald Tribune*, October 10, 1957.

Little, Brown and Company for the selection from *Invasion from Mars*, by Howard Koch, Copyright 1940 by Hadley Cantril, © renewed 1967 by Howard Koch. The text is included in *The Panic Broadcast*, by Howard Koch, to be published by Little, Brown and Company (Inc.), Copyright © 1970 by Howard Koch.

Louis E. Lomax for "The Negro Revolt Against 'The Negro Leaders'," from the June 1960 issue of *Harper's Magazine*, Copyright © 1960 by Harper's Magazine, Inc.

MCA Music for "Joe Hill," by Earl Robinson and Alfred Hayes, © Copyright 1938 MCA Music, a division of MCA, Inc., Copyright renewed and assigned 1965 to MCA Music, a division of MCA, Inc., 445 Park Avenue, New York, New York.

Mrs. Ellen C. Masters for "Anne Rutledge," from *Spoon River Anthology*, by Edgar Lee Masters, Copyright 1914, 1915, 1916, 1942 by Edgar Lee Masters.

The Nation for "Revolution Is Our Business," by William O. Douglas, from *The Nation*, May 31, 1952, Copyright 1952 by The Nation Associates, Inc.

The National Review, 105 E. 35th St., New York, N.Y. 10016, for "Political Assassination: Two Historical Types," by Will Herberg, from *National Review*, April 2, 1968, © National Review, Inc., 1968.

The New Republic for "Sherman Adams," by TRB, from *New Republic*, June 30, 1958, © 1958, Harrison-Blaine of New Jersey, Inc. Also for "Following Mr. K.," by TRB, from *New Republic*, September 28, 1959, © 1959, Harrison-Blaine of New Jersey, Inc. Also for "What Hath Dodd Wrought?" by Robert Yoakum, from *New Republic*, April 8, 1967, © 1967, Harrison-Blaine of New Jersey, Inc.

The New York Times for "Proprietary Group Assails Drug Bill," © 1951 by The New York Times Company. Also for "Alabama: Racism vs. Reason," © 1965 by The New York Times Company. Also for "Pilots Agree to Fly Higher Over Home of a Protestor," by David Binder, © 1967 by The New York Times Company. Also for "Dumplings Do It Again; Copters to Fly Higher," © 1967 by The New York Times Company.

Newsweek for "Medicine: Drugs," condensed from *Newsweek*, November 12, 1951, Copyright Newsweek, Inc., 1951.

Norwegian-American Historical Association for Letter by Ole M. Raeder, from *America in the Forties: The Letters of Ole Munch Raeder*, tr. and ed. by Gunnar J. Malmin.

Franklin D. Roosevelt Library for "Exchange of Communications Between the President of the United States and Maxim Litvinov of the Union of Soviet Socialist Republics, November 16, 1933."

Roosevelt University, Labor Education Division for "Bread and Roses," from *Songs of Work and Freedom*, ed. by Edith Fowke and Joe Glazer.

Culver Pictures, Inc.: fol. 333 (bottom rt.); fol. 419 (bottom rt.); 684

Courtesy of Detroit Public Library, Burton Historical Collection: 72

George Eastman House: fol. 253 (bottom rt.); Mrs. Ralph Mackay—134; Richard Parker—148

Photoworld: fol. 419 (top rt.); 433; fol. 451 (bottom l.); fol. 467 (bottom rt.); fol. 557 (top l.); 690

General Tire and Rubber Company: 491

Granger Collection: 149; fol. 149 (top rt.); 249; fol. 317 (bottom l.)

Rapho Guillumette: Don Getsug—fol. 593 (top l.); Ted Spiegel—fol. 577 (top l.)

Historical Society of Delaware: 42

Historical Society of Pennsylvania: fol. 69 (bottom rt.)

Kramer Hofmester: 475

Henry E. Huntington Library and Art Gallery: fol. 69 (bottom c.)

Illinois State Highway Department: 745

Imperial War Museum: fol. 403 (top rt.)

Independence National Historical Park: fol. 99 (rt. c.); 664

Joslyn Art Museum, Northern Natural Gas Co. Collection: fol. 149 (top l.)

Kansas State Historical Society: 216

Keystone Press Agency, Inc.: 474

Library of Congress: 2; 4; fol. 17 bottom l.); fol. 51 (top l., c.l., top rt. and c.rt.); 58; fol. 69 (bottom l. and c. rt.); 70; 94; 95; 98; fol. 99 (top rt. and bottom rt.); fol. 117 (bottom l. and bottom rt.); 125; fol. 133 (bottom l. and top rt.); 147; 150; fol. 163 (top l. and bottom rt.); 166; fol. 179 (top l., bottom l., and c.rt.); fol. 195 (top l., c.l., bottom l. and bottom rt.); 196; 197; fol. 211 (bottom rt.); 215; fol. 219 (bottom rt.); 220; 237; 250; 251; fol. 253 (top c.) fol. 269 (top l., bottom l., top rt., c., and bottom rt.) fol. 285 (bottom l., top rt., c., and bottom rt.); 290; 291; fol. 301 (c., bottom l., top l., and bottom rt.); fol. 317 (top l., c., and top rt.); 318; fol. 333 (top l., c., bottom l. and top rt.); fol. 349 (top rt., and bottom rt.); 350 (bottom l. and rt.); 351; fol. 365 (top l.); 383; 384; 403; fol. 403 (bottom l.); fol. 419 (bottom l.); fol. 451 (bottom rt.); 472; 473; fol. 485 (bottom l.); 646 (bottom); 650; 661 (top and bottom); 663 (bottom); 678; 706; 720; 728 (above and rt.); 740; 758 (top, l. and bottom); 759 (l.)

"Life," © Time Inc.: Stan Wayman—574-575

Lightfoot Collection: 194; fol. 349 (top l.); fol. 419 (top l.)

"Los Angeles Times" Syndicate: Hugh Haynie—fol. 627 (bottom c.)

McNaught Syndicate, Inc.: Courtesy, Reg Manning—fol. 611 (c.)

Magnum Photos: Bruce Davidson—726; Elliott Erwitt—746; Bert Glinn—fol. 557 (bottom rt.); Danny Lyon —572; Burk Uzzle—573; Inge Morath—fol. 577 (bottom l.)

From the Collection of the Maryland Historical Society: fol. 117 (rt. c.)

Massachusetts Historical Society: fol. 29 (top c. and top rt.); fol. 69 (top l.); fol. 99 (top c.) 757 (bottom); Adams Papers—728 (above right)

Metropolitan Museum of Art: fol. 163 (bottom l.); fol. 179 (top c.); fol. 211 (c.rt.); Gift of J. Pierpont Morgan—fol. 17 (top l.); Bequest of Charles Allen Munn—fol. 29 (top rt.); Stokes-Hawes Gift—fol. 133 (bottom rt.)

"The Milwaukee Journal": Courtesy, Ross Lewis—fol. 557 (top rt.)

J. P. Morgan Library: 644

Courtesy, Museum of Fine Arts, Boston, M. & M. Karolik Collection: fol. 219 (top l.)

Museum of the City of New York: Davies Collection—fol. 163 (top rt.); Harry T. Peters Collection— fol. 219 (top rt.)

National Academy of Design: fol. 195 (top rt.)

National Aeronautics and Space Administration: fol. 627 (bottom rt.)

National Archives: fol. 99 (bottom l.); fol. 253 (top l. and top rt.); 663 (rt.); Navy Dept.—fol. 485 (rt.)

National Gallery of Art: fol. 149 (c.); Garbisch Collection—748

National Maritime Museum: 638

National Portrait Gallery: fol. 69 (c.l.)

Kenneth Nebenzahl, Inc., Chicago: 642-643

Other Merriam-Webster Dictionaries of Special Usefulness:

Webster's Third New International This is the latest Merriam-Webster unabridged dictionary. A masterpiece of modern defining, every definition is given in a single phrase of precise meaning. 200,000 usage examples, primarily from well-known persons and publications, demonstrate word usage to make meanings clearly understandable. More than 450,000 entries, including 100,000 new words or new meanings never before covered in the unabridged Merriam-Webster. 3,000 terms illustrated, with 20 true-to-life plates in color. Simplified pronunciation key, clear and informative etymologies, 1,000 synonym articles. The ultimate in dictionary ownership. 2,728 pages.

Webster's Seventh New Collegiate This new desk dictionary is the latest in the famous Merriam-Webster Collegiate series, the outstanding favorite in schools, homes, and offices. 130,000 entries include 20,000 new words and new meanings for more complete coverage than any other desk dictionary. Precise, clear definitions with 10,000 usage examples assure full understanding and accurate use of words. 1,244 pages. Every year over a million people buy this Webster's.

Webster's New Dictionary of Synonyms When a thesaurus is needed, this is the book to ask for. It quickly shows how to use the right word in the right place by defining, discriminating, and illustrating word meanings. Unlike any thesaurus, it contains thousands of illustrative quotations which make shades of meaning crystal clear. Its alphabetical arrangement saves hunting through an index. It shows clearly which word to use to express precisely the meaning you want. 942 pages.

Webster's Biographical Dictionary The most inclusive single volume of biographical reference. In this handy book are concise biographies of more than 40,000 men and women from all walks of life, every historical period, every nationality. Birth dates, important accomplishments, influence on history, with name pronunciations.

Webster's Geographical Dictionary This unusual book lists 40,000 of the world's important places with concise information about each— exact locations, physical features, economic data, historical notes. For businessman or traveler, for following the day's news, for helping children in their schoolwork, here is quick, accurate information.

G. & C. MERRIAM CO.
Springfield, Mass. 01101